The Norton Introduction to Literature

SHORTER EIGHTH EDITION

The Norton Introduction to

Literature

SHORTER EIGHTH EDITION

Jerome Beaty
LATE OF EMORY UNIVERSITY

Alison Booth
UNIVERSITY OF VIRGINIA

J. Paul Hunter
EMERITUS, UNIVERSITY OF CHICAGO
UNIVERSITY OF VIRGINIA

Kelly J. Mays
UNIVERSITY OF NEVADA, LAS VEGAS

W. W. NORTON & COMPANY
NEW YORK · LONDON

Since this page cannot legibly accommodate all the copyright notices, pp. A95–
A106 constitute an extension of the copyright page.

The text of this book is composed in Optima and Stone Serif, with the display set
in Optima and Stone Serif.
Composition by Binghamton Valley.
Manufacturing by R. R. Donnelly & Sons.
Book design by Joan Greenfield.

Editor: Peter Simon
Developmental Editor: Kurt Wildermuth
Associate Managing Editor: Marian Johnson
Production Manager: Diane O'Connor
Editorial Assistant: Isobel Evans
Permissions Manager: Nancy Rodwan
Cover Design: Debra Morton Hoyt
Art Research: Neil Ryder Hoos

Library of Congress Cataloging-in-Publication Data

The Norton introduction to literature / [edited by] J. Paul Hunter, Alison Booth,
Kelly J. Mays.—Shorter 8th ed.
    p. cm.
  Includes bibliographical references and index.

  ISBN 0-393-97743-9 (pbk.)

    1. Literature—Collections. I. Hunter, J. Paul, date. II. Booth, Alison. III. Mays,
Kelly J.

PN6014.N67 2001b
808—dc21   2001040325

W. W. Norton & Company, Inc., 500 Fifth Avenue, New York, N.Y. 10110
www.wwnorton. com

W. W. Norton & Company Ltd., Castle House, 75/76 Wells Street,
                    London W1T 3QT

6 7 8 9 0

Contents

Fiction

Exploring Contexts 320

Exploring Contexts 830

Evaluating Poetry 956

Reading More Poetry 967

Drama

Drama: Reading, Responding, Writing 1016

Understanding the Text 1043

Exploring Contexts 1216

Evaluating Drama 1670

Appendices

Writing about Literature A3

Glossary A53

Biographical Sketches A64

Preface

Through eight editions, *The Norton Introduction to Literature* has been committed to helping students learn to read and enjoy literature. This edition, like those before it, offers many different ways of building and reinforcing the skills of reading; in addition to studying literature in terms of its elements, our book emphasizes reading works in different contexts—authorial, historical, cultural, and critical. For this edition, we have provided many new selections and have strengthened our contextual groups by adding a new chapter, "The Author's Work as Context: William Shakespeare," which calls attention to stylistic and thematic currents running through Shakespeare's work and encourages students to read Shakespeare actively and critically.

The Shorter Eighth Edition, like its predecessors, offers in a single volume a complete course in reading and writing about literature. It is both an anthology and a textbook—a teaching anthology—for the indispensable course in which, together with a college teacher, a college student begins to read literature, and to write about it, seriously. To that end, we have added a new introduction, "What Is Literature?," which grapples with questions concerning the nature of literature, the value of reading it and writing about it, and the history of the canon.

The works are arranged in order to introduce a reader to the study of literature. Each genre is approached in three logical steps. Fiction, for example, is introduced by *Fiction: Reading, Responding, Writing,* which treats the purpose and nature of fiction, the reading experience, and the first steps one takes to begin writing about fiction. This is followed by the seven-chapter section called *Understanding the Text,* in which stories are analyzed in terms of craft, the so-called elements of fiction; this section ends with "The Whole Text," a chapter that uses the analytical aids offered in the previous chapters, putting them together to view the work as a whole. The third section, *Exploring Contexts,* suggests some ways of seeing a work of literature interacting with its temporal and cultural contexts and reaching out beyond the page.

The sections on reading, analyzing, and placing the work in context are followed, in each genre, by guidance in taking that final and extremely difficult step—evaluation. *Evaluating Poetry,* for example, demonstrates how to assess the merits of two poems; rather than offering definitive judgments, a litmus test, or even a checklist or formula, it discusses ways of bringing to consciousness, defining, modifying, articulating, and negotiating one's judgments about a work of literature. *Evaluating Fiction* and *Evaluating Drama* have been further refined in this edition to guide students toward determining and declaring *on what basis* they make their evaluative judgments.

Ending the fiction and poetry sections, *Reading More* _____ is a reservoir of additional examples, for independent study or a different approach. The book's arrangement facilitates the reader's movement from narrower to broader questions, mirroring the way people read—wanting to learn more as they experience more.

In the section called *Writing about Literature,* we deal with both the writing process as applied to literary works—choosing a topic, gathering evidence, developing an argument, and so forth—and with the varieties of a reader's written responses, from copying and paraphrasing to analysis and interpretation. We explore not merely the hows but also the whats and whys. In addition, we discuss critical approaches, providing a basic overview of contemporary critical theory and an introduction to its terminology, and we cover the use and citation of secondary sources. This section, when coupled with the student research paper on page 466, provides a brief reference for writers of literary research papers.

The Shorter Eighth Edition includes forty-nine stories, fourteen of which are new; 317 poems, 101 of which are new; and fourteen plays, five of which are new.

In the fiction section, we have added stories by Jorge Luis Borges, Stephen Crane, Jhumpa Lahiri, Ursula K. Le Guin, Herman Melville, Lorrie Moore, Katherine Anne Porter, Carol Shields, Elizabeth Tallent, and William Carlos Williams.

The poetry section has been similarly infused with new selections by Virginia Hamilton Adair, Thomas Bastard, Eavan Boland, Francis William Bourdillon, Lee Ann Brown, Thomas Campion, Kelly Cherry, Marilyn Chin, Mary Coleridge, Martha Collins, Emily Dickinson, John Donne, Bob Dylan, David Ferry, Emily Grosholz, Thom Gunn, Robert Hayden, Felicia Dorothea Hemans, Langston Hughes, Ben Jonson, John Keats, D. H. Lawrence, Lady Mary Wortley Montagu, Marilyn Nelson, Willie Perdomo, Sylvia Plath, Thomas Randolph, Christina Rossetti, Alfred Tennyson, Derek Walcott, Phyllis Wheatley, and W. B. Yeats.

New to the drama section are Lillian Hellman's *The Children's Hour,* Henrik Ibsen's *A Doll House,* and August Wilson's *The Piano Lesson.*

We have retained our editorial procedures, which proved their usefulness in earlier editions. First of all, we have annotated the works, as is customary in Norton anthologies; our notes are informational and not interpretive, for their purpose is to help readers understand and appreciate the work, not to dictate a meaning or a response. Second, to avoid giving the impression that all literature was written at the same time, we have noted at the right margin after each selection the date of first book publication; or, when preceded by a *p,* first periodical publication; or, when the date appears at the left margin, the year of composition. Finally, in a glossary at the back we define the literary terms used throughout the book.

One exciting feature of *The Norton Introduction to Literature* isn't bound into the book itself. *LitWeb,* a Web-based companion to the text, prepared by Annette Woodlief of Virginia Commonwealth University, provides students and teachers with in-depth reading prompts and exercises designed to inspire creative reading of and writing about literature, as well as links to useful literary resources. To view this unique ancillary, visit *www.wwnorton.com/introlit.*

Also, because nearly any reading experience can be enhanced by an accompanying *listening* experience, all copies of *The Norton Introduction to Literature* will include a CD audio companion, offering readings and performances in each of the genres.

In all our work on this edition, we have been guided by teachers in other English departments and in our own, by students who used the textbook and wrote us, and by students in our own classes. We hope that with such capable help we have been able to offer you a solid and stimulating introduction to the experience of literature.

The occasion of the Shorter Eighth Edition of *The Norton Introduction to Literature* is both a celebratory and a sad one. Two wonderful new editors, Alison Booth and Kelly Mays, have joined the editorial team for this edition, and readers will quickly see the enlarged vision and range, as well as extensive knowledge and sheer intelligence, that they bring to the study of literature. But we also suffered a powerful loss when—in January of 2000—founding editor Jerome Beaty died after a courageous fight against cancer. New and old, we all miss the wit, judgment, good humor, and constant challenge of his fierce and loving intelligence. His imprint will be here for editions to come.

Acknowledgments We would like to thank our teachers, for their example in the love of literature and in the art of sharing that love; our students, for their patience as we learn from them to be better teachers of literature; and our families, for their understanding when the work of preparing this book made us seem less than perfectly loving and attentive toward them.

We would also like to thank our colleagues, many of whom have taught our book and evaluated our efforts, for their constant encouragement and enlightenment. Of our colleagues, we would like especially to thank Jonathan Martin, Robert von Hallberg, Michelle Hawley, Anne Elizabeth Murdy, Janel Mueller, Vicky Olwell, Richard Strier, and John Wright (all at the University of Chicago); Gwin Griesbeck and the students in "Introduction to Literature" (University of Virginia); Franny Nudelman, Steve Arata, Christopher Jackson, Julie Pal, Matthew Davis, and Amanda French—as fellow teachers and collaborators in creating this edition—and the members of the Graduate Pedagogy Workshop in 1999 (University of Virginia). For their help in selecting papers by student writers, we would like to thank Geneva Ballard, Theresa Budniakiewicz, Rebecca S. Ries, and Avantika Rohatgi (all at Indiana University–Purdue University at Indianapolis), and Thomas Miller, Tilly Warnock, Lisa-Anne Culp, Loren Goodman, Brendan McBryde, and Ruthe Thompson (all at the University of Arizona). We also thank the students whose papers we include: Daniel Bronson, Geoffrey Clement, Willow D. Crystal, Teri Garrity, Meaghan E. Parker, Sara Rosen, Sherry Schnake, Kimberly Smith, Thaddeus Smith, Jeanette Sperhac, and Caryl Zook. For her work on the *Instructor's Guide,* we thank Kelly Hager, Simmons College.

We would like to thank the many teachers whose comments on the Seventh Edition have helped us plan the Eighth: Professor Lisa Ashby, Concordia University; Dr. Mary Bagley, Missouri Baptist College; Professor Beverly Bailey, Seminole Community College; Professor Charles Bailey, San Jacinto College Central; Professor Carolyn Baker, San Antonio College; Professor Abby Bardi, Prince George's Community College; Professor Joseph Bathanti, Mitchell Community College; Professor Jim Beggs, Rodesto Junior College; Professor Elaine Bender, El Camino College; Professor Gerri Black, Atlantic-Cape Community College; Professor Tom Caldwell, Lake Land College; Professor Joe Cambridge, Tompkins Cortland Community College; Dr. Peggy Cole, Arapahoe Community College; Professor Daniel Colvin, Western Illinois University; Professor Ruth Corson, Norwalk Community Technical College; Professor Janis Crowe, Furman University; Professor Bonnie Davids, Missouri Valley College; Professor Al Davis, Moorhead State University; Professor Kathleen De Grave, Pittsburg State University; Professor Dixie Durham, Chapman University; Dr. Lamona Evans, University of Central Oklahoma; Professor Susan Fitzgerald, University of Memphis; Professor Julie Fleenes, Harper College; Dr. Deborah Ford, University of Southern Mississippi; Professor Kim Gardner, University of Memphis; Professor John Gery, University of New Orleans; Professor Joseph Green, Lower Columbia College; Dr. Loren Gruber, Missouri Valley College; Professor James Guimond, Rider University; Professor Andrew Gutteridge, Trinity Western University; Professor Janice Hall, St. Petersburg Junior College; Professor Sidney Harrison, Manatee College; Professor Jim Hauser, William Patterson University; Dr. Philip Heldrich, Emporia State University; Professor Jonathan Hershey, Floyd College; Professor Lin Humphrey, Citrus College; Dr. Vernon Ingraham, University of Massachussets, Dartmouth; Professor

Claudia Jannone, University of South Florida; Professor Charles Jimenez, Hillsborough Community College; Professor Sally Joranko, John Carroll University; Professor P. Kelly Joyner, George Mason University; Professor Josephine King, Georgia Central and Southern University; Professor Dennis Kriewald, Laredo Community College; Dr. Katherine Leffel, University of Alabama, Birmingham; Professor Jerri Lindblad, Frederick Community College; Professor Eileen Maguire, University of North Florida; Professor Paul Marx, University of New Haven; Professor Susan McClure, Indiana University of Pennsylvania; Dr. Nellie McCrory, Gaston College; Professor Darlene McElfresh, Northern Kentucky University; Professor Jim McKeown, McLennan Community College; Professor Robert McPhillips, Iona College; Professor Karen Miller, St. Petersburg Junior College; Professor Joseph Mills, North Carolina School of the Arts; Dr. Craig Monk, University of Lethbridge; Professor Paul Munn, Saginaw Valley State University; Professor Solveig Nelson, Grand View College; Professor James Obertino, Central Missouri State University; Professor Jeannette Palmer, Motlow State Community College; Professor Leland Person, University of Alabama, Birmingham; Professor Robert Petersen, Middle Tennessee State University; Dr. Rhonda Pettit, University of Cincinnati, Raymond Walters College; Professor Sylvia Rackow, Baruch College; Professor Daniel Robinson, Colorado State University; Professor Marti Robinson, Ulster County Community College; Professor Victoria Rosner, Texas A&M University; Professor Mike Runyan, Saddleback College; Professor Harold Schneider, American River College; Dr. Beverly Schneller, Millersville University; Professor Donald Schweda, Quincy University; Professor Judith Seagle, East Tennessee State University; Professor Karen Sidwell, St. Petersburg Junior College; Professor Judy Sieg, Spartanburg Technical College; Dr. Stephen Sparacio, St. John's University; Professor Linda Stolhancke, University of West Florida; Professor Debra Sutton, Jefferson College; Professor Burt Thorp, University of North Dakota; Professor James Thorson, University of New Mexico; Professor James Tomck, Delta State University; Professor Susan Trudell, Scott Community College; Professor Richard Turner, Indiana UniversityPurdue University at Indianapolis; Dr. Von Underwood, Cameron University; Professor John Valone, Sacramento City College; Professor Michael Weiser, Thomas Nelson Community College; Professor Sallie Wolf, Arapahoe Community College; Professor Clarence Wolfshehl, William Woods University; Professor Whitney Womack, Miami University, Ohio; Professor David Zimmerman, Amarillo College.

What Is Literature?

What is literature? Does it include: (a) a novel written by a French person in 1885, (b) a sermon delivered by a Scotsman in 1640, (c) a long poem developed orally by an ancient culture, (d) letters or diaries found in someone's attic, (e) the archive of an online chatroom, (f) the tape-recorded memories of Carolina sharecroppers, (g) a video documentary, (h) a horror movie, (i) all of the above? If you answered "all of the above," you're right. Of course, people could have interesting debates about particular examples or general kinds of works and whether they rank as literature. The list could go on, as well; you may have thought of other possibilities. Some people would stretch the definition of literature to include any kind of organized human expression, from ballet to advertising, that can be "read" in ways similar to the ways we read a story or a poem. Others would just say literature is anything cataloged under "P" in the Library of Congress system, and still others would hang onto a more familiar definition, something like "Literature is creative writing." This book can't define literature—no one can answer the question "What is literature?" once and for all—but it can help you come closer to your own definition of what literature is, how it works, and how some varieties of it have changed over time.

Before you opened this book, you probably could guess that it would contain the sorts of stories, poems, and plays you have encountered in English classes or in the literature section of a library or bookstore. Perhaps that suggests a working definition of literature: the three kinds of writing or genres that we select for *The Norton Introduction to Literature* form the heart of literature as it has been defined in schools and universities for over a century. Yet even in college classrooms literature often also includes works of nonfiction. You may be assigned essays or autobiographies in an English class; no one would object to calling these literature. *The Oxford English Dictionary (OED)* defines literature as "writing which has claim to consideration on the ground of beauty of form or emotional effect." The key elements in this definition may be *writing*—after all, the words *literature* and *letters* have roots in common—and *beauty* and *emotion*. But we sometimes use the word *literature* to refer to writing that has little to do with feelings or artful form, as in scientific literature—the articles on a particular subject— or campaign literature. And at least some of the nonfictional works studied in literature classrooms—Martin Luther King Jr.'s "Letter from Birmingham Jail," for example—were originally intended as "campaign literature" of one sort or another.

Could literature, then, include *anything* written? Or could it include works that do not depend on written words? (Look back at examples f–h in the first paragraph; although each involves written transcripts or scripts, the media of audio- and videotape and film are nonverbal.) Every society has forms of oral storytelling or poetry, and some peoples do not write down the cherished myths and traditions that are their "literature." If you go on to take more classes in literature or to major in English or another language, you might encounter texts that stretch the concept of literature still further: Web sites or performances, for example. As Alvin Kernan puts it in *The Death of Literature* (1990), literature has become "only . . . one among many . . . modes, print, television, radio, VCR, cassette, record, and CD, by which information can be assembled, organized, and transmitted effectively."

While Kernan and others worry that the ongoing expansion of literature may mean its death, the concept as we know it is fairly new. Two hundred years ago, before universities were open to women or people of color, a small elite of men studied the ancient classics in Greek and Latin, never dreaming of taking college courses about poetry or fiction or drama written in the modern languages they used every day. Before modern literature became part of the college curriculum, the word *literature* itself had to be invented. At first, it referred to the cultivation of reading or the practice of writing ("he was a man of much literature"). Only later did it refer to a specialized category of works. Over time, this category narrowed more and more, eventually designating only a special set of imaginative writings, particularly associated with a language and nation (as in "English," "American," or "French" literature). Roughly speaking, by 1900 a college student could take a course in English literature, and the syllabus would exclude most nonfictional forms of writing, from travel writing and journalism to biography, history, or philosophy. Literature had become a walled-in flower garden filled with works of beauty, pleasure, imagination.

> *Literature is not things but a way to comprehend things.*
> —NORMAN N. HOLLAND

Of course, that garden always had gates and doors out. For example, some early and mid twentieth-century literature professors studied Gibbon's histories or the essays of Carlyle and Emerson; others pursued their own kinds of scientific scholarship. But now, as you begin this introduction to literature in the twenty-first century, the walls of that garden have come down. Literature today generally encompasses oral and even visual forms (film and video being closely related to drama, of course); it takes in, as it did long ago, writings of diverse design and purpose, including nonfiction. As a twenty-first-century student of literature, you may feel the pleasure of reading the best imaginative writings of the past, hoping with the speaker of Keats's "Ode on Melancholy" to "burst Joy's grape against" your "palate fine." As a reader, you may learn to test your palate or taste for the beauty of language and form, the joy of stirring theme and action. Yet you may also discover a new joy in the expanding horizons of literature. The garden reserved for beautiful poetry, fiction, and drama is flourishing. In it, historically authenticated varieties are planted next to new hybrids, the ancient and exquisite bonzai tree next to that beautiful intruder some might call a weed—all there for you to notice and appreciate. But the fields beyond the unwalled garden are wild and inviting as well.

Though no book can fully represent every species in this flourishing garden, this collection can and will introduce you to both classic writers and fresh voices; to both tradition and experimentation. Since there has never been absolute, lasting agreement about *what* counts as literature, why not consider instead *how* and *why* we look at particular forms of expression? A song lyric, a screenplay, a supermarket romance, a novel by Toni Morrison or Thomas Mann, and a poem by Walt Whitman or Katherine Philips may each be interpreted *in a literary way* and may thus yield insights and pleasures. Honing your skills at this kind of interpretation is the primary purpose of this book. By learning to recognize how a story, poem, or play works, you should gain interpretative skills that you can take with you when you explore zones outside the garden of literature. Yet the best way to become a *person of much literature* is to enhance the skills you already have as a reader of poetry, fiction, and drama, three of the most important forms of literature in its standard sense. Each work included here holds its own rewards of form and feeling, beauty and pleasure, but what makes the work *effective?* By learning the skills and strategies that help you defend your opinion of a work's effectiveness, you will be able to support your *evaluation* of any work.

BUT WHY READ LITERATURE? WHY STUDY IT?

In the opening chapters of Charles Dickens's novel *Hard Times* (1854), the Utilitarian politician Mr. Thomas Gradgrind warns the pupils at his "model" school to avoid using their imaginations. "Teach these boys and girls nothing but Facts. Facts alone are wanted in life," exclaims Mr. Gradgrind to the schoolmaster, Mr. M'Chaokumchild. To press his point, Mr. Gradgrind asks "girl number twenty," Sissy Jupe, whose father performs in the circus, to define a horse. When she cannot, Gradgrind turns to Bitzer, a pale, lifeless boy who "looked as though, if he were cut, he would bleed white." A "model" student of this "model" school, Bitzer gives exactly the kind of definition to satisfy Mr. Gradgrind:

"Quadruped. Graminivorous. Forty teeth, namely, twenty-four grinders, four eye-teeth, and twelve incisive. Sheds coat in spring; in marshy countries, sheds hoofs." . . . Thus (and much more) Bitzer. "Now girl number twenty," said Mr. Gradgrind. "You know what a horse is."

Anyone who has any sense of what a horse is rebels against Bitzer's lifeless version of that animal and against the "Gradgrind" view of reality. Like The Grinch Who Stole Christmas, or like Dickens's own Ebenezer Scrooge, Gradgrind wants to kill the irrational spirit; he wants to deal only with material things that can be bought and sold and with qualities that can be measured and counted. As this first scene leads us to expect, in the course of *Hard Times* the fact-grinding Mr. Gradgrind learns that human beings cannot live on facts alone; that it is dangerous to stunt the faculties of imagination and feeling; that, in the words of one of the novel's more lovable characters, "People must be amused." Through the downfall of an exaggerated enemy of imagination, Dickens reminds us why we like and even *need* to read fiction.

Through the ages, people like Gradgrind have dismissed literature as a luxury, a frivolous pastime, or even a sinful indulgence. Pretending to agree with the Gradgrinds of the world, Oscar Wilde asserted that "all art is quite useless"; but by this Wilde was suggesting that beauty and pleasure are the sole aims of the arts, including imaginative literature. Others (including Dickens himself) have argued for a kind of middle ground between the positions of a Gradgrind or a Wilde, insisting that literature should and does instruct as well as entertain.

Wonderfully, instruction and delight often go hand in hand in our experience of literature: we learn from what delights us or what leads us to appreciate new kinds of delight. The pleasure of reading comes in many varieties, however, and sometimes the best pleasures require an effort that beginners tend to call pain. A lot of poetry, fiction, and drama, including some in this collection, is at first difficult for any reader to grasp. Twentieth-century writer and critic T. S. Eliot even went so far as to say that "literature must be difficult." The modern short story, a form that arose less than two hundred years ago and came of age in the twentieth century, thrives on compactness; oblique suggestiveness; emotional, intellectual, and moral ambiguity. The reader is invited to collaborate in creating its meanings, as if to dine at a gourmet table of small portions beautifully served, rather than grabbing the Big Gulp on the run. Meanwhile, works from centuries ago might seem to most contemporary readers to be written in a foreign language.

If we read literature only for pleasure, why would we bother with any piece of writing that requires such effort? One answer is that new kinds of literary pleasure open up through that effort. As we read more and more, we become able to extend ourselves further, like athletes who train for heavier weights or longer jumps with repeated practice. Another answer came from Wilde himself, for whom literature is of supreme importance precisely because it frees us from the utilitarian preoccupations and activities of daily life. We value literature (all art, really) for breaking the rules of the ordinary. In some kinds of written entertainment, we find immediate "escape," but even imaginative writing that is more difficult to read and understand than a John Grisham or Patricia Cornwell novel offers escape of a sort: it takes us beyond familiar ways of thinking. A realistic story, poem, or play can satisfy a desire for broader experience, even unpleasant experience; we can learn what it might be like to grow up on a Canadian fox farm, for example, or to clean toilets in the Singapore airport. We yearn for such knowledge in a very personal way, as though we can know our own identities and experiences only by overleaping the boundaries that usually separate us from other selves and worlds. As Wilde might have conceded, literature seems extremely *useful* in this respect.

Ultimately, it is impossible to separate knowledge from imagination, instruction from pleasure. For many ages, different peoples have affirmed that while imaginative writing may be like playing, such play is the closest we come to grappling with the complexity of life, the pressure and dread of death. Perhaps nothing is more important; perhaps literature is the very thing humanity can least afford to do without. Albert Einstein considered himself something of an artist: "Knowledge is limited. Imagination encircles the world." To approach that encircling vision, a person needs not only literacy but a comprehension of diverse writings and arts. A well-read person has powers of comprehension, perspective, reasoning, and insight that may be lacking in a person who relies on the daily media or on personal experience. Literature itself provides many examples of characters or even real people who gain a feeling of mastery as well as a claim to civil rights and respect through learning to read and to write. Take a famous episode in *The Autobiography of Malcolm X* (1964). Malcolm X, in prison, with only an eighth grade education, realizes he needs to learn standard written and spoken English if he is to succeed as a leader. He begins by copying every word in the dictionary and soon moves to absorbing the books on history and religion in the prison's extensive library. What were the fruits of this labor? "I had never been so truly free in my life. . . . [A] new world opened to me, of being able to read and *understand*." Literacy and a wide knowledge of literature of various kinds can be a sort of franchise, like the vote, and can launch a career.

> *Poets are the unacknowledged legislators of the world.*
>
> —PERCY BYSSHE SHELLEY

You may already feel the power and pleasure to be gained from challenging reading. Why not simply enjoy it in solitude, on your own free time? Because reading is only one of the activities involved in gaining a full understanding of literature. Literature has a history, and learning that history makes all the difference in the pleasure you can derive from literature. By studying different genres and different works from various times in history and from various national traditions—by becoming familiar with the conventions of writing a sonnet in seventeenth-century England or of writing a short story in 1920s America—you can come to appreciate and even love works that you might have disliked if you simply read them on your own. Discussing works with your teachers and other students, and writing about them, will give you practice in analyzing them in greater depth. A clear understanding of the aims and designs of a story, poem, or play never falls like a bolt out of the blue. Instead, it emerges from a process that often involves comparing this work with other works of its genre, trying to put into words *how* and *why* this work had such an effect on you, and responding to what others say or write about it. One of the great benefits of a literature course is that your own writing, for any purpose, will improve. You will write more effectively because you have paid attention to the way authors use words and because you have tried to convey to *your* readers the way a particular writer's words—an image, a turn of phrase, a dramatic speech—have affected you.

Yet studying literature involves more than cultivating your own skills and insights. Reading can open worlds and change a person's life, but literature also has political effects (government censors through the ages have taken the power of literature very seriously). The international best-seller *Uncle Tom's Cabin* (1852), for example, helped create such strong antislavery sentiments before the U.S. Civil War that Abraham Lincoln reportedly described its author, Harriet Beecher Stowe, as "the little lady who caused the big war." The personal and the political effects of literature intertwine. A sense of self and an identity as part of a group or a nationality are shaped and reinforced by respected traditions, and many groups and nations now try to recover and protect their own literary traditions rather than be misrepresented by the writings of others. Margaret Atwood has claimed that when Canadian literature was ignored, for instance, Canada itself seemed to have forgotten its identity. Since the 1970s, Canada and many other former colonies of European countries have recovered and developed thriving literatures of their own. Instead of one **canon**— or a single selective list of the most-recognized or -esteemed works—there are now many canons of literature written in English.

> *Americans and Canadians are not the same. . . . Put simply, south of you you have Mexico and south of us we have you.*
>
> —MARGARET ATWOOD

WHY NOT STICK TO THE CANON?

Although the definition of literature has changed across centuries, and opinions have differed about the value and function of various kinds of writing, until recently most people agreed that reading and studying the most revered authors and works of the past was an essential part of education. Controversy now rages about the canon, but the many heated arguments are too complex to review here. To simplify: defenders of the canon insist that only the study of "the best that is known and thought in the world" (in the words of the nineteenth-century poet and critic Matthew Arnold) can guide us to become better readers, thinkers, and writers. Critics of the canon tend to argue, instead, that we must enlarge or entirely abandon the canon if we are to achieve the goal of education: to broaden experience and to open minds. Defenders of the canon understandably fear that the best literature will be forgotten. Their critics express the equally valid fear that if we concentrate on only a traditional canon we neglect vast numbers of texts (many that were influential in their time and place) and, in the process, ignore vast stretches of human experience. They insist that we should both respond critically to *all* texts and scrutinize the standards by which certain works have been designated great. Many, however, believe that the most productive path

> *[The Native American] oral tradition . . . is the source of their identity as a people and as individuals. . . . When that wellspring of identity is tampered with, the sense of self is also tampered with.*
>
> —PAULA GUNN ALLEN

lies somewhere between extreme traditionalism and canon-bashing. A good grounding in traditional forms of literature prepares you both to encounter all varieties of human expression and to make your own informed decisions about the relative worth of particular forms and particular works.

Although this debate has many dimensions, it is often reduced to questions about which authors should be included in literature courses and anthologies: why Dryden and Pope but not Aphra Behn; why Ralph Ellison and not Zora Neale Hurston; why Joseph Conrad or Doris Lessing and not V. S. Naipaul or Bessie Head? *Whom* we publish and teach matters, because our choices convey certain messages about the many kinds of people who have made an art of writing. This collection represents a diverse array of authors both ancient and modern, but it does not treat an assortment of types of authors as an end in itself. The works included here are *good*—each after its kind is a splendid creation—but of course such a judgment of quality requires some supporting evidence. For this reason, many historical varieties of literature and many valid approaches to literary interpretation coexist here, and some added guidelines regarding the latter appear in the appendix "Critical Approaches." As you read, you can gather the most telling evidence, identify your own standards for judging texts, define your own approaches to interpreting them, and finally decide for yourself whether these works belong in the book or in your personal "canon." Because the pleasure of reading unfamiliar works depends so much on understanding changing conventions and historical contexts, the "contextual" chapters offer information on authors' lives, on time periods, on writing trends during those periods, and so on.

Debates about the canon and about whom we should include on the list of literary "greats" won't end soon, but such debates are only the latest version of a discussion as old as literature itself. Considering how recently literature was defined in the modern sense (as the artful, fictitious prose or poetry of a nation), it is all the more remarkable that we persist in wanting to read what was written as long ago as the fifth century B.C. (in this collection, Sophocles) or before the first permanent European settlements in North America (Shakespeare's *A Midsummer Night's Dream*). Defenders of a canon should find comfort both in the staying power of many works and in the fact that some alien weeds that seemed distinctly threatening at first have turned out to be lovely additions to the literary garden.

Each new technology that permits unsupervised communications with strangers raises fears about harmful effects on the young or uninitiated. In the early 1800s, many people decried the seductive influence of novel-reading, especially on girls. Such warnings closely resemble those we hear today about television, video games, and the Internet. By 1900, both the novel and the short story were recognized as forms of great artistic worth. Because standards of literary value inevitably change, we should keep an open mind about the possibility of modifying our own views. By 2050, the video games of the early 2000s may be considered an art form (as well as entertainment). Meanwhile, your children will still be able to appreciate, as you can, the great pleasures and insights at the imaginative heart of literature: short fiction, poetry, and drama.

The Norton Introduction to Literature

SHORTER EIGHTH EDITION

Fiction

Fiction: Reading, Responding, Writing

SPENCER HOLST

The Zebra Storyteller

Once upon a time there was a Siamese cat who pretended to be a lion and spoke inappropriate Zebraic.

That language is whinnied by the race of striped horses in Africa.

Here now: An innocent zebra is walking in a jungle and approaching from another direction is the little cat; they meet.

"Hello there!" says the Siamese cat in perfectly pronounced Zebraic. "It certainly is a pleasant day, isn't it? The sun is shining, the birds are singing, isn't the world a lovely place to live today!"

5   The zebra is so astonished at hearing a Siamese cat speaking like a zebra, why—he's just fit to be tied.

So the little cat quickly ties him up, kills him, and drags the better parts of the carcass back to his den.

The cat successfully hunted zebras many months in this manner, dining on filet mignon of zebra every night, and from the better hides he made bow neckties and wide belts after the fashion of the decadent princes of the Old Siamese court.

He began boasting to his friends he was a lion, and he gave them as proof the fact that he hunted zebras.

The delicate noses of the zebras told them there was really no lion in the neighborhood. The zebra deaths caused many to avoid the region. Superstitious, they decided the woods were haunted by the ghost of a lion.

10   One day the storyteller of the zebras was ambling, and through his mind ran plots for stories to amuse the other zebras, when suddenly his eyes brightened, and he said, "That's it! I'll tell a story about a Siamese cat who learns to speak our language! What an idea! That'll make 'em laugh!"

Just then the Siamese cat appeared before him, and said, "Hello there! Pleasant day today, isn't it!"

The zebra storyteller wasn't fit to be tied at hearing a cat speaking his language, because he'd been thinking about that very thing.

He took a good look at the cat, and he didn't know why, but there was some-thing about his looks he didn't like, so he kicked him with a hoof and killed him. That is the function of the storyteller.

1971

The Zebra Storyteller" suggests that the purpose of stories is to prepare us for the unexpected. Though the storyteller thinks he is just spinning stories out of his own imagination in order to amuse, his stories prove to be practical. When the extraordinary occurs—like a Siamese cat speaking Zebraic—the storyteller is prepared because he has already imagined it, and he alone is able to protect his tribe against the unheard-of.

Other storytellers make the function of fiction less extraordinary. According to them, fiction enables readers to avoid projecting false hopes and fears (such as the zebras' superstitious belief that they are being preyed on by the ghost of a lion) and shows them what they can actually expect in their everyday lives, so that they can prepare them-selves. In George Eliot's novel *Adam Bede*, Hetty Sorrel is being paid admiring attention by the young squire, and she dreams of elopement, marriage, all sorts of vague pleasures. She does not dream that she will be seduced, made pregnant, abandoned. Her imagi-nation has not been trained to project any "narrative" other than her dreams: "Hetty had never read a novel," George Eliot tells us, "[so] how could she find a shape for her expectations?"

We are all storytellers, then, of one stripe or another. Whenever we plan the future or ponder a decision, we are telling stories—projecting expectations through narrative. Whether we tell stories or read them, we are educating our imaginations, either extend-ing our mental experience in the actual, as Hetty might have done by reading novels, or preparing ourselves for the extraordinary and unexpected, like the zebra storyteller.

The actual and the extraordinary suggest two different uses readers make of fiction. Sometimes we want to read about people like ourselves, or about places, experiences, and ideas that are familiar and agreeable. Most of us initially prefer American literature and twentieth-century literature to literature remote in time or place. Indeed, stories must somehow be related to our own lives before we can find them intellectually or emotionally meaningful. No matter what our literary experience and taste, most of us relate in a special way to stories about people like us, experiences like our own, and especially to a story that mentions our hometown or neighborhood or the name of the street that we used to walk along on our way to school. No one would deny that one of the many things that fiction may be "for" is learning about ourselves and the world around us.

But occasionally the last thing we want is a story about people like ourselves, expe-riences like those of our everyday lives, and places and times like here and now. On such occasions we want (or are accused of wanting) to escape. If fiction must be relevant enough to relate meaningfully to us, it must also be "irrelevant," different, strange—as strange, perhaps, as a Siamese cat speaking Zebraic. It must take us out of ourselves, out of the confining vision of our own eyes, which is conditioned by our own back-ground and experience, and show us that there are ways of looking at the world other than our own. So, in addition to many stories about approximately our own time and place, this collection includes a sprinkling of stories written in the last century, a few written in vastly different cultures, and a few written about worlds that have not existed or do not (yet) exist.

What a story shows us or teaches us we may call its **message**—an objective, universal truth that we were unaware of before reading the story. We gradually learn, however, that stories tell us not so much what life means as what it's like. Rather than abstract or "objective" truths, stories deal with perceptions. These perceptions may be translated into messages, but we soon discover that the messages boil down to things like "There's good and there's bad in everybody," "Hurting people is wrong," and "Everything is not what it seems"—messages we do not need literature to deliver. Indeed, we do not have to agree with what a story says or shows so long as we are convinced that if we had *those* eyes and were *there,* this is what we might see.

Whenever we can say yes, we are convinced, then we have been able to go beyond the limitations of our own vision, our own past and conditions. We are able to see a new world, or the same old world in a new way. And by recognizing that we can see things differently, we realize that things we used to think were fixed, objective entities "out there," were fixed only in our perceptions. Or, as is too often the case, we realize that we have been accepting things at face value; we have been perceiving what habit and convention have told us is "really there." Stories, then, may awaken us to look at things for ourselves. For example, we "know" that most ordinary tabletops are rectangular, but in a story we may be told that such a tabletop is diamond-shaped. We understand that if we were to look at the tabletop from a certain angle it would appear diamond-shaped. But doesn't that mean that the tabletop is rectangular only when we look at it from a certain angle? How often do we look at a tabletop from that angle? We look again, and we recognize that though we've always "known" such a tabletop is rectangular, we may have never actually *seen* it as one. The story has not only allowed us to see reality from another angle, but it has helped us to sharpen our own vision, our own experience.

In reading a story, you are also telling a story or many stories, projecting the possible futures of the events and the characters' lives much as you project your own future actions in the "story" of your own life. Your projection of the story's future—what is going to happen next—is conditioned by the details, including the specific words, of the story. But it is also conditioned by your life experience (your sense of what life is like) and by your reading experience (your sense of what stories are like). When, as the story unfolds, your **expectations** are modified or the unexpected occurs, fiction and your reality interact: you may simply reject the story's version of what life or the world is like—it's only fiction, after all—or you may reexamine your own views, adding possibilities or at least tentatively questioning what you formerly took for granted (do I really see a rectangle when I look at the tabletop?).

In the story that follows, both the eighteen-year-old narrator and Jack are storytellers: each projects a future. The story, however, remains in the present, so we cannot tell which projection is right. Like the characters, we are more or less in the middle of our own lives. Though they may not get to know the future, both Jack and the narrator learn through their storytelling that more than one scenario of the future can be projected. Even if we think the narrator as naive as George Eliot's Hetty, projecting a dream rather than a possible reality, she has now at least "read Jack's novel," so she knows there are alternative futures. And so do we.

ELIZABETH TALLENT

No One's a Mystery

For my eighteenth birthday Jack gave me a five-year diary with a latch and a little key, light as a dime. I was sitting beside him scratching at the lock, which didn't seem to want to work, when he thought he saw his wife's Cadillac in the distance, coming toward us. He pushed me down onto the dirty floor of the pickup and kept one hand on my head while I inhaled the musk of his cigarettes in the dashboard ashtray and sang along with Rosanne Cash on the tape deck. We'd been drinking tequila and the bottle was between his legs, resting up against his crotch, where the seam of his Levi's was bleached linen-white, though the Levi's were nearly new. I don't know why his Levi's always bleached like that, along the seams and at the knees. In a curve of cloth his zipper glinted, gold.

"It's her," he said. "She keeps the lights on in the daytime. I can't think of a single habit in a woman that irritates me more than that." When he saw that I was going to stay still he took his hand from my head and ran it through his own dark hair.

"Why does she?" I said.

"She thinks it's safer. Why does she need to be safer? She's driving exactly fifty-five miles an hour. She believes in those signs: 'Speed Monitored by Aircraft.' It doesn't matter that you can look up and see that the sky is empty."

"She'll see your lips move, Jack. She'll know you're talking to someone."   5

"She'll think I'm singing along with the radio."

He didn't lift his head, just raised the fingers in salute while the pressure of his palm steadied the wheel, and I heard the Cadillac honk twice, musically; he was driving easily eighty miles an hour. I studied his boots. The elk heads stitched into the leather were bearded with frayed thread, the toes were scuffed, and there was a compact wedge of muddy manure between the heel and the sole—the same boots he'd been wearing for the two years I'd known him. On the tape deck Rosanne Cash sang, "Nobody's into me, no one's a mystery."

"Do you think she's getting famous because of who her daddy is or for herself?" Jack said.

"There are about a hundred pop tops on the floor, did you know that? Some little kid could cut a bare foot on one of these, Jack."

"No little kids get into this truck except for you."   10

"How come you let it get so dirty?"

" 'How come,' " he mocked. "You even sound like a kid. You can get back into the seat now, if you want. She's not going to look over her shoulder and see you."

"How do you know?"

"I just know," he said. "Like I know I'm going to get meat loaf for supper. It's in the air. Like I know what you'll be writing in that diary."

"What will I be writing?" I knelt on my side of the seat and craned around to   15
look at the butterfly of dust printed on my jeans. Outside the window Wyoming was dazzling in the heat. The wheat was fawn and yellow and parted smoothly

by the thin dirt road. I could smell the water in the irrigation ditches hidden in the wheat.

"Tonight you'll write, 'I love Jack. This is my birthday present from him. I can't imagine anybody loving anybody more than I love Jack.' "

"I can't."

"In a year you'll write. 'I wonder what I ever really saw in Jack. I wonder why I spent so many days just riding around in his pickup. It's true he taught me something about sex. It's true there wasn't ever much else to do in Cheyenne.' "

"I won't write that."

20   "In two years you'll write, 'I wonder what that old guy's name was, the one with the curly hair and the filthy dirty pickup truck and time on his hands.' "

"I won't write that."

"No?"

"Tonight I'll write, 'I love Jack. This is my birthday present from him. I can't imagine anybody loving anybody more than I love Jack.' "

"No, you can't," he said. "You can't imagine it."

25   "In a year I'll write. 'Jack should be home any minute now. The table's set— my grandmother's linen and her old silver and the yellow candles left over from the wedding—but I don't know if I can wait until after the trout à la Navarra to make love to him.' "

"It must have been a fast divorce."

"In two years I'll write, 'Jack should be home by now. Little Jack is hungry for his supper. He said his first word today besides "Mama" and "Papa." He said "kaka." ' "

Jack laughed. "He was probably trying to finger-paint with kaka on the bathroom wall when you heard him say it."

"In three years I'll write, 'My nipples are a little sore from nursing Eliza Rosamund.' "

30   "Rosamund. Every little girl should have a middle name she hates."

" 'Her breath smells like vanilla and her eyes are just Jack's color of blue.' "

"That's nice," Jack said.

"So, which one do you like?"

"I like yours," he said. "But I believe mine."

35   "It doesn't matter. I believe mine."

"Not in your heart of hearts, you don't."

"You're wrong."

"I'm not wrong," he said. "And her breath would smell like your milk, and it's kind of a bittersweet smell, if you want to know the truth."

1985

One of the pleasures of reading and one of the ways of penetrating the meaning and effectiveness of stories is through our emotional responses, which often begin with our rooting for, identifying with, admiring, or despising one character or the other, wishing for one outcome or another. Our wishes and fears, our expectations and emotions, and the kind of world we imagine that the characters inhabit make up the major register of our emotional responses to fiction. And one of the first moves from reading to writing about fiction may well involve this "partisanship."

There are two views emphasized in "No One's a Mystery," two main characters you might identify or side with. How do you feel about the narrator? You may think she's a fool for getting involved with a married man, or immoral, and so perhaps you feel bitter about her projections of a married life with Jack, and believe they will never come true. Or you may identify with her, and find her dreams poignant (if hopeless) or uplifting (if you think they might come true), while you may view Jack as either realistic or cynical. An early paper in a literature course may have you defend the projections into the future of Jack or the narrator. You may wish to argue that both are wrong, both right, or that the truth lies somewhere in between. Or you may argue for the story's third character, the wife, who, though not embodied, may nevertheless elicit your sympathy. Try writing down your view of a story like this in essay form before discussing it with others. You will then have a record of your uninfluenced, unchallenged view. Later, you may be surprised to find that some of your classmates do not agree with you. But in discussing or arguing for your views you may discover not only that there are reasonable differences of opinion, but that what a person believes about the future beyond the story reveals something about that person. A second paper may be either an argument with someone else's position or a composite or new view based on your discussion and exchange with classmates. And you may want to look at what you learned about yourself from your arguments about the story.

These ideas for papers are meant to be more than suggested writing assignments. They also suggest one *way* of writing about literature and are meant to show that writing about a story is not some special or arcane art but just a somewhat more formal, responsible, committed way of talking about what you have read. Think of the last time you saw a movie with a friend and left the theater discussing the film. If you were to put such responses down on paper, look at them carefully, think about them a bit, and try to make your views or responses convincing, you would be taking the first step toward writing about literature. You could even call it literary criticism.

Writing about the characters and events in stories as if they were real people and real happenings, and writing about your responses to and opinions about them, is only one kind of writing about literature. You can only write such a paper *after* you have read the whole story and formed an opinion, and your "argument" will involve going back to the story seeking out details to support your position, and, perhaps, situating where you are coming from in terms of personal experience, moral or religious views, and so on. But reading a story is not just something to argue or even think about after you have read it. It is first of all an experience—made up of thoughts and feelings—that happens *while you are in the very act of reading.*

One of the things most of us do when we are actively engaged in reading a story is to anticipate or interpret: what will happen next? what kind of person is a given character? how is the world of the story related to the world as I know it? what kind of a story is it? will it end happily or not? You will notice two aspects to such anticipation. One involves our experience, direct or indirect, in the world, and may be thought of as referential or representational; that is, we take the nouns to refer to real things—the word *table* calls up a more or less concrete image of a table—and from the words describing characters we imagine more or less real people and their actions and choices as potentially if not actually real. The other aspect is literary. We pay attention to the words themselves, to their sounds, their connotations, their relation to other words that look or sound like them, and not just to what they denote—tables or diaries or jewels. Stories can even play with these referential and literary aspects of words, surprising us by shifting from one aspect to another. The zebra who did not tell stories was astonished, and the words say "he's just fit to be tied." This is a common figure of speech, and we do not expect to take the words "seriously" or referentially. We are surprised, then, when the story does: "So the little cat quickly ties him up. . . ."

We are aware that a story is a story and that telling a story involves certain conventions—for example, stories are generally written in the past tense, though we like to imagine them as happening in a kind of present, with the end not yet known. Different kinds of stories, too, have their own conventions: fairy tales and sometimes other fantasies, like "The Zebra Storyteller," begin with "Once upon a time"; in ghost stories and certain other scary stories there is almost always a beautiful young woman threatened by danger; these stories, adventure stories, and comic stories almost always end happily; and so on.

Anticipation begins at the beginning—or even earlier. As soon as we read the title of the story that follows, "The Jewelry," we start: will it be lost? stolen? inherited? Our anticipation is channeled by first- or secondhand life experience—how we think jewelry functions in "the real world." Notice that this anticipation is triggered by the title. Life experiences do not come with titles to guide us, but our reading experience tells us that titles are significant, worth paying attention to if we are to anticipate and understand. Perhaps not as early as our reading of the title, but soon, we begin to anticipate a shape or configuration of the entire story. Based on our own real experiences and what we've read, we project a vague shape early on, frequently adjusting it as we proceed through the story, but always connected to it as we read on. With the first sentence of "The Jewelry"—"Having met the girl one evening, at the house of the office-superintendent, M. Lantin became enveloped in love as in a net"—we begin casting our own net. The story will involve love. What do we know or believe about love? about different kinds of love? about the possible outcomes of falling in love? What is the connection between love and jewelry? We are not yet prepared to define that connection, but we may have tentative expectations about it. Though the first sentence may be summarized in "real" or experiential terms as "M. Lantin has fallen (deeply) in love," the precise *words* in the sentence that describe falling in love are "became enveloped in love as in a net." Does this merely emphasize how deeply he has fallen in love, or is there something uncomfortable, painful, even ominous about the words—note, about the *words*—"enveloped as in a net"? How we anticipate and interpret what the story "means" or "says about life" will be conditioned throughout by our life experience, by such literary "devices" as the title, by the precise words of the story, and by our experience with kinds of stories and what usually happens and eventuates in such stories. We must remain tentative in our expectations, however, and alert to changes and modifications, as this story will show. For example, when the fourth paragraph concludes with "and [he] married her," we must abandon the love-and-courtship story we anticipated and imagine an entirely new set of possibilities.

GUY DE MAUPASSANT

The Jewelry[1]

Having met the girl one evening, at the house of the office-superintendent, M. Lantin became enveloped in love as in a net.

1. Translated by Lafcadio Hearn.

She was the daughter of a country-tutor, who had been dead for several years. Afterward she had come to Paris with her mother, who made regular visits to several bourgeois families of the neighborhood, in hopes of being able to get her daughter married. They were poor and respectable, quiet and gentle. The young girl seemed to be the very ideal of that pure good woman to whom every young man dreams of entrusting his future. Her modest beauty had a charm of angelic shyness; and the slight smile that always dwelt about her lips seemed a reflection of her heart.

Everybody sang her praises; all who knew her kept saying: "The man who gets her will be lucky. No one could find a nicer girl than that."

M. Lantin, who was then chief clerk in the office of the Minister of the Interior, with a salary of 3,500 francs a year,[2] demanded her hand, and married her.

He was unutterably happy with her. She ruled his home with an economy so adroit that they really seemed to live in luxury. It would be impossible to conceive of any attentions, tendernesses, playful caresses which she did not lavish upon her husband; and such was the charm of her person that, six years after he married her, he loved her even more than he did the first day.

There were only two points upon which he ever found fault with her—her love of the theater, and her passion for false jewelry.

Her lady-friends (she was acquainted with the wives of several small office holders) were always bringing her tickets for the theaters; whenever there was a performance that made a sensation, she always had her *loge* secured, even for first performances; and she would drag her husband with her to all these entertainments, which used to tire him horribly after his day's work. So at last he begged her to go to the theater with some lady-acquaintances who would consent to see her home afterward. She refused for quite a while—thinking it would not look very well to go out thus unaccompanied by her husband. But finally she yielded, just to please him; and he felt infinitely grateful to her therefor.

Now this passion for the theater at last evoked in her the desire of dress. It was true that her toilette remained simple, always in good taste, but modest; and her sweet grace, her irresistible grace, ever smiling and shy, seemed to take fresh charm from the simplicity of her robes. But she got into the habit of suspending in her pretty ears two big cut pebbles, fashioned in imitation of diamonds; and she wore necklaces of false pearls, bracelets of false gold, and haircombs studded with paste-imitations of precious stones.

Her husband, who felt shocked by this love of tinsel and show, would often say—"My dear, when one has not the means to afford real jewelry, one should appear adorned with one's natural beauty and grace only—and these gifts are the rarest of jewels."

But she would smile sweetly and answer: "What does it matter? I like those things—that is my little whim. I know you are right; but one can't make oneself over again. I've always loved jewelry so much!"

And then she would roll the pearls of the necklaces between her fingers, and make the facets of the cut crystals flash in the light, repeating: "Now look at them—see how well the work is done. You would swear it was real jewelry."

2. A midlevel bureaucratic wage, perhaps about $25,000 to $30,000 today.

He would then smile in his turn, and declare to her: "You have the tastes of a regular Gypsy."

Sometimes, in the evening, when they were having a chat by the fire, she would rise and fetch the morocco box in which she kept her "stock" (as M. Lantin called it)—would put it on the tea-table, and begin to examine the false jewelry with passionate delight, as if she experienced some secret and mysterious sensations of pleasure in their contemplation; and she would insist on putting one of the necklaces round her husband's neck, and laugh till she couldn't laugh any more, crying out: "Oh! how funny you look!" Then she would rush into his arms, and kiss him furiously.

One winter's night, after she had been to the Opera, she came home chilled through, and trembling. Next day she had a bad cough. Eight days after that, she died of pneumonia.

15   Lantin was very nearly following her into the tomb. His despair was so frightful that in one single month his hair turned white. He wept from morning till night, feeling his heart torn by inexpressible suffering—ever haunted by the memory of her, by the smile, by the voice, by all the charm of the dead woman.

Time did not assuage his grief. Often during office hours his fellow-clerks went off to a corner to chat about this or that topic of the day—his cheeks might have been seen to swell up all of a sudden, his nose wrinkle, his eyes fill with water— he would pull a frightful face, and begin to sob.

He had kept his dead companion's room just in the order she had left it, and he used to lock himself up in it every evening to think about her—all the furniture, and even all her dresses, remained in the same place they had been on the last day of her life.

But life became hard for him. His salary, which, in his wife's hands, had amply sufficed for all household needs, now proved scarcely sufficient to supply his own few wants. And he asked himself in astonishment how she had managed always to furnish him with excellent wines and with delicate eating which he could not now afford at all with his scanty means.

He got a little into debt, like men obliged to live by their wits. At last one morning that he happened to find himself without a cent in his pocket, and a whole week to wait before he could draw his monthly salary, he thought of selling something; and almost immediately it occurred to him to sell his wife's "stock"— for he had always borne a secret grudge against the flash-jewelry that used to annoy him so much in former days. The mere sight of it, day after day, somewhat spoiled the sad pleasure of thinking of his darling.

20   He tried a long time to make a choice among the heap of trinkets she had left behind her—for up to the very last day of her life she had kept obstinately buying them, bringing home some new thing almost every night—and finally he resolved to take the big pearl necklace which she used to like the best of all, and which he thought ought certainly to be worth six or eight francs, as it was really very nicely mounted for an imitation necklace.

He put it in his pocket, and walked toward the office, following the boulevards, and looking for some jewelry-store on the way, where he could enter with confidence.

Finally he saw a place and went in; feeling a little ashamed of thus exposing his misery, and of trying to sell such a trifling object.

"Sir," he said to the jeweler, "please tell me what this is worth."

The jeweler took the necklace, examined it, weighed it, took up a magnifying glass, called his clerk, talked to him in whispers, put down the necklace on the counter, and drew back a little bit to judge of its effect at a distance.

M. Lantin, feeling very much embarrassed by all these ceremonies, opened his   25
mouth and began to declare—"Oh! I know it can't be worth much" . . . when the jeweler interrupted him saying:

"Well, sir, that is worth between twelve and fifteen thousand francs; but I cannot buy it unless you can let me know exactly how you came by it."

The widower's eyes opened enormously, and he stood gaping—unable to understand. Then after a while he stammered out: "You said? . . . Are you sure?" The jeweler, misconstruing the cause of this astonishment, replied in a dry tone— "Go elsewhere if you like, and see if you can get any more for it. The very most I would give for it is fifteen thousand. Come back and see me again, if you can't do better."

M. Lantin, feeling perfectly idiotic, took his necklace and departed; obeying a confused desire to find himself alone and to get a chance to think.

But the moment he found himself in the street again, he began to laugh, and he muttered to himself: "The fool!—oh! what a fool; If I had only taken him at his word. Well, well!—a jeweler who can't tell paste from real jewelry!"

And he entered another jewelry-store, at the corner of the Rue de la Paix. The   30
moment the jeweler set eyes on the necklace, he examined—"Hello! I know that necklace well—it was sold here!"

M. Lantin, very nervous, asked:

"What's it worth?"

"Sir, I sold it for twenty-five thousand francs. I am willing to buy it back again for eighteen thousand—if you can prove to me satisfactorily, according to legal presciptions, how you came into possession of it"—This time, M. Lantin was simply paralyzed with astonishment. He said: "Well . . . but please look at it again, sir. I always thought until now that it was . . . was false."

The jeweler said:

"Will you give me your name, sir?"   35

"Certainly. My name is Lantin; I am employed at the office of the Minister of the Interior. I live at No. 16, Rue des Martyrs."

The merchant opened the register, looked, and said: "Yes; this necklace was sent to the address of Madame Lantin, 16 Rue des Martyrs, on July 20th, 1876."

And the two men looked into each other's eyes—the clerk wild with surprise; the jeweler suspecting he had a thief before him.

The jeweler resumed:

"Will you be kind enough to leave this article here for twenty-four hours   40
only—I'll give you a receipt."

M. Lantin stuttered: "Yes-ah! certainly." And he went out folding up the receipt, which he put in his pocket.

Then he crossed the street, went the wrong way, found out his mistake, returned by way of the Tuileries, crossed the Seine, found out he had taken the wrong road again, and went back to the Champs-Élysées without being able to get one clear idea into his head. He tried to reason, to understand. His wife could never have bought so valuable an object as that. Certainly not. But then, it must have been a present! . . . A present from whom? What for?

He stopped and stood stock-still in the middle of the avenue.

A horrible suspicion swept across his mind. . . . She? . . . But then all those other pieces of jewelry must have been presents also! . . . Then it seemed to him that the ground was heaving under his feet; that a tree, right in front of him, was falling toward him; he thrust out his arms instinctively, and fell senseless.

He recovered his consciousness again in a drug-store to which some bystanders had carried him. He had them lead him home, and he locked himself into his room.

Until nightfall he cried without stopping, biting his handkerchief to keep himself from screaming out. Then, completely worn out with grief and fatigue, he went to bed, and slept a leaden sleep.

A ray of sunshine awakened him, and he rose and dressed himself slowly to go to the office. It was hard to have to work after such a shock. Then he reflected that he might be able to excuse himself to the superintendent, and he wrote to him. Then he remembered he would have to go back to the jeweler's; and shame made his face purple. He remained thinking a long time. Still he could not leave the necklace there; he put on his coat and went out.

It was a fine day; the sky extended all blue over the city, and seemed to make it smile. Strollers were walking aimlessly about, with their hands in their pockets.

Lantin thought as he watched them passing: "How lucky the men are who have fortunes! With money a man can even shake off grief—you can go where you please—travel—amuse yourself! Oh! if I were only rich!"

He suddenly discovered he was hungry—not having eaten anything since the evening before. But his pockets were empty; and he remembered the necklace. Eighteen thousand francs! Eighteen thousand francs!—that was a sum—that was!

He made his way to the Rue de la Paix and began to walk backward and forward on the sidewalk in front of the store. Eighteen thousand francs! Twenty times he started to go in; but shame always kept him back.

Still he was hungry—very hungry—and had not a cent. He made one brusque resolve, and crossed the street almost at a run, so as not to let himself have time to think over the matter; and he rushed into the jeweler's.

As soon as he saw him, the merchant hurried forward, and offered him a chair with smiling politeness. Even the clerks came forward to stare at Lantin, with gaiety in their eyes and smiles about their lips.

The jeweler said: "Sir, I made inquiries; and if you are still so disposed, I am ready to pay you down the price I offered you."

The clerk stammered: "Why, yes—sir, certainly."

The jeweler took from a drawer eighteen big bills,[3] counted them, and held

---

3. French paper money varies in size; the larger the bill, the larger the denomination.

them out to Lantin, who signed a little receipt, and thrust the money feverishly into his pocket.

Then, as he was on the point of leaving, he turned to the ever-smiling merchant, and said, lowering his eyes: "I have some—I have some other jewelry, which came to me in the same—from the same inheritance. Would you purchase them also from me?"

The merchant bowed, and answered: "Why, certainly, sir—certainly. . . ." One of the clerks rushed out to laugh at his ease; another kept blowing his nose as hard as he could.

Lantin, impassive, flushed and serious, said: "I will bring them to you."

And he hired a cab to get the jewelry.   60

When he returned to the store, an hour later, he had not yet breakfasted. They examined the jewelry—piece by piece—putting a value on each. Nearly all had been purchased from that very house.

Lantin, now, disputed estimates made, got angry, insisted on seeing the books, and talked louder and louder the higher the estimates grew.

The big diamond earrings were worth 20,000 francs; the bracelets, 35,000; the brooches, rings and medallions, 16,000; a set of emeralds and sapphires, 14,000; solitaire, suspended to a gold neckchain, 40,000; the total value being estimated at 196,000 francs.

The merchant observed with mischievous good nature: "The person who owned these must have put all her savings into jewelry."

Lantin answered with gravity: "Perhaps that is as good a way of saving money   65
as any other." And he went off, after having agreed with the merchant that an expert should make a counter-estimate for him the next day.

When he found himself in the street again, he looked at the Column Vendôme[4] with the desire to climb it, as if it were a May pole. He felt jolly enough to play leapfrog over the Emperor's head—up there in the blue sky.

He breakfasted at Voisin's[5] restaurant, and ordered wine at 20 francs a bottle.

Then he hired a cab and drove out to the Bois.[6] He looked at the carriages passing with a sort of contempt, and a wild desire to yell out to the passers-by: "I am rich, too—I am! I have 200,000 francs!"

The recollection of the office suddenly came back to him. He drove there, walked right into the superintendent's private room, and said: "Sir, I come to give you my resignation. I have just come into a fortune of *three* hundred thousand francs." Then he shook hands all round with his fellow-clerks; and told them all about his plans for a new career. Then he went to dinner at the Café Anglais.

Finding himself seated at the same table with a man who seemed to him quite   70
genteel, he could not resist the itching desire to tell him, with a certain air of coquetry, that he had just inherited a fortune of *four* hundred thousand francs.

For the first time in his life he went to the theater without feeling bored by the performance; and he passed the night in revelry and debauch.

4. Famous column with a statue of Napoleon at the top.   5. Like the Café Anglais below, a well-known and high-priced restaurant.   6. Large Parisian park where the rich took their outings.

Six months after he married again. His second wife was the most upright of spouses, but had a terrible temper. She made his life very miserable.

1883

Stories are not always written. Ballads and even epics were sung, plays are still acted out on the stage, and most cultures have or had oral storytellers. Writing, however, makes a difference. Oral or dramatic "readings" or performances are communal, the responses tend to be uniform (though there's always the person in the audience who laughs at the wrong time), and the purpose of the performances is more overtly to move or persuade the group or community. They have a closer relation to classical rhetoric, political speeches, or concerts than written narrative does. We read, usually, alone, most of the time silently, and if there are—and there usually are—emotions, they are deeply personal, not shared. There is a tendency, then, in literary criticism, and in reading for and discussing literature in class, to stress interpretation, the "ideas" in literary texts, or the formal structures, and to slight somewhat the emotional or affective aspect of our essentially solitary literary experience. But though it may be difficult to develop the vocabulary needed to talk about literature (we have to get beyond "I liked it" and "I didn't like it"), we must never forget the deeply stirring response that literature engenders and the differences in kinds and depths of response that different works stimulate.

QUESTIONS

1. What specific words or phrases in the first two paragraphs of "The Jewelry" alert you to the possibility that all may not be as it seems? How are these expectations or fears allayed in the next few paragraphs? What new fears or expectations are aroused very soon thereafter?
2. Since the story is called "The Jewelry" and life does not come wrapped in such convenient titles, you may come to suspect the truth before M. Lantin does. How does your attitude toward him change?

WRITING SUGGESTIONS

1. Stop "The Zebra Storyteller" after paragraph 5 ("... fit to be tied"), and in five to ten paragraphs write your own ending.
2. Write a parody or imitation of "No One's a Mystery," giving it the same title as a recent song.
3. Write a two- or three-page scene of Jack (from "No One's a Mystery") and his wife at home.
4. Write an "off-stage" scene that shows how Lantin's first wife got one or more pieces of the jewelry.

Understanding the Text

PLOT

In "The Zebra Storyteller" you can see the skeleton of the typical short story **plot** or **plot structure.** *Plot* simply means the arrangement of the **action,** an imagined event or a series of such events.

Action usually involves **conflict,** a struggle between opposing forces, and it often falls into something like the same five parts that we find in a play: exposition, rising action, turning point (or climax), falling action, conclusion. The conflict in this little tale is between the Siamese cat and the zebras, especially the zebra storyteller. The first part of the action, called the **exposition,** introduces the characters, situation, and, usually, time and place. The exposition here is achieved in three sentences: the time is "once upon a," the place Africa, the characters a Siamese cat who speaks Zebraic and an innocent zebra, and the situation their meeting. We then enter the second part of the plot, the **rising action:** events that complicate the situation and intensify or complicate the conflict or introduce new ones. The first event here is the meeting between an innocent zebra and the Zebraic-speaking cat. That initial conflict of zebra and cat is over in a hurry—the zebra who is "fit to be tied" is tied up and eaten. Complications build with the cat's continuing success in killing zebras, and the zebras' growing fears and consequent superstitious belief that the ghost of a lion haunts the region preying on zebras. The **turning point** or **climax** of the action is the third part of the story, the appearance of the zebra storyteller: until now the cat has had it all his way, but his luck is about to change. From this point on the complications that grew in the first part of the story are untangled—the zebra storyteller, for example, is not surprised when he meets a Siamese cat speaking Zebraic "because he'd been thinking about that very thing"; this is the fourth part of the story, the reverse movement or **falling action.** The story ends at the fifth part, the **conclusion:** the point at which the situation that was destabilized at the beginning of the story (when the Zebraic-speaking cat appeared) becomes stable once more: Africa is again free of cats speaking the language of zebras.

This typical arrangement of the action of a story is not just a formula for composing a narrative or for critical analysis; it also has its emotional and intellectual effect on your responses as reader. The exposition invites you to begin immediately building images of the time and place of the action, the people, the situation, and the issues involved, and even to identify with or root for one or more of the participants. You choose to be on the side of the zebras or the Siamese cat (though your choice is guided by the language and details of the story: the cat speaks "inappropriate" Zebraic; the zebra is introduced as "innocent"). As the situation becomes more complicated during the rising action, you are led to be increasingly concerned with how "your" zebras, the "good guys," are going to get out of this worsening situation (the cat eating more and more zebras), or, if the complications of the rising action are positive (as in the marriage and prosperity and happiness of M. Lantin in "The Jewelry"), you become more and more concerned about what is going to happen to turn things around (for even if you do not know about turning points in narrative, you know that sometimes things in stories and even in real life—knock on wood—seem too good to be true or too good to last). Consciously or unconsciously you become involved in the story, trying to anticipate how the complications will unravel, how everything will come out.

Another aspect of structure that affects you, the reader, is the order in which the events are told. In life, actions occur one after the other, sequentially. Not all stories, however, describe events chronologically. It is then, when historical order is disturbed, that a plot is created. "The king died and then the queen died," to use one critic's example, is not a plot, for it has not been "tampered with." "The queen died after the king died" includes the same historical events, but the order in which they are reported has been changed. The reader of the first sentence focuses on the king first; the reader of the second sentence focuses on the queen. While essentially the same thing has been said, the difference in focus and emphasis changes the effect and, in the broadest sense, the meaning as well. The **history** has been structured into plot.

The ordering of events, then, provides stories with structure and plot, and has its consequences in effect and meaning. The first opportunity for **structuring** a story is at the beginning, and beginnings are consequently particularly sensitive and important. Why does a story begin where it does? No event (at least since the Big Bang) is a true beginning; your own life story begins before you were born and even before you were conceived. So to begin a story the author has to make a **selection,** to indicate that for the purposes of this story the beginning is a given point rather than any other. "Having met the girl one evening, at the house of the office-superintendent, M. Lantin became enveloped in love as in a net." That first sentence of "The Jewelry" seems a perfectly natural and "innocent" way to begin a story that will involve Lantin and his wife. But why not begin with a slightly modified paragraph 5: "M. Lantin was perfectly happy in his marriage"? or with paragraph 9, inserting a new first sentence: "M. Lantin was perfectly happy with his wife and smiled at her two little faults: her love of the theater, and her passion for false jewelry. He felt shocked by . . ."? After all, this last sentence would immediately introduce the jewelry that gives the story its title. Or the story could begin with the death of the girl's father, her move with her mother to Paris, and so on. These are the earliest events mentioned in the exposition, and so in the unstructured history they would come first. In searching for a reason for Maupassant's beginning, we might look at what we learn and what is emphasized in the beginning as it now stands: the class of Lantin and his income; the girl's beauty, modesty, respectability, and poverty; her mother's search for a husband for her; Lantin's falling in love as if into a "net." It might be useful to consider on your own or in an assigned essay how the details in these first eight paragraphs affect your reading, responding, and understanding of the people, events, and "meaning" of the story. Or you might want to explain why John Cheever's "The Country Husband," in this chapter, begins, "To begin at the beginning, the airplane from Minneapolis in which Francis Weed was traveling East ran into heavy weather," rather than with, say, paragraph 11, when the Weeds are preparing to go out on the evening on which Francis meets the baby-sitter; or even, with a few adjustments, with paragraph 15, when the baby-sitter opens the door and Francis sees her for the first time, for it is with their encounter that the story seems truly to begin.

The point at which a story ends is also a sensitive and meaningful aspect of its structure. A typical beginning—first sentence (Lantin meets the girl) or first **discriminated occasion** (the first encounter of a zebra with the Zebraic-speaking cat)—destabilizes the history: something happens that changes the ordinary life of one or more characters and sets off a new course of events, which constitute the story. A typical ending either re-establishes the old order (no more cats eating zebras) or establishes a new one (Lantin remarried). Endings, like beginnings, affect the reader and suggest meaning. And like beginnings, they are arbitrary structures that interrupt history, for all stories (or more precisely, histories) about individuals end the same way, as Margaret Atwood somewhat cynically suggests in "Happy Endings": *"John and Mary die. John and Mary die. John and Mary die."* That is true, of course, only if you equate the story with the history, for the history extends not only backward as far as you can see but also forward to the end of the lives of those in the story. (And why not the lives of their children, grandchildren, and so on?) Not all stories end with the deaths of the characters who interest us; in fact, of the stories in this and the introductory chapters only Atwood's ends with the deaths of both its major characters, while "The Zebra Storyteller" ends with the death of the Zebraic-speaking cat. Where a story ends goes a long way to determining how it affects us and what we make of it. "The Zebra Storyteller" ends with the triumph of the zebra over the Siamese cat, leaving us with the feeling that good guys win, and with a moral that leads us to the "point" or meaning of the story. "No One's a Mystery" leaves us without an answer and pushes us back into our own experiences and beliefs to judge who is right and who is wrong about the couple's future.

All questions about the effect or meaning of beginnings and endings follow from an assumption that we must now recognize: there are reasons for the structures of the narrative. Indeed, in a short story, in part because of its brevity, every detail, every arrangement or ordering must "count." One writer has said that if there is a gun on the wall at the beginning of a story, it must be fired by the end. The relevance of events or details is not limited, however, merely to future action—events in the plot—for most seem to have relevance in other ways. In paragraph 9 of "The Country Husband," for example, Francis Weed listens to "the evening sounds of Shady Hill." These include a door slamming, the sound of someone cutting grass—which do not lead to events but may establish the nature of the suburban setting—and the sound of someone playing (badly) Beethoven's *Moonlight Sonata*, which may on the one hand reinforce Weed's thoughtful or dreamy mood or introduce "romance" into the story, and on the other hand, because of the petulant and self-pitying performance, show why Weed is dissatisfied with the shallowness of his suburban neighbors and perhaps suburban life. Notice the "may" and the "perhaps" in the previous sentence. The relevancy of a detail to a story is not always as simple and incontrovertible as the inevitable shooting of the gun. Though you ought to be alert as to how the details function in affecting you or contributing to your visualization or understanding of the people, incidents, and issues of the story, there is not necessarily a precise answer to the question of how a detail functions. In Cheever's story, why does Mr. Nixon shout "Varmints! Rascals! . . . Avaunt and quit my sight!" at the squirrels? What does it add? What would be lost

> *"The king died, and then the queen died" is a story. "The king died, and then the queen died of grief" is a plot.*
>
> —E. M. FORSTER

without it? You may see the effects and implications differently from your classmates; indeed you may not have chosen this detail to interrogate at all. These differences of selection and explanation may shed light on why readers respond to, understand, and judge stories differently.

Structuring a story is not just a matter of choosing where to begin or end it, or of choosing or inventing affective and meaningful details, but also of ordering all the events in between. Sometimes, as Atwood says, the plot is "just one thing after another, a what and a what and a what." Even when that is the case, sometimes the reader is forced to think back to prior events. In a detective story, for example, the crime has usually been committed before the story begins, in the history and not in the plot. At the end, when the detective explains "who done it," you must think back not only to the crime, but to all the hints or clues that you have been given, including false clues or "red herrings" that make you look in the wrong direction. In such a story we expect the ending to explain what happened earlier. Sometimes, however, a story moves back; that is, instead of making you think of earlier events, it actually breaks into its own order, reaches back into the history, and presents or dramatizes a scene that happened before the fictional present. In James Baldwin's "Sonny's Blues," for example, there is such a replay or **flashback** (or rather a series of flashbacks). There is a very brief scene from the past triggered by the word "safe" (paragraph 79), the narrator recalling his father's words, which then leads to a specific dramatized scene—the last time the narrator talked to his mother. This is followed by another scene—the narrator's conversation with Sonny after their mother's funeral. This scene of course follows the previous one, but in terms of where the story began (the fictional present) it is in the past and, therefore, is in fact a flashback. Nor does the story return to the fictional present for some time—"I read about Sonny's trouble in the spring. Little Grace died in the fall . . ." (paragraph 177)—when Sonny has been living with the narrator for two weeks, and it proceeds from that point to the end.

One reason for structuring the history into plot is to engage the reader's attention, to make the reader read on. This can be done not only by arousing the reader's expectations of what will happen next but also by generating **curiosity**—the desire to know what is happening or has happened. It is the sheer power of curiosity, for example, that keeps us reading intensely when we know as little as Watson or Sherlock Holmes himself at the beginning of a story or "case." But it is not only the detective story that plays upon our curiosity. "Sonny's Blues" begins, "I read about it in the paper . . . ," and that "it" without antecedent is repeated seven times in the first paragraph and first two sentences of the second paragraph. Read those first two paragraphs and stop. If you try at this point to examine what is going on in your mind, you more than likely will find that you are asking yourself what "it" might refer to, and you will probably have framed for yourself several possible answers. It may be in part for this reason that Baldwin begins how and where he does, getting you engaged in the story, so that you will read on. Even a title, such as "The Zebra Storyteller," "A Very Old Man with Enormous Wings," or "The Rocking-Horse Winner," can make us curious enough to pick up a story; after that, it's up to the story to keep us engaged.

Perhaps stronger than curiosity is **suspense**—that particular kind of expectation involving anticipation of and doubt about what is going to happen next (as differentiated from expectations about what a character is like, what the theme is or how it will develop, and so on). Even in reading a little fable like "The Zebra Storyteller" our minds are—or should be—at work: a cat speaking Zebraic is killing zebras; the zebra storyteller thinking of plots comes up with the idea of a story about a cat that learns to speak Zebraic: "What an idea! That'll make 'em laugh!" he tells himself. Then he meets the cat—what will happen next? How many possibilities did you or can you anticipate? Even though you now know the ending, you could go back to this point in the story and, recalling your expectations, reconstruct or reinvent the rest of the story.

Sometimes the suspense is generated and defined not so much by what happens within the story as it is by what we expect from stories. In "The Jewelry," for example, when Lantin's wife dies so early in the story, we know this is not the end; something is going to happen or be revealed because there are several pages left and stories do not go on unless something is going to happen. But what? Lantin grieves so intensely, locks himself in her room. Will her ghost return? He is going bankrupt, he looks over his wife's jewelry, and when he goes to sell a piece he finds it is not mere costume jewelry, but real. How much sooner than Lantin himself do you realize the source of the jewelry? There is a certain satisfaction in seeing the truth before he does. But *then* what do you expect to happen next? Do you anticipate his debauching? How did you expect the story to end?

If you were to pause just before reading the final paragraph of the Maupassant story and consciously explore your expectations, you would see that these are based on both fictional and actual conventions—indeed, most of us would probably assume the story could have ended with the word "debauch," without the final brief paragraph, and that the story would end with the irony of Lantin's getting pleasure out of his having been betrayed. We can accept this even within our conventional moral terms—he may get bitter pleasures for a time, but he will soon tire of such pleasures or be undone by them.

The final paragraph, however, if it does not contradict, deepens the irony: now he has a truly "upright" wife—and he is miserable. Our conventional expectations that morality brings happiness, that infidelity and debauchery lead to various kinds of ruin, are wrenched into question. He has tired of debauchery, but is he better off leading a moral life? Is the world amoral—or even immoral? Do good guys finish last? We do not have to believe this, but to read the story fully we need to call our perhaps more opti-mistic and conventional views into question.

In order to keep you engaged and alert, a story must make you ask questions about what will happen or what will be revealed next. To respond fully to a story you must be alert to the signals and guess along with the author. One way of seeing whether and how your mind is engaged in your reading is to pause at crucial points in the story and consciously explore what you think is coming. At least in one aspect, fiction is a guessing game.

Like all guessing games, from quiz shows to philosophy, the plot game in fiction has certain guidelines. A well-structured plot will play fair with you, offering at appropriate points all the necessary indications or clues to what will happen next, not just springing new and essential information on you at the last minute ("Meanwhile, unknown to our hero, the Marines were just on the other side of the hill . . ."). It is this playing fair that makes the ending of a well-structured story satisfying or, when you look back on it, inevitable. Most stories also offer a number of reasonable but false signals (red herrings) to get you off the scent, so that in a well-structured story the ending, though inevitable, is also surprising. And though there is usually an overarching action from beginning to end, in many stories there are layers of expectation or suspense, so that as soon as one question is answered another comes forth to replace it, keeping you in doubt as to the final outcome.

Unlike most guessing games, however, the reward is not for the right guess—antic-ipating the outcome before the final paragraph—but for the number of guesses, right *and* wrong, that you make, the number of signals you respond to. If you are misled by none of the false signals in the early pages of a story—by Sonny's friend saying, " 'Listen. They'll let him out and then it'll just start all over again' " (paragraph 36), for example— you may be closer to being "right," but you have missed many of the implications of the story. But, more important, you have missed the pleasure of *learning* the "truth" a story has to offer, and you know how much less meaningful it is to be told something than to learn for yourself, through your own experience. Fiction is a way of transmitting not just perception but experience.

Though plot is the structuring of events, an event can be an outcome or consequence as well as a happening, and the expectation, surprise, and perception surrounding plot structure can involve meaning as well as action, as we have seen in the worldview suggested by the ending of "The Jewelry." Maupassant's ending upsets our conventional thinking about human conduct and morality. Though expectations based on social, moral, or literary conventions that support the ordinary are not so consciously aroused as are those aroused by action and adventure—the kind of expectation described by the term *suspense*—their fulfillment, modification, or contradiction is a significant aim and effect of many stories. Fiction is in part a guessing game, but it is not merely a game. Many stories seek to give new insights into human perception, experience, meaning, or at least to challenge our more or less unconsciously held beliefs. They strive to tell truths—new, subjective truths, but truths—even though they "lie" about the actuality of the people and events represented. But first they have to get your attention, and one way is by arousing your curiosity and exciting your anticipation. That is one of the primary functions of plot. Looking for signals, anticipating what is to come next, and remembering what has been said and signaled earlier are essential to fully appreciating and understanding stories and their structures. That is how you should function as a reader of plot.

MARGARET ATWOOD

Happy Endings

John and Mary meet.
What happens next?
If you want a happy ending, try A.

A. John and Mary fall in love and get married. They both have worthwhile and remunerative jobs which they find stimulating and challenging. They buy a charming house. Real estate values go up. Eventually, when they can afford live-in help, they have two children, to whom they are devoted. The children turn out well. John and Mary have a stimulating and challenging sex life and worthwhile friends. They go on fun vacations together. They retire. They both have hobbies which they find stimulating and challenging. Eventually they die. This is the end of the story.

5   B. Mary falls in love with John but John doesn't fall in love with Mary. He merely uses her body for selfish pleasure and ego gratification of a tepid kind. He comes to her apartment twice a week and she cooks him dinner, you'll notice that he doesn't even consider her worth the price of a dinner out, and after he's eaten the dinner he fucks her and after that he falls asleep, while

she does the dishes so he won't think she's untidy, having all those dirty dishes lying around, and puts on fresh lipstick so she'll look good when he wakes up, but when he wakes up he doesn't even notice, he puts on his socks and his shorts and his pants and his shirt and his tie and his shoes, the reverse order from the one in which he took them off. He doesn't take off Mary's clothes, she takes them off herself, she acts as if she's dying for it every time, not because she likes sex exactly, she doesn't, but she wants John to think she does because if they do it often enough surely he'll get used to her, he'll come to depend on her and they will get married, but John goes out the door with hardly so much as a good-night and three days later he turns up at six o'clock and they do the whole thing over again.

Mary gets run-down. Crying is bad for your face, everyone knows that and so does Mary but she can't stop. People at work notice. Her friends tell her John is a rat, a pig, a dog, he isn't good enough for her, but she can't believe it. Inside John, she thinks, is another John, who is much nicer. This other John will emerge like a butterfly from a cocoon, a Jack from a box, a pit from a prune, if the first John is only squeezed enough.

One evening John complains about the food. He has never complained about the food before. Mary is hurt.

Her friends tell her they've seen him in a restaurant with another woman, whose name is Madge. It's not even Madge that finally gets to Mary: it's the restaurant. John has never taken Mary to a restaurant. Mary collects all the sleeping pills and aspirins she can find, and takes them and a half a bottle of sherry. You can see what kind of a woman she is by the fact that it's not even whiskey. She leaves a note for John. She hopes he'll discover her and get her to the hospital in time and repent and then they can get married, but this fails to happen and she dies.

John marries Madge and everything continues as in A.

C.   John, who is an older man, falls in love with Mary, and Mary, who is only   10
twenty-two, feels sorry for him because he's worried about his hair falling out. She sleeps with him even though she's not in love with him. She met him at work. She's in love with someone called James, who is twenty-two also and not yet ready to settle down.

John on the contrary settled down long ago: this is what is bothering him. John has a steady, respectable job and is getting ahead in his field, but Mary isn't impressed by him, she's impressed by James, who has a motorcycle and a fabulous record collection. But James is often away on his motorcycle, being free. Freedom isn't the same for girls, so in the meantime Mary spends Thursday evenings with John. Thursdays are the only days John can get away.

John is married to a woman called Madge and they have two children, a charming house which they bought just before the real estate values went up, and hobbies which they find stimulating and challenging, when they have the time. John tells Mary how important she is to him, but of course he can't leave his wife because a commitment is a commitment. He goes on about this more than is necessary and Mary finds it boring, but older men can keep it up longer so on the whole she has a fairly good time.

One day James breezes in on his motorcycle with some top-grade California hybrid and James and Mary get higher than you'd believe possible and they climb into bed. Everything becomes very underwater, but along comes John, who has a key to Mary's apartment. He finds them stoned and entwined. He's hardly in any position to be jealous, considering Madge, but nevertheless he's overcome with despair. Finally he's middle-aged, in two years he'll be bald as an egg and he can't stand it. He purchases a handgun, saying he needs it for target practice—this is the thin part of the plot, but it can be dealt with later—and shoots the two of them and himself.

Madge, after a suitable period of mourning, marries an understanding man called Fred and everything continues as in A, but under different names.

15   D.   Fred and Madge have no problems. They get along exceptionally well and are good at working out any little difficulties that may arise. But their charming house is by the seashore and one day a giant tidal wave approaches. Real estate values go down. The rest of the story is about what caused the tidal wave and how they escape from it. They do, though thousands drown, but Fred and Madge are virtuous and lucky. Finally on high ground they clasp each other, wet and dripping and grateful, and continue as in A.

E.   Yes, but Fred has a bad heart. The rest of the story is about how kind and understanding they both are until Fred dies. Then Madge devotes herself to charity work until the end of A. If you like, it can be "Madge," "cancer," "guilty and confused," and "bird watching."

F.   If you think this is all too bourgeois, make John a revolutionary and Mary a counterespionage agent and see how far that gets you. Remember, this is Canada. You'll still end up with A, though in between you may get a lustful brawling saga of passionate involvement, a chronicle of our times, sort of.

You'll have to face it, the endings are the same however you slice it. Don't be deluded by any other endings, they're all fake, either deliberately fake, with malicious intent to deceive, or just motivated by excessive optimism if not by downright sentimentality.

The only authentic ending is the one provided here:

20   *John and Mary die. John and Mary die. John and Mary die.*

So much for endings. Beginnings are always more fun. True connoisseurs, however, are known to favor the stretch in between, since it's the hardest to do anything with.

That's about all that can be said for plots, which anyway are just one thing after another, a what and a what and a what.

Now try How and Why.

1983

JOHN CHEEVER

The Country Husband

To begin at the beginning, the airplane from Minneapolis in which Francis Weed was traveling East ran into heavy weather. The sky had been a hazy blue, with the clouds below the plane lying so close together that nothing could be seen of the earth. The mist began to form outside the windows, and they flew into a white cloud of such density that it reflected the exhaust fires. The color of the cloud darkened to gray, and the plane began to rock. Francis had been in heavy weather before, but he had never been shaken up so much. The man in the seat beside him pulled a flask out of his pocket and took a drink. Francis smiled at his neighbor, but the man looked away; he wasn't sharing his pain killer with anyone. The plane began to drop and flounder wildly. A child was crying. The air in the cabin was overheated and stale, and Francis' left foot went to sleep. He read a little from a paper book that he had bought at the airport, but the violence of the storm divided his attention. It was black outside the ports. The exhaust fires blazed and shed sparks in the dark, and, inside, the shaded lights, the stuffiness, and the window curtains gave the cabin an atmosphere of intense and misplaced domesticity. Then the light flickered and went out. "You know what I've always wanted to do?" the man beside Francis said suddenly. "I've always wanted to buy a farm in New Hampshire and raise beef cattle." The stewardess announced that they were going to make an emergency landing. All but the children saw in their minds the spreading wings of the Angel of Death. The pilot could be heard singing faintly, "I've got sixpence, jolly, jolly sixpence. I've got sixpence to last me all my life . . ."[1] There was no other sound.

The loud groaning of the hydraulic valves swallowed up the pilot's song, and there was a shrieking high in the air, like automobile brakes, and the plane hit flat on its belly in a cornfield and shook them so violently that an old man up forward howled, "Me kidneys! Me kidneys!" The stewardess flung open the door, and someone opened an emergency door at the back, letting in the sweet noise of their continuing mortality—the idle splash and smell of a heavy rain. Anxious for their lives, they filed out of the doors and scattered over the cornfield in all directions, praying that the thread would hold. It did. Nothing happened. When it was clear that the plane would not burn or explode, the crew and the stewardess gathered the passengers together and led them to the shelter of a barn. They were not far from Philadelphia, and in a little while a string of taxis took them into the city. "It's just like the Marne,"[2] someone said, but there was surprisingly little relaxation of that suspiciousness with which many Americans regard their fellow travelers.

In Philadelphia, Francis Weed got a train to New York. At the end of that journey, he crossed the city and caught just as it was about to pull out the com-

---

1. Song popular with Allied troops in World War II.   2. On September 8, 1914, over one thousand Paris taxicabs were requisitioned to move troops to the Marne River to halt the encircling Germans.

muting train that he took five nights a week to his home in Shady Hill.

He sat with Trace Bearden. "You know, I was in that plane that just crashed outside Philadelphia," he said. "We came down in a field . . ." He had traveled faster than the newspapers or the rain, and the weather in New York was sunny and mild. It was a day in late September, as fragrant and shapely as an apple. Trace listened to the story, but how could he get excited? Francis had no powers that would let him re-create a brush with death—particularly in the atmosphere of a commuting train, journeying through a sunny countryside where already, in the slum gardens, there were signs of harvest. Trace picked up his newspaper, and Francis was left alone with his thoughts. He said good night to Trace on the platform at Shady Hill and drove in his secondhand Volkswagen up to the Blen-hollow neighborhood, where he lived.

5   The Weeds' Dutch Colonial house was larger than it appeared to be from the driveway. The living room was spacious and divided like Gaul,[3] into three parts. Around an ell to the left as one entered from the vestibule was the long table, laid for six, with candles and a bowl of fruit in the center. The sounds and smells that came from the open kitchen door were appetizing, for Julia Weed was a good cook. The largest part of the living room centered on a fireplace. On the right were some bookshelves and a piano. The room was polished and tranquil, and from the windows that opened to the west there was some late-summer sunlight, brilliant and as clear as water. Nothing here was neglected; nothing had not been burnished. It was not the kind of household where, after prying open a stuck cigarette box, you would find an old shirt button and a tarnished nickel. The hearth was swept, the roses on the piano were reflected in the polish of the broad top, and there was an album of Schubert waltzes on the rack. Louisa Weed, a pretty girl of nine, was looking out the western windows. Her young brother Henry was standing beside her. Her still younger brother, Toby, was studying the figures of some tonsured monks drinking beer on the polished brass of the woodbox. Francis, taking off his hat and putting down his paper, was not consciously pleased with the scene; he was not that reflective. It was his element, his creation, and he returned to it with that sense of lightness and strength with which any creature returns to his home. "Hi, everybody," he said. "The plane from Minneapolis . . ."

Nine times out of ten, Francis would be greeted with affection, but tonight the children are absorbed in their own antagonisms. Francis had not finished his sentence about the plane crash before Henry plants a kick in Louisa's behind. Louisa swings around, saying, "*Damn you!*" Francis makes the mistake of scolding Louisa for bad language before he punishes Henry. Now Louisa turns on her father and accuses him of favoritism. Henry is always right; she is persecuted and lonely; her lot is hopeless. Francis turns to his son, but the son has justification for the kick—she hit him first; she hit him on the ear, which is dangerous. Louisa agrees with this passionately. She hit him on the ear, and she *meant* to hit him on the ear, because he messed up her china collection. Henry says that this is a lie. Little Toby turns away from the woodbox to throw in some evidence for Louisa. Henry

---

3. Ancient France (Gaul) is so described by Julius Caesar in *The Gallic War*.

claps his hand over little Toby's mouth. Francis separates the two boys but accidentally pushes Toby into the woodbox. Toby begins to cry. Louisa is already crying. Just then, Julia Weed comes into that part of the room where the table is laid. She is a pretty, intelligent woman, and the white in her hair is premature. She does not seem to notice the fracas. "Hello, darling," she says serenely to Francis. "Wash your hands, everyone. Dinner is ready." She strikes a match and lights the six candles in this vale of tears.[4]

This simple announcement, like the war cries of the Scottish chieftains, only refreshes the ferocity of the combatants. Louisa gives Henry a blow on the shoulder. Henry, although he seldom cries, has pitched nine innings and is tired. He bursts into tears. Little Toby discovers a splinter in his hand and begins to howl. Francis says loudly that he has been in a plane crash and that he is tired. Julia appears again from the kitchen and, still ignoring the chaos, asks Francis to go upstairs and tell Helen that everything is ready. Francis is happy to go; it is like getting back to headquarters company.[5] He is planning to tell his oldest daughter about the airplane crash, but Helen is lying on her bed reading a *True Romance* magazine, and the first thing Francis does is to take the magazine from her hand and remind Helen that he has forbidden her to buy it. She did not buy it, Helen replies. It was given to her by her best friend, Bessie Black. Everybody reads *True Romance*. Bessie Black's father reads *True Romance*. There isn't a girl in Helen's class who doesn't read *True Romance*. Francis expresses his detestation of the magazine and then tells her that dinner is ready—although from the sounds downstairs it doesn't seem so. Helen follows him down the stairs. Julia has seated herself in the candlelight and spread a napkin over her lap. Neither Louisa nor Henry has come to the table. Little Toby is still howling, lying face down on the floor. Francis speaks to him gently: "Daddy was in a plane crash this afternoon, Toby. Don't you want to hear about it?" Toby goes on crying. "If you don't come to the table now, Toby," Francis says, "I'll have to send you to bed without any supper." The little boy rises, gives him a cutting look, flies up the stairs to his bedroom, and slams the door. "Oh, dear," Julia says, and starts to go after him. Francis says that she will spoil him. Julia says that Toby is ten pounds underweight and has to be encouraged to eat. Winter is coming, and he will spend the cold months in bed unless he has his dinner. Julia goes upstairs. Francis sits down at the table with Helen. Helen is suffering from the dismal feeling of having read too intently on a fine day, and she gives her father and the room a jaded look. She doesn't understand about the plane crash, because there wasn't a drop of rain in Shady Hill.

Julia returns with Toby, and they all sit down and are served. "Do I have to look at that big, fat slob?" Henry says, of Louisa. Everybody but Toby enters into this skirmish, and it rages up and down the table for five minutes. Toward the end, Henry puts his napkin over his head and, trying to eat that way, spills spinach all over his shirt. Francis asks Julia if the children couldn't have their dinner earlier. Julia's guns are loaded for this. She can't cook two dinners and lay two

---

4. Common figurative reference to earthly life (vale is valley), though here the tears are literal.   5. That is, like escaping from combat to relative safety behind the lines.

tables. She paints with lightning strokes that panorama of drudgery in which her youth, her beauty, and her wit have been lost. Francis says that he must be understood; he was nearly killed in an airplane crash, and he doesn't like to come home every night to a battlefield. Now Julia is deeply concerned. Her voice trembles. He doesn't come home every night to a battlefield. The accusation is stupid and mean. Everything was tranquil until he arrived. She stops speaking, puts down her knife and fork, and looks into her plate as if it is a gulf. She begins to cry. "Poor Mummy!" Toby says, and when Julia gets up from the table, drying her tears with a napkin, Toby goes to her side. "Poor Mummy," he says. "Poor Mummy!" And they climb the stairs together. The other children drift away from the battlefield, and Francis goes into the back garden for a cigarette and some air.

It was a pleasant garden, with walks and flower beds and places to sit. The sunset had nearly burned out, but there was still plenty of light. Put into a thoughtful mood by the crash and the battle, Francis listened to the evening sounds of Shady Hill. "Varmints! Rascals!" old Mr. Nixon shouted to the squirrels in his bird-feeding station. "Avaunt and quit my sight!" A door slammed. Someone was cutting grass. Then Donald Goslin, who lived at the corner, began to play the "Moonlight Sonata."[6] He did this nearly every night. He threw the tempo out the window and played it *rubato*[7] from beginning to end, like an outpouring of tearful petulance, lonesomeness, and self-pity—of everything it was Beethoven's greatness not to know. The music rang up and down the street beneath the trees like an appeal for love, for tenderness, aimed at some lovely housemaid—some fresh-faced, homesick girl from Galway, looking at old snapshots in her third-floor room. "Here, Jupiter, here, Jupiter," Francis called to the Mercers' retriever. Jupiter crashed through the tomato vines with the remains of a felt hat in his mouth.

10   Jupiter was an anomaly. His retrieving instincts and his high spirits were out of place in Shady Hill. He was as black as coal, with a long, alert, intelligent, rakehell face. His eyes gleamed with mischief, and he held his head high. It was the fierce, heavily collared dog's head that appears in heraldry, in tapestry, and that used to appear on umbrella handles and walking sticks. Jupiter went where he pleased, ransacking wastebaskets, clotheslines, garbage pails, and shoe bags. He broke up garden parties and tennis matches, and got mixed up in the processional at Christ Church on Sunday, barking at the men in red dresses.[8] He crashed through old Mr. Nixon's rose garden two or three times a day, cutting a wide swath through the Condesa de Sastagos,[9] and as soon as Donald Goslin lighted his barbecue fire on Thursday nights, Jupiter would get the scent. Nothing the Goslins did could drive him away. Sticks and stones and rude commands only moved him to the edge of the terrace, where he remained, with his gallant and heraldic muzzle, waiting for Donald Goslin to turn his back and reach for the salt. Then he would spring onto the terrace, lift the steak lightly off the fire, and run

6. Beethoven's *Sonata Quasi una Fantasia* (1802), a famous and frequently sentimentalized piano composition.   7. With intentional deviations from strict tempo.   8. Probably the choir.   9. Uncommon yellow and red roses, difficult to grow.

away with the Goslins' dinner. Jupiter's days were numbered. The Wrightsons' German gardener or the Farquarsons' cook would soon poison him. Even old Mr. Nixon might put some arsenic in the garbage that Jupiter loved. "Here, Jupiter, Jupiter!" Francis called, but the dog pranced off, shaking the hat in his white teeth. Looking at the windows of his house, Francis saw that Julia had come down and was blowing out the candles.

Julia and Francis Weed went out a great deal. Julia was well liked and gregarious, and her love of parties sprang from a most natural dread of chaos and loneliness. She went through the morning mail with real anxiety, looking for invitations, and she usually found some, but she was insatiable, and if she had gone out seven nights a week, it would not have cured her of a reflective look— the look of someone who hears distant music—for she would always suppose that there was a more brilliant party somewhere else. Francis limited her to two weeknight parties, putting a flexible interpretation on Friday, and rode through the weekend like a dory in a gale. The day after the airplane crash, the Weeds were to have dinner with the Farquarsons.

Francis got home late from town, and Julia got the sitter while he dressed, and then hurried him out of the house. The party was small and pleasant, and Francis settled down to enjoy himself. A new maid passed the drinks. Her hair was dark, and her face was round and pale and seemed familiar to Francis. He had not developed his memory as a sentimental faculty. Wood smoke, lilac, and other such perfumes did not stir him, and his memory was something like his appendix—a vestigial repository. It was not his limitation at all to be unable to escape the past; it was perhaps his limitation that he had escaped it so successfully. He might have seen the maid at other parties, he might have seen her taking a walk on Sunday afternoons, but in either case he would not be searching his memory now. Her face was, in a wonderful way, a moon face—Norman or Irish—but it was not beautiful enough to account for his feeling that he had seen her before, in circumstances that he ought to be able to remember. He asked Nellie Farquarson who she was. Nellie said that the maid had come through an agency, and that her home was Trénon, in Normandy—a small place with a church and a restaurant that Nellie had once visited. While Nellie talked on about her travels abroad, Francis realized where he had seen the woman before. It had been at the end of the war. He had left a replacement depot with some other men and taken a three-day pass in Trénon. On their second day, they had walked out to a crossroads to see the public chastisement of a young woman who had lived with the German commandant during the Occupation.

It was a cool morning in the fall. The sky was overcast, and poured down onto the dirt crossroads a very discouraging light. They were on high land and could see how like one another the shapes of the clouds and the hills were as they stretched off toward the sea. The prisoner arrived sitting on a three-legged stool in a farm cart. She stood by the cart while the Mayor read the accusation and the sentence. Her head was bent and her face was set in that empty half smile behind which the whipped soul is suspended. When the Mayor was finished, she undid her hair and let it fall across her back. A little man with a gray mustache cut off her hair with shears and dropped it on the ground. Then, with a bowl of soapy water and a straight razor, he shaved her skull clean. A woman approached and began to undo the fastenings of her clothes, but the prisoner pushed her aside and undressed herself. When she pulled her chemise over her head and threw it on the ground, she was naked. The women jeered; the men were still. There was no change in the falseness or the plaintiveness of the prisoner's smile. The cold wind made her white skin rough and hardened the nipples of her breasts. The jeering ended gradually, put down by the recognition of their common humanity. One woman spat on her, but some inviolable grandeur in her nakedness lasted through the ordeal. When the crowd was quiet, she turned—she had begun to cry—and, with nothing on but a pair of worn black shoes and stockings, walked down the dirt road alone away from the village. The round white face had aged a little, but there was no question but that the maid who passed his cocktails and later served Francis his dinner was the woman who had been punished at the crossroads.

The war seemed now so distant and that world where the cost of partisanship had been death or torture so long ago. Francis had lost track of the men who had been with him in Vésey. He could not count on Julia's discretion. He could not tell anyone. And if he had told the story now, at the dinner table, it would have been a social as well as a human error. The people in the Farquarsons' living room seemed united in their tacit claim that there had been no past, no war—that there was no danger or trouble in the world. In the recorded history of human arrangements, this extraordinary meeting would have fallen into place, but the atmosphere of Shady Hill made the memory unseemly and impolite. The prisoner withdrew after passing the coffee, but the encounter left Francis feeling languid; it had opened his memory and his senses, and left them dilated. Julia went into the house. Francis stayed in the car to take the sitter home.

15   Expecting to see Mrs. Henlein, the old lady who usually stayed with the children, he was surprised when a young girl opened the door and came out onto the lighted stoop. She stayed in the light to count her textbooks. She was frowning and beautiful. Now, the world is full of beautiful young girls, but Francis saw here the difference between beauty and perfection. All those endearing flaws, moles, birthmarks, and healed wounds were missing, and he experienced in his consciousness that moment when music breaks glass, and felt a pang of recognition as strange, deep and wonderful as anything in his life. It hung from her frown, from an impalpable darkness in her face—a look that impressed him as a direct appeal for love. When she had counted her books, she came down the steps and opened the car door. In the light, he saw that her cheeks were wet. She got in and shut the door.

"You're new," Francis said.

"Yes. Mrs. Henlein is sick. I'm Anne Murchison."

"Did the children give you any trouble?"

"Oh, no, no." She turned and smiled at him unhappily in the dim dashboard light. Her light hair caught on the collar of her jacket, and she shook her head to set it loose.

20   "You've been crying."

"Yes."

"I hope it was nothing that happened in our house."

"No, no, it was nothing that happened in your house." Her voice was bleak. "It's no secret. Everybody in the village knows. Daddy's an alcoholic, and he just called me from some saloon and gave me a piece of his mind. He thinks I'm immoral. He called just before Mrs. Weed came back."

"I'm sorry."

"Oh, *Lord!*" She gasped and began to cry. She turned toward Francis, and he took her in his arms and let her cry on his shoulder. She shook in his embrace, and this movement accentuated his sense of the fineness of her flesh and bone. The layers of their clothing felt thin, and when her shuddering began to diminish, it was so much like a paroxysm of love that Francis lost his head and pulled her roughly against him. She drew away. "I live on Belleview Avenue," she said. "You go down Lansing Street to the railroad bridge."

"All right." He started the car.

"You turn left at that traffic light. . . . Now you turn right here and go straight on toward the tracks."

The road Francis took brought him out of his own neighborhood, across the tracks, and toward the river, to a street where the near-poor lived, in houses whose peaked gables and trimmings of wooden lace conveyed the purest feelings of pride and romance, although the houses themselves could not have offered much privacy or comfort, they were all so small. The street was dark, and, stirred by the grace and beauty of the troubled girl, he seemed, in turning into it, to have come into the deepest part of some submerged memory. In the distance, he saw a porch light burning. It was the only one, and she said that the house with the light was where she lived. When he stopped the car, he could see beyond the porch light into a dimly lighted hallway with an old-fashioned clothes tree. "Well, here we are," he said, conscious that a young man would have said something different.

She did not move her hands from the books, where they were folded, and she turned and faced him. There were tears of lust in his eyes. Determinedly—not sadly—he opened the door on his side and walked around to open hers. He took her free hand, letting his fingers in between hers, climbed at her side the two concrete steps, and went up a narrow walk through a front garden where dahlias, marigolds, and roses—things that had withstood the light frosts—still bloomed, and made a bittersweet smell in the night air. At the steps, she freed her hand and then turned and kissed him swiftly. Then she crossed the porch and shut the door. The porch light went out, then the light in the hall. A second later, a light went on upstairs at the side of the house, shining into a tree that was still covered with leaves. It took her only a few minutes to undress and get into bed, and then the house was dark.

Julia was asleep when Francis got home. He opened a second window and got into bed to shut his eyes on that night, but as soon as they were shut—as soon as he had dropped off to sleep—the girl entered his mind, moving with perfect freedom through its shut doors and filling chamber after chamber with her light, her perfume, and the music of her voice. He was crossing the Atlantic with her on the old *Mauretania*[1] and, later, living with her in Paris. When he woke from his dream, he got up and smoked a cigarette at the open window. Getting back into bed, he cast around in his mind for something he desired to do that would injure no one, and he thought of skiing. Up through the dimness in his mind rose the image of a mountain deep in snow. It was late in the day. Wherever his eyes looked, he saw broad and heartening things. Over his shoulder, there was a snow-filled valley, rising into wooded hills where the trees dimmed the whiteness like a sparse coat of hair. The cold deadened all sound but the loud, iron clanking of the lift machinery. The light on the trails was blue, and it was harder than it had been a minute or two earlier to pick the turns, harder to judge—now that the snow was all deep blue—the crust, the ice, the bare spots, and the deep piles of dry powder. Down the mountain he swung, matching his speed against the contours of a slope that had been formed in the first ice age, seeking with ardor some simplicity of feeling and circumstance. Night fell then, and he drank a Martini with some old friend in a dirty country bar.

In the morning, Francis' snow-covered mountain was gone, and he was left with his vivid memories of Paris and the *Mauretania*. He had been bitten gravely. He washed his body, shaved his jaws, drank his coffee, and missed the seventy-thirty-one. The train pulled out just as he brought his car to the station, and the longing he felt for the coaches as they drew stubbornly away from him reminded him of the humors of love. He waited for the eight-two, on what was now an empty platform. It was a clear morning; the morning seemed thrown like a gleaming bridge of light over his mixed affairs. His spirits were feverish and high. The image of the girl seemed to put him into a relationship to the world that was mysterious and enthralling. Cars were beginning to fill up the parking lot, and he noticed that those that had driven down from the high land above Shady Hill were white with hoarfrost. This first clear sign of autumn thrilled him. An express train—a night train from Buffalo or Albany—came down the tracks between the platforms, and he saw that the roofs of the foremost cars were covered with a skin of ice. Struck by the miraculous physicalness of everything, he smiled at the passengers in the dining car, who could be seen eating eggs and wiping their mouths with napkins as they traveled. The sleeping-car compartments, with their soiled bed linen, trailed through the fresh morning like a string of rooming-house windows. Then he saw an extraordinary thing; at one of the bedroom windows sat an unclothed woman of exceptional beauty, combing her golden hair. She passed like an apparition through Shady Hill, combing and combing her hair, and Francis followed her with his eyes until she was out of sight. Then old Mrs. Wrightson joined him on the platform and began to talk.

"Well, I guess you must be surprised to see me here the third morning in a row," she said, "but because of my window curtains I'm becoming a regular commuter. The curtains I bought on Monday I returned on Tuesday, and the curtains I bought Tuesday I'm returning today. On Monday, I got exactly what I wanted—it's a wool tapestry with roses and birds—but when I got them home, I found

---

1. The original *Mauretania* (1907–1935), sister ship of the *Lusitania*, which was sunk by the Germans in 1915, was the most famous transatlantic liner of its day.

they were the wrong length. Well, I exchanged them yesterday, and when I got them home, I found they were still the wrong length. Now I'm praying to high heaven that the decorator will have them in the right length, because you know my house, you *know* my living-room windows, and you can imagine what a problem they present. I don't know what to do with them."

"I know what to do with them," Francis said.

"What?"

"Paint them black on the inside, and shut up."

There was a gasp from Mrs. Wrightson, and Francis looked down at her to be sure that she knew he meant to be rude. She turned and walked away from him, so damaged in spirit that she limped. A wonderful feeling enveloped him, as if light were being shaken about him, and he thought again of Venus combing and combing her hair as she drifted through the Bronx. The realization of how many years had passed since he had enjoyed being deliberately impolite sobered him. Among his friends and neighbors, there were brilliant and gifted people—he saw that—but many of them, also, were bores and fools, and he had made the mistake of listening to them all with equal attention. He had confused a lack of discrimination with Christian love, and the confusion seemed general and destructive. He was grateful to the girl for this bracing sensation of independence. Birds were singing—cardinals and the last of the robins. The sky shone like enamel. Even the smell of ink from his morning paper honed his appetite for life, and the world that was spread out around him was plainly a paradise.

If Francis had believed in some hierarchy of love—in spirits armed with hunting bows, in the capriciousness of Venus and Eros[2]—or even in magical potions, philters, and stews, in scapulae and quarters of the moon,[3] it might have explained his susceptibility and his feverish high spirits. The autumnal loves of middle age are well publicized, and he guessed that he was face to face with one of these, but there was not a trace of autumn in what he felt. He wanted to sport in the green woods, scratch where he itched, and drink from the same cup.

His secretary, Miss Rainey, was late that morning—she went to a psychiatrist three mornings a week—and when she came in, Francis wondered what advice a psychiatrist would have for him. But the girl promised to bring back into his life something like the sound of music. The realization that this music might lead him straight to a trial for statutory rape at the country courthouse collapsed his happiness. The photograph of his four children laughing into the camera on the beach at Gay Head reproached him. On the letterhead of his firm there was a drawing of the Laocoön,[4] and the figure of the priest and his sons in the coils of the snake appeared to him to have the deepest meaning.

He had lunch with Pinky Trabert. At a conversational level, the mores of his friends were robust and elastic, but he knew that the moral card house would

2. Roman name for the goddess of love (Greek: *Aphrodite*) and Greek name for her son (Roman: *Cupid*).   3. Love-inducing and predictive magic. *Scapulae:* shoulderblades or bones of the back. 4. Famous Greek statue, described here, now in the Vatican museum; the "meaning" for Weed seems to reside in the physical struggle, not in the legend (in which the priest and his sons were punished for warning the Trojans about the wooden horse).

come down on them all—on Julia and the children as well—if he got caught taking advantage of a baby-sitter. Looking back over the recent history of Shady Hill for some precedent, he found there was none. There was no turpitude; there had not been a divorce since he lived there; there had not even been a breath of scandal. Things seemed arranged with more propriety even than in the Kingdom of Heaven. After leaving Pinky, Francis went to a jeweler's and bought the girl a bracelet. How happy this clandestine purchase made him, how stuffy and comical the jeweler's clerks seemed, how sweet the women who passed at his back smelled! On Fifth Avenue, passing Atlas with his shoulders bent under the weight of the world,[5] Francis thought of the strenuousness of containing his physicalness within the patterns he had chosen.

40   He did not know when he would see the girl next. He had the bracelet in his inside pocket when he got home. Opening the door of his house, he found her in the hall. Her back was to him, and she turned when she heard the door close. Her smile was open and loving. Her perfection stunned him like a fine day—a day after a thunderstorm. He seized her and covered her lips with his, and she struggled but she did not have to struggle for long, because just then little Gertrude Flannery appeared from somewhere and said, "Oh, Mr. Weed . . ."

Gertrude was a stray. She had been born with a taste for exploration, and she did not have it in her to center her life with her affectionate parents. People who did not know the Flannerys concluded from Gertrude's behavior that she was the child of a bitterly divided family, where drunken quarrels were the rule. This was not true. The fact that little Gertrude's clothing was ragged and thin was her own triumph over her mother's struggle to dress her warmly and neatly. Garrulous, skinny, and unwashed, she drifted from house to house around the Blenhollow neighborhood, forming and breaking alliances based on an attachment to babies, animals, children her own age, adolescents, and sometimes adults. Opening your front door in the morning, you would find Gertrude sitting on your stoop. Going into the bathroom to shave, you would find Gertrude using the toilet. Looking into your son's crib, you would find it empty, and, looking further, you would find that Gertrude had pushed him in his baby carriage into the next village. She was helpful, pervasive, honest, hungry, and loyal. She never went home of her own choice. When the time to go arrived, she was indifferent to all its signs. "Go home, Gertrude," people could be heard saying in one house or another, night after night. "Go home, Gertrude. It's time for you to go home now, Gertrude." "You had better go home and get your supper, Gertrude." "I told you to go home twenty minutes ago, Gertrude." "Your mother will be worrying about you, Gertrude." "Go home, Gertrude, go home."

There are times when the lines around the human eye seem like shelves of eroded stone and when the staring eye itself strikes us with such a wilderness of animal feeling that we are at a loss. The look Francis gave the little girl was ugly and queer, and it frightened her. He reached into his pockets—his hands were shaking—and took out a quarter. "Go home, Gertrude, go home, and don't tell

5. In Greek legend the Titan Atlas supported the heavens on his shoulders, but he has come to be depicted as bearing the globe; the statue is at Rockefeller Center.

anyone, Gertrude. Don't—" He choked and ran into the living room as Julia called down to him from upstairs to hurry and dress.

The thought that he would drive Anne Murchison home later that night ran like a golden thread through the events of the party that Francis and Julia went to, and he laughed uproariously at dull jokes, dried a tear when Mabel Mercer told him about the death of her kitten, and stretched, yawned, sighed, and grunted like any other man with a rendezvous at the back of his mind. The bracelet was in his pocket. As he sat talking, the smell of grass was in his nose, and he was wondering where he would park the car. Nobody lived in the old Parker mansion, and the driveway was used as a lovers' lane. Townsend Street was a dead end, and he could park there, beyond the last house. The old lane that used to connect Elm Street to the riverbanks was overgrown, but he had walked there with his children, and he could drive his car deep enough into the brushwoods to be concealed.

The Weeds were the last to leave the party, and their host and hostess spoke of their own married happiness while they all four stood in the hallway saying good night. "She's my girl," their host said, squeezing his wife. "She's my blue sky. After sixteen years, I still bite her shoulders. She makes me feel like Hannibal crossing the Alps."[6]

The Weeds drove home in silence. Francis brought the car up the driveway and sat still, with the motor running. "You can put the car in the garage," Julia said as she got out. "I told the Murchison girl she could leave at eleven. Someone drove her home." She shut the door, and Francis sat in the dark. He would be spared nothing then, it seemed, that a fool was not spared: ravening lewdness, jealousy, this hurt to his feelings that put tears in his eyes, even scorn—for he could see clearly the image he now presented, his arms spread over the steering wheel and his head buried in them for love.

Francis had been a dedicated Boy Scout when he was young, and, remembering the precepts of his youth, he left his office early the next afternoon and played some round-robin squash, but, with his body toned up by exercise and a shower, he realized that he might better have stayed at his desk. It was a frosty night when he got home. The air smelled sharply of change. When he stepped into the house, he sensed an unusual stir. The children were in their best clothes, and when Julia came down, she was wearing a lavender dress and her diamond sunburst. She explained the stir: Mr. Hubber was coming at seven to take their photograph for the Christmas card. She had put out Francis' blue suit and a tie with some color in it, because the picture was going to be in color this year. Julia was lighthearted at the thought of being photographed for Christmas. It was the kind of ceremony she enjoyed.

Francis went upstairs to change his clothes. He was tired from the day's work and tired with longing, and sitting on the edge of the bed had the effect of deepening his weariness. He thought of Anne Murchison, and the physical need to

6. The Carthaginian general (274–183 B.C.) attacked the Romans from the rear by crossing the Alps, considered impregnable, with the use of elephants.

express himself, instead of being restrained by the pink lamps of Julia's dressing table, engulfed him. He went to Julia's desk, took a piece of writing paper, and began to write on it. "Dear Anne, I love you, I love you, I love you . . ." No one would see the letter, and he used no restraint. He used phrases like "heavenly bliss," and "love nest." He salivated, sighed, and trembled. When Julia called him to come down, the abyss between his fantasy and the practical world opened so wide that he felt it affected the muscles of his heart.

Julia and the children were on the stoop, and the photographer and his assistant had set up a double battery of floodlights to show the family and the architectural beauty of the entrance to their house. People who had come home on a late train slowed their cars to see the Weeds being photographed for their Christmas card. A few waved and called to the family. It took half an hour of smiling and wetting their lips before Mr. Hubber was satisfied. The heat of the lights made an unfresh smell in the frosty air, and when they were turned off, they lingered on the retina of Francis' eyes.

Later that night, while Francis and Julia were drinking their coffee in the living room, the doorbell rang. Julia answered the door and let in Clayton Thomas. He had come to pay for some theatre tickets that she had given his mother some time ago, and that Helen Thomas had scrupulously insisted on paying for, though Julia had asked her not to. Julia invited him in to have a cup of coffee. "I won't have any coffee," Clayton said, "but I will come in for a minute." He followed her into the living room, said good evening to Francis, and sat awkwardly in a chair.

50   Clayton's father had been killed in the war, and the young man's fatherlessness surrounded him like an element. This may have been conspicuous in Shady Hill because the Thomases were the only family that lacked a piece; all the other marriages were intact and productive. Clayton was in his second or third year of college, and he and his mother lived alone in a large house, which she hoped to sell. Clayton had once made some trouble. Years ago, he had stolen some money and run away; he had got to California before they caught up with him. He was tall and homely, wore horn-rimmed glasses, and spoke in a deep voice.

"When do you go back to college, Clayton?" Francis asked.

"I'm not going back," Clayton said. "Mother doesn't have the money, and there's no sense in all this pretense. I'm going to get a job, and if we sell the house, we'll take an apartment in New York."

"Won't you miss Shady Hill?" Julia asked.

"No," Clayton said. "I don't like it."

55   "Why not?" Francis asked.

"Well, there's a lot here I don't approve of," Clayton said gravely. "Things like the club dances. Last Saturday night, I looked in toward the end and saw Mr. Granner trying to put Mrs. Minot into the trophy case. They were both drunk. I disapprove of so much drinking."

"It was Saturday night," Francis said.

"And all the dovecotes are phony," Clayton said. "And the way people clutter up their lives. I've thought about it a lot, and what seems to me to be really wrong with Shady Hill is that it doesn't have any future. So much energy is spent in perpetuating the place—in keeping out undesirables, and so forth—that the only idea of the future anyone has is just more and more commuting trains and more parties. I don't think that's healthy. I think people ought to be able to dream big dreams about the future. I think people ought to be able to dream great dreams."

"It's too bad you couldn't continue with college," Julia said.

"I want to go to divinity school," Clayton said.   60

"What's your church?" Francis asked.

"Unitarian, Theosophist, Transcendentalist, Humanist,"[7] Clayton said.

"Wasn't Emerson a transcendentalist?" Julia asked.

"I mean the English transcendentalists," Clayton said. "All the American transcendentalists were goops."

"What kind of job do you expect to get?" Francis asked.   65

"Well, I'd like to work for a publisher," Clayton said, "but everyone tells me there's nothing doing. But it's the kind of thing I'm interested in. I'm writing a long verse play about good and evil. Uncle Charlie might get me into a bank, and that would be good for me. I need the discipline. I have a long way to go in forming my character. I have some terrible habits. I talk too much. I think I ought to take vows of silence. I ought to try not to speak for a week, and discipline myself. I've thought of making a retreat at one of the Episcopalian monasteries, but I don't like Trinitarianism."

"Do you have any girl friends?" Francis asked.

"I'm engaged to be married," Clayton said. "Of course, I'm not old enough or rich enough to have my engagement observed or respected or anything, but I bought a simulated emerald for Anne Murchison with the money I made cutting lawns this summer. We're going to be married as soon as she finishes school."

Francis recoiled at the mention of the girl's name. Then a dingy light seemed to emanate from his spirit, showing everything—Julia, the boy, the chairs—in their true colorlessness. It was like a bitter turn of the weather.

"We're going to have a large family," Clayton said. "Her father's a terrible   70
rummy, and I've had my hard times, and we want to have lots of children. Oh, she's wonderful, Mr. and Mrs. Weed, and we have so much in common. We like all the same things. We sent out the same Christmas card last year without planning it, and we both have an allergy to tomatoes, and our eyebrows grow together in the middle. Well, goodnight."

Julia went to the door with him. When she returned, Francis said that Clayton was lazy, irresponsible, affected, and smelly. Julia said that Francis seemed to be getting intolerant; the Thomas boy was young and should be given a chance. Julia had noticed other cases where Francis had been short-tempered. "Mrs. Wrightson has asked everyone in Shady Hill to her anniversary party but us," she said.

"I'm sorry, Julia."

"Do you know why they didn't ask us?"

"Why?"

---

7. All are deviations from orthodox Christianity and tend to be more human- than God-oriented, though their differences hardly seem reconcilable; the American transcendentalists (see below) tended to change the emphasis from the study of thought to belief in "intuition."

75   "Because you insulted Mrs. Wrightson."

"Then you know about it?"

"June Masterson told me. She was standing behind you."

Julia walked in front of the sofa with a small step that expressed, Francis knew, a feeling of anger.

"I did insult Mrs. Wrightson, Julia, and I meant to. I've never liked her parties, and I'm glad she's dropped us."

80   "What about Helen?"

"How does Helen come into this?"

"Mrs. Wrightson's the one who decides who goes to the assemblies."

"You mean she can keep Helen from going to the dances?"

"Yes."

85   "I hadn't thought of that."

"Oh. I knew you hadn't thought of it," Julia cried, thrusting hiltdeep into this chink of his armor. "And it makes me furious to see this kind of stupid thoughtlessness wreck everyone's happiness."

"I don't think I've wrecked anyone's happiness."

"Mrs. Wrightson runs Shady Hill and has run it for the last forty years. I don't know what makes you think that in a community like this you can indulge every impulse you have to be insulting, vulgar, and offensive."

"I have very good manners," Francis said, trying to give the evening a turn toward the light.

90   "Damn you, Francis Weed!" Julia cried, and the spit of her words struck him in the face. "I've worked hard for the social position we enjoy in this place, and I won't stand by and see you wreck it. You must have understood when you settled here that you couldn't expect to live like a bear in a cave."

"I've got to express my likes and dislikes."

"You can conceal your dislikes. You don't have to meet everything head on, like a child. Unless you're anxious to be a social leper. It's no accident that we get asked out a great deal! It's no accident that Helen has so many friends. How would you like to spend your Saturday nights at the movies? How would you like to spend your Sunday raking up dead leaves? How would you like it if your daughter spent the assembly nights sitting at her window, listening to the music from the club? How would you like it—" He did something then that was, after all, not so unaccountable, since her words seemed to raise up between them a wall so deadening that he gagged. He struck her full in the face. She staggered and then, a moment later, seemed composed. She went up the stairs to their room. She didn't slam the door. When Francis followed, a few minutes later, he found her packing a suitcase.

"Julia, I'm very sorry."

"It doesn't matter," she said. She was crying.

95   "Where do you think you're going?"

"I don't know. I just looked at a timetable. There's an eleven-sixteen into New York. I'll take that."

"You can't go, Julia."

"I can't stay. I know that."

"I'm sorry about Mrs. Wrightson, Julia, and I'm—"

"It doesn't matter about Mrs. Wrightson. That isn't the trouble." 100

"What is the trouble?"

"You don't love me."

"I do love you, Julia."

"No, you don't."

"Julia, I do love you, and I would like to be as we were—sweet and bawdy and 105 dark—but now there are so many people."

"You hate me."

"I don't hate you, Julia."

"You have no idea of how much you hate me. I think it's subconscious. You don't realize the cruel things you've done."

"What cruel things, Julia?"

"The cruel acts your subconscious drives you to in order to express your hatred 110 of me."

"What, Julia?"

"I've never complained."

"Tell me."

"You don't know what you're doing."

"Tell me." 115

"Your clothes."

"What do you mean?"

"I mean the way you leave your dirty clothes around in order to express your subconscious hatred of me."

"I don't understand."

"I mean your dirty socks and your dirty pajamas and your dirty underwear and 120 your dirty shirts!" She rose from kneeling by the suitcase and faced him, her eyes blazing and her voice ringing with emotion. "I'm talking about the fact that you've never learned to hang up anything. You just leave your clothes all over the floor where they drop, in order to humiliate me. You do it on purpose!" She fell on the bed, sobbing.

"Julia, darling!" he said, but when she felt his hand on her shoulder she got up.

"Leave me alone," she said. "I have to go." She brushed past him to the closet and came back with a dress. "I'm not taking any of the things you've given me," she said. "I'm leaving my pearls and the fur jacket."

"Oh, Julia!" Her figure, so helpless in its self-deceptions, bent over the suitcase made him nearly sick with pity. She did not understand how desolate her life would be without him. She didn't understand the hours that working women have to keep. She didn't understand that most of her friendships existed within the framework of their marriage, and that without this she would find herself alone. She didn't understand about travel, about hotels, about money. "Julia, I can't let you go! What you don't understand, Julia, is that you've come to be dependent on me."

She tossed her head back and covered her face with her hands. "Did you say that I was dependent on you?" she asked. "Is that what you said? And who is it that tells you what time to get up in the morning and when to go to bed at night? Who is it that prepares your meals and picks up your dirty clothes and invites your friends to dinner? If it weren't for me, your neckties would be greasy and your clothing would be full of moth holes. You were alone when I met you, Francis Weed, and you'll be alone when I leave. When Mother asked you for a list to send out invitations to our wedding, how many names did you have to give her? Fourteen!"

125   "Cleveland wasn't my home, Julia."

"And how many of your friends came to the church? Two!"

"Cleveland wasn't my home, Julia."

"Since I'm not taking the fur jacket," she said quietly, "you'd better put it back into storage. There's an insurance policy on the pearls that comes due in January. The name of the laundry and maid's telephone number—all those things are in my desk. I hope you won't drink too much, Francis. I hope that nothing bad will happen to you. If you do get into serious trouble, you can call me."

"Oh, my darling, I can't let you go!" Francis said. "I can't let you go, Julia!" He took her in his arms.

130   "I guess I'd better stay and take care of you for a little while longer," she said.

Riding to work in the morning, Francis saw the girl walk down the aisle of the coach. He was surprised; he hadn't realized that the school she went to was in the city, but she was carrying books, she seemed to be going to school. His surprise delayed his reaction, but then he got up clumsily and stepped into the aisle. Several people had come between them, but he could see her ahead of him, waiting for someone to open the car door, and then, as the train swerved, putting out her hand to support herself as she crossed the platform into the next car. He followed her through that car and halfway through another before calling her name—"Anne! Anne!"—but she didn't turn. He followed her into still another car, and she sat down in an aisle seat. Coming up to her, all his feelings warm and bent in her direction, he put his hand on the back of her seat—even this touch warmed him—and leaning down to speak to her, he saw that it was not Anne. It was an older woman wearing glasses. He went on deliberately into another car, his face red with embarrassment and the much deeper feeling of having his good sense challenged; for if he couldn't tell one person from another, what evidence was there that his life with Julia and the children had as much reality as his dreams of iniquity in Paris or the litter, the grass smell, and the cave-shaped trees in Lovers' Lane.

Late that afternoon, Julia called to remind Francis that they were going out for dinner. A few minutes later, Trace Bearden called. "Look, fellar," Trace said. "I'm calling for Mrs. Thomas. You know? Clayton, that boy of hers, doesn't seem able to get a job, and I wondered if you could help. If you'd call Charlie Bell—I know he's indebted to you—and say a good word for the kid, I think Charlie would—"

"Trace, I hate to say this," Francis said, "but I don't feel that I can do anything for that boy. The kid's worthless. I know it's a harsh thing to say, but it's a fact. Any kindness done for him would backfire in everybody's face. He's just a worthless kid, Trace, and there's nothing else to be done about it. Even if we got him a job, he wouldn't be able to keep it for a week. I know that to be a fact. It's an awful thing, Trace, and I know it is, but instead of recommending that kid, I'd feel obligated to warn people against him—people who knew his father and would naturally want to step in and do something. I'd feel obliged to warn them. He's a thief . . ."

The moment this conversation was finished, Miss Rainey came in and stood by his desk. "I'm not going to be able to work for you any more, Mr. Weed," she said. "I can stay until the seventeenth if you need me, but I've been offered a whirlwind of a job, and I'd like to leave as soon as possible."

She went out, leaving him to face alone the wickedness of what he had done to the Thomas boy. His children in their photograph laughed and laughed, glazed with all the bright colors of summer, and he remembered that they had met a bagpiper on the beach that day and he had paid the piper a dollar to play them a battle song of the Black Watch.[8] The girl would be at the house when he got home. He would spend another evening among his kind neighbors, picking and choosing dead-end streets, cart tracks, and the driveways of abandoned houses. There was nothing to mitigate his feeling—nothing that laughter or a game of softball with the children would change—and, thinking back over the plane crash, the Farquarsons' new maid, and Anne Murchison's difficulties with her drunken father, he wondered how he could have avoided arriving at just where he was. He was in trouble. He had been lost once in his life, coming back from a trout stream in the north woods, and he had now the same bleak realization that no amount of cheerfulness or hopefulness or valor or perseverance could help him find, in the gathering dark, the path that he'd lost. He smelled the forest. The feeling of bleakness was intolerable, and he saw clearly that he had reached the point where he would have to make a choice.

He could go to a psychiatrist, like Miss Rainey; he could go to church and confess his lusts; he could go to a Danish-massage parlor[9] in the West Seventies that had been recommended by a salesman; he could rape the girl or trust that he would somehow be prevented from doing this; or he could get drunk. It was his life, his boat, and, like every other man, he was made to be the father of thousands, and what harm could there be in a tryst that would make them both feel more kindly toward the world? This was the wrong train of thought, and he came back to the first, the psychiatrist. He had the telephone number of Miss Rainey's doctor, and he called and asked for an immediate appointment. He was insistent with the doctor's secretary—it was his manner in business—and when she said that the doctor's schedule was full for the next few weeks, Francis demanded an appointment that day and was told to come at five.

The psychiatrist's office was in a building that was used mostly by doctors and dentists, and the hallways were filled with the candy smell of mouthwash and memories of pain. Francis' character had been formed upon a series of private resolves—resolves about cleanliness, about going off the high diving board or repeating any other feat that challenged his courage, about punctuality, honesty, and virtue. To abdicate the perfect loneliness in which he had made his most vital

8. Originally a British Highland regiment that became a line regiment and distinguished itself in battle.
9. Sometimes fronts for houses of prostitution.

decisions shattered his concept of character and left him now in a condition that felt like shock. He was stupefied. The scene for his *miserere mei Deus*[1] was, like the waiting room of so many doctor's offices, a crude token gesture toward the sweets of domestic bliss: a place arranged with antiques, coffee tables, potted plants, and etchings of snow-covered bridges and geese in flight, although there were no children, no marriage bed, no stove, even, in this travesty of a house, where no one had ever spent the night and where the curtained windows looked straight onto a dark air shaft. Francis gave his name and address to a secretary and then saw, at the side of the room, a policeman moving toward him. "Hold it, hold it," the policeman said. "Don't move. Keep your hands where they are."

"I think it's all right, Officer," the secretary began. "I think it will be—"

"Let's make sure," the policeman said, and he began to slap Francis' clothes, looking for what—pistols, knives, an icepick? Finding nothing, he went off and the secretary began a nervous apology: "When you called on the telephone, Mr. Weed, you seemed very excited, and one of the doctor's patients has been threatening his life, and we have to be careful. If you want to go in now?" Francis pushed open a door connected to an electrical chime, and in the doctor's lair sat down heavily, blew his nose into a handkerchief, searched in his pockets for cigarettes, for matches, for something, and said hoarsely, with tears in his eyes, "I'm in love, Dr. Herzog."

140 It is a week or ten days later in Shady Hill. The seven-fourteen has come and gone, and here and there dinner is finished and the dishes are in the dish-washing machine. The village hangs, morally and economically, from a thread; but it hangs by its thread in the evening light. Donald Goslin has begun to worry the "Moonlight Sonata" again. *Marcato ma sempre pianissimo!*[2] He seems to be wringing out a wet bath towel, but the housemaid does not heed him. She is writing a letter to Arthur Godfrey.[3] In the cellar of his house, Francis Weed is building a coffee table. Dr. Herzog recommends woodwork as a therapy, and Francis finds some true consolation in the simple arithmetic involved and in the holy smell of new wood. Francis is happy. Upstairs, little Toby is crying, because he is tired. He puts off his cowboy hat, gloves, and fringed jacket, unbuckles the belt studded with gold and rubies, the silver bullets and holsters, slips off his suspenders, his checked shirt, and Levi's, and sits on the edge of his bed to pull off his high boots. Leaving this equipment in a heap, he goes to the closet and takes his space suit off a nail. It is a struggle for him to get into the long tights, but he succeeds. He loops the magic cape over his shoulders and, climbing onto the footboard of his bed, he spreads his arms and flies the short distance to the floor, landing with a thump that is audible to everyone in the house but himself.

"Go home, Gertrude, go home," Mrs. Masterson says. "I told you to go home an hour ago, Gertrude. It's way past your suppertime, and your mother will be worried. Go home!" A door on the Babcocks' terrace flies open, and out comes Mrs. Babcock without any clothes on, pursued by a naked husband. (Their chil-

---

1. Have mercy upon me, O God; first words of Psalm 51.   2. Stressed but always very softly.   3. At the time of the story, host of a daytime radio program especially popular with housewives.

dren are away at boarding school, and their terrace is screened by a hedge.) Over the terrace they go and in at the kitchen door, as passionate and handsome a nymph and satyr as you will find on any wall in Venice. Cutting the last of the roses in her garden, Julia hears old Mr. Nixon shouting at the squirrels in his bird-feeding station. "Rapscallions! Varmints! Avaunt and quit my sight!" A miserable cat wanders into the garden, sunk in spiritual and physical discomfort. Tied to its head is a small straw hat—a doll's hat—and it is securely buttoned into a doll's dress, from the skirts of which protrudes its long, hairy tail. As it walks, it shakes its feet, as if it had fallen into water.

"Here, pussy, pussy, pussy!" Julia calls.

"Here, pussy, here, poor pussy!" But the cat gives her a skeptical look and stumbles away in its skirts. The last to come is Jupiter. He prances through the tomato vines, holding in his generous mouth the remains of an evening slipper. Then it is dark; it is a night where kings in golden suits ride elephants over the mountains.[4]

1958

JAMES BALDWIN

Sonny's Blues

I read about it in the paper, in the subway, on my way to work. I read it, and I couldn't believe it, and I read it again. Then perhaps I just stared at it, at the newsprint spelling out his name, spelling out the story. I stared at it in the swinging lights of the subway car, and in the faces and bodies of the people, and in my own face, trapped in the darkness which roared outside.

It was not to be believed and I kept telling myself that, as I walked from the subway station to the high school. And at the same time I couldn't doubt it. I was scared, scared for Sonny. He became real to me again. A great block of ice got settled in my belly and kept melting there slowly all day long, while I taught my classes algebra. It was a special kind of ice. It kept melting, sending trickles of ice water all up and down my veins, but it never got less. Sometimes it hardened and seemed to expand until I felt my guts were going to come spilling out or that I was going to choke or scream. This would always be at a moment when I was remembering some specific thing Sonny had once said or done.

When he was about as old as the boys in my classes his face had been bright and open, there was a lot of copper in it; and he'd had wonderfully direct brown eyes, and great gentleness and privacy. I wondered what he looked like now. He

---

4. See Sinclair Lewis, *Main Street* (1920), in which the protagonist finds the small town of Gopher Prairie stifling and leaves with her son for Washington, D.C., where, she tells him, " 'We're going to find elephants with golden howdahs from which peep young maharanees with necklaces of rubies. . . .' "

had been picked up, the evening before, in a raid on an apartment downtown, for peddling and using heroin.

I couldn't believe it: but what I mean by that is that I couldn't find any room for it anywhere inside me. I had kept it outside me for a long time. I hadn't wanted to know. I had had suspicions, but I didn't name them, I kept putting them away. I told myself that Sonny was wild, but he wasn't crazy. And he'd always been a good boy, he hadn't ever turned hard or evil or disrespectful, the way kids can, so quick, so quick, especially in Harlem. I didn't want to believe that I'd ever see my brother going down, coming to nothing, all that light in his face gone out, in the condition I'd already seen so many others. Yet it had happened and here I was, talking about algebra to a lot of boys who might, every one of them for all I knew, be popping off needles every time they went to the head.[1] Maybe it did more for them than algebra could.

5   I was sure that the first time Sonny had ever had horse,[2] he couldn't have been much older than these boys were now. These boys, now, were living as we'd been living then, they were growing up with a rush and their heads bumped abruptly against the low ceiling of their actual possibilities. They were filled with rage. All they really knew were two darknesses, the darkness of their lives, which was now closing in on them, and the darkness of the movies, which had blinded them to that other darkness, and in which they now, vindictively, dreamed, at once more together than they were at any other time, and more alone.

When the last bell rang, the last class ended, I let out my breath. It seemed I'd been holding it for all that time. My clothes were wet—I may have looked as though I'd been sitting in a steam bath, all dressed up, all afternoon. I sat alone in the classroom a long time. I listened to the boys outside, downstairs, shouting and cursing and laughing. Their laughter struck me for perhaps the first time. It was not the joyous laughter which—God knows why—one associates with children. It was mocking and insular, its intent was to denigrate. It was disenchanted, and in this, also, lay the authority of their curses. Perhaps I was listening to them because I was thinking about my brother and in them I heard my brother. And myself.

One boy was whistling a tune, at once very complicated and very simple, it seemed to be pouring out of him as though he were a bird, and it sounded very cool and moving through all that harsh, bright air, only just holding its own through all those other sounds.

I stood up and walked over to the window and looked down into the courtyard. It was the beginning of the spring and the sap was rising in the boys. A teacher passed through them every now and again, quickly, as though he or she couldn't wait to get out of that courtyard, to get those boys out of their sight and off their minds. I started collecting my stuff. I thought I'd better get home and talk to Isabel.

The courtyard was almost deserted by the time I got downstairs. I saw this boy standing in the shadow of a doorway, looking just like Sonny. I almost called his name. Then I saw that it wasn't Sonny, but somebody we used to know, a boy

1. Lavatory.   2. Heroin.

from around our block. He'd been Sonny's friend. He'd never been mine, having been too young for me, and, anyway, I'd never liked him. And now, even though he was a grown-up man, he still hung around that block, still spent hours on the street corners, was always high and raggy. I used to run into him from time to time and he'd often work around to asking me for a quarter or fifty cents. He always had some real good excuse, too, and I always gave it to him. I don't know why.

But now, abruptly, I hated him. I couldn't stand the way he looked at me, partly like a dog, partly like a cunning child. I wanted to ask him what the hell he was doing in the school courtyard. 10

He sort of shuffled over to me, and he said, "I see you got the papers. So you already know about it."

"You mean about Sonny? Yes, I already know about it. How come they didn't get you?"

He grinned. It made him repulsive and it also brought to mind what he'd looked like as a kid. "I wasn't there. I stay away from them people."

"Good for you." I offered him a cigarette and I watched him through the smoke. "You come all the way down here just to tell me about Sonny?"

"That's right." He was sort of shaking his head and his eyes looked strange, as 15 though they were about to cross. The bright sun deadened his damp dark brown skin and it made his eyes look yellow and showed up the dirt in his kinked hair. He smelled funky. I moved a little away from him and I said, "Well, thanks. But I already know about it and I got to get home."

"I'll walk you a little ways," he said. We started walking. There were a couple of kids still loitering in the courtyard and one of them said goodnight to me and looked strangely at the boy beside me.

"What're you going to do?" he asked me. "I mean, about Sonny?"

"Look. I haven't seen Sonny for over a year, I'm not sure I'm going to do anything. Anyway, what the hell *can* I do?"

"That's right," he said quickly, "ain't nothing you can do. Can't much help old Sonny no more, I guess."

It was what I was thinking and so it seemed to me he had no right to say it. 20

"I'm surprised at Sonny, though," he went on—he had a funny way of talking, he looked straight ahead as though he were talking to himself—"I thought Sonny was a smart boy, I thought he was too smart to get hung."

"I guess he thought so too," I said sharply, "and that's how he got hung. And how about you? You're pretty goddamn smart, I bet."

Then he looked directly at me, just for a minute. "I ain't smart," he said. "If I was smart, I'd have reached for a pistol a long time ago."

"Look. Don't tell *me* your sad story, if it was up to me, I'd give you one." Then I felt guilty—guilty, probably, for never having supposed that the poor bastard *had* a story of his own, much less a sad one, and I asked, quickly, "What's going to happen to him now?"

He didn't answer this. He was off by himself some place. 25

"Funny thing," he said, and from his tone we might have been discussing the quickest way to get to Brooklyn, "when I saw the papers this morning, the first thing I asked myself was if I had anything to do with it. I felt sort of responsible."

I began to listen more carefully. The subway station was on the corner, just before us, and I stopped. He stopped, too. We were in front of a bar and he ducked slightly, peering in, but whoever he was looking for didn't seem to be there. The juke box was blasting away with something black and bouncy and I half watched the barmaid as she danced her way from the juke box to her place behind the bar. And I watched her face as she laughingly responded to something someone said to her, still keeping time to the music. When she smiled one saw the little girl, one sensed the doomed, still-struggling woman beneath the battered face of the semi-whore.

"I never *give* Sonny nothing," the boy said finally, "but a long time ago I come to school high and Sonny asked me how it felt." He paused, I couldn't bear to watch him, I watched the barmaid, and I listened to the music which seemed to be causing the pavement to shake. "I told him it felt great." The music stopped, the barmaid paused and watched the juke box until the music began again. "It did."

All this was carrying me some place I didn't want to go. I certainly didn't want to know how it felt. It filled everything, the people, the houses, the music, the dark, quicksilver barmaid, with menace; and this menace was their reality.

30   "What's going to happen to him now?" I asked again.

"They'll send him away some place and they'll try to cure him." He shook his head. "Maybe he'll even think he's kicked the habit. Then they'll let him loose"— he gestured, throwing his cigarette into the gutter. "That's all."

"What do you mean, that's *all?*"

But I knew what he meant.

"I *mean*, that's *all*." He turned his head and looked at me, pulling down the corners of his mouth. "Don't you know what I mean?" he asked, softly.

35   "How the hell *would* I know what you mean?" I almost whispered it, I don't know why.

"That's right," he said to the air, "how would *he* know what I mean?" He turned toward me again, patient and calm, and yet I somehow felt him shaking, shaking as though he were going to fall apart. I felt that ice in my guts again, the dread I'd felt all afternoon; and again I watched the barmaid, moving about the bar, washing glasses, and singing. "Listen. They'll let him out and then it'll just start all over again. That's what I mean."

"You mean—they'll let him out. And then he'll just start working his way back in again. You mean he'll never kick the habit. Is that what you mean?"

"That's right," he said, cheerfully. "*You* see what I mean."

"Tell me," I said at last, "why does he want to die? He must want to die, he's killing himself, why does he want to die?"

40   He looked at me in surprise. He licked his lips. "He don't want to die. He wants to live. Don't nobody want to die, ever."

Then I wanted to ask him—too many things. He could not have answered, or if he had, I could not have borne the answers. I started walking. "Well, I guess it's none of my business."

"It's going to be rough on old Sonny," he said. We reached the subway station.

"This is your station?" he asked. I nodded. I took one step down. "Damn!" he said, suddenly. I looked up at him. He grinned again. "Damn it if I didn't leave all my money home. You ain't got a dollar on you, have you? Just for a couple of days, is all."

All at once something inside gave and threatened to come pouring out of me. I didn't hate him any more. I felt that in another moment I'd start crying like a child.

"Sure," I said. "Don't sweat." I looked in my wallet and didn't have a dollar, I only had a five. "Here," I said. "That hold you?"

He didn't look at it—he didn't want to look at it. A terrible, closed look came over his face, as though he were keeping the number on the bill a secret from him and me. "Thanks," he said, and now he was dying to see me go. "Don't worry about Sonny. Maybe I'll write him or something."

"Sure," I said. "You do that. So long."

"Be seeing you," he said. I went on down the steps.

And I didn't write Sonny or send him anything for a long time. When I finally did, it was just after my little girl died, and he wrote me back a letter which made me feel like a bastard.

Here's what he said:

Dear brother,

You don't know how much I needed to hear from you. I wanted to write you many a time but I dug how much I must have hurt you and so I didn't write. But now I feel like a man who's been trying to climb up out of some deep, real deep and funky hole and just saw the sun up there, outside. I got to get outside.

I can't tell you much about how I got here. I mean I don't know how to tell you. I guess I was afraid of something or I was trying to escape from something and you know I have never been very strong in the head (smile). I'm glad Mama and Daddy are dead and can't see what's happened to their son and I swear if I'd known what I was doing I would never have hurt you so, you and a lot of other fine people who were nice to me and who believed in me.

I don't want you to think it had anything to do with me being a musician. It's more than that. Or maybe less than that. I can't get anything straight in my head down here and I try not to think about what's going to happen to me when I get outside again. Sometime I think I'm going to flip and *never* get outside and sometime I think I'll come straight back. I tell you one thing, though, I'd rather blow my brains out than go through this again. But that's what they all say, so they tell me. If I tell you when I'm coming to New York and if you could meet me, I sure would appreciate it. Give my love to Isabel and the kids and I was sure sorry to hear about little Gracie. I wish I could be like Mama and say the Lord's will be done, but I don't know it seems to me that trouble is the one thing that never does get stopped and I don't know what good it does to blame it on the Lord. But maybe it does some good if you believe it.

Your brother,
Sonny

Then I kept in constant touch with him and I sent him whatever I could and I went to meet him when he came back to New York. When I saw him many things I thought I had forgotten came flooding back to me. This was because I had begun, finally, to wonder about Sonny, about the life that Sonny lived inside. This life, whatever it was, had made him older and thinner and it had deepened the distant stillness in which he had always moved. He looked very unlike my baby brother. Yet, when he smiled, when we shook hands, the baby brother I'd never known looked out from the depths of his private life, like an animal waiting to be coaxed into the light.

"How you been keeping?" he asked me.

55   "All right. And you?"

"Just fine." He was smiling all over his face. "It's good to see you again."

"It's good to see you."

The seven years' difference in our ages lay between us like a chasm: I wondered if these years would ever operate between us as a bridge. I was remembering, and it made it hard to catch my breath, that I had been there when he was born; and I had heard the first words he had ever spoken. When he started to walk, he walked from our mother straight to me. I caught him just before he fell when he took the first steps he ever took in this world.

"How's Isabel?"

60   "Just fine. She's dying to see you."

"And the boys?"

"They're fine, too. They're anxious to see their uncle."

"Oh, come on. You know they don't remember me."

"Are you kidding? Of course they remember you."

65   He grinned again. We got into a taxi. We had a lot to say to each other, far too much to know how to begin.

As the taxi began to move, I asked, "You still want to go to India?"

He laughed. "You still remember that. Hell, no. This place is Indian enough for me."

"It used to belong to them," I said.

And he laughed again. "They damn sure knew what they were doing when they got rid of it."

70   Years ago, when he was around fourteen, he'd been all hipped on the idea of going to India. He read books about people sitting on rocks, naked, in all kinds of weather, but mostly bad, naturally, and walking barefoot through hot coals and arriving at wisdom. I used to say that it sounded to me as though they were getting away from wisdom as fast as they could. I think he sort of looked down on me for that.

"Do you mind," he asked, "if we have the driver drive alongside the park? On the west side—I haven't seen the city in so long."

"Of course not," I said. I was afraid that I might sound as though I were humoring him, but I hoped he wouldn't take it that way.

So we drove along, between the green of the park and the stony, lifeless elegance of hotels and apartment buildings, toward the vivid, killing streets of our childhood. These streets hadn't changed, though housing projects jutted up out of them now like rocks in the middle of a boiling sea. Most of the houses in which we had grown up had vanished, as had the stores from which we had stolen, the basements in which we had first tried sex, the rooftops from which we had hurled tin cans and bricks. But houses exactly like the houses of our past yet dominated the landscape, boys exactly like the boys we once had been found themselves smothering in these houses, came down into the streets for light and air and found themselves encircled by disaster. Some escaped the trap, most didn't. Those who got out always left something of themselves behind, as some animals amputate a leg and leave it in the trap. It might be said, perhaps, that I had escaped, after all, I was a school teacher; or that Sonny had, he hadn't lived in Harlem for years. Yet, as the cab moved uptown through streets which seemed, with a rush, to darken with dark people, and as I covertly studied Sonny's face, it came to me that what we both were seeking through our separate cab windows was that part of ourselves which had been left behind. It's always at the hour of trouble and confrontation that the missing member aches.

We hit 110th Street and started rolling up Lenox Avenue. And I'd known this avenue all my life, but it seemed to me again, as it had seemed on the day I'd first heard about Sonny's trouble, filled with a hidden menace which was its very breath of life.

"We almost there," said Sonny.   75

"Almost." We were both too nervous to say anything more.

We live in a housing project. It hasn't been up long. A few days after it was up it seemed uninhabitably new, now, of course, it's already rundown. It looks like a parody of the good, clean, faceless life—God knows the people who live in it do their best to make it a parody. The beat-looking grass lying around isn't enough to make their lives green, the hedges will never hold out the streets, and they know it. The big windows fool no one, they aren't big enough to make space out of no space. They don't bother with the windows, they watch the TV screen instead. The playground is most popular with the children who don't play at jacks, or skip rope, or roller skate, or swing, and they can be found in it after dark. We moved in partly because it's not too far from where I teach, and partly for the kids; but it's really just like the houses in which Sonny and I grew up. The same things happen, they'll have the same things to remember. The moment Sonny and I started into the house I had the feeling that I was simply bringing him back into the danger he had almost died trying to escape.

Sonny has never been talkative. So I don't know why I was sure he'd be dying to talk to me when supper was over the first night. Everything went fine, the oldest boy remembered him, and the youngest boy liked him, and Sonny had remembered to bring something for each of them; and Isabel, who is really much nicer than I am, more open and giving, had gone to a lot of trouble about dinner and was genuinely glad to see him. And she's always been able to tease Sonny in a way that I haven't. It was nice to see her face so vivid again and to hear her laugh and watch her make Sonny laugh. She wasn't, or, anyway, she didn't seem to be, at all uneasy or embarrassed. She chatted as though there were no subject which had to be avoided and she got Sonny past his first, faint stiffness. And thank God she was there, for I was filled with that icy dread again. Everything I did seemed awkward to me, and everything I said sounded freighted with hidden meaning. I was trying to remember everything I'd heard about dope addiction and I couldn't help watching Sonny for signs. I wasn't doing it out of malice. I was trying to find out something about my brother. I was dying to hear him tell me he was safe.

"Safe!" my father grunted, whenever Mama suggested trying to move to a neighborhood which might be safer for children. "Safe, hell! Ain't no place safe for kids, nor nobody."

80   He always went on like this, but he wasn't, ever, really as bad as he sounded, not even on weekends, when he got drunk. As a matter of fact, he was always on the lookout for "something a little better," but he died before he found it. He died suddenly, during a drunken weekend in the middle of the war, when Sonny was fifteen. He and Sonny hadn't ever got on too well. And this was partly because Sonny was the apple of his father's eye. It was because he loved Sonny so much and was frightened for him, that he was always fighting with him. It doesn't do any good to fight with Sonny. Sonny just moves back, inside himself, where he can't be reached. But the principal reason that they never hit it off is that they were so much alike. Daddy was big and rough and loud-talking, just the opposite of Sonny, but they both had—that same privacy.

Mama tried to tell me something about this, just after Daddy died. I was home on leave from the army.

This was the last time I ever saw my mother alive. Just the same, this picture gets all mixed up in my mind with pictures I had of her when she was younger. The way I always see her is the way she used to be on a Sunday afternoon, say, when the old folks were talking after the big Sunday dinner. I always see her wearing pale blue. She'd be sitting on the sofa. And my father would be sitting in the easy chair, not far from her. And the living room would be full of church folks and relatives. There they sit, in chairs all around the living room, and the night is creeping up outside, but nobody knows it yet. You can see the darkness growing against the windowpanes and you hear the street noises every now and again, or maybe the jangling beat of a tambourine from one of the churches close by, but it's real quiet in the room. For a moment nobody's talking, but every face looks darkening, like the sky outside. And my mother rocks a little from the waist, and my father's eyes are closed. Everyone is looking at something a child can't see. For a minute they've forgotten the children. Maybe a kid is lying on the rug, half asleep. Maybe somebody's got a kid in his lap and is absent-mindedly stroking the kid's head. Maybe there's a kid, quiet and big-eyed, curled up in a big chair in the corner. The silence, the darkness coming, and the darkness in the faces frighten the child obscurely. He hopes that the hand which strokes his forehead will never stop—will never die. He hopes that there will never come a time when the old folks won't be sitting around the living room, talking about where they've come from, and what they've seen, and what's happened to them and their kinfolk.

But something deep and watchful in the child knows that this is bound to end, is already ending. In a moment someone will get up and turn on the light. Then the old folks will remember the children and they won't talk any more that day. And when light fills the room, the child is filled with darkness. He knows that every time this happens he's moved just a little closer to that darkness outside. The darkness outside is what the old folks have been talking about. It's what they've come from. It's what they endure. The child knows that they won't talk any more because if he knows too much about what's happened to *them*, he'll know too much too soon, about what's going to happen to *him*.

The last time I talked to my mother, I remember I was restless. I wanted to get out and see Isabel. We weren't married then and we had a lot to straighten out between us.

There Mama sat, in black, by the window. She was humming an old church song, *Lord, you brought me from a long ways off.* Sonny was out somewhere. Mama kept watching the streets.

"I don't know," she said, "if I'll ever see you again, after you go off from here. But I hope you'll remember the things I tried to teach you."

"Don't talk like that," I said, and smiled. "You'll be here a long time yet."

She smiled, too, but she said nothing. She was quiet for a long time. And I said, "Mama, don't you worry about nothing. I'll be writing all the time, and you be getting the checks. . . ."

"I want to talk to you about your brother," she said, suddenly. "If anything happens to me he ain't going to have nobody to look out for him."

"Mama," I said, "ain't nothing going to happen to you or Sonny. Sonny's all right. He's a good boy and he's got good sense."

"It ain't a question of his being a good boy," Mama said, "nor of his having good sense. It ain't only the bad ones, nor yet the dumb ones that gets sucked under." She stopped, looking at me. "Your Daddy once had a brother," she said, and she smiled in a way that made me feel she was in pain. "You didn't never know that, did you?"

"No," I said, "I never knew that," and I watched her face.

"Oh, yes," she said, "your Daddy had a brother." She looked out of the window again. "I know you never saw your Daddy cry. But *I* did—many a time, through all these years."

I asked her, "What happened to his brother? How come nobody's ever talked about him?"

This was the first time I ever saw my mother look old.

"His brother got killed," she said, "when he was just a little younger than you are now. I knew him. He was a fine boy. He was maybe a little full of the devil, but he didn't mean nobody no harm."

Then she stopped and the room was silent, exactly as it had sometimes been on those Sunday afternoons. Mama kept looking out into the streets.

"He used to have a job in the mill," she said, "and, like all young folks, he just liked to perform on Saturday nights. Saturday nights, him and your father would drift around to different places, go to dances and things like that, or just sit around with people they knew, and your father's brother would sing, he had a fine voice, and play along with himself on his guitar. Well, this particular Saturday night, him and your father was coming home from some place, and they were both a little drunk and there was a moon that night, it was bright like day. Your father's brother was feeling kind of good, and he was whistling to himself, and he had his guitar slung over his shoulder. They was coming down a hill and beneath them was a road that turned off from the highway. Well, your father's brother, being always kind of frisky, decided to run down this hill, and he did, with that guitar banging and clanging behind him, and he ran across the road, and he was making water behind a tree. And your father was sort of amused at him and he was still coming down the hill, kind of slow. Then he heard a car motor and that same minute his brother stepped from behind the tree, into the road, in the moonlight. And he started to cross the road. And your father started to run down the hill, he says he don't know why. This car was full of white men. They was all drunk, and when they seen your father's brother they let out a great whoop and holler and they aimed the car straight at him. They was having fun, they just wanted to scare him, the way they do sometimes, you know. But they was drunk. And I guess the boy, being drunk, too, and scared, kind of lost his head. By the time he jumped it was too late. Your father says he heard his brother scream when the car rolled over him, and he heard the wood of that guitar when it give, and he heard them strings go flying, and he heard them white men shouting, and the car kept on a-going and it ain't stopped till this day. And, time your father got down the hill, his brother weren't nothing but blood and pulp."

Tears were gleaming on my mother's face. There wasn't anything I could say.

"He never mentioned it," she said, "because I never let him mention it before you children. Your Daddy was like a crazy man that night and for many a night thereafter. He says he never in his life seen anything as dark as that road after the lights of that car had gone away. Weren't nothing, weren't nobody on that road, just your Daddy and his brother and that busted guitar. Oh, yes. Your Daddy never did really get right again. Till the day he died he weren't sure but that every white man he saw was the man that killed his brother."

She stopped and took out her handkerchief and dried her eyes and looked at me.

"I ain't telling you all this," she said, "to make you scared or bitter or to make you hate nobody. I'm telling you this because you got a brother. And the world ain't changed."

I guess I didn't want to believe this. I guess she saw this in my face. She turned away from me, toward the window again, searching those streets.

"But I praise my Redeemer," she said at last, "that He called your Daddy home before me. I ain't saying it to throw no flowers at myself, but, I declare, it keeps me from feeling too cast down to know I helped your father get safely through this world. Your father always acted like he was the roughest, strongest man on earth. And everybody took him to be like that. But if he hadn't had me there— to see his tears!"

She was crying again. Still, I couldn't move. I said, "Lord, Lord, Mama, I didn't know it was like that."

"Oh, honey," she said, "there's a lot that you don't know. But you are going to find out." She stood up from the window and came over to me. "You got to hold on to your brother," she said, "and don't let him fall, no matter what it looks like is happening to him and no matter how evil you gets with him. You going to be evil with him many a time. But don't you forget what I told you, you hear?"

"I won't forget," I said. "Don't you worry, I won't forget. I won't let nothing happen to Sonny."

My mother smiled as though she was amused at something she saw in my face. Then, "You may not be able to stop nothing from happening. But you got to let him know you's *there*."

Two days later I was married, and then I was gone. And I had a lot of things on my mind and I pretty well forgot my promise to Mama until I got shipped home on a special furlough for her funeral.

And, after the funeral, with just Sonny and me alone in the empty kitchen, I tried to find out something about him.

"What do you want to do?" I asked him.

"I'm going to be a musician," he said.

For he had graduated, in the time I had been away, from dancing to the juke box to finding out who was playing what, and what they were doing with it, and he had bought himself a set of drums.

"You mean, you want to be a drummer?" I somehow had the feeling that being a drummer might be all right for other people but not for my brother Sonny.

"I don't think," he said, looking at me very gravely, "that I'll ever be a good drummer. But I think I can play a piano."

I frowned. I'd never played the role of the oldest brother quite so seriously before, had scarcely ever, in fact, *asked* Sonny a damn thing. I sensed myself in the presence of something I didn't really know how to handle, didn't understand. So I made my frown a little deeper as I asked: "What kind of musician do you want to be?"

He grinned. "How many kinds do you think there are?"

"Be *serious*," I said.

He laughed, throwing his head back, and then looked at me. "I *am* serious."

"Well, then, for Christ's sake, stop kidding around and answer a serious question. I mean, do you want to be a concert pianist, you want to play classical music and all that, or—or what?" Long before I finished he was laughing again. "For Christ's *sake*, Sonny!"

He sobered, but with difficulty. "I'm sorry. But you sound so—*scared!*" and he was off again.

"Well, you may think it's funny now, baby, but it's not going to be so funny when you have to make your living at it, let me tell you *that*." I was furious because I knew he was laughing at me and I didn't know why.

"No," he said, very sober now, and afraid, perhaps, that he'd hurt me, "I don't want to be a classical pianist. That isn't what interests me. I mean"—he paused, looking hard at me, as though his eyes would help me to understand, and then gestured helplessly, as though perhaps his hand would help—"I mean, I'll have a lot of studying to do, and I'll have to study *everything*, but, I mean, I want to play *with*—jazz musicians." He stopped. "I want to play jazz," he said.

Well, the word had never before sounded as heavy, as real, as it sounded that afternoon in Sonny's mouth. I just looked at him and I was probably frowning a real frown by this time. I simply couldn't see why on earth he'd want to spend his time hanging around nightclubs, clowning around on bandstands, while people pushed each other around a dance floor. It seemed—beneath him, somehow. I had never thought about it before, had never been forced to, but I suppose I had always put jazz musicians in a class with what Daddy called "good-time people."

125   "Are you *serious?*"

"Hell, *yes,* I'm serious."

He looked more helpless than ever, and annoyed, and deeply hurt.

I suggested, helpfully: "You mean—like Louis Armstrong?"

His face closed as though I'd struck him. "No. I'm not talking about none of that old-time, down home crap."

130   "Well, look, Sonny, I'm sorry, don't get mad. I just don't altogether get it, that's all. Name somebody—you know, a jazz musician you admire."

"Bird."

"Who?"

"Bird! Charlie Parker![3] Don't they teach you nothing in the goddamn army?"

I lit a cigarette. I was surprised and then a little amused to discover that I was trembling. "I've been out of touch," I said. "You'll have to be patient with me. Now. Who's this Parker character?"

135   "He's just one of the greatest jazz musicians alive," said Sonny, sullenly, his hands in his pockets, his back to me. "Maybe *the* greatest," he added, bitterly, "that's probably why *you* never heard of him."

"All right," I said, "I'm ignorant. I'm sorry. I'll go out and buy all the cat's records right away, all right?"

"It don't," said Sonny, with dignity, "make any difference to me. I don't care what you listen to. Don't do me no favors."

I was beginning to realize that I'd never seen him so upset before. With another part of my mind I was thinking that this would probably turn out to be one of those things kids go through and that I shouldn't make it seem important by pushing it too hard. Still, I didn't think it would do any harm to ask: "Doesn't all this take a lot of time? Can you make a living at it?"

He turned back to me and half leaned, half sat, on the kitchen table. "Everything takes time," he said, "and—well, yes, sure, I can make a living at it. But what I don't seem to be able to make you understand is that it's the only thing I want to do."

140   "Well, Sonny," I said gently, "you know people can't always do exactly what they *want* to do—"

"*No,* I don't know that," said Sonny, surprising me. "I think people *ought* to do what they want to do, what else are they alive for?"

"You getting to be a big boy," I said desperately, "it's time you started thinking about your future."

"I'm thinking about my future," said Sonny, grimly. "I think about it all the time."

I gave up. I decided, if he didn't change his mind, that we could always talk

3. Charlie ("Bird") Parker (1920–1955), brilliant saxophonist and innovator of jazz; working in New York in the mid-1940s, he developed, with Dizzy Gillespie and others, the style of jazz called "bebop." He was a narcotics addict.

about it later. "In the meantime," I said, "you got to finish school." We had already decided that he'd have to move in with Isabel and her folks. I knew this wasn't the ideal arrangement because Isabel's folks are inclined to be dicty[4] and they hadn't especially wanted Isabel to marry me. But I didn't know what else to do. "And we have to get you fixed up at Isabel's."

There was a long silence. He moved from the kitchen table to the window.   145
"That's a terrible idea. You know it yourself."

"Do you have a *better* idea?"

He just walked up and down the kitchen for a minute. He was as tall as I was. He had started to shave. I suddenly had the feeling that I didn't know him at all.

He stopped at the kitchen table and picked up my cigarettes. Looking at me with a kind of mocking, amused defiance, he put one between his lips. "You mind?"

"You smoking already?"

He lit the cigarette and nodded, watching me through the smoke. "I just   150
wanted to see if I'd have the courage to smoke in front of you." He grinned and blew a great cloud of smoke to the ceiling. "It was easy." He looked at my face. "Come on, now. I bet you was smoking at my age, tell the truth."

I didn't say anything but the truth was on my face, and he laughed. But now there was something very strained in his laugh. "Sure. And I bet that ain't all you was doing."

He was frightening me a little. "Cut the crap," I said. "We already decided that you was going to go and live at Isabel's. Now what's got into you all of a sudden?"

"*You* decided it," he pointed out. "*I* didn't decide nothing." He stopped in front of me, leaning against the stove, arms loosely folded. "Look, brother. I don't want to stay in Harlem no more, I really don't." He was very earnest. He looked at me, then over toward the kitchen window. There was something in his eyes I'd never seen before, some thoughtfulness, some worry all his own. He rubbed the muscle of one arm. "It's time I was getting out of here."

"Where do you want to *go*, Sonny?"

"I want to join the army. Or the navy, I don't care. If I say I'm old enough,   155
they'll believe me."

Then I got mad. It was because I was so scared. "You must be crazy. You goddamn fool, what the hell do you want to go and join the *army* for?"

"I just told you. To get out of Harlem."

"Sonny, you haven't even finished *school*. And if you really want to be a musician, how do you expect to study if you're in the *army*?"

He looked at me, trapped, and in anguish. "There's ways. I might be able to work out some kind of deal. Anyway, I'll have the G.I. Bill when I come out."

"*If* you come out." We stared at each other. "Sonny, please. Be reasonable. I   160
know the setup is far from perfect. But we got to do the best we can."

"I ain't learning nothing in school," he said. "Even when I go." He turned away from me and opened the window and threw his cigarette out into the narrow alley. I watched his back. "At least, I ain't learning nothing you'd want me

4. Snobbish, bossy.

to learn." He slammed the window so hard I thought the glass would fly out, and turned back to me. "And I'm sick of the stink of these garbage cans!"

"Sonny," I said, "I know how you feel. But if you don't finish school now, you're going to be sorry later that you didn't." I grabbed him by the shoulders. "And you only got another year. It ain't so bad. And I'll come back and I swear I'll help you do *whatever* you want to do. Just try to put up with it till I come back. Will you please do that? For me?"

He didn't answer and he wouldn't look at me.

"Sonny. You hear me?"

165   He pulled away. "I hear you. But you never hear anything *I* say."

I didn't know what to say to that. He looked out of the window and then back at me. "OK," he said, and sighed. "I'll try."

Then I said, trying to cheer him up a little, "They got a piano at Isabel's. You can practice on it."

And as a matter of fact, it did cheer him up for a minute. "That's right," he said to himself. "I forgot that." His face relaxed a little. But the worry, the thoughtfulness, played on it still, the way shadows play on a face which is staring into the fire.

But I thought I'd never hear the end of that piano. At first, Isabel would write me, saying how nice it was that Sonny was so serious about his music and how, as soon as he came in from school, or wherever he had been when he was supposed to be at school, he went straight to that piano and stayed there until suppertime. And, after supper, he went back to that piano and stayed there until everybody went to bed. He was at the piano all day Saturday and all day Sunday. Then he bought a record player and started playing records. He'd play one record over and over again, all day long sometimes, and he'd improvise along with it on the piano. Or he'd play one section of the record, one chord, one change, one progression, then he'd do it on the piano. Then back to the record. Then back to the piano.

170   Well, I really don't know how they stood it. Isabel finally confessed that it wasn't like living with a person at all, it was like living with sound. And the sound didn't make any sense to her, didn't make any sense to any of them—naturally. They began, in a way, to be afflicted by this presence that was living in their home. It was as though Sonny were some sort of god, or monster. He moved in an atmosphere which wasn't like theirs at all. They fed him and he ate, he washed himself, he walked in and out of their door; he certainly wasn't nasty or unpleasant or rude, Sonny isn't any of those things; but it was as though he were all wrapped up in some cloud, some fire, some vision all his own; and there wasn't any way to reach him.

At the same time, he wasn't really a man yet, he was still a child, and they had to watch out for him in all kinds of ways. They certainly couldn't throw him out. Neither did they dare to make a great scene about that piano because even they dimly sensed, as I sensed, from so many thousands of miles away, that Sonny was at that piano playing for his life.

But he hadn't been going to school. One day a letter came from the school board and Isabel's mother got it—there had, apparently, been other letters but

Sonny had torn them up. This day, when Sonny came in, Isabel's mother showed him the letter and asked where he'd been spending his time. And she finally got it out of him that he'd been down in Greenwich Village, with musicians and other characters, in a white girl's apartment. And this scared her and she started to scream at him and what came up, once she began—though she denies it to this day—was what sacrifices they were making to give Sonny a decent home and how little he appreciated it.

Sonny didn't play the piano that day. By evening, Isabel's mother had calmed down but then there was the old man to deal with, and Isabel herself. Isabel says she did her best to be calm but she broke down and started crying. She says she just watched Sonny's face. She could tell, by watching him, what was happening with him. And what was happening was that they penetrated his cloud, they had reached him. Even if their fingers had been a thousand times more gentle than human fingers ever are, he could hardly help feeling that they had stripped him naked and were spitting on that nakedness. For he also had to see that his presence, that music, which was life or death to him, had been torture for them and that they had endured it, not at all for his sake, but only for mine. And Sonny couldn't take that. He can take it a little better today than he could then but he's still not very good at it and, frankly, I don't know anybody who is.

The silence of the next few days must have been louder than the sound of all the music ever played since time began. One morning, before she went to work, Isabel was in his room for something and she suddenly realized that all of his records were gone. And she knew for certain that he was gone. And he was. He went as far as the navy would carry him. He finally sent me a postcard from some place in Greece and that was the first I knew that Sonny was still alive. I didn't see him any more until we were both back in New York and the war had long been over.

He was a man by then, of course, but I wasn't willing to see it. He came by the house from time to time, but we fought almost every time we met. I didn't like the way he carried himself, loose and dreamlike all the time, and I didn't like his friends, and his music seemed to be merely an excuse for the life he led. It sounded just that weird and disordered.

Then we had a fight, a pretty awful fight, and I didn't see him for months. By and by I looked him up, where he was living, in a furnished room in the Village, and I tried to make it up. But there were lots of other people in the room and Sonny just lay on his bed, and he wouldn't come downstairs with me, and he treated these other people as though they were his family and I weren't. So I got mad and then he got mad, and then I told him that he might just as well be dead as live the way he was living. Then he stood up and he told me not to worry about him any more in life, that he *was* dead as far as I was concerned. Then he pushed me to the door and the other people looked on as though nothing were happening, and he slammed the door behind me. I stood in the hallway, staring at the door. I heard somebody laugh in the room and then the tears came to my eyes. I started down the steps, whistling to keep from crying, I kept whistling to myself, *You going to need me, baby, one of these cold, rainy days.*

I read about Sonny's trouble in the spring. Little Grace died in the fall. She was a beautiful little girl. But she only lived a little over two years. She died of polio and she suffered. She had a slight fever for a couple of days, but it didn't seem like anything and we just kept her in bed. And we would certainly have called the doctor, but the fever dropped, she seemed to be all right. So we thought it had just been a cold. Then, one day, she was up, playing, Isabel was in the kitchen fixing lunch for the two boys when they'd come in from school, and she heard Grace fall down in the living room. When you have a lot of children you don't always start running when one of them falls, unless they start screaming or something. And, this time, Gracie was quiet. Yet, Isabel says that when she heard that *thump* and then that silence, something happened to her to make her afraid. And she ran to the living room and there was little Grace on the floor, all twisted up, and the reason she hadn't screamed was that she couldn't get her breath. And when she did scream, it was the worst sound, Isabel says, that she'd ever heard in all her life, and she still hears it sometimes in her dreams. Isabel will sometimes wake me up with a low, moaning, strangling sound and I have to be quick to awaken her and hold her to me and where Isabel is weeping against me seems a mortal wound.

I think I may have written Sonny the very day that little Grace was buried. I was sitting in the living room in the dark, by myself, and I suddenly thought of Sonny. My trouble made his real.

One Saturday afternoon, when Sonny had been living with us, or anyway, been in our house, for nearly two weeks, I found myself wandering aimlessly about the living room, drinking from a can of beer, and trying to work up courage to search Sonny's room. He was out, he was usually out whenever I was home, and Isabel had taken the children to see their grandparents. Suddenly I was standing still in front of the living room window, watching Seventh Avenue. The idea of searching Sonny's room made me still. I scarcely dared to admit to myself what I'd be searching for. I didn't know what I'd do if I found it. Or if I didn't.

180   On the sidewalk across from me, near the entrance to a barbecue joint, some people were holding an old-fashioned revival meeting. The barbecue cook, wearing a dirty white apron, his conked[5] hair reddish and metallic in the pale sun, and a cigarette between his lips, stood in the doorway, watching them. Kids and older people paused in their errands and stood there, along with some older men and a couple of very tough-looking women who watched everything that happened on the avenue, as though they owned it, or were maybe owned by it. Well, they were watching this, too. The revival was being carried on by three sisters in black, and a brother. All they had were their voices and their Bibles and a tambourine. The brother was testifying[6] and while he testified two of the sisters stood together, seeming to say, amen, and the third sister walked around with the tambourine outstretched and a couple of people dropped coins into it. Then the brother's testimony ended and the sister who had been taking up the collection dumped the coins into her palm and transferred them to the pocket of her long black robe. Then she raised both hands, striking the tambourine against the air,

---

5. Processed: straightened and greased.   6. Publicly professing belief.

and then against one hand, and she started to sing. And the two other sisters and the brother joined in.

It was strange, suddenly, to watch, though I had been seeing these meetings all my life. So, of course, had everybody else down there. Yet, they paused and watched and listened and I stood still at the window. " 'Tis the old ship of Zion," they sang, and the sister with the tambourine kept a steady, jangling beat, "it has rescued many a thousand!" Not a soul under the sound of their voices was hearing this song for the first time, not one of them had been rescued. Nor had they seen much in the way of rescue work being done around them. Neither did they especially believe in the holiness of the three sisters and the brother, they knew too much about them, knew where they lived, and how. The woman with the tambourine, whose voice dominated the air, whose face was bright with joy, was divided by very little from the woman who stood watching her, a cigarette between her heavy, chapped lips, her hair a cuckoo's nest, her face scarred and swollen from many beatings, and her black eyes glittering like coal. Perhaps they both knew this, which was why, when, as rarely, they addressed each other, they addressed each other as Sister. As the singing filled the air the watching, listening faces underwent a change, the eyes focusing on something within; the music seemed to soothe a poison out of them; and time seemed, nearly, to fall away from the sullen, belligerent, battered faces, as though they were fleeing back to their first condition, while dreaming of their last. The barbecue cook half shook his head and smiled, and dropped his cigarette and disappeared into his joint. A man fumbled in his pockets for change and stood holding it in his hand impatiently, as though he had just remembered a pressing appointment further up the avenue. He looked furious. Then I saw Sonny, standing on the edge of the crowd. He was carrying a wide, flat notebook with a green cover, and it made him look, from where I was standing, almost like a schoolboy. The coppery sun brought out the copper in his skin, he was very faintly smiling, standing very still. Then the singing stopped, the tambourine turned into a collection plate again. The furious man dropped in his coins and vanished, so did a couple of the women, and Sonny dropped some change in the plate, looking directly at the woman with a little smile. He started across the avenue, toward the house. He has a slow, loping walk, something like the way Harlem hipsters walk, only he's imposed on this his own half-beat. I had never really noticed it before.

I stayed at the window, both relieved and apprehensive. As Sonny disappeared from my sight, they began singing again. And they were still singing when his key turned in the lock.

"Hey," he said.

"Hey, yourself. You want some beer?"

"No. Well, maybe." But he came up to the window and stood beside me, looking out. "What a warm voice," he said.

They were singing *If I could only hear my mother pray again!*

"Yes," I said, "and she can sure beat that tambourine."

"But what a terrible song," he said, and laughed. He dropped his notebook on the sofa and disappeared into the kitchen. "Where's Isabel and the kids?"

"I think they went to see their grandparents. You hungry?"

190   "No." He came back into the living room with his can of beer. "You want to come some place with me tonight?"

I sensed, I don't know how, that I couldn't possibly say no. "Sure. Where?"

He sat down on the sofa and picked up his notebook and started leafing through it. "I'm going to sit in with some fellows in a joint in the Village."

"You mean, you're going to play, tonight?"

"That's right." He took a swallow of his beer and moved back to the window. He gave me a sidelong look. "If you can stand it."

195   "I'll try," I said.

He smiled to himself and we both watched as the meeting across the way broke up. The three sisters and the brother, heads bowed, were singing *God be with you till we meet again*. The faces around them were very quiet. Then the song ended. The small crowd dispersed. We watched the three women and the lone man walk slowly up the avenue.

"When she was singing before," said Sonny, abruptly, "her voice reminded me for a minute of what heroin feels like sometimes—when it's in your veins. It makes you feel sort of warm and cool at the same time. And distant. And—and sure." He sipped his beer, very deliberately not looking at me. I watched his face. "It makes you feel—in control. Sometimes you've got to have that feeling."

"Do you?" I sat down slowly in the easy chair.

"Sometimes." He went to the sofa and picked up his notebook again. "Some people do."

200   "In order," I asked, "to play?" And my voice was very ugly, full of contempt and anger.

"Well"—he looked at me with great, troubled eyes, as though, in fact, he hoped his eyes would tell me things he could never otherwise say—"they *think* so. And *if* they think so—!"

"And what do *you* think?" I asked.

He sat on the sofa and put his can of beer on the floor. "I don't know," he said, and I couldn't be sure if he were answering my question or pursuing his thoughts. His face didn't tell me. "It's not so much to *play*. It's to *stand* it, to be able to make it at all. On any level." He frowned and smiled: "In order to keep from shaking to pieces."

"But these friends of yours," I said, "they seem to shake themselves to pieces pretty goddamn fast."

205   "Maybe." He played with the notebook. And something told me that I should curb my tongue, that Sonny was doing his best to talk, that I should listen. "But of course you only know the ones that've gone to pieces. Some don't—or at least they haven't *yet* and that's just about all *any* of us can say." He paused. "And then there are some who just live, really, in hell, and they know it and they see what's happening and they go right on. I don't know." He sighed, dropped the notebook, folded his arms. "Some guys, you can tell from the way they play, they on something *all* the time. And you can see that, well, it makes something real for them. But of course," he picked up his beer from the floor and sipped it and put the can

down again, "they *want* to, too, you've got to see that. Even some of them that say they don't—*some,* not all."

"And what about you?" I asked—I couldn't help it. "What about you? Do *you* want to?"

He stood up and walked to the window and I remained silent for a long time. Then he sighed. "Me," he said. Then: "While I was downstairs before, on my way here, listening to that woman sing, it struck me all of a sudden how much suffering she must have had to go through—to sing like that. It's *repulsive* to think you have to suffer that much."

I said: "But there's no way not to suffer—is there, Sonny?"

"I believe not," he said and smiled, "but that's never stopped anyone from trying." He looked at me. "Has it?" I realized, with this mocking look, that there stood between us, forever, beyond the power of time or forgiveness, the fact that I had held silence—so long!—when he had needed human speech to help him. He turned back to the window. "No, there's no way not to suffer. But you try all kinds of ways to keep from drowning in it, to keep on top of it, and to make it seem—well, like *you.* Like you did something, all right, and now you're suffering for it. You know?" I said nothing. "Well you know," he said, impatiently, "why *do* people suffer? Maybe it's better to do something to give it a reason, *any* reason."

"But we just agreed," I said, "that there's no way not to suffer. Isn't it better, then, just to—take it?"   210

"But nobody just takes it," Sonny cried, "that's what I'm telling you! *Everybody* tries not to. You're just hung up on the *way* some people try—it's not *your* way!"

The hair on my face began to itch, my face felt wet. "That's not true," I said, "that's not true. I don't give a damn what other people do, I don't even care how they suffer. I just care how *you* suffer." And he looked at me. "Please believe me," I said, "I don't want to see you—die—trying not to suffer."

"I won't," he said flatly, "die trying not to suffer. At least, not any faster than anybody else."

"But there's no need," I said, trying to laugh, "is there? in killing yourself."

I wanted to say more, but I couldn't. I wanted to talk about will power and   215
how life could be—well, beautiful. I wanted to say that it was all within; but was it? or, rather, wasn't that exactly the trouble? And I wanted to promise that I would never fail him again. But it would all have sounded—empty words and lies.

So I made the promise to myself and prayed that I would keep it.

"It's terrible sometimes, inside," he said, "that's what's the trouble. You walk these streets, black and funky and cold, and there's not really a living ass to talk to, and there's nothing shaking, and there's no way of getting it out—that storm inside. You can't talk it and you can't make love with it, and when you finally try to get with it and play it, you realize *nobody's* listening. So *you've* got to listen. You got to find a way to listen."

And then he walked away from the window and sat on the sofa again, as though all the wind had suddenly been knocked out of him. "Sometimes you'll do *anything* to play, even cut your mother's throat." He laughed and looked at me. "Or your brother's." Then he sobered. "Or your own." Then: "Don't worry. I'm all right now and I think I'll *be* all right. But I can't forget—where I've been. I don't mean just the physical place I've been, I mean where I've *been*. And *what* I've been."

"What have you been, Sonny?" I asked.

220   He smiled—but sat sideways on the sofa, his elbow resting on the back, his fingers playing with his mouth and chin, not looking at me. "I've been something I didn't recognize, didn't know I could be. Didn't know anybody could be." He stopped, looking inward, looking helplessly young, looking old. "I'm not talking about it now because I feel *guilty* or anything like that—maybe it would be better if I did, I don't know. Anyway, I can't really talk about it. Not to you, not to anybody," and now he turned and faced me. "Sometimes, you know, and it was actually when I was most *out* of the world, I felt that I was in it, that I was *with* it, really, and I could play or I didn't really have to *play*, it just came out of me, it was there. And I don't know how I played, thinking about it now, but I know I did awful things, those times, sometimes, to people. Or it wasn't that I *did* anything to them—it was that they weren't real." He picked up the beer can; it was empty; he rolled it between his palms: "And other times—well, I needed a fix, I needed to find a place to lean, I needed to clear a space to *listen*—and I couldn't find it, and I—went crazy, I did terrible things to *me*, I was terrible *for* me." He began pressing the beer can between his hands, I watched the metal begin to give. It glittered, as he played with it like a knife, and I was afraid he would cut himself, but I said nothing. "Oh well. I can never tell you. I was all by myself at the bottom of something, stinking and sweating and crying and shaking, and I smelled it, you know? *my* stink, and I thought I'd die if I couldn't get away from it and yet, all the same, I knew that everything I was doing was just locking me in with it. And I didn't know," he paused, still flattening the beer can, "I didn't know, I still *don't* know, something kept telling me that maybe it was good to smell your own stink, but I didn't think that *that* was what I'd been trying to do—and—who can stand it?" and he abruptly dropped the ruined beer can, looking at me with a small, still smile, and then rose, walking to the window as though it were the lodestone rock. I watched his face, he watched the avenue. "I couldn't tell you when Mama died—but the reason I wanted to leave Harlem so bad was to get away from drugs. And then, when I ran away, that's what I was running from— really. When I came back, nothing had changed, *I* hadn't changed, I was just— older." And he stopped, drumming with his fingers on the windowpane. The sun had vanished, soon darkness would fall. I watched his face. "It can come again," he said, almost as though speaking to himself. Then he turned to me. "It can come again," he repeated. "I just want you to know that."

"All right," I said, at last. "So it can come again. All right."

He smiled, but the smile was sorrowful. "I had to try to tell you," he said.

"Yes," I said. "I understand that."

"You're my brother," he said, looking straight at me, and not smiling at all.

225   "Yes," I repeated, "yes. I understand that."

He turned back to the window, looking out. "All that hatred down there," he said, "all that hatred and misery and love. It's a wonder it doesn't blow the avenue apart."

We went to the only nightclub on a short, dark street, downtown. We squeezed through the narrow, chattering, jampacked bar to the entrance of the big room, where the bandstand was. And we stood there for a moment, for the lights were very dim in this room and we couldn't see. Then, "Hello, boy," said the voice and an enormous black man, much older than Sonny or myself, erupted out of all that atmospheric lighting and put an arm around Sonny's shoulder. "I been sitting right here," he said, "waiting for you."

He had a big voice, too, and heads in the darkness turned toward us.

Sonny grinned and pulled a little away, and said, "Creole, this is my brother. I told you about him."

Creole shook my hand. "I'm glad to meet you, son," he said, and it was clear   230 that he was glad to meet me *there*, for Sonny's sake. And he smiled, "You got a real musician in *your* family," and he took his arm from Sonny's shoulder and slapped him, lightly, affectionately, with the back of his hand.

"Well. Now I've heard it all," said a voice behind us. This was another musician, and a friend of Sonny's, a coal-black, cheerful-looking man, built close to the ground. He immediately began confiding to me, at the top of his lungs, the most terrible things about Sonny, his teeth gleaming like a lighthouse and his laugh coming up out of him like the beginning of an earthquake. And it turned out that everyone at the bar knew Sonny, or almost everyone; some were musicians, working there, or nearby, or not working, some were simply hangers-on, and some were there to hear Sonny play. I was introduced to all of them and they were all very polite to me. Yet, it was clear that, for them, I was only Sonny's brother. Here, I was in Sonny's world. Or, rather: his kingdom. Here, it was not even a question that his veins bore royal blood.

They were going to play soon and Creole installed me, by myself, at a table in a dark corner. Then I watched them, Creole, and the little black man, and Sonny, and the others, while they horsed around, standing just below the bandstand. The light from the bandstand spilled just a little short of them and, watching them laughing and gesturing and moving about, I had the feeling that they, nevertheless, were being most careful not to step into that circle of light too suddenly; that if they moved into the light too suddenly, without thinking, they would perish in flame. Then, while I watched, one of them, the small black man, moved into the light and crossed the bandstand and started fooling around with his drums. Then—being funny and being, also, extremely ceremonious—Creole took Sonny by the arm and led him to the piano. A woman's voice called Sonny's name and a few hands started clapping. And Sonny, also being funny and being ceremonious, and so touched, I think, that he could have cried, but neither hiding it nor showing it, riding it like a man, grinned, and put both hands to his heart and bowed from the waist.

Creole then went to the bass fiddle and a lean, very bright-skinned brown man jumped up on the bandstand and picked up his horn. So there they were, and the atmosphere on the bandstand and in the room began to change and tighten. Someone stepped up to the microphone and announced them. Then there were all kinds of murmurs. Some people at the bar shushed others. The waitress ran around, frantically getting in the last orders, guys and chicks got closer to each other, and the lights on the bandstand, on the quartet, turned to a kind of indigo. Then they all looked different there. Creole looked about him for the last time, as though he were making certain that all his chickens were in the coop, and then he—jumped and struck the fiddle. And there they were.

All I know about music is that not many people ever really hear it. And even then, on the rare occasions when something opens within, and the music enters, what we mainly hear, or hear corroborated, are personal, private, vanishing evocations. But the man who creates the music is hearing something else, is dealing with the roar rising from the void and imposing order on it as it hits the air. What is evoked in him, then, is of another order, more terrible because it has no words, and triumphant, too, for that same reason. And his triumph, when he triumphs, is ours. I just watched Sonny's face. His face was troubled, he was working hard, but he wasn't with it. And I had the feeling that, in a way, everyone on the bandstand was waiting for him, both waiting for him and pushing him along. But as I began to watch Creole, I realized that it was Creole who held them all back. He had them on a short rein. Up there, keeping the beat with his whole body, wailing on the fiddle, with his eyes half closed, he was listening to everything, but he was listening to Sonny. He was having a dialogue with Sonny. He wanted Sonny to leave the shoreline and strike out for the deep water. He was Sonny's witness that deep water and drowning were not the same thing—he had been there, and he knew. And he wanted Sonny to know. He was waiting for Sonny to do the things on the keys which would let Creole know that Sonny was in the water.

235   And, while Creole listened, Sonny moved, deep within, exactly like someone in torment. I had never before thought of how awful the relationship must be between the musician and his instrument. He has to fill it, this instrument, with the breath of life, his own. He has to make it do what he wants it to do. And a piano is just a piano. It's made out of so much wood and wires and little hammers and big ones, and ivory. While there's only so much you can do with it, the only way to find this out is to try; to try and make it do everything.

And Sonny hadn't been near a piano for over a year. And he wasn't on much better terms with his life, not the life that stretched before him now. He and the piano stammered, started one way, got scared, stopped; started another way, panicked, marked time, started again; then seemed to have found a direction, panicked again, got stuck. And the face I saw on Sonny I'd never seen before. Everything had been burned out of it, and, at the same time, things usually hidden were being burned in, by the fire and fury of the battle which was occurring in him up there.

Yet, watching Creole's face as they neared the end of the first set, I had the feeling that something had happened, something I hadn't heard. Then they finished, there was scattered applause, and then, without an instant's warning, Creole started into something else, it was almost sardonic, it was *Am I Blue.*[7] And, as though he commanded, Sonny began to play. Something began to happen. And Creole let out the reins. The dry, low, black man said something awful on the drums, Creole answered, and the drums talked back. Then the horn insisted, sweet and high, slightly detached perhaps, and Creole listened, commenting now and then, dry, and driving, beautiful and calm and old. Then they all came together again, and Sonny was part of the family again. I could tell this from his face. He seemed to have found, right there beneath his fingers, a damn brand-new piano. It seemed that he couldn't get over it. Then, for a while, just being happy with Sonny, they seemed to be agreeing with him that brand-new pianos certainly were a gas.

Then Creole stepped forward to remind them that what they were playing was the blues. He hit something in all of them, he hit something in me, myself, and the music tightened and deepened, apprehension began to beat the air. Creole began to tell us what the blues were all about. They were not about anything very new. He and his boys up there were keeping it new, at the risk of ruin, destruction, madness, and death, in order to find new ways to make us listen. For, while the tale of how we suffer, and how we are delighted, and how we may triumph is never new, it always must be heard. There isn't any other tale to tell, it's the only light we've got in all this darkness.

And this tale, according to that face, that body, those strong hands on those strings, has another aspect in every country, and a new depth in every generation. Listen, Creole seemed to be saying, listen. Now these are Sonny's blues. He made the little black man on the drums know it, and the bright, brown man on the horn. Creole wasn't trying any longer to get Sonny in the water. He was wishing him Godspeed. Then he stepped back, very slowly, filling the air with the immense suggestion that Sonny speak for himself.

Then they all gathered around Sonny and Sonny played. Every now and again one of them seemed to say, amen. Sonny's fingers filled the air with life, his life. But that life contained so many others. And Sonny went all the way back, he really began with the spare, flat statement of the opening phrase of the song. Then he began to make it his. It was very beautiful because it wasn't hurried and it was no longer a lament. I seemed to hear with what burning he had made it his, and what burning we had yet to make it ours, how we could cease lamenting. Freedom lurked around us and I understood, at last, that he could help us to be free if we would listen, that he would never be free until we did. Yet, there was no battle in his face now, I heard what he had gone through, and would continue to go through until he came to rest in earth. He had made it his: that long line, of which we knew only Mama and Daddy. And he was giving it back, as everything must be given back, so that, passing through death, it can live forever. I saw my mother's face again, and felt, for the first time, how the stones of the road she had walked on must have bruised her feet. I saw the moonlit road where my father's brother died. And it brought something else back to me, and carried me

240

7. A favorite jazz standard, brilliantly recorded by Billie Holiday.

past it, I saw my little girl again and felt Isabel's tears again, and I felt my own tears begin to rise. And I was yet aware that this was only a moment, that the world waited outside, as hungry as a tiger, and that trouble stretched above us, longer than the sky.

Then it was over. Creole and Sonny let out their breath, both soaking wet, and grinning. There was a lot of applause and some of it was real. In the dark, the girl came by and I asked her to take drinks to the bandstand. There was a long pause, while they talked up there in the indigo light and after awhile I saw the girl put a Scotch and milk on top of the piano for Sonny. He didn't seem to notice it, but just before they started playing again, he sipped from it and looked toward me, and nodded. Then he put it back on top of the piano. For me, then, as they began to play again, it glowed and shook above my brother's head like the very cup of trembling.[8]

1957

QUESTIONS

1. We are advised by Margaret Atwood that if we want a happy ending, to try her sketch A. Does it have a happy ending? What does she claim is the only authentic ending for a story? What is the difference between the way Atwood uses the word "plot" and the way it is used in the introduction to this chapter?
2. Rearrange the incidents in "The Country Husband" in chronological order. The structured story begins, "To begin at the beginning . . ." and tells about the near-crash of Francis's plane. Why is that the beginning? What is it the beginning of?
3. Describe the location, appearance, and socioeconomic makeup of Shady Hill in "The Country Husband." Why is the dog Jupiter "an anomaly" (paragraph 10)? Why do Clayton Thomas and Anne also not "belong"? Who wins the struggle between Francis Weed and Shady Hill?
4. The opening scene of "Sonny's Blues" is not the first incident in Sonny and his brother's relationship. Why does the story begin here? Does this story have a "happy ending"? According to Atwood, Baldwin should, in all honesty, carry on with the story until both Sonny and his brother die. Why does Baldwin's story end here?
5. In "Sonny's Blues," how is the first-person narrator, the person telling the story, identified or characterized in the first sentence? in the first paragraph? in the first couple pages? in the story as a whole?

WRITING SUGGESTIONS

1. Choose one of Atwood's "stories" (or conflate two or three) and write a scene or two illustrating the "How" or the "Why."
2. Compare the treatment of marital infidelity in Cheever's "The Country Husband" and Maupassant's "The Jewelry," or one or more of the sketches in Atwood's "Happy Endings."
3. Write a story or a sketch or the outline of a story centering on the same situation in "The Country Husband" but set in the 1990s (or 2000s) and in a place you know.

---

8. See Isaiah 51.17, 22–23: "Awake, awake, stand up, O Jerusalem, which hast drunk at the hand of the Lord the cup of his fury; thou hast drunken the dregs of the cup of trembling, and wrung them out. . . . Behold, I have taken out of thine hand the cup of trembling, even the dregs of the cup of my fury; thou shalt no more drink it again: But I will put it into the hand of them that afflict thee; . . ."

4. Rearrange the episodes in "Sonny's Blues" as they would appear in the hypothetical history—that is, in chronological order. Pick the three or four changes that seem to you most important. Describe the difference in effect and significance that Baldwin has achieved with his structuring or rearrangement.

2

NARRATION AND POINT OF VIEW

Structuring involves more than plot and the ordering of events; selection involves more than the choosing or inventing of incidents. What would "Sonny's Blues" be like seen through the eyes of Sonny? What incidents might he choose to tell? In what order might he arrange them?

Who is telling us the story—whose words are we reading? Where does this person stand in relation to what is going on in the story? In drama, events appear before us directly. Narrative, unlike drama, is always mediated. In narrative, someone is always *between* us and the events—a viewer, a speaker, or both. The way a story is mediated is a key element in fictional structure. This mediation involves both the angle of vision— the point from which the people, events, and other details are viewed—and the words in which the story is embodied. The viewing aspect is called the **focus,** and the verbal aspect the **voice.** Both are generally lumped together in the term **point of view.** The teller of a story or novel—the voice that speaks *all* the words we read in it—is called the **narrator.**

Focus acts much as a camera does, choosing what we can look at and the angle at which we can view it, framing, proportioning, emphasizing—even distorting. Plot is a structure that places us in a time relationship to the history; focus places us in a spatial relationship.

We must pay careful attention to the focus at any given point in a story. Is it fixed or mobile? Does it stay at more or less the same angle to, and at the same distance from, the characters and action, or does it move around or in and out? When the focus centers on a single individual in the story, or relies on that character's voice or thoughts, we say that the point of view is **limited.** When that person leaves the room, the camera must go too, and if we are to know what happens in the room when the focal character is gone, some means of bringing that information must be devised, such as a letter or a report by another character. When stories or novels have several focal characters, the point of view is said to be **unlimited.** The camera is free not only to pull back from a character but also to follow scenes when that character is absent, and to record the perceptions and internal voices of new characters. **Third-person narrators** ("he" or "she") with unlimited access to the thoughts of characters are often called **omniscient** (meaning "all-knowing").

Identifying the particular kind of narration and point of view an author has chosen for a story is much more than a technical exercise. When you pick up a story or novel, among the first questions you should ask are "Who is telling this?" and "Who sees or knows what?" As you find answers, you begin to locate what makes this story unique. The events in the characters' lives could be presented in a variety of ways, but a different kind of narrator or point of view would change the story utterly. You might want to test this by imagining "The Jewelry" as a first-person story narrated by the wife, or "The Country Husband" in the voice and focus of Anne, the baby-sitter, or Francis Weed's wife.

Point of view may be limited to a **first-person narrator** ("I"), such as Montresor in Edgar Allan Poe's "The Cask of Amontillado." Sometimes such a narrator addresses an **auditor,** an audience within the fiction whose possible reaction is part of the story. Montresor is telling someone what happened one evening fifty years ago. (The beginning of the second sentence, "You, who so well know the nature of my soul," suggests that Montresor is speaking to a friend.) Poe's story, then, is controlled by Montresor's point of view: both what he perceived during his act of revenge and what he says about it years later. The reader never knows what the victim, Fortunato, is thinking, but can only guess through what Montresor tells his listener about Fortunato's appearance and behavior. It is true that at one point, as the two men are probing further and further into the caves of wine bottles and bones, the narrator temporarily speaks as though he and Fortunato share the focus: "we perceived a still interior crypt or recess. . . . Its termination the feeble light did not enable us to see" (paragraphs 68–69). But the joke is on the unfortunate Fortunato. He will end up where no one, certainly not the reader, can see or hear him.

Montresor has the last word, but he does not see some aspects of his own tale. If you listened to your friend explaining something he did in the past, you would want to sympathize, but you would also judge his possible motives and the accuracy of his account. In this way, reading stories told in the first person resembles our everyday efforts to understand what people tell us about themselves. In a story, we can find signals that suggest the right mixture of sympathy and distrust to give the speaker. Often a first-person narrator unintentionally condemns herself—the reader can see her flaws—as she tries to be impressive. Sometimes a first-person narrator gives false or distorted information. Some fictions are narrated by villains (Montresor surely counts), insane people, fools, liars, or hypocrites. When we resist a narrator's point of view and judge his or her flaws or misperceptions, we call that narrator **unreliable.** Successful first-person fictions often leave us undecided about the reliability of their narrators or speakers. When you encounter them later in this book, ask yourself how much you trust Sister in Eudora Welty's "Why I Live at the P.O.," the lawyer in Herman Melville's "Bartleby, the Scrivener," the townspeople in William Faulkner's "A Rose for Emily," and the Duke of Ferrara in Robert Browning's poem "My Last Duchess."

First-person narration isn't the only type that gives us a limited focus on one character, of course. Readers can gain a privileged insight into one character's experiences through third-person narration as well. Many narratives, from novels to short stories to films, focus on a **centered** or **central consciousness,** filtering things, people, and events through an individual character's perceptions and responses. The modern short story, with its tightly controlled range, often centers on one character's changing state of mind in an ordinary situation during a brief period of time. In third-person narratives, a reader may identify, close-up, with a complex personality but also take in the whole picture, with a bit of distance or perspective on that personality. In John Cheever's "The Country Husband," for example, the narrator slides easily from describing the outer world of a suburban morning to stating the perceptions, feelings, and thoughts of Francis Weed: "The sky shone like enamel. Even the smell of ink from his morning paper honed his appetite for life, and the world that was spread out around him was plainly a paradise" (paragraph 36). This narrator shows us a realistic world that is far from paradise, while also sympathetically tracing the way that Francis glorifies ordinary things around him because he thinks he has fallen in love.

Some stories are more interested in setting contradictory versions of reality side by side than in creating a realistic narrative of one person's psychological development. "The Zebra Storyteller," like a fable, uses unlimited narration to dramatize what happens when cultures, languages, and ways of seeing the world clash. We are with the first zebra (who is killed) when he meets a cat speaking Zebraic and are told he is "astonished." We learn that the zebras can smell no lion and so "decided the woods were haunted by the ghost of a lion," and we get inside the mind of the storyteller and "hear" him speaking to himself. Throughout, the story seems free to see matter from one focus or another and even to dip inside a character's mind.

Readers quickly learn the rules that each story will follow, and can tolerate different sorts of rules within one story or among different stories. After all, this is fiction. If animals can talk, they can talk. If a story settles in on a central consciousness at the beginning, we are surprised by a shift to someone else later on.

There are stories in this book ("The Most Dangerous Game," "Barn Burning," and "The Lame Shall Enter First," for example) in which the point of view does shift—or jump—from a previously established centered consciousness. The shift may strike us as breaking the rules of the story, or we may need to revise our understanding of what the story is trying to do. Some stories make a point of asking us to revise our expectations, to bend our rules both for reality and for storytelling. If the narrator refuses to choose what "really" happened, as in Margaret Atwood's "Happy Endings" or Lorrie Moore's "How," we as readers must think about alternatives; the story may be *about* making choices in life and in stories.

"How" has a consistent, limited focus on a central consciousness, but instead of being told in the third person and past tense like "The Country Husband," Moore's story uses **second-person narration,** mostly in the future tense. (Other authors—notably, Jay McInerney, in his novel *Bright Lights, Big City* [1984]—have employed the second-person voice, creating an effect similar to conversational anecdotes. Contemporary stories often use present tense, but the future tense is extremely rare.) "How" is designed as a parody of a self-help book, offering advice or instructions to "you." At times, you, the flesh-and-blood reader, may identify yourself as the person addressed, even if you are not a young, urban woman who works in an office and seeks relationships other than marriage. At other times, you may imagine "you" as a character acting out a probable story about trying to escape a relationship with a man who is seriously ill. Will the auditor, "you," follow the unidentified narrator's advice? Which choices will she make? Is this a clever game played with fiction, or does it convey the difficulty of living out one's own indecisive and conflicted experience?

"How" may be limited to a central consciousness, but that individual is deliberately generic: "you" might be anyone with a certain lifestyle. Ernest Hemingway's "Hills Like White Elephants" takes a different tack to portray generic players engaged in aimless pursuits. Hemingway's third-person narrator takes an unlimited or objective position outside *all* the characters. "Hills Like White Elephants" is a masterpiece of external narration; it seems odd to apply the term *omniscient* to a narrator who knows—or is willing to tell us—so little about the characters. Neither the American nor the girl is a favorite or focal character. True, we see what the girl sees when she looks at the landscape, but we hear only what she says, not what she thinks. In a long paragraph at the end, the narrative camera follows the American as he goes to the bar alone, but it does not report his feelings about the recent argument. The effect of this method is both close-up—as though we too were at the station, eavesdropping on the couple—and remote, *almost* as out of touch as the lives of these two transients. Almost, because minimal, precise clues help us decipher the young woman's pain and the couple's denial. Thus the narration and point of view are exactly right for this incisive but detached story.

Similarly, Timothy Findley's "Dreams" chooses the appropriate narration and point of view for its purpose: third-person unlimited, with alternating internal voice and focus of several characters. The mystery of Dr. Everett Menlo's insomnia is more effective because we begin with the point of view of his wife, Dr. Mimi Menlo, and only later discover what has invaded the husband's dreams. The focus is not even limited by consciousness, for we are party to some of the character's dreams; nor, indeed, is it limited to "characters" in the usual sense since we are given even the dog Thurber's dreams and thoughts (see, for example, paragraphs 6, 54, 167). If Margaret Atwood's "Happy Endings" is about plot structure, "Dreams," in its way, is about focus. The focus of the narrative is unlimited because the very concept of the limited focus or perspective of the individual mind is made doubtful. Not only may we be able to dream each other's dreams, but our very minds or consciousness may be someone else's dream!

To appreciate and enjoy a story, then, you need to find out how it is being told and by whom: you should identify the narrator and the point of view. Sometimes the narrator is a character, like Montresor in Poe's story, and sometimes the narrator has a clear personality even if he or she played no part in the events. At other times, readers may answer the question "Who is telling this story?" with the name of the author. It may seem, for example, that Cheever himself is the narrator of "The Country Husband." This can be misleading, however. We can dig up a few facts about the author's life and read them into the story, or, worse, read the character or detail of the story into the author's life. It is more prudent, therefore, especially on the basis of a single story, to speak not of the author but of the author's **persona,** the voice or figure of the author who tells and structures the story, who may or may not resemble in nature or values the actual person of the author. Mary Anne Evans wrote novels under the name George Eliot; her first-person narrator speaks of "himself." That male narrator may be a good example of the persona or representative that most authors construct to "write" their stories.

We say *write* the stories. But just as poets write of singing their songs (poems), so we often speak of telling a story, and we speak of a narrator, which means a teller. There are stories, usually with first-person narrators, that make much of the convention of oral storytelling—Louise Erdrich's "Love Medicine," later in this book, for example. Stories with auditors, such as "The Cask of Amontillado" or Eudora Welty's "Why I Live at the P.O.," also have a kind of "oral" feeling. They may remind us of the acts of telling and listening that are so basic to human communities and communication. Children love to hear a story read aloud, even if they have already read it to themselves many times. Older readers, too, enjoy imagining a narrative as a scene of telling. We know that we are only reading words on a page, but we imagine the narrator speaking to us, giving shape, focus, and voice to a particular history.

EDGAR ALLAN POE

The Cask of Amontillado

The thousand injuries of Fortunato I had borne as I best could, but when he ventured upon insult I vowed revenge. You, who so well know the nature of my soul, will not suppose, however, that I gave utterance to a threat. *At length* I would be avenged; this was a point definitively settled—but the very definitiveness with which it was resolved precluded the idea of risk. I must not only punish but punish with impunity. A wrong is unredressed when retribution overtakes its redresser. It is equally unredressed when the avenger fails to make himself felt as such to him who has done the wrong.

It must be understood that neither by word nor deed had I given Fortunato cause to doubt my good will. I continued, as was my wont, to smile in his face, and he did not perceive that my smile *now* was at the thought of his immolation.

He had a weak point—this Fortunato—although in other regards he was a man to be respected and even feared. He prided himself upon his connoisseurship in wine. Few Italians have the true virtuoso spirit. For the most part their enthusiasm is adopted to suit the time and opportunity, to practice imposture upon the British and Austrian *millionaires*. In painting and gemmary, Fortunato, like his country-men, was a quack, but in the matter of old wines he was sincere. In this respect I did not differ from him materially;—I was skilful in the Italian vintages myself, and bought largely whenever I could.

It was about dusk, one evening during the supreme madness of the carnival season, that I encountered my friend. He accosted me with excessive warmth, for he had been drinking much. The man wore motley. He had on a tight-fitting parti-striped dress,[1] and his head was surmounted by the conical cap and bells. I was so pleased to see him that I should never have done wringing his hand.

5   I said to him—"My dear Fortunato, you are luckily met. How remarkably well you are looking to-day. But I have received a pipe[2] of what passes for Amontillado, and I have my doubts."

"How?" said he. "Amontillado? A pipe? Impossible! And in the middle of the carnival!"

"I have my doubts," I replied; "and I was silly enough to pay the full Amon-tillado price without consulting you in the matter. You were not to be found, and I was fearful of losing a bargain."

"Amontillado!"

"I have my doubts."

10   "Amontillado!"

"And I must satisfy them."

"Amontillado!"

"As you are engaged, I am on my way to Luchresi. If any one has a critical turn it is he. He will tell me——"

1. Fortunato wears a jester's costume or outfit, not a woman's dress.   2. A cask holding 126 gallons.

"Luchresi cannot tell Amontillado from Sherry."

"And yet some fools will have it that his taste is a match for your own."   15

"Come, let us go."

"Whither?"

"To your vaults."

"My friend, no; I will not impose upon your good nature. I perceive you have an engagement. Luchresi——"

"I have no engagement;—come."   20

"My friend, no. It is not the engagement, but the severe cold with which I perceive you are afflicted. The vaults are insufferably damp. They are encrusted with nitre."

"Let us go, nevertheless. The cold is merely nothing. Amontillado! You have been imposed upon. And as for Luchresi, he cannot distinguish Sherry from Amontillado."

Thus speaking, Fortunato possessed himself of my arm; and putting on a mask of black silk and drawing a *roquelaire*[3] closely about my person, I suffered him to hurry me to my palazzo.

There were no attendants at home; they had absconded to make merry in honour of the time. I had told them that I should not return until the morning, and had given them explicit orders not to stir from the house. These orders were sufficient, I well knew, to insure their immediate disappearance, one and all, as soon as my back was turned.

I took from their sconces two flambeaux, and giving one to Fortunato, bowed   25
him through several suites of rooms to the archway that led into the vaults. I passed down a long and winding staircase, requesting him to be cautious as he followed. We came at length to the foot of the descent, and stood together upon the damp ground of the catacombs of the Montresors.

The gait of my friend was unsteady, and the bells upon his cap jingled as he strode.

"The pipe," said he.

"It is farther on," said I; "but observe the white web-work which gleams from these cavern walls."

He turned towards me, and looked into my eyes with two filmy orbs that distilled the rheum of intoxication.

"Nitre?" he asked, at length.   30

"Nitre," I replied. "How long have you had that cough?"

"Ugh! ugh! ugh!—ugh! ugh! ugh!—ugh! ugh! ugh!—ugh! ugh! ugh!—ugh! ugh! ugh!"

My poor friend found it impossible to reply for many minutes.

"It is nothing," he said, at last.

"Come," I said, with decision, "we will go back; your health is precious. You   35
are rich, respected, admired, beloved; you are happy, as once I was. You are a man to be missed. For me it is no matter. We will go back; you will be ill, and I cannot be responsible. Besides, there is Luchresi——"

3. Man's heavy, knee-length cloak.

"Enough," he said; "the cough is a mere nothing; it will not kill me. I shall not die of a cough."

"True—true," I replied; "and, indeed, I had no intention of alarming you unneccessarily—but you should use all proper caution. A draught of this Medoc⁴ will defend us from the damps."

Here I knocked off the neck of a bottle which I drew from a long row of its fellows that lay upon the mould.

"Drink," I said, presenting him the wine.

He raised it to his lips with a leer. He paused and nodded to me familiarly, while his bells jingled.

"I drink," he said, "to the buried that repose around us."

"And I to your long life."

He again took my arm, and we proceeded.

"These vaults," he said, "are extensive."

"The Montresors," I replied, "were a great and numerous family."

"I forget your arms."

"A huge human foot d'or,⁵ in a field azure; the foot crushes a serpent rampant whose fangs are imbedded in the heel."

"And the motto?"

*"Nemo me impune lacessit."*⁶

"Good!" he said.

The wine sparkled in his eyes and the bells jingled. My own fancy grew warm with the Medoc. We had passed through long walls of piled skeletons, with casks and puncheons intermingling, into the inmost recesses of the catacombs. I paused again, and this time I made bold to seize Fortunato by an arm above the elbow.

"The nitre!" I said; "see, it increases. It hangs like moss upon the vaults. We are below the river's bed. The drops of moisture trickle among the bones. Come, we will go back ere it is too late. Your cough——"

"It is nothing," he said; "let us go on. But first, another draught of the Medoc."

I broke and reached him a flaçon of De Grâve. He emptied it at a breath. His eyes flashed with a fierce light. He laughed and threw the bottle upwards with a gesticulation I did not understand.

I looked at him in surprise. He repeated the movement—a grotesque one.

"You do not comprehend?" he said.

"Not I," I replied.

"Then you are not of the brotherhood."

"How?"

"You are not of the masons."⁷

"Yes, yes," I said; "yes, yes."

"You? Impossible! A mason?"

"A mason," I replied.

"A sign," he said, "a sign."

---

4. Like De Grâve (below), a French wine.   5. Of gold.   6. No one provokes me with impunity.
7. Masons or Freemasons, an international secret society condemned by the Catholic Church. Montresor means by mason one who builds with stone, brick, etc.

"It is this," I answered producing from beneath the folds of my *roquelaire* a   65
trowel.

"You jest," he exclaimed, recoiling a few paces. "But let us proceed to the
Amontillado."

"Be it so," I said, replacing the tool beneath the cloak and again offering him
my arm. He leaned upon it heavily. We continued our route in search of the
Amontillado. We passed through a range of low arches, descended, passed on,
and descending again, arrived at a deep crypt, in which the foulness of the air
caused our flambeaux rather to glow than flame.

At the most remote end of the crypt there appeared another less spacious. Its
walls had been lined with human remains, piled to the vault overhead, in the
fashion of the great catacombs of Paris. Three sides of this interior crypt were still
ornamented in this manner. From the fourth side the bones had been thrown
down, and lay promiscuously upon the earth, forming at one point a mound of
some size. Within the wall thus exposed by the displacing of the bones, we perceived a still interior crypt or recess, in depth about four feet, in width three, in
height six or seven. It seemed to have been constructed for no especial use within
itself, but formed merely the interval between two of the colossal supports of the
roof of the catacombs, and was backed by one of their circumscribing walls of
solid granite.

It was in vain that Fortunato, uplifting his dull torch, endeavoured to pry into
the depth of the recess. Its termination the feeble light did not enable us to see.

"Proceed," I said; "herein is the Amontillado. As for Luchresi——"   70

"He is an ignoramus," interrupted my friend, as he stepped unsteadily forward,
while I followed immediately at his heels. In an instant he had reached the
extremity of the niche, and finding his progress arrested by the rock, stood stupidly bewildered. A moment more and I had fettered him to the granite. In its
surface were two iron staples, distant from each other about two feet, horizontally.
From one of these depended a short chain, from the other a padlock. Throwing
the links about his waist, it was but the work of a few seconds to secure it. He was
too much astounded to resist. Withdrawing the key I stepped back from the recess.

"Pass your hand," I said, "over the wall; you cannot help feeling the nitre.
Indeed, it is *very* damp. Once more let me *implore* you to return. No? Then I must
positively leave you. But I will first render you all the little attentions in my
power."

"The Amontillado!" ejaculated my friend, not yet recovered from his
astonishment.

"True," I replied; "the Amontillado."

As I said these words I busied myself among the pile of bones of which I have   75
before spoken. Throwing them aside, I soon uncovered a quantity of building
stone and mortar. With these materials and with the aid of my trowel, I began
vigorously to wall up the entrance of the niche.

I had scarcely laid the first tier of the masonry when I discovered that the
intoxication of Fortunato had in great measure worn off. The earliest indication
I had of this was a low moaning cry from the depth of the recess. It was *not* the
cry of a drunken man. There was then a long and obstinate silence. I laid the

second tier, and the third, and the fourth; and then I heard the furious vibration of the chain. The noise lasted for several minutes, during which, that I might hearken to it with the more satisfaction, I ceased my labours and sat down upon the bones. When at last the clanking subsided, I resumed the trowel, and finished without interruption the fifth, the sixth, and the seventh tier. The wall was now nearly upon a level with my breast. I again paused, and holding the flambeaux over the mason-work, threw a few feeble rays upon the figure within.

A succession of loud and shrill screams, bursting suddenly from the throat of the chained form, seemed to thrust me violently back. For a brief moment I hesitated, I trembled. Unsheathing my rapier, I began to grope with it about the recess; but the thought of an instant reassured me. I placed my hand upon the solid fabric of the catacombs and felt satisfied. I reapproached the wall. I replied to the yells of him who clamoured. I re-echoed, I aided, I surpassed them in volume and in strength. I did this, and the clamourer grew still.

It was now midnight, and my task was drawing to a close. I had completed the eighth, the ninth and the tenth tier. I had finished a portion of the last and the eleventh; there remained but a single stone to be fitted and plastered in. I struggled with its weight; I placed it partially in its destined position. But now there came from out the niche a low laugh that erected the hairs upon my head. It was succeeded by a sad voice, which I had difficulty in recognizing as that of the noble Fortunato. The voice said—

"Ha! ha! ha!—he! he! he!—a very good joke, indeed—an excellent jest. We will have many a rich laugh about it at the palazzo—he! he! he!—over our wine—he! he! he!"

80   "The Amontillado!" I said.

"He! he! he!—he! he! he!—yes, the Amontillado. But is it not getting late? Will not they be awaiting us at the palazzo—the Lady Fortunato and the rest? Let us be gone."

"Yes," I said, "let us be gone."

"For the love of God, Montresor!"

"Yes," I said, "for the love of God!"

85   But to these words I hearkened in vain for a reply. I grew impatient. I called aloud—

"Fortunato!"

No answer. I called again—

"Fortunato!"

No answer still. I thrust a torch through the remaining aperture and let it fall within. There came forth in return only a jingling of the bells. My heart grew sick; it was the dampness of the catacombs that made it so. I hastened to make an end of my labour. I forced the last stone into its position; I plastered it up. Against the new masonry I re-erected the old rampart of bones. For the half of a century no mortal has disturbed them. *In pace requiescat!*[8]

1846

8. May he rest in peace!

ERNEST HEMINGWAY

Hills Like White Elephants

The hills across the valley of the Ebro[1] were long and white. On this side there was no shade and no trees and the station was between two lines of rails in the sun. Close against the side of the station there was the warm shadow of the building and a curtain, made of strings of bamboo beads, hung across the open door into the bar, to keep out flies. The American and the girl with him sat at a table in the shade, outside the building. It was very hot and the express from Barcelona would come in forty minutes. It stopped at this junction for two minutes and went on to Madrid.

"What should we drink?" the girl asked. She had taken off her hat and put it on the table.

"It's pretty hot," the man said.

"Let's drink beer."

"Dos cervezas," the man said into the curtain.   5

"Big ones?" a woman asked from the doorway.

"Yes. Two big ones."

The woman brought two glasses of beer and two felt pads. She put the felt pads and the beer glasses on the table and looked at the man and the girl. The girl was looking off at the line of hills. They were white in the sun and the country was brown and dry.

"They look like white elephants," she said.

"I've never seen one," the man drank his beer.   10

"No, you wouldn't have."

"I might have," the man said. "Just because you say I wouldn't have doesn't prove anything."

The girl looked at the bead curtain. "They've painted something on it," she said. "What does it say?"

"Anis del Toro. It's a drink."

"Could we try it?"   15

The man called "Listen" through the curtain. The woman came out from the bar.

"Four reales."[2]

"We want two Anis del Toro."

"With water?"

"Do you want it with water?"   20

"I don't know," the girl said. "Is it good with water?"

"It's all right."

"You want them with water?" asked the woman.

"Yes, with water."

"It tastes like licorice," the girl said and put the glass down.   25

---

1. River in northern Spain.   2. Spanish coins.

"That's the way with everything."

"Yes," said the girl. "Everything tastes of licorice. Especially all the things you've waited so long for, like absinthe."

"Oh, cut it out."

"You started it," the girl said. "I was being amused. I was having a fine time."

30   "Well, let's try and have a fine time."

"All right. I was trying. I said the mountains looked like white elephants. Wasn't that bright?"

"That was bright."

"I wanted to try this new drink. That's all we do, isn't it—look at things and try new drinks?"

"I guess so."

35   The girl looked across at the hills.

"They're lovely hills," she said. "They don't really look like white elephants. I just meant the coloring of their skin through the trees."

"Should we have another drink?"

"All right."

The warm wind blew the bead curtain against the table.

40   "The beer's nice and cool," the man said.

"It's lovely," the girl said.

"It's really an awfully simple operation, Jig," the man said. "It's not really an operation at all."

The girl looked at the ground the table legs rested on.

"I know you wouldn't mind it, Jig. It's really not anything. It's just to let the air in."

45   The girl did not say anything.

"I'll go with you and I'll stay with you all the time. They just let the air in and then it's all perfectly natural."

"Then what will we do afterward?"

"We'll be fine afterward. Just like we were before."

"What makes you think so?"

50   "That's the only thing that bothers us. It's the only thing that's made us unhappy."

The girl looked at the bead curtain, put her hand out and took hold of two of the strings of beads.

"And you think then we'll be all right and be happy."

"I know we will. You don't have to be afraid. I've known lots of people that have done it."

"So have I," said the girl. "And afterward they were all so happy."

55   "Well," the man said, "if you don't want to you don't have to. I wouldn't have you do it if you didn't want to. But I know it's perfectly simple."

"And you really want to?"

"I think it's the best thing to do. But I don't want you to do it if you don't really want to."

"And if I do it you'll be happy and things will be like they were and you'll love me?"

"I love you now. You know I love you."

"I know. But if I do it, then it will be nice again if I say things are like white   60
elephants, and you'll like it?"

"I'll love it. I love it now but I just can't think about it. You know how I get
when I worry."

"If I do it you won't ever worry?"

"I won't worry about that because it's perfectly simple."

"Then I'll do it. Because I don't care about me."

"What do you mean?"   65

"I don't care about me."

"Well, I care about you."

"Oh, yes. But I don't care about me. And I'll do it and then everything will be
fine."

"I don't want you to do it if you feel that way."

The girl stood up and walked to the end of the station. Across, on the other   70
side, were fields of grain and trees along the banks of the Ebro. Far away, beyond
the river, were mountains. The shadow of a cloud moved across the field of grain
and she saw the river through the trees.

"And we could have all this," she said. "And we could have everything and
every day we make it more impossible."

"What did you say?"

"I said we could have everything."

"We can have everything."

"No, we can't."   75

"We can have the whole world."

"No, we can't."

"We can go everywhere."

"No, we can't. It isn't ours any more."

"It's ours."   80

"No, it isn't. And once they take it away, you never get it back."

"But they haven't taken it away."

"We'll wait and see."

"Come on back in the shade," he said. "You mustn't feel that way."

"I don't feel any way," the girl said. "I just know things."   85

"I don't want you to do anything that you don't want to do—"

"Nor that isn't good for me," she said. "I know. Could we have another beer?"

"All right. But you've got to realize—"

"I realize," the girl said. "Can't we maybe stop talking?"

They sat down at the table and the girl looked across at the hills on the dry   90
side of the valley and the man looked at her and at the table.

"You've got to realize," he said, "that I don't want you to do it if you don't
want to. I'm perfectly willing to go through with it if it means anything to you."

"Doesn't it mean anything to you? We could get along."

"Of course it does. But I don't want anybody but you. I don't want any one
else. And I know it's perfectly simple."

"Yes, you know it's perfectly simple."

95   "It's all right for you to say that, but I do know it."
        "Would you do something for me now?"
        "I'd do anything for you."
        "Would you please please please please please please please stop talking?"
        He did not say anything but looked at the bags against the wall of the station.
There were labels on them from all the hotels where they had spent nights.
100   "But I don't want you to," he said, "I don't care anything about it."
        "I'll scream," the girl said.
        The woman came out through the curtains with two glasses of beer and put
them down on the damp felt pads. "The train comes in five minutes," she said.
        "What did she say?" asked the girl.
        "That the train is coming in five minutes."
105   The girl smiled brightly at the woman, to thank her.
        "I'd better take the bags over to the other side of the station," the man said.
She smiled at him.
        "All right. Then come back and we'll finish the beer."
        He picked up the two heavy bags and carried them around the station to the
other tracks. He looked up the tracks but could not see the train. Coming back,
he walked through the barroom, where people waiting for the train were drinking.
He drank an Anis at the bar and looked at the people. They were all waiting
reasonably for the train. He went out through the bead curtain. She was sitting
at the table and smiled at him.
        "Do you feel better?" he asked.
110   "I feel fine," she said. "There's nothing wrong with me. I feel fine."

                                                                              1927

LORRIE MOORE
────────────

How

So all things limp together for the only possible.
                                                    —*Beckett*
                                                    Murphy[1]

Begin by meeting him in a class, in a bar, at a rummage sale. Maybe he teaches
sixth grade. Manages a hardware store. Foreman at a carton factory. He will be a
good dancer. He will have perfectly cut hair. He will laugh at your jokes.

---

1. Samuel Beckett (1906–1989), Nobel Prize–winning Irish novelist and playwright who lived in France.
This epigraph, from his 1938 novel, *Murphy*, is representative of Beckett's absurdist vision and verbal
experimentation, perhaps best known today through his play *Waiting for Godot*.

A week, a month, a year. Feel discovered, comforted, needed, loved, and start sometimes, somehow, to feel bored. When sad or confused, walk uptown to the movies. Buy popcorn. These things come and go. A week, a month, a year.

Make attempts at a less restrictive arrangement. Watch them sputter and deflate like balloons. He will ask you to move in. Do so hesitantly, with ambivalence. Clarify: rents are high, nothing long-range, love and all that, hon, but it's footloose. Lay out the rules with much elocution. Stress openness, nonexclusivity. Make room in his closet, but don't rearrange the furniture.

And yet from time to time you will gaze at his face or his hands and want nothing but him. You will feel passing waves of dependency, devotion, and sentimentality. A week, a month, a year, and he has become your family. Let's say your real mother is a witch. Your father a warlock. Your brothers twin hunchbacks of Notre Dame. They all live in a cave together somewhere.

His name means savior. He rolls into your arms like Ozzie and Harriet, the whole Nelson genealogy. He is living rooms and turkey and mantels and Vicks, a nip at the collarbone and you do a slow syrup sink into those arms like a hearth, into those living rooms, well hello Mary Lou.[2]

Say you work in an office but you have bigger plans. He wants to go with you. He wants to be what it is that you want to be. Say you're an aspiring architect. Playwright. Painter. He shows you his sketches. They are awful. What do you think?

Put on some jazz. Take off your clothes. Carefully. It is a craft. He will lie on the floor naked, watching, his arms crossed behind his head. Shirt: brush on snare, steady. Skirt: the desultory talk of piano keys, rocking slow, rambling. Dance together in the dark though it is only afternoon.

Go to a wedding. His relatives. Everyone will compare weight losses and gains. Maiden cousins will be said to have fattened embarrassingly. His mother will be a bookkeeper or a dental hygienist. She will introduce you as his *girl*. Try not to protest. They will have heard a lot about you. Uncles will take him aside and query, What is keeping you, boy? Uncomfortable, everywhere, women in stiff blue taffeta will eye you pitifully, then look quickly away. Everyone will polka. Someone will flash a fifty to dance with the bride and she will hike up her gown and flash back: freshly shaven legs, a wide rolled-out-barrel of a grin. Feel spared. Thought you two'd be doing this by now, you will hear again. Smile. Shrug. Shuffle back for more potato salad.

2. A popular song by Ricky Nelson includes the refrain "So hello Mary Lou / Goodbye heart." The leading characters in *Ozzie and Harriet*, a popular TV show starring Nelson, his parents, and his brother, now stand for a 1950s ideal of family roles.

It hits you more insistently. A restlessness. A virus of discontent. When you pass other men in the street, smile and stare them straight in the eye, straight in the belt buckle.

10   Somehow—in a restaurant or a store—meet an actor. From Vassar or Yale. He can quote Coriolanus's mother.[3] This will seem good. Sleep with him once and ride home at 5 a.m. crying in a taxicab. Or: don't sleep with him. Kiss him good night at Union Square and run for your life.

Back at home, days later, feel cranky and tired. Sit on the couch and tell him he's stupid. That you bet he doesn't know who Coriolanus is. That since you moved in you've noticed he rarely reads. He will give you a hurt, hungry-to-learn look, with his James Cagney[4] eyes. He will try to kiss you. Turn your head. Feel suffocated.

When he climbs onto the covers, naked and hot for you, unleash your irritation in short staccato blasts. Show him your book. Your aspirin. Your clock on the table reading 12:45. He will flop back over to his side of the bed, exasperated. Maybe he'll say something like: Christ, what's wrong? Maybe he won't. If he spends too long in the bathroom, don't ask questions.

The touchiest point will always be this: he craves a family, a neat nest of human bowls; he wants to have your children. On the street he pats their heads. In the supermarket they gather around him by the produce. They form a tight little cluster of cheeks and smiles and hopes. They look like grapes. It will all be for you, baby; reel, sway backward into the frozen foods. An unwitting sigh will escape from your lips like gas. He will begin to talk about a movie camera and children's encyclopedias, picking up size-one shoes in department stores and marveling in one high, amazed whistle. Avoid shopping together.

He will have a nephew named Bradley Bob. Or perhaps a niece named Emily who is always dressed in pink and smells of milk and powder and dirty diapers, although she is already three. At visits she will prance and squeal. She will grab his left leg like a tree trunk and not let go. She will call him nunko. He will know tricks: pulling dimes from her nose, quarters from her ears. She will shriek with glee, flapping her hands in front of her. Leg released, he will pick her up, carry her around like a prize. He is the best nunko in town.

15   Think about leaving. About packing a bag and slithering off, out the door.
        But it is hot out there. And dry. And he can look somehow good to you, like Robert Goulet in a bathing suit.[5]
        No, it wouldn't be in summer.[5]

3. *Coriolanus* is a rarely performed, disturbing tragedy by William Shakespeare.   4. Early Hollywood movie star (1899–1986), more tough guy than romantic lead.   5. Robert Goulet starred as Lancelot in the 1960s musical *Camelot*; the lyrics for his role included "If ever I would leave you, / How could it be in summer . . . or winter or fall?"

Escape into books. When he asks what you're reading, hold it up without comment. The next day look across to the brown chair and you will see him reading it too. A copy from the library that morning. He has seven days. He will look over the top and wink, saying: Beat you.

He will seem to be listening to the classical music station, glancing quickly at you for approval.

At the theater he will chomp Necco wafers loudly and complain about the head in front of him. 20

He will ask you what *supercilious* means.

He will ask you who Coriolanus is.

He might want to know where Sardinia is located.

What's a *croissant?*

Begin to plot your getaway. Envision possibilities for civility. These are only possibilities. 25

A week, a month, a year: Tell him you've changed. You no longer like the same music, eat the same food. You dress differently. The two of you are incongruous together. When he tells you that he is changing too, that he loves your records, your teas, your falafel, your shoes, tell him: See, that's the problem. Endeavor to baffle.

Pace around in the kitchen and say that you are unhappy.
But I love you, he will say in his soft, bewildered way, stirring the spaghetti sauce but not you, staring into the pan as if waiting for something, a magic fish, to rise from it and say: That is always enough, why is that not always enough?

You will forget whoever it was that said never trust a thought that doesn't come while walking. But clutch at it. Apartments can shrink inward like drying ponds. You will gasp. Say: I am going for a walk. When he follows you to the door, buzzing at your side like a fly by a bleeding woman, add: *alone.* He will look surprised and hurt and you will hate him. Slam the door, out, down, hurry, it will be colder than you thought, but not far away will be a bar, smoky and dark and sticky with spilled sours. The bartender will be named Rusty or Max and he will know you. A flashy jukebox will blare Jimmy Webb.[6] A balding, purple-shirted man to your left will try to get your attention, mouthing, singing drunkenly.

6. Jimmy Webb (1946–), American songwriter who won many Grammys in the later 1960s for such hits as "By the Time I Get to Phoenix," "Wichita Lineman," and "Up, Up and Away," sung by Glen Campbell, the Fifth Dimension, and others. His "MacArthur Park," a seven-minute elaborate production with orchestra and choir, sung by the actor Richard Harris, was a hit that broke the mold of AM popular radio.

Someone to your right will sniffle to the music. Blink into your drink. Hide behind your hair. Sweet green icing will be flowing down.[7] Flowing, baby, like the Mississippi.

30   Next: there are medical unpleasantries. Kidneys. He will pee blood. Say you can't believe it. When he shows you later, it will be dark, the color of meat drippings. A huge invisible fist will torpedo through your gut, your face, your pounding heart.

This is no time to leave.

There will be doctor's appointments, various opinions. There is nothing conclusive, just an endless series of tests. He will have jarred urine specimens in the refrigerator among the eggs and peanut butter. Some will be in salad dressing bottles. They will be different colors: some green, some purple, some brown. Ask which is the real salad dressing. He will point it out and smile helplessly. Smile back. He will begin to laugh and so will you. Collapse. Roll. Roar together on the floor until you cannot laugh anymore. Bury your face in the crook of his neck. There will be nothing else in the world you can do. That night lie next to each other, silent, stiff, silvery-white in bed. Lie like sewing needles.

Continue to doctor-hop. Await the reports. Look at your watch. If ever you would leave him. Look at your calendar. It wouldn't be in autumn.

There is never anything conclusive, just an endless series of tests.

35   Once a week you will feel in love with him again. Massage his lower back when it is aching. Lay your cheek against him, feeling, listening for his kidneys. Stay like that all night, never quite falling asleep, never quite wanting to.

The thought will occur to you that you are waiting for him to die.

You will meet another actor. Or maybe it's the same one. Begin to have an affair. Begin to lie. Have dinner with him and his Modigliani-necked mother.[8] She will smoke cigars, play with the fondue, discuss the fallacy of feminine maternal instinct. Afterward, you will all get high.

There is never anything conclusive, just an endless series of tests.

And could you leave him tripping merrily through the snow?

7. Webb's "MacArthur Park" is notorious for such lyrics as: "MacArthur's Park is melting in the dark, / All the sweet green icing flowing down."   8. Amedeo Modigliani (1884–1920), Italian painter famous for elongated nudes.

You will fantasize about a funeral. At that you could cry. It would be a study   40
in post-romantic excess, something vaguely Wagnerian.[9] You would be comforted
by his lugubrious sisters and his dental hygienist mom. The four of you in the
cemetery would throw yourselves at his grave's edge, heaving and sobbing like
old Israeli women. You, in particular, would shout, bare your wrists, shake them
at the sky, foam at the mouth. There would be no shame, no dignity. You would
fly immediately to Acapulco and lounge drunk and malodorous in the casinos
until three.

After dinners with the actor: creep home. Your stomach will get fluttery, your
steps smaller as you approach the door. Neighbors will be playing music you recall
from your childhood—an opera about a pretty lady who was bad and cut a man's
hair in his sleep.[1] You recall, recall your grandfather playing it with a sort of wrath,
his visage laminated with Old Testament righteousness, the violins warming, the
scenario unfolding now as you stand outside the door. Ray pawned off my ten
dresses: it cascades like a waterfall. Dolly-la, Dolly-la: it is the wail, the next to the
last good solo of a doomed man.

Tiptoe. It won't matter. He will be sitting up in bed looking empty. Kiss him,
cajole him. Make love to him like never before. At four in the morning you will
still be awake, staring at the ceiling. You will horrify yourself.

Thoughts of leaving will move in, bivouac throughout the living room; they
will have eyes like rodents and peer out at you from under the sofa, in the dark,
from under the sink, luminous glass beads positioned in twos. The houseplants
will appear to have chosen sides. Some will thrust stems at you like angry limbs.
They will seem to caw like crows. Others will simply sag.

When you go out, leave him with a sinkful of dirty dishes. He will slowly
dry them with paper towels, his skin scalded red beneath the wet, flattened
hair of his forearms. You will be tempted to tell him to leave them, or to use
the terrycloth in the drawer. But you won't. You will put on your coat and
hurry away.

When you return, the bathroom light will be on. You will see blouses of yours   45
that he has washed by hand. They will hang in perfect half-inches, dripping,
scolding from the shower curtain rod. They will be buttoned with his Cagney
eyes, faintly hooded, the twinkle sad and dulled.
Slip quietly under the covers; hold his sleeping hand.
There is never anything conclusive.

9. Richard Wagner (1813–1883), German composer of massive, stormy operas.   1. Delilah cut the Old
Testament hero Samson's hair while he slept. An opera in French, *Samson et Dalila*, by Camille Saint-
Saëns (1835–1921), first performed in 1877, includes lyrics that a child might put into English as "Ray
pawned off my ten dresses" and "Dolly-la."

At work you will be lachrymose and distracted. You will shamble through the hall like a legume with feet. People will notice.

Nightmares have seasons like hurricanes. Be prepared. You will dream that someone with a violin case is trailing you through the city. Little children come at you with grins and grenades. You may bolt awake with a spasm, reach for him, and find he is not there, but lost in his own sleep, somnambulant, is roaming through the apartment like an old man, babbling gibberish, bumping into tables and lamps, a blanket he has torn from the bed wrapped clumsily around him, toga-style. Get up. Go to him. Touch him. At first he will look at you, wide-eyed, and not see. Put your arms around his waist. He will wake and gasp and cry into your hair. In a minute he will know where he is.

50   Dream about rainbows, about escapes, about wizards. Your past will fly by you, event by event, like Dorothy's tornadoed neighborhood, past the blown-out window.[2] Airborne. One by one. Wave hello, good-bye. Practice.

Begin to call in sick. Make sure it is after he has already left for work. Sit in a rocking chair. Stare around at the apartment. It will be mid-morning and flooded in a hush of sunlight. You rarely see it like this. It will seem strangely deserted, premonitory. There will be apricots shrunk to buttons on the windowsill. A fly will bang stupidly against the panes. The bed will lie open, revealed, like something festering, the wrinkles in the sheets marking time, marking territory like the capillaries of a map. Rock. Hush. Breathe.

On the night you finally tell him, take him out to dinner. Translate the entrees for him. When you are home, lying in bed together, tell him that you are going to leave. He will look panicked, but not surprised. Perhaps he will say, Look, I don't care who else you're seeing or anything: what is your reason?

Do not attempt to bandy words. Tell him you do not love him anymore. It will make him cry, rivulets wending their way into his ears. You will start to feel sick. He will say something like: Well, you lose some, you lose some. You are supposed to laugh. Exhale. Blow your nose. Flick off the light. Have a sense of humor, he will whisper into the black. Have a heart.

Make him breakfast. He will want to know where you will go. Reply: To the actor. Or: To the hunchbacks. He will not eat your breakfast. He will glare at it, stir it around the plate with a fork, and then hurl it against the wall.

55   When you walk up Third Avenue toward the IRT,[3] do it quickly. You will have a full bag. People will seem to know what you have done, where you are going. They will have his eyes, the same pair, passed along on the street from face to face, like secrets, like glasses at the opera.

2. In the film *The Wizard of Oz*, Dorothy dreams of a place "somewhere over the rainbow," and her home is struck by a tornado.   3. One of the lines of the New York City subway system.

This is how you are.
Rushing downstairs into the steamy burn of the subway.
Unable to look a panhandler in the pan.

You will never see him again. Or perhaps you will be sitting in Central Park one April eating your lunch and he will trundle by on roller skates. You will greet him with a wave and a mouth full of sandwich. He will nod, but he will not stop.

There will be an endless series of tests.   60

A week, a month, a year. The sadness will die like an old dog. You will feel nothing but indifference. The logy whine of a cowboy harmonica, plaintive, weary, it will fade into the hills slow as slow Hank Williams.[4] One of those endings.

1985

TIMOTHY FINDLEY

Dreams

For R. E. Turner

Doctor Menlo was having a problem: he could not sleep and his wife—the other Doctor Menlo—was secretly staying awake in order to keep an eye on him. The trouble was that, in spite of her concern and in spite of all her efforts, Doctor Menlo—whose name was Mimi—was always nodding off because of her exhaustion.

She had tried drinking coffee, but this had no effect. She detested coffee and her system had a built-in rejection mechanism. She also prescribed herself a week's worth of Dexedrine to see if that would do the trick. *Five mg*[1] *at bedtime*—all to no avail. And even though she put the plastic bottle of small orange hearts beneath her pillow and kept augmenting her intake, she would wake half an hour later with a dreadful start to discover the night was moving on to morning.

Everett Menlo had not yet declared the source of his problem. His restless condition had begun about ten days ago and had barely raised his interest. Soon, however, the time spent lying awake had increased from one to several hours and then, on Monday last, to all-night sessions. Now he lay in a state of rigid apprehension—eyes wide open, arms above his head, his hands in fists—like a man in pain unable to shut it out. His neck, his back and his shoulders constantly harried him with cramps and spasms. Everett Menlo had become a full-blown insomniac.

4. (Hiram) Hank Williams (1923–1953), pioneer of American country music, had many hits in his short, hard life, including "Lovesick Blues" (1949) and "Your Cheatin' Heart" (1953).   1. Milligrams.

Clearly, Mimi Menlo concluded, her husband was refusing to sleep because he believed something dreadful was going to happen the moment he closed his eyes. She had encountered this sort of fear in one or two of her patients. Everett, on the other hand, would not discuss the subject. If the problem had been hers, he would have said *such things cannot occur if you have gained control of yourself.*

Mimi began to watch for the dawn. She would calculate its approach by listening for the increase of traffic down below the bedroom window. The Menlos' home was across the road from The Manulife Centre—corner of Bloor and Bay streets. Mimi's first sight of daylight always revealed the high, white shape of its terraced storeys. Their own apartment building was of a modest height and colour—twenty floors of smoky glass and polished brick. The shadow of the Manulife would crawl across the bedroom floor and climb the wall behind her, grey with fatigue and cold.

The Menlo beds were an arm's length apart, and lying like a rug between them was the shape of a large, black dog of unknown breed. All night long, in the dark of his well, the dog would dream and he would tell the content of his dreams the way that victims in a trance will tell of being pursued by posses of their nameless fears. He whimpered, he cried and sometimes he howled. His legs and his paws would jerk and flail and his claws would scrabble desperately against the parquet floor. Mimi—who loved this dog—would lay her hand against his side and let her fingers dabble in his coat in vain attempts to soothe him. Sometimes, she had to call his name in order to rouse him from his dreams because his heart would be racing. Other times, she smiled and thought: *at least there's one of us getting some sleep.* The dog's name was Thurber and he dreamed in beige and white.

Everett and Mimi Menlo were both psychiatrists. His field was schizophrenia; hers was autistic children. Mimi's venue was the Parkin Institute at the University of Toronto; Everett's was the Queen Street Mental Health Centre. Early in their marriage they had decided never to work as a team and not—unless it was a matter of financial life and death—to accept employment in the same institution. Both had always worked with the kind of physical intensity that kills, and yet they gave the impression this was the only tolerable way in which to function. It meant there was always a sense of peril in what they did, but the peril—according to Everett—made their lives worth living. This, at least, had been his theory twenty years ago when they were young.

Now, for whatever unnamed reason, peril had become his enemy and Everett Menlo had begun to look and behave and lose his sleep like a haunted man. But he refused to comment when Mimi asked him what was wrong. Instead, he gave the worst of all possible answers a psychiatrist can hear who seeks an explanation of a patient's silence: he said there was *absolutely nothing wrong.*

"You're sure you're not coming down with something?"

"Yes."

"And you wouldn't like a massage?"

"I've already told you: no."

"Can I get you anything?"

"No."

"And you don't want to talk?"   15

"That's right."

"Okay, Everett . . ."

"Okay, what?"

"Okay, nothing. I only hope you get some sleep tonight."

Everett stood up. "Have you been spying on me, Mimi?"   20

"What do you mean by *spying*?"

"Watching me all night long."

"Well, Everett, I don't see how I can fail to be aware you aren't asleep when we share this bedroom. I mean—I can hear you grinding your teeth. I can see you lying there wide awake."

"When?"

"All the time. You're staring at the ceiling."   25

"I've never stared at the ceiling in my whole life. I sleep on my stomach."

"You sleep on your stomach *if* you sleep. But you have not been sleeping. Period. No argument."

Everett Menlo went to his dresser and got out a pair of clean pyjamas. Turning his back on Mimi, he put them on.

Somewhat amused at the coyness of this gesture, Mimi asked what he was hiding.

"Nothing!" he shouted at her.   30

Mimi's mouth fell open. Everett never yelled. His anger wasn't like that; it manifested itself in other ways, in silence and withdrawal, never shouts.

Everett was staring at her defiantly. He had slammed the bottom drawer of his dresser. Now he was fumbling with the wrapper of a pack of cigarettes.

Mimi's stomach tied a knot.

Everett hadn't touched a cigarette for weeks.

"Please don't smoke those," she said. "You'll only be sorry if you do."   35

"And you," he said, "will be sorry if I don't."

"But, dear . . ." said Mimi.

"Leave me for Christ's sake alone!" Everett yelled.

Mimi gave up and sighed and then she said: "all right. Thurber and I will go and sleep in the living-room. Good-night."

Everett sat on the edge of his bed. His hands were shaking.   40

"Please," he said—apparently addressing the floor. "Don't leave me here alone. I couldn't bear that."

This was perhaps the most chilling thing he could have said to her. Mimi was alarmed; her husband was genuinely terrified of something and he would not say what it was. If she had not been who she was—if she had not known what she knew—if her years of training had not prepared her to watch for signs like this, she might have been better off. As it was, she had to face the possibility the strongest, most sensible man on earth was having a nervous breakdown of major proportions. Lots of people have breakdowns, of course; but not, she had thought, the gods of reason.

"All right," she said—her voice maintaining the kind of calm she knew a child afraid of the dark would appreciate. "In a minute I'll get us something to drink. But first, I'll go and change. . . ."

Mimi went into the sanctum of the bathroom, where her nightgown waited for her—a portable hiding-place hanging on the back of the door. "You stay there," she said to Thurber, who had padded after her. "Mama will be out in just a moment."

45   Even in the dark, she could gauge Everett's tension. His shadow—all she could see of him—twitched from time to time and the twitching took on a kind of lurching rhythm, something like the broken clock in their living-room.

Mimi lay on her side and tried to close her eyes. But her eyes were tied to a will of their own and would not obey her. Now she, too, was caught in the same irreversible tide of sleeplessness that bore her husband backward through the night. Four or five times she watched him lighting cigarettes—blowing out the matches, courting disaster in the bedclothes—conjuring the worst of deaths for the three of them: a flaming pyre on the twentieth floor.

All this behaviour was utterly unlike him; foreign to his code of discipline and ethics; alien to everything he said and believed. *Openness, directness, sharing of ideas, encouraging imaginative response to every problem. Never hide troubles. Never allow despair* . . . These were his directives in everything he did. Now, he had thrown them over.

One thing was certain. She was not the cause of his sleeplessness. She didn't have affairs and neither did he. He might be ill—but whenever he'd been ill before, there had been no trauma; never a trauma like this one, at any rate. Perhaps it was something about a patient—one of his tougher cases; a wall in the patient's condition they could not break through; some circumstance of someone's lack of progress—a sudden veering towards a catatonic state, for instance—something that Everett had not foreseen that had stymied him and was slowly . . . what? Destroying his sense of professional control? His self-esteem? His scientific certainty? If only he would speak.

Mimi thought about her own worst case: a child whose obstinate refusal to communicate was currently breaking her heart and, thus, her ability to help. If ever she had needed Everett to talk to, it was now. All her fellow doctors were locked in a battle over this child; they wanted to take him away from her. Mimi refused to give him up; he might as well have been her own flesh and blood. Everything had been done—from gentle holding sessions to violent bouts of manufactured anger—in her attempt to make the child react. She was staying with him every day from the moment he was roused to the moment he was induced to sleep with drugs.

50   His name was Brian Bassett and he was eight years old. He sat on the floor in the furthest corner he could achieve in one of the observation-isolation rooms where all the autistic children were placed when nothing else in their treatment—nothing of love or expertise—had managed to break their silence. Mostly, this was a signal they were coming to the end of life.

There in his four-square, glass-box room, surrounded by all that can tempt a child if a child can be tempted—toys and food and story-book companions—Brian Bassett was in the process, now, of fading away. His eyes were never closed and his arms were restrained. He was attached to three machines that nurtured him with all that science can offer. But of course, the spirit and the will to live cannot be fed by force to those who do not want to feed.

Now, in the light of Brian Bassett's utter lack of willing contact with the world around him—his utter refusal to communicate—Mimi watched her husband through the night. Everett stared at the ceiling, lit by the Manulife building's distant lamps, borne on his back further and further out to sea. She had lost him, she was certain.

When, at last, he saw that Mimi had drifted into her own and welcome sleep, Everett rose from his bed and went out into the hall, past the simulated jungle of the solarium, until he reached the dining-room. There, all the way till dawn, he amused himself with two decks of cards and endless games of Dead Man's Solitaire.

Thurber rose and shuffled after him. The dining-room was one of Thurber's favourite places in all his confined but privileged world, for it was here—as in the kitchen—that from time to time a hand descended filled with the miracle of food. But whatever it was that his master was doing up there above him on the table-top, it wasn't anything to do with feeding or with being fed. The playing cards had an old and dusty dryness to their scent and they held no appeal for the dog. So he once again lay down and he took up his dreams, which at least gave his paws some exercise. This way, he failed to hear the advent of a new dimension to his master's problem. This occurred precisely at 5:45 A.M. when the telephone rang and Everett Menlo, having rushed to answer it, waited breathless for a minute while he listened and then said: "yes" in a curious, strangulated fashion. Thurber—had he been awake—would have recognized in his master's voice the signal for disaster.

For weeks now, Everett had been working with a patient who was severely and uniquely schizophrenic. This patient's name was Kenneth Albright, and while he was deeply suspicious, he was also oddly caring. Kenneth Albright loved the detritus of life, such as bits of woolly dust and wads of discarded paper. He loved all dried-up leaves that had drifted from their parent trees and he loved the dead bees that had curled up to die along the window-sills of his ward. He also loved the spiderwebs seen high up in the corners of the rooms where he sat on plastic chairs and ate with plastic spoons.

Kenneth Albright talked a lot about his dreams. But his dreams had become, of late, a major stumbling block in the process of his recovery. Back in the days when Kenneth had first become Doctor Menlo's patient, the dreams had been overburdened with detail: "over-cast," as he would say, "with characters" and over-produced, again in Kenneth's phrase, "as if I were dreaming the dreams of Cecil B. de Mille."[2]

2. Cecil Blount DeMille (1881–1959), American motion-picture producer and director best known for his lavishly spectacular films on biblical subjects.

Then he had said: "but a person can't really dream someone else's dreams. Or can they, Doctor Menlo?"

"No" had been Everett's answer—definite and certain.

Everett Menlo had been delighted, at first, with Kenneth Albright's dreams. They had been immensely entertaining—complex and filled with intriguing detail. Kenneth himself was at a loss to explain the meaning of these dreams, but as Everett had said, it wasn't Kenneth's job to explain. That was Everett's job. His job and his pleasure. For quite a long while, during these early sessions, Everett had written out the dreams, taken them home and recounted them to Mimi.

60   Kenneth Albright was a paranoid schizophrenic. Four times now, he had attempted suicide. He was a fiercely angry man at times—and at other times as gentle and as pleasant as a docile child. He had suffered so greatly, in the very worst moments of his disease, that he could no longer work. His job—it was almost an incidental detail in his life and had no importance for him, so it seemed—was returning reference books, in the Metro Library, to their places in the stacks. Sometimes—mostly late of an afternoon—he might begin a psychotic episode of such profound dimensions that he would attempt his suicide right behind the counter and even once, in the full view of everyone, while riding in the glass-walled elevator. It was after this last occasion that he was brought, in restraints, to be a resident patient at the Queen Street Mental Health Centre. He had slashed his wrists with a razor—but not before he had also slashed and destroyed an antique copy of *Don Quixote,* the pages of which he pasted to the walls with blood.

For a week thereafter, Kenneth Albright—just like Brian Bassett—had refused to speak or to move. Everett had him kept in an isolation cell, force-fed and drugged. Slowly, by dint of patience, encouragement and caring even Kenneth could recognize as genuine, Everett Menlo had broken through the barrier. Kenneth was removed from isolation, pampered with food and cigarettes, and he began relating his dreams.

At first there seemed to be only the dreams and nothing else in Kenneth's memory. Broken pencils, discarded toys and the telephone directory all had roles to play in these dreams but there were never any people. All the weather was bleak and all the landscapes were empty. Houses, motor cars and office buildings never made an appearance. Sounds and smells had some importance; the wind would blow, the scent of unseen fires was often described. Stairwells were plentiful, leading nowhere, all of them rising from a subterranean world that Kenneth either did not dare to visit or would not describe.

The dreams had little variation, one from another. The themes had mostly to do with loss and with being lost. The broken pencils were all given names and the discarded toys were given to one another as companions. The telephone books were the sources of recitations—hours and hours of repeated names and numbers, some of which—Everett had noted with surprise—were absolutely accurate.

All of this held fast until an incident occurred one morning that changed the face of Kenneth Albright's schizophrenia forever; an incident that stemmed—so it seemed—from something he had dreamed the night before.

65   Bearing in mind his previous attempts at suicide, it will be obvious that Ken-

neth Albright was never far from sight at the Queen Street Mental Health Centre. He was, in fact, under constant observation; constant, that is, as human beings and modern technology can manage. In the ward to which he was ultimately consigned, for instance, the toilet cabinets had no doors and the shower-rooms had no locks. Therefore, a person could not ever be alone with water, glass or shaving utensils. (All the razors were cordless automatics.) Scissors and knives were banned, as were pieces of string and rubber bands. A person could not even kill his feet and hands by binding up his wrists or ankles. Nothing poisonous was anywhere available. All the windows were barred. All the double doors between this ward and the corridors beyond were doors with triple locks and a guard was always near at hand.

Still, if people want to die, they will find a way. Mimi Menlo would discover this to her everlasting sorrow with Brian Bassett. Everett Menlo would discover this to his everlasting horror with Kenneth Albright.

On the morning of April 19th, a Tuesday, Everett Menlo, in the best of health, had welcomed a brand-new patient into his office. This was Anne Marie Wilson, a young and brilliant pianist whose promising career had been halted mid-flight by a schizophrenic incident involving her ambition. She was, it seemed, no longer able to play and all her dreams were shattered. The cause was simple, to all appearances: Anne Marie had a sense of how, precisely, the music should be and she had not been able to master it accordingly. "Everything I attempt is terrible," she had said—in spite of all her critical accolades and all her professional success. Other doctors had tried and failed to break the barriers in Anne Marie, whose hands had taken on a life of their own, refusing altogether to work for her. Now it was Menlo's turn and hope was high.

Everett had been looking forward to his session with this prodigy. He loved all music and had thought to find some means within its discipline to reach her. She seemed so fragile, sitting there in the sunlight, and he had just begun to take his first notes when the door flew open and Louise, his secretary, had said: "I'm sorry, Doctor Menlo. There's a problem. Can you come with me at once?"

Everett excused himself.

Anne Marie was left in the sunlight to bide her time. Her fingers were moving around in her lap and she put them in her mouth to make them quiet. 70

Even as he'd heard his secretary speak, Everett had known the problem would be Kenneth Albright. Something in Kenneth's eyes had warned him there was trouble on the way: a certain wariness that indicated all was not as placid as it should have been, given his regimen of drugs. He had stayed long hours in one position, moving his fingers over his thighs as if to dry them on his trousers; watching his fellow patients come and go with abnormal interest—never, however, rising from his chair. An incident was on the horizon and Everett had been waiting for it, hoping it would not come.

Louise had said that Doctor Menlo was to go at once to Kenneth Albright's ward. Everett had run the whole way. Only after the attendant had let him in past the double doors, did he slow his pace to a hurried walk and wipe his brow.

He didn't want Kenneth to know how alarmed he had been.

Coming to the appointed place, he paused before he entered, closing his eyes, preparing himself for whatever he might have to see. *Other people have killed themselves: I've seen it often enough,* he was thinking. *I simply won't let it affect me.* Then he went in.

The room was small and white—a dining-room—and Kenneth was sitting down in a corner, his back pressed out against the walls on either side of him. His head was bowed and his legs drawn up and he was obviously trying to hide without much success. An intern was standing above him and a nurse was kneeling down beside him. Several pieces of bandaging with blood on them were scattered near Kenneth's feet and there was a white enamel basin filled with pinkish water on the floor beside the nurse.

75 "Morowetz," Everett said to the intern. "Tell me what has happened here." He said this just the way he posed such questions when he took the interns through the wards at examination time, quizzing them on symptoms and prognoses.

But Morowetz the intern had no answer. He was puzzled. What had happened had no sane explanation.

Everett turned to Charterhouse, the nurse.

"On the morning of April 19th, at roughly ten-fifteen, I found Kenneth Albright covered with blood," Ms Charterhouse was to write in her report. "His hands, his arms, his face and his neck were stained. I would say the blood was fresh and the patient's clothing—mostly his shirt—was wet with it. Some—a very small amount of it—had dried on his forehead. The rest was uniformly the kind of blood you expect to find free-flowing from a wound. I called for assistance and meanwhile attempted to ascertain where Mister Albright might have been injured. I performed this examination without success. I could find no source of bleeding anywhere on Mister Albright's body."

Morowetz concurred.

80 The blood was someone else's.

"Was there a weapon of any kind?" Doctor Menlo had wanted to know.

"No, sir. Nothing," said Charterhouse.

"And was he alone when you found him?"

"Yes, sir. Just like this in the corner."

85 "And the others?"

"All the patients in the ward were examined," Morowetz told him.

"And?"

"Not one of them was bleeding."

Everett said: "I see."

90 He looked down at Kenneth.

"This is Doctor Menlo, Kenneth. Have you anything to tell me?"

Kenneth did not reply.

Everett said: "When you've got him back in his room and tranquillized, will you call me, please?"

Morowetz nodded.

95 The call never came. Kenneth had fallen asleep. Either the drugs he was given

had knocked him out cold, or he had opted for silence. Either way, he was incommunicado.

No one was discovered bleeding. Nothing was found to indicate an accident, a violent attack, an epileptic seizure. A weapon was not located. Kenneth Albright had not a single scratch on his flesh from stem, as Everett put it, to gudgeon. The blood, it seemed, had fallen like the rain from heaven: unexplained and inexplicable.

Later, as the day was ending, Everett Menlo left the Queen Street Mental Health Centre. He made his way home on the Queen streetcar and the Bay bus. When he reached the apartment, Thurber was waiting for him. Mimi was at a god-damned meeting.

That was the night Everett Menlo suffered the first of his failures to sleep. It was occasioned by the fact that, when he wakened sometime after three, he had just been dreaming. This, of course, was not unusual—but the dream itself was perturbing. There was someone lying there, in the bright white landscape of a hospital dining-room. Whether it was a man or a woman could not be told, it was just a human body, lying down in a pool of blood.

Kenneth Albright was kneeling beside this body, pulling it open the way a child will pull a Christmas present open—yanking at its strings and ribbons, wanting only to see the contents. Everett saw this scene from several angles, never speaking, never being spoken to. In all the time he watched—the usual dream eternity—the silence was broken only by the sound of water dripping from an unseen tap. Then, Kenneth Albright rose and was covered with blood, the way he had been that morning. He stared at Doctor Menlo, looked right through him and departed. Nothing remained in the dining-room but plastic tables and plastic chairs and the bright red thing on the floor that once had been a person. Everett Menlo did not know and could not guess who this person might have been. He only knew that Kenneth Albright had left this person's body in Everett Menlo's dream.

Three nights running, the corpse remained in its place and every time that 100 Everett entered the dining-room in the nightmare he was certain he would find out who it was. On the fourth night, fully expecting to discover he himself was the victim, he beheld the face and saw it was a stranger.

But there are no strangers in dreams; he knew that now after twenty years of practice. *There are no strangers; there are only people in disguise.*

Mimi made one final attempt in Brian Bassett's behalf to turn away the fate to which his other doctors—both medical and psychiatric—had consigned him. Not that, as a group, they had failed to expend the full weight of all they knew and all they could do to save him. One of his medical doctors—a woman whose name was Juliet Bateman—had moved a cot into his isolation room and stayed with him twenty-four hours a day for over a week. But her health had been undermined by this and when she succumbed to the Shanghai flu she removed herself for fear of infecting Brian Bassett.

The parents had come and gone on a daily basis for months in a killing routine of visits. But parents, their presence and their loving, are not the answer when a child has fallen into an autistic state. They might as well have been strangers. And so they had been advised to stay away.

Brian Bassett was eight years old—*unlucky eight,* as one of his therapists had said—and in every other way, in terms of physical development and mental capability, he had always been a perfectly normal child. Now, in the final moments of his life, he weighed a scant thirty pounds, when he should have weighed twice that much.

105   Brian had not been heard to speak a single word in over a year of constant observation. Earlier—long ago as seven months—a few expressions would visit his face from time to time. Never a smile—but often a kind of sneer, a passing of judgment, terrifying in its intensity. Other times, a pinched expression would appear—a signal of the shyness peculiar to autistic children, who think of light as being unfriendly.

Mimi's militant efforts in behalf of Brian had been exemplary. Her fellow doctors thought of her as *Bassett's crazy guardian angel.* They begged her to remove herself in order to preserve her health. Being wise, being practical, they saw that all her efforts would not save him. But Mimi's version of being a guardian angel was more like being a surrogate warrior: a hired gun or a samurai. Her cool determination to thwart the enemies of silence, stillness and starvation gave her strengths that even she had been unaware were hers to command.

Brian Bassett, seated in his corner on the floor, maintained a solemn composure that lent his features a kind of unearthly beauty. His back was straight, his hands were poised, his hair was so fine he looked the very picture of a spirit waiting to enter a newborn creature. Sometimes Mimi wondered if this creature Brian Bassett waited to inhabit could be human. She thought of all the animals she had ever seen in all her travels and she fell upon the image of a newborn fawn as being the most tranquil and the most in need of stillness in order to survive. If only all the natural energy and curiosity of a newborn beast could have entered into Brian Bassett, surely, they would have transformed the boy in the corner into a vibrant, joyous human being. But it was not to be.

On the 29th of April—one week and three days after Everett had entered into his crisis of insomnia—Mimi sat on the floor in Brian Bassett's isolation room, gently massaging his arms and legs as she held him in her lap.

His weight, by now, was shocking—and his skin had become translucent. His eyes had not been closed for days—for weeks—and their expression might have been carved in stone.

110   "Speak to me. Speak," she whispered to him as she cradled his head beneath her chin. "Please at least speak before you die."

Nothing happened. Only silence.

Juliet Bateman—wrapped in a blanket—was watching through the observation glass as Mimi lifted up Brian Bassett and placed him in his cot. The cot had metal sides—and the sides were raised. Juliet Bateman could see Brian Bassett's eyes and his hands as Mimi stepped away.

Mimi looked at Juliet and shook her head. Juliet closed her eyes and pulled her blanket tighter like a skin that might protect her from the next five minutes.

Mimi went around the cot to the other side and dragged the IV stand in closer to the head. She fumbled for a moment with the long plastic lifelines—anti-dehydrants, nutrients—and she adjusted the needles and brought them down inside the nest of the cot where Brian Bassett lay and she lifted up his arm in order to insert the tubes and bind them into place with tape.

This was when it happened—just as Mimi Menlo was preparing to insert the second tube.   115

Brian Bassett looked at her and spoke.

"No," he said. "Don't."

Don't meant death.

Mimi paused—considered—and set the tube aside. Then she withdrew the tube already in place and she hung them both on the IV stand.

All right, she said to Brian Bassett in her mind, *you win.*   120

She looked down then with her arm along the side of the cot—and one hand trailing down so Brian Bassett could touch it if he wanted to. She smiled at him and said to him: "not to worry. Not to worry. None of us is ever going to trouble you again." He watched her carefully. "Goodbye, Brian," she said. "I love you."

Juliet Bateman saw Mimi Menlo say all this and was fairly sure she had read the words on Mimi's lips just as they had been spoken.

Mimi started out the room. She was determined now there was no turning back and that Brian Bassett was free to go his way. But just as she was turning the handle and pressing her weight against the door—she heard Brian Bassett speak again.

"Goodbye," he said.

And died.   125

Mimi went back and Juliet Bateman, too, and they stayed with him another hour before they turned out his lights. "Someone else can cover his face," said Mimi. "I'm not going to do it." Juliet agreed and they came back out to tell the nurse on duty that their ward had died and their work with him was over.

On the 30th of April—a Saturday—Mimi stayed home and made her notes and she wondered if and when she would weep for Brian Bassett. Her hand, as she wrote, was steady and her throat was not constricted and her eyes had no sensation beyond the burning itch of fatigue. She wondered what she looked like in the mirror, but resisted that discovery. Some things could wait. Outside it rained. Thurber dreamed in the corner. Bay Street rumbled in the basement.

Everett, in the meantime, had reached his own crisis and because of his desperate straits a part of Mimi Menlo's mind was on her husband. Now he had not slept for almost ten days. *We really ought to consign ourselves to hospital beds,* she thought. Somehow, the idea held no persuasion. It occurred to her that laughter might do a better job, if only they could find it. The brain, when over-extended, gives us the most surprisingly simple propositions, she concluded. *Stop,* it says to us. *Lie down and sleep.*

Five minutes later, Mimi found herself still sitting at the desk, with her fountain pen capped and her fingers raised to her lips in an attitude of gentle prayer. It required some effort to re-adjust her gaze and re-establish her focus on the surface of the window glass beyond which her mind had wandered. Sitting up, she had been asleep.

130   Thurber muttered something and stretched his legs and yawned, still asleep. Mimi glanced in his direction. *We've both been dreaming,* she thought, *but his dream continues.*

Somewhere behind her, the broken clock was attempting to strike the hour of three. Its voice was dull and rusty, needing oil.

Looking down, she saw the words BRIAN BASSETT written on the page before her and it occurred to her that, without his person, the words were nothing more than extrapolations from the alphabet—something fanciful we call a "name" in the hope that, one day, it will take on meaning.

She thought of Brian Bassett with his building blocks—pushing the letters around on the floor and coming up with more acceptable arrangements: *TINA STERABBS . . . IAN BRETT BASS . . . BEST STAB the RAIN:* a sentence. He had known all along, of course, that *BRIAN BASSETT* wasn't what he wanted because it wasn't what he was. He had come here against his will, was held here against his better judgment, fought against his captors and finally escaped.

But where was here to Ian Brett Bass? Where was here to Tina Sterabbs? Like Brian Bassett, they had all been here in someone else's dreams, and had to wait for someone else to wake before they could make their getaway.

135   Slowly, Mimi uncapped her fountain pen and drew a firm, black line through Brian Bassett's name. *We dreamed him,* she wrote, *that's all. And then we let him go.*

Seeing Everett standing in the doorway, knowing he had just returned from another Kenneth Albright crisis, she had no sense of apprehension. All this was only as it should be. Given the way that everything was going, it stood to reason Kenneth Albright's crisis had to come in this moment. If he managed, at last, to kill himself then at least her husband might begin to sleep again.

Far in the back of her mind a carping, critical voice remarked that any such thoughts were *deeply unfeeling and verging on the barbaric.* But Mimi dismissed this voice and another part of her brain stepped forward in her defence. *I will weep for Kenneth Albright,* she thought, *when I can weep for Brian Bassett. Now, all that matters is that Everett and I survive.*

Then she strode forward and put out her hand for Everett's briefcase, set the briefcase down and helped him out of his topcoat. She was playing wife. It seemed to be the thing to do.

For the next twenty minutes Everett had nothing to say, and after he had poured himself a drink and after Mimi had done the same, they sat in their chairs and waited for Everett to catch his breath.

140   The first thing he said when he finally spoke was: "finish your notes?"

"Just about," Mimi told him. "I've written everything I can for now." She did not elaborate. "You're home early," she said, hoping to goad him into saying something new about Kenneth Albright.

"Yes," he said. "I am." But that was all.

Then he stood up—threw back the last of his drink and poured another. He lighted a cigarette and Mimi didn't even wince. He had been smoking now three days. The atmosphere between them had been, since then, enlivened with a magnetic kind of tension. But it was a moribund tension, slowly beginning to dissipate.

Mimi watched her husband's silent torment now with a kind of clinical detachment. This was the result, she liked to tell herself, of her training and her discipline. The lover in her could regard Everett warmly and with concern, but the psychiatrist in her could also watch him as someone suffering a nervous breakdown, someone who could not be helped until the symptoms had multiplied and declared themselves more openly.

Everett went into the darkest corner of the room and sat down hard in one of   145
Mimi's straight-backed chairs: the ones inherited from her mother. He sat, prim, like a patient in a doctor's office, totally unrelaxed and nervy; expressionless. Either he had come to receive a deadly diagnosis, or he would get a clean bill of health.

Mimi glided over to the sofa in the window, plush and red and deeply comfortable; a place to recuperate. The view—if she chose to turn only slightly sideways—was one of the gentle rain that was falling onto Bay Street. Sopping-wet pigeons huddled on the window-sill; people across the street in the Manulife building were turning on their lights.

A renegade robin, nesting in their eaves, began to sing.

Everett Menlo began to talk.

"Please don't interrupt," he said at first.

"You know I won't," said Mimi. It was a rule that neither one should interrupt   150
the telling of a case until they had been invited to do so.

Mimi put her fingers into her glass so the ice-cubes wouldn't click. She waited.

Everett spoke—but he spoke as if in someone else's voice, perhaps the voice of Kenneth Albright. This was not entirely unusual. Often, both Mimi and Everett Menlo spoke in the voices of their patients. What was unusual, this time, was that, speaking in Kenneth's voice, Everett began to sweat profusely—so profusely that Mimi was able to watch his shirt front darkening with perspiration.

"As you know," he said, "I have not been sleeping."

This was the understatement of the year. Mimi was silent.

"I have not been sleeping because—to put it in a nutshell—I have been afraid   155
to dream."

Mimi was somewhat startled by this. Not by the fact that Everett was afraid to dream, but only because she had just been thinking of dreams herself.

"I have been afraid to dream, because in all my dreams there have been bodies. Corpses. Murder victims."

Mimi—not really listening—idly wondered if she had been one of them.

"In all my dreams, there have been corpses," Everett repeated. "But I am not the murderer. Kenneth Albright is the murderer, and, up to this moment, he has left behind him fifteen bodies: none of them people I recognize."

Mimi nodded. The ice-cubes in her drink were beginning to freeze her fingers.   160
Any minute now, she prayed, they would surely melt.

"I gave up dreaming almost a week ago," said Everett, "thinking that if I did, the killing pattern might be altered; broken." Then he said tersely; "it was not. The killings have continued. . . ."

"How do you know the killings have continued, Everett, if you've given up your dreaming? Wouldn't this mean he had no place to hide the bodies?"

In spite of the fact she had disobeyed their rule about not speaking, Everett answered her.

"I know they are being continued because I have seen the blood."

165   "Ah, yes. I see."

"No, Mimi. No. You do not see. The blood is not a figment of my imagination. The blood, in fact, is the only thing not dreamed." He explained the stains on Kenneth Albright's hands and arms and clothes and he said: "It happens every day. We have searched his person for signs of cuts and gashes—even for internal and rectal bleeding. Nothing. We have searched his quarters and all the other quarters in his ward. His ward is locked. His ward is isolated in the extreme. None of his fellow patients was ever found bleeding—never had cause to bleed. There were no injuries—no self-inflicted wounds. We thought of animals. Perhaps a mouse—a rat. But nothing. Nothing. Nothing . . . We also went so far as to strip-search all the members of the staff who entered that ward and I, too, offered myself for this experiment. Still nothing. Nothing. No one had bled."

Everett was now beginning to perspire so heavily he removed his jacket and threw it on the floor. Thurber woke and stared at it, startled. At first, it appeared to be the beast that had just pursued him through the woods and down the road. But, then, it sighed and settled and was just a coat; a rumpled jacket lying down on the rug.

Everett said: "We had taken samples of the blood on the patient's hands—on Kenneth Albright's hands and on his clothing and we had these samples analysed. No. It was not his own blood. No, it was not the blood of an animal. No, it was not the blood of a fellow patient. No, it was not the blood of any members of the staff. . . ."

Everett's voice had risen.

170   "Whose blood was it?" he almost cried. "Whose the hell was it?"

Mimi waited.

Everett Menlo lighted another cigarette. He took a great gulp of his drink.

"Well . . ." He was calmer now; calmer of necessity. He had to marshall the evidence. He had to put it all in order—bring it into line with reason. "Did this mean that—somehow—the patient had managed to leave the premises—do some bloody deed and return without our knowledge of it? That is, after all, the only possible explanation. Isn't it?"

Mimi waited.

175   "Isn't it?" he repeated.

"Yes," she said. "It's the only possible explanation."

"Except there is no way out of that place. There is absolutely no way out."

Now, there was a pause.

"But one," he added—his voice, again, a whisper.

180   *Mimi* was silent. Fearful—watching his twisted face.

"Tell me," Everett Menlo said—the perfect innocent, almost the perfect child in quest of forbidden knowledge. "Answer me this—be honest: is there blood in dreams?"

Mimi could not respond. She felt herself go pale. Her husband—after all, the sanest man alive—had just suggested something so completely mad he might as well have handed over his reason in a paper bag and said to her, *burn this.*

"The only place that Kenneth Albright goes, I tell you, is into dreams," Everett said. "That is the only place beyond the ward into which the patient can or does escape."

Another—briefer—pause.

"It is real blood, Mimi. Real. And he gets it all from dreams. *My dreams.*"

They waited for this to settle.

Everett said: "I'm tired. I'm tired. I cannot bear this any more. I'm tired. . . ."

Mimi thought, *good. No matter what else happens, he will sleep tonight.*

He did. And so, at last, did she.

Mimi's dreams were rarely of the kind that engender fear. She dreamt more gentle scenes with open spaces that did not intimidate. She would dream quite often of water and of animals. Always, she was nothing more than an observer; roles were not assigned her; often, this was sad. Somehow, she seemed at times locked out, unable to participate. These were the dreams she endured when Brian Bassett died: field trips to see him in some desert setting; underwater excursions to watch him floating amongst the seaweed. He never spoke, and, indeed, he never appeared to be aware of her presence.

That night, when Everett fell into his bed exhausted and she did likewise, Mimi's dream of Brian Bassett was the last she would ever have of him and somehow, in the dream, she knew this. What she saw was what, in magical terms, would be called a disappearing act. Brian Bassett vanished. Gone.

Sometime after midnight on May Day morning, Mimi Menlo awoke from her dream of Brian to the sound of Thurber thumping the floor in a dream of his own.

Everett was not in his bed and Mimi cursed. She put on her wrapper and her slippers and went beyond the bedroom into the hall.

No lights were shining but the street lamps far below and the windows gave no sign of stars.

Mimi made her way past the jungle, searching for Everett in the living-room. He was not there. She would dream of this one day; it was a certainty.

"Everett?"

He did not reply.

Mimi turned and went back through the bedroom.

"Everett?"

She heard him. He was in the bathroom and she went in through the door.

"Oh," she said, when she saw him. "Oh, my God."

Everett Menlo was standing in the bathtub, removing his pyjamas. They were soaking wet, but not with perspiration. They were soaking wet with blood.

For a moment, holding his jacket, letting its arms hang down across his belly and his groin, Everett stared at Mimi, blank-eyed from his nightmare.

Mimi raised her hands to her mouth. She felt as one must feel, if helpless, watching someone burn alive.

205 Everett threw the jacket down and started to remove his trousers. His pyjamas, made of cotton, had been green. His eyes were blinded now with blood and his hands reached out to find the shower taps.

"Please don't look at me," he said. "I . . . Please go away."

Mimi said: "no." She sat on the toilet seat. "I'm waiting here," she told him, "until we both wake up."

1988

QUESTIONS

1. Who is the auditor, the "You," addressed in the first paragraph of "The Cask of Amontillado"? (You may want to wait until you have finished the last sentence of the story before answering.) When is the story being told? Why? How does your knowledge of the auditor and the occasion influence the story's effect?

2. In "How," several phrases repeat, mostly notably "A week, a month, a year" and "just an endless series of tests." Locate each place that these phrases occur. How does their meaning change? What is the effect of the repetition?

3. What does the last sentence in "Dreams"—" 'I'm waiting here,' she told him, 'until we both wake up' "—mean or suggest? (This question does not imply that there is only one meaning or implication.) How are the meanings related to point of view? For example, if the entire story is a dream of Mimi's, then hers is the only center of consciousness (or unconsciousness). Other meanings also seem to require a specific point of view.

4. In paragraph 133, Mimi makes other names and phrases out of the letters of Brian Bassett's name, then adds, "He had known all along, of course, that BRIAN BASSETT wasn't what he wanted because it wasn't what he was. He had come here against his will, was held here against his better judgment, fought against his captors and finally escaped." In the next paragraph, she adds that he had "been here in someone else's dreams, and had to wait for someone else to wake before [he] could make [his] getaway." She also assumes that there was a "here" for the others—Ian Brett Bass, Tina Sterabbs—who are just names made from the letters of his. What is Mimi saying here? What seems to be her sense of reality? Of the relation of body and spirit? (Paragraph 107 might also be helpful in trying to answer these questions.) Can you find other significant patterns in the names in this story?

5. Find the first indication in "Hills Like White Elephants" that the "American" and the "girl" are not getting along. What is the first clue about the exact nature of their conflict? Why are they going to Madrid? What is the tone of the man's repeated assurance, "it's perfectly simple"?

WRITING SUGGESTIONS

1. Write a parody of "The Cask of Amontillado" set in modern times, perhaps on a college campus ("A Barrel of Bud"?).

2. In "How," the man that "you" lives with "craves a family" and plays well with children.

Notice other details of his domestic behavior. "You" is referred to as a woman, but does she do some things that are usually thought of as masculine? Discuss the ways that the story works against expectations about women's and men's roles in relationships.

3. Compare the second-person voice and imperatives in "How" with the similar technique in Jamaica Kincaid's "Girl" (see chapter 10) or the choices offered to the reader in Atwood's "Happy Endings." What activities or responses are expected of "you," as reader or auditor in each story? Comment on the differences.

4. Carry a notebook or tape recorder with you for a day or two, and note any stories you tell or hear, such as in daydreams, in conversation, on the phone, or through email. Consider what makes stories; your transcripts may be short, and may consist of memories, observations about your own character or those of people around you, plans, or predictions about the future. Choose two and modify them into plot summaries (no more than a paragraph each), using the first or the third person, the present or the past tense. Add a note as to whether a full version of each story should give the inner thoughts of one or more characters, and why.

3

CHARACTER

In a good many stories the narrator is a disembodied offstage speaker, without a personal history, without influence on the action, without a personality other than that suggested by voice and style. So it is in some of the earlier stories in this volume—"The Zebra Storyteller," "The Jewelry," "Dreams." In "The Cask of Amontillado," however, Poe's narrator both tells us the story and plays a part in the action within the story. Without him, we would lack not only a storyteller, but also a story (for any narrator) to tell. In addition to being the narrator, he is a **character:** someone who acts, appears, or is referred to as playing a part in a literary work.

> The foundation of good fiction is character-creation and nothing else. . . . Style counts; plot counts; originality of outlook counts. But none of these counts anything like so much as the convincingness of the characters.
>
> —ARNOLD BENNETT

The most common term for the character with the leading male role is **hero,** the "good guy," who opposes the **villain,** or "bad guy." The leading female character is the **heroine.** Heroes and heroines are usually larger than life, stronger or better than most human beings, almost godlike. In most modern fiction, however, the leading character is much more ordinary, more like the rest of us. Such a character is sometimes called an **antihero,** not because he opposes the hero but because he is not heroic in stature or perfection, is not so clearly or simply a "good guy." An older and more neutral term than hero for the leading character, a term that does not imply either the presence or the absence of outstanding virtue (and that has the added advantage of referring equally to male and female characters), is **protagonist,** whose opponent is the **antagonist.** You might get into long and pointless arguments by calling Lantin or Montresor a hero, but most would agree that each is his story's protagonist. (This is not to say, however, that some stories don't leave open to debate the question of which character most deserves the title of protagonist. Is Sonny or his brother the protagonist of "Sonny's Blues"?)

The **major** or **main characters** are those we see more of over a longer period of time; we learn more about them, and we think of them as more complex and, therefore, frequently more "realistic" than the **minor characters,** the figures who fill out the story. These major characters can grow and change, as Lantin does and as Judith does in Doris Lessing's "Our Friend Judith"; by the end of these stories both protagonists have acted unpredictably based on what we learned earlier in the story about them and their past actions.

Yet while minor characters may be less prominent and less complex, they are ultimately just as important to a story as major characters. In fact, minor characters often play a key role in shaping our interpretations of, and attitudes toward, the major characters and in precipitating the changes that major characters undergo. In Herman Melville's "Bartleby, the Scrivener," for example, "flighty" Turkey and "fiery" Nippers help us, as well as the story's narrator, to recognize the uniqueness of the "singularly sedate" Bartleby (paragraph 16). Like many a minor character, then, Turkey and Nippers might be described as **foils** to this major character in the sense that they serve as a contrast, throwing into relief the traits that distinguish and define him. In "Sonny's Blues," to take a different example, the "three sisters in black, and a brother" singing spirituals on a street corner do a great deal to foster change in the narrator (paragraph 177): helping him to appreciate in a new way the expressive power of music, these characters pave the way for the ultimate transformation of the narrator's attitudes toward both Sonny and the way of life Sonny represents.

Characters like Baldwin's narrator, who can thus "surprise convincingly," an influential critic says, are **round characters,** whereas characters that, like Turkey and Nippers, are not very complex and do not change in surprising ways, are **flat.** But we must be careful not to let terms like *flat* and *round* or *major* and *minor* turn into value judgments. Because flat characters are less complex than round ones, it is easy to assume they are artistically inferior; we need only to think of the characters of Charles Dickens, almost all of whom are flat, to realize that this is not always true.

The terms *flat* and *round,* like the terms *hero* and *antihero,* are not absolute or precise. They designate extremes or tendencies, not pigeonholes. Is Poe's Montresor or Melville's Nippers entirely flat? Is Shakespeare's Falstaff? Little Orphan Annie? Bart Simpson? Are all these characters equally flat? We will probably agree that Baldwin's Sonny is a round character, but what about Findley's Mimi or Everett Menlo? Cheever's Francis Weed? Melville's Bartleby? Are they all equally round? Our answers are less important than our looking carefully at these characters to see what we know about each of them, to what degree they can be summed up in a phrase or a sentence; to discover how we learned what we know about them and how our judgment has been shaped by the story; to think about and perhaps judge the assumptions about human motivation, behavior, and nature that underlie the character and his or her characterization. Flat and round are useful as categories but are even more useful as tools of investigation, as ways of focusing our attention and sharpening our perception.

Though most of Dickens's flat characters are highly individualized, not to say unique, some, like Fagin, the avaricious Jewish moneylender of *Oliver Twist,* are **stereotypes:** characters based on conscious or unconscious cultural assumptions that sex, age, ethnicity or nationality, occupation, marital status, and so on are predictably accompanied by certain character traits, actions, even values.

The stereotype may be very useful in creating a round character, one who can surprise convincingly: Judith, according to a Canadian woman, is "one of your typical English spinsters." Judith, however, acts in ways that defy the limitations of the stereotype. A stereotype is, after all, only a quick—and superficial—form of classification, and classification is a common first step in definitions. One of the chief ways we have of describing or defining is by placing the thing to be defined in a category or class and then distinguishing it from the other members of that class. A good deal of **characterization**— the art, craft, method of presentation, or creation of fictional personages—involves a similar process. Characters are almost inevitably identified by category—by sex, age, nationality, occupation, and so on. We learn that the narrator of "Why I Live at the P.O." is a woman, relatively young, who lives in a small town in Mississippi.

Paradoxically, in fiction, as in life, the more groups a character is placed in, the more individual he or she becomes. Sonny, for example, is simultaneously an African American, a man, a blues musician, a heroin addict, a younger brother, an ex-convict, and a resident of an inner-city neighborhood. As a result, our interpretation of Sonny is shaped not only by our assumptions about each of these social groups, but also by our sense of the way belonging to all of these groups helps to make Sonny who he is. Thus the story asks us to think about how Sonny's choice to be a blues musician relates to the fact that he is African American, about the way inner-city life has shaped Sonny's experience of being African American, and so on.

Not all generalizations involve cultural stereotypes, of course. Some may involve generalized character traits that the story or narrator defines for us (and that we must accept unless events in the story prove otherwise). Physical characteristics, for example, also serve as categories. As with stereotypes, when physical characteristics are multiplied, the result is more and more particularizing or individualizing. The detailed physical description of Judith makes it possible to visualize her rather fully, almost to recognize her as an individual:

> Judith is tall, small-breasted, slender. Her light brown hair is parted in the centre and cut straight around her neck. A high straight forehead, straight nose, and full grave mouth are setting for her eyes, which are green, large and prominent. Her lids are very white, fringed with gold, and moulded close over the eyeball. . . . (paragraph 7)

At the same time, however, the very physical attributes that individualize Judith also encourage us to see her as a certain type of person and, in this case, may confirm for us that she does conform to our stereotype: "small-breasted" and "slender," with "straight" features, a "grave" mouth, and a severe haircut, Judith does, indeed, *look* as straitlaced, prudish, and conventional as we might expect a "typical English spinster" to be.

In most cases we not only see what characters look like, but also see what they do and hear what they say; we sometimes learn what they think, and what other people think or say about them; we often know what kind of clothes they wear, what and how much they own, treasure, or covet; we may be told about their childhood, parents, or some parts of their past. And all of this information combines to shape our sense of the character. We learn a little about Eudora Welty's "Sister" from her age, her sex, and where she lives. We learn a good deal more from the way she talks to her family and they to her, how she decides what she owns, and what she chooses to take with her when she moves. Yet as the enigmatic Bartleby may suggest, what we don't know about a character can be as significant and revealing as what we do know. What, for example, is the effect of the fact that we never learn the narrator's name in either "Bartleby, the Scrivener" or "Sonny's Blues"? that we know only the nicknames of Nippers and Turkey, as well as Welty's "Sister"? that we never know for certain whether Shirley-T. is adopted or not?

The fact that what characters like "Sister" or Bartleby do (or don't do) is as much a part of characterization as what they look like or say may help to remind us once again that the elements of fiction are abstractions, useful for analysis but not truly separable. Throughout a story, plot (or incident) and character are fused. As novelist Henry James has said,

> What is character but the determination of incident? What is incident but the illustration of character? . . . It is an incident for a woman to stand up with her hand resting on a table

and look at you in a certain way; or if it is not an incident I think it will be hard to say what it is. At the same time it is an expression of character. If you say you don't see it, . . . this is exactly what the artist who has reasons of his own for thinking he *does* see it undertakes to show you.

Though characterization is gradual, taking place sequentially through the story, it is not, as it may seem natural to assume, entirely cumulative. We do not begin with an empty space called Judith or Francis Weed or Sonny and fill it in gradually by adding physical traits, habitual actions, ways of speaking, and so on. Our imagination does not work that way. Rather, just as at each point in the action we project some sort of configuration of how the story will come out or what the world of the story will be like or mean, so we project a more or less complete image of each character at the point at which he or she is first mentioned or appears. The image is based on the initial reference in the text, our reading, and our life experiences and associations. (Don't you have an image of a Herb? a Maude? a spinster?) The next time the character is mentioned, or when he or she speaks or acts, we do not so much "adjust" our first impression as we project a new image (just as in the plot we project a new series of developments and a new outcome). As our sense of a character develops and grows, information that we received early in the story thus tends to take on a different significance. When we first read the physical description of Judith, for example, we probably assign most importance to those features that make her seem straitlaced and rigid, yet by the end of the story we may well both remember and pay more attention to the narrator's remark that those features merely serve as a "setting" for Judith's vibrant green eyes.

There may be some carryover between our initial and later impressions, but we do not in the course of the story put the character together like a Mr. Potato Head. Instead, we overlay one image on the other, and though the final image may be the most enduring, the early images do not all disappear: our view of the character is multidimensional, flickering, like a time-lapse photograph. Perhaps that is why it is rare that any actor in a film based on a novel or story matches the way we imagined that character if we have read the book or story first—our imagination has not one image but rather a sequence of images associated with that character. It is also why some of us feel that seeing the film before reading the book hobbles the imagination. A particular character's physical attributes, for example, may not be described in a novel until after that character has been involved in some incident; the reader may then need to adjust his or her earlier vision of that character, which is not an option for the viewer of a film. It is thus the reader, rather than a casting director, who finalizes a character in his or her own imagination.

For no matter how many methods of characterization are employed, at some point the definition of the individual stops. No matter how individualized the character may be, he or she remains a member of a number of groups, and we make certain assumptions about that character based on our fixed or stereotyped notions of those groups. To destroy a stereotype, a story must introduce a stereotype to destroy. And somehow the destereotyped character, no matter how particularized, remains to some degree representative. This representativeness makes characters meaningful to us—helps us to both relate to, and learn from, them. If Judith turns out to be not as prudish and prissy as the stereotype of the English spinster has led us to believe, we may well conclude that the stereotype is false and that Judith is more representative of the real English spinster than the stereotype is. Indeed, this tendency to generalize from the particulars of a story sometimes also or instead extends beyond cultural groups such as "English spinsters" or "heroin addicts" to human characters at large: if Sonny can change his ways after years of habitual conduct, then human character, the story might seem to say, is not permanently fixed at birth, in infancy, childhood, ever.

One of the reasons it is so difficult to discuss character is precisely that the principles of definition and evaluation of fictional characters (not of their characterizations, the way they are presented) are the same as those we use for real people, an area of violent controversy and confusion. The very term *character,* when it refers not to a fictional personage but to a combination of qualities in a human being, is somewhat ambiguous. It usually has moral overtones, often favorable (a man of character); it is sometimes neutral but evaluative (character reference). Judgment about character usually involves moral terms like *good* and *bad* and *strong* and *weak.* **Personality** usually implies that which distinguishes or individualizes a person, and the judgment called for is not so much moral as social—*pleasing* or *displeasing.* An older term, **nature** (it is in one's nature to be so or do such), usually implies something inherent or inborn, something fixed and thus predictable. The **existential character** implies the opposite; that is, whatever our past, our conditioning, our pattern of previous behavior, we can, by choice, by free will, change all that right this minute, as Sonny does.

> A man, woman or child, cannot buy a morsel of pickled salmon, look at his shoe, or bring in a mug of ale; a solitary object cannot pass on the other side of the way; a boy cannot take a bite at a turnip or hold a horse; a bystander cannot answer the simplest question; a dog cannot fall into a doze; a bird cannot whet his bill; a pony cannot have a peculiar nose, nor a pig one ear, but out peeps the first germ of "character."
>
> —R. H. HORNE

We must not forget the distinction between the character and the characterization, the method by which he or she is presented; so we must be careful to distinguish the *good character,* meaning someone whom, if real, we would consider virtuous, and the *good characterization,* meaning a fictional person who, no matter what his or her morality or behavior, is well presented. Just as an actor receives a best-actor award for playing a character well rather than for playing a good character, so an author may be recognized for good characterization even if we do not like or admire the character the author has created. Often the "bad" or at least morally complex characters (or those that, like Sonny or Bartleby, challenge our sense of what is and is not virtuous) interest and teach us the most.

Effective characterization can encourage us to identify so completely with certain characters that they seem to be part of the history that lies behind the story or beyond the story as part of our own world, to exist in a reality that is detachable from the words and events of the story in which they appear. We feel we might recognize Jane Eyre, Sherlock Holmes, or "Sister" on the street, and we might be able to anticipate what they would say or do in *our* world, outside the story. But fictional characters are neither real nor detachable, and they exist only in the words of the works in which they are presented. We must recognize that characters have roles, functions, limitations, and their very existence only in the context of the story; we must not confuse fictional characters with real people. This is not to say, however, that we may not learn about real people from characters in fiction or learn to understand fictional characters in part from what we know about real people. For real people, too, exist in a context of other people and other elements, their history and geography and their "narrator," the one who is representing them—that is, *you.* Indeed, it may be worth paying particular attention to how stories create the images of people and what those images assume about human character precisely because this process is so similar to the way we get to know and understand real people and because we, too, constantly make and act on assumptions about human character. For we are all artists representing reality to ourselves. If we study the art of characterization and think about the way we interpret fictional characters, we may become better artists, able to enrich our reading both of fictional texts and of real people and situations.

EUDORA WELTY

Why I Live at the P.O.

I was getting along fine with Mama, Papa-Daddy, and Uncle Rondo until my sister Stella-Rondo just separated from her husband and came back home again. Mr. Whitaker! Of course I went with Mr. Whitaker first, when he first appeared here in China Grove, taking "Pose Yourself" photos, and Stella-Rondo broke us up. Told him I was one-sided. Bigger on one side than the other, which is a deliberate, calculated falsehood: I'm the same. Stella-Rondo is exactly twelve months to the day younger than I am and for that reason she's spoiled.

She's always had anything in the world she wanted and then she'd throw it away. Papa-Daddy give her this gorgeous Add-a-Pearl necklace when she was eight years old and she threw it away playing baseball when she was nine, with only two pearls.

So as soon as she got married and moved away from home the first thing she did was separate! From Mr. Whitaker! This photographer with the popeyes she said she trusted. Came home from one of those towns up in Illinois and to our complete surprise brought this child of two.

Mama said she like to make her drop dead for a second. "Here you had this marvelous blonde child and never so much as wrote your mother a word about it," says Mama. "I'm thoroughly ashamed of you." But of course she wasn't.

Stella-Rondo just calmly takes off this *hat,* I wish you could see it. She says, 5
"Why, Mama, Shirley-T.'s adopted, I can prove it."

"How?" says Mama, but all I says was, "H'm!" There I was over the hot stove, trying to stretch two chickens over five people and a completely unexpected child into the bargain without one moment's notice.

"What do you mean—'H'm'?" says Stella-Rondo, and Mama says, "I heard that, Sister."

I said that oh, I didn't mean a thing, only that whoever Shirley-T. was, she was the spit-image of Papa-Daddy if he'd cut off his beard, which of course he'd never do in the world. Papa-Daddy's Mama's papa and sulks.

Stella-Rondo got furious! She said, "Sister, I don't need to tell you you got a lot of nerve and always did have and I'll thank you to make no future reference to my adopted child whatsoever."

"Very well," I said. "Very well, very well. Of course I noticed at once she looks 10
like Mr. Whitaker's side too. That frown. She looks like a cross between Mr. Whitaker and Papa-Daddy."

"Well, all I can say is she isn't."

"She looks exactly like Shirley Temple to me," says Mama, but Shirley-T. just ran away from her.

So the first thing Stella-Rondo did at the table was turn Papa-Daddy against me.

"Papa-Daddy," she says. He was trying to cut up his meat. "Papa-Daddy!" I was taken completely by surprise. Papa-Daddy is about a million years old and's got this long-long beard. "Papa-Daddy, Sister says she fails to understand why you don't cut off your beard."

15   So Papa-Daddy l-a-y-s down his knife and fork! He's real rich. Mama says he is, he says he isn't. So he says, "Have I heard correctly? You don't understand why I don't cut off my beard?"

"Why," I says, "Papa-Daddy, of course I understand, I did not say any such a thing, the idea!"

He says, "Hussy!"

I says, "Papa-Daddy, you know I wouldn't any more want you to cut off your beard than the man in the moon. It was the farthest thing from my mind! Stella-Rondo sat there and made that up while she was eating breast of chicken."

But he says, "So the postmistress fails to understand why I don't cut off my beard. Which job I got you through my influence with the government. 'Bird's nest'—is that what you call it?"

20   Not that it isn't the next to smallest P.O. in the entire state of Mississippi.

I says, "Oh, Papa-Daddy," I says, "I didn't say any such a thing, I never dreamed it was a bird's nest, I have always been grateful though this is the next to smallest P.O. in the state of Mississippi, and I do not enjoy being referred to as a hussy by my own grandfather."

But Stella-Rondo says, "Yes, you did say it too. Anybody in the world could of heard you, that had ears."

"Stop right there," says Mama, looking at *me*.

So I pulled my napkin straight back through the napkin ring and left the table.

25   As soon as I was out of the room Mama says, "Call her back, or she'll starve to death," but Papa-Daddy says, "This is the beard I started growing on the Coast when I was fifteen years old." He would of gone on till nightfall if Shirley-T. hadn't lost the Milky Way she ate in Cairo.

So Papa-Daddy says, "I am going out and lie in the hammock, and you can all sit here and remember my words: I'll never cut off my beard as long as I live, even one inch, and I don't appreciate it in you at all." Passed right by me in the hall and went straight out and got in the hammock.

It would be a holiday. It wasn't five minutes before Uncle Rondo suddenly appeared in the hall in one of Stella-Rondo's flesh-colored kimonos, all cut on the bias, like something Mr. Whitaker probably thought was gorgeous.

"Uncle Rondo!" I says. "I didn't know who that was! Where are you going?"

"Sister," he says, "get out of my way, I'm poisoned."

30   "If you're poisoned stay away from Papa-Daddy," I says. "Keep out of the hammock. Papa-Daddy will certainly beat you on the head if you come within forty miles of him. He thinks I deliberately said he ought to cut off his beard after he

got me the P.O., and I've told him and told him and told him, and he acts like he just don't hear me. Papa-Daddy must of gone stone deaf."

"He picked a fine day to do it then," says Uncle Rondo, and before you could say "Jack Robinson" flew out in the yard.

What he'd really done, he'd drunk another bottle of that prescription. He does it every single Fourth of July as sure as shooting, and it's horribly expensive. Then he falls over in the hammock and snores. So he insisted on zigzagging right on out to the hammock, looking like a half-wit.

Papa-Daddy woke with this horrible yell and right there without moving an inch he tried to turn Uncle Rondo against me. I heard every word he said. Oh, he told Uncle Rondo I didn't learn to read till I was eight years old and he didn't see how in the world I ever got the mail put up at the P.O., much less read it all, and he said if Uncle Rondo could only fathom the lengths he had gone to get me that job! And he said on the other hand he thought Stella-Rondo had a brilliant mind and deserved credit for getting out of town. All the time he was just lying there swinging as pretty as you please and looping out his beard, and poor Uncle Rondo was *pleading* with him to slow down the hammock, it was making him as dizzy as a witch to watch it. But that's what Papa-Daddy likes about a hammock. So Uncle Rondo was too dizzy to get turned against me for the time being. He's Mama's only brother and is a good case of a one-track mind. Ask anybody. A certified pharmacist.

Just then I heard Stella-Rondo raising the upstairs window. While she was married she got this peculiar idea that it's cooler with the windows shut and locked. So she has to raise the window before she can make a soul hear her outdoors.

So she raises the window and says, "*Oh!*" You would have thought she was mortally wounded.

Uncle Rondo and Papa-Daddy didn't even look up, but kept right on with what they were doing. I had to laugh.

I flew up the stairs and threw the door open! I says, "What in the wide world's the matter, Stella-Rondo? You mortally wounded?"

"No," she says, "I am not mortally wounded but I wish you would do me the favor of looking out that window there and telling me what you see."

So I shade my eyes and look out the window.

"I see the front yard," I says.

"Don't you see any human beings?"

"I see Uncle Rondo trying to run Papa-Daddy out of the hammock," I says. "Nothing more. Naturally, it's so suffocating-hot in the house, with all the windows shut and locked, everybody who cares to stay in their right mind will have to go out and get in the hammock before the Fourth of July is over."

"Don't you notice anything different about Uncle Rondo?" asks Stella-Rondo.

"Why, no, except he's got on some terrible-looking flesh-colored contraption I wouldn't be found dead in, is all I can see," I says.

"Never mind, you won't be found dead in it, because it happens to be part of my trousseau, and Mr. Whitaker took several dozen photographs of me in it," says Stella-Rondo. "What on earth could uncle Rondo *mean* by wearing part of my trousseau out in the broad open daylight without saying so much as 'Kiss my foot,' *knowing* I only got home this morning after my separation and hung my negligee up on the bathroom door, just as nervous as I could be?"

"I'm sure I don't know, and what do you expect me to do about it?" I says. "Jump out the window?"

"No, I expect nothing of the kind. I simply declare that Uncle Rondo looks like a fool in it, that's all," she says. "It makes me sick to my stomach."

"Well, he looks as good as he can," I says. "As good as anybody in reason could." I stood up for Uncle Rondo, please remember. And I said to Stella-Rondo, "I think I would do well not to criticize so freely if I were you and came home with a two-year-old child I had never said a word about, and no explanation whatever about my separation."

"I asked you the instant I entered this house not to refer one more time to my adopted child, and you gave me your word of honor you would not," was all Stella-Rondo would say, and started pulling out every one of her eyebrows with some cheap Kress tweezers.

50   So I merely slammed the door behind me and went down and made some green-tomato pickle. Somebody had to do it. Of course Mama had turned both the Negroes loose; she always said no earthly power could hold one anyway on the Fourth of July, so she wouldn't even try. It turned out that Jaypan fell in the lake and came within a very narrow limit of drowning.

So Mama trots in. Lifts up the lid and says, "H'm! Not very good for your Uncle Rondo in his precarious condition, I must say. Or poor little adopted Shirley-T. Shame on you!"

That made me tired. I says, "Well, Stella-Rondo had better thank her lucky stars it was her instead of me came trotting in with that very peculiar-looking child. Now if it had been me that trotted in from Illinois and brought a peculiar-looking child or two, I shudder to think of the reception I'd of got, much less controlled the diet of an entire family."

"But you must remember, Sister, that you were never married to Mr. Whitaker in the first place and didn't go up to Illinois to live," says Mama, shaking a spoon in my face. "If you had I would of been just as overjoyed to see you and your little adopted girl as I was to see Stella-Rondo, when you wound up with your separation and came on back home."

"You would not," I says.

55   "Don't contradict me, I would," says Mama.

But I said she couldn't convince me though she talked till she was blue in the face. Then I said, "Besides, you know as well as I do that that child is not adopted."

"She most certainly is adopted," says Mama, stiff as a poker.

I says, "Why, Mama, Stella-Rondo had her just as sure as anything in this world, and just too stuck up to admit it."

"Why, Sister," said Mama. "Here I thought we were going to have a pleasant Fourth of July, and you start right out not believing a word your own baby sister tells you!"

60   "Just like Cousin Annie Flo. Went to her grave denying the facts of life," I reminded Mama.

"I told you if you ever mentioned Annie Flo's name I'd slap your face," says Mama, and slaps my face.

"All right, you wait and see," I says.

"I," says Mama, "I prefer to take my children's word for anything when it's humanly possible." You ought to see Mama, she weighs two hundred pounds and has real tiny feet.

Just then something perfectly horrible occurred to me.

"Mama," I says, "can that child talk?" I simply had to whisper! "Mama, I won-   65
der if that child can be—you know—in any way? Do you realize?" I says, "that she hasn't spoke one single, solitary word to a human being up to this minute? This is the way she looks," I says, and I looked like this.

Well, Mama and I just stood there and stared at each other. It was horrible!

"I remember well that Joe Whitaker frequently drank like a fish," says Mama. "I believed to my soul he drank *chemicals*." And without another word she marches to the foot of the stairs and calls Stella-Rondo.

"Stella-Rondo? O-o-o-o-o! Stella-Rondo!"

"What?" says Stella-Rondo from upstairs. Not even the grace to get up off the bed.

"Can that child of yours talk?" asks Mama.   70

Stella-Rondo says, "Can she what?"

"Talk! Talk!" says Mama. "Burdyburdyburdyburdy!"

So Stella-Rondo yells back, "Who says she can't talk?"

"Sister says so," says Mama.

"You didn't have to tell me, I know whose word of honor don't mean a thing   75
in this house," says Stella-Rondo.

And in a minute the loudest Yankee voice I ever heard in my life yells out, "OE'm Pop-OE the Sailor-r-r Ma-a-an!" and then somebody jumps up and down in the upstairs hall. In another second the house would of fallen down.

"Not only talks, she can tap-dance!" calls Stella-Rondo. "Which is more than some people I won't name can do."

"Why, the little precious darling thing!" Mama says, so surprised. "Just as smart as she can be!" Starts talking baby talk right there. Then she turns on me. "Sister, you ought to be thoroughly ashamed! Run upstairs this instant and apologize to Stella-Rondo and Shirley-T."

"Apologize for what?" I says. "I merely wondered if the child was normal, that's all. Now that she's proved she is, why, I have nothing further to say."

But Mama just turned on her heel and flew out, furious. She ran right upstairs   80
and hugged the baby. She believed it was adopted. Stella-Rondo hadn't done a thing but turn her against me from upstairs while I stood there helpless over the hot stove. So that made Mama, Papa-Daddy, and the baby all on Stella-Rondo's side.

Next, Uncle Rondo.

I must say that Uncle Rondo has been marvelous to me at various times in the past and I was completely unprepared to be made to jump out of my skin, the way it turned out. Once Stella-Rondo did something perfectly horrible to him—

broke a chain letter from Flanders Field—and he took the radio back he had given her and gave it to me. Stella-Rondo was furious! For six months we all had to call her Stella instead of Stella-Rondo, or she wouldn't answer. I always thought Uncle Rondo had all the brains of the entire family. Another time he sent me to Mammoth Cave with all expenses paid.

But this would be the day he was drinking that prescription, the Fourth of July.

So at supper Stella-Rondo speaks up and says she thinks Uncle Rondo ought to try to eat a little something. So finally Uncle Rondo said he would try a little cold biscuits and ketchup, but that was all. So *she* brought it to him.

85 "Do you think it wise to disport with ketchup in Stella-Rondo's flesh-colored kimono?" I says. Trying to be considerate! If Stella-Rondo couldn't watch out for her trousseau, somebody had to.

"Any objections?" asks Uncle Rondo, just about to pour out all of the ketchup.

"Don't mind what she says, Uncle Rondo," says Stella-Rondo. "Sister has been devoting this solid afternoon to sneering out my bedroom window at the way you look."

"What's that?" says Uncle Rondo. Uncle Rondo has got the most terrible temper in the world. Anything is liable to make him tear the house down if it comes at the wrong time.

So Stella-Rondo says, "Sister says, 'Uncle Rondo certainly does look like a fool in that pink kimono!' "

90 Do you remember who it was really said that?

Uncle Rondo spills out all the ketchup and jumps out of his chair and tears off the kimono and throws it down on the dirty floor and puts his foot on it. It had to be sent all the way to Jackson to the cleaners and re-pleated.

"So that's your opinion of your Uncle Rondo, is it?" he says. "I look like a fool, do I? Well, that's the last straw. A whole day in this house with nothing to do, and then to hear you come out with a remark like that behind my back!"

"I didn't say any such of a thing, Uncle Rondo," I says, "and I'm not saying who did, either. Why, I think you look all right. Just try to take care of yourself and not talk and eat at the same time," I says. "I think you better go lie down."

"Lie down my foot," says Uncle Rondo. I ought to of known by that he was fixing to do something perfectly horrible.

95 So he didn't do anything that night in the precarious state he was in—just played Casino with Mama and Stella-Rondo and Shirley-T. and gave Shirley-T. a nickel with a head on both sides. It tickled her nearly to death, and she called him "Papa." But at 6:30 A.M. the next morning, he threw a whole five-cent package of some unsold one-inch firecrackers from the store as hard as he could into my bedroom and they every one went off. Not one bad one in the string. Anybody else, there'd be one that wouldn't go off.

Well, I'm just terribly susceptible to noise of any kind, the doctor has always told me I was the most sensitive person he had ever seen in his whole life, and I was simply prostrated. I couldn't eat! People tell me they heard it as far as the cemetery, and old Aunt Jep Patterson, that had been holding her own so good, thought it was Judgment Day and she was going to meet her whole family. It's usually so quiet here.

And I'll tell you it didn't take me any longer than a minute to make up my mind what to do. There I was with the whole entire house on Stella-Rondo's side and turned against me. If I have anything at all I have pride.

So I just decided I'd go straight down to the P.O. There's plenty of room there in the back, I says to myself.

Well! I made no bones about letting the family catch on to what I was up to. I didn't try to conceal it.

The first thing they knew, I marched in where they were all playing Old Maid and pulled the electric oscillating fan out by the plug, and everything got real hot. Next I snatched the pillow I'd done the needlepoint on right off the daven-port from behind Papa-Daddy. He went "Ugh!" I beat Stella-Rondo up the stairs and finally found my charm bracelet in her bureau drawer under a picture of Nelson Eddy.[1]

"So that's the way the land lies," says Uncle Rondo. There he was, piecing on the ham. "Well, Sister, I'll be glad to donate my army cot if you got any place to set it up, providing you'll leave right this minute and let me get some peace." Uncle Rondo was in France.

"Thank you kindly for the cot and 'peace' is hardly the word I would select if I had to resort to firecrackers at 6:30 A.M. in a young girl's bedroom," I says to him. "And as to where I intend to go, you seem to forget my position as post-mistress of China Grove, Mississippi," I says. "I've always got the P.O."

Well, that made them all sit up and take notice.

I went out front and started digging up some four-o'clocks to plant around the P.O.

"Ah-ah-ah!" says Mama, raising the window. "Those happen to be my four-o'clocks. Everything planted in that star is mine. I've never known you to make anything grow in your life."

"Very well," I says. "But I take the fern. Even you, Mama, can't stand there and deny that I'm the one watered that fern. And I happen to know where I can send in a box top and get a packet of one thousand mixed seeds, no two the same kind, free."

"Oh, where?" Mama wants to know.

But I says, "Too late. You 'tend to your house, and I'll 'tend to mine. You hear things like that all the time if you know how to listen to the radio. Perfectly marvelous offers. Get anything you want free."

So I hope to tell you I marched in and got that radio, and they could of all bit a nail in two, especially Stella-Rondo, that it used to belong to, and she well knew she couldn't get it back, I'd sue for it like a shot. And I very politely took the sewing-machine motor I helped pay the most on to give Mama for Christmas back in 1929, and a good big calendar, with the first-aid remedies on it. The thermometer and the Hawaiian ukulele certainly were rightfully mine, and I stood on the step-ladder and got all my watermelon-rind preserves and every fruit and

1. Opera singer (1901–1967) who enjoyed phenomenal popularity in the 1930s and 1940s when he costarred in several film musicals with Jeanette MacDonald. The two were known as "America's Singing Sweethearts."

vegetable I'd put up, every jar. Then I began to pull the tacks out of the bluebird wall vases on the archway to the dining room.

110   "Who told you you could have those, Miss Priss?" says Mama, fanning as hard as she could.

"I bought 'em and I'll keep track of 'em," I says. "I'll tack 'em up one on each side of the post-office window, and you can see 'em when you come to ask me for your mail, if you're so dead to see 'em."

"Not I! I'll never darken the door to that post office again if I live to be a hundred," Mama says. "Ungrateful child! After all the money we spent on you at the Normal."[2]

"Me either," says Stella-Rondo. "You can just let my mail lie there and *rot*, for all I care. I'll never come and relieve you of a single, solitary piece."

"I should worry," I says. "And who you think's going to sit down and write you all those big fat letters and postcards, by the way? Mr. Whitaker? Just because he was the only man ever dropped down in China Grove and you got him—unfairly—is he going to sit down and write you a lengthy correspondence after you come home giving no rhyme nor reason whatsoever for your separation and no explanation for the presence of that child? I may not have your brilliant mind, but I fail to see it."

115   So Mama says, "Sister, I've told you a thousand times that Stella-Rondo simply got homesick, and this child is far too big to be hers," and she says, "Now, why don't you just sit down and play Casino?"

Then Shirley-T. sticks out her tongue at me in this perfectly horrible way. She has no more manners than the man in the moon. I told her she was going to cross her eyes like that some day and they'd stick.

"It's too late to stop me now," I says. "You should have tried that yesterday. I'm going to the P.O. and the only way you can possibly see me is to visit me there."

So Papa-Daddy says, "You'll never catch me setting foot in that post office, even if I should take a notion into my head to write a letter some place." He says, "I won't have you reachin' out of that little old window with a pair of shears and cuttin' off any beard of mine. I'm too smart for you!"

"We all are," says Stella-Rondo.

120   But I said, "If you're so smart, where's Mr. Whitaker?"

So then Uncle Rondo says, "I'll thank you from now on to stop reading all the orders I get on postcards and telling everybody in China Grove what you think is the matter with them," but I says, "I draw my own conclusions and will continue in the future to draw them." I says, "If people want to write their innermost secrets on penny postcards, there's nothing in the wide world you can do about it, Uncle Rondo."

"And if you think we'll ever *write* another postcard you're sadly mistaken," says Mama.

"Cutting off your nose to spite your face then," I says. "But if you're all deter-

2. That is, normal school (teachers' college).

mined to have no more to do with the U.S. mail, think of this: What will Stella-Rondo do now, if she wants to tell Mr. Whitaker to come after her?"

"Wah!" says Stella-Rondo. I knew she'd cry. She had a conniption fit right there in the kitchen.

"It will be interesting to see how long she holds out," I says. "And now—I am leaving." 125

"Good-bye," says Uncle Rondo.

"Oh, I declare," says Mama, "to think that a family of mine should quarrel on the Fourth of July, or the day after, over Stella-Rondo leaving old Mr. Whitaker and having the sweetest little adopted child! It looks like we'd all be glad!"

"Wah!" says Stella-Rondo, and has a fresh conniption fit.

"He left *her*—you mark my words," I says. "That's Mr. Whitaker. I know Mr. Whitaker. After all, I knew him first. I said from the beginning he'd up and leave her. I foretold every single thing that's happened."

"Where did he go?" asks Mama. 130

"Probably to the North Pole, if he knows what's good for him," I says.

But Stella-Rondo just bawled and wouldn't say another word. She flew to her room and slammed the door.

"Now look what you've gone and done, Sister," says Mama. "You go apologize."

"I haven't the time, I'm leaving," I says.

"Well, what are you waiting around for?" asks Uncle Rondo. 135

So I just picked up the kitchen clock and marched off, without saying, "Kiss my foot," or anything, and never did tell Stella-Rondo good-bye.

There was a girl going along on a little wagon right in front.

"Girl," I says, "come help me haul these things down the hill, I'm going to live in the post office."

Took her nine trips in her express wagon. Uncle Rondo came out on the porch and threw her a nickel.

And that's the last I've laid eyes on any of my family or my family laid eyes on 140 me for five solid days and nights. Stella-Rondo may be telling the most horrible tales in the world about Mr. Whitaker, but I haven't heard them. As I tell everybody, I draw my own conclusions.

But oh, I like it here. It's ideal, as I've been saying. You see, I've got everything cater-cornered, the way I like it. Hear the radio? All the war news. Radio, sewing machine, book ends, ironing board and that great big piano lamp—peace, that's what I like. Butter-bean vines planted all along the front where the strings are.

Of course, there's not much mail. My family are naturally the main people in China Grove, and if they prefer to vanish from the face of the earth, for all the mail they get or the mail they write, why, I'm not going to open my mouth. Some of the folks here in town are taking up for me and some turned against me. I know which is which. There are always people who will quit buying stamps just to get on the right side of Papa-Daddy.

But here I am, and here I'll stay. I want the world to know I'm happy.

And if Stella-Rondo should come to me this minute, on bended knees, and *attempt* to explain the incidents of her life with Mr. Whitaker, I'd simply put my fingers in both my ears and refuse to listen.

1941

Bartleby, the Scrivener

A Story of Wall Street

I am a rather elderly man. The nature of my avocations for the last thirty years has brought me into more than ordinary contact with what would seem an interesting and somewhat singular set of men, of whom as yet nothing that I know of has ever been written:—I mean the law-copyists or scriveners. I have known very many of them, professionally and privately, and if I pleased, could relate divers histories, at which good-natured gentlemen might smile, and sentimental souls might weep. But I waive the biographies of all other scriveners for a few passages in the life of Bartleby, who was a scrivener the strangest I ever saw or heard of. While of other law-copyists I might write the complete life, of Bartleby nothing of that sort can be done. I believe that no materials exist for a full and satisfactory biography of this man. It is an irreparable loss to literature. Bartleby was one of those beings of whom nothing is ascertainable, except from the original sources, and in his case those are very small. What my own astonished eyes saw of Bartleby, *that* is all I know of him, except, indeed, one vague report which will appear in the sequel.

Ere introducing the scrivener, as he first appeared to me, it is fit I make some mention of myself, my *employées,* my business, my chambers, and general surroundings; because some such description is indispensable to an adequate understanding of the chief character about to be presented.

Imprimis:[1] I am a man who, from his youth upwards, has been filled with a profound conviction that the easiest way of life is the best. Hence, though I belong to a profession proverbially energetic and nervous, even to turbulence, at times, yet nothing of that sort have I ever suffered to invade my peace. I am one of those unambitious lawyers who never addresses a jury, or in any way draws down public applause; but in the cool tranquillity of a snug retreat, do a snug business among rich men's bonds and mortgages and title-deeds. All who know me, consider me an eminently *safe* man. The late John Jacob Astor,[2] a personage little given to poetic enthusiasm, had no hesitation in pronouncing my first grand point to be

1. In the first place.   2. New York fur merchant and landowner (1763–1848) who died the richest man in the United States.

prudence; my next, method. I do not speak it in vanity, but simply record the fact, that I was not unemployed in my profession by the late John Jacob Astor; a name which, I admit, I love to repeat, for it hath a rounded and orbicular sound to it, and rings like unto bullion. I will freely add that I was not insensible to the late John Jacob Astor's good opinion.

Some time prior to the period at which this little history begins, my avocations had been largely increased. The good old office, now extinct in the State of New York, of a Master in Chancery[3] had been conferred upon me. It was not a very arduous office, but very pleasantly remunerative. I seldom lose my temper; much more seldom indulge in dangerous indignation at wrongs and outrages; but I must be permitted to be rash here and declare, that I consider the sudden and violent abrogation of the office of Master in Chancery, by the new Constitution, as a— premature act; inasmuch as I had counted upon a life-lease of the profits, whereas I only received those of a few short years. But this is by the way.

My chambers were up stairs at No. —— Wall Street. At one end they looked   5 upon the white wall of the interior of a spacious skylight shaft, penetrating the building from top to bottom. This view might have been considered rather tame than otherwise, deficient in what landscape painters call "life." But if so, the view from the other end of my chambers offered, at least, a contrast, if nothing more. In that direction my windows commanded an unobstructed view of a lofty brick wall, black by age and everlasting shade; which wall required no spyglass to bring out its lurking beauties, but for the benefit of all near-sighted spectators, was pushed up to within ten feet of my window panes. Owing to the great height of the surrounding buildings, and my chambers being on the second floor, the in- terval between this wall and mine not a little resembled a huge square cistern.

At the period just preceding the advent of Bartleby, I had two persons as copy- ists in my employment, and a promising lad as an office-boy. First, Turkey; sec- ond, Nippers, third, Ginger Nut. These may seem names the like of which are not usually found in the Directory.[4] In truth they were nicknames, mutually conferred upon each other by my three clerks, and were deemed expressive of their respec- tive persons or characters. Turkey was a short, pursy[5] Englishman of about my own age, that is, somewhere not far from sixty. In the morning, one might say, his face was of a fine florid hue, but after twelve o'clock, meridian—his dinner hour—it blazed like a grate full of Christmas coals; and continued blazing—but, as it were, with a gradual wane—till 6 o'clock, P.M. or thereabouts, after which I saw no more of the proprietor of the face, which gaining its meridian with the sun, seemed to set with it, to rise, culminate, and decline the following day, with the like regularity and undiminished glory. There are many singular coincidences I have known in the course of my life, not the least among which was the fact, that exactly when Turkey displayed his fullest beams from his red and radiant countenance, just then, too, at that critical moment, began the daily period when I considered his business capacities as seriously disturbed for the remainder of the twenty-four hours. Not that he was absolutely idle, or averse to business then; far

3. A court of chancery can temper the law, applying "dictates of conscience" or "the principles of natural justice"; the office of Master was abolished in 1847.   4. Post Office Directory.   5. Fat, short-winded.

from it. The difficulty was, he was apt to be altogether too energetic. There was a strange, inflamed, flurried, flighty recklessness of activity about him. He would be incautious in dipping his pen into his inkstand. All his blots upon my documents were dropped there after twelve o'clock, meridian. Indeed, not only would he be reckless and sadly given to making blots in the afternoon, but some days he went further, and was rather noisy. At such times, too, his face flamed with augmented blazonry, as if cannel coal had been heaped on anthracite.[6] He made an unpleasant racket with his chair; spilled his sand-box; in mending his pens, impatiently split them all to pieces, and threw them on the floor in a sudden passion; stood up and leaned over his table, boxing his papers about in a most indecorous manner, very sad to behold in an elderly man like him. Nevertheless, as he was in many ways a most valuable person to me, and all the time before twelve o'clock, meridian, was the quickest, steadiest creature too, accomplishing a great deal of work in a style not easy to be matched—for these reasons, I was willing to overlook his eccentricities, though indeed, occasionally, I remonstrated with him. I did this very gently, however, because, though the civilest, nay, the blandest and most reverential of men in the morning, yet in the afternoon he was disposed, upon provocation, to be slightly rash with his tongue, in fact, insolent. Now, valuing his morning services as I did, and resolved not to lose them; yet, at the same time made uncomfortable by his inflamed ways after twelve o'clock; and being a man of peace, unwilling by my admonitions to call forth unseemly retorts from him; I took upon me, one Saturday noon (he was always worse on Saturdays), to hint to him, very kindly, that perhaps now that he was growing old, it might be well to abridge his labors; in short, he need not come to my chambers after twelve o'clock, but, dinner over, had best go home to his lodgings and rest himself till tea-time. But no; he insisted upon his afternoon devotions. His countenance became intolerably fervid, as he oratorically assured me—gesticulating with a long ruler at the other end of the room—that if his services in the morning were useful, how indispensable, then, in the afternoon?

"With submission, sir," said Turkey on this occasion, "I consider myself your right-hand man. In the morning I but marshal and deploy my columns; but in the afternoon I put myself at their head, and gallantly charge the foe, thus!"—and he made a violent thrust with the ruler.

"But the blots, Turkey," intimated I.

"True,—but, with submission, sir, behold these hairs! I am getting old. Surely, sir, a blot or two of a warm afternoon is not to be severely urged against gray hairs. Old age—even if it blot the page—is honorable. With submission, sir, we *both* are getting old."

10   This appeal to my fellow-feeling was hardly to be resisted. At all events, I saw that go he would not. So I made up my mind to let him stay, resolving, nevertheless, to see to it, that during the afternoon he had to do with my less important papers.

Nippers, the second on my list, was a whiskered, sallow, and, upon the whole, rather piratical-looking young man of about five and twenty. I always deemed

6. A fast, bright-burning coal heaped on slow-burning, barely glowing coal.

him the victim of two evil powers—ambition and indigestion. The ambition was evinced by a certain impatience of the duties of a mere copyist, an unwarrantable usurpation of strictly professional affairs, such as the original drawing up of legal documents. The indigestion seemed betokened in an occasional nervous testiness and grinning irritability, causing the teeth to audibly grind together over mistakes committed in copying; unnecessary maledictions, hissed, rather than spoken, in the heat of business; and especially by a continual discontent with the height of the table where he worked. Though of a very ingenious mechanical turn, Nippers could never get this table to suit him. He put chips under it, blocks of various sorts, bits of pasteboard, and at last went so far as to attempt an exquisite adjustment by final pieces of folded blotting-paper. But no invention would answer. If, for the sake of easing his back, he brought the table lid at a sharp angle well up towards his chin, and wrote there like a man using the steep roof of a Dutch house for his desk:—then he declared that it stopped the circulation in his arms. If now he lowered the table to his waistbands, and stooped over it in writing, then there was a sore aching in his back. In short, the truth of the matter was, Nippers knew not what he wanted. Or, if he wanted any thing, it was to be rid of a scrivener's table altogether. Among the manifestations of his diseased ambition was a fondness he had for receiving visits from certain ambiguous-looking fellows in seedy coats, whom he called his clients. Indeed I was aware that not only was he, at times, considerable of a ward-politician, but he occasionally did a little business at the Justices' courts, and was not unknown on the steps of the Tombs.[7] I have good reason to believe, however, that one individual who called upon him at my chambers, and who, with a grand air, he insisted was his client, was no other than a dun,[8] and the alleged title-deed, a bill. But with all his failings, and the annoyances he caused me, Nippers, like his compatriot Turkey, was a very useful man to me; wrote a neat, swift hand; and, when he chose, was not deficient in a gentlemanly sort of deportment. Added to this, he always dressed in a gentlemanly sort of way: and so, incidentally, reflected credit upon my chambers. Whereas with respect to Turkey, I had much ado to keep him from being a reproach to me. His clothes were apt to look oily and smell of eating-houses. He wore his pantaloons very loose and baggy in summer. His coats were execrable; his hat not to be handled. But while the hat was a thing of indifference to me, inasmuch as his natural civility and deference, as a dependent Englishman, always led him to doff it the moment he entered the room, yet his coat was another matter. Concerning his coats, I reasoned with him; but with no effect. The truth was, I suppose, that a man with so small an income, could not afford to sport such a lustrous face and a lustrous coat at one and the same time. As Nippers once observed, Turkey's money went chiefly for red ink. One winter day I presented Turkey with a highly-respectable looking coat of my own, a padded gray coat, of a most comfortable warmth, and which buttoned straight up from the knee to the neck. I thought Turkey would appreciate the favor, and abate his rashness and obstreperousness of afternoons. But no. I verily believe that buttoning himself up in so downy and blanket-like a coat had a pernicious effect upon him; upon the same principle

---

7. Prison in New York City.   8. Bill collector.

that too much oats are bad for horses. In fact, precisely as a rash, restive horse is said to feel his oats, so Turkey felt his coat. It made him insolent. He was a man whom prosperity harmed.

Though concerning the self-indulgent habits of Turkey I had my own private surmises, yet touching Nippers I was well persuaded that whatever might be his faults in other respects, he was, at least, a temperate young man. But indeed, nature herself seemed to have been his vintner,[9] and at his birth charged him so thoroughly with an irritable, brandy-like disposition, that all subsequent potations were needless. When I consider how, amid the stillness of my chambers, Nippers would sometimes impatiently rise from his seat, and stooping over his table, spread his arms wide apart, seize the whole desk, and move it, and jerk it, with a grim, grinding motion on the floor, as if the table were a perverse voluntary agent, intent on thwarting and vexing him; I plainly perceive that for Nippers, brandy and water were altogether superfluous.

It was fortunate for me that, owing to its peculiar cause—indigestion—the irritability and consequent nervousness of Nippers, were mainly observable in the morning, while in the afternoon he was comparatively mild. So that Turkey's paroxysms only coming on about twelve o'clock, I never had to do with their eccentricities at one time. Their fits relieved each other like guards. When Nippers' was on, Turkey's was off; and *vice versa*. This was a good natural arrangement under the circumstances.

Ginger Nut, the third on my list, was a lad some twelve years old. His father was a carman,[1] ambitious of seeing his son on the bench instead of a cart, before he died. So he sent him to my office as student at law, errand boy, and cleaner and sweeper, at the rate of one dollar a week. He had a little desk to himself, but he did not use it much. Upon inspection, the drawer exhibited a great array of the shells of various sorts of nuts. Indeed, to this quick-witted youth the whole noble science of the law was contained in a nutshell. Not the least among the employments of Ginger Nut, as well as one which he discharged with the most alacrity, was his duty as cake and apple purveyor for Turkey and Nippers. Copying law papers being proverbially a dry, husky sort of business, my two scriveners were fain to moisten their mouths very often with Spitzenbergs[2] to be had at the numerous stalls nigh the Custom House and Post Office. Also, they sent Ginger Nut very frequently for that peculiar cake—small, flat, round, and very spicy—after which he had been named by them. Of a cold morning when business was but dull, Turkey would gobble up scores of these cakes, as if they were mere wafers—indeed they sell them at the rate of six or eight for a penny—the scrape of his pen blending with the crunching of the crisp particles in his mouth. Of all the fiery afternoon blunders and flurried rashnesses of Turkey, was his once moistening a ginger-cake between his lips, and clapping it on to a mortgage for a seal. I came within an ace of dismissing him then. But he mollified me by making an oriental bow, and saying—"With submission, sir, it was generous of me to find you in[3] stationery on my own account."

9. Wine seller.   1. Driver of wagon or cart that hauls goods.   2. Red-and-yellow American apple.
3. Supply you with.

Now my original business—that of a conveyancer and title hunter,[4] and   15
drawer-up of recondite documents of all sorts—was considerably increased by
receiving the master's office. There was now great work for scriveners. Not only
must I push the clerks already with me, but I must have additional help. In answer
to my advertisement, a motionless young man one morning stood upon my office
threshold, the door being open, for it was summer. I can see that figure now—
pallidly neat, pitiably respectable, incurably forlorn! It was Bartleby.

After a few words touching his qualifications, I engaged him, glad to have
among my corps of copyists a man of so singularly sedate an aspect, which I
thought might operate beneficially upon the flighty temper of Turkey, and the
fiery one of Nippers.

I should have stated before that ground glass folding-doors divided my premises into two parts, one of which was occupied by my scriveners, the other by
myself. According to my humor I threw open these doors, or closed them. I resolved to assign Bartleby a corner by the folding-doors, but on my side of them,
so as to have this quiet man within easy call, in case any trifling thing was to be
done. I placed his desk close up to a small side-window in that part of the room,
a window which originally had afforded a lateral view of certain grimy backyards
and bricks, but which, owing to subsequent erections, commanded at present no
view at all, though it gave some light. Within three feet of the panes was a wall,
and the light came down from far above, between two lofty buildings, as from a
very small opening in a dome. Still further to a satisfactory arrangement, I procured a high green folding screen, which might entirely isolate Bartleby from my
sight, though not remove him from my voice. And thus, in a manner, privacy
and society were conjoined.

At first Bartleby did an extraordinary quantity of writing. As if long famishing
for something to copy, he seemed to gorge himself on my documents. There was
no pause for digestion. He ran a day and night line, copying by sunlight and by
candlelight. I should have been quite delighted with his application, had he been
cheerfully industrious. But he wrote on silently, palely, mechanically.

It is, of course, an indispensable part of a scrivener's business to verify the
accuracy of his copy, word by word. Where there are two or more scriveners in
an office, they assist each other in this examination, one reading from the copy,
the other holding the original. It is a very dull, wearisome, and lethargic affair. I
can readily imagine that to some sanguine temperaments it would be altogether
intolerable. For example, I cannot credit that the mettlesome poet Byron would
have contentedly sat down with Bartleby to examine a law document of, say, five
hundred pages, closely written in a crimpy hand.

Now and then, in the haste of business, it had been my habit to assist in   20
comparing some brief document myself, calling Turkey or Nippers for this purpose. One object I had in placing Bartleby so handy to me behind the screen, was
to avail myself of his services on such trivial occasions. It was on the third day, I
think, of his being with me, and before any necessity had arisen for having his

4. Lawyer who draws up deeds for transferring property, and one who searches out legal control of title
deeds.

own writing examined, that, being much hurried to complete a small affair I had in hand, I abruptly called to Bartleby. In my haste and natural expectancy of instant compliance, I sat with my head bent over the original on my desk, and my right hand sideways, and somewhat nervously extended with the copy, so that immediately upon emerging from his retreat, Bartleby might snatch it and proceed to business without the least delay.

In this very attitude did I sit when I called to him, rapidly stating what it was I wanted him to do—namely, to examine a small paper with me. Imagine my surprise, nay, my consternation, when without moving from his privacy, Bartleby, in a singularly mild, firm voice, replied, "I would prefer not to."

I sat awhile in perfect silence, rallying my stunned faculties. Immediately it occurred to me that my ears had deceived me, or Bartleby had entirely misunderstood my meaning. I repeated my request in the clearest tone I could assume. But in quite as clear a one came the previous reply, "I would prefer not to."

"Prefer not to," echoed I, rising in high excitement, and crossing the room with a stride. "What do you mean? Are you moon-struck?[5] I want you to help me compare this sheet here—take it," and I thrust it towards him.

"I would prefer not to," said he.

25   I looked at him steadfastly. His face was leanly composed; his gray eye dimly calm. Not a wrinkle of agitation rippled him. Had there been the least uneasiness, anger, impatience or impertinence in his manner; in other words, had there been anything ordinarily human about him, doubtless I should have violently dismissed him from the premises. But as it was, I should have as soon thought of turning my pale plaster-of-paris bust of Cicero[6] out-of-doors. I stood gazing at him awhile, as he went on with his own writing, and then reseated myself at my desk. This is very strange, thought I. What had one best do? But my business hurried me. I concluded to forget the matter for the present, reserving it for my future leisure. So calling Nippers from the other room, the paper was speedily examined.

A few days after this, Bartleby concluded four lengthy documents, being quadruplicates of a week's testimony taken before me in my High Court of Chancery. It became necessary to examine them. It was an important suit, and great accuracy was imperative. Having all things arranged I called Turkey, Nippers and Ginger Nut from the next room, meaning to place the four copies in the hands of my four clerks, while I should read from the original. Accordingly Turkey, Nippers and Ginger Nut had taken their seats in a row, each with his document in hand, when I called to Bartleby to join this interesting group.

"Bartleby! quick, I am waiting."

I heard a slow scrape of his chair legs on the uncarpeted floor, and soon he appeared standing at the entrance of his hermitage.

"What is wanted?" said he mildly.

30   "The copies, the copies," said I hurriedly. "We are going to examine them. There"—and I held towards him the fourth quadruplicate.

---

5. Crazy.   6. Marcus Tullius Cicero (106–43 B.C.), pro-republican Roman statesman, barrister, writer, and orator.

"I would prefer not to," he said, and gently disappeared behind the screen.

For a few moments I was turned into a pillar of salt,[7] standing at the head of my seated column of clerks. Recovering myself, I advanced towards the screen, and demanded the reason for such extraordinary conduct.

"*Why* do you refuse?"

"I would prefer not to."

With any other man I should have flown outright into a dreadful passion, scorned all further words, and thrust him ignominiously from my presence. But there was something about Bartleby that not only strangely disarmed me, but in a wonderful manner touched and disconcerted me. I began to reason with him.

"These are your own copies we are about to examine. It is labor saving to you, because one examination will answer for your four papers. It is common usage. Every copyist is bound to help examine his copy. Is it not so? Will you not speak? Answer!"

"I prefer not to," he replied in a flute-like tone. It seemed to me that while I had been addressing him, he carefully revolved every statement that I made; fully comprehended the meaning; could not gainsay the irresistible conclusion; but, at the same time, some paramount consideration prevailed with him to reply as he did.

"You are decided, then, not to comply with my request—a request made according to common usage and common sense?"

He briefly gave me to understand that on that point my judgment was sound. Yes: his decision was irreversible.

It is not seldom the case that when a man is browbeaten in some unprecedented and violently unreasonable way, he begins to stagger in his own plainest faith. He begins, as it were, vaguely to surmise that, wonderful as it may be, all the justice and all the reason is on the other side. Accordingly, if any disinterested persons are present, he turns to them for some reinforcement for his own faltering mind.

"Turkey," said I, "what do you think of this? Am I not right?"

"With submission, sir," said Turkey, with his blandest tone, "I think that you are."

"Nippers," said I, "what do *you* think of it?"

"I think I should kick him out of the office."

(The reader of nice perceptions will here perceive that, it being morning, Turkey's answer is couched in polite and tranquil terms, but Nippers replies in ill-tempered ones. Or, to repeat a previous sentence, Nippers's ugly mood was on duty, and Turkey's off.)

"Ginger Nut," said I, willing to enlist the smallest suffrage[8] in my behalf, "what do *you* think of it?"

"I think, sir, he's a little *luny*," replied Ginger Nut, with a grin.

"You hear what they say," said I, turning towards the screen, "come forth and do your duty."

35

40

45

7. Struck dumb; in Genesis 19.26, Lot's wife, defying God's command, "looked back from behind him, and she became a pillar of salt."   8. Favorable vote.

But he vouchsafed no reply. I pondered a moment in sore perplexity. But once more business hurried me. I determined again to postpone the consideration of this dilemma to my future leisure. With a little trouble we made out to examine the papers without Bartleby, though at every page or two, Turkey deferentially dropped his opinion that this proceeding was quite out of the common; while Nippers, twitching in his chair with a dyspeptic nervousness, ground out between his set teeth occasional hissing maledictions against the stubborn oaf behind the screen. And for his (Nippers's) part, this was the first and the last time he would do another man's business without pay.

50   Meanwhile Bartleby sat in his hermitage, oblivious to everything but his own peculiar business there.

Some days passed, the scrivener being employed upon another lengthy work. His late remarkable conduct led me to regard his ways narrowly. I observed that he never went to dinner; indeed that he never went anywhere. As yet I had never of my personal knowledge known him to be outside of my office. He was a perpetual sentry in the corner. At about eleven o'clock though, in the morning, I noticed that Ginger Nut would advance toward the opening in Bartleby's screen, as if silently beckoned thither by a gesture invisible to me where I sat. The boy would then leave the office jingling a few pence, and reappear with a handful of ginger-nuts which he delivered in the hermitage, receiving two of the cakes for his trouble.

He lives, then, on ginger-nuts, thought I; never eats a dinner, properly speaking; he must be a vegetarian then; but no; he never eats even vegetables, he eats nothing but ginger-nuts. My mind then ran on in reveries concerning the probable effects upon the human constitution of living entirely on ginger-nuts. Ginger-nuts are so called because they contain ginger as one of their peculiar constituents, and the final flavoring one. Now what was ginger? A hot, spicy thing. Was Bartleby hot and spicy? Not at all. Ginger, then, had no effect upon Bartleby. Probably he preferred it should have none.

Nothing so aggravates an earnest person as a passive resistance. If the individual so resisted be of a not inhumane temper, and the resisting one perfectly harmless in his passivity; then, in the better moods of the former, he will endeavor charitably to construe to his imagination what proves impossible to be solved by his judgment. Even so, for the most part, I regarded Bartleby and his ways. Poor fellow! thought I, he means no mischief; it is plain he intends no insolence; his aspect sufficiently evinces that his eccentricities are involuntary. He is useful to me. I can get along with him. If I turn him away, the chances are he will fall in with some less indulgent employer, and then he will be rudely treated, and perhaps driven forth miserably to starve. Yes. Here I can cheaply purchase a delicious self-approval. To befriend Bartleby; to humor him in his strange wilfulness, will cost me little or nothing, while I lay up in my soul what will eventually prove a sweet morsel for my conscience. But this mood was not invariable with me. The passiveness of Bartleby sometimes irritated me. I felt strangely goaded on to encounter him in new opposition, to elicit some angry spark from him answerable to my own. But indeed I might as well have essayed to strike fire with my knuckles against a bit of Windsor soap.[9] But one afternoon the evil impulse in me mastered me, and the following little scene ensued:

"Bartleby," said I, "when those papers are all copied, I will compare them with you."

"I would prefer not to."   55

"How? Surely you do not mean to persist in that mulish vagary?"

No answer.

I threw open the folding-doors near by, and turning upon Turkey and Nippers, exclaimed in an excited manner—

"He says, a second time, he won't examine his papers. What do you think of it, Turkey?"

It was afternoon, be it remembered. Turkey sat glowing like a brass boiler, his   60
bald head steaming, his hands reeling among his blotted papers.

"Think of it?" roared Turkey; "I think I'll just step behind his screen, and black his eyes for him!"

So saying, Turkey rose to his feet and threw his arms into a pugilistic position. He was hurrying away to make good his promise, when I detained him, alarmed at the effect of incautiously rousing Turkey's combativeness after dinner.

"Sit down, Turkey," said I, "and hear what Nippers has to say. What do you think of it, Nippers? Would I not be justified in immediately dismissing Bartleby?"

"Excuse me, that is for you to decide, sir. I think his conduct quite unusual, and indeed unjust, as regards Turkey and myself. But it may only be a passing whim."

"Ah," exclaimed I, "you have strangely changed your mind then—you speak   65
very gently of him now."

"All beer," cried Turkey; "gentleness is effects of beer—Nippers and I dined together today. You see how gentle *I* am, sir. Shall I go and black his eyes?"

"You refer to Bartleby, I suppose. No, not today, Turkey," I replied; "pray, put up your fists."

I closed the doors, and again advanced towards Bartleby. I felt additional incentives tempting me to my fate. I burned to be rebelled against again. I remembered that Bartleby never left the office.

"Bartleby," said I, "Ginger Nut is away; just step round to the Post Office, won't you? (it was but a three minutes' walk,) and see if there is anything for me."

"I would prefer not to."   70

"You *will* not?"

"I *prefer* not."

I staggered to my desk, and sat there in a deep study. My blind inveteracy returned. Was there any other thing in which I could procure myself to be ignominiously repulsed by this lean, penniless wight?—my hired clerk? What added thing is there, perfectly reasonable, that he will be sure to refuse to do?

"Bartleby!"

No answer.   75

9. Scented soap, usually brown.

"Bartleby," in a louder tone.

No answer.

"Bartleby," I roared.

Like a very ghost, agreeably to the laws of magical invocation, at the third summons, he appeared at the entrance of his hermitage.

80 "Go to the next room, and tell Nippers to come to me."

"I prefer not to," he respectfully and slowly said, and mildly disappeared.

"Very good, Bartleby," said I, in a quiet sort of serenely severe self-possessed tone, intimating the unalterable purpose of some terrible retribution very close at hand. At the moment I half intended something of the kind. But upon the whole, as it was drawing towards my dinner-hour, I thought it best to put on my hat and walk home for the day, suffering much from perplexity and distress of mind.

Shall I acknowledge it? The conclusion of this whole business was, that it soon became a fixed fact of my chambers, that a pale young scrivener, by the name of Bartleby, had a desk there; that he copied for me at the usual rate of four cents a folio (one hundred words); but he was permanently exempt from examining the work done by him, that duty being transferred to Turkey and Nippers, one of compliment doubtless to their superior acuteness; moreover, said Bartleby was never on any account to be dispatched on the most trivial errand of any sort; and that even if entreated to take upon him such a matter, it was generally understood that he would prefer not to—in other words, that he would refuse point-blank.

As days passed on, I became considerably reconciled to Bartleby. His steadiness, his freedom from all dissipation, his incessant industry (except when he chose to throw himself into a standing revery behind his screen), his great stillness, his unalterableness of demeanor under all circumstances, made him a valuable acquisition. One prime thing was this,—*he was always there;*—first in the morning, continually through the day, and the last at night. I had a singular confidence in his honesty. I felt my most precious papers perfectly safe in his hands. Sometimes to be sure I could not, for the very soul of me, avoid falling into sudden spasmodic passions with him. For it was exceeding difficult to bear in mind all the time those strange peculiarities, privileges, and unheard of exemptions, forming the tacit stipulations on Bartleby's part under which he remained in my office. Now and then, in the eagerness of dispatching pressing business, I would inadvertently summon Bartleby, in a short, rapid tone, to put his finger, say, on the incipient tie of a bit of red tape with which I was about compressing some papers. Of course, from behind the screen the usual answer, "I prefer not to," was sure to come; and then, how could a human creature with the common infirmities of our nature, refrain from bitterly exclaiming upon such perverseness—such unreasonableness? However, every added repulse of this sort which I received only tended to lessen the probability of my repeating the inadvertence.

85 Here it must be said, that according to the custom of most legal gentlemen occupying chambers in densely-populated law buildings, there were several keys to my door. One was kept by a woman residing in the attic, which person weekly scrubbed and daily swept and dusted my apartments. Another was kept by Turkey

for convenience sake. The third I sometimes carried in my own pocket. The fourth I knew not who had.

Now, one Sunday morning I happened to go to Trinity Church, to hear a celebrated preacher, and finding myself rather early on the ground, I thought I would walk round to my chambers for a while. Luckily I had my key with me; but upon applying it to the lock, I found it resisted by something inserted from the inside. Quite surprised, I called out; when to my consternation a key was turned from within; and thrusting his lean visage at me, and holding the door ajar, the apparition of Bartleby appeared, in his shirt sleeves, and otherwise in a strangely tattered dishabille, saying quietly that he was sorry, but he was deeply engaged just then, and—preferred not admitting me at present. In a brief word or two, he moreover added, that perhaps I had better walk round the block two or three times, and by that time he would probably have concluded his affairs.

Now, the utterly unsurmised appearance of Bartleby, tenanting my law-chambers of a Sunday morning, with his cadaverously gentlemanly *nonchalance,* yet withal firm and self-possessed, had such a strange effect upon me, that incontinently I slunk away from my own door, and did as desired. But not without sundry twinges of impotent rebellion against the mild effrontery of this unaccountable scrivener. Indeed, it was his wonderful mildness, chiefly, which not only disarmed me, but unmanned me, as it were. For I consider that one, for the time, is sort of unmanned when he tranquilly permits his hired clerk to dictate to him, and order him away from his own premises. Furthermore, I was full of uneasiness as to what Bartleby could possibly be doing in my office in his shirt sleeves, and in an otherwise dismantled condition of a Sunday morning. Was anything amiss going on? Nay, that was out of the question. It was not to be thought of for a moment that Bartleby was an immoral person. But what could he be doing there?—copying? Nay again, whatever might be his eccentricities, Bartleby was an eminently decorous person. He would be the last man to sit down to his desk in any state approaching to nudity. Besides, it was Sunday; and there was something about Bartleby that forbade the supposition that he would by any secular occupation violate the proprieties of the day.

Nevertheless, my mind was not pacified; and full of a restless curiosity, at last I returned to the door. Without hindrance I inserted my key, opened it, and entered. Bartleby was not to be seen. I looked round anxiously, peeped behind his screen; but it was very plain that he was gone. Upon more closely examining the place, I surmised that for an indefinite period Bartleby must have ate, dressed, and slept in my office, and that too without plate, mirror, or bed. The cushioned seat of a ricketty old sofa in one corner bore the faint impress of a lean, reclining form. Rolled away under his desk, I found a blanket under the empty grate, a blacking box[1] and brush; on a chair, a tin basin, with soap and a ragged towel; in a newspaper a few crumbs of ginger-nuts and a morsel of cheese. Yes, thought I, it is evident enough that Bartleby has been making his home here, keeping bachelor's hall all by himself. Immediately then the thought came sweeping across

---

1. Box of black shoe polish.

me, What miserable friendlessness and loneliness are here revealed! His poverty is great; but his solitude, how horrible! Think of it. Of a Sunday, Wall Street is deserted as Petra;[2] and every night of every day it is an emptiness. This building too, which of weekdays hums with industry and life, at nightfall echoes with sheer vacancy, and all through Sunday is forlorn. And here Bartleby makes his home; sole spectator of a solitude which he has seen all populous—a sort of innocent and transformed Marius brooding among the ruins of Carthage![3]

For the first time in my life a feeling of overpowering stinging melancholy seized me. Before, I had never experienced aught but a not-unpleasing sadness. The bond of a common humanity now drew me irresistibly to gloom. A fraternal melancholy! For both I and Bartleby were sons of Adam. I remembered the bright silks and sparkling faces I had seen that day, in gala trim, swan-like sailing down the Mississippi of Broadway; and I contrasted them with the pallid copyist, and thought to myself, Ah, happiness courts the light, so we deem the world is gay; but misery hides aloof, so we deem that misery there is none. These sad fancyings—chimeras, doubtless, of a sick and silly brain—led on to other and more special thoughts, concerning the eccentricities of Bartleby. Presentiments of strange discoveries hovered round me. The scrivener's pale form appeared to me laid out, among uncaring strangers, in its shivering winding sheet.

90   Suddenly I was attracted by Bartleby's closed desk, the key in open sight left in the lock.

I mean no mischief, seek the gratification of no heartless curiosity, thought I; besides, the desk is mine, and its contents too, so I will make bold to look within. Everything was methodically arranged, the papers smoothly placed. The pigeon-holes were deep, and removing the files of documents, I groped into their recesses. Presently I felt something there, and dragged it out. It was an old bandanna hand-kerchief, heavy and knotted. I opened it, and saw it was a savings' bank.

I now recalled all the quiet mysteries which I had noted in the man. I remembered that he never spoke but to answer; that though at intervals he had considerable time to himself, yet I had never seen him reading—no, not even a newspaper; that for long periods he would stand looking out, at his pale window behind the screen, upon the dead brick wall; I was quite sure he never visited any refectory or eating house; while his pale face clearly indicated that he never drank beer like Turkey, or tea and coffee even, like other men; that he never went anywhere in particular that I could learn; never went out for a walk, unless indeed that was the case at present; that he had declined telling who he was, or whence he came, or whether he had any relatives in the world; that though so thin and pale, he never complained of ill health. And more than all, I remembered a certain unconscious air of pallid—how shall I call it?—of pallid haughtiness, say, or rather

2. Once a flourishing Middle Eastern trade center, long in ruins.   3. Gaius (or Caius) Marius (157–86 B.C.), Roman consul and general, expelled from Rome in 88 B.C. by Sulla; when an officer of Sextilius, the governor, forbade him to land in Africa, Marius replied, "Go tell him that you have seen Caius Marius sitting in exile among the ruins of Carthage," applying the example of the fortune of that city to the change of his own condition. The image was so common that a few years after "Bartleby," Dickens apologizes for using it: "like that lumbering Marius among the ruins of Carthage, who has sat heavy on a thousand millions of similes" ("The Calais Night-Mail," in *The Uncommercial Traveler*).

an austere reserve about him, which had positively awed me into my tame compliance with his eccentricities, when I had feared to ask him to do the slightest incidental thing for me, even though I might know, from his long-continued motionlessness, that behind his screen he must be standing in one of those dead-wall reveries of his.

Revolving all these things, and coupling them with the recently discovered fact that he made my office his constant abiding place and home, and not forgetful of his morbid moodiness; revolving all these things, a prudential feeling began to steal over me. My first emotions had been those of pure melancholy and sincerest pity; but just in proportion as the forlornness of Bartleby grew and grew to my imagination, did that same melancholy merge into fear, that pity into repulsion. So true it is, and so terrible too, that up to a certain point the thought or sight of misery enlists our best affections; but, in certain special cases, beyond that point it does not. They err who would assert that invariably this is owing to the inherent selfishness of the human heart. It rather proceeds from a certain hopelessness of remedying excessive and organic ill. To a sensitive being, pity is not seldom pain. And when at last it is perceived that such pity cannot lead to effectual succor, common sense bids the soul be rid of it. What I saw that morning persuaded me that the scrivener was the victim of innate and incurable disorder. I might give alms to his body; but his body did not pain him; it was his soul that suffered, and his soul I could not reach.

I did not accomplish the purpose of going to Trinity Church that morning. Somehow, the things I had seen disqualified me for the time from churchgoing. I walked homeward, thinking what I would do with Bartleby. Finally, I resolved upon this;—I would put certain calm questions to him the next morning, touching his history, &c., and if he declined to answer them openly and unreservedly (and I supposed he would prefer not), then to give him a twenty-dollar bill over and above whatever I might owe him, and tell him his services were no longer required; but that if in any other way I could assist him, I would be happy to do so, especially if he desired to return to his native place, wherever that might be, I would willingly help to defray the expenses. Moreover, if, after reaching home, he found himself at any time in want of aid, a letter from him would be sure of a reply.

The next morning came.   95

"Bartleby," said I, gently calling to him behind his screen.

No reply.

"Bartleby," said I, in a still gentler tone, "come here; I am not going to ask you to do anything you would prefer not to do—I simply wish to speak to you."

Upon this he noiselessly slid into view.

"Will you tell me, Bartleby, where you were born?"   100

"I would prefer not to."

"Will you tell me *anything* about yourself?"

"I would prefer not to."

"But what reasonable objection can you have to speak to me? I feel friendly towards you."

He did not look at me while I spoke, but kept his glance fixed upon my bust   105 of Cicero, which as I then sat, was directly behind me, some six inches above my head.

"What is your answer, Bartleby?" said I, after waiting a considerable time for a reply, during which his countenance remained immovable, only there was the faintest conceivable tremor of the white attenuated mouth.

"At present I prefer to give no answer," he said, and retired into his hermitage.

It was rather weak in me I confess, but his manner on this occasion nettled me. Not only did there seem to lurk in it a certain calm disdain, but his perverseness seemed ungrateful, considering the undeniable good usage and indulgence he had received from me.

Again I sat ruminating what I should do. Mortified as I was at his behavior, and resolved as I had been to dismiss him when I entered my office, nevertheless I strangely felt something superstitious knocking at my heart, and forbidding me to carry out my purpose, and denouncing me for a villain if I dared to breathe one bitter word against this forlornest of mankind. At last, familiarly drawing my chair behind his screen, I sat down and said: "Bartleby, never mind then about revealing your history; but let me entreat you, as a friend, to comply as far as may be with the usages of this office. Say now you will help to examine papers tomorrow or next day: in short, say now that in a day or two you will begin to be a little reasonable:—say so, Bartleby."

110   "At present I would prefer not to be a little reasonable," was his mildly cadaverous reply.

Just then the folding-doors opened, and Nippers approached. He seemed suffering from an unusually bad night's rest, induced by severer indigestion than common. He overheard those final words of Bartleby.

"*Prefer not*, eh?" gritted Nippers—"I'd *prefer* him, if I were you, sir," addressing me—"I'd *prefer* him; I'd give him preferences, the stubborn mule! What is it, sir, pray, that he *prefers* not to do now?"

Bartleby moved not a limb.

"Mr. Nippers," said I, "I'd prefer that you would withdraw for the present."

115   Somehow, of late I had got into the way of involuntarily using this word "prefer" upon all sorts of not exactly suitable occasions. And I trembled to think that my contact with the scrivener had already and seriously affected me in a mental way. And what further and deeper aberration might it not yet produce? This apprehension had not been without efficacy in determining me to summary means.

As Nippers, looking very sour and sulky, was departing, Turkey blandly and deferentially approached.

"With submission, sir," said he, "yesterday I was thinking about Bartleby here, and I think that if he would but prefer to take a quart of good ale every day, it would do much towards mending him and enabling him to assist in examining his papers."

"So you have got the word too," said I, slightly excited.

"With submission, what word, sir?" asked Turkey, respectfully crowding himself into the contracted space behind the screen, and by so doing making me jostle the scrivener. "What word, sir?"

"I would prefer to be left alone here," said Bartleby, as if offended at being mobbed in his privacy. 120

"That's the word, Turkey," said I—"*that's* it."

"Oh, *prefer?* oh yes—queer word. I never use it myself. But, sir, as I was saying, if he would but prefer—"

"Turkey," interrupted I, "you will please withdraw."

"Oh certainly, sir, if you prefer that I should."

As he opened the folding-door to retire, Nippers at his desk caught a glimpse 125 of me, and asked whether I would prefer to have a certain paper copied on blue paper or white. He did not in the least roguishly accent the word *prefer*. It was plain that it involuntarily rolled from his tongue. I thought to myself, surely I must get rid of a demented man, who already has in some degree turned the tongues, if not the heads of myself and clerks. But I thought it prudent not to break the dismission at once.

The next day I noticed that Bartleby did nothing but stand at his window in his dead-wall revery. Upon asking him why he did not write, he said that he had decided upon doing no more writing.

"Why, how now? what next?" exclaimed I, "do no more writing?"

"No more."

"And what is the reason?"

"Do you not see the reason for yourself," he indifferently replied. 130

I looked steadfastly at him, and perceived that his eyes looked dull and glazed. Instantly it occurred to me, that his unexampled diligence in copying by his dim window for the first few weeks of his stay with me might have temporarily impaired his vision.

I was touched. I said something in condolence with him. I hinted that of course he did wisely in abstaining from writing for a while; and urged him to embrace that opportunity of taking wholesome exercise in the open air. This, however, he did not do. A few days after this, my other clerks being absent, and being in a great hurry to dispatch certain letters by the mail, I thought that, having nothing else earthly to do, Bartleby would surely be less inflexible than usual, and carry these letters to the post office. But he blankly declined. So, much to my inconvenience, I went myself.

Still added days went by. Whether Bartleby's eyes improved or not, I could not say. To all appearance, I thought they did. But when I asked him if they did, he vouchsafed no answer. At all events, he would do no copying. At last, in reply to my urgings, he informed me that he had permanently given up copying.

"What!" exclaimed I; "suppose your eyes should get entirely well—better than ever before—would you not copy then?"

"I have given up copying," he answered, and slid aside. 135

He remained, as ever, a fixture in my chamber. Nay—if that were possible— he became still more of a fixture than before. What was to be done? He would do nothing in the office: why should he stay there? In plain fact, he had now become a millstone[4] to me, not only useless as a necklace, but afflictive to bear. Yet I was sorry for him. I speak less than truth when I say that, on his own account, he occasioned me uneasiness. If he would but have named a single relative or friend, I would instantly have written, and urged their taking the poor fellow away to some convenient retreat. But he seemed alone, absolutely alone in the universe. A bit of wreck in the mid-Atlantic. At length, necessities connected with my business tyrannized over all other considerations. Decently as I could, I told Bartleby that in six days' time he must unconditionally leave the office. I warned him to take measures, in the interval, for procuring some other abode. I offered to assist him in this endeavor, if he himself would but take the first step towards a removal. "And when you finally quit me, Bartleby," added I, "I shall see that you go not away entirely unprovided. Six days from this hour, remember."

At the expiration of that period, I peeped behind the screen, and lo! Bartleby was there.

I buttoned up my coat, balanced myself; advanced slowly towards him, touched his shoulder, and said, "The time has come; you must quit this place; I am sorry for you; here is money; but you must go."

"I would prefer not," he replied, with his back still towards me.

140   "You *must*."

He remained silent.

Now I had an unbounded confidence in this man's common honesty. He had frequently restored to me sixpences and shillings[5] carelessly dropped upon the floor, for I am apt to be very reckless in such shirt-button affairs. The proceeding then which followed will not be deemed extraordinary.

"Bartleby," said I, "I owe you twelve dollars on account; here are thirty-two; the odd twenty are yours.—Will you take it?" and I handed the bills towards him.

But he made no motion.

145   "I will leave them here then," putting them under a weight on the table. Then taking my hat and cane and going to the door I tranquilly turned and added— "After you have removed your things from these offices, Bartleby, you will of course lock the door—since everyone is now gone for the day but you—and if you please, slip your key underneath the mat, so that I may have it in the morning. I shall not see you again; so good-bye to you. If hereafter in your new place of abode I can be of any service to you, do not fail to advise me by letter. Good-bye, Bartleby, and fare you well."

But he answered not a word; like the last column of some ruined temple, he remained standing mute and solitary in the middle of the otherwise deserted room.

As I walked home in a pensive mood, my vanity got the better of my pity. I could not but highly plume myself on my masterly management in getting rid of Bartleby. Masterly I call it, and such it must appear to any dispassionate thinker.

4. Heavy stone for grinding grain. See Matthew 18.6: "But whoso shall offend one of these little ones which believe in me, it were better for him that a millstone were hanged about his neck, and that he were drowned in the depth of the sea."   5. Coins now worth six cents and twelve cents but once worth twice that.

The beauty of my procedure seemed to consist in its perfect quietness. There was no vulgar bullying, no bravado of any sort, no choleric hectoring, and striding to and fro across the apartment, jerking out vehement commands for Bartleby to bundle himself off with his beggarly traps.[6] Nothing of the kind. Without loudly bidding Bartleby depart—as an inferior genius might have done—I *assumed* the ground that depart he must; and upon that assumption built all I had to say. The more I thought over my procedure, the more I was charmed with it. Nevertheless, next morning, upon awakening, I had my doubts,—I had somehow slept off the fumes of vanity. One of the coolest and wisest hours a man has is just after he awakes in the morning. My procedure seemed as sagacious as ever,—but only in theory. How it would prove in practice—there was the rub. It was truly a beautiful thought to have assumed Bartleby's departure; but, after all, that assumption was simply my own, and none of Bartleby's. The great point was, not whether I had assumed that he would quit me, but whether he would prefer so to do. He was more a man of preferences than assumptions.

After breakfast, I walked downtown, arguing the probabilities *pro* and *con*. One moment I thought it would prove a miserable failure, and Bartleby would be found all alive at my office as usual; the next moment it seemed certain that I should see his chair empty. And so I kept veering about. At the corner of Broadway and Canal Street, I saw quite an excited group of people standing in earnest conversation.

"I'll take odds he doesn't," said a voice as I passed.

"Doesn't go?—done!" said I, "put up your money."

I was instinctively putting my hand in my pocket to produce my own, when I remembered that this was an election day. The words I had overheard bore no reference to Bartleby, but to the success or non-success of some candidate for the mayoralty. In my intent frame of mind, I had, as it were, imagined that all Broadway shared in my excitement, and were debating the same question with me. I passed on, very thankful that the uproar of the street screened my momentary absent-mindedness.

As I had intended, I was earlier than usual at my office door. I stood listening for a moment. All was still. He must be gone. I tried the knob. The door was locked. Yes, my procedure had worked to a charm; he indeed must be vanished. Yet a certain melancholy mixed with this: I was almost sorry for my brilliant success. I was fumbling under the door mat for the key, which Bartleby was to have left there for me, when accidentally my knee knocked against a panel, producing a summoning sound, and in response a voice came to me from within—"Not yet; I am occupied."

It was Bartleby.

I was thunderstruck. For an instant I stood like the man who, pipe in mouth, was killed one cloudless afternoon long ago in Virginia, by summer lightning; at his own warm open window he was killed, and remained leaning out there upon the dreamy afternoon, till some one touched him, when he fell.

"Not gone!" I murmured at last. But again obeying that wondrous ascendancy

150

155

6. Personal belongings, luggage.

which the inscrutable scrivener had over me, and from which ascendency, for all my chafing, I could not completely escape, I slowly went downstairs and out into the street, and while walking round the block, considered what I should next do in this unheard-of perplexity. Turn the man out by an actual thrusting I could not; to drive him away by calling him hard names would not do; calling in the police was an unpleasant idea; and yet, permit him to enjoy his cadaverous triumph over me,—this too I could not think of. What was to be done? or, if nothing could be done, was there anything further that I could *assume* in the matter? Yes, as before I had prospectively assumed that Bartleby would depart, so now I might retrospectively assume that departed he was. In the legitimate carrying out of this assumption, I might enter my office in a great hurry, and pretending not to see Bartleby at all, walk straight against him as if he were air. Such a proceeding would in a singular degree have the appearance of a home-thrust.[7] It was hardly possible that Bartleby could withstand such an application of the doctrine of assumptions. But upon second thoughts the success of the plan seemed rather dubious. I resolved to argue the matter over with him again.

"Bartleby," said I, entering the office, with a quietly severe expression, "I am seriously displeased. I am pained, Bartleby. I had thought better of you. I had imagined you of such a gentlemanly organization, that in any delicate dilemma a slight hint would suffice—in short, an assumption. But it appears I am deceived. Why," I added, unaffectedly starting, "you have not even touched that money yet," pointing to it, just where I had left it the evening previous.

He answered nothing.

"Will you, or will you not, quit me?" I now demanded in a sudden passion, advancing close to him.

"I would prefer *not* to quit you," he replied, gently emphasizing the *not*.

160   "What earthly right have you to stay here? Do you pay any rent? Do you pay my taxes? Or is this property yours?"

He answered nothing.

"Are you ready to go on and write now? Are your eyes recovered? Could you copy a small paper for me this morning? or help examine a few lines? or step round to the post office? In a word, will you do anything at all, to give a coloring to your refusal to depart the premises?"

He silently retired into his hermitage.

I was now in such a state of nervous resentment that I thought it but prudent to check myself at present from further demonstrations. Bartleby and I were alone. I remembered the tragedy of the unfortunate Adams and the still more unfortunate Colt in the solitary office of the latter;[8] and how poor Colt, being dreadfully incensed by Adams, and imprudently permitting himself to get wildly excited, was at unawares hurried into his fatal act—an act which certainly no man could possibly deplore more than the actor himself. Often it had occurred to me in my ponderings upon the subject, that had that altercation taken place in the public street, or at a private residence, it would not have terminated as it did. It was the

---

7. Thrust that reaches its mark.   8. In 1841, John C. Colt, brother of the famous gunmaker, unintentionally killed Samuel Adams, a printer, when he hit him on the head during a fight.

circumstance of being alone in a solitary office, up stairs, of a building entirely unhallowed by humanizing domestic associations—an uncarpeted office, doubt-less, of a dusty, haggard sort of appearance;—this it must have been, which greatly helped to enhance the irritable desperation of the hapless Colt.

But when this old Adam[9] of resentment rose in me and tempted me concerning   165 Bartleby, I grappled him and threw him. How? Why, simply by recalling the divine injunction: "A new commandment[1] give I unto you, that ye love one an-other." Yes, this it was that saved me. Aside from higher considerations, charity often operates as a vastly wise and prudent principle—a great safeguard to its possessor. Men have committed murder for jealousy's sake, and anger's sake, and hatred's sake, and selfishness' sake, and spiritual pride's sake; but no man that ever I heard of, ever committed a diabolical murder for sweet charity's sake. Mere self-interest, then, if no better motive can be enlisted, should, especially with high-tempered men, prompt all beings to charity and philanthropy. At any rate, upon the occasion in question, I strove to drown my exasperated feelings towards the scrivener by benevolently construing his conduct. Poor fellow, poor fellow! thought I, he don't mean anything; and besides, he has seen hard times, and ought to be indulged.

I endeavored also immediately to occupy myself, and at the same time to com-fort my despondency. I tried to fancy that in the course of the morning, at such time as might prove agreeable to him, Bartleby, of his own free accord, would emerge from his hermitage, and take up some decided line of march in the direc-tion of the door. But no. Half-past twelve o'clock came; Turkey began to glow in the face, overturn his inkstand, and become generally obstreperous; Nippers abated down into quietude and courtesy; Ginger Nut munched his noon apple; and Bartleby remained standing at his window in one of his profoundest dead-wall reveries. Will it be credited? Ought I to acknowledge it? That afternoon I left the office without saying one further word to him.

Some days now passed, during which, at leisure intervals I looked a little into "Edwards on the Will," and "Priestley on Necessity."[2] Under the circumstances, those books induced a salutary feeling. Gradually I slid into the persuasion that these troubles of mine touching the scrivener, had been all predestinated from eternity, and Bartleby was billeted upon me for some mysterious purpose of an all-wise Providence, which it was not for a mere mortal like me to fathom. Yes, Bartleby, stay there behind your screen, thought I; I shall persecute you no more; you are harmless and noiseless as any of these old chairs; in short, I never feel so private as when I know you are here. At least I see it, I feel it; I penetrate to the

9. Sinful element in human nature, see e.g., "Invocation of Blessing on the Child," in the *Book of Common Prayer:* "Grant that the old Adam in this child may be so buried, that the new man may be raised up in him." Christ is sometimes called the "new Adam."   1. In John 13.34, where, however, the phrasing is "I give unto . . ."   2. Jonathan Edwards (1703–1758), New England Calvinist theologian and revivalist, in *The Freedom of the Will* (1754), argued that human beings are not in fact free, for though they choose according to the way they see things, that way is predetermined (by biography, environment, and char-acter), and they act out of personality rather than by will. Joseph Priestley (1733–1804), Dissenting preacher, scientist, grammarian, and philosopher, in *The Doctrine of Philosophical Necessity* (1777), argued that free will is theologically objectionable, metaphysically incomprehensible, and morally undesirable.

predestinated purpose of my life. I am content. Others may have loftier parts to enact; but my mission in this world, Bartleby, is to furnish you with office-room for such period as you may see fit to remain.

I believe that this wise and blessed frame of mind would have continued with me, had it not been for the unsolicited and uncharitable remarks obtruded upon me by my professional friends who visited the rooms. But thus it often is, that the constant friction of illiberal minds wears out at last the best resolves of the more generous. Though to be sure, when I reflected upon it, it was not strange that people entering my office should be struck by the peculiar aspect of the unaccountable Bartleby, and so be tempted to throw out some sinister observations concerning him. Sometimes an attorney having business with me, and calling at my office, and finding no one but the scrivener there, would undertake to obtain some sort of precise information from him touching my whereabouts; but without heeding his idle talk, Bartleby would remain standing immovable in the middle of the room. So after contemplating him in that position for a time, the attorney would depart, no wiser than he came.

Also, when a Reference[3] was going on, and the room full of lawyers and witnesses and business was driving fast; some deeply occupied legal gentleman present, seeing Bartleby wholly unemployed, would request him to run round to his (the legal gentleman's) office and fetch some papers for him. Thereupon, Bartleby would tranquilly decline, and yet remain idle as before. Then the lawyer would give a great stare, and turn to me. And what could I say? At last I was made aware that all through the circle of my professional acquaintance, a whisper of wonder was running round, having reference to the strange creature I kept at my office. This worried me very much. And as the idea came upon me of his possibly turning out a long-lived man, and keep occupying my chambers, and denying my authority; and perplexing my visitors; and scandalizing my professional reputation; and casting a general gloom over the premises; keeping soul and body together to the last upon his savings (for doubtless he spent but half a dime a day), and in the end perhaps outlive me, and claim possession of my office by right of his perpetual occupancy: as all these dark anticipations crowded upon me more and more, and my friends continually intruded their relentless remarks upon the apparition in my room; a great change was wrought in me. I resolved to gather all my faculties together, and forever rid me of this intolerable incubus.

170 Ere revolving any complicated project, however, adapted to this end, I first simply suggested to Bartleby the propriety of his permanent departure. In a calm and serious tone, I commended the idea to his careful and mature consideration. But having taken three days to meditate upon it, he apprised me that his original determination remained the same; in short, that he still preferred to abide with me.

What shall I do? I now said to myself, buttoning up my coat to the last button. What shall I do? what ought I to do? what does conscience say I *should* do with this man, or rather ghost. Rid myself of him, I must; go, he shall. But how? You will not thrust him, the poor, pale, passive mortal,—you will not thrust such a

3. Consultation or committee meeting.

helpless creature out of your door? you will not dishonor yourself by such cruelty? No, I will not, I cannot do that. Rather would I let him live and die here, and then mason up his remains in the wall. What then will you do? For all your coaxing, he will not budge. Bribes he leaves under your own paperweight on your table; in short, it is quite plain that he prefers to cling to you.

Then something severe, something unusual must be done. What! surely you will not have him collared by a constable, and commit his innocent pallor to the common jail? And upon what ground could you procure such a thing to be done?—a vagrant, is he? What! he a vagrant, a wanderer, who refuses to budge? It is because he will *not* be a vagrant, then, that you seek to count him *as* a vagrant. That is too absurd. No visible means of support: there I have him. Wrong again: for indubitably he *does* support himself, and that is the only unanswerable proof that any man can show of his possessing the means so to do. No more then. Since he will not quit me, I must quit him. I will change my offices; I will move else-where; and give him fair notice, that if I find him on my new premises I will then proceed against him as a common trespasser.

Acting accordingly, next day I thus addressed him: "I find these chambers too far from the City Hall; the air is unwholesome. In a word, I propose to remove my offices next week, and shall no longer require your services. I tell you this now, in order that you may seek another place."

He made no reply, and nothing more was said.

On the appointed day I engaged carts and men, proceeded to my chambers, and having but little furniture, everything was removed in a few hours. Through-out, the scrivener remained standing behind the screen, which I directed to be removed the last thing. It was withdrawn; and being folded up like a huge folio, left him the motionless occupant of a naked room. I stood in the entry watching him a moment, while something from within me upbraided me.

I re-entered, with my hand in my pocket—and—and my heart in my mouth.

"Good-bye, Bartleby; I am going—good-bye, and God some way bless you; and take that," slipping something in his hand. But it dropped upon the floor, and then,—strange to say—I tore myself from him whom I had so longed to be rid of.

Established in my new quarters, for a day or two I kept the door locked, and started at every footfall in the passages. When I returned to my rooms after any little absence, I would pause at the threshold for an instant, and attentively listen, ere applying my key. But these fears were needless. Bartleby never came nigh me.

I thought all was going well, when a perturbed-looking stranger visited me, inquiring whether I was the person who had recently occupied rooms at No. —— Wall Street.

Full of forebodings, I replied that I was.

"Then sir," said the stranger, who proved a lawyer, "you are responsible for the man you left there. He refuses to do any copying; he refuses to do anything; he says he prefers not to; and he refuses to quit the premises."

"I am very sorry, sir," said I, with assumed tranquillity, but an inward tremor, "but, really, the man you allude to is nothing to me—he is no relation or appren-tice of mine, that you should hold me responsible for him."

"In mercy's name, who is he?"

"I certainly cannot inform you. I know nothing about him. Formerly I employed him as a copyist; but he has done nothing for me now for some time past."

185   "I shall settle him then,—good morning, sir."

Several days passed, and I heard nothing more; and though I often felt a charitable prompting to call at the place and see poor Bartleby, yet a certain squeamishness of I know not what withheld me.

All is over with him, by this time, thought I at last, when through another week no further intelligence reached me. But coming to my room the day after, I found several persons waiting at my door in a high state of nervous excitement.

"That's the man—here he comes," cried the foremost one, whom I recognized as the lawyer who had previously called upon me alone.

"You must take him away, sir, at once," cried a portly person among them, advancing upon me, and whom I knew to be the landlord of No. —— Wall Street. "These gentlemen, my tenants, cannot stand it any longer; Mr. B——" pointing to the lawyer, "has turned him out of his room, and he now persists in haunting the building generally, sitting upon the banisters of the stairs by day, and sleeping in the entry by night. Everybody is concerned; clients are leaving the offices; some fears are entertained of a mob; something you must do, and that without delay."

190   Aghast at this torrent, I fell back before it, and would fain have locked myself in my new quarters. In vain I persisted that Bartleby was nothing to me—no more than to anyone else. In vain:—I was the last person known to have anything to do with him, and they held me to the terrible account. Fearful then of being exposed in the papers (as one person present obscurely threatened) I considered the matter, and at length said, that if the lawyer would give me a confidential interview with the scrivener, in his (the lawyer's) own room, I would that afternoon strive my best to rid them of the nuisance they complained of.

Going upstairs to my old haunt, there was Bartleby silently sitting upon the banister at the landing.

"What are you doing here, Bartleby?" said I.

"Sitting upon the banister," he mildly replied.

I motioned him into the lawyer's room, who then left us.

195   "Bartleby," said I, "are you aware that you are the cause of great tribulation to me, by persisting in occupying the entry after being dismissed from the office?"

No answer.

"Now one of two things must take place. Either you must do something, or something must be done to you. Now what sort of business would you like to engage in? Would you like to re-engage in copying for someone?"

"No; I would prefer not to make any change."

"Would you like a clerkship in a drygoods store?"

200   "There is too much confinement about that. No, I would not like a clerkship; but I am not particular."

"Too much confinement," I cried, "why you keep yourself confined all the time!"

"I would prefer not to take a clerkship," he rejoined, as if to settle that little item at once.

"How would a bartender's business suit you? There is no trying of the eyesight in that."

"I would not like it at all; though, as I said before, I am not particular."

His unwonted wordiness inspirited me. I returned to the charge. 205

"Well then, would you like to travel through the country collecting bills for the merchants? That would improve your health."

"No, I would prefer to be doing something else."

"How then would going as a companion to Europe, to entertain some young gentleman with your conversation,—how would that suit you?"

"Not at all. It does not strike me that there is anything definite about that. I like to be stationary. But I am not particular."

"Stationary you shall be then," I cried, now losing all patience, and for the first 210 time in all my exasperating connection with him fairly flying into a passion. "If you do not go away from these premises before night, I shall feel bound—indeed I *am* bound—to—to—to quit the premises myself!" I rather absurdly concluded, knowing not with what possible threat to try to frighten his immobility into compliance. Despairing of all further efforts, I was precipitately leaving him, when a final thought occurred to me—one which had not been wholly unindulged before.

"Bartleby," said I, in the kindest tone I could assume under such exciting circumstances, "will you go home with me now—not to my office, but my dwelling—and remain there till we can conclude upon some convenient arrangement for you at our leisure? Come, let us start now, right away."

"No: at present I would prefer not to make any change at all."

I answered nothing; but effectually dodging everyone by the suddenness and rapidity of my flight, rushed from the building, ran up Wall Street toward Broadway, and jumping into the first omnibus was soon removed from pursuit. As soon as tranquillity returned I distinctly perceived that I had now done all that I possibly could, both in respect to the demands of the landlord and his tenants, and with regard to my own desire and sense of duty, to benefit Bartleby, and shield him from rude persecution. I now strove to be entirely carefree and quiescent; and my conscience justified me in the attempt; though indeed it was not so successful as I could have wished. So fearful was I of being again hunted out by the incensed landlord and his exasperated tenants, that, surrendering my business to Nippers, for a few days I drove about the upper part of the town and through the suburbs, in my rockaway; crossed over to Jersey City and Hoboken, and paid fugitive visits to Manhattanville and Astoria. In fact I almost lived in my rockaway for the time.

When again I entered my office, lo, a note from the landlord lay upon the desk. I opened it with trembling hands. It informed me that the writer had sent to the police, and had Bartleby removed to the Tombs as a vagrant. Moreover, since I knew more about him than anyone else, he wished me to appear at that place, and make a suitable statement of the facts. These tidings had a conflicting effect upon me. At first I was indignant; but at last almost approved. The landlord's energetic, summary disposition had led him to adopt a procedure which I do not think I would have decided upon myself; and yet as a last resort, under such peculiar circumstances, it seemed the only plan.

As I afterwards learned, the poor scrivener, when told that he must be con- 215 ducted to the Tombs, offered not the slightest obstacle, but in his pale unmoving way, silently acquiesced.

Some of the compassionate and curious bystanders joined the party; and headed by one of the constables arm in arm with Bartleby, the silent procession filed its way through all the noise, and heat, and joy of the roaring thoroughfares at noon.

The same day I received the note I went to the Tombs, or to speak more properly, the Halls of Justice. Seeking the right officer, I stated the purpose of my call, and was informed that the individual I described was indeed within. I then assured the functionary that Bartleby was a perfectly honest man, and greatly to be compassionated, however unaccountably eccentric. I narrated all I knew, and closed by suggesting the idea of letting him remain in as indulgent confinement as possible till something less harsh might be done—though indeed I hardly knew what. At all events, if nothing else could be decided upon, the alms-house must receive him. I then begged to have an interview.

Being under no disgraceful charge, and quite serene and harmless in all his ways, they had permitted him freely to wander about the prison, and especially in the inclosed grass-platted yards thereof. And so I found him there, standing all alone in the quietest of the yards, his face towards a high wall, while all around, from the narrow slits of the jail windows, I thought I saw peering out upon him the eyes of murderers and thieves.

"Bartleby!"

220   "I know you," he said, without looking round,—"and I want nothing to say to you."

"It was not I that brought you here, Bartleby," said I, keenly pained at his implied suspicion. "And to you, this should not be so vile a place. Nothing reproachful attaches to you by being here. And see, it is not so sad a place as one might think. Look, there is the sky, and here is the grass."

"I know where I am," he replied, but would say nothing more, and so I left him.

As I entered the corridor again, a broad meat-like man, in an apron, accosted me, and jerking his thumb over his shoulder said—"Is that your friend?"

"Yes."

225   "Does he want to starve? If he does, let him live on the prison fare, that's all."

"Who are you?" asked I, not knowing what to make of such an unofficially-speaking person in such a place.

"I am the grub-man. Such gentlemen as have friends here, hire me to provide them with something good to eat."

"Is this so?" said I, turning to the turnkey.

He said it was.

230   "Well then," said I, slipping some silver into the grub-man's hands (for so they called him). "I want you to give particular attention to my friend there; let him have the best dinner you can get. And you must be as polite to him as possible."

"Introduce me, will you?" said the grub-man, looking at me with an expression which seemed to say he was all impatience for an opportunity to give a specimen of his breeding.

Thinking it would prove of benefit to the scrivener, I acquiesced; and asking the grub-man his name, went up with him to Bartleby.

"Bartleby, this is Mr. Cutlets; you will find him very useful to you."

"Your sarvant, sir, your sarvant," said the grub-man, making a low salutation behind his apron. "Hope you find it pleasant here, sir;—spacious grounds—cool apartments, sir—hope you'll stay with us some time—try to make it agreeable. May Mrs. Cutlets and I have the pleasure of your company to dinner, sir, in Mrs. Cutlets' private room?"

"I prefer not to dine today," said Bartleby, turning away. "It would disagree   235 with me; I am unused to dinners." So saying he slowly moved to the other side of the inclosure, and took up a position fronting the dead-wall.

"How's this?" said the grub-man, addressing me with a stare of astonishment. "He's odd, ain't he?"

"I think he is a little deranged," said I, sadly.

"Deranged? deranged is it? Well now, upon my word, I thought that friend of yourn was a gentleman forger; they are always pale and genteel-like, them forgers. I can't help pity 'em—can't help it, sir. Did you know Monroe Edwards?" he added touchingly, and paused. Then laying his hand pityingly on my shoulder, sighed, "he died of consumption at Sing Sing. So you weren't acquainted with Monroe?"

"No, I was never socially acquainted with any forgers. But I cannot stop longer. Look to my friend yonder. You will not lose by it. I will see you again."

Some few days after this, I again obtained admission to the Tombs, and went   240 through the corridors in quest of Bartleby; but without finding him.

"I saw him coming from his cell not long ago," said a turnkey, "may be he's gone to loiter in the yards."

So I went in that direction.

"Are you looking for the silent man?" said another turnkey passing me. "Yonder he lies—sleeping in the yard there. 'Tis not twenty minutes since I saw him lie down."

The yard was entirely quiet. It was not accessible to the common prisoners. The surrounding walls, of amazing thickness, kept off all sounds behind them. The Egyptian character of the masonry weighed upon me with its gloom. But a soft imprisoned turf grew under foot. The heart of the eternal pyramids, it seemed, wherein, by some strange magic, through the clefts, grass seed, dropped by birds, had sprung.

Strangely huddled at the base of the wall, his knees drawn up, and lying on   245 his side, his head touching the cold stones, I saw the wasted Bartleby. But nothing stirred. I paused; then went close up to him; stooped over, and saw that his dim eyes were open; otherwise he seemed profoundly sleeping. Something prompted me to touch him. I felt his hand, when a tingling shiver ran up my arm and down my spine to my feet.

The round face of the grub-man peered upon me now. "His dinner is ready. Won't he dine today, either? Or does he live without dining?"

"Lives without dining," said I, and closed the eyes.

"Eh!—He's asleep, ain't he?"

"With kings and counsellors,"[4] murmured I.

---

4. I.e., dead. See Job 3.13–14: "then had I been at rest, With kings and counsellors of the earth, which built desolate places for themselves."

250   There would seem little need for proceeding further in this history. Imagination will readily supply the meager recital of poor Bartleby's interment. But ere parting with the reader, let me say, that if this little narrative has sufficiently interested him, to awaken curiosity as to who Bartleby was, and what manner of life he led prior to the present narrator's making his acquaintance, I can only reply, that in such curiosity I fully share, but am wholly unable to gratify it. Yet here I hardly know whether I should divulge one little item of rumor, which came to my ear a few months after the scrivener's decease. Upon what basis it rested, I could never ascertain; and hence, how true it is I cannot now tell. But inasmuch as this vague report has not been without a certain strange suggestive interest to me, however sad, it may prove the same with some others; and so I will briefly mention it. The report was this: that Bartleby had been a subordinate clerk in the Dead Letter Office at Washington, from which he had been suddenly removed by a change in the administration. When I think over this rumor, I cannot adequately express the emotions which seize me. Dead letters! does it not sound like dead men? Conceive a man by nature and misfortune prone to a pallid hopelessness, can any business seem more fitted to heighten it than that of continually handling these dead letters, and assorting them for the flames? For by the cartload they are annually burned. Sometimes from out the folded paper the pale clerk takes a ring:—the finger it was meant for, perhaps, molders in the grave; a banknote sent in swiftest charity:—he whom it would relieve, nor eats nor hungers any more; pardon for those who died despairing; hope for those who died unhoping; good tidings for those who died stifled by unrelieved calamities. On errands of life, these letters speed to death.

Ah Bartleby! Ah humanity!

p. 1853

DORIS LESSING
_____

Our Friend Judith

I stopped inviting Judith to meet people when a Canadian woman remarked, with the satisfied fervour of one who has at last pinned a label on a rare specimen: "She is, of course, one of your typical English spinsters."

This was a few weeks after an American sociologist, having elicited from Judith the facts that she was fortyish, unmarried, and living alone, had enquired of me: "I suppose she has given up?" "Given up what?" I asked; and the subsequent discussion was unrewarding.

Judith did not easily come to parties. She would come after pressure, not so much—one felt—to do one a favour, but in order to correct what she believed to be a defect in her character. "I really ought to enjoy meeting new people more than I do," she said once. We reverted to an earlier pattern of our friendship: odd evenings together, an occasional visit to the cinema, or she would telephone to say: "I'm on my way past you to the British Museum. Would you care for a cup of coffee with me? I have twenty minutes to spare."

It is characteristic of Judith that the word "spinster," used of her, provoked fascinated speculation about other people. There are my aunts, for instance: aged seventy-odd, both unmarried, one an ex-missionary from China, one a retired matron of a famous London hospital. These two old ladies live together under the shadow of the cathedral in a country town. They devote much time to the Church, to good causes, to letter writing with friends all over the world, to the grandchildren and the great-grandchildren of relatives. It would be a mistake, however, on entering a house in which nothing has been moved for fifty years, to diagnose a condition of fossilised late-Victorian integrity. They read every book review in the *Observer* or the *Times*,[1] so that I recently got a letter from Aunt Rose enquiring whether I did not think that the author of *On the Road*[2] was not—perhaps?—exaggerating his difficulties. They know a good deal about music, and write letters of encouragement to young composers they feel are being neglected—"You must understand that anything new and original takes time to be understood." Well-informed and critical Tories, they are as likely to dispatch telegrams of protest to the Home Secretary[3] as letters of support. These ladies, my aunts Emily and Rose, are surely what is meant by the phrase "English spinster." And yet, once the connection has been pointed out, there is no doubt that Judith and they are spiritual cousins, if not sisters. Therefore it follows that one's pitying admiration for women who have supported manless and uncomforted lives needs a certain modification?

One will, of course, never know; and I feel now that it is entirely my fault that I shall never know. I had been Judith's friend for upward of five years before the incident occurred which I involuntarily thought of—stupidly enough—as the first time Judith's mask slipped.

A mutual friend, Betty, had been given a cast-off Dior[4] dress. She was too short for it. Also she said: "It's not a dress for a married woman with three children and a talent for cooking. I don't know why not, but it isn't." Judith was the right build. Therefore one evening the three of us met by appointment in Judith's bedroom, with the dress. Neither Betty nor I was surprised at the renewed discovery that Judith was beautiful. We had both often caught each other, and ourselves, in moments of envy when Judith's calm and severe face, her undemonstratively perfect body, succeeded in making everyone else in a room or a street look cheap.

Judith is tall, small-breasted, slender. Her light brown hair is parted in the centre and cut straight around her neck. A high straight forehead, straight nose, a full grave mouth are setting for her eyes, which are green, large and prominent.

5

---

1. Prestigious London newspapers representing roughly the younger, more liberal establishment and the Establishment proper, respectively.   2. Jack Kerouac (1922–1969), a leading writer of the Beat Generation, 1950s forerunners of the hippies. Kerouac heroes felt themselves completely cut off from and victimized by American society.   3. Head of the British government department responsible for domestic matters.   4. Famous French designer of high fashions.

Her lids are very white, fringed with gold, and moulded close over the eyeball, so that in profile she has the look of a staring gilded mask. The dress was of dark green glistening stuff, cut straight, with a sort of loose tunic. It opened simply at the throat. In it Judith could of course evoke nothing but classical images. Diana, perhaps, back from the hunt, in a relaxed moment? A rather intellectual wood nymph who had opted for an afternoon in the British Museum Reading Room? Something like that. Neither Betty nor I said a word, since Judith was examining herself in a long mirror, and must know she looked magnificent.

Slowly she drew off the dress and laid it aside. Slowly she put on the old cord skirt and woollen blouse she had taken off. She must have surprised a resigned glance between us, for she then remarked, with the smallest of mocking smiles: "One surely ought to stay in character, wouldn't you say?" She added, reading the words out of some invisible book, written not by her, since it was a very vulgar book, but perhaps by one of us: "It does everything *for* me, I must admit."

"After seeing you in it," Betty cried out, defying her, "I can't bear for anyone else to have it. I shall simply put it away." Judith shrugged, rather irritated. In the shapeless skirt and blouse, and without makeup, she stood smiling at us, a woman at whom forty-nine out of fifty people would not look twice.

10   A second revelatory incident occurred soon after. Betty telephoned me to say that Judith had a kitten. Did I know that Judith adored cats? "No, but of course she would," I said.

Betty lived in the same street as Judith and saw more of her than I did. I was kept posted about the growth and habits of the cat and its effect on Judith's life. She remarked for instance that she felt it was good for her to have a tie and some responsibility. But no sooner was the cat out of kittenhood than all the neighbours complained. It was a tomcat, ungelded, and making every night hideous. Finally the landlord said that either the cat or Judith must go, unless she was prepared to have the cat "fixed."[5] Judith wore herself out trying to find some person, anywhere in Britain, who would be prepared to take the cat. This person would, however, have to sign a written statement not to have the cat "fixed." When Judith took the cat to the vet to be killed, Betty told me she cried for twenty-four hours.

"She didn't think of compromising? After all, perhaps the cat might have preferred to live, if given the choice?"

"Is it likely I'd have the nerve to say anything so sloppy to Judith? It's the nature of a male cat to rampage lustfully about, and therefore it would be morally wrong for Judith to have the cat fixed, simply to suit her own convenience."

"She said that?"

15   "She wouldn't have to *say* it, surely?"

A third incident was when she allowed a visiting young American, living in Paris, the friend of a friend and scarcely known to her, to use her flat while she visited her parents over Christmas. The young man and his friends lived it up for ten days of alcohol and sex and marijuana, and when Judith came back it took a week to get the place clean again and the furniture mended. She telephoned twice

---

5. Gelded, castrated.

to Paris, the first time to say that he was a disgusting young thug and if he knew what was good for him he would keep out of her way in the future; the second time to apologise for losing her temper. "I had a choice either to let someone use my flat, or to leave it empty. But having chosen that you should have it, it was clearly an unwarrantable infringement of your liberty to make any conditions at all. I do most sincerely ask your pardon." The moral aspects of the matter having been made clear, she was irritated rather than not to receive letters of apology from him—fulsome, embarrassed, but above all, baffled.

It was the note of curiosity in the letters—he even suggested coming over to get to know her better—that irritated her most. "What do you suppose he means?" she said to me. "He lived in my flat for ten days. One would have thought that should be enough, wouldn't you?"

The facts about Judith, then, are all in the open, unconcealed, and plain to anyone who cares to study them; or, as it became plain she feels, to anyone with the intelligence to interpret them.

She has lived for the last twenty years in a small two-roomed flat high over a busy West London street. The flat is shabby and badly heated. The furniture is old, was never anything but ugly, is now frankly rickety and fraying. She has an income of two hundred pounds[6] a year from a dead uncle. She lives on this and what she earns from her poetry, and from lecturing on poetry to night classes and extramural university classes.

She does not smoke or drink, and eats very little, from preference, not self-discipline.   20

She studied poetry and biology at Oxford, with distinction.

She is a Castlewell. That is, she is a member of one of the academic upper-middleclass families, which have been producing for centuries a steady supply of brilliant but sound men and women who are the backbone of the arts and sciences in Britain. She is on cool good terms with her family, who respect her and leave her alone.

She goes on long walking tours, by herself, in such places as Exmoor or West Scotland.

Every three or four years she publishes a volume of poems.

The walls of her flat are completely lined with books. They are scientific, clas-   25
sical and historical; there is a great deal of poetry and some drama. There is not one novel. When Judith says: "Of course I don't read novels," this does not mean that novels have no place, or a small place, in literature; or that people should not read novels; but that it must be obvious she can't be expected to read novels.

I had been visiting her flat for years before I noticed two long shelves of books, under a window, each shelf filled with the works of a single writer. The two writers are not, to put it at the mildest, the kind one would associate with Judith. They are mild, reminiscent, vague and whimsical. Typical English *belles-lettres*, in fact, and by definition abhorrent to her. Not one of the books in the two shelves has been read; some of the pages are still uncut. Yet each book is inscribed or dedicated to her: gratefully, admiringly, sentimentally and, more than once, amorously. In

6. About one-third or even one-half of a subsistence income.

short, it is open to anyone who cares to examine these two shelves, and to work out dates, to conclude that Judith from the age of fifteen to twenty-five had been the beloved young companion of one elderly literary gentleman, and from twenty-five to thirty-five the inspiration of another.

During all that time she had produced her own poetry, and the sort of poetry, it is quite safe to deduce, not at all likely to be admired by her two admirers. Her poems are always cool and intellectual; that is their form, which is contradicted or supported by a gravely sensuous texture. They are poems to read often; one has to, to understand them.

I did not ask Judith a direct question about these two eminent but rather fusty lovers. Not because she would not have answered, or because she would have found the question impertinent, but because such questions are clearly unnecessary. Having those two shelves of books where they are, and books she could not conceivably care for, for their own sake, is publicly giving credit where credit is due. I can imagine her thinking the thing over, and deciding it was only fair, or perhaps honest, to place the books there; and this despite the fact that she would not care at all for the same attention to be paid to her. There is something almost contemptuous in it. For she certainly despises people who feel they need attention.

For instance, more than once a new emerging wave of "modern" young poets have discovered her as the only "modern" poet among their despised and well-credited elders. This is because, since she began writing at fifteen, her poems have been full of scientific, mechanical and chemical imagery. This is how she thinks, or feels.

30   More than once has a young poet hastened to her flat, to claim her as an ally, only to find her totally and by instinct unmoved by words like "modern," "new," "contemporary." He has been outraged and wounded by her principle, so deeply rooted as to be unconscious, and to need no expression but a contemptuous shrug of the shoulders, that publicity seeking or to want critical attention is despicable. It goes without saying that there is perhaps one critic in the world she has any time for. He has sulked off, leaving her on her shelf, which she takes it for granted is her proper place, to be read by an appreciative minority.

Meanwhile she gives her lectures, walks alone through London, writes her poems, and is seen sometimes at a concert or a play with a middleaged professor of Greek, who has a wife and two children.

Betty and I had speculated about this professor, with such remarks as: Surely she must sometimes be lonely? Hasn't she ever wanted to marry? What about that awful moment when one comes in from somewhere at night to an empty flat?

It happened recently that Betty's husband was on a business trip, her children visiting, and she was unable to stand the empty house. She asked Judith for a refuge until her own home filled again.

Afterwards Betty rang me up to report: "Four of the five nights Professor Adams came in about ten or so."

35   "Was Judith embarrassed?"

"Would you expect her to be?"

"Well, if not embarrassed, at least conscious there was a situation?"

"No, not at all. But I must say I don't think he's good enough for her. He can't possibly understand her. He calls her Judy."

"Good God."

"Yes. But I was wondering. Suppose the other two called her Judy—'little Judy'—imagine it! Isn't it awful? But it does rather throw a light on Judith?"

"It's rather touching."

"I suppose it's touching. But *I* was embarrassed—oh, not because of the situation. Because of how she was, with him. 'Judy, is there another cup of tea in that pot?' And she, rather daughterly and demure, pouring him one."

"Well yes, I can see how you felt."

"Three of the nights he went to her bedroom with her—very casual about it, because she was being. But he was not there in the mornings. So I asked her. You know how it is when you ask her a question. As if you've been having long conversations on that very subject for years and years, and she is merely continuing where you left off last. So when she says something surprising, one feels such a fool to be surprised?"

"Yes. And then?"

"I asked her if she was sorry not to have children. She said yes, but one couldn't have everything."

"One can't have everything, she said?"

"Quite clearly feeling she *has* nearly everything. She said she thought it was a pity, because she would have brought up children very well."

"When you come to think of it, she would, too."

"I asked about marriage, but she said on the whole the role of a mistress suited her better."

"She used the word 'mistress'?"

"You must admit it's the accurate word."

"I suppose so."

"And then she said that while she liked intimacy and sex and everything, she enjoyed waking up in the morning alone and *her own person.*"

"Yes, *of course.*"

"Of course. But now she's bothered because the professor would like to marry her. Or he feels he ought. At least, he's getting all guilty and obsessive about it. She says she doesn't see the point of divorce, and anyway, surely it would be very hard on his poor old wife after all these years, particularly after bringing up two children so satisfactorily. She talks about his wife as if she's a kind of nice old charwoman, and it wouldn't be *fair* to sack her, you know. Anyway. What with one thing and another. Judith's going off to Italy soon in order *to collect herself.*"

"But how's she going to pay for it?"

"Luckily the Third Programme's[7] commissioning her to do some arty pro-

7. British Broadcasting Corporation public radio service (and now also television channel) specializing in classical music, literature and plays, lectures, etc.

grammes. They offered her a choice of The Cid—El Thid[8] you know—and the Borgias. Well, the Borghese, then. And Judith settled for the Borgias."

"The Borgias," I said, *"Judith?"*

60 "Yes, quite. I said that too, in that tone of voice. She saw my point. She says the epic is right up her street, whereas the Renaissance has never been on her wave length. Obviously it couldn't be, all the magnificence and cruelty and *dirt*. But of course chivalry and a high moral code and all those idiotically noble goings-on are right on her wave length."

"Is the money the same?"

"Yes. But is it likely Judith would let money decide? No, she said that one should always choose something new, that isn't up one's street. Well, because it's better for her character, and so on, to get herself unsettled by the Renaissance. She didn't say *that*, of course."

"Of course not."

Judith went to Florence; and for some months postcards informed us tersely of her doings. Then Betty decided she must go by herself for a holiday. She had been appalled by the discovery that if her husband was away for a night she couldn't sleep; and when he went to Australia for three weeks, she stopped living until he came back. She had discussed this with him, and he had agreed that if she really felt the situation to be serious, he would despatch her by air, to Italy, in order to recover her self-respect. As she put it.

65 I got this letter from her: "It's no use, I'm coming home. I might have known. Better face it, once you're really married you're not fit for man nor beast. And if you remember what I used to be like! *Well!* I moped around Milan. I sunbathed in Venice, then I thought my tan was surely worth something, so I was on the point of starting an affair with another lonely soul, but I lost heart, and went to Florence to see Judith. She wasn't there. She'd gone to the Italian Riviera. I had nothing better to do, so I followed her. When I saw the place I wanted to laugh, it's so much not Judith, you know, all those palms and umbrellas and gaiety at all costs and ever such an ornamental blue sea. Judith is in an enormous stone room up on the hillside above the sea, with grape vines all over the place. You should see her, she's got beautiful. It seems for the last fifteen years she's been going to Soho[9] every Saturday morning to buy food at an Italian shop. I must have looked surprised, because she explained she liked Soho. I suppose because all that dreary vice and nudes and prostitutes and everything prove how right she is to be as she is? She told the people in the shop she was going to Italy, and the *signora*[1] said, what a coincidence, she was going back to Italy too, and she did hope an old friend like Miss Castlewell would visit her there. Judith said to me: 'I felt lacking, when she used the word friend. Our relations have always been formal. Can you understand it?' she said to me. 'For fifteen years,' I said to her. She said: 'I think I must feel it's a kind of imposition, don't you know, expecting

8. Castilian, standard Spanish, pronunciation of El Cid (rhymes with *steed*), the title of an eleventh-century soldier-hero and hero of many works of literature.   9. A section of London roughly equivalent to Greenwich Village in New York—haunt of writers, painters, and so forth—known for foreign restaurants and groceries but also prostitutes and pornography.   1. Proprietress.

people to feel friendship for one.' *Well*. I said: 'You ought to understand it, because you're like that yourself.' 'Am I?' she said. 'Well, think about it,' I said. But I could see she didn't want to think about it. Anyway, she's here, and I've spent a week with her. The widow Maria Rineiri inherited her mother's house, so she came home, from Soho. On the ground floor is a tatty little *rosticceria*[2] patronised by the neighbours. They are all working people. This isn't tourist country, up on the hill. The widow lives above the shop with her little boy, a nasty little brat of about ten. Say what you like, the English are the only people who know how to bring up children, I don't care if that's insular. Judith's room is at the back, with a balcony. Underneath her room is the barber's shop, and the barber is Luigi Rineiri, the widow's younger brother. Yes, I was keeping him until the last. He is about forty, tall dark handsome, a great *bull*, but rather a sweet fatherly bull. He has cut Judith's hair and made it lighter. Now it looks like a sort of gold helmet. Judith is all brown. The widow Rineiri has made her a white dress and a green dress. They fit, for a change. When Judith walks down the street to the lower town, all the Italian males take one look at the golden girl and melt in their own oil like ice cream. Judith takes all this in her stride. She sort of acknowledges the homage. Then she strolls into the sea and vanishes into the foam. She swims five miles every day. *Naturally*. I haven't asked Judith whether she has collected herself, because you can see she hasn't. The widow Rineiri is matchmaking. When I noticed this I wanted to laugh, but luckily I didn't because Judith asked me, really wanting to know: 'Can you see me married to an Italian barber?' (Not being snobbish, but stating the position, so to speak.) 'Well yes,' I said, 'you're the only woman I know who I can see married to an Italian barber.' Because it wouldn't matter who she married, she'd always be her *own person*. 'At any rate, for a time,' I said. At which she said, asperously,[3] 'You can use phrases like for a time in England but not in Italy.' Did you ever see England, at least London, as the home of licence, liberty and free love? No, neither did I, but of course she's right. Married to Luigi it would be the family, the neighbours, the church and the *bambini*.[4] All the same she's thinking about it, believe it or not. Here she's quite different, all relaxed and free. She's melting in the attention she gets. The widow mothers her and makes her coffee all the time, and listens to a lot of good advice about how to bring up that nasty brat of hers. Unluckily she doesn't take it. Luigi is crazy for her. At mealtimes she goes to the *trattoria*[5] in the upper square and all the workmen treat her like a goddess. Well, a film star then. I said to her, you're mad to come home. For one thing her rent is ten bob[6] a week, and you eat *pasta* and drink red wine till you bust for about one and sixpence. No, she said, it would be nothing but self-indulgence to stay. Why? I said. She said, she's got nothing to stay for. (Ho ho.) And besides, she's done her research on the Borghese, though so far she can't see her way to an honest presentation of the facts. What made these people tick? she wants to know. And so she's only staying because of the cat. I forgot to mention the cat. This is a town of cats. The Italians here love their cats. I wanted to feed a stray cat at the table, but the waiter said no; and after

2. Grill.   3. Sharply, harshly.   4. Children.   5. Inexpensive restaurant.   6. Shillings. There were twenty shillings to the pound; *one and sixpence*, below, is one and a half shillings.

lunch, all the waiters came with trays crammed with leftover food and stray cats came from everywhere to eat. And at dark when the tourists go in to feed and the beach is empty—you know how empty and forlorn a beach is at dusk?—well cats appear from everywhere. The beach seems to move, then you see it's cats. They go stalking along the thin inch of grey water at the edge of the sea, shaking their paws crossly at each step, snatching at the dead little fish, and throwing them with their mouths up on to the dry stand. Then they scamper after them. You've never seen such a snarling and fighting. At dawn when the fishing boats come in to the empty beach, the cats are there in dozens. The fishermen throw them bits of fish. The cats snarl and fight over it. Judith gets up early and goes down to watch. Sometimes Luigi goes too, being tolerant. Because what he really likes is to join the evening promenade with Judith on his arm around and around the square of the upper town. Showing her off. Can you *see* Judith? But she does it. Being tolerant. But she smiles and enjoys the attention she gets, there's no doubt about it.

"She has a cat in her room. It's a kitten really, but it's pregnant. Judith says she can't leave until the kittens are born. The cat is too young to have kittens. Imagine Judith. She sits on her bed in that great stone room, with her bare feet on the stone floor, and watches the cat, and tries to work out why a healthy uninhibited Italian cat always fed on the best from the *rosticceria* should be neurotic. Because it is. When it sees Judith watching it gets nervous and starts licking at the roots of its tail. But Judith goes on watching, and says about Italy that the reason why the English love the Italians is because the Italians make the English feel superior. They have no discipline. And that's a despicable reason for one nation to love another. Then she talks about Luigi and says he has no sense of guilt, but a sense of sin; whereas she has no sense of sin but she has guilt. I haven't asked her if this has been an insuperable barrier, because judging from how she looks, it hasn't. She says she would rather have a sense of sin, because sin can be atoned for, and if she understood sin, perhaps she would be more at home with the Renaissance. Luigi is very healthy, she says, and not neurotic. He is a Catholic of course. He doesn't mind that she's an atheist. His mother has explained to him that the English are all pagans, but good people at heart. I suppose he thinks a few smart sessions with the local priest would set Judith on the right path for good and all. Meanwhile the cat walks nervously around the room, stopping to lick, and when it can't stand Judith watching it another second, it rolls over on the floor, with its paws tucked up, and rolls up its eyes, and Judith scratches its lumpy pregnant stomach and tells it to relax. It makes *me* nervous to see her, it's not like her, I don't know why. Then Luigi shouts up from the barber's shop, then he comes up and stands at the door laughing, and Judith laughs, and the widow says: Children, enjoy yourselves. And off they go, walking down to the town eating ice cream. The cat follows them. It won't let Judith out of its sight, like a dog. When she swims miles out to sea, the cat hides under a beach hut until she comes back. Then she carries it back up the hill, because that nasty little boy chases it. *Well.* I'm coming home tomorrow thank God, to my dear old Billy, I was mad ever to leave him. There is something about Judith and Italy that has upset me, I don't know what. The point is, what on earth can Judith and Luigi *talk* about? Nothing. How can they? And of course it doesn't matter. So I turn out to be a prude as well. See you next week."

It was my turn for a dose of the sun, so I didn't see Betty. On my way back from Rome I stopped off in Judith's resort and walked up through narrow streets to the upper town, where, in the square with the vine-covered *trattoria* at the corner, was a house with ROSTICCERIA written in black paint on a cracked wooden board over a low door. There was a door curtain of red beads, and flies settled on the beads. I opened the beads with my hands and looked into a small dark room with a stone counter. Loops of salami hung from metal hooks. A glass bell covered some plates of cooked meats. There were flies on the salami and on the glass bell. A few tins on the wooden shelves, a couple of pale loaves, some wine casks and an open case of sticky pale green grapes covered with fruit flies seemed to be the only stock. A single wooden table with two chairs stood in a corner, and two workmen sat there, eating lumps of sausage and bread. Through another bead curtain at the back came a short, smoothly fat, slender-limbed woman with greying hair. I asked for Miss Castlewell, and her face changed. She said in an offended, offhand way: "Miss Castlewell left last week." She took a white cloth from under the counter, and flicked at the flies on the glass bell. "I'm a friend of hers," I said, and she said: *Si,*[7] and put her hands palm down on the counter and looked at me, expressionless. The workmen got up, gulped down the last of their wine, nodded and went. She *ciao*'d[8] them; and looked back at me. Then, since I didn't go, she called: "Luigi!" A shout came from the back room, there was a rattle of beads, and in came first a wiry sharp-faced boy, and then Luigi. He was tall, heavy-shouldered, and his black rough hair was like a cap, pulled low over his brows. He looked good-natured, but at the moment uneasy. His sister said something, and he stood beside her, an ally, and confirmed: "Miss Castlewell went away." I was on the point of giving up, when through the bead curtain that screened off a dazzling light eased a thin tabby cat. It was ugly and it walked uncomfortably, with its back quarters bunched up. The child suddenly let out a "Ssssss" through his teeth, and the cat froze. Luigi said something sharp to the child, and something encouraging to the cat, which sat down, looked straight in front of it, then began frantically licking at its flanks. "Miss Castlewell was offended with us," said Mrs. Rineiri suddenly, and with dignity. "She left early one morning. We did not expect her to go." I said: "Perhaps she had to go home and finish some work."

Mrs. Rineiri shrugged, then sighed. Then she exchanged a hard look with her brother. Clearly the subject had been discussed, and closed forever.

"I've known Judith a long time," I said, trying to find the right note. "She's a remarkable woman. She's a poet." But there was no response to this at all. Meanwhile the child, with a fixed bared-teeth grin, was staring at the cat, narrowing his eyes. Suddenly he let out another "Ssssssss" and added a short high yelp. The cat shot backwards, hit the wall, tried desperately to claw its way up the wall, came to its senses and again sat down and began its urgent, undirected licking at its fur. This time Luigi cuffed the child, who yelped in earnest, and then ran out into the street past the cat. Now that the way was clear the cat shot across the

7. Yes.   8. Said good-bye to.

floor, up onto the counter, and bounded past Luigi's shoulder and straight through the bead curtain into the barber's shop, where it landed with a thud.

70 "Judith was sorry when she left us," said Mrs. Rineiri uncertainly. "She was crying."

"I'm sure she was."

"And so," said Mrs. Rineiri, with finality, laying her hands down again, and looking past me at the bead curtain. That was the end. Luigi nodded brusquely at me, and went into the back. I said goodbye to Mrs. Rineiri and walked back to the lower town. In the square I saw the child, sitting on the running board of a lorry[9] parked outside the *trattoria*, drawing in the dust with his bare toes, and directing in front of him a blank, unhappy stare.

I had to go through Florence, so I went to the address Judith had been at. No, Miss Castlewell had not been back. Her papers and books were still here. Would I take them back with me to England? I made a great parcel and brought them back to England.

I telephoned Judith and she said she had already written for the papers to be sent, but it was kind of me to bring them. There had seemed to be no point, she said, in returning to Florence.

75 "Shall I bring them over?"

"I would be very grateful, of course."

Judith's flat was chilly, and she wore a bunchy sage-green woollen dress. Her hair was still a soft gold helmet, but she looked pale and rather pinched. She stood with her back to a single bar of electric fire—lit because I demanded it—with her legs apart and her arms folded. She contemplated me.

"I went to the Rineiris' house."

"Oh. Did you?"

80 "They seemed to miss you."

She said nothing.

"I saw the cat too."

"Oh. Oh, I suppose you and Betty discussed it?" This was with a small unfriendly smile.

"Well, Judith, you must see we were likely to?"

85 She gave this her consideration and said: "I don't understand why people discuss other people. Oh—I'm not criticising you. But I don't see why you are so interested. I don't understand human behaviour and I'm not particularly interested."

"I think you should write to the Rineiris."

"I wrote and thanked them, of course."

"I don't mean that."

"You and Betty have worked it out?"

90 "Yes, we talked about it. We thought we should talk to you, so you should write to the Rineiris."

"Why?"

9. Truck.

"For one thing, they are both very fond of you."

"Fond," she said smiling.

"Judith, I've never in my life felt such an atmosphere of being let down."

Judith considered this. "When something happens that shows one there is really a complete gulf in understanding, what is there to say?"

"It could scarcely have been a complete gulf in understanding. I suppose you are going to say we are being interfering?"

Judith showed distaste. "That is a very stupid word. And it's a stupid idea. No one can interfere with me if I don't let them. No, it's that I don't understand people. I don't understand why you or Betty should care. Or why the Rineiris should, for that matter," she added with the small tight smile.

"Judith!"

"If you've behaved stupidly, there's no point in going on. You put an end to it."

"What happened? Was it the cat?"

"Yes, I suppose so. But it's not important." She looked at me, saw my ironical face, and said: "The cat was too young to have kittens. That is all there was to it."

"Have it your way. But that is obviously not all there is to it."

"What upsets me is that I don't understand at all why I was so upset then."

"What happened? Or don't you want to talk about it?"

"I don't give a damn whether I talk about it or not. You really do say the most extraordinary things, you and Betty. If you want to know, I'll tell you. What does it matter?"

"I would like to know, of course."

"*Of course!*" she said. "In your place I wouldn't care. Well, I think the essence of the thing was that I must have had the wrong attitude to that cat. Cats are supposed to be independent. They are supposed to go off by themselves to have their kittens. This one didn't. It was climbing up on to my bed all one night and crying for attention. I don't like cats on my bed. In the morning I saw she was in pain. I stayed with her all that day. Then Luigi—he's the brother, you know."

"Yes."

"Did Betty mention him? Luigi came up to say it was time I went for a swim. He said the cat should look after itself. I blame myself very much. That's what happens when you submerge yourself in somebody else."

Her look at me was now defiant; and her body showed both defensiveness and aggression. "Yes. It's true. I've always been afraid of it. And in the last few weeks I've behaved badly. It's because I let it happen."

"Well, go on."

"I left the cat and swam. It was late, so it was only for a few minutes. When I came out of the sea the cat had followed me and had had a kitten on the beach. That little beast Michele—the son, you know?—well, he always teased the poor thing, and now he had frightened her off the kitten. It was dead, though. He held it up by the tail and waved it at me as I came out of the sea. I told him to bury it. He scooped two inches of sand away and pushed the kitten in—on the beach, where people are all day. So I buried it properly. He had run off. He was chasing the poor cat. She was terrified and running up the town. I ran too. I caught Michele and I was so angry I hit him. I don't believe in hitting children. I've been feeling beastly about it ever since."

"You were angry."

"It's no excuse. I would never have believed myself capable of hitting a child. I hit him very hard. He went off, crying. The poor cat had got under a big lorry parked in the square. Then she screamed. And then a most remarkable thing happened. She screamed just once, and all at once cats just materialised. One minute there was just one cat, lying under a lorry, and the next, dozens of cats. They sat in a big circle around the lorry, all quite still, and watched my poor cat."

115   "Rather moving," I said.

"Why?"

"There is no evidence one way or the other," I said in inverted commas, "that the cats were there out of concern for a friend in trouble."

"No," she said energetically. "There isn't. It might have been curiosity. Or anything. How do we know? However, I crawled under the lorry. There were two paws sticking out of the cat's back end. The kitten was the wrong way round. It was stuck. I held the cat down with one hand and I pulled the kitten out with the other." She held out her long white hands. They were still covered with fading scars and scratches. "She bit and yelled, but the kitten was alive. She left the kitten and crawled across the square into the house. Then all the cats got up and walked away. It was the most extraordinary thing I've ever seen. They vanished again. One minute they were all there, and then they had vanished. I went after the cat, with the kitten. Poor little thing, it was covered with dust—being wet, don't you know. The cat was on my bed. There was another kitten coming, but it got stuck too. So when she screamed and screamed I just pulled it out. The kittens began to suck. One kitten was very big. It was a nice fat black kitten. It must have hurt her. But she suddenly bit out—snapped, don't you know, like a reflex action, at the back of the kitten's head. It died, just like that. Extraordinary, isn't it?" she said, blinking hard, her lips quivering. "She was its mother, but she killed it. Then she ran off the bed and went downstairs into the shop under the counter. I called to Luigi. You know, he's Mrs. Rineiri's brother."

"Yes, I know."

120   "He said she was too young, and she was badly frightened and very hurt. He took the alive kitten to her but she got up and walked away. She didn't want it. Then Luigi told me not to look. But I followed him. He held the kitten by the tail and he banged it against the wall twice. Then he dropped it into the rubbish heap. He moved aside some rubbish with his toe, and put the kitten there and pushed rubbish over it. Then Luigi said the cat should be destroyed. He said she was badly hurt and it would always hurt her to have kittens."

"He hasn't destroyed her. She's still alive. But it looks to me as if he were right."

"Yes, I expect he was."

"What upset you—that he killed the kitten?"

"Oh no, I expect the cat would if he hadn't. But that isn't the point, is it?"

125   "What is the point?"

"I don't think I really know." She had been speaking breathlessly, and fast.

Now she said slowly: "It's not a question of right or wrong, is it? Why should it be? It's a question of what one is. That night Luigi wanted to go promenading with me. For him, that was *that*. Something had to be done, and he'd done it. But I felt ill. He was very nice to me. He's a very good person," she said, defiantly.

"Yes, he looks it."

"That night I couldn't sleep. I was blaming myself. I should never have left the cat to go swimming. Well, and then I decided to leave the next day. And I did. And that's all. The whole thing was a mistake, from start to finish."

"Going to Italy at all?"

"Oh, to go for a holiday would have been all right."   130

"You've done all that work for nothing? You mean you aren't going to make use of all that research?"

"No. It was a mistake."

"Why don't you leave it a few weeks and see how things are then?"

"Why?"

"You might feel differently about it."   135

"What an extraordinary thing to say. Why should I? Oh, you mean, time passing, healing wounds—that sort of thing? What an extraordinary idea. It's always seemed to me an extraordinary idea. No, right from the beginning I've felt ill at ease with the whole business, not myself at all."

"Rather irrationally, I should have said."

Judith considered this, very seriously. She frowned while she thought it over. Then she said: "But if one cannot rely on what one feels, what can one rely on?"

"On what one thinks, I should have expected you to say."

"Should you? Why? Really, you people are all very strange. I don't understand 140 you." She turned off the electric fire, and her face closed up. She smiled, friendly and distant, and said: "I don't really see any point at all in discussing it."

1963

QUESTIONS

1. What image do you have of Sister, the narrator of "Why I Live at the P.O.," after the first ten paragraphs? How do paragraphs 37–49 sharpen, confirm, modify, expand, or change your image? paragraphs 63–68, 94–95? 99 and 108–10? 128–30? 136–38? Is she reliable? Compare paragraphs 8 and 14, and paragraphs 47 and 89, but remember that all the words of the story are Sister's. What is the effect of the contradictions on your view of the characters? on your expectations? on your response to the story? When in relation to the time of the actions is Sister telling this story? When would you date actions of the story? based on what evidence?

2. In some ways, Bartleby is a character defined negatively rather than positively—by the things he doesn't do, by the fact that he seldom talks, by all the information about his inner life and his past that neither the reader nor the characters have. Yet Bartleby's very inaction and silence provoke a great deal of talk and activity in the other characters. Why and how? One of the few things that Bartleby does say (again and again) is that he would "prefer not to," a phrase that provokes a great deal of commentary: Turkey insists he "never use[s]" that "queer word" *prefer*; Nippers uses the word in a different sense than Bartleby

does; and the narrator finds himself "involuntarily using this word" after hearing Bartleby say it so often. What might these various responses to Bartleby's statement tell us about each of the characters? about what Bartleby comes to represent to them?

3. Because we are told the story of "our friend Judith" by a friend, we never get to know Judith from the inside and are never very close to the action. This seems to have the effect of lessening the suspense and perhaps even our interest in or feelings for Judith. What is gained by this focus and voice? How does it change the meaning of the story? The friend says she blundered and lost her opportunity to find out what Judith and her life were really like. How did she lose the opportunity? Was it really a blunder? Could she have found out what she wanted to know if she had not "blundered"? What is the friend "really" like?

WRITING SUGGESTIONS

1. In paragraph 63 of "Why I Live at the P.O.," after Mama says that she prefers to believe her children, the narrator tells us that Mama weighs two hundred pounds and has small feet. What is the effect of this peculiar shift from one sentence to the next? What does it contribute to your image of Sister? Find several more such non sequiturs and analyze their effect. Write a brief essay on the relationship between style and humor in "Why I Live at the P.O."

2. Write an essay analyzing the changes that the narrator undergoes in "Bartleby, the Scrivener." How exactly does Bartleby inspire those changes? In these terms, what might be the significance of the last line of the story? What might the narrator have learned, through Bartleby, about "humanity"?

3. Write an analysis of the character of the narrator of "Our Friend Judith." Base your interpretation solidly on specific passages, incidents, and attitudes in the story.

4. Write for or against one of these two interpretations of Judith's character. Or show why neither is satisfactory:
   a. Judith seems to be cool, intellectual, and respectable, but she's really fiery and passionate. She's hypocritical, since she lives one kind of life in the open and another in secret.
   b. Judith is her own woman and does not need a man to lean on or depend on. She has her own full life and her profession, and does things her own way, the way men are praised for doing but women are often condemned for doing.

4

SETTING

All stories, like all individuals, are embedded in a context or **setting**—a time and place. The time can be contemporary ("Dreams") or historical ("The Cask of Amontillado") or even mythically vague ("The Zebra Storyteller"). It can be very limited, only a few minutes elapsing ("An Occurrence at Owl Creek Bridge") or some years ("Sonny's Blues"). The place can be rather fixed and interior ("No One's a Mystery") or varied ("Our Friend Judith"). It can be foreign ("The Cask of Amontillado") or American ("The Country Husband") or tied to a region ("Why I Live at the P.O." and the South) or a locale ("Sonny's Blues" and Harlem). Just as character and plot are so closely interrelated as to be ultimately indistinguishable (see chapter 3), so too are character, plot, and setting. Paradoxically, to see this interpenetration, we must think of them first as separable elements. The individuals in the stories are embedded in the specific context, and the more we know of the setting, and of the relationship of the character to the setting, the more likely we are to understand the character and the story.

Maupassant's "The Jewelry" is set in Paris in the late 1870s. Naturally, you might say, since it was written by a Frenchman in the early 1880s; he's just writing about his own time and place. True enough, but the cynicism, the somewhat bitter irony of the story set among the bourgeoisie and the bureaucracy, owes a good deal of its tone to the recent (1870–71) defeat of France and the siege and occupation of Paris by the Prussian Bismarck. (France paid Germany a billion dollars in reparations, an unheard-of amount in those days, and did so, to the world's astonishment, in just three years. Might this have something to do with the emphasis on money in the story?) The interaction of tone and times, setting and situation, are fused in this story in a way that would scarcely be possible in another context.

John Cheever's "The Country Husband" is set in the early to middle 1950s, close enough to our time so that we know the important things about the period—Elvis, Marilyn, all that. World War II seems distant, but not too distant: a man in midlife crisis served in the army during that time. It is set in suburban New York, not too remote or exotic a setting, since it has many of the qualities of the suburbs of any contemporary city. Yet the story is still somewhat of a period piece. The myth of the calm, comfortable good life—peace and plenty in the suburbs after the decades of Depression and war, the milieu of "Leave It to Beaver" and "Father Knows Best"—still prevailed. Airplane accidents and alcoholic fathers and memories of war were banned. And it seemed, at certain times, boring, almost unbearably so. All the excitement, all the romance of life, was gone, kept away by rows of white picket fences. Yes, we have suburbs like Shady Hill, but not many of the wives stay at home like Julia Weed and we no longer believe they are fenced off from the problems and promises of the Big City. The setting of this 1958 story makes of Francis a "weed," and though there are still crabgrass and dandelions in some of our finest neighborhoods, he and history would be difficult to transplant.

"The Country Husband" is, despite its relative modernity, a historical story. Its time, place, and historical setting interact with its narrative. Some stories are more overtly historical, and their milieu—or the stereotypes associated with it—are more obviously significant than those in Cheever's tale. The protagonist and the plot of "The Cask of Amontillado" are Machiavellian (characterized by subtle or unscrupulous cunning; after the Italian Renaissance politician and writer Niccolò Machiavelli, 1469–1527), and the story is set in Italy during the Renaissance. The Puritan goodman Brown lives in the reign of King William (1689–1702) in Salem, Massachusetts, where in 1692 the famous witch trials were held—what better place and time for a story whose subject is a witches' meeting and whose theme has to do with humanity's natural depravity? An *English* "spinster" seems (or seemed) much more prudish and virginal than just any old spinster, Italian lovers more sensual than Anglo-Saxon ones, and in "Our Friend Judith" testing those conventions is, virtually, the story.

In some stories setting, even when appropriate and natural, can symbolize whole ways of life or value systems. In "The Lady with the Dog," Yalta with its fruit, seashore, and semitropical climate exemplifies a more passionate, pleasurable, exciting life than the cold and cloudy, bureaucratic, intellectually rarefied air and routine of Moscow. The plot, therefore, cannot be entirely understood in isolation from the setting and the characters' relation to the setting.

Jing-Mei Woo, the narrator of "A Pair of Tickets," explores the relation of place, heritage, and ethnic identity. Living in San Francisco she had, at fifteen, "vigorously denied that I had any Chinese whatsoever below my skin," but at thirty-six, as she crosses the border from Hong Kong into China, she finds that she is "becoming Chinese." In Guangzhou, however, she discovers that within the vast change of place and cultures, in the modern world, at least among the privileged, there is a homogeneity: though men and women are working without safety belts or helmets on a scaffold made of bamboo held together with plastic strips, the hotel she is taken to "looks like a grander version of the Hyatt Regency." There are "shopping arcades and restaurants all encased in granite and glass," and in the rooms color television, a wet bar, Coke Classic, M & M's, Johnnie Walker Red, and so on. Her father's family circumvents her plan to have a Chinese feast, and they dine on hamburgers, french fries, apple pie à la mode, delivered by room service. In the modern city of Shanghai, meeting her twin half-sisters for the first time, she finds she is Chinese not because of place or face, but because of "blood." But within this story is another story, her mother's story, with another setting in time and conditions. Fleeing from Kweilin and the advance of the Japanese army in 1944, Jing-Mei's mother was forced by overwhelming circumstances to abandon her twin babies. Jing-Mei can now explain a good deal about her own past, about her mother and their relationship, from the story of her actions and the historical circumstances of the war.

If one of the functions of literature is to help us understand others and the way they see the world, setting—the time and place in which the fictional characters and action are embedded—is an essential element.

AMY TAN

A Pair of Tickets

The minute our train leaves the Hong Kong border and enters Shenzhen, China, I feel different. I can feel the skin on my forehead tingling, my blood rushing through a new course, my bones aching with a familiar old pain. And I think, My mother was right. I am becoming Chinese.

"Cannot be helped," my mother said when I was fifteen and had vigorously denied that I had any Chinese whatsoever below my skin. I was a sophomore at Galileo High in San Francisco, and all my Caucasian friends agreed: I was about as Chinese as they were. But my mother had studied at a famous nursing school in Shanghai, and she said she knew all about genetics. So there was no doubt in her mind, whether I agreed or not: Once you are born Chinese, you cannot help but feel and think Chinese.

"Someday you will see," said my mother. "It's in your blood, waiting to be let go."

And when she said this, I saw myself transforming like a werewolf, a mutant tag of DNA suddenly triggered, replicating itself insidiously into a *syndrome*, a cluster of telltale Chinese behaviors, all those things my mother did to embarrass me—haggling with store owners, pecking her mouth with a toothpick in public, being color-blind to the fact that lemon yellow and pale pink are not good combinations for winter clothes.

But today I realize I've never really known what it means to be Chinese. I am thirty-six years old. My mother is dead and I am on a train, carrying with me her dreams of coming home. I am going to China.

We are going to Guangzhou, my seventy-two-year-old father, Canning Woo, and I, where we will visit his aunt, whom he has not seen since he was ten years old. And I don't know whether it's the prospect of seeing his aunt or if it's because he's back in China, but now he looks like he's a young boy, so innocent and happy I want to button his sweater and pat his head. We are sitting across from each other, separated by a little table with two cold cups of tea. For the first time I can ever remember, my father has tears in his eyes, and all he is seeing out the train window is a sectioned field of yellow, green, and brown, a narrow canal flanking the tracks, low rising hills, and three people in blue jackets riding an ox-driven cart on this early October morning. And I can't help myself. I also have misty eyes, as if I had seen this a long, long time ago, and had almost forgotten.

In less than three hours, we will be in Guangzhou, which my guidebook tells me is how one properly refers to Canton these days. It seems all the cities I have heard of, except Shanghai, have changed their spellings. I think they are saying China has changed in other ways as well. Chungking is Chongqing. And Kweilin is Guilin. I have looked these names up, because after we see my father's aunt in Guangzhou, we will catch a plane to Shanghai, where I will meet my two half-sisters for the first time.

They are my mother's twin daughters from her first marriage, little babies she was forced to abandon on a road as she was fleeing Kweilin for Chungking in 1944. That was all my mother had told me about these daughters, so they had remained babies in my mind, all these years, sitting on the side of a road, listening to bombs whistling in the distance while sucking their patient red thumbs.

And it was only this year that someone found them and wrote with this joyful news. A letter came from Shanghai, addressed to my mother. When I first heard about this, that they were alive, I imagined my identical sisters transforming from little babies into six-year-old girls. In my mind, they were seated next to each other at a table, taking turns with the fountain pen. One would write a neat row of characters: *Dearest Mama. We are alive.* She would brush back her wispy bangs and hand the other sister the pen, and she would write: *Come get us. Please hurry.*

10   Of course they could not know that my mother had died three months before, suddenly, when a blood vessel in her brain burst. One minute she was talking to my father, complaining about the tenants upstairs, scheming how to evict them under the pretense that relatives from China were moving in. The next minute she was holding her head, her eyes squeezed shut, groping for the sofa, and then crumpling softly to the floor with fluttering hands.

So my father had been the first one to open the letter, a long letter it turned out. And they did call her Mama. They said they always revered her as their true mother. They kept a framed picture of her. They told her about their life, from the time my mother last saw them on the road leaving Kweilin to when they were finally found.

And the letter had broken my father's heart so much—these daughters calling my mother from another life he never knew—that he gave the letter to my mother's old friend Auntie Lindo and asked her to write back and tell my sisters, in the gentlest way possible, that my mother was dead.

But instead Auntie Lindo took the letter to the Joy Luck Club and discussed with Auntie Ying and Auntie An-mei what should be done, because they had known for many years about my mother's search for her twin daughters, her endless hope. Auntie Lindo and the others cried over this double tragedy, of losing my mother three months before, and now again. And so they couldn't help but think of some miracle, some possible way of reviving her from the dead, so my mother could fulfill her dream.

So this is what they wrote to my sisters in Shanghai: "Dearest Daughters, I too have never forgotten you in my memory or in my heart. I never gave up hope that we would see each other again in a joyous reunion. I am only sorry it has been too long. I want to tell you everything about my life since I last saw you. I want to tell you this when our family comes to see you in China. . . ." They signed it with my mother's name.

15   It wasn't until all this had been done that they first told me about my sisters, the letter they received, the one they wrote back.

"They'll think she's coming, then," I murmured. And I had imagined my sisters now being ten or eleven, jumping up and down, holding hands, their pigtails bouncing, excited that their mother—*their* mother—was coming, whereas my mother was dead.

"How can you say she is not coming in a letter?" said Auntie Lindo. "She is their mother. She is your mother. You must be the one to tell them. All these years, they have been dreaming of her." And I thought she was right.

But then I started dreaming, too, of my mother and my sisters and how it would be if I arrived in Shanghai. All these years, while they waited to be found, I had lived with my mother and then had lost her. I imagined seeing my sisters at the airport. They would be standing on their tiptoes, looking anxiously, scanning from one dark head to another as we got off the plane. And I would recognize them instantly, their faces with the identical worried look.

"*Jyejye, Jyejye.* Sister, Sister. We are here," I saw myself saying in my poor version of Chinese.

"Where is Mama?" they would say, and look around, still smiling, two flushed   20 and eager faces. "Is she hiding?" And this would have been like my mother, to stand behind just a bit, to tease a little and make people's patience pull a little on their hearts. I would shake my head and tell my sisters she was not hiding.

"Oh, that must be Mama, no?" one of my sisters would whisper excitedly, pointing to another small woman completely engulfed in a tower of presents. And that, too, would have been like my mother, to bring mountains of gifts, food, and toys for children—all bought on sale—shunning thanks, saying the gifts were nothing, and later turning the labels over to show my sisters, "Calvin Klein, 100% wool."

I imagined myself starting to say, "Sisters, I am sorry, I have come alone . . ." and before I could tell them—they could see it in my face—they were wailing, pulling their hair, their lips twisted in pain, as they ran away from me. And then I saw myself getting back on the plane and coming home.

After I had dreamed this scene many times—watching their despair turn from horror into anger—I begged Auntie Lindo to write another letter. And at first she refused.

"How can I say she is dead? I cannot write this," said Auntie Lindo with a stubborn look.

"But it's cruel to have them believe she's coming on the plane," I said. "When   25 they see it's just me, they'll hate me."

"Hate you? Cannot be." She was scowling. "You are their own sister, their only family."

"You don't understand," I protested.

"What I don't understand?" she said.

And I whispered, "They'll think I'm responsible, that she died because I didn't appreciate her."

And Auntie Lindo looked satisfied and sad at the same time, as if this were true   30 and I had finally realized it. She sat down for an hour, and when she stood up she handed me a two-page letter. She had tears in her eyes. I realized that the very thing I had feared, she had done. So even if she had written the news of my mother's death in English, I wouldn't have had the heart to read it.

"Thank you," I whispered.

The landscape has become gray, filled with low flat cement buildings, old factories, and then tracks and more tracks filled with trains like ours passing by in the opposite direction. I see platforms crowded with people wearing drab Western clothes, with spots of bright colors: little children wearing pink and yellow, red and peach. And there are soldiers in olive green and red, and old ladies in gray tops and pants that stop mid-calf. We are in Guangzhou.

Before the train even comes to a stop, people are bringing down their belongings from above their seats. For a moment there is a dangerous shower of heavy suitcases laden with gifts to relatives, half-broken boxes wrapped in miles of string to keep the contents from spilling out, plastic bags filled with yarn and vegetables and packages of dried mushrooms, and camera cases. And then we are caught in a stream of people rushing, shoving, pushing us along, until we find ourselves in one of a dozen lines waiting to go through customs. I feel as if I were getting on a number 30 Stockton bus in San Francisco. I am in China, I remind myself. And somehow the crowds don't bother me. It feels right. I start pushing too.

I take out the declaration forms and my passport. "Woo," it says at the top, and below that, "June May," who was born in "California, U.S.A.," in 1951. I wonder if the customs people will question whether I'm the same person as in the passport photo. In this picture, my chin-length hair is swept back and artfully styled. I am wearing false eyelashes, eye shadow, and lip liner. My cheeks are hollowed out by bronze blusher. But I had not expected the heat in October. And now my hair hangs limp with the humidity. I wear no makeup; in Hong Kong my mascara had melted into dark circles and everything else had felt like layers of grease. So today my face is plain, unadorned except for a thin mist of shiny sweat on my forehead and nose.

35   Even without makeup, I could never pass for true Chinese. I stand five-foot-six, and my head pokes above the crowd so that I am eye level only with other tourists. My mother once told me my height came from my grandfather, who was a northerner, and may have even had some Mongol blood. "This is what your grandmother once told me," explained my mother. "But now it is too late to ask her. They are all dead, your grandparents, your uncles, and their wives and children, all killed in the war, when a bomb fell on our house. So many generations in one instant."

She had said this so matter-of-factly that I thought she had long since gotten over any grief she had. And then I wondered how she knew they were all dead.

"Maybe they left the house before the bomb fell," I suggested.

"No," said my mother. "Our whole family is gone. It is just you and I."

"But how do you know? Some of them could have escaped."

40   "Cannot be," said my mother, this time almost angrily. And then her frown was washed over by a puzzled blank look, and she began to talk as if she were trying to remember where she had misplaced something. "I went back to that house. I kept looking up to where the house used to be. And it wasn't a house, just the sky. And below, underneath my feet, were four stories of burnt bricks and wood, all the life of our house. Then off to the side I saw things blown into the yard, nothing valuable. There was a bed someone used to sleep in, really just a metal frame twisted up at one corner. And a book, I don't know what kind, because every page had turned black. And I saw a teacup which was unbroken but filled with ashes. And then I found my doll, with her hands and legs broken,

her hair burned off. . . . When I was a little girl, I had cried for that doll, seeing it all alone in the store window, and my mother had bought it for me. It was an American doll with yellow hair. It could turn its legs and arms. The eyes moved up and down. And when I married and left my family home, I gave the doll to my youngest niece, because she was like me. She cried if that doll was not with her always. Do you see? If she was in the house with that doll, her parents were there, and so everybody was there, waiting together, because that's how our family was."

The woman in the customs booth stares at my documents, then glances at me briefly, and with two quick movements stamps everything and sternly nods me along. And soon my father and I find ourselves in a large area filled with thousands of people and suitcases. I feel lost and my father looks helpless.

"Excuse me," I say to a man who looks like an American. "Can you tell me where I can get a taxi?" He mumbles something that sounds Swedish or Dutch.

"Syau Yen! Syau Yen!" I hear a piercing voice shout from behind me. An old woman in a yellow knit beret is holding up a pink plastic bag filled with wrapped trinkets. I guess she is trying to sell us something. But my father is staring down at this tiny sparrow of a woman, squinting into her eyes. And then his eyes widen, his face opens up and he smiles like a pleased little boy.

"*Aiyi! Aiyi!*"—Auntie Auntie!—he says softly.

"Syau Yen!" coos my great-aunt. I think it's funny she has just called my father "Little Wild Goose." It must be his baby milk name, the name used to discourage ghosts from stealing children.   45

They clasp each other's hands—they do not hug—and hold on like this, taking turns saying, "Look at you! You are so old. Look how old you've become!" They are both crying openly, laughing at the same time, and I bite my lip, trying not to cry. I'm afraid to feel their joy. Because I am thinking how different our arrival in Shanghai will be tomorrow, how awkward it will feel.

Now Aiyi beams and points to a Polaroid picture of my father. My father had wisely sent pictures when he wrote and said we were coming. See how smart she was, she seems to intone as she compares the picture to my father. In the letter, my father had said we would call her from the hotel once we arrived, so this is a surprise, that they've come to meet us. I wonder if my sisters will be at the airport.

It is only then that I remember the camera. I had meant to take a picture of my father and his aunt the moment they met. It's not too late.

"Here, stand together over here," I say, holding up the Polaroid. The camera flashes and I hand them the snapshot. Aiyi and my father still stand close together, each of them holding a corner of the picture, watching as their images begin to form. They are almost reverentially quiet. Aiyi is only five years older than my father, which makes her around seventy-seven. But she looks ancient, shrunken, a mummified relic. Her thin hair is pure white, her teeth are brown with decay. So much for stories of Chinese women looking young forever, I think to myself.

Now Aiyi is crooning to me: "*Jandale.*" So big already. She looks up at me, at   50
my full height, and then peers into her pink plastic bag—her gifts to us, I have

figured out—as if she is wondering what she will give to me, now that I am so old and big. And then she grabs my elbow with her sharp pincerlike grasp and turns me around. A man and a woman in their fifties are shaking hands with my father, everybody smiling and saying, "Ah! Ah!" They are Aiyi's oldest son and his wife, and standing next to them are four other people, around my age, and a little girl who's around ten. The introductions go by so fast, all I know is that one of them is Aiyi's grandson, with his wife, and the other is her granddaughter, with her husband. And the little girl is Lili, Aiyi's great-granddaughter.

Aiyi and my father speak the Mandarin dialect from their childhood, but the rest of the family speaks only the Cantonese of their village. I understand only Mandarin but can't speak it that well. So Aiyi and my father gossip unrestrained in Mandarin, exchanging news about people from their old village. And they stop only occasionally to talk to the rest of us, sometimes in Cantonese, sometimes in English.

"Oh, it is as I suspected," says my father, turning to me. "He died last summer." And I already understood this. I just don't know who this person, Li Gong, is. I feel as if I were in the United Nations and the translators had run amok.

"Hello," I say to the little girl. "My name is Jing-mei." But the little girl squirms to look away, causing her parents to laugh with embarrassment. I try to think of Cantonese words I can say to her, stuff I learned from friends in Chinatown, but all I can think of are swear words, terms for bodily functions, and short phrases like "tastes good," "tastes like garbage," and "she's really ugly." And then I have another plan: I hold up the Polaroid camera, beckoning Lili with my finger. She immediately jumps forward, places one hand on her hip in the manner of a fashion model, juts out her chest, and flashes me a toothy smile. As soon as I take the picture she is standing next to me, jumping and giggling every few seconds as she watches herself appear on the greenish film.

By the time we hail taxis for the ride to the hotel, Lili is holding tight onto my hand, pulling me along.

55   In the taxi, Aiyi talks nonstop, so I have no chance to ask her about the different sights we are passing by.

"You wrote and said you would come only for one day," says Aiyi to my father in an agitated tone. "One day! How can you see your family in one day! Toishan is many hours' drive from Guangzhou. And this idea to call us when you arrive. This is nonsense. We have no telephone."

My heart races a little. I wonder if Auntie Lindo told my sisters we would call from the hotel in Shanghai?

Aiyi continues to scold my father. "I was so beside myself, ask my son, almost turned heaven and earth upside down trying to think of a way! So we decided the best was for us to take the bus from Toishan and come into Guangzhou— meet you right from the start."

And now I am holding my breath as the taxi driver dodges between trucks and buses, honking his horn constantly. We seem to be on some sort of long freeway overpass, like a bridge above the city. I can see row after row of apartments, each floor cluttered with laundry hanging out to dry on the balcony.

We pass a public bus, with people jammed in so tight their faces are nearly wedged against the window. Then I see the skyline of what must be downtown Guangzhou. From a distance, it looks like a major American city, with highrises and construction going on everywhere. As we slow down in the more congested part of the city, I see scores of little shops, dark inside, lined with counters and shelves. And then there is a building, its front laced with scaffolding made of bamboo poles held together with plastic strips. Men and women are standing on narrow platforms, scraping the sides, working without safety straps or helmets. Oh, would OSHA[1] have a field day here, I think.

Aiyi's shrill voice rises up again: "So it is a shame you can't see our village, our house. My sons have been quite successful, selling our vegetables in the free market. We had enough these last few years to build a big house, three stories, all of new brick, big enough for our whole family and then some. And every year, the money is even better. You Americans aren't the only ones who know how to get rich!" 60

The taxi stops and I assume we've arrived, but then I peer out at what looks like a grander version of the Hyatt Regency. "This is communist China?" I wonder out loud. And then I shake my head toward my father. "This must be the wrong hotel." I quickly pull out our itinerary, travel tickets, and reservations. I had explicitly instructed my travel agent to choose something inexpensive, in the thirty-to-forty-dollar range. I'm sure of this. And there it says on our itinerary: Garden Hotel, Huanshi Dong Lu. Well, our travel agent had better be prepared to eat the extra, that's all I have to say.

The hotel is magnificent. A bellboy complete with uniform and sharp-creased cap jumps forward and begins to carry our bags into the lobby. Inside, the hotel looks like an orgy of shopping arcades and restaurants all encased in granite and glass. And rather than be impressed, I am worried about the expense, as well as the appearance it must give Aiyi, that we rich Americans cannot be without our luxuries even for one night.

But when I step up to the reservation desk, ready to haggle over this booking mistake, it is confirmed. Our rooms are prepaid, thirty-four dollars each. I feel sheepish, and Aiyi and the others seem delighted by our temporary surroundings. Lili is looking wide-eyed at an arcade filled with video games.

Our whole family crowds into one elevator, and the bellboy waves, saying he will meet us on the eighteenth floor. As soon as the elevator door shuts, everybody becomes very quiet, and when the door finally opens again, everybody talks at once in what sounds like relieved voices. I have the feeling Aiyi and the others have never been on such a long elevator ride.

Our rooms are next to each other and are identical. The rugs, drapes, bedspreads are all in shades of taupe. There's a color television with remote-control panels built into the lamp table between the two twin beds. The bathroom has marble walls and floors. I find a built-in wet bar with a small refrigerator stocked with Heineken beer, Coke Classic, and Seven-Up, mini-bottles of Johnnie Walker 65

1. Occupational Safety and Health Administration.

Red, Bacardi rum, and Smirnoff vodka, and packets of M & M's, honey-roasted cashews, and Cadbury chocolate bars. And again I say out loud, "This is communist China?"

My father comes into my room. "They decided we should just stay here and visit," he says, shrugging his shoulders. "They say, Less trouble that way. More time to talk."

"What about dinner?" I ask. I have been envisioning my first real Chinese feast for many days already, a big banquet with one of those soups steaming out of a carved winter melon, chicken wrapped in clay, Peking duck, the works.

My father walks over and picks up a room service book next to a *Travel & Leisure* magazine. He flips through the pages quickly and then points to the menu. "This is what they want," says my father.

So it's decided. We are going to dine tonight in our rooms, with our family, sharing hamburgers, french fries, and apple pie à la mode.

70   Aiyi and her family are browsing the shops while we clean up. After a hot ride on the train, I'm eager for a shower and cooler clothes.

The hotel has provided little packets of shampoo which, upon opening, I discover is the consistency and color of hoisin sauce.[2] This is more like it, I think. This is China. And I rub some in my damp hair.

Standing in the shower, I realize this is the first time I've been by myself in what seems like days. But instead of feeling relieved, I feel forlorn. I think about what my mother said, about activating my genes and becoming Chinese. And I wonder what she meant.

Right after my mother died, I asked myself a lot of things, things that couldn't be answered, to force myself to grieve more. It seemed as if I wanted to sustain my grief, to assure myself that I had cared deeply enough.

But now I ask the questions mostly because I want to know the answers. What was that pork stuff she used to make that had the texture of sawdust? What were the names of the uncles who died in Shanghai? What had she dreamt all these years about her other daughters? All the times when she got mad at me, was she really thinking about them? Did she wish I were they? Did she regret that I wasn't?

------

75   At one o'clock in the morning, I awake to tapping sounds on the window. I must have dozed off and now I feel my body uncramping itself. I'm sitting on the floor, leaning against one of the twin beds. Lili is lying next to me. The others are asleep, too, sprawled out on the beds and floor. Aiyi is seated at a little table, looking very sleepy. And my father is staring out the window, tapping his fingers on the glass. The last time I listened my father was telling Aiyi about his life since he last saw her. How he had gone to Yenching University, later got a post with a newspaper in Chungking, met my mother there, a young widow. How they later fled together to Shanghai to try to find my mother's family house, but there was

---

2. Sweet brownish-red sauce made from soybeans, sugar, water, spices, garlic, and chili.

nothing there. And then they traveled eventually to Canton and then to Hong Kong, then Haiphong and finally to San Francisco. . . .

"Suyuan didn't tell me she was trying all these years to find her daughters," he is now saying in a quiet voice. "Naturally, I did not discuss her daughters with her. I thought she was ashamed she had left them behind."

"Where did she leave them?" asks Aiyi. "How were they found?"

I am wide awake now. Although I have heard parts of this story from my mother's friends.

"It happened when the Japanese took over Kweilin," says my father.

"Japanese in Kweilin?" says Aiyi. "That was never the case. Couldn't be. The   80
Japanese never came to Kweilin."

"Yes, that is what the newspapers reported. I know this because I was working for the news bureau at the time. The Kuomintang[3] often told us what we could say and could not say. But we knew the Japanese had come into Kwangsi Province. We had sources who told us how they had captured the Wuchang-Canton railway. How they were coming overland, making very fast progress, marching toward the provincial capital."

Aiyi looks astonished. "If people did not know this, how could Suyuan know the Japanese were coming?"

"An officer of the Kuomintang secretly warned her," explains my father. "Suyuan's husband also was an officer and everybody knew that officers and their families would be the first to be killed. So she gathered a few possessions and, in the middle of the night, she picked up her daughters and fled on foot. The babies were not even one year old."

"How could she give up those babies!" sighs Aiyi. "Twin girls. We have never had such luck in our family." And then she yawns again.

"What were they named?" she asks. I listen carefully. I had been planning on   85
using just the familiar "Sister" to address them both. But now I want to know how to pronounce their names.

"They have their father's surname, Wang," says my father. "And their given names are Chwun Yu and Chwun Hwa."

"What do the names mean?" I ask.

"Ah." My father draws imaginary characters on the window. "One means 'Spring Rain,' the other 'Spring Flower,' " he explains in English, "because they born in the spring, and of course rain come before flower, same order these girls are born. Your mother like a poet, don't you think?"

I nod my head. I see Aiyi nod her head forward, too. But it falls forward and stays there. She is breathing deeply, noisily. She is asleep.

"And what does Ma's name mean?" I whisper.   90

" 'Suyuan,' " he says, writing more invisible characters on the glass. "The way she write it in Chinese, it mean 'Long-Cherished Wish.' Quite a fancy name, not so ordinary like flower name. See this first character, it mean something like 'Forever Never Forgotten.' But there is another way to write 'Suyuan.' Sound exactly the same, but the meaning is opposite." His finger creates the brushstrokes of

3. National People's Party, led by Generalissimo Chiang Kai-shek (1887–1975).

another character. "The first part look the same: 'Never Forgotten.' But the last part add to first part make the whole word mean 'Long-Held Grudge.' Your mother get angry with me, I tell her her name should be Grudge."

My father is looking at me, moist-eyed. "See, I pretty clever, too, hah?"

I nod, wishing I could find some way to comfort him. "And what about my name," I ask, "what does 'Jing-mei' mean?"

"Your name also special," he says. I wonder if any name in Chinese is not something special. " 'Jing' like excellent *jing*. Not just good, it's something pure, essential, the best quality. *Jing* is good leftover stuff when you take impurities out of something like gold, or rice, or salt. So what is left—just pure essence. And 'Mei,' this is common *mei*, as in *meimei*, 'younger sister.' "

95   I think about this. My mother's long-cherished wish. Me, the younger sister who was supposed to be the essence of the others. I feed myself with the old grief, wondering how disappointed my mother must have been. Tiny Aiyi stirs suddenly, her head rolls and then falls back, her mouth opens as if to answer my question. She grunts in her sleep, tucking her body more closely into the chair.

"So why did she abandon those babies on the road?" I need to know, because now I feel abandoned too.

"Long time I wondered this myself," says my father. "But then I read that letter from her daughters in Shanghai now, and I talk to Auntie Lindo, all the others. And then I knew. No shame in what she done. None."

"What happened?"

"Your mother running away—" begins my father.

100   "No, tell me in Chinese," I interrupt. "Really, I can understand."

He begins to talk, still standing at the window, looking into the night.

———————

After fleeing Kweilin, your mother walked for several days trying to find a main road. Her thought was to catch a ride on a truck or wagon, to catch enough rides until she reached Chungking, where her husband was stationed.

She had sewn money and jewelry into the lining of her dress, enough, she thought, to barter rides all the way. If I am lucky, she thought, I will not have to trade the heavy gold bracelet and jade ring. These were things from her mother, your grandmother.

By the third day, she had traded nothing. The roads were filled with people, everybody running and begging for rides from passing trucks. The trucks rushed by, afraid to stop. So your mother found no rides, only the start of dysentery pains in her stomach.

105   Her shoulders ached from the two babies swinging from scarf slings. Blisters grew on the palms from holding two leather suitcases. And then the blisters burst and began to bleed. After a while, she left the suitcases behind, keeping only the food and a few clothes. And later she also dropped the bags of wheat flour and rice and kept walking like this for many miles, singing songs to her little girls, until she was delirious with pain and fever.

Finally, there was not one more step left in her body. She didn't have the strength to carry those babies any farther. She slumped to the ground. She knew she would die of her sickness, or perhaps from thirst, from starvation, or from the Japanese, who she was sure were marching right behind her.

She took the babies out of the slings and sat them on the side of the road, then lay down next to them. You babies are so good, she said, so quiet. They smiled back, reaching their chubby hands for her, wanting to be picked up again. And then she knew she could not bear to watch her babies die with her.

She saw a family with three young children in a cart going by. "Take my babies, I beg you," she cried to them. But they stared back with empty eyes and never stopped.

She saw another person pass and called out again. This time a man turned around, and he had such a terrible expression—your mother said it looked like death itself—she shivered and looked away.

When the road grew quiet, she tore open the lining of her dress, and stuffed jewelry under the shirt of one baby and money under the other. She reached into her pocket and drew out the photos of her family, the picture of her father and mother, the picture of herself and her husband on their wedding day. And she wrote on the back of each the names of the babies and this same message: "Please care for these babies with the money and valuables provided. When it is safe to come, if you bring them to Shanghai, 9 Weichang Lu, the Li family will be glad to give you a generous reward. Li Suyuan and Wang Fuchi."

And then she touched each baby's cheek and told her not to cry. She would go down the road to find them some food and would be back. And without looking back, she walked down the road, stumbling and crying, thinking only of this one last hope, that her daughters would be found by a kindhearted person who would care for them. She would not allow herself to imagine anything else.

She did not remember how far she walked, which direction she went, when she fainted, or how she was found. When she awoke, she was in the back of a bouncing truck with several other sick people, all moaning. And she began to scream, thinking she was now on a journey to Buddhist hell. But the face of an American missionary lady bent over her and smiled, talking to her in a soothing language she did not understand. And yet she could somehow understand. She had been saved for no good reason, and it was now too late to go back and save her babies.

When she arrived in Chungking, she learned her husband had died two weeks before. She told me later she laughed when the officers told her this news, she was so delirious with madness and disease. To come so far, to lose so much and to find nothing.

I met her in a hospital. She was lying on a cot, hardly able to move, her dysentery had drained her so thin. I had come in for my foot, my missing toe, which was cut off by a piece of falling rubble. She was talking to herself, mumbling.

"Look at these clothes," she said, and I saw she had on a rather unusual dress for wartime. It was silk satin, quite dirty, but there was no doubt it was a beautiful dress.

"Look at this face," she said, and I saw her dusty face and hollow cheeks, her eyes shining black. "Do you see my foolish hope?"

"I thought I had lost everything, except these two things," she murmured. "And I wondered which I would lose next. Clothes or hope? Hope or clothes?"

"But now, see here, look what is happening," she said, laughing, as if all her prayers had been answered. And she was pulling hair out of her head as easily as one lifts new wheat from wet soil.

It was an old peasant woman who found them. "How could I resist?" the peasant woman later told your sisters when they were older. They were still sitting obediently near where your mother had left them, looking like little fairy queens waiting for their sedan to arrive.

120   The woman, Mei Ching, and her husband, Mei Han, lived in a stone cave. There were thousands of hidden caves like that in and around Kweilin so secret that the people remained hidden even after the war ended. The Meis would come out of their cave every few days and forage for food supplies left on the road, and sometimes they would see something that they both agreed was a tragedy to leave behind. So one day they took back to their cave a delicately painted set of rice bowls, another day a little footstool with a velvet cushion and two new wedding blankets. And once, it was your sisters.

They were pious people, Muslims, who believed the twin babies were a sign of double luck, and they were sure of this when, later in the evening, they discovered how valuable the babies were. She and her husband had never seen rings and bracelets like those. And while they admired the pictures, knowing the babies came from a good family, neither of them could read or write. It was not until many months later that Mei Ching found someone who could read the writing on the back. By then, she loved these baby girls like her own.

In 1952 Mei Han, the husband, died. The twins were already eight years old, and Mei Ching now decided it was time to find your sisters' true family.

She showed the girls the picture of their mother and told them they had been born into a great family and she would take them back to see their true mother and grandparents. Mei Ching told them about the reward, but she swore she would refuse it. She loved these girls so much, she only wanted them to have what they were entitled to—a better life, a fine house, educated ways. Maybe the family would let her stay on as the girls' amah. Yes, she was certain they would insist.

Of course, when she found the place at 9 Weichang Lu, in the old French Concession, it was something completely different. It was the site of a factory building, recently constructed, and none of the workers knew what had become of the family whose house had burned down on that spot.

125   Mei Ching could not have known, of course, that your mother and I, her new husband, had already returned to that same place in 1945 in hopes of finding both her family and her daughters.

Your mother and I stayed in China until 1947. We went to many different cities—back to Kweilin, to Changsha, as far south as Kunming. She was always looking out of one corner of her eye for twin babies, then little girls. Later we went to Hong Kong, and when we finally left in 1949 for the United States, I think she was even looking for them on the boat. But when we arrived, she no longer talked about them. I thought, At last, they have died in her heart.

When letters could be openly exchanged between China and the United States, she wrote immediately to old friends in Shanghai and Kweilin. I did not know she did this. Auntie Lindo told me. But of course, by then, all the street names had changed. Some people had died, others had moved away. So it took many years to find a contact. And when she did find an old schoolmate's address and wrote asking her to look for her daughters, her friend wrote back and said this was impossible, like looking for a needle on the bottom of the ocean. How did she know her daughters were in Shanghai and not somewhere else in China? The friend, of course, did not ask, How do you know your daughters are still alive?

So her schoolmate did not look. Finding babies lost during the war was a matter of foolish imagination, and she had no time for that.

But every year, your mother wrote to different people. And this last year, I think she got a big idea in her head, to go to China and find them herself. I remember she told me, "Canning, we should go, before it is too late, before we are too old." And I told her we were already too old, it was already too late.

I just thought she wanted to be a tourist! I didn't know she wanted to go and look for her daughters. So when I said it was too late, that must have put a terrible thought in her head that her daughters might be dead. And I think this possibility grew bigger and bigger in her head, until it killed her.

Maybe it was your mother's dead spirit who guided her Shanghai schoolmate to find her daughters. Because after your mother died, the schoolmate saw your sisters, by chance, while shopping for shoes at the Number One Department Store on Nanjing Dong Road. She said it was like a dream, seeing these two women who looked so much alike, moving down the stairs together. There was something about their facial expressions that reminded the schoolmate of your mother.

She quickly walked over to them and called their names, which of course, they did not recognize at first, because Mei Ching had changed their names. But your mother's friend was so sure, she persisted. "Are you not Wang Chwun Yu and Wang Chwun Hwa?" she asked them. And then these double-image women became very excited, because they remembered the names written on the back of an old photo, a photo of a young man and woman they still honored, as their much-loved first parents, who had died and become spirit ghosts still roaming the earth looking for them.

————————

At the airport, I am exhausted. I could not sleep last night. Aiyi had followed me into my room at three in the morning, and she instantly fell asleep on one of the twin beds, snoring with the might of a lumberjack. I lay awake thinking about my mother's story, realizing how much I have never known about her, grieving that my sisters and I had both lost her.

And now at the airport, after shaking hands with everybody, waving good-bye, I think about all the different ways we leave people in this world. Cheerily waving good-bye to some at airports, knowing we'll never see each other again. Leaving others on the side of the road, hoping that we will. Finding my mother in my father's story and saying good-bye before I have a chance to know her better.

Aiyi smiles at me as we wait for our gate to be called. She is so old. I put one arm around her and one arm around Lili. They are the same size, it seems. And then it's time. As we wave good-bye one more time and enter the waiting area, I get the sense I am going from one funeral to another. In my hand I'm clutching a pair of tickets to Shanghai. In two hours we'll be there.

The plane takes off. I close my eyes. How can I describe to them in my broken Chinese about our mother's life? Where should I begin?

"Wake up, we're here," says my father. And I awake with my heart pounding in my throat. I look out the window and we're already on the runway. It's gray outside.

And now I'm walking down the steps of the plane, onto the tarmac and toward the building. If only, I think, if only my mother had lived long enough to be the one walking toward them. I am so nervous I cannot even feel my feet. I am just moving somehow.

Somebody shouts, "She's arrived!" And then I see her. Her short hair. Her small body. And that same look on her face. She has the back of her hand pressed hard against her mouth. She is crying as though she had gone through a terrible ordeal and were happy it is over.

140 And I know it's not my mother, yet it is the same look she had when I was five and had disappeared all afternoon, for such a long time, that she was convinced I was dead. And when I miraculously appeared, sleepy-eyed, crawling from underneath my bed, she wept and laughed, biting the back of her hand to make sure it was true.

And now I see her again, two of her, waving, and in one hand there is a photo, the Polaroid I sent them. As soon as I get beyond the gate, we run toward each other, all three of us embracing, all hesitations and expectations forgotten.

"Mama, Mama," we all murmur, as if she is among us.

My sisters look at me, proudly. *"Meimei jandale,"* says one sister proudly to the other. "Little Sister has grown up." I look at their faces again and I see no trace of my mother in them. Yet they still look familiar. And now I also see what part of me is Chinese. It is so obvious. It is my family. It is in our blood. After all these years, it can finally be let go.

My sisters and I stand, arms around each other, laughing and wiping the tears from each other's eyes. The flash of the Polaroid goes off and my father hands me the snapshot. My sisters and I watch quietly together, eager to see what develops.

145 The gray-green surface changes to the bright colors of our three images, sharpening and deepening all at once. And although we don't speak, I know we all see it: Together we look like our mother. Her same eyes, her same mouth, open in surprise to see, at last, her long-cherished wish.

1989

ANTON CHEKHOV

The Lady with the Dog[1]

I

It was said that a new person had appeared on the sea-front: a lady with a little dog. Dmitri Dmitritch Gurov, who had by then been a fortnight at Yalta,[2] and so was fairly at home there, had begun to take an interest in new arrivals. Sitting in Verney's pavilion, he saw, walking on the sea-front, a fair-haired young lady of medium height, wearing a *béret*; a white Pomeranian dog was running behind her.

And afterwards he met her in the public gardens and in the square several times a day. She was walking alone, always wearing the same *béret*, and always with the same white dog; no one knew who she was, and every one called her simply "the lady with the dog."

"If she is here alone without a husband or friends, it wouldn't be amiss to make her acquaintance," Gurov reflected.

He was under forty, but he had a daughter already twelve years old, and two sons at school. He had been married young, when he was a student in his second year, and by now his wife seemed half as old again as he. She was a tall, erect woman with dark eyebrows, staid and dignified, and, as she said of herself, intellectual. She read a great deal, used phonetic spelling, called her husband, not Dmitri, but Dimitri, and he secretly considered her unintelligent, narrow, inelegant, was afraid of her, and did not like to be at home. He had begun being unfaithful to her long ago—had been unfaithful to her often, and, probably on that account, almost always spoke ill of women, and when they were talked about in his presence, used to call them "the lower race."

It seemed to him that he had been so schooled by bitter experience that he might call them what he liked, and yet he could not get on for two days together without "the lower race." In the society of men he was bored and not himself, with them he was cold and uncommunicative; but when he was in the company of women he felt free, and knew what to say to them and how to behave; and he was at ease with them even when he was silent. In his appearance, in his character, in his whole nature, there was something attractive and elusive which allured women and disposed them in his favour; he knew that, and some force seemed to draw him, too, to them.

Experience often repeated, truly bitter experience, had taught him long ago that with decent people, especially Moscow people—always slow to move and irresolute—every intimacy, which at first so agreeably diversifies life and appears a light and charming adventure, inevitably grows into a regular problem of extreme intricacy, and in the long run the situation becomes unbearable. But at every fresh meeting with an interesting woman this experience seemed to slip

5

1. Translated by Constance Garnett.   2. Russian city on the Black Sea; a resort for southern vacations.

out of his memory, and he was eager for life, and everything seemed simple and amusing.

One evening he was dining in the gardens, and the lady in the *béret* came up slowly to take the next table. Her expression, her gait, her dress, and the way she did her hair told him that she was a lady, that she was married, that she was in Yalta for the first time and alone, and that she was dull there. . . . The stories told of the immorality in such places as Yalta are to a great extent untrue; he despised them, and knew that such stories were for the most part made up by persons who would themselves have been glad to sin if they had been able; but when the lady sat down at the next table three paces from him, he remembered these tales of easy conquests, of trips to the mountains, and the tempting thought of a swift, fleeting love affair, a romance with an unknown woman, whose name he did not know, suddenly took possession of him.

He beckoned coaxingly to the Pomeranian, and when the dog came up to him he shook his finger at it. The Pomeranian growled: Gurov shook his finger at it again.

The lady looked at him and at once dropped her eyes.

10 "He doesn't bite," she said, and blushed.

"May I give him a bone?" he asked; and when she nodded he asked courteously, "Have you been long in Yalta?"

"Five days."

"And I have already dragged out a fortnight here."

There was a brief silence.

15 "Time goes fast, and yet it is so dull here!" she said, not looking at him.

"That's only the fashion to say it is dull here. A provincial will live in Belyov or Zhidra and not be dull, and when he comes here it's 'Oh, the dulness! Oh, the dust!' One would think he came from Grenada."[3]

She laughed. Then both continued eating in silence, like strangers, but after dinner they walked side by side; and there sprang up between them the light jesting conversation of people who are free and satisfied, to whom it does not matter where they go or what they talk about. They walked and talked of the strange light on the sea: the water was of a soft warm lilac hue, and there was a golden streak from the moon upon it. They talked of how sultry it was after a hot day. Gurov told her that he came from Moscow, that he had taken his degree in Arts, but had a post in a bank; that he had trained as an opera-singer, but had given it up, that he owned two houses in Moscow. . . . And from her he learnt that she had grown up in Petersburg, but had lived in S—— since her marriage two years before, that she was staying another month in Yalta, and that her husband, who needed a holiday too, might perhaps come and fetch her. She was not sure whether her husband had a post in a Crown Department[4] or under the Provincial Council—and was amused by her own ignorance. And Gurov learnt, too, that she was called Anna Sergeyevna.

Afterwards he thought about her in his room at the hotel—thought she would

3. Romantic city in southern Spain.   4. Department appointed by the czar or an elective local council (*zemstvo*).

certainly meet him next day; it would be sure to happen. As he got into bed he thought how lately she had been a girl at school, doing lessons like his own daughter; he recalled the diffidence, the angularity, that was still manifest in her laugh and her manner of talking with a stranger. This must have been the first time in her life she had been alone in surroundings in which she was followed, looked at, and spoken to merely from a secret motive which she could hardly fail to guess. He recalled her slender, delicate neck, her lovely grey eyes.

"There's something pathetic about her, anyway," he thought, and fell asleep.

II

A week had passed since they had made acquaintance. It was a holiday. It was   20
sultry indoors, while in the street the wind whirled the dust round and round, and blew people's hats off. It was a thirsty day, and Gurov often went into the pavilion, and pressed Anna Sergeyevna to have syrup and water or an ice. One did not know what to do with oneself.

In the evening when the wind had dropped a little, they went out on the groyne to see the steamer come in. There were a great many people walking about the harbour; they had gathered to welcome some one, bringing bouquets. And two peculiarities of a well-dressed Yalta crowd were very conspicuous: the elderly ladies were dressed like young ones, and there were great numbers of generals.

Owing to the roughness of the sea, the steamer arrived late, after the sun had set, and it was a long time turning about before it reached the groyne. Anna Sergeyevna looked through her lorgnette at the steamer and the passengers as though looking for acquaintances, and when she turned to Gurov her eyes were shining. She talked a great deal and asked disconnected questions, forgetting next moment what she had asked; then she dropped her lorgnette in the crush.

The festive crowd began to disperse; it was too dark to see people's faces. The wind had completely dropped, but Gurov and Anna Sergeyevna still stood as though waiting to see some one else come from the steamer. Anna Sergeyevna was silent now, and sniffed the flowers without looking at Gurov.

"The weather is better this evening," he said. "Where shall we go now? Shall we drive somewhere?"

She made no answer.   25

Then he looked at her intently, and all at once put his arm round her and kissed her on the lips, and breathed in the moisture and the fragrance of the flowers; and he immediately looked round him, anxiously wondering whether any one had seen them.

"Let us go to your hotel," he said softly. And both walked quickly.

The room was close and smelt of the scent she had bought at the Japanese shop. Gurov looked at her and thought: "What different people one meets in the world!" From the past he preserved memories of careless, good-natured women, who loved cheerfully and were grateful to him for the happiness he gave them, however brief it might be; and of women like his wife who loved without any genuine feeling, with superfluous phrases, affectedly, hysterically, with an expression that suggested that it was not love nor passion, but something more significant; and of two or three others, very beautiful, cold women, on whose faces he had caught a glimpse of a rapacious expression—an obstinate desire to snatch from life more than it could give, and these were capricious, unreflecting, domineering, unintelligent women not in their first youth, and when Gurov grew cold to them their beauty excited his hatred, and the lace on their linen seemed to him like scales.

But in this case there was still the diffidence, the angularity of inexperienced youth, an awkward feeling; and there was a sense of consternation as though some one had suddenly knocked at the door. The attitude of Anna Sergeyevna— "the lady with the dog"—to what had happened was somehow peculiar, very grave, as though it were her fall—so it seemed, and it was strange and inappropriate. Her face dropped and faded, and on both sides of it her long hair hung down mournfully; she mused in a dejected attitude like "the woman who was a sinner" in an old-fashioned picture.

30   "It's wrong," she said. "You will be the first to despise me now."

There was a water-melon on the table. Gurov cut himself a slice and began eating it without haste. There followed at least half an hour of silence.

Anna Sergeyevna was touching; there was about her the purity of a good, simple woman who had seen little of life. The solitary candle burning on the table threw a faint light on her face, yet it was clear that she was very unhappy.

"How could I despise you?" asked Gurov. "You don't know what you are saying."

"God forgive me," she said, and her eyes filled with tears. "It's awful."

35   "You seem to feel you need to be forgiven."

"Forgiven? No. I am a bad, low woman; I despise myself and don't attempt to justify myself. It's not my husband but myself I have deceived. And not only just now; I have been deceiving myself for a long time. My husband may be a good, honest man, but he is a flunkey! I don't know what he does there, what his work is, but I know he is a flunkey! I was twenty when I was married to him. I have been tormented by curiosity; I wanted something better. 'There must be a different sort of life,' I said to myself. I wanted to live! To live, to live! . . . I was fired by curiosity . . . you don't understand it, but, I swear to God, I could not control myself; something happened to me: I could not be restrained. I told my husband I was ill, and came here. . . . And here I have been walking about as though I were dazed, like a mad creature; . . . and now I have become a vulgar, contemptible woman whom any one may despise."

Gurov felt bored already, listening to her. He was irritated by the naïve tone, by this remorse, so unexpected and inopportune; but for the tears in her eyes, he might have thought she was jesting or playing a part.

"I don't understand," he said softly. "What is it you want?"

She hid her face on his breast and pressed close to him.

40   "Believe me, believe me, I beseech you . . ." she said. "I love a pure, honest life, and sin is loathsome to me. I don't know what I am doing. Simple people say: 'The Evil One has beguiled me.' And I may say of myself now that the Evil One has beguiled me."

"Hush, hush! . . ." he muttered.

He looked at her fixed, scared eyes, kissed her, talked softly and affectionately, and by degrees she was comforted, and her gaiety returned; they both began laughing.

Afterwards when they went out there was not a soul on the sea-front. The town with its cypresses had quite a deathlike air, but the sea still broke noisily on the shore; a single barge was rocking on the waves, and a lantern was blinking sleepily on it.

They found a cab and drove to Oreanda.

"I found out your surname in the hall just now: it was written on the board— 45
Von Diderits," said Gurov. "Is your husband a German?"

"No; I believe his grandfather was a German, but he is an Orthodox Russian himself."

At Oreanda they sat on a seat not far from the church, looked down at the sea, and were silent. Yalta was hardly visible through the morning mist; white clouds stood motionless on the mountain-tops. The leaves did not stir on the trees, grass-hoppers chirruped, and the monotonous hollow sound of the sea rising up from below, spoke of the peace, of the eternal sleep awaiting us. So it must have sounded when there was no Yalta, no Oreanda here; so it sounds now, and it will sound as indifferently and monotonously when we are all no more. And in this constancy, in this complete indifference to the life and death of each of us, there lies hid, perhaps, a pledge of our eternal salvation, of the unceasing movement of life upon earth, of unceasing progress towards perfection. Sitting beside a young woman who in the dawn seemed so lovely, soothed and spellbound in these magical surroundings—the sea, mountains, clouds, the open sky—Gurov thought how in reality everything is beautiful in this world when one reflects: everything except what we think or do ourselves when we forget our human dignity and the higher aims of our existence.

A man walked up to them—probably a keeper—looked at them and walked away. And this detail seemed mysterious and beautiful, too. They saw a steamer come from Theodosia, with its lights out in the glow of dawn.

"There is dew on the grass," said Anna Sergeyevna, after a silence.

"Yes. It's time to go home."   50

They went back to the town.

Then they met every day at twelve o'clock on the sea-front, lunched and dined together, went for walks, admired the sea. She complained that she slept badly, that her heart throbbed violently; asked the same questions, troubled now by jealousy and now by the fear that he did not respect her sufficiently. And often in the square or gardens, when there was no one near them, he suddenly drew her to him and kissed her passionately. Complete idleness, these kisses in broad daylight while he looked round in dread of some one's seeing them, the heat, the smell of the sea, and the continual passing to and fro before him of idle, well-dressed, well-fed people, made a new man of him; he told Anna Sergeyevna how beautiful she was, how fascinating. He was impatiently passionate, he would not move a step away from her, while she was often pensive and continually urged him to confess that he did not respect her, did not love her in the least, and thought of her as nothing but a common woman. Rather late almost every evening they drove somewhere out of town, to Oreanda or to the waterfall; and the expedition was always a success, the scenery invariably impressed them as grand and beautiful.

They were expecting her husband to come, but a letter came from him, saying that there was something wrong with his eyes, and he entreated his wife to come home as quickly as possible. Anna Sergeyevna made haste to go.

"It's a good thing I am going away," she said to Gurov. "It's the finger of destiny!"

She went by coach and he went with her. They were driving the whole day. When she had got into a compartment of the express, and when the second bell had rung, she said:

"Let me look at you once more . . . look at you once again. That's right."

She did not shed tears, but was so sad that she seemed ill, and her face was quivering.

"I shall remember you . . . think of you," she said. "God be with you; be happy. Don't remember evil against me. We are parting forever—it must be so, for we ought never to have met. Well, God be with you."

The train moved off rapidly, its lights soon vanished from sight, and a minute later there was no sound of it, as though everything had conspired together to end as quickly as possible that sweet delirium, that madness. Left alone on the platform, and gazing into the dark distance, Gurov listened to the chirrup of the grasshoppers and the hum of the telegraph wires, feeling as though he had only just waked up. And he thought, musing, that there had been another episode or adventure in his life, and it, too, was at an end, and nothing was left of it but a memory. . . . He was moved, sad, and conscious of a slight remorse. This young woman whom he would never meet again had not been happy with him; he was genuinely warm and affectionate with her, but yet in his manner, his tone, and his caresses there had been a shade of light irony, the coarse condescension of a happy man who was, besides, almost twice her age. All the time she had called him kind, exceptional, lofty; obviously he had seemed to her different from what he really was, so he had unintentionally deceived her. . . .

Here at the station was already a scent of autumn; it was a cold evening.

"It's time for me to go north," thought Gurov as he left the platform. "High time!"

III

At home in Moscow everything was in its winter routine; the stoves were heated, and in the morning it was still dark when the children were having breakfast and getting ready for school, and the nurse would light the lamp for a short time. The frosts had begun already. When the first snow has fallen, on the first day of sledge-driving it is pleasant to see the white earth, the white roofs, to draw soft, delicious breath, and the season brings back the days of one's youth. The old limes and birches, white with hoar-frost, have a good-natured expression; they are nearer to one's heart than cypresses and palms, and near them one doesn't want to be thinking of the sea and the mountains.

Gurov was Moscow born; he arrived in Moscow on a fine frosty day, and when he put on his fur coat and warm gloves, and walked along Petrovka, and when on Saturday evening he heard the ringing of the bells, his recent trip and the places he had seen lost all charm for him. Little by little he became absorbed in Moscow life, greedily read three newspapers a day, and declared he did not read the Moscow papers on principle! He already felt a longing to go to restaurants, clubs, dinner-parties, anniversary celebrations, and he felt flattered at entertaining distinguished lawyers and artists, and at playing cards with a professor at the doctors' club. He could already eat a whole plateful of salt fish and cabbage. . . .

In another month, he fancied, the image of Anna Sergeyevna would be shrouded in a mist in his memory, and only from time to time would visit him in his dreams with a touching smile as others did. But more than a month passed, real winter had come, and everything was still clear in his memory as though he had parted with Anna Sergeyevna only the day before. And his memories glowed more and more vividly. When in the evening stillness he heard from his study the voices of his children, preparing their lessons, or when he listened to a song or the organ at the restaurant, or the storm howled in the chimney, suddenly everything would rise up in his memory: what had happened on the groyne, and the early morning with the mist on the mountains, and the steamer coming from Theodosia, and the kisses. He would pace a long time about his room, remembering it all and smiling; then his memories passed into dreams, and in his fancy the past was mingled with what was to come. Anna Sergeyevna did not visit him in dreams, but followed him about everywhere like a shadow and haunted him. When he shut his eyes he saw her as though she were living before him, and she seemed to him lovelier, younger, tenderer than she was; and he imagined himself finer than he had been in Yalta. In the evenings she peeped out at him from the bookcase, from the fireplace, from the corner—he heard her breathing, the caressing rustle of her dress. In the street he watched the women, looking for some one like her.

He was tormented by an intense desire to confide his memories to some one. 65 But in his home it was impossible to talk of his love, and he had no one outside; he could not talk to his tenants nor to any one at the bank. And what had he to talk of? Had he been in love, then? Had there been anything beautiful, poetical, or edifying or simply interesting in his relations with Anna Sergeyevna? And there was nothing for him but to talk vaguely of love, of woman, and no one guessed what it meant; only his wife twitched her black eyebrows, and said: "The part of a lady-killer does not suit you at all, Dimitri."

One evening, coming out of the doctors' club with an official with whom he had been playing cards, he could not resist saying:

"If only you knew what a fascinating woman I made the acquaintance of in Yalta!"

The official got into his sledge and was driving away, but turned suddenly and shouted:

"Dmitri Dmitritch!"

"What?" 70

"You were right this evening: the sturgeon was a bit too strong!"

These words, so ordinary, for some reason moved Gurov to indignation, and struck him as degrading and unclean. What savage manners, what people! What senseless nights, what uninteresting, uneventful days! The rage for card-playing, the gluttony, the drunkenness, the continual talk always about the same thing. Useless pursuits and conversations always about the same things absorb the better part of one's time, the better part of one's strength, and in the end there is left a life grovelling and curtailed, worthless and trivial, and there is no escaping or getting away from it—just as though one were in a madhouse or a prison.

Gurov did not sleep all night, and was filled with indignation. And he had a headache all next day. And the next night he slept badly; he sat up in bed, thinking, or paced up and down his room. He was sick of his children, sick of the bank; he had no desire to go anywhere or to talk of anything.

In the holidays in December he prepared for a journey, and told his wife he was going to Petersburg to do something in the interests of a young friend—and he set off for S——. What for? He did not very well know himself. He wanted to see Anna Sergeyevna and to talk with her—to arrange a meeting, if possible.

75   He reached S—— in the morning, and took the best room at the hotel, in which the floor was covered with grey army cloth, and on the table was an inkstand, grey with dust and adorned with a figure on horseback, with its hat in its hand and its head broken off. The hotel porter gave him the necessary information; Von Diderits lived in a house of his own in Old Gontcharny Street—it was not far from the hotel: he was rich and lived in good style, and had his own horses; every one in the town knew him. The porter pronounced the name "Dridirits."

Gurov went without haste to Old Gontcharny Street and found the house. Just opposite the house stretched a long grey fence adorned with nails.

"One would run away from a fence like that," thought Gurov, looking from the fence to the windows of the house and back again.

He considered: to-day was a holiday, and the husband would probably be at home. And in any case it would be tactless to go into the house and upset her. If he were to send her a note it might fall into her husband's hands, and then it might ruin everything. The best thing was to trust to chance. And he kept walking up and down the street by the fence, waiting for the chance. He saw a beggar go in at the gate and dogs fly at him; then an hour later he heard a piano, and the sounds were faint and indistinct. Probably it was Anna Sergeyevna playing. The front door suddenly opened, and an old woman came out, followed by the familiar white Pomeranian. Gurov was on the point of calling to the dog, but his heart began beating violently, and in his excitement he could not remember the dog's name.

He walked up and down, and loathed the grey fence more and more, and by now he thought irritably that Anna Sergeyevna had forgotten him, and was perhaps already amusing herself with some one else, and that that was very natural in a young woman who had nothing to look at from morning till night but that confounded fence. He went back to his hotel room and sat for a long while on the sofa, not knowing what to do, then he had dinner and a long nap.

80   "How stupid and worrying it is!" he thought when he woke and looked at the

dark windows: it was already evening. "Here I've had a good sleep for some reason. What shall I do in the night?"

He sat on the bed, which was covered by a cheap grey blanket, such as one sees in hospitals, and he taunted himself in his vexation:

"So much for the lady with the dog . . . so much for the adventure. . . . You're in a nice fix. . . ."

That morning at the station a poster in large letters had caught his eye. "The Geisha"[5] was to be performed for the first time. He thought of this and went to the theatre.

"It's quite possible she may go to the first performance," he thought.

The theatre was full. As in all provincial theatres, there was a fog above the chandelier, the gallery was noisy and restless; in the front row the local dandies were standing up before the beginning of the performance, with their hands behind them; in the Governor's box the Governor's daughter, wearing a boa, was sitting in the front seat, while the Governor himself lurked modestly behind the curtain with only his hands visible; the orchestra was a long time tuning up; the stage curtain swayed. All the time the audience were coming in and taking their seats Gurov looked at them eagerly.

Anna Sergeyevna, too, came in. She sat down in the third row, and when Gurov looked at her his heart contracted, and he understood clearly that for him there was in the whole world no creature so near, so precious, and so important to him; she, this little woman, in no way remarkable, lost in a provincial crowd, with a vulgar lorgnette in her hand, filled his whole life now, was his sorrow and his joy, the one happiness that he now desired for himself, and to the sounds of the inferior orchestra, of the wretched provincial violins, he thought how lovely she was. He thought and dreamed.

A young man with small side-whiskers, tall and stooping, came in with Anna Sergeyevna and sat down beside her; he bent his head at every step and seemed to be continually bowing. Most likely this was the husband whom at Yalta, in a rush of bitter feeling, she had called a flunkey. And there really was in his long figure, his side-whiskers, and the small bald patch on his head, something of the flunkey's obsequiousness; his smile was sugary, and in his buttonhole there was some badge of distinction like the number on a waiter.

During the first interval the husband went away to smoke; she remained alone in her stall. Gurov, who was sitting in the stalls, too, went up to her and said in a trembling voice, with a forced smile:

"Good-evening."

She glanced at him and turned pale, then glanced again with horror, unable to believe her eyes, and tightly gripped the fan and the lorgnette in her hands, evidently struggling with herself not to faint. Both were silent. She was sitting, he was standing, frightened by her confusion and not venturing to sit down beside her. The violins and the flute began tuning up. He felt suddenly frightened; it seemed as though all the people in the boxes were looking at them. She got up

85

90

5. Operetta by Sidney Jones (1861–1946) that toured eastern Europe in 1898–99.

and went quickly to the door; he followed her, and both walked senselessly along passages, and up and down stairs, and figures in legal, scholastic, and civil service uniforms, all wearing badges, flitted before their eyes. They caught glimpses of ladies, of fur coats hanging on pegs; the draughts blew on them, bringing a smell of stale tobacco. And Gurov, whose heart was beating violently, thought:

"Oh, heavens! Why are these people here and this orchestra! . . ."

And at that instant he recalled how when he had seen Anna Sergeyevna off at the station he had thought that everything was over and they would never meet again. But how far they were still from the end!

On the narrow, gloomy staircase over which was written "To the Amphi-theatre," she stopped.

"How you have frightened me!" she said, breathing hard, still pale and over-whelmed. "Oh, how you have frightened me! I am half dead. Why have you come? Why?"

95   "But do understand, Anna, do understand . . ." he said hastily in a low voice. "I entreat you to understand. . . ."

She looked at him with dread, with entreaty, with love; she looked at him intently, to keep his features more distinctly in her memory.

"I am so unhappy," she went on, not heeding him. "I have thought of nothing but you all the time; I live only in the thought of you. And I wanted to forget, to forget you; but why, oh, why, have you come?"

On the landing above them two schoolboys were smoking and looking down, but that was nothing to Gurov; he drew Anna Sergeyevna to him, and began kissing her face, her cheeks, and her hands.

"What are you doing, what are you doing!" she cried in horror, pushing him away. "We are mad. Go away to-day; go away at once. . . . I beseech you by all that is sacred, I implore you. . . . There are people coming this way!"

100   Some one was coming up the stairs.

"You must go away," Anna Sergeyevna went on in a whisper. "Do you hear, Dmitri Dmitritch? I will come and see you in Moscow. I have never been happy; I am miserable now, and I never, never shall be happy, never! Don't make me suffer still more! I swear I'll come to Moscow. But now let us part. My precious, good, dear one, we must part!"

She pressed his hand and began rapidly going downstairs, looking round at him, and from her eyes he could see that she really was unhappy. Gurov stood for a little while, listened, then, when all sound had died away, he found his coat and left the theatre.

IV

And Anna Sergeyevna began coming to see him in Moscow. Once in two or three months she left S——, telling her husband that she was going to consult a doctor about an internal complaint—and her husband believed her, and did not believe her. In Moscow she stayed at the Slaviansky Bazaar hotel, and at once sent a man in a red cap to Gurov. Gurov went to see her, and no one in Moscow knew of it.

Once he was going to see her in this way on a winter morning (the messenger had come the evening before when he was out). With him walked his daughter, whom he wanted to take to school: it was on the way. Snow was falling in big wet flakes.

"It's three degrees above freezing-point, and yet it is snowing," said Gurov to his daughter. "The thaw is only on the surface of the earth; there is quite a different temperature at a greater height in the atmosphere." 105

"And why are there no thunderstorms in the winter, father?"

He explained that, too. He talked, thinking all the while that he was going to see *her*, and no living soul knew of it, and probably never would know. He had two lives: one, open, seen and known by all who cared to know, full of relative truth and of relative falsehood, exactly like the lives of his friends and acquaintances; and another life running its course in secret. And through some strange, perhaps accidental, conjunction of circumstances, everything that was essential, of interest and of value to him, everything in which he was sincere and did not deceive himself, everything that made the kernel of his life, was hidden from other people; and all that was false in him, the sheath in which he hid himself to conceal the truth—such, for instance, as his work in the bank, his discussions at the club, his "lower race," his presence with his wife at anniversary festivities— all that was open. And he judged of others by himself, not believing in what he saw, and always believing that every man had his real, most interesting life under the cover of secrecy and under the cover of night. All personal life rested on secrecy, and possibly it was partly on that account that civilised man was so nervously anxious that personal privacy should be respected.

After leaving his daughter at school, Gurov went on to the Slaviansky Bazaar. He took off his fur coat below, went upstairs, and softly knocked at the door. Anna Sergeyevna, wearing his favourite grey dress, exhausted by the journey and the suspense, had been expecting him since the evening before. She was pale; she looked at him, and did not smile, and he had hardly come in when she fell on his breast. Their kiss was slow and prolonged, as though they had not met for two years.

"Well, how are you getting on there?" he asked. "What news?"

"Wait; I'll tell you directly. . . . I can't talk." 110

She could not speak; she was crying. She turned away from him, and pressed her handkerchief to her eyes.

"Let her have her cry out. I'll sit down and wait," he thought, and he sat down in an arm-chair.

Then he rang and asked for tea to be brought him, and while he drank his tea she remained standing at the window with her back to him. She was crying from emotion, from the miserable consciousness that their life was so hard for them; they could only meet in secret, hiding themselves from people, like thieves! Was not their life shattered?

"Come, do stop!" he said.

It was evident to him that this love of theirs would not soon be over, that he could not see the end of it. Anna Sergeyevna grew more and more attached to him. She adored him, and it was unthinkable to say to her that it was bound to have an end some day; besides, she would not have believed it! 115

He went up to her and took her by the shoulders to say something affectionate and cheering, and at that moment he saw himself in the looking-glass.

His hair was already beginning to turn grey. And it seemed strange to him that he had grown so much older, so much plainer during the last few years. The shoulders on which his hands rested were warm and quivering. He felt compassion for this life, still so warm and lovely, but probably already not far from beginning to fade and wither like his own. Why did she love him so much? He always seemed to women different from what he was, and they loved in him not himself, but the man created by their imagination, whom they had been eagerly seeking all their lives; and afterwards, when they noticed their mistake, they loved him all the same. And not one of them had been happy with him. Time passed, he had made their acquaintance, got on with them, parted, but he had never once loved; it was anything you like, but not love.

And only now when his head was grey he had fallen properly, really in love—for the first time in his life.

Anna Sergeyevna and he loved each other like people very close and akin, like husband and wife, like tender friends; it seemed to them that fate itself had meant them for one another, and they could not understand why he had a wife and she a husband; and it was as though they were a pair of birds of passage, caught and forced to live in different cages. They forgave each other for what they were ashamed of in their past, they forgave everything in the present, and felt that this love of theirs had changed them both.

120   In moments of depression in the past he had comforted himself with any arguments that came into his mind, but now he no longer cared for arguments; he felt profound compassion, he wanted to be sincere and tender. . . .

"Don't cry, my darling," he said. "You've had your cry; that's enough. . . . Let us talk now, let us think of some plan."

Then they spent a long while taking counsel together, talked of how to avoid the necessity for secrecy, for deception, for living in different towns and not seeing each other for long at a time. How could they be free from this intolerable bondage?

"How? How?" he asked, clutching his head. "How?"

And it seemed as though in a little while the solution would be found, and then a new and splendid life would begin; and it was clear to both of them that they had still a long, long road before them, and that the most complicated and difficult part of it was only just beginning.

1899

QUESTIONS

1. The mother of Jing-mei Woo, in "A Pair of Tickets," told her that being Chinese is a matter of genetics, and Jing-mei finds that that is true. What is the role of place and time (history), then, in this story?

2. Yalta, where "The Lady with the Dog" opens, is a resort on the Black Sea; Moscow, where Gurov lives, is described at the beginning of section III. To what extent do the settings

relate to the events and emotions of the story? How do other details—such as the water-melon in section II (Yalta) and the slightly "off" sturgeon in section III (Moscow)—relate to the settings and the attitudes and feelings associated with the places? Which are con-ventionally assumed to be more real, the feelings we have on holiday or those in our everyday lives? How is this convention related to our expectations about the outcome of the story? to the meaning of the story?

WRITING SUGGESTIONS

1. Compare the use of episodes from World War II in "The Country Husband" and "A Pair of Tickets."
2. Write a personal narrative about a visit to a place important in your family history that you had never visited before and how you felt about your relation to that place; or about an episode that made you recognize or affirm your ethnic identity or heritage.
3. Write a fifth section of "The Lady with the Dog."

5

SYMBOL

One of the chief devices for bridging the gap between the writer's vision and the reader's is the **symbol,** commonly defined as something that stands for something else: a flower, for example, may be seen as a symbol of a particular state. Symbols are generally **figurative;** that is, they compare or put together two *unlike* things. A senator, on the other hand, represents a state *literally:* the state is a governmental unit, and the senator is a member of the government. But the flower has nothing to do with government and so represents the state only figuratively.

But why speak of anything in terms of something else? Why should snakes commonly be symbolic of evil? Sure, some snakes are poisonous, but for some people so are bees, and a lot of snakes are not only harmless but actually helpful ecologically. (In Kipling's *The Jungle Book* the python Ka, while frightening, is on the side of law and order.) Through repeated use over the centuries, the snake has become a traditional symbol of evil—not just danger, sneakiness, and repulsiveness, but theological, absolute evil. Had Peyton Farquhar, in "An Occurrence at Owl Creek Bridge," been confronted by a snake when he was thrown ashore, we would not necessarily have said, "Aha—snake, symbol of Evil," though that potential meaning might have hovered around the incident and sent us looking backward and forward in the story for supporting evidence that this snake was being used symbolically. However, when we discover that the stranger in "Young Goodman Brown" has a walking stick upon which is carved the image of a snake, we are much more likely to find it such a symbol because of other, related potential symbols or meanings in the context: the term *goodman,* used throughout the story, suggests the distinct possibility that Brown (a common name) stands for more than a "mere" individual young man. Brown's bride is named Faith—a common name among the early Puritans, but together with *goodman,* suggesting symbolic possibilities. Then, just before the stranger with the walking stick appears, Brown says, "What if the devil himself should be at my very elbow!"

A single item, even something as traditionally fraught with meaning as a snake or a rose, becomes a symbol only when its potentially symbolic meaning is confirmed by something else in the story, just as a point needs a second point to define a line. Multiple symbols, potential symbols, direct and indirect hints such as Brown's mention of the devil: these are among the ways in which details may be identified as symbols (for interpreting symbols is relatively easy once you know what is and what probably is not a symbol).

One form of what may be called an indirect hint is repetition. That an "old maid" like Judith should have a cat seems so ordinary it borders on the trite. But when she chooses to have her male cat put to death rather than neutered, it is likely to make some of us sit up and take notice. This choice may suggest something about the unconventional in her character, but we probably don't think of the cat as itself representing anything. What happens, though, when there appears another cat, a female this time, whose sex life calls forth strange behavior on Judith's part? And when the killing of a kitten interrupts Judith's affair with Luigi? It is difficult to say when or if the literal cats shade off into symbols, for they remain so solidly cats in the story. All we can say for sure is that cats become more important in reading and understanding Lessing's story than, say, the cask of Amontillado does in Poe's story. The cask remains a thing pure and simple. Repetition, then, calls attention to details and may alert us to potential symbolic overtones, but it does not necessarily turn a thing into a symbol; as long as we get the suggestions of significance, however, agreeing on exactly what—or when—something may be called a symbol is not important.

> *You can't give a great symbol a "meaning," anymore than you can give a cat a "meaning." Symbols are organic units of consciousness with a life of their own, and you can never explain them away. . . . An allegorical image has a meaning . . . ; symbols . . . don't "mean something." They stand for units of human feeling, human experience. A complex of emotional experience is a symbol.*
>
> —D. H. LAWRENCE

Direct hints may take the form of explicit statements. (Authors are not so anxious to hide their meanings as some readers are prone to believe.) We also may be alerted to the fact that something is standing for something else when it does not by itself seem to make literal sense. It does not take us long to realize that "Young Goodman Brown" is not entirely as realistic a story as "Sonny's Blues" or "The Lady with the Dog," and despite the amount of explicit detail about the "art" of fasting and the seriousness of the "artist's" thoughts about what he is doing, the events of "A Hunger Artist" seem so bizarre that most readers begin looking around for some kind of explanation or interpretation, for some kind of symbolism. For when things do not seem explicable in terms of everyday reality, we often look beyond them for some meaning.

We must remember, however, that symbols do not exist solely for the transmission of a meaning we can paraphrase; they do not disappear from the story, our memory, or our response once their "meaning" has been sucked out of them. Faith's pink ribbons and Judith's cats are objects in their stories, whatever meanings or suggestions of meanings they give rise to.

Few symbols can be exhausted or neatly translated into an abstract phrase or equivalent: the "something else" that the "something" stands for is ultimately elusive. After you have read Ann Beattie's "Janus," try to paraphrase just what the bowl stands for. Or explain with certainty what Faith's pink ribbon symbolizes in "Young Goodman Brown." It is not that the bowl and the ribbon mean nothing, but that they mean so many things that no single equivalence will do; even an abstract statement seems to reduce rather than fully explain the significance to the reader. The noun in the title of "A Hunger Artist" suggests a simple "clue" to the symbolic "meaning" of the story. Indeed, since virtually every detail in the story—the artist caring only for his art, not money, fame, and so on; the commercial presenter of the art, here the "impresario," caring for the popular success and not the art itself—relates to the nature of art and the artist, we inevitably equate the strange hunger artist to the artist in general. So, when the panther is surprisingly, almost arbitrarily introduced at the end of the story, after the first shock, we inevitably try to make him "fit into" the simple symbolic meaning. What we may find is that the story not only represents but also *defines* the "true" nature of art and the artist.

When a figure is expressed as an explicit comparison, often signaled by *like* or *as*, it is called a **simile:** "eyes as blue as the sky"; "the baby brother I'd never known looked out from the depths of his private life, like an animal waiting to be coaxed into the light" ("Sonny's Blues"). An implicit comparison or identification of one thing with another unlike itself, without a verbal signal but just seeming to say "A *is* B," is called a **metaphor:** "Her hair was still a soft gold helmet" ("Our Friend Judith"); " . . . the girl entered his mind, moving with perfect freedom through its shut doors and filling chamber after chamber with her light . . . " ("The Country Husband"). Sometimes all figures are loosely referred to as metaphors.

An **allegory** is like a metaphor in that one thing (usually nonrational, abstract, religious) is implicitly spoken of in terms of something that is concrete and usually sensuous (perceptible by the senses), but the comparison in allegory is extended to include a whole work or a large portion of a work. *The Pilgrim's Progress* is probably the most famous prose allegory in English; its central character is named Christian; he was born in the City of Destruction and sets out for the Celestial City, passes through the Slough of Despond and Vanity Fair, meets men named Pliable and Obstinate, and so on.

When an entire story, like "Young Goodman Brown" or "A Hunger Artist," is symbolic, it is sometimes called a **myth.** *Myth* originally meant a story of communal origin that provided an explanation or religious interpretation of man, nature, the universe, and the relation between them. When used by one culture to describe the stories of another culture, the word usually implies that the stories are false: we speak of classical myths, but Christians do not speak of Christian myth. We also apply the term *myth* now to stories by individuals, sophisticated authors, but often there is still the implication that the mythic story relates to a communal or group experience, whereas a symbolic story may be more personal or private. It is hard to draw the line firmly: "A Hunger Artist" relates to a Western, if not universal, conception of art; "Young Goodman Brown" appears to have clearly national, American, and thus mythic, implications; "Janus" seems primarily personal and thus symbolic. A plot or character element that recurs in cultural or cross-cultural myths, such as images of the devil as in "Young Goodman Brown," is now widely called an **archetype.**

A symbol can be as brief and local as a metaphor or as extended as an allegory. Like an allegory, it usually speaks in concrete terms of the non- or superrational, the abstract, that which is not immediately perceived by the senses. Though some allegories can be complex, with paraphrasable equivalences, allegory usually implies one-to-one relationships (as do the names from *The Pilgrim's Progress*), and literary symbols usually have highly complex or even inexpressible equivalences, as in "Janus." "Janus" is complexly symbolic in that there are areas of meaning or implication that cannot be rendered in other terms or conveniently separated from the particulars of the story. The ultimate unparaphrasable nature of most symbolic images or stories is not vagueness but richness, not disorder but complexity.

NATHANIEL HAWTHORNE

Young Goodman Brown

Young goodman Brown came forth, at sunset, into the street of Salem village,[1] but put his head back, after crossing the threshold, to exchange a parting kiss with his young wife. And Faith, as the wife was aptly named, thrust her own pretty head into the street, letting the wind play with the pink ribbons of her cap, while she called to goodman Brown.

"Dearest heart," whispered she, softly and rather sadly, when her lips were close to his ear, "pr'y thee, put off your journey until sunrise, and sleep in your own bed to-night. A lone woman is troubled with such dreams and such thoughts, that she's afeard of herself, sometimes. Pray, tarry with me this night, dear husband, of all nights in the year!"

"My love and my Faith," replied young goodman Brown, "of all nights in the year, this one night must I tarry away from thee. My journey, as thou callest it, forth and back again, must needs be done 'twixt now and sunrise. What, my sweet, pretty wife, dost thou doubt me already, and we but three months married!"

"Then, God bless you!" said Faith, with the pink ribbons, "and may you find all well, when you come back."

"Amen!" cried goodman Brown. "Say thy prayers, dear Faith, and go to bed at dusk, and no harm will come to thee."

So they parted; and the young man pursued his way, until, being about to turn the corner by the meeting-house, he looked back, and saw the head of Faith still peeping after him, with a melancholy air, in spite of her pink ribbons.

"Poor little Faith!" thought he, for his heart smote him. "What a wretch am I, to leave her on such an errand! She talks of dreams, too. Methought, as she spoke, there was trouble in her face, as if a dream had warned her what work is to be done to-night. But, no, no! 't would kill her to think it. Well; she's a blessed angel on earth; and after this one night, I'll cling to her skirts and follow her to Heaven."

With this excellent resolve for the future, goodman Brown felt himself justified in making more haste on his present evil purpose. He had taken a dreary road, darkened by all the gloomiest trees of the forest, which barely stood aside to let the narrow path creep through, and closed immediately behind. It was all as lonely as could be; and there is this peculiarity in such a solitude, that the traveler knows not who may be concealed by the innumerable trunks and the thick boughs overhead; so that, with lonely footsteps, he may yet be passing through an unseen multitude.

"There may be a devilish Indian behind every tree," said goodman Brown, to himself; and he glanced fearfully behind him, as he added, "What if the devil himself should be at my very elbow!"

5

---

1. Salem, Massachusetts, Hawthorne's birthplace (1804), was the scene of the famous witch trials of 1692; *goodman:* husband, master of household.

10   His head being turned back, he passed a crook of the road, and looking forward again, beheld the figure of a man, in grave and decent attire, seated at the foot of an old tree. He arose, at goodman Brown's approach, and walked onward, side by side with him.

"You are late, goodman Brown," said he. "The clock of the Old South was striking as I came through Boston; and that is full fifteen minutes agone."

"Faith kept me back awhile," replied the young man, with a tremor in his voice, caused by the sudden appearance of his companion, though not wholly unexpected.

It was now deep dusk in the forest, and deepest in that part of it where these two were journeying. As nearly as could be discerned, the second traveler was about fifty years old, apparently in the same rank of life as goodman Brown, and bearing a considerable resemblance to him, though perhaps more in expression than features. Still, they might have been taken for father and son. And yet, though the elder person was as simply clad as the younger, and as simple in manner too, he had an indescribable air of one who knew the world, and would not have felt abashed at the governor's dinner-table, or in king William's[2] court, were it possible that his affairs should call him thither. But the only thing about him, that could be fixed upon as remarkable, was his staff, which bore the likeness of a great black snake, so curiously wrought, that it might almost be seen to twist and wriggle itself, like a living serpent. This, of course, must have been an ocular deception, assisted by the uncertain light.

"Come, goodman Brown!" cried his fellow-traveler, "this is a dull pace for the beginning of a journey. Take my staff, if you are so soon weary."

15   "Friend," said the other, exchanging his slow pace for a full stop, "having kept covenant by meeting thee here, it is my purpose now to return whence I came. I have scruples, touching the matter thou wot'st of."

"Sayest thou so?" replied he of the serpent, smiling apart. "Let us walk on, nevertheless, reasoning as we go, and if I convince thee not, thou shalt turn back. We are but a little way in the forest, yet."

"Too far, too far!" exclaimed the goodman, unconsciously resuming his walk. "My father never went into the woods on such an errand, nor his father before him. We have been a race of honest men and good Christians, since the days of the martyrs. And shall I be the first of the name of Brown, that ever took this path, and kept"—

"Such company, thou wouldst say," observed the elder person, interpreting his pause. "Good, goodman Brown! I have been as well acquainted with your family as with ever a one among the Puritans; and that's no trifle to say. I helped your grandfather, the constable, when he lashed the Quaker woman so smartly through the streets of Salem. And it was I that brought your father a pitch-pine knot, kindled at my own hearth, to set fire to an Indian village, in king Philip's[3] war. They were my good friends, both; and many a pleasant walk have we had

2. William III (1650–1702), ruler of England from 1689 to 1702, until 1694 jointly with his wife, Mary II.   3. Metacom or Metacomet, chief of the Wampanoag Indians, known as King Philip, led a war against the New England colonists in 1675–76 that devastated many frontier communities.

along this path, and returned merrily after midnight. I would fain be friends with
you, for their sake."

"If it be as thou sayest," replied goodman Brown, "I marvel they never spoke
of these matters. Or, verily, I marvel not, seeing that the least rumor of the sort
would have driven them from New-England. We are a people of prayer, and good
works, to boot, and abide no such wickedness."

"Wickedness or not," said the traveler with the twisted staff, "I have a very   20
general acquaintance here in New-England. The deacons of many a church have
drunk the communion wine with me; the selectmen, of divers towns, make me
their chairman; and a majority of the Great and General Court are firm supporters
of my interest. The governor and I, too—but these are state-secrets."

"Can this be so!" cried goodman Brown, with a stare of amazement at his
undisturbed companion. "Howbeit, I have nothing to do with the governor and
council; they have their own ways, and are no rule for a simple husbandman, like
me. But, were I to go on with thee, how should I meet the eye of that good old
man, our minister, at Salem village? Oh, his voice would make me tremble, both
Sabbath-day and lecture-day!"[4]

Thus far, the elder traveler had listened with due gravity, but now burst into a
fit of irrepressible mirth, shaking himself so violently, that his snake-like staff
actually seemed to wriggle in sympathy.

"Ha! ha! ha!" shouted he, again and again; then composing himself, "Well, go
on, goodman Brown, go on; but, pr'y thee, don't kill me with laughing!"

"Well, then, to end the matter at once," said goodman Brown, considerably
nettled, "there is my wife, Faith. It would break her dear little heart; and I'd rather
break my own!"

"Nay, if that be the case," answered the other, "e'en[5] go thy ways, goodman   25
Brown. I would not, for twenty old women like the one hobbling before us, that
Faith should come to any harm."

As he spoke, he pointed his staff at a female figure on the path, in whom
goodman Brown recognized a very pious and exemplary dame, who had taught
him his catechism, in youth, and was still his moral and spiritual adviser, jointly
with the minister and deacon Gookin.

"A marvel, truly, that goody[6] Cloyse should be so far in the wilderness, at nightfall!" said he. "But, with your leave, friend, I shall take a cut through the woods,
until we have left this Christian woman behind. Being a stranger to you, she
might ask whom I was consorting with, and whither I was going."

"Be it so," said his fellow-traveler. "Betake you to the woods, and let me keep
the path."

Accordingly, the young man turned aside, but took care to watch his companion, who advanced softly along the road, until he had come within a staff's length
of the old dame. She, meanwhile, was making the best of her way, with singular
speed for so aged a woman, and mumbling some indistinct words, a prayer, doubt-

---

4. The day for an informal sermon; in the New England colonies, this was usually a Thursday.
5. Just.   6. Short for "goodwife" or housewife.

less, as she went. The traveler put forth his staff, and touched her withered neck with what seemed the serpent's tail.

30   "The devil!" screamed the pious old lady.

"Then goody Cloyse knows her old friend?" observed the traveler, confronting her, and leaning on his writhing stick.

"Ah, forsooth, and is it your worship, indeed?" cried the good dame. "Yea, truly is it, and in the very image of my old gossip, goodman Brown, the grandfather of the silly fellow that now is. But, would your worship believe it? my broomstick hath strangely disappeared, stolen, as I suspect, by that unhanged witch, goody Cory, and that, too, when I was all anointed with the juice of smallage and cinque-foil and wolf's-bane"[7]—

"Mingled with fine wheat and the fat of a new-born babe," said the shape of old goodman Brown.

"Ah, your worship knows the receipt," cried the old lady, cackling aloud. "So, as I was saying, being all ready for the meeting, and no horse to ride on, I made up my mind to foot it; for they tell me, there is a nice young man to be taken into communion to-night. But now your good worship will lend me your arm, and we shall be there in a twinkling."

35   "That can hardly be," answered her friend. "I may not spare you my arm, goody Cloyse, but here is my staff, if you will."

So saying, he threw it down at her feet, where, perhaps, it assumed life, being one of the rods which its owner had formerly lent to the Egyptian Magi.[8] Of this fact, however, goodman Brown could not take cognizance. He had cast up his eyes in astonishment, and looking down again, beheld neither goody Cloyse nor the serpentine staff, but his fellow-traveler alone, who waited for him as calmly as if nothing had happened.

"That old woman taught me my catechism!" said the young man; and there was a world of meaning in this simple comment.

They continued to walk onward, while the elder traveler exhorted his companion to make good speed and persevere in the path, discoursing so aptly, that his arguments seemed rather to spring up in the bosom of his auditor, than to be suggested by himself. As they went, he plucked a branch of maple, to serve for a walking-stick, and began to strip it of the twigs and little boughs, which were wet with evening dew. The moment his fingers touched them, they became strangely withered and dried up, as with a week's sunshine. Thus the pair proceeded, at a good free pace, until suddenly, in a gloomy hollow of the road, goodman Brown sat himself down on the stump of a tree, and refused to go any farther.

"Friend," said he, stubbornly, "my mind is made up. Not another step will I budge on this errand. What if a wretched old woman do choose to go to the devil, when I thought she was going to Heaven! Is that any reason why I should quit my dear Faith, and go after her?"

7. Plants traditionally associated with witchcraft.   8. In Exodus 7.8–12, The Lord instructs Moses to have his brother Aaron, high priest of the Hebrews, throw down his rod before the pharaoh, whereupon it will be turned into a serpent. The pharaoh has his magicians (magi) do likewise, "but Aaron's rod swallowed up their rods."

"You will think better of this, by-and-by," said his acquaintance, composedly.   40
"Sit here and rest yourself awhile; and when you feel like moving again, there is
my staff to help you along."

Without more words, he threw his companion the maple stick, and was as
speedily out of sight, as if he had vanished into the deepening gloom. The young
man sat a few moments, by the roadside, applauding himself greatly, and thinking
with how clear a conscience he should meet the minister, in his morning-walk,
nor shrink from the eye of good old deacon Gookin. And what calm sleep would
be his, that very night, which was to have been spent so wickedly, but purely and
sweetly now, in the arms of Faith! Amidst these pleasant and praiseworthy meditations, goodman Brown heard the tramp of horses along the road, and deemed
it advisable to conceal himself within the verge of the forest, conscious of the
guilty purpose that had brought him thither, though now so happily turned from
it.

On came the hoof-tramps and the voices of the riders, two grave old voices,
conversing soberly as they drew near. These mingled sounds appeared to pass
along the road, within a few yards of the young man's hiding-place; but owing,
doubtless, to the depth of the gloom, at that particular spot, neither the travelers
nor their steeds were visible. Though their figures brushed the small boughs by
the way-side, it could not be seen that they intercepted, even for a moment, the
faint gleam from the strip of bright sky, athwart which they must have passed.
Goodman Brown alternately crouched and stood on tip-toe, pulling aside the
branches, and thrusting forth his head as far as he durst, without discerning so
much as a shadow. It vexed him the more, because he could have sworn, were
such a thing possible, that he recognized the voices of the minister and deacon
Gookin, jogging along quietly, as they were wont to do, when bound to some
ordination or ecclesiastical council. While yet within hearing, one of the riders
stopped to pluck a switch.

"Of the two, reverend Sir," said the voice like the deacon's, "I had rather miss
an ordination-dinner than to-night's meeting. They tell me that some of our community are to be here from Falmouth[9] and beyond, and others from Connecticut
and Rhode-Island; besides several of the Indian powows, who, after their fashion,
know almost as much deviltry as the best of us. Moreover, there is a goodly young
woman to be taken into communion."

"Mighty well, deacon Gookin!" replied the solemn old tones of the minister.
"Spur up, or we shall be late. Nothing can be done, you know, until I get on the
ground."

The hoofs clattered again, and the voices, talking so strangely in the empty   45
air, passed on through the forest, where no church had ever been gathered, nor
solitary Christian prayed. Whither, then, could these holy men be journeying, so
deep into the heathen wilderness? Young goodman Brown caught hold of a tree,
for support, being ready to sink down on the ground, faint and overburthened
with the heavy sickness of his heart. He looked up to the sky, doubting whether

---

9. A port in extreme southern Massachusetts; Salem is in northern Massachusetts.

there really was a Heaven above him. Yet, there was the blue arch, and the stars brightening in it.

"With Heaven above, and Faith below, I will yet stand firm against the devil!" cried goodman Brown.

While he still gazed upward, into the deep arch of the firmament, and had lifted his hands to pray, a cloud, though no wind was stirring, hurried across the zenith, and hid the brightening stars. The blue sky was still visible, except directly overhead, where this black mass of cloud was sweeping swiftly northward. Aloft in the air, as if from the depths of the cloud, came a confused and doubtful sound of voices. Once, the listener fancied that he could distinguish the accents of town's-people of his own, men and women, both pious and ungodly, many of whom he had met at the communion-table, and had seen others rioting at the tavern. The next moment, so indistinct were the sounds, he doubted whether he had heard aught but the murmur of the old forest, whispering without a wind. Then came a stronger swell of those familiar tones, heard daily in the sunshine, at Salem village, but never, until now, from a cloud of night. There was one voice, of a young woman, uttering lamentations, yet with an uncertain sorrow, and entreating for some favor, which, perhaps, it would grieve her to obtain. And all the unseen multitude, both saints and sinners, seemed to encourage her onward.

"Faith!" shouted goodman Brown, in a voice of agony and desperation; and the echoes of the forest mocked him, crying—"Faith! Faith!" as if bewildered wretches were seeking her, all through the wilderness.

The cry of grief, rage, and terror, was yet piercing the night, when the unhappy husband held his breath for a response. There was a scream, drowned immediately in a louder murmur of voices, fading into far-off laughter, as the dark cloud swept away, leaving the clear and silent sky above goodman Brown. But something fluttered lightly down through the air, and caught on the branch of a tree. The young man seized it, and beheld a pink ribbon.

50   "My Faith is gone!" cried he, after one stupefied moment. "There is no good on earth; and sin is but a name. Come, devil! for to thee is this world given."

And maddened with despair, so that he laughed loud and long, did goodman Brown grasp his staff and set forth again, at such a rate, that he seemed to fly along the forest-path, rather than to walk or run. The road grew wilder and drearier, and more faintly traced, and vanished at length, leaving him in the heart of the dark wilderness, still rushing onward, with the instinct that guides mortal man to evil. The whole forest was peopled with frightful sounds; the creaking of the trees, the howling of wild beasts, and the yell of Indians; while, sometimes, the wind tolled like a distant church-bell, and sometimes gave a broad roar around the traveler, as if all Nature were laughing him to scorn. But he was himself the chief horror of the scene, and shrank not from its other horrors.

"Ha! ha! ha!" roared goodman Brown, when the wind laughed at him. "Let us hear which will laugh loudest! Think not to frighten me with your deviltry! Come witch, come wizard, come Indian powow, come devil himself! and here come goodman Brown. You may as well fear him as he fear you!"

In truth, all through the haunted forest, there could be nothing more frightful than the figure of goodman Brown. On he flew, among the black pines, brandishing his staff with frenzied gestures, now giving vent to an inspiration of horrid blasphemy, and now shouting forth such laughter, as set all the echoes of the forest laughing like demons around him. The fiend in his own shape is less hideous, than when he rages in the breast of man. Thus sped the demoniac on his course, until, quivering among the trees, he saw a red light before him, as when the felled trunks and branches of a clearing have been set on fire, and throw up their lurid blaze against the sky, at the hour of midnight. He paused, in a lull of the tempest that had driven him onward, and heard the swell of what seemed a hymn, rolling solemnly from a distance, with the weight of many voices. He knew the tune; it was a familiar one in the choir of the village meeting-house. The verse died heavily away, and was lengthened by a chorus, not of human voices, but of all the sounds of the benighted wilderness, pealing in awful harmony together. Goodman Brown cried out; and his cry was lost to his own ear, by its unison with the cry of the desert.

In the interval of silence, he stole forward, until the light glared full upon his eyes. At one extremity of an open space, hemmed in by the dark wall of the forest, arose a rock, bearing some rude, natural resemblance either to an altar or a pulpit, and surrounded by four blazing pines, their tops aflame, their stems untouched, like candles at an evening meeting. The mass of foliage, that had overgrown the summit of the rock, was all on fire, blazing high into the night, and fitfully illuminating the whole field. Each pendent twig and leafy festoon was in a blaze. As the red light arose and fell, a numerous congregation alternately shone forth, then disappeared in shadow, and again grew, as it were, out of the darkness, peopling the heart of the solitary woods at once.

"A grave and dark-clad company!" quoth goodman Brown.   55

In truth, they were such. Among them, quivering to-and-fro, between gloom and splendor, appeared faces that would be seen, next day, at the council-board of the province, and others which, Sabbath after Sabbath, looked devoutly heavenward, and benignantly over the crowded pews, from the holiest pulpits in the land. Some affirm, that the lady of the governor was there. At least, there were high dames well known to her, and wives of honored husbands, and widows, a great multitude, and ancient maidens, all of excellent repute, and fair young girls, who trembled, lest their mothers should espy them. Either the sudden gleams of light, flashing over the obscure field, bedazzled goodman Brown, or he recognized a score of the church-members of Salem village, famous for their especial sanctity. Good old deacon Gookin had arrived, and waited at the skirts of that venerable saint, his revered pastor. But, irreverently consorting with these grave, reputable, and pious people, these elders of the church, these chaste dames and dewy virgins, there were men of dissolute lives and women of spotted fame, wretches given over to all mean and filthy vice, and suspected even of horrid crimes. It was strange to see, that the good shrank not from the wicked, nor were the sinners abashed by the saints. Scattered, also, among their pale-faced enemies, were the Indian priests, or powows, who had often scared their native forest with more hideous incantations than any known to English witchcraft.

"But, where is Faith?" thought goodman Brown; and, as hope came into his heart, he trembled.

Another verse of the hymn arose, a slow and solemn strain, such as the pious love, but joined to words which expressed all that our nature can conceive of sin, and darkly hinted at far more. Unfathomable to mere mortals is the lore of fiends. Verse after verse was sung, and still the chorus of the desert swelled between, like the deepest tone of a mighty organ. And, with the final peal of that dreadful anthem, there came a sound, as if the roaring wind, the rushing streams, the howling beasts, and every other voice of the unconverted wilderness, were mingling and according with the voice of guilty man, in homage to the prince of all. The four blazing pines threw up a loftier flame, and obscurely discovered shapes and visages of horror on the smoke-wreaths, above the impious assembly. At the same moment, the fire on the rock shot redly forth, and formed a glowing arch above its base, where now appeared a figure. With reverence be it spoken, the apparition bore no slight similitude, both in garb and manner, to some grave divine of the New-England churches.

"Bring forth the converts!" cried a voice, that echoed through the field and rolled into the forest.

At the word, goodman Brown stept forth from the shadow of the trees, and approached the congregation, with whom he felt a loathful brotherhood, by the sympathy of all that was wicked in his heart. He could have well nigh sworn, that the shape of his own dead father beckoned him to advance, looking downward from a smoke-wreath, while a woman, with dim features of despair, threw out her hand to warn him back. Was it his mother? But he had no power to retreat one step, nor to resist, even in thought, when the minister and good old deacon Gookin, seized his arms, and led him to the blazing rock. Thither came also the slender form of a veiled female, led between goody Cloyse, that pious teacher of the catechism, and Martha Carrier, who had received the devil's promise to be queen of hell. A rampant hag was she! And there stood the proselytes, beneath the canopy of fire.

"Welcome, my children," said the dark figure, "to the communion of your race! Ye have found, thus young, your nature and your destiny. My children, look behind you!"

They turned; and flashing forth, as it were, in a sheet of flame, the fiend-worshippers were seen; the smile of welcome gleamed darkly on every visage.

"There," resumed the sable form, "are all whom ye have reverenced from youth. Ye deemed them holier than yourselves, and shrank from your own sin, contrasting it with their lives of righteousness, and prayerful aspirations heavenward. Yet, here are they all, in my worshipping assembly! This night it shall be granted you to know their secret deeds; how hoary-bearded elders of the church have whispered wanton words to the young maids of their households; how many a woman, eager for widow's weeds, has given her husband a drink at bed-time, and let him sleep his last sleep in her bosom; how beardless youths have made haste to inherit their fathers' wealth; and how fair damsels—blush not, sweet ones!—have dug little graves in the garden, and bidden me, the sole guest, to an infant's funeral. By the sympathy of your human hearts for sin, ye shall scent out all the places—whether in church, bed-chamber, street, field, or forest—where crime has been committed, and shall exult to behold the whole earth one stain of guilt, one mighty blood-spot. Far more than this! It shall be yours to penetrate, in every bosom, the deep mystery of sin, the fountain of all wicked arts, and which, inexhaustibly supplies more evil impulses than human power—than my power, at its utmost!—can make manifest in deeds. And now, my children, look upon each other."

They did so; and, by the blaze of the hell-kindled torches, the wretched man beheld his Faith, and the wife her husband, trembling before that unhallowed altar.

"Lo! there ye stand, my children," said the figure, in a deep and solemn tone, almost sad, with its despairing awfulness, as if his once angelic nature could yet mourn for our miserable race. "Depending upon one another's hearts, ye had still hoped, that virtue were not all a dream. Now are ye undeceived! Evil is the nature of mankind. Evil must be your only happiness. Welcome, again, my children, to the communion of your race!" 65

"Welcome!" repeated the fiend-worshippers, in one cry of despair and triumph.

And there they stood, the only pair, as it seemed, who were yet hesitating on the verge of wickedness, in this dark world. A basin was hollowed, naturally, in the rock. Did it contain water, reddened by the lurid light? or was it blood? or, perchance, a liquid flame? Herein did the Shape of Evil dip his hand, and prepare to lay the mark of baptism upon their foreheads, that they might be partakers of the mystery of sin, more conscious of the secret guilt of others, both in deed and thought, than they could now be of their own. The husband cast one look at his pale wife, and Faith at him. What polluted wretches would the next glance shew them to each other, shuddering alike at what they disclosed and what they saw!

"Faith! Faith!" cried the husband. "Look up to Heaven, and resist the Wicked One!"

Whether Faith obeyed, he knew not. Hardly had he spoken, when he found himself amid calm night and solitude, listening to a roar of the wind, which died heavily away through the forest. He staggered against the rock and felt it chill and damp, while a hanging twig, that had been all on fire, besprinkled his cheek with the coldest dew.

The next morning, young goodman Brown came slowly into the street of Salem 70 village, staring around him like a bewildered man. The good old minister was taking a walk along the graveyard, to get an appetite for breakfast and meditate his sermon, and bestowed a blessing, as he passed, on goodman Brown. He shrank from the venerable saint, as if to avoid an anathema. Old deacon Gookin was at domestic worship, and the holy words of his prayer were heard through the open window. "What God doth the wizard pray to?" quoth goodman Brown. Goody Cloyse, that excellent old Christian, stood in the early sunshine, at her own lattice, catechising a little girl, who had brought her a pint of morning's milk. Goodman Brown snatched away the child, as from the grasp of the fiend himself. Turning the corner by the meeting-house, he spied the head of Faith, with the pink ribbons, gazing anxiously forth, and bursting into such joy at sight of him, that she skipt along the street, and almost kissed her husband before the whole village. But, goodman Brown looked sternly and sadly into her face, and passed on without a greeting.

Had goodman Brown fallen asleep in the forest, and only dreamed a wild dream of a witch-meeting?

Be it so, if you will. But, alas! it was a dream of evil omen for young goodman Brown. A stern, a sad, a darkly meditative, a distrustful, if not a desperate man, did he become, from the night of that fearful dream. On the Sabbath-day, when the congregation were singing a holy psalm, he could not listen, because an anthem of sin rushed loudly upon his ear, and drowned all the blessed strain. When the minister spoke from the pulpit, with power and fervid eloquence, and, with his hand on the open bible, of the sacred truths of our religion, and of saint-like lives and triumphant deaths, and of future bliss or misery unutterable, then did goodman Brown turn pale, dreading, lest the roof should thunder down upon the gray blasphemer and his hearers. Often, awakening suddenly at midnight, he shrank from the bosom of Faith, and at morning or eventide, when the family knelt down at prayer, he scowled, and muttered to himself, and gazed sternly at his wife, and turned away. And when he had lived long, and was borne to his grave, a hoary corpse, followed by Faith, an aged woman, and children and grand-children, a goodly procession, besides neighbors, not a few, they carved no hopeful verse upon his tomb-stone; for his dying hour was gloom.

1835

FRANZ KAFKA

A Hunger Artist [1]

During these last decades the interest in professional fasting has markedly diminished. It used to pay very well to stage such great performances under one's own management, but today that is quite impossible. We live in a different world now. At one time the whole town took a lively interest in the hunger artist; from day to day of his fast the excitement mounted; everybody wanted to see him at least once a day; there were people who bought season tickets for the last few days and sat from morning till night in front of his small barred cage; even in the nighttime there were visiting hours, when the whole effect was heightened by torch flares; on fine days the cage was set out in the open air, and then it was the children's special treat to see the hunger artist; for their elders he was often just a joke that happened to be in fashion, but the children stood open-mouthed, holding each other's hands for greater security, marveling at him as he sat there pallid in black tights, with his ribs sticking out so prominently, not even on a seat but down among straw on the ground, sometimes giving a courteous nod, answering questions with a constrained smile, or perhaps stretching an arm through the bars so that one might feel how thin it was, and then again withdrawing deep into him-

1. Translated by Edwin and Willa Muir.

self, paying no attention to anyone or anything, not even to the all-important striking of the clock that was the only piece of furniture in his cage, but merely staring into vacancy with half shut eyes, now and then taking a sip from a tiny glass of water to moisten his lips.

Besides casual onlookers there were also relays of permanent watchers selected by the public, usually butchers, strangely enough, and it was their task to watch the hunger artist day and night, three of them at a time, in case he should have some secret recourse to nourishment. This was nothing but a formality, instituted to reassure the masses, for the initiates knew well enough that during his fast the artist would never in any circumstances, not even under forcible compulsion, swallow the smallest morsel of food: the honor of his profession forbade it. Not every watcher, of course, was capable of understanding this, there were often groups of night watchers who were very lax in carrying out their duties and deliberately huddled together in a retired corner to play cards with great absorption, obviously intending to give the hunger artist the chance of a little refreshment, which they supposed he could draw from some private hoard. Nothing annoyed the artist more than such watchers; they made him miserable; they made his fast seem unendurable; sometimes he mastered his feebleness sufficiently to sing during their watch for as long as he could keep going, to show them how unjust their suspicions were. But that was of little use; they only wondered at his cleverness in being able to fill his mouth even while singing. Much more to his taste were the watchers who sat close up to the bars, who were not content with the dim night lighting of the hall but focused him in the full glare of the electric pocket torch given them by the impresario. The harsh light did not trouble him at all, in any case he could never sleep properly, and he could always drowse a little, whatever the light, at any hour, even when the hall was thronged with noisy onlookers. He was quite happy at the prospect of spending a sleepless night with such watchers; he was ready to exchange jokes with them, to tell them stories out of his nomadic life, anything at all to keep them awake and demonstrate to them again that he had no eatables in his cage and that he was fasting as not one of them could fast. But his happiest moment was when the morning came and an enormous breakfast was brought them, at his expense, on which they flung themselves with the keen appetite of healthy men after a weary night of wakefulness. Of course there were people who argued that this breakfast was an unfair attempt to bribe the watchers, but that was going rather too far, and when they were invited to take on a night's vigil without a breakfast, merely for the sake of the cause, they made themselves scarce, although they stuck stubbornly to their suspicions.

Such suspicions, anyhow, were a necessary accompaniment to the profession of fasting. No one could possibly watch the hunger artist continuously, day and night, and so no one could produce first-hand evidence that the fast had really been rigorous and continuous; only the artist himself could know that, he was therefore bound to be the sole completely satisfied spectator of his own fast. Yet for other reasons he was never satisfied; it was not perhaps mere fasting that had brought him to such skeleton thinness that many people had regretfully to keep away from his exhibitions, because the sight of him was too much for them, perhaps it was dissatisfaction with himself that had worn him down. For he alone knew, what no other initiate knew, how easy it was to fast. It was the easiest thing in the world. He made no secret of this, yet people did not believe him, at the best they set him down as modest, most of them, however, thought he was out for publicity or else was some kind of cheat who found it easy to fast because he had discovered a way of making it easy, and then had the impudence to admit the fact, more or less. He had to put up with all that, and in the course of time had got used to it, but his inner dissatisfaction always rankled, and never yet, after any term of fasting—this must be granted to his credit—had he left the cage of his own free will. The longest period of fasting was fixed by his impresario at forty days, beyond that term he was not allowed to go, not even in great cities, and there was good reason for it, too. Experience had proved that for about forty days the interest of the public could be stimulated by a steadily increasing pressure of advertisement, but after that the town began to lose interest, sympathetic support began notably to fall off; there were of course local variations as between one town and another or one country and another, but as a general rule forty days marked the limit. So on the fortieth day the flower-bedecked cage was opened, enthusiastic spectators filled the hall, a military band played, two doctors entered the cage to measure the results of the fast, which were announced through a megaphone, and finally two young ladies appeared, blissful at having been selected for the honor, to help the hunger artist down the few steps leading to a small table on which was spread a carefully chosen invalid repast. And at this very moment the artist always turned stubborn. True, he would entrust his bony arms to the outstretched helping hands of the ladies bending over him, but stand up he would not. Why stop fasting at this particular moment, after forty days of it? He had held out for a long time, an illimitably long time; why stop now, when he was in his best fasting form, or rather, not yet quite in his best fasting form? Why should he be cheated of the fame he would get for fasting longer, for being not only the record hunger artist of all time, which presumably he was already, but for beating his own record by a performance beyond human imagination, since he felt that there were no limits to his capacity for fasting? His public pretended to admire him so much, why should it have so little patience with him; if he could endure fasting longer, why shouldn't the public endure it? Besides, he was tired, he was comfortable sitting in the straw, and now he was supposed to lift himself to his full height and go down to a meal the very thought of which gave him a nausea that only the presence of the ladies kept him from betraying, and even that with an effort. And he looked up into the eyes of the ladies who were apparently so friendly and in reality so cruel, and shook his head, which felt too heavy on its strengthless neck. But then there happened yet again what always happened. The impresario came forward, without a word—for the band made speech impossible—lifted his arms in the air above the artist, as if inviting Heaven to look down upon its creature here in the straw, this suffering martyr, which indeed he was, although in quite another sense; grasped him round the emaciated waist, with exaggerated caution, so that the frail condition he was in might be appreciated; and committed him to the care of the blenching ladies, not without secretly giving him a shaking so that his legs and body tottered and swayed. The artist now submitted completely; his head lolled on his breast as if it had landed there by chance; his body was hollowed out; his legs in a spasm of self-preservation clung close to each other at the knees, yet scraped on the ground as if it were not really solid ground, as if they were only trying to find solid ground; and the whole weight of his body, a feather-weight after all, relapsed onto one of the ladies, who, looking round for help and panting a little—this post of honor was not at all what she had expected it to be—first stretched her neck as far as she could to keep her face at least free from contact with the artist, when finding this impossible, and her more fortunate companion not coming to her aid but merely holding extended on her own trembling hand the little bunch of knuckle-bones that was the artist's, to the great delight of the spectators burst into tears and had to be replaced by an attendant who had long been stationed in readiness. Then came the food, a little of which the impresario managed to get between the artist's lips, while he sat in a kind of half-fainting trance, to the accompaniment of cheerful patter designed to distract the public's attention from the artist's condition; after that, a toast was drunk to the public, supposedly prompted by a whisper from the artist in the impresario's ear; the band confirmed it with a mighty flourish, the spectators melted away, and no one had any cause to be dissatisfied with the proceedings, no one except the hunger artist himself, he only, as always.

So he lived for many years, with small regular intervals of recuperation, in visible glory, honored by the world, yet in spite of that troubled in spirit, and all the more troubled because no one would take his trouble seriously. What comfort could he possibly need? What more could he possibly wish for? And if some good-natured person, feeling sorry for him, tried to console him by pointing out that his melancholy was probably caused by fasting, it could happen, especially when he had been fasting for some time, that he reacted with an outburst of fury and to the general alarm began to shake the bars of his cage like a wild animal. Yet the impresario had a way of punishing these outbreaks which he rather enjoyed putting into operation. He would apologize publicly for the artist's behavior, which was only to be excused, he admitted, because of the irritability caused by fasting; a condition hardly to be understood by well-fed people; then by natural transition he went on to mention the artist's equally incomprehensible boast that he could fast for much longer than he was doing; he praised the high ambition, the good will, the great self-denial undoubtedly implicit in such a statement; and then quite simply countered it by bringing out photographs, which were also on sale to the public, showing the artist on the fortieth day of a fast lying in bed almost dead from exhaustion. This perversion of the truth, familiar to the artist though it was, always unnerved him afresh and proved too much for him. What was a consequence of the premature ending of his fast was here presented as the cause of it! To fight against this lack of understanding, against a whole world of non-understanding, was impossible. Time and again in good faith he stood by the bars listening to the impresario, but as soon as the photographs appeared he always let go and sank with a groan back on to his straw, and the reassured public could once more come close and gaze at him.

A few years later when the witnesses of such scenes called them to mind, they often failed to understand themselves at all. For meanwhile the aforementioned change in public interest had set in; it seemed to happen almost overnight; there may have been profound causes for it, but who was going to bother about that; at any rate the pampered hunger artist suddenly found himself deserted one fine day by the amusement seekers, who went streaming past him to other more favored attractions. For the last time the impresario hurried him over half Europe to discover whether the old interest might still survive here and there; all in vain; everywhere, as if by secret agreement, a positive revulsion from professional fasting was in evidence. Of course it could not really have sprung up so suddenly as all that, and many premonitory symptoms which had not been sufficiently remarked or suppressed during the rush and glitter of success now came retrospectively to mind, but it was now too late to take any countermeasures. Fasting would surely come into fashion again at some future date, yet that was no comfort for those living in the present. What, then, was the hunger artist to do? He had been applauded by thousands in his time and could hardly come down to showing himself in a street booth at village fairs, and as for adopting another profession, he was not only too old for that but too fanatically devoted to fasting. So he took leave of the impresario, his partner in an unparalleled career, and hired himself to a large circus; in order to spare his own feelings he avoided reading the conditions of his contract.

A large circus with its enormous traffic in replacing and recruiting men, animals and apparatus can always find a use for people at any time, even for a hunger artist, provided of course that he does not ask too much, and in this particular case anyhow it was not only the artist who was taken on but his famous and long-known name as well, indeed considering the peculiar nature of his performance, which was not impaired by advancing age, it could not be objected that here was an artist past his prime, no longer at the height of his professional skill, seeking a refuge in some quiet corner of a circus; on the contrary, the hunger artist averred that he could fast as well as ever, which was entirely credible, he even alleged that if he were allowed to fast as he liked, and this was at once promised him without more ado, he could astound the world by establishing a record never yet achieved, a statement which certainly provoked a smile among the other professionals, since it left out of account the change in public opinion, which the hunger artist in his zeal conveniently forgot.

He had not, however, actually lost his sense of the real situation and took it as a matter of course that he and his cage should be stationed, not in the middle of the ring as a main attraction, but outside, near the animal cages, on a site that was after all easily accessible. Large and gaily painted placards made a frame for the cage and announced what was to be seen inside it. When the public came thronging out in the intervals to see the animals, they could hardly avoid passing the hunger artist's cage and stopping there for a moment, perhaps they might even have stayed longer had not those pressing behind them in the narrow gangway, who did not understand why they should be held up on their way toward the excitements of the menagerie, made it impossible for anyone to stand gazing quietly for any length of time. And that was the reason why the hunger artist, who had of course been looking forward to these visiting hours as the main achievement of his life, began instead to shrink from them. At first he could hardly wait for the intervals; it was exhilarating to watch the crowds come streaming his way, until only too soon—not even the most obstinate self-deception, clung to almost consciously, could hold out against the fact—the conviction was borne in upon him that these people, most of them, to judge from their actions, again and again, without exception, were all on their way to the menagerie. And the first sight of them from the distance remained the best. For when they reached his cage he was at once deafened by the storm of shouting and abuse that arose from the two contending factions, which renewed themselves continuously, of those who wanted to stop and stare at him—he soon began to dislike them more than the others—not out of real interest but only out of obstinate self-assertiveness, and those who wanted to go straight on to the animals. When the first great rush was past, the stragglers came along, and these, whom nothing could have prevented from stopping to look at him as long as they had breath, raced past with long strides, hardly even glancing at him, in their haste to get to the menagerie in time. And all too rarely did it happen that he had a stroke of luck, when some father of a family fetched up before him with his children, pointed a finger at the hunger artist and explained at length what the phenomenon meant, telling stories of earlier years when he himself had watched similar but much more thrilling performances, and the children, still rather uncomprehending, since neither inside nor outside school had they been sufficiently prepared for this lesson—what did they care about fasting?—yet showed by the brightness of their intent eyes that new and better times might be coming. Perhaps, said the hunger artist to himself many a time, things would be a little better if his cage were set not quite so near the menagerie. That made it too easy for people to make their choice, to say nothing of what he suffered from the stench of the menagerie, the animals' restlessness by night, the carrying past of raw lumps of flesh for the beasts of prey, the roaring at feeding times, which depressed him continually. But he did not dare to lodge a complaint with the management; after all, he had the animals to thank for the troops of people who passed his cage, among whom there might always be one here and there to take an interest in him, and who could tell where they might seclude him if he called attention to his existence and thereby to the fact that, strictly speaking, he was only an impediment on the way to the menagerie.

A small impediment, to be sure, one that grew steadily less. People grew familiar with the strange idea that they could be expected, in times like these, to take an interest in a hunger artist, and with this familiarity the verdict went out against him. He might fast as much as he could, and he did so; but nothing could save him now, people passed him by. Just try to explain to anyone the art of fasting! Anyone who has no feeling for it cannot be made to understand it. The fine placards grew dirty and illegible, they were torn down; the little notice board telling the number of fast days achieved, which at first was changed carefully every day, had long stayed at the same figure, for after the first few weeks even this small task seemed pointless to the staff; and so the artist simply fasted on and on, as he had once dreamed of doing, and it was no trouble to him, just as he had always foretold, but no one counted the days, no one, not even the artist himself, knew what records he was already breaking, and his heart grew heavy. And when once in a time some leisurely passer-by stopped, made merry over the old figure on the board and spoke of swindling, that was in its way the stupidest lie ever invented by indifference and inborn malice, since it was not the hunger artist who was cheating; he was working honestly, but the world was cheating him of his reward.

Many more days went by, however, and that too came to an end. An overseer's eye fell on the cage one day and he asked the attendants why this perfectly good cage should be left standing there unused with dirty straw inside it; nobody knew, until one man, helped out by the notice board, remembered about the hunger artist. They poked into the straw with sticks and found him in it. "Are you still fasting?" asked the overseer. "When on earth do you mean to stop?" "Forgive me, everybody," whispered the hunger artist; only the overseer, who had his ear to the bars, understood him. "Of course," said the overseer, and tapped his forehead with a finger to let the attendants know what state the man was in, "we forgive you." "I always wanted you to admire my fasting," said the hunger artist. "We do admire it," said the overseer, affably. "But you shouldn't admire it," said the hunger artist. "Well, then we don't admire it," said the overseer, "but why shouldn't we admire it?" "Because I have to fast, I can't help it," said the hunger artist. "What a fellow you are," said the overseer, "and why can't you help it?" "Because," said the hunger artist, lifting his head a little and speaking, with his lips pursed, as if for a kiss, right into the overseer's ear, so that no syllable might be lost, "because I couldn't find the food I liked. If I had found it, believe me, I should have made no fuss and stuffed myself like you or anyone else." These were his last words, but in his dimming eyes remained the firm though no longer proud persuasion that he was still continuing to fast.

10   "Well, clear this out now!" said the overseer, and they buried the hunger artist, straw and all. Into the cage they put a young panther. Even the most insensitive felt it refreshing to see this wild creature leaping around the cage that had so long been dreary. The panther was all right. The food he liked was brought him without hesitation by the attendants; he seemed not even to miss his freedom; his noble body, furnished almost to the bursting point with all that it needed, seemed to carry freedom around with it too; somewhere in his jaws it seemed to lurk; and the joy of life streamed with such ardent passion from his throat that for the onlookers it was not easy to stand the shock of it. But they braced themselves, crowded round the cage, and did not want ever to move away.

1924

ANN BEATTIE

Janus

The bowl was perfect. Perhaps it was not what you'd select if you faced a shelf of bowls, and not the sort of thing that would inevitably attract a lot of attention at a crafts fair, yet it had real presence. It was as predictably admired as a mutt who has no reason to suspect he might be funny. Just such a dog, in fact, was often brought out (and in) along with the bowl.

Andrea was a real estate agent, and when she thought that some prospective buyers might be dog lovers, she would drop off her dog at the same time she placed the bowl in the house that was up for sale. She would put a dish of water in the kitchen for Mondo, take his squeaking plastic frog out of her purse and drop it on the floor. He would pounce delightedly, just as he did every day at home, batting around his favorite toy. The bowl usually sat on a coffee table, though recently she had displayed it on top of a pine blanket chest and on a lacquered table. It was once placed on a cherry table beneath a Bonnard[1] still life, where it held its own.

Everyone who has purchased a house or who has wanted to sell a house must be familiar with some of the tricks used to convince a buyer that the house is quite special: a fire in the fireplace in early evening; jonquils in a pitcher on the kitchen counter, where no one ordinarily has space to put flowers; perhaps the slight aroma of spring, made by a single drop of scent vaporizing from a lamp bulb.

The wonderful thing about the bowl, Andrea thought, was that it was both subtle and noticeable—a paradox of a bowl. Its glaze was the color of cream and seemed to glow no matter what light it was placed in. There were a few bits of color in it—tiny geometric flashes—and some of these were tinged with flecks of silver. They were as mysterious as cells seen under a microscope; it was difficult not to study them, because they shimmered, flashing for a split second, and then resumed their shape. Something about the colors and their random placement suggested motion. People who liked country furniture always commented on the bowl, but then it turned out that people who felt comfortable with Biedermeier[2] loved it just as much. But the bowl was not at all ostentatious, or even so notice-able that anyone would suspect that it had been put in place deliberately. They might notice the height of the ceiling on first entering a room, and only when their eye moved down from that, or away from the refraction of sunlight on a pale wall, would they see the bowl. Then they would go immediately to it and comment. Yet they always faltered when they tried to say something. Perhaps it was because they were in the house for a serious reason, not to notice some object.

Once, Andrea got a call from a woman who had not put in an offer on a house she had shown her. That bowl, she said—would it be possible to find out where

1. Pierre Bonnard (1867–1947), French painter.   2. Unpretentious Central European furniture made primarily between 1820 and 1840.

the owners had bought that beautiful bowl? Andrea pretended that she did not know what the woman was referring to. A bowl, somewhere in the house? Oh, on a table under the window. Yes, she would ask, of course. She let a couple of days pass, then called back to say that the bowl had been a present and the people did not know where it had been purchased.

When the bowl was not being taken from house to house, it sat on Andrea's coffee table at home. She didn't keep it carefully wrapped (although she transported it that way, in a box); she kept it on the table, because she liked to see it. It was large enough so that it didn't seem fragile, or particularly vulnerable if anyone sideswiped the table or Mondo blundered into it at play. She had asked her husband to please not drop his house key in it. It was meant to be empty.

When her husband first noticed the bowl, he had peered into it and smiled briefly. He always urged her to buy things she liked. In recent years, both of them had acquired many things to make up for all the lean years when they were graduate students, but now that they had been comfortable for quite a while, the pleasure of new possessions dwindled. Her husband had pronounced the bowl "pretty," and he had turned away without picking it up to examine it. He had no more interest in the bowl than she had in his new Leica.[3]

She was sure that the bowl brought her luck. Bids were often put in on houses where she had displayed the bowl. Sometimes the owners, who were always asked to be away or to step outside when the house was being shown, didn't even know that the bowl had been in their house. Once—she could not imagine how—she left it behind, and then she was so afraid that something might have happened to it that she rushed back to the house and sighed with relief when the woman owner opened the door. The bowl, Andrea explained—she had purchased a bowl and set it on the chest for safekeeping while she toured the house with the prospective buyers, and she . . . She felt like rushing past the frowning woman and seizing her bowl. The owner stepped aside, and it was only when Andrea ran to the chest that the lady glanced at her a little strangely. In the few seconds before Andrea picked up the bowl, she realized that the owner must have just seen that it had been perfectly placed, that the sunlight struck the bluer part of it. Her pitcher had been moved to the far side of the chest, and the bowl predominated. All the way home, Andrea wondered how she could have left the bowl behind. It was like leaving a friend at an outing—just walking off. Sometimes there were stories in the paper about families forgetting a child somewhere and driving to the next city. Andrea had only gone a mile down the road before she remembered.

In time, she dreamed of the bowl. Twice, in a waking dream—early in the morning, between sleep and a last nap before rising—she had a clear vision of it. It came into sharp focus and startled her for a moment—the same bowl she looked at every day.

10   She had a very profitable year selling real estate. Word spread, and she had more clients than she felt comfortable with. She had the foolish thought that if only the bowl were an animate object she could thank it. There were times when she

3. An expensive German camera.

wanted to talk to her husband about the bowl. He was a stockbroker, and sometimes told people that he was fortunate to be married to a woman who had such
a fine aesthetic sense and yet could also function in the real world. They were a
lot alike, really—they had agreed on that. They were both quiet people—reflective, slow to make value judgments, but almost intractable once they had come
to a conclusion. They both liked details, but while ironies attracted her, he was
more impatient and dismissive when matters became many sided or unclear. But
they both knew this; it was the kind of thing they could talk about when they
were alone in the car together, coming home from a party or after a weekend
with friends. But she never talked to him about the bowl. When they were at
dinner, exchanging their news of the day, or while they lay in bed at night listening to the stereo and murmuring sleepy disconnections, she was often tempted
to come right out and say that she thought that the bowl in the living room, the
cream-colored bowl, was responsible for her success. But she didn't say it. She
couldn't begin to explain it. Sometimes in the morning, she would look at him
and feel guilty that she had such a constant secret.

Could it be that she had some deeper connection with the bowl—a relationship of some kind? She corrected her thinking: how could she imagine such a
thing, when she was a human being and it was a bowl? It was ridiculous. Just
think of how people lived together and loved each other . . . But was that always
so clear, always a relationship? She was confused by these thoughts, but they
remained in her mind. There was something within her now, something real,
that she never talked about.

The bowl was a mystery, even to her. It was frustrating, because her involvement with the bowl contained a steady sense of unrequited good fortune; it would
have been easier to respond if some sort of demand were made in return. But that
only happened in fairy tales. The bowl was just a bowl. She did not believe that
for one second. What she believed was that it was something she loved.

In the past, she had sometimes talked to her husband about a new property
she was about to buy or sell—confiding some clever strategy she had devised to
persuade owners who seemed ready to sell. Now she stopped doing that, for all
her strategies involved the bowl. She became more deliberate with the bowl, and
more possessive. She put it in houses only when no one was there, and removed
it when she left the house. Instead of just moving a pitcher or a dish, she would
remove all the other objects from a table. She had to force herself to handle them
carefully, because she didn't really care about them. She just wanted them out of
sight.

She wondered how the situation would end. As with a lover, there was no exact
scenario of how matters would come to a close. Anxiety became the operative
force. It would be irrelevant if the lover rushed into someone else's arms, or wrote
her a note and departed to another city. The horror was the possibility of the
disappearance. That was what mattered.

She would get up at night and look at the bowl. It never occurred to her that
she might break it. She washed and dried it without anxiety, and she moved it
often, from coffee table to mahogany corner table or wherever, without fearing
an accident. It was clear that she would not be the one who would do anything

to the bowl. The bowl was only handled by her, set safely on one surface or another; it was not very likely that anyone would break it. A bowl was a poor conductor of electricity: it would not be hit by lightning. Yet the idea of damage persisted. She did not think beyond that—to what her life would be without the bowl. She only continued to fear that some accident would happen. Why not, in a world where people set plants where they did not belong, so that visitors touring a house would be fooled into thinking that dark corners got sunlight—a world full of tricks?

She had first seen the bowl several years earlier, at a crafts fair she had visited half in secret, with her lover. He had urged her to buy the bowl. She didn't *need* any more things, she told him. But she had been drawn to the bowl, and they had lingered near it. Then she went on to the next booth, and he came up behind her, tapping the rim against her shoulder as she ran her fingers over a wood carving. "You're still insisting that I buy that?" she said. "No," he said. "I bought it for you." He had bought her other things before this—things she liked more, at first—the child's ebony-and-turquoise ring that fitted her little finger; the wooden box, long and thin, beautifully dovetailed, that she used to hold paper clips; the soft gray sweater with a pouch pocket. It was his idea that when he could not be there to hold her hand she could hold her own—clasp her hands inside the lone pocket that stretched across the front. But in time she became more attached to the bowl than to any of his other presents. She tried to talk herself out of it. She owned other things that were more striking or valuable. It wasn't an object whose beauty jumped out at you; a lot of people must have passed it by before the two of them saw it that day.

Her lover had said that she was always too slow to know what she really loved. Why continue with her life the way it was? Why be two-faced, he asked her. He had made the first move toward her. When she would not decide in his favor, would not change her life and come to him, he asked her what made her think she could have it both ways. And then he made the last move and left. It was a decision meant to break her will, to shatter her intransigent ideas about honoring previous commitments.

Time passed. Alone in the living room at night, she often looked at the bowl sitting on the table, still and safe, unilluminated. In its way, it was perfect: the world cut in half, deep and smoothly empty. Near the rim, even in dim light, the eye moved toward one small flash of blue, a vanishing point on the horizon.

1986

QUESTIONS

1. Why does goodman Brown go to a witches' meeting?
2. Why does Faith Brown, his wife, wear pink ribbons?
3. In reading "Janus," what impression do you get of Andrea—and her attachment to the bowl—in the first half of the story? What expectations—if any—are aroused by that first half? What does it mean to you that Andrea thought the bowl was meant to be empty (paragraph 6)? What other qualities of the bowl seem to suggest something about Andrea or her life? In paragraph 14, Andrea wonders how the situation would end. This probably

makes some readers, perhaps most, think about how this story is going to end. How does it? Where did Andrea get the bowl? How significant is that? Why is the story called "Janus"?

4. Assuming the hunger artist is representative of artists of all kinds, who or what is the "impresario"? the panther who replaces the dead artist? What are the qualities of the panther that make it an appropriate replacement? What are the implications of the first sentence about how appreciation of art has changed in recent times?

WRITING SUGGESTIONS

1. Write a parody of "Young Goodman Brown" or an imitation, perhaps in the style of Stephen King or Anne Rice.
2. Write an analysis of the symbolism used in one of the stories in "Fiction: Reading, Responding, Writing" or in one of the stories in the first three chapters of this textbook.
3. Paraphrase several possible meanings of the bowl in "Janus." Argue for one or explain how the symbol of the bowl may be meaningful and yet elude any possible paraphrase of its meaning.
4. Write an essay suggesting how details from "A Hunger Artist" define the nature of "art."
5. Write an essay arguing that "A Hunger Artist" is or is not an allegory by looking at details that do not seem to suggest an obvious meaning—such as the butchers who sit up with the artist all night tempting him to sneak food—and explaining how these details either "fit" an allegorical reading (perhaps defining certain aspects of the artist or society) or resist such a reading.

STUDENT WRITING

Geoffrey Clement's essay responds to the second writing suggestion, above. In it, he deftly traces in "Sonny's Blues" (from chapter 1) the symbolism and the thematic and evaluative force of images of water in its solid (ice), liquid, and gaseous (steam, boiling) states.

The Struggle to Surface in the Water of "Sonny's Blues"

Geoffrey Clement

In "Sonny's Blues," James Baldwin employs water as a symbol that enables him to concentrate more clearly on the lack of and the crucial need for a real sense of communication among members of society. As Baldwin captures the intensity of Sonny's and his brother's struggles to understand their situation, he vividly depicts a society that seeks to swallow up the souls of its inhabitants and gradually to drown them spiritually. Thus, Baldwin illustrates quite clearly his sense of the hopelessness in man's plight. In portraying the struggle of street life in Harlem, he uses water in its opposite forms--frozen water and boiling water--and toward the end of the story, as Sonny's and his brother's revelations help to resolve the conflict, the water becomes calm.

Initially, and as a result of Sonny's arrest, Sonny's brother gradually realizes that he has not fulfilled his promise and that his feelings of love for his brother have certainly gone unexpressed, if indeed they exist. As a result, he feels physically the coldness that has permeated his emotional life: "It was a special kind of ice. It kept melting, sending trickles of ice water all up and down my veins, but it never got less. Sometimes it hardened and seemed to expand . . ." (par. 2). So the ice represents his guilt and his fears, both of which will lessen little. Although he learns to adapt to these feelings, they occasionally resurface. Upon Sonny's return from prison, for example, his brother thinks, "and thank God she [his wife] was there, for I was filled with that icy dread again. Everything I did seemed awkward to me, and everything I said sounded freighted with hidden meaning. . . . I was dying to hear him tell me he was safe" (par. 78). In addition to this guilt, Sonny's brother experiences much of the same emotional turmoil that Sonny has endured. In this passage in particular, he is seeking reassurance that there is a way to survive their imprisonment without having to feel the pain Sonny felt. Baldwin not only uses ice to show the brother's disappointment in his failures as a brother but also to point to the brother's own struggle for security, identity, and communication.

As Sonny's brother begins to realize that within him there has grown a heart hardened and haunted by the cold darkness of Harlem's streets, he also begins to recognize many of the realities that his brother has faced and that he too must eventually face. Sonny's brother is spiritually walking through "the vivid, killing streets of our childhood. These streets hadn't changed, though housing projects jutted up out of them now like rocks in the middle of a boiling sea" (par. 73). Here, Baldwin paints an almost hellish picture of pain and suffering, of emotional torment and fears, and of spiritual drowning and isolation, all of which slowly become real in the mind of Sonny's brother. He begins to feel for the first time in his life the depth of his denial of his brother. Tragically, he finds that when he is ready to reach out to help Sonny, he cannot, for he is even more lost and confused than Sonny himself. Sonny's brother wants desperately to save Sonny from the inevitable struggle, yet he learns from Sonny that "the storm inside" (par. 217) will pass over only with the constant expression of love. Clearly, the process of revelation is a very dramatic one, since Sonny's brother comes to understand Sonny's need for a giving, communicating, responsible relationship, a commitment filled with careful listening, compassion, and understanding. Sonny does not believe he can make his brother understand his experiences with drugs: "I can never tell you. I was all by myself at the bottom of something . . . . and I thought I'd die if I couldn't get away from it and yet, all the same, I knew that everything I was doing was just locking me in with it" (par. 220). Once his brother grasps the importance of listening with love and understanding, however, Sonny is finally able to reach out.

Toward the end of the story, the ice and the boiling sea come together, and there is peace; Sonny is able to reach out, and he starts to swim in the calmer water. Now, he finds freedom in expressing his struggles through his music, while at the same time alerting his audience to the lessons he has learned. Creole "wanted Sonny to leave the shoreline and strike out for the deep water. He was Sonny's witness that deep water and drowning were not the same thing" (par. 234). As Sonny ventures further and further into his own understanding of life's struggles, he tries, his brother tells us, "to find new ways to make us listen. For, while the tale of how we suffer, and how we are delighted, and how we may triumph is never new, it always must be heard . . . it's the only light we've got in all this darkness" (par. 238). In a powerful way, Sonny taught the audience to listen: "Freedom lurked around us and I understood, at last, that he could help us be free if we would listen, that we would never be free until we did" (par. 240). The boiling rage of the streets and the coldness within his heart are reconciled as the brother finally witnesses "Sonny's world" (par. 231). Finally, he recognizes that Sonny has found the strength of knowing that he has discovered in music the outlet through which he can express himself and warn others of his mistakes. He sends up to the bandstand not water, not ice, but Scotch and milk. Sonny sips it in a sort of communion and puts it back on top of the piano, where "it glowed and shook above [his] head like the very cup of trembling" (par. 241).

Throughout his story, Baldwin stresses the lack of companionship to try to manipulate the reader's emotions. Playing on the contrasts between forms of water, he draws parallels to the theme of emotional conflict within the minds of Sonny and his brother. While the sea is calmer toward the end, there is still a sense of rage, because only in the expression of his struggle is Sonny able to find meaning, satisfaction, and forgiveness for his brother. The streets, society's common ground, still try to isolate its members as each person individually struggles to reach the surface. But if the struggler can find a listening helper, which Sonny finds in his brother, then he will reach the surface and breathe the fulfilling breath of love. The cup of trembling will be taken out of the struggler's hand, the Bible tells us, and will be put "into the hand of them that afflict thee" (p. 70n.). Light gracefully touches and penetrates the surface of the water, and the cup of trembling is still.

6

THEME

If you ask what a story is "about," an author is likely to answer by telling you the **subject.** Indeed, many authors tell you the subject in their titles: "An Occurrence at Owl Creek Bridge," "A Conversation with My Father." Though a subject is always concrete, it may be stated at greater length than the few words of a title: "a man's thoughts as he faces execution for spying during the Civil War" ("An Occurrence at Owl Creek Bridge"); "A dying father's request for his daughter to write a simple story spotlights their different views on life and fiction" ("A Conversation with My Father").

A friend might be more likely to tell you what a story is about by giving you a summary of the action: During World War II, a Chinese woman who is fleeing the Japanese has to abandon her twin daughters. Having escaped, she searches for them but cannot find them. She moves to America and there has another daughter. The mother

> *To Generalize is to be an Idiot.*
> *To Particularize is the Alone*
> *Distinction of Merit. General*
> *Knowledges are those*
> *Knowledges that Idiots*
> *possess.*
>
> —WILLIAM BLAKE

dies, and not long after, a letter from China reveals that the twins have been found, alive and grown up. The "American" daughter—who does not identify herself as "Chinese-American" but just American—goes to China, finds her sisters, and sees the resemblance to her and her mother in their faces. She knows now that she "is Chinese." (We sometimes call this a **plot summary,** but you will notice that this summary describes the history, the events, in more or less chronological order, while the plot arranges or structures the history differently. In "A Pair of Tickets," remember, Jing-Mei Woo does not know the story of her mother's wartime experience or about the survival of her sisters until the latter part of the story.)

Your teacher may well explain a story by summarizing its **theme.** Some refer to the central idea, the thesis, or even the message of the story, and that is roughly what we mean by theme: a generalization or abstraction from the story. Thus the subject of "Young Goodman Brown" may be said to be a coven (witches' meeting) or, more fully, "a young colonial New England husband is driven mad by finding everyone he thought good and pure attending a witches' meeting." The theme may be "everyone partakes of evil" or, more succinctly, "the Fall." There are, as you can see, degrees of generalization and abstraction; subject (a young man finds that everyone is evil) shades off into theme, which itself can be more or less general and abstract.

Discussions of literature in or out of class sometimes seem to suggest that stories exist for their themes, that we read only to get the "point" or message. But most themes are less than earth-shattering. That all men and women are evil may be debatable, but it certainly isn't news. That not all unmarried women of a certain age are prudish, dried up, and repressed—an apparent theme of "Our Friend Judith"—is widely recognized, something we scarcely need a dozen or so pages of fiction to find out. No wonder, then, that some skeptics contend that stories are only elaborate ways of "saying something simple," that literature is a game in which authors hide their meanings under shells of words. Of course, reading a dozen or so pages of a story like "Our Friend Judith" can be enjoyable. Could it be that we really read fiction for fun, and all our talk about themes is just hiding from our puritan natures the fact that we are goofing off? But articulating the theme of a story is neither the purpose of nor the excuse for reading fiction, nor do authors hide their meanings like Easter eggs. In order to relate his or her unique vision of reality to an absent and unknown reader, a writer must find a way of communicating—some common ground on which to meet the various individuals who will read the story.

Common experiences, common assumptions, common language, and common places offer such ground. Readers reach out from their own subjective worlds toward that new and different vision of the author with the help of the common elements (the general), and especially through the commonplaces of theme, bringing back the particulars and generalizations of the story to their own reading and living experience. In "Janus," the reader sees a successful suburban real estate agent who is married to a stockbroker but who has lost her lover, a man she truly loved, because she could not or would not decide to leave her husband; a woman whose world is "perfect," but cut in half and empty, like the beloved bowl her lover picked out for her and gave her. Generalizing from plot and character, setting and symbol, the

> *Every description in words . . . is a generalization. That is the nature of words. There are no individuals conveyed in words but only more or less specific generalizations. . . .*
> —WILLIAM WIMSATT

reader may conclude that what the story says (its theme) is that a full or happy life is more than convention and material success. More specifically, "Janus" seems to warn us about leading a two-faced existence: we may purchase the "perfect" house with the right objects in it but forfeit the really important contents or meaning of a home: feelings, memory, love. Although the theme in fiction usually relates closely to plot and character, every detail in a short story contributes to our interpretation of theme. In "Janus," the narration and point of view, the structure and details, in addition to what happens to Andrea, her husband, and her lover, add to the theme of material well-being and emotional lack. The delay in revealing the history of the bowl seems to reflect Andrea's own refusal to admit what she is missing. Like the bowl, the story circles back to its beginning (and tells the earliest events last). Andrea can neither let go of feelings nor face them, and the voice keeps repeating terms for deception: "tricks," "secret." The first sentence itself, "The bowl was perfect," changes slightly but crucially at the end: "In its way, it was perfect."

Though the reader's own situation and choices may be considerably different from those of the protagonist in "Janus," he or she may be led by Beattie's story to ponder what is truly important and valuable in life, and, whether he or she agrees with the conclusions of the story or not, to come to a fuller understanding of the issues and theme. The significance of any story is modified to some extent by the reader's experience of books and life. You should not reduce every story to the dimensions of what you already know and feel, but you should reach out to the story and bring it back to you as an addition to and modification of your own experience.

Stories, novels, and films often capture our imaginations because they depict ways of life we have never experienced. Since the earliest oral storytelling, human beings have had an appetite to hear about other lands and other peoples. Although today travel writing, ethnography, history, and other forms of nonfiction partially satisfy this appetite, fiction remains one of the best ways to convey the subtleties of interaction among people of different races and cultures. Conflicts, revelations—the kinds of problems and developments that make a good story—arise, for example, when a person from one country visits or moves to another, or when people of two different ethnic groups or cultures interact. The three stories in this chapter emphasize cultural and social differences and prejudices, while at the same time pondering estrangement or loss within families or between lovers. Each story conveys a powerful sense of place or of local culture, as well as of great distances traveled between cultures. The point of view may be that of an insider who is strangely attracted to a troubled visitor: think of the focal character, Mr. Kapasi, in Jhumpa Lahiri's "Interpreter of Maladies." Or the point of view may be that of an outsider or sojourner, as in the first-person retrospective of Angela Carter's "A Souvenir of Japan," or the present-tense narration by the widow in Bharati Mukherjee's "The Management of Grief."

In "A Souvenir of Japan," the narrator is a tall, blue-eyed, blond woman who recalls a time when she lived in a vast Japanese city as the lover of a younger Japanese man. From the first half of the first sentence ("When I went outside to see if he was coming home"), we focus on a love story, an unstable passion: he is always leaving her alone in the little home that she rents for them. Later passages in the story focus on this love story. But the title of the story and the second half of the first sentence turn the reader's attention to the customs of the country. The narrator, who seems to be writing to a fellow Westerner—"If you plan to come and live in Japan" (paragraph 20)—offers a "souvenir" in the form of exquisite descriptions of fireworks and neighborhood customs. On a first reading, we may feel disoriented, like a traveler. The unusual mixture of travelogue and love story calls our attention to a main point the story tries to make—a theme. One way to state that theme is that two cultures may love and desire each other, like incompatible lovers, but can never unite. As the last sentence declares, "try as we might to possess the essence of each other's otherness, we would inevitably fail." This is a type of failure that we recognize all too well: the sort of theme, difficult to summarize, that makes a story matter.

In distinctive ways, the other two stories also convey failures of understanding across cultural gaps. Each of the titles refers to an effort to keep emotion and experience at a distance through language: "The Management of Grief" suggests the official or public way of dealing with death; "Interpreter of Maladies" designates both a tour guide's second job as translator in a doctor's office and his role in figuring out what ails a young family of Indian-Americans. A terrorist bombing of an airliner over Ireland eliminates the family of Mukherjee's narrator, Shaila Bhave, who describes the aftermath in a numb and quiet present tense. She must serve as go-between and translator—interpreter of maladies, perhaps—having been left behind to "complete" the process of building a life in a new world. In Lahiri's "Interpreter of Maladies" an unhappily married woman seeks relief in telling her secret to a convenient listener. "Interpreter of Maladies," like Flannery O'Connor's "A Good Man Is Hard to Find," represents a family car trip as a distorted pilgrimage, though the perspective of the multilingual driver, Mr. Kapasi, serves as a gentler lens through which we observe a less violent revelation than in O'Connor's story. Mr. and Mrs. Das have adapted to North American culture so thoroughly that they act like ignorant tourists in India, the land their parents grew up in and have now returned to. As Mr. Kapasi subtly interprets their maladies, they are a family of siblings and consumers, their values as jumbled as the trash and treats in Mrs. Das's straw bag. Each of these stories, then, treats the theme of cultural difference. To locate this theme is not to close the "case," but rather to begin a more searching investigation of the details that make each story vivid and unique. After all, a statement that can do justice to all the complexity and all the particulars of a story is not likely to take the simple form of a message. Indeed, it is the complex particularity of literature, its ultimate irreducibility, that makes critics and teachers reject *message* (which suggests a simple packaged statement) as a suitable term even for the paraphrasable thematic content of a story.

"Young Goodman Brown" is an allegorical story whose details do function as symbols with paraphrasable meanings, yet even its theme refuses to be reduced to a simple statement. The theme relates to spiritual evil, the kind of evil suggested by the snake and Satan figures. But this theme is not entirely portable: it cannot be taken out of the story and used as a substitute for what the story "means"; nor can it, without qualification, be used to explain all the significant details in the story. The facts that Brown is a newlywed, that Faith wears pink (coquettish?) ribbons, and that she, whom Brown thought so pure and innocent, shows up at the meeting of witches and sinners, suggest a more specific kind of evil than the spiritual or theological evil suggested by the snake and Satan: moral or, even more specifically, sexual evil. This means we must modify our definition of the theme. But how? What does the story imply about the relationship of sex and evil? Is all sex evil? Is Original Sin sexual? Some details—the snake, the Satanic guide—suggest a theme; other details modify it; still others—Brown's behavior after the night of the witches' meeting—may modify it further, so that the theme, though an approximate version of it may be abstracted from the story, remains embedded in it, ultimately inseparable from the details of plot, character, setting, and symbol.

To some readers, inferring themes seems like pulling rabbits out of hats. Not too much conjuring is needed, however, to infer the theme of "Young Goodman Brown": we can derive the theme of theological evil from the symbols (the snake-staff, Satan figure, names) and test physical details—like pink ribbons and the narrative situation (the three-month marriage)—that have sexual implications against the theme to see if we must modify our paraphrase. There are, of course, other ways that details suggest generalizations or meaning, and other ways to abstract meaning from detail. Aided by footnotes, perhaps, you likely noticed the **allusions**—references to history, the Bible, literature, paintings, and so on—in "Young Goodman Brown." The scene is Salem in the time of King William—that is, about the time of the Salem witch trials—and the stranger's serpentine staff is related to those of the pharaoh's Egyptian magi, which turn to snakes. So allusion as well as symbols, plot, focus and voice, and character are elements that contribute to and must be accounted for in paraphrasing a theme. That is why theme is important and why it comes last in a discussion of the elements of fiction.

But remember, the theme is an inadequate abstraction from the story; the story and its details do not disappear or lose significance once distilled into theme, nor could you reconstruct a story merely from its paraphrased theme. Indeed, theme and story, history and structure, do not so much interact, are not so much interrelated, as they are fused, inseparable.

ANGELA CARTER

A Souvenir of Japan

When I went outside to see if he was coming home, some children dressed ready for bed in cotton nightgowns were playing with sparklers in the vacant lot on the corner. When the sparks fell down in beards of stars, the smiling children cooed softly. Their pleasure was very pure because it was so restrained. An old woman said: "And so they pestered their father until he bought them fireworks." In their language, fireworks are called *hannabi,* which means "flower fire." All through summer, every evening, you can see all kinds of fireworks, from the humblest to the most elaborate, and once we rode the train out of Shinjuku for an hour to watch one of the public displays which are held over rivers so that the dark water multiplies the reflections.

By the time we arrived at our destination, night had already fallen. We were in the suburbs. Many families were on their way to enjoy the fireworks. Their mothers had scrubbed and dressed up the smallest children to celebrate the treat. The little girls were especially immaculate in pink and white cotton kimonos tied with fluffy sashes like swatches of candy floss. Their hair had been most beautifully brushed, arranged in sleek, twin bunches and decorated with twists of gold and silver thread. These children were all on their best behavior, because they were staying up late, and held their parents' hands with a charming propriety. We followed the family parties until we came to some fields by the river and saw, high in the air, fireworks already opening out like variegated parasols. They were visible from far away and, as we took the path that led through the fields towards their source, they seemed to occupy more and more of the sky.

Along the path were stalls where shirtless cooks with sweatbands round their heads roasted corncobs and cuttlefish over charcoal. We bought cuttlefish on skewers and ate them as we walked along. They had been basted with soy sauce and were very good. There were also stalls selling goldfish in plastic bags and others for big balloons with rabbit ears. It was like a fairground—but such a well-ordered fair! Even the patrolling policemen carried colored paper lanterns instead of torches.[1] Everything was altogether quietly festive. Ice-cream sellers wandered among the crowd, ringing handbells. Their boxes of wares smoked with cold and they called out in plaintive voices, "Icy, icy, icy cream!" When young lovers dispersed discreetly down the tracks in the sedge, the shadowy, indefatigable salesmen pursued them with bells, lamps and mournful cries.

By now, a great many people were walking towards the fireworks but their steps fell so softly and they chatted in such gentle voices there was no more noise than a warm, continual, murmurous humming, the cozy sound of shared happiness, and the night filled with a muted, bourgeois yet authentic magic. Above our heads, the fireworks hung dissolving earrings on the night. Soon we lay down

---

1. Flashlights (British).

in a stubbled field to watch the fireworks. But, as I expected, he very quickly grew restive.

"Are you happy?" he asked. "Are you sure you're happy?" I was watching the fireworks and did not reply at first although I knew how bored he was and, if he was himself enjoying anything, it was only the idea of my pleasure—or, rather, the idea that he enjoyed my pleasure, since this would be a proof of love. I became guilty and suggested we return to the heart of the city. We fought a silent battle of self-abnegation and I won it, for I had the stronger character. Yet the last thing in the world that I wanted was to leave the scintillating river and the gentle crowd. But I knew his real desire was to return and so return we did, although I do not know if it was worth my small victory of selflessness to bear his remorse at cutting short my pleasure, even if to engineer this remorse had, at some subterranean level, been the whole object of the outing.

Nevertheless, as the slow train nosed back into the thickets of neon, his natural liveliness returned. He could not lose his old habit of walking through the streets with a sense of expectation, as if a fateful encounter might be just around the corner, for, the longer one stayed out, the longer something remarkable might happen and, even if nothing ever did, the chance of it appeased the sweet ache of his boredom for a little while. Besides, his duty by me was done. He had taken me out for the evening and now he wanted to be rid of me. Or so I saw it. The word for wife, *okusan*, means the person who occupies the inner room and rarely, if ever, comes out of it. Since I often appeared to be his wife, I was frequently subjected to this treatment, though I fought against it bitterly.

But I usually found myself waiting for him to come home knowing, with a certain resentment, that he would not; and that he would not even telephone me to tell me he would be late, either, for he was far too guilty to do so. I had nothing better to do than to watch the neighborhood children light their sparklers and giggle; the old woman stood beside me and I knew she disapproved of me. The entire street politely disapproved of me. Perhaps they thought I was contributing to the delinquency of a juvenile for he was obviously younger than I. The old woman's back was bowed almost to a circle from carrying, when he was a baby, the father who now supervised the domestic fireworks in his evening *déshabillé* of loose, white, crepe drawers, naked to the waist. Her face had the seamed reserve of the old in this country. It was a neighborhood poignantly rich in old ladies.

At the corner shop, they put an old lady outside on an upturned beer crate each morning, to air. I think she must have been the household grandmother. She was so old she had lapsed almost entirely into a somnolent plant life. She was of neither more nor less significance to herself or to the world than the pot of morning glories which blossomed beside her and perhaps she had less significance than the flowers, which would fade before lunch was ready. They kept her very clean. They covered her pale cotton kimono with a spotless pinafore trimmed with coarse lace and she never dirtied it because she did not move. Now and then, a child came out to comb her hair. Her consciousness was quite beclouded by time and, when I passed by, her rheumy eyes settled upon me always with the same, vague, disinterested wonder, like that of an Eskimo watching a train. When she whispered, *Irrasyaimase,* the shopkeeper's word of welcome, in the ghostliest of whispers, like the rustle of a paper bag, I saw her teeth were rimmed with gold.

The children lit sparklers under a mouse-colored sky and, because of the pollution in the atmosphere, the moon was mauve. The cicadas throbbed and shrieked in the backyards. When I think of this city, I shall always remember the cicadas who whirr relentlessly all through the summer nights, rising to a piercing crescendo in the subfusc dawn. I have heard cicadas even in the busiest streets, though they thrive best in the back alleys, where they ceaselessly emit that scarcely tolerable susurration which is like a shrill intensification of extreme heat.

A year before, on such a throbbing, voluptuous, platitudinous, subtropical night, we had been walking down one of these shady streets together, in and out of the shadows of the willow trees, looking for somewhere to make love. Morning glories climbed the lattices which screened the low, wooden houses, but the darkness hid the tender colors of these flowers, which the Japanese prize because they fade so quickly. He soon found a hotel, for the city is hospitable to lovers. We were shown into a room like a paper box. It contained nothing but a mattress spread on the floor. We lay down immediately and began to kiss one another. Then a maid soundlessly opened the sliding door and, stepping out of her slippers, crept in on stockinged feet, breathing apologies. She carried a tray which contained two cups of tea and a plate of candies. She put the tray down on the matted floor beside us and backed, bowing and apologizing, from the room while our uninterrupted kiss continued. He started to unfasten my shirt and then she came back again. This time, she carried an armful of towels. I was stripped stark naked when she returned for a third time to bring the receipt for his money. She was clearly a most respectable woman and, if she was embarrassed, she did not show it by a single word or gesture.

I learned his name was Taro. In a toy store, I saw one of those books for children with pictures which are cunningly made of paper cut-outs so that, when you turn the page, the picture springs up in the three stylized dimensions of a backdrop in Kabuki. It was the story of Momotaro, who was born from a peach. Before my eyes, the paper peach split open and there was the baby, where the stone should have been. He, too, had the inhuman sweetness of a child born from something other than a mother, a passive, cruel sweetness I did not immediately understand, for it was that of the repressed masochism which, in my country, is usually confined to women.

Sometimes he seemed to possess a curiously unearthly quality when he perched upon the mattress with his knees drawn up beneath his chin in the attitude of a pixie on a doorknocker. At these times, his face seemed somehow both too flat and too large for his elegant body which had such curious, androgynous grace with its svelte, elongated spine, wide shoulders and unusually well developed pectorals, almost like the breasts of a girl approaching puberty. There was a subtle lack of alignment between face and body and he seemed almost goblin, as if he might have borrowed another person's head, as Japanese goblins do, in order to perform some devious trick. These impressions of a weird visitor were fleeting yet haunting. Sometimes, it was possible for me to believe he had practiced an enchantment upon me, as foxes in this country may, for, here, a fox can masquerade as human and at the best of times the high cheekbones gave to his face the aspect of a mask.

His hair was so heavy his neck drooped under its weight and was of a black so deep it turned purple in sunlight. His mouth also was purplish and his blunt, bee-stung lips those of Gauguin's Tahitians. The touch of his skin was as smooth as water as it flows through the fingers. His eyelids were retractable, like those of a cat, and sometimes disappeared completely. I should have liked to have had him embalmed and been able to keep him beside me in a glass coffin, so that I could watch him all the time and he would not have been able to get away from me.

As they say, Japan is a man's country. When I first came to Tokyo, cloth carps fluttered from poles in the gardens of the families fortunate enough to have borne boy children, for it was the time of the annual festival, Boys Day. At least they do not disguise the situation. At least one knows where one is. Our polarity was publicly acknowledged and socially sanctioned. As an example of the use of the word *dewa,* which occasionally means, as far as I can gather, "in," I once found in a textbook a sentence which, when translated, read: "In a society where men dominate, they value women only as the object of men's passions." If the only conjunction possible to us was that of the death-defying double-somersault of love, it is, perhaps, a better thing to be valued only as an object of passion than never to be valued at all. I had never been so absolutely the mysterious other. I had become a kind of phoenix, a fabulous beast; I was an outlandish jewel. He found me, I think, inexpressibly exotic. But I often felt like a female impersonator in Japan.

In the department store there was a rack of dresses labeled: "For Young and Cute Girls Only." When I looked at them, I felt as gross as Glumdalclitch.[2] I wore men's sandals because they were the only kind that fitted me and, even so, I had to take the largest size. My pink cheeks, blue eyes and blatant yellow hair made of me, in the visual orchestration of this city in which all heads were dark, eyes brown and skin monotone, an instrument which played upon an alien scale. In a sober harmony of subtle plucked instruments and wistful flutes, I blared. I proclaimed myself like in a perpetual fanfare. He was so delicately put together that I thought his skeleton must have the airy elegance of a bird's and I was sometimes afraid that I might smash him. He told me that when he was in bed with me, he felt like a small boat upon a wide, stormy sea.

We pitched our tent in the most unlikely surroundings. We were living in a room furnished only by passion amongst homes of the most astounding respectability. The sounds around us were the swish of brooms upon *tatami* matting and the clatter of demotic Japanese. On all the window ledges, prim flowers bloomed in pots. Every morning, the washing came out on the balconies at seven. Early one morning, I saw a man washing the leaves of his tree. Quilts and mattresses went out to air at eight. The sunlight lay thick enough on these unpaved alleys to lay the dust and somebody always seemed to be practicing Chopin in one or

15

2. In Jonathan Swift's *Gulliver's Travels,* Glumdalclitch is a giantess of Brobdingnag. She is Gulliver's nurse and, though only nine years old, is nearly forty feet tall.

another of the flimsy houses, so lightly glued together from plywood it seemed they were sustained only by willpower. Once I was at home, however, it was as if I occupied the inner room and he did not expect me to go out of it, although it was I who paid the rent.

Yet, when he was away from me, he spent much of the time savoring the most annihilating remorse. But this remorse or regret was the stuff of life to him and out he would go again the next night, or, if I had been particularly angry, he would wait until the night after that. And, even if he fully intended to come back early and had promised me he would do so, circumstances always somehow denied him and once more he would contrive to miss the last train. He and his friends spent their nights in a desultory progression from coffee shop to bar to *pachinko* parlor to coffee shop again, with the radiant aimlessness of the pure existential hero. They were connoisseurs of boredom. They savored the various bouquets of the subtly differentiated boredoms which rose from the long, wasted hours at the dead end of night. When it was time for the first train in the morning, he would go back to the mysteriously deserted, Piranesi[3] perspectives of the station, discolored by dawn, exquisitely tortured by the notion—which probably contained within it a damped-down spark of hope—that, this time, he might have done something irreparable.

I speak as if he had no secrets from me. Well, then, you must realize that I was suffering from love and I knew him as intimately as I knew my own image in a mirror. In other words, I knew him only in relation to myself. Yet, on those terms, I knew him perfectly. At times, I thought I was inventing him as I went along, however, so you will have to take my word for it that we existed. But I do not want to paint our circumstantial portraits so that we both emerge with enough well-rounded, spuriously detailed actuality that you are forced to believe in us. I do not want to practice such sleight of hand. You must be content only with glimpses of our outlines, as if you had caught sight of our reflections in the looking-glass of somebody else's house as you passed by the window. His name was not Taro. I only called him Taro so that I could use the conceit of the peach boy, because it seemed appropriate.

Speaking of mirrors, the Japanese have a great respect for them and, in old-fashioned inns, one often finds them hooded with fabric covers when not in use. He said: "Mirrors make a room uncozy." I am sure there is more to it than that although they love to be cozy. One must love coziness if one is to live so close together. But, as if in celebration of the thing they feared, they seemed to have made the entire city into a cold hall of mirrors which continually proliferated whole galleries of constantly changing appearances, all marvelous but none tangible. If they did not lock up the real looking-glasses, it would be hard to tell what was real and what was not. Even buildings one had taken for substantial had a trick of disappearing overnight. One morning, we woke to find the house next door reduced to nothing but a heap of sticks and a pile of newspapers neatly tied with string, left out for the garbage collector.

---

3. Giambattista Piranesi (1720–1778), Italian architect, painter, and engraver famous for exaggerated (oversized), dramatic, mysterious, almost dreamlike prints of Roman architecture and ruins.

I would not say that he seemed to me to possess the same kind of insubstantiality although his departure usually seemed imminent, until I realized he was as erratic but as inevitable as the weather. If you plan to come and live in Japan, you must be sure you are stoical enough to endure the weather. No, it was not insubstantiality; it was a rhetoric valid only on its own terms. When I listened to his protestations, I was prepared to believe he believed in them, although I knew perfectly well they meant nothing. And that isn't fair. When he made them, he believed in them implicitly. Then, he was utterly consumed by conviction. But his dedication was primarily to the idea of himself in love. This idea seemed to him magnificent, even sublime. He was prepared to die for it, as one of Baudelaire's dandies[4] might have been prepared to kill himself in order to preserve himself in the condition of a work of art, for he wanted to make this experience a masterpiece of experience which absolutely transcended the everyday. And this would annihilate the effects of the cruel drug, boredom, to which he was addicted although, perhaps, the element of boredom which is implicit in an affair so isolated from the real world was its principal appeal for him. But I had no means of knowing how far his conviction would take him. And I used to turn over in my mind from time to time the question: how far does a pretense of feeling, maintained with absolute conviction, become authentic?

This country has elevated hypocrisy to the level of the highest style. To look at a samurai, you would not know him for a murderer, or a geisha for a whore. The magnificence of such objects hardly pertains to the human. They live only in a world of icons and there they participate in rituals which transmute life itself to a series of grand gestures, as moving as they are absurd. It was as if they all thought, if we believe in something hard enough, it will come true and, lo and behold! they had and it did. Our street was in essence a slum but, in appearance, it was a little enclave of harmonious quiet and, *mirabile dictu*, it was the appearance which was the reality, because they all behaved so well, kept everything so clean and lived with such rigorous civility. What terrible discipline it takes to live harmoniously. They had crushed all their vigor in order to live harmoniously and now they had the wistful beauty of flowers pressed dry in an enormous book.

But repression does not necessarily give birth only to severe beauties. In its programmed interstices, monstrous passions bloom. They torture trees to make them look more like the formal notion of a tree. They paint amazing pictures on their skins with awl and gouge, sponging away the blood as they go; a tattooed man is a walking masterpiece of remembered pain. They boast the most passionate puppets in the world who mimic love suicides in a stylized fashion, for here there is no such comfortable formula as "happy ever after." And, when I remembered the finale of the puppet tragedies, how the wooden lovers cut their throats together, I felt the beginnings of unease, as if the hieratic imagery of the country might overwhelm me, for his boredom had reached such a degree that he was insulated against everything except the irritation of anguish. If he valued me as

4. Charles Baudelaire (1821–1867), French writer who lived a life of excess and debauchery and took such a lifestyle, the life of a "dandy," as a theme for his infamous poetic work *Les fleurs du mal (The Flowers of Evil)* (1857).

an object of passion, he had reduced the word to its root, which derives from the Latin, *patior,* I suffer. He valued me as an instrument which would cause him pain.

So we lived under a disoriented moon which was as angry a purple as if the sky had bruised its eye, and, if we made certain genuine intersections, these only took place in darkness. His contagious conviction that our love was unique and desperate infected me with an anxious sickness; soon we would learn to treat one another with the circumspect tenderness of comrades who are amputees, for we were surrounded by the most moving images of evanescence, fireworks, morning glories, the old, children. But the most moving of these images were the intangible reflections of ourselves we saw in one another's eyes, reflections of nothing but appearances, in a city dedicated to seeming, and, try as we might to possess the essence of each other's otherness, we would inevitably fail.

1974

BHARATI MUKHERJEE

The Management of Grief

A woman I don't know is boiling tea the Indian way in my kitchen. There are a lot of women I don't know in my kitchen, whispering, and moving tactfully. They open doors, rummage through the pantry, and try not to ask me where things are kept. They remind me of when my sons were small, on Mother's Day or when Vikram and I were tired, and they would make big, sloppy omelets. I would lie in bed pretending I didn't hear them.

Dr. Sharma, the treasurer of the Indo-Canada Society, pulls me into the hall-way. He wants to know if I am worried about money. His wife, who has just come up from the basement with a tray of empty cups and glasses, scolds him. "Don't bother Mrs. Bhave with mundane details." She looks so monstrously pregnant her baby must be days overdue. I tell her she shouldn't be carrying heavy things. "Shaila," she says, smiling, "this is the fifth." Then she grabs a teenager by his shirttails. He slips his Walkman off his head. He has to be one of her four children, they have the same domed and dented foreheads. "What's the official word now?" she demands. The boy slips the headphones back on. "They're acting evasive, Ma. They're saying it could be an accident or a terrorist bomb."

All morning, the boys have been muttering, Sikh Bomb, Sikh Bomb. The men, not using the word, bow their heads in agreement. Mrs. Sharma touches her fore-head at such a word. At least they've stopped talking about space debris and Russian lasers.

Two radios are going in the dining room. They are tuned to different stations. Someone must have brought the radios down from my boys' bedrooms. I haven't gone into their rooms since Kusum came running across the front lawn in her bathrobe. She looked so funny, I was laughing when I opened the door.

The big TV in the den is being whizzed through American networks and cable   5
channels.

"Damn!" some man swears bitterly. "How can these preachers carry on like nothing's happened?" I want to tell him we're not that important. You look at the audience, and at the preacher in his blue robe with his beautiful white hair, the potted palm trees under a blue sky, and you know they care about nothing.

The phone rings and rings. Dr. Sharma's taken charge. "We're with her," he keeps saying. "Yes, yes, the doctor has given calming pills. Yes, yes, pills are having necessary effect." I wonder if pills alone explain this calm. Not peace, just a deadening quiet. I was always controlled, but never repressed. Sound can reach me, but my body is tensed, ready to scream. I hear their voices all around me. I hear my boys and Vikram cry, "Mommy, Shaila!" and their screams insulate me, like headphones.

The woman boiling water tells her story again and again. "I got the news first. My cousin called from Halifax before six A.M., can you imagine? He'd gotten up for prayers and his son was studying for medical exams and he heard on a rock channel that something had happened to a plane. They said first it had disappeared from the radar, like a giant eraser just reached out. His father called me, so I said to him, what do you mean, 'something bad'? You mean a hijacking? And he said, *behn*,[1] there is no confirmation of anything yet, but check with your neighbors because a lot of them must be on that plane. So I called poor Kusum straightaway. I knew Kusum's husband and daughter were booked to go yesterday."

Kusum lives across the street from me. She and Satish had moved in less than a month ago. They said they needed a bigger place. All these people, the Sharmas and friends from the Indo-Canada Society had been there for the housewarming. Satish and Kusum made homemade tandoori on their big gas grill and even the white neighbors piled their plates high with that luridly red, charred, juicy chicken. Their younger daughter had danced, and even our boys had broken away from the Stanley Cup telecast to put in a reluctant appearance. Everyone took pictures for their albums and for the community newspapers—another of our families had made it big in Toronto—and now I wonder how many of those happy faces are gone. "Why does God give us so much if all along He intends to take it away?" Kusum asks me.

I nod. We sit on carpeted stairs, holding hands like children. "I never once told   10
him that I loved him," I say. I was too much the well brought up woman. I was so well brought up I never felt comfortable calling my husband by his first name.

"It's all right," Kusum says. "He knew. My husband knew. They felt it. Modern young girls have to say it because what they feel is fake."

Kusum's daughter, Pam, runs in with an overnight case. Pam's in her McDonald's uniform. "Mummy! You have to get dressed!" Panic makes her cranky. "A reporter's on his way here."

"Why?"

---

1. No.

"You want to talk to him in your bathrobe?" She starts to brush her mother's long hair. She's the daughter who's always in trouble. She dates Canadian boys and hangs out in the mall, shopping for tight sweaters. The younger one, the goody-goody one according to Pam, the one with a voice so sweet that when she sang *bhajans*[2] for Ethiopian relief even a frugal man like my husband wrote out a hundred dollar check, *she* was on that plane. *She* was going to spend July and August with grandparents because Pam wouldn't go. Pam said she'd rather wait-ress at McDonald's. "If it's a choice between Bombay and Wonderland, I'm pick-ing Wonderland," she'd said.

15   "Leave me alone," Kusum yells. "You know what I want to do? If I didn't have to look after you now, I'd hang myself."

Pam's young face goes blotchy with pain. "Thanks," she says, "don't let me stop you."

"Hush," pregnant Mrs. Sharma scolds Pam. "Leave your mother alone. Mr. Sharma will tackle the reporters and fill out the forms. He'll say what has to be said."

Pam stands her ground. "You think I don't know what Mummy's thinking? *Why her?* that's what. That's sick! Mummy wishes my little sister were alive and I were dead."

Kusum's hand in mine is trembly hot. We continue to sit on the stairs.

20   She calls before she arrives, wondering if there's anything I need. Her name is Judith Templeton and she's an appointee of the provincial government. "Multi-culturalism?" I ask, and she says, "partially," but that her mandate is bigger. "I've been told you knew many of the people on the flight," she says. "Perhaps if you'd agree to help us reach the others . . . ?"

She gives me time at least to put on tea water and pick up the mess in the front room. I have a few *samosas*[3] from Kusum's housewarming that I could fry up, but then I think, why prolong this visit?

Judith Templeton is much younger than she sounded. She wears a blue suit with a white blouse and a polka dot tie. Her blond hair is cut short, her only jewelry is pearl drop earrings. Her briefcase is new and expensive looking, a gleam-ing cordovan leather. She sits with it across her lap. When she looks out the front windows onto the street, her contact lenses seem to float in front of her light blue eyes.

"What sort of help do you want from me?" I ask. She has refused the tea, out of politeness, but I insist, along with some slightly stale biscuits.

"I have no experience," she admits. "That is, I have an MSW and I've worked in liaison with accident victims, but I mean I have no experience with a tragedy of this scale—"

25   "Who could?" I ask.

"—and with the complications of culture, language, and customs. Someone mentioned that Mrs. Bhave is a pillar—because you've taken it more calmly."

At this, perhaps I frown, for she reaches forward, almost to take my hand. "I

2. Hymns.   3. Fried turnovers filled with meat or vegetable mixtures.

hope you understand my meaning, Mrs. Bhave. There are hundreds of people in Metro directly affected, like you, and some of them speak no English. There are some widows who've never handled money or gone on a bus, and there are old parents who still haven't eaten or gone outside their bedrooms. Some houses and apartments have been looted. Some wives are still hysterical. Some husbands are in shock and profound depression. We want to help, but our hands are tied in so many ways. We have to distribute money to some people, and there are legal documents—these things can be done. We have interpreters, but we don't always have the human touch, or maybe the right human touch. We don't want to make mistakes, Mrs. Bhave, and that's why we'd like to ask you to help us."

"More mistakes, you mean," I say.

"Police matters are not in my hands," she answers.

"Nothing I can do will make any difference," I say. "We must all grieve in our   30 own way."

"But you are coping very well. All the people said, Mrs. Bhave is the strongest person of all. Perhaps if the others could see you, talk with you, it would help them."

"By the standards of the people you call hysterical, I am behaving very oddly and very badly, Miss Templeton." I want to say to her, *I wish I could scream, starve, walk into Lake Ontario, jump from a bridge.* "They would not see me as a model. I do not see myself as a model."

I am a freak. No one who has ever known me would think of me reacting this way. This terrible calm will not go away.

She asks me if she may call again, after I get back from a long trip that we all must make. "Of course," I say. "Feel free to call, anytime."

Four days later, I find Kusum squatting on a rock overlooking a bay in Ireland. It   35 isn't a big rock, but it juts sharply out over water. This is as close as we'll ever get to them. June breezes balloon out her sari and unpin her knee-length hair. She has the bewildered look of a sea creature whom the tides have stranded.

It's been one hundred hours since Kusum came stumbling and screaming across my lawn. Waiting around the hospital, we've heard many stories. The police, the diplomats, they tell us things thinking that we're strong, that knowledge is helpful to the grieving, and maybe it is. Some, I know, prefer ignorance, or their own versions. The plane broke into two, they say. Unconsciousness was instantaneous. No one suffered. My boys must have just finished their breakfasts. They loved eating on planes, they loved the smallness of plates, knives, and forks. Last year they saved the airline salt and pepper shakers. Half an hour more and they would have made it to Heathrow.

Kusum says that we can't escape our fate. She says that all those people—our husbands, my boys, her girl with the nightingale voice, all those Hindus, Christians, Sikhs, Muslims, Parsis, and atheists on that plane—were fated to die together off this beautiful bay. She learned this from a swami in Toronto.

I have my Valium.

Six of us "relatives"—two widows and four widowers—choose to spend the day today by the waters instead of sitting in a hospital room and scanning photographs of the dead. That's what they call us now: relatives. I've looked through twenty-seven photos in two days. They're very kind to us, the Irish are very understanding. Sometimes understanding means freeing a tourist bus for this trip to the bay, so we can pretend to spy our loved ones through the glassiness of waves or in sunspeckled cloud shapes.

40   I could die here, too, and be content.

"What is that, out there?" She's standing and flapping her hands and for a moment I see a head shape bobbing in the waves. She's standing in the water, I, on the boulder. The tide is low, and a round, black, headsized rock has just risen from the waves. She returns, her sari end dripping and ruined and her face is a twisted remnant of hope, the way mine was a hundred hours ago, still laughing but inwardly knowing that nothing but the ultimate tragedy could bring two women together at six o'clock on a Sunday morning. I watch her face sag into blankness.

"That water felt warm, Shaila," she says at length.

"You can't," I say. "We have to wait for our turn to come."

I haven't eaten in four days, haven't brushed my teeth.

45   "I know," she says. "I tell myself I have no right to grieve. They are in a better place than we are. My swami says I should be thrilled for them. My swami says depression is a sign of our selfishness."

Maybe I'm selfish. Selfishly I break away from Kusum and run, sandals slapping against stones, to the water's edge. What if my boys aren't lying pinned under the debris? What if they aren't stuck a mile below that innocent blue chop? What if, given the strong currents. . . .

Now I've ruined my sari, one of my best. Kusum has joined me, knee-deep in water that feels to me like a swimming pool. I could settle in the water, and my husband would take my hand and the boys would slap water in my face just to see me scream.

"Do you remember what good swimmers my boys were, Kusum?"

"I saw the medals," she says.

50   One of the widowers, Dr. Ranganathan from Montreal, walks out to us, carrying his shoes in one hand. He's an electrical engineer. Someone at the hotel mentioned his work is famous around the world, something about the place where physics and electricity come together. He has lost a huge family, something indescribable. "With some luck," Dr. Ranganathan suggests to me, "a good swimmer could make it safely to some island. It is quite possible that there may be many, many microscopic islets scattered around."

"You're not just saying that?" I tell Dr. Ranganathan about Vinod, my elder son. Last year he took diving as well.

"It's a parent's duty to hope," he says. "It is foolish to rule out possibilities that have not been tested. I myself have not surrendered hope."

Kusum is sobbing once again. "Dear lady," he says, laying his free hand on her arm, and she calms down.

"Vinod is how old?" he asks me. He's very careful, as we all are. *Is*, not was.

55   "Fourteen. Yesterday he was fourteen. His father and uncle were going to take him down to the Taj and give him a big birthday party. I couldn't go with them

because I couldn't get two weeks off from my stupid job in June." I process bills for a travel agent. June is a big travel month.

Dr. Ranganathan whips the pockets of his suit jacked inside out. Squashed roses, in darkening shades of pink, float on the water. He tore the roses off creepers in somebody's garden. He didn't ask anyone if he could pluck the roses, but now there's been an article about it in the local papers. When you see an Indian person, it says, please give him or her flowers.

"A strong youth of fourteen," he says, "can very likely pull to safety a younger one."

My sons, though four years apart, were very close. Vinod wouldn't let Mithun drown. *Electrical engineering*, I think, foolishly perhaps: this man knows important secrets of the universe, things closed to me. Relief spins me lightheaded. No wonder my boys' photographs haven't turned up in the gallery of photos of the recovered dead. "Such pretty roses," I say.

"My wife loved pink roses. Every Friday I had to bring a bunch home. I used to say, why? After twenty-odd years of marriage you're still needing proof positive of my love?" He has identified his wife and three of his children. Then others from Montreal, the lucky ones, intact families with no survivors. He chuckles as he wades back to shore. Then he swings around to ask me a question. "Mrs. Bhave, you are wanting to throw in some roses for your loved ones? I have two big ones left."

But I have other things to float: Vinod's pocket calculator; a half-painted model B-52 for my Mithun. They'd want them on their island. And for my husband? For him I let fall into the calm, glassy waters a poem I wrote in the hospital yesterday. Finally he'll know my feelings for him. 60

"Don't tumble, the rocks are slippery," Dr. Ranganathan cautions. He holds out a hand for me to grab.

Then it's time to get back on the bus, time to rush back to our waiting posts on hospital benches.

Kusum is one of the lucky ones. The lucky ones flew here, identified in multiplicate their loved ones, then will fly to India with the bodies for proper ceremonies. Satish is one of the few males who surfaced. The photos of faces we saw on the walls in an office at Heathrow and here in the hospital are mostly of women. Women have more body fat, a nun said to me matter-of-factly. They float better. Today I was stopped by a young sailor on the street. He had loaded bodies, he'd gone into the water when—he checks my face for signs of strength—when the sharks were first spotted. I don't blush, and he breaks down. "It's all right," I say. "Thank you." I had heard about the sharks from Dr. Ranganathan. In his orderly mind, science brings understanding, it holds no terror. It is the shark's duty. For every deer there is a hunter, for every fish a fisherman.

The Irish are not shy; they rush to me and give me hugs and some are crying. 65 I cannot imagine reactions like that on the streets of Toronto. Just strangers, and I am touched. Some carry flowers with them and give them to any Indian they see.

After lunch, a policeman I have gotten to know quite well catches hold of me.

He says he thinks he has a match for Vinod. I explain what a good swimmer Vinod is.

"You want me with you when you look at photos?" Dr. Ranganathan walks ahead of me into the picture gallery. In these matters, he is a scientist, and I am grateful. It is a new perspective. "They have performed miracles," he says. "We are indebted to them."

The first day or two the policemen showed us relatives only one picture at a time; now they're in a hurry, they're eager to lay out the possibles, and even the probables.

The face on the photo is of a boy much like Vinod; the same intelligent eyes, the same thick brows dipping into a V. But this boy's features, even his cheeks, are puffier, wider, mushier.

70   "No." My gaze is pulled by other pictures. There are five other boys who look like Vinod.

The nun assigned to console me rubs the first picture with a fingertip. "When they've been in the water for a while, love, they look a little heavier." The bones under the skin are broken, they said on the first day—try to adjust your memories. It's important.

"It's not him. I'm his mother. I'd know."

"I know this one!" Dr. Ranganathan cries out suddenly from the back of the gallery. "And this one!" I think he senses that I don't want to find my boys. "They are the Kutty brothers. They were also from Montreal." I don't mean to be crying. On the contrary, I am ecstatic. My suitcase in the hotel is packed heavy with dry clothes for my boys.

The policeman starts to cry. "I am so sorry, I am so sorry, ma'am. I really thought we had a match."

75   With the nun ahead of us and the policeman behind, we, the unlucky ones without our children's bodies, file out of the makeshift gallery.

From Ireland most of us go on to India. Kusum and I take the same direct flight to Bombay, so I can help her clear customs quickly. But we have to argue with a man in uniform. He has large boils on his face. The boils swell and glow with sweat as we argue with him. He wants Kusum to wait in line and he refuses to take authority because his boss is on a tea break. But Kusum won't let her coffins out of sight, and I shan't desert her though I know that my parents, elderly and diabetic, must be waiting in a stuffy car in a scorching lot.

"You bastard!" I scream at the man with the popping boils. Other passengers press closer. "You think we're smuggling contraband in those coffins!"

Once upon a time we were well brought up women; we were dutiful wives who kept our heads veiled, our voices shy and sweet.

In India, I become, once again, an only child of rich, ailing parents. Old friends of the family come to pay their respects. Some are Sikh, and inwardly, involuntarily, I cringe. My parents are progressive people; they do not blame communities for a few individuals.

80   In Canada it is a different story now.

"Stay longer," my mother pleads. "Canada is a cold place. Why would you want to be all by yourself?" I stay.

Three months pass. Then another.

"Vikram wouldn't have wanted you to give up things!" they protest. They call my husband by the name he was born with. In Toronto he'd changed to Vik so the men he worked with at his office would find his name as easy as Rod or Chris. "You know, the dead aren't cut off from us!"

My grandmother, the spoiled daughter of a rich *zamindar*,[4] shaved her head with rusty razor blades when she was widowed at sixteen. My grandfather died of childhood diabetes when he was nineteen, and she saw herself as the harbinger of bad luck. My mother grew up without parents, raised indifferently by an uncle, while her true mother slept in a hut behind the main estate house and took her food with the servants. She grew up a rationalist. My parents abhor mindless mortification.

The zamindar's daughter kept stubborn faith in Vedic rituals; my parents rebelled. I am trapped between two modes of knowledge. At thirty-six, I am too old to start over and too young to give up. Like my husband's spirit, I flutter between worlds.

Courting aphasia, we travel. We travel with our phalanx of servants and poor relatives. To hill stations and to beach resorts. We play contract bridge in dusty gymkhana clubs. We ride stubby ponies up crumbly mountain trails. At tea dances, we let ourselves be twirled twice round the ballroom. We hit the holy spots we hadn't made time for before. In Varanasi, Kalighat, Rishikesh, Hardwar, astrologers and palmists seek me out and for a fee offer me cosmic consolations.

Already the widowers among us are being shown new bride candidates. They cannot resist the call of custom, the authority of their parents and older brothers. They must marry; it is the duty of a man to look after a wife. The new wives will be young widows with children, destitute but of good family. They will make loving wives, but the men will shun them. I've had calls from the men over crackling Indian telephone lines. "Save me," they say, these substantial, educated, successful men of forty. "My parents are arranging a marriage for me." In a month they will have buried one family and returned to Canada with a new bride and partial family.

I am comparatively lucky. No one here thinks of arranging a husband for an unlucky widow.

Then, on the third day of the sixth month into this odyssey, in an abandoned temple in a tiny Himalayan village, as I make my offering of flowers and sweet-meats to the god of a tribe of animists, my husband descends to me. He is squatting next to a scrawny *sadhu* in moth-eaten robes. Vikram wears the vanilla suit he wore the last time I hugged him. The *sadhu* tosses petals on a butter-fed flame, reciting Sanskrit mantras and sweeps his face of flies. My husband takes my hands in his.

You're beautiful, he starts. Then, *What are you doing here?*

85

90

4. Landowner.

Shall I stay? I ask. He only smiles, but already the image is fading. *You must finish alone what we started together.* No seaweed wreathes his mouth. He speaks too fast just as he used to when we were an envied family in our pink split-level. He is gone.

In the windowless altar room, smoky with joss sticks and clarified butter lamps, a sweaty hand gropes for my blouse. I do not shriek. The *sadhu* arranges his robe. The lamps hiss and sputter out.

When we come out of the temple, my mother says, "Did you feel something weird in there?"

My mother has no patience with ghosts, prophetic dreams, holy men, and cults.

95   "No," I lie. "Nothing."

But she knows that she's lost me. She knows that in days I shall be leaving.

Kusum's put her house up for sale. She wants to live in an ashram in Hardwar. Moving to Hardwar was her swami's idea. Her swami runs two ashrams, the one in Hardwar and another here in Toronto.

"Don't run away," I tell her.

"I'm not running away," she says. "I'm pursuing inner peace. You think you or that Ranganathan fellow are better off?"

100   Pam's left for California. She wants to do some modelling, she says. She says when she comes into her share of the insurance money she'll open a yoga-cum-aerobics studio in Hollywood. She sends me postcards so naughty I daren't leave them on the coffee table. Her mother has withdrawn from her and the world.

The rest of us don't lose touch, that's the point. Talk is all we have, says Dr. Ranganathan, who has also resisted his relatives and returned to Montreal and to his job, alone. He says, whom better to talk with than other relatives? We've been melted down and recast as a new tribe.

He calls me twice a week from Montreal. Every Wednesday night and every Saturday afternoon. He is changing jobs, going to Ottawa. But Ottawa is over a hundred miles away, and he is forced to drive two hundred and twenty miles a day. He can't bring himself to sell his house. The house is a temple, he says; the king-sized bed in the master bedroom is a shrine. He sleeps on a folding cot. A devotee.

There are still some hysterical relatives. Judith Templeton's list of those needing help and those who've "accepted" is in nearly perfect balance. Acceptance means you speak of your family in the past tense and you make active plans for moving ahead with your life. There are courses at Seneca and Ryerson[5] we could be taking. Her gleaming leather briefcase is full of college catalogues and lists of cultural societies that need our help. She has done impressive work, I tell her.

"In the textbooks on grief management," she replies—I am her confidante, I

5. Seneca College of Applied Arts and Technology, in Willowdale; Ryerson Polytechnical Institute, Toronto.

realize, one of the few whose grief has not sprung bizarre obsessions—"there are stages to pass through: rejection, depression, acceptance, reconstruction." She has compiled a chart and finds that six months after the tragedy, none of us still reject reality, but only a handful are reconstructing. "Depressed Acceptance" is the plateau we've reached. Remarriage is a major step in reconstruction (though she's a little surprised, even shocked, over *how* quickly some of the men have taken on new families). Selling one's house and changing jobs and cities is healthy.

How do I tell Judith Templeton that my family surrounds me, and that like   105
creatures in epics, they've changed shapes? She sees me as calm and accepting but worries that I have no job, no career. My closest friends are worse off than I. I cannot tell her my days, even my nights, are thrilling.

She asks me to help with families she can't reach at all. An elderly couple in Agincourt whose sons were killed just weeks after they had brought their parents over from a village in Punjab. From their names, I know they are Sikh. Judith Templeton and a translator have visited them twice with offers of money for air fare to Ireland, with bank forms, power-of-attorney forms, but they have refused to sign, or to leave their tiny apartment. Their sons' money is frozen in the bank. Their sons' investment apartments have been trashed by tenants, the furnishings sold off. The parents fear that anything they sign or any money they receive will end the company's or the country's obligations to them. They fear they are selling their sons for two airline tickets to a place they've never seen.

The high-rise apartment is a tower of Indians and West Indians, with a sprinkling of Orientals. The nearest bus stop kiosk is lined with women in saris. Boys practice cricket in the parking lot. Inside the building, even I wince a bit from the ferocity of onion fumes, the distinctive and immediate Indianness of frying *ghee,* but Judith Templeton maintains a steady flow of information. These poor old people are in imminent danger of losing their place and all their services.

I say to her, "They are Sikh. They will not open up to a Hindu woman." And what I want to add is, as much as I try not to, I stiffen now at the sight of beards and turbans. I remember a time when we all trusted each other in this new country, it was only the new country we worried about.

The two rooms are dark and stuffy. The lights are off, and an oil lamp sputters on the coffee table. The bent old lady has let us in, and her husband is wrapping a white turban over his oiled, hip-length hair. She immediately goes to the kitchen, and I hear the most familiar sound of an Indian home, tap water hitting and filling a teapot.

They have not paid their utility bills, out of fear and the inability to write a   110
check. The telephone is gone; electricity and gas and water are soon to follow. They have told Judith their sons will provide. They are good boys, and they have always earned and looked after their parents.

We converse a bit in Hindi. They do not ask about the crash and I wonder if I should bring it up. If they think I am here merely as a translator, then they may feel insulted. There are thousands of Punjabi-speakers, Sikhs, in Toronto to do a better job. And so I say to the old lady, "I too have lost my sons, and my husband, in the crash."

Her eyes immediately fill with tears. The man mutters a few words which sound like a blessing. "God provides and God takes away," he says.

I want to say, but only men destroy and give back nothing. "My boys and my husband are not coming back," I say. "We have to understand that."

Now the old woman responds. "But who is to say? Man alone does not decide these things." To this her husband adds his agreement.

115   Judith asks about the bank papers, the release forms. With a stroke of the pen, they will have a provincial trustee to pay their bills, invest their money, send them a monthly pension.

"Do you know this woman?" I ask them.

The man raises his hand from the table, turns it over and seems to regard each finger separately before he answers. "This young lady is always coming here, we make tea for her and she leaves papers for us to sign." His eyes scan a pile of papers in the corner of the room. "Soon we will be out of tea, then will she go away?"

The old lady adds, "I have asked my neighbors and no one else gets *angrezi*[6] visitors. What have we done?"

"It's her job," I try to explain. "The government is worried. Soon you will have no place to stay, no lights, no gas, no water."

120   "Government will get its money. Tell her not to worry, we are honorable people."

I try to explain the government wishes to give money, not take. He raises his hand. "Let them take," he says. "We are accustomed to that. That is no problem."

"We are strong people," says the wife. "Tell her that."

"Who needs all this machinery?" demands the husband. "It is unhealthy, the bright lights, the cold air on a hot day, the cold food, the four gas rings. God will provide, not government."

"When our boys return," the mother says. Her husband sucks his teeth. "Enough talk," he says.

125   Judith breaks in. "Have you convinced them?" The snaps on her cordovan briefcase go off like firecrackers in that quiet apartment. She lays the sheaf of legal papers on the coffee table. "If they can't write their names, an X will do—I've told them that."

Now the old lady has shuffled to the kitchen and soon emerges with a pot of tea and two cups. "I think my bladder will go first on a job like this," Judith says to me, smiling. "If only there was some way of reaching them. Please thank her for the tea. Tell her she's very kind."

I nod in Judith's direction and tell them in Hindi, "She thanks you for the tea. She thinks you are being very hospitable but she doesn't have the slightest idea what it means."

I want to say, humor her. I want to say, my boys and my husband are with me too, more than ever. I look in the old man's eyes and I can read his stubborn, peasant's message: *I have protected this woman as best I can. She is the only person I have left. Give to me or take from me what you will, but I will not sign for it. I will not pretend that I accept.*

6. English, Anglo.

In the car, Judith says, "You see what I'm up against? I'm sure they're lovely people, but their stubbornness and ignorance are driving me crazy. They think signing a paper is signing their sons' death warrants, don't they?"

I am looking out the window. I want to say, *In our culture, it is a parent's duty to hope.*   130

"Now Shaila, this next woman is a real mess. She cries day and night, and she refuses all medical help. We may have to—"

"—Let me out at the subway," I say.

"I beg your pardon?" I can feel those blue eyes staring at me.

It would not be like her to disobey. She merely disapproves, and slows at a corner to let me out. Her voice is plaintive. "Is there anything I said? Anything I did?"

I could answer her suddenly in a dozen ways, but I choose not to. "Shaila?   135
Let's talk about it," I hear, then slam the door.

A wife and mother begins her new life in a new country, and that life is cut short. Yet her husband tells her: Complete what we have started. We, who stayed out of politics and came halfway around the world to avoid religious and political feuding have been the first in the New World to die from it. I no longer know what we started, nor how to complete it. I write letters to the editors of local papers and to members of Parliament. Now at least they admit it was a bomb. One MP answers back, with sympathy, but with a challenge. You want to make a difference? Work on a campaign. Work on mine. Politicize the Indian voter.

My husband's old lawyer helps me set up a trust. Vikram was a saver and a careful investor. He had saved the boys' boarding school and college fees. I sell the pink house at four times what we paid for it and take a small apartment downtown. I am looking for a charity to support.

We are deep in the Toronto winter, gray skies, icy pavements. I stay indoors, watching television. I have tried to assess my situation, how best to live my life, to complete what we began so many years ago. Kusum has written me from Hardwar that her life is now serene. She has seen Satish and has heard her daughter sing again. Kusum was on a pilgrimage, passing through a village when she heard a young girl's voice, singing one of her daughter's favorite *bhajans*. She followed the music through the squalor of a Himalayan village, to a hut where a young girl, an exact replica of her daughter, was fanning coals under the kitchen fire. When she appeared, the girl cried out, "Ma!" and ran away. What did I think of that?

I think I can only envy her.

Pam didn't make it to California, but writes me from Vancouver. She works in   140
a department store, giving make-up hints to Indian and Oriental girls. Dr. Ranganathan has given up his commute, given up his house and job, and accepted an academic position in Texas where no one knows his story and he has vowed not to tell it. He calls me now once a week.

I wait, I listen, and I pray, but Vikram has not returned to me. The voices and the shapes and the nights filled with visions ended abruptly several weeks ago.

I take it as a sign.

One rare, beautiful, sunny day last week, returning from a small errand on Yonge Street, I was walking through the park from the subway to my apartment. I live equidistant from the Ontario Houses of Parliament and the University of Toronto. The day was not cold, but something in the bare trees caught my attention. I looked up from the gravel, into the branches and the clear blue sky beyond. I thought I heard the rustling of larger forms, and I waited a moment for voices. Nothing.

"What?" I asked.

145   Then as I stood in the path looking north to Queen's Park and west to the university, I heard the voices of my family one last time. *Your time has come*, they said. *Go, be brave.*

I do not know where this voyage I have begun will end. I do not know which direction I will take. I dropped the package on a park bench and started walking.

1988

JHUMPA LAHIRI

Interpreter of Maladies

At the tea stall Mr. and Mrs. Das bickered about who should take Tina to the toilet. Eventually Mrs. Das relented when Mr. Das pointed out that he had given the girl her bath the night before. In the rearview mirror Mr. Kapasi watched as Mrs. Das emerged slowly from his bulky white Ambassador, dragging her shaved, largely bare legs across the back seat. She did not hold the little girl's hand as they walked to the rest room.

They were on their way to see the Sun Temple at Konarak.[1] It was a dry, bright Saturday, the mid-July heat tempered by a steady ocean breeze, ideal weather for sightseeing. Ordinarily Mr. Kapasi would not have stopped so soon along the way, but less than five minutes after he'd picked up the family that morning in front of Hotel Sandy Villa, the little girl complained. The first thing Mr. Kapasi had noticed when he saw Mr. and Mrs. Das, standing with their children under the portico of the hotel, was that they were very young, perhaps not even thirty. In addition to Tina they had two boys, Ronny and Bobby, who appeared very close in age and had teeth covered in a network of flashing silver wires. The family looked Indian but dressed as foreigners did, the children in stiff, brightly colored clothing and caps with translucent visors. Mr. Kapasi was accustomed to foreign tourists; he was assigned to them regularly because he could speak English. Yes-

---

1. Below, the story provides an accurate history and description of the Sun Temple at Konark (or Konarak), still a pilgrimage as well as tourist site near the east coast in the Orissa region of India. According to legend, the temple was built because Samba, son of Lord Krishna, was cured of leprosy by Surya, the sun god.

terday he had driven an elderly couple from Scotland, both with spotted faces and fluffy white hair so thin it exposed their sunburnt scalps. In comparison, the tanned, youthful faces of Mr. and Mrs. Das were all the more striking. When he'd introduced himself, Mr. Kapasi had pressed his palms together in greeting, but Mr. Das squeezed hands like an American so that Mr. Kapasi felt it in his elbow. Mrs. Das, for her part, had flexed one side of her mouth, smiling dutifully at Mr. Kapasi, without displaying any interest in him.

As they waited at the tea stall, Ronny, who looked like the older of the two boys, clambered suddenly out of the back seat, intrigued by a goat tied to a stake in the ground.

"Don't touch it," Mr. Das said. He glanced up from his paperback tour book, which said "INDIA" in yellow letters and looked as if it had been published abroad. His voice, somehow tentative and a little shrill, sounded as though it had not yet settled into maturity.

"I want to give it a piece of gum," the boy called back as he trotted ahead. 5

Mr. Das stepped out of the car and stretched his legs by squatting briefly to the ground. A clean-shaven man, he looked exactly like a magnified version of Ronny. He had a sapphire blue visor, and was dressed in shorts, sneakers, and a T-shirt. The camera slung around his neck, with an impressive telephoto lens and numerous buttons and markings, was the only complicated thing he wore. He frowned, watching as Ronny rushed toward the goat, but appeared to have no intention of intervening. "Bobby, make sure that your brother doesn't do anything stupid."

"I don't feel like it," Bobby said, not moving. He was sitting in the front seat beside Mr. Kapasi, studying a picture of the elephant god taped to the glove compartment.

"No need to worry," Mr. Kapasi said. "They are quite tame." Mr. Kapasi was forty-six years old, with receding hair that had gone completely silver, but his butterscotch complexion and his unlined brow, which he treated in spare moments to dabs of lotus-oil balm, made it easy to imagine what he must have looked like at an earlier age. He wore gray trousers and a matching jacket-style shirt, tapered at the waist, with short sleeves and a large pointed collar, made of a thin but durable synthetic material. He had specified both the cut and the fabric to his tailor—it was his preferred uniform for giving tours because it did not get crushed during his long hours behind the wheel. Through the windshield he watched as Ronny circled around the goat, touched it quickly on its side, then trotted back to the car.

"You left India as a child?" Mr. Kapasi asked when Mr. Das had settled once again into the passenger seat.

"Oh, Mina and I were both born in America," Mr. Das announced with an air 10
of sudden confidence. "Born and raised. Our parents live here now, in Assansol.[2] They retired. We visit them every couple years." He turned to watch as the little

---

2. Or Asonsol, a city in northeastern India, not far from Calcutta and about three hundred miles from Puri, the coastal city in Orissa that the Das family is visiting. Puri is both a tourist resort and a Hindu holy city, said to be dominated by the forces of both God and humanity.

girl ran toward the car, the wide purple bows of her sundress flopping on her narrow brown shoulders. She was holding to her chest a doll with yellow hair that looked as if it had been chopped, as a punitive measure, with a pair of dull scissors. "This is Tina's first trip to India, isn't it, Tina?"

"I don't have to go to the bathroom anymore," Tina announced.

"Where's Mina?" Mr. Das asked.

Mr. Kapasi found it strange that Mr. Das should refer to his wife by her first name when speaking to the little girl. Tina pointed to where Mrs. Das was purchasing something from one of the shirtless men who worked at the tea stall. Mr. Kapasi heard one of the shirtless men sing a phrase from a popular Hindi love song as Mrs. Das walked back to the car, but she did not appear to understand the words of the song, for she did not express irritation, or embarrassment, or react in any other way to the man's declarations.

He observed her. She wore a red-and-white-checkered skirt that stopped above her knees, slip-on shoes with a square wooden heel, and a close-fitting blouse styled like a man's undershirt. The blouse was decorated at chest-level with a calico appliqué in the shape of a strawberry. She was a short woman, with small hands like paws, her frosty pink fingernails painted to match her lips, and was slightly plump in her figure. Her hair, shorn only a little longer than her husband's, was parted far to one side. She was wearing large dark brown sunglasses with a pinkish tint to them, and carried a big straw bag, almost as big as her torso, shaped like a bowl, with a water bottle poking out of it. She walked slowly, carrying some puffed rice tossed with peanuts and chili peppers in a large packet made from newspapers. Mr. Kapasi turned to Mr. Das.

15   "Where in America do you live?"

"New Brunswick, New Jersey."

"Next to New York?"

"Exactly. I teach middle school there."

"What subject?"

20   "Science. In fact, every year I take my students on a trip to the Museum of Natural History in New York City. In a way we have a lot in common, you could say, you and I. How long have you been a tour guide, Mr. Kapasi?"

"Five years."

Mrs. Das reached the car. "How long's the trip?" she asked, shutting the door.

"About two and a half hours," Mr. Kapasi replied.

At this Mrs. Das gave an impatient sigh, as if she had been traveling her whole life without pause. She fanned herself with a folded Bombay film magazine written in English.

25   "I thought that the Sun Temple is only eighteen miles north of Puri," Mr. Das said, tapping on the tour book.

"The roads to Konarak are poor. Actually it is a distance of fifty-two miles," Mr. Kapasi explained.

Mr. Das nodded, readjusting the camera strap where it had begun to chafe the back of his neck.

Before starting the ignition, Mr. Kapasi reached back to make sure the cranklike locks on the inside of each of the back doors were secured. As soon as the car began to move the little girl began to play with the lock on her side, clicking it with some effort forward and backward, but Mrs. Das said nothing to stop her. She sat a bit slouched at one end of the back seat, not offering her puffed rice to anyone. Ronny and Tina sat on either side of her, both snapping bright green gum.

"Look," Bobby said as the car began to gather speed. He pointed with his finger to the tall trees that lined the road. "Look."

"Monkeys!" Ronny shrieked. "Wow!"   30

They were seated in groups along the branches, with shining black faces, silver bodies, horizontal eyebrows, and crested heads. Their long gray tails dangled like a series of ropes among the leaves. A few scratched themselves with black leathery hands, or swung their feet, staring as the car passed.

"We call them the hanuman," Mr. Kapasi said. "They are quite common in the area."

As soon as he spoke, one of the monkeys leaped into the middle of the road, causing Mr. Kapasi to brake suddenly. Another bounced onto the hood of the car, then sprang away. Mr. Kapasi beeped his horn. The children began to get excited, sucking in their breath and covering their faces partly with their hands. They had never seen monkeys outside of a zoo, Mr. Das explained. He asked Mr. Kapasi to stop the car so that he could take a picture.

While Mr. Das adjusted his telephoto lens, Mrs. Das reached into her straw bag and pulled out a bottle of colorless nail polish, which she proceeded to stroke on the tip of her index finger.

The little girl stuck out a hand. "Mine too. Mommy, do mine too."   35

"Leave me alone," Mrs. Das said, blowing on her nail and turning her body slightly. "You're making me mess up."

The little girl occupied herself by buttoning and unbuttoning a pinafore on the doll's plastic body.

"All set," Mr. Das said, replacing the lens cap.

The car rattled considerably as it raced along the dusty road, causing them all to pop up from their seats every now and then, but Mrs. Das continued to polish her nails. Mr. Kapasi eased up on the accelerator, hoping to produce a smoother ride. When he reached for the gearshift the boy in front accommodated him by swinging his hairless knees out of the way. Mr. Kapasi noted that this boy was slightly paler than the other children. "Daddy, why is the driver sitting on the wrong side in this car, too?" the boy asked.

"They all do that here, dummy," Ronny said.   40

"Don't call your brother a dummy," Mr. Das said. He turned to Mr. Kapasi. "In America, you know . . . it confuses them."

"Oh yes, I am well aware," Mr. Kapasi said. As delicately as he could, he shifted gears again, accelerating as they approached a hill in the road. "I see it on *Dallas*, the steering wheels are on the left-hand side."

"What's *Dallas?*" Tina asked, banging her now naked doll on the seat behind Mr. Kapasi.

"It went off the air," Mr. Das explained. "It's a television show."[3]

45   They were all like siblings, Mr. Kapasi thought as they passed a row of date trees. Mr. and Mrs. Das behaved like an older brother and sister, not parents. It seemed that they were in charge of the children only for the day; it was hard to believe they were regularly responsible for anything other than themselves. Mr. Das tapped on his lens cap, and his tour book, dragging his thumbnail occasionally across the pages so that they made a scraping sound. Mrs. Das continued to polish her nails. She had still not removed her sunglasses. Every now and then Tina renewed her plea that she wanted her nails done, too, and so at one point Mrs. Das flicked a drop of polish on the little girl's finger before depositing the bottle back inside her straw bag.

"Isn't this an air-conditioned car?" she asked, still blowing on her hand. The window on Tina's side was broken and could not be rolled down.

"Quit complaining," Mr. Das said. "It isn't so hot."

"I told you to get a car with air-conditioning," Mrs. Das continued. "Why do you do this, Raj, just to save a few stupid rupees. What are you saving us, fifty cents?"

Their accents sounded just like the ones Mr. Kapasi heard on American television programs, though not like the ones on *Dallas*.

50   "Doesn't it get tiresome, Mr. Kapasi, showing people the same thing every day?" Mr. Das asked, rolling down his own window all the way. "Hey, do you mind stopping the car. I just want to get a shot of this guy."

Mr. Kapasi pulled over to the side of the road as Mr. Das took a picture of a barefoot man, his head wrapped in a dirty turban, seated on top of a cart of grain sacks pulled by a pair of bullocks. Both the man and the bullocks were emaciated. In the back seat Mrs. Das gazed out another window, at the sky, where nearly transparent clouds passed quickly in front of one another.

"I look forward to it, actually," Mr. Kapasi said as they continued on their way. "The Sun Temple is one of my favorite places. In that way it is a reward for me. I give tours on Fridays and Saturdays only. I have another job during the week."

"Oh? Where?" Mr. Das asked.

"I work in a doctor's office."

55   "You're a doctor?"

"I am not a doctor. I work with one. As an interpreter."

"What does a doctor need an interpreter for?"

"He has a number of Gujarati patients. My father was Gujarati, but many people do not speak Gujarati in this area,[4] including the doctor. And so the doctor asked me to work in his office, interpreting what the patients say."

"Interesting. I've never heard of anything like that," Mr. Das said.

60   Mr. Kapasi shrugged. "It is a job like any other."

---

3. Reruns of this American television show (1978–91), featuring the rich, dysfunctional Ewing family of Dallas, continue worldwide.   4. Gujarat is a northwestern region of India, on the Arabian Sea. Mr. Kapasi speaks several of India's disparate regional languages—those of Bengal and Orissa, near where he lives, and Gujarati, from the opposite coast—along with the more widespread Hindi and English.

"But so romantic," Mrs. Das said dreamily, breaking her extended silence. She lifted her pinkish brown sunglasses and arranged them on top of her head like a tiara. For the first time, her eyes met Mr. Kapasi's in the rearview mirror: pale, a bit small, their gaze fixed but drowsy.

Mr. Das craned to look at her. "What's so romantic about it?"

"I don't know. Something." She shrugged, knitting her brows together for an instant. "Would you like a piece of gum, Mr. Kapasi?" she asked brightly. She reached into her straw bag and handed him a small square wrapped in green-and-white-striped paper. As soon as Mr. Kapasi put the gum in his mouth a thick sweet liquid burst onto his tongue.

"Tell us more about your job, Mr. Kapasi," Mrs. Das said.

"What would you like to know, madame?"   65

"I don't know," she shrugged, munching on some puffed rice and licking the mustard oil from the corners of her mouth. "Tell us a typical situation." She settled back in her seat, her head tilted in a patch of sun, and closed her eyes. "I want to picture what happens."

"Very well. The other day a man came in with a pain in his throat."

"Did he smoke cigarettes?"

"No. It was very curious. He complained that he felt as if there were long pieces of straw stuck in his throat. When I told the doctor he was able to prescribe the proper medication."

"That's so neat."   70

"Yes," Mr. Kapasi agreed after some hesitation.

"So these patients are totally dependent on you," Mrs. Das said. She spoke slowly, as if she were thinking aloud. "In a way, more dependent on you than the doctor."

"How do you mean? How could it be?"

"Well, for example, you could tell the doctor that the pain felt like a burning, not straw. The patient would never know what you had told the doctor, and the doctor wouldn't know that you had told the wrong thing. It's a big responsibility."

"Yes, a big responsibility you have there, Mr. Kapasi," Mr. Das agreed.   75

Mr. Kapasi had never thought of his job in such complimentary terms. To him it was a thankless occupation. He found nothing noble in interpreting people's maladies, assiduously translating the symptoms of so many swollen bones, count-less cramps of bellies and bowels, spots on people's palms that changed color, shape, or size. The doctor, nearly half his age, had an affinity for bell-bottom trousers and made humorless jokes about the Congress party.[5] Together they worked in a stale little infirmary where Mr. Kapasi's smartly tailored clothes clung to him in the heat, in spite of the blackened blades of a ceiling fan churning over their heads.

5. The Indian National Congress party, founded in 1885, led the movement for independence from Britain (gained in 1947) through the successive leadership of Mohandas Gandhi and Jawaharlal Nehru. The party divided and subdivided, but a faction once led by Indira Gandhi dominated through the 1980s and much of the '90s, despite being constantly accused of corruption and of using violent tactics. The fiasco of Indian government would be a grim joke.

The job was a sign of his failings. In his youth he'd been a devoted scholar of foreign languages, the owner of an impressive collection of dictionaries. He had dreamed of being an interpreter for diplomats and dignitaries, resolving conflicts between people and nations, settling disputes of which he alone could understand both sides. He was a self-educated man. In a series of notebooks, in the evenings before his parents settled his marriage, he had listed the common etymologies of words, and at one point in his life he was confident that he could converse, if given the opportunity, in English, French, Russian, Portuguese, and Italian, not to mention Hindi, Bengali, Orissi, and Gujarati. Now only a handful of European phrases remained in his memory, scattered words for things like saucers and chairs. English was the only non-Indian language he spoke fluently anymore. Mr. Kapasi knew it was not a remarkable talent. Sometimes he feared that his children knew better English than he did, just from watching television. Still, it came in handy for the tours.

He had taken the job as an interpreter after his first son, at the age of seven, contracted typhoid—that was how he had first made the acquaintance of the doctor. At the time Mr. Kapasi had been teaching English in a grammar school, and he bartered his skills as an interpreter to pay the increasingly exorbitant medical bills. In the end the boy had died one evening in his mother's arms, his limbs burning with fever, but then there was the funeral to pay for, and the other children who were born soon enough, and the newer, bigger house, and the good schools and tutors, and the fine shoes and the television, and the countless other ways he tried to console his wife and to keep her from crying in her sleep, and so when the doctor offered to pay him twice as much as he earned at the grammar school, he accepted. Mr. Kapasi knew that his wife had little regard for his career as an interpreter. He knew it reminded her of the son she'd lost, and that she resented the other lives he helped, in his own small way, to save. If ever she referred to his position, she used the phrase "doctor's assistant," as if the process of interpretation were equal to taking someone's temperature, or changing a bedpan. She never asked him about the patients who came to the doctor's office, or said that his job was a big responsibility.

For this reason it flattered Mr. Kapasi that Mrs. Das was so intrigued by his job. Unlike his wife, she had reminded him of its intellectual challenges. She had also used the word "romantic." She did not behave in a romantic way toward her husband, and yet she had used the word to describe him. He wondered if Mr. and Mrs. Das were a bad match, just as he and his wife were. Perhaps they, too, had little in common apart from three children and a decade of their lives. The signs he recognized from his own marriage were there—the bickering, the indifference, the protracted silences. Her sudden interest in him, an interest she did not express in either her husband or her children, was mildly intoxicating. When Mr. Kapasi thought once again about how she had said "romantic," the feeling of intoxication grew.

80   He began to check his reflection in the rearview mirror as he drove, feeling grateful that he had chosen the gray suit that morning and not the brown one, which tended to sag a little in the knees. From time to time he glanced through the mirror at Mrs. Das. In addition to glancing at her face he glanced at the

strawberry between her breasts, and the golden brown hollow in her throat. He decided to tell Mrs. Das about another patient, and another: the young woman who had complained of a sensation of raindrops in her spine, the gentleman whose birthmark had begun to sprout hairs. Mrs. Das listened attentively, stroking her hair with a small plastic brush that resembled an oval bed of nails, asking more questions, for yet another example. The children were quiet, intent on spotting more monkeys in the trees, and Mr. Das was absorbed by his tour book, so it seemed like a private conversation between Mr. Kapasi and Mrs. Das. In this manner the next half hour passed, and when they stopped for lunch at a roadside restaurant that sold fritters and omelette sandwiches, usually something Mr. Kapasi looked forward to on his tours so that he could sit in peace and enjoy some hot tea, he was disappointed. As the Das family settled together under a magenta umbrella fringed with white and orange tassels, and placed their orders with one of the waiters who marched about in tricornered caps, Mr. Kapasi reluctantly headed toward a neighboring table.

"Mr. Kapasi, wait. There's room here," Mrs. Das called out. She gathered Tina onto her lap, insisting that he accompany them. And so, together, they had bottled mango juice and sandwiches and plates of onions and potatoes deep-fried in graham-flour batter. After finishing two omelette sandwiches Mr. Das took more pictures of the group as they ate.

"How much longer?" he asked Mr. Kapasi as he paused to load a new roll of film in the camera.

"About half an hour more."

By now the children had gotten up from the table to look at more monkeys perched in a nearby tree, so there was a considerable space between Mrs. Das and Mr. Kapasi. Mr. Das placed the camera to his face and squeezed one eye shut, his tongue exposed at one corner of his mouth. "This looks funny. Mina, you need to lean in closer to Mr. Kapasi."

She did. He could smell a scent on her skin, like a mixture of whiskey and rosewater. He worried suddenly that she could smell his perspiration, which he knew had collected beneath the synthetic material of his shirt. He polished off his mango juice in one gulp and smoothed his silver hair with his hands. A bit of the juice dripped onto his chin. He wondered if Mrs. Das had noticed.

She had not. "What's your address, Mr. Kapasi?" she inquired, fishing for something inside her straw bag.

"You would like my address?"

"So we can send you copies," she said. "Of the pictures." She handed him a scrap of paper which she had hastily ripped from a page of her film magazine. The blank portion was limited, for the narrow strip was crowded by lines of text and a tiny picture of a hero and heroine embracing under a eucalyptus tree.

The paper curled as Mr. Kapasi wrote his address in clear, careful letters. She would write to him, asking about his days interpreting at the doctor's office, and he would respond eloquently, choosing only the most entertaining anecdotes, ones that would make her laugh out loud as she read them in her house in New Jersey. In time she would reveal the disappointment of her marriage, and he his. In this way their friendship would grow, and flourish. He would possess a picture

of the two of them, eating fried onions under a magenta umbrella, which he
would keep, he decided, safely tucked between the pages of his Russian grammar.
As his mind raced, Mr. Kapasi experienced a mild and pleasant shock. It was
similar to a feeling he used to experience long ago when, after months of translating with the aid of a dictionary, he would finally read a passage from a French
novel, or an Italian sonnet, and understand the words, one after another, unencumbered by his own efforts. In those moments Mr. Kapasi used to believe that
all was right with the world, that all struggles were rewarded, that all of life's
mistakes made sense in the end. The promise that he would hear from Mrs. Das
now filled him with the same belief.

90   When he finished writing his address Mr. Kapasi handed her the paper, but as
soon as he did so he worried that he had either misspelled his name, or accidentally reversed the numbers of his postal code. He dreaded the possibility of a lost
letter, the photograph never reaching him, hovering somewhere in Orissa, close
but ultimately unattainable. He thought of asking for the slip of paper again, just
to make sure he had written his address accurately, but Mrs. Das had already
dropped it into the jumble of her bag.

They reached Konarak at two-thirty. The temple, made of sandstone, was a massive pyramid-like structure in the shape of a chariot. It was dedicated to the great
master of life, the sun, which struck three sides of the edifice as it made its journey
each day across the sky. Twenty-four giant wheels were carved on the north and
south sides of the plinth. The whole thing was drawn by a team of seven horses,
speeding as if through the heavens. As they approached, Mr. Kapasi explained
that the temple had been built between A.D. 1243 and 1255, with the efforts of
twelve hundred artisans, by the great ruler of the Ganga dynasty, King Narasim-
hadeva the First, to commemorate his victory against the Muslim army.

"It says the temple occupies about a hundred and seventy acres of land," Mr.
Das said, reading from his book.

"It's like a desert," Ronny said, his eyes wandering across the sand that
stretched on all sides beyond the temple.

"The Chandrabhaga River once flowed one mile north of here. It is dry now,"
Mr. Kapasi said, turning off the engine.

95   They got out and walked toward the temple, posing first for pictures by the
pair of lions that flanked the steps. Mr. Kapasi led them next to one of the wheels
of the chariot, higher than any human being, nine feet in diameter.

" 'The wheels are supposed to symbolize the wheel of life,' " Mr. Das read.
" 'They depict the cycle of creation, preservation, and achievement of realization.'
Cool." He turned the page of his book. " 'Each wheel is divided into eight thick
and thin spokes, dividing the day into eight equal parts. The rims are carved with
designs of birds and animals, whereas the medallions in the spokes are carved
with women in luxurious poses, largely erotic in nature.' "

What he referred to were the countless friezes of entwined naked bodies, making love in various positions, women clinging to the necks of men, their knees
wrapped eternally around their lovers' thighs. In addition to these were assorted
scenes from daily life, of hunting and trading, of deer being killed with bows and

arrows and marching warriors holding swords in their hands.

It was no longer possible to enter the temple, for it had filled with rubble years ago, but they admired the exterior, as did all the tourists Mr. Kapasi brought there, slowly strolling along each of its sides. Mr. Das trailed behind, taking pictures. The children ran ahead, pointing to figures of naked people, intrigued in particular by the Nagamithunas, the half-human, half-serpentine couples who were said, Mr. Kapasi told them, to live in the deepest waters of the sea. Mr. Kapasi was pleased that they liked the temple, pleased especially that it appealed to Mrs. Das. She stopped every three or four paces, staring silently at the carved lovers, and the processions of elephants, and the topless female musicians beating on two-sided drums.

Though Mr. Kapasi had been to the temple countless times, it occurred to him, as he, too, gazed at the topless women, that he had never seen his own wife fully naked. Even when they had made love she kept the panels of her blouse hooked together, the string of her petticoat knotted around her waist. He had never admired the backs of his wife's legs the way he now admired those of Mrs. Das, walking as if for his benefit alone. He had, of course, seen plenty of bare limbs before, belonging to the American and European ladies who took his tours. But Mrs. Das was different. Unlike the other women, who had an interest only in the temple, and kept their noses buried in a guidebook, on their eyes behind the lens of a camera, Mrs. Das had taken an interest in him.

Mr. Kapasi was anxious to be alone with her, to continue their private con- 100 versation, yet he felt nervous to walk at her side. She was lost behind her sunglasses, ignoring her husband's requests that she pose for another picture, walking past her children as if they were strangers. Worried that he might disturb her, Mr. Kapasi walked ahead, to admire, as he always did, the three life-sized bronze avatars of Surya, the sun god, each emerging from its own niche on the temple facade to greet the sun at dawn, noon, and evening. They wore elaborate headdresses, their languid, elongated eyes closed, their bare chests draped with carved chains and amulets. Hibiscus petals, offerings from previous visitors, were strewn at their gray-green feet. The last statue, on the northern wall of the temple, was Mr. Kapasi's favorite. This Surya had a tired expression, weary after a hard day of work, sitting astride a horse with folded legs. Even his horse's eyes were drowsy. Around his body were smaller sculptures of women in pairs, their hips thrust to one side.

"Who's that?" Mrs. Das asked. He was startled to see that she was standing beside him.

"He is the Astachala-Surya," Mr. Kapasi said. "The setting sun."

"So in a couple of hours the sun will set right here?" She slipped a foot out of one of her square-heeled shoes, rubbed her toes on the back of her other leg.

"That is correct."

She raised her sunglasses for a moment, then put them back on again. "Neat." 105

Mr. Kapasi was not certain exactly what the word suggested, but he had a feeling it was a favorable response. He hoped that Mrs. Das had understood Surya's beauty, his power. Perhaps they would discuss it further in their letters. He would explain things to her, things about India, and she would explain things to him about America. In its own way this correspondence would fulfill his dream, of serving as an interpreter between nations. He looked at her straw bag, delighted that his address lay nestled among its contents. When he pictured her so many thousands of miles away he plummeted, so much so that he had an overwhelming urge to wrap his arms around her, to freeze with her, even for an instant, in an embrace witnessed by his favorite Surya. But Mrs. Das had already started walking.

"When do you return to America?" he asked, trying to sound placid.

"In ten days."

He calculated: A week to settle in, a week to develop the pictures, a few days to compose her letter, two weeks to get to India by air. According to his schedule, allowing room for delays, he would hear from Mrs. Das in approximately six weeks' time.

110   The family was silent as Mr. Kapasi drove them back, a little past four-thirty, to Hotel Sandy Villa. The children had bought miniature granite versions of the chariot's wheels at a souvenir stand, and they turned them round in their hands. Mr. Das continued to read his book. Mrs. Das untangled Tina's hair with her brush and divided it into two little ponytails.

Mr. Kapasi was beginning to dread the thought of dropping them off. He was not prepared to begin his six-week wait to hear from Mrs. Das. As he stole glances at her in the rearview mirror, wrapping elastic bands around Tina's hair, he wondered how he might make the tour last a little longer. Ordinarily he sped back to Puri using a shortcut, eager to return home, scrub his feet and hands with sandalwood soap, and enjoy the evening newspaper and a cup of tea that his wife would serve him in silence. The thought of that silence, something to which he'd long been resigned, now oppressed him. It was then that he suggested visiting the hills at Udayagiri and Khandagiri, where a number of monastic dwellings were hewn out of the ground, facing one another across a defile. It was some miles away, but well worth seeing, Mr. Kapasi told them.

"Oh yeah, there's something mentioned about it in this book," Mr. Das said. "Built by a Jain king or something."[6]

"Shall we go then?" Mr. Kapasi asked. He paused at a turn in the road. "It's to the left."

Mr. Das turned to look at Mrs. Das. Both of them shrugged.

115   "Left, left," the children chanted.

Mr. Kapasi turned the wheel, almost delirious with relief. He did not know what he would do or say to Mrs. Das once they arrived at the hills. Perhaps he would tell her what a pleasing smile she had. Perhaps he would compliment her strawberry shirt, which he found irresistibly becoming. Perhaps, when Mr. Das was busy taking a picture, he would take her hand.

He did not have to worry. When they got to the hills, divided by a steep path thick with trees, Mrs. Das refused to get out of the car. All along the path, dozens of monkeys were seated on stones, as well as on the branches of the trees. Their

6. This site is not a major tourist attraction; "giri" means mountain. Jainism, one of the several main religions of India, is an atheist sect that emerged from Hinduism around 580 B.C., at about the same time as Buddhism.

hind legs were stretched out in front and raised to shoulder level, their arms resting on their knees.

"My legs are tired," she said, sinking low in her seat. "I'll stay here."

"Why did you have to wear those stupid shoes?" Mr. Das said. "You won't be in the pictures."

"Pretend I'm there."   120

"But we could use one of these pictures for our Christmas card this year. We didn't get one of all five of us at the Sun Temple. Mr. Kapasi could take it."

"I'm not coming. Anyway, those monkeys give me the creeps."

"But they're harmless," Mr. Das said. He turned to Mr. Kapasi. "Aren't they?"

"They are more hungry than dangerous," Mr. Kapasi said. "Do not provoke them with food, and they will not bother you."

Mr. Das headed up the defile with the children, the boys at his side, the little   125 girl on his shoulders. Mr. Kapasi watched as they crossed paths with a Japanese man and woman, the only other tourists there, who paused for a final photograph, then stepped into a nearby car and drove away. As the car disappeared out of view some of the monkeys called out, emitting soft whooping sounds, and then walked on their flat black hands and feet up the path. At one point a group of them formed a little ring around Mr. Das and the children. Tina screamed in delight. Ronny ran in circles around his father. Bobby bent down and picked up a fat stick on the ground. When he extended it, one of the monkeys approached him and snatched it, then briefly beat the ground.

"I'll join them," Mr. Kapasi said, unlocking the door on his side. "There is much to explain about the caves."

"No. Stay a minute," Mrs. Das said. She got out of the back seat and slipped in beside Mr. Kapasi. "Raj has his dumb book anyway." Together, through the windshield, Mrs. Das and Mr. Kapasi watched as Bobby and the monkey passed the stick back and forth between them.

"A brave little boy," Mr. Kapasi commented.

"It's not so surprising," Mrs. Das said.

"No?"   130

"He's not his."

"I beg your pardon?"

"Raj's. He's not Raj's son."

Mr. Kapasi felt a prickle on his skin. He reached into his shirt pocket for the small tin of lotus-oil balm he carried with him at all times, and applied it to three spots on his forehead. He knew that Mrs. Das was watching him, but he did not turn to face her. Instead he watched as the figures of Mr. Das and the children grew smaller, climbing up the steep path, pausing every now and then for a picture, surrounded by a growing number of monkeys.

"Are you surprised?" The way she put it made him choose his words with care.   135

"It's not the type of thing one assumes," Mr. Kapasi replied slowly. He put the tin of lotus-oil balm back in his pocket.

"No, of course not. And no one knows, of course. No one at all. I've kept it a secret for eight whole years." She looked at Mr. Kapasi, tilting her chin as if to gain a fresh perspective. "But now I've told you."

Mr. Kapasi nodded. He felt suddenly parched, and his forehead was warm and slightly numb from the balm. He considered asking Mrs. Das for a sip of water, then decided against it.

"We met when we were very young," she said. She reached into her straw bag in search of something, then pulled out a packet of puffed rice. "Want some?"

"No, thank you."

She put a fistful in her mouth, sank into the seat a little, and looked away from Mr. Kapasi, out the window on her side of the car. "We married when we were still in college. We were in high school when he proposed. We went to the same college, of course. Back then we couldn't stand the thought of being separated, not for a day, not for a minute. Our parents were best friends who lived in the same town. My entire life I saw him every weekend, either at our house or theirs. We were sent upstairs to play together while our parents joked about our marriage. Imagine! They never caught us at anything, though in a way I think it was all more or less a setup. The things we did those Friday and Saturday nights, while our parents sat downstairs drinking tea . . . I could tell you stories, Mr. Kapasi."

As a result of spending all her time in college with Raj, she continued, she did not make many close friends. There was no one to confide in about him at the end of a difficult day, or to share a passing thought or a worry. Her parents now lived on the other side of the world, but she had never been very close to them, anyway. After marrying so young she was overwhelmed by it all, having a child so quickly, and nursing, and warming up bottles of milk and testing their temperature against her wrist while Raj was at work, dressed in sweaters and corduroy pants, teaching his students about rocks and dinosaurs. Raj never looked cross or harried, or plump as she had become after the first baby.

Always tired, she declined invitations from her one or two college girlfriends, to have lunch or shop in Manhattan. Eventually the friends stopped calling her, so that she was left at home all day with the baby, surrounded by toys that made her trip when she walked or wince when she sat, always cross and tired. Only occasionally did they go out after Ronny was born, and even more rarely did they entertain. Raj didn't mind; he looked forward to coming home from teaching and watching television and bouncing Ronny on his knee. She had been outraged when Raj told her that a Punjabi friend,[7] someone whom she had once met but did not remember, would be staying with them for a week for some job interviews in the New Brunswick area.

Bobby was conceived in the afternoon, on a sofa littered with rubber teething toys, after the friend learned that a London pharmaceutical company had hired him, while Ronny cried to be freed from his playpen. She made no protest when the friend touched the small of her back as she was about to make a pot of coffee, then pulled her against his crisp navy suit. He made love to her swiftly, in silence, with an expertise she had never known, without the meaningful expressions and smiles Raj always insisted on afterward. The next day Raj drove the friend to JFK.[8] He was married now, to a Punjabi girl, and they lived in London still, and every

---

7. A person from the Punjab, a northern region of India, near Pakistan.   8. John F. Kennedy International Airport, in New York City.

year they exchanged Christmas cards with Raj and Mina, each couple tucking photos of their families into the envelopes. He did not know that he was Bobby's father. He never would.

"I beg your pardon, Mrs. Das, but why have you told me this information?" 145 Mr. Kapasi asked when she had finally finished speaking, and had turned to face him once again.

"For God's sake, stop calling me Mrs. Das. I'm twenty-eight. You probably have children my age."

"Not quite." It disturbed Mr. Kapasi to learn that she thought of him as a parent. The feeling he had had toward her, that had made him check his reflection in the rearview mirror as they drove, evaporated a little.

"I told you because of your talents." She put the packet of puffed rice back into her bag without folding over the top.

"I don't understand," Mr. Kapasi said.

"Don't you see? For eight years I haven't been able to express this to anybody, 150 not to friends, certainly not to Raj. He doesn't even suspect it. He thinks I'm still in love with him. Well, don't you have anything to say?"

"About what?"

"About what I've just told you. About my secret, and about how terrible it makes me feel. I feel terrible looking at my children, and at Raj, always terrible. I have terrible urges, Mr. Kapasi, to throw things away. One day I had the urge to throw everything I own out of the window, the television, the children, everything. Don't you think it's unhealthy?"

He was silent.

"Mr. Kapasi, don't you have anything to say? I thought that was your job."

"My job is to give tours, Mrs. Das." 155

"Not that. Your other job. As an interpreter."

"But we do not face a language barrier. What need is there for an interpreter?"

"That's not what I mean. I would never have told you otherwise. Don't you realize what it means for me to tell you?"

"What does it mean?"

"It means that I'm tired of feeling so terrible all the time. Eight years, Mr. 160 Kapasi, I've been in pain eight years. I was hoping you could help me feel better, say the right thing. Suggest some kind of remedy."

He looked at her, in her red plaid skirt and strawberry T-shirt, a woman not yet thirty, who loved neither her husband nor her children, who had already fallen out of love with life. Her confession depressed him, depressed him all the more when he thought of Mr. Das at the top of the path, Tina clinging to his shoulders, taking pictures of ancient monastic cells cut into the hills to show his students in America, unsuspecting and unaware that one of his sons was not his own. Mr. Kapasi felt insulted that Mrs. Das should ask him to interpret her common, trivial little secret. She did not resemble the patients in the doctor's office, those who came glassy-eyed and desperate, unable to sleep or breathe or urinate with ease, unable, above all, to give words to their pains. Still, Mr. Kapasi believed it was his duty to assist Mrs. Das. Perhaps he ought to tell her to confess the truth to Mr. Das. He would explain that honesty was the best policy. Honesty, surely, would help her feel better, as she'd put it. Perhaps he would offer to preside over the discussion, as a mediator. He decided to begin with the most obvious question, to get to the heart of the matter, and so he asked, "Is it really pain you feel, Mrs. Das, or is it guilt?"

She turned to him and glared, mustard oil thick on her frosty pink lips. She opened her mouth to say something, but as she glared at Mr. Kapasi some certain knowledge seemed to pass before her eyes, and she stopped. It crushed him; he knew at that moment that he was not even important enough to be properly insulted. She opened the car door and began walking up the path, wobbling a little on her square wooden heels, reaching into her straw bag to eat handfuls of puffed rice. It fell through her fingers, leaving a zigzagging trail, causing a monkey to leap down from a tree and devour the little white grains. In search of more, the monkey began to follow Mrs. Das. Others joined him, so that she was soon being followed by about half a dozen of them, their velvety tails dragging behind.

Mr. Kapasi stepped out of the car. He wanted to holler, to alert her in some way, but he worried that if she knew they were behind her, she would grow nervous. Perhaps she would lose her balance. Perhaps they would pull at her bag or her hair. He began to jog up the path, taking a fallen branch in his hand to scare away the monkeys. Mrs. Das continued walking, oblivious, trailing grains of puffed rice. Near the top of the incline, before a group of cells fronted by a row of squat stone pillars, Mr. Das was kneeling on the ground, focusing the lens of his camera. The children stood under the arcade, now hiding, now emerging from view.

"Wait for me," Mrs. Das called out. "I'm coming."

165   Tina jumped up and down. "Here comes Mommy!"

"Great," Mr. Das said without looking up. "Just in time. We'll get Mr. Kapasi to take a picture of the five of us."

Mr. Kapasi quickened his pace, waving his branch so that the monkeys scampered away, distracted, in another direction.

"Where's Bobby?" Mrs. Das asked when she stopped.

Mr. Das looked up from the camera. "I don't know. Ronny, where's Bobby?"

170   Ronny shrugged. "I thought he was right here."

"Where is he?" Mrs. Das repeated sharply. "What's wrong with all of you?"

They began calling his name, wandering up and down the path a bit. Because they were calling, they did not initially hear the boy's screams. When they found him, a little farther down the path under a tree, he was surrounded by a group of monkeys, over a dozen of them, pulling at his T-shirt with their long black fingers. The puffed rice Mrs. Das had spilled was scattered at his feet, raked over by the monkeys' hands. The boy was silent, his body frozen, swift tears running down his startled face. His bare legs were dusty and red with welts from where one of the monkeys struck him repeatedly with the stick he had given to it earlier.

"Daddy, the monkey's hurting Bobby," Tina said.

Mr. Das wiped his palms on the front of his shorts. In his nervousness he accidentally pressed the shutter on his camera; the whirring noise of the advancing film excited the monkeys, and the one with the stick began to beat Bobby more intently. "What are we supposed to do? What if they start attacking?"

"Mr. Kapasi," Mrs. Das shrieked, noticing him standing to one side. "Do some- 175 thing, for God's sake, do something!"

Mr. Kapasi took his branch and shooed them away, hissing at the ones that remained, stomping his feet to scare them. The animals retreated slowly, with a measured gait, obedient but unintimidated. Mr. Kapasi gathered Bobby in his arms and brought him back to where his parents and siblings were standing. As he carried him he was tempted to whisper a secret into the boy's ear. But Bobby was stunned, and shivering with fright, his legs bleeding slightly where the stick had broken the skin. When Mr. Kapasi delivered him to his parents, Mr. Das brushed some dirt off the boy's T-shirt and put the visor on him the right way. Mrs. Das reached into her straw bag to find a bandage which she taped over the cut on his knee. Ronny offered his brother a fresh piece of gum. "He's fine. Just a little scared, right, Bobby?" Mr. Das said, patting the top of his head.

"God, let's get out of here," Mrs. Das said. She folded her arms across the strawberry on her chest. "This place gives me the creeps."

"Yeah. Back to the hotel, definitely," Mr. Das agreed.

"Poor Bobby," Mrs. Das said. "Come here a second. Let Mommy fix your hair." Again she reached into her straw bag, this time for her hairbrush, and began to run it around the edges of the translucent visor. When she whipped out the hairbrush, the slip of paper with Mr. Kapasi's address on it fluttered away in the wind. No one but Mr. Kapasi noticed. He watched as it rose, carried higher and higher by the breeze, into the trees where the monkeys now sat, solemnly observing the scene below. Mr. Kapasi observed it too, knowing that this was the picture of the Das family he would preserve forever in his mind.

1999

QUESTIONS

1. Imagine a Japanese person reading "A Souvenir of Japan" (in English or translated), or a Sikh in India reading "The Management of Grief" (in English or translated). How might this person's response differ from that of a reader who shares the narrator's nationality, English or Indo-Canadian?
2. "A Souvenir of Japan" is at once a love story, an analysis of Japanese culture as seen by an outsider, and a questioning of the nature of feelings and perception—are they "real" or constructed? The third sentence of the story sets up its subtleties, twists, paradoxes: "[The children's] pleasure was very pure because it was so restrained." Go through the story and find several instances of such arresting, puzzling statements. How does paragraph 18, in which the narrator analyzes how she is telling the story, relate to the theme? How do the fireworks of the first paragraph relate to the theme?
3. The tour in "Interpreter of Maladies" makes two stops at significant sites: the original destination, the Sun Temple, and a detour to the hills at Udayagiri and Khandagiri. In what ways do these different settings and experiences contribute to the theme or themes of the story? How do the specific details of the design of the Sun Temple relate to the secret that Mrs. Das confesses to Mr. Kapasi? Look closely at what happens after Mr. Kapasi uses the word "guilt," and note exactly what each adult does to make the encounter with the monkeys better or worse. How do these actions relate to the idea of guilt? to the theme of cultural difference? Why is it significant that Mr. Das kneels before a "group of cells" for a religious community? Does Mr. Kapasi learn anything from the Das family's American values?

4. The characters in "Interpreter of Maladies" seem to change back and forth from young to old, in their own or in each other's views. Find all the moments when the question of age comes up: why is it an issue in each instance? Do older or younger people, whether male or female, have more attractiveness, status, power? Can you explain how the question of youth or maturity connects with the cultural theme of the story?

WRITING SUGGESTIONS

1. Rewrite the first seven paragraphs of "A Souvenir of Japan," using another focus and voice.
2. The narrator in "The Management of Grief" says, "Acceptance means you speak of your family in the past tense and you make active plans for moving ahead with your life" (paragraph 103). Write a short essay focusing on this statement as a key to the theme of the story. Is this the narrator's own view, or is she paraphrasing the advice of Judith Templeton, the government appointee for "multiculturalism" and social services? Does the story suggest it is possible to accept the death of children and spouse?
3. Write a narrative or an essay on one of the provocative phrases or sentences in "A Souvenir of Japan," such as "He . . . had the inhuman sweetness of a child born from something other than a mother, a passive, cruel sweetness I did not immediately understand, for it was that of the repressed masochism which, in my country, is usually confined to women" (paragraph 11); "how far does a pretense of feeling, maintained with absolute conviction, become authentic?" (paragraph 20); "soon we would learn to treat one another with the circumspect tenderness of comrades who are amputees" (paragraph 23).

7

THE WHOLE TEXT

Plot, point of view, character, setting, symbol, and theme are useful concepts. But they do not really exist as discrete parts in a finished work. Analyzing a story means thinking about issues smaller than the whole story—asking questions about some particulars before trying to consider the story as a whole. Analyzing may be enhanced by talking or writing about a story in terms of its "elements," but we must remain aware of the arbitrariness of those distinctions and of the integrity of the story as a whole. As you read the stories that follow in this chapter, apply all that you have learned about the history, the structure, and the elements of fiction, but be especially alert as to how the elements interact. Notice how, after taking it apart in order to analyze it, we can put the story back together.

Discussing story-writing in terms of plot, character, and theme is like trying to describe the expression on a face by saying where the eyes, nose, and mouth are.

—FLANNERY O'CONNOR

JOSEPH CONRAD

The Secret Sharer

I

On my right hand there were lines of fishing-stakes resembling a mysterious system of half-submerged bamboo fences, incomprehensible in its division of the domain of tropical fishes, and crazy[1] of aspect as if abandoned for ever by some nomad tribe of fishermen now gone to the other end of the ocean; for there was no sign of human habitation as far as the eye could reach. To the left a group of barren islets, suggesting ruins of stone walls, towers, and blockhouses, had its

1. Irregular, rickety.

foundations set in a blue sea that itself looked solid, so still and stable did it lie below my feet; even the track of light from the westering sun shone smoothly, without that animated glitter which tells of an imperceptible ripple. And when I turned my head to take a parting glance at the tug which had just left us anchored outside the bar, I saw the straight line of the flat shore joined to the stable sea, edge to edge, with a perfect and unmarked closeness, in one leveled floor half brown, half blue under the enormous dome of the sky. Corresponding in their insignificance to the islets of the sea, two small clumps of trees, one on each side of the only fault in the impeccable joint, marked the mouth of the river Meinam[2] we had just left on the first preparatory stage of our homeward journey; and, far back on the inland level, a larger and loftier mass, the grove surrounding the great Paknam pagoda, was the only thing on which the eye could rest from the vain task of exploring the monotonous sweep of the horizon. Here and there gleams as of a few scattered pieces of silver marked the windings of the great river; and on the nearest of them, just within the bar, the tug steaming right into the land became lost to my sight, hull and funnel and masts, as though the impassive earth had swallowed her up without an effort, without a tremor. My eye followed the light cloud of her smoke, now here, now there, above the plain, according to the devious curves of the stream, but always fainter and farther away, till I lost it at last behind the mitre-shaped hill of the great pagoda. And then I was left alone with my ship, anchored at the head of the Gulf of Siam.

She floated at the starting-point of a long journey, very still in an immense stillness, the shadows of her spars flung far to the eastward by the setting sun. At that moment I was alone on her decks. There was not a sound in her—and around us nothing moved, nothing lived, not a canoe on the water, not a bird in the air, not a cloud in the sky. In this breathless pause at the threshold of a long passage we seemed to be measuring our fitness for a long and arduous enterprise, the appointed task of both our existences to be carried out, far from all human eyes, with only sky and sea for spectators and for judges.

There must have been some glare in the air to interfere with one's sight, because it was only just before the sun left us that my roaming eyes made out beyond the highest ridge of the principal islet of the group something which did away with the solemnity of perfect solitude. The tide of darkness flowed on swiftly; and with tropical suddenness a swarm of stars came out above the shadowy earth, while I lingered yet, my hand resting lightly on my ship's rail as if on the shoulder of a trusted friend. But, with all that multitude of celestial bodies staring down at one, the comfort of quiet communion with her was gone for good. And there were also disturbing sounds by this time—voices, footsteps forward; the steward flitted along the main deck, a busily ministering spirit; a handbell tinkled urgently under the poop deck. . . .

I found my two officers waiting for me near the supper table, in the lighted cuddy. We sat down at once, and as I helped the chief mate, I said:

2. The Menan (Chao Phraya) runs through Bangkok, Thailand, into the Gulf of Siam. The Paknam Pagoda stands at the mouth of the river.

"Are you aware that there is a ship anchored inside the islands? I saw her mast-   5
heads above the ridge as the sun went down."

He raised sharply his simple face, overcharged by a terrible growth of whisker,
and emitted his usual ejaculations, "Bless my soul, sir! You don't say so!"

My second mate was a round-cheeked, silent young man, grave beyond his
years, I thought; but as our eyes happened to meet I detected a slight quiver on
his lips. I looked down at once. It was not my part to encourage sneering on board
my ship. It must be said, too, that I knew very little of my officers. In consequence
of certain events of no particular significance, except to myself, I had been
appointed to the command only a fortnight before. Neither did I know much of
the hands forward. All these people had been together for eighteen months or so,
and my position was that of the only stranger on board. I mention this because
it has some bearing on what is to follow. But what I felt most was my being a
stranger to the ship; and if all the truth must be told, I was somewhat of a stranger
to myself. The youngest man on board (barring the second mate), and untried as
yet by a position of the fullest responsibility, I was willing to take the adequacy
of the others for granted. They had simply to be equal to their tasks; but I wondered how far I should turn out faithful to that ideal conception of one's own
personality every man sets up for himself secretly.

Meantime the chief mate, with an almost visible effect of collaboration on the
part of his round eyes and frightful whiskers, was trying to evolve a theory of the
anchored ship. His dominant trait was to take all things into earnest consideration. He was of a painstaking turn of mind. As he used to say, he "liked to account
to himself" for practically everything that came in his way, down to a miserable
scorpion he had found in his cabin a week before. The why and the wherefore of
that scorpion—how it got on board and came to select his room rather than the
pantry (which was a dark place and more what a scorpion would be partial to),
and how on earth it managed to drown itself in the inkwell of his writing-desk—
had exercised him infinitely. The ship within the islands was much more easily
accounted for; and just as we were about to rise from table he made his pronouncement. She was, he doubted not, a ship from home lately arrived. Probably
she drew too much water to cross the bar except at the top of spring tides.
Therefore she went into that natural harbor to wait for a few days in preference
to remaining in an open roadstead.

"That's so," confirmed the second mate suddenly, in his slightly hoarse voice.
"She draws over twenty feet. She's the Liverpool ship *Sephora* with a cargo of coal.
Hundred and twenty-three days from Cardiff."

We looked at him in surprise.   10

"The tugboat skipper told me when he come on board for your letters, sir,"
explained the young man. "He expects to take her up the river the day after
tomorrow."

After thus overwhelming us with the extent of his information he slipped out
of the cabin. The mate observed regretfully that he "could not account for that
young fellow's whims." What prevented him telling us all about it at once, he
wanted to know.

I detained him as he was making a move. For the last two days the crew had

had plenty of hard work, and the night before they had very little sleep. I felt painfully that I—a stranger—was doing something unusual when I directed him to let all hands turn in without setting an anchor-watch.[3] I proposed to keep on deck myself till one o'clock or thereabouts. I would get the second mate to relieve me at that hour.

"He will turn out the cook and the steward at four," I concluded, "and then give you a call. Of course at the slightest sign of any sort of wind we'll have the hands up and make a start at once."

15   He concealed his astonishment. "Very well, sir." Outside the cuddy he put his head in the second mate's door to inform him of my unheard-of caprice to take a five hours' anchor-watch on myself. I heard the other raise his voice incredulously—"What? The captain himself?" Then a few more murmurs, a door closed, then another. A few moments later I went on deck.

My strangeness, which had made me sleepless, had prompted that unconventional arrangement, as if I had expected in those solitary hours of the night to get on terms with the ship of which I knew nothing, manned by men of whom I knew very little more. Fast alongside a wharf, littered like any ship in port with a tangle of unrelated things, invaded by unrelated shore people, I had hardly seen her yet properly. Now, as she lay cleared for sea, the stretch of her main deck seemed to me very fine under the stars. Very fine, very roomy for her size, and very inviting. I descended the poop and paced the waist, my mind picturing to myself the coming passage through the Malay Archipelago, down the Indian Ocean, and up the Atlantic. All its phases were familiar enough to me, every characteristic, all the alternatives which were likely to face me on the high seas— everything! . . . except the novel responsibility of command. But I took heart from the reasonable thought that the ship was like other ships, the men like other men, and that the sea was not likely to keep any special surprises expressly for my discomfiture.

Arrived at that comforting conclusion, I bethought myself of a cigar and went below to get it. All was still down there. Everybody at the after end of the ship was sleeping profoundly. I came out again on the quarter-deck, agreeably at ease in my sleeping suit on that warm, breathless night, barefooted, a glowing cigar in my teeth, and, going forward, I was met by the profound silence of the fore end of the ship. Only as I passed the door of the forecastle I heard a deep, quiet, trustful sigh of some sleeper inside. And suddenly I rejoiced in the great security of the sea as compared with the unrest of the land, in my choice of that untempted life presenting no disquieting problems, invested with an elementary moral beauty by the absolute straightforwardness of its appeal and by the singleness of its purpose.

The riding-light[4] in the fore-rigging burned with a clear, untroubled, as if symbolic, flame, confident and bright in the mysterious shades of the night. Passing on my way aft along the other side of the ship, I observed that the rope side-ladder, put over, no doubt, for the master of the tug when he came to fetch away

3. A detachment of seamen kept on deck while the ship lies at anchor.   4. Special light displayed by a ship while ("riding") at anchor.

our letters, had not been hauled in as it should have been. I became annoyed at this, for exactitude in small matters is the very soul of discipline. Then I reflected that I had myself peremptorily dismissed my officers from duty, and by my own act had prevented the anchor-watch being formally set and things properly attended to. I asked myself whether it was wise ever to interfere with the established routine of duties even from the kindest of motives. My action might have made me appear eccentric. Goodness only knew how that absurdly whiskered mate would "account" for my conduct, and what the whole ship thought of that informality of their new captain. I was vexed with myself.

Not from compunction certainly, but, as it were mechanically, I proceeded to get the ladder in myself. Now a side-ladder of that sort is a light affair and comes in easily, yet my vigorous tug, which should have brought it flying on board, merely recoiled upon my body in a totally unexpected jerk. What the devil! . . . I was so astounded by the immovableness of that ladder that I remained stockstill, trying to account for it to myself like that imbecile mate of mine. In the end, of course, I put my head over the rail.

The side of the ship made an opaque belt of shadow on the darkling glassy shimmer of the sea. But I saw at once something elongated and pale floating very close to the ladder. Before I could form a guess a faint flash of phosphorescent light, which seemed to issue suddenly from the naked body of a man, flickered in the sleeping water with the elusive, silent play of summer lightning in a night sky. With a gasp I saw revealed to my stare a pair of feet, the long legs, a broad livid back immersed right up to the neck in a greenish cadaverous glow. One hand, awash, clutched the bottom rung of the ladder. He was complete but for the head. A headless corpse! The cigar dropped out of my gaping mouth with a tiny plop and a short hiss quite audible in the absolute stillness of all things under heaven. At that I suppose he raised up his face, a dimly pale oval in the shadow of the ship's side. But even then I could only barely make out down there the shape of his black-haired head. However, it was enough for the horrid, frost-bound sensation which had gripped me about the chest to pass off. The moment of vain exclamations was past too. I only climbed on the spare spar and leaned over the rail as far as I could, to bring my eyes nearer to that mystery floating alongside.

As he hung by the ladder, like a resting swimmer, the sea-lightning played about his limbs at every stir; and he appeared in it ghastly, silvery, fish-like. He remained as mute as a fish, too. He made no motion to get out of the water, either. It was inconceivable that he should not attempt to come on board, and strangely troubling to suspect that perhaps he did not want to. And my first words were prompted by just that troubled incertitude.

"What's the matter?" I asked in my ordinary tone, speaking down to the face upturned exactly under mine.

"Cramp," it answered, no louder. Then slightly anxious, "I say, no need to call any one."

"I was not going to," I said.

"Are you alone on deck?"

"Yes."

20

25

I had somehow the impression that he was on the point of letting go the ladder to swim away beyond my ken—mysterious as he came. But, for the moment, this being appearing as if he had risen from the bottom of the sea (it was certainly the nearest land to the ship) wanted only to know the time. I told him. And he, down there, tentatively:

"I suppose your captain's turned in?"

"I am sure he isn't," I said.

30   He seemed to struggle with himself, for I heard something like the low, bitter murmur of doubt. "What's the good?" His next words came out with a hesitating effort.

"Look here, my man. Could you call him out quietly?"

I thought the time had come to declare myself.

"*I* am the captain."

I heard a "By Jove!" whispered at the level of the water. The phosphorescence flashed in the swirl of the water all about his limbs, his other hand seized the ladder.

35   "My name's Leggatt."

The voice was calm and resolute. A good voice. The self-possession of that man had somehow induced a corresponding state in myself. It was very quietly that I remarked:

"You must be a good swimmer."

"Yes. I've been in the water practically since nine o'clock. The question for me now is whether I am to let go this ladder and go on swimming till I sink from exhaustion or—to come on board here."

I felt this was no mere formula of desperate speech, but a real alternative in the view of a strong soul. I should have gathered from this that he was young; indeed, it is only the young who are ever confronted by such clear issues. But at the time it was pure intuition on my part. A mysterious communication was established already between us two—in the face of that silent, darkened tropical sea. I was young, too; young enough to make no comment. The man in the water began suddenly to climb up the ladder, and I hastened away from the rail to fetch some clothes.

40   Before entering the cabin I stood still, listening in the lobby at the foot of the stairs. A faint snore came through the closed door of the chief mate's room. The second mate's door was on the hook, but the darkness in there was absolutely soundless. He, too, was young and could sleep like a stone. Remained the steward, but he was not likely to wake up before he was called. I got a sleeping suit out of my room, and, coming back on deck, saw the naked man from the sea sitting on the main-hatch, glimmering white in the darkness, his elbows on his knees and his head in his hands. In a moment he had concealed his damp body in a sleeping suit of the same gray-stripe pattern as the one I was wearing, and followed me like my double on the poop. Together we moved right aft, barefooted, silent.

"What is it?" I asked in a deadened voice, taking the lighted lamp out of the binnacle, and raising it to his face.

"An ugly business."

He had rather regular features; a good mouth; light eyes under somewhat heavy, dark eyebrows; a smooth, square forehead; no growth on his cheeks; a small, brown mustache, and a well-shaped, round chin. His expression was concentrated, meditative, under the inspecting light of the lamp I held up to his face; such as a man thinking hard in solitude might wear. My sleeping suit was just right for his size. A well-knit young fellow of twenty-five at most. He caught his lower lip with the edge of white, even teeth.

"Yes," I said, replacing the lamp in the binnacle. The warm, heavy tropical night closed upon his head again.

"There's a ship over there," he murmured. 45

"Yes, I know. The *Sephora*. Did you know of us?"

"Hadn't the slightest idea. I am the mate of her—" He paused and corrected himself. "I should say I *was*."

"Aha! Something wrong?"

"Yes. Very wrong indeed. I've killed a man."

"What do you mean? Just now?" 50

"No, on the passage. Weeks ago. Thirty-nine south. When I say a man—"

"Fit of temper," I suggested confidently.

The shadowy, dark head, like mine, seemed to nod imperceptibly above the ghostly gray of my sleeping suit. It was, in the night, as though I had been faced by my own reflection in the depths of a sombre and immense mirror.

"A pretty thing to have to own up to for a Conway[5] boy," murmured my double distinctly.

"You're a Conway boy?" 55

"I am," he said, as if startled. Then, slowly . . . "Perhaps you too . . ."

It was so; but being a couple of years older I had left before he joined. After a quick interchange of dates a silence fell; and I thought suddenly of my absurd mate with his terrific whiskers and the "Bless my soul—you don't say so" type of intellect. My double gave me an inkling of his thoughts by saying:

"My father's a parson in Norfolk. Do you see me before a judge and jury on that charge? For myself I can't see the necessity. There are fellows that an angel from heaven—And I am not that. He was one of those creatures that are just simmering all the time with a silly sort of wickedness. Miserable devils that have no business to live at all. He wouldn't do his duty and wouldn't let anybody else do theirs. But what's the good of talking! You know well enough the sort of ill-conditioned snarling cur . . ."

He appealed to me as if our experiences had been as identical as our clothes. And I knew well enough the pestiferous danger of such a character where there are no means of legal repression. And I knew well enough also that my double there was no homicidal ruffian. I did not think of asking him for details, and he told me the story roughly in brusque, disconnected sentences. I needed no more. I saw it all going on as though I were myself inside that other sleeping suit.

"It happened while we were setting a reefed foresail, at dusk. Reefed foresail! 60

5. The wooden battleship *Conway* was used to train young officers for the Royal Navy and merchant service.

You understand the sort of weather. The only sail we had left to keep the ship running; so you may guess what it had been like for days. Anxious sort of job, that. He gave me some of his cursed insolence at the sheet.[6] I tell you I was overdone with this terrific weather that seemed to have no end to it. Terrific, I tell you—and a deep ship. I believe the fellow himself was half crazed with funk. It was no time for gentlemanly reproof, so I turned round and felled him like an ox. He up and at me. We closed just as an awful sea made for the ship. All hands saw it coming and took to the rigging, but I had him by the throat, and went on shaking him like a rat, the men above us yelling. 'Look out! Look out!' Then a crash as if the sky had fallen on my head. They say that for over ten minutes hardly anything was to be seen of the ship—just the three masts and a bit of the forecastle head and of the poop all awash driving along in a smother of foam. It was a miracle that they found us, jammed together behind the forebits. It's clear that I meant business, because I was holding him by the throat still when they picked us up. He was black in the face. It was too much for them. It seems they rushed us aft together, gripped as we were, screaming 'Murder!' like a lot of luna-tics, and broke into the cuddy. And the ship running for her life, touch and go all the time, any minute her last in a sea fit to turn your hair gray only a-looking at it. I understand that the skipper, too, started raving like the rest of them. The man had been deprived of sleep for more than a week, and to have this spring on him at the height of a furious gale nearly drove him out of his mind. I wonder they didn't fling me overboard after getting the carcass of their precious shipmate out of my fingers. They had rather a job to separate us, I've been told. A sufficiently fierce story to make an old judge and a respectable jury sit up a bit. The first thing I heard when I came to myself was the maddening howling of that endless gale, and on that the voice of the old man. He was hanging on to my bunk, staring into my face out of his sou'wester.

" 'Mr. Leggatt, you have killed a man. You can act no longer as chief mate of this ship.' "

His care to subdue his voice made it sound monotonous. He rested a hand on the end of the skylight to steady himself with, and all that time did not stir a limb, so far as I could see. "Nice little tale for a quiet tea party," he concluded in the same tone.

One of my hands, too, rested on the end of the skylight; neither did I stir a limb, so far as I knew. We stood less than a foot from each other. It occurred to me that if old "Bless my soul—you don't say so" were to put his head up the companion and catch sight of us, he would think he was seeing double, or imag-ine himself come upon a scene of weird witchcraft: the strange captain having a quiet confabulation by the wheel with his own gray ghost. I became very much concerned to prevent anything of the sort. I heard the other's soothing undertone:

"My father's a parson in Norfolk," it said. Evidently he had forgotten he had told me this important fact before. Truly a nice little tale.

"You had better slip down into my stateroom now," I said, moving off stealth-

65

---

6. Rope or chain attached to the lower corner of a sail used for shortening or slackening it.

ily. My double followed my movements; our bare feet made no sound; I let him in, closed the door with care, and, after giving a call to the second mate, returned on deck for my relief.

"Not much sign of any wind yet," I remarked when he approached.

"No, sir. Not much," he assented sleepily in his hoarse voice, with just enough deference, no more, and barely suppressing a yawn.

"Well, that's all you have to look out for. You have got your orders."

"Yes, sir."

I paced a turn or two on the poop and saw him take up his position face forward   70 with his elbow in the ratlines of the mizzen-rigging before I went below. The mate's faint snoring was still going on peacefully. The cuddy lamp was burning over the table on which stood a vase with flowers, a polite attention from the ship's provision merchant—the last flowers we should see for the next three months at the very least. Two bunches of bananas hung from the beam symmetrically, one on each side of the rudder-casing. Everything was as before in the ship—except that two of her captain's sleeping suits were simultaneously in use, one motionless in the cuddy, the other keeping very still in the captain's stateroom.

It must be explained here that my cabin had the form of the capital letter L, the door being within the angle and opening into the short part of the letter. A couch was to the left, the bedplace to the right; my writing-desk and the chronometers' table faced the door. But any one opening it, unless he stepped right inside, had no view of what I call the long (or vertical) part of the letter. It contained some lockers surmounted by a bookcase; and a few clothes, a thick jacket or two, caps, oilskin coat, and such-like, hung on hooks. There was at the bottom of that part a door opening into my bathroom, which could be entered also directly from the saloon. But that way was never used.

The mysterious arrival had discovered the advantage of this particular shape. Entering my room, lighted strongly by a big bulkhead lamp swung on gimbals above my writing-desk, I did not see him anywhere till he stepped out quietly from behind the coats hung in the recessed part.

"I heard somebody moving about, and went in there at once," he whispered.

I, too, spoke under my breath.

"Nobody is likely to come in here without knocking and getting permis-   75 sion."

He nodded. His face was thin and the sunburn faded, as though he had been ill. And no wonder. He had been, I heard presently, kept under arrest in his cabin for nearly nine weeks. But there was nothing sickly in his eyes or in his expression. He was not a bit like me, really; yet, as we stood leaning over my bedplace, whispering side by side, with our dark heads together and our backs to the door, anybody bold enough to open it stealthily would have been treated to the uncanny sight of a double captain busy talking in whispers with his other self.

"But all this doesn't tell me how you came to hang on to our side-ladder," I inquired, in the hardly audible murmurs we used, after he had told me something more of the proceedings on board the *Sephora* once the bad weather was over.

"When we sighted Java Head[7] I had had time to think all those matters out several times over. I had six weeks of doing nothing else, and with only an hour or so every evening for a tramp on the quarterdeck."

He whispered, his arms folded on the side of my bedplace, staring through the open port. And I could imagine perfectly the manner of this thinking out—a stubborn if not a steadfast operation; something of which I should have been perfectly incapable.

80 "I reckoned it would be dark before we closed with the land," he continued, so low that I had to strain my hearing, near as we were to each other, shoulder touching shoulder almost. "So I asked to speak to the old man. He always seemed very sick when he came to see me—as if he could not look me in the face. You know, that foresail saved the ship. She was too deep to have run long under bare poles. And it was I that managed to set it for him. Anyway, he came. When I had him in my cabin—he stood by the door looking at me as if I had the halter round my neck already—I asked him right away to leave my cabin door unlocked at night while the ship was going through Sunda Straits. There would be the Java coast within two or three miles, off Anjer Point. I wanted nothing more. I've had a prize for swimming my second year in the Conway."

"I can believe it," I breathed out.

"God only knows why they locked me in every night. To see some of their faces you'd have thought they were afraid I'd go about at night strangling people. Am I a murdering brute? Do I look it? By Jove! if I had been he wouldn't have trusted himself like that into my room. You'll say I might have chucked him aside and bolted out, there and then—it was dark already. Well, no. And for the same reason I wouldn't think of trying to smash the door. There would have been a rush to stop me at the noise, and I did not mean to get into a confounded scrimmage. Somebody else might have got killed—for I would not have broken out only to get chucked back, and I did not want any more of that work. He refused, looking more sick than ever. He was afraid of the men, and also of that old second mate of his who had been sailing with him for years—a gray-headed old humbug; and his steward, too, had been with him devil knows how long—seventeen years or more—a dogmatic sort of loafer who hated me like poison, just because I was the chief mate. No chief mate ever made more than one voyage in the *Sephora*, you know. Those two old chaps ran the ship. Devil only knows what the skipper wasn't afraid of (all his nerve went to pieces altogether in that hellish spell of bad weather we had)—of what the law would do to him—of his wife, perhaps. Oh yes! she's on board. Though I don't think she would have meddled. She would have been only too glad to have me out of the ship in any way. The 'brand of Cain'[8] business, don't you see? That's all right. I was ready enough to go off wandering on the face of the earth—and that was price enough to pay for an Abel of that sort. Anyhow, he wouldn't listen to me. 'This thing must take its course. I represent the law here.' He was shaking like a leaf. 'So you won't?' 'No!' 'Then I

7. A famous landmark for clipper ships engaged in the China trade on the western end of Java, the southern entrance to the Sunda Straits mentioned below; the killing thus took place some fifteen hundred miles south of the present scene.   8. Genesis 4.15.

hope you will be able to sleep on that," I said, and turned my back on him. 'I wonder that *you* can,' cries he, and locks the door.

"Well, after that, I couldn't. Not very well. That was three weeks ago. We have had a slow passage through the Java Sea; drifted about Carimata[9] for ten days. When we anchored here they thought, I suppose, it was all right. The nearest land (and that's five miles) is the ship's destination; the consul would soon set about catching me; and there would have been no object in bolting to these islets there. I don't suppose there's a drop of water on them. I don't know how it was, but tonight that steward, after bringing me my supper, went out to let me eat it, and left the door unlocked. And I ate it—all there was, too. After I had finished I strolled out on the quarterdeck. I don't know that I meant to do anything. A breath of fresh air was all I wanted, I believe. Then a sudden temptation came over me. I kicked off my slippers and was in the water before I had made up my mind fairly. Somebody heard the splash and they raised an awful hullabaloo. "He's gone! Lower the boats! He's committed suicide! No, he's swimming.' Certainly I was swimming. It's not easy for a swimmer like me to commit suicide by drowning. I landed on the nearest islet before the boat left the ship's side. I heard them pulling about in the dark, hailing, and so on, but after a bit they gave up. Everything quieted down and the anchorage became as still as death. I sat down on a stone and began to think. I felt certain they would start searching for me at daylight. There was no place to hide on those stony things—and if there had been, what would have been the good? But now I was clear of that ship I was not going back. So after a while I took off all my clothes, tied them up in a bundle with a stone inside, and dropped them in the deep water on the outer side of that islet. That was suicide enough for me. Let them think what they liked, but I didn't mean to drown myself. I meant to swim till I sank—but that's not the same thing. I struck out for another of these little islands, and it was from that one that I first saw your riding-light. Something to swim for. I went on easily, and on the way I came upon a flat rock a foot or two above water. In the daytime, I dare say, you might make it out with a glass from your poop. I scrambled up on it and rested myself for a bit. Then I made another start. That last spell must have been over a mile."

His whisper was getting fainter and fainter, and all the time he stared straight out through the porthole, in which there was not even a star to be seen. I had not interrupted him. There was something that made comment impossible, in his narrative, or perhaps in himself; a sort of feeling, a quality, which I can't find a name for. And when he ceased, all I found was a futile whisper, "So you swam for our light?"

"Yes—straight for it. It was something to swim for. I couldn't see any stars low down because the coast was in the way, and I couldn't see the land, either. The water was like glass. One might have been swimming in a confounded thousand feet deep cistern with no place for scrambling out anywhere; but what I didn't like was the notion of swimming round and round like a crazed bullock before I

85

---

9. The Karimata Islands in the straits between Borneo and Sumatra, some three hundred miles northeast of the Sunda Straits.

gave out; and as I didn't mean to go back . . . No. Do you see me being hauled back, stark naked, off one of these little islands by the scruff of the neck and fighting like a wild beast? Somebody would have got killed for certain, and I did not want any of that. So I went on. Then your ladder—"

"Why didn't you hail the ship?" I asked, a little louder.

He touched my shoulder lightly. Lazy footsteps came right over our heads and stopped. The second mate had crossed from the other side of the poop and might have been hanging over the rail, for all we knew.

"He couldn't hear us talking—could he?" My double breathed into my very ear anxiously.

His anxiety was an answer, a sufficient answer, to the question I had put to him. An answer containing all the difficulty of that situation. I closed the porthole quietly, to make sure. A louder word might have been overheard.

90 "Who's that?" he whispered then.

"My second mate. But I don't know much more of the fellow than you do."

And I told him a little about myself. I had been appointed to take charge while I least expected anything of the sort, not quite a fortnight ago. I didn't know either the ship or the people. Hadn't had the time in port to look about me or size anybody up. And as to the crew, all they knew was that I was appointed to take the ship home. For the rest, I was almost as much of a stranger on board as himself, I said. And at the moment I felt it most acutely. I felt that it would take very little to make me a suspect person in the eyes of the ship's company.

He had turned about meantime; and we, the two strangers in the ship, faced each other in identical attitudes.

"Your ladder—" he murmured, after a silence. "Who'd have thought of finding a ladder hanging over at night in a ship anchored out here! I felt just then a very unpleasant faintness. After the life I've been leading for nine weeks, anybody would have got out of condition. I wasn't capable of swimming round as far as your rudder-chains. And, lo and behold! there was a ladder to get hold of. After I gripped it I said to myself, "What's the good?' When I saw a man's head looking over I thought I would swim away presently and leave him shouting—in whatever language it was. I didn't mind being looked at. I—I liked it. And then you speaking to me so quietly—as if you had expected me—made me hold on a little longer. It had been a confounded lonely time—I don't mean while swimming. I was glad to talk a little to somebody that didn't belong to the *Sephora*. As to asking for the captain, that was a mere impulse. It could have been no use, with all the ship knowing about me and the other people pretty certain to be round here in the morning. I don't know—I wanted to be seen, to talk with somebody, before I went on. I don't know what I would have said. . . . 'Fine night, isn't it?' or something of the sort."

95 "Do you think they will be round here presently?" I asked, with some incredulity.

"Quite likely," he said faintly.

He looked extremely haggard all of a sudden. His head rolled on his shoulders.

"H'm. We shall see then. Meantime get into that bed," I whispered. "Want help? There."

It was a rather high bedplace with a set of drawers underneath. This amazing swimmer really needed the lift I gave him by seizing his leg. He tumbled in, rolled over on his back, and flung one arm across his eyes. And then, with his face nearly hidden, he must have looked exactly as I used to look in that bed. I gazed upon my other self for a while before drawing across carefully the two green serge curtains which ran on a brass rod. I thought for a moment of pinning them together for greater safety, but I sat down on the couch, and once there I felt unwilling to rise and hunt for a pin. I would do it in a moment. I was extremely tired, in a peculiarly intimate way, by the strain of stealthiness, by the effort of whispering, and the general secrecy of this excitement. It was three o'clock by now, and I had been on my feet since nine, but I was not sleepy; I could not have gone to sleep. I sat there, fagged out, looking at the curtains, trying to clear my mind of the confused sensation of being in two places at once, and greatly bothered by an exasperating knocking in my head. It was a relief to discover suddenly that it was not in my head at all, but on the outside of the door. Before I could collect myself, the words "Come in" were out of my mouth, and the steward entered with a tray, bringing in my morning coffee. I had slept, after all, and I was so frightened that I shouted, "This way! I am here, steward," as though he had been miles away. He put down the tray on the table next the couch and only then said, very quietly, "I can see you are here, sir." I felt him give me a keen look, but I dared not meet his eyes just then. He must have wondered why I had drawn the curtains of my bed before going to sleep on the couch. He went out, hooking the door open as usual.

I heard the crew washing decks above me. I knew I would have been told at once if there had been any wind. Calm, I thought, and I was doubly vexed. Indeed, I felt dual more than ever. The steward reappeared suddenly in the doorway. I jumped up from the couch so quickly that he gave a start.

"What do you want here?"

"Close your port, sir—they are washing decks."

"It is closed," I said, reddening.

"Very well, sir." But he did not move from the doorway and returned my stare in an extraordinary, equivocal manner for a time. Then his eyes, wavered, all his expression changed, and in a voice unusually gentle, almost coaxingly.

"May I come in to take the empty cup away, sir?"

"Of course!" I turned my back on him while he popped in and out. Then I unhooked and closed the door and even pushed the bolt. This sort of thing could not go on very long. The cabin was as hot as an oven, too. I took a peep at my double, and discovered that he had not moved; his arm was still over his eyes; but his chest heaved, his hair was wet, his chin glistened with perspiration. I reached over him and opened the port.

"I must show myself on deck," I reflected.

Of course, theoretically, I could do what I liked, with no one to say nay to me within the whole circle of the horizon; but to lock my cabin door and take the key away I did not dare. Directly I put my head out of the companion I saw the group of my two officers, the second mate barefooted, the chief mate in long india-rubber boots, near the break of the poop, and the steward half-way down

100

105

the poop ladder talking to them eagerly. He happened to catch sight of me and dived, the second ran down on the main deck shouting some order or other, and the chief mate came to meet me, touching his cap.

There was a sort of curiosity in his eye that I did not like. I don't know whether the steward had told them that I was "queer" only, or downright drunk, but I know the man meant to have a good look at me. I watched him coming with a smile which, as he got into point-blank range, took effect and froze his very whiskers. I did not give him time to open his lips.

110   "Square the yards by lifts and braces before the hands go to breakfast."

It was the first particular order I had given on board that ship; and I stayed on deck to see it executed too. I had felt the need of asserting myself without loss of time. That sneering young cub got taken down a peg or two on that occasion, and I also seized the opportunity of having a good look at the face of every fore-mast man as they filed past me to go to the after braces. At breakfast time, eating nothing myself, I presided with such frigid dignity that the two mates were only too glad to escape from the cabin as soon as decency permitted; and all the time the dual working of my mind distracted me almost to the point of insanity. I was constantly watching myself, my secret self, as dependent on my actions as my own personality, sleeping in that bed, behind that door which faced me as I sat at the head of the table. It was very much like being mad, only it was worse, because one was aware of it.

I had to shake him for a solid minute, but when at last he opened his eyes it was in the full possession of his senses, with an inquiring look.

"All's well so far," I whispered. "Now you must vanish into the bathroom."

He did so, as noiseless as a ghost, and I then rang for the steward, and facing him boldly, directed him to tidy up my stateroom while I was having my bath—"and be quick about it." As my tone admitted of no excuses, he said, "Yes, sir," and ran off to fetch his dustpan and brushes. I took a bath and did most of my dressing, splashing, and whistling softly for the steward's edification, while the secret sharer of my life stood drawn bolt upright in that little space, his face looking very sunken in daylight, his eyelids lowered under the stern, dark line of his eyebrows drawn together by a slight frown.

115   When I left him there to go back to my room the steward was finishing dusting. I sent for the mate and engaged him in some insignificant conversation. It was, as it were, trifling with the terrific character of his whiskers; but my object was to give him an opportunity for a good look at my cabin. And then I could at last shut, with a clear conscience, the door of my stateroom and get my double back into the recessed part. There was nothing else for it. He had to sit still on a small folding stool, half smothered by the heavy coats hanging there. We listened to the steward going into the bathroom out of the saloon, filling the water-bottles there, scrubbing the bath, setting things to rights, whisk, bang, clatter—out again into the saloon—turn the key—click. Such was my scheme for keeping my second self invisible. Nothing better could be contrived under the circumstances. And there we sat: I at my writing-desk ready to appear busy with some papers, he behind me, out of sight of the door. It would not have been prudent to talk in daytime; and I could not have stood the excitement of that queer sense of whis-

pering to myself. Now and then, glancing over my shoulder, I saw him far back there, sitting rigidly on the low stool, his bare feet close together, his arms folded, his head hanging on his breast—and perfectly still. Anybody would have taken him for me.

I was fascinated by it myself. Every moment I had to glance over my shoulder. I was looking at him when a voice outside the door said:

"Beg pardon, sir."

"Well!" . . . I kept my eyes on him, and so when the voice outside the door announced, "There's a ship's boat coming our way, sir," I saw him give a start—the first movement he had made for hours. But he did not raise his bowed head.

"All right. Get the ladder over."

I hesitated. Should I whisper something to him? But what? His immobility   120
seemed to have been never disturbed. What could I tell him he did not know already? . . . Finally I went on deck.

II

The skipper of the *Sephora* had a thin, red whisker all round his face, and the sort of complexion that goes with hair of that color; also the particular, rather smeary shade of blue in the eyes. He was not exactly a showy figure; his shoulders were high, his stature but middling—one leg slightly more bandy than the other. He shook hands, looking vaguely around. A spiritless tenacity was his main characteristic, I judged. I behaved with a politeness which seemed to disconcert him. Perhaps he was shy. He mumbled to me as if he were ashamed of what he was saying; gave his name (it was something like Archbold—but at this distance of years I hardly am sure), his ship's name, and a few other particulars of that sort, in the manner of a criminal making a reluctant and doleful confession. He had had terrible weather on the passage out—terrible—terrible—wife aboard, too.

By this time we were seated in the cabin and the steward brought in a tray with a bottle and glasses. "Thanks! No." Never took liquor. Would have some water, though. He drank two tumblerfuls. Terrible thirsty work. Ever since daylight had been exploring the islands round his ship.

"What was that for—fun?" I asked with an appearance of polite interest.

"No!" He sighed. "Painful duty."

As he persisted in his mumbling and I wanted my double to hear every word,   125
I hit upon the notion of informing him that I regretted to say I was hard of hearing.

"Such a young man too!" he nodded, keeping his smeary, blue, unintelligent eyes fastened upon me. "What was the cause of it—some disease?" he inquired, without the least sympathy and as if he thought that, if so, I'd got no more than I deserved.

"Yes; disease," I admitted in a cheerful tone which seemed to shock him. But my point was gained, because he had to raise his voice to give me his tale. It is not worth while to record that version. It was just over two months since all this had happened, and he had thought so much about it that he seemed completely muddled as to its bearings, but still immensely impressed.

"What would you think of such a thing happening on board your own ship? I've had the *Sephora* for these fifteen years. I am a well-known shipmaster."

He was densely distressed—and perhaps I should have sympathized with him if I had been able to detach my mental vision from the unsuspected sharer of my cabin as though he were my second self. There he was on the other side of the bulkhead, four or five feet from us, no more, as we sat in the saloon. I looked politely at Captain Archbold (if that was his name), but it was the other I saw, in a gray sleeping suit, seated on a low stool, his bare feet close together, his arms folded, and every word said between us falling into the ears of his dark head bowed on his chest.

130 "I have been at sea now, man and boy, for seven and thirty years, and I've never heard of such a thing happening in an English ship. And that it should be my ship. Wife on board, too."

I was hardly listening to him.

"Don't you think," I said, "that the heavy sea which, you told me, came aboard just then might have killed the man? I have seen the sheer weight of a sea kill a man very neatly, by simply breaking his neck."

"Good God!" he uttered impressively, fixing his smeary blue eyes on me. "The sea! No man killed by the sea ever looked like that." He seemed positively scandalized at my suggestion. And as I gazed at him, certainly not prepared for anything original on his part, he advanced his head close to mine and thrust his tongue out at me so suddenly that I couldn't help starting back.

After scoring over my calmness in this graphic way he nodded wisely. If I had seen the sight, he assured me, I would never forget it as long as I lived. The weather was too bad to give the corpse a proper sea burial. So next day at dawn they took it up on the poop, covering its face with a bit of bunting; he read a short prayer, and then, just as it was, in its oilskins and long boots, they launched it amongst those mountainous seas that seemed ready every moment to swallow up the ship herself and the terrified lives on board of her.

135 "That reefed foresail saved you," I threw in.

"Under God—it did," he exclaimed fervently. "It was by a special mercy, I firmly believe, that it stood some of those hurricane squalls."

"It was the setting of that sail which—" I began.

"God's own hand in it," he interrupted me. "Nothing less could have done it. I don't mind telling you that I hardly dared give the order. It seemed impossible that we could touch anything without losing it, and then our last hope would have been gone."

The terror of that gale was on him yet. I let him go on for a bit, then said casually—as if returning to a minor subject:

140 "You were very anxious to give up your mate to the shore people, I believe?"

He was. To the law. His obscure tenacity on that point had in it something incomprehensible and a little awful; something, as it were, mystical, quite apart from his anxiety that he should not be suspected of "countenancing any doings of that sort." Seven and thirty virtuous years at sea, of which over twenty of immaculate command, and the last fifteen in the *Sephora*, seemed to have laid him under some pitiless obligation.

"And you know," he went on, groping shamefacedly amongst his feelings, "I did not engage that young fellow. His people had some interest with my owners. I was in a way forced to take him on. He looked very smart, very gentlemanly, and all that. But do you know—I never liked him, somehow. I am a plain man. You see, he wasn't exactly the sort for the chief mate of a ship like the *Sephora*."

I had become so connected in thoughts and impressions with the secret sharer of my cabin that I felt as if I, personally, were being given to understand that I, too, was not the sort that would have done for the chief mate of a ship like the *Sephora*. I had no doubt of it in my mind.

"Not at all the style of man. You understand," he insisted superfluously, looking hard at me.

I smiled urbanely. He seemed at a loss for a while.   145

"I suppose I must report a suicide."

"Beg pardon?"

"Sui-cide! That's what I'll have to write to my owners directly I get in."

"Unless you manage to recover him before tomorrow," I assented dispassionately. . . . "I mean, alive."

He mumbled something which I really did not catch, and I turned my ear to   150
him in a puzzled manner. He fairly bawled:

"The land—I say, the mainland is at least seven miles off my anchorage."

"About that."

My lack of excitement, of curiosity, of surprise, of any sort of pronounced interest, began to arouse his distrust. But except for the felicitous pretense of deafness I had not tried to pretend anything. I had felt utterly incapable of playing the part of ignorance properly, and therefore was afraid to try. It is also certain that he had brought some ready-made suspicions with him, and that he viewed my politeness as a strange and unnatural phenomenon. And yet how else could I have received him? Not heartily! That was impossible for psychological reasons, which I need not state here. My only object was to keep off his inquiries. Surlily? Yes, but surliness might have provoked a point-blank question. From its novelty to him and from its nature, punctilious courtesy was the manner best calculated to restrain the man. But there was the danger of his breaking through my defense bluntly. I could not, I think, have met him by a direct lie, also for psychological (not moral) reasons. If he had only known how afraid I was of his putting my feeling of identity with the other to the test! But, strangely enough (I thought of it only afterward), I believe that he was not a little disconcerted by the reverse side of that weird situation, by something in me that reminded him of the man he was seeking—suggested a mysterious similitude to the young fellow he had distrusted and disliked from the first.

However that might have been the silence was not very prolonged. He took another oblique step.

"I reckon I had no more than a two-mile pull to your ship. Not a bit more."   155

"And quite enough, too, in this awful heat," I said.

Another pause full of mistrust followed. Necessity, they say, is mother of invention, but fear, too, is not barren of ingenious suggestions. And I was afraid he would ask me point-blank for news of my other self.

"Nice little saloon, isn't it?" I remarked, as if noticing for the first time the way his eyes roamed from one closed door to the other. "And very well fitted out, too. Here, for instance," I continued, reaching over the back of my seat negligently and flinging the door open, "is my bathroom."

He made an eager movement, but hardly gave it a glance. I got up, shut the door of the bathroom, and invited him to have a look round, as if I were very proud of my accommodation. He had to rise and be shown round, but he went through the business without any raptures whatever.

160 "And now we'll have a look at my stateroom," I declared, in a voice as loud as I dared to make it, crossing the cabin to the starboard side with purposely heavy steps.

He followed me in and gazed around. My intelligent double had vanished. I played my part.

"Very convenient—isn't it?"

"Very nice. Very comf . . ." He didn't finish, and went out brusquely as if to escape from some unrighteous wiles of mine. But it was not to be. I had been too frightened not to feel vengeful; I felt I had him on the run, and I meant to keep him on the run. My polite insistence must have had something menacing in it, because he gave in suddenly. And I did not let him off a single item: mates' rooms, pantry, storerooms, the very sail-locker, which was also under the poop—he had to look into them all. When at last I showed him out on the quarter-deck he drew a long, spiritless sigh, and mumbled dismally that he must really be going back to his ship now. I desired my mate, who had joined us, to see to the captain's boat.

The man of whiskers gave a blast on the whistle which he used to wear hanging round his neck, and yelled, "*Sephora*'s away!" My double down there in my cabin must have heard, and certainly could not feel more relieved than I. Four fellows came running out from somewhere forward and went over the side, while my own men, appearing on deck too, lined the rail. I escorted my visitor to the gang-way ceremoniously, and nearly overdid it. He was a tenacious beast. On the very ladder he lingered, and in that unique, guiltily conscientious manner of sticking to the point:

165 "I say . . . you . . . you don't think that—"

I covered his voice loudly.

"Certainly not. . . . I am delighted. Goodbye."

I had an idea of what he meant to say, and just saved myself by the privilege of defective hearing. He was too shaken generally to insist, but my mate, close witness of that parting, looked mystified and his face took on a thoughtful cast. As I did not want to appear as if I wished to avoid all communication with my officers, he had the opportunity to address me.

"Seems a very nice man. His boat's crew told our chaps a very extraordinary story, if what I am told by the steward is true. I suppose you had it from the captain, sir?"

170 "Yes. I had a story from the captain."

"A very horrible affair—isn't it, sir?"

"It is."

"Beats all these tales we hear about murders in Yankee ships."

"I don't think it beats them. I don't think it resembles them in the least."

"Bless my soul—you don't say so! But of course I've no acquaintance whatever   175
with American ships, not I, so I couldn't go against your knowledge. It's horrible
enough for me. . . . But the queerest part is that those fellows seemed to have
some idea the man was hidden aboard here. They had really. Did you ever hear
of such a thing?"

"Preposterous—isn't it?"

We were walking to and fro athwart the quarter-deck. No one of the crew
forward could be seen (the day was Sunday), and the mate pursued:

"There was some little dispute about it. Our chaps took offense. 'As if we would
harbor a thing like that,' they said. 'Wouldn't you like to look for him in our coal-
hole?' Quite a tiff. But they made it up in the end. I suppose he did drown himself.
Don't you, sir?"

"I don't suppose anything."

"You have no doubt in the matter, sir?"   180

"None whatever."

I left him suddenly. I felt I was producing a bad impression, but with my double
down there it was most trying to be on deck. And it was almost as trying to be
below. Altogether a nerve-trying situation. But on the whole I felt less torn in two
when I was with him. There was no one in the whole ship whom I dared take
into my confidence. Since the hands had got to know his story, it would have
been impossible to pass him off for any one else, and an accidental discovery was
to be dreaded now more than ever. . . .

The steward being engaged in laying the table for dinner, we could talk only
with our eyes when I first went down. Later in the afternoon we had a cautious
try at whispering. The Sunday quietness of the ship was against us; the stillness
of air and water around her was against us; the elements, the men were against
us—everything was against us in our secret partnership; time itself—for this could
not go on for ever. The very trust in Providence was, I supposed, denied to his
guilt. Shall I confess that this thought cast me down very much? And as to the
chapter of accidents which counts for so much in the book of success, I could
only hope that it was closed. For what favorable accident could be expected?

"Did you hear everything?" were my first words as soon as we took up our
position side by side, leaning over my bedplace.

He had. And the proof of it was his earnest whisper, "The man told you he   185
hardly dared to give the order."

I understood the reference to be to that saving foresail.

"Yes. He was afraid of it being lost in the setting."

"I assure you he never gave the order. He may think he did, but he never gave
it. He stood there with me on the break of the poop after the maintopsail blew
away, and whimpered about our last hope—positively whimpered about it and
nothing else—and the night coming on! To hear one's skipper go on like that in
such weather was enough to drive any fellow out of his mind. It worked me up
into a sort of desperation. I just took it into my own hands and went away from
him, boiling, and—But what's the use telling you? You know! . . . Do you think

that if I had not been pretty fierce with them I should have got the men to do anything? Not it! The boss'en[1] perhaps? Perhaps! It wasn't a heavy sea—it was a sea gone mad! I suppose the end of the world will be something like that; and a man may have the heart to see it coming once and be done with it—but to have to face it day after day . . . I don't blame anybody. I was precious little better than the rest. Only—I was an officer of that old coal-wagon, anyhow. . . ."

"I quite understand," I conveyed that sincere assurance into his ear. He was out of breath with whispering; I could hear him pant slightly. It was all very simple. The same strung-up force which had given twenty-four men a chance, at least, for their lives had, in a sort of recoil, crushed an unworthy mutinous existence.

190   But I had no leisure to weigh the merits of the matter—footsteps in the saloon, a heavy knock. "There's enough wind to get under way with, sir." Here was the call of a new claim upon my thoughts and even upon my feelings.

"Turn the hands up," I cried through the door. "I'll be on deck directly."

I was going out to make the acquaintance of my ship. Before I left the cabin our eyes met—the eyes of the only two strangers on board. I pointed to the recessed part where the little camp-stool awaited him and laid my finger on my lips. He made a gesture—somewhat vague—a little mysterious, accompanied by a faint smile, as if of regret.

This is not the place to enlarge upon the sensations of a man who feels for the first time a ship move under his feet to his own independent word. In my case they were not unalloyed. I was not wholly alone with my command; for there was that stranger in my cabin. Or, rather, I was not completely and wholly with her. Part of me was absent. That mental feeling of being in two places at once affected me physically as if the mood of secrecy had penetrated my very soul. Before an hour had elapsed since the ship had begun to move, having occasion to ask the mate (he stood by my side) to take a compass bearing of the Pagoda, I caught myself reaching up to his ear in whispers. I say I caught myself, but enough had escaped to startle the man. I can't describe it otherwise than by saying that he shied. A grave, preoccupied manner, as though he were in possession of some perplexing intelligence, did not leave him henceforth. A little later I moved away from the rail to look at the compass with such a stealthy gait that the helmsman noticed it—and I could not help noticing the unusual roundness of his eyes. These are trifling instances, though it's to no commander's advantage to be suspected of ludicrous eccentricities. But I was also more seriously affected. There are to a seaman certain words, gestures, that should in given conditions come as naturally, as instinctively, as the winking of a menaced eye. A certain order should spring on to his lips without thinking; a certain sign should get itself made, so to speak, without reflection. But all unconscious alertness had abandoned me. I had to make an effort of will to recall myself back (from the cabin) to the conditions of the moment. I felt that I was appearing an irresolute commander to those people who were watching me more or less critically.

And, besides, there were the scares. On the second day out, for instance, com-

1. *Bosun* or *boatswain:* a petty officer in charge of the deck crew and of the rigging.

ing off the deck in the afternoon (I had straw slippers on my bare feet) I stopped
at the open pantry door and spoke to the steward. He was doing something there
with his back to me. At the sound of my voice he nearly jumped out of his skin,
as the saying is, and incidentally broke a cup.

"What on earth's the matter with you?" I asked, astonished.   195

He was extremely confused. "Beg your pardon, sir. I made sure you were in
your cabin."

"You see I wasn't."

"No, sir. I could have sworn I had heard you moving in there not a moment
ago. It's most extraordinary . . . very sorry, sir."

I passed on with an inward shudder. I was so identified with my secret double
that I did not even mention the fact in those scanty, fearful whispers we
exchanged. I suppose he had made some slight noise of some kind or other. It
would have been miraculous if he hadn't at one time or another. And yet, haggard
as he appeared, he looked always perfectly self-controlled, more than calm—
almost invulnerable. On my suggestion he remained almost entirely in the bathroom, which, upon the whole, was the safest place. There could be really no
shadow of an excuse for any one ever wanting to go in there, once the steward
had done with it. It was a very tiny place. Sometimes he reclined on the floor, his
legs bent, his head sustained on one elbow. At others I would find him on the
camp-stool, sitting in his gray sleeping suit and with his cropped dark hair like a
patient, unmoved convict. At night I would smuggle him into my bedplace, and
we would whisper together, with the regular footfalls of the officer of the watch
passing and repassing over our heads. It was an infinitely miserable time. It was
lucky that some tins of fine preserves were stowed in a locker in my stateroom;
hard bread I could always get hold of; and so he lived on stewed chicken, pâté
de foie gras, asparagus, cooked oysters, sardines—on all sorts of abominable sham-
delicacies out of tins. My early morning coffee he always drank; and it was all I
dared do for him in that respect.

Every day there was the horrible maneuvering to go through so that my room   200
and then the bathroom should be done in the usual way. I came to hate the sight
of the steward, to abhor the voice of that harmless man. I felt that it was he who
would bring on the disaster of discovery. It hung like a sword over our heads.

The fourth day out, I think (we were then working down the east side of the
Gulf of Siam, tack for tack,[2] in light winds and smooth water)—the fourth day, I
say, of this miserable juggling with the unavoidable, as we sat at our evening meal,
that man, whose slightest movement I dreaded, after putting down the dishes ran
up on deck busily. This could not be dangerous. Presently he came down again;
and then it appeared that he had remembered a coat of mine which I had thrown
over a rail to dry after having been wetted in a shower which had passed over the
ship in the afternoon. Sitting stolidly at the head of the table I became terrified
at the sight of the garment on his arm. Of course he made for my door. There
was no time to lose.

"Steward!" I thundered. My nerves were so shaken that I could not govern my

2. By a series of shiftings back and forth of sails.

voice and conceal my agitation. This was the sort of thing that made my terrifi-cally whiskered mate tap his forehead with his forefinger. I had detected him using that gesture while talking on deck with a confidential air to the carpenter. It was too far to hear a word, but I had no doubt that this pantomime could only refer to the strange new captain.

"Yes, sir," the pale-faced steward turned resignedly to me. It was this madden-ing course of being shouted at, checked without rhyme or reason, arbitrarily chased out of my cabin, suddenly called into it, sent flying out of his pantry on incomprehensible errands, that accounted for the growing wretchedness of his expression.

"Where are you going with that coat?"

205 "To your room, sir."

"Is there another shower coming?"

"I'm sure I don't know, sir. Shall I go up again and see, sir?"

"No! never mind."

My object was attained, as of course my other self in there would have heard everything that passed. During this interlude my two officers never raised their eyes off their respective plates; but the lip of that confounded cub, the second mate, quivered visibly.

210 I expected the steward to hook my coat on and come out at once. He was very slow about it; but I dominated my nervousness sufficiently not to shout after him. Suddenly I became aware (it could be heard plainly enough) that the fellow for some reason or other was opening the door of the bathroom. It was the end. The place was literally not big enough to swing a cat in. My voice died in my throat and I went stony all over. I expected to hear a yell of surprise and terror, and made a movement, but had not the strength to get on my legs. Everything remained still. Had my second self taken the poor wretch by the throat? I don't know what I could have done next moment if I had not seen the steward come out of my room, close the door, and then stand quietly by the sideboard.

"Saved," I thought. "But, no! Lost! Gone! He was gone!"

I laid my knife and fork down and leaned back in my chair. My head swam. After a while, when sufficiently recovered to speak in a steady voice, I instructed my mate to put the ship round at eight o'clock himself.

"I won't come on deck," I went on. "I think I'll turn in, and unless the wind shifts I don't want to be disturbed before midnight. I feel a bit seedy."

"You did look middling bad a little while ago," the chief mate remarked with-out showing any great concern.

215 They both went out, and I stared at the steward clearing the table. There was nothing to be read on that wretched man's face. But why did he avoid my eyes? I asked myself. Then I thought I should like to hear the sound of his voice.

"Steward!"

"Sir!" Startled as usual.

"Where did you hang up that coat?"

"In the bathroom, sir." The usual anxious tone. "It's not quite dry yet, sir."

220 For some time longer I sat in the cuddy. Had my double vanished as he had

come? But of his coming there was an explanation, whereas his disappearance would be inexplicable. . . . I went slowly into my dark room, shut the door, lighted the lamp, and for a time dared not turn round. When at last I did I saw him standing bolt upright in the narrow recessed part. It would not be true to say I had a shock, but an irresistible doubt of his bodily existence flitted through my mind. Can it be, I asked myself, that he is not visible to other eyes than mine? It was like being haunted. Motionless, with a grave face, he raised his hands slightly at me in a gesture which meant clearly, "Heavens! what a narrow escape!" Narrow indeed. I think I had come creeping quietly as near insanity as any man who has not actually gone over the border. That gesture restrained me, so to speak.

The mate with the terrific whiskers was now putting the ship on the other tack. In the moment of profound silence which follows upon the hands going to their stations I heard on the poop his raised voice: "Hard alee!"[3] and the distant shout of the order repeated on the main deck. The sails, in that light breeze, made but a faint fluttering noise. It ceased. The ship was coming round slowly; I held my breath in the renewed stillness of expectation; one wouldn't have thought that there was a single living soul on her decks. A sudden brisk shout, "Mainsail haul!" broke the spell, and in the noisy cries and rush overhead of the men running away with the main brace we two, down in my cabin, came together in our usual position by the bedplace.

He did not wait for my question. "I heard him fumbling here and just managed to squat myself down in the bath," he whispered to me. "The fellow only opened the door and put his arm in to hang the coat up. All the same. . . ."

"I never thought of that," I whispered back, even more appalled than before at the closeness of the shave, and marveling at that something unyielding in his character which was carrying him through so finely. There was no agitation in his whisper. Whoever was being driven distracted, it was not he. He was sane. And the proof of his sanity was continued when he took up the whispering again.

"It would never do for me to come to life again."

It was something that a ghost might have said. But what he was alluding to   225
was his old captain's reluctant admission of the theory of suicide. It would obviously serve his turn—if I had understood at all the view which seemed to govern the unalterable purpose of his action.

"You must maroon me as soon as ever you can get amongst these islands off the Cambodje[4] shore," he went on.

"Maroon you! We are not living in a boy's adventure tale," I protested. His scornful whispering took me up.

"We aren't indeed! There's nothing of a boy's tale in this. But there's nothing else for it. I want no more. You don't suppose I am afraid of what can be done to me? Prison or gallows or whatever they may please. But you don't see me coming back to explain such things to an old fellow in a wig and twelve respectable tradesmen, do you? What can they know whether I am guilty or not—or of *what* I am

3. That is, put the helm all the way over to the side away from the wind.   4. Cambodian.

guilty, either? That's my affair. What does the Bible say? 'Driven off the face of the earth.'[5] Very well. I am off the face of the earth now. As I came at night so I shall go."

"Impossible!" I murmured. "You can't."

230   "Can't? . . . . Not naked like a soul on the Day of Judgment. I shall freeze on to this sleeping suit. The Last Day is not yet—and . . . you have understood thoroughly. Didn't you?"

I felt suddenly ashamed of myself. I may say truly that I understood—and my hesitation in letting that man swim away from my ship's side had been a mere sham sentiment, a sort of cowardice.

"It can't be done now till next night," I breathed out. "The ship is on the offshore tack and the wind may fail us."

"As long as I know that you understand," he whispered. "But of course you do. It's a great satisfaction to have got somebody to understand. You seem to have been there on purpose." And in the same whisper, as if we two whenever we talked had to say things to each other which were not fit for the world to hear, he added, "It's very wonderful."

We remained side by side talking in our secret way—but sometimes silent or just exchanging a whispered word or two at long intervals. And as usual he stared through the port. A breath of wind came now and again into our faces. The ship might have been moored in dock, so gently and on an even keel she slipped through the water, that did not murmur even at our passage, shadowy and silent like a phantom sea.

235   At midnight I went on deck, and to my mate's great surprise put the ship round on the other tack. His terrible whiskers flitted round me in silent criticism. I certainly should not have done it if it had been only a question of getting out of that sleepy gulf as quickly as possible. I believe he told the second mate, who relieved him, that it was a great want of judgment. The other only yawned. That intolerable cub shuffled about so sleepily and lolled against the rails in such a slack, improper fashion that I came down on him sharply.

"Aren't you properly awake yet?"

"Yes, sir! I am awake."

"Well, then, be good enough to hold yourself as if you were. And keep a look out. If there's any current we'll be closing with some islands long before daylight."

The east side of the gulf is fringed with islands, some solitary, others in groups. On the blue background of the high coast they seem to float on silvery patches of calm water, arid and gray, or dark green and rounded like clumps of evergreen bushes, with the larger ones, a mile or two long, showing the outlines of ridges, ribs of gray rock under the dank mantle of matted leafage. Unknown to trade, to travel, almost to geography, the manner of life they harbor is an unsolved secret. There must be villages—settlements of fishermen at least—on the largest of them, and some communication with the world is probably kept up by native craft. But all that forenoon, as we headed for them, fanned along by the faintest of breezes,

5. Genesis 4.14.

I saw no sign of man or canoe in the field of the telescope I kept on pointing at the scattered group.

At noon I gave no orders for a change of course, and the mate's whiskers became much concerned and seemed to be offering themselves unduly to my notice. At last I said:

"I am going to stand right in. Quite in—as far as I can take her."

The stare of extreme surprise imparted an air of ferocity also to his eyes, and he looked truly terrific for a moment.

"We're not doing well in the middle of the gulf," I continued casually. "I am going to look for the land breezes tonight."

"Bless my soul! Do you mean, sir, in the dark amongst the lot of all them islands and reefs and shoals?"

"Well, if there are any regular land breezes at all on this coast one must get close inshore to find them—mustn't one?"

"Bless my soul!" he exclaimed again under his breath. All that afternoon he wore a dreamy, comtemplative appearance which in him was a mark of perplexity. After dinner I went into my stateroom as if I meant to take some rest. There we two bent our dark heads over a half-unrolled chart lying on my bed.

"There," I said. "It's got to be Koh-ring.[6] I've been looking at it ever since sunrise. It has got two hills and a low point. It must be inhabited. And on the coast opposite there is what looks like the mouth of a biggish river—with some town, no doubt, not far up. It's the best chance for you that I can see."

"Anything. Koh-ring let it be."

He looked thoughtfully at the chart as if surveying chances and distances from a lofty height—and following with his eyes his own figure wandering on the blank land of Cochin-China, and then passing off that piece of paper clean out of sight into uncharted regions. And it was as if the ship had two captains to plan her course for her. I had been so worried and restless running up and down that I had not had the patience to dress that day. I had remained in my sleeping suit, with straw slippers and a soft floppy hat. The closeness of the heat in the gulf had been most oppressive, and the crew were used to see me wandering in that airy attire.

"She will clear the south point as she heads now," I whispered into his ear. "Goodness only knows when, though—but certainly after dark. I'll edge her in to half a mile, as far as I may be able to judge in the dark . . ."

"Be careful," he murmured warningly—and I realized suddenly that all my future, the only future for which I was fit, would perhaps go irretrievably to pieces in any mishap to my first command.

I could not stop a moment longer in the room. I motioned him to get out of sight and made my way on the poop. That unplayful cub had the watch. I walked up and down for a while thinking things out, then beckoned him over.

"Send a couple of hands to open the two quarter-deck ports," I said mildly.

He actually had the impudence, or else so forgot himself in his wonder at such an incomprehensible order, as to repeat:

6. *Koh* or *Ko* means *island;* there are a large number of islands with that prefix at the head of the Gulf of Siam, but not, apparently, a Koh-ring.

255   "Open the quarter-deck ports! What for, sir?"

"The only reason you need concern yourself about is because I tell you to do so. Have them opened wide and fastened properly."

He reddened and went off, but I believe made some jeering remark to the carpenter as to the sensible practice of ventilating a ship's quarter-deck. I know he popped into the mate's cabin to impart the fact to him, because the whiskers came on deck, as it were by chance, and stole glances at me from below—for signs of lunacy or drunkenness, I suppose.

A little before supper, feeling more restless than ever, I rejoined, for a moment, my second self. And to find him sitting so quietly was surprising, like something against nature, inhuman.

I developed my plan in a hurried whisper.

260   "I shall stand in as close as I dare and then put her round. I shall presently find means to smuggle you out of here into the sail-locker, which communicates with the lobby. But there is an opening, a sort of square for hauling the sails out, which gives straight on the quarterdeck and which is never closed in fine weather, so as to give air to the sails. When the ship's way is deadened in stays[7] and all the hands are aft at the main braces you shall have a clear road to slip out and get overboard through the open quarter-deck port. I've had them both fastened up. Use a rope's end to lower yourself into the water so as to avoid a splash—you know. It could be heard and cause some beastly complication."

He kept silent for a while, then whispered, "I understand."

"I won't be there to see you go," I began with an effort. "The rest . . . I only hope I have understood too."

"You have. From first to last"—and for the first time there seemed to be a faltering, something strained in his whisper. He caught hold of my arm, but the ringing of the supper bell made me start. He didn't though; he only released his grip.

After supper I didn't come below again till well past eight o'clock. The faint, steady breeze was loaded with dew; and the wet, darkened sails held all there was of propelling power in it. The night, clear and starry, sparkled darkly, and the opaque, lightless patches shifting slowly amongst the low stars were the drifting islets. On the port bow there was a big one more distant and shadowily imposing by the great space of sky it eclipsed.

265   On opening the door I had a back view of my very own self looking at a chart. He had come out of the recess and was standing near the table.

"Quite dark enough," I whispered.

He stepped back and leaned against my bed with a level, quiet glance. I sat on the couch. We had nothing to say to each other. Over our heads the officer of the watch moved here and there. Then I heard him move quickly. I knew what that meant. He was making for the companion; and presently his voice was outside my door.

"We are drawing in pretty fast, sir. Land looks rather close."

7. When the ship's forward motion is slowed or stopped while its head is being turned toward the wind for the purpose of shifting the sail.

"Very well," I answered. "I am coming on deck directly."

I waited till he was gone out of the cuddy, then rose. My double moved too. 270
The time had come to exchange our last whispers, for neither of us was ever to
hear each other's natural voice.

"Look here!" I opened a drawer and took out three sovereigns. "Take this,
anyhow. I've got six and I'd give you the lot, only I must keep a little money to
buy some fruit and vegetables for the crew from native boats as we go through
Sunda Straits."

He shook his head.

"Take it," I urged him, whispering desperately. "No one can tell what . . ."

He smiled and slapped meaningly the only pocket of the sleeping jacket. It was
not safe, certainly. But I produced a large old silk handkerchief of mine, and tying
the three pieces of gold in a corner, pressed it on him. He was touched, I suppose,
because he took it at last and tied it quickly round his waist under the jacket, on
his bare skin.

Our eyes met; several seconds elapsed, till, our glances still mingled, I extended 275
my hand and turned the lamp out. Then I passed through the cuddy, leaving the
door of my room wide open. . . . "Steward!"

He was still lingering in the pantry in the greatness of his zeal, giving a rub-up
to a plated cruet stand the last thing before going to bed. Being careful not to
wake up the mate, whose room was opposite, I spoke in an undertone.

He looked round anxiously. "Sir!"

"Can you get me a little hot water from the galley?"

"I am afraid, sir, the galley fire's been out for some time now."

"Go and see." 280

He fled up the stairs.

"Now," I whispered loudly into the saloon—too loudly, perhaps, but I was
afraid I couldn't make a sound. He was by my side in an instant—the double
captain slipped past the stairs—through a tiny dark passage . . . a sliding door.
We were in the sail-locker, scrambling on our knees over the sails. A sudden
thought struck me. I saw myself wandering barefooted, bareheaded, the sun beating on my dark poll. I snatched off my floppy hat and tried hurriedly in the dark
to ram it on my other self. He dodged and fended off silently. I wonder what he
thought had come to me before he understood and suddenly desisted. Our hands
met gropingly, lingered united in a steady, motionless clasp for a second. . . . No
word was breathed by either of us when they separated.

I was standing quietly by the pantry door when the steward returned.

"Sorry, sir. Kettle barely warm. Shall I light the spirit-lamp?"

"Never mind." 285

I came out on deck slowly. It was now a matter of conscience to shave the land
as close as possible—for now he must go overboard whenever the ship was
put in stays. Must! There could be no going back for him. After a moment I walked
over to leeward and my heart flew into my mouth at the nearness of the land on
the bow. Under any other circumstances I would not have held on a minute
longer. The second mate had followed me anxiously.

I looked on till I felt I could command my voice.

"She will weather," I said then in a quiet tone.

"Are you going to try that, sir?" he stammered out incredulously.

290 I took no notice of him and raised my tone just enough to be heard by the helmsman.

"Keep her good full."[8]

"Good full, sir."

The wind fanned my cheek, the sails slept, the world was silent. The strain of watching the dark loom of the land grow bigger and denser was too much for me. I had to shut my eyes—because the ship must go closer. She must! The stillness was intolerable. Were we standing still?

When I opened my eyes the second view started my heart with a thump. The black southern hill of Koh-ring seemed to hang right over the ship like a towering fragment of the everlasting night. On that enormous mass of blackness there was not a gleam to be seen, not a sound to be heard. It was gliding irresistibly towards us and yet seemed already within reach of the hand. I saw the vague figures of the watch grouped in the waist, gazing in awed silence.

295 "Are you going on, sir?" inquired an unsteady voice at my elbow.

I ignored it. I had to go on.

"Keep her full. Don't check her way. That won't do now," I said warningly.

"I can't see the sails very well," the helmsman answered me, in strange, quavering tones.

Was she close enough? Already she was, I won't say in the shadow of the land, but in the very blackness of it, already swallowed up as it were, gone too close to be recalled, gone from me altogether.

300 "Give the mate a call," I said to the young man who stood at my elbow as still as death. "And turn all hands up."

My tone had a borrowed loudness reverberated from the height of the land. Several voices cried out together, "We are all on deck, sir."

Then stillness again, with the great shadow gliding closer, towering higher, without a light, without a sound. Such a hush had fallen on the ship that she might have been a bark of the dead floating in slowly under the very gate of Erebus.

"My God! Where are we?"

It was the mate moaning at my elbow. He was thunderstruck, and as it were deprived of the moral support of his whiskers. He clapped his hands and absolutely cried out, "Lost!"

305 "Be quiet," I said sternly.

He lowered his tone, but I saw the shadowy gesture of his despair. "What are we doing here?"

"Looking for the land wind."

He made as if to tear his hair, and addressed me recklessly.

"She will never get out. You have done it, sir. I knew it'd end in something like this. She will never weather, and you are too close now to stay. She'll drift ashore before she's round. O my God!"

---

8. That is, keep the ship's sails filled with wind.

I caught his arm as he was raising it to batter his poor devoted head, and shook   310
it violently.

"She's ashore already," he wailed, trying to tear himself away.

"Is she? . . . Keep good full there!"

"Good full, sir," cried the helmsman in a frightened, thin, childlike voice.

I hadn't let go the mate's arm and went on shaking it. "Ready about,[9] do you
hear? You go forward"—shake—"and stop there"—shake—"and hold your
noise"—shake—"and see these head-sheets properly overhauled"—shake, shake—
shake.

And all the time I dared not look towards the land lest my heart should fail   315
me. I released my grip at last and he ran forward as if fleeing for dear life.

I wondered what my double there in the sail-locker thought of this commotion. He was able to hear everything—and perhaps he was able to understand
why, on my conscience, it had to be thus close—no less. My first order "Hard
alee!" re-echoed ominously under the towering shadow of Koh-ring as if I had
shouted in a mountain gorge. And then I watched the land intently. In that
smooth water and light wind it was impossible to feel the ship coming-to.[1] No! I
could not feel her. And my second self was making now ready to slip out and
lower himself overboard. Perhaps he was gone already . . . ?

The great black mass brooding over our very mast-heads began to pivot away
from the ship's side silently. And now I forgot the secret stranger ready to depart,
and remembered only that I was a total stranger to the ship. I did not know her.
Would she do it? How was she to be handled?

I swung the mainyard and waited helplessly. She was perhaps stopped, and
her very fate hung in the balance, with the black mass of Koh-ring like the gate
of the everlasting night towering over her taffrail. What would she do now? Had
she way on her[2] yet? I stepped to the side swiftly, and on the shadowy water I
could see nothing except a faint phosphorescent flash revealing the glassy
smoothness of the sleeping surface. It was impossible to tell—and I had not
learned yet the feel of my ship. Was she moving? What I needed was something
easily seen, a piece of paper, which I could throw overboard and watch. I had
nothing on me. To run down for it I didn't dare. There was no time. All at once
my strained, yearning stare distinguished a white object floating within a yard of
the ship's side—white, on the black water. A phosphorescent flash passed under
it. What was that thing? . . . I recognized my own floppy hat. It must have fallen
off his head . . . and he didn't bother. Now I had what I wanted—the saving mark
for my eyes. But I hardly thought of my other self, now gone from the
ship, to be hidden for ever from all friendly faces, to be a fugitive and a vagabond
on the earth, with no brand of the curse on his sane forehead to stay a slaying
hand . . . too proud to explain.

And I watched the hat—the expression of my sudden pity for his mere flesh.
It had been meant to save his homeless head from the dangers of the sun. And

9. That is, be ready to shift the sails (tack). The head-sheets, below, are the lines attached to the sails of
the forward mast, and to overhaul is to slacken a rope by pulling it in the opposite direction to that used
in hoisting a sail and thus loosening the blocks.   1. Coming to a standstill.   2. Was she moving?

now—behold—it was saving the ship, by serving me for a mark to help out the ignorance of my strangeness. Ha! It was drifting forward, warning me just in time that the ship had gathered sternway.

320   "Shift the helm," I said in a low voice to the seaman standing still like a statue.

The man's eyes glistened wildly in the binnacle light as he jumped round to the other side and spun round the wheel.

I walked to the break of the poop. On the overshadowed deck all hands stood by the forebraces waiting for my order. The stars ahead seemed to be gliding from right to left. And all was so still in the world that I heard the quiet remark, "She's round," passed in a tone of intense relief between two seamen.

"Let go and haul."

The foreyards ran round with a great noise, amidst cheery cries. And now the frightful whiskers made themselves heard giving various orders. Already the ship was drawing ahead. And I was alone with her. Nothing! no one in the world should stand now between us, throwing a shadow on the way of silent knowledge and mute affection; the perfect communion of a seaman with his first command.

325   Walking to the taffrail, I was in time to make out, on the very edge of a darkness thrown by a towering black mass like the very gateway of Erebus—yes, I was in time to catch an evanescent glimpse of my white hat left behind to mark the spot where the secret sharer of my cabin and of my thoughts, as though he were my second self, had lowered himself into the water to take his punishment: a free man, a proud swimmer striking out for a new destiny.

1912

The first paragraph of the story clearly functions as exposition, especially in describing the **setting**—the place and time of day. Its last sentence suggests something of the situation: the speaker is alone with *his* ship. It also establishes the focus and voice. In the description of the scene in the Gulf of Siam, there are some words that, though appropriate, are not necessarily inevitable. These are words that might not be used by just any narrator or in just any circumstances and so may characterize the speaker or his situation. In the first sentence alone you may notice "mysterious," "incomprehensible," even "crazy," which, though it deals with the physical irregularity of the fences, also suggests the irrational. These words arouse suspense and so further the plot, but they may also suggest something of the theme. And, since another speaker would be likely to see things somewhat differently and use different words, his choices may also characterize the speaker. Some of the details of the paragraph may also be symbolic.

QUESTIONS AND WRITING SUGGESTIONS

1. How does the second paragraph further advance the description of setting, of situation, of theme? Are any of the details here symbolic or potentially symbolic? The last sentence of this paragraph seems to relate directly to theme, though it may also help characterize the narrator. There are many such sentences in the story—an example might be "And suddenly I rejoiced in the great security of the sea . . ." (paragraph 17). Collect five or

six such sentences and see how they relate not only to theme but to other elements.

2. How does paragraph 7 characterize the second mate, explain the narrator's situation, and further arouse suspense and define the theme?

3. How does the description of the episode with the scorpion (paragraph 8) characterize the chief mate and, when looked back upon later, further the plot and suspense? How does the chief mate's propensity for logical explanations relate to the theme?

4. How does the "unconventional arrangement" of the narrator-captain's standing the first anchor-watch relate to his character? to the plot? to the theme(s)?

5. When the narrator notices that the rope side-ladder has not been hauled in, he blames himself for having disturbed the ship's routine and conjectures about how he will look in the eyes of the officers and crew and how his conduct will be "accounted" for by the chief mate. All this relates to the characters of the two men, the plot or suspense, and the theme. It is just then that "the secret sharer" appears at the very end of that same ladder. Is he, then, in some way symbolic? If so, how? In the light of all that follows, is it good or bad to break the rules? Does following or breaking rules seem to have anything to do with being a captain? Explain.

6. What is the effect of paragraph 20, in which "something elongated and pale" appears at the bottom of the ladder? How many elements are involved in that description (including the first sentence of the next paragraph)?

7. When Leggatt is aboard and dressed in the captain's sleeping suit, he is described as looking like the captain's "double." That, plus Leggatt's arriving from the sea naked, looking like a fish, being phosphorescent and oblong, together with the title of the story and the narrator's seeing his first command as a test, has led a substantial number of critics and other readers to view these details as Freudian symbols and to attribute to this story a Freudian, or at least a psychological, theme. Make out the best case you can for such a reading of the story. What happens to the specifics of the situation, the characters, the plot? Which details are symbolic in your version, and which are not? Now make out the best case *against* such a reading. If you are so committed to one position or the other that you cannot see how there can be another side, pair yourself off with someone else in the class who has made the best counterargument.

8. When Leggatt tells his story, there is a shift in the focus and voice. How does this story within a story function in the plot of "The Secret Sharer"? How does it help define the character of Leggatt? How does it relate to the theme of "the double" in the larger story?

9. Why does the captain hide Leggatt rather than turn him in? How do all the elements of the story contribute to your answering this question?

10. The captain of the *Sephora* tells his version of Leggatt's crime, but the narrator says, "It is not worth while to record that version. It was just over two months since all this had happened, and . . . he seemed completely muddled" (paragraph 127). Yet the narrator is telling his and Leggatt's story at a "distance of years," and there is a bit of Archbold's story in the paragraphs that follow. Write a fuller (two- or three-page) version of how the *Sephora* captain would tell the story. How does this shift in focus and voice affect the plot? the characterization of the captain of the *Sephora?* of Leggatt? of the narrator of "The Secret Sharer"? the theme?

11. Archbold believes Leggatt was too gentlemanly to be chief mate of the *Sephora,* and the narrator, so identified now with Leggatt, thinks Archbold would not consider the narrator himself a suitable chief mate (much less captain). How would you analyze this notion in terms of focus? character? symbol? theme?

12. There seems to be a turn in the story after Archbold leaves: ironically, Leggatt seems more of a burden to the narrator, who now seems to see himself in his role as captain: "I was not wholly alone with my command; for there was that stranger in my cabin. . . . Part of me was absent" (paragraph 193). What is the effect of this feeling of split identity on the plot? How does it relate to focus? The whole story can be read as the initiation of the narrator into leadership or captaincy. How does Leggatt figure in that initiation

theme? How does his character relate to it? Is he a symbol? If you think he is, of what is he a symbol? How do the final episode and final two paragraphs of the story relate to this portion of the plot, this view of Leggatt, this theme? Can you imagine this story— the story of a new captain taking over command of a strange ship, with mates not of his own choosing and not of his own "kind," of the strained relations between the new captain and the other officers, of his routine and unroutine orders, of his emotional state, and of his first daring act of seamanship, of all this—without any mention of, or presence of, or story of, a Leggatt, a secret sharer? Write a brief synopsis of such a story. Is there some way in which you might still call it "The Secret Sharer"? Who has the secret and with whom does he share it?

13. How does the captain's giving Leggatt his hat figure in the plot? What does it suggest about the narrator's character and feelings? Of what, if anything, might it be a symbol?

14. Write a sequel to "The Secret Sharer" about what happens to Leggatt after he leaves the ship, using as much evidence as you can from the elements and details of Conrad's story but with a new focus and voice.

The story that follows is funnier than, but just as meaningful as, "The Secret Sharer." It is the title story, or chapter, of a work that calls itself a novel but can also be seen as a collection of related but separable stories (indeed, many of the chapters were first published separately as stories, and an expanded edition of *Love Medicine* adds four new stories or chapters and rearranges the original sequence). Reading the whole novel or collection may enrich your understanding and enjoyment of the parts, but this story is, as you will see, quite wonderful, enjoyable, and understandable by itself. It is a somewhat unfamiliar world you will be entering; though nearer to us in time and space, it is perhaps even stranger than the world of "The Secret Sharer." Stop reading after paragraph 18, look at the first of the Questions and Writing Suggestions on page 319, and get your bearings.

LOUISE ERDRICH

Love Medicine

I never really done much with my life, I suppose. I never had a television. Grandma Kashpaw had one inside her apartment at the Senior Citizens, so I used to go there and watch my favorite shows. For a while she used to call me the biggest waste on the reservation and hark back to how she saved me from my own mother, who wanted to tie me in a potato sack and throw me in a slough. Sure, I was grateful to Grandma Kashpaw for saving me like that, for raising me, but gratitude gets old. After a while, stale. I had to stop thanking her. One day I told her I had paid her back in full by staying at her beck and call. I'd do anything for Grandma. She knew that. Besides, I took care of Grandpa like nobody else could, on account of what a handful he'd gotten to be.

But that was nothing. I know the tricks of mind and body inside out without ever having trained for it, because I got the touch. It's a thing you got to be born with. I got secrets in my hands that nobody ever knew to ask. Take Grandma

Kashpaw with her tired veins all knotted up in her legs like clumps of blue snails. I take my fingers and I snap them on the knots. The medicine flows out of me. The touch. I run my fingers up the maps of those rivers of veins or I knock very gentle above their hearts or I make a circling motion on their stomachs, and it helps them. They feel much better. Some women pay me five dollars.

I couldn't do the touch for Grandpa, though. He was a hard nut. You know, some people fall right through the hole in their lives. It's invisible, but they come to it after time, never knowing where. There is this woman here, Lulu Lamartine, who always had a thing for Grandpa. She loved him since she was a girl and always said he was a genius. Now she says that his mind got so full it exploded.

How can I doubt that? I know the feeling when your mental power builds up too far. I always used to say that's why the Indians got drunk. Even statistically we're the smartest people on the earth. Anyhow with Grandpa I couldn't hardly believe it, because all my youth he stood out as a hero to me. When he started getting toward second childhood he went through different moods. He would stand in the woods and cry at the top of his shirt. It scared me, scared everyone, Grandma worst of all.

Yet he was so smart—do you believe it?—that he *knew* he was getting foolish.   5

He said so. He told me that December I failed school and come back on the train to Hoopdance. I didn't have nowhere else to go. He picked me up there and he said it straight out: "I'm getting into my second childhood." And then he said something else I still remember: "I been chosen for it. I couldn't say no." So I figure that a man so smart all his life—tribal chairman and the star of movies and even pictured in the statehouse and on cans of snuff—would know what he's doing by saying yes. I think he was called to second childhood like anybody else gets a call for the priesthood or the army or whatever. So I really did not listen too hard when the doctor said this was some kind of disease old people got eating too much sugar. You just can't tell me that a man who went to Washington and gave them bureaucrats what for could lose his mind from eating too much Milky Way. No, he put second childhood on himself.

Behind those songs he sings out in the middle of Mass, and back of those stories that everybody knows by heart, Grandpa is thinking hard about life. I know the feeling. Sometimes I'll throw up a smokescreen to think behind. I'll hitch up to Winnipeg and play the Space Invaders for six hours, but all the time there and back I will be thinking some fairly deep thoughts that surprise even me, and I'm used to it. As for him, if it was just the thoughts there wouldn't be no problem. Smokescreen is what irritates the social structure, see, and Grandpa has done things that just distract people to the point they want to throw him in the cookie jar where they keep the mentally insane. He's far from that, I know for sure, but even Grandma had trouble keeping her patience once he started sneaking off to Lamartine's place. He's not supposed to have his candy, and Lulu feeds it to him. That's *one* of the reasons why he goes.

Grandma tried to get me to put the touch on Grandpa soon after he began stepping out. I didn't want to, but before Grandma started telling me again what a bad state my bare behind was in when she first took me home, I thought I should at least pretend.

I put my hands on either side of Grandpa's head. You wouldn't look at him and say he was crazy. He's a fine figure of a man, as Lamartine would say, with all his hair and half his teeth, a beak like a hawk, and cheeks like the blades of a hatchet. They put his picture on all the tourist guides to North Dakota and even copied his face for artistic paintings. I guess you could call him a monument all of himself. He started grinning when I put my hands on his templates, and I knew right then he knew how come I touched him. I knew the smokescreen was going to fall.

10   And I was right: just for a moment it fell.

"Let's pitch whoopee," he said across my shoulder to Grandma.

They don't use that expression much around here anymore, but for damn sure it must have meant something. It got her goat right quick.

She threw my hands off his head herself and stood in front of him, over-matching him pound for pound, and taller too, for she had a growth spurt in middle age while he had shrunk, so now the length and breadth of her surpassed him. She glared and spoke her piece into his face about how he was off at all hours tomcatting and chasing Lamartine again and making a damn old fool of himself.

"And you got no more whoopee to pitch anymore anyhow!" she yelled at last, surprising me so my jaw just dropped, for us kids all had pretended for so long that those rustling sounds we heard from their side of the room at night never happened. She sure had pretended it, up till now, anyway. I saw that tears were in her eyes. And that's when I saw how much grief and love she felt for him. And it gave me a real shock to the system. You see I thought love got easier over the years so it didn't hurt so bad when it hurt, or feel so good when it felt good. I thought it smoothed out and old people hardly noticed it. I thought it curled up and died, I guess. Now I saw it rear up like a whip and lash.

15   She loved him. She was jealous. She mourned him like the dead.

And he just smiled into the air, trapped in the seams of his mind.

So I didn't know what to do. I was in a laundry then. They was like parents to me, the way they had took me home and reared me. I could see her point for wanting to get him back the way he was so at least she could argue with him, sleep with him, not be shamed out by Lamartine. She'd always love him. That hit me like a ton of bricks. For one whole day I felt this odd feeling that cramped my hands. When you have the touch, that's where longing gets you. I never loved like that. It made me feel all inspired to see them fight, and I wanted to go out and find a woman who I would love until one of us died or went crazy. But I'm not like that really. From time to time I heal a person all up good inside, however when it comes to the long shot I doubt that I got staying power.

And you need that, staying power, going out to love somebody. I knew this quality was not going to jump on me with no effort. So I turned my thoughts back to Grandma and Grandpa. I felt her side of it with my hands and my tangled guts, and I felt his side of it within the stretch of my mentality. He had gone out to lunch one day and never came back. He was fishing in the middle of Matchi-manito. And there was big thoughts on his line, and he kept throwing them back for even bigger ones that would explain to him, say, the meaning of how we got here and why we have to leave so soon. All in all, I could not see myself treating

Grandpa with the touch, bringing him back, when the real part of him had chose to be off thinking somewhere. It was only the rest of him that stayed around causing trouble, after all, and we could handle most of it without any problem.

Besides, it was hard to argue with his reasons for doing some things. Take Holy Mass. I used to go there just every so often, when I got frustrated mostly, because even though I know the Higher Power dwells everyplace, there's something very calming about the cool greenish inside of our mission. Or so I thought, anyway. Grandpa was the one who stripped off my delusions in this matter, for it was he who busted right through what Father calls the sacred serenity of the place.

We filed in that time. Me and Grandpa. We sat down in our pews. Then the 20 rosary got started up pre-Mass and that's when Grandpa filled up his chest and opened his mouth and belted out them words.

HAIL MARIE FULL OF GRACE.

He had a powerful set of lungs.

And he kept on like that. He did not let up. He hollered and he yelled them prayers, and I guess people was used to him by now, because they only muttered theirs and did not quit and gawk like I did. I was getting red-faced, I admit. I give him the elbow once or twice, but that wasn't nothing to him. He kept on. He shrieked to heaven and he pleaded like a movie actor and he pounded his chest like Tarzan in the Lord I Am Not Worthies. I thought he might hurt himself. Then after a while I guess I got used to it, and that's when I wondered: how come?

So afterwards I out and asked him. "How come? How come you yelled?"

"God don't hear me otherwise," said Grandpa Kashpaw. 25

I sweat. I broke right into a little cold sweat at my hairline because I knew this was perfectly right and for years not one damn other person had noticed it. God's been going deaf. Since the Old Testament, God's been deafening up on us. I read, see. Besides the dictionary, which I'm constantly in use of, I had this Bible once. I read it. I found there was discrepancies between then and now. It struck me. Here God used to raineth bread from clouds, smite the Phillipines, sling fire down on red-light districts where people got stabbed. He even appeared in person every once in a while. God used to pay attention, is what I'm saying.

Now there's your God in the Old Testament and there is Chippewa Gods as well. Indian Gods, good and bad, like tricky Nanabozho or the water monster, Missepeshu, who lives over in Matchimanito. That water monster was the last God I ever heard to appear. It had a weakness for young girls and grabbed one of the Pillagers off her rowboat. She got to shore all right, but only after this monster had its way with her. She's an old lady now. Old Lady Pillager. She still doesn't like to see her family fish that lake.

Our Gods aren't perfect, is what I'm saying, but at least they come around. They'll do a favor if you ask them right. You don't have to yell. But you do have to know, like I said, how to ask in the right way. That makes problems, because to ask proper was an art that was lost to the Chippewas once the Catholics gained ground. Even now, I have to wonder if Higher Power turned it back, if we got to yell, or if we just don't speak its language.

I looked around me. How else could I explain what all I had seen in my short life—King smashing his fist in things, Gordie drinking himself down to the Bismarck hospitals, or Aunt June left by a white man to wander off in the snow. How else to explain the times my touch don't work, and farther back, to the oldtime Indians who was swept away in the outright germ warfare and dirty-dog killing of the whites. In those times, us Indians was so much kindlier than now.

30   We took them in.

Oh yes, I'm bitter as an old cutworm just thinking of how they done to us and doing still.

So Grandpa Kashpaw just opened my eyes a little there. Was there any sense relying on a God whose ears was stopped? Just like the government? I says then, right off, maybe we got nothing but ourselves. And that's not much, just personally speaking. I know I don't got the cold hard potatoes it takes to understand everything. Still, there's things I'd like to do. For instance, I'd like to help some people like my Grandpa and Grandma Kashpaw get back some happiness within the tail ends of their lives.

I told you once before I couldn't see my way clear to putting the direct touch on Grandpa's mind, and I kept my moral there, but something soon happened to make me think a little bit of mental adjustment wouldn't do him and the rest of us no harm.

It was after we saw him one afternoon in the sunshine courtyard of the Senior Citizens with Lulu Lamartine. Grandpa used to like to dig there. He had his little dandelion fork out, and he was prying up them dandelions right and left while Lamartine watched him.

35   "He's scratching up the dirt, all right," said Grandma, watching Lamartine watch Grandpa out the window.

Now Lamartine was about half the considerable size of Grandma, but you would never think of sizes anyway. They were different in an even more noticeable way. It was the difference between a house fixed up with paint and picky fence, and a house left to weather away into the soft earth, is what I'm saying. Lamartine was jacked up, latticed, shuttered, and vinyl sided, while Grandma sagged and bulged on her slipped foundations and let her hair go the silver gray of rain-dried lumber. Right now, she eyed the Lamartine's pert flowery dress with such a look it despaired me. I knew what this could lead to with Grandma. Alternating tongue storms and rock-hard silences was hard on a man, even one who didn't notice, like Grandpa. So I went fetching him.

But he was gone when I popped through the little screen door that led out on the courtyard. There was nobody out there either, to point which way they went. Just the dandelion fork quibbling upright in the ground. That gave me an idea. I snookered over to the Lamartine's door and I listened in first, then knocked. But nobody. So I went walking through the lounges and around the card tables. Still nobody. Finally it was my touch that led me to the laundry room. I cracked the door. I went in. There they were. And he was really loving her up good, boy, and she was going hell for leather. Sheets was flapping on the lines above, and washcloths, pillowcases, shirts was also flying through the air, for they was trying to clear out a place for themselves in a high-heaped but shallow laundry cart. The washers and dryers was all on, chock-full of quarters, shaking and moaning. I couldn't hear what Grandpa and the Lamartine was billing and cooing, and they couldn't hear me.

I didn't know what to do, so I went inside and shut the door.

The Lamartine wore a big curly light-brown wig. Looked like one of them squeaky little white-people dogs. Poodles they call them. Anyway, that wig is what saved us from the worse. For I could hardly shout and tell them I was in there, no more could I try and grab him. I was trapped where I was. There was nothing I could really do but hold the door shut. I was scared of somebody else upsetting in and really getting an eyeful. Turned out though, in the heat of the clinch, as I was trying to avert my eyes you see, the Lamartine's curly wig jumped off her head. And if you ever been in the midst of something and had a big change like that occur in the someone, you can't help know how it devastates your basic urges. Not only that, but her wig was almost with a life of its own. Grandpa's eyes were bugging at the change already, and swear to God if the thing didn't rear up and pop him in the face like it was going to start something. He scrambled up, Grandpa did, and the Lamartine jumped up after him all addled looking. They just stared at each other, huffing and puffing, with quizzical expression. The surprise seemed to drive all sense completely out of Grandpa's mind.

"The letter was what started the fire," he said. "I never would have done it."   40

"What letter?" said the Lamartine. She was stiff-necked now, and elegant, even bald, like some alien queen. I gave her back the wig. The Lamartine replaced it on her head, and whenever I saw her after that, I couldn't help thinking of her bald, with special powers, as if from another planet.

"That was a close call," I said to Grandpa after she had left.

But I think he had already forgot the incident. He just stood there all quiet and thoughtful. You really wouldn't think he was crazy. He looked like he was just about to say something important, explaining himself. He said something, all right, but it didn't have nothing to do with anything that made sense.

He wondered where the heck he put his dandelion fork. That's when I decided about the mental adjustment.

Now what was mostly our problem was not so much that he was not all there,   45 but that what was there of him often hankered after Lamartine. If we could put a stop to that, I thought, we might be getting someplace. But here, see, my touch was of no use. For what could I snap my fingers at to make him faithful to Grandma? Like the quality of staying power, this faithfulness was invisible. I know it's something that you got to acquire, but I never known where from. Maybe there's no rhyme or reason to it, like my getting the touch, and then again maybe it's a kind of magic.

It was Grandma Kashpaw who thought of it in the end. She knows things. Although she will not admit she has a scrap of Indian blood in her, there's no doubt in my mind she's got some Chippewa. How else would you explain the way she'll be sitting there, in front of her TV story, rocking in her armchair and suddenly she turns on me, her brown eyes hard as lake-bed flint.

"Lipsha Morrissey," she'll say, "you went out last night and got drunk."

How did she know that? I'll hardly remember it myself. Then she'll say she just had a feeling or ache in the scar of her hand or a creak in her shoulder. She is constantly being told things by little aggravations in her joints or by her household appliances. One time she told Gordie never to ride with a crazy Lamartine boy. She had seen something in the polished-up tin of her bread toaster. So he didn't. Sure enough, the time came we heard how Lyman and Henry went out of control in their car, ending up in the river. Lyman swam to the top, but Henry never made it.

Thanks to Grandma's toaster, Gordie was probably spared.

50   Someplace in the blood Grandma Kashpaw knows things. She also remembers things, I found. She keeps things filed away. She's got a memory like them video games that don't forget your score. One reason she remembers so many details about the trouble I gave her in early life is so she can flash back her total when she needs to.

Like now. Take the love medicine. I don't know where she remembered that from. It came tumbling from her mind like an asteroid off the corner of the screen.

Of course she starts out by mentioning the time I had this accident in church and did she leave me there with wet overhalls? No she didn't. And ain't I glad? Yes I am. Now what you want now, Grandma?

But when she mentions them love medicines, I feel my back prickle at the danger. These love medicines is something of an old Chippewa specialty. No other tribe has got them down so well. But love medicines is not for the layman to handle. You don't just go out and get one without paying for it. Before you get one, even, you should go through one hell of a lot of mental condensation. You got to think it over. Choose the right one. You could really mess up your life grinding up the wrong little thing.

So anyhow, I said to Grandma I'd give this love medicine some thought. I knew the best thing was to go ask a specialist like Old Lady Pillager, who lives up in a tangle of bush and never shows herself. But the truth is I was afraid of her, like everyone else. She was known for putting the twisted mouth on people, seizing up their hearts. Old Lady Pillager was serious business, and I have always thought it best to steer clear of that whenever I could. That's why I took the powers in my own hands. That's why I did what I could.

55   I put my whole mentality to it, nothing held back. After a while I started to remember things I'd heard gossiped over.

I heard of this person once who carried a charm of seeds that looked like baby pearls. They was attracted to a metal knife, which made them powerful. But I didn't know where them seeds grew. Another love charm I heard about I couldn't go along with, because how was I suppose to catch frogs in the act, which it required. Them little creatures is slippery and fast. And then the powerfullest of all, the most extreme, involved nail clips and such. I wasn't anywhere near asking Grandma to provide me all the little body bits that this last love recipe called for. I went walking around for days just trying to think up something that would work.

Well I got it. If it hadn't been the early fall of the year, I never would have got it. But I was sitting underneath a tree one day down near the school just watching people's feet go by when something tells me, look up! Look up! So I look up, and I see two honkers, Canada geese, the kind with little masks on their faces, a bird what mates for life. I see them flying right over my head naturally preparing to land in some slough on the reservation, which they certainly won't get off of alive.

It hits me, anyway. Them geese, they mate for life. And I think to myself, just what if I went out and got a pair? And just what if I fed some part—say the goose heart—of the female to Grandma and Grandpa ate the other heart? Wouldn't that work? Maybe it's all invisible, and then maybe again it's magic. Love is a stony road. We know that for sure. If it's true that the higher feelings of devotion get lodged in the heart like people say, then we'd be home free. If not, eating goose heart couldn't harm nobody anyway. I thought it was worth my effort, and Grandma Kashpaw thought so, too. She had always known a good idea when she heard one. She borrowed me Grandpa's gun.

So I went out to this particular slough, maybe the exact same slough I never got thrown in by my mother, thanks to Grandma Kashpaw, and I hunched down in a good comfortable pile of rushes. I got my gun loaded up. I ate a few of these soft baloney sandwiches Grandma made me for lunch. And then I waited. The cattails blown back and forth above my head. Them stringy blue herons was spearing up their prey. The thing I know how to do best in this world, the thing I been training for all my life, is to wait. Sitting there and sitting there was no hardship on me. I got to thinking about some funny things that happened. There was this one time that Lulu Lamartine's little blue tweety bird, a paraclete, I guess you'd call it, flown up inside her dress and got lost within there. I recalled her running out into the hallway trying to yell something, shaking. She was doing a right good jig there, cutting the rug for sure, and the thing is it *never* flown out. To this day people speculate where it went. They fear she might perhaps of crushed it in her corsets. It sure hasn't ever yet been seen alive. I thought of funny things for a while, but then I used them up, and strange things that happened started weaseling their way into my mind.

I got to thinking quite naturally of the Lamartine's cousin named Wristwatch. I never knew what his real name was. They called him Wristwatch because he got his father's broken wristwatch as a young boy when his father passed on. Never in his whole life did Wristwatch take his father's watch off. He didn't care if it worked, although after a while he got sensitive when people asked what time it was, teasing him. He often put it to his ear like he was listening to the tick. But it was broken for good and forever, people said so, at least that's what they thought.

Well I saw Wristwatch smoking in his pickup one afternoon and by nine that evening he was dead.

He died sitting at the Lamartine's table, too. As she told it, Wristwatch had just eaten himself a good-size dinner and she said would he take seconds on the hot dish when he fell over to the floor. They turnt him over. He was gone. But here's the strange thing: when the Senior Citizen's orderly took the pulse he noticed that the wristwatch Wristwatch wore was now working. The moment he died the wristwatch started keeping perfect time. They buried him with the watch still ticking on his arm.

I got to thinking. What if some gravediggers dug up Wristwatch's casket in two hundred years and that watch was still going? I thought what question they would ask and it was this: Whose hand wound it?

I started shaking like a piece of grass at just the thought.

65   Not to get off the subject or nothing. I was still hunkered in the slough. It was passing late into the afternoon and still no honkers had touched down. Now I don't need to tell you that the waiting did not get to me, it was the chill. The rushes was very soft, but damp. I was getting cold and debating to leave, when they landed. Two geese swimming here and there as big as life, looking deep into each other's little pinhole eyes. Just the ones I was looking for. So I lifted Grandpa's gun to my shoulder and I aimed perfectly, and *blam! Blam!* I delivered two accurate shots. But the thing is, them shots missed. I couldn't hardly believe it. Whether it was that the stock had warped or the barrel got bent someways, I don't quite know, but anyway them geese flown off into the dim sky, and Lipsha Morrissey was left there in the rushes with evening fallen and his two cold hands empty. He had before him just the prospect of another day of bone-cracking chill in them rushes, and the thought of it got him depressed.

Now it isn't my style, in no way, to get depressed.

So I said to myself, Lipsha Morrissey, you're a happy S.O.B. who could be covered up with weeds by now down at the bottom of this slough, but instead you're alive to tell the tale. You might have problems in life, but you still got the touch. You got the power, Lipsha Morrissey. Can't argue that. So put your mind to it and figure out how not to be depressed.

I took my advice. I put my mind to it. But I never saw at the time how my thoughts led me astray toward a tragic outcome none could have known. I ignored all the danger, all the limits, for I was tired of sitting in the slough and my feet were numb. My face was aching. I was chilled, so I played with fire. I told myself love medicine was simple. I told myself the old superstitions was just that—strange beliefs. I told myself to take the ten dollars Mary MacDonald had paid me for putting the touch on her arthritis joint, and the other five I hadn't spent yet from winning bingo last Thursday. I told myself to go down to the Red Owl store.

And here is what I did that made the medicine backfire. I took an evil shortcut. I looked at birds that was dead and froze.

70   All right. So now I guess you will say, "Slap a malpractice suit on Lipsha Morrissey."

I heard of those suits. I used to think it was a color clothing quack doctors had to wear so you could tell them from the good ones. Now I know better that it's law.

As I walked back from the Red Owl with the rock-hard, heavy turkeys, I argued to myself about malpractice. I thought of faith. I thought to myself that faith could be called belief against the odds and whether or not there's any proof. How does that sound? I thought how we might have to yell to be heard by Higher Power, but that's not saying it's not *there*. And that is faith for you. It's belief even when the goods don't deliver. Higher Power makes promises we all know they can't back up, but anybody ever go and slap an old malpractice suit on God? Or the U.S. government? No they don't. Faith might be stupid, but it gets us through. So what I'm heading at is this. I finally convinced myself that the real actual power to the love medicine was not the goose heart itself but the faith in the cure.

I didn't believe it, I knew it was wrong, but by then I had waded so far into my lie I was stuck there. And then I went one step further.

The next day, I cleaned the hearts away from the paper packages of gizzards inside the turkeys. Then I wrapped them hearts with a clean hankie and brung them both to get blessed up at the mission. I wanted to get official blessings from the priest, but when Father answered the door to the rectory, wiping his hands on a little towel, I could tell he was a busy man.

"Booshoo,[1] Father," I said. "I got a slight request to make of you this   75
afternoon."

"What is it?" he said.

"Would you bless this package?" I held out the hankie with the hearts tied inside it.

He looked at the package, questioning it.

"It's turkey hearts," I honestly had to reply.

A look of annoyance crossed his face.   80

"Why don't you bring this matter over to Sister Martin," he said. "I have duties."

And so, although the blessing wouldn't be as powerful, I went over to the Sisters with the package.

I rung the bell, and they brought Sister Martin to the door. I had her as a music teacher, but I was always so shy then. I never talked out loud. Now, I had grown taller than Sister Martin. Looking down, I saw that she was not feeling up to snuff. Brown circles hung under her eyes.

"What's the matter?" she said, not noticing who I was.

"Remember me, Sister?"   85

She squinted up at me.

"Oh yes," she said after a moment. "I'm sorry, you're the youngest of the Kashpaws. Gordie's brother."

Her face warmed up.

"Lipsha," I said, "that's my name."

"Well, Lipsha," she said, smiling broad at me now, "what can I do for you?"   90

They always said she was the kindest-hearted of the Sisters up the hill, and she was. She brought me back into their own kitchen and made me take a big yellow wedge of cake and a glass of milk.

"Now tell me," she said, nodding at my package. "What have you got wrapped up so carefully in those handkerchiefs?"

Like before, I answered honestly.

---

1. *Bonjour,* French for "good day."

"Ah," said Sister Martin. "Turkey hearts." She waited.

95 "I hoped you could bless them."

She waited some more, smiling with her eyes. Kindhearted though she was, I began to sweat. A person could not pull the wool down over Sister Martin. I stumbled through my mind for an explanation, quick, that wouldn't scare her off.

"They're a present," I said, "for Saint Kateri's statue."

"She's not a saint yet."

"I know," I stuttered on. "In the hopes they will crown her."

100 "Lipsha," she said, "I never heard of such a thing."

So I told her. "Well the truth is," I said, "it's a kind of medicine."

"For what?"

"Love."

"Oh Lipsha," she said after a moment, "you don't need any medicine. I'm sure any girl would like you exactly the way you are."

105 I just sat there. I felt miserable, caught in my pack of lies.

"Tell you what," she said, seeing how bad I felt, "my blessing won't make any difference anyway. But there is something you can do."

I looked up at her, hopeless.

"Just be yourself."

I looked down at my plate. I knew I wasn't much to brag about right then, and I shortly became even less. For as I walked out the door I stuck my fingers in the cup of holy water that was sacred from their touches. I put my fingers in and blessed the hearts, quick, with my own hand.

110 I went back to Grandma and sat down in her little kitchen at the Senior Citizens. I unwrapped them hearts on the table, and her hard agate eyes went soft. She said she wasn't even going to cook those hearts up but eat them raw so their power would go down strong as possible.

I couldn't hardly watch when she munched hers. Now that's true love. I was worried about how she would get Grandpa to eat his, but she told me she'd think of something and don't worry. So I did not. I was supposed to hide off in her bedroom while she put dinner on a plate for Grandpa and fixed up the heart so he'd eat it. I caught a glint of the plate she was making for him. She put that heart smack on a piece of lettuce like in a restaurant and then attached to it a little heap of boiled peas.

He sat down. I was listening in the next room.

She said, "Why don't you have some mash potato?" So he had some mash potato. Then she gave him a little piece of boiled meat. He ate that. Then she said, "Why you didn't never touch your salad yet. See that heart? I'm feeding you it because the doctor said your blood needs building up."

I couldn't help it, at that point I peeked through a crack in the door.

115 I saw Grandpa picking at that heart on his plate with a certain look. He didn't look appetized at all, is what I'm saying. I doubted our plan was going to work. Grandma was getting worried, too. She told him one more time, loudly, that he had to eat that heart.

"Swallow it down," she said. "You'll hardly notice it."

He just looked at her straight on. The way he looked at her made me think I was going to see the smokescreen drop a second time, and sure enough it happened.

"What you want me to eat this for so bad?" he asked her uncannily.

Now Grandma knew the jig was up. She knew that he knew she was working medicine. He put his fork down. He rolled the heart around his saucer plate.

"I don't want to eat this," he said to Grandma. "It don't look good." 120

"Why it's fresh grade-A," she told him. "One hundred percent."

He didn't ask percent what, but his eyes took on an even more warier look.

"Just go on and try it," she said, taking the salt shaker up in her hand. She was getting annoyed. "Not tasty enough? You want me to salt it for you?" She waved the shaker over his plate.

"All right, skinny white girl!" She had got Grandpa mad. Oopsy-daisy, he popped the heart into his mouth. I was about to yawn loudly and come out of the bedroom. I was about ready for this crash of wills to be over, when I saw he was still up to his old tricks. First he rolled it into one side of his cheek. "Mmmmm," he said. Then he rolled it into the other side of his cheek. "Mmmmmmm," again. Then he stuck his tongue out with the heart on it and put it back, and there was no time to react. He had pulled Grandma's leg once too far. Her goat was got. She was so mad she hopped up quick as a wink and slugged him between the shoulderblades to make him swallow.

Only thing is, he choked. 125

He choked real bad. A person can choke to death. You ever sit down at a restaurant table and up above you there is a list of instructions what to do if something slides down the wrong pipe? It sure makes you chew slow, that's for damn sure. When Grandpa fell off his chair better believe me that little graphic illustrated poster fled into my mind. I jumped out the bedroom. I done everything within my power that I could do to unlodge what was choking him. I squeezed underneath his rib cage. I socked him in the back. I was desperate. But here's the factor of decision: he wasn't choking on the heart alone. There was more to it than that. It was other things that choked him as well. It didn't seem like he wanted to struggle or fight. Death came and tapped his chest, so he went just like that. I'm sorry all through my body at what I done to him with that heart, and there's those who will say Lipsha Morrissey is just excusing himself off the hook by giving song and dance about how Grandpa gave up.

Maybe I can't admit what I did. My touch had gone worthless, that is true. But here is what I seen while he lay in my arms.

You hear a person's life will flash before their eyes when they're in danger. It was him in danger, not me, but it was *his* life come over me. I saw him dying, and it was like someone pulled the shade down in a room. His eyes clouded over and squeezed shut, but just before that I looked in. He was still fishing in the middle of Matchimanito. Big thoughts was on his line and he had half a case of beer in the boat. He waved at me, grinned, and then the bobber went under.

Grandma had gone out of the room crying for help. I bunched my force up in my hands and I held him. I was so wound up I couldn't even breathe. All the moments he had spent with me, all the times he had hoisted me on his shoulders or pointed into the leaves was concentrated in that moment. Time was flashing back and forth like a pinball machine. Lights blinked and balls hopped and rubber bands chirped, until suddenly I realized the last ball had gone down the drain and there was nothing. I felt his force leaving him, flowing out of Grandpa never to return. I felt his mind weakening. The bobber going under in the lake. And I felt the touch retreat back into the darkness inside my body, from where it came.

130   One time, long ago, both of us were fishing together. We caught a big old snapper what started towing us around like it was a motor. "This here fishline is pretty damn good," Grandpa said. "Let's keep this turtle on and see where he takes us." So we rode along behind that turtle, watching as from time to time it surfaced. The thing was just about the size of a washtub. It took us all around the lake twice, and as it was traveling, Grandpa said something as a joke. "Lipsha," he said, "we are glad your mother didn't want you because we was always looking for a boy like you who would tow us around the lake."

"I ain't no snapper. Snappers is so stupid they stay alive when their head's chopped off," I said.

"That ain't stupidity," said Grandpa. "Their brain's just in their heart, like yours is."

When I looked up, I knew the fuse had blown between my heart and my mind and that a terrible understanding was to be given.

Grandma got back into the room and I saw her stumble. And then she went down too. It was like a house you can't hardly believe has stood so long, through years of record weather, suddenly goes down in the worst yet. It makes sense, is what I'm saying, but you still can't hardly believe it. You think a person you know has got through death and illness and being broke and living on commodity rice will get through anything. Then they fold and you see how fragile were the stones that underpinned them. You see how instantly the ground can shift you thought was solid. You see the stop signs and the yellow dividing markers of roads you traveled and all the instructions you had played according to vanish. You see how all the everyday things you counted on was just a dream you had been having by which you run your whole life. She had been over me, like a sheer overhang of rock dividing Lipsha Morrissey from outer space. And now she went underneath. It was as though the banks gave way on the shores of Matchimanito, and where Grandpa's passing was just the bobber swallowed under by his biggest thought, her fall was the house and the rock under it sliding after, sending half the lake splashing up to the clouds.

135   Where there was nothing.

You play them games never knowing what you see. When I fell into the dream alongside of both of them I saw that the dominions I had defended myself from anciently was but delusions of the screen. Blips of light. And I was scot-free now, whistling through space.

I don't know how I come back. I don't know from where. They was slapping my face when I arrived back at Senior Citizens and they was oxygenating her. I saw her chest move, almost unwilling. She sighed the way she would when somebody bothered her in the middle of a row of beads she was counting. I think it irritated her to no end that they brought her back. I knew from the way she looked after they took the mask off, she was not going to forgive them disturbing her restful peace. Nor was she forgiving Lipsha Morrissey. She had been stepping out onto the road of death, she told the children later at the funeral. I asked was there any stop signs or dividing markers on that road, but she clamped her lips in a vise the way she always done when she was mad.

Which didn't bother me. I knew when things had cleared out she wouldn't have no choice. I was not going to speculate where the blame was put for Grandpa's death. We was in it together. She had slugged him between the shoulders. My touch had failed him, never to return.

All the blood children and the took-ins, like me, came home from Minneapolis and Chicago, where they had relocated years ago. They stayed with friends on the reservation or with Aurelia or slept on Grandma's floor. They were struck down with grief and bereavement to be sure, every one of them. At the funeral I sat down in the back of the church with Albertine. She had gotten all skinny and ragged haired from cramming all her years of study into two or three. She had decided that to be a nurse was not enough for her so she was going to be a doctor. But the way she was straining her mind didn't look too hopeful. Her eyes were bloodshot from driving and crying. She took my hand. From the back we watched all the children and the mourners as they hunched over their prayers, their hands stuffed full of Kleenex. It was someplace in that long sad service that my vision shifted. I began to see things different, more clear. The family kneeling down turned to rocks in a field. It struck me how strong and reliable grief was, and death. Until the end of time, death would be our rock.

So I had perspective on it all, for death gives you that. All the Kashpaw children had done various things to me in their lives—shared their folks with me, loaned me cash, beat me up in secret—and I decided, because of death, then and there I'd call it quits. If I ever saw King again, I'd shake his hand. Forgiving somebody else made the whole thing easier to bear.

Everybody saw Grandpa off into the next world. And then the Kashpaws had to get back to their jobs, which was numerous and impressive. I had a few beers with them and I went back to Grandma, who had sort of got lost in the shuffle of everybody being sad about Grandpa and glad to see one another.

Zelda had sat beside her the whole time and was sitting with her now. I wanted to talk to Grandma, say how sorry I was, that it wasn't her fault, but only mine. I would have, but Zelda gave me one of her looks of strict warning as if to say, "I'll take care of Grandma. Don't horn in on the women."

If only Zelda knew, I thought, the sad realities would change her. But of course I couldn't tell the dark truth.

It was evening, late. Grandma's light was on underneath a crack in the door. About a week had passed since we buried Grandpa. I knocked first but there wasn't no answer, so I went right in. The door was unlocked. She was there but she didn't notice me at first. Her hands were tied up in her rosary, and her gaze was fully absorbed in the easy chair opposite her, the one that had always been Grandpa's favorite. I stood there, staring with her, at the little green nubs in the cloth and plastic armrest covers and the sad little hair-tonic stain he had made on the white doily where he laid his head. For the life of me I couldn't figure what she was staring at. Thin space. Then she turned.

145   "He ain't gone yet," she said.

Remember that chill I luckily didn't get from waiting in the slough? I got it now. I felt it start from the very center of me, where fear hides, waiting to attack. It spiraled outward so that in minutes my fingers and teeth were shaking and clattering. I knew she told the truth. She seen Grandpa. Whether or not he had been there is not the point. She had *seen* him, and that meant anybody else could see him, too. Not only that but, as is usually the case with these here ghosts, he had a certain uneasy reason to come back. And of course Grandma Kashpaw had scanned it out.

I sat down. We sat together on the couch watching his chair out of the corner of our eyes. She had found him sitting in his chair when she walked in the door.

"It's the love medicine, my Lipsha," she said. "It was stronger than we thought. He came back even after death to claim me to his side."

I was afraid. "We shouldn't have tampered with it," I said. She agreed. For a while we sat still. I don't know what she thought, but my head felt screwed on backward. I couldn't accurately consider the situation, so I told Grandma to go to bed. I would sleep on the couch keeping my eye on Grandpa's chair. Maybe he would come back and maybe he wouldn't. I guess I feared the one as much as the other, but I got to thinking, see, as I lay there in darkness, that perhaps even through my terrible mistakes some good might come. If Grandpa did come back, I thought he'd return in his right mind. I could talk with him. I could tell him it was all my fault for playing with power I did not understand. Maybe he'd forgive me and rest in peace. I hoped this. I calmed myself and waited for him all night.

150   He fooled me though. He knew what I was waiting for, and it wasn't what he was looking to hear. Come dawn I heard a blood-splitting cry from the bedroom and I rushed in there. Grandma turnt the lights on. She was sitting on the edge of the bed and her face looked harsh, pinched-up, gray.

"He was here," she said. "He came and laid down next to me in bed. And he touched me."

Her heart broke down. She cried. His touch was so cold. She laid back in bed after a while, as it was morning, and I went to the couch. As I lay there, falling asleep, I suddenly felt Grandpa's presence and the barrier between us like a swollen river. I felt how I had wronged him. How awful was the place where I had sent him. Behind the wall of death, he'd watched the living eat and cry and get drunk. He was lonesome, but I understood he meant no harm.

"Go back," I said to the dark, afraid and yet full of pity. "You got to be with your own kind now," I said. I felt him retreating, like a sigh, growing less. I felt his spirit as it shrunk back through the walls, the blinds, the brick courtyard of Senior Citizens. "Look up Aunt June," I whispered as he left.

I slept late the next morning, a good hard sleep allowing the sun to rise and warm the earth. It was past noon when I awoke. There is nothing, to my mind, like a long sleep to make those hard decisions that you neglect under stress of wake-fulness. Soon as I woke up that morning, I saw exactly what I'd say to Grandma. I had gotten humble in the past week, not just losing the touch but getting jolted into the understanding that would prey on me from here on out. Your life feels different on you, once you greet death and understand your heart's position. You wear your life like a garment from the mission bundle sale ever after—lightly because you realize you never paid nothing for it, cherishing because you know you won't ever come by such a bargain again. Also you have the feeling someone wore it before you and someone will after. I can't explain that, not yet, but I'm putting my mind to it.

"Grandma," I said, "I got to be honest about the love medicine."   155

She listened. I knew from then on she would be listening to me the way I had listened to her before. I told her about the turkey hearts and how I had them blessed. I told her what I used as love medicine was purely a fake, and then I said to her what my understanding brought me.

"Love medicine ain't what brings him back to you, Grandma. No, it's some-thing else. He loved you over time and distance, but he went off so quick he never got the chance to tell you how he loves you, how he doesn't blame you, how he understands. It's true feeling, not no magic. No supermarket heart could have brung him back."

She looked at me. She was seeing the years and days I had no way of knowing, and she didn't believe me. I could tell this. Yet a look came on her face. It was like the look of mothers drinking sweetness from their children's eyes. It was tenderness.

"Lipsha," she said, "you was always my favorite."

She took the beads off the bedpost, where she kept them to say at night, and   160
she told me to put out my hand. When I did this, she shut the beads inside of my fist and held them there a long minute, tight, so my hand hurt. I almost cried when she did this. I don't really know why. Tears shot up behind my eyelids, and yet it was nothing. I didn't understand, except her hand was so strong, squeezing mine.

The earth was full of life and there were dandelions growing out the window, thick as thieves, already seeded, fat as big yellow plungers. She let my hand go. I got up. "I'll go out and dig a few dandelions," I told her.

Outside, the sun was hot and heavy as a hand on my back. I felt it flow down my arms, out my fingers, arrowing through the ends of the fork into the earth. With every root I prized up there was return, as if I was kin to its secret lesson. The touch got stronger as I worked through the grassy afternoon. Uncurling from me like a seed out of the blackness where I was lost, the touch spread. The spiked leaves full of bitter mother's milk. A buried root. A nuisance people dig up and throw in the sun to wither. A globe of frail seeds that's indestructible.

1982

QUESTIONS AND WRITING SUGGESTIONS

1. In the first dramatized scene, Lipsha, the narrator, at Grandma Kashpaw's request, tries to "put the touch" on Grandpa. By this time, some seventeen or eighteen paragraphs into the story, focus and voice and the setting and situation have been established; you should be getting a good idea of Lipsha's character, you should be forming some fairly definite expectations about the plot, and, with the help of the title, you should have some glimmers about the developing theme. Write down what you have observed of the structure and elements of the story and what you expect to happen. As you read on, note how your expectations are fulfilled or modified: in what ways are these surprises or changes in expectations related to plot? character? theme? and how do they define the world of the fiction? differ from your prior view of the world? To what extent are they convincing?

2. Voice is a dominant element in this story, and it is in large measure through Lipsha's voice that we infer his character. His language is ungrammatical—the story opens with "I never really *done* much" and is full of phrases like "I don't got"—and his malapropisms (ludicrous misuse of words)—"templates" for "temples," "laundry" for "quandary," and "Phillipines" for "Philistines"—tend to undercut his apparent confidence in his literary skills ("Besides the dictionary, which I'm constantly in use of, I had this Bible once. I read it" [paragraph 26]). His limitations, skillfully indicated, extend to his somewhat naive view of reality—or causality: for example, his version of why Grandpa has symptoms of senility, his "thoughtful" acceptance of Grandpa's illuminating insight that God is going deaf. These errors, attitudes, and views, however, are endearing and often quite funny. Some of them will turn out, in strange ways, to seem almost wise. His kindness and good nature show through the errors and naivete, and he is capable of insights that, though naive and tender, are not ludicrous: "I thought love got easier over the years so it didn't hurt so bad when it hurt, or feel so good when it felt good" (paragraph 14); "From time to time I heal a person all up good inside, however when it comes to the long shot I doubt I got staying power. / And you need that, staying power, going out to love somebody" (paragraphs 17 and 18). His voice reveals character and theme, and his character is instrumental in this plot. Write a paper that shows how the theme is presented in this story through a character who is not well educated or intellectually profound and how the character's very limitations contribute meaning and force to that theme.

3. How is "love medicine" related to the plot? to Grandma's and Lipsha's characters? to theme? In what way(s) may it be considered a symbol?

4. Lipsha tells the stories of Lulu's "tweety bird" that disappeared up her dress and of Wristwatch, whose broken watch started keeping time after its owner dropped dead. He then says, "Not to get off the subject or nothing" (paragraph 65). Are these stories off the subject? How do they arouse expectations? How do they function in the plot? What do they tell you of Lipsha's character? of the nature of the people on the reservation? Are they related to the theme? if so, how? When he thinks of Wristwatch's grave being dug up in two hundred years, the watch still running, and the diggers asking, "Whose hand wound it?" he says he "started shaking like a piece of grass at just the thought" (paragraph 64). Is it with awe and fear or with laughter? Do you find it awesome or funny? If there is a difference between how you feel and how you believe Lipsha feels, what is the effect? What is the relationship of this difference to plot, character, voice, and the other elements of the story? How is this episode related to the "subject" he does not mean to be getting off of when the story continues: for example, he says he fires two "accurate" shots at the geese but the shots miss; how does this affect your view of his "reliability" and thus your reading of character? plot? theme? How does it affect your reading of his glance forward, "I never saw at the time how my thoughts led me astray toward a tragic outcome none could have known" (paragraph 68)? There is a death involved. Is it "tragic"? How do you respond to it? He says he took "an evil shortcut" in practicing love medicine: does that mean that he has discovered that the old beliefs are not "superstitions" or "strange" as he thought at the time?

5. Toward the end of the story, Lipsha tells Grandma that it was not "love medicine" that

brought Grandpa's ghost back to her but love itself, not magic but feeling. Grandma looks at him tenderly and says, " 'Lipsha, . . . you was always my favorite' " (paragraph 159). Explain this passage in terms of the plot (but be sure to remember Lulu); in terms of Lipsha's character; in terms of Grandma's; in terms of theme (and you might even want to think of "love medicine" as symbol).

"The Open Boat" is a very different kind of story. It engages, from the very beginning, a powerful sense of fear and impending tragedy; the story's major effects involve suspense over whether the four men in a boat can survive in their battle with the raging seas. As in "Love Medicine," the effects depend heavily on the narrative point of view, our knowing events from the "inside" as they happen rather than from a larger, or longer, perspective on them. Thinking about the elements of a story—plot, character, setting, symbol, and theme as well as point of view—can be very helpful here in sorting out how the story generates its strong sense of anxiety and potential doom. The plot is, in one sense, very simple—four men in a boat trying to get to shore safely after a shipwreck—and the theme can also be phrased simply and in several different ways: as humanity against nature, for example, or the trial of human experience and ingenuity, or the way community is formed in the face of common peril. And from the first words, the setting—the stormy seas off the coast of Florida—is presented in the bleakest terms. Setting or location, here, *is* fate, or we might say it is plot and character combined. The accident of being in the wrong place at the wrong time, yet of continuing among the survivors, becomes a relentless test of character and a suspension of outcome. The waves constantly shifting the angles of their challenge seem to symbolize the life-or-death *itproblem the men face in their small boat. Although the necessary basic knowledge about each element is presented within the opening paragraphs, notice, as you read, how details accumulate to enrich and complicate each of the elements as the story proceeds. It might even be a good idea to jot down, or mark in the margins, the various elaborations of detail that further each element.

STEPHEN CRANE

The Open Boat

A Tale Intended to Be after the Fact:[1] Being the Experience of Four Men from the Sunk Steamer Commodore

I

None of them knew the color of the sky. Their eyes glanced level and were fastened upon the waves that swept toward them. These waves were of the hue of slate, save for the tops, which were of foaming white, and all of the men knew the colors of the sea. The horizon narrowed and widened, and dipped and rose,

1. Crane had an experience very like the one here re-created in fiction. The autobiographical account of his sea experience was published in the New York *Press* on January 7, 1897.

and at all times its edge was jagged with waves that seemed thrust up in points like rocks.

Many a man ought to have a bathtub larger than the boat which here rode upon the sea. These waves were most wrongfully and barbarously abrupt and tall, and each froth-top was a problem in small-boat navigation.

The cook squatted in the bottom, and looked with both eyes at the six inches of gunwale which separated him from the ocean. His sleeves were rolled over his fat forearms, and the two flaps of his unbuttoned vest dangled as he bent to bail out the boat. Often he said, "Gawd! that was a narrow clip." As he remarked it he invariably gazed eastward over the broken sea.

The oiler, steering with one of the two oars in the boat, sometimes raised himself suddenly to keep clear of water that swirled in over the stern. It was a thin little oar, and it seemed often ready to snap.

5   The correspondent, pulling at the other oar, watched the waves and wondered why he was there.

The injured captain, lying in the bow, was at this time buried in that profound dejection and indifference which comes, temporarily at least, to even the bravest and most enduring when, willy-nilly, the firm fails, the army loses, the ship goes down. The mind of the master of a vessel is rooted deep in the timbers of her, though he command for a day or a decade; and this captain had on him the stern impression of a scene in the grays of dawn of seven turned faces, and later a stump of a topmast with a white ball on it, that slashed to and fro at the waves, went low and lower, and down. Thereafter there was something strange in his voice. Although steady, it was deep with mourning, and of a quality beyond oration or tears.

"Keep 'er a little more south, Billie," said he.

"A little more south, sir," said the oiler in the stern.

A seat in his boat was not unlike a seat upon a bucking broncho, and by the same token a broncho is not much smaller. The craft pranced and reared and plunged like an animal. As each wave came, and she rose for it, she seemed like a horse making at a fence outrageously high. The manner of her scramble over these walls of water is a mystic thing, and, moreover, at the top of them were ordinarily these problems in white water, the foam racing down from the summit of each wave requiring a new leap, and a leap from the air. Then, after scornfully bumping a crest, she would slide and race and splash down a long incline, and arrive bobbing and nodding in front of the next menace.

10   A singular disadvantage of the sea lies in the fact that after successfully surmounting one wave you discover that there is another behind it just as important and just as nervously anxious to do something effective in the way of swamping boats. In a ten-foot dinghy one can get an idea of the resources of the sea in the line of waves that is not probable to the average experience, which is never at sea in a dinghy. As each slaty wall of water approached, it shut all else from the view of the men in the boat, and it was not difficult to imagine that this particular wave was the final outburst of the ocean, the last effort of the grim water. There was a terrible grace in the move of the waves, and they came in silence, save for the snarling of the crests.

In the wan light the faces of the men must have been gray. Their eyes must have glinted in strange ways as they gazed steadily astern. Viewed from a balcony, the whole thing would, doubtless, have been weirdly picturesque. But the men in the boat had no time to see it, and if they had had leisure, there were other things to occupy their minds. The sun swung steadily up the sky, and they knew it was broad day because the color of the sea changed from slate to emerald-green streaked with amber lights, and the foam was like tumbling snow. The process of the breaking day was unknown to them. They were aware only of this effect upon the color of the waves that rolled toward them.

In disjointed sentences the cook and the correspondent argued as to the difference between a life-saving station and a house of refuge. The cook had said: "There's a house of refuge just north of the Mosquito Inlet Light, and as soon as they see us they'll come off in their boat and pick us up."

"As soon as who see us?" said the correspondent.

"The crew," said the cook.

"Houses of refuge don't have crews," said the correspondent. "As I understand   15
them, they are only places where clothes and grub are stored for the benefit of shipwrecked people. They don't carry crews."

"Oh, yes, they do," said the cook.

"No, they don't," said the correspondent.

"Well, we're not there yet, anyhow," said the oiler, in the stern.

"Well," said the cook, "perhaps it's not a house of refuge that I'm thinking of as being near Mosquito Inlet Light; perhaps it's a life-saving station."

"We're not there yet," said the oiler in the stern.   20

II

As the boat bounced from the top of each wave the wind tore through the hair of the hatless men, and as the craft plopped her stern down again the spray slashed past them. The crest of each of these waves was a hill, from the top of which the men surveyed for a moment a broad tumultuous expanse, shining and wind-riven. It was probably splendid, it was probably glorious, this play of the free sea, wild with lights of emerald and white and amber.

"Bully good thing it's an on-shore wind," said the cook. "If not, where would we be? Wouldn't have a show."

"That's right," said the correspondent.

The busy oiler nodded his assent.

Then the captain, in the bow, chuckled in a way that expressed humor, con-   25
tempt, tragedy, all in one. "Do you think we've got much of a show now, boys?" said he.

Whereupon the three were silent, save for a trifle of hemming and hawing. To express any particular optimism at this time they felt to be childish and stupid, but they all doubtless possessed this sense of the situation in their minds. A young man thinks doggedly at such times. On the other hand, the ethics of their condition was decidedly against any open suggestion of hopelessness. So they were silent.

"Oh, well," said the captain, soothing his children, "we'll get ashore all right."

But there was that in his tone which made them think; so the oiler quoth, "Yes! if this wind holds."

The cook was bailing. "Yes! if we don't catch hell in the surf."

Canton-flannel[2] gulls flew near and far. Sometimes they sat down on the sea, near patches of brown seaweed that rolled over the waves with a movement like carpets on a line in a gale. The birds sat comfortably in groups, and they were envied by some in the dinghy, for the wrath of the sea was no more to them than it was to a covey of prairie chickens a thousand miles inland. Often they came very close and stared at the men with black bead-like eyes. At these times they were uncanny and sinister in their unblinking scrutiny, and the men hooted angrily at them, telling them to be gone. One came, and evidently decided to alight on the top of the captain's head. The bird flew parallel to the boat and did not circle, but made short sidelong jumps in the air in chicken fashion. His black eyes were wistfully fixed upon the captain's head. "Ugly brute," said the oiler to the bird. "You look as if you were made with a jackknife." The cook and the correspondent swore darkly at the creature. The captain naturally wished to knock it away with the end of the heavy painter, but he did not dare do it, because anything resembling an emphatic gesture would have capsized this freighted boat; and so, with his open hand, the captain gently and carefully waved the gull away. After it had been discouraged from the pursuit the captain breathed easier on account of his hair, and others breathed easier because the bird struck their minds at this time as being somehow gruesome and ominous.

In the meantime the oiler and the correspondent rowed; and also they rowed. They sat together in the same seat, and each rowed an oar. Then the oiler took both oars; then the correspondent took both oars, then the oiler; then the correspondent. They rowed and they rowed. The very ticklish part of the business was when the time came for the reclining one in the stern to take his turn at the oars. By the very last star of truth, it is easier to steal eggs from under a hen than it was to change seats in the dinghy. First the man in the stern slid his hand along the thwart and moved with care, as if he were of Sèvres.[3] Then man in the rowing-seat slid his hand along the other thwart. It was all done with the most extraordinary care. As the two sidled past each other, the whole party kept watchful eyes on the coming wave, and the captain cried: "Look out, now! Steady, there!"

The brown mats of seaweed that appeared from time to time were like islands, bits of earth. They were travelling, apparently, neither one way nor the other. They were, to all intents, stationary. They informed the men in the boat that it was making progress slowly toward the land.

The captain, rearing cautiously in the bow after the dinghy soared on a great swell, said that he had seen the lighthouse at Mosquito Inlet. Presently the cook remarked that he had seen it. The correspondent was at the oars then, and for some reason he too wished to look at the lighthouse; but his back was toward the far shore, and the waves were important, and for some time he could not seize an opportunity to turn his head. But at last there came a wave more gentle than

---

2. Actually a plain-weave cotton fabric.   3. A type of fine china.

the others, and when at the crest of it he swiftly scoured the western horizon.

"See it?" said the captain.

"No," said the correspondent, slowly; "I didn't see anything."   35

"Look again," said the captain. He pointed. "It's exactly in that direction."

At the top of another wave the correspondent did as he was bid, and this time his eyes chanced on a small, still thing on the edge of the swaying horizon. It was precisely like the point of a pin. It took an anxious eye to find a lighthouse so tiny.

"Think we'll make it, Captain?"

"If this wind holds and the boat don't swamp, we can't do much else," said the captain.

The little boat, lifted by each towering sea and splashed viciously by the crests,   40 made progress that in the absence of seaweed was not apparent to those in her. She seemed just a wee thing wallowing, miraculously top up, at the mercy of five oceans. Occasionally a great spread of water, like white flames, swarmed into her.

"Bail her, cook," said the captain, serenely.

"All right, Captain," said the cheerful cook.

III

It would be difficult to describe the subtle brotherhood of men that was here established on the seas. No one said that it was so. No one mentioned it. But it dwelt in the boat, and each man felt it warm him. They were a captain, an oiler, a cook, and a correspondent, and they were friends—friends in a more curiously iron-bound degree than may be common. The hurt captain, lying against the water jar in the bow, spoke always in a low voice and calmly; but he could never command a more ready and swiftly obedient crew than the motley three of the dinghy. It was more than a mere recognition of what was best for the common safety. There was surely in it a quality that was personal and heart-felt. And after this devotion to the commander of the boat, there was this comradeship, that the correspondent, for instance, who had been taught to be cynical of men, knew even at the time was the best experience of his life. But no one said that it was so. No one mentioned it.

"I wish we had a sail," remarked the captain. "We might try my overcoat on the end of an oar, and give you two boys a chance to rest." So the cook and the correspondent held the mast and spread wide the overcoat; the oiler steered; and the little boat made good way with her new rig. Sometimes the oiler had to scull sharply to keep a sea from breaking into the boat, but otherwise sailing was a success.

Meanwhile the lighthouse had been growing slowly larger. It had now almost   45 assumed color, and appeared like a little gray shadow on the sky. The man at the oars could not be prevented from turning his head rather often to try for a glimpse of this little gray shadow.

At last, from the top of each wave, the men in the tossing boat could see land. Even as the lighthouse was an upright shadow on the sky, this land seemed but a long black shadow on the sea. It certainly was thinner than paper. "We must be about opposite New Smyrna,"[4] said the cook, who had coasted this shore often in schooners. "Captain, by the way, I believe they abandoned that life-saving station there about a year ago."

"Did they?" said the captain.

The wind slowly died away. The cook and the correspondent were not now obliged to slave in order to hold high the oar. But the waves continued their old impetuous swooping at the dinghy, and the little craft, no longer underway, struggled woundily over them. The oiler or the correspondent took the oars again.

Shipwrecks are *apropos* of nothing. If men could only train for them and have them occur when the men had reached pink condition, there would be less drowning at sea. Of the four in the dinghy none had slept any time worth mentioning for two days and two nights previous to embarking in the dinghy, and in the excitement of clambering about the deck of a foundering ship they had also forgotten to eat heartily.

50   For these reasons, and for others, neither the oiler nor the correspondent was fond of rowing at this time. The correspondent wondered ingenuously how in the name of all that was sane could there be people who thought it amusing to row a boat. It was not an amusement; it was a diabolical punishment, and even a genius of mental aberrations could never conclude that it was anything but a horror to the muscles and a crime against the back. He mentioned to the boat in general how the amusement of rowing struck him, and the weary-faced oiler smiled in full sympathy. Previously to the foundering, by the way, the oiler had worked a double watch in the engine-room of the ship.

"Take her easy, now, boys," said the captain. "Don't spend yourselves. If we have to run a surf you'll need all your strength, because we'll sure have to swim for it. Take your time."

Slowly the land arose from the sea. From a black line it became a line of black and a line of white—trees and sand. Finally the captain said that he could make out a house on the shore. "That's the house of refuge, sure," said the cook. "They'll see us before long, and come out after us."

The distant lighthouse reared high. "The keeper ought to be able to make us out now, if he's looking through a glass," said the captain. "He'll notify the life-saving people."

"None of those other boats could have got ashore to give word of the wreck," said the oiler, in a low voice, "else the life-boat would be out hunting us."

55   Slowly and beautifully the land loomed out of the sea. The wind came again. It had veered from the northeast to the southeast. Finally a new sound struck the ears of the men in the boat. It was the low thunder of the surf on the shore. "We'll never be able to make the lighthouse now," said the captain. "Swing her head a little more north, Billie."

"A little more north, sir," said the oiler.

Whereupon the little boat turned her nose once more down the wind, and all but the oarsman watched the shore grow. Under the influence of this expansion doubt and direful apprehension were leaving the minds of the men. The man-

4. Town on the Florida coast.

agement of the boat was still most absorbing, but it could not prevent a quiet cheerfulness. In an hour, perhaps, they would be ashore.

Their backbones had become thoroughly used to balancing in the boat, and they now rode this wild colt of a dinghy like circus men. The correspondent thought that he had been drenched to the skin, but happening to feel in the top pocket of his coat, he found therein eight cigars. Four of them were soaked with sea-water; four were perfectly scatheless. After a search, somebody produced three dry matches; and thereupon the four waifs rode impudently in their little boat and, with an assurance of an impending rescue shining in their eyes, puffed at the big cigars, and judged well and ill of all men. Everybody took a drink of water.

IV

"Cook," remarked the captain, "there don't seem to be any signs of life about your house of refuge."

"No," replied the cook. "Funny they don't see us!"

A broad stretch of lowly coast lay before the eyes of the men. It was of low dunes topped with dark vegetation. The roar of the surf was plain, and sometimes they could see the white lip of a wave as it spun up the beach. A tiny house was blocked out black upon the sky. Southward, the slim lighthouse lifted its little gray length.

Tide, wind, and waves were swinging the dinghy northward. "Funny they don't see us," said the men.

The surf's roar was here dulled, but its tone was nevertheless thunderous and mighty. As the boat swam over the great rollers the men sat listening to this roar. "We'll swamp sure," said everybody.

It is fair to say here that there was not a life-saving station within twenty miles in either direction; but the men did not know this fact, and in consequence they made dark and opprobrious remarks concerning the eyesight of the nation's life-savers. Four scowling men sat in the dinghy and surpassed records in the invention of epithets.

"Funny they don't see us."

The light-heartedness of a former time had completely faded. To their sharpened minds it was easy to conjure pictures of all kinds of incompetency and blindness and, indeed, cowardice. There was the shore of the populous land, and it was bitter and bitter to them that from it came no sign.

"Well," said the captain, ultimately, "I suppose we'll have to make a try for ourselves. If we stay out here too long, we'll none of us have strength left to swim after the boat swamps."

And so the oiler, who was at the oars, turned the boat straight for the shore. There was a sudden tightening of muscles. There was some thinking.

"If we don't all get ashore," said the captain—"if we don't all get ashore, I suppose you fellows know where to send news of my finish?"

They then briefly exchanged some addresses and admonitions. As for the reflections of the men, there was a great deal of rage in them. Perchance they might be formulated thus: "If I am going to be drowned—if I am going to be drowned—if I am going to be drowned, why, in the name of the seven mad gods who rule the sea, was I allowed to come thus far and contemplate sand and trees? Was I brought here merely to have my nose dragged away as I was about to nibble the sacred cheese of life? It is preposterous. If this old ninny-woman, Fate, cannot do better than this, she should be deprived of the management of men's fortunes. She is an old hen who knows not her intention. If she has decided to drown me, why did she not do it in the beginning and save me all this trouble? The whole affair is absurd. . . . But no; she cannot mean to drown me. She dare not drown me. She cannot drown me. Not after all this work." Afterward the man might have had an impulse to shake his fist at the clouds. "Just you drown me, now, and then hear what I call you!"

The billows that came at this time were more formidable. They seemed always just about to break and roll over the little boat in a turmoil of foam. There was a preparatory and long growl in the speech of them. No mind unused to the sea would have concluded that the dinghy could ascend these sheer heights in time. The shore was still afar. The oiler was a wily surfman. "Boys," he said, swiftly, "she won't live three minutes more, and we're too far out to swim. Shall I take her to sea again, Captain?"

"Yes; go ahead!" said the captain.

This oiler, by a series of quick miracles and fast and steady oarsmanship, turned the boat in the middle of the surf and took her safely to sea again.

There was a considerable silence as the boat bumped over the furrowed sea to deeper water. Then somebody in gloom spoke: "Well, anyhow, they must have seen us from the shore by now."

75   The gulls went in slanting flight up the wind toward the gray, desolate east. A squall, marked by dingy clouds and clouds brick-red, like smoke from a burning building, appeared from the southeast.

"What do you think of those life-saving people? Ain't they peaches?"

"Funny they haven't seen us."

"Maybe they think we're out here for sport! Maybe they think we're fishin'. Maybe they think we're damned fools."

It was a long afternoon. A changed tide tried to force them southward, but wind and wave said northward. Far ahead, where coast-line, sea, and sky formed their mighty angle, there were little dots which seemed to indicate a city on the shore.

80   "St. Augustine."

The captain shook his head. "Too near Mosquito Inlet."

And the oiler rowed, and then the correspondent rowed; then the oiler moved. It was a weary business. The human back can become the seat of more aches and pains than are registered in books for the composite anatomy of a regiment. It is a limited area, but it can become the theatre of innumerable muscular conflicts, tangles, wrenches, knots, and other comforts.

"Did you ever like to row, Billie?" asked the correspondent.

"No," said the oiler; "hang it!"

85   When one exchanged the rowing-seat for a place in the bottom of the boat, he suffered a bodily depression that caused him to be careless of everything save

an obligation to wiggle one finger. There was cold sea-water swashing to and fro in the boat, and he lay in it. His head, pillowed on a thwart, was within an inch of the swirl of a wave-crest, and sometimes a particularly obstreperous sea came inboard and drenched him once more. But these matters did not annoy him. It is almost certain that if the boat had capsized he would have tumbled comfortably out upon the ocean as if he felt sure that it was a great soft mattress.

"Look! There's a man on the shore!"

"There? See 'im? See 'im?"

"Yes, sure! He's walking along."

"Now he's stopped. Look! He's facing us!"

"He's waving at us!"   90

"So he is! By thunder!"

"Ah, now we're all right! Now we're all right! There'll be a boat out here for us in half an hour."

"He's going on. He's running. He's going up to that house there."

The remote beach seemed lower than the sea, and it required a searching glance to discern the little black figure. The captain saw a floating stick, and they rowed to it. A bath towel was by some weird chance in the boat, and, tying this on the stick, the captain waved it. The oarsman did not dare turn his head, so he was obliged to ask questions.

"What's he doing now?"   95

"He's standing still again. He's looking, I think. . . . There he goes again— toward the house. . . . Now he's stopped again."

"Is he waving at us?"

"No, not now; he was, though."

"Look! There comes another man!"

"He's running."   100

"Look at him go, would you!"

"Why, he's on a bicycle. Now he's met the other man. They're both waving at us. Look!"

"There comes something up the beach."

"What the devil is that thing?"

"Why, it looks like a boat."   105

"Why, certainly, it's a boat."

"No; it's on wheels."

"Yes, so it is. Well, that must be the life-boat. They drag them along shore on a wagon."

"That's the life-boat, sure."

"No, by God, it's—it's an omnibus."   110

"I tell you it's a life-boat."

"It is not! It's an omnibus. I can see it plain. See? One of these big hotel omnibuses."

"By thunder, you're right. It's an omnibus, sure as fate. What do you suppose they are doing with an omnibus? Maybe they are going around collecting the life-crew, hey?"

"That's it, likely. Look! There's a fellow waving a little black flag. He's standing on the steps of the omnibus. There comes those other two fellows. Now they're all talking together. Look at the fellow with the flag. Maybe he ain't waving it!"

115 "That ain't a flag, is it? That's his coat. Why, certainly, that's his coat."

"So it is: it's his coat. He's taken it off and is waving it around his head. But would you look at him swing it!"

"Oh, say, there isn't any life-saving station there. That's just a winter-resort."

"What's that idiot with the coat mean? What's he signaling, anyhow?"

"It looks as if he were trying to tell us to go north. There must be a life-saving station up there."

120 "No; he thinks we're fishing. Just giving us a merry hand. See? Ah, there, Willie!"

"Well, I wish I could make something out of those signals. What do you suppose he means?"

"He don't mean anything; he's just playing."

"Well, if he'd just signal us to try the surf again, or to go to sea and wait, or go north, or go south, or go to hell, there would be some reason in it. But look at him! He just stands there and keeps his coat revolving like a wheel. The ass!"

"There come more people."

125 "Now there's quite a mob. Look! Isn't that a boat?"

"Where? Oh, I see where you mean. No, that's no boat."

"That fellow is still waving his coat."

"He must think we like to see him to do that. Why don't he quit? It don't mean anything."

"I don't know. I think he is trying to make us go north. It must be that there's a life-saving station there somewhere."

130 "Say, he ain't tired yet. Look at 'im wave!"

"Wonder how long he can keep that up. He's been revolving his coat ever since he caught sight of us. He's an idiot. Why aren't they getting men to bring a boat out? A fishing boat—one of those big yawls—could come out here all right. Why don't he do something?"

"Oh, it's all right now."

"They'll have a boat out here for us in less than no time, now that they've seen us."

A faint yellow tone came into the sky over the low land. The shadows on the sea slowly deepened. The wind bore coldness with it, and the men began to shiver.

135 "Holy smoke!" said one, allowing his voice to express his impious mood, "if we keep on monkeying out here! If we've got to flounder out here all night!"

"Oh, we'll never have to stay here all night! Don't you worry. They've seen us now, and it won't be long before they'll come chasing out after us."

The shore grew dusky. The man waving a coat blended gradually into this gloom, and it swallowed in the same manner the omnibus and the group of people. The spray, when it dashed uproariously over the side, made the voyagers shrink and swear like men who were being branded.

"I'd like to catch the chump who waved the coat. I feel like socking him one, just for luck."

"Why? What did he do?"

"Oh, nothing, but then he seemed so damned cheerful."   140

In the meantime the oiler rowed, and then the correspondent rowed, and then the oiler rowed. Gray-faced and bowed forward, they mechanically, turn by turn, plied the leaden oars. The form of the lighthouse had vanished from the southern horizon, but finally a pale star appeared, just lifting from the sea. The streaked saffron in the west passed before the all-merging darkness, and the sea to the east was black. The land had vanished, and was expressed only by the low and drear thunder of the surf.

"If I am going to be drowned—if I am going to be drowned—if I am going to be drowned, why, in the name of the seven mad gods who rule the sea, was I allowed to come thus far and contemplate sand and trees? Was I brought here merely to have my nose dragged away as I was about to nibble the sacred cheese of life?"

The patient captain, drooped over the water-jar, was sometimes obliged to speak to the oarsman.

"Keep her head up! Keep her head up!"

"Keep her head up, sir." The voices were weary and low.   145

This was surely a quiet evening. All save the oarsman lay heavily and listlessly in the boat's bottom. As for him, his eyes were just capable of noting the tall black waves that swept forward in a most sinister silence, save for an occasional subdued growl of a crest.

The cook's head was on a thwart, and he looked without interest at the water under his nose. He was deep in other scenes. Finally he spoke. "Billie," he murmured, dreamfully, "what kind of pie do you like best?"

V

"Pie!" said the oiler and the correspondent, agitatedly. "Don't talk about those things, blast you!"

"Well," said the cook, "I was just thinking about ham sandwiches, and——"

A night on the sea in an open boat is a long night. As darkness settled finally,   150
the shine of the light, lifting from the sea in the south, changed to full gold. On the northern horizon a new light appeared, a small bluish gleam on the edge of the waters. These two lights were the furniture of the world. Otherwise there was nothing but waves.

Two men huddled in the stern, and distances were so magnificent in the dinghy that the rower was enabled to keep his feet partly warm by thrusting them under his companions. Their legs indeed extended far under the rowing-seat until they touched the feet of the captain forward. Sometimes, despite the efforts of the tired oarsman, a wave came piling into the boat, an icy wave of the night, and the chilling water soaked them anew. They would twist their bodies for a moment and groan, and sleep the dead sleep once more, while the water in the boat gurgled about them as the craft rocked.

The plan of the oiler and the correspondent was for one to row until he lost the ability, and then arouse the other from his sea-water couch in the bottom of the boat.

The oiler plied the oars until his head drooped forward and the overpowering sleep blinded him; and he rowed yet afterward. Then he touched a man in the bottom of the boat, and called his name. "Will you spell me for a little while?" he said meekly.

"Sure, Billie," said the correspondent, awaking and dragging himself to a sitting position. They exchanged places carefully, and the oiler, cuddling down in the sea-water at the cook's side, seemed to go to sleep instantly.

155   The particular violence of the sea had ceased. The waves came without snarling. The obligation of the man at the oars was to keep the boat headed so that the tilt of the rollers would not capsize her, and to preserve her from filling when the crests rushed past. The black waves were silent and hard to be seen in the darkness. Often one was almost upon the boat before the oarsman was aware.

In a low voice the correspondent addressed the captain. He was not sure that the captain was awake, although this iron man seemed to be always awake. "Captain, shall I keep her making for that light north, sir?"

The same steady voice answered him. "Yes. Keep it about two points off the port bow."

The cook had tied a life-belt around himself in order to get even the warmth which this clumsy cork contrivance could donate, and he seemed almost stove-like when a rower, whose teeth invariably chattered wildly as soon as he ceased his labor, dropped down to sleep.

The correspondent, as he rowed, looked down at the two men sleeping underfoot. The cook's arm was around the oiler's shoulders, and, with their fragmentary clothing and haggard faces, they were the babes of the sea—a grotesque rendering of the old babes in the wood.

160   Later he must have grown stupid at his work, for suddenly there was a growling of water, and a crest came with a roar and a swash into the boat, and it was a wonder that it did not set the cook afloat in his life-belt. The cook continued to sleep, but the oiler sat up, blinking his eyes and shaking with the new cold.

"Oh, I'm awful sorry, Billie," said the correspondent, contritely.

"That's all right, old boy," said the oiler, and lay down again and was asleep.

Presently it seemed that even the captain dozed, and the correspondent thought that he was the one man afloat on all the ocean. The wind had a voice as it came over the waves, and it was sadder than the end.

There was a long, loud swishing astern of the boat, and a gleaming trail of phosphorescence, like blue flame, was furrowed on the black waters. It might have been made by a monstrous knife.

165   Then there came a stillness, while the correspondent breathed with open mouth and looked at the sea.

Suddenly there was another swish and another long flash of bluish light, and this time it was alongside the boat, and might almost have been reached with an oar. The correspondent saw an enormous fin speed like a shadow through the water, hurling the crystalline spray and leaving the long glowing trail.

The correspondent looked over his shoulder at the captain. His face was hidden, and he seemed to be asleep. He looked at the babes of the sea. They certainly were asleep. So, being bereft of sympathy, he leaned a little way to one side and swore softly into the sea.

But the thing did not then leave the vicinity of the boat. Ahead or astern, on one side or the other, at intervals long or short, fled the long sparkling streak, and there was to be heard the *whirroo* of the dark fin. The speed and power of the thing was greatly to be admired. It cut the water like a gigantic and keen projectile.

The presence of this biding thing did not affect the man with the same horror that it would if he had been a picnicker. He simply looked at the sea dully and swore in an undertone.

Nevertheless, it is true that he did not wish to be alone with the thing. He 170
wished one of his companions to awake by chance and keep him company with it. But the captain hung motionless over the water-jar and the oiler and the cook in the bottom of the boat were plunged in slumber.

VI

"If I am going to be drowned—if I am going to be drowned—if I am going to be drowned, why, in the name of the seven mad gods who rule the sea, was I allowed to come thus far and contemplate sand and trees?"

During this dismal night, it may be remarked that a man would conclude that it was really the intention of the seven mad gods to drown him, despite the abominable injustice of it. For it was certainly an abominable injustice to drown a man who had worked so hard, so hard. The man felt it would be a crime most unnatural. Other people had drowned at sea since galleys swarmed with painted sails, but still——

When it occurs to a man that nature does not regard him as important, and that she feels she would not maim the universe by disposing of him, he at first wishes to throw bricks at the temple, and he hates deeply the fact that there are no bricks and no temples. Any visible expression of nature would surely be pelleted with his jeers.

Then, if there be no tangible thing to hoot, he feels, perhaps, the desire to confront a personification and indulge in pleas, bowed to one knee, and with hands supplicant, saying, "Yes, but I love myself."

A high cold star on a winter's night is the word he feels that she says to him. 175
Thereafter he knows the pathos of his situation.

The men in the dinghy had not discussed these matters, but each had, no doubt, reflected upon them in silence and according to his mind. There was seldom any expression upon their faces save the general one of complete weariness. Speech was devoted to the business of the boat.

To chime the notes of his emotions, a verse mysteriously entered the correspondent's head. He had even forgotten that he had forgotten this verse, but it suddenly was in his mind.

> A soldier of the Legion lay dying in Algiers;
> There was lack of woman's nursing, there was dearth of woman's tears;
> But a comrade stood beside him, and he took the comrade's hand,
> And he said, "I never more shall see my own, my native land."[5]

5. From "Bingen on the Rhine," by Caroline Norton (1808–1877).

In his childhood the correspondent had been made acquainted with the fact that a soldier of the Legion lay dying in Algiers, but he had never regarded it as important. Myriads of his schoolfellows had informed him of the soldier's plight, but the dinning had naturally ended by making him perfectly indifferent. He had never considered it his affair that a soldier of the Legion lay dying in Algiers, nor had it appeared to him as a matter for sorrow. It was less to him than the breaking of a pencil's point.

Now, however, it quaintly came to him as a human, living thing. It was no longer merely a picture of a few throes in the breast of a poet, meanwhile drinking tea and warming his feet at the grate; it was an actuality—stern, mournful, and fine.

The correspondent plainly saw the soldier. He lay on the sand with his feet out straight and still. While his pale left hand was upon his chest in an attempt to thwart the going of his life, the blood came between his fingers. In the far Algerian distance, a city of low square forms was set against a sky that was faint with the last sunset hues. The correspondent, plying the oars and dreaming of the slow and slower movements of the lips of the soldier, was moved by a profound and perfectly impersonal comprehension. He was sorry for the soldier of the Legion who lay dying in Algiers.

180   The thing which had followed the boat and waited had evidently grown bored at the delay. There was no longer to be heard the slash of the cutwater, and there was no longer the flame of the long trail. The light in the north still glimmered, but it was apparently no nearer to the boat. Sometimes the boom of the surf rang in the correspondent's ears, and he turned the craft seaward then and rowed harder. Southward, some one had evidently built a watch-fire on the beach. It was too low and too far to be seen, but it made a shimmering, roseate reflection upon the bluff in back of it, and this could be discerned from the boat. The wind came stronger, and sometimes a wave suddenly raged out like a mountain-cat, and there was to be seen the sheen and sparkle of a broken crest.

The captain, in the bow, moved on his water-jar and sat erect. "Pretty long night," he observed to the correspondent. He looked at the shore. "Those life-saving people take their time."

"Did you see that shark playing around?"

"Yes, I saw him. He was a big fellow, all right."

"Wish I had known you were awake."

185   Later the correspondent spoke into the bottom of the boat. "Billie!" There was a slow and gradual disentanglement. "Billie, will you spell me?"

"Sure," said the oiler.

As soon as the correspondent touched the cold, comfortable seawater in the bottom of the boat and had huddled close to the cook's life-belt he was deep in sleep, despite the fact that his teeth played all the popular airs. This sleep was so good to him that it was but a moment before he heard a voice call his name in a tone that demonstrated the last stages of exhaustion. "Will you spell me?"

"Sure, Billie."

The light in the north had mysteriously vanished, but the correspondent took his course from the wide-awake captain.

90   Later in the night they took the boat farther out to sea, and the captain directed

the cook to take one oar at the stern and keep the boat facing the seas. He was to call out if he should hear the thunder of the surf. This plan enabled the oiler and the correspondent to get respite together. "We'll give those boys a chance to into shape again," said the captain. They curled down and, after a few preliminary chatterings and trembles, slept once more the dead sleep. Neither knew they had bequeathed to the cook the company of another shark, or perhaps the same shark.

As the boat caroused on the waves, spray occasionally bumped over the side and gave them a fresh soaking, but this had no power to break their repose. The ominous slash of the wind and the water affected them as it would have affected mummies.

"Boys," said the cook, with the notes of every reluctance in his voice, "she's drifted in pretty close. I guess one of you had better take her to sea again." The correspondent, aroused, heard the crash of the toppled crests.

As he was rowing, the captain gave him some whiskey-and-water, and this steadied the chills out of him. "If I ever get ashore and anybody shows me even a photograph of an oar——"

At last there was a short conversation.

"Billie! . . . Billie, will you spell me?"   195

"Sure," said the oiler.

VII

When the correspondent again opened his eyes, the sea and the sky were each of the gray hue of the dawning. Later, carmine and gold was painted upon the waters. The morning appeared finally, in its splendor, with a sky of pure blue, and the sunlight flamed on the tips of the waves.

On the distant dunes were set many little black cottages, and a tall white wind-mill reared above them. No man, nor dog, nor bicycle appeared on the beach. The cottages might have formed a deserted village.

The voyagers scanned the shore. A conference was held in the boat. "Well," said the captain, "if no help is coming, we might better try a run through the surf right away. If we stay out here much longer we will be too weak to do anything for ourselves at all." The others silently acquiesced in this reasoning. The boat was headed for the beach. The correspondent wondered if none ever ascended the tall wind-tower, and if then they never looked seaward. This tower was a giant, standing with its back to the plight of the ants. It represented in a degree, to the correspondent, the serenity of nature amid the struggles of the individual—nature in the wind, and nature in the vision of men. She did not seem cruel to him then, nor beneficent, nor treacherous, nor wise. But she was indifferent, flatly indiffer-ent. It is, perhaps, plausible that a man in this situation, impressed with the unconcern of the universe, should see the innumerable flaws of his life, and have them taste wickedly in his mind, and wish for another chance. A distinction between right and wrong seems absurdly clear to him, then, in this new ignorance of the grave-edge, and he understands that if he were given another opportunity he would mend his conduct and his words, and be better and brighter during an introduction or at a tea.

200 "Now, boys," said the captain, "she is going to swamp sure. All we can do is to work her in as far as possible, and then when she swamps, pile out and scramble for the beach. Keep cool now, and don't jump until she swamps sure."

The oiler took the oars. Over his shoulders he scanned the surf. "Captain," he said, "I think I'd better bring her about and keep her head-on to the seas and back her in."

"All right, Billie," said the captain. "Back her in." The oiler swung the boat then, and, seated in the stern, the cook and the correspondent were obliged to look over their shoulders to contemplate the lonely and indifferent shore.

The monstrous inshore rollers heaved the boat high until the men were again enabled to see the white sheets of water scudding up the slanted beach. "We won't get in very close," said the captain. Each time a man could wrest his attention from the rollers, he turned his glance toward the shore, and in the expression of the eyes during this contemplation there was a singular quality. The correspondent, observing the others, knew that they were not afraid, but the full meaning of their glances was shrouded.

As for himself, he was too tired to grapple fundamentally with the fact. He tried to coerce his mind into thinking of it, but the mind was dominated at this time by the muscles, and the muscles said they did not care. It merely occurred to him that if he should drown it would be a shame.

205 There were no hurried words, no pallor, no plain agitation. The men simply looked at the shore. "Now, remember to get well clear of the boat when you jump," said the captain.

Seaward the crest of a roller suddenly fell with a thunderous crash, and the long white comber came roaring down upon the boat.

"Steady now," said the captain. The men were silent. They turned their eyes from the shore to the comber and waited. The boat slid up the incline, leaped at the furious top, bounced over it, and swung down the long back of the wave. Some water had been shipped, and the cook bailed it out.

But the next crest crashed also. The tumbling, boiling flood of white water caught the boat and whirled it almost perpendicular. Water swarmed in from all sides. The correspondent had his hands on the gunwale at this time, and when the water entered at that place he swiftly withdrew his fingers, as if he objected to wetting them.

The little boat, drunken with this weight of water, reeled and snuggled deeper into the sea.

210 "Bail her out, cook! Bail her out!" said the captain.

"All right, Captain," said the cook.

"Now, boys, the next one will do for us sure," said the oiler. "Mind to jump clear of the boat."

The third wave moved forward, huge, furious, implacable. It fairly swallowed the dinghy, and almost simultaneously the men tumbled into the sea. A piece of life-belt had lain in the bottom of the boat, and as the correspondent went overboard he held this to his chest with his left hand.

The January water was icy, and reflected immediately that it was colder than he had expected to find it off the coast of Florida. This appeared to his dazed mind as a fact important enough to be noted at the time. The coldness of the water was sad; it was tragic. This fact was somehow mixed and confused with his opinion of his own situation, so that it seemed almost a proper reason for tears. The water was cold.

When he came to the surface he was conscious of little but the noisy water. Afterward he saw his companions in the sea. The oiler was ahead in the race. He was swimming strongly and rapidly. Off to the correspondent's left, the cook's great white and corked back bulged out of the water, and in the rear the captain was hanging with his one good hand to the keel of the overturned dinghy.

There is a certain immovable quality to a shore, and the correspondent wondered at it amid the confusion of the sea.

It seemed also very attractive; but the correspondent knew that it was a long journey, and he paddled leisurely. The piece of life-preserver lay under him, and sometimes he whirled down the incline of a wave as if he were on a hand-sled.

But finally he arrived at a place in the sea where travel was beset with difficulty. He did not pause swimming to inquire what manner of current had caught him, but there his progress ceased. The shore was set before him like a bit of scenery on a stage, and he looked at it and understood with his eyes each detail of it.

As the cook passed, much farther to the left, the captain was calling to him, "Turn over on your back, cook! Turn over on your back and use the oar."

"All right, sir." The cook turned on his back, and, paddling with an oar, went ahead as if he were a canoe.

Presently the boat also passed to the left of the correspondent, with the captain clinging with one hand to the keel. He would have appeared like a man raising himself to look over a board fence if it were not for the extraordinary gymnastics of the boat. The correspondent marvelled that the captain could still hold to it.

They passed on nearer to shore—the oiler, the cook, the captain—and following them went the water-jar, bouncing gaily over the seas.

The correspondent remained in the grip of this strange new enemy, a current. The shore, with its white slope of sand and its green bluff topped with little silent cottages, was spread like a picture before him. It was very near to him then, but he was impressed as one who, in a gallery, looks at a scene from Brittany or Algiers.

He thought: "I am going to drown? Can it be possible? Can it be possible? Can it be possible?" Perhaps an individual must consider his own death to be the final phenomenon of nature.

But later a wave perhaps whirled him out of this small deadly current, for he found suddenly that he could again make progress toward the shore. Later still he was aware that the captain, clinging with one hand to the keel of the dinghy, had his face turned away from the shore and toward him, and was calling his name. "Come to the boat! Come to the boat!"

In his struggle to reach the captain and the boat, he reflected that when one gets properly wearied drowning must really be a comfortable arrangement—a cessation of hostilities accompanied by a large degree of relief; and he was glad of it, for the main thing in his mind for some moments had been horror of the temporary agony; he did not wish to be hurt.

Presently he saw a man running along the shore. He was undressing with most remarkable speed. Coat, trousers, shirt, everything flew magically off him.

"Come to the boat!" called the captain.

"All right, Captain." As the correspondent paddled, he saw the captain let himself down to bottom and leave the boat. Then the correspondent performed his one little marvel of the voyage. A large wave caught him and flung him with ease and supreme speed completely over the boat and far beyond it. It struck him even then as an event in gymnastics and a true miracle of the sea. An overturned boat in the surf is not a plaything to a swimming man.

230   The correspondent arrived in water that reached only to his waist, but his condition did not enable him to stand for more than a moment. Each wave knocked him into a heap, and the undertow pulled at him.

Then he saw the man who had been running and undressing, and undressing and running, come bounding into the water. He dragged ashore the cook, and then waded toward the captain; but the captain waved him away and sent him to the correspondent. He was naked—naked as a tree in winter; but a halo was about his head, and he shone like a saint. He gave a strong pull, and a long drag, and a bully heave at the correspondent's hand. The correspondent, schooled in the minor formulae, said, "Thanks, old man." But suddenly the man cried, "What's that?" He pointed a swift finger. The correspondent said, "Go."

In the shallows, face downward, lay the oiler. His forehead touched sand that was periodically, between each wave, clear of the sea.

The correspondent did not know all that transpired afterward. When he achieved safe ground he fell, striking the sand with each particular part of his body. It was as if he had dropped from a roof, but the thud was grateful to him.

It seems that instantly the beach was populated with men with blankets, clothes, and flasks, and women with coffee-pots and all the remedies sacred to their minds. The welcome of the land to the men from the sea was warm and generous; but a still and dripping shape was carried slowly up the beach, and the land's welcome for it could only be the different and sinister hospitality of the grave.

235   When it came night, the white waves paced to and fro in the moonlight, and the wind brought the sound of the great sea's voice to the men on the shore, and they felt that they could then be interpreters.

1898

QUESTIONS AND WRITING SUGGESTIONS

1. When do you become aware that your view of events is limited to things seen and heard by the four men in the boat? How important is that to the story's effect? In what specific ways? How much of the story's suspense depends on this point of view? How would the story differ in its effects if it were told autobiographically through a first-person narrator?
2. Examine the language of the story's first paragraph. What specific colors are mentioned or implied here? How is the contrast between the sea and the sky significant? How much differentiation in color is discernible to the men? What angles of vision are implied by the color imagery? What details about body posture and fatigue are implied? By which specific words and phrases?
3. How much plot detail do you know by the end of the third paragraph? What crucial

information is, at this point, not yet clear? Note carefully all the points in the text where additional plot facts are presented.

4. Examine carefully paragraphs 3–6, then differentiate as fully as you can the four men. Which ones are most alike? What distinguishing features help you keep them straight as the narrative proceeds? What additional facts are provided later about each of the men? Mark the passages where additions to the characterizations occur. How do you account for the general agreeableness of the group toward the individual needs of each other? How does the captain set himself apart from the rest? How important is the sense of hierarchy in the group? How is it signaled? How might the plot differ if the makeup of the group were to change?

5. In some ways the story seems almost timeless as the relentless waves threaten the men and the boat. What narrative devices are used to keep the dangers from seeming monotonous? How much time actually passes? How is the passing of time recorded? In what ways are the threats to life different in different parts of the story? At which points in the story does the men's weariness outweigh their sense of danger? How are these points signaled by the language? What functions does the repetitive language perform?

6. At what points in the story does the perspective "expand" to include larger reflections and generalizations? Mark as many of these observations as you can find. How are they justified by the narrative's point of view? Describe the "voice" in these comments. What is their tone? In which of the men do you become most interested as the story develops? Point to textual indications that the point of view gradually narrows to increasingly suggest an individual voice rather than the collective one of the four men. Why does such a narrowing occur? What effect does this narrowing point of view have on the story's conclusion?

7. Look carefully at paragraphs later in the story in which different "elements" (such as plot, character, language, setting, and so on) seem purposely merged or fused. How is such interaction accomplished? Choose a single paragraph that illustrates the close interaction of different elements, and write a two-page analytical paper showing how the paragraph works to make the story's narrative presentation seem holistic.

8. How important is it that the threat to the men involves a natural force? How would the story's theme differ if the threat were caused by human beings? How would the symbolism differ? Describe as exactly as you can what the changing waves symbolize. How does the language in the story support this symbolism? How much does the story's symbolic effect depend upon the traditional "life as voyage" metaphor?

Exploring Contexts

8

THE AUTHOR'S WORK AS CONTEXT: FLANNERY O'CONNOR

Even if it were desirable to read a story as a thing in itself, separate from everything else we had ever read or seen and from everything else the author had written, this is in practice impossible. We can read Faulkner or Welty or Poe for the first time only once. After we read a second and then a third story by an author, we begin to recognize the voice and have a sense of familiarity, as we would with a growing acquaintance. Each story is part of the author's entire body of work—the **oeuvre** or **canon**—which, taken together, forms something like a huge single entity, a vision, a world, a "superwork."

The author's voice and vision soon create in us certain expectations—of action, structure, characterization, worldview, language. We come to expect short sentences from Hemingway, long ones from Faulkner, a certain amount of violence from both. We are not surprised if a Conrad story is set in Africa or Asia or aboard ship, but we are surprised if a Faulkner story takes place outside Mississippi (his portion of which, we soon learn, he calls Yoknapatawpha).

When we find an author's vision attractive or challenging, we naturally want to find out more about it, reading not only the literary works in the canon but the author's nonfictional prose—essays, letters, anything we can find that promises a fuller or clearer view of that unique way of looking at the world. Such knowledge is helpful—within limits. D. H. Lawrence warned us to trust the tale and not the teller. A statement of beliefs or of intentions is not necessarily the same as what a given work may show or achieve; and, on the other hand, writers often embody in their art what they cannot articulate, what indeed may not be expressible, in discursive prose.

In this chapter we will look briefly but closely at the work of Flannery O'Connor. We will look both at the differences and the similarities among three of her works.

The short stories and brief selections from O'Connor's letters and essays in this chapter are meant to make you feel more at home (and interested) in O'Connor's world and to raise questions about the relationship of the individual work to an author's work as a whole.

In this chapter we offer three of Flannery O'Connor's stories, including the title stories of her first collection, *A Good Man Is Hard to Find* (1955), and her last, *Everything That Rises Must Converge* (published posthumously in 1965). Her career was short, its latter stages hampered by periodic, intensifying, painful, and debilitating bouts of lupus, but her accomplishments were considerable: she died at thirty-nine, having published some thirty-one stories, two novels, essays, and reviews.

O'Connor's fiction is set most often in the American South, rural or urban, and her characters most often Southerners, white or black. Consequently, her subject is often racism. O'Connor has a keen eye for realistic detail, for her characters' self-deception, and for the truth that lies beneath the surface of language and self-image. Her means of releasing this inner truth is often, as in Faulkner, violence, which shocks the reader into looking beyond the surface and the conventional to discover a truth, often an uncomfortable truth, that lies within. Though O'Connor is a deeply religious and serious writer, her stories are replete with irony and wit, and are sometimes downright funny. Indeed, as you will see, she is not above mixing comedy and horror or using comic pratfalls seriously.

The central, sometimes obsessive concerns and assumptions that permeate an author's work not only relate the individual stories to each other, mutually illuminating and enriching them; they also serve as the author's trademark. It is not difficult to recognize or even parody a story by O'Connor.

Embodying these larger concerns and underlying such larger structures as plot, focus, and voice are the basic characteristics of the author's language, such as **diction,** the

Flannery O'Connor

choice and use of words; sentence structure; **rhetorical tropes,** figures of thought and speech; **imagery;** and **rhythm**—in other words, the author's **style.**

Perhaps because of the uniqueness of style, the vocabulary for discussing stylistic elements is not precise or accessible. We can broadly characterize diction as **formal** ("The Cask of Amontillado") or **informal** (most of the stories in this book), and within the broad term *informal* we can identify a level of language that approximates the speech of ordinary people and call it **colloquial** ("Why I Live at the P.O."). But to characterize precisely an author's diction so that it adequately describes his or her work and marks it off from the work of contemporaries is a difficult task indeed.

Diction and sentence structure contribute to the **tone** of a work, or the implied attitude or stance of the author toward the characters and events, an aspect somewhat analogous to tone of voice. When what is being said and the tone are consistent, it is difficult to separate one from the other; when there seems to be a discrepancy, we have some words that are useful to describe the difference. If the language seems exaggerated, we call it **overstatement,** or **hyperbole.** Sometimes it will be the narrator, sometimes a character, who uses language so intensive or exaggerated that we must read it at a discount, as it were, and judge the speaker's accuracy or honesty in the process. When Julian's mother, in "Everything That Rises Must Converge," says, " 'I've always had a great respect for my colored friends. . . . I'd do anything in the world for them' " (paragraph 32), we know she protests too much, that she is exaggerating, and we see her racism through or underneath her language. When Sister in "Why I Live at the P.O." says, "I do not enjoy being referred to as a hussy by my own grandfather," we know that she means to express her dislike of being called a hussy much more forcefully than she does. She is indulging in a bit of obvious **understatement,** or **litotes.** When a word or expression carries not only its literal meaning but a different meaning for the speaker as well, we have an example of **verbal irony.** When Fortunato says, "I shall not die of a cough," Montresor's "True—true" may seem reassuring, but we learn later in the story why it is both accurate and ominous. There are also nonverbal forms of irony, the most common of which is **dramatic irony,** in which a character holds a position or has an expectation that is reversed or fulfilled in an unexpected way. In D. H. Lawrence's "Odour of Chrysanthemums" (see "Reading More Fiction"), Elizabeth Bates knows her husband's habit of drinking himself into unconsciousness and expects him to be brought home like a log. How is her expectation fulfilled? She had also said bitterly, "But he needn't come rolling in here in his pit-dirt, for *I* won't wash him" (paragraph 78), and yet she does. Why is her determination altered? As you read "Odour of Chrysanthemums," watch for other reversed or unexpectedly fulfilled expectations. Close to dramatic irony but not involving outcome, close to verbal irony but not entirely embedded in words, is a kind of irony created by the gap between the character's and the narrator's (and reader's) interpretation or values. In "A Good Man Is Hard to Find," the grandmother's careful attention to her dress, she believes, assures respect: "In case of an accident, anyone seeing her dead on the highway would know at once that she was a lady" (paragraph 12). She takes this seriously; most readers find it ludicrous or pathetic. This gap is frequently present in O'Connor's stories. It is not demeaning to her characters, but testimony both to her keen realistic observation and to her knowledge of her characters from the inside.

Another, highly emphasized element of style is **imagery.** In its broadest sense imagery includes any sensory detail or evocation in a work. Note how much more imagery in that sense we find in "Janus" than in, say, "The Zebra Storyteller." Imagery in this broad sense, however, is so prevalent in literature that it would take exhaustive statistics to differentiate styles by counting the number of sensory elements per hundred or thousand words, categorizing the images as primarily visual, tactile, and so forth. In a more restricted sense, imagery refers to figurative language (see chapter 5, "Symbol"), particularly that which defines an abstraction or any emotional or psychological state with a sensory comparison. The opening paragraph of "Odour of Chrysanthemums" illustrates the broader definition of imagery, and this passage from later in the same story may represent the figurative sense: "Life with its smoky burning gone from him, had left him apart. . . . In her womb was ice of fear" (paragraph 218).

We might say that if an author's vision gives us his or her profile, the style gives us a fingerprint—though the fingerprint is unique and definitive, it is also harder to come by than a glimpse of a profile. Ultimately, however, vision and style are less distinguishable from each other than the profile-fingerprint image suggests. For vision and style, just like history and structure, do more than interact: they are inextricably fused or compounded.

FLANNERY O'CONNOR

A Good Man Is Hard to Find

The grandmother didn't want to go to Florida. She wanted to visit some of her connections in east Tennessee and she was seizing at every chance to change Bailey's mind. Bailey was the son she lived with, her only boy. He was sitting on the edge of his chair at the table, bent over the orange sports section of the *Journal.* "Now look here, Bailey," she said, "see here, read this," and she stood with one hand on her thin hip and the other rattling the newspaper at his bald head. "Here this fellow that calls himself The Misfit is aloose from the Federal Pen and headed toward Florida and you read here what it says he did to these people. Just you read it. I wouldn't take my children in any direction with a criminal like that aloose in it. I couldn't answer to my conscience if I did."

Bailey didn't look up from his reading so she wheeled around then and faced the children's mother, a young woman in slacks, whose face was as broad and innocent as a cabbage and was tied around with a green head-kerchief that had two points on the top like a rabbit's ears. She was sitting on the sofa, feeding the baby his apricots out of a jar. "The children have been to Florida before," the old lady said. "You all ought to take them somewhere else for a change so they would see different parts of the world and be broad. They never have been to east Tennessee."

The children's mother didn't seem to hear her but the eight-year-old boy, John Wesley, a stocky child with glasses, said, "If you don't want to go to Florida, why dontcha stay at home?" He and the little girl, June Star, were reading the funny papers on the floor.

"She wouldn't stay at home to be queen for a day," June Star said without raising her yellow head.

5   "Yes and what would you do if this fellow, The Misfit, caught you?" the grandmother asked.

"I'd smack his face," John Wesley said.

"She wouldn't stay at home for a million bucks," June Star said. "Afraid she'd miss something. She has to go everywhere we go."

"All right, Miss," the grandmother said. "Just remember that the next time you want me to curl your hair."

June Star said her hair was naturally curly.

10   The next morning the grandmother was the first one in the car, ready to go. She had her big black valise that looked like the head of a hippopotamus in one corner, and underneath it she was hiding a basket with Pitty Sing,[1] the cat, in it. She didn't intend for the cat to be left alone in the house for three days because he would miss her too much and she was afraid he might brush against one of the gas burners and accidentally asphyxiate himself. Her son, Bailey, didn't like to arrive at a motel with a cat.

She sat in the middle of the back seat with John Wesley and June Star on either side of her. Bailey and the children's mother and the baby sat in front and they left Atlanta at eight forty-five with the mileage on the car at 55890. The grandmother wrote this down because she thought it would be interesting to say how many miles they had been when they got back. It took them twenty minutes to reach the outskirts of the city.

The old lady settled herself comfortably, removing her white cotton gloves and putting them up with her purse on the shelf in front of the back window. The children's mother still had on slacks and still had her head tied up in a green kerchief, but the grandmother had on a navy blue straw sailor hat with a bunch of white violets on the brim and a navy blue dress with a small white dot in the print. Her collars and cuffs were white organdy trimmed with lace and at her neckline she had pinned a purple spray of cloth violets containing a sachet. In case of an accident, anyone seeing her dead on the highway would know at once that she was a lady.

She said she thought it was going to be a good day for driving, neither too hot nor too cold, and she cautioned Bailey that the speed limit was fifty-five miles an hour and that the patrolmen hid themselves behind billboards and small clumps of trees and sped out after you before you had a chance to slow down. She pointed out interesting details of the scenery: Stone Mountain; the blue granite that in some places came up to both sides of the highway; the brilliant red clay banks slightly streaked with purple; and the various crops that made rows of green lacework on the ground. The trees were full of silver-white sunlight and the meanest of them sparkled. The children were reading comic magazines and their mother had gone back to sleep.

"Let's go through Georgia fast so we won't have to look at it much," John Wesley said.

15   "If I were a little boy," said the grandmother, "I wouldn't talk about my native

1. Named after Pitti-Sing, one of the "three little maids from school" in Gilbert and Sullivan's operetta *The Mikado* (1885).

state that way. Tennessee has the mountains and Georgia has the hills."

"Tennessee is just a hillbilly dumping ground," John Wesley said, "and Georgia is a lousy state too."

"You said it," June Star said.

"In my time," said the grandmother, folding her thin veined fingers, "children were more respectful of their native states and their parents and everything else. People did right then. Oh look at the cute little pickaninny!" she said and pointed to a Negro child standing in the door of a shack. "Wouldn't that make a picture, now?" she asked and they all turned and looked at the little Negro out of the back window. He waved.

"He didn't have any britches on," June Star said.

"He probably didn't have any," the grandmother explained. "Little niggers in   20 the country don't have things like we do. If I could paint, I'd paint that picture," she said.

The children exchanged comic books.

The grandmother offered to hold the baby and the children's mother passed him over the front seat to her. She set him on her knee and bounced him and told him about the things they were passing. She rolled her eyes and screwed up her mouth and stuck her leathery thin face into his smooth bland one. Occasionally he gave her a faraway smile. They passed a large cotton field with five or six graves fenced in the middle of it, like a small island. "Look at the graveyard!" the grandmother said, pointing it out. "That was the old family burying ground. That belonged to the plantation."

"Where's the plantation?" John Wesley asked.

"Gone With the Wind," said the grandmother. "Ha. Ha."

When the children finished all the comic books they had brought, they opened   25 the lunch and ate it. The grandmother ate a peanut butter sandwich and an olive and would not let the children throw the box and the paper napkins out the window. When there was nothing else to do they played a game by choosing a cloud and making the other two guess what shape it suggested. John Wesley took one the shape of a cow and June Star guessed a cow and John Wesley said, no, an automobile, and June Star said he didn't play fair, and they began to slap each other over the grandmother.

The grandmother said she would tell them a story if they would keep quiet. When she told a story, she rolled her eyes and waved her head and was very dramatic. She said once when she was a maiden lady she had been courted by a Mr. Edgar Atkins Teagarden from Jasper, Georgia. She said he was a very good-looking man and a gentleman and that he brought her a watermelon every Saturday afternoon with his initials cut in it, E. A. T. Well, one Saturday, she said, Mr. Teagarden brought the watermelon and there was nobody at home and he left it on the front porch and returned in his buggy to Jasper, but she never got the watermelon, she said, because a nigger boy ate it when he saw the initials, E. A. T.! This story tickled John Wesley's funny bone and he giggled and giggled but June Star didn't think it was any good. She said she wouldn't marry a man that just brought her a watermelon on Saturday. The grandmother said she would have done well to marry Mr. Teagarden because he was a gentleman and had bought Coca-Cola stock when it first came out and that he had died only a few years ago, a very wealthy man.

They stopped at The Tower for barbecued sandwiches. The Tower was a part stucco and part wood filling station and dance hall set in a clearing outside of Timothy. A fat man named Red Sammy Butts ran it and there were signs stuck here and there on the building and for miles up and down the highway saying, TRY RED SAMMY'S FAMOUS BARBECUE. NONE LIKE FAMOUS RED SAMMY'S! RED SAM! THE FAT BOY WITH THE HAPPY LAUGH! A VETERAN! RED SAMMY'S YOUR MAN!

Red Sammy was lying on the bare ground outside The Tower with his head under a truck while a gray monkey about a foot high, chained to a small china-berry tree, chattered nearby. The monkey sprang back into the tree and got on the highest limb as soon as he saw the children jump out of the car and run toward him.

Inside, The Tower was a long dark room with a counter at one end and tables at the other and dancing space in the middle. They all sat down at a board table next to the nickelodeon[2] and Red Sam's wife, a tall burnt-brown woman with hair and eyes lighter than her skin, came and took their order. The children's mother put a dime in the machine and played "The Tennessee Waltz," and the grand-mother said that tune always made her want to dance. She asked Bailey if he would like to dance but he only glared at her. He didn't have a naturally sunny disposition like she did and trips made him nervous. The grandmother's brown eyes were very bright. She swayed her head from side to side and pretended she was dancing in her chair. June Star said play something she could tap to so the children's mother put in another dime and played a fast number and June Star stepped out onto the dance floor and did her tap routine.

30   "Ain't she cute?" Red Sam's wife said, leaning over the counter. "Would you like to come be my little girl?"

"No I certainly wouldn't," June Star said. "I wouldn't live in a broken-down place like this for a million bucks!" and she ran back to the table.

"Ain't she cute?" the woman repeated, stretching her mouth politely.

"Aren't you ashamed?" hissed the grandmother.

Red Sam came in and told his wife to quit lounging on the counter and hurry up with these people's order. His khaki trousers reached just to his hip bones and his stomach hung over them like a sack of meal swaying under his shirt. He came over and sat down at a table nearby and let out a combination sigh and yodel. "You can't win," he said. "You can't win," and he wiped his sweating red face off with a gray handkerchief. "These days you don't know who to trust," he said. "Ain't that the truth?"

35   "People are certainly not nice like they used to be," said the grandmother.

"Two fellers come in here last week," Red Sammy said, "driving a Chrysler. It was a old beat-up car but it was a good one and these boys looked all right to me. Said they worked at the mill and you know I let them fellers charge the gas they bought? Now why did I do that?"

2. Jukebox.

"Because you're a good man!" the grandmother said at once.

"Yes'm, I suppose so," Red Sam said as if he were struck with this answer.

His wife brought the orders, carrying the five plates all at once without a tray, two in each hand and one balanced on her arm. "It isn't a soul in this green world of God's that you can trust," she said. "And I don't count nobody out of that, not nobody," she repeated, looking at Red Sammy.

"Did you read about that criminal, The Misfit, that's escaped?" asked the grandmother.   40

"I wouldn't be a bit surprised if he didn't attact this place right here," said the woman. "If he hears about it being here, I wouldn't be none surprised to see him. If he hears it's two cent in the cash register, I wouldn't be a tall surprised if he . . ."

"That'll do," Red Sam said. "Go bring these people their Co'-Colas," and the woman went off to get the rest of the order.

"A good man is hard to find," Red Sammy said. "Everything is getting terrible. I remember the day you could go off and leave your screen door unlatched. Not no more."

He and the grandmother discussed better times. The old lady said that in her opinion Europe was entirely to blame for the way things were now. She said the way Europe acted you would think we were made of money and Red Sam said it was no use talking about it, she was exactly right. The children ran outside into the white sunlight and looked at the monkey in the lacy chinaberry tree. He was busy catching fleas on himself and biting each one carefully between his teeth as if it were a delicacy.

They drove off again into the hot afternoon. The grandmother took cat naps   45
and woke up every few minutes with her own snoring. Outside of Toombsboro she woke up and recalled an old plantation that she had visited in this neighborhood once when she was a young lady. She said the house had six white columns across the front and that there was an avenue of oaks leading up to it and two little wooden trellis arbors on either side in front where you sat down with your suitor after a stroll in the garden. She recalled exactly which road to turn off to get to it. She knew that Bailey would not be willing to lose any time looking at an old house, but the more she talked about it, the more she wanted to see it once again and find out if the little twin arbors were still standing. "There was a secret panel in this house," she said craftily, not telling the truth but wishing that she were, "and the story went that all the family silver was hidden in it when Sherman came through but it was never found . . ."

"Hey!" John Wesley said. "Let's go see it! We'll find it! We'll poke all the woodwork and find it! Who lives there? Where do you turn off at? Hey Pop, can't we turn off there?"

"We never have seen a house with a secret panel!" June Star shrieked. "Let's go to the house with the secret panel! Hey Pop, can't we go see the house with the secret panel!"

"It's not far from here, I know," the grandmother said. "It wouldn't take over twenty minutes."

Bailey was looking straight ahead. His jaw was as rigid as a horseshoe. "No," he said.

50   The children began to yell and scream that they wanted to see the house with the secret panel. John Wesley kicked the back of the front seat and June Star hung over her mother's shoulder and whined desperately into her ear that they never had any fun even on their vacation, that they could never do what THEY wanted to do. The baby began to scream and John Wesley kicked the back of the seat so hard that his father could feel the blows in his kidney.

"All right!" he shouted and drew the car to a stop at the side of the road. "Will you all shut up? Will you all just shut up for one second? If you don't shut up, we won't go anywhere."

"It would be very educational for them," the grandmother murmured.

"All right," Bailey said, "but get this: this is the only time we're going to stop for anything like this. This is the one and only time."

"The dirt road that you have to turn down is about a mile back," the grandmother directed. "I marked it when we passed."

55   "A dirt road," Bailey groaned.

After they had turned around and were headed toward the dirt road, the grandmother recalled other points about the house, the beautiful glass over the front doorway and the candle-lamp in the hall. John Wesley said that the secret panel was probably in the fireplace.

"You can't go inside this house," Bailey said. "You don't know who lives there."

"While you all talk to the people in front, I'll run around behind and get in a window," John Wesley suggested.

"We'll all stay in the car," his mother said.

60   They turned onto the dirt road and the car raced roughly along in a swirl of pink dust. The grandmother recalled the times when there were no paved roads and thirty miles was a day's journey. The dirt road was hilly and there were sudden washes in it and sharp curves on dangerous embankments. All at once they would be on a hill, looking down over the blue tops of trees for miles around, then the next minute, they would be in a red depression with the dust-coated trees looking down on them.

"This place had better turn up in a minute," Bailey said, "or I'm going to turn around."

The road looked as if no one had traveled on it in months.

"It's not much farther," the grandmother said and just as she said it, a horrible thought came to her. The thought was so embarrassing that she turned red in the face and her eyes dilated and her feet jumped up, upsetting her valise in the corner. The instant the valise moved, the newspaper top she had over the basket under it rose with a snarl and Pitty Sing, the cat, sprang onto Bailey's shoulder.

The children were thrown to the floor and their mother, clutching the baby, out the door onto the ground; the old lady was thrown into the front seat. The car turned over once and landed right-side-up in a gulch off the side of the road. Bailey remained in the driver's seat with the cat—gray-striped with a broad white face and an orange nose—clinging to his neck like a caterpillar.

65   As soon as the children saw they could move their arms and legs, they scrambled out of the car, shouting, "We've had an ACCIDENT!" The grandmother was curled up under the dashboard, hoping she was injured so that Bailey's wrath

would not come down on her all at once. The horrible thought she had had before the accident was that the house she had remembered so vividly was not in Georgia but in Tennessee.

Bailey removed the cat from his neck with both hands and flung it out the window against the side of a pine tree. Then he got out of the car and started looking for the children's mother. She was sitting against the side of the red gutted ditch, holding the screaming baby, but she only had a cut down her face and a broken shoulder. "We've had an ACCIDENT!" the children screamed in a frenzy of delight.

"But nobody's killed," June Star said with disappointment as the grandmother limped out of the car, her hat still pinned to her head but the broken front brim standing up at a jaunty angle and the violet spray hanging off the side. They all sat down in the ditch, except the children, to recover from the shock. They were all shaking.

"Maybe a car will come along," said the children's mother hoarsely.

"I believe I have injured an organ," said the grandmother, pressing her side, but no one answered her. Bailey's teeth were clattering. He had on a yellow sport shirt with bright blue parrots designed in it and his face was as yellow as the shirt. The grandmother decided that she would not mention that the house was in Tennessee.

The road was about ten feet above and they could see only the tops of the trees on the other side of it. Behind the ditch they were sitting in there were more woods, tall and dark and deep. In a few minutes they saw a car some distance away on top of a hill, coming slowly as if the occupants were watching them. The grandmother stood up and waved both arms dramatically to attract their attention. The car continued to come on slowly, disappeared around a bend and appeared again, moving even slower, on top of the hill they had gone over. It was a big black battered hearselike automobile. There were three men in it.

It came to a stop just over them and for some minutes, the driver looked down with a steady expressionless gaze to where they were sitting, and didn't speak. Then he turned his head and muttered something to the other two and they got out. One was a fat boy in black trousers and a red sweat shirt with a silver stallion embossed on the front of it. He moved around on the right side of them and stood staring, his mouth partly open in a kind of loose grin. The other had on khaki pants and a blue striped coat and a gray hat pulled down very low, hiding most of his face. He came around slowly on the left side. Neither spoke.

The driver got out of the car and stood by the side of it, looking down at them. He was an older man than the other two. His hair was just beginning to gray and he wore silver-rimmed spectacles that gave him a scholarly look. He had a long creased face and didn't have on any shirt or undershirt. He had on blue jeans that were too tight for him and was holding a black hat and a gun. The two boys also had guns.

"We've had an ACCIDENT!" the children screamed.

The grandmother had the peculiar feeling that the bespectacled man was someone she knew. His face was as familiar to her as if she had known him all her life but she could not recall who he was. He moved away from the car and began to come down the embankment, placing his feet carefully so that he wouldn't slip. He had on tan and white shoes and no socks, and his ankles were red and thin. "Good afternoon," he said. "I see you all had you a little spill."

75 "We turned over twice!" said the grandmother.

"Oncet," he corrected. "We seen it happen. Try their car and see will it run, Hiram," he said quietly to the boy with the gray hat.

"What you got that gun for?" John Wesley asked. "Whatcha gonna do with that gun?"

"Lady," the man said to the children's mother, "would you mind calling them children to sit down by you? Children make me nervous. I want all you all to sit down right together there where you're at."

"What are you telling US what to do for?" June Star asked.

80 Behind them the line of woods gaped like a dark open mouth. "Come here," said their mother.

"Look here now," Bailey began suddenly, "we're in a predicament! We're in . . ."

The grandmother shrieked. She scrambled to her feet and stood staring. "You're The Misfit!" she said. "I recognized you at once!"

"Yes'm," the man said, smiling slightly as if he were pleased in spite of himself to be known, "but it would have been better for all of you, lady, if you hadn't of reckernized me."

Bailey turned his head sharply and said something to his mother that shocked even the children. The old lady began to cry and The Misfit reddened.

85 "Lady," he said, "don't you get upset. Sometimes a man says things he don't mean. I don't reckon he meant to talk to you thataway."

"You wouldn't shoot a lady, would you?" the grandmother said and removed a clean handkerchief from her cuff and began to slap at her eyes with it.

The Misfit pointed the toe of his shoe into the ground and made a little hole and then covered it up again. "I would hate to have to," he said.

"Listen," the grandmother almost screamed, "I know you're a good man. You don't look a bit like you have common blood. I know you must come from nice people!"

"Yes mam," he said, "finest people in the world." When he smiled he showed a row of strong white teeth. "God never made a finer woman than my mother and my daddy's heart was pure gold," he said. The boy with the red sweat shirt had come around behind them and was standing with his gun at his hip. The Misfit squatted down on the ground. "Watch them children, Bobby Lee," he said. "You know they make me nervous." He looked at the six of them huddled together in front of him and he seemed to be embarrassed as if he couldn't think of anything to say. "Ain't a cloud in the sky," he remarked, looking up at it. "Don't see no sun but don't see no cloud neither."

90 "Yes, it's a beautiful day," said the grandmother. "Listen," she said, "you shouldn't call yourself The Misfit because I know you're a good man at heart. I can just look at you and tell."

"Hush!" Bailey yelled. "Hush! Everybody shut up and let me handle this!" He was squatting in the position of a runner about to sprint forward but he didn't move.

"I pre-chate that, lady," The Misfit said and drew a little circle in the ground with the butt of his gun.

"It'll take a half a hour to fix this here car," Hiram called, looking over the raised hood of it.

"Well, first you and Bobby Lee get him and that little boy to step over yonder with you," The Misfit said, pointing to Bailey and John Wesley. "The boys want to ast you something," he said to Bailey. "Would you mind stepping back in them woods there with them?"

"Listen," Bailey began, "we're in a terrible predicament! Nobody realizes what this is," and his voice cracked. His eyes were as blue and intense as the parrots in his shirt and he remained perfectly still.

The grandmother reached up to adjust her hat brim as if she were going to the woods with him but it came off in her hand. She stood staring at it and after a second she let it fall on the ground. Hiram pulled Bailey up by the arm as if he were assisting an old man. John Wesley caught hold of his father's hand and Bobby Lee followed. They went off toward the woods and just as they reached the dark edge, Bailey turned and supporting himself against a gray naked pine trunk, he shouted, "I'll be back in a minute, Mamma, wait on me!"

"Come back this instant!" his mother shrilled but they all disappeared into the woods.

"Bailey Boy!" the grandmother called in a tragic voice but she found she was looking at The Misfit squatting on the ground in front of her. "I just know you're a good man," she said desperately. "You're not a bit common!"

"Nome, I ain't a good man," The Misfit said after a second as if he had considered her statement carefully, "but I ain't the worst in the world neither. My daddy said I was a different breed of dog from my brothers and sisters. 'You know,' Daddy said, 'it's some that can live their whole life out without asking about it and it's others has to know why it is, and this boy is one of the latters. He's going to be into everything!' " He put on his black hat and looked up suddenly and then away deep into the woods as if he were embarrassed again. "I'm sorry I don't have on a shirt before you ladies," he said, hunching his shoulders slightly. "We buried our clothes that we had on when we escaped and we're just making do until we can get better. We borrowed these from some folks we met," he explained.

"That's perfectly all right," the grandmother said. "Maybe Bailey has an extra shirt in his suitcase."

"I'll look and see terrectly," The Misfit said.

"Where are they taking him?" the children's mother screamed.

"Daddy was a card himself," The Misfit said. "You couldn't put anything over on him. He never got in trouble with the Authorities though. Just had the knack of handling them."

"You could be honest too if you'd only try," said the grandmother. "Think how wonderful it would be to settle down and live a comfortable life and not have to think about somebody chasing you all the time."

105   The Misfit kept scratching in the ground with the butt of his gun as if he were thinking about it. "Yes'm, somebody is always after you," he murmured.

The grandmother noticed how thin his shoulder blades were just behind his hat because she was standing up looking down on him. "Do you ever pray?" she asked.

He shook his head. All she saw was the black hat wiggle between his shoulder blades. "Nome," he said.

There was a pistol shot from the woods, followed closely by another. Then silence. The old lady's head jerked around. She could hear the wind move through the tree tops like a long satisfied insuck of breath. "Bailey Boy!" she called.

"I was a gospel singer for a while," The Misfit said. "I been most everything. Been in the arm service, both land and sea, at home and abroad, been twict married, been an undertaker, been with the railroads, plowed Mother Earth, been in a tornado, seen a man burnt alive oncet," and looked up at the children's mother and the little girl who were sitting close together, their faces white and their eyes glassy; "I even seen a woman flogged," he said.

110   "Pray, pray," the grandmother began, "pray, pray . . ."

"I never was a bad boy that I remember of," The Misfit said in an almost dreamy voice, "but somewheres along the line I done something wrong and got sent to the penitentiary. I was buried alive," and he looked up and held her attention to him by a steady stare.

"That's when you should have started to pray," she said. "What did you do to get sent to the penitentiary that first time?"

"Turn to the right, it was a wall," The Misfit said, looking up again at the cloudless sky. "Turn to the left, it was a wall. Look up it was a ceiling, look down it was a floor. I forgot what I done, lady. I set there and set there, trying to remember what it was I done and I ain't recalled it to this day. Oncet in a while, I would think it was coming to me, but it never come."

"Maybe they put you in by mistake," the old lady said vaguely.

115   "Nome," he said. "It wasn't no mistake. They had the papers on me."

"You must have stolen something," she said.

The Misfit sneered slightly. "Nobody had nothing I wanted," he said. "It was a head-doctor at the penitentiary said what I had done was kill my daddy but I known that for a lie. My daddy died in nineteen ought nineteen of the epidemic flu and I never had a thing to do with it. He was buried in the Mount Hopewell Baptist churchyard and you can go there and see for yourself."

"If you would pray," the old lady said, "Jesus would help you."

"That's right," The Misfit said.

120   "Well then, why don't you pray?" she asked trembling with delight suddenly.

"I don't want no hep," he said. "I'm doing all right by myself."

Bobby Lee and Hiram came ambling back from the woods. Bobby Lee was dragging a yellow shirt with bright blue parrots in it.

"Thow me that shirt, Bobby Lee," The Misfit said. The shirt came flying at him and landed on his shoulder and he put it on. The grandmother couldn't name what the shirt reminded her of. "No, lady," The Misfit said while he was buttoning it up, "I found out the crime don't matter. You can do one thing or you can do another, kill a man or take a tire off his car, because sooner or later you're going to forget what it was you done and just be punished for it."

The children's mother had begun to make heaving noises as if she couldn't get her breath. "Lady," he asked, "would you and that little girl like to step off yonder with Bobby Lee and Hiram and join your husband?"

"Yes, thank you," the mother said faintly. Her left arm dangled helplessly and   125
she was holding the baby, who had gone to sleep, in the other. "Hep that lady up, Hiram," The Misfit said as she struggled to climb out of the ditch, "and Bobby Lee, you hold onto that little girl's hand."

"I don't want to hold hands with him," June Star said. "He reminds me of a pig."

The fat boy blushed and laughed and caught her by the arm and pulled her off into the woods after Hiram and her mother.

Alone with The Misfit, the grandmother found that she had lost her voice. There was not a cloud in the sky nor any sun. There was nothing around her but woods. She wanted to tell him that he must pray. She opened and closed her mouth several times before anything came out. Finally she found herself saying, "Jesus, Jesus," meaning, Jesus will help you, but the way she was saying it, it sounded as if she might be cursing.

"Yes'm," The Misfit said as if he agreed. "Jesus thown everything off balance. It was the same case with Him as with me except He hadn't committed any crime and they could prove I had committed one because they had the papers on me. Of course," he said, "they never shown me my papers. That's why I sign myself now. I said long ago, you get you a signature and sign everything you do and keep a copy of it. Then you'll know what you done and you can hold up the crime to the punishment and see do they match and in the end you'll have something to prove you ain't been treated right. I call myself The Misfit," he said, "because I can't make what all I done wrong fit what all I gone through in punishment."

There was a piercing scream from the woods, followed closely by a pistol report.   130
"Does it seem right to you, lady, that one is punished a heap and another ain't punished at all?"

"Jesus!" the old lady cried. "You've got good blood! I know you wouldn't shoot a lady! I know you come from nice people! Pray! Jesus, you ought not to shoot a lady. I'll give you all the money I've got!"

"Lady," The Misfit said, looking beyond her far into the woods, "there never was a body that give the undertaker a tip."

There were two more pistol reports and the grandmother raised her head like a parched old turkey hen crying for water and called, "Bailey Boy, Bailey Boy!" as if her heart would break.

"Jesus was the only One that ever raised the dead." The Misfit continued, "and He shouldn't have done it. He thown everything off balance. If He did what He said, then it's nothing for you to do but thow away everything and follow Him, and if He didn't, then it's nothing for you to do but enjoy the few minutes you got left the best way you can—by killing somebody or burning down his house or doing some other meanness to him. No pleasure but meanness," he said and his voice had become almost a snarl.

135   "Maybe He didn't raise the dead," the old lady mumbled, not knowing what she was saying and feeling so dizzy that she sank down in the ditch with her legs twisted under her.

"I wasn't there so I can't say He didn't," The Misfit said. "I wisht I had of been there," he said, hitting the ground with his fist. "It ain't right I wasn't there because if I had of been there I would of known. Listen lady," he said in a high voice, "if I had of been there I would of known and I wouldn't be like I am now." His voice seemed about to crack and the grandmother's head cleared for an instant. She saw the man's face twisted close to her own as if he were going to cry and she murmured, "Why you're one of my babies. You're one of my own children!" She reached out and touched him on the shoulder. The Misfit sprang back as if a snake had bitten him and shot her three times through the chest. Then he put his gun down on the ground and took off his glasses and began to clean them.

Hiram and Bobby Lee returned from the woods and stood over the ditch, looking down at the grandmother who half sat and half lay in a puddle of blood with her legs crossed under her like a child's and her face smiling up at the cloudless sky.

Without his glasses, The Misfit's eyes were red-rimmed and pale and defenseless-looking. "Take her off and thow her where you thown the others," he said, picking up the cat that was rubbing itself against his leg.

"She was a talker, wasn't she?" Bobby Lee said, sliding down the ditch with a yodel.

140   "She would of been a good woman," The Misfit said, "if it had been somebody there to shoot her every minute of her life."

"Some fun!" Bobby Lee said.

"Shut up, Bobby Lee," The Misfit said. "It's no real pleasure in life."

1955

FLANNERY O'CONNOR

The Lame Shall Enter First

Sheppard sat on a stool at the bar that divided the kitchen in half, eating his cereal out of the individual pasteboard box it came in. He ate mechanically, his eyes on the child, who was wandering from cabinet to cabinet in the panelled kitchen, collecting the ingredients for his breakfast. He was a stocky blond boy of ten. Sheppard kept his intense blue eyes fixed on him. The boy's future was written in his face. He would be a banker. No, worse. He would operate a small loan company. All he wanted for the child was that he be good and unselfish and neither seemed likely. Sheppard was a young man whose hair was already white. It stood up like a narrow brush halo over his pink sensitive face.

The boy approached the bar with the jar of peanut butter under his arm, a plate with a quarter of a small chocolate cake on it in one hand and the ketchup bottle in the other. He did not appear to notice his father. He climbed up on the stool and began to spread peanut butter on the cake. He had very large round ears that leaned away from his head and seemed to pull his eyes slightly too far apart. His shirt was green but so faded that the cowboy charging across the front of it was only a shadow.

"Norton," Sheppard said, "I saw Rufus Johnson yesterday. Do you know what he was doing?"

The child looked at him with a kind of half attention, his eyes forward but not yet engaged. They were a paler blue than his father's as if they might have faded like the shirt; one of them listed, almost imperceptibly, toward the outer rim.

"He was in an alley," Sheppard said, "and he had his hand in a garbage can.   5 He was trying to get something to eat out of it." He paused to let this soak in. "He was hungry," he finished, and tried to pierce the child's conscience with his gaze.

The boy picked up the piece of chocolate cake and began to gnaw it from one corner.

"Norton," Sheppard said, "do you have any idea what it means to share?"

A flicker of attention. "Some of it's yours," Norton said.

"Some of it's *his,*" Sheppard said heavily. It was hopeless. Almost any fault would have been preferable to selfishness—a violent temper, even a tendency to lie.

The child turned the bottle of ketchup upside down and began thumping   10 ketchup onto the cake.

Sheppard's look of pain increased. "You are ten and Rufus Johnson is fourteen," he said. "Yet I'm sure your shirts would fit Rufus." Rufus Johnson was a boy he had been trying to help at the reformatory for the past year. He had been released two months ago. "When he was in the reformatory, he looked pretty good, but when I saw him yesterday, he was skin and bones. He hasn't been eating cake with peanut butter on it for breakfast."

The child paused. "It's stale," he said. "That's why I have to put stuff on it."

Sheppard turned his face to the window at the end of the bar. The side lawn, green and even, sloped fifty feet or so down to a small suburban wood. When his wife was living, they had often eaten outside, even breakfast, on the grass. He had never noticed then that the child was selfish. "Listen to me," he said, turning back to him, "look at me and listen."

The boy looked at him. At least his eyes were forward.

"I gave Rufus a key to this house when he left the reformatory—to show my   15 confidence in him and so he would have a place he could come to and feel welcome any time. He didn't use it, but I think he'll use it now because he's seen me and he's hungry. And if he doesn't use it, I'm going out and find him and bring him here. I can't see a child eating out of garbage cans."

The boy frowned. It was dawning upon him that something of his was threatened.

Sheppard's mouth stretched in disgust. "Rufus's father died before he was born," he said. "His mother is in the state penitentiary. He was raised by his grandfather in a shack without water or electricity and the old man beat him every day. How would you like to belong to a family like that?"

"I don't know," the child said lamely.

"Well, you might think about it sometime," Sheppard said.

20   Sheppard was City Recreational Director. On Saturdays he worked at the reformatory as a counselor, receiving nothing for it but the satisfaction of knowing he was helping boys no one else cared about. Johnson was the most intelligent boy he had worked with and the most deprived.

Norton turned what was left of the cake over as if he no longer wanted it.

"Maybe he won't come," the child said and his eyes brightened slightly.

"Think of everything you have that he doesn't!" Sheppard said. "Suppose you had to root in garbage cans for food? Suppose you had a huge swollen foot and one side of you dropped lower than the other when you walked?"

The boy looked blank, obviously unable to imagine such a thing.

25   "You have a healthy body," Sheppard said, "a good home. You've never been taught anything but the truth. Your daddy gives you everything you need and want. You don't have a grandfather who beats you. And your mother is not in the state penitentiary."

The child pushed his plate away. Sheppard groaned aloud.

A knot of flesh appeared below the boy's suddenly distorted mouth. His face became a mass of lumps with slits for eyes. "If she was in the penitentiary," he began in a kind of racking bellow, "I could go to seeeeee her." Tears rolled down his face and the ketchup dribbled on his chin. He looked as if he had been hit in the mouth. He abandoned himself and howled.

Sheppard sat helpless and miserable, like a man lashed by some elemental force of nature. This was not a normal grief. It was all part of his selfishness. She had been dead for over a year and a child's grief should not last so long. "You're going on eleven years old," he said reproachfully.

The child began an agonizing high-pitched heaving noise.

30   "If you stop thinking about yourself and think what you can do for somebody else," Sheppard said, "then you'll stop missing your mother."

The boy was silent but his shoulders continued to shake. Then his face collapsed and he began to howl again.

"Don't you think I'm lonely without her too?" Sheppard said. "Don't you think I miss her at all? I do, but I'm not sitting around moping. I'm busy helping other people. When do you see me just sitting around thinking about my troubles?"

The boy slumped as if he were exhausted but fresh tears streaked his face.

"What are you going to do today?" Sheppard asked, to get his mind on something else.

35   The child ran his arm across his eyes. "Sell seeds," he mumbled.

Always selling something. He had four quart jars full of nickels and dimes he had saved and he took them out of his closet every few days and counted them. "What are you selling seeds for?"

"To win a prize."

"What's the prize?"

"A thousand dollars."

40   "And what would you do if you had a thousand dollars?"

"Keep it," the child said and wiped his nose on his shoulder.

"I feel sure you would," Sheppard said. "Listen," he said and lowered his voice to an almost pleading tone, "suppose by some chance you did win a thousand dollars. Wouldn't you like to spend it on children less fortunate than yourself? Wouldn't you like to give some swings and trapezes to the orphanage? Wouldn't you like to buy poor Rufus Johnson a new shoe?"

The boy began to back away from the bar. Then suddenly he leaned forward and hung with his mouth open over his plate. Sheppard groaned again. Everything came up, the cake, the peanut butter, the ketchup—a limp sweet batter. He hung over it gagging, more came, and he waited with his mouth open over the plate as if he expected his heart to come up next.

"It's all right," Sheppard said, "it's all right. You couldn't help it. Wipe your mouth and go lie down."

The child hung there a moment longer. Then he raised his face and looked blindly at his father.   45

"Go on," Sheppard said. "Go on and lie down."

The boy pulled up the end of his t-shirt and smeared his mouth with it. Then he climbed down off the stool and wandered out of the kitchen.

Sheppard sat there staring at the puddle of half-digested food. The sour odor reached him and he drew back. His gorge rose. He got up and carried the plate to the sink and turned the water on it and watched grimly as the mess ran down the drain. Johnson's sad thin hand rooted in garbage cans for food while his own child, selfish, unresponsive, greedy, had so much that he threw it up. He cut off the faucet with a thrust of his fist. Johnson had a capacity for real response and had been deprived of everything from birth; Norton was average or below and had had every advantage.

He went back to the bar to finish his breakfast. The cereal was soggy in the cardboard box but he paid no attention to what he was eating. Johnson was worth any amount of effort because he had the potential. He had seen it from the time the boy had limped in for his first interview.

Sheppard's office at the reformatory was a narrow closet with one window and   50
a small table and two chairs in it. He had never been inside a confessional but he thought it must be the same kind of operation he had here, except that he explained, he did not absolve. His credentials were less dubious than a priest's; he had been trained for what he was doing.

When Johnson came in for his first interview, he had been reading over the boy's record—senseless destruction, windows smashed, city trash boxes set afire, tires slashed—the kind of thing he found where boys had been transplanted abruptly from the country to the city as this one had. He came to Johnson's I. Q. score. It was 140. He raised his eyes eagerly.

The boy sat slumped on the edge of his chair, his arms hanging between his thighs. The light from the window fell on his face. His eyes, steel-colored and very still, were trained narrowly forward. His thin dark hair hung in a flat forelock across the side of his forehead, not carelessly like a boy's, but fiercely like an old man's. A kind of fanatic intelligence was palpable in his face.

Sheppard smiled to diminish the distance between them.

The boy's expression did not soften. He leaned back in his chair and lifted a monstrous club foot to his knee. The foot was in a heavy black battered shoe with a sole four or five inches thick. The leather parted from it in one place and the end of an empty sock protruded like a gray tongue from a severed head. The case was clear to Sheppard instantly. His mischief was compensation for the foot.

55   "Well Rufus," he said, "I see by the record here that you don't have but a year to serve. What do you plan to do when you get out?"

"I don't make no plans," the boy said. His eyes shifted indifferently to something outside the window behind Sheppard in the far distance.

"Maybe you ought to," Sheppard said and smiled.

Johnson continued to gaze beyond him.

"I want to see you make the most of your intelligence," Sheppard said. "What's most important to you? Let's talk about what's important to *you.*" His eyes dropped involuntarily to the foot.

60   "Study it and git your fill," the boy drawled.

Sheppard reddened. The black deformed mass swelled before his eyes. He ignored the remark and the leer the boy was giving him. "Rufus," he said, "you've got into a lot of senseless trouble but I think when you understand why you do these things, you'll be less inclined to do them." He smiled. They had so few friends, saw so few pleasant faces, that half his effectiveness came from nothing more than smiling at them. "There are a lot of things about yourself that I think I can explain to you," he said.

Johnson looked at him stonily. "I ain't asked for no explanation," he said. "I already know why I do what I do."

"Well good!" Sheppard said. "Suppose you tell me what's made you do the things you've done?"

A black sheen appeared in the boy's eyes. "Satan," he said. "He has me in his power."

65   Sheppard looked at him steadily. There was no indication on the boy's face that he had said this to be funny. The line of his thin mouth was set with pride. Sheppard's eyes hardened. He felt a momentary dull despair as if he were faced with some elemental warping of nature that had happened too long ago to be corrected now. This boy's questions about life had been answered by signs nailed on the pine trees: DOES SATAN HAVE YOU IN HIS POWER? REPENT OR BURN IN HELL. JESUS SAVES. He would know the Bible with or without reading it. His despair gave way to outrage. "Rubbish!" he snorted. "We're living in the space age! You're too smart to give me an answer like that."

Johnson's mouth twisted slightly. His look was contemptuous but amused. There was a glint of challenge in his eyes.

Sheppard scrutinized his face. Where there was intelligence anything was possible. He smiled again, a smile that was like an invitation to the boy to come into a school room with all its windows thrown open to the light. "Rufus," he said, "I'm going to arrange for you to have a conference with me once a week. Maybe there's an explanation for your explanation. Maybe I can explain your devil to you."

After that he had talked to Johnson every Saturday for the rest of the year. He talked at random, the kind of talk the boy would never have heard before. He talked a little above him to give him something to reach for. He roamed from simple psychology and the dodges of the human mind to astronomy and the space capsules that were whirling around the earth faster than the speed of sound and would soon encircle the stars. Instinctively he concentrated on the stars. He wanted to give the boy something to reach for besides his neighbor's goods. He wanted to stretch his horizons. He wanted him to *see* the universe, to see that the darkest parts of it could be penetrated. He would have given anything to be able to put a telescope in Johnson's hands.

Johnson said little and what he did say, for the sake of his pride, was in dissent or senseless contradiction, with the clubfoot raised always to his knee like a weapon ready for use, but Sheppard was not deceived. He watched his eyes and every week he saw something in them crumble. From the boy's face, hard but shocked, braced against the light that was ravaging him, he could see that he was hitting dead center.

Johnson was free now to live out of garbage cans and rediscover his old igno-   70
rance. The injustice of it was infuriating. He had been sent back to the grand-father; the old man's imbecility could only be imagined. Perhaps the boy had by now run away from him. The idea of getting custody of Johnson had occurred to Sheppard before, but the fact of the grandfather had stood in the way. Nothing excited him so much as thinking what he could do for such a boy. First he would have him fitted for a new orthopedic shoe. His back was thrown out of line every time he took a step. Then he would encourage him in some particular intellectual interest. He thought of the telescope. He could buy a second-hand one and they could set it up in the attic window. He sat for almost ten minutes thinking what he could do if he had Johnson here with him. What was wasted on Norton would cause Johnson to flourish. Yesterday when he had seen him with his hand in the garbage can, he had waved and started forward. Johnson had seen him, paused a split-second, then vanished with the swiftness of a rat, but not before Sheppard had seen his expression change. Something had kindled in the boy's eyes, he was sure of it, some memory of the lost light.

He got up and threw the cereal box in the garbage. Before he left the house, he looked into Norton's room to be sure he was not still sick. The child was sitting cross-legged on his bed. He had emptied the quart jars of change into one large pile in front of him, and was sorting it out by nickels and dimes and quarters.

That afternoon Norton was alone in the house, squatting on the floor of his room arranging packages of flower seeds in rows around himself. Rain slashed against the window panes and rattled in the gutters. The room had grown dark but every few minutes it was lit by silent lightning and the seed packages showed up gaily on the floor. He squatted motionless like a large pale frog in the midst of this potential garden. All at once his eyes became alert. Without warning the rain had stopped. The silence was heavy as if the downpour had been hushed by violence. He remained motionless, only his eyes turning.

Into the silence came the distinct click of a key turning in the front door lock. The sound was a very deliberate one. It drew attention to itself and held it as if it were controlled more by a mind than by a hand. The child leapt up and got into the closet.

The footsteps began to move in the hall. They were deliberate and irregular, a light and then a heavy one, then a silence as if the visitor had paused to listen himself or to examine something. In a minute the kitchen door screeked. The footsteps crossed the kitchen to the refrigerator. The closet wall and the kitchen wall were the same. Norton stood with his ear pressed against it. The refrigerator door opened. There was a prolonged silence.

75   He took off his shoes and then tiptoed out of the closet and stepped over the seed packages. In the middle of the room, he stopped and remained where he was, rigid. A thin bony-face boy in a wet black suit stood in his door, blocking his escape. His hair was flattened to his skull by the rain. He stood there like an irate drenched crow. His look went through the child like a pin and paralyzed him. Then his eyes began to move over everything in the room—the unmade bed, the dirty curtains on the one large window, a photograph of a wide-faced young woman that stood up in the clutter on top of the dresser.

The child's tongue suddenly went wild. "He's been expecting you, he's going to give you a new shoe because you have to eat out of garbage cans!" he said in a kind of mouse-like shriek.

"I eat out of garbage cans," the boy said slowly with a beady stare, "because I like to eat out of garbage cans. See?"

The child nodded.

"And I got ways of getting my own shoe. See?"

80   The child nodded, mesmerized.

The boy limped in and sat down on the bed. He arranged a pillow behind him and stretched his short leg out so that the big black shoe rested conspicuously on a fold of the sheet.

Norton's gaze settled on it and remained immobile. The sole was as thick as a brick.

Johnson wiggled it slightly and smiled. "If I kick somebody *once* with this," he said, "it learns them not to mess with me."

The child nodded.

85   "Go in the kitchen," Johnson said, "and make me a sandwich with some of that rye bread and ham and bring me a glass of milk."

Norton went off like a mechanical toy, pushed in the right direction. He made a large greasy sandwich with ham hanging out the sides of it and poured out a glass of milk. Then he returned to the room with the glass of milk in one hand and the sandwich in the other.

Johnson was leaning back regally against the pillow. "Thanks, waiter," he said and took the sandwich.

Norton stood by the side of the bed, holding the glass.

The boy tore into the sandwich and ate steadily until he finished it. Then he took the glass of milk. He held it with both hands like a child and when he lowered it for breath, there was a rim of milk around his mouth. He handed Norton the empty glass. "Go get me one of them oranges in there, waiter," he said hoarsely.

90   Norton went to the kitchen and returned with the orange. Johnson peeled it

with his fingers and let the peeling drop in the bed. He ate it slowly, spitting the seeds out in front of him. When he finished, he wiped his hands on the sheet and gave Norton a long appraising stare. He appeared to have been softened by the service. "You're his kid all right," he said. "You got the same stupid face."

The child stood there stolidly as if he had not heard.

"He don't know his left hand from his right," Johnson said with a hoarse pleasure in his voice.

The child cast his eyes a little to the side of the boy's face and looked fixedly at the wall.

"Yaketty yaketty yak," Johnson said, "and never says a thing."

The child's upper lip lifted slightly but he didn't say anything.   95

"Gas," Johnson said. "Gas."

The child's face began to have a wary look of belligerence. He backed away slightly as if he were prepared to retreat instantly. "He's good," he mumbled. "He helps people."

"Good!" Johnson said savagely. He thrust his head forward. "Listen here," he hissed, "I don't care if he's good or not. He ain't *right!*"

Norton looked stunned.

The screen door in the kitchen banged and someone entered. Johnson sat   100 forward instantly. "Is that him?" he said.

"It's the cook," Norton said. "She comes in the afternoon."

Johnson got up and limped into the hall and stood in the kitchen door and Norton followed him.

The colored girl was at the closet taking off a bright red raincoat. She was a tall light-yellow girl with a mouth like a large rose that had darkened and wilted. Her hair was dressed in tiers on top of her head and leaned to the side like the Tower of Pisa.

Johnson made a noise through his teeth. "Well look at Aunt Jemima," he said.

The girl paused and trained an insolent gaze on them. They might have been   105 dust on the floor.

"Come on," Johnson said, "let's see what all you got besides a nigger." He opened the first door to his right in the hall and looked into a pink-tiled bath-room. "A pink can!" he murmured.

He turned a comical face to the child. "Does he sit on that?"

"It's for company," Norton said, "but he sits on it sometimes."

"He ought to empty his head in it," Johnson said.

The door was open to the next room. It was the room Sheppard had slept in   110 since his wife died. An ascetic-looking iron bed stood on the bare floor. A heap of Little League baseball uniforms was piled in one corner. Papers were scattered over a large roll-top desk and held down in various places by his pipes. Johnson stood looking into the room silently. He wrinkled his nose. "Guess who?" he said.

The door to the next room was closed but Johnson opened it and thrust his head into the semi-darkness within. The shades were down and the air was close with a faint scent of perfume in it. There was a wide antique bed and a mammoth dresser whose mirror glinted in the half light. Johnson snapped the light switch by the door and crossed the room to the mirror and peered into it. A silver comb and brush lay on the linen runner. He picked up the comb and began to run it through his hair. He combed it straight down on his forehead. Then he swept it to the side, Hitler fashion.

"Leave her comb alone!" the child said. He stood in the door, pale and breathing heavily as if he were watching sacrilege in a holy place.

Johnson put the comb down and picked up the brush and gave his hair a swipe with it.

"She's dead," the child said.

"I ain't afraid of dead people's things," Johnson said. He opened the top drawer and slid his hand in.

"Take your big fat dirty hands off my mother's clothes!" the child said in a high suffocated voice.

"Keep your shirt on, sweetheart," Johnson murmured. He pulled up a wrinkled red polka dot blouse and dropped it back. Then he pulled out a green silk kerchief and whirled it over his head and let it float to the floor. His hand continued to plow deep into the drawer. After a moment it came up gripping a faded corset with four dangling metal supporters. "Thisyer must be her saddle," he observed.

He lifted it gingerly and shook it. Then he fastened it around his waist and jumped up and down, making the metal supporters dance. He began to snap his fingers and turn his hips from side to side. "Gonter rock, rattle and roll," he sang. "Gonter rock, rattle and roll. Can't please that woman, to save my doggone soul." He began to move around, stamping the good foot down and slinging the heavy one to the side. He danced out the door, past the stricken child and down the hall toward the kitchen.

A half hour later Sheppard came home. He dropped his raincoat on a chair in the hall and came as far as the parlor door and stopped. His face was suddenly transformed. It shone with pleasure. Johnson sat, a dark figure, in a high-backed pink upholstered chair. The wall behind him was lined with books from floor to ceiling. He was reading one. Sheppard's eyes narrowed. It was a volume of the Encyclopedia Britannica. He was so engrossed in it that he did not look up. Sheppard held his breath. This was the perfect setting for the boy. He had to keep him here. He had to manage it somehow.

"Rufus!" he said, "it's good to see you boy!" and he bounded forward with his arm outstretched.

Johnson looked up, his face blank. "Oh hello," he said. He ignored the hand as long as he was able but when Sheppard did not withdraw it, he grudgingly shook it.

Sheppard was prepared for this kind of reaction. It was part of Johnson's make-up never to show enthusiasm.

"How are things?" he said. "How's your grandfather treating you?" He sat down on the edge of the sofa.

"He dropped dead," the boy said indifferently.

"You don't mean it!" Sheppard cried. He got up and sat down on the coffee table nearer the boy.

"Naw," Johnson said, "he ain't dropped dead. I wisht he had."

"Well where is he?" Sheppard muttered.

"He's gone with a remnant to the hills," Johnson said. "Him and some others. They're going to bury some Bibles in a cave and take two of different kinds of animals and all like that. Like Noah. Only this time it's going to be fire, not flood."

Sheppard's mouth stretched wryly. "I see," he said. Then he said, "In other words the old fool has abandoned you?"

"He ain't no fool," the boy said in an indignant tone.   130

"Has he abandoned you or not?" Sheppard asked impatiently.

The boy shrugged.

"Where's your probation officer?"

"I ain't supposed to keep up with him," Johnson said. "He's supposed to keep up with me."

Sheppard laughed. "Wait a minute," he said. He got up and went into the hall   135
and got his raincoat off the chair and took it to the hall closet to hang it up. He had to give himself time to think, to decide how he could ask the boy so that he would stay. He couldn't force him to stay. It would have to be voluntary. Johnson pretended not to like him. That was only to uphold his pride, but he would have to ask him in such a way that his pride could still be upheld. He opened the closet door and took out a hanger. An old gray winter coat of his wife's still hung there. He pushed it aside but it didn't move. He pulled it open roughly and winced as if he had seen the larva inside a cocoon. Norton stood in it, his face swollen and pale, with a drugged look of misery on it. Sheppard stared at him. Suddenly he was confronted with a possibility. "Get out of there," he said. He caught him by the shoulder and propelled him firmly into the parlor and over to the pink chair where Johnson was sitting with the encyclopedia in his lap. He was going to risk everything in one blow.

"Rufus," he said, "I've got a problem. I need your help."

Johnson looked up suspiciously.

"Listen," Sheppard said, "we need another boy in the house." There was a genuine desperation in his voice. "Norton here has never had to divide anything in his life. He doesn't know what it means to share. And I need somebody to teach him. How about helping me out? Stay here for a while with us, Rufus. I need your help." The excitement in his voice made it thin.

The child suddenly came to life. His face swelled with fury. "He went in her room and used her comb!" he screamed, yanking Sheppard's arm. "He put on her corset and danced with Leola, he . . ."

"Stop this!" Sheppard said sharply. "Is tattling all you're capable of? I'm not   140
asking you for a report on Rufus's conduct. I'm asking you to make him welcome here. Do you understand?

"You see how it is?" he asked, turning to Johnson.

Norton kicked the leg of the pink chair viciously, just missing Johnson's swollen foot. Sheppard yanked him back.

"He said you weren't nothing but gas!" the child shrieked.

A sly look of pleasure crossed Johnson's face.

Sheppard was not put back. These insults were part of the boy's defensive   145
mechanism. "What about it, Rufus?" he said. "Will you stay with us for a while?"

Johnson looked straight in front of him and said nothing. He smiled slightly and appeared to gaze upon some vision of the future that pleased him.

"I don't care," he said and turned a page of the encyclopedia. "I can stand anywhere."

"Wonderful." Sheppard said. "Wonderful."

"He said," the child said in a throaty whisper, "you didn't know your left hand from your right."

150   There was a silence.

Johnson wet his finger and turned another page of the encyclopedia.

"I have something to say to both of you," Sheppard said in a voice without inflection. His eyes moved from one to the other of them and he spoke slowly as if what he was saying he would say only once and it behooved them to listen. "If it made any difference to me what Rufus thinks of me," he said, "then I wouldn't be asking him here. Rufus is going to help me out and I'm going to help him out and we're both going to help you out. I'd simply be selfish if I let what Rufus thinks of me interfere with what I can do for Rufus. If I can help a person, all I want is to do it. I'm above and beyond simple pettiness."

Neither of them made a sound. Norton stared at the chair cushion. Johnson peered closer at some fine print in the encyclopedia. Sheppard was looking at the tops of their heads. He smiled. After all, he had won. The boy was staying. He reached out and ruffled Norton's hair and slapped Johnson on the shoulder. "Now you fellows sit here and get acquainted," he said gaily and started toward the door. "I'm going to see what Leola left us for supper."

When he was gone, Johnson raised his head and looked at Norton. The child looked back at him bleakly. "God, kid," Johnson said in a cracked voice, "how do you stand it?" His face was stiff with outrage. "He thinks he's Jesus Christ!"

II

155   Sheppard's attic was a large unfinished room with exposed beams and no electric light. They had set the telescope up on a tripod in one of the dormer windows. It pointed now toward the dark sky where a sliver of moon, as fragile as an egg shell, had just emerged from behind a cloud with a brilliant silver edge. Inside, a kerosene lantern set on a trunk cast their shadows upward and tangled them, wavering slightly, in the joints overhead. Sheppard was sitting on a packing box, looking through the telescope, and Johnson was at his elbow, waiting to get at it. Sheppard had bought it for fifteen dollars two days before at a pawn shop.

"Quit hoggin it," Johnson said.

Sheppard got up and Johnson slid onto the box and put his eye to the instrument.

Sheppard sat down on a straight chair a few feet away. His face was flushed with pleasure. This much of his dream was a reality. Within a week he had made it possible for this boy's vision to pass through a slender channel to the stars. He looked at Johnson's bent back with complete satisfaction. The boy had on one of Norton's plaid shirts and some new khaki trousers he had bought him. The shoe would be ready next week. He had taken him to the brace shop the day after he came and had him fitted for a new shoe. Johnson was as touchy about the foot as if it were a sacred object. His face had been glum while the clerk, a young man with a bright pink bald head, measured the foot with his profane hands. The shoe was going to make the greatest difference in the boy's attitude. Even a child with normal feet was in love with the world after he had got a new pair of shoes. When Norton got a new pair, he walked around for days with his eyes on his feet.

Sheppard glanced across the room at the child. He was sitting on the floor against a trunk, trussed up in a rope he had found and wound around his legs from his ankles to his knees. He appeared so far away that Sheppard might have been looking at him through the wrong end of the telescope. He had had to whip him only once since Johnson had been with them—the first night when Norton had realized that Johnson was going to sleep in his mother's bed. He did not believe in whipping children, particularly in anger. In this case, he had done both and with good results. He had had no more trouble with Norton.

The child hadn't shown any positive generosity toward Johnson but what he couldn't help, he appeared to be resigned to. In the mornings Sheppard sent the two of them to the Y swimming pool, gave them money to get their lunch at the cafeteria and instructed them to meet him in the park in the afternoon to watch his Little League baseball practice. Every afternoon they had arrived at the park, shambling, silent, their faces closed each on his own thoughts as if neither were aware of the other's existence. At least he could be thankful there were no fights. 160

Norton showed no interest in the telescope. "Don't you want to get up and look through the telescope, Norton?" he said. It irritated him that the child showed no intellectual curiosity whatsoever. "Rufus is going to be way ahead of you."

Norton leaned forward absently and looked at Johnson's back.

Johnson turned around from the instrument. His face had begun to fill out again. The look of outrage had retreated from his hollow cheeks and was shored up now in the caves of his eyes, like a fugitive from Sheppard's kindness. "Don't waste your valuable time, kid," he said. "You seen the moon once, you seen it."

Sheppard was amused by these sudden turns of perversity. The boy resisted whatever he suspected was meant for his improvement and contrived when he was vitally interested in something to leave the impression he was bored. Sheppard was not deceived. Secretly Johnson was learning what he wanted him to learn—that his benefactor was impervious to insult and that there were no cracks in his armor of kindness and patience where a successful shaft could be driven. "Some day you may go to the moon," he said. "In ten years men will probably be making round trips there on schedule. Why you boys may be spacemen. Astronauts!"

"Astro-nuts," Johnson said. 165

"Nuts or nauts," Sheppard said, "it's perfectly possible that you, Rufus Johnson, will go to the moon."

Something in the depths of Johnson's eyes stirred. All day his humor had been glum. "I ain't going to the moon and get there alive," he said, "and when I die I'm going to hell."

"It's at least possible to get to the moon," Sheppard said dryly. The best way to handle this kind of thing was with gentle ridicule. "We can see it. We know it's there. Nobody has given any reliable evidence there's a hell."

"The Bible has give the evidence," Johnson said darkly, "and if you die and go there you burn forever."

170   The child leaned forward.

"Whoever says it ain't a hell," Johnson said, "is contradicting Jesus. The dead are judged and the wicked are damned. They weep and gnash their teeth while they burn," he continued, "and it's everlasting darkness."

The child's mouth opened. His eyes appeared to grow hollow.

"Satan runs it," Johnson said.

Norton lurched up and took a hobbled step toward Sheppard. "Is she there?" he said in a loud voice. "Is she there burning up?" He kicked the rope off his feet. "Is she on fire?"

175   "Oh my God," Sheppard muttered. "No no," he said, "of course she isn't. Rufus is mistaken. Your mother isn't anywhere. She's not unhappy. She just isn't." His lot would have been easier if when his wife died he had told Norton she had gone to heaven and that some day he would see her again, but he could not allow himself to bring him up on a lie.

Norton's face began to twist. A knot formed in his chin.

"Listen," Sheppard said quickly and pulled the child to him, "your mother's spirit lives on in other people and it'll live on in you if you're good and generous like she was."

The child's pale eyes hardened in disbelief.

Sheppard's pity turned to revulsion. The boy would rather she be in hell than nowhere. "Do you understand?" he said. "She doesn't exist." He put his hand on the child's shoulder. "That's all I have to give you," he said in a softer, exasperated tone, "the truth."

180   Instead of howling, the boy wrenched himself away and caught Johnson by the sleeve. "Is she there, Rufus?" he said. "Is she there, burning up?"

Johnson's eyes glittered. "Well," he said, "she is if she was evil. Was she a whore?"

"Your mother was not a whore," Sheppard said sharply. He had the sensation of driving a car without brakes. "Now let's have no more of this foolishness. We were talking about the moon."

"Did she believe in Jesus?" Johnson asked.

Norton looked blank. After a second he said, "Yes," as if he saw that this was necessary. "She did," he said. "All the time."

185   "She did not," Sheppard muttered.

"She did all the time," Norton said. "I heard her say she did all the time."

"She's saved," Johnson said.

The child still looked puzzled. "Where?" he said. "Where is she at?"

"On high," Johnson said.

190   "Where's that?" Norton gasped.

"It's in the sky somewhere," Johnson said, "but you got to be dead to get there. You can't go in no space ship." There was a narrow gleam in his eyes now like a beam holding steady on its target.

"Man's going to the moon," Sheppard said grimly, "is very much like the first fish crawling out of the water onto land billions and billions of years ago. He didn't have an earth suit. He had to grow his adjustments inside. He developed lungs."

"When I'm dead will I go to hell or where she is?" Norton asked.

"Right now you'd go where she is," Johnson said, "but if you live long enough, you'll go to hell."

Sheppard rose abruptly and picked up the lantern. "Close the window, Rufus," he said. "It's time we went to bed."   195

On the way down the attic stairs he heard Johnson say in a loud whisper behind him, "I'll tell you all about it tomorrow, kid, when Himself has cleared out."

The next day when the boys came to the ball park, he watched them as they came from behind the bleachers and around the edge of the field. Johnson's hand was on Norton's shoulder, his head bent toward the younger boy's ear, and on the child's face there was a look of complete confidence, of dawning light. Sheppard's grimace hardened. This would be Johnson's way of trying to annoy him. But he would not be annoyed. Norton was not bright enough to be damaged much. He gazed at the child's dull absorbed little face. Why try to make him superior? Heaven and hell were for the mediocre, and he was that if he was anything.

The two boys came into the bleachers and sat down about ten feet away, facing him, but neither gave him any sign of recognition. He cast a glance behind him where the Little Leaguers were spread out in the field. Then he started for the bleachers. The hiss of Johnson's voice stopped as he approached.

"What have you fellows been doing today?" he asked genially.

"He's been telling me . . ." Norton started.   200

Johnson pushed the child in the ribs with his elbow. "We ain't been doing nothing," he said. His face appeared to be covered with a blank glaze but through it a look of complicity was blazoned forth insolently.

Sheppard felt his face grow warm, but he said nothing. A child in a Little League uniform had followed him and was nudging him in the back of the leg with a bat. He turned and put his arm around the boy's neck and went with him back to the game.

That night when he went to the attic to join the boys at the telescope, he found Norton there alone. He was sitting on the packing box, hunched over, looking intently through the instrument. Johnson was not there.

"Where's Rufus?" Sheppard asked.

"I said where's Rufus?" he said louder.   205

"Gone somewhere," the child said without turning around.

"Gone where?" Sheppard asked.

"He just said he was going somewhere. He said he was fed up looking at stars."

"I see," Sheppard said glumly. He turned and went back down the stairs. He searched the house without finding Johnson. Then he went to the living room and sat down. Yesterday he had been convinced of his success with the boy. Today he faced the possibility that he was failing with him. He had been over-lenient,

too concerned to have Johnson like him. He felt a twinge of guilt. What difference
did it make if Johnson liked him or not? What was that to him? When the boy
came in, they would have a few things understood. As long as you stay here
there'll be no going out at night by yourself, do you understand?

210   I don't have to stay here. It ain't nothing to me staying here.

Oh my God, he thought. He could not bring it to that. He would have to be
firm but not make an issue of it. He picked up the evening paper. Kindness and
patience were always called for but he had not been firm enough. He sat holding
the paper but not reading it. The boy would not respect him unless he showed
firmness. The doorbell rang and he went to answer it. He opened it and stepped
back, with a pained disappointed face.

A large dour policeman stood on the stoop, holding Johnson by the elbow. At
the curb a patrol car waited. Johnson looked very white. His jaw was thrust forward as if to keep from trembling.

"We brought him here first because he raised such a fit," the policeman said,
"but now that you've seen him, we're going to take him to the station and ask
him a few questions."

"What happened?" Sheppard muttered.

215   "A house around the corner from here," the policeman said. "A real smash job,
dishes broken all over the floor, furniture turned upside down . . ."

"I didn't have a thing to do with it!" Johnson said. "I was walking along minding my own bidnis when this cop came up and grabbed me."

Sheppard looked at the boy grimly. He made no effort to soften his expression.

Johnson flushed. "I was just walking along," he muttered, but with no conviction in his voice.

"Come on, bud," the policeman said.

220   "You ain't going to let him take me, are you?" Johnson said. "You believe me,
don't you?" There was an appeal in his voice that Sheppard had not heard there
before.

This was crucial. The boy would have to learn that he could not be protected
when he was guilty. "You'll have to go with him, Rufus," he said.

"You're going to let him take me and I tell you I ain't done a thing?" Johnson
said shrilly.

Sheppard's face became harder as his sense of injury grew. The boy had failed
him even before he had had a chance to give him the shoe. They were to have
got it tomorrow. All his regret turned suddenly on the shoe; his irritation at the
sight of Johnson doubled.

"You made out like you had all this confidence in me," the boy mumbled.

225   "I did have," Sheppard said. His face was wooden.

Johnson turned away with the policeman but before he moved, a gleam of
pure hatred flashed toward Sheppard from the pits of his eyes.

Sheppard stood in the door and watched them get into the patrol car and drive
away. He summoned his compassion. He would go to the station tomorrow and
see what he could do about getting him out of trouble. The night in jail would
not hurt him and the experience would teach him that he could not treat with
impunity someone who had shown him nothing but kindness. Then they would

go get the shoe and perhaps after a night in jail it would mean even more to the boy.

The next morning at eight o'clock the police sergeant called and told him he could come pick Johnson up. "We booked a nigger on that charge," he said. "Your boy didn't have nothing to do with it."

Sheppard was at the station in ten minutes, his face hot with shame. Johnson sat slouched on a bench in a drab outer office, reading a police magazine. There was no one else in the room. Sheppard sat down beside him and put his hand tentatively on his shoulder.

The boy glanced up—his lip curled—and back to the magazine. 230

Sheppard felt physically sick. The ugliness of what he had done bore in upon him with a sudden dull intensity. He had failed him at just the point where he might have turned him once and for all in the right direction. "Rufus," he said, "I apologize. I was wrong and you were right. I misjudged you."

The boy continued to read.

"I'm sorry."

The boy wet his finger and turned a page.

Sheppard braced himself. "I was a fool, Rufus," he said. 235

Johnson's mouth slid slightly to the side. He shrugged without raising his head from the magazine.

"Will you forget it, this time?" Sheppard said. "It won't happen again."

The boy looked up. His eyes were bright and unfriendly. "I'll forget it," he said, "but you better remember it." He got up and stalked toward the door. In the middle of the room he turned and jerked his arm at Sheppard and Sheppard jumped up and followed him as if the boy had yanked an invisible leash.

"Your shoe," he said eagerly, "today is the day to get your shoe!" Thank God for the shoe!

But when they went to the brace shop, they found that the shoe had been 240 made two sizes too small and a new one would not be ready for another ten days. Johnson's temper improved at once. The clerk had obviously made a mistake in the measurements but the boy insisted the foot had grown. He left the shop with a pleased expression, as if, in expanding, the foot had acted on some inspiration of its own. Sheppard's face was haggard.

After this he redoubled his efforts. Since Johnson had lost interest in the telescope, he bought a microscope and a box of prepared slides. If he couldn't impress the boy with immensity, he would try the infinitesimal. For two nights Johnson appeared absorbed in the new instrument, then he abruptly lost interest in it, but he seemed content to sit in the living room in the evening and read the encyclopedia. He devoured the encyclopedia as he devoured his dinner, steadily and without dint to his appetite. Each subject appeared to enter his head, be ravaged, and thrown out. Nothing pleased Sheppard more than to see the boy slouched on the sofa, his mouth shut, reading. After they had spent two or three evenings like this, he began to recover his vision. His confidence returned. He knew that some day he would be proud of Johnson.

On Thursday night Sheppard attended a city council meeting. He dropped the boys off at a movie on his way and picked them up on his way back. When they reached home, an automobile with a single red eye above its windshield was waiting in front of the house. Sheppard's lights as he turned into the driveway illuminated two dour faces in the car.

"The cops!" Johnson said. "Some nigger has broke in somewhere and they've come for me again."

"We'll see about that," Sheppard muttered. He stopped the car in the driveway and switched off the lights. "You boys go in the house and go to bed," he said. "I'll handle this."

245   He got out and strode toward the squad car. He thrust his head in the window. The two policemen were looking at him with silent knowledgeable faces. "A house on the corner of Shelton and Mills," the one in the driver's seat said. "It looks like a train run through it."

"He was in the picture show downtown," Sheppard said. "My boy was with him. He had nothing to do with the other one and he had nothing to do with this one. I'll be responsible."

"If I was you," the one nearest him said, "I wouldn't be responsible for any little bastard like him."

"I said I'd be responsible," Sheppard repeated coldly. "You people made a mistake the last time. Don't make another."

The policemen looked at each other. "It ain't our funeral," the one in the driver's seat said, and turned the key in the ignition.

250   Sheppard went in the house and sat down in the living room in the dark. He did not suspect Johnson and he did not want the boy to think he did. If Johnson thought he suspected him again, he would lose everything. But he wanted to know if his alibi was airtight. He thought of going to Norton's room and asking him if Johnson had left the movie. But that would be worse. Johnson would know what he was doing and would be incensed. He decided to ask Johnson himself. He would be direct. He went over in his mind what he was going to say and then he got up and went to the boy's door.

It was open as if he had been expected but Johnson was in bed. Just enough light came in from the hall for Sheppard to see his shape under the sheet. He came in and stood at the foot of the bed. "They've gone," he said. "I told them you had nothing to do with it and that I'd be responsible."

There was a muttered "Yeah," from the pillow.

Sheppard hesitated. "Rufus," he said, "you didn't leave the movie for anything at all, did you?"

"You make out like you got all this confidence in me!" a sudden outraged voice cried, "and you ain't got any! You don't trust me no more now than you did then!" The voice, disembodied, seemed to come more surely from the depths of Johnson than when his face was visible. It was a cry of reproach, edged slightly with contempt.

255   "I do have confidence in you," Sheppard said intensely. "I have every confidence in you. I believe in you and I trust you completely."

"You got your eye on me all the time," the voice said sullenly. "When you get through asking me a bunch of questions, you're going across the hall and ask Norton a bunch of them."

"I have no intention of asking Norton anything and never did," Sheppard said gently. "And I don't suspect you at all. You could hardly have got from the picture show downtown and out here to break in a house and back to the picture show in the time you had."

"That's why you believe me!" the boy cried, "—because you think I couldn't have done it."

"No, no!" Sheppard said. "I believe you because I believe you've got the brains and the guts not to get in trouble again. I believe you know yourself well enough now to know that you don't have to do such things. I believe that you can make anything of yourself that you set your mind to."

Johnson sat up. A faint light shone on his forehead but the rest of his face was invisible. "And I could have broke in there if I'd wanted to in the time I had," he said.

"But I know you didn't," Sheppard said. "There's not the least trace of doubt in my mind."

There was a silence. Johnson lay back down. Then the voice, low and hoarse, as if it were being forced out with difficulty, said, "You don't want to steal and smash up things when you've got everything you want already."

Sheppard caught his breath. The boy was thanking him! He was thanking him! There was gratitude in his voice. There was appreciation. He stood there, smiling foolishly in the dark, trying to hold the moment in suspension. Involuntarily he took a step toward the pillow and stretched out his hand and touched Johnson's forehead. It was cold and dry like rusty iron.

"I understand. Good night, son," he said and turned quickly and left the room. He closed the door behind him and stood there, overcome with emotion.

Across the hall Norton's door was open. The child lay on the bed on his side, looking into the light from the hall.

After this, the road with Johnson would be smooth.

Norton sat up and beckoned to him.

He saw the child but after the first instant, he did not let his eyes focus directly on him. He could not go in and talk to Norton without breaking Johnson's trust. He hesitated, but remained where he was a moment as if he saw nothing. Tomorrow was the day they were to go back for the shoe. It would be a climax to the good feeling between them. He turned quickly and went back into his own room.

The child sat for some time looking at the spot where his father had stood. Finally his gaze became aimless and he lay back down.

The next day Johnson was glum and silent as if he were ashamed that he had revealed himself. His eyes had a hooded look. He seemed to have retired within himself and there to be going through some crisis of determination. Sheppard could not get to the brace shop quickly enough. He left Norton at home because he did not want his attention divided. He wanted to be free to observe Johnson's reaction minutely. The boy did not seem pleased or even interested in the prospect of the shoe, but when it became an actuality, certainly then he would be moved.

The brace shop was a small concrete warehouse lined and stacked with the equipment of affliction. Wheel chairs and walkers covered most of the floor. The walls were hung with every kind of crutch and brace. Artificial limbs were stacked on the shelves, legs and arms and hands, claws and hooks, straps and human harnesses and unidentifiable instruments for unnamed deformities. In a small clearing in the middle of the room there was a row of yellow plastic-cushioned chairs and a shoe-fitting stool. Johnson slouched down in one of the chairs and set his foot up on the stool and sat with his eyes on it moodily. What was roughly the toe had broken open again and he had patched it with a piece of canvas; another place he had patched with what appeared to be the tongue of the original shoe. The two sides were laced with twine.

There was an excited flush on Sheppard's face; his heart was beating unnaturally fast.

The clerk appeared from the back of the shop with the new shoe under his arm. "Got her right this time!" he said. He straddled the shoe-fitting stool and held the shoe up, smiling as if he had produced it by magic.

It was a black slick shapeless object, shining hideously. It looked like a blunt weapon, highly polished.

275   Johnson gazed at it darkly.

"With this shoe," the clerk said, "you won't know you're walking. You'll think you're riding!" He bent his bright pink bald head and began gingerly to unlace the twine. He removed the old shoe as if he were skinning an animal still half alive. His expression was strained. The unsheathed mass of foot in the dirty sock made Sheppard feel queasy. He turned his eyes away until the new shoe was on. The clerk laced it up rapidly. "Now stand up and walk around," he said, "and see if that ain't power glide." He winked at Sheppard. "In that shoe," he said, "he won't know he don't have a normal foot."

Sheppard's face was bright with pleasure.

Johnson stood up and walked a few yards away. He walked stiffly with almost no dip in his short side. He stood for a moment, rigid, with his back to them.

"Wonderful!" Sheppard said. "Wonderful." It was as if he had given the boy a new spine.

280   Johnson turned around. His mouth was set in a thin icy line. He came back to the seat and removed the shoe. He put his foot in the old one and began lacing it up.

"You want to take it home and see if it suits you first?" the clerk murmured.

"No," Johnson said. "I ain't going to wear it at all."

"What's wrong with it?" Sheppard said, his voice rising.

"I don't need no new shoe," Johnson said. "And when I do, I got ways of getting my own." His face was stony but there was a glint of triumph in his eyes.

285   "Boy," the clerk said, "is your trouble in your foot or in your head?"

"Go soak your skull," Johnson said. "Your brains are on fire."

The clerk rose glumly but with dignity and asked Sheppard what he wanted done with the shoe, which he dangled dispiritedly by the lace.

Sheppard's face was a dark angry red. He was staring straight in front of him at a leather corset with an artificial arm attached.

The clerk asked him again.

290   "Wrap it up," Sheppard muttered. He turned his eyes to Johnson. "He's not mature enough for it yet," he said. "I had thought he was less of a child."

The boy leered. "You been wrong before," he said.

That night they sat in the living room and read as usual. Sheppard kept himself glumly entrenched behind the Sunday New York *Times*. He wanted to recover his good humor, but every time he thought of the rejected shoe, he felt a new charge of irritation. He did not trust himself even to look at Johnson. He realized that the boy had refused the shoe because he was insecure. Johnson had been frightened by his own gratitude. He didn't know what to make of the new self he was becoming conscious of. He understood that something he had been was threatened and he was facing himself and his possibilities for the first time. He was questioning his identity. Grudgingly, Sheppard felt a slight return of sympathy for the boy. In a few minutes, he lowered his paper and looked at him.

Johnson was sitting on the sofa, gazing over the top of the encyclopedia. His expression was trancelike. He might have been listening to something far away. Sheppard watched him intently but the boy continued to listen, and did not turn his head. The poor kid is lost, Sheppard thought. Here he had sat all evening, sullenly reading the paper, and had not said a word to break the tension. "Rufus," he said.

Johnson continued to sit, stock-still, listening.

"Rufus," Sheppard said in a slow hypnotic voice, "you can be anything in the world you want to be. You can be a scientist or an architect or an engineer or whatever you set your mind to, and whatever you set your mind to be, you can be the best of its kind." He imagined his voice penetrating to the boy in the black caverns of his psyche. Johnson leaned forward but his eyes did not turn. On the street a car door closed. There was a silence. Then a sudden blast from the door bell. 295

Sheppard jumped up and went to the door and opened it. The same policeman who had come before stood there. The patrol car waited at the curb.

"Lemme see that boy," he said.

Sheppard scowled and stood aside. "He's been here all evening," he said. "I can vouch for it."

The policeman walked into the living room. Johnson appeared engrossed in his book. After a second he looked up with an annoyed expression, like a great man interrupted at his work.

"What was that you were looking at in that kitchen window over on Winter Avenue about a half hour ago, bud?" the policeman asked. 300

"Stop persecuting this boy!" Sheppard said. "I'll vouch for the fact he was here. I was here with him."

"You heard him," Johnson said. "I been here all the time."

"It ain't everybody makes tracks like you," the policeman said and eyed the clubfoot.

"They couldn't be his tracks," Sheppard growled, infuriated. "He's been here all the time. You're wasting your own time and you're wasting ours." He felt the *ours* seal his solidarity with the boy. "I'm sick of this," he said. "You people are too damn lazy to go out and find whoever is doing these things. You come here automatically."

The policeman ignored this and continued looking through Johnson. His eyes were small and alert in his fleshy face. Finally he turned toward the door. "We'll get him sooner or later," he said, "with his head in a window and his tail out." 305

Sheppard followed him to the door and slammed it behind him. His spirits were soaring. This was exactly what he had needed. He returned with an expectant face.

Johnson had put the book down and was sitting there, looking at him slyly. "Thanks," he said.

Sheppard stopped. The boy's expression was predatory. He was openly leering.

"You ain't such a bad liar yourself," he said.

310 "Liar?" Sheppard murmured. Could the boy have left and come back? He felt himself sicken. Then a rush of anger sent him forward. "Did you leave?" he said furiously. "I didn't see you leave."

The boy only smiled.

"You went up in the attic to see Norton," Sheppard said.

"Naw," Johnson said, "that kid is crazy. He don't want to do nothing but look through that stinking telescope."

"I don't want to hear about Norton," Sheppard said harshly. "Where were you?"

315 "I was sitting on that pink can by my ownself," Johnson said. "There wasn't no witnesses."

Sheppard took out his handkerchief and wiped his forehead. He managed to smile.

Johnson rolled his eyes. "You don't believe in me," he said. His voice was cracked the way it had been in the dark room two nights before. "You make out like you got all this confidence in me but you ain't got any. When things get hot, you'll fade like the rest of them." The crack became exaggerated, comic. The mockery in it was blatant. "You don't believe in me. You ain't got no confidence," he wailed. "And you ain't any smarter than that cop. All that about tracks—that was a trap. There wasn't any tracks. That whole place is concreted in the back and my feet were dry."

Sheppard slowly put the handkerchief back in his pocket. He dropped down on the sofa and gazed at the rug beneath his feet. The boy's clubfoot was set within the circle of his vision. The pieced-together shoe appeared to grin at him with Johnson's own face. He caught hold of the edge of the sofa cushion and his knuckles turned white. A chill of hatred shook him. He hated the shoe, hated the foot, hated the boy. His face paled. Hatred choked him. He was aghast at himself.

He caught the boy's shoulder and gripped it fiercely as if to keep himself from falling. "Listen," he said, "you looked in that window to embarrass me. That was all you wanted—to shake my resolve to help you, but my resolve isn't shaken. I'm stronger than you are. I'm stronger than you are and I'm going to save you. The good will triumph."

320 "Not when it ain't true," the boy said. "Not when it ain't right."

"My resolve isn't shaken," Sheppard repeated. "I'm going to save you."

Johnson's look became sly again. "You ain't going to save me," he said. "You're going to tell me to leave this house. I did those other two jobs too—the first one as well as the one I done when I was supposed to be in the picture show."

"I'm not going to tell you to leave," Sheppard said. His voice was toneless, mechanical. "I'm going to save you."

Johnson thrust his head forward. "Save yourself," he hissed. "Nobody can save me but Jesus."

Sheppard laughed curtly. "You don't deceive me," he said. "I flushed that out   325
of your head in the reformatory. I saved you from that, at least."

The muscles in Johnson's face stiffened. A look of such repulsion hardened on his face that Sheppard drew back. The boy's eyes were like distorting mirrors in which he saw himself made hideous and grotesque. "I'll show you," Johnson whispered. He rose abruptly and started headlong for the door as if he could not get out of Sheppard's sight quick enough, but it was the door to the back hall he went through, not the front door. Sheppard turned on the sofa and looked behind him where the boy had disappeared. He heard the door to his room slam. He was not leaving. The intensity had gone out of Sheppard's eyes. They looked flat and lifeless as if the shock of the boy's revelation were only now reaching the center of his consciousness. "If he would only leave," he murmured. "If he would only leave now of his own accord."

The next morning Johnson appeared at the breakfast table in the grandfather's suit he had come in. Sheppard pretended not to notice but one look told him what he already knew, that he was trapped, that there could be nothing now but a battle of nerves and that Johnson would win it. He wished he had never laid eyes on the boy. The failure of his compassion numbed him. He got out of the house as soon as he could and all day he dreaded to go home in the evening. He had a faint hope that the boy might be gone when he returned. The grandfather's suit might have meant he was leaving. The hope grew in the afternoon. When he came home and opened the front door, his heart was pounding.

He stopped in the hall and looked silently into the living room. His expectant expression faded. His face seemed suddenly as old as his white hair. The two boys were sitting close together on the sofa, reading the same book. Norton's cheek rested against the sleeve of Johnson's black suit. Johnson's finger moved under the lines they were reading. The elder brother and the younger. Sheppard looked woodenly at this scene for almost a minute. Then he walked into the room and took off his coat and dropped it on a chair. Neither boy noticed him. He went on to the kitchen.

Leola left the supper on the stove every afternoon before she left and he put it on the table. His head ached and his nerves were taut. He sat down on the kitchen stool and remained there, sunk in his depression. He wondered if he could infuriate Johnson enough to make him leave of his own accord. Last night what had enraged him was the Jesus business. It might enrage Johnson, but it depressed him. Why not simply tell the boy to go? Admit defeat. The thought of facing Johnson again sickened him. The boy looked at him as if he were the guilty one, as if he were a moral leper. He knew without conceit that he was a good man, that he had nothing to reproach himself with. His feelings about Johnson now were involuntary. He would like to feel compassion for him. He would like to be able to help him. He longed for the time when there would be no one but himself and Norton in the house, when the child's simple selfishness would be all he had to contend with, and his own loneliness.

330   He got up and took three serving dishes off the shelf and took them to the stove. Absently he began pouring the butterbeans and the hash into the dishes. When the food was on the table, he called them in.

They brought the book with them. Norton pushed his place setting around to the same side of the table as Johnson's and moved his chair next to Johnson's chair. They sat down and put the book between them. It was a black book with red edges.

"What's that you're reading?" Sheppard asked, sitting down.

"The Holy Bible," Johnson said.

God give me strength, Sheppard said under his breath.

335   "We lifted it from a ten cent store," Johnson said.

"We?" Sheppard muttered. He turned and glared at Norton. The child's face was bright and there was an excited sheen to his eyes. The change that had come over the boy struck him for the first time. He looked alert. He had on a blue plaid shirt and his eyes were a brighter blue than he had ever seen them before. There was a strange new life in him, the sign of new and more rugged vices. "So now you steal?" he said, glowering. "You haven't learned to be generous but you have learned to steal."

"No he ain't," Johnson said. "I was the one lifted it. He only watched. He can't sully himself. It don't make any difference about me. I'm going to hell anyway."

Sheppard held his tongue.

"Unless," Johnson said, "I repent."

340   "Repent, Rufus," Norton said in a pleading voice. "Repent, hear? You don't want to go to hell."

"Stop talking this nonsense," Sheppard said, looking sharply at the child.

"If I do repent, I'll be a preacher," Johnson said. "If you're going to do it, it's no sense in doing it halfway."

"What are you going to be, Norton," Sheppard asked in a brittle voice, "a preacher too?"

There was a glitter of wild pleasure in the child's eyes. "A space man!" he shouted.

345   "Wonderful," Sheppard said bitterly.

"Those space ships ain't going to do you any good unless you believe in Jesus," Johnson said. He wet his finger and began to leaf through the pages of the Bible. "I'll read you where it says so," he said.

Sheppard leaned forward and said in a low furious voice, "Put that Bible up, Rufus, and eat your dinner."

Johnson continued searching for the passage.

"Put that Bible up!" Sheppard shouted.

350   The boy stopped and looked up. His expression was startled but pleased.

"That book is something for you to hide behind," Sheppard said. "It's for cowards, people who are afraid to stand on their own feet and figure things out for themselves."

Johnson's eyes snapped. He backed his chair a little way from the table. "Satan has you in his power," he said. "Not only me. You too."

Sheppard reached across the table to grab the book but Johnson snatched it and put it in his lap.

Sheppard laughed. "You don't believe in that book and you know you don't believe in it!"

"I believe it!" Johnson said. "You don't know what I believe and what I don't."   355

Sheppard shook his head. "You don't believe it. You're too intelligent."

"I ain't too intelligent," the boy muttered. "You don't know nothing about me. Even if I didn't believe it, it would still be true."

"You don't believe it!" Sheppard said. His face was a taunt.

"I believe it!" Johnson said breathlessly. "I'll show you I believe it!" He opened the book in his lap and tore out a page of it and thrust it into his mouth. He fixed his eyes on Sheppard. His jaws worked furiously and the paper crackled as he chewed it.

"Stop this," Sheppard said in a dry, burnt-out voice. "Stop it."   360

The boy raised the Bible and tore out a page with his teeth and began grinding it in his mouth, his eyes burning.

Sheppard reached across the table and knocked the book out of his hand. "Leave the table," he said coldly.

Johnson swallowed what was in his mouth. His eyes widened as if a vision of splendor were opening up before him. "I've eaten it!" he breathed. "I've eaten it like Ezekiel and it was honey to my mouth!"[1]

"Leave this table," Sheppard said. His hands were clenched beside his plate.

"I've eaten it!" the boy cried. Wonder transformed his face. "I've eaten it like   365 Ezekiel and I don't want none of your food after it nor no more ever."

"Go then," Sheppard said softly. "Go. Go."

The boy rose and picked up the Bible and started toward the hall with it. At the door he paused, a small black figure on the threshold of some dark apocalypse. "The devil has you in his power," he said in a jubilant voice and disappeared.

After supper Sheppard sat in the living room alone. Johnson had left the house but he could not believe that the boy had simply gone. The first feeling of release had passed. He felt dull and cold as at the onset of an illness and dread had settled in him like a fog. Just to leave would be too anticlimactic an end for Johnson's taste; he would return and try to prove something. He might come back a week later and set fire to the place. Nothing seemed too outrageous now.

He picked up the paper and tried to read. In a moment he threw it down and got up and went into the hall and listened. He might be hiding in the attic. He went to the attic door and opened it.

The lantern was lit, casting a dim light on the stairs. He didn't hear anything.   370 "Norton," he called, "are you up there?" There was no answer. He mounted the narrow stairs to see.

Amid the strange vine-like shadows cast by the lantern, Norton sat with his

---

1. Ezekiel 3.1–3. The Lord in a vision told Ezekiel to eat a roll and go speak to the captive Israelites; when he ate, "it was in my mouth as honey for sweetness."

eye to the telescope. "Norton," Sheppard said, "do you know where Rufus went?"

The child's back was to him. He was sitting hunched, intent, his large ears directly above his shoulders. Suddenly he waved his hand and crouched closer to the telescope as if he could not get near enough to what he saw.

"Norton!" Sheppard said in a loud voice.

The child didn't move.

375   "Norton!" Sheppard shouted.

Norton started. He turned around. There was an unnatural brightness about his eyes. After a moment he seemed to see that it was Sheppard. "I've found her!" he said breathlessly.

"Found who?" Sheppard said.

"Mamma!"

Sheppard steadied himself in the door way. The jungle of shadows around the child thickened.

380   "Come and look!" he cried. He wiped his sweaty face on the tail of his plaid shirt and then put his eye back to the telescope. His back became fixed in a rigid intensity. All at once he waved again.

"Norton," Sheppard said, "you don't see anything in the telescope but star clusters. Now you've had enough of that for one night. You'd better go to bed. Do you know where Rufus is?"

"She's there!" he cried, not turning around from the telescope. "She waved at me!"

"I want you in bed in fifteen minutes," Sheppard said. After a moment he said, "Do you hear me, Norton?"

The child began to wave frantically.

385   "I mean what I say," Sheppard said. "I'm going to call in fifteen minutes and see if you're in bed."

He went down the steps again and returned to the parlor. He went to the front door and cast a cursory glance out. The sky was crowded with the stars he had been fool enough to think Johnson could reach. Somewhere in the small wood behind the house, a bull frog sounded a low hollow note. He went back to his chair and sat a few minutes. He decided to go to bed. He put his hands on the arms of the chair and leaned forward and heard, like the first shrill note of a disaster warning, the siren of a police car, moving slowly into the neighborhood and nearer until it subsided with a moan outside the house.

He felt a cold weight on his shoulders as if an icy cloak had been thrown about him. He went to the door and opened it.

Two policemen were coming up the walk with a dark snarling Johnson between them, handcuffed to each. A reporter jogged alongside and another policeman waited in the patrol car.

"Here's your boy," the dourest of the policemen said. "Didn't I tell you we'd get him?"

390   Johnson jerked his arm down savagely. "I was waitin for you!" he said. "You wouldn't have got me if I hadn't of wanted to get caught. It was my idea." He was addressing the policemen but leering at Sheppard.

Sheppard looked at him coldly.

"Why did you want to get caught?" the reporter asked, running around to get beside Johnson. "Why did you deliberately want to get caught?"

The question and the sight of Sheppard seemed to throw the boy into a fury. "To show up that big tin Jesus!" he hissed and kicked his leg out at Sheppard. "He thinks he's God. I'd rather be in the reformatory than in his house, I'd rather be in the pen! The Devil has him in his power. He don't know his left hand from his right, he don't have as much sense as his crazy kid!" He paused and then swept on to his fantastic conclusion. "He made suggestions to me!"

Sheppard's face blanched. He caught hold of the door facing.

"Suggestions?" the reporter said eagerly, "what kind of suggestion?"   395

"Immor'l suggestions!" Johnson said. "What kind of suggestions do you think? But I ain't having none of it, I'm a Christian, I'm . . ."

Sheppard's face was tight with pain. "He knows that's not true," he said in a shaken voice. "He knows he's lying. I did everything I knew how for him. I did more for him than I did for my own child. I hoped to save him and I failed, but it was an honorable failure. I have nothing to reproach myself with. I made no suggestions to him."

"Do you remember the suggestions?" the reporter asked. "Can you tell us exactly what he said?"

"He's a dirty atheist," Johnson said. "He said there wasn't no hell."

"Well, they seen each other now," one of the policemen said with a knowing   400
sigh. "Let's us go."

"Wait," Sheppard said. He came down one step and fixed his eyes on Johnson's eyes in a last desperate effort to save himself. "Tell the truth, Rufus," he said. "You don't want to perpetrate this lie. You're not evil, you're mortally confused. You don't have to make up for that foot, you don't have to . . ."

Johnson hurled himself forward. "Listen at him!" he screamed. "I lie and steal because I'm good at it! My foot don't have a thing to do with it! The lame shall enter first! The halt'll be gathered together. When I get ready to be saved, Jesus'll save me, not that lying stinking atheist, not that . . ."

"That'll be enough out of you," the policeman said and yanked him back. "We just wanted you to see we got him," he said to Sheppard, and the two of them turned around and dragged Johnson away, half turned and screaming back at Sheppard.

"The lame'll carry off the prey!" he screeched, but his voice was muffled inside the car. The reporter scrambled into the front seat with the driver and slammed the door and the siren wailed into the darkness.

Sheppard remained there, bent slightly like a man who has been shot but   405
continues to stand. After a minute he turned and went back in the house and sat down in the chair he had left. He closed his eyes on a picture of Johnson in a circle of reporters at the police station, elaborating his lies. "I have nothing to reproach myself with," he murmured. His every action had been selfless, his one aim had been to save Johnson for some decent kind of service, he had not spared himself, he had sacrificed his reputation, he had done more for Johnson than he had done for his own child. Foulness hung about him like an odor in the air, so close that it seemed to come from his own breath. "I have nothing to reproach

myself with," he repeated. His voice sounded dry and harsh. "I did more for him than I did for my own child." He was swept with a sudden panic. He heard the boy's jubilant voice. Satan has you in his power.

"I have nothing to reproach myself with," he began again. "I did more for him than I did for my own child." He heard his voice as if it were the voice of his accuser. He repeated the sentence silently.

Slowly his face drained of color. It became almost gray beneath the white halo of his hair. The sentence echoed in his mind, each syllable like a dull blow. His mouth twisted and he closed his eyes against the revelation. Norton's face rose before him, empty, forlorn, his left eye listing almost imperceptibly toward the outer rim as if it could not bear a full view of grief. His heart constricted with a repulsion for himself so clear and intense that he gasped for breath. He had stuffed his own emptiness with good works like a glutton. He had ignored his own child to feed his vision of himself. He saw the clear-eyed Devil, the sounder of hearts, leering at him from the eyes of Johnson. His image of himself shrivelled until everything was black before him. He sat there paralyzed, aghast.

He saw Norton at the telescope, all back and ears, saw his arm shoot up and wave frantically. A rush of agonizing love for the child rushed over him like a transfusion of life. The little boy's face appeared to him transformed; the image of his salvation; all light. He groaned with joy. He would make everything up to him. He would never let him suffer again. He would be mother and father. He jumped up and ran to his room, to kiss him, to tell him that he loved him, that he would never fail him again.

The light was on in Norton's room but the bed was empty. He turned and dashed up the attic stairs and at the top reeled back like a man on the edge of a pit. The tripod had fallen and the telescope lay on the floor. A few feet over it, the child hung in the jungle of shadows, just below the beam from which he had launched his flight into space.

1965

FLANNERY O'CONNOR

Everything That Rises Must Converge

Her doctor had told Julian's mother that she must lose twenty pounds on account of her blood pressure, so on Wednesday nights Julian had to take her downtown on the bus for a reducing class at the Y. The reducing class was designed for working girls over fifty, who weighed from 165 to 200 pounds. His mother was one of the slimmer ones, but she said ladies did not tell their age or weight. She would not ride the buses by herself at night since they had been integrated, and because the reducing class was one of her few pleasures, necessary for her health, and *free,* she said Julian could at least put himself out to take her, considering all she did for him. Julian did not like to consider all she did for him, but every Wednesday night he braced himself and took her.

She was almost ready to go, standing before the hall mirror, putting on her hat, while he, his hands behind him, appeared pinned to the door frame, waiting like Saint Sebastian for the arrows to begin piercing him.[1] The hat was new and had cost her seven dollars and a half. She kept saying, "Maybe I shouldn't have paid that for it. No, I shouldn't have. I'll take it off and return it tomorrow. I shouldn't have bought it."

Julian raised his eyes to heaven. "Yes, you should have bought it," he said. "Put it on and let's go." It was a hideous hat. A purple velvet flap came down on one side of it and stood up on the other; the rest of it was green and looked like a cushion with the stuffing out. He decided it was less comical than jaunty and pathetic. Everything that gave her pleasure was small and depressed him.

She lifted the hat one more time and set it down slowly on top of her head. Two wings of gray hair protruded on either side of her florid face, but her eyes, sky-blue, were as innocent and untouched by experience as they must have been when she was ten. Were it not that she was a widow who had struggled fiercely to feed and clothe and put him through school and who was supporting him still, "until he got on his feet," she might have been a little girl that he had to take to town.

"It's all right, it's all right," he said. "Let's go." He opened the door himself and started down the walk to get her going. The sky was a dying violet and the houses stood out darkly against it, bulbous liver-colored monstrosities of a uniform ugliness though no two were alike. Since this had been a fashionable neighborhood forty years ago, his mother persisted in thinking they did well to have an apartment in it. Each house had a narrow collar of dirt around it in which sat, usually, a grubby child. Julian walked with his hands in his pockets, his head down and thrust forward and his eyes glazed with the determination to make himself completely numb during the time he would be sacrificed to her pleasure.

The door closed and he turned to find the dumpy figure, surmounted by the atrocious hat, coming toward him. "Well," she said, "you only live once and paying a little more for it, I at least won't meet myself coming and going."

"Some day I'll start making money," Julian said gloomily—he knew he never would—"and you can have one of those jokes whenever you take the fit." But first they would move. He visualized a place where the nearest neighbors would be three miles away on either side.

"I think you're doing fine," she said, drawing on her gloves. "You've only been out of school a year. Rome wasn't built in a day."

She was one of the few members of the Y reducing class who arrived in hat and gloves and who had a son who had been to college. "It takes time," she said, "and the world is in such a mess. This hat looked better on me than any of the others, though when she brought it out I said, 'Take that thing back. I wouldn't

5

---

1. Discovered to be a Christian, Sebastian, Roman commander in Milan, was tied to a tree, shot with arrows, and left for dead. (He recovered, but when he reasserted his faith he was clubbed to death.)

have it on my head,' and she said, 'Now wait till you see it on,' and when she put it on me, I said, 'We-ull,' and she said, 'If you ask me, that hat does something for you and you do something for the hat, and besides,' she said, 'with that hat, you won't meet yourself coming and going.' "

10   Julian thought he could have stood his lot better if she had been selfish, if she had been an old hag who drank and screamed at him. He walked along, saturated in depression, as if in the midst of his martyrdom he had lost his faith. Catching sight of his long, hopeless, irritated face, she stopped suddenly with a grief-stricken look, and pulled back on his arm. "Wait on me," she said. "I'm going back to the house and take this thing off and tomorrow I'm going to return it. I was out of my head. I can pay the gas bill with that seven-fifty."

He caught her arm in a vicious grip. "You are not going to take it back," he said. "I like it."

"Well," she said, "I don't think I ought . . ."

"Shut up and enjoy it," he muttered, more depressed than ever.

"With the world in the mess it's in," she said, "it's a wonder we can enjoy anything. I tell you, the bottom rail is on the top."

15   Julian sighed.

"Of course," she said, "if you know who are you, you can go anywhere." She said this every time he took her to the reducing class. "Most of them in it are not our kind of people," she said, "but I can be gracious to anybody. I know who I am."

"They don't give a damn for your graciousness," Julian said savagely. "Knowing who you are is good for one generation only. You haven't the foggiest idea where you stand now or who you are."

She stopped and allowed her eyes to flash at him. "I most certainly do know who I am," she said, "and if you don't know who you are, I'm ashamed of you."

"Oh hell," Julian said.

20   "Your great-grandfather was a former governor of this state," she said. "Your grandfather was a prosperous land-owner. Your grandmother was a Godhigh."

"Will you look around you," he said tensely, "and see where you are now?" and he swept his arm jerkily out to indicate the neighborhood, which the growing darkness at least made less dingy.

"You remain what you are," she said. "Your great-grandfather had a plantation and two hundred slaves."

"There are no more slaves," he said irritably.

"They were better off when they were," she said. He groaned to see that she was off on that topic. She rolled onto it every few days like a train on an open track. He knew every stop, every junction, every swamp along the way, and knew the exact point at which her conclusion would roll majestically into the station: "It's ridiculous. It's simply not realistic. They should rise, yes, but on their own side of the fence."

25   "Let's skip it," Julian said.

"The ones I feel sorry for," she said, "are the ones that are half white. They're tragic."

"Will you skip it?"

"Suppose we were half white. We would certainly have mixed feelings."

"I have mixed feelings now," he groaned.

"Well let's talk about something pleasant," she said. "I remember going to Grandpa's when I was a little girl. Then the house had double stairways that went up to what was really the second floor—all the cooking was done on the first. I used to like to stay down in the kitchen on account of the way the walls smelled. I would sit with my nose pressed against the plaster and take deep breaths. Actually the place belonged to the Godhighs but your grandfather Chestny paid the mortgage and saved it for them. They were in reduced circumstances," she said, "but reduced or not, they never forgot who they were."

"Doubtless that decayed mansion reminded them," Julian muttered. He never spoke of it without contempt or thought of it without longing. He had seen it once when he was a child before it had been sold. The double stairways had rotted and been torn down. Negroes were living in it. But it remained in his mind as his mother had known it. It appeared in his dreams regularly. He would stand on the wide porch, listening to the rustle of oak leaves, then wander through the high-ceilinged hall into the parlor that opened onto it and gaze at the worn rugs and faded draperies. It occurred to him that it was he, not she, who could have appreciated it. He preferred its threadbare elegance to anything he could name and it was because of it that all the neighborhoods they had lived in had been a torment to him—whereas she had hardly known the difference. She called her insensitivity "being adjustable."

"And I remember the old darky who was my nurse, Caroline. There was no better person in the world. I've always had a great respect for my colored friends," she said. "I'd do anything in the world for them and they'd . . ."

"Will you for God's sake get off that subject?" Julian said. When he got on a bus by himself, he made it a point to sit down beside a Negro, in reparation as it were for his mother's sins.

"You're mighty touchy tonight," she said. "Do you feel all right?"

"Yes I feel all right," he said. "Now lay off."

She pursed her lips. "Well, you certainly are in a vile humor," she observed. "I just won't speak to you at all."

They had reached the bus stop. There was no bus in sight and Julian, his hands still jammed in his pockets and his head thrust forward, scowled down the empty street. The frustration of having to wait on the bus as well as ride on it began to creep up his neck like a hot hand. The presence of his mother was borne in upon him as she gave a pained sigh. He looked at her bleakly. She was holding herself very erect under the preposterous hat, wearing it like a banner of her imaginary dignity. There was in him an evil urge to break her spirit. He suddenly unloosened his tie and pulled it off and put it in his pocket.

She stiffened. "Why must you look like *that* when you take me to town?" she said. "Why must you deliberately embarrass me?"

"If you'll never learn where you are," he said, "you can at least learn where I am."

"You look like a—thug," she said.

"Then I must be one," he murmured.

"I'll just go home," she said. "I will not bother you. If you can't do a little thing like that for me . . ."

Rolling his eyes upward, he put his tie back on. "Restored to my class," he muttered. He thrust his face toward her and hissed, "True culture is in the mind, the *mind*," he said, and tapped his head, "the mind."

"It's in the heart," she said, "and in how you do things and how you do things is because of who you *are*."

45   "Nobody in the damn bus cares who you are."

"I care who I am," she said icily.

The lighted bus appeared on top of the next hill and as it approached, they moved out into the street to meet it. He put his hand under her elbow and hoisted her up on the creaking step. She entered with a little smile, as if she were going into a drawing room where everyone had been waiting for her. While he put in the tokens, she sat down on one of the broad front seats for three which faced the aisle. A thin woman with protruding teeth and long yellow hair was sitting on the end of it. His mother moved up beside her and left room for Julian beside herself. He sat down and looked at the floor across the aisle where a pair of thin feet in red and white canvas sandals were planted.

His mother immediately began a general conversation meant to attract anyone who felt like talking. "Can it get any hotter?" she said and removed from her purse a folding fan, black with a Japanese scene on it, which she began to flutter before her.

"I reckon it might could," the woman with the protruding teeth said, "but I know for a fact my apartment couldn't get no hotter."

50   "It must get the afternoon sun," his mother said. She sat forward and looked up and down the bus. It was half filled. Everybody was white. "I see we have the bus to ourselves," she said. Julian cringed.

"For a change," said the woman across the aisle, the owner of the red and white canvas sandals. "I come on one the other day and they were thick as fleas—up front and all through."

"The world is in a mess everywhere," his mother said. "I don't know how we've let it get in this fix."

"What gets my goat is all those boys from good families stealing automobile tires," the woman with the protruding teeth said. "I told my boy, I said you may not be rich but you been raised right and if I ever catch you in any such mess, they can send you on to the reformatory. Be exactly where you belong."

"Training tells," his mother said. "Is your boy in high school?"

55   "Ninth grade," the woman said.

"My son just finished college last year. He wants to write but he's selling typewriters until he gets started," his mother said.

The woman leaned forward and peered at Julian. He threw her such a malevolent look that she subsided against the seat. On the floor across the aisle there was an abandoned newspaper. He got up and got it and opened it out in front of him. His mother discreetly continued the conversation in a lower tone but the woman across the aisle said in a loud voice, "Well that's nice. Selling typewriters is close to writing. He can go right from one to the other."

"I tell him," his mother said, "that Rome wasn't built in a day."

Behind the newspaper Julian was withdrawing into the inner compartment of his mind where he spent most of his time. This was a kind of mental bubble in which he established himself when he could not bear to be a part of what was going on around him. From it he could see out and judge but in it he was safe from any kind of penetration from without. It was the only place where he felt free of the general idiocy of his fellows. His mother had never entered it but from it he could see her with absolute clarity.

The old lady was clever enough and he thought that if she had started from any of the right premises, more might have been expected of her. She lived according to the laws of her own fantasy world, outside of which he had never seen her set foot. The law of it was to sacrifice herself for him after she had first created the necessity to do so by making a mess of things. If he had permitted her sacrifices, it was only because her lack of foresight had made them necessary. All of her life had been a struggle to act like a Chestny without the Chestny goods, and to give him everything she thought a Chestny ought to have; but since, said she, it was fun to struggle, why complain? And when you had won, as she had won, what fun to look back on the hard times! He could not forgive her that she had enjoyed the struggle and that she thought *she* had won.

What she meant when she said she had won was that she had brought him up successfully and had sent him to college and that he had turned out so well— good looking (her teeth had gone unfilled so that his could be straightened), intelligent (he realized he was too intelligent to be a success), and with a future ahead of him (there was of course no future ahead of him). She excused his gloominess on the grounds that he was still growing up and his radical ideas on his lack of practical experience. She said he didn't yet know a thing about "life," that he hadn't even entered the real world—when already he was as disenchanted with it as a man of fifty.

The further irony of all this was that in spite of her, he had turned out so well. In spite of going to only a third-rate college, he had, on his own initiative, come out with a first-rate education; in spite of growing up dominated by a small mind, he had ended up with a large one; in spite of all her foolish views, he was free of prejudice and unafraid to face facts. Most miraculous of all, instead of being blinded by love for her as she was for him, he had cut himself emotionally free of her and could see her with complete objectivity. He was not dominated by his mother.

The bus stopped with a sudden jerk and shook him from his meditation. A woman from the back lurched forward with little steps and barely escaped falling in his newspaper as she righted herself. She got off and a large Negro got on. Julian kept his paper lowered to watch. It gave him a certain satisfaction to see injustice in daily operation. It confirmed his view that with a few exceptions there was no one worth knowing within a radius of three hundred miles. The Negro was well dressed and carried a briefcase. He looked around and then sat down on the other end of the seat where the woman with the red and white canvas sandals was sitting. He immediately unfolded a newspaper and obscured himself behind it. Julian's mother's elbow at once prodded insistently into his ribs. "Now you see why I won't ride on these buses by myself," she whispered.

The woman with the red and white canvas sandals had risen at the same time the Negro sat down and had gone further back in the bus and taken the seat of the woman who had got off. His mother leaned forward and cast her an approving look.

65   Julian rose, crossed the aisle, and sat down in the place of the woman with the canvas sandals. From this position, he looked serenely across at his mother. Her face had turned an angry red. He stared at her, making his eyes the eyes of a stranger. He felt his tension suddenly lift as if he had openly declared war on her.

He would have liked to get in conversation with the Negro and to talk with him about art or politics or any subject that would be above the comprehension of those around them, but the man remained entrenched behind his paper. He was either ignoring the change of seating or had never noticed it. There was no way for Julian to convey his sympathy.

His mother kept her eyes fixed reproachfully on his face. The woman with the protruding teeth was looking at him avidly as if he were a type of monster new to her.

"Do you have a light?" he asked the Negro.

Without looking away from his paper, the man reached in his pocket and handed him a packet of matches.

70   "Thanks," Julian said. For a moment he held the matches foolishly. A NO SMOK-ING sign looked down upon him from over the door. This alone would not have deterred him; he had no cigarettes. He had quit smoking some months before because he could not afford it. "Sorry," he muttered and handed back the matches. The Negro lowered the paper and gave him an annoyed look. He took the matches and raised the paper again.

His mother continued to gaze at him but she did not take advantage of his momentary discomfort. Her eyes retained their battered look. Her face seemed to be unnaturally red, as if her blood pressure had risen. Julian allowed no glimmer of sympathy to show on his face. Having got the advantage, he wanted desperately to keep it and carry it through. He would have liked to teach her a lesson that would last her a while, but there seemed no way to continue the point. The Negro refused to come out from behind his paper.

Julian folded his arms and looked stolidly before him, facing her but as if he did not see her, as if he had ceased to recognize her existence. He visualized a scene in which, the bus having reached their stop, he would remain in his seat and when she said, "Aren't you going to get off?" he would look at her as a stranger who had rashly addressed him. The corner they got off on was usually deserted, but it was well lighted and it would not hurt her to walk by herself the four blocks to the Y. He decided to wait until the time came and then decide whether or not he would let her get off by herself. He would have to be at the Y at ten to bring her back, but he could leave her wondering if he was going to show up. There was no reason for her to think she could always depend on him.

He retired again into the high-ceilinged room sparsely settled with large pieces of antique furniture. His soul expanded momentarily but then he became aware of his mother across from him and the vision shriveled. He studied her coldly. Her feet in little pumps dangled like a child's and did not quite reach the floor. She was training on him an exaggerated look of reproach. He felt completely detached from her. At that moment he could with pleasure have slapped her as he would have slapped a particularly obnoxious child in his charge.

He began to imagine various unlikely ways by which he could teach her a lesson. He might make friends with some distinguished Negro professor or lawyer and bring him home to spend the evening. He would be entirely justified but her blood pressure would rise to 300. He could not push her to the extent of making her have a stroke, and moreover, he had never been successful at making any Negro friends. He had tried to strike up an acquaintance on the bus with some of the better types, with ones that looked like professors or ministers or lawyers. One morning he had sat down next to a distinguished-looking dark brown man who had answered his questions with a sonorous solemnity but who had turned out to be an undertaker. Another day he had sat down beside a cigar-smoking Negro with a diamond ring on his finger, but after a few stilted pleasantries, the Negro had rung the buzzer and risen, slipping two lottery tickets into Julian's hand as he climbed over him to leave.

He imagined his mother lying desperately ill and his being able to secure only   75
a Negro doctor for her. He toyed with that idea for a few minutes and then dropped it for a momentary vision of himself participating as a sympathizer in a sit-in demonstration. This was possible but he did not linger with it. Instead, he approached the ultimate horror. He brought home a beautiful suspiciously Negroid woman. Prepare yourself, he said. There is nothing you can do about it. This is the woman I've chosen. She's intelligent, dignified, even good, and she's suffered and she hasn't thought it *fun*. Now persecute us, go ahead and persecute us. Drive her out of here, but remember, you're driving me too. His eyes were narrowed and through the indignation he had generated, he saw his mother across the aisle, purple-faced, shrunken to the dwarf-like proportions of her moral nature, sitting like a mummy beneath the ridiculous banner of her hat.

He was tilted out of his fantasy again as the bus stopped. The door opened with a sucking hiss and out of the dark a large, gaily dressed, sullen-looking colored woman got on with a little boy. The child, who might have been four, had on a short plaid suit and a Tyrolean hat with a blue feather in it. Julian hoped that he would sit down beside him and that the woman would push in beside his mother. He could think of no better arrangement.

As she waited for her tokens, the woman was surveying the seating possibilities—he hoped with the idea of sitting where she was least wanted. There was something familiar-looking about her but Julian could not place what it was. She was a giant of a woman. Her face was set not only to meet opposition but to seek it out. The downward tilt of her large lower lip was like a warning sign: DON'T TAMPER WITH ME. Her bulging figure was encased in a green crepe dress and her feet overflowed in red shoes. She had on a hideous hat. A purple velvet flap came down on one side of it and stood up on the other; the rest of it was green and looked like a cushion with the stuffing out. She carried a mammoth red pocket-book that bulged throughout as if it were stuffed with rocks.

To Julian's disappointment, the little boy climbed up on the empty seat beside his mother. His mother lumped all children, black and white, into the common category, "cute," and she thought little Negroes were on the whole cuter than little white children. She smiled at the little boy as he climbed on the seat.

Meanwhile the woman was bearing down upon the empty seat beside Julian. To his annoyance, she squeezed herself into it. He saw his mother's face change as the woman settled herself next to him and he realized with satisfaction that this was more objectionable to her than it was to him. Her face seemed almost gray and there was a look of dull recognition in her eyes, as if suddenly she had sickened at some awful confrontation. Julian saw that it was because she and the woman had, in a sense, swapped sons. Though his mother would not realize the symbolic significance of this, she would feel it. His amusement showed plainly on his face.

80   The woman next to him muttered something unintelligible to herself. He was conscious of a kind of bristling next to him, a muted growling like that of an angry cat. He could not see anything but the red pocketbook upright on the bulging green thighs. He visualized the woman as she had stood waiting for her tokens—the ponderous figure, rising from the red shoes upward over the solid hips, the mammoth bosom, the haughty face, to the green and purple hat.

His eyes widened.

The vision of the two hats, identical, broke upon him with the radiance of a brilliant sunrise. His face was suddenly lit with joy. He could not believe that Fate had thrust upon his mother such a lesson. He gave a loud chuckle so that she would look at him and see that he saw. She turned her eyes on him slowly. The blue in them seemed to have turned a bruised purple. For a moment he had an uncomfortable sense of her innocence, but it lasted only a second before principle rescued him. Justice entitled him to laugh. His grin hardened until it said to her as plainly as if he were saying aloud: Your punishment exactly fits your pettiness. This should teach you a permanent lesson.

Her eyes shifted to the woman. She seemed unable to bear looking at him and to find the woman preferable. He became conscious again of the bristling presence at his side. The woman was rumbling like a volcano about to become active. His mother's mouth began to twitch slightly at one corner. With a sinking heart, he saw incipient signs of recovery on her face and realized that this was going to strike her suddenly as funny and was going to be no lesson at all. She kept her eyes on the woman and an amused smile came over her face as if the woman were a monkey that had stolen her hat. The little Negro was looking up at her with large fascinated eyes. He had been trying to attract her attention for some time.

"Carver!" the woman said suddenly. "Come heah!"

85   When he saw that the spotlight was on him at last, Carver drew his feet up and turned himself toward Julian's mother and giggled.

"Carver!" the woman said. "You heah me? Come heah!"

Carver slid down from the seat but remained squatting with his back against the base of it, his head turned slyly around toward Julian's mother, who was smiling at him. The woman reached a hand across the aisle and snatched him to her. He righted himself and hung backwards on her knees, grinning at Julian's mother. "Isn't he cute?" Julian's mother said to the woman with the protruding teeth.

"I reckon he is," the woman said without conviction.

The Negress yanked him upright but he eased out of her grip and shot across the aisle and scrambled, giggling wildly, onto the seat beside his love.

"I think he likes me," Julian's mother said, and smiled at the woman. It was   90 the smile she used when she was being particularly gracious to an inferior. Julian saw everything was lost. The lesson had rolled off her like rain on a roof.

The woman stood up and yanked the little boy off the seat as if she were snatching him from contagion. Julian could feel the rage in her at having no weapon like his mother's smile. She gave the child a sharp slap across his leg. He howled once and then thrust his head into her stomach and kicked his feet against her shins. "Behave," she said vehemently.

The bus stopped and the Negro who had been reading the newspaper got off. The woman moved over and set the little boy down with a thump between herself and Julian. She held him firmly by the knee. In a moment he put his hands in front of his face and peeped at Julian's mother through his fingers.

"I see yoooooooo!" she said and put her hand in front of her face and peeped at him.

The woman slapped his hand down. "Quit yo' foolishness," she said, "before I knock the living Jesus out of you!"

Julian was thankful that the next stop was theirs. He reached up and pulled   95 the cord. The woman reached up and pulled it at the same time. Oh my God, he thought. He had the terrible intuition that when they got off the bus together, his mother would open her purse and give the little boy a nickel. The gesture would be as natural to her as breathing. The bus stopped and the woman got up and lunged to the front, dragging the child, who wished to stay on, after her. Julian and his mother got up and followed. As they neared the door, Julian tried to relieve her of her pocketbook.

"No," she murmured, "I want to give the little boy a nickel."

"No!" Julian hissed. "No!"

She smiled down at the child and opened her bag. The bus door opened and the woman picked him up by the arm and descended with him, hanging at her hip. Once in the street she set him down and shook him.

Julian's mother had to close her purse while she got down the bus step but as soon as her feet were on the ground, she opened it again and began to rummage inside. "I can't find but a penny," she whispered, "but it looks like a new one."

"Don't do it!" Julian said fiercely between his teeth. There was a streetlight on   100 the corner and she hurried to get under it so that she could better see into her pocketbook. The woman was heading off rapidly down the street with the child still hanging backward on her hand.

"Oh little boy!" Julian's mother called and took a few quick steps and caught up with them just beyond the lamppost. "Here's a bright new penny for you," and she held out the coin, which shone bronze in the dim light.

The huge woman turned and for a moment stood, her shoulders lifted and her face frozen with frustrated rage, and stared at Julian's mother. Then all at once she seemed to explode like a piece of machinery that had been given one ounce of pressure too much. Julian saw the black fist swing out with the red pocketbook. He shut his eyes and cringed as he heard the woman shout, "He don't take nobody's pennies!" When he opened his eyes, the woman was disappearing down the street with the little boy staring wide-eyed over her shoulder. Julian's mother was sitting on the sidewalk.

"I told you not to do that," Julian said angrily. "I told you not to do that!"

He stood over her for a minute, gritting his teeth. Her legs were stretched out in front of her and her hat was on her lap. He squatted down and looked her in the face. It was totally expressionless. "You got exactly what you deserved," he said. "Now get up."

105   He picked up her pocketbook and put what had fallen out back in it. He picked the hat up off her lap. The penny caught his eye on the sidewalk and he picked that up and let it drop before her eyes into the purse. Then he stood up and leaned over and held his hands out to pull her up. She remained immobile. He sighed. Rising above them on either side were black apartment buildings, marked with irregular rectangles of light. At the end of the block a man came out of a door and walked off in the opposite direction. "All right," he said, "suppose somebody happens by and wants to know why you're sitting on the sidewalk?"

She took the hand and, breathing hard, pulled heavily up on it and then stood for a moment, swaying slightly as if the spots of light in the darkness were circling around her. Her eyes, shadowed and confused, finally settled on his face. He did not try to conceal his irritation. "I hope this teaches you a lesson," he said. She leaned forward and her eyes raked his face. She seemed trying to determine his identity. Then, as if she found nothing familiar about him, she started off with a headlong movement in the wrong direction.

"Aren't you going on to the Y?" he asked.

"Home," she muttered.

"Well, are we walking?"

110   For answer she kept going. Julian followed along, his hands behind him. He saw no reason to let the lesson she had had go without backing it up with an explanation of its meaning. She might as well be made to understand what had happened to her. "Don't think that was just an uppity Negro woman," he said. "That was the whole colored race which will no longer take your condescending pennies. That was your black double. She can wear the same hat as you, and to be sure," he added gratuitously (because he thought it was funny), "it looked better on her than it did on you. What all this means," he said, "is that the old world is gone. The old manners are obsolete and your graciousness is not worth a damn." He thought bitterly of the house that had been lost for him. "You aren't who you think you are," he said.

She continued to plow ahead, paying no attention to him. Her hair had come undone on one side. She dropped her pocketbook and took no notice. He stooped and picked it up and handed it to her but she did not take it.

"You needn't act as if the world had come to an end," he said, "because it hasn't. From now on you've got to live in a new world and face a few realities for a change. Buck up," he said, "it won't kill you."

She was breathing fast.

"Let's wait on the bus," he said.

"Home," she said thickly.   115

"I hate to see you behave like this," he said. "Just like a child. I should be able to expect more of you." He decided to stop where he was and make her stop and wait for a bus. "I'm not going any farther," he said stopping. "We're going on the bus."

She continued to go on as if she had not heard him. He took a few steps and caught her arm and stopped her. He looked into her face and caught his breath. He was looking into a face he had never seen before. "Tell Grandpa to come get me," she said.

He stared, stricken.

"Tell Caroline to come get me," she said.

Stunned, he let her go and she lurched forward again, walking as if one leg   120 were shorter than the other. A tide of darkness seemed to be sweeping her from him. "Mother!" he cried. "Darling, sweetheart, wait!" Crumpling, she fell to the pavement. He dashed forward and fell at her side, crying, "Mamma, Mamma!" He turned her over. Her face was fiercely distorted. One eye, large and staring, moved slightly to the left as if it had become unmoored. The other remained fixed on him, raked his face again, found nothing and closed.

"Wait here, wait here!" he cried and jumped up and began to run for help toward a cluster of lights he saw in the distance ahead of him. "Help, help!" he shouted, but his voice was thin, scarcely a thread of sound. The lights drifted farther away the faster he ran and his feet moved numbly as if they carried him nowhere. The tide of darkness seemed to sweep him back to her, postponing from moment to moment his entry into the world of guilt and sorrow.

1965

<hr />

FLANNERY O'CONNOR

Passages from Essays and Letters

From "The Fiction Writer and His Country" (1957)

... [W]hen I look at stories I have written I find that they are, for the most part, about people who are poor, who are afflicted in both mind and body, who have little—or at best a distorted—sense of spiritual purpose, and whose actions do not apparently give the reader a great assurance of the joy of life.

Yet how is this? For I am no disbeliever in spiritual purpose and no vague believer. I see from the standpoint of Christian orthodoxy. This means that for me the meaning of life is centered in our Redemption by Christ and what I see in the world I see in its relation to that.

Some may blame preoccupation with the grotesque on the fact that here we have a Southern writer and that this is just the type of imagination that Southern life fosters. . . . I find it hard to believe that what is observable behavior in one section can be entirely without parallel in another. At least, of late, Southern writers have had the opportunity of pointing out that none of us invented Elvis Presley and that that youth is himself probably less an occasion for concern than his popularity, which is not restricted to the Southern part of the country.

When you can assume that your audience holds the same beliefs you do, you can relax a little and use more normal means of talking to it; when you have to assume that it does not, then you have to make your vision apparent by shock—to the hard of hearing you shout, and for the almost-blind you draw large and startling figures.

From "The Grotesque in Southern Fiction" (written 1960; posthumously published in 1965)

All novelists are fundamentally seekers and describers of the real, but the realism of each novelist will depend on his view of the ultimate reaches of reality. . . . If the novelist is in tune with this [modern scientific] spirit, if he believes that actions are predetermined by psychic make-up or the economic situation or some other determinable factor, then he will be concerned above all with an accurate reproduction of the things that most immediately concern man, with the natural forces that he feels control his destiny. . . .

On the other hand, if the writer believes that our life is and will remain essentially mysterious, . . . then what he sees on the surface will be of interest to him only as he can go through it into an experience of mystery itself. . . . [F]or this kind of writer, the meaning of a story does not begin except at a depth where adequate motivation and adequate psychology and the various determinations have been exhausted. Such a writer will be interested in what we don't understand rather than in what we do.

From "The Nature and Aim of Fiction"[1] (posthumously published in 1972)

. . . The beginning of human knowledge is through the senses, and the fiction writer begins where human perception begins. He appeals through the senses, and you cannot appeal to the senses with abstractions. . . . [F]iction is so very much an incarnational art.

---

1. These selections and those that follow (from "Writing Short Stories") are composites, edited from O'Connor manuscripts by Sally and Robert Fitzgerald in *Mystery and Manners*.

Now the word *symbol* scares a good many people off, just as the word *art* does. They seem to feel that a symbol is some mysterious thing put in arbitrarily by the writer to frighten the common reader—sort of a literary Masonic grip that is only for the initiated. They seem to think that it is a way of saying something that you aren't actually saying, and so . . . they approach it as if it were a problem in algebra. Find *x*. And when they do find or think they find this abstraction, *x*, then they go off with an elaborate sense of satisfaction and the notion that they have "understood" the story. . . .

I think for the fiction writer himself, symbols are something he uses simply as a matter of course. You might say that these are details that, while having their essential place in the literal level of the story, operate in depth as well as on the surface, increasing the story in every direction.

People have a habit of saying, "What is the theme of your story?" and they expect you to give them a statement. . . . And when they've got a statement . . . , they go off happy and feel it is no longer necessary to read the story . . . , but for the fiction writer himself the whole story is the meaning, because it is an experience, not an abstraction.

From "Writing Short Stories" (posthumously published in 1972)

. . . A story is a complete dramatic action—and in good stories, the characters are shown through the action and the action is controlled through the characters, and the result of this is meaning that derives from the whole presented experience.

. . . Nothing essential to the main experience can be left out of a short story. All the action has to be satisfactorily accounted for in terms of motivation, and there has to be a beginning, a middle, and an end, though not necessarily in that order.

. . . I prefer to talk about the meaning in a story rather than the theme of a story. People talk about the theme of a story as if the theme were like the string that a sack of chicken feed is tied with. They think that if you can pick out the theme, the way you pick the right thread in the chicken-feed sack, you can rip the story open and feed the chickens. But this is not the way meaning works in fiction.

When you can state the theme of a story, when you can separate it from the story itself, then you can be sure the story is not a very good one. The meaning of a story has to be embodied in it, has to be made concrete in it. A story is a way to say something that can't be said any other way, and it takes every word in the story to say what the meaning is. You tell a story because a statement would be inadequate.

An idiom characterizes a society, and when you ignore the idiom, you are very likely ignoring the whole social fabric that could make a meaningful character. You can't cut characters off from their society and say much about them as individuals. You can't say anything meaningful about the mystery of a personality unless you put that personality in a believable and significant social context.

O'Connor alongside self-portrait with peacock

From "On Her Own Work" (posthumously published in 1972)

In most English classes the short story has become a kind of literary specimen to be dissected. Every time a story of mine appears in a Freshman anthology, I have a vision of it, with its little organs laid open, like a frog in a bottle.

I realize that a certain amount of this what-is-the-significance has to go on, but I think something has gone wrong in the process when, for so many students, the story becomes simply a problem to be solved, something which you evaporate to get Instant Enlightenment.

A story isn't any good unless it successfully resists paraphrase, unless it hangs on and expands in the mind. Properly, you analyze to enjoy, but it's equally true that to analyze with any discrimination, you have to have enjoyed already, and I think that the best reason to hear a story read is that it should stimulate that primary enjoyment.

I often ask myself what makes a story work, and what makes it hold up as a story, and I have decided that it is probably some action, some gesture of a character that is unlike any other in the story, one which indicates where the real heart of the story lies. This would have to be an action or a gesture which was both totally right and totally unexpected; it would have to be one that was both in character and beyond character; it would have to suggest both the world and eternity. The action or gesture I'm talking about would have to be on the anagogical level, that is, the level which has to do with the Divine life and our participation in it. It would be a gesture that transcended any neat allegory that might have been intended or any pat moral categories a reader could make. It would be a gesture which somehow made contact with mystery.

. . . [I]n my own stories I have found that violence is strangely capable of returning my characters to reality and preparing them to accept their moment of grace. . . .

We hear many complaints about the prevalence of violence in modern fiction, and it is always assumed that this violence is a bad thing and meant to be an end in itself. With the serious writer, violence is never an end in itself. It is the extreme situation that best reveals what we are essentially. . . .

From "Novelist and Believer" (written 1963; posthumously published in 1972)

. . . Great fiction . . . is not simply an imitation of feeling. The good novelist not only finds a symbol for feeling, he finds a symbol and a way of lodging it which tells the intelligent reader whether this feeling is adequate or inadequate, whether it is moral or immoral, whether it is good or evil. And his theology, even in its most remote reaches, will have a direct bearing on this.

. . . The artist penetrates the concrete world in order to find at its depths the image of its source, the image of ultimate reality. This in no way hinders his perception of evil but rather sharpens it, for only when the natural world is seen as good does evil become intelligible as a destructive force and a necessary result of our freedom.

From the Letters

To a Professor of English, 28 March 1961

The meaning of a story should go on expanding for the reader the more he thinks about it, but meaning cannot be captured in an interpretation. If teachers are in the habit of approaching a story as if it were a research problem for which any answer is believable so long as it is not obvious, then I think students will never learn to enjoy fiction. Too much interpretation is certainly worse than too little, and where feeling for a story is absent, theory will not supply it.

To Louise and Tom Gossett, 10 April 1961

I have just read a review of my book [The Violent Bear It Away], long and damming [sic], which says it don't give us hope and courage and that all novels should give us hope and courage. I think if the novel is to give us virtue the selection of hope and courage is rather arbitrary—why not charity, peace, patience, joy, benignity, long-suffering and fear of the Lord? Or faith? The fact of the matter is that the modern mind opposes courage to faith. It also demands that the novel provide us with gifts that only religion can give. I don't think the novel can offend against the truth, but I think its truths are more particular than general. But this is a large subject and I ain't no aesthetician.

TO ROSLYN BARNES, 17 JUNE 1961

Can you tell me if the statement: "everything that rises must converge" is a true proposition in physics? I can easily see its moral, historical and evolutionary significance, but I want to know if it is also a correct physical statement.

TO "A," 22 JULY 1961

I had a story that I had written a first draft sort of on and Caroline thought as usual that it wasn't dramatic enough (and she was right) and told me all the things that I tell you when I read one of yours. She did think the structure was good and the situation. All I got to do is write the story. This one is called "The Lame Shall Enter First."

TO "A," 16 SEPTEMBER 1961

The thing I am writing now is surely going to convince Jack [the author John Hawkes] that I am of the Devil's party. It is out of hand right now but I am hoping I can bring it into line. It is a composite of all the eccentricities of my writing and for this reason may not be any good, maybe almost a parody. But what you start, you ought to carry through and if it is no good, I don't have to publish it. I am thinking of changing the title to "The Lame Will Carry Off the Prey."

TO JOHN HAWKES, 28 NOVEMBER 1961

You haven't convinced me that I write with the Devil's will or belong in the romantic tradition and I'm prepared to argue some more with you on this if I can remember where we left off at. I think the reason we can't agree on this is because there is a difference in our two devils. My Devil has a name, a history and a definite plan. His name is Lucifer, he's a fallen angel, his sin is pride, and his aim is the destruction of the Divine plan. Now I judge that your Devil is co-equal to God, not his creature: that pride is his virtue not his sin; and that his aim is not to destroy the Divine plan because there isn't any Divine plan to destroy. My Devil is objective and yours is subjective. You say one becomes "evil" when one leaves the herd. I say that depends entirely on what the herd is doing.

TO "A," 9 DECEMBER 1961

Some friends of mine in Texas wrote me that a friend of theirs went into a bookstore looking for a paperback copy of A Good Man. The clerk said, "We don't have that one but we have another by that author, called The Bear That Ran Away With It. I foresee the trouble I am going to have with "Everything That Rises Must Converge"—"Every Rabbit That Rises Is a Sage."

TO CECIL DAWKINS, 6 SEPTEMBER 1962

About the story ["The Lame Shall Enter First"] I certainly agree that it don't work and have never felt that it did, but in heaven's name where do you get the idea that Sheppard represents Freud? Freud never entered my mind and looking back over it, I can't make him fit now. The story is about a man who thought he was good and thought he was doing good when he wasn't. Freud was a great one, wasn't he, for bringing home to people the fact that they weren't what they thought they were, so if Freud were in this, which he is not, he would certainly be on the other side of the fence from Shepp. The story doesn't work because I don't know, don't sympathize, don't like Mr. Sheppard in the way that I know and like most of my other characters. This is a story, not a statement. I think you ought to look for simpler explanations of why things don't work and not mess around with philosophical ideas where they haven't been intended or don't apply. There's nothing in the story that could possibly suggest that Sheppard represents Freud. This is some theory of which you are possessed. I am wondering if this kind of theorizing could be what is interfering with your getting going on some writing. Don't mix up thought-knowledge with felt-knowledge. If Sheppard represents anything here, it is, as he realizes at the end of the story, the empty man who fills up his emptiness with good works.

To "A," 3 November 1962
    . . . In that story of mine ["The Lame Shall Enter First"] . . . the little boy wouldn't have been looking for his mother if she hadn't been a good one when she was alive. This of course could be debated, but it's nowhere suggested in the story that she wasn't a good one.

To Marion Montgomery, 16 June 1963
    I never wrote and thanked you for innerducing me at Georgia or for the copy of *The Sermon of Introduction*, but I liked them. They made up for my present lack of popularity with the *Atlanta Journal-Constitution* book page, that alert sheet of Sunday criticism. Did you ever see their mention of "Everything That Rises Must Converge"? Unsigned. I suspect somebody from Atlanta U. did it.

To "A," 1 September 1963
    The topical is poison. I got away with it in "Everything That Rises" but only because I say a plague on everybody's house as far as the race business goes.

QUESTIONS

1. What does the scene at Red Sam's Barbecue in "A Good Man Is Hard to Find" add to the story? How does it contribute to the characterization of the main characters? help define the society and its values? prepare for what follows?
2. How does Sheppard explain why Norton throws up ("The Lame Shall Enter First," paragraph 48)? Why do you think Norton throws up (other than his putting peanut butter and ketchup on his cake)?
3. What internal evidence is there that "The Lame Shall Enter First," "A Good Man Is Hard to Find," and "Everything That Rises Must Converge" are by the same author?

WRITING SUGGESTIONS

1. Write a character sketch of the grandmother in "A Good Man Is Hard to Find," and indicate how and why your response to the grandmother changes, shifts, or is intensified from the beginning to the end of the story.

2. Chart and analyze your responses to "A Good Man Is Hard to Find."
3. Briefly retell the story of "Everything That Rises Must Converge" from the point of view, perhaps even in the voice, of the African American woman who is wearing "*the* hat."
4. Compare the function of money in "The Lame Shall Enter First" and Guy de Maupassant's "The Jewelry."

9

LITERARY KIND AS CONTEXT: INITIATION STORIES

Themes are useful for grouping stories together for comparison, both to highlight similarities and to reveal differences in history and structure and so to discover the uniqueness of the work. Types of characters—stereotypes—are useful for the same purpose: to show both the common qualities and the unique combination of qualities in a particular character in a story. Though grouping and classification, used poorly, can blur distinctions and make all members of a group seem the same, when used well they do not blur but bring into focus the individuality of each member.

Because literary criticism lacks the specific and agreed-on system of classification used in biology, its terms are not so fixed as *phylum, genus, species.* In this book, we use the term **genre** for the largest commonly agreed-on categories: fiction, poetry, drama. We use the term **subgenre** for the divisions within a genre—subgenres of fiction, for example, are novel, novella, short story, and so on. A **kind** is a species or subcategory within a subgenre. (You may, however, see these terms used differently in other contexts; literary critics often, for example, refer to the novel or the short story as a genre and refer to particular kinds, like the Gothic novel or mystery novel, as subgenres.)

One kind of short story, so common that some maintain it is not a kind but is equivalent to the subgenre short story itself, is the **initiation story,** in which a character—often but not always a child or young person—first learns, or is "initiated into," a significant truth about the universe, reality, society, people, himself or herself. Such a subject tends to dictate the main outlines of the story's action: it begins with the protagonist in a state of innocence or mistaken belief (exposition); it leads up to the moment of illumination or the discovery of the or a truth (rising action to climax or turning point); and it ends usually (but not always) with some indication of the result of that discovery (falling action to conclusion). This kind is particularly suitable to a short story because it lends itself to brief treatment: the illumination is more or less sudden—there is no need for lengthy development, for multiple scenes or settings, for much time to pass, for too many complications of action or a large cast of characters—yet it can encapsulate a whole life or important segment of a life and wide-ranging, significant themes.

If you've been reading this book from the beginning, you have already run into a number of initiation stories, and you may have some idea of what sorts of truths their protagonists discover. Young goodman Brown discovers that all people are capable of evil. The captain in "The Secret Sharer" discovers that someone very much like him, virtually his double and therefore probably he himself, is not only capable of murder but may, under certain circumstances and in his capacity as a captain or leader, consciously choose murder as the lesser of evils. Just as the "adult" knowledge into which characters are initiated differs widely, so, too, do their responses: one may retreat from the truth physically or psychologically, as does Brown, or remain unchanged, or revert to one's former state. Such stories suggest, however, that even if we choose to retreat from a newly perceived truth, we can never completely return to our former innocence.

Since to the young all things seem possible—one can be a doctor, novelist, tennis pro, rock star, and saint, serially or simultaneously—many of the truths learned in initiation stories have to do with limitation. The girl in "Boys and Girls" learns that she is "only a girl," the boy in "Araby" that he is merely "a creature driven" by romantic dreams that can never be realized. Sometimes a child learns the difference between words and reality in the adult world, as Hazel does in "Gorilla, My Love."

By the time you finish this chapter, you should have some idea of the variations possible within the initiation story, and, as you look back to such stories as "Sonny's Blues," "The Country Husband," and "The Lame Shall Enter First," you should have a still better idea of the range of stories in this kind. Adults may be initiated as well as children and adolescents; the truths may be bitter or pleasing, cosmic, social, psychological; the initiates may change forever, retreat, shrug off what they have learned. By seeing all these stories as part of the large group of initiation stories, you may the more readily notice the differences in the protagonists, the learning experiences, and the effects of the initiations on the protagonists, whether they are permanent or temporary, life-denying or life-enhancing. You may, in other words, have gone a long way toward defining the unique vision of the story, its precise and individual illumination of reality, its particular definitions of illusion and truth, of childlike innocence and adult wisdom. And that's the function of classification in the first place.

TONI CADE BAMBARA

Gorilla, My Love

That was the year Hunca Bubba changed his name. Not a change up, but a change back, since Jefferson Winston Vale was the name in the first place. Which was news to me cause he'd been my Hunca Bubba my whole lifetime, since I couldn't manage Uncle to save my life. So far as I was concerned it was a change completely to somethin soundin very geographical weatherlike to me, like somethin you'd find in a almanac. Or somethin you'd run across when you sittin in the navigator seat with a wet thumb on the map crinkly in your lap, watchin the roads and signs so when Granddaddy Vale say "Which way, Scout," you got sense enough to say take the next exit or take a left or whatever it is. Not that Scout's my name. Just the name Granddaddy call whoever sittin in the navigator seat. Which is usually me cause I don't feature sittin in the back with the pecans. Now, you figure pecans all right to be sittin with. If you thinks so, that's your business. But they dusty sometime and make you cough. And they got a way of slidin around and dippin down sudden, like maybe a rat in the buckets. So if you scary like me, you sleep with the lights on and blame it on Baby Jason and, so as not to waste good electric, you study the maps. And that's how come I'm in the navigator seat most times and get to be called Scout.

So Hunca Bubba in the back with the pecans and Baby Jason, and he in love. And we got to hear all this stuff about this woman he in love with and all. Which really ain't enough to keep the mind alive, though Baby Jason got no better sense than to give his undivided attention and keep grabbin at the photograph which is just a picture of some skinny woman in a countrified dress with her hand shot up to her face like she shame fore cameras. But there's a movie house in the background which I ax about. Cause I am a movie freak from way back, even though it do get me in trouble sometime.

Like when me and Big Brood and Baby Jason was on our own last Easter and couldn't go to the Dorset cause we'd seen all the Three Stooges they was. And the RKO Hamilton was closed readying up for the Easter Pageant that night. And the West End, the Regun and the Sunset was too far, less we had grownups with us which we didn't. So we walk up Amsterdam Avenue to the Washington and *Gorilla, My Love* playin, they say, which suit me just fine, though the "my love" part kinda drag Big Brood some. As for Baby Jason, shoot, like Granddaddy say, he'd follow me into the fiery furnace if I say come on. So we go in and get three bags of Havmore potato chips which not only are the best potato chips but the best bags for blowin up and bustin real loud so the matron come trottin down the aisle with her chunky self, flashin that flashlight dead in your eye so you can give her some lip, and if she answer back and you already finish seein the show anyway, why then you just turn the place out. Which I love to do, no lie. With Baby Jason kickin at the seat in front, egging me on, and Big Brood mumblin bout what fiercesome things we goin do. Which means me. Like when the big boys come up on us talkin bout Lemme a nickel. It's me that hide the money. Or when the bad boys in the park take Big Brood's Spaudeen[1] way from him. It's me that jump on they back and fight awhile. And it's me that turns out the show if the matron get too salty.

So the movie come on and right away it's this churchy music and clearly not about no gorilla. Bout Jesus. And I am ready to kill, not cause I got anything gainst Jesus. Just that when you fixed to watch a gorilla picture you don't wanna get messed around with Sunday School stuff. So I am mad. Besides, we see this rag-gedy old brown film *King of Kings*[2] every year and enough's enough. Grownups figure they can treat you just anyhow. Which burns me up. There I am, my feet up and my Havmore potato chips really salty and crispy and two jawbreakers in my lap and the money safe in my shoe from the big boys, and there comes this Jesus stuff. So we all go wild. Yellin, booin, stompin and carrying on. Really to wake the man in the booth up there who musta went to sleep and put on the wrong reels. But no, cause he holler down to shut up and then he turn the sound up so we really gotta holler like crazy to even hear ourselves good. And the matron

---

1. Probably refers to "Spaldeen," the small pink rubber ball made by the Spalding company and used for stick ball.   2. Although there is a 1961 version, this probably refers to the silent movie made in the 1920s.

ropes off the children section and flashes her light all over the place and we yell some more and some kids slip under the rope and run up and down the aisle just to show it take more than some dusty ole velvet rope to tie us down. And I'm flingin the kid in front of me's popcorn. And Baby Jason kickin seats. And it's really somethin. Then here come the big and bad matron, the one they let out in case of emergency. And she totin that flashlight like she gonna use it on some-body. This here the colored matron Brandy and her friends call Thunderbuns. She do not play. She do not smile. So we shut up and watch the simple ass picture.

5   Which is not so simple as it is stupid. Cause I realized that just about anybody in my family is better than this god they always talkin about. My daddy wouldn't stand for nobody treatin any of us that way. My mama specially. And I can just see it now, Big Brood up there on the cross talkin bout Forgive them Daddy cause they don't know what they doin. And my Mama say Get on down from there you big fool, whatcha think this is, playtime? And my Daddy yellin to Grand-daddy to get him a ladder cause Big Brood actin the fool, his mother side of the family showin up. And my mama and her sister Daisy jumpin on them Romans beatin them with they pocketbooks. And Hunca Bubba tellin them folks on they knees they better get out the way and go get some help or they goin to get tram-pled on. And Granddaddy Vale sayin Leave the boy alone, if that's what he wants to do with his life we ain't got nothin to say about it. Then Aunt Daisy givin him a taste of that pocketbook, fussin bout what a damn fool old man Granddaddy is. Then everybody jumpin in his chest like the time Uncle Clayton went in the army and come back with only one leg and Granddaddy say somethin stupid about that's life. And by this time Big Brood off the cross and in the park playin handball or skully[3] or somethin. And the family in the kitchen throwin dishes at each other, screamin bout if you hadn't done this I wouldn't had to do that. And me in the parlor trying to do my arithmetic yellin Shut it off.

Which is what I was yellin all by myself which make me a sittin target for Thunderbuns. But when I yell We want our money back, that gets everybody in chorus. And the movie windin up with this heavenly cloud music and the smart-ass up there in his hole in the wall turns up the sound again to drown us out. Then there comes Bugs Bunny which we already seen so we know we been had. No gorilla my nuthin. And Big Brood say Awwww sheeet, we goin to see the manager and get our money back. And I know from this we business. So I brush the potato chips out of my hair which is where Baby Jason like to put em, and I march myself up the aisle to deal with the manager who is a crook in the first place for lyin out there sayin *Gorilla, My Love* playin. And I never did like the man cause he oily and pasty at the same time like the bad guy in the serial, the one that got a hideout behind a push-button bookcase and play "Moonlight Sonata"[4] with gloves on. I knock on the door and I am furious. And I am alone, too. Cause Big Brood suddenly got to go so bad even though my mama told us bout goin in them nasty bathrooms. And I hear him sigh like he disgusted when he get to

---

3. A basketball game that tests shooting skill and can be played alone or as a contest between two peo-ple.   4. Popular name for Beethoven's *Piano Sonata in C Sharp Minor*, Opus 27, No. 2. The "bad guy" who plays this piece is the Phantom of the Opera.

the door and see only a little kid there. And now I'm really furious cause I get so tired grownups messin over kids cause they little and can't take em to court. What is it, he say to me like I lost my mittens or wet myself or am somebody's retarded child. When in reality I am the smartest kid P.S. 186 ever had in its whole lifetime and you can ax anybody. Even them teachers that don't like me cause I won't sing them Southern songs or back off when they tell me my questions are out of order. And cause my Mama come up there in a minute when them teachers start playin the dozens[5] behind colored folks. She stalks in with her hat pulled down bad and that Persian lamb coat draped back over one hip on account of she got her fist planted there so she can talk that talk which gets us all hypnotized, and teacher be comin undone cause she know this could be her job and her behind cause Mama got pull with the Board and bad by her own self anyhow.

So I kick the door open wider and just walk right by him and sit down and tell the man about himself and that I want my money back and that goes for Baby Jason and Big Brood too. And he still trying to shuffle me out the door even though I'm sittin which shows him for the fool he is. Just like them teachers do fore they realize Mama like a stone on that spot and ain't backin up. So he ain't gettin up off the money. So I was forced to leave, takin the matches from under his ashtray, and set a fire under the candy stand, which closed the raggedy ole Washington down for a week. My Daddy had the suspect it was me cause Big Brood got a big mouth. But I explained right quick what the whole thing was about and I figured it was even-steven. Cause if you say Gorilla, My Love, you supposed to mean it. Just like when you say you goin to give me a party on my birthday, you gotta mean it. And if you say me and Baby Jason can go South pecan haulin with Granddaddy Vale, you better not be comin up with no stuff about the weather look uncertain or did you mop the bathroom or any other trickified business. I mean even gangsters in the movies say My word is my bond. So don't nobody get away with nothin far as I'm concerned. So Daddy put his belt back on. Cause that's the way I was raised. Like my Mama say in one of them situations when I won't back down, Okay Badbird, you right. Your point is well-taken. Not that Badbird my name, just what she say when she tired arguin and know I'm right. And Aunt Jo, who is the hardest head in the family and worse even than Aunt Daisy, she say, You absolutely right Miss Muffin, which also ain't my real name but the name she gave me one time when I got some medicine shot in my behind and wouldn't get up off her pillows for nothin. And even Granddaddy Vale—who got no memory to speak of, so sometime you can just plain lie to him, if you want to be like that— he say, Well if that's what I said, then that's it. But this name business was different they said. It wasn't like Hunca Bubba had gone back on his word or anything. Just that he was thinkin bout gettin married and was usin his real name now. Which ain't the way I saw it at all.

So there I am in the navigator seat. And I turned to him and just plain ole ax

5. Ritualized game or contest in which two participants exchange insults directed against each other's relatives.

him. I mean I come right on out with it. No sense goin all around that barn the old folks talk about. And like my mama say, Hazel—which is my real name and what she remembers to call me when she bein serious—when you got somethin on your mind, speak up and let the chips fall where they may. And if anybody don't like it, tell em to come see your mama. And Daddy look up from the paper and say, You hear your Mama good, Hazel. And tell em to come see me first. Like that. That's how I was raised.

So I turn clear round in the navigator seat and say, "Look here, Hunca Bubba or Jefferson Windsong Vale or whatever your name is, you gonna marry this girl?"

10 "Sure am," he say, all grins.

And I say, "Member that time you was baby-sittin me when we lived at four-o-nine and there was this big snow and Mama and Daddy got held up in the country so you had to stay for two days?"

And he say, "Sure do."

"Well. You remember how you told me I was the cutest thing that ever walked the earth?"

"Oh, you were real cute when you were little," he say, which is supposed to be funny. I am not laughin.

15 "Well. You remember what you said?"

And Granddaddy Vale squintin over the wheel and axin Which way, Scout. But Scout is busy and don't care if we all get lost for days.

"Watcha mean, Peaches?"

"My name is Hazel. And what I mean is you said you were going to marry *me* when I grew up. You were going to wait. That's what I mean, my dear Uncle Jefferson." And he don't say nuthin. Just look at me real strange like he never saw me before in life. Like he lost in some weird town in the middle of night and lookin for directions and there's no one to ask. Like it was me that messed up the maps and turned the road posts round. "Well, you said it, didn't you?" And Baby Jason lookin back and forth like we playin ping-pong. Only I ain't playin. I'm hurtin and I can hear that I am screamin. And Granddaddy Vale mumblin how we never gonna get to where we goin if I don't turn around and take my navigator job serious.

"Well, for cryin out loud, Hazel, you just a little girl. And I was just teasin."

20 " 'And I was just teasin,' " I say back just how he said it so he can hear what a terrible thing it is. Then I don't say nuthin. And he don't say nuthin. And Baby Jason don't say nuthin nohow. Then Granddaddy Vale speak up. "Look here, Precious, it was Hunca Bubba what told you them things. This here, Jefferson Winston Vale." And Hunca Bubba say, "That's right. That was somebody else. I'm a new somebody."

"You a lyin dawg," I say, when I meant to say treacherous dog, but just couldn't get hold of the word. It slipped away from me. And I'm crying and crumplin down in the seat and just don't care. And Granddaddy say to hush and steps on the gas. And I'm losin my bearins and don't even know where to look on the map cause I can't see for cryin. And Baby Jason cryin too. Cause he is my blood brother and understands that we must stick together or be forever lost, what with grownups playin change-up and turnin you round every which way so bad. And don't even say they sorry.

1972

ALICE MUNRO

Boys and Girls

My father was a fox farmer. That is, he raised silver foxes, in pens; and in the fall and early winter, when their fur was prime, he killed them and skinned them and sold their pelts to the Hudson's Bay Company or the Montreal Fur Traders. These companies supplied us with heroic calendars to hang, one on each side of the kitchen door. Against a background of cold blue sky and black pine forests and treacherous northern rivers, plumed adventurers planted the flags of England or of France; magnificent savages bent their backs to the portage.

For several weeks before Christmas, my father worked after supper in the cellar of our house. The cellar was white-washed, and lit by a hundred-watt bulb over the worktable. My brother Laird and I sat on the top step and watched. My father removed the pelt inside-out from the body of the fox, which looked surprisingly small, mean and rat-like, deprived of its arrogant weight of fur. The naked, slippery bodies were collected in a sack and buried at the dump. One time the hired man, Henry Bailey, had taken a swipe at me with this sack, saying, "Christmas present!" My mother thought that was not funny. In fact she disliked the whole pelting operation—that was what the killing, skinning, and preparation of the furs was called—and wished it did not have to take place in the house. There was the smell. After the pelt had been stretched inside-out on a long board my father scraped away delicately, removing the little clotted webs of blood vessels, the bubbles of fat; the smell of blood and animal fat, with the strong primitive odour of the fox itself, penetrated all parts of the house. I found it reassuringly seasonal, like the smell of oranges and pine needles.

Henry Bailey suffered from bronchial troubles. He would cough and cough until his narrow face turned scarlet, and his light blue, derisive eyes filled up with tears; then he took the lid off the stove, and, standing well back, shot out a great clot of phlegm—hsss—straight into the heart of the flames. We admired him for this performance and for his ability to make his stomach growl at will, and for his laughter, which was full of high whistlings and gurglings and involved the whole faulty machinery of his chest. It was sometimes hard to tell what he was laughing at, and always possible that it might be us.

After we had been sent to bed we could still smell fox and still hear Henry's laugh, but these things, reminders of the warm, safe, brightly lit downstairs world, seemed lost and diminished, floating on the stale cold air upstairs. We were afraid at night in the winter. We were not afraid of *outside* though this was the time of year when snowdrifts curled around our house like sleeping whales and the wind harassed us all night, coming up from the buried fields, the frozen swamp, with its old bugbear chorus of threats and misery. We were afraid of *inside*, the room where we slept. At this time the upstairs of our house was not finished. A brick chimney went up one wall. In the middle of the floor was a square hole, with a wooden railing around it; that was where the stairs came up. On the other side of the stairwell were the things that nobody had any use for any more—a soldiery roll of linoleum, standing on end, a wicker baby carriage, a fern basket, china jugs and basins with cracks in them, a picture of the Battle of Balaclava,[1] very sad to look at. I had told Laird, as soon as he was old enough to understand such things, that bats and skeletons lived over there; whenever a man escaped from the county jail, twenty miles away, I imagined that he had somehow let himself in the window and was hiding behind the linoleum. But we had rules to keep us safe. When the light was on, we were safe as long as we did not step off the square of worn carpet which defined our bedroom-space; when the light was off no place was safe but the beds themselves. I had to turn out the light kneeling on the end of my bed, and stretching as far as I could to reach the cord.

5   In the dark we lay on our beds, our narrow life rafts, and fixed our eyes on the faint light coming up the stairwell, and sang songs. Laird sang "Jingle Bells," which he would sing any time, whether it was Christmas or not, and I sang "Danny Boy." I loved the sound of my own voice, frail and supplicating, rising in the dark. We could make out the tall frosted shapes of the windows now, gloomy and white. When I came to the part, *When I am dead, as dead I well may be*—a fit of shivering caused not by the cold sheets but by pleasurable emotion almost silenced me. *You'll kneel and say, an Ave there above me*—What was an Ave? Every day I forgot to find out.

Laird went straight from singing to sleep. I could hear his long, satisfied, bubbly breaths. Now for the time that remained to me, the most perfectly private and perhaps the best time of the whole day, I arranged myself tightly under the covers and went on with one of the stories I was telling myself from night to night. These stories were about myself, when I had grown a little older; they took place in a world that was recognizably mine, yet one that presented opportunities for courage, boldness and self-sacrifice, as mine never did. I rescued people from a bombed building (it discouraged me that the real war had gone on so far away from Jubilee). I shot two rabid wolves who were menacing the schoolyard (the teachers cowered terrified at my back). I rode a fine horse spiritedly down the main street of Jubilee, acknowledging the townspeople's gratitude for some yet-to-be-worked-out piece of heroism (nobody ever rode a horse there, except King Billy in the Orangemen's Day[2] parade). There was always riding and shooting in these stories, though I had only been on a horse twice—bareback because we did

---

1. An indecisive Crimean War battle fought on October 25, 1854.   2. The Orange Society is an Irish Protestant group named after William of Orange, who, as King William III of England, defeated the Catholic James II. The society sponsors an annual procession on July 12 to commemorate the victory of William III at the Battle of the Boyne (1690).

not own a saddle—and the second time I had slid right around and dropped under the horse's feet; it had stepped placidly over me. I really was learning to shoot, but I could not hit anything yet, not even tin cans on fence posts.

Alive, the foxes inhabited a world my father made for them. It was surrounded by a high guard fence, like a medieval town, with a gate that was padlocked at night. Along the streets of this town were ranged large, sturdy pens. Each of them had a real door that a man could go through, a wooden ramp along the wire, for the foxes to run up and down on, and a kennel—something like a clothes chest with airholes—where they slept and stayed in winter and had their young. There were feeding and watering dishes attached to the wire in such a way that they could be emptied and cleaned from the outside. The dishes were made of old tin cans, and the ramps and kennels of odds and ends of old lumber. Everything was tidy and ingenious; my father was tirelessly inventive and his favourite book in the world was *Robinson Crusoe*.[3] He had fitted a tin drum on a wheelbarrow, for bringing water down to the pens. This was my job in summer, when the foxes had to have water twice a day. Between nine and ten o'clock in the morning, and again after supper, I filled the drum at the pump and trundled it down through the barnyard to the pens, where I parked it, and filled my watering can and went along the streets. Laird came too, with his little cream and green gardening can, filled too full and knocking against his legs and slopping water on his canvas shoes. I had the real watering can, my father's, though I could only carry it three-quarters full.

The foxes all had names, which were printed on a tin plate and hung beside their doors. They were not named when they were born, but when they survived the first year's pelting and were added to the breeding stock. Those my father had named were called names like Prince, Bob, Wally and Betty. Those I had named were called Star or Turk, or Maureen or Diana. Laird named one Maud after a hired girl we had when he was little, one Harold after a boy at school, and one Mexico, he did not say why.

Naming them did not make pets out of them, or anything like it. Nobody but my father ever went into the pens, and he had twice had blood-poisoning from bites. When I was bringing them their water they prowled up and down on the paths they had made inside their pens, barking seldom—they saved that for night-time, when they might get up a chorus of community frenzy—but always watching me, their eyes burning, clear gold, in their pointed, malevolent faces. They were beautiful for their delicate legs and heavy, aristocratic tails and the bright fur sprinkled on dark down their backs—which gave them their name—but especially for their faces, drawn exquisitely sharp in pure hostility, and their golden eyes.

Besides carrying water I helped my father when he cut the long grass, and the 10 lamb's quarter and flowering money-musk, that grew between the pens. He cut with the scythe and I raked into piles. Then he took a pitchfork and threw fresh-

3. Novel (1719) by Daniel Defoe about a man shipwrecked on a desert island; it goes into great detail about his ingenious contraptions.

cut grass all over the top of the pens, to keep the foxes cooler and shade their coats, which were browned by too much sun. My father did not talk to me unless it was about the job we were doing. In this he was quite different from my mother, who, if she was feeling cheerful, would tell me all sorts of things—the name of a dog she had had when she was a little girl, the names of boys she had gone out with later on when she was grown up, and what certain dresses of hers had looked like—she could not imagine now what had become of them. Whatever thoughts and stories my father had were private, and I was shy of him and would never ask him questions. Nevertheless I worked willingly under his eyes, and with a feeling of pride. One time a feed salesman came down into the pens to talk to him and my father said, "Like to have you meet my new hired man." I turned away and raked furiously, red in the face with pleasure.

"Could of fooled me," said the salesman. "I thought it was only a girl."

After the grass was cut, it seemed suddenly much later in the year. I walked on stubble in the earlier evening, aware of the reddening skies, the entering silences, of fall. When I wheeled the tank out of the gate and put the padlock on, it was almost dark. One night at this time I saw my mother and father standing talking on the little rise of ground we called the gangway, in front of the barn. My father had just come from the meathouse; he had his stiff bloody apron on, and a pail of cut-up meat in his hand.

It was an odd thing to see my mother down at the barn. She did not often come out of the house unless it was to do something—hang out the wash or dig potatoes in the garden. She looked out of place, with her bare lumpy legs, not touched by the sun, her apron still on and damp across the stomach from the supper dishes. Her hair was tied up in a kerchief, wisps of it falling out. She would tie her hair up like this in the morning, saying she did not have time to do it properly, and it would stay tied up all day. It was true, too; she really did not have time. These days our back porch was piled with baskets of peaches and grapes and pears, bought in town, and onions and tomatoes and cucumbers grown at home, all waiting to be made into jelly and jam and preserves, pickles and chili sauce. In the kitchen there was a fire in the stove all day, jars clinked in boiling water, sometimes a cheesecloth bag was strung on a pole between two chairs, straining blue-black grape pulp for jelly. I was given jobs to do and I would sit at the table peeling peaches that had been soaked in the hot water, or cutting up onions, my eyes smarting and streaming. As soon as I was done I ran out of the house, trying to get out of earshot before my mother thought of what she wanted me to do next. I hated the hot dark kitchen in summer, the green blinds and the flypapers, the same old oilcloth table and wavy mirror and bumpy linoleum. My mother was too tired and preoccupied to talk to me, she had no heart to tell about the Normal School Graduation Dance; sweat trickled over her face and she was always counting under her breath, pointing at jars, dumping cups of sugar. It seemed to me that work in the house was endless, dreary and peculiarly depressing; work done out of doors, and in my father's service, was ritualistically important.

I wheeled the tank up to the barn, where it was kept, and I heard my mother saying, "Wait till Laird gets a little bigger, then you'll have a real help."

What my father said I did not hear. I was pleased by the way he stood listening, politely as he would to a salesman or a stranger, but with an air of wanting to get on with his real work. I felt my mother had no business down here and I wanted him to feel the same way. What did she mean about Laird? He was no help to anybody. Where was he now? Swinging himself sick on the swing, going around in circles, or trying to catch caterpillars. He never once stayed with me till I was finished.

"And then I can use her more in the house," I heard my mother say. She had a dead-quiet, regretful way of talking about me that always made me uneasy. "I just get my back turned and she runs off. It's not like I had a girl in the family at all."

I went and sat on a feed bag in the corner of the barn, not wanting to appear when this conversation was going on. My mother, I felt, was not to be trusted. She was kinder than my father and more easily fooled, but you could not depend on her, and the real reasons for the things she said and did were not to be known. She loved me, and she sat up late at night making a dress of the difficult style I wanted, for me to wear when school started, but she was also my enemy. She was always plotting. She was plotting now to get me to stay in the house more, although she knew I hated it (*because* she knew I hated it) and keep me from working for my father. It seemed to me she would do this simply out of perversity, and to try her power. It did not occur to me that she could be lonely, or jealous. No grown-up could be; they were too fortunate. I sat and kicked my heels monotonously against a feedbag, raising dust, and did not come out till she was gone.

At any rate, I did not expect my father to pay any attention to what she said. Who could imagine Laird doing my work—Laird remembering the padlock and cleaning out the watering-dishes with a leaf on the end of a stick, or even wheeling the tank without it tumbling over? It showed how little my mother knew about the way things really were.

I have forgotten to say what the foxes were fed. My father's bloody apron reminded me. They were fed horsemeat. At this time most farmers still kept horses, and when a horse got too old to work, or broke a leg or got down and would not get up, as they sometimes did, the owner would call my father, and he and Henry went out to the farm in the truck. Usually they shot and butchered the horse there, paying the farmer from five to twelve dollars. If they had already too much meat on hand, they would bring the horse back alive, and keep it for a few days or weeks in our stable, until the meat was needed. After the war the farmers were buying tractors and gradually getting rid of horses altogether, so it sometimes happened that we got a good healthy horse, that there was just no use for any more. If this happened in the winter we might keep the horse in our stable till spring, for we had plenty of hay and if there was a lot of snow—and the plow did not always get our road cleared—it was convenient to be able to go to town with a horse and cutter.[4]

The winter I was eleven years old we had two horses in the stable. We did not know what names they had had before, so we called them Mack and Flora. Mack

20

4. A small, light sleigh.

was an old black workhorse, sooty and indifferent. Flora was a sorrel mare, a driver. We took them both out in the cutter. Mack was slow and easy to handle. Flora was given to fits of violent alarm, veering at cars and even at other horses, but we loved her speed and high-stepping, her general air of gallantry and abandon. On Saturdays we went down to the stable and as soon as we opened the door on its cosy, animal-smelling darkness Flora threw up her head, rolled her eyes, whinnied despairingly and pulled herself through a crisis of nerves on the spot. It was not safe to go into her stall; she would kick.

This winter also I began to hear a great deal more on the theme my mother had sounded when she had been talking in front of the barn. I no longer felt safe. It seemed that in the minds of the people around me there was a steady undercurrent of thought, not to be deflected, on this one subject. The word *girl* had formerly seemed to me innocent and unburdened, like the world *child;* now it appeared that it was no such thing. A girl was not, as I had supposed, simply what I was; it was what I had to become. It was a definition, always touched with emphasis, with reproach and disappointment. Also it was a joke on me. Once Laird and I were fighting, and for the first time ever I had to use all my strength against him; even so, he caught and pinned my arm for a moment, really hurting me. Henry saw this, and laughed, saying, "Oh, that there Laird's gonna show you, one of these days!" Laird was getting a lot bigger. But I was getting bigger too.

My grandmother came to stay with us for a few weeks and I heard other things. "Girls don't slam doors like that." "Girls keep their knees together when they sit down." And worse still, when I asked some questions, "That's none of girls' business." I continued to slam the doors and sit as awkwardly as possible, thinking that by such measures I kept myself free.

When spring came, the horses were let out in the barnyard. Mack stood against the barn wall trying to scratch his neck and haunches, but Flora trotted up and down and reared at the fences, clattering her hooves against the rails. Snow drifts dwindled quickly, revealing the hard grey and brown earth, the familiar rise and fall of the ground, plain and bare after the fantastic landscape of winter. There was a great feeling of opening-out, of release. We just wore rubbers now, over our shoes; our feet felt ridiculously light. One Saturday we went out to the stable and found all the doors open, letting in the unaccustomed sunlight and fresh air. Henry was there, just idling around looking at his collection of calendars which were tacked up behind the stalls in a part of the stable my mother had probably never seen.

"Come to say goodbye to your old friend Mack?" Henry said. "Here, you give him a taste of oats." He poured some oats into Laird's cupped hands and Laird went to feed Mack. Mack's teeth were in bad shape. He ate very slowly, patiently shifting the oats around in his mouth, trying to find a stump of a molar to grind it on. "Poor old Mack," said Henry mournfully. "When a horse's teeth's gone, he's gone. That's about the way."

25   "Are you going to shoot him today?" I said. Mack and Flora had been in the stable so long I had almost forgotten they were going to be shot.

Henry didn't answer me. Instead he started to sing in a high, trembly, mocking-sorrowful voice, *Oh, there's no more work, for poor Uncle Ned, he's gone where the good darkies go.*[5] Mack's thick, blackish tongue worked diligently at Laird's hand. I went out before the song was ended and sat down on the gangway.

I had never seen them shoot a horse, but I knew where it was done. Last summer Laird and I had come upon a horse's entrails before they were buried. We had thought it was a big black snake, coiled up in the sun. That was around in the field that ran up beside the barn. I thought that if we went inside the barn, and found a wide crack or knothole to look through we would be able to see them do it. It was not something I wanted to see; just the same, if a thing really happened, it was better to see it, and know.

My father came down from the house, carrying the gun.

"What are you doing here?" he said.

"Nothing."   30

"Go on up and play around the house."

He sent Laird out of the stable. I said to Laird, "Do you want to see them shoot Mack?" and without waiting for an answer led him around to the front door of the barn, opened it carefully, and went in. "Be quiet or they'll hear us," I said. We could hear Henry and my father talking in the stable, then the heavy, shuffling steps of Mack being backed out of his stall.

In the loft it was cold and dark. Thin, crisscrossed beams of sunlight fell through the cracks. The hay was low. It was a rolling country, hills and hollows, slipping under our feet. About four feet up was a beam going around the walls. We piled hay up in one corner and I boosted Laird up and hoisted myself. The beam was not very wide; we crept along it with our hands flat on the barn walls. There were plenty of knotholes, and I found one that gave me the view I wanted— a corner of the barnyard, the gate, part of the field. Laird did not have a knothole and began to complain.

I showed him a widened crack between two boards. "Be quiet and wait. If they hear you you'll get us in trouble."

My father came in sight carrying the gun. Henry was leading Mack by the   35 halter. He dropped it and took out his cigarette papers and tobacco; he rolled cigarettes for my father and himself. While this was going on Mack nosed around in the old, dead grass along the fence. Then my father opened the gate and they took Mack through. Henry led Mack way from the path to a patch of ground and they talked together, not loud enough for us to hear. Mack again began searching for a mouthful of fresh grass, which was not to be found. My father walked away in a straight line, and stopped short at a distance which seemed to suit him. Henry was walking away from Mack too, but sideways, still negligently holding on to the halter. My father raised the gun and Mack looked up as if he had noticed something and my father shot him.

Mack did not collapse at once but swayed, lurched sideways and fell, first on his side; then he rolled over on his back and, amazingly, kicked his legs for a few seconds in the air. At this Henry laughed, as if Mack had done a trick for him. Laird, who had drawn a long, groaning breath of surprise when the shot was fired, said out loud, "He's not dead." And it seemed to me it might be true. But his legs

---

5. Lines from the Stephen Foster song "Old Uncle Ned."

stopped, he rolled on his side again, his muscles quivered and sank. The two men walked over and looked at him in a businesslike way; they bent down and examined his forehead where the bullet had gone in, and now I saw his blood on the brown grass.

"Now they just skin him and cut him up," I said. "Let's go." My legs were a little shaky and I jumped gratefully down into the hay. "Now you've seen how they shoot a horse," I said in a congratulatory way, as if I had seen it many times before. "Let's see if any barn cat's had kittens in the hay." Laird jumped. He seemed young and obedient again. Suddenly I remembered how, when he was little, I had brought him into the barn and told him to climb the ladder to the top beam. That was in the spring, too, when the hay was low. I had done it out of a need for excitement, a desire for something to happen so that I could tell about it. He was wearing a little bulky brown and white checked coat, made down from one of mine. He went all the way up, just as I told him, and sat down on the top beam with the hay far below him on one side, and the barn floor and some old machinery on the other. Then I ran screaming to my father, "Laird's up on the top beam!" My father came, my mother came, my father went up the ladder talking very quietly and brought Laird down under his arm, at which my mother leaned against the ladder and began to cry. They said to me, "Why weren't you watching him?" but nobody ever knew the truth. Laird did not know enough to tell. But whenever I saw the brown and white checked coat hanging in the closet, or at the bottom of the rag bag, which was where it ended up, I felt a weight in my stomach, the sadness of unexorcised guilt.

I looked at Laird who did not even remember this, and I did not like the look on this thin, winter-pale face. His expression was not frightened or upset, but remote, concentrating. "Listen," I said, in an unusually bright and friendly voice, "you aren't going to tell, are you?"

"No," he said absently.

40   "Promise."

"Promise," he said. I grabbed the hand behind his back to make sure he was not crossing his fingers. Even so, he might have a nightmare; it might come out that way. I decided I had better work hard to get all thoughts of what he had seen out of his mind—which, it seemed to me, could not hold very many things at a time. I got some money I had saved and that afternoon we went into Jubilee and saw a show, with Judy Canova,[6] at which we both laughed a great deal. After that I thought it would be all right.

Two weeks later I knew they were going to shoot Flora. I knew from the night before, when I heard my mother ask if the hay was holding out all right, and my father said, "Well, after to-morrow there'll just be the cow, and we should be able to put her out to grass in another week." So I knew it was Flora's turn in the morning.

This time I didn't think of watching it. That was something to see just one time. I had not thought about it very often since, but sometimes when I was busy, working at school, or standing in front of the mirror combing my hair and won-

6. American comedian (1913–1983) best known for her yodeling in hillbilly movies of the 1940s.

dering if I would be pretty when I grew up, the whole scene would flash into my mind: I would see the easy, practised way my father raised the gun, and hear Henry laughing when Mack kicked his legs in the air. I did not have any great feeling of horror and opposition, such as a city child might have had; I was too used to seeing the death of animals as a necessity by which we lived. Yet I felt a little ashamed, and there was a new wariness, a sense of holding-off, in my attitude to my father and his work.

It was a fine day, and we were going around the yard picking up tree branches that had been torn off in winter storms. This was something we had been told to do, and also we wanted to use them to make a teepee. We heard Flora whinny, and then my father's voice and Henry's shouting, and we ran down to the barnyard to see what was going on.

The stable door was open. Henry had just brought Flora out, and she had   45
broken away from him. She was running free in the barnyard, from one end to the other. We climbed up on the fence. It was exciting to see her running, whinnying, going up on her hind legs, prancing and threatening like a horse in a Western movie, an unbroken ranch horse, though she was just an old driver, an old sorrel mare. My father and Henry ran after her and tried to grab the dangling halter. They tried to work her into a corner, and they had almost succeeded when she made a run between them, wild-eyed, and disappeared around the corner of the barn. We heard the rails clatter down as she got over the fence, and Henry yelled, "She's into the field now!"

That meant she was in the long L-shaped field that ran up by the house. If she got around the center, heading towards the lane, the gate was open; the truck had been driven into the field this morning. My father shouted to me, because I was on the other side of the fence, nearest the lane, "Go shut the gate!"

I could run very fast. I ran across the garden, past the tree where our swing was hung, and jumped across a ditch into the lane. There was the open gate. She had not got out, I could not see her up on the road; she must have run to the other end of the field. The gate was heavy. I lifted it out of the gravel and carried it across the roadway. I had it half-way across when she came in sight, galloping straight towards me. There was just time to get the chain on. Laird came scrambling through the ditch to help me.

Instead of shutting the gate, I opened it as wide as I could. I did not make any decision to do this, it was just what I did. Flora never slowed down; she galloped straight past me, and Laird jumped up and down, yelling, "Shut it, shut it!" even after it was too late. My father and Henry appeared in the field a moment too late to see what I had done. They only saw Flora heading for the township road. They would think I had not got there in time.

They did not waste any time asking about it. They went back to the barn and got the gun and the knives they used, and put these in the truck; then they turned the truck around and came bouncing up the field toward us. Laird called to them, "Let me go too, let me go too!" and Henry stopped the truck and they took him in. I shut the gate after they were all gone.

I supposed Laird would tell. I wondered what would happen to me. I had never   50
disobeyed my father before, and I could not understand why I had done it. Flora

would not really get away. They would catch up with her in the truck. Or if they did not catch her this morning somebody would see her and telephone us this afternoon or tomorrow. There was no wild country here for her to run to, only farms. What was more, my father had paid for her, we needed the meat to feed the foxes, we needed the foxes to make our living. All I had done was make more work for my father who worked hard enough already. And when my father found out about it he was not going to trust me any more; he would know that I was not entirely on his side. I was on Flora's side, and that made me no use to anybody, not even to her. Just the same, I did not regret it; when she came running at me and I held the gate open, that was the only thing I could do.

I went back to the house, and my mother said, "What's all the commotion?" I told her that Flora had kicked down the fence and got away. "Your poor father," she said, "now he'll have to go chasing over the countryside. Well, there isn't any use planning dinner before one." She put up the ironing board. I wanted to tell her, but thought better of it and went upstairs and sat on my bed.

Lately I had been trying to make my part of the room fancy, spreading the bed with old lace curtains, and fixing myself a dressing-table with some leftovers of cretonne for a skirt. I planned to put up some kind of barricade between my bed and Laird's, to keep my section separate from his. In the sunlight, the lace curtains were just dusty rags. We did not sing at night any more. One night when I was singing Laird said, "You sound silly," and I went right on but the next night I did not start. There was not so much need to anyway, we were no longer afraid. We knew it was just old furniture over there, old jumble and confusion. We did not keep to the rules. I still stayed awake after Laird was asleep and told myself stories, but even in these stories something different was happening, mysterious alterations took place. A story might start off in the old way, with a spectacular danger, a fire or wild animals, and for a while I might rescue people; then things would change around, and instead, somebody would be rescuing me. It might be a boy from our class at school, or even Mr. Campbell, our teacher, who tickled girls under the arms. And at this point the story concerned itself at great length with what I looked like—how long my hair was, and what kind of dress I had on; by the time I had these details worked out the real excitement of the story was lost.

It was later than one o'clock when the truck came back. The tarpaulin was over the back, which meant there was meat in it. My mother had to heat dinner up all over again. Henry and my father had changed from their bloody overalls into ordinary working overalls in the barn, and they washed their arms and necks and faces at the sink, and splashed water on their hair and combed it. Laird lifted his arm to show off a streak of blood. "We shot old Flora," he said, "and cut her up in fifty pieces."

"Well I don't want to hear about it," my mother said. "And don't come to my table like that."

55   My father made him go and wash the blood off.

We sat down and my father said grace and Henry pasted his chewing-gum on the end of his fork, the way he always did; when he took it off he would have us admire the pattern. We began to pass the bowls of steaming, overcooked vegetables. Laird looked across the table at me and said proudly, distinctly, "Anyway it was her fault Flora got away."

"What?" my father said.

"She could of shut the gate and she didn't. She just open' it up and Flora run out."

"Is that right?" my father said.

Everybody at the table was looking at me. I nodded, swallowing food with great difficulty. To my shame, tears flooded my eyes.

My father made a curt sound of disgust. "What did you do that for?"

I did not answer. I put down my fork and waited to be sent from the table, still not looking up.

But this did not happen. For some time nobody said anything, then Laird said matter-of-factly, "She's crying."

"Never mind," my father said. He spoke with resignation, even good humour, the words which absolved and dismissed me for good. "She's only a girl," he said.

I didn't protest that, even in my heart. Maybe it was true.

1968

JAMES JOYCE

Araby

North Richmond Street, being blind,[1] was a quiet street except at the hour when the Christian Brothers' School set the boys free. An uninhabited house of two storeys stood at the blind end, detached from its neighbours in a square ground. The other houses of the street, conscious of decent lives within them, gazed at one another with brown imperturbable faces.

The former tenant of our house, a priest, had died in the back drawing-room. Air, musty from having been long enclosed, hung in all the rooms, and the waste room behind the kitchen was littered with old useless papers. Among these I found a few paper-covered books, the pages of which were curled and damp: *The Abbot*, by Walter Scott, *The Devout Communicant* and *The Memoirs of Vidocq*.[2] I liked the last best because its leaves were yellow. The wild garden behind the house contained a central apple tree and a few straggling bushes, under one of which I found the late tenant's rusty bicycle-pump. He had been a very charitable

---

1. Dead-end street.   2. The "memoirs" were probably *not* written by François Vidocq (1775–1857), a French criminal who became chief of detectives and who died poor and disgraced for his part in a crime that he solved; the 1820 novel by Sir Walter Scott (1771–1834) is a romance about the Catholic Mary, Queen of Scots (1542–1587), who was beheaded; *The Devout Communicant: or Pious Mediations and Aspirations for the Three Days Before and Three Days After Receiving the Holy Eucharist* (1813) is a Catholic religious tract.

priest; in his will he had left all his money to institutions and the furniture of his house to his sister.

When the short days of winter came, dusk fell before we had well eaten our dinners. When we met in the street the houses had grown sombre. The space of sky above us was the colour of ever-changing violet and towards it the lamps of the street lifted their feeble lanterns. The cold air stung us and we played till our bodies glowed. Our shouts echoed in the silent street. The career of our play brought us through the dark muddy lanes behind the houses, where we ran the gauntlet of the rough tribes from the cottages, to the back doors of the dark dripping gardens where odours arose from the ashpits,[3] to the dark odorous stables where a coachman smoothed and combed the horse or shook music from the buckled harness. When we returned to the street, light from the kitchen windows had filled the areas. If my uncle was seen turning the corner, we hid in the shadow until we had seen him safely housed. Or if Mangan's sister came out on the doorstep to call her brother in to his tea, we watched her from our shadow peer up and down the street. We waited to see whether she would remain or go in and, if she remained, we left our shadow and walked up to Mangan's steps resignedly. She was waiting for us, her figure defined by the light from the half-opened door. Her brother always teased her before he obeyed, and I stood by the railings looking at her. Her dress swung as she moved her body, and the soft rope of her hair tossed from side to side.

Every morning I lay on the floor in the front parlour watching her door. The blind was pulled down to within an inch of the sash so that I could not be seen. When she came out on the doorstep my heart leaped. I ran to the hall, seized my books and followed her. I kept her brown figure always in my eye and, when we came near the point at which our ways diverged, I quickened my pace and passed her. This happened morning after morning. I had never spoken to her, except for a few casual words, and yet her name was like a summons to all my foolish blood.

5   Her image accompanied me even in places the most hostile to romance. On Saturday evenings when my aunt went marketing I had to go to carry some of the parcels. We walked through the flaring streets, jostled by drunken men and bargaining women, amid the curses of labourers, the shrill litanies of shop-boys who stood on guard by the barrels of pigs' cheeks, the nasal chanting of street-singers, who sang a *come-all-you* about O'Donovan Rossa,[4] or a ballad about the troubles in our native land. These noises converged in a single sensation of life for me: I imagined that I bore my chalice safely through a throng of foes. Her name sprang to my lips at moments in strange prayers and praises which I myself did not understand. My eyes were often full of tears (I could not tell why) and at times a flood from my heart seemed to pour itself out into my bosom. I thought little of the future. I did not know whether I would ever speak to her or not or, if I spoke to her, how I would tell her of my confused adoration. But my body was like a harp and her words and gestures were like fingers running upon the wires.

3. Where fireplace ashes were dumped.   4. Jeremiah O'Donovan (1831–1915) was a militant Irish nationalist who fought on despite terms in prison and banishment. *Come-all-you:* A song, of which there were many, that began "Come, all you Irishmen."

One evening I went into the back drawing-room in which the priest had died. It was a dark rainy evening and there was no sound in the house. Through one of the broken panes I heard the rain impinge upon the earth, the fine incessant needles of water playing in the sodden beds. Some distant lamp or lighted window gleamed below me. I was thankful that I could see so little. All my senses seemed to desire to veil themselves and, feeling that I was about to slip from them, I pressed the palms of my hands together until they trembled, murmuring: *"O love! O love!"* many times.

At last she spoke to me. When she addressed the first words to me I was so confused that I did not know what to answer. She asked me was I going to *Araby*.[5] I forgot whether I answered yes or no. It would be a splendid bazaar, she said; she would love to go.

"And why can't you?" I asked.

While she spoke she turned a silver bracelet round and round her wrist. She could not go, she said, because there would be a retreat that week in her convent. Her brother and two other boys were fighting for their caps and I was alone at the railings. She held one of the spikes, bowing her head towards me. The light from the lamp opposite our door caught the white curve of her neck, lit up her hair that rested there and, falling, lit up the hand upon the railing. It fell over one side of her dress and caught the white border of a petticoat, just visible as she stood at ease.

"It's well for you," she said.

"If I go," I said, "I will bring you something."

What innumerable follies laid waste my waking and sleeping thoughts after that evening! I wished to annihilate the tedious intervening days. I chafed against the work of school. At night in my bedroom and by day in the classroom her image came between me and the page I strove to read. The syllables of the word *Araby* were called to me through the silence in which my soul luxuriated and cast an Eastern enchantment over me. I asked for leave to go to the bazaar on Saturday night. My aunt was surprised and hoped it was not some Freemason[6] affair. I answered few questions in class. I watched my master's face pass from amiability to sternness; he hoped I was not beginning to idle. I could not call my wandering thoughts together. I had hardly any patience with the serious work of life which, now that it stood between me and my desire, seemed to me child's play, ugly monotonous child's play.

On Saturday morning I reminded my uncle that I wished to go to the bazaar in the evening. He was fussing at the hallstand, looking for the hat-brush, and answered me curtly:

"Yes, boy, I know."

As he was in the hall I could not go into the front parlour and lie at the window. I left the house in bad humour and walked slowly towards the school. The air was pitilessly raw and already my heart misgave me.

When I came home to dinner my uncle had not yet been home. Still it was

5. A bazaar billed as a "Grand Oriental Fête," Dublin, May 1894. 6. Freemasons—members of a major, secretive, and highly ritualistic fraternal organization—were considered enemies of the Catholics.

early. I sat staring at the clock for some time and, when its ticking began to irritate me, I left the room. I mounted the staircase and gained the upper part of the house. The high, cold, empty, gloomy rooms liberated me and I went from room to room singing. From the front window I saw my companions playing below in the street. Their cries reached me weakened and indistinct and, leaning my forehead against the cool glass, I looked over at the dark house where she lived. I may have stood there for an hour, seeing nothing but a brown-clad figure cast by my imagination, touched discreetly by the lamplight at the curved neck, at the hand upon the railings and at the border below the dress.

When I came downstairs again I found Mrs. Mercer sitting at the fire. She was an old, garrulous woman, a pawnbroker's widow, who collected used stamps for some pious purpose. I had to endure the gossip of the tea-table. The meal was prolonged beyond an hour and still my uncle did not come. Mrs. Mercer stood up to go: she was sorry she couldn't wait any longer, but it was after eight o'clock and she did not like to be out late, as the night air was bad for her. When she had gone I began to walk up and down the room, clenching my fists. My aunt said:

"I'm afraid you may put off your bazaar for this night of Our Lord."

At nine o'clock I heard my uncle's latchkey in the hall door. I heard him talking to himself and heard the hallstand rocking when it had received the weight of his overcoat. I could interpret these signs. When he was midway through his dinner I asked him to give me the money to go to the bazaar. He had forgotten.

20   "The people are in bed and after their first sleep now," he said.

I did not smile. My aunt said to him energetically:

"Can't you give him the money and let him go? You've kept him late enough as it is."

My uncle said he was very sorry he had forgotten. He said he believed in the old saying: "All work and no play makes Jack a dull boy." He asked me where I was going and, when I had told him a second time, he asked me did I know *The Arab's Farewell to his Steed*.[7] When I left the kitchen he was about to recite the opening lines of the piece to my aunt.

I held a florin[8] tightly in my hand as I strode down Buckingham Street towards the station. The sight of the streets thronged with buyers and glaring with gas recalled to me the purpose of my journey. I took my seat in a third-class carriage of a deserted train. After an intolerable delay the train moved out of the station slowly. It crept onward among ruinous houses and over the twinkling river. At Westland Row Station a crowd of people pressed to the carriage doors; but the porters moved them back, saying that it was a special train for the bazaar. I remained alone in the bare carriage. In a few minutes the train drew up beside an improvised wooden platform. I passed out on to the road and saw by the lighted dial of a clock that it was ten minutes to ten. In front of me was a large building which displayed the magical name.

25   I could not find any sixpenny entrance and, fearing that the bazaar would be closed, I passed in quickly through a turnstile, handing a shilling to a weary-

---

7. Or *The Arab's Farewell to His Horse*, a sentimental nineteenth-century poem by Caroline Norton. The speaker has sold the horse.   8. Two-shilling piece; thus four times the "sixpenny entrance" fee.

looking man. I found myself in a big hall girdled at half its height by a gallery. Nearly all the stalls were closed and the greater part of the hall was in darkness. I recognized a silence like that which pervades a church after a service. I walked into the centre of the bazaar timidly. A few people were gathered about the stalls which were still open. Before a curtain, over which the words *Café Chantant*[9] were written in coloured lamps, two men were counting money on a salver. I listened to the fall of the coins.

Remembering with difficulty why I had come I went over to one of the stalls and examined porcelain vases and flowered tea-sets. At the door of the stall a young lady was talking and laughing with two young gentlemen. I remarked their English accents and listened vaguely to their conversation.

"O, I never said such a thing!"

"O, but you did!"

"O, but I didn't!"

"Didn't she say that?"   30

"Yes. I heard her."

"O, there's a . . . fib!"

Observing me, the young lady came over and asked me did I wish to buy anything. The tone of her voice was not encouraging; she seemed to have spoken to me out of a sense of duty. I looked humbly at the great jars that stood like eastern guards at either side of the dark entrance to the stall and murmured:

"No, thank you."

The young lady changed the position of one of the vases and went back to the   35
two young men. They began to talk of the same subject. Once or twice the young lady glanced at me over her shoulder.

I lingered before her stall, though I knew my stay was useless, to make my interest in her wares seem the more real. Then I turned away slowly and walked down the middle of the bazaar. I allowed the two pennies to fall against the sixpence in my pocket. I heard a voice call from one end of the gallery that the light was out. The upper part of the hall was now completely dark.

Gazing up into the darkness I saw myself as a creature driven and derided by vanity; and my eyes burned with anguish and anger.

                                                                                                                  1914

QUESTIONS

1. What is the nature of the initiation in "Gorilla, My Love"? in "Boys and Girls"? How are the two initiation experiences similar? How do they differ?

2. The phrase "only a girl" appears twice in Alice Munro's story. How do the contexts differ? How do the implications of the phrase differ at each appearance (that is, what does it mean or suggest each time)?

3. In paragraph 5 of "Araby," the protagonist-narrator describes himself as carrying with him

---

9. Café with music.

the image of Mangan's sister "even in places the most hostile to romance." Why might "romance" be a particularly appropriate word, or what various meanings of the term "romance" might come into play here? What is the significance of the narrator's vision of himself as bearing a "chalice safely through a throng of foes" (same paragraph)? How might this image relate to other direct and indirect references to religion found elsewhere in the story? How do religious terms and images help to shape our sense of the nature and significance of the initiation depicted?

WRITING SUGGESTIONS

1. Using "Gorilla, My Love" as a model, write a personal narrative in which you describe an initiation (real or fictional) in your own life.
2. The initiation in "Boys and Girls" hinges upon its protagonists' discoveries about what it means to be a girl; to what extent might the initiation in "Araby" take the shape it does because of the protagonist's gender? In a few paragraphs discuss why and how it does and doesn't matter that the protagonist of "Araby" is male, or write an essay comparing these two stories and considering the role that gender plays in shaping each protagonist's initiation experience.
3. Identify a group of related words or images that recurs in one of the stories in this chapter. Relate the pattern to the story's theme, citing evidence from the story.

10

FORM AS CONTEXT: THE SHORT SHORT STORY

The short short story, a story of about two thousand words or fewer, has been around for a long time, but has suddenly become popular. There have been many attempts to explain this phenomenon, explanations ranging from the shrinking attention span "caused" by television, to the hurried, fragmented nature of contemporary life, to our disenchantment with lengthy explanations of behavior by psychologists, politicians, and novelists. There have also been attempts to define the form generically. Its boundaries have been those of the anecdote, the vignette, the parable, the poem, the short story proper; yet all these borders have been contested.

Length is not just an aspect of form, however; it also contributes significantly to a story's effect and to your consequent response. You rarely read a full-length novel in a single sitting, so not only is there a momentary recapitulation in your mind as you pick up the narrative again—something like the excerpts from the previous episode in a television miniseries—but you have lived another period of your life outside the narrative. When you sit down to read again you are not exactly the same repository of experiences as when you put the book down, and not only are you at a different point in your life, but your mood may have drastically changed. The novel has advantages, however, in its duration and in the times of your readings and departures: you are likely to recall the characters, scenes, and incidents, in one order or another, in more or less accurate detail, from time to time during the period you are away from the text. The novel thereby gets a texture, layers of memories and views from different angles, that is rarely obtained by a short story, and never by a short short story. You usually read a short story in a single sitting, and though it has an immediate and concentrated impact and you pause a moment and savor its emotional and intellectual effect, you can rarely recall all its detail; yet rarely, too, do you immediately begin at the beginning and read it through once again. The effect of the short short story is stronger; even if the aftereffect is of the same duration (and it often is longer, because its economy has left so much out that you have to supply a great deal yourself), it is stronger compared to the length of time of your reading. You can remember almost all, if not all, the details. Yet, if you are strongly impressed, you may read the story again immediately. So novels, short stories, and short short stories differ not merely in formal length but in the way we read and respond to them.

Although you may be able to read four or five short short stories in the time it takes to read one short story, you will probably find the experience overwhelming rather than satisfying. The effects of short short stories are so strong and so concentrated that reading several is likely to overcharge your response system. You might take a break after each story in this chapter, using the time to rehearse the story in your mind, to recall its details and its language, and to fill in the particulars that the story's conciseness can only imply. And when one of these stories affects you, you may want to write an account of your emotive and intellectual responses, what you recall, and what you choose to supply.

The stories in this chapter represent some of the variety of the short short form. (Other stories in the book that fit or approach the definition are "The Zebra Storyteller," "Happy Endings," "The Cask of Amontillado," "A Conversation with My Father," and "Hills Like White Elephants.") Kate Chopin's "Story of an Hour" ends with the ironic reversal that perhaps comes from Maupassant, though Chopin's story, as the title indicates, takes place in only an hour of fictional time. In contrast, Gabriel Garcia Márquez's "Very Old man with Enormous Wings" covers years, defying any unity or constriction of time the brevity of the narrative might lead you to expect. Jamaica Kincaid's "Girl" does not seem so much to span time as to compact it. The story is largely the words of mother to daughter (with two brief responses by the daughter). The near-monologue does not take place at one moment, however; rather, we can infer—in part from the repetition, in part from memories of our own childhood—that its instructions were repeated time and time again over the years the girl was growing up. William Carlos Williams's "The Use of Force" could also be titled "The Story of an Hour," whereas Ursula K. Le Guin's "She Unnames Them," reimagining the Creation, employs a greater mythic span than does Garcia Márquez's story. The short short story can be just the right form to achieve *either* a great concentration *or* a vast expansion of time.

In addition to a variety of temporal scales, these short short stories exhibit widely different treatments of physical space and realistic detail. Though Mrs. Mallard's catastrophe in "The Story of an Hour" may seem improbable, it is psychologically and even medically realistic, and Chopin's story takes place as much in an everyday, familiar world as do the struggles of doctor and patient in "The Use of Force," or the preparation for a day at work in Nicholson Baker's "Pants on Fire." As in many modern and contemporary stories, the laws of physics apply here. But other stories aim more at the heightened effects of poetry or the imaginative freedom of fantasy. "A Very Old Man with Enormous Wings" represents the many short short tales that are fantasies—written in a literary mode involving the consciously unreal—about places, societies, or beings that never existed, do not exist, or do not yet exist, or with qualities that are beyond or counter to the ordinary or commonsensical. Often such fantasies tease us with the possibilities of allegory but are more than likely symbolic—untranslatable into "messages" or ordinary "meaning." In "She Unnames Them," Le Guin humorously adopts the point of view of Eve in the Garden of Eden and thus challenges *man's* domination of the world through the power of language. Her serious argument nevertheless gains a poetic magic similar to that of Yasunari Kawabata's meticulously beautiful descriptions of children's lanterns in "The Grasshopper and the Bell Cricket." Is Kawabata's text a novel of fewer than fifteen hundred words, or is it an expanded haiku? All you have learned of history and structure, focus and voice, characterization, symbol, and theme are needed to articulate the explicit *and* subtle effects here and in the other superb short short stories.

KATE CHOPIN

The Story of an Hour

Knowing that Mrs. Mallard was afflicted with a heart trouble, great care was taken to break to her as gently as possible the news of her husband's death.

It was her sister Josephine who told her, in broken sentences; veiled hints that revealed in half concealing. Her husband's friend Richards was there, too, near her. It was he who had been in the newspaper office when intelligence of the railroad disaster was received, with Brently Mallard's name leading the list of "killed." He had only taken the time to assure himself of its truth by a second telegram, and had hastened to forestall any less careful, less tender friend in bearing the sad message.

She did not hear the story as many women have heard the same, with a paralyzed inability to accept its significance. She wept at once, with sudden, wild abandonment, in her sister's arms. When the storm of grief had spent itself she went away to her room alone. She would have no one follow her.

There stood, facing the open window, a comfortable, roomy armchair. Into this she sank, pressed down by a physical exhaustion that haunted her body and seemed to reach into her soul.

She could see in the open square before her house the tops of trees that were all aquiver with the new spring life. The delicious breath of rain was in the air. In the street below a peddler was crying his wares. The notes of a distant song which some one was singing reached her faintly, and countless sparrows were twittering in the eaves.   5

There were patches of blue sky showing here and there through the clouds that had met and piled one above the other in the west facing her window.

She sat with her head thrown back upon the cushion of the chair, quite motionless, except when a sob came up into her throat and shook her, as a child who has cried itself to sleep continues to sob in its dreams.

She was young, with a fair, calm face, whose lines bespoke repression and even a certain strength. But now there was a dull stare in her eyes, whose gaze was fixed away off yonder on one of those patches of blue sky. It was not a glance of reflection, but rather indicated a suspension of intelligent thought.

There was something coming to her and she was waiting for it, fearfully. What was it? She did not know; it was too subtle and elusive to name. But she felt it, creeping out of the sky, reaching toward her through the sounds, the scents, the color that filled the air.

Now her bosom rose and fell tumultuously. She was beginning to recognize   10
this thing that was approaching to possess her, and she was striving to beat it back with her will—as powerless as her two white slender hands would have been.

When she abandoned herself a little whispered word escaped her slightly parted lips. She said it over and over under her breath: "free, free, free!" The vacant stare and the look of terror that had followed it went from her eyes.

They stayed keen and bright. Her pulses beat fast, and the coursing blood warmed and relaxed every inch of her body.

She did not stop to ask if it were or were not a monstrous joy that held her. A clear and exalted perception enabled her to dismiss the suggestion as trivial.

She knew that she would weep again when she saw the kind, tender hands folded in death; the face that had never looked save with love upon her, fixed and gray and dead. But she saw beyond that bitter moment a long procession of years to come that would belong to her absolutely. And she opened and spread her arms out to them in welcome.

There would be no one to live for her during those coming years; she would live for herself. There would be no powerful will bending hers in that blind persistence with which men and women believe they have a right to impose a private will upon a fellow-creature. A kind intention or a cruel intention made the act seem no less a crime as she looked upon it in that brief moment of illumination.

15   And yet she had loved him—sometimes. Often she had not. What did it matter! What could love, the unsolved mystery, count for in face of this possession of self-assertion which she suddenly recognized as the strongest impulse of her being!

"Free! Body and soul free!" she kept whispering.

Josephine was kneeling before the closed door with her lips to the keyhole, imploring for admission. "Louise, open the door! I beg; open the door—you will make yourself ill. What are you doing, Louise? For heaven's sake open the door."

"Go away. I am not making myself ill." No; she was drinking in a very elixir of life through that open window.

Her fancy was running riot along those days ahead of her. Spring days, and summer days, and all sorts of days that would be her own. She breathed a quick prayer that life might be long. It was only yesterday she had thought with a shudder that life might be long.

20   She arose at length and opened the door to her sister's importunities. There was a feverish triumph in her eyes, and she carried herself unwittingly like a goddess of Victory. She clasped her sister's waist, and together they descended the stairs. Richards stood waiting for them at the bottom.

Some one was opening the front door with a latchkey. It was Brently Mallard who entered, a little travel-stained, composedly carrying his grip-sack and umbrella. He had been far from the scene of accident, and did not even know there had been one. He stood amazed at Josephine's piercing cry; at Richards' quick motion to screen him from the view of his wife.

But Richards was too late.

When the doctors came they said she had died of heart disease—of joy that kills.

                                                                            1891

GABRIEL GARCÍA MÁRQUEZ

A Very Old Man with Enormous Wings[1]

A Tale for Children

On the third day of rain they had killed so many crabs inside the house that Pelayo had to cross his drenched courtyard and throw them into the sea, because the newborn child had a temperature all night and they thought it was due to the stench. The world had been sad since Tuesday. Sea and sky were a single ash-gray thing and the sands of the beach, which on March nights glimmered like powdered light, had become a stew of mud and rotten shellfish. The light was so weak at noon that when Pelayo was coming back to the house after throwing away the crabs, it was hard for him to see what it was that was moving and groaning in the rear of the courtyard. He had to go very close to see that it was an old man, a very old man, lying face down in the mud, who, in spite of his tremendous efforts, couldn't get up, impeded by his enormous wings.

Frightened by that nightmare, Pelayo ran to get Elisenda, his wife, who was putting compresses on the sick child, and he took her to the rear of the courtyard. They both looked at the fallen body with mute stupor. He was dressed like a ragpicker. There were only a few faded hairs left on his bald skull and very few teeth in his mouth, and his pitiful condition of a drenched great-grandfather had taken away any sense of grandeur he might have had. His huge buzzard wings, dirty and half-plucked, were forever entangled in the mud. They looked at him so long and so closely that Pelayo and Elisenda very soon overcame their surprise and in the end found him familiar. Then they dared speak to him, and he answered in an incomprehensible dialect with a strong sailor's voice. That was how they skipped over the inconvenience of the wings and quite intelligently concluded that he was a lonely castaway from some foreign ship wrecked by the storm. And yet, they called in a neighbor woman who knew everything about life and death to see him, and all she needed was one look to show them their mistake.

"He's an angel," she told them. "He must have been coming for the child, but the poor fellow is so old that the rain knocked him down."

On the following day everyone knew that a flesh-and-blood angel was held captive in Pelayo's house. Against the judgment of the wise neighbor woman, for whom angels in those times were the fugitive survivors of a celestial conspiracy, they did not have the heart to club him to death. Pelayo watched over him all afternoon from the kitchen, armed with his bailiff's club, and before going to bed he dragged him out of the mud and locked him up with the hens in the wire chicken coop. In the middle of the night, when the rain stopped, Pelayo and Elisenda were still killing crabs. A short time afterward the child woke up without a fever and with a desire to eat. Then they felt magnanimous and decided to put the angel on a raft with fresh water and provisions for three days and leave him

1. Translated by Gregory Rabassa.

to his fate on the high seas. But when they went out into the courtyard with the first light of dawn, they found the whole neighborhood in front of the chicken coop having fun with the angel, without the slightest reverence, tossing him things to eat through the openings in the wire as if he weren't a supernatural creature but a circus animal.

5   Father Gonzaga arrived before seven o'clock, alarmed at the strange news. By that time onlookers less frivolous than those at dawn had already arrived and they were making all kinds of conjectures concerning the captive's future. The simplest among them thought that he should be named mayor of the world. Others of sterner mind felt that he should be promoted to the rank of five-star general in order to win all wars. Some visionaries hoped that he could be put to stud in order to implant on earth a race of winged wise men who could take charge of the universe. But Father Gonzaga, before becoming a priest, had been a robust woodcutter. Standing by the wire, he reviewed his catechism in an instant and asked them to open the door so that he could take a close look at that pitiful man who looked more like a huge decrepit hen among the fascinated chickens. He was lying in a corner drying his open wings in the sunlight among the fruit peels and breakfast leftovers that the early risers had thrown him. Alien to the impertinences of the world, he only lifted his antiquarian eyes and murmured something in his dialect when Father Gonzaga went into the chicken coop and said good morning to him in Latin. The parish priest had his first suspicion of an imposter when he saw that he did not understand the language of God or know how to greet His ministers. Then he noticed that seen close up he was much too human: he had an unbearable smell of the outdoors, the back side of his wings was strewn with parasites and his main feathers had been mistreated by terrestrial winds, and nothing about him measured up to the proud dignity of angels. Then he came out of the chicken coop and in a brief sermon warned the curious against the risks of being ingenuous. He reminded them that the devil had the bad habit of making use of carnival tricks in order to confuse the unwary. He argued that if wings were not the essential element in determining the difference between a hawk and an airplane, they were even less so in the recognition of angels. Nevertheless, he promised to write a letter to his bishop so that the latter would write to his primate so that the latter would write to the Supreme Pontiff in order to get the final verdict from the highest courts.

His prudence fell on sterile hearts. The news of the captive angel spread with such rapidity that after a few hours the courtyard had the bustle of a marketplace and they had to call in troops with fixed bayonets to disperse the mob that was about to knock the house down. Elisenda, her spine all twisted from sweeping up so much marketplace trash, then got the idea of fencing in the yard and charging five cents admission to see the angel.

The curious came from far away. A traveling carnival arrived with a flying acrobat who buzzed over the crowd several times, but no one paid any attention to him because his wings were not those of an angel but, rather, those of a sidereal bat. The most unfortunate invalids on earth came in search of health: a poor woman who since childhood had been counting her heartbeats and had run out of numbers; a Portuguese man who couldn't sleep because the noise of the stars disturbed him; a sleepwalker who got up at night to undo the things he had done while awake; and many others with less serious ailments. In the midst of that shipwreck disorder that made the earth tremble, Pelayo and Elisenda were happy with fatigue, for in less than a week they had crammed their rooms with money and the line of pilgrims waiting their turn to enter still reached beyond the horizon.

The angel was the only one who took no part in his own act. He spent his time trying to get comfortable in his borrowed nest, befuddled by the hellish heat of the oil lamps and sacramental candles that had been placed along the wire. At first they tried to make him eat some mothballs, which, according to the wisdom of the wise neighbor woman, were the food prescribed for angels. But he turned them down, just as he turned down the papal lunches[2] that the penitents brought him, and they never found out whether it was because he was an angel or because he was an old man that in the end he ate nothing but eggplant mush. His only supernatural virtue seemed to be patience. Especially during the first days, when the hens pecked at him, searching for the stellar parasites that proliferated in his wings, and the cripples pulled out feathers to touch their defective parts with, and even the most merciful threw stones at him, trying to get him to rise so they could see him standing. The only time they succeeded in arousing him was when they burned his side with an iron for branding steers, for he had been motionless for so many hours that they thought he was dead. He awoke with a start, ranting in his hermetic language and with tears in his eyes, and he flapped his wings a couple of times, which brought on a whirlwind of chicken dung and lunar dust and a gale of panic that did not seem to be of this world. Although many thought that his reaction had been one not of rage but of pain, from then on they were careful not to annoy him, because the majority understood that his passivity was not that of a hero taking his ease but that of a cataclysm in repose.

Father Gonzaga held back the crowd's frivolity with formulas of maidservant inspiration while awaiting the arrival of a final judgment on the nature of the captive. But the mail from Rome showed no sense of urgency. They spent their time finding out if the prisoner had a navel, if his dialect had any connection with Aramaic, how many times he could fit on the head of a pin, or whether he wasn't just a Norwegian with wings. Those meager letters might have come and gone until the end of time if a providential event had not put an end to the priest's tribulations.

It so happened that during those days, among so many other carnival attrac-   10
tions, there arrived in town the traveling show of the woman who had been changed into a spider for having disobeyed her parents. The admission to see her was not only less than the admission to see the angel, but people were permitted to ask her all manner of questions about her absurd state and to examine her up and down so that no one would ever doubt the truth of her horror. She was a frightful tarantula the size of a ram and with the head of a sad maiden. What was most heart-rending, however, was not her outlandish shape but the sincere affliction with which she recounted the details of her misfortune. While still practically

2. Choice, extremely expensive meals.

a child she had sneaked out of her parents' house to go to a dance, and while she was coming back through the woods after having danced all night without permission, a fearful thunderclap rent the sky in two and through the crack came the lightning bolt of brimstone that changed her into a spider. Her only nourishment came from the meatballs that charitable souls chose to toss into her mouth. A spectacle like that, full of so much human truth and with such a fearful lesson, was bound to defeat without even trying that of a haughty angel who scarcely deigned to look at mortals. Besides, the few miracles attributed to the angel showed a certain mental disorder, like the blind man who didn't recover his sight but grew three new teeth, or the paralytic who didn't get to walk but almost won the lottery, and the leper whose sores sprouted sunflowers. Those consolation miracles, which were more like mocking fun, had already ruined the angel's reputation when the woman who had been changed into a spider finally crushed him completely. That was how Father Gonzaga was cured forever of his insomnia and Pelayo's courtyard went back to being as empty as during the time it had rained for three days and crabs walked through the bedrooms.

The owners of the house had no reason to lament. With the money they saved they built a two-story mansion with balconies and gardens and high netting so that crabs wouldn't get in during the winter, and with iron bars on the windows so that angels wouldn't get in. Pelayo also set up a rabbit warren close to town and gave up his job as bailiff for good, and Elisenda bought some satin pumps with high heels and many dresses of iridescent silk, the kind worn on Sunday by the most desirable women in those times. The chicken coop was the only thing that didn't receive any attention. If they washed it down with creolin[3] and burned tears of myrrh inside it every so often, it was not in homage to the angel but to drive away the dungheap stench that still hung everywhere like a ghost and was turning the new house into an old one. At first, when the child learned to walk, they were careful that he not get too close to the chicken coop. But then they began to lose their fears and got used to the smell, and before the child got his second teeth he'd gone inside the chicken coop to play, where the wires were falling apart. The angel was no less standoffish with him than with other mortals, but he tolerated the most ingenious infamies with the patience of a dog who had no illusions. They both came down with chicken pox at the same time. The doctor who took care of the child couldn't resist the temptation to listen to the angel's heart, and he found so much whistling in the heart and so many sounds in his kidneys that it seemed impossible for him to be alive. What surprised him most, however, was the logic of his wings. They seemed so natural on that completely human organism that he couldn't understand why other men didn't have them too.

When the child began school it had been some time since the sun and rain had caused the collapse of the chicken coop. The angel went dragging himself about here and there like a stray dying man. They would drive him out of the bedroom with a broom and a moment later find him in the kitchen. He seemed to be in so many places at the same time that they grew to think that he'd been duplicated, that he was reproducing himself all through the house, and the exas-

---

3. A disinfectant.

perated and unhinged Elisenda shouted that it was awful living in that hell full of angels. He could scarcely eat and his antiquarian eyes had also become so foggy that he went about bumping into posts. All he had left were the bare cannulae of his last feathers. Pelayo threw a blanket over him and extended him the charity of letting him sleep in the shed, and only then did they notice that he had a temperature at night, and was delirious with the tongue twisters of an old Norwegian. That was one of the few times they became alarmed, for they thought he was going to die and not even the wise neighbor woman had been able to tell them what to do with dead angels.

And yet he not only survived his worst winter, but seemed improved with the first sunny days. He remained motionless for several days in the farthest corner of the courtyard, where no one would see him, and at the beginning of December some large, stiff feathers began to grow on his wings, the feathers of a scarecrow, which looked more like another misfortune of decrepitude. But he must have known the reason for those changes, for he was quite careful that no one should notice them, that no one should hear the sea chanteys that he sometimes sang under the stars. One morning Elisenda was cutting some bunches of onions for lunch when a wind that seemed to come from the high seas blew into the kitchen. Then she went to the window and caught the angel in his first attempts at flight. They were so clumsy that his fingernails opened a furrow in the vegetable patch and he was on the point of knocking the shed down with the ungainly flapping that slipped on the light and couldn't get a grip on the air. But he did manage to gain altitude. Elisenda let out a sign of relief, for herself and for him, when she saw him pass over the last houses, holding himself up in some way with the risky flapping of a senile vulture. She kept watching him even when she was through cutting the onions and she kept on watching until it was no longer possible for her to see him, because then he was no longer an annoyance in her life but an imaginary dot on the horizon of the sea.

1968

JAMAICA KINCAID

Girl

Wash the white clothes on Monday and put them on the stone heap; wash the color clothes on Tuesday and put them on the clothesline to dry; don't walk barehead in the hot sun; cook pumpkin fritters in very hot sweet oil; soak your little cloths right after you take them off; when buying cotton to make yourself a nice blouse, be sure that it doesn't have gum on it, because that way it won't hold up well after a wash; soak salt fish overnight before you cook it; is it true that you sing benna[1] in Sunday school?; always eat your food in such a way that

1. Sing popular music, calypso.

it won't turn someone else's stomach; on Sundays try to walk like a lady and not like the slut you are so bent on becoming; don't sing benna in Sunday school; you mustn't speak to wharf-rat boys, not even to give directions; don't eat fruits on the street—flies will follow you; *but I don't sing benna on Sundays at all and never in Sunday school;* this is how to sew on a button; this is how to make a buttonhole for the button you have just sewed on; this is how to hem a dress when you see the hem coming down and so to prevent yourself from looking like the slut I know you are so bent on becoming; this is how you iron your father's khaki shirt so that it doesn't have a crease; this is how you iron your father's khaki pants so that they don't have a crease; this is how you grow okra—far from the house, because okra tree harbors red ants; when you are growing dasheen, make sure it gets plenty of water or else it makes your throat itch when you are eating it; this is how you sweep a corner; this is how you sweep a whole house; this is how you sweep a yard; this is how you smile to someone you don't like too much; this is how you smile to someone you don't like at all; this is how you smile to someone you like completely; this is how you set a table for tea; this is how you set a table for dinner; this is how you set a table for dinner with an important guest; this is how you set a table for lunch; this is how you set a table for breakfast; this is how to behave in the presence of men who don't know you very well, and this way they won't recognize immediately the slut I have warned you against becoming; be sure to wash every day, even if it is with your own spit; don't squat down to play marbles—you are not a boy, you know; don't pick people's flowers— you might catch something; don't throw stones at blackbirds, because it might not be a blackbird at all; this is how to make a bread pudding; this is how to make doukona;[2] this is how to make pepper pot; this is how to make a good medicine for a cold; this is how to make a good medicine to throw away a child before it even becomes a child; this is how to catch a fish; this is how to throw back a fish you don't like, and that way something bad won't fall on you; this is how to bully a man; this is how a man bullies you; this is how to love a man, and if this doesn't work there are other ways, and if they don't work don't feel too bad about giving up; this is how to spit up in the air if you feel like it, and this is how to move quick so that it doesn't fall on you; this is how to make ends meet; always squeeze bread to make sure it's fresh; *but what if the baker won't let me feel the bread?;* you mean to say that after all you are really going to be the kind of woman who the baker won't let near the bread?

1983

NICHOLSON BAKER

Pants on Fire

I can remember the day that my life as an adult began. I was four months into my first year as a businessman, so I had only five shirts. Each of them could be

2. A spicy pudding, often made from plantain and wrapped in a plantain or banana leaf.

worn, at the very most, three times, except for the blue, which continued to look sharp well into the fourth wearing, as long as none of the previous wearings had been on unusually hot days. The cleaners would accept no fewer than three shirts at a time, and laundry took four days, so frequently there would be a single shirt hanging in my large, resonant closet when I came home from work.

On the morning of my adulthood, I had on my bureau an unopened brown paper parcel containing three clean shirts. I pried off the string (for it never paid to try to snap the string that early in the morning, or to fiddle with the excellent dry cleaner's knot) and let string and paper fall at my feet. When I was a boy, my mother had sometimes brought home paper parcels of thinly sliced Westphalian ham and allowed me to open them, and this first moment of shirt disclosure had something of the Westphalian experience, yet was perhaps even more pleasing because in this case I was rediscovering my old buddies—articles of clothing I'd worn and worn, now in a condition of almost unrecognizable freshness. The familiar puffy wrinkles inside the elbows and around the waist, where I had tucked and retucked the tails, were replaced by new, good kinds of semi-intentional knife-edge wrinkles here and there that only heightened the impression of ironedness, having come about either from the indiscriminate force of pressing machines (those crow's-feet on the sleeve near the cuffs) or as part of the final folding. And the shirts weren't merely folded: strips of light-blue paper held them tightly and individually to their stored state, with their arms impossibly bent behind them as if concealing a present.

I looked at the three of them—two whites and the long-running blue—and I decided I would wear my slightly older (four months old) white. Four months a businessman! When I looked closely, I was sure I could detect a slight aging of the cotton—it seemed to be taking the starch more crisply than the newer white shirt could. I snapped the blue paper strip and pulled out the shirt cardboard just as you used to pull the old kind of Polaroid film from the camera through rollers that squeezed a cool, chemical jelly over the face-down snapshot, which you saw only after the anxious ten count. The cardboard went on top of the stack of cardboards (quite a stack). I saved them partly because I had always liked drawing on the shirt cardboards saved from my father's shirts. Also, a shirt cardboard, curved into a trough, makes a nice receptacle to hold under your chin while you trim your beard—something I had been doing more frequently since starting the job. Now I held the freed shirt in the air with a little finger hooked under the collar and shook it once. It made the sound of a flag flying outside the consulate of a small, rich country. Now—was I ready to put it on?

My T-shirt, of course, was already tucked in my shorts; a few weeks into the job I had discovered that this small act of foresight made the rest of the business day much more comfortable. And my pants were on but not fastened. I *was* ready. The shirt was always colder than expected. I started work at the second button from the top, braving the minor pain in my thumb tip as I pushed that button through and heard the minuscule creaking or winching sound that its edge made in clearing the densely stitched perimeter. From there I progressed right down the central strip of buttons, did up my pants, and moved on to the cuffs. These two buttons were naturally the hardest, because you could use only one hand and the starch was always heaviest in that region, but I had gotten to a point where I could fasten them almost without thinking. You upend the right cuff button with your thumbnail and crack the starch-fused buttonhole apart over it and close your fingers hypodermically to propel it into place; then you repeat the procedure with the other cuff. Speeded up, the two symmetrical cuff-buttoning sequences would look like a Highland reel.[1]

5   The top button called me to the mirror, where I saw my chin jut up into a bulldog expression to make way for the fists at my neck. Then the tie, the belt, the shoes—all automatic subroutines.

I had my coat on when I remembered that I'd forgotten to put on antiperspirant. This was a setback. I contemplated undoing the belt, untucking the shirt, untucking the T-shirt from the shorts. Was it worth it? I was running late.

Here was where I made a discovery. An image came to me—Ingres's portrait of Napoleon.[2] Displacing my tie, I undid a single middle button. Yes, it was quite possible to get at your underarm by entering the shirt through the gap made by one undone button and then working the stick of antiperspirant up the pleural cavity between T-shirt and shirt until you were able to snag the sleevelet of the T-shirt with a finger and pull it past the seam where your shirtsleeve began, thereby exposing the area you needed to reach. I felt like Balboa or Copernicus.[3] In college I had been amazed to see women take off bras without removing their sweatshirts, by unfastening the rear bra-catch through the material, pushing one sleeve up far enough to slip off one strap, and, after a few arousing shrugs of their shoulders, pulling the whole wriggling thing nonchalantly out of the opposite sleeve. My own antiperspirant discovery had some of the topologically revelatory flavor of those bra removals.

I walked to the subway very pleased with myself. My business shoes (my one pair) made a nice granular sound on the sidewalk. The subway wasn't crowded, and I got a standing spot I liked and had room to bend to put my briefcase between my ankles. It was one of those good rides, where the motion of the train is soothing and the car temperature is pleasantly warm but not hot. The phrase "You can taste it with your eyes" came into my head; being mildly hungry, I ran with it. It was a shame that white bread had fallen into disfavor, I decided, since only white bread looks really good as toast, and only white bread looks good when cut diagonally. I remembered the strange steamy feeling of white toast at the moment you remove it from the toaster (no matter how crumby or disreputable the toaster is, the toast always comes out smooth and clean), and the many styles of buttering you can use. You can scrape lightly, keeping to the surface, or if you have cold butter you may be obliged to crush into the softer region below the crust as you

1. An image for the quick movements of both arms from side to side in a traditional Scottish dance.   2. The French painter Jean-Auguste-Dominique Ingres (1780–1867) painted Napoleon twice. In *Bonaparte as First Consul* (1804), Napoleon's left fist is tucked into his partially buttoned red jacket. In another famous image, *Napoleon in His Study* (1812) by the French painter Jacques-Louis David (1748–1825), the emperor's right hand is tucked inside the unbuttoned middle of his white vest.   3. Vasco Núñez de Balboa (1475–1519), a Spanish explorer, the first European to discover the Pacific Ocean (1513); Nicolaus Copernicus (1473–1543), Polish astronomer and clergyman, whose Latin treatise *Six Books Concerning the Revolutions of the Heavenly Orbs* revolutionized astronomy by placing the sun (not the Earth) at the center of the cosmos, with the Earth and other planets orbiting it.

force the butter to spread. You can tap little chips of butter onto the toast without spreading them at all, and then place the two pieces of toast face to face and cut them in half diagonally, so that the pressure of the knife helps the melting of the butter in addition to halving the bread. Now, why is diagonal cutting better than cutting straight across? Because the corner of a triangularly cut slice gives you an ideal first bite. With rectangularly cut toast, you have to angle the shape into your mouth, as if you were angling a big dresser through a hall doorway: you have to catch one corner of your mouth with one corner of the toast and then slightly and carefully *turn* the toast, drawing the mouth open with it so that the far corner of the toast can clear; only then do you chomp down. Also, with the diagonal slice, most of the tapered bite is situated right up near the front of your mouth, where you want it to be as you begin to chew. With the rectangular slice, a cumbersome fraction is riding out of control, high on the dome of the tongue. One subway stop before mine, I concluded that there had been a logic behind the progress away from the parallel and toward the diagonal cut of toast, and that this hypotenusal expedient is not, as it may first have appeared to be, merely an affectation of short-order cooks.

I became curious about how late I was going to be. My watch had been stolen by threat of force a week before, but I glanced hopefully down the diminishing perspective of hands and wrists hanging from the metal loops of the subway car. I spotted many watches, women's and men's, but on this particular morning they were all unreadable. The buckle, and not the face, of one pointed my way; some were too far off; the women's were too small; several lacked all circumferential points of reference, and thus remained Necco wafers[4] to all but their wearers; some were oriented so that the slightest gleam from their crystals obscured the hands or the diodes beneath. A wristwatch less than a foot from my head, worn by a too carefully shaven man reading a newspaper folded into tiny segments, was exactly half visible; the left, or up-arm, half eclipsed by his cuff, so that while I could easily make out the terminal "-get" of the tall-lettered trademark, and even notice for the first time the microscopic vibration of the sweep hand following its tiny jolt to the next-adjoining second, all the timepiece could tell me was that it was not yet past nine o'clock. The cuff was possibly more expertly starched than my own.

And this was when I realized abruptly that, as of that minute (I am sorry I can't say exactly which minute), I had finished with whatever major growth I was going to have as a human being, and that I was now forever arrested at an intermediate stage of personal development. I did not move or flinch or make any outward sign. Actually, once the first horrible moment of raw surprise had passed, the sensation was exciting. I was set: I was the sort of person who said "actually" too much. I was the sort of person who thought about buttered toast on the subway— buttered *raisin* toast, if it came to that: the way the high, crisp scrape of the butter knife is muted by its passage over the heat-blimped form of a raisin, and the way, if you cut across a raisin, it will sometimes fall out, still intact though dented, as you lift the slice from the plate. I was the sort of person whose biggest discoveries

10

4. Disk-shaped candies.

were likely to be tricks to applying toiletries while fully dressed. I was a man, but not quite the magnitude of man I had hoped to be.

As the train slowed for my stop, I tried to stretch out the initial pain of this discovery for as long as I could, because I hadn't had too many such moments of truth in my life. Back at street level, I decided that I had undergone a trial sufficiently out of the ordinary to justify my taking the time, late or not, to get some breakfast to go, at the good coffee place. Once there, however, as I watched the woman behind the counter open a beautiful small white bag for my coffee and tissue-wrapped muffin with the same loose-wristed flip she would use if she were shaking down a thermometer, I felt a sudden impatience to get to the office. I hurried toward my building. I was looking forward to the morning show-and-tell period, when I would describe, leaning in various doorways or on modular dividers, how my personality had ground to an amazing halt, right on the subway, and had left me a brand-new adult. I shot my cuffs and pushed through the revolving door to work.

1986

YASUNARI KAWABATA

The Grasshopper and the Bell Cricket[1]

Walking along the tile-roofed wall of the university, I turned aside and approached the upper school. Behind the white board fence of the school playground, from a dusky clump of bushes under the black cherry trees, an insect's voice could be heard. Walking more slowly and listening to that voice, and furthermore reluctant to part with it, I turned right so as not to leave the playground behind. When I turned to the left, the fence gave way to an embankment planted with orange trees. At the corner, I exclaimed with surprise. My eyes gleaming at what they saw up ahead, I hurried forward with short steps.

At the base of the embankment was a bobbing cluster of beautiful varicolored lanterns, such as one might see at a festival in a remote country village. Without going any farther, I knew that it was a group of children on an insect chase among the bushes of the embankment. There were about twenty lanterns. Not only were there crimson, pink, indigo, green, purple, and yellow lanterns, but one lantern glowed with five colors at once. There were even some little red store-bought lanterns. But most of the lanterns were beautiful square ones which the children had made themselves with love and care. The bobbing lanterns, the coming together of children on this lonely slope—surely it was a scene from a fairy tale?

One of the neighborhood children had heard an insect sing on this slope one night. Buying a red lantern, he had come back the next night to find the insect. The night after that, there was another child. This new child could not buy a

1. Translated by Lane Dunlop.

lantern. Cutting out the back and front of a small carton and papering it, he placed a candle on the bottom and fastened a string to the top. The number of children grew to five, and then to seven. They learned how to color the paper that they stretched over the windows of the cutout cartons, and to draw pictures on it. Then these wise child-artists, cutting out round, three-cornered, and lozenge leaf shapes in the cartons, coloring each little window a different color, with circles and diamonds, red and green, made a single and whole decorative pattern. The child with the red lantern discarded it as a tasteless object that could be bought at a store. The child who had made his own lantern threw it away because the design was too simple. The pattern of light that one had had in hand the night before was unsatisfying the morning after. Each day, with cardboard, paper, brush, scissors, penknife, and glue, the children made new lanterns out of their hearts and minds. Look at my lantern! Be the most unusually beautiful! And each night, they had gone out on their insect hunts. These were the twenty children and their beautiful lanterns that I now saw before me.

Wide-eyed, I loitered near them. Not only did the square lanterns have old-fashioned patterns and flower shapes, but the names of the children who had made them were cut out in squared letters of the syllabary. Different from the painted-over red lanterns, others (made of thick cutout cardboard) had their designs drawn onto the paper windows, so that the candle's light seemed to emanate from the form and color of the design itself. The lanterns brought out the shadows of the bushes like dark light. The children crouched eagerly on the slope wherever they heard an insect's voice.

"Does anyone want a grasshopper?" A boy, who had been peering into a bush   5
about thirty feet away from the other children, suddenly straightened up and shouted.

"Yes! Give it to me!" Six or seven children came running up. Crowding behind the boy who had found the grasshopper, they peered into the bush. Brushing away their outstretched hands and spreading out his arms, the boy stood as if guarding the bush where the insect was. Waving the lantern in his right hand, he called again to the other children.

"Does anyone want a grasshopper? A grasshopper!"

"I do! I do!" Four or five more children came running up. It seemed you could not catch a more precious insect than a grasshopper. The boy called out a third time.

"Doesn't anyone want a grasshopper?"

Two or three more children came over.   10

"Yes. I want it."

It was a girl, who just now had come up behind the boy who'd discovered the insect. Lightly turning his body, the boy gracefully bent forward. Shifting the lantern to his left hand, he reached his right hand into the bush.

"It's a grasshopper."

"Yes. I'd like to have it."

The boy quickly stood up. As if to say "Here!" he thrust out his fist that held   15
the insect at the girl. She, slipping her left wrist under the string of her lantern, enclosed the boy's fist with both hands. The boy quietly opened his fist. The insect

was transferred to between the girl's thumb and index finger.

"Oh! It's not a grasshopper. It's a bell cricket." The girl's eyes shone as she looked at the small brown insect.

"It's a bell cricket! It's a bell cricket!" The children echoed in an envious chorus.

"It's a bell cricket. It's a bell cricket."

Glancing with her bright intelligent eyes at the boy who had given her the cricket, the girl opened the little insect cage hanging at her side and released the cricket in it.

20   "It's a bell cricket."

"Oh, it's a bell cricket," the boy who'd captured it muttered. Holding up the insect cage close to his eyes, he looked inside it. By the light of his beautiful many-colored lantern, also held up at eye level, he glanced at the girl's face.

Oh, I thought. I felt slightly jealous of the boy, and sheepish. How silly of me not to have understood his actions until now! Then I caught my breath in surprise. Look! It was something on the girl's breast which neither the boy who had given her the cricket, nor she who had accepted it, nor the children who were looking at them noticed.

In the faint greenish light that fell on the girl's breast, wasn't the name "Fujio" clearly discernible? The boy's lantern, which he held up alongside the girl's insect cage, inscribed his name, cut out in the green papered aperture, onto her white cotton kimono. The girl's lantern, which dangled loosely from her wrist, did not project its pattern so clearly, but still one could make out, in a trembling patch of red on the boy's waist, the name "Kiyoko." This chance interplay of red and green—if it was chance or play—neither Fujio nor Kiyoko knew about.

Even if they remembered forever that Fujio had given her the cricket and that Kiyoko had accepted it, not even in dreams would Fujio ever know that his name had been written in green on Kiyoko's breast or that Kiyoko's name had been inscribed in red on his waist, nor would Kiyoko ever know that Fujio's name had been inscribed in green on her breast or that her own name had been written in red on Fujio's waist.

25   Fujio! Even when you have become a young man, laugh with pleasure at a girl's delight when, told that it's a grasshopper, she is given a bell cricket; laugh with affection at a girl's chagrin when, told that it's a bell cricket, she is given a grasshopper.

Even if you have the wit to look by yourself in a bush away from the other children, there are not many bell crickets in the world. Probably you will find a girl like a grasshopper whom you think is a bell cricket.

And finally, to your clouded, wounded heart, even a true bell cricket will seem like a grasshopper. Should that day come, when it seems to you that the world is only full of grasshoppers, I will think it a pity that you have no way to remember tonight's play of light, when your name was written in green by your beautiful lantern on a girl's breast.

1988

WILLIAM CARLOS WILLIAMS

The Use of Force

They were new patients to me, all I had was the name, Olson. Please come down as soon as you can, my daughter is very sick. When I arrived I was met by the mother, a big startled looking woman, very clean and apologetic who merely said, Is this the doctor? and let me in. In the back, she added. You must excuse us, doctor, we have her in the kitchen where it is warm. It is very damp here sometimes.

The child was fully dressed and sitting on her father's lap near the kitchen table. He tried to get up, but I motioned for him not to bother, took off my overcoat and started to look things over. I could see that they were all very nervous, eyeing me up and down distrustfully. As often, in such cases, they weren't telling me more than they had to, it was up to me to tell them; that's why they were spending three dollars on me.

The child was fairly eating me up with her cold, steady eyes, and no expression to her face whatever. She did not move and seemed, inwardly, quiet; an unusually attractive little thing, and as strong as a heifer in appearance. But her face was flushed, she was breathing rapidly, and I realized that she had a high fever. She had magnificent blonde hair, in profusion. One of those picture children often reproduced in advertising leaflets and the photogravure sections of the Sunday papers.

She's had a fever for three days, began the father and we don't know what it comes from. My wife has given her things, you know, like people do, but it don't do no good. And there's been a lot of sickness around. So we tho't you'd better look her over and tell us what is the matter.

As doctors often do I took a trial shot at it as a point of departure. Has she had a sore throat?   5

Both parents answered me together, No . . . No, she says her throat don't hurt her.

Does your throat hurt you? added the mother to the child. But the little girl's expression didn't change nor did she move her eyes from my face.

Have you looked?

I tried to, said the mother, but I couldn't see.

As it happens we had been having a number of cases of diphtheria in the school   10
to which this child went during that month and we were all, quite apparently, thinking of that, though no one had as yet spoken of the thing.

Well, I said, suppose we take a look at the throat first. I smiled in my best professional manner and asking for the child's first name I said, come on, Mathilda, open your mouth and let's take a look at your throat.

Nothing doing.

Aw, come on, I coaxed, just open your mouth wide and let me take a look. Look, I said opening both hands wide, I haven't anything in my hands. Just open up and let me see.

Such a nice man, put in the mother. Look how kind he is to you. Come on, do what he tells you to. He won't hurt you.

15   At that I ground my teeth in disgust. If only they wouldn't use the word "hurt" I might be able to get somewhere. But I did not allow myself to be hurried or disturbed but speaking quietly and slowly I approached the child again.

As I moved my chair a little nearer suddenly with one catlike movement both her hands clawed instinctively for my eyes and she almost reached them too. In fact she knocked my glasses flying and they fell, though unbroken, several feet away from me on the kitchen floor.

Both the mother and father almost turned themselves inside out in embarrassment and apology. You bad girl, said the mother, taking her and shaking her by one arm. Look what you've done. The nice man . . . .

For heaven's sake, I broke in. Don't call me a nice man to her. I'm here to look at her throat on the chance that she might have diphtheria and possibly die of it. But that's nothing to her. Look here, I said to the child, we're going to look at your throat. You're old enough to understand what I'm saying. Will you open it now by yourself or shall we have to open it for you?

Not a move. Even her expression hadn't changed. Her breaths however were coming faster and faster. Then the battle began. I had to do it. I had to have a throat culture for her own protection. But first I told the parents that it was entirely up to them. I explained the danger but said that I would not insist on a throat examination so long as they would take the responsibility.

20   If you don't do what the doctor says you'll have to go to the hospital, the mother admonished her severely.

Oh yeah? I had to smile to myself. After all, I had already fallen in love with the savage brat, the parents were contemptible to me. In the ensuing struggle they grew more and more abject, crushed, exhausted while she surely rose to magnificent heights of insane fury of effort bred of her terror of me.

The father tried his best, and he was a big man but the fact that she was his daughter, his shame at her behavior and his dread of hurting her made him release her just at the critical times when I had almost achieved success, till I wanted to kill him. But his dread also that she might have diphtheria made him tell me to go on, go on though he himself was almost fainting, while the mother moved back and forth behind us raising and lowering her hands in an agony of apprehension.

Put her in front of you on your lap, I ordered, and hold both her wrists.

But as soon as he did the child let out a scream. Don't, you're hurting me. Let go of my hands. Let them go I tell you. Then she shrieked terrifyingly, hysterically. Stop it! Stop it! You're killing me!

25   Do you think she can stand it, doctor! said the mother.

You get out, said the husband to his wife. Do you want her to die of diphtheria?

Come on now, hold her, I said.

Then I grasped the child's head with my left hand and tried to get the wooden tongue depressor between her teeth. She fought, with clenched teeth, desperately! But now I also had grown furious—at a child. I tried to hold myself down but I couldn't. I know how to expose a throat for inspection. And I did my best. When finally I got the wooden spatula behind the last teeth and just the point of it into the mouth cavity, she opened up for an instant but before I could see anything she came down again and gripping the wooden blade between her molars she reduced it to splinters before I could get it out again.

Aren't you ashamed, the mother yelled at her. Aren't you ashamed to act like that in front of the doctor?

Get me a smooth-handled spoon of some sort, I told the mother. We're going through with this. The child's mouth was already bleeding. Her tongue was cut and she was screaming in wild hysterical shrieks. Perhaps I should have desisted and come back in an hour or more. No doubt it would have been better. But I have seen at least two children lying dead in bed of neglect in such cases, and feeling that I must get a diagnosis now or never I went at it, again. But the worst of it was that I too had got beyond reason. I could have torn the child apart in my own fury and enjoyed it. It was a pleasure to attack her. My face was burning with it. 30

The damned little brat must be protected against her own idiocy, one says to one's self at such times. Others must be protected against her. It is a social necessity. And all these things are true. But a blind fury, a feeling of adult shame, bred of a longing for muscular release are the operatives. One goes on to the end.

In the final unreasoning assault I overpowered the child's neck and jaws. I forced the heavy silver spoon back of her teeth and down her throat till she gagged. And there it was—both tonsils covered with membrane. She had fought valiantly to keep me from knowing her secret. She had been hiding that sore throat for three days at least and lying to her parents in order to escape just such an outcome as this.

Now truly she was furious. She had been on the defensive before but now she attacked. Tried to get off her father's lap and fly at me while tears of defeat blinded her eyes.

1938

URSULA K. LE GUIN

She Unnames Them

Most of them accepted namelessness with the perfect indifference with which they had so long accepted and ignored their names. Whales and dolphins, seals and sea otters consented with particular grace and alacrity, sliding into anonymity as into their element. A faction of yaks, however, protested. They said that "yak" sounded right, and that almost everyone who knew they existed called them that. Unlike the ubiquitous creatures such as rats and fleas, who had been called by hundreds or thousands of different names since Babel, the yaks could truly say, they said, that they had a *name*. They discussed the matter all summer. The councils of the elderly females finally agreed that though the name might be useful to others it was so redundant from the yak point of view that they never spoke it themselves and hence might as well dispense with it. After they presented the argument in this light to their bulls, a full consensus was delayed only by the onset of severe early blizzards. Soon after the beginning of the thaw, their agreement was reached and the designation "yak" was returned to the donor.

Among the domestic animals, few horses had cared what anybody called them since the failure of Dean Swift's attempt to name them from their own vocabulary.[1] Cattle, sheep, swine, asses, mules, and goats, along with chickens, geese, and turkeys, all agreed enthusiastically to give their names back to the people to whom—as they put it—they belonged.

A couple of problems did come up with pets. The cats, of course, steadfastly denied ever having had any name other than those self-given, unspoken, effan-ineffably personal names which, as the poet named Eliot[2] said, they spend long hours daily contemplating—though none of the contemplators has ever admitted that what they contemplate is their names and some onlookers have wondered if the object of that meditative gaze might not in fact be the Perfect, or Platonic, Mouse.[3] In any case, it is a moot point now. It was with the dogs, and with some parrots, lovebirds, ravens, and mynahs, that the trouble arose. These verbally talented individuals insisted that their names were important to them, and flatly refused to part with them. But as soon as they understood that the issue was precisely one of individual choice, and that anybody who wanted to be called Rover, or Froufrou, or Polly, or even Birdie in the personal sense, was perfectly free to do so, not one of them had the least objection to parting with the lowercase (or, as regards German creatures, uppercase) generic appellations "poodle," "parrot," "dog," or "bird," and all the Linnaean qualifiers[4] that had trailed along behind them for two hundred years like tin cans tied to a tail.

The insects parted with their names in vast clouds and swarms of ephemeral syllables buzzing and stinging and humming and flitting and crawling and tunneling away.

5   As for the fish of the sea, their names dispersed from them in silence throughout the oceans like faint, dark blurs of cuttlefish ink, and drifted off on the currents without a trace.

None were left now to unname, and yet how close I felt to them when I saw one of them swim or fly or trot or crawl across my way or over my skin, or stalk me in the night, or go along beside me for a while in the day. They seemed far closer than when their names had stood between myself and them like a clear barrier: so close that my fear of them and their fear of me became one same fear. And the attraction that many of us felt, the desire to smell one another's smells, feel or

1. In *Gulliver's Travels* (1726), Part IV, Jonathan Swift (1667–1745), dean of St. Patrick's Cathedral, Dublin, gave the name *Houyhnhnms*—which sounds like a horse neighing—to a race of rational, talking horses.   2. British (American-born) poet T. S. Eliot (1888–1965), in *The Naming of Cats* (1939), where he coined the word *effanineffable*.   3. That is, the ideal form of a mouse; the Greek philosopher Plato (ca. 428–348 or 347 B.C.) argued that archetypes existed for all material things.   4. Swedish botanist and taxonomist Carolus Linnaeus (1707–1778) originated the modern scientific classification of plants and animals.

rub or caress one another's scales or skin or feathers or fur, taste one another's blood or flesh, keep one another warm—that attraction was now all one with the fear, and the hunter could not be told from the hunted, nor the eater from the food.

This was more or less the effect I had been after. It was somewhat more powerful than I had anticipated, but I could not now, in all conscience, make an exception for myself. I resolutely put anxiety away, went to Adam,[5] and said, "You and your father lent me this—gave it to me, actually. It's been really useful, but it doesn't exactly seem to fit very well lately. But thanks very much! It's really been very useful."

It is hard to give back a gift without sounding peevish or ungrateful, and I did not want to leave him with that impression of me. He was not paying much attention, as it happened, and said only, "Put it down over there, O.K.?" and went on with what he was doing.

One of my reasons for doing what I did was that talk was getting us nowhere, but all the same I felt a little let down. I had been prepared to defend my decision. And I thought that perhaps when he did notice he might be upset and want to talk. I put some things away and fiddled around a little, but he continued to do what he was doing and to take no notice of anything else. At last I said, "Well, goodbye, dear. I hope the garden key turns up."

He was fitting parts together, and said, without looking around, "O.K., fine, dear. When's dinner?" 10

"I'm not sure," I said. "I'm going now. With the—" I hesitated, and finally said, "With them, you know," and went on out. In fact, I had only just then realized how hard it would have been to explain myself. I could not chatter away as I used to do, taking it all for granted. My words now must be as slow, as new, as single, as tentative as the steps I took going down the path away from the house, between the dark-branched, tall dancers motionless against the winter shining.

1985

QUESTIONS

1. How do the details in paragraphs 5 through 10 in "The Story of an Hour" prepare for the reversal that comes in paragraph 11? Did you find the turn surprising? convincing?
2. What humorous elements do you find in "A Very Old Man with Enormous Wings"? How do they function? Is the old man a symbol? If so, does he "stand for" something you can name or paraphrase? If you cannot say what he stands for, how can he be a symbol? If we do not read this story symbolically, how can we deal with its fantastic elements? take the story seriously as "literature"?
2. What images of the characters of the girl and her mother emerge from your reading of "Girl"? How are those images created?
4. The narrator of "Pants on Fire" announces that his story is about "the day that my life as

---

5. See Genesis, esp. 2.19 ("So out of the ground the Lord God formed every beast of the field and every bird of the air and brought them to the man to see what he would call them") and 3.20 ("The man called his wife's name Eve, because she was the mother of all living").

an adult began," and at the end he plans to tell his office-mates about "how my personality had ground to an amazing halt, right on the subway." What is he going to tell his cowork-ers? Is the revelation sufficiently dramatic for a story of initiation or changed identity? What patterns can you find in the kinds of things he describes and the ways he describes them? What does his fixation on small details tell you about him?

5. What does the narrator contribute to the meaning and effect of "The Grasshopper and the Bell Cricket"? (Try to imagine the story without him.) What is the effect of the relatively lengthy description of the varied lanterns? To what extent are the meanings of "grasshop-per" and "bell cricket" paraphrasable? What is the tone, effect, and meaning of the last two paragraphs?

WRITING SUGGESTIONS

1. Compare "A Very Old Man with Enormous Wings" and "A Hunger Artist" as "meaningful fantasies."

2. Write a personal essay called "Boy" or "Another Girl" that deals with the oft-repeated and multiple instructions, advice, and commands of a parent (not necessarily a mother).

3. The introduction to the chapter states that all you have learned about the elements of fiction may be, perhaps must be, brought to bear on these short short stories. Write an analysis of "The Grasshopper and the Bell Cricket" as if for the earlier chapter called "The Whole Text."

4. In "The Use of Force," the narrator says, "But the worst of it was that I too had got beyond reason. . . . It was a pleasure to attack her" (paragraph 30). Without the title and the doctor's reflections on his own reactions, this might be merely a minor, unpleasant inci-dent. Discuss the effect of the first-person point of view in this story, examining what the doctor tells us about the scene and his feelings. Although there are no quotation marks, try to distinguish dialogue and narration from the narrator's thoughts. Why does it matter that the patient is a pretty little girl, the family poor (possibly immigrants), the doctor a man who values his reason?

5. Compare the power of naming or language in "She Unnames Them" and in "A Zebra Storyteller."

11

CRITICAL CONTEXTS:
A FICTION CASEBOOK

We have already seen that although stories may be read as if they stand alone, they are enriched by being situated in authorial, literary, or cultural and historical contexts. Once a work has earned a place in the literature, it is also surrounded by a critical context—readers who write about the work and others who engage those readers or critics in dialogue about that work. To write critically about a work is to engage not only the text, but also those who have written about the text. It is always advisable, however, to read the story first, reread it, and read it still more times until you have come to terms with it; that is, settled in your own mind what you think about the story and how you evaluate it. Then—and only then—should you go to other critics, "secondary sources." Often when you read criticism before you have made up your own mind, *all* the critics seem "right" (and the most recently read the "most clearly right"), and your own responses are dulled or lost. On the other hand, when you have settled on your own responses to the story, you can read critics and pick up *additional* information or insights that can enrich rather than erase your own response and judgment. Reading criticism should be an enriching experience, not one that robs you of your individual responses.

The story that stands here in the middle of critical discussion is William Faulkner's popular, classic, and controversial "A Rose for Emily." It is followed by a student paper in which the author was asked to come to terms with the story before reading the critical discussions that have surrounded it almost since its first publication seventy years ago. There are hundreds of critical essays and commentaries on this story—a recent online search of the Modern Language Association bibliography yielded eighty-three studies of the story and Faulkner's "Southern gothic" published since 1981, some in Japanese. It is virtually impossible, then, to fully "report" the history of the

> In each [literary work] there is something (an individual intuition—or a concept which can never be expressed in other terms). It is like the square root of two or like π, which cannot be expressed by rational numbers but only as their limit. Criticism of [literature] is like 1.414 . . . or 3.1415. . . . not all it would be, yet all that can be had and very useful.
>
> —WILLIAM WIMSATT

critical discussion of this fascinating story. The four critical pieces reprinted here are not necessarily the best (and not necessarily not the best), nor do they fully represent the spectrum of comment and argument about the story. They do, instead, suggest some of the approaches or the aspects of a story that have been singled out for analysis, response, judgment.

Lawrence R. Rodgers's "'We all said, "she will kill herself"'": The Narrator/Detective in William Faulkner's 'A Rose for Emily,'" situates Faulkner's story in a literary kind, the detective story, matching details of the story to generally accepted definitions of the ingredients of detective fiction.

George L. Dillon's "Styles of Reading," though it first appeared in a highly theoretical "professional" journal, groups a variety of actual student responses into three categories, and many students who have read this essay agree that it represents the way they read and the kinds of questions they ask of a text. The essay is abbreviated here (we use ellipses to indicate our deletions): in its original form it demonstrated with long passages from other critics that student approaches were analogous to professional critical readings. Its purpose here is to represent and clarify various ways students or professional critics read this—or any—story, and to make students more conscious of what they are doing and what they might do in reading fiction.

The third piece, Judith Fetterley's "A Rose for 'A Rose for Emily,'" is adapted from her book *The Resisting Reader: A Feminist Approach to American Fiction*, and, as the title of the book suggests, it is because Emily is a woman—indeed, a lady—that the revelation of what she has done seems grotesque. Faulkner, she says, sees Emily as "a woman victimized and betrayed by the system of sexual politics, who nevertheless has discovered, within the structures that victimize her, sources of power for herself." Faulkner has implied this, she says, indicating but not quoting occasional comments of his. Other passages from Faulkner's conversations, however, scarcely identify him as a feminist. Two such passages appear, for example, in *The Paris Review Interviews: Writers at Work*, first series (Baltimore: Penguin, 1958). The first quotation suggests that "the perfect milieu for the artist to work in" is a brothel. The house is quiet in the mornings—the best time to write—the work is easy, and the pay adequate; the job offers him whatever social life he wants, "gives him a certain standing in his society," and "all the inmates of the house are female and would defer to him and call him 'sir'" (124). The second statement is more sweeping and perhaps more outrageous: "Success is feminine and like a woman; if you cringe before her, she will override you. So the way to treat her is to show her the back of your hand" (125). This is not to discount Fetterley's feminist reading of the story, but only to make you wary of trusting what an author says about his or her own work—trust the tale and not the teller. We naturally and properly read stories as if they are communications from another human mind and experience that we are trying to understand (reading, as one critic has suggested, as a member of the "authorial audience"). And all readings must begin with this intention. But even our friends sometimes tell us things about themselves, their attitudes and actions, that they do not know they are revealing, and sometimes claim intentions or accomplishments that we know not to be "true." We must be alert to the possibility that even authors cannot always distinguish between what they meant and what they have said. We must, then, see a work, another critic has said, "as it cannot see itself." It is only proper to acknowledge the profundity and power of an author's vision and art but probably not a good idea to claim to know fully the author's "intention" (even if you've read a quotation by the author that purports to define that intention).

When a work has engaged a number of critics, and especially when something in the work is difficult or controversial, subsequent commentaries need to acknowledge the previous readings and, by contradicting or modifying their conclusions with new evidence or more persuasive argument, justify still another essay on the oft-debated topic. Gene M. Moore's "Of Time and Its Mathematical Progression: Problems of Chronology in Faulkner's 'A Rose for Emily'" is just such an essay. It raises once again perhaps the most frequently discussed aspect of Faulkner's story: the precise dating of the events (including Emily's dates of birth and death). Moore cuts some knots and tightens others, establishing a new chronology, and, while admitting residual inconsistencies, offers an explanation of how these came about. It should serve here as an exemplary critical argument—engaging both the story and its commentators.

A NOTE ON DOCUMENTATION

Alert readers will notice that these commentaries use different forms of documentation. Dillon's essay was published in 1982 and Fetterley's book in 1978. Both give their references in notes at the end of their article—for example, "1. Brooke-Rose, 'The Readerhood of Man,' in *The Reader in the Text,* ed. Susan R. Suleiman and Inge Crosman (Princeton: Princeton University Press, 1980), 120–48" (Dillon); "See *Faulkner in the University: Class Conferences at the University of Virginia 1957–1958,* edited by Frederick L. Gwynn and Joseph L. Blotner (Charlottesville: University of Virginia Press, 1959), 87–88; *Faulkner at Nagano,* edited by Robert A. Jeliffe (Tokyo: Kenkyusha, 1956), 71" (Fetterley)—and neither gives a bibliography or a list of "works cited." The essays of Rodgers and Moore—published in 1995 and 1992, respectively—give such a list and interpolate the references with the page number(s) in the text parenthetically—for example, "(Going 53)," "(Wilson 56)." The suggested standard form for literary essays and books is set by the Modern Language Association; between the publication of the earlier and the later essays, MLA changed the form it recommended. Not everyone uses the newer form. But it is not only for that reason that the older form has been left here in the older essays: whenever you do literary research in books and articles from earlier decades, you will run into this earlier form, so it is just as well to be familiar with it. Note that while this documentation is standard for *literary* commentary, critical and scholarly works in other disciplines—psychology, chemistry, and so forth—use other forms. One of the best sources for all the major forms—and for other assistance in research methods and the writing of research papers—is Melissa Walker's *Writing Research Papers,* fourth edition (New York: Norton, 1997).

WILLIAM FAULKNER

A Rose for Emily

I

When Miss Emily Grierson died, our whole town went to her funeral: the men through a sort of respectful affection for a fallen monument, the women mostly out of curiosity to see the inside of her house, which no one save an old man-servant—a combined gardener and cook—had seen in at least ten years.

It was a big, squarish frame house that had once been white, decorated with cupolas and spires and scrolled balconies in the heavily lightsome style of the seventies, set on what had once been our most select street. But garages and cotton gins had encroached and obliterated even the august names of that neighborhood; only Miss Emily's house was left, lifting its stubborn and coquettish decay above the cotton wagons and the gasoline pumps—an eyesore among eyesores. And now Miss Emily had gone to join the representatives of those august names where they lay in the cedar-bemused cemetery among the ranked and anonymous graves of Union and Confederate soldiers who fell at the battle of Jefferson.

Alive, Miss Emily had been a tradition, a duty, and a care; a sort of hereditary obligation upon the town, dating from that day in 1894 when Colonel Sartoris, the mayor—he who fathered the edict that no Negro woman should appear on the streets without an apron—remitted her taxes, the dispensation dating from the death of her father on into perpetuity. Not that Miss Emily would have accepted charity. Colonel Sartoris invented an involved tale to the effect that Miss Emily's father had loaned money to the town, which the town, as a matter of business, preferred this way of repaying. Only a man of Colonel Sartoris' generation and thought could have invented it, and only a woman could have believed it.

When the next generation, with its more modern ideas, became mayors and aldermen, this arrangement created some little dissatisfaction. On the first of the year they mailed her a tax notice. February came, and there was no reply. They wrote her a formal letter, asking her to call at the sheriff's office at her convenience. A week later the mayor wrote her himself, offering to call or to send his car for her, and received in reply a note on paper of an archaic shape, in a thin, flowing calligraphy in faded ink, to the effect that she no longer went out at all. The tax notice was also enclosed, without comment.

5   They called a special meeting of the Board of Aldermen. A deputation waited upon her, knocked at the door through which no visitor had passed since she ceased giving china-painting lessons eight or ten years earlier. They were admitted by the old Negro into a dim hall from which a stairway mounted into still more shadow. It smelled of dust and disuse—a close, dank smell. The Negro led them into the parlor. It was furnished in heavy, leather-covered furniture. When the Negro opened the blinds of one window, a faint dust rose sluggishly about their thighs, spinning with slow motes in the single sun-ray. On a tarnished gilt easel before the fireplace stood a crayon portrait of Miss Emily's father.

They rose when she entered—a small, fat woman in black, with a thin gold chain descending to her waist and vanishing into her belt, leaning on an ebony cane with a tarnished gold head. Her skeleton was small and spare; perhaps that was why what would have been merely plumpness in another was obesity in her. She looked bloated, like a body long submerged in motionless water, and of that pallid hue. Her eyes, lost in the fatty ridges of her face, looked like two small pieces of coal pressed into a lump of dough as they moved from one face to another while the visitors stated their errand.

She did not ask them to sit. She just stood in the door and listened quietly until the spokesman came to a stumbling halt. Then they could hear the invisible watch ticking at the end of the gold chain.

Her voice was dry and cold. "I have no taxes in Jefferson. Colonel Sartoris explained it to me. Perhaps one of you can gain access to the city records and satisfy yourselves."

"But we have. We are the city authorities, Miss Emily. Didn't you get a notice from the sheriff, signed by him?"

"I received a paper, yes," Miss Emily said. "Perhaps he considers himself the   10 sheriff. . . . I have no taxes in Jefferson."

"But there is nothing on the books to show that, you see. We must go by the—"

"See Colonel Sartoris. I have no taxes in Jefferson."

"But, Miss Emily—"

"See Colonel Sartoris." (Colonel Sartoris had been dead almost ten years.) "I have no taxes in Jefferson. Tobe!" The Negro appeared. "Show these gentlemen out."

II

So she vanquished them, horse and foot, just as she had vanquished their fathers   15 thirty years before about the smell. That was two years after her father's death and a short time after her sweetheart—the one we believed would marry her— had deserted her. After her father's death she went out very little; after her sweetheart went away, people hardly saw her at all. A few of the ladies had the temerity to call, but were not received, and the only sign of life about the place was the Negro man—a young man then—going in and out with a market basket.

"Just as if a man—any man—could keep a kitchen properly," the ladies said; so they were not surprised when the smell developed. It was another link between the gross, teeming world and the high and mighty Griersons.

A neighbor, a woman, complained to the mayor, Judge Stevens, eighty years old.

"But what will you have me do about it, madam?" he said.

"Why, send her word to stop it," the woman said. "Isn't there a law?"

"I'm sure that won't be necessary," Judge Stevens said. "It's probably just a   20 snake or a rat that nigger of hers killed in the yard. I'll speak to him about it."

The next day he received two more complaints, one from a man who came in diffident deprecation. "We really must do something about it, Judge. I'd be the last one in the world to bother Miss Emily, but we've got to do something." That night the Board of Aldermen met—three gray-beards and one younger man, a member of the rising generation.

"It's simple enough," he said. "Send her word to have her place cleaned up. Give her a certain time to do it in, and if she don't . . ."

"Dammit, sir," Judge Stevens said, "will you accuse a lady to her face of smelling bad?"

So the next night, after midnight, four men crossed Miss Emily's lawn and slunk about the house like burglars, sniffing along the base of the brickwork and at the cellar openings while one of them performed a regular sowing motion with his hand out of a sack slung from his shoulder. They broke open the cellar door and sprinkled lime there, and in all the outbuildings. As they recrossed the lawn, a window that had been dark was lighted and Miss Emily sat in it, the light behind her, and her upright torso motionless as that of an idol. They crept quietly across the lawn and into the shadow of the locusts that lined the street. After a week or two the smell went away.

25   That was when people had begun to feel really sorry for her. People in our town, remembering how old lady Wyatt, her great-aunt, had gone completely crazy at last, believed that the Griersons held themselves a little too high for what they really were. None of the young men were quite good enough for Miss Emily and such. We had long thought of them as a tableau; Miss Emily a slender figure in white in the background, her father a spraddled silhouette in the foreground, his back to her and clutching a horsewhip, the two of them framed by the back-flung front door. So when she got to be thirty and was still single, we were not pleased exactly, but vindicated; even with insanity in the family she wouldn't have turned down all of her chances if they had really materialized.

When her father died, it got about that the house was all that was left to her; and in a way, people were glad. At last they could pity Miss Emily. Being left alone, and a pauper, she had become humanized. Now she too would know the old thrill and the old despair of a penny more or less.

The day after his death all the ladies prepared to call at the house and offer condolence and aid, as is our custom. Miss Emily met them at the door, dressed as usual and with no trace of grief on her face. She told them that her father was not dead. She did that for three days, with the ministers calling on her, and the doctors, trying to persuade her to let them dispose of the body. Just as they were about to resort to law and force, she broke down, and they buried her father quickly.

We did not say she was crazy then. We believed she had to do that. We remembered all the young men her father had driven away, and we knew that with nothing left, she would have to cling to that which had robbed her, as people will.

III

She was sick for a long time. When we saw her again, her hair was cut short, making her look like a girl, with a vague resemblance to those angels in colored church windows—sort of tragic and serene.

30   The town had just let the contracts for paving the sidewalks, and in the summer after her father's death they began to work. The construction company came with niggers and mules and machinery, and a foreman named Homer Barron, a Yankee—a big, dark, ready man, with a big voice and eyes lighter than his face. The little boys would follow in groups to hear him cuss the niggers, and the niggers singing in time to the rise and fall of picks. Pretty soon he knew everybody in town. Whenever you heard a lot of laughing anywhere about the square, Homer Barron would be in the center of the group. Presently we began to see him and Miss Emily on Sunday afternoons driving in the yellow-wheeled buggy and the matched team of bays from the livery stable.

At first we were glad that Miss Emily would have an interest, because the ladies all said, "Of course a Grierson would not think seriously of a Northerner, a day laborer." But there were still others, older people, who said that even grief could not cause a real lady to forget *noblesse oblige*—without calling it *noblesse oblige*. They just said, "Poor Emily. Her kinsfolk should come to her." She had some kin in Alabama; but years ago her father had fallen out with them over the estate of old lady Wyatt, the crazy woman, and there was no communication between the two families. They had not even been represented at the funeral.

And as soon as the old people said, "Poor Emily," the whispering began. "Do you suppose it's really so?" they said to one another. "Of course it is. What else could . . ." This behind their hands; rustling of craned silk and satin behind jalousies closed upon the sun of Sunday afternoon as the thin, swift clop-clop-clop of the matched team passed: "Poor Emily."

She carried her head high enough—even when we believed that she was fallen. It was as if she demanded more than ever the recognition of her dignity as the last Grierson; as if it had wanted that touch of earthiness to reaffirm her imperviousness. Like when she bought the rat poison, the arsenic. That was over a year after they had begun to say "Poor Emily," and while the two female cousins were visiting her.

"I want some poison," she said to the druggist. She was over thirty then, still a slight woman, though thinner than usual, with cold, haughty black eyes in a face the flesh of which was strained across the temples and about the eyesockets as you imagine a lighthouse-keeper's face ought to look. "I want some poison," she said.

"Yes, Miss Emily. What kind? For rats and such? I'd recom—"   35

"I want the best you have. I don't care what kind."

The druggist named several. "They'll kill anything up to an elephant. But what you want is—"

"Arsenic," Miss Emily said. "Is that a good one?"

"Is . . . arsenic? Yes ma'am. But what you want—"

"I want arsenic."   40

The druggist looked down at her. She looked back at him, erect, her face like a strained flag. "Why, of course," the druggist said. "If that's what you want. But the law requires you to tell what you are going to use it for."

Miss Emily just stared at him, her head tilted back in order to look him eye for eye, until he looked away and went and got the arsenic and wrapped it up. The Negro delivery boy brought her the package; the druggist didn't come back. When she opened the package at home there was written on the box, under the skull and bones: "For rats."

IV

So the next day we all said, "She will kill herself"; and we said it would be the best thing. When she had first begun to be seen with Homer Barron, we had said, "She will marry him." Then we said, "She will persuade him yet," because Homer himself had remarked—he liked men, and it was known that he drank with the younger men in the Elk's Club—that he was not a marrying man. Later we said,

"Poor Emily," behind the jalousies as they passed on Sunday afternoon in the glittering buggy, Miss Emily with her head high and Homer Barron with his hat cocked and a cigar in his teeth, reins and whip in a yellow glove.

Then some of the ladies began to say that it was a disgrace to the town and a bad example to the young people. The men did not want to interfere, but at last the ladies forced the Baptist minister—Miss Emily's people were Episcopal—to call upon her. He would never divulge what happened during that interview, but he refused to go back again. The next Sunday they again drove about the streets, and the following day the minister's wife wrote to Miss Emily's relations in Alabama.

45   So she had blood-kin under her roof again and we sat back to watch developments. At first nothing happened. Then we were sure that they were to be married. We learned that Miss Emily had been to the jeweler's and ordered a man's toilet set in silver, with the letters H. B. on each piece. Two days later we learned that she had bought a complete outfit of men's clothing, including a nightshirt, and we said, "They are married." We were really glad. We were glad because the two female cousins were even more Grierson than Miss Emily had ever been.

So we were not surprised when Homer Barron—the streets had been finished some time since—was gone. We were a little disappointed that there was not a public blowing-off, but we believed that he had gone on to prepare for Miss Emily's coming, or to give her a chance to get rid of the cousins. (By that time it was a cabal, and we were all Miss Emily's allies to help circumvent the cousins.) Sure enough, after another week they departed. And, as we had expected all along, within three days Homer Barron was back in town. A neighbor saw the Negro man admit him at the kitchen door at dusk one evening.

And that was the last we saw of Homer Barron. And of Miss Emily for some time. The Negro man went in and out with the market basket, but the front door remained closed. Now and then we would see her at a window for a moment, as the men did that night when they sprinkled the lime, but for almost six months she did not appear on the streets. Then we knew that this was to be expected too; as if that quality of her father which had thwarted her woman's life so many times had been too virulent and too furious to die.

When we next saw Miss Emily, she had grown fat and her hair was turning gray. During the next few years it grew grayer and grayer until it attained an even pepper-and-salt iron-gray, when it ceased turning. Up to the day of her death at seventy-four it was still that vigorous iron-gray, like the hair of an active man.

From that time on her front door remained closed, save for a period of six or seven years, when she was about forty, during which she gave lessons in china-painting. She fitted up a studio in one of the downstairs rooms, where the daughters and grand-daughters of Colonel Sartoris' contemporaries were sent to her with the same regularity and in the same spirit that they were sent on Sundays with a twenty-five cent piece for the collection plate. Meanwhile her taxes had been remitted.

50   Then the newer generation became the backbone and the spirit of the town, and the painting pupils grew up and fell away and did not send their children to

her with boxes of color and tedious brushes and pictures cut from the ladies' magazines. The front door closed upon the last one and remained closed for good. When the town got free postal delivery Miss Emily alone refused to let them fasten the metal numbers above her door and attach a mailbox to it. She would not listen to them.

Daily, monthly, yearly we watched the Negro grow grayer and more stooped, going in and out with the market basket. Each December we sent her a tax notice, which would be returned by the post office a week later, unclaimed. Now and then we would see her in one of the downstairs windows—she had evidently shut up the top floor of the house—like the carven torso of an idol in a niche, looking or not looking at us, we could never tell which. Thus she passed from generation to generation—dear, inescapable, impervious, tranquil, and perverse.

And so she died. Fell ill in the house filled with dust and shadows, with only a doddering Negro man to wait on her. We did not even know she was sick; we had long since given up trying to get any information from the Negro. He talked to no one, probably not even to her, for his voice had grown harsh and rusty, as if from disuse.

She died in one of the downstairs rooms, in a heavy walnut bed with a curtain, her gray head propped on a pillow yellow and moldy with age and lack of sunlight.

V

The Negro met the first of the ladies at the front door and let them in, with their hushed, sibilant voices and their quick, curious glances, and then he disappeared. He walked right through the house and out the back and was not seen again.

The two female cousins came at once. They held the funeral on the second day, with the town coming to look at Miss Emily beneath a mass of bought flowers, with the crayon face of her father musing profoundly above the bier and the ladies sibilant and macabre; and the very old men—some in their brushed Confederate uniforms—on the porch and the lawn, talking of Miss Emily as if she had been a contemporary of theirs, believing that they had danced with her and courted her perhaps, confusing time with its mathematical progression, as the old do, to whom all the past is not a diminishing road, but, instead, a huge meadow which no winter ever quite touches, divided from them now by the narrow bottleneck of the most recent decade of years.

Already we knew that there was one room in that region above stairs which no one had seen in forty years, and which would have to be forced. They waited until Miss Emily was decently in the ground before they opened it.

The violence of breaking down the door seemed to fill this room with pervading dust. A thin, acrid pall as of the tomb seemed to lie everywhere upon this room decked and furnished as for a bridal: upon the valance curtains of faded rose color, upon the rose-shaded lights, upon the dressing table, upon the delicate array of crystal and the man's toilet things backed with tarnished silver, silver so tarnished that the monogram was obscured. Among them lay a collar and tie, as if they had just been removed, which, lifted, left upon the surface a pale crescent in the dust. Upon a chair hung the suit, carefully folded; beneath it the two mute shoes and the discarded socks.

The man himself lay in the bed.

For a long while we just stood there, looking down at the profound and flesh-less grin. The body had apparently once lain in the attitude of an embrace, but now the long sleep that outlasts love, that conquers even the grimace of love, had cuckolded him. What was left of him, rotted beneath what was left of the night-shirt, had become inextricable from the bed in which he lay; and upon him and upon the pillow beside him lay that even coating of the patient and biding dust.

60   Then we noticed that in the second pillow was the indentation of a head. One of us lifted something from it, and leaning forward, that faint and invisible dust dry and acrid in the nostrils, we saw a long strand of iron-gray hair.

1931

STUDENT WRITING

Daniel Bronson's paper is a direct (unresearched) response to "A Rose for Emily." In his paper, Daniel traces the theme of resistance to change in the story, which he supports with examples from the text.

"Like the Sand of the Hourglass . . ."

Daniel Bronson

The year 1865 saw the end of the Civil War between the Union and the Confederacy, and saw the beginning of a "New South." With the many changes pressed upon the South, the so-called "Old South" could no longer exist. For example, people could not own slaves as they had in the past, and they couldn't survive anymore simply by belonging to a family with an "august name." These changes didn't happen overnight however; they took many years to occur. In William Faulkner's "A Rose for Emily," we are shown the transition from Old South to New South as it takes place in the little town of Jefferson, and we see how Miss Emily Grierson, survivor of the Old South, resists these changes.

Jefferson was once inhabited by many well-off families who were members of the Old South's aristocratic class. As time, and the Reconstruction, marched on, these families slowly disappeared. Eventually, the last true living legacy of the Old South in Jefferson was Miss Emily Grierson. She had been raised to be a Southern Belle, an upstanding member of society, and she clung to her world of the Old South. She kept a black servant, Tobe, who did everything for her, just

433

as if he were a slave, and she lived in "a big, squarish frame house
that had once been white, decorated with cupolas and spires and
scrolled balconies in the heavily lightsome style of the seventies, set
on what had once been our most select street" (par. 2). With the
infiltration of the New South, however, "garages and cotton gins . . .
encroached and obliterated even the august names of that neighborhood"
(par. 2). Yet the house remained, "lifting its stubborn and coquettish
decay above the cotton wagons and the gasoline pumps," just as its
willful inhabitant "carried her head high . . . even when we believed
that she was fallen" (par. 33).

The house was all that Miss Emily really had left after her father
died. When he passed away, Miss Emily spent three days denying his
death and not letting the doctors and ministers dispose of the body.
Though it is not told first in the story, this was the first time Miss
Emily had rejected the truth in order to retain her world of the past:
a world in which other members of the Old South, such as Colonel
Sartoris, lived on after they too had died.

Colonel Sartoris also represented the Old South, and he protected
Emily when her father died. As mayor of Jefferson at the time, he
remitted her taxes, and since no aristocratic woman such as Miss Emily
could possibly lower herself to accept charity, came up with a story of
how her father had loaned money to Jefferson and this was how Miss
Emily was to be repaid. "Only a man of Colonel Sartoris' generation
and thought could have invented it, and only a woman could have
believed it" (par. 3). So when Miss Emily was later approached by
members of the generation of city authorities who wanted her taxes, she
held onto the past and told them repeatedly to see Colonel Sartoris,
even though he had been dead for almost ten years. Furthermore, when
city authorities asked her whether or not she received "a notice from
the sheriff, signed by him," she remarks, "Perhaps he considers himself
the sheriff" (pars. 9, 10). Obviously, Miss Emily didn't accept that
whoever was the new sheriff was really the sheriff. As far as she was
concerned, the sheriff was still the same person it was several years
ago.

We are shown not only the government of the Old South Jefferson, when
it sided with Miss Emily, and the government of the New South
Jefferson, when it was against Miss Emily, but we also catch a glimpse

of Jefferson's government when it was still under transition. About two
years after her father's death, a smell developed around Miss Emily's
house. The "member of the rising generation" on the Board of Aldermen
said that the solution to the problem was "'simple enough. . . . Send
her word to have her place cleaned up. Give her a certain time to do it
in, and if she don't . . .'" At that point the remaining Old South
revealed itself when the eighty-year-old mayor, Judge Stevens, irately
asked, " '[W]ill you accuse a lady to her face of smelling bad?' "
(pars. 22, 23). It is apparent that though there were some old-timers
left, just as Jefferson changed, so did its people.

Members of the Old South were very honorable, graceful and above all,
dignified. They had great respect for each other and for each other's
feelings, and were quick to help one another whenever possible. Most
importantly, however, they always retained their dignity, no matter
what. Miss Emily preserved her world of the Old South by hanging on to
her dignity. It was because her dignity was so essential to her that a
major conflict arose when Miss Emily met Homer Barron. Homer was a
personification of Reconstruction and was Miss Emily's opposite in every
way. He was a Yankee, a solicializer, a member of the vulgar, haphazard
post-war generation, and "a day laborer," having been hired to build
Jefferson's sidewalks and thereby contribute to the urbanization of the
town.

When opposites attracted however, Miss Emily put her dignity on the
line and was seen "on Sunday afternoons driving in the yellow-wheeled
buggy and the matched team of bays from the livery stable" with Homer
(par. 30). The ladies of the town said, "'Of course a Grierson would
not think seriously of a Northerner,'" and the "older people," those of
the Old South, "said that even grief could not cause a real lady to
forget *noblesse oblige*--without calling it *noblesse oblige*" (par. 31).
As time passed, Homer and Miss Emily were seen again and again, until
finally, "some of the ladies began to say that it was a disgrace to the
town and a bad example to the young people. The men did not want to
interfere, but at last the ladies forced the Baptist minister . . . to
call upon her" (par. 44). Then "the minister's wife wrote to Miss
Emily's relations in Alabama" (par. 44). When they arrived, Miss Emily
realized she had to do something to preserve the dignity and pride that
kept her Old South alive.

Her choices were few: marry Homer, or separate from him completely. At first it appeared that Miss Emily and Homer were either married or getting ready to be married, for she "ordered a man's toilet set in silver, with the letters H. B. on each piece" and she "bought a complete outfit of men's clothing, including a nightshirt" (par. 45). Unfortunately, while this may have kept her reputation from being tarnished as far as the New South people were concerned, it was still not enough for Miss Emily's Old South dignity. It demanded that she never demean herself by being married to a Northerner. Therefore, in order to keep Homer, but not what he was or what he stood for, Miss Emily killed him, then kept him in a bed where she could be with him when she chose without "compromising her dignity." This violence and necrophilia reflect her wish to hold onto the South's dead past as well as her own and the price she pays to do so.

Miss Emily retained her sense of her dignity and her private version of the world of the Old South for the rest of her life. She was a "monument," "a tradition, a duty, and a care" (pars. 1, 3). Living secluded, she surrounded herself as best as she could by locking herself in her old house with only her memories and her black servant. When she died, she did so in dignity, "in a heavy walnut bed with a curtain, her gray head propped on a pillow" (par. 53). With her death went her Old South world as well, leaving behind only "the very old men--some in their brushed Confederate uniforms" to remind the New South of the past (par. 55) and to offer a rose of remembrance and respect for Emily.

LAWRENCE R. RODGERS

"We all said, 'she will kill herself'": The Narrator/Detective in William Faulkner's "A Rose for Emily"*

William Faulkner's most famous short story, "A Rose for Emily," is a classic expression of American gothicism. Rich in interpretive possibility and long a critical

*From *Clues: A Journal of Detection* 16 (1995): 117–29.

favorite, this 1929 story is a dark parable of the decline of southern sensibility. Its impact relies on a slow accretion of atmospheric detail, with each new detail further illuminating the many mysteries surrounding the life of confederate matriarch Emily Grierson. The story also may be read within the framework of a related popular genre, the classical detective story, whose American origins are traced to Edgar Allan Poe. It is commonly known that Faulkner learned much about genre-writing from his fellow southerner. He capitalized on Poe's legacy in novels such as *Intruder in the Dust* (1948) and *Knight's Gambit* (1949) as well as in "An Error in Chemistry," his 1946 short story published in *Ellery Queen's Mystery Magazine.* Faulkner's ability to expand and rework the devices of the detective story in these later works makes him a worthy successor to Poe.[1] But it is in the earlier, less straightforward story of detection, "A Rose for Emily," that Faulkner's lifelong interest in shaping his fiction around the theme of detection can be observed in its nascent form, and the important presence of the detective figure throughout his fiction can begin to be more fully appreciated.

While it might initially seem surprising that 20th-century America's premier novelist would draw so freely from the conventions of formula fiction, Faulkner was, to his frustration, well-versed with the necessities of writing with mass publication in mind. Any number of his works betray his willingness to annex popular conventions. His sixth novel, *Sanctuary,* is a case in point.[2] Frustrated by a mounting stack of what he considered brilliant fiction with no press to publish it, he sat down in late January of 1929 and in four months completed the sensational *Sanctuary,* which would remain his bleakest, most unrelentingly ruthless examination of the modern world. As he would later tell an audience, the novel was "basely conceived . . . I thought of the most horrific idea I could think of and wrote it" with the goal of making money (qtd. in Minter 107). Shortly after *Sanctuary's* acceptance, in April 1930, while the near-broke writer was still awaiting royalties, "A Rose for Emily" appeared in *The Forum.* Having already had it rejected by *Scribner's,* Faulkner was thrilled to receive his first short story publication, less for the honor than for the fact that he desperately needed money to pay mounting medical costs and back bills for materials used in restoring his home, Rowen Oak.

Following the example of "A Rose for Emily," the bulk of Faulkner's short fiction was produced in assembly-line spurts of productivity and aimed toward quick publication in national magazines, which, in turn, helped finance the slower pace of his more involved, less marketable novels. Biographer Frederick Karl notes that Faulkner earned more from selling four short stories to *Saturday Evening Post* than from the combined royalties of his first four novels (401). Nonetheless, the shy southerner much preferred to don the guise of the solitary romantic artist laboring purely for the sake of his craft. But in light of his lifelong financial difficulties, such a pose merely placated his ongoing taste for self-invention. However much he scorned the popular marketplace in favor of writing what he viewed as Art with a capital A, he always maintained close contact with a broad-based, "nonliterary" readership.[3]

In his well-known discussion of detective story conventions in *Adventure, Mystery and Romance,* John Cawelti provides a useful, simple litmus test for establishing whether a text follows the classical detective formula. In his scheme, there are three conditions that must be met: 1) the story must have a mystery that needs solving; 2) there must be concealed facts that a detective has to explore; and 3) these facts must become clear in the end (132). "A Rose for Emily" easily satisfies these conditions. Homer Barron, a laborer from the North, comes to work in the tightly knit community of Jefferson, Mississippi. After he is seen in the company of Emily, the eccentric daughter of one of Jefferson's finest families, Homer's courtship fuels town gossip. Various loosely related details soon mount up to suggest something is seriously amiss. Homer mysteriously disappears, re-appears and then disappears again not long after Miss Emily purchases rat poison. A foul smell emanates from her old home, causing some men from the town to sneak into her yard to sprinkle it with lime. Emily herself goes through profound physical changes, growing fat and grey-headed. Finally, after her death, Homer's disappearance is solved in what Irving Howe has wryly noted makes for a hair-raising conclusion (265). Miss Emily, aware of the town's penchant for judgment, ruled by the codes of etiquette of a once-proud lineage, and unable to fathom the changing conditions of the new South, has indeed poisoned Homer and retreated (with his corpse) into the recesses of her attic, where, liberated from prying eyes, she has been allowed to carry on her illicit love affair in post-mortem privacy. The evidence betraying her necrophilia is a single strand of iron-grey hair lying on a head-shaped indentation next to the corpse, which, much like the values that Emily tried to uphold by removing her affairs from public view, has become a grotesque, rotted perversion of its former self.

In light of all the praise given over to the originality, ambiguity, technical merit, and skillful manipulation of discontinuous, fragmentary narrative time in "A Rose for Emily," it is, within these considerations, an interestingly conven-tional detective tale. Its pattern of action is ordered around the basic elements of the popular genre: a southern setting circumscribing an eerie, decaying mansion; a curious disappearance; portents of a murder, in this case a poisoning; an unlikely, peculiar suspect, and a mysterious locked room whose assortment of clues turns up a corpse, a murderer and, finally, a solution to a macabre but oddly plausible crime. What appears to be missing here is the detective, the detached figure whose analytic insight allows him (or, more rarely, her) to solve the crime and thus restore rationality and a sense of order to a world of uncertainty.

However, on examination, we find that Faulkner (who made a career of stretch-ing the boundaries of convention, literary and otherwise, to suit his own needs) provides a kind of detective, but with an inventive twist. Cawelti notes that a detective story need not contain a professional crime solver like a Maigret, a Dupin or a Holmes as long as some character "performs the role of successful inquirer" (132).

In "A Rose for Emily" the unnamed narrator that pieces together the frag-mented decline of the Grierson lineage plays just such a role. More originally, this narrator/detective is also an unknowing driving force behind Emily's crime. Speaking in the "we" voice, the narrator, an overwhelming presence throughout the narrative, embodies the town's shared sentiments toward Emily. Having spent years not only observing but also commenting and rendering judgment upon the woman described as "a tradition, a duty, and a care,"[4] this *vox populi* is so per-sistent in assuming its natural right to intrude on Emily's life, that she—obsessively mindful of the need to honor the town's, and her father's, rigid code of genteel behavior—chooses murder rather than a public flouting of the town's values. The dramatic distance on display here provides an ironic layer to the narrative. As the observers of the conflict between the teller-of-tale's desire to solve the curious mysteries that surround Emily's life—indeed, his complicity in shaping them—and his undetective-like detachment from her crimes, readers occupy the tantalizing position of having insight into unraveling the mystery which the narrator lacks.

A classical detective story, quite simply, begins with an unsolved crime and moves toward its solution. Introduced into a world of ambiguity, mystery, and multiple possibilities, the reader is steadily made aware of key details that eventually allow a series of events to be placed into a comprehendable order. In "A Rose for Emily" the air of mystery commences with the first sentence: "When Miss Emily Grierson died, our whole town went to her funeral: the men through a sort of respectful affection for a fallen monument, the women mostly out of curiosity to see the inside of her house, which no one save an old manservant . . . had seen in at least ten years" (119). Playing off the detective convention of entering a locked room and delaying the revelation of its contents until the story's conclusion, this teasing beginning invites the reader to participate in unraveling the mysteries that have led up to Emily's funeral. However, making order out of Emily's life is a complicated matter, since the narrator recalls the details through a non-linear filter.

Cloaking an additional layer of mystery on Emily's story, the narrator's disjointed, associational recollection of details has led readers and critics to become the surrogate detectives of Faulkner's world. They have tried to "unscramble" the chronology and thus "solve" the structural ambiguities of the story by reconstructing Faulkner's calendar.[5] With evidence sparse and at times contradictory, these attempts, relying on close reading, conjecture, and extra-textual evidence, have yielded several slightly different time-lines. Although these time-lines claim to be pedagogically useful in allowing students to grasp "the elusive, illusive quality of time that lies at the heart of the story" (Going 53), their more immediate appeal is as a kind of armchair detective's game. They offer the challenge of taking the story's one exact reference to time (the remitting of Colonel Sartoris' taxes "in 1894") and combining it with the two dozen or so more approximate references to come up with a set of dates corresponding to the major events of Emily's life. Since the temporal world of Faulkner's Yoknapatawpha County remains relatively consistent (if inexact) throughout his entire corpus, other texts besides "A Rose for Emily," like his 1929 novel *Sartoris,* also help provide clues. Thus the more familiar the detective-critic becomes with the entire Faulkner corpus, the more equipped he or she is to place the events of Emily's life in the context of Yoknapatawpha County's overall pattern of myth.

But beyond offering superficial clarification about the plot, an exact chronology hardly seems to matter. As is invariably the case with Faulkner, appreciating the text's brilliance only begins with comprehending the plot, however ordered. Reduced to its basic situation, "A Rose for Emily" is fairly standard melodrama, probably loosely based on a conflation of actual odd events that occurred around

Oxford in the 1920s (cf. Cullen and Watkins 70–71). Faulkner's plots can be brilliantly imagined, but what infuses this particular story with its force is the *manner* in which the plot is related to us by the purportedly innocuous observer of Emily's life. In other words, Faulkner conceives of "A Rose for Emily" quite cunningly by bending the traditional presentation of the detective. The narrative's overwhelming presence is the narrator himself, speaking as a representative voice of Jefferson (or, in using the "we" pronoun throughout, perhaps even as the collective voice of the town). In culling the data of Emily's life, the narrator/detective's favored posture is, in the classic mode of the genre, one of surveillance and, less classically, one of judgment. From the initial sentence, the narrator demands not just to retell the events of Emily's life, but to relish the manner in which the town intrudes upon them. Town members try to collect her taxes, insist on burying her father, attempt to rid her house of its odor, force the Baptist minister and her Alabama relatives into her home, and, after her death, eagerly break into her mysterious upstairs room.

Fully in keeping with the town's invasive aesthetic of observation, the narrator/detective's willingness to pass judgment on all he witnesses so completely overturns the illusion of objectivity that he speaks, if you will, not as the detached soloist of a Greek chorus, but as a prime participant in the tragic drama he relates. The ways of interpreting Emily's decision to murder Homer are numerous, as the many critical pieces on the story bear out. For simple clarification, they can be summarized along two lines. One group finds the murder growing out of Emily's demented attempt to forestall the inevitable passage of time—toward her abandonment by Homer, toward her own death, and toward the steady encroachment of the North and the New South on something loosely defined as the "tradition" of the Old South. Another view sees the murder in more psychological terms. It grows out of Emily's complex relationship to her father, who, by elevating her above all of the eligible men of Jefferson, insured that to yield to what one commentator called the "normal emotions" associated with desire, his daughter had to "retreat into a marginal world, into fantasy" (O'Connor 184).

These lines of interpretation complement more than critique each other, and collectively they offer an interesting range of views on the story. Together, they de-emphasize the element of detection, viewing the murder and its solution not as the central action but as manifestations of the principal element, the decline of the Grierson lineage and all it represents. Recognizing the way in which the story makes use of the detective genre, however, adds another interpretive layer to the story by making the narrator—or more precisely, the collective sensibility the narrator represents—a central player in the pattern of action. Detective stories typically place less emphasis on the crime, the criminal, and the victim than on the detective. Detectives such as Dupin, Holmes, Poirot, Sergeant Cuff, Dr. Gideon Fell, and Nero Wolfe may be detached from the society they observe but they still rest at the center of the author's narrative world. Faulkner bends his narrator/detective in some obvious ways away from these more traditional examples. Strictly speaking, his detective is no nearer Poe's Dupin than Emily is a re-creation of Minister D, the master criminal of "The Purloined Letter." But the narrative is an ongoing investigation of Emily's life and the narrator is the principal detective in this investigation.

Much of the story's action is centered around the combination of Emily's desire to remain isolated and the narrator and his fellow townsfolk's refusal to honor that desire. Consider, among many examples, the language of intrusion and judgment implied in the following passages.

> They were not surprised when the smell developed.

> That was when people had begun to feel really sorry for her. People in our town . . . believed that the Griersons held themselves a little too high for what they really were.

> So when she got to be thirty and was still single, we were not pleased exactly, but vindicated.

> When her father died, it got about that the house was all that was left to her; and in a way, people were glad. At last they could pity Miss Emily.

> We did not say she was crazy then. We believed she had to do that.

> As soon as the old people said, "Poor Emily," the whispering began.

> She carried her head high enough—even when we believed that she was fallen.

And finally, the story's most startling and significant statement made shortly after Emily purchases rat poison: "So the next day we all said, 'she will kill herself'; and *we said it would be the best thing*" (my emphasis, 121–26). The town, it is evident, has made Emily its obsession, with every detail of her life subject to discussion, speculation and assessment. Without means by which to carry on her affair in public (and a noticeably diminishing lack of interest on Homer's part, since he "liked men" and was not ready to settle down), Emily insures her isolation in a cunningly ironic and comic verbal reversal on the town's recommendation of suicide; she herself kills Homer Barron, and from the town's point of view, it was the best thing.

"The detective novel features two expulsions of 'bad' or socially unfit characters: the victim and the murderer" (Grella 49). In the context of the genre, as George Grella describes it, Homer is a classic victim because he is guilty of an unpardonable crime against the community. He was born in the North, which in the world of Jefferson, Mississippi, since the days of the Civil War, has been a capital offense. After he disappears, no more attention is paid to him ("that was the last we saw of Homer Barron" [127]). The town's purported lack of interest can be formally explained as a crafty plotting device of Faulkner's to draw suspicion away from the existence of the murder (which is further obscured by the temporal shifts in the narrative). To this end, the narrator casually mentions Homer for the first time in the story as the "sweetheart" who "deserted" Emily. But it is also significant that as a northerner—as well as a common day-laborer—Homer represents the kind of unwelcomed resident and ineligible mate the town wants to repel if it is to preserve its traditional arrangements. His very proximity to Emily is, according to Jefferson's ladies, "a disgrace to the town and a bad example to the young people" (126). Homer is, to echo Grella's apt phrase, "an exceptionally murderable man" (49)—a victim whose disappearance invites a conspiracy of silence.

The very failure of the narrator and the town to "solve" the crime until the murderer herself has died indicates much about the true nature of the society in which the murder occurred. If we assume that the narrator/detective and other townsfolk know about the crime (although the textual evidence for this can only be ambiguously inferred), we also realize that for the town to reveal Emily's crime and indicate what it will do in response is far more complicated than silently ignoring the entire matter. For the people of Jefferson, the illusion of *noblesse oblige* is to be preserved at all costs, whether it means remitting Emily's taxes, inviting her Alabama kinfolk to come to Jefferson and regulate her embarrassing courtship, or ignoring a murder by passing off the foul smell emanating from her house shortly after Homer's disappearance as "probably just a snake or a rat."

This conveniently evasive speculation comes from Judge Stevens (whose son is likely Gavin Stevens, the detective/lawyer/chess aficionado in *Knight's Gambit*). The statement can be read several ways. It emphasizes Emily's status as a Poe-like "least-likely" criminal, a misfit so unsuited for the role of murderer that the town's leading citizen does not suspect her. In this light, the Judge's pronouncement is not a red herring, but its opposite, a statement that has the effect of allowing a very real clue to be introduced before allowing a purportedly disinterested observer to shift the narrative's emphasis away from the crime. However, it can also be suggested that, given the facts at hand (e.g., Emily's resistance to allowing her father to be buried and Stevens' reluctance to accuse a "lady" of smelling bad), Stevens' statement is not the naive observation of a casual onlooker but a conveniently calculating means on his part of preserving order, glossing over the rather obvious fact that a well-known citizen has a murder victim rotting inside her house. Where the reader stands in relation to the very tangible clue of the smell depends on his or her willingness to accept the judge's explanation at face value. Like the best detective writers, Faulkner is able to offer pieces of information about the crime, thus putting the careful reader on equal footing with characters in the story, but to do so in such a way as to delay the obvious solution until more substantial proof of the murder comes forth.

That proof comes in the story's final three paragraphs, beginning with the one-sentence paragraph: "The man himself lay in the bed." The crime is both confirmed and solved; the detective pattern is compressed into one climactic scene, which inventively re-imagines a version of Poe's "locked room" mystery, "The Murders in the Rue Morgue." In the classic locked-room story, Dupin unravels the story behind a mother and daughter's murder, which has occurred in an apartment where all the windows and doors are sealed from the inside. In Faulkner's version, a victim's body is similarly discovered inside a mysterious upstairs room, whose door has to be broken down to gain admittance. But since the killer's identity and the mechanism of the murder are readily apparent, the narrator's puzzle is not solved simply by answering "who done it" and "how she done it." The narrator has the more challenging goal of comprehending the gruesome spectacle in the context of the town's obsession with Emily's entire life. This is accomplished with the minuscule clue of a single strand of hair, a temporarily "hidden object" that once detected sets Emily's disturbed mind state into stark relief and provides the town with just the kind of hindsight evidence it needs to justify all of the attention it paid to her over the years.

Finally, in a single sentence, Faulkner skillfully brings the mystery to a close and leaves the reader to reflect upon the narrator/detective's involvement in Emily's deranged decision to murder Homer Barron. As an inventive precursor to Faulkner's own later detective characters, this narrator is an example of how the author, rather than simply mimicking other detective stories, re-worked the classical devices of detection to suit his own ends. "A Rose for Emily" is a notable example of Faulkner's talent for taking the raw materials of his surroundings and working them into original forms—whether this meant drawing from his literary antecedents, re-configuring actual events, or delving into his own considerable imagination. John T. Irwin, in his discussion of *Knight's Gambit,* sets Faulkner next to Poe as a "worthy successor" and a "formidable competitor to the [detective] genre's originator" (173). When viewed as a detective story, "A Rose for Emily" helps buttress this claim and thereby furthers our appreciation of Faulkner's life-long interest in laying out and then solving the many curious mysteries of what he famously termed his "own little postage stamp of native soil" (qtd. in Minter 76).

NOTES

1. For discussions of Faulkner's debt to Poe, see especially Irwin Cawelti, 134; and Stronks, 11.
2. *Sanctuary* exhibits its own interesting connections to the classical detective story. In his famous 1933 preface to the novel French novelist André Malraux remarked that *Sanctuary* was "a novel with a detective-story atmosphere but without detectives"; qtd. in Sundquist, 47.
3. For a thorough discussion of Faulkner and popular short fiction see Matthews, 3–37.
4. All subsequent quotes from the primary text are from *Collected Stories of William Faulkner,* 119–30, and will be cited internally by page number.
5. In the Merrill Literary Casebook series for "A Rose for Emily," editor M. Thomas Inge reprints four articles that posit slightly different time-lines, all of which focus on the story's chronology: see 34, 50–53, 83, 84–86, 90–92.

WORKS CITED

Cawelti, John G. *Adventure, Mystery, and Romance: Formula Stories as Art and Popular Culture.* Chicago: U of Chicago P, 1976.
Cullen, John B., and Floyd C. Watkins, *Old Times in the Faulkner Country.* Chapel Hill: U of North Carolina P, 1961.
Faulkner, William. *Collected Stories of William Faulkner.* New York: Vintage, 1977.
Going, William T. "Chronology in Teaching 'A Rose for Emily.'" *A Rose for Emily.* Ed. M. Thomas Inge. Columbus: Merrill, 1970. 50–53.
Grella, George. "Murder and Manners: The Formal Detective Novel." *Dimensions of Detective Fiction.* Ed. Larry N. Landrum, Pat Browne, and Ray B. Browne. Bowling

Green, OH: Bowling Green State U Popular P, 1976. 37–57.

Howe, Irving. *William Faulkner: A Critical Study.* New York: Vintage, 1962.

Inge, M. Thomas, ed. *A Rose for Emily.* Columbus: Merrill, 1970.

Irwin, John T. *"Knight's Gambit:* Poe, Faulkner, and the Tradition of the Detective Story." *Faulkner and the Short Story.* Ed. Evans Harrington and Ann J. Abadie. Jackson: U of Mississippi P, 1992. 149–73.

Karl, Frederick R. *William Faulkner: An American Writer.* New York: Weidenfeld and Nicolson, 1989.

Matthews, John T. "Shortened Stories: Faulkner and the Market." *Faulkner and the Short Story.* Ed. Evans Harrington and Ann J. Abadie. Jackson: UP of Mississippi. 3–37.

Minter, David. *William Faulkner: His Life and Work.* Baltimore: Johns Hopkins UP, 1980.

O'Connor, William. "The State of Faulkner Criticism." *Sewanee Review* 60 (1952): 184.

Stronks, James. "A Poe Source for Faulkner? 'To Helen' and 'A Rose for Emily.'" *Poe Newsletter* I (Apr. 1968): 11.

Sundquist, Eric. *Faulkner: The House Divided.* Baltimore: Johns Hopkins UP, 1983.

GEORGE L. DILLON

*Styles of Reading**

One of the things readers do with stories is to talk about them. These stories have not said it all, and readers derive evident pleasure from completing them, commenting on them, making them their own in various ways. Christine Brooke-Rose has recently called attention to the strategic incompleteness of good stories—spelling everything out treats the reader as stupid—and has suggested a classification of stories according to the tasks they leave to readers, or in which they entangle readers.[1] If we look at actual, published discussions of a story, however, we find no two of them answering the same set of questions, which suggests that we should look for questions (pre)inscribed in the reader as well as the text—the text, it is a matter of fact, has not very narrowly constrained the set of questions the readers have posed. As soon as we raise the matter of the actual performance of readers, however, we encounter a plethora of variables, and it has become something of a fashion in discussions of reading to enumerate them, often, it seems, to frighten scholars back to the study of narrative competence and the ways texts constrain, or should constrain interpretations. . . . If we are concerned with how people actually do read stories, however, these lists outline an area for research. . . . Perhaps there are underlying regularities which *in fact* shape readers' performances; perhaps there are none. In this article, I will examine readings of Faulkner's "A Rose for Emily," and focus initially on one area of variation—the answers readers have given to questions about the chronological sequence, or "event chain," of the story—to see how wild the variation is and what hope there may be of identifying regularities of performance.

*From *Poetics Today* 3.2 (1982):77–88. Copyright 1982 by The Porter Institute for Poetics and Semiotics, Tel Aviv University. Reprinted by permission.

One reason for focusing on event chains is that these have been among the most intensively studied of the many aspects of story comprehension. . . . Readers employ two basic operations in building event chains: connection and inference. No story I know of spells out all of the terms and connections in an event chain (Miss Emily's motive for murdering Homer Barron, for example, is left for the reader to infer, as is the connection of the arsenic to the murder), and a story that did spell them all out would treat the reader as inconceivably stupid. Two distinctions are in order here: event chains are not precisely chronological, though I think they do correspond closely to . . . chronological sequences, that is, a certain sequentiality is implicit in the notions of motive, action, cause, response, and consequence, but not necessarily clock or calendar time, nor do pieces of the overall chain have to be strictly ordered; different sequences may overlap. This point is quite clear in regard to "A Rose for Emily": it seems possible to establish a chronology of the story that orders all of its major incidents, though it is very difficult to do so,[2] and it is not necessary to have worked out such a time scheme in order to get major portions of the event chain straight. Second, event chains are not "plots." . . . That is, they are shapeless and open-ended; they do not account for any sense of beginning, climax, or conclusion. . . . [E]vent chains are part of the comprehension of all narratives; indeed, of all happenings, not just stories. . . .

When we survey the published criticism of "A Rose for Emily," we find a large and bewildering array of questions about the event chain that have been answered. These include:

1. Why weren't there suitable suitors for Emily?
2. How does Emily respond to being denied suitors?
3. Why does Emily take up with Homer Barron?
4. What happened when he left? Did he abandon her? Why did he come back?
5. Why did she kill him?
6. Why did the smell disappear after only one week?
7. What did Miss Emily think of the men scattering lime around her house?
8. How did the hair come to be on the pillow? How much hair is a *strand?*
9. What was her relationship to Tobe?
10. Did she lie beside the corpse? How often, for what period of years?
11. Why did she not leave the house for the last decade of her life?
12. Did she not know Colonel Sartoris had been dead ten years when she faced down the Aldermen?
13. How crazy was she (unable to distinguish fantasy from reality)?
14. Why does she allow so much dust in her house?

There is also one question that has been asked but not answered, as far as I know: What transpired when the Baptist minister visited her? As the specialists in story comprehension have noted, once we realize that a Story Comprehender must have the power to carry out inferences in order to comprehend even the simplest story and give it that power, the problem becomes one of limiting the inferences drawn to some "relevant" subset of the possible ones. . . . [B]ut it is not clear how to apply this principle [of relevance] to the fourteen questions and answers, since every one of those questions was answered by at least one critic who felt the answer was relevant to the interpretation of the story—relevant to determining her motives, naming her actions, and so on. Of course, some of these event-chain inferences are stimulated by the particular interpretation a critic is putting forth, but there does not seem to be any basis on which to separate those inferences that are made independent of an interpretation from those which are not. . . . People do not agree on the story to then disagree on the interpretation. It is simply not true that, as Wolfgang Iser claims, "On the level of plot, then, there is a high degree of intersubjective consensus," with subjective variation arising at the level of significance.[3] In fact, when we look at the list of questions that have been answered, the construction of event chains seems wildly unconstrained.

If we look at whole readings, however, some system and pattern does emerge. There are two surveys of the criticism of this story, and both find it fairly easy to group the readings into three classes (though the classes are somewhat differently defined).[4] We could group the readings according to what one might call "approaches," suggesting by that term some set of general questions readers taking a particular approach tend to pose of texts they read. This notion can be pushed in two, opposite directions. Taking it one way, we could argue that the variation considered so far does not directly reflect the way readers read but the way critics write about stories when they have an eye toward publication. . . . Taken the other way, these approaches could be viewed as personal styles or preferences in reading that happen to have acquired some public sanction. We generally have some style of reading before we know much about "approaches," after all, though we may learn other questions to ask when we study literature. In any case, one must have learned the approach in order to use it. . . . Some light on the matter is shed, I think, by the very copious transcripts of interviews with undergraduate English majors about "A Rose for Emily" published by Norman Holland in *5 Readers Reading*.

Holland's students also show three distinct approaches, and these approaches match up with the types of approaches in the published criticism[, t]hough . . . they do seem to be giving what they feel are their own responses and to be responding in somewhat original—but consistent—ways to his questions. Also, . . . the criticism they chose to be influenced by as much reflects their cognitive styles as it determines them. Holland's study strongly suggests that there are styles of reading stories, characteristic ways that readers interrogate texts, and that the "approaches" in the criticism are indeed rooted in the critics' own styles of reading and appeal to like-minded readers. I will illustrate this correspondence for three basic styles, which I will call the Character-Action-Moral (CAM) style, the Digger for Secrets style, and the Anthropologist style.

The CAM style differs markedly from the other two in treating the meaning (or significance) as more or less evident in the story: the reader makes the text his own, and makes the reading more apparent, by elaborating the event chain in the direction of the main character's traits, motives, thoughts, responses, and choices. To do this, CAM readers treat the world of the text as an extension or portion of the real world, the characters as real persons, so that we will recognize the experience of characters as being like our own experience; hence it can be understood or explained just as we would understand our own experience. Thus, the inferences they draw are based on commonsense notions of the way the world is, people are, etc. The other two styles appropriate the text not by immersion, but by analytic distance, probing and abstracting behind what is said; they assume that the world of the text is an edited version of our world—a *structure* rather than a glimpse or fragment. The CAM reader works by amalgamating the story into the body of his own beliefs and practical axioms about how life is or should be, the analytic styles by postulating the otherness or strangeness of the text.

The standard CAM reading contains lists of traits that account for the actions of the main character in a straightforward evaluative fashion. . . . The actions are assumed to be pointers toward relatively permanent and pervasive characteristics, and one often finds "it could be otherwise" speculations in CAM readings (e.g., "A Rose for Emily" could have had a happy outcome if Homer Barron had been a marrying man—West;[5] if another man had proposed to Emily after she finished with Homer, she would have declined the offer because she felt herself already married—Sam, in Holland [pp. 138–39]). That is, the notion of character seems to presuppose the freedom of individuals to choose their responses to their situations, and stories like "A Rose for Emily" are treated as collisions between characters and situations—as *tragedies,* in the traditional Butcher/Bradley sense:

> Perhaps the horrible and the admirable aspects of Miss Emily's final deed arise from the same basic fact of her character: she insists on meeting the world on her own terms. She never cringes, she never begs for sympathy, she refuses to shrink into an amiable old maid, she never accepts the community's ordinary judgments or values. This independence of spirit and pride can, and does in her case, twist the individual into a sort of monster, but, at the same time, this refusal to accept the hero values carries with it a dignity and courage.[6] . . .

. . . We can see here the way the common notion of tragedy directs the reading toward character analysis; it also introduces three other questions, namely, those of awareness, tragic flaw, and moral. The evoking or constructing of character seems to lead directly to inference o[f] the character's thoughts. When done naïvely, the results are fairly obtrusive, as when Holland's Sam says Emily has an awareness that "things were moving on, that things were changing, and yet, a similar awareness that she was unable to change along with them" (p. 137). More subtle is a partial merging of reader's and character's points of view. The reader talks about the character in terms the character himself might use: "She lost her honor, and what else could she do but keep him [Homer] forever, make him hers in the only way she possibly could?" (Sam. p. 137). . . .

This construction of an inner logic for the character is essential to the drawing of the moral: once we have realized the character's viewpoint, we can see the fatal flaw, the impulses or tendencies in ourselves that we should not give in to. If this immersion and identification with the character (which is plainly the identification of the character with the reader, in terms of himself) fails, . . . the CAM reader must direct his attention away from the details that suggest Miss Emily is not "like us" (above all, the questions about sleeping next to the corpse).

In sum, then, the CAM style is not afraid to state the obvious; it does not try to be ingenious or clever, but solid and useful; it does not assume the author is fashioning puzzles for us to solve, or playing tricks on us. The story conceals nothing—it is merely, of necessity, incomplete. For Diggers for Secrets, however, the story enwraps secrets, the narrator hides them[,] . . . and the reader must uncover them. The title of Edward Stone's *A Certain Morbidness* suggests how he will read "A Rose for Emily."[7] Diggers for Secrets expect narrators to screen us from the "reality,"

> But when, during her early spinsterhood, her father dies and she refuses for three days to hand his putrefying body over for burial, we are shocked by this irrational action, even though in keeping with his standpoint of noncommitment Faulkner tries to minimize it ("We remembered all the young men her father had driven away, and we knew that with nothing left, she would have to cling to that which had robbed her, as people will"). (Stone, 96)

and expect the author only to give us clues:

> For Faulkner, so far from withholding all clues to Homer Barron's whereabouts, scatters them with a precise prodigality; since his is a story primarily of character, it is to his purpose to saturate our awareness of Miss Emily's abnormality as he goes, so that the last six shocking words merely put the final touch on that purpose. (p. 65)

Sebastian, who is Holland's Digger, also comments on the evenhandedness of the narrator, whom he describes as switching sides (p. 177), and he too finds the maxim about holding on to that which robbed her a screen rather than an explanation: "Shouldn't have put that in, Bill," he says (p. 186). He even proposes to see through the author: "I wanted to see what unconscious things he would reveal about the South" (p. 186).

When Diggers for Secrets explain the psychology of characters, they employ the categories of depth and abnormal psychology . . . and frequently "diagnose" motives the characters would not be aware of and in terms they might well not accept. Sebastian uses the terms *sexuality, obsession,* and *necrophilia* heavily and confidently, but he still falls short, in eloquence at least, of . . . Edward Stone:

> Her passionate, almost sexual relationship with her dead father forces her to distrust the living body of Homer and to kill him so that he will resemble the dead father she can never forget.
>
> Not only does this obsessed spinster continue for some years to share a marriage bed with the body of the man she poisoned—she evidently derives either erotic gratification or spiritual sustenance (both?) from these ghastly nuptials. She becomes, in short, a necrophile or a veritable saprophytic organism; for we learn that the "slender figure in white" that was the young Miss Emily becomes, as though with the middle-aged propriety that the marriage customarily brings, fat! (Stone, 96)

. . . In a similar vein, Sebastian draws numerous inferences about the Negro servant Tobe's complicity in Emily's crime, about her "affair" with Homer, about the details of her sleeping with his corpse (how can a woman perform an act of necrophilia on a man?), and so on.

Symbolism being a ready avenue to non-obvious meanings, these readers find symbolic significances and secrets in details that the CAM readers either pass over or handle prosaically: Miss Emily's house for Stone is an isolated fortress, a forbidden, majestic stronghold; . . . for Sebastian, the title is richly ironic, "an unforgiveable irony in one sense: 'A Rose by any other name would not smell half as sweet!' There's not much sweetness about *her* rose. So I think the title refers to the decomposition of living matter, and so I take it ironically" (p. 182). . . . One expects such ironies from an author presumed to conceal.

An interesting feature of "A Rose for Emily" is that it contains not only a literal hidden secret (which Sebastian objects to as a bit too overt) but a "reader" as well (the narrator). That is, people who habitually look for the dirty reality behind appearances are open to the charge of prurience, a charge that would be easy to level at these readers, and one that the story conveniently allows us to displace onto the narrator ("the community") instead. So the taint of corruption spreads to the town, all these readers say, but, of course, not to *us*.[8] Thus in a sense, the abnormal becomes normal, and the story acquires the universality that raises it from case history to literature. The search for the abnormal and perverse finally leads back to the unacknowledged parts of our selves.

Though the Diggers for Secrets make use of abstractive codes that explain what is going on in the story, their interest in "what's really going on" does, as we have seen, lead to inferences elaborating the event chain. The third group, the Anthropologists, have much less to say about events than either of the first two groups. Their interest, rather, is in identifying the cultural norms and values that explain what characters indisputably do and say. Like Diggers for Secrets, these readers go beneath the surface and state things that are implicit and not said, though what they bring out is not a secret, but the general principles and values which the story illustrates as an example. To some degree, early readings that talk of a conflict in "A Rose for Emily" between the North and the South, or old versus new South, outline this approach, but these readings tended to be brief and schematic, as if critics were not willing to reopen old wounds.[9] And, too, Faulkner was on record as not intending such an interpretation.[10] When a reader is especially engaged in the critique of the norms and values of American society, however, the story takes on interest as an extended exemplum. Thus the two instances of this style of reading, Holland's Shep and Judith Fetterley, are both radicals. For Shep, who is Holland's example of a sixties radical, the characters and events of the story exemplify forces of social struggle—class struggle, racial struggle, and above all the struggle between true and false values. Thus he says Emily's father represents the old code, the dead hand of the past; Homer Barron represents the forces of aimless technology; Emily herself was, he says, "perpetuating the same ethos in which her father lived" (p. 61); "In a way, Miss Emily is a descendant of the culture hero, except that she's a descendant of the culture hero in his waning phase" (p. 166); "They had a very rigid formal code and it was perhaps very much a dead code by the time she got her hands on it, but it represented something which the new people weren't able to offer an adequate substitute for" (p. 161). Proceeding at such a lofty plane, he is fairly indifferent to the detailed goings-on of the event chain, though he does infer Emily's response to the lime-scattering incident—namely, scorn for the men—and he is willing to speculate under Holland's urging. He offers two motives for the murder, first, simple revenge, to keep him from leaving her; but he also evolves a second, mythic explanation, which I quote at some length:

> She can reverse the social decay process by putting her lover, representative of all of them ["the newcomers"] through a physical decay process and coming to relish the sight. This would also give some sort of, quote, explanation, unquote, for her necrophilic hangups. The fact that she wanted her father's body around to . . . preserve it from decay—she was denying the end of the line thing symbolized by putting it underground and letting the earth have it. (p. 171)

. . . So there is a double or triple pattern of explanation here—commonsense psychology (she wanted revenge), operation of social forces, and mythic patterns; these explanations seem somewhat detached from each other and so the reading is not completely totalized.

If Shep is an example of a sixties radical, then Judith Fetterley, in her book *The Resisting Reader*,[11] represents a kind of seventies version of the same basic style of reading. Fetterley focuses on stating the social norms and codes that explain the events of the story—there is very little in the way of constructive activity of motives, actions, responses, and consequences, except for a brief discussion of the lime-scattering incident. She also offers two motives for the murder: first, that Emily murdered Homer because she had to have a man (thus illustrating the brainwashing of the code); but she also offers the following symbolic/mythic account:

> Having been consumed by her father, Emily in turn feeds off Homer Barron, becoming, after his death, suspiciously fat. Or, to put it another way, it is as if, after her father's death, she has reversed his act of incorporating her by incorporating and becoming him, metamorphosed from the slender figure in white to the obese figure in black whose hair is "a vigorous iron-gray, like the hair of an active man." She has taken into herself the violence in him which thwarted her and has reenacted it upon Homer Barron. (pp. 42–43)

On first reading, this seems very much like Stone's celebration of Faulkner's "ghoulish evolution" of the gothic, but on closer examination, the passage is really suggesting a crude form of retributive justice, a pointed, if lurid, warning to the upholders of patriarchy. It is striking that the same elementary operations— *connecting* her growing fat to Homer's murder and *inferring* a causal link—result in such different explanations.

Like Shep, Fetterley makes heavy use of symbolic interpretation and the logic of example: Emily's confinement by her father represents confinement of women by patriarchy; the remission of taxes signifies continued dependence of women on men; the men's treatment of her, and her ability to buffalo them and commit murder without punishment, are explained in terms of the code of the "lady" who is assumed to be out of touch with reality, and must be kept so; Emily represents the town itself, and in discovering her nature, they discover their own.

The focus of Fetterley's interest is in flushing the codes out of hiding and explaining what happens in terms of them, though it is not a totalizing reading in that she doesn't claim to have explained everything in the story in terms of the codes; this treatment represents the extreme of abstraction away from the events and surface of the story toward allegory and parable. That's what it means to be a Resisting Reader: to refuse to give yourself to the work, to accept any of its givens—and in fact, to bring precisely those axioms into question.

Clearly, then, these three styles or approaches are asking different questions of the text, and constructing what are to various degrees different stories in the course of answering them. . . . Readers predisposed to a certain style of reading[, however,] will, when faced with the same text, come up with some very similar stories along with some very similar explanations.

. . . [T]he notion that these styles are, or can become, general patterns of thinking, rather than a learned decorum of literary criticism, seems to derive support from the consideration that we also exhibit differences of styles in thinking about real people and events. We think of ourselves and others as conscious, moral agents shaping our destinies in situations benign and hostile, but also as mysteries to ourselves and others, and/or as enacting typical social roles and attitudes. There is some basis for concluding that we understand literature and life in the same or similar ways, and that some of the ways we read literature will be applied in reading others of life's texts.

NOTES

1. Brooke-Rose, "The Readerhood of Man," in *The Reader in the Text,* ed. Susan R. Suleiman and Inge Crosman (Princeton: Princeton University Press, 1980), 120–48.

2. At least five chronologies have appeared in print, all differing: William T. Going, "Chronology in Teaching 'A Rose for Emily.'" *Exercise Exchange* 5 (1958): 8–11; Robert W. Woodward, "The Chronology of 'A Rose for Emily,'" *Exercise Exchange* 13 (1966): 17–19; Paul D. McGlynn, "The Chronology of 'A Rose for Emily,'" *Studies in Short Fiction* 6 (1969): 461–62; Helen E. Nebeker, "Chronology Revisited," *Studies in Short Fiction* 8 (1971): 471–73; and Menakhem Perry, "Literary Dynamics: How the Order of a Text Creates Its Meaning," *Poetics Today* 1 (1979): 35–63; 311–61.

3. Wolfgang Iser, *The Act of Reading* (Baltimore: Johns Hopkins University Press, 1978), 123. Iser's definition of *significance* as "the reader's absorption of the meaning into his own existence" (p. 151) leaves us in need of an intermediate term between it and *plot* (event chains)—something like *explanation,* which is constructed to account for events (e.g., in terms of character traits, maxims of behavior, mythic patterns, etc.) but which is not necessarily the amalgamation of the story into the reader's subjectivity. For one thing, explanation need not be evaluative. I am using *interpretation* in a broad sense here to mean the reader's commentary minus any plot summary, though even the latter is usually tailored to fit the commentary.

4. See Norman Holland, *5 Readers Reading* (New Haven: Yale University Press, 1975), 21–24 (cited in the text as Holland, or Holland's Sam); and Perry, "Literary Dynamics," 62–63 et passim.

5. Ray B. West, "Atmosphere and Theme in Faulkner's 'A Rose for Emily,'" in *William Faulkner: Four Decades of Criticism,* ed. Linda W. Wagner (East Lansing: Michigan State University Press, 1973), 192–98. Cited in the text as West.

6. Cleanth Brooks and Robert Penn Warren, *Understanding Fiction* (New York: Crofts, 1948), . . . [413].

7. Stone, *A Certain Morbidness* (Carbondale: Southern Illinois University Press, 1969). Cited in the text as Stone.

8. For Ruth Sullivan, however, the narrator is a prying, probing voyeur, and so are we readers. See "The Narrators in 'A Rose for Emily,'" *Journal of Narrative Technique* 1 (1971): 159–78.

9. Frederick Gwynn and Joseph L. Blotner, *Faulkner in the University* (New York: Vintage Books, 1965), 47–48.

10. There is one style which I find attested only in Holland's interviews (and in some of the papers of David Bleich's students), that we might call the Visualizer style, the style of Holland's Sandra, whose comments . . . are strongly weighted to descriptions of characters' expressions and feelings, decors and other physical details and commentary on the suitability of words, images and tonal effects in the narration. This is perhaps the most surface- or craft-conscious of the styles, and the reason it does not appear in the published readings is that it is more a style of appreciation than explanation, or, to put it another way, it is more concerned with explaining the details of the style and presentation . . . than with the story. . . .

11. Fetterley, *The Resisting Reader* (Bloomington and London: Indiana University Press, 1978).

JUDITH FETTERLEY

A Rose for "A Rose for Emily"*

In "A Rose for Emily" . . . grotesque reality . . . becomes explicit. Justifying Faulkner's use of the grotesque has been a major concern of critics who have written on the story. If, however, one approaches "A Rose for Emily" from a feminist perspective, one notices that the grotesque aspects of the story are a result of its violation of the expectations generated by the conventions of sexual politics. The ending shocks us not simply by its hint of necrophilia; more shocking is the fact that it is a woman who provides the hint. It is one thing for Poe to spend his nights in the tomb of Annabel Lee and another thing for Miss Emily Grierson to deposit a strand of iron-gray hair on the pillow beside the rotted corpse of Homer Barron. Further, we do not expect to discover that a woman has murdered a man. . . . To reverse [the] "natural" pattern inevitably produces the grotesque.

Faulkner, however, is not interested in invoking the kind of grotesque which is the consequence of reversing the clichés of sexism for the sake of a cheap thrill.

*From *The Resisting Reader: A Feminist Approach to American Fiction,* by Judith Fetterley (Bloomington and London: Indiana U P, 1978). Copyright 1978 by Judith Fetterley. Reprinted by permission.

. . . Rather, Faulkner invokes the grotesque in order to illuminate and define the true nature of the conventions on which it depends. "A Rose for Emily" is a story not of a conflict between the South and the North or between the old order and the new; it is a story of the patriarchy North and South, new and old, and of the sexual conflict within it. As Faulkner himself has implied,[1] it is a story of a woman victimized and betrayed by the system of sexual politics, who nevertheless has discovered, within the structures that victimize her, sources of power for herself. . . . "A Rose for Emily" is the story of how to murder your gentleman caller and get away with it. Faulkner's story is an analysis of how men's attitudes toward women turn back upon themselves; it is a demonstration of the thesis that it is impossible to oppress without in turn being oppressed, it is impossible to kill without creating the conditions for your own murder. "A Rose for Emily" is the story of a *lady* and of her revenge for that grotesque identity.

"When Miss Emily Grierson died, our whole town went to her funeral." The public and communal nature of Emily's funeral, a festival that brings the town together, clarifying its social relationships and revitalizing its sense of the past, indicates her central role in Jefferson. Alive, Emily is town property and the subject of shared speculation; dead, she is town history and the subject of legend. It is her value as a symbol, however obscure and however ambivalent, of something that is of central significance to the identity of Jefferson and to the meaning of its history that compels the narrator to assume a communal voice to tell her story. For Emily . . . is a man-made object, a cultural artifact, and what she is reflects and defines the culture that has produced her.

The history the narrator relates to us reveals Jefferson's continuous emotional involvement with Emily. Indeed, though she shuts herself up in a house which she rarely leaves and which no one enters, her furious isolation is in direct proportion to the town's obsession with her: . . . she is the object of incessant attention; her every act is immediately consumed by the town for gossip and seized on to justify their interference in her affairs. Her private life becomes a public document that the town folk feel free to interpret at will, and they are alternately curious, jealous, spiteful, pitying, partisan, proud, disapproving, admiring, and vindicated. Her funeral is not simply a communal ceremony; it is also the climax of their invasion of her private life and the logical extension of their voyeuristic attitude toward her. Despite the narrator's demurral, getting inside Emily's house is the all-consuming desire of the town's population, both male and female; while the men may wait a little longer, their motive is still prurient curiosity: "Already we knew that there was one room in that region above stairs which no one had seen in forty years, and which would have to be forced. They waited until Miss Emily was decently in the ground before they opened it."

In a context in which the overtones of violation and invasion are so palpable, the word "decently" has that ironic ring which gives the game away. When the men finally do break down the door, they find that Emily has satisfied their prurience with a vengeance and in doing so has created for them a mirror image of themselves. The true nature of Emily's relation to Jefferson is contained in the analogies between what those who break open that room see in it and what has brought them there to see it. The perverse, violent, and grotesque aspects of the sight of Homer Barron's rotted corpse in a room decked out for a bridal and now faded and covered in dust reflects back to them the perverseness of their own prurient interest in Emily, the violence implicit in their continued invasions of her life, and the grotesqueness of the symbolic artifact they have made of her—their monument, their idol, their lady. Thus, the figure that Jefferson places at the center of its legendary history does indeed contain the clue to the meaning of that history—a history which began long before Emily's funeral and long before Homer Barron's disappearance or appearance and long before Colonel Sartoris' fathering of edicts and remittances. It is recorded in that emblem which lies at the heart of the town's memory and at the heart of patriarchal culture: "We had long thought of them as a tableau, Miss Emily a slender figure in white in the background, her father a spraddled silhouette in the foreground, his back to her and clutching a horsewhip, the two of them framed by the back-flung front door."

The importance of Emily's father in shaping the quality of her life is insistent throughout the story. Even in her death the force of his presence is felt; above her dead body sits "the crayon face of her father musing profoundly," symbolic of the degree to which he has dominated and shadowed her life, "as if that quality of her father which had thwarted her woman's life so many times had been too virulent and too furious to die." The violence of this consuming relationship is made explicit in the imagery of the tableau. Although the violence is apparently directed outward—the upraised horsewhip against the would-be suitor—the real object of it is the woman-daughter, forced into the background and dominated by the phallic figure of the spraddled father whose back is turned on her and who prevents her from getting out at the same time that he prevents them from getting in. [Emily's] . . . spatial confinement [is] . . . a metaphor for her psychic confinement: her identity is determined by the constructs of her father's mind, and she can no more escape from his creation of her as "a slender figure in white" than she can escape his house.

What is true for Emily in relation to her father is equally true for her in relation to Jefferson: her status as a lady is a cage from which she cannot escape. To them she is always *Miss* Emily; she is never referred to and never thought of as otherwise. In omitting her title from his, Faulkner emphasizes the point that the real violence done to Emily is in making her a "Miss"; the omission is one of his roses for her. Because she is *Miss* Emily *Grierson,* Emily's father dresses her in white, places her in the background, and drives away her suitors. Because she is Miss Emily Grierson, the town invests her with that communal significance which makes her the object of their obsession and the subject of their incessant scrutiny. And because she is a lady, the town is able to impose a particular code of behavior on her ("But there were still others, older people, who said that even grief could not cause a real lady to forget *noblesse oblige*") and to see in her failure to live up to that code an excuse for interfering in her life. As a lady, Emily is venerated, but veneration results in the more telling emotions of envy and spite: "It was another link between the gross, teeming world and the high and mighty Griersons"; "People . . . believed that the Griersons held themselves a little too high for what they really were." The violence implicit in the desire to see the monument fall and reveal itself for clay suggests the violence inherent in the original impulse to venerate.

The violence behind veneration is emphasized through another telling emblem in the story. Emily's position as a hereditary obligation upon the town dates from "that day in 1894 when Colonel Sartoris, the mayor—he who fathered the edict that no Negro woman should appear on the streets without an apron on— remitted her taxes, the dispensation dating from the death of her father on into perpetuity." The conjunction of these two actions in the same syntactic unit is crucial, for it insists on their essential similarity. It indicates that the impulse to exempt is analogous to the desire to restrict, and that what appears to be a kindness or an act of veneration is in fact an insult. Sartoris' remission of Emily's taxes is a public declaration of the fact that a lady is not considered to be, and hence not allowed or enabled to be, economically independent (consider, in this connection, Emily's lessons in china painting; they are a latter-day version of Sartoris' "charity" and a brilliant image of Emily's economic uselessness). His act is a public statement of the fact that a lady, if she is to survive, must have either husband or father, and that, because Emily has neither, the town must assume responsibility for her. The remission of taxes that defines Emily's status dates from the death of her father, and she is handed over from one patron to the next, the town instead of husband taking on the role of father. Indeed, the use of the word "fathered" in describing Sartoris' behavior as mayor underlines the fact that his chivalric attitude toward Emily is simply a subtler and more dishonest version of her father's horsewhip.

The narrator is the last of the patriarchs who take upon themselves the burden of defining Emily's life, and his violence toward her is the most subtle of all. His tone of incantatory reminiscence and nostalgic veneration seems free of the taint of horsewhip and edict. Yet a thoroughgoing contempt for the "ladies" who spy and pry and gossip out of their petty jealousy and curiosity is one of the clearest strands in the narrator's consciousness. Emily is exempted from the general indictment because she is a *real* lady—that is, eccentric, slightly crazy, obsolete, a "stubborn and coquettish decay," absurd but indulged; "dear, inescapable, impervious, tranquil, and perverse"; indeed, anything and everything but human.

Not only does "A Rose for Emily" expose the violence done to a woman by making her a lady; it also explores the particular form of power the victim gains from this position and can use on those who enact this violence. "A Rose for Emily" is concerned with the consequences of violence for both the violated and the violators. One of the most striking aspects of the story is the disparity between Miss Emily Grierson and the Emily to whom Faulkner gives his rose in ironic imitation of the chivalric behavior the story exposes. The form of Faulkner's title establishes a camaraderie between author and protagonist and signals that a distinction must be made between the story Faulkner is telling and the story the narrator is telling. This distinction is of major importance because it suggests, of course, that the narrator, looking through a patriarchal lens, does not see Emily at all but rather a figment of his own imagination created in conjunction with the cumulative imagination of the town: . . . nobody sees *Emily*. And because nobody sees *her*, she can literally get away with murder. Emily is characterized by her ability to understand and utilize the power that accrues to her from the fact that men do not see her but rather their concept of her: "'I have no taxes in Jefferson. Colonel Sartoris explained it to me. . . . Tobe! . . . Show these gentlemen out." Relying on the conventional assumptions about ladies who are expected to be neither reasonable nor in touch with reality, Emily presents an impregnable front that vanquishes the men "horse and foot, just as she had vanquished their fathers thirty years before." In spite of their "modern" ideas, this new generation, when faced with Miss Emily, are as much bound by the code of gentlemanly behavior as their fathers were ("They rose when she entered"). This code gives Emily a power that renders the gentlemen unable to function in a situation in which a lady neither sits down herself nor asks them to. They are brought to a "stumbling halt" and can do nothing when confronted with her refusal to engage in rational discourse. Their only recourse in the face of such eccentricity is to engage in behavior unbecoming to gentlemen, and Emily can count on their continuing to see themselves as gentlemen and her as a lady and on their returning a verdict of helpless noninterference.

It is in relation to Emily's disposal of Homer Barron, however, that Faulkner demonstrates most clearly the power of conventional assumptions about the nature of ladies to blind the town to what is going on and to allow Emily to murder with impunity. When Emily buys the poison, it never occurs to anyone that she intends to use it on Homer, so strong is the presumption that ladies when jilted commit suicide, not murder. And when her house begins to smell, the women blame it on the eccentricity of having a man servant rather than a woman, "as if a man—any man—could keep a kitchen properly." And then they hint that her eccentricity may have shaded over into madness, "remembering how old lady Wyatt, her great aunt, had gone completely crazy at last." The presumption of madness, that preeminently female response to bereavement, can be used to explain away much in the behavior of ladies whose activities seem a bit odd.

But even more pointed is what happens when the men try not to explain but to do something about the smell: "'Dammit, sir,' Judge Stevens said, 'will you accuse a lady to her face of smelling bad?'" But if a lady cannot be told that she smells, then the cause of the smell cannot be discovered and so her crime is "perfect." Clearly, the assumptions behind the Judge's outraged retort go beyond the myth that ladies are out of touch with reality. His outburst insists that it is the responsibility of gentlemen to make them so. Ladies must not be confronted with facts; they must be shielded from all that is unpleasant. Thus Colonel Sartoris remits Emily's taxes with a palpably absurd story, designed to protect her from an awareness of her poverty and her dependence on charity, and to protect him from having to confront her with it. And thus Judge Stevens will not confront Emily with the fact that her house stinks, though she is living in it and can hardly be unaware of the odor. Committed as they are to the myth that ladies and bad smells cannot coexist, these gentlemen insulate themselves from reality. And by defining a lady as a subhuman and hence sublegal entity, they have created a situation their laws can't touch. They have made it possible for Emily to be extra-legal: "'Why, of course,' the druggist said, 'If that's what you want. But the law requires you to tell what you are going to use it for.' Miss Emily just stared at him, her head tilted back in order to look him eye for eye, until he looked away and went and got the arsenic and wrapped it up." And, finally, they have created a situation in which they become the criminals: "So the next night, after midnight, four men crossed Miss Emily's lawn and slunk about the house like burglars." Above them, "her upright torso motionless as that of an idol," sits Emily, observing them act out their charade of chivalry. As they leave, she confronts them with the reality they are trying to protect her from: she turns on the light so that they may see her watching them. One can only wonder at the fact, and regret, that she didn't call the sheriff and have them arrested for trespassing.

Not only is "A Rose for Emily" a supreme analysis of what men do to women by making them ladies; it is also an exposure of how this act in turn defines and recoils upon men. This is the significance of the dynamic that Faulkner establishes between Emily and Jefferson. And it is equally the point of the dynamic implied between the tableau of Emily and her father and the tableau which greets the men who break down the door of that room in the region above the stairs. When the would-be "suitors" finally get into her father's house, they discover the consequences of his oppression of her, for the violence contained in the rotted corpse of Homer Barron is the mirror image of the violence represented in the tableau, the back-flung front door flung back with a vengeance. Having been consumed by her father, Emily in turn feeds off Homer Barron, becoming, after his death, suspiciously fat. Or, to put it another way, it is as if, after her father's death, she has reversed his act of incorporating her by incorporating and becoming him, metamorphosed from the slender figure in white to the obese figure in black whose hair is "a vigorous iron-gray, like the hair of an active man." She has taken into herself the violence in him which thwarted her and has reenacted it upon Homer Barron.

That final encounter, however, is not simply an image of the reciprocity of violence. Its power of definition also derives from its grotesqueness, which makes finally explicit the grotesqueness that has been latent in the description of Emily throughout the story: "Her skeleton was small and spare; perhaps that was why what would have been merely plumpness in another was obesity in her. She looked bloated, like a body long submerged in motionless water, and of that pallid hue. Her eyes, lost in the fatty ridges of her face, looked like two small pieces of coal pressed into a lump of dough." The impact of this description depends on the contrast it establishes between Emily's reality as a fat, bloated figure in black and the conventional image of a lady—expectations that are fostered in the town by its emblematic memory of Emily as a slender figure in white and in us by the narrator's tone of romantic invocation and by the passage itself. Were she not expected to look so diferent, were her skeleton not small and spare, Emily would not be so grotesque. Thus, the focus is on the grotesqueness that results when stereotypes are imposed upon reality. And the implication of this focus is that the real grotesque is the stereotype itself. If Emily is both lady and grotesque, then the syllogism must be completed thus: the idea of a lady is grotesque. So Emily is metaphor and mirror for the town of Jefferson; and when, at the end, the town folk finally discover who and what she is, they have in fact encountered who and what they are. . . . [T]he efforts to read "A Rose for Emily" as a parable of the relations between North and South, or as a conflict between an old order and a new, or as a story about the human relation to Time, don't work because the attempt to make Emily representative of such concepts stumbles over the fact that woman's condition is not the "human" condition.[2] To understand Emily's experience requires a primary awareness of the fact that she is a woman.

But, more important, Faulkner provides us with an image of retaliation. [Emily] does not simply acquiesce; she prefers to murder rather than to die. In this respect she is a welcome change from the image of woman as willing victim that fills the pages of our literature. . . . Nevertheless, Emily's action is still reaction. "A Rose for Emily" exposes the poverty of a situation in which turnabout is the only possibility and in which one's acts are neither self-generated nor self-determined but are simply a response to and a reflection of forces outside oneself. Though Emily may be proud, strong, and indomitable, her murder of Homer Barron is finally an indication of the severely limited nature of the power women can wrest from the system that oppresses them. . . . Emily's act . . . is possible only because it can be kept secret; and it can be kept secret only at the cost of exploiting her image as a lady. . . .

Patriarchal culture is based to a considerable extent on the argument that men and women are made for each other and on the conviction that "masculinity" and "feminity" are the natural reflection of that divinely ordained complement. Yet, if one reads . . . "A Rose for Emily" as [an] analys[i]s of the consequences of a massive differentiation of everything according to sex, one sees that in reality a sexist culture is one in which men and women are not simply incompatible but murderously so. . . . Emily murders Homer Barron because she must at any cost get a man. The [gap] . . . between cultural myth and cultural reality . . . suggest[s] that in this disparity is the ultimate grotesque.

NOTES

1. See *Faulkner in the University: Class Conferences at the University of Virginia 1957–1958,* edited by Frederick L. Gwynn and Joseph I. Blotner (Charlottesville: University of Virginia Press, 1959), 87–88; *Faulkner at Nagamo,* edited by Robert A. Jeliffe (Tokyo: Kenkyusha, 1956), 71.
2. For a sense of some of the difficulties involved in reading the story in these terms, I refer the reader to the collection of criticism edited by M. Thomas Inge, *A Rose for Emily* (Columbus, Ohio: Merrill, 1970).

GENE M. MOORE

Of Time and Its Mathematical Progression: Problems of Chronology in Faulkner's "A Rose for Emily"*

Over the past 30 years, no fewer than *eight* different chronologies have been proposed to account for the events occurring in William Faulkner's celebrated short story "A Rose for Emily."[1] These chronologies cover a span of 14 years (Miss Emily was born between 1850 and 1864, and died between 1924 and 1938), and they make use of many different kinds of evidence: not only internal temporal references and cross-references in the story, but also historical, biographical, canonical, and even forensic evidence. Given the amount of interest generated by this question and the range of evidence employed in the various arguments, it is remarkable that no one seems ever to have regarded the original manuscript as a possible source of chronological information; in fact, evidence from the manuscript makes it possible to solve some of the problems of Miss Emily's chronology by fixing the date of her father's death.

While critics have recognized the importance of time to a proper understanding of the story[,] . . . they have also complained, in strong and vivid language, of the difficulty of establishing a consistent chronology: "Faulkner destroys chronological time in his story" (Magalaner and Volpe, cited in Inge 63); he uses "a complicatedly disjunctive time scheme" (Wilson 56) that "twists chronology almost beyond recognition" (Sullivan 167); his technique is an "abandonment of chronology" (A. M. Wright, cited in Sullivan 167). Yet whether the story of Miss Emily Grierson is to be understood in terms of conflict between the North and the South, between the Old South and the New South, or between the "past" and the "present," for the sake of all these arguments it is vitally important to establish her own chronological place in the historical context of the passing generations. What dates are carved on Miss Emily's tombstone?

The task at hand has never been stated more simply than by William T. Going in the earliest of the chronologies: "By means of internal or external evidence, date the major events of Emily Grierson's life" (8). Yet in practice it is often difficult to distinguish "internal" from "external" evidence. Is evidence from the unrevised manuscript of "A Rose for Emily" internal or external? What about

---

*From *Studies in Short Fiction* 29 (Spring 1992): 195–204. All notes are Moore's; some of his works cited have been omitted.   1. These chronologies were proposed by—in chronological order—Going (1958), Hagopian et al. (1964), Woodward (1966), McGlynn (1969), Nebeker (1970 and 1971), Wilson (1972), Brooks (1978), and Perry (1979). The first four were reprinted in Inge's 1970 casebook. Cleanth Brooks refers to five chronologies in this casebook (382n), but I have only been able to discover four, and my count is confirmed by the list in one of the suggestions for short papers at the end of Inge's volume (127). Helen E. Nebeker has proposed two different chronologies (the first in "Emily's Rose . . . : Thematic Implications" and the second in "Emily's Rose . . . : A Postscript" and "Chronology Revised"). Although different evidence is used, Nebeker's second chronology agrees with that proposed by Hagopian et al.

references to Judge Stevens or Colonel Sartoris in other works by Faulkner? In general, what constitutes legitimate chronological evidence? In cases of conflict, what forms of evidence should take precedence over others? The "internal" chronology of a given work may or may not prove to be consistent, and may or may not be attached (consistently or inconsistently) to a variety of "external" chronologies based on information such as references occurring in other works by the same author (*canonical* evidence), or what we know about the author's life (*biographical* evidence) or the context of history in general (*historical* evidence). In each case, specific chronological references can be either *absolute,* in the form of dates (such as the single reference to 1894 in "A Rose for Emily"); *relative* to other references (e.g., "the summer after her father's death," "thirty years before"); or *contextual,* establishing a measure of time with reference to historical or natural codes of temporality outside the text (e.g., allusions to the Civil War signify 1861–65; the graying of Miss Emily's hair is a gradual process; dead bodies decompose at a certain rate under certain conditions, etc.). The discrepancies among the eight chronologies are largely a result of underlying differences of opinion about the relative weights to be accorded these various kinds of evidence.

The specific difficulty of establishing a chronology for Miss Emily arises largely because the first half of her story is told essentially in reverse chronological order, and the events in it are described not in terms of dates or specific historical references, but most often in terms of her age at the time. Anchoring this "internal" chronology in history requires, in effect, that we find at least one point of attachment between "internal" references to Miss Emily's age or activities, and "external" references to dates or known historical events.

Most of the discussion in the eight chronologies has centered upon two problematic events in her life: the remission of her taxes by Colonel Sartoris in 1894 [paragraph 3], and the period of china-painting lessons "when she was about forty" [paragraph 49]. 1894 is the only date mentioned in the story, but its exact position in Miss Emily's life (i.e., her age at the time) is by no means certain. In the third paragraph of the story, reference is made to "that day in 1894 when Colonel Sartoris, the mayor . . . remitted her taxes, the dispensation dating from the death of her father on into perpetuity." . . . This means, at the least, that her father died no later than 1894. We are told that at the time of her father's death Miss Emily had "got to be thirty and was still single" [paragraph 25]; and when she buys the poison about two years later, the narrator reminds us that "She was over thirty then" [paragraph 34]. The year 1864 is thus a *terminus ad quem* for Miss Emily's birth, and is respected as such by all the chronologists.

Some, however, have taken 1894 as the point of attachment between Emily's life and historical chronology, assuming that her taxes were remitted immediately following her father's death, and that he accordingly died that same year (McGlynn, Wilson). Her age at the time is taken as 30 (McGlynn) or 32 (Wilson), indicating that she was born in 1862 or 1864 and died in 1936 or 1938. However, "A Rose for Emily" was first published in 1930, creating a "glaring discrepancy" that led Helen E. Nebeker to revise her original chronology ("Chronology Revised" 471), and that in Menakhem Perry's opinion leads to "absurd conclusions" (344n26). Nebeker and Perry take 1930, the date of publication, as a *ter-*

minus ad quem for Miss Emily's death, which means that the year 1856 becomes the corresponding *terminus* for her birth.[2]

The remission of Miss Emily's taxes is mentioned twice in the story: first as occurring in 1894, and second in connection with the period of her china-painting lessons "when she was about forty": the narrator ends the paragraph describing these lessons with the remark that "Meanwhile her taxes had been remitted" (128). Some chronologists have taken this "Meanwhile" to mean that Miss Emily must have been "about forty" in 1894, and that she was therefore born in 1854 and died in 1928 (Hagopian et al., Nebeker, "Emily's Rose . . . : A Postscript" and "Chronology Revised"). Brooks's chronology is a numerical compromise between those of Going and Hagopian et al., according to which Miss Emily, born in 1852, would have been 42 in 1894. Perry also takes this "Meanwhile" as indicative of simultaneity: "She was exempted from taxation in the period when she gave china-painting lessons" (344n26). In other words, much of the discrepancy among the various chronologies can be understood as a result of the choice of where to attach the historical "anchor" of the remission of taxes in 1894: to the death of Miss Emily's father when she was "over thirty," or to the china-painting period when she was "about forty"?

Surprisingly, what no one seems to have noticed or taken seriously is that in the original manuscript Faulkner assigned a different date to the remission of Miss Emily's taxes and a specific date to her father's death: the corresponding passage in the manuscript speaks of "that day in 1904 when Colonel Sartoris . . . remitted her taxes dating from the death of her father 16 years back, on into perpetuity" (Inge 8).[3] One can only speculate about why Faulkner found it necessary to shift the date of Colonel Sartoris's gallant action back ten years from 1904 to 1894, and to delete all reference to the "16 years" since the father's death. Perhaps 16 years seemed too long for Miss Emily to remain actively on the minds of city officials? In any event, it is clear that when Faulkner originally committed the story to paper, her taxes were remitted not in 1894 but in 1904, 16 years after the death of her father in 1888. Restoring Faulkner's alterations and deletions may seem to run counter to the editorial principle of respecting the author's final intentions; but keeping the original dates in mind can help untangle the story's chronology.

The altered date and the omission of the reference to "16 years back" in the typescript version need not mean that Faulkner had necessarily changed his mind about the date of Miss Emily's father's death. Had he moved it back the same 10 years, she would have to have been born before 1848 to have been over 30 by

---

2. The provisional futurism of a situation in which Miss Emily dies fictionally some years after the announcement of her death in the "real" world, as posited in half of the published chronologies (those of Woodward, McGlynn, Nebeker ["Emily's Rose . . . : Thematic Implications"], and Wilson), is not without literary precedent. . . . In the case of "A Rose for Emily," the "inconvenience" indeed exists only if one claims to identify the fictional world of Miss Emily with the historical world of William Faulkner; but this claim is at the origin of any attempt to set up a chronology.   3. This oversight is all the more remarkable in view of the fact that a quite legible reproduction of the first manuscript page was printed as an illustration in Inge's 1970 casebook, which all the later critics have cited as a reference.

1878, and would thus have been of the same generation as the Civil War veterans who attend her funeral. As Brooks noted,

> The "very old men—some in their brushed Confederate uniforms" who, at the funeral, talked "of Miss Emily as if she had been a contemporary of theirs, believing that they had danced with her and courted her" must have been a number of years older than she. (*WF: Toward Yoknapatawpha and Beyond* 383)[4]

However, in the earliest of the chronologies, William T. Going invoked Faulkner's authority to the effect that Miss Emily was born in 1850 and died in 1924, since 1924 was the date assigned to "A Rose for Emily" in Malcolm Cowley's Viking Portable edition of Faulkner's works (1946), in which Cowley noted editorially that dates were assigned "with the author's consent and later with his advice at doubtful points" (cited in Inge 51).[5] Going set the date of her father's death as early as 1882.

Manuscript evidence cannot solve all the chronological problems, since the china-painting period is defined not only in connection with Miss Emily's being "about forty," but also retrospectively, working backward from later events: the death of Colonel Sartoris, the visit of the tax delegation, and her own death. We are told that no one had seen the house's interior for "at least ten years" before she died [paragraph 1], and that the visit of the tax delegation (which may or may not have been the last visit before her death, but is in any case the only visit we are told about) took place "eight or ten years" after she ceased giving china-painting lessons [paragraph 5] and "almost ten years" after the death of Colonel Sartoris [paragraph 14].[6] In other words, she died at least 18 years after the last lessons were given: 18 years before her death at age 74, Miss Emily would have been 56 years old, so that if the lessons lasted for "a period of six or seven years" [paragraph 49], Miss Emily could not have been "about forty" at the time, but would instead have been about 50. Paul D. McGlynn has attempted to disregard this problem by suggesting that "Of course 'about forty' might well be a genteel euphemism for 'about fifty'" (Inge 91; cf. Wilson 59); but this suggestion still does not explain why the narrator would protect Miss Emily's age only at this particular point and not elsewhere. Would anyone wish to read the narrator's two references to her being "over thirty" as genteel euphemisms for "over forty," or the announcement of her "death at seventy-four" as a coded euphemism for 84? In effect, the chronology to be established by tracing the course of Miss Emily's life forward from the time of her father's death fails to square with the chronology to be derived retrospectively from the time of her own death.

Interpreting the reference to "at least ten years" as possibly allowing for as

---

4. On similar historical gounds, one could argue that the Homer Barron episode must be set much later, since the actual streets of Oxford were not paved until the 1920s (Cullen and Watkins 71, cited in Inge 17).   5. Cowley also acknowledged in his Introduction that "As one book leads into another, Faulkner sometimes falls into inconsistencies of detail." He added that "these errors are comparatively few and inconsequential. . . . I should judge that most of them are afterthoughts rather than oversights" (Cowley 7–8).   6. In the place of the reference to the china-painting lessons as having ceased "eight or ten years earlier" (120), the unrevised manuscript reads "6 or 7 years ago" (Faulkner, *Manuscripts* 189).

much as 20 years is also no solution, since the visit of the tax delegation is the peg from which the date of the smell "thirty years before" is hung. Internal references indicate that Homer Barron must have died when Miss Emily was about 33 or 34 years old: at least 40 years before her own death (equal to the "at least ten years" since the last visit plus the 30 years since the smell), and two years after her father's death, which occurred when she was already at least 30. A limit is thereby set to the range of time included in "at least": her last visit had to occur "at least ten years" and at most 12 years before her death, since if it occurred more than 12 years earlier, she would have been under 30 when her father died.

In summary, the chronologies can be divided roughly into two groups: one group—Woodward, McGlynn, Nebeker ("Emily's Rose . . . : Thematic Implications"), and Wilson—connects the tax remission of 1894 with her father's death (Emily is between 30 and 34 in 1894); while the other—Going, Hagopian et al., Nebeker ("Emily's Rose . . . : A Postscript" and "Chronology Revised"), Brooks, and Perry—links the reference to 1894 with the period of china-painting (i.e., Emily is "about forty," or between 39 and 42, in 1894). The first group tends to disregard the narrator's reference to the remission of taxes as being retroactive: "the dispensation dating from the death of her father on into perpetuity" [paragraph 3]. Taxes are collected annually—"On the first of the year they mailed her a tax notice" [paragraph 4]—so that if Miss Emily's taxes were remitted the same year her father died, the narrator's reference to the retroactive nature of the remission would appear to be unnecessary.

This much can be determined on the basis of "internal" references alone; but the references to Colonel Sartoris and to Judge Stevens lead us outside the story to look for external canonical evidence in the form of references to these gentlemen in other works by Faulkner. If Judge Stevens was already 80 years old and mayor at the time of the smell (which the chronologies date variously between 1884 and 1896), then he is probably too old to be Judge Lemuel Stevens, the father of Gavin Stevens, who is mentioned in Faulkner's late works: he would have been between 102 and 114 years old at the time of his death in 1918— perhaps not an altogether impossible age, but one remarkable enough to be worth mentioning. Nevertheless, most of the glossaries and indexes have identified the elderly Judge Stevens of "A Rose for Emily" with Judge Lemuel . . . .

Similar problems arise with the reference to a Colonel Sartoris who was mayor in 1894 and who died "almost ten years" before the visit of the tax delegation (and thus about 20 years before Miss Emily's death, when she was about 54). Once again, there is some doubt about which Colonel Sartoris is meant: Faulkner has described the early history of the Sartoris family more thoroughly than that of the Stevenses, so that it appears correspondingly more difficult to imagine a strange new Colonel Sartoris, unique to "A Rose for Emily" and unmentioned elsewhere, who could have been mayor in 1894. Faulkner's works mention two Colonel Sartorises: Colonel John Sartoris, who dies too early to have been Miss Emily's mayor in 1894, and his son Bayard—"the banker with his courtesy title acquired partly by inheritance and partly by propinquity" (*Reivers* 74)—who dies too late. . . .

However, the original date of 1904 for the mayoral edict may help to solve this problem as well, since young Bayard Sartoris could well have been mayor at that time. We are told in *The Reivers* of his propensity for passing edicts, although he is not specifically named as mayor; when his matched carriage horses are startled by a home-made automobile, "by the next night there was formally recorded into the archives of Jefferson a city ordinance against the operation of any mechanically propelled vehicle inside the corporate limits" (27–28); additional information in *The Reivers* makes it possible to date this incident as having occurred in 1904. The Colonel's tendency to govern by radical edict is mentioned in "A Rose for Emily" as well, since it was "he who fathered the edict that no Negro woman should appear on the streets without an apron" (par. 3).

In conclusion, the neglected manuscript evidence, by allowing us to fix the date of the death of Miss Emily's father in 1888, makes it possible to establish a chronology that is different from the eight that have been suggested previously (although it differs from that of Perry by only one year). Perhaps when Faulkner decided to move the time of Miss Emily's tax remission back by ten years, he simply failed to consider the consequences of this alteration for the rest of the chronology. Yet whether the year in question is 1894 or 1904, the internal inconsistency of the period of her china-painting remains, together with the canonical inconsistencies concerning the identities of Judge Stevens and Colonel Sartoris. The ancient Civil War veterans who try to remember Miss Emily are not alone in having to cope with the problem of "confusing time with its mathematical progression."

APPENDIX: A CHRONOLOGY FOR MISS EMILY GRIERSON

1856: Miss Emily is born; the narrator never mentions her birth directly, but his reference to "the day of her death at seventy-four" (127–28) defines the parameters of any chronology in terms of a span of 74 years.

1870–1879: The Grierson house is built "in the heavily lightsome style of the seventies" (119), thus presumably during the 1870s.

1888: Her father dies after "she got to be thirty" (123).

1889: She meets Homer Barron "the summer after her father's death" (124).

1890: She buys arsenic from the druggist "over a year after they had begun to say 'Poor Emily'. . . . She was over thirty then" (125). She poisons Homer Barron, who disappears "two years after her father's death"; a smell is noticed "a short time after" (122), which is also "thirty years before" the tax visit (121).

1893–1900: Miss Emily is "about forty"; she gives lessons in china-painting "for a period of six or seven years" (128).

1894: "Meanwhile" (119, 128) Colonel Sartoris, the mayor, remits her taxes.

1920: She is visited by a deputation of the Board of Aldermen "eight or ten years" after she stops giving china-painting lessons (120) and "almost ten years" (121) after the death of Colonel Sartoris.

1930: She dies "at least ten years" (119) since her last visit, presumably from the tax deputation; after her funeral, the room, "which no one had seen in forty years" (129), is opened.

WORKS CITED

Brooks, Cleanth. *William Faulkner: The Yoknapatawpha Country.* New Haven: Yale UP, 1963.

———. *William Faulkner: Toward Yoknapatawpha and Beyond.* New Haven: Yale UP, 1978.

Cowley, Malcolm. Introduction. *The Portable Faulkner.* New York: Viking, 1946. 1–24.

Cullen, John B., and Floyd C. Watkins. "Miss Emily." *Old Times in the Faulkner Country.* Chapel Hill: U of North Carolina P, 1961. 70–71. Rpt. in Inge 17–18.

Faulkner, William. *Collected Stories of William Faulkner.* New York: Random, 1950.

———. *Flags in the Dust.* New York: Random, 1973.

———. *Requiem for a Nun.* New York: Random, 1950.

———. *The Reivers.* New York: Random, 1962.

———. "A Rose for Emily." *Collected Stories* 119–30.

———. *The Unvanquished.* New York: Random, 1938.

———. *William Faulkner Manuscripts: These 13.* Ed. Noel Polk. New York: Garland, 1985. 188–214.

Ford, Margaret Patricia, and Suzanne Kincaid. *Who's Who in Faulkner.* N.p.: Louisiana State UP, 1963.

Going, William T. "Chronology in Teaching 'A Rose for Emily.'" *Exercise Exchange* 5 (February 1958): 8–11. Rpt. in Inge 50–53.

Hagopian, John V., W. Gordon Cunliffe, and Martin Dolch. "A Rose for Emily," *Insight I: Analyses of American Literature.* Frankfurt: Hirschgraben, 1964. 43–50. Rpt. in Inge 76–83.

Inge, M. Thomas. *William Faulkner: A Rose for Emily.* The Charles E. Merrill Literary Casebook Series. Columbus, OH: Merrill, 1970.

Kirk, Robert W., and Marvin Klotz. *Faulkner's People: A Complete Guide and Index to Characters in the Fiction of William Faulkner.* Berkeley: U of California P, 1963.

McGlynn, Paul D. "The Chronology of 'A Rose for Emily.'" *Studies in Short Fiction* 6 (1969): 461–62. Rpt. in Inge 90–92.

Nebeker, Helen E. "Emily's Rose of Love: Thematic Implications of Point of View in Faulkner's 'A Rose for Emily.'" *Bulletin of the Rocky Mountain Modern Language Association* 24 (1970): 3–13.

———. "Emily's Rose of Love: A Postscript." *Bulletin of the Rocky Mountain Modern Language Association* 24 (1970): 190–91.

———. "Chronology Revised." *Studies in Short Fiction* 8 (1971): 471–73.

Perry, Menakhem. "Literary Dynamics: How the Order of a Text Creates its Meanings [With an Analysis of Faulkner's 'A Rose for Emily']." *Poetics Today* 1:1–2 (Autumn 1979): 35–64, 311–61.

Runyan, Harry. *A Faulkner Glossary.* New York: Citadel, 1964.

Sullivan, Ruth. "The Narrator in 'A Rose for Emily.'" *Journal of Narrative Technique* 1 (1971): 159–78.

Wilson, G. R., Jr. "The Chronology of Faulkner's 'A Rose for Emily' Again." *Notes on Mississippi Writers* 5 (Fall 1972): 56, 44, 58–62.

Woodward, Robert H. "The Chronology of 'A Rose for Emily.'" *Exercise Exchange* 8 (March 1966): 17–19. Rpt. in Inge 84–86.

Willow D. Crystal

Professor Akerley

English 1002

23 April 2001

"One of us . . . .": Concepts of the Private and the Public

in William Faulkner's "A Rose for Emily"

Throughout "A Rose for Emily," William Faulkner introduces a tension between what is private, or belongs to the individual, and what is public, or the possession of the group. "When Miss Emily Grierson died," the tale begins,

> our whole town went to her funeral: the men through a sort of
> respectful affection for a fallen monument, the women mostly
> out of curiosity to see the inside of her house. . . . (119)

The men of the small town of Jefferson, Mississippi, are motivated to attend Miss Emily's funeral for "public" reasons; the women, to see "the inside of her house," that private realm which has remained inaccessible for "at least ten years."

This opposition of the private with the public has intrigued critics of Faulkner's tale since the story was first published. Distinctions between the private and the public are central to Lawrence R. Rodgers's argument in his essay "'We all said, "she will kill herself"': The Narrator / Detective in William Faulkner's 'A Rose for Emily.'" The very concept of the detective genre demands that there "be concealed facts . . . [which] must become clear in the end" (Rodgers 119), private actions which become public knowledge. In her feminist tribute—"A Rose for 'A Rose for Emily'"—Judith Fetterley uses the private / public dichotomy to demonstrate the "grotesque reality" (Fetterley 34) of the patriarchal social system in Faulkner's story. According to Fetterley, Miss Emily's "*private* life becomes a *public* document that the town folk feel free to interpret at will" (36, emphasis added). Thus, while critics such as Rodgers and Fetterley offer convincing—if divergent—interpretations of "A Rose for Emily," it is necessary first to understand in Faulkner's eerie and enigmatic story the relationship between the public and the private, and the consequences of this relationship within the story and on the reader.

The most explicit illustration of the opposition between the public and the private occurs in the social and economic interactions between the town of Jefferson, represented by the narrator's "we," and the reclusive Miss Emily. "Alive," the narrator explains, "Miss Emily had been a tradition, a duty, and a care; a sort of hereditary obligation upon the town, dating from that day in 1894 when Colonel Sartoris, the mayor, . . . remitted her taxes, the dispensation dating from the death of her father on into perpetuity" (120). Ironically (and this is one of the prime examples of the complexity of the relationship of private and public in the story), the price of privacy for Miss Emily becomes the loss of that very privacy. Despite--or perhaps because of--her refusal to buy into the community, the citizens of Jefferson determine that it is their "duty," their "hereditary obligation," to oversee her activities. When, for example, Miss Emily's house begins to emit an unpleasant smell, the town officials decide to solve the problem by dusting her property with lime. When she refuses to provide a reason why she wants to buy poison, the druggist scrawls "'For rats'" (126) across the package, literally and protectively overwriting her silence.

Arguably, the townspeople's actions serve to protect Miss Emily's privacy--by preserving her perceived gentility--as much as they effectively destroy it with their intrusive zeal. But in this very act of protection they reaffirm the town's proprietary relation to the public "monument" which is Miss Emily and, consequently, reinforce her inability to make decisions for herself.

While the communal narrator and Miss Emily appear to be polar opposites--one standing for the public while the other fiercely defends her privacy--the two are united when an outsider such as Homer Barron appears in their midst. If Miss Emily serves as a representation--an icon, an inactive "tableau," an "idol"--of traditional antebellum southern values, then Homer represents all that is new and different. A "'day laborer'" (124) from the North, Homer comes to Jefferson to pave the sidewalks, a task which itself suggests the modernization of the town.

The secret and destructive union between these two representational figures implies a complex relationship between the private and the public. When Miss Emily kills Homer and confines his remains to a room in her attic, where, according to Lawrence R. Rodgers, "she has been allowed to carry on her illicit love affair in post-mortem privacy" (119), this grotesque act ironically suggests that she has capitulated to the code of gentility that Jefferson imagines her to embody. This code demands the end of a romantic affair which some residents deemed "a disgrace to the town and a bad example to the young people" (126), thus placing traditions and the good of the community above Miss Emily's own wishes. Through its insistence on Miss Emily's symbolic relation to a bygone era, the town--via the narrator-- becomes "an unknowing driving force behind Emily's crime" (Rodgers 120). Her private act is both the result of and a support for public norms and expectations.

At the same time, however, the act of murder also marks Miss Emily's corruption of that very code. By killing Homer in private, Miss Emily deliberately flouts public norms, and by eluding explicit detection until after her own death, she asserts the primacy of the private. The murder of the outsider in their midst thus leads Miss Emily to achieve paradoxically both a more complete privacy--a marriage of sorts without a husband--and a role in the preservation of the community.

Yet the elaborate relationship between Jefferson and Miss Emily is not the only way in which Homer's murder may be understood as a casualty of the tension between the public and the private. When Miss Emily kills Homer, Rodgers contends,

> from the town's point of view, it was the best thing. . . . Homer represents the kind of unwelcome resident and ineligible mate the town wants to repel if it is to preserve its traditional arrangements. (125)

The people of Jefferson and Miss Emily join in a struggle to "repel" the outside and to ensure a private, inner order and tradition. This complicity creates intriguing parallels among the illicit, fatal union of Homer and Miss Emily, the reunion of the North and the South following the Civil War. In this reformulation of the private and the public, Miss Emily becomes, as Fetterley notes, a "metaphor and mirror for the town of Jefferson" (43). Miss Emily's honor is the townspeople's honor, her preservation their preservation.

Finally, the parallels between Miss Emily's secretive habits and the narrator's circuitous presentation of the story lead to a third dimension of the negotiations between the private and the public in "A Rose for Emily," a dimension in which Faulkner as author and the collective "we" as narrator confront their public consumers, the readers. Told by the anonymous narrator as if retrospectively, "A Rose for Emily" skips forward and backward in time, omitting details and deferring revelations to such a degree that many critics have gone to extreme lengths to establish reliable chronologies for the tale.[1] The much-debated "we" remains anonymous and unreachable throughout the tale--maintaining a virtually unbreachable privacy--even as it invites the public (the reader) to participate in the narrator's acts of detection and revelation. "The dramatic distance on display here," Rodgers observes,

> provides an ironic layer to the narrative. As the observers
> of the conflict between the teller-of-tale's desire to solve
> the curious mysteries that surround Emily's life--indeed, his
> [*sic*] complicity in shaping them--and his undetective-like
> detachment from her crimes, readers occupy the tantalizing
> position of having insight into unraveling the mystery which
> the narrator lacks. (120-21)

The reader is thus a member of the communal "we"--party to the narrator's investigation and Jefferson's voyeuristic obsession with Miss Emily--but also apart, removed to a plane from which "insight" into and observation of the narrator's own actions and motives become possible. The reader, just like Miss Emily, Homer, and the town of Jefferson itself, becomes a crucial element in the tension between the public and the private.

Thus, public and private are, in the end, far from exclusive categories. And for all of its literal as well as figurative insistence on opposition and either/or structures, Faulkner's "A Rose for Emily" enacts the provocative idea of being "[o]ne of us" (Faulkner 130), of being both an individual *and* a member of a community, both a private entity *and* a participant in the public sphere.

---

[1] Gene M. Moore's essay "Of Time and Its Mathematical Progression: Problems of Chronology in Faulkner's 'A Rose for Emily'" documents the proliferation of such chronologies.

Works Cited

Faulkner, William. "A Rose for Emily." *Collected Stories of William Faulkner*. New York: Random, 1950. 119-30.

Fetterley, Judith. "A Rose for 'A Rose for Emily.' " *The Resisting Reader: A Feminist Approach to American Fiction*. Bloomington: Indiana UP, 1978. 34-45.

Moore, Gene M. "Of Time and Its Mathematical Progression: Problems of Chronology in Faulkner's 'A Rose for Emily.' " *Studies in Short Fiction* 29 (Spring 1992): 195-204.

Rodgers, Lawrence R. " 'We all said, "she will kill herself" ': The Narrator / Detective in William Faulkner's 'A Rose for Emily.' " *Clues: A Journal of Detection* 16 (1995): 117-29.

Evaluating Fiction

To evaluate a work of literature—to assess its worth or quality—is one of the most fundamental, significant, and difficult activities in literary study. It is impossible to dodge such questions as "Is this story good?" "Is it great?" "Is it better than that one? . . . that other one?" "Is it worth reading? studying?" It is equally impossible to answer such questions definitively, for all time and for all readers.

It is, however, usually possible to answer the question "Do you like this story?" and often possible to answer "Do you like this one more than or less than that other?" Whether you like a story or not when you first read it is therefore probably the proper place to *begin*. But it is a dangerous place to *stop* the process of evaluation. If our appreciation and understanding of literature is to grow, and if we are not content simply to stick with our own prejudices or to rely on the authority of "those who know best," we must learn to specify what it is *we* like about a story and to search out in our minds and experience the reasons *we* like it. We must listen to other readers' responses too— those of our classmates, professors, professional critics like those in the previous chapter—responses that may reinforce our own, may show us things to appreciate in the story that we missed, or may challenge the viability of our reasons, if not that of our responses.

GRACE PALEY

A Conversation with My Father

My father is eighty-six years old and in bed. His heart, that bloody motor, is equally old and will not do certain jobs any more. It still floods his head with brainy light. But it won't let his legs carry the weight of his body around the house. Despite my metaphors, this muscle failure is not due to his old heart, he says, but to a potassium shortage. Sitting on one pillow, leaning on three, he offers last-minute advice and makes a request.

"I would like you to write a simple story just once more," he says, "the kind de Maupassant wrote, or Chekhov, the kind you used to write. Just recognizable people and then write down what happened to them next."

I say, "Yes, why not? That's possible." I want to please him, though I don't remember writing that way. I *would* like to try to tell such a story, if he means the kind that begins: "There was a woman . . ." followed by plot, the absolute line between two points which I've always despised. Not for literary reasons, but because it takes all hope away. Everyone, real or invented, deserves the open destiny of life.

Finally I thought of a story that had been happening for a couple of years right across the street. I wrote it down, then read it aloud. "Pa," I said, "how about this? Do you mean something like this?"

5   Once in my time there was a woman and she had a son. They lived nicely, in a small apartment in Manhattan. This boy at about fifteen became a junkie, which is not unusual in our neighborhood. In order to maintain her close friendship with him, she became a junkie too. She said it was part of the youth culture, with which she felt very much at home. After a while, for a number of reasons, the boy gave it all up and left the city and his mother in disgust. Hopeless and alone, she grieved. We all visit her.

"O.K., Pa, that's it," I said, "an unadorned and miserable tale."

"But that's not what I mean," my father said. "You misunderstood me on purpose. You know there's a lot more to it. You know that. You left everything out. Turgenev[1] wouldn't do that. Chekhov wouldn't do that. There are in fact Russian writers you never heard of, you don't have an inkling of, as good as anyone, who can write a plain ordinary story, who would not leave out what you have left out. I object not to facts but to people sitting in trees talking senselessly, voices from who knows where . . ."

"Forget that one, Pa, what have I left out now? In this one?"

"Her looks, for instance."

10   "Oh. Quite handsome, I think. Yes."

"Her hair?"

"Dark, with heavy braids, as though she were a girl or a foreigner."

"What were her parents like, her stock? That she became such a person. It's interesting, you know."

"From out of town. Professional people. The first to be divorced in their county. How's that? Enough?" I asked.

15   "With you, it's all a joke," he said. "What about the boy's father. Why didn't you mention him? Who was he? Or was the boy born out of wedlock?"

"Yes," I said. "He was born out of wedlock."

"For Godsakes, doesn't anyone in your stories get married? Doesn't anyone have the time to run down to City Hall before they jump into bed?"

"No," I said. "In real life, yes. But in my stories, no."

"Why do you answer me like that?"

20   "Oh, Pa, this is a simple story about a smart woman who came to N.Y.C. full of interest love trust excitement very up to date, and about her son, what a hard

1. Ivan Sergeyevich Turgenev (1818–1883); his best-known novel, *Fathers and Sons,* deals with the conflict between generations.

time she had in this world. Married or not, it's of small consequence."

"It is of great consequence," he said.

"O.K.," I said.

"O.K. O.K. yourself," he said, "but listen. I believe you that she's good-looking, but I don't think she was so smart."

"That's true," I said. "Actually that's the trouble with stories. People start out fantastic. You think they're extraordinary, but it turns out as the work goes along, they're just average with a good education. Sometimes the other way around, the person's a kind of dumb innocent, but he outwits you and you can't even think of an ending good enough."

"What do you do then?" he asked. He had been a doctor for a couple of decades   25
and then an artist for a couple of decades and he's still interested in details, craft, technique.

"Well, you just have to let the story lie around till some agreement can be reached between you and the stubborn hero."

"Aren't you talking silly, now?" he asked. "Start again," he said. "It so happens I'm not going out this evening. Tell the story again. See what you can do this time."

"O.K.," I said. "But it's not a five-minute job." Second attempt:

> Once, across the street from us, there was a fine handsome woman, our neighbor. She had a son whom she loved because she'd known him since birth (in helpless chubby infancy, and in the wrestling, hugging ages, seven to ten, as well as earlier and later). This boy, when he fell into the fist of adolescence, became a junkie. He was not a hopeless one. He was in fact hopeful, an ideologue and successful converter. With his busy brilliance, he wrote persuasive articles for his high-school newspaper. Seeking a wider audience, using important connections, he drummed into Lower Manhattan newsstand distribution a periodical called *Oh! Golden Horse!*[2]
>
> In order to keep him from feeling guilty (because guilt is the stony heart of nine   30
> tenths of all clinically diagnosed cancers in America today, she said), and because she had always believed in giving bad habits room at home where one could keep an eye on them, she too became a junkie. Her kitchen was famous for a while—a center for intellectual addicts who knew what they were doing. A few felt artistic like Coleridge and others were scientific and revolutionary like Leary.[3] Although she was often high herself, certain good mothering reflexes remained, and she saw to it that there was lots of orange juice around and honey and milk and vitamin pills. However, she never cooked anything but chili, and that no more than once a week. She explained, when we talked to her, seriously, with neighborly concern, that it was her part in the youth culture and she would rather be with the young, it was an honor, than with her own generation.
>
> One week, while nodding through an Antonioni[4] film, this boy was severely

2. *Horse* is slang term for heroin.   3. Timothy Leary (1920–1996), American psychologist, promoted the use of psychedelic drugs; Samuel Taylor Coleridge (1772–1834), English Romantic poet, claimed that his poem *Kubla Khan* recorded what he remembered of a dream stimulated by opium.   4. Michelangelo Antonioni (1912–), Italian director *(Blow-Up, Zabriskie Point)*. *Nodding:* a slang term referring to the narcotic effect of heroin.

jabbed by the elbow of a stern and proselytizing girl, sitting beside him. She offered immediate apricots and nuts for his sugar level, spoke to him sharply, and took him home.

She had heard of him and his work and she herself published, edited, and wrote a competitive journal called *Man Does Live By Bread Alone*. In the organic heat of her continuous presence he could not help but become interested once more in his muscles, his arteries, and nerve connections. In fact he began to love them, treasure them, praise them with funny little songs in *Man Does Live . . .*

> the fingers of my flesh transcend
> my transcendental soul
> the tightness in my shoulders end
> my teeth have made me whole

To the mouth of his head (that glory of will and determination) he brought hard apples, nuts, wheat germ, and soybean oil. He said to his old friends, From now on, I guess I'll keep my wits about me. I'm going on the natch. He said he was about to begin a spiritual deep-breathing journey. How about you too, Mom? he asked kindly.

His conversion was so radiant, splendid, that neighborhood kids his age began to say that he had never been a real addict at all, only a journalist along for the smell of the story. The mother tried several times to give up what had become without her son and his friends a lonely habit. This effort only brought it to supportable levels. The boy and his girl took their electronic mimeograph and moved to the bushy edge of another borough. They were very strict. They said they would not see her again until she had been off drugs for sixty days.

35   At home alone in the evening, weeping, the mother read and reread the seven issues of *Oh! Golden Horse!* They seemed to her as truthful as ever. We often crossed the street to visit and console. But if we mentioned any of our children who were at college or in the hospital or dropouts at home, she would cry out, My baby! My baby! and burst into terrible, face-scarring, time-consuming tears. The End.

First my father was silent, then he said, "Number One: You have a nice sense of humor. Number Two: I see you can't tell a plain story. So don't waste time." Then he said sadly, "Number Three: I suppose that means she was alone, she was left like that, his mother. Alone. Probably sick?"

I said, "Yes."

"Poor woman. Poor girl, to be born in a time of fools, to live among fools. The end. The end. You were right to put that down. The end."

I didn't want to argue, but I had to say, "Well, it is not necessarily the end, Pa."

40   "Yes," he said, "what a tragedy. The end of a person."

"No, Pa," I begged him. "It doesn't have to be. She's only about forty. She could be a hundred different things in this world as time goes on. A teacher or a social worker. An ex-junkie! Sometimes it's better than having a master's in education."

"Jokes," he said. "As a writer that's your main trouble. You don't want to recognize it. Tragedy! Plain tragedy! Historical tragedy! No hope. The end."

"Oh, Pa," I said. "She could change."

"In your own life, too, you have to look it in the face." He took a couple of nitroglycerin.[5] "Turn to five," he said, pointing to the dial on the oxygen tank. He inserted the tubes into his nostrils and breathed deep. He closed his eyes and said, "No."

I had promised the family to always let him have the last word when arguing, but in this case I had a different responsibility. That woman lives across the street. She's my knowledge and my invention. I'm sorry for her. I'm not going to leave her there in that house crying. (Actually neither would Life, which unlike me has no pity.)

Therefore: She did change. Of course her son never came home again. But right now, she's the receptionist in a storefront community clinic in the East Village. Most of the customers are young people, some old friends. The head doctor said to her, "If we only had three people in this clinic with your experiences . . ."

"The doctor said that?" My father took the oxygen tubes out of his nostrils and said, "Jokes. Jokes again."

"No, Pa, it could really happen that way, it's a funny world nowadays."

"No," he said. "Truth first. She will slide back. A person must have character. She does not."

"No, Pa," I said. "That's it. She's got a job. Forget it. She's in that storefront working."

"How long will it be?" he asked. "Tragedy! You too. When will you look it in the face?"

1974

As we noted in chapter two, some short stories include an auditor who is also a character, as they reenact the oral tradition of telling stories. Grace Paley's narrator, evidently a fiction writer very much like the author, tells us, in first-person present tense, about a visit with her dying father. In a "simple story" that appears casually factual (this might be Paley's memory of a conversation with her real father), Paley dramatizes the process of building fiction and of evaluating it. The woman and her father collaborate in shaping a story based on actual lives ("That woman lives across the street. She's my knowledge and my invention" [paragraph 45]), though they disagree on matters of fact as well as style. The father, an experienced reader of fiction by the Russian masters, demands psychological realism. Each character should have a detailed past, complex motives, a network of social relations and material conditions, as in a story by Chekhov. Above all, a story should remind readers of the world of cause and effect, without miracles. All life ends in death, a "tragedy," as he insists. The narrator, being younger and more given to humor (" 'Jokes. . . . As a writer that's your main trouble' "[paragraph 42]), sometimes likes magical or fantastic effects. At least once, she wrote a story with " 'people sitting in trees talking senselessly, voices from who knows where' " (paragraph 7), that the father objected to strongly. On previous occasions, however, she has written the sort of story her father likes. Though she is trying to keep her father happy, trying to avoid a conflict as he lies dying, she nevertheless cannot resist defying him, tossing out the " 'unadorned and miserable tale' " in paragraph 5. On a second try, she does tell a story he likes; his

---

5. Medicine for certain heart conditions.

responses in paragraphs 36–40 show that he has been engaged and moved by the narrative. But the parent and child who share an addiction to fiction rather than to heroin— both stories and drugs can relieve pain—still differ when it comes to endings: should they be tragic or comic? The writer wants life to continue beyond the last word of a story: addicts can recover, new generations bring hope, as the genre of comedy affirms. Yet the father has the last word in this story, with his question about death: " 'When will you look it in the face?' "

"A Conversation with My Father" is a short "frame" story, or story within a story. The teller and auditor provide the first frame. But yet an outer frame or level can be detected, that of the author's persona and the readers of the story. Readers can respond to the whole text almost as an allegory about the writing of fiction. In this reading, the author may be implying that readers are as difficult yet as important to please as one's own dying father; she may be indicating that reviewers want contradictory things: old-fashioned realism, fantasy, humor. She may want to soften the blow of mortality with comic effects—with the wry humor and ethnic flavor of the dialogue between the narrator and the father. She may want to combine metaphors and facts, as the first paragraph signals: the imaginative daughter claims that "[h]is heart, that bloody motor . . . floods his head with brainy light," but the father, a former doctor, says it is really just "a potassium shortage." She may want readers to enjoy the fiction as a clever artifice *and* to feel with her characters as though they were real people. Notice the comments on "craft, technique" in paragraphs 24–26 that tell us this writer sees characters as both made-up and alive, independent of their author: " 'that's the trouble with stories. People start out fantastic . . . but it turns out . . . they're just average. . . . Sometimes the other way around . . . and you can't think of an ending good enough. . . . [Y]ou just have to let the story lie around till some agreement can be reached between you and the stubborn hero.' " The drug-addicted mother and son in the internal story and the contentious father and daughter in the frame story may seem worse or no better than average, far from heroic, but somehow stubbornly alive. Altogether, "A Conversation with My Father," as a story, demonstrates its point about our *need* to tell stories. A dying man devotes precious time to stories because they rouse the feelings of connection to others—interest, sympathy—that sustain human life. It would be hard to find a good reason to alter a word in Paley's story—one standard of evaluation for a story that *works on its own terms.*

Now, that is one evaluation of this story. But readers can add different frames of interpretation, with varying evaluations of the story. Some readers may be like the father, a Chekhov fan wanting an unobtrusive narrator quietly presenting realistic character development. Others may want this story to experiment further with storytelling technique instead of appealing to sentiment about mothers and sons, fathers and daughters, illness and addiction. Some readers may have a general distaste for this and other Paley stories because of the setting and culture: without being anti-Semitic or elitist, readers may feel they can't identify with these characters—lower-middle-class urban Jews and bohemians—or may fail to catch the tone. (Have you ever mistaken another family's style of playful argument for actual rage or cruelty, or their ordinary speech patterns for rudeness? Or have you ever missed a severe reproach or insult in a family that has very placid manners?) Still other readers may argue that Paley's story is flawed because it never clarifies the terms of its debate about styles and modes of fiction. That is, the narrator deliberately misunderstands the father's request for "a simple story" like Maupassant's or Chekhov's. These writers did not tell only "the absolute line" of plot. Some traditional stories allow the comic, ongoing ending, "the open destiny of life," that the narrator insists on, and this objection might lead readers to decide that Paley's story is clever, amusing, but muddled on the theme of fiction writing. Just as the father and daughter seem to relish their disagreements and to respect each other's expertise, we can learn from and enjoy such disagreements about the qualities and merits of fiction. Evaluations that support their assertions with detailed evidence from the text can even persuade us to like a story more or less.

The story that follows has little in common with "A Conversation with My Father." Certainly, it is not about the writing of fiction in any conspicuous way, although a character in it, General Zaroff, likes to plot deadly games. "The Most Dangerous Game" has aroused a wide range of responses. After reading it once, take some time—maybe enough to reread the story—and consider your own response and evaluation, perhaps writing them down. Then go on to read the responses and evaluation that follow.

RICHARD CONNELL

The Most Dangerous Game

"Off there to the right—somewhere—is a large island," said Whitney. "It's rather a mystery—"

"What island is it?" Rainsford asked.

"The old charts call it 'Ship-Trap Island,'" Whitney replied. "A suggestive name, isn't it? Sailors have a curious dread of the place. I don't know why. Some superstition—"

"Can't see it," remarked Rainsford, trying to peer through the dank tropical night that was palpable as it pressed its thick warm blackness in upon the yacht.

"You've good eyes," said Whitney, with a laugh, "and I've seen you pick off a   5 moose moving in the brown fall bush at four hundred yards, but even you can't see four miles or so through a moonless Caribbean night."

"Nor four yards," admitted Rainsford. "Ugh! It's like moist black velvet."

"It will be light in Rio," promised Whitney. "We should make it in a few days. I hope the jaguar guns have come from Purdey's. We should have some good hunting up the Amazon. Great sport, hunting."

"The best sport in the world," agreed Rainsford.

"For the hunter," amended Whitney. "Not for the jaguar."

"Don't talk rot, Whitney," said Rainsford. "You're a big-game hunter, not a   10 philosopher. Who cares how a jaguar feels?"

"Perhaps the jaguar does," observed Whitney.

"Bah! They've no understanding."

"Even so, I rather think they understand one thing—fear. The fear of pain and the fear of death."

"Nonsense," laughed Rainsford. "This hot weather is making you soft, Whitney. Be a realist. The world is made up of two classes—the hunters and the huntees. Luckily, you and I are hunters. Do you think we've passed that island yet?"

"I can't tell in the dark. I hope so."   15

"Why?" asked Rainsford.

"The place has a reputation—a bad one."

"Cannibals?" suggested Rainsford.

"Hardly. Even cannibals wouldn't live in such a God-forsaken place. But it's gotten into sailor lore, somehow. Didn't you notice that the crew's nerves seemed a bit jumpy today?"

20 "They were a bit strange, now you mention it. Even Captain Nielsen—"

"Yes, even that tough-minded old Swede, who'd go up to the devil himself and ask him for a light. Those fishy blue eyes held a look I never saw there before. All I could get out of him was: 'This place has an evil name among sea-faring men, sir.' Then he said to me, very gravely: 'Don't you feel anything?'—as if the air about us was actually poisonous. Now, you mustn't laugh when I tell you this— I did feel something like a sudden chill.

"There was no breeze. The sea was as flat as a plate-glass window. We were drawing near the island then. What I felt was a—a mental chill; a sort of sudden dread."

"Pure imagination," said Rainsford. "One superstitious sailor can taint the whole ship's company with his fear."

"Maybe. But sometimes I think sailors have an extra sense that tells them when they are in danger. Sometimes I think evil is a tangible thing—with wave lengths, just as sound and light have. An evil place can, so to speak, broadcast vibrations of evil. Anyhow, I'm glad we're getting out of this zone. Well, I think I'll turn in now, Rainsford."

25 "I'm not sleepy," said Rainsford. "I'm going to smoke another pipe up on the after deck."

"Good night, then, Rainsford. See you at breakfast."

"Right. Good night, Whitney."

There was no sound in the night as Rainsford sat there, but the muffled throb of the engine that drove the yacht swiftly through the darkness, and the swish and ripple of the wash of the propeller.

Rainsford, reclining in a steamer chair, indolently puffed on his favorite brier. The sensuous drowsiness of the night was on him. "It's so dark," he thought, "that I could sleep without closing my eyes; the night would be my eyelids—"

30 An abrupt sound startled him. Off to the right he heard it, and his ears, expert in such matters, could not be mistaken. Again he heard the sound, and again. Somewhere, off in the blackness, some one had fired a gun three times.

Rainsford sprang up and moved quickly to the rail, mystified. He strained his eyes in the direction from which the reports had come, but it was like trying to see through a blanket. He leaped upon the rail and balanced himself there, to get greater elevation; his pipe, striking a rope, was knocked from his mouth. He lunged for it; a short, hoarse cry came from his lips as he realized he had reached too far and had lost his balance. The cry was pinched off short as the bloodwarm waters of the Caribbean Sea closed over his head.

He struggled up to the surface and tried to cry out, but the wash from the speeding yacht slapped him in the face and the salt water in his open mouth made him gag and strangle. Desperately he struck out with strong strokes after the receding lights of the yacht, but he stopped before he had swum fifty feet. A certain cool-headedness had come to him; it was not the first time he had been in a tight place. There was a chance that his cries could be heard by some one aboard the yacht, but that chance was slender, and grew more slender as the yacht raced on. He wrestled himself out of his clothes, and shouted with all his power. The lights of the yacht became faint and ever-vanishing fireflies; then they were blotted out entirely by the night.

Rainsford remembered the shots. They had come from the right, and doggedly he swam in that direction, swimming with slow, deliberate strokes, conserving his strength. For a seemingly endless time he fought the sea. He began to count his strokes; he could do possibly a hundred more and then—

Rainsford heard a sound. It came out of the darkness, a high screaming sound, the sound of an animal in an extremity of anguish and terror.

He did not recognize the animal that made the sound; he did not try to; with fresh vitality he swam toward the sound. He heard it again; then it was cut short by another noise, crisp, staccato.

"Pistol shot," muttered Rainsford, swimming on.

Ten minutes of determined effort brought another sound to his ears—the most welcome he had ever heard—the muttering and growling of the sea breaking on a rocky shore. He was almost on the rocks before he saw them; on a night less calm he would have been shattered against them. With his remaining strength he dragged himself from the swirling waters. Jagged crags appeared to jut into the opaqueness; he forced himself upward, hand over hand. Gasping, his hands raw, he reached a flat place at the top. Dense jungle came down to the very edge of the cliffs. What perils that tangle of trees and underbrush might hold for him did not concern Rainsford just then. All he knew was that he was safe from his enemy, the sea, and that utter weariness was on him. He flung himself down at the jungle edge and tumbled headlong into the deepest sleep of his life.

When he opened his eyes he knew from the position of the sun that it was late in the afternoon. Sleep had given him new vigor; a sharp hunger was picking at him. He looked about him, almost cheerfully.

"Where there are pistol shots, there are men. Where there are men, there is food," he thought. But what kind of men, he wondered, in so forbidding a place? An unbroken front of snarled and ragged jungle fringed the shore.

He saw no sign of a trail through the closely knit web of weeds and trees; it was easier to go along the shore, and Rainsford floundered along by the water. Not far from where he had landed, he stopped.

Some wounded thing, by the evidence a large animal, had thrashed about in the underbrush; the jungle weeds were crushed down and the moss was lacerated; one patch of weeds was stained crimson. A small, glittering object not far away caught Rainsford's eye and he picked it up. It was an empty cartridge.

"A twenty-two," he remarked. "That's odd. It must have been a fairly large animal too. The hunter had his nerve with him to tackle it with a light gun. It's clear that the brute put up a fight. I suppose the first three shots I heard was when the hunter flushed his quarry and wounded it. The last shot was when he trailed it here and finished it."

He examined the ground closely and found what he had hoped to find—the print of hunting boots. They pointed along the cliff in the direction he had been going. Eagerly, he hurried along, now slipping on a rotten log or a loose stone, but making headway; night was beginning to settle down on the island.

Bleak darkness was blacking out the sea and jungle when Rainsford sighted the lights. He came upon them as he turned a crook in the coast line, and his first thought was that he had come upon a village, for there were many lights. But as he forged along he saw to his great astonishment that all the lights were in one enormous building—a lofty structure with pointed towers plunging upward into the gloom. His eyes made out the shadowy outlines of a palatial château; it was set on a high bluff, and on three sides of it cliffs dived down to where the sea licked greedy lips in the shadows.

45   "Mirage," thought Rainsford. But it was no mirage, he found, when he opened the tall spiked iron gate. The stone steps were real enough; the massive door with a leering gargoyle for a knocker was real enough; yet about it all hung an air of unreality.

He lifted the knocker, and it creaked up stiffly, as if it had never before been used. He let it fall, and it startled him with its booming loudness. He thought he heard steps within; the door remained closed. Again Rainsford lifted the heavy knocker, and let it fall. The door opened then, opened as suddenly as if it were on a spring, and Rainsford stood blinking in the river of glaring gold light that poured out. The first thing Rainsford's eyes discerned was the largest man Rainsford had ever seen—a gigantic creature, solidly made and blackbearded to the waist. In his hand the man held a long-barreled revolver, and he was pointing it straight at Rainsford's heart.

Out of the snarl of beard two small eyes regarded Rainsford.

"Don't be alarmed," said Rainsford, with a smile which he hoped was disarming. "I'm no robber. I fell off a yacht. My name is Sanger Rainsford of New York City."

The menacing look in the eyes did not change. The revolver pointed as rigidly as if the giant were a statue. He gave no sign that he understood Rainsford's words, or that he had even heard them. He was dressed in uniform, a black uniform trimmed with gray astrakhan.

50   "I'm Sanger Rainsford of New York," Rainsford began again. "I fell off a yacht. I am hungry."

The man's only answer was to raise with his thumb the hammer of his revolver. Then Rainsford saw the man's free hand go to his forehead in a military salute, and he saw him click his heels together and stand at attention. Another man was coming down the broad marble steps, an erect, slender man in evening clothes. He advanced to Rainsford and held out his hand.

In a cultivated voice marked by a slight accent that gave it added precision and deliberateness, he said: "It is a very great pleasure and honor to welcome Mr. Sanger Rainsford, the celebrated hunter, to my home."

Automatically Rainsford shook the man's hand.

"I've read your book about hunting snow leopards in Tibet, you see" explained the man. "I am General Zaroff."

Rainsford's first impression was that the man was singularly handsome; his second was that there was an original, almost bizarre quality about the general's face. He was a tall man past middle age, for his hair was a vivid white; but his thick eyebrows and pointed military mustache were as black as the night from which Rainsford had come. His eyes, too, were black and very bright. He had high cheek bones, a sharp-cut nose, a spare, dark face, the face of a man used to giving orders, the face of an aristocrat. Turning to the giant in uniform, the general made a sign. The giant put away his pistol, saluted, withdrew.

"Ivan is an incredibly strong fellow," remarked the general, "but he has the misfortune to be deaf and dumb. A simple fellow, but, I'm afraid, like all his race, a bit of a savage."

"Is he Russian?"

"He is a Cossack," said the general, and his smile showed red lips and pointed teeth. "So am I."

"Come," he said, "we shouldn't be chatting here. We can talk later. Now you want clothes, food, rest. You shall have them. This is a most restful spot."

Ivan had reappeared, and the general spoke to him with lips that moved but gave forth no sound.

"Follow Ivan, if you please, Mr. Rainsford," said the general. "I was about to have my dinner when you came. I'll wait for you. You'll find that my clothes will fit you, I think."

It was to a huge, beam-ceilinged bedroom with a canopied bed big enough for six men that Rainsford followed the silent giant. Ivan laid out an evening suit, and Rainsford, as he put it on, noticed that it came from a London tailor who ordinarily cut and sewed for none below the rank of duke.

The dining room to which Ivan conducted him was in many ways remarkable. There was a medieval magnificence about it; it suggested a baronial hall of feudal times with its oaken panels, its high ceiling, its vast refectory table where twoscore men could sit down to eat. About the hall were the mounted heads of many animals—lions, tigers, elephants, moose, bears; larger or more perfect specimens Rainsford had never seen. At the great table the general was sitting, alone.

"You'll have a cocktail, Mr. Rainsford," he suggested. The cocktail was surpassingly good; and, Rainsford noted, the table appointments were of the finest—the linen, the crystal, the silver, the china.

They were eating *borsch,* the rich, red soup with whipped cream so dear to Russian palates. Half apologetically General Zaroff said: "We do our best to preserve the amenities of civilization here. Please forgive any lapses. We are well off the beaten track, you know. Do you think the champagne has suffered from its long ocean trip?"

"Not in the least," declared Rainsford. He was finding the general a most thoughtful and affable host, a true cosmopolite. But there was one small trait of the general's that made Rainsford uncomfortable. Whenever he looked up from his plate he found the general studying him, appraising him narrowly.

"Perhaps," said General Zaroff, "you were surprised that I recognized your name. You see, I read all books on hunting published in English, French, and Russian. I have but one passion in my life, Mr. Rainsford, and it is the hunt."

"You have some wonderful heads here," said Rainsford as he ate a particularly well cooked filet mignon. "That Cape buffalo is the largest I ever saw."

"Oh, that fellow. Yes, he was a monster."

70   "Did he charge you?"

"Hurled me against a tree," said the general. "Fractured my skull. But I got the brute."

"I've always thought," said Rainsford, "that the Cape buffalo is the most dangerous of all big game."

For a moment the general did not reply; he was smiling his curious red-lipped smile. Then he said slowly: "No. You are wrong, sir. The Cape buffalo is not the most dangerous big game." He sipped his wine. "Here in my preserve on this island," he said in the same slow tone, "I hunt more dangerous game."

Rainsford expressed his surprise. "Is there big game on this island?"

75   The general nodded. "The biggest."

"Really?"

"Oh, it isn't here naturally, of course. I have to stock the island."

"What have you imported, general?" Rainsford asked. "Tigers?"

The general smiled. "No," he said. "Hunting tigers ceased to interest me some years ago. I exhausted their possibilities, you see. No thrill left in tigers, no real danger. I live for danger, Mr. Rainsford."

80   The general took from his pocket a gold cigarette case and offered his guest a long black cigarette with a silver tip; it was perfumed and gave off a smell like incense.

"We will have some capital hunting, you and I," said the general. "I shall be most glad to have your society."

"But what game—" began Rainsford.

"I'll tell you," said the general. "You will be amused, I know. I think I may say, in all modesty, that I have done a rare thing. I have invented a new sensation. May I pour you another glass of port, Mr. Rainsford?"

"Thank you, general."

85   The general filled both glasses, and said: "God makes some men poets. Some He makes kings, some beggars. Me He made a hunter. My hand was made for the trigger, my father said. He was a very rich man with a quarter of a million acres in the Crimea, and he was an ardent sportsman. When I was only five years old he gave me a little gun, specially made in Moscow for me, to shoot sparrows with. When I shot some of his prize turkeys with it, he did not punish me; he complimented me on my marksmanship. I killed my first bear in the Caucasus when I was ten. My whole life has been one prolonged hunt. I went into the army—it was expected of noblemen's sons—and for a time commanded a division of Cossack cavalry, but my real interest was always the hunt. I have hunted every kind of game in every land. It would be impossible for me to tell you how many animals I have killed."

The general puffed at his cigarette.

"After the debacle in Russia[1] I left the country, for it was imprudent for an

---

1. The Revolution of 1917, which overthrew the czar and prepared the way for Communist rule.

officer of the Czar to stay there. Many noble Russians lost everything. I, luckily, had invested heavily in American securities, so I shall never have to open a tea room in Monte Carlo or drive a taxi in Paris. Naturally, I continued to hunt— grizzlies in your Rockies, crocodiles in the Ganges, rhinoceroses in East Africa. It was in Africa that the Cape buffalo hit me and laid me up for six months. As soon as I recovered I started for the Amazon to hunt jaguars, for I had heard they were unusually cunning. They weren't." The Cossack sighed. "They were no match at all for a hunter with his wits about him, and a high-powered rifle. I was bitterly disappointed. I was lying in my tent with a splitting headache one night when a terrible thought pushed its way into my mind. Hunting was beginning to bore me! And hunting, remember, had been my life. I have heard that in America business men often go to pieces when they give up the business that has been their life."

"Yes, that's so," said Rainsford.

The general smiled. "I had no wish to go to pieces," he said. "I must do something. Now, mine is an analytical mind, Mr. Rainsford. Doubtless that is why I enjoy the problems of the chase."

"No doubt, General Zaroff."   90

"So," continued the general, "I asked myself why the hunt no longer fascinated me. You are much younger than I am, Mr. Rainsford, and have not hunted as much, but you perhaps can guess the answer."

"What was it?"

"Simply this: hunting had ceased to be what you call 'a sporting proposition.' It had become too easy. I always got my quarry. Always. There is no greater bore than perfection."

The general lit a fresh cigarette.

"No animal had a chance with me any more. That is no boast; it is a mathe-   95 matical certainty. The animal had nothing but his legs and his instinct. Instinct is no match for reason. When I thought of this it was a tragic moment for me, I can tell you."

Rainsford leaned across the table, absorbed in what his host was saying.

"It came to me as an inspiration what I must do," the general went on.

"And that was?"

The general smiled the quiet smile of one who had faced an obstacle and surmounted it with success. "I had to invent a new animal to hunt," he said.

"A new animal? You're joking."   100

"Not at all," said the general. "I never joke about hunting. I needed a new animal. I found one. So I bought this island, built this house, and here I do my hunting. The island is perfect for my purposes—there are jungles with a maze of trails in them, hills, swamps—"

"But the animal, General Zaroff?"

"Oh," said the general, "it supplies me with the most exciting hunting in the world. No other hunting compares with it for an instant. Every day I hunt, and I never grow bored now, for I have a quarry with which I can match my wits."

Rainsford's bewilderment showed in his face.

"I wanted the ideal animal to hunt," explained the general. "So I said: 'What   105 are the attributes of an ideal quarry?' And the answer was, of course: 'It must have courage, cunning, and, above all, it must be able to reason.' "

"But no animal can reason," objected Rainsford.

"My dear fellow," said the general, "there is one that can."

"But you can't mean—" gasped Rainsford.

"And why not?"

110   "I can't believe you are serious, General Zaroff. This is a grisly joke."

"Why should I not be serious? I am speaking of hunting."

"Hunting? Good God, General Zaroff, what you speak of is murder."

The general laughed with entire good nature. He regarded Rainsford quizzically. "I refuse to believe that so modern and civilized a young man as you seem to be harbors romantic ideas about the value of human life. Surely your experiences in the war—"

"Did not make me condone cold-blooded murder," finished Rainsford stiffly.

115   Laughter shook the general. "How extraordinarily droll you are!" he said. "One does not expect nowadays to find a young man of the educated class, even in America, with such a naïve, and, if I may say so, mid-Victorian point of view. It's like finding a snuff-box in a limousine. Ah, well, doubtless you had Puritan ancestors. So many Americans appear to have had. I'll wager you'll forget your notions when you go hunting with me. You've a genuine new thrill in store for you, Mr. Rainsford."

"Thank you, I'm a hunter, not a murderer."

"Dear me," said the general, quite unruffled, "again that unpleasant word. But I think I can show you that your scruples are quite ill founded."

"Yes?"

"Life is for the strong, to be lived by the strong, and, if need be, taken by the strong. The weak of the world were put here to give the strong pleasure. I am strong. Why should I not use my gift? If I wish to hunt, why should I not? I hunt the scum of the earth—sailors from tramp ships—lascars, blacks, Chinese, whites, mongrels—a thoroughbred horse or hound is worth more than a score of them."

120   "But they are men," said Rainsford hotly.

"Precisely," said the general. "That is why I use them. It gives me pleasure. They can reason, after a fashion. So they are dangerous."

"But where do you get them?"

The general's left eyelid fluttered down in a wink. "This island is called Ship-Trap," he answered. "Sometimes an angry god of the high seas sends them to me. Sometimes, when Providence is not so kind, I help Providence a bit. Come to the window with me."

Rainsford went to the window and looked out toward the sea.

125   "Watch! Out there!" exclaimed the general, pointing into the night. Rainsford's eyes saw only blackness, and then, as the general pressed a button, far out to sea Rainsford saw the flash of lights.

The general chuckled. "They indicate a channel," he said, "where there's none: giant rocks with razor edges crouch like a sea monster with wide-open jaws. They can crush a ship as easily as I crush this nut." He dropped a walnut on the hardwood floor and brought his heel grinding down on it. "Oh, yes," he said, casually, as if in answer to a question, "I have electricity. We try to be civilized here."

"Civilized? And you shoot down men?"

A trace of anger was in the general's black eyes, but it was there for but a second, and he said, in his most pleasant manner: "Dear me, what a righteous young man you are! I assure you I do not do the thing you suggest. That would be barbarous. I treat these visitors with every consideration. They get plenty of good food and exercise. They get into splendid physical condition. You shall see for yourself tomorrow."

"What do you mean?"

"We'll visit my training school," smiled the general. "It's in the cellar. I have about a dozen pupils down there now. They're from the Spanish bark San Lucar that had the bad luck to go on the rocks out there. A very inferior lot, I regret to say. Poor specimens and more accustomed to the deck than to the jungle."

He raised his hand, and Ivan, who served as waiter, brought thick Turkish coffee. Rainsford, with an effort, held his tongue in check.

"It's a game, you see," pursued the general blandly. "I suggest to one of them that we go hunting. I give him a supply of food and an excellent hunting knife. I give him three hours' start. I am to follow, armed only with a pistol of the smallest caliber and range. If my quarry eludes me for three whole days, he wins the game. If I find him"—the general smiled—"he loses."

"Suppose he refuses to be hunted?"

"Oh," said the general, "I give him his option, of course. He need not play that game if he doesn't wish to. If he does not wish to hunt, I turn him over to Ivan. Ivan once had the honor of serving as official knouter to the Great White Czar,[2] and he has his own ideas of sport. Invariably, Mr. Rainsford, invariably they choose the hunt."

"And if they win?"

The smile on the general's face widened. "To date I have not lost," he said.

Then he added, hastily: "I don't wish you to think me a braggart, Mr. Rainsford. Many of them afford only the most elementary sort of problem. Occasionally I strike a tartar. One almost did win. I eventually had to use the dogs."

"The dogs?"

"This way, please. I'll show you."

The general steered Rainsford to a window. The lights from the windows sent a flickering illumination that made grotesque patterns on the courtyard below, and Rainsford could see moving about there a dozen or so huge black shapes; as they turned toward him, their eyes glittered greenly.

"A rather good lot, I think," observed the general. "They are let out at seven every night. If anyone should try to get into my house—or out of it—something extremely regrettable would occur to him." He hummed a snatch of song from the Folies Bergère.[3]

"And now," said the general, "I want to show you my new collection of heads. Will you come with me to the library?"

---

2. Probably Nicholas II (1868–1918), who was overthrown by the Revolution and executed; White designates those opposed to the Communists, or Reds.   3. Paris theater and music hall.

"I hope," said Rainsford, "that you will excuse me tonight, General Zaroff. I'm really not feeling at all well."

"Ah, indeed?" the general inquired solicitously. "Well, I suppose that's only natural, after your long swim. You need a good, restful night's sleep. Tomorrow you'll feel like a new man, I'll wager. Then we'll hunt, eh? I've one rather promising prospect—"

145   Rainsford was hurrying from the room.

"Sorry you can't go with me tonight," called the general. "I expect rather fair sport—a big, strong black. He looks resourceful—Well, good night, Mr. Rainsford; I hope you have a good night's rest."

The bed was good, and the pajamas of the softest silk, and he was tired in every fiber of his being, but nevertheless Rainsford could not quiet his brain with the opiate of sleep. He lay, eyes wide open. Once he thought he heard stealthy steps in the corridor outside his room. He sought to throw open the door; it would not open. He went to the window and looked out. His room was high up in one of the towers. The lights of the château were out now; and it was dark and silent, but there was a fragment of sallow moon, and by its wan light he could see, dimly, the courtyard; there, weaving in and out in the pattern of shadow, were black, noiseless forms; the hounds heard him at the window and looked up, expectantly, with their green eyes. Rainsford went back to bed and lay down. By many methods he tried to put himself to sleep. He had achieved a doze when, just as morning began to come, he heard, far off in the jungle, the faint report of a pistol.

General Zaroff did not appear until luncheon. He was dressed faultlessly in the tweeds of a country squire. He was solicitous about the state of Rainsford's health.

"As for me," sighed the general, "I do not feel so well. I am worried, Mr. Rainsford. Last night I detected traces of my old complaint."

150   To Rainsford's questioning glance the general said: "Ennui. Boredom."

Then, taking a second helping of *crêpes suzette,* the general explained: "The hunting was not good last night. The fellow lost his head. He made a straight trail that offered no problems at all. That's the trouble with these sailors; they have dull brains to begin with, and they do not know how to get about in the woods. They do excessively stupid and obvious things. It's most annoying. Will you have another glass of Chablis, Mr. Rainsford?"

"General," said Rainsford firmly, "I wish to leave this island at once."

The general raised his thickets of eyebrows; he seemed hurt. "But, my dear fellow," the general protested, "you've only just come. You've had no hunting—"

"I wish to go today," said Rainsford. He saw the dead black eyes of the general on him, studying him. General Zaroff's face suddenly brightened.

155   He filled Rainsford's glass with venerable Chablis[4] from a dusty bottle.

"Tonight," said the general, "we will hunt—you and I."

Rainsford shook his head. "No, general," he said, "I will not hunt."

The general shrugged his shoulders and delicately ate a hothouse grape. "As you wish, my friend," he said. "The choice rests entirely with you. But may I not

---

4. A very dry white Burgundy table wine; Veuve Cliquot, below, is a fine champagne.

venture to suggest that you will find my idea of sport more diverting than Ivan's?"

He nodded toward the corner to where the giant stood, scowling, his thick arms crossed on his hogshead of a chest.

"You don't mean—" cried Rainsford.   160

"My dear fellow," said the general, "have I not told you I always mean what I say about hunting? This is really an inspiration. I drink to a foeman worthy of my steel—at last."

The general raised his glass, but Rainsford sat staring at him.

"You'll find this game worth playing," the general said enthusiastically. "Your brain against mine. Your woodcraft against mine. Your strength and stamina against mine. Outdoor chess! And the stake is not without value, eh?"

"And if I win—" began Rainsford huskily.

"I'll cheerfully acknowledge myself defeated if I do not find you by midnight   165 of the third day," said General Zaroff. "My sloop will place you on the mainland near a town."

The general read what Rainsford was thinking.

"Oh, you can trust me," said the Cossack. "I will give you my word as a gentleman and a sportsman. Of course you, in turn, must agree to say nothing of your visit here."

"I'll agree to nothing of the kind," said Rainsford.

"Oh," said the general, "in that case—But why discuss that now? Three days hence we can discuss it over a bottle of Veuve Cliquot, unless—"

The general sipped his wine.   170

Then a businesslike air animated him. "Ivan," he said to Rainsford, "will supply you with hunting clothes, food, a knife. I suggest you wear moccasins; they leave a poorer trail. I suggest too that you avoid the big swamp in the southeast corner of the island. We call it Death Swamp. There's quicksand there. One foolish fellow tried it. The deplorable part of it was that Lazarus followed him. You can imagine my feelings, Mr. Rainsford. I loved Lazarus; he was the finest hound in my pack. Well, I must beg you to excuse me now. I always take a siesta after lunch. You'll hardly have time for a nap, I fear. You'll want to start, no doubt. I shall not follow till dusk. Hunting at night is so much more exciting than by day, don't you think? Au revoir, Mr. Rainsford, au revoir."

General Zaroff, with a deep, courtly bow, strolled from the room.

From another door came Ivan. Under one arm he carried khaki hunting clothes, a haversack of food, a leather sheath containing a long-bladed hunting knife; his right hand rested on a cocked revolver thrust in the crimson sash about his waist. . . .

Rainsford had fought his way through the bush for two hours. "I must keep my nerve. I must keep my nerve," he said through tight teeth.

He had not been entirely clear-headed when the château gates snapped shut   175 behind him. His whole idea at first was to put distance between himself and General Zaroff, and, to this end, he had plunged along, spurred on by the sharp rowels of something very like panic. Now he had got a grip on himself, had stopped, and was taking stock of himself and the situation.

He saw that straight flight was futile; inevitably it would bring him face to face with the sea. He was in a picture with a frame of water, and his operations, clearly, must take place within that frame.

"I'll give him a trail to follow," muttered Rainsford, and he struck off from the rude paths he had been following into the trackless wilderness. He executed a series of intricate loops; he doubled on his trail again and again, recalling all the lore of the fox hunt, and all the dodges of the fox. Night found him leg-weary, with hands and face lashed by the branches, on a thickly wooded ridge. He knew it would be insane to blunder on through the dark, even if he had the strength. His need for rest was imperative and he thought: "I have played the fox, now I must play the cat of the fable."[5] A big tree with a thick trunk and outspread branches was nearby, and, taking care to leave not the slightest mark, he climbed up into the crotch, and stretching out on one of the broad limbs, after a fashion, rested. Rest brought him new confidence and almost a feeling of security. Even so zealous a hunter as General Zaroff could not trace him there, he told himself; only the devil himself could follow that complicated trail through the jungle after dark. But, perhaps, the general was a devil—

An apprehensive night crawled slowly by like a wounded snake, and sleep did not visit Rainsford, although the silence of a dead world was on the jungle. Toward morning when a dingy gray was varnishing the sky, the cry of some startled bird focused Rainsford's attention in that direction. Something was coming through the bush, coming slowly, carefully, coming by the same winding way Rainsford had come. He flattened himself down on the limb, and through a screen of leaves almost as thick as tapestry, he watched. The thing that was approaching was a man.

It was General Zaroff. He made his way along with his eyes fixed in utmost concentration on the ground before him. He paused, almost beneath the tree, dropped to his knees and studied the ground. Rainsford's impulse was to hurl himself down like a panther, but he saw that the general's right hand held something metallic—a small automatic pistol.

The hunter shook his head several times, as if he were puzzled. Then he straightened up and took from his case one of his black cigarettes; its pungent incense-like smoke floated up to Rainsford's nostrils.

Rainsford held his breath. The general's eyes had left the ground and were traveling inch by inch up the tree. Rainsford froze there, every muscle tensed for a spring. But the sharp eyes of the hunter stopped before they reached the limb where Rainsford lay; a smile spread over his brown face. Very deliberately he blew a smoke ring into the air; then he turned his back on the tree and walked carelessly away, back along the trail he had come. The swish of the underbrush against his hunting boots grew fainter and fainter.

The pent-up air burst hotly from Rainsford's lungs. His first thought made him feel sick and numb. The general could follow a trail through the woods at night;

5. The fox boasts of his many tricks to elude the hounds; the cat responds that he knows only one—to climb the nearest tree—but that this is worth more than all the fox's tricks.

he could follow an extremely difficult trail; he must have uncanny powers; only by the merest chance had the Cossack failed to see his quarry.

Rainsford's second thought was even more terrible. It sent a shudder of cold horror through his whole being. Why had the general smiled? Why had he turned back?

Rainsford did not want to believe what his reason told him was true, but the truth was as evident as the sun that had by now pushed through the morning mists. The general was playing with him! The general was saving him for another day's sport! The Cossack was the cat; he was the mouse. Then it was that Rainsford knew the full meaning of terror.

"I will not lose my nerve. I will not."

He slid down the tree, and struck off again into the woods. His face was set and he forced the machinery of his mind to function. Three hundred yards from his hiding place he stopped where a huge dead tree leaned precariously on a smaller, living one. Throwing off his sack of food, Rainsford took his knife from its sheath and began to work with all his energy.

The job was finished at last, and he threw himself down behind a fallen log a hundred feet away. He did not have to wait long. The cat was coming again to play with the mouse.

Following the trail with the sureness of a bloodhound, came General Zaroff. Nothing escaped those searching black eyes, no crushed blade of grass, no bent twig, no mark, no matter how faint, in the moss. So intent was the Cossack on his stalking that he was upon the thing Rainsford had made before he saw it. His foot touched the protruding bough that was the trigger. Even as he touched it, the general sensed his danger and leaped back with the agility of an ape. But he was not quite quick enough; the dead tree, delicately adjusted to rest on the cut living one, crashed down and struck the general a glancing blow on the shoulder as it fell; but for his alertness, he must have been smashed beneath it. He staggered, but he did not fall; nor did he drop his revolver. He stood there, rubbing his injured shoulder, and Rainsford, with fear again gripping his heart, heard the general's mocking laugh ring through the jungle.

"Rainsford," called the general, "if you are within sound of my voice, as I suppose you are, let me congratulate you. Not many men know how to make a Malay man-catcher. Luckily, for me, I too have hunted in Malacca. You are proving interesting, Mr. Rainsford. I am going now to have my wound dressed; it's only a slight one. But I shall be back. I shall be back."

When the general, nursing his bruised shoulder, had gone, Rainsford took up his flight again. It was flight now, a desperate, hopeless flight, that carried him on for some hours. Dusk came, then darkness, and still he pressed on. The ground grew softer under his moccasins; the vegetation grew ranker, denser; insects bit him savagely. Then, as he stepped forward, his foot sank into the ooze. He tried to wrench it back, but the muck sucked viciously at his foot as if it were a giant leech. With a violent effort, he tore his foot loose. He knew where he was now. Death Swamp and its quicksand.

His hands were tight closed as if his nerve were something tangible that someone in the darkness was trying to tear from his grip. The softness of the earth had given him an idea. He stepped back from the quicksand a dozen feet or so and, like some huge prehistoric beaver, he began to dig.

Rainsford had dug himself in in France[6] when a second's delay meant death. That had been a placid pastime compared to his digging now. The pit grew deeper; when it was above his shoulders, he climbed out and from some hard saplings cut stakes and sharpened them to a fine point. These stakes he planted in the bottom of the pit with the points sticking up. With flying fingers he wove a rough carpet of weeds and branches and with it he covered the mouth of the pit. Then, wet with sweat and aching with tiredness, he crouched behind the stump of a lightning-charred tree.

He knew his pursuer was coming; he heard the padding sound of feet on the soft earth, and the night breeze brought him the perfume of the general's cigarette. It seemed to Rainsford that the general was coming with unusual swiftness; he was not feeling his way along, foot by foot. Rainsford, crouching there, could not see the general, nor could he see the pit. He lived a year in a minute. Then he felt an impulse to cry aloud with joy, for he heard the sharp crackle of the breaking branches as the cover of the pit gave way; he heard the sharp scream of pain as the pointed stakes found their mark. He leaped up from his place of concealment. Then he cowered back. Three feet from the pit a man was standing, with an electric torch in his hand.

"You've done well, Rainsford," the voice of the general called. "Your Burmese tiger pit has claimed one of my best dogs. Again you score. I think, Mr. Rainsford, I'll see what you can do against my whole pack. I'm going home for a rest now. Thank you for a most amusing evening."

195   At daybreak Rainsford, lying near the swamp, was awakened by a sound that made him know that he had new things to learn about fear. It was a distant sound, faint and wavering, but he knew it. It was the baying of a pack of hounds.

Rainsford knew he could do one of two things. He could stay where he was and wait. That was suicide. He could flee. That was postponing the inevitable. For a moment he stood there, thinking. An idea that held a wild chance came to him, and, tightening his belt, he headed away from the swamp.

The baying of the hounds drew nearer, then still nearer, nearer, ever nearer. On a ridge Rainsford climbed a tree. Down a watercourse, not a quarter of a mile away, he could see the bush moving. Straining his eyes, he saw the lean figure of General Zaroff; just ahead of him Rainsford made out another figure whose wide shoulders surged through the tall jungle weeds; it was the giant Ivan, and he seemed pulled forward by some unseen force; Rainsford knew that Ivan must be holding the pack in leash.

They would be on him any minute now. His mind worked frantically. He thought of a native trick he had learned in Uganda. He slid down the tree. He caught hold of a springy young sapling and to it he fastened his hunting knife, with the blade pointing down the trail; with a bit of wild grapevine he tied back

---

6. During World War I he had quickly dug a hole or trench to shelter himself from exploding shells, bullets, and so forth.

the sapling. Then he ran for his life. The hounds raised their voices as they hit the fresh scent. Rainsford knew now how an animal at bay feels.

He had to stop to get his breath. The baying of the hounds stopped abruptly, and Rainsford's heart stopped too. They must have reached the knife.

He shinnied excitedly up a tree and looked back. His pursuers had stopped. 200 But the hope that was in Rainsford's brain when he climbed died, for he saw in the shallow valley that General Zaroff was still on his feet. But Ivan was not. The knife, driven by the recoil of the springing tree, had not wholly failed.

Rainsford had hardly tumbled to the ground when the pack took up the cry again.

"Nerve, nerve, nerve!" he panted, as he dashed along. A blue gap showed between the trees dead ahead. Ever nearer drew the hounds. Rainsford forced himself on toward that gap. He reached it. It was the shore of the sea. Across a cove he could see the gloomy gray stone of the château. Twenty feet below him the sea rumbled and hissed. Rainsford hesitated. He heard the hounds. Then he leaped far out into the sea. . . .

When the general and his pack reached the place by the sea, the Cossack stopped. For some minutes he stood regarding the blue-green expanse of water. He shrugged his shoulders. Then he sat down, took a drink of brandy from a silver flask, lit a perfumed cigarette, and hummed a bit from "Madame Butterfly."[7]

General Zaroff had an exceedingly good dinner in his great paneled dining hall that evening. With it he had a bottle of Pol Roger and half a bottle of Chambertin.[8] Two slight annoyances kept him from perfect enjoyment. One was the thought that it would be difficult to replace Ivan; the other was that his quarry had escaped him; of course the American hadn't played the game—so thought the general as he tasted his after-dinner liqueur. In his library he read, to soothe himself, from the works of Marcus Aurelius.[9] At ten he went up to his bedroom. He was deliciously tired, he said to himself, as he locked himself in. There was a little moonlight so, before turning on his light, he went to the window and looked down at the courtyard. He could see the great hounds, and he called: "Better luck another time," to them. Then he switched on the light.

A man, who had been hiding in the curtains of the bed, was standing there. 205 "Rainsford!" screamed the general. "How in God's name did you get here?"

"Swam," said Rainsford. "I found it quicker than walking through the jungle."

The general sucked in his breath and smiled. "I congratulate you," he said. "You have won the game."

Rainsford did not smile. "I am still a beast at bay," he said, in a low, hoarse voice. "Get ready, General Zaroff."

The general made one of his deepest bows. "I see," he said. "Splendid! One of 210

7. Opera (1904) by Giacomo Puccini (1858–1924).   8. A highly esteemed Red burgundy wine; Pol Roger is champagne.   9. Marcus Aurelius Antoninus (A.D. 121–180), Roman emperor (161–180), Stoic philosopher, writer, and humanitarian.

us is to furnish a repast for the hounds. The other will sleep in this very excellent bed. On guard, Rainsford. . . ."

He had never slept in a better bed, Rainsford decided.

1924

A good many readers like "The Most Dangerous Game." In class it is often a favorite, or even *the* favorite. Other readers recommend dropping this story from the anthology because it is "unworthy," not really literature. Is this simply ignorance on the one hand or snobbery on the other?

Here are two brief papers, somewhat like those a student might write in class, the first supporting "The Most Dangerous Game," the second responding to the first.

Why "The Most Dangerous Game" Is Good Literature

Thaddeus Smith

"The Most Dangerous Game" by Richard Connell is exciting. Things happen in it, and you want to read on because you want to find out what will happen next and how it will come out. Too often the things we need to read for class are boring, nothing happens, or, if something does happen, it happens inside somebody's head. But here things happen outside; I mean, there's real action.

Not only is there action, but that action is important, a real life-and-death struggle. This story is not just about whether somebody used the wrong fork or had a good time or didn't have a good time at a party.

The good guy wins, the story ends happily, and when you finish reading it, you feel good about things. Sometimes in class I think only real downers are supposed to be good stories, like life always has to be full of gloom and doom. Now all of us die sooner or later, of course, but that's only the end, a minute or a month or something, and there's all the rest of the time when we're not dead and not really in the process of dying. That's life, and that's what a good story should be about.

"The Most Dangerous Game" is fun to read. Sometimes I think that what
are supposed to be the "good" stories are the ones I don't like. But
popular stories can be good: there have been several movies made of
"The Most Dangerous Game" and several stories adapted from it with just
a few things changed. But, I'm told, the world of literature isn't a
democracy--you don't vote for what's Literature. When I say I like
Stephen King--and I'm sure not the only one, because he sells lots and
lots of book--teachers or English majors say wait fifty years and see if
his stuff is still around.

Well, "The Most Dangerous Game" is over seventy years old, older than
at least three-quarters of the stories in this book, so it's stood the
test of time, whatever that is.

Why "The Most Dangerous Game" Is Not Good Literature

Sara Rosen

Though "The Most Dangerous Game" may be "a good read," at least the
first time through, and I have nothing against someone reading it or
even liking it in its way, I don't think it ought to be in *The Norton
Introduction to Literature*. Being in the anthology gives it a status it
does not deserve. It makes it the subject of serious study by college
students, and college students ought to be engaged in more challenging
and thought-provoking reading material, even if outside of class they
are reading Stephen King and the likes of "The Most Dangerous Game."

Though it's true that a life-and-death struggle is important--for the
person involved--it has no relevance for us, no outreach: it does not
relate to our experience nor does it really illuminate anything about
our experience or the way we look at life. I don't mean that a worthy
story must have a "message," necessarily, but it should have a "theme,"
something that explores a significant area of human experience and
understanding.

I admit that there is something like suspense in Connell's story, but
that is not enough. There's nothing wrong with suspense in itself--

expectations of one sort or another are part of every good work--but here the suspense is manipulated at the price of consistency. Note how we're seeing things from Rainsford's perspective (not through his eyes and mind exactly, not in the first person, but over his shoulder) until near the end when he leaps into the sea. At that point, when we're supposed to want most to know what happens next, there's the more or less artificial suspense added by three dots and a break on the page, and then we're not with Rainsford but Zaroff, just to make us wonder if Rainsford did indeed die. It's a cheap trick. Besides, don't we know from the beginning that in this kind of story the hero never dies, so isn't the suspense really phony? What's wrong with stories like this is the unrealistic, wish-fulfilling way it looks at reality: it tells us that good guys always finish first; they win because they're good.

While good guys do sometimes finish first, and plenty of good stories end happily, more or less, like "Sonny Blues," and "The Secret Sharer," life is not always like that, and this victory seems a little too easy.

Finally, Rainsford has no "character"; he's just a good guy because he's an American and his life is threatened by a bad guy who's a Russian; and the bad guy is just a bad guy, with no redeeming human qualities--it's all about guys in white hats versus guys in black hats.

These are not polished and conclusive arguments, of course. Had the writer of the first paper read the response, he might have had more to say. About the alleged absence of theme in "The Most Dangerous Game," for example:

There is a theme in Connell's story. It is a very important one, one that you have to think about, and that some people will agree with, though it is not a theme that you necessarily have to agree with in order to appreciate the story. Notice it is set just after the Russian Revolution, and Zaroff (the "son of the czar") is a cruel aristocrat from the czarist regime who believes in power, believes that might-makes-right, and believes some people are better than others and have a right to do what they will with their "inferiors," even kill them for pleasure. Rainsford at the beginning is a hunter/exploiter, never thinking what the "inferior" beast, the hunted, feels like. Having been put in the place of the hunted he will no doubt learn to have more reverence for life, more sympathy for the underdog.

The opponent, hearing this contention that there is a significant theme in the story, might well respond that the theme as described is too pat, and that it is presented through too convenient (as well as unbelievable) a situation, too much of a setup.

This, then, is only one example of the kinds of arguments readers can use to support their judgments. We need to go on from there to consider what we read for ("a good read"? "an illumination of human life and experience"?), and what we mean by "the reader," the one judging the story to be "good."

Let us assume for the moment that "the readers" can be represented roughly by the people in this class—you, those who agree with you about stories, and those who, though they are more or less like you, do not always agree with you. We said earlier that if our appreciation and understanding of literature is to grow, and if we are not merely to accept what those considered "authorities" say is good or great, we must learn to isolate, analyze, and articulate what *we* like (or dislike) in a story. And, we said, we must listen to those with other responses as they articulate their reasons.

Now for the test. "Barn Burning" is one of William Faulkner's most admired stories. It has some of the same attractive qualities as "The Most Dangerous Game"—conflict, action, suspense—but some readers find it critically flawed. Regardless of which side we are on, we must take seriously people's reservations and questions, Faulkner's status as a Nobel laureate and much-revered writer, and the story's established reputation. But first, we must read it.

WILLIAM FAULKNER

Barn Burning

The store in which the Justice of the Peace's court was sitting smelled of cheese. The boy, crouched on his nail keg at the back of the crowded room, knew he smelled cheese, and more: from where he sat he could see the ranked shelves close-packed with the solid, squat, dynamic shapes of tin cans whose labels his stomach read, not from the lettering which meant nothing to his mind but from the scarlet devils and the silver curve of fish—this, the cheese which he knew he smelled and the hermetic meat which his intestines believed he smelled coming in intermittent gusts momentary and brief between the other constant one, the smell and sense just a little of fear because mostly of despair and grief, the old fierce pull of blood. He could not see the table where the Justice sat and before which his father and his father's enemy (*our enemy* he thought in that despair; *ourn! mine and hisn both! He's my father!*) stood, but he could hear them, the two of them that is, because his father had said no word yet:

"But what proof have you, Mr. Harris?"

"I told you. The hog got into my corn. I caught it up and sent it back to him. He had no fence that would hold it. I told him so, warned him. The next time I put the hog in my pen. When he came to get it I gave him enough wire to patch up his pen. The next time I put the hog up and kept it. I rode down to his house and saw the wire I gave him still rolled on to the spool in his yard. I told him he could have the hog when he paid me a dollar pound fee. That evening a nigger came with the dollar and got the hog. He was a strange nigger. He said, 'He say to tell you wood and hay kin burn.' I said, 'What?' 'That whut he say to tell you,' the nigger said. 'Wood and hay kin burn.' That night my barn burned. I got the stock out but I lost the barn."

"Where is the nigger? Have you got him?"

5   "He was a strange nigger, I tell you. I don't know what became of him."

"But that's not proof. Don't you see that's not proof?"

"Get that boy up here. He knows." For a moment the boy thought too that the man meant his older brother until Harris said, "Not him. The little one. The boy," and, crouching, small for his age, small and wiry like his father, in patched and faded jeans even too small for him, with straight, uncombed, brown hair and eyes gray and wild as storm scud, he saw the men between himself and the table part and become a lane of grim faces, at the end of which he saw the Justice, a shabby, collarless, graying man in spectacles, beckoning him. He felt no floor under his bare feet; he seemed to walk beneath the palpable weight of the grim turning faces. His father, stiff in his black Sunday coat donned not for the trial but for the moving, did not even look at him. *He aims for me to lie,* he thought, again with that frantic grief and despair. *And I will have to do hit.*

"What's your name, boy?" the Justice said.

"Colonel Sartoris Snopes," the boy whispered.

10   "Hey?" the Justice said. "Talk louder. Colonel Sartoris? I reckon anybody named for Colonel Sartoris in this country can't help but tell the truth, can they?" The boy said nothing. *Enemy! Enemy!* he thought; for a moment he could not even see, could not see that the Justice's face was kindly nor discern that his voice was troubled when he spoke to the man named Harris: "Do you want me to question this boy?" But he could hear, and during those subsequent long seconds while there was absolutely no sound in the crowded little room save that of quiet and intent breathing it was as if he had swung outward at the end of a grape vine, over a ravine, and at the top of the swing had been caught in a prolonged instant of mesmerized gravity, weightless in time.

"No!" Harris said violently, explosively. "Damnation! Send him out of here!" Now time, the fluid world, rushed beneath him again, the voices coming to him again through the smell of cheese and sealed meat, the fear and despair and the old grief of blood:

"This case is closed. I can't find against you, Snopes, but I can give you advice. Leave this country and don't come back to it."

His father spoke for the first time, his voice cold and harsh, level, without emphasis: "I aim to. I don't figure to stay in a country among people who . . ." he said something unprintable and vile, addressed to no one.

"That'll do," the Justice said. "Take your wagon and get out of this country before dark. Case dismissed."

15   His father turned, and he followed the stiff black coat, the wiry figure walking a little stiffly from where a Confederate provost's man's[1] musket ball had taken him in the heel on a stolen horse thirty years ago, followed the two backs now,

---

1. Military policeman's.

since his older brother had appeared from somewhere in the crowd, no taller than the father but thicker, chewing tobacco steadily, between the two lines of grim-faced men and out of the store and across the worn gallery and down the sagging steps and among the dogs and half-grown boys in the mild May dust, where as he passed a voice hissed:

"Barn burner!"

Again he could not see, whirling; there was a face in a red haze, moonlike, bigger than the full moon, the owner of it half again his size, he leaping in the red haze toward the face, feeling no blow, feeling no shock when his head struck the earth, scrabbling up and leaping again, feeling no blow this time either and tasting no blood, scrabbling up to see the other boy in full flight and himself already leaping into pursuit as his father's hand jerked him back, the harsh, cold voice speaking above him: "Go get in the wagon."

It stood in a grove of locusts and mulberries across the road. His two hulking sisters in their Sunday dresses and his mother and her sister in calico and sun-bonnets were already in it, sitting on and among the sorry residue of the dozen and more movings which even the boy could remember—the battered stove, the broken beds and chairs, the clock inlaid with mother-of-pearl, which would not run, stopped at some fourteen minutes past two o'clock of a dead and forgotten day and time, which had been his mother's dowry. She was crying, though when she saw him she drew her sleeve across her face and began to descend from the wagon. "Get back," the father said.

"He's hurt. I got to get some water and wash his . . ."

"Get back in the wagon," his father said. He got in too, over the tail-gate. His 20
father mounted to the seat where the older brother already sat and struck the gaunt mules two savage blows with the peeled willow, but without heat. It was not even sadistic; it was exactly that same quality which in later years would cause his descendants to overrun the engine before putting a motor car into motion, striking and reining back in the same movement. The wagon went on, the store with its quiet crowd of grimly watching men dropped behind; a curve in the road hid it. *Forever* he thought. *Maybe he's done satisfied now, now that he has . . .* stop-ping himself, not to say it aloud even to himself. His mother's hand touched his shoulder.

"Does hit hurt?" she said.

"Naw," he said. "Hit don't hurt. Lemme be."

"Can't you wipe some of the blood off before hit dries?"

"I'll wash to-night," he said. "Lemme be, I tell you."

The wagon went on. He did not know where they were going. None of them 25
ever did or ever asked, because it was always somewhere, always a house of sorts waiting for them a day or two days or even three days away. Likely his father had already arranged to make a crop on another farm before he . . . Again he had to stop himself. He (the father) always did. There was something about his wolf-like independence and even courage when the advantage was at least neutral which impressed strangers, as if they got from his latent ravening ferocity not so much a sense of dependability as a feeling that his ferocious conviction in the rightness of his own actions would be of advantage to all whose interest lay with his.

That night they camped, in a grove of oaks and beeches where a spring ran. The nights were still cool and they had a fire against it, of a rail lifted from a nearby fence and cut into lengths—a small fire, neat, niggard almost, a shrewd fire; such fires were his father's habit and custom always, even in freezing weather. Older, the boy might have remarked this and wondered why not a big one; why should not a man who had not only seen the waste and extravagance of war, but who had in his blood an inherent voracious prodigality with material not his own, have burned everything in sight? Then he might have gone a step farther and thought that that was the reason: that niggard blaze was the living fruit of nights passed during those four years in the woods hiding from all men, blue or gray,[2] with his strings of horses (captured horses, he called them). And older still, he might have divined the true reason: that the element of fire spoke to some deep mainspring of his father's being, as the element of steel or of powder spoke to other men, as the one weapon for the preservation of integrity, else breath were not worth the breathing, and hence to be regarded with respect and used with discretion.

But he did not think this now and he had seen those same niggard blazes all his life. He merely ate his supper beside it and was already half asleep over his iron plate when his father called him, and once more he followed the stiff back, the stiff and ruthless limp, up the slope and on to the starlit road where, turning, he could see his father against the stars but without face or depth—a shape black, flat, and bloodless as though cut from tin in the iron folds of the frock-coat which had not been made for him, the voice harsh like tin and without heat like tin:

"You were fixing to tell them. You would have told him." He didn't answer. His father struck him with the flat of his hand on the side of the head, hard but without heat, exactly as he had struck the two mules at the store, exactly as he would strike either of them with any stick in order to kill a horse fly, his voice still without heat or anger: "You're getting to be a man. You got to learn. You got to learn to stick to your own blood or you ain't going to have any blood to stick to you. Do you think either of them, any man there this morning, would? Don't you know all they wanted was a chance to get at me because they knew I had them beat? Eh?" Later, twenty years later, he was to tell himself, "If I had said they wanted only truth, justice, he would have hit me again." But now he said nothing. He was not crying. He just stood there. "Answer me," his father said.

"Yes," he whispered. His father turned.

30   "Get on to bed. We'll be there tomorrow."

Tomorrow they were there. In the early afternoon the wagon stopped before a paintless two-room house identical almost with the dozen others it had stopped before even in the boy's ten years, and again, as on the other dozen occasions, his mother and aunt got down and began to unload the wagon, although his two sisters and his father and brother had not moved.

"Likely hit ain't fitten for hawgs," one of the sisters said.

---

2. The colors of Union and Confederate Civil War (1861–65) uniforms, respectively.

"Nevertheless, fit it will and you'll hog it and like it," his father said. "Get out of them chairs and help your Ma unload."

The two sisters got down, big, bovine, in a flutter of cheap ribbons; one of them drew from the jumbled wagon bed a battered lantern, the other a worn broom. His father handed the reins to the older son and began to climb stiffly over the wheel. "When they get unloaded, take the team to the barn and feed them." Then he said, and at first the boy thought he was still speaking to his brother: "Come with me."

"Me?" he said.

"Yes," his father said. "You."   35

"Abner," his mother said. His father paused and looked back—the harsh level stare beneath the shaggy, graying, irascible brows.

"I reckon I'll have a word with the man that aims to begin to-morrow owning me body and soul for the next eight months."

They went back up the road. A week ago—or before last night, that is—he would have asked where they were going, but not now. His father had struck him before last night but never before had he paused afterward to explain why; it was as if the blow and the following calm, outrageous voice still rang, repercussed, divulging nothing to him save the terrible handicap of being young, the light weight of his few years, just heavy enough to prevent his soaring free of the world as it seemed to be ordered but not heavy enough to keep him footed solid in it, to resist it and try to change the course of its events.

Presently he could see the grove of oaks and cedars and the other flowering   40
trees and shrubs, where the house would be, though not the house yet. They walked beside a fence massed with honeysuckle and Cherokee roses and came to a gate swinging open between two brick pillars, and now, beyond a sweep of drive, he saw the house for the first time and at that instant he forgot his father and the terror and despair both, and even when he remembered his father again (who had not stopped) the terror and despair did not return. Because, for all the twelve movings, they had sojourned until now in a poor country, a land of small farms and fields and houses, and he had never seen a house like this before. *Hit's big as a courthouse* he thought quietly, with a surge of peace and joy whose reason he could not have thought into words, being too young for that: *They are safe from him. People whose lives are a part of this peace and dignity are beyond his touch, he no more to them than a buzzing wasp: capable of stinging for a little moment but that's all; the spell of this peace and dignity rendering even the barns and stable and cribs which belong to it impervious to the puny flames he might contrive* . . . this, the peace and joy, ebbing for an instant as he looked again at the stiff black back, the stiff and implacable limp of the figure which was not dwarfed by the house, for the reason that it had never looked big anywhere and which now, against the serene columned backdrop, had more than ever that impervious quality of something cut ruthlessly from tin, depthless, as though, sidewise to the sun, it would cast no shadow. Watching him, the boy remarked the absolutely undeviating course which his father held and saw the stiff foot come squarely down in a pile of fresh droppings where a horse had stood in the

drive and which his father could have avoided by a simple change of stride. But it ebbed only for a moment, though he could not have thought this into words either, walking on in the spell of the house, which he could even want but without envy, without sorrow, certainly never with that ravening and jealous rage which unknown to him walked in the ironlike black coat before him: *Maybe he will feel it too. Maybe it will even change him now from what maybe he couldn't help but be.*

They crossed the portico. Now he could hear his father's stiff foot as it came down on the boards with clocklike finality, a sound out of all proportion to the displacement of the body it bore and which was not dwarfed either by the white door before it, as though it had attained to a sort of vicious and ravening minimum not to be dwarfed by anything—the flat, wide, black hat, the formal coat of broadcloth which had once been black but which had now that friction-glazed greenish cast of the bodies of old house flies, the lifted sleeve which was too large, the lifted hand like a curled claw. The door opened so promptly that the boy knew the Negro must have been watching them all the time, an old man with neat grizzled hair, in a linen jacket, who stood barring the door with his body, saying, "Wipe yo foots, white man, fo you come in here. Major ain't home nohow."

"Get out of my way, nigger," his father said, without heat too, flinging the door back and the Negro also and entering, his hat still on his head. And now the boy saw the prints of the stiff foot on the doorjamb and saw them appear on the pale rug behind the machinelike deliberation of the foot which seemed to bear (or transmit) twice the weight which the body compassed. The Negro was shouting "Miss Lula! Miss Lula!" somewhere behind them, then the boy, deluged as though by a warm wave by a suave turn of carpeted stair and a pendant glitter of chandeliers and a mute gleam of gold frames, heard the swift feet and saw her too, a lady—perhaps he had never seen her like before either—in a gray, smooth gown with lace at the throat and an apron tied at the waist and the sleeves turned back, wiping cake or biscuit dough from her hands with a towel as she came up the hall, looking not at his father at all but at the tracks on the blond rug with an expression of incredulous amazement.

"I tried," the Negro cried. "I tole him to . . ."

"Will you please go away?" she said in a shaking voice. "Major de Spain is not at home. Will you please go away?"

45   His father had not spoken again. He did not speak again. He did not even look at her. He just stood stiff in the center of the rug, in his hat, the shaggy iron-gray brows twitching slightly above the pebble-colored eyes as he appeared to examine the house with brief deliberation. Then with the same deliberation he turned; the boy watched him pivot on the good leg and saw the stiff foot drag round the arc of the turning, leaving a final long and fading smear. His father never looked at it, he never once looked down at the rug. The Negro held the door. It closed behind them, upon the hysteric and indistinguishable woman-wail. His father stopped at the top of the steps and scraped his boot clean on the edge of it. At the gate he stopped again. He stood for a moment, planted stiffly on the stiff foot, looking back at the house. "Pretty and white, ain't it?" he said. "That's sweat.

Nigger sweat. Maybe it ain't white enough yet to suit him. Maybe he wants to mix some white sweat with it."

Two hours later the boy was chopping wood behind the house within which his mother and aunt and the two sisters (the mother and aunt, not the two girls, he knew that; even at this distance and muffled by walls the flat loud voices of the two girls emanated an incorrigible idle inertia) were setting up the stove to prepare a meal, when he heard the hooves and saw the linen-clad man on a fine sorrel mare, whom he recognized even before he saw the rolled rug in front of the Negro youth following on a fat bay carriage horse—a suffused, angry face vanishing, still at full gallop, beyond the corner of the house where his father and brother were sitting in the two tilted chairs; and a moment later, almost before he could have put the axe down, he heard the hooves again and watched the sorrel mare go back out of the yard, already galloping again. Then his father began to shout one of the sisters' names, who presently emerged backward from the kitchen door dragging the rolled rug along the ground by one end while the other sister walked behind it.

"If you ain't going to tote, go on and set up the wash pot," the first said.

"You, Sarty!" the second shouted. "Set up the wash pot!" His father appeared at the door, framed against that shabbiness, as he had been against that other bland perfection, impervious to either, the mother's anxious face at his shoulder.

"Go on," the father said. "Pick it up." The two sisters stooped, broad, lethargic; stooping, they presented an incredible expanse of pale cloth and a flutter of tawdry ribbons.

"If I thought enough of a rug to have to git hit all the way from France I wouldn't keep hit where folks coming in would have to tromp on hit," the first said. They raised the rug. 50

"Abner," the mother said. "Let me do it."

"You go back and git dinner," his father said. "I'll tend to this."

From the woodpile through the rest of the afternoon the boy watched them, the rug spread flat in the dust beside the bubbling wash-pot, the two sisters stooping over it with that profound and lethargic reluctance, while the father stood over them in turn, implacable and grim, driving them though never raising his voice again. He could smell the harsh homemade lye they were using; he saw his mother come to the door once and look toward them with an expression not anxious now but very like despair; he saw his father turn, and he fell to with the axe and saw from the corner of his eye his father raise from the ground a flattish fragment of field stone and examine it and return to the pot, and this time his mother actually spoke: "Abner. Abner. Please don't. Please, Abner."

Then he was done too. It was dusk; the whippoorwills had already begun. He could smell coffee from the room where they would presently eat the cold food remaining from the mid-afternoon meal, though when he entered the house he realized they were having coffee again probably because there was a fire on the hearth, before which the rug now lay spread over the backs of the two chairs. The tracks of his father's foot were gone. Where they had been were now long, water-cloudy scoriations resembling the sporadic course of a Lilliputian mowing machine.

55   It still hung there while they ate the cold food and then went to bed, scattered without order or claim up and down the two rooms, his mother in one bed, where his father would later lie, the older brother in the other, himself, the aunt, and the two sisters on pallets on the floor. But his father was not in bed yet. The last thing the boy remembered was the depthless, harsh silhouette of the hat and coat bending over the rug and it seemed to him that he had not even closed his eyes when the silhouette was standing over him, the fire almost dead behind it, the stiff foot prodding him awake. "Catch up the mule," his father said.

When he returned with the mule his father was standing in the black door, the rolled rug over his shoulder. "Ain't you going to ride?" he said.

"No. Give me your foot."

He bent his knee into his father's hand, the wiry, surprising power flowed smoothly, rising, he rising with it, on to the mule's bare back (they had owned a saddle once; the boy could remember it though not when or where) and with the same effortlessness his father swung the rug up in front of him. Now in the starlight they retraced the afternoon's path, up the dusty road rife with honeysuckle, through the gate and up the black tunnel of the drive to the lightless house, where he sat on the mule and felt the rough warp of the rug drag across his thighs and vanish.

"Don't you want me to help?" he whispered. His father did not answer and now he heard again that stiff foot striking the hollow portico with that wooden and clocklike deliberation, that outrageous overstatement of the weight it carried. The rug, hunched, not flung (the boy could tell that even in the darkness) from his father's shoulder struck the angle of wall and floor with a sound unbelievably loud, thunderous, then the foot again, unhurried and enormous; a light came on in the house and the boy sat, tense, breathing steadily and quietly and just a little fast, though the foot itself did not increase its beat at all, descending the steps now; now the boy could see him.

60   "Don't you want to ride now?" he whispered. "We kin both ride now," the light within the house altering now, flaring up and sinking. *He's coming down the stairs now,* he thought. He had already ridden the mule up beside the horse block; presently his father was up behind him and he doubled the reins over and slashed the mule across the neck, but before the animal could begin to trot the hard, thin arm came round him, the hard, knotted hand jerking the mule back to a walk.

In the first red rays of the sun they were in the lot, putting plow gear on the mules. This time the sorrel mare was in the lot before he heard it at all, the rider collarless and even bareheaded, trembling, speaking in a shaking voice as the woman in the house had done, his father merely looking up once before stooping again to the hame he was buckling, so that the man on the mare spoke to his stooping back:

"You must realize you have ruined that rug. Wasn't there anybody here, any of your women . . ." he ceased, shaking, the boy watching him, the older brother leaning now in the stable door, chewing, blinking slowly and steadily at nothing apparently. "It cost a hundred dollars. But you never had a hundred dollars. You never will. So I'm going to charge you twenty bushels of corn against your crop. I'll add it in your contract and when you come to the commissary you can sign it. That won't keep Mrs. de Spain quiet but maybe it will teach you to wipe your feet off before you enter her house again."

Then he was gone. The boy looked at his father, who still had not spoken or even looked up again, who was now adjusting the logger-head in the hame.

"Pap," he said. His father looked at him—the inscrutable face, the shaggy brows beneath which the gray eyes glinted coldly. Suddenly the boy went toward him, fast, stopping as suddenly. "You done the best you could!" he cried. "If he wanted hit done different why didn't he wait and tell you how? He won't git no twenty bushels! He won't git none! We'll gether hit and hide hit! I kin watch . . ."

"Did you put the cutter back in that straight stock like I told you?"   65

"No, sir," he said.

"Then go do it."

That was Wednesday. During the rest of that week he worked steadily, at what was within his scope and some which was beyond it, with an industry that did not need to be driven nor even commanded twice; he had this from his mother, with the difference that some at least of what he did he liked to do, such as splitting wood with the half-size axe which his mother and aunt had earned, or saved money somehow, to present him with at Christmas. In company with the two older women (and on one afternoon, even one of the sisters), he built pens for the shoat and the cow which were a part of his father's contract with the landlord, and one afternoon, his father being absent, gone somewhere on one of the mules, he went to the field.

They were running a middle buster[3] now, his brother holding the plow straight while he handled the reins, and walking beside the straining mule, the rich black soil shearing cool and damp against his bare ankles, he thought *Maybe this is the end of it. Maybe even that twenty bushels that seems hard to have to pay for just a rug will be a cheap price for him to stop forever and always from being what he used to be;* thinking, dreaming now, so that his brother had to speak sharply to him to mind the mule: *Maybe he even won't collect the twenty bushels. Maybe it will all add up and balance and vanish—corn, rug, fire; the terror and grief, the being pulled two ways like between two teams of horses—gone, done with for ever and ever.*

Then it was Saturday; he looked up from beneath the mule he was harnessing   70 and saw his father in the black coat and hat. "Not that," his father said. "The wagon gear." And then, two hours later, sitting in the wagon bed behind his father and brother on the seat, the wagon accomplished a final curve, and he saw the weathered paintless store with its tattered tobacco- and patent-medicine posters and the tethered wagons and saddle animals below the gallery. He mounted the gnawed steps behind his father and brother, and there again was the lane of quiet, watching faces for the three of them to walk through. He saw the man in spectacles sitting at the plank table and he did not need to be told this was a Justice of the Peace; he sent one glare of fierce, exultant, partisan defiance at the man in collar and cravat now, whom he had seen but twice before in his life, and that on a galloping horse, who now wore on his face an expression not of rage but of amazed unbelief which the boy could not have known was at the incredible cir-

---

3. A double moldboard plow that throws a ridge of earth both ways.

cumstance of being sued by one of his own tenants, and came and stood against his father and cried at the Justice: "He ain't done it! He ain't burnt . . ."

"Go back to the wagon," his father said.

"Burnt?" the Justice said. "Do I understand this rug was burned too?"

"Does anybody here claim it was?" his father said. "Go back to the wagon." But he did not, he merely retreated to the rear of the room, crowded as that other had been, but not to sit down this time, instead, to stand pressing among the motionless bodies, listening to the voices:

"And you claim twenty bushels of corn is too high for the damage you did to the rug?"

75   "He brought the rug to me and said he wanted the tracks washed out of it. I washed the tracks out and took the rug back to him."

"But you didn't carry the rug back to him in the same condition it was in before you made the tracks on it."

His father did not answer, and now for perhaps half a minute there was no sound at all save that of breathing, the faint, steady suspiration of complete and intent listening.

"You decline to answer that, Mr. Snopes?" Again his father did not answer. "I'm going to find against you, Mr. Snopes. I'm going to find that you were responsible for the injury to Major de Spain's rug and hold you liable for it. But twenty bushels of corn seems a little high for a man in your circumstances to have to pay. Major de Spain claims it cost a hundred dollars. October corn will be worth about fifty cents. I figure that if Major de Spain can stand a ninety-five dollar loss on something he paid cash for, you can stand a five-dollar loss you haven't earned yet. I hold you in damages to Major de Spain to the amount of ten bushels of corn over and above your contract with him, to be paid to him out of your crop at gathering time. Court adjourned."

It had taken no time hardly, the morning was but half begun. He thought they would return home and perhaps back to the field, since they were late, far behind all other farmers. But instead his father passed on behind the wagon, merely indicating with his hand for the older brother to follow with it, and crossed the road toward the blacksmith shop opposite, pressing on after his father, overtaking him, speaking, whispering up at the harsh, calm face beneath the weathered hat: "He won't git no ten bushels neither. He won't git one. We'll . . ." until his father glanced for an instant down at him, the face absolutely calm, the grizzled eyebrows tangled above the cold eyes, the voice almost pleasant, almost gentle:

80   "You think so? Well, we'll wait till October anyway."

The matter of the wagon—the setting of a spoke or two and the tightening of the tires—did not take long either, the business of the tires accomplished by driving the wagon into the spring branch behind the shop and letting it stand there, the mules nuzzling into the water from time to time, and the boy on the seat with the idle reins, looking up the slope and through the sooty tunnel of the shed where the slow hammer rang and where his father sat on an upended cypress bolt, easily, either talking or listening, still sitting there when the boy brought the dripping wagon up out of the branch and halted it before the door.

"Take them on to the shade and hitch," his father said. He did so and returned.

His father and the smith and a third man squatting on his heels inside the door were talking, about crops and animals; the boy, squatting too in the ammoniac dust and hoof-parings and scales of rust, heard his father tell a long and unhurried story out of the time before the birth of the older brother even when he had been a professional horsetrader. And then his father came up beside him where he stood before a tattered last year's circus poster on the other side of the store, gazing rapt and quiet at the scarlet horses, the incredible poisings and convolutions of tulle and tights and the painted leers of comedians, and said, "It's time to eat."

But not at home. Squatting beside his brother against the front wall, he watched his father emerge from the store and produce from a paper sack a segment of cheese and divide it carefully and deliberately into three with his pocket knife and produce crackers from the same sack. They all three squatted on the gallery and ate, slowly, without talking; then in the store again, they drank from a tin dipper tepid water smelling of the cedar bucket and of living beech trees. And still they did not go home. It was a horse lot this time, a tall rail fence upon and along which men stood and sat and out of which one by one horses were led, to be walked and trotted and then cantered back and forth along the road while the slow swapping and buying went on and the sun began to slant westward, they—the three of them—watching and listening, the older brother with his muddy eyes and his steady, inevitable tobacco, the father commenting now and then on certain of the animals, to no one in particular.

It was after sundown when they reached home. They ate supper by lamplight, then, sitting on the doorstep, the boy watched the night fully accomplish, listening to the whippoorwills and the frogs, when he heard his mother's voice: "Abner! No! No! Oh, God. Oh, God. Abner!" and he rose, whirled, and saw the altered light through the door where a candle stub now burned in a bottle neck on the table and his father, still in the hat and coat, at once formal and burlesque as though dressed carefully for some shabby and ceremonial violence, emptying the reservoir of the lamp back into the five-gallon kerosene can from which it had been filled, while the mother tugged at his arm until he shifted the lamp to the other hand and flung her back, not savagely or viciously, just hard, into the wall, her hands flung out against the wall for balance, her mouth open and in her face the same quality of hopeless despair as had been in her voice. Then his father saw him standing in the door.

"Go to the barn and get that can of oil we were oiling the wagon with," he said. The boy did not move. Then he could speak. 85

"What . . ." he cried. "What are you . . ."

"Go get that oil," his father said. "Go."

Then he was moving, running, outside the house, toward the stable: this the old habit, the old blood which he had not been permitted to choose for himself, which had been bequeathed him willy nilly and which had run for so long (and who knew where, battening on what of outrage and savagery and lust) before it came to him. *I could keep on,* he thought. *I could run on and on and never look back, never need to see his face again. Only I can't. I can't,* the rusted can in his hand now, the liquid sploshing in it as he ran back to the house and into it, into the sound of his mother's weeping in the next room, and handed the can to his father.

"Ain't you going to even send a nigger?" he cried. "At least you sent a nigger before!"

90   This time his father didn't strike him. The hand came even faster than the blow had, the same hand which had set the can on the table with almost excruciating care flashing from the can toward him too quick for him to follow it, gripping him by the back of his shirt and on to tiptoe before he had seen it quit the can, the face stooping at him in breathless and frozen ferocity, the cold, dead voice speaking over him to the older brother, who leaned against the table, chewing with that steady, curious, sidewise motion of cows:

"Empty the can into the big one and go on. I'll catch up with you."

"Better tie him up to the bedpost," the brother said.

"Do like I told you," the father said. Then the boy was moving, his bunched shirt and the hard, bony hand between his shoulder-blades, his toes just touching the floor, across the room and into the other one, past the sisters sitting with spread heavy thighs in the two chairs over the cold hearth, and to where his mother and aunt sat side by side on the bed, the aunt's arms about his mother's shoulders.

"Hold him," the father said. The aunt made a startled movement. "Not you," the father said. "Lennie. Take hold of him. I want to see you do it." His mother took him by the wrist. "You'll hold him better than that. If he gets loose don't you know what he is going to do? He will go up yonder." He jerked his head toward the road. "Maybe I'd better tie him."

95   "I'll hold him," his mother whispered.

"See you do then." Then his father was gone, the stiff foot heavy and measured upon the boards, ceasing at last.

Then he began to struggle. His mother caught him in both arms, he jerking and wrenching at them. He would be stronger in the end, he knew that. But he had no time to wait for it. "Lemme go!" he cried. "I don't want to have to hit you!"

"Let him go!" the aunt said. "If he don't go, before God, I am going up there myself!"

"Don't you see I can't?" his mother cried. "Sarty! Sarty! No! No! Help me, Lizzie!"

100   Then he was free. His aunt grasped at him but it was too late. He whirled, running, his mother stumbled forward on to her knees behind him, crying to the nearer sister: "Catch him, Net! Catch him!" But that was too late too, the sister (the sisters were twins, born at the same time, yet either of them now gave the impression of being, encompassing as much living meat and volume and weight as any other two of the family) not yet having begun to rise from the chair, her head, face, alone merely turned, presenting to him in the flying instant an astonishing expanse of young female features untroubled by any surprise even, wearing only an expression of bovine interest. Then he was out of the room, out of the house, in the mild dust of the starlit road and the heavy rifeness of honeysuckle, the pale ribbon unspooling with terrific slowness under his running feet, reaching the gate at last and turning in, running, his heart and lungs drumming, on up the drive toward the lighted house, the lighted door. He did not knock, he burst in, sobbing for breath, incapable for the moment of speech; he saw the

astonished face of the Negro in the linen jacket without knowing when the Negro had appeared.

"De Spain!" he cried, panted. "Where's . . ." then he saw the white man too emerging from a white door down the hall. "Barn!" he cried. "Barn!"

"What?" the white man said. "Barn?"

"Yes!" the boy cried. "Barn!"

"Catch him!" the white man shouted.

But it was too late this time too. The Negro grasped his shirt, but the entire sleeve, rotten with washing, carried away, and he was out that door too and in the drive again, and had actually never ceased to run even while he was screaming into the white man's face.

Behind him the white man was shouting, "My horse! Fetch my horse!" and he thought for an instant of cutting across the park and climbing the fence into the road, but he did not know the park nor how high the vine-massed fence might be and he dared not risk it. So he ran on down the drive, blood and breath roaring; presently he was in the road again though he could not see it. He could not hear either: the galloping mare was almost upon him before he heard her, and even then he held his course, as if the very urgency of his wild grief and need must in a moment more find his wings, waiting until the ultimate instant to hurl himself aside and into the weed-choked roadside ditch as the horse thundered past and on, for an instant in furious silhouette against the stars, the tranquil early summer night sky which, even before the shape of the horse and rider vanished, stained abruptly and violently upward: a long, swirling roar incredible and soundless, blotting the stars, and he springing up and into the road again, running again, knowing it was too late yet still running even after he heard the shot and, an instant later, two shots, pausing now without knowing he had ceased to run, crying "Pap! Pap!", running again before he knew he had begun to run, stumbling, tripping over something and scrabbling up again without ceasing to run, looking backward over his shoulder at the glare as he got up, running on among the invisible trees, panting, sobbing, "Father! Father!"

At midnight he was sitting on the crest of a hill. He did not know it was midnight and he did not know how far he had come. But there was no glare behind him now and he sat now, his back toward what he had called home for four days anyhow, his face toward the dark woods which he would enter when breath was strong again, small, shaking steadily in the chill darkness, hugging himself into the remainder of his thin, rotten shirt, the grief and despair now no longer terror and fear but just grief and despair. *Father. My father,* he thought. "He was brave!" he cried suddenly, aloud but not loud, no more than a whisper: "He was! He was in the war! He was in Colonel Sartoris' cav'ry!" not knowing that his father had gone to that war a private in the fine old European sense, wearing no uniform, admitting the authority of and giving fidelity to no man or army or flag, going to war as Malbrouck[4] himself did: for booty—it meant nothing and less than nothing to him if it were enemy booty or his own.

The slow constellations wheeled on. It would be dawn and then sun-up after

4. John Churchill, the first duke of Marlborough (1650–1722), an English general whose name became distorted as Malbrough and Malbrouch in English and French popular songs celebrating his exploits.

a while and he would be hungry. But that would be to-morrow and now he was only cold, and walking would cure that. His breathing was easier now and he decided to get up and go on, and then he found that he had been asleep because he knew it was almost dawn, the night almost over. He could tell that from the whippoorwills. They were everywhere now among the dark trees below him, constant and inflectioned and ceaseless, so that, as the instant for giving over to the day birds drew nearer and nearer, there was no interval at all between them. He got up. He was a little stiff, but walking would cure that too as it would the cold, and soon there would be the sun. He went on down the hill, toward the dark woods within which the liquid silver voices of the birds called unceasing—the rapid and urgent beating of the urgent and quiring heart of the late spring night. He did not look back.

1939

The most common reservations about this story can be summarized as three "charges":

1. Faulkner's style is bad. His sentences are often too long and complicated, vague, unnecessarily wordy, and sometimes hard to read.
2. The structure of the story seems almost haphazard: it wanders off the subject or out of focus.
3. The reasons the story gives—and insists upon—for people acting the way they do are unrealistic and shallow.

Can a story with a dubious style, form, theme, and vision of human actions and motives be good, much less great? Should we, must we, like it, or at least recognize its "literary value"?

Let us see a few examples of what those who find the story flawed might isolate, analyze, and articulate. We can begin with Faulkner's awkward and obscure style and pick out an early sentence—the second sentence of the story—as evidence:

> The boy, crouched on his nail keg at the back of the crowded room, knew he smelled cheese, and more: from where he sat he could see the ranked shelves close-packed with the solid, squat, dynamic shapes of tin cans whose labels his stomach read, not from the lettering which meant nothing to his mind but from the scarlet devils and the silver curve of fish—this, the cheese which he knew he smelled and the hermetic meat which his intestines believed he smelled coming in intermittent gusts momentary and brief between the other constant one, the smell and sense just a little of fear because mostly of despair and grief, the old fierce pull of blood.

Even those who do not mind taking some pains in reading will probably acknowledge that this sentence is not immediately clear. The chief problem is how to relate the final phrase, "the old fierce pull of blood," to the rest of the sentence, and so to discover what the sentence as a whole means. After a little work, we may decide that the sentence says there is not only the smell of cheese and the imagined smell of canned meat but also the smell of despair and grief and even some smell of fear; and that despair, grief, and fear are in the boy's "blood," that is, inherited, in his genes. We still cannot be sure whether this implies that acquired traits or experiences are hereditary or whether "blood" means something else, and we still cannot be sure whether the smell of fear is imaginary—like the smell of the meat in the cans—or real—like the smell of the cheese (perhaps the smell of the sweat that comes with fear, or the odor some say fear gives off). But even if we have successfully unravelled the thread, what is the value of a sentence that has to be worked over so much and whose meaning even then is doubtful?

Now as to the matter of form. One reason "The Most Dangerous Game" is just a slick adventure story, some people say, is that everything in it is manipulated to heighten suspense. But if we criticize Connell for shifting focus for his own purposes, what can we say about the shifting of focus in "Barn Burning"? One such shift occurs when the narrator is explaining why the man who burns other people's barns lights only a small neat fire when it is for his own use:

> Older, the boy might have remarked this and wondered why not a big one; why should not a man who had not only seen the waste and extravagance of war, but who had in his blood an inherent voracious prodigality with material not his own, have burned everything in sight? Then he might have gone a step farther and thought that that was the reason: that niggard blaze was the living fruit of nights passed during those four years in the woods hiding from all men, blue or gray, with his strings of horses (captured horses, he called them). And older still, he might have divined the true reason: that the element of fire spoke to some deep mainspring of his father's being, as the element of steel or of powder spoke to other men, as the one weapon for the preservation of integrity, else breath were not worth the breathing, and hence to be regarded with respect and used with discretion. (paragraph 26)

The boy who perceives the action of the rest of the story only "might" know what is revealed here. Is it okay to shift the focus temporally like this because the purpose of the shift is not "merely" to enhance the suspense but to clarify the meaning, to reveal "the true reason"?

Besides shifting to a time outside the story's present, sometimes the focus moves away from the boy's consciousness, which, like Rainsford's in "The Most Dangerous Game," dominates the rest of the story. When the father climbs aboard the wagon and immediately starts hitting the mules with a willow switch, the narrator comments,

> It was not even sadistic; it was exactly that same quality which in later years would cause his descendants to overrun the engine before putting a motor car into motion, striking and reining back in the same movement. (paragraph 20)

The time moves backward as well as forward, and it always seems to do so in order to clarify or emphasize the meaning or illustrate the concept of "blood"—inborn, inherited habits or feelings. So, when his father tells him to get a can of oil the boy knows will be used to burn still another barn, despite the boy's repugnance at the act, he does it:

> Then he was moving, running, outside the house, toward the stable: this the old habit, the old blood which he had not been permitted to choose for himself, which had been bequeathed him willy nilly and which had run for so long (and who knew where, battening on what of outrage and savagery and lust) before it came to him. *I could keep on,* he thought. *I could run on and on and never look back, never need to see his face again. Only I can't. I can't. . . .* (paragraph 88)

This passage leads us directly into the third reservation or question, that having to do with the story's vision of the springs of human action. Can we accept that such habits, such capacities or incapacities, are bred into the "blood"? Can we even take this concept seriously, even if we cannot accept it? And if it is a serious concept, to what does it lead? to genetic determinism of one kind or another? to justifying "class"? to racism?

And, to go back to the earlier passage about the fire: what does it mean that "the element of fire spoke to some deep mainspring of his father's being, as the element of steel or of powder spoke to other men"? And how is it that fire, swords, guns—violence—can be weapons "for the preservation of integrity," without which life is not worth living? What "integrity" is the father so intent on preserving? And what kind of "discretion" does the father show in his use of fire? Our accepting the meaning of this passage is crucial because that meaning is not embedded in the fiction, as part of the action and thoughts of the characters—the boy, let us say—but is separated from them by the shift in focus and by the flat statement that we are being given the "true reason"; so it has the authority of the author's persona, and we either have to believe it or discount the whole vision of the story.

And if we look beneath the surface of these "true reasons" and the "pull of blood" and look at the events of the story itself, we begin to suspect a "hidden agenda," an ideology that determines the characters' actions and motivations.

Why is it that the boy overcomes or betrays the "pull of blood" only when the "aristocratic" Major de Spain's barn is to be burned? Is the blood of the highborn somehow more valuable than that of the low? (Though the boy is a Snopes, his first name is that of the aristocrat Colonel Sartoris.) Is some blood better than others? Are some loyalties better than others? Or is property a higher good than blood?

The selection of certain key passages or incidents, the analysis and interpretation of the text, can be used to directly confront these critical comments and questions, as well as to explore other, more positive areas of the story and its accomplishment. And the objections themselves can be examined in terms of their hidden agendas and their unspoken assumptions about what makes a story good.

The long second sentence of "Barn Burning" puts extraordinary emphasis on "blood." The concept can stand such emphasis, even demands it, for "blood" is one of the forces that conflict within the boy. Therefore the sentence, though it is difficult, gives ready access to the meaning of the story by calling attention to one of its key elements. Part of the sentence's length, too, consists in magnificent particularizing detail, the kind that convinces you the author knows what he is talking about and really "sees" the scene. The density of detail also realizes (makes real) the boy's sensations. The detail and the focus of the sentence indicate where the significant action of the story will take place—that is, inside the boy—and so help us to understand and perhaps feel with him. Finally, the move from the smell of cheese to the "smells" of canned meat and fear is crucial: the smell of cheese is real. The smell of meat, though contained inside the can, is also real. So the boy's sensory imagination does not falsify; it penetrates into things beyond the immediate sense perceptions. This "power" gives reality to the smell of despair, grief, fear—not necessarily real to the senses, but really there beneath the surface, real to the imagination. Thus the sentence opens up our notions of reality to include not just what the senses tell us, but what the imagination can sense. And by doing this through sensory images that gradually shade off into the imaginative, it makes us feel that the imaginative is valid, rather than simply telling us that this is so. A sentence that seemed unnecessarily long, complex, and difficult turns out to do what no short sentence or series of sentences would be likely to manage.

Complexity, even obscurity, is not in all cases "bad"—as the criticism of the sentence seemed to assume. Literary value follows not necessarily from rules of usage but from questions of function—from whether language and detail work to create, reveal, intensify the meaning and effect of the story.

It may be precisely in this merging of the physical and the imaginative (moral or psychological) that one of the strengths of the story—and of Faulkner—lies. The force that opposes blood, we soon learn, is the boy's sense of right and wrong. Though the boy knows his father is guilty of maliciously burning down Mr. Harris's barn, he also knows that because he is tied to his father by "blood," he must lie to the judge. During the pause after the judge asks Harris if he really wants the boy questioned, "it was as if [the boy] had swung outward at the end of a grape vine, over a ravine, and at the top of the swing had been caught in a prolonged instant of mesmerized gravity, weightless in time" (paragraph 10). Most readers would acknowledge the appropriateness of the image both to the feeling of suspense and to the experience of the boy, and the intervention of the image suspends the meaning and imitates the boy's suspense. When Harris says the boy does not have to testify, "the smell of cheese and sealed meat, the fear and despair and the old grief of blood" return to the boy's consciousness. The importance and meaning of fear, despair, and grief in the "blood" is now a little clearer.

Faulkner's complexity, "idiosyncrasies" (what some call "flaws"), and difficulty (sometimes called "obscurity") usually come from this interpenetration of imagination and sensory reality or other things that we usually keep separate, like past and present. Each episode, character, detail is saturated with the full world of his fiction, and its function seems to be primarily to embody that world rather than to further the plot or make a statement. The present is informed by the past and informs the future. Characters (Major de Spain) and names (Colonel Sartoris) that are minor or casual here are central elsewhere in Faulkner's canon, as though they were actors in a repertory theater. The fiction is all one seamless, interconnected, timeless world. The interpenetration of community and generations is essential to the vision.

This reading gives both a smaller and a larger role to the concept of "blood." "Blood" alone—inherited traits, customs, motives—does not determine behavior, but it is one of the multitude of communal and traditional forces that condition behavior. Though "blood" can explain many acts and impulses, its force does not eliminate free will. The boy does, after all, choose to warn the Major of his father's intention, chooses morality over blood. To claim that it was only Major de Spain's class or property that moved the boy to consider betraying his father is to ignore the story's opening, where the boy is on the verge of doing so in the Harris case. The father's crimes went well beyond the destruction of property; indeed it was the primacy of property over principles in his scheme of values that led him to serve neither North nor South but Mammon (by being a nonpartisan horse thief) during the Civil War.

Explaining the function of what may at first have seemed defects does not close the discussion about the merits of a work or the nature and function of literature. To begin with, not all the "evidence" is always in the story, of course. Already we have seen that some of the response to Faulkner is ideological, based on social or political values that have little to do with focus shifts or sentence length. We must admit that some beauty is in the eyes of the beholder, as well. Let us constantly be aware of our own responses and try at the same time to account for those responses in terms of both the narrative strategies and our own prejudices or predispositions.

Evaluating a story, then, means reading carefully (and widely); learning as much as we can about the elements of fiction, about literary and cultural contexts, and about narrative strategies; articulating our analyses; being honest about our own responses and feeling responsible for articulating them as clearly and convincingly as possible; taking our opinions seriously but listening with attention and an open mind to the judgments and reasoning of other readers. It requires as well some examination and knowledge of ourselves—of what in ourselves conditions our responses to fiction—and a willingness to look at what underlies our judgments and how we might learn and grow. Assessing the value of a story is difficult and a firm evaluation elusive in part because it means examining more than words on a page: it means examining ideas, beliefs, and feelings we take for granted. It means examining and, to a degree, evaluating our outer world and inner selves.

Reading More Fiction

AMBROSE BIERCE

An Occurrence at Owl Creek Bridge

I

A man stood upon a railroad bridge in Northern Alabama, looking down into the swift waters twenty feet below. The man's hands were behind his back, the wrists bound with a cord. A rope loosely encircled his neck. It was attached to a stout cross-timber above his head, and the slack fell to the level of his knees. Some loose boards laid upon the sleepers supporting the metals of the railway supplied a footing for him and his executioners—two private soldiers of the Federal army, directed by a sergeant, who in civil life may have been a deputy sheriff. At a short remove upon the same temporary platform was an officer in the uniform of his rank, armed. He was a captain. A sentinel at each end of the bridge stood with his rifle in the position known as "support," that is to say, vertical in front of the left shoulder, the hammer resting on the forearm thrown straight across the chest—a formal and unnatural position, enforcing an erect carriage of the body. It did not appear to be the duty of these two men to know what was occurring at the centre of the bridge; they merely blockaded the two ends of the foot plank which traversed it.

Beyond one of the sentinels nobody was in sight; the railroad ran straight away into a forest for a hundred yards, then, curving, was lost to view. Doubtless there was an outpost further along. The other bank of the stream was open ground—a gentle acclivity crowned with a stockade of vertical tree trunks, loopholed for rifles, with a single embrasure through which protruded the muzzle of a brass cannon commanding the bridge. Midway of the slope between bridge and fort were the spectators—a single company of infantry in line, at "parade rest," the butts of the rifles on the ground, the barrels inclining slightly backward against the right shoulder, the hands crossed upon the stock. A lieutenant stood at the right of the line, the point of his sword upon the ground, his left hand resting upon his right. Excepting the group of four at the centre of the bridge not a man moved. The company faced the bridge, staring stonily, motionless. The sentinels, facing the banks of the stream, might have been statues to adorn the bridge. The captain stood with folded arms, silent, observing the work of his subordinates but making no sign. Death is a dignitary who, when he comes announced, is to be received with formal manifestations of respect, even by those most familiar with him. In the code of military etiquette silence and fixity are forms of deference.

The man who was engaged in being hanged was apparently about thirty-five years of age. He was a civilian, if one might judge from his dress, which was that of a planter. His features were good—a straight nose, firm mouth, broad forehead, from which his long, dark hair was combed straight back, falling behind his ears to the collar of his well-fitting frock coat. He wore a moustache and pointed beard, but no whiskers; his eyes were large and dark grey and had a kindly expression which one would hardly have expected in one whose neck was in the hemp. Evidently this was no vulgar assassin. The liberal military code makes provision for hanging many kinds of people, and gentlemen are not excluded.

The preparations being complete, the two private soldiers stepped aside and each drew away the plank upon which he had been standing. The sergeant turned to the captain, saluted and placed himself immediately behind that officer, who in turn moved apart one pace. These movements left the condemned man and the sergeant standing on the two ends of the same plank, which spanned three of the cross-ties of the bridge. The end upon which the civilian stood almost, but not quite, reached a fourth. This plank had been held in place by the weight of the captain; it was now held by that of the sergeant. At a signal from the former, the latter would step aside, the plank would tilt and the condemned man go down between two ties. The arrangement commended itself to his judgment as simple and effective. His face had not been covered nor his eyes bandaged. He looked a moment at his "unsteadfast footing," then let his gaze wander to the swirling water of the stream racing madly beneath his feet. A piece of dancing driftwood caught his attention and his eyes followed it down the current. How slowly it appeared to move! What a sluggish stream!

5   He closed his eyes in order to fix his last thoughts upon his wife and children. The water, touched to gold by the early sun, the brooding mists under the banks at some distance down the stream, the fort, the soldiers, the piece of drift—all had distracted him. And now he became conscious of a new disturbance. Striking through the thought of his dear ones was a sound which he could neither ignore nor understand, a sharp, distinct, metallic percussion like the stroke of a black-smith's hammer upon the anvil; it had the same ringing quality. He wondered what it was, and whether immeasurably distant or near by—it seemed both. Its recurrence was regular, but as slow as the tolling of a death knell. He awaited each stroke with impatience and—he knew not why—apprehension. The intervals of silence grew progressively longer, the delays became maddening. With their greater infrequency the sounds increased in strength and sharpness. They hurt his ear like the thrust of a knife; he feared he would shriek. What he heard was the ticking of his watch.

He unclosed his eyes and saw again the water below him. "If I could free my hands," he thought, "I might throw off the noose and spring into the stream. By diving I could evade the bullets, and, swimming vigorously, reach the bank, take to the woods, and get away home. My home, thank God, is as yet outside their lines; my wife and little ones are still beyond the invader's farthest advance."

As these thoughts, which have here to be set down in words, were flashed into the doomed man's brain rather than evolved from it, the captain nodded to the sergeant. The sergeant stepped aside.

II

Peyton Farquhar was a well-to-do planter, of an old and highly-respected Alabama family. Being a slave owner, and, like other slave owners, a politician, he was naturally an original secessionist and ardently devoted to the Southern cause. Circumstances of an imperious nature which it is unnecessary to relate here, had prevented him from taking service with the gallant army which had fought the disastrous campaigns ending with the fall of Corinth,[1] and he chafed under the inglorious restraint, longing for the release of his energies, the larger life of the soldier, the opportunity for distinction. That opportunity, he felt, would come, as it comes to all in war time. Meanwhile he did what he could. No service was too humble for him to perform in aid of the South, no adventure too perilous for him to undertake if consistent with the character of a civilian who was at heart a soldier, and who in good faith and without too much qualification assented to at least a part of the frankly villainous dictum that all is fair in love and war.

One evening while Farquhar and his wife were sitting on a rustic bench near the entrance to his grounds, a grey-clad soldier rode up to the gate and asked for a drink of water. Mrs. Farquhar was only too happy to serve him with her own white hands. While she was gone to fetch the water, her husband approached the dusty horseman and inquired eagerly for news from the front.

"The Yanks are repairing the railroads," said the man, "and are getting ready 10 for another advance. They have reached the Owl Creek bridge, put it in order, and built a stockade on the other bank. The commandant has issued an order, which is posted everywhere, declaring that any civilian caught interfering with the railroad, its bridges, tunnels, or trains, will be summarily hanged. I saw the order."

"How far is it to the Owl Creek bridge?" Farquhar asked.

"About thirty miles."

"Is there no force on this side the creek?"

"Only a picket post half a mile out, on the railroad, and a single sentinel at this end of the bridge."

"Suppose a man—a civilian and student of hanging—should elude the picket 15 post and perhaps get the better of the sentinel," said Farquhar, smiling, "what could he accomplish?"

The soldier reflected. "I was there a month ago," he replied. "I observed that the flood of last winter had lodged a great quantity of driftwood against the wooden pier at this end of the bridge. It is now dry and would burn like tow."

The lady had now brought the water, which the soldier drank. He thanked her ceremoniously, bowed to her husband, and rode away. An hour later, after nightfall, he repassed the plantation, going northward in the direction from which he had come. He was a Federal scout.

---

1. Corinth, Mississippi, captured by General Ulysses S. Grant in April 1862.

III

As Peyton Farquhar fell straight downward through the bridge, he lost consciousness and was as one already dead. From this state he was awakened—ages later, it seemed to him—by the pain of a sharp pressure upon his throat, followed by a sense of suffocation. Keen, poignant agonies seemed to shoot from his neck downward through every fibre of his body and limbs. These pains appeared to flash along well-defined lines of ramification, and to beat with an inconceivably rapid periodicity. They seemed like streams of pulsating fire heating him to an intolerable temperature. As to his head, he was conscious of nothing but a feeling of fullness—of congestion. These sensations were unaccompanied by thought. The intellectual part of his nature was already effaced; he had power only to feel, and feeling was torment. He was conscious of motion. Encompassed in a luminous cloud, of which he was now merely the fiery heart, without material substance, he swung through unthinkable arcs of oscillation, like a vast pendulum. Then all at once, with terrible suddenness, the light about him shot upward with the noise of a loud plash; a frightful roaring was in his ears, and all was cold and dark. The power of thought was restored; he knew that the rope had broken and he had fallen into the stream. There was no additional strangulation; the noose about his neck was already suffocating him, and kept the water from his lungs. To die of hanging at the bottom of a river!—the idea seemed to him ludicrous. He opened his eyes in the blackness and saw above him a gleam of light, but how distant, how inaccessible! He was still sinking, for the light became fainter and fainter until it was a mere glimmer. Then it began to grow and brighten, and he knew that he was rising toward the surface—knew it with reluctance, for he was now very comfortable. "To be hanged and drowned," he thought, "that is not so bad; but I do not wish to be shot. No; I will not be shot; that is not fair."

He was not conscious of an effort, but a sharp pain in his wrist apprised him that he was trying to free his hands. He gave the struggle his attention, as an idler might observe the feat of a juggler, without interest in the outcome. What splendid effort!—what magnificent, what superhuman strength! Ah, that was a fine endeavour! Bravo! The cord fell away; his arms parted and floated upward, the hands dimly seen on each side in the growing light. He watched them with a new interest as first one and then the other pounced upon the noose at his neck. They tore it away and thrust it fiercely aside, its undulations resembling those of a water-snake. "Put it back, put it back!" He thought he shouted these words to his hands, for the undoing of the noose had been succeeded by the direst pang which he had yet experienced. His neck ached horribly; his brain was on fire; his heart, which had been fluttering faintly, gave a great leap, trying to force itself out at his mouth. His whole body was racked and wrenched with an insupportable anguish! But his disobedient hands gave no heed to the command. They beat the water vigorously with quick, downward strokes, forcing him to the surface. He felt his head emerge; his eyes were blinded by the sunlight; his chest expanded convulsively, and with a supreme and crowning agony his lungs engulfed a great draught of air, which instantly he expelled in a shriek!

He was now in full possession of his physical senses. They were, indeed, preternaturally keen and alert. Something in the awful disturbance of his organic system had so exalted and refined them that they made record of things never before perceived. He felt the ripples upon his face and heard their separate sounds as they struck. He looked at the forest on the bank of the stream, saw the individual trees, the leaves and the veining of each leaf—the very insects upon them, the locusts, the brilliant-bodied flies, the grey spiders stretching their webs from twig to twig. He noted the prismatic colors in all the dewdrops upon a million blades of grass. The humming of the gnats that danced above the eddies of the stream, the beating of the dragon flies' wings, the strokes of the water spiders' legs, like oars which had lifted their boat—all these made audible music. A fish slid along beneath his eyes and he heard the rush of its body parting the water.

He had come to the surface facing down the stream; in a moment the visible world seemed to wheel slowly round, himself the pivotal point, and he saw the bridge, the fort, the soldiers upon the bridge, the captain, the sergeant, the two privates, his executioners. They were in silhouette against the blue sky. They shouted and gesticulated, pointing at him; the captain had drawn his pistol, but did not fire; the others were unarmed. Their movements were grotesque and horrible, their forms gigantic.

Suddenly he heard a sharp report and something struck the water smartly within a few inches of his head, spattering his face with spray. He heard a second report, and saw one of the sentinels with his rifle at his shoulder, a light cloud of blue smoke rising from the muzzle. The man in the water saw the eye of the man on the bridge gazing into his own through the sights of the rifle. He observed that it was a grey eye, and remembered having read that grey eyes were keenest and that all famous marksmen had them. Nevertheless, this one had missed.

A counter swirl had caught Farquhar and turned him half round; he was again looking into the forest on the bank opposite the fort. The sound of a clear, high voice in a monotonous singsong now rang out behind him and came across the water with a distinctness that pierced and subdued all other sounds, even the beating of the ripples in his ears. Although no soldier, he had frequented camps enough to know the dread significance of that deliberate, drawling, aspirated chant; the lieutenant on shore was taking a part in the morning's work. How coldly and pitilessly—with what an even, calm intonation, presaging and enforcing tranquillity in the men—with what accurately-measured intervals fell those cruel words:

"Attention, company. . . . Shoulder arms. . . . Ready. . . . Aim. . . . Fire."

Farquhar dived—dived as deeply as he could. The water roared in his ears like the voice of Niagara, yet he heard the dulled thunder of the volley, and rising again toward the surface, met shining bits of metal, singularly flattened, oscillating slowly downward. Some of them touched him on the face and hands, then fell away, continuing their descent. One lodged between his collar and neck; it was uncomfortably warm, and he snatched it out.

As he rose to the surface, gasping for breath, he saw that he had been a long time under water; he was perceptibly farther down stream—nearer to safety. The soldiers had almost finished reloading; the metal ramrods flashed all at once in the sunshine as they were drawn from the barrels, turned in the air, and thrust

25

into their sockets. The two sentinels fired again, independently and ineffectually.

The hunted man saw all this over his shoulder; he was now swimming vigorously with the current. His brain was as energetic as his arms and legs; he thought with the rapidity of lightning.

"The officer," he reasoned, "will not make that martinet's error a second time. It is as easy to dodge a volley as a single shot. He has probably already given the command to fire at will. God help me, I cannot dodge them all!"

An appalling plash within two yards of him, followed by a loud rushing sound, *diminuendo,* which seemed to travel back through the air to the fort and died in an explosion which stirred the very river to its deeps! A rising sheet of water, which curved over him, fell down upon him, blinded him, strangled him! The cannon had taken a hand in the game. As he shook his head free from the commotion of the smitten water, he heard the deflected shot humming through the air ahead, and in an instant it was cracking and smashing the branches in the forest beyond.

30 "They will not do that again," he thought; "the next time they will use a charge of grape. I must keep my eye upon the gun; the smoke will apprise me—the report arrives too late; it lags behind the missile. It is a good gun."

Suddenly he felt himself whirled round and round—spinning like a top. The water, the banks, the forest, the now distant bridge, fort and men—all were commingled and blurred. Objects were represented by their colors only; circular horizontal streaks of color—that was all he saw. He had been caught in a vortex and was being whirled on with a velocity of advance and gyration which made him giddy and sick. In a few moments he was flung upon the gravel at the foot of the left bank of the stream—the southern bank—and behind a projecting point which concealed him from his enemies. The sudden arrest of his motion, the abrasion of one of his hands on the gravel, restored him and he wept with delight. He dug his fingers into the sand, threw it over himself in handfuls and audibly blessed it. It looked like gold, like diamonds, rubies, emeralds; he could think of nothing beautiful which it did not resemble. The trees upon the bank were giant garden plants; he noted a definite order in their arrangement, inhaled the fragrance of their blooms. A strange, roseate light shone through the spaces among their trunks, and the wind made in their branches the music of æolian harps. He had no wish to perfect his escape, was content to remain in that enchanting spot until retaken.

A whizz and rattle of grapeshot among the branches high above his head roused him from his dream. The baffled cannoneer had fired him a random farewell. He sprang to his feet, rushed up the sloping bank, and plunged into the forest.

All that day he travelled, laying his course by the rounding sun. The forest seemed interminable; nowhere did he discover a break in it, not even a woodman's road. He had not known that he lived in so wild a region. There was something uncanny in the revelation.

By nightfall he was fatigued, footsore, famishing. The thought of his wife and children urged him on. At last he found a road which led him in what he knew to be the right direction. It was as wide and straight as a city street, yet it seemed untravelled. No fields bordered it, no dwelling anywhere. Not so much as the barking of a dog suggested human habitation. The black bodies of the great trees formed a straight wall on both sides, terminating on the horizon in a point, like a diagram in a lesson in perspective. Overhead, as he looked up through this rift in the wood, shone great golden stars looking unfamiliar and grouped in strange constellations. He was sure they were arranged in some order which had a secret and malign significance. The wood on either side was full of singular noises, among which—once, twice, and again—he distinctly heard whispers in an unknown tongue.

His neck was in pain, and, lifting his hand to it, he found it horribly swollen.   35
He knew that it had a circle of black where the rope had bruised it. His eyes felt congested; he could no longer close them. His tongue was swollen with thirst; he relieved its fever by thrusting it forward from between his teeth into the cool air. How softly the turf had carpeted the untravelled avenue! He could no longer feel the roadway beneath his feet!

Doubtless, despite his suffering, he fell asleep while walking, for now he sees another scene—perhaps he has merely recovered from a delirium. He stands at the gate of his own home. All is as he left it, and all bright and beautiful in the morning sunshine. He must have travelled the entire night. As he pushes open the gate and passes up the wide white walk, he sees a flutter of female garments; his wife, looking fresh and cool and sweet, steps down from the verandah to meet him. At the bottom of the steps she stands waiting, with a smile of ineffable joy, an attitude of matchless grace and dignity. Ah, how beautiful she is! He springs forward with extended arms. As he is about to clasp her, he feels a stunning blow upon the back of the neck; a blinding white light blazes all about him, with a sound like the shock of a cannon—then all is darkness and silence!

Peyton Farquhar was dead; his body, with a broken neck, swung gently from side to side beneath the timbers of the Owl Creek bridge.

1891

HENRY JAMES

The Real Thing

I

When the porter's wife, who used to answer the house-bell, announced "A gentleman and a lady, sir" I had, as I often had in those days—the wish being father to the thought—an immediate vision of sitters. Sitters my visitors in this case proved to be; but not in the sense I should have preferred. There was nothing at first however to indicate that they mightn't have come for a portrait. The gentleman, a man of fifty, very high and very straight, with a moustache slightly grizzled and a dark grey walking-coat admirably fitted, both of which I noted profession-

ally—I don't mean as a barber or yet as a tailor—would have struck me as a celebrity if celebrities often were striking. It was a truth of which I had for some time
been conscious that a figure with a good deal of frontage was, as one might say,
almost never a public institution. A glance at the lady helped to remind me of
this paradoxical law: she also looked too distinguished to be a "personality."
Moreover one would scarcely come across two variations together.

Neither of the pair immediately spoke—they only prolonged the preliminary
gaze suggesting that each wished to give the other a chance. They were visibly
shy; they stood there letting me take them in—which, as I afterwards perceived,
was the most practical thing they could have done. In this way their embarrassment served their cause. I had seen people painfully reluctant to mention that
they desired anything so gross as to be represented on canvas; but the scruples of
my new friends appeared almost insurmountable. Yet the gentleman might have
said "I should like a portrait of my wife," and the lady might have said "I should
like a portrait of my husband." Perhaps they weren't husband and wife—this
naturally would make the matter more delicate. Perhaps they wished to be done
together—in which case they ought to have brought a third person to break the
news.

"We come from Mr. Rivet," the lady finally said with a dim smile that had the
effect of a moist sponge passed over a "sunk"[1] piece of painting, as well as of a
vague allusion to vanished beauty. She was as tall and straight, in her degree, as
her companion, and with ten years less to carry. She looked as sad as a woman
could look whose face was not charged with expression; that is her tinted oval
mask showed waste as an exposed surface shows friction. The hand of time had
played over her freely, but to an effect of elimination. She was slim and stiff, and
so well-dressed, in dark blue cloth, with lappets and pockets and buttons, that it
was clear she employed the same tailor as her husband. The couple had an inde-
finable air of prosperous thrift—they evidently got a good deal of luxury for their
money. If I was to be one of their luxuries it would behove me to consider my
terms.

"Ah, Claude Rivet recommended me?" I echoed; and I added that it was very
kind of him, though I could reflect that, as he only painted landscape, this wasn't
a sacrifice.

5   The lady looked very hard at the gentleman, and the gentleman looked round
the room. Then staring at the floor a moment and stroking his moustache, he
rested his pleasant eyes on me with the remark: "He said you were the right one."

"I try to be, when people want to sit."

"Yes, we should like to," said the lady anxiously.

"Do you mean together?"

My visitors exchanged a glance. "If you could do anything with *me* I suppose
it would be double," the gentleman stammered.

10   "Oh yes, there's naturally a higher charge for two figures than for one."

"We should like to make it pay," the husband confessed.

1. When colors lose their brilliance after they have dried on the canvas, they have "sunk in."

"That's very good of you," I returned, appreciating so unwonted a sympathy—for I supposed he meant pay the artist.

A sense of strangeness seemed to draw on the lady.

"We mean for the illustrations—Mr. Rivet said you might put one in."

"Put in—an illustration?" I was equally confused.   15

"Sketch her off, you know," said the gentleman, colouring.

It was only then that I understood the service Claude Rivet had rendered me; he had told them how I worked in black-and-white, for magazines, for storybooks, for sketches of contemporary life, and consequently had copious employment for models. These things were true, but it was not less true—I may confess it now; whether because the aspiration was to lead to everything or to nothing I leave the reader to guess—that I couldn't get the honours, to say nothing of the emoluments, of a great painter of portraits out of my head. My "illustrations" were my pot-boilers; I looked to a different branch of art—far and away the most interesting it had always seemed to me—to perpetuate my fame. There was no shame in looking to it also to make my fortune; but that fortune was by so much further from being made from the moment my visitors wished to be "done" for nothing. I was disappointed; for in the pictorial sense I had immediately *seen* them. I had seized their type—I had already settled what I would do with it. Something that wouldn't absolutely have pleased them, I afterwards reflected.

"Ah you're—you're—a—?" I began as soon as I had mastered my surprise. I couldn't bring out the dingy word "models": it seemed so little to fit the case.

"We haven't had much practice," said the lady.

"We've got to *do* something, and we've thought that an artist in your line   20 might perhaps make something of us," her husband threw off. He further mentioned that they didn't know many artists and that they had gone first, on the off-chance—he painted views of course, but sometimes put in figures; perhaps I remembered—to Mr. Rivet, whom they had met a few years before at a place in Norfolk where he was sketching.

"We used to sketch a little ourselves," the lady hinted.

"It's very awkward, but we absolutely *must* do something," her husband went on.

"Of course we're not so *very* young," she admitted with a wan smile.

With the remark that I might as well know something more about them the husband had handed me a card extracted from a neat new pocket-book—their appurtenances were all of the freshest—and inscribed with the words "Major Monarch." Impressive as these words were they didn't carry my knowledge much further; but my visitor presently added: "I've left the army and we've had the misfortune to lose our money. In fact our means are dreadfully small."

"It's awfully trying—a regular strain," said Mrs. Monarch.   25

They evidently wished to be discreet—to take care not to swagger because they were gentlefolk. I felt them willing to recognise this as something of a drawback, at the same time that I guessed at an underlying sense—their consolation in adversity—that they *had* their points. They certainly had; but these advantages struck me as preponderantly social; such for instance as would help to make a drawing-room look well. However, a drawing-room was always, or ought to be, a picture.

In consequence of his wife's allusion to their age Major Monarch observed: "Naturally it's more for the figure that we thought of going in. We can still hold ourselves up." On the instant I saw that the figure was indeed their strong point. His "naturally" didn't sound vain, but it lighted up the question. "*She* has the best one," he continued, nodding at his wife with a pleasant after-dinner absence of circumlocution. I could only reply, as if we were in fact sitting over our wine, that this didn't prevent his own from being very good; which led him in turn to make answer: "We thought that if you ever have to do people like us we might be something like it. *She* particularly—for a lady in a book, you know."

I was so amused by them that, to get more of it, I did my best to take their point of view; and though it was an embarrassment to find myself appraising physically, as if they were animals on hire or useful blacks, a pair whom I should have expected to meet only in one of the relations in which criticism is tacit, I looked at Mrs. Monarch judicially enough to be able to exclaim after a moment with conviction: "Oh yes, a lady in a book!" She was singularly like a bad illustration.

"We'll stand up, if you like," said the Major; and he raised himself before me with a really grand air.

I could take his measure at a glance—he was six feet two and a perfect gentleman. It would have paid any club in process of formation and in want of a stamp to engage him at a salary to stand in the principal window. What struck me at once was that in coming to me they had rather missed their vocation; they could surely have been turned to better account for advertising purposes. I couldn't of course see the thing in detail, but I could see them make somebody's fortune—I don't mean their own. There was something in them for a waistcoat-maker, an hotel-keeper or a soap-vendor. I could imagine "We always use it" pinned on their bosoms with the greatest effect; I had a vision of the brilliancy with which they would launch a table d'hôte.

Mrs. Monarch sat still, not from pride but from shyness, and presently her husband said to her; "Get up, my dear, and show how smart you are." She obeyed, but she had no need to get up to show it. She walked to the end of the studio and then came back blushing, her fluttered eyes on the partner of her appeal. I was reminded of an incident I had accidentally had a glimpse of in Paris being with a friend there, a dramatist about to produce a play, when an actress came to him to ask to be entrusted with a part. She went through her paces before him, walked up and down as Mrs. Monarch was doing. Mrs. Monarch did it quite as well, but I abstained from applauding. It was very odd to see such people apply for such poor pay. She looked as if she had ten thousand a year. Her husband had used the word that described her: she was in the London current jargon essentially and typically "smart." Her figure was, in the same order of ideas, conspicuously and irreproachably "good." For a woman of her age her waist was surprisingly small; her elbow moreover had the orthodox crook. She held her head at the conventional angle, but why did she come to *me?* She ought to have tried on jackets at a big shop. I feared my visitors were not only destitute but "artistic"—which would be a great complication. When she sat down again I thanked her, observing that what a draughtsman most valued in his model was the faculty of keeping quiet.

"Oh *she* can keep quiet," said Major Monarch. Then he added jocosely: "I've always kept her quiet."

"I'm not a nasty fidget, am I?" It was going to wring tears from me, I felt, the way she hid her head, ostrich-like, in the other's broad bosom.

The owner of this expanse addressed his answer to me. "Perhaps it isn't out of place to mention—because we ought to be quite business-like, oughtn't we?—that when I married her she was known as the Beautiful Statue."

"Oh dear!" said Mrs. Monarch ruefully.   35

"Of course I should want a certain amount of expression," I rejoined.

"Of *course!*"—and I had never heard such unanimity.

"And then I suppose you know that you'll get awfully tired."

"Oh we *never* get tired!" they eagerly cried.

"Have you had any kind of practice?"   40

They hesitated—they looked at each other. "We've been photographed—*immensely*," said Mrs. Monarch.

"She means the fellows have asked us themselves," added the Major.

"I see—because you're so good-looking."

"I don't know what they thought, but they were always after us."

"We always got our photographs for nothing," smiled Mrs. Monarch.   45

"We might have brought some, my dear," her husband remarked.

"I'm not sure we have any left. We've given quantities away," she explained to me.

"With our autographs and that sort of thing," said the Major.

"Are they to be got in the shops?" I enquired as a harmless pleasantry.

"Oh yes, *hers*—they used to be."   50

"Not now," said Mrs. Monarch with her eyes on the floor.

II

I could fancy the "sort of thing" they put on the presentation copies of their photographs, and I was sure they wrote a beautiful hand. It was odd how quickly I was sure of everything that concerned them. If they were now so poor as to have to earn shillings and pence they could never have had much of a margin. Their good looks had been their capital, and they had good-humouredly made the most of the career that this resource marked out for them. It was in their faces, the blankness, the deep intellectual repose of the twenty years of country-house visiting that had given them pleasant intonations. I could see the sunny drawing-rooms, sprinkled with periodicals she didn't read, in which Mrs. Monarch had continuously sat; I could see the wet shrubberies in which she had walked, equipped to admiration for either exercise. I could see the rich covers[2] the Major had helped to shoot and the wonderful garments in which, late at night, he repaired to the smoking-room to talk about them. I could imagine their leggings

2. Flocks of game birds.

and waterproofs, their knowing tweeds and rugs, their rolls of sticks and cases of tackle and neat umbrellas; and I could evoke the exact appearance of their servants and the compact variety of their luggage on the platforms of country stations.

They gave small tips, but they were liked; they didn't do anything themselves, but they were welcome. They looked so well everywhere; they gratified the general relish for stature, complexion and "form." They knew it without fatuity or vulgarity, and they respected themselves in consequence. They weren't superficial; they were thorough and kept themselves up—it had been their line. People with such a taste for activity had to have some line. I could feel how even in a dull house they could have been counted on for the joy of life. At present something had happened—it didn't matter what, their little income had grown less, it had grown least—and they had to do something for pocket-money. Their friends could like them, I made out, without liking to support them. There was something about them that represented credit—their clothes, their manners, their type; but if credit is a large empty pocket in which an occasional chink reverberates, the chink at least must be audible. What they wanted of me was to help to make it so. Fortunately they had no children—I soon divined that. They would also perhaps wish our relations to be kept secret: this was why it was "for the figure"—the reproduction of the face would betray them.

I liked them—I felt, quite as their friends must have done—they were so simple; and I had no objection to them if they would suit. But somehow with all their perfections I didn't easily believe in them. After all they were amateurs, and the ruling passion of my life was the detestation of the amateur. Combined with this was another perversity—an innate preference for the represented subject over the real one: the defect of the real one was so apt to be a lack of representation. I liked things that appeared; then one was sure. Whether they *were* or not was a subordinate and almost always a profitless question. There were other considerations, the first of which was that I already had two or three recruits in use, notably a young person with big feet, in alpaca, from Kilburn, who for a couple of years had come to me regularly for my illustrations and with whom I was still—perhaps ignobly—satisfied. I frankly explained to my visitors how the case stood, but they had taken more precautions than I supposed. They had reasoned out their opportunity, for Claude Rivet had told them of the projected *édition de luxe* of one of the writers of our day—the rarest of the novelists—who, long neglected by the multitudinous vulgar and dearly prized by the attentive (need I mention Philip Vincent?) had had the happy fortune of seeing, late in life, the dawn and then the full light of a higher criticism; an estimate in which on the part of the public there was something really of expiation. The edition preparing, planned by a publisher of taste, was practically an act of high reparation; the wood-cuts with which it was to be enriched were the homage of English art to one of the most independent representatives of English letters. Major and Mrs. Monarch confessed to me they had hoped I might be able to work *them* into my branch of the enterprise. They knew I was to do the first of the books, "Rutland Ramsay," but I had to make clear to them that my participation in the rest of the affair—this first book was to be a test—must depend on the satisfaction I should give. If this should be limited my employers would drop me with scarce common forms. It was therefore a crisis for me, and naturally I was making special preparations, looking about for new people, should they be necessary, and securing the best types. I admitted however that I should like to settle down to two or three good models who would do for everything.

"Should we have often to—a—put on special clothes?" Mrs. Monarch timidly demanded.

"Dear yes—that's half the business."

"And should we be expected to supply our own costumes?"

"Oh no; I've got a lot of things. A painter's models put on—or put off—anything he likes."

"And you mean—a—the same?"

"The same?"

Mrs. Monarch looked at her husband again.

"Oh she was just wondering," he explained, "if the costumes are in *general* use." I had to confess that they were, and I mentioned further that some of them—I had a lot of genuine greasy last-century things—had served their time, a hundred years ago, on living world-stained men and women; on figures not perhaps so far removed, in that vanished world, from *their* type, the Monarchs', *quoi!*[3] of a breeched and bewigged age. "We'll put on anything that *fits*," said the Major.

"Oh I arrange that—they fit in the pictures."

"I'm afraid I should do better for the modern books. I'd come as you like," said Mrs. Monarch.

"She has got a lot of clothes at home: they might do for contemporary life," her husband continued.

"Oh I can fancy scenes in which you'd be quite natural." And indeed I could see the slipshod rearrangements of stale properties—the stories I tried to produce pictures for without the exasperation of reading them—whose sandy tracts the good lady might help to people. But I had to return to the fact that for this sort of work—the daily mechanical grind—I was already equipped: the people I was working with were fully adequate.

"We only thought we might be more like *some* characters," said Mrs. Monarch mildly, getting up.

Her husband also rose; he stood looking at me with a dim wistfulness that was touching in so fine a man.

"Wouldn't it be rather a pull sometimes to have—a—to have—?" He hung fire; he wanted me to help him by phrasing what he meant. But I couldn't—I didn't know. So he brought it out awkwardly: "The *real* thing; a gentleman, you know, or a lady." I was quite ready to give a general assent—I admitted that there was a great deal in that. This encouraged Major Monarch to say, following up his appeal with an unacted gulp: "It's awfully hard—we've tried everything." The gulp was communicative; it proved too much for his wife. Before I knew it Mrs. Monarch had dropped again upon a divan and burst into tears. Her husband sat down beside her, holding one of her hands; whereupon she quickly dried her eyes with

3. What! (French).

the other, while I felt embarrassed as she looked up at me. "There isn't a confounded job I haven't applied for—waited for—prayed for. You can fancy we'd
be pretty bad first. Secretaryships and that sort of thing? You might as well ask
for a peerage. I'd be *anything*—I'm strong; a messenger or a coalheaver. I'd put on
a gold-laced cap and open carriage-doors in front of the haberdasher's; I'd hang
about a station to carry portmanteaux; I'd be a postman. But they won't *look* at
you; there are thousands as good as yourself already on the ground. *Gentlemen,*
poor beggars, who've drunk their wine, who've kept their hunters!"

70   I was as reassuring as I knew how to be, and my visitors were presently on their
feet again while, for the experiment, we agreed on an hour. We were discussing
it when the door opened and Miss Churm came in with a wet umbrella. Miss
Churm had to take the omnibus to Maida Vale and then walk half a mile. She
looked a trifle blowsy and slightly splashed. I scarcely ever saw her come in without thinking fresh how odd it was that, being so little in herself, she should yet
be so much in others. She was a meagre little Miss Churm, but was such an ample
heroine of romance. She was only a freckled cockney, but she could represent
everything, from a fine lady to a shepherdess; she had the faculty as she might
have had a fine voice or long hair. She couldn't spell and she loved beer, but she
had two or three "points," and practice, and a knack, and mother-wit, and a
whimsical sensibility, and a love of the theatre, and seven sisters, and not an
ounce of respect, especially for the *h*.[4] The first thing my visitors saw was that her
umbrella was wet, and in their spotless perfection they visibly winced at it. The
rain had come on since their arrival.

    "I'm all in a soak; there *was* a mess of people in the 'bus. I wish you lived near
a stytion," said Miss Churm. I requested her to get ready as quickly as possible,
and she passed into the room in which she always changed her dress. But before
going out she asked me what she was to get into this time.

    "It's the Russian princess, don't you know?" I answered; "the one with the
'golden eyes,' in black velvet, for the long thing in the *Cheapside.*"

    "Golden eyes? I *say!*" cried Miss Churm, while my companions watched her
with intensity as she withdrew. She always arranged herself, when she was late,
before I could turn around; and I kept my visitors a little on purpose, so that they
might get an idea, from seeing her, what would be expected of themselves. I
mentioned that she was quite my notion of an excellent model—she was really
very clever.

    "Do you think she looks like a Russian princess?" Major Monarch asked with
lurking alarm.

75   "When I make her, yes."

    "Oh if you have to *make* her—!" he reasoned, not without point.

    "That's the most you can ask. There are so many who are not makeable."

    "Well now, *here's* a lady"—and with a persuasive smile he passed his arm into
his wife's—"who's already made!"

    "Oh I'm not a Russian princess," Mrs. Monarch protested a little coldly. I could

---

4. Working-class Londoners, especially in the East End (cockneys), drop *h*'s 'orribly.

see she had known some and didn't like them. There at once was a complication of a kind I never had to fear with Miss Churm.

This young lady came back in black velvet—the gown was rather rusty and very low on her lean shoulders—and with a Japanese fan in her red hands. I reminded her that in the scene I was doing she had to look over some one's head. "I forget whose it is; but it doesn't matter. Just look over a head." 80

"I'd rather look over a stove," said Miss Churm; and she took her station near the fire. She fell into position, settled herself into a tall attitude, gave a certain backward inclination to her head and a certain forward droop to her fan, and looked, at least to my prejudiced sense, distinguished and charming, foreign and dangerous. We left her looking so while I went downstairs with Major and Mrs. Monarch.

"I believe I could come about as near it as that," said Mrs. Monarch.

"Oh, you think she's shabby, but you must allow for the alchemy of art."

However, they went off with an evident increase of comfort founded on their demonstrable advantage in being the real thing. I could fancy them shuddering over Miss Churm. She was very droll about them when I went back, for I told her what they wanted.

"Well, if *she* can sit I'll tyke to bookkeeping," said my model. 85

"She's very ladylike," I replied as an innocent form of aggravation.

"So much the worse for *you*. That means she can't turn round."

"She'll do for the fashionable novels."

"Oh yes, she'll *do* for them!" my model humorously declared. "Ain't they bad enough without her?" I had often sociably denounced them to Miss Churm.

III

It was for the elucidation of a mystery in one of these works that I first tried Mrs. 90 Monarch. Her husband came with her, to be useful if necessary—it was sufficiently clear that as a general thing he would prefer to come with her. At first I wondered if this were for "propriety's" sake—if he were going to be jealous and meddling. The idea was too tiresome, and if it had been confirmed it would speedily have brought our acquaintance to a close. But I soon saw there was nothing in it and that if he accompanied Mrs. Monarch it was—in addition to the chance of being wanted—simply because he had nothing else to do. When they were separate his occupation was gone and they never *had* been separate. I judged rightly that in their awkward situation their close union was their main comfort and that this union had no weak spot. It was a real marriage, an encouragement to the hesitating, a nut for pessimists to crack. Their address was humble—I remember afterwards thinking it had been the only thing about them that was really professional—and I could fancy the lamentable lodgings in which the Major would have been left alone. He could sit there more or less grimly with his wife— he couldn't sit there anyhow without her.

He had too much tact to try and make himself agreeable when he couldn't be useful; so when I was too absorbed in my work to talk he simply sat and waited. But I liked to hear him talk—it made my work, when not interrupting it, less mechanical, less special. To listen to him was to combine the excitement of going out with the economy of staying at home. There was only one hindrance—that I seemed not to know any of the people this brilliant couple had known. I think he wondered extremely, during the term of our intercourse, whom the deuce I *did* know. He hadn't a stray sixpence of an idea to fumble for, so we didn't spin it very fine; we confined ourselves to questions of leather and even of liquor—saddlers and breeches-makers and how to get excellent claret cheap—and matters like "good trains" and the habits of small game. His lore on these last subjects was astonishing—he managed to interweave the station-master with the ornithologist. When he couldn't talk about greater things he could talk cheerfully about smaller, and since I couldn't accompany him into reminiscences of the fashionable world he could lower the conversation without a visible effort to my level.

So earnest a desire to please was touching in a man who could so easily have knocked one down. He looked after the fire and had an opinion on the draught of the stove without my asking him, and I could see that he thought many of my arrangements not half knowing. I remember telling him that if I were only rich I'd offer him a salary to come and teach me how to live. Sometimes he gave a random sigh of which the essence might have been: "Give me even such a bare old barrack as *this,* and I'd do something with it!" When I wanted to use him he came alone; which was an illustration of the superior courage of women. His wife could bear her solitary second floor, and she was in general more discreet; showing by various small reserves that she was alive to the propriety of keeping our relations markedly professional—not letting them slide into sociability. She wished it to remain clear that she and the Major were employed, not cultivated, and if she approved of me as a superior, who could be kept in his place, she never thought me quite good enough for an equal.

She sat with great intensity, giving the whole of her mind to it, and was capable of remaining for an hour almost as motionless as before a photographer's lens. I could see she had been photographed often, but somehow the very habit that made her good for that purpose unfitted her for mine. At first I was extremely pleased with her ladylike air, and it was a satisfaction, on coming to follow her lines, to see how good they were and how far they could lead the pencil. But after a little skirmishing I began to find her too insurmountably stiff; do what I would with it my drawing looked like a photograph or a copy of a photograph. Her figure had no variety of expression—she herself had no sense of variety. You may say that this was my business and was only a question of placing her. Yet I placed her in every conceivable position and she managed to obliterate their differences. She was always a lady certainly, and into the bargain was always the same lady. She was the real thing, but always the same thing. There were moments when I rather writhed under the serenity of her confidence that she *was* the real thing. All her dealings with me and all her husband's were an implication that this was lucky for *me.* Meanwhile I found myself trying to invent types that approached her own, instead of making her own transform itself—in the clever way that was not impossible for instance to poor Miss Churm. Arrange as I would and take the precautions I would, she always came out, in my pictures, too tall—landing me in the dilemma of having represented a fascinating woman as seven feet high, which (out of respect perhaps to my own very much scantier inches) was far from my idea of such personage.

The case was worse with the Major—nothing I could do would keep *him* down, so that he became useful only for representation of brawny giants. I adored variety and range, I cherished human accidents, the illustrative note; I wanted to characterise closely, and the thing in the world I most hated was the danger of being ridden by a type. I had quarrelled with some of my friends about it; I had parted company with them for maintaining that one *had* to be, and that if the type was beautiful—witness Raphael and Leonardo[5]—the servitude was only a gain. I was neither Leonardo nor Raphael—I might only be a presumptuous young modern searcher; but I held that everything was to be sacrificed sooner than character. When they claimed that the obsessional form could easily *be* character I retorted, perhaps superficially, "Whose?" It couldn't be everybody's—it might end in being nobody's.

After I had drawn Mrs. Monarch a dozen times I felt surer even than before   95 that the value of such a model as Miss Churm resided precisely in the fact that she had no positive stamp, combined of course with the other fact that what she did have was a curious and inexplicable talent for imitation. Her usual appearance was like a curtain which she could draw up at request for a capital performance. This performance was simply suggestive; but it was a word to the wise—it was vivid and pretty. Sometimes even I thought it, though she was plain herself, too insipidly pretty; I made it a reproach to her that the figures drawn from her were monotonously (*bêtement,*[6] as we used to say) graceful. Nothing made her more angry: it was so much of her pride to feel she could sit for characters that had nothing in common with each other. She would accuse me at such moments of taking away her "reputytion."

It suffered a certain shrinkage, this queer quantity, from the repeated visits of my new friends. Miss Churm was greatly in demand, never in want of employment, so I had no scruple in putting her off occasionally, to try them more at my ease. It was certainly amusing at first to do the real thing—it was amusing to do Major Monarch's trousers. They *were* the real thing, even if he did come out colossal. It was amusing to do his wife's back hair—it was so mathematically neat— and the particular "smart" tension of her tight stays. She lent herself especially to positions in which the face was somewhat averted or blurred; she abounded in ladylike back views and *profils perdus.*[7] When she stood erect she took naturally one of the attitudes in which court-painters represent queens and princesses; so that I found myself wondering whether, to draw out this accomplishment, I couldn't get the editor of the *Cheapside* to publish a really royal romance, "A Tale of Buckingham Palace." Sometimes however the real thing and the make-believe came into contact; by which I mean that Miss Churm, keeping an appointment or coming to make one on days when I had much work in hand, encountered

---

5. Raffaello Sanzio (1483–1520) and Leonardo da Vinci (1452–1519), famous Italian Renaissance painters. Leonardo was also an inventor, military engineer, architect, sculptor, anatomist, and so forth.
6. Foolishly.   7. Incomplete profiles, showing more of the back of the head and less of the face.

her invidious rivals. The encounter was not on their part, for they noticed her no more than if she had been the housemaid; not from intentional loftiness, but simply because as yet, professionally, they didn't know how to fraternise, as I could imagine they would have liked—or at least that the Major would. They couldn't talk about the omnibus—they always walked; and they didn't know what else to try—she wasn't interested in good trains or cheap claret. Besides, they must have felt—in the air—that she was amused at them, secretly derisive of their ever knowing how. She wasn't a person to conceal the limits of her faith if she had had a chance to show them. On the other hand Mrs. Monarch didn't think her tidy; for why else did she take pains to say to me—it was going out of the way, for Mrs. Monarch—that she didn't like dirty women?

One day when my young lady happened to be present with my other sitters— she even dropped in, when it was convenient, for a chat—I asked her to be so good as to lend a hand in getting tea, a service with which she was familiar and which was one of a class that, living as I did in a small way, with slender domestic resources, I often appealed to my models to render. They liked to lay hands on my property, to break the sitting, and sometimes the china—it made them feel Bohemian. The next time I saw Miss Churm after this incident she surprised me greatly by making a scene about it—she accused me of having wished to humiliate her. She hadn't resented the outrage at the time, but had seemed obliging and amused, enjoying the comedy of asking Mrs. Monarch, who sat vague and silent, whether she would have cream and sugar, and putting an exaggerated simper into the question. She had tried intonations—as if she too wished to pass for the real thing—till I was afraid my other visitors would take offence.

Oh they were determined not to do this, and their touching patience was the measure of their great need. They would sit by the hour, uncomplaining, till I was ready to use them; they would come back on the chance of being wanted and would walk away cheerfully if it failed. I used to go to the door with them to see in what magnificent order they retreated. I tried to find other employment for them—I introduced them to several artists. But they didn't "take," for reasons I could appreciate, and I became rather anxiously aware that after such disappointments they fell back upon me with a heavier weight. They did me the honor to think me most *their* form. They weren't romantic enough for the painters, and in those days there were few serious workers in black-and-white. Besides, they had an eye to the great job I had mentioned to them—they had secretly set their hearts on supplying the right essence for my pictorial vindication of our fine novelist. They knew that for this undertaking I should want no costume-effects, none of the frippery of past ages—that it was a case in which everything would be contemporary and satirical and presumably genteel. If I could work them into it their future would be assured, for the labour would of course be long and the occupation steady.

One day Mrs. Monarch came without her husband—she explained his absence by his having had to go to the City.[8] While she sat there in her usual relaxed majesty there came at the door a knock which I immediately recognised as the subdued appeal of a model out of work. It was followed by the entrance of a young

---

8. Financial and legal center of London.

man whom I at once saw to be a foreigner and who proved in fact an Italian acquainted with no English word but my name, which he uttered in a way that made it seem to include all others. I hadn't then visited his country, nor was I proficient in his tongue; but as he was not so meanly constituted—what Italian is?—as to depend only on that member for expression he conveyed to me, in familiar but graceful mimicry, that he was in search of exactly the employment in which the lady before me was engaged. I was not struck with him at first, and while I continued to draw I dropped few signs of interest or encouragement. He stood his ground however—not importunately, but with a dumb dog-like fidelity in his eyes that amounted to innocent impudence, the manner of a devoted servant—he might have been in the house for years—unjustly suspected. Suddenly it struck me that this very attitude and expression made a picture; whereupon I told him to sit down and wait till I should be free. There was another picture in the way he obeyed me, and I observed as I worked that there were others still in the way he looked wonderingly, with his head thrown back, about the high studio. He might have been crossing himself in Saint Peter's. Before I finished I said to myself "The fellow's a bankrupt orange-monger, but a treasure."

When Mrs. Monarch withdrew he passed across the room like a flash to open the door for her, standing there with the rapt pure gaze of the young Dante spellbound by the young Beatrice.[9] As I never insisted, in such situations, on the blankness of the British domestic, I reflected that he had the making of a servant—and I needed one, but couldn't pay him to be only that—as well as of a model; in short I resolved to adopt my bright adventurer if he would agree to officiate in the double capacity. He jumped at my offer, and in the event my rashness—for I had really known nothing about him—wasn't brought home to me. He proved a sympathetic though a desultory ministrant, and had in a wonderful degree the *sentiment de la pose*.[1] It was uncultivated, instinctive, a part of the happy instinct that had guided him to my door and helped him to spell out my name on the card nailed to it. He had had no other introduction to me than a guess, from the shape of my high north window, seen outside, that my place was a studio and that as a studio it would contain an artist. He had wandered to England in search of fortune, like other itinerants, and had embarked, with a partner and a small green hand-cart, on the sale of penny ices. The ices had melted away and the partner had dissolved in their train. My young man wore tight yellow trousers with reddish stripes and his name was Oronte. He was sallow but fair, and when I put him into some old clothes of my own he looked like an Englishman. He was as good as Miss Churm, who could look, when requested, like an Italian.

IV

I thought Mrs. Monarch's face slightly convulsed when, on her coming back with her husband, she found Oronte installed. It was strange to have to recognise in a scrap of a lazzarone[2] a competitor to her magnificent Major. It was she who

---

9. Dante Alighieri (1265–1321), Italian poet, author of *The Divine Comedy,* was inspired for life poetically and spiritually by Beatrice Portinari, whom he first saw when they were children and saw only infrequently thereafter.   1. Instinct for striking poses.   2. Street person.

scented danger first, for the Major was anecdotically unconscious. But Oronte gave us tea, with a hundred eager confusions—he had never been concerned in so queer a process—and I think she thought better of me for having at last an "establishment." They saw a couple of drawings that I had made of the establishment, and Mrs. Monarch hinted that it never would have struck her he had sat for them. "Now the drawings you make from *us,* they look exactly like us," she reminded me, smiling in triumph; and I recognized that this was indeed just their defect. When I drew the Monarchs I couldn't anyhow get away from them—get into the character I wanted to represent; and I hadn't the least desire my model should be discoverable in my picture. Miss Churm never was, and Mrs. Monarch thought I hid her, very properly, because she was vulgar; whereas if she was lost it was only as the dead who go to heaven are lost—in the gain of an angel the more.

By this time I had got a certain start with "Rutland Ramsay," the first novel in the great projected series; that is I had produced a dozen drawings, several with the help of the Major and his wife, and I had sent them in for approval. My understanding with the publishers, as I have already hinted, had been that I was to be left to do my work, in this particular case, as I liked, with the whole book committed to me; but my connexion with the rest of the series was only contingent. There were moments when, frankly, it *was* a comfort to have the real thing under one's hand; for there were characters in "Rutland Ramsay" that were very much like it. There were people presumably as erect as the Major and women of as good a fashion as Mrs. Monarch. There was a great deal of country-house life—treated, it is true, in a fine fanciful ironical generalised way—and there was a considerable implication of knickerbockers and kilts. There were certain things I had to settle at the outset; such things for instance as the exact appearance of the hero and the particular bloom and figure of the heroine. The author of course gave me a lead, but there was a margin for interpretation. I took the Monarchs into my confidence, I told them frankly what I was about, I mentioned my embarrassments and alternatives. "Oh take *him!*" Mrs. Monarch murmured sweetly, looking at her husband; and "What could you want better than my wife?" the Major enquired with the comfortable candour that now prevailed between us.

I wasn't obliged to answer these remarks—I was only obliged to place my sitters. I wasn't easy in mind, and I postponed a little timidly perhaps the solving of my question. The book was a large canvas, the other figures were numerous, and I worked off at first some of the episodes in which the hero and the heroine were not concerned. When once I had set *them* up I should have to stick to them—I couldn't make my young man seven feet high in one place and five feet nine in another. I inclined on the whole to the latter measurement, though the Major more than once reminded me that *he* looked about as young as any one. It was indeed quite possible to arrange him, for the figure, so that it would have been difficult to detect his age. After the spontaneous Oronte had been with me a month, and after I had given him to understand several times over that his native exuberance would presently constitute an insurmountable barrier to our further intercourse, I waked to a sense of his heroic capacity. He was only five feet seven, but the remaining inches were latent. I tried him almost secretly at first, for I was really rather afraid of the judgment my other models would pass on such a choice. If they regarded Miss Churm as little better than a snare what would they think of the representation by a person so little the real thing as an Italian street-vendor of a protagonist formed by a public school?

If I went a little in fear of them it wasn't because they bullied me, because they had got an oppressive foothold, but because in their really pathetic decorum and mysteriously permanent newness they counted on me so intensely. I was therefore very glad when Jack Hawley came home: he was always of such good counsel. He painted badly himself, but there was no one like him for putting his finger on the place. He had been absent from England for a year; he had been somewhere—I don't remember where—to get a fresh eye. I was in a good deal of dread of any such organ, but we were old friends; he had been away for months and a sense of emptiness was creeping into my life. I hadn't dodged a missile for a year.

He came back with a fresh eye, but with the same old black velvet blouse, and the first evening he spent in my studio we smoked cigarettes till the small hours. He had done no work himself, he had only got the eye; so the field was clear for the production of my little things. He wanted to see what I had produced for the *Cheapside,* but he was disappointed in the exhibition. That at least seemed the meaning of two or three comprehensive groans which, as he lounged on my big divan, his leg folded under him, looking at my latest drawings, issued from his lips with the smoke of the cigarette. 105

"What's the matter with you?" I asked.

"What's the matter with *you?*"

"Nothing save that I'm mystified."

"You are indeed. You're quite off the hinge. What's the meaning of this new fad?" And he tossed me, with visible irreverence, a drawing in which I happened to have depicted both my elegant models. I asked if he didn't think it good, and he replied that it struck him as execrable, given the sort of thing I had always represented myself to him as wishing to arrive at; but I let that pass—I was so anxious to see exactly what he meant. The two figures in the picture looked colossal, but I supposed this was *not* what he meant, inasmuch as, for aught he knew the contrary, I might have been trying for some such effect. I maintained that I was working exactly in the same way as when he last had done me the honour to tell me I might do something some day. "Well, there's a screw loose somewhere," he answered; "wait a bit and I'll discover it." I depended upon him to do so: where else was the fresh eye? But he produced at last nothing more luminous than "I don't know—I don't like your types." This was lame for a critic who had never consented to discuss with me anything but the question of execution, the direction of strokes and the mystery of values.

"In the drawings you've been looking at I think my types are very handsome." 110

"Oh they won't do!"

"I've been working with new models."

"I see you have. *They* won't do."

"Are you very sure of that?"

"Absolutely—they're stupid." 115

"You mean *I* am—for I ought to get round that."

"You *can't*—with such people. Who are they?"

I told him, so far as was necessary, and he concluded heartlessly: "Ce sont des gens qu'il faut mettre à la porte."[3]

"You've never seen them; they're awfully good"—I flew to their defence.

"Not seen them? Why all this recent work of yours drops to pieces with them. It's all I want to see of them."

"No one else has said anything against it—the *Cheapside* people are pleased."

"Everyone else is an ass, and the *Cheapside* people the biggest asses of all. Come, don't pretend at this time of day to have pretty illusions about the public, especially about publishers and editors. It's not for *such* animals you work—it's for those who know, *coloro che sanno;*[4] so keep straight for *me* if you can't keep straight for yourself. There was a certain sort of thing you used to try for—and a very good thing it was. But this twaddle isn't *in* it." When I talked with Hawley later about "Rutland Ramsay" and its possible successors he declared that I must get back into my boat again or I should go to the bottom. His voice in short was the voice of warning.

I noted the warning, but I didn't turn my friends out of doors. They bored me a good deal; but the very fact that they bored me admonished me not to sacrifice them—if there was anything to be done with them—simply to irritation. As I look back at this phase they seem to me to have pervaded my life not a little. I have a vision of them as most of the time in my studio, seated against the wall on an old velvet bench to be out of the way, and resembling the while a pair of patient courtiers in a royal ante-chamber. I'm convinced that during the coldest weeks of the winter they held their ground because it saved them fire. Their newness was losing its gloss, and it was impossible not to feel them objects of charity. Whenever Miss Churm arrived they went away, and after I was fairly launched in "Rutland Ramsay" Miss Churm arrived pretty often. They managed to express to me tacitly that they supposed I wanted her for the low life of the book, and I let them suppose it, since they had attempted to study the work—it was lying about the studio—without discovering that it dealt only with the highest circles. They had dipped into the most brilliant of our novelists without deciphering many passages. I still took an hour from them, now and again, in spite of Jack Hawley's warning: it would be time enough to dismiss them, if dismissal should be necessary, when the rigour of the season was over. Hawley had made their acquaintance—he had met them at my fireside—and thought them a ridiculous pair. Learning that he was a painter they tried to approach him, to show him too that they were the real thing; but he looked at them, across the big room, as if they were miles away: they were a compendium of everything he most objected to in the social system of his country. Such people as that, all convention and patent-leather, with ejaculations that stopped conversation, had no business in a studio. A studio was a place to learn to see, and how could you see through a pair of feather-beds?

3. That kind of person should be shown the door.   4. Actually, *color che sanno*—those who know (Dante, *The Divine Comedy*, "The Inferno," 4.131).

The main inconvenience I suffered at their hands was that at first
letting it break upon them that my artful little servant had begun to si^{of}
"Rutland Ramsay." They knew I had been odd enough—they were pre^r
this time to allow oddity to artists—to pick a foreign vagabond out of th^y
when I might have had a person with whiskers and credentials, but it wà
time before they learned how high I rated his accomplishments. They foun
in an attitude more than once, but they never doubted I was doing him ¿
organ-grinder. There were several things they never guessed, and one of them
that for a striking scene in the novel, in which a footman briefly figured,
occurred to me to make use of Major Monarch as the menial. I kept putting th.
off, I didn't like to ask him to don the livery—besides the difficulty of finding a
livery to fit him. At last, one day late in the winter, when I was at work on the
despised Oronte, who caught one's idea on the wing, and was in the glow of
feeling myself go very straight, they came in, the Major and his wife, with their
society laugh about nothing (there was less and less to laugh at); came on like
country-callers—they always reminded me of that—who have walked across the
park after church and are presently persuaded to stay to luncheon. Luncheon was
over, but they could stay to tea—I knew they wanted it. The fit was on me, however, and I couldn't let my ardour cool and my work wait, with the fading daylight, while my model prepared it. So I asked Mrs. Monarch if she would mind
laying it out—a request which for an instant brought all the blood to her face.
Her eyes were on her husband's for a second, and some mute telegraphy passed
between them. Their folly was over the next instant; his cheerful shrewdness put
an end to it. So far from pitying their wounded pride, I must add, I was moved
to give it as complete a lesson as I could. They bustled about together and got out
the cups and saucers and made the kettle boil. I know they felt as if they were
waiting on my servant, and when the tea was prepared I said: "He'll have a cup,
please—he's tired." Mrs. Monarch brought him one where he stood, and he took
it from her, as if he had been a gentleman at a party squeezing a crush-hat with
an elbow.

Then it came over me that she had made a great effort for me—made it with
a kind of nobleness—and that I owed her a compensation. Each time I saw her
after this I wondered what the compensation could be. I couldn't go on doing
the wrong thing to oblige them. Oh it *was* the wrong thing, the stamp of the
work for which they sat—Hawley was not the only person to say it now. I sent
in a large number of the drawings I had made for "Rutland Ramsay," and I
received a warning that was more to the point than Hawley's. The artistic adviser
of the house for which I was working was of opinion that many of my illustrations
were not what had been looked for. Most of these illustrations were the subjects
in which the Monarchs had figured. Without going into the question of what *had*
been looked for, I had to face the fact that at this rate I shouldn't get the other
books to do. I hurled myself in despair on Miss Churm—I put her through all her
paces. I not only adopted Oronte publicly as my hero, but one morning when
the Major looked in to see if I didn't require him to finish a *Cheapside* figure for
which he had begun to sit the week before, I told him I had changed my mind—
I'd do the drawing from my man. At this my visitor turned pale and stood looking

125

.r idea of an English gentleman?" he asked.

at me. ointed, I was nervous, I wanted to get on with my work; so I replied

I wa: "Oh my dear Major—I can't be ruined for *you!*" . . .

with orrid speech, but he stood another moment—after which, without a

I quitted the studio. I drew a long breath, for I said to myself that I

wo see him again. I hadn't told him definitely that I was in danger of

sh ny work rejected, but I was vexed at his not having felt the catastrophe

h air, read with me the moral of our fruitless collaboration, the lesson that

e deceptive atmosphere of art even the highest respectability may fail of

g plastic.

I didn't owe my friends money, but I did see them again. They reappeared together three days later, and, given all the other facts, there was something tragic in that one. It was a clear proof they could find nothing else in life to do. They had threshed the matter out in a dismal conference—they had digested the bad news that they were not in for the series. If they weren't useful to me even for the *Cheapside* their function seemed difficult to determine, and I could only judge at first that they had come, forgivingly, decorously, to take a last leave. This made me rejoice in secret that I had little leisure for a scene; for I had placed both my other models in position together and I was pegging away at a drawing from which I hoped to derive glory. It had been suggested by the passage in which Rutland Ramsay, drawing up a chair to Artemisia's piano-stool, says extraordinary things to her while she ostensibly fingers out a difficult piece of music. I had done Miss Churm at the piano before—it was an attitude in which she knew how to take on an absolutely poetic grace. I wished the two figures to "compose" together with intensity, and my little Italian had entered perfectly into my conception. The pair were vividly before me, the piano had been pulled out; it was a charming show of blended youth and murmured love, which I had only to catch and keep. My visitors stood and looked at it, and I was friendly to them over my shoulder.

They made no response, but I was used to silent company and went on with my work, only a little disconcerted—even though exhilarated by the sense that *this* was at least the ideal thing—at not having got rid of them after all. Presently I heard Mrs. Monarch's sweet voice beside or rather above me: "I wish her hair were a little better done." I looked up and she was staring with a strange fixedness at Miss Churm, whose back was turned to her. "Do you mind my just touching it?" she went on—a question which made me spring up for an instant as with the instinctive fear that she might do the young lady a harm. But she quieted me with a glance I shall never forget—I confess I should like to have been able to paint *that*—and went for a moment to my model. She spoke to her softly, laying a hand on her shoulder and bending over her; and as the girl, understanding, gratefully assented, she disposed her rough curls, with a few quick passes, in such a way as to make Miss Churm's head twice as charming. It was one of the most heroic personal services I've ever seen rendered. Then Mrs. Monarch turned away with a low sigh and, looking about her as if for something to do, stooped to the floor with a noble humility and picked up a dirty rag that had dropped out of my paint-box.

The Major meanwhile had also been looking for something to do, and, wandering to the other end of the studio, saw before him my breakfast-things neglected, unremoved. "I say, can't I be useful *here?*" he called out to me with an irrepressible quaver. I assented with a laugh that I fear was awkward, and for the next ten minutes, while I worked, I heard the light clatter of china and the tinkle of spoons and glass. Mrs. Monarch assisted her husband—they washed up my crockery, they put it away. They wandered off into my little scullery, and I afterwards found that they had cleaned my knives and that my slender stock of plate had an unprecedented surface. When it came over me, the latent eloquence of what they were doing, I confess that my drawing was blurred for a moment—the picture swam. They had accepted their failure, but they couldn't accept their fate. They had bowed their heads in bewilderment to the perverse and cruel law in virtue of which the real thing could be so much less precious than the unreal; but they didn't want to starve. If my servants were my models; then my models might be my servants. They would reverse the parts—the others would sit for the ladies and gentlemen and *they* would do the work. They would still be in the studio— it was an intense dumb appeal to me not to turn them out. "Take us on," they wanted to say—"we'll do *anything.*"

My pencil dropped from my hand; my sitting was spoiled and I got rid of my sitters, who were also evidently rather mystified and awestruck. Then, alone with the Major and his wife I had a most uncomfortable moment. He put their prayer into a single sentence: "I say, you know—just let *us* do for you, can't you?" I couldn't—it was dreadful to see them emptying my slops; but I pretended I could, to oblige them, for about a week. Then I gave them a sum of money to go away, and I never saw them again. I obtained the remaining books, but my friend Hawley repeats that Major and Mrs. Monarch did me a permanent harm, got me into false ways. If it be true I'm content to have paid the price—for the memory.

1892, 1909

CHARLOTTE PERKINS GILMAN

The Yellow Wallpaper

It is very seldom that mere ordinary people like John and myself secure ancestral halls for the summer.

A colonial mansion, a hereditary estate, I would say a haunted house, and reach the height of romantic felicity—but that would be asking too much of fate!

Still I will proudly declare that there is something queer about it.

Else, why should it be let so cheaply? And why have stood so long untenanted?

John laughs at me, of course, but one expects that in marriage.   5

John is practical in the extreme. He has no patience with faith, an intense horror of superstition, and he scoffs openly at any talk of things not to be felt and seen and put down in figures.

John is a physician, and *perhaps*—(I would not say it to a living soul, of course, but this is dead paper and a great relief to my mind—) *perhaps* that is one reason I do not get well faster.

You see he does not believe I am sick!

And what can one do?

If a physician of high standing, and one's own husband, assures friends and relatives that there is really nothing the matter with one but temporary nervous depression—a slight hysterical tendency—what is one to do?

My brother is also a physician, and also of high standing, and he says the same thing.

So I take phosphates or phosphites—whichever it is, and tonics, and journeys, and air, and exercise, and am absolutely forbidden to "work" until I am well again.

Personally, I disagree with their ideas.

Personally, I believe that congenial work, with excitement and change, would do me good.

But what is one to do?

I did write for a while in spite of them; but it *does* exhaust me a good deal—having to be so sly about it, or else meet with heavy opposition.

I sometimes fancy that in my condition if I had less opposition and more society and stimulus—but John says the very worst thing I can do is to think about my condition, and I confess it always makes me feel bad.

So I will let it alone and talk about the house.

The most beautiful place! It is quite alone, standing well back from the road, quite three miles from the village. It makes me think of English places that you read about, for there are hedges and walls and gates that lock, and lots of separate little houses for the gardeners and people.

There is a *delicious* garden! I never saw such a garden—large and shady, full of box-bordered paths, and lined with long grape-covered arbors with seats under them.

There were greenhouses, too, but they are all broken now.

There was some legal trouble, I believe, something about the heirs and co-heirs; anyhow, the place has been empty for years.

That spoils my ghostliness, I am afraid, but I don't care—there is something strange about the house—I can feel it.

I even said so to John one moonlight evening, but he said what I felt was a *draught,* and shut the window.

I get unreasonably angry with John sometimes. I'm sure I never used to be so sensitive. I think it is due to this nervous condition.

But John says if I feel so, I shall neglect proper self-control; so I take pains to control myself—before him, at least, and that makes me very tired.

I don't like our room a bit. I wanted one downstairs that opened on the piazza and had roses all over the window, and such pretty old-fashioned chintz hangings! but John would not hear of it.

He said there was only one window and not room for two beds, and no near room for him if he took another.

He is very careful and loving, and hardly lets me stir without special direction.

I have a schedule prescription for each hour in the day; he takes all care from me, and so I feel basely ungrateful not to value it more.

He said we came here solely on my account, that I was to have perfect rest and all the air I could get. "Your exercise depends on your strength, my dear," said he, "and your food somewhat on your appetite; but air you can absorb all the time." So we took the nursery at the top of the house.

It is a big, airy room, the whole floor nearly, with windows that look all ways, and air and sunshine galore. It was nursery first and then playroom and gymnasium, I should judge; for the windows are barred for little children, and there are rings and things in the walls.

The paint and paper look as if a boys' school had used it. It is stripped off— the paper—in great patches all around the head of my bed, about as far as I can reach, and in a great place on the other side of the room low down. I never saw a worse paper in my life.

One of those sprawling flamboyant patterns committing every artistic sin.

It is dull enough to confuse the eye in following, pronounced enough to constantly irritate and provoke study, and when you follow the lame uncertain curves for a little distance they suddenly commit suicide—plunge off at outrageous angles, destroy themselves in unheard of contradictions.

The color is repellant, almost revolting; a smouldering unclean yellow, strangely faded by the slow-turning sunlight.

It is a dull yet lurid orange in some places, a sickly sulphur tint in others.

No wonder the children hated it! I should hate it myself if I had to live in this room long.

There comes John, and I must put this away,—he hates to have me write a word.

We have been here two weeks, and I haven't felt like writing before, since that first day.

I am sitting by the window now, up in this atrocious nursery, and there is nothing to hinder my writing as much as I please, save lack of strength.

John is away all day, and even some nights when his cases are serious.

I am glad my case is not serious!

But these nervous troubles are dreadfully depressing.

John does not know how much I really suffer. He knows there is no *reason* to suffer, and that satisfies him.

Of course it is only nervousness. It does weigh on me so not to do my duty in any way!

I mean to be such a help to John, such a real rest and comfort, and here I am a comparative burden already!

Nobody would believe what an effort it is to do what little I am able,—to dress and entertain, and order things.

It is fortunate Mary is so good with the baby. Such a dear baby!

And yet I *cannot* be with him, it makes me so nervous.

I suppose John never was nervous in his life. He laughs at me so about this wallpaper!

At first he meant to repaper the room, but afterwards he said that I was letting it get the better of me, and that nothing was worse for a nervous patient than to give way to such fancies.

He said that after the wallpaper was changed it would be the heavy bedstead, and then the barred windows, and then that gate at the head of the stairs, and so on.

"You know the place is doing you good," he said, "and really, dear, I don't care to renovate the house just for a three months' rental."

"Then do let us go downstairs," I said, "there are such pretty rooms there."

Then he took me in his arms and called me a blessed little goose, and said he would go down cellar, if I wished, and have it whitewashed into the bargain.

But he is right enough about the beds and windows and things.

It is an airy and comfortable room as any one need wish, and, of course, I would not be so silly as to make him uncomfortable just for a whim.

I'm really getting quite fond of the big room, all but that horrid paper.

Out of one window I can see the garden, those mysterious deep-shaded arbors, the riotous old-fashioned flowers, and bushes and gnarly trees.

Out of another I get a lovely view of the bay and a little private wharf belonging to the estate. There is a beautiful shaded lane that runs down there from the house. I always fancy I see people walking in these numerous paths and arbors, but John has cautioned me not to give way to fancy in the least. He says that with my imaginative power and habit of story-making, a nervous weakness like mine is sure to lead to all manner of excited fancies, and that I ought to use my will and good sense to check the tendency. So I try.

I think sometimes that if I were only well enough to write a little it would relieve the press of ideas and rest me.

But I find I get pretty tired when I try.

It is so discouraging not to have any advice and companionship about my work. When I get really well, John says we will ask Cousin Henry and Julia down for a long visit; but he says he would as soon put fireworks in my pillow-case as to let me have those stimulating people about now.

I wish I could get well faster.

But I must not think about that. This paper looks to me as if it *knew* what a vicious influence it had!

There is a recurrent spot where the pattern lolls like a broken neck and two bulbous eyes stare at you upside down.

I get positively angry with the impertinence of it and the everlastingness. Up and down and sideways they crawl, and those absurd, unblinking eyes are everywhere. There is one place where two breadths didn't match, and the eyes go all up and down the line, one a little higher than the other.

I never saw so much expression in an inanimate thing before, and we all know how much expression they have! I used to lie awake as a child and get more entertainment and terror out of blank walls and plain furniture than most children could find in a toy-store.

I remember what a kindly wink the knobs of our big, old bureau used to have, and there was one chair that always seemed like a strong friend.

I used to feel that if any of the other things looked too fierce I could always hop into that chair and be safe.

The furniture in this room is no worse than inharmonious, however, for we had to bring it all from downstairs. I suppose when this was used as a playroom they had to take the nursery things out, and no wonder! I never saw such ravages as the children have made here.

The wallpaper, as I said before, is torn off in spots, and it sticketh closer than a brother—they must have had perseverance as well as hatred.

Then the floor is scratched and gouged and splintered, the plaster itself is dug out here and there, and this great heavy bed which is all we found in the room, looks as if it had been through the wars.

But I don't mind it a bit—only the paper.   75

There comes John's sister. Such a dear girl as she is, and so careful of me! I must not let her find me writing.

She is a perfect and enthusiastic housekeeper, and hopes for no better profession. I verily believe she thinks it is the writing which made me sick!

But I can write when she is out, and see her a long way off from these windows.

There is one that commands the road, a lovely shaded winding road, and one that just looks off over the country. A lovely country, too, full of great elms and velvet meadows.

This wallpaper has a kind of sub-pattern in a different shade, a particularly   80
irritating one, for you can only see it in certain lights, and not clearly then.

But in the places where it isn't faded and where the sun is just so—I can see a strange, provoking, formless sort of figure, that seems to skulk about behind that silly and conspicuous front design.

There's sister on the stairs!

Well, the Fourth of July is over! The people are all gone and I am tired out. John thought it might do me good to see a little company, so we just had mother and Nellie and the children down for a week.

Of course I didn't do a thing. Jennie sees to everything now.

But it tired me all the same.   85

John says if I don't pick up faster he shall send me to Weir Mitchell[1] in the fall.

But I don't want to go there at all. I had a friend who was in his hands once, and she says he is just like John and my brother, only more so!

Besides, it is such an undertaking to go so far.

I don't feel as if it was worth while to turn my hand over for anything, and I'm getting dreadfully fretful and querulous.

I cry at nothing, and cry most of the time.   90

Of course I don't when John is here, or anybody else, but when I am alone.

And I am alone a good deal just now. John is kept in town very often by serious

---

1. Silas Weir Mitchell (1829–1914), American physician, novelist, and specialist in nerve disorders, popularized the rest cure.

cases, and Jennie is good and lets me alone when I want her to.

So I walk a little in the garden or down that lovely lane, sit on the porch under the roses, and lie down up here a good deal.

I'm getting really fond of the room in spite of the wallpaper. Perhaps *because* of the wallpaper.

95   It dwells in my mind so!

I lie here on this great immovable bed—it is nailed down, I believe—and follow that pattern about by the hour. It is as good as gymnastics, I assure you. I start, we'll say, at the bottom, down in the corner over there where it has not been touched, and I determine for the thousandth time that I *will* follow that pointless pattern to some sort of conclusion.

I know a little of the principle of design, and I know this thing was not arranged on any laws of radiation, or alternation, or repetition, or symmetry, or anything else that I ever heard of.

It is repeated, of course, by the breadths, but not otherwise.

Looked at in one way each breadth stands alone, the bloated curves and flour-ishes—a kind of "debased Romanesque" with *delirium tremens*—go waddling up and down in isolated columns of fatuity.

100   But, on the other hand, they connect diagonally, and the sprawling outlines run off in great slanting waves of optic horror, like a lot of wallowing seaweeds in full chase.

The whole thing goes horizontally, too, at least it seems so, and I exhaust myself in trying to distinguish the order of its going in that direction.

They have used a horizontal breadth for a frieze, and that adds wonderfully to the confusion.

There is one end of the room where it is almost intact, and there, when the crosslights fade and the low sun shines directly upon it, I can almost fancy radi-ation after all,—the interminable grotesque seem to form around a common cen-ter and rush off in headlong plunges of equal distraction.

It makes me tired to follow it. I will take a nap I guess.

105   I don't know why I should write this.

I don't want to.

I don't feel able.

And I know John would think it absurd. But I *must* say what I feel and think in some way—it is such a relief!

But the effort is getting to be greater than the relief.

110   Half the time now I am awfully lazy, and lie down ever so much.

John says I mustn't lose my strength, and has me take cod liver oil and lots of tonics and things, to say nothing of ale and wine and rare meat.

Dear John! He loves me very dearly, and hates to have me sick. I tried to have a real earnest reasonable talk with him the other day, and tell him how I wish he would let me go and make a visit to Cousin Henry and Julia.

But he said I wasn't able to go, nor able to stand it after I got there; and I did not make out a very good case for myself, for I was crying before I had finished.

It is getting to be a great effort for me to think straight. Just this nervous weakness I suppose.

And dear John gathered me up in his arms, and just carried me upstairs and 115 laid me on the bed, and sat by me and read to me till it tired my head.

He said I was his darling and his comfort and all he had, and that I must take care of myself for his sake, and keep well.

He says no one but myself can help me out of it, that I must use my will and self-control and not let any silly fancies run away with me.

There's one comfort, the baby is well and happy, and does not have to occupy this nursery with the horrid wallpaper.

If we had not used it, that blessed child would have! What a fortunate escape! Why, I wouldn't have a child of mine, an impressionable little thing, live in such a room for worlds.

I never thought of it before, but it is lucky that John kept me here after all, I 120 can stand it so much easier than a baby, you see.

Of course I never mention it to them any more—I am too wise,—but I keep watch of it all the same.

There are things in that paper that nobody knows but me, or ever will.

Behind that outside pattern the dim shapes get clearer every day.

It is always the same shape, only very numerous.

And it is like a woman stooping down and creeping about behind that pattern. 125 I don't like it a bit. I wonder—I begin to think—I wish John would take me away from here!

It is so hard to talk with John about my case, because he is so wise, and because he loves me so.

But I tried it last night.

It was moonlight. The moon shines in all around just as the sun does.

I hate to see it sometimes, it creeps so slowly, and always comes in by one window or another.

John was asleep and I hated to waken him, so I kept still and watched the 130 moonlight on that undulating wallpaper till I felt creepy.

The faint figure behind seemed to shake the pattern, just as if she wanted to get out.

I got up softly and went to feel and see if the paper *did* move, and when I came back John was awake.

"What is it, little girl?" he said. "Don't go walking about like that—you'll get cold."

I thought it was a good time to talk, so I told him that I really was not gaining here, and that I wished he would take me away.

"Why, darling!" said he, "our lease will be up in three weeks, and I can't see 135 how to leave before.

"The repairs are not done at home, and I cannot possibly leave town just now. Of course if you were in any danger, I could and would, but you really are better, dear, whether you can see it or not. I am a doctor, dear, and I know. You are gaining flesh and color, your appetite is better, I feel really much easier about you."

"I don't weigh a bit more," said I, "nor as much; and my appetite may be better in the evening when you are here, but it is worse in the morning when you are away!"

"Bless her little heart!" said he with a big hug, "she shall be as sick as she pleases! But now let's improve the shining hours by going to sleep, and talk about it in the morning!"

"And you won't go away?" I asked gloomily.

140 "Why, how can I, dear? It is only three weeks more and then we will take a nice little trip of a few days while Jennie is getting the house ready. Really dear you are better!"

"Better in body perhaps—" I began, and stopped short, for he sat up straight and looked at me with such a stern, reproachful look that I could not say another word.

"My darling," said he, "I beg of you, for my sake and for our child's sake, as well as for your own, that you will never for one instant let that idea enter your mind! There is nothing so dangerous, so fascinating, to a temperament like yours. It is a false and foolish fancy. Can you not trust me as a physician when I tell you so?"

So of course I said no more on that score, and we went to sleep before long. He thought I was asleep first, but I wasn't, and lay there for hours trying to decide whether that front pattern and the back pattern really did move together or separately.

On a pattern like this, by daylight, there is a lack of sequence, a defiance of law, that is a constant irritant to a normal mind.

145 The color is hideous enough, and unreliable enough, and infuriating enough, but the pattern is torturing.

You think you have mastered it, but just as you get well underway in following, it turns a back-somersault and there you are. It slaps you in the face, knocks you down, and tramples upon you. It is like a bad dream.

The outside pattern is a florid arabesque, reminding one of a fungus. If you can imagine a toadstool in joints, an interminable string of toadstools, budding and sprouting in endless convolutions—why, that is something like it.

That is, sometimes!

There is one marked peculiarity about this paper, a thing nobody seems to notice but myself, and that is that it changes as the light changes.

150 When the sun shoots in through the east window—I always watch for that first long, straight ray—it changes so quickly that I never can quite believe it.

That is why I watch it always.

By moonlight—the moon shines in all night when there is a moon—I wouldn't know it was the same paper.

At night in any kind of light, in twilight, candlelight, lamplight, and worst of all by moonlight, it becomes bars! The outside pattern I mean, and the woman behind it is as plain as can be.

I didn't realize for a long time what the thing was that showed behind, that dim sub-pattern, but now I am quite sure it is a woman.

By daylight she is subdued, quiet. I fancy it is the pattern that keeps her so still. It is so puzzling. It keeps me quiet by the hour. 155

I lie down ever so much now. John says it is good for me, and to sleep all I can.

Indeed he started the habit by making me lie down for an hour after each meal.

It is a very bad habit I am convinced, for you see I don't sleep.

And that cultivates deceit, for I don't tell them I'm awake—O no!

The fact is I am getting a little afraid of John. 160

He seems very queer sometimes, and even Jennie has an inexplicable look.

It strikes me occasionally, just as a scientific hypothesis,—that perhaps it is the paper!

I have watched John when he did not know I was looking, and come into the room suddenly on the most innocent excuses, and I've caught him several times *looking at the paper!* And Jennie too. I caught Jennie with her hand on it once.

She didn't know I was in the room, and when I asked her in a quiet, a very quiet voice, with the most restrained manner possible, what she was doing with the paper—she turned around as if she had been caught stealing, and looked quite angry—asked me why I should frighten her so!

Then she said that the paper stained everything it touched, that she had found 165 yellow smooches on all my clothes and John's, and she wished we would be more careful!

Did not that sound innocent? But I know she was studying that pattern, and I am determined that nobody shall find it out but myself!

Life is very much more exciting now than it used to be. You see I have something more to expect, to look forward to, to watch. I really do eat better, and am more quiet than I was.

John is so pleased to see me improve! He laughed a little the other day, and said I seemed to be flourishing in spite of my wallpaper.

I turned it off with a laugh. I had no intention of telling him it was *because* of the wallpaper—he would make fun of me. He might even want to take me away.

I don't want to leave now until I have found it out. There is a week more, and 170 I think that will be enough.

I'm feeling ever so much better! I don't sleep much at night, for it is so interesting to watch developments; but I sleep a good deal in the daytime.

In the daytime it is tiresome and perplexing.

There are always new shoots on the fungus, and new shades of yellow all over it. I cannot keep count of them, though I have tried conscientiously.

It is the strangest yellow, that wallpaper! It makes me think of all the yellow things I ever saw—not beautiful ones like buttercups, but old foul, bad yellow things.

But there is something else about that paper—the smell! I noticed it the 175 moment we came into the room, but with so much air and sun it was not bad.

Now we have had a week of fog and rain, and whether the windows are open or not, the smell is here.

It creeps all over the house.

I find it hovering in the dining-room, skulking in the parlor, hiding in the hall, lying in wait for me on the stairs.

It gets into my hair.

Even when I go to ride, if I turn my head suddenly and surprise it—there is that smell!

Such a peculiar odor, too! I have spent hours in trying to analyze it, to find what it smelled like.

It is not bad—at first, and very gentle, but quite the subtlest, most enduring odor I ever met.

In this damp weather it is awful, I wake up in the night and find it hanging over me.

It used to disturb me at first. I thought seriously of burning the house—to reach the smell.

But now I am used to it. The only thing I can think of that it is like is the *color* of the paper! A yellow smell.

There is a very funny mark on this wall, low down, near the mopboard. A streak that runs round the room. It goes behind every piece of furniture, except the bed, a long, straight, even *smooch*, as if it had been rubbed over and over.

I wonder how it was done and who did it, and what they did it for. Round and round and round—round and round and round—it makes me dizzy!

I really have discovered something at last.

Through watching so much at night, when it changes so, I have finally found out.

The front pattern *does* move—and no wonder! The woman behind shakes it!

Sometimes I think there are a great many women behind, and sometimes only one, and she crawls around fast, and her crawling shakes it all over.

Then in the very bright spots she keeps still, and in the very shady spots she just takes hold of the bars and shakes them hard.

And she is all the time trying to climb through. But nobody could climb through that pattern—it strangles so; I think that is why it has so many heads.

They get through, and then the pattern strangles them off and turns them upside down, and makes their eyes white!

If those heads were covered or taken off it would not be half so bad.

I think that woman gets out in the daytime!

And I'll tell you why—privately—I've seen her!

I can see her out of every one of my windows!

It is the same woman, I know, for she is always creeping, and most women do not creep by daylight.

I see her in that long shaded lane, creeping up and down. I see her in those dark grape arbors, creeping all around the garden.

I see her on that long road under the trees, creeping along, and when a carriage   200
comes she hides under the blackberry vines.

I don't blame her a bit. It must be very humiliating to be caught creeping by
daylight!

I always lock the door when I creep by daylight. I can't do it at night, for I
know John would suspect something at once.

And John is so queer now, that I don't want to irritate him. I wish he would
take another room! Besides, I don't want anybody to get that woman out at night
but myself.

I often wonder if I could see her out of all the windows at once.

But, turn as fast as I can, I can only see out of one at one time.   205

And though I always see her, she *may* be able to creep faster than I can turn!

I have watched her sometimes away off in the open country, creeping as fast
as a cloud shadow in a high wind.

If only that top pattern could be gotten off from the under one! I mean to try it,
little by little.

I have found out another funny thing, but I shan't tell it this time! It does not
do to trust people too much.

There are only two more days to get this paper off, and I believe John is begin-   210
ning to notice. I don't like the look in his eyes.

And I heard him ask Jennie a lot of professional questions about me. She had
a very good report to give.

She said I slept a good deal in the daytime.

John knows I don't sleep very well at night, for all I'm so quiet!

He asked me all sorts of questions, too, and pretended to be very loving and
kind.

As if I couldn't see through him!   215

Still, I don't wonder he acts so, sleeping under this paper for three months.

It only interests me, but I feel sure John and Jennie are secretly affected by it.

Hurrah! This is the last day, but it is enough. John to stay in town over night, and
won't be out until this evening.

Jennie wanted to sleep with me—the sly thing! but I told her I should undoubtedly rest better for a night all alone.

That was clever, for really I wasn't alone a bit! As soon as it was moonlight and   220
that poor thing began to crawl and shake the pattern, I got up and ran to help
her.

I pulled and she shook, I shook and she pulled, and before morning we had
peeled off yards of that paper.

A strip about as high as my head and half around the room.

And then when the sun came and that awful pattern began to laugh at me, I
declared I would finish it to-day!

We go away to-morrow, and they are moving all my furniture down again to
leave things as they were before.

225   Jennie looked at the wall in amazement, but I told her merrily that I did it out of pure spite at the vicious thing.

She laughed and said she wouldn't mind doing it herself, but I must not get tired.

How she betrayed herself that time!

But I am here, and no person touches this paper but me,—not *alive!*

She tried to get me out of the room—it was too patent! But I said it was so quiet and empty and clean now that I believed I would lie down again and sleep all I could; and not to wake me even for dinner—I would call when I woke.

230   So now she is gone, and the servants are gone, and the things are gone, and there is nothing left but that great bedstead nailed down, with the canvas mattress we found on it.

We shall sleep downstairs to-night, and take the boat home to-morrow.

I quite enjoy the room, now it is bare again.

How those children did tear about here!

This bedstead is fairly gnawed!

235   But I must get to work.

I have locked the door and thrown the key down into the front path.

I don't want to go out, and I don't want to have anybody come in, till John comes.

I want to astonish him.

I've got a rope up here that even Jennie did not find. If that woman does get out, and tries to get away, I can tie her!

240   But I forgot I could not reach far without anything to stand on!

This bed will *not* move!

I tried to lift and push it until I was lame, and then I got so angry I bit off a little piece at one corner—but it hurt my teeth.

Then I peeled off all the paper I could reach standing on the floor. It sticks horribly and the pattern just enjoys it! All those strangled heads and bulbous eyes and waddling fungus growths just shriek with derision!

I am getting angry enough to do something desperate. To jump out of the window would be admirable exercise, but the bars are too strong even to try.

245   Besides I wouldn't do it. Of course not. I know well enough that a step like that is improper and might be misconstrued.

I don't like to *look* out of the windows even—there are so many of those creeping women, and they creep so fast.

I wonder if they all come out of that wallpaper as I did?

But I am securely fastened now by my well-hidden rope—you don't get *me* out in the road there!

I suppose I shall have to get back behind the pattern when it comes night, and that is hard!

250   It is so pleasant to be out in this great room and creep around as I please!

I don't want to go outside. I won't, even if Jennie asks me to.

For outside you have to creep on the ground, and everything is green instead of yellow.

But here I can creep smoothly on the floor, and my shoulder just fits in that long smooch around the wall, so I cannot lose my way.

Why there's John at the door!

It is no use, young man, you can't open it!   255

How he does call and pound!

Now he's crying for an axe.

It would be a shame to break down that beautiful door!

"John dear!" said I in the gentlest voice, "the key is down by the front steps, under a plantain leaf!"

That silenced him for a few moments.   260

Then he said—very quietly indeed, "Open the door, my darling!"

"I can't," said I. "The key is down by the front door under a plantain leaf!"

And then I said it again, several times, very gently and slowly, and said it so often that he had to go and see, and he got it of course, and came in. He stopped short by the door.

"What is the matter?" he cried. "For God's sake, what are you doing!"

I kept on creeping just the same, but I looked at him over my shoulder.   265

"I've got out at last," said I, "in spite of you and Jane. And I've pulled off most of the paper, so you can't put me back!"

Now why should that man have fainted? But he did, and right across my path by the wall, so that I had to creep over him every time!

1892

D. H. LAWRENCE

Odour of Chrysanthemums

I

The small locomotive engine, Number 4, came clanking, stumbling down from Selston with seven full waggons. It appeared round the corner with loud threats of speed, but the colt that it startled from among the gorse, which still flickered indistinctly in the raw afternoon, outdistanced it at a canter. A woman, walking up the railway line to Underwood, drew back into the hedge, held her basket aside, and watched the footplate of the engine advancing. The trucks thumped heavily past, one by one, with slow inevitable movement, as she stood insignificantly trapped between the jolting black waggons and the hedge; then they curved away towards the coppice where the withered oak leaves dropped noiselessly, while the birds, pulling at the scarlet hips beside the track, made off into the dusk that had already crept into the spinney. In the open, the smoke from the engine sank and cleaved to the rough grass. The fields were dreary and forsaken, and in the marshy strip that led to the whimsey, a reedy pit-pond, the fowls had already abandoned their run among the alders, to roost in the tarred fowl-house. The pit-bank loomed up beyond the pond, flames like red sores lick-ing its ashy sides, in the afternoon's stagnant light. Just beyond rose the tapering chimneys and the clumsy black headstocks of Brinsley Colliery. The two wheels were spinning fast up against the sky, and the winding-engine rapped out its little spasms. The miners were being turned up.

The engine whistled as it came into the wide bay of railway lines beside the colliery, where rows of trucks stood in harbour.

Miners, single, trailing and in groups, passed like shadows diverging home. At the edge of the ribbed level of sidings squat a low cottage, three steps down from the cinder track. A large bony vine clutched at the house, as if to claw down the tiled roof. Round the bricked yard grew a few wintry primroses. Beyond, the long garden sloped down to a bush-covered brook course. There were some twiggy apple trees, winter-crack trees, and ragged cabbages. Beside the path hung dishev-elled pink chrysanthemums, like pink cloths hung on bushes. A woman came stooping out of the felt-covered fowl-house, half-way down the garden. She closed and padlocked the door, then drew herself erect, having brushed some bits from her white apron.

She was a tall woman of imperious mien, handsome, with definite black eye-brows. Her smooth black hair was parted exactly. For a few moments she stood steadily watching the miners as they passed along the railway: then she turned towards the brook course. Her face was calm and set, her mouth was closed with disillusionment. After a moment she called:

5   "John!" There was no answer. She waited, and then said distinctly:

"Where are you?"

"Here!" replied a child's sulky voice from among the bushes. The woman looked piercingly through the dusk.

"Are you at that brook?" she asked sternly.

For answer the child showed himself before the raspberry-canes that rose like whips. He was a small, sturdy boy of five. He stood quite still, defiantly.

10   "Oh!" said the mother, conciliated. "I thought you were down at that wet brook—and you remember what I told you—"

The boy did not move or answer.

"Come, come on in," she said more gently, "it's getting dark. There's your grandfather's engine coming down the line!"

The lad advanced slowly, with resentful, taciturn movement. He was dressed in trousers and waistcoat of cloth that was too thick and hard for the size of the garments. They were evidently cut down from a man's clothes.

As they went slowly towards the house he tore at the ragged wisps of chrysan-themums and dropped the petals in handfuls along the path.

15   "Don't do that—it does look nasty," said his mother. He refrained, and she, suddenly pitiful, broke off a twig with three or four wan flowers and held them against her face. When mother and son reached the yard her hand hesitated, and instead of laying the flower aside, she pushed it in her apron-band. The mother and son stood at the foot of the three steps looking across the bay of lines at the passing home of the miners. The trundle of the small train was imminent.

Suddenly the engine loomed past the house and came to a stop opposite the gate.

The engine-driver, a short man with round grey beard, leaned out of the cab high above the woman.

"Have you got a cup of tea?" he said in a cheery, hearty fashion.

It was her father. She went in, saying she would mash.[1] Directly, she returned.

"I didn't come to see you on Sunday," began the little grey-bearded man.

"I didn't expect you," said his daughter.

The engine-driver winced; then, reassuming his cheery, airy manner, he said: "Oh, have you heard then? Well, and what do you think——?"

"I think it is soon enough," she replied.

At her brief censure the little man made an impatient gesture, and said coaxingly, yet with dangerous coldness:

"Well, what's a man to do? It's no sort of life for a man of my years, to sit at my own hearth like a stranger. And if I'm going to marry again it may as well be soon as late—what does it matter to anybody?"

The woman did not reply, but turned and went into the house. The man in the engine-cab stood assertive, till she returned with a cup of tea and a piece of bread and butter on a plate. She went up the steps and stood near the footplate of the hissing engine.

"You needn't 'a' brought me bread an' butter," said her father. "But a cup of tea"—he sipped appreciatively—"it's very nice." He sipped for a moment or two, then: "I hear as Walter's got another bout on," he said.

"When hasn't he?" said the woman bitterly.

"I heered tell of him in the 'Lord Nelson'[2] braggin' as he was going to spend that b—— afore he went: half a sovereign[3] that was."

"When?" asked the woman.

"A' Sat'day night—I know that's true."

"Very likely," she laughed bitterly. "He gives me twenty-three shillings."

"Aye, it's a nice thing, when a man can do nothing with his money but make a beast of himself!" said the grey-whiskered man. The woman turned her head away. Her father swallowed the last of his tea and handed her the cup.

"Aye," he sighed, wiping his mouth. "It's a settler, it is——"

He put his hand on the lever. The little engine strained and groaned, and the train rumbled towards the crossing. The woman again looked across the metals. Darkness was settling over the spaces of the railway and trucks: the miners, in grey sombre groups, were still passing home. The winding-engine pulsed hurriedly, with brief pauses. Elizabeth Bates looked at the dreary flow of men, then she went indoors. Her husband did not come.

The kitchen was small and full of firelight; red coals piled glowing up the chimney mouth. All the life of the room seemed in the white, warm hearth and

1. Prepare (tea).   2. A public house, pub.   3. A sovereign was about half a week's wage; there are twenty shillings (see below) to the pound.

the steel fender reflecting the red fire. The cloth was laid for tea; cups glinted in the shadows. At the back, where the lowest stairs protruded into the room, the boy sat struggling with a knife and a piece of white wood. He was almost hidden in the shadow. It was half-past four. They had but to await the father's coming to begin tea. As the mother watched her son's sullen little struggle with the wood, she saw herself in his silence and pertinacity; she saw the father in her child's indifference to all but himself. She seemed to be occupied by her husband. He had probably gone past his home, slunk past his own door, to drink before he came in, while his dinner spoiled and wasted in waiting. She glanced at the clock, then took the potatoes to strain them in the yard. The garden and fields beyond the brook were closed in uncertain darkness. When she rose with the saucepan, leaving the drain steaming into the night behind her, she saw the yellow lamps were lit along the high road that went up the hill away beyond the space of the railway lines and the field.

Then again she watched the men trooping home, fewer now and fewer.

Indoors the fire was sinking and the room was dark red. The woman put her saucepan on the hob, and set a batter pudding near the mouth of the oven. Then she stood unmoving. Directly, gratefully, came quick young steps to the door. Someone hung on the latch a moment, then a little girl entered and began pulling off her outdoor things, dragging a mass of curls, just ripening from gold to brown, over her eyes with her hat.

Her mother chid her for coming late from school, and said she would have to keep her at home the dark winter days.

40   "Why, mother, it's hardly a bit dark yet. The lamp's not lighted, and my father's not home."

"No, he isn't. But it's a quarter to five! Did you see anything of him?"

The child became serious. She looked at her mother with large, wistful blue eyes.

"No, mother, I've never seen him. Why? Has he come up an' gone past, to Old Brinsley? He hasn't, mother, 'cos I never saw him."

"He'd watch that," said the mother bitterly, "he'd take care as you didn't see him. But you may depend upon it, he's seated in the 'Prince o' Wales.' He wouldn't be this late."

45   The girl looked at her mother piteously.

"Let's have our teas, mother, should we?" said she.

The mother called John to table. She opened the door once more and looked out across the darkness of the lines. All was deserted: she could not hear the winding-engines.

"Perhaps," she said to herself, "he's stopped to get some ripping[4] done."

They sat down to tea. John, at the end of the table near the door, was almost lost in the darkness. Their faces were hidden from each other. The girl crouched against the fender slowly moving a thick piece of bread before the fire. The lad, his face a dusky mark on the shadow, sat watching her who was transfigured in the red glow.

4. Coal-mining term for taking down the roof of an underground road in order to make it higher.

"I do think it's beautiful to look in the fire," said the child.   50

"Do you?" said her mother. "Why?"

"It's so red, and full of little caves—and it feels so nice, and you can fair smell it."

"It'll want mending directly," replied her mother, "and then if your father comes he'll carry on and say there never is a fire when a man comes home sweating from the pit.—A public-house is always warm enough."

There was silence till the boy said complainingly: "Make haste, our Annie."

"Well, I am doing! I can't make the fire do it no faster, can I?"   55

"She keeps wafflin'⁵ it about so's to make 'er slow," grumbled the boy.

"Don't have such an evil imagination, child," replied the mother.

Soon the room was busy in the darkness with the crisp sound of crunching. The mother ate very little. She drank her tea determinedly, and sat thinking. When she rose her anger was evident in the stern unbending of her head. She looked at the pudding in the fender, and broke out:

"It is a scandalous thing as a man can't even come home to his dinner! If it's crozzled⁶ up to a cinder I don't see why I should care. Past his very door he goes to get to a public-house, and here I sit with his dinner waiting for him——"

She went out. As she dropped piece after piece of coal on the red fire, the   60
shadows fell on the walls, till the room was almost in total darkness.

"I canna see," grumbled the invisible John. In spite of herself, the mother laughed.

"You know the way to your mouth," she said. She set the dustpan outside the door. When she came again like a shadow on the hearth, the lad repeated, complaining sulkily:

"I canna see."

"Good gracious!" cried the mother irritably, "you're as bad as your father if it's a bit dusk!"

Nevertheless she took a paper spill from a sheaf on the mantelpiece and pro-   65
ceeded to light the lamp that hung from the ceiling in the middle of the room. As she reached up, her figure displayed itself just rounding with maternity.

"Oh, mother——!" exclaimed the girl.

"What?" said the woman, suspended in the act of putting the lamp-glass over the flame. The copper reflector shone handsomely on her, as she stood with uplifted arm, turning to face her daughter:

"You've got a flower in your apron!" said the child, in a little rapture at this unusual event.

"Goodness me!" exclaimed the woman, relieved. "One would think the house was afire." She replaced the glass and waited a moment before turning up the wick. A pale shadow was seen floating vaguely on the floor.

"Let me smell!" said the child, still rapturously, coming forward and putting   70
her face to her mother's waist.

"Go along, silly!" said the mother, turning up the lamp. The light revealed their suspense so that the woman felt it almost unbearable. Annie was still bend-

5. Waving.   6. Shriveled.

ing at her waist. Irritably, the mother took the flowers out from her apron-band.

"Oh, mother—don't take them out!" Annie cried, catching her hand and trying to replace the sprig.

"Such nonsense!" said the mother, turning away. The child put the pale chrysanthemums to her lips, murmuring:

"Don't they smell beautiful!"

75 Her mother gave a short laugh.

"No," she said, "not to me. It was chrysanthemums when I married him, and chrysanthemums when you were born, and the first time they ever brought him home drunk, he'd got brown chrysanthemums in his button-hole."

She looked at the children. Their eyes and their parted lips were wondering. The mother sat rocking in silence for some time. Then she looked at the clock.

"Twenty minutes to six!" In a tone of fine bitter carelessness she continued: "Eh, he'll not come now till they bring him. There he'll stick! But he needn't come rolling in here in his pit-dirt, for *I* won't wash him. He can lie on the floor ——Eh, what a fool I've been, what a fool! And this is what I came here for, to this dirty hole, rats and all, for him to slink past his very door. Twice last week—he's begun now——"

She silenced herself, and rose to clear the table.

80 While for an hour or more the children played, subduedly intent, fertile of imagination, united in fear of the mother's wrath, and in dread of their father's home-coming, Mrs. Bates sat in her rocking-chair making a "singlet" of thick cream-coloured flannel, which gave a dull wounded sound as she tore off the grey edge. She worked at her sewing with energy, listening to the children, and her anger wearied itself, lay down to rest, opening its eyes from time to time and steadily watching, its ears raised to listen. Sometimes even her anger quailed and shrank, and the mother suspended her sewing, tracing the footsteps that thudded along the sleepers outside; she would lift her head sharply to bid the children "hush," but she recovered herself in time, and the footsteps went past the gate, and the children were not flung out of their playworld.

But at last Annie sighed, and gave in. She glanced at her waggon of slippers, and loathed the game. She turned plaintively to her mother.

"Mother!"—but she was inarticulate.

John crept out like a frog from under the sofa. His mother glanced up.

"Yes," she said, "just look at those shirtsleeves!"

85 The boy held them out to survey them, saying nothing. Then somebody called in a hoarse voice away down the line, and suspense bristled in the room, till two people had gone by outside, talking.

"It is time for bed," said the mother.

"My father hasn't come," wailed Annie plaintively. But her mother was primed with courage.

"Never mind. They'll bring him when he does come—like a log." She meant there would be no scene. "And he may sleep on the floor till he wakes himself. I know he'll not go to work tomorrow after this!"

The children had their hands and faces wiped with a flannel.[7] They were very quiet. When they had put on their nightdresses, they said their prayers, the boy mumbling. The mother looked down at them, at the brown silken bush of intertwining curls in the nape of the girl's neck, at the little black head of the lad, and her heart burst with anger at their father who caused all three such distress. The children hid their faces in her skirts for comfort.

When Mrs. Bates came down, the room was strangely empty, with a tension 90
of expectancy. She took up her sewing and stitched for some time without raising her head. Meantime her anger was tinged with fear.

      II

The clock struck eight and she rose suddenly, dropping her sewing on her chair. She went to the stairfoot door, opened it, listening. Then she went out, locking the door behind her.

Something scuffled in the yard, and she started though she knew it was only the rats with which the place was overrun. The night was very dark. In the great bay of railway lines, bulked with trucks, there was no trace of light, only away back she could see a few yellow lamps at the pit-top, and the red smear of the burning pit-bank on the night. She hurried along the edge of the track, then, crossing the converging lines, came to the stile by the white gates, whence she emerged on the road. Then the fear which had led her shrank. People were walking up to New Brinsley; she saw the lights in the houses; twenty yards further on were the broad windows of the "Prince of Wales," very warm and bright, and the loud voices of men could be heard distinctly. What a fool she had been to imagine that anything had happened to him! He was merely drinking over there at the "Prince of Wales." She faltered. She had never yet been to fetch him, and she never would go. So she continued her walk towards the long straggling line of houses, standing blank on the highway. She entered a passage between the dwellings.

"Mr. Rigley?—Yes! Did you want him? No, he's not in at this minute."

The raw-boned woman leaned forward from her dark scullery and peered at the other, upon whom fell a dim light through the blind of the kitchen window.

"Is it Mrs. Bates?" she asked in a tone tinged with respect. 95

"Yes. I wondered if your Master was at home. Mine hasn't come yet."

" 'Asn't 'e! Oh, Jack's been 'ome an 'ad 'is dinner an' gone out. 'E's just gone for 'alf an hour afore bedtime. Did you call at the 'Prince of Wales'?"

"No——"

"No, you didn't like——! It's not very nice." The other woman was indulgent. There was an awkward pause. "Jack never said nothink about—about your Mester," she said.

"No!—I expect he's stuck in there!" 100

Elizabeth Bates said this bitterly, and with recklessness. She knew that the

7. Washrag.

woman across the yard was standing at her door listening, but she did not care. As she turned:

"Stop a minute! I'll just go an' ask Jack if 'e knows anythink," said Mrs. Rigley.

"Oh, no—I wouldn't like to put—!"

"Yes, I will, if you will just step inside an' see as th' childer doesn't come downstairs and set theirselves afire."

Elizabeth Bates, murmuring a remonstrance, stepped inside. The other woman apologized for the state of the room.

The kitchen needed apology. There were little frocks and trousers and childish undergarments on the squab[8] and on the floor, and a litter of playthings every-where. On the black American cloth[9] of the table were pieces of bread and cake, crusts, slops, and a teapot with cold tea.

"Eh, ours is just as bad," said Elizabeth Bates, looking at the woman, not at the house. Mrs. Rigley put a shawl over her head and hurried out, saying:

"I shanna be a minute."

The other sat, noting with faint disapproval the general untidiness of the room. Then she fell to counting the shoes of various sizes scattered over the floor. There were twelve. She sighed and said to herself, "No wonder!"—glanc-ing at the litter. There came the scratching of two pairs of feet on the yard, and the Rigleys entered. Elizabeth Bates rose. Rigley was a big man, with very large bones. His head looked particularly bony. Across his temple was a blue scar, caused by a wound got in the pit, a wound in which the coal-dust remained blue like tattooing.

" 'Asna 'e come whoam yit?" asked the man, without any form of greeting, but with deference and sympathy. "I couldna say wheer he is—'e's non ower theer!"—he jerked his head to signify the "Prince of Wales."

" 'E's 'appen[1] gone up to th' 'Yew,' " said Mrs. Rigley.

There was another pause. Rigley had evidently something to get off his mind:

"Ah left 'im finishin' a stint," he began. "Loose-all[2] 'ad bin gone about ten minutes when we com'n away, an' I shouted, 'Are ter comin', Walt?' an' 'e said 'Go on, Ah shanna be but a 'ef a minnit,' so we com'n ter th' bottom, me an' Browers, thinkin' as 'e wor just behint, an' 'ud come up i' th' next bantle[3]——"

He stood perplexed, as if answering a charge of deserting his mate. Elizabeth Bates, now again certain of disaster, hastened to reassure him:

"I expect 'e's gone up to th' 'Yew Tree,' as you say. It's not the first time. I've fretted myself into a fever before now. He'll come home when they carry him."

"Ay, isn't it too bad!" deplored the other woman.

"I'll just step up to Dick's an' see if 'e *is* theer," offered the man, afraid of appearing alarmed, afraid of taking liberties.

"Oh, I wouldn't think of bothering you that far," said Elizabeth Bates, with emphasis, but he knew she was glad of his offer.

As they stumbled up the entry, Elizabeth Bates heard Rigley's wife run across

---

8. Sofa.   9. Enameled oilcloth.   1. Perhaps.   2. Signal to quit work and come to the surface.
3. An open seat or car of the lift or elevator that takes the miners to the surface.

the yard and open her neighbour's door. At this, suddenly all the blood in her body seemed to switch away from her heart.

"Mind!" warned Rigley. "Ah've said many a time as Ah'd fill up them ruts in this entry, sumb'dy 'll be breakin' their legs yit."

She recovered herself and walked quickly along with the miner.

"I don't like leaving the children in bed, and nobody in the house," she said.

"No, you dunna!" he replied courteously. They were soon at the gate of the cottage.

"Well, I shanna be many minnits. Dunna you be frettin' now, 'e'll be all right," said the butty.[4]

"Thank you very much, Mr. Rigley," she replied.

"You're welcome!" he stammered, moving away. "I shanna be many minnits."

The house was quiet. Elizabeth Bates took off her hat and shawl, and rolled back the rug. When she had finished, she sat down. It was a few minutes past nine. She was startled by the rapid chuff of the winding-engine at the pit, and the sharp whirr of the brakes on the rope as it descended. Again she felt the painful sweep of her blood, and she put her hand to her side, saying aloud, "Good gracious!—it's only the nine o'clock deputy going down," rebuking herself.

She sat still, listening. Half an hour of this, and she was wearied out.

"What am I working up like this for?" she said pitiably to herself, "I s'll only be doing myself some damage."

She took out her sewing again.

At a quarter to ten there were footsteps. One person! She watched for the door to open. It was an elderly woman, in a black bonnet and a black woollen shawl—his mother. She was about sixty years old, pale, with blue eyes, and her face all wrinkled and lamentable. She shut the door and turned to her daughter-in-law peevishly.

"Eh, Lizzie, whatever shall we do, whatever shall we do!" she cried.

Elizabeth drew back a little, sharply.

"What is it, mother?" she said.

The elder woman seated herself on the sofa.

"I don't know, child, I can't tell you!"—she shook her head slowly. Elizabeth sat watching her, anxious and vexed.

"I don't know," replied the grandmother, sighing very deeply. "There's no end to my troubles, there isn't. The things I've gone through, I'm sure it's enough——!" She wept without wiping her eyes, the tears running.

"But, mother," interrupted Elizabeth, "what do you mean? What is it?"

The grandmother slowly wiped her eyes. The fountains of her tears were stopped by Elizabeth's directness. She wiped her eyes slowly.

"Poor child! Eh, you poor thing!" she moaned. "I don't know what we're going to do, I don't—and you as you are—it's a thing, it is indeed!"

Elizabeth waited.

"Is he dead?" she asked, and at the words her heart swung violently, though she felt a slight flush of shame at the ultimate extravagance of the question. Her

---

4. Buddy, fellow worker.

words sufficiently frightened the old lady, almost brought her to herself.

"Don't say so, Elizabeth! We'll hope it's not as bad as that; no, may the Lord spare us that, Elizabeth. Jack Rigley came just as I was sittin' down to a glass afore going to bed, an' 'e said, ' 'Appen you'll go down th' line, Mrs. Bates. Walt's had an accident. 'Appen you'll go an' sit wi' 'er till we can get him home.' I hadn't time to ask him a word afore he was gone. An' I put my bonnet on an' come straight down, Lizzie. I thought to myself, 'Eh, that poor blessed child, if anybody should come an' tell her of a sudden, there's no knowin'; what'll 'appen to 'er.' You mustn't let it upset you, Lizzie—or you know what to expect. How long is it, six months—or is it five, Lizzie? Ay!"—the old woman shook her head—"time slips on, it slips on! Ay!"

Elizabeth's thoughts were busy elsewhere. If he was killed—would she be able to manage on the little pension and what she could earn?—she counted up rapidly. If he was hurt—they wouldn't take him to the hospital—how tiresome he would be to nurse!—but perhaps she'd be able to get him away from the drink and his hateful ways. She would—while he was ill. The tears offered to come to her eyes at the picture. But what sentimental luxury was this she was beginning?—She turned to consider the children. At any rate she was absolutely necessary for them. They were her business.

"Ay!" repeated the old woman, "it seems but a week or two since he brought me his first wages. Ay—he was a good lad, Elizabeth, he was, in his way. I don't know why he got to be such a trouble, I don't. He was a happy lad at home, only full of spirits. But there's no mistake he's been a handful of trouble, he has! I hope the Lord'll spare him to mend his ways. I hope so, I hope so. You've had a sight o' trouble with him, Elizabeth, you have indeed. But he was a jolly enough lad wi' me, he was, I can assure you. I don't know how it is. . . ."

The old woman continued to muse aloud, a monotonous irritating sound, while Elizabeth thought concentratedly, startled once, when she heard the winding-engine chuff quickly, and the brakes skirr with a shriek. Then she heard the engine more slowly, and the brakes made no sound. The old woman did not notice. Elizabeth waited in suspense. The mother-in-law talked, with lapses into silence.

"But he wasn't your son, Lizzie, an' it makes a difference. Whatever he was, I remember him when he was little, an' I learned to understand him and to make allowances. You've got to make allowances for them—"

It was half-past ten, and the old woman was saying: "But it's trouble from beginning to end; you're never too old for trouble, never too old for that——" when the gate banged back, and there were heavy feet on the steps.

"I'll go, Lizzie, let me go," cried the old woman, rising. But Elizabeth was at the door. It was a man in pit-clothes.

"They're bringin' 'im, Missis," he said. Elizabeth's heart halted a moment. Then it surged on again, almost suffocating her.

"Is he—is it bad?" she asked.

The man turned away, looking at the darkness:

"The doctor says 'e'd been dead hours. 'E saw 'im i' th' lamp-cabin."

The old woman, who stood just behind Elizabeth, dropped into a chair and folded her hands, crying: "Oh, my boy, my boy!"

"Hush!" said Elizabeth, with a sharp twitch of a frown. "Be still, mother, don't   155
waken th' children: I wouldn't have them down for anything!"

The old woman moaned softly, rocking herself. The man was drawing away. Elizabeth took a step forward.

"How was it?" she asked.

"Well, I couldn't say for sure," the man replied, very ill at ease. " 'E wor finishin' a stint an' th' butties 'ad gone, an' a lot o' stuff come down atop 'n 'im."

"And crushed him?" cried the widow, with a shudder.

"No," said the man, "it fell at th' back of 'im. 'E wor under th' face, an' it niver   160
touched 'im. It shut 'im in. It seems 'e wor smothered."

Elizabeth shrank back. She heard the old woman behind her cry:

"What?—what did 'e say it was?"

The man replied, more loudly: "'E wor smothered!"

Then the old woman wailed aloud, and this relieved Elizabeth.

"Oh, mother," she said, putting her hands on the old woman, "don't waken   165
th' children, don't waken th' children."

She wept a little, unknowing, while the old mother rocked herself and moaned. Elizabeth remembered that they were bringing him home, and she must be ready. "They'll lay him in the parlour," she said to herself, standing a moment pale and perplexed.

Then she lighted a candle and went into the tiny room. The air was cold and damp, but she could not make a fire, there was no fireplace. She set down the candle and looked round. The candlelight glittered on the lustre-glasses,[5] on the two vases that held some of the pink chrysanthemums, and on the dark mahogany. There was a cold, deathly smell of chrysanthemums in the room. Elizabeth stood looking at the flowers. She turned away, and calculated whether there would be room to lay him on the floor, between the couch and the chiffonier. She pushed the chairs aside. There would be room to lay him down and to step round him. Then she fetched the old red tablecloth, and another old cloth, spreading them down to save her bit of carpet. She shivered on leaving the parlour; so, from the dresser-drawer she took a clean shirt and put it at the fire to air. All the time her mother-in-law was rocking herself in the chair and moaning.

"You'll have to move from there, mother," said Elizabeth. "They'll be bringing him in. Come in the rocker."

The old mother rose mechanically, and seated herself by the fire, continuing to lament. Elizabeth went into the pantry for another candle, and there, in the little penthouse[6] under the naked tiles, she heard them coming. She stood still in the pantry doorway, listening. She heard them pass the end of the house, and come awkwardly down the three steps, a jumble of shuffling footsteps and mut-

5. Glass pendants around the edge of an ornamental vase.   6. Structure, usually with a sloping roof, attached to a house.

tering voices. The old woman was silent. The men were in the yard.

170   Then Elizabeth heard Matthews, the manager of the pit, say: "You go in first, Jim. Mind!"

The door came open, and the two women saw a collier backing into the room, holding one end of a stretcher, on which they could see the nailed pitboots of the dead man. The two carriers halted, the man at the head stooping to the lintel of the door.

"Wheer will you have him?" asked the manager, a short, white-bearded man.

Elizabeth roused herself and came from the pantry carrying the unlighted candle.

"In the parlour," she said.

175   "In there, Jim!" pointed the manager, and the carriers backed round into the tiny room. The coat with which they had covered the body fell off as they awkwardly turned through the two doorways, and the women saw their man, naked to the waist, lying stripped for work. The old woman began to moan in a low voice of horror.

"Lay th' stretcher at th' side," snapped the manager, "an' put 'im on th' cloths. Mind now, mind! Look you now——!"

One of the men had knocked off a vase of chrysanthemums. He stared awkwardly, then they set down the stretcher. Elizabeth did not look at her husband. As soon as she could get in the room, she went and picked up the broken vase and the flowers.

"Wait a minute!" she said.

The three men waited in silence while she mopped up the water with a duster.

180   "Eh, what a job, what a job, to be sure!" the manager was saying, rubbing his brow with trouble and perplexity. "Never knew such a thing in my life, never! He'd no business to ha' been left. I never knew such a thing in my life! Fell over him clean as a whistle, an' shut him in. Not four foot of space, there wasn't—yet it scarce bruised him."

He looked down at the dead man, lying prone, half naked, all grimed with coal-dust.

" ' 'Sphyxiated,' the doctor said. It *is* the most terrible job I've ever known. Seems as if it was done o' purpose. Clean over him, an' shut 'im in, like a mousetrap"—he made a sharp, descending gesture with his hand.

The colliers standing by jerked aside their heads in hopeless comment.

The horror of the thing bristled upon them all.

185   Then they heard the girl's voice upstairs calling shrilly: "Mother, mother—who is it? Mother, who is it?"

Elizabeth hurried to the foot of the stairs and opened the door:

"Go to sleep!" she commanded sharply. "What are you shouting about? Go to sleep at once—there's nothing——"

Then she began to mount the stairs. They could hear her on the boards, and on the plaster floor of the little bedroom. They could hear her distinctly:

"What's the matter now?—what's the matter with you, silly thing?"—her voice was much agitated, with an unreal gentleness.

"I thought it was some men come," said the plaintive voice of the child. "Has   190
he come?"

"Yes, they've brought him. There's nothing to make a fuss about. Go to sleep
now, like a good child."

They could hear her voice in the bedroom, they waited whilst she covered the
children under the bedclothes.

"Is he drunk?" asked the girl, timidly, faintly.

"No! No—he's not! He's—he's asleep."

"Is he asleep downstairs?"   195

"Yes—and don't make a noise."

There was silence for a moment, then the men heard the frightened child
again:

"What's that noise?"

"It's nothing, I tell you, what are you bothering for?"

The noise was the grandmother moaning. She was oblivious of everything,   200
sitting on her chair rocking and moaning. The manager put his hand on her arm
and bade her "Sh-sh!!"

The old woman opened her eyes and looked at him. She was shocked by this
interruption, and seemed to wonder.

"What time is it?"—the plaintive thin voice of the child, sinking back unhappily into sleep, asked this last question.

"Ten o'clock," answered the mother more softly. Then she must have bent
down and kissed the children.

Matthews beckoned to the men to come away. They put on their caps, and
took up the stretcher. Stepping over the body, they tiptoed out of the house. None
of them spoke till they were far from the wakeful children.

When Elizabeth came down she found her mother alone on the parlour floor,   205
leaning over the dead man, the tears dropping on him.

"We must lay him out," the wife said. She put on the kettle, then returning
knelt at the feet, and began to unfasten the knotted leather laces. The room was
clammy and dim with only one candle, so that she had to bend her face almost
to the floor. At last she got off the heavy boots and put them away.

"You must help me now," she whispered to the old woman. Together they
stripped the man.

When they arose, saw him lying in the naïve dignity of death, the women
stood arrested in fear and respect. For a few moments they remained still, looking
down, the old mother whimpering. Elizabeth felt countermanded. She saw him,
how utterly inviolable he lay in himself. She had nothing to do with him. She
could not accept it. Stooping, she laid her hand on him, in claim. He was still
warm, for the mine was hot where he had died. His mother had his face between
her hands, and was murmuring incoherently. The old tears fell in succession as
drops from wet leaves; the mother was not weeping, merely her tears flowed.
Elizabeth embraced the body of her husband, with cheek and lips. She seemed to
be listening, inquiring, trying to get some connection. But she could not. She was
driven away. He was impregnable.

She rose, went into the kitchen, where she poured warm water into a bowl, brought soap and flannel and a soft towel.

210   "I must wash him," she said.

Then the old mother rose stiffly, and watched Elizabeth as she carefully washed his face, carefully brushing the big blonde moustache from his mouth with the flannel. She was afraid with a bottomless fear, so she ministered to him. The old woman, jealous, said:

"Let me wipe him!"—and she kneeled on the other side drying slowly as Elizabeth washed, her big black bonnet sometimes brushing the dark head of her daughter. They worked thus in silence for a long time. They never forgot it was death, and the touch of the man's dead body gave them strange emotions, different in each of the women; a great dread possessed them both, the mother felt the lie was given to her womb, she was denied; the wife felt the utter isolation of the human soul, the child within her was a weight apart from her.

At last it was finished. He was a man of handsome body, and his face showed no traces of drink. He was blonde, full-fleshed, with fine limbs. But he was dead.

"Bless him," whispered his mother, looking always at his face, and speaking out of sheer terror. "Dear lad—bless him!" She spoke in a faint sibilant ecstasy of fear and mother love.

215   Elizabeth sank down again to the floor, and put her face against his neck, and trembled and shuddered. But she had to draw away again. He was dead, and her living flesh had no place against his. A great dread and weariness held her: she was so unavailing. Her life was gone like this.

"White as milk he is, clear as a twelve-month baby, bless him, the darling!" the old mother murmured to herself. "Not a mark on him, clear and clean and white, beautiful as ever a child was made," she murmured with pride. Elizabeth kept her face hidden.

"He went peaceful, Lizzie—peaceful as sleep. Isn't he beautiful, the lamb? Ay— he must ha' made his peace, Lizzie. 'Appen he made it all right, Lizzie, shut in there. He'd have time. He wouldn't look like this if he hadn't made his peace. The lamb, the dear lamb. Eh, but he had a hearty laugh. I loved to hear it. He had the heartiest laugh, Lizzie, as a lad——"

Elizabeth looked up. The man's mouth was fallen back, slightly open under the cover of the moustache. The eyes, half shut, did not show glazed in the obscurity. Life with its smoky burning gone from him, had left him apart and utterly alien to her. And she knew what a stranger he was to her. In her womb was ice of fear, because of this separate stranger with whom she had been living as one flesh. Was this what it all meant—utter, intact separateness, obscured by heat of living? In dread she turned her face away. The fact was too deadly. There had been nothing between them, and yet they had come together, exchanging their nakedness repeatedly. Each time he had taken her, they had been two isolated beings, far apart as now. He was no more responsible than she. The child was like ice in her womb. For as she looked at the dead man, her mind, cold and detached, said clearly: "Who am I? What have I been doing? I have been fighting a husband who did not exist. *He* existed all the time. What wrong have I done? What was that I have been living with? There lies the reality, this man."—And her soul died in her for fear: she knew she had never seen him, he had never seen her, they had met in the dark and had fought in the dark, not knowing whom they met nor whom they fought. And now she saw, and turned silent in seeing. For she had been wrong. She had said he was something he was not; she had felt familiar with him. Whereas he was apart all the while, living as she never lived, feeling as she never felt.

In fear and shame she looked at his naked body, that she had known falsely. And he was the father of her children. Her soul was torn from her body and stood apart. She looked at his naked body and was ashamed, as if she had denied it. After all, it was itself. It seemed awful to her. She looked at his face, and she turned her own face to the wall. For his look was other than hers, his way was not her way. She had denied him what he was—she saw it now. She had refused him as himself.—And this had been her life, and his life.—She was grateful to death, which restored the truth. And she knew she was not dead.

And all the while her heart was bursting with grief and pity for him. What had he suffered? What stretch of horror for this helpless man! She was rigid with agony. She had not been able to help him. He had been cruelly injured, this naked man, this other being, and she could make no reparation. There were the children—but the children belonged to life. This dead man had nothing to do with them. He and she were only channels through which life had flowed to issue in the children. She was a mother—but how awful she knew it now to have been a wife. And he, dead now, how awful he must have felt it to be a husband. She felt that in her next world he would be a stranger to her. If they met there, in the beyond, they would only be ashamed of what had been before. The children had come, for some mysterious reason, out of both of them. But the children did not unite them. Now he was dead, she knew how eternally he was apart from her, how eternally he had nothing more to do with her. She saw this episode of her life closed. They had denied each other in life. Now he had withdrawn. An anguish came over her. It was finished then: it had become hopeless between them long before he died. Yet he had been her husband. But how little!

"Have you got his shirt, 'Lizabeth?"

Elizabeth turned without answering, though she strove to weep and behave as her mother-in-law expected. But she could not, she was silenced. She went into the kitchen and returned with the garment.

"It is aired," she said, grasping the cotton shirt here and there to try. She was almost ashamed to handle him; what right had she or anyone to lay hands on him; but her touch was humble on his body. It was hard work to clothe him. He was so heavy and inert. A terrible dread gripped her all the while: that he could be so heavy and utterly inert, unresponsive, apart. The horror of the distance between them was almost too much for her—it was so infinite a gap she must look across.

At last it was finished. They covered him with a sheet and left him lying, with his face bound. And she fastened the door of the little parlour, lest the children should see what was lying there. Then, with peace sunk heavy on her heart, she went about making tidy the kitchen. She knew she submitted to life, which was her immediate master. But from death, her ultimate master, she winced with fear and shame.

1914

KATHERINE ANNE PORTER

Flowering Judas

Braggioni sits heaped upon the edge of a straight-backed chair much too small for him, and sings to Laura in a furry, mournful voice. Laura has begun to find reasons for avoiding her own house until the latest possible moment, for Braggioni is there almost every night. No matter how late she is, he will be sitting there with a surly, waiting expression, pulling at his kinky yellow hair, thumbing the strings of his guitar, snarling a tune under his breath. Lupe the Indian maid meets Laura at the door, and says with a flicker of a glance towards the upper room, "He waits."

Laura wishes to lie down, she is tired of her hairpins and the feel of her long tight sleeves, but she says to him, "Have you a new song for me this evening?" If he says yes, she asks him to sing it. If he says no, she remembers his favorite one, and asks him to sing it again. Lupe brings her a cup of chocolate and a plate of rice, and Laura eats at the small table under the lamp, first inviting Braggioni, whose answer is always the same: "I have eaten, and besides, chocolate thickens the voice."

Laura says, "Sing, then," and Braggioni heaves himself into song. He scratches the guitar familiarly as though it were a pet animal, and sings passionately off key, taking the high notes in a prolonged painful squeal. Laura, who haunts the markets listening to the ballad singers, and stops every day to hear the blind boy playing his reed-flute in Sixteenth of September Street,[1] listens to Braggioni with pitiless courtesy, because she dares not smile at his miserable performance. Nobody dares to smile at him. Braggioni is cruel to everyone, with a kind of specialized insolence, but he is so vain of his talents, and so sensitive to slights, it would require a cruelty and vanity greater than his own to lay a finger on the vast cureless wound of his self-esteem. It would require courage, too, for it is dangerous to offend him, and nobody has this courage.

Braggioni loves himself with such tenderness and amplitude and eternal charity that his followers—for he is a leader of men, a skilled revolutionist, and his skin had been punctured in honorable warfare—warm themselves in the reflected glow, and say to each other: "He has a real nobility, a love of humanity raised above mere personal affections." The excess of this self-love has flowed out, inconveniently for her, over Laura, who, with so many others, owes her comfortable

---

1. Street in Morelia, a city in western Mexico.

situation and her salary to him. When he is in a very good humor, he tells her, "I am tempted to forgive you for being a *gringa. Gringita!*"[2] and Laura, burning, imagines herself leaning forward suddenly, and with a sound back-handed slap wiping the suety smile from his face. If he notices her eyes at these moments he gives no sign.

She knows what Braggioni would offer her, and she must resist tenaciously   5 without appearing to resist, and if she could avoid it she would not admit even to herself the slow drift of his intention. During these long evenings which have spoiled a long month for her, she sits in her deep chair with an open book on her knees, resting her eyes on the consoling rigidity of the printed page when the sight and sound of Braggioni singing threaten to identify themselves with all her remembered afflictions and to add their weight to her uneasy premonitions of the future. The gluttonous bulk of Braggioni has become a symbol of her many disillusions, for a revolutionist should be lean, animated by heroic faith, a vessel of abstract virtues. This is nonsense, she knows it now and is ashamed of it. Revolution must have leaders, and leadership is a career for energetic men. She is, her comrades tell her, full of romantic error, for what she defines as cynicism in them is merely "a developed sense of reality." She is almost too willing to say, "I am wrong, I suppose I don't really understand the principles," and afterward she makes a secret truce with herself, determined not to surrender her will to such expedient logic. But she cannot help feeling that she has been betrayed irreparably by the disunion between her way of living and her feeling of what life should be, and at times she is almost contented to rest in this sense of grievance as a private store of consolation. Sometimes she wishes to run away, but she stays. Now she longs to fly out of this room, down the narrow stairs, and into the street where the houses lean together like conspirators under a single mottled lamp, and leave Braggioni singing to himself.

Instead she looks at Braggioni, frankly and clearly, like a good child who understands the rules of behavior. Her knees cling together under sound blue serge, and her round white collar is not purposely nun-like. She wears the uniform of an idea, and has renounced vanities. She was born Roman Catholic, and in spite of her fear of being seen by someone who might make a scandal of it, she slips now and again into some crumbling little church, kneels on the chilly stone, and says a Hail Mary on the gold rosary she bought in Tehuantepec. It is no good and she ends by examining the altar with its tinsel flowers and ragged brocades, and feels tender about the battered doll-shape of some male saint whose white, lace-trimmed drawers hang limply around his ankles below the hieratic dignity of his velvet robe. She has encased herself in a set of principles derived from her early training, leaving no detail of gesture or of personal taste untouched, and for this reason she will not wear lace made on machines. This is her private heresy, for in her special group the machine is sacred, and will be the salvation of the workers. She loves fine lace, and there is a tiny edge of fluted cobweb on this collar, which is one of twenty precisely alike, folded in blue tissue paper in the upper drawer of her clothes chest.

2. Diminutive of *gringa:* non-Mexican woman, used pejoratively.

Braggioni catches her glance solidly as if he had been waiting for it, leans forward, balancing his paunch between his spread knees, and sings with tremendous emphasis, weighing his words. He has, the song relates, no father and no mother, nor even a friend to console him; lonely as a wave of the sea he comes and goes, lonely as a wave. His mouth opens round and yearns sideways, his balloon cheeks grow oily with the labor of song. He bulges marvelously in his expensive garments. Over his lavender collar, crushed upon a purple necktie, held by a diamond hoop: over his ammunition belt of tooled leather worked in silver, buckled cruelly around his gasping middle: over the tops of his glossy yellow shoes Braggioni swells with ominous ripeness, his mauve silk hose stretched taut, his ankles bound with the stout leather thongs of his shoes.

When he stretches his eyelids at Laura she notes again that his eyes are the true tawny yellow cat's eyes. He is rich, not in money, he tells her, but in power, and this power brings with it the blameless ownership of things, and the right to indulge his love of small luxuries. "I have a taste for the elegant refinements," he said once, flourishing a yellow silk handkerchief before her nose. "Smell that? It is Jockey Club, imported from New York." Nonetheless he is wounded by life. He will say so presently. "It is true everything turns to dust in the hand, to gall on the tongue." He sighs and his leather belt creaks like a saddle girth. "I am disappointed in everything as it comes. Everything." He shakes his head. "You, poor thing, you will be disappointed too. You are born for it. We are more alike than you realize in some things. Wait and see. Some day you will remember what I have told you, you will know that Braggioni was your friend."

Laura feels a slow chill, a purely physical sense of danger, a warning in her blood that violence, mutilation, a shocking death, wait for her with lessening patience. She has translated this fear into something homely, immediate, and sometimes hesitates before crossing the street. "My personal fate is nothing, except as the testimony of a mental attitude," she reminds herself, quoting from some forgotten philosophic primer, and is sensible enough to add, "Anyhow, I shall not be killed by an automobile if I can help it."

10   "It may be true I am as corrupt, in another way, as Braggioni," she thinks in spite of herself, "as callous, as incomplete," and if this is so, any kind of death seems preferable. Still she sits quietly, she does not run. Where could she go? Uninvited she has promised herself to this place; she can no longer imagine herself as living in another country, and there is no pleasure in remembering her life before she came here.

Precisely what is the nature of this devotion, its true motives, and what are its obligations? Laura cannot say. She spends part of her days in Xochimilco, near by, teaching Indian children to say in English, "The cat is on the mat." When she appears in the classroom they crowd about her with smiles on their wise, innocent, clay-colored faces, crying. "Good morning, my titcher!" in immaculate voices, and they make of her desk a fresh garden of flowers every day.

During her leisure she goes to union meetings and listens to busy important voices quarreling over tactics, methods, internal politics. She visits the prisoners of her own political faith in their cells, where they entertain themselves with counting cockroaches, repenting of their indiscretions, composing their memoirs, writing out manifestoes and plans for their comrades who are still walking about free, hands in pockets, sniffing fresh air. Laura brings them food and cigarettes and a little money, and she brings messages disguised in equivocal phrases from the men outside who dare not set foot in the prison for fear of disappearing into the cells kept empty for them. If the prisoners confuse night and day, and complain, "Dear little Laura, time doesn't pass in this infernal hole, and I won't know when it is time to sleep unless I have a reminder," she brings them their favorite narcotics, and says in a tone that does not wound them with pity, "Tonight will really be night for you," and though her Spanish amuses them, they find her comforting, useful. If they lose patience and all faith, and curse the slowness of their friends in coming to their rescue with money and influence, they trust her not to repeat everything, and if she inquires, "Where do you think we can find money, or influence?" they are certain to answer, "Well, there is Braggioni, why doesn't he do something?"

She smuggles letters from headquarters to men hiding from firing squads in back streets in mildewed houses, where they sit in tumbled beds and talk bitterly as if all Mexico were at their heels, when Laura knows positively they might appear at the band concert in the Alameda on Sunday morning, and no one would notice them. But Braggioni says, "Let them sweat a little. The next time they may be careful. It is very restful to have them out of the way for a while." She is not afraid to knock on any door in any street after midnight, and enter in the darkness, and say to one of these men who is really in danger: "They will be looking for you—seriously—tomorrow morning after six. Here is some money from Vicente. Go to Vera Cruz and wait."

She borrows money from the Roumanian agitator to give to his bitter enemy the Polish agitator. The favor of Braggioni is their disputed territory, and Braggioni holds the balance nicely, for he can use them both. The Polish agitator talks love to her over café tables, hoping to exploit what he believes is her secret sentimental preference for him, and he gives her misinformation which he begs her to repeat as the solemn truth to certain persons. The Roumanian is more adroit. He is generous with his money in all good causes, and lies to her with an air of ingenuous candor, as if he were her good friend and confidant. She never repeats anything they may say. Braggioni never asks questions. He has other ways to discover all that he wishes to know about them.

Nobody touches her, but all praise her gray eyes, and the soft, round under lip which promises gayety, yet is always grave, nearly always firmly closed: and they cannot understand why she is in Mexico. She walks back and forth on her errands, with puzzled eyebrows, carrying her little folder of drawings and music and school papers. No dancer dances more beautifully than Laura walks, and she inspires some amusing, unexpected ardors, which cause little gossip, because nothing comes of them. A young captain who had been a soldier in Zapata's[3] army attempted, during a horseback ride near Cuernavaca, to express his desire for her with the noble simplicity befitting a rude folk-hero: but gently, because he was gentle. This gentleness was his defeat, for when he alighted, and removed her

15

3. Emiliano Zapata (1879–1919), Mexican peasant-revolutionary general.

foot from the stirrup, and essayed to draw her down into his arms, her horse, ordinarily a tame one, shied fiercely, reared and plunged away. The young hero's horse careered blindly after his stable-mate, and the hero did not return to the hotel until rather late that evening. At breakfast he came to her table in full charro[4] dress, gray buckskin jacket and trousers with strings of silver buttons down the leg, and he was in a humorous, careless mood. "May I sit with you?" and "You are a wonderful rider. I was terrified that you might be thrown and dragged. I should never have forgiven myself. But I cannot admire you enough for your riding!"

"I learned to ride in Arizona," said Laura.

"If you will ride with me again this morning, I promise you a horse that will not shy with you," he said. But Laura remembered that she must return to Mexico City at noon.

Next morning the children made a celebration and spent their playtime writing on the blackboard, "We lov ar ticher," and with tinted chalks they drew wreaths of flowers around the words. The young hero wrote her a letter: "I am a very foolish, wasteful, impulsive man. I should have first said I love you, and then you would not have run away. But you shall see me again." Laura thought, "I must send him a box of colored crayons," but she was trying to forgive herself for having spurred her horse at the wrong moment.

A brown, shock-haired youth came and stood in her patio one night and sang like a lost soul for two hours, but Laura could think of nothing to do about it. The moonlight spread a wash of gauzy silver over the clear spaces of the garden, and the shadows were cobalt blue. The scarlet blossoms of the Judas tree were dull purple, and the names of the colors repeated themselves automatically in her mind, while she watched not the boy, but his shadow, fallen like a dark garment across the fountain rim, trailing in the water. Lupe came silently and whispered expert counsel in her ear: "If you will throw him one little flower, he will sing another song or two and go away." Laura threw the flower, and he sang a last song and went away with the flower tucked in the band of his hat. Lupe said, "He is one of the organizers of the Typographers Union, and before that he sold corridos[5] in the Merced market, and before that, he came from Guanajuato, where I was born. I would not trust any man, but I trust least those from Guanajuato."

20 She did not tell Laura that he would be back again the next night, and the next, nor that he would follow her at a certain fixed distance around the Merced market, through the Zócalo, up Francisco I. Madero Avenue, and so along the Paseo de la Reforma to that Chapultepec Park, and into the Philosopher's Footpath, still with that flower withering in his hat, and an indivisible attention in his eyes.

Now Laura is accustomed to him, it means nothing except that he is nineteen years old and is observing a convention with all propriety, as though it were founded on a law of nature, which in the end it might well prove to be. He is beginning to write poems which he prints on a wooden press, and he leaves them stuck like handbills in her door. She is pleasantly disturbed by the abstract, un-

---

4. Costume worn by peasant horsemen of special status.   5. Popular ballads.

hurried watchfulness of his black eyes which will in time turn easily towards another object. She tells herself that throwing the flower was a mistake, for she is twenty-two years old and knows better; but she refuses to regret it, and persuades herself that her negation of all external events as they occur is a sign that she is gradually perfecting herself in the stoicism she strives to cultivate against that disaster she fears, though she cannot name it.

She is not at home in the world. Every day she teaches children who remain strangers to her, though she loves their tender round hands and their charming opportunist savagery. She knocks at unfamiliar doors not knowing whether a friend or a stranger shall answer, and even if a known face emerges from the sour gloom of that unknown interior, still it is the face of a stranger. No matter what this stranger says to her, nor what her message to him, the very cells of her flesh reject knowledge and kinship in one monotonous word. No. No. No. She draws her strength from this one holy talismanic word which does not suffer her to be led into evil. Denying everything, she may walk anywhere in safety, she looks at everything without amazement.

No, repeats this firm unchanging voice of her blood; and she looks at Braggioni without amazement. He is a great man, he wishes to impress this simple girl who covers her great round breasts with thick dark cloth, and who hides long, invaluably beautiful legs under a heavy skirt. She is almost thin except for the incomprehensible fullness of her breasts, like a nursing mother's, and Braggioni, who considers himself a judge of women, speculates again on the puzzle of her notorious virginity, and takes the liberty of speech which she permits without a sign of modesty, indeed, without any sort of sign, which is disconcerting.

"You think you are so cold, *gringita!* Wait and see. You will surprise yourself some day! May I be there to advise you!" He stretches his eyelids at her, and his ill-humored cat's eyes waver in a separate glance for the two points of light marking the opposite ends of a smoothly drawn path between the swollen curve of her breasts. He is not put off by that blue serge, nor by her resolutely fixed gaze. There is all the time in the world. His cheeks are bellying with the wind of song. "O girl with the dark eyes," he sings, and reconsiders. "But yours are not dark. I can change all that. O girl with the green eyes, you have stolen my heart away!" then his mind wanders to the song, and Laura feels the weight of his attention being shifted elsewhere. Singing thus, he seems harmless, he is quite harmless, there is nothing to do but sit patiently and say "No," when the moment comes. She draws a full breath, and her mind wanders also, but not far. She dares not wander too far.

Not for nothing has Braggioni taken pains to be a good revolutionist and a   25
professional lover of humanity. He will never die of it. He has the malice, the cleverness, the wickedness, the sharpness of wit, the hardness of heart, stipulated for loving the world profitably. *He will never die of it.* He will live to see himself kicked out from his feeding trough by other hungry world-saviors. Traditionally he must sing in spite of his life which drives him to bloodshed, he tells Laura, for his father was a Tuscany[6] peasant who drifted to Yucatan and married a Maya

6. Region in northern Italy.

woman: a woman of race, an aristocrat. They gave him the love and knowledge of music, thus: and under the rip of his thumbnail, the strings of the instrument complain like exposed nerves.

Once he was called Delgadito by all the girls and married women who ran after him; he was so scrawny all his bones showed under his thin cotton clothing, and he could squeeze his emptiness to the very backbone with his two hands. He was a poet and the revolution was only a dream then; too many women loved him and sapped away his youth, and he could never find enough to eat anywhere, anywhere! Now he is a leader of men, crafty men who whisper in his ear, hungry men who wait for hours outside his office for a word with him, emaciated men with wild faces who waylay him at the street gate with a timid, "Comrade, let me tell you . . ." and they blow the foul breath from their empty stomachs in his face.

He is always sympathetic. He gives them handfuls of small coins from his own pocket, he promises them work, there will be demonstrations, they must join the unions and attend the meetings, above all they must be on the watch for spies. They are closer to him than his own brothers, without them he can do nothing— until tomorrow, comrade!

Until tomorrow. "They are stupid, they are lazy, they are treacherous, they would cut my throat for nothing," he says to Laura. He has good food and abundant drink, he hires an automobile and drives in the Paseo on Sunday morning, and enjoys plenty of sleep in a soft bed beside a wife who dares not disturb him; and he sits pampering his bones in easy billows of fat, singing to Laura, who knows and thinks these things about him. When he was fifteen, he tried to drown himself because he loved a girl, his first love, and she laughed at him. "A thousand women have paid for that," and his tight little mouth turns down at the corners. Now he perfumes his hair with Jockey Club, and confides to Laura: "One woman is really as good as another for me, in the dark. I prefer them all."

His wife organizes unions among the girls in the cigarette factories, and walks in picket lines, and even speaks at meetings in the evening. But she cannot be brought to acknowledge the benefits of true liberty. "I tell her I must have my freedom, net. She does not understand my point of view." Laura has heard this many times. Braggioni scratches the guitar and meditates. "She is an instinctively virtuous woman, pure gold, no doubt of that. If she were not, I should lock her up, and she knows it."

30   His wife, who works so hard for the good of the factory girls, employs part of her leisure lying on the floor weeping because there are so many women in the world, and only one husband for her, and she never knows where nor when to look for him. He told her: "Unless you can learn to cry when I am not here, I must go away for good." That day he went away and took a room at the Hotel Madrid.

It is this month of separation for the sake of higher principles that has been spoiled not only for Mrs. Braggioni, whose sense of reality is beyond criticism, but for Laura, who feels herself bogged in a nightmare. Tonight Laura envies Mrs. Braggioni, who is alone, and free to weep as much as she pleases about a concrete wrong. Laura has just come from a visit to the prison, and she is waiting for tomorrow with a bitter anxiety as if tomorrow may not come, but time may be caught immovably in this hour, with herself transfixed, Braggioni singing on forever, and Eugenio's body not yet discovered by the guard.

Braggioni says: "Are you going to sleep?" Almost before she can shake her head, he begins telling her about the May-day disturbances coming on in Morelia, for the Catholics hold a festival in honor of the Blessed Virgin, and the Socialists celebrate their martyrs on that day. "There will be two independent processions, starting from either end of town, and they will march until they meet, and the rest depends . . ." He asks her to oil and load his pistols. Standing up, he unbuckles his ammunition belt, and spreads it laden across her knees. Laura sits with the shells slipping through the cleaning cloth dipped in oil, and he says again he cannot understand why she works so hard for the revolutionary idea unless she loves some man who is in it. "Are you not in love with someone?" "No," says Laura. "And no one is in love with you?" "No." "Then it is your own fault. No woman need go begging. Why, what is the matter with you? The legless beggar woman in the Alameda has a perfectly faithful lover. Did you know that?"

Laura peers down the pistol barrel and says nothing, but a long, slow faintness rises and subsides in her; Braggioni curves his swollen fingers around the throat of the guitar and softly smothers the music out of it, and when she hears him again he seems to have forgotten her, and is speaking in the hypnotic voice he uses when talking in small rooms to a listening, close-gathered crowd. Some day this world, now seemingly so composed and eternal, to the edges of every sea shall be merely a tangle of gaping trenches, of crashing walls and broken bodies. Everything must be torn from its accustomed place where it has rotted for centuries, hurled skyward and distributed, cast down again clean as rain, without separate identity. Nothing shall survive that the stiffened hands of poverty have created for the rich and no one shall be left alive except the elect spirits destined to procreate a new world cleansed of cruelty and injustice, ruled by benevolent anarchy: "Pistols are good, I love them, cannon are even better, but in the end I pin my faith to good dynamite," he concludes, and strokes the pistol lying in her hands. "Once I dreamed of destroying this city, in case it offered resistance to General Ortíz, but it fell into his hands like an overripe pear."

He is made restless by his own words, rises and stands waiting. Laura holds up the belt to him: "Put that on, and go kill somebody in Morelia, and you will be happier," she says softly. The presence of death in the room makes her bold. "Today, I found Eugenio going into a stupor. He refused to allow me to call the prison doctor. He had taken all the tablets I brought him yesterday. He said he took them because he was bored."

"He is a fool, and his death is his own business," says Braggioni, fastening his   35
belt carefully.

"I told him if he had waited only a little while longer, you would have got him set free," says Laura. "He said he did not want to wait."

"He is a fool and we are well rid of him," says Braggioni, reaching for his hat.

He goes away. Laura knows his mood has changed, she will not see him any more for a while. He will send word when he needs her to go on errands into strange streets, to speak to the strange faces that will appear, like clay masks with the power of human speech, to mutter their thanks to Braggioni for his help. Now she is free, and she thinks, I must run while there is time. But she does not go.

Braggioni enters his own house where for a month his wife has spent many hours every night weeping and tangling her hair upon her pillow. She is weeping now, and she weeps more at the sight of him, the cause of all her sorrows. He looks about the room. Nothing is changed, the smells are good and familiar, he is well acquainted with the woman who comes toward him with no reproach except grief on her face. He says to her tenderly: "You are so good, please don't cry any more, you dear good creature." She says, "Are you tired, my angel? Sit here and I will wash your feet." She brings a bowl of water, and kneeling, unlaces his shoes, and when from her knees she raises her sad eyes under her blackened lids, he is sorry for everything, and bursts into tears. "Ah, yes, I am hungry, I am tired, let us eat something together," he says, between sobs. His wife leans her head on his arm and says, "Forgive me!" and this time he is refreshed by the solemn, endless rain of her tears.

40   Laura takes off her serge dress and puts on a white linen nightgown and goes to bed. She turns her head a little to one side, and lying still, reminds herself that it is time to sleep. Numbers tick in her brain like little clocks, soundless doors close of themselves around her. If you would sleep, you must not remember anything, the children will say tomorrow, good morning, my teacher, the poor prisoners who come every day brining flowers to their jailor. 1-2-3-4-5—it is monstrous to confuse love with revolution, night with day, life with death—ah, Eugenio!

The tolling of the midnight bell is a signal, but what does it mean? Get up, Laura, and follow me: come out of your sleep, out of your bed, out of this strange house. What are you doing in this house? Without a word, without fear she rose and reached for Eugenio's hand, but he eluded her with a sharp, sly smile and drifted away. This is not all, you shall see—Murderer, he said, follow me, I will show you a new country, but it is far away and we must hurry. No, said Laura, not unless you take my hand, no; and she clung first to the stair rail, and then to the topmost branch of the Judas tree that bent down slowly and set her upon the earth, and then to the rocky ledge of a cliff, and then to the jagged wave of a sea that was not water but a desert of crumbling stone. Where are you taking me, she asked in wonder but without fear. To death, and it is a long way off, and we must hurry, said Eugenio. No, said Laura, not unless you take my hand. Then eat these flowers, poor prisoner, said Eugenio in a voice of pity, take and eat: and from the Judas tree he stripped the warm bleeding flowers, and held them to her lips. She saw that his hand was fleshless, a cluster of small white petrified branches, and his eye sockets were without light, but she ate the flowers greedily for they satisfied both hunger and thirst. Murderer! said Eugenio, and Cannibal! This is my body and my blood. Laura cried No! and at the sound of her own voice, she awoke trembling, and was afraid to sleep again.

1929, 1930

JORGE LUIS BORGES

The Garden of Forking Paths[1]

On page 22 of Liddell Hart's *History of World War I* you will read that an attack against the Serre-Montauban line by thirteen British divisions (supported by 1,400 artillery pieces), planned for the 24th of July, 1916, had to be postponed until the morning of the 29th. The torrential rains, Captain Liddell Hart comments, caused this delay, an insignificant one, to be sure.

The following statement, dictated, reread and signed by Dr. Yu Tsun, former professor of English at the *Hochschule* at Tsingtao,[2] throws an unsuspected light over the whole affair. The first two pages of the document are missing.

" . . . and I hung up the receiver. Immediately afterwards, I recognized the voice that had answered in German. It was that of Captain Richard Madden. Madden's presence in Viktor Runeberg's apartment meant the end of our anxieties and—but this seemed, *or should have seemed,* very secondary to me—also the end of our lives. It meant that Runeberg had been arrested or murdered.[3] Before the sun set on that day, I would encounter the same fate. Madden was implacable. Or rather, he was obliged to be so. An Irishman at the service of England, a man accused of laxity and perhaps of treason, how could he fail to seize and be thankful for such a miraculous opportunity: the discovery, capture, maybe even the death of two agents of the German Reich? I went up to my room; absurdly I locked the door and threw myself on my back on the narrow iron cot. Through the window I saw the familiar roofs and the cloud-shaded six o'clock sun. It seemed incredible to me that that day without premonitions or symbols should be the one of my inexorable death. In spite of my dead father, in spite of having been a child in a symmetrical garden of Hai Feng, was I—now—going to die? Then I reflected that everything happens to a man precisely, precisely *now.* Centuries of centuries and only in the present do things happen; countless men in the air, on the face of the earth and the sea, and all that really is happening is happening to me . . . The almost intolerable recollection of Madden's horselike face banished these wanderings. In the midst of my hatred and terror (it means nothing to me now to speak of terror, now that I have mocked Richard Madden, now that my throat yearns for the noose) it occurred to me that that tumultuous and doubtless happy warrior did not suspect that I possessed the Secret. The name of the exact location of the new British artillery park on the River Ancre. A bird streaked across the gray sky and blindly I translated it into an airplane and that airplane into many (against the French sky) annihilating the artillery station with vertical bombs. If only my mouth, before a bullet shattered it, could cry out that secret name so it could be heard in Germany . . . My human voice was very weak. How

---

1. Translated by Donald A. Yates.   2. Major port in east China on the Yellow Sea controlled and developed by Germany in the early 1900s. *Hochschule:* university (German).   3. A hypothesis both hateful and odd. The Prussian spy Hans Rabener, alias Viktor Runeberg, attacked with drawn automatic the bearer of the warrant for his arrest, Captain Richard Madden. The latter, in self-defense, inflicted the wound which brought about Runeberg's death. (Editor's note.) [This note is by Borges as "Editor."]

might I make it carry to the ear of the Chief? To the ear of that sick and hateful man who knew nothing of Runeberg and me save that we were in Stafford shire[4] and who was waiting in vain for our report in his arid office in Berlin, endlessly examining newspapers . . . I said out loud: *I must flee.* I sat up noiselessly, in a useless perfection of silence, as if Madden were already lying in wait for me. Something—perhaps the mere vain ostentation of proving my resources were nil—made me look through my pockets. I found what I knew I would find. The American watch, the nickel chain and the square coin, the key ring with the incriminating useless keys to Runeberg's apartment, the notebook, a letter which I resolved to destroy immediately (and which I did not destroy), a crown, two shillings and a few pence, the red and blue pencil, the handkerchief, the revolver with one bullet. Absurdly, I took it in my hand and weighed it in order to inspire courage within myself. Vaguely I thought that a pistol report can be heard at a great distance. In ten minutes my plan was perfected. The telephone book listed the name of the only person capable of transmitting the message; he lived in a suburb of Fenton, less than a half hour's train ride away.

I am a cowardly man. I say it now, now that I have carried to its end a plan whose perilous nature no one can deny. I know its execution was terrible. I didn't do it for Germany, no. I care nothing for a barbarous country which imposed upon me the abjection of being a spy. Besides, I know of a man from England— a modest man—who for me is no less great than Goethe.[5] I talked with him for scarcely an hour, but during that hour he was Goethe . . . I did it because I sensed that the Chief somehow feared people of my race—for the innumerable ancestors who merge within me. I wanted to prove to him that a yellow man could save his armies. Besides, I had to flee from Captain Madden. His hands and his voice could call at my door at any moment. I dressed silently, bade farewell to myself in the mirror, went downstairs, scrutinized the peaceful street and went out. The station was not far from my home, but I judged it wise to take a cab. I argued that in this way I ran less risk of being recognized; the fact is that in the deserted street I felt myself visible and vulnerable, infinitely so. I remember that I told the cab driver to stop a short distance before the main entrance. I got out with voluntary, almost painful slowness; I was going to the village of Ashgrove but I bought a ticket for a more distant station. The train left within a very few minutes, at eight-fifty. I hurried; the next one would leave at nine-thirty. There was hardly a soul on the platform. I went through the coaches; I remember a few farmers, a woman dressed in mourning, a young boy who was reading with fervor the *Annals* of Tacitus,[6] a wounded and happy soldier. The coaches jerked forward at last. A man whom I recognized ran in vain to the end of the platform. It was Captain Richard Madden. Shattered, trembling, I shrank into the far corner of the seat, away from the dreaded window.

5   From this broken state I passed into an almost abject felicity. I told myself that the duel had already begun and that I had won the first encounter by frustrating, even if for forty minutes, even if by a stroke of fate, the attack of my adversary. I

---

4. County in west-central England.   5. Johann Wolfgang von Goethe (1749–1832), German poet and dramatist, author of *Faust.*   6. Cornelius Tacitus (A.D. 55–117), Roman historian.

argued that this slightest of victories foreshadowed a total victory. I argued (no less fallaciously) that my cowardly felicity proved that I was a man capable of carrying out the adventure successfully. From this weakness I took strength that did not abandon me. I foresee that man will resign himself each day to more atrocious undertakings; soon there will be no one but warriors and brigands; I give them this counsel: *The author of an atrocious undertaking ought to imagine that he has already accomplished it, ought to impose upon himself a future as irrevocable as the past.* Thus I proceeded as my eyes of a man already dead registered the elapsing of that day, which was perhaps the last, and the diffusion of the night. The train ran gently along, amid ash trees. It stopped, almost in the middle of the fields. No one announced the name of the station. "Ashgrove?" I asked a few lads on the platform. "Ashgrove," they replied. I got off.

A lamp enlightened the platform but the faces of the boys were in shadow. One questioned me, "Are you going to Dr. Stephen Albert's house?" Without waiting for my answer, another said, "The house is a long way from here, but you won't get lost if you take this road to the left and at every crossroads turn again to your left." I tossed them a coin (my last), descended a few stone steps and started down the solitary road. It went downhill, slowly. It was of elemental earth; overhead the branches were tangled; the low, full moon seemed to accompany me.

For an instant, I thought that Richard Madden in some way had penetrated my desperate plan. Very quickly, I understood that that was impossible. The instructions to turn always to the left reminded me that such was the common procedure for discovering the central point of certain labyrinths. I have some understanding of labyrinths: not for nothing am I the great grandson of that Ts'ui Pên who was governor of Yunnan and who renounced worldly power in order to write a novel that might be even more populous than the *Hung Lu Meng*[7] and to construct a labyrinth in which all men would become lost. Thirteen years he dedicated to these heterogeneous tasks, but the hand of a stranger murdered him—and his novel was incoherent and no one found the labyrinth. Beneath English trees I meditated on that lost maze: I imagined it inviolate and perfect at the secret crest of a mountain; I imagined it erased by rice fields or beneath the water; I imagined it infinite, no longer composed of octagonal kiosks and return-ing paths, but of rivers and provinces and kingdoms . . . I thought of a labyrinth of labyrinths, of one sinuous spreading labyrinth that would encompass the past and the future and in some way involve the stars. Absorbed in these illusory images, I forgot my destiny of one pursued. I felt myself to be, for an unknown period of time, an abstract perceiver of the world. The vague, living countryside, the moon, the remains of the day worked on me, as well as the slope of the road which eliminated any possibility of weariness. The afternoon was intimate, infi-nite. The road descended and forked among the now confused meadows. A high-pitched, almost syllabic music approached and receded in the shifting of the wind, dimmed by leaves and distance. I thought that a man can be an enemy of other men, of the moments of other men, but not of a country: not of fireflies,

7. *The Story of the Stone* (1791), a panoramic Chinese novel that features more than 430 characters.

words, gardens, streams of water, sunsets. Thus I arrived before a tall, rusty gate. Between the iron bars I made out a poplar grove and a pavilion. I understood suddenly two things, the first trivial, the second almost unbelievable: the music came from the pavilion, and the music was Chinese. For precisely that reason I had openly accepted it without paying it any heed. I do not remember whether there was a bell or whether I knocked with my hand. The sparkling of the music continued.

From the rear of the house within a lantern approached: a lantern that the trees sometimes striped and sometimes eclipsed, a paper lantern that had the form of a drum and the color of the moon. A tall man bore it. I didn't see his face for the light blinded me. He opened the door and said slowly, in my own language: "I see that the pious Hsi P'êng persists in correcting my solitude. You no doubt wish to see the garden?"

I recognized the name of one of our consuls and I replied, disconcerted, "The garden?"

"The garden of forking paths."

Something stirred in my memory and I uttered with incomprehensible certainty, "The garden of my ancestor Ts'ui Pên."

"Your ancestor? Your illustrious ancestor? Come in."

The damp path zigzagged like those of my childhood. We came to a library of Eastern and Western books. I recognized bound in yellow silk several volumes of the Lost Encyclopedia, edited by the Third Emperor of the Luminous Dynasty but never printed.[8] The record on the phonograph revolved next to a bronze phoenix. I also recall a *famille rose* vase and another, many centuries older, of that shade of blue which our craftsmen copied from the potters of Persia . . .

Stephen Albert observed me with a smile. He was, as I have said, very tall, sharp-featured, with gray eyes and a gray beard. He told me that he had been a missionary in Tientsin "before aspiring to become a Sinologist."

We sat down—I on a long, low divan, he with his back to the window and a tall circular clock. I calculated that my pursuer, Richard Madden, could not arrive for at least an hour. My irrevocable determination could wait.

"An astounding fate, that of Ts'ui Pên," Stephen Albert said. "Governor of his native province, learned in astronomy, in astrology and in the tireless interpretation of the canonical books, chess player, famous poet and calligrapher—he abandoned all this in order to compose a book and a maze. He renounced the pleasures of both tyranny and justice, of his populous couch, of his banquets and even of erudition—all to close himself up for thirteen years in the Pavilion of the Limpid Solitude. When he died, his heirs found nothing save chaotic manuscripts. His family, as you may be aware, wished to condemn them to the fire; but his executor—a Taoist or Buddhist monk—insisted on their publication."

"We descendants of Ts'ui Pên," I replied, "continue to curse that monk. Their publication was senseless. The book is an indeterminate heap of contradictory

---

8. A massive encyclopedia commissioned in the early 1400s by the Yung-lo emperor of the Ming dynasty. One copy of the 11,095 manuscript volumes was made in the mid 1500s, the original was destroyed, and only 370 volumes of the copy remain today.

drafts. I examined it once: in the third chapter the hero dies, in the fourth he is alive. As for the other undertaking of Ts'ui Pên, his labyrinth . . . "

"Here is Ts'ui Pên's labyrinth," he said, indicating a tall lacquered desk.

"An ivory labyrinth!" I exclaimed. "A minimum labyrinth."

"A labyrinth of symbols," he corrected. "An invisible labyrinth of time. To me, a barbarous Englishman, has been entrusted the revelation of this diaphanous mystery. After more than a hundred years, the details are irretrievable; but it is not hard to conjecture what happened. Ts'ui Pên must have said once: *I am withdrawing to write a book.* And another time: *I am withdrawing to construct a labyrinth.* Every one imagined two works; to no one did it occur that the book and the maze were one and the same thing. The Pavilion of the Limpid Solitude stood in the center of a garden that was perhaps intricate; that circumstance could have suggested to the heirs a physical labyrinth. Ts'ui Pên died; no one in the vast territories that were his came upon the labyrinth; the confusion of the novel suggested to me that *it* was the maze. Two circumstances gave me the correct solution of the problem. One: the curious legend that Ts'ui Pên had planned to create a labyrinth which would be strictly infinite. The other: a fragment of a letter I discovered."

Albert rose. He turned his back on me for a moment; he opened a drawer of the black and gold desk. He faced me and in his hands he held a sheet of paper that had once been crimson, but was now pink and tenuous and cross-sectioned. The fame of Ts'ui Pên as a calligrapher had been justly won. I read, uncomprehendingly and with fervor, these words written with a minute brush by a man of my blood: *I leave to the various futures (not to all) my garden of forking paths.* Wordlessly, I returned the sheet. Albert continued:

"Before unearthing this letter, I had questioned myself about the ways in which a book can be infinite. I could think of nothing other than a cyclic volume, a circular one. A book whose last page was identical with the first, a book which had the possibility of continuing indefinitely. I remembered too that night which is at the middle of the Thousand and One Nights[9] when Scheherazade (through a magical oversight of the copyist) begins to relate word for word the story of the Thousand and One Nights, establishing the risk of coming once again to the night when she must repeat it, and thus on to infinity. I imagined as well a Platonic, hereditary work, transmitted from father to son, in which each new individual adds a chapter or corrects with pious care the pages of his elders. These conjectures diverted me; but none seemed to correspond, not even remotely, to the contradictory chapters of Ts'ui Pên. In the midst of this perplexity, I received from Oxford the manuscript you have examined. I lingered, naturally, on the sentence: *I leave to the various futures (not to all) my garden of forking paths.* Almost instantly, I understood: 'The garden of forking paths' was the chaotic novel; the phrase 'the various futures (not to all)' suggested to me the forking in time, not in space. A broad rereading of the work confirmed the theory. In all fictional works, each time a man is confronted with several alternatives, he chooses one and eliminates

9. Also known as the *Arabian Nights*, a thousand and one tales told by Scheherazade to her husband, Shahrayar, king of Samarkind, to postpone her execution.

the others; in the fiction of Ts'ui Pên, he chooses—simultaneously—all of them. *He creates*, in this way, diverse futures, diverse times which themselves also proliferate and fork. Here, then, is the explanation of the novel's contradictions. Fang, let us say, has a secret; a stranger calls at his door; Fang resolves to kill him. Naturally, there are several possible outcomes: Fang can kill the intruder, the intruder can kill Fang, they both can escape, they both can die, and so forth. In the work of Ts'ui Pên, all possible outcomes occur; each one is the point of departure for other forkings. Sometimes, the paths of this labyrinth converge: for example, you arrive at this house, but in one of the possible pasts you are my enemy, in another, my friend. If you will resign yourself to my incurable pronunciation, we shall read a few pages."

His face, within the vivid circle of the lamplight, was unquestionably that of an old man, but with something unalterable about it, even immortal. He read with slow precision two versions of the same epic chapter. In the first, an army marches to a battle across a lonely mountain; the horror of the rocks and shadows makes the men undervalue their lives and they gain an easy victory. In the second, the same army traverses a palace where a great festival is taking place; the resplendent battle seems to them a continuation of the celebration and they win the victory. I listened with proper veneration to these ancient narratives, perhaps less admirable in themselves than the fact that they had been created by my blood and were being restored to me by a man of a remote empire, in the course of a desperate adventure, on a Western isle. I remember the last words, repeated in each version like a secret commandment: *Thus fought the heroes, tranquil their admirable hearts, violent their swords, resigned to kill and to die.*

From that moment on, I felt about me and within my dark body an invisible, intangible swarming. Not the swarming of the divergent, parallel and finally coalescent armies, but a more inaccessible, more intimate agitation that they in some manner prefigured. Stephen Albert continued:

25   "I don't believe that your illustrious ancestor played idly with these variations. I don't consider it credible that he would sacrifice thirteen years to the infinite execution of a rhetorical experiment. In your country, the novel is a subsidiary form of literature; in Ts'ui Pên's time it was a despicable form. Ts'ui Pên was a brilliant novelist, but he was also a man of letters who doubtless did not consider himself a mere novelist. The testimony of his contemporaries proclaims—and his life fully confirms—his metaphysical and mystical interests. Philosophic controversy usurps a good part of the novel. I know that of all problems, none disturbed him so greatly nor worked upon him so much as the abysmal problem of time. Now then, the latter is the only problem that does not figure in the pages of the *Garden*. He does not even use the word that signifies *time*. How do you explain this voluntary omission?"

I proposed several solutions—all unsatisfactory. We discussed them. Finally, Stephen Albert said to me:

"In a riddle whose answer is chess, what is the only prohibited word?"

I thought a moment and replied, "The word *chess*."

"Precisely," said Albert. "*The Garden of Forking Paths* is an enormous riddle, or parable, whose theme is time; this recondite cause prohibits its mention. To omit a word always, to resort to inept metaphors and obvious periphrases, is perhaps the most emphatic way of stressing it. That is the tortuous method preferred, in each of the meanderings of his indefatigable novel, by the oblique Ts'ui Pên. I have compared hundreds of manuscripts, I have corrected the errors that the negligence of the copyists has introduced, I have guessed the plan of this chaos, I have re-established—I believe I have re-established—the primordial organization, I have translated the entire work: it is clear to me that not once does he employ the word 'time.' The explanation is obvious: *The Garden of Forking Paths* is an incomplete, but not false, image of the universe as Ts'ui Pên conceived it. In contrast to Newton and Schopenhauer,[1] your ancestor did not believe in a uniform, absolute time. He believed in an infinite series of times, in a growing, dizzying net of divergent, convergent and parallel times. This network of times which approached one another, forked, broke off, or were unaware of one another for centuries, embraces *all* possibilities of time. We do not exist in the majority of these times; in some you exist, and not I; in others I, and not you; in others, both of us. In the present one, which a favorable fate has granted me, you have arrived at my house; in another, while crossing the garden, you found me dead; in still another, I utter these same words, but I am a mistake, a ghost."

"In every one," I pronounced, not without a tremble to my voice, "I am grateful to you and revere you for your re-creation of the garden of Ts'ui Pên."

"Not in all," he murmured with a smile. "Time forks perpetually toward innumerable futures. In one of them I am your enemy."

Once again I felt the swarming sensation of which I have spoken. It seemed to me that the humid garden that surrounded the house was infinitely saturated with invisible persons. Those persons were Albert and I, secret, busy and multiform in other dimensions of time. I raised my eyes and the tenuous nightmare dissolved. In the yellow and black garden there was only one man; but this man was as strong as a statue . . . this man was approaching along the path and he was Captain Richard Madden.

"The future already exists," I replied, "but I am your friend. Could I see the letter again?"

Albert rose. Standing tall, he opened the drawer of the tall desk; for the moment his back was to me. I had readied the revolver. I fired with extreme caution. Albert fell uncomplainingly, immediately. I swear his death was instantaneous—a lightning stroke.

The rest is unreal, insignificant. Madden broke in, arrested me. I have been condemned to the gallows. I have won out abominably; I have communicated to Berlin the secret name of the city they must attack. They bombed it yesterday; I read it in the same papers that offered to England the mystery of the learned Sinologist Stephen Albert who was murdered by a stranger, one Yu Tsun. The Chief had deciphered this mystery. He knew my problem was to indicate (through the uproar of the war) the city called Albert, and that I had found no other means

30

35

---

1. Arthur Schopenhauer (1788–1860), German philosopher; Sir Isaac Newton (1642–1727), English mathematician and physicist.

to do so than to kill a man of that name. He does not know (no one can know) my innumerable contrition and weariness.

For Victoria Ocampo

1941

RAYMOND CARVER

Cathedral

This blind man, an old friend of my wife's, he was on his way to spend the night. His wife had died. So he was visiting the dead wife's relatives in Connecticut. He called my wife from his in-laws'. Arrangements were made. He would come by train, a five-hour trip, and my wife would meet him at the station. She hadn't seen him since she worked for him one summer in Seattle ten years ago. But she and the blind man had kept in touch. They made tapes and mailed them back and forth. I wasn't enthusiastic about his visit. He was no one I knew. And his being blind bothered me. My idea of blindness came from the movies. In the movies, the blind moved slowly and never laughed. Sometimes they were led by seeing-eye dogs. A blind man in my house was not something I looked forward to.

That summer in Seattle she had needed a job. She didn't have any money. The man she was going to marry at the end of the summer was in officers' training school. He didn't have any money, either. But she was in love with the guy, and he was in love with her, etc. She'd seen something in the paper: HELP WANTED— *Reading to Blind Man,* and a telephone number. She phoned and went over, was hired on the spot. She'd worked with this blind man all summer. She read stuff to him, case studies, reports, that sort of thing. She helped him organize his little office in the county social-service department. They'd become good friends, my wife and the blind man. How do I know these things? She told me. And she told me something else. On her last day in the office, the blind man asked if he could touch her face. She agreed to this. She told me he touched his fingers to every part of her face, her nose—even her neck! She never forgot it. She even tried to write a poem about it. She was always trying to write a poem. She wrote a poem or two every year, usually after something really important had happened to her.

When we first started going out together, she showed me the poem. In the poem, she recalled his fingers and the way they had moved around over her face. In the poem, she talked about what she had felt at the time, about what went through her mind when the blind man touched her nose and lips. I can remember I didn't think much of the poem. Of course, I didn't tell her that. Maybe I just don't understand poetry. I admit it's not the first thing I reach for when I pick up something to read.

Anyway, this man who'd first enjoyed her favors, the officer-to-be, he'd been her childhood sweetheart. So okay. I'm saying that at the end of the summer she let the blind man run his hands over her face, said goodbye to him, married her childhood etc., who was now a commissioned officer, and she moved away from Seattle. But they'd kept in touch, she and the blind man. She made the first contact after a year or so. She called him up one night from an Air Force base in Alabama. She wanted to talk. They talked. He asked her to send him a tape and tell him about her life. She did this. She sent the tape. On the tape, she told the blind man about her husband and about their life together in the military. She told the blind man she loved her husband but she didn't like it where they lived and she didn't like it that he was a part of the military-industrial thing. She told the blind man she'd written a poem and he was in it. She told him that she was writing a poem about what it was like to be an Air Force officer's wife. The poem wasn't finished yet. She was still writing it. The blind man made a tape. He sent her the tape. She made a tape. This went on for years. My wife's officer was posted to one base and then another. She sent tapes from Moody AFB, McGuire, Mc-Connell, and finally Travis, near Sacramento, where one night she got to feeling lonely and cut off from people she kept losing in that moving-around life. She got to feeling she couldn't go it another step. She went in and swallowed all the pills and capsules in the medicine chest and washed them down with a bottle of gin. Then she got into a hot bath and passed out.

But instead of dying, she got sick. She threw up. Her officer—why should he have a name? he was the childhood sweetheart, and what more does he want?—came home from somewhere, found her, and called the ambulance. In time, she put it all on a tape and sent the tape to the blind man. Over the years, she put all kinds of stuff on tapes and sent the tapes off lickety-split. Next to writing a poem every year, I think it was her chief means of recreation. On one tape, she told the blind man she'd decided to live away from her officer for a time. On another tape, she told him about her divorce. She and I began going out, and of course she told her blind man about it. She told him everything, or so it seemed to me. Once she asked me if I'd like to hear the latest tape from the blind man. This was a year ago. I was on the tape, she said. So I said okay, I'd listen to it. I got us drinks and we settled down in the living room. We made ready to listen. First she inserted the tape into the player and adjusted a couple of dials. Then she pushed a lever. The tape squeaked and someone began to talk in this loud voice. She lowered the volume. After a few minutes of harmless chitchat, I heard my own name in the mouth of this stranger, this blind man I didn't even know! And then this: "From all you've said about him, I can only conclude—" But we were interrupted, a knock at the door, something, and we didn't ever get back to the tape. Maybe it was just as well. I'd heard all I wanted to.

Now this same blind man was coming to sleep in my house.

"Maybe I could take him bowling," I said to my wife. She was at the draining board doing scalloped potatoes. She put down the knife she was using and turned around.

"If you love me," she said, "you can do this for me. If you don't love me, okay. But if you had a friend, any friend, and the friend came to visit, I'd make him feel

5

comfortable." She wiped her hands with the dish towel.

"I don't have any blind friends," I said.

10   "You don't have *any* friends," she said. "Period. Besides," she said, "goddamn it, his wife's just died! Don't you understand that? The man's lost his wife!"

I didn't answer. She'd told me a little about the blind man's wife. Her name was Beulah. Beulah! That's a name for a colored woman.

"Was his wife a Negro?" I asked.

"Are you crazy?" my wife said. "Have you just flipped or something?" She picked up a potato. I saw it hit the floor, then roll under the stove. "What's wrong with you?" she said. "Are you drunk?"

"I'm just asking," I said.

15   Right then my wife filled me in with more detail than I cared to know. I made a drink and sat at the kitchen table to listen. Pieces of the story began to fall into place.

Beulah had gone to work for the blind man the summer after my wife had stopped working for him. Pretty soon Beulah and the blind man had themselves a church wedding. It was a little wedding—who'd want to go to such a wedding in the first place?—just the two of them, plus the minister and the minister's wife. But it was a church wedding just the same. It was what Beulah had wanted, he'd said. But even then Beulah must have been carrying the cancer in her glands. After they had been inseparable for eight years—my wife's word, *inseparable*—Beulah's health went into a rapid decline. She died in a Seattle hospital room, the blind man sitting beside the bed and holding on to her hand. They'd married, lived and worked together, slept together—had sex, sure—and then the blind man had to bury her. All this without his having ever seen what the goddamned woman looked like. It was beyond my understanding. Hearing this, I felt sorry for the blind man for a little bit. And then I found myself thinking what a pitiful life this woman must have led. Imagine a woman who could never see herself as she was seen in the eyes of her loved one. A woman who could go on day after day and never receive the smallest compliment from her beloved. A woman whose husband could never read the expression on her face, be it misery or something better. Someone who could wear makeup or not—what difference to him? She could, if she wanted, wear green eye-shadow around one eye, a straight pin in her nostril, yellow slacks and purple shoes, no matter. And then to slip off into death, the blind man's hand on her hand, his blind eyes streaming tears—I'm imagining now—her last thought maybe this: that he never even knew what she looked like, and she on an express to the grave. Robert was left with a small insurance policy and half of a twenty-peso Mexican coin. The other half of the coin went into the box with her. Pathetic.

So when the time rolled around, my wife went to the depot to pick him up. With nothing to do but wait—sure, I blamed him for that—I was having a drink and watching the TV when I heard the car pull into the drive. I got up from the sofa with my drink and went to the window to have a look.

I saw my wife laughing as she parked the car. I saw her get out of the car and shut the door. She was still wearing a smile. Just amazing. She went around to the other side of the car to where the blind man was already starting to get out. This blind man, feature this, he was wearing a full beard! A beard on a blind man!

Too much, I say. The blind man reached into the back seat and dragged out a suitcase. My wife took his arm, shut the car door, and, talking all the way, moved him down the drive and then up the steps to the front porch. I turned off the TV. I finished my drink, rinsed the glass, dried my hands. Then I went to the door.

My wife said, "I want you to meet Robert. Robert, this is my husband. I've told you all about him." She was beaming. She had this blind man by his coat sleeve.

The blind man let go of his suitcase and up came his hand.   20

I took it. He squeezed hard, held my hand, and then he let it go.

"I feel like we've already met," he boomed.

"Likewise," I said. I didn't know what else to say. Then I said, "Welcome. I've heard a lot about you." We began to move then, a little group, from the porch into the living room, my wife guiding him by the arm. The blind man was carrying his suitcase in his other hand. My wife said things like, "To your left here, Robert. That's right. Now watch it, there's a chair. That's it. Sit down right here. This is the sofa. We just bought this sofa two weeks ago."

I started to say something about the old sofa. I'd liked that old sofa. But I didn't say anything. Then I wanted to say something else, small-talk, about the scenic ride along the Hudson. How going *to* New York, you should sit on the right-hand side of the train, and coming *from* New York, the left-hand side.

"Did you have a good train ride?" I said. "Which side of the train did you sit   25
on, by the way?"

"What a question, which side!" my wife said. "What's it matter which side?" she said.

"I just asked," I said.

"Right side," the blind man said. "I hadn't been on a train in nearly forty years. Not since I was a kid. With my folks. That's been a long time. I'd nearly forgotten the sensation. I have winter in my beard now," he said. "So I've been told, anyway. Do I look distinguished, my dear?" the blind man said to my wife.

"You look distinguished, Robert," she said. "Robert," she said. "Robert, it's just so good to see you."

My wife finally took her eyes off the blind man and looked at me. I had the   30
feeling she didn't like what she saw. I shrugged.

I've never met, or personally known, anyone who was blind. This blind man was late forties, a heavy-set, balding man with stooped shoulders, as if he carried a great weight there. He wore brown slacks, brown shoes, a light-brown shirt, a tie, a sports coat. Spiffy. He also had this full beard. But he didn't use a cane and he didn't wear dark glasses. I'd always thought dark glasses were a must for the blind. Fact was, I wished he had a pair. At first glance, his eyes looked like anyone else's eyes. But if you looked close, there was something different about them. Too much white in the iris, for one thing, and the pupils seemed to move around in the sockets without his knowing it or being able to stop it. Creepy. As I stared at his face, I saw the left pupil turn in toward his nose while the other made an effort to keep in one place. But it was only an effort, for that eye was on the roam without his knowing it or wanting it to be.

I said, "Let me get you a drink. What's your pleasure? We have a little of everything. It's one of our pastimes."

"Bub, I'm a Scotch man myself," he said fast enough in this big voice.

"Right," I said. Bub! "Sure you are. I knew it."

35   He let his fingers touch his suitcase, which was sitting alongside the sofa. He was taking his bearings. I didn't blame him for that.

"I'll move that up to your room," my wife said.

"No, that's fine," the blind man said loudly. "It can go up when I go up."

"A little water with the Scotch?" I said.

"Very little," he said.

40   "I knew it," I said.

He said, "Just a tad. The Irish actor, Barry Fitzgerald? I'm like that fellow. When I drink water, Fitzgerald said, I drink water. When I drink whiskey, I drink whiskey." My wife laughed. The blind man brought his hand up under his beard. He lifted his beard slowly and let it drop.

I did the drinks, three big glasses of Scotch with a splash of water in each. Then we made ourselves comfortable and talked about Robert's travels. First the long flight from the West Coast to Connecticut, we covered that. Then from Connecticut up here by train. We had another drink concerning that leg of the trip.

I remembered having read somewhere that the blind didn't smoke because, as speculation had it, they couldn't see the smoke they exhaled. I thought I knew that much and that much only about blind people. But this blind man smoked his cigarette down to the nubbin and then lit another one. This blind man filled his ashtray and my wife emptied it.

When we sat down at the table for dinner, we had another drink. My wife heaped Robert's plate with cube steak, scalloped potatoes, green beans. I buttered him up two slices of bread. I said, "Here's bread and butter for you." I swallowed some of my drink. "Now let us pray," I said, and the blind man lowered his head. My wife looked at me, her mouth agape. "Pray the phone won't ring and the food doesn't get cold," I said.

45   We dug in. We ate everything there was to eat on the table. We ate like there was no tomorrow. We didn't talk. We ate. We scarfed. We grazed that table. We were into serious eating. The blind man had right away located his foods, he knew just where everything was on his plate. I watched with admiration as he used his knife and fork on the meat. He'd cut two pieces of meat, fork the meat into his mouth, and then go all out for the scalloped potatoes, the beans next, and then he'd tear off a hunk of buttered bread and eat that. He'd follow this up with a big drink of milk. It didn't seem to bother him to use his fingers once in a while, either.

We finished everything, including half a strawberry pie. For a few moments, we sat as if stunned. Sweat beaded on our faces. Finally, we got up from the table and left the dirty plates. We didn't look back. We took ourselves into the living room and sank into our places again. Robert and my wife sat on the sofa. I took the big chair. We had us two or three more drinks while they talked about the major things that had come to pass for them in the past ten years. For the most part, I just listened. Now and then I joined in. I didn't want him to think I'd left the room, and I didn't want her to think I was feeling left out. They talked of things that had happened to them—to them!—these past ten years. I waited in vain to hear my name on my wife's sweet lips: "And then my dear husband came into my life"—something like that. But I heard nothing of the sort. More talk of Robert. Robert had done a little of everything, it seemed, a regular blind jack-of-all-trades. But most recently he and his wife had had an Amway distributorship, from which, I gathered, they'd earned their living, such as it was. The blind man was also a ham radio operator. He talked in his loud voice about conversations he'd had with fellow operators in Guam, in the Philippines, in Alaska, and even in Tahiti. He said he'd have a lot of friends there if he ever wanted to go visit those places. From time to time, he'd turn his blind face toward me, put his hand under his beard, ask me something. How long had I been in my present position? (Three years.) Did I like my work? (I didn't.) Was I going to stay with it? (What were the options?) Finally, when I thought he was beginning to run down, I got up and turned on the TV.

My wife looked at me with irritation. She was heading toward a boil. Then she looked at the blind man and said, "Robert, do you have a TV?"

The blind man said, "My dear, I have two TVs. I have a color set and a black-and-white thing, an old relic. It's funny, but if I turn the TV on, and I'm always turning it on, I turn on the color set. It's funny, don't you think?"

I didn't know what to say to that. I had absolutely nothing to say to that. No opinion. So I watched the news program and tried to listen to what the announcer was saying.

"This is a color TV," the blind man said. "Don't ask me how, but I can tell." 50

"We traded up a while ago," I said.

The blind man had another taste of his drink. He lifted his beard, sniffed it, and let it fall. He leaned forward on the sofa. He positioned his ashtray on the coffee table, then put the lighter to his cigarette. He leaned back on the sofa and crossed his legs at the ankles.

My wife covered her mouth, and then she yawned. She stretched. She said, "I think I'll go upstairs and put on my robe. I think I'll change into something else. Robert, you make yourself comfortable," she said.

"I'm comfortable," the blind man said.

"I want you to feel comfortable in this house," she said. 55

"I am comfortable," the blind man said.

After she'd left the room, he and I listened to the weather report and then to the sports roundup. By that time, she'd been gone so long I didn't know if she was going to come back. I thought she might have gone to bed. I wished she'd come back downstairs. I didn't want to be left alone with a blind man. I asked him if he wanted another drink, and he said sure. Then I asked if he wanted to smoke some dope with me. I said I'd just rolled a number. I hadn't, but I planned to do so in about two shakes.

"I'll try some with you," he said.

"Damn right," I said. "That's the stuff."

I got our drinks and sat down on the sofa with him. Then I rolled us two fat 60 numbers. I lit one and passed it. I brought it to his fingers. He took it and inhaled.

"Hold it as long as you can," I said. I could tell he didn't know the first thing.

My wife came back downstairs wearing her pink robe and her pink slippers.

"What do I smell?" she said.

"We thought we'd have us some cannabis," I said.

65   My wife gave me a savage look. Then she looked at the blind man and said, "Robert, I didn't know you smoked."

He said, "I do now, my dear. There's a first time for everything. But I don't feel anything yet."

"This stuff is pretty mellow," I said. "This stuff is mild. It's dope you can reason with," I said. "It doesn't mess you up."

"Not much it doesn't, bub," he said, and laughed.

My wife sat on the sofa between the blind man and me. I passed her the number. She took it and toked and then passed it back to me. "Which way is this going?" she said. Then she said, "I shouldn't be smoking this. I can hardly keep my eyes open as it is. That dinner did me in. I shouldn't have eaten so much."

70   "It was the strawberry pie," the blind man said. "That's what did it," he said, and he laughed his big laugh. Then he shook his head.

"There's more strawberry pie," I said.

"Do you want some more, Robert?" my wife said.

"Maybe in a little while," he said.

We gave our attention to the TV. My wife yawned again. She said, "Your bed is made up when you feel like going to bed, Robert. I know you must have had a long day. When you're ready to go to bed, say so." She pulled his arm. "Robert?"

75   He came to and said, "I've had a real nice time. This beats tapes, doesn't it?"

I said, "Coming at you," and I put the number between his fingers. He inhaled, held the smoke, and then let it go. It was like he'd been doing it since he was nine years old.

"Thanks, bub," he said. "But I think this is all for me. I think I'm beginning to feel it," he said. He held the burning roach out for my wife.

"Same here," she said. "Ditto. Me, too." She took the roach and passed it to me. "I may just sit here for a while between you two guys with my eyes closed. But don't let me bother you, okay? Either one of you. If it bothers you, say so. Otherwise, I may just sit here with my eyes closed until you're ready to go to bed," she said. "Your bed's made up, Robert, when you're ready. It's right next to our room at the top of the stairs. We'll show you up when you're ready. You wake me up now, you guys, if I fall asleep." She said that and then she closed her eyes and went to sleep.

The news program ended. I got up and changed the channel. I sat back down on the sofa. I wished my wife hadn't pooped out. Her head lay across the back of the sofa, her mouth open. She'd turned so that her robe had slipped away from her legs, exposing a juicy thigh. I reached to draw her robe back over her, and it was then that I glanced at the blind man. What the hell! I flipped the robe open again.

80   "You say when you want some strawberry pie," I said.

"I will," he said.

I said, "Are you tired? Do you want me to take you up to your bed? Are you ready to hit the hay?"

"Not yet," he said. "No, I'll stay up with you, bub. If that's all right. I'll stay up until you're ready to turn in. We haven't had a chance to talk. Know what I mean? I feel like me and her monopolized the evening." He lifted his beard and he let it fall. He picked up his cigarettes and his lighter.

"That's all right," I said. Then I said, "I'm glad for the company."

And I guess I was. Every night I smoked dope and stayed up as long as I could before I fell asleep. My wife and I hardly ever went to bed at the same time. When I did go to sleep, I had these dreams. Sometimes I'd wake up from one of them, my heart going crazy.

Something about the church and the Middle Ages was on the TV. Not your run-of-the-mill TV fare. I wanted to watch something else. I turned to the other channels. But there was nothing on them, either. So I turned back to the first channel and apologized.

"Bub, it's all right," the blind man said. "It's fine with me. Whatever you want to watch is okay. I'm always learning something. Learning never ends. It won't hurt me to learn something tonight. I got ears," he said.

We didn't say anything for a time. He was leaning forward with his head turned at me, his right ear aimed in the direction of the set. Very disconcerting. Now and then his eyelids drooped and then they snapped open again. Now and then he put his fingers into his beard and tugged, like he was thinking about something he was hearing on the television.

On the screen, a group of men wearing cowls was being set upon and tormented by men dressed in skeleton costumes and men dressed as devils. The men dressed as devils wore devil masks, horns, and long tails. This pageant was part of a procession. The Englishman who was narrating the thing said it took place in Spain once a year. I tried to explain to the blind man what was happening.

"Skeletons," he said. "I know about skeletons," he said, and he nodded.

The TV showed this one cathedral. Then there was a long, slow look at another one. Finally, the picture switched to the famous one in Paris, with its flying buttresses and its spires reaching up to the clouds. The camera pulled away to show the whole of the cathedral rising above the skyline.

There were times when the Englishman who was telling the thing would shut up, would simply let the camera move around over the cathedrals. Or else the camera would tour the countryside, men in fields walking behind oxen. I waited as long as I could. Then I felt I had to say something. I said, "They're showing the outside of this cathedral now. Gargoyles. Little statues carved to look like monsters. Now I guess they're in Italy. Yeah, they're in Italy. There's paintings on the walls of this one church."

"Are those fresco paintings, bub?" he asked, and he sipped from his drink.

I reached for my glass. But it was empty. I tried to remember what I could remember. "You're asking me are those frescoes?" I said. "That's a good question. I don't know."

The camera moved to a cathedral outside Lisbon. The differences in the Portuguese cathedral compared with the French and Italian were not that great. But they were there. Mostly the interior stuff. Then something occurred to me, and I said, "Something has occurred to me. Do you have any idea what a cathedral is?

What they look like, that is? Do you follow me? If somebody says cathedral to you, do you have any notion what they're talking about? Do you know the difference between that and a Baptist church, say?"

He let the smoke dribble from his mouth. "I know they took hundreds of workers fifty or a hundred years to build," he said. "I just heard the man say that, of course. I know generations of the same families worked on a cathedral. I heard him say that, too. The men who began their life's work on them, they never lived to see the completion of their work. In that wise, bub, they're no different from the rest of us, right?" He laughed. Then his eyelids drooped again. His head nodded. He seemed to be snoozing. Maybe he was imagining himself in Portugal. The TV was showing another cathedral now. This one was in Germany. The Englishman's voice droned on. "Cathedrals," the blind man said. He sat up and rolled his head back and forth. "If you want the truth, bub, that's about all I know. What I just said. What I heard him say. But maybe you could describe one to me? I wish you'd do it. I'd like that. If you want to know, I really don't have a good idea."

I stared hard at the shot of the cathedral on the TV. How could I even begin to describe it? But say my life depended on it. Say my life was being threatened by an insane guy who said I had to do it or else.

I stared some more at the cathedral before the picture flipped off into the countryside. There was no use. I turned to the blind man and said, "To begin with, they're very tall." I was looking around the room for clues. "They reach way up. Up and up. Toward the sky. They're so big, some of them, they have to have these supports. To help hold them up, so to speak. These supports are called buttresses. They remind me of viaducts, for some reason. But maybe you don't know viaducts, either? Sometimes the cathedrals have devils and such carved into the front. Sometimes lords and ladies. Don't ask me why this is," I said.

He was nodding. The whole upper part of his body seemed to be moving back and forth.

100   "I'm not doing so good, am I?" I said.

He stopped nodding and leaned forward on the edge of the sofa. As he listened to me, he was running his fingers through his beard. I wasn't getting through to him, I could see that. But he waited for me to go on just the same. He nodded, like he was trying to encourage me. I tried to think what else to say. "They're really big," I said. "They're massive. They're built of stone. Marble, too, sometimes. In those olden days, when they built cathedrals, men wanted to be close to God. In those olden days, God was an important part of everyone's life. You could tell this from their cathedral-building. I'm sorry," I said, "but it looks like that's the best I can do for you. I'm just no good at it."

"That's all right, bub," the blind man said. "Hey, listen. I hope you don't mind my asking you. Can I ask you something? Let me ask you a simple question, yes or no. I'm just curious and there's no offense. You're my host. But let me ask if you are in any way religious? You don't mind my asking?"

I shook my head. He couldn't see that, though. A wink is the same as a nod to a blind man. "I guess I don't believe in it. In anything. Sometimes it's hard. You know what I'm saying?"

"Sure, I do," he said.

"Right," I said.   105

The Englishman was still holding forth. My wife sighed in her sleep. She drew a long breath and went on with her sleeping.

"You'll have to forgive me," I said. "But I can't tell you what a cathedral looks like. It just isn't in me to do it. I can't do any more than I've done."

The blind man sat very still, his head down, as he listened to me.

I said, "The truth is, cathedrals don't mean anything special to me. Nothing. Cathedrals. They're something to look at on late-night TV. That's all they are."

It was then that the blind man cleared his throat. He brought something up.   110 He took a handkerchief from his back pocket. Then he said, "I get it, bub. It's okay. It happens. Don't worry about it," he said. "Hey, listen to me. Will you do me a favor? I got an idea. Why don't you find us some heavy paper? And a pen. We'll do something. We'll draw one together. Get us a pen and some heavy paper. Go on, bub, get the stuff," he said.

So I went upstairs. My legs felt like they didn't have any strength in them. They felt like they did after I'd done some running. In my wife's room, I looked around. I found some ballpoints in a little basket on her table. And then I tried to think where to look for the kind of paper he was talking about.

Downstairs, in the kitchen, I found a shopping bag with onion skins in the bottom of the bag. I emptied the bag and shook it. I brought it into the living room and sat down with it near his legs. I moved some things, smoothed the wrinkles from the bag, spread it out on the coffee table.

The blind man got down from the sofa and sat next to me on the carpet.

He ran his fingers over the paper. He went up and down the sides of the paper. The edges, even the edges. He fingered the corners.

"All right," he said. "All right, let's do her."   115

He found my hand, the hand with the pen. He closed his hand over my hand. "Go ahead, bub, draw," he said. "Draw. You'll see. I'll follow along with you. It'll be okay. Just begin now like I'm telling you. You'll see. Draw," the blind man said.

So I began. First I drew a box that looked like a house. It could have been the house I lived in. Then I put a roof on it. At either end of the roof, I drew spires. Crazy.

"Swell," he said. "Terrific. You're doing fine," he said. "Never thought anything like this could happen in your lifetime, did you, bub? Well, it's a strange life, we all know that. Go on now. Keep it up."

I put in windows with arches. I drew flying buttresses. I hung great doors. I couldn't stop. The TV station went off the air. I put down the pen and closed and opened my fingers. The blind man felt around over the paper. He moved the tips of his fingers over the paper, all over what I had drawn, and he nodded.

"Doing fine," the blind man said.   120

I took up the pen again, and he found my hand. I kept at it. I'm no artist. But I kept drawing just the same.

My wife opened up her eyes and gazed at us. She sat up on the sofa, her robe hanging open. She said, "What are you doing? Tell me, I want to know."

I didn't answer her.

The blind man said, "We're drawing a cathedral. Me and him are working on it. Press hard," he said to me. "That's right. That's good," he said. "Sure. You got it, bub. I can tell. You didn't think you could. But you can, can't you? You're cooking with gas now. You know what I'm saying? We're going to really have us something here in a minute. How's the old arm?" he said. "Put some people in there now. What's a cathedral without people?"

125 My wife said, "What's going on? Robert, what are you doing? What's going on?"

"It's all right," he said to her. "Close your eyes now," the blind man said to me.

I did it. I closed them just like he said.

"Are they closed?" he said. "Don't fudge."

"They're closed," I said.

130 "Keep them that way," he said. He said, "Don't stop now. Draw."

So we kept on with it. His fingers rode my fingers as my hand went over the paper. It was like nothing else in my life up to now.

Then he said, "I think that's it. I think you got it," he said. "Take a look. What do you think?"

But I had my eyes closed. I thought I'd keep them that way for a little longer. I thought it was something I ought to do.

"Well?" he said. "Are you looking?"

135 My eyes were still closed. I was in my house. I knew that. But I didn't feel like I was inside anything.

"It's really something," I said.

1983

CAROL SHIELDS

Dressing Down

You might say that my grandfather carried the idea of "dressing down" to new heights.

He was, of course, a social activist of national reputation and, as well, the first serious nudist in southern Ontario, the founder of Club Soleil, which is still in existence, still thriving, on the shores of Lake Simcoe, just north of Toronto. You'll recognize his name at once if you're up on your twentieth-century history.

His biography came out too late—he had been dead for some years by then—for him to comment on or defend his own beliefs as a naturist, not that he would have done so, not that he would have entertained for two minutes the rude intervention of a press interview. *But how do you carry your wallet, sir? What do you do, sir, about, um, the male body's sudden embarrassments?*

Please, he would have said to the journalists from the *Toronto Star* or the *Globe* or the *Telegram* or whatever, please! The exposure of the skin to the sun and air is a private matter, and your interest in the project, gentlemen, ladies, is—forgive me—entirely prurient.

These same questions, I confess, also occurred to me as a young boy. How had my grandfather become a nudist in the first place and what did it mean to him to shuck off his clothes, all his clothes, for one month of the year? Was it so he could feel the gaze of a hot July afternoon spreading across the square lean acreage of his chest, and, in softer shadows, onto those other less talked about areas? And, another question, how did he reconcile his nudist yearnings with his Wesleyan calling, with his eleven-months-a-year job as YMCA director for eastern Canada?

If you drive the highway to Lake Simcoe today, you'll be struck by the variety of signs greeting you left and right between the groves of pine and birch: one by one they gesture toward green-leafed darkness, offering winding trails, gravel roads, pointing the way to countless small hidden lakes, beaches, and stretches of inspirational shore. "Awake-Again Bible Conference." "Bide-a-Wee Housekeeping Cottages, Reasonable Rates." "The Merit Institute. Absolutely Private." "Fish 'n' Fun with Mike and Hank." "Stop and Say Hello—Ted and Tina." "ADX Yoga and More." And, finally, "Club Soleil."

Club Soleil has never, not since its founding in 1926, had more than the most discreet of highway signs, hand-painted, black on white, a single board nailed to the trunk of a long-lived elm, with a roughly fashioned arrow tip pointing eastward toward a trail, one that discouraged (yet allowed) wheeled traffic.

Campers at Club Soleil slept in tents in the early years. Meals, vegetarian, were taken beneath the shade of an immense canvas structure known as The Meeting Place. Why vegetarian? Why Carrot Soufflé on Monday, Parsnip Purée on Tuesday, Swiss Chard Pie on Wednesday, and so on and so on? My grandfather was a meat eater for the rest of the year, but in July he lived on leaves, roots, seeds, the only nourishment going at Club Soleil.

The prohibition against the eating of flesh might seem to some visitors a contradiction when human flesh was everywhere displayed on the Club Soleil lawns and on the narrow strip of beach running around a promontory called The Point. The living hams and haunches of middle-aged men made their way between mixed flower and vegetable beds, another of my grandfather's innovations. And so did the necks, shoulders, throats, and bellies of their wives. White jellied breast flesh jiggled in the Ontario sunlight, tested it, defied it. Buttocks. Thighs. Calves. Fragile ankle bones belonging to city lawyers, physicians, charity organizers, household matriarchs. Patrician feet stepped carefully across the beach pebbles and drummed up and down on the grass where a volleyball court had been set up for the young people.

My grandmother had difficulty with all this. It was only after she and my grandfather were married that he told her how he had been taken by friends soon after finishing university to a naturist beach on the Atlantic coast of France. He had greeted the new experience as a door swinging wide open in his existence. Some men are brought to life by the sexual spasm; my grandfather tasted ecstasy for the first time as he lowered his trousers on the slope of a French sand dune, then, more cautiously, dropping his underwear as well, then stepping free. Dry heat and sunlight penetrated his dark manly parts, which since birth had been confined. A hundred other bathers looked on, or rather, they *didn't* look on, that was the wonder of it, that they never so much as glanced in his direction.

He had not expected in his life to feel a breeze pass over his nether regions—this is the untethering miracle he tried to explain to my grandmother, and later to her son, my father. The pleasure was intense and yet subtle. It resonated across the width of his skin, the entire human envelope electrified—here was paradise. And it was in accord with nature's design, as he saw it. It was true; he was able to see nothing perverse about his reaction. How could it be so when he became at that pants-dropping moment larger, stronger, nobler, a man charged with a new range of moral duty? The Protestant God of shame had nodded in response, nodded and smiled and drifted away, and my grandfather, so unexpectedly twitched into life, announced himself an instant convert. He walked straight into the sea, then, where the cold salt water flowed around every mound and recess of his body and completed the arc of liberation.

But how was he to bring the same set of circumstances and appreciations to rigid Ontario? And how, a year later, to explain his passion to his young bride, my gently brought up grandmother?

He was a man, however, who took for granted his right to make his dreams come true. Ever methodical in his dealings, he sent away to the International Naturism Institute in Switzerland for information, then began to look for a piece of well-sheltered lake property which he was able to purchase with part of his inheritance. Next he carefully sounded out a few of his more worldly friends. Might they be interested? Had they discovered for themselves the health-giving benefits of naturism, psychological as well as physical, the mind and body unfettered and fused? Did they know of others who might be interested in the venture? Discretion would rule the day, of course. Privacy, sanctuary, a quiet bond between comrades, an agreement to give one's self up to the pleasures that God Himself had provided.

Yes, my grandmother said, but this is not the sort of thing that remains secret, no matter how circumspect one is.

15   She was right. Word got around. It was inevitable. But her husband's passion for health and sun, his annual indulgence, only enhanced his dignity. It seemed he could do no wrong in those days. The imagined presence of this young, muscular, unclothed body, released to nature, to prelapsarian abandonment, and its contrast to the suited, shirted, necktied manliness he presented to the world as he went about lecturing on social justice or presiding over his YMCA duties—this misalignment only gave him a beguiling, eccentric edge, arousing even in the straitlaced a shrugging admiration and making of him an exceptional being, freeminded, liberal, a man of virility, who also happened to be clever and compelling—especially to women. He became, in the puritanical society he inhabited, rather famous.

My grandmother's disinclination for nudity would not have surprised those who knew her well. Her interest was in covering up, not stripping down. The same week she married my grandfather she'd had curtains and heavy draperies made for the windows of the house they bought on Macklin Avenue. By the following

summer slipcovers dressed the wicker porch furniture. Scarves in broiderie an-
glaise[1] adorned every bureau. Pillows in my grandparents' house were fitted with
undercovers as well as overcovers, and she herself sewed a sort of skirt in flowered
chintz, which was tied prettily with bias tape around the wringer washing
machine when it was not in use. Lace doilies sat on the arms and back of every
chair. Woolen throws were flung across the various sofas. Rugs lay scattered everywhere upon the thick carpets. Fullness, plumpness, doubleness. Hers was a house
where one could imagine the possibility of suffocation.

Her own clothing, needless to say, comprised layers of underclothes, foundation garments, garters and stockings, brassieres, camisoles, slips, blouses, cardi-
gans, lined skirts, aprons, and even good aprons worn over the everyday aprons.
Her mind drifted toward texture, fabric, protection, and warmth, as though she
could never burrow deeply enough into the folds of herself.

Which was why she had so much difficulty taking part in the annual July rites
at Lake Simcoe. Naturism was not her nature. Nudity was the cross she bore.

At first she tried to make bargains with her husband. "I'll go," she told him, "but
don't expect me to go around with *my* clothes off."

He reasoned with her gently, reminding her that nudity was an activity that, [20]
once established, did not allow abstentions. Nudity implied community. The
effort to throw off cultural ignorance was so difficult, he explained, that reinforcement was ever needed. A single clothed person creates a rebuke to the unclothed.
One person walking across the Club Soleil lawn in a summer dress and sandals
and underpants is enough to unsettle others in the matter of the choice they had
taken.

But going without clothes was unhygienic, she argued.

No, he said, not at all. (He had read his material from the International Naturism Institute closely.) Woven cloth harbors mites, molds, dust, germs. Whereas
nothing is easier to keep clean than human skin, which is, in fact, self-cleaning.

Infection, my grandmother pointed out. From others.

Not a chance, he argued. Not when every camper is issued a clean towel at the
beginning of the day, and this towel is used on the various benches and ham-
mocks at Club Soleil, and even carried into the dining hall and spread on the
chair before the diner sits down.

"It's different for women," she protested, gesturing awkwardly, miserably. [25]
"Women have special problems."

My grandfather explained that when women campers were "having their
time," they had only to wear a short pleated skirt, rather like a tennis skirt. No
one thought a thing of it, six days, seven days, nature's timetable. There was, of
course, no reason to cover the breasts or shoulders.

"I can't imagine Mrs. Archie Hammond going around naked, not with her sags
and bags." My grandmother said this with uncharacteristic bitterness.

"Kate and Archie have both signed up."

"Naked? Those two?"

---

1. Decorative fabric popular in the nineteenth century.

30   "Of course, naked. Though naked, my love, is not really a word that naturists use."

"Yes, you've told me. A hundred times. But naked is naked."

"Semantics." (My grandfather, it must be remembered, lived in the day when to snort out the word *semantics* was enough to win any quarrel.)

"You do know what people will say, don't you?"

"Of course I know. They'll say that visitors to Camp Soleil are licentious. That we are seekers of sexual pleasure, and that the removal of the artificial barrier of clothing will only inflame our lust. But these people will be wrong."

35   "I'm not so sure of that," she said. "I know Archie Hammond. I've seen how he looks at women, even with their clothes on."

"Our bodies are God's gifts. There are those who believe that our bodies are holy temples."

"Then why," she asked cannily, "don't you ever see pictures of Jesus without *his* clothes on? He's always got that big brown robe wrapped around him. Even on the cross he had a little piece of cloth—"

"This discussion is going nowhere."

Indeed this discussion would have gone nowhere. It would have vanished into historical silence, except that my grandfather confided its essence to his adult son—my own father—years later, where it was received, as such parental offerings are, with huge embarrassment and rejection. How could such a private argument have taken place between one's own mother and father? Why this mention of the unmentionables between them, infidelities, monthlies—was it really necessary?

40   "Don't you see," my grandmother, not yet thirty years old, said to her husband, "how humiliating this is for me? A grown-up woman. Playing Adam and Eve at the beach."

He was touched by the Adam and Eve reference. It brought a smile to his lips, threw him off course. This was not what she intended.

"Do it for me," he pleaded. He had a slow, rich, persuasive way of speaking. "Please just try it for me."

"Would you love me less if I refused?"

"No," he replied. But he had let slip a small pause before he spoke, and this was registered on my grandmother's consciousness.

45   "It's wrong, you know it's wrong. It fans those instincts of ours that belong to, well . . ."

"To what? Say it."

"To barnyard animals."

"Ah!"

"I can't help it. That's what I think."

50   "We are animals, my precious love."

"You know what I mean."

"Why don't we make a bargain, then?"

She was suspicious of bargains. She came from a wealthy Ontario family (cheese, walnuts, whiskey) where bad bargains had been made between brother and sister, father and son. "What kind of bargain?" she asked.

"You're crying."

"I have to know. I need to know." 55

"I propose that during the month of July we abstain."

"Abstain?"

"From sexual intercourse."

"But"—she must have paused at this point, hating this term *sexual intercourse,* and yet shocked that her husband would relinquish so easily their greatest personal pleasure—"why?"

"To prove to you, conclusively, that going unclothed among those we trust 60 has nothing to do with the desires of the flesh."

"I see."

My grandmother was a passionate woman, but probably shy about the verbal expression of passion—and not sure how to show her shocked disappointment in the proposed accommodation. "I don't know what to think," she said, tears lining her lashes, knowing she had somehow been trapped in her own objections.

And so she was now faced with a dilemma. Her husband had countered each of her arguments about Club Soleil, and had even offered the ultimate sacrifice, an abstention from intimate relations during the unclothed month of July. She was cornered. She must respond, somehow, and of course she was at an age when people believe they will become more and not less than they are.

"All right," she said to the proposed bargain. "All right."

Did she say it crossly or tenderly? With a sense of defeat or victory? The par- 65 ticular tone of the story has not come down to me.

And so the long succession of summers began, the humiliation of July first when my grandmother's favorite flowered dresses came off, her girdle, her hose, her underpants. There is a certain sharp irony to be felt when cast in a role one can't quite occupy, and for my grandmother a jolt of anger must surely have accompanied her acquiescence, the beginning of a longer anger. She found a way to walk on the beach with reasonable dignity, but never with ease, and she learned to stand nodding and chatting with Kate Hammond and the other women, blocking out the sight of their bared, softening flesh, discussing the weather, the children, the latest movies and books. She never, apparently, became accustomed to her exposed body with its pale protrusions, its slopes and meadows and damp cavities. Her fair face lightly perspired in the fresh breeze. Always she carried herself with an air of dolefulness, her eyes wary, her hands crossed stiffly over the region of her pubis. Stiff with love and suffering and absence.

This went on for years. My grandparents and the other original members grew older. Some of them retired and moved to Florida, but a new and younger set of naturists joined the ranks. Archie Hammond died of a heart attack, though Kate Hammond remained a loyal summer camper, moving from a tent into one of the newer cabins. The tennis courts were upgraded. A vegetarian chef was brought from Banff.[2]

2. Mountain-resort town in Alberta, Canada.

Then, suddenly one summer, my grandmother refused to take part. The cause of her refusal was me, her ten-year-old grandson, who was to be taken to Club Soleil for the first time. It was one thing, she felt, to take off her clothes in front of her husband and friends; she had hardened herself to the shame of it. But she would not become a naked grandmother, she would not allow herself to surrender to this ultimate indignity. This was asking too much.

She remained in Toronto that summer, and the rupture between herself and my grandfather was never completely mended.

70   It might be wondered why I was not introduced to Club Soleil until I was ten years old. I loved my grandparents, and had often wondered where they disappeared to each summer. I sensed some reticence, distaste even, on my father's part when it came to discussing the matter. *Soleil* was a French word, he explained carefully, meaning sunshine. Our own vacations—my mother, father, and I, their only child—were taken at Muskoka Lodge, where the wearing of clothes was unquestioned, and indeed may have been part of the reason for going there. It was a fashionable place in those days, and a full wardrobe of "resort apparel" was de rigueur. I remember that my mother possessed a pale peach dress with a little "bolero" that floated behind her as she stood leaning on the porch rail during the evening cocktail hour. My father, of course, ended each day by exchanging his golf clothes for a white dinner jacket.

Then one year they decided to go to Europe instead, and someone suggested that I should stay behind and join my grandparents at Club Soleil. The idea of perpetual *soleil* was appealing, especially since our own Muskoka Lodge summers were often cloudy or rain-soaked.

At this point the real nature of the enterprise was explained to me, and I remember my father's words as he struggled to fill me in. "It is a place," he said, "where people go about in their birthday suits."

I knew what birthday suits meant. It was one of the jokes of the schoolyard. Birthday suits meant buck-naked, stark-naked. Starkers.

"You mean with nothing on?" I was deeply shocked, though I later wondered if part of my shock was rehearsed and just slightly augmented for effect.

75   My father coughed slightly. "It's believed, you see, to be good for the health. Vitamin D, the sunshine vitamin."

"Not even their swimming suits?" This came out in a theatrical squeal. It seemed important to reach a full understanding at once, to get it over with.

"I know it's difficult to imagine." He patted me on the shoulder then, a rare gesture from a man who lacked any real sense of physical warmth.

Oddly, the thought of my grandmother's naked body lay well within my powers of imagination. I had inspected the plump nylon-encased feet and legs of my mother, so rosy, sleek, and unscented, and I'd also seen the statues in the park and at the art gallery, the smooth marble parts of women, unblemished and still and lacking human orifices. What shocked me far more was thinking of my unclothed grandfather, a man who had always seemed to me *more* clothed than other men. His dark business suits were thicker of fabric and more closely woven. And there were his tight collars, black hose, serious oxfords, and the silk scarf he tucked in the neck of his woolen overcoat so that not an inch of flesh, except for his hands and face, was available for scrutiny. But this was my winter grandfather, the only one I had ever seen. Could he possibly have, tucked between his trousered legs, what my father had, what I had?

Yes, it turned out that he did, but instead of hiding these parts behind a bath towel as I was taught to do at home, he strolled the grounds of Club Soleil, an elegant man at home in his own aging, pickled-in-brine skin, a revered ascetic and—it was clear—lord of his own domain, majestic in his entitlement, patting the heads of children and stopping to chat with Kate Hammond at the edge of the archery range. "You must not be afraid," he said to me kindly on the day of my arrival, "to follow the rituals we observe in our summer community."

To be encouraged in such sanctified naughtiness was beyond any dream a ten-year-old boy might have. I learned. I learned fast, but at the same time I understood that the world was subtly spoiled. People with their limbs and creases and folds were more alike than I thought. Skin tones, hairy patches—that was all they had. Take off your clothes and you were left with your dull suit of invisibility.   80

What I witnessed led me into a distress I couldn't account for or explain, but which involved a feverish disowning of my own naked body and a frantic plummeting into willed blindness. I was launched into the long business of shame, accumulating the mingled secrets of disgust and longing, that eventually formed a kind of rattling carapace that restricted natural movement and ease.

"I'm only sorry," my grandfather said often that summer, "that your grandmother is not here to see how brown and strong you've grown."

When my grandfather died he was buried in a plain pine coffin, just as the instructions in his will outlined.

And his tall and by now greatly withered body was laid out on the bare floor of the coffin without a stitch to conceal his nakedness and not even a blanket or sheet for comfort's sake. This was not his request, but my grandmother's, grimly decreed when the family gathered to discuss the "arrangements." She insisted it would have been what he wanted, and since the coffin was to be closed, what difference did it make. She also insisted that Mrs. Kate Hammond be barred from the funeral.

"It is impossible to bar anyone from a public funeral," my father insisted.   85

"Then she is not to be invited to stay for coffee afterward," my grandmother said. "She will probably come anyway, but she is not to be explicitly invited." She said this sternly, punitively it seemed to her family, in an attempt to outflank her dead husband, but by then all of us had learned to shrink from the anger that deformed her last years.

Her own death, pneumonia, occurred a mere eighteen months after my grandfather's. She too had specified in her will a plain pine box, with the additional written request that her body be put to rest unclothed and that the coffin be left open at the funeral.

It was as though she had hungered for this lewd indiscretion, as though some large smoldering ugliness had offered itself to her in her last days and she had been unable to resist. That's what I thought at the time.

Now I think of that final gesture differently. (Needless to say, the family did *not* honor her final request, the pine coffin, yes, and yes to the naked body, but the lid was firmly closed.) It seems to me now that an offering was made on her part, heartbreaking in its impropriety and wish for amends. This desire perhaps had acquired a grotesque life of its own, with a vividness that could find no form of expression in the scanable universe. "The unclothed body," she might have said, pouring into that vessel of a word a metaphorical cleansing, "is all we're allowed to take away with us."

90   The rest must have fallen away in the same moment she wrote down the words of her will: the draperies, the coverings, the fringe and feathers, the wrappings, the linings, the stuffings and stitching. Good-bye, she must have said to what couldn't be helped. Good-bye to the circular life of shame and its infinite regress.

She must have thought she could get everything back by a single act of acquiescence. In the next world, just a breath away, the two of them would greet each other rapturously. Their revealed limbs would flash among the bright vegetation, at home in the green-clothed world, and embracing each other without restraint.

She would have forgotten that nature's substance is gnarled and knotted in its grain, so that no absolutely straight thing can come of it. They should have understood that all along, those two. It might have become one of their perishable secrets, part of the bliss they would one day gladly surrender.

1999

Poetry

Poetry: Reading, Responding, Writing

If you're already a reader of poetry, you know: poetry reading is not just an intellectual and bookish activity; it is about feeling. Reading poetry well means responding to it: if you respond on a feeling level, you are likely to read more accurately, with deeper understanding, and with greater pleasure. And, conversely, if you read poetry accurately, and with attention to detail, you will almost certainly respond—or learn how to respond—to it on an emotional level. Reading poetry involves conscious articulation

> *Poetry is a way of taking life by the throat.*
>
> —ROBERT FROST

through language, and reading and responding come to be, for experienced readers of poetry, very nearly one. But those who teach poetry—and there are a lot of us, almost all enthusiasts about both poetry as a subject and reading as a craft—have discovered something else: writing about poetry helps both the reading and the responding processes. Responding involves remembering and reflecting as well. As you recall your own past and make associations between things in the text and things you already know and feel, you will not only respond more fully to a particular poem, but improve your reading skills more generally. Your knowledge and life experience inform your reading of what is before you and allow you to connect things within the text—events, images, words, sounds—so that meanings and feelings develop and accumulate. Prior learning creates expectations: of pattern, repetition, association, or causality. Reflecting on the text—and on expectations produced by themes and ideas in the text—re-creates old feelings but directs them in new, often unusual ways. Poems, even when they are about things we have no experience of, connect to things we do know and order our memories, thoughts, and feelings in new and newly challenging ways.

A course in reading poetry can ultimately enrich your life by helping you become more articulate and more sensitive to both ideas and feelings: that's the larger goal. But the more immediate goal—and the route to the larger one—is to make you a better reader of texts and a more precise and careful writer yourself. Close attention to one text makes you appreciate, and understand, textuality and its possibilities more generally. Texts may be complex and even unstable in some ways; they do not affect all readers the same way, and they work through language that has its own volatilities and complexities. But paying attention to how you read—developing specific questions to ask and working on your reading skills systematically—can take a lot of the guesswork out of reading texts and give you a sense of greater satisfaction in your interpretations.

600

READING

Poems, perhaps even more than other texts, can sharpen your reading skills because they tend to be so compact, so fully dependent on concise expressions of feeling. In poems, ideas and feelings are packed tightly into just a few lines. The experiences of life are very concentrated here, and meanings emerge quickly, word by word. Poems often show us the very process of putting feelings into a language that can be shared with others—to *say* feelings in a communicable way. Poetry can be intellectual too, explaining and exploring ideas, but its focus is more often on how people feel than how they think. Poems work out a shareable language for feeling, and one of poetry's most insistent virtues involves its attempt to express the inexpressible. How can anyone, for example, put into words what it means to be in love or how it feels to lose someone one cares about? Poetry tries, and it often captures a shade of emotion that feels just right to a reader. No single poem can be said to represent all the things that love or death feels like or means, but one of the joys of experiencing poetry occurs when we read a poem and want to say, "Yes, that is just what it is like; I know exactly what that line means but I've never been able to express it so well." Poetry can be the voice of our feelings even when our minds are speechless with grief or joy. Reading is no substitute for living, but it can make living more abundant and more available.

Here are two poems that talk about the sincerity and depth of love between two people. Each is written as if it were spoken by one person to his or her lover, and each is definite and powerful about the intensity and quality of love; but the poems work in quite different ways—the first one asserting the strength and depth of love, the second implying intense feeling by reminiscing about earlier events in the relationship between the two people.

ELIZABETH BARRETT BROWNING

How Do I Love Thee?

How do I love thee? Let me count the ways.
I love thee to the depth and breadth and height
My soul can reach, when feeling out of sight
For the ends of Being and ideal Grace.
I love thee to the level of every day's   5
Most quiet need, by sun and candlelight.
I love thee freely, as men strive for Right;
I love thee purely, as they turn from Praise;
I love thee with the passion put to use
In my old griefs, and with my childhood's faith.   10
I love thee with a love I seemed to lose
With my lost saints—I love thee with the breath,
Smiles, tears of all my life!—and, if God choose,
I shall but love thee better after death.   1850

JAROLD RAMSEY

The Tally Stick

Here from the start, from our first of days, look:
I have carved our lives in secret on this stick
of mountain mahogany the length of your arms
outstretched, the wood clear red, so hard and rare.
It is time to touch and handle what we know we share.

Near the butt, this intricate notch where the grains
converge and join: it is our wedding.
I can read it through with a thumb and tell you now
who danced, who made up the songs, who meant us joy.
These little arrowheads along the grain,
they are the births of our children. See,
they make a kind of design with these heavy crosses,
the deaths of our parents, the loss of friends.

Over it all as it goes, of course, I
have chiseled Events, History—random
hashmarks cut against the swirling grain.
See, here is the Year the World Went Wrong,
we thought, and here the days the Great Men fell.
The lengthening runes of our lives run through it all.

See, our tally stick is whittled nearly end to end;
delicate as scrimshaw, it would not bear you up.
Regrets have polished it, hand over hand.
Yet let us take it up, and as our fingers
like children leading on a trail cry back
our unforgotten wonders, sign after sign,
we will talk softly as of ordinary matters,
and in one another's blameless eyes go blind.   p. 1977

"How Do I Love Thee?" is direct but fairly abstract. It lists several ways in which the poet feels love and connects them to some noble ideas of higher obligations—to justice (line 7), for example, and to spiritual aspiration (lines 2–4). It suggests a wide range of things that love can mean and notices a variety of emotions. It is an ardent statement of feeling and asserts a permanence that will extend even beyond death. It contains admirable thoughts and memorable phrases that many lovers would like to hear said to themselves. What it does not do is say very much about what the relationship between the two lovers is like on an everyday basis, what experiences they have had together, what distinguishes their relationship from that of other devoted or ideal lovers. Its appeal is to our general sense of what love is like and how intense feelings can be; it does not offer details.

"The Tally Stick" is much more concrete. The whole poem concentrates on a single object that, like "How Do I Love Thee?," "counts" or "tallies" the ways in which this couple love one another. This stick stands for their love and becomes a kind of physical reminder of it: its natural features (lines 6, 10, and 12) and the marks carved on it (lines 15–16, 20–21) indicate events in the story of the relationship. We could say that the stick *symbolizes* their love—later on, we will look at terms like this that make it easier to talk about poems—but for now it is enough to notice that the stick serves the lovers as a marker and a reminder of some specific details of their love. It is a special kind of reminder because its language is "secret" (line 2), something they can share privately (except that we as readers of the poem are sort of looking over their shoulders, not intruding but sharing their secret). The poet interprets the particular features of the stick as standing for particular events—their wedding and the births of their children, for example—and carves marks into it as reminders of other events (lines 15 ff.). The stick itself becomes a very personal object, and in the last stanza of the poem it is as if we watch the lovers touching the stick together and reminiscing over it, gradually dissolving into their emotions and each other as they recall the "unforgotten wonders" (line 25) of their lives together.

Both poems are powerful statements of feelings, each in its own way. Various readers will respond differently to each poem; the effect these poems have on their readers will lead some to prefer one and some the other. Personal preference does not mean that objective standards for poetry cannot be found—some poems are better than others, and later we will look in detail at features that help us to evaluate poems—but we need have no preconceived standards as to what poetry must be or how it must work. Some good poems are quite abstract, others quite specific. Any poem that helps us to articulate and clarify human feelings and ideas has a legitimate claim on us as readers.

Both "How Do I Love Thee?" and "The Tally Stick" are written as if they were addressed to the partner in the love relationship, and both talk directly about the intensity of the love, as does the following poem:

LINDA PASTAN

love poem

<pre>
I want to write you
a love poem as headlong
as our creek
after thaw
when we stand   5
on its dangerous
banks and watch it carry
with it every twig
every dry leaf and branch
in its path   10
every scruple
when we see it
so swollen
with runoff
that even as we watch   15
</pre>

we must grab
each other
and step back
we must grab each
20   other or
get our shoes
soaked we must
grab each other   1988

The directness and simplicity of this poem suggest how the art and craft of poems work. The poem expresses the desire to write a love poem even as the love poem itself begins to proceed; the desire and the resultant poem exist side by side, and in reading the poem we seem to watch and hear the poet's creative process at work in developing appropriate metaphors and means of expression. The poem must be "headlong" (line 2), to match the power of a love that needs to be compared to the irresistible forces of nature. The poem should, like the love it expresses and the swollen creek it describes, sweep everything along, and it should represent (and reproduce) the sense of watching that the lovers have when they observe natural processes at work. The poem, like the action it represents, has to suggest to readers the kind of desire that grabbing each other means to the lovers.

The lovers in this poem seem, at least to themselves, to own the world they observe, but in fact they are controlled by it. The creek on whose banks they stand is "our creek" (line 3), but what they observe as they watch its rising currents requires them ("must," lines 16, 19, 22) to "grab each other" over and over again. It is as if their love is part of nature itself, which subjects them to forces larger than themselves. Everything—twigs, leaves, branches, scruples—is carried along by the powerful currents after the "thaw" (line 4), and the poem replicates the repeated action of the lovers as if to power along observant readers just as the lovers are powered along by what they see. But the poem (and their love) admits dangers, too; it is the fact of danger that propels the lovers to each other. The poem suggests that love provides a kind of haven, but the haven hardly involves passivity or peace; instead, it requires the kind of grabbing that means activity and boldness and deep passion. Love here is no quiet or simple matter even if the expression of it in poems can be direct and based on a simple observation of experience. The "love poem" itself—linked as it is with the headlong currents of the creek from which the lovers are protecting themselves—even represents that which is beyond love and that, therefore, both threatens it and at the same time makes it happen. The power of poetry is thus affirmed at the center of the poem, but what poetry is about (love and life) is suggested to be more important. Poetry makes things happen but is not itself a substitute for life, just a means to make life more energetic and meaningful.

The next poem talks only indirectly about the quality and intensity of love. It is written as if it were a letter from a woman to her husband, who has gone on a long journey on business. It directly expresses how much she misses him and indirectly suggests how much she cares about him.

EZRA POUND

The River-Merchant's Wife: A Letter

(after Rihaku[1])

While my hair was still cut straight across my forehead
I played about the front gate, pulling flowers.
You came by on bamboo stilts, playing horse,
You walked about my seat, playing with blue plums.
And we went on living in the village of Chokan: 5
Two small people, without dislike or suspicion.

At fourteen I married My Lord you.
I never laughed, being bashful.
Lowering my head, I looked at the wall.
Called to, a thousand times, I never looked back.   10

At fifteen I stopped scowling,
I desired my dust to be mingled with yours
For ever and for ever and for ever.
Why should I climb the look out?

At sixteen you departed,   15
You went into far Ku-to-yen, by the river of swirling eddies,
And you have been gone five months.
The monkeys make sorrowful noise overhead.

You dragged your feet when you went out.
By the gate now, the moss is grown, the different mosses,   20
Too deep to clear them away!

The leaves fall early this autumn, in wind.
The paired butterflies are already yellow with August
Over the grass in the West garden;
They hurt me. I grow older.   25
If you are coming down through the narrows of the river Kiang,
Please let me know beforehand,
And I will come out to meet you
　　As far as Cho-fu-Sa.   1915

The "letter" tells us only a few facts about the nameless merchant's wife: that she is about sixteen and a half years old, that she married at fourteen and fell in love with her husband a year later, that she is now very lonely. About their relationship we know only that they were childhood playmates in a small Chinese village, that their marriage originally was not a matter of personal choice, and that the husband unwillingly went away on a long journey five months ago. But the words tell us a great deal about how the

1. The Japanese name for Li Po, an eighth-century Chinese poet. Pound's poem is a loose paraphrase of Li Po's.

young wife feels, and the simplicity of her language suggests her sincere and deep longing. The daily noises she hears seem "sorrowful" (line 18), and she worries about the dangers of the faraway place where her husband is, thinking of it in terms of its perilous "river of swirling eddies" (line 16). She thinks of how moss has grown up over the unused gate, and more time seems to her to have passed than actually has (lines 22–25). Nostalgically she remembers their innocent childhood, when they played together without deeper love or commitment (lines 1–6), and contrasts that with her later satisfaction in their love (lines 11–14) and with her present anxiety, loneliness, and desire. We do not need to know the geography of the river Kiang or how far Cho-fu-Sa is to sense that her wish to see him is very strong, that her desire is powerful enough to make her venture beyond the ordinary geographical bounds of her existence so that their reunion will happen sooner. The closest she comes to a direct statement about her love is "I desired my dust to be mingled with yours / For ever and for ever and for ever" (lines 12–13). But her single-minded vision of the world, her perception of even the beauty of nature as only a record of her husband's absence and the passage of time, and her plain, apparently uncalculated language about her rejection of other suitors and her shutting out of the rest of the world all show her to be committed, desirous, nearly desperate for his presence. In a different sense, she has also counted the ways that she loves her man.

Here is another poem about marriage that expresses a very different set of attitudes and feelings.

DENISE LEVERTOV

Wedding-Ring

My wedding-ring lies in a basket
as if at the bottom of a well.
Nothing will come to fish it back up
and onto my finger again.
5   It lies
among keys to abandoned houses,
nails waiting to be needed and hammered
into some wall,
telephone numbers with no names attached,
10   idle paperclips.
                        It can't be given away
for fear of bringing ill-luck.
                        It can't be sold
for the marriage was good in its own
15   time, though that time is gone.
                        Could some artificer
beat into it bright stones, transform it
into a dazzling circlet no one could take
for solemn betrothal or to make promises
20   living will not let them keep? Change it
into a simple gift I could give in friendship?   1978

The artifact—the ring—at the center of this poem is out-of-date and abandoned, standing for a worn-out and terminated marriage. Unlike the eager and committed voice in the previous poem, the voice here is tired, resigned, sad; the poem's speaker seems willing to try for a new and better relationship but is also hesitant, cautious, and perhaps somewhat disillusioned by previous experience. This, too, is a poem about love, but the moment of love has long since passed, and the poem focuses on the feelings of aftermath.

Poems can be about the meaning of a relationship or about disappointment just as easily as about emotional fulfillment, and poets are often very good at suggesting the contradictions and uncertainties in relationships. Poets often find love quaint or downright funny, too, mainly because it involves human beings who, however serious their intentions and concerns, are often inept, uncertain, and self-contradictory—in short, human. Showing us ourselves as others see us is one of the more useful tasks that poems perform, but the poems that result can be just as entertaining and pleasurable—and sometimes amusing—as they are educational. The love poems gathered at the end of this chapter suggest both the intensities and the foibles of human relationships, and sometimes the analysis can be complicated or harsh as well as touching or reverential. The poetry of love is as complicated as love itself.

RESPONDING

The poems we have looked at so far all describe, though in quite different ways, feelings associated with loving or being attached to someone and the expression—either physical or verbal—of those feelings. Watching how poems work out a language for feeling can help us to work out a language for our own feelings, but the process is also reciprocal: being conscious of feelings we already have can lead us into poems more surely and with more satisfaction. Readers with a strong romantic bent—and with strong yearnings or positive memories of desire—will be likely to find "The Tally Stick" and "The River-Merchant's Wife: A Letter" easy to respond to and like, while those more skeptical of human institutions and male habits may find the disillusionment and resignation of "Wedding-Ring" more satisfying.

> *If I feel physically as if the top of my head were taken off, I know that is poetry.*
>
> —EMILY DICKINSON

Poems can be about all kinds of experiences, and not all the things we find in them will replicate (or even relate to) experiences we may have individually had. But sharing through language will often enable us to get in touch with feelings—of love or anger, fear or confidence—we did not know we had. The next few poems involve another, far less pleasant set of feelings than those usually generated by love, but even here, where our experience may be limited, we are able to respond, to feel the tug of emotions within us that we may not be fully aware of. In the following poem, a father struggles to understand and control his grief over the death of a seven-year-old son. We don't have to be a father or to have lost a loved one to be aware of—and even share—the speaker's pain because our own experiences will have given us some idea of what such a loss would feel like. And the words and strategies of the poem may activate expectations created by our previous experiences.

BEN JONSON

On My First Son

Farewell, thou child of my right hand,[1] and joy;
My sin was too much hope of thee, loved boy:
Seven years thou wert lent to me, and I thee pay,
Exacted by thy fate, on the just[2] day.
O could I lose all father now! for why
Will man lament the state he should envý,
To have so soon 'scaped world's and flesh's rage,
And, if no other misery, yet age?
Rest in soft peace, and asked, say, "Here doth lie
Ben Jonson his[3] best piece of poetry."
For whose sake henceforth all his vows be such
As what he loves may never like too much.

                                            1616

This poem's attempts to rationalize the boy's death are quite conventional. Although the father tries to be comforted by pious thoughts, his feelings keep showing through. The poem's beginning—with its formal "farewell" and the rather distant-sounding address to the dead boy ("child of my right hand")—cannot be sustained for long: both of the first two lines end with bursts of emotion. It is as if the father is trying to explain the death to himself and to keep his emotions under control, but cannot quite manage it. Even the punctuation suggests the way his feelings compete with conventional attempts to put the death into some sort of perspective that will soften the grief, and the comma near the end of each of the first two lines marks a pause that cannot quite hold back the overflowing emotion. But finally the only "idea" that the poem supports is that the father wishes he did not feel so intensely; in the fifth line he fairly blurts that he wishes he could lose his fatherly emotions, and in the final lines he resolves never again to "like" so much that he can be this deeply hurt. Philosophy and religion offer their useful counsels in this poem, but they prove far less powerful than feeling. Rather than drawing some kind of moral about what death means, the poem presents the actuality of feeling as inevitable and nearly all-consuming.

The poem that follows also tries to suppress the rawness of feelings about the death of a loved one, but here the survivor is haunted by memories of his wife when he sees a physical object—a vacuum cleaner—that he associates with her.

1. A literal translation of the son's name, Benjamin.   2. Exact; the son died on his seventh birthday, in 1603.   3. Ben Jonson's (a common Renaissance form of the possessive).

HOWARD NEMEROV

The Vacuum

The house is so quiet now
The vacuum cleaner sulks in the corner closet,
Its bag limp as a stopped lung, its mouth
Grinning into the floor, maybe at my
Slovenly life, my dog-dead youth.   5

I've lived this way long enough,
But when my old woman died her soul
Went into that vacuum cleaner, and I can't bear
To see the bag swell like a belly, eating the dust
And the woolen mice, and begin to howl   10

Because there is old filth everywhere
She used to crawl, in the corner and under the stair.
I know now how life is cheap as dirt,
And still the hungry, angry heart
Hangs on and howls, biting at air.   1955   15

The poem is about a vacuum in the husband's life, but the title refers most obviously to the vacuum cleaner that, like the tally stick we looked at earlier, seems to stand for many of the things that were once important in the life he had together with his wife. The cleaner is a reminder of the dead wife ("my old woman," line 7) because of her devotion to cleanliness. But to the surviving husband buried in the filth of his life it seems as if the machine has become almost human, a kind of ghost of her: it "sulks" (line 2), it has lungs and a mouth (line 3), and it seems to grin, making fun of what has become of him. He "can't bear" (line 8) to see it in action because it then seems too much alive, too much a reminder of her life. The poem records his paralysis, his inability to do more than discover that life is "cheap as dirt" without her ordering and cleansing presence for him. At the end it is *his* angry heart that acts like the haunting machine, howling and biting at air as if he has merged with her spirit and the physical object that memorializes her. This poem puts a strong emphasis on the stillness of death and the way it makes things seem to stop; it captures in words the hurt, the anger, the inability to understand, the vacuum that remains when a loved one dies and leaves a vacant space. But here we do not see the body or hear a direct good-bye to the dead person; rather we encounter the feeling that lingers and won't go away, recalled through memory by an especially significant object, a mere thing but one that has been personalized to the point of becoming nearly human in itself. (The event described here is, by the way, fictional; the poet's wife did not in fact die. Like a dramatist or writer of fiction, the poet may simply *imagine* an event in order to analyze and articulate how such an event might feel in certain circumstances.)

Here is another poem about a death:

SEAMUS HEANEY

Mid-Term Break

I sat all morning in the college sick bay
Counting bells knelling classes to a close.
At two o'clock our neighbors drove me home.

In the porch I met my father crying—
5   He had always taken funerals in his stride—
And Big Jim Evans saying it was a hard blow.

The baby cooed and laughed and rocked the pram
When I came in, and I was embarrassed
By old men standing up to shake my hand

10 And tell me they were "sorry for my trouble,"
Whispers informed strangers I was the eldest,
Away at school, as my mother held my hand

In hers and coughed out angry tearless sighs.
At ten o'clock the ambulance arrived
15 With the corpse, stanched and bandaged by the nurses.

Next morning I went up into the room. Snowdrops
And candles soothed the bedside; I saw him
For the first time in six weeks. Paler now,

Wearing a poppy bruise on his left temple,
20 He lay in the four foot box as in his cot.
No gaudy scars, the bumper knocked him clear.

A four foot box, a foot for every year.   1966

If, in "The Vacuum," the grief is displaced onto an object left behind, here grief seems almost wordless. The speaker of the poem, the older brother of the dead four-year-old, cannot really articulate his grief and instead provides a lot of meticulous detail, as if giving us information can substitute for an expression of feeling. He is "embarrassed" (line 8) by the attempts of others to say how they feel and to empathize with him. He records the feelings of other family members in detail, but never fully expresses his own feelings, as if he has taken on a kind of deadness of his own that eludes, and substitutes for, articulation. Only when he confronts the bruised body itself can he begin to come to terms with the loss, and even there he resorts to a kind of mathematical formula to displace the feeling so that he doesn't have to talk about it. Though the feelings in the poem are extremely powerful, the power is expressed (as in the Jonson poem above) by suppression. It is not restraint that holds back the young man's grief, but a silence that cannot be put into any words except those of enumerated facts.

Sometimes poems are a way of confronting feelings. Sometimes they explore feelings in detail and try to intellectualize or rationalize them. At other times, poems generate responses by recalling an experience many years in the past. In the following two poems, for example, memories of childhood provide perspective on two very different events. In the first, written as if the person speaking the poem were in the fifth grade, a child's sense of death is portrayed through her exploration of a photograph that makes her grandfather's presence vivid to her memory—a memory that lingers primarily through smell and touch. In the second poem, another childhood memory—this time of over-shoes—takes an adult almost physically back into childhood. As you read the two poems, keep track of (or perhaps even jot down) your responses. How much of your feeling is due to your own past experiences? In which specific places? What family photographs do you remember most vividly? What feelings did they invoke that make them so memorable? How are your memories different from those expressed in "Fifth Grade Autobiography"? in "The Fury of Overshoes"? Which feelings expressed in each poem are similar to your own? Where do your feelings differ most strongly? How would you articulate your responses to memories differently? In what ways does an awareness of your similar—and different—experiences and feelings make you a better reader of the poem?

RITA DOVE

Fifth Grade Autobiography

I was four in this photograph fishing
with my grandparents at a lake in Michigan.
My brother squats in poison ivy.
His Davy Crockett cap
sits squared on his head so the raccoon tail   5
flounces down the back of his sailor suit.

My grandfather sits to the far right
in a folding chair,
and I know his left hand is on
the tobacco in his pants pocket   10
because I used to wrap it for him
every Christmas. Grandmother's hips
bulge from the brush, she's leaning
into the ice chest, sun through the trees
printing her dress with soft   15
luminous paws.

I am staring jealously at my brother;
the day before he rode his first horse, alone.
I was strapped in a basket
behind my grandfather.   20
He smelled of lemons. He's died—

but I remember his hands.   1989

ANNE SEXTON

The Fury of Overshoes

They sit in a row
outside the kindergarten,
black, red, brown, all
with those brass buckles.
5   Remember when you couldn't
buckle your own
overshoe
or tie your own
shoe
10   or cut your own meat
and the tears
running down like mud
because you fell off your
tricycle?
15   Remember, big fish,
when you couldn't swim
and simply slipped under
like a stone frog?
The world wasn't
20   yours.
It belonged to
the big people.
Under your bed
sat the wolf
25   and he made a shadow
when cars passed by
at night.
They made you give up
your nightlight
30   and your teddy
and your thumb.
Oh overshoes,
don't you
remember me,
35   pushing you up and down
in the winter snow?
Oh thumb,
I want a drink,
it is dark,
40   where are the big people,
when will I get there,
taking giant steps
all day,
each day
45   and thinking
nothing of it?

1974

There is much more going on in the poems we have glanced at than we have taken time to consider, but even the quickest look at these poems suggests the range of feelings that poems offer—the depth of feeling, the clarity, the experience that may be articulately and precisely shared. Not all poems are as accessible as those we've looked at so far, and even the accessible ones yield themselves to us more readily and more fully if we approach them systematically by developing specific reading habits and skills—just as someone learning to play tennis or to make pottery systematically learns the rules, the techniques, the things to watch out for that are distinctive to the pleasures and hazards of that skill or craft. It helps if you develop a sense of what to expect, and the chapters that follow will show you the things that poets can do—and thus what poems can do for you.

But knowing what to expect isn't everything. As a reader of poetry, you should always be open—to new experiences, new feelings, new ideas. Every poem is a potential new experience, and no matter how sophisticated you become, you can still be surprised (and delighted) by new poems—and by rereading old ones. Good poems bear many, many rereadings, and often one discovers something new with every new reading: there is no such thing as "mastering" a poem, and good poems are not exhausted by repeated readings. Let poems surprise you when you come to them, let them come on their own terms, let them be themselves. If you are open to poetry, you are also open to much more that the world can offer you.

No one can give you a method that will offer you total experience of all poems. But because individual poems often share characteristics with other poems, the following guidelines can prompt you to ask the right questions:

1. *Read the syntax literally.* What the words say literally in normal sentences is only a starting point, but it is the place to start. Not all poems use normal prose syntax, but most of them do, and you can save yourself embarrassment by paraphrasing accurately (that is, rephrasing what the poem literally says, in plain prose) and not simply free-associating from an isolated word or phrase.

2. *Articulate for yourself what the title, subject, and situation make you expect.* Poets often use false leads and try to surprise you by doing shocking things, but defining expectation lets you be conscious of where you are when you begin.

3. *Identify the poem's situation.* What is said is often conditioned by where it is said and by whom. Identifying the speaker and his or her place in the situation puts what he or she says in perspective.

4. *Find out what is implied by the traditions behind the poem.* Verse forms, poetic kinds, and metrical patterns all have a frame of reference, traditions of the way they are usually used and for what. For example, the anapest (two unstressed syllables followed by a stressed one, as in the word *Tennessee*) is usually used for comic poems, and when poets use it "straight" they are probably making a point with this "departure."

5. *Bother the reference librarian.* Look up anything you don't understand: an unfamiliar word (or an ordinary word used in an unfamiliar way), a place, a person, a myth, an idea—anything the poem uses. When you can't find what you need or don't know where to look, ask for help.

6. *Remember that poems exist in time, and times change.* Not only the meanings of words, but whole ways of looking at the universe vary in different ages. Consciousness of time works two ways: your knowledge of history provides a context for reading the poem, and the poem's use of a word or idea may modify your notion of a particular age.

7. *Take a poem on its own terms.* Adjust to the poem; don't make the poem adjust to

you. Be prepared to hear things you do not want to hear. Not all poems are about your ideas, nor will they always present emotions you want to feel. But be tolerant and listen to the poem's ideas, not only to your desire to revise them for yourself.

8. *Be willing to be surprised.* Things often happen in poems that turn them around. A poem may seem to suggest one thing at first, then persuade you of its opposite, or at least of a significant qualification or variation.

9. *Assume there is a reason for everything.* Poets do make mistakes, but when a poem shows some degree of verbal control it is usually safest to assume that the poet chose each word carefully; if the choice seems peculiar, you may be missing something. Try to account for everything in a poem, see what kind of sense you can make of it, and figure out a coherent pattern that explains the text as it stands.

10. *Argue.* Discussion usually results in clarification and keeps you from being too dependent on personal biases and preoccupations that sometimes mislead even the best readers. Talking a poem over with someone else (especially someone who thinks very differently) can expand your perspective.

WRITING ABOUT POEMS

If you have been keeping notes on your personal responses to the poems you've read, you have already taken an important step toward writing about them. There are many different ways to write about poems, just as there are many different things to say. (The chapter in the back of the book called "Writing about Literature" suggests many different kinds of topics.) But all writing begins from a clear sense of the poem itself and your responses to it, so the first steps (long before formally sitting down to write) are to read the poem over several times and keep notes on the things that strike you and the questions that remain.

Formulating a clear series of questions will usually suggest an appropriate approach to the poem and a good topic. Learning to ask the right questions can save you a lot of time. Some questions—the kinds of questions implied in the ten guidelines for reading listed above—are basic and more or less apply to all poems. But each poem makes demands of its own, too, because of its distinctive way of going about its business, so you will usually want to list what seem to you the crucial questions for that poem. Here, just to give you an example, are some questions that could lead you to a paper topic on the first poem on the next page:

1. How does the title affect your reading of and response to the poem?
2. What is the poem about?
3. What makes the poem interesting?
4. Who is the speaker? What role does the speaker have?
5. What effect does the poem have on you? Do you think the poet intended such an effect?
6. What is distinctive about the poet's use of language? Which words especially contribute to the poem's effect?

What *is* poetry? Let your definition be cumulative as you read more and more poems. No dictionary definition will cover all that you find, and it is better to discover for yourself poetry's many ingredients, its many effects, its many ways of acting. What can it do for you? Wait and see. Add up its effects after you have read carefully—after you have studied and reread—a hundred or so poems; then add to that total as you continue to read new poems or reread old ones.

PRACTICING READING: SOME POEMS ON LOVE

W. H. AUDEN

[Stop all the clocks, cut off the telephone]

Stop all the clocks, cut off the telephone,
Prevent the dog from barking with a juicy bone,
Silence the pianos and with muffled drum
Bring out the coffin, let the mourners come.

Let aeroplanes circle moaning overhead   5
Scribbling on the sky the message He Is Dead,
Put crêpe bows round the white necks of the public doves,
Let the traffic policemen wear black cotton gloves.

He was my North, my South, my East and West,
My working week and my Sunday rest,   10
My noon, my midnight, my talk, my song;
I thought that love would last for ever: I was wrong.

The stars are not wanted now: put out every one;
Pack up the moon and dismantle the sun;
Pour away the ocean and sweep up the wood;   15
For nothing now can ever come to any good.

ca. 1936

ANNE BRADSTREET

To My Dear and Loving Husband

If ever two were one, then surely we.
If ever man were loved by wife, then thee;
If ever wife was happy in a man,
Compare with me ye women if you can.
I prize thy love more than whole mines of gold,   5
Or all the riches that the East doth hold.
My love is such that rivers cannot quench,
Nor aught but love from thee give recompense.
Thy love is such I can no way repay;
The heavens reward thee manifold, I pray.   10
Then while we live, in love let's so persever,
That when we live no more we may live ever.

1678

WILLIAM SHAKESPEARE

[*Let me not to the marriage of true minds*]

Let me not to the marriage of true minds
Admit impediments.[1] Love is not love
Which alters when it alteration finds,
Or bends with the remover to remove:
Oh, no! it is an ever-fixéd mark,
That looks on tempests and is never shaken;
It is the star to every wandering bark,
Whose worth's unknown, although his height be taken.[2]
Love's not Time's fool, though rosy lips and cheeks
Within his bending sickle's compass come;
Love alters not with his brief hours and weeks,
But bears it out even to the edge of doom.
If this be error and upon me proved,
I never writ, nor no man ever loved.

1609

EDNA ST. VINCENT MILLAY

[*What lips my lips have kissed, and where, and why*]

What lips my lips have kissed, and where, and why,
I have forgotten, and what arms have lain
Under my head till morning; but the rain
Is full of ghosts tonight, that tap and sigh
Upon the glass and listen for reply,
And in my heart there stirs a quiet pain
For unremembered lads that not again
Will turn to me at midnight with a cry.
Thus in the winter stands the lonely tree,
Nor knows what birds have vanished one by one,
Yet knows its boughs more silent than before:
I cannot say what loves have come and gone;
I only know that summer sang in me
A little while, that in me sings no more.

1923

1. The Marriage Service contains this address to the witnesses: "If any of you know cause or just impediments why these persons should not be joined together. . . ."   2. That is, measuring the altitude of
stars (for purposes of navigation) is not a way to measure value.

MARY, LADY CHUDLEIGH

To the Ladies

Wife and servant are the same,
But only differ in the name:
For when that fatal knot is tied,
Which nothing, nothing can divide,
When she the word *Obey* has said,   5
And man by law supreme has made,
Then all that's kind is laid aside,
And nothing left but state and pride.
Fierce as an eastern prince he grows,
And all his innate rigor shows: 10
Then but to look, to laugh, or speak,
Will the nuptial contract break.
Like mutes, she signs alone must make,
And never any freedom take,
But still be governed by a nod,   15
And fear her husband as her god:
Him still must serve, him still obey,
And nothing act, and nothing say,
But what her haughty lord thinks fit,
Who, with the power, has all the wit.   20
Then shun, oh! shun that wretched state,
And all the fawning flatterers hate.
Value yourselves, and men despise:
You must be proud, if you'll be wise.   1703

W. B. YEATS

A Last Confession

What lively lad most pleasured me
Of all that with me lay?
I answer that I gave my soul
And loved in misery,
But had great pleasure with a lad   5
That I loved bodily.

Flinging from his arms I laughed
To think his passion such
He fancied that I gave a soul
Did but our bodies touch,   10

And laughed upon his breast to think
Beast gave beast as much.

I gave what other women gave
That stepped out of their clothes,
15   But when this soul, its body off,
Naked to naked goes,
He it has found shall find therein
What none other knows,

And give his own and take his own
20   And rule in his own right;
And though it loved in misery
Close and cling so tight,
There's not a bird of day that dare
Extinguish that delight.   1933

QUESTIONS

1. Which love poem in this chapter seems to you the most effective? the most moving? the most accurate in its representation of emotions? the most beautiful in its sentiments? Pick out specific things in each poem you have chosen that help to make it work. Did you choose the same poem to answer each question? What did you learn about your own tastes and judgments from comparing the answers you gave to each question?
2. Compare the method of summing up ways of loving in "How Do I Love Thee?" (Browning) with those in "The Tally Stick" (Ramsey).
3. What, exactly, do we know about the person who has just died in Auden's "Stop all the clocks"? What different strategies does the speaker of the poem use to convey the depth of his emotion? In what sense is this a love poem?
4. Did "To the Ladies," or your response to it, surprise you? Did you notice that it was published in 1703? If not, does that date modify your response? Why?

WRITING SUGGESTIONS

1. Of all the love poems in this chapter, which one would you most like to have addressed to you? which least? Write a prose answer to the author of either poem you have chosen, explaining what seemed to you most (or least) complimentary in what the poem said about you.
2. Paraphrase—that is, put into different words line by line and stanza by stanza—Yeats's "A Last Confession." Summarize the poem's basic statement in one sentence. How accurately do your paraphrase and summary represent the feelings recorded in the poem?
3. Jot down your responses to all the marriage poems in this chapter. Which one most accurately expresses your ideal of a good marriage? Why do you think so? What does your choice say about you?

Understanding the Text

12

TONE

Poetry is full of surprises. Poems express anger or outrage just as effectively as love or sadness, and good poems can be written about going to a rock concert or having lunch or cutting the lawn, as well as about making love or smelling flowers or listening to Beethoven. Even poems on "predictable" subjects can surprise us with unpredicted attitudes, unusual events, or sudden twists. Knowing that a poem is about some particular subject—love, for example, or death—may give us a general idea of what to expect, but it never tells us altogether what we will find in a particular poem. Responding to a poem fully means being open to the poem and its surprises, letting the poem guide us to its own stances, feelings, and ideas—to an explanation of a topic that may be very different from what we expect or what we think. Letting a poem speak to us means listening to *how* the poem says what it says—hearing the tone of voice implied in the way the words are spoken. *What* a poem says involves its **theme,** a statement about its subject. *How* a poem makes that statement involves its **tone,** the attitude or feelings it expresses about the theme.

The following two poems—one about death and one about love—express attitudes and feelings different from those in the poems we have read so far.

MARGE PIERCY

Barbie Doll

This girlchild was born as usual
and presented dolls that did pee-pee
and miniature GE stoves and irons
and wee lipsticks the color of cherry candy.
Then in the magic of puberty, a classmate said: 5
You have a great big nose and fat legs.

She was healthy, tested intelligent,
possessed strong arms and back,
abundant sexual drive and manual dexterity.

10   She went to and fro apologizing.
      Everyone saw a fat nose on thick legs.

      She was advised to play coy,
      exhorted to come on hearty,
      exercise, diet, smile and wheedle.
15   Her good nature wore out
      like a fan belt.
      So she cut off her nose and her legs
      and offered them up.

      In the casket displayed on satin she lay
20   with the undertaker's cosmetics painted on,
      a turned-up putty nose,
      dressed in a pink and white nightie.
      Doesn't she look pretty? everyone said.
      Consummation at last.
25   To every woman a happy ending.   1973

W. D. SNODGRASS

Leaving the Motel

      Outside, the last kids holler
      Near the pool: they'll stay the night.
      Pick up the towels; fold your collar
      Out of sight.

5   Check: is the second bed
      Unrumpled, as agreed?
      Landlords have to think ahead
      In case of need,

      Too. Keep things straight: don't take
10   The matches, the wrong keyrings—
      We've nowhere we could keep a keepsake—
      Ashtrays, combs, things

      That sooner or later others
      Would accidentally find.
15   Check: take nothing of one another's
      And leave behind

      Your license number only,
      Which they won't care to trace;
      We've paid. Still, should such things get lonely,
20   Leave in their vase

      An aspirin to preserve
      Our lilacs, the wayside flowers

We've gathered and must leave to serve
A few more hours;

That's all. We can't tell when   25
We'll come back, can't press claims,
We would no doubt have other rooms then,
Or other names.   1968

The first poem, "Barbie Doll," has the strong note of sadness that characterizes many death poems, but it emphasizes not the girl's death but the disappointments in her life. The only "scene" in the poem (lines 19–23) portrays the unnamed girl at rest in her casket, but the still body in the casket contrasts not with vitality but with frustration and anxiety: her life since puberty (lines 5–6) had been full of apologies and attempts to change her physical appearance and emotional makeup. The rest she achieves in death is not, however, a triumph, despite what people say (line 23). Although the poem's last two words are "happy ending," this girl without a name has died in embarrassment and without fulfillment, and the final lines are ironic, questioning the whole idea of what "happy" means. The cheerful comments at the end lack force and truth because of what we already know; we understand them as ironic because they underline how unhappy the girl was and how false her cosmeticized corpse is to the sad truth of her life.

The poem suggests the falsity and destructiveness of those standards of female beauty that have led to the tragedy of the girl's life. In an important sense, the poem is not really *about* death at all in spite of the fact that the girl's death and her repaired corpse are central to it. As the title suggests, the poem dramatizes how standardized, commercialized notions of femininity and prettiness can be painful and destructive to those whose bodies do not precisely fit the conformist models, and the poem attacks vigorously those conventional standards and the widespread, unthinking acceptance of them.

"Leaving the Motel" similarly goes in quite a different direction from many poems on the subject of love. Instead of expressing assurance about how love lasts and endures, or about the sincerity and depth of affection, this poem describes a parting of lovers after a brief, surreptitious sexual encounter. But it does not emphasize sexuality or eroticism in the meeting of the nameless lovers (we see them only as they prepare to leave), nor does it suggest why or how they have found each other, or what either of them is like as a person. It focuses on how careful they must be not to get caught, how exact and calculating they must be in their planning, how finite and limited their encounter must be, how sealed off this encounter is from the rest of their lives. The poem relates the tiny details the lovers must think of, the agreements they must observe, and the ritual checklist of their duties ("Check . . . Keep things straight . . . Check . . . ," lines 5, 9, 15). Affection and sentiment have their small place in the poem (notice the care for the flowers, lines 19–24, and the thought of "press[ing] claims," line 26), but the emphasis is on temporariness, uncertainty, and limits. Although it is about an illicit, perhaps adulterous, sexual encounter, there is no sex in the poem, only a kind of archaeological record of lust.

Labeling a poem a "love poem" or a "death poem" is primarily a matter of convenience; such categories indicate the **subject** of a poem or the event or **topic** it chooses to engage. But as the poems we have been looking at suggest, poems that may be loosely called love poems or death poems may differ widely from one another, express totally different attitudes or ideas, and concentrate on very different aspects of the subject. The main advantages of grouping poems in this way for study is that a reader can become conscious of individual differences: a reading of two poems side by side may suggest how each is distinctive in what it has to say and how it says it.

The theme of a poem may be expressed in several different ways, and poems often have more than one theme. We could say, for example, that the theme of "Leaving the Motel" is that illicit love is secretive, careful, transitory, and short on emotion and sentiment, or that secret sexual encounters tend to be brief, calculated, and characterized by restrained or hesitant feelings. "Barbie Doll" suggests that commercialized standards destroy human values; that rigid and idealized notions of normality cripple those who are different; that people are easily and tragically led to accept evaluations thrust upon them by others; that American consumers tend to be conformists, easily influenced in their outlook by advertising and by commercial products; that children who do not conform to middle-class standards and notions don't have a chance. The poem implies each of these statements, and all are quite central to it. But none of these statements individually nor all of them together would fully express or explain the poem itself. To state the themes in such a brief and abstract way—though it may help to clarify what the poem does and does not say—does not do justice to the experience of the poem, the way it works on us as readers, the way we respond. Poems affect us in all sorts of ways—emotional and psychological as well as rational—and often a poem's dramatization of a story, an event, or a moment bypasses our rational responses and affects us far more deeply than a clear and logical argument would.

Here is a poem even more directly about desire and its implications. It too is cautious, even critical, but it represents the appeal of both drugs and sex as powerfully as it depicts the fear of their consequences. The "Plague" is the AIDS epidemic in America, especially among gay men, in the early 1990s.

THOM GUNN

In Time of Plague

My thoughts are crowded with death
and it draws so oddly on the sexual
that I am confused
confused to be attracted
5   by, in effect, my own annihilation.
Who are these two, these fiercely attractive men
who want me to stick their needle in my arm?
They tell me they are called Brad and John,
one from here, one from Denver, sitting the same
10   on the bench as they talk to me,
their legs spread apart, their eyes attentive.
I love their daring, their looks, their jargon,
and what they have in mind.

Their mind is the mind of death.
15   They know it, and do not know it,
and they are like me in that
(I know it, and do not know it)

and like the flow of people through this bar.
Brad and John thirst heroically together
for euphoria—for a state of ardent life   20
in which we could all stretch ourselves
and lose our differences. I seek
to enter their minds: am I a fool,
and they direct and right, properly
testing themselves against risk,   25
as a human must, and does,
or are they the fools, their alert faces
mere death's heads lighted glamorously?

I weigh possibilities
till I am afraid of the strength   30
of my own health
and of their evident health.

They get restless at last with my indecisiveness
and so, first one, and then the other,
move off into the moving concourse of people   35
who are boisterous and bright
carrying in their faces and throughout their bodies
the news of life and death.   1992

Delicate subject, sensitive poem. The situation and narrative here are quite clear, and the speaker is plainly attracted by the two men and "what they have in mind" (line 13), but the poem is about a mental state rather than action. The tone is carefully poised between excitement and fear—so much so that the two emotions don't just coexist but are nearly one, and a lust for life and attraction to death are very close. The speaker realizes that he is "attracted by . . . my own annihilation" (lines 4–5), and his vacillation about action involves a kind of internal debate ("I weigh possibilities," line 29) between desire and self-protection. The tone of voice here is both excited and cautionary—and at the same time.

Poems, then, differ widely from one another even when they share a common subject. And the subjects of poetry also vary widely. It isn't true that certain subjects are "poetic" and that others aren't appropriate to poetry. Any human activity, thought, or feeling can be the subject of poetry. Poetry often deals with beauty and the softer, more attractive human emotions, but it can deal with ugliness and unattractive human conduct as well, for poetry seeks to represent human beings and human events, showing us ourselves not only as we would like to be but as we are. Good poetry gets written about all kinds of topics, in all kinds of forms, with all kinds of attitudes. Here, for example, is a poem about a prison inmate—and about the conflict between individual and societal values.

ETHERIDGE KNIGHT

Hard Rock Returns to Prison from the Hospital for the Criminal Insane

Hard Rock was "known not to take no shit
From nobody," and he had the scars to prove it:
Split purple lips, lumped ears, welts above
His yellow eyes, and one long scar that cut
5   Across his temple and plowed through a thick
Canopy of kinky hair.

The WORD was that Hard Rock wasn't a mean nigger
Anymore, that the doctors had bored a hole in his head,
Cut out part of his brain, and shot electricity
10   Through the rest. When they brought Hard Rock back,
Handcuffed and chained, he was turned loose,
Like a freshly gelded stallion, to try his new status.
And we all waited and watched, like indians at a corral,
To see if the WORD was true.

15   As we waited we wrapped ourselves in the cloak
Of his exploits: "Man, the last time, it took eight
Screws to put him in the Hole."[1] "Yeah, remember when he
Smacked the captain with his dinner tray?" "He set
The record for time in the Hole—67 straight days!"
20   "Ol Hard Rock! man, that's one crazy nigger."
And then the jewel of a myth that Hard Rock had once bit
A screw on the thumb and poisoned him with syphilitic spit.

The testing came, to see if Hard Rock was really tame.
A hillbilly called him a black son of a bitch
25   And didn't lose his teeth, a screw who knew Hard Rock
From before shook him down and barked in his face.
And Hard Rock did *nothing*. Just grinned and looked silly,
His eyes empty like knot holes in a fence.

And even after we discovered that it took Hard Rock
30   Exactly 3 minutes to tell you his first name,
We told ourselves that he had just wised up,
Was being cool; but we could not fool ourselves for long,
And we turned away, our eyes on the ground. Crushed.
He had been our Destroyer, the doer of things
35   We dreamed of doing but could not bring ourselves to do,
The fears of years, like a biting whip,
Had cut grooves too deeply across our backs.   1968

---

1. Solitary confinement. *Screws:* guards.

The picture of Hard Rock as a kind of hero to other prison inmates is established early in the poem through a retelling of the legends circulated about him; the straight-forward chronology of the poem sets up the mystery of how he will react after his "treatment" in the hospital. The poem identifies with those who wait; they are hopeful that Hard Rock's spirit has not been broken by surgery or shock treatments, and the lines crawl almost to a stop with disappointment in stanza 4. The *"nothing"* (line 27) of Hard Rock's response to teasing and taunting and the emptiness of his eyes ("like knot holes in a fence," line 28) reduce the heroic hopes and illusions to despair. The final stanza recounts the observers' attempts to reinterpret, to hang onto hope that their symbol of heroism could stand up against the best efforts to tame him, but the spirit has gone out of the hero-worshipers, too, and the poem records them as beaten, conformed, deprived of their spirit as Hard Rock has been of his. The poem records the despair of the hopeless, and it protests against the cruel exercise of power that can curb even as rebellious a figure as Hard Rock.

The following poem is equally full of anger and disappointment, but it expresses its attitudes in a very different way.

WILLIAM BLAKE

London

I wander through each chartered street,
Near where the chartered Thames does flow,
And mark in every face I meet
Marks of weakness, marks of woe.

In every cry of every man,
In every Infant's cry of fear,
In every voice, in every ban,
The mind-forged manacles I hear.

How the Chimney-sweeper's cry
Every black'ning Church appalls;
And the hapless Soldier's sigh
Runs in blood down Palace walls.

But most through midnight streets I hear
How the youthful Harlot's curse
Blasts the new-born Infant's tear,
And blights with plagues the Marriage hearse.   1794

The poem gives a strong sense of how London feels to this particular observer; it is cluttered, constricting, oppressive. The wordplay here articulates and connects the strong emotions he associates with London experiences. The repeated words—"every," for example, and "cry"—intensify the sense of total despair in the city and weld con-nections between things not necessarily related, such as the cries of street vendors with the cries for help. The twice-used word "chartered" implies strong feelings, too. The streets, instead of seeming alive with people or bustling with movement, are rigidly, coldly determined, controlled, cramped. Likewise the river seems as if it were planned, programmed, laid out by an oppressor. In actual fact, the course of the Thames through the city had been altered (slightly) by the government before Blake's time, but most important is the word's emotional force, the sense it projects of constriction and artificiality: the speaker experiences London as if human artifice had totally altered nature. Moreover, according to the poem, people are victimized, "marked" by their confrontations with urbanness and the power of institutions: the "Soldier's sigh" that "runs in blood down Palace walls" vividly suggests, through a metaphor that visually depicts the speaker's feelings, both the powerlessness of the individual and the callousness of power. The "description" of the city has clearly become, by now, a subjective, highly emotional, and vivid expression of how the speaker feels about London and what it represents to him.

> *Poetry makes nothing happen.*
>
> —W. H. AUDEN

Another thing about "London": at first it looks like an account of a personal experience, as if the speaker is describing and interpreting as he goes along: "I wander through each chartered street." But soon it is clear that he is describing many wanderings, putting together impressions from many walks, re-creating a typical walk—which shows him "every" person in the streets, allows him to generalize about the churches being "appalled" (literally, made white) by the cry of the representative Chimney-sweeper, and leads to his conclusions about soldiers, prostitutes, and infants. We receive not a personal record of an event, but a representation of it, as it seems in retrospect—not a story, not a narrative or chronological account of events, but a dramatization of self that compresses many experiences into one.

> *When power leads man toward arrogance, poetry reminds him of his limitations. When power narrows the areas of man's concern, poetry reminds him of the richness and diversity of his existence. When power corrupts, poetry cleanses.*
>
> —JOHN F. KENNEDY

"London" is somber in spite of the poet's playfulness with words. Wordplay may be witty and funny if it calls attention to its own cleverness, but here it involves the discovery of unsuspected (but meaningful) connections between things. The tone of the poem is sad, despairing, and angry; reading it aloud, one would try to show in the tone of one's voice the strong feelings that the poem expresses, just as one would try to reproduce tenderness and caring and passion in reading aloud "The Tally Stick" or "How Do I Love Thee?"

The following two poems are "about" animals, although both of them place their final emphasis on what human beings are like: the animal in each case is only the means to the end of exploring human nature. The poems share a common assumption that animal behavior may appear to reflect human habits and conduct and may reveal much about ourselves, and in each case the character central to the poem is revealed to be surprisingly unlike the way she thinks of herself. But the poems are very different from one another. Read each poem aloud, and try to imagine what each main character is like. What tones of voice do you use to help express the character of the "killer" (line 24) in the first poem? What demands on your voice does the second poem make?

MAXINE KUMIN

Woodchucks

Gassing the woodchucks didn't turn out right.
The knockout bomb from the Feed and Grain Exchange
was featured as merciful, quick at the bone
and the case we had against them was airtight,
both exits shoehorned shut with puddingstone,[2]   5
but they had a sub-sub-basement out of range.

Next morning they turned up again, no worse
for the cyanide than we for our cigarettes
and state-store Scotch, all of us up to scratch.
They brought down the marigolds as a matter of course   10
and then took over the vegetable patch
nipping the broccoli shoots, beheading the carrots.

The food from our mouths, I said, righteously thrilling
to the feel of the .22, the bullets' neat noses.
I, a lapsed pacifist fallen from grace   15
puffed with Darwinian pieties for killing,
now drew a bead on the littlest woodchuck's face.
He died down in the everbearing roses.

Ten minutes later I dropped the mother. She
flipflopped in the air and fell, her needle teeth   20
still hooked in a leaf of early Swiss chard.
Another baby next. O one-two-three
the murderer inside me rose up hard,
the hawkeye killer came on stage forthwith.

There's one chuck left. Old wily fellow, he keeps   25
me cocked and ready day after day after day.
All night I hunt his humped-up form. I dream
I sight along the barrel in my sleep.
If only they'd all consented to die unseen
gassed underground the quiet Nazi way.   1972   30

2. A mixture of cement, pebbles, and gravel.

ADRIENNE RICH

Aunt Jennifer's Tigers

Aunt Jennifer's tigers prance across a screen,
Bright topaz denizens of a world of green.
They do not fear the men beneath the tree;
They pace in sleek chivalric certainty.

5   Aunt Jennifer's fingers fluttering through her wool
Find even the ivory needle hard to pull.
The massive weight of Uncle's wedding band
Sits heavily upon Aunt Jennifer's hand.

When Aunt is dead, her terrified hands will lie
10   Still ringed with ordeals she was mastered by.
The tigers in the panel that she made
Will go on prancing, proud and unafraid.   1951

If you read "Woodchucks" aloud, how would your tone of voice change from beginning to end? What tone would you use to read the ending? How does the hunter feel about her increasing attraction to violence? Why does the poem begin by calling the gassing of the woodchucks "merciful" and end by describing it as "the quiet Nazi way"? What names does the hunter call herself? How does the name-calling affect your feelings about her? Exactly when does the hunter begin to *enjoy* the feel of the gun and the idea of killing? How does the poet make that clear?

Why are tigers a particularly appropriate contrast to the quiet and subdued manner of Aunt Jennifer? What words used to describe the tigers seem particularly significant? In what ways is the tiger an opposite of Aunt Jennifer? In what ways does it externalize her secrets? Why are Aunt Jennifer's hands described as "terrified"? What clues does the poem give about why Aunt Jennifer is so afraid? How does the poem make you feel about Aunt Jennifer? about her tigers? about her life? How would you describe the tone of the poem? How does the poet feel about Aunt Jennifer?

Twenty years after writing "Aunt Jennifer's Tigers," Adrienne Rich said this about the poem:

> In writing this poem, composed and apparently cool as it is, I thought I was creating a portrait of an imaginary woman. But this woman suffers from the opposition of her imagination, worked out in tapestry, and her life style, "ringed with ordeals she was mastered by." It was important to me that Aunt Jennifer was a person as distinct from myself as possible—distanced by the formalism of the poem, by its objective, observant tone—even by putting the woman in a different generation. In those years formalism was part of the strategy—like asbestos gloves, it allowed me to handle materials I couldn't pick up bare-handed.[3]

3. From "When We Dead Awaken: Writing as Re-Vision," a talk given in December 1971 at the Women's Forum of the Modern Language Association.

Not often do we have such an explicit comment on a poem by its author, and (although such a statement may clarify why the author chose particular modes of presentation and how the poem fits into the author's own patterns of thinking and growing) we don't actually need it to understand and experience the force of the poem. Most poems contain within them all we need to tap the human and artistic resources they offer us.

Subject, theme, and tone: each of these categories gives us a way to begin considering poems and showing how one poem differs from another. Comparing poems on the same subject or with a similar theme or tone can lead to a clearer understanding of each individual poem and can refine our responses to the subtleties of individual differences. The title of a poem ("Leaving the Motel," for example) or the way the poem first introduces its subject often can give us a sense of what to expect, but we must be open to surprise, too. No two poems affect us in exactly the same way; the variety of possible poems multiplies when you think of all the possible themes and tones that can be explored within any single subject. Varieties of feeling often coincide with varieties of thinking, and readers open to the pleasures of the unexpected may find themselves learning, growing, becoming more sensitive to ideas and human issues as well as more articulate about feelings and thoughts they already have.

MANY TONES: POEMS ABOUT
FAMILY RELATIONSHIPS

GALWAY KINNELL

After Making Love We Hear Footsteps

For I can snore like a bullhorn
or play loud music
or sit up talking with any reasonably sober Irishman
and Fergus will only sink deeper
5   into his dreamless sleep, which goes by all in one flash,
but let there be that heavy breathing
or a stifled come-cry anywhere in the house
and he will wrench himself awake
and make for it on the run—as now, we lie together,
10   after making love, quiet, touching along the length of our bodies,
familiar touch of the long-married,
and he appears—in his baseball pajamas, it happens,
the neck opening so small
he has to screw them on, which one day may make him wonder
15   about the mental capacity of baseball players—
and says, "Are you loving and snuggling? May I join?"
He flops down between us and hugs us and snuggles himself to sleep,
his face gleaming with satisfaction at being this very child.

In the half darkness we look at each other
20   and smile
and touch arms across his little, startlingly muscled body—
this one whom habit of memory propels to the ground of his making,
sleeper only the mortal sounds can sing awake,
this blessing love gives again into our arms.   1980

EMILY GROSHOLZ

Eden

In lurid cartoon colors, the big baby
dinosaur steps backwards under the shadow
of an approaching tyrannosaurus rex.

"His mommy going to fix it," you remark,
serenely anxious, hoping for the best.   5

After the big explosion, after the lights
go down inside the house and up the street,
we rush outdoors to find a squirrel stopped
in straws of half-gnawed cable. I explain,
trying to fit the facts, "The squirrel is dead."   10

No, you explain it otherwise to me.
"He's sleeping. And his mommy going to come."
Later, when the squirrel has been removed,
"His mommy fix him," you insist, insisting
on the right to know what you believe.   15

The world is truly full of fabulous
great and curious small inhabitants,
and you're the freshly minted, unashamed
Adam in this garden. You preside,
appreciate, and judge our proper names.   20

Like God, I brought you here.
Like God, I seem to be omnipotent,
mostly helpful, sometimes angry as hell.
I fix whatever minor faults arise
with bandaids, batteries, masking tape, and pills.   25

But I am powerless, as you must know,
to chase the serpent sliding in the grass,
or the tall angel with the flaming sword
who scares you when he rises suddenly
behind the gates of sunset.   1992   30

EAVAN BOLAND

The Necessity for Irony

On Sundays,
when the rain held off,
after lunch or later,
I would go with my twelve year old
daughter into town,   5
and put down the time
at junk sales, antique fairs.

There I would
lean over tables,
absorbed by   10

lace, wooden frames,
glass. My daughter stood
at the other end of the room,
her flame-coloured hair
15 obvious whenever—
which was not often—

I turned around.
I turned around.
She was gone.
20 Grown. No longer ready
to come with me, whenever
a dry Sunday
held out its promises
of small histories. Endings.

25 When I was young
I studied styles: their use
and origin. Which age
was known for which
ornament: and was always drawn
30 to a lyric speech, a civil tone.
But never thought
I would have the need,
as I do now, for a darker one:

Spirit of irony,
35 my caustic author
of the past, of memory,—
and of its pain, which returns
hurts, stings—reproach me now,
remind me
40 that I was in those rooms,
with my child,
with my back turned to her,
searching—oh irony!—
for beautiful things.

1998

LI-YOUNG LEE
_____

Persimmons

In sixth grade Mrs. Walker
slapped the back of my head
and made me stand in the corner
for not knowing the difference
5 between *persimmon* and *precision*.
How to choose

persimmons. This is precision.
Ripe ones are soft and brown-spotted.
Sniff the bottoms. The sweet one
will be fragrant. How to eat: 10
put the knife away, lay down newspaper.
Peel the skin tenderly, not to tear the meat.
Chew the skin, suck it,
and swallow. Now, eat
the meat of the fruit,   15
so sweet,
all of it, to the heart.

Donna undresses, her stomach is white.
In the yard, dewy and shivering
with crickets, we lie naked,   20
face-up, face-down.
I teach her Chinese.
Crickets: *chiu chiu*. Dew: I've forgotten.
Naked: I've forgotten.
Ni, wo: you and me.   25
I part her legs,
remember to tell her
she is beautiful as the moon.

Other words
that got me into trouble were   30
fight and *fright, wren* and *yarn*.
Fight was what I did when I was frightened,
fright was what I felt when I was fighting.
Wrens are small, plain birds,
yarn is what one knits with.   35
Wrens are soft as yarn.
My mother made birds out of yarn.
I loved to watch her tie the stuff;
a bird, a rabbit, a wee man.

Mrs. Walker brought a persimmon to class   40
and cut it up
so everyone could taste
a *Chinese apple*. Knowing
it wasn't ripe or sweet, I didn't eat
but watched the other faces.   45

My mother said every persimmon has a sun
inside, something golden, glowing,
warm as my face.

Once, in the cellar, I found two wrapped in newspaper,
forgotten and not yet ripe.   50
I took them and set both on my bedroom windowsill,
where each morning a cardinal
sang, *The sun, the sun.*

55
Finally understanding
he was going blind,
my father sat up all one night
waiting for a song, a ghost.
I gave him the persimmons,
swelled, heavy as sadness,
60
and sweet as love.

This year, in the muddy lighting
of my parents' cellar, I rummage, looking
for something I lost.
My father sits on the tired, wooden stairs,
65
black cane between his knees,
hand over hand, gripping the handle.

He's so happy that I've come home.
I ask how his eyes are, a stupid question.
All gone, he answers.

70
Under some blankets, I find a box.
Inside the box I find three scrolls.
I sit beside him and untie
three paintings by my father:
Hibiscus leaf and a white flower.
75
Two cats preening.
Two persimmons, so full they want to drop from the cloth.

He raises both hands to touch the cloth,
asks, *Which is this?*

This is persimmons, Father.

80
Oh, the feel of the wolftail on the silk,
the strength, the tense
precision in the wrist.
I painted them hundreds of times
eyes closed. These I painted blind.
85
Some things never leave a person:
scent of the hair of one you love,
the texture of persimmons,
in your palm, the ripe weight.   1986

ROBERT HAYDEN

Those Winter Sundays

Sundays too my father got up early
and put his clothes on in the blueblack cold,
then with cracked hands that ached

from labor in the weekday weather made
banked fires blaze. No one ever thanked him.   5

I'd wake and hear the cold splintering, breaking.
When the rooms were warm, he'd call,
and slowly I would rise and dress,
fearing the chronic angers of that house,

Speaking indifferently to him,   10
who had driven out the cold
and polished my good shoes as well.
What did I know, what did I know
of love's austere and lonely offices?   1966

SUSAN MUSGRAVE

You Didn't Fit

for my father

You wouldn't fit in your coffin
but to me it was no surprise.
All your life you had never fit in
anywhere; you saw no reason to
begin fitting now.   5

When I was little I remember
a sheriff coming. You were
taken to court because your
false teeth didn't fit and you
wouldn't pay the dentist. It was   10
your third set, you said none of them
fit properly. I was afraid then
that something would take you from me
as it has done now: death
with a bright face and teeth that   15
fit perfectly.

A human smile that shuts me out.
The Court, I remember, returned
your teeth, now marked an exhibit.
You were dismissed with costs—   20
I never understood. The teeth were
terrible. We liked you better
without them.

We didn't fit, either, into your
life or your loneliness, though you   25
tried, and we did too. Once

30

I wanted to marry you, and then left;
I'm still the child who won't fit
into the arms of anyone, but is
always reaching.

I was awkward for years, my bones
didn't fit in my body but stuck out
like my heart—people used to comment
on it. They said I was very good

35

at office parties where you took me
and let others do the talking—the
crude jokes, the corny men—I saw
how they hurt you and I loved you
harder than ever.

40

Because neither of us fit. Later you
blamed me, said "You must fit in,"
but I didn't and I still think
it made you secretly happy.

45

Like I am now: you won't fit in your
coffin. My mother, after a life
of it, says, "This is the last straw."
And it is. We're all clutching.

1985

ALAN DUGAN

Elegy

I know but will not tell
you, Aunt Irene, why there
are soapsuds in the whiskey:
Uncle Robert had to have

5

a drink while shaving. May
there be no bloodshed in your house
this morning of my father's death
and no unkept appearance
in the living, since he has

10

to wear the rouge and lipstick
of your ceremony, mother,
for the first and last time:
father, hello and goodbye.

1963

KELLY CHERRY

Alzheimer's

He stands at the door, a crazy old man
Back from the hospital, his mind rattling
Like the suitcase, swinging from his hand,
That contains shaving cream, a piggy bank,
A book he sometimes pretends to read,   5
His clothes. On the brick wall beside him
Roses and columbine slug it out for space, claw the mortar.
The sun is shining, as it does late in the afternoon
In England, after rain.
Sun hardens the house, reifies it,   10
Strikes the iron grillwork like a smithy
And sparks fly off, burning in the bushes—
The rosebushes—
While the white wood trim defines solidity in space.
This is his house. He remembers it as his,   15
Remembers the walkway he built between the front room
And the garage, the rhododendron he planted in back,
The car he used to drive. He remembers himself,
A younger man, in a tweed hat, a man who loved
Music. There is no time for that now. No time for music,   20
The peculiar screeching of strings, the luxurious
Fiddling with emotion.
Other things have become more urgent.
Other matters are now of greater import, have more
Consequence, must be attended to. The first   25
Thing he must do, now that he is home, is decide who
This woman is, this old, white-haired woman
Standing here in the doorway,
Welcoming him in.   1997

AGHA SHAHID ALI

Postcard from Kashmir

(for Pavan Sahgal)

Kashmir shrinks into my mailbox,
my home a neat four by six inches.

I always loved neatness. Now I hold
the half-inch Himalayas in my hand.

⁵ This is home. And this the closest
I'll ever be to home. When I return,
the colors won't be so brilliant,
the Jhelum's waters[1] so clean,
so ultramarine. My love
¹⁰ so overexposed.

And my memory will be a little
out of focus, in it
a giant negative, black
and white, still undeveloped.   1987

JIMMY SANTIAGO BACA

Green Chile

I prefer red chile over my eggs
and potatoes for breakfast.
Red chile *ristras*[2] decorate my door,
dry on my roof, and hang from eaves.
⁵ They lend open-air vegetable stands
historical grandeur, and gently swing
with an air of festive welcome.
I can hear them talking in the wind,
haggard, yellowing, crisp, rasping
¹⁰ tongues of old men, licking the breeze.

       But grandmother loves green chile.
When I visit her,
she holds the green chile pepper
in her wrinkled hands.
¹⁵ Ah, voluptuous, masculine,
an air of authority and youth simmers
from its swan-neck stem, tapering to a flowery
collar, fermenting resinous spice.
A well-dressed gentleman at the door
²⁰ my grandmother takes sensuously in her hand,
rubbing its firm glossed sides,
caressing the oily rubbery serpent,
with mouth-watering fulfillment,
fondling its curves with gentle fingers.
²⁵ Its bearing magnificent and taut
as flanks of a tiger in mid-leap,
she thrusts her blade into
and cuts it open, with lust

---

1. The river Jhelum runs through Kashmir and Pakistan.   2. Braided strings of peppers.

on her hot mouth, sweating over the stove,
bandanna round her forehead,   30
mysterious passion on her face
and she serves me green chile con carne
between soft warm leaves of corn tortillas,
with beans and rice—her sacrifice
to her little prince.   35
I slurp from my plate
with last bit of tortilla, my mouth burns
and I hiss and drink a tall glass of cold water.

All over New Mexico, sunburned men and women
drive rickety trucks stuffed with gunny-sacks   40
of green chile, from Belen, Veguita, Willard, Estancia,
San Antonio y Socorro, from fields
to roadside stands, you see them roasting green chile
in screen-sided homemade barrels, and for a dollar a bag,
we relive this old, beautiful ritual again and again.   1989   45

QUESTIONS

1. Consider carefully how the tone of Hayden's "Those Winter Sundays" is created. What activities of the father inspire the son's admiration? Which words of the son are especially effective in suggesting his attitude toward his father? Why is the phrase "what did I know" repeated in line 13? What are the connotations of the word "austere" in line 14? How old does the son seem to be at the time the poem is written? How can you tell?

2. What attitude does Dugan's "Elegy" take toward Aunt Irene? toward Uncle Robert? toward the mother? toward the father? How can you tell about the attitudes toward each? What individual words or factual details help to suggest the attitudes? Is "Elegy" an appropriate title for the poem? Why?

3. Compare the ideas of motherhood in Grosholz's "Eden" and Boland's "The Necessity for Irony." What different kinds of things do the two speakers remember about their children? How much of the difference can be accounted for by time and perspective? By the children's ages? By the mothers' personalities?

4. What different qualities do the red and green chiles have in Baca's "Green Chiles"? How fully do they reflect the differences between the speaker and his grandmother? Which words in the poem help to personify the chiles? What purposes do this kind of language serve?

WRITING SUGGESTIONS

1. Read aloud Kinnell's "After Making Love We Hear Footsteps" and Musgrave's "You Didn't Fit." Pick out three or four key words from each poem that seem to control the tone of voice you use. Then, concentrating on the words you have isolated, write an essay of no more than six hundred words in which you compare the tones of the two poems.

2. Cherry's "Alzheimer's" uses contrasts—especially before and after—to characterize the ravages of Alzheimer's disease. What evidence does the poem provide about what the man used to be like? What specific changes have come about? How does the setting of the poem suggest some of those changes? In what ways do the stabilities of house, landscape, and other people clarify what has happened? Write an essay of three hundred to five hundred words about the function of the poem's setting.

13

SPEAKER: WHOSE VOICE DO WE HEAR?

Poems are personal. The thoughts and feelings they express belong to a specific person, and however general or universal their sentiments seem to be, poems come to us as the expression of an individual human voice. That voice is often the voice of the poet. But not always. Poets sometimes create "characters" just as writers of fiction or drama do—people who speak for them only indirectly. A character may, in fact, be very different from the poet, just as a character in a play or story is different from the author, and that person, the **speaker** of the poem, may express ideas or feelings very different from the poet's own. In the following poem, rather than himself speaking directly to us, the poet has created two speakers, both female, each of whom has a distinctive voice, personality, and character.

THOMAS HARDY

The Ruined Maid

"O 'Melia,[1] my dear, this does everything crown!
Who could have supposed I should meet you in Town?
And whence such fair garments, such prosperi-ty?"—
"O didn't you know I'd been ruined?" said she.

5   —"You left us in tatters, without shoes or socks,
Tired of digging potatoes, and spudding up docks;[2]
And now you've gay bracelets and bright feathers three!"—
"Yes: that's how we dress when we're ruined," said she.

—"At home in the barton[3] you said 'thee' and 'thou,'
10   And 'thik oon,' and 'theäs oon,' and 't'other'; but now

1. Short for Amelia.   2. Spading up weeds.   3. Farmyard.

Your talking quite fits 'ee for high compa-ny!"—
"Some polish is gained with one's ruin," said she.

—"Your hands were like paws then, your face blue and bleak
But now I'm bewitched by your delicate cheek,
And your little gloves fit as on any la-dy!"—   15
"We never do work when we're ruined," said she.

—"You used to call home-life a hag-ridden dream,
And you'd sigh, and you'd sock;[4] but at present you seem
To know not of megrims[5] or melancho-ly!"—
"True. One's pretty lively when ruined," said she.   20

—"I wish I had feathers, a fine sweeping gown,
And a delicate face, and could strut about Town!"—
"My dear—a raw country girl, such as you be,
Cannot quite expect that. You ain't ruined," said she.

1866

The first voice, that of a young woman who has remained back on the farm, is designated typographically (that is, by the way the poem is printed): there are dashes at the beginning and end of all but the first of her speeches. She speaks the first part of each **stanza** (a stanza is a section of a poem designated by spacing), usually the first three lines. The second young woman, a companion and coworker on the farm in years gone by, regularly gets the last line in each stanza (and in the last stanza, two lines), so it is clear who is talking at every point. Also, the two speakers are just as clearly distinguished by what they say, how they say it, and what sort of person each proves to be. The nameless stay-at-home shows little knowledge of the world, and everything surprises her: seeing her former companion at all, but especially seeing her well clothed, cheerful, and polished; and as the poem develops she shows increasing envy of her more worldly friend. She is the "raw country girl" (line 23) that the other speaker says she is, and she still speaks the country dialect ("fits 'ee," line 11, for example) that she notices her friend has lost (lines 9–11). The "ruined" young woman ('Melia), on the other hand, says little except the refrain about having been ruined, but even the slight variations she plays on that theme suggest her sophistication and amusement at her rural friend, although she still uses a country "ain't" at the end. We are not told the full story of their lives (was the "ruined" young woman thrown out? did she run away from home or work?), but we know enough (that they've been separated for some time, that the stay-at-home did not know where the other had gone) to allow the dialogue to articulate the contrast between them: one is still rural, inexperienced, and innocent; the other is sophisticated, citified, and "ruined." Each speaker's style of speech then does the rest.

It is equally obvious that there is a speaker (or, in this case, a singer) in stanzas 2 through 9 of the following poem:

4. Deliver angry blows.   5. Migraine headaches.

X. J. KENNEDY

In a Prominent Bar in Secaucus One Day

*To the tune of "The Old Orange Flute" or the tune of
"Sweet Betsy from Pike"*

In a prominent bar in Secaucus[6] one day
Rose a lady in skunk with a topheavy sway,
Raised a knobby red finger—all turned from their beer—
While with eyes bright as snowcrust she sang high and clear:

5　"Now who of you'd think from an eyeload of me
That I once was a lady as proud as could be?
Oh I'd never sit down by a tumbledown drunk
If it wasn't, my dears, for the high cost of junk.

"All the gents used to swear that the white of my calf
10　Beat the down of a swan by a length and a half.
In the kerchief of linen I caught to my nose
Ah, there never fell snot, but a little gold rose.

"I had seven gold teeth and a toothpick of gold.
My Virginia cheroot was a leaf of it rolled
15　And I'd light it each time with a thousand in cash—
Why the bums used to fight if I flicked them an ash.

"Once the toast of the Biltmore,[7] the belle of the Taft,
I would drink bottle beer at the Drake, never draft,
And dine at the Astor on Salisbury steak
20　With a clean tablecloth for each bite I did take.

"In a car like the Roxy[8] I'd roll to the track,
A steel-guitar trio, a bar in the back,
And the wheels made no noise, they turned over so fast,
Still it took you ten minutes to see me go past.

25　"When the horses bowed down to me that I might choose,
I bet on them all, for I hated to lose.
Now I'm saddled each night for my butter and eggs
And the broken threads race down the backs of my legs.

"Let you hold in mind, girls, that your beauty must pass
30　Like a lovely white clover that rusts with its grass.
Keep your bottoms off barstools and marry you young
Or be left—an old barrel with many a bung.

"For when time takes you out for a spin in his car
You'll be hard-pressed to stop him from going too far

6. A small town on the Hackensack River in New Jersey, a few miles west of Manhattan.　7. Like the
Taft, Drake, and Astor, a once-fashionable New York hotel.　8. A luxurious old New York theater and
movie house, the site of many "world premieres" in the heyday of Hollywood.

And be left by the roadside, for all your good deeds,   35
Two toadstools for tits and a face full of weeds."

All the house raised a cheer, but the man at the bar
Made a phonecall and up pulled a red patrol car
And she blew us a kiss as they copped her away
From that prominent bar in Secaucus, N.J.   1961   40

Again, we learn about the character primarily through her own words, although we may not believe everything she tells us about her past. From her introduction in the first stanza we get some general notion of her appearance and condition, but it is she who tells us that she is a junkie (line 8) and a prostitute (line 27) and that her face and figure have seen better days (lines 32, 36). That information could make her a sad case, and the poem might lament her state or allow us to lament it, but instead she presents herself in a light, friendly and theatrical way. She is anxious to give advice and sound righteous (line 31, for example), but she's also enormously cheerful about herself, and her spirit repeatedly bursts through her song. Her performance gives her a lot of pleasure as she exaggerates outrageously about her former luxury and prominence, and even her departure in a patrol car she chooses to treat as a grand exit, throwing a kiss to her audience. The comedy is bittersweet, perhaps, but she is allowed to present herself, through her own words and attitudes, as a likable character—someone who has survived life's disappointments and retained her dignity. The glorious fiction of her life, narrated with energy and polish in the manner of a practiced and accomplished liar, betrays some rather naive notions of good taste and luxurious living (lines 18–26). But this "lady in skunk" has a picturesque and engaging style, a refreshing sense of humor about herself, and a flair for drama. Like the cheap fur she wears, her experiences in what she considers high life satisfy her sense of style and celebration. The self-portrait accumulates, almost completely through how she talks about herself, and the poet develops our attitude toward her by allowing her to recount her story herself, in her own words—or rather in words chosen for her by the author.

The following poem uses the idea of speaker in a very different way and for quite different tonal purposes:

ADRIENNE RICH

Letters in the Family

I: Catalonia, 1936

Dear Parents:
            I'm the daughter
you didn't bless when she left,
an unmarried woman wearing a khaki knapsack   5
with a poor mark in Spanish.
                    I'm writing now
from a plaster-dusted desk in a town

pocked street by street with hand grenades,
some of them, dear ones, thrown by me.
This is a school: the children are at war.
You don't need honors in schoolroom Spanish here
to be of use and my right arm
's as strong as anyone's. I sometimes think
all languages are spoken here,
even mine, which you got zero in.
Don't worry. Don't try to write. I'm happy,
if you could know it.
                                        Rochelle.

II: Yugoslavia, 1944[9]

Dear Chana,
                        where are you now?
Am sending this pocket-to-pocket
(though we both know pockets we'd hate to lie in).
They showed me that poem you gave Reuven,
about the match:
Chana, you know, I never was
for martyrdom. I thought we'd try our best,
ragtag mission that we were,
then clear out if the signals looked too bad.
Something in you drives things ahead for me
but if I can I mean to stay alive.
We're none of us giants, you know,
just small, frail, inexperienced romantic people.
But there are things we learn.
You know the sudden suck of empty space
between the jump and the ripcord pull?
I hate it. I hate it so,
I've hated you for your dropping
ecstatically in free-fall, in the training,
your look, dragged on the ground, of knowing
precisely why you were there.
                                        My mother's
still in Palestine. And yours
still there in Hungary. Well, there we are.
When this is over—
                        I'm

9. See *Hannah Senesh: Her Life and Diary* (New York: Schocken, 1973). Born in Budapest, 1921, Hannah Senesh became a Zionist and emigrated to Palestine at the age of eighteen; her mother and brother remained in Europe. In 1943, she joined an expedition of Jews who trained under the British to parachute behind Nazi lines in Europe and connect with the partisan underground, to rescue Jews in Hungary, Romania, and Czechoslovakia. She was arrested by the Nazis, imprisoned, tortured, and executed in November 1944. Like the other letter-writers, 'Esther' is an imagined person.
    See also Ruth Whitman's long poem, *The Testing of Hannah Senesh* (Detroit: Wayne State University Press, 1986) [Rich's note].

your earthbound friend to the end, still yours—
                                        Esther.

III: Southern Africa, 1986   50

Dear children:
            We've been walking nights
a long time over rough terrain,
sometimes through marshes. Days we hide
under what bushes we can find.   55
Our stars steer us. I write
on my knee by a river with a weary hand,
and the weariness will come through
this letter that should tell you
nothing but love. I can't say where we are,   60
what weeds are in bloom, what birds cry at dawn.
The less you know the safer.
But not to know how you are going on—
Matile's earache, Emma's lessons, those tell-tale
eyes and tongues, so quick—are you remembering   65
to be brave and wise and strong?
At the end of this hard road
we'll sit all together at one meal
and I'll tell you everything: the names
of our comrades, how the letters   70
were routed to you, why I left.
And I'll stop and say, "Now you,
grown so big, how was it for you, those times?
Look, I know you in detail, every inch of each
sweet body, haven't I washed and dried you   75
a thousand times?"
            And we'll eat and tell our stories
together. That is my reason.
            Ma.   1989

Like Hardy's "The Ruined Maid," this poem uses different voices, and here they are clearly distinguished as different "historical" characters—Rochelle, Esther, and "Ma," women from three separate places and times who in letter form tell their own stories. In each case, the individual story is part of some larger historical moment, and although all three characters are (as the author's footnote points out) fictional, the three stories together present a kind of history of female heroism in difficult cultural moments.

Try reading the poem aloud so you can hear how different in tone the three voices sound; each woman has distinctive expressions and syntax of her own. All are in part defined by their relationships to families left behind, but all are defined even more fully by their own idealistic determination to resist the larger social and political forces in the cultures where they are at the time they write their letters. Telling stories, the pleasure identified by the third speaker as the ultimate purpose of her actions (lines 56–62), is important to all three speakers as a way of defining themselves in relation to their families; to the poem, the telling of separate stories by the different speakers becomes the collective means to exemplify the power of historical women in action.

Historical speakers like these can present special interpretive problems because we as readers may lack information relevant to their characters. In the following poem, for example, the Canadian poet Margaret Atwood draws heavily upon facts and traditions about a nineteenth-century émigré from Scotland to Canada:

MARGARET ATWOOD

Death of a Young Son by Drowning

He, who navigated with success
the dangerous river of his own birth
once more set forth

on a voyage of discovery
5   into the land I floated on
but could not touch to claim.

His feet slid on the bank,
the currents took him;
he swirled with ice and trees in the swollen water

10   and plunged into distant regions,
his head a bathysphere;
through his eyes' thin glass bubbles

he looked out, reckless adventurer
on a landscape stranger than Uranus
15   we have all been to and some remember.

There was an accident; the air locked,
he was hung in the river like a heart.
They retrieved the swamped body,

cairn of my plans and future charts,
20   with poles and hooks
from among the nudging logs.

It was spring, the sun kept shining, the new grass
leapt to solidity;
my hands glistened with details.

25   After the long trip I was tired of waves.
My foot hit rock. The dreamed sails
collapsed, ragged.

I planted him in this country
like a flag.   1970

The poem comes from a volume called *The Journals of Susanna Moodie: Poems by Margaret Atwood* (1970). A kind of frontier pioneer, Moodie herself had written two books about Canada, *Roughing It in the Bush* and *Life in the Clearings,* and Atwood found their observations rather stark and disorganized. She wrote her Susanna Moodie poems to refocus the "character" and to reconstruct Moodie's actual geographical exploration and self-discovery. To truly understand these thoughts and meditations, then, we need to know their historical referent. Read in context, they present very powerful psychological and cultural analyses.

Some speakers in poems are not, however, nearly so heroic or attractive, and some poems create a speaker who makes us dislike him or her, also because of what the poet makes him or her say, as the following poem does. Here the speaker, as the title implies, is a monk, but he shows himself to be most unspiritual: mean, self-righteous, and despicable.

ROBERT BROWNING

Soliloquy of the Spanish Cloister

Gr-r-r—there go, my heart's abhorrence!
   Water your damned flower-pots, do!
If hate killed men, Brother Lawrence,
   God's blood, would not mine kill you!
What? your myrtle-bush wants trimming?   5
   Oh, that rose has prior claims—
Needs its leaden vase filled brimming?
   Hell dry you up with its flames!

At the meal we sit together:
   Salve tibi![1] I must hear   10
Wise talk of the kind of weather,
   Sort of season, time of year:
Not a plenteous cork-crop: scarcely
   Dare we hope oak-galls,[2] *I doubt:*
What's the Latin name for "parsley"?   15
   What's the Greek name for Swine's Snout?

Whew! We'll have our platter burnished,
   Laid with care on our own shelf!
With a fire-new spoon we're furnished,
   And a goblet for ourself,   20
Rinsed like something sacrificial
   Ere 'tis fit to touch our chaps[3]—
Marked with L. for our initial!
   (He-he! There his lily snaps!)

---

1. Hail to thee (Latin). Italics usually indicate the words of Brother Lawrence.   2. Abnormal growth on oak trees, used for tanning.   3. Jaws.

Saint, forsooth! While brown Dolores 25
   —Squats outside the Convent bank
With Sanchicha, telling stories,
   Steeping tresses in the tank,
Blue-black, lustrous, thick like horsehairs,
   —Can't I see his dead eye glow, 30
Bright as 'twere a Barbary corsair's?[4]
   (That is, if he'd let it show!)

When he finishes refection,
   Knife and fork he never lays
Cross-wise, to my recollection, 35
   As do I, in Jesu's praise.
I the Trinity illustrate,
   Drinking watered orange-pulp—
In three sips the Arian[5] frustrate;
   —While he drains his at one gulp. 40

Oh, those melons? If he's able
   We're to have a feast! so nice!
One goes to the Abbot's table,
   All of us get each a slice.
How go on your flowers? None double? 45
   Not one fruit-sort can you spy?
Strange!—And I, too, at such trouble,
   —Keep them close-nipped on the sly!

There's a great text in Galatians,
   Once you trip on it, entails 50
Twenty-nine distinct damnations,[6]
   One sure, if another fails:
If I trip him just a-dying,
   Sure of heaven as sure can be,
Spin him round and send him flying 55
   Off to hell, a Manichee?[7]

Or, my scrofulous French novel
   On gray paper with blunt type!
Simply glance at it, you grovel
   Hand and foot in Belial's gripe:[8] 60
If I double down its pages
   At the woeful sixteenth print,
When he gathers his greengages,
   Ope a sieve and slip it in't?

Or, there's Satan!—one might venture 65
   Pledge one's soul to him, yet leave

---

4. African pirate's.   5. A heretical sect that denied the Trinity.   6. Galatians 5.15–23 provides a long list of possible offenses, but they do not add up to twenty-nine.   7. A heretic. According to the Manichean heresy, the world was divided into the forces of good and evil, equally powerful.   8. In the clutches of Satan.

Such a flaw in the indenture
　　—As he'd miss till, past retrieve,
Blasted lay that rose-acacia
　　We're so proud of! *Hy, Zy, Hine . . .*[9]
'St, there's Vespers! *Plena gratiâ*
　　Ave, Virgo.[1] Gr-r-r—you swine!

70

1842

Not many poems begin with a growl, and this harsh sound turns out to be fair warning that we are about to meet a real beast, even though he is in the clothing of a religious man. In line 1 he shows himself to hold a most uncharitable attitude toward his fellow monk, Brother Lawrence, and by line 4 he has uttered two profanities and admitted his intense feelings of hatred and vengefulness. His ranting and roaring is full of exclamation points (four in the first stanza!), and he reveals his own personality and character when he imagines curses and unflattering nicknames for Brother Lawrence or plots malicious jokes on him. By the end, we have accumulated no knowledge of Brother Lawrence that makes him seem a fit target for such rage (except that he is pious, dutiful, and pleasant—perhaps enough to make this sort of speaker despise him), but we have discovered the speaker to be lecherous (stanza 4), full of false piety (stanza 5), malicious in trivial matters (stanza 6), ready to use his theological learning to sponsor damnation rather than salvation (stanza 7), a closet reader and viewer of pornography within the monastery (stanza 8)—even willing to risk his own soul in order to torment Brother Lawrence (last stanza).

The speaker characterizes himself; the details accrue and accumulate into a fairly full portrait, and here we do not have even an opening and closing "objective" description (as in Kennedy's "In a Prominent Bar") or another speaker (as in Hardy's "The Ruined Maid") to give us perspective. Except for the moments when the speaker mimics or parodies Brother Lawrence (usually in italic type), we have only the speaker's own words and thoughts. But that is enough; the poet has controlled them so carefully that we know what he thinks of the speaker—that he is a mean-spirited, vengeful hypocrite, a thoroughly disreputable and unlikable character. The whole poem has been about him and his attitudes; the point has been to characterize the speaker and develop in us a dislike of him and what he stands for—total hypocrisy.

In reading a poem like this aloud, we would want our voice to suggest all the unlikable features of a hypocrite. We would also need to suggest, through tone of voice, the author's contemptuous mocking of the rage and hypocrisy, and we would want, like an actor, to create strong disapproval in the hearer. The poem's words (the ones the author has given to the speaker) clearly imply those attitudes, and we would want our voice to express them. Usually there is much more to a poem than the identification and characterization of the speaker, but in many cases it is necessary to identify the speaker and determine his or her character before we can appreciate what else goes on in the poem. And sometimes, as here, in looking for the speaker of the poem, we approach the center of the poem itself.

Sometimes the effect of a poem depends on our recognizing the temporal position of the speaker as well as her or his identity. The following poem, for example, quickly makes plain that a childhood experience is at the center of the action and that the speaker is female:

---

9. Possibly the beginning of an incantation or curse.　1. The opening words of the *Ave Maria*, here reversed: "Full of grace, Hail, Virgin" (Latin).

TESS GALLAGHER

Sudden Journey

Maybe I'm seven in the open field—
the straw-grass so high
only the top of my head makes a curve
of brown in the yellow. Rain then.
5   First a little. A few drops on my
wrist, the right wrist. More rain.
My shoulders, my chin. Until I'm looking up
to let my eyes take the bliss.
I open my face. Let the teeth show. I
10   pull my shirt down past the collar-bones.
I'm still a boy under my breast spots.
I can drink anywhere. The rain. My
skin shattering. Up suddenly, needing
to gulp, turning with my tongue, my arms out
15   running, running in the hard, cold plenitude
of all those who reach earth by falling.   1984

The sense of adventure and wonder here has a lot to do with the childlike sentence structure and choice of words at the beginning of the poem. Sentences are short, observations direct and simple. The rain becomes exciting and blissful and totally absorbing as the child's actions and reactions take over the poem in lines 2–13. But not all of the poem takes place in a child's mind in spite of the precise and impressive re-creation of childish responses and feelings. The opening line makes clear that we are sliding into a supposition of the past; "maybe I'm seven" makes clear that we, as conspiring adults, are pretending ourselves into earlier time. And at the end the word "plenitude"—crucial to interpreting the poem's full effect and meaning—makes clear that we are finding an adult perspective on the incident. Elsewhere, too, the adult world gives the incident meaning. In line 12, for example, the joke about being able to drink anywhere depends on an adult sense of what being a boy might mean. The "journey" of the poem's title is not only the little girl's running in the rain, but also the adult movement into a past re-created and newly understood.

The speaker in the following poem positions herself very differently, but we do not get a full sense of her until the poem is well along. As you read, try to imitate the tone of voice you think this person would use. Exactly when do you begin to know what she is like?

DOROTHY PARKER

A Certain Lady

Oh, I can smile for you, and tilt my head,
    And drink your rushing words with eager lips,

And paint my mouth for you a fragrant red,
   And trace your brows with tutored finger-tips.
When you rehearse your list of loves to me,   5
   Oh, I can laugh and marvel, rapturous-eyed.
And you laugh back, nor can you ever see
   The thousand little deaths my heart has died.
And you believe, so well I know my part,
   That I am gay as morning, light as snow,   10
And all the straining things within my heart
   You'll never know.

Oh, I can laugh and listen, when we meet,
   And you bring tales of fresh adventurings—
Of ladies delicately indiscreet,   15
   Of lingering hands, and gently whispered things.
And you are pleased with me, and strive anew
   To sing me sagas of your late delights.
Thus do you want me—marveling, gay, and true—
   Nor do you see my staring eyes of nights.   20
And when, in search of novelty, you stray,
   Oh, I can kiss you blithely as you go . . .
And what goes on, my love, while you're away,
   You'll never know.   1937

    To whom does the speaker seem to be talking? What sort of person is he? How do you feel about him? Which habits and attitudes of his do you like least? How soon can you tell that the speaker is not altogether happy about his conversation and conduct? In what tone of voice would you read the first twenty-two lines aloud? What attitude would you try to express toward the person spoken to? What tone would you use for the last two lines? How would you describe the speaker's personality? What aspects of her behavior are most crucial to the poem's effect?

    It is easy to assume that the speaker in a poem is an extension of the poet. Is the speaker in this poem Dorothy Parker? Maybe. A lot of Parker's poems present a similar world-weary posture and a kind of cynicism about romantic love. But the poem is hardly an example of self-revelation, a giving away of personal secrets. If it were, it would be silly, not to say risky, to address her lover in a way that gives damaging facts about a pose she has been so careful to set up.

    In poems such as "The Ruined Maid," "In a Prominent Bar," and "Soliloquy of the Spanish Cloister," we are in no danger of mistaking the speaker for the poet, once we have recognized that poets may create speakers who participate in specific situations much as in fiction or drama. When there is a pointed discrepancy between the speaker and what we know of the poet—when the speaker is a woman, for example, and the poet is a man—we know we have a created speaker to contend with and that the point (or at least *one* point) in the poem is to observe the characterization carefully. In "A Certain Lady" we may be less sure, and in other poems the discrepancy between speaker and poet may be even more uncertain. What are we to make, for example, of the speaker in "Woodchucks" in the previous chapter? Is that speaker the real Maxine Kumin? At best (without knowing something quite specific about the author) we can only say "maybe" to that question. What we can be sure of is the sort of person the speaker is portrayed to be—someone (a man? a woman?) surprised to discover feelings and attitudes that contradict values apparently held confidently. And that is exactly what we need to know for the poem to have its effect.

A similar kind of self-mocking of the speaker is present in the following poem, but here the mockery is put to less revelatory, more comic ends.

A. R. AMMONS

Needs

I want something suited to my special needs
I want chrome hubcaps, pin-on attachments
and year round use year after year
I want a workhorse with smooth uniform cut,
5   dozer blade and snow blade & deluxe steering
wheel
I want something to mow, throw snow, tow
and sow with
I want precision reel blades
10   I want a console styled dashboard
I want an easy spintype recoil starter
I want combination bevel and spur gears, 14
gauge stamped steel housing and
washable foam element air cleaner
15   I want a pivoting front axle and extrawide
turf tires
I want an inch of foam rubber inside a vinyl
covering
and especially if it's not too much, if I
20   can deserve it, even if I can't pay for it
I want to mow while riding.   1970

The poet here may be teasing himself about his desire for comfort and ease—and showing how readily advertisements and catalog descriptions manipulate us. But the speaker doesn't have to be the author for the teasing to work. In fact, the effect is to tease those attitudes no matter who holds them by teasing a speaker who illustrates the attitudes. It doesn't matter to the poem whether the speaker is the poet himself or some totally invented character. If the speaker is a version of the poet himself—perhaps a *side* of his personality that he is exploring—the portrait is still fictional in an important sense. The poem presents not a whole human being (*no* poem could do that) but only a part or version of him—a mood perhaps, an aspect, an attitude, a role. The poet presents someone with an obsession, in this case a small and not very damaging one, and allows him to spout phrases as if he were reciting from an ad or a sales catalog. The "portrait" is made more comic by a clear sense the poem projects that what we have here is only a part of the person, an interest grown too intense, gone askew, gotten out of proportion, something that happens to most of us from time to time. All we know about the speaker is that he has a one-track mind, that he is obsessed by his own luxurious comfort. He may not even be a "he": there is nothing in the poem that makes us certain that the speaker is male. It is customary to think of the speaker in a poem written by a man as "he" and in a poem written by a woman as "she" (as in Maxine Kumin's "Woodchucks") unless the poem presents contrary evidence; but it is merely a convenience, a habit, nothing more.

Even when poets present themselves as if they were speaking directly to us in their own voices, their poems present only a partial portrait, something considerably less than the full personality and character of the poet. Even when there is not an obviously created character—someone with distinct characteristics that are different from those of the poet—strategies of characterization are used to present the person speaking in one way and not another. Even in a poem like the following one, which contains identifiable autobiographical details, it is still a good idea to think of the speaker instead of the poet, although here the poet is probably writing about a personal, actual experience, and he is certainly making a character of himself—that is, characterizing himself in a certain way, emphasizing some parts of himself and not others.

WILLIAM WORDSWORTH

She Dwelt among the Untrodden Ways

She dwelt among the untrodden ways
    Beside the springs of Dove,[2]
A Maid whom there were none to praise
    And very few to love:

A violet by a mossy stone   5
    Half hidden from the eye!
—Fair as a star, when only one
    Is shining in the sky.

She lived unknown, and few could know
    When Lucy ceased to be;   10
But she is in her grave, and, oh,
    The difference to me!   1800

Is this poem more about Lucy or about the speaker's feelings concerning her death? Though her simple life, far removed from fame and known only to a few, is said to have been beautiful, we know little about her beyond her name and where she lived, in a beautiful but then-isolated section of northern England. We don't know if she was young or old, only that the speaker thinks of her as "fair" and compares her to a "violet by a mossy stone." We do know that the speaker is deeply pained by her death, so deeply that he is almost inarticulate with grief, lapsing into simple exclamation ("oh," line 11) and unable to articulate the "difference" that her death makes.

2. A small stream in the Lake District in northern England, near where Wordsworth lived in Dove Cottage at Grasmere.

Did Lucy actually live? Was she a friend of the poet? We don't know; the poem doesn't tell us, and even biographers of Wordsworth are unsure. What we do know is that Wordsworth was able to represent grief over the death very powerfully. Whether the speaker is the historical Wordsworth or not, that speaker is a major focus of the poem, and it is his feelings that the poem isolates and expresses. We need to recognize some characteristics of the speaker and be sensitive to his feelings for the poem to work.

The poems we have looked at in this chapter—and the group that follows at the end of the chapter—all suggest the value of beginning the reading of any poem with simple questions: Who is speaking? What do we know about him or her? What kind of person is she or he? Putting together the evidence that the poem presents in answer to such questions can often take us a long way into the poem. For some poems, such questions won't help a great deal because the speaking voice is too indistinct or the character behind the poem too scantily presented. But starting with such questions will often lead you toward the central experience the poem offers. At the very least, the question of speaker helps clarify the tone of voice, and it often provides guidance to the larger situation the poem explores.

• • •

ANDREW HUDGINS

Praying Drunk

Our Father who art in heaven, I am drunk.
Again. Red wine. For which I offer thanks.
I ought to start with praise, but praise
comes hard to me. I stutter. Did I tell you
5   about the woman whom I taught, in bed,
this prayer? It starts with praise; the simple form
keeps things in order. I hear from her sometimes.
Do you? And after love, when I was hungry,
I said, *Make me something to eat.* She yelled,
10   *Poof! You're a casserole!*—and laughed so hard
she fell out of the bed. Take care of her.

Next, confession—the dreary part. At night
deer drift from the dark woods and eat my garden.
They're like enormous rats on stilts except,
15   of course, they're beautiful. But why? What *makes*
them beautiful? I haven't shot one yet.
I might. When I was twelve, I'd ride my bike
out to the dump and shoot the rats. It's hard
to kill your rats, our Father. You have to use
20   a hollow point and hit them solidly.
A leg is not enough. The rat won't pause.
Yeep! Yeep! it screams, and scrabbles, three-legged, back
into the trash, and I would feel a little bad
to kill something that wants to live
25   more savagely than I do, even if

it's just a rat. My garden's vanishing.
Perhaps I'll merely plant more beans, though that
might mean more beautiful and hungry deer.
Who knows?
        I'm sorry for the times I've driven   30
home past a black, enormous, twilight ridge.
Crested with mist, it looked like a giant wave
about to break and sweep across the valley,
and in my loneliness and fear I've thought,
O let it come and wash the whole world clean.   35
Forgive me. This is my favorite sin: despair—
whose love I celebrate with wine and prayer.

Our Father, thank you for all the birds and trees,
that nature stuff. I'm grateful for good health,
food, air, some laughs, and all the other things   40
I'm grateful that I've never had to do
without. I have confused myself. I'm glad
there's not a rattrap large enough for deer.
While at the zoo last week, I sat and wept
when I saw one elephant insert his trunk   45
into another's ass, pull out a lump,
and whip it back and forth impatiently
to free the goodies hidden in the lump.
I could have let it mean most anything,
but I was stunned again at just how little   50
we ask for in our lives. *Don't look! Don't look!*
Two young nuns tried to herd their giggling
schoolkids away. *Line up,* they called. *Let's go
and watch the monkeys in the monkey house.*
I laughed, and got a dirty look. Dear Lord,   55
we lurch from metaphor to metaphor,
which is—let it be so—a form of praying.

I'm usually asleep by now—the time
for supplication. Requests. As if I'd stayed
up late and called the radio and asked   60
they play a sentimental song. Embarrassed.
I want a lot of money and a woman.
And, also, I want vanishing cream. You know—
a character like Popeye rubs it on
and disappears. Although you see right through him,   65
he's there. He chuckles, stumbles into things,
and smoke that's clearly visible escapes
from his invisible pipe. It makes me think,
sometimes, of you. What makes me think of me
is the poor jerk who wanders out on air   70
and then looks down. Below his feet, he sees
eternity, and suddenly his shoes
no longer work on nothingness, and down
he goes. As I fall past, remember me.   1991

AUDRE LORDE

Hanging Fire

I am fourteen
and my skin has betrayed me
the boy I cannot live without
still sucks his thumb
5   in secret
how come my knees are
always so ashy
what if I die
before morning
10   and momma's in the bedroom
with the door closed.

I have to learn how to dance
in time for the next party
my room is too small for me
15   suppose I die before graduation
they will sing sad melodies
but finally
tell the truth about me
There is nothing I want to do
20   and too much
that has to be done
and momma's in the bedroom
with the door closed.

Nobody even stops to think
25   about my side of it
I should have been on Math Team
my marks were better than his
why do I have to be
the one
30   wearing braces
I have nothing to wear tomorrow
will I live long enough
to grow up
and momma's in the bedroom
35   with the door closed.   1978

SIR THOMAS WYATT

They Flee from Me

They flee from me, that sometime did me seek,
With naked foot stalking in my chamber.

I have seen them, gentle, tame, and meek,
That now are wild, and do not remember
That sometime they put themselves in danger   5
To take bread at my hand; and now they range,
Busily seeking with a continual change.

Thankéd be Fortune it hath been otherwise,
Twenty times better; but once in special,
In thin array, after a pleasant guise,   10
When her loose gown from her shoulders did fall,
And she me caught in her arms long and small.[3]
And therewith all sweetly did me kiss
And softly said, "Dear heart, how like you this?"

It was no dream, I lay broad waking.   15
But all is turned, thorough[4] my gentleness,
Into a strange fashion of forsaking;
And I have leave to go, of her goodness,
And she also to use newfangleness.[5]
But since that I so kindely[6] am servéd,   20
I fain[7] would know what she hath deservéd.   1557

MARY COLERIDGE

The Poison Flower

The poison flower that in my garden grew
Killed all the other flowers beside.
They withered off and died,
Because their fiery foe sucked up the dew.

When the sun shone, the poison flower breathed cold   5
And spread a chilly mist of dull disgrace.
They could not see his face,
Roses and lilies languished and grew old.

Wherefore I tore that flower up by the root,
And flung it on the rubbish heap to fade   10
Amid the havoc that itself had made.
I did not leave one shoot.

Fair is my garden as it once was fair.
Lilies and roses reign.
They drink the dew, they see the sun again;   15
But I rejoice no longer, walking there.

3. Slender.   4. Through.   5. Fondness for novelty.   6. That is, in kind.   7. Eagerly.

GWENDOLYN BROOKS

We Real Cool

THE POOL PLAYERS,
SEVEN AT THE GOLDEN SHOVEL.

We real cool. We
Left school. We

Lurk late. We
Strike straight. We

5   Sing sin. We
Thin gin. We

Jazz June. We
Die soon.   1950

WALT WHITMAN

[*I celebrate myself, and sing myself*]

I celebrate myself, and sing myself,
And what I assume you shall assume,
For every atom belonging to me as good belongs to you.
I loafe and invite my soul,
5   I lean and loafe at my ease observing a spear of summer grass.

My tongue, every atom of my blood, form'd from this soil, this air,
Born here of parents born here from parents the same, and their parents
the same,
I, now thirty-seven years old in perfect health begin,
Hoping to cease not till death.
10 Creeds and schools in abeyance,
Retiring back a while sufficed at what they are, but never forgotten,
I harbor for good or bad, I permit to speak at every hazard,
Nature without check with original energy.   1855, 1881

QUESTIONS

1. What, precisely, do we know about the speaker in Lorde's "Hanging Fire"? How much self-confidence does she have? How can you tell? How does she feel about herself?
2. How fully does the speaker characterize himself in "Praying Drunk"? What facts and phrases seem especially revealing? What details of his past? How important is his sense of humor and self-deprecation? How does the disarming early admission that "I am drunk" (line 1) work as the "prayer" goes on? How do your normal expectations of what a prayer consists of work here?

WRITING SUGGESTION

1. The speaker in Ammons's "Needs" reveals himself to have desires and needs that he is not himself fully conscious of. Analyze carefully just what elements in the poem make clear to us the "secret" aspects of his character. Compare the character of the speaker (and the strategies used to characterize her) in Maxine Kumin's "Woodchucks" (chapter 12). Compare "Needs" in detail with "Woodchucks," and write a six- or seven-hundred-word essay in which you characterize the speakers in the two poems, making clear what kind of attitude each poem develops toward its speaker.

14

SITUATION AND SETTING: WHAT HAPPENS? WHERE? WHEN?

Questions about the speaker ("Who" questions) in a poem almost always lead to questions of "Where?" "When?" and "Why?" Identifying the speaker usually is, in fact, part of a larger process of defining the entire imagined **situation** in a poem: What is happening? Where is it happening? Who is the speaker speaking to? Who else is present? Why is this event occurring? In order to understand the dialogue in Hardy's "The

> It is difficult / to get the news
> from poems / yet men die
> miserably every day / for lack /
> of what is found there.
>
> —WILLIAM CARLOS WILLIAMS

Ruined Maid," for example, we need to recognize that the friends are meeting after an extended period of separation, and that they meet in a town setting rather than the rural area in which they grew up together. We infer (from the opening lines) that the meeting is accidental, and that no other friends are present for the conversation. The poem's whole "story" depends on their situation: after leading sepa-

rate lives for some time they have some catching up to do. We don't know what specific town, year, season, or time of day is involved because those details are not important to the poem's effect. But crucial to the poem are the where and when questions that define the situation and relationship of the two speakers, and the answer to the why question—that the meeting is by chance—is important, too. In another poem we looked at in the previous chapter, Parker's "A Certain Lady," the specific moment and place are not important, but we do need to notice that the "lady" is talking to (or having an imaginary conversation with) her lover and that they are talking about a relationship of some duration.

Sometimes a *specific* time and place (**setting**) may be important. X. J. Kennedy's "lady in skunk" sings her life story "in a prominent bar in Secaucus," a smelly and unfashionable town in New Jersey, but on no particular occasion ("one day"). In Browning's "Soliloquy of the Spanish Cloister," the setting (a monastery) adds to the irony because of the gross inappropriateness of such sentiments and attitudes in a supposedly holy place, just as the setting of Betjeman's "In Westminster Abbey" (below, page 684) similarly helps us to judge the speaker's ideas, attitudes, and self-conception.

The title of the following poem suggests that place may be important, and it is, although you may be surprised to discover exactly what exists at this address and what uses the speaker makes of it.

JAMES DICKEY

Cherrylog Road

Off Highway 106
At Cherrylog Road I entered
The '34 Ford without wheels,
Smothered in kudzu,
With a seat pulled out to run   5
Corn whiskey down from the hills,

And then from the other side
Crept into an Essex
With a rumble seat of red leather
And then out again, aboard   10
A blue Chevrolet, releasing
The rust from its other color,

Reared up on three building blocks.
None had the same body heat;
I changed with them inward, toward   15
The weedy heart of the junkyard,
For I knew that Doris Holbrook
Would escape from her father at noon

And would come from the farm
To seek parts owned by the sun   20
Among the abandoned chassis,
Sitting in each in turn
As I did, leaning forward
As in a wild stock-car race

In the parking lot of the dead.   25
Time after time, I climbed in
And out the other side, like
An envoy or movie star
Met at the station by crickets.
A radiator cap raised its head,   30

Become a real toad or a kingsnake
As I neared the hub of the yard,
Passing through many states,
Many lives, to reach
Some grandmother's long Pierce-Arrow   35
Sending platters of blindness forth

From its nickel hubcaps
And spilling its tender upholstery
On sleepy roaches,
The glass panel in between   40
Lady and colored driver
Not all the way broken out,

The back-seat phone
Still on its hook.
45   I got in as though to exclaim,
"Let us go to the orphan asylum,
John; I have some old toys
For children who say their prayers."

I popped with sweat as I thought
50   I heard Doris Holbrook scrape
Like a mouse in the southern-state sun
That was eating the paint in blisters
From a hundred car tops and hoods.
She was tapping like code,

55   Loosening the screws,
Carrying off headlights,
Sparkplugs, bumpers,
Cracked mirrors and gear-knobs,
Getting ready, already,
60   To go back with something to show

Other than her lips' new trembling
I would hold to me soon, soon,
Where I sat in the ripped back seat
Talking over the interphone,
65   Praying for Doris Holbrook
To come from her father's farm

And to get back there
With no trace of me on her face
To be seen by her red-haired father
70   Who would change, in the squalling barn,
Her back's pale skin with a strop,
Then lay for me

In a bootlegger's roasting car
With a string-triggered 12-gauge shotgun
75   To blast the breath from the air.
Not cut by the jagged windshields,
Through the acres of wrecks she came
With a wrench in her hand,

Through dust where the blacksnake dies
80   Of boredom, and the beetle knows
The compost has no more life.
Someone outside would have seen
The oldest car's door inexplicably
Close from within:

85   I held her and held her and held her,
Convoyed at terrific speed
By the stalled, dreaming traffic around us,
So the blacksnake, stiff

With inaction, curved back
Into life, and hunted the mouse   90

With deadly overexcitement,
The beetles reclaimed their field
As we clung, glued together,
With the hooks of the seat springs
Working through to catch us red-handed   95
Amidst the gray breathless batting

That burst from the seat at our backs.
We left by separate doors
Into the changed, other bodies
Of cars, she down Cherrylog Road   100
And I to my motorcycle
Parked like the soul of the junkyard

Restored, a bicycle fleshed
With power, and tore off
Up Highway 106, continually   105
Drunk on the wind in my mouth,
Wringing the handlebar for speed,
Wild to be wreckage forever.   1964

The *exact* location of the junkyard is not important (there is no Highway 106 near the real Cherrylog Road in North Georgia), but we do need to know that the setting is rural, that the time is summer and the summer is hot, and that moonshine whiskey is native to the area. Following the story is no problem once we have sorted out these few facts, and we are prepared to meet the cast of characters: Doris Holbrook, her red-haired father, and the speaker. About each we learn just enough to appreciate the sense of vitality, adventure, power, and disengagement that constitute the major effects of the poem.

The situation of lovemaking in a setting other than the junkyard would not produce the same effects, and the exotic sense of a forbidden meeting in this unlikely place helps to re-create the speaker's sense of the episode. For him, it is memorable (notice all the tiny details he recalls), powerful (notice his reaction when he gets back on his motorcycle), dreamlike (notice the sense of time standing still, especially in lines 85–89), and important (notice how the speaker perceives his environment as changed by their lovemaking, lines 88–91 and 98–100). The wealth of details about setting also helps us to raise other, related questions. Why does the speaker fantasize about being shot by the father (lines 72–75)? Why, in a poem so full of details, do we find out so little about what Doris Holbrook looks like and thinks about? What gives us the sense that this incident is a composite of episodes, an event that was repeated many times? What gives us the impression that the events occurred long ago? What makes the speaker feel so powerful at the end? What does he mean when he talks of himself as being "wild to be wreckage forever"? All of the poem's attention to the speaker's reactions, reflections, and memories is intricately tied up with the particulars of setting. Making love in a junkyard is crucial to the speaker's sense of both power and wreckage, and to him Doris is merely a matter of excitement, adventure, and pale skin, appreciated because she makes the world seem different and because she is willing to take risks and to suffer for meeting him like this. The more we probe the poem with questions about situation, the more likely we are to catch the poem's full effect.

The plot of "Cherrylog Road" is fairly easy to sort out, but its effect is more complex than the simple story suggests. The next poem we will look at is initially much more difficult to follow. Part of the difficulty is that the poem comes from an earlier age and its language and sentence structure are a bit unfamiliar, and part is that the action in the poem is so closely connected to what is being said. But its opening lines—addressed to someone who is resisting the speaker's suggestions—disclose the situation, and gradually we figure out the scene: a man, trying to convince a woman that they should make love, uses a nearby flea for an unlikely example; it becomes part of his argument. And once we recognize the situation, we can readily follow (and be amused by) the speaker's witty and intricate argument.

JOHN DONNE

The Flea

Mark but this flea, and mark in this[1]
How little that which thou deny'st me is;
It sucked me first, and now sucks thee,
And in this flea our two bloods mingled be;
Thou know'st that this cannot be said
A sin, nor shame, nor loss of maidenhead.
    Yet this enjoys before it woo,
    And pampered[2] swells with one blood made of two,
    And this, alas, is more than we would do.[3]

Oh stay, three lives in one flea spare,
Where we almost, yea more than, married are.
This flea is you and I, and this
Our marriage bed, and marriage temple is;
Though parents grudge, and you, we're met
And cloistered in these living walls of jet.
    Though use[4] make you apt to kill me,
    Let not to that, self-murder added be,
    And sacrilege, three sins in killing three.

Cruel and sudden, hast thou since
Purpled thy nail in blood of innocence?
Wherein could this flea guilty be,
Except in that drop which it sucked from thee?
Yet thou triumph'st, and say'st that thou
Find'st not thyself, nor me, the weaker now;

1. Medieval preachers and rhetoricians asked their hearers to "mark" (look at) an object that illustrated a moral or philosophical lesson they wished to emphasize.   2. Fed luxuriously.   3. According to contemporary medical theory, conception involved the literal mingling of the lovers' blood. 4. Habit.

'Tis true; then learn how false, fears be;   25
Just so much honor, when thou yield'st to me,
Will waste, as this flea's death took life from thee.   1633

The scene in "The Flea" develops, action occurs, even as the poem unfolds. Between stanzas 1 and 2, the woman makes a move to kill the flea (as stanza 2 opens, the speaker is trying to stop her), and between stanzas 2 and 3 she has squashed the flea with her fingernail. Once we make sense of what the speaker says, the action is just as clear from the words as if we had stage directions in the margin. All of the speaker's verbal cleverness and all of his specious arguments follow from the situation, and in this poem (as in Browning's "Soliloquy of the Spanish Cloister") we watch as if we were observing a scene in a play. The speaker is, in effect, giving a dramatic monologue for our benefit.

Neither time nor place is important to "The Flea," except that we assume the speaker and his friend are in the same place and have the leisure for some playfulness. The situation could occur anywhere a man, a woman, and a flea could be together: indoors, outdoors, morning, evening, city, country, in cottage or palace, on a boat or in a bedroom. We know, from the date of publication, that Donne was writing about people of almost four centuries ago, but the conduct he describes might equally happen in later ages. Only the habits of language (and perhaps the speaker's religious attitudes) date the poem.

The two poems that follow have simpler plots, but in each case the heart of the poem is in the basic situation:

RITA DOVE

Daystar

She wanted a little room for thinking:
but she saw diapers steaming on the line,
a doll slumped behind the door.

So she lugged a chair behind the garage
to sit out the children's naps.   5

Sometimes there were things to watch—
the pinched armor of a vanished cricket,
a floating maple leaf. Other days
she stared until she was assured
when she closed her eyes   10
she'd see only her own vivid blood.

She had an hour, at best, before Liza appeared
pouting from the top of the stairs.
And just *what* was mother doing
out back with the field mice? Why,   15

building a palace. Later
that night when Thomas rolled over and
lurched into her, she would open her eyes
and think of the place that was hers
20   for an hour—where
she was nothing,
pure nothing, in the middle of the day.   1986

LINDA PASTAN

To a Daughter Leaving Home

When I taught you
at eight to ride
a bicycle, loping along
beside you
5   as you wobbled away
on two round wheels,
my own mouth rounding
in surprise when you pulled
ahead down the curved
10   path of the park,
I kept waiting
for the thud
of your crash as I
sprinted to catch up,
15   while you grew
smaller, more breakable
with distance,
pumping, pumping
for your life, screaming
20   with laughter,
the hair flapping
behind you like a
handkerchief waving
goodbye.   1988

Both poems involve motherhood, but they take entirely different stances about it and have very different tones. The mother in Dove's "Daystar" is overwhelmed by the demands of young children and needs a room of her own. All she can manage, however, is a brief hour of respite. The situation is virtually the whole story here. Nothing really happens except that daily events (washing diapers, picking up toys, looking at crickets and leaves, explaining the world to children, having sex) crowd her brief private hour and make it precious. Being "nothing" (lines 21 and 22) takes on great value in these circumstances, and the poem makes much of the setting: an isolated chair behind the garage. Setting in poems often means something much more specific about a particular culture or social history, but here time and place are given value by the circumstances of the situation for one frazzled mother.

The particulars of time and place in Pastan's "To a Daughter Leaving Home" are even less specific; the incident the poem describes happened a long time ago, and its vividness is a function of memory. The speaker here thinks back nostalgically to a moment when her daughter made an earlier (but briefer) departure from the home. Though we learn very little about the speaker, at least directly, we may infer quite a bit about her— her affection for her daughter, the kind of mother she has been, her anxiety at the new departure that seems to reflect the earlier wobbly ride into the distance. The daughter is now, the poem implies, old enough to "leave" home in a full sense, but we do not know the specific reason or what the present circumstances are. Only the title tells us the situation, and (like "Daystar") the poem is all situation.

Some poems, however, depend heavily on historical specifics. In the preceding chapter, for example, we saw how Margaret Atwood based "Death of a Young Son by Drowning" on an actual person's journal entries. While the following poem refers to a particular event, it also draws on the parallels between that event and circumstances surrounding the poet and his immediate readers:

JOHN MILTON

On the Late Massacre in Piedmont

Avenge, O Lord, thy slaughtered saints, whose bones
 Lie scattered on the Alpine mountains cold;
 Even them who kept thy truth so pure of old
 When all our fathers worshiped stocks and stones,[5]
Forget not: in thy book record their groans   5
 Who were thy sheep and in their ancient fold
 Slain by the bloody Piemontese that rolled
 Mother with infant down the rocks. Their moans
The vales redoubled to the hills, and they
 To heaven. Their martyred blood and ashes sow   10
 O'er all th' Italian fields, where still doth sway
The triple tyrant:[6] that from these may grow
 A hundredfold, who having learnt thy way
 Early may fly the Babylonian woe.[7]

1655

The "slaughtered saints" were members of the Waldensians—a heretical sect that had long been settled in southern France and northern Italy (the Piedmont). Though a

5. Idols of wood and stone.   6. The pope's tiara featured three crowns.   7. In Milton's day, Protestants often likened the Roman Church to Babylonian decadence, called the church "the whore of Babylon," and read Revelation 17 and 18 as an allegory of its coming destruction.

minority, the Waldensians were allowed freedom of worship until 1655, when their protection under the law was taken away and locals attacked them, killing large numbers. This poem, then, is not a private meditation, but rather a public statement about a well-known "news" event. The reader, to fully understand the poem and respond to it meaningfully, must therefore be acquainted with its historical context, including the massacre itself and the significance it had for Milton and his English audience.

Milton wrote the poem shortly after the massacre became known in England, and implicit in its "meaning" is a parallel Milton's readers would have felt between events in the Piedmont and current English politics. Milton signals the analogy early on by calling the dead Piedmontese "saints," the term then regularly used by English Protestants of the Puritan stamp to describe themselves and to thereby assert their belief that every individual Christian—not just those few "special" religious heroes singled out in the Catholic tradition—lived a heroic life. By identifying the Waldensians with the English Puritans—their beliefs were in some ways quite similar, and both were minorities in a larger political and cultural context—Milton was warning his fellow Puritans that, if the Stuart monarchy were reestablished, what had just happened to the Waldensians could happen to them as well. Following the Restoration in 1660, tight restrictions were in fact placed on the Puritan "sects" under the new monarchy. In lines 12 and 14, the poem alludes to dangers of religious rule by dominant groups by invoking standard images of Catholic power and persecution; the heir to the English throne (who succeeded to the throne as Charles II in 1660) was spending his exile in Catholic Europe and was, because of his sympathetic treatment of Catholic associates and friends, suspected of being a Catholic. Chauvinistic Englishmen, who promoted rivalries with Catholic powers like France, considered him a traitor.

Many poems, like this one, make use of historical occurrences and situations to create a widely evocative set of angers, sympathies, and conclusions. Sometimes a poet's intention in recording a particular moment or event is to commemorate it or comment upon it. A poem written about a specific occasion is usually called an **occasional poem,** and such a poem is **referential;** that is, it *refers* to a certain historical time or event. Sometimes, it is hard to place ourselves fully enough in another time or place to imagine sympathetically what a particular historical moment would have been like, and even the best poetic efforts do not necessarily transport us there. For such poems we need, at the least, specific historical information—plus a willingness on our part as readers to be transported, by a name, a date, or a dramatic situation.

Time or place may, of course, be used much less specifically and still be important to a poem; frequently a poem's setting draws upon common notions of a particular time or place. Setting a poem in a garden, for example, or writing about apples almost inevitably reminds many readers of the Garden of Eden because it is part of the Western heritage of belief or knowledge. Even people who don't read at all or who lack Judeo-Christian religious commitments are likely to know about Eden, and a poet writing in our culture can count on that. An **allusion** is a reference to something outside the poem that carries a history of meaning and strong emotional associations. (For a longer account of allusion, see chapter 22.) For example, gardens may carry suggestions of innocence and order, or temptation and the Fall, or both, depending on how the poem handles the allusion. Well-known places from history or myth may be popularly associated with particular ideas or values or ways of life.

The place involved in a poem is its **spatial setting,** and the time is its **temporal setting.** The temporal setting may involve a specific date or an era, a season of the year or a time of day. We tend, for example, to think of spring as a time of discovery and growth, and poems set in spring are likely to make use of that association; morning usually suggests discovery as well—beginnings, vitality, the world fresh and new—even to those of us who in reality take our waking slow. Temporal or spatial setting often influences our expectation of theme and tone, although a poet may surprise us by making something very different of our expectation. Setting is often an important factor in creating the mood in poems just as in stories, plays, or films. Often the details of setting have a lot to do with the way we ultimately respond to the poem's subject or theme, as in this poem:

SYLVIA PLATH

Point Shirley

From Water-Tower Hill to the brick prison
The shingle booms, bickering under
The sea's collapse.
Snowcakes break and welter. This year
The gritted wave leaps   5
The seawall and drops onto a bier
Of quahog chips,[8]
Leaving a salty mash of ice to whiten

In my grandmother's sand yard. She is dead,
Whose laundry snapped and froze here, who   10
Kept house against
What the sluttish, rutted sea could do.
Squall waves once danced
Ship timbers in through the cellar window;
A thresh-tailed, lanced   15
Shark littered in the geranium bed—

Such collusion of mulish elements
She wore her broom straws to the nub.
Twenty years out
Of her hand; the house still hugs in each drab   20
Stucco socket
The purple egg-stones: from Great Head's knob
To the filled-in Gut
The sea in its cold gizzard ground those rounds.

Nobody wintering now behind   25
The planked-up windows where she set
Her wheat loaves
And apple cakes to cool. What is it
Survives, grieves
So, over this battered, obstate spit   30
Of gravel? The waves'
Spewed relics clicker masses in the wind,

8. Chips from quahog clamshells, common on the New England coast.

Gray waves the stub-necked eiders ride.
A labor of love, and that labor lost.
35   Steadily the sea
Eats at Point Shirley. She died blessed,
And I come by
Bones, bones only, pawed and tossed,
A dog-faced sea.
40   The sun sinks under Boston, bloody red.

I would get from these dry-papped stones
The milk your love instilled in them.
The black ducks dive.
And though your graciousness might stream,
45   And I contrive,
Grandmother, stones are nothing of home
To that spumiest dove.
Against both bar and tower the black sea runs.   1960

One does not have to know the New England coast by personal experience to find it vividly re-created in Plath's poem. A reader who knows that coast or another like it may have an advantage in being able to respond more quickly to the poem's precise description, but the poem does not depend on the reader's having such knowledge. The exact location of Point Shirley, near Boston, is not especially important, but visualization of the setting is. Crucial to the poem's tone and mood is the sense of the sea as aggressor, a force powerful enough to change the contours of the coast and invade the privacy of yards and homes. The energy, relentlessness, and impersonality of the sea met their match, though only temporarily, in the speaker's grandmother, who "[k]ept house against / What the sluttish, rutted sea could do" (lines 11–12). The grandmother *belonged* in this setting, and it seemed hers, but twenty years of her absence (since her death) now begin to show. Still, the marks of her obstinacy and love remain, although ultimately they are doomed by the sea's more enduring power.

Details—and how they are amassed—matter here rather than historic particulars of time and place. The grays and whites and drab colors of the sea and its leavings provide both a visual sense of the scene and the mood for the poem. The stubbornness that the speaker admired in the grandmother seems a part of that tenacious grayness. Nothing happens rapidly here; things wear down. Even the "bloody red" (line 40) of the sun's setting—an ominous sign that adds a vivid fright to the dullness rather than brightening it—makes promises that seem slow and long-term. The toughness of the boarded-up house is a monument to the grandmother's loving care and becomes a way for the speaker to touch her human spirit, but the poem finally emphasizes the relentless black sea, which runs against the landmarks and fortresses that had been identified with the setting in the very first line.

Queries about situation and setting begin as simple questions of identification, but frequently become more complex when we sort out all the implications. Often it takes only a moment to determine a poem's situation, but it may take much longer to discover all the implications of time and place, for their meanings may depend upon visual details, or upon actual historical occurrences, or upon habitual ways of thinking about certain times and places—or all three at once. As you read the following poem, notice how the setting—another shore—prepares us for the speaker's moods and ideas, and then watch how the movement of his mind is affected by what he sees.

MATTHEW ARNOLD

Dover Beach[9]

The sea is calm tonight.
The tide is full, the moon lies fair
Upon the straits; on the French coast the light
Gleams and is gone; the cliffs of England stand,
Glimmering and vast, out in the tranquil bay.   5
Come to the window, sweet is the night-air!
Only, from the long line of spray
Where the sea meets the moon-blanched land,
Listen! you hear the grating roar
Of pebbles which the waves draw back, and fling,   10
At their return, up the high strand,
Begin, and cease, and then again begin,
With tremulous cadence slow, and bring
The eternal note of sadness in.

Sophocles long ago   15
Heard it on the Aegean, and it brought
Into his mind the turbid ebb and flow
Of human misery;[1] we
Find also in the sound a thought,
Hearing it by this distant northern sea.   20

The Sea of Faith
Was once, too, at the full, and round earth's shore
Lay like the folds of a bright girdle furled.
But now I only hear
Its melancholy, long, withdrawing roar,   25
Retreating, to the breath
Of the night-wind, down the vast edges drear
And naked shingles[2] of the world.

Ah, love, let us be true
To one another! for the world, which seems   30
To lie before us like a land of dreams,
So various, so beautiful, so new,
Hath really neither joy, nor love, nor light,

9. At the narrowest point on the English Channel. The light on the French coast (lines 3–4) would be about twenty miles away.   1. In Sophocles' *Antigone*, lines 637–46, the chorus compares the fate of the house of Oedipus to the waves of the sea.   2. Pebble-strewn beaches.

35   Nor certitude, nor peace, nor help for pain;
        And we are here as on a darkling plain
        Swept with confused alarms of struggle and flight,
        Where ignorant armies clash by night.

    ca. 1851

Exactly what is the dramatic situation in "Dover Beach"? How soon are you aware that someone is being spoken to? How much do you learn about the person spoken to? How would you describe the speaker's mood? What does the speaker's mood have to do with time and place? Do any details of present time and place help to account for his tendency to talk repeatedly of the past and the future? How important is it to the poem's total effect that the beach here involves an international border? What particulars of Dover Beach seem especially important to the poem's themes? to its emotional effects?

Not all poems have an identifiable situation or setting, just as not all poems have a speaker who is entirely distinct from the author. Poems that simply present a series of thoughts and feelings directly, in a contemplative, meditative, or reflective way, may not set up any kind of action, plot, or situation at all, preferring to speak directly without the intermediary of a dramatic device. But most poems depend crucially upon a sense of place, a sense of time, and an understanding of human interaction in scenes that resemble the strategies of drama or film. And questions about these matters will often lead you to define not only the "facts" but also the feelings central to the design a poem has upon its readers.

SITUATIONS

MARILYN NELSON

How I Discovered Poetry

It was like soul-kissing, the way the words
filled my mouth as Mrs. Purdy read from her desk.
All the other kids zoned an hour ahead to 3:15,
but Mrs. Purdy and I wandered lonely as clouds borne
by a breeze off Mount Parnassus. She must have seen   5
the darkest eyes in the room brim: The next day
she gave me a poem she'd chosen especially for me
to read to the all except for me white class.
She smiled when she told me to read it, smiled harder,
said oh yes I could. She smiled harder and harder   10
until I stood and opened my mouth to banjo playing
darkies, pickaninnies, disses and dats. When I finished
my classmates stared at the floor. We walked silent
to the buses, awed by the power of words.

                                                                1997

EMILY BRONTË

The Night-Wind

In summer's mellow midnight,
A cloudless moon shone through
Our open parlor window
And rosetrees wet with dew.

I sat in silent musing,   5
The soft wind waved my hair:
It told me Heaven was glorious,
And sleeping Earth was fair.

I needed not its breathing
To bring such thoughts to me,   10
But still it whispered lowly,
"How dark the woods will be!

"The thick leaves in my murmur
Are rustling like a dream,

15 And all their myriad voices
    Instinct[1] with spirit seem."

    I said, "Go, gentle singer,
    Thy wooing voice is kind,
    But do not think its music
20 Has power to reach my mind.

    "Play with the scented flower,
    The young tree's supple bough,
    And leave my human feelings
    In their own course to flow."

25 The wanderer would not leave me;
    Its kiss grew warmer still—
    "O come," it sighed so sweetly,
    "I'll win thee 'gainst thy will.

    "Have we not been from childhood friends?
30 Have I not loved thee long?
    As long as thou hast loved the night
    Whose silence wakes my song.

    "And when thy heart is laid at rest
    Beneath the church-yard stone
35 I shall have time enough to mourn
    And thou to be alone."

September 11, 1840

ANDREW MARVELL

To His Coy Mistress

    Had we but world enough, and time,
    This coyness,[2] lady, were no crime.
    We would sit down, and think which way
    To walk, and pass our long love's day.
5   Thou by the Indian Ganges' side
    Shouldst rubies[3] find: I by the tide
    Of Humber would complain.[4] I would
    Love you ten years before the Flood,
    And you should if you please refuse
10 Till the conversion of the Jews.[5]

---

1. Infused.   2. Hesitancy, modesty (not necessarily suggesting calculation).   3. Talismans that are supposed to preserve virginity.   4. Write love complaints, conventional songs lamenting the cruelty of love. *Humber:* a small river that flows through Marvell's hometown of Hull.   5. Which, according to popular Christian belief, will occur just before the end of the world.

My vegetable love[6] should grow
Vaster than empires, and more slow;
An hundred years should go to praise
Thine eyes, and on thy forehead gaze;
Two hundred to adore each breast,   15
But thirty thousand to the rest.
An age at least to every part,
And the last age should show your heart.
For, lady, you deserve this state;[7]
Nor would I love at lower rate.   20
   But at my back I always hear
Time's wingéd chariot hurrying near;
And yonder all before us lie
Deserts of vast eternity.
Thy beauty shall no more be found,   25
Nor, in thy marble vault, shall sound
My echoing song; then worms shall try
That long preserved virginity,
And your quaint honor turn to dust,
And into ashes all my lust: 30
The grave's a fine and private place,
But none, I think, do there embrace.
   Now therefore, while the youthful hue
Sits on thy skin like morning dew,[8]
And while thy willing soul transpires[9]   35
At every pore with instant fires,
Now let us sport us while we may,
And now, like am'rous birds of prey,
Rather at once our time devour
Than languish in his slow-chapped[1] pow'r.   40
Let us roll all our strength and all
Our sweetness up into one ball,
And tear our pleasures with rough strife
Thorough[2] the iron gates of life.
Thus, though we cannot make our sun   45
Stand still,[3] yet we will make him run.[4]   1681

6. Which is capable only of passive growth, not of consciousness. The "vegetable soul" is lower than the
other two divisions of the soul, "animal" and "rational."   7. Dignity.   8. The text reads "glew." "Lew"
(warmth) has also been suggested as an emendation.   9. Breathes forth.   1. Slow-jawed. Chronos
(Time), ruler of the world in early Greek myth, devoured all of his children except Zeus, who was hidden.
Later, Zeus seized power (see line 46 and note).   2. Through.   3. To lengthen his night of love with
Alcmene, Zeus made the sun stand still.   4. Each sex act was believed to shorten life by one day.

MARILYN CHIN

Summer Love

The black smoke rising means that I am cooking
dried lotus, bay oysters scrambled with eggs.
If this doesn't please you, too bad, it's all I have.
I don't mind your staying for breakfast—but, please—do not linger;
5   nothing worse in the morning than last night's love.

Your belly is flat and your skin—milk in the moonlight.
I notice your glimmer among a thousand tired eyes.
When we dance closely, fog thickens, all distinctions falter.
I let you touch me where I am most vulnerable,
10   heart of the vulva, vulva of the heart.

Perhaps, I fear, there will not be another like you.
Or you might walk away in the same face of the others—
    —blue with scorn and a troubled life.
But, for now, let the summers be savored and the centuries be forgiven.
15   Two lovers in a field of floss and iris—
where nothing else matters but the dew and the light.   1994

VIRGINIA HAMILTON ADAIR

Peeling an Orange

Between you and a bowl of oranges I lie nude
Reading *The World's Illusion* through my tears.
You reach across me hungry for global fruit,
Your bare arm hard, furry and warm on my belly.
5   Your fingers pry the skin of a navel orange
Releasing tiny explosions of spicy oil.
You place peeled disks of gold in a bizarre pattern
On my white body. Rearranging, you bend and bite
The disks to release further their eager scent.
10   I say "Stop, you're tickling," my eyes still on the page.
Aromas of groves arise. Through green leaves
Glow the lofty snows. Through red lips
Your white teeth close on a translucent segment.
Your face over my face eclipses *The World's Illusion*.
15   Pulp and juice pass into my mouth from your mouth.
We laugh against each other's lips. I hold my book
Behind your head, still reading, still weeping a little.
You say "Read on, I'm just an illusion," rolling

Over upon me soothingly, gently moving,
Smiling greenly through long lashes. And soon   20
I say "Don't stop. Don't disillusion me."
Snows melt. The mountain silvers into many a stream.
The oranges are golden worlds in a dark dream.   1996

HOWARD NEMEROV

A Way of Life

It's been going on a long time.
For instance, these two guys, not saying much, who slog
Through sun and sand, fleeing the scene of their crime,
Till one turns, without a word, and smacks
His buddy flat with the flat of an axe,   5
Which cuts down on the dialogue
Some, but is viewed rather as normal than sad
By me, as I wait for the next ad.

It seems to me it's been quite a while
Since the last vision of blonde loveliness   10
Vanished, her shampoo and shower and general style
Replaced by this lean young lunk-
head parading along with a gun in his back to confess
How yestereve, being drunk
And in a state of existential despair,   15
He beat up his grandma and pawned her invalid chair.

But here at last is a pale beauty
Smoking a filter beside a mountain stream,
Brief interlude, before the conflict of love and duty
Gets moving again, as sheriff and posse expound,   20
Between jail and saloon, the American Dream
Where Justice, after considerable horsing around,
Turns out to be Mercy; when the villain is knocked off,
A kindly uncle offers syrup for my cough.

And now these clean-cut athletic types   25
In global hats are having a nervous debate
As they stand between their individual rocket ships
Which have landed, appropriately, on some rocks
Somewhere in Space, in an atmosphere of hate
Where one tells the other to pull up his socks   30
And get going, he doesn't say where; they fade,
And an angel food cake flutters in the void.

I used to leave now and again;
No more. A lot of violence in American life

35   These days, mobsters and cops all over the scene.
        But there's a lot of love, too, mixed with the strife,
        And kitchen-kindness, like a bedtime story
        With rich food and a more kissable depilatory.
        Still, I keep my weapons handy, sitting here
40   Smoking and shaving and drinking the dry beer.   1967

TIMES

WILLIAM SHAKESPEARE

[*Full many a glorious morning have I seen*]

Full many a glorious morning have I seen
Flatter the mountain-tops with sovereign eye,
Kissing with golden face the meadows green,
Gilding pale streams with heavenly alchymy;
Anon permit the basest clouds to ride   5
With ugly rack[1] on his celestial face,
And from the forlorn world his visage hide,
Stealing unseen to west with this disgrace:
Even so my sun one early morn did shine,
With all-triumphant splendor on my brow;   10
But, out! alack! he was but one hour mine,
The region cloud hath mask'd him from me now.
   Yet him for this my love no whit disdaineth;
   Suns of the world may stain when heaven's sun staineth.   1609

JOHN DONNE

The Good-Morrow

I wonder, by my troth, what thou and I
   Did, till we loved? were we not weaned till then?
But sucked on country pleasures, childishly?
   Or snorted we in the Seven Sleepers' den?[2]
'Twas so; but[3] this, all pleasures fancies be.   5
If ever any beauty I did see,
Which I desired, and got,[4] twas but a dream of thee.

And now good-morrow to our waking souls,
   Which watch not one another out of fear;
For love, all love of other sights controls,   10
   And makes one little room an everywhere.
Let sea-discoverers to new worlds have gone,

---

1. Moss.   2. According to legend, seven Christian youths escaped Roman persecution by sleeping in a cave for 187 years. *Snorted:* snored.   3. Except for.   4. Sexually possessed. *Beauty:* Beautiful woman.

Let maps to other,[5] worlds on worlds have shown,
Let us possess one world, each hath one, and is one.

15   My face in thine eye, thine in mine appears,[6]
    And true plain hearts do in the faces rest;
Where can we find two better hemispheres,
    Without sharp north, without declining west?
    Whatever dies was not mixed equally,[7]
20   If our two loves be one, or, thou and I
Love so alike that none do slacken, none can die.

1633

SYLVIA PLATH

Morning Song

Love set you going like a fat gold watch.
The midwife slapped your footsoles, and your bald cry
Took its place among the elements.

Our voices echo, magnifying your arrival. New statue.
5   In a drafty museum, your nakedness
Shadows our safety. We stand round blankly as walls.

I'm no more your mother
Than the cloud that distils a mirror to reflect its own slow
Effacement at the wind's hand.

10   All night your moth-breath
Flickers among the flat pink roses. I wake to listen:
A far sea moves in my ear.

One cry, and I stumble from bed, cow-heavy and floral
In my Victorian nightgown.
15   Your mouth opens clean as a cat's. The window square

Whitens and swallows its dull stars. And now you try
Your handful of notes;
The clear vowels rise like balloons.

1961

5. Other people.   6. That is, each is reflected in the other's eyes.   7. Perfectly mixed elements, according to scholastic philosophy, were stable and immortal.

JONATHAN SWIFT

A Description of the Morning

Now hardly here and there a hackney-coach[8]
Appearing, showed the ruddy morn's approach.
Now Betty[9] from her master's bed had flown,
And softly stole to discompose her own.
The slip shod 'prentice from his master's door   5
Had pared the dirt, and sprinkled round the floor.
Now Moll had whirled her mop with dext'rous airs,
Prepared to scrub the entry and the stairs.
The youth with broomy stumps began to trace
The kennel-edge[1] where wheels had worn the place.   10
The small-coal man[2] was heard with cadence deep,
Till drowned in shriller notes of chimney-sweep:
Duns[3] at his lordship's gate began to meet;
And brick-dust Moll had screamed through half the street.[4]
The turnkey now his flock returning sees,   15
Duly let out a-nights to steal for fees.[5]
The watchful bailiffs take their silent stands,[6]
And schoolboys lag with satchels in their hands.   p. 1709

KAREN VOLKMAN

Evening

The child calling and calling
his lost dog home on the long
suburban block, doesn't know he is part
of a peculiar orchestration,
along with traffic, and the predictable   5
humming of my fridge, and the tick
of the clock still not set back
from daylight savings—a music
specific to a private
kitchen view, in the unfolding   10
dimensions of a sepia twilight

8. Hired coach. *Hardly:* scarcely; that is, they are just beginning to appear.   9. A stock name for a servant girl. Moll (lines 7, 14) is a frequent lower-class nickname.   1. Edge of the gutter that ran down the middle of the street. *Trace:* To find old nails [Swift's note].   2. A seller of coal and charcoal.   3. Bill collectors.   4. Selling powdered brick that was used to clean knives.   5. Jailers collected fees from prisoners for their keep and often let them out at night so they could steal to pay expenses.   6. Looking for those on their "wanted" lists.

from which comes, again
and again, the high far note
of the child in his chanting,
15   so natural and knowing that it
might happen every dusk,
as if loss were an inevitable
condition of nightfall,
spread from streets and houses
20   to an open, barren hill, and to
the hulking, enigmatic water-
tower, bulbous, beneath which
a frail white dog must be asleep.   1996

ARCHIBALD LAMPMAN

Winter Evening

To-night the very horses springing by
Toss gold from whitened nostrils. In a dream
The streets that narrow to the westward gleam
Like rows of golden palaces; and high
5   From all the crowded chimneys tower and die
A thousand aureoles. Down in the west
The brimming plains beneath the sunset rest,
One burning sea of gold. Soon, soon shall fly
The glorious vision, and the hours shall feel
10   A mightier master; soon from height to height,
With silence and the sharp unpitying stars,
Stern creeping frosts, and winds that touch like steel,
Out of the depth beyond the eastern bars,
Glittering and still shall come the awful night.   1899

PLACES

MARY OLIVER

Singapore

In Singapore, in the airport,
a darkness was ripped from my eyes.
In the women's restroom, one compartment stood open.
A woman knelt there, washing something
   in the white bowl.   5

Disgust argued in my stomach
and I felt, in my pocket, for my ticket.

A poem should always have birds in it.
Kingfishers, say, with their bold eyes and gaudy wings.
Rivers are pleasant, and of course trees.   10
A waterfall, or if that's not possible, a fountain
   rising and falling.
A person wants to stand in a happy place, in a poem.

When the woman turned I could not answer her face.
Her beauty and her embarrassment struggled together, and   15
   neither could win.
She smiled and I smiled. What kind of nonsense is this?
Everybody needs a job.

Yes, a person wants to stand in a happy place, in a poem.
But first we must watch her as she stares down at her labor,   20
   which is dull enough.
She is washing the tops of the airport ashtrays, as big as
   hubcaps, with a blue rag.
Her small hands turn the metal, scrubbing and rinsing.
She does not work slowly, nor quickly, but like a river.   25
Her dark hair is like the wing of a bird.

I don't doubt for a moment that she loves her life.
And I want her to rise up from the crust and the slop
   and fly down to the river.
This probably won't happen.   30
But maybe it will.
If the world were only pain and logic, who would want it?

Of course, it isn't.
Neither do I mean anything miraculous, but only
the light that can shine out of a life. I mean   35
the way she unfolded and refolded the blue cloth,

the way her smile was only for my sake; I mean
the way this poem is filled with trees, and birds.

1990

JOHN BETJEMAN

In Westminster Abbey[1]

Let me take this other glove off
  As the *vox humana*[2] swells,
And the beauteous fields of Eden
  Bask beneath the Abbey bells.
5 Here, where England's statesmen lie,
Listen to a lady's cry.

Gracious Lord, oh bomb the Germans.
  Spare their women for Thy Sake,
And if that is not too easy
10 We will pardon Thy Mistake.
But, gracious Lord, whate'er shall be,
Don't let anyone bomb me.

Keep our Empire undismembered
  Guide our Forces by Thy Hand,
15 Gallant blacks from far Jamaica,
  Honduras and Togoland;
Protect them Lord in all their fights,
And, even more, protect the whites.

Think of what our Nation stands for,
20 Books from Boots[3] and country lanes,
Free speech, free passes, class distinction,
  Democracy and proper drains.
Lord, put beneath Thy special care
One-eighty-nine Cadogan Square.[4]

25 Although dear Lord I am a sinner,
  I have done no major crime;
Now I'll come to Evening Service
  Whensoever I have the time.
So, Lord, reserve for me a crown,
30 And do not let my shares go down.

I will labor for Thy Kingdom,
  Help our lads to win the war,

1. Gothic church in London in which English monarchs are crowned and many famous Englishmen are buried (see lines 5, 39–40).   2. Organ tones that resemble the human voice.   3. A chain of London pharmacies.   4. Presumably where the speaker lives, in a fashionable section of central London.

Send white feathers to the cowards[5]
  Join the Women's Army Corps,[6]
Then wash the Steps around Thy Throne   35
In the Eternal Safety Zone.

Now I feel a little better,
  What a treat to hear Thy Word
Where the bones of leading statesmen,
  Have so often been interred.   40
And now, dear Lord, I cannot wait
Because I have a luncheon date.   1940

THOM GUNN

A Map of the City

I stand upon a hill and see
A luminous country under me,
Through which at two the drunk must weave;
The transient's pause, the sailor's leave.

I notice, looking down the hill,   5
Arms braced upon a window sill;
And on the web of fire escapes
Move the potential, the grey shapes.

I hold the city here, complete:
And every shape defined by light   10
Is mine, or corresponds to mine,
Some flickering or some steady shine.

This map is ground of my delight.
Between the limits, night by night,
I watch a malady's advance,   15
I recognize my love of chance.

By the recurrent lights I see
Endless potentiality,
The crowded, broken, and unfinished!
I would not have the risk diminished.   1954   20

---

5. White feathers were sometimes given or sent to men not in uniform to suggest that they were cowards and should join the armed forces.   6. The speaker uses the old World War I name (Women's Army Auxiliary Corps) of the Auxiliary Territorial Service, an organization that performed domestic (and some foreign) defense duties.

DEREK WALCOTT

Midsummer

Certain things here[7] are quietly American—
that chain-link fence dividing the absent roars
of the beach from the empty ball park, its holes
muttering the word umpire instead of empire;
the gray, metal light where an early pelican
coasts, with its engine off, over the pink fire
of a sea whose surface is as cold as Maine's.
The light warms up the sides of white, eager Cessnas[8]
parked at the airstrip under the freckling hills
of St. Thomas. The sheds, the brown, functional hangar,
are like those of the Occupation in the last war.
The night left a rank smell under the casuarinas,
the villas have fenced-off beaches where the natives walk,
illegal immigrants from unlucky islands
who envy the smallest polyp its right to work.
Here the wetback crab and the mollusc are citizens,
and the leaves have green cards. Bulldozers jerk
and gouge out a hill, but we all know that the dust
is industrial and must be suffered. Soon—
the sea's corrugations are sheets of zinc
soldered by the sun's steady acetylene. This
drizzle that falls now is American rain,
stitching stars in the sand. My own corpuscles
are changing as fast. I fear what the migrant envies:
the starry pattern they make—the flag on the post office—
the quality of the dirt, the fealty changing under my foot.

1984

QUESTIONS

1. Compare the tones of the two Donne poems, "The Flea" and "The Good-Morrow."
2. Why is the specific city important to the total effect of Mary Oliver's "Singapore"? What does the fact that the poem's central event takes place in an airport imply about the speaker?
3. What historical "facts" about Westminster Abbey contribute to the irony of Betjeman's "In Westminster Abbey"?

WRITING SUGGESTIONS

1. Try to connect one of the poems in this chapter to an experience in your life that has helped you appreciate the poem. Write a page or two explaining how the poem speaks to your situation.
2. What, exactly, happens in Donne's "The Good-Morrow"? How does the speaker feel about his lover? about the night of love? about himself? What is the evidence for his

---

7. In Trinidad.   8. Small airplanes.

feelings about each of these things? What does the dawn have to do with the speaker's state of mind? with the tone of the poem? Write a two-page paper about the significance of the time setting.

3. Compare the definitions of *aubade* and *aube* in at least three handbooks of literary terms. Consider the morning poems by Shakespeare, Donne, Swift, and Plath. Choose *one* of these poems, then analyze how closely it relates to the tradition of morning poems described in the handbooks. Write an essay of no more than two pages in which you explain how the poem employs, modifies, and/or rejects the standard expectations of how mornings should be described in poetry.

4. Consult a handbook of classical literature to find out how Roman poets represented sunrises mythologically. (Hint: look up Phoebus, then—guided by the handbook or a reference librarian—read several poems that describe Phoebus or his fiery chariot in detail.) Consider carefully the opening lines of Swift's "A Description of the Morning." Write an account—no more than three paragraphs—of how Swift's first two lines work: in what ways do they use and modify the standard mythological expectations? What do you make of the comparison of ordinary modern life to mythic patterns? What evaluation of modern life (or of mythology) is implied?

STUDENT WRITING

Below is an excerpt from one student's first response to Linda Pastan's "To a Daughter Leaving Home." The student's assignment was similar to Writing Suggestion 1. Note how she asks Pastan questions about meaning as a way of articulating her own response to and questions about the poem.

A Letter to an Author

Kimberly Smith

Dear Linda,

I read your poem "To a Daughter Leaving Home" and it really grabbed my attention. I felt as if I were in your head knowing exactly how you felt when you wrote it. It was a feeling that a father, mother or even a child could understand. I also understand that you were born in New York, as I was. After reading the poem and finding out that we were born in the same place, I felt a connection to you. I came to Tucson from New Jersey and it was a very big culture shock. Knowing you are from the east gave me an easy feeling, a feeling of home.

I can remember back when I learned how to ride a bike. My father gave me the incentive that if I could ride to him without falling, then he would take me out for a lobster dinner. So, I did. I was ten and I got on that bike and peddled away until I could catch my balance and my Dad could let me go. I know now that learning to ride my bike meant more than my father watching me ride down the road. It was a symbol of freedom and growing up. It was time for my parents to let go a little more. I saw that same feeling in your poem also. Is that what you meant? Did you intend the bike image to portray a feeling of growing up and moving along in life?

It seemed to me that you wrote the poem to represent stages of a child's life. The first stage is from the beginning to the line "on two round wheels" (line 6). This stage, I believe, is when a baby is learning to walk and he or she wobbles around until getting the hang of it. The second stage is until the line "sprinted to catch up" (line 14). These are the elementary years and maybe junior high, when the child is trying to be on her own and do things for herself. I can remember this stage very well. I thought that I was at an age where I did not need my parents' help anymore. I used to say, "Mom, I am eleven years old and I am old enough to stay alone. I don't need a baby-sitter." The next stage, which I believe is one of the biggest changes in a child's life, ends at the line "with laughter" (line 20). This stage, to me, is very clearly marked high school. The idea about growing more distant I related to very well. That is because I definitely grew up a lot and learned a lot during high school. I got a car and finally felt like an individual, with her own mind. I was able to make my own decisions which was very important to me.

The language you have chosen is very simple, just like the stages of a child's life. Your sentences are short and to the point. I believe that you arranged the poem in the way you did to show a balance. The arrangement of the poem on paper is straight, just like a bike ride and just as parents want their child's life to be. I believe that you chose your words very carefully. For example, "thud" (line 12) has a deep and powerful meaning. It coincides with the last word of the poem, "goodbye" (line 24). Thud is a very final word as if you fell and you heard a big thud. "Goodbye" (line 24) has that same meaning here. You get a feeling of the end instead of just a new beginning. That is what I felt when I read those words. Did you intend to show that same connection between the words "thud" (line 12) and "goodbye" (line 24) that I saw?

There is one impression that I am getting from you in your poem that I do not agree with. I am not sure if you are intending this, but I got the feeling that you have the idea that as children go farther away that they become more fragile. That may be true in some cases, but if children are brought up in an environment that is like a glass box, then they definitely need to move out on their own. Everyone makes mistakes, but they only mean something if you can fix them yourself. I always tell my father that I appreciate his advice but sometimes I need to figure things out on my own and that growing up is all about making mistakes.

I learned a lot from your poem. I hope you enjoy my comments and feelings.

Yours truly,

Kimberly Smith

15

LANGUAGE

Fiction and drama depend upon language just as poetry does, but in a poem almost everything comes down to the particular meanings and implications of individual words. When we read stories and plays, we generally focus our attention on character and plot, and although words determine how we imagine those characters and how we respond to what happens to them, we are not as likely to pause over any one word as we may need to when reading a poem. Because poems often are short, a lot depends on every word in them. Sometimes, as though they are prose that has been distilled, poems contain only the essential words. They say just barely enough to communicate in the most basic way, using elemental signs—with each chosen for exactly the right shade of meaning or feeling or both. But elemental does not necessarily mean simple, and these signs may be very rich in their meanings and complex in their effects.

PRECISION AND AMBIGUITY

Let's look first at poems that create some of their effects by examining—or playing with—a single word. Often multiple meanings or shiftiness and uncertainty of a word are at issue. The following short poem, for example, depends almost entirely on the way we use the word *play*.

SARAH CLEGHORN

[*The golf links lie so near the mill*]

The golf links lie so near the mill
That almost every day
The laboring children can look out
And see the men at play.

p. 1915

While traveling in the American South, Cleghorn had seen a textile mill, which at the time employed quite young children, right next to a golf course. Her poem doesn't *say* that we expect men to work and children to play; it just assumes our expectation and builds an effect of **dramatic irony**—an incongruity between what we expect and what actually occurs—out of the observation. The poem saves almost all of its devastating effect for the final word, after the situation has been carefully described and the irony set up.

In the following two poems, a word used over and over acquires multiple meanings and refuses to be limited to a single one.

ANNE FINCH, COUNTESS OF WINCHELSEA

There's No To-Morrow

A Fable imitated from Sir Roger L'Estrange

Two long had Lov'd, and now the Nymph desir'd,
The Cloak of Wedlock, as the Case requir'd;
Urg'd that, the Day he wrought her to this Sorrow,
He Vow'd, that he wou'd marry her To-Morrow.
5   Agen he Swears, to shun the present Storm,
That he, To-Morrow, will that Vow perform.
The Morrows in their due Successions came;
Impatient still on Each, the pregnant Dame
Urg'd him to keep his Word, and still he swore the same.
10   When tir'd at length, and meaning no Redress,
But yet the Lye not caring to confess,
He for his Oath this Salvo chose to borrow,
That he was Free, since there was no To-Morrow;
For when it comes in Place to be employ'd,
15   'Tis then To-Day; To-Morrow's ne'er enjoy'd.
The Tale's a Jest, the Moral is a Truth;
To-Morrow and To-Morrow, cheat our Youth:
In riper Age, To-Morrow still we cry,
Not thinking, that the present Day we Dye;
20   Unpractis'd all the Good we had Design'd;
There's No To-Morrow to a Willing Mind.   1713

CHARLES BERNSTEIN

Of Time and the Line

George Burns[1] likes to insist that he always
takes the straight lines; the cigar in his mouth
is a way of leaving space between the
lines for a laugh. He weaves lines together
by means of a picaresque narrative;   5
not so Hennie Youngman,[2] whose lines are strict-
ly paratactic. My father pushed a
line of ladies' dresses—not down the street
in a pushcart but upstairs in a fact'ry
office. My mother has been more concerned   10
with her hemline. Chairman Mao[3] put forward
Maoist lines, but that's been abandoned (mostly) for the East-West line of malarkey
so popular in these parts. The prestige
of the iambic line has recently   15
suffered decline, since it's no longer so
clear who "I" am, much less who *you* are. When
making a line, better be double sure
what you're lining in & what you're lining
out & which side of the line you're on; the   20
world is made up so (Adam didn't so much
name as delineate). Every poem's got
a prosodic lining, some of which will
unzip for summer wear. The lines of an
imaginary are inscribed on the   25
social flesh by the knifepoint of history.
Nowadays, you can often spot a work
of poetry by whether it's in lines
or no; if it's in prose, there's a good chance
it's a poem. While there is no lesson in   30
the line more useful than that of the pick-
et line, the line that has caused the most adversity is the bloodline. In Russia
everyone is worried about long lines;
back in the USA, it's strictly soup-   35
lines. "Take a chisel to write," but for an
actor a line's got to be cued. Or, as
they say in math, it takes two lines to make
an angle but only one lime to make
a Margarita.   1991   40

1. American comedian (1896–1996), who played straight man to his wife, Gracie Allen.   2. American comedian (1906–1998).   3. Mao Zedong (1893–1976), leader of the revolution that established China as a communist nation.

The Finch poem repeatedly explores the shifting sands of the word "to-morrow," first noting how different people may think of its meanings differently, then showing how these shifts are anchored in time and the whole process of meaning. The Bernstein poem finds a great variety of completely different meanings of the word "line." How many different meanings can you distinguish in the poem? What does "Time" (in the title) have to do with the poem?

Here is a far more personal and emotional poem, which uses a single word, "terminal," to explore the changing relationship between two people—a father (who speaks the poem) and daughter.

YVOR WINTERS

At the San Francisco Airport

to my daughter, 1954

This is the terminal: the light
Gives perfect vision, false and hard;
The metal glitters, deep and bright.
Great planes are waiting in the yard—
5   They are already in the night.

And you are here beside me, small,
Contained and fragile, and intent
On things that I but half recall—
Yet going whither you are bent—
10   I am the past, and that is all.

But you and I in part are one:
The frightened brain, the nervous will,
The knowledge of what must be done,
The passion to acquire the skill
15   To face that which you dare not shun.

The rain of matter upon sense
Destroys me momently. The score:
There comes what will come. The expense
Is what one thought, and something more—
20   One's being and intelligence.

This is the terminal, the break.
Beyond this point, on lines of air,
You take the way that you must take;
And I remain in light and stare—
25   In light, and nothing else, awake.
      1954

In this case, the poem soberly and thoughtfully probes the several possible meanings of its key word. The importance of the word involves its **ambiguity** (an ability to mean more than one thing) rather than its **precision** (exactness).

What does it *mean* to be in a place called a "terminal"? As the parting of father and daughter is explored carefully, the place of parting and the means of transportation take on meanings larger than their simple referential ones. The poem presents contrasts— young and old, light and dark, past and present, security and adventure. The father ("I am the past," line 10) remains in the light, among known objects and experience familiar to his many years; the daughter is about to depart into the night, the unknown, the uncertain future. But they both share a sense of the necessity of the parting, of the need for the daughter to mature, gain knowledge, acquire experience. Is she going off to school? to college? to her first job? We don't know, but her plane ride clearly means a new departure and a clean break with childhood, dependency, the past.

So much depends upon the word "terminal." It refers to the airport building, of course, but it also implies a boundary, an extremity, a terminus, something that is limited, a junction, a place where a connection may be broken. Important as well is the unambiguous meaning of certain words, that is, what these other words **denote.** The final stanza is articulated flatly, as if the speaker has recovered from the momentary confusion of stanza 4, when "being and intelligence" are lost in the emotion of the parting itself. The words "break," "point," "way," and "remain" are almost unemotional and colorless; they do not make value judgments or offer personal views, but rather define and describe. The sharp articulation of the last stanza stresses the **denotations** of the words employed, as though the speaker is trying to disengage himself from the emotion of the situation and just give the facts.

Words, however, are more than hard blocks of meaning on whose sense everyone agrees. They also have a more personal side, and they carry emotional force and shades of suggestion. The words we use indicate not only what we mean but how we feel about it, and we choose words that we hope will engage others emotionally and persuasively, in conversation and daily usage as well as in poems. A person who holds office is, quite literally (and unemotionally), an *office-holder*—the word denotes what he or she does.

> *A poet is, before anything else,*
> *a person who is passionately*
> *in love with language.*
>
> —W. H. AUDEN

But if we want to convey that a particular officeholder is wise, trustworthy, and deserving of political support we may call that person a *civil servant,* a *political leader,* or an *elected official,* whereas if we want to promote distrust or contempt of that same office-holder we might say *politician* or *bureaucrat* or *political hack.* These latter words have clear **connotations**—suggestions of emotional coloration that imply our attitude and invite a similar one on the part of our hearers. What words **connote** can be just as important to a poem as what they denote, although some poems depend primarily on denotation and some more on connotation.

"At the San Francisco Airport" depends primarily on denotation; the speaker tries to *specify* the meanings and implications of the parting with his daughter, and his tendency to split categories neatly for the two of them at first contributes to the sense of clarity and certainty he wants to project. He is the past (line 10) and what remains (line 24); he has age and experience, his life is the known quantity, he stands in the light. She, on the other hand, is committed to the adventure of going into the night; she seems small, fragile, and her identity exists in the uncertain future. Yet the connotations of some words carry strong emotional force as well as clear definition: that the daughter seems "small" and "fragile" to the speaker suggests his fear for her, something quite different from her sense of adventure. The neat, clean categories keep breaking down, and the speaker's feelings keep showing through. In stanza 1, the light in the terminal gives "perfect vision," but the speaker also notices, indirectly, its artificial quality: it is "false" and "hard," suggesting the limits of the rationalism he tries to maintain. That artificial light shines over most of the poem and honors the speaker's effort, but the whole poem represents his struggle, and in stanza 4 the signals of disturbance are very strong as, despite an insistence on a vocabulary of calculation, his rational facade collapses completely. If we have observed his verbal strategies carefully, we should not be surprised to find him at the end just *staring* in the artificial light, merely awake, although the poem has shown him to be unconsciously awake to much more than he will candidly admit.

"At the San Francisco Airport" is an unusually intricate and complicated poem, and it offers us, if we are willing to examine precisely its carefully crafted fabric, rich insight into how complex it is to be human and to have human feelings and foibles when we think we must be rational machines. But connotations can work more simply. The following epitaph, for example, even though it describes the mixed feelings one person has about another, depends heavily on the connotations of fairly common words.

WALTER DE LA MARE

Slim Cunning Hands

Slim cunning hands at rest, and cozening eyes—
Under this stone one loved too wildly lies;
How false she was, no granite could declare;
    Nor all earth's flowers, how fair.   1950

What the speaker in "Slim Cunning Hands" remembers about the dead woman— her hands, her eyes—tells part of the story; her physical presence was clearly important to him. The poem's other nouns—stone, granite, flowers—all remind us of her death and its finality. All these words denote objects having to do with rituals that memorialize a departed life. Granite and stone connote finality as well, and flowers connote fragility and suggest the shortness of life (which is why they have become the symbolic language of funerals). The way the speaker talks about the woman expresses, in just a few words, the complexity of his love for her. She was loved, he says, too "wildly"—by him perhaps, and apparently by others. The excitement she offered is suggested by the word, and also the lack of control. The words "cunning" and "cozening" help us interpret both her wildness and her falsity; they suggest her calculation, cleverness, and untrustworthiness as well as her skill, persuasiveness, and ability to please. Too, coming at the end of the second line the word "lies" has more than one meaning. The body "lies" under the stone, but the woman's falsity has by now become too prominent to ignore as a second meaning. And the word "fair," a simple yet very inclusive word, suggests how totally attractive the speaker finds her: her beauty is just as incapable of being expressed by flowers as her fickleness is of being expressed in something as permanent as stone. But the word "fair," in the emphatic position as the final word, also implies two other meanings that seem to resonate, ironically, with what we have already learned about her from the speaker: "impartial" and "just." "Impartial" she may be in her preferences (as the word "false" suggests), but to the speaker she is hardly "just," and the final defining word speaks both to her appearance and (ironically) to her character. Simple words here tell us perhaps all we need to know of a long story—or at least the speaker's version of it.

Words like "fair" and "cozening" are clearly loaded; they imply more emotionally than they literally mean. They have strong, clear connotations; they tell us what to think, what evaluation to make; and they suggest the basis for the evaluation. Both words in the title of the following poem similarly turn out to be key ones to its meaning and effect:

PAT MORA

Gentle Communion

Even the long-dead are willing to move.
Without a word, she came with me from the desert.
Mornings she wanders through my rooms
making beds, folding socks.

Since she can't hear me anymore,   5
Mamande[4] ignores the questions I never knew
to ask, about her younger days, her red
hair, the time she fell and broke her nose
in the snow. I will never know.

When I try to make her laugh,   10
to disprove her sad album face, she leaves
the room, resists me as she resisted
grinning for cameras, make-up, English.

While I write, she sits and prays,
feet apart, legs never crossed,   15
the blue housecoat buttoned high
as her hair dries white, girlish
around her head and shoulders.

She closes her eyes, bows her head,
and like a child presses her hands together,   20
her patient flesh steeple, the skin
worn, like the pages of her prayer book.

Sometimes I sit in her wide-armed
chair as I once sat in her lap.
Alone, we played a quiet I Spy.   25
She peeled grapes I still taste.

She removes the thin skin, places
the luminous coolness on my tongue.
I know not to bite or chew. I wait
for the thick melt,   30
our private green honey.   1991

4. A child's conflation of *mama grande* (Spanish for "grandmother").

Neither of the words in the title appears in the text itself, but both resonate throughout the poem. "Communion" is the more powerful of the words; here, it comes to imply the close ritualized relationship between the speaker and "Mamande." Mamande has long been dead but now returns, recalling to the speaker a host of memories and providing a sense of history and family identity. To the speaker, the reunion has a powerful value, reminding her of rituals, habits, and beliefs that "place" her and affirm her heritage. The past is strong in the speaker's mind and in the poem. Many details are recalled from album photographs—the blue housecoat (line 16), the sad face (line 11), the white hair that was once red (lines 7–8 and 17), the posture at prayer (lines 19–22), the big chair (lines 23–24), the plain old-fashioned style (line 13)—and the speaker's childhood memories fade into them as she recalls a specific intimate moment.

The full effect of the word "communion"—which describes an intimate moment of union and a ritual—comes only in the final lines, when the speaker remembers the secret of the grapes and recalls their sensuous feel and taste. The moment brings together the experience of different generations and cultures and represents a sacred sharing: the Spanish grandmother had resisted English, modernity, and show (line 13), and the speaker is a poet, writing (and publishing) in English, but the two have a common "private" (line 31) moment ritually shared and forever memorable. At the end, too, the full sense of "gentle" becomes evident—a word that sums up the softness, quietness, and understatedness of the experience, the personal qualities of "Mamande," and the unpretentious but dignified social level of the family heritage. Throughout the text, other words—ordinary, simple, and precise—suggest the sense of personal dignity, revealed identity, and verbal power that the speaker comes to accept as her own. Look especially at the words "move" (line 1), "steeple" (line 21), and "luminous" (line 28).

Words are the starting point for all poetry, and almost every word is likely to be significant, either denotatively or connotatively or both. Poets who know their craft pick each word with care to express exactly what needs to be expressed and to suggest every emotional shade that the poem is calculated to evoke in us. Often individual words qualify and amplify one another—suggestions clarify other suggestions, and meanings grow upon meanings—and thus the way the words are put together can be important, too. Notice, for example, that in "Slim Cunning Hands" the final emphasis is on how *fair* in appearance the woman was; the speaker's last word describes the quality he can't forget in spite of her lack of a different kind of fairness and his distrust of her, the quality that, even though it doesn't justify everything else, mitigates all the disappointment and hurt.

That word does not stand all by itself, however, any more than any other word in a poem can be considered all alone. Every word exists within larger units of meaning— sentences, patterns of comparisons and contrasts, the whole poem—and where the word is and how it is used are often important. The final word or words may be especially emphatic (as in "Slim Cunning Hands"), and words that are repeated take on a special intensity, as "terminal" does in "At the San Francisco Airport" or as "chartered" and "cry" do in "London" (chapter 12). Certain words often stand out, because they are used in an unusual way (like "chartered" in "London") or because they are given an artificial prominence—through unusual sentence structure, for example, or because the title calls special attention to them.

Sometimes word choice in poems is less dramatic and less obviously "significant" but equally important. Often, in fact, simple appropriateness makes the words in a poem work, and words that do not call special attention to themselves can be the most effective. Precision of denotation may be just as impressive and productive of specific effects as the resonance or ambiguous suggestiveness of connotation. Often poems achieve their power by a combination of verbal effects, setting off elaborate figures of speech (which we will discuss shortly) or other complicated strategies with simple words chosen to mark exact actions, moments, or states of mind. Notice, for example, how carefully the following poem produces its complex description of emotional patterns by delineating and then elaborating precise stages of feeling.

EMILY DICKINSON

[*After great pain, a formal feeling comes*—]

After great pain, a formal feeling comes—
The Nerves sit ceremonious, like Tombs—
The stiff Heart questions was it He, that bore,
And Yesterday, or Centuries before?

The Feet, mechanical, go round—   5
Of Ground, or Air, or Ought—
A Wooden way
Regardless grown,
A Quartz contentment, like a stone—

This is the Hour of Lead—   10
Remembered, if outlived,
As Freezing Persons recollect the Snow—
First—Chill—then Stupor—then the letting go—

  ca. 1862

As you read the following poem, notice how the title calls upon us to wonder, from the beginning, how playful and how patterned the boy's bedtime romp with his father is. Try to be conscious of the emotional effects created by what seem to be the key words. Which words establish the bond between the two males?

THEODORE ROETHKE

My Papa's Waltz

The whiskey on your breath
Could make a small boy dizzy;
But I hung on like death:
Such waltzing was not easy.

We romped until the pans   5
Slid from the kitchen shelf;

My mother's countenance
Could not unfrown itself.

The hand that held my wrist
10   Was battered on one knuckle;
At every step you missed
My right ear scraped a buckle.

You beat time on my head
With a palm caked hard by dirt,
15   Then waltzed me off to bed
Still clinging to your shirt.   1948

Exactly what is the situation in "My Papa's Waltz"? What are the family's economic circumstances? How can you tell? What indications are there of the family's social class? of the father's line of work? How would you characterize the speaker? How does the poem indicate his pleasure in the bedtime ritual? Which words suggest the boy's excitement? Which suggest his anxiety? How can you tell the speaker's feelings about his father? What clues are there about what the mother is like? How can you tell that the experience is remembered at some years' distance? What clues are there in the word choice that an adult is remembering a childhood experience? How scared was the boy at the time? How does the grown adult now evaluate his emotions when he was a boy? In what sense is the poem a tribute to memories of the father? How would you describe the poem's tone?

The subtlety and force of word choice is sometimes very much affected by **word order,** the way the sentences are put together. Some poems employ unusual word order because of the demands of rhyme and meter, but ordinarily poets use word order very much as prose writers do, to create a particular emphasis. When you find an unusual word order, you can be pretty sure that something there merits special attention. Notice the odd constructions in the second and third stanzas of "My Papa's Waltz"—the way the speaker talks about the abrasion of buckle on ear in line 12, for example. He does not say that the buckle scraped his ear, but rather puts it the other way round—a big difference in the kind of effect created, for it avoids placing blame and refuses to specify any unpleasant effect. Had he said that the buckle scraped his ear—the normal way of putting it—we would have to worry about the fragile ear. The **syntax** (sentence structure) of the poem channels our feeling and helps to control what we think of the "waltz."

In the most curious part of the poem, the second stanza, the silent mother appears, and the syntax is peculiar in two places. In lines 5–6, the connection between the romping and the pans falling is stated oddly: "We romped *until* the pans / Slid from the kitchen shelf" (emphasis added). The speaker does not say that they knocked down the pans or imply awkwardness, but he does suggest energetic activity and duration. He implies intensity, almost design—as though the romping would not be complete until the pans fell. And the sentence about the mother—odd but effective—makes her position clear. A silent bystander in this male ritual, she doesn't seem frightened or angry. She seems to be holding a frown, or having it molded on her face, as though it were part of her own ritual, as well as perhaps a facet of her stern character. The syntax implies that she *has to* maintain the frown, and the falling of the pans almost seems to be for her benefit. She disapproves, but she remains their audience.

Sometimes poems create, as well, a powerful sense of the way minds and emotions work by varying normal syntactical order in special ways. Listen, for example, in the following poem to the speaker's sudden loss of vocal control in the midst of what seems to be a calm analysis of her feelings about sexual behavior.

SHARON OLDS

Sex without Love

How do they do it, the ones who make love
without love? Beautiful as dancers,
gliding over each other like ice-skaters
over the ice, fingers hooked
inside each other's bodies, faces   5
red as steak, wine, wet as the
children at birth whose mothers are going to
give them away. How do they come to the
come to the   come to the   God   come to the
still waters, and not love   10
the one who came there with them, light
rising slowly as steam off their joined
skin? These are the true religious,
the purists, the pros, the ones who will not
accept a false Messiah, love the   15
priest instead of the God. They do not
mistake the lover for their own pleasure,
they are like great runners: they know they are alone
with the road surface, the cold, the wind,
the fit of their shoes, their over-all cardio-   20
vascular health—just factors, like the partner
in the bed, and not the truth, which is the
single body alone in the universe
against its own best time.   1984

The poem starts calmly enough, with a simple rhetorical question implying that the speaker just cannot understand sex without love. Lines 2–4 compare such sexual activity with some distant aesthetic, with two carefully delineated examples, and the speaker—although plainly disapproving—seems coolly, almost chillingly, in control of the analysis and evaluation. But by the end of the fourth line, something begins to seem odd: "hooked" seems too ugly and extreme a way to characterize the lovers' fingers, however much the speaker may disapprove, and by line 6 the syntax seems to break down. How does "wine" fit the syntax of the line? Is it parallel with "steak," another example of redness? or is it somehow related to the last part of the sentence, parallel with "faces"? Neither of these possibilities quite works. At best, the punctuation is faulty; at worst, the speaker's mind is working too fast for the language it can generate, scrambling its images. We can't yet be quite sure what is going on, but by the ninth line the lack of control is manifest with the compulsive repeating (three times) of "come to the" and the interjected "God."

Such verbal behavior—here concretized by the way the poem orders its words—invites us to reevaluate the speaker's moralism relative to her emotional involvement with the issues and with her representation of sexuality itself. The speaker's values, as well as those who have sex without love, become a subject for evaluation.

Words, the basic building materials of poetry, come in many kinds and can be used in many different ways and in different—sometimes surprising—combinations. They are seldom simple or transparent, even when we know their meanings and recognize their syntax as ordinary and conventional. Carefully examining them individually and collectively is a crucial part of the process of reading poems, and learning exactly what kinds of questions to ask about the words that poems use and how poems use them is one of the most basic—and rewarding—skills a reader of poetry can develop.

• • •

MARTHA COLLINS

Lies

Anyone can get it wrong, laying low
when she ought to lie, but is it a lie
for her to say she laid him when we know
he wouldn't lie still long enough to let
5   her do it? A good lay is not a song,
not anymore; a good lie is something
else: lyrics, lines, what if you say *dear sister*
when you have no sister, what if you say *guns*
when you saw no guns, though you know
10   they're there? *She laid down her arms; she lay*
down, her arms by her sides. If we don't know,
do we lie if we say? If we don't say, do we lie
down on the job? To arms! in any case
dear friends. If we must lie, let's not lie around.   1999

EMILY DICKINSON

[I dwell in Possibility—]

I dwell in Possibility—
A fairer House than Prose—
More numerous of Windows—
Superior—for Doors—

Of Chambers as the Cedars—   5
Impregnable of Eye—
And for an Everlasting Roof
The Gambrels[5] of the Sky—

Of Visitors—the fairest—
For Occupation—This—   10
The spreading wide my narrow Hands
To gather Paradise—

ca. 1862

WILLIAM CARLOS WILLIAMS

The Red Wheelbarrow

so much depends
upon

a red wheel
barrow

glazed with rain   5
water

beside the white
chickens.   1923

This Is Just to Say

I have eaten
the plums
that were in
the icebox

and which   5
you were probably
saving
for breakfast

Forgive me
they were delicious   10
so sweet
and so cold   1934

5. Roofs with double slopes.

GERARD MANLEY HOPKINS

Pied Beauty[6]

Glory be to God for dappled things—
    For skies of couple-color as a brinded[7] cow;
      For rose-moles all in stipple[8] upon trout that swim;
Fresh-firecoal chestnut-falls;[9] finches' wings;
5   Landscape plotted and pieced—fold, fallow, and plow;
      And all trades, their gear and tackle and trim.
All things counter, original, spare, strange;
    Whatever is fickle, freckled (who knows how?)
      With swift, slow; sweet, sour; adazzle, dim;
10 He fathers-forth whose beauty is past change;
      Praise him.   1887

E. E. CUMMINGS

[in Just-][1]

in Just-
spring   when the world is mud-
luscious the little
lame balloonman

5 whistles   far   and wee

and eddieandbill come
running from marbles and
piracies and it's
spring

10 when the world is puddle-wonderful

the queer
old balloonman whistles
far   and   wee
and bettyandisbel come dancing

15 from hop-scotch and jump-rope and
it's
spring
and

---

6. Particolored beauty: having patches or sections of more than one color.   7. Streaked or spotted.   8. Rose-colored dots or flecks.   9. Fallen chestnuts as red as burning coals.   1. The first poem
in the series *Chansons innocentes*.

                the
                        goat-footed   20

balloonMan   whistles
far
and
wee²   1923

BEN JONSON

*Still to Be Neat*³

Still⁴ to be neat, still to be dressed,
As you were going to a feast;
Still to be powdered, still perfumed;
Lady, it is to be presumed,
Though art's hid causes are not found,   5
All is not sweet, all is not sound.

Give me a look, give me a face
That makes simplicity a grace;
Robes loosely flowing, hair as free;
Such sweet neglect more taketh me   10
Than all th' adulteries of art.
They strike mine eyes, but not my heart.   1609

ROBERT HERRICK

Delight in Disorder

A sweet disorder in the dress
Kindles in clothes a wantonness.
A lawn⁵ about the shoulders thrown
Into a fine distractiön;
An erring lace, which here and there   5
Enthralls the crimson stomacher,⁶
A cuff neglectful, and thereby

---

2. Pan, whose Greek name means "everything," is traditionally represented with a syrinx (or the pipes of Pan). The upper half of his body is human, the lower half goat, and as the father of Silenus he is associated with the spring rites of Dionysus.   3. A song from Jonson's play *The Silent Woman* (1609–10).   4. Continually.   5. Scarf of fine linen.   6. Ornamental covering for the breasts.

Ribbands[7] to flow confusedly;
A winning wave, deserving note,
10 In the tempestuous petticoat;
A careless shoestring, in whose tie
I see a wild civility;
Do more bewitch me than when art
Is too precise[8] in every part.   1648

JOHN MILTON

From Paradise Lost[9]

I

Of man's first disobedience, and the fruit[1]
Of that forbidden tree whose mortal taste
Brought death into the world, and all our woe,
With loss of Eden, till one greater Man
5   Restore us, and regain the blissful seat,
Sing, Heav'nly Muse,[2] that, on the secret top
Of Oreb, or of Sinai, didst inspire
That shepherd who first taught the chosen seed
In the beginning how the Heav'ns and Earth
10   Rose out of Chaos: or, if Sion hill
Delight thee more, and Siloa's brook that flowed
Fast[3] by the oracle of God, I thence
Invoke thy aid to my adventurous song,
That with no middle flight intends to soar

7. Ribbons.   8. In the sixteenth and seventeenth centuries, Puritans were often called Precisians because of their fastidiousness.   9. The opening lines of Books I and II and a short passage from Book III. The first passage states the poem's subject, and the second describes Satan's beginning address to the council of fallen angels meeting to discuss strategy; in the third, God is looking down from Heaven at his new human creation and watching Satan approaching the Earth.   1. The apple, but also the consequences.   2. Addressing one of the Muses and asking for aid is a convention for the opening lines of an epic; Milton complicates the standard procedure here by describing sources and circumstances of Judeo-Christian revelation rather than specifically invoking one of the nine classical Muses. Sinai is the spur of Mount Oreb, where Moses ("That shepherd," line 8), who was traditionally regarded as author of the first five books of the Bible) received the Law; Sion hill and Siloa (lines 10–11), near Jerusalem, correspond to the traditional mountain (Helicon) and springs of classical tradition. Later, in Book VII, Milton calls upon Urania, the Muse of astronomy, but he does not mention by name the Muse of epic poetry, Calliope.   3. Close.

Above th' Aonian mount,[4] while it pursues   15
Things unattempted yet in prose or rhyme.
And chiefly thou, O Spirit,[5] that dost prefer
Before all temples th' upright heart and pure,
Instruct me, for thou know'st; thou from the first
Wast present, and, with mighty wings outspread,   20
Dovelike sat'st brooding on the vast abyss,
And mad'st it pregnant: what in me is dark
Illumine; what is low, raise and support;
That, to the height of this great argument,[6]
I may assert Eternal Providence,   25
And justify the ways of God to men.
   Say first (for Heav'n hides nothing from thy view,
Nor the deep tract of Hell), say first what cause
Moved our grand parents, in that happy state,
Favored of Heav'n so highly, to fall off   30
From their Creator, and transgress his will
For one restraint, lords of the world besides?[7]
Who first seduced them to that foul revolt?
Th' infernal serpent; he it was, whose guile,
Stirred up with envy and revenge, deceived   35
The mother of mankind, what time[8] his pride
Had cast him out from Heav'n, with all his host
Of rebel angels, by whose aid, aspiring
To set himself in glory above his peers,
He trusted to have equaled the Most High,   40
If he opposed; and with ambitious aim
Against the throne and monarchy of God,
Raised impious war in Heav'n and battle proud,
With vain attempt. Him the Almighty Power
Hurled headlong flaming from th' ethereal sky,   45
With hideous ruin and combustion down
To bottomless perdition, there to dwell
In adamantine chains and penal fire,
Who durst defy th' Omnipotent to arms.[9]

* * *

II

High on a throne of royal state, which far
Outshone the wealth of Ormus and of Ind,[1]
Or where the gorgeous East with richest hand
Show'rs on her kings barbaric pearl and gold,

---

4. Mount Helicon, home of the classical Muses.   5. The divine voice that inspired the Hebrew prophets. Genesis 1.2 says that "the spirit of God moved upon the face of the waters" as part of the process of Creation; Milton follows tradition in making the inspirational and communicative function of God present in Creation itself. The passage echoes and merges many biblical references to Creation and divine revelation.   6. Subject.   7. In all other respects. *For:* because of.   8. When.   9. After invoking the Muse and giving a brief summary of the poem's subject, an epic regularly begins *in medias res* ("in the midst of things").   1. India. *Ormus:* Hormuz, an island in the Persian Gulf, famous for pearls.

5   Satan exalted sat, by merit raised
      To that bad eminence; and, from despair
      Thus high uplifted beyond hope, aspires
      Beyond thus high, insatiate to pursue
      Vain war with Heav'n, and by success[2] untaught,
10   His proud imaginations thus displayed:
         "Powers and Dominions, Deities of Heav'n,
      For since no deep within her gulf can hold
      Immortal vigor, though oppressed and fall'n,
      I give not Heav'n for lost. From this descent
15   Celestial virtues rising will appear
      More glorious and more dread than from no fall,
      And trust themselves to fear no second fate.
      Me though just right and the fixed laws of Heav'n
      Did first create your leader, next, free choice,
20   With what besides, in council or in fight,
      Hath been achieved of merit, yet this loss,
      Thus far at least recovered, hath much more
      Established in a safe unenvied throne
      Yielded with full consent. The happier state
25   In Heav'n, which follows dignity, might draw
      Envy from each inferior; but who here
      Will envy whom the highest place exposes
      Foremost to stand against the Thunderer's aim
      Your bulwark, and condemns to greatest share
30   Of endless pain? Where there is then no good
      For which to strive, no strife can grow up there
      From faction; for none sure will claim in hell
      Precédence, none, whose portion is so small
      Of present pain, that with ambitious mind
35   Will covet more. With this advantage then
      To union, and firm faith, and firm accord,
      More than can be in Heav'n, we now return
      To claim our just inheritance of old,
      Surer to prosper than prosperity
40   Could have assured us; and by what best way,
      Whether of open war or covert guile,
      We now debate; who can advise, may speak."

                         * * *

            III

                         * * *

56   Now had th' Almighty Father from above,
      From the pure empyrean where he sits
      High throned above all height, bent down his eye,
      His own works and their works at once to view:

---

2. Outcome, either good or bad.

About him all the sanctities of Heav'n[3]   60
Stood thick as stars, and from his sight received
Beatitude past utterance; on his right
The radiant image of his glory sat,
His only Son. On earth he first beheld
Our two first parents, yet the only two   65
Of mankind, in the happy garden placed,
Reaping immortal fruits of joy and love,
Uninterrupted joy, unrivaled love,
In blissful solitude. He then surveyed
Hell and the gulf between, and Satan there   70
Coasting the wall of Heav'n on this side Night
In the dun air sublime,[4] and ready now
To stoop[5] with wearied wings and willing feet
On the bare outside of this world, that seemed
Firm land embosomed without firmament,   75
Uncertain which, in ocean or in air.   1667

THOMAS BASTARD

De Puero Balbutiente[6]

Methinks 'tis pretty sport to hear a child
Rocking a word in mouth yet undefiled;
The tender racquet rudely plays the sound
Which, weakly bandied, cannot back rebound
And the soft air the softer roof doth kiss   5
With a sweet dying and a pretty miss,
Which hears no answer yet from the white rank
Of teeth not risen from their coral bank.
The alphabet is searched for letters soft
To try a word before it can be wrought;   10
And when it slideth forth, it goes as nice[7]
As when a man doth walk upon the ice.   1598

---

3. The hierarchies of angels.   4. A loft in the twilight atmosphere.   5. Swoop down, like a bird of prey.
6. On a Child Learning to Talk.   7. Carefully.

PICTURING: THE LANGUAGES OF DESCRIPTION

The language of poetry is almost always visual and pictorial. Rather than depending primarily on abstract ideas and elaborate reasoning, poems depend mainly on concrete and specific words that create images in our minds. Poems thus help us to see things afresh and anew or to feel them suggestively through our other physical senses, such as hearing or touch. But most often, poetry uses the sense of sight in that it helps us form, in our minds, visual impressions, images that communicate more directly than concepts. We "see" yellow leaves on a branch, a father and son waltzing precariously, or two lovers sitting together on the bank of a stream, so that our response begins from a vivid impression of exactly what is happening. Some people think that those media and arts that challenge the imagination of a hearer or reader—radio drama, for example, or poetry—allow us to respond more fully than those (such as television or theater) that actually show things more fully to our physical senses. Certainly they leave more to our imagination, to our mind's eye.

Visual applications of language stem from the nature and direction of the poetic process itself, and some of them have to do with how poems are conceived and then, gradually, become fleshed out in words. Poems are sometimes quite abstract—they can even be *about* abstractions. But they usually are not; they are quite concrete in what they ask us to see. One reason is that they often begin in a poet's mind with a picture or an image: of a person, a place, an event, or an object of observation. That image may be based on something the poet has seen—that is, it may be a picture of something remembered by the poet—but it may also be totally imaginary and only based on the "real world" in the sense that it draws on the poet's physical sense of what the world (and people and things in it) are like. Sometimes a poet represents an imagined scene or object in a highly stylized or feeling-centered way, as do, for example, impressionist or surrealist painters. But that process often begins from a quite specific image in the poet's mind that he or she then tries to **represent,** in words, in such a way that readers can "see" it also—or almost see it through the poet's vivid verbal representation of what he or she has already "seen" (imaged) in the mind.

Think of it this way: a painter or sculptor uses strategies of form, color, texture, angle, and relationship to create a visual idea, and so the viewer begins with an *actual* image, something that can be seen physically (though the viewer's understanding and interpretation may be many steps away). Even when a poet begins with an imagining that draws on visual experience, however, the reader still has to *imagine* (through the poem's words) an image, some person or thing or action that the poem describes. The poet must help the reader to flesh out that mental image on the basis of the words he or she uses. In a sense, then, the reader becomes a visual artist, but the poet explains how the visualization is to be done by evoking specific responses through words. *How* that happens can involve quite complicated verbal strategies—or even *visual* ones that draw on the possibilities of print (see chapter 18).

The languages of description are quite varied. The visual qualities of poetry result partly from the two aspects of poetic language described in the previous section: the precision of individual words and (its opposite) the reach, richness, and ambiguity of suggestion that words sometimes accrue. Visualization can also derive from some quite sophisticated rhetorical and literary devices (figures of speech and symbols, for example, as we will see later in this chapter). But often description involves first of all simply naming, providing the word—a noun, a verb, an adjective or adverb—that will trigger familiar knowledge from a reader's experience. A reader can readily imagine a *dog* or *cat* or *house* or *flower* when the word for each is named, but not all readers will have the same kind of dog or flower come to mind (because of our individual experiences) until the word is qualified in some way. So the poet may specify that the dog is a greyhound or poodle, or that the flower is a daffodil or a lilac or Queen Anne's lace; or the poet may provide colors, sizes, specific movements, or particular identifying features. Such description can involve either narrowing by category or expansion through detail, and often comparisons are either explicitly or implicitly involved. In Richard Wilbur's "The Beautiful Changes," for example, the similarity between wading through flowers in a meadow and wading among waves in the sea helps to suggest how the first experience feels as well as to etch it visually in our minds. More than just a matter of naming, being precise in individual words, and providing basic information, description involves qualification and comparison; sometimes the poet needs to tell us what a picture is not, dissociating what the poem is about to describe from other possible images we may expect or have in mind. Notice, for example, how Ben Jonson's "To Penshurst" begins by telling us how this building and this estate are different from other great houses we might be thinking of. Different features in the language of description add up to something that describes a whole—a picture or scene—as well as a series of individualized objects.

Seeing in the mind's eye—the re-creation of visual experience—requires different skills from poets and readers. Poets use all the language strategies they can think of to re-create for us something they have already "seen." Poets depend on our having had a rich variety of visual experiences and try to draw on those experiences by using common, evocative words and then refining the process through more elaborate verbal devices. We as readers inhabit the process the other way round, trying to draw on our previous knowledge so that we can "see" by following verbal clues. In the poems that follow, notice the ways that description leads to specific images, and pay attention to how shape, color, relationship, and perspective become clear, not only through individual words but also through combinations of words and phrases that suggest appearance and motion.

GAIL MAZUR

Bluebonnets

I lay down by the side of the road
in a meadow of bluebonnets, I broke
the unwritten law of Texas. My brother

was visiting, he'd been tired, afraid of
his tiredness as we'd driven toward Bremen,   5
so we stopped for the blue relatives

of lupine, we left the car on huge feet
we'd inherited from our lost father,
our Polish grandfather. Those flowers

were too beautiful to only look at;   10
we walked on them, stood in the middle
of them, threw ourselves down,

15

crushing them in their one opportunity
to thrive and bloom. We lay like angels
forgiven our misdeeds, transported

to azure fields, the only word for
the color eluded me—delft, indigo,
sapphire, some heavenly word you might

20

speak to a sky. I led my terrestrial brother
there to make him smile and this
is my only record of the event.

We took no pictures, we knew no camera
could fathom that blue. I brushed
the soft spikes, I fingered lightly

25

the delicate earthly petals, I thought,
This is what my hands do well
isn't it, touch things about to vanish.   1995

RICHARD WILBUR

The Beautiful Changes

One wading a Fall meadow finds on all sides
The Queen Anne's Lace[1] lying like lilies
On water; it glides
So from the walker, it turns

5

Dry grass to a lake, as the slightest shade of you
Valleys my mind in fabulous blue Lucernes.[2]

The beautiful changes as a forest is changed
By a chameleon's tuning his skin to it;
As a mantis, arranged

10

On a green leaf, grows
Into it, makes the leaf leafier, and proves
Any greenness is deeper than anyone knows.

Your hands hold roses always in a way that says
They are not only yours; the beautiful changes

15

In such kind ways,
Wishing ever to sunder
Things and things' selves for a second finding, to lose
For a moment all that it touches back to wonder.   1947

1. A delicate-looking plant, with finely divided leaves and flat clusters of small white flowers, sometimes called "wild carrot."   2. Alfalfa, a plant resembling clover, with small purple flowers. Lake Lucerne is famed for deep blue color and its picturesque Swiss setting amid limestone mountains.

ANDREW MARVELL

On a Drop of Dew

See how the orient[3] dew
Shed from the bosom of the morn
   Into the blowing roses,
Yet careless of its mansion new
For[4] the clear region where 'twas born   5
   Round in itself incloses,
   And in its little globe's extent
Frames as it can its native element;
   How it the purple flow'r does slight,
   Scarce touching where it lies,   10
But gazing back upon the skies,
   Shines with a mournful light
      Like its own tear,
Because so long divided from the sphere.[5]
   Restless it rolls and unsecure,   15
      Trembling lest it grow impure,

   Till the warm sun pity its pain,
And to the skies exhale it back again.
      So the soul, that drop, that ray
Of the clear fountain of eternal day,   20
Could it within the human flower be seen,
   Rememb'ring still its former height,
   Shuns the sweet leaves and blossoms green;
   And, recollecting its own light,
Does, in its pure and circling thoughts, express   25
The greater Heaven in an Heaven less.
   In how coy[6] a figure wound,
   Every way it turns away;
   So the world excluding round,
   Yet receiving in the day: 30
   Dark beneath, but bright above,
   Here disdaining, there in love.

   How loose and easy hence to go,
   How girt and ready to ascend;
   Moving but on a point below,   35
    It all about does upwards bend.
Such did the manna's sacred dew distill,
White and entire, though congealed and chill;[7]
Congealed on earth, but does, dissolving, run
Into the glories of th' almighty sun.   1681   40

---

3. Shining.   4. By reason of.   5. Of heaven.   6. Reserved, withdrawn, modest.   7. In the wilderness, the Israelites fed upon manna from heaven (distilled from the dew; see Exodus 16.10–21); manna became a traditional symbol for divine grace.

BEN JONSON

To Penshurst[8]

Thou art not, Penshurst, built to envious show,
Of touch[9] or marble; nor canst boast a row
Of polished pillars, or a roof of gold;
Thou hast no lantern[1] whereof tales are told,
5   Or stair, or courts; but stand'st an ancient pile,
And, these grudged at, art reverenced the while.[2]
Thou joy'st in better marks, of soil, of air,
Of wood, of water; therein thou art fair.
Thou hast thy walks for health, as well as sport;
10   Thy mount, to which the dryads do resort,
Where Pan and Bacchus[3] their high feasts have made
Beneath the broad beech and the chestnut shade,
That taller tree, which of a nut was set
At his great birth[4] where all the Muses met.
15   There in the writhéd bark are cut the names
Of many a sylvan, taken with his flames;[5]
And thence the ruddy satyrs oft provoke
The lighter fauns to reach thy Lady's Oak.[6]
Thy copse too, named of Gamage,[7] thou hast there,
20   That never fails to serve thee seasoned deer
When thou wouldst feast, or exercise, thy friends.
The lower land, that to the river bends,
Thy sheep, thy bullocks, kine, and calves do feed;
The middle grounds thy mares and horses breed.
25   Each bank doth yield thee conies;[8] and the tops,
Fertile of wood, Ashore and Sidney's copse,
To crown thy open table, doth provide
The purpled pheasant with the speckled side;
The painted partridge lies in every field,
30   And for thy mess is willing to be killed.
And if the high-swollen Medway[9] fail thy dish,
Thou hast thy ponds that pay thee tribute fish,
Fat agéd carps that run into thy net,
And pikes, now weary their own kind to eat,

8. The country seat (in Kent) of the Sidney family, owned by Sir Robert, brother of the poet, Sir Philip. Jonson's celebration of the estate is one of the earliest "house" poems and a prominent example of topographical or didactic-descriptive poetry.   9. Touchstone: basanite, a smooth dark stone similar to black marble.   1. A glassed or open tower or dome atop the roof.   2. I.e., although these (more pretentious structures) are envied anyway.   3. Ancient gods of nature and wine, both associated with spectacular feasting and celebration.   4. Sir Philip Sidney's, on November 30, 1554; the tree stood for nearly 150 years.   5. Inspired by Sidney's love poetry.   6. Where, according to legend, a former lady of the house (Lady Leicester) began labor pains. *Satyrs:* half-men, half-goats who participated in the rites of Bacchus.   7. The maiden name of the owner's wife. *Copse:* thicket.   8. Rabbits.   9. A river bordering the estate.

As loath the second draught or cast to stay,[1]   35
Officiously[2] at first themselves betray;
Bright eels that emulate them, and leap on land
Before the fisher, or into his hand.
Then hath thy orchard fruit, thy garden flowers,
Fresh as the air, and new as are the hours.   40
The early cherry, with the later plum,
Fig, grape, and quince, each in his time doth come:
The blushing apricot and woolly peach
Hang on thy walls, that every child may reach.
And though thy walls be of the country stone,   45
They're reared with no man's ruin, no man's groan;
There's none that dwell about them wish them down,
But all come in, the farmer and the clown,[3]
And no one empty-handed, to salute
Thy lord and lady, though they have no suit.[4]   50
Some bring a capon, some a rural cake,
Some nuts, some apples; some that think they make
The better cheeses bring 'em, or else send
By their ripe daughters, whom they would commend
This way to husbands, and whose baskets bear   55
An emblem of themselves in plum or pear.
But what can this (more than express their love)
Add to thy free[5] provisions, far above
The need of such? whose liberal board doth flow
With all that hospitality doth know;   60
Where comes no guest but is allowed to eat,
Without his fear, and of thy lord's own meat;
Where the same beer and bread, and selfsame wine,
That is his lordship's shall be also mine.
And I not fain[6] to sit (as some this day   65
At great men's tables), and yet dine away.[7]
Here no man tells[8] my cups; nor, standing by,
A waiter doth my gluttony envý,
But gives me what I call, and lets me eat;
He knows below he shall find plenty of meat.   70
Thy tables hoard not up for the next day;
Nor, when I take my lodging, need I pray
For fire, or lights, or livery;[9] all is there,
As if thou then wert mine, or I reigned here:
There's nothing I can wish, for which I stay.   75
That found King James when hunting late this way
With his brave son, the prince,[1] they saw thy fires
Shine bright on every hearth, as the desires
Of thy Penates[2] had been set on flame

---

1. Await. *Draught:* drawing in of a net.   2. Obligingly.   3. Rustic, peasant.   4. Request for favors.
5. Generous.   6. Obliged.   7. Possibly, "elsewhere," because they do not get enough to eat; or
"away" in the sense of far from the party of honor.   8. Counts.   9. Provisions (or, possibly, servants).   1. Prince Henry, who died in 1612.   2. Roman household gods.

80   To entertain them; or the country came
        With all their zeal to warm their welcome here.
        What (great I will not say, but) sudden cheer
        Didst thou then make 'em! and what praise was heaped
        On thy good lady then! who therein reaped
85   The just reward of her high housewifery;[3]
        To have her linen, plate, and all things nigh,
        When she was far; and not a room but dressed
        As if it had expected such a guest!
        These, Penshurst, are thy praise, and yet not all.
90   Thy lady's noble, fruitful, chaste withal.
        His children thy great lord may call his own,
        A fortune in this age but rarely known.
        They are, and have been, taught religion; thence
        Their gentler spirits have sucked innocence.
95   Each morn and even they are taught to pray,
        With the whole household, and may, every day,
        Read in their virtuous parents' noble parts
        The mysteries of manners, arms, and arts.
        Now, Penshurst, they that will proportion[4] thee
100   With other edifices, when they see
        Those proud, ambitious heaps, and nothing else,
        May say, their lords have built, but thy lord dwells.   1616

---

3. Domestic economy.   4. Compare.

METAPHOR AND SIMILE

Being visual does not just mean describing; telling us facts; indicating shapes, colors, and specific details; and giving us precise discriminations through exacting verbs, nouns, adverbs, and adjectives. Often the vividness of the picture in our minds depends upon comparisons through **figures of speech.** What we are trying to imagine is pictured in terms of something else familiar to us, and we are asked to think of one thing as if it were something else. Many such comparisons, in which something is pictured or figured forth in terms of something already familiar to us, are taken for granted in daily life. Things we can't see or that aren't familiar to us are imaged as things we already know; for example, God is said to be like a father; Italy is said to be shaped like a boot; life is compared to a forest, a journey, or a sea. When the comparison is explicit—that is, when one thing is directly compared to something else—the figure is called a **simile.** When the comparison is implicit, with something described as if it were something else, it is called a **metaphor.**

Poems use **figurative language** much of the time. A poem may insist that death is like a sunset or sex like an earthquake or that the way to imagine how it feels to be spiritually secure is to think of the way a shepherd takes care of his sheep. The pictorialness of our imagination may *clarify* things for us—scenes, states of mind, ideas—but at the same time it stimulates us to think of how those pictures make us *feel*. Pictures, even when they are mental pictures or imagined visions, may be both denotative and connotative, just as individual words are: they may clarify and make precise, and they may channel our feelings. In the poem that follows, the poet helps us visualize the old age and approaching death of the speaker by making comparisons with familiar things—the coming of winter, the approach of sunset, and the dying embers of a fire.

WILLIAM SHAKESPEARE

[*That time of year thou mayst in me behold*]

That time of year thou mayst in me behold
When yellow leaves, or none, or few, do hang
Upon those boughs which shake against the cold,
Bare ruined choirs, where late the sweet birds sang.
In me thou see'st the twilight of such day   5
As after sunset fadeth in the west;
Which by and by[1] black night doth take away,
Death's second self,[2] that seals up all in rest.
In me thou see'st the glowing of such fire,
That on the ashes of his youth doth lie,   10
As the deathbed whereon it must expire,
Consumed with that which it was nourished by.
This thou perceiv'st, which makes thy love more strong,
To love that well which thou must leave ere long.   1609

1. Shortly.   2. Sleep.

The first four lines of "That time of year" evoke images of the late autumn; but notice that the poet does not have the speaker say directly that his physical condition and age make him resemble autumn. He draws the comparison without stating it as a comparison: you can see, he says, my own state in the coming of winter, when almost all the leaves have fallen from the trees. The speaker portrays himself *indirectly* by talking about the passing of the year. The poem uses metaphor; that is, one thing is pictured *as if* it were something else. "That time of year" goes on to another metaphor in lines 5–8 and still another in lines 9–12, and each metaphor contributes to our understanding of the speaker's sense of his old age and approaching death. More important, however, is the way the metaphors give us feelings, an emotional sense of the speaker's age and of his own attitude toward aging. Through the metaphors we come to understand, appreciate, and to some extent share the increasing sense of anxiety and urgency that the poem expresses. Our emotional sense of the poem depends largely on the way each metaphor is developed and by the way each metaphor leads, with its own kind of internal logic, to another.

The images of late autumn in the first four lines all suggest loneliness, loss, and nostalgia for earlier times. As in the rest of the poem, the speaker presents our eyes as the main vehicle for noticing his age and condition; in the phrase "thou mayst in me behold" (line 1) he introduces what he is asking to see, and in both lines 5 and 9 he tells us similarly "[i]n me thou see'st. . . ." The picture of the trees shedding their leaves suggests that autumn is nearly over, and we can imagine trees either with yellow leaves, or without leaves, or with just a trace of foliage remaining—the latter perhaps most feelingly suggesting the bleakness and loneliness that characterize the change of seasons, the ending of the life cycle. But other senses are invoked, too. The boughs shaking against the cold represent an appeal to our tactile sense, and the next line appeals to our sense of hearing, although only as a reminder that the birds no longer sing. (Notice how exact the visual representation is of the bare, or nearly bare, limbs, even as the speaker notes the cold and the lack of birds; birds lined up like a choir on risers would have made a striking visual image on the barren limbs one above the other, but now there is only the *reminder* of what used to be. The present is quiet, bleak, trembly, and lonely; it is the absence of color, song, and life that creates the strong visual impression, a reminder of what formerly was.)

The next four lines have a slightly different tone, and the color changes. From a black-and-white landscape with a few yellow leaves, we come upon a rich and almost warm reminder of a faded sunset. But a somber note enters the poem in these lines through another figure of speech, **personification,** which involves treating an abstraction, such as death or justice or beauty, as if it were a person. As the poem talks about the coming of night and of sleep, Sleep is personified and identified as the "second self" of Death (that is, as a kind of "double" for death). The main emphasis is on how night and sleep close in on our sense of twilight, and only secondarily does a reminder of death enter the poem. But it does enter.

The third metaphor—that of the dying embers of a fire—begins in line 9 and continues to color and warm the bleak cold that the poem began with, but it also sharpens the reminder of death. The three main metaphors in the poem work in a way to make our sense of old age and approaching death more familiar but also more immediate: moving from barren trees, to fading twilight, to dying embers suggests a sensuous increase of color and warmth but also an increasing urgency. The first metaphor involves a whole season, or at least a segment of one, a matter of days or possibly weeks; the second involves the passing of a single day, reducing the time scale to a matter of minutes, and the third draws our attention to that split second when a glowing ember fades into a gray ash. The final part of the fire metaphor introduces the most explicit sense of death so far, as the metaphor of embers shifts into a direct reminder of death. Embers, which had been a metaphor of the speaker's aging body, now themselves become, metaphorically, a deathbed; the vitality that nourishes youth is used up just as a log in a fire is. The urgency of the reminder of coming death has now peaked. It is friendlier but now seems immediate and inevitable, a natural part of the life process, and the final two lines then offer an explicit plea to make good and intense use of the remaining moments of human relationship.

"That time of year" represents an unusually intricate use of images to organize a poem and focus its emotional impact. Not all poems are so skillfully made, and not all depend on such a full and varied use of metaphor. But most poems use metaphors for at least part of their effect, and often a poem fully develops a single metaphor as its major way of making a statement and an impact, as in the following poem about the role of a mother and wife.

LINDA PASTAN

Marks

My husband gives me an A
for last night's supper,
an incomplete for my ironing,
a B plus in bed.
My son says I am average,   5
an average mother, but if
I put my mind to it
I could improve.
My daughter believes
in Pass / Fail and tells me   10
I pass. Wait 'til they learn
I'm dropping out.   1978

The speaker in "Marks" is obviously not thrilled with the idea of continually being judged, and the metaphor of marks (or grades) as a way of talking about her performance of roles in the family suggests her irritation. The list of the roles implies the many things expected of her, and the three different systems of marking (letter grades, categories to be checked off on a chart, and pass/fail) detail the difficulties of multiple standards. The poem retains the language of schooldays all the way to the end ("learn," line 11; "dropping out," line 12), and the major effect of the poem depends on the irony of the speaker's surrendering to the metaphor the family has thrust upon her; if she is to be judged as if she were a student, she retains the right to leave the system. Ironically, she joins the system (adopts the metaphor for herself) in order to defeat it.

The following poem depends from the beginning—even from its title—on a single metaphor and the values associated with it.

DAVID WAGONER

My Father's Garden

On his way to the open hearth where white-hot steel
Boiled against furnace walls in wait for his lance
To pierce the fireclay and set loose demons
And dragons in molten tons, blazing
Down to the huge satanic caldrons,   5
Each day he would pass the scrapyard, his kind of garden.

In rusty rockeries of stoves and brake drums,
In grottoes of sewing machines and refrigerators,
He would pick flowers for us: small gears and cogwheels
With teeth like petals, with holes for anthers,   10
Long stalks of lead to be poured into toy soldiers,
Ball bearings as big as grapes to knock them down.

He was called a melter. He tried to keep his brain
From melting in those tyger-mouthed mills
Where the same steel reappeared over and over   15
To be reborn in the fire as something better
Or worse: cannons or cars, needles or girders,
Flagpoles, swords, or plowshares.

But it melted. His classical learning ran
Down and away from him, not burning bright.   20
His fingers culled a few cold scraps of Latin
And Greek, *magna sine laude*,[3] for crosswords
And brought home lumps of tin and sewer grills
As if they were his ripe prize vegetables.   1987

This poem plays tribute to the speaker's father and the things the father understands and values in his ordinary, workingman's life. The father, a "melter" (line 13) in the steel mills (lines 14–15), values things made from what he helps produce. His avocation has developed from his vocation: he collects metal objects from the scrapyard and brings them home just as another man might pick flowers for his family. The scrapyard is, says the speaker, "his kind of garden" (line 6). The father has led a hard life, but he shows love for his children in the only way he knows how—by bringing home things that mean something to him and that can be made into toys his children will come to value. Describing these scraps as the products of his garden—"As if they were his ripe prize vegetables" (line 24)—makes them seem homegrown, carefully tended, nurtured by the father into a useful beauty. Instead of crude and ugly pieces of scrap, they become— through the metaphor of the poem—examples of value and beauty corresponding to the warm feelings the speaker has for a father who did what he could with what he knew and what he had.

3. Without great distinction; a reversal of the usual *magna cum laude*.

Poets often use metaphoric language self-consciously and explicitly, and sometimes (as in the following poem) they celebrate the richness of language that makes their art possible:

ROBERT FRANCIS

Hogwash

The tongue that mothered such a metaphor
Only the purest purist could despair of.

Nobody ever called swill sweet but isn't
Hogwash a daisy in a field of daisies?

What beside sports and flowers could you find   5
To praise better than the American language?

Bruised by American foreign policy
What shall I soothe me, what defend me with

But a handful of clean unmistakable words—
Daisies, daisies, in a field of daisies?   1965   10

The poet here claims little for his own invention and not much for the art of poetry, insisting that the American language itself is responsible for miraculous conceptions. The poet plays cheerfully here with what words offer—the pun on "purest" and "purist" (line 2), for example, and the taunting (but misleading) similarity of the beginnings of "swill" and "sweet" (line 3)—but insists that poems and poets only articulate things already realized in common speech, where metaphors are "mothered" (line 1). "Hogwash," although never explicitly glossed or discussed in the poem, is the primary example: What *does* "hogwash" mean? How do hogs wash themselves and in what? to what purpose and effect? How did the term get invented as a metaphor, and what are its visual implications? And what is it doing as an example of beauty in a poem about "clean unmistakable words" (line 9)? But then the poem plays even more fully with "daisy" (lines 4 and 10) as metaphor and idiomatic expression. A "daisy" is a great success, a breakthrough, a beaut, a perfect example, and the word "hogwash" is such a daisy, an instance of such a success: a "daisy in a field of daisies," a success of successes, a wonder in a language full of wonders.

Not everything American, according to this poem, is as praiseworthy as its language, and the word "hogwash" ultimately has its context established in the poem's fourth stanza, when the speaker finally tells us why the word is so soothing and so pertinent. Poets, the poem says, need words and metaphors that are not always images of beauty because the world is full of things that are not altogether beautiful, and metaphors of ugliness can be "daisies," too.

Not all poets feel as positive as Francis claims to be here about the raw materials they have to work with in language. Ultimately, of course, the modesty of the poet's claims here about his own inventiveness becomes as comic as the metaphor of "hog-wash" itself and the poem's characterization of foreign policy, for it is the poem that makes this particular use of the metaphor, no matter where or when the metaphor was invented: the wit belongs to the poem, not the language. Poets make use of whatever idioms, expressions, inherited metaphors, and traditions of language come their way, and they turn them to their own uses, sometimes quite surprisingly.

The difficulty of conveying what some experiences are like and how we feel about them sometimes leads poets to startling comparisons and figures of speech that may at first seem far-fetched but that, in one way or another, do in fact suggest the quality of the experience or the feelings associated with it. Sometimes poets use a series of metaphors, as if no single act of visualization will serve but several together may suggest the full complexity of the experience or cumulatively define the feeling precisely. Metaphors open up virtually endless possibilities of comparison, giving words a chance to be more than words, offering our mind's eye a challenge to keep up with the fertile and articulate imagination of writers who make it their business to see things that ordinary people miss, noticing the most surprising likenesses and conveying feelings more powerfully than politicians usually do.

Sometimes, in poetry as in prose, comparisons are made explicitly, as in the following poem:

ROBERT BURNS

A Red, Red Rose

O, my luve's like a red, red rose
That's newly sprung in June.
O, my luve is like the melodie
That's sweetly played in tune.

5   As fair art thou, my bonnie lass,
So deep in luve am I;
And I will luve thee still, my dear,
Till a' the seas gang⁴ dry.

Till a' the seas gang dry, my dear,
10   And the rocks melt wi' the sun;
And I will luve thee still, my dear,
While the sands o' life shall run.

And fare thee weel, my only luve,
And fare thee weel a while!
15   And I will come again, my luve,
Though it were ten thousand mile.   1796

_____
4. Go.

The first four lines make two explicit comparisons: the speaker says that his love is "like a . . . rose" and "like [a] melodie." As we noted earlier, such *explicit* comparison is called a simile, and usually (as here) the comparison involves the word *like* or the word *as*. Similes work much as do metaphors, except that they usually are used more passingly, more incidentally; they make a quick comparison and usually do not elaborate, whereas metaphors often extend over a long section of a poem (in which case they are called **extended metaphors**) or even over the whole poem, as in "Marks" (in which case they are called **controlling metaphors**).

The two similes in "A Red, Red Rose" assume that we already have a favorable opinion of roses and of melodies. Here the poet does not develop the comparison or even remind us of attractive details about roses or tunes. He pays the quick compliment and moves on. Similes sometimes develop more elaborate comparisons than this and occasionally even control long sections of a poem (in which case they are called **analogies**), but usually a simile is briefer and relies more fully on something we already know. The speaker in "My Papa's Waltz" says that he hung on "like death"; he doesn't have to explain or elaborate the comparison: we know the anxiety he refers to.

Like metaphors, similes may imply both meaning and feeling; they may both explain something and invoke feelings about it. All figurative language involves an attempt to clarify something *and* to help readers feel a certain way about it. Saying that one's love is like a rose implies a delicate and fragile beauty and invites our senses into play so that we can share sensuously a response to fragrant appeal and soft touch, just as the shivering boughs and dying embers in "That time of year" explain separation and loss at the same time that they invite us to share the cold sense of loneliness and the warmth of old friendship.

Once you start looking for them, you will find figures of speech in poem after poem; they are among the most common devices through which poets share their vision with us.

The following poem uses a variety of metaphors to describe sexual experiences:

ADRIENNE RICH

Two Songs

1

Sex, as they harshly call it,
I fell into this morning
at ten o'clock, a drizzling hour
of traffic and wet newspapers.
I thought of him who yesterday   5
clearly didn't
turn me to a hot field
ready for plowing,
and longing for that young man
piercéd me to the roots   10
bathing every vein, etc.[5]

---

5. See the opening lines of the Prologue to Chaucer's *Canterbury Tales*.

All day he appears to me
touchingly desirable,
a prize one could wreck one's peace for.
I'd call it love if love
didn't take so many years
but lust too is a jewel
a sweet flower and what
pure happiness to know
all our high-toned questions
breed in a lively animal.

                    2

That "old last act"!
And yet sometimes
all seems post coitum triste[6]
and I a mere bystander.
Somebody else is going off,
getting shot to the moon.
Or, a moon-race!
Split seconds after
my opposite number lands
I make it—
we lie fainting together
at a crater-edge
heavy as mercury in our moonsuits
till he speaks
in a different language
yet one I've picked up
through cultural exchanges . . .
we murmur the first moonwords:
Spasibo.[7] *Thanks. O.K.*   1964

The first "song" begins straightforwardly as narration ("Sex . . . I fell into this morning / at ten o'clock"), but the vividness of sex and desire is communicated mostly by figure. The speaker describes her body as "a hot field / ready for plowing" (lines 7–8)—quite unlike her resistant body yesterday—and also describes her longing by metaphor, in this case an elaborate one borrowed from another poem. After so sensual and urgent a beginning, the song turns more thoughtful and philosophical, but even the intellectual sorting between love and lust comes to depend on figures: lust is a "jewel" (line 17) and a "flower" (line 18). After the opening pace and excitement, those later metaphors seem calm and tame, moving the poem from the lust of its beginning to a contemplative reflection on the value and beauty of momentary physical pleasures.

The second song depends on two closely related metaphors, and here the metaphors for sex are highly self-conscious and a little comic. The song begins on a plaintive note, considering the classic melancholic feeling after sex; the speaker pictures herself as

6. Sadness after sexual union.   7. Russian for "thanks."

725 METAPHOR AND SIMILE 725

isolated, left out, "a bystander" (line 25), while someone else is having sexual pleasure. She describes the pleasure of others through two colloquial expressions (both metaphors) for sexual climax: "going off" (line 26) and "getting shot to the moon" (line 27). Suddenly the narrator pretends to take sex as space travel seriously and creates a metaphor of her own: sexual partners running a "moon-race" (line 28). In the rest of the poem, she presents the metaphor in the context of the space race between the United States and Russia in the early 1960s, and she describes the race, not exactly even but close enough, in detail. These are international relations, foreign affairs, and the lovers appropriately say their thank-yous separately in Russian and English, then communicate an international *"O.K."*

• • •

ANONYMOUS[8]

The Twenty-third Psalm

The Lord is my shepherd; I shall not want.
He maketh me to lie down in green pastures: he leadeth me beside
    the still waters.
He restoreth my soul: he leadeth me in the paths of righteousness
    for his name's sake.
Yea, though I walk through the valley of the shadow of death,
    I will fear no evil: for thou art with me;
    thy rod and thy staff they comfort me.
Thou preparest a table before me in the presence of mine enemies:
    thou anointest my head with oil; my cup runneth over.   5
Surely goodness and mercy shall follow me all the days of my life:
    and I will dwell in the house of the Lord for ever.

8. Traditionally attributed to King David. This English translation is from the King James Version of the Bible.

JOHN DONNE

[*Batter my heart, three-personed God; for You*][9]

Batter my heart, three-personed God; for You
As yet but knock, breathe, shine, and seek to mend;
That I may rise and stand, o'erthrow me, and bend
Your force, to break, blow, burn, and make me new.
5   I, like an usurped town, to another due,
Labor to admit You, but Oh, to no end!
Reason, Your viceroy[1] in me, me should defend,
But is captived, and proves weak or untrue.
Yet dearly I love You, and would be loved fain,[2]
10   But am betrothed unto Your enemy:
Divorce me, untie or break that knot again,
Take me to You, imprison me, for I,
Except You enthrall me, never shall be free,
Nor ever chaste, except You ravish me.   1633

The Computation

For the first twenty years, since yesterday,
I scarce believed thou couldst be gone away;
For forty more, I fed on favours past,
And forty on hopes—that thou wouldst, they might, last.
5   Tears drowned one hundred, and sighs blew out two;
A thousand, I did neither think, nor do,
Or not divide, all being one thought of you;
Or in a thousand more forgot that too.
Yet call not this long life, but think that I
10   Am, by being dead, immortal. Can ghosts die?   1633

DAVID FERRY

At the Hospital

She was the sentence the cancer spoke at last,
Its blurred grammar finally clarified.   1983

---

9. *Holy Sonnets*, 14.   1. One who rules as the representative of a higher power.   2. Gladly.

RANDALL JARRELL

The Death of the Ball Turret Gunner[3]

From my mother's sleep I fell into the State,
And I hunched in its belly till my wet fur froze.
Six miles from earth, loosed from its dream of life,
I woke to black flak and the nightmare fighters.
When I died they washed me out of the turret with a hose.   1945   5

FRANCIS WILLIAM BOURDILLON

The Night Has a Thousand Eyes

The night has a thousand eyes,
    And the day but one;
Yet the light of the bright world dies
    With the dying sun.

The mind has a thousand eyes,   5
    And the heart but one;
Yet the light of a whole life dies
    When the love is gone.   1889

3. A ball turrett was a plexiglass sphere set into the belly of a B-17 or B-24 and inhabited by two .50 caliber machine-guns and one man, a short, small man. When this gunner tracked with his machine-guns a fighter attacking his bomber from below, he revolved with the turret; hunched upside-down in his little sphere, he looked like the foetus in the womb. The fighters which attacked him were armed with cannon firing explosive shells. The hose was a steam hose [Jarrell's note].

EMILY DICKINSON

[*Wild Nights—Wild Nights!*]

Wild Nights—Wild Nights!
Were I with thee
Wild Nights should be
Our luxury!

5   Futile—the Winds—
To a Heart in port—
Done with the Compass—
Done with the Chart!

Rowing in Eden—
10   Ah, the Sea!
Might I but moor—Tonight—
In Thee!

ca. 1861

SYMBOL

The word *symbol* is often used sloppily and sometimes pretentiously, but properly used the term suggests one of the most basic things about poems—their ability to get beyond what words signify and make larger claims about meanings in the verbal world. All words go beyond themselves. They are not simply a collection of sounds: they signify something beyond their sounds, often things or actions or ideas. Words describe not only a verbal universe but also a world in which actions occur, acts have implications, and events mean. Sometimes words signify something beyond themselves, say a rock or a tree or a cloud, and symbolize something as well, such as solidity or life or dreams. Words can—when their implications are agreed on by tradition, convention, or habit—stand for things beyond their most immediate meanings or significations and become symbols, and even simple words that have accumulated no special power from previous use may be given special significance in special circumstances—either in poetry or in life itself.

A **symbol** is, put simply, something that stands for something else. The everyday world is full of common examples; a flag, a logo, a trademark, or a skull and crossbones all suggest things beyond themselves, and everyone likely understands what their display indicates, whether or not each viewer shares a commitment to what the object represents. In common usage a prison symbolizes confinement, constriction, and loss of freedom, and in specialized traditional usage a cross may symbolize oppression, cruelty, suffering, death, resurrection, triumph, or the intersection of two separate things, traditions, or ideas (as in crossroads and crosscurrents, for example). The specific symbolic significance depends on the context; a reader, for example, might determine significance by looking at contiguous details in a poem and by examining the poem's attitude toward a particular tradition or body of beliefs. A star means one thing to a Jewish poet and something else to a Christian poet, still something else to a sailor or an actor. In a very literal sense, words themselves are all symbols (they stand for an object, action, or quality, not just for letters or sounds), but symbols in poetry are said to be those words and groups of words that have a range of reference beyond their literal signification or denotation.

Poems sometimes create a symbol out of a thing, action, or event that has no previously agreed on symbolic significance. The following poem, for example, gives a seemingly random gesture symbolic significance:

SHARON OLDS

Leningrad Cemetery, Winter of 1941[1]

That winter, the dead could not be buried.
The ground was frozen, the gravediggers weak from hunger,
the coffin wood used for fuel. So they were covered with something

1. The nine-hundred-day siege of Leningrad (now Saint Petersburg) during World War II began in September 1941.

5
10
15

and taken on a child's sled to the cemetery
in the sub-zero air. They lay on the soil,
some of them wrapped in dark cloth
bound with rope like the tree's ball of roots
when it waits to be planted; others wound in sheets,
their pale, gauze, tapered shapes
stiff as cocoons that will split down the center
when the new life inside is prepared;
but most lay like corpses, their coverings
coming undone, naked calves
hard as corded wood spilling
from under a cloak, a hand reaching out
with no sign of peace, wanting to come back
even to the bread made of glue and sawdust,
even to the icy winter, and the siege.   p. 1979

All of these corpses—frozen, neglected, beginning to be in disarray—vividly stamp
upon our minds a picture of the horrors of war, one likely to stay in our minds long after
we have finished reading the poem. Several details are striking, and the poem's language
heightens our sense of them. The corpses wound in sheets, for example, are described
in "their pale, gauze, tapered shapes" (line 9), and they are compared to cocoons that
one day will split and emit new life; and the limbs that dangle loose when the coverings
come undone are "hard as corded wood spilling" (line 14). But clearly the most memorable sight is the hand dangling from one corpse that is coming unwrapped, for the
poet invests that hand with special significance, giving its gesture *meaning*. The hand
is "reaching out . . . wanting to come back" (lines 15–16): it is as if the dead can still
gesture even if they cannot speak, and the gesture seems to signify the desire of the dead
to return at any price. They would be glad to live, even under the grim conditions that
attend the living in Leningrad during the war. Suddenly the grimness that we—living—
have been witnessing pales by comparison with what the dead have lost simply by
being dead. The hand has been made to *symbolize* the desire of the dead to return, to
live, to be still among us, anywhere. The hand reaches out in the poem as a gesture that
means; the poet has made it a symbol of desire.

The whole array of dead bodies in the poem might be called symbolic as well. As a
group, they stand for the human waste that the war has produced, and their dramatic
visual presence provides the poem with a dramatic visualization of how war and its
requirements have no time for decency, not even the decency of burial. The bodies are
a symbol in the sense that they stand for what the poem as a whole asserts.

The following poem also arises out of a historical moment. Here, however, the poet
gives significance to a personal event by the interpretation he puts upon it.

JAMES DICKEY

The Leap

The only thing I have of Jane MacNaughton
Is one instant of a dancing-class dance.
She was the fastest runner in the seventh grade,
My scrapbook says, even when boys were beginning
To be as big as the girls,   5
But I do not have her running in my mind,
Though Frances Lane is there, Agnes Fraser,
Fat Betty Lou Black in the boys-against-girls
Relays we ran at recess: she must have run

Like the other girls, with her skirts tucked up   10
So they would be like bloomers,
But I cannot tell; that part of her is gone.
What I do have is when she came,
With the hem of her skirt where it should be
For a young lady, into the annual dance   15
Of the dancing class we all hated, and with a light
Grave leap, jumped up and touched the end
Of one of the paper-ring decorations

To see if she could reach it. She could,
And reached me now as well, hanging in my mind   20
From a brown chain of brittle paper, thin
And muscular, wide-mouthed, eager to prove
Whatever it proves when you leap
In a new dress, a new womanhood, among the boys
Whom you easily left in the dust   25
Of the passionless playground. If I said I saw
In the paper where Jane MacNaughton Hill,

Mother of four, leapt to her death from a window
Of a downtown hotel, and that her body crushed-in
The top of a parked taxi, and that I held   30
Without trembling a picture of her lying cradled
In that papery steel as though lying in the grass,
One shoe idly off, arms folded across her breast,
I would not believe myself. I would say
The convenient thing, that it was a bad dream   35
Of maturity, to see that eternal process

Most obsessively wrong with the world
Come out of her light, earth-spurning feet
Grown heavy: would say that in the dusty heels
Of the playground some boy who did not depend   40
On speed of foot, caught and betrayed her.
Jane, stay where you are in my first mind:
It was odd in that school, at that dance.

I and the other slow-footed yokels sat in corners
45   Cutting rings out of drawing paper

Before you leapt in your new dress
And touched the end of something I began,
Above the couples struggling on the floor,
New men and women clutching at each other
50   And prancing foolishly as bears: hold on
To that ring I made for you, Jane—
My feet are nailed to the ground
By dust I swallowed thirty years ago—
While I examine my hands.   1967

Memory is crucial to "The Leap." The fact that Jane MacNaughton's graceful leap in dancing class has stuck in the speaker's mind all these years means that this leap was important to him, meant something to him, stood for something in his mind. For the speaker, the leap is an "instant" and the "only thing" he has of Jane. He remembers its grace and ease, and he struggles at several points to articulate its meaning (lines 15–26, 44–50), but even without articulation or explanation it remains in his head as a visual memory, a symbol of something beyond himself, something he cannot do, something he wanted to be. What that leap stood for, or symbolized, was boldness, confidence, accomplishment, maturity, Jane's ability to go beyond her fellow students in dancing class—the transcending of childhood by someone entering adulthood. Her feet now seem "earth-spurning" (line 38) in that original leap, and they separate her from everyone else. Jane MacNaughton was beyond the speaker's abilities and any attempt he could make to articulate his hopes, but she was not beyond his dreams. And even before articulation, she symbolized a dream.

The leap to her death seems cruelly inappropriate and ironic in the context of her earlier leap. In memory she is suspended in air, as if there were no gravity, no coming back to earth, as if life could exist as dream. And so the photograph, re-created in precise detail, is a cruel dashing of the speaker's dream—a detailed record of the ending of a leap, a denial of the suspension in which his memory had held her. His dream is grounded; her mortality is insistent. But the speaker still wants to hang on to (line 42) that symbolic moment, which he confronts in a more mature context but which he will never altogether replace or surrender.

The leap is ultimately symbolic in the *poem*, too, not just in the speaker's mind. In the poem (and for us as readers) its symbolism is double: the first leap symbolizes aspiration, and the second symbolizes the frustration and grounding of high hopes; the two are complementary, one impossible to imagine without the other. The poem is horrifying in some ways, a dramatic reminder that human beings don't ultimately transcend their mortality, their limits, no matter how heroic or unencumbered by gravity they may seem to an observer. But it is not altogether sad and despairing, partly because it notices and affirms the validity of the original leap and partly because it creates and elaborates another symbol: the paper chain.

The chain connects Jane to the speaker both literally and figuratively. It is, in part, *his* paper chain that she had leaped to touch in dancing class (lines 18–19), and he thinks of her first leap as "touch[ing] the end of something I began" (line 47). He and the other "slow-footed," earthbound "yokels" (line 44) made the chain, and it connects them to her original leap, just as a photograph glimpsed in the paper connects the speaker to her second leap. The paper in the chain is "brittle" (line 21), and its creators seem dull artisans compared to the artistic performer that Jane was. They are heavy and "left in the dust" (lines 25, 52–53), but she is "light" (line 16) and able to transcend them, even in transcendence touching their lives and what they can do. And so the paper chain becomes the poem's symbol of linkage, connecting lower accomplishment to higher possibility, the artisan to the artist, material substance to the act of imagination. And at the end the speaker examines the hands that made the chain because those hands certify his connection to her and the imaginative leap she had made for him. The chain thus symbolizes not only the lower capabilities of those who cannot leap like the budding Jane could, but (later) the connection with her leap as both transcendence and mortality. Like the leap itself, the chain has been elevated to special meaning, given symbolic significance, by the poet's treatment of it. A leap and a chain have no necessary significance in themselves to most of us—at least no significance that we have all agreed on—but they may take on significance in specific circumstances or a specific text.

Other objects and acts have a significance built in because of past usage in literature, or tradition, or the stories a culture develops to explain itself and its values. Over the years some things have acquired an agreed-on significance, an accepted value in our minds. They already stand for something before the poet cites them; they are **traditional symbols.** Their uses in poetry have to do with the fact that poets can count on a recognition of their traditional suggestions and meanings outside the poem, and the poem does not have to propose or argue a particular symbolic value. Birds, for example, traditionally symbolize flight, freedom from confinement, detachment from earthbound limits, the ability to soar beyond rationality and transcend mortal limits. Traditionally, birds have also been linked with imagination, especially poetic imagination, and poets often identify with them as pure and ideal singers of songs, as in Keats's "Ode to a Nightingale" (see chapter 20). One of the most traditional symbols, the rose, may be a simple and fairly plentiful flower in its season, but it has stood for particular qualities so long that to name it raises predictable expectations. Its beauty, delicacy, fragility, shortness of life, and depth of color have made it a symbol of the transitoriness of beauty, and countless poets have counted on its accepted symbolism—sometimes to compliment a friend (as Burns does in "A Red, Red Rose") or sometimes to make a point about the nature of symbolism. The following poem draws, in a quite traditional way, on the traditional meanings.

EDMUND WALLER

Song

Go, lovely rose!
Tell her that wastes her time and me
    That now she knows,
When I resemble² her to thee,
How sweet and fair she seems to be.   5

    Tell her that's young,
And shuns to have her graces spied,
    That hadst thou sprung

2. Compare.

10 In deserts, where no men abide,
    Thou must have uncommended died.

        Small is the worth
    Of beauty from the light retired;
        Bid her come forth,
    Suffer herself to be desired,
15 And not blush so to be admired.

        Then die! that she
    The common fate of all things rare
        May read in thee;
    How small a part of time they share
    That are so wondrous sweet and fair!   1645

    The speaker in "Song" sends the rose to his love in order to have it speak its traditional
meanings involving not only beauty but also transitoriness. He counts on accepted symbolism to make his point and hurry her into acceptance of his advances. Likewise, the
poet does not elaborate or argue these things; he counts on the tradition, habits of mind
built on familiarity and repetition (though, of course, readers unfamiliar with the tradition
will not respond in the same way—that is one reason it is difficult to read with full
appreciation texts from another linguistic or cultural tradition).
    Poets may use traditional symbols to invoke predictable responses—in effect using
shortcuts to meaning and power by repeating acts of signification and symbolization
sanctioned by time and cultural habit. But often poets examine the tradition even as
they employ it, and sometimes they revise or reverse meanings built into the tradition.
Symbols do not necessarily stay the same over time, and poets often turn even the most
traditional symbols to their own original uses. Knowing the traditions of poetry—reading
a lot of poems and observing how they tend to use certain words, metaphors, and
symbols—can be very useful in reading new poems, but traditions modify and individual
poems do highly individual things. Knowing the past never means being able to predict
new texts with confidence. Symbolism makes things happen, but individual poets and
texts determine what will happen and how. The following two poems work important
variations on the traditional associations of roses:

D. H. LAWRENCE

I Am Like a Rose

    I am myself at last; now I achieve
    My very self. I, with the wonder mellow,
    Full of fine warmth, I issue forth in clear
    And single me, perfected from my fellow.

5   Here I am all myself. No rose-bush heaving
    Its limpid sap to culmination has brought
    Itself more sheer and naked out of the green
    In stark-clear roses, than I to myself am brought.   1917

DOROTHY PARKER

One Perfect Rose

A single flow'r he sent me, since we met.
    All tenderly his messenger he chose;
Deep-hearted, pure, with scented dew still wet—
    One perfect rose.

I knew the language of the floweret;   5
    "My fragile leaves," it said, "his heart enclose."
Love long has taken for his amulet
    One perfect rose.

Why is it no one ever sent me yet
    One perfect limousine, do you suppose?   10
Ah no, it's always just my luck to get
    One perfect rose.   1937

Sometimes symbols—traditional or not—become so insistent in the world of a poem that the larger referential world is left almost totally behind. In such cases the symbol is everything, and the poem does not just *use* symbols but becomes a **symbolic poem,** usually a highly individualized one dependent on an internal system introduced by the individual poet.

Here is an example of such a poem:

WILLIAM BLAKE

The Sick Rose[3]

O rose, thou art sick.
The invisible worm
That flies in the night
In the howling storm

Has found out thy bed   5
Of crimson joy,
And his dark secret love
Does thy life destroy.   1794

---

3. In Renaissance emblem books, the scarab beetle, worm, and rose are closely associated: the beetle feeds on dung, and the smell of the rose is fatal to it.

The poem does not seem to be about a rose, but about what the rose represents—not in this case something altogether understandable through the traditional meanings of *rose*.

We usually associate the rose with beauty and love, often with sex; and here several key terms have sexual connotations: "worm," "bed," and "crimson joy." The violation of the rose by the worm is the poem's main concern; the violation seems to have involved secrecy, deceit, and "dark" motives, and the result is sickness rather than the joy of love. The poem is sad; it involves a sense of hurt and tragedy, nearly of despair. The poem cries out against the misuse of the rose, against its desecration, implying that instead of a healthy joy in sensuality and sexuality, there has been in this case destruction and hurt because of misunderstanding and repression and lack of sensitivity.

But to say so much about this poem we have to extrapolate from other poems by Blake, and we have to introduce information from outside the poem. Fully symbolic poems often require that, and thus they ask us to go beyond the formal procedures of reading that we have discussed so far. As presented in this poem, the rose is not part of the normal world that we ordinarily see, and it is symbolic in a special sense. The poet does not simply take an object from that everyday world and give it special significance, making it a symbol in the same sense that the leap or the corpse's hand is a symbol. Here the rose seems to belong to its own world, a world made entirely inside the poem or the poet's head. The rose is not referential, or not primarily so. The whole poem is symbolic; it is not paraphrasable; it lives in its own world. But what is the rose here a symbol of? In general terms, we can say from what the poem tells us; but we may not be as confident as we can be in the more nearly everyday world of "The Leap" or "Leningrad Cemetery, Winter of 1941," poems that contain actions we recognize from the world of probabilities in which we live. In "The Sick Rose," it seems inappropriate to ask the standard questions: What rose? Where? Which worm? What are the particulars here? In the world of this poem worms can fly and may be invisible. We are altogether in a world of meanings that have been formulated according to a particular system of knowledge and code of belief. We will feel comfortable and confident in that world only if we read many poems written by the poet (in this case William Blake) within the same symbolic system.

Negotiation of meanings in symbolic poems can be very difficult indeed. Reading symbolic poems is an advanced skill that depends on special knowledge of authors and of the special traditions they work from. But usually the symbols you will find in poems *are* referential, and you can readily discover their meanings by carefully studying the poems themselves.

· · ·

ROBERT FROST

Fireflies in the Garden

Here come real stars to fill the upper skies,
And here on earth come emulating flies,
That though they never equal stars in size,
(And they were never really stars at heart)
Achieve at times a very star-like start. 5
Only, of course, they can't sustain the part. 1928

ADRIENNE RICH

Diving into the Wreck

First having read the book of myths,
and loaded the camera,
and checked the edge of the knife-blade,
I put on
the body-armor of black rubber 5
the absurd flippers
the grave and awkward mask.
I am having to do this
not like Cousteau[4] with his
assiduous team 10
aboard the sun-flooded schooner
but here alone.

There is a ladder.
The ladder is always there
hanging innocently 15
close to the side of the schooner.
We know what it is for,
we who have used it.
Otherwise
it's a piece of maritime floss 20
some sundry equipment.

I go down.
Rung after rung and still
the oxygen immerses me
the blue light 25
the clear atoms

---

4. Jacques-Yves Cousteau (1910–1997), French underwater explorer and writer.

of our human air.
I go down.
My flippers cripple me,
30 I crawl like an insect down the ladder
and there is no one
to tell me when the ocean
will begin.

First the air is blue and then
35 it is bluer and then green and then
black I am blacking out and yet
my mask is powerful
it pumps my blood with power
the sea is another story
40 the sea is not a question of power
I have to learn alone
to turn my body without force
in the deep element.

And now: it is easy to forget
45 what I came for
among so many who have always
lived here
swaying their crenellated fans
between the reefs
50 and besides
you breathe differently down here.

I came to explore the wreck.
The words are purposes.
The words are maps.
55 I came to see the damage that was done
and the treasures that prevail.
I stroke the beam of my lamp
slowly along the flank
of something more permanent
60 than fish or weed

the thing I came for:
the wreck and not the story of the wreck
the thing itself and not the myth
the drowned face always staring
65 toward the sun
the evidence of damage
worn by salt and sway into this threadbare beauty
the ribs of the disaster
curving their assertion
70 among the tentative haunters.

This is the place.
And I am here, the mermaid whose dark hair
streams black, the merman in his armored body

We circle silently
about the wreck   75
we dive into the hold.
I am she: I am he

whose drowned face sleeps with open eyes
whose breasts still bear the stress
whose silver, copper, vermeil cargo lies   80
obscurely inside barrels
half-wedged and left to rot
we are the half-destroyed instruments
that once held to a course
the water-eaten log   85
the fouled compass

We are, I am, you are
by cowardice or courage
the one who find our way
back to this scene   90
carrying a knife, a camera
a book of myths
in which
our names do not appear.

1972   1973

ROO BORSON

After a Death

Seeing that there's no other way,
I turn his absence into a chair.
I can sit in it,
gaze out through the window.
I can do what I do best   5
and then go out into the world.
And I can return then with my useless love,
to rest,
because the chair is there.   1989

HOWARD NEMEROV

The Town Dump

"The art of our necessities is strange,
That can make vile things precious."[5]

A mile out in the marshes, under a sky
Which seems to be always going away
In a hurry, on that Venetian land threaded
With hidden canals, you will find the city
5   Which seconds ours (so cemeteries, too,
Reflect a town from hillsides out of town),
Where Being most Becomingly[6] ends up
Becoming some more. From cardboard tenements,
Windowed with cellophane, or simply tenting
10   In paper bags, the angry mackerel eyes
Glare at you out of stove-in, sunken heads
Far from the sea; the lobster, also, lifts
An empty claw in his most minatory
Of gestures; oyster, crab, and mussel shells
15   Lie here in heaps, savage as money hurled
Away at the gate of hell. If you want results,
These are results.
                Objects of value or virtue,
However, are also to be picked up here,
20   Though rarely, lying with bones and rotten meat,
Eggshells and mouldy bread, banana peels
No one will skid on, apple cores that caused
Neither the fall of man nor a theory
Of gravitation.[7] People do throw out
25   The family pearls by accident, sometimes,
Not often; I've known dealers in antiques
To prowl this place by night, with flashlights, on
The off-chance of somebody's having left
Derelict chairs which will turn out to be
30   By Hepplewhite,[8] a perfect set of six
Going to show, I guess, that in any sty
Someone's heaven may open and shower down
Riches responsive to the right dream; though
It is a small chance, certainly, that sends

---

5. *King Lear* 3.2.70–71.   6. "Being" and "Becoming" have been, since Heraclitus (ca. 540–ca. 480 B.C.),
the standard antinomies in Western philosophy, standing for (respectively) the eternal and that which
changes.   7. According to legend, Sir Isaac Newton's discovery of the principle of gravitation followed
his being hit on the head by a falling apple.   8. A late-eighteenth-century cabinetmaker and furniture
designer, famed for his simplification of neoclassic lines. No pieces known to have been made by Hepplewhite survive.

The ghostly dealer, heavy with fly-netting   35
Over his head, across these hills in darkness,
Stumbling in cut-glass goblets, lacquered cups,
And other products of his dreamy midden[9]
Penciled with light and guarded by the flies.

For there are flies, of course. A dynamo   40
Composed, by thousands, of our ancient black
Retainers, hums here day and night, steady
As someone telling[1] beads, the hum becoming
A high whine at any disturbance; then,
Settled again, they shine under the sun   45
Like oil-drops, or are invisible as night,
By night.
        All this continually smoulders,
Crackles, and smokes with mostly invisible fires
Which, working deep, rarely flash out and flare,   50
And never finish. Nothing finishes;
The flies, feeling the heat, keep on the move.
Among the flies, the purifying fires,
The hunters by night, acquainted with the art
Of our necessities, and the new deposits   55
That each day wastes with treasure, you may say
There should be ratios. You may sum up
The results if you want results. But I will add
That wild birds, drawn to the carrion and flies,
Assemble in some numbers here, their wings   60
Shining with light, their flight enviably free,
Their music marvelous, though sad, and strange.   1958

QUESTIONS

1. List all the neologisms and other unusual words in Hopkins's "Pied Beauty." Find the most precise synonym you can for each. How can you tell exactly what these words contribute to the poem? Explain the effects of the repeated consonant sounds (alliteration) and repeated vowel sounds (assonance) in the poem. What are the advantages of making up original words to describe highly individualized effects? What are the disadvantages?

2. Compare Dickinson's "I dwell in Possibility—" with two of her other poems, "A narrow Fellow in the Grass" (chapter 16) and "Wild Nights—Wild Nights!" (this chapter). What patterns of word use do you see in the three poems? What kinds of vocabulary do they have in common? what patterns of syntax? what strategies of organization?

3. Read aloud the passages from Milton's *Paradise Lost*. Then ask a friend to read the passages aloud as well. As the friend reads, note which words—and which choices of word order—provide especially useful guides for reading aloud. Make a list of all the lines in which the "normal" word order would be different if the poem were not written in a metrical form designed for reading aloud. In each case in which the poem uses unusual word order, try to figure out exactly what effect is produced by the variation.

---

9. Refuse heap. The term usually describes those primitive refuse heaps that have been untouched for centuries and in which archaeologists dig for shards and artifacts of older cultures.   1. Counting.

4. Characterize as fully as you can the speaker in Donne's "Batter my heart, three-personed God." Explain how the metaphor of invasion and resistance works in the poem. What effect does this central metaphor have on our conception of the speaker? Explain the terms "imprison" (line 12) and "enthrall" (line 13). Explain "chaste" and "ravish" (line 14). How do these two sets of terms relate to the poem's central metaphor?

5. List every term in "The Twenty-third Psalm" that relates to the central metaphor of shepherding. Explain the metaphors of anointing and the overfull cup in line 5. (If you have trouble with this metaphor and do not understand the historical/cultural reference, ask a reference librarian to guide you to biblical commentaries that explain the practices referred to here.) What is the "house of the Lord" (line 6), and how does it relate to the basic metaphor of the psalm? (Again, if you are not sure of the historical/cultural reference, consult biblical commentaries or other historical sources on social and economic structures of the ancient Middle East.)

WRITING SUGGESTIONS

1. Choose one poem you have read so far in the course in which a single word seems crucial to that poem's total effect. Write a short essay in which you work out carefully how the poem's meaning and tone depend on that one word.

2. With the help of a reference librarian, find several pictures of B-17 bombers, then study carefully the design and appearance of the ball turret. Try to find a picture of the gunner at work in the turret, and note carefully his body position. Explain, in a paragraph, how Jarrell's poem "The Death of the Ball Turret Gunner" uses the visual details of the ball turret to create the fetal and birth metaphors in the poem.

3. With the help of a reference librarian, find at least six more poems that are about roses. After reading them carefully, list all the things that the rose seems to stand for in the poems. Write a paragraph about each poem showing how it establishes specific symbolism for the rose.

16

THE SOUNDS OF POETRY

A lot of what happens in a poem happens in your mind's eye, but some of it happens in your voice. Poems are full of sounds and silences as well as words and sentences that are meaningful. Besides choosing words for their meanings, poets sometimes choose words because they have certain sounds, and poems use sound effects to create a mood or establish a tone, just as films do. Sometimes the sounds of words are crucial to what is happening in the text of the poem.

The following poem explores the sounds of a particular word, tries them on, and analyzes them in relation to the word itself.

HELEN CHASIN

The Word Plum

The word *plum* is delicious

pout and push, luxury of
self-love, and savoring murmur

full in the mouth and falling
like fruit   5

taut skin
pierced, bitten, provoked into
juice, and tart flesh

question
and reply, lip and tongue   10
of pleasure.   1968

The poem savors the sounds of the word as well as the taste and feel of the fruit itself. It is almost as if the poem is tasting the sounds and rolling them carefully on the tongue. The second and third lines even replicate the *p, l, uh,* and *m* sounds of the word while at the same time imitating the squishy sounds of eating the fruit. Words like "delicious" and "luxury" sound juicy, and other words imitate sounds of satisfaction and pleasure— "murmur," for example. Even the process of eating is in part re-created aurally. The tight, clipped sounds of "taut skin / pierced" suggest the way teeth sharply break the skin and slice quickly into the solid flesh of a plum, and as they describe the tartness, the words ("provoked," "question") force the lips to pucker and the tongue and palate to meet and hold, as if the mouth were savoring a tart fruit. The poet is having fun here re-creating the various sense appeals of a plum, teasing the sounds and meanings out of available words. The words must mean something appropriate and describe something accurately first of all, of course, but when they can also imitate the sounds and feel of the process, they can do double duty. Not many poems manipulate sound as intensely or as fully as "The Word *Plum,*" but many poems at least contain passages in which the sounds of life are reproduced by the human voice reading the poem. To get the full effect of this poem— and of many others—you must read aloud; that way, you can pay attention to the vocal rhythms and articulate the sounds as the poem calls for them to be reproduced by the human voice.

> *Poetry is a comforting piece of fiction set to more or less lascivious music.*
>
> —H. L. MENCKEN

You will almost always enhance a poem's effect by reading aloud, using your voice to pronounce the words so that the poem becomes a spoken communication. Historically, poetry began as an oral phenomenon, and often poems that seem very difficult when looked at silently come alive when turned into sound. Early bards in many cultures chanted or recited their verses, and the music of poetry—its cadences and rhythms— developed from this kind of performance. Often performances of primitive poetry (sometimes in later ages) were accompanied by some kind of musical instrument. The rhythms of any poem become clearer when you say or hear them.

Poetry is almost always a vocal art, dependent on the human voice to become its full self (for some exceptions look at the shaped verse in chapter 18). In a sense, it begins to exist as a real phenomenon when a reader reads and actualizes it. Poems don't really achieve their full meaning when they exist merely on a page; a poem on a page is more a score or set of stage directions for a poem than a poem itself. Sometimes, in fact, it is hard to experience the poem at all unless you hear it; the actual experience of saying the words aloud or hearing them spoken is very good practice for learning to hear in your mind's ear when you read silently. A good poetry reading might easily convince you of the importance of a good voice sensitive to the poem's requirements, but you can also persuade yourself by reading poems aloud in the privacy of your own room. An audience is even better, however, because it provides someone to share the pleasure in the sounds themselves and consider what they imply. At its oral best, much poetry is communal.

MONA VAN DUYN

What the Motorcycle Said

Br-r-r-am-m-m, rackety-am-m, OM, *Am:*
All—r-r-room, r-r-ram, ala-bas-ter—
Am, the world's my oyster.

I hate plastic, wear it black and slick,
hate hardhats, wear one on my head,   5
that's what the motorcycle said.

Passed phonies in Fords, knocked down billboards, landed
on the other side of The Gap, and Whee,
bypassed history.

When I was born (The Past), baby knew best.   10
They shook when I bawled, took Freud's path,
threw away their wrath.

R-r-rackety-am-m. *Am.* War, rhyme,
soap, meat, marriage, the Phantom Jet
are shit, and like that.   15

Hate pompousness, punishment, patience, am into Love,
hate middle-class moneymakers, live on Dad,
that's what the motorcycle said.

Br-r-r-am-m-m. It's Nowsville, man. Passed Oldies, Uglies,
Straighties, Honkies. I'll never be   20
mean, tired or unsexy.

Passed cigarette suckers, souses, mother-fuckers,
losers, went back to Nature and found
how to get VD, stoned.

Passed a cow, too fast to hear her moo, "*I* rolled   25
our leaves of grass into one ball.
I am the grassy All."

Br-r-r-am-m-m, rackety-am-m, OM, *Am:*
All—gr-r-rin, oooohgah, gl-l-utton—
Am, the world's my smilebutton.   1973   30

Saying this poem as if you were a motorcycle with the power of speech (sort of) is part
of the poem's fun, and the rich, loud sounds of a motorcycle revving up concentrate
and intensify the effect and enrich the pleasure. It's a shame not to hear a poem like
this aloud; you miss a lot if you don't try to imitate the sounds or to pick up the motor's
rhythms. A performance here is clearly worth it: a human being as motorcycle, motorcycle as human being.

And it's a good poem, too. It does something interesting, important, and maybe a bit
subversive. The speaking motorcycle seems to take on the values of some of its riders,
the noisy and obtrusive ones that readers most likely associate with motorcycles. The

types of riders made fun of here are themselves sort of mindless and mechanical; they have cult feelings about their group, they travel in packs, and they live no life beyond their machines. The speaking motorcycle, like such riders, grooves on power and speed, lives for the moment, and has little respect for people, the past, institutions, or anything beyond its own small world. It is self-centered, modish, ignorant, and inarticulate; but it is proud as well, mighty proud, and feels important in its own sounds. That's what the motorcycle says.

The following poem uses sound effects efficiently, too.

KENNETH FEARING

Dirge

1-2-3 was the number he played but today the number came 3-2-1;
Bought his Carbide at 30, and it went to 29; had the favorite at Bowie[1]
    but the track was slow—

O executive type, would you like to drive a floating-power, knee-
    action, silk-upholstered six? Wed a Hollywood star? Shoot the course
    in 58? Draw to the ace, king, jack?
O fellow with a will who won't take no, watch out for three cigarettes
    on the same, single match; O democratic voter born in August under
    Mars, beware of liquidated rails—

Denouement to denouement, he took a personal pride in the certain,
5   certain way he lived his own, private life,
But nevertheless, they shut off his gas; nevertheless, the bank foreclosed;
    nevertheless, the landlord called; nevertheless, the radio broke,

And twelve o'clock arrived just once too often,
Just the same he wore one gray tweed suit, bought one straw hat, drank
    one straight Scotch, walked one short step, took one long look, drew one
    deep breath,
Just one too many,

10   And wow he died as wow he lived,
Going whop to the office and blooie home to sleep and biff got married
    and bam had children and oof got fired,
Zowie did he live and zowie did he die,

With who the hell are you at the corner of his casket, and where the
    hell're we going on the right-hand silver knob, and who the hell cares
    walking second from the end with an American Beauty[2] wreath from why
    the hell not,

Very much missed by the circulation staff of the New York Evening Post;
    deeply, deeply mourned by the B.M.T.[3]
15   Wham, Mr. Roosevelt; pow, Sears Roebuck; awk, big dipper; bop, summer
    rain; Bong, Mr., bong, Mr., bong, Mr., bong.

1935

---

1. A racetrack in Maryland. *Carbide:* stock in the Union Carbide Corporation.   2. A variety of rose.
3. A New York City subway line.

As the title implies, "Dirge" is a kind of musical lament, in this case for a certain sort of businessman who took many chances and saw his investments and life go down the drain in the depression of the early 1930s. Reading this poem aloud helps a lot, in part because of the expressive cartoon words here that echo the action, words like "oof" and "blooie" (which primarily carry their meaning in their sounds, for they have practically no literal or referential meaning). Reading aloud also helps us notice that the poem employs rhythms much as a song would and that it frequently shifts its pace and mood. Notice how carefully the first two lines are balanced, and then how quickly the rhythm shifts as the "executive type" is addressed directly in line 3. (Line 2 is long and dribbles over in the narrow pages of a book like this; the especially long lines and irregular line lengths here create some of the poem's special sound effects.) In the direct address, the poem first picks up a series of advertising features, which it recites in rapid-fire order rather like the advertising phrases in Ammons's "Needs" (chapter 13). In stanza 3 here, the rhythm shifts again, but the poem gives us helpful clues about how to read. Line 5 sounds like prose and is long, drawn out, and rather dull (rather like its subject), but line 6 sets up a regular (and monotonous) rhythm with its repeated

> *There are only three things . . .*
> *that a poem must reach: the*
> *eye, the ear, and what we may*
> *call the heart or the mind. It is*
> *the most important of all to*
> *reach the heart of the reader.*
> *And the surest way to reach*
> *the heart is through the ear.*
>
> —ROBERT FROST

"nevertheless," which punctuates the rhythm like a drumbeat: "But nevertheless, *tuh-tuh-tuh-tuh-tuh;* nevertheless, *tuh-tuh-tuh-tuh;* nevertheless, *tuh-tuh-tuh-tuh;* nevertheless, *tuh-tuh-tuh-tuh-tuh.*" In the next stanza, the repetitive phrasing comes again, this time guided by the word "one" in cooperation with other words of one syllable: "wore *one* gray tweed suit, bought *one* straw hat, *tuh* one *tuh-tuh, tuh* one *tuh-tuh, tuh* one *tuh-tuh, tuh* one *tuh-tuh.*" And then a new rhythm and a new technique begin in stanza 5, which imitates the language of comic books to describe in violent, exaggerated terms the routine of the businessman's life. You have to say words like "whop" and "zowie" aloud and in the rhythm of the whole sentence to get the full effect of how boring his life is, no matter how he tries to jazz it up with exciting words. And so it goes—repeated words, shifting rhythms, emphasis on routine and averageness—until the final bell ("Bong . . . bong . . . bong . . . bong") tolls rhythmically for the dead man in the final clanging line.

Sometimes sounds in poems just provide special effects, rather like a musical score behind a film, setting mood and getting us into an appropriate frame of mind. But often sound and meaning go hand in hand, and the poet finds words that in their sounds echo the action. A word that captures or approximates the sound of what it describes, such as "splash" or "squish" or "murmur," is an **onomatopoeic** word, and the device itself is **onomatopoeia.** And poets can do similar things with pacing and rhythm, sounds and pauses. The punctuation, the length of vowels, and the combination of consonant sounds help to control the way we read so that we use our voice to imitate what is being described. The poems at the end of this chapter suggest several ways that such imitations of pace and pause may occur: by echoing the lapping of waves on a shore, for example ("Like as the waves"), or reproducing the rhythms of a musical style ("Dear John, Dear Coltrane").

Here is a classic passage in which a skillful poet talks about the virtues of making the sound echo the sense—and shows at the same time how to do it:

ALEXANDER POPE

Sound and Sense[4]

337   But most by numbers[5] judge a poet's song,
        And smooth or rough, with them, is right or wrong;
        In the bright muse though thousand charms conspire,[6]
340   Her voice is all these tuneful fools admire,
        Who haunt Parnassus[7] but to please their ear,
        Not mend their minds; as some to church repair,
        Not for the doctrine, but the music there.
        These, equal syllables[8] alone require,
345   Though oft the ear the open vowels tire,
        While expletives[9] their feeble aid do join,
        And ten low words oft creep in one dull line,
        While they ring round the same unvaried chimes,
        With sure returns of still expected rhymes.
350   Where'er you find "the cooling western breeze,"
        In the next line, it "whispers through the trees";
        If crystal streams "with pleasing murmurs creep,"
        The reader's threatened (not in vain) with "sleep."
        Then, at the last and only couplet fraught
355   With some unmeaning thing they call a thought,
        A needless Alexandrine[1] ends the song,
        That, like a wounded snake, drags its slow length along.
        Leave such to tune their own dull rhymes, and know
        What's roundly smooth, or languishingly slow;
360   And praise the easy vigor of a line,
        Where Denham's strength and Waller's[2] sweetness join.
        True ease in writing comes from art, not chance,
        As those move easiest who have learned to dance.
        'Tis not enough no harshness gives offense,
365   The sound must seem an echo to the sense:
        Soft is the strain when Zephyr[3] gently blows,
        And the smooth stream in smoother numbers flows;
        But when loud surges lash the sounding shore,
        The hoarse, rough verse should like the torrent roar.
370   When Ajax[4] strives, some rock's vast weight to throw,
        The line too labors, and the words move slow;

4. From *An Essay on Criticism*, Pope's poem on the art of poetry and the problems of literary criticism. The passage excerpted here follows a discussion of several common weaknesses of critics—failure to regard an author's intention, for example, or overemphasis on clever metaphors and ornate style.   5. Meter, rhythm, sound.   6. Unite.   7. A mountain in Greece, traditionally associated with the Muses and considered the seat of poetry and music.   8. Regular accents.   9. Filler words, such as "do."   1. A line of six metrical feet, sometimes used in pentameter poems to vary the pace mechanically. Line 357 is an alexandrine.   2. Sir John Denham and Edmund Waller, seventeenth-century poets credited with perfecting the heroic couplet.   3. The west wind.   4. A Greek hero of the Trojan War, noted for his strength.

Not so, when swift Camilla[5] scours the plain,
Flies o'er th' unbending corn, and skims along the main.
Hear how Timotheus'[6] varied lays surprise,
And bid alternate passions fall and rise!   375
While, at each change, the son of Libyan Jove[7]
Now burns with glory, and then melts with love;
Now his fierce eyes with sparkling fury glow,
Now sighs steal out, and tears begin to flow:
Persians and Greeks like turns of nature[8] found,   380
And the world's victor stood subdued by sound!
The pow'r of music all our hearts allow,
And what Timotheus was, is DRYDEN now.   1711

A lot of things are going on here simultaneously. The poem uses a number of echoic
or onomatopoeic words, and in some lines pleasant and unpleasant consonant sounds
underline a particular point or add some mood music. When the poet talks about a
particular weakness in poetry, he illustrates it at the same time—by using open vowels
(line 345), expletives (line 346), monosyllabic words (line 347), predictable rhymes
(lines 350–53), or long, slow lines (line 357). And the good qualities of poetry he talks
about and illustrates as well (line 360, for example). But the main effects of the passage
come from an interaction of several strategies at once. The effects are fairly simple and
easy to spot, but their causes involve a lot of poetic ingenuity. In line 340, for example,
Pope achieves a careful cacophonous effect by repeating the o͞o vowel sound and
repeating the *l* consonant sound together with (twice) interrupting the rough *f* sound in
the middle; no one wants to be caught admiring that music, but the careful harmony of
the preceding sounds has set us up beautifully. And the pace of lines 347, 357, and 359
is carefully controlled by clashing consonant sounds as well as by the use of long vowels.
Line 347 moves incredibly slowly and seems much longer than it is because almost all
the one-syllable words end in a consonant that refuses to blend with the beginning of
the next word, making the words hard to say without distinct, awkward pauses between
them. In lines 357 and 359, long vowels such as those in "wounded," "snake," "slow,"
"along," "roundly," and "smooth" help to slow down the pace, and awkward, unpro-
nounceable consonants are again juxtaposed. The commas also provide nearly a full
stop in the midst of these lines to slow us down still more. Similarly, the harsh lashing
of the shore in lines 368–69 is accomplished partly by onomatopoeia, partly by a shift
in the pattern of stress, which creates irregular waves in line 368, and partly by the
dominance of rough consonants in line 369. (In Pope's time, the English *r* was still trilled
gruffly so that it could be made to sound extremely rrrough and harrrsh.) Almost every
line in this passage demonstrates how to make sound echo sense.

   As "Sound and Sense" and "Dirge" suggest, poets most effectively manipulate sound
by carefully controlling the rhythm of the voice so that not only are the proper sounds
heard, but they are heard at precisely the right moment. Pace and rhythm are nearly as

5. A woman warrior in Virgil's *Aeneid*.   6. The court musician of Alexander the Great, celebrated in a
famous poem by Dryden (see line 383) for the power of his music over Alexander's emotions.   7. In
Greek tradition, the chief god of any people was often given the name Zeus (Jove), and the chief god of
Libya (the Greek name for all of Africa) was called Zeus Ammon. Alexander visited his oracle and was
proclaimed son of the god.   8. Similar alternations of emotion.

important to a good poem as they are to a good piece of music. The human voice naturally develops certain rhythms in speech; some syllables and some words receive more stress than others. Just as multisyllabic words put more stress on some syllables than others (dictionaries always indicate which syllables are stressed), words in the context of a sentence receive more or less stress, depending on meaning. One-syllable words are thus sometimes stressed and sometimes not. A careful poet controls the flow of stresses so that, in many poems, a certain basic rhythm (or **meter**) develops almost like a quiet percussion instrument in the background. Not all poems have meter, and not all metered poems follow a single dominant rhythm, but many poems employ one pervasive pattern, and it is useful to look for patterns of stress.

Here is a poem that names and illustrates many of the meters. If someone read it aloud and you charted the stressed (¯) and unstressed (˘) syllables, you would have a chart similar to that done by the poet himself in the text.

SAMUEL TAYLOR COLERIDGE

Metrical Feet

Lesson for a Boy

Trōchĕe trīps frŏm lōng tŏ shōrt;[9]
From long to long in solemn sort
Slōw Spōndēe stālks; strōng fōōt! yet ill able
Ēvĕr tŏ cōme ŭp wĭth Dāctȳl trĭsȳllăblĕ.
Ĭāmbĭcs mārch frŏm shōrt tŏ lōng—
Wĭth ă lēap ănd ă bōūnd thĕ swĭft Ānăpĕsts thrōng;
One syllable long, with one short at each side,
Ămphībrăchȳs hāstes wĭth ă stātelȳ stride—
Fīrst ănd lāst bēĭng lōng, mīddlĕ shōrt, Amphĭmācer
Strīkes hĭs thūndĕrĭng hōōfs līke ă prōūd hīgh-brĕd Rācer.
If Derwent[1] be innocent, steady, and wise,
And delight in the things of earth, water, and skies;
Tender warmth at his heart, with these meters to show it,
With sound sense in his brains, may make Derwent a poet—
May crown him with fame, and must win him the love
Of his father on earth and his Father above.
My dear, dear child!
Could you stand upon Skiddaw,[2] you would not from its whole ridge
See a man who so loves you as your fond S. T. COLERIDGE.

1806

The following poem exemplifies **dactylic** rhythm (¯ ˘ ˘, or a stressed syllable followed by two unstressed ones).

9. The long and short marks over syllables are Coleridge's. 1. Written originally for Coleridge's son Hartley, the poem was later adapted for his younger son, Derwent. 2. A mountain in the lake country of northern England (where Coleridge lived in his early years), near the town of Derwent.

WENDY COPE

Emily Dickinson

Higgledy-piggledy
Emily Dickinson
Liked to use dashes
Instead of full stops.

Nowadays, faced with such   5
Idiosyncrasy,
Critics and editors
Send for the cops.   1986

Limericks rely on **anapestic** meter (˘ ˘ ¯, or two unstressed syllables followed by a stressed one), although usually the first two syllables are in iambic meter (see below).

ANONYMOUS

[There was a young lady of Riga]

There was a young lady of Riga
Who went for a ride on a tiger;
  They returned from the ride
  With the lady inside,
And a smile on the face of the tiger.   5

The following poem is composed in the more common **trochaic** meter (¯ ˘, a stressed syllable followed by an unstressed one).

SIR JOHN SUCKLING

Song

Why so pale and wan, fond Lover?
  Prithee why so pale?
Will, when looking well can't move her,
  Looking ill prevail?
  Prithee why so pale?   5

Why so dull and mute, young Sinner?
   Prithee why so mute?
Will, when speaking well can't win her,
   Saying nothing do 't?
10   Prithee why so mute?

Quit, quit, for shame, this will not move,
   This cannot take her;
If of her self she will not love,
   Nothing can make her,
15   The Devil take her.   1646

Like "Sound and Sense," the following poem employs the most common meter in Anglophone poetry, **iambic** (˘ ¯, an unstressed syllable followed by a stressed one, which some would argue is the most "natural" rhythm for the English language).

JOHN DRYDEN
_____

To the Memory of Mr. Oldham[3]

Farewell, too little, and too lately known,
Whom I began to think and call my own;
For sure our souls were near allied, and thine
Cast in the same poetic mold with mine.
5 One common note on either lyre did strike,
And knaves and fools we both abhorred alike.
To the same goal did both our studies drive;
The last set out the soonest did arrive.
Thus Nisus fell upon the slippery place,
10 While his young friend performed and won the race.[4]
O early ripe! to thy abundant store
What could advancing age have added more?
It might (what nature never gives the young)
Have taught the numbers[5] of thy native tongue.
15 But satire needs not those, and wit will shine
Through the harsh cadence of a rugged line.[6]
A noble error, and but seldom made,
When poets are by too much force betrayed.
Thy generous fruits, though gathered ere their prime,
20 Still showed a quickness; and maturing time

3. John Oldham (1653–1683), who like Dryden (see lines 3–6) wrote satiric poetry.   4. In Virgil's *Aeneid* (Book 5), Nisus (who is leading the race) falls and then trips the second runner so that his friend Euryalus can win.   5. Rhythms.   6. In Dryden's time, the English *r* was pronounced with a harsh, trilling sound.

But mellows what we write to the dull sweets of rhyme.
Once more, hail and farewell; farewell, thou young,
But ah too short, Marcellus[7] of our tongue;
Thy brows with ivy, and with laurels bound;
But fate and gloomy night encompass thee around.   1684   25

Scanning a poem line by line—that is, sorting out its metrical pattern—can be hard work, and few people enjoy the process (which is called **scansion**). Doing it right involves listening carefully to your voice as you read aloud, marking the stressed and unstressed syllables, counting the syllables and feet, and checking the rhyme patterns. But there is no easy substitute for this work, and there is often a major payoff in seeing the subtleties of a poet's craft as well as in hearing the poetry itself more fully and resonantly. If, for example, you chart "To the Memory of Mr. Oldham," you will notice some extraordinary variations in the basic iambic pattern, variations that signal special emphasis on certain key terms and that indicate structural changes and directions. Even the first line is highly irregular—even though no pattern has yet been established in our ears. (Often, in fact, you will need to scan several lines before you can be sure of the "controlling" metrical pattern of a poem.) Possibly as many as seven syllables in this first line are stressed, rather than the expected five in a regular iambic pentameter line, and the effect is both to strongly emphasize Oldham's relatively unknown status (*too lit*-tle *and too late*-ly *known*) and to draw out, lengthily, in conjunction with the use of a series of long vowels, the reading of the line. (For an exemplary analysis of metrical variations in this poem, see the sample essay at the end of this chapter.)

Hearing a poem properly involves practice. Practice, practice, practice. And do it aloud, so that you get used to hearing your voice, so that you become self-conscious about where the stresses fall, and so that the rhythms begin to play themselves out "naturally." Your dictionary will show you the stresses for every word of more than one syllable, and the governing stress of individual words will largely control the patterns in a line: if you read a line for its basic sense (almost, for a moment, as if it were prose), you will usually see the line's basic pattern. But single-syllable words can be a challenge because they may or may not get a stress depending on their syntactic function and the full meaning of the sentence. Normally, important functional words, such as nouns and verbs of one syllable, get stressed (as in normal conversation or in prose); but conjunctions (such as *and* or *but*), prepositions (such as *on* or *with*), and articles (such as *an* or *the*) do not. But you often need to make decisions as you say words aloud, decisions based on what the words actually say and what the sentence means. Listen to yourself as you read aloud and be prepared for uncertainties. Sometimes you will even find your "normal" pronunciation being influenced or modified by the pattern your voice develops as you hear basic rhythms. The way you actually read a line, once you have "heard" the basic rhythm, is influenced by two factors: normal pronunciations and prose sense (on the one hand) and the dominating pattern of the poem (on the other). Since these two forces are constantly in tension and are sometimes contradictory, you can almost never fully predict the actual reading of a line, and good reading aloud (like every other art) depends less on formula than on subtlety and flexibility.

Because scanning lines is an imprecise craft, sometimes very good readers plausibly

7. Nephew of the Roman emperor Augustus who died at twenty, celebrated by Virgil in the *Aeneid*, Book 6.

disagree about whether or not to stress certain syllables. Then, too, some stresses are stronger than others: the convention of calling syllables "stressed" or "unstressed" fails to measure degrees of stress—and meaning often dictates that some syllables be stressed *much* more heavily than others.

In addition, not every poem relies on a formal pattern of stresses. As we saw in "Sound and Sense" and "To the Memory of Mr. Oldham," a poem dominated by iambic meter might incorporate trochaic, anapestic, spondaic, or dactylic feet in one place or another to create a stylistic effect. Beyond that, a poet tired of or resistant to traditional vocal patterns might follow or create other patterns—or employ patternlessness—to form the sound of a poem. Counting only the number of syllables (and *not* stresses) in a line is one common variation, which early-twentieth-century poets such as Marianne Moore were especially fond of. Even more widespread is **free verse,** which does without any governing pattern of stresses or line lengths.

EDGAR ALLAN POE

The Raven

Once upon a midnight dreary, while I pondered, weak and weary,
Over many a quaint and curious volume of forgotten lore,
While I nodded, nearly napping, suddenly there came a tapping,
As of some one gently rapping, rapping at my chamber door.
5   " 'Tis some visitor," I muttered, "tapping at my chamber door—
            Only this, and nothing more."

Ah, distinctly I remember it was in the bleak December,
And each separate dying ember wrought its ghost upon the floor.
Eagerly I wished the morrow;—vainly I had sought to borrow
10   From my books surcease of sorrow—sorrow for the lost Lenore—
For the rare and radiant maiden whom the angels name Lenore—
            Nameless here for evermore.

And the silken sad uncertain rustling of each purple curtain
Thrilled me—filled me with fantastic terrors never felt before;
15   So that now, to still the beating of my heart, I stood repeating
" 'Tis some visitor entreating entrance at my chamber door;—
Some late visitor entreating entrance at my chamber door;—
            This it is, and nothing more."

Presently my soul grew stronger; hesitating then no longer,
20   "Sir," said I, "or Madam, truly your forgiveness I implore;
But the fact is I was napping, and so gently you came rapping,
And so faintly you came tapping, tapping at my chamber door,
That I scarce was sure I heard you"—here I opened wide the door;—
            Darkness there, and nothing more.

25   Deep into that darkness peering, long I stood there wondering, fearing,
Doubting, dreaming dreams no mortal ever dared to dream before;
But the silence was unbroken, and the darkness gave no token,

And the only word there spoken was the whispered word, "Lenore!"
This I whispered, and an echo murmured back the word, "Lenore!"—
                Merely this, and nothing more.   30

Back into the chamber turning, all my soul within me burning,
Soon I heard again a tapping somewhat louder than before.
"Surely," said I, "surely that is something at my window lattice;
Let me see, then, what thereat is, and this mystery explore—
Let my heart be still a moment and this mystery explore;—   35
             'Tis the wind and nothing more!"

Open here I flung the shutter, when, with many a flirt and flutter,
In there stepped a stately raven of the saintly days of yore;
Not the least obeisance made he; not an instant stopped or stayed he;
But, with mien of lord or lady, perched above my chamber door—   40
Perched upon a bust of Pallas[8] just above my chamber door—
          Perched, and sat, and nothing more.

Then this ebony bird beguiling my sad fancy into smiling,
By the grave and stern decorum of the countenance it wore,
"Though thy crest be shorn and shaven, thou," I said, "art sure no
    craven,   45
Ghastly grim and ancient raven wandering from the Nightly shore—
Tell me what thy lordly name is on the Night's Plutonian[9] shore!"
          Quoth the raven, "Nevermore."

Much I marvelled this ungainly fowl to hear discourse so plainly,
Though its answer little meaning—little relevancy bore,   50
For we cannot help agreeing that no living human being
Ever yet was blessed with seeing bird above his chamber door—
Bird or beast upon the sculptured bust above his chamber door,
         With such name as "Nevermore."

But the raven, sitting lonely on the placid bust, spoke only   55
That one word, as if his soul in that one word he did outpour.
Nothing farther then he uttered—not a feather then he fluttered—
Till I scarcely more than muttered "Other friends have flown before—
On the morrow *he* will leave me, as my hopes have flown before."
         Then the bird said "Nevermore."   60

Startled at the stillness broken by reply so aptly spoken,
"Doubtless," said I, "what it utters is its only stock and store
Caught from some unhappy master whom unmerciful Disaster
Followed fast and followed faster till his songs one burden bore—
Till the dirges of his Hope that melancholy burden bore   65
         Of 'Never—nevermore.' "

But the raven still beguiling all my sad soul into smiling,
Straight I wheeled a cushioned seat in front of bird and bust and door;
Then, upon the velvet sinking, I betook myself to linking
Fancy unto fancy, thinking what this ominous bird of yore—   70

---

8. Athena, the Greek goddess of wisdom.   9. Dark; Pluto was god of the underworld.

What this grim, ungainly, ghastly, gaunt, and ominous bird of yore
     Meant in croaking "Nevermore."

This I sat engaged in guessing, but no syllable expressing
To the fowl whose fiery eyes now burned into my bosom's core;
This and more I sat divining, with my head at ease reclining
On the cushion's velvet lining that the lamplight gloated o'er,
But whose velvet violet lining with the lamplight gloating o'er,
     She shall press, ah, nevermore!

Then, methought, the air grew denser, perfumed from an unseen censer
Swung by angels whose faint foot-falls tinkled on the tufted floor.
"Wretch," I cried, "thy God hath lent thee—by these angels he hath sent thee
Respite—respite and nepenthe[1] from thy memories of Lenore!
Quaff, oh quaff this kind nepenthe and forget this lost Lenore!"
     Quoth the raven, "Nevermore."

"Prophet!" said I, "thing of evil!—prophet still, if bird or devil!—
Whether Tempter sent, or whether tempest tossed thee here ashore,
Desolate, yet all undaunted, on this desert land enchanted—
On this home by Horror haunted—tell me truly, I implore—
Is there—*is* there balm in Gilead?[2]—tell me—tell me, I implore!"
     Quoth the raven, "Nevermore."

"Prophet!" said I, "thing of evil—prophet still, if bird or devil!
By that Heaven that bends above us—by that God we both adore—
Tell this soul with sorrow laden if, within the distant Aidenn,
It shall clasp a sainted maiden whom the angels name Lenore—
Clasp a rare and radiant maiden whom the angels name Lenore."
     Quoth the raven, "Nevermore."

"Be that word our sign of parting, bird or fiend!" I shrieked upstarting—
"Get thee back into the tempest and the Night's Plutonian shore!
Leave no black plume as a token of that lie thy soul hath spoken!
Leave my loneliness unbroken!—quit the bust above my door!
Take thy beak from out my heart, and take thy form from off my door!"
     Quoth the raven, "Nevermore."

And the raven, never flitting, still is sitting, still is sitting
On the pallid bust of Pallas just above my chamber door;
And his eyes have all the seeming of a demon's that is dreaming,
And the lamp-light o'er him streaming throws his shadow on the floor;
And my soul from out that shadow that lies floating on the floor
     Shall be lifted—nevermore!   1844

---

1. A drug reputed by the Greeks to cause forgetfulness or sorrow. 2. Cf. Jeremiah 8.22.

WILLIAM SHAKESPEARE

[*Like as the waves make towards the pebbled shore*]

Like as the waves make towards the pebbled shore,
So do our minutes hasten to their end,
Each changing place with that which goes before,
In sequent toil all forwards do contend.[3]
Nativity, once in the main[4] of light,   5
Crawls to maturity, wherewith being crowned,
Crooked[5] eclipses 'gainst his glory fight,
And Time that gave doth now his gift confound.[6]
Time doth transfix[7] the flourish set on youth
And delves the parallels[8] in beauty's brow,   10
Feeds on the rarities of nature's truth,
And nothing stands but for his scythe to mow.
And yet to times in hope[9] my verse shall stand,
Praising thy worth, despite his cruel hand.   1609

JAMES MERRILL

Watching the Dance

1. BALANCHINE'S[1]

Poor savage, doubting that a river flows
But for the myriad eddies made
By unseen powers twirling on their toes,

Here in this darkness it would seem
You had already died, and were afraid.   5
Be still. Observe the powers. Infer the stream.

2. DISCOTHÈQUE

Having survived entirely your own youth,
Last of your generation, purple gloom
Investing you, sit, Jonah,[2] beyond speech,

And let towards the brute volume VOOM whale mouth   10
VAM pounding viscera VAM VOOM
A teenage plankton luminously twitch.   1967

3. Struggle. *Sequent:* successive.   4. High seas. *Nativity:* newborn life.   5. Perverse.   6. Bring to nothing.   7. Pierce.   8. Lines, wrinkles.   9. In the future.   1. George Balanchine (1904–1983), Russian-
born ballet choreographer and teacher.   2. According to Jonah 4, Jonah sat in gloom near Nineveh after
its residents repented and God decided to spare the city from destruction.

GERARD MANLEY HOPKINS

Spring and Fall:

to a young child

Márgarét áre you gríeving
Over Goldengrove unleaving?
Leáves, like the things of man, you
With your fresh thoughts care for, can you?
5 Áh! ás the heart grows older
It will come to such sights colder
By and by, nor spare a sigh
Though worlds of wanwood leafmeal[3] lie;
And yet you wíll weep and know why.
10 Now no matter, child, the name:
Sórrow's spríngs áre the same.
Nor mouth had, no nor mind, expressed
What heart heard of, ghost[4] guessed:
It ís the blight man was born for,
15 It is Margaret you mourn for.

1880

LEE ANN BROWN

Foolproof Loofah

Lo! I fill prol pills
Poof! I rail pro lolls
Fool! I ill for lips
O Pale! I foil frail profs
5 Fop! I frill pale roils—
So! I proof oil spills

April Fool's!   1999

EMILY DICKINSON

[A narrow Fellow in the Grass]

A narrow Fellow in the Grass
Occasionally rides—

---

3. Broken up, leaf by leaf (analogous to "piecemeal"). *Wanwood:* pale, gloomy woods.   4. Soul.

You may have met Him—did you not
His notice sudden is—

The Grass divides as with a Comb—   5
A spotted shaft is seen—
And then it closes at your feet
And opens further on—

He likes a Boggy Acre
A Floor too cool for Corn—   10
Yet when a Boy, and Barefoot—
I more than once at Noon

Have passed, I thought, a Whip lash
Unbraiding in the Sun
When stooping to secure it   15
It wrinkled, and was gone—

Several of Nature's People
I know, and they know me—
I feel for them a transport
Of cordiality—   20

But never met this Fellow
Attended, or alone
Without a tighter breathing
And Zero at the Bone—   1866

WORDS AND MUSIC

People often associate poetry with music, and there are good reasons—both historical and theoretical—for doing so. The word **lyric,** for example—the standard term for a short, harmonious, pleasant, and often romantic poem—derives from the ancient Greeks' practice of reciting or singing (and perhaps composing) certain poems to the accompaniment of a stringed, harplike musical instrument, the lyre. Throughout history, poems have been set to music for voices or instruments, and many "lyrics" have been created specifically to fit musical compositions. Many poems, especially during the Renaissance, were simply called "Song" (or "Chanson" or "Lied" or similar terms in other languages), and some were constructed in hybrid musical-poetic forms such as the madrigal, the dirge, the hymn, and so on.

The most fundamental link between poetry and music involves their almost equal dependence on the principles of rhythm. Both genres have a basis in mathematics—a regular beat or syncopated sound pattern predicts (and to some extent determines) their phrasing and formal movement. Not all composers of either poetry or music have mathematical knowledge, but their crafts depend on an ability to hear (almost instinctively and certainly habitually) pacings, pauses, alternations, and relationships. Just as good musicians learn to listen and count so easily that it seems "natural," poets often develop an ear for rhythm that makes their sound choices effortless and, seemingly, automatic. Readers, too, can develop such an ear, and hearing the rhythms of poems can be crucial to the total effects they create.

There are movements, of course, in both poetry and music to suppress or ignore regular patterns in favor of "freer" sounds and repetitions, but the tendency of both arts to use rhythm predictably makes some comparisons (and some common terminology) desirable and useful for describing strategies and effects. But the parallels are often *not* precise, the relationships metaphoric rather than actual. Both poetry and music use representational or imitative strategies to create the illusion of sounds—bells, waves, locomotives, for example—but words operate referentially in a way that sounds normally do not, and their syntax is of a different kind from that in musical composition. Readers can better appreciate sound effects in poetry by hearing musical relationships, but the referential fact of language almost always alters the "pure" effects of sound (except in nonsense lyrics or in poems like "Joy Sonnet in a Random Universe" or "What the Motorcycle Said," where simple sounds or tonal expressions are simply recorded and transliterated).

Poems composed to or for music tend to differ from poems that produce or rely on rhythmic, harmonic, or musical effects created solely by words themselves. Reading the lyrics of a song you know well (so that you, in effect, "hear" the music as you read the words) is quite different from reading words that have for you no musical association or history. You probably cannot stop yourself from hearing the music that accompanies lyrics by, say, the Beatles, and the music thus becomes for you, even when you just *read* the words, part of the total effect. But the "music" (or more exactly the percussive rhythms) created by a poem itself can work in a similar way when there is no musical "source" or co-creation. To say that a poem makes or uses "music" can mean many different things.

The poems that follow were all written for, in conjunction with, or to imitate music. If you "update" this collection with lyrics from your favorite contemporary singers and groups, you may find that some lyrics that are very good when sung do not work well as "separate" poetic texts, whereas some make very good poems indeed. Can you, in the lyrics you know well, separate the actual musical implications from those of the words alone?

THOMAS RANDOLPH

A Song

Music, thou queen of souls, get up and string
Thy powerful lute, and some sad requiem sing,
Till rocks requite thy echo with a groan,
And the dull cliffs repeat the duller tone.
5 Then on a sudden with a nimble hand
Run gently o'er the chords, and so command
The pine to dance, the oak his roots forgo,
The holm and aged elm to foot it too;
Myrtles shall caper, lofty cedars run,
10 And call the courtly palm to make up one.
Then, in the midst of all their jolly train,
Strike a sad note, and fix 'em trees again.

1638

THOMAS CAMPION

When to Her Lute Corinna Sings

When to her lute Corinna sings,
Her voice revives the leaden[5] strings,
And doth in highest notes appear
As any challenged[6] echo clear;
But when she doth of mourning speak,   5
Ev'n with her sighs the strings do break.

And as her lute doth live or die,
Led by her passion, so must I:
For when of pleasure she doth sing,
My thoughts enjoy a sudden spring;   10
But if she doth of sorrow speak,
Ev'n from my heart the strings do break.   1601

ROBERT HAYDEN

Homage to the Empress of the Blues[7]

Because there was a man somewhere in a candystripe silk shirt,
gracile and dangerous as a jaguar and because a woman moaned
for him in sixty-watt gloom and mourned him Faithless Love
Twotiming Love Oh Love Oh Careless Aggravating Love,

    She came out on the stage in yards of pearls, emerging like   5
    a favorite scenic view, flashed her golden smile and sang.

Because grey laths began somewhere to show from underneath
torn hurdygurdy[8] lithographs of dollfaced heaven;
and because there were those who feared alarming fists of snow
on the door and those who feared the riot-squad of statistics,   10

    She came out on the stage in ostrich feathers, beaded satin,
    and shone that smile on us and sang.   1962

---

5. That is, heavy.   6. Aroused.   7. Bessie Smith (1894 [or 1898?]–1937); legendary blues singer whose theatrical style grew out of the black American vaudeville tradition.   8. A disreputable kind of dance hall.

MICHAEL HARPER

Dear John, Dear Coltrane

a love supreme, a love supreme
a love supreme, a love supreme[9]

Sex fingers toes
in the marketplace
near your father's church
in Hamlet, North Carolina—[1]
witness to this love
in this calm fallow
of these minds,
there is no substitute for pain:
genitals gone or going,
seed burned out,
you tuck the roots in the earth,
turn back, and move
by river through the swamps,
singing: *a love supreme, a love supreme;*
what does it all mean?
Loss, so great each black
woman expects your failure
in mute change, the seed gone.
You plod up into the electric city—
your song now crystal and
the blues. You pick up the horn
with some will and blow
into the freezing night:
a love supreme, a love supreme—

Dawn comes and you cook
up the thick sin 'tween
impotence and death, fuel
the tenor sax cannibal
heart, genitals and sweat
that makes you clean—
a love supreme, a love supreme—

Why you so black?
cause I am
why you so funky?
cause I am
why you so black

9. Coltrane wrote "A Love Supreme" in response to a spiritual experience in 1957 that also led to his quitting heroin and alcohol. The record was released in 1965.   1. Coltrane's birthplace. His family shared a house with Coltrane's grandfather, who was the minister of St. Stephen's AME Zion Church there.

cause I am
why you so sweet?
cause I am
why you so black?   40
cause I am
a love supreme, a love supreme:

So sick
you couldn't play *Naima*,[2]
so flat we ached   45
for song you'd concealed
with your own blood,
your diseased liver gave
out its purity,
the inflated heart   50
pumps out, the tenor kiss,
tenor love:
a love supreme, a love supreme—
a love supreme, a love supreme—   1970

BOB DYLAN

Mr. Tambourine Man

Hey! Mr. Tambourine Man, play a song for me,
I'm not sleepy and there is no place I'm going to.
Hey! Mr. Tambourine Man, play a song for me,
In the jingle jangle morning I'll come followin' you.

Though I know that evenin's empire has returned into sand,   5
Vanished from my hand,
Left me blindly here to stand but still not sleeping.
My weariness amazes me, I'm branded on my feet,
I have no one to meet
And the ancient empty street's too dead for dreaming.   10

Hey! Mr. Tambourine Man, play a song for me,
I'm not sleepy and there is no place I'm going to.
Hey! Mr. Tambourine Man, play a song for me,
In the jingle jangle morning I'll come followin' you.

Take me on a trip upon your magic swirlin' ship,   15
My senses have been stripped, my hands can't feel to grip,
My toes too numb to step, wait only for my boot heels

---

2. A song Coltrane wrote for and named after his wife, recorded in 1959.

To be wanderin'.
I'm ready to go anywhere, I'm ready for to fade
20   Into my own parade, cast your dancing spell my way,
I promise to go under it.

Hey! Mr. Tambourine Man, play a song for me,
I'm not sleepy and there is no place I'm going to.
Hey! Mr. Tambourine Man, play a song for me,
25   In the jingle jangle morning I'll come followin' you.

Though you might hear laughin', spinnin', swingin' madly across the
        sun,
It's not aimed at anyone, it's just escapin' on the run
And but for the sky there are no fences facin'.
And if you hear vague traces of skippin' reels of rhyme
30   To your tambourine in time, it's just a ragged clown behind,
I wouldn't pay it any mind, it's just a shadow you're
Seein' that he's chasing.

Hey! Mr. Tambourine Man, play a song for me,
I'm not sleepy and there is no place I'm going to.
35   Hey! Mr. Tambourine Man, play a song for me,
In the jingle jangle morning I'll come followin' you.

Then take me disappearin' through the smoke rings of my mind,
Down the foggy ruins of time, far past the frozen leaves,
The haunted, frightened trees, out to the windy beach,
40   Far from the twisted reach of crazy sorrow.
Yes, to dance beneath the diamond sky with one hand waving free,
Silhouetted by the sea, circled by the circus sands,
With all memory and fate driven deep beneath the waves,
Let me forget about today until tomorrow.

45   Hey! Mr. Tambourine Man, play a song for me,
I'm not sleepy and there is no place I'm going to.
Hey! Mr. Tambourine Man, play a song for me,
In the jingle jangle morning I'll come followin' you.   1964

WILLIE PERDOMO

123rd Street Rap

A day on
123rd Street

goes a little
something like
5   this:

Automatic bullets bounce
off stoop steps

It's about time to pay
all my debts

Church bells bong for   10
for drunken mourners

Baby men growing on
all the corners

Money that
ain't mine   15

Sun that
don't shine

Trees that
don't grow

Wind that   20
won't blow

Drug posses
ready to rumble

Ceilings starting
to crumble   25

Abuelas[3] close
eyes and pray

While they watch
the children play

Not much I   30
can say

Except day turns
to night

And I can't tell what's
wrong from what's right   35

on 123rd Street   1996

3. Grandmothers.

QUESTIONS

1. Read Lee's "Persimmons" (chapter 12) and compare its sound effects with those in Chasin's "The Word *Plum*." How visual an image does each poem create? To what purposes does Lee put the visual qualities of the persimmon? Which other of the five senses are evoked in each poem? to what specific purpose?
2. Read "Watching the Dance" and "The Raven" aloud. As you read each, be especially conscious of the way punctuation and spacing guide your pauses and of the pace you develop as you become accustomed to the prevailing rhythms of the poem. What function does repetition have in the reading aloud of each poem?
3. Scan—that is, mark all of the stressed syllables and chart their pattern in—Shakespeare's "Like as the waves make towards the pebbled shore." What variations do you find on the basic iambic pentameter pattern? What functions do the variations perform in each case?

WRITING SUGGESTIONS

1. Read Pope's "Sound and Sense" over carefully twice—once silently and once aloud—and then mark the stressed and unstressed syllables. Draw up a chart indicating, line by line, exactly what the patterns of stress are, and then single out all the lines that have major variations from the basic iambic pentameter pattern. Pick out six lines with variations that seem to you worthy of comment, and write a paragraph on each in which you show how the varied metrical pattern contributes to the specific effects achieved in that line. (You will probably notice that in most of the lines other strategies also contribute to the sound effects, but confine your discussion to the achievement through metrical pattern.)
2. Try your hand at writing limericks in imitation of "There was a young lady of Riga"; study the rhythmic patterns and line lengths carefully, and imitate them exactly in your poem. Begin your limerick with "There once was a —— from ——" (using a place for which you think you can find a comic rhyme).
3. Scan line by line Suckling's "Song." In an essay of no more than five hundred words, show in detail how the varied metrical pattern in the final stanza abruptly changes the tone of the poem and reverses the poem's direction.
4. Read Birney's "Anglosaxon Street" (chapter 18) aloud. Then go through the poem line by line and pick out half a dozen words and patterns of sound that seem to you especially effective in creating vocal effects. Analyze carefully the effects created by each of these words or word groups and try to account for exactly how the passage works. Then, using these examples as the primary (though not necessarily the exclusive) basis, write a three-page paper on the uses of sound in the poem.

STUDENT WRITING

This essay not only scans the Dryden poem but also uses metrical analysis to inform structural and tonal analyses.

Metrical Variation and Meaning
in "To the Memory of Mr. Oldham"

Christine Woodside

In his poem "To the Memory of Mr. Oldham," John Dryden rationalizes the death of a fellow satirist by comparing himself to the dead men. He begins by saying they were "cast in the same poetic mold," then considers the fact that Oldham's youth did not prevent him from reaching the "same goal" before the older speaker. Dryden also notes that while age--and thus experience--would have given Oldham a smoother command of the English language, satire and wit do not need such polishing and will "shine" through a less-experienced poet's "rugged line." He points out the possible stagnant quality that experience can nurture and seems to imply both that experience is unnecessary to produce good satire and that Oldham's death was timely, since he had already succeeded. Still, the poem ends in a tired, labored farewell, suggesting that Oldham's death was not timely, and that "fate and gloomy night" surround him. Since this poem is a single stanza, the shifts in thought and tone are subtle. The occasional exceptions to the iambic pentameter emphasize the different themes Dryden addresses. Although the variations in meter do not drastically alter the poem's significance, they do clarify some of the main ideas in the poem.

The first notable idea is the alliance Dryden feels with Oldham, which is emphasized by four separate metrical variations. The word "allied" in the third line is accented on the first syllable, which disturbs the metrical flow that requires a stress on the second. In the next line, "cast in the same" throws off the iambic rhythm with an unexpected stress on the word "cast." (This also highlights the word "same," since two small words are unaccented between the two.) A third metrical surprise is in the fifth line, where the first three words, "One common note," receive accents. These accents not only emphasize the words, but actually slow down the reader. Another emphasis on unity is in the seventh line, where the first two words yield to stresses on the third and fourth in "[t]o the same goal." All of these unsettling accent changes illustrate Dryden's conviction that both he and Oldham had the same goals in their poetry.

There are two variances in meter that emphasize youth. The first of these occurs when Dryden mentions that Oldham has surpassed his older and more experienced ally in a short amount of time: "While his young friend performed and won the race." Here the word "young" receives the unexpected accent. Not surprisingly, Dryden goes on to discuss Oldham's youth and youth's lack of control over the language. The second metrical variation deals with this inexperience with language, saying that a young poet's work must show "[t]hrough the harsh cadence of a rugged line." By position, neither "harsh" nor "cadence" would normally receive the accent, but both stand out noticeably. Interestingly, Dryden chooses to emphasize, metrically, youthful inexperience while at the same time saying that satire does not need an experienced control of the language. By doing this, he is contending that youth is not a handicap, at least not in satire. Still, he does choose to emphasize the "harsh cadence" (the consonants are hard to pronounce) of inexperienced work.

The next three metrical variations shift the attention to experience, which, he says, only "mellows what we write to the dull sweets of rhyme." The word "dull" receives an unexpected accent and, together with "sweets," gives the line a tired, heavy quality. This mirrors Dryden's thought that "maturing time" will only make his work "dull." (Also, as he mentions that rhyme can become stagnant, he has just completed three consecutive rhyming lines; the pattern calls for two.) The second "dull" metrical difference appears in line 22. "Once more, hail" is also slow and heavy because all three words need an accent. Finally, the last line contains six iambic feet instead of five, and the last word is redundant: "But fate and gloomy night encompass thee around." To say "encompass thee" would imply the word "around"; the last word does not change or clarify anything. It merely shows that Dryden allows the "dull sweets of rhyme" to control his choice of words! In the three metrical variations above, Dryden generates the very dullness he criticizes as characteristic of an older, experienced poet such as himself.

This poem discusses the "one common note" Dryden shares with Oldham; it then considers Oldham's youth; then deals with Dryden's age and experience in relation to the dead man's youth. All three of these ideas are reflected in the variations of the iambic pentameter, and the variations strengthen their impact.

17

INTERNAL STRUCTURE

"Proper words in proper places": that is how one great writer of English prose, Jonathan Swift, described good writing. A good poet finds appropriate words, and already we have looked at some implications for readers of the verbal choices a poet makes. But the poet must also decide where to put those words—how to arrange them for maximum effect—because individual words, metaphors, and symbols exist not only within phrases and sentences and rhythmic patterns but also within the larger whole of the poem. How should the words be arranged and the poem organized? What comes first and what last? Will the poem have a "plot"? What principle or idea of organization will inform it? How can words, sentences, images, ideas, and feelings be combined into a structure that holds together, seems complete, and affects readers?

Considering these questions from the poet's point of view (What shall I plan? Where shall I begin?) can help us notice the effects of structural choices. Every poem works differently from every other one, and therefore every poet must make independent decisions about how to organize an individual poem. But poems do fall into patterns of organization, sometimes because of subject matter, sometimes because of effects intended, sometimes for other reasons. A poet may consciously decide on a particular strategy, may reach instinctively for one, or may happen into one that suits the needs of the moment—a framework onto which words and sentences will hang, one by one and group by group.

When a poem tells a story, the organization may be fairly straightforward. The following poem, for example, tells a simple story largely in chronological order (first . . . and then . . .):

EDWIN ARLINGTON ROBINSON

Mr. Flood's Party

Old Eben Flood, climbing alone one night
Over the hill between the town below
And the forsaken upland hermitage

That held as much as he should ever know
On earth again of home, paused warily. 5
The road was his and not a native near;
And Eben, having leisure, said aloud,
For no man else in Tilbury Town to hear:

"Well, Mr. Flood, we have the harvest moon
Again, and we may not have many more; 10
The bird is on the wing, the poet says,[1]
And you and I have said it here before.
Drink to the bird." He raised up to the light
The jug that he had gone so far to fill,
And answered huskily: "Well, Mr. Flood, 15
Since you propose it, I believe I will."

Alone, as if enduring to the end
A valiant armor of scarred hopes outworn
He stood there in the middle of the road
Like Roland's ghost winding a silent horn.[2] 20
Below him, in the town among the trees,
Where friends of other days had honored him,
A phantom salutation of the dead
Rang thinly till old Eben's eyes were dim.

Then, as a mother lays her sleeping child 25
Down tenderly, fearing it may awake
He set the jug down slowly at his feet
With trembling care, knowing that most things break;
And only when assured that on firm earth
It stood, as the uncertain lives of men 30
Assuredly did not, he paced away,
And with his hand extended paused again:

"Well, Mr. Flood, we have not met like this
In a long time; and many a change has come
To both of us, I fear, since last it was 35
We had a drop together. Welcome home!"
Convivially returning with himself,
Again he raised the jug up to the light;
And with an acquiescent quaver said:
"Well, Mr. Flood, if you insist, I might. 40

"Only a very little, Mr. Flood—
For auld lang syne. No more, sir; that will do."
So, for the time, apparently it did,
And Eben evidently thought so too;
For soon amid the silver loneliness 45

1. Edward FitzGerald, in "The Rubáiyát of Omar Khayyám" (more or less a translation of an Arab original), so describes the "Bird of Time." 2. According to French legend, Roland used his powerful ivory horn to warn his allies of impending attack.

Of night he lifted up his voice and sang,
Secure, with only two moons listening,
Until the whole harmonious landscape rang—

"For auld lang syne." The weary throat gave out,
50   The last word wavered, and the song was done.
He raised again the jug regretfully
And shook his head, and was again alone.
There was not much that was ahead of him,
And there was nothing in the town below—
55   Where strangers would have shut the many doors
That many friends had opened long ago.   1921

    The fairly simple **narrative structure** here is based on the gradual unfolding of the story. After old Eben is introduced and "placed" in relation to the town and his home, the "plot" unfolds: he sits down in the road, reviews his life, reflects on the present, and has a drink—several drinks, in fact, as he thinks about passing time and growing old; then he sings and considers going "home." Not much happens, really; we get a vignette of Mr. Flood between two places and two times. But there *is* action, and the poem's movement—its organization and structure—depends on it: Mr. Flood in motion, in stasis, and then, again, contemplating motion. This counts as event, and a certain, limited chronological movement. We could say that a spare sort of story takes place, like that in Dickey's "Cherrylog Road" (chapter 14). The poem's organization—its structural principle—involves the passing of time, action moving forward, a larger story being revealed by the few moments depicted here.

    "Mr. Flood's Party" presents about as much story as a short poem ever does, but like most poems it doesn't really emphasize the developing action—which all seems fairly predictable once we "get" who Eben is, how old he is, and what "position" he occupies in the communal memory of Tilbury Town and vice versa. Rather, the movement forward in time dictates the shape of the poem, determines the way it presents its images, ideas, themes. Nearly everything takes place within an easy-to-follow chronology.

    But even here, in this most simple narrative structure, we note complications. One complication is in the use of time itself, for "old" time and "present" time seem posed against each other as a structural principle, too, one in tension with the chronological movement: Eben's past, as contrasted with his present and limited future, focuses the poem's attention, and in some ways the contrast between what was and what is seems even more important than the brief movement through present time that gets the most obvious attention in the poem. Then, too, "character"—Eben's character and that of the townspeople of later generations—gets a lot of attention, even as the chronology moves forward. More than one structural principle is at work here. We may identify the main movement of the poem as chronological and its principal structure as narrative, but to be fair and full in our discussion we have to note several other competing organizational forces at work—principles of comparison and contrast, for example, and of descriptive elaboration.

    Most poems work with this kind of complexity, and identifying a single structure behind any poem involves a sense of what kind of organizational principle makes it work, while at the same time recognizing that other principles repeatedly, perhaps continually, compete for our attention. A poem's structure involves its conceptual framework—what principle best explains its organization and movement—and it is often useful to identify one dominating kind of structure, such as narrative structure, that gives the poem its shape. But we need to recognize from the start that most poems follow paradigmatic models loosely. Finding an appropriate label to describe the structure of a particular poem can help in analyzing the poem's other aspects, but the label itself has no magic.

> *Back of the idea of organic*
> *form is the concept that there*
> *is a form in all things (and in*
> *our experience) which the poet*
> *can discover and reveal.*
>
> —DENISE LEVERTOV

Purely narrative poems are often very long, much longer than can be included in a book like this, and often include many features that are not, strictly speaking, closely connected to the narrative or linked to a strict chronology. Very often a poem moves from a narrative of an event to some sort of commentary or reflection on it, as in Larkin's "Church Going". Reflection can be included along the way or may be implicit in the way the story is narrated, as in Kumin's "Woodchucks" (chapter 12), where we focus more on the narrator and her responses than on the events in the story as such.

Just as poems sometimes take on a structure like that of a story, they sometimes borrow the structures of plays. The following poem has a **dramatic structure;** it consists of a series of scenes, each of which is presented vividly and in detail, as if on a kind of stage or place of public display.

HOWARD NEMEROV

The Goose Fish

On the long shore, lit by the moon
To show them properly alone,
Two lovers suddenly embraced
So that their shadows were as one.
The ordinary night was graced   5
For them by the swift tide of blood
That silently they took at flood.
And for a little time they prized
    Themselves emparadised.

Then, as if shaken by stage-fright   10
Beneath the hard moon's bony light,
They stood together on the sand
Embarrassed in each other's sight
But still conspiring hand in hand,
Until they saw, there underfoot,   15
As though the world had found them out,
The goose fish turning up, though dead,
    His hugely grinning head.

There in the china light he lay,
Most ancient and corrupt and gray.   20
They hesitated at his smile,

Wondering what it seemed to say
To lovers who a little while
Before had thought to understand,
25   By violence upon the sand,
The only way that could be known
        To make a world their own.

It was a wide and moony grin
Together peaceful and obscene;
30   They knew not what he would express,
So finished a comedian
He might mean failure or success,
But took it for an emblem of
Their sudden, new and guilty love
35   To be observed by, when they kissed,
        That rigid optimist.

So he became their patriarch,
Dreadfully mild in the half-dark.
His throat that the sand seemed to choke,
40   His picket teeth, these left their mark
But never did explain the joke
That so amused him, lying there
While the moon went down to disappear
Along the still and tilted track
45   That bears the zodiac.   1955

The first stanza sets the scene—a sandy shore in moonlight—and presents, in fact, the major action of the poem. The rest of the poem dramatizes the lovers' reactions: their initial embarrassment and feelings of guilt (stanza 2), their attempt to interpret the goose fish's smile (stanza 3), their decision to make him, whatever his meaning, the "emblem" of their love (stanza 4), and their acceptance of the fish's ambiguity and of their own relationship (stanza 5). The five stanzas do not exactly present five different scenes or angles on the action, but they do present separate dramatic moments, even if only a few minutes apart. Almost like a play of five very short acts, the poem traces the drama of the lovers' discovery of themselves, of their coming to terms with the meaning of their action. As in many plays, the central event (their lovemaking) is not the central focus of the drama, although the drama is based upon that event and could not take place without it. The poem depicts that event swiftly but very vividly through figurative language: "they took at flood" the "swift tide of blood." The lovers then briefly feel "emparadised," but the poem concentrates on their later reactions.

Their sudden discovery of the fish, a rude shock, injects a grotesque, almost macabre, note into the poem. From a vision of paradise, the poem seems for a moment to turn toward gothic horror when the lovers discover that they have, after all, been seen—and by such a ghoulish spectator. The last three stanzas gradually re-create the intruder in their minds, as they admit that their act of love exists not in isolation, but rather as part of a continuum, as part of their relationship to the larger world, even (at the end) within the context of the rotating world, its seasons, and the zodiac. In retrospect, we can see that even at the moment of passion the lovers were in touch with larger processes controlled by the presiding mood ("the swift *tide* of blood"), but neither they nor we had understood their act as such then, and the poem is about this gradual recognition of their "place" in time and space.

Stages of feeling and knowing rather than specific visual scenes determine the poem's progress, and its dramatic structure depends upon internal perceptions and internal states of mind rather than dialogue and events. Visualization and images help to organize the poem, too. Notice in particular how the two most striking visual features—the fish and the moon—are presented stanza by stanza. In stanza 1, the fish does not appear, and the moon exists plain; it is only mentioned, not described, and its light provides a stage spotlight to assure not center-stage attention, but rather total privacy: the moon serves as a lookout for the lovers. The stage imagery, barely suggested by the light in stanza 1, is articulated in stanza 2, and there the moon is "hard" and its light "bony"; its characteristics seem more appropriate to the fish, which has now become visible. In stanza 3, the moon's light comes to seem fragile ("china") as it exposes the fish directly; the moon's role as lookout and protector seems abandoned, or at least endangered. No moon appears in stanza 4, but the fish's grin is "wide and moony," almost as if the two onlookers, one earthly and dead, the other heavenly and eternal, have merged, as they nearly were by the imagery in stanza 2. And in stanza 5, the fish becomes a friend, a comedian, an optimist, an emblem, and a patriarch of their love—and his new position in collaboration with the lovers is presided over by the moon going about its eternal business. The moon—providing the stage light for the poem and the means by which not only the fish but the meaning of the lovers' act is discovered—has also helped to organize the poem, partly as a dramatic accessory, partly as imagery.

The following dramatic poem represents a composite of several similar experiences (compare Blake's "London" [chapter 12] and Dickey's "Cherrylog Road" [chapter 14]) rather than a single event—a fairly common pattern in dramatic poems:

PHILIP LARKIN

Church Going

Once I am sure there's nothing going on
I step inside, letting the door thud shut.
Another church: matting, seats, and stone,
And little books; sprawlings of flowers, cut
For Sunday, brownish now; some brass and stuff   5
Up at the holy end; the small neat organ;
And a tense, musty, unignorable silence,
Brewed God knows how long. Hatless, I take off
My cycle-clips in awkward reverence,

Move forward, run my hand around the font.   10
From where I stand, the roof looks almost new—
Cleaned, or restored? Someone would know: I don't.
Mounting the lectern, I peruse a few
Hectoring large-scale verses, and pronounce

15   "Here endeth" much more loudly than I'd meant.
        The echoes snigger briefly. Back at the door
        I sign the book, donate an Irish sixpence,
        Reflect the place was not worth stopping for.

        Yet stop I did: in fact I often do,
20   And always end much at a loss like this,
        Wondering what to look for; wondering, too,
        When churches fall completely out of use
        What we shall turn them into, if we shall keep
        A few cathedrals chronically on show,
25   Their parchment, plate and pyx in locked cases,
        And let the rest rent-free to rain and sheep.
        Shall we avoid them as unlucky places?

        Or, after dark, will dubious women come
        To make their children touch a particular stone;
30   Pick simples[3] for a cancer; or on some
        Advised night see walking a dead one?
        Power of some sort or other will go on
        In games, in riddles, seemingly at random;
        But superstition, like belief, must die,
35   And what remains when disbelief has gone?
        Grass, weedy pavement, brambles, buttress, sky,

        A shape less recognizable each week,
        A purpose more obscure. I wonder who
        Will be the last, the very last, to seek
40   This place for what it was; one of the crew
        That tap and jot and know what rood-lofts[4] were?
        Some ruin-bibber,[5] randy for antique,
        Or Christmas-addict, counting on a whiff
        Of gown-and-bands and organ-pipes and myrrh?
45   Or will he be my representative,

        Bored, uninformed, knowing the ghostly silt
        Dispersed, yet tending to this cross of ground
        Through suburb scrub because it held unspilt
        So long and equably what since is found
50   Only in separation—marriage, and birth,
        And death, and thoughts of these—for whom was built
        This special shell? For, though I've no idea
        What this accoutered frowsty barn is worth,
        It pleases me to stand in silence here;

55   A serious house on serious earth it is,
        In whose blent air all our compulsions meet,
        Are recognized, and robed as destinies.
        And that much never can be obsolete,

---

3. Medicinal herbs.   4. Galleries atop the screens (on which crosses are mounted) that divide the naves or main bodies of churches from the choirs or chancels.   5. Literally, ruin-drinker: someone extremely attracted to antiquarian objects.

Since someone will forever be surprising
A hunger in himself to be more serious,   60
And gravitating with it to this ground,
Which, he once heard, was proper to grow wise in,
If only that so many dead lie round.   1955

Ultimately, the poem focuses on what it means to visit churches, what sort of phenomenon church buildings represent, and what we should make of the fact that "church going" (in the usual sense of the word) has declined so much. The poem uses a *different* sort of church going (visitation by tourists) to consider larger questions about the relationship of religion to culture and history. The poem is, finally, a rather philosophical one about the directions of English culture, and through an enumeration of religious objects and rituals it reviews part of the history of that culture. It tells a kind of story first, through one lengthy dramatized scene, in order to comment later on what the place and the experience may mean, and the larger conclusion derives from the particulars of what the speaker does and touches. By the end of stanza 2 the action is over, but that action, we are told, stands for many such visits to similar churches; after that, the next five stanzas present reflection and discussion.

"Church Going" is a curious poem in many ways. It goes to a lot of trouble to characterize its speaker, who seems a rather odd choice as a commentator on the state of religion. His informal attire (he takes off his cycle-clips at the end of stanza 1) and his less than worshipful behavior do not at first make him seem like a serious philosopher. He is not disrespectful or sacrilegious, and before the end of stanza 1 he has tried to describe the "awkward reverence" he feels; but his overly somber imitation of part of the service stamps him as playful, a little satirical, and as a tourist here, not someone who regularly drops in for prayer or meditation in the usual sense. And yet those early details give him credentials, in a way; he knows the names of religious objects and has some history of churches in his grasp. Clearly he does this sort of church going often ("Yet stop I did: in fact I often do," line 19) because he wonders seriously what it all means—now—in comparison to what it meant to religious worshipers in times past. Ultimately, he takes the church, its cultural meaning, and its function seriously (lines 55 ff.), and he understands the importance of the church in the history of his culture. Thus the relatively brief drama provides a context for the more digressive and rambling free-floating reflections that grow out of the speaker's dramatic experience.

Sometimes poems are organized by contrasts, and they conveniently set one thing up against another that is quite different. Notice, for example, how the following poem carefully contrasts two worlds:

PAT MORA

Sonrisas

I live in a doorway
between two rooms, I hear
quiet clicks, cups of black
coffee, *click, click* like facts

5
       budgets, tenure, curriculum,
from careful women in crisp beige
suits, quick beige smiles
that seldom sneak into their eyes.

10
I peek
in the other room señoras
in faded dresses stir sweet
milk coffee, laughter whirls
with steam from fresh *tamales*
    sh, sh, mucho ruido,[6]

15
they scold one another,
press their lips, trap smiles
in their dark, Mexican eyes.
                         1986

Here different words, habits, and values characterize the worlds of the two sets of characters, and the poem is organized largely through the contrasts between them. The meaning of the poem (the difference between the two worlds) is very nearly the same as the structure.

Poems often have **discursive structures,** too; that is, they may be organized like a treatise, an argument, or an essay. "First," they say, "and second . . . and third. . . ." This sort of 1-2-3 structure takes a variety of forms depending on what is being enumerated or argued. The following poem, for example, honors three people who have died, but it makes clear and sharp distinctions among them. Depending on the person about to be described, the earth is "sweet," "bright," or "dark," and in this way the structure itself suggests comparisons and contrasts. As you read the poem, try to articulate just what sort of person each of the three is.

JAMES WRIGHT

Arrangements with Earth for Three Dead Friends

Sweet earth, he ran and changed his shoes to go
Outside with other children through the fields.
He panted up the hills and swung from trees
Wild as a beast but for the human laughter

5
That tumbled like a cider down his cheeks.
Sweet earth, the summer has been gone for weeks,
And weary fish already sleeping under water
Below the banks where early acorns freeze.
Receive his flesh and keep it cured of colds.

10
Button his coat and scarf his throat from snow.

6. A lot of noise.

And now, bright earth, this other is out of place
In what, awake, we speak about as tombs.
He sang in houses when the birds were still
And friends of his were huddled round till dawn
After the many nights to hear him sing.   15
Bright earth, his friends remember how he sang
Voices of night away when wind was one.
Lonely the neighborhood beneath your hill
Where he is waved away through silent rooms.
Listen for music, earth, and human ways.   20

Dark earth, there is another gone away,
But she was not inclined to beg of you
Relief from water falling or the storm.
She was aware of scavengers in holes
Of stone, she knew the loosened stones that fell   25
Indifferently as pebbles plunging down a well
And broke for the sake of nothing human souls.
Earth, hide your face from her where dark is warm.
She does not beg for anything, who knew
The change of tone, the human hope gone gray.   1957   30

Why, in stanza 1, is the earth represented as a parent? What does addressing the earth here as "sweet" seem to mean? How does the address to earth as "bright" fit the dead person described in stanza 2? In what different senses is the person described in stanza 3 "dark"? Why is the earth asked to give attention secretly to this person? Exactly what kind of person was she? How does the poem make you feel about her? Is there any cumulative point in describing three such different people in the same poem? What is accomplished by having the poem's three stanzas addressed to various aspects of earth? Similar discursive structures help organize poems such as Shelley's "Ode to the West Wind" (later in this chapter), where the wind drives a leaf in Part I, a cloud in Part II, a wave in Part III, and then, after a summary and statement of the speaker's ambitious hope in Part IV, is asked to make the speaker a lyre in Part V.

Poems may borrow their organizational strategies from many places, imitating chronological, visual, or discursive shapes in reality or in other works of art. Sometimes poems strive to be almost purely descriptive of someone or something (using **descriptive structures**), in which case poets have to make organizational decisions much as painters or photographers would, deciding first how a whole scene should look, then putting the parts into proper place for the whole. Of course, poems must present their details sequentially, not all at once as actual pictures more or less can, so poets must decide where to start a description (at the left? center? top?) and what sort of movement to use (linear across the scene? clockwise?). But if having words instead of paint or film has some disadvantages, it also has particular assets: figurative language can be a part of description, or an adjunct to it. Poets can insert comparisons at any point without necessarily disturbing the unity of their descriptions.

Some poems use **imitative structures,** mirroring as exactly as possible the structure of something that already exists as an object and can be seen—another poem perhaps, as in Koch's "Variations on a Theme by William Carlos Williams" (chapter 23). Other poems use **reflective** (or **meditative**) **structures,** pondering a subject, theme, or event, and letting the mind play with it, skipping (sometimes illogically but still usefully) from one sound to another, or to related thoughts or objects as the mind receives them.

Although this poem employs several organizational principles, it ultimately takes its structure from an important shift in the speaker's attitude as she reviews, ponders, and rethinks events of long ago.

SHARON OLDS

The Victims

When Mother divorced you, we were glad. She took it and
took it, in silence, all those years and then
kicked you out, suddenly, and her
kids loved it. Then you were fired, and we
5   grinned inside, the way people grinned when
Nixon's helicopter lifted off the South
Lawn for the last time.[7] We were tickled
to think of your office taken away,
your secretaries taken away,
10   your lunches with three double bourbons,
your pencils, your reams of paper. Would they take your
suits back, too, those dark
carcasses hung in your closet, and the black
noses of your shoes with their large pores?
15   She had taught us to take it, to hate you and take it
until we pricked with her for your
annihilation, Father. Now I
pass the bums in doorways, the white
slugs of their bodies gleaming through slits in their
20   suits of compressed silt, the stained
flippers of their hands, the underwater
fire of their eyes, ships gone down with the
lanterns lit, and I wonder who took it and
took it from them in silence until they had
25   given it all away and had nothing
left but this.   1984

"The Victims" divides basically into two parts. In the first two-thirds of the poem (from line 1 to the middle of line 17), the speaker evokes her father (the "you" of lines 1, 3, and so forth), who had been guilty of terrible habits and behavior when the speaker was young and was kicked out suddenly and divorced by the speaker's mother (lines 1–3). He was then fired from his job (line 4) and lost his whole way of life (lines 8–12), and the speaker (taught by the mother, lines 15–17) recalls celebrating every defeat and

7. When Richard Nixon resigned the U.S. presidency on August 8, 1974, his exit from the White House (by helicopter from the lawn) was televised live.

every loss ("we pricked with her for your annihilation," lines 16–17). The mother is regarded as a victim ("She took it and took it, in silence, all those years" [lines 1–2]), and the speaker forms an indivisible unit with her and the other children ("her kids," lines 3–4). They are the "we" of the first part of the poem. They were "glad" (line 1) at the divorce; they "loved it" (line 4) when the mother kicked out the father; they "grinned" (line 5) when the father was fired; they were "tickled" (line 7) when he lost his job, his secretaries, and his daily life. Only at the end of the first section does the speaker (now older but remembering what it was like to be a child) recognize that the mother was responsible for the easy, childish vision of the father's guilt ("She had taught us to take it, to hate you and take it" [line 15]); nevertheless, all sympathy in this part of the poem is with the mother and her children, while all of the imagery is entirely unfavorable to the father. The family reacted to the father's misfortunes the way observers responded to the retreat in disgrace of Richard Nixon from the U.S. presidency. The father seems to have led a luxurious and insensitive life, with lots of support in his office (lines 8–11), fancy clothes (lines 12–14), and decadent lunches (line 10); his artificial identity seemed haunting and daunting (lines 11–14) to the speaker as child.

But in line 17, the poem shifts focus and shifts gears. The "you" in the poem is now, suddenly, "Father." A bit of sympathy begins to surface for "bums in doorways" (line 18), who begin to seem like victims, too; their bodies are "slugs" (line 19), their suits are made of residual waste pressed into regimented usefulness (lines 19–20), and their hands are constricted into mechanical "flippers" (line 21). Their eyes contain fire (line 22), but it is as if they retain only a spark of life in their submerged and dying state. The speaker has not forgotten the cruelty and insensitivity remembered in the first part of the poem, but the blame seems to have shifted somewhat and the father is not the only villain, nor are the mother and children the only victims. Look carefully at how the existence of street people recalls earlier details about the father, how sympathy for his plight is elicited from us, and how the definition of victim shifts.

Imagery, words, attitudes, and narrative are different in the two parts of the poem, and the second half carefully qualifies the first, as if to illustrate the more mature and considered attitudes of the speaker in her older years—a qualification of the easy imitation of the earlier years, when the mother's views were thoroughly dominant and seemed sensible and adequate. Change has governed the poem's structure here; differences in age, attitude, and tone are supported by entirely different sets of terms, attitudes, and versions of causality.

The paradigms (or models) for organizing poems are, finally, not all that different from those of prose. It may be easier to organize something short rather than something long, but the question of intensity becomes comparatively more important in shorter works. Basically, the problem of how to organize one's material is, for the writer, first of all a matter of deciding what kind of thing one wants to create, of having its purposes and effects clearly in mind. That means that every poem will differ somewhat from every other, but it also means that patterns of purpose—narrative, dramatic, discursive, descriptive, imitative, or reflective—may help writers organize and formulate their ideas. A consciousness of purpose and effect can help the reader see *how* a poem proceeds toward its goal. Seeing how a poem is organized is, in turn, often a good way of seeing where it is going and what its real concerns and purposes may be. Often a poem's organization helps to make clear the particular effects that the poet wishes to generate. In a good poem, means and end are closely related, and a reader who is a good observer of one will be able to discover the other.

• • •

ANONYMOUS

Sir Patrick Spens

The king sits in Dumferling toune,[8]
   Drinking the blude-reid[9] wine:
"O whar will I get guid sailor,
   To sail this ship of mine?"

5   Up and spake an eldern knicht,
   Sat at the king's richt knee:
"Sir Patrick Spens is the best sailor
   That sails upon the sea."

The king has written a braid[1] letter
10   And signed it wi' his hand,
And sent it to Sir Patrick Spens,
   Was walking on the sand.

The first line that Sir Patrick read,
   A loud lauch[2] lauched he;
15   The next line that Sir Patrick read,
   The tear blinded his ee.[3]

"O wha is this has done this deed,
   This il deed done to me,
To send me out this time o' the year,
20   To sail upon the sea?

"Make haste, make haste, my merry men all,
   Our guid ship sails the morn."
"O say na sae,[4] my master dear,
   For I fear a deadly storm.

25   "Late, late yestre'en I saw the new moon
   Wi' the auld moon in her arm,
And I fear, I fear, my dear mastér,
   That we will come to harm."

O our Scots nobles were richt laith[5]
30   To weet their cork-heeled shoon,[6]
But lang owre a'[7] the play were played
   Their hats they swam aboon.[8]

O lang, lang, may their ladies sit,
   Wi' their fans into their hand,
35   Or ere they see Sir Patrick Spens
   Come sailing to the land.

---

8. Town.   9. Blood-red.   1. Broad: explicit.   2. Laugh.   3. Eye.   4. Not so.   5. Right loath: very reluctant.   6. To wet their cork-heeled shoes. Cork was expensive, and, therefore, such shoes were a mark of wealth and status.   7. Before all.   8. Their hats swam above them.

O lang, lang, may the ladies stand
  Wi' their gold kems[9] in their hair,
Waiting for their ain[1] dear lords,
  For they'll see them na mair.   40

Half o'er, half o'er to Aberdour
  It's fifty fadom deep,
And there lies guid Sir Patrick Spens
  Wi' the Scots lords at his feet.

probably thirteenth century

WILLIAM CARLOS WILLIAMS

The Dance

In Brueghel's great picture, The Kermess,[2]
the dancers go round, they go round and
around, the squeal and the blare and the
tweedle of bagpipes, a bugle and fiddles
tipping their bellies (round as the thick-   5
sided glasses whose wash they impound)
their hips and their bellies off balance
to turn them. Kicking and rolling about
the Fair Grounds, swinging their butts, those
shanks must be sound to bear up under such   10
rollicking measures, prance as they dance
in Brueghel's great picture, The Kermess.   1944

EMILY DICKINSON

[The Wind begun to knead the Grass—]

The Wind begun to knead the Grass—
As Women do a Dough—
He flung a Hand full at the Plain—
A Hand full at the Sky—
The Leaves unhooked themselves from Trees—   5
And started all abroad—
The Dust did scoop itself like Hands—
And throw away the Road—
The Wagons quickened on the Street—

9. Combs.   1. Own.   2. A painting by Pieter Brueghel the Elder (1525?–1569).

10   The Thunders gossiped low—
      The Lightning showed a Yellow Head—
      And then a livid Toe—
      The Birds put up the Bars to Nests—
      The Cattle flung to Barns—
15   Then came one drop of Giant Rain—
      And then, as if the Hands
      That held the Dams—had parted hold—
      The Waters Wrecked the Sky—
      But overlooked my Father's House—
20   Just Quartering a Tree—

          1864

ROO BORSON

Save Us From

      Save us from night,
      from bleak open highways
      without end, and the fluorescent
      oases of gas stations,
5   from the gunning of immortal
      engines past midnight,
      when time has no meaning,
      from all-night cafés,
      their ghoulish slices of pie,
10   and the orange ruffle on the
      apron of the waitress,
      the matching plastic chairs,
      from orange and brown and
      all unearthly colors,
15   banish them back to the test tube,
      save us from them,
      from those bathrooms with a
      moonscape of skin in the mirror,
      from fatigue, its merciless brightness,
20   when each cell of the body stands on end,
      and the sensation of teeth,
      and the mind's eternal sentry,
      and the unmapped city
      with its cold bed.
25   Save us from insomnia,
      its treadmill,
      its school bells and factory bells,
      from living-rooms like the tomb,
      their plaid chesterfields

and galaxies of dust, 30
from chairs without arms,
from any matched set of furniture,
from floor-length drapes which
close out the world,
from padded bras and rented suits, 35
from any object in which horror is concealed.
Save us from waking after nightmares,
save us from nightmares,
from other worlds,
from the mute, immobile contours 40
of dressers and shoes,
from another measureless day, save us.   1989

PERCY BYSSHE SHELLEY

Ode to the West Wind

I

O wild West Wind, thou breath of Autumn's being,
Thou, from whose unseen presence the leaves dead
Are driven, like ghosts from an enchanter fleeing,

Yellow, and black, and pale, and hectic red,
Pestilence-stricken multitudes: O thou, 5
Who chariotest to their dark wintry bed

The wingéd seeds, where they lie cold and low,
Each like a corpse within its grave, until
Thine azure sister of the Spring shall blow

Her clarion[3] o'er the dreaming earth, and fill 10
(Driving sweet buds like flocks to feed in air)
With living hues and odors plain and hill:

Wild Spirit, which art moving everywhere;
Destroyer and preserver; hear, oh, hear!

II

Thou on whose stream, mid the steep sky's commotion,
Loose clouds like earth's decaying leaves are shed, 15
Shook from the tangled boughs of Heaven and Ocean,

Angels[4] of rain and lightning: there are spread
On the blue surface of thine aëry surge,
Like the bright hair uplifted from the head 20

---

3. Trumpet call.   4. Messengers.

Of some fierce Maenad,[5] even from the dim verge
Of the horizon to the zenith's height,
The locks of the approaching storm. Thou dirge

Of the dying year, to which this closing night
25   Will be the dome of a vast sepulcher,
Vaulted with all thy congregated might

Of vapors, from whose solid atmosphere
Black rain, and fire, and hail will burst: oh, hear!

III

Thou who didst waken from his summer dreams
30   The blue Mediterranean, where he lay,
Lulled by the coil of his crystálline streams,

Beside a pumice isle in Baiae's bay,[6]
And saw in sleep old palaces and towers
Quivering within the wave's intenser day,

35   All overgrown with azure moss and flowers
So sweet, the sense faints picturing them! Thou
For whose path the Atlantic's level powers

Cleave themselves into chasms, while far below
The sea-blooms and the oozy woods which wear
40   The sapless foliage of the ocean, know

Thy voice, and suddenly grow gray with fear,
And tremble and despoil themselves:[7] oh, hear!

IV

If I were a dead leaf thou mightest bear;
If I were a swift cloud to fly with thee;
45   A wave to pant beneath thy power, and share

The impulse of thy strength, only less free
Than thou, O uncontrollable! If even
I were as in my boyhood, and could be

The comrade of thy wanderings over Heaven,
50   As then, when to outstrip thy skyey speed
Scarce seemed a vision; I would ne'er have striven

As thus with thee in prayer in my sore need.
Oh, lift me as a wave, a leaf, a cloud!
I fall upon the thorns of life! I bleed!

5. A frenzied female votary of Dionysus, the Greek god of vegetation and fertility who was supposed to die in the fall and rise again each spring.   6. Where Roman emperors had erected villas, west of Naples. 7. The vegetation at the bottom of the sea . . . sympathizes with that of the land in the change of seasons [Shelley's note].

A heavy weight of hours has chained and bowed   55
One too like thee: tameless, and swift, and proud.

                    V

Make me thy lyre, even as the forest is:
What if my leaves are falling like its own!
The tumult of thy mighty harmonies

Will take from both a deep, autumnal tone,   60
Sweet though in sadness. Be thou, Spirit fierce,
My spirit! Be thou me, impetuous one!

Drive my dead thoughts over the universe
Like withered leaves to quicken a new birth!
And, by the incantation of this verse,   65

Scatter, as from an unextinguished hearth
Ashes and sparks, my words among mankind!
Be through my lips to unawakened earth

The trumpet of a prophecy! O Wind,
If Winter comes, can Spring be far behind?   1820   70

W. H. AUDEN
_____

In Memory of W. B. Yeats

(d. January, 1939)

                    I

He disappeared in the dead of winter:
The brooks were frozen, the airports almost deserted,
And snow disfigured the public statues;
The mercury sank in the mouth of the dying day.
What instruments we have agree   5
The day of his death was a dark cold day.

Far from his illness
The wolves ran on through the evergreen forests,
The peasant river was untempted by the fashionable quays;
By mourning tongues   10
The death of the poet was kept from his poems.

But for him it was his last afternoon as himself,
An afternoon of nurses and rumors;
The provinces of his body revolted,

15   The squares of his mind were empty,
       Silence invaded the suburbs,
       The current of his feeling failed; he became his admirers.

       Now he is scattered among a hundred cities
       And wholly given over to unfamiliar affections,
20   To find his happiness in another kind of wood
       And be punished under a foreign code of conscience.
       The words of a dead man
       Are modified in the guts of the living.

       But in the importance and noise of tomorrow
25   When the brokers are roaring like beasts on the floor of the Bourse,[8]
       And the poor have the sufferings to which they are fairly accustomed,
       And each in the cell of himself is almost convinced of his freedom,
       A few thousand will think of this day
       As one thinks of a day when one did something slightly unusual.
30   What instruments we have agree
       The day of his death was a dark cold day.

                    II

       You were silly like us; your gift survived it all:
       The parish of rich women, physical decay,
       Yourself. Mad Ireland hurt you into poetry.
35   Now Ireland has her madness and her weather still,
       For poetry makes nothing happen: it survives
       In the valley of its making where executives
       Would never want to tamper, flows on south
       From ranches of isolation and the busy griefs,
40   Raw towns that we believe and die in; it survives,
       A way of happening, a mouth.

                    III

       Earth, receive an honored guest:
       William Yeats is laid to rest.
       Let the Irish vessel lie
45   Emptied of its poetry.

       In the nightmare of the dark
       All the dogs of Europe bark,
       And the living nations wait,
       Each sequestered in its hate;

50   Intellectual disgrace
       Stares from every human face,
       And the seas of pity lie
       Locked and frozen in each eye.

8. The Paris stock exchange.

Follow, poet, follow right
To the bottom of the night,   55
With your unconstraining voice
Still persuade us to rejoice;

With the farming of a verse
Make a vineyard of the curse,
Sing of human unsuccess   60
In a rapture of distress;

In the deserts of the heart
Let the healing fountain start,
In the prison of his days
Teach the free man how to praise.   65

1939

QUESTIONS

1. How many different "scenes" can you identify in "Sir Patrick Spens"? Where does each scene begin and end? How are the transitions made from scene to scene? How is the "fading" effect between scenes accomplished?
2. Why does the last line of Williams's "The Dance" repeat the first line? How do the line breaks early in the poem help control the poem's rhythm and pace? What differences do you notice in the choice of words early in the poem and then later? How is the poem organized?
3. What words and patterns are repeated in the different stanzas of Shelley's "Ode to the West Wind"? What differences are there from stanza to stanza? What "progress" does the poem make? In what sense is the poem "revolutionary" or "cyclical"? What contribution to the structure of the poem do the sound patterns make? How do the rhymes and repeated stanza patterns contribute to the tone of the poem? to its meaning?
4. Pick out one of the poems you have read earlier in the course that seems particularly effective in the way it is put together. Read it over several times and consider carefully how it is organized, that is, what structural principles it uses. What do the choices of speaker, situation, and setting have to do with the poem's structure? What other artistic decisions contribute to its structure?

WRITING SUGGESTIONS

1. After doing the reading and analysis suggested in question 4 above, write a detailed essay in which you consider fully the structural principles at work in the poem. The length of your essay will depend on both the length of the poem you choose and the complexity of its structure, but try to choose a poem that you can discuss fully in less than a thousand words.
2. Carefully reread Dickey's "Cherrylog Road" (chapter 14). Then find another poem in this book in which memory of a much earlier event plays an important structural function. Compare the poems in detail, noting how (in each case) memory influences the way the event is reconstructed. What details of the event are in each case omitted in the retelling? What parts are lengthened or dwelt upon? What, in each case, is the point of having the event recalled later rather than from an immediate recollection?

   Write a three- or four-page essay comparing the structuring function of memory in the two poems, noting in each case exactly how the structural principles at work in the poem help to create the poem's final tone.

STUDENT WRITING

This essay discusses structure and relates other elements, such as language and speaker, to it.

Language and Structure in Sharon Olds's "The Victims"

Carol Lin

Sharon Olds's poem "The Victims" plays with forms of the verb "to take." The infinitive and its forms have multiple meanings, but two distinct ones resonate throughout Olds's poem, helping to structure the poem's "story" and ultimately its most important emotional effects. An examination of the use and meaning of "to take" reveals much about the speaker's position and feelings within "The Victims."

In the first line the speaker addresses her father directly. From the opening sentence--"When mother divorced you, we were glad" (line 1)--one immediately gains a sense of the family relationship. A form of the verb "to take" surfaces in the second sentence as the speaker says, "She took it and / took it" (lines 1-2). Here, "took" conveys a slang meaning of "to take"; it presents an inverse of the action of taking, namely receiving. Via this meaning, the speaker expresses the frustration and troubles that the mother suffered through; it was not actual things that the mother took. Thus, here the word depicts victimization of the mother rather than an assertive act.

In lines 8-9, the past participle of "to take" presents another instance of victimization and powerlessness. Here, the father experiences helplessness and powerlessness when "[his] office [was] taken away, / [his] secretaries [were] taken away." The father is in a passive position as things are taken away from him; he does not have control or power. Those who "take" become ominous forces as the speaker asks rhetorically, "Would they take your / suits back, too, those dark / carcasses hung in your closet, and the black / noses of your shoes with their large pores?" (lines 11-14). If "they" did take those suits and shoes, one senses, it would be an ultimate loss of control and power for the father.

Repeated use of the verb "to take" allows one to gauge shifts in the speaker's point of view. To begin with, the mother now seems to be one of "them": she "took it"--took "the underwater / fire of [his] eyes" (lines 21-22)--as she "kicked [him] out" (line 3). In addition, the mother victimized the speaker in that she "taught [her] to take it, to hate [him] and take it" (line 15). Thus the speaker, like the mother, both took abuse and was abusive, "prick[ing] with her for [his] / annihilation" (lines 16-17). Once the speaker has revealed her own role as "taker" and has felt sympathy for the father, she wonders "who took it and / took it" (lines 23-24) from "the bums in doorways" (line 18), her range of sympathy widening to include the larger world of men who "had given it all away" (lines 24-25).

The use of "took" in these final lines refers back to the start of the poem. "The bums" may be powerless automatons--"ships gone down" (line 22)--like the father. But when the speaker wonders "who took it and / took it from them in silence" (lines 23-24), one recalls that the mother also "took it and / took it, in silence" (lines 1-2) from the father. This resonance crystallizes the transitions within the speaker's point of view.

At the beginning of "The Victims," the speaker tells the father about what he could not see and what the speaker could not say when the events occurred. As the poem progresses, the speaker realizes and works through the anger and frustration involved in being so one-sided and unsympathetic. Though she had been swayed by the mother, she now has grown to see from a different perspective, one that allows sympathy for many people. Through her multiple uses of the verb "to take," the speaker both remains true to her earlier feelings and reveals a great change in attitude.

18

EXTERNAL FORM

Most poems of more than a few lines are divided into stanzas, groups of lines divided from other groups by white space on the page. Putting some space between groupings of lines has the effect of sectioning a poem, giving its physical appearance a series of divisions that often mark breaks in thought, changes of scene or image, or other shifts in structure or direction. In Donne's "The Flea" (chapter 14), for example, the stanza divisions mark distinct stages in the action: between the first and second stanzas, the speaker stops his companion from killing the flea; between the second and third stanzas, the companion follows through on her intention and kills the flea. In Nemerov's "The Goose Fish" (chapter 17), the stanzas mark stages in the self-perception of the lovers; each stanza is a more or less distinct scene, and the scenes unfold almost like a series of slides. Not all stanzas are quite so neatly patterned as these, but any formal division of a poem into stanzas is important to consider: what appear to be gaps or silences may be structural indicators.

Historically, stanzas have most often been organized by patterns of rhyme, and thus stanza divisions have been a visual indicator of patterns in sound. In most traditional stanza forms, the pattern of rhyme is repeated in stanza after stanza throughout the poem, until voice and ear become familiar with the pattern and come to expect and, in a sense, depend on it. The accumulation of pattern allows us to "hear" variations as well, just as we do in music. The rhyme thus becomes an organizational device in the poem—a formal, external determiner of organization, as distinguished from the internal, structural determiners we considered in chapter 17—and ordinarily the metrical patterns stay constant from stanza to stanza. In Shelley's "Ode to the West Wind," for example, the first and third lines in each stanza rhyme, and the middle line then rhymes with the first and third lines of the next stanza. (In indicating rhyme, we conventionally use a different letter of the alphabet to represent each sound; in the following example, if we begin with "being" as *a* and "dead" as *b*, then "fleeing" is also *a*, and "red" and "bed" are *b*.)

O wild West Wind, thou breath of Autumn's being,	*a*
Thou, from whose unseen presence the leaves dead	*b*
Are driven, like ghosts from an enchanter fleeing,	*a*
Yellow, and black, and pale, and hectic red,	*b*
Pestilence-stricken multitudes: O thou,	*c*
Who chariotest to their dark wintry bed	*b*

The wingéd seeds, where they lie cold and low,	c
Each like a corpse within its grave, until	d
Thine azure sister of the Spring shall blow	c

In this stanza form, known as **terza rima,** the stanzas are linked to each other by a common sound: one rhyme sound from each stanza is picked up in the next stanza, and so on to the end of the poem (though sometimes poems have sections that use varied rhyme schemes). This stanza form was used by Dante in *The Divine Comedy,* written in Italian in the early 1300s. Terza rima is not all that common in English because it is a rhyme-rich stanza form—that is, it requires many rhymes, and thus many different rhyme words—and English is, relatively speaking, a rhyme-poor language (not as rich in rhyme possibilities as Italian or French). One reason for this is that English derives from so many different language families that it has fewer similar word endings than languages that have remained "pure"—that is, more dependent for vocabulary on the roots and patterns found in a single language family.

Contemporary poets use rhyme sparingly, finding it neither necessary nor appealing, but until the twentieth century the music of rhyme was central to both the sound and the formal conception of most poems. Because poetry was originally an oral art (and its texts not always written down), various kinds of **memory devices** (sometimes called **mnemonic devices**) were built into poems to help reciters remember them. Rhyme was one such device, and most people still find it easier to memorize poetry that rhymes. The simple pleasure of hearing familiar sounds repeated at regular intervals may also help to account for the traditional popularity of rhyme, and perhaps plain habit (for both poets and hearers) had a lot to do with why rhyme flourished for so many centuries as a standard expectation. Rhyme also helps to give poetry a special aural quality that distinguishes it from prose, a significant advantage in ages that worry about decorum and propriety and are anxious to preserve a strong sense of poetic tradition. Some ages have been very concerned that poetry should not in any way be mistaken for prose or made to serve prosaic functions, and the literary critics and theorists in those ages made extraordinary efforts to emphasize the distinctions between poetry, which was thought to be artistically superior, and prose, which was thought to be primarily utilitarian. A pride in elitism and a fear that an expanded reading public could ultimately dilute the possibilities of traditional art forms have been powerful cultural forces in Western civilization, and if such forces were not themselves responsible for creating rhyme in poetry, they at least helped to preserve a sense of its necessity. But rhyme and other patterns of repeated sounds are also important, for various historical and cultural reasons, to non-Western languages and poetic traditions as well.

There are at least two other reasons for rhyme. One is complex and hard to state justly without long explanations. It involves traditional ideas about the symmetrical relationship of different aspects of the world and the function of poetry to reflect the universe as human learning has understood it. Many cultures (especially in earlier centuries) have assumed that rhyme was proper to verse, perhaps even essential. Poets in these ages and cultures would have felt themselves eccentric to compose poems any other way. Some English poets (especially in the Renaissance) did experiment—very successfully—with **blank verse** (that is, verse that did not rhyme but that nevertheless had strict metrical requirements), but the cultural pressure for rhyme was almost constant. Why? As noted above, custom or habit may account for part of the assumption that rhyme was necessary, but probably not all of it. Rather, the poets' sense that poetry was an imitation of larger relationships in the universe made it seem natural to use rhyme to represent or re-create a sense of harmony, correspondence, symmetry, and order. The sounds of poetry were thus (they thought) reminders of the harmonious cosmos, of the music of the spheres that animated the planets, the processes of nature, the interrelationship of all created things and beings. Probably no poet ever thought, "I shall now tunefully emulate the harmony of God's carefully ordered universe," but the tendency to use rhyme and other repetitions or re-echoings of sound (such as **alliteration** or **assonance**) nevertheless stemmed ultimately from basic assumptions about how the universe worked. In a modern world increasingly perceived as fragmented, rambling, and unrelated, there is of course less of a tendency to testify to a sense of harmony and symmetry. It would be too easy and too mechanical to think that rhyme in a poem specifically means that the poet has a firm sense of cosmic order, and that an unrhymed poem testifies to chaos, but cultural assumptions do affect the expectations of both poets and readers, and cultural tendencies create a kind of pressure on the individual creator. If you take a survey course (or a series of related "period" courses) in English or American literature, you will readily notice the diminishing sense of the need for—or relevance of—rhyme. And other linguistic and national traditions similarly vary usages in different times, depending on the philosophical and cultural assumptions of the time and place.

One other reason for using rhyme is that it provides a kind of discipline for the poet, a way of harnessing poetic talents and keeping a rein on the imagination, so that the results are ordered, controlled, put into some kind of meaningful and recognizable form. Robert Frost said that writing poems without rhyme or rhythm was like playing tennis without a net. Writing good poetry does require a lot of discipline, and Frost speaks for many (perhaps most) traditional poets in suggesting that rhyme or rhythm can be a major source of that discipline. But neither one is the only possible source, and more recent poets have usually felt they would rather play by new rules or invent their own as they go along; they have, therefore, sought their sources of discipline elsewhere, preferring the sparer tones that unrhymed poetry provides. It is not that contemporary poets cannot think of rhyme words or that they do not care about the sounds of their poetry; rather, recent poets have consciously decided not to work with rhyme and to use instead other aural and metrical devices and other strategies

> *Concentration is the very essence of poetry.*
>
> —AMY LOWELL

for organizing stanzas, just as they have chosen to work with experimental and variable rhythms instead of writing necessarily in the traditional English meters. Some modern poets, though, have protested the abandonment of rhyme and have continued to write rhymed verse successfully in a more or less traditional way.

The amount and density of rhyme vary widely in stanza and verse forms, from elaborate and intricate patterns of rhyme to more casual or spare sound repetitions. The **Spenserian stanza,** for example, is even more rhyme-rich than terza rima, using only three rhyme sounds in nine rhymed lines, as in Keats's *The Eve of St. Agnes:*

Her falt'ring hand upon the balustrade,	*a*
Old Angela was feeling for the stair,	*b*
When Madeline, St. Agnes' charméd maid,	*a*
Rose, like a missioned spirit, unaware:	*b*
With silver taper's light, and pious care,	*b*
She turned, and down the agéd gossip led	*c*
To a safe level matting. Now prepare,	*b*
Young Porphyro, for gazing on that bed;	*c*
She comes, she comes again, like ring dove frayed and fled	*c*

On the other hand, the **ballad stanza** (as in "Sir Patrick Spens") has only one set of rhymes in four lines; lines 1 and 3 in each stanza do not rhyme at all:

> The king sits in Dumferling toune,   *a*
> Drinking the blude-reid wine: *b*
> "O whar will I get guid sailor,   *c*
> To sail this ship of mine?"   *b*

Most stanza forms use a metrical pattern as well as a rhyme scheme. Terza rima, for example, involves iambic meter (unstressed and stressed syllables alternating regularly), and each line has five beats (pentameter). Most of the Spenserian stanza (the first eight lines) is also in iambic pentameter, but the ninth line in each stanza has one extra foot (thus, the last line is in iambic hexameter). The ballad stanza, also iambic, as are most English stanza and verse forms, alternates three-beat and four-beat lines; lines 1 and 3 are unrhymed iambic tetrameter (four beats), and lines 2 and 4 are rhymed iambic trimeter (three beats).

THE SONNET

The **sonnet,** one of the most persistent verse forms, originated in the Middle Ages as a prominent form in Italian and French poetry. It dominated English poetry in the late sixteenth and early seventeenth centuries and then was revived several times from the early-nineteenth century onward. Except for some early experiments with length, the sonnet has always been fourteen lines long, and it usually is written in iambic pentameter. It is most often printed as if it were a *single* stanza, although it actually has several formal divisions that represent its rhyme schemes and formal breaks. As a popular and traditional verse form in English for more than four centuries, the sonnet has been surprisingly resilient even in ages that largely reject rhyme. It continues to attract a variety of poets, including (curiously) radical and even revolutionary poets, who find its formal demands, discipline, and set outcome very appealing. Its uses, although quite varied, can be illustrated fairly precisely. As a verse form, the sonnet is contained, compact, demanding; whatever it does, it must do concisely and quickly. To be effective, it must take advantage of the possibilities inherent in its shortness and its relative rigidity. It is best suited to intensity of feeling and concentration of expression. Not too surprisingly, one subject it frequently discusses is confinement itself.

WILLIAM WORDSWORTH

Nuns Fret Not

> Nuns fret not at their convent's narrow room;
> And hermits are contented with their cells;
> And students with their pensive citadels;
> Maids at the wheel, the weaver at his loom,

Sit blithe and happy; bees that soar for bloom,   5
High as the highest Peak of Furness-fells,[1]
Will murmur by the hour in foxglove bells:
In truth the prison, unto which we doom
Ourselves, no prison is: and hence for me,
In sundry moods, 'twas pastime to be bound   10
Within the sonnet's scanty plot of ground;
Pleased if some souls (for such there needs must be)
Who have felt the weight of too much liberty,
Should find brief solace there, as I have found.   1807

Most sonnets are structured according to one of two principles of division. On one principle, the sonnet divides into three units of four lines each and a final unit of two lines, and sometimes the line spacing reflects this division. On the other, the fundamental break is between the first eight lines (called an octave) and the last six (called a sestet). The 4-4-4-2 sonnet is usually called the **English** or **Shakespearean sonnet,** and ordinarily its rhyme scheme reflects the structure: the scheme of *abab cdcd efef gg* is the classic one, but many variations from that pattern still reflect the basic 4-4-4-2 division. The 8-6 sonnet is usually called the **Italian** or **Petrarchan sonnet** (the Italian poet Petrarch was an early master of this structure), and its "typical" rhyme scheme is *abbaabba cdecde,* although it too produces many variations that still reflect the basic division into two parts.

The two kinds of sonnet structures are useful for two different sorts of argument. The 4-4-4-2 structure works very well for constructing a poem that wants to make a three-step argument (with a quick summary at the end), or for setting up brief, cumulative images. "That time of year thou mayst in me behold" (page 717), for example, uses the 4-4-4-2 structure to mark the progressive steps toward death and the parting of friends by using three distinct images, then summarizing. "Let me not to the marriage of true minds" (page 616) works very similarly, following the kind of organization that in chapter 17 was referred to as the 1-2-3 structure—and doing it compactly and economically.

Here, on the other hand, is a poem that uses the 8-6 pattern:

HENRY CONSTABLE

[*My lady's presence makes the roses red*]

My lady's presence makes the roses red,
Because to see her lips they blush for shame.
The lily's leaves, for envy, pale became,
And her white hands in them this envy bred.
The marigold the leaves abroad doth spread,   5
Because the sun's and her power is the same.

---

1. Mountains in England's Lake District, where Wordsworth lived.

> The violet of purple colour came,
> Dyed in the blood she made my heart to shed.
> In brief: all flowers from her their virtue take;
10 From her sweet breath their sweet smells do proceed;
> The living heat which her eyebeams doth make
> Warmeth the ground and quickeneth the seed.
> The rain, wherewith she watereth the flowers,
> Falls from mine eyes, which she dissolves in showers.   1594

The first eight lines argue that the lady's presence is responsible for the color of all of nature's flowers, and the final six lines summarize and extend that argument to smells and heat—and finally to the rain that the lady draws from the speaker's eyes. That kind of two-part structure, in which the octave states a proposition or generalization and the sestet provides a particularization or application of it, has a variety of uses. The final lines may, for example, reverse the first eight and achieve a paradox or irony in the poem, or the poem may nearly balance two comparable arguments. Basically, the 8-6 structure lends itself to poems with two points to make, or to those that wish to make one point and then illustrate it.

Sometimes the neat and precise structure is altered—either slightly, as in Wordsworth's "Nuns Fret Not," above (where the 8-6 structure is more of an $8\frac{1}{2}$-$5\frac{1}{2}$ structure), or more radically as particular needs or effects may demand. And the two basic structures certainly do not define all the structural possibilities within a fourteen-line poem, even if they do suggest the most traditional ways of taking advantage of the sonnet's compact and well-kept container.

During the Renaissance, poets regularly employed the sonnet for love poems, and many modern sonnets continue to be about love or private life. And many continue to use a personal, apparently open and sincere tone. But poets often find the sonnet's compact form and rigid demands equally useful for many varieties of subject, theme, and tone. Besides love, sonnets often treat other subjects: politics, philosophy, discovery of a new world. And tones vary widely too, from the anger and remorse of "Th' expense of spirit in a waste of shame" (page 959) and righteous outrage of "On the Late Massacre in Piedmont" (page 667) to the tender awe of "How Do I Love Thee?" (page 601). Many poets seem to take the kind of comfort Wordsworth describes in the careful limits of the form, finding in its two basic variations (the English sonnet, such as "That time of year," and the Italian sonnet, such as "On First Looking into Chapman's Homer" [page 832]) a sufficiency of ways to organize their materials into coherent structures.

• • •

JOHN KEATS

On the Sonnet

If by dull rhymes our English must be chained,
And like Andromeda,[2] the sonnet sweet
Fettered, in spite of painéd loveliness,
Let us find, if we must be constrained,
Sandals more interwoven and complete   5
To fit the naked foot of Poesy:[3]
Let us inspect the lyre, and weigh the stress
Of every chord,[4] and see what may be gained
By ear industrious, and attention meet;
Misers of sound and syllable, no less   10
Than Midas[5] of his coinage, let us be
Jealous of dead leaves in the bay-wreath crown;[6]
So, if we may not let the Muse be free,
She will be bound with garlands of her own.

1819

CLAUDE McKAY

The White House

Your door is shut against my tightened face,
And I am sharp as steel with discontent;
But I possess the courage and the grace
To bear my anger proudly and unbent.
The pavement slabs burn loose beneath my feet,   5
And passion rends my vitals as I pass,
A chafing savage, down the decent street,
Where boldly shines your shuttered door of glass.
Oh, I must search for wisdom every hour,
Deep in my wrathful bosom sore and raw,   10
And find in it the superhuman power
To hold me to the letter of your law!
Oh, I must keep my heart inviolate
Against the poison of your deadly hate.   1937

2. Who, according to Greek myth, was chained to a rock so that she would be devoured by a sea monster. She was rescued by Perseus, who married her. When she died she was placed among the stars.   3. In a letter that contained this sonnet, Keats expressed impatience with the traditional Petrarchan and Shakespearean sonnet forms: "I have been endeavoring to discover a better sonnet stanza than we have."   4. Lyre string.   5. The legendary king of Phrygia who asked, and got, the power to turn all he touched to gold.   6. The bay tree was sacred to Apollo, god of poetry, and bay wreaths came to symbolize true poetic achievement. The withering of the bay tree is sometimes considered an omen of death. *Jealous:* suspiciously watchful.

JOHN MILTON

[*When I consider how my light is spent*]

When I consider how my light is spent,
   Ere half my days, in this dark world and wide,
   And that one talent which is death to hide[7]
   Lodged with me useless, though my soul more bent
5   To serve therewith my Maker, and present
   My true account, lest he returning chide;
   "Doth God exact day-labor, light denied?"
   I fondly ask; but Patience to prevent[8]
That murmur, soon replies, "God doth not need
10   Either man's work or his own gifts; who best
   Bear his mild yoke, they serve him best. His state
Is kingly. Thousands at his bidding speed
   And post o'er land and ocean without rest:
   They also serve who only stand and wait."

1652?

WILLIAM WORDSWORTH

London, 1802

Milton! thou should'st be living at this hour:
England hath need of thee: she is a fen
Of stagnant waters: altar, sword, and pen,
Fireside, the heroic wealth of hall and bower,
5   Have forfeited their ancient English dower
Of inward happiness. We are selfish men;
Oh! raise us up, return to us again;
And give us manners, virtue, freedom, power.
Thy soul was like a star, and dwelt apart:
10   Thou hadst a voice whose sound was like the sea:
Pure as the naked heavens, majestic, free,
So didst thou travel on life's common way,
In cheerful godliness; and yet thy heart
The lowliest duties on herself did lay.

1802

7. In the parable of the talents (Matthew 25), the servants who earned interest on their master's money (his talents) while he was away were called "good and faithful"; the one who hid the money and simply returned it was condemned and sent away. Usury, a deadly sin under Catholicism, was regarded by Puritans as a metaphor for attaining salvation.   8. Forestall. *Fondly:* foolishly.

CHRISTINA ROSSETTI

In an Artist's Studio

One face looks out from all his canvases,
   One selfsame figure sits or walks or leans;
   We found her hidden just behind those screens,
That mirror gave back all her loveliness.
A queen in opal or in ruby dress,   5
   A nameless girl in freshest summer-greens,
   A saint, an angel—every canvass means
The same one meaning, neither more nor less.
He feeds upon her face by day and night,
   And she with true kind eyes looks back on him   10
Fair as the moon and joyful as the light:
   Not wan with waiting, not with sorrow dim;
Not as she is, but was when hope shone bright;
   Not as she is, but as she fills his dream.   1856

SIR CHARLES G. D. ROBERTS

The Potato Harvest

A high bare field, brown from the plough, and borne
   Aslant from sunset; amber wastes of sky
   Washing the ridge; a clamor of crows that fly
In from the wide flats where the spent tides mourn
To yon their rocking roosts in pines wind-torn;   5
   A line of grey snake-fence that zigzags by
   A pond and cattle; from the homestead nigh
The long deep summonings of the supper horn.
Black on the ridge, against that lonely flush,
   A cart, and stoop-necked oxen; ranged beside   10
     Some barrels; and the day-worn harvest-folk,
Here emptying their baskets, jar the hush
   With hollow thunders. Down the dusk hillside
     Lumbers the wain; and day fades out like smoke.   1886

GWENDOLYN BROOKS

First Fight. Then Fiddle.

First fight. Then fiddle. Ply the slipping string
With feathery sorcery; muzzle the note
With hurting love; the music that they wrote
Bewitch, bewilder. Qualify to sing
Threadwise. Devise no salt, no hempen thing
For the dear instrument to bear. Devote
The bow to silks and honey. Be remote
A while from malice and from murdering.
But first to arms, to armor. Carry hate
In front of you and harmony behind.
Be deaf to music and to beauty blind.
Win war. Rise bloody, maybe not too late
For having first to civilize a space
Wherein to play your violin with grace.

1949

ROBERT FROST

Range-Finding

The battle rent a cobweb diamond-strung
And cut a flower beside a groundbird's nest
Before it stained a single human breast.
The stricken flower bent double and so hung.
And still the bird revisited her young.
A butterfly its fall had dispossessed,
A moment sought in air his flower of rest,
Then slightly stooped to it and fluttering clung.
On the bare upland pasture there had spread
O'ernight 'twixt mullein stalks a wheel of thread
And straining cables wet with silver dew.
A sudden passing bullet shook it dry.
The indwelling spider ran to greet the fly,
But finding nothing, sullenly withdrew.

1916

COUNTEE CULLEN

Yet Do I Marvel

I doubt not God is good, well-meaning, kind,
And did He stoop to quibble could tell why
The little buried mole continues blind,
Why flesh that mirrors Him must some day die,
Make plain the reason tortured Tantalus[9]   5
Is baited by the fickle fruit, declare
If merely brute caprice dooms Sisyphus[1]
To struggle up a never-ending stair.
Inscrutable His ways are, and immune
To catechism by a mind too strewn   10
With petty cares to slightly understand
What awful brain compels His awful hand.
Yet do I marvel at this curious thing:
To make a poet black, and bid him sing!   1925

HELEN CHASIN

Joy Sonnet in a Random Universe

Sometimes I'm happy: la la la la la la la
la la la la la la la la la la la la la la la la la
la la la la. Tum tum ti tum. La la la la la la
la la la la la la la la la la la la la la la la la.
Hey nonny nonny. La la la la la la la la la   5
la la la la la la la la la la la la. Vo do di o do.
Poo poo pi doo. La la la la la la la la la la
la la la la la la la la la la la la la la la la la la
la la. Whack a doo. La la la la la la la. Sh-
boom, sh-boom. La la la la la la la la la la   10
la la la la la la la la la la la la la la la la la la
la la. Dum di dum. La la la la la la la la la
la la la la la la la la la la. Tra la la. Tra la la
la la la la la la la la la la la. Yeah yeah yeah.   1968

9. In Greek myth he was condemned, for ambiguous reasons, to stand up to his neck in water he couldn't
drink and to be within sight of fruit he couldn't reach to eat.   1. The king of Corinth who, in Greek
myth, was condemned eternally to roll a huge stone uphill.

STANZA FORMS

Many stanza forms are represented in this book. Some have names, because they have been used over and over by different poets. Others were invented for a particular use in a particular poem and may never be repeated again. Most traditional stanzas are based on rhyme schemes, but some use other kinds of predictable sound patterns; early English poetry, for example, used alliteration to construct a balance between the first and second half of each line (see Earle Birney's "Anglosaxon Street" [chapter 18] for a modern imitation of this principle). Sometimes, especially when poets interact with each other within a strong community, highly elaborate *verse forms* have been developed that set up stanzas as part of a scheme for the whole poem. The poets of medieval Provence were especially inventive, subtle, and elaborate in their construction of complex verse forms, some of which have been copied by poets ever since. The **sestina,** for example, depends on the measured repetition of words (rather than just sounds) in particular places; see, for example, Bishop's "Sestina" (later in this chapter) and try to decipher the pattern. (There are also double and even triple sestinas, tough tests of a poet's ingenuity.) And the **villanelle,** another Provençal form, depends on the patterned repetition of whole lines (see Dylan Thomas's "Do Not Go Gentle into That Good Night" [next page]). Different cultures and different languages develop their own patterns and measures—not all poetries are parallel to English poetry—and they vary from age to age as well as nation to nation.

You can probably deduce the principles involved in each of the following stanza or verse forms by looking carefully at a poem that uses it; if you have trouble, look at the definitions in the glossary.

heroic couplet	"Sound and Sense"	chapter 16
tetrameter couplet	"To His Coy Mistress"	chapter 14
limerick	"There was a young lady of Riga"	chapter 16
free verse	"Dirge"	chapter 16
blank verse	from *Paradise Lost*	chapter 15

What are stanza forms good for? What use is it to recognize them? Why do poets bother? Matters discussed in this chapter so far have suggested two reasons: (1) Breaks between stanzas provide convenient pauses for reader and writer, something roughly equivalent to paragraphs in prose. The eye thus picks up the places where some kind of pause or break or change of focus occurs. (2) Poets sometimes use stanza forms, as they do rhyme itself, as a discipline: writing in a certain kind of stanza form imposes a shape on the act of imagination. But visual spaces and unexpected print divisions also mean that poems sometimes *look* unusual and require special visual attention, attention that does not always follow the logic of sound patterns or syntax. After the following poems illustrating some common stanza forms, you will find a section on poems that employ special configurations and shapes, using spaces and print in other ways, to establish their meanings and effects.

• • •

DYLAN THOMAS

Do Not Go Gentle into That Good Night[1]

Do not go gentle into that good night,
Old age should burn and rave at close of day;
Rage, rage against the dying of the light.

Though wise men at their end know dark is right,
Because their words had forked no lightning they   5
Do not go gentle into that good night.

Good men, the last wave by, crying how bright
Their frail deeds might have danced in a green bay,
Rage, rage against the dying of the light.

Wild men who caught and sang the sun in flight,   10
And learn, too late, they grieved it on its way,
Do not go gentle into that good night.

Grave men, near death, who see with blinding sight
Blind eyes could blaze like meteors and be gay,
Rage, rage against the dying of the light.   15

And you, my father, there on the sad height,
Curse, bless, me now with your fierce tears, I pray.
Do not go gentle into that good night.
Rage, rage against the dying of the light.   1952

MARIANNE MOORE

Poetry

I, too, dislike it: there are things that are important beyond all this
    fiddle.
    Reading it, however, with a perfect contempt for it, one discovers in
    it after all, a place for the genuine.
        Hands that can grasp, eyes
        that can dilate, hair that can rise   5
            if it must, these things are important not because a

high-sounding interpretation can be put upon them but because they
    are
    useful. When they become so derivative as to become unintelligible,
    the same thing may be said for all of us, that we

---

1. Written during the final illness of the poet's father.

10   do not admire what
            we cannot understand: the bat
               holding on upside down or in quest of something to

       eat, elephants pushing, a wild horse taking a roll, a tireless wolf under
         a tree, the immovable critic twitching his skin like a horse that feels a
         flea, the base-
15   ball fan, the statistician—
           nor is it valid
               to discriminate against "business documents and

       school-books"[2]; all these phenomena are important. One must make a
         distinction
         however: when dragged into prominence by half poets, the result is
         not poetry,
20   nor till the poets among us can be
          "literalists of
            the imagination"[3]—above
               insolence and triviality and can present

       for inspection, "imaginary gardens with real toads in them," shall we
         have
25   it. In the meantime, if you demand on the one hand,
         the raw material of poetry in
          all its rawness and
           that which is on the other hand
             genuine, you are interested in poetry.   1921

ELIZABETH BISHOP

Sestina

September rain falls on the house.
In the failing light, the old grandmother
sits in the kitchen with the child
beside the Little Marvel Stove,
5 reading the jokes from the almanac,
laughing and talking to hide her tears.

---

2. *Diary of Tolstoy* (Dutton), p. 84. "Where the boundary between prose and poetry lies, I shall never be able to understand. The question is raised in manuals of style, yet the answer to it lies beyond me. Poetry is verse: Prose is not verse. Or else poetry is everything with the exception of business documents and school books" [Moore's note].   3. Yeats, *Ideas of Good and Evil* (A. H. Bullen, 1903), p. 182. "The limitation of [William Blake's] view was from the very intensity of his vision; he was a too literal realist of imagination, as others are of nature; and because he believed that the figures seen by the mind's eye, when exalted by inspiration, were 'eternal existences,' symbols of divine essences, he hated every grace of style that might obscure their lineaments" [Moore's note].

She thinks that her equinoctial tears
and the rain that beats on the roof of the house
were both foretold by the almanac,
but only known to a grandmother.   10
The iron kettle sings on the stove.
She cuts some bread and says to the child,

It's time for tea now; but the child
is watching the teakettle's small hard tears
dance like mad on the hot black stove,   15
the way the rain must dance on the house.
Tidying up, the old grandmother
hangs up the clever almanac

on its string. Birdlike, the almanac
hovers half open above the child,   20
hovers above the old grandmother
and her teacup full of dark brown tears.
She shivers and says she thinks the house
feels chilly, and puts more wood in the stove.

It was to be, says the Marvel Stove.   25
I know what I know, says the almanac.
With crayons the child draws a rigid house
and a winding pathway. Then the child
puts in a man with buttons like tears
and shows it proudly to the grandmother.   30

But secretly, while the grandmother
busies herself about the stove,
the little moons fall down like tears
from between the pages of the almanac
into the flower bed the child   35
has carefully placed in the front of the house.

Time to plant tears, says the almanac.
The grandmother sings to the marvellous stove
and the child draws another inscrutable house.   1965

ARCHIBALD MacLEISH
_____

Ars Poetica[4]

A poem should be palpable and mute
As a globed fruit,

Dumb
As old medallions to the thumb,

_____

4. "The Art of Poetry," title of a poetical treatise by the Roman poet Horace (65–8 B.C.).

5   Silent as the sleeve-worn stone
    Of casement ledges where the moss has grown—

    A poem should be wordless
    As the flight of birds.

    A poem should be motionless in time
10   As the moon climbs.

    Leaving, as the moon releases
    Twig by twig the night-entangled trees,

    Leaving, as the moon behind the winter leaves,
    Memory by memory the mind—

15   A poem should be motionless in time
    As the moon climbs.

    A poem should be equal to:
    Not true.

    For all the history of grief
20   An empty doorway and a maple leaf.

    For love
    The leaning grasses and two lights above the sea—

    A poem should not mean
    But be.   1926

THE WAY A POEM LOOKS

Stanza breaks and other kinds of print spaces are important, primarily to guide the voice and mind to a clearer sense of sound and meaning. But there are exceptions. A few poems are written to be seen rather than heard, and their appearance on the page is crucial to their effect. Cummings's poem "l(a," for example, tries to visualize typographically what the poet asks you to see in your mind's eye.

E. E. CUMMINGS

[l(a]

l(a

le
af
fa

ll   5

s)
one
l

iness   1958

Occasionally, too, poems are composed in a specific shape so that they look like physical objects. The poems that follow in this chapter—some very old, some more recent—illustrate ways in which visual effects may be created. Even though poetry has traditionally been thought of as oral—words to be said, sung, or performed rather than looked at—the idea that poems can also be related to painting and the visual arts is an old one. Theodoric in ancient Greece is credited with inventing **technopaegnia**—that is, the construction of poems with visual appeal. Once, the shaping of words to resemble an object was thought to have mystical power, but more recent attempts at **concrete poetry** or **shaped verse** are usually playful exercises (such as Hollander's "You Too? Me Too—Why Not? Soda Pop" [chapter 22]) that attempt to supplement (or replace) verbal meanings with devices from painting and sculpture.

Reading a poem like Herbert's "Easter Wings" aloud wouldn't make much sense. Our eyes are everything for a poem like that. A more frequent poetic device involves asking the eyes to become a guide for the voice. The following poem depends on recognition of some standard typographical symbols and knowledge of their names. We have to say those names to read the poem.

FRANKLIN P. ADAMS

Composed in the Composing Room

At stated .ic times
I love to sit and—off rhymes
Till ,tose at last I fall
Exclaiming "I don't ∧ all."

5   Though I'm an * objection
By running this in this here §
This ☞ of the Fleeting Hour,
This lofty -ician Tower—

10 A ¶er's hope dispels
All fear of deadly ‖.
You think these [ ] are a pipe?
Well, not on your †eotype.

1914

We create the right term here when we verbalize, putting the visual signs together with the words or letters printed in the poem, for example making the word "periodic" out of ".ic" or "high Phoenician" out of "-ician." Like "Easter Wings," "Composed in the Composing Room" uses typography in an extreme way; here the eyes (and mind) are drawn into a punlike game that offers more puzzle-solving pleasure than emotional effect. More often poets give us—by the visual placement of sounds—a guide to reading, inviting us to regulate the pace of our reading, notice pauses or silences, pay attention both to the syntax of the poem and to the rhetoric of the voice, thus providing us a kind of musical score for reading.

E. E. CUMMINGS

[Buffalo Bill 's][1]

Buffalo Bill 's
defunct
          who used to
          ride a watersmooth-silver
5   stallion
and break onetwothreefourfive pigeonsjustlikethat
                                        Jesus

he was a handsome man
                        and what i want to know is

1. *Portraits* XXI.

how do you like your blueeyed boy   10
Mister Death   1923

The unusual spacing of words here, with some run together and others widely separated, provides a guide to reading, regulating both speed and sense, so that the poem
can capture aloud some of the excitement and wonder of a boy's enthusiasm for a
theatrical act as spectacular as that of Buffalo Bill. A good reader-aloud, with only this
typographical guidance, can capture some of the wide-eyed boy's responses, remembered now in retrospect from a later perspective (notice how the word "defunct" helps
to set the time and point of view).

In prose, syntax and punctuation are the main guides to the voice of a reader, providing indicators of emphasis, pace, and speed; in poetry as well they are more conventional and more common guides than extreme forms of typography, such as in
"Buffalo Bill 's." Reading a poem sensitively is in some ways a lot like reading a piece
of prose sensitively: one has to pay close attention to the way the sentences are put
together and how they are punctuated. A good reader makes use of appropriate pauses
as well as thundering emphasis; silence as well as sound is part of any poem, and reading
punctuation is as important as knowing how to say the words.

Beyond punctuation, the placement and spacing of lines on the page may be helpful
to a reader even when that placement is not as radical as it is in "Buffalo Bill 's." The
fact that poetry looks different from prose is not an accident; decisions to make lines
one length instead of another have as much to do with vocal breaks and phrasing as
with functions of syntax or meaning. In a good poem, there are few accidents, not even
in the way the poem meets the eye, for as readers our eyes are the most direct route to
our voices; they are our scanner and director, our prompter and guide.

The eye also may help the ear in another way—guiding us to notice repeated sounds
by repeated visual patterns in letters. The most common rhymes in poems occur at the
ends of lines, and the arrangement of lines (the typography of the poem) often calls
attention to the pattern of sounds because of the similar appearance of line-ending
words, as in sonnets and other traditional verse forms and sometimes in radically unconventional patterns. Not all words that rhyme have similar spellings, of course, but similarities of word appearance seem to imply a relationship of sound, too, and many poems
hint at their stanza patterns and verse forms by their spatial arrangement and repeated
patterns at ends of lines. The following poem takes advantage of such expectations and
plays with them by forcing a letter into arbitrary line relationships, forcing words ("stew,"
line 2) in order to create rhymes, setting up rhyme patterns and then breaking them (lines
9–11), using false or near rhymes (lines 10–11), and creating long lines with multisyllabic
rhymes that seem silly (the final two lines).

STEVIE SMITH

The Jungle Husband

Dearest Evelyn, I often think of you
Out with the guns in the jungle stew
Yesterday I hittapotamus

I put the measurements down for you but they got lost in the fuss
It's not a good thing to drink out here
You know, I've practically given it up dear.
Tomorrow I am going alone a long way
Into the jungle. It is all grey
But green on top
Only sometimes when a tree has fallen
The sun comes down plop, it is quite appalling.
You never want to go in a jungle pool
In the hot sun, it would be the act of a fool
Because it's always full of anacondas, Evelyn, not looking ill-fed
I'll say. So no more now, from your loving husband, Wilfred.   1957

Visual devices can be entertainments to amuse, puzzle, or tease readers of poetry whose chief expectations concern sound, but sometimes poets achieve surprising (and lasting) original effects by manipulations of print space. Stanzas—visual breaks in poems that indicate some kind of unit of meaning or measurement—ultimately are more than visual devices, for they point to structural questions and ultimately frame and formalize the content of poems. But they involve—as do the similar visual patterns of words that rhyme—part of the "score" of poems, and suggest one more way that sight becomes a guide to sound in many poems.

• • •

GEORGE HERBERT

Easter Wings

Lord, who createdst man in wealth and store,[2]
Though foolishly he lost the same,
Decaying more and more,
Till he became
Most poor:
With thee
O let me rise
As larks,[3] harmoniously,
And sing this day thy victories:
Then shall the fall further the flight in me.

My tender age in sorrow did begin;
And still with sicknesses and shame
Thou didst so punish sin,
That I became
Most thin.
With thee
Let me combine,
And feel this day thy victory;
For, if I imp[4] my wing on thine,
Affliction shall advance the flight in me.

1633

2. In plenty.   3. Which herald the morning.   4. Engraft. In falconry, to engraft feathers in a damaged wing, so as to restore the powers of flight (*OED*).

EARLE BIRNEY

Anglosaxon Street

Dawn drizzle ended   dampness steams from
blotching brick and   blank plasterwaste
Faded housepatterns   hoary and finicky
unfold stuttering   stick like a phonograph

Here is a ghetto   gotten for goyim   5
O with care denuded   of nigger and kike
No coonsmell rankles   reeks only cellarrot
Ottar[5] of carexhaust   catcorpse and cookinggrease

Imperial hearts   heave in this haven
Cracks across windows   are welded with slogans   10
There'll Always Be An England   enhances geraniums
and V's for Victory   vanquish the housefly

Ho! with climbing sun   march the bleached beldames
festooned with shopping bags   farded[6] flatarched
bigthewed Saxonwives   stepping over buttrivers   15
waddling back wienerladen   to suckle smallfry

Hoy! with sunslope   shrieking over hydrants
flood from learninghall   the lean fingerlings
Nordic nobblecheeked[7]   not all clean of nose
leaping Commandowise   into leprous lanes   20

What! after whistleblow!   spewed from wheelboat
after daylight doughtiness   dire handplay
in sewertrench or sandpit   come Saxonthegns
Junebrown Jutekings[8]   jawslack for meat

Sit after supper   on smeared doorsteps   25
not humbly swearing   hatedeeds on Huns
profiteers politicians   pacifists Jews

Then by twobit magic   to muse in movie
unlock picturehoard   or lope to alehall
soaking bleakly   in beer skittleless   30

Home again to hotbox   and humid husbandhood
in slumbertrough adding   sleepily to Anglekin
Alongside in lanenooks   carling and leman[9]
caterwaul and clip[1]   careless of Saxonry
with moonglow and haste   and a higher heartbeat   35

---

5. Roselike fragrance.   6. Rouged.   7. Pimpled.   8. The Jutes were the German tribe that invaded England in the fifth century and spearheaded the Anglo-Saxon conquest. *Saxonthegns:* freemen who provided military services for the Saxon lords.   9. Lover. *Carling:* old woman.   1. Embrace.

Slumbers now slumtrack   unstinks cooling
waiting brief for milkmaid   mornstar and worldrise

Toronto 1942, revised 1966

DAVID FERRY

Evening News

We have been there.
                                   and seen nothing
Nothing has been there
                                   for us to see
In what a beautiful silence
                                   the death is inflicted
In a dazzling distance
                                   in the fresh dews
And morning lights
                                   how radiantly
In the glistening
                                   the village is wasted.
It is by such sights
                                   the eye is instructed.   1983

QUESTIONS

1. Chart the rhyme scheme of Keats's "On the Sonnet," and then, after a careful reading aloud of the poem, mark the major structural breaks in the poem. At what points do the structural breaks and the breaks in rhyme pattern coincide? At what points do they conflict? Can you account for the variations in terms of the poem's meaning?
2. Describe the structure of Wordsworth's "London, 1802." In what sense is it an Italian sonnet? Describe the rhyme scheme of this sonnet, and justify (if you can) its unusual pattern.
3. Is Chasin's "Joy Sonnet in a Random Universe" a sonnet? On what grounds can you justify calling it a sonnet?
4. What principles determine the form of Birney's "Anglosaxon Street"? How do sound patterns in the poem relate to its form?

WRITING SUGGESTIONS

1. Consider the structure of McKay's "The White House" and the poem's themes of confinement and exclusion. In what specific ways does the poem use the tight restrictions of the sonnet form? Write an essay of about two pages on the way content and form interact in the poem.
2. Consider carefully the structure and sequencing in Brooks's "First Fight. Then Fiddle." Notice how various uses of sound in the poem (rhyme, onomatopoeia, and alliteration, for example) help to enforce its themes and tones. In an essay of about six hundred words, show the relationship between "sound and sense" in the poem.

19

THE WHOLE TEXT

In the previous seven chapters, we have been thinking about one thing at a time—setting, word choice, symbolism, meter, stanza form, and so on—and we have discussed each poem primarily in terms of a single issue. Learning to deal with one problem at a time is good educational practice and in the long run will make you a more careful and more effective reader of poems. Still, the elements of poems do not work individually but in combination, and in considering even the simplest elements (speaker, for example, or setting) we have noticed how categories overlap—how, for example, the question of setting in Dickey's "Cherrylog Road" quickly merges into questions about the speaker, his state of mind, his personality, his distance from the central

> *All good poetry . . . is forged*
> *slowly and patiently, and link*
> *by link with sweat and blood*
> *and tears.*
>
> —LORD ALFRED DOUGLAS

events in the poem. Thinking about a single issue never does complete justice to an individual poem; no poem depends for all its effects on just one device or one element of craft. Poems are complex wholes that demand varieties of attention, and ultimately, to read any poem fully and well you need to ask all the questions about craft, form, and tradition that you can think of, all the ones we've asked so far, and many others you may learn to ask on the basis of more experience in reading poems. Not all questions are equally relevant to all poems, of course, but moving systematically through your whole list of questions will enable you to get beyond the fragmentation of particular issues and approach the whole poem and its multiple ways of creating effects. In this chapter we will consider how the various elements of poems work together.

On the next page is a short poem in which several issues we have considered come up almost simultaneously.

ELIZABETH JENNINGS

Delay

The radiance of that star that leans on me
Was shining years ago. The light that now
Glitters up there my eye may never see
And so the time lag teases me with how

5   Love that loves now may not reach me until
Its first desire is spent. The star's impulse
Must wait for eyes to claim it beautiful
And love arrived may find us somewhere else.   1953

In most poems, several issues come up more or less at once, and the analytic practice of separating issues is a convenience rather than an assertion of priority or order. In "Delay," a lot of the basic questions (about speaker, situation, and setting, for example) seem to be put on hold in the beginning, but if we proceed systematically the poem opens itself to us. The first line identifies the "I" (or rather, in this case, "me") of the poem as an observer of the bright star that is the main object in the poem and the principal source of its imagery, its "plot," and its analogical argument. But we learn little about the speaker. She surfaces again in lines 4 and 5 and with someone else ("us") in line 8, but she is always in the objective case—acted on rather than acting. All we know for certain about her is that she can speak about the time it takes light from the stars to reach her and that she contemplates deeply and at length about the meaning and effect of such time lags. We know even less about the setting and situation; somewhere the speaker watches a bright star and meditates on the fact that she is seeing it long, long after its actual light was sent forth. Her location is not specified, and the time, though probably night, could be any night (in the age of modern astronomy, that is, because the speaker knows about the speed of light and the distance of the stars from Earth); the only other explicit clues we have about the situation involve the "us" of the final line and the fact that the speaker's concern with time seems oddly personal, something that matters to her emotional life—not merely a matter of stellar knowledge.

The poem's language helps us understand much more about the speaker and her situation, as do the poem's structure and stanza form. The most crucial word in the first stanza is probably the verb "leans" (line 1); certainly it is the most unusual and surprising word. Because a star cannot literally *lean* on its observer, the word seems to suggest the speaker's perception of her relationship to the star. Perhaps she feels that the star impinges on her, that she is somehow *subject* to its influence, though not in the popular, astrological sense. Here the star influences the speaker because she understands something about the way the universe works and can apply her knowledge of light and light years in an analogical way to her own life: it "leans" because it tells her something about how observers are affected by their relationships to what they observe. And it is worth noticing how fully the speaker thinks of herself as object rather than actor. Here, as throughout the poem, she is acted upon; things happen *to* her—the star leans on her, the time lag teases her (line 4), love may not reach her (line 5), and she (along with someone else) is the object sought in the final line.

Other crucial words also help clarify the speaker and her situation. The words "radiance" (line 1) and "[g]litters" (line 3) are fairly standard ones to describe stars, but here their standard meanings are carefully qualified by their position in time. The radiance comes from years ago and seems to be unavailable to the speaker, who now sees only glitter, something far less warm and resonant. And the word "impulse" in line 6 invokes technical knowledge about light. Rather than being impulsive or quickly spent, a star must "wait" for its reception in the eye of the beholder, where it becomes "beautiful"; in physics, an impulse combines force and duration. Hence, the receiver of light—the beholder, the acted-upon—becomes important, and we begin to see why the speaker always appears as object: she is the receiver and interpreter, and the light is not complete—its duration not established—until she receives and interprets it. The star does, after all, "lean" on (depend on) her in some objective sense as well as the subjective one in which she first seems to report it.

The stanza form suggests that the poem may have stages and that its meaning may emerge in two parts, a suggestion confirmed by the poem's form and structure. The first stanza is entirely about stars and stargazing, but the second stanza establishes the analogy with love that becomes the poem's central metaphor. Now, too, more becomes clear about the speaker and her situation. Her concern is about delay, "time lag" (line 4), and the fact that "[l]ove that loves now may not reach me until / Its first desire is spent" (lines 5–6), a strong indication that her initial observation of the star is driven by feeling and her emotional context. Her attempt to put the remoteness of feeling into a perspective that will enable understanding and patience becomes the "plot" of the poem, and her final calm recognition about "us"—that "love arrived may find us somewhere else"—is, if not comforting, nevertheless a recognition that patience is important and that some things do last. Even the sounds of the poem—in this case the way rhyme is used—help support the meaning of the poem and the tone it achieves. The rhymes in the first part of the poem reflect perfectly the stable sense of ancient stars, while in the second stanza the sounds involve near-rhyme: there is harmony here, but in human life and emotion nothing is quite perfect.

Here is another short poem whose several elements deserve detailed attention:

ANONYMOUS

Western Wind

Western wind, when wilt thou blow,
  The small rain down can rain?
Christ, if my love were in my arms
  And I in my bed again!

fifteenth century

Perhaps the most obvious thing here is the poem's structure: its first two lines seem to have little to do with the last two. How can we account for these two distinct and apparently unrelated directions, the calm concern with natural processes in the first part and the emotional outburst about loneliness and lovelessness in the second? The best route to the whole poem is still to begin with the most simple of questions—who? when? where? what is happening?—and proceed to more difficult and complex ones.

As in Jennings's "Delay," the speaker here offers little explicit autobiography. The first two lines provide no personal information, but ask a question that could be delivered quite impersonally; they could be part of a philosophical meditation. The abbreviated syntax at the end of line 1 (the question of causality is not fully stated, and we have to supply the "so that" implied at the end of the line) may suggest strong feeling and emotional upset, but it tells us nothing intimate, only that the time is spring (which is when the western wind blows). No place is indicated, no year, no particulars of situation. But lines 3–4, while remaining inexplicit about exact details, make the speaker's situation clear enough: his love is no longer in his arms, and he wishes she were. (We don't really know genders here, but we guess based on what we think of as typical practice in fifteenth-century England.)

The poem's language, a study in contrast, guides us to see the two-part structure clearly. The question asked of the wind in lines 1–2 involves straightforward, steady language, but line 3 bursts with agony and personal despair. The power of the first word of line 3—especially in an age of belief—suggests a speaker ready to state his loss in the strongest possible terms, and the parallel statements of loss in lines 3 and 4 suggest not only the speaker's physical relationship to his love but also his displacement from home: he is deprived of both place and love, human contact and contact with his past. His longing for a world ordered according to his past experience is structured to parallel his longing for the spring wind that brings the world back to life. The two parts of the poem both express a desire for return—to life, to order, to causal relationships within the world. Setting has in fact become a central theme in the poem, and what the poem expresses tonally involves a powerful desire for stability and belonging—an effect that grows out of our sense of the speaker's situation and character. Speaker, setting, language, and structure here intertwine to create the intense focus of the poem.

In the following short poem, several elements likewise interrelate:

ROBERT HERRICK

Upon Julia's Clothes

Whenas in silks my Julia goes
Then, then, methinks, how sweetly flows
That liquefaction of her clothes.

Next, when I cast mine eyes, and see
That brave[1] vibration, each way free,
O, how that glittering taketh me!

5

1648

The poem is unabashed in its admiration of the way Julia looks, and nearly everything in its six short lines contributes to its celebratory tone. Perhaps the most striking thing about the poem is its unusual, highly suggestive use of words. "[G]oes" at the end of line 1 may be the first word to call special attention to itself, though we will return in a minute to the very first word of the poem. "Walks" or "moves" would seem to be more

---

1. Handsome, showy.

obvious choices; "goes" is more neutral and less specific and in most circumstances would seem an inferior choice, but here the point seems to be to describe Julia in a kind of seamless and unspecified motion and from a specific angle, because the poem wants to record the effect of Julia's movement on the speaker (already a second element becomes crucial) rather than the specifics of Julia herself. Another word that seems especially important is "liquefaction" (line 3), also an unusual and suggestive word about motion. Again it implies no specific kind of motion, just smoothness and seamlessness, and it applies not to Julia but to her clothes—the kind of indirection that doesn't really fool anybody. Other words that might repay a close look include "vibration" in line 5 (the speaker is finally a little more direct); "brave" and "free," also in line 5; and "glittering" and "taketh" in line 6.

Had we begun conventionally by thinking about speaker, situation, and setting, we would have quickly noticed the precise way that the speaker clothes Julia: "in silks," which move almost as one with her body. And we would have noticed that the speaker positions himself almost as voyeur (standing for us as observers, of course, but also for himself as the central figure in the poem). Not much detail about situation or setting is given (and the speaker is characterized only as a viewer and appreciator), but one thing about the scene is crucial, and this takes us back to the first word of the poem, "whenas." The slightly quaint quality of the word may at first obscure, to a modern reader, just what it tells us about the situation, that it is a *kind* of scene rather than a single event. "Whenas" is very close to "whenever"; the speaker's claim seems to be that he responds this way *whenever* Julia dons her silks—apparently fairly often, at least in his memory or imagination.

Most of the speaker's language is sensual and rather provocative (he is anxious to share his responses with others so that *everyone* will know just how "taking" Julia is), but one rather elaborate (though somewhat disguised) metaphor suggests his awareness of his own calculation and its consequences. In the beginning of the second stanza he describes how he "cast" his eyes: it is a metaphor from fishing, a frequent one in love poetry about luring, chasing, and catching. Julia is the object. The metaphor continues two lines later, but the angler has caught himself: he is taken by the "glittering" lure. This turning of the tables, drawing as it does on a traditional, common image that is then modified to help characterize the speaker, gives a little depth to the show: whatever the slither and glitter, there is not just showing off and sensuality but a catch in this angling.

Many other elements deserve comment, especially because they quickly relate to each other. Consider the way the poet uses sounds, first of all in picking words like "liquefaction" that are themselves almost onomatopoeic, but then also using rhyme very cleverly. There are only two rhyme sounds in the poem, one in the first stanza, the other in the second. The long *ee* of the second becomes almost exclamatory, and the three words of the first seem to become linked in a kind of separate grammar of their own, as if "goes," "flows," and "clothes" were all part of a single action—pretty much what the poem claims on a thematic level. A lot happens in this short and simple poem, and although a reader can get at it step by step by thinking about element after element, the interlocking of the elements is finally the most impressive aspect. Although the plot reenacts familiar stances of woman as object and man as gazer, our analysis and reading need to be flexible enough to consider not only all the analytical categories, but also the ways in which they work together.

Going back to poems read earlier in the book—with the methods and approaches you have learned since then—can help you see how different elements of poems interrelate. Look, for example, at the stanza divisions in Dickey's "Cherrylog Road" (chapter 14) and consider how the neatly spaced, apparently discrete units work against the sometimes frantic pacing of the poem. Or consider the character of the speaker, or the fundamental metaphor of "wreckage" that sponsors the poem, relative to the idea of the speaker. Go back and read Kumin's "Woodchucks" (page 627) while thinking about structural questions; or consider how the effaced speaker works in Rich's "Aunt Jennifer's Tigers" (page 628); or think about metaphor in Nemerov's "The Vacuum" (page 609).

Here are several new poems to analyze. As you read them, think about the elements discussed in the previous seven chapters—but rather than thinking about a single element at a time, try to consider relationships, how the different elements combine to make you respond not to a single device but to a complex set of strategies and effects.

• • •

W. H. AUDEN

Musée des Beaux Arts[2]

About suffering they were never wrong,
The Old Masters: how well they understood
Its human position; how it takes place
While someone else is eating or opening a window or just walking
    dully along;
5 How, when the aged are reverently, passionately waiting
For the miraculous birth, there always must be
Children who did not specially want it to happen, skating
On a pond at the edge of the wood:
They never forgot
10 That even the dreadful martyrdom must run its course
Anyhow in a corner, some untidy spot
Where the dogs go on with their doggy life and the torturer's horse
Scratches its innocent behind on a tree.

In Brueghel's *Icarus*,[3] for instance: how everything turns away
15 Quite leisurely from the disaster; the plowman may
Have heard the splash, the forsaken cry,
But for him it was not an important failure; the sun shone
As it had to on the white legs disappearing into the green
Water; and the expensive delicate ship that must have seen
20 Something amazing, a boy falling out of the sky,
Had somewhere to get to and sailed calmly on.

1938

2. The Museum of the Fine Arts, in Brussels.   3. *Landscape with the Fall of Icarus*, by Pieter Brueghel the Elder (1525?–1569), located in the Brussels museum. According to Greek myth, Daedalus and his son, Icarus, escaped from imprisonment by using homemade wings of feathers and wax; but Icarus flew too near the sun, the wax melted, and he fell into the sea and drowned. In the Brueghel painting the central figure is a peasant plowing, and several other figures are more immediately noticeable than Icarus, who, disappearing into the sea, is easy to miss in the lower right-hand corner. Equally ignored by the figures is a dead body in the woods.

GEORGE HERBERT

The Collar

I struck the board[4] and cried, "No more;
      I will abroad!
What? shall I ever sigh and pine?
My lines[5] and life are free, free as the road,
  Loose as the wind, as large as store.[6]   5
      Shall I be still in suit?[7]
Have I no harvest but a thorn
To let me blood, and not restore
What I have lost with cordial[8] fruit?
      Sure there was wine   10
Before my sighs did dry it; there was corn
  Before my tears did drown it.
Is the year only lost to me?
  Have I no bays[9] to crown it,
No flowers, no garlands gay? All blasted?   15
      All wasted?
Not so, my heart; but there is fruit,
      And thou hast hands.
Recover all thy sigh-blown age
On double pleasures: leave thy cold dispute   20
Of what is fit, and not. Forsake thy cage,
      Thy rope of sands,[1]
Which petty thoughts have made, and made to thee
  Good cable, to enforce and draw,
      And be thy law,   25
While thou didst wink[2] and wouldst not see.
      Away! take heed;
      I will abroad.
Call in thy death's-head[3] there; tie up thy fears.
      He that forbears   30
  To suit and serve his need,
      Deserves his load."
But as I raved and grew more fierce and wild
      At every word,
Methought I heard one calling, *Child!*   35
      And I replied, *My Lord.*   1633

---

4. Table.   5. Lot.   6. A storehouse; that is, in abundance.   7. In service to another.
8. Reviving, restorative.   9. Laurel wreaths of triumph.   1. Moral restrictions.   2. That is, close
your eyes to the weaknesses of such restrictions.   3. *Memento mori*, a skull intended to remind people
of their mortality.

ROBERT FROST

Design

I found a dimpled spider, fat and white,
On a white heal-all,[4] holding up a moth
Like a white piece of rigid satin cloth—
Assorted characters of death and blight
5   Mixed ready to begin the morning right,
Like the ingredients of a witches' broth—
A snow-drop spider, a flower like a froth,
And dead wings carried like a paper kite.

What had that flower to do with being white,
10   The wayside blue and innocent heal-all?
What brought the kindred spider to that height,
Then steered the white moth thither in the night?
What but design of darkness to appall?—
If design govern in a thing so small.

1936

EMILY DICKINSON

[My Life had stood—a Loaded Gun—]

My Life had stood—a Loaded Gun—
In Corners—till a Day
The Owner passed—identified—
And carried Me away—

5   And now We roam in Sovereign Woods—
And now We hunt the Doe—
And every time I speak for Him—
The Mountains straight reply—

And do I smile, such cordial light
10   Upon the Valley glow—
It is as a Vesuvian face
Had let its pleasure through—

And when at Night—Our good Day done—
I guard My Master's Head—
15   'Tis better than the Eider-Duck's
Deep Pillow—to have shared—

To foe of His—I'm deadly foe—
None stir the second time—

4. A plant, also called the "all-heal" and "self-heal," with tightly clustered violet-blue flowers.

On whom I lay a Yellow Eye—
Or an emphatic Thumb—   20

Though I than He—may longer live
He longer must—than I—
For I have but the power to kill,
Without—the power to die—

ca. 1863

BEN JONSON

Epitaph on Elizabeth, L. H.

Wouldst thou hear what man can say
In a little? Reader, stay.
Underneath this stone doth lie
As much beauty as could die;
Which in life did harbor give   5
To more virtue than doth live.
If at all she had a fault,
Leave it buried in this vault.
One name was Elizabeth;
Th' other, let it sleep with death: 10
Fitter, where it died, to tell,
Than that it lived at all. Farewell.   1616

QUESTIONS

1. Consider the setting of Auden's "Musée des Beaux Arts" in the sense of both the painting and its location in the museum. In what different ways do the two settings become important? How does the use of setting relate to the way the speaker is conceived? Define the role or roles played by all the other characters in the poem, including the people on the ship. Whose attitudes (or perhaps words) are being echoed or parodied in line 20? Describe the poem's structure.
2. Consider the elements of speaker and situation simultaneously as you analyze Herbert's "The Collar."
3. Consider the interrelation of the elements of speaker, words and word order, and stanza form in Dickinson's "My Life had stood—a Loaded Gun—."
4. Consider the interrelationships among speaker, structure, stanza form, and tone in Frost's "Design."

WRITING SUGGESTIONS

1. Find a reproduction of the Brueghel painting on which Auden's poem "Musée des Beaux Arts" is based. "Read" the painting carefully and notice which details Auden mentions and which he does not. What aspect(s) of the painting does he emphasize? What does he

ignore? Write a three-page essay in which you show exactly how Auden *uses* the Brueghel painting in his poem.

2. Consider Frost's "Design" as a sonnet. What features of the sonnet seem especially important to the effects Frost achieves here? Consider the structure, rhyme scheme, and imagery. Now look at Frost's "Range-Finding" (chapter 18), and ask the same questions about this poem. Which poem uses the sonnet form more effectively? Why?

Write a four- to five-page essay comparing the two poems and evaluating their use of the sonnet form.

STUDENT WRITING

Below is a whole-text analysis of Maxine Kumin's "Woodchucks" (chapter 12). In it, the writer addresses the setting, language, tone, structure, rhythm, and, finally, the meaning of the poem.

Tragedy in Five Stanzas: "Woodchucks"

Meaghan E. Parker

Maxine Kumin's poem "Woodchucks" is not, as the title might suggest, about cute, furry woodchucks, but instead describes how the speaker changes as she tries to kill them, revealing aspects of human attitudes toward killing. The speaker undergoes an internal conflict as she realizes her capacity for murder during her battle with the woodchucks. She is caught up in the age-old struggle of humans against nature, except that this time, it takes place in the modern, technological world. This battle is presented in five dramatic scenes, marked by six-line stanzas; the poem's structure echoes the format of a classical tragedy in five acts. The poem is subtly organized, each stanza rhyming *abcacb*, and more or less employing a pentameter line, mixing iambs with anapests. Although the rhyme and meter remain mostly constant over the course of this highly structured poem, the tone and pacing change with each stanza, as the speaker's attitudes transform during the struggle with the woodchucks. Kumin indicates the development of the speaker's internal conflict by employing word choice to change the tone from slightly humorous and relaxed to indignant martial righteousness and finally to a harsh and primitive hunter's voice, and by utilizing pacing and meter to build the action to its climax.

The poem is set in small-town North America, where the speaker grows marigolds, broccoli, carrots, roses, and chard in her garden. Although the speaker buys the gas bomb from the "Feed and Grain Exchange," she is not a farmer, since she has only a "vegetable patch" (lines 2 and 11). Therefore, her killing of the woodchucks is not an occupational or economic necessity; the woodchucks were merely a nuisance, and the speaker is sort of dabbling in killing. The first line states that the "gassing . . . didn't turn out right," not that it didn't work, emphasizing with this understatement the dilettantish air of the speaker's activities (line 1). The first stanza employs a playful humor: the gas is called a "knockout bomb," like some comic-book weapon, and the speaker puns on the word "airtight" (lines 2–4). The store "featured" the bomb, as if it were displayed and advertised as a consumer desirable, not as an agent of death (line 3). Line 3 utilizes anapestic feet to add to the humorous tone, and most of the lines of stanza 1 are composed of long clauses, creating an even, calm pacing. That the speaker and her compatriots ("we") had made a "case against them" suggests that the decision to kill the woodchucks was a calm, rational, legal event, yet the woodchucks evade the law by escaping "out of range" underground (lines 4–6). The escalation of the battle is indicated by the military term "range" and the woodchucks' refusal to play by the rules (line 6).

The second stanza is less lighthearted; even though the irrepressible woodchucks "turned up again" "up to scratch," they are now unmistakably opponents to the "we," who attacked them with "cyanide" (lines 7–9). The weapon seems more sinister now; not just gas from a "merciful" "knockout bomb," but murderous cyanide. The last three lines are a litany of the woodchuck's crimes against nature, each one described as increasing in savagery and wanton destruction. First, they merely "brought down the marigolds," but in a "matter of course," thoughtless way; then they "took over" the vegetables, as if they were marauding bandits conquering the speaker's territory (lines 10–11). The speaker is horrified at the "nipping" and "beheading" of the vegetables; the use

of the execution-related word "beheading" to create indignation
at the death of a plant is ironic, probably consciously on the part of
the speaker, since she had tried to execute the woodchuck (line 12).
The litany of crimes is reeled off in quick anapestic feet, subtly
hinting at the irony of the speaker's anger at the woodchucks and the
ridiculousness of the escalating battle.

The action picks up pace in stanza 3, the center of the poem and the
point at which the speaker makes her transformation from silent killer
to murderous hunter. She indignantly implies that the woodchucks would
steal "the food from our mouths": a cliché that is supposed to indicate
what heartless criminals the woodchucks are, even though the poem does
not indicate that the speaker is a subsistence farmer who would starve
without the vegetables (line 13). Even so, she enjoys the feel of the
gun, "righteously thrilling" to have the weapon of her justified revenge
in her hands (line 13). The ".22" and the "bullets' neat noses" feel
right and good, and while the woodchucks are depersonalized into the
enemy, the bullets gain "noses" (line 14). The killer is "righteous,"
"fallen from grace" and "puffed with Darwinian pieties"; these heavy-
handed, Bible-thumping words echo religious and political leaders'
sermons against evil enemies. The pace of the first four lines of this
stanza is heavy and martial, booming with polysyllabic words and
stirring phrases. The meter here is the most irregular, with the two
stressed syllables and similar sounds of "*lapsed*" and "*pacifist*"
pounding home the contrast between the speaker's current manifestation
as righteous killer and her former beliefs (line 15). Lines 15 and 16
begin with a stress, on "I" and "puffed"; the majority of the other
lines in the poem begin with an unstressed syllable, so this pair of
exceptions stands out, at the exact center of the poem, and presents
the turning point of the speaker's attitudes toward killing. Now
"fallen from grace," she is "puffed" like a self-righteous windbag and
exchanges her pacifism for the maxim of survival of the fittest (lines 15–
16). Line 17 begins the switch in tone from martial sloganeering to
impersonal, hunting slang, as the speaker "dr[aws] a bead" on a
woodchuck and kills him. His death is contrasted with the perennialness
of the "everbearing roses," for whose sake he dies; this phrase

indicates an undercurrent of regret at the killing of the woodchuck
(line 18).

The fourth stanza speeds up, using short, harsh, clashing words in
short simple clauses, instead of the sermonizing phrases of the last
stanza. The speaker says she "dropped the mother": "drop," a crude,
impersonal, and unfeeling word for "shot dead," indicates the speaker's
new callous attitude toward the killing of the woodchucks (line 19).
Similarly, the description of the woodchuck "flipflopp[ing] in the air"
is gratuitous and violent, and the stress on "flip," since the first
syllable of the line should be unstressed, emphasizes the visual image
of the helpless, blown-away woodchuck (line 20). The speaker
immediately moves on: "another baby next" is killed without comment
(line 22). In the same line, she counts down "O one-two-three" for the
three woodchucks she's killed, and the three strong stresses lead into
the climax of the poem, where she announces what she's become:
"murderer" and "hawkeye killer" (lines 23-24). The killer comes "on
stage forthwith," as the speaker appears fully transformed by her
killing, her capability for murderous action arising from her nature to
triumph over her professed pacifism. The stage metaphor reinforces the
five-act tragic structure that the poem mirrors, and line 24 brings the
poem to its climax in the fourth stanza.

Throughout the poem, the poet uses the directions down and up to
contrast life and death. The woodchucks "turn up" alive (line 7), "up
to scratch" (line 9) from their "sub-sub-basement," but then they
"brought down the marigolds" (line 10), so they "died down in the . . .
roses" (line 18), "flipflopped and fell" after being "dropped" (lines 19-
20). The speaker, on the other hand, was "up to scratch" (line 9) but
"[fell] from grace" (line 15), so the "murderer inside [her] rose up
hard," as her former pacifist self died down and was reborn as a killer
(line 23). In the final stanza, the speaker, now living as this new
self, describes her continuing struggle with the woodchuck and the
tolls this battle is taking on her, as she remains "cocked and ready
day after day after day" and her obsession with hunting this elusive
prey keeps her awake at night, dreaming of shooting (lines 26-28). The
pacing slows, as the action falls from the climax, and an unspecified

amount of time elapses, but still there is no resolution and thus no victory; the speaker realizes she has lost already to the woodchucks; the tragedy is that, since they have stolen her innocence of killing, now she will never have peace.

The final two lines echo the beginning of the poem: "gassing" from line 1 and "gassed" from line 30 are each stressed syllables beginning a line, thus neatly bookending the poem. The speaker suggests that if the woodchucks had died from the gas, she would not have directly confronted them and their deaths and thus would not have undergone this tragic change into an obsessive hunter. However, this statement contains a telling historical allusion, which suggests that the gassing wouldn't have been an easy moral way out either: the speaker wishes they had died "gassed underground the quiet Nazi way" (line 30). If the deaths had been quiet, efficient, clean, nonconfrontational and unwitnessed by her, the speaker could deny any complicity to her conscience. The contradiction here is important: no matter how "merciful," gassing is still murder, as the Nazis made abundantly clear. Kumin draws a parallel between what we consider the "mercy killing" of animals and the "murder" of human beings, and thus her poem describes how delusions of righteousness cause people to wield unnecessary power over others, and how this damages and changes their sense of self as they realize and accept the human capability for acts of murder.

Exploring Contexts

20

THE AUTHOR'S WORK AS CONTEXT: JOHN KEATS

Poems are not all written in the same style, as if they were produced by a corporation or put together in a committee. Even though all poets share the same medium (language) and usually have some common notions of their craft, they put the unique resources of their individual minds and consciousnesses into what they create. A poet may rely on tradition extensively and use devices that others have developed without surrendering his or her individuality, just as an individual's integrity and uniqueness are not compromised by characteristics the individual may share with others—political affiliations, religious beliefs, tastes in clothes and music. Sometimes people's uniqueness is hard to define—what exactly constitutes the singular personality of an individual?—but it is always there, and we recognize and depend on it in our relationships with other people. And so with poets: most don't make a conscious effort to put an individual stamp on their work; they don't have to. The stamp is there, just in the way they choose subjects, words, configurations. Every individual's consciousness uniquely marks what it records, imagines, and decides to print. In this chapter, after considering what makes the poems of any poet distinctive, we will look at the features of John Keats's poems that stamp them specifically as his own, and in the next chapter (on the poems of Adrienne Rich), we will look at how development and change occur over the course of a poet's career even though the author's character and integrity remain constant.

Experienced readers can often identify a poem as the distinctive work of an individual poet even though they may never have seen the poem before, much as experienced listeners can identify a particular composer, singer, or group after hearing only a few phrases of a piece of new music. Such an ability depends on a lot of reading or a lot of listening to music, but any reasonably sensitive reader can learn, over time, to do it with great accuracy. Developing this ability, however, is not really an end in itself; rather, it is a by-product of learning to notice the particular, distinctive qualities in the style of any poet. Once you've read several poems by the same poet, you will usually see some features that the poems all share, and gradually you may come to think of those features as characteristic. Many people have favorite poets—just as they may have favorite rock groups—whose sounds and themes and style are attractive, familiar, and identifiable to them. To perform an experiment, consult the Index of Authors at the back of this book to locate the following poems by Howard Nemerov: "The Vacuum," "The Town Dump," "The Goose Fish," and "Boom!" After reading these poems, list the similarities you find in all of them. Then look at Nemerov's "A Way of Life." (You can also perform this experiment on other poets whose work appears in the book several times, such as Emily Dickinson and John Donne.)

In what ways is "A Way of Life" like the other Nemerov poems? The concern with contemporary life, the tendency to concentrate on modern conveniences and luxuries, and the interest in isolating and defining aspects of the distinctively modern sensibility are all characteristic of Nemerov, as is the tendency to create a short drama, with a speaker who is not altogether admirable. Several of Nemerov's other poems also share an attitude that seems deeply imbedded in this poem, a kind of antiromanticism that emerges when someone tries to sound or feel *too* proud or cheerful and is shown, by events in the poem, to be part of a grimmer reality instead. The concentration upon one or more physical objects is also characteristic, and often (as in "The Vacuum") the main object is a mechanical one that symbolizes modernity and our modern dependency on things rather than our concern with human relationships. Americanness is emphasized here, too, as if the poem were concerned with helping us define our culture, its habits, and its values. The mood of loneliness is typical of Nemerov, and so is the poem's witty conversational style. The verbal

John Keats

wit here—although not as prominent as the puns and double entendres of "Boom!"—is characteristically informal. Often it seems to derive from the language of commercials and street speech, and Nemerov's undercutting of this language—having a paranoid and simpleminded speaker talk about a gangster in "a state of existential despair"—resembles the strategy of "Boom!" or "The Vacuum." The regular stanzas, rhymed but not in a traditional or regular way and with a number of near-rhymes, are also typical (compare, for example, "The Goose Fish"). In short, "A Way of Life" encapsulates Nemerov's thematic interests and ideas, his verbal style, and his cast of mind.

That some poems have common features does not mean that every poem by a particular author will be predictable and contain all these features. Most poets like to experiment with subjects, tones, forms, strategies, and devices. But the work of any writer will display a characteristic way of thinking—the distinct stamp imposed by a unique consciousness. It will have certain identifiable *tendencies,* although not all of them will show up in any one poem.

Of what practical use is it to notice the distinctive voice and mind of a particular poet? One use (though not the most important one for the casual reader) is the pleasant surprise that occurs when you recognize something familiar. Reading a new poem by a familiar poet can be like meeting an old friend whose face or conversation reminds you of experiences you have had together. In fact, poetic friendships can be treasures just as personal friendships are, even though they are necessarily more distant and somewhat more abstract. Just as novelty—meeting something or someone altogether new to you—provides one kind of pleasure, so revisiting or recalling the familiar provides another, its equal and opposite. Just *knowing* and *recognizing* often feel good in and of themselves.

In addition, just as you learn from watching other people—seeing how they react and respond to people and events, observing how they cope with various situations—you also learn from watching poets at work, seeing how they learn and develop, how they change their minds, how they discover the reach and limits of their imaginations and talents, how they find their distinctive voices and come to terms with their own identities. Watching a poet at work over a period of years (as you can Adrienne Rich in the next chapter) is a little like watching an autobiography unfold, except that the individual poems exist separately and for themselves at the same time that they record a distinctive but changing and perhaps evolving consciousness.

Finally, the more you know about a poet (and the more poems you read by that poet), the better a reader you will likely be of any individual poem by the poet. External facts of the writer's life may enter whatever he or she writes—be it a poem, an essay, a letter, or an autobiography—but beyond that, when you grow accustomed to a writer's habits and manners and means of expression, you learn what to expect. Coming to a new poem by a poet you already know, you adjust faster, know what to look for, and have expectations (although they may be unconscious and unarticulated) of what the poem will be like.

On First Looking into Chapman's Homer[1]

Much have I traveled in the realms of gold,
And many goodly states and kingdoms seen;
Round many western islands have I been
Which bards in fealty to Apollo[2] hold.
5   Oft of one wide expanse had I been told
That deep-browed Homer ruled as his demesne;
Yet did I never breathe its pure serene[3]
Till I heard Chapman speak out loud and bold:
Then felt I like some watcher of the skies
10   When a new planet swims into his ken;[4]
Or like stout Cortez[5] when with eagle eyes
He stared at the Pacific—and all his men
Looked at each other with a wild surmise—
Silent, upon a peak in Darien.

                                                            1816

1. George Chapman's were among the most famous Renaissance translations; he completed his *Iliad* in 1611, his *Odyssey* in 1616. Keats wrote the sonnet after being led to Chapman by a former teacher and reading the *Iliad* all night long.   2. Greek god of poetry and music. *Fealty:* literally, the loyalty owed by a vassal to his feudal lord.   3. Atmosphere.   4. Range of vision.   5. Actually, Balboa; he first viewed the Pacific from Darien, in Panama.

On the Grasshopper and the Cricket

The poetry of earth is never dead:
When all the birds are faint with the hot sun,
And hide in cooling trees, a voice will run
From hedge to hedge about the new-mown mead;
That is the grasshopper's—he takes the lead   5
In summer luxury—he has never done
With his delights; for when tired out with fun
He rests at ease beneath some pleasant weed.
The poetry of earth is ceasing never:
On a lone winter evening, when the frost   10
Has wrought a silence, from the stove there shrills
The cricket's song, in warmth increasing ever,
And seems to one in drowsiness half lost,
The grasshopper's among some grassy hills.

December 30, 1816

From *Endymion (Book 1)*[6]

A thing of beauty is a joy for ever:
Its loveliness increases; it will never
Pass into nothingness; but still will keep
A bower quiet for us, and a sleep
Full of sweet dreams, and health, and quiet breathing.   5
Therefore, on every morrow, are we wreathing
A flowery band to bind us to the earth,
Spite of despondence, of the inhuman dearth
Of noble natures, of the gloomy days,
Of all the unhealthy and o'er-darkened ways   10
Made for our searching: yes, in spite of all,
Some shape of beauty moves away the pall
From our dark spirits. Such the sun, the moon,
Trees old, and young sprouting a shady boon
For simple sheep; and such are daffodils   15
With the green world they live in; and clear rills
That for themselves a cooling covert make
'Gainst the hot season; the mid forest brake,[7]
Rich with a sprinkling of fair musk-rose blooms:
And such too is the grandeur of the dooms[8]   20
We have imagined for the mighty dead;
All lovely tales that we have heard or read:

---

6. Keats's long poem about the myth of a mortal (Endymion) loved by the goddess of the moon.
7. Thicket.   8. Judgments.

An endless fountain of immortal drink,
Pouring unto us from the heaven's brink.
25   Nor do we merely feel these essences
For one short hour; no, even as the trees
That whisper round a temple become soon
Dear as the temple's self, so does the moon,
The passion poesy, glories infinite,
30   Haunt us till they become a cheering light
Unto our souls, and bound to us so fast,
That, whether there be shine, or gloom o'ercast,
They always must be with us, or we die.

1817

Ode to a Nightingale

I

My heart aches, and a drowsy numbness pains
    My sense, as though of hemlock I had drunk,
Or emptied some dull opiate to the drains
    One minute past, and Lethe-wards⁹ had sunk:
5 'Tis not through envy of thy happy lot,
    But being too happy in thine happiness,
        That thou, light-wingéd Dryad¹ of the trees,
            In some melodious plot
Of beechen green, and shadows numberless,
10   Singest of summer in full-throated ease.

II

O, for a draught of vintage! that hath been
    Cooled a long age in the deep-delvéd earth,
Tasting of Flora² and the country green,
    Dance, and Provençal song,³ and sunburnt mirth!
15 O for a beaker full of the warm South,
    Full of the true, the blushful Hippocrene,⁴
        With beaded bubbles winking at the brim,
            And purple-stainéd mouth;
That I might drink, and leave the world unseen,
20   And with thee fade away into the forest dim:

III

Fade far away, dissolve, and quite forget
    What thou among the leaves hast never known,

9. Toward the river of forgetfulness (Lethe) in Hades.   1. Wood nymph.   2. Roman goddess of flowers.
3. The medieval troubadours of Provence were famous for their love songs.   4. The fountain of the
Muses on Mt. Helicon, whose waters bring poetic inspiration.

The weariness, the fever, and the fret
  Here, where men sit and hear each other groan;
Where palsy shakes a few, sad, last gray hairs,   25
    Where youth grows pale, and specter-thin, and dies;
      Where but to think is to be full of sorrow
        And leaden-eyed despairs,
    Where Beauty cannot keep her lustrous eyes,
      Or new Love pine at them beyond tomorrow.   30

IV

Away! away! for I will fly to thee,
  Not charioted by Bacchus and his pards,[5]
But on the viewless[6] wings of Poesy,
  Though the dull brain perplexes and retards:
Already with thee! tender is the night,   35
    And haply the Queen-Moon is on her throne,
      Clustered around by all her starry Fays;[7]
        But here there is no light,
Save what from heaven is with the breezes blown
    Through verdurous glooms and winding mossy ways.   40

V

I cannot see what flowers are at my feet,
  Nor what soft incense hangs upon the boughs,
But, in embalméd[8] darkness, guess each sweet
  Wherewith the seasonable month endows
The grass, the thicket, and the fruit-tree wild;   45
    White hawthorn, and the pastoral eglantine;[9]
      Fast fading violets covered up in leaves;
        And mid-May's eldest child,
The coming musk-rose, full of dewy wine,
    The murmurous haunt of flies on summer eves.   50

VI

Darkling[1] I listen; and, for many a time
  I have been half in love with easeful Death,
Called him soft names in many a muséd rhyme,
  To take into the air my quiet breath;
Now more than ever seems it rich to die,   55
    To cease upon the midnight with no pain,
      While thou art pouring forth thy soul abroad
        In such an ecstasy!
Still wouldst thou sing, and I have ears in vain—
    To thy high requiem become a sod.   60

5. The Roman god of wine was sometimes portrayed in a chariot drawn by leopards.
6. Invisible.   7. Fairies.   8. Fragrant, aromatic.   9. Sweetbriar or honeysuckle.   1. In the dark.

VII

Thou wast not born for death, immortal Bird!
  No hungry generations tread thee down;
The voice I hear this passing night was heard
  In ancient days by emperor and clown:
Perhaps the selfsame song that found a path
  Through the sad heart of Ruth,[2] when, sick for home,
    She stood in tears amid the alien corn;
      The same that ofttimes hath
Charmed magic casements, opening on the foam
    Of perilous seas, in faery lands forlorn.

VIII

Forlorn! the very word is like a bell
  To toll me back from thee to my sole self!
Adieu! the fancy cannot cheat so well
  As she is famed to do, deceiving elf.
Adieu! adieu! thy plaintive anthem fades
  Past the near meadows, over the still stream,
    Up the hillside; and now 'tis buried deep
      In the next valley-glades:
Was it a vision, or a waking dream?
    Fled is that music:—Do I wake or sleep?

May 1819

Ode on a Grecian Urn

I

Thou still unravished bride of quietness,
  Thou foster-child of silence and slow time,
Sylvan historian, who canst thus express
  A flowery tale more sweetly than our rhyme:
What leaf-fringed legend haunts about thy shape
  Of deities or mortals, or of both,
    In Tempe or the dales of Arcady?[3]
What men or gods are these? What maidens loath?
  What mad pursuit? What struggle to escape?
    What pipes and timbrels? What wild ecstasy?

---

2. A virtuous Moabite widow who, according to the Old Testament Book of Ruth, left her own country to accompany her mother-in-law, Naomi, back to Naomi's native land. She supported herself as a gleaner.
3. Arcadia. Tempe is a beautiful valley near Mt. Olympus in Greece, and the valley ("dales") of Arcadia a picturesque section of the Peloponnesus; both came to be associated with the pastoral ideal.

II

Heard melodies are sweet, but those unheard
  Are sweeter; therefore, ye soft pipes, play on;
Not to the sensual[4] ear, but, more endeared,
  Pipe to the spirit ditties of no tone:
Fair youth, beneath the trees, thou canst not leave   15
  Thy song, nor ever can those trees be bare;
    Bold Lover, never, never canst thou kiss,
Though winning near the goal—yet, do not grieve;
  She cannot fade, though thou hast not thy bliss,
    For ever wilt thou love, and she be fair!   20

III

Ah, happy, happy boughs! that cannot shed
  Your leaves, nor ever bid the Spring adieu;
And, happy melodist, unweariéd,
  For ever piping songs for ever new;
More happy love! more happy, happy love!   25
  For ever warm and still to be enjoyed,
    For ever panting, and for ever young;
All breathing human passion far above,
  That leaves a heart high-sorrowful and cloyed,
    A burning forehead, and a parching tongue.   30

IV

Who are these coming to the sacrifice?
  To what green altar, O mysterious priest,
Lead'st thou that heifer lowing at the skies,
  And all her silken flanks with garlands dressed?
What little town by river or sea shore,   35
  Or mountain-built with peaceful citadel,
    Is emptied of this folk, this pious morn?
And, little town, thy streets for evermore
  Will silent be; and not a soul to tell
    Why thou art desolate, can e'er return.   40

V

O Attic shape! Fair attitude! with brede[5]
  Of marble men and maidens overwrought,[6]
With forest branches and the trodden weed;
  Thou, silent form, dost tease us out of thought
As doth eternity: Cold Pastoral!   45
  When old age shall this generation waste,
    Thou shalt remain, in midst of other woe
Than ours, a friend to man, to whom thou say'st,

---

4. Of the senses, as distinguished from the "ear" of the spirit or imagination.   5. Woven pattern. *Attic:* Attica was the district of ancient Greece surrounding Athens.   6. Ornamented all over.

Beauty is truth, truth beauty[7]—that is all
50   Ye know on earth, and all ye need to know.

May 1819

To Autumn

I

Season of mists and mellow fruitfulness,
    Close bosom-friend of the maturing sun;
Conspiring with him how to load and bless
    With fruit the vines that round the thatch-eves run;
5 To bend with apples the mossed cottage-trees,
    And fill all fruit with ripeness to the core;
        To swell the gourd, and plump the hazel shells
With a sweet kernel; to set budding more,
    And still more, later flowers for the bees,
10   Until they think warm days will never cease,
        For Summer has o'er-brimmed their clammy cells.

II

Who hath not seen thee oft amid thy store?
    Sometimes whoever seeks abroad may find
Thee sitting careless on a granary floor,
15   Thy hair soft-lifted by the winnowing wind;[8]
Or on a half-reaped furrow sound asleep,
    Drowsed with the fume of poppies, while thy hook[9]
        Spares the next swath and all its twinèd flowers:
And sometimes like a gleaner thou dost keep
20   Steady thy laden head across a brook;
    Or by a cider-press, with patient look,
        Thou watchest the last oozings hours by hours.

III

Where are the songs of Spring? Ay, where are they?
    Think not of them, thou hast thy music too—
25 While barrèd clouds bloom the soft-dying day,
    And touch the stubble-plains with rosy hue;
Then in a wailful choir the small gnats mourn
    Among the river sallows, borne aloft
        Or sinking as the light wind lives or dies;

7. In some texts of the poem "Beauty is truth, truth beauty" is in quotation marks and in some texts it is not, leading to critical disagreements about whether the last line and a half are also inscribed on the urn or spoken by the poet.   8. Which sifts the grain from the chaff.   9. Scythe or sickle.

And full-grown lambs loud bleat from hilly bourn;[1]   30
Hedge-crickets sing; and now with treble soft
The red-breast whistles from a garden-croft;[2]
And gathering swallows twitter in the skies.

September 19, 1819

PASSAGES FROM LETTERS AND THE PREFACE TO *ENDYMION*

From *Letter to Benjamin Bailey, November 22, 1817*[1]

. . . I am certain of nothing but of the holiness of the Heart's affections and the truth of Imagination—What the imagination seizes as Beauty must be truth—whether it existed before or not—for I have the same Idea of all our Passions as of Love they are all in their sublime, creative of essential Beauty. . . . The Imagination may be compared to Adam's dream[2]—he awoke and found it truth. I am the more zealous in this affair, because I have never yet been able to perceive how any thing can be known for truth by consequitive reasoning—and yet it must be—Can it be that even the greatest Philosopher ever ~~when~~ arrived at his goal without putting aside numerous objections—However it may be, O for a Life of Sensations rather than of Thoughts! It is "a Vision in the form of Youth" a Shadow of reality to come—and this consideration has further conv[i]nced me for it has come as auxiliary to another favorite Speculation of mine, that we shall enjoy ourselves here after by having what we called happiness on Earth repeated in a finer tone and so repeated—And yet such a fate can only befall those who delight in sensation rather than hunger as you do after Truth—Adam's dream will do here and seems to be a conviction that Imagination and its empyreal reflection is the same as human Life and its spiritual repetition. But as I was saying—the simple imaginative Mind may have its rewards in the repeti[ti]on of its own silent Working coming continually on the spirit with a fine suddenness—to compare great things with small—have you never by being surprised with an old Melody—in a delicious place—by a delicious voice, fe[l]t over again your very speculations and surmises at the time it first operated on your soul—do you not remember forming to yourself the singer's face more beautiful that [*for* than] it was possible and yet with the elevation of the Moment you did not think so—even then you were mounted on the Wings of Imagination so high—that the Prototype must be here after—that delicious face you will see—What a time! I am continually running away from the subject—sure this cannot be exactly the case with a complex Mind—one that is imaginative and at the same time careful of its fruits—who

---

1. Domain.   2. An enclosed garden near a house.   1. Keats's private letters, often carelessly written, are reprinted uncorrected.   2. In *Paradise Lost* 7.460–90.

would exist partly on sensation partly on thought—to whom it is necessary that years should bring the philosophic Mind—such an one I consider your's and therefore it is necessary to your eternal Happiness that you not only ~~have~~ drink this old Wine of Heaven which I shall call the redigestion of our most ethereal Musings on Earth; but also increase in knowledge and know all things. . . .

From *Letter to George and Thomas Keats, December 21, 1817*

. . . I spent Friday evening with Wells[3] & went the next morning to see *Death on the Pale horse.*[4] It is a wonderful picture, when West's age is considered; But there

George Keats

Thomas Keats

is nothing to be intense upon; no women one feels mad to kiss, no face swelling into reality. the excellence of every Art is its intensity, capable of making all disagreeables evaporate, from their being in close relationship with Beauty & Truth— Examine King Lear & you will find this exemplified throughout; but in this picture we have unpleasantness without any momentous depth of speculation excited, in which to bury its repulsiveness—The picture is larger than Christ rejected—I dined with Haydon the sunday after you left, & had a very pleasant day, I dined too (for I have been out too much lately) with Horace Smith & met his two Brothers with Hill & Kingston & one Du Bois,[5] they only served to convince me, how superior humour is to wit in respect to enjoyment—These men say things which make one start, without making one feel, they are all alike; their manners are alike; they all know fashionables; they have a mannerism in their very eating & drinking, in their mere handling a Decanter—They talked of Kean[6] & his low company—Would I were with that company instead of yours said I to myself! I know such like acquaintance will never do for me & yet I am going to Reynolds, on wednesday—Brown & Dilke walked with me & back from the Christmas pantomime. I had not a dispute but a disquisition

3. Charles Wells (1800–1879), an author.   4. By Benjamin West (1738–1820), American painter and president of the Royal Academy; *Christ Rejected* (mentioned below) is also by West.   5. Thomas Hill (1760–1840), a book collector, and Edward duBois (1774–1850), a journalist.   6. Edmund Kean (1789– 1833), a famous Shakespearean actor.

with Dilke, on various subjects; several things dovetailed in my mind, & at once it struck me, what quality went to form a Man of Achievement especially in Literature & which Shakespeare posessed so enormously—I mean *Negative Capability*, that is when man is capable of being in uncertainties, Mysteries, doubts, without any irritable reaching after fact & reason—Coleridge, for instance, would let go by a fine isolated verisimilitude caught from the Penetralium of mystery, from being incapable of remaining content with half knowledge. This pursued through Volumes would perhaps take us no further than this, that with a great poet the sense of Beauty overcomes every other consideration, or rather obliterates all consideration.

Letter to John Hamilton Reynolds, February 19, 1818

I have an idea that a Man might pass a very pleasant life in this manner—let him on any certain day read a certain Page of full Poesy or distilled Prose and let him wander with it, and muse upon it, and reflect from it, and bring home to it, and prophesy upon it, and dream upon it—untill it becomes stale— but when will it do so? Never—When Man has arrived at a certain ripeness in intellect any one grand and spiritual passage serves him as a starting post towards all "the two-and-thirty Pallaces"[7] How happy is such a "voyage of conception," what delicious diligent Indolence! A doze upon a Sofa does not hinder it, and a nap upon Clover engenders ethereal finger-pointings —the prattle of a child gives it wings, and the converse of middle age a strength to beat them—a strain of musick conducts to "an odd angle of the Isle",[8] and when the leaves whisper it puts a "girdle round the earth",[9] Nor will this sparing touch of noble Books be any irreverance to their

John Hamilton Reynolds

Writers—for perhaps the honors paid by Man to Man are trifles in comparison to the Benefit done by great Works to the "Spirit and pulse of good" by their mere passive existence. Memory should not be called knowledge—Many have original minds who do not think it—they are led away by Custom—Now it appears to me that almost any Man may like the Spider spin from his own inwards his own airy Citadel—the points of leaves and twigs on which the Spider begins her work are few and she fills the Air with a beautiful circuiting: man should be content with as few points to tip with the fine Webb of his Soul and weave a tapestry empyr-

---

7. "Places of delight" in Buddhism.   8. *The Tempest* 2.2.224.   9. *A Midsummer Night's Dream* 2.1.175–76: "I'll put a girdle round about the earth / In forty minutes."

ean—full of Symbols for his spiritual eye, of softness for his spiritual touch, of space for his wandering of distinctness for his Luxury—But the Minds of Mortals are so different and bent on such diverse Journeys that it may at first appear impossible for any common taste and fellowship to exist bettween between two or three under these suppositions—It is however quite the contrary—Minds would leave each other in contrary directions, traverse each other in Numberless points, and all [*for* at] last greet each other at the Journeys end—An old Man and a child would talk together and the old Man be led on his Path, and the child left thinking—Man should not dispute or assert but whisper results to his neighbor, and thus by every germ of Spirit sucking the Sap from mould ethereal every human might become great, and Humanity instead of being a wide heath of Furse[1] and Briars with here and there a remote Oak or Pine, would become a grand democracy of Forest Trees. It has been an old Comparison for our urging on—the Bee hive—however it seems to me that we should rather be the flower than the Bee—for it is a false notion that more is gained by receiving than giving —no, the receiver and the giver are equal in their benefits—The f[l]ower I doubt not receives a fair guerdon from the Bee—its leaves blush deeper in the next spring —and who shall say between Man and Woman which is the most delighted? Now it is more noble to sit like Jove that [*for* than] to fly like Mercury—let us not therefore go hurrying about and collecting honey bee like, buzzing here and there impatiently from a knowledge of what is to be arrived at; but let us open our leaves like a flower and be passive and receptive—budding patiently under the eye of Apollo and taking hints from every noble insect that favors us with a visit— sap will be given us for Meat and dew for drink—I was led into these thoughts, my dear Reynolds, by the beauty of the morning operating on a sense of Idleness —I have not read any Books—the Morning said I was right—I had no Idea but of the Morning, and the Thrush said I was right—seeming to say—

> O thou whose face hath felt the Winter's wind,
> Whose eye has seen the snow-clouds hung in mist,
> And the black elm tops 'mong the freezing stars,
> To thee the spring will be a harvest-time.
> O thou, whose only book has been the light
> Of supreme darkness which thou feddest on
> Night after night when Phœbus was away,
> To thee the spring shall be a triple morn.
> O fret not after knowledge—I have none,
> And yet my song comes native with the warmth.
> O fret not after knowledge—I have none,
> And yet the Evening listens. He who saddens
> At thought of idleness cannot be idle,
> And he's awake who thinks himself asleep.

Now I am sensible all this is a mere sophistication, however it may neighbor to any truths, to excuse my own indolence—so I will not deceive myself that Man

---

1. *The Tempest* 1.1.58–59.

should be equal with jove—but think himself very well off as a sort of scullion-Mercury, or even a humble Bee—It is not [*for* no] matter whether I am right or wrong either one way or another, if there is sufficient to lift a little time from your Shoulders.

From *Letter to John Taylor, February 27, 1818*

. . . It is a sorry thing for me that any one should have to overcome Prejudices in reading my Verses—that affects me more than any hyper-criticism on any particular Passage. In *Endymion* I have most likely but moved into the Go-cart from the leading strings. In Poetry I have a few Axioms, and you will see how far I am from their Centre. 1st I think Poetry should surprise by a fine excess and not by Singularity—it should strike the Reader as a wording of his own highest thoughts, and appear almost a Remembrance—2nd Its touches of Beauty should never be half way therby making the reader breathless instead of content: the rise, the progress, the setting of imagery should like the Sun come natural natural too him—shine over him and set soberly although in magnificence leaving him in the Luxury of twilight—but it is easier to think what Poetry should be than to write it—and this leads me on to another axiom. That if Poetry comes not as naturally as the Leaves to a tree it had better not come at all. However it may be with me I cannot help looking into new countries with "O for a Muse of fire to ascend!"[2]—If Endymion serves me as a Pioneer perhaps I ought to be content. I have great reason to be content, for thank God I can read and perhaps understand Shakspeare to his depths, and I have I am sure many friends, who, if I fail, will attribute any change in my Life and Temper to Humbleness rather than to Pride—to a cowering under the Wings of great Poets rather than to a Bitterness that I am not appreciated. I am anxious to get Endymion printed that I may forget it and proceed. . . .

From *the Preface to* Endymion, *dated April 10, 1818*

The imagination of a boy is healthy, and the mature imagination of a man is healthy; but there is a space of life between, in which the soul is in a ferment, the character undecided, the way of life uncertain, the ambition thick-sighted: thence proceeds mawkishness, and all the thousand bitters which those men I speak of must necessarily taste in going over the following pages.

I hope I have not in too late a day touched the beautiful mythology of Greece, and dulled its brightness: for I wish to try once more, before I bid it farewell.

---

2. *Henry V* Prologue 1: "O for a muse of fire, that would ascend."

CHRONOLOGY

1795 John Keats born October 31 at Finsbury, just north of London, the eldest child of Thomas and Frances Jennings Keats. Thomas Keats was head ostler at a livery stable.

1797–1803 Birth of three brothers and sisters: George in 1797, Thomas in 1799, Frances Mary (Fanny) in 1803.

1803 With George, begins school in Enfield.

1804 Father killed by a fall from his horse, April 15. On June 27 his mother remarries, and the children go to live with their maternal grandparents at Enfield. The grandfather dies a year later, and the children move with their grandmother to Lower Edmonton.

1809 Begins a literary friendship with Charles Cowden Clarke, the son of the headmaster at the Enfield school, and develops a strong interest in reading.

1810 Mother dies of tuberculosis, after a long illness.

1811 Leaves school to become apprenticed to an apothecary-surgeon in Edmonton; completes a prose translation of the *Aeneid,* begun at school.

1814 Earliest known attempts at writing verse. In December his grandmother dies, and the family home is broken up.

1815 In October moves to next stage of his medical training at Guy's Hospital, south of the Thames in London.

1816 On May 5 his first published poem, "O Solitude," appears in Leigh Hunt's *Examiner.* In October writes "On First Looking into Chapman's Homer," published in December. Meets Hunt, Benjamin Haydon, John Hamilton Reynolds, and Shelley. By the spring of 1817, gives up the idea of medical practice.

1817 In March, moves with brothers to Hampstead, sees the Elgin Marbles with Haydon, and publishes his first collection, *Poems.* Composes *Endymion* between April and November. Reads Milton, Shakespeare, and Coleridge and rereads Wordsworth during the year.

1818 *Endymion* published in April, unfavorably reviewed in September, defended by Reynolds in October. During the summer goes on walking tour of the Lake Country and Scotland, but returns to London in mid-August with a sore throat and severe chills. His brother Tom is also seriously ill by late summer, dying on December 1. In September, Keats first meets Fanny Brawne (eighteen years old), with whom he arrives at an "understanding" by Christmas.

1819 Writes *The Eve of St. Agnes* in January, revises it in September. In April Fanny Brawne and her mother move into the other half of the double house in which Keats lives. During April and May writes "La Belle Dame sans Merci" and all the major odes except "To Autumn," written in September. Rental arrangements force separation from Fanny Brawne during the summer (Keats on Isle of Wight from June to August), and in the fall he tries to break his dependence on her, but they become engaged by Christmas. Earlier in December suffers a recurrence of his sore throat.

1820 In February has a severe hemorrhage and in June an attack of blood-spitting. In July his doctor orders him to Italy for the winter; he sails in September and finally arrives in Rome on November 15. In July a volume of poems published, *Lamia, Isabella, The Eve of St. Agnes and Other Poems.* Fanny Brawne nurses him through the late summer.

1821 Dies at 11 P.M., February 23. Buried in the English Cemetery at Rome.

QUESTIONS

1. Once you have read at least half a dozen poems by Keats, list the ideas that you have found in more than one poem. Also list any distinctive stylistic features you have noticed. What kinds of experiences or events does he tend to write about? Does he follow any pattern in his use of speaker? Does he have favorite words that he uses in a particular way? What about metaphors? What are his habits in putting poems together? Which poems make you want to know more about the author and his experiences before you try to interpret them?

2. What stanza forms does Keats seem to like? How do you explain his fondness for repeated rhymes? What kinds of tonal effects are produced by the rhyme-rich sound patterns of the poems? What effect on meaning does the emphasis on rhyme have?

3. What kinds of images dominate Keats's poems? What kinds of settings? Do Keats's poems tend to have a distinctive, describable speaker? What tones are characteristic of Keats?

WRITING SUGGESTION

Pick out one poem that seems "typical" in that it uses many of the strategies found in other poems by Keats and displays themes that seem central to his work. Write a detailed paper (of eight to ten pages) in which you analyze the poem, showing in exactly what ways it is typical of Keats's work. Be sure to cite specific passages in other poems (as well as details from the main poem you are writing about) to prove your points.

21

THE AUTHOR'S WORK IN CONTEXT: ADRIENNE RICH

The poet featured in this chapter, Adrienne Rich, has had a long and very distinguished career. Many readers and critics regard her as the best poet writing today. And a careful reader of her work will find similarities of interest, strategy, and taste from her earliest poems—published shortly after World War II, in 1951—to her newest ones. A distinctive mind and orientation are at work in all her poems; we can speak about characteristic features in Rich's poetry just as surely as we do about characteristic features in Keats's work even though she has already written many more poems over a much longer period of years. Throughout her career, Rich has, for example, steadfastly remained interested in social and political issues and has often concentrated on themes relating to women's consciousness and the societal roles of women. She has always conceived her poems with a powerful sense of functional structure and cast them in lyric modes that sensitively reflect their moods and tones. And her poetic voice has always been firm and clear, setting out images vividly and taking a stand in matters of conscience. But over the years the voice has changed quite a lot, too, and Rich's views on a number of issues have

The fear of poetry is an indication that we are cut off from our own reality.

—MURIEL RUKEYSER

modified and developed. Many of the changes in Rich's ideas and attitudes reflect changing concerns among American intellectuals (especially women) in the second half of the twentieth century, and her poems represent both changed social conditions and sharply altered social, political, and philosophical attitudes. But they also reflect altered personal circumstances and changes in lifestyle and expressions of sexual preference. Rich married in her early twenties and had three children by the time she was thirty; many of her early poems are about heterosexual love, and some of them are quite explicitly about sex (see, for example, "Two Songs," chapter 15). More recently, she has been involved in a long-term lesbian relationship and has written, again quite explicitly, about sex between women (see, for example, "My mouth hovers across your breasts," this chapter). In her poems, not only can we trace the contours of her evolving personal and political life and commitments, but (even more important for the study of poetry generally) we can see how changes *within* the poet and *in her social and cultural context* alter the themes and directions of her work and even change the formal nature of what she does.

One way to study Rich as an "author in context" is to read carefully what she says about herself and her poems: she is unusually straightforward, explicit, and articulate, and to read her describing her own development is to be guided carefully through her changing ideas about what is important both to the individual subjective consciousness and to societal attitudes and changing roles. Gathered at the end of this chapter are excerpts from Rich's writing about herself and about poetry more generally, and you can use these self-conscious reflections as a kind of commentary on the poems included here and elsewhere in the book. (Consult the Index of Authors for Rich poems in other chapters.) You can (1) read the commentary, then the poems; (2) read the poems, then the commentary; or (3) read the poems and commentary intermixed, in chronological order.

Adrienne Rich circa 1970

An even better way to study Adrienne Rich is to go to the library and read all (or as much as you can find) of her writing and consider in detail how the various texts interact. Most poets—even John Keats, who lived only to age twenty-five—change a lot during their careers, and many of the changes correspond to larger social and cultural changes in their own times and nations. Reading as much as possible of a poet's work (along with that of relevant contemporaries) and watching the poet develop within various traditions and contexts can lead to a relatively balanced assessment of a particular career and also to a more exact assessment of what poetry is about in a particular time, era, or culture.

Studying Rich's career in context suggests a number of larger literary, cultural, and historical issues—the kinds of issues we will explore more fully in the next two chapters. You might want to think about Adrienne Rich again after you have read those chapters—especially the "Constructing Identity, Exploring Gender" section of chapter 23.

At a Bach Concert

Coming by evening through the wintry city
We said that art is out of love with life.
Here we approach a love that is not pity.

This antique discipline, tenderly severe,
Renews belief in love yet masters feeling,   5
Asking of us a grace in what we bear.

Form is the ultimate gift that love can offer—
The vital union of necessity
With all that we desire, all that we suffer.

A too-compassionate art is half an art.   10
Only such proud restraining purity
Restores the else-betrayed, too-human heart.   1951

Storm Warnings

The glass has been falling all the afternoon,
And knowing better than the instrument
What winds are walking overhead, what zone
Of gray unrest is moving across the land,
5   I leave the book upon a pillowed chair
And walk from window to closed window, watching
Boughs strain against the sky

And think again, as often when the air
Moves inward toward a silent core of waiting,
10   How with a single purpose time has traveled
By secret currents of the undiscerned
Into this polar realm. Weather abroad
And weather in the heart alike come on
Regardless of prediction.

15   Between foreseeing and averting change
Lies all the mastery of elements
Which clocks and weatherglasses cannot alter.
Time in the hand is not control of time,
Nor shattered fragments of an instrument
20   A proof against the wind; the wind will rise,
We can only close the shutters.

I draw the curtains as the sky goes black
And set a match to candles sheathed in glass
Against the keyhole draught, the insistent whine
25   Of weather through the unsealed aperture.
This is our sole defense against the season;
These are the things that we have learned to do
Who live in troubled regions.   1951

Snapshots of a Daughter-in-Law

1

You, once a belle in Shreveport,
with henna-colored hair, skin like a peachbud,
still have your dresses copied from that time,
and play a Chopin prelude
5   called by Cortot: *"Delicious recollections*
float like perfume through the memory."

Your mind now, mouldering like wedding-cake,
heavy with useless experience, rich
with suspicion, rumor, fantasy,
10   crumbling to pieces under the knife-edge
of mere fact. In the prime of your life.

Nervy, glowering, your daughter
wipes the teaspoons, grows another way.

2

Banging the coffee-pot into the sink
she hears the angels chiding, and looks out   15
past the raked gardens to the sloppy sky.
Only a week since They said: *Have no patience.*

The next time it was: *Be insatiable.*
Then: *Save yourself; others you cannot save.*[1]
Sometimes she's let the tapstream scald her arm,   20
a match burn to her thumbnail,

or held her hand above the kettle's snout
right in the woolly steam. They are probably angels,
since nothing hurts her any more, except
each morning's grit blowing into her eyes.   25

3

A thinking woman sleeps with monsters.
The beak that grips her, she becomes. And Nature,
that sprung-lidded, still commodious
steamer-trunk of *tempora* and *mores*[2]
gets stuffed with it all: the mildewed orange-flowers,   30
the female pills, the terrible breasts
of Boadicea[3] beneath flat foxes' heads and orchids.

Two handsome women, gripped in argument,
each proud, acute, subtle, I hear scream
across the cut glass and majolica   35
like Furies[4] cornered from their prey:
The argument *ad feminam,*[5] all the old knives
that have rusted in my back, I drive in yours,
ma semblable, ma soeur![6]

4

Knowing themselves too well in one another: 40
their gifts no pure fruition, but a thorn,
the prick filed sharp against a hint of scorn . . .

1. According to Matthew 27.42, the chief priests, scribes, and elders mocked the crucified Jesus by saying, "He saved others; himself he cannot save."   2. Times and customs.   3. Queen of the ancient Britons. When her husband died, the Romans seized the territory he ruled and scourged Boadicea; she then led a heroic but ultimately unsuccessful revolt. *Female pills:* patent medicines for "female trouble."   4. In Roman mythology, the three sisters were the avenging spirits of retributive justice.   5. To the woman (Latin). The *argumentum ad hominem* (literally, argument to the man) is (in logic) an argument aimed at a person's individual prejudices or special interests.   6. My mirror-image (or "double"), my sister. Baudelaire, in the prefatory poem to *Les Fleurs du Mal,* addresses (and attacks) his "hypocrite reader" as "mon semblable, mon frère" (my double, my brother).

Reading while waiting
for the iron to heat,
45   writing, *My Life had stood—a Loaded Gun—*[7]
in that Amherst pantry while the jellies boil and scum,
or, more often,
iron-eyed and beaked and purposed as a bird,
dusting everything on the whatnot every day of life.

5

50   *Dulce ridens, dulce loquens,*[8]
she shaves her legs until they gleam
like petrified mammoth-tusk.

6

When to her lute Corinna sings[9]
neither words nor music are her own;
55   only the long hair dipping
over her cheek, only the song
of silk against her knees
and these
adjusted in reflections of an eye.

60   Poised, trembling and unsatisfied, before
an unlocked door, that cage of cages,
tell us, you bird, you tragical machine—
is this *fertilisante douleur?*[1] Pinned down
by love, for you the only natural action,
65   are you edged more keen
to prise the secrets of the vault? has Nature shown
her household books to you, daughter-in-law,
that her sons never saw?

7

"To have in this uncertain world some stay
70   *which cannot be undermined, is*
of the utmost consequence."[2]
                              Thus wrote
a woman, partly brave and partly good,
who fought with what she partly understood.
75   Few men about her would or could do more,
hence she was labeled harpy, shrew and whore.

---

7. "My Life had stood—a Loaded Gun—" [Poem No. 754], Emily Dickinson, *Complete Poems,* ed. T. H. Johnson, 1960, p. 369. [Rich's note]. See chapter 19.   8. Sweet (or "winsome") laughter, sweet chatter. The phrase (slightly modified here) concludes Horace's *Ode* 1.22, describing the appeal of a mistress. 9. The opening line of a lyric by Thomas Campion (1567–1620). See chapter 16.   1. Enriching pain (French).   2. ". . . is of the utmost consequence," from Mary Wollstonecraft, *Thoughts on the Education of Daughters,* London, 1787 [Rich's note].

8

"You all die at fifteen," said Diderot,[3]
and turn part legend, part convention.
Still, eyes inaccurately dream
behind closed windows blankening with steam.   80
Deliciously, all that we might have been,
all that we were—fire, tears,
wit, taste, martyred ambition—
stirs like the memory of refused adultery
the drained and flagging bosom of our middle years.   85

9

Not that it is done well, but
that it is done at all?[4] Yes, think
of the odds! or shrug them off forever.
This luxury of the precocious child,
Time's precious chronic invalid,—   90
would we, darlings, resign it if we could?
Our blight has been our sinecure:
mere talent was enough for us—
glitter in fragments and rough drafts.

Sigh no more, ladies.   95
                    Time is male
and in his cups drinks to the fair.
Bemused by gallantry, we hear
our mediocrities over-praised,
indolence read as abnegation,   100
slattern thought styled intuition,
every lapse forgiven, our crime
only to cast too bold a shadow
or smash the mould straight off.

For that, solitary confinement,   105
tear gas, attrition shelling.
Few applicants for that honor.

10

                    Well,
she's long about her coming, who must be

3. "Vous mourez toutes a quinze ans," from the *Lettres à Sophie Volland,* quoted by Simone de Beauvoir in *Le Deuxième Sexe,* vol. II, pp. 123–4 [Rich's note]. Editor of the *Encyclopédie* (the central document of the French Enlightenment), Denis Diderot (1713–1784) became disillusioned with the traditional education of women and undertook an experimental education for his own daughter.   4. Samuel Johnson's comment on women preachers: "Sir, a woman's preaching is like a dog's walking on his hinder legs. It is not done well, but you are surprised to find it done at all" (Boswell's *Life of Johnson,* ed. L. F. Powell and G. B. Hill [Oxford: Clarendon, 1934–64], 1.463).

110   more merciless to herself than history.[5]
      Her mind full to the wind, I see her plunge
      breasted and glancing through the currents,
      taking the light upon her
      at least as beautiful as any boy
115   or helicopter,
                        poised, still coming,
      her fine blades making the air wince

      but her cargo
      no promise then:
120   delivered
      palpable
      ours.

      1958–1960

In her 1972 essay *When We Dead Awaken,* Rich describes her consciousness during
the time she was writing this poem:

> Over two years I wrote a 10-part poem called "Snapshots of a Daughter-in-Law," in a
> longer, looser mode than I've ever trusted myself with before. It was an extraordinary relief
> to write that poem. It strikes me now as too literary, too dependent on allusion; I hadn't
> found the courage yet to do without authorities, or even to use the pronoun "I"—the
> woman in the poem is always "she." One section of it, #2, concerns a woman who thinks
> she is going mad; she is haunted by voices telling her to resist and rebel, voices which
> she can hear but not obey.

Planetarium

> (*Thinking of Caroline Herschel, 1750–1848, astronomer, sister of
> William; and others*)

      A woman in the shape of a monster
      a monster in the shape of a woman
      the skies are full of them

      a woman   "in the snow
5   among the Clocks and instruments
      or measuring the ground with poles"

      in her 98 years to discover
      8 comets

5. Cf. *Le Deuxième Sexe,* vol. II, p. 574: ". . . elle arrive du fond des ages, de Thèbes, de Minos, de Chichen
Itza; et elle est aussi le totem planté au coeur de la brousse africaine; c'est un helicoptère et c'est un oiseau;
et voilà la plus grande merveille: sous ses cheveux peints le bruissement des feuillages devient une pensée
et des paroles s'échappent de ses seins" [Rich's note].

she whom the moon ruled
like us   10
levitating into the night sky
riding the polished lenses

Galaxies of women, there
doing penance for impetuousness
ribs chilled   15
in those spaces   of the mind

An eye,
          "virile, precise and absolutely certain"
          from the mad webs of Uranisborg[6]
                                    encountering the NOVA   20
every impulse of light exploding
from the core
as life flies out of us

          Tycho whispering at last
          "Let me not seem to have lived in vain"   25

What we see, we see
and seeing is changing

the light that shrivels a mountain
and leaves a man alive

Heartbeat of the pulsar   30
heart sweating through my body

The radio impulse
pouring in from Taurus
          I am bombarded yet   I stand

I have been standing all my life in the   35
direct path of a battery of signals
the most accurately transmitted most
untranslatable language in the universe
I am a galactic cloud so deep   so invo-
luted that a light wave could take 15   40
years to travel through me   And has
taken   I am an instrument in the shape
of a woman trying to translate pulsations
into images   for the relief of the body
and the reconstruction of the mind.   45

1968

6. Actually Uraniborg, the elaborate palace-laboratory-observatory of Danish astronomer Tycho Brahe (1546–1601), whose cosmology tried to fuse the Ptolemaic and Copernican systems. Brahe discovered and described (in *De Nova Stella*, 1573) a new star in what had previously been considered a fixed-star system.

For the Record

The clouds and the stars didn't wage this war
the brooks gave no information
if the mountain spewed stones of fire into the river
it was not taking sides
5   the raindrop faintly swaying under the leaf
had no political opinions

and if here or there a house
filled with backed-up raw sewage
or poisoned those who lived there
10 with slow fumes, over years
the houses were not at war
nor did the tinned-up buildings

intend to refuse shelter
to homeless old women and roaming children
15 they had no policy to keep them roaming
or dying, no, the cities were not the problem
the bridges were non-partisan
the freeways burned, but not with hatred

Even the miles of barbed-wire
20 stretched around crouching temporary huts
designed to keep the unwanted
at a safe distance, out of sight
even the boards that had to absorb
year upon year, so many human sounds

25 so many depths of vomit, tears
slow-soaking blood
had not offered themselves for this
The trees didn't volunteer to be cut into boards
nor the thorns for tearing flesh
30 Look around at all of it

and ask whose signature
is stamped on the orders, traced
in the corner of the building plans
Ask where the illiterate, big-bellied
35 women were, the drunks and crazies,
the ones you fear most of all: ask where you were.   1983

[My mouth hovers across your breasts][7]

My mouth hovers across your breasts
in the short grey winter afternoon

---

7. This is poem three in Rich's series "Tracking Poems."

in this bed   we are delicate
and tough   so hot with joy we amaze ourselves
tough   and delicate   we play rings   5
around each other   our daytime candle burns
with its peculiar light   and if the snow
begins to fall outside   filling the branches
and if the night falls   without announcement
these are the pleasures of winter   10
sudden, wild and delicate   your fingers
exact   my tongue exact at the same moment
stopping to laugh at a joke
my love   hot on your scent   on the cusp of winter   1986

History[8]

Should I simplify my life for you?
Don't ask how I began to love men.
Don't ask how I began to love women.
Remember the forties songs, the slowdance numbers
the small sex-filled gas-rationed Chevrolet?   5
Remember walking in the snow and who was gay?
Cigarette smoke of the movies, silver-and-gray
profiles, dreaming the dreams of he-and-she
breathing the dissolution of the wisping silver plume?
Dreaming that dream we leaned applying lipstick   10
by the gravestone's mirror when we found ourselves
playing in the cemetery. In Current Events she said
the war in Europe is over, the Allies
and she wore no lipstick have won the war
and we raced screaming out of Sixth Period.   15

Dreaming that dream
we had to maze our ways through a wood
where lips were knives breasts razors and I hid
in the cage of my mind scribbling
this map stops where it all begins   20
into a red-and-black notebook.
Remember after the war when peace came down
as plenty for some and they said we were saved
in an eternal present and we knew the world could end?
—remember after the war when peace rained down   25
on the winds from Hiroshima Nagasaki Utah Nevada?[9]
and the socialist queer Christian teacher jumps from the hotel window?
and L.G. saying *I want to sleep with you but not for sex*
and the red-and-black enamelled coffee-pot dripped slow through the
dark grounds
—appetite terror power tenderness   30

8. This is poem four in Rich's series "Inscriptions."   9. Sites of atomic-bomb explosions, the first two in Japan near the end of World War II, the last two at test sites in the desert.

the long kiss in the stairwell the switch thrown
on two Jewish Communists[1] married to each other
the definitive crunch of glass at the end of the wedding?
(When shall we learn, what should be clear as day,
35   *We cannot choose what we are free to love?)*

1995

Modotti[2]

Your footprints of light on sensitive paper
that typewriter you made famous
my footsteps following you up stairwells of scarred oak and shredded newsprint
5   these windowpanes smeared with stifled breaths
corridors of tile and jaundiced plaster
if this is where I must look for you
then this is where I'll find you

From a streetlamp's wet lozenge bent
10   on a curb plastered with newsprint
the headlines aiming straight at your eyes
to a room's dark breath-smeared light
these footsteps I'm following you with
down tiles of a red corridor
15   if this is a way to find you
of course this is how I'll find you

Your negatives pegged to dry in a darkroom
rigged up over a bathtub's lozenge
your footprints of light on sensitive paper
20   stacked curling under blackened panes
the always upstairs of your hideout
the stern exposure of your brows
—these footsteps I'm following you with
aren't to arrest you

25   The bristling hairs of your eyeflash
that typewriter you made famous
your enormous will to arrest and frame
what was, what is, still liquid, flowing
your exposure of manifestos, your

1. Julius and Ethel Rosenberg, executed as spies by the United States in 1953.   2. Tina Modotti (1896–1942): photographer, political activist, revolutionary. Her most significant artistic work was done in Mexico in the 1920s, including a study of the typewriter belonging to her lover, the Cuban revolutionary Julio Antonio Mella. Framed for his murder by the fascists in 1929, she was expelled from Mexico in 1930. After some years of political activity in Berlin, the Soviet Union, and Spain, she returned incognito to Mexico, where she died in 1942.

In my search for Modotti I had to follow clues she left; I did not want to iconize her but to imagine critically the traps and opportunities of her life and choices [Rich's note].

lightbulb in a scarred ceiling   30
well if this is how I find you
Modotti so I find you

In the red wash of your darkroom
from your neighborhood of volcanoes
to the geranium nailed in a can   35
on the wall of your upstairs hideout
in the rush of breath a window
of revolution allowed you
on this jaundiced stair in this huge lashed eye

                                        these   40
footsteps I'm following you with

1996   1999

PERSONAL REFLECTIONS

From *When We Dead Awaken: Writing as Re-Vision*[1]

Most, if not all, human lives are full of fantasy—passive daydreaming which need not be acted on. But to write poetry or fiction, or even to think well, is not to fantasize, or to put fantasies on paper. For a poem to coalesce, for a character or an action to take shape, there has to be an imaginative transformation of reality which is in no way passive. And a certain freedom of the mind is needed—freedom to press on, to enter the currents of your thought like a glider pilot, knowing that your motion can be sustained, that the buoyancy of your attention will not be suddenly snatched away. Moreover, if the imagination is to transcend and transform experience it has to question, to challenge, to conceive of alternatives, perhaps to the very life you are living at that moment. You have to be free to play around with the notion that day might be night, love might be hate, nothing can be too sacred for the

Adrienne Rich in 1978

1. First published in *College English* in 1972; this version, slightly revised, is included in *On Lies, Secrets, and Silence: Selected Prose: 1966–1978* (1979).

imagination to turn into its opposite or to call experimentally by another name. For writing is re-naming. Now, to be maternally with small children all day in the old way, to be with a man in the old way of marriage, requires a holding-back, a putting-aside of that imaginative activity, and demands instead a kind of conservatism. I want to make it clear that I am *not* saying that in order to write well, or think well, it is necessary to become unavailable to others, or to become a devouring ego. This has been the myth of the masculine artist and thinker; and I do not accept it. But to be a female human being trying to fulfill traditional female functions in a traditional way *is* in direct conflict with the subversive function of the imagination. The word traditional is important here. There must be ways, and we will be finding out more and more about them, in which the energy of creation and the energy of relation can be united. But in those earlier years I always felt the conflict as a failure of love in myself. I had thought I was choosing a full life: the life available to most men, in which sexuality, work, and parenthood could coexist. But I felt, at twenty-nine, guilt toward the people closest to me, and guilty toward my own being.

I wanted, then, more than anything, the one thing of which there was never enough: time to think, time to write. The fifties and early sixties were years of rapid revelations: the sit-ins and marches in the South, the Bay of Pigs, the early antiwar movement, raised large questions—questions for which the masculine world of the academy around me seemed to have expert and fluent answers. But I needed to think for myself—about pacifism and dissent and violence, about poetry and society, and about my own relationship to all these things. For about ten years I was reading in fierce snatches, scribbling in notebooks, writing poetry in fragments; I was looking desperately for clues, because if there were no clues then I thought I might be insane. I wrote in a notebook about this time:

> Paralyzed by the sense that there exists a mesh of relationships—e.g., between my anger at the children, my sensual life, pacifism, sex (I mean sex in its broadest significance, not merely sexual desire)—an interconnectedness which, if I could see it, make it valid, would give me back myself, make it possible to function lucidly and passionately. Yet I grope in and out among these dark webs.

I think I began at this point to feel that politics was not something "out there" but something "in here" and of the essence of my condition.

In the late fifties I was able to write, for the first time, directly about experiencing myself as a woman. The poem was jotted in fragments during children's naps, brief hours in a library, or at 3 A.M. after rising with a wakeful child. I despaired of doing any continuous work at this time. Yet I began to feel that my fragments and scraps had a common consciousness and a common theme, one which I would have been very unwilling to put on paper at an earlier time because I had been taught that poetry should be "universal," which meant, of course, nonfemale. Until then I had tried very much *not* to identify myself as a female poet.

How Does a Poet Put Bread on the Table?[2]

But how does a poet put bread on the table? Rarely, if ever, by poetry alone. Of the four lesbian poets at the Nuyorican Poets Café about whose lives I know something, one directs an underfunded community arts project, two are untenured college teachers, one an assistant dean of students at a state university. Of other poets I know, most teach, often part time, without security but year round; two are on disability; one does clerical work; one cleans houses; one is a paid organizer; one has a paid editing job. Whatever odd money comes in erratically from readings and workshops, grants, permissions fees, royalties, prizes can be very odd money indeed, never to be counted on and almost always small: checks have to be chased down, grants become fewer and more competitive in a worsening political and economic climate. Most poets who teach at universities are untenured, without pension plans or group health insurance, or are employed at public and community colleges with heavy teaching loads and low salaries. Many give unpaid readings and workshops as part of their political "tithe."

Inherited wealth accounts for the careers of some poets: to inherit wealth is to inherit time. Most of the poets I know, hearing of a sum of money, translate it not into possessions, but into time—that precious immaterial necessity of our lives. It's true that a poem can be attempted in brief interstitial moments, pulled out of the pocket and worked on while waiting for a bus or riding a train or while children nap or while waiting for a new batch of clerical work or blood samples to come in. But only certain kinds of poems are amenable to these conditions. Sometimes the very knowledge of coming interruption dampens the flicker. And there is a difference between the ordinary "free" moments stolen from exhausting family strains, from alienating labor, from thought chained by material anxiety, and those other moments that sometimes arrive in a life being lived at its height though under extreme tension; perhaps we are waiting to initiate some act we believe will catalyze change but whose outcome is uncertain; perhaps we are facing personal or communal crisis in which everything unimportant seems to fall away and we are left with our naked lives, the brevity of life itself, and words. At such times we may experience a speeding-up of our imaginative powers, images and voices rush together in a kind of inevitability, what was externally fragmented is internally recognized, and the hand can barely keep pace.

But such moments presuppose other times: when we could simply stare into the wood grain of a door, or the trace of bubbles in a glass of water as long as we wanted to, *almost* secure in the knowledge that there would be no interruption— times of slowness, or purposelessness.

Often such time feels like a luxury, guiltily seized when it can be had, fearfully taken because it does not seem like work, this abeyance, but like "wasting time" in a society where personal importance—even job security—can hinge on acting busy, where the phrase "keeping busy" is a common idiom, where there is, for activists, so much to be done.

---

2. From *What Is Found There: Notebooks on Poetry and Politics* (1993).

Most, if not all, of the names we know in North American poetry are the names of people who have had some access to freedom in time—that privilege of some which is actually a necessity for all. The struggle to limit the working day is a sacred struggle for the worker's freedom in time. To feel herself or himself, for a few hours or a weekend, as a free being with choices—to plant vegetables and later sit on the porch with a cold beer, to write poetry or build a fence or fish or play cards, to walk without a purpose, to make love in the daytime. To sleep late. Ordinary human pleasures, the self's re-creation. Yet every working generation has to reclaim that freedom in time, and many are brutally thwarted in the effort. Capitalism is based on the abridgment of that freedom.

Poets in the United States have either had some kind of private means, or help from people with private means, have held full-time, consuming jobs, or have chosen to work in low-paying, part-time sectors of the economy, saving their creative energies for poetry, keeping their material wants simple. Interstitial living, where the art itself is not expected to bring in much money, where the artist may move from a clerical job to part-time, temporary teaching to subsistence living on the land to waitressing or doing construction or translating, typesetting, or ghostwriting. In the 1990s this kind of interstitial living is more difficult, risky, and wearing than it has ever been, and this is a loss to all the arts—as much as the shrinkage of arts funding, the censorship-by-clique, the censorship by the Right, the censorship by distribution.

A Communal Poetry[3]

One day in New York in the late 1980s, I had lunch with a poet I'd known for more than twenty years. Many of his poems were—are—embedded in my life.

Adrienne Rich in the 1990s

We had read together at the antiwar events of the Vietnam years. Then, for a long time, we hardly met. As a friend, he had seemed to me withheld, defended in a certain way I defined as masculine and with which I was becoming in general impatient; yet often, in their painful beauty, his poems told another story. On this day, he was as I had remembered him: distant, stiff, shy perhaps. The conversation stumbled along as we talked about our experiences with teaching poetry, which seemed a safe ground. I made some remark about how long it was since last we'd talked. Suddenly, his whole manner changed: *You disappeared! You simply disappeared.* I realized he meant not so

3. From *What Is Found There: Notebooks on Poetry and Politics* (1993).

much from his life as from a landscape of poetry to which he thought we both belonged and were in some sense loyal.

If anything, those intervening years had made me feel more apparent, more visible—to myself and to others—as a poet. The powerful magnet of the women's liberation movement—and the women's poetry movement it released—had drawn me to coffeehouses where women were reading new kinds of poems; to emerging "journals of liberation" that published women's poems, often in a context of political articles and the beginnings of feminist criticism; to bookstores selling chapbooks and pamphlets from the new women's presses; to a woman poet's workshops with women in prison; to meetings with other women poets in Chinese restaurants, coffee shops, apartments, where we talked not only of poetry, but of the conditions that make it possible or impossible. It had never occurred to me that I was disappearing—rather, that I was, along with other women poets, beginning to appear. In fact, we were taking part in an immense shift in human consciousness.

My old friend had, I believe, not much awareness of any of this. It was, for him, so off-to-the-edge, so out-of-the-way; perhaps so dangerous, it seemed I had sunk, or dived, into a black hole. Only later, in a less constrained and happier meeting, were we able to speak of the different ways we had perceived that time.

He thought there had been a known, defined poetic landscape and that as poetic contemporaries we simply shared it. But whatever poetic "generation" I belonged to, in the 1950s I was a mother, under thirty, raising three small children. Notwithstanding the prize and the fellowship to Europe that my first book of poems had won me, there was little or no "appearance" I then felt able to claim as a poet, against that other profound and as yet unworded reality.

Why I Refused the National Medal for the Arts [4]

July 3, 1997

Jane Alexander, Chair
The National Endowment for the Arts
1100 Pennsylvania Avenue
Washington, D.C. 20506

Dear Jane Alexander,

I just spoke with a young man from your office, who informed me that I had been chosen to be one of twelve recipients of the National Medal for the Arts at a ceremony at the White House in the fall. I told him at once that I could not accept such an award from President Clinton or this White House because the

4. From *Arts of the Possible: Essays and Conversations* (2001).
    After the text of my letter to Jane Alexander, then chair of the National Endowment for the Arts, had been fragmentarily quoted in various news stories, Steve Wasserman, editor of the *Los Angeles Times Book Review*, asked me for an article expanding on my reasons. Herewith the letter and the article [Rich's note].

very meaning of art, as I understand it, is incompatible with the cynical politics of this administration. I want to clarify to you what I meant by my refusal.

Anyone familiar with my work from the early sixties on knows that I believe in art's social presence—as breaker of official silences, as voice for those whose voices are disregarded, and as a human birthright. In my lifetime I have seen the space for the arts opened by movements for social justice, the power of art to break despair. Over the past two decades I have witnessed the increasingly brutal impact of racial and economic injustice in our country.

There is no simple formula for the relationship of art to justice. But I do know that art—in my own case the art of poetry—means nothing if it simply decorates the dinner table of power that holds it hostage. The radical disparities of wealth and power in America are widening at a devastating rate. A president cannot meaningfully honor certain token artists while the people at large are so dishonored.

I know you have been engaged in a serious and disheartening struggle to save government funding for the arts, against those whose fear and suspicion of art is nakedly repressive. In the end, I don't think we can separate art from overall human dignity and hope. My concern for my country is inextricable from my concerns as an artist. I could not participate in a ritual that would feel so hypocritical to me.

Sincerely,
Adrienne Rich

cc: President Clinton

The invitation from the White House came by telephone on July 3. After several years' erosion of arts funding and hostile propaganda from the religious right and the Republican Congress, the House vote to end the National Endowment for the Arts was looming. That vote would break as news on July 10; my refusal of the National Medal for the Arts would run as a sidebar story alongside in the *New York Times* and the *San Francisco Chronicle*.

In fact, I was unaware of the timing. My refusal came directly out of my work as a poet and essayist and citizen drawn to the interfold of personal and public experience. I had recently been thinking and writing about the shrinking of the social compact, of whatever it was this country had ever meant when it called itself a democracy: the shredding of the vision of *government of the people, by the people, for the people.*

"We the people—still an excellent phrase," said the playwright Lorraine Hansberry in 1962, well aware who had been excluded, yet believing the phrase might someday come to embrace us all. And I had for years been feeling both personal and public grief, fear, hunger, and the need to render this, my time, in the language of my art.

Whatever was "newsworthy" about my refusal was not about a single individual—not myself, not President Clinton. Nor was it about a single political party. Both major parties have displayed a crude affinity for the interests of corporate power, while deserting the majority of the people, especially the most vulnerable. Like so many others, I've watched the dismantling of our public education, the steep rise in our incarceration rates, the demonization of our young black men, the accusations against our teen-age mothers, the selling of health care—public and private—to the highest bidders, the export of subsistence-level jobs in the United States to even lower-wage countries, the use of below-minimum-wage prison labor to break strikes and raise profits, the scapegoating of immigrants, the denial of dignity and minimal security to working and poor people. At the same time, we've witnessed the acquisition of publishing houses, once risk-taking conduits of creativity, by conglomerates driven single-mindedly to fast profits, the acquisition of major communications and media by those same interests, the sacrifice of the arts and public libraries in stripped-down school and civic budgets, and, most recently, the evisceration of the National Endowment for the Arts. Piece by piece the democratic process has been losing ground to the accumulation of private wealth.

There is no political leadership in the White House or the Congress that has spoken to and for the people who, in a very real sense, have felt abandoned by their government.

Lorraine Hansberry spoke her words about government during the Cuban missile crisis, at a public meeting in New York to abolish the House Un-American Activities Committee. She also said in that speech, "My government is wrong." She did not say, I abhor all government. She claimed her government as a citizen, African American, and female, and she challenged it. (I listened to her words again, on an old vinyl recording, this past Fourth of July.)

In a similar spirit many of us today might wish to hold government accountable, to challenge the agendas of private power and wealth that have displaced historical tendencies toward genuinely representative government in the United States. We might still wish to claim our government, to say, *This belongs to us—* we, the people, as we are now.

We would have to start asking questions that have been defined as nonquestions—or as naive, childish questions. In the recent official White House focus on race, it goes consistently unsaid that the all-embracing enterprise of our early history was the slave trade, which left nothing, no single life, untouched, and was, along with the genocide of the native population and the seizure of their lands, the foundation of our national prosperity and power. Promote dialogues on race? apologize for slavery? We would need to perform an autopsy on capitalism itself.

Marxism has been declared dead. Yet the questions Marx raised are still alive and pulsing, however the language and the labels have been co-opted and abused. What is social wealth? How do the conditions of human labor infiltrate other social relationships? What would it require for people to live and work together in conditions of radical equality? How much inequality will we tolerate in the world's richest and most powerful nation? Why and how have these and similar questions become discredited in public discourse?

And what about art? Mistrusted, adored, pietized, condemned, dismissed as entertainment, commodified, auctioned at Sotheby's, purchased by investment-seeking celebrities, it dies into the "art object" of a thousand museum basements. It's also reborn hourly in prisons, women's shelters, small-town garages, community-college workshops, halfway houses, wherever someone picks up a pencil, a wood-burning tool, a copy of *The Tempest,* a tag-sale camera, a whittling knife, a stick of charcoal, a pawnshop horn, a video of *Citizen Kane,* whatever lets you know again that this deeply instinctual yet self-conscious expressive language, this regenerative process, could help you save your life. "If there were no poetry on any day in the world," the poet Muriel Rukeyser wrote, "poetry would be invented that day. For there would be an intolerable hunger." In an essay on the Caribbean poet Aimé Césaire, Clayton Eshleman names this hunger as "the desire, the need, for a more profound and ensouled world." There is a continuing dynamic between art repressed and art reborn, between the relentless marketing of the superficial and the "spectral and vivid reality that employs all means" (Rukeyser again) to reach through armoring, resistances, resignation, to recall us to desire.

Art is both tough and fragile. It speaks of what we long to hear and what we dread to find. Its source and native impulse, the imagination, may be shackled in early life, yet may find release in conditions offering little else to the spirit. For a recent document on this, look at Phyllis Kornfeld's *Cellblock Visions: Prison Art in America,* notable for the variety and emotional depth of the artworks reproduced, the words of the inmate artists, and for Kornfeld's unsentimental and lucid text. Having taught art to inmates for fourteen years, in eighteen institutions (including maximum-security units), she sees recent incarceration policy as rapidly devolving from rehabilitation to dehumanization, including the dismantling of prison arts programs.

Art can never be totally legislated by any system, even those that reward obedience and send dissident artists to hard labor and death; nor can it, in our specifically compromised system, be really free. It may push up through cracked macadam, by the merest means, but it needs breathing space, cultivation, protection to fulfill itself. Just as people do. New artists, young or old, need education in their art, the tools of their craft, chances to study examples from the past and meet practitioners in the present, get the criticism and encouragement of mentors, learn that they are not alone. As the social compact withers, fewer and fewer people will be told *Yes, you can do this; this also belongs to you.* Like government, art needs the participation of the many in order not to become the property of a powerful and narrowly self-interested few.

Art is our human birthright, our most powerful means of access to our own and another's experience and imaginative life. In continually rediscovering and recovering the humanity of human beings, art is crucial to the democratic vision. A government tending further and further away from the search for democracy will see less and less "use" in encouraging artists, will see art as obscenity or hoax.

In 1987, the late Justice William Brennan spoke of "formal reason severed from the insights of passion" as a major threat to due-process principles. "Due process asks whether government has treated someone fairly, whether individual dignity has been honored, whether the worth of an individual has been acknowledged.

Officials cannot always silence these questions by pointing to rational action taken according to standard rules. They must plumb their conduct more deeply, seeking answers in the more complex equations of human nature and experience."

It is precisely where fear and hatred of art join the pull toward quantification and abstraction, where the human face is mechanically deleted, that human dignity disappears from the social equation. Because it is to those "complex equations of human nature and experience" that art addresses itself.

In a society tyrannized by the accumulation of wealth as Eastern Europe was tyrannized by its own false gods of concentrated power, recognized artists have, perhaps, a new opportunity: to work out our connectedness, *as artists,* with other people who are beleaguered, suffering, disenfranchised—precariously employed workers, trashed elders, rejected youth, the "unsuccessful," and the art they too are nonetheless making and seeking.

I wish I didn't feel the necessity to say here that none of this is about imposing ideology or style or content on artists; it's about the inseparability of art from acute social crisis in this century and the one now approaching.

We have a short-lived model, in our history, for the place of art in relation to government. During the Depression of the 1930s, under New Deal legislation, thousands of creative and performing artists were paid modest stipends to work in the Federal Writers Project, the Federal Theatre Project, the Federal Art Project. Their creativity, in the form of novels, murals, plays, performances, public monuments, the providing of music and theater to new audiences, seeded the art and the consciousness of succeeding decades. By 1939 this funding was discontinued.

Federal funding for the arts, like the philanthropy of private arts patrons, can be given and taken away. In the long run art needs to grow organically out of a social compost nourishing to everyone, a literate citizenry, a free, universal, public education complex with art as an integral element, a society honoring both human individuality and the search for a decent, sustainable common life. In such conditions, art would still be a voice of hunger, desire, discontent, passion, reminding us that the democratic project is never-ending.

For that to happen, what else would have to change?

1997

CHRONOLOGY

1929   Born in Baltimore, Maryland, May 16. Began writing poetry as a child under the encouragement and supervision of her father, Dr. Arnold Rich, from whose "very Victorian, pre-Raphaelite" library, Rich later recalled, she read Tennyson, Keats, Arnold, Blake, Rossetti, Swinburne, Carlyle, and Pater.

1951   A.B., Radcliffe College. *A Change of World* chosen by W. H. Auden for publication in the Yale Younger Poets series.

1952–1953   Guggenheim Fellowship; travel in Europe and England. Marriage to Alfred H. Conrad, an economist who taught at Harvard. Residence in Cambridge, Massachusetts, 1953–66.

1955   Birth of David Conrad. Publication of *The Diamond Cutters and Other Poems.*

1957	Birth of Paul Conrad.
1959	Birth of Jacob Conrad.
1960	National Institute of Arts and Letters Award for poetry.
1961–1962	Guggenheim Fellowship; residence with family in the Netherlands.
1962	Bollingen Foundation grant for translation of Dutch poetry.
1962–1963	Amy Lowell Travelling Fellowship.
1963	*Snapshots of a Daughter-in-Law* published. Bess Hokin Prize of *Poetry* magazine.
1966	*Necessities of Life* published. Move to New York City; residence there from 1966 on. Increasingly active politically in protests against the war in Vietnam.
1966–1968	Lecturer at Swarthmore College.
1967–1969	Adjunct Professor of Writing in the Graduate School of the Arts, Columbia University.
1968	Began teaching in the SEEK and Open Admissions Programs at City College of New York.
1969	*Leaflets* published.
1970	Death of Alfred Conrad.
1971	*The Will to Change* published. Increasingly active in the women's movement.
1972–1973	Fannie Hurst Visiting Professor of Creative Literature at Brandeis University.
1973	*Diving into the Wreck* published.
1974	National Book Award for *Diving into the Wreck*. Rich rejects the award as an individual, but accepts it, in a statement written with Audre Lorde and Alice Walker, two other nominees, in the name of all women. Professor of English, City College of New York.
1975	*Poems: Selected and New* published.
1976	Professor of English at Douglass College. *Of Woman Born: Motherhood as Experience and Institution* published. *Twenty-one Love Poems* published.
1978	*The Dream of a Common Language: Poems 1974–1977* published.
1979	*On Lies, Secrets, and Silence: Selected Prose 1966–1978* published. Leaves Douglass College and New York City; moves to Montague, Massachusetts; edits, with Michelle Cliff, the lesbian-feminist journal *Sinister Wisdom*.
1981	*A Wild Patience Has Taken Me This Far: Poems 1978–1981* published.
1984	*The Fact of a Doorframe: Poems Selected and New 1950–1984* published. Moves to Santa Cruz, California. Professor of English, San Jose State University.
1986	*Blood, Bread, and Poetry: Selected Prose 1979–1985* published. Professor of English, Stanford University.
1989	*Time's Power: Poems 1985–1988* published.
1991	*An Atlas of the Difficult World: Poems 1988–1991* published.
1992	Wins *Los Angeles Times* Book Prize for *An Atlas of the Difficult World: Poems 1988–1991,* the Lenore Marshall/*Nation* Prize for Poetry, and Nicholas Roerich Museum Poet's Prize; is co-winner of the Frost Silver Medal for distinguished lifetime achievement.
1993	*What Is Found There: Notebooks on Poetry and Politics* published.
1994	Awarded MacArthur fellowship.
1995	*Dark Fields of the Republic: Poems 1991–1995* published.
1996	Awarded the Tanning Prize, given by the Academy of American Poets.
1999	Elected a chancellor of the Academy. Received Lannan Foundation's Lifetime Achievement Award. *Midnight Salvage: Poems 1995–1998* published.

QUESTION

What significant differences do you notice among the poems by Adrienne Rich that appear throughout this book? Can you quickly tell an early Rich poem from a later one? What are the differences in subject matter? in style? in situation? in strategies of argument? Try to read all the Rich poems in the book at one sitting, working in poems from other chapters in the appropriate chronological places. Characterize, as fully as you can, the voice of the poems written in the 1950s; in the 1960s; 1970s; 1980s; 1990s. In what ways does the voice change? What similarities do you find from beginning to end?

WRITING SUGGESTIONS

1. In what sense is "At a Bach Concert" typical of Rich's early poetry? Compare "Storm Warnings" and "Aunt Jennifer's Tigers" in terms of the comments Rich makes about her early work in the passage quoted from *When We Dead Awaken: Writing as Re-Vision* (page 628). What "typical" features do the poems share? Write a detailed analysis (about fifteen hundred words) of "At a Bach Concert."
2. Carefully considering plot, characterization, and structure, write an essay in which you detail the ways "Diving into the Wreck" (chapter 15) is and is not typical of Rich's work. (Alternate version: Do other poems strike you as more typical of Rich? If so, choose one and show how it is characteristic of Rich's ideas and strategies.)

22

LITERARY TRADITION AS CONTEXT

The more poetry you read, the better a reader of poetry you will likely be. This is not just because your skills will improve and develop, but also because you will come to know more about poetic traditions and can thus understand more fully how poets draw upon each other. Poets are conscious of other poets, and often they refer to each other's work or use it as a starting point for their own in ways that may not be immediately obvious to an outsider. Poetry can be thought of as a form of argument: poets agree or disagree over basic matters. Sometimes a quiet (or even noisy) competitiveness underlies their concern with what other poets have done or can do; at other times, playfulness and a sense of humor about poetic possibilities take over, and the competitiveness dwindles to fun and poetic games. And often poets want to tap the rich mine of artistic expression in order to share in the bounty of our heritage. In any case, a poet's consciousness of what others have done leads to a sense of tradition that is often hard to articulate but nevertheless is very important to the effects of poetry—and this sense of tradition is something of a problem for a relatively new reader of poetry. How can I possibly read this poem intelligently, we are likely to ask sometimes in exasperation, until I've read all the other poems that inspired it? It's a real problem. Poets don't expect their readers to have Ph.D.s in literature, but sometimes it *seems* as if they do. For some poets—John Milton, T. S. Eliot, and Richard Wilbur are examples—it does help if one has read practically everything imaginable.

Why are poets so dependent on each other? What is the point of their relentless consciousness of what has already been done by others? Why do they repeatedly answer, allude to, and echo other poems? Why does tradition matter to them?

A sense of common task, a kind of communality of purpose, accounts for some traditional poetic practice, and the competitive desire of individual poets to achieve a place in the English and American poetic tradition accounts for more. Many poets strive to be counted among those who achieve, through their writing, a place in history; and a way of establishing that place is to define for oneself the relationship between one's own work and that of others whose place is already secure. Poets may share and wish to pass on a serious and abiding cultural tradition, but they may also share a sense of playfulness, a kind of poetic gamesmanship. Making words dance on the page or in our heads provides in itself a satisfaction and

> The truest poetry is the most feigning.
>
> —WILLIAM SHAKESPEARE

delight for many writers—pride in craft that is like the pride of a painter or potter or tennis player. Often poets set themselves a particular task to see what they can do. One way of doing that is to introduce a standard traditional **motif** (a recurrent device, formula, or situation that deliberately connects a poem with common patterns of existing thought), and then to play variations on it much as a musician might do. Another way is to provide an alternative answer to a question that has repeatedly been asked and answered in a traditional way. Poetic playfulness by no means excludes serious intention—the poems in this chapter often make important statements about their subject, however humorous they may be in their method. Some teasing of the tradition and of other poets is pure fun, a kind of kidding among good friends; some is harsher and represents an attempt to see the world very differently—to define and articulate a very different set of attitudes and values.

The Anglophone poetic tradition is a rich and varied heritage, and individual poets draw upon it in countless ways. You have probably noticed, in the poems you have read so far, a number of allusions, glances at the tradition or at individual expressions of it. The more poems you read, the more you will notice and the more you will yourself become a comfortable member of the audience poets write for. Poets expect a lot from readers—not always, but often enough to make a new reader feel nervous and sometimes inadequate. The other side of that discomfort comes when you begin to notice things that other readers don't. The groups of poems in this chapter illustrate some of the ways that the tradition energizes individual poets and suggest some of the things poets like to do with their heritage.

ECHO AND ALLUSION

The poems in this group illustrate the familiar poetic strategy of echoing or alluding to other texts as a way of importing meaning into a particular poem, similar to the strategy of "sampling" words or sounds in contemporary music. An **echo** may simply recall a word, phrase, or sound in another text as a way of associating what is going on in *this* poem with something in another, familiar text. The familiarity itself may sometimes be the point: writers often like to associate what they do with what has already been thought or expressed, especially if their work sounds like a text that is already much admired. Echoes of Shakespeare, for example, may imply that this new text shares concerns (and, therefore, insight or quality?) with Shakespeare. An **allusion** more insistently connects a particular word, phrase, or section of a poem with some similar formulation in a previous text; it *invokes* a previous text as a kind of gloss on this one—that is, it asks the reader to interpret this text in the light of some previous one, depending explicitly on the reader's recognition of the previous text and asking for interpretation based on the implied similarity.

Strategies of echo and allusion can be very complicated, for the question of just how much of one text can carry over—or be forcibly brought over—into another one cannot be answered categorically.

Often poets quote—or echo with variations—a passage from another text in order to suggest some thematic, ideological, tonal, or other link. Sometimes the purpose is simply to invoke an idea or attitude from another text, another place, or another culture. In "Two Songs" (chapter 15), for example, Adrienne Rich employs Chaucer's familiar formulation of the rites of spring (with its description of all things coming to life, their vital juices flowing, as they follow the natural progress of the seasons) to suggest the way the sap rises and bodies merge in ordinary lusty human beings. The quotation thus puts the speaker's attraction to a lover into a larger human perspective, and her sense of herself as a subject and object of lust comes to seem ordinary, part of the natural course of events.

The first poem in "Echo and Allusion" belongs, uncomfortably, in the *carpe diem* ("seize the day") tradition; but unlike ordinary *carpe diem* poems, it is moralistic. It undercuts the speaker by having him allude to familiar biblical passages that imply a condemnation of live-for-today attitudes and ideas. By echoing Satan's tempting addresses to Eve in Genesis, the speaker in Jonson's "Come, my Celia" condemns himself in the eyes of readers and becomes a seducer-tempter instead of a libertine-hero. The other poems here variously recall individual lines, passages, poems, ideas, or traditions in order to establish a particular stance or develop a position or attitude. The meaning of each poem derives primarily from a sorting through of the allusion.

Poems do not necessarily need earlier texts to exist or have meaning, but prior texts may set up what happens in a particular poem or govern how we construe it. Allusion— the strategy of using one text to comment on and influence the interpretation of another—is one of the most popular and familiar strategies that poets use.

BEN JONSON

[*Come, my Celia, let us prove*][1]

Come, my Celia, let us prove,[2]
While we can, the sports of love;
Time will not be ours forever:
He at length our good will sever.
5 Spend not, then, his gifts in vain;
Suns that set may rise again,
But if once we lose this light,
'Tis with us perpetual night.
Why should we defer our joys?
10 Fame and rumor are but toys.
Cannot we delude the eyes
Of a few poor household spies?
Or his easier ears beguile,
Thus removéd by our wile?
15 'Tis no sin love's fruits to steal,
But the sweet thefts to reveal;
To be taken, to be seen,
These have crimes accounted been.

1606

1. A song from *Volpone*, sung by the play's villain and would-be seducer. Part of the poem paraphrases Catullus, poem 5.   2. Experience.

WILLIAM BLAKE

The Lamb

Little Lamb, who made thee?
Dost thou know who made thee?
Gave thee life, and bid thee feed
By the stream and o'er the mead;
Gave thee clothing of delight,   5
Softest clothing woolly bright;
Gave thee such a tender voice,
Making all the vales rejoice?
    Little Lamb, who made thee?
    Dost thou know who made thee?   10

Little Lamb, I'll tell thee!
Little Lamb, I'll tell thee:
He is calléd by thy name,
For he calls himself a Lamb,
He is meek and he is mild;   15
He became a little child.
I a child and thou a lamb,
We are calléd by his name.
    Little Lamb, God bless thee!
    Little Lamb, God bless thee!   1789   20

HOWARD NEMEROV

Boom!

Sees Boom in Religion, too

Atlantic City, June 23, 1957 (AP).—*President Eisenhower's pastor said
tonight that Americans are living in a period of "unprecedented religious
activity" caused partially by paid vacations, the eight-hour day and
modern conveniences.*

   *"These fruits of material progress," said the Rev. Edward L. R. Elson
of the National Presbyterian Church, Washington, "have provided the
leisure, the energy, and the means for a level of human and spiritual
values never before reached."*

Here at the Vespasian-Carlton,[3] it's just one
religious activity after another; the sky

---

3. Vespasian was emperor of Rome A.D. 69–79, shortly after the reign of Nero. In French, *vespasienne*
means "public toilet."

is constantly being crossed by cruciform
airplanes, in which nobody disbelieves
5   for a second and the tide, the tide
of spiritual progress and prosperity
miraculously keeps rising, to a level
never before attained. The churches are full,
the beaches are full, and the filling-stations
10   are full, God's great ocean is full
of paid vacationers praying an eight-hour day
to the human and spiritual values, the fruits,
the leisure, the energy, and the means, Lord,
the means for the level, the unprecedented level,
15   and the modern conveniences, which also are full.
Never before, O Lord, have the prayers and praises
from belfry and phonebooth, from ballpark and barbecue
the sacrifices, so endlessly ascended.

It was not thus when Job in Palestine
20   sat in the dust and cried, cried bitterly;[4]
when Damien kissed the lepers on their wounds
it was not thus;[5] it was not thus
when Francis worked a fourteen-hour day
strictly for the birds;[6] when Dante took
25   a week's vacation without pay and it rained
part of the time,[7] O Lord, it was not thus.

But now the gears mesh and the tires burn
and the ice chatters in the shaker and the priest
in the pulpit and Thy Name, O Lord,
30   is kept before the public, while the fruits
ripen and religion booms and the level rises
and every modern convenience runneth over,
that it may never be with us as it hath been
with Athens and Karnak and Nagasaki,[8]
35   nor Thy sun for one instant refrain from shining
on the rainbow Buick by the breezeway
or the Chris Craft with the uplift life raft;
that we may continue to be the just folks we are,
plain people with ordinary superliners and

4. According to the Book of Job, he was afflicted with the loss of prosperity, children, and health as a test of his faith. His name means, in Hebrew, "he cries"; see especially Job 2.7–13.   5. "Father Damien" (Joseph Damien de Veuster, 1840–1889), a Roman Catholic missionary from Belgium, was known for his work among lepers in Hawaii; he ultimately contracted leprosy himself and died there.   6. St. Francis of Assisi, thirteenth-century founder of the Franciscan order, was noted for his love of all living things, and one of the most famous stories about him tells of his preaching to the birds. *Strictly for the birds:* a mid-twentieth-century expression for worthless or unfashionable activity.   7. Dante's journey through Hell, Purgatory, and Paradise (in *The Divine Comedy*) takes a week, beginning on Good Friday, 1300. It rains in the third chasm of Hell.   8. A large Japanese port city, virtually destroyed by a U.S. atomic bomb in 1945. *Athens:* the cultural center of ancient Greek civilization. *Karnak:* a village on the Nile, built on the site of ancient Thebes.

disposable diaperliners, people of the stop'n'shop   40
'n'pray as you go, of hotel, motel, boatel,
the humble pilgrims of no deposit no return
and please adjust thy clothing, who will give to Thee,
if Thee will keep us going, our annual
Miss Universe, for Thy Name's Sake, Amen.   1960   45

MARIANNE MOORE

Love in America?

Whatever it is, it's a passion—
a benign dementia that should be
engulfing America, fed in a way
   the opposite of the way
in which the Minotaur[9] was fed.   5
It's a Midas[1] of tenderness;
   from the heart;
nothing else. From one with ability
to bear being misunderstood—
   take the blame, with "nobility   10
   that is action,"[2] identifying itself with
pioneer unperfunctoriness

without brazenness[3] or
bigness of overgrown
undergrown shallowness.   15

Whatever it is, let it be without
   affectation.

Yes, yes, yes, *yes*.   1967

9. The Minotaur demanded a virgin to devour once a year [Moore's note; notes 1–3 are also Moore's].
1. Midas, who had the golden touch, was inconvenienced when eating or picking things up.   2. Una-
muno said that what we need as a cure for unruly youth is "nobility that is action."   3. *without brazenness or bigness* . . . Winston Churchill: "Modesty becomes a man."

ROBERT HOLLANDER

You Too? Me Too—Why Not? Soda Pop

<pre>
                      I am
                      look
                      ing at
                      the Co
                      caCola
                      bottle
                      which is
                      green wi
                      th ridges
                      just–like
                   c   c   c
                   o   o   o
                   l   l   l
                   u   u   u
                   m   m   m
                   n   n   n
                   s   s   s
                and on itself it says

                   COCA-COLA
                   reg.u.s.pat.off.
</pre>

exactly like an art pop
statue of that kind of
bottle but not so green
that the juice inside
gives other than the co-
lor it has when I pour
it out in a clear glass
glass on this table top
(It's making me thirsty
all this winking and
beading of Hippocrene
please let me pause drinking the fluid in)
ah! it is enticing how each
color is the same
brown in green bottle
brown in uplifted glass
making each utensil on
the table laid a brown
fork in a brown shade
making me long to watch
them harvesting the crop
which makes the deep-aged
rich brown wine of America
that is to say which makes
soda   pop

p. 1968

WILLIAM SHAKESPEARE

[*Not marble, nor the gilded monuments*]

Not marble, nor the gilded monuments
Of princes, shall outlive this powerful rhyme;
But you shall shine more bright in these conténts
Than unswept stone, besmeared with sluttish time.
When wasteful war shall statues overturn,   5
And broils root out the work of masonry,
Nor Mars his sword nor war's quick fire shall burn
The living record of your memory.
'Gainst death and all-oblivious enmity
Shall you pace forth; your praise shall still find room   10
Even in the eyes of all posterity
That wear this world out to the ending doom.[4]
So, till the judgment that yourself arise,
You live in this, and dwell in lovers' eyes.   1609

4. Judgment Day.

POETIC "KINDS"

By now you have experienced all sorts of poems, on a variety of subjects and with all kinds of tones—short poems, long poems, poems that rhyme and poems that don't. And there are, of course, many other sorts of poems that we haven't looked at. Some poems, for example, have thousands of lines and differ substantially from the poems that can be included in a book like this.

Poems may be classified in a variety of ways—by subject, topic, or theme; by their length, appearance, and formal features; by the way they are organized; by the level of language they use; by the poet's intention and what kinds of effects the poem tries to generate.

Classification may be, of course, simply an intellectual exercise. Recognizing that a poem is, for example, an elegy, a parody, or a satire may provide a satisfaction like that of identifying a scarlet tanager, a weeping willow, a French phrase, or a 1967 Ford Thunderbird. Just *knowing* what others don't know may give us a sense of importance, accomplishment, and power. But we can also experience a poem more fully if we understand early on what kind of poem it is, and if we know that the poet has consciously played by certain rules. The **conventions** a poet employs indicate certain standard ways of saying things to achieve certain expected effects, and thus the **tradition** involved in a particular poetic kind yields certain standard responses—or variations on them, depending on a particular poem's relation to that tradition. For example, the humor and fun of the following poem depend entirely on readers' recognizing the *kind* of poem they are reading.

CHRISTOPHER MARLOWE

The Passionate Shepherd to His Love

Come live with me and be my love,
And we will all the pleasures prove[1]
That valleys, groves, hills, and fields,
Woods, or steepy mountain yields.

5   And we will sit upon the rocks,
Seeing the shepherds feed their flocks,
By shallow rivers to whose falls
Melodious birds sing madrigals.

And I will make thee beds of roses
10 And a thousand fragrant posies,
A cap of flowers, and a kirtle[2]
Embroidered all with leaves of myrtle;

A gown made of the finest wool
Which from our pretty lambs we pull;

1. Experience.   2. Gown.

Fair lined slippers for the cold,   15
With buckles of the purest gold;

A belt of straw and ivy buds,
With coral clasps and amber studs:
And if these pleasures may thee move,
Come live with me, and be my love.   20

The shepherd swains[3] shall dance and sing
For thy delight each May morning:
If these delights thy mind may move,
Then live with me and be my love.   1600

A beginning reader of poetry might easily protest that a plea such as this one is unrealistic and fanciful, and thus feel unsure of the poem's tone. What could such a reader think of a speaker who constructs his argument in such a dreamlike way? But the traditions behind the poem and the conventions of the poetic kind make its intention and effects clear. "The Passionate Shepherd to His Love" is a **pastoral poem,** a poetic kind that concerns itself with the simple life of country folk and describes that life in stylized, idealized terms. The people in a pastoral poem are usually (as here) shepherds, although they may be fishermen or other rustics who lead an outdoor life and tend to basic human needs in a simplified society; the world of the poem is one of simplicity, beauty, music, and love. Life always seems timeless in pastoral; people are eternally young, and the season is always spring, usually May. Nature seems endlessly green and the future entirely golden. Difficulty, frustration, disappointment, and obligation do not exist in this world, which is blissfully free of problems. Shepherds sing instead of tending sheep, and they make love and play music instead of having to watch out for wolves in the night. If only the shepherd boy and shepherd girl can agree with each other to make love joyously and passionately, they will live happily ever after. Their language, though informal and fairly simple, always seems a bit more sophisticated than that of real shepherds with real problems and real sheep.

Unrealistic? Of course. No real shepherd spends even a single day like that, and certainly the world of simple country folk includes ferocities of nature, human falsehood and knavery, disease, bad weather, old age, moments that are not all green and gold. Probably no poet ever thought that shepherds really live that way, but it is an attractive fantasy, and poets who write pastoral simply choose this one formulaic way to isolate a series of idealized moments. Fantasies can be personal and private, of course, but a certain pleasure comes from shared public fantasies, such as the central moment when two people first contemplate the joys of ecstatic love. To present a certain tone, attitude, and wholeness, poets self-consciously construct this vision of a world that is self-existent, self-contained, and self-referential.

Other poetic kinds exemplified in this book are:

epic	From *Paradise Lost*	p. 706
lyric	"The Lamb"	p. 871
ballad	"Sir Patrick Spens"	p. 782

3. Youths.

aubade	"The Sun Rising"	p. 972
meditation	"Love Calls Us to the Things of This World"	p. 1001
dramatic monologue	"My Last Duchess"	p. 915
soliloquy	"Soliloquy of the Spanish Cloister"	p. 647
confessional	"Skunk Hour"	p. 984
protest	"Hard Rock Returns . . . "	p. 624

You will find definitions and brief descriptions of them in the glossary. Each kind has its own characteristics and conventions—established by tradition, repetition, and habit—each deserves detailed study and discussion. Meanwhile, in the following section we will examine and provide examples of yet another poetic kind:

HAIKU

The **haiku,** an import into the English poetic tradition, has a long history in its original-language tradition, Japanese. Originally, the haiku (then called *hokku*) was a short section of a longer poem (called a *renga* or *haikai*) composed by several poets who wrote segments in response to one another in a long, cumulative poetic exercise or game. But early on, at least as early as the seventeenth century, the distinctive subject matter and mode of the haiku, together with the creative discipline required by its formal demands, made it an attractive form in itself, and several major poets built their reputations largely on the basis of their skill in the form.

Traditionally, the Japanese haiku was an unrhymed poem consisting of seventeen sounds (or, rather, characters representing seventeen sounds) and distributed over three lines in a five, seven, five pattern—that is, five distinctive sounds in the first line, seven in the second, and five in the third. "Sounds" in the Japanese language are not exactly the same as "syllables" in English, but there is a rough parallel—close enough so that when English writers began to write haiku about a century ago, they ordinarily translated the sound requirement into syllables. Here, for example, is a haiku (in translation) that conforms in its Japanese original to the standard formal definition:

CHIYOJO

[*Whether astringent*][1]

Whether astringent
I do not know. This is my first
Persimmon picking.

Haiku aim for conciseness and compression. They leave a lot unsaid, suggesting connections and causes but seldom making them explicit. Typically, haiku describe a

---

1. Chiyojo (1703–1775) is probably the most famous Japanese woman haiku poet. Tradition has it that she wrote this poem at the time of (and about) her engagement. Translation by Daniel C. Buchanan.

natural object—a flower, say, or an animal, or a place—and imply a relationship between that perception and some human feeling or state of mind. Haiku thus depend heavily on emotive language, and they try not to be definitive. Instead of conclusions, summaries, closures, and neat answers, haiku seek openings up; they alert the mind to possibility.

Three other traditional characteristics of haiku affect readers' expectations. First, haiku have a "seasonal" requirement, so that each poem associates itself with one season of the year and thus "dates" itself in relation to a predictable, revolving pattern of change. This seasonal association may be quite subtle and indirect—through, for example, some flower, event, or condition normally connected with a particular season. Second, haiku more generally involve descriptions of nature: a poem often begins with the observation of a specific natural phenomenon—a plant, an animal, or an aspect of landscape—that becomes connected, implicitly or explicitly, with a human feeling or emotion. This use of nature develops out of the Buddhist sense of nature as orderly and benign but also contingent and transient. Since human beings are a part of that unified order, other parts of nature serve as "natural" reflections of human states. Haiku adapted into other languages and cultures cannot, of course, rely on the same religious assumptions or worldview, but most haiku strive to retain a sense of the human and natural as being mutually reflective and interdependent. Third, haiku often connect the "natural" and the human through a combination of observation and imagination. They blur the Western distinction between seeing something literally and having some "vision" of its end or meaning, though they seldom explicitly articulate that claim to a larger, visionary perspective.

Some of the traditional "masters" of haiku from the seventeenth to the early twentieth century—Bashō and Buson, for example—are represented (in English translations) in the examples that follow. But haiku has become an international form, and during the last half century or so, poets around the world have made conscious, concentrated attempts to create a haiku tradition in at least fifty languages. The habits and traditions of different languages and literatures have influenced and modified the way haiku are written, something that might offend some traditional masters of haiku, just as it would amuse others to see their work so readily but loosely adapted. Later poets and even translators of classic verses have not always observed the seventeen-syllable and three-line requirements, for example. As in any other poetic kind, the conventions prove both demanding and adaptable to the particular needs of different situations, different languages, and different individual poets. (If you would like to try writing haiku, you might consult one of the guides written for this purpose, such as William S. Higginson's *Haiku Handbook: How to Write, Share, and Teach Haiku* [1992].)

BASHŌ

[*A village without bells*—][2]

A village without bells—
    how do they live?
      spring dusk.

2. Matsuo Bashō (1644–1694) is usually considered the first great master poet of haiku. Translations by Robert Hass.

[This road—]

This road—
no one goes down it,
autumn evening.

BUSON

[Coolness—]³

Coolness—
the sound of the bell
as it leaves the bell.

[Listening to the moon]

Listening to the moon,
gazing at the croaking of frogs
in a field of ripe rice.

SEIFŪ

[The faces of dolls]⁴

The faces of dolls.
In unavoidable ways
I must have grown old.

Perhaps the single most famous haiku poem is by Bashō. Here are four different translations into English of that poem. (The source of these poems, Hiroaki Sato's *One Hundred Frogs: From Matsu [i.e. Matsuo] Basho to Allen Ginsberg*, contains an even greater variety of examples.)

3. Yosa Buson (1716–1783). Translations by Robert Hass. 4. Seifū (1650–1721) was a nun. Translation by Daniel C. Buchanan.

LAFCADIO HEARN

[Old pond— . . .]

Old pond—frogs jumped in—sound of water.   1898

CLARA A. WALSH

[An old-time pond, from off whose shadowed depth]

An old-time pond, from off whose shadowed depth
Is heard the splash where some lithe frog leaps in.   1910

EARL MINER

[The still old pond]

The still old pond
and as a frog leaps in it
    the sound of a splash.   1979

ALLEN GINSBERG

[The old pond]

The old pond—a frog jumps in, kerplunk!   1979

The following haiku poems were all written in English:

BABETTE DEUTSCH

[*The falling flower*][5]

The falling flower
I saw drift back to the branch
Was a butterfly.   1957

ETHERIDGE KNIGHT

[*Eastern guard tower*]

Eastern guard tower
glints in sunset; convicts rest
like lizards on rocks.   1960

RICHARD WRIGHT

[*In the falling snow*]

In the falling snow
A laughing boy holds out his palms
Until they are white.   1960

JAMES A. EMANUEL

Ray Charles

His get-aboard smile,
picnic knees, back-up bounce: JAZZ,
all there, ounce by ounce.   1999

5. An adaptation of a sixteenth-century poem by Arakida Moritake (1473–1549).

IMITATING AND ANSWERING

A poem will often respond directly—sometimes point by point or even line by line or word by word—to another poem. The tactic may be teasing or comic, but often, too, a real issue exists behind such a facetious answer, a serious criticism perhaps of the first poem's point or the tradition it represents, or an attempt to provide a different perspective. While it may follow its model slavishly, the poem may also alter key words or details so that readers will easily notice the differences in tone or attitude.

The result seems self-conscious, as if the poet were trying to do something a little bit different in light of the shared tradition. However "sincere" the poem may be, its sense of play is equally important. The first three poems below, for example, playfully pick on Marlowe's "The Passionate Shepherd to His Love" (earlier in this chapter). In effect, all of them provide "answers" to that poem. It is as if his "love" were telling the shepherd what is wrong with his argument, and the poets are answering Marlowe, too. These poets know full well what Marlowe was doing in the fantasy of his original poem, and they clearly have a lot of fun telling him how people in various circumstances might feel about his fantasy. There is in the end a lot of joy and not much hostility in their "realistic" deflation of his magic. The poems by Koch and Skirrow poke gentle fun at other famous works, offering a summary or another version of what might have happened in each (see, respectively, Williams's "This Is Just to Say," in chapter 15, and Keats's "Ode on a Grecian Urn," in chapter 20).

Strictly speaking, only one of the poems that follow (the one by Koch) is a **parody**—that is, it pretends to write in the style of the original poem but comically exaggerates that style and changes the content. The others make fun of an original in less direct phraseological ways, but they share a similar objective of answering an original, even though they use very different styles to alter the poetic intention of that original.

SIR WALTER RALEGH

The Nymph's Reply to the Shepherd

If all the world and love were young,
And truth in every shepherd's tongue,
These pretty pleasures might me move
To live with thee and be thy love.

Time drives the flocks from field to fold,   5
When rivers rage, and rocks grow cold,
And Philomel[1] becometh dumb;
The rest complain of cares to come.

The flowers do fade, and wanton fields
To wayward winter reckoning yields: 10
A honey tongue, a heart of gall,
Is fancy's spring, but sorrow's fall.

1. The nightingale.

Thy gowns, thy shoes, thy beds of roses,
Thy cap, thy kirtle, and thy posies
15   Soon break, soon wither, soon forgotten;
In folly ripe, in reason rotten.

Thy belt of straw and ivy buds,
Thy coral clasps and amber studs,
All these in me no means can move
20   To come to thee and be thy love.

But could youth last, and love still breed,
Had joys no date,[2] nor age no need,
Then these delights my mind might move
To live with thee and be thy love.   1600

WILLIAM CARLOS WILLIAMS

Raleigh Was Right

We cannot go to the country
for the country will bring us no peace
What can the small violets tell us
that grow on furry stems in
5   the long grass among lance shaped leaves?

Though you praise us
and call to mind the poets
who sung of our loveliness
it was long ago!
10   long ago! when country people
would plow and sow with
flowering minds and pockets at ease—
if ever this were true.

Not now. Love itself a flower
15   with roots in a parched ground.
Empty pockets make empty heads.
Cure it if you can but
do not believe that we can live
today in the country
20   for the country will bring us no peace.   1941

2. End.

E. E. CUMMINGS

[(*ponder,darling,these busted statues*]

(ponder,darling,these busted statues
of yon motheaten forum be aware
notice what hath remained
—the stone cringes
clinging to the stone,how obsolete   5

lips utter their extant smile. . . .
remark

a few deleted of texture
or meaning monuments and dolls

resist Them Greediest Paws of careful   10
time all of which is extremely
unimportant)whereas Life

matters if or

when the your- and my-
idle vertical worthless   15
self unite in a peculiarly
momentary

partnership(to instigate
constructive
                Horizontal   20
business. . . . even so,let us make haste
—consider well this ruined aqueduct

lady,
which used to lead something into somewhere)   1926

ALLEN GINSBERG

A Further Proposal

Come live with me and be my love,
And we will some old pleasures prove.
Men like me have paid in verse
This costly courtesy, or curse;

But I would bargain with my art   5
(As to the mind, now to the heart),
My symbols, images, and signs
Please me more outside these lines.

For your share and recompense,
10   You will be taught another sense:
The wisdom of the subtle worm
Will turn most perfect in your form.

Not that your soul need tutored be
By intellectual decree,
15   But graces that the mind can share
Will make you, as more wise, more fair,

Till all the world's devoted thought
Find all in you it ever sought,
And even I, of skeptic mind,
20   A Resurrection of a kind.

This compliment, in my own way,
For what I would receive, I pay;
Thus all the wise have writ thereof,
And all the fair have been their love.

1947

KENNETH KOCH

Variations on a Theme by William Carlos Williams

1

I chopped down the house that you had been saving to live in next
   summer.
I am sorry, but it was morning, and I had nothing to do
and its wooden beams were so inviting.

2

We laughed at the hollyhocks together
5   and then I sprayed them with lye.
Forgive me. I simply do not know what I am doing.

3

I gave away the money that you had been saving to live on for the
   next ten years.
The man who asked for it was shabby
and the firm March wind on the porch was so juicy and cold.

4

10   Last evening we went dancing and I broke your leg.
Forgive me. I was clumsy, and
I wanted you here in the wards, where I am the doctor!   1962

DESMOND SKIRROW

Ode on a Grecian Urn Summarized

Gods chase
Round vase.
What say?
What play?
Don't know.   5
Nice, though.   p. 1960

CULTURAL BELIEF AND TRADITION

The poems in this group draw on a tradition that is larger than just "literary." Mythologies involve whole systems of belief, usually cultural in scope, and the familiar literary formulations of these mythologies are just the surface articulations of a larger view of why the world works the way it does.

Every culture develops stories to explain itself. These stories, about who we are and why we are the way we are, constitute what are often called **myths.** Calling something a myth does not mean that it is false. In fact, it means nearly the opposite, for cultures that subscribe to various myths, or that have ever subscribed to particular myths about culture or history, become infused with and defined by those views. Myth, in the sense in which it is used here, involves explanations of life that are more or less universally believed within a particular culture; it is a frame of reference that people within the culture understand and share. This sharing of a frame of reference does not mean that all people within a culture are carbon copies of each other or that popular stereotypes represent reality accurately, nor does it mean that every individual in the culture *knows* the perceived history and can articulate its events, ideas, and values. But it does mean that a shared history and a shared set of symbols lie behind any particular culture and that the culture is to some extent aware of its distinctiveness from other cultures.

A **culture** may be of many sizes and shapes. Often we think of a nation as a culture (and so speak of American culture, American history, the myth of America, the American dream, the American frame of reference), and we may make smaller and larger divisions—as long as the group has some common history and a somewhat cohesive purpose. We speak of southern culture, for example, or of urban culture, or of the drug culture, or of the various popular-music cultures, or of a culture associated with a particular political belief, economic class, or social group. Most of us belong, willingly or not, to a number of such cultures at one time, and to some extent our identities and destinies are linked with the distinctive features of those cultures and with the ways each culture perceives its identity, values, and history. Some of these cultures we choose to join; some are thrust upon us by birth and circumstances. It is these larger and more persistent forms of culture—not those chosen by an individual—that we illustrate in this section.

Poets aware of their heritage often like to probe its history and beliefs and plumb its depths, just as they like to articulate and play variations on the poetic tradition they feel a part of. For poetry written in the English language over the last four hundred years or so, both the Judeo-Christian frame of reference and the classical frame of reference (drawing on the civilizations of ancient Greece and Rome) have been quite important. Western culture, a broad culture that includes many nations and many religious and social groups, is largely defined within these two frames of reference—or it has been until quite recently. As religious belief in the West has eroded over the past two or three centuries, and as classical civilization has been less emphasized and less studied, poets have felt increasingly less comfortable in assuming that their audiences share a knowledge of their systems, but they have often continued to use them to isolate and articulate human traits that have cultural continuity and importance. More recently, poets have drawn on other cultural myths—Native American, African, and Asian, for example—to expand our sense of common heritage and give new meaning to the "American" and "Western" experience. The poems that follow draw on details from different myths and do so in a variety of ways and tones.

JOHN HOLLANDER

Adam's Task

*And Adam gave names to all cattle, and to the fowl of the air, and to
every beast of the field . . .*

—*Gen. 2:20*

Thou, paw-paw-paw; thou, glurd; thou, spotted
   Glurd; thou, whitestap, lurching through
The high-grown brush; thou, pliant-footed,
   Implex; thou, awagabu.

Every burrower, each flier   5
   Came for the name he had to give:
Gay, first work, ever to be prior,
   Not yet sunk to primitive.

Thou, verdle; thou, McFleery's pomma;
   Thou; thou; thou—three types of grawl;   10
Thou, flisket; thou, kabasch; thou, comma-
   Eared mashawk; thou, all; thou, all.

Were, in a fire of becoming,
   Laboring to be burned away,
Then work, half-measuring, half-humming,   15
   Would be as serious as play.

Thou, pambler; thou, rivarn; thou, greater
   Wherret, and thou, lesser one;
Thou, sproal; thou, zant; thou, lily-eater.
   Naming's over. Day is done.   1971   20

SUSAN DONNELLY

Eve Names the Animals

To me, *lion* was sun on a wing
over the garden. *Dove,*
a burrowing, blind creature.

I swear that man
never knew animals. Words   5
he lined up according to size,

while elephants slipped flat-eyed
through water

and trout
10   hurtled from the underbrush, tusked
and ready for battle.

The name he gave me stuck
me to him. He did it to comfort me,
for not being first.

15   Mornings, while he slept,
I got away. Pickerel
hopped on the branches above me.
Only spider accompanied me,
nosing everywhere,
20   running up to lick my hand.

Poor finch. I suppose I was
woe to him—
the way he'd come looking for me,
not wanting either of us
25   to be ever alone

But to myself I was
palomino
        raven
            fox . . .

30   I strung words
by their stems and wore them
as garlands on my long walks.

The next day
I'd find them withered.

35   I liked change.   1985

H. D. (HILDA DOOLITTLE)

Helen

All Greece[1] hates
the still eyes in the white face,
the luster as of olives
where she stands,
5   and the white hands.

All Greece reviles
the wan face when she smiles,

---

1. Helen's husband, Menelaus, was king of Sparta, an ancient Greek city. The Greeks attacked the city of Troy to get her back from Paris, son of the Trojan King.

hating it deeper still
when it grows wan and white,
remembering past enchantments   10
and past ills.

Greece sees unmoved
God's daughter, born of love,[2]
the beauty of cool feet
and slenderest of knees,   15
could love indeed the maid,
only if she were laid,
white ash amid funereal cypresses.   1924

MIRIAM WADDINGTON

Ulysses Embroidered

You've come
at last from
all your journeying
to the old blind woman
in the tower,   5
Ulysses.[3]

After all adventurings
through seas and
mountains through
giant battles,   10
storms and death,
from pinnacles
to valleys;

Past sirens
naked on rocks   15
between Charybdis
and Scylla, from
dragons' teeth,
from sleep in
stables choking   20
on red flowers
walking through weeds
and through shipwreck.

2. Helen was the daughter of Zeus, king of the gods, and Leda, a mortal. (See W. B. Yeats's poem "Leda and the Swan.")   3. After the end of the Trojan War, Ulysses (or Odysseus), king of Ithaca and one of the Greek heroes of the war, returned to his island home and to his wife, Penelope. To ward off suitors, Penelope had craftily been weaving and unraveling a tapestry that had to be finished before she would remarry. See Homer's *Odyssey* for accounts of these events and others mentioned in the poem.

And now you are
25   climbing the stairs,
taking shape,
a figure in shining
thread rising from
a golden shield:
30   a medallion
emblazoned in
tapestry you grew
from the blind hands
of Penelope.

35   Her tapestry
saw everything,
her stitches
embroidered the
painful colors
40   of her breath the
long sighing touch
of her hands.

She made many
journeys.   1992

ALFRED, LORD TENNYSON

The Kraken

Below the thunders of the upper deep,
Far, far beneath in the abysmal sea,
His ancient, dreamless, uninvaded sleep
The Kraken[4] sleepeth: faintest sunlights flee
5   About his shadowy sides; above him swell
Huge sponges of millennial growth and height;
And far away into the sickly light,
From many a wondrous grot and secret cell
Unnumbered and enormous polypi[5]
10   Winnow with giant arms the slumbering green.
There hath he lain for ages, and will lie
Battening upon huge sea worms in his sleep,
Until the latter fire[6] shall heat the deep;
Then once by man and angels to be seen,
15   In roaring he shall rise and on the surface die.   1830

4. A gigantic mythical sea beast.   5. Octopuses.   6. According to the biblical Book of Revelation, fire that will consume the world.

LANGSTON HUGHES

The Negro Speaks of Rivers

I've known rivers:
I've known rivers ancient as the world and older than the flow of
    human blood in human veins.

My soul has grown deep like the rivers.

I bathed in the Euphrates when dawns were young.
I built my hut near the Congo and it lulled me to sleep.   5
I looked upon the Nile and raised the pyramids above it.
I heard the singing of the Mississippi when Abe Lincoln went down to
    New Orleans, and I've seen its muddy bosom turn all golden in the
    sunset.

I've known rivers:
Ancient, dusky rivers.

My soul has grown deep like the rivers.   1926   10

PHYLLIS WHEATLEY

On Being Brought from Africa to America

'Twas mercy brought me from my Pagan land,
Taught my benighted soul to understand
That there's a God, that there's a Saviour too:
Once I redemption neither sought nor knew.
Some view our sable race with scornful eye,   5
"Their colour is a diabolic die."
Remember, Christians, Negroes, black as Cain,[7]
May be refin'd, and join th' angelic train.   1773

JUNE JORDAN

Something Like a Sonnet for
Phillis Miracle Wheatley

Girl from the realm of birds florid and fleet
flying full feather in far or near weather

---

7. One of Adam's sons, he killed his brother Abel. See Genesis 4.

Who fell to a dollar lust coffled like meat
Captured by avarice and hate spit together
5   Trembling asthmatic alone on the slave block
built by a savagery travelling by carriage
viewed like a species of flaw in the livestock
A child without safety of mother or marriage

Chosen by whimsy but born to surprise
10   They taught you to read but you learned how to write
Begging the universe into your eyes:
They dressed you in light but you dreamed with the night.
From Africa singing of justice and grace,
Your early verse sweetens the fame of our Race.   1989

MAYA ANGELOU

Africa

Thus she had lain
sugar cane sweet
deserts her hair
golden her feet
5   mountains her breasts
two Niles her tears
Thus she has lain
Black through the years.

Over the white seas
10   rime white and cold
brigands ungentled
icicle bold
took her young daughters
sold her strong sons
15   churched her with Jesus
bled her with guns.
Thus she has lain.

Now she is rising
remember her pain
20   remember the losses
her screams loud and vain
remember her riches
her history slain
now she is striding
25   although she had lain.   1975

DEREK WALCOTT

A Far Cry from Africa

A wind is ruffling the tawny pelt
Of Africa. Kikuyu,[8] quick as flies,
Batten upon the bloodstreams of the veldt.[9]
Corpses are scattered through a paradise.
Only the worm, colonel of carrion, cries: 5
"Waste no compassion on these separate dead!"
Statistics justify and scholars seize
The salients of colonial policy.
What is that to the white child hacked in bed?
To savages, expendable as Jews?   10

Threshed out by beaters,[1] the long rushes break
In a white dust of ibises whose cries
Have wheeled since civilization's dawn
From the parched river or beast-teeming plain.
The violence of beast on beast is read   15
As natural law, but upright man
Seeks his divinity by inflicting pain.
Delirious as these worried beasts, his wars
Dance to the tightened carcass of a drum,
While he calls courage still that native dread   20
Of the white peace contracted by the dead.

Again brutish necessity wipes its hands
Upon the napkin of a dirty cause, again
A waste of our compassion, as with Spain,[2]
The gorilla wrestles with the superman.   25
I who am poisoned with the blood of both,
Where shall I turn, divided to the vein?
I who have cursed
The drunken officer of British rule, how choose
Between this Africa and the English tongue I love?   30
Betray them both, or give back what they give?
How can I face such slaughter and be cool?
How can I turn from Africa and live?   1962

8. An East African tribe whose members, as Mau Mau fighters, conducted an eight-year terrorist campaign against British colonial settlers in Kenya.   9. Open country, neither cultivated nor forest (Afrikaans). 1. In big-game hunting, natives are hired to beat the brush, driving birds—such as ibises—and animals into the open.   2. The Spanish Civil War (1936–39), in which the Loyalists were supported by liberals in the West and militarily by Soviet Communists, and the rebels by Nazi Germany and Fascist Italy.

ALBERTO ALVARO RÍOS

Advice to a First Cousin

The way the world works is like this:
for the bite of scorpions, she says,
my grandmother to my first cousin,
because I might die and someone must know,
5   go to the animal jar
the one with the soup of green herbs
mixed with the scorpions I have been putting in
still alive. Take one out
put it on the bite. It has had time to think
10 there with the others—put the lid back tight—
and knows that a biting is not the way to win
a finger or a young girl's foot.
It will take back into itself the hurting
the redness and the itching and its marks.

15 But the world works like this, too:
look out for the next scorpion you see,
she says, and makes a big face to scare me
thereby instructing my cousin, look out!
for one of the scorpion's many
20 illegitimate and unhappy sons.
It will be smarter, more of the devil.
It will have lived longer than these dead ones.
It will know from them something more
about the world, in the way mothers know
25 when something happens to a child, or how
I knew from your sadness you had been bitten.
It will learn something stronger than biting.
Look out most for that scorpion, she says,
making a big face to scare me again and it works
30 I go—crying—she lets me go—they laugh,
the way you must look out for men
who have not yet bruised you.

1985

LOUISE ERDRICH

Jacklight

The same Chippewa word is used both for flirting and hunting game,
while another Chippewa word connotes both using force in intercourse
and also killing a bear with one's bare hands.   —DUNNING 1959

We have come to the edge of the woods,
out of brown grass where we slept, unseen,
out of knotted twigs, out of leaves creaked shut,
out of hiding.

At first the light wavered, glancing over us.   5
Then it clenched to a fist of light that pointed,
searched out, divided us.
Each took the beams like direct blows the heart answers.
Each of us moved forward alone.

We have come to the edge of the woods,   10
drawn out of ourselves by this night sun,
this battery of polarized acids,
that outshines the moon.

We smell them behind it
but they are faceless, invisible,   15
We smell the raw steel of their gun barrels,
mink oil on leather, their tongues of sour barley.
We smell their mother buried chin-deep in wet dirt.

We smell their fathers with scoured knuckles,
teeth cracked from hot marrow.   20
We smell their sisters of crushed dogwood, bruised apples,
of fractured cups and concussions of burnt hooks.

We smell their breath steaming lightly behind the jacklight.
We smell the itch underneath the caked guts on their clothes.
We smell their minds like silver hammers   25
cocked back, held in readiness
for the first of us to step into the open.

We have come to the edge of the woods,
out of brown grass where we slept, unseen,
out of leaves creaked shut, out of our hiding.   30
We have come here too long.

It is their turn now,
their turn to follow us. Listen,
they put down their equipment.
It is useless in the tall brush.   35
And now they take the first steps, not knowing
how deep the woods are and lightless.
How deep the woods are.   1984

QUESTIONS

1. How, specifically, is the speaker undercut in Jonson's "Come, my Celia, let us prove"? Explain how the strategy of allusion works in the poem.
2. Are Moore's notes to "Love in America?" adequate to explain the allusions in her poem? What other information do you wish to have? After you have unearthed that information in your college library, show in detail how each separate allusion works. How would you paraphrase the poem? Why does the poem's title end with a question mark?
3. Read Cummings's "(ponder, darling, these busted statues" closely in relation to Marvell's "To His Coy Mistress." In what specific ways does it echo Marvell's poem? Which images are specifically derived from Marvell? In what specific ways does the Cummings poem undercut the argument of the Marvell poem? In what ways does it undercut its own argument? to what purpose? In what ways does Ginsberg's "A Further Proposal" differ from the other poems written in imitation of Marvell?
4. Indicate the specific ways in which Ralegh's poem "replies" to Marlowe's. In what points does Williams agree with Ralegh? What, exactly, is "unfair" about Skirrow's summary of Keats? How would Keats have justified his poem against Skirrow's summary?
5. What attitudes toward Adam and Eve do the Donnelly and Hollander poems display? How are those attitudes projected by devices within the poems?
6. Which poems that draw from classical mythology develop the strongest negative attitudes toward their "heroes" and "heroines"?
7. What values do the Hughes and Angelou poems associate with Africa?

WRITING SUGGESTIONS

1. In what specific ways is Marvell's "To His Coy Mistress" anchored to its historical or cultural context? to its philosophical and thematic contexts? Can you tell that it is written by a seventeenth-century poet? How? What historical or cultural "allusions" anchor the poem to its time? In what specific ways does the Cummings poem establish itself as contemporary? Write a five- to seven-hundred word essay in which you show how Cummings undercuts the assumptions of Marvell.
2. Using a poetry index (available in the reference section of your college library), find half a dozen poems that have the word *elegy* in their titles. Compare their tones and strategies. Decide which features and expectations are central to the poetic kind. Then look back at Jonson's "On My First Son" (page 608), often said to be a typical elegy, and write a two-page analysis of the poem in which you show how it uses and transforms the expectations associated with the elegy as a poetic kind.
3. In an essay of about three pages, show how the primary effects of Waddington's "Ulysses Embroidered" or Erdrich's "Jacklight" relate to its cultural myths.

23

CULTURAL AND HISTORICAL CONTEXT

The more you know, the better a reader of poetry you will likely be. And that goes for general knowledge as well as knowledge of other poetry and literary traditions. Poems often draw on a larger fund of human knowledge about all sorts of things, asking us to bring to bear on a poem facts and values we have taken on from earlier reading or from our experiences in the world more generally. In the previous nine chapters, we have looked at how practice and the learning of specific skills make interpretation easier and better, but in this "contextual" section we are concerned with information you need to read richly and fully: information about authors, about events that influenced them or became the inspiration or basis for their writing, and about literary traditions that provide a context for their work. Poets always write in a specific time, under particular circumstances, and with some awareness of the world around them, whether or not they specifically refer to contemporary matters in a particular poem. In this chapter, we will discuss the specifically cultural and historical—events, movements, ideas that directly influence poets or that poets in some way represent in the poems they write.

Very little that you know will ultimately go to waste in your reading of poetry. The best potential reader of poetry has already developed reading skills to perfection, read everything, thought deeply about all kinds of things, and is wise beyond belief—wise enough to know exactly how to apply specific knowledge to a given text. We all strive to be that ideal reader, but none of us actually is. Of course, no poet really expects any reader to be all those things, but poems themselves can make demands: they may require readers to know as much about history, for example, as about the intricacies of language and form. Poems not only *refer* to people, places, and events—things that exist in time—but they also are products of given moments, participating in both the potentialities and the limitations of the times in which they are created.

Things that happen every day frequently find their way into poetry in an easy and yet often forceful manner. Making love in a junkyard, as in Dickey's "Cherrylog Road" (chapter 14) is one kind of example; a reader doesn't need to know what particular junkyard was involved—or imaginatively involved—in order to understand the poem, but that reader does need to know what an auto junkyard was like in the mid-twentieth century, with more or less whole car bodies being scattered in various states of disarray over a large plot of ground. But what if, over the next generation or two, junkyards completely disappear as we find other ways to dispose of old cars? Already a lot of old cars are crushed into small metal blocks, especially in large cities. But what if the metal is all melted down, or the junk is orbited into space? If that should happen, readers then may have never seen a junkyard, and they will need a footnote to explain what such junkyards were like. The history of junkyards will not be lost—people will view the pictures, films, and records and write definitive books about the forms and functions of junkyards, probably even including the fact that lovers occasionally visited them—but the public memory of junkyards will soon disappear. No social customs, nothing that is made, no institutions or sites last forever.

Readers may still be able to experience "Cherrylog Road" when junkyards disappear, but they will need some help, and they may think its particulars a little quaint, much as we regard literature that involves a horse and buggy—or even making love in the back-seat of a parked car—as quaint now. Institutions change, habits change, times change, places and settings change—all kinds of particulars change, even when people's wants, needs, and foibles pretty much go on in the same way. Footnotes never provide a precise or adequate substitute for the ease and pleasure that come from already knowing, but they can help us understand and pave the way for feeling and experience. With the aid of footnotes, poems can stimulate in readers a kind of imaginative historical sympathy, for poems from earlier times that refer to specific contemporary details (and that have now become to us, in our own time, *historical* details) often describe human nature and human experiences very much as we still know and experience them. Today's poem may need tomorrow's footnote, but the poem need not be tomorrow's puzzle or only a curiosity or fossil.

The following poem, not that many years old, already requires some explanation. Many readers will not know the factual details of its occasion, and (even more important) most readers will not recall the powerful reaction throughout the United States to the event.

JAMES A. EMANUEL

Emmett Till[1]

I hear a whistling
Through the water.
Little Emmett
Won't be still.
5 He keeps floating
Round the darkness,
Edging through
The silent chill.
Tell me, please,
10 That bedtime story
Of the fairy
River Boy

1. In 1955, Till, a fourteen-year-old from Chicago, was lynched in Mississippi for allegedly making sexual advances toward a white woman.

Who swims forever,
Deep in treasures,
Necklaced in   15
A coral toy.   1968

How do you know what you need to know? The easiest clue is your own puzzlement. When something that you don't recognize happens in a poem—and yet the poem seems not to clarify it—you have a clue that readers at the time the poem was written must have recognized something that is not now common knowledge. Once you know you don't know, it takes only a little work to find out: most college libraries contain far more information than you will ever need, and the trick is to search efficiently. Your ability to find the information will depend upon how well you know the written reference materials and computer searches available to you. Practice helps. Knowledge accumulates. Most poems printed in textbooks like this one will be annotated for you with basic facts, but often you will need additional information to interpret a poem's full meaning and resonance. An editor, trying to satisfy the needs of a variety of readers, may not always write the note you in particular need, so you may have to do some digging in the library for any poem you read—certainly for those you come upon in magazines and unannotated collections. Few poets like to annotate their own work (they'd rather let you struggle a little to appreciate it), and besides, many things that now need notes didn't when they were written.

The two poems that follow both require from the reader some specific "referential" information, but they differ considerably in their emphasis on the particularities of time and place. The first poem reflects and refers to a moment just before the outbreak of World War I when British naval forces were preparing for combat by taking gunnery practice in the English Channel. The second reflects a longer cultural moment in which attitudes and assumptions, rather than some specific event, are at stake.

THOMAS HARDY

Channel Firing

That night your great guns, unawares,
Shook all our coffins as we lay,
And broke the chancel window squares,[2]
We thought it was the Judgment-day

And sat upright. While drearisome   5
Arose the howl of wakened hounds:
The mouse let fall the altar-crumb,[3]
The worms drew back into the mounds,

---

2. The windows near the altar in a church.   3. Breadcrumbs from the sacrament of Communion.

The glebe cow[4] drooled. Till God called, "No;
10   It's gunnery practice out at sea
Just as before you went below;
The world is as it used to be:

"All nations striving strong to make
Red war yet redder. Mad as hatters
15   They do no more for Christés sake
Than you who are helpless in such matters.

"That this is not the judgment-hour
For some of them's a blessed thing,
For if it were they'd have to scour
20   Hell's floor for so much threatening . . .

"Ha, ha. It will be warmer when
I blow the trumpet (if indeed
I ever do; for you are men,
And rest eternal sorely need)."

25   So down we lay again. "I wonder,
Will the world ever saner be,"
Said one, "than when He sent us under
In our indifferent century!"

And many a skeleton shook his head.
30   "Instead of preaching forty year,"
My neighbor Parson Thirdly said,
"I wish I had stuck to pipes and beer."

Again the guns disturbed the hour,
Roaring their readiness to avenge.
35   As far inland as Stourton Tower,
And Camelot, and starlit Stonehenge.[5]

April 1914

SANDRA GILBERT

Sonnet: The Ladies' Home Journal

The brilliant stills of food, the cozy
glossy, bygone life—mashed potatoes
posing as whipped cream, a neat mom

4. Parish cow pastured on the meadow next to the churchyard.   5. A circular formation of upright stones dating from about 1800 B.C., on Salisbury Plain, Wiltshire; it is thought to have been a ceremonial site for political and religious occasions or an early scientific experiment in astronomy. *Stourton Tower*, built in the eighteenth century to commemorate King Alfred's ninth-century victory over the Danes, in Stourhead Park, Wiltshire. *Camelot:* the legendary site of King Arthur's court, said to have been in Cornwall or Somerset.

conjuring shapes from chaos, trimming the flame—
how we ached for all that,   5
that dance of love in the living room,
those paneled walls, that kitchen golden
as the inside of a seed: how we leaned
on those shiny columns of advice,
stroking the *thank yous*, the firm thighs, the wise   10
closets full of soap.

But even then
we knew it was the lies we loved, the lies
we wore like Dior coats,[6] the clean-cut airtight
lies that laid out our lives in black and white.   1984   15

"Channel Firing" is not ultimately *about* World War I, for it presumes that human behavior stays the same from age to age, but it begins from a particular historical vantage point. The composition date was recorded by the author on the manuscript and is considered part of the poem, but even with that clue a reader would not be able to make much sense of the poem without recognizing the specific reference—the dramatic situation here (with a waking corpse as the main speaker) is difficult enough to sort out. The firing of the guns has awakened the dead who are buried near the channel, and in their puzzlement they assume it is Judgment Day, time for them to arise, until God enters and tells them what is happening. Much of the poem's effect depends on character portrayal—a God who laughs and sounds cynical, a parson who regrets his selfless life and wishes he had indulged himself more—as well as the sense that nothing ever changes. But particularity of time and place are crucial to this sense of changelessness; even so important a contemporary moment as the beginning of a world war—a moment viewed by most people at the time as unique and world-changing—fades into a timeless parade of moments that stretches over centuries of history. The geographical particulars cited at the end—as the sound of the guns moves inland to be heard in place after place—make the same point. Great moments in history are all encompassed in the sound of the guns and its message about human behavior. Times, places, and events, however important they seem, all become part of some larger pattern that denies individuality or uniqueness.

The particulars in "Sonnet: The Ladies' Home Journal" work differently—not to remind us of a specific time that readers need to identify but to characterize a way of seeing and thinking. The referentiality here is more cultural than historical; it is based more on ideas and attitudes characteristic of a particular period than on a specific moment or location. The pictures in the *Ladies' Home Journal* stand for a whole way of thinking about women that was characteristic of the time—the mid-twentieth century—when this popular magazine flourished. The poem implicitly contrasts the "lies" (line 13) of the magazine with the truth of the present—that women's lives and values don't reside in some fantasized sense of beautiful food, motherhood, social rituals, and commercial products. Two vastly different cultural attitudes—that of the poem's present, with its skeptical view of women's traditional roles, and that of a past in which superficial glossy photographs represented gender identity—are at the heart of the poem. Readers

6. Designer coats by Christian Dior.

need to know what the *Ladies' Home Journal* was like in order to understand the poem; we do not need to know the date or contents of a specific issue, only that this magazine reflected the attitudes and values of a whole age and culture. The referentiality here involves information about ideas and consciousness—about cultural attitudes and their effects on actual human beings—more than time and event.

To get at appropriate factual, cultural, and historical information, we need to ask three kinds of questions. One kind is obvious: it is the "Do I understand the reference to . . . ?" kind. When events, places, or people unfamiliar to you come up, you will need to find out what, where, or who they are. The second kind of question is more difficult: How do you know, in a poem that does *not* refer specifically to events, people, or ideas that you do not recognize, that you *need* to know more? When a poem has no specific references to look up, no people or events to identify, how do you know that it has a specific context? To deal with this sort of question, you have to trust two people: the poet and yourself. Usually, good poets will not puzzle you more than necessary, so you can safely assume that something not self-explanatory will merit close attention and possibly some digging in the library. (Poets do make mistakes and miscalculations about their readers, but at the start we should assume they know what they are doing and why they are doing it.) References that are not in themselves clear provide a strong clue that you need more information. And so you need to trust yourself: when something doesn't click, when the information given you does not seem enough, you need to trust your puzzlement and try to find the missing facts that will allow the poem to make sense. But how? Often the date of the poem helps; sometimes the title gives a clue or a point of departure; sometimes you can uncover, by reading about the author, some of the things he or she was interested in or concerned about. There is no single all-purpose way to discover what to look for, but that kind of research—looking for clues, adding up the evidence—can be interesting in itself and very rewarding when it is successful. Meanwhile, the third question is why? For every factual reference, you need to ask why. Why does the poem refer to this particular person instead of some other? What function does the reference serve?

Beyond simply understanding that a particular poem is about an event or place or movement, you often must develop a full sense of historical context, a sense of the larger significance and resonance of the historical occurrence or attitude referred to. A poem may expect you to already have some sense of that significance; just as often it works to continue your education, telling you more, wanting you to understand and appreciate—on the level of feeling—some further things about this occurrence.

What we need to bring to our reading varies from poem to poem. For example, Wilfred Owen's "Dulce et Decorum Est" (this chapter) needs our knowledge that poison gas was used in World War I; the green tint through which the speaker sees the world

> *When I came to poetry it was through the struggles of tribal peoples to assert our human rights, to secure our sovereign rights as nations in the early seventies. It was the struggle begun by my grandmothers and grandfathers when they fought the move from our homelands in the Southeast to Indian Territory. This, too, was my personal struggle as a poet. It was in this wave of cultural renaissance for Indian peoples in this country that I heard the poetry that would change me, a poetry that could have been written those mornings of creation from childhood. This poetry named me as it jolted the country into sharp consciousness.*
>
> —JOY HARJO

in lines 13–14 comes from green glass in the goggles of the gas mask he has just put on. But some broader issues matter as well. Harder to specify but probably even more important is the climate of opinion that surrounded the war. To idealists, it was "the war to end all wars," and many participants—as well as politicians and propagandists—considered it a sacred mission, regarding the threat of Germany's expansionist policy as dangerous to Western civilization. No doubt you will read the poem more intelligently—and with more feeling—the more you know about the context, and the same is true of any poem with a cultural or historical referent. But at the same time, your sense of these subjects will grow as a result of reading sensitively and thoughtfully the poems themselves. Facts are no substitute for skills. Once you have read individually the poems in this section, try taking a breather; and then at one sitting read them all again. Reading poetry can be a form of gaining knowledge as well as an aesthetic experience. Although we don't generally go to poetry for information as such, poems often give us more than we come for. The ways to wisdom are paved with facts, and although poetry is not primarily a data-conscious art, it often requires us to be aware, sometimes in detail, of its referents in the real world.

TIMES, PLACES, AND EVENTS

MILLER WILLIAMS

Thinking about Bill, Dead of AIDS

We did not know the first thing about
how blood surrenders to even the smallest threat
when old allergies turn inside out,

the body rescinding all its normal orders
5   to all defenders of flesh, betraying the head,
pulling its guards back from all its borders.

Thinking of friends afraid to shake your hand,
we think of your hand shaking, your mouth set,
your eyes drained of any reprimand.

10   Loving, we kissed you, partly to persuade
both you and us, seeing what eyes had said,
that we were loving and were not afraid.

If we had had more, we would have given more.
As it was we stood next to your bed,
15   stopping, though, to set our smiles at the door.

Not because we were less sure at the last.
Only because, not knowing anything yet,
we didn't know what look would hurt you least.   1989

IRVING LAYTON

From Colony to Nation

A dull people,
but the rivers of this country
are wide and beautiful

A dull people
5   enamoured of childish games,
but food is easily come by
and plentiful

Some with a priest's voice
in their cage of ribs: but
10   on high mountain-tops and in thunderstorms
the chirping is not heard

Deferring to beadle and censor;
not ashamed for this,
but given over to horseplay,
the making of money   15

A dull people, without charm or
ideas,
settling into the clean empty look
of a Mountie or dairy farmer
as into a legacy   20

One can ignore them
(the silences, the vast distances help)
and suppose them at the bottom
of one of the meaner lakes,
their bones not even picked for souvenirs.   1956   25

MARY JO SALTER

Welcome to Hiroshima

is what you first see, stepping off the train:
a billboard brought to you in living English
by Toshiba Electric. While a channel
silent in the TV of the brain

projects those flickering re-runs of a cloud   5
that brims its risen columnful like beer
and, spilling over, hangs its foamy head,
you feel a thirst for history: what year

it started to be safe to breathe the air,
and when to drink the blood and scum afloat   10
on the Ohta River. But no, the water's clear,
they pour it for your morning cup of tea

in one of the countless sunny coffee shops
whose plastic dioramas advertise
mutations of cuisine behind the glass: 15
a pancake sandwich; a pizza someone tops

with a maraschino cherry. Passing by
the Peace Park's floral hypocenter (where
how bravely, or with what mistaken cheer,
humanity erased its own erasure),   20

you enter the memorial museum
and through more glass are served, as on a dish
of blistered grass, three mannequins. Like gloves
a mother clips to coatsleeves, strings of flesh

25   hang from their fingertips; or as if tied
to recall a duty for us, *Reverence*
the dead whose mourners too shall soon be dead,
but all commemoration's swallowed up

in questions of bad taste, how re-created
30   horror mocks the grim original,
and thinking at last *They should have left it all*
you stop. This is the wristwatch of a child.

Jammed on the moment's impact, resolute
to communicate some message, although mute,
35   it gestures with its hands at eight-fifteen
and eight-fifteen and eight-fifteen again

while tables of statistics on the wall
update the news by calling on a roll
of tape, death gummed on death, and in the case
40   adjacent, an exhibit under glass

is glass itself: a shard the bomb slammed in
a woman's arm at eight-fifteen, but some
three decades on—as if to make it plain
hope's only as renewable as pain,

45   and as if all the unsung
debasements of the past may one day come
rising to the surface once again—
worked its filthy way out like a tongue.   1984

LANGSTON HUGHES

Harlem (A Dream Deferred)

What happens to a dream deferred?

     Does it dry up
     like a raisin in the sun?
     Or fester like a sore—
5   And then run?
     Does it stink like rotten meat?
     Or crust and sugar over—
     like a syrupy sweet?

     Maybe it just sags
10   like a heavy load.

     Or does it explode?   1951

ROBERT HAYDEN

Frederick Douglass

When it is finally ours, this freedom,[1] this liberty, this beautiful
and terrible thing, needful to man as air,
usable as earth; when it belongs at last to all,
when it is truly instinct, brain matter, diastole, systole,
reflex action; when it is finally won; when it is more   5
than the gaudy mumbo jumbo of politicians:
this man, this Douglass, this former slave, this Negro
beaten to his knees, exiled, visioning a world
where none is lonely, none hunted, alien,
this man, superb in love and logic, this man   10
shall be remembered. Oh, not with statues' rhetoric,
not with legends and poems and wreaths of bronze alone,
but with the lives grown out of his life, the lives
fleshing his dream of the beautiful, needful thing.   1966

FELICIA DOROTHEA HEMANS

Casabianca[2]

The boy stood on the burning deck
    Whence all but he had fled;
The flame that lit the battle's wreck
    Shone round him o'er the dead.

Yet beautiful and bright he stood,   5
    As born to rule the storm;
A creature of heroic blood,
    A proud, though childlike form.

The flames roll'd on—he would not go
    Without his father's word;   10
That father, faint in death below,
    His voice no longer heard.

He call'd aloud:—"Say, Father, say
    If yet my task is done?"

1. Frederick Douglass (1817–1895), an escaped slave, was involved in the Underground Railroad and became publisher of the famous abolitionist newspaper the *North Star*, in Rochester, New York.
2. Young Casabianca, a boy about thirteen years old, son to the Admiral of the *Orient*, remained at his post (in the Battle of the Nile [1798]) after the ship had taken fire, and all the guns had been abandoned; and perished in the explosion of the vessel, when the flames had reached the powder [Hemans's note].

15   He knew not that the chieftain lay
            Unconscious of his son.

        "Speak, Father!" once again he cried,
            "If I may yet be gone!"
        And but the booming shots replied,
20   And fast the flames roll'd on.

        Upon his brow he felt their breath,
            And in his waving hair,
        And look'd from that lone post of death
            In still, yet brave despair.

25   And shouted but once more aloud,
            "My Father! must I stay?"
        While o'er him fast, through sail and shroud,
            The wreathing fires made way.

        They wrapt the ship in splendour wild,
30   They caught the flag on high,
        And stream'd above the gallant child,
            Like banners in the sky.

        There came a burst of thunder sound—
            The boy—oh! where was he?
35   Ask of the winds that far around
            With fragments strew'd the sea!—

        With mast, and helm, and pennon fair,
            That well had borne their part,
        But the noblest thing which perish'd there
40   Was that young faithful heart   1829

ELIZABETH BISHOP

Casabianca

        Love's the boy stood on the burning deck
        trying to recite "The boy stood on
        the burning deck." Love's the son
            stood stammering elocution
5   while the poor ship in flames went down.

        Love's the obstinate boy, the ship,
        even the swimming sailors, who
        would like a schoolroom platform, too,
            or an excuse to stay
10   on deck. And love's the burning boy.   1946

WILFRED OWEN

Dulce et Decorum Est[3]

Bent double, like old beggars under sacks,
Knock-kneed, coughing like hags, we cursed through sludge,
Till on the haunting flares we turned our backs
And towards our distant rest began to trudge.
Men marched asleep. Many had lost their boots   5
But limped on, blood-shod. All went lame; all blind;
Drunk with fatigue; deaf even to the hoots
Of disappointed shells that dropped behind.

Gas! Gas! Quick, boys!—An ecstasy of fumbling,
Fitting the clumsy helmets just in time;   10
But someone still was yelling out and stumbling
And floundering like a man in fire or lime.—
Dim, through the misty panes and thick green light
As under a green sea, I saw him drowning.

In all my dreams, before my helpless sight,   15
He plunges at me, guttering, choking, drowning.

If in some smothering dreams you too could pace
Behind the wagon that we flung him in,
And watch the white eyes writhing in his face,
His hanging face, like a devil's sick of sin;   20
If you could hear, at every jolt, the blood
Come gargling from the froth-corrupted lungs,
Obscene as cancer, bitter as the cud
Of vile, incurable sores on innocent tongues,—
My friend, you would not tell with such high zest   25
To children ardent for some desperate glory,
The old Lie: Dulce et decorum est
Pro patria mori.

1917

---

3. Part of a phrase from Horace (Roman poet and satirist, 65–8 B.C.), quoted in full in the last lines: "It is sweet and proper to die for one's country."

DUDLEY RANDALL

Ballad of Birmingham

(On the bombing of a church in Birmingham, Alabama, 1963)

"Mother dear, may I go downtown
Instead of out to play,
And march the streets of Birmingham
In a Freedom March today?"

5   "No, baby, no, you may not go,
For the dogs are fierce and wild,
And clubs and hoses, guns and jails
Aren't good for a little child."

"But, mother, I won't be alone.
10 Other children will go with me,
And march the streets of Birmingham
To make our country free."

"No, baby, no, you may not go,
For I fear those guns will fire.
15 But you may go to church instead
And sing in the children's choir."

She has combed and brushed her night-dark hair,
And bathed rose petal sweet,
And drawn white gloves on her small brown hands,
20 And white shoes on her feet.

The mother smiled to know her child
Was in the sacred place,
But that smile was the last smile
To come upon her face.

25 For when she heard the explosion,
Her eyes grew wet and wild.
She raced through the streets of Birmingham
Calling for her child.

She clawed through bits of glass and brick,
30 Then lifted out a shoe.
"Oh, here's the shoe my baby wore,
But, baby, where are you?"

1969

CONSTRUCTING IDENTITY, EXPLORING GENDER

ELIZABETH BISHOP

Exchanging Hats

Unfunny uncles who insist
in trying on a lady's hat,
—oh, even if the joke falls flat,
we share your slight transvestite twist

in spite of our embarrassment.   5
Costume and custom are complex.
The headgear of the other sex
inspires us to experiment.

Anandrous[1] aunts, who, at the beach
with paper plates upon your laps,   10
keep putting on the yachtsmen's caps
with exhibitionistic screech,

the visors hanging o'er the ear
so that the golden anchors drag,
—the tides of fashion never lag.   15
Such caps may not be worn next year.

Or you who don the paper plate
itself, and put some grapes upon it,
or sport the Indian's feather bonnet,
—perversities may aggravate   20

the natural madness of the hatter.
And if the opera hats collapse
and crowns grow draughty, then, perhaps,
he thinks what might a miter matter?

Unfunny uncle, you who wore a   25
hat too big, or one too many,
tell us, can't you, are there any
stars inside your black fedora?

Aunt exemplary and slim,
with avernal[2] eyes, we wonder   30
what slow changes they see under
their vast, shady, turned-down brim.   1956

1. Literally, belonging to the category of male.   2. Infernal.

MARIE HOWE

Practicing

I want to write a love poem for the girls I kissed in seventh grade,
a song for what we did on the floor in the basement

of somebody's parents' house, a hymn for what we didn't say but
    thought:
That feels good or *I like that,* when we learned how to open each other's
    mouths

how to move our tongues to make somebody moan. We called it practicing, and
one was the boy, and we paired off—maybe six or eight girls—and turned
    out

the lights and kissed and kissed until we were stoned on kisses, and lifted
    our
nightgowns or let the straps drop, and, Now you be the boy:

concrete floor, sleeping bag or couch, playroom, game room, train room,
    laundry.
Linda's basement was like a boat with booths and portholes

instead of windows. Gloria's father had a bar downstairs with stools that
    spun,
plush carpeting. We kissed each other's throats.

We sucked each other's breasts, and we left marks, and never spoke of it
    upstairs
outdoors, in daylight, not once. We did it, and it was

practicing, and slept, sprawled so our legs still locked or crossed, a hand
    still lost
in someone's hair . . . and we grew up and hardly mentioned who

the first kiss really was—a girl like us, still sticky with the moisturizer
    we'd
shared in the bathroom. I want to write a song

for that thick silence in the dark, and the first pure thrill of unreluctant
    desire,
just before we made ourselves stop.

1998

RICHARD LOVELACE

Song: To Lucasta, Going to the Wars

Tell me not, sweet, I am unkind,
   That from the nunnery
Of thy chaste breast and quiet mind
   To war and arms I fly.

True: a new mistress now I chase,   5
   The first foe in the field;
And with a stronger faith embrace
   A sword, a horse, a shield.

Yet this inconstancy is such
   As you too shall adore;   10
I could not love thee, dear, so much,
   Loved I not honor more.   1649

ROBERT BROWNING

My Last Duchess

Ferrara[3]

That's my last Duchess painted on the wall,
Looking as if she were alive. I call
That piece a wonder, now: Frà Pandolf's hands[4]
Worked busily a day, and there she stands.
Will't please you sit and look at her? I said   5
"Frà Pandolf" by design, for never read
Strangers like you that pictured countenance,
The depth and passion of its earnest glance,
But to myself they turned (since none puts by
The curtain I have drawn for you, but I)   10
And seemed as they would ask me, if they durst,
How such a glance came there; so, not the first
Are you to turn and ask thus. Sir, 'twas not
Her husband's presence only, called that spot

3. Alfonso II, duke of Ferrara in Italy in the mid sixteenth century, is the presumed speaker of the poem, which is loosely based on historical events. The duke's first wife—whom he had married when she was fourteen—died under suspicious circumstances at seventeen, and he then negotiated through an agent (to whom the poem is spoken) for the hand of the niece of the count of Tyrol in Austria.   4. Frà Pandolf is, like Claus (line 56), fictitious.

15   Of joy into the Duchess' cheek: perhaps
      Frà Pandolf chanced to say "Her mantle laps
      Over my lady's wrist too much," or "Paint
      Must never hope to reproduce the faint
      Half-flush that dies along her throat": such stuff
20   Was courtesy, she thought, and cause enough
      For calling up that spot of joy. She had
      A heart—how shall I say?—too soon made glad,
      Too easily impressed; she liked whate'er
      She looked on, and her looks went everywhere.
25   Sir, 'twas all one! My favor at her breast,
      The dropping of the daylight in the West,
      The bough of cherries some officious fool
      Broke in the orchard for her, the white mule
      She rode with round the terrace—all and each
30   Would draw from her alike the approving speech,
      Or blush, at least. She thanked men,—good! but thanked
      Somehow—I know not how—as if she ranked
      My gift of a nine-hundred-years-old name
      With anybody's gift. Who'd stoop to blame
35   This sort of trifling? Even had you skill
      In speech—which I have not—to make your will
      Quite clear to such an one, and say, "Just this
      Or that in you disgusts me; here you miss,
      Or there exceed the mark"—and if she let
40   Herself be lessoned so, nor plainly set
      Her wits to yours, forsooth, and made excuse,
      —E'en then would be some stooping; and I choose
      Never to stoop. Oh sir, she smiled, no doubt,
      Whene'er I passed her; but who passed without
45   Much the same smile? This grew; I gave commands;
      Then all smiles stopped together. There she stands
      As if alive. Will't please you rise? We'll meet
      The company below, then. I repeat,
      The Count your master's known munificence
50   Is ample warrant that no just pretense
      Of mine for dowry will be disallowed;
      Though his fair daughter's self, as I avowed
      At starting, is my object. Nay, we'll go
      Together down, sir. Notice Neptune, though,
55   Taming a sea-horse, thought a rarity,
      Which Claus of Innsbruck cast in bronze for me!   1842

ELIZABETH BARRETT BROWNING

To George Sand

A Desire

Thou large-brained woman and large-hearted man,
Self-called George Sand[5] whose soul, amid the lions
Of thy tumultuous senses, moans defiance
And answers roar for roar, as spirits can:
I would some mild miraculous thunder ran   5
Above the applauded circus,[6] in appliance
Of thine own nobler nature's strength and science,
Drawing two pinions, white as wings of swan,
From thy strong shoulders, to amaze the place
With holier light! that thou to woman's claim   10
And man's, mightst join beside the angel's grace
Of a pure genius sanctified from blame,
Till child and maiden pressed to thine embrace
To kiss upon thy lips a stainless fame.   1844

To George Sand

A Recognition

True genius, but true woman! dost deny
The woman's nature with a manly scorn,
And break away the gauds and armlets worn
By weaker women in captivity?
Ah, vain denial! that revolted cry   5
Is sobbed in by a woman's voice forlorn,—
Thy woman's hair, my sister, all unshorn
Floats back dishevelled strength in agony,
Disproving thy man's name: and while before
The world thou burnest in a poet-fire,   10
We see thy woman-heart beat evermore
Through the large flame. Beat purer, heart, and higher,
Till God unsex thee on the heavenly shore
Where unincarnate spirits purely aspire!   1844

5. Pseudonym of Amandine-Aurore-Lucie (or -Lucille) Dupin, baronne Dudevant (1804–1876), French Romantic novelist, famous for her unconventional ideas and behavior.   6. Roman spectacle involving gladiatorial games, brutal athletic contests, and the killing of Christian slaves by lions.

LADY MARY WORTLEY MONTAGU

Written the First Year I Was Marry'd

While thirst of power, and desire of fame,
In every age is every woman's aim;
Of beauty vain, of silly toasters proud,
Fond of a train, and happy in a crowd,
On every fop bestowing a kind glance,   5
Each conquest owing to some loose advance,
Affect to fly, in hopes to be persu'd,
And think they're virtuous, if not grossly lewd:
Let this sure maxim be my virtue's guide,
In part to blame she is, who has been try'd;   10
Too near he has approach'd, who is deny'd.

1712–13

MARGE PIERCY

What's That Smell in the Kitchen?

All over America women are burning dinners.
It's lambchops in Peoria; it's haddock
in Providence; it's steak in Chicago;
tofu delight in Big Sur; red
rice and beans in Dallas.   5
All over America women are burning
food they're supposed to bring with calico
smile on platters glittering like wax.
Anger sputters in her brainpan, confined
but spewing out missiles of hot fat.   10
Carbonized despair presses like a clinker
from a barbecue against the back of her eyes.
If she wants to grill anything, it's
her husband spitted over a slow fire.
If she wants to serve him anything   15
it's a dead rat with a bomb in its belly
ticking like the heart of an insomniac.
Her life is cooked and digested,
nothing but leftovers in Tupperware.
Look, she says, once I was roast duck   20
on your platter with parsley but now I am Spam.
Burning dinner is not incompetence but war.

1983

PAULETTE JILES

Paper Matches

My aunts washed dishes while the uncles
squirted each other on the lawn with
   garden hoses. Why are we in here,
I said, and they are out there.
   That's the way it is,   5
   said Aunt Hetty, the shrivelled-up one.
   I have the rages that small animals have,
being small, being animal.
   Written on me was a message,
"At Your Service" like a book of   10
paper matches. One by one we were
taken out and struck.
   We come bearing supper.
our heads on fire.   1973

EDNA ST. VINCENT MILLAY

[*Women have loved before as I love now*]

Women have loved before as I love now;
At least, in lively chronicles of the past—
Of Irish waters by a Cornish prow
Or Trojan waters by a Spartan mast
Much to their cost invaded—here and there,   5
Hunting the amorous line, skimming the rest,
I find some woman bearing as I bear
Love like a burning city in the breast.
I think however that of all alive
I only in such utter, ancient way   10
Do suffer love; in me alone survive
The unregenerate passions of a day
When treacherous queens, with death upon the tread,
Heedless and wilful, took their knights to bed.   1931

[*I, being born a woman and distressed*]

I, being born a woman and distressed
By all the needs and notions of my kind,
Am urged by your propinquity to find

Your person fair, and feel a certain zest
5   To bear your body's weight upon my breast:
So subtly is the fume of life designed,
To clarify the pulse and cloud the mind,
And leave me once again undone, possessed.
Think not for this, however, the poor treason
10   Of my stout blood against my staggering brain,
I shall remember you with love, or season
My scorn with pity,—let me make it plain:
I find this frenzy insufficient reason
For conversation when we meet again.   1923

AMY LOWELL

The Lonely Wife[7]

The mist is thick. On the wide river, the water-plants float smoothly.
No letters come; none go.
There is only the moon, shining through the clouds of a hard, jade-
    green sky,
Looking down at us so far divided, so anxiously apart.
All day, going about my affairs, I suffer and grieve, and press the
5   thought of you closely to my heart.
My eyebrows are locked in sorrow, I cannot separate them.
Nightly, nightly, I keep ready half the quilt,
And wait for the return of that divine dream which is my Lord.

Beneath the quilt of the Fire-Bird, on the bed of the Silver-Crested Love-
    Pheasant,
10   Nightly, nightly, I drowse alone.
The red candles in the silver candlesticks melt, and the wax runs from
    them,
As the tears of your so Unworthy One escape and continue constantly
    to flow.
A flower face endures but a short season,
Yet still he drifts along the river Hsiao and the river Hsiang.
As I toss on my pillow, I hear the cold, nostalgic sound of the water-
15   clock:
Shêng! Shêng! it drips, cutting my heart in two.

I rise at dawn. In the Hall of Pictures
They come and tell me that the snow-flowers are falling.
The reed-blind is rolled high, and I gaze at the beautiful, glittering,
    primeval snow,
20   Whitening the distance, confusing the stone steps and the courtyard.

7. A translation/adaptation of a poem by the Chinese poet Li Po (A.D. 701–762).

The air is filled with its shining, it blows far out like the smoke of a
  furnace.
The grass-blades are cold and white, like jade girdle pendants.
Surely the Immortals in Heaven must be crazy with wine to cause such
  disorder,
Seizing the white clouds, crumpling them up, destroying them.

                                                                      1921

LIZ ROSENBERG

The Silence of Women

Old men, as time goes on, grow softer, sweeter,
while their wives get angrier.
You see them hauling the men across the mall
or pushing them down on chairs,
"Sit there! and don't you move!"   5
A lifetime of *yes* has left them
hissing bent as snakes.
It seems even their bones will turn
against them, once the fruitful years are gone.
Something snaps off the houselights,   10
and the cells go dim;
the chicken hatching back into the egg.

Oh lifetime of silence!
words scattered like a sibyl's leaves.
Voice thrown into a baritone storm—   15
whose shrilling is a soulful wind
blown through an instrument
that cannot beat time

but must make music
any way it can.   1994   20

THOM GUNN

A Blank

The year of griefs being through, they had to merge
In one last grief, with one last property;
To view itself like loosened cloud lose edge,
And pull apart, and leave a voided sky.

Watching Victorian porches through the glass,   5
From the 6 bus, I caught sight of a friend
Stopped on a corner-kerb to let us pass,

A four-year-old blond child tugging his hand,
Which tug he held against with a slight smile.
10   I knew the smile from certain passages
Two years ago, thus did not know him well,
Since they took place in my bedroom and his.

A sturdy-looking admirable young man.
He said "I chose to do this with my life."
15   Casually met he said it of the plan
He undertook without a friend or wife.

Now visibly tugged upon by his decision,
Wayward and eager. So this was his son!
What I admired about his self-permission
20   Was that he turned from nothing he had done,
Or was, or had been, even while he transposed
The expectations he took out at dark
—Of Eros playing, features undisclosed—
Into another pitch, where he might work
25   With the same melody, and opted so
To educate, permit, guide, feed, keep warm,
And love a child to be adopted, though
The child was still a blank then on a form.

The blank was flesh now, running on its nerve,
30   This fair-topped organism dense with charm,
Its braided muscle grabbing what would serve,
His countering pull, his own devoted arm.   1992

QUESTIONS

1. What additional information would you like to have about the events referred to in Hayden's "Frederick Douglass" and Randall's "Ballad of Birmingham"? What details in these poems call for additional information about the events on which each is based? What details about the life and writings of Frederick Douglass, and about his character, would help your reading of the poem named for him? What do you make of the mention of "dogs," "clubs," and "hoses" in "Ballad of Birmingham"? What did "Freedom March" mean in 1969? Given the poem's structure and its portrayal of children's voices and attitudes, what difference might it make to your reading if you had factual information about the actual casualties of the bombing? If you were editing this poem, what other footnotes would you provide? Reread "Sir Patrick Spens" (chapter 17). In what ways does Randall's poem allude to it? Why?

2. What details about the physical suffering from poison gas are specifically suggested in Owen's "Dulce et Decorum Est"? what details about the physical effects of atomic explosions in Salter's "Welcome to Hiroshima"? How accurate are these representations? Using the reference resources in your college library, look up news accounts of gassings in World War I and the atomic bombing of Hiroshima, and compare the journalistic details with those given in the poems. How careful does each poet seem to have been in representing historical events? What evidence do you find of distortion or "poetic license"? Which details are specifically chosen for powerful rhetorical effects in each poem?

3. Compare the images of fire and burning in Piercy's "What's That Smell in the Kitchen?" and Jiles's "Paper Matches." How are the images used differently in each poem? What common thread of meaning informs the images in these poems? On what kind of cultural assumptions about women and their roles do these images seem to be based? In what ways are these images like other images of passion in other poems you have read? In what ways are the images like other images of destruction?
4. Which poems in the "Constructing Identity, Exploring Gender" group concern the importance of physical space? In what ways do they portray its absence? In what ways do they represent the male sense of a woman's "place"?
5. What images of women's passivity, deferentiality, and compliance can you find within the poems in this group? How is each image treated in the individual poem? In what ways do images of assertion and resistance compete with these images? What differences in imagery do you notice between men's portrayal of women and women's portrayal of women?

WRITING SUGGESTIONS

1. Using reference materials available in your college library, construct a detailed narrative (of about five hundred to seven hundred words) of the Birmingham bombing. Then "read" the poem in the context of the full story, showing how the poem uses specific details of the incident to create its effects.
2. Which poem in the "Constructing Identity, Exploring Gender" group most effectively describes how men construct their gender and identity? Which most successfully describes how women do? Pick one of the two poems and, in an essay of about five hundred words, discuss the devices it uses to accomplish this task.

24

CRITICAL CONTEXTS: A POETRY CASEBOOK

As the previous context chapters have suggested, poems draw on all kinds of earlier texts, experiences, and events. But they also produce new contexts of discussion and interpretation, ongoing conversations about the poems themselves. Because readers of poems see different things in them, and because readers bring different interests to their readings, differences and disagreements develop about how poems should be experienced, interpreted, and evaluated. Just as what you say about a poem differs from what your classmates say, and just as the paper you write about a poem differs from—and often disagrees with—what other students will write, various observations and comments develop around any poem that is read repeatedly by various readers. Many of those interpretations are published in specialized journals and books (the selections that follow are all reprinted from published sources), and a kind of dialogue develops among readers, producing a body of interpretations and commentaries about the poem. Professional interpreters of texts are often called **literary critics,** and the textual analysis they provide is called **criticism**—not because their work is necessarily negative or corrective, but because they ask hard, analytical, "critical" questions and interpret texts through a wide variety of literary, historical, biographical, psychological, aesthetic, moral, political, or social perspectives.

Your own interpretive work may seem to you more private and far removed from such "professional" writing about poems. But once you engage in class discussion with your teacher or even talk informally with a fellow student about a poem, you are in effect practicing your own literary criticism—offering comments, analyzing, judging, putting the poem into some kind of perspective that makes it more knowable and understandable to yourself or to other readers. You are, in effect, joining the ongoing conversation about the poem. The accumulated criticism on any particular poem is, in fact, basically just public conversation and discussion—give and take, competing interpretations, accumulation of relevant facts and information—on the topic of how that poem should be experienced, interpreted, and evaluated. And when you *write* about the poem, you may often engage specifically the opinions of others—your teacher, fellow students, or published "criticism." You may not have the experience or specific expertise of professional critics, but you can modify or answer the work of others and use it in your own work.

There are many different ways to engage literary criticism and put it to work for you. The most common is to draw on published work for specific information about the poem: glossings of particular terms; explanations of references or situations you don't recognize; accounts of how, when, and under what circumstances the poem was written. Another common use is as a springboard for your own interpretation, either building upon what someone else has said or using it as a point of departure to disagree and launch a different view. In either case, your own paper may readily develop out of your reading or out of a class lecture or class discussion, which you may draw on just as you would written accounts. When you use the work of others, you must give full credit, carefully detailing the source of all direct quotations and all borrowed ideas. You must always tell your reader exactly how to find the material you have quoted or summarized. Usually, you do this through careful notes and a list of citations (or bibliography) at the end of your paper. Your instructor will guide you to handbooks—for example, the *MLA Handbook* or *The Chicago Manual of Style*—that demonstrate how to cite each item in the appropriate style.

It can seem intimidating to become involved in critical dialogue, especially with those who are "authorities" or "experts" whose work has been published and widely read. But your own reading experience gives you a legitimate perspective, too, and often you can sharpen your skills by arguing out your views against those with extensive interpretive experience. Besides, as you will quickly discover when you read several critical pieces on a particular poem, even the experts disagree.

Procedurally, it is usually best to do your own extensive analysis of a poem *before* consulting what other critics have said. That way, you can confront other views from a firm (though tentative) position. You always want to take in new information and to challenge both your first impressions and your considered analyses, but don't be too quick to adopt somebody else's ideas. The best way to test the views of others is to compare them critically to your own conclusions, which you might then want to supplement, refine, extend, or even scrap altogether. In other words, proceed just as you have been proceeding—asking the questions you have learned to ask, sorting out the evidence you have noticed, and moving toward an integrated interpretation of the poem.

Before you read the criticism on Sylvia Plath's "Daddy" reprinted in this chapter, carefully read the poem itself several times. Ask all the analytical questions you have found useful in other cases: Who is speaking? To whom? When? Under what conditions? What is the full dramatic situation behind the poem? What kind of language does the poem use? To what effect? How does the poem use metaphor? allusion? historical reference? What strategies of rhythm and sound does the poem use? To what effect? What is the poem's tone? In what ways is this poem like other poems or other texts on similar topics? When was the poem written? What do you know about the person who wrote the poem? In what ways is this poem like others you have read by this poet or by this poet's contemporaries? How do the poem's themes and attitudes reflect the culture and times in which it was written?

SYLVIA PLATH

Daddy[1]

You do not do, you do not do
Any more, black shoe
In which I have lived like a foot
For thirty years, poor and white,
5   Barely daring to breathe or Achoo.

Daddy, I have had to kill you.
You died before I had time—
Marble-heavy, a bag full of God,
Ghastly statue with one gray toe
10   Big as a Frisco seal

And a head in the freakish Atlantic
Where it pours bean green over blue
In the waters off beautiful Nauset.[2]
I used to pray to recover you.
15   Ach, du.[3]

In the German tongue, in the Polish town
Scraped flat by the roller
Of wars, wars, wars.
But the name of the town is common.
20   My Polack friend

Says there are a dozen or two.
So I never could tell where you
Put your foot, your root,
I never could talk to you.
25   The tongue stuck in my jaw.

It stuck in a barb wire snare.
Ich, ich, ich, ich,
I could hardly speak.
I thought every German was you.
30   And the language obscene

An engine, an engine
Chuffing me off like a Jew.
A Jew to Dachau, Auschwitz, Belsen.[4]
I began to talk like a Jew.
35   I think I may well be a Jew.

The snows of the Tyrol, the clear beer of Vienna[5]
Are not very pure or true.

---

1. First published in *Ariel*, a volume of poems that appeared two years after Plath's suicide.   2. An inlet on Cape Cod.   3. Oh, you (German). Plath often portrays herself as Jewish and her oppressors as German. *Ich* (below, line 27): German for "I."   4. Sites of World War II Nazi death camps.   5. The snow in the Tyrol (an Alpine region in Austria and northern Italy) is, legendarily, as pure as the beer is clear in Vienna.

With my gypsy-ancestress and my weird luck
And my Taroc[6] pack and my Taroc pack
I may be a bit of a Jew.   40

I have always been scared of *you,*
With your Luftwaffe,[7] your gobbledygoo.
And your neat moustache
And your Aryan eye, bright blue.
Panzer-man, panzer-man, O You—   45

Not God but a swastika
So black no sky could squeak through.
Every woman adores a Fascist,
The boot in the face, the brute
Brute heart of a brute like you.   50

You stand at the blackboard, daddy,
In the picture I have of you,
A cleft in your chin instead of your foot
But no less a devil for that, no not
Any less the black man who   55

Bit my pretty red heart in two.
I was ten when they buried you.
At twenty I tried to die
And get back, back, back to you.
I thought even the bones would do   60

But they pulled me out of the sack,
And they stuck me together with glue.
And then I knew what to do.
I made a model of you,
A man in black with a Meinkampf[8] look   65

And a love of the rack and the screw.
And I said I do, I do.
So daddy, I'm finally through.
The black telephone's off at the root,
The voices just can't worm through.   70

If I've killed one man, I've killed two—
The vampire who said he was you
And drank my blood for a year,
Seven years, if you want to know.
Daddy, you can lie back now.   75

There's a stake in your fat black heart
And the villagers never liked you.
They are dancing and stamping on you.
They always *knew* it was you.
Daddy, daddy, you bastard, I'm through.   1966   80

6. Tarot, playing cards used mainly for fortune-telling.   7. The German air force.   8. The title of
Adolf Hitler's autobiography and manifesto (1925–27); German for "my struggle."

Once you have a "reading" of your own and have made extensive notes about your conclusions, look at the selections that follow. You can read them in a variety of ways:

- skim them all quickly, and look for things that surprise you or that provide you with specific challenges; or
- read each critical piece carefully, one by one, and keep close track of all the things with which you agree and (even more important) of those things with which you disagree; or
- look specifically for facts or apparently crucial information new to you, examine and question the information carefully, and see how it affects the interpretation you have previously decided on; or
- look for points of disagreement in the different interpretations, make a list of the most important issues raised, and look for the crucial parts of the poem where the basis for these disagreements occurs.

You will also find your own ways to respond to and use the various critical views you come upon here. Working the views of others into your own arguments and your own writing is complicated; while supporting your own conclusions, you must be fair to what others say. But learning to use the facts, opinions, and interpretations of others will clarify your own thoughts, hone or add to your analytical skills, and deepen your views. And participating in the larger conversation about a specific poem—or about poetry in general—will help you read, respond, and write more effectively.

Sylvia Plath

Sylvia Plath's father, Otto Plath

GEORGE STEINER

*Dying Is an Art**

. . . [N]o group of poems since Dylan Thomas' *Deaths and Entrances* has had as vivid and disturbing an impact on English critics and readers as has *Ariel*. Sylvia Plath's last poems have already passed into legend as both representative of our present tone of emotional life and unique in their implacable, harsh brilliance. Those among the young who read new poetry will know "Daddy," "Lady Laza- rus," and "Death & Co." almost by heart, and reference to Sylvia Plath is constant where poetry and the conditions of its present existence are discussed.

The spell does not lie wholly in the poems themselves. The suicide of Sylvia Plath at the age of thirty-one in 1963, and the personality of this young woman who had come from Massachusetts to study and live in England (where she mar- ried Ted Hughes, himself a gifted poet), are vital parts of it. To those who knew her and to the greatly enlarged circle who were electrified by her last poems and sudden death, she had come to signify the specific honesties and risks of the poet's condition. Her personal style, and the price in private harrowing she so obviously paid to achieve the intensity and candor of her principal poems, have taken on their own dramatic authority.

All this makes it difficult to judge the poems. I mean that the vehemence and intimacy of the verse is such as to constitute a very powerful rhetoric of sincerity. The poems play on our nerves with their own proud nakedness, making claims so immediate and sharply urged that the reader flinches, embarrassed by the rou- tine discretions and evasions of his own sensibility. Yet if these poems are to take life among us, if they are to be more than exhibits in the history of modern psychological stress, they must be read with all the intelligence and scruple we can muster. They are too honest, they have cost too much, to be yielded to myth.

. . . It requires no biographical impertinence to realize that Sylvia Plath's life was harried by bouts of physical pain, that she sometimes looked on the accumulated exactions of her own nerve and body as "a trash To annihilate each decade." She was haunted by the piecemeal, strung-together mechanics of the flesh, by what could be so easily broken and then mended with such searing ingenuity. The hospital ward was her exemplary ground:

> My patent leather overnight case like a black pillbox,
> My husband and child smiling out of the family photo;
> Their smiles catch onto my skin, little smiling hooks.

This brokenness, so sharply feminine and contemporary, is, I think, her prin- cipal realization. It is by the graphic expression she gave to it that she will be

---

* From George Steiner, *Language and Silence: Essays on Language, Literature, and the Inhuman* (1967; New York: Atheneum, 1974), pp. 295–302.

judged and remembered. Sylvia Plath carries forward, in an intensely womanly and aggravated note, from Robert Lowell's *Life Studies,* a book that obviously had a great impact on her. This new frankness of women about the specific hurts and tangles of their nervous-physiological makeup is as vital to the poetry of Sylvia Plath as it is to the tracts of Simone de Beauvoir or to the novels of Edna O'Brien and Brigid Brophy. Women speak out as never before:

> The womb
> Rattles its pod, the moon
> Discharges itself from the tree with nowhere to go.
>
> ("Childless Woman")

> They have swabbed me clear of my loving associations.
> Scared and bare on the green plastic-pillowed trolley. . . .
>
> ("Tulips")

It is difficult to think of a precedent to the fearful close of "Medusa" (the whole poem is extraordinary):

> I shall take no bite of your body,
> Bottle in which I live,
>
> Ghastly Vatican.
> I am sick to death of hot salt.
> Green as eunuchs, your wishes
> Hiss at my sin.
> Off, off, eely tentacle!
>
> There is nothing between us.

The ambiguity and dual flash of insight in this final line are of a richness and obviousness that only a very great poem can carry off.

The progress registered between the early and the mature poems is one of concretion. The general Gothic means with which Sylvia Plath was so fluently equipped become singular to herself and therefore fiercely honest. What had been style passes into need. It is the need of a superbly intelligent, highly literate young woman to cry out about her especial being, about the tyrannies of blood and gland, of nervous spasm and sweating skin, the rankness of sex and childbirth in which a woman is still compelled to be wholly of her organic condition. Where Emily Dickinson could—indeed was obliged to—shut the door on the riot and humiliations of the flesh, thus achieving her particular dry lightness, Sylvia Plath "fully assumed her own condition." This alone would assure her of a place in modern literature. But she took one step further, assuming a burden that was not naturally or necessarily hers.

Born in Boston in 1932 of German and Austrian parents, Sylvia Plath had no personal, immediate contact with the world of the concentration camps. I may be mistaken, but so far as I know there was nothing Jewish in her background. But her last, greatest poems culminate in an act of identification, of total communion with those tortured and massacred. The poet sees herself on

An engine, an engine
Chuffing me off like a Jew.
A Jew to Dachau, Auschwitz, Belsen.
I began to talk like a Jew.
I think I may well be a Jew.

The snows of the Tyrol, the clear beer of Vienna
Are not very pure or true.
With my gypsy ancestress and my weird luck

And my Tarot pack and my Tarot pack
I may be a bit of a Jew.

Distance is no help; nor the fact that one is "guilty of nothing." The dead men cry out of the yew hedges. The poet becomes the loud cry of their choked silence:

Herr God, Herr Lucifer
Beware
Beware.
Out of the ash
I rise with my red hair
And I eat men like air.

Here the almost surrealistic wildness of the gesture is kept in place by the insistent obviousness of the language and beat; a kind of Hieronymus Bosch[1] nursery rhyme.

Sylvia Plath is only one of a number of young contemporary poets, novelists, and playwrights, themselves in no way implicated in the actual holocaust, who have done most to counter the general inclination to forget the death camps. Perhaps it is only those who had no part in the events who *can* focus on them rationally and imaginatively; to those who experienced the thing, it has lost the hard edges of possibility, it has stepped outside the real.

Committing the whole of her poetic and formal authority to the metaphor, to the mask of language, Sylvia Plath *became* a woman being transported to Auschwitz on the death trains. The notorious shards of massacre seemed to enter into her own being:

A cake of soap,
A wedding ring,
A gold filling.

In "Daddy" she wrote one of the very few poems I know of in any language to come near the last horror. It achieves the classic act of generalization, translating a private, obviously intolerable hurt into a code of plain statement, of instantaneously public images which concern us all. It is the "Guernica"[2] of modern poetry. And it is both histrionic and, in some ways, "arty," as is Picasso's outcry.

---

1. A fifteenth-century Netherlandish artist whose nightmarish paintings are filled with obscure symbolism.   2. Picasso's famous painting (1937) depicting the brutalities of war.

Are these final poems entirely legitimate? In what sense does anyone, himself uninvolved and long after the event, commit a subtle larceny when he invokes the echoes and trappings of Auschwitz and appropriates an enormity of ready emotion to his own private design? Was there latent in Sylvia Plath's sensibility, as in that of many of us who remember only by fiat of imagination, a fearful envy, a dim resentment at not having been there, of having missed the rendezvous with hell? In "Lady Lazarus" and "Daddy" the realization seems to me so complete, the sheer rawness and control so great, that only irresistible need could have brought it off. These poems take tremendous risks, extending Sylvia Plath's essentially austere manner to the very limit. They are a bitter triumph, proof of the capacity of poetry to give to reality the greater permanence of the imagined. She could not return from them.

IRVING HOWE

*The Plath Celebration: A Partial Dissent**

. . . Sylvia Plath's most famous poem, adored by many sons and daughters, is "Daddy." It is a poem with an affecting theme, the feelings of the speaker as she regathers the pain of her father's premature death and her persuasion that he has betrayed her by dying:

> I was ten when they buried you.
> At twenty I tried to die
> And get back, back, back to you.

In the poem Sylvia Plath identifies the father (we recall his German birth) with the Nazis ("Panzer-man, panzer-man, O You") and flares out with assaults for which nothing in the poem (nor, so far as we know, in Sylvia Plath's own life) offers any warrant: "A cleft in your chin instead of your foot / But no less a devil for that. . . ." Nor does anything in the poem offer warrant, other than the free-flowing hysteria of the speaker, for the assault of such lines as, "There's a stake in your fat black heart / And the villagers never liked you." Or for the snappy violence of

> Every woman adores a Fascist,
> The boot in the face, the brute
> Brute heart of a brute like you.

What we have here is a revenge fantasy, feeding upon filial love-hatred, and thereby mostly of clinical interest. But seemingly aware that the merely clinical can't provide the materials for a satisfying poem, Sylvia Plath tries to enlarge upon

---

* From Irving Howe, *The Critical Point of Literature and Culture* (1973; New York: Horizon Press, 1977), pp. 231–33.

the personal plight, give meaning to the personal outcry, by fancying the girl as victim of a Nazi father:

> An engine, an engine
> Chuffing me off like a Jew.
> A Jew to Dachau, Auschwitz, Belsen.
> I began to talk like a Jew.
> I think I may well be a Jew.

The more sophisticated admirers of this poem may say that I fail to see it as a dramatic presentation, a monologue spoken by a disturbed girl not necessarily to be identified with Sylvia Plath, despite the similarities of detail between the events of the poem and the events of her life. I cannot accept this view. The personal-confessional element, strident and undisciplined, is simply too obtrusive to suppose the poem no more than a dramatic picture of a certain style of disturbance. If, however, we did accept such a reading of "Daddy," we would fatally narrow its claims to emotional or moral significance, for we would be confining it to a mere vivid imagining of pathological state. That, surely, is not how its admirers really take the poem.

It is clearly not how the critic George Steiner takes the poem when he calls it "the 'Guernica' of modern poetry." But then, in an astonishing turn, he asks: "In what sense does anyone, himself uninvolved and long after the event, commit a subtle larceny when he invokes the echoes and trappings of Auschwitz and appropriates an enormity of ready emotion to his own private design?" The question is devastating to his early comparison with "Guernica." Picasso's painting objectifies the horrors of Guernica, through the distancing of art; no one can suppose that he shares or participates in them. Plath's poem aggrandizes on the "enormity of ready emotion" invoked by references to the concentration camps, in behalf of an ill-controlled if occasionally brilliant outburst. There is something monstrous, utterly disproportionate, when tangled emotions about one's father are deliberately compared with the historical fate of the European Jews; something sad, if the comparison is made spontaneously. "Daddy" persuades once again, through the force of negative example, of how accurate T. S. Eliot was in saying, "The more perfect the artist, the more completely separate in him will be the man who suffers and the mind which creates."

A. ALVAREZ

Sylvia Plath*

. . . The reasons for Sylvia Plath's images are always there, though sometimes you have to work hard to find them. She is, in short, always in intelligent control of her feelings. Her work bears out her theories:

* From A. Alvarez, *Beyond All This Fiddle* (London: Penguin, 1968), pp. 56–57.

I think my poems come immediately out of the sensuous and emotional experiences I have, but I must say I cannot sympathise with these cries from the heart
that are informed by nothing except a needle or a knife or whatever it is. I believe
that one should be able to control and manipulate experiences, even the most
terrifying—like madness, being tortured, this kind of experience—and one should
be able to manipulate these experiences with an informed and intelligent mind. I
think that personal experience shouldn't be a kind of shut box and mirror-looking
narcissistic experience. I believe it should be generally relevant, to such things as
Hiroshima and Dachau, and so on.

It seems to me that it was only by her determination both to face her most inward
and terrifying experiences and to use her intelligence in doing so—so as not to
be overwhelmed by them—that she managed to write these extraordinary last
poems, which are at once deeply autobiographical and yet detached, generally
relevant.

"Lady Lazarus" is a stage further on from "Fever 103°"; its subject is the total
purification of achieved death. It is also far more intimately concerned with the
drift of Sylvia Plath's life. The deaths of Lady Lazarus correspond to her own crises:
the first just after her father died, the second when she had her nervous breakdown, the third perhaps a presentiment of the death that was shortly to come.
Maybe this closeness of the subject helped make the poem so direct. The details
don't clog each other: they are swept forward by the current of immediate feeling,
marshalled by it and ordered. But what is remarkable about the poem is the objectivity with which she handles such personal material. She is not just talking about
her own private suffering. Instead, it is the very closeness of her pain which gives
it a general meaning; through it she assumes the suffering of all the modern
victims. Above all, she becomes an imaginary Jew. I think this is a vitally important element in her work. For two reasons. First, because anyone whose subject
is suffering has a ready-made modern example of hell on earth in the concentration camps. And what matters in them is not so much the physical torture—since
sadism is general and perennial—but the way modern, as it were industrial, techniques can be used to destroy utterly the human identity. Individual suffering
can be heroic provided it leaves the person who suffers a sense of his own individuality—provided, that is, there is an illusion of choice remaining to him. But
when suffering is mass-produced, men and women become as equal and identity-
less as objects on an assembly line, and nothing remains—certainly no values, no
humanity. This anonymity of pain, which makes all dignity impossible, was Sylvia Plath's subject. Second, she seemed convinced, in these last poems, that the
root of her suffering was the death of her father, whom she loved, who abandoned
her, and who dragged her after him into death. And in her fantasies her father
was pure German, pure Aryan, pure anti-semite.

It all comes together in the most powerful of her last poems, "Daddy" . . . ,
about which she wrote the following bleak note:

The poem is spoken by a girl with an Electra complex. Her father died while she
thought he was God. Her case is complicated by the fact that her father was also a
Nazi and her mother very possibly part Jewish. In the daughter the two strains

marry and paralyse each other—she has to act out the awful little allegory once over before she is free of it.[1]

. . . What comes through most powerfully, I think, is the terrible *unforgivingness* of her verse, the continual sense not so much of violence—although there is a good deal of that—as of violent resentment that this should have been done to *her.* What she does in the poem is, with a weird detachment, to turn the violence against herself so as to show that she can equal her oppressors with her self-inflicted oppression. And this is the strategy of the concentration camps. When suffering is there whatever you do, by inflicting it upon yourself you achieve your identity, you set yourself free.

Yet the tone of the poem, like its psychological mechanisms, is not single or simple, and she uses a great deal of skill to keep it complex. Basically, her trick is to tell this horror story in a verse form as insistently jaunty and ritualistic as a nursery rhyme. And this helps her to maintain towards all the protagonists—her father, her husband and herself—a note of hard and sardonic anger, as though she were almost amused that her own suffering should be so extreme, so grotesque. The technical psychoanalytic term for this kind of insistent gaiety to protect you from what, if faced nakedly, would be insufferable, is "manic defence." But what, in a neurotic, is a means of avoiding reality can become, for an artist, a source of creative strength, a way of handling the unhandleable, and presenting the situation in all its fullness. When she first read me the poem a few days after she wrote it, she called it a piece of "light verse." It obviously isn't, yet equally obviously it also isn't the racking personal confession that a mere description or précis of it might make it sound.

Yet neither is it unchangingly vindictive or angry. The whole poem works on one single, returning note and rhyme, echoing from start to finish:

> You do not do, you do not do . . .
> . . . I used to pray to recover you.
> Ach, du . . .

There is a kind of cooing tenderness in this which complicates the other, more savage note of resentment. It brings in an element of pity, less for herself and her own suffering than for the person who made her suffer. Despite everything, "Daddy" is a love poem.

1. From the introductory notes to "New Poems," a reading prepared for the BBC Third Programme but never broadcast [Alvarez's note].

JUDITH KROLL

Rituals of Exorcism: "Daddy" *

Poems explicitly about the protagonist's father, read in order of composition, show that the attitude toward him evolves from nostalgic mournfulness, regret, and guilt, to resentment and a bitter resolve to break his hold on her. . . .

The recital of the myth in "Daddy" ends in a ritual intended to cancel the earlier "sacred marriage" which has suffocated her:

> You do not do, you do not do
> Any more, black shoe
> In which I have lived like a foot
> For thirty years, poor and white,
> Barely daring to breathe or Achoo.[1]

In this image of passive and victimized domesticity, the speaker implicitly compares her past self to the "old woman who lived in a shoe" who "didn't know what to do"; now, however, she makes it clear that she does know what to do.

As a preamble to the exorcism, she recounts the development of her father's image, beginning with his earlier status as a "bag full of God, / Ghastly statue" (that is, a godlike colossus—mentioning the ghastliness, the ghostly, deathlike, pallid nature of the statue, anticipates the inversions to come) and then introduces the revised images: "panzer-man," "swastika," "Fascist," "brute," "devil," "bastard." Daddy must be cast in this new light, transformed from god to devil, if he is to be successfully expelled, but there must also be some real basis for it. To be effectively exposed, he must first appear as godly. But the speaker soon shows that she now attributes his godliness in part to his authoritarianism and personal inaccessibility—qualities which became intensified through his death, and which later became transferred to "a model of you"—her husband. Both men are really variations on a familiar type, even a stereotype: the "god" who, like Marco the "woman-hater" in *The Bell Jar,* is "chock-full of power" . . . over women precisely because of his deadness, or ultimate inaccessibility, to them. Loving a man literally or metaphorically dead ("The face that lived in this mirror is the face of a dead man" ["The Courage of Shutting-Up"]) becomes a kind of persecution or punishment; and so, by the end of the incantation, Daddy deserves to be cast out. The "black telephone . . . off at the root," conveys the finality of the intended exorcism.

The "venomousness," ambiguous from the beginning, is not the whole story. "Daddy" is not primarily a poem of "father-hatred" or abuse as Robert Lowell, Elizabeth Hardwick, and others have contended. The need for exorcising her

---

* From Judith Kroll, *Chapters in a Mythology: The Poetry of Sylvia Plath* (New York: Harper & Row, 1976), pp. 122–26. Unless otherwise specified, all notes are Kroll's.   1. When Plath introduced "Daddy" as being about "a girl with an Electra complex" (with, in effect, the female version of an Oedipus complex), she gave a clue to what may be a play on words in the poem. "Oedipus" means "swell-foot," and therefore the speaker's identification of herself as a "foot" may be a private way of saying "I am Oedipus" and incorporating into the poem an allusion to the Electra complex.

father's ghost lies, after all, in the extremity of her attachment to him. Alvarez very justly remarks that

> The whole poem works on one single, returning note and rhyme, echoing from start to finish:
>
>> You do not do, you do not do . . .
>> . . . I used to pray to recover you.
>> Ach, du . . .
>
> There is a kind of cooing tenderness in this which complicates the other, more savage note of resentment. It brings in an element of pity, less for herself and her own suffering than for the person who made her suffer. Despite everything, "Daddy" is a love poem.[2]

The love is not merely conveyed by the rhythm and sound of the poem, it is a necessary part of the poem's meaning, a part of the logic of its act.

The exorcism serves another purpose because through it she attempts to reject the pattern of being abandoned and made to suffer by a god, a man who is "chock-full of power": she creates "a model of you"—an image of her father—and marries this proxy. Then she kills both father and husband at once, magically using each as the other's representative.[3] Each death entails that of the other: the stake in her father's heart also kills the "vampire who said he was you"; and the killing of her marriage (for which she now claims to take responsibility, as she does for having allowed her marriage to perpetuate, by proxy, her relationship to her father) finally permits Daddy to "lie back." Formerly an acquiescent victim, she now vengefully cancels that role. The marriage to and killing of her father by proxy are acts of what Frazer[4] calls "sympathetic magic," in which "things act on each other at a distance through a secret sympathy" . . . . Such magic, which assumes that human beings can either directly influence the course of nature or can induce gods to influence nature in the desired way, nearly always constitutes the logic of the rituals Frazer discusses. The ritual marriage of a Whitsun bride and bridegroom, for example, aims at assuring abundant crops by sympathetically encouraging a marriage between the powers of fertility. Likewise, diseases may be either inflicted or drawn off by sympathetic magic on the principle that "as the image suffers, so does the man" . . . .

Plath was familiar with and used such ideas; for example, she transcribed, from *The Golden Bough*, Frazer's remark about the fertility or barrenness of a man's wife affecting his garden; and she echoes Frazer again in a line, excised from her poem "The Other," in which opening doors and windows is connected with the facilitation of childbirth. (Also, being "lame in the memory" and self, associated with the lameness and death of her father, is at once a homeopathic wound and a sympathetic attachment to him.) The notion that "as the image suffers, so does the man"—affecting the real subject through a proxy—nicely describes marriage to a model of Daddy, and explains why "If I've killed one man, I've killed two."

---

2. Alvarez, "Sylvia Plath," p. 66.   3. The biographical basis for this identification is evident in *Letters Home*. . . .   4. Sir James George Frazer (1854–1941), Scottish anthropologist whose book, *The Golden Bough*, analyzes early religious and magical practices [Editor's note].

The earlier attempt of the speaker in "Daddy" to recover her father also involved sympathetic magic; she had tried to rejoin him by dying and becoming like him:

> At twenty I tried to die
> And get back, back, back to you.

She finally exorcises her father as if he were a scapegoat invested with the evils of her spoiled history. Frazer's discussion of rituals in which the dying god is also a scapegoat is germane here. He conjectures that two originally separate rituals merged to form this combination, and the father in "Daddy" may well be described as such a divine scapegoat figure.[5]

Sometimes it is a place from which a devil must be cast out, but usually it is a person who is possessed. In Plath's mythology the speaker is not possessed by her father in this sense, but by the false self who is in his thrall. That is why the true self is released (as in "Purdah" and "Lady Lazarus") when the oppressor is made hateful, and thereby overthrown. Rituals of exorcism in Plath's poetry therefore inherently involve the idea of rebirth. When exorcism, or attempted exorcism, of father or proxy occurs, it is preliminary to a rebirth which will entail expulsion of the false self and spoiled history. And even when a ritual of rebirth does not involve an explicit exorcism, one is usually implied.

The logic of sympathetic magic, which appears widely in Plath's late poetry, might well be called one of the physical laws of her poems. . . . Such a logic seems poetically appropriate for a mythology: that the Moon-muse (or one of her agents, such as "The Rival") governs and affects her by a "secret sympathy" seems natural to a mythic drama.

The motifs "released"—or triggered—in her late poems contain the potential for a sympathetic association of those details which express the same motif. Because the details are not incidental, called forth as they are by her mythology, the sympathy is in a sense guaranteed. The images of blood, violent death, and red poppies, all of which release the death and rebirth motif, have the potential for sympathetically affecting one another through their family resemblance. "Tulips" contains an example of the secret sympathy which operates through such resemblance (that is, through expressing the same motif):

> The tulips are too red in the first place, they hurt me.
> . . .
> Their redness talks to my wound, it corresponds.[6]

---

5. Frazer says: "If we ask why a dying god should be chosen to take upon himself and carry away the sins and sorrows of the people, it may be suggested that in the practice of using the divinity as a scapegoat we have a combination of two customs. . . . [T]he result would be the employment of the dying god as a scapegoat. He was killed, not originally to take away sin, but to save the divine life from the degeneracy of old age; but, since he had to be killed at any rate, people may have thought that they might as well seize the opportunity to lay upon him the burden of their sufferings and sins, in order that he might bear it away with him to the unknown world beyond the grave." [Pp. 667–68] . . .   6. By the time "Tulips" was written, she had clearly developed much of the technique, imagery, and themes (such as the logic of sympathetic magic) of the late poems.

The word "corresponds" refers both to the communication between tulips and wound and to their underlying likeness. The tulips stand in the same relation to the incipient health or normalcy of the speaker that the poppies in later poems do to her suppressed true self, to (or with) which the poppies correspond. In a sense, this correspondence, and the contrast between it and the speaker's death-in-life existence, *is* the underlying motif in these poems.

It has already been suggested that the Moon-muse has a "sympathetic"—even though not entirely welcome—relation with the speaker[7] (as mother, totem, familiar, emblem) which can be activated without her consent, just as in "Tulips" she cannot prevent her wound from corresponding with the red flowers. Similarly, the coldness and sterility of the Moon-muse may infect the speaker, causing and not merely representing her state of being. The Moon therefore functions as both "emblem" and "real agent."

MARY LYNN BROE

From *Protean Poetic**

Among the other poems that display the performing self, "Daddy" and "Lady Lazarus" are two of the most often quoted, but most frequently misunderstood, poems in the Plath canon. The speaker in "Daddy" performs a mock poetic exorcism of an event that has already happened—the death of her father, who she feels withdrew his love from her by dying prematurely: "Daddy, I have had to kill you. / You died before I had time—."

The speaker attempts to exorcise not just the memory of her father but her own *Mein Kampf* model of him as well as her inherited behavioral traits that lead her graveward under the Freudian banner of death instinct or Thanatos's libido. But her ritual reenactment simply does not take. The event comically backfires as pure self-parody: the metaphorical murder of the father dwindles into Hollywood spectacle, while the poet is lost in the clutter of the collective unconscious.

Early in the poem, the ritual gets off on the wrong foot both literally and figuratively. A sudden rhythmic break midway through the first stanza interrupts the insistent and mesmeric chant of the poet's own freedom:

7. The belief Frazer mentions, that "a barren wife infects her husband's garden with her own sterility," is the sort of contagion that occurs in *Three Women*, in which the Secretary has been infected by the Moon's sterility and by that of the men with whom she works. Men, who cannot bear children, have the disease of "flatness," for they create only negations of and abstractions about life rather than life itself. This disease can (through the mediumship of the Moon) be caught from men, and it is therefore also an inversion or parody of conception. Referring to her miscarriage, the Secretary says: "I watched the men walk about me in the office. They were so flat! / There was something about them like cardboard, and now I had caught it. . . ."

* From Mary Lynn Broe, *Protean Poetic: The Poetry of Sylvia Plath* (Columbia and London: University of Missouri Press, 1980), pp. 172–75.

> You do not do, you do not do
> Any more, black shoe
> In which I have lived like a foot
> For thirty years, poor and white,
> Barely daring to breathe or Achoo.

The break suggests, on the one hand, that the nursery-rhyme world of contained terror is here abandoned; on the other, that the poet-exorcist's mesmeric control is superficial, founded in a shaky faith and an unsure heart—the worst possible state for the strong, disciplined exorcist.

At first she kills her father succinctly with her own words, demythologizing him to a ludicrous piece of statuary that is hardly a Poseidon or the Colossus of Rhodes:[1]

> Marble-heavy, a bag full of God,
> Ghastly statue with one grey toe
> Big as a Frisco seal
>
> And a head in the freakish Atlantic
> Where it pours bean green over blue
> In the waters off beautiful Nauset.
> I used to pray to recover you.
> Ach, du.

Then as she tries to patch together the narrative of him, his tribal myth (the "common" town, the "German tongue," the war-scraped culture), she begins to lose her own powers of description to a senseless Germanic prattle ("The tongue stuck in my jaw. / It stuck in a barb wire snare. / Ich, ich, ich, ich"). The individual man is absorbed by his inhuman archetype, the "panzer man," "an engine / Chuffing me off like a Jew." Losing the exorcist's power that binds the spirit and then casts out the demon, she is the classic helpless victim of the swastika man. As she culls up her own picture of him as a devil, he refuses to adopt this stereotype. Instead he jumbles his trademark:

> A cleft in your chin instead of your foot
> But no less a devil for that, no not
> Any less the black man who
>
> Bit my pretty red heart in two.

The overt Nazi-Jew allegory throughout the poem suggests that, by a simple inversion of power, father and daughter grow more alike. But when she tries to imitate his action of dying, making all the appropriate grand gestures, she once again fails: "but they pulled me out of the sack, / And they stuck me together with glue." She retreats to a safe world of icons and replicas, but even the doll image she constructs turns out to be "the vampire who said he was you." At last, she

---

1. One of the seven wonders of the ancient world, a gigantic statue of the Greek sun god, Helios; *Poseidon:* the chief sea god in the Greek pantheon [Editor's note].

abandons her father to the collective unconscious where it is *he* who is finally recognized ("they always *knew* it was you"). *She* is lost, impersonally absorbed by his irate persecutors, bereft of both her power and her conjuror's discipline, and possessed by the incensed villagers. The exorcist's ritual, one of purifying, cleansing, commanding silence and then ordering the evil spirit's departure, has dwindled to a comic picture from the heart of darkness. Mad villagers stamp on the devil-vampire creation.

In the course of performing the imaginative "killing," the speaker moves through a variety of emotions, from viciousness ("a stake in your fat black heart"), to vengefulness ("You bastard, I'm through"), finally to silence ("the black telephone's off at the root"). It would seem that the real victim is the poet-performer who, despite her straining toward identification with the public events of holocaust and destruction of World War II, becomes more murderously persecuting than the "panzer-man" who smothered her, and who abandoned her with a paradoxical love, guilt, and fear. Unlike him, she kills three times: the original subject, the model to whom she said "I do, I do," and herself, the imitating victim. But each of these killings is comically inverted. Each backfires. Instead of successfully binding the spirits, commanding them to remain silent and cease doing harm, and then ordering them to an appointed place, the speaker herself is stricken dumb.

The failure of the exorcism and the emotional ambivalence are echoed in the curious rhythm. The incantatory safety of the nursery-rhyme thump (seemingly one of controlled, familiar terrors) also suggests some sinister brooding by its repetition. The poem opens with a suspiciously emphatic protest, a kind of psychological whistling-in-the-dark. As it proceeds, "Daddy" 's continuous life-rhythms—the assonance, consonance, and especially the sustained *oo* sounds—triumph over either the personal or the cultural-historical imagery. The sheer sense of organic life in the interwoven sounds carries the verse forward in boisterous spirit and communicates an underlying feeling of comedy that is also echoed in the repeated failure of the speaker to perform her exorcism.

Ultimately, "Daddy" is like an emotional, psychological, and historical autopsy, a final report. There is no real progress. The poet is in the same place in the beginning as in the end. She begins the poem as a hesitant but familiar fairy-tale daughter who parodies her attempt to reconstruct the myth of her father. Suffocating in her shoe house, she is unable to do much with that "bag full of God." She ends as a murderous member of a mythical community enacting the ritual or vampire killing, but only for a surrogate vampire, not the real thing ("the vampire who said he was you"). Although it seems that the speaker has moved from identification with the persecuted to identity as persecutor, Jew to vampire-killer, powerless to powerful, she has simply enacted a performance that allows her to live with what is unchangeable. She has used her art to stave off suffocation, and performs her self-contempt with a degree of bravado.[2]

---

2. What remains the most thorough and enlightening account of the poem is A. R. Jones, "On 'Daddy,' " *The Art of Sylvia Plath,* [ed. Newman], pp. 230–36 [Broe's note].

MARGARET HOMANS

From *A Feminine Tradition**

To place an exclusive valuation on the literal, expecially to identify the self as literal, is simply to ratify women's age-old and disadvantageous position as the other and the object. Contemporary poetry by women that takes up this self-defeating strategy risks encounters with death that are destructive both poetically and actually. The current belief in a literal "I" present in poetry is responsible for the popular superstition that Sylvia Plath's death was the purposeful completion of her poetry's project, the assumption being that if the speaker is precisely the same as the biographical Plath, the poetry's self-destructive violence is directed toward Plath herself, not toward an imagined speaker. This reading of Plath is unfair to the woman and, by calling it merely unmediated self-expression, obscures her poetry's real power. In poem after poem depicting or wishing for physical violence, the imagery of violence is part of a symmetrical figurative system, and death is figured as a way of achieving rebirth or some other transcendence.[1] Plath's project may not thus be very different from that of Dickinson, who speaks quite often from beyond the grave, reimagining and repossessing death as her own in order to dispel the terrors of literal death. However, within that figurative system the poet embraces a self-destructive program that must soon have been poetically terminal, even if it did not bring about the actual death.

Several of Plath's late poems come to terms with a father figure (who may include the poetic fathers she acknowledges in *The Colossus*), whose crime, no different from that identified by nineteenth-century women, is of attempting to transform the feminine self into objects. "Lady Lazarus" borrows the most appalling of Nazi imagery to accuse a generalized figure of male power of the ultimate reification. Not only is the dead victim of "Herr Doktor" and "Herr Enemy" an object in being dead, but she is also reduced to the actual physical objects from which the Nazis profited by destroying human bodies: "a Nazi lampshade,"

> A cake of soap,
> A wedding ring,
> A gold filling.

The poem combines the tradition of woman as medium of exchange with that of woman as object to produce a desperately concise picture of literalization.

---

* From Margaret Homans, *Women Writers and Poetic Identity: Dorothy Wordsworth, Emily Brontë, and Emily Dickinson* (Princeton: Princeton University Press, 1982), pp. 218–21.   1. I am indebted here, for their persuasively positive readings of Plath, to Judith Kroll, *Chapters in a Mythology: The Poetry of Sylvia Plath* (New York: Harper & Row, 1976), and to Stacy Pies, "Coming Clear of the Shadow: The Poetry of Sylvia Plath," unpublished essay (Yale University, 1979) [Homans's note].

I am your opus,
I am your valuable,
The pure gold baby

That melts to a shriek.

Though the poet is here objecting to literalization, not embracing it, the poetic myth of suicide through which the oppression may be lifted amounts to the same thing: the speaker must submit to this literalization in order to transcend it.

Out of the ash
I rise with my red hair
And I eat men like air.

Their death costs her death, and powerful though the poem is, this is an extraordinarily high price for retribution. And as always, it is the process of objectification that makes up the poem, not the final, scarcely articulable transcendence.

"Daddy" uses Nazi imagery to make the same accusation about objectification brought against men as oppressors in "Lady Lazarus" and makes the corollary accusation against the father (and the husband modelled after him) that objectification has silenced her:

I never could talk to you.
The tongue stuck in my jaw.

It stuck in a barb wire snare.
Ich, ich, ich, ich,
I could hardly speak.

In this context defiance and retribution take the form of her speaking, but again this counterattack is counterproductive. Punning on the expression "being through" to mean both establishing a telephone connection and being finished, she at once makes and conclusively severs communication:

So daddy, I'm finally through.
The black telephone's off at the root,
The voices just can't worm through.

The poem concludes, "Daddy, daddy, you bastard, I'm through." Suppressing the power of the one who silenced her, she simultaneously returns herself to the silence that the poem came into being to protest.

PAMELA J. ANNAS

From *A Disturbance in Mirrors**

. . . [T]he particular sexual metaphor in "Daddy" is sado-masochism, which stands for the authority structure of a partriarchal and war-making society. . . . "Daddy" is an analysis of the structure of the society in which the individual is enmeshed. Intertwined with the image of sadist and masochist in "Daddy" is a parallel image of vampire and victim. In "Daddy," father, husband, and a larger patriarchal and competitive authority structure, which the speaker of the poem sees as having been responsible for the various imperialisms of the twentieth century, all melt together and become demonic, finally a gigantic vampire figure. In the modulation from one image to another to form an accumulated image that is characteristic of many of Plath's late poems, the male figure at the center of "Daddy" takes four major forms: the statue, the Gestapo officer, the professor, and the vampire. The poem begins, however, with an image of a black shoe, an image which, like the black shoe in "The Munich Mannequins" and like the black suit in "The Applicant," can be seen to stand for corporate man. The second stanza of the poem refers back to the title poem of *The Colossus*, where the speaker's father, representative of a gigantic male other, so dominated her world that her horizon was bounded by his scattered pieces. In "Daddy," she describes him as:

> Marble-heavy, a bag full of God,
> Ghastly statue with one grey toe
> Big as a Frisco seal

> And a head in the freakish Atlantic
> Where it pours bean green over blue
> In the waters off beautiful Nauset.

Between "The Colossus" and "Daddy" there has been a movement from a mythic and natural landscape to one with social and political boundaries. Here the image of her father, grown larger than the earlier Colossus of Rhodes, stretches across and subsumes the whole of the United States, from the Pacific to the Atlantic ocean.

The next seven stanzas of "Daddy" construct the image of the Gestapo officer, using her family background—her parents were both of German origin—to mediate between her personal sense of suffocation and the social history of the Nazi invasions. The black shoe of the first stanza in which she says she has been wedged like a foot "barely daring to breathe" becomes in stanza ten, at the end of the Nazi section, a larger social image of suffocation: "Not God but a swastika / So black no sky could squeak through." The Gestapo figure recurs briefly three stan-

* From Pamela J. Annas, *A Disturbance in Mirrors: The Poetry of Sylvia Plath*, Contributions in Women's Studies no. 89 (New York, Westport, and London: Greenwood Press, 1988), pp. 139–43. All notes are Annas's.

zas later as the speaker of the poem transfers the image from father to husband and incidentally suggests that the victim has some control in a brutalized association—at least to the extent she chooses to be there.[1]

> I made a model of you,
> A man in black with a Meinkampf look
>
> And a love of the rack and the screw.
> And I said I do, I do.

The Gestapo figure becomes "Herr Professor" in stanza eleven, an actual image of Plath's father, and also an image of what has for centuries been seen as the prototypical and even ideal relationship between a man and a woman.[2] The professor, who is a man, talks and is active; the woman, who is a student, listens and is passive. A patriarchal social structure is at its purest and, superficially, at its most benign in the stereotyped relationship of male teacher and female student and is a stock romantic fantasy even in women's literature—Emma and Mr. Knightley, Lucy Snowe and the professor in *Villette*.[3] But Plath places this image between the images of Nazi/Jew and vampire/victim so that it becomes the center of a series. Indeed, the image of daddy as teacher turns almost immediately into a devil/demon/vampire:

> A cleft in your chin instead of your foot
> But no less a devil for that, no not
> Any less the black man who
>
> Bit my pretty red heart in two.

The last two stanzas of "Daddy" are like the conclusion of "Lady Lazarus" in their assertion that the speaker of the poem is breaking out of the cycle and that, in order to do so, she must turn on and kill Herr God, Herr Lucifer in the one poem, and Daddy in his final metamorphosis as vampire in the other poem. Plath explained this in Freudian terms in an introductory note to the poem for a BBC Third Programme reading:

1. See Wilhelm Reich's *The Mass Psychology of Fascism* (New York: Simon and Schuster, 1969), particularly his chapter on "The Authoritarian Personality," for an analysis of how an oppressed class can contribute to its own oppression. Judith Lewis Herman, in *Father-Daughter Incest* (Cambridge, Mass.: Harvard University Press, 1981), discusses the history of the suppression of incest beginning with Freud and continuing into contemporary psychological literature, the attribution of reports of incest to hysterical female oedipal fantasizing or, when the fact of incest is impossible to deny, assigning blame to the victim: what Herman calls the Seductive Daughter and/or the Collusive Mother (Chapter 1, "A Common Occurence"). Writing in the early 1960s and familiar with some of these attitudes, . . . Plath [not surprisingly] assigns some culpability to the victim. Herman goes on to say, "Even when the girl does give up her erotic attachment to her father, she is encouraged to persist in the fantasy that some other man, like her father, will some day take possession of her, raising her above the common lot of womankind" (p. 57).

I am not of course suggesting that Plath literally had an incestuous relationship with her father—there is no evidence one way or the other—but she does make recurrent use of father/daughter incest as a symbol for male/female relations in a patriarchal society. . . .   2. This photograph of Otto Plath is reproduced on page 17 of *Letters Home*.   3. [Mary] Ellmann, *Thinking About Women* [New York: Harcourt Brace Jovanovich, 1968], pp. 119–23.

The poem is spoken by a girl with an Electra complex. The father died while she thought he was God. Her case is complicated by the fact that her father was also a Nazi and her mother very possibly part Jewish. In the daughter the two strains marry and paralyze each other—she has to act out the awful little allegory once over before she is free of it.[4]

This reenacting of the allegory becomes at the end of "Daddy" a frenzied communal ritual of exorcism.

> Daddy, you can lie back now.
>
> There's a stake in your fat black heart
> And the villagers never liked you.
> They are dancing and stamping on you.
> They always *knew* it was you.
> Daddy, daddy, you bastard, I'm through.

This cycle of victim/vampire is, left alone, a closed and repetitive cycle, like the repeated suicides of "Lady Lazarus." According to the legends and the Hollywood film versions of these legends we all grew up on, once consumed by a vampire, one dies and is reborn a vampire and preys upon others, who in their turn die and become vampires. The vampire imagery in Sylvia Plath's poetry intersects on one level with her World War II imagery and its exploitation and victimization and on another level intersects with her images of a bureaucratic, fragmented, and dead—in the sense of numbed and unaware—society. The connections are sometimes confused, but certainly World War II is often imaged in her poetry as a kind of grisly, vampiric feast. . . .

The whole of "Daddy" is an exorcism to banish the demon, put a stake through the vampire's heart, and thus break the cycle of vampire→victim. It is crucial to the poem that the exorcism is accomplished through communal action by the "villagers." The rhythm of the poem is powerfully and deliberately primitive: a child's chant, a formal curse. The hard sounds, short lines, and repeated rhymes of "do," "you," "Jew," and "through" give a hard pounding quality to the poem that is close to the sound of a heart beat. "Daddy," as well as "Lady Lazarus" and, to a lesser extent, "Fever 103°," is structured as a magical formula or incantation. In the *Colossus* poems, Plath also used poetry as a ritual incantation, but in those early poems it was most often directed toward transformation of self. By 1961, she is less often attempting to transform self into some other, but rather attempting to rid herself and her world of demons. That is, rebirth cannot occur until after the demons have been exorcised. In all three of these poems, the possibilities of the individual are very much tied to those of her society.

Purity, which is what exorcism aims at, is for Plath an ambiguous concept. On the one hand it means integrity of self, wholeness rather than fragmentation, as unspoiled state of being, rest, perfection, aesthetic beauty, and loss of self through transformation into some reborn other. On the other hand, it also means absence, isolation, blindness, a kind of autism which shuts out the world, stasis and death,

---

4. Quoted in [M. L.] Rosenthal, *The New Poets* [New York: Oxford University Press, 1967], p. 82.

and a loss of self through dispersal into some other. In "Lady Lazarus" and "Fever 103°'" the emphasis is on exorcising the poet's previous selves, though within a social context that makes that unlikely. "Daddy," however, is a purification of the world; in "Daddy" it is the various avatars of the other—the male figure who represents the patriarchal society she lives in—that are being exorcised. In all three cases, the exorcism is violent and, perhaps, provisional. Does she believe, in any of these cases, that a rebirth under such conditions is really possible, that an exorcism is truly taking place, that once the allegory is reenacted, she will be rid of it? The more the speaker of the poems defines her situation as desperate, the more violent and vengeful becomes the agent of purification and trans- formation. All three of these poems are retaliatory fantasies: in "Lady Lazarus" she swallows men, in "Fever 103°'" she leaves them behind, in "Daddy" she kills them. . . .

STEVEN GOULD AXELROD

*Jealous Gods**

. . . [Although "Daddy"] has traditionally been read as "personal" (Aird 78)[1] or "confessional" (M. L. Rosenthal 82),[2] Margaret Homans has more recently sug- gested that it concerns a woman's dislocated relations to speech (*Women Writers* 220–21).[3] Plath herself introduced it on the BBC as the opposite of confession, as a constructed fiction: "Here is a poem spoken by a girl with an Electra complex. Her father died while she thought he was God. Her case is complicated by the fact that her father was also a Nazi and her mother very possibly part Jewish. In the daughter the two strains marry and paralyze each other—she has to act out the awful little allegory once over before she is free of it" (*CP* 293).[4] We might interpret this preface as an accurate retelling of the poem; or we might regard it as a case of an author's estrangement from her text, on the order of Coleridge's preface to "Kubla Khan" in which he claims to be unable to finish the poem, having forgotten what it was about. However we interpret Plath's preface, we must agree that "Daddy" is dramatic and allegorical, since its details depart freely from the facts of her biography. In this poem she again figures her unresolved conflicts with paternal authority as a textual issue. Significantly, her father was a published writer, and his successor, her husband, was also a writer. Her preface asserts that the poem concerns a young woman's paralyzing self-division, which she can defeat only through allegorical representation. Recalling that paralysis was one of

* From Steven Gould Axelrod, *Sylvia Plath: The Wound and the Cure of Words* (Baltimore and London: Johns Hopkins University Press, 1990), pp. 51–70, 237. Unless otherwise indicated, all notes are Axel- rod's.   1. Eileen Aird, *Sylvia Plath: Her Life and Work* (New York: Harper & Row, 1973).   2. M. L. Rosenthal, *The New Poets: American and British Poetry since World War II* (London: Oxford University Press, 1967).   3. Margaret Homans, *Women Writers and Poetic Identity: Dorothy Wordsworth, Emily Brontë, and Emily Dickinson* (Princeton: Princeton University Press, 1980).   4. *CP=The Collected Poems*.

Plath's main tropes for literary incapacity, we begin to see that the poem evokes the female poet's anxiety of authorship and specifically Plath's strategy of delivering herself from that anxiety by making it the topic of her discourse. Viewed from this perspective, "Daddy" enacts the woman poet's struggle with "daddy-poetry." It represents her effort to eject the "buried male muse" from her invention process and the "jealous gods" from her audience (*J* 223;[5] *CP* 179).

Plath wrote "Daddy" several months after Hughes left her, on the day she learned that he had agreed to a divorce (October 12, 1962). George Brown and Tirril Harris have shown that early loss makes one especially vulnerable to subsequent loss (Bowlby 250–59),[6] and Plath seems to have defended against depression by almost literally throwing herself into her poetry. She followed "Daddy" with a host of poems that she considered her greatest achievement to date: "Medusa," "The Jailer," "Lady Lazarus," "Ariel," the bee sequence, and others. The letters she wrote to her mother and brother on the day of "Daddy," and then again four days later, brim with a sense of artistic self-discovery: "Writing like mad. . . . Terrific stuff, as if domesticity had choked me" (*LH* 466).[7] Composing at the "still blue, almost eternal hour before the baby's cry, before the glassy music of the milkman, settling his bottles" (quoted in Alvarez, *Savage God* 21),[8] she experienced an "enormous" surge in creative energy (*LH* 467). Yet she also expressed feelings of misery: "The half year ahead seems like a lifetime, and the half behind an endless hell" (*LH* 468). She was again contemplating things German: a trip to the Austrian Alps, a renewed effort to learn the language. If "German" was Randall Jarrell's "favorite country," it was not hers, yet it returned to her discourse like clock work at times of psychic distress. Clearly Plath was attempting to find and to evoke in her art what she could not find or communicate in her life. She wished to compensate for her fragmenting social existence by investing herself in her texts: "Hope, when free, to write myself out of this hole" (*LH* 466). Desperately eager to sacrifice her "flesh," which was "wasted," to her "mind and spirit," which were "fine" (*LH* 470), she wrote "Daddy" to demonstrate the existence of her voice, which had been silent or subservient for so long. She wrote it to prove her "genius" (*LH* 468).

Plath projected her struggle for textual identity onto the figure of a partly Jewish young woman who learns to express her anger at the patriarch and at his language of male mastery, which is as foreign to her as German, as "obscene" as murder (st. 6), and as meaningless as "gobbledygoo" (st. 9). The patriarch's death "off beautiful Nauset" (st. 3) recalls Plath's journal entry in which she associated the "green seaweeded water" at "Nauset Light" with "the deadness of a being . . . who no longer creates" (*J* 164). Daddy's deadness—suggesting Plath's unwillingness to let her father, her education, her library, or her husband inhibit her any longer—inspires the poem's speaker to her moment of illumination. At a basic level, "Daddy" concerns its own violent, transgressive birth as a text, its origin in a culture that regards it as illegitimate—a judgment the speaker hurls back on the

5. *J* = *The Journals.*   6. John Bowlby, *Attachment and Loss,* III: *Loss: Sadness and Depression* (London: Hogarth, 1980).   7. *LH* = *Letters Home.*   8. A. Alvarez, *The Savage God: A Study of Suicide* (1971; New York, Bantam, 1973).

patriarch himself when she labels *him* a bastard (st. 16). Plath's unaccommodating worldview, which was validated by much in her childhood and adult experience, led her to understand literary tradition not as an expanding universe of beneficial influence (as depicted in Eliot's "Tradition and the Individual Talent") but as a closed universe in which every addition required a corresponding subtraction— a Spencerian agon in which only the fittest survived. If Plath's speaker was to be born as a poet, a patriarch must die.

As in "The Colossus," the father here appears as a force or an object rather than as a person. Initially he takes the form of an immense "black shoe," capable of stamping on his victim (st. 1). Immediately thereafter he becomes a marble "statue" (st. 2), cousin to the monolith of the earlier poem. He then transforms into Nazi Germany (st. 6–7, 9–10), the archetypal totalitarian state. When the protagonist mentions Daddy's "boot in the face" (st. 10), she may be alluding to Orwell's comment in *1984*, "If you want a picture of the future, imagine a boot stomping on a human face—forever" (3.3). Eventually the father declines in stature from God (st. 2) to a devil (st. 11) to a dying vampire (st. 15). Perhaps he shrinks under the force of his victim's denunciation, which de-creates him as a power as it creates him as figure. But whatever his size, he never assumes human dimensions, aspirations, and relations—except when posing as a teacher in a photograph (st. 11). Like the colossus, he remains figurative and symbolic, not individual.

Nevertheless, the male figure of "Daddy" does differ significantly from that of "The Colossus." In the earlier poem, which emphasizes his lips, mouth, throat, tongue, and voice, the colossus allegorically represents the power of speech, however fragmented and resistant to the protagonist's ministrations. In the later poem Daddy remains silent, apart from the gobbledygoo attributed to him once (st. 9). He uses his mouth primarily for biting and for drinking blood. The poem emphasizes his feet and, implicitly, his phallus. He is a "black shoe" (st. 1), a statue with "one gray toe" (st. 2), a "boot" (st. 10). The speaker, estranged from him by fear, could never tell where he put his "foot," his "root" (st. 5). Furthermore, she is herself silenced by his shoe: "I never could talk to you" (st. 5). Daddy is no "male muse" (*J* 223), not even one in ruins, but frankly a male censor. His boot in the face of "every woman" is presumably lodged in her mouth (st. 10). He stands for all the elements in the literary situation and in the female ephebe's internalization of it, that prevent her from producing any words at all, even copied or subservient ones. Appropriately, Daddy can be killed only by being stamped on: he lives and dies by force, not language. If "The Colossus" tells a tale of the patriarch's speech, his grunts and brays, "Daddy" tells a tale of the daughter's effort to speak.

Thus we are led to another important difference between the two poems. The "I" of "The Colossus" acquires her identity only through serving her "father," whereas the "I" of "Daddy" actuates her gift only through opposition to him. The latter poem precisely inscribes the plot of Plath's dream novel of 1958: "a girl's search for her dead father—for an outside authority which must be developed, instead, from the inside" (*J* 258). As the child of a Nazi, the girl could "hardly speak" (st. 6), but as a Jew she begins "to talk" and to acquire an identity (st. 7). In Plath's allegory, the outsider Jew corresponds to "the rebel, the artist, the odd"

(*JP* 55),[9] and particularly to the woman artist. Otto Rank's *Beyond Psychology*,[1] which had a lasting influence on her, explicitly compares women to Jews, since "woman . . . has suffered from the very beginning a fate similar to that of the Jew, namely, suppression, slavery, confinement, and subsequent persecution" (287–88). Rank, whose discourse I would consider tainted by anti-Semitism, argues that Jews speak a language of pessimistic "self-hatred" that differs essentially from the language of the majority cultures in which they find themselves (191, 281–84). He analogously, though more sympathetically, argues that woman speaks in a language different from man's, and that as a result of man's denial of woman's world, "woman's 'native tongue' has hitherto been unknown or at least unheard" (248). Although Rank's essentializing of woman's "nature" lapses into the sexist clichés of his time ("intuitive," "irrational" [249]), his idea of linguistic difference based on gender and his analogy between Jewish and female speech seem to have embedded themselves in the substructure of "Daddy" (and in many of Plath's other texts as well). For Plath, as later for Adrienne Rich, the Holocaust and the patriarchy's silencing of women were linked outcomes of the masculinist interpretation of the world. Political insurrection and female self-assertion also interlaced symbolically. In "Daddy," Plath's speaker finds her voice and motive by identifying herself as antithetical to her Fascist father. Rather than getting the colossus "glued" and properly jointed, she wishes to stick herself "together with glue" (st. 13), an act that seems to require her father's dismemberment. Previously devoted to the patriarch—both in "The Colossus" and in memories evoked in "Daddy" of trying to "get back" to him (st. 12)—she now seeks only to escape from him and to see him destroyed.

Plath has unleashed the anger, normal in mourning as well as in revolt, that she suppressed in the earlier poem. But she has done so at a cost. Let us consider her childlike speaking voice. The language of "Daddy," beginning with its title, is often regressive. The "I" articulates herself by moving backward in time, using the language of nursery rhymes and fairy tales (the little old woman who lived in a shoe, the black man of the forest). Such language accords with a child's conception of the world, not an adult's. Plath's assault on the language of "daddy-poetry" has turned inward, on the language of her own poem, which teeters precariously on the edge of a preverbal abyss—represented by the eerie, keening "oo" sound with which a majority of the verses end. And then let us consider the play on "through" at the poem's conclusion. Although that last line allows for multiple readings, one interpretation is that the "I" has unconsciously carried out her father's wish: her discourse, by transforming itself into cathartic oversimplifications, has undone itself.

Yet the poem does contain its verbal violence by means more productive than silence. In a letter to her brother, Plath referred to "Daddy" as "gruesome" (*LH* 472), while on almost the same day she described it to A. Alvarez as a piece of "light verse" (Alvarez, *Beyond* 56).[2] She later read it on the BBC in a highly ironic tone of voice. The poem's unique spell derives from its rhetorical complexity: its

9. *JP=Johnny Panic and the Bible of Dreams.*   1. Otto Rank, *Beyond Psychology* (Baltimore: Johns Hopkins University Press, 1990).   2. A. Alvarez, *Beyond All This Fiddle* (London: Allen Lane–Penguin, 1968).

variegated and perhaps bizarre fusion of the horrendous and the comic. As Uroff has remarked, it both shares and remains detached from the fixation of its protagonist (159).[3] The protagonist herself seems detached from her own fixation. She is "split in the most complex fashion," as Plath wrote of Ivan Karamazov[4] in her Smith College honors thesis. Plath's speaker uses potentially self-mocking melodramatic terms to describe both her opponent ("so black no sky could squeak through" [st. 10]) and herself ("poor and white" [st. 1]). While this aboriginal speaker quite literally expresses black-and-white thinking, her civilized double possesses a sensibility sophisticated enough to subject such thinking to irony. Thus the poem expresses feelings that it simultaneously parodies—it may be parodying the very idea of feeling. The tension between erudition and simplicity in the speaker's voice appears in her pairings that juxtapose adult with childlike diction: "breathe or Achoo," "your Luftewaffe, your gobbledygoo" (st. 1, 9). She can expound such adult topics as Taroc packs, Viennese beer, and Tyrolean snowfall; can specify death camps by name; and can employ an adult vocabulary of "recover," "ancestress," "Aryan," *"Meinkampf,"* "obscene," and "bastard." Yet she also has recourse to a more primitive lexicon that includes "chuffing," "your fat black heart," and "my pretty red heart." She proves herself capable of careful intellectual discriminations ("so I never could tell" [st. 5]), conventionalized description ("beautiful Nauset" [st. 3]), and moral analogy ("if I've killed one man, I've killed two" [st. 15], while also exhibiting regressive fantasies (vampires), repetitions ("wars, wars, wars" [st. 4]), and inarticulateness ("panzer-man, panzer-man, O You—" [st. 9]). She oscillates between calm reflection ("You stand at the blackboard, daddy, / In the picture I have of you" [st. 11]) and mad incoherence ("Ich, ich, ich, ich" [st. 6]). Her sophisticated language puts her wild language in an ironic perspective, removing the discourse from the control of the archaic self who understands experience only in extreme terms.

The ironies in "Daddy" proliferate in unexpected ways, however. When the speaker proclaims categorically that "every woman adores a Fascist" (st. 10), she is subjecting her victimization to irony by suggesting that sufferers choose, or at least accommodate themselves to, their suffering. But she is also subjecting her authority to irony, since her claim about "every woman" is transparently false. It simply parodies patriarchal commonplaces, such as those advanced by Helene Deutsch concerning "feminine masochism" (192–99, 245–85).[5] The adult, sophisticated self seems to be speaking here: Who else would have the confidence to make a sociological generalization? Yet the content of the assertion, if taken straightforwardly, returns us to the regressive self who is dominated by extravagant emotions she cannot begin to understand. Plath's mother wished that Plath would write about "decent, courageous people" (*LH* 477), and she herself heard an inner voice demanding that she be a perfect "paragon" in her language and feeling (*J* 176). But in the speaker of "Daddy," she inscribed the opposite of such

3. Margaret Dickie Uroff, *Sylvia Plath and Ted Hughes* (Urbana: University of Illinois Press, 1979). 4. A character in Fyodor Dostoyevsky's novel *The Brothers Karamazov* who suffers debilitating guilt for having wished for his father's death [Editor's note]. 5. Helen Deutsch, *The Psychology of Women*, I: *Girlhood* (1944; repr. New York: Bantam, 1973).

a paragon: a divided self whose veneer of civilization is breached and infected by unhealthy instincts.

Plath's irony cuts both ways. At the same time that the speaker's sophisticated voice undercuts her childish voice, reducing its melodrama to comedy, the childish or maddened voice undercuts the pretensions of the sophisticated voice, revealing the extremity of suffering masked by its ironies. While demonstrating the inadequacy of thinking and feeling in opposites, the poem implies that such a mode can locate truths denied more complex cognitive and affective systems. The very moderation of the normal adult intelligence, its tolerance of ambiguity, its defenses against the primal energies of the id, results in falsification. Reflecting Schiller's idea that the creative artist experiences a "momentary and passing madness" (quoted by Freud in a passage of *The Interpretation of Dreams* [193][6] that Plath underscored), "Daddy" gives voice to that madness. Yet the poem's sophisticated awareness, its comic vision, probably wins out in the end, since the poem concludes by curtailing the power of its extreme discourse . . . . Furthermore, Plath distanced herself from the poem's aboriginal voice by introducing her text as "a poem spoken by a girl with an Electra complex"—that is, as a study of the *girl's* pathology rather than her father's—and as an allegory that will "free" her from that pathology. She also distanced herself by reading the poem in a tone that emphasized its irony. And finally, she distanced herself by laying the poem's wild voice permanently to rest after October. The aboriginal vision was indeed purged. "Daddy" represents not Dickinson's madness that is divinest sense, but rather an entry into a style of discourse and a mastery of it. The poem realizes the trope of suffering by means of an inherent irony that both questions and validates the trope in the same gestures, and that finally allows the speaker to conclude the discourse and to remove herself from the trope with a sense of completion rather than wrenching, since the irony was present from the very beginning.

Plath's poetic revolt in "Daddy" liberated her pent-up creativity, but the momentary success sustained her little more than self-sacrifice had done. "Daddy" became another stage in her development, an unrepeatable experiment, a vocal opening that closed itself at once. The poem is not only an elegy for the power of "daddy-poetry" but for the powers of speech Plath discovered in composing it.

When we consider "Daddy" generically, a further range of implications presents itself. Although we could profitably consider the poem as the dramatic monologue Plath called it in her BBC broadcast, let us regard it instead as the kind of poem most readers have taken it to be: a domestic poem. I have chosen this term, rather than M. L. Rosenthal's better-known "confessional poem" or the more neutral "autobiographical poem," because "confessional poem" implies a confession rather than a making (though Steven Hoffman[7] and Lawrence Kramer[8] have recently indicated the mode's conventions) and because "autobiographical

6. Sigmund Freud, *The Interpretation of Dreams*, ed. James Strachey, Standard Edition, IV (1900; New York: Norton, 1976).   7. Steven Hoffman, "Impersonal Personalism: The Making of a Confessional Poetic," *English Literary History* 45 (Winter 1978): 687–709.   8. Lawrence Kramer, "Freud and the Skunks: Genre and Language in *Life Studies*," in *Robert Lowell: Essays on the Poetry*, ed. Steven Gould Axelrod and Helen Deese (New York: Cambridge University Press, 1986).

poem" is too general for our purpose. I shall define the domestic poem as one that represents and comments on a protagonist's relationship to one or more family members, usually a parent, child, or spouse. To focus our discussion even further, I shall emphasize poetry that specifically concerns a father.

. . . In the 1950s the "domestic poem" proper appeared on the scene, with its own conventions and expectations, and with its own complex cultural and literary reasons for being. Perhaps the precursive poems made the genre's eventual flowering inevitable, while its precise timing depended on a reaction against modernism's aesthetic of impersonality. Theodore Roethke wrote several early poems that initiated the genre: "My Papa's Waltz" (1948), "The Lost Son" (1948), and "Where Knock Is Open Wide" (1951). Lowell's "Life Studies" sequence (1959) was, and is, the genre's most prominent landmark. Other poems in the genre include John Berryman's *The Dream Songs* (1969); Frank Bidart's "Golden State" (1973) and "Confessional" (1983); Robert Duncan's "My Mother Would Be a Falconress" (1968); Allen Ginsberg's *Kaddish* (1960); Randall Jarrell's "The Lost World" (1965); Maxine Kumin's "The Thirties Revisited" (1975), "My Father's Neckties" (1978), and "Marianne, My Mother, and Me" (1989); Stanley Kunitz's "Father and Son" (1958) and "The Testing Tree" (1971); Lowell's "To Mother" (1977), "Robert T. S. Lowell" (1977), and "Unwanted" (1977); James Merrill's "Scenes of Childhood" (1962); Adrienne Rich's "After Dark" (1966); Anne Sexton's "Division of the Parts" (1960) and "The Death of the Fathers" (1972); W. D. Snodgrass' "Heart's Needle" (1959); Diane Wakoski's "The Father of My Country" (1968); and of course Sylvia Plath's "Daddy" (1962). In all these poems, the parent-child relationship serves as a locus for psychological investigation. In many of them it also serves as a means of representing the acquisition of poetic identity and of exploring the bounds of textuality itself. Because later writers were conscious of the Roethke-Lowell domestic poem as at least a genre in embryo, they chose to use its features, or perhaps the power of the genre was such that the features chose them. The "domestic poem" became a system of signs in which each individual text's adherence to the system and deviations within the system produced its particular literary meaning.

In 1959 Plath did not consciously attempt to write in the domestic poem genre, perhaps because she was not yet ready to assume her majority. Her journal entries of that period bristle with an impatience at herself that may derive from this reluctance. She may have feared asserting her "I am I am I am," which seemed to carry with it a countervailing impulse of self-retribution. But by fall 1962, when she had already lost so much, she was ready to chance tackling poetic tradition, and specifically her chief male instructors, Roethke and Lowell. In "Daddy" she achieved her victory in two ways. First, as we have seen, she symbolically assaults a father figure who is identified with male control of language. All her anxiety of influence comes to the fore in the poem: her sense of belatedness, her awareness of constraint, her fears of inadequacy, her furious need to overcome her dependency, her guilt at her own aggressivity. Since the precursors "do not do / Any more" (st. 1), she wishes to escape their paralyzing influence and to empty the "bag full of God" that has kept her tongue stuck in her jaw for so long (st. 2, 5). The father whose power she attacks is not simply Roethke or Lowell, or even Hughes or Otto Plath, but a literary character who includes reference to all of them as categories of masculine authority. Although the Daddy of poetry has already "died" (st. 2)—the fate of all published texts in Plath's postromantic perspective—the speaker must symbolically "kill" him from her own discourse. The poem ironically depicts poetry as both an aggression and a suicide. The female ephebe herself becomes a "brute" in the act of voicing (st. 10), just as have her teachers before her. But the aggression of her speech yields to the self-annihilation of language. By the end of the poem she too, like her male precursors, is "through." The speaker's textual life will be misread on innumerable occasions in innumerable ways, whereas her own misreading and miswriting of the precursors is finished. In its conclusion, the poem acknowledges its alienation from itself, confessing the transitoriness of its unbounded power.

In addition to killing the father in its fictional plot, the poem seeks to discredit the forefathers through its status as poetic act. Taking a genre established by Roethke and Lowell, "Daddy" fundamentally alters it through antithesis and parody. Like all strong poems, it transforms its genre and therefore the way we perceive the precursive examples, making them seem not fulfillments but anticipations. Thus the later work projects its anxiety retrospectively back through its predecessors. Haunted by fears of inadequacy and redundancy, it seeks to make the earlier poems seem incompetent by comparison—a kind of juvenilia in the career of the genre, to represent the final possible stroke, or at the very least to inaugurate some new and important genre, of which the whole domestic genre was but a foreshadowing.

This point comes clearer if we compare "Daddy" with two analogues, Roethke's "The Lost Son" (1948) and Lowell's "Commander Lowell" (1959). In the Freudian drama of "The Lost Son," the protagonist subjectively relives his childhood fears and fantasies. Like the speaker of the companion piece, "My Papa's Waltz," he is still enmeshed in the family romance, remembering the father ambivalently as powerful, protective, and threatening. After locating himself at his father's grave, where he feels both grief and estrangement (in a scene that adumbrates "Electra on Azalea Path"), he descends into his unconscious, seeking, as Roethke later explained, "some clue to existence" (*Poet* 38).[9] He encounters his death wish, his memory of his father as "Father Fear," his sexual anxieties, and finally the "dark swirl" of a blackout, after which a childhood memory of his "Papa" shouting "order" in German returns him to consciousness. Although the figure of "Papa" blends earthly and heavenly father (*Poet* 39), he also symbolizes the superego, restoring order to a psyche and a poem that had fallen into chaos. At the poem's conclusion, as the "lost son" waits for his "understandable spirit" to revive, he appears to be purged, though not cured, of the conflicts that incapacitated him.

The speaker of "Commander Lowell," in contrast, is objective, precise, and witty. His discourse reflects a detached perspective on the past rather than a psy-

---

9. *On the Poet and His Craft: Selected Prose of Theodore Roethke*, ed. Ralph J. Mills, Jr. (Seattle and London: University of Washington Press, 1965).

chic reimmersion in it. He portrays his father as one who threatened him only through weakness. This father "was nothing to shout / about to the summer colony at 'Matt' "; took "four shots with his putter to sink his putt"; sang "Anchors Aweigh" in the bathtub; was fired from his job; and squandered his inheritance. Whereas Roethke's poem represents a cathartic experience, Lowell's converts chaotic feelings into intellectual irony. Whereas Roethke's poem can be read as an allegory of man's relationship to God or as a model of the Freudian psyche, Lowell's remains a realistic narrative, though it does suggest the cultural and financial decline of a social class.

Plath's poem combines features of both of these precursors: Roethke's evocation of a German-speaking authoritarian with Lowell's sarcastic deflation of a man without qualities; Roethke's subjective anguish with Lowell's social comedy. Like Roethke's Papa, Plath's title character is an intimidating patriarch; like Lowell's Father, he is a buffoon ("big as a Frisco seal"). Finally, Plath's poem, like those of her predecessors, has little to do with psychological cure: the speaker's defenses remain in place. But in a deeper sense, "Daddy" swerves sharply from its precursors, curtailing their power. It turns the psychological depth of Roethke's poem and the ironically detached surface of Lowell's poem into a fury of denunciation, an extravagance of emotion, an exaggeration of acts and effects, perhaps revealing the subtexts of both precursors. If in a sense the texts by Roethke and Lowell constitute what Ned Lukacher[1] might term the primal scene of "Daddy," the latter poem's raw intensity succeeds in reversing the relationship, making itself resemble *their* primal scene. It unmasks Roethke's implicitly oppressive father figure as a monster and Lowell's sophisticated comedy as slapstick. It transforms the domestic genre alternately into a horror show, encapsulating every political, cultural, and familial atrocity of the age, and a theater of cruelty, evoking nervous laughter. "Daddy" takes the genre as far as it can go—and then further.

---

1. Ned Lukacher, *Primal Scenes: Literature, Philosophy, Psychoanalysis* (Ithaca and London: Cornell University Press, 1986).

Evaluating Poetry

How do you know a good poem when you see one? This is not an easy question to answer—partly because deciding about the *value* of poems is a complex, difficult, and often lengthy process, and partly because no single and absolute criterion will measure texts and neatly divide the good from the not so good. People who long for a nice, infallible sorter—some test that will automatically pick out the best poems and distinguish variations of quality much as a litmus test separates acids from bases—often bemoan the "relativity" in evaluating poems. But even if no simple and absolute standard exists, we nevertheless can make distinctions. Some poems are better—that is, more consistently effective with talented and experienced readers—than others. Even if we cannot sensibly rate poems on a 1-to-10 scale or universally agree on the excellence of a single poem, we still can set out criteria to help readers who have not yet developed confidence in their own judgments. As a reader, of course, you don't need to spend all your time asking about quality and being judgmental about poetry. But because life isn't long enough to read everything, you often must separate those poems likely to be worth your time from those that aren't. Besides, the process of sorting—in which you begin to articulate your own judgments and poetic values—can help make you a better reader and a more informed, sophisticated, and wiser person. Evaluating poems can be, among other things, a way to learn about yourself, for what you like in poetry says a lot about where your values lie.

> *Poetry is a language that tells us, through a more or less emotional reaction, something that cannot be said.*
>
> —EDWIN ARLINGTON ROBINSON

"I like it." That simple, unreflective statement about a poem can begin your articulation of standards—as long as you next ask yourself why. Answers to *why* may be, at first, quite basic, even from experienced and sophisticated readers. "I like the way it sounds" or "I like its rhythm and pace" might be good, if partial, reasons for liking a poem. The popularity of nursery rhymes, simple childish ditties, or even Poe's "The Raven" owes a lot (if not necessarily everything) to the use of sound. Another frequent answer might be "Because it is true" or "Because I agree with what it says." We all tend to like sentiments or ideas that resemble our own more than those that challenge or disturb us, though bad formulations of some idea we treasure, like bad behavior in someone we love, can prove more embarrassing than comforting. But the longer we struggle with our reasons for liking a poem, the more complex and revealing our answers will likely be: "I like the *way* it expresses something I had thought but never quite articulated." "I like the way its sounds and rhythms imitate the sounds of what is being described." "I like the way it presents conflicting emotions, balancing negative and positive feelings that seem to exist at the same time in about equal intensity." "I like its precision in describing just how something like that affects a person." Such statements as "I like . . ." quietly cross the border into the area of "I admire," and when you include a second clause, beginning with "because" and offering complex reasons for that admiration, you move into the process of critical evaluation.

What reasons might different readers agree on? *Groups* of readers might agree on certain ideas—questions of politics or economics or religion, for example—but not readers across the board. More likely to generate consensus are technical criteria, questions of craft. How precise are the word choices at crucial moments in the poem? How rich, suggestive, and resonant are the words that open up the poem to larger statements and claims? How appropriate, original, and imaginative are the metaphors and other figures of speech? How carefully and clearly is the poem's situation set up? How fully and appropriately is the speaker characterized? How well matched are the speaker, situation, and setting with the poem's sentiments and ideas? How consistent and appropriate to its themes is the poem's tone? How carefully worked out is the poem's structure? How appropriate to the desired effects are the line breaks, the stanza breaks, and the pattern of rhythms and sounds?

Sometimes you can see how good a poem is in its various aspects by looking at what it is not—considering the choices *not* made by the poet. Often you can consider what a poem would be like if a different artistic choice had been made, as a way of seeing the importance of the choice actually made. What if, for example, Sylvia Plath had described a black *crow* in rainy weather instead of a rook? What if William Carlos Williams had described a *white* wheelbarrow? Sometimes you have the benefit, by referring to a working manuscript or an autobiographical account of composition, of actually watching the process of selection. Look, for example, at the several drafts of the first stanza of Richard Wilbur's "Love Calls Us to the Things of This World":

(a) My eyes came open to the squeak of pulleys
My spirit, shocked from the brothel of itself

(b) My eyes came open to the shriek of pulleys,
And the soul, spirited from its proper wallow,
Hung in the air as bodiless and hollow

(c) My eyes came open to the pulleys' cry.
The soul, spirited from its proper wallow,
Hung in the air as bodiless and hollow
As light that frothed upon the wall opposing;
But what most caught my eyes at their unclosing
Was two gray ropes that yanked across the sky.
One after one into the window frame
. . . the hosts of laundry came

(d) The eyes open to a cry of pulleys,
And the soul, so suddenly spirited from sleep,
As morning sunlight frothing on the floor,
while just outside the window
The air is solid with a dance of angels.

(e) The eyes open to a cry of pulleys,
And spirited from sleep, the astounded soul
Hangs for a moment bodiless and simple
As dawn light in the moment of its breaking:

            Outside the open window
            The air is crowded with a

(f)   The eyes open to a cry of pulleys,
       And spirited from sleep, the astounded soul
       Hangs for a moment bodiless and simple
       As false dawn
          Outside the open window,
       Their air is leaping with a rout of angels.
          Some are in bedsheets, some are in dresses,
          it does not seem to matter

Notice how much more appropriate to the total poem is the choice of "cry" over "shriek" or "squeak" to describe the sound of pulleys or how much more effective than the metaphor of a spirit's "brothel" is the image of the soul hanging "bodiless." Notice the things Wilbur excised from the early drafts as well as the things he added when the poem became clearer and more of a piece in his mind.

Let's look again at one of the first poems we discussed, Adrienne Rich's "Aunt Jennifer's Tigers" (chapter 12). This poem gets some of its power from the poet's clear and sympathetic engagement with Aunt Jennifer's situation, but its effects derive from a series of specific technical choices. Rich may or may not have made all these choices consciously; her later comments on the poem suggest that her creative instincts, as well as her then-repressed sense of gender, may have governed some decisions. But however conscious, the choices of speaker, situation, metaphor, and connotative words work brilliantly together to create a strong feminist statement, almost a manifesto on the subject of mastery and compliance, even while (at the same time) making powerful assertions about the power of art to overcome human circumstances.

In a sense this poem has no speaker, no specified personality—only a faceless niece who observes the central character—but the effacing of this speaker in the light of the vivid Jennifer amounts to a brilliant artistic decision. Jennifer, powerless to articulate and possibly even to understand her own plight, nevertheless almost speaks for herself, primarily through her hands. The narrator's seeming refusal to do more than simply describe Jennifer's hands and their product gives Jennifer the crucial central role; she is the center of attention throughout, and the poem emphasizes only what can be seen, with little apparent "editorial" comment (though the speaker does make three evaluative statements, saying that Jennifer was "mastered" by her ordeals [line 10], and noting that her hands are "terrified" [line 9] and that the wedding band "sits heavily" [line 8] on one of them). The tigers are ultimately more eloquent than the speaker: they "prance" (lines 1 and 12) and "pace" (line 4), and they are "proud" (line 12) and unafraid of men (lines 3 and 12), embodying the guarded message Jennifer sends to the world even though she herself is "mastered" and "ringed" (line 10). The brightly conceived colors in the tapestry, the expressive description of Jennifer's fingers and hands (note especially the excitement implied in "fluttering" [line 5]), and the action of the panel itself combine with the characterization of Jennifer to present a strong statement of generational repression—and boldness. The image of knitting as art, suggesting the way the classical Fates determine the future and the nature of things, also hints at what is involved in Rich's art. The quality of the poem lies in the precision and imaginativeness of Rich's craft. In later years, Rich has become clearer and more vocal about her values, but the direction and intensity of her vision are already apparent in this excellent poem taken from her first book, published half a century ago.

The following celebrated poem similarly accomplishes a great deal in a short space:

WILLIAM SHAKESPEARE

[*Th' expense of spirit in a waste of shame*]

Th' expense of spirit in a waste[1] of shame
Is lust in action; and, till action, lust
Is perjured, murderous, bloody, full of blame,
Savage, extreme, rude, cruel, not to trust;
Enjoyed no sooner but despiséd straight: 5
Past reason hunted; and no sooner had,
Past reason hated, as a swallowed bait,
On purpose laid to make the taker mad:
Mad in pursuit, and in possession so;
Had, having, and in quest to have, extreme;   10
A bliss in proof;[2] and proved, a very woe;
Before, a joy proposed; behind, a dream.
All this the world well knows; yet none knows well
To shun the heaven that leads men to this hell.   1609

This poem fully characterizes its speaker, and it does so with economical skill. It sets up the situation slowly and, at first, somewhat unclearly, but the delay in clarity serves a purpose: we know that whatever disturbs the speaker concerns "lust in action" (line 2); we don't know what the disturbance is, but we gather that it stems from personal experience. Because the two explosive *p*'s in the first half of the first line start the poem swiftly and powerfully, we know that the speaker has strong feelings, and by the fourth line he has listed nine separate unpleasant human characteristics driven by lust. He virtually spits them out.

But the speaker expresses more than just anger and negativity. He admits that lust has definite, and powerful, pleasures: it is anticipated with pleasure ("a joy proposed," line 12) and "enjoyed" (line 5) at the time ("a bliss in proof," line 11). Such inconsistencies (or at least complexities) in the speaker's opinion give the poem its unique flavor. His views—like lust itself, according to him—are "extreme" (line 10). The first twelve lines present no easy conclusions, only a confusing vacillation between positives and negatives. The strong condemnation of lust in the beginning—detailed in terms of how it makes people feel about themselves and how it affects their actions—quickly shifts into admissions of pleasure and joy, then shifts back again. No opinion sticks for long, except for the speaker's certainty about the power of lust to drive people to behavior they may love or hate. The "moral" he offers at the end will comfort no one. Everyone agrees with what I've been saying, he concludes, but no one knows how to avoid lust

1. Using up; also, desert. *Expense:* expending.   2. In the act.

and its consequences because its pleasures are so sensational, both in prospect and in actuality ("the heaven that leads men to this hell").

The speaker's vacillating opinions and moods are not the only confusing thing about the poem's organization. His account of lust repeatedly shifts in time. Does he mean lust as it is being satisfied ("lust in action")? Or does he mean desire and anticipation? Or does he mean what happens afterward? He discusses all three, and hardly system-atically. The first line and a half describe the present, and the meter of the first line even imitates the rhythms and force of male ejaculation: note how the basic iambic-pentameter strategy of the poem does not regularize until near the end of the second line. But by line 2 he is talking about what happens before lust in action ("till action"), and by line 5, after. Lines 6 and 7 contrast before and after, and line 9 compares before and during. Line 10 describes all three posi-tions in time ("Had, having, and in quest to have"). Line 11 compares during and after; line 12, before and after. The speaker seems unable to decide exactly what he wants to talk about and what he thinks of his subject.

Poems may or may not follow classical patterns—they explode out of everyday experience.

—DOROTHY LIVESAY

All this shifting around in focus and in feelings could be regarded as a serious flaw. Don't we expect a short poem, especially a sonnet, to be carefully organized and focused toward a single end? Shouldn't the poet make up his mind about what he thinks and what the poem is about? We could easily construct an argument, on the basis of consistency or clarity of purpose, that this is not a very good poem, that perhaps the greatest poet in the English language was not, here, at the top of his form. But doing so would ignore the power of the poem's effects and underrate another principle of con-sistency—that of character. If we regard the poem as representative of a mind wrestling with the complex feelings brought about by lust—someone out of control because of lust, conscious enough to see his plight but unable to do anything about it—we can see a higher consistency that explains the poem's grip on many readers. This is an account of a human mind grappling with an often-repeated human truism, the subject of many much longer works of literature: lust is beautiful but terrifying, certainly to be avoided but impossible to avoid. Shakespeare has managed, in the unlikely space of fourteen lines and in a form in which we expect tight organization and intense focus, to portray succinctly the human recognition of confusion and powerlessness in the face of a pas-sion larger than our ability to control it.

Here is another poem that is something of a challenge to evaluate:

JOHN DONNE

Song

Go, and catch a falling star,
  Get with child a mandrake root,[3]
Tell me, where all past years are,

3. The forked mandrake root looks vaguely human.

Or who cleft the devil's foot,
Teach me to hear mermaids singing   5
Or to keep off envy's stinging,
    And find
    What wind
Serves to advance an honest mind.

If thou beest born to strange sights,[4]   10
    Things invisible to see,
Ride ten thousand days and nights,
    Till age snow white hairs on thee;
Thou, when thou return'st, wilt tell me
All strange wonders that befell thee,   15
    And swear
    No where
Lives a woman true, and fair.

If thou find'st one, let me know:
    Such a pilgrimage were sweet.   20
Yet do not, I would not go,
    Though at next door we might meet:
Though she were true when you met her,
And last till you write your letter,
    Yet she   25
    Will be
False, ere I come, to two, or three.   1633

First we need to consider the irregular, jerky rhythm. Since the poem is called "Song," we expect music, harmony, something pleasant and (within limits) predictable in its rhythm and movement. But this "song" presents nothing like that. At first its message sounds lyrical and romantic: to go and catch a falling star is, if impossible, a romantic thing to propose, a motif that often comes up (and has for centuries) in love poems and popular songs; and lines 3 and 5 propose similar traditional romantic activities that evoke wonder and pleasure in contemplation. But the activities suggested in the alternate lines (2, 4, and 6) contrast sharply; they are just as bold in their unromantic or antiromantic sentiments. Making a mandrake root pregnant does not sound like an especially pleasant activity, however much such a root may look like a female body, and knowledge of the devil's cleft foot or envy's stinging are not usually the stuff of romantic poems or songs. Besides, the strange interruptions of easy rhythm (indicated by commas) in otherwise pleasant lines like 1 and 3 suggest that something less than lyrical goes on there, too.

By the time we reach the last stanza, what is going on has become clearer. We have here a portrait of an angry and disillusioned man who is obsessed with the infidelity of women. He is talking to another man, apparently someone who has far more positive, perhaps even romantic, notions of women, and the poem is a kind of argument, except that the disillusioned speaker does all the talking. He pretends to take into account some traditional romantic rhetoric, but turns it all on its head, intermixing the traditional

---

4. That is, if you have supernatural powers.

impossible quests of lovers with a quest of his own—to find a "woman true, and fair" (line 18). But he knows cynically—he would probably say from experience, though he offers no evidence of his experience and no account of why he feels the way he does— that all these quests are impossible. A bitter man, he wants nothing to do with love or romance.

If we were to evaluate this "song" on the basis of harmonic and romantic expectations, looking for evenness of rhythms, pleasant sounds, and an attractive series of images consonant with romantic attitudes, we would certainly find it wanting. But again (as with the Shakespeare poem above) a larger question of appropriateness begs to be applied. Do the sounds, tone, images, and organization of the poem "work" in terms of the speaker portrayed here and the kind of artistic project this poem represents? The displeasure we feel in the speaker's words, images, feelings, and attitudes ultimately needs to be directed toward the speaker; the poet has done a good job of portraying a character whose bitterness, however generated, is unpleasant and off-putting. The poem "works" on its own terms. We may or may not like to hear attitudes like this expressed in a poem; we may or may not approve of using a pretended "song" to mouth such sentiments. But whether or not we "like" the poem in terms of what it says, we can evaluate, through close analysis of its several different elements (much as we have been doing analytically in earlier chapters), how *well* it does what it does. Remaining, of course, are still larger questions of whether what it tries to do is worth doing, and readers of different philosophical or political persuasions may differ widely in their opinions and evaluations of that matter.

Different people admire different things, and when we talk about criteria for evaluating poetry, we talk about, at best, elements that a fairly large number of people have, over a long period of time, agreed on as important. A substantial agreement about political or social values may exist within a particular group—misogynists or feminists, say, may reach a consensus among themselves about the value of Donne's "Song." But more general agreements that bridge social and ideological divisions will more likely involve the kinds of matters that have come up for analysis in earlier chapters, matters involving how well a poem *works,* how well it uses the resources within its conceptual limits. For some readers, ideology is everything, and quality has no meaning beyond political views or moral conclusions. But for others, different, more pluralistic evaluations can be made about accomplishment and quality. You need to decide on your own criteria.

Consistency. Appropriateness. Coherence. Effectiveness. Such terms play key roles in most readers' evaluations—as they have done in this discussion. But individual critics or readers will have their own emphases, their own highly personal preferences, their own axes to grind. For some critics in past generations, *organic unity*—whether a poem achieved, like something grown in nature, a wholeness of conception and effect—was the key to all evaluation. With experience, you will develop your own set of criteria, which may or may not involve a single ruling concept or term—*tension* or *ambiguity* or *complexity* or *simplicity* or *authenticity* or *cultural truth* or *representation* or *psychological accuracy.* But wherever (and whenever) you come out, you will learn something about yourself and your values in the process of articulating exactly what you like and admire—and why.

• • •

GALWAY KINNELL

Blackberry Eating

I love to go out in late September
among the fat, overripe, icy, black blackberries
to eat blackberries for breakfast,
the stalks very prickly, a penalty
they earn for knowing the black art   5
of blackberry-making; and as I stand among them
lifting the stalks to my mouth, the ripest berries
fall almost unbidden to my tongue,
as words sometimes do, certain peculiar words
like *strengths* or *squinched*,   10
many-lettered, one-syllabled lumps,
which I squeeze, squinch open, and splurge well
in the silent, startled, icy, black language
of blackberry-eating in late September.   1980

EMILY DICKINSON

[The Brain—is wider than the Sky—]

The Brain—is wider than the Sky—
For—put them side by side—
The one the other will contain
With ease—and You—beside—

The Brain is deeper than the sea—   5
For—hold them—Blue to Blue—
The one the other will absorb—
As Sponges—Buckets—do—

The Brain is just the weight of God—
For—Heft them—Pound for Pound—   10
And they will differ—if they do—
As Syllable from Sound—

ca. 1862

WALLACE STEVENS

Anecdote of the Jar

I placed a jar in Tennessee,
And round it was, upon a hill.
It made the slovenly wilderness
Surround that hill.

5 The wilderness rose up to it,
And sprawled around, no longer wild.
The jar was round upon the ground
And tall and of a port in air.

It took dominion everywhere.
10 The jar was gray and bare.
It did not give of bird or bush,
Like nothing else in Tennessee.

1923

JOHN CROWE RANSOM

Bells for John Whiteside's Daughter

There was such speed in her little body,
And such lightness in her footfall,
It is no wonder her brown study[5]
Astonishes us all.

5 Her wars were bruited in our high window.
We looked among orchard trees and beyond
Where she took arms against her shadow,
Or harried unto the pond

The lazy geese, like a snow cloud
10 Dripping their snow on the green grass,
Tricking and stopping, sleepy and proud,
Who cried in goose, Alas,

For the tireless heart within the little
Lady with rod that made them rise
15 From their noon apple-dreams and scuttle
Goose-fashion under the skies!

5. Stillness, as if in meditation or deep thought.

But now go the bells, and we are ready,
In one house we are sternly stopped
To say we are vexed at her brown study,
Lying so primly propped.   20

1924

MICHAEL ONDAATJE

King Kong Meets Wallace Stevens

Take two photographs—
Wallace Stevens and King Kong
(Is it significant that I eat bananas as I write this?)

Stevens is portly, benign, a white brush cut
striped tie. Businessman but   5
for the dark thick hands, the naked brain
the thought in him.

Kong is staggering
lost in New York streets again
a spawn of annoyed cars at his toes.   10
The mind is nowhere.
Fingers are plastic, electric under the skin.
He's at the call of Metro-Goldwyn-Mayer.

Meanwhile W. S. in his suit
is thinking chaos is thinking fences.   15
In his head—the seeds of fresh pain
his exorcising,
the bellow of locked blood.

The hands drain from his jacket,
pose in the murderer's shadow.   1979   20

QUESTIONS

1. What is the single most important factor in whether you like or dislike a poem? Read back over the poems that you have liked most; what do they have in common?
2. How adaptable are you in adjusting to a poem's emphases? Which poems have you liked though you didn't especially like the conclusions they came to?
3. How important to you is the *precision* of words in a poem? Do you tend to like poems better if they are definite and explicit in what they say? if they are ambiguous, uncertain, or complex?
4. Which issues and concepts in chapters 12 through 19 have you found most useful? most surprising? Which chapters did you enjoy most? From which did you learn the most about yourself and your tastes and values?
5. What do you value most in poetry generally? Do you read poems that are not assigned? How do you choose them? Do you read poems outside this textbook or outside the course?

If so, what kinds of poems do you seek out? Do specific titles draw you in? particular subjects, topics, or themes?

6. How important to you is the *tone* of a poem? Do you tend to like funny poems more than serious ones? tragic situations more than comic ones? unusual treatments of standard or predictable subjects and themes?

7. Which poem in this chapter did you most enjoy? Which one did you like best after reading the commentary about it? Have you violently disliked any poems you have read this term? What about them particularly irritated you? Have you changed your mind about some poems after you have reread or discussed them? How did your criteria change?

8. Are certain subjects or themes always appealing to you? always unappealing?

WRITING SUGGESTIONS

1. Choose one poem that you especially admire and one that you do not. Write a two- or three-page essay about each in which you show what specific accomplishments (or lack of them) led you to your evaluative conclusions. Treat each poem in detail, and suggest fully not only how but *why* things "work"—or don't work. Try to construct your argument as "objectively" as possible so that you are not simply pitting your personal judgment against someone else's. (Alternative: find two poems that are very much alike in subject matter, theme, or situation, but that seem unequally successful. Write one *comparative* essay in which you account for the difference in quality by showing in detail the difference between what works and what does not.)

2. Discuss with classmates a variety of poems you have read this term, and choose one poem about which a number of you disagree. Discuss among yourselves the different perspectives you have on the poem, and try to sort out in the discussion exactly what issues are at stake. Take notes on the discussion, trying to be clear about how your position differs from that of other students. Once you believe that you have the issues sorted out and can be clear about your own position, write a two- or three-page personal letter to your instructor in which you outline a position contrary to your own and then answer it point by point. Be sure to make clear in your letter the *grounds* for your evaluative position, positive or negative—that is, the principles or values on which you base your evaluation. (Hint: in the conversation with classmates, try to steer the discussion to a clear disagreement on no more than two or three points, and in your letter focus carefully on these points. State the arguments of your classmates as effectively and forcefully as you can so that your own argument will be as probing and sophisticated as you can make it.)

3. Choose a poem you have read this term that you admire but really don't like very much. In thinking over the poem again, try to account for the conflict between your feelings and your intellectual judgment: what questions of content or form, social or political assumption, personal style, or manner of argument in the poem make it less attractive to you? In a personal letter to a friend who is not in the class and who thus has not heard the class discussions of the issues, describe your dilemma, being careful to first outline why you think the poem is admirable. Say frankly what your personal reservations about the poem are, and at the end use the discussion of the poem to talk about your own values, as they pertain to poetry in general.

Reading More Poetry

WILLIAM BLAKE

The Tyger

Tyger! Tyger! burning bright
In the forests of the night,
What immortal hand or eye
Could frame thy fearful symmetry?

In what distant deeps or skies   5
Burnt the fire of thine eyes?
On what wings dare he aspire?
What the hand dare seize the fire?

And what shoulder, & what art,
Could twist the sinews of thy heart?   10
And when thy heart began to beat,
What dread hand? & what dread feet?

What the hammer? what the chain?
In what furnace was thy brain?
What the anvil? what dread grasp   15
Dare its deadly terrors clasp?

When the stars threw down their spears
And water'd heaven with their tears,
Did he smile his work to see?
Did he who made the Lamb make thee?   20

Tyger! Tyger! burning bright
In the forests of the night,
What immortal hand or eye
Dare frame thy fearful symmetry?   1790

GWENDOLYN BROOKS

To the Diaspora

you did not know you were Afrika

When you set out for Afrika
you did not know you were going.
Because
you did not know you were Afrika.
5   You did not know the Black continent
that had to be reached
was you.

I could not have told you then that some sun
would come,
10 somewhere over the road,
would come evoking the diamonds
of you, the Black continent—
somewhere over the road.
You would not have believed my mouth.

15 When I told you, meeting you somewhere close
to the heat and youth of the road,
liking my loyalty, liking belief,
you smiled and you thanked me but very little believed me.

Here is some sun. Some.
20 Now off into the places rough to reach.
Though dry, though drowsy, all unwillingly a-wobble,
into the dissonant and dangerous crescendo.
Your work, that was done, to be done to be done to be done.   1981

SAMUEL TAYLOR COLERIDGE

Kubla Khan

Or, a Vision in a Dream[1]

In Xanadu did Kubla Khan
A stately pleasure-dome decree:
Where Alph, the sacred river, ran
Through caverns measureless to man

---

1. Coleridge said he wrote this fragment immediately after waking from an opium dream and that after he was interrupted by a caller he was unable to finish the poem.

Down to a sunless sea.   5
So twice five miles of fertile ground
With walls and towers were girdled round:
And here were gardens bright with sinuous rills
Where blossomed many an incense-bearing tree;
And here were forests ancient as the hills,   10
Enfolding sunny spots of greenery.

But oh! that deep romantic chasm which slanted
Down the green hill athwart a cedarn cover!²
A savage place! as holy and enchanted
As e'er beneath a waning moon was haunted   15
By woman wailing for her demon-lover!³
And from this chasm, with ceaseless turmoil seething,
As if this earth in fast thick pants were breathing,
A mighty fountain momently was forced,
Amid whose swift half-intermitted burst   20
Huge fragments vaulted like rebounding hail,
Or chaffy grain beneath the thresher's flail:
And 'mid these dancing rocks at once and ever
It flung up momently the sacred river.
Five miles meandering with a mazy motion   25
Through wood and dale the sacred river ran,
Then reached the caverns measureless to man,
And sank in tumult to a lifeless ocean:
And 'mid this tumult Kubla heard from far
Ancestral voices prophesying war!   30

    The shadow of the dome of pleasure
    Floated midway on the waves;
    Where was heard the mingled measure
    From the fountain and the caves.
It was a miracle of rare device,   35
A sunny pleasure-dome with caves of ice!

    A damsel with a dulcimer
    In a vision once I saw:
    It was an Abyssinian maid,
    And on her dulcimer she played,   40
    Singing of Mount Abora.
    Could I revive within me
    Her symphony and song,
    To such a deep delight 'twould win me,
That with music loud and long,   45
I would build that dome in air,
That sunny dome! those caves of ice!
And all who heard should see them there,

2. From side to side of a cover of cedar trees.   3. In a famous and often-imitated German ballad, the
lady Lenore is carried off on horseback by the specter of her lover and married to him at his grave.

And all should cry, Beware! Beware!
50   His flashing eyes, his floating hair!
Weave a circle round him thrice,
And close your eyes with holy dread,
For he on honey-dew hath fed,
And drunk the milk of Paradise.

1798

EMILY DICKINSON

[*Because I could not stop for Death—*]

Because I could not stop for Death—
He kindly stopped for me—
The Carriage held but just Ourselves—
And Immortality.

5   We slowly drove—He knew no haste
And I had put away
My labor and my leisure too,
For His Civility—

We passed the School, where Children strove
10   At Recess—in the Ring—
We passed the Fields of Gazing Grain—
We passed the Setting Sun—

Or rather—He passed Us—
The Dews drew quivering and chill—
15   For only Gossamer,⁴ my Gown—
My Tippet—only Tulle⁵—

We paused before a House that seemed
A Swelling of the Ground—
The Roof was scarcely visible—
20   The Cornice—in the Ground—

Since then—'tis Centuries—and yet
Feels shorter than the Day
I first surmised the Horses' Heads
Were toward Eternity—

ca. 1863

---

4. A soft, sheer fabric.   5. A fine net fabric. *Tippet:* scarf.

[*I stepped from Plank to Plank*]

I stepped from Plank to Plank
A slow and cautious way
The Stars about my Head I felt
About my Feet the Sea.

I knew not but the next   5
Would be my final inch—
This gave me that precarious Gait
Some call Experience.

ca. 1864

[*It dropped so low—in my Regard—*]

It dropped so low—in my Regard—
I heard it hit the Ground—
And go to pieces on the Stones
At bottom of my Mind—

Yet blamed the Fate that flung it—*less*   5
Than I denounced Myself,
For entertaining Plated Wares
Upon my Silver Shelf—

ca. 1863

[*We do not play on Graves—*]

We do not play on Graves—
Because there isn't Room—
Besides—it isn't even—it slants
And People come—

And put a Flower on it—   5
And hang their faces so—
We're fearing that their Hearts will drop—
And crush our pretty play—

And so we move as far
As Enemies—away—   10
Just looking round to see how far
It is—Occasionally—

ca. 1862

[*She dealt her pretty words like Blades—*]

She dealt her pretty words like Blades—
How glittering they shone—
And every One unbared a Nerve
Or wantoned with a Bone—

5   She never deemed—she hurt—
That—is not Steel's Affair—
A vulgar grimace in the Flesh—
How ill the Creatures bear—

To Ache is human—not polite—
10   The Film upon the eye
Mortality's old Custom—
Just locking up—to Die.

1862

JOHN DONNE

[*Death, be not proud, though some have callèd thee*]

Death, be not proud, though some have callèd thee
Mighty and dreadful, for thou art not so;
For those whom thou think'st thou dost overthrow
Die not, poor Death, nor yet canst thou kill me.
5   From rest and sleep, which but thy pictures[6] be,
Much pleasure; then from thee much more must flow,
And soonest[7] our best men with thee do go,
Rest of their bones, and soul's delivery.[8]
Thou art slave to Fate, Chance, kings, and desperate men,
10 And dost with Poison, War, and Sickness dwell;
And poppy or charms can make us sleep as well,
And better than thy stroke; why swell'st[9] thou then?
One short sleep past, we wake eternally
And death shall be no more; Death, thou shalt die.

1633

The Sun Rising

Busy old fool, unruly sun,
Why dost thou thus,
Through windows, and through curtains, call on us?

6. Likenesses.   7. Most willingly.   8. Deliverance.   9. Puff with pride.

Must to thy motions lovers' seasons run?
        Saucy pedantic wretch, go chide   5
        Late schoolboys, and sour prentices,[1]
Go tell court-huntsmen that the king will ride,
    Call country ants[2] to harvest offices;
Love, all alike, no season knows, nor clime,
Nor hours, days, months, which are the rags of time.   10
        Thy beams, so reverend and strong
        Why shouldst thou think?
I could eclipse and cloud them with a wink,
But that I would not lose her sight so long:
        If her eyes have not blinded thine,   15
        Look, and tomorrow late, tell me
Whether both the Indias[3] of spice and mine
Be where thou left'st them, or lie here with me.
Ask for those kings whom thou saw'st yesterday,
And thou shalt hear, all here in one bed lay.   20

        She is all states, and all princes I,
        Nothing else is.
Princes do but play us; compared to this,
All honor's mimic, all wealth alchemy.[4]
        Thou, sun, art half as happy as we,   25
        In that the world's contracted thus;
Thine age asks[5] ease, and since thy duties be
To warm the world, that's done in warming us.
Shine here to us, and thou art every where;
This bed thy center[6] is, these walls thy sphere.   1633   30

A Valediction: Forbidding Mourning

As virtuous men pass mildly away,
    And whisper to their souls to go,
Whilst some of their sad friends do say,
    "The breath goes now," and some say, "No,"

So let us melt, and make no noise,   5
    No tear-floods, nor sigh-tempests move;
'Twere profanation of our joys
    To tell the laity our love.

Moving of the earth[7] brings harms and fears,
    Men reckon what it did and meant;   10
But trepidation of the spheres,[8]
    Though greater far, is innocent.

1. Apprentices.   2. Farmworkers.   3. The East and West Indies, commercial sources of spices and gold.
4. Imposture, like the "scientific" procedures for turning base metals into gold. *Mimic:* hypocritical.
5. Requires.   6. Of orbit.   7. Earthquakes.   8. The Renaissance hypothesis that the celestial spheres trembled and thus caused unexpected variations in their orbits. Such movements are "innocent" because earthlings do not observe or fret about them.

Dull sublunary[9] lovers' love
    (Whose soul is sense) cannot admit
15   Absence, because it doth remove
        Those things which elemented[1] it.

But we, by a love so much refined
    That our selves know not what it is,
Inter-assured of the mind,
20   Care less, eyes, lips, and hands to miss.

Our two souls therefore, which are one,
    Though I must go, endure not yet
A breach, but an expansion,
        Like gold to airy thinness beat.

25   If they be two, they are two so
    As stiff twin compasses are two:
Thy soul, the fixed foot, makes no show
    To move, but doth, if the other do;

And though it in the center sit,
30   Yet when the other far doth roam,
It leans, and hearkens after it,
    And grows erect, as that comes home.

Such wilt thou be to me, who must,
    Like the other foot, obliquely run;
35   Thy firmness makes my circle[2] just,
    And makes me end where I begun.

    1611?

PAUL LAURENCE DUNBAR

Sympathy

I know what the caged bird feels, alas!
    When the sun is bright on the upland slopes;
When the wind stirs soft through the springing grass,
And the river flows like a stream of glass;
5   When the first bird sings and the first bud opens,
And the faint perfume from its chalice steals—
I know what the caged bird feels!

I know why the caged bird beats his wing
    Till its blood is red on the cruel bars;

---

9. Below the moon—that is, changeable. According to the traditional cosmology that Donne invokes here, the moon was considered the dividing line between the immutable celestial world and the earthly mortal one.   1. Comprised.   2. A traditional symbol of perfection.

For he must fly back to his perch and cling 10
When he fain would be on the bough a-swing;
   And a pain still throbs in the old, old scars
And they pulse again with a keener sting—
I know why he beats his wing!

I know why the caged bird sings, ah me, 15
   When his wing is bruised and his bosom sore,—
When he beats his bars and he would be free;
It is not a carol of joy or glee,
   But a prayer that he sends from his heart's deep core,
But a plea, that upward to Heaven he flings— 20
I know why the caged bird sings! 1893

We Wear the Mask

We wear the mask that grins and lies,
It hides our cheeks and shades our eyes,—
This debt we pay to human guile;
With torn and bleeding hearts we smile,
And mouth with myriad subtleties. 5

Why should the world be over-wise,
In counting all our tears and sighs?
Nay, let them only see us, while
   We wear the mask.

We smile, but, O great Christ, our cries 10
To thee from tortured souls arise.
We sing, but oh the clay is vile
Beneath our feet, and long the mile;
But let the world dream otherwise,
   We wear the mask! 1896 15

T. S. ELIOT

Journey of the Magi[3]

"A cold coming we had of it,
Just the worst time of the year
For a journey, and such a long journey:
The ways deep and the weather sharp,
The very dead of winter."[4] 5

3. The wise men who followed the star of Bethlehem. See Matthew 2.1–12.   4. An adaptation of a passage from a 1622 sermon by Lancelot Andrews.

And the camels galled, sore-footed, refractory,
Lying down in the melting snow.
There were times we regretted
The summer palaces on slopes, the terraces,
10 And the silken girls bringing sherbet.
Then the camel men cursing and grumbling
And running away, and wanting their liquor and women,
And the night-fires going out, and the lack of shelters,
And the cities hostile and the towns unfriendly
15 And the villages dirty and charging high prices:
A hard time we had of it.
At the end we preferred to travel all night,
Sleeping in snatches,
With the voices singing in our ears, saying
20 That this was all folly.

Then at dawn we came down to a temperate valley,
Wet, below the snow line, smelling of vegetation;
With a running stream and a water-mill beating the darkness,
And three trees on the low sky,[5]
25 And an old white horse galloped away in the meadow.
Then we came to a tavern with vine-leaves over the lintel,
Six hands at an open door dicing for pieces of silver,
And feet kicking the empty wine-skins.
But there was no information, and so we continued
30 And arrived at evening, not a moment too soon
Finding the place; it was (you may say) satisfactory.

All this was a long time ago, I remember,
And I would do it again, but set down
This set down
35 This: were we led all that way for
Birth or Death? There was a Birth, certainly,
We had evidence and no doubt. I had seen birth and death,
But had thought they were different; this Birth was
Hard and bitter agony for us, like Death, our death.
40 We returned to our places, these Kingdoms,[6]
But no longer at ease here, in the old dispensation,
With an alien people clutching their gods.
I should be glad of another death.

                                                              1927

5. Suggesting the three crosses of the Crucifixion (Luke 23.32–33). The Magi see several objects that suggest later events in Christ's life: pieces of silver (see Matthew 26.14–16), the dicing (see Matthew 27.35), the white horse (see Revelation 6.2 and 19.11–16), and the empty wine skins (see Matthew 9.17, possibly relevant also to lines 41–42).   6. The Bible identifies the wise men only as "from the east," and subsequent tradition has made them kings. In Persia, magi were members of an ancient priestly caste.

ROBERT FROST

The Road Not Taken

Two roads diverged in a yellow wood,
And sorry I could not travel both
And be one traveler, long I stood
And looked down one as far as I could
To where it bent in the undergrowth;   5

Then took the other, as just as fair,
And having perhaps the better claim,
Because it was grassy and wanted wear;
Though as for that the passing there
Had worn them really about the same,   10

And both that morning equally lay
In leaves no step had trodden black.
Oh, I kept the first for another day!
Yet knowing how way leads on to way,
I doubted if I should ever come back.   15

I shall be telling this with a sigh
Somewhere ages and ages hence:
Two roads diverged in a wood, and I—
I took the one less traveled by,
And that has made all the difference.   1916   20

Stopping by Woods on a Snowy Evening

Whose woods these are I think I know.
His house is in the village, though;
He will not see me stopping here
To watch his woods fill up with snow.

My little horse must think it queer   5
To stop without a farmhouse near
Between the woods and frozen lake
The darkest evening of the year.

He gives his harness bells a shake
To ask if there is some mistake.   10
The only other sound's the sweep
Of easy wind and downy flake.

The woods are lovely, dark, and deep,
But I have promises to keep,
And miles to go before I sleep,   15
And miles to go before I sleep.   1923

THOMAS GRAY

Elegy Written in a Country Churchyard

The curfew tolls the knell of parting day,
  The lowing herd wind slowly o'er the lea,
The plowman homeward plods his weary way,
  And leaves the world to darkness and to me.

Now fades the glimmering landscape on the sight,
  And all the air a solemn stillness holds,
Save where the beetle wheels his droning flight,
  And drowsy tinklings lull the distant folds;

Save that from yonder ivy-mantled tower
  The moping owl does to the moon complain
Of such, as wandering near her secret bower,
  Molest her ancient solitary reign.

Beneath those rugged elms, that yew tree's shade,
  Where heaves the turf in many a moldering heap,
Each in his narrow cell forever laid,
  The rude⁷ forefathers of the hamlet sleep.

The breezy call of incense-breathing Morn,
  The swallow twittering from the straw-built shed,
The cock's shrill clarion, or the echoing horn.⁸
  No more shall rouse them from their lowly bed.

For them no more the blazing hearth shall burn,
  Or busy housewife ply her evening care;
No children run to lisp their sire's return,
  Or climb his knees the envied kiss to share.

Oft did the harvest to their sickle yield,
  Their furrow oft the stubborn glebe⁹ has broke;
How jocund did they drive their team afield!
  How bowed the woods beneath their sturdy stroke!

Let not Ambition mock their useful toil,
  Their homely joys, and destiny obscure;
Nor Grandeur hear with a disdainful smile
  The short and simple annals of the poor.

The boast of heraldry,¹ the pomp of power,
  And all that beauty, all that wealth e'er gave,
Awaits alike the inevitable hour.
  The paths of glory lead but to the grave.

Nor you, ye proud, impute to these the fault,
  If Memory o'er their tomb no trophies² raise,

---

7. Unlearned.   8. The hunter's horn.   9. Soil.   1. Noble birth.   2. An ornamental or symbolic
group of figures depicting the achievements of the deceased.

Where through the long-drawn aisle and fretted[3] vault
    The pealing anthem swells the note of praise   40

Can storied urn or animated[4] bust
    Back to its mansion call the fleeting breath?
Can Honor's voice provoke the silent dust,
    Or Flattery soothe the dull cold ear of Death?

Perhaps in this neglected spot is laid   45
    Some heart once pregnant with celestial fire;
Hands that the rod of empire might have swayed,
    Or waked to ecstasy the living lyre.

But Knowledge to their eyes her ample page
    Rich with the spoils of time did ne'er unroll;   50
Chill Penury repressed their noble rage,
    And froze the genial current of the soul.

Full many a gem of purest ray serene,
    The dark unfathomed caves of ocean bear:
Full many a flower is born to blush unseen,   55
    And waste its sweetness on the desert air.

Some village Hampden,[5] that with dauntless breast
    The little tyrant of his fields withstood;
Some mute inglorious Milton[6] here may rest,
    Some Cromwell[7] guiltless of his country's blood.   60

The applause of listening senates to command,
    The threats of pain and ruin to despise,
To scatter plenty o'er a smiling land,
    And read their history in a nation's eyes,

Their lot forbade: nor circumscribed alone   65
    Their growing virtues, but their crimes confined;
Forbade to wade through slaughter to a throne,
    And shut the gates of mercy on mankind,

The struggling pangs of conscious truth to hide,
    To quench the blushes of ingenuous shame,   70
Or heap the shrine of Luxury and Pride
    With incense kindled at the Muse's flame.

Far from the madding crowd's ignoble strife,
    Their sober wishes never learned to stray;
Along the cool sequestered vale of life   75
    They kept the noiseless tenor of their way.

Yet even these bones from insult to protect
    Some frail memorial still erected nigh,

3. Decorated with intersecting lines in relief.   4. Lifelike. *Storied urn:* a funeral urn with an epitaph or pictured story inscribed on it.   5. John Hampden (1594–1643), who, both as a private citizen and as a member of Parliament, zealously defended the rights of the people against the autocratic policies of Charles I.   6. John Milton (1608–1674), great English poet.   7. Oliver Cromwell (1599–1658), lord protector of England during the Interregnum, noted for military genius but also cruelty and intolerance.

With uncouth rhymes and shapeless sculpture decked,[8]
    Implores the passing tribute of a sigh.

Their name, their years, spelt by the unlettered Muse,
    The place of fame and elegy supply:
And many a holy text around she strews,
    That teach the rustic moralist to die.

For who to dumb Forgetfulness a prey,
    This pleasing anxious being e'er resigned,
Left the warm precincts of the cheerful day,
    Nor cast one longing lingering look behind?

On some fond breast the parting soul relies,
    Some pious drops the closing eye requires;
Even from the tomb the voice of Nature cries,
    Even in our ashes live their wonted fires.

For thee, who mindful of the unhonored dead
    Dost in these lines their artless tale relate;
If chance, by lonely contemplation led,
    Some kindred spirit shall inquire thy fate,

Haply some hoary-headed swain may say,
    "Oft have we seen him at the peep of dawn
Brushing with hasty steps the dews away
    To meet the sun upon the upland lawn.

"There at the foot of yonder nodding beech
    That wreathes its old fantastic roots so high,
His listless length at noontide would he stretch,
    And pore upon the brook that babbles by.

"Hard by yon wood, now smiling as in scorn,
    Muttering his wayward fancies he would rove,
Now drooping, woeful wan, like one forlorn,
    Or crazed with care, or crossed in hopeless love.

"One morn I missed him on the customed hill,
    Along the heath and near his favorite tree;
Another came; nor yet beside the rill,
    Nor up the lawn, nor at the wood was he;

"The next with dirges due in sad array
    Slow through the churchway path we saw him borne.
Approach and read (for thou canst read) the lay,
    Graved on the stone beneath yon aged thorn."

The Epitaph

Here rests his head upon the lap of Earth
A youth to Fortune and to Fame unknown.

8. Cf. the "storied urn or animated bust" (line 41) dedicated inside the church to the "proud" (line 37).

Fair Science[9] frowned not on his humble birth,
    And Melancholy marked him for her own.   120

Large was his bounty, and his soul sincere,
    Heaven did a recompense as largely send:
He gave to Misery all he had, a tear,
    He gained from Heaven ('twas all he wished) a friend.

No farther seek his merits to disclose,   125
    Or draw his frailties from their dread abode
(There they alike in trembling hope repose),
    The bosom of his Father and his God.   1751

GERARD MANLEY HOPKINS

God's Grandeur

The world is charged with the grandeur of God.
    It will flame out, like shining from shook foil;[1]
    It gathers to a greatness, like the ooze of oil
Crushed. Why do men then now not reck his rod?[2]
Generations have trod, have trod, have trod;   5
    And all is seared with trade; bleared, smeared with toil;
    And wears man's smudge and shares man's smell: the soil
Is bare now, nor can foot feel, being shod.

And for all this, nature is never spent;
    There lives the dearest freshness deep down things;   10
And though the last lights off the black West went
    Oh, morning, at the brown brink eastward, springs—
Because the Holy Ghost over the bent
    World broods with warm breast and with ah! bright wings.   1918

The Windhover[3]

To Christ our Lord

I caught this morning morning's minion,[4] king-
    dom of daylight's dauphin,[5] dapple-dawn-drawn Falcon, in his riding
    Of the rolling level underneath him steady air, and striding

9. Learning.   1. "I mean foil in its sense of leaf or tinsel. . . . Shaken goldfoil gives off broad glares like sheet lightning and also, and this is true of nothing else, owing to its zig-zag dints and creasings and network of small many cornered facets, a sort of fork lightning too" (*Letters of Gerard Manley Hopkins to Robert Bridges,* ed. C. C. Abbott [1955], p. 169).   2. Heed his authority.   3. A small hawk, the kestrel, which habitually hovers in the air, headed into the wind.   4. Favorite, beloved.   5. Heir to regal splendor.

High there, how he rung upon the rein of a wimpling[6] wing
In his ecstasy! then off, off forth on swing,
    As a skate's heel sweeps smooth on a bow-bend: the hurl and gliding
    Rebuffed the big wind. My heart in hiding
Stirred for a bird,—the achieve of, the mastery of the thing!

Brute beauty and valor and act, oh, air, pride, plume, here
    Buckle![7] AND the fire that breaks from thee then, a billion
Times told lovelier, more dangerous, O my chevalier![8]

    No wonder of it: shéer plód makes plow down sillion[9]
Shine, and blue-bleak embers, ah my dear,
    Fall, gall themselves, and gash gold-vermilion.

1877

LANGSTON HUGHES

I, Too

I, too, sing America.

I am the darker brother.
They send me to eat in the kitchen
When company comes,
But I laugh,
And eat well,
And grow strong.

Tomorrow,
I'll sit at the table.
When company comes
Nobody'll dare
Say to me,
"Eat in the kitchen,"
Then.

Besides,
They'll see how beautiful I am
And be ashamed—

I, too, am America.

1932

---

6. Rippling.   7. Several meanings may apply: to join closely, to prepare for battle, to grapple with, to collapse.   8. Horseman, knight.   9. The narrow strip of land between furrows in an open field divided for separate cultivation.

Theme for English B

The instructor said,

> Go home and write
> a page tonight.
> And let that page come out of you—
> Then, it will be true.   5

I wonder if it's that simple?
I am twenty-two, colored, born in Winston-Salem.
I went to school there, then Durham,[1] then here
to this college[2] on the hill above Harlem.
I am the only colored student in my class.   10
The steps from the hill lead down into Harlem,
through a park, then I cross St. Nicholas,[3]
Eighth Avenue, Seventh, and I come to the Y,
the Harlem Branch Y, where I take the elevator
up to my room, sit down, and write this page: 15

It's not easy to know what is true for you or me
at twenty-two, my age. But I guess I'm what
I feel and see and hear, Harlem, I hear you:
hear you, hear me—we two—you, me, talk on this page.
(I hear New York, too.) Me—who?   20

Well, I like to eat, sleep, drink, and be in love.
I like to work, read, learn, and understand life.
I like a pipe for a Christmas present,
or records—Bessie,[4] bop, or Bach.
I guess being colored doesn't make me *not* like   25
the same things other folks like who are other races.
So will my page be colored that I write?

Being me, it will not be white.
But it will be
a part of you, instructor.   30
You are white—
yet a part of me, as I am a part of you.
That's American.
Sometimes perhaps you don't want to be a part of me.
Nor do I often want to be a part of you.   35
But we are, that's true!
As I learn from you,
I guess you learn from me—
although you're older—and white—
and somewhat more free.   40

This is my page for English B.   1959

---

1. Winston-Salem and Durham are cities in North Carolina.   2. Columbia University.   3. An avenue
east of Columbia University.   4. Bessie Smith (1894 [or 1898?]–1937), famous blues singer.

ROBERT LOWELL

Skunk Hour

for Elizabeth Bishop

Nautilus Island's hermit
heiress still lives through winter in her Spartan cottage;
her sheep still graze above the sea.
Her son's a bishop. Her farmer
5   is first selectman[5] in our village,
she's in her dotage.

Thirsting for
the hierarchic privacy
of Queen Victoria's century,
10   she buys up all
the eyesores facing her shore,
and lets them fall.

The season's ill—
we've lost our summer millionaire,
15   who seemed to leap from an L. L. Bean[6]
catalogue. His nine-knot yawl
was auctioned off to lobstermen.
A red fox stain covers Blue Hill.

And now our fairy
20   decorator brightens his shop for fall,
his fishnet's filled with orange cork,
orange, his cobbler's bench and awl,
there is no money in his work,
he'd rather marry.

25   One dark night,
my Tudor Ford climbed the hill's skull,
I watched for love-cars. Lights turned down,
they lay together, hull to hull,
where the graveyard shelves on the town. . . .
30   My mind's not right.

A car radio bleats,
"Love, O careless Love. . . ."[7] I hear
my ill-spirit sob in each blood cell,
as if my hand were at its throat. . . .
35   I myself am hell;
nobody's here—

5. An elected New England town official.   6. Famous old Maine sporting goods firm.   7. A popular
song.

only skunks, that search
in the moonlight for a bite to eat.
They march on their soles up Main Street:
white stripes, moonstruck eyes' red fire   40
under the chalk-dry and spar spire
of the Trinitarian Church.

I stand on top
of our back steps and breathe the rich air—
a mother skunk with her column of kittens swills the garbage pail.   45
She jabs her wedge head in a cup
of sour cream, drops her ostrich tail,
and will not scare.   1959

ANDREW MARVELL

The Garden

   How vainly men themselves amaze[8]
To win the palm, the oak, or bays,[9]
And their incessant labors see
Crowned from some single herb, or tree,
Whose short and narrow-vergèd[1] shade   5
Does prudently their toils upbraid;
While all flowers and all trees do close[2]
To weave the garlands of repose!

   Fair Quiet, have I found thee here,
And Innocence, thy sister dear?   10
Mistaken long, I sought you then
In busy companies of men.
Your sacred plants,[3] if here below,
Only among the plants will grow;
Society is all but rude[4]   15
To[5] this delicious solitude.

   No white nor red was ever seen
So am'rous as this lovely green.
Fond lovers, cruel as their flame,
Cut in these trees their mistress' name: 20
Little, alas, they know, or heed
How far these beauties hers exceed!
Fair trees, wheresoe'er your barks I wound,
No name shall but your own be found.

---

8. Become frenzied.   9. Awards for athletic, civic, and literary achievements.   1. Narrowly cropped.
2. Unite.   3. Cuttings.   4. Barbarous.   5. Compared to.

25   When we have run our passion's heat,
      Love hither makes his best retreat.
      The gods, that mortal beauty chase,
      Still in a tree did end their race:
      Apollo hunted Daphne so,
30   Only that she might laurel grow;
      And Pan did after Syrinx speed,
      Not as a nymph, but for a reed.[6]

      What wondrous life is this I lead!
      Ripe apples drop about my head;
35   The luscious clusters of the vine
      Upon my mouth do crush their wine;
      The nectarine and curious[7] peach
      Into my hands themselves do reach;
      Stumbling on melons, as I pass,
40   Insnared with flowers, I fall on grass.

      Meanwhile the mind, from pleasure less,
      Withdraws into its happiness;[8]
      The mind, that ocean where each kind
      Does straight its own resemblance find;[9]
45   Yet it creates, transcending these,
      Far other worlds and other seas,
      Annihilating[1] all that's made
      To a green thought in a green shade.

      Here at the fountain's sliding foot,
50   Or at some fruit tree's mossy root,
      Casting the body's vest[2] aside,
      My soul into the boughs does glide:
      There, like a bird, it sits and sings,
      Then whets[3] and combs its silver wings,
55   And, till prepared for longer flight,
      Waves in its plumes the various[4] light.

      Such was that happy garden-state,
      While man there walked without a mate:
      After a place so pure, and sweet,
60   What other help could yet be meet![5]
      But 'twas beyond a mortal's share
      To wander solitary there:
      Two paradises 'twere in one
      To live in paradise alone.

---

6. In Ovid's *Metamorphoses,* Daphne, pursued by Apollo, is turned into a laurel, and Syrinx, pursued by Pan, into a reed that Pan makes into a flute.   7. Exquisite.   8. That is, the mind withdraws from lesser-sense pleasure into contemplation.   9. All land creatures supposedly had corresponding sea creatures. 1. Reducing to nothing by comparison.   2. Vestment, clothing; the flesh is being considered as simply clothing for the soul.   3. Preens.   4. Many-colored.   5. Appropriate.

How well the skillful gardener drew   65
Of flowers and herbs this dial[6] new,
Where, from above, the milder sun
Does through a fragrant zodiac run;
And as it works, th' industrious bee
Computes its time as well as we!   70
How could such sweet and wholesome hours
Be reckoned but with herbs and flowers?   1681

SHARON OLDS

I Go Back to May 1937

I see them standing at the formal gates of their colleges,
I see my father strolling out
under the ochre sandstone arch, the
red tiles glinting like bent
plates of blood behind his head, I   5
see my mother with a few light books at her hip
standing at the pillar made of tiny bricks with the
wrought-iron gate still open behind her, its
sword-tips black in the May air,
they are about to graduate, they are about to get married,   10
they are kids, they are dumb, all they know is they are
innocent, they would never hurt anybody.
I want to go up to them and say Stop,
don't do it—she's the wrong woman,
he's the wrong man, you are going to do things   15
you cannot imagine you would ever do,
you are going to do bad things to children,
you are going to suffer in ways you never heard of,
you are going to want to die. I want to go
up to them there in the late May sunlight and say it,   20
her hungry pretty blank face turning to me,
her pitiful beautiful untouched body,
his arrogant handsome blind face turning to me,
his pitiful beautiful untouched body,
but I don't do it. I want to live. I   25
take them up like the male and female
paper dolls and bang them together
at the hips like chips of flint as if to
strike sparks from them, I say
Do what you are going to do, and I will tell about it.   1987   30

_____
6. A garden planted in the shape of a sundial, complete with zodiac.

The Lifting

Suddenly my father lifted up his nightie, I
turned my head away but he cried out
Shar!, my nickname, so I turned and looked.
He was sitting in the high cranked-up hospital bed with the
5   gown up, around his neck,
to show me the weight he had lost. I looked
where his solid ruddy stomach had been
and I saw the skin fallen into loose
soft hairy rippled folds
10   lying in a pool of folds
down at the base of his abdomen,
the gaunt torso of a big man
who will die soon. Right away
I saw how much his hips are like mine,
15   the long, white angles, and then
how much his pelvis is shaped like my daughter's,
a chambered whelk-shell hollowed out,
I saw the folds of skin like something
poured, a thick batter, I saw
20   his rueful smile, the cast-up eyes as he
shows me his old body, he knows
I will be interested, he knows I will find him
appealing. If anyone had told me I would sit
by him and he would pull up his nightie and I would look
25   at him, his naked body, the thick
bud of his glans, his penis in all that
dark hair, look at him
in affection and uneasy wonder
I would not have believed it. But now I can still
30   see the tiny snowflakes, white and
night-blue, on the cotton of the gown as it
rises the way we were promised at death it would rise,
the veils would fall from our eyes, we would know everything.   1990

SYLVIA PLATH

Barren Woman

Empty, I echo to the least footfall,
Museum without statues, grand with pillars, porticoes, rotundas.
In my courtyard a fountain leaps and sinks back into itself,
Nun-hearted and blind to the world. Marble lilies
5   Exhale their pallor like scent.

I imagine myself with a great public,
Mother of a white Nike and several bald-eyed Apollos.[7]
Instead, the dead injure me with attentions, and nothing can happen.
The moon lays a hand on my forehead,
Blank-faced and mum as a nurse.   10

February 21, 1963

Black Rook in Rainy Weather

On the stiff twig up there
Hunches a wet black rook
Arranging and rearranging its feathers in the rain.
I do not expect a miracle
Or an accident   5

To set the sight on fire
In my eye, nor seek
Any more in the desultory weather some design,
But let spotted leaves fall as they fall,
Without ceremony, or portent   10

Although, I admit, I desire,
Occasionally, some backtalk
From the mute sky, I can't honestly complain:
A certain minor light may still
Leap incandescent   15

Out of kitchen table or chair
As if a celestial burning took
Possession of the most obtuse objects now and then—
Thus hallowing an interval
Otherwise inconsequent   20

By bestowing largesse, honor,
One might say love. At any rate, I now walk
Wary (for it could happen
Even in this dull, ruinous landscape); skeptical,
Yet politic; ignorant   25

Of whatever angel may choose to flare
Suddenly at my elbow. I only know that a rook
Ordering its black feathers can so shine
As to seize my senses, haul
My eyelids up, and grant   30

A brief respite from fear
Of total neutrality. With luck,
Trekking stubborn through this season

---

7. That is, gods of poetic inspiration. *Nike:* goddess of victory.

Of fatigue, I shall
35   Patch together a content

Of sorts. Miracles occur,
If you care to call those spasmodic
Tricks of radiance miracles. The wait's begun again,
The long wait for the angel,
40   For that rare, random descent.[8]   1960

EZRA POUND
_____

In a Station of the Metro[9]

The apparition of these faces in the crowd;
Petals on a wet, black bough.   p. 1913

A Virginal

No, no! Go from me. I have left her lately.
I will not spoil my sheath with lesser brightness,
For my surrounding air hath a new lightness;
Slight are her arms, yet they have bound me straitly
5   And left me cloaked as with a gauze of aether;
As with sweet leaves; as with a subtle clearness.
Oh, I have picked up magic in her nearness
To sheathe me half in half the things that sheathe her.
No, no! Go from me, I have still the flavor,
10   Soft as spring wind that's come from birchen bowers.
Green come the shoots, aye April in the branches,
As winter's wound with her sleight hand she staunches,
Hath of the trees a likeness of the savor:
As white their bark, so white this lady's hours.   1912

WALLACE STEVENS
_____

The Emperor of Ice-Cream

Call the roller of big cigars,
The muscular one, and bid him whip

8. According to Acts 2, the Holy Ghost at Pentecost descended like a tongue of fire upon Jesus' disciples.
9. The Paris subway.

In kitchen cups concupiscent curds.[1]
Let the wenches dawdle in such dress
As they are used to wear, and let the boys   5
Bring flowers in last month's newspapers.
Let be be finale of seem.[2]
The only emperor is the emperor of ice-cream.

Take from the dresser of deal,
Lacking the three glass knobs, that sheet   10
On which she embroidered fantails[3] once
And spread it so as to cover her face.
If her horny feet protrude, they come
To show how cold she is, and dumb.
Let the lamp affix its beam.   15
The only emperor is the emperor of ice-cream.   1923

Sunday Morning

I

Complacencies of the peignoir, and late
Coffee and oranges in a sunny chair,
And the green freedom of a cockatoo
Upon a rug mingle to dissipate
The holy hush of ancient sacrifice.   5
She dreams a little, and she feels the dark
Encroachment of that old catastrophe,[4]
As a calm darkens among water-lights.
The pungent oranges and bright, green wings
Seem things in some procession of the dead,   10
Winding across wide water, without sound,
The day is like wide water, without sound,
Stilled for the passing of her dreaming feet
Over the seas, to silent Palestine,
Dominion of the blood and sepulchre.   15

II

Why should she give her bounty to the dead?
What is divinity if it can come
Only in silent shadows and in dreams?
Shall she not find in comforts of the sun,

---

1. "The words 'concupiscent curds' have no genealogy; they are merely expressive: at least, I hope they are expressive. They express the concupiscence of life, but, by contrast with the things in relation in the poem, they express or accentuate life's destitution, and it is this that gives them something more than a cheap lustre" (*Letters of Wallace Stevens,* ed. Holly Stevens [1966], p. 500).   2. "[T]he true sense of Let be be the finale of seem is let being become the conclusion of denouement of appearing to be: in short, ice cream is an absolute good. The poem is obviously not about ice cream, but about being as distinguished from seeming to be" (*Letters,* p. 341).   3. Fantail pigeons.   4. The Crucifixion.

20   In pungent fruit and bright, green wings, or else
      In any balm or beauty of the earth,
      Things to be cherished like the thought of heaven.
      Divinity must live within herself:
      Passions of rain, or moods in falling snow;
25   Grievings in loneliness, or unsubdued
      Elations when the forest blooms; gusty
      Emotions on wet roads on autumn nights;
      All pleasures and all pains, remembering
      The bough of summer and the winter branch.
30   These are the measures destined for her soul.

                        III

      Jove in the clouds has his inhuman birth.
      No mother suckled him, no sweet land gave
      Large-mannered motions to his mythy mind
      He moved among us, as a muttering king,
35   Magnificent, would move among his hinds,[5]
      Until our blood, commingling, virginal,
      With heaven, brought such requital to desire
      The very hinds discerned it, in a star.[6]
      Shall our blood fail? Or shall it come to be
40   The blood of paradise? And shall the earth
      Seem all of paradise that we shall know?
      The sky will be much friendlier then than now,
      A part of labor and a part of pain,
      And next in glory to enduring love,
45   Not this dividing and indifferent blue.

                        IV

      She says, "I am content when wakened birds,
      Before they fly, test the reality
      Of misty fields, by their sweet questionings;
      But when the birds are gone, and their warm fields
50   Return no more, where, then, is paradise?"
      There is not any haunt of prophecy,
      Nor any old chimera of the grave,
      Neither the golden underground, nor isle
      Melodious, where spirits gat[7] them home,
55   Nor visionary south, nor cloudy palm
      Remote on heaven's hill, that has endured
      As April's green endures, or will endure
      Like her remembrance of awakened birds,
      Or her desire for June and evening, tipped
60   By the consummation of the swallow's wings.

---

5. Lowliest rural subjects.   6. The star of Bethlehem.   7. Got.

V

She says, "But in contentment I still feel
The need of some imperishable bliss."
Death is the mother of beauty; hence from her,
Alone, shall come fulfillment to our dreams
And our desires. Although she strews the leaves   65
Of sure obliteration on our paths,
The path sick sorrow took, the many paths
Where triumph rang its brassy phrase, or love
Whispered a little out of tenderness,
She makes the willow shiver in the sun   70
For maidens who were wont to sit and gaze
Upon the grass, relinquished to their feet.
She causes boys to pile new plums and pears
On disregarded plate.[8] The maidens taste
And stray impassioned in the littering leaves.   75

VI

Is there no change of death in paradise?
Does ripe fruit never fall? Or do the boughs
Hang always heavy in that perfect sky,
Unchanging, yet so like our perishing earth,
With rivers like our own that seek for seas   80
They never find, the same receding shores
That never touch with inarticulate pang?
Why set the pear upon those river-banks
Or spice the shores with odors of the plum?
Alas, that they should wear our colors there,   85
The silken weavings of our afternoons,
And pick the strings of our insipid lutes!
Death is the mother of beauty, mystical,
Within whose burning bosom we devise
Our earthly mothers awaiting, sleeplessly.   90

VII

Supple and turbulent, a ring of men
Shall chant in orgy[9] on a summer morn
Their boisterous devotion to the sun,
Not as a god, but as a god might be,
Naked among them, like a savage source.   95
Their chant shall be a chant of paradise,
Out of their blood, returning to the sky;

8. "Plate is used in the sense of so-called family plate. Disregarded refers to the disuse into which things fall that have been possessed for a long time. I mean, therefore, that death releases and renews. What the old have come to disregard, the young inherit and make use of" (*Letters*, pp. 183–84).   9. Ceremonial revelry.

And in their chant shall enter, voice by voice,
The windy lake wherein their lord delights,
100   The trees, like serafin,[1] and echoing hills,
That choir among themselves long afterward.
They shall know well the heavenly fellowship
Of men that perish and of summer morn.
And whence they came and whither they shall go
105   The dew upon their feet shall manifest.

VIII

She hears, upon that water without sound,
A voice that cries, "The tomb in Palestine
Is not the porch of spirits lingering.
It is the grave of Jesus, where he lay."
110   We live in an old chaos of the sun,
Or old dependency of day and night,
Or island solitude, unsponsored, free,
Of that wide water, inescapable.
Deer walk upon our mountains, and the quail
115   Whistle about us their spontaneous cries;
Sweet berries ripen in the wilderness;
And, in the isolation of the sky,
At evening, casual flocks of pigeons make
Ambiguous undulations as they sink,
120   Downward to darkness, on extended wings.

1915

ALFRED, LORD TENNYSON

Now Sleeps the Crimson Petal[2]

Now sleeps the crimson petal, now the white;
Nor waves the cypress in the palace walk;
Nor winks the gold fin in the porphyry font;[3]
The firefly wakens; waken thou with me.

5   Now droops the milk-white peacock like a ghost,
And like a ghost she glimmers on to me.

Now lies the Earth all Danaë[4] to the stars,
And all thy heart lies open unto me.

---

1. Seraphim, the highest of the nine orders of angels.   2. A song from *The Princess,* a long narrative
poem about what the mid nineteenth century called the "new woman."   3. Stone fishbowl. *Porphyry:*
a red stone containing fine white crystals.   4. A princess in Greek mythology, seduced by Zeus after he
became a shower of gold to enter the tower in which she was confined.

Now slides the silent meteor on, and leaves
A shining furrow, as thy thoughts in me.   10

Now folds the lily all her sweetness up,
And slips into the bosom of the lake;
So fold thyself, my dearest, thou, and slip
Into my bosom and be lost in me.   1847

Tears, Idle Tears[5]

Tears, idle tears, I know not what they mean,
Tears from the depth of some divine despair
Rise in the heart, and gather to the eyes,
In looking on the happy autumn-fields,
And thinking of the days that are no more.   5

Fresh as the first beam glittering on a sail,
That brings our friends up from the underworld,
Sad as the last which reddens over one
That sinks with all we love below the verge;
So sad, so fresh, the days that are no more.   10

Ah, sad and strange as in dark summer dawns
The earliest pipe of half-awakened birds
To dying ears, when unto dying eyes
The casement slowly grows a glimmering square;
So sad, so strange, the days that are no more.   15

Dear as remembered kisses after death,
And sweet as those by hopeless fancy feigned
On lips that are for others; deep as love,
Deep as first love, and wild with all regret;
O Death in Life, the days that are no more!   20

1847

Ulysses[6]

It little profits that an idle king,
By this still hearth, among these barren crags,
Matched with an agéd wife,[7] I mete and dole
Unequal laws unto a savage race,
That hoard, and sleep, and feed, and know not me.   5

5. A song from *The Princess*.   6. After the end of the Trojan War, Ulysses (or Odysseus), king of Ithaca
and one of the Greek heroes of the war, returned to his island home (line 34). Homer's account of the
situation is in the *Odyssey* 11, but Dante's account of Ulysses in the *Inferno* 26 is the more immediate
background of the poem.   7. Penelope.

I cannot rest from travel; I will drink
Life to the lees.[8] All times I have enjoyed
Greatly, have suffered greatly, both with those
That loved me, and alone; on shore, and when
10   Through scudding drifts the rainy Hyades[9]
Vexed the dim sea. I am become a name;
For always roaming with a hungry heart
Much have I seen and known—cities of men
And manners, climates, councils, governments,
15   Myself not least, but honored of them all—
And drunk delight of battle with my peers,
Far on the ringing plains of windy Troy.
I am a part of all that I have met;
Yet all experience is an arch wherethrough
20   Gleams that untraveled world, whose margin fades
For ever and for ever when I move.
How dull it is to pause, to make an end,
To rust unburnished, not to shine in use!
As though to breathe were life. Life piled on life
25   Were all too little, and of one to me
Little remains; but every hour is saved
From that eternal silence, something more,
A bringer of new things; and vile it were
For some three suns to store and hoard myself,
30   And this gray spirit yearning in desire
To follow knowledge like a sinking star,
Beyond the utmost bound of human thought.

This is my son, mine own Telemachus,
To whom I leave the scepter and the isle—
35   Well-loved of me, discerning to fulfill
This labor by slow prudence to make mild
A rugged people, and through soft degrees
Subdue them to the useful and the good.
Most blameless is he, centered in the sphere
40   Of common duties, decent not to fail
In offices of tenderness, and pay
Meet adoration to my household gods,
When I am gone. He works his work, I mine.

There lies the port; the vessel puffs her sail:
45   There gloom the dark, broad seas. My mariners,
Souls that have toiled, and wrought, and thought with me—
That ever with a frolic welcome took
The thunder and the sunshine, and opposed
Free hearts, free foreheads—you and I are old;

8. All the way down to the bottom of the cup.   9. A group of stars that were supposed to predict rain
when they rose at the same time as the sun.

Old age hath yet his honor and his toil.   50
Death closes all; but something ere the end,
Some work of noble note, may yet be done,
Not unbecoming men that strove with Gods.
The lights begin to twinkle from the rocks;
The long day wanes; the slow moon climbs; the deep   55
Moans round with many voices. Come, my friends.
'Tis not too late to seek a newer world.
Push off, and sitting well in order smite
The sounding furrows; for my purpose holds
To sail beyond the sunset, and the baths   60
Of all the western stars, until I die.
It may be that the gulfs will wash us down;[1]
It may be we shall touch the Happy Isles,[2]
And see the great Achilles, whom we knew.
Though much is taken, much abides; and though   65
We are not now that strength which in old days
Moved earth and heaven, that which we are, we are:
One equal temper of heroic hearts,
Made weak by time and fate, but strong in will
To strive, to seek, to find, and not to yield.   70

1833

DYLAN THOMAS

Fern Hill

Now as I was young and easy under the apple boughs
About the lilting house and happy as the grass was green,
  The night above the dingle starry,
    Time let me hail and climb
  Golden in the heydays of his eyes,   5
And honored among wagons I was prince of the apple towns
And once below a time I lordly had the trees and leaves
    Trail with daisies and barley
  Down the rivers of the windfall light.

And as I was green and carefree, famous among the barns   10
About the happy yard and singing as the farm was home,
  In the sun that is young once only,
    Time let me play and be
  Golden in the mercy of his means,

1. Beyond the Gulf of Gibraltar was supposed to be a chasm that led to Hades.   2. Elysium, the Islands of the Blessed, where heroes like Achilles (line 64) abide after death.

15   And green and golden I was huntsman and herdsman, the calves
        Sang to my horn, the foxes on the hills barked clear and cold,
                And the sabbath rang slowly
        In the pebbles of the holy streams.

        All the sun long it was running, it was lovely, the hay
20   Fields high as the house, the tunes from the chimneys, it was air
                And playing, lovely and watery
                        And fire green as grass.
        And nightly under the simple stars
        As I rode to sleep the owls were bearing the farm away,
25   All the moon long I heard, blessed among stables, the nightjars[3]
                Flying with the ricks,[4] and the horses
                        Flashing into the dark.

        And then to awake, and the farm, like a wanderer white
        With the dew, come back, the cock on his shoulder: it was all
30   Shining, it was Adam and maiden,
                        The sky gathered again
        And the sun grew round that very day.
        So it must have been after the birth of the simple light
        In the first, spinning place, the spellbound horses walking warm
35   Out of the whinnying green stable
                        On to the fields of praise.

        And honored among foxes and pheasants by the gay house
        Under the new made clouds and happy as the heart was long,
                In the sun born over and over,
40   I ran my heedless ways,
                My wishes raced through the house-high hay
        And nothing I cared, at my sky-blue trades, that time allows
        In all his tuneful turning so few and such morning songs
                Before the children green and golden
45   Follow him out of grace,

        Nothing I cared, in the lamb white days, that time would take me
        Up to the swallow-thronged loft by the shadow of my hand,
                In the moon that is always rising,
                        Nor that riding to sleep
50   I should hear him fly with the high fields
        And wake to the farm forever fled from the childless land.
        Oh as I was young and easy in the mercy of his means,
                Time held me green and dying
                Though I sang in my chains like the sea.   1946

3. Birds.   4. Haystacks.

JEAN TOOMER

Song of the Son[5]

Pour O pour that parting soul in song,
O pour it in the sawdust glow of night,
Into the velvet pine-smoke air tonight,
And let the valley carry it along.
And let the valley carry it along.   5

O land and soil, red soil and sweet-gum tree,
So scant of grass, so profligate of pines,
Now just before an epoch's sun declines
Thy son, in time, I have returned to thee,
Thy son, I have in time returned to thee.   10

In time, for though the sun is setting on
A song-lit race of slaves, it has not set;
Though late, O soil, it is not too late yet
To catch thy plaintive soul, leaving, soon gone,
Leaving, to catch thy plaintive soul soon gone.   15

O Negro slaves, dark purple ripened plums,
Squeezed, and bursting in the pine-wood air,
Passing, before they strip the old tree bare
One plum was saved for me, one seed becomes

An everlasting song, a singing tree,   20
Caroling softly souls of slavery,
What they were, and what they are to me,
Caroling softly souls of slavery.   1923

WALT WHITMAN

Facing West from California's Shores

Facing west, from California's shores,
Inquiring, tireless, seeking what is yet unfound,
I, a child, very old, over waves, towards the house of maternity,[6] the
    land of migrations, look afar,
Look off the shores of my Western sea, the circle almost circled:
For starting westward from Hindustan, from the vales of Kashmere,   5
From Asia, from the north, from the God, the sage, and the hero,
From the south, from the flowery peninsulas and the spice islands,
Long having wandered since, round the earth having wandered,

5. From the novel *Cane*.   6. Asia, as the supposed birthplace of the human race.

Now I face home again, very pleased and joyous;
10   (But where is what I started for, so long ago?
And why is it yet unfound?)   1860

I Hear America Singing

I hear America singing, the varied carols I hear,
Those of mechanics, each one singing his as it should be blithe and
        strong,
The carpenter singing his as he measures his plank or beam,
The mason singing his as he makes ready for work, or leaves off work,
The boatman singing what belongs to him in his boat, the deckhand
5   singing on the steamboat deck,
The shoemaker singing as he sits on his bench, the hatter singing as he
        stands,
The wood-cutter's song, the ploughboy's on his way in the morning, or
        at noon intermission or at sundown,
The delicious singing of the mother, or of the young wife at work, or of
        the girl sewing or washing,
Each singing what belongs to him or her and to none else,
The day what belongs to the day—at night the party of young fellows,
10   robust, friendly,
Singing with open mouths their strong melodious songs.   1860

A Noiseless Patient Spider

A noiseless patient spider,
I marked where on a little promontory it stood isolated,
Marked how to explore the vacant vast surrounding,
It launched forth filament, filament, filament, out of itself,
5   Ever unreeling them, ever tirelessly speeding them.

And you O my soul where you stand,
Surrounded, detached, in measureless oceans of space,
Ceaselessly musing, venturing, throwing, seeking the spheres to connect
        them,
Till the bridge you will need be formed, till the ductile anchor hold,
10   Till the gossamer thread you fling catch somewhere, O my soul.
                                                              1881

RICHARD WILBUR

Museum Piece

The good gray guardians of art
Patrol the halls on spongy shoes,
Impartially protective, though
Perhaps suspicious of Toulouse.[7]

Here dozes one against the wall,   5
Disposed upon a funeral chair.
A Degas[8] dancer pirouettes
Upon the parting of his hair.

See how she spins! The grace is there,
But strain as well is plain to see.   10
Degas loved the two together:
Beauty joined to energy.

Edgar Degas purchased once
A fine El Greco,[9] which he kept
Against the wall beside his bed   15
To hang his pants on while he slept.   1950

Love Calls Us to the Things of This World

    The eyes open to a cry of pulleys,
And spirited from sleep, the astounded soul
Hangs for a moment bodiless and simple
As false dawn.
            Outside the open window   5
The morning air is all awash with angels.

    Some are in bed-sheets, some are in blouses,
Some are in smocks: but truly there they are.
Now they are rising together in calm swells
Of halcyon[1] feeling, filling whatever they wear   10
With the deep joy of their impersonal breathing;
    Now they are flying in place,[2] conveying
The terrible speed of their omnipresence, moving
And staying like white water; and now of a sudden

7. Henri-Marie-Raymond de Toulouse-Lautrec (1864–1901), French painter famous for his posters, drawings, and paintings of singers, dancers, and actresses.   8. Edgar Degas (1834–1917), French impressionist, usually considered the master of the human figure in movement.   9. El Greco (1541–1614), Cretan-born Spanish painter, known for the mannered disproportion of his figures.   1. Serene.
2. Like planes in a formation.

15 They swoon down into so rapt a quiet
That nobody seems to be there.
                    The soul shrinks

     From all that it is about to remember,
From the punctual rape of every blessed day,
20 And cries,
                    "Oh, let there be nothing on earth but laundry,
Nothing but rosy hands in the rising steam
And clear dances done in the sight of heaven."

     Yet, as the sun acknowledges
25 With a warm look the world's hunks and colors,
The soul descends once more in bitter love
To accept the waking body, saying now
In a changed voice as the man yawns and rises,

     "Bring them down from their ruddy gallows;
30 Let there be clean linen for the backs of thieves;
Let lovers go fresh and sweet to be undone,
And the heaviest nuns walk in a pure floating
Of dark habits,
                    keeping their difficult balance."   1956

WILLIAM WORDSWORTH

Lines Written a Few Miles above Tintern Abbey, On Revisiting the Banks of the Wye during a Tour, July 13, 1798[3]

     Five years have passed; five summers, with the length
Of five long winters! and again I hear
These waters, rolling from their mountain-springs
With a soft inland murmur. Once again
5 Do I behold these steep and lofty cliffs,
That on a wild secluded scene impress
Thoughts of more deep seclusion; and connect
The landscape with the quiet of the sky.
The day is come when I again repose
10 Here, under this dark sycamore, and view
These plots of cottage-ground, these orchard tufts,
Which at this season, with their unripe fruits,
Are clad in one green hue, and lose themselves

---

3. Wordsworth had first visited the Wye valley and the ruins of the medieval abbey there in 1793, while on a solitary walking tour. He was twenty-three then, twenty-eight when he wrote this poem.

'Mid groves and copses.[4] Once again I see
These hedge-rows, hardly hedge-rows, little lines 15
Of sportive wood run wild: these pastoral farms,
Green to the very door; and wreaths of smoke
Sent up, in silence, from among the trees!
With some uncertain notice, as might seem
Of vagrant dwellers in the houseless woods, 20
Or of some hermit's cave, where by his fire
The hermit sits alone.

           These beauteous forms,
Through a long absence, have not been to me
As is a landscape to a blind man's eye;
But oft, in lonely rooms, and 'mid the din 25
Of towns and cities, I have owed to them,
In hours of weariness, sensations sweet,
Felt in the blood, and felt along the heart;
And passing even into my purer mind,
With tranquil restoration—feelings too 30
Of unremembered pleasure: such, perhaps,
As have no slight or trivial influence
On that best portion of a good man's life,
His little, nameless, unremembered acts
Of kindness and of love. Nor less, I trust, 35
To them I may have owed another gift,
Of aspect more sublime; that blessèd mood,
In which the burthen[5] of the mystery,
In which the heavy and the weary weight
Of all this unintelligible world, 40
Is lightened—that serene and blessèd mood,
In which the affections gently lead us on—
Until, the breath of this corporeal frame
And even the motion of our human blood
Almost suspended, we are laid asleep 45
In body, and become a living soul;
While with an eye made quiet by the power
Of harmony, and the deep power of joy,
We see into the life of things.

              If this
Be but a vain belief, yet, oh! how oft— 50
In darkness and amid the many shapes
Of joyless daylight; when the fretful stir
Unprofitable, and the fever of the world,
Have hung upon the beatings of my heart—
How oft, in spirit, have I turned to thee, 55
O sylvan Wye! thou wanderer through the woods,
How often has my spirit turned to thee!

4. Thickets.   5. Burden.

And now, with gleams of half-extinguished thought,
With many recognitions dim and faint,
60   And somewhat of a sad perplexity,
The picture of the mind revives again;
While here I stand, not only with the sense
Of present pleasure, but with pleasing thoughts
That in this moment there is life and food
65   For future years. And so I dare to hope,
Though changed, no doubt, from what I was when first
I came among these hills; when like a roe
I bounded o'er the mountains, by the sides
Of the deep rivers, and the lonely streams,
70   Wherever nature led: more like a man
Flying from something that he dreads than one
Who sought the thing he loved. For nature then
(The coarser[6] pleasures of my boyish days,
And their glad animal movements all gone by)
75   To me was all in all—I cannot paint
What then I was. The sounding cataract
Haunted me like a passion; the tall rock,
The mountain, and the deep and gloomy wood,
Their colors and their forms, were then to me
80   An appetite; a feeling and a love,
That had no need of a remoter charm.
By thought supplied, nor any interest
Unborrowed from the eye. That time is past,
And all its aching joys are now no more,
85   And all its dizzy raptures. Not for this
Faint I,[7] nor mourn nor murmur; other gifts
Have followed; for such loss, I would believe,
Abundant recompense. For I have learned
To look on nature, not as in the hour
90   Of thoughtless youth; but hearing oftentimes
The still, sad music of humanity,
Nor harsh nor grating, though of ample power
To chasten and subdue. And I have felt
A presence that disturbs me with the joy
95   Of elevated thoughts, a sense sublime
Of something far more deeply interfused,
Whose dwelling is the light of setting suns,
And the round ocean and the living air,
And the blue sky, and in the mind of man:
100   A motion and a spirit, that impels
All thinking things, all objects of all thought,
And rolls through all things. Therefore am I still
A lover of the meadows and the woods
And mountains; and of all that we behold

6. Physical.   7. Am I discouraged.

From this green earth; of all the mighty world   105
Of eye, and ear—both what they half create,
And what perceive; well pleased to recognize
In nature and the language of the sense
The anchor of my purest thoughts, the nurse,
The guide, the guardian of my heart, and soul   110
Of all my moral being.

              Nor perchance,
If I were not thus taught, should I the more
Suffer my genial spirits[8] to decay:
For thou art with me here upon the banks
Of this fair river; thou my dearest Friend,[9]   115
My dear, dear Friend; and in thy voice I catch
The language of my former heart, and read
My former pleasures in the shooting lights
Of thy wild eyes. Oh! yet a little while
May I behold in thee what I was once,   120
My dear, dear Sister! and this prayer I make,
Knowing that Nature never did betray
The heart that loved her; 'tis her privilege,
Through all the years of this our life, to lead
From joy to joy: for she can so inform   125
The mind that is within us, so impress
With quietness and beauty, and so feed
With lofty thoughts, that neither evil tongues,
Rash judgments, nor the sneers of selfish men,
Nor greetings where no kindness is, nor all   130
The dreary intercourse of daily life,
Shall e'er prevail against us, or disturb
Our cheerful faith that all which we behold
Is full of blessings. Therefore let the moon
Shine on thee in thy solitary walk;   135
And let the misty mountain-winds be free
To blow against thee: and, in after years,
When these wild ecstasies shall be matured
Into a sober pleasure; when thy mind
Shall be a mansion for all lovely forms,   140
Thy memory be as a dwelling-place
For all sweet sounds and harmonies; oh! then,
If solitude, or fear, or pain, or grief,
Should be thy portion, with what healing thoughts
Of tender joy wilt thou remember me,   145
And these my exhortations! No, perchance—
If I should be where I no more can hear
Thy voice, nor catch from thy wild eyes these gleams
Of past existence—wilt thou then forget
That on the banks of this delightful stream   150

8. Natural disposition; that is, the spirits that are part of his individual genius.   9. His sister Dorothy.

We stood together; and that I, so long
A worshiper of Nature, hither came
Unwearied in that service; rather say
With warmer love—oh! with far deeper zeal
155   Of holier love. Nor wilt thou then forget,
That after many wanderings, many years
Of absence, these steep woods and lofty cliffs,
And this green pastoral landscape, were to me
More dear, both for themselves and for thy sake!   1798

W. B. YEATS

The Lake Isle of Innisfree[1]

I will arise and go now, and go to Innisfree,
And a small cabin build there, of clay and wattles made,
Nine bean-rows will I have there, a hive for the honey-bee,
And live alone in the bee-loud glade.

5   And I shall have some peace there, for peace comes dropping slow,
Dropping from the veils of the morning to where the cricket sings;
There midnight's all a glimmer, and noon a purple glow,
And evening full of the linnet's wings.

I will arise and go now, for always night and day
10   I hear lake water lapping with low sounds by the shore;
While I stand on the roadway, or on the pavements grey,
I hear it in the deep heart's core.

1890

Easter 1916[2]

I have met them at close of day
Coming with vivid faces
From counter or desk among gray
Eighteenth-century houses.
5   I have passed with a nod of the head
Or polite meaningless words,
Or have lingered awhile and said
Polite meaningless words,

---

1. Island in Lough Gill, County Sligo, Ireland.   2. On Easter Monday, 1916, nationalist leaders proclaimed an Irish Republic. After a week of street fighting, the British government put down the Easter
Rebellion and executed a number of prominent nationalists, including the four leaders mentioned in
lines 75–76, all of whom Yeats knew personally.

And thought before I had done
Of a mocking tale or a gibe   10
To please a companion
Around the fire at the club,
Being certain that they and I
But lived where motley is worn:
All changed, changed utterly: 15
A terrible beauty is born.

That woman's[3] days were spent
In ignorant good-will,
Her nights in argument
Until her voice grew shrill.   20
What voice more sweet than hers
When, young and beautiful,
She rode to harriers?
This man[4] had kept a school
And rode our wingéd horse;[5]   25
This other[6] his helper and friend
Was coming into his force;
He might have won fame in the end,
So sensitive his nature seemed,
So daring and sweet his thought.   30
This other man[7] I had dreamed
A drunken, vainglorious lout.
He had done most bitter wrong
To some who are near my heart,
Yet I number him in the song;   35
He, too, has resigned his part
In the casual comedy;
He, too, has been changed in his turn,
Transformed utterly:
A terrible beauty is born.   40

Hearts with one purpose alone
Through summer and winter seem
Enchanted to a stone
To trouble the living stream.
The horse that comes from the road,   45
The rider, the birds that range
From cloud to tumbling cloud,
Minute by minute they change;

3. Countess Constance Georgina Markiewicz, a beautiful and well-born young woman from County Sligo who became a vigorous and bitter nationalist. At first condemned to death, she later had her sentence commuted to life imprisonment, and she gained amnesty in 1917.   4. Patrick Pearse, who led the assault on the Dublin Post Office, from which the proclamation of a republic was issued. A schoolmaster by profession, he had vigorously supported the restoration of the Gaelic language in Ireland and was an active political writer and poet.   5. Pegasus, a traditional symbol of poetic inspiration.   6. Thomas MacDonagh, also a writer and teacher.   7. Major John MacBride, who had married Yeats's beloved Maud Gonne in 1903 but separated from her two years later.

50 A shadow of cloud on the stream
Changes minute by minute;
A horse-hoof slides on the brim,
And a horse plashes within it;
The long-legged moor-hens dive,
And hens to moor-cocks call;
55 Minute by minute they live:
The stone's in the midst of all.

Too long a sacrifice
Can make a stone of the heart.
O when may it suffice?
60 That is Heaven's part, our part
To murmur name upon name,
As a mother names her child
When sleep at last has come
On limbs that had run wild.
65 What is it but nightfall?
No, no, not night but death;
Was it needless death after all?
For England may keep faith[8]
For all that is done and said.
70 We know their dream; enough
To know they dreamed and are dead;
And what if excess of love
Bewildered them till they died?
I write it out in a verse—
75 MacDonagh and MacBride
And Connolly[9] and Pearse
Now and in time to be,
Wherever green is worn,
Are changed, changed utterly;
80 A terrible beauty is born.

1916

The Second Coming[1]

Turning and turning in the widening gyre[2]
The falcon cannot hear the falconer;
Things fall apart; the center cannot hold;
Mere anarchy is loosed upon the world,

8. Before the uprising the English had promised eventual home rule to Ireland.   9. James Connolly, the leader of the Easter uprising.   1. The Second Coming of Christ, according to Matthew 24.29–44, will come after a time of "tribulation." Disillusioned by Ireland's continued civil strife, Yeats saw his time as the end of another historical cycle. In *A Vision* (1937), Yeats describes his view of history as dependent on cycles of about two thousand years: the birth of Christ had ended the cycle of Greco-Roman civilization, and now the Christian cycle seemed near an end, to be followed by an antithetical cycle, ominous in its portents.   2. Literally, the widening spiral of a falcon's flight. "Gyre" is Yeats's term for a cycle of history, which he diagrammed as a series of interpenetrating cones.

The blood-dimmed tide is loosed, and everywhere 5
The ceremony of innocence is drowned;
The best lack all conviction, while the worst
Are full of passionate intensity.
Surely some revelation is at hand;
Surely the Second Coming is at hand. 10
The Second Coming! Hardly are those words out
When a vast image out of *Spiritus Mundi*[3]
Troubles my sight: somewhere in sands of the desert
A shape with lion body and the head of a man,
A gaze blank and pitiless as the sun, 15
Is moving its slow thighs, while all about it
Reel shadows of the indignant desert birds.[4]
The darkness drops again; but now I know
That twenty centuries of stony sleep
Were vexed to nightmare by a rocking cradle, 20
And what rough beast, its hour come round at last,
Slouches towards Bethlehem to be born?

January 1919

Leda and the Swan[5]

A sudden blow: the great wings beating still
Above the staggering girl, her thighs caressed
By the dark webs, her nape caught in his bill,
He holds her helpless breast upon his breast.

How can those terrified vague fingers push 5
The feathered glory from her loosening thighs?
And how can body, laid in that white rush,
But feel the strange heart beating where it lies?

A shudder in the loins engenders there
The broken wall, the burning roof and tower 10
And Agamemnon dead.
                    Being so caught up,
So mastered by the brute blood of the air,
Did she put on his knowledge with his power
Before the indifferent beak could let her drop?

1923

3. Or *Anima Mundi*, the spirit or soul of the world. Yeats considered this universal consciousness or memory a fund from which poets drew their images and symbols. 4. Yeats later wrote of the "brazen winged beast . . . described in my poem *The Second Coming*" as "associated with laughing, ecstatic destruction." 5. According to Greek myth, Zeus took the form of a swan to fornicate with Leda, who became the mother of Helen of Troy; of Castor; and also of Clytemnestra, Agamemnon's wife and murderer. Helen's abduction from her husband, Menelaus, brother of Agamemnon, began the Trojan War (line 10). Yeats described the visit of Zeus to Leda as an annunciation like that to Mary (see Luke 1.26–38): "I imagine the annunciation that founded Greece as made to Leda" (*A Vision*).

Sailing to Byzantium[6]

I

That[7] is no country for old men. The young
In one another's arms, birds in the trees
—Those dying generations—at their song,
The salmon-falls, the mackerel-crowded seas
5   Fish, flesh, or fowl, commend all summer long
Whatever is begotten, born, and dies.
Caught in that sensual music all neglect
Monuments of unaging intellect.

II

An aged man is but a paltry thing,
10   A tattered coat upon a stick, unless
Soul clap its hands and sing, and louder sing
For every tatter in its mortal dress,
Nor is there singing school but studying
Monuments of its own magnificence;
15   And therefore I have sailed the seas and come
To the holy city of Byzantium.

III

O sages standing in God's holy fire
As in the gold mosaic of a wall,
Come from the holy fire, perne in a gyre,[8]
20   And be the singing-masters of my soul.
Consume my heart away; sick with desire
And fastened to a dying animal
It knows not what it is; and gather me
Into the artifice of eternity.

IV

25   Once out of nature I shall never take
My bodily form from any natural thing,
But such a form as Grecian goldsmiths make
Of hammered gold and gold enameling

6. The ancient name of Istanbul, the capital and holy city of Eastern Christendom from the late fourth century until 1453. It was famous for its stylized and formal mosaics; its symbolic, nonnaturalistic art; and its highly developed intellectual life. Yeats repeatedly uses it to symbolize a world of artifice and timelessness, free from the decay and death of the natural and sensual world.   7. Ireland, as an instance of the natural, temporal world.   8. That is, whirl in a coiling motion, so that his soul may merge with its motion as the timeless world invades the cycles of history and nature. "Perne" is Yeats's coinage (from the noun *pirn*): to spin around in the kind of spiral pattern that thread makes as it comes off a bobbin or spool.

To keep a drowsy Emperor awake;[9]
Or set upon a golden bough[1] to sing   30
To lords and ladies of Byzantium
Of what is past, or passing, or to come.   1927

Among School Children

I

I walk through the long schoolroom questioning;
A kind old nun in a white hood replies;
The children learn to cipher and to sing,
To study reading-books and history,
To cut and sew, be neat in everything   5
In the best modern way—the children's eyes
In momentary wonder stare upon
A sixty-year-old smiling public man.[2]

II

I dream of a Ledaean body,[3] bent
Above a sinking fire, a tale that she   10
Told of a harsh reproof, or trivial event
That changed some childish day to tragedy—
Told, and it seemed that our two natures blent
Into a sphere from youthful sympathy,
Or else, to alter Plato's parable,   15
Into the yolk and white of the one shell.[4]

III

And thinking of that fit of grief or rage
I look upon one child or t'other there
And wonder if she stood so at that age—
For even daughters of the swan can share   20
Something of every paddler's heritage—
And had that color upon cheek or hair,
And thereupon my heart is driven wild:
She stands before me as a living child.

9. "I have read somewhere that in the Emperor's palace at Byzantium was a tree made of gold and silver, and artificial birds that sang" [Yeats's note].   1. In Book 6 of the *Aeneid*, the sibyl tells Aeneas that he must pluck a golden bough from a nearby tree in order to descend to Hades. Each time Aeneas plucks the one such branch there, an identical one takes its place.   2. At sixty (in 1925), Yeats had been a senator of the Irish Free State.   3. Like that of Helen of Troy, daughter of Leda. The memory dream is of Maud Gonne (see also lines 29–30), with whom Yeats had long been hopelessly in love.   4. In Plato's *Symposium*, the origin of human love is explained by parable: Human beings were once spheres, but Zeus feared their power and cut them in half; now each half longs to be reunited with its missing half. Helen and Pollux were hatched from one of two eggs born to Leda after her union with Zeus in the form of a swan; the other contained Castor and Clytemnestra. According to Yeats in *A Vision*, "from one of [Leda's] eggs came Love and from the other War."

IV

25   Her present image floats into the mind—
Did Quattrocento finger⁵ fashion it
Hollow of cheek as though it drank the wind
And took a mess of shadows for its meat?
And I though never of Ledaean kind
30   Had pretty plumage once—enough of that,
Better to smile on all that smile, and show
There is a comfortable kind of old scarecrow.

V

What youthful mother, a shape upon her lap
Honey of generation⁶ had betrayed,
35   And that must sleep, shriek, struggle to escape
As recollection or the drug decide,
Would think her son, did she but see that shape
With sixty or more winters on its head,
A compensation for the pang of his birth,
40   Or the uncertainty of his setting forth?

VI

Plato thought nature but a spume that plays
Upon a ghostly paradigm of things;⁷
Solider Aristotle played the taws
Upon the bottom of a king of kings;⁸
45   World-famous golden-thighed Pythagoras⁹
Fingered upon a fiddle-stick or strings
What a star sang and careless Muses heard:
Old clothes upon old sticks to scare a bird.

VII

Both nuns and mothers worship images,
50   But those the candles light are not as those
That animate a mother's reveries
But keep a marble or a bronze repose.
And yet they too break hearts—O Presences
That passion, piety or affection knows,

5. The hand of a fifteenth-century artist. Yeats especially admired Botticelli, and in *A Vision* praises his "deliberate strangeness everywhere [that] gives one an emotion of mystery which is new to painting." 6. Porphyry, a third-century Greek scholar and Neoplatonic philosopher, says "honey of generation" means the "pleasure arising from copulation" that draws souls "downward" to generation.   7. Plato considered the real world an imperfect and illusory copy of the ideal world.   8. Aristotle, the teacher of Alexander the Great, disciplined him with a strap ("taws," line 43). His philosophy, insisting on the interdependence of form and matter, took the real world far more seriously than did Plato's.   9. Highly revered Greek mathematician and philosopher (580?–500? B.C.); one legend describes his godlike golden thighs.

And that all heavenly glory symbolize—   55
O self-born mockers of man's enterprise;

VIII

Labor is blossoming or dancing where
The body is not bruised to pleasure soul,
Nor beauty born out of its own despair,
Nor blear-eyed wisdom out of midnight oil.   60
O chestnut-tree, great-rooted blossomer,
Are you the leaf, the blossom or the bole?
O body swayed to music, O brightening glance,
How can we know the dancer from the dance?   1927

Drama

Drama:
Reading, Responding, Writing

Plays are generally written to be performed—by actors, on a stage, for an audience. Playwrights create plays fully conscious of the possibilities that go beyond words and texts and extend to physical actions, stage devices, and other bits of theatricality that can be used to create special effects and modify responses. Consequently, responding to a stage production of a play involves physical senses as well as the imagination. Furthermore, your responses are not wholly a private matter but are, in part, communal: you respond not just as an individual but as part of an audience sharing the moment.

To attend a play—to see and hear it as part of an audience—represents a different kind of experience from the usually solitary act of reading. A live audience of real people responds directly and immediately to the play, whereas a text may lie silent and undisturbed in a book for days or even years at a time. On the stage, real live human beings, standing for imaginary characters, deliver lines and perform actions that you listen to and watch. Beyond the stage, you and the other members of the audience have, at a single instant, a common experience that you have deliberately sought: you have assembled for the explicit purpose of seeing a play.

> On the stage it is always now; the personages are standing on that razor-edge, between the past and the future, which is the essential character of conscious being; the words are rising to their lips in immediate spontaneity.
>
> —THORNTON WILDER

But you do not directly experience the author's text. It has been mediated by the director and actors who have brought it to the stage and to your eyes and ears. These mediators interpret the play, and they perform for viewers part of the act of imagination that readers must perform for themselves. In stories and poems, only the written text stands between author and reader; but in plays, all the people involved in a particular production—the director, producer, actors, even stage designers—help interpret the author's text for a specific audience. Consciously or not, every director interprets every scene by the way he or she stages the action; timing, casting, set design, physical interaction, and the phrasing and tone of every speech affect how the play comes across. Every syllable uttered by every actor in some sense affects the outcome; tone of voice and the slightest body gesture equal, for an actor, the choices of words and sentence rhythms for a writer.

Every performance uniquely expresses that collaborative effort. Actors must remember hundreds of lines and perform movements on stage at precise times; the stagehands must change sets and install props between scenes; light and sound effects must occur on certain visual and aural cues. In any of these areas a single change or error—a new inflection at the end of a line or a misplaced prop—guarantees that a given performance will be unique. Similarly, no two audiences are the same, and the character of an audience inevitably affects the performance. A warm, responsive audience brings out the best in performers, as any actor will tell you, while a crowd's cold indifference often results in a tepid or stiff production. For these reasons, no staged realization of a play can ever duplicate another.

Just as no two single performances can be identical, no two interpretations can be exactly the same. We speak of Olivier's Hamlet (meaning the performance of the title role by Sir Laurence Olivier), of Dame Maggie Smith's or Glenda Jackson's Hedda Gabler, or of Zeffirelli's *Romeo and Juliet* (meaning the film directed by Franco Zeffirelli), because in each case the hand of the actor or director leads to a distinctive interpretation of the play. In the written text Hamlet may seem indecisive, melancholy, conniving, mad, vindictive, ambitious, or some combination of these things; individual performances emphasize one attribute or another, always at some expense to other characteristics and interpretations. No play can be all things to an audience in any one performance or run. And no two members of the audience will respond to all of these signals in exactly the same way.

This limitation of the performed play, its multiple variables but necessary restriction of the several possible meanings of the work to one interpretation, led the nineteenth-century writer Charles Lamb to come home from the theater vowing never to see another play of Shakespeare's on the stage. He found that no matter how good the performance, the enacted play restricted his imagination and robbed the play of some of the richness he found in reading it—and imagining it—for himself.

Without renouncing the theater or depriving ourselves of the thrilling experience of a brilliantly directed and performed interpretation of a play, we can reassert the quite different claims of reading drama as *literature,* as something written. Rather than being a poor substitute for seeing a play, reading drama is simply a different kind of experience, literary rather than theatrical.

In some ways reading a play is the same as reading a story or novel. In both cases we anticipate what will happen next and what it all means. We imagine the characters, setting, action; we respond to the symbolic suggestiveness of images; and we project configurations of thematic significance. The chief difference between narrative and drama on the page is the absence, in drama, of a mediator, someone standing between the reader and the work and helping us relate to the characters, actions, and meanings. For this reason, reading drama may place a greater strain on the imagination: the reader must be his or her own mediator, narrator, and interpreter.

Even the strain put upon our imaginations may prove rewarding, however. For not only are we freer to incorporate the play into our beings, but in becoming our own mediators we see how our imaginations or our responses to storytelling really work. Customarily we speak of "casting" characters in our minds, painting in scenic backdrops, placing furniture and props, and choreographing action. While we no doubt do some of this, most of our imaginations are not so well stocked, so we do not fully re-create what the playwright had in her or his mind's eye. While we might ask ourselves who should play Hamlet or Hedda Gabler, most of us do not have a full and fixed visual image of a character: we place a shape here, a profile there, and add a feature, mannerism, or gesture as we read on, mainly on the basis of suggestions in the text, though sometimes according to memories of theatrical performances or movies seen previously.

In reading drama dependent on dialogue, we construct character and personality from what a character says; we do this by relating our own experiences to what we read, responding in terms of expectations based on what we have felt in comparable situations. We've known someone who said things like this, or remember another play or story that suggests such attitudes and statements. So what we imagine as we read depends greatly upon our repertoire of experiences of life and literature. A character, even at the end of a play, is less a solid construction (or reconstruction) than a series of frames like those that make up a movie, each a little different. When we have seen an actor playing Blanche DuBois in *A Streetcar Named Desire* and see her as we read the play, we no longer simply read that play but watch it mentally, more or less remembering the play we once saw.

To say this is not necessarily to agree with Charles Lamb—an actor *can* show us something in a part we might not have seen for ourselves. If we go to the theater often, we have layers of performances that lend depth to our reading. But to read a play we have never seen is not to watch in the mind's eye a single, well-defined figure incorporating a character throughout the one, three, or five acts. We *watch* plays, but we *read* drama. Though we must take every opportunity to see a play performed to enrich our own reading of it, and though we should take advantage of our silent reading to include all the alternatives we can, each time we read a play we do our own interpreting, make our own choices and omissions. Reading, we perform all the parts, and we may want to ask ourselves how we would act this or that role, read this or that line; what kind of person we should try to imagine ourselves being; what, if we were that person, our motivations might be, and so on. But most important, perhaps, we want to consider what choices are available and what making one choice or another means.

As with fiction and poetry, writing about drama usually sharpens your responses and focuses your reading. When you write about drama, in a very real sense you perform the role that directors and actors take on in a stage performance: you give your "reading" of the text, interpreting it to guide other readers' responses. But as when you write about a story or a poem, you also mold your own response, by forcing yourself to be clear about just what your response is. The virtue of writing about drama, as in writing about any text, lies mainly in your having to be precise and articulate about how the text affects you. Normally, you consider what a play says to you and how the theatrical or imagined action should be interpreted before you actually write about it, but the act of writing will shape your initial impressions and lead to further reflection and insight. Your reading of drama (and fiction and poetry) will be considerably enhanced by your writing about it, just as the process of responding itself may be clarified by your putting into words what has happened to you as a result of confronting a given text.

And as writing about a play after you have read it may help you formulate or clarify your response, jotting down your thoughts before you've finished it may help you clarify your expectations. If when someone speaks you always finish his or her sentences, you are not being a good listener, but if when reading you always project forward, to what may happen next, or what a certain character will become, or what a play will show or suggest, you are being a good reader. As with fiction and poetry, expectation or anticipation should always be part of your response. One way to capture this kind of response is to stop your reading at some reasonable point—the end of a scene or an act, or when you are puzzled, or where the action seems to pause briefly—and write out how you think the action will proceed, how the play will end, what its characters will ultimately seem like to you, and what the play will say or show.

When you begin reading the short play that follows, Susan Glaspell's *Trifles*, even the title may raise certain expectations: Is the play a light comedy, something "trifling"?

The list of characters that follows the title, however, includes a sheriff and his wife and a county attorney, suggesting, perhaps a different kind of play. You could at this point jot down your expectations or questions about what kind of a play this is. You might pause again when, just a few lines into the play, the county attorney asks Mr. Hale to "tell just what happened," and examine your expectations at that point.

As you read, mark points in the play where your expectations are confirmed or altered, and where you find answers to your questions about what kind of play it is, how it will end, and what themes it has.

SUSAN GLASPELL

Trifles

CHARACTERS

SHERIFF	MRS. PETERS, *Sheriff's wife*
COUNTY ATTORNEY	MRS. HALE
HALE	

SCENE: *The kitchen in the now abandoned farmhouse of* JOHN WRIGHT, *a gloomy kitchen, and left without having been put in order—unwashed pans under the sink, a loaf of bread outside the bread-box, a dish-towel on the table—other signs of incompleted work. At the rear the outer door opens and the* SHERIFF *comes in followed by the* COUNTY ATTORNEY *and* HALE. *The* SHERIFF *and* HALE *are men in middle life, the* COUNTY ATTORNEY *is a young man; all are much bundled up and go at once to the stove. They are followed by the two women—the* SHERIFF's *wife first; she is a slight wiry woman, a thin nervous face.* MRS. HALE *is larger and would ordinarily be called more comfortable looking, but she is disturbed now and looks fearfully about as she enters. The women have come in slowly, and stand close together near the door.*

COUNTY ATTORNEY: [*Rubbing his hands.*] This feels good. Come up to the fire, ladies.

MRS. PETERS: [*After taking a step forward.*] I'm not—cold.

SHERIFF: [*Unbuttoning his overcoat and stepping away from the stove as if to mark the beginning of official business.*] Now, Mr. Hale, before we move things about, you explain to Mr. Henderson just what you saw when you came here yesterday morning.

COUNTY ATTORNEY: By the way, has anything been moved? Are things just as you left them yesterday?

SHERIFF: [*Looking about.*] It's just the same. When it dropped below zero last night I thought I'd better send Frank out this morning to make a fire for us—no use getting pneumonia with a big case on, but I told him not to touch anything except the stove—and you know Frank.

COUNTY ATTORNEY: Somebody should have been left here yesterday.

SHERIFF: Oh—yesterday. When I had to send Frank to Morris Center for that man who went crazy—I want you to know I had my hands full yesterday. I knew you could get back from Omaha by today and as long as I went over everything here myself—

COUNTY ATTORNEY: Well, Mr. Hale, tell just what happened when you came here yesterday morning.

HALE: Harry and I had started to town with a load of potatoes. We came along the road from my place and as I got here I said, "I'm going to see if I can't get John Wright to go in with me on a party telephone." I spoke to Wright about it once before and he put me off, saying folks talked too much anyway, and all he asked was peace and quiet—I guess you know about how much he talked himself; but I thought maybe if I went to the house and talked about it before his wife, though I said to Harry that I didn't know as what his wife wanted made much difference to John—

COUNTY ATTORNEY: Let's talk about that later, Mr. Hale. I do want to talk about that, but tell now just what happened when you got to the house.

HALE: I didn't hear or see anything; I knocked at the door, and still it was all quiet inside. I knew they must be up, it was past eight o'clock. So I knocked again, and I thought I heard somebody say, "Come in." I wasn't sure, I'm not sure yet, but I opened the door—this door [*Indicating the door by which the two women are still standing.*] and there in that rocker—[*Pointing to it.*] sat Mrs. Wright.

[*They all look at the rocker.*]

COUNTY ATTORNEY: What—was she doing?

HALE: She was rockin' back and forth. She had her apron in her hand and was kind of—pleating it.

COUNTY ATTORNEY: And how did she—look?

HALE: Well, she looked queer.

COUNTY ATTORNEY: How do you mean—queer?

HALE: Well, as if she didn't know what she was going to do next. And kind of done up.

COUNTY ATTORNEY: How did she seem to feel about your coming?

HALE: Why, I don't think she minded—one way or other. She didn't pay much attention. I said, "How do, Mrs. Wright, it's cold, ain't it?" And she said, "Is it?"—and went on kind of pleating at her apron. Well, I was surprised; she didn't ask me to come up to the stove, or to set down, but just sat there, not even looking at me, so I said, "I want to see John." And then she—laughed. I guess you would call it a laugh. I thought of Harry and the team outside, so I said a little sharp: "Can't I see John?" "No," she says, kind o' dull like. "Ain't he home?" says I. "Yes," says she, "he's home." "Then why can't I see him?" I asked her, out of patience. " 'Cause he's dead," says she. *"Dead?"* says I. She just nodded her head, not getting a bit excited, but rockin' back and forth. "Why—where is he?" says I, not knowing what to say. She just pointed upstairs—like that. [*Himself pointing to the room above.*] I got up, with the idea of going up there. I walked from there to here—then I says, "Why, what did he die of?" "He died of a rope round his neck," says she, and just went on pleatin' at her apron. Well, I went out and called Harry. I thought I might—need help. We went upstairs and there he was lyin'—

COUNTY ATTORNEY: I think I'd rather have you go into that upstairs, where you can point it all out. Just go on now with the rest of the story.

HALE: Well, my first thought was to get that rope off. It looked . . . [*Stops, his face twitches.*] . . . but Harry, he went up to him, and he said, "No, he's dead all right, and we'd better not touch anything." So we went back down stairs. She was still sitting that same way. "Has anybody been notified?" I asked. "No," says she unconcerned. "Who did this, Mrs. Wright?" said Harry. He said it business-like—and she stopped pleatin' of her apron. "I don't know," she says. "You don't *know?*" says Harry. "No," says she. "Weren't you sleepin' in the bed with him?" says Harry. "Yes," says she, "but I was on the inside." "Somebody slipped a rope round his neck and strangled him and you didn't wake up?" says Harry. "I didn't wake up," she said after him. We must 'a looked as if we didn't see how that could be, for after a minute she said, "I sleep sound." Harry was going to ask her more questions but I said maybe we ought to let her tell her story first to the coroner, or the sheriff, so Harry went fast as he could to Rivers' place, where there's a telephone.

COUNTY ATTORNEY: And what did Mrs. Wright do when she knew that you had gone for the coroner?

HALE: She moved from that chair to this one over here [*Pointing to a small chair in the corner.*] and just sat there with her hands held together and looking down. I got a feeling that I ought to make some conversation, so I said I had come in to see if John wanted to put in a telephone, and at that she started to laugh, and then she stopped and looked at me—scared. [*The* COUNTY ATTORNEY, *who has had his notebook out, makes a note.*] I dunno, maybe it wasn't scared. I wouldn't like to say it was. Soon Harry got back, and then Dr. Lloyd came, and you, Mr. Peters, and so I guess that's all I know that you don't.

COUNTY ATTORNEY: [*Looking around.*] I guess we'll go upstairs first—and then out to the barn and around there. [*To the* SHERIFF.] You're convinced that there was nothing important here—nothing that would point to any motive?

SHERIFF: Nothing here but kitchen things.

[*The* COUNTY ATTORNEY, *after again looking around the kitchen, opens the door of a cupboard closet. He gets up on a chair and looks on a shelf. Pulls his hand away, sticky.*]

COUNTY ATTORNEY: Here's a nice mess.

[*The women draw nearer.*]

MRS. PETERS: [*To the other woman.*] Oh, her fruit; it did freeze. [*To the* LAWYER.] She worried about that when it turned so cold. She said the fire'd go out and her jars would break.

SHERIFF: Well, can you beat the women! Held for murder and worryin' about her preserves.

COUNTY ATTORNEY: I guess before we're through she may have something more serious than preserves to worry about.

HALE: Well, women are used to worrying over trifles.

[*The two women move a little closer together.*]

COUNTY ATTORNEY: [*With the gallantry of a young politician.*] And yet, for all their worries, what would we do without the ladies? [*The women do not unbend. He goes to the sink, takes a dipperful of water from the pail and pouring it into a basin, washes his hands. Starts to wipe them on the roller-towel, turns it for a cleaner place.*] Dirty towels! [*Kicks his foot against the pans under the sink.*] Not much of a housekeeper, would you say, ladies?

MRS. HALE: [*Stiffly.*] There's a great deal of work to be done on a farm.

COUNTY ATTORNEY: To be sure. And yet [*With a little bow to her.*] I know there are some Dickson county farmhouses which do not have such roller towels. [*He gives it a pull to expose its length again.*]

MRS. HALE: Those towels get dirty awful quick. Men's hands aren't always as clean as they might be.

COUNTY ATTORNEY: Ah, loyal to your sex, I see. But you and Mrs. Wright were neighbors. I suppose you were friends, too.

MRS. HALE: [*Shaking her head.*] I've not seen much of her of late years. I've not been in this house—it's more than a year.

COUNTY ATTORNEY: And why was that? You didn't like her?

MRS. HALE: I liked her all well enough. Farmers' wives have their hands full, Mr. Henderson. And then—

COUNTY ATTORNEY: Yes—?

MRS. HALE: [*Looking about.*] It never seemed a very cheerful place.

COUNTY ATTORNEY: No—it's not cheerful. I shouldn't say she had the homemaking instinct.

MRS. HALE: Well, I don't know as Wright had, either.

COUNTY ATTORNEY: You mean that they didn't get on very well?

MRS. HALE: No, I don't mean anything. But I don't think a place'd be any cheerfuller for John Wright's being in it.

COUNTY ATTORNEY: I'd like to talk more of that a little later. I want to get the lay of things upstairs now. [*He goes to the left, where three steps lead to a stair door.*]

SHERIFF: I suppose anything Mrs. Peters does'll be all right. She was to take in some clothes for her, you know, and a few little things. We left in such a hurry yesterday.

COUNTY ATTORNEY: Yes, but I would like to see what you take, Mrs. Peters, and keep an eye out for anything that might be of use to us.

MRS. PETERS: Yes, Mr. Henderson. [*The women listen to the men's steps on the stairs, then look about the kitchen.*]

MRS. HALE: I'd hate to have men coming into my kitchen, snooping around and criticizing. [*She arranges the pans under sink which the* LAWYER *had shoved out of place.*]

MRS. PETERS: Of course it's no more than their duty.

MRS. HALE: Duty's all right, but I guess that deputy sheriff that came out to make the fire might have got a little of this on. [*Gives the roller towel a pull.*] Wish I'd thought of that sooner. Seems mean to talk about her for not having things slicked up when she had to come away in such a hurry.

MRS. PETERS: [*Who has gone to a small table in the left rear corner of the room, and lifted one end of a towel that covers a pan.*] She had bread set. [*Stands still.*]

MRS. HALE: [*Eyes fixed on a loaf of bread beside the bread box, which is on a low shelf at the other side of the room. Moves slowly toward it.*] She was going to put this in there. [*Picks up loaf, then abruptly drops it. In a manner of returning to familiar things.*] It's a shame about her fruit. I wonder if it's all gone. [*Gets up on the chair and looks.*] I think there's some here that's all right, Mrs. Peters. Yes— here; [*Holding it toward the window.*] this is cherries, too. [*Looking again.*] I declare I believe that's the only one. [*Gets down, bottle in her hand. Goes to the sink and wipes it off on the outside.*] She'll feel awful bad after all her hard work in the hot weather. I remember the afternoon I put up my cherries last summer. [*She puts the bottle on the big kitchen table, center of the room. With a sigh, is about to sit down in the rocking-chair. Before she is seated realizes what chair it is; with a slow look at it, steps back. The chair, which she has touched, rocks back and forth.*]

MRS. PETERS: Well, I must get those things from the front room closet. [*She goes to the door at the right, but after looking into the other room, steps back.*] You coming with me, Mrs. Hale? You could help me carry them. [*They go in the other room; reappear,* MRS. PETERS *carrying a dress and skirt,* MRS. HALE *following with a pair of shoes.*] My, it's cold in there. [*She puts the clothes on the big table, and hurries to the stove.*]

MRS. HALE: [*Examining the skirt.*] Wright was close. I think maybe that's why she kept so much to herself. She didn't even belong to the Ladies Aid. I suppose she felt she couldn't do her part, and then you don't enjoy things when you feel shabby. She used to wear pretty clothes and be lively, when she was Minnie Foster, one of the town girls singing in the choir. But that—oh, that was thirty years ago. This all you was to take in?

MRS. PETERS: She said she wanted an apron. Funny thing to want, for there isn't much to get you dirty in jail, goodness knows. But I suppose just to make her feel more natural. She said they was in the top drawer in this cupboard. Yes, here. And then her little shawl that always hung behind the door. [*Opens stair door and looks.*] Yes, here it is. [*Quickly shuts door leading upstairs.*]

MRS. HALE: [*Abruptly moving toward her.*] Mrs. Peters?

MRS. PETERS: Yes, Mrs. Hale?

MRS. HALE: Do you think she did it?

MRS. PETERS: [*In a frightened voice.*] Oh, I don't know.

MRS. HALE: Well, I don't think she did. Asking for an apron and her little shawl. Worrying about her fruit.

MRS. PETERS: [*Starts to speak, glances up, where footsteps are heard in the room above. In a low voice.*] Mr. Peters says it looks bad for her. Mr. Henderson is awful sarcastic in a speech and he'll make fun of her sayin' she didn't wake up.

MRS. HALE: Well, I guess John Wright didn't wake when they was slipping that rope under his neck.

MRS. PETERS: No, it's strange. It must have been done awful crafty and still. They say it was such a—funny way to kill a man, rigging it all up like that.

MRS. HALE: That's just what Mr. Hale said. There was a gun in the house. He says that's what he can't understand.

MRS. PETERS: Mr. Henderson said coming out that what was needed for the case was a motive; something to show anger, or—sudden feeling.

MRS. HALE: [*Who is standing by the table.*] Well, I don't see any signs of anger around here. [*She puts her hand on the dish towel which lies on the table, stands looking down at table, one half of which is clean, the other half messy.*] It's wiped to here. [*Makes a move as if to finish work, then turns and looks at loaf of bread outside the bread box. Drops towel. In that voice of coming back to familiar things.*] Wonder how they are finding things upstairs. I hope she had it a little more red-up[1] up there. You know, it seems kind of *sneaking.* Locking her up in town and then coming out here and trying to get her own house to turn against her!

MRS. PETERS: But Mrs. Hale, the law is the law.

MRS. HALE: I s'pose 'tis. [*Unbuttoning her coat.*] Better loosen up your things, Mrs. Peters. You won't feel them when you go out.

[MRS. PETERS *takes off her fur tippet, goes to hang it on hook at back of room, stands looking at the under part of the small corner table.*]

MRS. PETERS: She was piecing a quilt. [*She brings the large sewing basket and they look at the bright pieces.*]

MRS. HALE: It's log cabin pattern. Pretty, isn't it? I wonder if she was goin' to quilt it or just knot it?

[*Footsteps have been heard coming down the stairs. The* SHERIFF *enters followed by* HALE *and the* COUNTY ATTORNEY.]

SHERIFF: They wonder if she was going to quilt it or just knot it!

[*The men laugh, the women look abashed.*]

COUNTY ATTORNEY: [*Rubbing his hands over the stove.*] Frank's fire didn't do much up there, did it? Well, let's go out to the barn and get that cleared up.

[*The men go outside.*]

MRS. HALE: [*Resentfully.*] I don't know as there's anything so strange, our takin' up our time with little things while we're waiting for them to get the evidence. [*She sits down at the big table smoothing out a block with decision.*] I don't see as it's anything to laugh about.

MRS. PETERS: [*Apologetically.*] Of course they've got awful important things on their minds. [*Pulls up a chair and joins* MRS. HALE *at the table.*]

MRS. HALE: [*Examining another block.*] Mrs. Peters, look at this one. Here, this is the one she was working on, and look at the sewing! All the rest of it has been so nice and even. And look at this! It's all over the place! Why, it looks as if she didn't know what she was about! [*After she has said this they look at each other, then start to glance back at the door. After an instant* MRS. HALE *has pulled at a knot and ripped the sewing.*]

1. Tidied up.

MRS. PETERS: Oh, what are you doing, Mrs. Hale?

MRS. HALE: [*Mildly.*] Just pulling out a stitch or two that's not sewed very good. [*Threading the needle.*] Bad sewing always made me fidgety.

MRS. PETERS: [*Nervously.*] I don't think we ought to touch things.

MRS. HALE: I'll just finish up this end. [*Suddenly stopping and leaning forward.*] Mrs. Peters?

MRS. PETERS: Yes, Mrs. Hale?

MRS. HALE: What do you suppose she was so nervous about?

MRS. PETERS: Oh—I don't know. I don't know as she was nervous. I sometimes sew awful queer when I'm just tired. [MRS. HALE *starts to say something, looks at* MRS. PETERS, *then goes on sewing.*] Well I must get these things wrapped up. They may be through sooner than we think. [*Putting apron and other things together.*] I wonder where I can find a piece of paper, and string.

MRS. HALE: In that cupboard, maybe.

MRS. PETERS: [*Looking in cupboard.*] Why, here's a bird-cage. [*Holds it up.*] Did she have a bird, Mrs. Hale?

MRS. HALE: Why, I don't know whether she did or not—I've not been here for so long. There was a man around last year selling canaries cheap, but I don't know as she took one; maybe she did. She used to sing real pretty herself.

MRS. PETERS: [*Glancing around.*] Seems funny to think of a bird here. But she must have had one, or why would she have a cage? I wonder what happened to it.

MRS. HALE: I s'pose maybe the cat got it.

MRS. PETERS: No, she didn't have a cat. She's got that feeling some people have about cats—being afraid of them. My cat got in her room and she was real upset and asked me to take it out.

MRS. HALE: My sister Bessie was like that. Queer, ain't it?

MRS. PETERS: [*Examining the cage.*] Why, look at this door. It's broke. One hinge is pulled apart.

MRS. HALE: [*Looking too.*] Looks as if someone must have been rough with it.

MRS. PETERS: Why, yes. [*She brings the cage forward and puts it on the table.*]

MRS. HALE: I wish if they're going to find any evidence they'd be about it. I don't like this place.

MRS. PETERS: But I'm awful glad you came with me, Mrs. Hale. It would be lonesome for me sitting here alone.

MRS. HALE: It would, wouldn't it? [*Dropping her sewing.*] But I tell you what I do wish, Mrs. Peters. I wish I had come over sometimes when *she* was here. I—[*Looking around the room.*]—wish I had.

MRS. PETERS: But of course you were awful busy, Mrs. Hale—your house and your children.

MRS. HALE: I could've come. I stayed away because it weren't cheerful—and that's why I ought to have come. I—I've never liked this place. Maybe because it's down in a hollow and you don't see the road. I dunno what it is, but it's a lonesome place and always was. I wish I had come over to see Minnie Foster sometimes. I can see now—[*Shakes her head.*]

MRS. PETERS: Well, you mustn't reproach yourself, Mrs. Hale. Somehow we just don't see how it is with other folks until—something comes up.

MRS. HALE: Not having children makes less work—but it makes a quiet house, and

Wright out to work all day, and no company when he did come in. Did you know John Wright, Mrs. Peters?

MRS. PETERS: Not to know him; I've seen him in town. They say he was a good man.

MRS. HALE: Yes—good; he didn't drink, and kept his word as well as most, I guess, and paid his debts. But he was a hard man, Mrs. Peters. Just to pass the time of day with him—[*Shivers.*] Like a raw wind that gets to the bone. [*Pauses, her eye falling on the cage.*] I should think she would 'a wanted a bird. But what do you suppose went with it?

MRS. PETERS: I don't know, unless it got sick and died. [*She reaches over and swings the broken door, swings it again, both women watch it.*]

MRS. HALE: You weren't raised round here, were you? [MRS. PETERS *shakes her head.*] You didn't know—her?

MRS. PETERS: Not till they brought her yesterday.

MRS. HALE: She—come to think of it, she was kind of like a bird herself—real sweet and pretty, but kind of timid and—fluttery. How—she—did—change. [*Silence; then as if struck by a happy thought and relieved to get back to everyday things.*] Tell you what, Mrs. Peters, why don't you take the quilt in with you? It might take up her mind.

MRS. PETERS: Why, I think that's a real nice idea, Mrs. Hale. There couldn't possibly be any objection to it, could there? Now, just what would I take? I wonder if her patches are in here—and her things. [*They look in the sewing basket.*]

MRS. HALE: Here's some red. I expect this has got sewing things in it. [*Brings out a fancy box.*] What a pretty box. Looks like something somebody would give you. Maybe her scissors are in here. [*Opens box. Suddenly puts her hand to her nose.*] Why— [MRS. PETERS *bends nearer, then turns her face away.*] There's something wrapped up in this piece of silk.

MRS. PETERS: Why, this isn't her scissors.

MRS. HALE: [*Lifting the silk.*] Oh, Mrs. Peters—it's—

[MRS. PETERS *bends closer.*]

MRS. PETERS: It's the bird.

MRS. HALE: [*Jumping up.*] But, Mrs. Peters—look at it! Its neck! Look at its neck! It's all—other side *to.*

MRS. PETERS: Somebody—wrung—its—neck.

[*Their eyes meet. A look of growing comprehension, of horror. Steps are heard outside.* MRS. HALE *slips box under quilt pieces, and sinks into her chair. Enter* SHERIFF *and* COUNTY ATTORNEY. MRS. PETERS *rises.*]

COUNTY ATTORNEY: [*As one turning from serious things to little pleasantries.*] Well ladies, have you decided whether she was going to quilt it or knot it?

MRS. PETERS: We think she was going to—knot it.

COUNTY ATTORNEY: Well, that's interesting, I'm sure. [*Seeing the bird-cage.*] Has the bird flown?

MRS. HALE: [*Putting more quilt pieces over the box.*] We think the—cat got it.

COUNTY ATTORNEY: [*Preoccupied.*] Is there a cat?

[MRS. HALE *glances in a quick covert way at* MRS. PETERS.]

MRS. PETERS: Well, not *now*. They're superstitious, you know. They leave.

COUNTY ATTORNEY: [*To* SHERIFF PETERS, *continuing an interrupted conversation.*] No sign at all of anyone having come from the outside. Their own rope. Now let's go up again and go over it piece by piece. [*They start upstairs.*] It would have to have been someone who knew just the—

[MRS. PETERS *sits down. The two women sit there not looking at one another, but as if peering into something and at the same time holding back. When they talk now it is in the manner of feeling their way over strange ground, as if afraid of what they are saying, but as if they cannot help saying it.*]

MRS. HALE: She liked the bird. She was going to bury it in that pretty box.

MRS. PETERS: [*In a whisper.*] When I was a girl—my kitten—there was a boy took a hatchet, and before my eyes—and before I could get there—[*Covers her face an instant.*] If they hadn't held me back I would have—[*Catches herself, looks upstairs where steps are heard, falters weakly.*]—hurt him.

MRS. HALE: [*With a slow look around her.*] I wonder how it would seem never to have had any children around. [*Pause.*] No, Wright wouldn't like the bird— a thing that sang. She used to sing. He killed that, too.

MRS. PETERS: [*Moving uneasily.*] We don't know who killed the bird.

MRS. HALE: I knew John Wright.

MRS. PETERS: It was an awful thing was done in this house that night, Mrs. Hale. Killing a man while he slept, slipping a rope around his neck that choked the life out of him.

MRS. HALE: His neck. Choked the life out of him. [*Her hand goes out and rests on the bird-cage.*]

MRS. PETERS: [*With rising voice.*] We don't know who killed him. We don't *know*.

MRS. HALE: [*Her own feeling not interrupted.*] If there's been years and years of nothing, then a bird to sing to you, it would be awful—still, after the bird was still.

MRS. PETERS: [*Something within her speaking.*] I know what stillness is. When we homesteaded in Dakota, and my first baby died—after he was two years old, and me with no other then—

MRS. HALE: [*Moving.*] How soon do you suppose they'll be through, looking for the evidence?

MRS. PETERS: I know what stillness is. [*Pulling herself back.*] The law has got to punish crime, Mrs. Hale.

MRS. HALE: [*Not as if answering that.*] I wish you'd seen Minnie Foster when she wore a white dress with blue ribbons and stood up there in the choir and sang. [*A look around the room.*] Oh, I *wish* I'd come over here once in a while! That was a crime! That was a crime! Who's going to punish that?

MRS. PETERS: [*Looking upstairs.*] We mustn't—take on.

MRS. HALE: I might have known she needed help! I know how things can be—for women. I tell you, it's queer, Mrs. Peters. We live close together and we live far apart. We all go through the same things—it's all just a different kind of the same thing. [*Brushes her eyes, noticing the bottle of fruit, reaches out for it.*] If I was you, I wouldn't tell her her fruit was gone. Tell her it *ain't*. Tell her it's all right. Take this in to prove it to her. She—she may never know whether it was broke or not.

MRS. PETERS: [*Takes the bottle, looks about for something to wrap it in; takes petticoat from the clothes brought from the other room, very nervously begins winding this around the bottle. In a false voice.*] My, it's a good thing the men couldn't hear us. Wouldn't they just laugh! Getting all stirred up over a little thing like a— dead canary. As if that could have anything to do with—with—wouldn't they *laugh!*

[*The men are heard coming down stairs.*]

MRS. HALE: [*Under her breath.*] Maybe they would—maybe they wouldn't.

COUNTY ATTORNEY: No, Peters, it's all perfectly clear except a reason for doing it. But you know juries when it comes to women. If there was some definite thing. Something to show—something to make a story about—a thing that would connect up with this strange way of doing it—

[*The women's eyes meet for an instant. Enter HALE from outer door.*]

HALE: Well, I've got the team around. Pretty cold out there.

COUNTY ATTORNEY: I'm going to stay here a while by myself. [*To the SHERIFF.*] You can send Frank out for me, can't you? I want to go over everything. I'm not satisfied that we can't do better.

SHERIFF: Do you want to see what Mrs. Peters is going to take in?

[*The LAWYER goes to the table, picks up the apron, laughs.*]

COUNTY ATTORNEY: Oh, I guess they're not very dangerous things the ladies have picked out. [*Moves a few things about, disturbing the quilt pieces which cover the box. Steps back.*] No, Mrs. Peters doesn't need supervising. For that matter, a sheriff's wife is married to the law. Ever think of it that way, Mrs. Peters?

MRS. PETERS: Not—just that way.

SHERIFF: [*Chuckling.*] Married to the law. [*Moves toward the other room.*] I just want you to come in here a minute, George. We ought to take a look at these windows.

COUNTY ATTORNEY: [*Scoffingly.*] Oh, windows!

SHERIFF: We'll be right out, Mr. Hale.

[HALE *goes outside. The* SHERIFF *follows the* COUNTY ATTORNEY *into the other room. Then* MRS. HALE *rises, hands tight together, looking intensely at* MRS. PETERS, *whose eyes make a slow turn, finally meeting* MRS. HALE's. *A moment* MRS. HALE *holds her, then her own eyes point the way to where the box is concealed. Suddenly* MRS. PETERS *throws back quilt pieces and tries to put the box in the bag she is wearing. It is too big. She opens box, starts to take bird out, cannot touch it, goes to pieces, stands there helpless. Sound of a knob*] *turning in the other room.* MRS. HALE *snatches the box and puts it in the pocket of her big coat. Enter* COUNTY ATTORNEY *and* SHERIFF.]

COUNTY ATTORNEY: [*Facetiously.*] Well, Henry, at least we found out that she was not going to quilt it. She was going to—what is it you call it, ladies?
MRS. HALE: [*Her hand against her pocket.*] We call it—knot it, Mr. Henderson.

CURTAIN

1920

Now that you have finished reading the play, you might look back over your reading notes and trace how your expectations developed, how they were fulfilled or disappointed, how your focus moved from the murder plot to the feminist theme, how your view of certain characters—especially, perhaps, Mrs. Peters, the sheriff's wife—changed. One pattern of response may resemble the following:

When very early in the play Hale "tell[s] just what happened," his story initially generates curiosity rather than expectation: Mrs. Wright's conduct at first seems strange—at least to the point where she says her husband "died of a rope round his neck"—and then seems suspicious. Could she actually have slept so soundly that she didn't know someone had put a rope around his neck and pulled him upright, killing him? Though we remain curious about what actually happened and anticipate the discovery of the murderer—or perhaps wonder how the men will discover that Mrs. Wright is the murderer—we are distracted by another facet of the action: Hale's sexist remark that "women are used to worrying over trifles," and later the men's scoffing laughter at the women's conjecture as to whether Mrs. Wright was going to hand-quilt or knot the quilt she was making. In fact, our responses may differ according to gender. Some women might pick up the sexism earlier, in the county attorney's refusal to listen when Hale suggests that Mrs. Wright's desires may not have been very important to Wright, or the sheriff's dismissive remark that there is "[n]othing here but kitchen things."

The situation now raises a number of questions. How offensive are these remarks? When did you notice that the "submissive" Mrs. Peters was shifting her allegiance from her husband to Mrs. Hale? To what extent do the remarks justify the women's suppression of evidence (which the men might not have thought "real" evidence in any case)? Where do your sympathies lie? Should Mrs. Wright get away with it? Is it justifiable homicide? Does the play strongly suggest an answer to these questions? Does the answer make you like or dislike the play? How important is your acceptance or rejection of the social theme to your emotional response to the play?

There is nothing particularly difficult or unfamiliar about *Trifles* as a "story." (Glaspell did, indeed, turn the play into a story, called "A Jury of Her Peers.") It is a detective story and includes a murder, evidence, and interpretation—or "detection"—from the evidence, though unlike most other detective or murder stories, it asks not "who done it?" but why the murder was committed. Its **mode** of representation is a familiar type—domestic realism—in which the places, people, and even events are more or less ordinary (unfortunately, domestic violence and murder are not extraordinary). Its staging is also conventional in the modern theater: it has an imaginary wall separating the stage from the auditorium that acts as a frame (the **proscenium arch**). It also has—though somewhat in miniature—the traditional five-part structure: the **exposition**—the situation at the beginning of a play: here Mr. Hale's description of what happened; the **rising**

action—the complicating of the plot; the **climax**—the turning point: here, perhaps, the discovery of the dead bird; the **falling action**—the unwinding of the plot toward the conclusion: here the women covering up the "trifling" evidence; and the **conclusion.** This does not suggest that the play is trite or dull, but only that its type, subject matter, manner of presentation, and form are familiar—which might also be said, for example, of *Oedipus* or *Hamlet.*

The next play, David Ives's *Sure Thing,* is entirely different. It does not have a plot in the usual sense, but consists of a series of discrete, causally unconnected—indeed, "alternative"—scenes or portions of the scene involving the same two characters in the same situation speaking similar but not identical dialogue, with—with one exception— similar outcomes. A bit of "stage business"—the clang of a bell—signals that a "substitute" conversation will be offered. Although it is a funny play to read, it probably is funnier on the stage, where we actually *see* the same actors in the identical situation saying different lines. Though the alternative lines follow each other immediately after the word "[*Bell.*]," as readers we adjust time sequences from paragraph to paragraph or chapter to chapter so that the sequence has less immediacy on the page than it would have on the stage.

DAVID IVES

Sure Thing

CHARACTERS

BETTY   BILL

BETTY, *a woman in her late twenties, is reading at a café table. An empty chair is opposite her.* BILL, *same age, enters.*

BILL: Excuse me. Is this chair taken?
BETTY: Excuse me?
BILL: Is this taken?
BETTY: Yes it is.
BILL: Oh. Sorry.
BETTY: Sure thing.

[*A bell rings softly.*]

BILL: Excuse me. Is this chair taken?
BETTY: Excuse me?
BILL: Is this taken?
BETTY: No, but I'm expecting somebody in a minute.
BILL: Oh. Thanks anyway.
BETTY: Sure thing.

[*A bell rings softly.*]

BILL: Excuse me. Is this chair taken?

BETTY: No, but I'm expecting somebody very shortly.

BILL: Would you mind if I sit here till he or she or it comes?

BETTY: [*Glances at her watch.*] They do seem to be pretty late. . . .

BILL: You never know who you might be turning down.

BETTY: Sorry. Nice try, though.

BILL: Sure thing.

    [*Bell.*]

    Is this seat taken?

BETTY: No it's not.

BILL: Would you mind if I sit here?

BETTY: Yes I would.

BILL: Oh.

    [*Bell.*]

    Is this chair taken?

BETTY: No it's not.

BILL: Would you mind if I sit here?

BETTY: No. Go ahead.

BILL: Thanks. [*He sits. She continues reading.*] Everyplace else seems to be taken.

BETTY: Mm-hm.

BILL: Great place.

BETTY: Mm-hm.

BILL: What's the book?

BETTY: I just wanted to read in quiet, if you don't mind.

BILL: No. Sure thing.

    [*Bell.*]

BILL: Everyplace else seems to be taken.

BETTY: Mm-hm.

BILL: Great place for reading.

BETTY: Yes, I like it.

BILL: What's the book?

BETTY: *The Sound and the Fury.*

BILL: Oh. Hemingway.

    [*Bell.*]

    What's the book?

BETTY: *The Sound and the Fury.*

BILL: Oh. Faulkner.

BETTY: Have you read it?

BILL: Not . . . actually. I've sure read *about* it, though. It's supposed to be great.

BETTY: It is great.

BILL: I hear it's great. [*Small pause.*] Waiter?

[*Bell.*]

What's the book?
BETTY: *The Sound and the Fury.*
BILL: Oh. Faulkner.
BETTY: Have you read it?
BILL: I'm a Mets fan, myself.

[*Bell.*]

BETTY: Have you read it?
BILL: Yeah, I read it in college.
BETTY: Where was college?
BILL: I went to Oral Roberts University.

[*Bell.*]

BETTY: Where was college?
BILL: I was lying. I never really went to college. I just like to party.

[*Bell.*]

BETTY: Where was college?
BILL: Harvard.
BETTY: Do you like Faulkner?
BILL: I love Faulkner, I spent a whole winter reading him once.
BETTY: I've just started.
BILL: I was so excited after ten pages that I went out and bought everything else he wrote. One of the greatest reading experiences of my life. I mean, all that incredible psychological understanding. Page after page of gorgeous prose. His profound grasp of the mystery of time and human existence. The smells of the earth . . . What do you think?
BETTY: I think it's pretty boring.

[*Bell.*]

BILL: What's the book?
BETTY: *The Sound and the Fury.*
BILL: Oh! Faulkner!
BETTY: Do you like Faulkner?
BILL: I love Faulkner.
BETTY: He's incredible.
BILL: I spent a whole winter reading him once.
BETTY: I was so excited after ten pages that I went out and bought everything else he wrote.
BILL: All that incredible psychological understanding.
BETTY: And the prose is so gorgeous.
BILL: And the way he's grasped the mystery of time—
BETTY: —and human existence. I can't believe I've waited this long to read him.
BILL: You never know. You might not have liked him before.

BETTY: That's true.

BILL: You might not have been ready for him. You have to hit these things at the right moment or it's no good.

BETTY: That's happened to me.

BILL: It's all in the timing. [*Small pause.*] My name's Bill, by the way.

BETTY: I'm Betty.

BILL: Hi.

BETTY: Hi. [*Small pause.*]

BILL: Yes I thought reading Faulkner was . . . a great experience.

BETTY: Yes. [*Small pause.*]

BILL: *The Sound and the Fury* . . . [*Another small pause.*]

BETTY: Well. Onwards and upwards. [*She goes back to her book.*]

BILL: Waiter—?

[*Bell.*]

You have to hit these things at the right moment or it's no good.

BETTY: That's happened to me.

BILL: It's all in the timing. My name's Bill, by the way.

BETTY: I'm Betty.

BILL: Hi.

BETTY: Hi.

BILL: Do you come in here a lot?

BETTY: Actually I'm just in town for two days from Pakistan.

BILL: Oh. Pakistan.

[*Bell.*]

My name's Bill, by the way.

BETTY: I'm Betty.

BILL: Hi.

BETTY: Hi.

BILL: Do you come in here a lot?

BETTY: Every once in a while. Do you?

BILL: Not so much anymore. Not as much as I used to. Before my nervous breakdown.

[*Bell.*]

Do you come in here a lot?

BETTY: Why are you asking?

BILL: Just interested.

BETTY: Are you really interested, or do you just want to pick me up?

BILL: No, I'm really interested.

BETTY: Why would you be interested in whether I come in here a lot?

BILL: I'm just . . . getting acquainted.

BETTY: Maybe you're only interested for the sake of making small talk long enough to ask me back to your place to listen to some music, or because you've just rented this great tape for your VCR, or because you've got some terrific

unknown Django Reinhardt[1] record, only all you really want to do is fuck—
which you won't do very well—after which you'll go into the bathroom and
pee very loudly, then pad into the kitchen and get yourself a beer from the
refrigerator without asking me whether I'd like anything, and then you'll
proceed to lie back down beside me and confess that you've got a girlfriend
named Stephanie who's away at medical school in Belgium for a year, and
that you've been involved with her—*off and on*—in what you'll call a very
"intricate" relationship, for the past *seven YEARS*. None of which *interests* me,
mister!

BILL: Okay.

   [*Bell.*]

Do you come in here a lot?

BETTY: Every other day, I think.

BILL: I come in here quite a lot and I don't remember seeing you.

BETTY: I guess we must be on different schedules.

BILL: Missed connections.

BETTY: Yes. Different time zones.

BILL: Amazing how you can live right next door to somebody in this town and
never even know it.

BETTY: I know.

BILL: City life.

BETTY: It's crazy.

BILL: We probably pass each other in the street every day. Right in front of this
place, probably.

BETTY: Yep.

BILL: [*Looks around.*] Well the waiters here sure seem to be in some different time
zone. I can't seem to locate one anywhere. . . . Waiter! [*He looks back.*] So what
do you— [*He sees that she's gone back to her book.*]

BETTY: I beg pardon?

BILL: Nothing. Sorry.

   [*Bell.*]

BETTY: I guess we must be on different schedules.

BILL: Missed connections.

BETTY: Yes. Different time zones.

BILL: Amazing how you can live right next door to somebody in this town and
never even know it.

BETTY: I know.

BILL: City life.

BETTY: It's crazy.

BILL: You weren't waiting for somebody when I came in, were you?

BETTY: Actually I was.

BILL: Oh. Boyfriend?

---

1. Belgian-born French guitarist (1910–1953), Europe's first acclaimed jazz musician.

BETTY: Sort of.

BILL: What's a sort-of boyfriend?

BETTY: My husband.

BILL: Ah-ha.

[*Bell.*]

You weren't waiting for somebody when I came in, were you?

BETTY: Actually I was.

BILL: Oh. Boyfriend?

BETTY: Sort of.

BILL: What's a sort-of boyfriend?

BETTY: We were meeting here to break up.

BILL: Mm-hm . . .

[*Bell.*]

What's a sort-of boyfriend?

BETTY: My lover. Here she comes right now!

[*Bell.*]

BILL: You weren't waiting for somebody when I came in, were you?

BETTY: No, just reading.

BILL: Sort of a sad occupation for a Friday night, isn't it? Reading here, all by yourself?

BETTY: Do you think so?

BILL: Well sure. I mean, what's a good-looking woman like you doing out alone on a Friday night?

BETTY: Trying to keep away from lines like that.

BILL: No, listen—

[*Bell.*]

You weren't waiting for somebody when I came in, were you?

BETTY: No, just reading.

BILL: Sort of a sad occupation for a Friday night, isn't it? Reading here all by yourself?

BETTY: I guess it is, in a way.

BILL: What's a good-looking woman like you doing out alone on a Friday night anyway? No offense, but . . .

BETTY: I'm out alone on a Friday night for the first time in a very long time.

BILL: Oh.

BETTY: You see, I just recently ended a relationship.

BILL: Oh.

BETTY: Of rather long standing.

BILL: I'm sorry. [*Small pause.*] Well listen, since reading by yourself *is* such a sad occupation for a Friday night, would you like to go elsewhere?

BETTY: No . . .

BILL: Do something else?

BETTY: No thanks.

BILL: I was headed out to the movies in a while anyway.

BETTY: I don't think so.

BILL: Big chance to let Faulkner catch his breath. All those long sentences get him pretty tired.

BETTY: Thanks anyway.

BILL: Okay.

BETTY: I appreciate the invitation.

BILL: Sure thing.

> [*Bell.*]

You weren't waiting for somebody when I came in, were you?

BETTY: No, just reading.

BILL: Sort of a sad occupation for a Friday night, isn't it? Reading here all by yourself?

BETTY: I guess I was trying to think of it as existentially romantic. You know— cappuccino, great literature, rainy night . . .

BILL: That only works in Paris. We *could* hop the late plane to Paris. Get on a Concorde. Find a café . . .

BETTY: I'm a little short on plane fare tonight.

BILL: Darn it, so am I.

BETTY: To tell you the truth, I was headed to the movies after I finished this section. Would you like to come along? Since you can't locate a waiter?

BILL: That's a very nice offer, but . . .

BETTY: Uh-huh. Girlfriend?

BILL: Two, actually. One of them's pregnant, and Stephanie—

> [*Bell.*]

BETTY: Girlfriend?

BILL: No, I don't have a girlfriend. Not if you mean the castrating bitch I dumped last night.

> [*Bell.*]

BETTY: Girlfriend?

BILL: Sort of. Sort of.

BETTY: What's a sort-of girlfriend?

BILL: My mother.

> [*Bell.*]

I just ended a relationship, actually.

BETTY: Oh.

BILL: Of rather long standing.

BETTY: I'm sorry to hear it.

BILL: This is my first night out alone in a long time. I feel a little bit at sea, to tell you the truth.

BETTY: So you didn't stop to talk because you're a Moonie, or you have some weird political affiliation—?

BILL: Nope. Straight-down-the-ticket Republican.

[*Bell.*]

Straight-down-the-ticket Democrat.

[*Bell.*]

Can I tell you something about politics?

[*Bell.*]

I like to think of myself as a citizen of the universe.

[*Bell.*]

I'm unaffiliated.

BETTY: That's a relief. So am I.

BILL: I vote my beliefs.

BETTY: Labels are not important.

BILL: Labels are not important, exactly. Take me, for example. I mean, what does it matter if I had a two-point at—

[*Bell.*]

three-point at—

[*Bell*]

four-point at college? Or if I did come from Pittsburgh—

[*Bell.*]

Cleveland—

[*Bell.*]

Westchester County?

BETTY: Sure.

BILL: I believe that a man is what he is.

[*Bell.*]

A person is what he is.

[*Bell.*]

A person is . . . what they are.

BETTY: I think so too.

BILL: So what if I admire Trotsky?

[*Bell.*]

So what if I once had a total-body liposuction?

[*Bell.*]

So what if I don't have a penis?

[*Bell.*]

So what if I spent a year in the Peace Corps? I was acting on my convictions.

BETTY: Sure.

BILL: You just can't hang a sign on a person.

BETTY: Absolutely. I'll bet you're a Scorpio.

[*Many bells ring.*]

Listen, I was headed to the movies after I finished this section. Would you like to come along?

BILL: That sounds like fun. What's playing?

BETTY: A couple of the really early Woody Allen movies.

BILL: Oh.

BETTY: You don't like Woody Allen?

BILL: Sure. I like Woody Allen.

BETTY: But you're not crazy about Woody Allen.

BILL: Those early ones kind of get on my nerves.

BETTY: Uh-huh.

[*Bell.*]

BILL: Y'know I was headed to the—

BETTY: [*Simultaneously.*] I was thinking about—

BILL: I'm sorry.

BETTY: No, go ahead.

BILL: I was going to say that I was headed to the movies in a little while, and . . .

BETTY: So was I.

BILL: The Woody Allen festival?

BETTY: Just up the street.

BILL: Do you like the early ones?

BETTY: I think anybody who doesn't ought to be run off the planet.

BILL: How many times have you seen *Bananas*?

BETTY: Eight times.

BILL: Twelve. So are you still interested? [*Long pause.*]

BETTY: Do you like Entenmann's crumb cake . . . ?

BILL: Last night I went out at two in the morning to get one. Did you have an Etch-a-Sketch as a child?

BETTY: Yes! And do you like Brussels sprouts? [*Pause.*]

BILL: No, I think they're disgusting.

BETTY: They *are* disgusting!

BILL: Do you still believe in marriage in spite of current sentiments against it?

BETTY: Yes.

BILL: And children?

BETTY: Three of them.

BILL: Two girls and a boy.

BETTY: Harvard, Vassar, and Brown.

BILL: And will you love me?

BETTY: Yes.

BILL: And cherish me forever?

BETTY: Yes.

BILL: Do you still want to go to the movies?

BETTY: Sure thing.

BILL AND BETTY: [*Together.*] *Waiter!*

BLACKOUT

1989

QUESTIONS

1. All three of the men in *Trifles* seem sexist; indicate at least one bit of dialogue by each that would support this judgment. What do you learn of the character and attitudes of John Wright, the murdered man? How does the situation in the Wright household reflect on the relations among Peters, Hale, and their wives? Describe the differences between Mrs. Peters and Mrs. Hale; how does Mrs. Wright resemble them and differ from them? What is the effect of the last exchange of the play?
2. The characters in each exchange in *Sure Thing* are Betty and Bill. Do you assume each is the same character throughout the play, or do you think that, despite their names, they represent different people or types? If you see each as different, chose three or more bits of dialogue that suggest this, then describe and document the differences. If you were acting the part of Betty—or Bill—how would you play different portions of the play differently?

WRITING SUGGESTIONS

1. (a) Write a brief sketch of the trial of Mrs. Wright, or
   (b) write a brief of your case for or against, or
   (c) write a brief parody of the "feminism" of *Trifles*, or
   (d) describe an incident in the play in which male chauvinism (sexism) causes a blunder or oversight.
2. Argue that Caryl Zook's reading of the play (following) is too insistently feminist; that Henderson, for example, is being not dominant but polite in inviting (not ordering) the "ladies" to come up to the fire; that the sheriff's saying there's "[n]othing here but kitchen things" is not dismissive of women but just a direct response to the question of what he saw in the kitchen; and so forth. (Or, counter such a counterargument.)
3. Sometimes, before we talk to someone, stranger or friend, we mentally rehearse how that person might respond to us, even imagining several possibilities. Write such a scenario using *Sure Thing* as a model, preferably choosing a situation different from that in Ives's play. If you base your paper on a real episode, indicate how the actual conversation then went and analyze why the response matched one you predicted or differed from anything you projected.
4. Write a parody of or a response to *Sure Thing* in which the ages or races of the characters are different—for example, Betty and Bill as senior citizens—or in which their ages and races differ from each other, or in which the two characters are of the same gender.

STUDENT WRITING

In the following paper, Caryl Zook examines each twist in the action of *Trifles* in terms of the behavior demonstrated by the men and the women. Her style and tone are informal, but her feelings about the play are strong, and she convincingly uses details to support her reading.

<u>Trifles</u>

Caryl Zook

<u>Trifles</u>: The title is at once descriptive and ironic. The males in the play are, in varying degrees, patronizing to the women and self-important in all they do. While the men assume that all women's concerns are trifles, the women solve the case through their understanding of the importance of the little things. It is therefore easy for them to hide the evidence necessary to solve the case from the men.

The county attorney, Mr. Henderson, asserts his dominance from the first lines of the play, when he almost orders them to "[c]ome up to the fire, ladies." Mrs. Peters, the more timid of the two women in the scenes and trained to obey, starts to comply, then answers, "I'm not--cold."

Sheriff Peters says, "Nothing here but kitchen things," implying that these are "women's" things, things of no significance. The county attorney checks a high shelf and pulls his hand away, sticky. "Here's a nice mess," he says, attaching no significance to this "trifle."

Mrs. Peters realizes that almost all of Mrs. Wright's preserves had frozen and broken, as Mrs. Wright had anticipated and feared. She tells her husband, but he says, "Well, can you beat the women!" (interesting choice of words). "Held for murder and worryin' about her preserves." Hale adds, "Well, women are used to worrying over trifles." Like food, like the long hours of labor this woman must have invested to preserve a winter's worth of food for the family. Trifles. Furthermore, it was because of the sheriff's failure to keep a fire at the house that the jars froze and broke.

The men get a good laugh over the women, who discover that Mrs. Wright was piecing a quilt, when the sheriff says, "They wonder if she was going to quilt it or just knot it!" as if this were obviously a ridiculously trivial issue. It is a little pleasantry, a diversion for the county attorney to use as small talk. "Well, ladies, have you decided whether she was going to quilt it or knot it?" Mrs. Peters says, "We think she was going to--knot it." Is she reluctant to talk about Minnie Wright's knot-tying abilities? "Well, that's interesting, I'm sure," says the county attorney. He, of course, cares about more pressing matters, such as how to prove who tied the knot in the rope around John Wright's neck.

Ironically, while the men parade around being important and humorous at the expense of "the ladies," the ladies solve the crime. Mrs. Hale realizes that it may have been the deputy who got the towel dirty. Mrs. Peters discovers a canary with a broken neck. They conclude that Mr. Wright killed it and that this was the motive for the crime. They decide that justice will be best served, however, by removing this evidence in a show of solidarity with another mistreated, overworked, underappreciated female. Perhaps the attitude of the males on the scene --including their belittling definition of "women's work" as "trifles"-- is another motivation for the protective actions the women take on behalf of a victimized sister. Anything the women did or do is unimportant by comparison to what the men do. The long, hot hours spent canning and the months spent quilting a cover, rather than knotting it, are trifles also. Even if the men knew that Minnie Foster had loved to sing and that she bought a canary to bring some small joy into her childless life and that John Wright killed the songbird precisely because it made her happy, would they see it as a motive for murder? Or would they dismiss it as "trifles"?

Glaspell has woven a tightly bound plot. The major elements of the mystery are interconnected. John Wright died, according to Mrs. Wright, "of a rope around his neck." The women figure out that Mrs. Wright had bought a canary so that it would sing, as she used to sing, and that Mr. Wright had strangled it to death. She was, they determined, going to knot the quilt. Perhaps she could knot a rope when she wanted to. But let's not tell the men.

Understanding the Text

Although it has been possible in previous chapters to represent the elements of fiction and poetry by devoting a chapter to each major element and giving full-length texts as examples, it is not possible to do so with drama. In this chapter, we consider the basic *elements of drama*—character, structure, setting, tone, and theme—together. As we have indicated in the fiction and poetry chapters called "The Whole Text," the basic elements of literary works are not really so distinct from one another, but instead work together to form a whole: character is shown in action, action or plot relates to setting, setting relates to tone, and theme involves all elements at once.

Before reading the four full-length plays that follow and analyzing their elements and how they interrelate, for a few moments let us look back at *Trifles*. The setting in Glaspell's play is the kitchen of a midwestern farmhouse in which a murder has occurred. Having the action unfold in the kitchen, traditionally considered the woman's part of the house, relates to the play's theme or central idea—that men and women have different views of reality, that women viewing "trifles," like details in a kitchen, can discover truths as well as or better than men who believe themselves to be concerned only with more important matters. The plot—the finding of the "trifling" bits of evidence that implicate Mrs. Wright in the murder of her husband and the suggestions of John Wright's abusive behavior that lead the women to band together in her defense and to suppress evidence that the men would think trifling—depends on the setting and embodies the theme. The characters of Mrs. Peters, the sheriff's wife, and of Mrs. Hale are interrelated with plot and theme. Mrs. Hale is the more observant of the women and less subordinate to her husband and a man's way of looking at things, while Mrs. Peters is more conventional, less willing to defy male authority. In convincing Mrs. Peters, Mrs. Hale and the evidence convince most viewers that Mrs. Wright had good reason to murder her husband.

As you can see, the "elements" of drama exist primarily in cooperation with one another, not in isolation. We cannot put the elements together to understand a text as a whole, however, unless we first have some knowledge of the terms, distinctions, issues, and range of effects involved in considering such elements. Let us prepare to read the plays that follow, then, by briefly considering some of these elements.

CHARACTER

Someone who appears in a work is called a **character,** the same word we use to refer to those qualities of mind, spirit, and behavior that make one individual different from every other. The identity of terms is not mere coincidence, for the creation of an imaginary character by author and reader is almost always based on some conception of human character and of individual differences.

Plays have a special engagement with character because of the visual and concrete manner in which they portray people on the stage. Stories or poems may comment on a character or editorialize rather directly, but plays have to *reveal* character—that is, let characters dramatize the kind of people they are by their own words and actions. Other characters may, of course, express opinions about a particular character, and our feelings as readers or members of the audience may be influenced by such rumor and innuendo, but all characters who appear on the stage or on the drama's page ultimately have to be credible in their own terms.

Not all plays focus on characters, though all involve characters and characterization. The reader, without the image of a living actor in view, must imaginatively create or re-create that image. Or, to be more precise, the reader must build, project, revise, compound, and complicate the image of the characters throughout the reading of the play, imagining what the actors, directors, and stage managers would provide in a staged performance. A good performance can suggest things the reader might have overlooked; many good performances over time may reveal a richness the single reader might have missed. But a good reading may also be richer than any one performance. Making sense of characters is an interpretive act that draws most immediately on what the text or performance tells us. As readers, we also draw on things we know or assume—what we infer from language, action, and reaction and what we already believe about human psychology and how a person's past affects present and future behavior. As viewers, in addition, we are guided by and interact with what the director, actors, and stage managers assume, believe, or know.

The titles of such plays as *Hamlet, Antigone,* and *Oedipus the King* imply that the play will center on a single character, and most plays fulfill the expectations created by their titles: the main character (or **protagonist**) is not only at the center of the action, but is also the chief object of the playwright's (and the reader's or audience's) concern. Defining the character of the protagonist (sometimes by comparison with a competitor, or **antagonist**) often becomes the consuming interest of the play, and the action seems designed to illustrate, or clarify, or develop that character, or sometimes to make him or her a complex, unfathomable, mysterious being. Even titles that do not use proper names can indicate focus on a single character or character type—*Death of a Salesman,* for example, which suggests that the emphasis is on a type rather than an individual.

Art always aims at the individual. What the artist fixes on his canvas is something he has seen at a certain spot, on a certain day, at a certain hour, with a colouring that will never be seen again. What the poet sings of is a certain mood which was his, and his alone, and will never return. . . . Nothing could be more unique than the character of Hamlet. Though he may resemble other men in some respects, it is clearly not on that account that he interests us most.

—HENRI BERGSON

Characterization in a play involves more than protagonists or antagonists, **heroes** and **heroines** or **villains.** To imagine the play vividly and make sense of the action, structure, and themes of the work, we must pay attention to the supporting or minor characters as well as to the leading figures: plays (like films) tend to emphasize the distinctions between major characters, whose actions and fate are the focus of the plot, and minor ones, who facilitate what happens. But characters can also be categorized by what they require of those who are to act them. There are demanding and challenging roles; juicy parts and dull or routine ones; roles for stars, character actors, comedians, and novices. Characters can also be categorized by their cultural identities (Jewish mothers, Romanian raven-haired beauties, pious frauds, social climbers). These sometimes verge on (or are subsumed by) **stereotypes:** characters based on conscious or unconscious cultural assumptions that sex, age, ethnic or national identification, occupation, marital status, and so on are predictably accompanied by certain character traits, actions, even values. Stereotypes, especially disparaging ones, can be a weakness in a play if they involve important characters who do not develop or become individualized, or whose motives are inadequately explored. However, no matter how individualized characters ultimately turn out to be, they often begin as some identifiable "type" of person that the audience will recognize and have certain expectations about.

Playwrights often overturn or modify these expectations of character to surprise a reader or audience, or to make the character a deeper, more interesting study. In *A Doll House,* Nora Helmer seems at first to be something of an airhead—spoiled, superficial in her emotional commitments, inept with money, incapable of taking care of herself. It is as if she is playing house, and (as the play's title suggests) the kind of artificial, miniaturized, let's-pretend environment appears to stand for the way she and her dominating husband play out their marriage and family. Attractive but fragile, Nora strikes us as a doll with little beyond surface appeal; her children seem to be merely props. Gradually, however, the greater depths of her mind and character become visible, and the contrasts with her seemingly more worldly and upright husband break down and then reverse. Similarly, the male characters in *Trifles* stereotype Mrs. Peters and Mrs. Hale as interested only in kitchen things and other "trifles" because they are women and, therefore, not serious thinkers. The thrust of the play overturns such a stereotype. In *A Streetcar Named Desire,* Stella may seem to typify the southern aristocrat who has lost wealth, status, and her "mansion" in the Civil War and is abused by the postwar, newly rich bourgeoisie, but she differs greatly from the stereotype.

No matter how magnificent a performance may be, the actors must make choices— how to read a line, what body language to use, what gestures, if any, or stage "business" to bring to bear. Of course this means choosing how *not* to perform a scene as well, though some other way may be equally true to the text and equally or similarly effective. A performance is an interpretation, a "reading" of the play one way rather than another.

How would you play Nora, for example? How would you suggest the greater complexity of her character? How early would you suggest it?

Every production of a play (and, in a sense, every performance) is an interpretation. Not just "adaptations"—setting Greek or Elizabethan plays in modern times and performing in modern dress, for example—but even productions and performances that seek the "heart" or "essence" of a play are "readings," diagnoses and analyses of just what is vital and essential in the play. Interpretation does not necessarily mean getting the author's "intention," however. John Malkovich, in the 1983–84 production of *Death of a Salesman,* did not project Biff Loman as an outgoing, successful, hail-fellow-well-met jock, though that is what Arthur Miller intended and how he wanted the part played. Malkovich saw Biff as only pretending, playing the part of the jock. Big-time athletes, he insisted, don't glad-hand people; they wait for people to come to them. The actor did not change the author's words, but by body language, stage business, and carriage suggested his own view of the character's nature.

In a play performed on the stage we in the audience have a role, but a somewhat reduced role: actors tell us that no two performances are exactly alike, in part due to the nature of the audience. However, the actors and director have made choices and limited our freedom to interpret. Though as readers we may be the poorer for lacking the inspired insights of a great director and great actors, we are the richer for not being subjected to someone else's choices, for not having to settle on one interpretation, for the opportunity to hold complex, even contradictory, possibilities in mind, to "change character" as the words shift, while retaining all the possibilities we have gone through.

STRUCTURE

An important part of any storyteller's task, whether the story is narrative or dramatic, is the invention, selection, and arrangement of the action. What will happen—including the introduction of characters, the unfolding of events, the development of theme, and the resolution of situational problems—cannot properly be called a full-scale **plot** until some principles of order and organization are introduced and questions of character, story line, and theme are somehow brought together.

Judge not the play before the play is done:

Her plot hath many changes.

—FRANCIS QUARLES

Plot in plays usually involves a conflict, and dramatic structure centrally concerns the presentation— quite literally the embodiment or fleshing out—of that conflict. A conflict whose outcome is never in doubt may have other kinds of interest, but it is not truly dramatic. In a dramatic conflict each of the opposing forces—whether one character versus another, one group of characters versus another group, the values of an individual versus those of a group or society or nature, or one idea or ideology versus another one—at one point or another seems likely to triumph. In *Hamlet,* for example, our interest in the struggle between Hamlet and Claudius depends on their being evenly matched. Claudius has possession of the throne and the queen, but Hamlet's relation to the late king and his popularity with the people offset his opponent's strengths. As we have seen in "Drama: Reading, Responding, Writing," the typical structure of a dramatic plot involves five stages in the progression of the conflict: exposition, rising action, climax, falling action, and conclusion, and even a short play such as *Trifles* contains all five stages.

There are other structural devices by which a play can be organized and made meaningful and effective. Thematic concerns, for example, often hold together varieties of characters and winding plots. In *The Piano Lesson,* for example, the desire to define family, ancestry, and identity brings together the various kinds of conflict—between races, classes, generations, genders, individuals, and ways of life. Careful and intricate plot calculations, in which difficult situations keep in tension the precise strengths and weaknesses of crucial characters, also structure plays in subtle but analyzable ways, as do theme, symbol, and setting. In *The Piano Lesson,* for example, the constant presence of the piano on stage reminds us of the family's past and its relationship to the concept of human beings as property. The struggle over whether it will be sold or remain where it is as a reminder of the past brings out different values in the characters—Boy Willie is content to let the past go if he can trade it for land of his own, while Berniece insists on the value of knowing the past and keeping its lesson alive in the present. The piano— even more than the ghost of Sutter—watches over the play as the various characters act out their present values and needs. In *A Doll House,* Mrs. Linde's complex past (and her involvement with Krogstad) makes possible the conflict between employment at the bank and personal values and also enables the later "solution" between Nora and Krogstad over the old loan. And Torvald's insistence on abstract principles (but actual dedication to the importance of moral appearances) leads both to the complications of the loan and, ultimately, Nora's liberation.

Another structural device involves **dramatic irony,** the fulfillment of a plan, action, or expectation in a surprising way, often the opposite of what the characters intend. One example occurs in *Trifles,* when the women keep noticing all the everyday things in the house while the official investigators—the men—keep looking for large and unusual things. Finding "nothing . . . but kitchen things," and thinking they have no clues at all, the men condescend to the women's concerns: "Women are used to worrying about trifles." It is, of course, the women's "trifles" that reveal the truth about the murder that the men's search for "significant" evidence misses. Of course, the women's "trifles" have revealed the truth about the murder, while the men's search for "significant" evidence has missed it. Similarly, in *A Doll House,* Nora's simple and innocent belief in the fairness of laws comes to demonstrate its superiority over the calculated legal morality of her husband.

Besides structures like dramatic irony or thematic coherence that pull parts of a play together, and the five structural stages that shape dramatic action, most plays also have formal divisions, such as acts and scenes. In the Greek theater, scenes were separated by choral odes (see, for example, *Oedipus the King*). In many French plays, a new scene begins with any significant entrance or exit. Many "classic" plays, like *Hamlet,* have five acts, but modern plays tend to have two or three acts. Formal divisions are the result of the content of the individual play—where sharp breaks can be emotionally effective by creating suspense or giving readers a relief from tension—or the conventions of the period: the expectation in the modern theater, for example, that audiences will have one or two intermissions in a public performance. Divisions may vary, from the one-act, one-scene play—such as *Sure Thing*—to such long multiact plays as Eugene O'Neill's *Mourning Becomes Electra.*

STAGES, SETS, AND SETTING

Most of us have been to a theater at one time or another, if only for a school play, and we know what a conventional modern stage—the proscenium stage—looks like. It's like a room with the wall missing between us and it. So when we read a modern play— that is, one written during the past two or three hundred years—and imagine it taking place before us, we think of its happening on such a stage. There are other types of modern stages—the **thrust stage,** where the audience sits around three sides of the major acting area, and the **arena stage,** where the audience sits all the way around the acting area and players make their entrances and their exits through the auditorium—but most plays are staged on a proscenium stage. Twelve of the sixteen plays in this text can readily be imagined to be taking place on such a stage. The two Shakespeare plays and the two Greek plays here were staged quite differently, and if we imagine them on the proscenium stage, at times we will likely be a bit confused. In the Greek theater, the audience sat on a raised semicircle of seats **(amphitheater)** halfway around a circular area **(orchestra)** used primarily for dancing by the chorus. At the back of the orchestra was the **skene,** or stage house, representing the palace or temple before which the action took place. Shakespeare's stage, in contrast, basically involved a rectangular area built inside one end of a generally round enclosure, so that the audience was on three sides of the principal acting area. There were additional acting areas on either side of this stage, as well as a recessed area at the back of the stage (which could represent Gertrude's chamber in *Hamlet,* for example) and an upper acting area (which could serve as Juliet's balcony).

The conventions of dramatic writing and stage production have, of course, changed considerably since the advent of theater. These conventions involve, for instance, the way playwrights convey the notion of place. Usually the stage represents a particular place, or **setting.** The audience knows that the stage is a stage, but they accept it as a public square or a room in a castle or an empty road. In *Trifles,* remember, we accept the stage as a kitchen in a midwest farmhouse. Likewise, *Oedipus the King* takes place entirely before the palace at Thebes. Following the general convention of Greek drama, the play never changes place. When the action demands the presence of Teiresias, for example, the scene does not shift to him, but instead escorts bring him to the front of the palace.

In Shakespeare's theater the conventions of place are quite different: the acting area does not represent a specific place, but assumes a temporary identity according to the characters who inhabit it, their costumes, and their speeches. At the opening of *Hamlet* we know we are at a sentry station because a man dressed as a soldier challenges two others. By line 15, we know that we are in Denmark because the actors profess to be "liegemen to the Dane." At the end of the scene the actors leave the stage and in a sense take the sentry station with them. Shortly a group of people dressed in court costumes and a man and a woman wearing crowns appear. As a theater audience, we must surmise, from costumes and dialogue, that the acting area has now become a "chamber of state"; as readers of the text, we could also infer the change of place from the identity of the characters and their words, but our text provides more information than a performance can, identifying the changed place in a stage direction. The changes of scene in modern plays involve lowering a curtain or darkening the stage while different sets and props are arranged. **Sets** (the design, decoration, and scenery) and **props** (articles or objects used on the stage) vary greatly in modern productions of plays from all periods. Sometimes space is merely suggested—a circle of sand at one end of the stage, a blank wall behind—but typically a set involves some more or less realistic aids to the imagination. The farmhouse kitchen setting in *Trifles,* for example, is represented by a door leading to the outside of the house, another leading to the upstairs, and a third leading to another room. There must be at least a sink, a cupboard, a stove, a small table, a large kitchen table, and a rocking chair.

Dramatic conventions represent time and the changing of times as well as space and the changing of space, and these conventions, too, have changed over the years. Renaissance commentators on classical drama argued that in order to insure maximum dramatic impact, the action of a play should represent a very short time—sometimes as short as the actual performance (two or three hours), and certainly no longer than a single day. This **unity of time,** one of the so-called **classical unities,** impels a dramatist to select the moment when a stable situation should change and to fill in the necessary prior details by exposition or even by some more elaborate device, such as the enacted dreams and memories in *Death of a Salesman.* The action from the beginning to the end of the play thus can represent a rather long time span, even years, in a very short period of actual time.

Even classical drama, with its restricted time span, has conventions to mark the passing of represented time when it is supposed to pass at a greater rate than that of viewing or reading time. The choral odes in *Oedipus the King* are an example of one convention for representing the passage of time.

In Elizabethan drama the break between scenes covers whatever time is necessary without a formal device like the choral odes. Sometimes the time is short, like the break between Hamlet's departure to see his mother at the end of act 3, scene 2, and the entrance of the king with Rosencrantz and Guildenstern at the beginning of the next scene; at other times the elapsed time might be as long as that between scenes 4 and 5 of act 4, during which the news of Polonius's death reaches Paris and Laertes returns to Denmark and there rallies his friends.

Once again, we must remember, drama is both a literary and a performed art, and a play exists separately on page and stage. In reading plays, we use our imaginations much as we do when portraying to ourselves the unfolding of action in stories, but there is a difference. When we read stories, we have a mediator, a narrator to guide us. When we read plays, we know that in another manifestation they are staged, produced, performed, and that another set of consciousnesses would mediate if we were viewing the plays in performance. As readers, we take all the roles ourselves and do not portion them out to actors; we set the stage in our own minds. We become, in effect, our own producers, directors, and actors, but with the reader's latitude to keep multiple possibilities in mind. We become not just viewers of a staged production created by an intermediary, but imagining readers of a play—staging and restaging it in the mind's eye, mediated by our producer-selves.

TONE

It is difficult to define, describe, and, especially, demonstrate **tone**. A dictionary definition—"style or manner of expression in writing"—while "true," is so general or vague ("style," "manner," and "expression" can all use their own definitions) that it does not help us very much when we deal with the specifics of a text. We are more used to the concept of tone in spoken rather than written language, however; we think we know what "tone of voice" is, and we can identify someone's tone of voice when he or she says something to us. Because we often associate tone with dialogue, then, it is more crucial, or at least more of a presence, in drama than in other genres. The actor—and the reader, especially one who wants to render the words of a play aloud—must infer from the playwright's written language just how to read a line, what "tone of voice" to use. For a similar reason, tone is also more subjective, its nuances or subtleties a "negotiation" between the actor/reader and the author/playwright. The power of the reader/actor has limits, though: it would be difficult without parody to read Hamlet's famous soliloquy "To be or not to be" as comedy, for example. At times the playwright will help out the actor (or dictate to him or her) with a stage direction. In *Trifles,* for example, when the sheriff hears the women discussing the quilt Mrs. Wright had been making, he tells the other men, "They wonder if she was going to quilt or just knot it!" He clearly mocks the women, and the stage direction that follows suggests his tone and its effect: "[*The men laugh, the women look abashed.*]" At the climax of the play, Mrs. Peters finds the strangled bird that suggests Mrs. Wright's motivation in strangling her husband. As the men approach—they have been fruitlessly searching the barn for real or "untrifling" clues—Mrs. Hale hides the bird under the quilt pieces. The County Attorney says, "Well ladies, have you decided whether she was going to quilt it or knot it?" The dramatic irony here—the women and their trifles have figured out what happened, the men and their "serious" search have not—is underscored by the stage direction telling the actor how to read the line in such a way as to emphasize the irony: "[*As one turning from serious things to little pleasantries.*]"

Dramatic irony, where the reader or audience knows what the character does not, is relative easy to detect; **verbal irony,** especially without stage directions to help, can be fairly subtle and easy to miss. Near the end of *A Doll House,* for example, Torvald says, without a trace of intended irony: "You loved me the way a wife ought to love her husband. It's simply the means that you couldn't judge. But you think I love you any the less for not knowing how to handle your affairs? No, no—just lean on me; I'll guide you and teach you. I wouldn't be a man if this feminine helplessness didn't make you twice as attractive to me" (page 1146). By this point in the play, we are way ahead of him, seeing how helpless and hopeless he really is, and we understand, as he does not, Nora's superiority to him. To hear him mouth sexist platitudes only underscores his fundamental stupidity and lack of perception; we hear in his words a meaning he does not mean or hear for himself. The tone thus alters the meaning of the words. Indeed, it is chiefly when, as in this case, a discrepancy exists between the tone and the normal meaning of the words that tone is most identifiable—and important for our understanding. At other times, however, tone reinforces the language, action, and situation of a whole play or a major portion of it.

THEME

Tone may modulate the meaning of a few words, dominate an entire act, or pervade virtually an entire play. **Theme**—usually defined as a generalized or abstract paraphrase of the subject of a work—is by its very nature the most comprehensive of the elements, embracing, as its definition suggests, the entire work. In a very real sense theme is not actually part of the work, but is abstracted from the work by the readers or audience. Since we, as interpreters, infer the theme and define it in our own words, we understandably often disagree about nuances of emphasis or phrasing or even entire conceptions. The theme of *The Children's Hour,* for example, involves questions of innocence and knowledge. Initially, the apparent innocence of children turns into ugly, "knowing" revelations motivated entirely by selfishness and retribution. Mary's manipulativeness seems all the more corrupt and surprising because she is so young, and (indeed) she gets away with her revelations largely because some naïve adults assume a child to be innocent and incapable of malicious feigning. We feel enormous relief when she is unmasked, though subsequent revelations call into question not only the assumptions of most characters in the play but also our assumptions and sympathies. The ending of *A Doll House* similarly bends the theme: instead of the way that irresponsibility and naïveté can lead to exposure and near financial and emotional disaster, the play suddenly considers instinctive feelings and actions as they lead to freedom from crippling secrets and rigid moral presuppositions.

It is ironic (there's that word again) that because theme is pervasive, involving the entire work, we can say relatively little about it in general—that is, without discussing specific plays. The other elements—character, structure, setting, tone, as well as imagery, symbol, and so on—all contribute to this overarching element. So when we discuss theme, we must discuss the other elements and the specific details of the text.

LILLIAN HELLMAN

The Children's Hour

For D. Hammett with thanks

CHARACTERS

PEGGY ROGERS	MARY TILFORD
MRS. LILY MORTAR	KAREN WRIGHT
EVELYN MUNN	MARTHA DOBIE
HELEN BURTON	DOCTOR JOSEPH CARDIN
LOIS FISHER	AGATHA
CATHERINE	MRS. AMELIA TILFORD
ROSALIE WELLS	A GROCERY BOY

SCENE

ACT ONE
Living room of the Wright-Dobie School. Late afternoon in April.

ACT TWO
Scene I. Living room at Mrs. Tilford's. A few hours later.
Scene II. The same. Later that evening.

ACT THREE
The same as Act One. November.

ACT I

SCENE: *A room in the Wright-Dobie School for girls, a converted farm-house eighteen miles from the town of Lancet. It is a comfortable, unpretentious room used as an afternoon study-room and at all other times as the living room.*

A large door Left Center faces the audience. There is a single door Right. Against both back walls are bookcases. A large desk is at Right; a table, two sofas, and eight or ten chairs.

It is early in an afternoon in April.

AT RISE: MRS. LILY MORTAR *is sitting in a large chair Right Center, with her head back and her eyes closed. She is a plump, florid woman of forty-five with obviously touched-up hair. Her clothes are too fancy for a classroom.*

Seven girls, from twelve to fourteen years old, are informally grouped on chairs and sofa. Six of them are sewing with no great amount of industry on pieces of white material. One of the others, EVELYN MUNN, *is using her scissors to trim the hair of* ROSALIE, *who sits, nervously, in front of her. She has* ROSALIE'S *head bent back at an awkward angle and is enjoying herself.*

The eighth girl, PEGGY ROGERS, *is sitting in a higher chair than the others. She is reading aloud from a book. She is bored and she reads in a singsong, tired voice.*

PEGGY: [*Reading.*][1] "It is twice blest; it blesseth him that gives and him that takes: 'tis mightiest in the mightiest; it becomes the throned monarch better than his crown; his sceptre shows the force of temporal power, the attribute to awe and majesty, wherein . . ." [MRS. MORTAR *suddenly opens her eyes and stares at the haircutting. The children make efforts to warn* EVELYN. PEGGY *raises her voice until she is shouting.*] "doth sit the dread and fear of kings; but mercy is above . . ."

MRS. MORTAR: Evelyn! What are you doing?

EVELYN: [*Inanely. She lisps.*] Uh—nothing, Mrs. Mortar.

MRS. MORTAR: You are certainly doing something. You are ruining the scissors for one thing.

PEGGY: [*Loudly.*] "But mercy is above. It . . ."

MRS. MORTAR: Just a moment, Peggy. It is very unfortunate that you girls cannot sit quietly with your sewing and drink in the immortal words of the immortal bard. [*She sighs.*] Evelyn, go back to your sewing.

EVELYN: I can't get the hem thtraight. Honeth, I've been trying for three weekth, but I jutht can't do it.

MRS. MORTAR: Helen, please help Evelyn with the hem.

HELEN: [*Rises, holding up the garment* EVELYN *has been working on. It is soiled and shapeless, and so much has been cut off that it is now hardly large enough for a child of five. Giggling.*] She can't ever wear *that,* Mrs. Mortar.

MRS. MORTAR: [*Vaguely.*] Well, try to do something with it. Make some handkerchiefs or something. Be clever about it. Women must learn these tricks. [*To* PEGGY.] Continue. "Mightiest in the mightiest."

PEGGY: " 'Tis mightiest in the mightiest; it becomes the throned monarch better than his crown; his sceptre—his sceptre shows the force of temporal power, the attribute to awe and majesty, wherein—"

LOIS: [*From the back of the room chants softly and monotonously through the previous speech.*] Ferebam, ferebas, ferebat, ferebamus, ferebatis, fere, fere—

CATHERINE: [*Two seats away, the book propped in front of her.*] Fere*bant.*

LOIS: Ferebamus, ferebatis, fere*bant.*

MRS. MORTAR: Who's doing that?

PEGGY: [*The noise ceases. She hurries on.*] "Wherein doth sit the dread and fear of kings; but mercy is above this sceptred sway, it is enthroned in the hearts of kings, it is an attribute to God himself—"

MRS. MORTAR: [*Sadly, reproachfully.*] Peggy, can't you imagine yourself as Portia? Can't you read the lines with some feeling, some pity? [*Dreamily.*] Pity. Ah! As Sir Henry said to me many's the time, pity makes the actress. Now, why can't *you* feel pity?

1. From Shakespeare's *Merchant of Venice.*

PEGGY: I guess I feel pity.

LOIS: Ferebamus, ferebatis, fere—fere—fere—

CATHERINE: Fere*bant*, stupid.

MRS. MORTAR: How many people in this room are talking? Peggy, read the line again. I'll give you the cue.

PEGGY: What's a cue?

MRS. MORTAR: A cue is a line or word given the actor or actress to remind them of their next speech.

HELEN: [*Softly.*] To remind *him* or *her.*

ROSALIE: [*A fattish girl with glasses.*] Weren't you ever in the movies, Mrs. Mortar?

MRS. MORTAR: I had many offers, my dear. But the cinema is a shallow art. It has no—no—[*Vaguely.*] no fourth dimension. Now, Peggy, if you would only try to submerge yourself in this problem. You are pleading for the life of a man. [*She rises and there are faint sighs from the girls, who stare at her with blank, bored faces. She recites hammily, with gestures.*] "But mercy is above this sceptred sway; it is enthroned in the hearts of kings, it is an attribute to God himself; and earthly power doth then show likest God's when mercy seasons justice."

LOIS: [*almost singing it.*] Utor, fruor, fungor, potior, and vescor take the dative.

CATHERINE: Take the *ablative.*

LOIS: Oh, dear. Utor, fruor, fung—

MRS. MORTAR: [*To* LOIS, *with sarcasm.*] You have something to tell the class?

LOIS: [*Apologetically.*] We've got a Latin exam this afternoon.

MRS. MORTAR: And you intend to occupy the sewing and elocution hour learning what should have been learnt yesterday?

CATHERINE: [*Wearily.*] It takes her more than yesterday to learn it.

MRS. MORTAR: Well, I cannot allow you to interrupt us like this.

CATHERINE: But we're finished sewing.

LOIS: [*Admiringly.*] I bet you were good at Latin, Mrs. Mortar.

MRS. MORTAR: [*Conciliated.*] Long ago, my dear, long ago. Now, take your book over by the window and don't disturb our enjoyment of Shakespeare. [CATHERINE *and* LOIS *rise, go to window, stand mumbling and gesturing.*] Let us go back again. "It is an attribute of—" [*At this point the door opens far enough to let* MARY TILFORD, *clutching a slightly faded bunch of wild flowers, squeeze cautiously in. She is fourteen, neither pretty nor ugly. She is an undistinguished-looking girl, except for the sullenly dissatisfied expression on her face.*] "And earthly power doth then show likest God's when mercy seasons justice. We do pray for mercy, and that same prayer doth teach—"

PEGGY: [*Happily.*] You've skipped three lines.

MRS. MORTAR: In my entire career I've never missed a line.

PEGGY: But you did skip three lines. [*Goes to* MRS. MORTAR *with book.*] See?

MRS. MORTAR: [*Seeing* MARY *sidling along wall toward other end of the room, turns to her to avoid* PEGGY *and the book.*] Mary!

HELEN: [*In whisper to* MARY.] You're going to catch it now.

MRS. MORTAR: Mary!

MARY: Yes, Mrs. Mortar?

MRS. MORTAR: This is a pretty time to be coming to your sewing class, I must say.

Even if you have no interest in your work you might at least remember that you owe me a little courtesy. Courtesy is breeding. Breeding is an excellent thing. [*Turns to class.*] Always remember that.

ROSALIE: Please, Mrs. Mortar, can I write that down?

MRS. MORTAR: Certainly. Suppose you all write it down.

PEGGY: But we wrote it down last week.

[MARY *giggles.*]

MRS. MORTAR: Mary, I am still awaiting your explanation. Where have you been?

MARY: I took a walk.

MRS. MORTAR: So you took a walk. And may I ask, young lady, are we in the habit of taking walks when we should be at our classes?

MARY: I am sorry, Mrs. Mortar, I went to get you these flowers. I thought you would like them and I didn't know it would take so long to pick them.

MRS. MORTAR: [*Flattered.*] Well, well.

MARY: [*Almost in tears.*] You were telling us last week how much you liked flowers, and I thought that I would bring you some and—

MRS. MORTAR: That was very sweet of you, Mary; I always like thoughtfulness. But you must not allow anything to interfere with your classes. Now run along, dear, and get a vase and some water to put my flowers in. [MARY *turns, sticks out her tongue at* HELEN, *says:* "A-a-a," *and exits Left.*] You may put that book away, Peggy. I am sure your family need never worry about your going on the stage.

PEGGY: I don't want to go on the stage. I want to be a lighthouse-keeper's wife.

MRS. MORTAR: Well, I certainly hope you won't read to him.

[*The laughter of the class pleases her.* PEGGY *sits down among the other girls, who are making a great show of doing nothing.* MRS. MORTAR *returns to her chair, puts her head back, closes her eyes.*]

CATHERINE: How much longer, O Cataline, are you going to abuse our patience? [*To* LOIS.] Now translate it, and for goodness' sakes try to get it right this time.

MRS. MORTAR: [*For no reason.*] "One master passion in the breast, like Aaron's serpent, swallows all the rest."

[*She and* LOIS *are murmuring during* KAREN WRIGHT'S *entrance.* KAREN *is an attractive woman of twenty-eight, casually pleasant in manner, without sacrifice of warmth or dignity. She smiles at the girls, goes to the desk. With her entrance there is an immediate change in the manner of the girls: they are fond of her and they respect her. She gives* MORTAR, *whose quotation has reached her, an annoyed look.*]

LOIS: "Quo usque tandem a*butere*. . . ."

KAREN: [*Automatically.*] "Abutere." [*Opens drawer in desk.*] What's happened to your hair, Rosalie?

ROSALIE: It got cut, Miss Wright.

KAREN: [*Smiling.*] I can see that. A new style? Looks as though it has holes in it.

EVELYN: [*Giggling.*] I didn't mean to do it that bad, Mith Wright, but Rothalie'th got funny hair. I thaw a picture in the paper, and I wath trying to do it that way.

ROSALIE: [*Feels her hair, looks pathetically at* KAREN.] Oh, what shall I do, Miss Wright? [*Gesturing.*] It's long here, and it's short here and—

KAREN: Never mind. Come up to my room later and I'll see if I can fix it for you.

MRS. MORTAR: And hereafter we'll have no more haircutting.

KAREN: Helen, have you found your bracelet?

HELEN: No, I haven't, and I've looked everywhere.

KAREN: Have another look. It must be in your room somewhere.

[MARY *comes in Right, with her flowers in a vase. When she sees* KAREN, *she loses some of her assurance.* KAREN *looks at the flowers in surprise.*]

MARY: Good afternoon, Miss Wright. [*Sits down, looks at* KAREN, *who is staring hard at the flowers.*]

KAREN: Hello, Mary.

MRS. MORTAR: [*Fluttering around.*] Peggy has been reading Portia for us.

[PEGGY *sighs.*]

KAREN: [*Smiling.*] Peggy doesn't like Portia?

MRS. MORTAR: I don't think she quite appreciates it, but—

KAREN: [*Patting* PEGGY *on the head.*] Well, I didn't either. I don't think I do yet. Where'd you get those flowers, Mary?

MRS. MORTAR: She picked them for me. [*Hurriedly.*] It made her a little late to class, but she heard me say I loved flowers, and she went to get them for me. [*With a sigh.*] The first wild flowers of the season.

KAREN: But not the very first, are they, Mary?

MARY: I don't know.

KAREN: Where did you get them?

MARY: Near Conway's cornfield, I think.

KAREN: It wasn't necessary to go so far. There was a bunch exactly like this in the garbage can this morning.

MRS. MORTAR: [*After a second.*] Oh, I can't believe it! What a nasty thing to do! [*To* MARY.] And I suppose you have just as fine an excuse for being an hour late to breakfast this morning, and last week— [*To* KAREN.] I haven't wanted to tell you these things before, but—

KAREN: [*Hurriedly, as a bell rings off stage.*] There's the bell.

LOIS: [*Walking toward door.*] Ad, ab, ante, in, de, inter, con, post, præ— [*Looks up at* KAREN.] I *can't* seem to remember the rest.

KAREN: Præ, pro, sub, super. Don't worry, Lois. You'll come out all right. [LOIS *smiles, exits.* MARY *attempts to make a quick exit.*] Wait a minute, Mary. [*Reluctantly* MARY *turns back as the girls file out.* KAREN *moves the small chairs, clearing the room as she talks.*] Mary, I've had the feeling—and I don't think I'm wrong—that the girls here were happy; that they liked Miss Dobie and me, that they liked the school. Do you think that's true?

MARY: Miss Wright, I have to get my Latin book.

KAREN: I thought it was true until you came here a year ago. I don't think you're very happy here, and I'd like to find out why. [*Looks at* MARY, *waits for an answer, gets none, shakes her head.*] Why, for example, do you find it necessary to lie to us so often?

MARY: [*Without looking up.*] I'm not lying. I went out walking and I saw the flowers and they looked pretty and I didn't know it was so late.

KAREN: [*Impatiently.*] Stop it, Mary! I'm not interested in hearing that foolish story again. I *know* you got the flowers out of the garbage can. What I do want to know is why you feel you have to lie out of it.

MARY: [*Beginning to whimper.*] I *did* pick the flowers near Conway's. You never believe me. You believe everybody but me. It's always like that. Everything I say you fuss at me about. Everything I do is wrong.

KAREN: You know that isn't true. [*Goes to* MARY, *puts her arm around her, waits until the sobbing has stopped.*] Look, Mary, look at me. [*Raises* MARY'S *face with her hand.*] Let's try to understand each other. If you feel that you *have* to take a walk, or that you just *can't* come to class, or that you'd like to go into the village by yourself, come and tell me—I'll try and understand. [*Smiles.*] I don't say that I'll always agree that you should do exactly what you want to do, but I've had feelings like that, too—everybody has—and I won't be unreasonable about yours. But this way, this kind of lying you do, makes everything wrong.

MARY: [*Looking steadily at* KAREN.] I got the flowers near Conway's cornfield.

KAREN: [*Looks at* MARY, *sighs, moves back toward desk and stands there for a moment.*] Well, there doesn't seem to be any other way with you; you'll have to be punished. Take your recreation periods alone for the next two weeks. No horseback-riding and no hockey. Don't leave the school grounds for any reason whatsoever. Is that clear?

MARY: [*Carefully.*] Saturday, too?

KAREN: Yes.

MARY: But you said I could go to the boat-races.

KAREN: I'm sorry, but you can't go.

MARY: I'll tell my grandmother. I'll tell her how everybody treats me here and the way I get punished for every little thing I do. I'll tell her, I'll—

MRS. MORTAR: Why, I'd slap her hands!

KAREN: [*Turning back from door, ignoring* MRS. MORTAR'S *speech. To* MARY.] Go upstairs, Mary.

MARY: I don't feel well.

KAREN: [*Wearily.*] Go upstairs now.

MARY: I've got a pain. I've had it all morning. It hurts right here. [*Pointing vaguely in the direction of her heart.*] Really it does.

KAREN: Ask Miss Dobie to give you some hot water and bicarbonate of soda.

MARY: It's a bad pain. I've never had it before.

KAREN: I don't think it can be very serious.

MARY: My heart! It's my heart! It's stopping or something. I can't breathe. [*She takes a long breath and falls awkwardly to the floor.*]

KAREN: [*Sighs, shakes her head, kneels beside* MARY. *To* MRS. MORTAR.] Ask Martha to phone Joe.

MRS. MORTAR: [*Going out.*] Do you think—? Heart trouble is very serious in a child.

[KAREN *picks* MARY *up from the floor and carries her off Right. After a moment* MARTHA DOBIE *enters Center. She is about the same age as* KAREN. *She is a nervous, high-strung woman.*]

KAREN: [*Enters Right.*] Did you get Joe?

MARTHA: [*Nodding.*] What happened to her? She was perfectly well a few hours ago.

KAREN: She probably still is. I told her she couldn't go to the boat-races and she had a heart attack.

MARTHA: Where is she?

KAREN: In there. Mortar's with her.

MARTHA: Anything really wrong with her?

KAREN: I doubt it. [*Sits down at desk and begins to mark papers.*] She's a problem, that kid. Her latest trick was kidding your aunt out of a sewing lesson with those faded flowers we threw out. Then she threatened to go to her grandmother with some tale about being mistreated.

MARTHA: And, please God, Grandma would believe her and take her away.

KAREN: Which would give the school a swell black eye. But we ought to do something.

MARTHA: How about having a talk with Mrs. Tilford?

KAREN: [*Smiling*] You want to do it? [MARTHA *shakes her head.*] I hate to do it. She's been so nice to us. [*Shrugging her shoulders.*] Anyway, it wouldn't do any good. She's too crazy about Mary to see her faults very clearly—and the kid knows it.

MARTHA: How about asking Joe to say something to her? She'd listen to him.

KAREN: That would be admitting that we can't do the job ourselves.

MARTHA: Well, we can't, and we might as well admit it. We've tried everything we can think of. She's had more attention than any other three kids put together. And we still haven't the faintest idea what goes on inside her head.

KAREN: She's a strange girl.

MARTHA: That's putting it mildly.

KAREN: [*Laughs.*] It's funny. We always talk about the child as if she were a grown woman.

MARTHA: It's not so funny. There's something the matter with the kid. That's been true ever since the first day she came. She causes trouble here; she's bad for the other girls. I don't know what it is—it's a feeling I've got that it's wrong somewhere—

KAREN: All right, all right, we'll talk it over with Joe. Now what about our other pet nuisance?

MARTHA: [*Laughs.*] My aunt the actress? What's she been up to now?

KAREN: Nothing unusual. Last night at dinner she was telling the girls about the time she lost her trunks in Butte, Montana, and how she gave her best performance of Rosalind during a hurricane. Today in the kitchen you could hear her on what Sir Henry[2] said to her.

---

2. The esteemed English actor and theater manager Sir Henry Irving (1838–1905). *Rosalind:* The heroine of Shakespeare's *As You Like It.*

MARTHA: Wait until she does Hedda Gabler[3] standing on a chair. Sir Henry taught her to do it that way. He said it was a test of great acting.

KAREN: You must have had a gay childhood.

MARTHA: [Bitterly.] Oh, I did. I did, indeed. God, how I used to hate all that—

KAREN: Couldn't we get rid of her soon, Martha? I hate to make it hard on you, but she really ought not to be here.

MARTHA: [After a moment.] I know.

KAREN: We can scrape up enough money to send her away. Let's do it.

MARTHA: [Goes to her, affectionately pats her head.] You've been very patient about it. I'm sorry and I'll talk to her today. It'll probably be a week or two before she can be ready to leave. Is that all right?

KAREN: Of course. [Looks at her watch.] Did you get Joe himself on the phone?

MARTHA: He was already on his way. Isn't he always on his way over here?

KAREN: [Laughs.] Well, I'm going to marry him some day, you know.

MARTHA: [Looking at her.] You haven't talked of marriage for a long time.

KAREN: I've talked of it with Joe.

MARTHA: Then you are thinking about it—soon?

KAREN: Perhaps when the term is over. By that time we ought to be out of debt, and the school should be paying for itself.

MARTHA: [Nervously playing with a book on the table.] Then we won't be taking our vacation together?

KAREN: Of course we will. The three of us.

MARTHA: I had been looking forward to some place by the lake—just you and me— the way we used to at college.

KAREN: [Cheerfully.] Well, now there will be three of us. That'll be fun, too.

MARTHA: [After a pause.] Why haven't you told me this before?

KAREN: I'm not telling you anything we haven't talked about often.

MARTHA: But you're talking about it as soon now.

KAREN: I'm glad to be able to. I've been in love with Joe a long time. [MARTHA crosses to window and stands looking out, her back to KAREN. KAREN finishes marking papers and rises.] It's a big day for the school. Rosalie's finally put an "l" in could.

MARTHA: [In a dull, bitter tone, not turning from window.] You really are going to leave, aren't you?

KAREN: I'm not going to leave, and you know it. Why do you say things like that? We agreed a long time ago that my marriage wasn't going to make any difference to the school.

MARTHA: But it will. You know it will. It can't help it.

KAREN: That's nonsense. Joe doesn't want me to give up here.

MARTHA: [Turning from window.] I don't understand you. It's been so damned hard building this thing up, slaving and going without things to make ends meet— think of having a winter coat without holes in the lining again!—and now when we're getting on our feet, you're all ready to let it go to hell.

KAREN: This is a silly argument, Martha. Let's quit it. You haven't listened to a word I've said. I'm not getting married tomorrow, and when I do, it's not going to interfere with my work here. You're making something out of nothing.

3. Titular heroine of a famous play by Henrik Ibsen.

MARTHA: It's going to be hard going on alone afterward.

KAREN: For God's sake, do you expect me to give up my marriage?

MARTHA: I don't mean that, but it's so—

[*Door Center opens and* DOCTOR JOSEPH CARDIN *comes in. He is a large, pleasant-looking, carelessly dressed man of about thirty-five.*]

CARDIN: Hello, darling. Hi, Martha. What's the best news?

MARTHA: Hello, Joe.

KAREN: We tried to get you on the phone. Come in and look at your little cousin.

CARDIN: Sure. What's the matter with her now? I stopped at Vernie's on the way over to look at that little black bull he bought. He's a baby! There's going to be plenty of good breeding done in these hills.

KAREN: You'd better come and see her. She says she has a pain in her heart. [*Goes out Right.*]

CARDIN: [*Stopping to light a cigarette.*] Our little Mary pops up in every day's dispatches.

MARTHA: [*Impatiently.*] Go and see her. Heart attacks are nothing to play with.

CARDIN [*Looks at her.*] Never played with one in my life. [*Exits Right.*]

[MARTHA *walks around room and finally goes to stare out window.* MRS. MORTAR *enters Right.*]

MRS. MORTAR: *I* was asked to leave the room. [MARTHA *pays no attention.*] It seems that I'm not wanted in the room during the examination.

MARTHA: [*Over her shoulder.*] What difference does it make?

MRS. MORTAR: What difference does it make? Why, it was a deliberate snub.

MARTHA: There's very little pleasure in watching a man use a stethoscope.

MRS. MORTAR: Isn't it natural that the child should have me with her? Isn't it natural that an older woman should be present? [*No answer.*] Very well, if you are so thick-skinned that you don't resent these things—

MARTHA: What are you talking about? Why, in the name of heaven, should *you* be with her?

MRS. MORTAR: It—it's customary for an older woman to be present during an examination.

MARTHA: [*Laughs.*] Tell that to Joe. Maybe he'll give you a job as duenna for his office.

MRS. MORTAR: [*Reminiscently.*] It was I who saved Delia Lampert's life the time she had that heart attack in Buffalo. We almost lost her that time. Poor Delia! We went over to London together. She married Robert Laffonne. Not seven months later he left her and ran away with Eve Cloun, who was playing the Infant Phenomenon[4] in Birmingham—

MARTHA: Console yourself. If you've seen one heart attack, you've seen them all.

MRS. MORTAR: So you don't resent your aunt being snubbed and humiliated?

MARTHA: Oh, Aunt Lily!

MRS. MORTAR: Karen is consistently rude to me, and you know it.

---

4. Byname of the fictional child performer Ninetta Crummles in Charles Dickens's 1839 novel *Nicholas Nickleby*, which was adapted for the stage.

MARTHA: I know that she is very polite to you, and—what's more important—very patient.

MRS. MORTAR: Patient with me? *I*, who have worked my fingers to the bone!

MARTHA: Don't tell yourself that too often, Aunt Lilly; you'll come to believe it.

MRS. MORTAR: I *know* it's true. Where could you have gotten a woman of my reputation to give these children voice lessons, elocution lessons? Patient with me! Here I've donated my services—

MARTHA: I was under the impression you were being paid.

MRS. MORTAR: That small thing! I used to earn twice that for one performance.

MARTHA: The gilded days. It was very extravagant of them to pay you so much. [*Suddenly tired of the whole thing.*] You're not very happy here, are you, Aunt Lily?

MRS. MORTAR: Satisfied enough, I guess, for a poor relation.

MARTHA: [*Makes a motion of distaste.*] But you don't like the school or the farm or—

MRS. MORTAR: I told you at the beginning you shouldn't have bought a place like this. Burying yourself on a farm! You'll regret it.

MARTHA: We like it here. [*After a moment.*] Aunt Lily, you've talked about London for a long time. Would you like to go over?

MRS. MORTAR: [*With a sigh.*] It's been twenty years, and I shall never live to see it again.

MARTHA: Well, you can go any time you like. We can spare the money now, and it will do you a lot of good. You pick out the boat you want and I'll get the passage. [*She has been talking rapidly, anxious to end the whole thing.*] Now that's all fixed. You'll have a grand time seeing all your old friends, and if you live sensibly I ought to be able to let you have enough to get along on. [*She begins to gather books, notebooks, and pencils.*]

MRS. MORTAR: [*Slowly.*] So you want me to leave?

MARTHA: That's not the way to put it. You've wanted to go ever since I can remember.

MRS. MORTAR: You're trying to get rid of me.

MARTHA: That's it. We don't want you around when we dig up the buried treasure.

MRS. MORTAR: So? You're turning me out? At my age! Nice, grateful girl you are.

MARTHA: Oh, my God, how can anybody deal with you? You're going where you want to go, and we'll be better off alone. That suits everybody. You complain about the farm, you complain about the school, you complain about Karen, and now you have what you want and you're still looking for something to complain about.

MRS. MORTAR: [*With dignity.*] Please do not raise your voice.

MARTHA: You ought to be glad I don't do worse.

MRS. MORTAR: I absolutely refuse to be shipped off three thousand miles away. I'm not going to England. I shall go back to the stage. I'll write to my agents tomorrow, and as soon as they have something good for me—

MARTHA: The truth is I'd like you to leave soon. The three of us can't live together, and it doesn't make any difference whose fault it is.

MRS. MORTAR: You wish me to go tonight?

MARTHA: Don't act, Aunt Lily. Go as soon as you've found a place you like. I'll put the money in the bank for you tomorrow.

MRS. MORTAR: You think I'd take your money? I'd rather scrub floors first.

MARTHA: I imagine you'll change your mind.

MRS. MORTAR: I should have known by this time that the wise thing is to stay out of your way when *he's* in the house.

MARTHA: What are you talking about now?

MRS. MORTAR: Never mind. I should have known better. You always take your spite out on me.

MARTHA: Spite? [*Impatiently.*] Oh, don't let's have any more of this today. I'm tired. I've been working since six o'clock this morning.

MRS. MORTAR: Any day that he's in the house is a bad day.

MARTHA: When *who* is in the house?

MRS. MORTAR: Don't think you're fooling me, young lady. I wasn't born yesterday.

MARTHA: Aunt Lily, the amount of disconnected unpleasantness that goes on in your head could keep a psychologist busy for years. Now go take your nap.

MRS. MORTAR: I know what I know. Every time that man comes into this house, you have a fit. It seems like you just can't stand the idea of them being together. God knows what you'll do when they get married. You're jealous of him, that's what it is.

MARTHA: [*Her voice is tense and the previous attitude of good-natured irritation is gone.*] I'm very fond of Joe, and you know it.

MRS. MORTAR: You're fonder of Karen, and I know that. And it's unnatural, just as unnatural as it can be. You don't like their being together. You were always like that even as a child. If you had a little girl friend, you always got mad when she liked anybody else. Well, you'd better get a beau of your own now— a woman of your age.

MARTHA: The sooner you get out of here, the better. Your vulgarities are making me sick and I won't stand for them any longer. I want you to leave—

> [*At this point there is a sound outside the large doors Center.* MARTHA *breaks off, angry and ashamed. After a moment she crosses to the door and opens it.* EVELYN *and* PEGGY *are to be seen on the staircase. For a second she stands still as they stop and look at her. Then, afraid that her anger with her aunt will color anything she might say to the children, she crosses the room again and stands with her back to them.*]

MARTHA: What were you doing outside the door?

EVELYN: [*Hurriedly.*] We were going upthtairth, Mith Dobie.

PEGGY: We came down to see how Mary was.

MARTHA: And you stopped long enough to see how we were. Did you deliberately listen?

PEGGY: We didn't mean to. We heard voices and we couldn't help—

MRS. MORTAR: [*Fake social tone.*] Eavesdropping is something nice young ladies just don't do.

MARTHA: [*Turning to face the children.*] Go upstairs now. We'll talk about this later. [*Slowly shuts door as they begin to climb the stairs.*]

MRS. MORTAR: You mean to say you're not going to do anything about that? [*No answer. She laughs nastily.*] That's the trouble with these new-fangled notions of discipline and—

MARTHA: [*Thoughtfully.*] You know, it's really bad having you around children.

MRS. MORTAR: What exactly does that mean?

MARTHA: It means that I don't like them hearing the things you say. Oh, I'll "do something about it," but the truth is that this is their home, and things shouldn't be said in it that they can't hear. When you're at your best, you're not for tender ears.

MRS. MORTAR: So now it's my fault, is it? Just as I said, whenever he's in the house you think you can take it out on me. You've got to have some way to let out steam and—

[*Door opens Right and* CARDIN *comes in.*]

MARTHA: How is Mary?

[MRS. MORTAR, *head in air, gives* MARTHA *a malicious half-smile and makes what she thinks is majestic exit Center.*]

MRS. MORTAR: Good day, Joseph.

CARDIN: What's the matter with the Duchess? [*Nods at door Center.*]

MARTHA: Just keeping her hand in, in case Sir Henry's watching her from above. What about Mary?

CARDIN: Nothing. Absolutely nothing.

MARTHA: [*Sighs.*] I thought so.

CARDIN: I could have managed a better faint than that when I was six years old.

MARTHA: Nothing the matter with her at all, then?

CARDIN: [*Laughs.*] No, ma'am, not a thing. Just a little something she thought up.

MARTHA: But it's such a silly thing to do. She knew we'd have you in. [*Sighs.*] Maybe she's not so bright. Any idiots in your family, Joe? Any inbreeding?

CARDIN: Don't blame her on me. It's another side of the family. [*Laughs.*] You can look at Aunt Amelia and tell: old New England stock; never married out of Boston; still thinks honor is honor and dinner's at eight thirty. Yes, ma'am, we're a proud old breed.

MARTHA: The Jukes were an old family, too. Look, Joe, have you any idea what is the matter with Mary? I mean, has she always been like this?

CARDIN: She's always been a honey. Aunt Amelia's spoiling hasn't helped any, either.

MARTHA: We're reaching the end of our rope with her. This kind of thing—

CARDIN: [*Looking at her.*] Aren't you taking this too seriously?

MARTHA: [*After a second.*] I guess I am. But you stay around kids long enough and you won't know what to take seriously, either. But I do think somebody ought to talk to Mrs. Tilford about her.

CARDIN: You wouldn't be meaning me now, would you, Miss Dobie?

MARTHA: Well, Karen and I were talking about it this afternoon and—

CARDIN: Listen, friend, I'm marrying Karen, but I'm not writing Mary Tilford in the contract. [*Martha moves slightly.* CARDIN *takes her by the shoulders and turns her around to face him again. His face is grave, his voice gentle.*] Forget Mary for a minute. You and I have got something to fight about. Every time anything's said about marrying—about Karen marrying me—you— [*She winces.*] There it is. I'm fond of you. I always thought you liked me. What is it? I know how fond you are of Karen, but our marriage oughtn't to make a great deal of difference—

MARTHA: [*Pushing his hands from her shoulders.*] God damn you. I wish— [*She puts her face in her hands.* CARDIN *watches her in silence, mechanically lighting a cigarette. When she takes her hands from her face, she holds them out to him. Contritely.*] Joe, please, I'm sorry. I'm a fool, a nasty, bitter—

CARDIN: [*Takes her hands in one of his, patting them with his other hand.*] Aw, shut up. [*He puts an arm around her, and she leans her head against his lapel. They are standing like that when* KAREN *comes in Right.*]

MARTHA: [*To* KAREN, *as she wipes her eyes.*] Your friend's got a nice shoulder to weep on.

KAREN: He's an admirable man in every way. Well, the angel child is now putting her clothes back on.

MARTHA: The angel child's influence is abroad even while she's unconscious. Her room-mates were busy listening at the door while Aunt Lily and I were yelling at each other.

KAREN: We'll have to move those girls away from one another.

[*A bell rings from the rear of the house.*]

MARTHA: That's my class. I'll send Peggy and Evelyn down. You talk to them.

KAREN: All right. [*As* MARTHA *exits Center,* KAREN *goes toward door Right. As she passes* CARDIN *she kisses him.*] Mary!

[MARY *opens door, comes in, stands buttoning the neck of her dress.*]

CARDIN: [*To* MARY.] How's it feel to be back from the grave?

MARY: My heart hurts.

CARDIN: [*Laughing. To* KAREN.] Science has failed. Try a hairbrush.

MARY: It's *my* heart, and it hurts.

KAREN: Sit down.

MARY: I want to see my grandmother. I want to—

[EVELYN *and* PEGGY *timidly enter Center.*]

KAREN: Sit down, girls, I want to talk to you.

PEGGY: We're awfully sorry, really. We just didn't think and—

KAREN: I'm sorry too, Peggy. [*Thoughtfully.*] You and Evelyn never used to do things like this. We'll have to separate you three.

EVELYN: Ah, Mith Wright, we've been together almotht a year.

KAREN: It was evidently too long. Now, don't let's talk about it. Peggy, you will move into Lois's room, and Lois will move in with Evelyn. Mary will go in with Rosalie.

MARY: Rosalie hates me.

KAREN: That's a very stupid thing to say. I can't imagine Rosalie hating anyone.

MARY: [*Starting to cry.*] And it's all because I had a pain. If anybody else was sick they'd be put to bed and petted. You're always mean to me. I get blamed and punished for everything. [*To* CARDIN.] I do, Cousin Joe. All the time for everything.

> [MARY *by now is crying violently and as* KAREN *half moves toward her,* CARDIN, *who has been frowning, picks* MARY *up and puts her down on the couch.*]

CARDIN: You've been unpleasant enough to Miss Wright. Lie here until you've stopped working yourself into a fit. [*Picks up his hat and bag, smiles at* KAREN.] I've got to go now. She's not going to hurt herself crying. The next time she faints, I'd wait until she got tired lying on the floor. [*Passing* MARY, *he pats her head. She jerks away from him.*]

KAREN: Wait a minute. I'll walk to the car with you. [*To girls.*] Go up now and move your things. Tell Lois to get her stuff ready.

> [*She and* CARDIN *exit Center. A second after the door is closed,* MARY *springs up and throws a cushion at the door.*]

EVELYN: Don't do that. She'll hear you.

MARY: Who cares if she does? [*Kicks table.*] And she can hear that, too.

> [*Small ornament falls off table and breaks on floor.* EVELYN *and* PEGGY *gasp, and* MARY'S *bravado disappears for a moment.*]

EVELYN: [*Frightened.*] Now what are you going to do?

PEGGY: [*Stooping down in a vain effort to pick up the pieces.*] You'll get the devil now. Dr. Cardin gave it to Miss Wright. I guess it was kind of a lover's gift. People get awfully angry about a lover's gift.

MARY: Oh, leave it alone. She'll never know we did it.

PEGGY: *We* didn't do it. You did it yourself.

MARY: And what will you do if I say *we* did do it? [*Laughs.*] Never mind, I'll think of something else. The wind could've knocked it over.

EVELYN: Yeh. She'th going to believe that one.

MARY: Oh, stop worrying about it. I'll get out of it.

EVELYN: Did you really have a pain?

MARY: I fainted, didn't I?

PEGGY: I wish I could faint sometimes. I've never even worn glasses, like Rosalie.

MARY: A lot it'll get you to faint.

EVELYN: What did Mith Wright do to you when the clath left?

MARY: Told me I couldn't go to the boat-races.

EVELYN: Whew!

PEGGY: But we'll remember everything that happens and we'll give you all the souvenirs and things.

MARY: I won't let you go if I can't go. But I'll find some way to go. What were *you* doing?

PEGGY: I guess we shouldn't have done it, really. We came down to see what was happening to you, but the doors were closed and we could hear Miss Dobie

and Mortar having an awful row. Then Miss Dobie opens the door and there
we were.

MARY: And a lot of crawling and crying you both did too, I bet.

EVELYN: We were thort of thorry about lithening. I gueth it wathn't—

MARY: Ah, you're always sorry about everything. What were they saying?

PEGGY: What was who saying?

MARY: Dobie and Mortar, silly.

PEGGY: [*Evasively.*] Just talking, I guess.

EVELYN: Fighting, you mean.

MARY: About what?

EVELYN: Well, they were talking about Mortar going away to England and—

PEGGY: You know, it really wasn't very nice to've listened, and I think it's worse
to tell.

MARY: You do, do you? You just don't tell me and see what happens.

[PEGGY *sighs.*]

EVELYN: Mortar got awful thore at that and thaid they juth wanted to get rid of
her, and then they thtarted talking about Dr. Cardin.

MARY: What about him?

PEGGY: We'd better get started moving; Miss Wright will be back first thing we
know.

MARY: [*Fiercely.*] Shut up! Go on, Evelyn.

EVELYN: They're going to be married.

MARY: Everybody knows that.

PEGGY: But everybody doesn't know that Miss Dobie doesn't want them to get
married. How do you like that?

[*The door opens and* ROSALIE WELLS *sticks her head in.*]

ROSALIE: I have a class soon. If you're going to move your things—

MARY: Close that door, you idiot. [ROSALIE *closes door, stands near it.*] What do you
want?

ROSALIE: I'm trying to tell you. If you're going to move your things—not that I
want you in with me—you'd better start right now. Miss Wright's coming in
a minute.

MARY: Who cares if she is?

ROSALIE: [*Starts for door.*] I'm just telling you for your own good.

PEGGY: [*Getting up.*] We're coming.

MARY: No. Let Rosalie move our things.

ROSALIE: You crazy?

PEGGY: [*Nervously.*] It's all right. Evelyn and I'll get your things. Come on, Evelyn.

MARY: Trying to get out of telling me, huh? Well, you won't get out of it that way.
Sit down and stop being such a sissy. Rosalie, you go on up and move my
things and don't say a word about our being down here.

ROSALIE: And who was your French maid yesterday, Mary Tilford?

MARY: [*Laughing.*] You'll do for today. Now go on, Rosalie, and fix our things.

ROSALIE: You crazy?

MARY: And the next time we go into town, I'll let you wear my gold locket and buckle. You'll like that, won't you, Rosalie?

ROSALIE: [*Draws back, moves her hands nervously.*] I don't know what you're talking about.

MARY: Oh, I'm not talking about anything in particular. You just run along now and remind me the next time to get my buckle and locket for you.

ROSALIE: [*Stares at her a moment.*] All right, I'll do it this time, but just 'cause I got a good disposition. But don't think you're going to boss me around, Mary Tilford.

MARY: [*Smiling.*] No, indeed. [ROSALIE *starts for door.*] And get the things done neatly, Rosalie. Don't muss my white linen bloomers—

[*The door slams as* MARY *laughs.*]

EVELYN: Now what do you think of that? What made her tho agreeable?

MARY: Oh, a little secret we got. Go on, now, what else did they say?

PEGGY: Well, Mortar said that Dobie was jealous of them, and that she was like that when she was a little girl, and that she'd better get herself a beau of her own because it was unnatural, and that she never wanted anybody to like Miss Wright, and that was unnatural. Boy! Did Miss Dobie get sore at that!

EVELYN: Then we didn't hear any more. Peggy dropped a book.

MARY: What'd she mean Dobie was jealous?

PEGGY: What's unnatural?

EVELYN: Un for not. Not natural.

PEGGY: It's funny, because everybody gets married.

MARY: A lot of people don't—they're too ugly.

PEGGY: [*Jumps up, claps her hand to her mouth.*] Oh, my God! Rosalie'll find that copy of *Mademoiselle de Maupin*. She'll blab like the dickens.

MARY: Ah, she won't say a word.

EVELYN: Who getth the book when we move?

MARY: You can have it. That's what I was doing this morning—finishing it. There's one part in it—

PEGGY: What part?

[MARY *laughs.*]

EVELYN: Well, what wath it?

MARY: Wait until you read it.

EVELYN: Don't forget to give it to me.

PEGGY: It's a shame about being moved. I've got to go in with Helen, and she blows her nose all night. Lois told me.

MARY: It was a dirty trick making us move. She just wants to see how much fun she can take away from me. She hates me.

PEGGY: No, she doesn't, Mary. She treats you just like the rest of us—almost better.

MARY: That's right, stick up for your crush. Take her side against mine.

PEGGY: I didn't mean it that way.

EVELYN: [*Looks at her watch.*] We'd better get upthtairth.

MARY: I'm not going.

PEGGY: Rosalie isn't so bad.

EVELYN: What you going to do about the vathe?

MARY: I don't care about Rosalie and I don't care about the vase. I'm not going to be here.

EVELYN *and* PEGGY: [*Together.*] Not going to be here! What do you mean?

MARY: [*Calmly.*] I'm going home.

PEGGY: Oh, Mary—

EVELYN: You can't do that.

MARY: Can't I? You just watch. [*Begins to walk around the room.*] I'm not staying here. I'm going home and tell Grandma I'm not staying any more. [*Smiles to herself.*] I'll tell her I'm not happy. They're scared of Grandma—she helped 'em when they first started, you know—and when she tells 'em something, believe me, they'll sit up and listen. They can't get away with treating me like this, and they don't have to think they can.

PEGGY: [*Appalled.*] You just going to walk out like that?

EVELYN: What you going to tell your grandmother?

MARY: Oh, who cares? I'll think of something to tell her. I can always do it better on the spur of the moment.

PEGGY: She'll send you right back.

MARY: You let me worry about that. Grandma's very fond of me, on account my father was her favorite son. I can manage *her* all right.

PEGGY: I don't think you ought to go, really, Mary. It's just going to make an awful lot of trouble.

EVELYN: What'th going to happen about the vathe?

MARY: Say I did it—it doesn't make a bit of difference any more to me. Now listen, you two got to help. They won't miss me before dinner if you make Rosalie shut the door and keep it shut. Now, I'll go through the field to French's, and then I can get the bus to Homestead.

EVELYN: How you going to get to the thtreet-car?

MARY: Taxi, idiot.

PEGGY: How are you going to get out of here in the first place?

MARY: I'm going to walk out. You know where the front door is, or are you too dumb even for that? Well, I'm going right out that front door.

EVELYN: Gee, I wouldn't have the nerve.

MARY: Of course you wouldn't. You'd let 'em do anything to you they want. Well, they can't do it to me. Who's got any money?

EVELYN: Not me. Not a thent.

MARY: I've got to have at least a dollar for the taxi and a dime for the bus.

EVELYN: And where you going to find it?

PEGGY: See? Why don't you just wait until your allowance comes Monday, and then you can go any place you want. Maybe by that time—

MARY: I'm going today. *Now.*

EVELYN: You can't *walk* to Lanthet.

MARY: [*Goes to* PEGGY.] You've got money. You've got two dollars and twenty-five cents.

PEGGY: I—I—

MARY: Go get it for me.

PEGGY: No! No! I won't get it for you.

EVELYN: You can't have *that* money, Mary—

MARY: Get it for me.

PEGGY: [*Cringes, her voice is scared.*] I won't. I won't. Mamma doesn't send me much allowance—not half as much as the rest of you get—I saved this so long— you took it from me last time—

EVELYN: Ah, she wantth that bithycle tho bad.

PEGGY: I haven't gone to the movies, I haven't had any candy, I haven't had anything the rest of you get all the time. It took me so long to save that and I—

MARY: Go upstairs and get me the money.

PEGGY: [*Hysterically, backing away from her.*] I won't. I won't. I won't.

> [MARY *makes a sudden move for her, grabs her left arm, and jerks it back, hard and expertly.* PEGGY *screams softly.* EVELYN *tries to take* MARY'S *arm away. Without releasing her hold on* PEGGY, MARY *slaps* EVELYN'S *face.* EVELYN *begins to cry.*]

MARY: Just say when you've had enough.

PEGGY: [*Softly, stifling.*] All—all right—I'll get it.

> [MARY *smiles, nods her head as the Curtain falls.*]

ACT II

SCENE I

> SCENE: *Living room at* MRS TILFORD'S. *It is a formal room, without being cold or elegant. The furniture is old, but excellent. The exit to the hall is Left; glass doors Right lead to a dining room that cannot be seen.*

> AT RISE: *Stage is empty. Voices are heard in the hall.*

AGATHA: [*Off-stage.*] What are you doing here? Well, come on in—don't stand there gaping at me. Have they given you a holiday or did you just decide you'd get a better dinner here? [AGATHA *enters Left, followed by* MARY. AGATHA *is a sharp-faced maid, not young, with a querulous voice.*] Can't you even say hello?

MARY: Hello, Agatha. You didn't give me a chance. Where's Grandma?

AGATHA: Why aren't you in school? Look at your face and clothes. Where have you been?

MARY: I got a little dirty coming home. I walked part of the way through the woods.

AGATHA: Why didn't you put on your middy blouse and your old brown coat?

MARY: Oh, stop asking me questions. Where's Grandma?

AGATHA: Where ought any clean person be at this time of day? She's taking a bath.

MARY: Is anybody coming for dinner?

AGATHA: She didn't say anything about you coming.

MARY: How could she, stupid? She didn't know.

AGATHA: Then what are you doing here?

MARY: Leave me alone. I don't feel well.

AGATHA: Why don't you feel well? Who ever heard of a person going for a walk in the woods when they didn't feel well?

MARY: Oh, leave me alone. I came home because I was sick.

AGATHA: You look all right.

MARY: But I don't feel all right. [*Whining.*] I can't even come home without everybody nagging at me.

AGATHA: Don't think you're fooling me, young lady. You might pull the wool over some people's eyes, but—I bet you've been up to something again. [*Stares suspiciously at* MARY, *who says nothing.*] Well, you wait right here till I tell your grandmother. And if you feel so sick, you certainly won't want any dinner. A good dose of rhubarb and soda will fix you up. [*Exits Left.*]

[MARY *makes a face in the direction* AGATHA *has gone and stops sniffling. She looks nervously around the room, then goes to a low mirror and tries several experiments with her face in an attempt to make it look sick and haggard.*

MRS. TILFORD, *followed by* AGATHA, *enters Left.* MRS. TILFORD *is a large, dignified woman in her sixties, with a pleasant, strong face.*]

AGATHA: [*To* MRS. TILFORD, *as she follows her into the room.*] Why didn't you put some cold water on your chest? Do you want to catch your death of cold at your age? Did you have to hurry so?

MRS. TILFORD: Mary, what are you doing home?

[MARY *rushes to her and buries her head in* MRS. TILFORD'S *dress, crying.* MRS. TILFORD *lets her cry for a moment while she pats her head, then puts an arm around the child and leads her to a sofa.*]

MRS. TILFORD: Never mind, dear; now stop crying and tell me what is the matter.

MARY: [*Gradually stops crying, fondling* MRS. TILFORD'S *hand.*] It's so good to see you, Grandma. You didn't come to visit me all last week.

MRS. TILFORD: I couldn't, dear. But I was coming tomorrow.

MARY: I missed you so. [*Smiling up at* MRS. TILFORD.] I was awful homesick.

MRS. TILFORD: I'm glad that's all it was. I was frightened when Agatha said you were not well.

AGATHA: Did I say that? I said she needed a good dose of rhubarb and soda. Most likely she only came home for Wednesday night fudge cake.

MRS. TILFORD: We all get homesick. But how did you get here? Did Miss Karen drive you over?

MARY: I—I walked most of the way, and then a lady gave me a ride and—[*Looks timidly at* MRS. TILFORD.]

AGATHA: Did she have to walk through the woods in her very best coat?

MRS. TILFORD: Mary! Do you mean you left without permission?

MARY: [*Nervously.*] I ran away, Grandma. They didn't know—

MRS. TILFORD: That was a very bad thing to do, and they'll be worried. Agatha, phone Miss Wright and tell her Mary is here. John will drive her back before dinner.

MARY: [*As* AGATHA *starts toward telephone.*] No, Grandma, don't do that. Please don't do that. Please let me stay.

MRS. TILFORD: But, darling, you can't leave school any time you please.

MARY: Oh, please, Grandma, don't send me back right away. You don't know how they'll punish me.

MRS. TILFORD: I don't think they'll be that angry. Come, you're acting like a foolish little girl.

MARY: [*Hysterically, as she sees* AGATHA *about to pick up the telephone.*] Grandma! Please! I can't go back! I can't! They'll kill me! They will, Grandma! They'll kill me!

> [MRS. TILFORD *and* AGATHA *stare at* MARY *in amazement. She puts her head in* MRS. TILFORD'S *lap and sobs.*]

MRS. TILFORD: [*Motioning with a hand for* AGATHA *to leave the room.*] Never mind phoning now, Agatha.

AGATHA: If you're going to let her—

> [MRS. TILFORD *repeats the gesture.* AGATHA *exists Right, with offended dignity.*]

MRS. TILFORD: Stop crying, Mary.

MARY: [*Raising her head from* MRS. TILFORD'S *lap.*] It's so nice here, Grandma.

MRS. TILFORD: I'm glad you like being home with me, but at your age you can hardly— [*More seriously.*] What made you say such a terrible thing about Miss Wright and Miss Dobie? You know they wouldn't hurt you.

MARY: Oh, but they would. They—I— [*Breaks off, looks around as if hunting for a clue to her next word; then dramatically.*] I fainted today!

MRS. TILFORD: [*Alarmed.*] Fainted?

MARY: Yes, I did. My heart—I had a pain in my heart. I couldn't help having a pain in my heart, and when I fainted right in class, they called Cousin Joe and he said I didn't. He said it was maybe only that I ate my breakfast too fast and Miss Wright blamed me for it.

MRS. TILFORD: [*Relieved.*] I'm sure if Joseph said it wasn't serious, it wasn't.

MARY: But I did have a pain in my heart—honest.

MRS. TILFORD: Have you still got it?

MARY: I guess I haven't got it much any more, but I feel a little weak, and I was so scared of Miss Wright being so mean to me just because I was sick.

MRS. TILFORD: Scared of Karen? Nonsense. It's perfectly possible that you had a pain, but if you had really been sick your Cousin Joseph would certainly have known it. It's not nice to frighten people by pretending to be sick when you aren't.

MARY: I didn't *want* to be sick, but I'm always getting punished for everything.

MRS. TILFORD: [*Gently.*] You mustn't imagine things like that, child, or you'll grow up to be a very unhappy woman. I'm not going to scold you any more for coming home this time, though I suppose I should. Run along upstairs and wash your face and change your dress, and after dinner John will drive you back. Run along.

MARY: [*Happily.*] I can stay for dinner?

MRS. TILFORD: Yes.

MARY: Maybe I could stay till the first of the week. Saturday's your birthday and I could be here with you.

MRS. TILFORD: We don't celebrate my birthday, dear. You'll have to go back to school after dinner.

MARY: But— [*She hesitates, then goes up to* MRS. TILFORD *and puts her arms around the older woman's neck. Softly.*] How much do you love me?

MRS. TILFORD: [*Smiling.*] As much as all the words in all the books in all the world.

MARY: Remember when I was little and you used to tell me that right before I went to sleep? And it was a rule nobody could say another single word after you finished? You used to say: "Wor-rr-ld," and then I had to shut my eyes tight.

MRS. TILFORD: And sometimes you were naughty and didn't shut them.

MARY: I miss you an awful lot, Grandma.

MRS. TILFORD: And I miss you, but I'm afraid my Latin is too rusty—you'll learn it better in school.

MARY: But couldn't I stay out the rest of this term? After the summer maybe I won't mind it so much. I'll study hard, honest, and—

MRS. TILFORD: You're an earnest little coaxer, but it's out of the question. Back you go tonight. [*Gives* MARY *a playful slap.*] Let's not have any more talk about it now, and let's have no more running away from school ever.

MARY: [*Slowly.*] Then I really have to go back there tonight?

MRS. TILFORD: Of course.

MARY: You don't love me. You don't care whether they kill me or not.

MRS. TILFORD: Mary.

MARY: You don't! You don't! You don't care what happens to me.

MRS. TILFORD: [*Sternly.*] But I *do* care that you're talking this way.

MARY: [*Meekly.*] I'm sorry I said that, Grandma. I didn't mean to hurt your feelings. [*Puts her arms around* MRS. TILFORD'S *neck.*] Forgive me?

MRS. TILFORD: What made you talk like that?

MARY: [*In a whisper.*] I'm scared, Grandma, I'm scared. They'll do dreadful things to me.

MRS. TILFORD: Dreadful? Nonsense. They'll punish you for running away. You deserve to be punished.

MARY: It's not that. It's not anything I do. It never is. They—they just punish me anyhow, just like they got something against me. I'm afraid of them, Grandma.

MRS. TILFORD: That's ridiculous. What have they ever done to you that is so terrible?

MARY: A lot of things—all the time. Miss Wright says I can't go to the boat-races and— [*Realizing the inadequacy of this reply, she breaks off, hesitates, hunting for a more telling reply, and finally stammers*] It's—it's after what happened today.

MRS. TILFORD: You mean something else besides your naughtiness in pretending to faint and then running away?

MARY: I *did* faint. I didn't pretend. They just said that to make me feel bad. Anyway, it wasn't anything that I did.

MRS. TILFORD: What was it, then?

MARY: I can't tell you.

MRS. TILFORD: Why?

MARY: [*Sulkily.*] Because you're just going to take their part.

MRS. TILFORD: [*A little annoyed.*] Very well. Now run upstairs and get ready for dinner.

MARY: It was—it was all about Miss Dobie and Mrs. Mortar. They were talking awful things and Peggy and Evelyn heard them and Miss Dobie found out, and then they made us move our rooms.

MRS. TILFORD: What has that to do with you? I don't understand a word you're saying.

MARY: They made us move our rooms. They said we couldn't be together any more. They're afraid to have us near them, that's what it is, and they're taking it out on me. They're scared of you.

MRS. TILFORD: For a little girl you're imagining a lot of big things. Why should they be scared of me? Am I such an unpleasant old lady?

MARY: They're afraid you'll find out.

MRS. TILFORD: Find out what?

MARY: [*Vaguely.*] Things.

MRS. TILFORD: Run along, Mary. I hope you'll get more coherent as you get older.

MARY: [*Slowing starting for door.*] All right. But there're a lot of things. They have secrets or something, and they're afraid I'll find out and tell you.

MRS. TILFORD: There's not necessarily anything wrong with people having secrets.

MARY: [*Coming back in the room again.*] But they've got funny ones. Peggy and Evelyn heard Mrs. Mortar telling Miss Dobie that she was jealous of Miss Wright marrying Cousin Joe.

MRS. TILFORD: You shouldn't repeat things like that.

MARY: But that's what she said, Grandma. She said it was unnatural for a girl to feel that way.

MRS. TILFORD: What?

MARY: I'm just telling you what she said. She said there was something funny about it, and that Miss Dobie had always been like that, even when she was a little girl, and that it was unnatural—

MRS. TILFORD: Stop using that silly word, Mary.

MARY: [*Vaguely realizing that she is on the right track, hurries on.*] But that was the word *she* kept using, Grandma, and then they got mad and told Mrs. Mortar she'd have to get out.

MRS. TILFORD: That was probably not the reason at all.

MARY: [*Nodding vigorously.*] I bet it was, because honestly, Miss Dobie does get cranky and mean every time Cousin Joe comes, and today I heard her say to him: "God damn you," and then she said she was just a jealous fool and—

MRS. TILFORD: You have picked up some very fine words, haven't you, Mary?

MARY: That's just what she said, Grandma, and one time Miss Dobie was crying in Miss Wright's room, and Miss Wright was trying to stop her, and she said that all right, maybe she wouldn't get married right away if—

MRS. TILFORD: How do you know all this?

MARY: We couldn't help hearing because they—I mean Miss Dobie—was talking awful loud, and their room is right next to ours.

MRS. TILFORD: Whose room?

MARY: Miss Wright's room, I mean, and you can just ask Peggy and Evelyn whether we didn't hear. Almost always Miss Dobie comes in after we go to bed and stays a long time. I guess that's why they want to get rid of us—of me— because we hear things. That's why they're making us move our room, and they punish me all the time for—

MRS. TILFORD: For eavesdropping, I should think. [*She has said this mechanically. With nothing definite in her mind, she is making an effort to conceal the fact that* MARY'S *description of the life at school has shocked her.*] Well, now I think we've had enough gossip, don't you? Dinner's almost ready, and I can't eat with a girl who has such a dirty face.

MARY: [*Softly.*] I've heard other things, too.

MRS. TILFORD: [*Abstractedly.*] What? What did you say?

MARY: I've heard other things. Plenty of other things, Grandma.

MRS. TILFORD: What things?

MARY: Bad things.

MRS. TILFORD: Well, what were they?

MARY: I can't tell you.

MRS. TILFORD: Mary, you're annoying me very much. If you have anything to say, then say it and stop acting silly.

MARY: I mean I can't say it out loud.

MRS. TILFORD: There couldn't possibly be anything so terrible that you couldn't say it out loud. Now either tell the truth or be still.

MARY: Well, a lot of things I don't understand. But it's awful, and sometimes they fight and then they make up, and Miss Dobie cries and Miss Wright gets mad, and then they make up again, and there are funny noises and we get scared.

MRS. TILFORD: Noises? I suppose you girls have a happy time imagining a murder.

MARY: And we've seen things, too. Funny things. [*Sees the impatience of her grandmother.*] I'd tell you, but I got to whisper it.

MRS. TILFORD: Why must you whisper it?

MARY: I don't know. I just got to. [*Climbs on the sofa next to* MRS. TILFORD *and begins whispering. At first the whisper is slow and hesitant, but it gradually works itself up to fast, excited talking. In the middle of it* MRS. TILFORD *stops her.*]

MRS. TILFORD: [*Trembling.*] Do you know what you're saying? [*Without answering,* MARY *goes back to the whispering until the older woman takes her by the shoulders and turns her around to stare in her face.*] Mary? Are you telling me the truth?

MARY: Honest, honest. You just ask Peggy and Evelyn and— [*After a moment* MRS. TILFORD *gets up and begins to pace about the room. She is no longer listening to* MARY, *who keeps up a running fire of conversation.*] They know too. And maybe there're other kids who know, but we've always been frightened and so we didn't ask, and one night I was going to go and find out, but I got scared and we went to bed early so we wouldn't hear, but sometimes I couldn't help it, but we never talked about it much, because we thought they'd find out and—Oh, Grandma, don't make me go back to that awful place.

MRS. TILFORD: [*Abstractedly.*] What? [*Starts to move about again.*]

MARY: Don't make me back to that place. I just couldn't stand it any more. Really, Grandma, I'm so unhappy there, and if only I could stay out the rest of the term, why, then—

MRS. TILFORD: [*Makes irritated gesture.*] Be still a minute. [*After a moment.*] No, you won't have to go back.

MARY: [*Surprised.*] Honest?

MRS. TILFORD: Honest.

MARY: [*Hugging* MRS. TILFORD.] You're the nicest, loveliest grandma in all the world. You—you're not mad at me?

MRS. TILFORD: I'm not mad at you. Now go upstairs and get ready for dinner. [MARY *kisses her and runs happily out Left.* MRS. TILFORD *stands staring after her for a long moment; then, very slowly, she puts on her eyeglasses and crosses to the phone. She dials a number.*] Is Miss Wright—is Miss Wright in? [*Waits a second, hurriedly puts down the receiver.*] Never mind, never mind. [*Dials another number.*] Dr. Cardin, please. Mrs. Tilford. [*She remains absolutely motionless while she waits. When she does speak, her voice is low and tense.*] Joseph? Joseph? Can you come to see me right away? Yes, I'm perfectly well. No, but it's important, Joseph, very important. I must see you right away. I—I can't tell you over the phone. Can't you come sooner? it's not about Mary's fainting—I said it's not about Mary, Joseph; in one way it's about Mary— [*Suddenly quiet.*] But will the hospital take so long? Very well, Joseph, make it as soon as you can. [*Hangs up the receiver, sits for a moment undecided. Then, taking a breath, she dials another number.*] Mrs. Munn, please. This is Mrs. Tilford. Miriam? This is Amelia Tilford. I have something to tell you—something very shocking, I'm afraid—something about the school and Evelyn and Mary—

CURTAIN

SCENE II

SCENE: *The same as Scene I. The curtain has been lowered to mark the passing of a few hours.*

AT RISE: MARY *is lying on the floor playing with a puzzle.* AGATHA *appears lugging blankets and pillows across the room. Almost at the door, she stops and gives* MARY *an annoyed look.*

AGATHA: And see to it that she doesn't get my good quilt all dirty, and let her wear your green pajamas.

MARY: Who?

AGATHA: Who? Don't you ever keep your ears open? Rosalie Wells is coming over to spend the night with you.

MARY: You mean she's going to sleep *here?*

AGATHA: You heard me.

MARY: What for?

AGATHA: Do I know all the crazy things that are happening around here? Your grandmother phones Mrs. Wells all the way to New York, three dollars and eighty-five cents and families starving, and Mrs. Wells wanted to know if Rosalie could stay here until tomorrow.

MARY: [*Relieved.*] Oh. Couldn't Evelyn Munn come instead?

AGATHA: Sure. We'll have the whole town over to entertain you.

MARY: I won't let Rosalie Wells wear my new pajamas.

AGATHA: [*Exits as the front door-bell rings.*] Don't tell me what you won't do. You'll act like a lady for once in your life. [*Off-stage.*] Come on in, Rosalie. Just go on in there and make yourself at home. Have you had your dinner?

ROSALIE: [*Off-stage.*] Good evening. Yes'm.

AGATHA: [*Off-stage.*] Hang up your pretty coat. Have you had your bath?

ROSALIE: [*Off-stage.*] Yes, ma'am. This morning.

AGATHA: [*Off-stage.*] Well, you better have another one.

> [*She is climbing the stairs as* ROSALIE *comes into the room.* MARY, *lying in front of the couch, is hidden from her. Gingerly* ROSALIE *sits down on a chair.*]

MARY: [*Softly.*] Whooooooo. [ROSALIE *jumps.*] Whooooooo. [ROSALIE, *frightened, starts hurriedly for the door.* MARY *sits up, laughs.*] You're a goose.

ROSALIE: [*Belligerently.*] Oh, so it's you. Well, who likes to hear funny noises at night? You could have been a werewolf.

MARY: A werewolf wouldn't want you.

ROSALIE: You know everything, don't you? [MARY *laughs.* ROSALIE *comes over, stands staring at puzzle.*] Isn't it funny about school?

MARY: What's funny about it?

ROSALIE: Don't act like you can come home every night.

MARY: Maybe I can from now on. [*Rolls over on her back luxuriously.*] Maybe I'm never going back.

ROSALIE: Am I going back? I don't want to stay home.

MARY: What'll you give to know?

ROSALIE: Nothing. I'll ask Mamma.

MARY: Will you give me a free T. L.[5] if I tell you?

ROSALIE: [*Thinks for a moment.*] All right. Lois Fisher told Helen that you were very smart.

MARY: That's an old one. I won't take it.

ROSALIE: You got to take it.

MARY: Nope.

ROSALIE: [*Laughs.*] You don't know, anyway.

---

5. Trade-last; that is, will you give me a compliment in trade?

MARY: I know what I heard, and I know Grandma phoned your mother in New York to come and get you right away. You're just going to spend the night here. I wish Evelyn could come instead of you.

ROSALIE: But what's happened? Peggy and Helen and Evelyn and Lois went home tonight, too. Do you think somebody's got scarlet fever or something?

MARY: No.

ROSALIE: Do *you* know what it is? How'd you find out? [*No answer.*] You're always pretending you know everything. You're just faking. [*Flounces away.*] Never mind, don't bother telling me. I think curiosity is very unladylike, anyhow. I have no concern with your silly secrets.

MARY: Suppose I told you that I just may have said that you were in on it?

ROSALIE: In on what?

MARY: The secret. Suppose I told you that I *may have* said that you told me about it?

ROSALIE: Why, Mary Tilford! You can't do a thing like that. I didn't tell you about anything. [MARY *laughs.*] Did you tell your grandmother such a thing?

MARY: Maybe.

ROSALIE: Did you?

MARY: Maybe.

ROSALIE: Well, I'm going right up to your grandmother and tell her I didn't tell you anything—whatever it is. You're just trying to get me into trouble and I'm not going to let you. [*Starts for door.*]

MARY: Wait a minute, I'll come with you.

ROSALIE: What for?

MARY: I want to tell her about Helen Burton's bracelet.

ROSALIE: [*Sits down suddenly.*] What about it?

MARY: Just that you stole it.

ROSALIE: Shut up. I didn't do any such thing.

MARY: Yes, you did.

ROSALIE: [*Tearfully.*] You made it up. You're always making things up.

MARY: You can't call me a fibber, Rosalie Wells. That's a kind of a dare and I won't take a dare. I guess I'll go tell Grandma, anyway. Then she can call the police and they'll come for you and you'll spend the rest of your life in one of those solitary prisons and you'll get older and older, and when you're very old and can't see anymore, they'll let you out maybe with a big sign on your back saying you're a thief, and your mother and father will be dead and you won't have any place to go and you'll beg on the streets—

ROSALIE: I didn't steal anything. I borrowed the bracelet and I was going to put it back as soon as I'd worn it to the movies. I never meant to keep it.

MARY: Nobody'll believe that, least of all the police. You're just a common, ordinary thief. Stop that bawling. You'll have the whole house down here in a minute.

ROSALIE: You won't tell? Say you won't tell.

MARY: Am I a fibber?

ROSALIE: No.

MARY: Then say: "I apologize on my hands and knees."

ROSALIE: I apologize on my hands and knees. Let's play with the puzzle.

MARY: Wait a minute. Say: "From now on, I, Rosalie Wells, am the vassal of Mary Tilford and will do and say whatever she tells me under the solemn oath of a knight."

ROSALIE: I won't say that. That's the worse oath there is. [MARY *starts for the door.*] Mary! Please don't—

MARY: Will you swear it?

ROSALIE: [*Sniffling.*] But then you could tell me to do anything.

MARY: And you'd have to do it. Say it quick or I'll—

ROSALIE: [*Hurriedly.*] From now on, I, Rosalie Wells, am the vassal of Mary Tilford and will do and say whatever she tells me under the solemn oath of a knight. [*She gasps, and sits up straight as* MRS. TILFORD *enters.*]

MARY: Don't forget that.

MRS. TILFORD: Good evening, Rosalie, you're looking very well.

ROSALIE: Good evening, Mrs. Tilford.

MARY: She's getting fatter every day.

MRS. TILFORD: [*Abstractedly.*] Then it's very becoming. [*Door-bell rings.*] That must be Joseph. Mary, take Rosalie into the library. There's some fruit and milk on the table. Be sure you're both fast asleep by half past ten. [*Leans down, kisses them both.* ROSALIE *starts to exit Right, sees* MARY, *stops and hesitates.*]

MARY: Go on, Rosalie. [*Waits until* ROSALIE *reluctantly exits.*] Grandma.

MRS. TILFORD: Yes?

MARY: Grandma, Cousin Joe'll say I've got to go back. He'll say I really wasn't—

[CARDIN *enters and she runs from the room.*]

CARDIN: Hello, Amelia. [*Looks curiously at the fleeing* MARY.] Mary home, eh?

MRS. TILFORD: [*Watching* MARY *as she leaves.*] Hello, Joseph. Sit down. [*He sits down, looks at her curiously, waits for her to speak.*] Whisky?

CARDIN: Please. How are you feeling? Headaches again?

MRS. TILFORD: [*Puts drink on table.*] No.

CARDIN: Those are good powders. Bicarbonate of soda and water. Never hurt anybody yet.

MRS. TILFORD: Yes. How have you been, Joseph?

CARDIN: My good health is monotonous.

MRS. TILFORD: [*Vaguely, sparring for time.*] I haven't seen you the last few weeks. Agatha misses you for Sunday dinners.

CARDIN: I've been busy. We're getting the results from the mating-season right about now.

MRS. TILFORD: Did I take you away from a patient?

CARDIN: No. I was at the hospital.

MRS. TILFORD: How's it getting on?

CARDIN: Just the same. No money, badly equipped, a lousy laboratory, everybody growling at everybody else—Amelia, you didn't bring me here to talk about the hospital. We're talking like people waiting for the muffins to be passed around. What's the matter with you?

MRS. TILFORD: I—I have something to tell you.

CARDIN: Well, out with it.

MRS. TILFORD: It's a very hard thing to say, Joseph.

CARDIN: Hard for you to say to *me*? [*No answer.*] Don't be worried about Mary. I guessed that she ran home to tell you about her faint. It was caused by nothing but bad temper and was very clumsily managed, at that. Amelia, she's a terribly spoilt—

MRS. TILFORD: I heard about the faint. That's not what is worrying me.

CARDIN: [*Gently.*] Are you in some trouble?

MRS. TILFORD: We all are in trouble. Bad trouble.

CARDIN: We? Me, you mean? Nothing's the matter with me.

MRS. TILFORD: When did you last see Karen?

CARDIN: Today. This afternoon.

MRS. TILFORD: Oh. Not since seven o'clock?

CARDIN: What's happened since seven o'clock?

MRS. TILFORD: Joseph, you've been engaged to Karen for a long time. Are your plans any more definite than they were a year ago?

CARDIN: You can get ready to buy the wedding present. We'll have the wedding here, if you don't mind. The smell of clean little girls and boiled linen would worry me.

MRS. TILFORD: Why has Karen decided so suddenly to make it definite?

CARDIN: She has not suddenly decided anything. The school is pretty well on its feet, and now that Mrs. Mortar is leaving—

MRS. TILFORD: I've heard about their putting Mrs. Mortar out.

CARDIN: Putting her out? Well, maybe. But a nice sum for a trip and a promise that a good niece will support you the rest of your life is an enviable way of being put out.

MRS. TILFORD: [*Slowly.*] Don't you find it odd, Joseph, that they want so much to get rid of that silly, harmless woman?

CARDIN: I don't know what you're talking about, but it isn't odd at all. Lily Mortar is not a harmless woman, although God knows she's silly enough. She's a nasty, tiresome, spoilt old bitch. If you're forming a Mortar Welfare society, you're wasting your time. [*Gets up, puts down his glass.*] It's not like you to waste your time. Now, what's it that's really on your mind?

MRS. TILFORD: You must not marry Karen.

CARDIN: [*Shocked, he grins.*] You're a very impertinent lady. Why must I— [*Imitates her.*] not marry Karen?

MRS. TILFORD: Because there's something wrong with Karen—something horrible.

[*The door-bell is heard to ring loud and long.*]

CARDIN: I don't think I can allow you to say things like that, Amelia.

MRS. TILFORD: I have good reason for saying it. [*Breaks off as she hears voices off-stage.*] Who is that?

KAREN: [*Off-stage.*] Mrs. Tilford, Agatha. Is she in?

AGATHA: [*Off-stage.*] Yes'm. Come on in.

MRS. TILFORD: I won't have her here.

CARDIN: [*Angrily.*] What are you talking about?

MRS. TILFORD: I won't have her here.

CARDIN: [*Picks up his hat.*] Then you don't want me here either. [*Turns to face* KAREN, *who, with* MARTHA, *has rushed in.*] Darling, what—?

KAREN: [*Stops when she sees him, puts her hand over her eyes.*] Is it a joke, Joe?

MARTHA: [*With great force to* MRS. TILFORD.] We've come to find out what you are doing.

CARDIN: [*Kissing* KAREN.] What is it?

KAREN: It's crazy! It's crazy! What did she do it for?

CARDIN: What are you talking about? What do you mean?

MRS. TILFORD: You shouldn't have come here.

CARDIN: What is all this? What's happened?

KAREN: I tried to reach you. Hasn't she told you?

CARDIN: Nobody's told me anything. I haven't heard anything but wild talk. What is it, Karen? [*She starts to speak, then dumbly shakes her head.*] What's happened, Martha?

MARTHA: [*Violently.*] An insane asylum has been let loose. How do we know what's happened?

CARDIN: What was it?

KAREN: We didn't know what it was. Nobody would talk to us, nobody would tell us anything.

MARTHA: I'll tell you, I'll tell you. You see if you can make any sense out of it. At dinner-time Mrs. Munn's chauffeur said that Evelyn must be sent home right away. At half past seven Mrs. Burton arrived to tell us that she wanted Helen's things packed and that she'd wait outside because she didn't want to enter a place like ours. Five minutes later the Wells's butler came for Rosalie.

CARDIN: What was it?

MARTHA: It was a madhouse. People rushing in and out, the children being pushed into cars—

KAREN: [*Quiet now, takes his hand.*] Mrs. Rogers finally told us.

CARDIN: What? What?

KAREN: That—that Martha and I are—in love with each other. In love with each other. Mrs. Tilford told them.

CARDIN: [*For a moment stands staring at her incredulously. Then he walks across the room, stares out of the window, and finally turns to* MRS. TILFORD.] Did you tell them that?

MRS. TILFORD: Yes.

CARDIN: Are you sick?

MRS. TILFORD: You know I'm not sick.

CARDIN: [*Snapping the words out.*] Then what did you do it for?

MRS. TILFORD: [*Slowly.*] Because it's true.

KAREN: [*Incredulously.*] You think it's true, then?

MARTHA: You fool! You damned, vicious—

KAREN: Do you realize what you're saying?

MRS. TILFORD: I realize it very well. And—

MARTHA: You realize nothing, nothing, nothing.

MRS. TILFORD: And that's why I don't think you should have come here. [*Quietly, with a look at* MARTHA.] I shall not call you names, and I will not allow you to call me names. It comes to this: I can't trust myself to talk about it with you now or ever.

KAREN: What's she talking about, Joe? What's she mean? What is she trying to do to us? What is everybody doing to us?

MARTHA: [*Softly, as though to herself.*] Pushed around. We're being pushed around by crazy people. [*Shakes herself slightly.*] That's an awful thing. And we're standing here— [CARDIN *puts his arm around* KAREN, *walks with her to the window. They stand there together.*] We're standing here taking it. [*Suddenly with violence.*] Didn't you know we'd come here? Were we supposed to lie down and grin while you kicked us around with these lies?

MRS. TILFORD: This can't do any of us any good, Miss Dobie.

MARTHA: [*Scornfully imitating her.*] "This can't do any of us any good." Listen, listen. Try to understand this: you're not playing with paper dolls. We're human beings, see? It's our lives you're fooling with. *Our* lives. That's serious business for us. Can you understand that?

MRS. TILFORD: [*For the first time she speaks angrily.*] I can understand that, and I understand a lot more. *You've* been playing with a lot of children's lives, and that's why I stopped you. [*More calmly.*] I know how serious this is for you, how serious it is for all of us.

CARDIN: [*Bitterly.*] I don't think you do know.

MRS. TILFORD: I wanted to avoid this meeting because it can't do any good. You came here to find out if I had made the charge. You've found out. Let's end it there. *I don't want you in this house.* I'm sorry this had to be done to you, Joseph.

CARDIN: I don't like your sympathy.

MRS. TILFORD: Very well. There's nothing I mean to do, nothing I want to do. There's nothing anybody can do.

CARDIN: [*Carefully.*] You have already done a terrible thing.

MRS. TILFORD: I have done what I had to do. What they are may possibly be their own business. It becomes a great deal more than that when children are involved.

KAREN: [*Wildly.*] It's not true. Not a word of it is true; can't you understand that?

MRS. TILFORD: There won't be any punishment for either of you. But there mustn't be any punishment for me, either—and that's what this meeting is. This— this thing is your own. Go away with it. I don't understand it and I don't want any part of it.

MARTHA: [*Slowly.*] So you thought we would go away?

MRS. TILFORD: I think that's best for you.

MARTHA: There must be something we can do to you, and, whatever it is, we'll find it.

MRS. TILFORD: That will be very unwise.

KAREN: You are right to be afraid.

MRS. TILFORD: I am not afraid, Karen.

CARDIN: But you *are* old—and you *are* irresponsible.

MRS. TILFORD: [*Hurt.*] You know that's not true.

KAREN: [*Goes to her.*] I don't want to have anything to do with your mess, do you hear me? It makes me feel dirty and sick to be forced to say this, but here it is: there isn't a single word of truth in anything you've said. We're standing here defending ourselves—and against what? Against a lie. A great, awful lie.

MRS. TILFORD: I'm sorry that I can't believe that.

KAREN: Damn you!

CARDIN: But you can believe this: they've worked eight long years to save enough money to buy that farm, to start that school. They did without everything that young people ought to have. You wouldn't know about that. That school meant things to them: self-respect, and bread and butter, and honest work. Do you know what it is to try so hard for anything? Well, now it's gone. [*Suddenly hits the side of the table with his hand.*] What the hell did you do it for?

MRS. TILFORD: [*Softly.*] It had to be done.

CARDIN: Righteousness is a great thing.

MRS. TILFORD: [*Gently.*] I know how you must feel.

CARDIN: You don't know anything about how I feel. And you don't know how they feel, either.

MRS. TILFORD: I've loved you as much as I loved my own boys. I wouldn't have spared them; I couldn't spare you.

CARDIN: [*Fiercely.*] I believe you.

MARTHA: What is there to do to you? What can we do to you? There must be something—something that makes you feel the way we do tonight. You don't want any part of this, you said. But you'll get a part. More than you bargained for. [*Suddenly.*] Listen: are you willing to stand by everything you've said tonight?

MRS. TILFORD: Yes.

MARTHA: All right. That's fine. But don't get the idea we'll let you whisper this lie: you made it and you'll come out with it. Shriek it to your town of Lancet. We'll *make* you shriek it—and we'll make you do it in a court room. [*Quietly.*] Tomorrow, Mrs. Tilford, you will have a libel suit on your hands.

MRS. TILFORD: That will be very unwise.

KAREN: Very unwise—for you.

MRS. TILFORD: It is you I am thinking of. I am frightened for you. It was wrong of you to brazen it out here tonight; it would be criminally foolish of you to brazen it out in public. That can bring you nothing but pain. I am an old woman, Miss Dobie, and I have seen too many people, out of pride, act on that pride. In the end they punish themselves.

MARTHA: And you feel that you are too old to be punished? That we should spare you?

MRS. TILFORD: You know that is not what I meant.

CARDIN: [*Turns from the window.*] So you took a child's word for it?

MARTHA: [*Looks at him, shakes her head.*] I knew it, too.

KAREN: That is really where you got it? I can't believe—it couldn't be. Why, she's a child.

MARTHA: She's not a child any longer.

KAREN: Oh, my God, it all fits so well now. That girl has hated us for a long time. We never knew why, we never could find out. There didn't seem to be any reason—

MARTHA: There wasn't any reason. She hates everybody and everything.

KAREN: Your Mary's a strange girl, a bad girl. There's something very awful the matter with her.

MRS. TILFORD: I was waiting for you to say that, Miss Wright.

KAREN: I'm telling you the truth. We should have told it to you long ago. [*Stops, sighs.*] It's no use.

MARTHA: Where is she? Bring her out here and let us hear what she has to say.

MRS. TILFORD: You cannot see her.

CARDIN: Where is she?

MRS. TILFORD: I won't have that, Joseph.

CARDIN: I'm going to talk to her.

MRS. TILFORD: *I won't have her go through with that again.* [*To* KAREN *and* MARTHA.] You came here demanding explanations. It was I who should have asked them from you. You attack me, you attack Mary. I've told you I didn't mean you any harm. I still don't. You claim that it isn't true; it may be natural that you should say that, but I *know* that it is true. No matter what you say, you know very well I wouldn't have acted until I was absolutely sure. All I wanted was to get those children away. That has been done. There won't be any talk about it or about you—I'll see to that. You have been in my house long enough. Get out.

KAREN: [*Gets up.*] The wicked very young, and the wicked very old. Let's go home.

CARDIN: Sit down. [*To* MRS. TILFORD.] When two people come here with their lives spread on the table for you to cut to pieces, then the only honest thing to do is to give them a chance to come out whole. Are you honest?

MRS. TILFORD: I've always thought so.

CARDIN: Then where is Mary? [*After a moment she moves her head to door Right. Quickly* CARDIN *goes to the door and opens it.*] Mary! Come here.

[*After a moment* MARY *appears, stands nervously near door. Her manner is shy and afraid.*]

MRS. TILFORD: [*Gently.*] Sit down, dear, and don't be afraid.

MARTHA: [*Her lips barely moving.*] Make her tell the truth.

CARDIN: [*Walking about in front of* MARY.] Look: everybody lies all the time. Sometimes they have to, sometimes they don't. I've lied myself for a lot of different reasons, but there was never a time when, if I'd been given a second chance, I wouldn't have taken back the lie and told the truth. You're lucky if you ever get that chance. I'm telling you this because I'm about to ask you a question. Before you answer the question, I want to tell you that if you've l—if you made a mistake, you must take this chance and say so. You won't be punished for it. Do you get all that?

MARY: [*Timidly.*] Yes, Cousin Joe.

CARDIN: [*Grimly.*] All right, let's get started. Were you telling your grandmother the truth this afternoon? The exact truth about Miss Wright and Miss Dobie?

MARY: [*Without hesitation.*] Oh, yes.

> [KAREN *sighs deeply,* MARTHA, *her fists closed tight, turns her back to the child.* CARDIN *smiles as he looks at* MARY.]

CARDIN: All right, Mary, that was your chance; you passed it up. [*Pulls up a chair, sits down in front of her.*] Now let's find out things.

MRS. TILFORD: She's told you. Aren't you through?

CARDIN: Not by a long shot. You've started something, and I'm going to finish it for you. Will you answer some more questions, Mary?

MARY: Yes, Cousin Joe.

MARTHA: Stop that sick sweet tone.

> [MRS. TILFORD *half rises;* CARDIN *motions her back.*]

CARDIN: Why don't you like Miss Dobie and Miss Wright?

MARY: Oh, I do like them. They just don't like me. They never have liked me.

CARDIN: How do you know?

MARY: They're always picking on me. They're always punishing me for everything that happens. No matter what happens, it's always me.

CARDIN: Why do you think they do that?

MARY: Because—because they're—because they— [*Stops, turns.*] Grandma, I—

CARDIN: All right, we'll skip that one. Did you get punished today?

MARY: Yes, and it was just because Peggy and Evelyn heard them and so they took it out on me.

KAREN: That's a lie.

CARDIN: Sssh. Heard what, Mary?

MARY: Mrs. Mortar told Miss Dobie that there was something funny about her. She said that she had a funny feeling about her. She said that she had a funny feeling about Miss Wright, and Mrs. Mortar said that was unnatural. That was why we got punished, just because—

KAREN: That was not the reason they got punished.

MRS. TILFORD: [*To* MARTHA.] Miss Dobie?

MARTHA: My aunt is a stupid woman. What she said was unpleasant; it was said to annoy me. It meant nothing more than that.

MARY: And, Cousin Joe, she said every time you came to the school Miss Dobie got jealous, and that she didn't want you to get married.

MARTHA: [*To* CARDIN.] She said that, too. For God's sake, can't you see what's happening? This—this child is taking little things, little family things, and making them have meanings that— [*Stops, suddenly regards* MARY *with a combination of disgust and interest.*] Where did you learn so much in so little time?

CARDIN: What do you think Mrs. Mortar meant by all that, Mary?

MRS. TILFORD: Stop it, Joseph!

MARY: I don't know, but it was always kind of funny and she always said things like that and all the girls would talk about it when Miss Dobie went and visited Miss Wright late at night—

KAREN: [*Angrily.*] And we go to the movies at night and sometimes we read at night and sometimes we drink tea at night. Those are guilty things, too, Mrs. Tilford.

MARY: And there are always funny sounds and we'd stay awake and listen because we couldn't help hearing and I'd get frightened because the sounds were like—

MARTHA: Be still!

KAREN: [*With violence.*] No, no. You don't want her still now. What else did you hear?

MARY: Grandma, I—

MRS. TILFORD: [*Bitterly to* CARDIN.] You are trying to make her name it, aren't you?

CARDIN: [*Ignoring her, speaks to* MARY.] Go on.

MARY: I don't know; there were just sounds.

CARDIN: But what did you think they were? Why did they frighten you?

MARY: [*Weakly.*] I don't know.

CARDIN: [*Smiles at* MRS. TILFORD.] She doesn't know.

MARY: [*Hastily.*] I saw things, too. One night there was so much noise I thought somebody was sick or something and I looked through the keyhole and they were kissing and saying things and then I got scared because it was different sort of and I—

MARTHA: [*Her face distorted, turns to* MRS. TILFORD.] That child—that child is sick.

KAREN: Ask her again how she could see us.

CARDIN: How could you see Miss Dobie and Miss Wright?

MARY: I—I—

MRS. TILFORD: Tell him what you whispered to me.

MARY: It was at night and I was leaning down by the keyhole.

KAREN: *There's no keyhole on my door.*

MRS. TILFORD: What?

KAREN: There—is—no—keyhole—on—my—door.

MARY: [*Quickly.*] It wasn't her room, Grandma, it was the other room, I guess. It was *Miss Dobie's* room. I saw them through the keyhole in Miss Dobie's room.

CARDIN: How did you know anybody was in Miss Dobie's room?

MARY: I told you, I told you. Because we heard them. Everybody heard them—

MARTHA: I share a room with my aunt. It is on the first floor at the other end of the house. It is impossible to hear anything from there. [*To* CARDIN.] Tell her to come and see for herself.

MRS. TILFORD: [*Her voice shaken.*] What is this, Mary? Why did you say you saw through a keyhole? *Can* you hear from your room—?

MARY: [*Starts to cry.*] Everybody is yelling at me. I don't know what I'm saying with everybody mixing me all up. I did see it! I did see it!

MRS. TILFORD: *What* did you see? *Where* did you see it? I want the truth, now. The truth, whatever it is.

CARDIN: [*Gets up, moves his chair back.*] We can go home. We are finished here. [*Looks around.*] It's not a pleasant place to be.

MRS. TILFORD: [*Angrily.*] Stop that crying, Mary. Stand up.

[MARY *gets up, head down, still crying hysterically.* MRS. TILFORD *goes and stands directly in front of her.*]

MRS. TILFORD: *I want the truth.*

MARY: All—all right.

MRS. TILFORD: What is the truth?

MARY: It was Rosalie who saw them. I just said it was me so I wouldn't have to tattle on Rosalie.

CARDIN: [*Wearily.*] Oh, my God!

MARY: It *was* Rosalie, Grandma, she told us all about it. She said she had read about it in a book and she knew. [*Desperately.*] You ask Rosalie. You just ask Rosalie. She'll tell you. We used to talk about it all the time. That's the truth, that's the honest truth. She said it was when the door was open once and she told us all about it. I was just trying to save Rosalie, and everybody jumps on me.

MRS. TILFORD: [*To* CARDIN.] Please wait a minute. [*Goes to library door.*] Rosalie!

CARDIN: You're giving yourself an awful beating, Amelia, and you deserve whatever you get.

MRS. TILFORD: [*Stands waiting for* ROSALIE, *passes her hand over her face.*] I don't know. I don't know, any more. Maybe it's what I do deserve. [*As Rosalie, frightened, appears at the door, making bows to everybody, she takes the child gently by the hand, brings her down Center, talking nervously.*] I'm sorry to keep you up so late, Rosalie. You must be tired. [*Speaks rapidly.*] Mary says there's been a lot of talk in the school lately about Miss Wright and Miss Dobie. Is that true?

ROSALIE: I—I don't know what you mean.

MRS. TILFORD: That things have been said among you girls.

ROSALIE: [*Wide-eyed, frightened.*] What things? I never—I—I—

KAREN: [*Gently.*] Don't be frightened.

MRS. TILFORD: What was the talk about, Rosalie?

ROSALIE: [*Utterly bewildered.*] I don't know what she means, Miss Wright.

KAREN: Rosalie, Mary has told her grandmother that certain things at school have been—er—puzzling you girls. You, particularly.

ROSALIE: History puzzles me. I guess I'm not very good at history, and Helen helps me sometimes, if that—

KAREN: No, that's not what she meant. She says that you told her that you saw certain—certain acts between Miss Dobie and myself. She says that once, when the door was open, you saw us kissing each other in a way that— [*Unable to bear the child's look, she turns her back.*] women don't kiss one another.

ROSALIE: Oh, Miss Wright, I didn't, didn't, I didn't. I *never* said such a thing.

MRS. TILFORD: [*Grimly.*] That's true, my dear?

ROSALIE: I never saw any such thing. Mary always makes things up about me and everybody else. [*Starts to weep in excitement.*] I never said any such thing ever. Why, I never even could have thought of—

MARY: [*Staring at her, speaks very slowly.*] Yes, you did, Rosalie. You're just trying to get out of it. I remember just when you said it. I remember it, because it was the day Helen Burton's bracelet was—

ROSALIE: [*Stands fascinated and fearful, looking at* MARY.] I never did. I—I—you're just—

MARY: It was the day Helen's bracelet was stolen, and nobody knew who did it, and Helen said that if her mother found out, she'd have the thief put in jail.

KAREN: [*Puzzled, as are the others, by the sudden change in* ROSALIE'S *manner.*] There's nothing to cry about. You must help us by telling the truth. Why, what's the matter, Rosalie?

MARY: Grandma, there's something I've got to tell you that—

ROSALIE: [*With a shrill cry.*] Yes. Yes. I did see it. I told Mary. What Mary said was right. I said it, I said it—

[*Throws herself on the couch, weeping hysterically;* MARTHA *stands leaning against the door;* KAREN, CARDIN *and* MRS. TILFORD *are staring at* ROSALIE; MARY *slowly sits down as the Curtain falls.*]

ACT III

SCENE: *The same as Act One. Living room of the school.*

AT RISE: *The room has changed. It is not dirty, but it is dull and dark and uncared for. The windows are tightly shut, the curtains tightly drawn.* KAREN *is sitting in a large chair, Right Center, feet flat on floor.* MARTHA *is lying on the couch, her face buried against the pillows, her back to* KAREN. *It is a minute or two after the rise of the curtain before either speaks.*

MARTHA: It's cold in here.

KAREN: Yes.

MARTHA: What time is it?

KAREN: I don't know. What's the difference?

MARTHA: None. I was hoping it was time for my bath.

KAREN: Take it early today.

MARTHA: [*Laughs.*] Oh, I couldn't do that. I look forward all day to that bath. It's my last touch with the full life. It makes me feel important to know that there's one thing ahead of me, one thing I've *got* to do. You ought to get yourself something like that. I tell you, at five o'clock every day you comb your hair. How's that? It's better for you, take my word. You wake up in the morning and you say to yourself, the day's not entirely empty, life is rich and full; at five o'clock I'll comb my hair.

[*They fall back into silence. A moment later the phone rings. Neither of them pays the slightest attention to it. But the ringing becomes too insistent.* KAREN *rises, takes the receiver off, goes back to her chair and sits down.*]

KAREN: It's raining.

MARTHA: Hungry?

KAREN: No. You?

MARTHA: No, but I'd like to be hungry again. Remember how much we used to eat at college?

KAREN: That was ten years ago.

MARTHA: Well, maybe we'll be hungry in another ten years. It's cheaper this way.

KAREN: What's the old thing about time being more nourishing than bread?

MARTHA: Yeah? Maybe.

KAREN: Joe's late today. What time is it?

MARTHA: [*Turns again to lie on her side.*] We've been sitting here for eight days asking each other the time. Haven't you heard? There isn't any time any more.

KAREN: It's been days since we've been out of this house.

MARTHA: Well, we'll have to get off these chairs sooner or later. In a couple of months they'll need dusting.

KAREN: What'll we do when we get off?

MARTHA: God knows.

KAREN: [*Almost in a whisper.*] It's awful.

MARTHA: Let's not talk about it. [*After a moment.*] What about eggs for dinner?

KAREN: All right.

MARTHA: I'll make some potatoes with onions, the way you used to like them.

KAREN: It's a week ago Thursday. It never seemed real until the last day. It seems real enough now, all right.

MARTHA: Now and forever after.

KAREN: [*Suddenly.*] Let's go out.

MARTHA: [*Turns over, stares at her.*] Where to?

KAREN: We'll take a walk.

MARTHA: Where'll we walk?

KAREN: Why shouldn't we take a walk? We won't see anybody, and suppose we do, what of it? We'll jus—

MARTHA: [*Slowly gets up.*] Come on. We'll go through the park.

KAREN: They might see us. [*They stand looking at each other.*] Let's not go. [MARTHA *goes back, lies down again*] We'll go tomorrow.

MARTHA: [*Laughs.*] Stop kidding yourself.

KAREN: But Joe says we've got to go out. He says that all the people who don't think it's true will begin to wonder if we keep hiding this way.

MARTHA: If it makes you feel better to think there *are* such people, go ahead.

KAREN: He says we ought to go into town and go shopping and act as though—

MARTHA: Shopping? That's a sound idea. There aren't three stores in Lancet that would sell us anything. Hasn't he heard about the ladies' clubs and their meetings and their circulars and their visits and their—

KAREN: [*Softly.*] Don't tell him.

MARTHA: [*Gently.*] I won't. [*There are footsteps in the hall, and the sound of something being dragged.*] There's our friend.

> [A GROCERY BOY *appears lugging a box. He brings it into the room, stands staring at them, giggles a little. Walks toward* KAREN, *stops, examines her. She sits tense, looking away from him. Without taking his eyes from* KAREN, *he speaks.*]

GROCERY BOY: I knocked on the kitchen door but nobody answered.

MARTHA: You said that yesterday. All right. Thanks. Good-bye.

KAREN: [*Unable any longer to stand the stare.*] Make him stop it.

GROCERY BOY: Here are the things. [*Giggles, moves toward* MARTHA, *stands looking at her. Suddenly* MARTHA *thrusts her hand in the air.*]

MARTHA: I've got eight fingers, see? I'm a freak.

GROCERY BOY: [*Giggling.*] There's a car comin' here. [*Gets no answer, starts backing out of door, still looking. Familiarly.*] Good-bye. [*Exits.*]

MARTHA: [*Bitterly.*] You still think we should go into town?

KAREN: I don't know. I don't know about anything any more. [*After a moment.*] Martha, Martha, Martha—

MARTHA: [*Gently.*] What is it, Karen?

KAREN: What are we going to do? It's all so cold and unreal and— It's like that dark hour of the night when, half awake, you struggle through the black mess you've been dreaming. Then, suddenly, you wake up and you see your own bed or your own nightgown and you know you're back again in a solid world. But now it's all the nightmare; there is no solid world. Oh. Martha, *why* did it happen? *What* happened? What are we doing here like this?

MARTHA: Waiting.

KAREN: For what?

MARTHA: I don't know.

KAREN: We've got to get out of this place. I can't stand it any more.

MARTHA: You'll be getting married soon. Everything will be all right then.

KAREN: [*Vaguely.*] Yes.

MARTHA: [*Looks up at the tone.*] What is it?

KAREN: Nothing.

MARTHA: There mustn't be anything wrong between you and Joe. Never.

KAREN: [*Without conviction.*] Nothing's wrong. [*As footsteps are heard in the hall, her face lights up.*] There's Joe now.

[MRS. MORTAR, *small suitcase in hand, stands in the doorway, her face pushed coyly forward.*]

MRS. MORTAR: And here I am. Hello, hello.

MARTHA: [*She has turned over on her back and is staring at her aunt. She speaks to* KAREN.] The Duchess, isn't it? Returned at long last. [*Too jovially.*] Come on in. We're delighted to see you. Are you tired from your journey? Is there something I can get you?

MRS. MORTAR: [*Surprised.*] I'm very glad to see you both, and [*Looks around.*] I'm very glad to see the old place again. How is everything?

MARTHA: Everything's fine. We're splendid, thank you. You're just in time for tea.

MRS. MORTAR: You know, I should like some tea, if it isn't too much trouble.

MARTHA: No trouble at all. Some small sandwiches and a little brandy?

MRS. MORTAR: [*Puzzled finally.*] Why, Martha.

MARTHA: Where the hell have you been?

MRS. MORTAR: Around, around. I had a most interesting time. Things—

MARTHA: Why didn't you answer my telegrams?

MRS. MORTAR: Things have changed in the theater—drastically changed, I might say.

MARTHA: *Why didn't you answer my telegrams?*

MRS. MORTAR: Oh, Martha, there's your temper again.

MARTHA: Answer me and don't bother about my temper.

MRS. MORTAR: [*Nervously.*] I was moving around a great deal. [*Conversationally.*] You know, I think it will throw a very revealing light on the state of the new theater when I tell you that the Lyceum in Rochester now has a toilet back stage.

MARTHA: To hell with the toilet in Rochester. Where were you?

MRS. MORTAR: Moving around, I tell you.

KAREN: What difference does it all make now?

MRS. MORTAR: Karen is quite right. Let bygones be bygones. As I was saying, there's an effete something in the theater now, and that accounts for—

MARTHA: [*To* KAREN.] Isn't she wonderful? [*To* MRS. MORTAR.] Why did you refuse to come back here and testify for us?

MRS. MORTAR: Why, Martha, I didn't refuse to come back at all. That's the wrong way to look at it. I was on a tour; that's a moral obligation, you know. Now don't let's talk about unpleasant things any more. I'll go up and unpack a few things; tomorrow's plenty of time to get my trunk.

KAREN: [*Laughs.*] Things have changed here, you know.

MARTHA: She doesn't know. She expected to walk right up to a comfortable fire and sit down and she very carefully waited until the whole thing was over. [*Leans forward, speaking to* MRS. MORTAR.] Listen, Karen Wright and Martha Dobie brought a libel suit against a woman called Tilford because her grand-child had accused them of having what the judge called "sinful sexual knowl-edge of one another." [MRS. MORTAR *holds up her hand in protest, and* MARTHA *laughs.*] Don't like that, do you? Well, a great part of the defense's case was based on remarks made by Lily Mortar, actress in the toilets of Rochester, against her niece, Martha. And a greater part of the defense's case rested on the telling fact that Mrs. Mortar would not appear in court to deny or explain those remarks. Mrs. Mortar had a moral obligation to the theater. As you probably read in the papers, we lost the case.

MRS. MORTAR: I didn't think of it that way, Martha. It couldn't have done any good for all of us to get mixed up in that unpleasant notoriety— [*Sees* MARTHA'S *face. Hastily.*] But now that you've explained it, why, I do see it your way, and I'm sorry I didn't come back. But now that I am here, I'm going to stand shoulder to shoulder with you. I know what you've gone through, but the body and heart *do* recover, you know. I'll be here working right along with you and we'll—

MARTHA: There's an eight o'clock train. Get on it.

MRS. MORTAR: Martha.

MARTHA: You've come back to pick the bones dry. Well, there aren't even bones anymore. There's nothing here for you.

MRS. MORTAR: [*Sniffling a little.*] How can you talk to me like that?

MARTHA: Because I hate you. I've always hated you.

MRS. MORTAR: [*Gently.*] God will punish you for that.

MARTHA: He's been doing all right.

MRS. MORTAR: When you wish to apologize, I will be temporarily in my room. [*Starts to exit, almost bumps into* CARDIN, *steps back with dignity.*] How do you do?

CARDIN: [*Laughs.*] Look who's here. A little late, aren't you?

MRS. MORTAR: So it's you. Now, I call *that* loyal. A lot of men wouldn't still be here. They would have felt—

MARTHA: Get out of here.

KAREN: [*Opening door.*] I'll call you when it's time for your train.

[MRS. MORTAR *looks at her, exits.*]

CARDIN: Now, what do you think brought her back?

KAREN: God knows.

MARTHA: I know. She was broke.

CARDIN: [*Pats* MARTHA *on the shoulder.*] Don't let her worry you this time, Martha. We'll give her some money and get rid of her. [*Pulls* KAREN *to him.*] Been out today, darling?

KAREN: We started to go out.

CARDIN: [*Shakes his head.*] Feel all right?

[KAREN *leans over to kiss him. Almost imperceptibly he pulls back.*]

KAREN: Why did you do that?

MARTHA: Karen.

CARDIN: Do what?

KAREN: Draw back that way.

CARDIN: [*Laughs, kisses her.*] If we sit around here much longer, we'll all be bats. I sold my place today to Foster.

KAREN: You did what?

CARDIN: We're getting married this week. Then we're going away—all three of us.

KAREN: You can't leave here. I won't have you do this for me. What about the hospital and—

CARDIN: Shut up, darling, it's all fixed. We're going to Vienna and we're going quick. Fischer wrote that I can have my old place back.

KAREN: No! No! I'm not going to let you.

CARDIN: It's already done. Fischer can't pay me much, but it'll be enough for the three of us. Plenty if we live cheap.

MARTHA: I couldn't go with you, Joe.

CARDIN: Nonsense, Martha, we're all going. We're going to have fun again.

KAREN: [*Slowly.*] You don't want to go back to Vienna.

CARDIN: No.

KAREN: Then why?

CARDIN: Look: I don't want to go to Vienna; I'd rather have stayed here. But then you don't want to go to Vienna; you'd rather have stayed here. Well, to hell with that. We *can't* stay here, and Vienna offers enough to eat and sleep and drink beer on. Now don't object any more, please, darling. All right?

KAREN: All right.

MARTHA: I can't go. It's better for all of us if I don't.

CARDIN: [*Puts his arm around her.*] Not now. You stay with us now. Later on, if you want it that way. All right?

MARTHA: [*Smiles.*] All right.

CARDIN: Swell. I'll buy you good coffee cakes and take you both to Ischl for a honeymoon.

MARTHA: [*Picking up grocery box, she starts for door.*] A big coffee cake with a lot of raisins. It would be nice to like something again. [*Exits.*]

CARDIN: [*With a slightly forced heartiness.*] I'll be going back with a pretty girl who belongs to me. I'll show you off all over the place—to Dr. Engelhardt, and the nurse at the desk, and to the fat gal in the cake shop, and to Fischer. [*Laughs.*] The last time I saw him was at the railroad station. He took me back of the baggage car. [*With an imitation of an accent.*] "Joseph," he said, "you'll be a good doctor; I would trust you to cut up my Minna. But you're not a great doctor, and you never will be. Go back where you were born and take care of your sick. Leave the fancy work to the others." I came home.

KAREN: You'll be coming home again some day.

CARDIN: No. Let's not talk about it. [*After a moment.*] You'll need some clothes?

KAREN: A few. Oh, your Dr. Fischer was so right. This is where you belong.

CARDIN: I need an overcoat and a suit. You'll need a lot of things—heavy things. It's cold there now, much colder than you'd expect—

KAREN: I've done this to you. I've taken you away from everything you want.

CARDIN: But it's lovely in the mountains, and that's where we'll go for a month.

KAREN: They—*they've* done it. They've taken away every chance we had. Everything we wanted, everything we were going to be.

CARDIN: And we've got to stop talking like that. [*Takes her by the shoulder.*] We've got a chance. But it's just one chance, and if we miss it we're done for. It means that we've got to start putting the whole business behind us now. *Now*, Karen. What you've done, you've done—and that's that.

KAREN: What *I've* done?

CARDIN: [*Impatiently.*] What's been done to you.

KAREN: What did you mean? [*When there is no answer.*] What did you mean when you said: "What you've done"?

CARDIN: [*Shouting.*] Nothing. Nothing. [*Then very quietly.*] Karen, there are a lot of people in this world who've had bad trouble in their lives. We're three of those people. We could sit around the rest of our lives and exist on that trouble, until in the end we had nothing else and we'd want nothing else. That's something I'm not coming to and I'm not going to let you come to.

KAREN: I know. I'm sorry. [*After a moment.*] Joe, can we have a baby right away?

CARDIN: [*Vaguely.*] Yes, I guess so. Although we won't have much money now.

KAREN: You used to want one right away. You always said that was the way you wanted it. There's some reason for your changing.

CARDIN: My God, we *can't* go on like this. Everything I say to you is made to mean something else. We don't talk like people any more. Oh, let's get out of here as fast as we can.

KAREN: [*As though she is finishing the sentence for him.*] And every word will have a new meaning. You think we'll be able to run away from that? Woman, child, love, lawyer—no words that we can use in safety any more. [*Laughs bitterly.*] Sick, high-tragic people. That's what we'll be.

CARDIN: [*Gently.*] No, we won't, darling. Love is casual—that's the way it should be. We must find that out all over again. We must learn again to live and love like other people.

KAREN: It won't work.

CARDIN: What?

KAREN: The two of us together.

CARDIN: [*Sharply.*] Stop talking like that.

KAREN: It's true. [*Suddenly.*] I want you to say it now.

CARDIN: I don't know what you're talking about.

KAREN: Yes, you do. We've both known for a long time. I knew surely the day we lost the case. I was watching your face in court. It was ashamed—and sad at being ashamed. Say it now, Joe. Ask it now.

CARDIN: I have nothing to ask. Nothing— [*Quickly.*] All right. Is it—was it ever—

KAREN: [*Puts her hand over his mouth.*] No. Martha and I have never touched each other. [*Pulls his head down on her shoulder.*] That's all right, darling. I'm glad you asked. I'm not mad a bit, really.

CARDIN: I'm sorry, Karen, I'm sorry. I didn't mean to hurt you, I—

KAREN: I know. You wanted to wait until it was all over, you really never wanted to ask at all. You didn't know for sure; you thought there might be just a little truth in it all. [*With great feeling.*] You've been good to me and loyal. You're a fine man. [*Afraid of tears, she pats him, walks away.*] Now go and sit down, Joe. I have things to say. They're all mixed up and I must get them clear.

CARDIN: Don't let's talk any more. Let's forget and go ahead.

KAREN: [*Puzzled.*] Go ahead?

CARDIN: Yes, Karen.

KAREN: You believe me, then?

CARDIN: Of course I believe you. I only had to hear you say it.

KAREN: No, no, no. That isn't the way things work. Maybe you believe me. I'd never know whether you did or not. You'd never know whether you did, either. We couldn't do it that way. Can't you see what would happen? We'd be hounded by it all our lives. I'd be frightened, always, and in the end my own fright would make me—would make me hate you. [*Sees slight movement he makes.*] Yes, it would; I know it would. I'd hate you for what I thought I'd done to you. And I'd hate myself, too. It would grow and grow until we'd be ruined by it. [*Sees him about to speak.*] Ah, Joe, you've seen all that yourself. You knew it first.

CARDIN: [*Softly.*] I didn't mean it that way; I don't now.

KAREN: [*Smiles.*] You're still trying to spare me, still trying to tell yourself that we might be all right again. But we won't be all right. Not ever, ever, ever. I don't know all the reasons why. Look, I'm standing here. I haven't changed. [*Holds out her hands.*] My hands look just the same, my face is the same, even my dress is old. We're in a room we've been in so many times before; you're sitting where you always sit; it's nearly time for dinner. I'm like everybody else. I can have all the things that everybody has. I can have you and a baby, and I can go to market, and we can go to the movies, and people will talk to me and— [*Suddenly notices the pain in his face.*] Oh, I'm sorry. I mustn't talk like that. That couldn't be true any more.

CARDIN: It could be, Karen. We'll make it be like that.

KAREN: No. That's only what we'd like to have had. It's what we can't have now. Go home, darling.

CARDIN: [*With force.*] Don't talk like that. No matter what it is, we can't leave each other. I can't leave you—

KAREN: Joe, Joe. Let's do it now and quick; it will be too hard later on.

CARDIN: No, no, no. We love each other. [*His voice breaks.*] I'd give anything not to have asked questions, Karen.

KAREN: It had to be asked sooner or later—and answered. You're a good man—the best I'll ever know—and you've been better to me than— But it's no good now, for either of us; you can see that.

CARDIN: It can be. You say I helped you. Help me now; help me to be strong and good enough to— [*Goes toward her with his arms out.*] Karen!

KAREN: [*Drawing back.*] No, Joe! [*Then, as he stops.*] Will you do something for me?

CARDIN: No. I won't—

KAREN: Will you—will you go away for two days—a day—and think this all over by yourself—away from me and love and pity? Will you? And then decide.

CARDIN: [*After a long pause.*] Yes, if you want, but it won't make any difference. We will—

KAREN: Don't say anything. Please go now. [*She sits down, smiles, closes her eyes. For a moment he stands looking at her, then slowly puts on his hat.*] And all my heart goes with you.

CARDIN: [*At door, leaving.*] I'll be coming back. [*Exits, slowly, reluctantly, closing door.*]

KAREN: [*A moment after he has gone.*] No, you won't. Never, darling. [*Stays as she is until* MARTHA *enters Right.*]

MARTHA: [*Goes to lamp, lights it.*] It gets dark so early now. [*Sits down, stretches, laughs.*] Cooking always makes me feel better. Well, I guess we'll have to give the Duchess some dinner. When the hawks descend, you've got to feed 'em. Where's Joe? [*No answer.*] Where's Joe?

KAREN: Gone.

MARTHA: A patient? Will he be back in time for dinner?

KAREN: No.

MARTHA: [*Watching her.*] We'll save dinner for him, then. Karen! What's the matter?

KAREN: [*In a dull tone.*] He won't be back any more.

MARTHA: [*Speaking slowly and carefully.*] You mean he won't be back any more tonight.

KAREN: He won't be back at all.

MARTHA: [*Quickly, walks to* KAREN.] What happened? [KAREN *shakes her head.*] What happened, Karen?

KAREN: He thought that we had been lovers.

MARTHA: [*Tensely.*] I don't believe you.

[*Wearily* KAREN *turns her head away.*]

KAREN: All right.

MARTHA: [*Automatically.*] I don't believe it. He's never said a word all these months, all during the trial— [*Suddenly grabs* KAREN *by the shoulder, shakes her.*] Didn't you tell him? For God's sake, didn't you tell him it wasn't true?

KAREN: Yes.

MARTHA: He didn't believe you?

KAREN: I guess he believed me.

MARTHA: [*Angrily.*] Then what have you done?

KAREN: What had to be done.

MARTHA: It's all wrong. It's silly. He'll be back in a little while and you'll clear it all up— [*Realizes why that can't be, covers her mouth with her hand.*] Oh, God, I wanted that for you so much.

KAREN: Don't. I feel sick to my stomach.

MARTHA: [*Goes to couch opposite* KAREN, *puts her head in her arms.*] What's happened to us? What's really happened to us?

KAREN: I don't know. I want to be sleepy. I want to go to sleep.

MARTHA: Go back to Joe. He's strong; he'll understand. It's too much for you this way.

KAREN: [*Irritably.*] Stop talking about it. Let's pack and get out of here. Let's take the train in the morning.

MARTHA: The train to where?

KAREN: I don't know. Some place; any place.

MARTHA: A job? Money?

KAREN: In a big place we could get something to do.

MARTHA: They'd know about us. We've been famous.

KAREN: A small town, then.

MARTHA: They'd know more about us.

KAREN: [*As a child would say it.*] Isn't there anywhere to go?

MARTHA: No. There'll never be any place for us to go. We're bad people. We'll sit. We'll be sitting the rest of our lives wondering what's happened to us. You think this scene is strange? Well, get used to it; we'll be here for a long time. [*Suddenly pinches* KAREN *on the arm.*] Let's pinch each other sometimes. We can tell whether we're still living.

KAREN: [*Shivers, listlessly gets up, starts making a fire in the fireplace.*] But this isn't a new sin they tell us we've done. Other people aren't destroyed by it.

MARTHA: They are the people who believe in it, who want it, who've chosen it. We aren't like that. We don't love each other. [*Suddenly stops, crosses to fireplace, stands looking, abstractedly at* KAREN. *Speaks casually.*] I don't love you. We've been very close to each other, of course. I've loved you like a friend, the way thousands of women feel about other women.

KAREN: [*Only half listening.*] Yes.

MARTHA: Certainly that doesn't mean anything. There's nothing wrong about that. It's perfectly natural that I should be fond of you, that I should—

KAREN: [*Listlessly.*] Why are you saying all this to me?

MARTHA: Because I love you.

KAREN: [*Vaguely.*] Yes, of course.

MARTHA: I love you that way—maybe the way they said I loved you. I don't know. [*Waits, gets no answer, kneels down next to* KAREN.] Listen to me!

KAREN: What?

MARTHA: *I have loved you the way they said.*

KAREN: You're crazy.

MARTHA: There's always been something wrong. Always—as long as I can remember. But I never knew it until all this happened.

KAREN: [*For the first time looks up, horrified.*] Stop it!

MARTHA: You're afraid of hearing it; I'm more afraid than you.

KAREN: [*Puts her hands over her ears.*] I won't listen to you.

MARTHA: Take your hands down. [*Leans over, pulls* KAREN'S *hands away.*] You've got to know it. I can't keep it any longer. I've got to tell you how guilty I am.

KAREN: [*Deliberately.*] You are guilty of nothing.

MARTHA: I've been telling myself that since the night we heard the child say it; I've been praying I could convince myself of it. I can't, I can't any longer. It's there. I don't know how, I don't know why. But I did love you. I do love you. I resented your marriage; maybe because I wanted you; maybe I wanted you all along; maybe I couldn't call it by a name; maybe it's been there ever since I first knew you—

KAREN: [*Tensely.*] It's a lie. You're telling yourself a lie. We never thought of each other that way.

MARTHA: [*Bitterly.*] No, of course *you* didn't. But who says I didn't? I never felt that way about anybody but you. I've never loved a man— [*Stops. Softly.*] I never knew why before. Maybe it's that.

KAREN: [*Carefully.*] You are tired and sick.

MARTHA: [*As though she were talking to herself.*] It's funny; it's all mixed up. There's something in you, and you don't know it and you don't do anything about it. Suddenly a child gets bored and lies—and there you are, seeing it for the first time. [*Closes her eyes.*] I don't know. It all seems to come back to *me.* In some way I've ruined your life. I've ruined my own. I didn't even *know.* [*Smiles.*] There's a big difference between us now, Karen. I feel all dirty and— [*Puts out her hand, touches* KAREN'S *head.*] I can't stay with you any more, darling.

KAREN: [*In a shaken, uncertain tone.*] All this isn't true. You've never said it; we'll forget it by tomorrow—

MARTHA: Tomorrow? That's a funny word. Karen, we would have had to invent a new language, as children do, without words like tomorrow.

KAREN: [*Crying.*] Go and lie down, Martha. You'll feel better.

> [MARTHA *looks around the room, slowly, carefully. She is very quiet. Exits Right, stands at door for a second looking at* KAREN, *then slowly shuts the door behind her.*
>
> KAREN *sits alone without moving. There is no sound in the house until, a few minutes after* MARTHA'S *exit, a shot is heard. The sound of the shot should not be too loud or too strong. For a few seconds after the noise has died out,* KAREN *does not move. Then, suddenly, she springs from the chair, crosses the room, pulls open door Right. Almost at the same moment footsteps are heard on the staircase.*]

MRS. MORTAR: What was that? Where is it? [*Enters door Center, frightened, aimlessly moving about.*] Karen! Martha! Where are you? I heard a shot. What was—

[*Stops as she sees* KAREN *reappear Right. Walks toward her, still talking. Stops when she sees* KAREN'S *face.*] What—what is it? [KAREN *moves her hands, shakes her head slightly, passes* MRS. MORTAR, *and goes toward window.* MRS. MORTAR *stares at her for a moment, rushes past her through door Right. Left alone,* KAREN *leans against the window.* MRS. MORTAR *re-enters crying. After a minute.*] What shall we do? What shall we do?

KAREN: [*In a toneless voice.*] Nothing.

MRS. MORTAR: We've got to get a doctor—right away. [*Goes to phone, nervously, fumblingly starts to dial.*]

KAREN: [*Without turning.*] There isn't any use.

MRS. MORTAR: We've got to do something. Oh, it's awful. Poor Martha. I don't know what we can do— [*Puts phone down, collapses in chair, sobs quietly.*] You think she's dea—

KAREN: Yes.

MRS. MORTAR: Poor, poor Martha. I can't realize it's true. Oh, how could she—she was so—I don't know what— [*Looks up, still crying, surprised*] I'm—I'm frightened.

KAREN: Don't cry.

MRS. MORTAR: I can't help it. How can I help it? [*Gradually the sobs cease, and she sits rocking herself*] I'll never forgive myself for the last words I said to her. But I was good to her, Karen, and you know God will excuse me for that once. I always tried to do everything I could. [*Suddenly.*] Suicide's a sin. [*No answer. Timidly.*] Shouldn't we call somebody to—

KAREN: In a little while.

MRS. MORTAR: She shouldn't have done it, she shouldn't have done it. It was because of all this awful business. She would have got a job and started all over again—she was just worried and sick and—

KAREN: That isn't the reason she did it.

MRS. MORTAR: What—why—?

KAREN: [*Wearily.*] What difference does it make now?

MRS. MORTAR: [*Reproachfully.*] You're not crying.

KAREN: No.

MRS. MORTAR: What will happen to me? I haven't anything. Poor Martha—

KAREN: She was very good to you; she was good to us all.

MRS. MORTAR: Oh, I know she was, Karen, and I was good to her too. I did everything I could. I—I haven't any place to go. [*After a few seconds of silence.*] I'm afraid. It seems so queer—in the next room. [*Shivers.*]

KAREN: Don't be afraid.

MRS. MORTAR: It's different for you. You're young.

KAREN: Not any more.

[*The sound of the door-bell ringing.* MRS. MORTAR *jumps.* KAREN *doesn't move. It rings again.*]

MRS. MORTAR: [*Nervously.*] Who is it? [*The bell rings again.*] Shall I answer it? [KAREN *shrugs.*] I think we'd better. [*Exits down the hall through Center doors. Returns in a minute followed by* MRS. TILFORD'S *maid,* AGATHA, *who stands in the door.*] It's a woman. [*No answer.*] It's a woman to see you, Karen. [*Getting no answer, she turns to* AGATHA.] You can't come in now; we've had a—we've had trouble here.

AGATHA: Miss Karen, I've got to speak to you.

KAREN: [*Turns slowly, mechanically.*] Agatha.

AGATHA: [*Goes to* KAREN.] Please, Miss Karen. We've tried so hard to get you. I been phoning here all the time. Trying to get you. Phoning and phoning. Please, please let her come in. Just for a minute, Miss Karen. Please—

MRS. MORTAR: Who wants to come in here?

AGATHA: Mrs. Tilford. [*Looks at* KAREN.] Don't you feel well? [KAREN *shakes her head.*] You ain't mad at *me?*

MRS. MORTAR: That woman can't come in here. She caused all—

KAREN: I'm not mad at you, Agatha.

AGATHA: Can I—can I get you something?

KAREN: No.

AGATHA: You poor child. You look like you got a pain somewhere. [*Hesitates, takes* KAREN'S *hands.*] I only came cause she's so bad off. She's got to see you, Miss Karen, she's just got to. She's been sittin' outside in the car, hoping you'd come out. She can't get Dr. Joe. He—he won't talk to her any more. I wouldn't a come—I always been on your side—but she's sick. If only you could see her, you'd let her come for just a minute.

KAREN: I couldn't do that, Agatha.

AGATHA: I don't blame you. But I had to tell you. She's old. It's going to kill her.

KAREN: [*Bitterly.*] Kill her? Where is Mrs. Tilford?

AGATHA: Outside.

KAREN: All right.

AGATHA: [*Presses* KAREN'S *arm.*] You always been a good girl. [*Hurriedly exits.*]

MRS. MORTAR: You going to allow that woman to come in here? With Martha lying there? How can you be so feelingless? [*She starts to cry.*] I won't stay and see it. I won't have anything to do with it. I'll never let that woman— [*Rushes sobbing from the room.*]

[*A second after,* MRS. TILFORD *appears in the doorway Center. Her face, her walk, her voice have changed. She is feeble.*]

MRS. TILFORD: Karen, let me come in.

[*Without turning,* KAREN *bows her head.* MRS. TILFORD *enters, stands staring at the floor.*]

KAREN: Why have you come here?

MRS. TILFORD: I had to come. [*Stretches out her hand to* KAREN, *who does not turn. She drops her hand.*] I know *now;* I know it wasn't true.

KAREN: What?

MRS. TILFORD: [*Carefully.*] I know it wasn't true, Karen.

KAREN: [*Stares at her, shudders.*] You know it wasn't true? I don't care what you know. It doesn't matter any more. If that's what you had to say, you've said it. Go away.

MRS. TILFORD: [*Puts her hand to her throat.*] I've got to tell you.

KAREN: I don't want to hear you.

MRS. TILFORD: Last Tuesday Mrs. Wells found a bracelet in Rosalie's room. The bracelet had been hidden for several months. We found out that Rosalie had taken the bracelet from another girl, and that Mary— [*Closes her eyes.*] that Mary knew that and used it to force Rosalie into saying that she had seen you and Miss Dobie together. I—I've talked to Mary. I've found out. [KAREN *suddenly begins to laugh, high and sharp.*] Don't do that, Karen. I have only a little more to say, I've talked to Judge Potter. He will make all arrangements. There will be a public apology and an explanation. The damage suit will be paid to you in full and—and any more that you will be kind enough to take from me. I—I must see that you won't suffer any more.

KAREN: We're not going to suffer any more. Martha is dead. [MRS. TILFORD *gasps, shakes her head as though to shake off the truth, feebly falls into a chair, and covers her face.* KAREN *watches her for a minute.*] So you've come here to relieve your conscience? Well, I won't be your confessor. It's choking you, is it? [*Violently.*] And you want to stop the choking, don't you? You've done a wrong and you have to right that wrong or you can't rest your head again. You want to be "just," don't you, and you wanted us to help you be just? You've come to the wrong place for help. You want to be a "good" woman again, don't you? [*Bitterly.*] Oh, I know. You told us that night that you had to do what you did. Now you "have" to do this. A public apology and money paid, and you can sleep again and eat again. That done and there'll be peace for you. You're old, and the old are callous. Ten, fifteen years left for you. But what of me? It's a whole life for me. A whole God-damned life. [*Suddenly quiet, points to door Right.*] And what of her?

MRS. TILFORD: [*She is crying.*] You are still living.

KAREN: Yes. I guess so.

MRS. TILFORD: [*With a tremendous effort to control herself.*] I didn't come here to relieve myself. I swear to God I didn't. I came to try—to try anything. I knew there wasn't any relief for me, Karen, and that there never would be again. [*Tensely.*] But what I am or why I came doesn't matter. The only thing that matters is you and— You, now.

KAREN: There's nothing for me.

MRS. TILFORD: Oh, let's try to make something for you. You're young and I—I can help you.

KAREN: [*Smiles.*] You can help me?

MRS. TILFORD: [*With great feeling.*] Take whatever I can give you. Take it for yourself and use it for yourself. It won't bring me peace, if that's what's worrying you. [*Smiles.*] Those ten or fifteen years you talk about! They will be bad years.

KAREN: I'm tired, Mrs. Tilford. [*Almost tenderly.*] You will have a hard time ahead, won't you?

MRS. TILFORD: Yes.

KAREN: Mary?

MRS. TILFORD: I don't know.

KAREN: You can send her away.

MRS. TILFORD: No. I could never do that. Whatever she does, it must be to me and no one else. She's—she's——

KAREN: Yes. Your very own, to live with the rest of your life. [*For a moment she watches* MRS. TILFORD'S *face.*] It's over for me now, but it will never end for you. She's harmed us both, but she's harmed you more, I guess. [*Sits down beside* MRS. TILFORD.] I'm sorry.

MRS. TILFORD: [*Clings to her.*] Then you'll try for yourself.

KAREN: All right.

MRS. TILFORD: You and Joe.

KAREN: No. We're not together anymore.

MRS. TILFORD: [*Looks up at her.*] Did I do that, too?

KAREN: I don't think anyone did anything, any more.

MRS. TILFORD: [*Makes a half-movement to rise.*] I'll go to him right away.

KAREN: No, it's better now the way it is.

MRS. TILFORD: But he must know what I know, Karen. You must go back to him.

KAREN: [*Smiles.*] No, not any more.

MRS. TILFORD: You must, you must— [*Sees her face, hesitates.*] Perhaps later, Karen?

KAREN: Perhaps.

MRS. TILFORD: [*After a moment in which they both sit silent.*] Come away from here now, Karen. [KAREN *shakes her head.*] You can't stay with— [*Moves her hand toward door Right.*]

KAREN: When she is buried, then I will go.

MRS. TILFORD: You'll be all right?

KAREN: I'll be all right, I suppose. Good-bye, now.

[*They both rise.* MRS. TILFORD *speaks, pleadingly.*]

MRS. TILFORD: You'll let me help you? You'll let me try?

KAREN: Yes, if it will make you feel better.

MRS. TILFORD: [*With great feeling.*] Oh, yes, oh, yes, Karen.

[*Unconsciously* KAREN *begins to walk toward the window.*]

KAREN: [*Suddenly.*] Is it nice out?

MRS. TILFORD: It's been cold. [KAREN *opens the window slightly, sits on the ledge.* MRS. TILFORD *with surprise.*] It seems a little warmer, now.

KAREN: It feels very good.

[*They smile at each other.*]

MRS. TILFORD: You'll write me some time?

KAREN: If I ever have anything to say. Good-bye, now.

MRS. TILFORD: You will have. I know it. Good-bye, my dear.

[KAREN *smiles, shakes her head as* MRS. TILFORD *exits. She does not turn, but a minute later she raises her hand.*]

KAREN: Good-bye.

CURTAIN

1934

QUESTIONS

1. How much of act 1 seems to be exposition? Exactly what are we told and by whom? At what point in act 1 do you sense what individual characters are like and how they are related to each other? Where does the rising action begin?
2. Exactly what part of act 2 constitutes the play's turning point? Where does the falling action begin? In what does the play's final stability consist?
3. Through what actions is Mary's character established in act 1? What are the stages of our understanding of her? How much of our response to her is based on the reactions of other characters? If you were staging the play, how would you play her initial appearance? How would you establish her intimidation of the other children? How would you establish her desire to seem loving and innocent?
4. Trace the steps by which Karen's character is established. Which actions make her seem especially likable? Which show her anxieties? How would you play Martha?
5. Which scenes establish Mrs. Mortar's character? In what ways is she like Mary? How would you establish these similarities through staging?
6. What features of Mrs. Mortar's character are crucial to the plot? What features of Mrs. Tilford's character are crucial to the plot?
7. Why does Mrs. Tilford choose to believe her granddaughter? List the strategies Mary uses to make her lies plausible.

WRITING SUGGESTIONS

1. Write a brief character sketch of Mary Tilford. In a paragraph, list all the characteristics of her personality that bear on her actions in the play. Then, in a second paragraph, briefly show how, in a scene of your choosing, she publicly "performs" that personality.
2. One theme of the play involves weaknesses of character. Which characters have the most blatant weaknesses? Which weaknesses overlap among different characters? Choose two characters whose weaknesses seem comparable, and in a two-page essay show how the play dramatizes their similarity.
3. Look up early reviews of the play in the library. (You might also look up reviews of the film based on the play.) Compare your own responses and those of your classmates to those featured in the reviews. How much of the difference derives from different historical attitudes toward homosexuality? Toward sexuality in general? Write a two-page essay about how attitudes one brings to this play affect responses to particular speeches and scenes in the play. Which characters seem especially to elicit different responses now from the ones they produced in early productions?

HENRIK IBSEN

A Doll House[1]

CHARACTERS

TORVALD HELMER, *a lawyer*	THE HELMERS' THREE SMALL CHILDREN
NORA, *his wife*	ANNE-MARIE, *their nurse*
DR. RANK	HELENE, *a maid*
MRS. LINDE	A DELIVERY BOY
NILS KROGSTAD, *a bank clerk*	

The action takes place in HELMER's *residence.*

ACT I

A comfortable room, tastefully but not expensively furnished. A door to the right in the back wall leads to the entryway; another to the left leads to HELMER's *study. Between these doors, a piano. Midway in the left-hand wall a door, and further back a window. Near the window a round table with an armchair and a small sofa. In the right-hand wall, toward the rear, a door, and nearer the foreground a porcelain stove with two armchairs and a rocking chair beside it. Between the stove and the side door, a small table. Engravings on the walls. An* etagère *with china figures and other small art objects; a small bookcase with richly bound books; the floor carpeted; a fire burning in the stove. It is a winter day.*

A bell rings in the entryway; shortly after we hear the door being unlocked. NORA *comes into the room, humming happily to herself; she is wearing street clothes and carries an armload of packages, which she puts down on the table to the right. She has left the hall door open; and through it a* DELIVERY BOY *is seen, holding a Christmas tree and a basket, which he gives to the* MAID *who let them in.*

NORA: Hide the tree well, Helene. The children mustn't get a glimpse of it till this evening, after it's trimmed. [*To the* DELIVERY BOY, *taking out her purse.*] How much?

DELIVERY BOY: Fifty, ma'am.

NORA: There's a crown. No, keep the change. [*The* BOY *thanks her and leaves.* NORA *shuts the door. She laughs softly to herself while taking off her street things. Drawing a bag of macaroons from her pocket, she eats a couple, then steals over and listens at her husband's study door.*] Yes, he's home. [*Hums again as she moves to the table right.*]

HELMER: [*From the study.*] Is that my little lark twittering out there?

NORA: [*Busy opening some packages.*] Yes, it is.

1. Translated by Rolf Fjelde.

HELMER: Is that my squirrel rummaging around?

NORA: Yes!

HELMER: When did my squirrel get in?

NORA: Just now. [*Putting the macaroon bag in her pocket and wiping her mouth.*] Do come in, Torvald, and see what I've bought.

HELMER: Can't be disturbed. [*After a moment he opens the door and peers in, pen in hand.*] Bought, you say? All that there? Has the little spendthrift been out throwing money around again?

NORA: Oh, but Torvald, this year we really should let ourselves go a bit. It's the first Christmas we haven't had to economize.

HELMER: But you know we can't go squandering.

NORA: Oh yes, Torvald, we can squander a little now. Can't we? Just a tiny, wee bit. Now that you've got a big salary and are going to make piles and piles of money.

HELMER: Yes—starting New Year's. But then it's a full three months till the raise comes through.

NORA: Pooh! We can borrow that long.

HELMER: Nora! [*Goes over and playfully takes her by the ear.*] Are your scatterbrains off again? What if today I borrowed a thousand crowns, and you squandered them over Christmas week, and then on New Year's Eve a roof tile fell on my head, and I lay there—

NORA: [*Putting her hand on his mouth.*] Oh! Don't say such things!

HELMER. Yes, but what if it happened—then what?

NORA: If anything so awful happened, then it just wouldn't matter if I had debts or not.

HELMER: Well, but the people I'd borrowed from?

NORA: Them? Who cares about them! They're strangers.

HELMER: Nora, Nora, how like a woman! No, but seriously, Nora, you know what I think about that. No debts! Never borrow! Something of freedom's lost— and something of beauty, too—from a home that's founded on borrowing and debt. We've made a brave stand up to now, the two of us; and we'll go right on like that the little while we have to.

NORA: [*Going toward the stove.*] Yes, whatever you say, Torvald.

HELMER: [*Following her.*] Now, now, the little lark's wings mustn't droop. Come on, don't be a sulky squirrel. [*Taking out his wallet.*] Nora, guess what I have here.

NORA: [*Turning quickly.*] Money!

HELMER: There, see. [*Hands her some notes.*] Good grief, I know how costs go up in a house at Christmastime.

NORA: Ten—twenty—thirty—forty. Oh, thank you, Torvald; I can manage no end on this.

HELMER: You really will have to.

NORA: Oh yes, I promise I will But come here so I can show you everything I bought. And so cheap! Look, new clothes for Ivar here—and a sword. Here a horse and a trumpet for Bob. And a doll and a doll's bed here for Emmy; they're nothing much, but she'll tear them to bits in no time anyway. And

here I have dress material and handkerchiefs for the maids. Old Anne-Marie
really deserves something more.

HELMER: And what's in that package there?

NORA: [*With a cry.*] Torvald, no! You can't see that till tonight!

HELMER: I see. But tell me now, you little prodigal, what have you thought of for
yourself?

NORA: For myself? Oh, I don't want anything at all.

HELMER: Of course you do. Tell me just what—within reason—you'd most like to
have.

NORA: I honestly don't know. Oh, listen, Torvald—

HELMER: Well?

NORA: [*Fumbling at his coat buttons, without looking at him.*] If you want to give me
something, then maybe you could—you could—

HELMER: Come, on, out with it.

NORA: [*Hurriedly.*] You could give me money, Torvald. No more than you think
you can spare; then one of these days I'll buy something with it.

HELMER: But Nora—

NORA: Oh, please, Torvald darling, do that! I beg you, please. Then I could hang
the bills in pretty gilt paper on the Christmas tree. Wouldn't that be fun?

HELMER: What are those little birds called that always fly through their fortunes?

NORA: Oh yes, spendthrifts; I know all that. But let's do as I say, Torvald; then I'll
have time to decide what I really need most. That's very sensible, isn't it?

HELMER: [*Smiling.*] Yes, very—that is, if you actually hung onto the money I give
you, and you actually used it to buy yourself something. But it goes for the
house and for all sorts of foolish things, and then I only have to lay out some
more.

NORA: Oh, but Torvald—

HELMER: Don't deny it, my dear little Nora. [*Putting his arm around her waist.*]
Spendthrifts are sweet, but they use up a frightful amount of money. It's
incredible what it costs a man to feed such birds.

NORA: Oh, how can you say that! Really, I save everything I can.

HELMER: [*Laughing.*] Yes, that's the truth. Everything you can. But that's nothing
at all.

NORA: [*Humming, with a smile of quiet satisfaction.*] Hm, if you only knew what
expenses we larks and squirrels have, Torvald.

HELMER: You're an odd little one. Exactly the way your father was. You're never
at a loss for scaring up money; but the moment you have it, it runs right out
through your fingers; you never know what you've done with it. Well, one
takes you as you are. It's deep in your blood. Yes, these things are hereditary,
Nora.

NORA: Ah, I could wish I'd inherited many of Papa's qualities.

HELMER: And I couldn't wish you anything but just what you are, my sweet little
lark. But wait; it seems to me you have a very—what should I call it?—a very
suspicious look today—

NORA: I do?

HELMER: You certainly do. Look me straight in the eye.

NORA: [*Looking at him.*] Well?

HELMER: [*Shaking an admonitory finger.*] Surely my sweet tooth hasn't been running riot in town today, has she?

NORA: No. Why do you imagine that?

HELMER: My sweet tooth really didn't make a little detour through the confectioner's?

NORA: No, I assure you, Torvald—

HELMER: Hasn't nibbled some pastry?

NORA: No, not at all.

HELMER: Not even munched a macaroon or two?

NORA: No, Torvald, I assure you, really—

HELMER: There, there now. Of course I'm only joking.

NORA: [*Going to the table, right.*] You know I could never think of going against you.

HELMER: No, I understand that; and you *have* given me your word. [*Going over to her.*] Well, you keep your little Christmas secrets to yourself, Nora darling. I expect they'll come to light this evening, when the tree is lit.

NORA: Did you remember to ask Dr. Rank?

HELMER: No. But there's no need for that; it's assumed he'll be dining with us. All the same, I'll ask him when he stops by here this morning. I've ordered some fine wine. Nora, you can't imagine how I'm looking forward to this evening.

NORA: So am I. And what fun for the children, Torvald!

HELMER: Ah, it's so gratifying to know that one's gotten a safe, secure job, and with a comfortable salary. It's a great satisfaction, isn't it?

NORA: Oh, it's wonderful!

HELMER: Remember last Christmas? Three whole weeks before, you shut yourself in every evening till long after midnight, making flowers for the Christmas tree, and all the other decorations to surprise us. Ugh, that was the dullest time I've ever lived through.

NORA: It wasn't at all dull for me.

HELMER: [*Smiling.*] But the outcome *was* pretty sorry, Nora.

NORA: Oh, don't tease me with that again. How could I help it that the cat came in and tore everything to shreds.

HELMER: No, poor thing, you certainly couldn't. You wanted so much to please us all, and that's what counts. But it's just as well that the hard times are past.

NORA: Yes, it's really wonderful.

HELMER: Now I don't have to sit here alone, boring myself, and you don't have to tire your precious eyes and your fair little delicate hands—

NORA: [*Clapping her hands.*] No, is it really true, Torvald, I don't have to? Oh, how wonderfully lovely to hear! [*Taking his arm.*] Now I'll tell you just how I've thought we should plan things. Right after Christmas—[*The doorbell rings.*] Oh, the bell. [*Straightening the room up a bit.*] Somebody would have to come. What a bore!

HELMER: I'm not at home to visitors, don't forget.

MAID: [*From the hall doorway.*] Ma'am, a lady to see you—

NORA: All right, let her come in.

MAID: [*To* HELMER.] And the doctor's just come too.

HELMER: Did he go right to my study?

MAID: Yes, he did.

> [HELMER *goes into his room. The* MAID *shows in* MRS. LINDE, *dressed in traveling clothes, and shuts the door after her.*]

MRS. LINDE: [*In a dispirited and somewhat hesitant voice.*] Hello, Nora.

NORA: [*Uncertain.*] Hello—

MRS. LINDE: You don't recognize me.

NORA: No, I don't know—but wait, I think—[*Exclaiming.*] What! Kristine! Is it really you?

MRS. LINDE: Yes, it's me.

NORA: Kristine! To think I didn't recognize you. But then, how could I? [*More quietly.*] How you've changed, Kristine!

MRS. LINDE: Yes, no doubt I have. In nine—ten long years.

NORA: Is it so long since we met! Yes, it's all of that. Oh, these last eight years have been a happy time, believe me. And so now you've come in to town, too. Made the long trip in the winter. That took courage.

MRS. LINDE: I just got here by ship this morning.

NORA: To enjoy yourself over Christmas, of course. Oh, how lovely! Yes, enjoy ourselves, we'll do that. But take your coat off. You're not still cold? [*Helping her.*] There now, let's get cozy here by the stove. No, the easy chair there! I'll take the rocker here. [*Seizing her hands.*] Yes, now you have your old look again; it was only in that first moment. You're a bit more pale, Kristine—and maybe a bit thinner.

MRS. LINDE: And much, much older, Nora.

NORA: Yes, perhaps a bit older; a tiny, tiny bit; not much at all. [*Stopping short; suddenly serious.*] Oh, but thoughtless me, to sit here, chattering away. Sweet, good Kristine, can you forgive me?

MRS. LINDE: What do you mean, Nora?

NORA: [*Softly.*] Poor Kristine, you've become a widow.

MRS. LINDE: Yes, three years ago.

NORA: Oh, I knew it, of course; I read it in the papers. Oh, Kristine, you must believe me; I often thought of writing you then, but I kept postponing it, and something always interfered.

MRS. LINDE: Nora dear, I understand completely.

NORA: No, it was awful of me, Kristine. You poor thing, how much you must have gone through. And he left you nothing?

MRS. LINDE: No.

NORA: And no children?

MRS. LINDE: No.

NORA: Nothing at all, then?

MRS. LINDE: Not even a sense of loss to feed on.

NORA: [*Looking incredulously at her.*] But Kristine, how could that be?

MRS. LINDE: [*Smiling wearily and smoothing her hair.*] Oh, sometimes it happens, Nora.

NORA: So completely alone. How terribly hard that must be for you. I have three lovely children. You can't see them now; they're out with the maid. But now you must tell me everything—

MRS. LINDE: No, no, no, tell me about yourself.

NORA: No, you begin. Today I don't want to be selfish. I want to think only of you today. But there *is* something I must tell you. Did you hear of the wonderful luck we had recently?

MRS. LINDE: No, what's that?

NORA: My husband's been made manager in the bank, just think!

MRS. LINDE: Your husband? How marvelous!

NORA: Isn't it? Being a lawyer is such an uncertain living, you know, especially if one won't touch any cases that aren't clean and decent. And of course Torvald would never do that, and I'm with him completely there. Oh, we're simply delighted, believe me! He'll join the bank right after New Year's and start getting a huge salary and lots of commissions. From now on we can live quite differently—just as we want. Oh, Kristine, I feel so light and happy! Won't it be lovely to have stacks of money and not a care in the world?

MRS. LINDE: Well, anyway, it would be lovely to have enough for necessities.

NORA: No, not just for necessities, but stacks and stacks of money!

MRS. LINDE: [*Smiling.*] Nora, Nora, aren't you sensible yet? Back in school you were such a free spender.

NORA: [*With a quiet laugh.*] Yes, that's what Torvald still says. [*Shaking her finger.*] But "Nora, Nora" isn't as silly as you all think. Really, we've been in no position for me to go squandering. We've had to work, both of us.

MRS. LINDE: You too?

NORA: Yes, at odd jobs—needlework, crocheting, embroidery, and such— [*Casually.*] and other things too. You remember that Torvald left the department when we were married? There was no chance of promotion in his office, and of course he needed to earn more money. But that first year he drove himself terribly. He took on all kinds of extra work that kept him going morning and night. It wore him down, and then he fell deathly ill. The doctors said it was essential for him to travel south.

MRS. LINDE: Yes, didn't you spend a whole year in Italy?

NORA: That's right. It wasn't easy to get away, you know. Ivar had just been born. But of course we had to go. Oh, that was a beautiful trip, and it saved Torvald's life. But it cost a frightful sum, Kristine.

MRS. LINDE: I can well imagine.

NORA: Four thousand, eight hundred crowns it cost. That's really a lot of money.

MRS. LINDE: But it's lucky you had it when you needed it.

NORA: Well, as it was, we got it from Papa.

MRS. LINDE: I see. It was just about the time your father died.

NORA: Yes, just about then. And, you know, I couldn't make that trip out to nurse him. I had to stay here, expecting Ivar any moment, and with my poor sick Torvald to care for. Dearest Papa, I never saw him again, Kristine. Oh, that was the worst time I've known in all my marriage.

MRS. LINDE: I know how you loved him. And then you went off to Italy?

NORA: Yes. We had the means now, and the doctors urged us. So we left a month after.

MRS. LINDE: And your husband came back completely cured?

NORA: Sound as a drum!

MRS. LINDE: But—the doctor?

NORA: Who?

MRS. LINDE: I thought the maid said he was a doctor, the man who came in with me.

NORA: Yes, that was Dr. Rank—but he's not making a sick call. He's our closest friend, and he stops by at least once a day. No, Torvald hasn't had a sick moment since, and the children are fit and strong, and I am, too. [*Jumping up and clapping her hands.*] Oh, dear God, Kristine, what a lovely thing to live and be happy! But how disgusting of me—I'm talking of nothing but my own affairs. [*Sits on a stool close by* KRISTINE, *arms resting across her knees.*] Oh, don't be angry with me! Tell me, is it really true that you weren't in love with your husband? Why did you marry him, then?

MRS. LINDE: My mother was still alive, but bedridden and helpless—and I had my two younger brothers to look after. In all conscience, I didn't think I could turn him down.

NORA: No, you were right there. But was he rich at the time?

MRS. LINDE: He was very well off, I'd say. But the business was shaky, Nora. When he died, it all fell apart, and nothing was left.

NORA: And then—?

MRS. LINDE: Yes, so I had to scrape up a living with a little shop and a little teaching and whatever else I could find. The last three years have been like one endless workday without a rest for me. Now it's over, Nora. My poor mother doesn't need me, for she's passed on. Nor the boys, either; they're working now and can take care of themselves.

NORA: How free you must feel—

MRS. LINDE: No—only unspeakably empty. Nothing to live for now. [*Standing up anxiously.*] That's why I couldn't take it any longer out in that desolate hole. Maybe here it'll be easier to find something to do and keep my mind occupied. If I could only be lucky enough to get a steady job, some office work—

NORA: Oh, but Kristine, that's so dreadfully tiring, and you already look so tired. It would be much better for you if you could go off to a bathing resort.

MRS. LINDE: [*Going toward the window.*] I have no father to give me travel money, Nora.

NORA: [*Rising.*] Oh, don't be angry with me.

MRS. LINDE: [*Going to her.*] Nora dear, don't you be angry with me. The worst of my kind of situation is all the bitterness that's stored away. No one to work for, and yet you're always having to snap up your opportunities. You have to live; and so you grow selfish. When you told me the happy change in your lot, do you know I was delighted less for your sakes than for mine?

NORA: How so? Oh, I see. You think maybe Torvald could do something for you.

MRS. LINDE: Yes, that's what I thought.

NORA: And he will, Kristine! Just leave it to me; I'll bring it up so delicately—find something attractive to humor him with. Oh, I'm so eager to help you.

MRS. LINDE: How very kind of you, Nora, to be so concerned over me—doubly kind, considering you really know so little of life's burdens yourself.

NORA: I—? I know so little—?

MRS. LINDE: [*Smiling.*] Well, my heavens—a little needlework and such—Nora, you're just a child.

NORA: [*Tossing her head and pacing the floor.*] You don't have to act so superior.

MRS. LINDE: Oh?

NORA: You're just like the others. You all think I'm incapable of anything serious—

MRS. LINDE: Come now—

NORA: That I've never had to face the raw world.

MRS. LINDE: Nora dear, you've just been telling me all your troubles.

NORA: Hm! Trivia! [*Quietly.*] I haven't told you the big thing.

MRS. LINDE: Big thing? What do you mean?

NORA: You look down on me so, Kristine, but you shouldn't. You're proud that you worked so long and hard for your mother.

MRS. LINDE: I don't look down on a soul. But it *is* true: I'm proud—and happy, too—to think it was given to me to make my mother's last days almost free of care.

NORA: And you're also proud thinking of what you've done for your brothers.

MRS. LINDE: I feel I've a right to be.

NORA: I agree. But listen to this, Kristine—I've also got something to be proud and happy for.

MRS. LINDE: I don't doubt it. But whatever do you mean?

NORA: Not so loud. What if Torvald heard! He mustn't, not for anything in the world. Nobody must know, Kristine. No one but you.

MRS. LINDE: But what is it, then?

NORA: Come here. [*Drawing her down beside her on the sofa.*] It's true—I've also got something to be proud and happy for. I'm the one who saved Torvald's life.

MRS. LINDE: Saved—? Saved how?

NORA: I told you about the trip to Italy. Torvald never would have lived if he hadn't gone south—

MRS. LINDE: Of course; your father gave you the means—

NORA: [*Smiling.*] That's what Torvald and all the rest think, but—

MRS. LINDE: But—?

NORA: Papa didn't give us a pin. I was the one who raised the money.

MRS. LINDE: You? That whole amount?

NORA: Four thousand, eight hundred crowns. What do you say to that?

MRS. LINDE: But Nora, how was it possible? Did you win the lottery?

NORA: [*Disdainfully.*] The lottery? Pooh! No art to that.

MRS. LINDE: But where did you get it from then?

NORA: [*Humming, with a mysterious smile.*] Hmm, tra-la-la-la.

MRS. LINDE: Because you couldn't have borrowed it.

NORA: No? Why not?

MRS. LINDE: A wife can't borrow without her husband's consent.

NORA: [*Tossing her head.*] Oh, but a wife with a little business sense, a wife who knows how to manage—

MRS. LINDE: Nora, I simply don't understand—

NORA: You don't have to. Whoever said I *borrowed* the money? I could have gotten it other ways. [*Throwing herself back on the sofa.*] I could have gotten it from some admirer or other. After all, a girl with my ravishing appeal—

MRS. LINDE: You lunatic.

NORA: I'll bet you're eaten up with curiosity, Kristine.

MRS. LINDE: Now listen here, Nora—you haven't done something indiscreet?

NORA: [*Sitting up again.*] Is it indiscreet to save your husband's life?

MRS. LINDE: I think it's indiscreet that without his knowledge you—

NORA: But that's the point: he mustn't know! My Lord, can't you understand? He mustn't ever know the close call he had. It was to *me* the doctors came to say his life was in danger—that nothing could save him but a stay in the south. Didn't I try strategy then! I began talking about how lovely it would be for me to travel abroad like other young wives; I begged and I cried; I told him please to remember my condition, to be kind and indulge me; and then I dropped a hint that he could easily take out a loan. But at that, Kristine, he nearly exploded. He said I was frivolous, and it was his duty as man of the house not to indulge me in whims and fancies—as I think he called them. Aha, I thought, now you'll just have to be saved—and that's when I saw my chance.

MRS. LINDE: And your father never told Torvald the money wasn't from him?

NORA: No, never. Papa died right about then. I'd considered bringing him into my secret and begging him never to tell. But he was too sick at the time—and then, sadly, it didn't matter.

MRS. LINDE: And you've never confided in your husband since?

NORA: For heaven's sake, no! Are you serious? He's so strict on that subject. Besides—Torvald, with all his masculine pride—how painfully humiliating for him if he ever found out he was in debt to me. That would just ruin our relationship. Our beautiful, happy home would never be the same.

MRS. LINDE: Won't you ever tell him?

NORA: [*Thoughtfully.*] Yes—maybe sometime years from now, when I'm no longer so attractive. Don't laugh! I only mean when Torvald loves me less than now, when he stops enjoying my dancing and dressing up and reciting for him. Then it might be wise to have something in reserve— [*Breaking off.*] How ridiculous! That'll never happen— Well, Kristine, what do you think of my big secret? I'm capable of something too, hm? You can imagine, of course, how this thing hangs over me. It really hasn't been easy meeting the payments on time. In the business world there's what they call quarterly interest and what they call amortization, and these are always so terribly hard to manage. I've had to skimp a little here and there, wherever I could, you know. I could hardly spare anything from my house allowance, because Torvald has to live well. I couldn't let the children go poorly dressed; whatever I got for them, I felt I had to use up completely—the darlings!

MRS. LINDE: Poor Nora, so it had to come out of your own budget, then?

NORA: Yes, of course. But I was the one most responsible, too. Every time Torvald gave me money for new clothes and such, I never used more than half; always bought the simplest, cheapest outfits. It was a godsend that everything looks so well on me that Torvald never noticed. But it did weigh me down at times, Kristine. It *is* such a joy to wear fine things. You understand.

MRS. LINDE: Oh, of course.

NORA: And then I found other ways of making money. Last winter I was lucky enough to get a lot of copying to do. I locked myself in and sat writing every evening till late in the night. Ah, I was tired so often, dead tired. But still it was wonderful fun, sitting and working like that, earning money. It was almost like being a man.

MRS. LINDE: But how much have you paid off this way so far?

NORA: That's hard to say, exactly. These accounts, you know, aren't easy to figure. I only know that I've paid out all I could scrape together. Time and again I haven't known where to turn. [*Smiling.*] Then I'd sit here dreaming of a rich old gentleman who had fallen in love with me—

MRS. LINDE: What! Who is he?

NORA: Oh, really! And that he'd died, and when his will was opened, there in big letters it said, "All my fortune shall be paid over in cash, immediately, to that enchanting Mrs. Nora Helmer."

MRS. LINDE: But Nora dear—who *was* this gentleman?

NORA: Good grief, can't you understand? The old man never existed; that was only something I'd dream up time and again whenever I was at my wits' end for money. But it makes no difference now; the old fossil can go where he pleases for all I care; I don't need him or his will—because now I'm free. [*Jumping up.*] Oh, how lovely to think of that, Kristine! Carefree! To know you're carefree, utterly carefree; to be able to romp and play with the children, and to keep up a beautiful, charming home—everything just the way Torvald likes it! And think, spring is coming, with big blue skies. Maybe we can travel a little then. Maybe I'll see the ocean again. Oh yes, it *is* so marvelous to live and be happy!

[*The front doorbell rings.*]

MRS. LINDE: [*Rising.*] There's the bell. It's probably best that I go.

NORA: No, stay. No one's expected. It must be for Torvald.

MAID: [*From the hall doorway.*] Excuse me, ma'am—there's a gentleman here to see Mr. Helmer, but I didn't know—since the doctor's with him—

NORA: Who is the gentleman?

KROGSTAD: [*From the doorway.*] It's me, Mrs. Helmer.

[MRS. LINDE *starts and turns away toward the window.*]

NORA: [*Stepping toward him, tense, her voice a whisper.*] You? What is it? Why do you want to speak to my husband?

KROGSTAD: Bank business—after a fashion. I have a small job in the investment bank, and I hear now your husband is going to be our chief—

NORA: In other words, it's—

KROGSTAD: Just dry business, Mrs. Helmer. Nothing but that.

NORA: Yes, then please be good enough to step into the study. [*She nods indifferently as she sees him out by the hall door, then returns and begins stirring up the stove.*]

MRS. LINDE: Nora—who was that man?

NORA: That was a Mr. Krogstad—a lawyer.

MRS. LINDE: Then it really was him.

NORA: Do you know that person?

MRS. LINDE: I did once—many years ago. For a time he was a law clerk in our town.

NORA: Yes, he's been that.

MRS. LINDE: How he's changed.

NORA: I understand he had a very unhappy marriage.

MRS. LINDE: He's a widower now.

NORA: With a number of children. There now, it's burning. [*She closes the stove door and moves the rocker a bit to one side.*]

MRS. LINDE: They say he has a hand in all kinds of business.

NORA: Oh? That may be true; I wouldn't know. But let's not think about business. It's so dull.

[DR. RANK *enters from* HELMER's *study.*]

RANK: [*Still in the doorway.*] No, no, really—I don't want to intrude, I'd just as soon talk a little while with your wife. [*Shuts the door, then notices* MRS. LINDE.] Oh, beg pardon. I'm intruding here too.

NORA: No, not at all. [*Introducing him.*] Dr. Rank, Mrs. Linde.

RANK: Well now, that's a name much heard in this house. I believe I passed the lady on the stairs as I came.

MRS. LINDE: Yes, I take the stairs very slowly. They're rather hard on me.

RANK: Uh-hm, some touch of internal weakness?

MRS. LINDE: More overexertion, I'd say.

RANK: Nothing else? Then you're probably here in town to rest up in a round of parties?

MRS. LINDE: I'm here to look for work.

RANK: Is that the best cure for overexertion?

MRS. LINDE: One has to live, Doctor.

RANK: Yes, there's a common prejudice to that effect.

NORA: Oh, come on, Dr. Rank—you really do want to live yourself.

RANK: Yes, I really do. Wretched as I am, I'll gladly prolong my torment indefinitely. All my patients feel like that. And it's quite the same, too, with the morally sick. Right at this moment there's one of those moral invalids in there with Helmer—

MRS. LINDE: [*Softly.*] Ah!

NORA: Who do you mean?

RANK: Oh, it's a lawyer, Krogstad, a type you wouldn't know. His character is rotten to the root—but even he began chattering all-importantly about how he had to *live.*

NORA: Oh? What did he want to talk to Torvald about?

RANK: I really don't know. I only heard something about the bank.

NORA: I didn't know that Krog—that this man Krogstad had anything to do with the bank.

RANK: Yes, he's gotten some kind of berth down there. [*To* MRS. LINDE.] I don't know if you also have, in your neck of the woods, a type of person who scuttles about breathlessly, sniffing out hints of moral corruption, and then maneuvers his victim into some sort of key position where he can keep an eye on him. It's the healthy these days that are out in the cold.

MRS. LINDE: All the same, it's the sick who most need to be taken in.

RANK: [*With a shrug.*] Yes, there we have it. That's the concept that's turning society into a sanatorium.

[NORA, *lost in her thoughts, breaks out into quiet laughter and claps her hands.*]

RANK: Why do you laugh at that? Do you have any real idea of what society is?

NORA: What do I care about dreary old society? I was laughing at something quite different—something terribly funny. Tell me, Doctor—is everyone who works in the bank dependent now on Torvald?

RANK: Is that what you find so terribly funny?

NORA: [*Smiling and humming.*] Never mind, never mind [*Pacing the floor.*] Yes, that's really immensely amusing: that we—that Torvald has so much power now over all those people. [*Taking the bag out of her pocket.*] Dr. Rank, a little macaroon on that?

RANK: See here, macaroons! I thought they were contraband here.

NORA: Yes, but these are some that Kristine gave me.

MRS. LINDE: What? I—?

NORA: Now, now, don't be afraid. You couldn't possibly know that Torvald had forbidden them. You see, he's worried they'll ruin my teeth. But hmp! Just this once! Isn't that so, Dr. Rank? Help yourself! [*Puts a macaroon in his mouth.*] And you too, Kristine. And I'll also have one, only a little one—or two, at the most. [*Walking about again.*] Now I'm really tremendously happy. Now there's just one last thing in the world that I have an enormous desire to do.

RANK: Well! And what's that?

NORA: It's something I have such a consuming desire to say so Torvald could hear.

RANK: And why can't you say it?

NORA: I don't dare. It's quite shocking.

MRS. LINDE: Shocking?

RANK: Well, then it isn't advisable. But in front of us you certainly can. What do you have such a desire to say so Torvald could hear?

NORA: I have such a huge desire to say—to hell and be damned!

RANK: Are you crazy?

MRS. LINDE: My goodness, Nora!

RANK: Go on, say it. Here he is.

NORA: [*Hiding the macaroon bag.*] Shh, shh, shh!

[HELMER *comes in from his study, hat in hand, overcoat over his arm.*]

NORA: [*Going toward him.*] Well, Torvald dear, are you through with him?

HELMER: Yes, he just left.

NORA: Let me introduce you—this is Kristine, who's arrived here in town.

HELMER: Kristine—? I'm sorry, but I don't know—

NORA: Mrs. Linde, Torvald dear. Mrs. Kristine Linde.

HELMER: Of course. A childhood friend of my wife's, no doubt?

MRS. LINDE: Yes, we knew each other in those days.

NORA: And just think, she made the long trip down here in order to talk with you.

HELMER: What's this?

MRS. LINDE: Well, not exactly—

NORA: You see, Kristine is remarkably clever in office work, and so she's terribly eager to come under a capable man's supervision and add more to what she already knows—

HELMER: Very wise, Mrs. Linde.

NORA: And then when she heard that you'd become a bank manager—the story was wired out to the papers—then she came in as fast as she could and— Really, Torvald, for my sake you can do a little something for Kristine, can't you?

HELMER: Yes, it's not at all impossible. Mrs. Linde, I suppose you're a widow?

MRS. LINDE: Yes.

HELMER: Any experience in office work?

MRS. LINDE: Yes, a good deal.

HELMER: Well, it's quite likely that I can make an opening for you—

NORA: [Clapping her hands.] You see, you see!

HELMER: You've come at a lucky moment, Mrs. Linde.

MRS. LINDE: Oh, how can I thank you?

HELMER: Not necessary. [Putting his overcoat on.] But today you'll have to excuse me—

RANK: Wait, I'll go with you. [He fetches his coat from the hall and warms it at the stove.]

NORA: Don't stay out long, dear.

HELMER: An hour; no more.

NORA: Are you going too, Kristine?

MRS. LINDE: [Putting on her winter garments.] Yes, I have to see about a room now.

HELMER: Then perhaps we can all walk together.

NORA: [Helping her.] What a shame we're so cramped here, but it's quite impossible for us to—

MRS. LINDE: Oh, don't even think of it! Good-bye, Nora dear, and thanks for everything.

NORA: Good-bye for now. Of course you'll be back this evening. And you too, Dr. Rank. What? If you're well enough? Oh, you've got to be! Wrap up tight now.

[In a ripple of small talk the company moves out into the hall; children's voices are heard outside on the steps.]

NORA: There they are! There they are! [She runs to open the door. The children come in with their nurse, ANNE-MARIE.] Come in, come in! [Bends down and kisses them.] Oh, you darlings—! Look at them, Kristine. Aren't they lovely!

RANK: No loitering in the draft here.

HELMER: Come, Mrs. Linde—this place is unbearable now for anyone but mothers.

[DR. RANK, HELMER, *and* MRS. LINDE *go down the stairs.* ANNE-MARIE *goes into the living room with the children.* NORA *follows, after closing the hall door.*]

NORA: How fresh and strong you look. Oh, such red cheeks you have! Like apples and roses. [*The children interrupt her throughout the following.*] And it was so much fun? That's wonderful. Really? You pulled both Emmy and Bob on the sled? Imagine, all together! Yes, you're a clever boy, Ivar. Oh, let me hold her a bit, Anne-Marie. My sweet little doll baby! [*Takes the smallest from the nurse and dances with her.*] Yes, yes, Mama will dance with Bob as well. What? Did you throw snowballs? Oh, if I'd only been there! No, don't bother, Anne-Marie—I'll undress them myself. Oh yes, let me. It's such fun. Go in and rest; you look half frozen. There's hot coffee waiting for you on the stove. [*The nurse goes into the room to the left.* NORA *takes the children's winter things off, throwing them about, while the children talk to her all at once.*] Is that so? A big dog chased you? But it didn't bite? No, dogs never bite little, lovely doll babies. Don't peek in the packages, Ivar! What is it? Yes, wouldn't you like to know. No, no, it's an ugly something. Well? Shall we play? What shall we play? Hide-and-seek? Yes, let's play hide-and-seek. Bob must hide first. I must? Yes, let me hide first. [*Laughing and shouting, she and the children play in and out of the living room and the adjoining room to the right. At last* NORA *hides under the table. The children come storming in, search, but cannot find her, then hear her muffled laughter, dash over to the table, lift the cloth up and find her. Wild shouting. She creeps forward as if to scare them. More shouts. Meanwhile, a knock at the hall door; no one has noticed it. Now the door half opens, and* KROGSTAD *appears. He waits a moment; the game goes on.*]

KROGSTAD: Beg pardon, Mrs. Helmer—

NORA: [*With a strangled cry, turning and scrambling to her knees.*] Oh! What do you want?

KROGSTAD: Excuse me. The outer door was ajar; it must be someone forgot to shut it—

NORA: [*Rising.*] My husband isn't home, Mr. Krogstad.

KROGSTAD: I know that.

NORA: Yes—then what do you want here?

KROGSTAD: A word with you.

NORA: With—? [*To the children, quietly.*] Go in to Anne-Marie. What? No, the strange man won't hurt Mama. When he's gone, we'll play some more. [*She leads the children into the room to the left and shuts the door after them. Then, tense and nervous:*] You want to speak to me?

KROGSTAD: Yes, I want to.

NORA: Today? But it's not yet the first of the month—

KROGSTAD: No, it's Christmas Eve. It's going to be up to you how merry a Christmas you have.

NORA: What is it you want? Today I absolutely can't—

KROGSTAD: We won't talk about that till later. This is something else. You do have a moment to spare, I suppose?

NORA: Oh yes, of course—I do, except—

KROGSTAD: Good. I was sitting over at Olsen's Restaurant when I saw your husband go down the street—

NORA: Yes?

KROGSTAD: With a lady.

NORA: Yes. So?

KROGSTAD: If you'll pardon my asking: wasn't that lady a Mrs. Linde?

NORA: Yes.

KROGSTAD: Just now come into town?

NORA: Yes, today.

KROGSTAD: She's a good friend of yours?

NORA: Yes, she is. But I don't see—

KROGSTAD: I also knew her once.

NORA: I'm aware of that.

KROGSTAD: Oh? You know all about it. I thought so. Well, then let me ask you short and sweet: is Mrs. Linde getting a job in the bank?

NORA: What makes you think you can cross-examine me, Mr. Krogstad—you, one of my husband's employees? But since you ask, you might as well know— yes, Mrs. Linde's going to be taken on at the bank. And I'm the one who spoke for her, Mr. Krogstad. Now you know.

KROGSTAD: So I guessed right.

NORA: [*Pacing up and down.*] Oh, one does have a tiny bit of influence, I should hope. Just because I am a woman, don't think it means that— When one has a subordinate position, Mr. Krogstad, one really ought to be careful about pushing somebody who—hm—

KROGSTAD: Who has influence?

NORA: That's right.

KROGSTAD: [*In a different tone.*] Mrs. Helmer, would you be good enough to use your influence on my behalf?

NORA: What? What do you mean?

KROGSTAD: Would you please make sure that I keep my subordinate position in the bank?

NORA: What does that mean? Who's thinking of taking away your position?

KROGSTAD: Oh, don't play the innocent with me. I'm quite aware that your friend would hardly relish the chance of running into me again; and I'm also aware now whom I can thank for being turned out.

NORA: But I promise you—

KROGSTAD: Yes, yes, yes, to the point: there's still time, and I'm advising you to use your influence to prevent it.

NORA: But Mr. Krogstad, I have absolutely no influence.

KROGSTAD: You haven't? I thought you were just saying—

NORA: You shouldn't take me so literally. I! How can you believe that I have any such influence over my husband?

KROGSTAD: Oh, I've known your husband from our student days. I don't think the great bank manager's more steadfast than any other married man.

NORA: You speak insolently about my husband, and I'll show you the door.

KROGSTAD: The lady has spirit.

NORA: I'm not afraid of you any longer. After New Year's, I'll soon be done with the whole business.

KROGSTAD: [*Restraining himself.*] Now listen to me, Mrs. Helmer. If necessary, I'll fight for my little job in the bank as if it were life itself.

NORA: Yes, so it seems.

KROGSTAD: It's not just a matter of income; that's the least of it. It's something else— All right, out with it! Look, this is the thing. You know, just like all the others, of course, that once, a good many years ago, I did something rather rash.

NORA: I've heard rumors to that effect.

KROGSTAD: The case never got into court; but all the same, every door was closed in my face from then on. So I took up those various activities you know about. I had to grab hold somewhere; and I dare say I haven't been among the worst. But now I want to drop all that. My boys are growing up. For their sakes, I'll have to win back as much respect as possible here in town. That job in the bank was like the first rung in my ladder. And now your husband wants to kick me right back down in the mud again.

NORA: But for heaven's sake, Mr. Krogstad, it's simply not in my power to help you.

KROGSTAD: That's because you haven't the will to—but I have the means to make you.

NORA: You certainly won't tell my husband that I owe you money?

KROGSTAD: Hm—what if I told him that?

NORA: That would be shameful of you. [*Nearly in tears.*] This secret—my joy and my pride—that he should learn it in such a crude and disgusting way—learn it from you. You'd expose me to the most horrible unpleasantness—

KROGSTAD: Only unpleasantness?

NORA: [*Vehemently.*] But go on and try. It'll turn out the worse for you, because then my husband will really see what a crook you are, and then you'll *never* be able to hold your job.

KROGSTAD: I asked if it was just domestic unpleasantness you were afraid of?

NORA: If my husband finds out, then of course he'll pay what I owe at once, and then we'd be through with you for good.

KROGSTAD: [*A step closer.*] Listen, Mrs. Helmer—you've either got a very bad memory, or else no head at all for business. I'd better put you a little more in touch with the facts.

NORA: What do you mean?

KROGSTAD: When your husband was sick, you came to me for a loan of four thousand, eight hundred crowns.

NORA: Where else could I go?

KROGSTAD: I promised to get you that sum—

NORA: And you got it.

KROGSTAD: I promised to get you that sum, on certain conditions. You were so involved in your husband's illness, and so eager to finance your trip, that I guess you didn't think out all the details. It might just be a good idea to remind you. I promised you the money on the strength of a note I drew up.

NORA: Yes, and that I signed.

KROGSTAD: Right. But at the bottom I added some lines for your father to guarantee the loan. He was supposed to sign down there.

NORA: Supposed to? He did sign.

KROGSTAD: I left the date blank. In other words, your father would have dated his signature himself. Do you remember that?

NORA: Yes, I think—

KROGSTAD: Then I gave you the note for you to mail to your father. Isn't that so?

NORA: Yes.

KROGSTAD: And naturally you sent it at once—because only some five, six days later you brought me the note, properly signed. And with that, the money was yours.

NORA: Well, then; I've made my payments regularly, haven't I?

KROGSTAD: More or less. But—getting back to the point—those were hard times for you then, Mrs. Helmer.

NORA: Yes, they were.

KROGSTAD: Your father was very ill, I believe.

NORA: He was near the end.

KROGSTAD: He died soon after?

NORA: Yes.

KROGSTAD: Tell me, Mrs. Helmer, do you happen to recall the date of your father's death? The day of the month, I mean.

NORA: Papa died the twenty-ninth of September.

KROGSTAD: That's quite correct; I've already looked into that. And now we come to a curious thing— [*Taking out a paper.*] which I simply cannot comprehend.

NORA: Curious thing? I don't know—

KROGSTAD: This is the curious thing: that your father co-signed the note for your loan three days after his death.

NORA: How—? I don't understand.

KROGSTAD: Your father died the twenty-ninth of September. But look. Here your father dated his signature October second. Isn't that curious, Mrs. Helmer? [NORA *is silent.*] Can you explain it to me? [NORA *remains silent.*] It's also remarkable that the words "October second" and the year aren't written in your father's hand, but rather in one that I think I know. Well, it's easy to understand. Your father forgot perhaps to date his signature, and then someone or other added it, a bit sloppily, before anyone knew of his death. There's nothing wrong in that. It all comes down to the signature. And there's no question about *that,* Mrs. Helmer. It really *was* your father who signed his own name here, wasn't it?

NORA: [*After a short silence, throwing her head back and looking squarely at him.*] No, it wasn't. *I* signed papa's name.

KROGSTAD: Wait, now—are you fully aware that this is a dangerous confession?

NORA: Why? You'll soon get your money.

KROGSTAD: Let me ask you a question—why didn't you send the paper to your father?

NORA: That was impossible. Papa was so sick. If I'd asked him for his signature, I also would have had to tell him what the money was for. But I couldn't tell him, sick as he was, that my husband's life was in danger. That was just impossible.

KROGSTAD: Then it would have been better if you'd given up the trip abroad.

NORA: I couldn't possibly. The trip was to save my husband's life. I couldn't give that up.

KROGSTAD: But didn't you ever consider that this was a fraud against me?

NORA: I couldn't let myself be bothered by that. You weren't any concern of mine. I couldn't stand you, with all those cold complications you made, even though you knew how badly off my husband was.

KROGSTAD: Mrs. Helmer, obviously you haven't the vaguest idea of what you've involved yourself in. But I can tell you this: it was nothing more and nothing worse that I once did—and it wrecked my whole reputation.

NORA: You? Do you expect me to believe that you ever acted bravely to save your wife's life?

KROGSTAD: Laws don't inquire into motives.

NORA: Then they must be very poor laws.

KROGSTAD: Poor or not—if I introduce this paper in court, you'll be judged according to law.

NORA: This I refuse to believe. A daughter hasn't a right to protect her dying father from anxiety and care? A wife hasn't a right to save her husband's life? I don't know much about laws, but I'm sure that somewhere in the books these things are allowed. And you don't know anything about it—you who practice the law? You must be an awful lawyer, Mr. Krogstad.

KROGSTAD: Could be. But business—the kind of business we two are mixed up in— don't you think I know about that? All right. Do what you want now. But I'm telling you *this:* if I get shoved down a second time, you're going to keep me company. [*He bows and goes out through the hall.*]

NORA: [*Pensive for a moment, then tossing her head.*] Oh, really! Trying to frighten me! I'm not so silly as all that. [*Begins gathering up the children's clothes, but soon stops.*] But—? No, but that's impossible! I did it out of love.

THE CHILDREN: [*In the doorway, left.*] Mama, that strange man's gone out the door.

NORA: Yes, yes, I know it. But don't tell anyone about the strange man. Do you hear? Not even Papa!

THE CHILDREN: No, Mama. But now will you play again?

NORA: No, not now.

THE CHILDREN: Oh, but Mama, you promised.

NORA: Yes, but I can't now. Go inside; I have too much to do. Go in, go in, my sweet darlings. [*She herds them gently back in the room and shuts the door after them. Settling on the sofa, she takes up a piece of embroidery and makes some stitches, but soon stops abruptly.*] No! [*Throws the work aside, rises, goes to the hall door and calls out.*] Helene! Let me have the tree in here. [*Goes to the table, left, opens the table drawer, and stops again.*] No, but that's utterly impossible!

MAID: [*With the Christmas tree.*] Where should I put it, ma'am?

NORA: There. The middle of the floor.

MAID: Should I bring anything else?

NORA: No, thanks. I have what I need.

[*The* MAID, *who has set the tree down, goes out.*]

NORA: [*Absorbed in trimming the tree.*] Candles here—and flowers here. That terrible creature! Talk, talk, talk! There's nothing to it at all. The tree's going to be lovely. I'll do anything to please you, Torvald. I'll sing for you, dance for you—

[HELMER *comes in from the hall, with a sheaf of papers under his arm.*]

NORA: Oh! You're back so soon?

HELMER: Yes. Has anyone been here?

NORA: Here? No.

HELMER: That's odd. I saw Krogstad leaving the front door.

NORA: So? Oh yes, that's true. Krogstad was here a moment.

HELMER: Nora, I can see by your face that he's been here, begging you to put in a good word for him.

NORA: Yes.

HELMER: And it was supposed to seem like your own idea? You were to hide it from me that he'd been here. He asked you that, too, didn't he?

NORA: Yes, Torvald, but—

HELMER: Nora, Nora, and you could fall for that? Talk with that sort of person and promise him anything? And then in the bargain, tell me an untruth.

NORA: An untruth—?

HELMER: Didn't you say that no one had been here? [*Wagging his finger.*] My little songbird must never do that again. A songbird needs a clean beak to warble with. No false notes. [*Putting his arm about her waist.*] That's the way it should be, isn't it? Yes, I'm sure of it. [*Releasing her.*] And so, enough of that. [*Sitting by the stove.*] Ah, how snug and cozy it is here. [*Leafing among his papers.*]

NORA: [*busy with the tree, after a short pause.*] Torvald!

HELMER: Yes.

NORA: I'm so much looking forward to the Stenborgs' costume party, day after tomorrow.

HELMER: And I can't wait to see what you'll surprise me with.

NORA: Oh, that stupid business!

HELMER: What?

NORA: I can't find anything that's right. Everything seems so ridiculous, so inane.

HELMER: So my little Nora's come to *that* recognition?

NORA: [*Going behind his chair, her arms resting on its back.*] Are you very busy, Torvald?

HELMER: Oh—

NORA: What papers are those?

HELMER: Bank matters.

NORA: Already?

HELMER: I've gotten full authority from the retiring management to make all necessary changes in personnel and procedure. I'll need Christmas week for that. I want to have everything in order by New Year's.

NORA: So that was the reason this poor Krogstad—

HELMER: Hm.

NORA: [*Still leaning on the chair and slowly stroking the nape of his neck.*] If you weren't so very busy, I would have asked you an enormous favor, Torvald.

HELMER: Let's hear. What is it?

NORA: You know, there isn't anyone who has your good taste—and I want so much to look well at the costume party. Torvald, couldn't you take over and decide what I should be and plan my costume?

HELMER: Ah, is my stubborn little creature calling for a lifeguard?

NORA: Yes, Torvald, I can't get anywhere without your help.

HELMER: All right—I'll think it over. We'll hit on something.

NORA: Oh, how sweet of you. [*Goes to the tree again. Pause.*] Aren't the red flowers pretty—? But tell me, was it really such a crime that this Krogstad committed?

HELMER: Forgery. Do you have any idea what that means?

NORA: Couldn't he have done it out of need?

HELMER: Yes, or thoughtlessness, like so many others. I'm not so heartless that I'd condemn a man categorically for just one mistake.

NORA: No, of course not, Torvald!

HELMER: Plenty of men have redeemed themselves by openly confessing their crimes and taking their punishment.

NORA: Punishment—?

HELMER: But now Krogstad didn't go that way. He got himself out by sharp practices, and that's the real cause of his moral breakdown.

NORA: Do you really think that would—?

HELMER: Just imagine how a man with that sort of guilt in him has to lie and cheat and deceive on all sides, has to wear a mask even with the nearest and dearest he has, even with his own wife and children. And with the children, Nora— that's where it's most horrible.

NORA: Why?

HELMER: Because that kind of atmosphere of lies infects the whole life of a home. Every breath the children take in is filled with the germs of something degenerate.

NORA: [*Coming closer behind him.*] Are you sure of that?

HELMER: Oh, I've seen it often enough as a lawyer. Almost everyone who goes bad early in life has a mother who's a chronic liar.

NORA: Why just—the mother?

HELMER: It's usually the mother's influence that's dominant, but the father's works in the same way, of course. Every lawyer is quite familiar with it. And still this Krogstad's been going home year in, year out, poisoning his own children with lies and pretense; that's why I call him morally lost. [*Reaching his hands out toward her.*] So my sweet little Nora must promise me never to plead his cause. Your hand on it. Come, come, what's this? Give me your hand. There, now. All settled. I can tell you it'd be impossible for me to work alongside of him. I literally feel physically revolted when I'm anywhere near such a person.

NORA: [*Withdraws her hand and goes to the other side of the Christmas tree.*] How hot it is here! And I've got so much to do.

HELMER: [*Getting up and gathering his papers.*] Yes, and I have to think about getting some of these read through before dinner. I'll think about your costume, too. And something to hang on the tree in gilt paper, I may even see about that. [*Putting his hand on her head.*] Oh you, my darling little songbird. [*He goes into his study and closes the door after him.*]

NORA: [*Softly, after a silence.*] Oh, really! it isn't so. It's impossible. It must be impossible.

ANNE-MARIE: [*in the doorway, left.*] The children are begging so hard to come in to Mama.

NORA: No, no, no, don't let them in to me! You stay with them, Anne-Marie.

ANNE-MARIE: Of course, ma'am. [*Closes the door.*]

NORA: [*Pale with terror*]. Hurt my children—! Poison my home? [*A moment's pause; then she tosses her head.*] That's not true. Never. Never in all the world.

ACT II

Same room. Beside the piano the Christmas tree now stands stripped of ornament, burned-down candle stubs on its ragged branches. NORA's *street clothes lie on the sofa.* NORA, *alone in the room, moves restlessly about; at last she stops at the sofa and picks up her coat.*

NORA: [*Dropping the coat again.*] Someone's coming! [*Goes toward the door, listens.*] No—there's no one. Of course—nobody's coming today, Christmas Day—or tomorrow, either. But maybe— [*Opens the door and looks out.*] No, nothing in the mailbox. Quite empty. [*Coming forward.*] What nonsense! He won't do anything serious. Nothing terrible could happen. It's impossible. Why, I have three small children.

[ANNE-MARIE, *with a large carton, comes in from the room to the left.*]

ANNE-MARIE: Well, at last I found the box with the masquerade clothes.

NORA: Thanks. Put it on the table.

ANNE-MARIE: [*Does so.*] But they're all pretty much of a mess.

NORA: Ahh! I'd love to rip them in a million pieces!

ANNE-MARIE: Oh, mercy, they can be fixed right up. Just a little patience.

NORA: Yes, I'll go get Mrs. Linde to help me.

ANNE-MARIE: Out again now? In this nasty weather? Miss Nora will catch cold— get sick.

NORA: Oh, worse things could happen— How are the children?

ANNE-MARIE: The poor mites are playing with their Christmas presents, but—

NORA: Do they ask for me much?

ANNE-MARIE: They're so used to having Mama around, you know.

NORA: Yes, but Anne-Marie, I *can't* be together with them as much as I was.

ANNE-MARIE: Well, small children get used to anything.

NORA: You think so? Do you think they'd forget their mother if she was gone for good?

ANNE-MARIE: Oh, mercy—gone for good!

NORA: Wait, tell me, Anne-Marie—I've wondered so often—how could you ever have the heart to give your child over to strangers?

ANNE-MARIE: But I had to, you know, to become little Nora's nurse.

NORA: Yes, but how could you *do* it?

ANNE-MARIE: When I could get such a good place? A girl who's poor and who's gotten in trouble is glad enough for that. Because that slippery fish, he didn't do a thing for me, you know.

NORA: But your daughter's surely forgotten you.

ANNE-MARIE: Oh, she certainly has not. She's written to me, both when she was confirmed and when she was married.

NORA: [*Clasping her about the neck.*] You old Anne-Marie, you were a good mother for me when I was little.

ANNE-MARIE: Poor little Nora, with no other mother but me.

NORA: And if the babies didn't have one, then I know that you'd— What silly talk! [*Opening the carton.*] Go in to them. Now I'll have to— Tomorrow you can see how lovely I'll look.

ANNE-MARIE: Oh, there won't be anyone at the party as lovely as Miss Nora. [*She goes off into the room, left.*]

NORA: [*Begins unpacking the box, but soon throws it aside.*] Oh, if I dared to go out. If only nobody would come. If only nothing would happen here while I'm out. What craziness—nobody's coming. Just don't think. This muff—needs a brushing. Beautiful gloves, beautiful gloves. Let it go. Let it go! One, two, three, four, five, six— [*With a cry.*] Oh, there they are! [*Poises to move toward the door, but remains irresolutely standing.* MRS. LINDE *enters from the hall, where she has removed her street clothes.*]

NORA: Oh, it's you, Kristine. There's no one else out there? How good that you've come.

MRS. LINDE: I hear you were up asking for me.

NORA: Yes, I just stopped by. There's something you really can help me with. Let's get settled on the sofa. Look, there's going to be a costume party tomorrow evening at the Stenborgs' right above us, and now Torvald wants me to go as a Neapolitan peasant girl and dance the tarantella that I learned in Capri.

MRS. LINDE: Really, are you giving a whole performance?

NORA: Torvald says yes, I should. See, here's the dress. Torvald had it made for me down there; but now it's all so tattered that I just don't know—

MRS. LINDE: Oh, we'll fix that up in no time. It's nothing more than the trimmings—they're a bit loose here and there. Needle and thread? Good, now we have what we need.

NORA: Oh, how sweet of you!

MRS. LINDE: [*Sewing.*] So you'll be in disguise tomorrow, Nora. You know what? I'll stop by then for a moment and have a look at you all dressed up. But listen, I've absolutely forgotten to thank you for that pleasant evening yesterday.

NORA: [*Getting up and walking about.*] I don't think it was as pleasant as usual yesterday. You should have come to town a bit sooner, Kristine— Yes, Torvald really knows how to give a home elegance and charm.

MRS. LINDE: And you do, too, if you ask me. You're not your father's daughter for nothing. But tell me, is Dr. Rank always so down in the mouth as yesterday?

NORA: No, that was quite an exception. But he goes around critically ill all the time—tuberculosis of the spine, poor man. You know, his father was a disgusting thing who kept mistresses and so on—and that's why the son's been sickly from birth.

MRS. LINDE: [*Lets her sewing fall to her lap.*] But my dearest Nora, how do you know about such things?

NORA: [*Walking more jauntily.*] Hmp! When you've had three children, then you've had a few visits from—from women who know something of medicine, and they tell you this and that.

MRS. LINDE: [*Resumes sewing; a short pause.*] Does Dr. Rank come here every day?

NORA: Every blessed day. He's Torvald's best friend from childhood, and *my* good friend, too. Dr. Rank almost belongs to this house.

MRS. LINDE: But tell me—is he quite sincere? I mean, doesn't he rather enjoy flattering people?

NORA: Just the opposite. Why do you think that?

MRS. LINDE: When you introduced us yesterday, he was proclaiming that he'd often heard my name in this house; but later I noticed that your husband hadn't the slightest idea who I really was. So how could Dr. Rank—?

NORA: But it's all true, Kristine. You see, Torvald loves me beyond words, and, as he puts it, he'd like to keep me all to himself. For a long time he'd almost be jealous if I even mentioned any of my old friends back home. So of course I dropped that. But with Dr. Rank I talk a lot about such things, because he likes hearing about them.

MRS. LINDE: Now listen, Nora; in many ways you're still like a child. I'm a good deal older than you, with a little more experience. I'll tell you something: you ought to put an end to all this with Dr. Rank.

NORA: What should I put an end to?

MRS. LINDE: Both parts of it, I think. Yesterday you said something about a rich admirer who'd provide you with money—

NORA: Yes, one who doesn't exist—worse luck. So?

MRS. LINDE: Is Dr. Rank well off?

NORA: Yes, he is.

MRS. LINDE: With no dependents?

NORA: No, no one. But—

MRS. LINDE: And he's over here every day?

NORA: Yes, I told you that.

MRS. LINDE: How can a man of such refinement be so grasping?

NORA: I don't follow you at all.

MRS. LINDE: Now don't try to hide it, Nora. You think I can't guess who loaned you the forty-eight hundred crowns?

NORA: Are you out of your mind? How could you think such a thing! A friend of ours, who comes here every single day. What an intolerable situation that would have been!

MRS. LINDE: Then it really wasn't him.

NORA: No, absolutely not. It never even crossed my mind for a moment— And he had nothing to lend in those days; his inheritance came later.

MRS. LINDE: Well, I think that was a stroke of luck for you, Nora dear.

NORA: No, it never would have occurred to me to ask Dr. Rank— Still, I'm quite sure that if I had asked him—

MRS. LINDE: Which you won't, of course.

NORA: No, of course not. I can't see that I'd ever need to. But I'm quite positive that if I talked to Dr. Rank—

MRS. LINDE: Behind your husband's back?

NORA: I've got to clear up this other thing; *that's* also behind his back. I've *got* to clear it all up.

MRS. LINDE: Yes, I was saying that yesterday, but—

NORA: [*Pacing up and down.*] A man handles these problems so much better than a woman—

MRS. LINDE: One's husband does, yes.

NORA: Nonsense. [*Stopping.*] When you pay everything you owe, then you get your note back, right?

MRS. LINDE: Yes, naturally.

NORA: And can rip it into a million pieces and burn it up—that filthy scrap of paper!

MRS. LINDE: [*Looking hard at her, laying her sewing aside, and rising slowly.*] Nora, you're hiding something from me.

NORA: You can see it in my face?

MRS. LINDE: Something's happened to you since yesterday morning. Nora, what is it?

NORA: [*Hurrying toward her.*] Kristine! [*Listening.*] Shh! Torvald's home. Look, go in with the children a while. Torvald can't bear all this snipping and stitching. Let Anne-Marie help you.

MRS. LINDE: [*Gathering up some of the things.*] All right, but I'm not leaving here until we've talked this out. [*She disappears into the room, left, as* TORVALD *enters from the hall.*]

NORA: Oh, how I've been waiting for you, Torvald dear.

HELMER: Was that the dressmaker?

NORA: No, that was Kristine. She's helping me fix up my costume. You know, it's going to be quite attractive.

HELMER: Yes, wasn't that a bright idea I had?

NORA: Brilliant! But then wasn't I good as well to give in to you?

HELMER: Good—because you give in to your husband's judgment? All right, you little goose, I know you didn't mean it like that. But I won't disturb you. You'll want to have a fitting, I suppose.

NORA: And you'll be working?

HELMER: Yes. [*Indicating a bundle of papers.*] See. I've been down to the bank. [*Starts toward his study.*]

NORA: Torvald.

HELMER: [*Stops.*] Yes.

NORA: If your little squirrel begged you, with all her heart and soul, for something—?

HELMER: What's that?

NORA: Then would you do it?

HELMER: First, naturally, I'd have to know what it was.

NORA: Your squirrel would scamper about and do tricks, if you'd only be sweet and give in.

HELMER: Out with it.

NORA: Your lark would be singing high and low in every room—

HELMER: Come on, she does that anyway.

NORA: I'd be a wood nymph and dance for you in the moonlight.

HELMER: Nora—don't tell me it's that same business from this morning?

NORA: [*Coming closer.*] Yes, Torvald, I beg you, please!

HELMER: And you actually have the nerve to drag that up again?

NORA: Yes, yes, you've got to give in to me; you *have* to let Krogstad keep his job in the bank.

HELMER: My dear Nora, I've slated his job for Mrs. Linde.

NORA: That's awfully kind of you. But you could just fire another clerk instead of Krogstad.

HELMER: This is the most incredible stubbornness! Because you go and give an impulsive promise to speak up for him, I'm expected to—

NORA: That's not the reason, Torvald. It's for your own sake. That man does writing for the worst papers; you said it yourself. He could do you any amount of harm. I'm scared to death of him—

HELMER: Ah, I understand. It's the old memories haunting you.

NORA: What do you mean by that?

HELMER: Of course, you're thinking about your father.

NORA: Yes, all right. Just remember how those nasty gossips wrote in the papers about Papa and slandered him so cruelly. I think they'd have had him dismissed if the department hadn't sent you up to investigate, and if you hadn't been so kind and open-minded toward him.

HELMER: My dear Nora, there's a notable difference between your father and me. Your father's official career was hardly above reproach. But mine is; and I hope it'll stay that way as long as I hold my position.

NORA: Oh, who can ever tell what vicious minds can invent? We could be so snug and happy now in our quiet, carefree home—you and I and the children, Torvald! That's why I'm pleading with you so—

HELMER: And just by pleading for him you make it impossible for me to keep him on. It's already known at the bank that I'm firing Krogstad. What if it's rumored around now that the new bank manager was vetoed by his wife—

NORA: Yes, what then—?

HELMER: Oh yes—as long as our little bundle of stubbornness gets her way—! I should go and make myself ridiculous in front of the whole office—give people the idea I can be swayed by all kinds of outside pressure. Oh, you can bet I'd feel the effects of that soon enough! Besides—there's something that rules Krogstad right out at the bank as long as I'm the manager.

NORA: What's that?

HELMER: His moral failings I could maybe overlook if I had to—

NORA: Yes, Torvald, why not?

HELMER: And I hear he's quite efficient on the job. But he was a crony of mine back in my teens—one of those rash friendships that crop up again and again to embarrass you later in life. Well, I might as well say it straight out: we're on a first-name basis. And that tactless fool makes no effort at all to hide it in front of others. Quite the contrary—he thinks that entitles him to take a familiar air around me, and so every other second he comes booming out with his "Yes, Torvald!" and "Sure thing, Torvald!" I tell you, it's been excruciating for me. He's out to make my place in the bank unbearable.

NORA: Torvald, you can't be serious about all this.

HELMER: Oh no? Why not?

NORA: Because these are such petty considerations.

HELMER: What are you saying? Petty? You think I'm petty!

NORA: No, just the opposite, Torvald dear. That's exactly why—

HELMER: Never mind. You call my motives petty; then I might as well be just that. Petty! All right! We'll put a stop to this for good. [*Goes to the hall door and calls.*] Helene!

NORA: What do you want?

HELMER: [*Searching among his papers.*] A decision. [*The* MAID *comes in.*] Look here; take this letter; go out with it at once. Get hold of a messenger and have him deliver it. Quick now. It's already addressed. Wait, here's some money.

MAID: Yes, sir. [*She leaves with the letter.*]

HELMER: [*Straightening his papers.*] There, now, little Miss Willful.

NORA: [*Breathlessly.*] Torvald, what was that letter?

HELMER: Krogstad's notice.

NORA: Call it back, Torvald! There's still time. Oh, Torvald, call it back! Do it for my sake—for your sake, for the children's sake! Do you hear, Torvald; do it! You don't know how this can harm us.

HELMER: Too late.

NORA: Yes, too late.

HELMER: Nora dear, I can forgive you this panic, even though basically you're insulting me. Yes, you are! Or isn't it an insult to think that *I* should be afraid of a courtroom hack's revenge? But I forgive you anyway, because this shows so beautifully how much you love me. [*Takes her in his arms.*] This is the way it should be, my darling Nora. Whatever comes, you'll see: when it really counts, I have strength and courage enough as a man to take on the whole weight myself.

NORA: [*Terrified.*] What do you mean by that?

HELMER: The whole weight, I said.

NORA: [*Resolutely.*] No, never in all the world.

HELMER: Good. So we'll share it, Nora, as man and wife. That's as it should be. [*Fondling her.*] Are you happy now? There, there, there—not these frightened dove's eyes. It's nothing at all but empty fantasies— Now you should run through your tarantella and practice your tambourine. I'll go to the inner office and shut both doors, so I won't hear a thing; you can make all the noise you like. [*Turning in the doorway.*] And when Rank comes, just tell him where he can find me. [*He nods to her and goes with his papers into the study, closing the door.*]

NORA: [*Standing as though rooted, dazed with fright, in a whisper.*] He really could do it. He will do it. He'll do it in spite of everything. No, not that, never, never! Anything but that! Escape! A way out— [*The doorbell rings.*] Dr. Rank! Anything but that! *Anything*, whatever it is! [*Her hands pass over her face, smoothing it; she pulls herself together, goes over and opens the hall door.* DR. RANK *stands outside, hanging his fur coat up. During the following scene, it begins getting dark.*]

NORA: Hello, Dr. Rank. I recognized your ring. But you mustn't go in to Torvald yet; I believe he's working.

RANK: And you?

NORA: For you, I always have an hour to spare—you know that. [*He has entered, and she shuts the door after him.*]

RANK: Many thanks. I'll make use of these hours while I can.

NORA: What do you mean by that? While you can?

RANK: Does that disturb you?

NORA: Well, it's such an odd phrase. Is anything going to happen?

RANK: What's going to happen is what I've been expecting so long—but I honestly didn't think it would come so soon.

NORA: [*Gripping his arm.*] What is it you've found out? Dr. Rank, you have to tell me!

RANK: [*Sitting by the stove.*] It's all over with me. There's nothing to be done about it.

NORA: [*Breathing easier.*] Is it you—then—?

RANK: Who else? There's no point in lying to one's self. I'm the most miserable of all my patients, Mrs. Helmer. These past few days I've been auditing my internal accounts. Bankrupt! Within a month I'll probably be laid out and rotting in the churchyard.

NORA: Oh, what a horrible thing to say.

RANK: The thing itself is horrible. But the worst of it is all the other horror before it's over. There's only one final examination left; when I'm finished with that, I'll know about when my disintegration will begin. There's something I want to say. Helmer with his sensitivity has such a sharp distaste for anything ugly. I don't want him near my sickroom.

NORA: Oh, but Dr. Rank—

RANK: I won't have him in there. Under no condition. I'll lock my door to him— As soon as I'm completely sure of the worst, I'll send you my calling card marked with a black cross, and you'll know then the wreck has started to come apart.

NORA: No, today you're completely unreasonable. And I wanted you so much to be in a really good humor.

RANK: With death up my sleeve? And then to suffer this way for somebody else's sins. Is there any justice in that? And in every single family, in some way or another, this inevitable retribution of nature goes on—

NORA: [*Her hands pressed over her ears.*] Oh, stuff! Cheer up! Please—be gay!

RANK: Yes, I'd just as soon laugh at it all. My poor, innocent spine, serving time for my father's gay army days.

NORA: [*By the table, left.*] He was so infatuated with asparagus tips and *pâté de foie gras*, wasn't that it?

RANK: Yes—and with truffles.

NORA: Truffles, yes. And then with oysters, I suppose?

RANK: Yes, tons of oysters, naturally.

NORA: And then the port and champagne to go with it. It's so sad that all these delectable things have to strike at our bones.

RANK: Especially when they strike at the unhappy bones that never shared in the fun.

NORA: Ah, that's the saddest of all.

RANK: [*Looks searchingly at her.*] Hm.

NORA: [*After a moment.*] Why did you smile?

RANK: No, it was you who laughed.

NORA: No, it was you who smiled, Dr. Rank!

RANK: [*Getting up.*] You're even a bigger tease than I'd thought.

NORA: I'm full of wild ideas today.

RANK: That's obvious.

NORA: [*Putting both hands on his shoulders.*] Dear, dear Dr. Rank, you'll never die for Torvald and me.

RANK: Oh, that loss you'll easily get over. Those who go away are soon forgotten.

NORA: [*Looks fearfully at him.*] You believe that?

RANK: One makes new connections, and then—

NORA: Who makes new connections?

RANK: Both you and Torvald will when I'm gone. I'd say you're well under way already. What was that Mrs. Linde doing here last evening?

NORA: Oh, come—you can't be jealous of poor Kristine?

RANK: Oh yes, I am. She'll be my successor here in the house. When I'm down under, that woman will probably—

NORA: Shh! Not so loud. She's right in there.

RANK: Today as well. So you see.

NORA: Only to sew on my dress. Good gracious, how unreasonable you are. [*Sitting on the sofa.*] Be nice now, Dr. Rank. Tomorrow you'll see how beautifully I'll dance; and you can imagine then that I'm dancing only for you—yes, and of course for Torvald, too—that's understood. [*Takes various items out of the carton.*] Dr. Rank, sit over here and I'll show you something.

RANK: [*Sitting.*] What's that?

NORA: Look here. Look.

RANK: Silk stockings.

NORA: Flesh-colored. Aren't they lovely? Now it's so dark here, but tomorrow— No, no, no, just look at the feet. Oh well, you might as well look at the rest.

RANK: Hm—

NORA: Why do you look so critical? Don't you believe they'll fit?

RANK: I've never had any chance to form an opinion on that.

NORA: [Glancing at him a moment.] Shame on you. [Hits him lightly on the ear with the stockings.] That's for you. [Puts them away again.]

RANK: And what other splendors am I going to see now?

NORA: Not the least bit more, because you've been naughty. [She hums a little and rummages among her things.]

RANK: [After a short silence.] When I sit here together with you like this, completely easy and open, then I don't know—I simply can't imagine—whatever would have become of me if I'd never come into this house.

NORA: [Smiling.] Yes, I really think you feel completely at ease with us.

RANK: [More quietly, staring straight ahead.] And then to have to go away from it all—

NORA: Nonsense, you're not going away.

RANK: [His voice unchanged.] —and not even be able to leave some poor show of gratitude behind, scarcely a fleeting regret—no more than a vacant place that anyone can fill.

NORA: And if I asked you now for—? No—

RANK: For what?

NORA: For a great proof of your friendship—

RANK: Yes, yes?

NORA: No, I mean—for an exceptionally big favor—

RANK: Would you really, for once, make me so happy?

NORA: Oh, you haven't the vaguest idea what it is.

RANK: All right, then tell me.

NORA: No, but I can't, Dr. Rank—it's all out of reason. It's advice and help, too— and a favor—

RANK: So much the better. I can't fathom what you're hinting at. Just speak out. Don't you trust me?

NORA: Of course. More than anyone else. You're my best and truest friend, I'm sure. That's why I want to talk to you. All right, then, Dr. Rank: there's something you can help me prevent. You know how deeply, how inexpressibly dearly Torvald loves me; he'd never hesitate a second to give up his life for me.

RANK: [Leaning close to her.] Nora—do you think he's the only one—

NORA: [With a slight start.] Who—?

RANK: Who'd gladly give up his life for you.

NORA: [Heavily.] I see.

RANK: I swore to myself you should know this before I'm gone. I'll never find a better chance. Yes, Nora, now you know. And also you know now that you can trust me beyond anyone else.

NORA: [*Rising, natural and calm.*] Let me by.

RANK: [*Making room for her, but still sitting.*] Nora—

NORA: [*In the hall doorway.*] Helene, bring the lamp in. [*Goes over to the stove.*] Ah, dear Dr. Rank, that was really mean of you.

RANK: [*Getting up.*] That I've loved you just as deeply as somebody else? Was *that* mean?

NORA: No, but that you came out and told me. That was quite unnecessary—

RANK: What do you mean? Have you known—?

[*The* MAID *comes in with the lamp, sets it on the table, and goes out again.*]

RANK: Nora—Mrs. Helmer—I'm asking you: have you known about it?

NORA: Oh, how can I tell what I know or don't know? Really, I don't know what to say— Why did you have to be so clumsy, Dr. Rank! Everything was so good.

RANK: Well, in any case, you now have the knowledge that my body and soul are at your command. So won't you speak out?

NORA: [*Looking at him.*] After that?

RANK: Please, just let me know what it is.

NORA: You can't know anything now.

RANK: I have to. You mustn't punish me like this. Give me the chance to do whatever is humanly possible for you.

NORA: Now there's nothing you can do for me. Besides, actually, I don't need any help. You'll see—it's only my fantasies. That's what it is. Of course! [*Sits in the rocker, looks at him, and smiles.*] What a nice one you are, Dr. Rank. Aren't you a little bit ashamed, now that the lamp is here?

RANK: No, not exactly. But perhaps I'd better go—for good?

NORA: No, you certainly can't do that. You must come here just as you always have. You know Torvald can't do without you.

RANK: Yes, but *you?*

NORA: You know how much I enjoy it when you're here.

RANK: That's precisely what threw me off. You're a mystery to me. So many times I've felt you'd almost rather be with me than with Helmer.

NORA: Yes—you see, there are some people that one loves most and other people that one would almost prefer being with.

RANK: Yes, there's something to that.

NORA: When I was back home, of course I loved Papa most. But I always thought it was so much fun when I could sneak down to the maids' quarters, because they never tried to improve me, and it was always so amusing, the way they talked to each other.

RANK: Aha, so it's *their* place that I've filled.

NORA: [*Jumping up and going to him.*] Oh, dear, sweet Dr. Rank, that's not what I meant at all. But you can understand that with Torvald it's just the same as with Papa—

[*The* MAID *enters from the hall.*]

MAID: Ma'am—please! [*She whispers to* NORA *and hands her a calling card.*]

NORA: [*Glancing at the card.*] Ah! [*Slips it into her pocket.*]

RANK: Anything wrong?

NORA: No, no, not at all. It's only some—it's my new dress—

RANK: Really? But—there's your dress.

NORA: Oh, that. But this is another one—I ordered it—Torvald mustn't know—

RANK: Ah, now we have the big secret.

NORA: That's right. Just go in with him—he's back in the inner study. Keep him there as long as—

RANK: Don't worry. He won't get away. [*Goes into the study.*]

NORA: [*To the* MAID.] And he's standing waiting in the kitchen?

MAID: Yes, he came up by the back stairs.

NORA: But didn't you tell him somebody was here?

MAID: Yes, but that didn't do any good.

NORA: He won't leave?

MAID: No, he won't go till he's talked with you, ma'am.

NORA: Let him come in, then—but quietly. Helene, don't breathe a word about this. It's a surprise for my husband.

MAID: Yes, yes, I understand— [*Goes out.*]

NORA: This horror—it's going to happen. No, no, no, it can't happen, it mustn't. [*She goes and bolts* HELMER's *door. The* MAID *opens the hall door for* KROGSTAD *and shuts it behind him. He is dressed for travel in a fur coat, boots, and a fur cap.*]

NORA: [*Going toward him.*] Talk softly. My husband's home.

KROGSTAD: Well, good for him.

NORA: What do you want?

KROGSTAD: Some information.

NORA: Hurry up, then. What is it?

KROGSTAD: You know, of course, that I got my notice.

NORA: I couldn't prevent it, Mr. Krogstad. I fought for you to the bitter end, but nothing worked.

KROGSTAD: Does your husband's love for you run so thin? He knows everything I can expose you to, and all the same he dares to—

NORA: How can you imagine he knows anything about this?

KROGSTAD: Ah, no—I can't imagine it either, now. It's not at all like my fine Torvald Helmer to have so much guts—

NORA: Mr. Krogstad, I demand respect for my husband!

KROGSTAD: Why, of course—all due respect. But since the lady's keeping it so carefully hidden, may I presume to ask if you've also a bit better informed than yesterday about what you've actually done?

NORA: More than you ever could teach me.

KROGSTAD: Yes, I *am* such an awful lawyer.

NORA: What is it you want from me?

KROGSTAD: Just a glimpse of how you are, Mrs. Helmer. I've been thinking about you all day long. A cashier, a night-court scribbler, a—well, a type like me also has a little of what they call a heart, you know.

NORA: Then show it. Think of my children.

KROGSTAD: Did you or your husband ever think of mine? But never mind. I simply wanted to tell you that you don't need to take this thing too seriously. For the present, I'm not proceeding with any action.

NORA: Oh no, really! Well—I knew that.

KROGSTAD: Everything can be settled in a friendly spirit. It doesn't have to get around town at all; it can stay just among us three.

NORA: My husband must never know anything of this.

KROGSTAD: How can you manage that? Perhaps you can pay me the balance?

NORA: No, not right now.

KROGSTAD: Or you know some way of raising the money in a day or two?

NORA: No way that I'm willing to use.

KROGSTAD: Well, it wouldn't have done you any good, anyway. If you stood in front of me with a fistful of bills, you still couldn't buy your signature back.

NORA: Then tell me what you're going to do with it.

KROGSTAD: I'll just hold onto it—keep it on file. There's no outsider who'll even get wind of it. So if you've been thinking of taking some desperate step—

NORA: I have.

KROGSTAD: Been thinking of running away from home—

NORA: I have!

KROGSTAD: Or even of something worse—

NORA: How could you guess that?

KROGSTAD: You can drop those thoughts.

NORA: How could you guess I was thinking of *that?*

KROGSTAD: Most of us think about *that* at first. I thought about it too, but I discovered I hadn't the courage—

NORA: [*Lifelessly.*] I don't either.

KROGSTAD: [*Relieved.*] That's true, you haven't the courage? You too?

NORA: I don't have it—I don't have it.

KROGSTAD: It would be terribly stupid, anyway. After that first storm at home blows out, why, then—I have here in my pocket a letter for your husband—

NORA: Telling everything?

KROGSTAD: As charitably as possible.

NORA: [*Quickly.*] He mustn't ever get that letter. Tear it up. I'll find some way to get money.

KROGSTAD: Beg pardon, Mrs. Helmer, but I think I just told you—

NORA: Oh, I don't mean the money I owe you. Let me know how much you want from my husband, and I'll manage it.

KROGSTAD: I don't want any money from your husband.

NORA: What do you want, then?

KROGSTAD: I'll tell you what. I want to recoup, Mrs. Helmer; I want to get on in the world—and there's where your husband can help me. For a year and a half I've kept myself clean of anything disreputable—all that time struggling with the worst conditions; but I was satisfied, working my way up step by step. Now I've been written right off, and I'm just not in the mood to come crawling back. I tell you, I want to move on. I want to get back in the bank—in a better position. Your husband can set up a job for me—

NORA: He'll never do that!

KROGSTAD: He'll do it. I know him. He won't dare breathe a word of protest. And once I'm in there together with him, you just wait and see! Inside of a year, I'll be the manager's right-hand man. It'll be Nils Krogstad, not Torvald Helmer, who runs the bank.

NORA: You'll never see the day!

KROGSTAD: Maybe you think you can—

NORA: I have the courage now—for *that*.

KROGSTAD: Oh, you don't scare me. A smart, spoiled lady like you—

NORA: You'll see; you'll see!

KROGSTAD: Under the ice, maybe? Down in the freezing, coal-black water? There, till you float up in the spring, ugly, unrecognizable, with your hair falling out—

NORA: You don't frighten me.

KROGSTAD: Nor do you frighten me. One doesn't do these things, Mrs. Helmer. Besides, what good would it be? I'd still have him safe in my pocket.

NORA: Afterwards? When I'm no longer—?

KROGSTAD: Are you forgetting that *I'll* be in control then over your final reputation? [NORA *stands speechless, staring at him.*] Good; now I've warned you. Don't do anything stupid. When Helmer's read my letter, I'll be waiting for his reply. And bear in mind that it's your husband himself who's forced me back to my old ways. I'll never forgive him for that. Good-bye, Mrs. Helmer. [*He goes out through the hall.*]

NORA: [*Goes to the hall door, opens it a crack, and listens.*] He's gone. Didn't leave the letter. Oh no, no, that's impossible too! [*Opening the door more and more.*] What's that? He's standing outside—not going downstairs. He's thinking it over? Maybe he'll—? [*A letter falls in the mailbox; then* KROGSTAD's *footsteps are heard, dying away down a flight of stairs.* NORA *gives a muffled cry and runs over toward the sofa table. A short pause.*] In the mailbox. [*Slips warily over to the hall door.*] It's lying there. Torvald, Torvald—now we're lost!

MRS. LINDE: [*Entering with the costume from the room, left.*] There now, I can't see anything else to mend. Perhaps you'd like to try—

NORA: [*In a hoarse whisper.*] Kristine, come here.

MRS. LINDE: [*Tossing the dress on the sofa.*] What's wrong? You look upset.

NORA: Come here. See that letter? *There!* Look—through the glass in the mailbox.

MRS. LINDE: Yes, yes, I see it.

NORA: That letter's from Krogstad—

MRS. LINDE: Nora—it's Krogstad who loaned you the money!

NORA: Yes, and now Torvald will find out everything.

MRS. LINDE: Believe me, Nora, it's best for both of you.

NORA: There's more you don't know. I forged a name.

MRS. LINDE: But for heaven's sake—?

NORA: I only want to tell you that, Kristine, so that you can be my witness.

MRS. LINDE: Witness? Why should I—?

NORA: If I should go out of my mind—it could easily happen—

MRS. LINDE: Nora!

NORA: Or anything else occurred—so I couldn't be present here—

MRS. LINDE: Nora, Nora, you aren't yourself at all!

NORA: And someone should try to take on the whole weight, all of the guilt, you follow me—

MRS. LINDE: Yes, of course, but why do you think—?

NORA: Then you're the witness that it isn't true, Kristine. I'm very much myself; my mind right now is perfectly clear; and I'm telling you: nobody else has known about this; I alone did everything. Remember that.

MRS. LINDE: I will. But I don't understand all this.

NORA: Oh, how could you ever understand it? It's the miracle now that's going to take place.

MRS. LINDE: The miracle?

NORA: Yes, the miracle. But it's so awful, Kristine. It mustn't take place, not for anything in the world.

MRS. LINDE: I'm going right over and talk with Krogstad.

NORA: Don't go near him; he'll do you some terrible harm!

MRS. LINDE: There was a time once when he'd gladly have done anything for me.

NORA: He?

MRS. LINDE: Where does he live?

NORA: Oh, how do I know? Yes. [*Searches in her pocket.*] Here's his card. But the letter, the letter—!

HELMER: [*From the study, knocking on the door.*] Nora!

NORA: [*With a cry of fear.*] Oh! What is it? What do you want?

HELMER: Now, now, don't be so frightened. We're not coming in. You locked the door—are you trying on the dress?

NORA: Yes, I'm trying it. I'll look just beautiful, Torvald.

MRS. LINDE: [*Who has read the card.*] He's living right around the corner.

NORA: Yes, but what's the use? We're lost. The letter's in the box.

MRS. LINDE: And your husband has the key?

NORA: Yes, always.

MRS. LINDE: Krogstad can ask for his letter back unread; he can find some excuse—

NORA: But it's just this time that Torvald usually—

MRS. LINDE: Stall him. Keep him in there. I'll be back as quick as I can. [*She hurries out through the hall entrance.*]

NORA: [*Goes to HELMER's door, opens it, and peers in.*] Torvald!

HELMER: [*From the inner study.*] Well—does one dare set foot in one's own living room at last? Come on, Rank, now we'll get a look— [*In the doorway.*] But what's this?

NORA: What, Torvald dear?

HELMER: Rank had me expecting some grand masquerade.

RANK: [*In the doorway.*] That was my impression, but I must have been wrong.

NORA: No one can admire me in my splendor—not till tomorrow.

HELMER: But Nora dear, you look so exhausted. Have you practiced too hard?

NORA: No, I haven't practiced at all yet.

HELMER: You know, it's necessary—

NORA: Oh, it's absolutely necessary, Torvald. But I can't get anywhere without your help. I've forgotten the whole thing completely.

HELMER: Ah, we'll soon take care of that.

NORA: Yes, take care of me, Torvald, please! Promise me that? Oh, I'm so nervous. That big party— You must give up everything this evening for me. No business—don't even touch your pen. Yes? Dear Torvald, promise?

HELMER: It's a promise. Tonight I'm totally at your service—you little helpless thing. Hm—but first there's one thing I want to— [Goes toward the hall door.]

NORA: What are you looking for?

HELMER: Just to see if there's any mail.

NORA: No, no, don't do that, Torvald!

HELMER: Now what?

NORA: Torvald, please. There isn't any.

HELMER: Let me look, though. [Starts out. NORA, at the piano, strikes the first notes of the tarantella. HELMER, at the door, stops.] Aha!

NORA: I can't dance tomorrow if I don't practice with you.

HELMER: [Going over to her.] Nora dear, are you really so frightened?

NORA: Yes, so terribly frightened. Let me practice right now; there's still time before dinner. Oh, sit down and play for me, Torvald. Direct me. Teach me, the way you always have.

HELMER: Gladly, if it's what you want. [Sits at the piano.]

NORA: [Snatches the tambourine up from the box, then a long, varicolored shawl, which she throws around herself, whereupon she springs forward and cries out:] Play for me now! Now I'll dance!

[HELMER plays and NORA dances. RANK stands behind HELMER at the piano and looks on.]

HELMER: [As he plays.] Slower. Slow down.

NORA: Can't change it.

HELMER: Not so violent, Nora!

NORA: Has to be just like this.

HELMER: [Stopping.] No, no, that won't do at all.

NORA: [Laughing and swinging her tambourine.] Isn't that what I told you?

RANK: Let me play for her.

HELMER: [Getting up.] Yes, go on. I can teach her more easily then.

[RANK sits at the piano and plays; NORA dances more and more wildly. HELMER has stationed himself by the stove and repeatedly gives her directions; she seems not to hear them; her hair loosens and falls over her shoulders; she does not notice, but goes on dancing. MRS. LINDE enters.]

MRS. LINDE: [Standing dumbfounded at the door.] Ah—!

NORA: [Still dancing.] See what fun, Kristine!

HELMER: But Nora darling, you dance as if your life were at stake.

NORA: And it is.

HELMER: Rank, stop! This is pure madness. Stop it, I say!

[RANK breaks off playing, and NORA halts abruptly.]

HELMER: [Going over to her.] I never would have believed it. You've forgotten everything I taught you.

NORA: [*Throwing away the tambourine.*] You see for yourself.

HELMER: Well, there's certainly room for instruction here.

NORA: Yes, you see how important it is. You've got to teach me to the very last minute. Promise me that, Torvald?

HELMER: You can bet on it.

NORA: You mustn't, either today or tomorrow, think about anything else but me; you mustn't open any letters—or the mailbox—

HELMER: Ah, it's still the fear of that man—

NORA: Oh yes, yes, that too.

HELMER: Nora, it's written all over you—there's already a letter from him out there.

NORA: I don't know. I guess so. But you mustn't read such things now; there mustn't be anything ugly between us before it's all over.

RANK: [*Quietly to* HELMER.] You shouldn't deny her.

HELMER: [*Putting his arm around her.*] The child can have her way. But tomorrow night, after you've danced—

NORA: Then you'll be free.

MAID: [*In the doorway, right.*] Ma'am, dinner is served.

NORA: We'll be wanting champagne, Helene.

MAID: Very good, ma'am. [*Goes out.*]

HELMER: So—a regular banquet, hm?

NORA: Yes, a banquet—champagne till daybreak! [*Calling out.*] And some macaroons, Helene. Heaps of them—just this once.

HELMER: [*Taking her hands.*] Now, now, now—no hysterics. Be my own little lark again.

NORA: Oh, I will soon enough. But go on in—and you, Dr. Rank. Kristine, help me put up my hair.

RANK: [*Whispering, as they go.*] There's nothing wrong—really wrong, is there?

HELMER: Oh, of course not. It's nothing more than this childish anxiety I was telling you about. [*They go out, right.*]

NORA: Well?

MRS. LINDE: Left town.

NORA: I could see by your face.

MRS. LINDE: He'll be home tomorrow evening. I wrote him a note.

NORA: You shouldn't have. Don't try to stop anything now. After all, it's a wonderful joy, this waiting here for the miracle.

MRS. LINDE: What is it you're waiting for?

NORA: Oh, you can't understand that. Go in to them; I'll be along in a moment.

[MRS. LINDE *goes into the dining room.* NORA *stands a short while as if composing herself; then she looks at her watch.*]

NORA: Five. Seven hours to midnight. Twenty-four hours to the midnight after, and then the tarantella's done. Seven and twenty-four? Thirty-one hours to live.

HELMER: [*In the doorway, right.*] What's become of the little lark?

NORA: [*Going toward him with open arms.*] Here's your lark!

ACT III

Same scene. The table, with chairs around it, has been moved to the center of the room. A lamp on the table is lit. The hall door stands open. Dance music drifts down from the floor above. MRS. LINDE *sits at the table, absently paging through a book, trying to read, but apparently unable to focus her thoughts. Once or twice she pauses, tensely listening for a sound at the outer entrance.*

MRS. LINDE: [*Glancing at her watch.*] Not yet—and there's hardly any time left. If only he's not— [*Listening again.*] Ah, there he is. [*She goes out in the hall and cautiously opens the outer door. Quiet footsteps are heard on the stairs. She whispers:*] Come in. Nobody's here.

KROGSTAD: [*In the doorway.*] I found a note from you at home. What's back of all this?

MRS. LINDE: I just *had* to talk to you.

KROGSTAD: Oh? And it just *had* to be here in this house?

MRS. LINDE: At my place it was impossible; my room hasn't a private entrance. Come in; we're all alone. The maid's asleep, and the Helmers are at the dance upstairs.

KROGSTAD: [*Entering the room.*] Well, well, the Helmers are dancing tonight? Really?

MRS. LINDE: Yes, why not?

KROGSTAD: How true—why not?

MRS. LINDE: All right, Krogstad, let's talk.

KROGSTAD: Do we two have anything more to talk about?

MRS. LINDE: We have a great deal to talk about.

KROGSTAD: I wouldn't have thought so.

MRS. LINDE: No, because you've never understood me, really.

KROGSTAD: Was there anything more to understand—except what's all too common in life? A calculating woman throws over a man the moment a better catch comes by.

MRS. LINDE: You think I'm so thoroughly calculating? You think I broke it off lightly?

KROGSTAD: Didn't you?

MRS. LINDE: Nils—is that what you really thought?

KROGSTAD: If you cared, then why did you write me the way you did?

MRS. LINDE: What else could I do? If I had to break off with you, then it was my job as well to root out everything you felt for me.

KROGSTAD: [*Wringing his hands.*] So that was it. And this—all this, simply for money!

MRS. LINDE: Don't forget I had a helpless mother and two small brothers. We couldn't wait for you, Nils; you had such a long road ahead of you then.

KROGSTAD: That may be; but you still hadn't the right to abandon me for somebody else's sake.

MRS. LINDE: Yes—I don't know. So many, many times I've asked myself if I did have that right.

KROGSTAD: [*More softly.*] When I lost you, it was as if all the solid ground dissolved from under my feet. Look at me; I'm a half-drowned man now, hanging onto a wreck.

MRS. LINDE: Help may be near.

KROGSTAD: It was near—but then you came and blocked it off.

MRS. LINDE: Without my knowing it, Nils. Today for the first time I learned that it's you I'm replacing at the bank.

KROGSTAD: All right—I believe you. But now that you know, will you step aside?

MRS. LINDE: No, because that wouldn't benefit you in the slightest.

KROGSTAD: Not "benefit" me, hm! I'd step aside anyway.

MRS. LINDE: I've learned to be realistic. Life and hard, bitter necessity have taught me that.

KROGSTAD: And life's taught me never to trust fine phrases.

MRS. LINDE: Then life's taught you a very sound thing. But you do have to trust in actions, don't you?

KROGSTAD: What does that mean?

MRS. LINDE: You said you were hanging on like a half-drowned man to a wreck.

KROGSTAD: I've good reason to say that.

MRS. LINDE: I'm also like a half-drowned woman on a wreck. No one to suffer with; no one to care for.

KROGSTAD: You made your choice

MRS. LINDE: There wasn't any choice then.

KROGSTAD: So—what of it?

MRS. LINDE: Nils, if only we two shipwrecked people could reach across to each other.

KROGSTAD: What are you saying?

MRS. LINDE: Two on one wreck are at least better off than each on his own.

KROGSTAD: Kristine!

MRS. LINDE: Why do you think I came into town?

KROGSTAD: Did you really have some thought of me?

MRS. LINDE: I have to work to go on living. All my born days, as long as I can remember, I've worked, and it's been my best and my only joy. But now I'm completely alone in the world; it frightens me to be so empty and lost. To work for yourself—there's no joy in that. Nils, give me something—someone to work for.

KROGSTAD: I don't believe all this. It's just some hysterical feminine urge to go out and make a noble sacrifice.

MRS. LINDE: Have you ever found me to be hysterical?

KROGSTAD: Can you honestly mean this? Tell me—do you know everything about my past?

MRS. LINDE: Yes.

KROGSTAD: And you know what they think I'm worth around here.

MRS. LINDE: From what you were saying before, it would seem that with me you could have been another person.

KROGSTAD: I'm positive of that.

MRS. LINDE: Couldn't it happen still?

KROGSTAD: Kristine—you're saying this in all seriousness? Yes, you are! I can see it in you. And do you really have the courage, then—?

MRS. LINDE: I need to have someone to care for; and your children need a mother. We both need each other. Nils, I have faith that you're good at heart—I'll risk everything together with you.

KROGSTAD: [Gripping her hands.] Kristine, thank you, thank you— Now I know I can win back a place in their eyes. Yes—but I forgot—

MRS. LINDE: [Listening.] Shh! The tarantella. Go now! Go on!

KROGSTAD: Why? What is it?

MRS. LINDE: Hear the dance up there? When that's over, they'll be coming down.

KROGSTAD: Oh, then I'll go. But—it's all pointless. Of course, you don't know the move I made against the Helmers.

MRS. LINDE: Yes, Nils, I know.

KROGSTAD: And all the same, you have the courage to—?

MRS. LINDE: I know how far despair can drive a man like you.

KROGSTAD: Oh, if I only could take it all back.

MRS. LINDE: You easily could—your letter's still lying in the mailbox.

KROGSTAD: Are you sure of that?

MRS. LINDE: Positive. But—

KROGSTAD: [Looks at her searchingly.] Is that the meaning of it, then? You'll save your friend at any price. Tell me straight out. Is that it?

MRS. LINDE: Nils—anyone who's sold herself for somebody else once isn't going to do it again.

KROGSTAD: I'll demand my letter back.

MRS. LINDE: No, no.

KROGSTAD: Yes, of course. I'll stay here till Helmer comes down; I'll tell him to give me my letter again—that it only involves my dismissal—that he shouldn't read it—

MRS. LINDE: No, Nils, don't call the letter back.

KROGSTAD: But wasn't that exactly why you wrote me to come here?

MRS. LINDE: Yes, in that first panic. But it's been a whole day and night since then, and in that time I've seen such incredible things in this house. Helmer's got to learn everything; this dreadful secret has to be aired; those two have to come to a full understanding; all these lies and evasions can't go on.

KROGSTAD: Well, then, if you want to chance it. But at least there's one thing I can do, and do right away—

MRS. LINDE: [Listening.] Go now, go, quick! The dance is over. We're not safe another second.

KROGSTAD: I'll wait for you downstairs.

MRS. LINDE: Yes, please do; take me home.

KROGSTAD: I can't believe it; I've never been so happy. [He leaves by way of the outer door; the door between the room and the hall stays open.]

MRS. LINDE: [Straightening up a bit and getting together her street clothes.] How different now! How different! Someone to work for, to live for—a home to build. Well, it is worth the try! Oh, if they'd only come! [Listening.] Ah, there they are. Bundle up. [She picks up her hat and coat. NORA's and HELMER's voices can be

heard outside; a key turns in the lock, and HELMER *brings* NORA *into the hall almost
by force. She is wearing the Italian costume with a large black shawl about her; he
has on evening dress, with a black domino open over it.*]

NORA: [*Struggling in the doorway.*] No, no, no, not inside! I'm going up again. I don't
want to leave so soon.

HELMER: But Nora dear—

NORA: Oh, I beg you, please, Torvald. From the bottom of my heart, *please*—only
an hour more!

HELMER: Not a single minute, Nora darling. You know our agreement. Come on,
in we go; you'll catch cold out here. [*In spite of her resistance, he gently draws
her into the room.*]

MRS. LINDE: Good evening.

NORA: Kristine!

HELMER: Why, Mrs. Linde—are you here so late?

MRS. LINDE: Yes, I'm sorry, but I did want to see Nora in costume.

NORA: Have you been sitting here, waiting for me?

MRS. LINDE: Yes. I didn't come early enough; you were all upstairs; and then I
thought I really couldn't leave without seeing you.

HELMER: [*Removing* NORA's *shawl.*] Yes, take a good look. She's worth looking at, I
can tell you that, Mrs. Linde. Isn't she lovely?

MRS. LINDE: Yes, I should say—

HELMER: A dream of loveliness, isn't she? That's what everyone thought at the
party, too. But she's horribly stubborn—this sweet little thing. What's to be
done with her? Can you imagine, I almost had to use force to pry her away.

NORA: Oh, Torvald, you're going to regret you didn't indulge me, even for just a
half hour more.

HELMER: There, you see. She danced her tarantella and got a tumultuous hand—
which was well earned, although the performance may have been a bit too
naturalistic—I mean it rather overstepped the proprieties of art. But never
mind—what's important is, she made a success, an overwhelming success.
You think I could let her stay on after that and spoil the effect? Oh no; I took
my lovely little Capri girl—my capricious little Capri girl, I should say—took
her under my arm; one quick tour of the ballroom, a curtsy to every side, and
then—as they say in novels—the beautiful vision disappeared. An exit should
always be effective, Mrs. Linde, but that's what I can't get Nora to grasp. Phew,
it's hot in here. [*Flings the domino on a chair and opens the door to his room.*]
Why's it dark in here? Oh yes, of course. Excuse me. [*He goes in and lights a
couple of candles.*]

NORA: [*In a sharp, breathless whisper.*] So?

MRS. LINDE: [*Quietly.*] I talked with him.

NORA: And—?

MRS. LINDE: Nora—you must tell your husband everything.

NORA: [*Dully.*] I knew it.

MRS. LINDE: You've got nothing to fear from Krogstad, but you have to speak out.

NORA: I won't tell.

MRS. LINDE: Then the letter will.

NORA: Thanks, Kristine. I know now what's to be done. Shh!

HELMER: [*Reentering.*] Well, then, Mrs. Linde—have you admired her?

MRS. LINDE: Yes, and now I'll say good night.

HELMER: Oh, come, so soon? Is this yours, this knitting?

MRS. LINDE: Yes, thanks. I nearly forgot it.

HELMER: Do you knit, then?

MRS. LINDE: Oh yes.

HELMER: You know what? You should embroider instead.

MRS. LINDE: Really? Why?

HELMER: Yes, because it's a lot prettier. See here, one holds the embroidery so, in
the left hand, and then one guides the needle with the right—so—in an easy,
sweeping curve—right?

MRS. LINDE: Yes, I guess that's—

HELMER: But, on the other hand, knitting—it can never be anything but ugly.
Look, see here, the arms tucked in, the knitting needles going up and down—
there's something Chinese about it. Ah, that was really a glorious champagne
they served.

MRS. LINDE: Yes, good night, Nora, and don't be stubborn anymore.

HELMER: Well put, Mrs. Linde!

MRS. LINDE: Good night, Mr. Helmer.

HELMER: [*Accompanying her to the door.*] Good night, good night. I hope you get
home all right. I'd be very happy to—but you don't have far to go. Good
night, good night. [*She leaves. He shuts the door after her and returns.*] There,
now, at last we got her out the door. She's a deadly bore, that creature.

NORA: Aren't you pretty tired, Torvald?

HELMER: No, not a bit.

NORA: You're not sleepy?

HELMER: Not at all. On the contrary, I'm feeling quite exhilarated. But you? Yes,
you really look tired and sleepy.

NORA: Yes, I'm very tired. Soon now I'll sleep.

HELMER: See! You see! I was right all along that we shouldn't stay longer.

NORA: Whatever you do is always right.

HELMER: [*Kissing her brow.*] Now my little lark talks sense. Say, did you notice what
a time Rank was having tonight?

NORA: Oh, was he? I didn't get to speak with him.

HELMER: I scarcely did either, but it's a long time since I've seen him in such high
spirits. [*Gazes at her a moment, then comes nearer her.*] Hm—it's marvelous,
though, to be back home again—to be completely alone with you. Oh, you
bewitchingly lovely young woman!

NORA: Torvald, don't look at me like that!

HELMER: Can't I look at my richest treasure? At all that beauty that's mine, mine
alone—completely and utterly.

NORA: [*Moving around to the other side of the table.*] You mustn't talk to me that way
tonight.

HELMER: [*Following her.*] The tarantella is still in your blood, I can see—and it makes
you even more enticing. Listen. The guests are beginning to go. [*Dropping his*

voice.] Nora—it'll soon be quiet through this whole house.

NORA: Yes, I hope so.

HELMER: You do, don't you, my love? Do you realize—when I'm out at a party like this with you—do you know why I talk to you so little, and keep such a distance away; just send you a stolen look now and then—you know why I do it? It's because I'm imagining then that you're my secret darling, my secret young bride-to-be, and that no one suspects there's anything between us.

NORA: Yes, yes; oh, yes, I know you're always thinking of me.

HELMER: And then when we leave and I place the shawl over those fine young rounded shoulders—over that wonderful curving neck—then I pretend that you're my young bride, that we're just coming from the wedding, that for the first time I'm bringing you into my house—that for the first time I'm alone with you—completely alone with you, your trembling young beauty! All this evening I've longed for nothing but you. When I saw you turn and sway in the tarantella—my blood was pounding till I couldn't stand it—that's why I brought you down here so early—

NORA: Go away, Torvald! Leave me alone. I don't want all this.

HELMER: What do you mean? Nora, you're teasing me. You will, won't you? Aren't I your husband—?

[*A knock at the outside door.*]

NORA: [*Startled.*] What's that?

HELMER: [*Going toward the half.*] Who is it?

RANK: [*Outside.*] It's me. May I come in a moment?

HELMER: [*With quiet irritation.*] Oh, what does he want now? [*Aloud.*] Hold on. [*Goes and opens the door.*] Oh, how nice that you didn't just pass us by!

RANK: I thought I heard your voice, and then I wanted so badly to have a look in. [*Lightly glancing about.*] Ah, me, these old familiar haunts. You have it snug and cozy in here, you two.

HELMER: You seemed to be having it pretty cozy upstairs, too.

RANK: Absolutely. Why shouldn't I? Why not take in everything in life? As much as you can, anyway, and as long as you can. The wine was superb—

HELMER: The champagne especially.

RANK: You noticed that too? It's amazing how much I could guzzle down.

NORA: Torvald also drank a lot of champagne this evening.

RANK: Oh?

NORA: Yes, and that always makes him so entertaining.

RANK: Well, why shouldn't one have a pleasant evening after a well-spent day?

HELMER: Well spent? I'm afraid I can't claim that.

RANK: [*Slapping him on the back.*] But I can, you see!

NORA: Dr. Rank, you must have done some scientific research today.

RANK: Quite so.

HELMER: Come now—little Nora talking about scientific research!

NORA: And can I congratulate you on the results?

RANK: Indeed you may.

NORA: Then they were good?

RANK: The best possible for both doctor and patient—certainty.

NORA: [*Quickly and searchingly.*] Certainty?

RANK: Complete certainty. So don't I owe myself a gay evening afterwards?

NORA: Yes, you're right, Dr. Rank.

HELMER: I'm with you—just so long as you don't have to suffer for it in the morning.

RANK: Well, one never gets something for nothing in life.

NORA: Dr. Rank—are you very fond of masquerade parties?

RANK: Yes, if there's a good array of odd disguises—

NORA: Tell me, what should we two go as at the next masquerade?

HELMER: You little featherhead—already thinking of the next!

RANK: We two? I'll tell you what: you must go as Charmed Life—

HELMER: Yes, but find a costume for *that!*

RANK: Your wife can appear just as she looks every day.

HELMER: That was nicely put. But don't you know what you're going to be?

RANK: Yes, Helmer, I've made up my mind.

HELMER: Well?

RANK: At the next masquerade I'm going to be invisible.

HELMER: That's a funny idea.

RANK: They say there's a hat—black, huge—have you never heard of the hat that makes you invisible? You put it on, and then no one on earth can see you.

HELMER: [*Suppressing a smile.*] Ah, of course.

RANK: But I'm quite forgetting what I came for. Helmer, give me a cigar, one of the dark Havanas.

HELMER: With the greatest pleasure. [*Holds out his case.*]

RANK: Thanks. [*Takes one and cuts off the tip.*]

NORA: [*Striking a match*] Let me give you a light.

RANK: Thank you. [*She holds the match for him; he lights the cigar.*] And now good-bye.

HELMER: Good-bye, good-bye, old friend.

NORA: Sleep well, Doctor.

RANK: Thanks for that wish.

NORA: Wish me the same.

RANK: You? All right, if you like— Sleep well. And thanks for the light. [*He nods to them both and leaves.*]

HELMER: [*His voice subdued.*] He's been drinking heavily.

NORA: [*Absently.*] Could be. [HELMER *takes his keys from his pocket and goes out in the hall.*] Torvald—what are you after?

HELMER: Got to empty the mailbox; it's nearly full. There won't be room for the morning papers.

NORA: Are you working tonight?

HELMER: You know I'm not. Why—what's this? Someone's been at the lock.

NORA: At the lock—?

HELMER: Yes, I'm positive. What do you suppose—? I can't imagine one of the maids—? Here's a broken hairpin. Nora, it's yours—

NORA: [*Quickly.*] Then it must be the children—

HELMER: You'd better break them of that. Hm, hm—well, opened it after all. [*Takes the contents out and calls into the kitchen.*] Helene! Helene, would you put out the lamp in the hall. [*He returns to the room, shutting the hall door, then displays the handful of mail.*] Look how it's piled up. [*Sorting through them.*] Now what's this?

NORA: [*At the window.*] The letter! Oh, Torvald, no!

HELMER: Two calling cards—from Rank.

NORA: From Dr. Rank?

HELMER: [*Examining them.*] "Dr. Rank, Consulting Physician." They were on top. He must have dropped them in as he left.

NORA: Is there anything on them?

HELMER: There's a black cross over the name. See? That's a gruesome notion. He could almost be announcing his own death.

NORA: That's just what he's doing.

HELMER: What! You've heard something? Something he's told you?

NORA: Yes. That when those cards came, he'd be taking his leave of us. He'll shut himself in now and die.

HELMER: Ah, my poor friend! Of course I knew he wouldn't be here much longer. But so soon— And then to hide himself away like a wounded animal.

NORA: If it has to happen, then it's best it happens in silence—don't you think so, Torvald?

HELMER: [*Pacing up and down.*] He'd grown right into our lives. I simply can't imagine him gone. He with his suffering and loneliness—like a dark cloud setting off our sunlit happiness. Well, maybe it's best this way. For him, at least. [*Standing still.*] And maybe for us too, Nora. Now we're thrown back on each other, completely. [*Embracing her.*] Oh you, my darling wife, how can I hold you close enough? You know what, Nora—time and again I've wished you were in some terrible danger, just so I could stake my life and soul and everything, for your sake.

NORA: [*Tearing herself away, her voice firm and decisive.*] Now you must read your mail, Torvald.

HELMER: No, no, not tonight. I want to stay with you, dearest.

NORA: With a dying friend on your mind?

HELMER: You're right. We've both had a shock. There's ugliness between us—these thoughts of death and corruption. We'll have to get free of them first. Until then—we'll stay apart.

NORA: [*Clinging about his neck.*] Torvald—good night! Good night!

HELMER: [*Kissing her on the cheek.*] Good night, little songbird. Sleep well, Nora. I'll be reading my mail now. [*He takes the letters into his room and shuts the door after him.*]

NORA: [*With bewildered glances, groping about, seizing* HELMER's *domino, throwing it around her, and speaking in short, hoarse, broken whispers.*] Never see him again. Never, never. [*Putting her shawl over her head.*] Never see the children either— them, too. Never, never. Oh, the freezing black water! The depths—down— Oh, I wish it were over— He has it now; he's reading it—now. Oh no, no, not yet. Torvald, good-bye, you and the children— [*She starts for the hall; as she does*, HELMER *throws open his door and stands with an open letter in his hand.*]

HELMER: Nora!

NORA: [*Screams.*] Oh—!

HELMER: What is this? You know what's in this letter?

NORA: Yes, I know. Let me go! Let me out!

HELMER: [*Holding her back.*] Where are you going?

NORA: [*Struggling to break loose.*] You can't save me, Torvald!

HELMER: [*Slumping back.*] True! Then it's true what he writes? How horrible! No, no, it's impossible—it can't be true.

NORA: It *is* true. I've loved you more than all this world.

HELMER: Ah, none of your slippery tricks.

NORA: [*Taking one step toward him.*] Torvald—!

HELMER: What *is* this you've blundered into!

NORA: Just let me loose. You're not going to suffer for my sake. You're not going to take on my guilt.

HELMER: No more playacting. [*Locks the hall door.*] You stay right here and give me a reckoning. You understand what you've done? Answer! You understand?

NORA: [*Looking squarely at him, her face hardening.*] Yes. I'm beginning to understand everything now.

HELMER: [*Striding about.*] Oh, what an awful awakening! In all these eight years— she who was my pride and joy—a hypocrite, a liar—worse, worse—a criminal! How infinitely disgusting it all is! The shame! [NORA *says nothing and goes on looking straight at him. He stops in front of her.*] I should have suspected something of the kind. I should have known. All your father's flimsy values— Be still! All your father's flimsy values have come out in you. No religion, no morals, no sense of duty— Oh, how I'm punished for letting him off! I did it for your sake, and you repay me like this.

NORA: Yes, like this.

HELMER: Now you've wrecked all my happiness—ruined my whole future. Oh, it's awful to think of. I'm in a cheap little grafter's hands; he can do anything he wants with me, ask for anything, play with me like a puppet—and I can't breathe a word. I'll be swept down miserably into the depths on account of a featherbrained woman.

NORA: When I'm gone from this world, you'll be free.

HELMER: Oh, quit posing. Your father had a mess of those speeches too. What good would that ever do me if you were gone from this world, as you say? Not the slightest. He can still make the whole thing known; and if he does, I could be falsely suspected as your accomplice. They might even think that I was behind it—that I put you up to it. And all that I can thank you for— you that I've coddled the whole of our marriage. Can you see now what you've done to me?

NORA: [*Icily calm.*] Yes.

HELMER: It's so incredible, I just can't grasp it. But we'll have to patch up whatever we can. Take off the shawl. I said, take it off! I've got to appease him somehow or other. The thing has to be hushed up at any cost. And as for you and me, it's got to seem like everything between us is just as it was—to the outside world, that is. You'll go right on living in this house, of course. But you can't be allowed to bring up the children; I don't dare trust you with them— Oh, to have to say this to someone I've loved so much, and that I still—! Well, that's done with. From now on happiness doesn't matter; all that matters is saving the bits and pieces, the appearance— [*The doorbell rings.* HELMER *starts.*] What's that? And so late. Maybe the worst—? You think he'd—? Hide, Nora! Say you're sick. [NORA *remains standing motionless.* HELMER *goes and opens the door.*]

MAID: [*Half dressed, in the hall.*] A letter for Mrs. Helmer.

HELMER: I'll take it. [*Snatches the letter and shuts the door.*] Yes, it's from him. You don't get it; I'm reading it myself.

NORA: Then read it.

HELMER: [*By the lamp.*] I hardly dare. We may be ruined, you and I. But—I've got to know. [*Rips open the letter, skims through a few lines, glances at an enclosure, then cries out joyfully.*] Nora! [NORA *looks inquiringly at him.*] Nora! Wait—better check it again—Yes, yes, it's true. I'm saved. Nora, I'm saved!

NORA: And I?

HELMER: You too, of course. We're both saved, both of us. Look. He's sent back your note. He says he's sorry and ashamed—that a happy development in his life—oh, who cares what he says! Nora, we're saved! No one can hurt you. Oh, Nora, Nora—but first, this ugliness all has to go. Let me see— [*Takes a look at the note.*] No, I don't want to see it; I want the whole thing to fade like a dream. [*Tears the note and both letters to pieces, throws them into the stove and watches them burn.*] There—now there's nothing left— He wrote that since Christmas Eve you— Oh, they must have been three terrible days for you, Nora.

NORA: I fought a hard fight.

HELMER: And suffered pain and saw no escape but— No, we're not going to dwell on anything unpleasant. We'll just be grateful and keep on repeating: it's over now, it's over! You hear me, Nora? You don't seem to realize—it's over. What's it mean—that frozen look? Oh, poor little Nora, I understand. You can't believe I've forgiven you. But I have, Nora; I swear I have. I know that what you did, you did out of love for me.

NORA: That's true.

HELMER: You loved me the way a wife ought to love her husband. It's simply the means that you couldn't judge. But you think I love you any the less for not knowing how to handle your affairs? No, no—just lean on me; I'll guide you and teach you. I wouldn't be a man if this feminine helplessness didn't make you twice as attractive to me. You mustn't mind those sharp words I said— that was all in the first confusion of thinking my world had collapsed. I've forgiven you, Nora; I swear I've forgiven you.

NORA: My thanks for your forgiveness. [*She goes out through the door, right.*]

HELMER: No, wait— [*Peers in.*] What are you doing in there?

NORA: [*Inside.*] Getting out of my costume.

HELMER: [*By the open door.*] Yes, do that. Try to calm yourself and collect your thoughts again, my frightened little songbird. You can rest easy now; I've got wide wings to shelter you with. [*Walking about close by the door.*] How snug and nice our home is, Nora. You're safe here; I'll keep you like a hunted dove I've rescued out of a hawk's claws. I'll bring peace to your poor, shuddering heart. Gradually it'll happen, Nora; you'll see. Tomorrow all this will look different to you; then everything will be as it was. I won't have to go on repeating I forgive you; you'll feel it for yourself. How can you imagine I'd ever conceivably want to disown you—or even blame you in any way? Ah, you don't know a man's heart, Nora. For a man there's something indescribably sweet and satisfying in knowing he's forgiven his wife—and forgiven her out of a full and open heart. It's as if she belongs to him in two ways now: in a sense he's given her fresh into the world again, and she's become his wife and his child as well. From now on that's what you'll be to me—you little, bewildered, helpless thing. Don't be afraid of anything, Nora; just open your heart to me, and I'll be conscience and will to you both— [NORA *enters in her regular clothes.*] What's this? Not in bed? You've changed your dress?

NORA: Yes, Torvald, I've changed my dress.

HELMER: But why now, so late?

NORA: Tonight I'm not sleeping.

HELMER: But Nora dear—

NORA: [*Looking at her watch.*] It's still not so very late. Sit down, Torvald; we have a lot to talk over. [*She sits at one side of the table.*]

HELMER: Nora—what is this? That hard expression—

NORA: Sit down. This'll take some time. I have a lot to say.

HELMER: [*Sitting at the table directly opposite her.*] You worry me, Nora. And I don't understand you.

NORA: No, that's exactly it. You don't understand me. And I've never understood you either—until tonight. No, don't interrupt. You can just listen to what I say. We're closing out accounts, Torvald.

HELMER: How do you mean that?

NORA: [*After a short pause.*] Doesn't anything strike you about our sitting here like this?

HELMER: What's that?

NORA: We've been married now eight years. Doesn't it occur to you that this is the first time we two, you and I, man and wife, have ever talked seriously together?

HELMER: What do you mean—seriously?

NORA: In eight whole years—longer even—right from our first acquaintance, we've never exchanged a serious word on any serious thing.

HELMER: You mean I should constantly go and involve you in problems you couldn't possibly help me with?

NORA: I'm not talking of problems. I'm saying that we've never sat down seriously together and tried to get to the bottom of anything.

HELMER: But dearest, what good would that ever do you?

NORA: That's the point right there: you've never understood me. I've been wronged greatly, Torvald—first by Papa, and then by you.

HELMER: What! By us—the two people who've loved you more than anyone else?

NORA: [*Shaking her head.*] You never loved me. You've thought it fun to be in love with me, that's all.

HELMER: Nora, what a thing to say!

NORA: Yes, it's true now, Torvald. When I lived at home with Papa, he told me all his opinions, so I had the same ones too; or if they were different I hid them, since he wouldn't have cared for that. He used to call me his doll-child, and he played with me the way I played with my dolls. Then I came into your house—

HELMER: How can you speak of our marriage like that?

NORA: [*Unperturbed.*] I mean, then I went from Papa's hands into yours. You arranged everything to your own taste, and so I got the same taste as you— or I pretended to; I can't remember. I guess a little of both, first one, then the other. Now when I look back, it seems as if I'd lived here like a beggar—just from hand to mouth. I've lived by doing tricks for you, Torvald. But that's the way you wanted it. It's a great sin what you and Papa did to me. You're to blame that nothing's become of me.

HELMER: Nora, how unfair and ungrateful you are! Haven't you been happy here?

NORA: No, never. I thought so—but I never have.

HELMER: Not—not happy!

NORA: No, only lighthearted. And you've always been so kind to me. But our home's been nothing but a playpen. I've been your doll-wife here, just as at home I was Papa's doll-child. And in turn the children have been my dolls. I thought it was fun when you played with me, just as they thought it fun when I played with them. That's been our marriage, Torvald.

HELMER: There's some truth in what you're saying—under all the raving exaggeration. But it'll all be different after this. Playtime's over; now for the schooling.

NORA: Whose schooling—mine or the children's?

HELMER: Both yours and the children's, dearest.

NORA: Oh, Torvald, you're not the man to teach me to be a good wife to you.

HELMER: And you can say that?

NORA: And I—how am I equipped to bring up children?

HELMER: Nora!

NORA: Didn't you say a moment ago that that was no job to trust me with?

HELMER: In a flare of temper! Why fasten on that?

NORA: Yes, but you were so very right. I'm not up to the job. There's another job I have to do first. I have to try to educate myself. You can't help me with that. I've got to do it alone. And that's why I'm leaving you now.

HELMER: [*Jumping up.*] What's that?

NORA: I have to stand completely alone, if I'm ever going to discover myself and the world out there. So I can't go on living with you.

HELMER: Nora, Nora!

NORA: I want to leave right away. Kristine should put me up for the night—

HELMER: You're insane! You've no right! I forbid you!

NORA: From here on, there's no use forbidding me anything. I'll take with me whatever is mine. I don't want a thing from you, either now or later.

HELMER: What kind of madness is this!

NORA: Tomorrow I'm going home—I mean, home where I came from. It'll be easier up there to find something to do.

HELMER: Oh, you blind, incompetent child!

NORA: I must learn to be competent, Torvald.

HELMER: Abandon your home, your husband, your children! And you're not even thinking what people will say.

NORA: I can't be concerned about that. I only know how essential this is.

HELMER: Oh, it's outrageous. So you'll run out like this on your most sacred vows.

NORA: What do you think are my most sacred vows?

HELMER: And I have to tell you that! Aren't they your duties to your husband and children?

NORA: I have other duties equally sacred.

HELMER: That isn't true. What duties are they?

NORA: Duties to myself.

HELMER: Before all else, you're a wife and a mother.

NORA: I don't believe in that anymore. I believe that, before all else, I'm a human being, no less than you—or anyway, I ought to try to become one. I know the majority thinks you're right, Torvald, and plenty of books agree with you, too. But I can't go on believing what the majority says, or what's written in books. I have to think over these things myself and try to understand them.

HELMER: Why can't you understand your place in your own home? On a point like that, isn't there one everlasting guide you can turn to? Where's your religion?

NORA: Oh, Torvald, I'm really not sure what religion is.

HELMER: What—?

NORA: I only know what the minister said when I was confirmed. He told me religion was this thing and that. When I get clear and away by myself, I'll go into that problem too. I'll see if what the minister said was right, or, in any case, if it's right for me.

HELMER: A young woman your age shouldn't talk like that. If religion can't move you, I can try to rouse your conscience. You do have some moral feeling? Or, tell me—has that gone too?

NORA: It's not easy to answer that, Torvald. I simply don't know. I'm all confused about these things. I just know I see them so differently from you. I find out, for one thing, that the law's not at all what I'd thought—but I can't get it through my head that the law is fair. A woman hasn't a right to protect her dying father or save her husband's life! I can't believe that.

HELMER: You talk like a child. You don't know anything of the world you live in.

NORA: No, I don't. But now I'll begin to learn for myself. I'll try to discover who's right, the world or I.

HELMER: Nora, you're sick; you've got a fever. I almost think you're out of your head.

NORA: I've never felt more clearheaded and sure in my life.

HELMER: And—clearheaded and sure—you're leaving your husband and children?

NORA: Yes.

HELMER: Then there's only one possible reason.

NORA: What?

HELMER: You no longer love me.

NORA: No. That's exactly it.

HELMER: Nora! You can't be serious!

NORA: Oh, this is so hard, Torvald—you've been so kind to me always. But I can't help it. I don't love you anymore.

HELMER: [Struggling for composure.] Are you also clearheaded and sure about that?

NORA: Yes, completely. That's why I can't go on staying here.

HELMER: Can you tell me what I did to lose your love?

NORA: Yes, I can tell you. It was this evening when the miraculous thing didn't come—then I knew you weren't the man I'd imagined.

HELMER: Be more explicit; I don't follow you.

NORA: I've waited now so patiently eight long years—for, my Lord, I know miracles don't come every day. Then this crisis broke over me, and such a certainty filled me: *now* the miraculous event would occur. While Krogstad's letter was lying out there, I never for an instant dreamed that you could give in to his terms. I was so utterly sure you'd say to him: go on, tell your tale to the whole wide world. And when he'd done that—

HELMER: Yes, what then? When I'd delivered my own wife into shame and disgrace—!

NORA: When he'd done that, I was so utterly sure that you'd step forward, take the blame on yourself and say: I am the guilty one.

HELMER: Nora—!

NORA: You're thinking I'd never accept such a sacrifice from you? No, of course not. But what good would my protests be against you? That was the miracle I was waiting for, in terror and hope. And to stave that off, I would have taken my life.

HELMER: I'd gladly work for you day and night, Nora—and take on pain and deprivation. But there's no one who gives up honor for love.

NORA: Millions of women have done just that.

HELMER: Oh, you think and talk like a silly child.

NORA: Perhaps. But you neither think nor talk like the man I could join myself to. When your big fright was over—and it wasn't from any threat against me, only for what might damage you—when all the danger was past, for you it was just as if nothing had happened. I was exactly the same, your little lark, your doll, that you'd have to handle with double care now that I'd turned out so brittle and frail. [Gets up.] Torvald—in that instant it dawned on me that for eight years I've been living here with a stranger, and that I'd even conceived three children—oh, I can't stand the thought of it! I could tear myself to bits.

HELMER: [*Heavily.*] I see. There's a gulf that's opened between us—that's clear. Oh, but Nora, can't we bridge it somehow?

NORA: The way I am now, I'm no wife for you.

HELMER: I have the strength to make myself over.

NORA: Maybe—if your doll gets taken away.

HELMER: But to part! To part from you! No, Nora, no—I can't imagine it.

NORA: [*Going out, right.*] All the more reason why it has to be. [*She reenters with her coat and a small overnight bag, which she puts on a chair by the table.*]

HELMER: Nora, Nora, not now! Wait till tomorrow.

NORA: I can't spend the night in a strange man's room.

HELMER: But couldn't we live here like brother and sister—

NORA: You know very well how long that would last. [*Throws her shawl about her.*] Good-bye, Torvald. I won't look in on the children. I know they're in better hands than mine. The way I am now, I'm no use to them.

HELMER: But someday, Nora—someday—?

NORA: How can I tell? I haven't the least idea what'll become of me.

HELMER: But you're my wife, now and wherever you go.

NORA: Listen, Torvald—I've heard that when a wife deserts her husband's house just as I'm doing, then the law frees him from all responsibility. In any case, I'm freeing you from being responsible. Don't feel yourself bound, any more than I will. There has to be absolute freedom for us both. Here, take your ring back. Give me mine.

HELMER: That too?

NORA: That too.

HELMER: There it is.

NORA: Good. Well, now it's all over. I'm putting the keys here. The maids know all about keeping up the house—better than I do. Tomorrow, after I've left town, Kristine will stop by to pack up everything that's mine from home. I'd like those things shipped up to me.

HELMER: Over! All over! Nora, won't you ever think about me?

NORA: I'm sure I'll think of you often, and about the children and the house here.

HELMER: May I write you?

NORA: No—never. You're not to do that.

HELMER: Oh, but let me send you—

NORA: Nothing. Nothing.

HELMER: Or help you if you need it.

NORA: No. I accept nothing from strangers.

HELMER: Nora—can I never be more than a stranger to you?

NORA: [*Picking up the overnight bag.*] Ah, Torvald—it would take the greatest miracle of all—

HELMER: Tell me the greatest miracle!

NORA: You and I both would have to transform ourselves to the point that— Oh, Torvald, I've stopped believing in miracles.

HELMER: But I'll believe. Tell me! Transform ourselves to the point that—?

NORA: That our living together could be a true marriage. [*She goes out down the hall.*]

HELMER: [*sinks down on a chair by the door, face buried in his hands.*] Nora! Nora! [*Looking about and rising.*] Empty. She's gone. [*A sudden hope leaps in him.*] The greatest miracle—?

[*From below, the sound of a door slamming shut.*]

1879

QUESTIONS

1. Act 1 shows Nora to be vulnerable in a number of ways, and her character seems quite superficial. What strategies contribute to this impression? What actions make her seem reckless with money (or at least oblivious to its uses)? How does the season of the year contribute to the sense of freedom from obligation?
2. In what ways do our first impressions of Nora depend on Torvald's attitudes? What terms does he use to describe her? What attitudes lie behind his "affectionate" nicknames? Why does Nora encourage the sense of herself as inept and irresponsible?
3. Why does the play, early on, emphasize the forbidden macaroons? Why does Torvald ban them? What is implied by Nora's attitude toward them? Mrs. Linde's?
4. How does the setting contribute to the characterization of Nora? Of Torvald? Describe how, if you were staging the play, you would use stage space to emphasize Torvald's aloofness. What strategies of costume would you use for Nora and Torvald to underscore their characters?
5. Exactly when do you sense that Nora is more than the lighthearted and scatterbrained person she at first appears to be? Trace her development from then on: What "character" words would you use to describe the woman who emerges by the end of the play?
6. Trace all the references Torvald makes to his own uprightness. Which of his speeches early on suggest something less than the probity he claims? What indications are there before act 3 that Krogstad might have redeeming features?
7. What functions does Dr. Rank perform for the plot?
8. List individually all the facts from the past that lead to the crisis of the play and those that lead to its denouement. What features of each main character contribute to the plot?
9. How does the onstage piano add to the play? Why does the celebratory dance—Nora's triumphal appearance—occur offstage? Is there an equivalent in Torvald's character to Nora's theatricality?
10. The shadow of death hangs over the play from almost the start. Trace all the references to sickness and mortality; how do these references suggest the way the difficulties will resolve themselves? When do you begin to suspect that Nora might commit suicide? Which of her own words contribute to that suspicion? When do you suspect that Nora will force some other solution? How crucial is Mrs. Linde's character to the ultimate outcome? Krogstad's? Rank's?

WRITING SUGGESTIONS

1. Much of the play turns on the differences between Torvald's ideas about morality and Nora's. Examine carefully all the speeches they make that establish their values. Then, using as many of their own words as possible, create for each a summary defense that argues for the correctness of his or her views.
2. Write a final letter that Nora might send to Torvald, explaining and justifying her actions from the beginning of her marriage to the play's end.

3. Look carefully at every appearance the Helmer children make in the play and at every reference to them. Then write a two-page essay about how the children contribute to the play's resolution.

4. Dr. Rank is one of the most mysterious figures in the play; his role in the Helmer household puzzles even some of the other characters. Write a "defense" of Rank and the role he plays in the household; cast it in the form of a three-hundred-word letter he might write in anticipation of his death.

5. Write a 750-word essay on the title of the play. Consider carefully both of the key words in the title: why is "house" thematically important to what the play accomplishes? What different senses does the term *doll* have in the play? Some translations of the play are titled *A Doll's House*. What different implications does that title have? Also, consider carefully the ways that Torvald and Nora's father resemble each other; interpret the play's resolution in terms of the title.

AUGUST WILSON

The Piano Lesson

Gin my cotton
Sell my seed
Buy my baby
Everything she need
—*Skip James*

CHARACTERS

DOAKER	MARETHA
BOY WILLIE	AVERY
LYMON	WINING BOY
BERNIECE	GRACE

THE SETTING: *The action of the play takes place in the kitchen and parlor of the house where* DOAKER CHARLES *lives with his niece,* BERNIECE, *and her eleven-year-old daughter,* MARETHA. *The house is sparsely furnished, and although there is evidence of a woman's touch, there is a lack of warmth and vigor.* BERNIECE *and* MARETHA *occupy the upstairs rooms.* DOAKER'S *room is prominent and opens onto the kitchen. Dominating the parlor is an old upright piano. On the legs of the piano, carved in the manner of African sculpture, are mask-like figures resembling totems. The carvings are rendered with a grace and power of invention that lifts them out of the realm of craftsmanship and into the realm of art. At left is a staircase leading to the upstairs.*

ACT I

SCENE 1

[*The lights come up on the Charles household. It is five o'clock in the morning. The dawn is beginning to announce itself, but there is something in the air that belongs to the night. A stillness that is a portent, a gathering, a coming together of something akin to a storm. There is a loud knock at the door.*]

BOY WILLIE: [*Off stage, calling.*] Hey, Doaker . . . Doaker! [*He knocks again and calls.*] Hey, Doaker! Hey, Berniece! Berniece!

[DOAKER *enters from his room. He is a tall, thin man of forty-seven, with severe features, who has for all intents and purposes retired from the world though he works full-time as a railroad cook.*]

DOAKER: Who is it?
BOY WILLIE: Open the door, nigger! It's me . . . Boy Willie!
DOAKER: Who?

BOY WILLIE: Boy Willie! Open the door!

[DOAKER *opens the door and* BOY WILLIE *and* LYMON *enter.* BOY WILLIE *is thirty years old. He has an infectious grin and a boyishness that is apt for his name. He is brash and impulsive, talkative and somewhat crude in speech and manner.* LYMON *is twenty-nine.* BOY WILLIE*'s partner, he talks little, and then with a straightforwardness that is often disarming.*]

DOAKER: What you doing up here?

BOY WILLIE: I told you, Lymon. Lymon talking about you might be sleep. This is Lymon. You remember Lymon Jackson from down home? This my Uncle Doaker.

DOAKER: What you doing up here? I couldn't figure out who that was. I thought you was still down in Mississippi.

BOY WILLIE: Me and Lymon selling watermelons. We got a truck out there. Got a whole truckload of watermelons. We brought them up here to sell. Where's Berniece? [*Calls.*] Hey, Berniece!

DOAKER: Berniece up there sleep.

BOY WILLIE: Well, let her get up. [*Calls.*] Hey, Berniece!

DOAKER: She got to go to work in the morning.

BOY WILLIE: Well she can get up and say hi. It's been three years since I seen her. [*Calls.*] Hey, Berniece! It's me . . . Boy Willie.

DOAKER: Berniece don't like all that hollering now. She got to work in the morning.

BOY WILLIE: She can go on back to bed. Me and Lymon been riding two days in that truck . . . the least she can do is get up and say hi.

DOAKER: [*Looking out the window.*] Where you all get that truck from?

BOY WILLIE: It's Lymon's. I told him let's get a load of watermelons and bring them up here.

LYMON: Boy Willie say he going back, but I'm gonna stay. See what it's like up here.

BOY WILLIE: You gonna carry me down there first.

LYMON: I told you I ain't going back down there and take a chance on that truck breaking down again. You can take the train. Hey, tell him Doaker, he can take the train back. After we sell them watermelons he have enough money he can buy him a whole railroad car.

DOAKER: You got all them watermelons stacked up there no wonder the truck broke down. I'm surprised you made it this far with a load like that. Where you break down at?

BOY WILLIE: We broke down three times! It took us two and a half days to get here. It's a good thing we picked them watermelons fresh.

LYMON: We broke down twice in West Virginia. The first time was just as soon as we got out of Sunflower. About forty miles out she broke down. We got it going and got all the way to West Virginia before she broke down again.

BOY WILLIE: We had to walk about five miles for some water.

LYMON: It got a hole in the radiator but it runs pretty good. You have to pump

the brakes sometime before they catch. Boy Willie have his door open and
be ready to jump when that happens.

BOY WILLIE: Lymon think that's funny. I told the nigger I give him ten dollars to
get the brakes fixed. But he thinks that funny.

LYMON: They don't need fixing. All you got to do is pump them till they catch.

[BERNIECE *enters on the stairs. Thirty-five years old, with an eleven-year-old
daughter, she is still in mourning for her husband after three years.*]

BERNIECE: What you doing all that hollering for?

BOY WILLIE: Hey, Berniece. Doaker said you was sleep. I said at least you could get
up and say hi.

BERNIECE: It's five o'clock in the morning and you come in here with all this noise.
You can't come like normal folks. You got to bring all that noise with you.

BOY WILLIE: Hell, I ain't done nothing but come in and say hi. I ain't got in the
house good.

BERNIECE: That's what I'm talking about. You start all that hollering and carry on
as soon as you hit the door.

BOY WILLIE: Aw hell, woman, I was glad to see Doaker. You ain't had to come down
if you didn't want to. I come eighteen hundred miles to see my sister I figure
she might want to get up and say hi. Other than that you can go back upstairs.
What you got, Doaker? Where your bottle? Me and Lymon want a drink. [*To*
BERNIECE.] This is Lymon. You remember Lymon Jackson from down home.

LYMON: How you doing, Berniece. You look just like I thought you looked.

BERNIECE: Why you all got to come in hollering and carrying on? Waking the
neighbors with all that noise.

BOY WILLIE: They can come over and join the party. We fixing to have a party.
Doaker, where your bottle? Me and Lymon celebrating. The Ghosts of the
Yellow Dog got Sutter.

BERNIECE: Say what?

BOY WILLIE: Ask Lymon, they found him the next morning. Say he drowned in his
well.

DOAKER: When this happen, Boy Willie?

BOY WILLIE: About three weeks ago. Me and Lymon was over in Stoner County
when we heard about it. We laughed. We thought it was funny. A great big
old three-hundred-and-forty-pound man gonna fall down his well.

LYMON: It remind me of Humpty Dumpty.

BOY WILLIE: Everybody say the Ghosts of the Yellow Dog pushed him.

BERNIECE: I don't want to hear that nonsense. Somebody down there pushing
them people in their wells.

DOAKER: What was you and Lymon doing over in Stoner County?

BOY WILLIE: We was down there working. Lymon got some people down there.

LYMON: My cousin got some land down there. We was helping him.

BOY WILLIE: Got near about a hundred acres. He got it set up real nice. Me and
Lymon was down there chopping down trees. We was using Lymon's truck
to haul the wood. Me and Lymon used to haul wood all around them parts.

[*To* BERNIECE.] Me and Lymon got a truckload of watermelons out there.

[BERNIECE *crosses to the window to the parlor.*]

Doaker, where your bottle? I know you got a bottle stuck up in your room. Come on, me and Lymon want a drink.

[DOAKER *exits into his room.*]

BERNIECE: Where you all get that truck from?

BOY WILLIE: I told you it's Lymon's.

BERNIECE: Where you get the truck from, Lymon?

LYMON: I bought it.

BERNIECE: Where he get that truck from, Boy Willie?

BOY WILLIE: He told you he bought it. Bought it for a hundred and twenty dollars. I can't say where he got that hundred and twenty dollars from . . . but he bought that old piece of truck from Henry Porter. [*To* LYMON.] Where you get that hundred and twenty dollars from, nigger?

LYMON: I got it like you get yours. I know how to take care of money.

[DOAKER *brings a bottle and sets it on the table.*]

BOY WILLIE: Aw hell, Doaker got some of that good whiskey. Don't give Lymon none of that. He ain't used to good whiskey. He liable to get sick.

LYMON: I done had good whiskey before.

BOY WILLIE: Lymon bought that truck so he have him a place to sleep. He down there wasn't doing no work or nothing. Sheriff looking for him. He bought that truck to keep away from the sheriff. Got Stovall looking for him too. He down there sleeping in that truck ducking and dodging both of them. I told him come on let's go up and see my sister.

BERNIECE: What the sheriff looking for you for, Lymon?

BOY WILLIE: The man don't want you to know all his business. He's my company. He ain't asking you no questions.

LYMON: It wasn't nothing. It was just a misunderstanding.

BERNIECE: He in my house. You say the sheriff looking for him, I wanna know what he looking for him for. Otherwise you all can go back out there and be where nobody don't have to ask you nothing.

LYMON: It was just a misunderstanding. Sometimes me and the sheriff we don't think alike. So we just got crossed on each other.

BERNIECE: Might be looking for him about that truck. He might have stole that truck.

BOY WILLIE: We ain't stole no truck, woman. I told you Lymon bought it.

DOAKER: Boy Willie and Lymon got more sense than to ride all the way up here in a stolen truck with a load of watermelons. Now they might have stole them watermelons, but I don't believe they stole that truck.

BOY WILLIE: You don't even know the man good and you calling him a thief. And we ain't stole them watermelons either. Them old man Pitterford's watermelons. He give me and Lymon all we could load for ten dollars.

DOAKER: No wonder you got them stacked up out there. You must have five hundred watermelons stacked up out there.

BERNIECE: Boy Willie, when you and Lymon planning on going back?

BOY WILLIE: Lymon say he staying. As soon as we sell them watermelons I'm going on back.

BERNIECE: [*Starts to exit up the stairs.*] That's what you need to do. And you need to do it quick. Come in here disrupting the house. I don't want all that loud carrying on around here. I'm surprised you ain't woke Maretha up.

BOY WILLIE: I was fixing to get her now. [*Calls.*] Hey, Maretha!

DOAKER: Berniece don't like all that hollering now.

BERNIECE: Don't you wake that child up!

BOY WILLIE: You going up there . . . wake her up and tell her her uncle's here. I ain't seen her in three years. Wake her up and send her down here. She can go back to bed.

BERNIECE: I ain't waking that child up . . . and don't you be making all that noise. You and Lymon need to sell them watermelons and go on back.

[BERNIECE *exits up the stairs.*]

BOY WILLIE: I see Berniece still try to be stuck up.

DOAKER: Berniece alright. She don't want you making all that noise. Maretha up there sleep. Let her sleep until she get up. She can see you then.

BOY WILLIE: I ain't thinking about Berniece. You hear from Wining Boy? You know Cleotha died?

DOAKER: Yeah, I heard that. He come by here about a year ago. Had a whole sack of money. He stayed here about two weeks. Ain't offered nothing. Berniece asked him for three dollars to buy some food and he got mad and left.

LYMON: Who's Wining Boy?

BOY WILLIE: That's my uncle. That's Doaker's brother. You heard me talk about Wining Boy. He play piano. He done made some records and everything. He still doing that, Doaker?

DOAKER: He made one or two records a long time ago. That's the only ones I ever known him to make. If you let him tell it he a big recording star.

BOY WILLIE: He stopped down home about two years ago. That's what I hear. I don't know. Me and Lymon was up on Parchman Farm doing them three years.

DOAKER: He don't never stay in one place. Now, he been here about eight months ago. Back in the winter. Now, you subject not to see him for another two years. It's liable to be that long before he stop by.

BOY WILLIE: If he had a whole sack of money you liable never to see him. You ain't gonna see him until he get broke. Just as soon as that sack of money is gone you look up and he be on your doorstep.

LYMON: [*Noticing the piano.*] Is that the piano?

BOY WILLIE: Yeah . . . look here, Lymon. See how it's carved up real nice and polished and everything? You never find you another piano like that.

LYMON: Yeah, that look real nice.

BOY WILLIE: I told you. See how it's polished? My mama used to polish it every day. See all them pictures carved on it? That's what I was talking about. You can get a nice price for that piano.

LYMON: That's all Boy Willie talked about the whole trip up here. I got tired of hearing him talk about the piano.

BOY WILLIE: All you want to talk about is women. You ought to hear this nigger, Doaker. Talking about all the women he gonna get when he get up here. He ain't had none down there but he gonna get a hundred when he get up here.

DOAKER: How your people doing down there, Lymon?

LYMON: They alright. They still there. I come up here to see what it's like up here. Boy Willie trying to get me to go back and farm with him.

BOY WILLIE: Sutter's brother selling the land. He say he gonna sell it to me. That's why I come up here. I got one part of it. Sell them watermelons and get me another part. Get Berniece to sell that piano and I'll have the third part.

DOAKER: Berniece ain't gonna sell that piano.

BOY WILLIE: I'm gonna talk to her. When she see I got a chance to get Sutter's land she'll come around.

DOAKER: You can put that thought out your mind. Berniece ain't gonna sell that piano.

BOY WILLIE: I'm gonna talk to her. She been playing on it?

DOAKER: You know she won't touch that piano. I ain't never known her to touch it since Mama Ola died. That's over seven years now. She say it got blood on it. She got Maretha playing on it though. Say Maretha can go on and do everything she can't do. Got her in an extra school down at the Irene Kaufman Settlement House. She want Maretha to grow up and be a schoolteacher. Say she good enough she can teach on the piano.

BOY WILLIE: Maretha don't need to be playing on no piano. She can play on the guitar.

DOAKER: How much land Sutter got left?

BOY WILLIE: Got a hundred acres. Good land. He done sold it piece by piece, he kept the good part for himself. Now he got to give that up. His brother come down from Chicago for the funeral . . . he up there in Chicago got some kind of business with soda fountain equipment. He anxious to sell the land, Doaker. He don't want to be bothered with it. He called me to him and said cause of how long our families done known each other and how we been good friends and all, say he wanted to sell the land to me. Say he'd rather see me with it than Jim Stovall. Told me he'd let me have it for two thousand dollars cash money. He don't know I found out the most Stovall would give him for it was fifteen hundred dollars. He trying to get that extra five hundred out of me telling me he doing me a favor. I thanked him just as nice. Told him what a good man Sutter was and how he had my sympathy and all. Told him to give me two weeks. He said he'd wait on me. That's why I come up here. Sell them watermelons. Get Berniece to sell that piano. Put them two parts with the part I done saved. Walk in there. Tip my hat. Lay my money down on the table. Get my deed and walk on out. This time I get to keep all the cotton. Hire me some men to work it for me. Gin my cotton. Get my seed. And I'll see you again next year. Might even plant some tobacco or some oats.

DOAKER: You gonna have a hard time trying to get Berniece to sell that piano. You know Avery Brown from down there don't you? He up here now. He followed Berniece up here trying to get her to marry him after Crawley got killed. He been up here about two years. He call himself a preacher now.

BOY WILLIE: I know Avery. I know him from when he used to work on the Willshaw place. Lymon know him too.

DOAKER: He after Berniece to marry him. She keep telling him no but he won't give up. He keep pressing her on it.

BOY WILLIE: Avery think all white men is bigshots. He don't know there some white men ain't got as much as he got.

DOAKER: He supposed to come past here this morning. Berniece going down to the bank with him to see if he can get a loan to start his church. That's why I know Berniece ain't gonna sell that piano. He tried to get her to sell it to help him start his church. Sent the man around and everything.

BOY WILLIE: What man?

DOAKER: Some white fellow was going around to all the colored people's houses looking to buy up musical instruments. He'd buy anything. Drums. Guitars. Harmonicas. Pianos. Avery sent him past here. He looked at the piano and got excited. Offered her a nice price. She turned him down and got on Avery for sending him past. The man kept on her about two weeks. He seen where she wasn't gonna sell it, he gave her his number and told her if she ever wanted to sell it to call him first. Say he'd go one better than what anybody else would give her for it.

BOY WILLIE: How much he offer her for it?

DOAKER: Now you know me. She didn't say and I didn't ask. I just know it was a nice price.

LYMON: All you got to do is find out who he is and tell him somebody else wanna buy it from you. Tell him you can't make up your mind who to sell it to, and if he like Doaker say, he'll give you anything you want for it.

BOY WILLIE: That's what I'm gonna do. I'm gonna find out who he is from Avery.

DOAKER: It ain't gonna do you no good. Berniece ain't gonna sell that piano.

BOY WILLIE: She ain't got to sell it. I'm gonna sell it. I own just as much of it as she does.

BERNIECE: [Offstage, hollers.] Doaker! Go on get away. Doaker!

DOAKER: [Calling.] Berniece?

[DOAKER and BOY WILLIE rush to the stairs, BOY WILLIE runs up the stairs, passing BERNIECE as she enters, running.]

DOAKER: Berniece, what's the matter? You alright? What's the matter?

[BERNIECE tries to catch her breath. She is unable to speak.]

DOAKER: That's alright. Take your time. You alright. What's the matter? [He calls.] Hey, Boy Willie?

BOY WILLIE: [*Offstage.*] Ain't nobody up here.

BERNIECE: Sutter . . . Sutter's standing at the top of the steps.

DOAKER: [*Calls.*] Boy Willie!

[LYMON *crosses to the stairs and looks up.* BOY WILLIE *enters from the stairs.*]

BOY WILLIE: Hey Doaker, what's wrong with her? Berniece, what's wrong? Who was you talking to?

DOAKER: She say she seen Sutter's ghost standing at the top of the stairs.

BOY WILLIE: Seen what? Sutter? She ain't seen no Sutter.

BERNIECE: He was standing right up there.

BOY WILLIE: [*Entering on the stairs.*] That's all in Berniece's head. Ain't nobody up there. Go on up there, Doaker.

DOAKER: I'll take your word for it. Berniece talking about what she seen. She say Sutter's ghost standing at the top of the steps. She ain't just make all that up.

BOY WILLIE: She up there dreaming. She ain't seen no ghost.

LYMON: You want a glass of water, Berniece? Get her a glass of water, Boy Willie.

BOY WILLIE: She don't need no water. She ain't seen nothing. Go on up there and look. Ain't nobody up there but Maretha.

DOAKER: Let Berniece tell it.

BOY WILLIE: I ain't stopping her from telling it.

DOAKER: What happened, Berniece?

BERNIECE: I come out my room to come back down here and Sutter was standing there in the hall.

BOY WILLIE: What he look like?

BERNIECE: He look like Sutter. He look like he always look.

BOY WILLIE: Sutter couldn't find his way from Big Sandy to Little Sandy. How he gonna find his way all the way up here to Pittsburgh? Sutter ain't never even heard of Pittsburgh.

DOAKER: Go on, Berniece.

BERNIECE: Just standing there with the blue suit on.

BOY WILLIE: The man ain't never left Marlin County when he was living . . . and he's gonna come all the way up here now that he's dead?

DOAKER: Let her finish. I want to hear what she got to say.

BOY WILLIE: I'll tell you this. If Berniece had seen him like she think she seen him she'd still be running.

DOAKER: Go on, Berniece. Don't pay Boy Willie no mind.

BERNIECE: He was standing there . . . had his hand on top of his head. Look like he might have thought if he took his hand down his head might have fallen off.

LYMON: Did he have on a hat?

BERNIECE: Just had on that blue suit . . . I told him to go away and he just stood there looking at me . . . calling Boy Willie's name.

BOY WILLIE: What he calling my name for?

BERNIECE: I believe you pushed him in the well.

BOY WILLIE: Now what kind of sense that make? You telling me I'm gonna go out there and hide in the weeds with all them dogs and things he got around there . . . I'm gonna hide and wait till I catch him looking down his well just right . . . then I'm gonna run over and push him in. A great big old three-hundred-and-forty-pound man.

BERNIECE: Well, what he calling your name for?

BOY WILLIE: He bending over looking down his well, woman . . . how he know who pushed him? It could have been anybody. Where was you when Sutter fell in his well? Where was Doaker? Me and Lymon was over in Stoner County. Tell her, Lymon. The Ghosts of the Yellow Dog got Sutter. That's what happened to him.

BERNIECE: You can talk all that Ghosts of the Yellow Dog stuff if you want. I know better.

LYMON: The Ghosts of the Yellow Dog pushed him. That's what the people say. They found him in his well and all the people say it must be the Ghosts of the Yellow Dog. Just like all them other men.

BOY WILLIE: Come talking about he looking for me. What he come all the way up here for? If he looking for me all he got to do is wait. He could have saved himself a trip if he looking for me. That ain't nothing but in Berniece's head. Ain't no telling what she liable to come up with next.

BERNIECE: Boy Willie, I want you and Lymon to go ahead and leave my house. Just go on somewhere. You don't do nothing but bring trouble with you every-where you go. If it wasn't for you Crawley would still be alive.

BOY WILLIE: Crawley what? I ain't had nothing to do with Crawley getting killed. Crawley three time seven. He had his own mind.

BERNIECE: Just go on and leave. Let Sutter go somewhere else looking for you.

BOY WILLIE: I'm leaving. Soon as we sell them watermelons. Other than that I ain't going nowhere. Hell, I just got here. Talking about Sutter looking for me. Sutter was looking for that piano. That's what he was looking for. He had to die to find out where that piano was at . . . If I was you I'd get rid of it. That's the way to get rid of Sutter's ghost. Get rid of that piano.

BERNIECE: I want you and Lymon to go on and take all this confusion out of my house!

BOY WILLIE: Hey, tell her, Doaker. What kind of sense that make? I told you, Lymon, as soon as Berniece see me she was gonna start something. Didn't I tell you that? Now she done made up that story about Sutter just so she could tell me to leave her house. Well, hell, I ain't going nowhere till I sell them watermelons.

BERNIECE: Well why don't you go out there and sell them! Sell them and go on back!

BOY WILLIE: We waiting till the people get up.

LYMON: Boy Willie say if you get out there too early and wake the people up they get mad at you and won't buy nothing from you.

DOAKER: You won't be waiting long. You done let the sun catch up with you. This the time everybody be getting up around here.

BERNIECE: Come on, Doaker, walk up here with me. Let me get Maretha up and get her started. I got to get ready myself. Boy Willie, just go on out there and sell them watermelons and you and Lymon leave my house.

[BERNIECE *and* DOAKER *exit up the stairs.*]

BOY WILLIE: [*Calling after them.*] If you see Sutter up there . . . tell him I'm down here waiting on him.

LYMON: What if she see him again?

BOY WILLIE: That's all in her head. There ain't no ghost up there. [*Calls.*] Hey, Doaker . . . I told you ain't nothing up there.

LYMON: I'm glad he didn't say he was looking for me.

BOY WILLIE: I wish I would see Sutter's ghost. Give me a chance to put a whupping on him.

LYMON: You ought to stay up here with me. You be down there working his land . . . he might come looking for you all the time.

BOY WILLIE: I ain't thinking about Sutter. And I ain't thinking about staying up here. You stay up here. I'm going back and get Sutter's land. You think you ain't got to work up here. You think this the land of milk and honey. But I ain't scared of work. I'm going back and farm every acre of that land.

[DOAKER *enters from the stairs.*]

I told you there ain't nothing up there, Doaker. Berniece dreaming all that.

DOAKER: I believe Berniece seen something. Berniece levelheaded. She ain't just made all that up. She say Sutter had on a suit. I don't believe she ever seen Sutter in a suit. I believe that's what he was buried in, and that's what Berniece saw.

BOY WILLIE: Well, let her keep on seeing him then. As long as he don't mess with me.

[DOAKER *starts to cook his breakfast.*]

I heard about you, Doaker. They say you got all the women looking out for you down home. They be looking to see you coming. Say you got a different one every two weeks. Say they be fighting one another for you to stay with them. [*To* LYMON.] Look at him, Lymon. He know it's true.

DOAKER: I ain't thinking about no women. They never get me tied up with them. After Coreen I ain't got no use for them. I stay up on Jack Slattery's place when I be down there. All them women want is somebody with a steady payday.

BOY WILLIE: That ain't what I hear. I hear every two weeks the women all put on their dresses and line up at the railroad station.

DOAKER: I don't get down there but once a month. I used to go down there every two weeks but they keep switching me around. They keep switching all the fellows around.

BOY WILLIE: Doaker can't turn that railroad loose. He was working the railroad when I was walking around crying for sugartit. My mama used to brag on him.

DOAKER: I'm cooking now, but I used to line track. I pieced together the Yellow

Dog stitch by stitch. Rail by rail. Line track all up around there. I lined track all up around Sunflower and Clarksdale. Wining Boy worked with me. He helped put in some of that track. He'd work it for six months and quit. Go back to playing piano and gambling.

BOY WILLIE: How long you been with the railroad now?

DOAKER: Twenty-seven years. Now, I'll tell you something about the railroad. What I done learned after twenty-seven years. See, you got North. You got West. You look over here you got South. Over there you got East. Now, you can start from anywhere. Don't care where you at. You got to go one of them four ways. And whichever way you decide to go they got a railroad that will take you there. Now, that's something simple. You think anybody would be able to understand that. But you'd be surprised how many people trying to go North get on a train going West. They think the train's supposed to go where they going rather than where it's going.

Now, why people going? Their sister's sick. They leaving before they kill somebody . . . and they sitting across from somebody who's leaving to keep from getting killed. They leaving cause they can't get satisfied. They going to meet someone. I wish I had a dollar for every time that someone wasn't at the station to meet them. I done seen that a lot. In between the time they sent the telegram and the time the person get there . . . they done forgot all about them.

They got so many trains out there they have a hard time keeping them from running into each other. Got trains going every whichaway. Got people on all of them. Somebody going where somebody just left. If everybody stay in one place I believe this would be a better world. Now what I done learned after twenty-seven years of railroading is this . . . if the train stays on the track . . . it's going to get where it's going. It might not be where you going. If it ain't, then all you got to do is sit and wait cause the train's coming back to get you. The train don't never stop. It'll come back every time. Now I'll tell you another thing . . .

BOY WILLIE: What you cooking over there, Doaker? Me and Lymon's hungry.

DOAKER: Go on down there to Wylie and Kirkpatrick to Eddie's restaurant. Coffee cost a nickel and you can get two eggs, sausage, and grits for fifteen cents. He even give you a biscuit with it.

BOY WILLIE: That look good what you got. Give me a little piece of that grilled bread.

DOAKER: Here . . . go on take the whole piece.

BOY WILLIE: Here you go, Lymon . . . you want a piece?

[He gives LYMON a piece of toast. MARETHA enters from the stairs.]

BOY WILLIE: Hey, sugar. Come here and give me a hug. Come on give Uncle Boy Willie a hug. Don't be shy. Look at her, Doaker. She done got bigger. Ain't she got big?

DOAKER: Yeah, she getting up there.

BOY WILLIE: How you doing, sugar?

MARETHA: Fine.

BOY WILLIE: You was just a little old thing last time I seen you. You remember me, don't you? This your Uncle Boy Willie from down South. That there's Lymon. He my friend. We come up here to sell watermelons. You like watermelons?

[MARETHA *nods*.]

We got a whole truckload out front. You can have as many as you want. What you been doing?

MARETHA: Nothing.

BOY WILLIE: Don't be shy now. Look at you getting all big. How old is you?

MARETHA: Eleven. I'm gonna be twelve soon.

BOY WILLIE: You like it up here? You like the North?

MARETHA: It's alright.

BOY WILLIE: That there's Lymon. Did you say hi to Lymon?

MARETHA: Hi.

LYMON: How you doing? You look just like your mama. I remember you when you was wearing diapers.

BOY WILLIE: You gonna come down South and see me? Uncle Boy Willie gonna get him a farm. Gonna get a great big old farm. Come down there and I'll teach you how to ride a mule. Teach you how to kill a chicken, too.

MARETHA: I seen my mama do that.

BOY WILLIE: Ain't nothing to it. You just grab him by his neck and twist it. Get you a real good grip and then you just wring his neck and throw him in the pot. Cook him up. Then you got some good eating. What you like to eat? What kind of food you like?

MARETHA: I like everything . . . except I don't like no black-eyed peas.

BOY WILLIE: Uncle Doaker tell me your mama got you playing that piano. Come on play something for me.

[BOY WILLIE *crosses over to the piano followed by* MARETHA.]

Show me what you can do. Come on now. Here . . . Uncle Boy Willie give you a dime . . . show me what you can do. Don't be bashful now. That dime say you can't be bashful.

[MARETHA *plays. It is something any beginner first learns.*]

Here, let me show you something.

[BOY WILLIE *sits and plays a simple boogie-woogie.*]

See that? See what I'm doing? That's what you call the boogie-woogie. See now . . . you can get up and dance to that. That's how good it sound. It sound like you wanna dance. You can dance to that. It'll hold you up. Whatever kind of dance you wanna do you can dance to that right there. See that? See how it go? Ain't nothing to it. Go on you do it.

MARETHA: I got to read it on the paper.

BOY WILLIE: You don't need no paper. Go on. Do just like that there.

BERNIECE: Maretha! You get up here and get ready to go so you be on time. Ain't no need you trying to take advantage of company.

MARETHA: I got to go.

BOY WILLIE: Uncle Boy Willie gonna get you a guitar. Let Uncle Doaker teach you how to play that. You don't need to read no paper to play the guitar. Your mama told you about that piano? You know how them pictures got on there?

MARETHA: She say it just always been like that since she got it.

BOY WILLIE: You hear that, Doaker? And you sitting up here in the house with Berniece.

DOAKER: I ain't got nothing to do with that. I don't get in the way of Berniece's raising her.

BOY WILLIE: You tell your mama to tell you about that piano. You ask her how them pictures got on there. If she don't tell you I'll tell you.

BERNIECE: Maretha!

MARETHA: I got to get ready to go.

BOY WILLIE: She getting big, Doaker. You remember her, Lymon?

LYMON: She used to be real little.

[*There is a knock on the door.* DOAKER *goes to answer it.* AVERY *enters. Thirty-eight years old, honest and ambitious, he has taken to the city like a fish to water, finding in it opportunities for growth and advancement that did not exist for him in the rural South. He is dressed in a suit and tie with a gold cross around his neck. He carries a small Bible.*]

DOAKER: Hey, Avery, come on in. Berniece upstairs.

BOY WILLIE: Look at him . . . look at him . . . he don't know what to say. He wasn't expecting to see me.

AVERY: Hey, Boy Willie. What you doing up here?

BOY WILLIE: Look at him, Lymon.

AVERY: Is that Lymon? Lymon Jackson?

BOY WILLIE: Yeah, you know Lymon.

DOAKER: Berniece be ready in a minute, Avery.

BOY WILLIE: Doaker say you a preacher now. What . . . we supposed to call you Reverend? You used to be plain old Avery. When you get to be a preacher, nigger?

LYMON: Avery say he gonna be a preacher so he don't have to work.

BOY WILLIE: I remember when you was down there on the Willshaw place planting cotton. You wasn't thinking about no Reverend then.

AVERY: That must be your truck out there. I saw that truck with them watermelons, I was trying to figure out what it was doing in front of the house.

BOY WILLIE: Yeah, me and Lymon selling watermelons. That's Lymon's truck.

DOAKER: Berniece say you all going down to the bank.

AVERY: Yeah, they give me a half day off work. I got an appointment to talk to the bank about getting a loan to start my church.

BOY WILLIE: Lymon say preachers don't have to work. Where you working at, nigger?

DOAKER: Avery got him one of them good jobs. He working at one of them sky-scrapers downtown.

AVERY: I'm working down there at the Gulf Building running an elevator. Got a pension and everything. They even give you a turkey on Thanksgiving.

LYMON: How you know the rope ain't gonna break? Ain't you scared the rope's gonna break?

AVERY: That's steel. They got steel cables hold it up. It take a whole lot of breaking to break that steel. Naw, I ain't worried about nothing like that. It ain't nothing but a little old elevator. Now, I wouldn't get in none of them airplanes. You couldn't pay me to do nothing like that.

LYMON: That be fun. I'd rather do that than ride in one of them elevators.

BOY WILLIE: How many of them watermelons you wanna buy?

AVERY: I thought you was gonna give me one seeing as how you got a whole truck full.

BOY WILLIE: You can get one, get two. I'll give you two for a dollar.

AVERY: I can't eat but one. How much are they?

BOY WILLIE: Aw, nigger, you know I'll give you a watermelon. Go on, take as many as you want. Just leave some for me and Lymon to sell.

AVERY: I don't want but one.

BOY WILLIE: How you get to be a preacher, Avery? I might want to be a preacher one day. Have everybody call me Reverend Boy Willie.

AVERY: It come to me in a dream. God called me and told me he wanted me to be a shepherd for his flock. That's what I'm gonna call my church . . . The Good Shepherd Church of God in Christ.

DOAKER: Tell him what you told me. Tell him about the three hobos.

AVERY: Boy Willie don't want to hear all that.

LYMON: I do. Lots a people say your dreams can come true.

AVERY: Naw. You don't want to hear all that.

DOAKER: Go on. I told him you was a preacher. He didn't want to believe me. Tell him about the three hobos.

AVERY: Well, it come to me in a dream. See . . . I was sitting out in this railroad yard watching the trains go by. The train stopped and these three hobos got off. They told me they had come from Nazareth and was on their way to Jerusalem. They had three candles. They gave me one and told me to light it . . . but to be careful that it didn't go out. Next thing I knew I was standing in front of this house. Something told me to go knock on the door. This old woman opened the door and said they had been waiting on me. Then she led me into this room. It was a big room and it was full of all kinds of different people. They looked like anybody else except they all had sheep heads and was making noise like sheep make. I heard somebody call my name. I looked around and there was these same three hobos. They told me to take off my clothes and they give me a blue robe with gold thread. They washed my feet and combed my hair. Then they showed me these three doors and told me to pick one.

I went through one of them doors and that flame leapt off that candle and it seemed like my whole head caught fire. I looked around and there was four or five other men standing there with these same blue robes on. Then we heard a voice tell us to look out across this valley. We looked out and saw the valley was full of wolves. The voice told us that these sheep people that

I had seen in the other room had to go over to the other side of this valley and somebody had to take them. Then I heard another voice say, "Who shall I send?" Next thing I knew I said, "Here I am. Send me." That's when I met Jesus. He say, "If you go, I'll go with you." Something told me to say, "Come on. Let's go." That's when I woke up. My head still felt like it was on fire . . . but I had a peace about myself that was hard to explain. I knew right then that I had been filled with the Holy Ghost and called to be a servant of the Lord. It took me a while before I could accept that. But then a lot of little ways God showed me that it was true. So I became a preacher.

LYMON: I see why you gonna call it the Good Shepherd Church. You dreaming about them sheep people. I can see that easy.

BOY WILLIE: Doaker say you sent some white man past the house to look at that piano. Say he was going around to all the colored people's houses looking to buy up musical instruments.

AVERY: Yeah, but Berniece didn't want to sell that piano. After she told me about it . . . I could see why she didn't want to sell it.

BOY WILLIE: What's this man's name?

AVERY: Oh, that's a while back now. I done forgot his name. He give Berniece a card with his name and telephone number on it, but I believe she throwed it away.

[BERNIECE *and* MARETHA *enter from the stairs.*]

BERNIECE: Maretha, run back upstairs and get my pocketbook. And wipe that hair grease off your forehead. Go ahead, hurry up.

[MARETHA *exits up the stairs.*]

How you doing, Avery? You done got all dressed up. You look nice. Boy Willie, I thought you and Lymon was going to sell them watermelons.

BOY WILLIE: Lymon done got sleepy. We liable to get some sleep first.

LYMON: I ain't sleepy.

DOAKER: As many watermelons as you got stacked up on that truck out there, you ought to have been gone.

BOY WILLIE: We gonna go in a minute. We going.

BERNIECE: Doaker. I'm gonna stop down there on Logan Street. You want anything?

DOAKER: You can pick up some ham hocks if you going down there. See if you can get the smoked ones. If they ain't got that get the fresh ones. Don't get the ones that got all that fat under the skin. Look for the long ones. They nice and lean. [*He gives her a dollar.*] Don't get the short ones lessen they smoked. If you got to get the fresh ones make sure that they the long ones. If they ain't got them smoked then go ahead and get the short ones. [*Pause.*] You may as well get some turnip greens while you down there. I got some buttermilk . . . if you pick up some cornmeal I'll make me some cornbread and cook up them turnip greens.

[MARETHA *enters from the stairs.*]

MARETHA: We gonna take the streetcar?

BERNIECE: Me and Avery gonna drop you off at the settlement house. You mind them people down there. Don't be going down there showing your color. Boy Willie, I done told you what to do. I'll see you later, Doaker.

AVERY: I'll be seeing you again, Boy Willie.

BOY WILLIE: Hey, Berniece . . . what's the name of that man Avery sent past say he want to buy the piano?

BERNIECE: I knew it. I knew it when I first seen you. I knew you was up to something.

BOY WILLIE: Sutter's brother say he selling the land to me. He waiting on me now. Told me he'd give me two weeks. I got one part. Sell them watermelons get me another part. Then we can sell that piano and I'll have the third part.

BERNIECE: I ain't selling that piano, Boy Willie. If that's why you come up here you can just forget about it. [*To* DOAKER.] Doaker, I'll see you later. Boy Willie ain't nothing but a whole lot of mouth. I ain't paying him no mind. If he come up here thinking he gonna sell that piano then he done come up here for nothing.

[BERNIECE, AVERY, *and* MARETHA *exit the front door.*]

BOY WILLIE: Hey, Lymon! You ready to go sell these watermelons.

[BOY WILLIE *and* LYMON *start to exit. At the door* BOY WILLIE *turns to* DOAKER.]

Hey, Doaker . . . if Berniece don't want to sell that piano . . . I'm gonna cut it in half and go on and sell my half.

[BOY WILLIE *and* LYMON *exit.*]

[*The lights go down on the scene.*]

SCENE 2

[*The lights come up on the kitchen. It is three days later.* WINING BOY *sits at the kitchen table. There is a half-empty pint bottle on the table.* DOAKER *busies himself washing pots.* WINING BOY *is fifty-six years old.* DOAKER's *older brother, he tries to present the image of a successful musician and gambler, but his music, his clothes, and even his manner of presentation are old. He is a man who looking back over his life continues to live it with an odd mixture of zest and sorrow.*]

WINING BOY: So the Ghosts of the Yellow Dog got Sutter. That just go to show you I believe I always lived right. They say every dog gonna have his day and time it go around it sure come back to you. I done seen that a thousand times. I know the truth of that. But I'll tell you outright . . . if I see Sutter's ghost I'll be on the first thing I find that got wheels on it.

[DOAKER *enters from his room.*]

DOAKER: Wining Boy!

WINING BOY: And I'll tell you another thing . . . Berniece ain't gonna sell that piano.

DOAKER: That's what she told him. He say he gonna cut it in half and go on and sell his half. They been around here three days trying to sell them watermelons. They trying to get out to where the white folks live but the truck keep breaking down. They go a block or two and it break down again. They trying to get out to Squirrel Hill and can't get around the corner. He say soon as he can get that truck empty to where he can set the piano up in there he gonna take it out of here and go sell it.

WINING BOY: What about them boys Sutter got? How come they ain't farming that land?

DOAKER: One of them going to school. He left down there and come North to school. The other one ain't got as much sense as that frying pan over yonder. That is the dumbest white man I ever seen. He'd stand in the river and watch it rise till it drown him.

WINING BOY: Other than seeing Sutter's ghost how's Berniece doing?

DOAKER: She doing alright. She still got Crawley on her mind. He been dead three years but she still holding on to him. She need to go out here and let one of these fellows grab a whole handful of whatever she got. She act like it done got precious.

WINING BOY: They always told me any fish will bite if you got good bait.

DOAKER: She stuck up on it. She think it's better than she is. I believe she messing around with Avery. They got something going. He a preacher now. If you let him tell it the Holy Ghost sat on his head and heaven opened up with thunder and lightning and God was calling his name. Told him to go out and preach and tend to his flock. That's what he gonna call his church. The Good Shepherd Church.

WINING BOY: They had that joker down in Spear walking around talking about he Jesus Christ. He gonna live the life of Christ. Went through the Last Supper and everything. Rented him a mule on Palm Sunday and rode through the town. Did everything . . . talking about he Christ. He did everything until they got up to that crucifixion part. Got up to that part and told everybody to go home and quit pretending. He got up to the crucifixion part and changed his mind. Had a whole bunch of folks come down there to see him get nailed to the cross. I don't know who's the worse fool. Him or them. Had all them folks come down there . . . even carried the cross up this little hill. People standing around waiting to see him get nailed to the cross and he stop everything and preach a little sermon and told everybody to go home. Had enough nerve to tell them to come to church on Easter Sunday to celebrate his resurrection.

DOAKER: I'm surprised Avery ain't thought about that. He trying every little thing to get him a congregation together. They meeting over at his house till he get him a church.

WINING BOY: Ain't nothing wrong with being a preacher. You got the preacher on one hand and the gambler on the other. Sometimes there ain't too much difference in them.

DOAKER: How long you been in Kansas City?

WINING BOY: Since I left here. I got tied up with some old gal down there. [Pause.] You know Cleotha died.

DOAKER: Yeah, I heard that last time I was down there. I was sorry to hear that.

WINING BOY: One of her friends wrote and told me. I got the letter right here. [*He takes the letter out of his pocket.*] I was down in Kansas City and she wrote and told me Cleotha had died. Name of Willa Bryant. She say she know cousin Rupert. [*He opens the letter and reads.*] Dear Wining Boy: I am writing this letter to let you know Miss Cleotha Holman passed on Saturday the first of May she departed this world in the loving arms of her sister Miss Alberta Samuels. I know you would want to know this and am writing as a friend of Cleotha. There have been many hardships since last you seen her but she survived them all and to the end was a good woman whom I hope have God's grace and is in His Paradise. Your cousin Rupert Bates is my friend also and he give me your address and I pray this reaches you about Cleotha. Miss Willa Bryant. A friend. [*He folds the letter and returns it to his pocket.*] They was nailing her coffin shut by the time I heard about it. I never knew she was sick. I believe it was that yellow jaundice. That's what killed her mama.

DOAKER: Cleotha wasn't but forty-some.

WINING BOY: She was forty-six. I got ten years on her. I met her when she was sixteen. You remember I used to run around there. Couldn't nothing keep me still. Much as I loved Cleotha I loved to ramble. Couldn't nothing keep me still. We got married and we used to fight about it all the time. Then one day she asked me to leave. Told me she loved me before I left. Told me, Wining Boy, you got a home as long as I got mine. And I believe in my heart I always felt that and that kept me safe.

DOAKER: Cleotha always did have a nice way about her.

WINING BOY: Man that woman was something. I used to thank the Lord. Many a night I sat up and looked out over my life. Said, well, I had Cleotha. When it didn't look like there was nothing else for me, I said, thank God, at least I had that. If ever I go anywhere in this life I done known a good woman. And that used to hold me till the next morning. [*Pause.*] What you got? Give me a little nip. I know you got something stuck up in your room.

DOAKER: I ain't seen you walk in here and put nothing on the table. You done sat there and drank up your whiskey. Now you talking about what you got.

WINING BOY: I got plenty money. Give me a little nip.

[DOAKER *carries a glass into his room and returns with it half-filled. He sets it on the table in front of* WINING BOY.]

WINING BOY: You hear from Coreen?

DOAKER: She up in New York. I let her go from my mind.

WINING BOY: She was something back then. She wasn't too pretty but she had a way of looking at you made you know there was a whole lot of woman there. You got married and snatched her out from under us and we all got mad at you.

DOAKER: She up in New York City. That's what I hear.

[*The door opens and* BOY WILLIE *and* LYMON *enter.*]

BOY WILLIE: Aw hell . . . look here! We was just talking about you. Doaker say you left out of here with a whole sack of money. I told him we wasn't going see you till you got broke.

WINING BOY: What you mean broke? I got a whole pocketful of money.

DOAKER: Did you all get that truck fixed?

BOY WILLIE: We got it running and got halfway out there on Centre and it broke down again. Lymon went out there and messed it up some more. Fellow told us we got to wait till tomorrow to get it fixed. Say he have it running like new. Lymon going back down there and sleep in the truck so the people don't take the watermelons.

LYMON: Lymon nothing. You go down there and sleep in it.

BOY WILLIE: You was sleeping in it down home, nigger! I don't know nothing about sleeping in no truck.

LYMON: I ain't sleeping in no truck.

BOY WILLIE: They can take all the watermelons. I don't care. Wining Boy, where you coming from? Where you been?

WINING BOY: I been down in Kansas City.

BOY WILLIE: You remember Lymon? Lymon Jackson.

WINING BOY: Yeah, I used to know his daddy.

BOY WILLIE: Doaker say you don't never leave no address with nobody. Say he got to depend on your whim. See when it strike you to pay a visit.

WINING BOY: I got four or five addresses.

BOY WILLIE: Doaker say Berniece asked you for three dollars and you got mad and left.

WINING BOY: Berniece try and rule over you too much for me. That's why I left. It wasn't about no three dollars.

BOY WILLIE: Where you getting all these sacks of money from? I need to be with you. Doaker say you had a whole sack of money . . . turn some of it loose.

WINING BOY: I was just fixing to ask you for five dollars.

BOY WILLIE: I ain't got no money. I'm trying to get some. Doaker tell you about Sutter? The Ghosts of the Yellow Dog got him about three weeks ago. Berniece done seen his ghost and everything. He right upstairs. [Calls.] Hey Sutter! Wining Boy's here. Come on, get a drink!

WINING BOY: How many that make the Ghosts of the Yellow Dog done got?

BOY WILLIE: Must be about nine or ten, eleven or twelve. I don't know.

DOAKER: You got Ed Saunders. Howard Peterson. Charlie Webb.

WINING BOY: Robert Smith. That fellow that shot Becky's boy . . . say he was stealing peaches . . .

DOAKER: You talking about Bob Mallory.

BOY WILLIE: Berniece say she don't believe all that about the Ghosts of the Yellow Dog.

WINING BOY: She ain't got to believe. You go ask them white folks in Sunflower County if they believe. You go ask Sutter if he believe. I don't care if Berniece believe or not. I done been to where the Southern cross the Yellow Dog and called out their names. They talk back to you, too.

LYMON: What they sound like? The wind or something?

BOY WILLIE: You done been there for real, Wining Boy?

WINING BOY: Nineteen thirty. July of nineteen thirty I stood right there on that spot. It didn't look like nothing was going right in my life. I said everything can't go wrong all the time . . . let me go down there and call on the Ghosts of the Yellow Dog, see if they can help me. I went down there and right there where them two railroads cross each other . . . I stood right there on that spot and called out their names. They talk back to you, too.

LYMON: People say you can ask them questions. They talk to you like that?

WINING BOY: A lot of things you got to find out on your own. I can't say how they talked to nobody else. But to me it just filled me up in a strange sort of way to be standing there on that spot. I didn't want to leave. It felt like the longer I stood there the bigger I got. I seen the train coming and it seem like I was bigger than the train. I started not to move. But something told me to go ahead and get on out the way. The train passed and I started to go back up there and stand some more. But something told me not to do it. I walked away from there feeling like a king. Went on and had a stroke of luck that run on for three years. So I don't care if Berniece believe or not. Berniece ain't got to believe. I know cause I been there. Now Doaker'll tell you about the Ghosts of the Yellow Dog.

DOAKER: I don't try and talk that stuff with Berniece. Avery got her all tied up in that church. She just think it's a whole lot of nonsense.

BOY WILLIE: Berniece don't believe in nothing. She just think she believe. She believe in anything if it's convenient for her to believe. But when that convenience run out then she ain't got nothing to stand on.

WINING BOY: Let's not get on Berniece now. Doaker tell me you talking about selling that piano.

BOY WILLIE: Yeah . . . hey, Doaker, I got the name of that man Avery was talking about. The man what's fixing the truck gave me his name. Everybody know him. Say he buy up anything you can make music with. I got his name and his telephone number. Hey, Wining Boy, Sutter's brother say he selling the land to me. I got one part. Sell them watermelons get me the second part. Then . . . soon as I get them watermelons out that truck I'm gonna take and sell that piano and get the third part.

DOAKER: That land ain't worth nothing no more. The smart white man's up here in these cities. He cut the land loose and step back and watch you and the dumb white man argue over it.

WINING BOY: How you know Sutter's brother ain't sold it already? You talking about selling the piano and the man's liable to sold the land two or three times.

BOY WILLIE: He say he waiting on me. He say he give me two weeks. That's two weeks from Friday. Say if I ain't back by then he might gonna sell it to somebody else. He say he wanna see me with it.

WINING BOY: You know as well as I know the man gonna sell the land to the first one walk up and hand him the money.

BOY WILLIE: That's just who I'm gonna be. Look, you ain't gotta know he waiting on me. I know. Okay. I know what the man told me. Stovall already done tried to buy the land from him and he told him no. The man say he waiting on me . . . he waiting on me. Hey, Doaker . . . give me a drink. I see Wining Boy got his glass.

[DOAKER *exits into his room.*]

Wining Boy, what you doing in Kansas City? What they got down there?

LYMON: I hear they got some nice-looking women in Kansas City. I sure like to go down there and find out.

WINING BOY: Man, the women down there is something else.

[DOAKER *enters with a bottle of whiskey. He sets it on the table with some glasses.*]

DOAKER: You wanna sit up here and drink up my whiskey, leave a dollar on the table when you get up.

BOY WILLIE: You ain't doing nothing but showing your hospitality. I know we ain't got to pay for your hospitality.

WINING BOY: Doaker say they had you and Lymon down on the Parchman Farm. Had you on my old stomping grounds.

BOY WILLIE: Me and Lymon was down there hauling wood for Jim Miller and keeping us a little bit to sell. Some white fellows tried to run us off of it. That's when Crawley got killed. They put me and Lymon in the penitentiary.

LYMON: They ambushed us right there where that road dip down and around that bend in the creek. Crawley tried to fight them. Me and Boy Willie got away but the sheriff got us. Say we was stealing wood. They shot me in my stomach.

BOY WILLIE: They looking for Lymon down there now. They rounded him up and put him in jail for not working.

LYMON: Fined me a hundred dollars. Mr. Stovall come and paid my hundred dollars and the judge say I got to work for him to pay him back his hundred dollars. I told them I'd rather take my thirty days but they wouldn't let me do that.

BOY WILLIE: As soon as Stovall turned his back, Lymon was gone. He down there living in that truck dodging the sheriff and Stovall. He got both of them looking for him. So I brought him up here.

LYMON: I told Boy Willie I'm gonna stay up here. I ain't going back with him.

BOY WILLIE: Ain't nobody twisting your arm to make you go back. You can do what you want to do.

WINING BOY: I'll go back with you. I'm on my way down there. You gonna take the train? I'm gonna take the train.

LYMON: They treat you better up here.

BOY WILLIE: I ain't worried about nobody mistreating me. They treat you like you let them treat you. They mistreat me I mistreat them right back. Ain't no difference in me and the white man.

WINING BOY: Ain't no difference as far as how somebody supposed to treat you. I agree with that. But I'll tell you the difference between the colored man and the white man. Alright. Now you take and eat some berries. They taste real good to you. So you say I'm gonna go out and get me a whole pot of these

berries and cook them up to make a pie or whatever. But you ain't looked to see them berries is sitting in the white fellow's yard. Ain't got no fence around them. You figure anybody want something they'd fence it in. Alright. Now the white man come along and say that's my land. Therefore everything that grow on it belong to me. He tell the sheriff, "I want you to put this nigger in jail as a warning to all the other niggers. Otherwise first thing you know these niggers have everything that belong to us."

BOY WILLIE: I'd come back at night and haul off his whole patch while he was sleep.

WINING BOY: Alright. Now Mr. So and So, he sell the land to you. And he come to you and say, "John, you own the land. It's all yours now. But them is my berries. And come time to pick them I'm gonna send my boys over. You got the land . . . but them berries, I'm gonna keep them. They mine." And he go and fix it with the law that them is his berries. Now that's the difference between the colored man and the white man. The colored man can't fix nothing with the law.

BOY WILLIE: I don't go by what the law say. The law's liable to say anything. I go by if it's right or not. It don't matter to me what the law say. I take and look at it for myself.

LYMON: That's why you gonna end up back down there on the Parchman Farm.

BOY WILLIE: I ain't thinking about no Parchman Farm. You liable to go back before me.

LYMON: They work you too hard down there. All that weeding and hoeing and chopping down trees. I didn't like all that.

WINING BOY: You ain't got to like your job on Parchman. Hey, tell him, Doaker, the only one got to like his job is the waterboy.

DOAKER: If he don't like his job he need to set that bucket down.

BOY WILLIE: That's what they told Lymon. They had Lymon on water and everybody got mad at him cause he was lazy.

LYMON: That water was heavy.

BOY WILLIE: They had Lymon down there singing:

[*Sings.*]

O Lord Berta Berta O Lord gal oh-ah
O Lord Berta Berta O Lord gal well

[LYMON *and* WINING BOY *join in.*]

Go 'head marry don't you wait on me oh-ah
Go 'head marry don't you wait on me well
Might not want you when I go free oh-ah
Might not want you when I go free well

BOY WILLIE: Come on, Doaker. Doaker know this one.

[*As* DOAKER *joins in the men stamp and clap to keep time. They sing in harmony with great fervor and style.*]

O Lord Berta Berta O Lord gal oh-ah
O Lord Berta Berta O Lord gal well

Raise them up higher, let them drop on down oh-ah
Raise them up higher, let them drop on down well
Don't know the difference when the sun go down oh-ah
Don't know the difference when the sun go down well

Berta in Meridan and she living at ease oh-ah
Berta in Meridan and she living at ease well
I'm on old Parchman, got to work or leave oh-ah
I'm on old Parchman, got to work or leave well

O Alberta, Berta, O Lord gal oh-ah
O Alberta, Berta, O Lord gal well

When you marry, don't marry no farming man oh-ah
When you marry, don't marry no farming man well
Everyday Monday, hoe handle in your hand oh-ah
Everyday Monday, hoe handle in your hand well

When you marry, marry a railroad man, oh-ah
When you marry, marry a railroad man, well
Everyday Sunday, dollar in your hand oh-ah
Everyday Sunday, dollar in your hand well

O Alberta, Berta, O Lord gal oh-ah
O Alberta, Berta, O Lord gal well

BOY WILLIE: Doaker like that part. He like that railroad part.

LYMON: Doaker sound like Tangleye.[1] He can't sing a lick.

BOY WILLIE: Hey, Doaker, they still talk about you down on Parchman. They ask me, "You Doaker Boy's nephew?" I say, "Yeah, me and him is family." They treated me alright soon as I told them that. Say, "Yeah, he my uncle."

DOAKER: I don't never want to see none of them niggers no more.

BOY WILLIE: I don't want to see them either. Hey, Wining Boy, come on play some piano. You a piano player, play some piano. Lymon wanna hear you.

WINING BOY: I give that piano up. That was the best thing that ever happened to me, getting rid of that piano. That piano got so big and I'm carrying it around on my back. I don't wish that on nobody. See, you think it's all fun being a recording star. Got to carrying that piano around and man did I get slow. Got just like molasses. The world just slipping by me and I'm walking around with that piano. Alright. Now, there ain't but so many places you can go. Only so many road wide enough for you and that piano. And that piano get heavier and heavier. Go to a place and they find out you play piano, the first thing they want to do is give you a drink, find you a piano, and sit you right

---

1. Or Tangle Eye, one of the prisoners field-recorded at Parchman Farm by Alan Lomax in the 1930s and '40s.

down. And that's where you gonna be for the next eight hours. They ain't gonna let you get up! Now, the first three or four years of that is fun. You can't get enough whiskey and you can't get enough women and you don't never get tired of playing that piano. But that only last so long. You look up one day and you hate the whiskey, and you hate the women, and you hate the piano. But that's all you got. You can't do nothing else. All you know how to do is play that piano. Now, who am I? Am I me? Or am I the piano player? Sometime it seem like the only thing to do is shoot the piano player cause he the cause of all the trouble I'm having.

DOAKER: What you gonna do when your troubles get like mine?

LYMON: If I knew how to play it, I'd play it. That's a nice piano.

BOY WILLIE: Whoever playing better play quick. Sutter's brother say he waiting on me. I sell them watermelons. Get Berniece to sell that piano. Put them two parts with the part I done saved . . .

WINING BOY: Berniece ain't gonna sell that piano. I don't see why you don't know that.

BOY WILLIE: What she gonna do with it? She ain't doing nothing but letting it sit up there and rot. That piano ain't doing nobody no good.

LYMON: That's a nice piano. If I had it I'd sell it. Unless I knew how to play like Wining Boy. You can get a nice price for that piano.

DOAKER: Now I'm gonna tell you something, Lymon don't know this . . . but I'm gonna tell you why me and Wining Boy say Berniece ain't gonna sell that piano.

BOY WILLIE: She ain't got to sell it! I'm gonna sell it! Berniece ain't got no more rights to that piano than I do.

DOAKER: I'm talking to the man . . . let me talk to the man. See, now . . . to understand why we say that . . . to understand about that piano . . . you got to go back to slavery time. See, our family was owned by a fellow named Robert Sutter. That was Sutter's grandfather. Alright. The piano was owned by a fellow named Joel Nolander. He was one of the Nolander brothers from down in Georgia. It was coming up on Sutter's wedding anniversary and he was looking to buy his wife . . . Miss Ophelia was her name . . . he was looking to buy her an anniversary present. Only thing with him . . . he ain't had no money. But he had some niggers. So he asked Mr. Nolander to see if maybe he could trade off some of his niggers for that piano. Told him he would give him one and a half niggers for it. That's the way he told him. Say he could have one full grown and one half grown. Mr. Nolander agreed only he say he had to pick them. He didn't want Sutter to give him just any old nigger. He say he wanted to have the pick of the litter. So Sutter lined up his niggers and Mr. Nolander looked them over and out of the whole bunch he picked my grandmother . . . her name was Berniece . . . same like Berniece . . . and he picked my daddy when he wasn't nothing but a little boy nine years old. They made the trade off and Miss Ophelia was so happy with that piano that it got to be just about all she would do was play on that piano.

WINING BOY: Just get up in the morning, get all dressed up and sit down and play on that piano.

DOAKER: Alright. Time go along. Time go along. Miss Ophelia got to missing my grandmother . . . the way she would cook and clean the house and talk to her and what not. And she missed having my daddy around the house to fetch things for her. So she asked to see if maybe she could trade back that piano and get her niggers back. Mr. Nolander said no. Said a deal was a deal. Him and Sutter had a big falling out about it and Miss Ophelia took sick to the bed. Wouldn't get out of the bed in the morning. She just lay there. The doctor said she was wasting away.

WINING BOY: That's when Sutter called our granddaddy up to the house.

DOAKER: Now, our granddaddy's name was Boy Willie. That's who Boy Willie's named after . . . only they called him Willie Boy. Now, he was a worker of wood. He could make you anything you wanted out of wood. He'd make you a desk. A table. A lamp. Anything you wanted. Them white fellows around there used to come up to Mr. Sutter and get him to make all kinds of things for them. Then they'd pay Mr. Sutter a nice price. See, everything my grand-daddy made Mr. Sutter owned cause he owned him. That's why when Mr. Nolander offered to buy him to keep the family together Mr. Sutter wouldn't sell him. Told Mr. Nolander he didn't have enough money to buy him. Now . . . am I telling it right, Wining Boy?

WINING BOY: You telling it.

DOAKER: Sutter called him up to the house and told him to carve my grandmother and my daddy's picture on the piano for Miss Ophelia. And he took and carved this . . .

[DOAKER *crosses over to the piano.*]

See that right there? That's my grandmother, Berniece. She looked just like that. And he put a picture of my daddy when he wasn't nothing but a little boy the way he remembered him. He made them up out of his memory. Only thing . . . he didn't stop there. He carved all this. He got a picture of his mama . . . Mama Esther . . . and his daddy, Boy Charles.

WINING BOY: That was the first Boy Charles.

DOAKER: Then he put on the side here all kinds of things. See that? That's when him and Mama Berniece got married. They called it jumping the broom. That's how you got married in them days. Then he got here when my daddy was born . . . and here he got Mama Esther's funeral . . . and down here he got Mr. Nolander taking Mama Berniece and my daddy away down to his place in Georgia. He got all kinds of things what happened with our family. When Mr. Sutter seen the piano with all them carvings on it he got mad. He didn't ask for all that. But see . . . there wasn't nothing he could do about it. When Miss Ophelia seen it . . . she got excited. Now she had her piano and her niggers too. She took back to playing it and played on it right up till the day she died. Alright . . . now see, our brother Boy Charles . . . that's Berniece and Boy Willie's daddy . . . he was the oldest of us three boys. He's dead now. But he would have been fifty-seven if he had lived. He died in 1911 when he was thirty-one years old. Boy Charles used to talk about that piano all the time. He never could get it off his mind. Two or three months go by and he be talking about it again. He be talking about taking it out of Sutter's house.

Say it was the story of our whole family and as long as Sutter had it . . . he had us. Say we was still in slavery. Me and Wining Boy tried to talk him out of it but it wouldn't do any good. Soon as he quiet down about it he'd start up again. We seen where he wasn't gonna get it off his mind . . . so, on the Fourth of July, 1911 . . . when Sutter was at the picnic what the county give every year . . . me and Wining Boy went on down there with him and took that piano out of Sutter's house. We put it on a wagon and me and Wining Boy carried it over into the next county with Mama Ola's people. Boy Charles decided to stay around there and wait until Sutter got home to make it look like business as usual.

Now, I don't know what happened when Sutter came home and found that piano gone. But somebody went up to Boy Charles's house and set it on fire. But he wasn't in there. He must have seen them coming cause he went down and caught the 3:57 Yellow Dog. He didn't know they was gonna come down and stop the train. Stopped the train and found Boy Charles in the boxcar with four of them hobos. Must have got mad when they couldn't find the piano cause they set the boxcar afire and killed everybody. Now, nobody know who done that. Some people say it was Sutter cause it was his piano. Some people say it was Sheriff Carter. Some people say it was Robert Smith and Ed Saunders. But don't nobody know for sure. It was about two months after that that Ed Saunders fell down his well. Just upped and fell down his well for no reason. People say it was the ghost of them men who burned up in the boxcar that pushed him in his well. They started calling them the Ghosts of the Yellow Dog. Now, that's how all that got started and that why we say Berniece ain't gonna sell that piano. Cause her daddy died over it.

BOY WILLIE: All that's in the past. If my daddy had seen where he could have traded that piano in for some land of his own, it wouldn't be sitting up here now. He spent his whole life farming on somebody else's land. I ain't gonna do that. See, he couldn't do no better. When he come along he ain't had nothing he could build on. His daddy ain't had nothing to give him. The only thing my daddy had to give me was that piano. And he died over giving me that. I ain't gonna let it sit up there and rot without trying to do something with it. If Berniece can't see that, then I'm gonna go ahead and sell my half. And you and Wining Boy know I'm right.

DOAKER: Ain't nobody said nothing about who's right and who's wrong. I was just telling the man about the piano. I was telling him why we say Berniece ain't gonna sell it.

LYMON: Yeah, I can see why you say that now. I told Boy Willie he ought to stay up here with me.

BOY WILLIE: You stay! I'm going back! That's what I'm gonna do with my life! Why I got to come up here and learn to do something I don't know how to do when I already know how to farm? You stay up here and make your own way if that's what you want to do. I'm going back and live my life the way I want to live it.

[WINING BOY *gets up and crosses to the piano.*]

WINING BOY: Let's see what we got here. I ain't played on this thing for a while.

DOAKER: You can stop telling that. You was playing on it the last time you was through here. We couldn't get you off of it. Go on and play something.

[WINING BOY *sits down at the piano and plays and sings. The song is one which has put many dimes and quarters in his pocket, long ago, in dimly remembered towns and way stations. He plays badly, without hesitation, and sings in a forceful voice.*]

WINING BOY: [*Singing.*]

I am a rambling gambling man
I gambled in many towns
I rambled this wide world over
I rambled this world around
I had my ups and downs in life
And bitter times I saw
But I never knew what misery was
Till I lit on old Arkansas.

I started out one morning
To meet that early train
He said, "You better work for me
I have some land to drain.
I'll give you fifty cents a day,
Your washing, board and all
And you shall be a different man
In the state of Arkansas."

I worked six months for the rascal
Joe Herrin was his name
He fed me old corn dodgers
They was hard as any rock
My tooth is all got loosened
And my knees begin to knock
That was the kind of hash I got
In the state of Arkansas.

Traveling man
I've traveled all around this world
Traveling man
I've traveled from land to land
Traveling man
I've traveled all around this world
Well it ain't no use
Writing no news
I'm a traveling man.

[*The door opens and* BERNIECE *enters with* MARETHA.]

BERNIECE: Is that . . . Lord, I know that ain't Wining Boy sitting there.
WINING BOY: Hey, Berniece.

BERNIECE: You all had this planned. You and Boy Willie had this planned.

WINING BOY: I didn't know he was gonna be here. I'm on my way down home. I stopped by to see you and Doaker first.

DOAKER: I told the nigger he left out of here with that sack of money, we thought we might never see him again. Boy Willie say he wasn't gonna see him till he got broke. I looked up and seen him sitting on the doorstep asking for two dollars. Look at him laughing. He know it's the truth.

BERNIECE: Boy Willie, I didn't see that truck out there. I thought you was out selling watermelons.

BOY WILLIE: We done sold them all. Sold the truck too.

BERNIECE: I don't want to go through none of your stuff. I done told you to go back where you belong.

BOY WILLIE: I was just teasing you, woman. You can't take no teasing?

BERNIECE: Wining Boy, when you get here?

WINING BOY: A little while ago. I took the train from Kansas City.

BERNIECE: Let me go upstairs and change and then I'll cook you something to eat.

BOY WILLIE: You ain't cooked me nothing when I come.

BERNIECE: Boy Willie, go on and leave me alone. Come on, Maretha, get up here and change your clothes before you get them dirty.

[BERNIECE *exits up the stairs, followed by* MARETHA.]

WINING BOY: Maretha sure getting big, ain't she, Doaker. And just as pretty as she want to be. I didn't know Crawley had it in him.

[BOY WILLIE *crosses to the piano.*]

BOY WILLIE: Hey, Lymon . . . get up on the other side of this piano and let me see something.

WINING BOY: Boy Willie, what is you doing?

BOY WILLIE: I'm seeing how heavy this piano is. Get up over there, Lymon.

WINING BOY: Go on and leave that piano alone. You ain't taking that piano out of here and selling it.

BOY WILLIE: Just as soon as I get them watermelons out that truck.

WINING BOY: Well, I got something to say about that.

BOY WILLIE: This my daddy's piano.

WINING BOY: He ain't took it by himself. Me and Doaker helped him.

BOY WILLIE: He died by himself. Where was you and Doaker at then? Don't come telling me nothing about this piano. This is me and Berniece's piano. Am I right, Doaker?

DOAKER: Yeah, you right.

BOY WILLIE: Let's see if we can lift it up, Lymon. Get a good grip on it and pick it up on your end. Ready? Lift!

[*As they start to move the piano, the sound of* SUTTER'S GHOST *is heard.* DOAKER *is the only one to hear it. With difficulty they move the piano a little bit so it is out of place.*]

BOY WILLIE: What you think?

LYMON: It's heavy . . . but you can move it. Only it ain't gonna be easy.

BOY WILLIE: It wasn't that heavy to me. Okay, let's put it back.

[*The sound of* SUTTER'S GHOST *is heard again. They all hear it as* BERNIECE *enters on the stairs.*]

BERNIECE: Boy Willie . . . you gonna play around with me one too many times. And then God's gonna bless you and West is gonna dress you. Now set that piano back over there. I done told you a hundred times I ain't selling that piano.

BOY WILLIE: I'm trying to get me some land, woman. I need that piano to get me some money so I can buy Sutter's land.

BERNIECE: Money can't buy what that piano cost. You can't sell your soul for money. It won't go with the buyer. It'll shrivel and shrink to know that you ain't taken on to it. But it won't go with the buyer.

BOY WILLIE: I ain't talking about all that, woman. I ain't talking about selling my soul. I'm talking about trading that piece of wood for some land. Get something under your feet. Land the only thing God ain't making no more of. You can always get you another piano. I'm talking about some land. What you get something out the ground from. That's what I'm talking about. You can't do nothing with that piano but sit up there and look at it.

BERNIECE: That's just what I'm gonna do. Wining Boy, you want me to fry you some pork chops?

BOY WILLIE: Now, I'm gonna tell you the way I see it. The only thing that make that piano worth something is them carvings Papa Willie Boy put on there. That's what make it worth something. That was my great-grandaddy. Papa Boy Charles brought that piano into the house. Now, I'm supposed to build on what they left me. You can't do nothing with that piano sitting up here in the house. That's just like if I let them watermelons sit out there and rot. I'd be a fool. Alright now, if you say to me, Boy Willie, I'm using that piano. I give out lessons on it and that help me make my rent or whatever. Then that be something else. I'd have to go on and say, well, Berniece using that piano. She building on it. Let her go on and use it. I got to find another way to get Sutter's land. But Doaker say you ain't touched that piano the whole time it's been up here. So why you wanna stand in my way? See, you just looking at the sentimental value. See, that's good. That's alright. I take my hat off whenever somebody say my daddy's name. But I ain't gonna be no fool about no sentimental value. You can sit up here and look at the piano for the next hundred years and it's just gonna be a piano. You can't make more than that. Now I want to get Sutter's land with that piano. I get Sutter's land and I can go down and cash in the crop and get my seed. As long as I got the land and the seed then I'm alright. I can always get me a little something else. Cause that land give back to you. I can make me another crop and cash that in. I still got the land and the seed. But that piano don't put out nothing else. You ain't got nothing working for you. Now, the kind of man my daddy was he would have understood that. I'm sorry you can't see it that way. But that's why I'm gonna take that piano out of here and sell it.

BERNIECE: You ain't taking that piano out of my house. [*She crosses to the piano.*]

Look at this piano. Look at it. Mama Ola polished this piano with her tears for seventeen years. For seventeen years she rubbed on it till her hands bled. Then she rubbed the blood in . . . mixed it up with the rest of the blood on it. Every day that God breathed life into her body she rubbed and cleaned and polished and prayed over it. "Play something for me, Berniece. Play something for me, Berniece." Every day. "I cleaned it up for you, play something for me, Berniece." You always talking about your daddy but you ain't never stopped to look at what his foolishness cost your mama. Seventeen years' worth of cold nights and an empty bed. For what? For a piano? For a piece of wood? To get even with somebody? I look at you and you're all the same. You, Papa Boy Charles, Wining Boy, Doaker, Crawley . . . you're all alike. All this thieving and killing and thieving and killing. And what it ever lead to? More killing and more thieving. I ain't never seen it come to nothing. People getting burned up. People getting shot. People falling down their wells. It don't never stop.

DOAKER: Come on now, Berniece, ain't no need in getting upset.

BOY WILLIE: I done a little bit of stealing here and there, but I ain't never killed nobody. I can't be speaking for nobody else. You all got to speak for yourself, but I ain't never killed nobody.

BERNIECE: You killed Crawley just as sure as if you pulled the trigger.

BOY WILLIE: See, that's ignorant. That's downright foolish for you to say something like that. You ain't doing nothing but showing your ignorance. If the nigger was here I'd whup his ass for getting me and Lymon shot at.

BERNIECE: Crawley ain't knew about the wood.

BOY WILLIE: We told the man about the wood. Ask Lymon. He knew all about the wood. He seen we was sneaking it. Why else we gonna be out there at night? Don't come telling me Crawley ain't knew about the wood. Them fellows come up on us and Crawley tried to bully them. Me and Lymon seen the sheriff with them and give in. Wasn't no sense in getting killed over fifty dollars' worth of wood.

BERNIECE: Crawley ain't knew you stole that wood.

BOY WILLIE: We ain't stole no wood. Me and Lymon was hauling wood for Jim Miller and keeping us a little bit on the side. We dumped our little bit down there by the creek till we had enough to make a load. Some fellows seen us and we figured we better get it before they did. We come up there and got Crawley to help us load it. Figured we'd cut him in. Crawley trying to keep the wolf from his door . . . we was trying to help him.

LYMON: Me and Boy Willie told him about the wood. We told him some fellows might be trying to beat us to it. He say let me go back and get my thirty-eight. That's what caused all the trouble.

BOY WILLIE: If Crawley ain't had the gun he'd be alive today.

LYMON: We had it about half loaded when they come up on us. We seen the sheriff with them and we tried to get away. We ducked around near the bend in the creek . . . but they was down there too. Boy Willie say let's give in. But Crawley pulled out his gun and started shooting. That's when they started shooting back.

BERNIECE: All I know is Crawley would be alive if you hadn't come up there and got him.

BOY WILLIE: I ain't had nothing to do with Crawley getting killed. That was his own fault.

BERNIECE: Crawley's dead and in the ground and you still walking around here eating. That's all I know. He went off to load some wood with you and ain't never come back.

BOY WILLIE: I told you, woman . . . I ain't had nothing to do with . . .

BERNIECE: He ain't here, is he? He ain't here!

[BERNIECE *hits* BOY WILLIE.]

I said he ain't here. Is he?

[BERNIECE *continues to hit* BOY WILLIE, *who doesn't move to defend himself, other than back up and turning his head so that most of the blows fall on his chest and arms.*]

DOAKER: [*Grabbing* BERNIECE.] Come on, Berniece . . . let it go, it ain't his fault.

BERNIECE: He ain't here, is he? Is he?

BOY WILLIE: I told you I ain't responsible for Crawley.

BERNIECE: He ain't here.

BOY WILLIE: Come on now, Berniece . . . don't do this now. Doaker get her. I ain't had nothing to do with Crawley . . .

BERNIECE: You come up there and got him!

BOY WILLIE: I done told you now. Doaker, get her. I ain't playing.

DOAKER: Come on. Berniece.

[MARETHA *is heard screaming upstairs. It is a scream of stark terror.*]

MARETHA: Mama! . . . Mama!

[*The lights go down to black. End of Act One.*]

ACT II

SCENE 1

[*The lights come up on the kitchen. It is the following morning.* DOAKER *is ironing the pants to his uniform. He has a pot cooking on the stove at the same time. He is singing a song. The song provides him with the rhythm for his work and he moves about the kitchen with the ease born of many years as a railroad cook*]

DOAKER:

Gonna leave Jackson Mississippi
And go to Memphis
And double back to Jackson
Come on down to Hattiesburg

Change cars on the Y.D.
Coming through the territory to
Meridian
And Meridian to Greenville
And Greenville to Memphis
I'm on my way and I know where

Change cars on the Katy
Leaving Jackson
And going through Clarksdale
Hello Winona!
Courtland!
Bateville!
Como!
Senitobia!
Lewisberg!
Sunflower!
Glendora!
Sharkey!
And double back to Jackson
Hello Greenwood
I'm on my way Memphis
Clarksdale
Moorhead
Indianola
Can a highball pass through?
Highball on through sir
Grand Carson!
Thirty First Street Depot
Fourth Street Depot
Memphis!

[WINING BOY *enters carrying a suit of clothes.*]

DOAKER: I thought you took that suit to the pawnshop?

WINING BOY: I went down there and the man tell me the suit is too old. Look at this suit. This is one hundred percent silk! How a silk suit gonna get too old? I know what it was he just didn't want to give me five dollars for it. Best he wanna give me is three dollars. I figure a silk suit is worth five dollars all over the world. I wasn't gonna part with it for no three dollars so I brought it back.

DOAKER: They got another pawnshop up on Wylie.

WINING BOY: I carried it up there. He say he don't take no clothes. Only thing he take is guns and radios. Maybe a guitar or two. Where's Berniece?

DOAKER: Berniece still at work. Boy Willie went down there to meet Lymon this morning. I guess they got that truck fixed, they had been out there all day and ain't come back yet. Maretha scared to sleep up there now. Berniece don't know, but I seen Sutter before she did.

WINING BOY: Say what?

DOAKER: About three weeks ago. I had just come back from down there. Sutter couldn't have been dead more than three days. He was sitting over there at the piano. I come out to go to work . . . and he was sitting right there. Had his hand on top of his head just like Berniece said. I believe he broke his neck when he fell in the well. I kept quiet about it. I didn't see no reason to upset Berniece.

WINING BOY: Did he say anything? Did he say he was looking for Boy Willie?

DOAKER: He was just sitting there. He ain't said nothing. I went on out the door and left him sitting there. I figure as long as he was on the other side of the room everything be alright. I don't know what I would have done if he had started walking toward me.

WINING BOY: Berniece say he was calling Boy Willie's name.

DOAKER: I ain't heard him say nothing. He was just sitting there when I seen him. But I don't believe Boy Willie pushed him in the well. Sutter here cause of that piano. I heard him playing on it one time. I thought it was Berniece but then she don't play that kind of music. I come out here and ain't seen nobody, but them piano keys was moving a mile a minute. Berniece need to go on and get rid of it. It ain't done nothing but cause trouble.

WINING BOY: I agree with Berniece. Boy Charles ain't took it to give it back. He took it cause he figure he had more right to it than Sutter did. If Sutter can't understand that . . . then that's just the way that go. Sutter dead and in the ground . . . don't care where his ghost is. He can hover around and play on the piano all he want. I want to see him carry it out the house. That's what I want to see. What time Berniece get home? I don't see how I let her get away from me this morning.

DOAKER: You up there sleep. Berniece leave out of here early in the morning. She out there in Squirrel Hill cleaning house for some bigshot down there at the steel mill. They don't like you to come late. You come late they won't give you your carfare. What kind of business you got with Berniece?

WINING BOY: My business. I ain't asked you what kind of business you got.

DOAKER: Berniece ain't got no money. If that's why you was trying to catch her. She having a hard enough time trying to get by as it is. If she go ahead and marry Avery . . . he working every day . . . she go ahead and marry him they could do alright for themselves. But as it stands she ain't got no money.

WINING BOY: Well, let me have five dollars.

DOAKER: I just give you a dollar before you left out of here. You ain't gonna take my five dollars out there and gamble and drink it up.

WINING BOY: Aw, nigger, give me five dollars. I'll give it back to you.

DOAKER: You wasn't looking to give me five dollars when you had that sack of money. You wasn't looking to throw nothing my way. Now you wanna come in here and borrow five dollars. If you going back with Boy Willie you need to be trying to figure out how you gonna get train fare.

WINING BOY: That's why I need the five dollars. If I had five dollars I could get me some money.

[DOAKER *goes into his pocket.*]

Make it seven.

DOAKER: You take this five dollars . . . and you bring my money back here too.

[BOY WILLIE *and* LYMON *enter. They are happy and excited. They have money in all of their pockets and are anxious to count it.*]

DOAKER: How'd you do out there?

BOY WILLIE: They was lining up for them.

LYMON: Me and Boy Willie couldn't sell them fast enough. Time we got one sold we'd sell another.

BOY WILLIE: I seen what was happening and told Lymon to up the price on them.

LYMON: Boy Willie say charge them a quarter more. They didn't care. A couple of people give me a dollar and told me to keep the change.

BOY WILLIE: One fellow bought five. I say now what he gonna do with five watermelons? He can't eat them all. I sold him the five and asked him did he want to buy five more.

LYMON: I ain't never seen nobody snatch a dollar fast as Boy Willie.

BOY WILLIE: One lady asked me say, "Is they sweet?" I told her say, "Lady, where we grow these watermelons we put sugar in the ground." You know, she believed me. Talking about she had never heard of that before. Lymon was laughing his head off. I told her, "Oh, yeah, we put the sugar right in the ground with the seed." She say, "Well, give me another one." Them white folks is something else . . . ain't they, Lymon?

LYMON: Soon as you holler watermelons they come right out their door. Then they go and get their neighbors. Look like they having a contest to see who can buy the most.

WINING BOY: I got something for Lymon.

[WINING BOY *goes to get his suit.* BOY WILLIE *and* LYMON *continue to count their money.*]

BOY WILLIE: I know you got more than that. You ain't sold all them watermelons for that little bit of money.

LYMON: I'm still looking. That ain't all you got either. Where's all them quarters?

BOY WILLIE: You let me worry about the quarters. Just put the money on the table.

WINING BOY: [*Entering with his suit.*] Look here, Lymon . . . see this? Look at his eyes getting big. He ain't never seen a suit like this. This is one hundred percent silk. Go ahead . . . put it on. See if it fit you.

[LYMON *tries the suit coat on.*]

Look at that. Feel it. That's one hundred percent genuine silk. I got that in Chicago. You can't get clothes like that nowhere but New York and Chicago. You can't get clothes like that in Pittsburgh. These folks in Pittsburgh ain't never seen clothes like that.

LYMON: This is nice, feel real nice and smooth.

WINING BOY: That's a fifty-five-dollar suit. That's the kind of suit the bigshots wear. You need a pistol and a pocketful of money to wear that suit. I'll let you have it for three dollars. The women will fall out their windows they see you in a suit like that. Give me three dollars and go on and wear it down the street and get you a woman.

BOY WILLIE: That looks nice, Lymon. Put the pants on. Let me see it with the pants.

[LYMON *begins to try on the pants.*]

WINING BOY: Look at that . . . see how it fits you? Give me three dollars and go on and take it. Look at that, Doaker . . . don't he look nice?

DOAKER: Yeah . . . that's a nice suit.

WINING BOY: Got a shirt to go with it. Cost you an extra dollar. Four dollars you got the whole deal.

LYMON: How this look, Boy Willie?

BOY WILLIE: That look nice . . . if you like that kind of thing. I don't like them dress-up kind of clothes. If you like it, look real nice.

WINING BOY: That's the kind of suit you need for up here in the North.

LYMON: Four dollars for everything? The suit and the shirt?

WINING BOY: That's cheap. I should be charging you twenty dollars. I give you a break cause you a homeboy. That's the only way I let you have it for four dollars.

LYMON: [*Going into his pocket.*] Okay . . . here go the four dollars.

WINING BOY: You got some shoes? What size you wear?

LYMON: Size nine.

WINING BOY: That's what size I got! Size nine. I let you have them for three dollars.

LYMON: Where they at? Let me see them.

WINING BOY: They real nice shoes, too. Got a nice tip to them. Got pointy toe just like you want.

[WINING BOY *goes to get his shoes.*]

LYMON: Come on, Boy Willie, let's go out tonight. I wanna see what it looks like up here. Maybe we go to a picture show. Hey, Doaker, they got picture shows up here?

DOAKER: The Rhumba Theater. Right down there on Fullerton Street. Can't miss it. Got the speakers outside on the sidewalk. You can hear it a block away. Boy Willie know where it's at.

[DOAKER *exits into his room.*]

LYMON: Let's go to the picture show, Boy Willie. Let's go find some women.

BOY WILLIE: Hey, Lymon, how many of them watermelons would you say we got left? We got just under a half a load . . . right?

LYMON: About that much. Maybe a little more.

BOY WILLIE: You think that piano will fit up in there?

LYMON: If we stack them watermelons you can sit it up in the front there.

BOY WILLIE: I'm gonna call that man tomorrow.

WINING BOY: [*Returns with his shoes.*] Here you go . . . size nine. Put them on. Cost you three dollars. That's a Florsheim shoe. That's the kind Staggerlee[2] wore.

LYMON: [*Trying on the shoes.*] You sure these size nine?

WINING BOY: You can look at my feet and see we wear the same size. Man, you put on that suit and them shoes and you got something there. You ready for whatever's out there. But is they ready for you? With them shoes on you be the King of the Walk. Have everybody stop to look at your shoes. Wishing they had a pair. I'll give you a break. Go on and take them for two dollars.

[LYMON *pays* WINING BOY *two dollars.*]

LYMON: Come on, Boy Willie . . . let's go find some women. I'm gonna go upstairs and get ready. I'll be ready to go in a minute. Ain't you gonna get dressed?

BOY WILLIE: I'm gonna wear what I got on. I ain't dressing up for these city niggers.

[LYMON *exits up the stairs.*]

That's all Lymon think about is women.

WINING BOY: His daddy was the same way. I used to run around with him. I know his mama too. Two strokes back and I would have been his daddy! His daddy's dead now . . . but I got the nigger out of jail one time. They was fixing to name him Daniel and walk him through the Lion's Den.[3] He got in a tussle with one of them white fellows and the sheriff lit on him like white on rice. That's how the whole thing come about between me and Lymon's mama. She knew me and his daddy used to run together and he got in jail and she went down there and took the sheriff a hundred dollars. Don't get me to lying about where she got it from. I don't know. The sheriff *looked at that hundred dollars and turned his nose up.* Told her, say, "That ain't gonna do him no good. You got to put another hundred on top of that." She come up *there and got me where I was playing at this saloon* . . . said she had all but fifty dollars and asked me if I could help. Now the way I figured it . . . without that fifty dollars the sheriff was gonna turn him over to Parchman. The sheriff turn him over to Parchman it be three years before anybody see him again. Now I'm gonna say it right . . . I will give anybody fifty dollars to keep them out of jail for three years. I give her the fifty dollars and she told me to come over to the house. I ain't asked her. I figure if she was nice enough to invite me I ought to go. I ain't had to say a word. She invited me over just as nice. Say, "Why don't you come over to the house?" She ain't had to say nothing else. Them words rolled off her tongue just as nice. I went on down there and sat about three hours. Started to leave and changed my mind. She grabbed hold to me and say, "Baby, it's all night long." That was one of the shortest nights I have ever spent on this earth! I could have used another eight hours. Lymon's daddy didn't even say nothing to me when he got out. He just looked at me funny. He had a good notion something had happened between me an' her. L. D. Jackson. That was one bad-luck nigger. Got killed at some dance.

---

2. In African American folklore, a flashy figure (also called Stagger Lee, Stagolee, Stagalee, Stackolee, Stack O'Lee, Stack-o-lee, and so on) who murdered the man who stole his Stetson hat. The story is frequently retold (and reinterpreted) in song.   3. See Daniel 6.

Fellow walked in and shot him thinking he was somebody else.

[DOAKER *enters from his room.*]

Hey, Doaker, you remember L. D. Jackson?

DOAKER: That's Lymon's daddy. That was one bad-luck nigger.

BOY WILLIE: Look like you ready to railroad some.

DOAKER: Yeah, I got to make that run.

[LYMON *enters from the stairs. He is dressed in his new suit and shoes, to which he has added a cheap straw hat.*]

LYMON: How I look?

WINING BOY: You look like a million dollars. Don't he look good, Doaker? Come on, let's play some cards. You wanna play some cards?

BOY WILLIE: We ain't gonna play no cards with you. Me and Lymon gonna find some women. Hey, Lymon, don't play no cards with Wining Boy. He'll take all your money.

WINING BOY: [*To* LYMON.] You got a magic suit there. You can get you a woman easy with that suit . . . but you got to know the magic words. You know the magic words to get you a woman?

LYMON: I just talk to them to see if I like them and they like me.

WINING BOY: You just walk right up to them and say, "If you got the harbor I got the ship." If that don't work ask them if you can put them in your pocket. The first thing they gonna say is, "It's too small." That's when you look them dead in the eye and say, "Baby, ain't nothing small about me." If that don't work then you move on to another one. Am I telling him right, Doaker?

DOAKER: That man don't need you to tell him nothing about no women. These women these days ain't gonna fall for that kind of stuff. You got to buy them a present. That's what they looking for these days.

BOY WILLIE: Come on, I'm ready. You ready, Lymon? Come on, let's go find some women.

WINING BOY: Here, let me walk out with you. I wanna see the women fall out their window when they see Lymon.

[*They all exit and the lights go down on the scene.*]

SCENE 2

[*The lights come up on the kitchen. It is late evening of the same day.* BERNIECE *has set a tub for her bath in the kitchen. She is heating up water on the stove. There is a knock at the door.*]

BERNIECE: Who is it?

AVERY: It's me, Avery.

[BERNIECE *opens the door and lets him in.*]

BERNIECE: Avery, come on in. I was just fixing to take my bath.

AVERY: Where Boy Willie? I see that truck out there almost empty. They done sold almost all them watermelons.

BERNIECE: They was gone when I come home. I don't know where they went off to. Boy Willie around here about to drive me crazy.

AVERY: They sell them watermelons . . . he'll be gone soon.

BERNIECE: What Mr. Cohen say about letting you have the place?

AVERY: He say he'll let me have it for thirty dollars a month. I talked him out of thirty-five and he say he'll let me have it for thirty.

BERNIECE: That's a nice spot next to Benny Diamond's store.

AVERY: Berniece . . . I be at home and I get to thinking you up here an' I'm down there. I get to thinking how that look to have a preacher that ain't married. It makes for a better congregation if the preacher was settled down and married.

BERNIECE: Avery . . . not now. I was fixing to take my bath.

AVERY: You know how I feel about you, Berniece. Now . . . I done got the place from Mr. Cohen. I get the money from the bank and I can fix it up real nice. They give me a ten cents a hour raise down there on the job . . . now Berniece, I ain't got much in the way of comforts. I got a hole in my pockets near about as far as money is concerned. I ain't never found no way through life to a woman I care about like I care about you. I need that. I need somebody on my bond side. I need a woman that fits in my hand.

BERNIECE: Avery, I ain't ready to get married now.

AVERY: You too young a woman to close up, Berniece.

BERNIECE: I ain't said nothing about closing up. I got a lot of woman left in me.

AVERY: Where's it at? When's the last time you looked at it?

BERNIECE: [*Stunned by his remark.*] That's a nasty thing to say. And you call yourself a preacher.

AVERY: Anytime I get anywhere near you . . . you push me away.

BERNIECE: I got enough on my hands with Maretha. I got enough people to love and take care of.

AVERY: Who you got to love you? Can't nobody get close enough to you. Doaker can't half say nothing to you. You jump all over Boy Willie. Who you got to love you, Berniece?

BERNIECE: You trying to tell me a woman can't be nothing without a man. But you alright, huh? You can just walk out of here without me—without a woman— and still be a man. That's alright. Ain't nobody gonna ask you, "Avery, who you got to love you?" That's alright for you. But everybody gonna be worried about Berniece. "How Berniece gonna take care of herself? How she gonna raise that child without a man? Wonder what she do with herself. How she gonna live like that?" Everybody got all kinds of questions for Berniece. Everybody telling me I can't be a woman unless I got a man. Well, you tell me, Avery—you know—how much woman am I?

AVERY: It wasn't me, Berniece. You can't blame me for nobody else. I'll own up to my own shortcomings. But you can't blame me for Crawley or nobody else.

BERNIECE: I ain't blaming nobody for nothing. I'm just stating the facts.

AVERY: How long you gonna carry Crawley with you, Berniece? It's been over three years. At some point you got to let go and go on. Life's got all kinds of twists and turns. That don't mean you stop living. That don't mean you cut yourself off from life. You can't go through life carrying Crawley's ghost with you. Crawley's been dead three years. Three years, Berniece.

BERNIECE: I know how long Crawley's been dead. You ain't got to tell me that. I just ain't ready to get married right now.

AVERY: What is you ready for, Berniece? You just gonna drift along from day to day. Life is more than making it from one day to another. You gonna look up one day and it's all gonna be past you. Life's gonna be gone out of your hands—there won't be enough to make nothing with. I'm standing here now, Berniece—but I don't know how much longer I'm gonna be standing here waiting on you.

BERNIECE: Avery, I told you . . . when you get your church we'll sit down and talk about this. I got too many other things to deal with right now. Boy Willie and the piano . . . and Sutter's ghost. I thought I might have been seeing things, but Maretha done seen Sutter's ghost, too.

AVERY: When this happen, Berniece?

BERNIECE: Right after I came home yesterday. Me and Boy Willie was arguing about the piano and Sutter's ghost was standing at the top of the stairs. Maretha scared to sleep up there now. Maybe if you bless the house he'll go away.

AVERY: I don't know, Berniece. I don't know if I should fool around with something like that.

BERNIECE: I can't have Maretha scared to go to sleep up there. Seem like if you bless the house he would go away.

AVERY: You might have to be a special kind of preacher to do something like that.

BERNIECE: I keep telling myself when Boy Willie leave he'll go on and leave with him. I believe Boy Willie pushed him in the well.

AVERY: That's been going on down there a long time. The Ghosts of the Yellow Dog been pushing people in their wells long before Boy Willie got grown.

BERNIECE: Somebody down there pushing them people in their wells. They ain't just upped and fell. Ain't no wind pushed nobody in their well.

AVERY: Oh, I don't know. God works in mysterious ways.

BERNIECE: He ain't pushed nobody in their wells.

AVERY: He caused it to happen. God is the Great Causer. He can do anything. He parted the Red Sea.[4] He say I will smite my enemies. Reverend Thompson used to preach on the Ghosts of the Yellow Dog as the hand of God.

BERNIECE: I don't care who preached what. Somebody down there pushing them people in their wells. Somebody like Boy Willie. I can see him doing something like that. You ain't gonna tell me that Sutter just upped and fell in his well. I believe Boy Willie pushed him so he could get his land.

AVERY: What Doaker say about Boy Willie selling the piano?

BERNIECE: Doaker don't want no part of that piano. He ain't never wanted no part of it. He blames himself for not staying behind with Papa Boy Charles.

4. See Exodus 14.

He washed his hands of that piano a long time ago. He didn't want me to bring it up here—but I wasn't gonna leave it down there.

AVERY: Well, it seems to me somebody ought to be able to talk to Boy Willie.

BERNIECE: You can't talk to Boy Willie. He been that way all his life. Mama Ola had her hands full trying to talk to him. He don't listen to nobody. He just like my daddy. He get his mind fixed on something and can't nobody turn him from it.

AVERY: You ought to start a choir at the church. Maybe if he seen you was doing something with it—if you told him you was gonna put it in my church—maybe he'd see it different. You ought to put it down in the church and start a choir. The Bible say "Make a joyful noise unto the Lord." Maybe if Boy Willie see you was doing something with it he'd see it different.

BERNIECE: I done told you I don't play on that piano. Ain't no need in you to keep talking this choir stuff. When my mama died I shut the top on that piano and I ain't never opened it since. I was only playing it for her. When my daddy died seem like all her life went into that piano. She used to have me playing on it . . . had Miss Eula come in and teach me . . . say when I played it she could hear my daddy talking to her. I used to think them pictures came alive and walked through the house. Sometime late at night I could hear my mama talking to them. I said that wasn't gonna happen to me. I don't play that piano cause I don't want to wake them spirits. They never be walking around in this house.

AVERY: You got to put all that behind you, Berniece.

BERNIECE: I got Maretha playing on it. She don't know nothing about it. Let her go on and be a schoolteacher or something. She don't have to carry all of that with her. She got a chance I didn't have. I ain't gonna burden her with that piano.

AVERY: You got to put all of that behind you. Berniece. That's the same thing like Crawley. Everybody got stones in their passway. You got to step over them or walk around them. You picking them up and carrying them with you. All you got to do is set them down by the side of the road. You ain't got to carry them with you. You can walk over there right now and play that piano. You can walk over there right now and God will walk over there with you. Right now you can set that sack of stones down by the side of the road and walk away from it. You don't have to carry it with you. You can do it right now.

[AVERY *crosses over to the piano and raises the lid.*]

Come on, Berniece . . . set it down and walk away from it. Come on, play "Old Ship of Zion." Walk over here and claim it as an instrument of the Lord. You can walk over here right now and make it into a celebration.

[BERNIECE *moves toward the piano.*]

BERNIECE: Avery . . . I done told you I don't want to play that piano. Now or no other time.

AVERY: The Bible say, "The Lord is my refuge . . . and my strength!" With the strength of God you can put the past behind you, Berniece. With the strength of God you can do anything! God got a bright tomorrow. God don't ask what you done . . . God ask what you gonna do. The strength of God can move mountains! God's got a bright tomorrow for you . . . all you got to do is walk over here and claim it.

BERNIECE: Avery, just go on and let me finish my bath. I'll see you tomorrow.

AVERY: Okay, Berniece. I'm gonna go home. I'm gonna go home and read up on my Bible. And tomorrow . . . if the good Lord give me strength tomorrow . . . I'm gonna come by and bless the house . . . and show you the power of the Lord.

[AVERY *crosses to the door.*]

It's gonna be alright, Berniece. God say he will soothe the troubled waters. I'll come by tomorrow and bless the house.

[*The lights go down to black.*]

SCENE 3

[*Several hours later. The house is dark.* BERNIECE *has retired for the night.* BOY WILLIE *enters the darkened house with* GRACE.]

BOY WILLIE: Come on in. This is my sister's house. My sister live here. Come on, I ain't gonna bite you.

GRACE: Put some light on. I can't see.

BOY WILLIE: You don't need to see nothing, baby. This here is all you need to see. All you need to do is see me. If you can't see me you can feel me in the dark. How's that, sugar? [*He attempts to kiss her.*]

GRACE: Go on now . . . wait!

BOY WILLIE: Just give me one little old kiss.

GRACE: [*Pushing him away.*] Come on, now. Where I'm gonna sleep at?

BOY WILLIE: We got to sleep out here on the couch. Come on, my sister don't mind. Lymon come back he just got to sleep on the floor. He run off with Dolly somewhere he better stay there. Come on, sugar.

GRACE: Wait now . . . you ain't told me nothing about no couch. I thought you had a bed. Both of us can't sleep on that little old couch.

BOY WILLIE: It don't make no difference. We can sleep on the floor. Let Lymon sleep on the couch.

GRACE: You ain't told me nothing about no couch.

BOY WILLIE: What difference it make? You just wanna be with me.

GRACE: I don't want to be with you on no couch. Ain't you got no bed?

BOY WILLIE: You don't need no bed, woman. My granddaddy used to take women on the backs of horses. What you need a bed for? You just want to be with me.

GRACE: You sure is country. I didn't know you was this country.

BOY WILLIE: There's a lot of things you don't know about me. Come on, let me show you what this country boy can do.

GRACE: Let's go to my place. I got a room with a bed if Leroy don't come back there.

BOY WILLIE: Who's Leroy? You ain't said nothing about no Leroy.

GRACE: He used to be my man. He ain't coming back. He gone off with some other gal.

BOY WILLIE: You let him have your key?

GRACE: He ain't coming back.

BOY WILLIE: Did you let him have your key?

GRACE: He got a key but he ain't coming back. He took off with some other gal.

BOY WILLIE: I don't wanna go nowhere he might come. Let's stay here. Come on, sugar. [*He pulls her over to the couch.*] Let me heist your hood and check your oil. See if your battery needs charged. [*He pulls her to him. They kiss and tug at each other's clothing. In their anxiety they knock over a lamp.*]

BERNIECE: Who's that . . . Wining Boy?

BOY WILLIE: It's me . . . Boy Willie. Go on back to sleep. Everything's alright. [*To* GRACE.] That's my sister. Everything's alright, Berniece. Go on back to sleep.

BERNIECE: What you doing down there? What you done knocked over?

BOY WILLIE: It wasn't nothing. Everything's alright. Go on back to sleep. [*To* GRACE.] That's my sister. We alright. She gone back to sleep.

[*They begin to kiss.* BERNIECE *enters from the stairs dressed in a nightgown. She cuts on the light.*]

BERNIECE: Boy Willie, what you doing down here?

BOY WILLIE: It was just that there lamp. It ain't broke. It's okay. Everything's alright. Go on back to bed.

BERNIECE: Boy Willie, I don't allow that in my house. You gonna have to take your company someplace else.

BOY WILLIE: It's alright. We ain't doing nothing. We just sitting here talking. This here is Grace. That's my sister Berniece.

BERNIECE: You know I don't allow that kind of stuff in my house.

BOY WILLIE: Allow what? We just sitting here talking.

BERNIECE: Well, your company gonna have to leave. Come back and talk in the morning.

BOY WILLIE: Go on back upstairs now.

BERNIECE: I got an eleven-year-old girl upstairs. I can't allow that around here.

BOY WILLIE: Ain't nobody said nothing about that. I told you we just talking.

GRACE: Come on . . . let's go to my place. Ain't nobody got to tell me to leave but once.

BOY WILLIE: You ain't got to be like that, Berniece.

BERNIECE: I'm sorry, Miss. But he know I don't allow that in here.

GRACE: You ain't got to tell me but once. I don't stay nowhere I ain't wanted.

BOY WILLIE: I don't know why you want to embarrass me in front of my company.

GRACE: Come on, take me home.

BERNIECE: Go on, Boy Willie. Just go on with your company.

[BOY WILLIE *and* GRACE *exit.* BERNIECE *puts the light on in the kitchen and puts on the teakettle. Presently there is a knock at the door.* BERNIECE *goes to answer it.* BERNIECE *opens the door.* LYMON *enters.*]

LYMON: How you doing, Berniece? I thought you'd be asleep. Boy Willie been back here?

BERNIECE: He just left out of here a minute ago.

LYMON: I went out to see a picture show and never got there. We always end up doing something else. I was with this woman she just wanted to drink up all my money. So I left her there and came back looking for Boy Willie.

BERNIECE: You just missed him. He just left out of here.

LYMON: They got some nice-looking women in this city. I'm gonna like it up here real good. I like seeing them with their dresses on. Got them high heels. I like that. Make them look like they real precious. Boy Willie met a real nice one today. I wish I had met her before he did.

BERNIECE: He come by here with some woman a little while ago. I told him to go on and take all that out of my house.

LYMON: What she look like, the woman he was with? Was she a brown-skinned woman about this high? Nice and healthy? Got nice hips on her?

BERNIECE: She had on a red dress.

LYMON: That's her! That's Grace. She real nice. Laugh a lot. Lot of fun to be with. She don't be trying to put on. Some of these woman act like they the Queen of Sheba. I don't like them kind. Grace ain't like that. She real nice with herself.

BERNIECE: I don't know what she was like. He come in here all drunk knocking over the lamp, and making all kind of noise. I told them to take that somewhere else. I can't really say what she was like.

LYMON: She real nice. I seen her before he did. I was trying not to act like I seen her. I wanted to look at her a while before I said something. She seen me when I come into the saloon. I tried to act like I didn't see her. Time I looked around Boy Willie was talking to her. She was talking to him kept looking at me. That's when her friend Dolly came. I asked her if she wanted to go to the picture show. She told me to buy her a drink while she thought about it. Next thing I knew she done had three drinks talking about she too tired to go. I bought her another drink, then I left. Boy Willie was gone and I thought he might have come back here. Doaker gone, huh? He say he had to make a trip.

BERNIECE: Yeah, he gone on his trip. This is when I can usually get me some peace and quiet, Maretha asleep.

LYMON: She look just like you. Got them big eyes. I remember her when she was in diapers.

BERNIECE: Time just keep on. It go on with or without you. She going on twelve.

LYMON: She sure is pretty. I like kids.

BERNIECE: Boy Willie say you staying . . . what you gonna do up here in this big city? You thought about that?

LYMON: They never get me back down there. The sheriff looking for me. All because they gonna try and make me work for somebody when I don't want to. They gonna try and make me work for Stovall when he don't pay nothing.

It ain't like that up here. Up here you more or less do what you want to. I figure I find me a job and try to get set up and then see what the year brings. I tried to do that two or three times down there . . . but it never would work out. I was always in the wrong place.

BERNIECE: This ain't a bad city once you get to know your way around.

LYMON: Up here is different. I'm gonna get me a job unloading boxcars or something. One fellow told me say he know a place. I'm gonna go over there with him next week. Me and Boy Willie finish selling them watermelons I'll have enough money to hold me for a while. But I'm gonna go over there and see what kind of jobs they have.

BERNIECE: You shouldn't have too much trouble finding a job. It's all in how you present yourself. See now, Boy Willie couldn't get no job up here. Somebody hire him they got a pack of trouble on their hands. Soon as they find that out they fire him. He don't want to do nothing unless he do it his way.

LYMON: I know. I told him let's go to the picture show first and see if there was any women down there. They might get tired of sitting at home and walk down to the picture show. He say he wanna look around first. We never did get down there. We tried a couple of places and then we went to this saloon where he met Grace. I tried to meet her before he did but he beat me to her. We left Wining Boy sitting down there running his mouth. He told me if I wear this suit I'd find me a woman. He was almost right.

BERNIECE: You don't need to be out there in them saloons. Ain't no telling what you liable to run into out there. This one liable to cut you as quick as that one shoot you. You don't need to be out there. You start out that fast life you can't keep it up. It makes you old quick. I don't know what them women out there be thinking about.

LYMON: Mostly they be lonely and looking for somebody to spend the night with them. Sometimes it matters who it is and sometimes it don't. I used to be the same way. Now it got to matter. That's why I'm here now. Dolly liable not to even recognize me if she sees me again. I don't like women like that. I like my women to be with me in a nice and easy way. That way we can both enjoy ourselves. The way I see it we the only two people like us in the world. We got to see how we fit together. A woman that don't want to take the time to do that I don't bother with. Used to. Used to bother with all of them. Then I woke up one time with this woman and I didn't know who she was. She was the prettiest woman I had ever seen in my life. I spent the whole night with her and didn't even know it. I had never taken the time to look at her. I guess she kinda knew I ain't never really looked at her. She must have known that cause she ain't wanted to see me no more. If she had wanted to see me I believe we might have got married. How come you ain't married? It seem like to me you would be married. I remember Avery from down home. I used to call him plain old Avery. Now he Reverend Avery. That's kinda funny about him becoming a preacher. I like when he told about how that come to him in a dream about them sheep people and them hobos. Nothing ever come to me in a dream like that. I just dream about women. Can't never seem to find the right one.

BERNIECE: She out there somewhere. You just got to get yourself ready to meet her. That's what I'm trying to do. Avery's alright. I ain't really got nobody in mind.

LYMON: I get me a job and a little place and get set up to where I can make a woman comfortable I might get married. Avery's nice. You ought to go ahead and get married. You be a preacher's wife you won't have to work. I hate living by myself. I didn't want to be no strain on my mama so I left home when I was about sixteen. Everything I tried seem like it just didn't work out. Now I'm trying this.

BERNIECE: You keep trying it'll work out for you.

LYMON: You ever go down there to the picture show?

BERNIECE: I don't go in for all that.

LYMON: Ain't nothing wrong with it. It ain't like gambling and sinning. I went to one down in Jackson once. It was fun.

BERNIECE: I just stay home most of the time. Take care of Maretha.

LYMON: It's getting kind of late. I don't know where Boy Willie went off to. He's liable not to come back. I'm gonna take off these shoes. My feet hurt. Was you in bed? I don't mean to be keeping you up.

BERNIECE: You ain't keeping me up. I couldn't sleep after that Boy Willie woke me up.

LYMON: You got on that nightgown. I likes women when they wear them fancy nightclothes and all. It makes their skin look real pretty.

BERNIECE: I got this at the five-and-ten-cents store. It ain't so fancy.

LYMON: I don't too often get to see a woman dressed like that. [*There is a long pause.* LYMON *takes off his suit coat.*] Well, I'm gonna sleep here on the couch. I'm supposed to sleep on the floor but I don't reckon Boy Willie's coming back tonight. Wining Boy sold me this suit. Told me it was a magic suit. I'm gonna put it on again tomorrow. Maybe it bring me a woman like he say. [*He goes into his coat pocket and takes out a small bottle of perfume.*] I almost forgot I had this. Some man sold me this for a dollar. Say it come from Paris. This is the same kind of perfume the Queen of France wear. That's what he told me. I don't know if it's true or not. I smelled it. It smelled good to me. Here . . . smell it see if you like it. I was gonna give it to Dolly. But I didn't like her too much.

BERNIECE: [*Takes the bottle.*] It smells nice.

LYMON: I was gonna give it to Dolly if she had went to the picture with me. Go on, you take it.

BERNIECE: I can't take it. Here . . . go on you keep it. You'll find somebody to give it to.

LYMON: I wanna give it to you. Make you smell nice. [*He takes the bottle and puts perfume behind* BERNIECE's *ear.*] They tell me you supposed to put it right here behind your ear. Say if you put it there you smell nice all day.

[BERNIECE *stiffens at his touch.* LYMON *bends down to smell her.*]

There . . . you smell real good now. [*He kisses her neck.*] You smell real good for Lymon.

[*He kisses her again.* BERNIECE *returns the kiss, then breaks the embrace and crosses to the stairs. She turns and they look silently at each other.* LYMON *hands her the bottle of perfume.* BERNIECE *exits up the stairs.* LYMON *picks up his suit coat and strokes it lovingly with the full knowledge that it is indeed a magic suit. The lights go down on the scene.*]

SCENE 4

[*It is late the next morning. The lights come up on the parlor.* LYMON *is asleep on the sofa.* BOY WILLIE *enters the front door.*]

BOY WILLIE: Hey, Lymon! Lymon, come on get up.

LYMON: Leave me alone.

BOY WILLIE: Come on, get up, nigger! Wake up, Lymon.

LYMON: What you want?

BOY WILLIE: Come on, let's go. I done called the man about the piano.

LYMON: What piano?

BOY WILLIE: [*Dumps* LYMON *on the floor.*] Come on, get up!

LYMON: Why you leave, I looked around and you was gone.

BOY WILLIE: I come back here with Grace, then I went looking for you. I figured you'd be with Dolly.

LYMON: She just want to drink and spend up your money. I come on back here looking for you to see if you wanted to go to the picture show.

BOY WILLIE: I been up at Grace's house. Some nigger named Leroy come by but I had a chair up against the door. He got mad when he couldn't get in. He went off somewhere and I got out of there before he could come back. Berniece got mad when we came here.

LYMON: She say you was knocking over the lamp busting up the place.

BOY WILLIE: That was Grace doing all that.

LYMON: Wining Boy seen Sutter's ghost last night.

BOY WILLIE: Wining Boy's liable to see anything. I'm surprised he found the right house. Come on, I done called the man about the piano.

LYMON: What he say?

BOY WILLIE: He say to bring it on out. I told him I was calling for my sister, Miss Berniece Charles. I told him some man wanted to buy it for eleven hundred dollars and asked him if he would go any better. He said yeah, he would give me eleven hundred and fifty dollars for it if it was the same piano. I described it to him again and he told me to bring it out.

LYMON: Why didn't you tell him to come and pick it up?

BOY WILLIE: I didn't want to have no problem with Berniece. This way we just take it on out there and it be out the way. He want to charge twenty-five dollars to pick it up.

LYMON: You should have told him the man was gonna give you twelve hundred for it.

BOY WILLIE: I figure I was taking a chance with that eleven hundred. If I had told him twelve hundred he might have run off. Now I wish I had told him twelve-fifty. It's hard to figure out white folks sometimes.

LYMON: You might have been able to tell him anything. White folks got a lot of money.

BOY WILLIE: Come on, let's get it loaded before Berniece come back. Get that end over there. All you got to do is pick it up on that side. Don't worry about this side. You wanna stretch you' back for a minute?

LYMON: I'm ready.

BOY WILLIE: Get a real good grip on it now.

[*The sound of* SUTTER'S GHOST *is heard. They do not hear it.*]

LYMON: I got this end. You get that end.

BOY WILLIE: Wait till I say ready now. Alright. You got it good? You got a grip on it?

LYMON: Yeah, I got it. You lift up on that end.

BOY WILLIE: Ready? Lift!

[*The piano will not budge.*]

LYMON: Man, this piano is heavy! It's gonna take more than me and you to move this piano.

BOY WILLIE: We can do it. Come on—we did it before.

LYMON: Nigger—you crazy! That piano weighs five hundred pounds!

BOY WILLIE: I got three hundred pounds of it! I know you can carry two hundred pounds! You be lifting them cotton sacks! Come on lift this piano!

[*They try to move the piano again without success.*]

LYMON: It's stuck. Something holding it.

BOY WILLIE: How the piano gonna be stuck? We just moved it. Slide you' end out.

LYMON: Naw—we gonna need two or three more people. How this big old piano get in the house?

BOY WILLIE: I don't know how it got in the house. I know how it's going out though! You get on this end. I'll carry three hundred and fifty pounds of it. All you got to do is slide your end out. Ready?

[*They switch sides and try again without success.* DOAKER *enters from his room as they try to push and shove it.*]

LYMON: Hey, Doaker . . . how this piano get in the house?

DOAKER: Boy Willie, what you doing?

BOY WILLIE: I'm carrying this piano out the house. What it look like I'm doing? Come on, Lymon, let's try again.

DOAKER: Go on let the piano sit there till Berniece come home.

BOY WILLIE: You ain't got nothing to do with this, Doaker. This my business.

DOAKER: This is my house, nigger! I ain't gonna let you or nobody else carry nothing out of it. You ain't gonna carry nothing out of here without my permission!

BOY WILLIE: This is my piano. I don't need your permission to carry my belongings out of your house. This is mine. This ain't got nothing to do with you.

DOAKER: I say leave it over there till Berniece come home. She got part of it too. Leave it set there till you see what she say.

BOY WILLIE: I don't care what Berniece say. Come on, Lymon. I got this side.

DOAKER: Go on and cut it half in two if you want to. Just leave Berniece's half sitting over there. I can't tell you what to do with your piano. But I can't let you take her half out of here.

BOY WILLIE: Go on, Doaker. You ain't got nothing to do with this. I don't want you starting nothing now. Just go on and leave me alone. Come on, Lymon. I got this end.

[DOAKER *goes into his room.* BOY WILLIE *and* LYMON *prepare to move the piano.*]

LYMON: How we gonna get it in the truck?

BOY WILLIE: Don't worry about how we gonna get it on the truck. You got to get it out the house first.

LYMON: It's gonna take more than me and you to move this piano.

BOY WILLIE: Just lift up on that end, nigger!

[DOAKER *comes to the doorway of his room and stands.*]

DOAKER: [*Quietly with authority.*] Leave that piano set over there till Berniece come back. I don't care what you do with it then. But you gonna leave it sit over there right now.

BOY WILLIE: Alright . . . I'm gonna tell you this, Doaker. I'm going out of here . . . I'm gonna get me some rope . . . find me a plank and some wheels . . . and I'm coming back. Then I'm gonna carry that piano out of here . . . sell it and give Berniece half the money. See . . . now that's what I'm gonna do. And you . . . or nobody else is gonna stop me. Come on, Lymon . . . let's go get some rope and stuff. I'll be back, Doaker.

[BOY WILLIE *and* LYMON *exit. The lights go down on the scene.*]

SCENE 5

[*The lights come up.* BOY WILLIE *sits on the sofa, screwing casters on a wooden plank.* MARETHA *is sitting on the piano stool.* DOAKER *sits at the table playing solitaire.*]

BOY WILLIE: [*To* MARETHA.] Then after that them white folks down around there started falling down their wells. You ever seen a well? A well got a wall around it. It's hard to fall down a well. You got to be leaning way over. Couldn't nobody figure out too much what was making these fellows fall down their well . . . so everybody says the Ghosts of the Yellow Dog must have pushed them. That's what everybody called them four men what got burned up in the boxcar.

MARETHA: Why they call them that?

BOY WILLIE: Cause the Yazoo Delta railroad got yellow boxcars. Sometime the way the whistle blow sound like an old dog howling so the people call it the Yellow Dog.

MARETHA: Anybody ever see the Ghosts?

BOY WILLIE: I told you they like the wind. Can you see the wind?

MARETHA: No.

BOY WILLIE: They like the wind you can't see them. But sometimes you be in trouble they might be around to help you. They say if you go where the Southern cross the Yellow Dog . . . you go to where them two railroads cross each other . . . and call out their names . . . they say they talk back to you. I don't know, I ain't never done that. But Uncle Wining Boy he say he been down there and talked to them. You have to ask him about that part.

[BERNIECE *has entered from the front door.*]

BERNIECE: Maretha, you go on and get ready for me to do your hair.

[MARETHA *crosses to the steps.*]

Boy Willie, I done told you to leave my house. [*To* MARETHA.] Go on, Maretha.

[MARETHA *is hesitant about going up the stairs.*]

BOY WILLIE: Don't be scared. Here, I'll go up there with you. If we see Sutter's ghost I'll put a whupping on him. Come on, Uncle Boy Willie going with you.

[BOY WILLIE *and* MARETHA *exit up the stairs.*]

BERNIECE: Doaker—what is going on here?

DOAKER: I come home and him and Lymon was moving the piano. I told them to leave it over there till you got home. He went out and got that board and them wheels. He say he gonna take that piano out of here and ain't nobody gonna stop him.

BERNIECE: I ain't playing with Boy Willie. I got Crawley's gun upstairs. He don't know but I'm through with it. Where Lymon go?

DOAKER: Boy Willie sent him for some rope just before you come in.

BERNIECE: I ain't studying Boy Willie or Lymon—or the rope. Boy Willie ain't taking that piano out this house. That's all there is to it.

[BOY WILLIE *and* MARETHA *enter on the stairs.* MARETHA *carries a hot comb and a can of hair grease.* BOY WILLIE *crosses over and continues to screw the wheels on the board.*]

MARETHA: Mama, all the hair grease is gone. There ain't but this little bit left.

BERNIECE: [*Gives her a dollar.*] Here . . . run across the street and get another can. You come straight back, too. Don't you be playing around out there. And watch the cars. Be careful when you cross the street.

[MARETHA *exits out the front door.*]

Boy Willie, I done told you to leave my house.

BOY WILLIE: I ain't in you' house. I'm in Doaker's house. If he ask me to leave then I'll go on and leave. But consider me done left your part.

BERNIECE: Doaker, tell him to leave. Tell him to go on.

DOAKER: Boy Willie ain't done nothing for me to put him out of the house. I told you if you can't get along just go on and don't have nothing to do with each other.

BOY WILLIE: I ain't thinking about Berniece. [*He gets up and draws a line across the floor with his foot.*] There! Now I'm out of your part of the house. Consider me done left your part. Soon as Lymon come back with that rope. I'm gonna take that piano out of here and sell it.

BERNIECE: You ain't gonna touch that piano.

BOY WILLIE: Carry it out of here just as big and bold. Do like my daddy would have done come time to get Sutter's land.

BERNIECE: I got something to make you leave it over there.

BOY WILLIE: It's got to come better than this thirty-two-twenty.[5]

DOAKER: Why don't you stop all that! Boy Willie, go on and leave her alone. You know how Berniece get. Why you wanna sit there and pick with her?

BOY WILLIE: I ain't picking with her. I told her the truth. She the one talking about what she got. I just told her what she better have.

BERNIECE: That's alright, Doaker. Leave him alone.

BOY WILLIE: She trying to scare me. Hell, I ain't scared of dying. I look around and see people dying every day. You got to die to make room for somebody else. I had a dog that died. Wasn't nothing but a puppy. I picked it up and put it in a bag and carried it up there to Reverend C. L. Thompson's church. I carried it up there and prayed and asked Jesus to make it live like he did the man in the Bible.[6] I prayed real hard. Knelt down and everything. Say ask in Jesus' name. Well, I must have called Jesus' name two hundred times. I called his name till my mouth got sore. I got up and looked in the bag and the dog still dead. It ain't moved a muscle! I say, "Well, ain't nothing precious." And then I went out and killed me a cat. That's when I discovered the power of death. See, a nigger that ain't afraid to die is the worse kind of nigger for the white man. He can't hold that power over you. That's what I learned when I killed that cat. I got the power of death too. I can command him. I can call him up. The white man don't like to see that. He don't like for you to stand up and look him square in the eye and say, "I got it too." Then he got to deal with you square up.

BERNIECE: That's why I don't talk to him, Doaker. You try and talk to him and that's the only kind of stuff that comes out his mouth.

DOAKER: You say Avery went home to get his Bible?

BOY WILLIE: What Avery gonna do? Avery can't do nothing with me. I wish Avery would say something to me about this piano.

DOAKER: Berniece ain't said about that. Avery went home to get his Bible. He coming by to bless the house see if he can get rid of Sutter's ghost.

BOY WILLIE: Ain't nothing but a house full of ghosts down there at the church. What Avery look like chasing away somebody's ghost?

[MARETHA *enters the front door.*]

BERNIECE: Light that stove and set that comb over there to get hot. Get something to put around your shoulders.

BOY WILLIE: The Bible say an eye for an eye, a tooth for a tooth, and a life for a

---

5. That is, this thirty-two-twenty-caliber gun I'm (figuratively) holding.   6. Lazarus, who was raised from the dead by Jesus; see John 2.

life. Tit for tat. But you and Avery don't want to believe that. You gonna pass up that part and pretend it ain't in there. Everything else you gonna agree with. But if you gonna agree with part of it you got to agree with all of it. You can't do nothing halfway. You gonna go at the Bible halfway. You gonna act like that part ain't in there. But you pull out the Bible and open it and see what it say. Ask Avery. He a preacher. He'll tell you it's in there. He the Good Shepherd. Unless he gonna shepherd you to heaven with half the Bible.

BERNIECE: Maretha, bring me that comb. Make sure it's hot.

[MARETHA *brings the comb.* BERNIECE *begins to do her hair.*]

BOY WILLIE: I will say this for Avery. He done figured out a path to go through life. I don't agree with it. But he done fixed it so he can go right through it real smooth. Hell, he liable to end up with a million dollars that he done got from selling bread and wine.

MARETHA: OWWWWWW!

BERNIECE: Be still, Maretha. If you was a boy I wouldn't be going through this.

BOY WILLIE: Don't you tell that girl that. Why you wanna tell her that?

BERNIECE: You ain't got nothing to do with this child.

BOY WILLIE: Telling her you wished she was a boy. How's that gonna make her feel?

BERNIECE: Boy Willie, go on and leave me alone.

DOAKER: Why don't you leave her alone? What you got to pick with her for? Why don't you go on out and see what's out there in the streets? Have something to tell the fellows down home.

BOY WILLIE: I'm waiting on Lymon to get back with that truck. Why don't you go on out and see what's out there in the streets? You ain't got to work tomorrow. Talking about me . . . why don't you go out there? It's Friday night.

DOAKER: I got to stay around here and keep you all from killing one another.

BOY WILLIE: You ain't got to worry about me. I'm gonna be here just as long as it takes Lymon to get back here with that truck. You ought to be talking to Berniece. Sitting up there telling Maretha she wished she was a boy. What kind of thing is that to tell a child? If you want to tell her something tell her about that piano. You ain't even told her about that piano. Like that's something to be ashamed of. Like she supposed to go off and hide somewhere about that piano. You ought to mark down on the calendar the day that Papa Boy Charles brought that piano into the house. You ought to mark that day down and draw a circle around it . . . and every year when it come up throw a party. Have a celebration. If you did that she wouldn't have no problem in life. She could walk around here with her head held high. I'm talking about a big party!

Invite everybody! Mark that day down with a special meaning. That way she know where she at in the world. You got her going out here thinking she wrong in the world. Like there ain't no part of it belong to her.

BERNIECE: Let me take care of my child. When you get one of your own then you can teach it what you want to teach it.

[DOAKER *exits into his room.*]

BOY WILLIE: What I want to bring a child into this world for? Why I wanna bring somebody else into all this for? I'll tell you this . . . If I was Rockefeller[7] I'd have forty or fifty. I'd make one every day. Cause they gonna start out in life with all the advantages. I ain't got no advantages to offer nobody. Many is the time I looked at my daddy and seen him staring off at his hands. I got a little older I know what he was thinking. He sitting there saying, "I got these big old hands but what I'm gonna do with them? Best I can do is make a fifty-acre crop for Mr. Stovall. Got these big old hands capable of doing anything. I can take and build something with these hands. But where's the tools? All I got is these hands. Unless I go out here and kill me somebody and take what they got . . . it's a long row to hoe for me to get something of my own. So what I'm gonna do with these big old hands? What would you do?"

See now . . . if he had his own land he wouldn't have felt that way. If he had something under his feet that belonged to him he could stand up taller. That's what I'm talking about. Hell, the land is there for everybody. All you got to do is figure out how to get you a piece. Ain't no mystery to life. You just got to go out and meet it square on. If you got a piece of land you'll find everything else fall right into place. You can stand right up next to the white man and talk about the price of cotton . . . the weather, and anything else you want to talk about. If you teach that girl that she living at the bottom of life, she's gonna grow up and hate you.

BERNIECE: I'm gonna teach her the truth. That's just where she living. Only she ain't got to stay there. [*To* MARETHA.] Turn you' head over to the other side.

BOY WILLIE: This might be your bottom but it ain't mine. I'm living at the top of life. I ain't gonna just take my life and throw it away at the bottom. I'm in the world like everybody else. The way I see it everybody else got to come up a little taste to be where I am.

BERNIECE: You right at the bottom with the rest of us.

BOY WILLIE: I'll tell you this . . . and ain't a living soul can put a come back on it. If you believe that's where you at then you gonna act that way. If you act that way then that's where you gonna be. It's as simple as that. Ain't no mystery to life. I don't know how you come to believe that stuff. Crawley didn't think like that. He wasn't living at the bottom of life. Papa Boy Charles and Mama Ola wasn't living at the bottom of life. You ain't never heard them say nothing like that. They would have taken a strap to you if they heard you say something like that.

[DOAKER *enters from his room.*]

Hey, Doaker . . . Berniece say the colored folks is living at the bottom of life. I tried to tell her if she think that . . . that's where she gonna be. You think

7. John D. Rockefeller, father (1839–1937) and son (1847–1960), American oil magnates and philanthropists.

you living at the bottom of life? Is that how you see yourself?

DOAKER: I'm just living the best way I know how. I ain't thinking about no top or no bottom.

BOY WILLIE: That's what I tried to tell Berniece. I don't know where she got that from. That sound like something Avery would say. Avery think cause the white man give him a turkey for Thanksgiving that makes him better than everybody else. That's gonna raise him out of the bottom of life. I don't need nobody to give me a turkey. I can get my own turkey. All you have to do is get out my way. I'll get me two or three turkeys.

BERNIECE: You can't even get a chicken let alone two or three turkeys. Talking about get out your way. Ain't nobody in your way. [*To* MARETHA.] Straighten your head, Maretha! Don't be bending down like that. Hold your head up! [*To* BOY WILLIE.] All you got going for you is talk. You' whole life that's all you ever had going for you.

BOY WILLIE: See now . . . I'll tell you something about me. I done strung along and strung along. Going this way and that. Whatever way would lead me to a moment of peace. That's all I want. To be as easy with everything. But I wasn't born to that. I was born to a time of fire.

The world ain't wanted no part of me. I could see that since I was about seven. The world say it's better off without me. See, Berniece accept that. She trying to come up to where she can prove something to the world. Hell, the world a better place cause of me. I don't see it like Berniece. I got a heart that beats here and it beats just as loud as the next fellow's. Don't care if he black or white. Sometime it beats louder. When it beats louder, then everybody can hear it. Some people get scared of that. Like Berniece. Some people get scared to hear a nigger's heart beating. They think you ought to lay low with that heart. Make it beat quiet and go along with everything the way it is. But my mama ain't birthed me for nothing. So what I got to do? I got to mark my passing on the road. Just like you write on a tree, "Boy Willie was here."

That's all I'm trying to do with that piano. Trying to put my mark on the road. Like my daddy done. My heart say for me to sell that piano and get me some land so I can make a life for myself to live in my own way. Other than that I ain't thinking about nothing Berniece got to say.

[*There is a knock at the door.* BOY WILLIE *crosses to it and yanks it open thinking it is* LYMON. AVERY *enters. He carries a Bible.*]

BOY WILLIE: Where you been, nigger? Aw . . . I thought you was Lymon. Hey, Berniece, look who's here.

BERNIECE: Come on in, Avery. Don't you pay Boy Willie no mind.

BOY WILLIE: Hey . . . Hey, Avery . . . tell me this . . . can you get to heaven with half the Bible?

BERNIECE: Boy Willie . . . I done told you to leave me alone.

BOY WILLIE: I just ask the man a question. He can answer. He don't need you to speak for him. Avery . . . if you only believe on half the Bible and don't want to accept the other half . . . you think God let you in heaven? Or do you got to have the whole Bible? Tell Berniece . . . if you only believe in part of it . . .

when you see God he gonna ask you why you ain't believed in the other part
... then he gonna send you straight to Hell.

AVERY: You got to be born again. Jesus say unless a man be born again he cannot
come unto the Father and who so ever heareth my words and believeth them
not shall be cast into a fiery pit.

BOY WILLIE: That's what I was trying to tell Berniece. You got to believe in it all.
You can't go at nothing halfway. She think she going to heaven with half
the Bible. [*To* BERNIECE.] You hear that ... Jesus say you got to believe in it
all.

BERNIECE: You keep messing with me.

BOY WILLIE: I ain't thinking about you.

DOAKER: Come on in, Avery, and have a seat. Don't pay neither one of them no
mind. They been arguing all day.

BERNIECE: Come on in, Avery.

AVERY: How's everybody in here?

BERNIECE: Here, set this comb back over there on that stove. [*To* AVERY.] Don't pay
Boy Willie no mind. He been around here bothering me since I come home
from work.

BOY WILLIE: Boy Willie ain't bothering you. Boy Willie ain't bothering nobody.
I'm just waiting on Lymon to get back. I ain't thinking about you. You heard
the man say I was right and you still don't want to believe it. You just wanna
go and make up anythin'. Well there's Avery ... there's the preacher ... go
on and ask him.

AVERY: Berniece believe in the Bible. She been baptized.

BOY WILLIE: What about that part that say an eye for an eye a tooth for a tooth
and a life for a life? Ain't that in there?

DOAKER: What they say down there at the bank, Avery?

AVERY: Oh, they talked to me real nice. I told Berniece ... they say maybe they
let me borrow the money. They done talked to my boss down at work and
everything.

DOAKER: That's what I told Berniece. You working every day you ought to be able
to borrow some money.

AVERY: I'm getting more people in my congregation every day. Berniece says she
gonna be the Deaconess. I get me my church I can get married and settled
down. That's what I told Berniece.

DOAKER: That be nice. You all ought to go ahead and get married. Berniece don't
need to be by herself. I tell her that all the time.

BERNIECE: I ain't said nothing about getting married. I said I was thinking about
it.

DOAKER: Avery get him his church you all can make it nice. [*To* AVERY.] Berniece
said you was coming by to bless the house.

AVERY: Yeah, I done read up on my Bible. She asked me to come by and see if I
can get rid of Sutter's ghost.

BOY WILLIE: Ain't no ghost in this house. That's all in Berniece's head. Go on up
there and see if you see him. I'll give you a hundred dollars if you see him.
That's all in her imagination.

DOAKER: Well, let her find that out then. If Avery blessing the house is gonna make her feel better . . . what you got to do with it?

AVERY: Berniece say Maretha seen him too. I don't know, but I found a part in the Bible to bless the house. If he is here then that ought to make him go.

BOY WILLIE: You worse than Berniece believing all that stuff. Talking about . . . if he here. Go on up there and find out. I been up there I ain't seen him. If you reading from that Bible gonna make him leave out of Berniece imagination, well, you might be right. But if you talking about . . .

DOAKER: Boy Willie, why don't you just be quiet? Getting all up in the man's business. This ain't got nothing to do with you. Let him go ahead and do what he gonna do.

BOY WILLIE: I ain't stopping him. Avery ain't got no power to do nothing.

AVERY: Oh, I ain't got no power. God got the power! God got power over everything in His creation. God can do anything. God say, "As I commandeth so it shall be." God said, "Let there be light," and there was light.[8] He made the world in six days and rested on the seventh. God's got a wonderful power. He got power over life and death. Jesus raised Lazareth from the dead.[9] They was getting ready to bury him and Jesus told him say, "Rise up and walk." He got up and walked and the people made great rejoicing at the power of God. I ain't worried about him chasing away a little old ghost!

[*There is a knock at the door.* BOY WILLIE *goes to answer it.* LYMON *enters carrying a coil of rope.*]

BOY WILLIE: Where you been? I been waiting on you and you run off somewhere.

LYMON: I ran into Grace. I stopped and bought her drink. She say she gonna go to the picture show with me.

BOY WILLIE: I ain't thinking about no Grace nothing.

LYMON: Hi, Berniece.

BOY WILLIE: Give me that rope and get up on this side of the piano.

DOAKER: Boy Willie, don't start nothing now. Leave the piano alone.

BOY WILLIE: Get that board there, Lymon. Stay out of this, Doaker.

[BERNIECE *exits up the stairs.*]

DOAKER: You just can't take the piano. How you gonna take the piano? Berniece ain't said nothing about selling that piano.

BOY WILLIE: She ain't got to say nothing. Come on, Lymon. We got to lift one end at a time up on the board. You got to watch so that the board don't slide up under there.

LYMON: What we gonna do with the rope?

BOY WILLIE: Let me worry about the rope. You just get up on this side over here with me.

[BERNIECE *enters from the stairs. She has her hand in her pocket where she has Crawley's gun.*]

8. See Genesis 1.3.   9. See note 6, p. 1203.

AVERY: Boy Willie . . . Berniece . . . why don't you all sit down and talk this out now?

BERNIECE: Ain't nothing to talk out.

BOY WILLIE: I'm through talking to Berniece. You can talk to Berniece till you get blue in the face, and it don't make no difference. Get up on that side, Lymon. Throw that rope around there and tie it to the leg.

LYMON: Wait a minute . . . wait a minute, Boy Willie. Berniece got to say. Hey, Berniece . . . did you tell Boy Willie he could take this piano?

BERNIECE: Boy Willie ain't taking nothing out of my house but himself. Now you let him go ahead and try.

BOY WILLIE: Come on, Lymon, get up on this side with me.

[LYMON *stands undecided.*]

Come on, nigger! What you standing there for?

LYMON: Maybe Berniece is right, Boy Willie. Maybe you shouldn't sell it.

AVERY: You all ought to sit down and talk it out. See if you can come to an agreement.

DOAKER: That's what I been trying to tell them. Seem like one of them ought to respect the other one's wishes.

BERNIECE: I wish Boy Willie would go on and leave my house. That's what I wish. Now, he can respect that. Cause he's leaving here one way or another.

BOY WILLIE: What you mean one way or another? What's that supposed to mean? I ain't scared of no gun.

DOAKER: Come on, Berniece, leave him alone with that.

BOY WILLIE: I don't care what Berniece say. I'm selling my half. I can't help it if her half got to go along with it. It ain't like I'm trying to cheat her out of her half. Come on, Lymon.

LYMON: Berniece . . . I got to do this . . . Boy Willie say he gonna give you half of the money . . . say he want to get Sutter's land.

BERNIECE: Go on, Lymon. Just go on . . . I done told Boy Willie what to do.

BOY WILLIE: Here, Lymon . . . put that rope up over there.

LYMON: Boy Willie, you sure you want to do this? The way I figure it . . . I might be wrong . . . but I figure she gonna shoot you first.

BOY WILLIE: She just gonna have to shoot me.

BERNIECE: Maretha, get on out the way. Get her out the way, Doaker.

DOAKER: Go on, do what your mama told you.

BERNIECE: Put her in your room.

[MARETHA *exits to Doaker's room.* BOY WILLIE *and* LYMON *try to lift the piano. The door opens and* WINING BOY *enters. He has been drinking.*]

WINING BOY: Man, these niggers around here! I stopped down there at Seefus. . . . These folks standing around talking about Patchneck Red's coming. They jumping back and getting off the sidewalk talking about Patchneck Red this and Patchneck Red that. Come to find out . . . you know who they was talking about? Old John D. from up around Tyler! Used to run around with Otis Smith. He got everybody scared of him. Calling him Patchneck Red. They don't know I whupped the nigger's head in one time.

BOY WILLIE: Just make sure that board don't slide, Lymon.

LYMON: I got this side. You watch that side.

WINING BOY: Hey, Boy Willie, what you got? I know you got a pint stuck up in your coat.

BOY WILLIE: Wining Boy, get out the way!

WINING BOY: Hey, Doaker. What you got? Gimme a drink. I want a drink.

DOAKER: It look like you had enough of whatever it was. Come talking about "What you got?" You ought to be trying to find somewhere to lay down.

WINING BOY: I ain't worried about no place to lay down. I can always find me a place to lay down in Berniece's house. Ain't that right, Berniece?

BERNIECE: Wining Boy, sit down somewhere. You been out there drinking all day. Come in here smelling like an old polecat. Sit on down there, you don't need nothing to drink.

DOAKER: You know Berniece don't like all that drinking.

WINING BOY: I ain't disrespecting Berniece. Berniece, am I disrespecting you? I'm just trying to be nice. I been with strangers all day and they treated me like family. I come in here to family and you treat me like a stranger. I don't need your whiskey. I can buy my own. I wanted your company, not your whiskey.

DOAKER: Nigger, why don't you go upstairs and lay down? You don't need nothing to drink.

WINING BOY: I ain't thinking about no laying down. Me and Boy Willie fixing to party. Ain't that right, Boy Willie? Tell him. I'm fixing to play me some piano. Watch this.

[WINING BOY *sits down at the piano.*]

BOY WILLIE: Come on, Wining Boy! Me and Lymon fixing to move the piano.

WINING BOY: Wait a minute . . . wait a minute. This a song I wrote for Cleotha. I wrote this song in memory of Cleotha. [*He begins to play and sing.*]

> Hey little woman what's the matter with you now
> Had a storm last night and blowed the line all down
>
> Tell me how long
> Is I got to wait
> Can I get it now
> Or must I hesitate
>
> It takes a hesitating stocking in her hesitating shoe
> It takes a hesitating woman wanna sing the blues
>
> Tell me how long
> Is I got to wait
> Can I kiss you now
> Or must I hesitate.

BOY WILLIE: Come on, Wining Boy, get up! Get up, Wining Boy! Me and Lymon's fixing to move the piano.

WINING BOY: Naw . . . Naw . . . you ain't gonna move this piano!

BOY WILLIE: Get out the way, Wining Boy.

[WINING BOY, *his back to the piano, spreads his arms out over the piano.*]

WINING BOY: You ain't taking this piano out the house. You got to take me with it!

BOY WILLIE: Get on out the way, Wining Boy! Doaker get him!

[*There is a knock on the door.*]

BERNIECE: I got him, Doaker. Come on, Wining Boy. I done told Boy Willie he ain't taking the piano.

[BERNIECE *tries to take* WINING BOY *away from the piano.*]

WINING BOY: He got to take me with it!

[DOAKER *goes to answer the door.* GRACE *enters.*]

GRACE: Is Lymon here?

DOAKER: Lymon.

WINING BOY: He ain't taking that piano.

BERNIECE: I ain't gonna let him take it.

GRACE: I thought you was coming back. I ain't gonna sit in that truck all day.

LYMON: I told you I was coming back.

GRACE: [*Sees* BOY WILLIE.] Oh, hi, Boy Willie. Lymon told me you was gone back down South.

LYMON: I said he was going back. I didn't say he had left already.

GRACE: That's what you told me.

BERNIECE: Lymon, you got to take your company someplace else.

LYMON: Berniece, this is Grace. That there is Berniece. That's Boy Willie's sister.

GRACE: Nice to meet you. [*To* LYMON.] I ain't gonna sit out in that truck all day. You told me you was gonna take me to the movie.

LYMON: I told you I had something to do first. You supposed to wait on me.

BERNIECE: Lymon, just go on and leave. Take Grace or whoever with you. Just go on get out my house.

BOY WILLIE: You gonna help me move this piano first, nigger!

LYMON: [*To* GRACE.] I got to help Boy Willie move the piano first.

[*Everybody but* GRACE *suddenly senses* SUTTER's *presence.*]

GRACE: I ain't waiting on you. Told me you was coming right back. Now you got to move a piano. You just like all the other men. [GRACE *now senses something.*] Something ain't right here. I knew I shouldn't have come back up in this house. [GRACE *exits.*]

LYMON: Hey, Grace! I'll be right back, Boy Willie.

BOY WILLIE: Where you going, nigger?

LYMON: I'll be back. I got to take Grace home.

BOY WILLIE: Come on, let's move the piano first!

LYMON: I got to take Grace home. I told you I'll be back.

[LYMON *exits.* BOY WILLIE *exits and calls after him.*]

BOY WILLIE: Come on, Lymon! Hey . . . Lymon! Lymon . . . come on!

[*Again, the presence of* SUTTER *is felt.*]

WINING BOY: Hey, Doaker, did you feel that? Hey, Berniece . . . did you get cold?
Hey, Doaker . . .
DOAKER: What you calling me for?
WINING BOY: I believe that's Sutter.
DOAKER: Well, let him stay up there. As long as he don't mess with me.
BERNIECE: Avery, go on and bless the house.
DOAKER: You need to bless that piano. That's what you need to bless. It ain't done
nothing but cause trouble. If you gonna bless anything go on and bless that.
WINING BOY: Hey, Doaker, if he gonna bless something let him bless everything.
The kitchen . . . the upstairs. Go on and bless it all.
BOY WILLIE: Ain't no ghost in this house. He need to bless Berniece's head. That's
what he need to bless.
AVERY: Seem like that piano's causing all the trouble. I can bless that. Berniece,
put me some water in that bottle.

[AVERY *takes a small bottle from his pocket and hands it to* BERNIECE, *who goes
into the kitchen to get water.* AVERY *takes a candle from his pocket and lights
it. He gives it to* BERNIECE *as she gives him the water.*]

Hold this candle. Whatever you do make sure it don't go out.
O Holy Father we gather here this evening in the Holy Name to cast out
the spirit of one James Sutter. May this vial of water be empowered with thy
spirit. May each drop of it be a weapon and a shield against the presence of
all evil and may it be a cleansing and blessing of this humble abode.
Just as Our Father taught us how to pray so He say, "I will prepare a table
for you in the midst of mine enemies," and in His hands we place ourselves
to come unto his presence. Where there is Good so shall it cause Evil to scatter
to the Four Winds. [*He throws water at the piano at each commandment.*] Get
thee behind me, Satan! Get thee behind the face of Righteousness as we Glo-
rify His Holy Name! Get thee behind the Hammer of Truth that breaketh
down the Wall of Falsehood! Father. Father. Praise. Praise. We ask in Jesus'
name and call forth the power of the Holy Spirit as it is written. . . . [*He opens
the Bible and reads from it.*] I will sprinkle clean water upon thee and ye shall
be clean.
BOY WILLIE: All this old preaching stuff. Hell, just tell him to leave.

[AVERY *continues reading throughout* BOY WILLIE's *outburst.*]

AVERY: I will sprinkle clean water upon you and you shall be clean: from all your
uncleanliness, and from all your idols, will I cleanse you. A new heart also
will I give you, and a new spirit will I put within you: and I will take out of
your flesh the heart of stone, and I will give you a heart of flesh. And I will

put my spirit within you, and cause you to walk in my statutes, and ye shall keep my judgments, and do them.

[BOY WILLIE *grabs a pot of water from the stove and begins to fling it around the room.*]

BOY WILLIE: Hey Sutter! Sutter! Get your ass out this house! Sutter! Come on and get some of this water! You done drowned in the well, come on and get some more of this water!

[BOY WILLIE *is working himself into a frenzy as he* runs around the room throwing water and calling SUTTER's *name.* AVERY *continues reading.*]

BOY WILLIE: Come on, Sutter! [*He starts up the stairs.*] Come on, get some water! Come on, Sutter!

[*The sound of* SUTTER's GHOST *is heard. As* BOY WILLIE *approaches the steps he is suddenly thrown back by the unseen force, which is choking him. As he struggles he frees himself, then dashes up the stairs.*]

BOY WILLIE: Come on, Sutter!

AVERY: [*Continuing.*] A new heart also will I give you and a new spirit will I put within you: and I will take out of your flesh the heart of stone, and I will give you a heart of flesh. And I will put my spirit within you, and cause you to walk in my statutes, and ye shall keep my judgments, and do them.

[*There are loud sounds heard from upstairs as* BOY WILLIE *begins to wrestle with* SUTTER's GHOST. *It is a life-and-death struggle fraught with perils and faultless terror.* BOY WILLIE *is thrown down the stairs.* AVERY *is stunned into silence.* BOY WILLIE *picks himself up and dashes back upstairs.*]

AVERY: Berniece, I can't do it.

[*There are more sounds heard from upstairs.* DOAKER *and* WINING BOY *stare at one another in stunned disbelief. It is in this moment, from somewhere old, that* BERNIECE *realizes what she must do. She crosses to the piano. She begins to play. The song is found piece by piece. It is an old urge to song that is both a commandment and a plea. With each repetition it gains in strength. It is intended as an exorcism and a dressing for battle. A rustle of wind blowing across two continents.*]

BERNIECE: [*Singing.*]

I want you to help me
I want you to help me
I want you to help me
I want you to help me
I want you to help me
I want you to help me
Mama Berniece

I want you to help me
Mama Esther
I want you to help me
Papa Boy Charles
I want you to help me
Mama Ola
I want you to help me

I want you to help me
I want you to help me
I want you to help me
I want you to help me
I want you to help me
I want you to help me
I want you to help me
I want you to help me

[*The sound of a train approaching is heard. The noise upstairs subsides.*]

BOY WILLIE: Come on, Sutter! Come back, Sutter!

[BERNIECE *begins to chant:*]

BERNIECE:

Thank you.
Thank you.
Thank you.

[*A calm comes over the house.* MARETHA *enters from* DOAKER'S *room.* BOY WILLIE *enters on the stairs. He pauses a moment to watch* BERNIECE *at the piano.*]

BERNIECE:

Thank you.
Thank you.
Thank you.

BOY WILLIE: Wining Boy, you ready to go back down home? Hey, Doaker, what time the train leave?
DOAKER: You still got time to make it.

[MARETHA *crosses and embraces* BOY WILLIE.]

BOY WILLIE: Hey Berniece . . . if you and Maretha don't keep playing on that piano . . . ain't no telling . . . me and Sutter both liable to be back. [*He exits.*]
BERNIECE: Thank you.

[*The lights go down to black.*]

1987

QUESTIONS

1. List all the ways that the onstage piano stands for the past. What different pasts does it represent for different characters? What, specifically, do the carvings on the piano represent? How important is the past ownership of the piano? the way the family acquired it? In what ways do different characters' attitudes toward the piano reveal their sense of the past? Beyond making the piano central visually on the stage, what other staging strategies would you use (if you were producing the play) to suggest its function as symbol and as a guide to character and theme?
2. Why is Boy Willie portrayed in the first scene as so loud and intrusive? What aspects of his character does the opening scene illustrate? What other aspects of his character are revealed later? What does "land" represent to Boy Willie?
3. What functions does Maretha have in the play? In what ways is her age important?
4. In what ways is geography important to the play? What does "Mississippi" represent to the different characters? What does "Pittsburgh" represent to the different characters? What does Doaker's continued employment with the railroad symbolize?
5. What does the truckload of watermelons represent to Boy Willie? to Lymon? In what senses does the offstage presence of the watermelons keep time for the play and suggest exactly where the plot is? Describe the rising action and climax of the play in relation to the truck's load.
6. Clearly the past—and an effort to come to terms with it—dominates Berniece's thinking, whereas Boy Willie believes he can transcend the past if he can reverse the historic sense of racial ownership. Describe the complications of this tension as they develop throughout the play. Where do other characters fit into the opposition. What role does Doaker perform?
7. What plot functions does Grace perform? In what ways does her presence complicate the play's gender themes?
8. How do the themes of past and place interrelate in the play?
9. What does "Lesson" in the title mean? What lesson does the piano teach each of the characters?

WRITING SUGGESTIONS

1. Pretend you are Boy Willie. Write a five-hundred-word "newsy" letter to a friend back in Mississippi describing the conflict with Berniece. Be sure to provide a full and explicit defense of Boy Willie's motives and desires and his version of what Berniece wants.
2. Pretend you are Berniece. Write a five-hundred-word letter to a friend explaining fully why it is so important to keep the piano in the family.
3. Pretend you are Maretha. In a three-hundred-word letter to a school friend, describe your understanding of the conflict between Boy Willie and Berniece.
4. Pretend you are Lymon. In a two-hundred-word letter to a friend back in Mississippi, explain why you are so determined to find a new life in Pittsburgh and explain the difference between your values and Boy Willie's.

Exploring Contexts

25

THE AUTHOR'S WORK AS CONTEXT: WILLIAM SHAKESPEARE

When we read, we inevitably compare. We compare the writer's style to the styles of other writers; we compare characters within a story or play to one another and to people we know; we compare our life experiences to the many imaginary experiences that unfold before us as we read. Our interpretations of literature are fueled by such comparisons.

Reading several works by a single author is one of the most rewarding and enlightening types of comparison we can employ as active readers of literature. Such comparisons serve a variety of purposes: they help us develop a sense of the overall shape of the writer's work (that is, the writer's oeuvre, or canon); they reveal the kinds of characters, plots, and dramatic situations the author likes to create; they offer a glimpse into the author's particular way of looking at the world. At the same time, such comparisons can enrich our understanding of any one work by drawing our attention to features we might not have thought much about otherwise.

William Shakespeare

This chapter offers you the opportunity to compare two plays by one of history's most vital and versatile playwrights: William Shakespeare. Shakespeare is a particularly enticing subject for this kind of comparative study in part because we know so little about him. While we can ease and enhance our reading of many writers by studying the letters, essays, diaries, and other documents in which the writers comment directly on their lives and works, Shakespeare left behind no such record. The only records that exist are official ones—marriage licenses, property deeds, and wills.

Shakespeare's birthplace

Those records tell a brief story. Shakespeare's origins were humble: his grandfather, Richard, rented the land he farmed, near the town of Stratford-upon-Avon. Richard's son, John, married the daughter of one of Richard's former landlords and moved to town. There he became a tradesman prosperous and respected enough both to buy quite a bit of property and to hold several civic offices, including that of mayor. The family's star was on the rise by the time William was born (sometime in April 1564). Though most likely neither of Shakespeare's parents could read or write (certainly they had no formal schooling), his father's involvement in city government brought with it the privilege of enrolling William in the local free grammar school. Here Shakespeare learned how to read and write, not only in English but also in Latin and Greek. His schoolmasters also probably required him to read such standard classical works as Ovid's *Metamorphoses* and the plays of Plautus and Terence (which greatly influenced the plays he would later write). In 1582, Shakespeare married Anne Hathaway, the daughter of a local farmer; in the next three years, the couple had three children, including a set of twins.

From the time of the twins' birth in 1585 until 1592, Shakespeare's life becomes—for us—a blank: all we know is that by the latter date he was a successful actor and playwright spending most of his time in London. (We know this, in part, because Shakespeare was prominent enough to be called an "upstart crow" in a book published by a rival playwright in 1592; apparently, this London-born, university-educated author felt a bit threatened by the

> *The man keeps his mask firmly in place; apart from the works themselves there is only silence.*
>
> —SAMUEL SCHOENBAUM

undereducated provincial.) Though, in 1594, the "upstart crow" achieved renown as a poet by publishing two lengthy narrative poems (*Venus and Adonis* and *The Rape of Lucrece*), his career from this time until his death centered mainly on his work with the

The Globe Theater

Lord Chamberlain's (later King's) Men—one of the two most prominent acting companies of his day. Shakespeare's work with the company was multifaceted: an actor with the troupe and its chief dramatist, he was also a shareholder who helped manage the troupe's affairs (including the building of the Globe Theater, on the South Bank of the Thames River, in 1599). Being a shareholder ensured that he prospered along with the company (especially after they secured the patronage of the king in 1603). As a result, Shakespeare enjoyed a level of economic prosperity and a kind of status that wouldn't have been possible to a mere actor, playwright, or poet. The Crown granted Shakespeare's father (and thus the playwright) the title of "gentleman" in the late 1590s. And at his death in 1616, Shakespeare left his family substantial property in both London and Stratford (where the family had continued to live).

Such facts remind us that Shakespeare was, after all, a real and in some ways rather ordinary person—who ultimately convinced audiences and rivals alike that he was more than an "upstart crow," but who did not, as a recent biographer reminds us, "in his own day inspire the mysterious veneration that afterwards came to surround him." These mundane facts tell us almost nothing, however, about the man's or the artist's inner life—his personal opinions, his motives, his loves, his dislikes, his politics, his "philosophy." These we can only infer, guess at, or imagine by reading and comparing his plays and poems. Luckily, Shakespeare left us a lot of these, including 154 sonnets (some of which are included in the poetry section of this book) and at least thirty-eight plays. (Scholars believe Shakespeare cowrote at least one more play, and others may yet be discovered and authenticated.)

Given that the plays include thirteen comedies, ten tragedies, ten English histories, and five romances, variety is a distinctive feature of Shakespeare's work as a playwright. It is fitting, then, that the two plays included in this chapter—A Midsummer Night's Dream and Hamlet—seem, at first glance, so different. A Midsummer Night's Dream, written around 1595, is generally considered one of the last of Shakespeare's "apprentice" plays—the work of a young writer just beginning to find his own voice and dramatic style, still quite dependent on classical models. Though written only a few years later (ca. 1599–1601), Hamlet is nonetheless regarded as one of the greatest works of a seasoned writer. Differences proliferate: Dream, a comedy, culminates in marriage (several marriages, in fact); Hamlet, a tragedy, concludes with the death and destruction of an entire royal family. Dream is among Shakespeare's shortest plays; Hamlet, among his longest. Hamlet focuses squarely—almost relentlessly—on its title character, whom we leave the play feeling that we know inside and out. Dream, in contrast, flits among many characters. Though we may fall in love with some of them, we probably will not feel that we truly know them. (Indeed, part of the play's humor comes from our having as hard a time as the characters do remembering who is who and who loves whom.)

But while the plays have important and revealing differences, they have equally significant similarities, and by attending to these similarities we may come to understand and appreciate Shakespeare's particular way of looking at the world. To begin with, we may approach such similarities (within these or any plays) by concentrating on their basic elements, looking for patterns in character, setting, structure, tone, and theme (remembering, of course, that these elements ultimately work together in our experience of any one play).

In thinking about character, for example, notice that both the protagonists and the antagonists of *A Midsummer Night's Dream* and *Hamlet* are persons of high birth and position. These characters' choices and behavior deeply affect the communities that they lead. In fact, both plays repeatedly remind us of the general effects and communal significance of such characters' actions, as when, for example, we are told in *A Midsummer Night's Dream* of the "progeny of evils" that come of the "debate" and "dissension" between Titania and Oberon (2.1.115–16). Like all Shakespeare's plays, this comedy and tragedy both take for granted the idea that "on [a leader's] choice depends / The safety and health of th[e] whole state" (*Hamlet* 2.3.20–21), and both trace the effects of the particular, often bad, choices made by kings, princes, and dukes.

Shakespeare and his contemporaries often compared the relationship between a king and his subjects to that between a father and his children or between a husband and his wife. For example, an early Shakespeare comedy, *The Taming of the Shrew,* concludes with a speech in which the tamed shrew declares, "Thy husband is thy lord, thy life, thy keeper, / Thy head, thy sovereign." Building on this idea, she argues both that a woman's duty to her husband is the same "as the subject owes the prince" and that a woman who refuses to obey her husband is exactly like "a foul contending rebel / And graceless traitor." We can see similar analogies at work in *A Midsummer Night's Dream* and *Hamlet:* one begins with a duke and a father provoking a group of young Athenians to rebel against them; the other shows us a son and prince struggling to choose the right response to the murder of a father who was also a king.

We pay attention to the effects of these high-born characters on their environments in part because Shakespeare's plays also include characters who occupy positions much lower on the social scale than the main characters do. In addition to Titania, Oberon, Theseus, and Hippolyta (rulers of the divine and human realms), *A Midsummer Night's Dream* introduces us to the Athenian craftsmen (or "mechanicals") led by the fittingly named Bottom. And while *Hamlet* focuses predominantly on members of the Danish royal court, one of the most memorable scenes in the play features a lowly gravedigger and the skeletal remains of a court jester named Yorick. As a result, the two plays demonstrate Shakespeare's tendency to people his plays with a socially diverse cast of characters and to thereby create a socially inclusive dramatic world.

As inclusive as Shakespeare's dramatic world is, it is far from *democratic* (as the speech from *The Taming of the Shrew* suggests). As you read more plays by Shakespeare, you will probably become more attuned to the different ways in which they depict "high" and "low" characters. *A Midsummer Night's Dream* is typical, for example, in the way it associates socially low characters with **low** or **physical comedy** (as opposed to **high** or **verbal comedy**). Bottom, after all, wears an ass's head for much of the play. Yet Bottom is also typical of Shakespeare's socially humble characters because he possesses a kind of wisdom lacking in his social betters. Certainly, he has more imagination and a much greater appreciation of art's power than Duke Theseus, who refuses to believe in "fables," thinks lovers and poets are no better than madmen (5.1.3), and rather heartlessly ridicules the mechanicals' artistic efforts.

Despite the tendency to distinguish high from low, then, Shakespearean drama draws our attention to fundamental human experiences that cut across social lines. *A Midsummer Night's Dream* reminds us that a fairy queen is no more immune to love's magic or

Bottom, from *Midsummer Night's Dream*

foolishness than the lowliest of mortals; *Hamlet,* that a king's life lasts no longer than a court jester's. The joys of love, the pain of death—these experiences link us and remind us of our common humanity.

Shakespeare suggests such links, in part, by structuring each play so that the main plot is complemented by parallel, yet often contrasting, secondary plots. *A Midsummer Night's Dream* offers at least four plots, each featuring a pair of lovers whose happiness is, or has been, threatened by their own failures to understand each other or by others' opposition to their relationship. *Hamlet* revolves around three intersecting, but distinct, plots featuring Hamlet, Laertes, and Fortinbras—three very different young men who must each figure out how to respond to, and perhaps avenge, his father's murder. In these, as in other Shakespeare plays, the secondary plots can be divided into **underplots,** which are romantic or parodic versions of the main plot, and **overplots,** which foreground its political dimensions. In *A Midsummer Night's Dream,* Bottom becomes the protagonist of the underplot, Theseus and Hippolyta (and, perhaps, Titania and Oberon) of the overplot(s). In *Hamlet,* the underplot focuses on Laertes; the overplot, on Fortinbras. However, all the secondary plots encourage us (and sometimes, as in *Hamlet,* the characters themselves) to compare the way different people handle similar situations and thus to evaluate various choices, various responses. The parallel plots serve simultaneously as a structural device, a potent means of characterization, and a way of drawing our attention to general issues and themes.

Reading *Hamlet* and *A Midsummer Night's Dream* side by side also may help us appreciate the tonal complexity of Shakespeare's plays—their incorporation of both comic and tragic elements. While *A Midsummer Night's Dream* plunges us into a nighttime world dominated by the intertwining forces of magic, love, and humor, it also continually reminds us of the dangerous aspects of the night, of the struggles that human beings endure in their pursuit of love and happiness, of the brevity and fragility of human joy and human life, of what Hamlet calls the "thousand natural shocks / That flesh is

Sir Laurence Olivier as Hamlet

heir to" (3.1.62–63). The specter of death hovers in the background of *A Midsummer Night's Dream* as surely as it occupies the foreground of *Hamlet*. And while *Hamlet*, like most tragedies, focuses primarily on mortality, violence, and time's destructive force, it also shows us the comic side of the human condition. In fact, one of the things that makes Hamlet such a sympathetic character is his sense of humor; he proves so adept at wordplay that we wish he could stick to that instead of resorting to swordplay.

Turning from tone to theme, we find that both *Hamlet* and *A Midsummer Night's Dream* say something about the order of things and the rhythm of life. Although *Hamlet* ends with a body-strewn stage, the play encourages us to see those deaths as the necessary prelude to a restoration of order and health to a kingdom diseased and disordered as a result of a sovereign's choices. For Claudius's crimes ultimately infect and poison everything and everyone, even innocent bystanders like Ophelia. Both to us and to Hamlet, Claudius's reign represents the triumph of humanity's worst impulses. By embracing his role as heaven's "scourge and minister" even at the risk of his own life (3.4.179), however, Hamlet reaffirms our faith in humanity's noblest qualities as he sets right all that is "rotten in Denmark" (1.4.90). In *A Midsummer Night's Dream*, we again see the actions of a sovereign turn the world upside down: the young rebel against the old, women chase men, old friends turn on each other, an ass consorts with a queen. Clearly, the kinds of dissension and disorder at work in *A Midsummer Night's Dream* make us laugh, while those in *Hamlet* make us cringe or cry. Yet the rhythm of both plays turns out to be surprisingly similar, tracing the movement from disorder to order, from dissension to harmony. In the process, both plays ask us to think about the nature and causes of social, political, and moral disorder, of dissension within states and families.

As you read *Hamlet* and *A Midsummer Night's Dream*, you will discover many more parallels of theme, character, setting, and structure whose significance you will want to ponder and investigate. But you may also want to think about another, perhaps more elusive element: language. Shakespeare is justly celebrated for his use of language, and we pay homage to it, unwittingly or not, every time we use any one of the many idiomatic expressions that originated in the plays. (If, for example, you conclude that Shakespeare is "Greek to me," you have proven otherwise by quoting directly from his play *Julius Caesar*.) In Shakespearean drama, language is never an end in itself but instead establishes character and tone, structures the play, shapes our emotional response to it, and enunciates theme. *Hamlet*, for example, characterizes both Polonius and Hamlet in part through their penchant for wordplay. But as Polonius suggests, Hamlet's wordplay is "pregnant" with significance in a way that his own is not (2.2.201). While Polonius's use of language arguably demonstrates both his facile nature and his fondness for sham and trickery, Hamlet's displays his preoccupation with probing beneath the surface of language and much else.

> *Shakespeare's plays are not in the rigorous critical sense either tragedies or comedies, but compositions of a distinct kind; exhibiting the real state of sublunary nature, which partakes of good and evil, joy and sorrow.*
>
> —SAMUEL JOHNSON

> *[W]hen you are really reading* Hamlet, *the action and the characters are not something which you conceive apart from the words; you apprehend them . . . in the words, and the words are expressions of them.*
>
> —A. C. BRADLEY

In both *Hamlet* and *A Midsummer Night's Dream* the musical and visual qualities of Shakespeare's language are integral to its meaning. Though written mainly in verse, Shakespeare's plays include prose passages; and though most of the poetry is *blank verse* (unrhymed iambic pentameter), Shakespeare also uses rhyme and rhythmic variation to great effect. As you read the plays, then, you will want to pay attention to the texture and rhythm of the language—to the effect of *sound* on *sense.* You will also want to attend to the way Shakespeare uses language to appeal to your eye, as well as your ear. For visual imagery, like sound, consistently serves both structural and thematic ends, linking various moments and ideas, actions and themes. In *A Midsummer Night's Dream*, for example, characters frequently refer to their eyes. Such references begin in the very first scene: when Hermia wishes that her father "look'd but with my eyes," Theseus responds that "your eyes must with his judgment look" (lines 56–57). These lines prepare us for a play in which eyes will play a major part, in which love and vision tend to go hand in hand, in which both love and vision often conflict with "judgment." Oberon's love potion, after all, works through the eyes, while Puck initially misapplies the potion largely because his eyes have deceived him. The characters' talk of eyes thus connects directly to the plot; through both, the play asks us to think about the tremendous power of vision and the dangers of relying on it.

Reading many plays by a single playwright will help you better recognize stylistic patterns as well as structural and thematic ones within each play: each additional Shakespeare play you read will bring you closer to an understanding and appreciation of his unique way of looking at the world and of the way his views and his technique changed over time. You will gain a sense of Shakespeare's development as a dramatist even as, ideally, you develop your own skills as a reader of drama.

WILLIAM SHAKESPEARE

A Midsummer Night's Dream[1]

CHARACTERS

THESEUS, *Duke of Athens*

EGEUS, *father to Hermia*

LYSANDER,   } *in love with Hermia*
DEMETRIUS,   }

PHILOSTRATE, *Master of the Revels to Theseus*

QUINCE, *a carpenter*

SNUG, *a joiner*

BOTTOM, *a weaver*

FLUTE, *a bellows-maker*

SNOUT, *a tinker*

STARVELING, *a tailor*

HIPPOLYTA, *Queen of the Amazons, betrothed to Theseus*

HERMIA, *daughter to Egeus, in love with Lysander*

HELENA, *in love with Demetrius*

OBERON, *King of the Fairies*

TITANIA, *Queen of the Fairies*

PUCK, *or Robin Goodfellow*

PEASEBLOSSOM,   }
COBWEB,   } *fairies*
MOTH,   }
MUSTARDSEED,   }

Other FAIRIES *attending their king and queen*

ATTENDANTS *on Theseus and Hippolyta*

---

1. Edited and annotated by David Bevington (except footnotes set in brackets).

SCENE: *Athens, and a wood near it.*

ACT I

SCENE 1[2]

Enter THESEUS, HIPPOLYTA, PHILOSTRATE, *with others.*

THESEUS: Now, fair Hippolyta, our nuptial hour
  Draws on apace. Four happy days bring in
  Another moon; but, O, methinks, how slow
  This old moon wanes! She lingers[3] my desires,
  Like to a step-dame or a dowager[4]   5
  Long withering out a young man's revenue.
HIPPOLYTA: Four days will quickly steep themselves in night,
  Four nights will quickly dream away the time;
  And then the moon, like to a silver bow
  New-bent in heaven, shall behold the night   10
  Of our solemnities.
THESEUS: Go, Philostrate,
  Stir up the Athenian youth to merriments,
  Awake the pert and nimble spirit of mirth,
  Turn melancholy forth to funerals;
  The pale companion is not for our pomp.[5]   *[Exit* PHILOSTRATE.]   15
  Hippolyta, I woo'd thee with my sword,[6]
  And won thy love doing thee injuries;
  But I will wed thee in another key,
  With pomp, with triumph,[7] and with reveling.

       [Enter EGEUS *and his daughter* HERMIA, *and* LYSANDER, *and* DEMETRIUS.]

EGEUS: Happy be Theseus, our renowned Duke!   20
THESEUS: Thanks, good Egeus. What's the news with thee?
EGEUS: Full of vexation come I, with complaint
  Against my child, my daughter Hermia.
  Stand forth, Demetrius. My noble lord,
  This man hath my consent to marry her.   25
  Stand forth, Lysander. And, my gracious Duke,
  This man hath bewitch'd the bosom of my child.
  Thou, thou, Lysander, thou hast given her rhymes
  And interchang'd love-tokens with my child.
  Thou hast by moonlight at her window sung   30

---

2. Location: Athens. The palace of Theseus.   3. Lengthens, protracts.   4. Widow with a jointure or dower. *Step-dame:* stepmother.   5. Ceremonial magnificence. *Companion:* fellow.   6. That is, in a military engagement against the Amazons, when Hippolyta was taken captive.   7. Public festivity.

With feigning[8] voice verses of feigning love,
And stol'n the impression of her fantasy[9]
With bracelets of thy hair, rings, gauds, conceits,[1]
Knacks,[2] trifles, nosegays, sweetmeats—messengers
35   Of strong prevailment in unhardened youth.
With cunning hast thou filch'd my daughter's heart,
Turn'd her obedience, which is due to me,
To stubborn harshness. And, my gracious Duke,
Be it so she will not here before your Grace
40   Consent to marry with Demetrius,
I beg the ancient privilege of Athens:
As she is mine, I may dispose of her,
Which shall be either to this gentleman
Or to her death, according to our law
45   Immediately[3] provided in that case.
THESEUS: What say you, Hermia? Be advis'd, fair maid.
To you your father should be as a god—
One that compos'd your beauties, yea, and one
To whom you are but as a form in wax
50   By him imprinted and within his power
To leave the figure or disfigure[4] it.
Demetrius is a worthy gentleman.
HERMIA: So is Lysander.
THESEUS: In himself he is;
But in this kind, wanting your father's voice,[5]
55   The other must be held the worthier.
HERMIA: I would my father look'd but with my eyes.
THESEUS: Rather your eyes must with his judgment look.
HERMIA: I do entreat your Grace to pardon me.
I know not by what power I am made bold,
60   Nor how it may concern[6] my modesty,
In such a presence here to plead my thoughts;
But I beseech your Grace that I may know
The worst that may befall me in this case,
If I refuse to wed Demetrius.
65   THESEUS: Either to die the death, or to abjure
Forever the society of men.
Therefore, fair Hermia, question your desires,
Know of your youth, examine well your blood,[7]
Whether, if you yield not to your father's choice,
70   You can endure the livery[8] of a nun,

---

8. (1) Counterfeiting; (2) faining, desirous.   9. Made her fall in love with you (imprinting your image on her imagination) by stealthy and dishonest means.   1. Fanciful trifles. *Gauds:* playthings.
2. Knickknacks.   3. Expressly.   4. Obliterate. *Leave:* that is, leave unaltered.   5. Approval. *Kind:* respect. *Wanting:* lacking.   6. Befit.   7. Passions.   8. Habit.

For aye to be in shady cloister mew'd,[9]
To live a barren sister all your life,
Chanting faint hymns to the cold fruitless moon.
Thrice blessed they that master so their blood
To undergo such maiden pilgrimage;   75
But earthlier happy[1] is the rose distill'd,
Than that which withering on the virgin thorn
Grows, lives, and dies in single blessedness.
HERMIA: So will I grow, so live, so die, my lord,
Ere I will yield my virgin patent[2] up   80
Unto his lordship, whose unwished yoke
My soul consents not to give sovereignty.
THESEUS: Take time to pause; and, by the next new moon—
The sealing-day betwixt my love and me,
For everlasting bond of fellowship—   85
Upon that day either prepare to die
For disobedience to your father's will,
Or[3] else to wed Demetrius, as he would,
Or on Diana's altar to protest[4]
For aye austerity and single life.   90
DEMETRIUS: Relent, sweet Hermia, and, Lysander, yield
Thy crazed[5] title to my certain right.
LYSANDER: You have her father's love, Demetrius;
Let me have Hermia's. Do you marry him.
EGEUS: Scornful Lysander! True, he hath my love,   95
And what is mine my love shall render him.
And she is mine, and all my right of her
I do estate unto[6] Demetrius.
LYSANDER: I am, my lord, as well deriv'd[7] as he,
As well possess'd;[8] my love is more than his;   100
My fortunes every way as fairly[9] rank'd,
If not with vantage,[1] as Demetrius';
And, which is more than all these boasts can be,
I am belov'd of beauteous Hermia.
Why should not I then prosecute my right?   105
Demetrius, I'll avouch it to his head,[2]
Made love to Nedar's daughter, Helena,
And won her soul; and she, sweet lady, dotes,
Devoutly dotes, dotes in idolatry,
Upon this spotted[3] and inconstant man.   110
THESEUS: I must confess that I have heard so much,

9. Shut in (said of a hawk, poultry, and so on). *Aye:* ever.   1. Happier as respects this world.   2. Privilege.   3. Either.   4. Vow.   5. Cracked, unsound.   6. Settle or bestow upon.   7. Descended; that is, as well born.   8. Endowed with wealth.   9. Handsomely.   1. Superiority.   2. That is, face.   3. That is, morally stained.

And with Demetrius thought to have spoke thereof;
But, being over-full of self-affairs,
My mind did lose it. But, Demetrius, come,
115 And come, Egeus, you shall go with me;
I have some private schooling for you both.
For you, fair Hermia, look you arm[4] yourself
To fit your fancies[5] to your father's will;
Or else the law of Athens yields you up—
120 Which by no means we may extenuate[6]—
To death, or to a vow of single life.
Come, my Hippolyta. What cheer, my love?
Demetrius and Egeus, go[7] along.
I must employ you in some business
125 Against[8] our nuptial, and confer with you
Of something nearly that[9] concerns yourselves.
EGEUS: With duty and desire we follow you.

                        [Exeunt (all but LYSANDER *and* HERMIA*).]*

LYSANDER: How now, my love, why is your cheek so pale?
    How chance the roses there do fade so fast?
130 HERMIA: Belike[1] for want of rain, which I could well
    Beteem[2] them from the tempest of my eyes.
LYSANDER: Ay me! For aught that I could ever read,
    Could ever hear by tale or history,
    The course of true love never did run smooth;
135 But either it was different in blood[3]—
HERMIA: O cross,[4] too high to be enthrall'd to low!
LYSANDER: Or else misgraffed[5] in respect of years—
HERMIA: O spite, too old to be engag'd to young!
LYSANDER: Or else it stood upon the choice of friends[6]—
140 HERMIA: O hell, to choose love by another's eyes!
LYSANDER: Or, if there were a sympathy in choice,
    War, death, or sickness did lay siege to it,
    Making it momentany[7] as a sound,
    Swift as a shadow, short as any dream,
145 Brief as the lightning in the collied[8] night,
    That, in a spleen, unfolds[9] both heaven and earth,
    And ere a man hath power to say "Behold!"
    The jaws of darkness do devour it up.
    So quick bright things come to confusion.[1]

---

4. Take care you prepare.   5. Likings, thoughts of love.   6. Mitigate.   7. That is, come.   8. In preparation for.   9. That closely.   1. Very likely.   2. Grant, afford.   3. Hereditary station. 4. Vexation.   5. Ill grafted, badly matched.   6. Relatives.   7. Lasting but a moment.   8. Blackened (as with coal dust), darkened.   9. Discloses. *In a spleen:* in a swift impulse, in a violent flash. 1. Ruin. *Quick:* quickly; or, perhaps, living, alive.

HERMIA: If then true lovers have been ever cross'd,[2]   150
 It stands as an edict in destiny.
 Then let us teach our trial patience,[3]
 Because it is a customary cross,
 As due to love as thoughts and dreams and sighs,
 Wishes and tears, poor fancy's[4] followers.   155
LYSANDER: A good persuasion. Therefore, hear me, Hermia.
 I have a widow aunt, a dowager
 Of great revenue, and she hath no child.
 From Athens is her house remote seven leagues;
 And she respects[5] me as her only son.   160
 There, gentle Hermia, may I marry thee,
 And to that place the sharp Athenian law
 Cannot pursue us. If thou lovest me, then,
 Steal forth thy father's house tomorrow night;
 And in the wood, a league without the town,   165
 Where I did meet thee once with Helena
 To do observance to a morn of May,[6]
 There will I stay for thee.
HERMIA: My good Lysander!
 I swear to thee, by Cupid's strongest bow,
 By his best arrow[7] with the golden head,   170
 By the simplicity of Venus' doves,[8]
 By that which knitteth souls and prospers loves,
 And by that fire which burn'd the Carthage queen,
 When the false Troyan[9] under sail was seen,
 By all the vows that ever men have broke,   175
 In number more than ever women spoke,
 In that same place thou hast appointed me
 Tomorrow truly will I meet with thee.
LYSANDER: Keep promise, love. Look, here comes Helena.

     [*Enter* HELENA.]

HERMIA: God speed fair[1] Helena, whither away?   180
HELENA: Call you me fair? That fair again unsay.
 Demetrius loves your fair. O happy fair![2]
 Your eyes are lodestars, and your tongue's sweet air[3]

---

2. Always thwarted.   3. That is, teach ourselves patience in this trial.   4. Amorous passion's.
5. Regards.   6. Perform the ceremonies of May Day.   7. [Cupid's best gold-pointed arrows were supposed to induce love; his blunt leaden arrows, aversion.]   8. That is, those that drew Venus's chariot.
Simplicity: innocence.   9. [Dido, queen of Carthage, immolated herself on a funeral pyre after having been deserted by the Trojan hero Aeneas.]   1. Fair-complexioned (generally regarded by the Elizabethans as more beautiful than dark complexion).   2. Lucky fair one! *Fair:* beauty (even though Hermia is dark-complexioned).   3. Music. *Lodestars:* guiding stars.

More tuneable[4] than lark to shepherd's ear
185   When wheat is green, when hawthorn buds appear.
Sickness is catching. O, were favor[5] so,
Yours would I catch, fair Hermia, ere I go;
My ear should catch your voice, my eye your eye,
My tongue should catch your tongue's sweet melody.
190   Were the world mine, Demetrius being bated,[6]
The rest I'd give to be to you translated.[7]
O, teach me how you look, and with what art
You sway the motion[8] of Demetrius' heart.
HERMIA: I frown upon him, yet he loves me still.
195   HELENA: O that your frowns would teach my smiles such skill!
HERMIA: I give him curses, yet he gives me love.
HELENA: O that my prayers could such affection move![9]
HERMIA: The more I hate, the more he follows me.
HELENA: The more I love, the more he hateth me.
200   HERMIA: His folly, Helena, is no fault of mine.
HELENA: None, but your beauty. Would that fault were mine!
HERMIA: Take comfort. He no more shall see my face.
Lysander and myself will fly this place.
Before the time I did Lysander see,
205   Seem'd Athens as a paradise to me.
O, then, what graces in my love do dwell,
That he hath turn'd a heaven unto a hell!
LYSANDER: Helen, to you our minds we will unfold.
Tomorrow night, when Phoebe[1] doth behold
210   Her silver visage in the wat'ry glass,[2]
Decking with liquid pearl the bladed grass,
A time that lovers' flights doth still[3] conceal,
Through Athens' gates have we devis'd to steal.
HERMIA: And in the wood, where often you and I
215   Upon faint[4] primrose beds were wont to lie,
Emptying our bosoms of their counsel[5] sweet,
There my Lysander and myself shall meet;
And thence from Athens turn away our eyes,
To seek new friends and stranger companies.
220   Farewell, sweet playfellow. Pray thou for us,
And good luck grant thee thy Demetrius!
Keep word, Lysander. We must starve our sight
From lovers' food till morrow deep midnight.
LYSANDER: I will, my Hermia.   [*Exit* HERMIA.]
Helena, adieu.

---

4. Tuneful, melodious.   5. Appearance, looks.   6. Excepted.   7. Transformed.   8. Impulse.
9. Arouse. *Affection:* passion.   1. Diana, the moon.   2. Mirror.   3. Always.   4. Pale.   5. Secret
thought.

As you on him, Demetrius dote on you! [*Exit.*] 225
HELENA: How happy some o'er other some can be![6]
Through Athens I am thought as fair as she.
But what of that? Demetrius thinks not so;
He will not know what all but he do know.
And as he errs, doting on Hermia's eyes, 230
So I, admiring of[7] his qualities.
Things base and vile, holding no quantity,[8]
Love can transpose to form and dignity.
Love looks not with the eyes, but with the mind,
And therefore is wing'd Cupid painted blind. 235
Nor hath Love's mind of any judgment taste;[9]
Wings, and no eyes, figure[1] unheedy haste.
And therefore is Love said to be a child,
Because in choice he is so oft beguil'd.
As waggish boys in game[2] themselves forswear, 240
So the boy Love is perjur'd everywhere.
For ere Demetrius look'd on Hermia's eyne,[3]
He hail'd down oaths that he was only mine;
And when this hail some heat from Hermia felt,
So he dissolv'd, and show'rs of oaths did melt. 245
I will go tell him of fair Hermia's flight.
Then to the wood will he tomorrow night
Pursue her; and for this intelligence[4]
If I have thanks, it is a dear expense.[5]
But herein mean I to enrich my pain, 250
To have his sight thither and back again. [*Exit.*]

SCENE 2[6]

Enter QUINCE *the Carpenter, and* SNUG *the Joiner, and* BOTTOM *the Weaver, and* FLUTE
the Bellows-mender, and SNOUT *the Tinker, and* STARVELING *the Tailor.*

QUINCE: Is all our company here?
BOTTOM: You were best to call them generally,[7] man by man, according to the
    scrip.[8]
QUINCE: Here is the scroll of every man's name which is thought fit, through all
    Athens, to play in our interlude before the Duke and the Duchess on his 5
    wedding-day at night.

---

6. Can be in comparison to some others.   7. Wondering at.   8. That is, unsubstantial, unshapely.
9. That is, nor has Love, which dwells in the fancy or imagination, any taste or least bit of judgment or
reason.   1. Are a symbol of.   2. Sport, jest.   3. Eyes (old form of plural).   4. Information.
5. That is, a trouble worth taking. *Dear:* costly.   6. Location: Athens. Quince's house (?).   7. [Bot-
tom's blunder for *individually.*]   8. Script, written list.

BOTTOM: First, good Peter Quince, say what the play treats on, then read the names of the actors, and so grow to⁹ a point.

QUINCE: Marry,¹ our play is "The most lamentable comedy and most cruel death
10   of Pyramus and Thisby."

BOTTOM: A very good piece of work, I assure you, and a merry. Now, good Peter Quince, call forth your actors by the scroll. Masters, spread yourselves.

QUINCE: Answer as I call you. Nick Bottom, the weaver.

BOTTOM: Ready. Name what part I am for, and proceed.

15 QUINCE: You, Nick Bottom, are set down for Pyramus.

BOTTOM: What is Pyramus? A lover, or a tyrant?

QUINCE: A lover, that kills himself most gallant for love.

BOTTOM: That will ask some tears in the true performing of it. If I do it, let the audience look to their eyes. I will move storms; I will condole² in some
20   measure. To the rest—yet my chief humor³ is for a tyrant. I could play Ercles rarely, or a part to tear a cat in, to make all split.⁴

> "The raging rocks
> And shivering shocks
> Shall break the locks
>   Of prison gates;
25
> And Phibbus' car⁵
> Shall shine from far
> And make and mar
>   The foolish Fates."

30   This was lofty! Now name the rest of the players. This is Ercles' vein, a tyrant's vein. A lover is more condoling.

QUINCE: Francis Flute, the bellows-mender.

FLUTE: Here, Peter Quince.

QUINCE: Flute, you must take Thisby on you.

35 FLUTE: What is Thisby? A wand'ring knight?

QUINCE: It is the lady that Pyramus must love.

FLUTE: Nay, faith, let not me play a woman. I have a beard coming.

QUINCE: That's all one.⁶ You shall play it in a mask, and you may speak as small⁷ as you will.

40 BOTTOM: An⁸ I may hide my face, let me play Thisby too. I'll speak in a monstrous little voice, "Thisne, Thisne!" "Ah, Pyramus, my lover dear! Thy Thisby dear, and lady dear!"

QUINCE: No, no; you must play Pyramus; and, Flute, you Thisby.

BOTTOM: Well, proceed.

---

9. Come to.   1. [A mild oath, originally the name of the Virgin Mary.]   2. Lament, arouse pity.
3. Inclination, whim.   4. That is, cause a stir, bring the house down. *Ercles:* Hercules (the tradition of ranting came from Seneca's *Hercules Furens*). *Tear a cat:* that is, rant.   5. Phoebus's, the sun-god's, chariot.   6. It makes no difference.   7. High-pitched.   8. If.

QUINCE: Robin Starveling, the tailor.   45

STARVELING: Here, Peter Quince.

QUINCE: Robin Starveling, you must play Thisby's mother. Tom Snout, the tinker.

SNOUT: Here, Peter Quince.

QUINCE: You, Pyramus' father; myself, Thisby's father; Snug, the joiner, you, the
lion's part; and I hope here is a play fitted.   50

    SNUG: Have you the lion's part written? Pray you, if it be, give it me, for I am
    slow of study.

QUINCE: You may do it extempore, for it is nothing but roaring.

BOTTOM: Let me play the lion too. I will roar that I will do any man's heart good
to hear me. I will roar that I will make the Duke say, "Let him roar again, let   55
him roar again."

QUINCE: An you should do it too terribly, you would fright the Duchess and the
ladies, that they would shriek; and that were enough to hang us all.

ALL: That would hang us, every mother's son.

BOTTOM: I grant you, friends, if you should fright the ladies out of their wits, they   60
would have no more discretion but to hang us; but I will aggravate[9] my voice
so that I will roar[1] you as gently as any sucking dove; I will roar you an 'twere
any nightingale.

QUINCE: You can play no part but Pyramus; for Pyramus is a sweet-fac'd man, a
proper[2] man as one shall see in a summer's day, a most lovely gentlemanlike   65
man. Therefore you must needs play Pyramus.

BOTTOM: Well, I will undertake it. What beard were I best to play it in?

QUINCE: Why, what you will.

BOTTOM: I will discharge it in either your[3] straw-color beard, your orange-tawny
beard, your purple-in-grain beard, or your French-crown-color[4] beard, your   70
perfect yellow.

QUINCE: Some of your French crowns[5] have no hair at all, and then you will play
barefac'd. But, masters, here are your parts. [He distributes parts.] And I am to
entreat you, request you, and desire you, to con[6] them by tomorrow night;
and meet me in the palace wood, a mile without the town, by moonlight.   75
There will we rehearse; for if we meet in the city, we shall be dogg'd with
company, and our devices[7] known. In the meantime I will draw a bill[8] of
properties, such as our play wants. I pray you, fail me not.

BOTTOM: We will meet, and there we may rehearse most obscenely[9] and coura-
geously. Take pains, be perfect;[1] adieu.   80

QUINCE: At the Duke's oak we meet.

BOTTOM: Enough. Hold, or cut bow-strings.[2]   [Exeunt.]

---

9. [Bottom's blunder for *diminish.*]   1. That is, roar for you.   2. Handsome.   3. That is, you know
the kind I mean. *Discharge:* perform.   4. That is, color of a French crown, a gold coin. *Purple-in-grain:*
dyed a very deep red (from *grain,* the name applied to the dried insect used to make the dye).   5. Heads
bald from syphilis, the "French disease."   6. Learn by heart.   7. Plans.   8. List.   9. [An unintentionally funny blunder, whatever Bottom meant to say.]   1. That is, letter-perfect in memorizing
your parts.   2. [An archer's expression not definitely explained, but probably meaning here "keep your
promises, or give up the play."]

ACT II

SCENE 1[3]

Enter a FAIRY *at one door, and Robin Goodfellow* (PUCK) *at another.*

PUCK: How now, spirit! Whither wander you?
FAIRY: Over hill, over dale,
    Thorough[4] bush, thorough brier,
    Over park, over pale,[5]
5   Thorough flood, thorough fire,
    I do wander every where,
    Swifter than the moon's sphere;
    And I serve the Fairy Queen,
    To dew her orbs[6] upon the green.
10   The cowslips tall her pensioners[7] be.
    In their gold coats spots you see;
    Those be rubies, fairy favors,[8]
    In those freckles live their savors.[9]
    I must go seek some dewdrops here
15   And hang a pearl in every cowslip's ear.
    Farewell, thou lob[1] of spirits; I'll be gone.
    Our Queen and all her elves come here anon.[2]
PUCK: The King doth keep his revels here tonight.
    Take heed the Queen come not within his sight.
20   For Oberon is passing fell and wrath,[3]
    Because that she as her attendant hath
    A lovely boy, stolen from an Indian king;
    She never had so sweet a changeling.[4]
    And jealous Oberon would have the child
25   Knight of his train, to trace[5] the forests wild.
    But she perforce[6] withholds the loved boy,
    Crowns him with flowers and makes him all her joy.
    And now they never meet in grove or green,
    By fountain[7] clear, or spangled starlight sheen,
30   But they do square,[8] that all their elves for fear
    Creep into acorn-cups and hide them there.
FAIRY: Either I mistake your shape and making quite,
    Or else you are that shrewd and knavish sprite[9]
    Call'd Robin Goodfellow. Are not you he

---

3. Location: a wood near Athens.   4. Through.   5. Enclosure.   6. Circles; that is, fairy rings.
7. Retainers, members of the royal bodyguard.   8. Love tokens.   9. Sweet smells.   1. Country
bumpkin.   2. At once.   3. Wrathful. *Fell:* exceedingly angry.   4. Child exchanged for another by
the fairies.   5. Range through.   6. Forcibly.   7. Spring.   8. Quarrel.   9. Spirit. *Shrewd:* mischievous.

That frights the maidens of the villagery,   35
Skim milk, and sometimes labor in the quern,[1]
And bootless[2] make the breathless huswife churn,
And sometime make the drink to bear no barm,[3]
Mislead night-wanderers, laughing at their harm?
Those that Hobgoblin call you and sweet Puck,   40
You do their work, and they shall have good luck.
Are you not he?
PUCK: Thou speakest aright;
I am that merry wanderer of the night.
I jest to Oberon and make him smile
When I a fat and bean-fed horse beguile,   45
Neighing in likeness of a filly foal;
And sometime lurk I in a gossip's[4] bowl,
In very likeness of a roasted crab,[5]
And when she drinks, against her lips I bob
And on her withered dewlap[6] pour the ale.   50
The wisest aunt, telling the saddest[7] tale,
Sometime for three-foot stool mistaketh me;
Then slip I from her bum, down topples she,
And "tailor"[8] cries, and falls into a cough;
And then the whole quire[9] hold their hips and laugh,   55
And waxen in their mirth and neeze[1] and swear
A merrier hour was never wasted there.
But, room, fairy! Here comes Oberon.
FAIRY: And here my mistress. Would that he were gone!

[*Enter* OBERON, *the King of Fairies, at one door, with his train; and* TITANIA,
the Queen, at another, with hers.]

OBERON: Ill met by moonlight, proud Titania.   60
TITANIA: What, jealous Oberon? Fairies, skip hence.
I have forsworn his bed and company.
OBERON: Tarry, rash wanton.[2] Am not I thy lord?
TITANIA: Then I must be thy lady; but I know
When thou hast stolen away from fairy land,   65
And in the shape of Corin[3] sat all day,
Playing on pipes of corn[4] and versing love
To amorous Phillida. Why art thou here,
Come from the farthest steep[5] of India,
But that, forsooth, the bouncing Amazon,   70

1. Handmill.   2. In vain.   3. Yeast, head on the ale.   4. Old woman's.   5. Crab apple.
6. Loose skin on neck.   7. Most serious. *Aunt:* old woman.   8. [Possibly because she ends up sitting
cross-legged on the floor, looking like a tailor.]   9. Company.   1. Sneeze. *Waxen:* increase.
2. Headstrong creature.   3. Corin and Phillida are conventional names of pastoral lovers.   4. [Here,
oat stalks.]   5. Mountain range.

Your buskin'd[6] mistress and your warrior love,
To Theseus must be wedded, and you come
To give their bed joy and prosperity.

OBERON: How canst thou thus for shame, Titania,

75 Glance at my credit with Hippolyta,[7]
Knowing I know thy love to Theseus?
Didst not thou lead him through the glimmering night
From Perigenia,[8] whom he ravished?
And make him with fair Aegles[9] break his faith,

80 With Ariadne and Antiopa?[1]

TITANIA: These are the forgeries of jealousy;
And never, since the middle summer's spring,[2]
Met we on hill, in dale, forest, or mead,
By paved fountain or by rushy[3] brook,

85 Or in the beached margent[4] of the sea,
To dance our ringlets[5] to the whistling wind,
But with thy brawls thou hast disturb'd our sport.
Therefore the winds, piping to us in vain,
As in revenge, have suck'd up from the sea

90 Contagious[6] fogs; which falling in the land
Hath every pelting[7] river made so proud
That they have overborne their continents.[8]
The ox hath therefore stretch'd his yoke in vain,
The ploughman lost his sweat, and the green corn[9]

95 Hath rotted ere his youth attain'd a beard;
The fold[1] stands empty in the drowned field,
And crows are fatted with the murrion[2] flock;
The nine men's morris[3] is fill'd up with mud,
And the quaint mazes in the wanton[4] green

100 For lack of tread are undistinguishable.
The human mortals want their winter[5] here;
No night is now with hymn or carol bless'd.

6. Wearing half boots called buskins.   7. Make insinuations about my favored relationship with Hippolyta.   8. That is, Perigouna, one of Theseus's conquests. (This and the following women are named in Thomas North's translation of Plutarch's *Life of Theseus*.)   9. That is, Aegle, for whom Theseus deserted Ariadne, according to some accounts.   1. Queen of the Amazons and wife of Theseus; elsewhere identified with Hippolyta, but here thought of as a separate woman. *Ariadne:* the daughter of Minos, king of Crete, who helped Theseus to escape the labyrinth after killing the Minotaur; later she was abandoned by Theseus.   2. Beginning of midsummer.   3. Bordered with rushes. *Paved:* with pebbled bottom.   4. Edge, border. *In:* on.   5. Dances in a ring. (See *orbs* in 2.1.9.)   6. Noxious.   7. Paltry; or striking, moving forcefully.   8. Banks that contain them.   9. Grain of any kind. 1. Pen for sheep or cattle.   2. Having died of the murrain, plague.   3. That is, portion of the village green marked out in a square for a game played with nine pebbles or pegs.   4. Luxuriant. *Mazes:* that is, intricate paths marked out on the village green to be followed rapidly on foot as a kind of contest. 5. That is, regular winter season; or proper observances of winter, such as the *hymn* or *carol* in the next line. *Want:* lack.

Therefore[6] the moon, the governess of floods,
Pale in her anger, washes all the air,
That rheumatic[7] diseases do abound.   105
And thorough this distemperature[8] we see
The seasons alter: hoary-headed frosts
Fall in the fresh lap of the crimson rose,
And on old Hiems'[9] thin and icy crown
An odorous chaplet of sweet summer buds   110
Is, as in mockery, set. The spring, the summer,
The childing[1] autumn, angry winter, change
Their wonted liveries, and the mazed[2] world,
By their increase,[3] now knows not which is which.
And this same progeny of evils comes   115
From our debate,[4] from our dissension;
We are their parents and original.[5]
OBERON: Do you amend it then; it lies in you.
    Why should Titania cross her Oberon?
    I do but beg a little changeling boy,   120
    To be my henchman.[6]
TITANIA: Set your heart at rest.
    The fairy land buys not the child of me.
    His mother was a vot'ress of my order,
    And, in the spiced Indian air, by night,
    Full often hath she gossip'd by my side,   125
    And sat with me on Neptune's yellow sands,
    Marking th' embarked traders on the flood,[7]
    When we have laugh'd to see the sails conceive
    And grow big-bellied with the wanton[8] wind;
    Which she, with pretty and with swimming gait,   130
    Following—her womb then rich with my young squire—
    Would imitate, and sail upon the land
    To fetch me trifles, and return again,
    As from a voyage, rich with merchandise.
    But she, being mortal, of that boy did die;   135
    And for her sake do I rear up her boy,
    And for her sake I will not part with him.
OBERON: How long within this wood intend you stay?
TITANIA: Perchance till after Theseus' wedding-day.
    If you will patiently dance in our round[9]   140
    And see our moonlight revels, go with us;
    If not, shun me, and I will spare[1] your haunts.

---

6. That is, as a result of our quarrel.   7. Colds, flu, and other respiratory infections.   8. Disturbance in nature.   9. The winter god's.   1. Fruitful, pregnant.   2. Bewildered. *Liveries:* usual apparel.
3. Their yield, what they produce.   4. Quarrel.   5. Origin.   6. Attendant, page.   7. Flood tide.
Traders: trading vessels.   8. Sportive.   9. Circular dance.   1. Shun.

OBERON: Give me that boy, and I will go with thee.

TITANIA: Not for thy fairy kingdom. Fairies, away!

145 We shall chide downright, if I longer stay. [*Exeunt* TITANIA *with her train.*]

OBERON: Well, go thy way. Thou shalt not from[2] this grove

Till I torment thee for this injury.

My gentle Puck, come hither. Thou rememb'rest

Since[3] once I sat upon a promontory,

150 And heard a mermaid on a dolphin's back

Uttering such dulcet and harmonious breath[4]

That the rude sea grew civil at her song

And certain stars shot madly from their spheres,

To hear the sea-maid's music?

PUCK: I remember.

155 OBERON: That very time I saw, but thou couldst not,

Flying between the cold moon and the earth,

Cupid all[5] arm'd. A certain aim he took

At a fair vestal[6] throned by the west,

And loos'd his love-shaft smartly from his bow,

160 As[7] it should pierce a hundred thousand hearts;

But I might[8] see young Cupid's fiery shaft

Quench'd in the chaste beams of the wat'ry moon,

And the imperial vot'ress passed on,

In maiden meditation, fancy-free.[9]

165 Yet mark'd I where the bolt of Cupid fell:

It fell upon a little western flower,

Before milk-white, now purple with love's wound,

And maidens call it love-in-idleness.[1]

Fetch me that flow'r; the herb I showed thee once.

170 The juice of it on sleeping eyelids laid

Will make or man or[2] woman madly dote

Upon the next live creature that it sees.

Fetch me this herb, and be thou here again

Ere the leviathan[3] can swim a league.

175 PUCK: I'll put a girdle round about the earth

In forty[4] minutes.

OBERON: Having once this juice,

I'll watch Titania when she is asleep,

And drop the liquor of it in her eyes.

The next thing then she waking looks upon,

180 Be it on lion, bear, or wolf, or bull,

On meddling monkey, or on busy ape,

---

2. Go from.   3. When.   4. Voice, song.   5. Fully.   6. Vestal virgin (contains a complimentary
allusion to Queen Elizabeth as a votaress of Diana and probably refers to an actual entertainment in her
honor at Elvetham in 1591).   7. As if.   8. Could.   9. Free of love's spell.   1. Pansy, heartsease.
2. Either . . . or.   3. Sea monster, whale.   4. [The time parameters are used indefinitely here.]

She shall pursue it with the soul of love.
And ere I take this charm from off her sight,
As I can take it with another herb,
I'll make her render up her page to me.   185
But who comes here? I am invisible,
And I will overhear their conference.

     [*Enter* DEMETRIUS, HELENA *following him.*]

DEMETRIUS: I love thee not, therefore pursue me not.
  Where is Lysander and fair Hermia?
  The one I'll slay, the other slayeth me.   190
  Thou told'st me they were stol'n unto this wood;
  And here am I, and wode[5] within this wood,
  Because I cannot meet my Hermia.
  Hence, get thee gone, and follow me no more.
HELENA: You draw me, you hard-hearted adamant;[6]   195
  But yet you draw not iron, for my heart
  Is true as steel. Leave[7] you your power to draw,
  And I shall have no power to follow you.
DEMETRIUS: Do I entice you? Do I speak you fair?[8]
  Or, rather, do I not in plainest truth   200
  Tell you I do not nor I cannot love you?
HELENA: And even for that do I love you the more.
  I am your spaniel; and, Demetrius,
  The more you beat me, I will fawn on you.
  Use me but as your spaniel, spurn me, strike me,   205
  Neglect me, lose me; only give me leave,
  Unworthy as I am, to follow you.
  What worser place can I beg in your love—
  And yet a place of high respect with me—
  Than to be used as you use your dog?   210
DEMETRIUS: Tempt not too much the hatred of my spirit,
  For I am sick when I do look on thee.
HELENA: And I am sick when I look not on you.
DEMETRIUS: You do impeach[9] your modesty too much
  To leave the city and commit yourself   215
  Into the hands of one that loves you not,
  To trust the opportunity of night
  And the ill counsel of a desert[1] place
  With the rich worth of your virginity.
HELENA: Your virtue is my privilege. For that[2]   220

---

5. Mad (pronounced *wood* and often spelled so).   6. Lodestone, magnet (with pun on *hard-hearted*, since adamant was also thought to be the hardest of all stones and was confused with the diamond). 7. Give up.   8. Courteously.   9. Call into question.   1. Deserted.   2. Because. *Virtue:* goodness or power to attract. *Privilege:* safeguard, warrant.

It is not night when I do see your face,
Therefore I think I am not in the night;
Nor doth this wood lack worlds of company,
For you in my respect[3] are all the world.
225   Then how can it be said I am alone,
When all the world is here to look on me?
DEMETRIUS: I'll run from thee and hide me in the brakes,[4]
And leave thee to the mercy of wild beasts.
HELENA: The wildest hath not such a heart as you.
230   Run when you will, the story shall be chang'd:
Apollo flies and Daphne holds the chase,[5]
The dove pursues the griffin, the mild hind[6]
Makes speed to catch the tiger—bootless[7] speed,
When cowardice pursues and valor flies.
235 DEMETRIUS: I will not stay thy questions.[8] Let me go!
Or if thou follow me, do not believe
But I shall do thee mischief in the wood.
HELENA: Ay, in the temple, in the town, the field,
You do me mischief. Fie, Demetrius!
240   Your wrongs do set a scandal on my sex.
We cannot fight for love, as men may do;
We should be woo'd and were not made to woo.   [*Exit* DEMETRIUS.]
I'll follow thee and make a heaven of hell,
To die upon[9] the hand I love so well.   [*Exit.*]
245 OBERON: Fare thee well, nymph. Ere he do leave this grove,
Thou shalt fly him and he shall seek thy love.

      [*Enter* PUCK.]

Hast thou the flower there? Welcome, wanderer.
PUCK: Ay, there it is.   [*Offers the flower.*]
OBERON: I pray thee, give it me.
I know a bank where the wild thyme blows,[1]
250   Where oxlips[2] and the nodding violet grows,
Quite over-canopied with luscious woodbine,[3]
With sweet musk-roses and with eglantine.[4]
There sleeps Titania sometime of the night,
Lull'd in these flowers with dances and delight;
255   And there the snake throws[5] her enamel'd skin,
Weed[6] wide enough to wrap a fairy in.

---

3. As far as I am concerned.   4. Thickets.   5. [In the ancient myth, Daphne fled from Apollo and was saved from rape by being transformed into a laurel tree; here it is the female who *holds the chase,* or pursues, instead of the male.]   6. Female deer. *Griffin:* a fabulous monster with the head of an eagle and the body of a lion.   7. Fruitless.   8. Talk or argument. *Stay:* wait for.   9. By.   1. Blooms. 2. Flowers resembling cowslip and primrose.   3. Honeysuckle.   4. Sweetbriar, a kind of rose. *Musk-rose:* a kind of large, sweet-scented rose.   5. Sloughs off, sheds.   6. Garment.

And with the juice of this I'll streak⁷ her eyes,
And make her full of hateful fantasies.
Take thou some of it, and seek through this grove.   [*Gives some love-juice.*]
A sweet Athenian lady is in love   260
With a disdainful youth. Anoint his eyes,
But do it when the next thing he espies
May be the lady. Thou shalt know the man
By the Athenian garments he hath on.
Effect it with some care, that he may prove   265
More fond on⁸ her than she upon her love;
And look thou meet me ere the first cock crow.
PUCK: Fear not, my lord, your servant shall do so.   [*Exeunt.*]

SCENE 2⁹

Enter TITANIA, *Queen of Fairies, with her train.*

TITANIA: Come, now a roundel¹ and a fairy song;
Then, for the third part of a minute, hence—
Some to kill cankers² in the musk-rose buds,
Some war with rere-mice³ for their leathern wings,
To make my small elves coats, and some keep back   5
The clamorous owl, that nightly hoots and wonders
At our quaint⁴ spirits. Sing me now asleep.
Then to your offices and let me rest.

        [FAIRIES *sing.*]

[FIRST FAIRY:]

You spotted snakes with double⁵ tongue,
Thorny hedgehogs, be not seen;   10
Newts⁶ and blindworms, do no wrong,
Come not near our fairy queen.
[*Chorus.*]   Philomel,⁷ with melody
Sing in our sweet lullaby;
Lulla, lulla, lullaby, lulla, lulla, lullaby.   15
Never harm,
Nor spell nor charm,
Come our lovely lady nigh.
So, good night, with lullaby.

7. Anoint, touch gently.   8. Doting on.   9. Location: the wood.   1. Dance in a ring.   2. Canker-
worms.   3. Bats.   4. Dainty.   5. Forked.   6. Water lizards (considered poisonous, as were *blindworms*—small snakes with tiny eyes—and spiders).   7. The nightingale (Philomela, daughter of King
Pandion, was transformed into a nightingale, according to Ovid's *Metamorphoses* 6, after she had been
raped by her sister Procne's husband, Tereus).

[FIRST FAIRY:]

20   Weaving spiders, come not here;
              Hence, you long-legg'd spinners, hence!
              Beetles black, approach not near;
                  Worm nor snail, do no offense.
      [*Chorus.*]   Philomel, with melody, etc.

                                                    [TITANIA *sleeps.*]

[SECOND FAIRY:]

25   Hence, away! Now all is well.
                  One aloof stand sentinel.

                                                    [*Exeunt* FAIRIES.]

          [*Enter* OBERON *and squeezes the flower on* TITANIA's *eyelids.*]

OBERON: What thou seest when thou dost wake,
          Do it for thy true-love take;
          Love and languish for his sake.
30   Be it ounce,[8] or cat, or bear,
          Pard,[9] or boar with bristled hair,
          In thy eye that shall appear
          When thou wak'st, it is thy dear.
          Wake when some vile thing is near.   [*Exit.*]

          [*Enter* LYSANDER *and* HERMIA.]

35   LYSANDER: Fair love, you faint with wand'ring in the wood;
          And to speak troth,[1] I have forgot our way.
          We'll rest us, Hermia, if you think it good,
          And tarry for the comfort of the day.
     HERMIA: Be 't so, Lysander. Find you out a bed,
40   For I upon this bank will rest my head.
     LYSANDER: One turf shall serve as pillow for us both,
          One heart, one bed, two bosoms, and one troth.[2]
     HERMIA: Nay, good Lysander; for my sake, my dear,
          Lie further off yet, do not lie so near.
45   LYSANDER: O, take the sense, sweet, of my innocence![3]
          Love takes the meaning in love's conference.[4]
          I mean, that my heart unto yours is knit
          So that but one heart we can make of it;
          Two bosoms interchained with an oath—
50   So then two bosoms and a single troth.
          Then by your side no bed-room me deny,
          For lying so, Hermia, I do not lie.[5]

---

8. Lynx.   9. Leopard.   1. Truth.   2. Faith, trothplight.   3. That is, interpret my intention as
innocent.   4. That is, when lovers confer, love teaches each lover to interpret the other's meaning
lovingly.   5. Tell a falsehood (with a pun on *lie*, recline).

HERMIA: Lysander riddles very prettily.
　　Now much beshrew[6] my manners and my pride
　　If Hermia meant to say Lysander lied.　　　　　　　　　　　　　　55
　　But, gentle friend, for love and courtesy
　　Lie further off, in human[7] modesty;
　　Such separation as may well be said
　　Becomes a virtuous bachelor and a maid,
　　So far be distant; and, good night, sweet friend.　　　　　　　　60
　　Thy love ne'er alter till thy sweet life end!
LYSANDER: Amen, amen, to that fair prayer, say I,
　　And then end life when I end loyalty!
　　Here is my bed. Sleep give thee all his rest!
HERMIA: With half that wish the wisher's eyes be press'd![8]　　　　65

　　　　[*They sleep, separated by a short distance. Enter* PUCK.]

PUCK: Through the forest have I gone,
　　But Athenian found I none
　　On whose eyes I might approve[9]
　　This flower's force in stirring love.
　　Night and silence.—Who is here?　　　　　　　　　　　　　70
　　Weeds of Athens he doth wear.
　　This is he, my master said,
　　Despised the Athenian maid;
　　And here the maiden, sleeping sound,
　　On the dank and dirty ground.　　　　　　　　　　　　　75
　　Pretty soul! She durst not lie
　　Near this lack-love, this kill-courtesy.
　　Churl, upon thy eyes I throw
　　All the power this charm doth owe.[1]　　　　　[*Applies the love-juice.*]
　　When thou wak'st, let love forbid　　　　　　　　　　　　80
　　Sleep his seat on thy eyelid.
　　So awake when I am gone,
　　For I must now to Oberon.　　　　　　　　　　　　　[*Exit.*]

　　　　[*Enter* DEMETRIUS *and* HELENA, *running.*]

HELENA: Stay, though thou kill me, sweet Demetrius.
DEMETRIUS: I charge thee, hence, and do not haunt me thus.　　85
HELENA: O, wilt thou darkling[2] leave me? Do not so.
DEMETRIUS: Stay, on thy peril![3] I alone will go.　　　　　　[*Exit.*]
HELENA: O, I am out of breath in this fond[4] chase!
　　The more my prayer, the lesser is my grace.[5]
　　Happy is Hermia, wheresoe'er she lies,[6]　　　　　　　　90

---

6. Curse (but mildly meant).　　7. Courteous.　　8. That is, may we share your wish, so that your eyes
too are *press'd*, closed, in sleep.　　9. Test.　　1. Own.　　2. In the dark.　　3. That is, on pain of danger
to you if you don't obey me and stay.　　4. Doting.　　5. The favor I obtain.　　6. Dwells.

For she hath blessed and attractive eyes.
How came her eyes so bright? Not with salt tears;
If so, my eyes are oft'ner wash'd than hers.
No, no, I am as ugly as a bear;
95   For beasts that meet me run away for fear.
Therefore no marvel though Demetrius
Do, as a monster, fly my presence thus.
What wicked and dissembling glass of mine
Made me compare with Hermia's sphery eyne?[7]
100   But who is here? Lysander, on the ground?
Dead, or asleep? I see no blood, no wound.
Lysander, if you live, good sir, awake.
LYSANDER: [*Awaking.*] And run through fire I will for thy sweet sake.
Transparent[8] Helena! Nature shows art,
105   That through thy bosom makes me see thy heart.
Where is Demetrius? O, how fit a word
Is that vile name to perish on my sword!
HELENA: Do not say so, Lysander, say not so.
What though he love your Hermia? Lord, what though?
110   Yet Hermia still loves you. Then be content.
LYSANDER: Content with Hermia? No! I do repent
The tedious minutes I with her have spent.
Not Hermia but Helena I love.
Who will not change a raven for a dove?
115   The will of man is by his reason sway'd,
And reason says you are the worthier maid.
Things growing are not ripe until their season;
So I, being young, till now ripe not to reason.[9]
And touching now the point of human skill,[1]
120   Reason becomes the marshal to my will
And leads me to your eyes, where I o'erlook[2]
Love's stories written in love's richest book.
HELENA: Wherefore was I to this keen mockery born?
When at your hands did I deserve this scorn?
125   Is 't not enough, is 't not enough, young man,
That I did never, no, nor never can,
Deserve a sweet look from Demetrius' eye,
But you must flout my insufficiency?
Good troth, you do me wrong, good sooth,[3] you do,
130   In such disdainful manner me to woo.
But fare you well. Perforce I must confess
I thought you lord of more true gentleness.[4]

---

7. Eyes as bright as stars in their spheres.   8. (1) Radiant; (2) able to be seen through.   9. Mature
enough to be reasonable.   1. Judgment. *Touching:* reaching. *Point:* summit.   2. Read.   3. That is,
indeed, truly.   4. Courtesy. *Lord of:* that is, possessor of.

O, that a lady, of⁵ one man refus'd,
Should of another therefore be abus'd!⁶   *[Exit.]*
LYSANDER: She sees not Hermia. Hermia, sleep thou there,   135
And never mayst thou come Lysander near!
For as a surfeit of the sweetest things
The deepest loathing to the stomach brings,
Or as the heresies that men do leave
Are hated most of those they did deceive,   140
So thou, my surfeit and my heresy,
Of all be hated, but the most of me!
And, all my powers, address your love and might
To honor Helen and to be her knight!   *[Exit.]*
HERMIA: [*Awaking.*] Help me, Lysander, help me! Do thy best   145
To pluck this crawling serpent from my breast!
Ay me, for pity! What a dream was here!
Lysander, look how I do quake with fear.
Methought a serpent eat⁷ my heart away,
And you sat smiling at his cruel prey.⁸   150
Lysander! What, remov'd? Lysander! Lord!
What, out of hearing? Gone? No sound, no word?
Alack, where are you? Speak, an if you hear.
Speak, of all loves!⁹ I swoon almost with fear.
No? Then I well perceive you are not nigh.   155
Either death, or you, I'll find immediately.

[*Exit. Manet* TITANIA *lying asleep.*]

ACT III

SCENE 1¹

Enter the Clowns (QUINCE, SNUG, BOTTOM, FLUTE, SNOUT, *and* STARVELING.)

BOTTOM: Are we all met?
QUINCE: Pat, pat; and here's a marvailes convenient place for our rehearsal. This
    green plot shall be our stage, this hawthorn brake our tiring-house,² and we
    will do it in action as we will do it before the Duke.
BOTTOM: Peter Quince?   5
QUINCE: What sayest thou, bully³ Bottom?
BOTTOM: There are things in this comedy of Pyramus and Thisby that will never
    please. First, Pyramus must draw a sword to kill himself, which the ladies
    cannot abide. How answer you that?
SNOUT: By 'r lakin, a parlous⁴ fear.   10

---

5. By.   6. Ill treated.   7. Ate (pronounced *et*).   8. Act of preying.   9. For all love's sake.
1. Location: scene continues.   2. Attiring area, hence backstage. *Brake:* thicket.   3. That is, worthy,
jolly, fine fellow.   4. Perilous. *By 'r lakin:* by our ladykin; that is, the Virgin Mary.

STARVELING: I believe we must leave the killing out, when all is done.[5]

BOTTOM: Not a whit. I have a device to make all well. Write me[6] a prologue; and let the prologue seem to say, we will do no harm with our swords and that Pyramus is not kill'd indeed; and, for the more better assurance, tell them that I Pyramus am not Pyramus, but Bottom the weaver. This will put them out of fear.

QUINCE: Well, we will have such a prologue, and it shall be written in eight and six.[7]

BOTTOM: No, make it two more; let it be written in eight and eight.

SNOUT: Will not the ladies be afeard of the lion?

STARVELING: I fear it, I promise you.

BOTTOM: Masters, you ought to consider with yourselves, to bring in—God shield us!—a lion among ladies,[8] is a most dreadful thing. For there is not a more fearful[9] wild-fowl than your lion living; and we ought to look to 't.

SNOUT: Therefore another prologue must tell he is not a lion.

BOTTOM: Nay, you must name his name, and half his face must be seen through the lion's neck, and he himself must speak through, saying thus, or to the same defect:[1] "Ladies"—or "Fair ladies—I would wish you"—or "I would request you"—or "I would entreat you—not to fear, not to tremble; my life for yours.[2] If you think I come hither as a lion, it were pity of my life.[3] No, I am no such thing; I am a man as other men are." And there indeed let him name his name, and tell them plainly he is Snug the joiner.

QUINCE: Well, it shall be so. But there is two hard things: that is, to bring the moonlight into a chamber; for, you know, Pyramus and Thisby meet by moonlight.

SNOUT: Doth the moon shine that night we play our play?

BOTTOM: A calendar, a calendar! Look in the almanac. Find out moonshine, find out moonshine. [*They consult an almanac.*]

QUINCE: Yes, it doth shine that night.

BOTTOM: Why then may you leave a casement of the great chamber window, where we play, open, and the moon may shine in at the casement.

QUINCE: Ay; or else one must come in with a bush of thorns and a lantern, and say he comes to disfigure,[4] or to present,[5] the person of Moonshine. Then there is another thing: we must have a wall in the great chamber; for Pyramus and Thisby, says the story, did talk through the chink of a wall.

SNOUT: You can never bring in a wall. What say you, Bottom?

BOTTOM: Some man or other must present Wall. And let him have some plaster,

---

5. That is, when all is said and done.   6. That is, write at my suggestion. (*Me* is the ethic dative.)
7. Alternate lines of eight and six syllables, a common ballad measure.   8. [A contemporary pamphlet tells how at the christening in 1594 of Prince Henry, eldest son of King James VI of Scotland, later James I of England, a "blackmoor" instead of a lion drew the triumphal chariot since the lion's presence might have "brought some fear to the nearest."]   9. Fear-inspiring.   1. [Bottom's blunder for *effect*.]
2. That is, I pledge my life to make your lives safe.   3. My life would be endangered.   4. [Quince's blunder for *prefigure*.] *Bush of thorns*: bundle of thornbush faggots (part of the accoutrements of the man in the moon, according to the popular notions of the time, along with his lantern and his dog).
5. Represent.

or some loam, or some roughcast[6] about him, to signify wall; and let him hold his fingers thus, and through that cranny shall Pyramus and Thisby whisper.   50

QUINCE: If that may be, then all is well. Come, sit down, every mother's son, and rehearse your parts. Pyramus, you begin. When you have spoken your speech, enter into that brake, and so every one according to his cue.

[*Enter Robin* (PUCK).]

PUCK: What hempen home-spuns have we swagg'ring here,
So near the cradle of the Fairy Queen?   55
What, a play toward?[7] I'll be an auditor;
An actor too perhaps, if I see cause.

QUINCE: Speak, Pyramus. Thisby, stand forth.

BOTTOM: "Thisby, the flowers of odious savors sweet,"—

QUINCE: Odors, odors.   60

BOTTOM: —"Odors savors sweet;
So hath thy breath, my dearest Thisby dear.
But hark, a voice! Stay thou but here awhile,
And by and by I will to thee appear."   [*Exit.*]

PUCK: A stranger Pyramus than e'er played here.[8]   [*Exit.*]   65

FLUTE: Must I speak now?

QUINCE: Ay, marry, must you; for you must understand he goes but to see a noise that he heard, and is to come again.

FLUTE: "Most radiant Pyramus, most lily-white of hue,
Of color like the red rose on triumphant brier,   70
Most brisky juvenal and eke most lovely Jew,[9]
As true as truest horse that yet would never tire.
I'll meet thee, Pyramus, at Ninny's tomb."

QUINCE: "Ninus'[1] tomb," man. Why, you must not speak that yet. That you answer to Pyramus. You speak all your part at once, cues and all. Pyramus,   75
enter. Your cue is past; it is, "never tire."

FLUTE: O—"As true as truest horse, that yet would never tire."

[*Enter* PUCK, *and* BOTTOM *as Pyramus with the ass head.*][2]

BOTTOM: "If I were fair,[3] Thisby, I were only thine."

QUINCE: O monstrous! O strange! We are haunted. Pray, masters! Fly, masters! Help!   [*Exeunt* QUINCE, SNUG, FLUTE, SNOUT, *and* STARVELING.]   80

PUCK: I'll follow you, I'll lead you about a round,[4]
Through bog, through bush, through brake, through brier.

6. A mixture of lime and gravel used to plaster the outside of buildings.   7. About to take place.
8. That is, in this theater (?).   9. [Probably an absurd repetition of the first syllable of *juvenal*.] *Briskly
juvenal:* brisk youth. *Eke:* also.   1. Mythical founder of Nineveh (whose wife, Semiramis, was supposed
to have built the walls of Babylon, where the story of Pyramis and Thisbe [Thisby] takes place).   2. [This
stage direction, taken from the Folio, presumably refers to a standard stage property.]   3. Handsome.
4. Roundabout.

Sometime a horse I'll be, sometime a hound,
   A hog, a headless bear, sometime a fire;[5]
85 And neigh, and bark, and grunt, and roar, and burn,
   Like horse, hound, hog, bear, fire, at every turn.   [*Exit.*]
BOTTOM: Why do they run away? This is a knavery of them to make me afeard.

      [*Enter* SNOUT.]

SNOUT: O Bottom, thou art chang'd! what do I see on thee?
BOTTOM: What do you see? You see an ass-head of your own, do you?

                                                              [*Exit* SNOUT.]

      [*Enter* QUINCE.]

90 QUINCE: Bless thee, Bottom, bless thee! Thou art translated.[6]   [*Exit.*]
BOTTOM: I see their knavery. This is to make an ass of me, to fright me, if they
      could. But I will not stir from this place, do what they can. I will walk up
      and down here, and will sing, that they shall hear I am not afraid.

[*Sings.*]

         The woosel cock[7] so black of hue,
95   With orange-tawny bill,
         The throstle[8] with his note so true,
            The wren with little quill[9]—

TITANIA: [*Awaking.*] What angel wakes me from my flow'ry bed?

[BOTTOM *sings.*]

         The finch, the sparrow, and the lark,
100   The plain-song[1] cuckoo grey,
         Whose note full many a man doth mark,
            And dares not answer nay[2]—

      For, indeed, who would set his wit to so foolish a bird? Who would give a
      bird the lie,[3] though he cry "cuckoo" never so?[4]
105 TITANIA: I pray thee, gentle mortal, sing again.
   Mine ear is much enamored of thy note;
   So is mine eye enthralled to thy shape;
   And thy fair virtue's force[5] perforce doth move me
   On the first view to say, to swear, I love thee.
110 BOTTOM: Methinks, mistress, you should have little reason for that. And yet, to
      say the truth, reason and love keep little company together nowadays. The
      more the pity that some honest neighbors will not make them friends. Nay,
      I can gleek[6] upon occasion.

---

5. Will-o'-the-wisp.   6. Transformed.   7. Male ousel or ouzel, blackbird.   8. Song thrush.
9. [Literally, a reed pipe; hence, the bird's piping song.]   1. Singing a melody without variations.
2. That is, cannot deny that he is a cuckold.   3. Call the bird a liar.   4. Ever so much.   5. The
power of your beauty.   6. Scoff, jest.

TITANIA: Thou art as wise as thou art beautiful.

BOTTOM: Not so, neither. But if I had wit enough to get out of this wood, I have   115
enough to serve mine own turn.[7]

TITANIA: Out of this wood do not desire to go.
Thou shalt remain here, whether thou wilt or no.
I am a spirit of no common rate.[8]
The summer still doth tend upon my state;[9]   120
And I do love thee. Therefore, go with me.
I'll give thee fairies to attend on thee,
And they shall fetch thee jewels from the deep,
And sing while thou on pressed flowers dost sleep.
And I will purge thy mortal grossness so   125
That thou shalt like an airy spirit go.
Peaseblossom, Cobweb, Moth,[1] and Mustardseed!

[*Enter four* FAIRIES (PEASEBLOSSOM, COBWEB, MOTH, and MUSTARDSEED).]

PEASEBLOSSOM: Ready.

COBWEB: And I.

MOTH: And I.

MUSTARDSEED: And I.

ALL: Where shall we go?

TITANIA: Be kind and courteous to this gentleman.
Hop in his walks and gambol in his eyes;   130
Feed him with apricocks and dewberries,
With purple grapes, green figs, and mulberries;
The honey-bags steal from the humble-bees,
And for night-tapers crop their waxen thighs
And light them at the fiery glow-worm's eyes,   135
To have my love to bed and to arise;
And pluck the wings from painted butterflies
To fan the moonbeams from his sleeping eyes.
Nod to him, elves, and do him courtesies.

PEASEBLOSSOM: Hail, mortal!   140

COBWEB: Hail!

MOTH: Hail!

MUSTARDSEED: Hail!

BOTTOM: I cry your worships mercy, heartily. I beseech your worship's name.

COBWEB: Cobweb.   145

BOTTOM: I shall desire you of more acquaintance, good Master Cobweb. If I cut
my finger, I shall make bold with you.[2] Your name, honest gentleman?

PEASEBLOSSOM: Peaseblossom.

BOTTOM: I pray you, commend me to Mistress Squash,[3] your mother, and to Master

7. Answer my purpose.   8. Rank, value.   9. Waits upon me as a part of my royal retinue. *Still:* ever,
always.   1. That is, mote, speck. (The two words *moth* and *mote* were pronounced alike.)   2. [Cob-
webs were used to stanch bleeding.]   3. Unripe pea pod.

150   Peascod,[4] your father. Good Master Peaseblossom, I shall desire you of more
    acquaintance too. Your name, I beseech you, sir?
MUSTARDSEED: Mustardseed.
BOTTOM: Good Master Mustardseed, I know your patience well.[5] That same cow-
    ardly, giant-like ox-beef hath devour'd many a gentleman of your house. I
155   promise you your kindred hath made my eyes water ere now. I desire you of
    more acquaintance, good Master Mustardseed.
TITANIA: Come wait upon him; lead him to my bower.
    The moon methinks looks with a wat'ry eye;
    And when she weeps,[6] weeps every little flower,
160   Lamenting some enforced[7] chastity.
    Tie up my lover's tongue, bring him silently.   [*Exeunt.*]

SCENE 2[8]

Enter OBERON, *King of Fairies.*

OBERON: I wonder if Titania be awak'd;
    Then, what it was that next came in her eye,
    Which she must dote on in extremity.

    [*Enter Robin Goodfellow* (PUCK).]

    Here comes my messenger. How now, mad spirit?
5   What night-rule[9] now about this haunted grove?
PUCK: My mistress with a monster is in love.
    Near to her close[1] and consecrated bower,
    While she was in her dull[2] and sleeping hour,
    A crew of patches, rude mechanicals,[3]
10   That work for bread upon Athenian stalls,
    Were met together to rehearse a play
    Intended for great Theseus' nuptial day.
    The shallowest thick-skin of that barren sort,[4]
    Who Pyramus presented,[5] in their sport
15   Forsook his scene[6] and ent'red in a brake.
    When I did him at this advantage take,
    An ass's nole[7] I fixed on his head.
    Anon his Thisby must be answered,
    And forth my mimic[8] comes. When they him spy,
20   As wild geese that the creeping fowler eye,

---

4. Ripe pea pod.   5. What you have endured.   6. That is, she causes dew.   7. Forced, violated, or,
possibly, constrained (since Titania at this moment is hardly concerned about chastity).   8. Location:
the wood.   9. Much frequented. *Night-rule:* diversion for the night.   1. Secret, private.
2. Drowsy.   3. Ignorant artisans. *Patches:* clowns, fools.   4. Stupid company or crew.   5. Acted.
6. Playing area.   7. Noddle, head.   8. Burlesque actor.

Or russet-pated choughs, many in sort,[9]
Rising and cawing at the gun's report,
Sever[1] themselves and madly sweep the sky,
So, at his sight, away his fellows fly;
And, at our stamp, here o'er and o'er one falls;   25
He murder cries and help from Athens calls.
Their sense thus weak, lost with their fears thus strong,
Made senseless things begin to do them wrong,
For briers and thorns at their apparel snatch;
Some, sleeves—some, hats; from yielders all things catch.   30
I led them on in this distracted fear
And left sweet Pyramus translated there,
When in that moment, so it came to pass,
Titania wak'd and straightway lov'd an ass.
OBERON: This falls out better than I could devise.   35
    But hast thou yet latch'd[2] the Athenian's eyes
    With the love-juice, as I did bid thee do?
PUCK: I took him sleeping—that is finish'd too—
    And the Athenian woman by his side,
    That, when he wak'd, of force[3] she must be ey'd.   40

        [*Enter* DEMETRIUS *and* HERMIA.]

OBERON: Stand close. This is the same Athenian.
PUCK: This is the woman, but not this the man.   [*They stand aside.*]
DEMETRIUS: O, why rebuke you him that loves you so?
    Lay breath so bitter on your bitter foe.
HERMIA: Now I but chide; but I should use thee worse,   45
    For thou, I fear, hast given me cause to curse.
    If thou hast slain Lysander in his sleep,
    Being o'er shoes in blood, plunge in the deep,
    And kill me too.
    The sun was not so true unto the day   50
    As he to me. Would he have stolen away
    From sleeping Hermia? I'll believe as soon
    This whole[4] earth may be bor'd and that the moon
    May through the center creep and so displease
    Her brother's noontide with th' Antipodes.[5]   55
    It cannot be but thou hast murd'red him;
    So should a murderer look, so dead,[6] so grim.
DEMETRIUS: So should the murdered look, and so should I,
    Pierc'd through the heart with your stern cruelty.
    Yet you, the murderer, look as bright, as clear,   60

---

9. In a flock. *Russet-pated choughs:* gray-headed jackdaws.   1. That is, scatter.   2. Moistened,
anointed.   3. Perforce.   4. Solid.   5. The people on the opposite side of the Earth. *Her brother's:*
that is, the sun's.   6. Deadly, or deathly pale.

As yonder Venus in her glimmering sphere.
HERMIA: What's this to my Lysander? Where is he?
    Ah, good Demetrius, wilt thou give him me?
DEMETRIUS: I had rather give his carcass to my hounds.
65 HERMIA: Out, dog! Out, cur! Thou driv'st me past the bounds
    Of maiden's patience. Hast thou slain him, then?
    Henceforth be never numb'red among men!
    O, once tell true, tell true, even for my sake!
    Durst thou have look'd upon him being awake,
70 And hast thou kill'd him sleeping? O brave touch![7]
    Could not a worm,[8] an adder, do so much?
    An adder did it; for with doubler tongue
    Than thine, thou serpent, never adder stung.
DEMETRIUS: You spend your passion on a mispris'd mood.[9]
75 I am not guilty of Lysander's blood,
    Nor is he dead, for aught that I can tell.
HERMIA: I pray thee, tell me then that he is well.
DEMETRIUS: An if I could, what should I get therefore?
HERMIA: A privilege never to see me more.
80 And from thy hated presence part I so.
    See me no more, whether he be dead or no.   [Exit.]
DEMETRIUS: There is no following her in this fierce vein.
    Here therefore for a while I will remain.
    So sorrow's heaviness doth heavier[1] grow
85 For debt that bankrupt[2] sleep doth sorrow owe;
    Which now in some slight measure it will pay,
    If for his tender here I make some stay.[3]   [He lies down and sleeps.]
OBERON: What hast thou done? Thou hast mistaken quite
    And laid the love-juice on some true-love's sight.
90 Of thy misprision[4] must perforce ensue
    Some true love turn'd and not a false turn'd true.
PUCK: Then fate o'er-rules, that, one man holding troth,[5]
    A million fail, confounding[6] oath on oath.
OBERON: About the wood go swifter than the wind,
95 And Helena of Athens look thou find.
    All fancy-sick she is and pale of cheer[7]
    With sighs of love, that cost the fresh blood[8] dear.
    By some illusion see thou bring her here.
    I'll charm his eyes against she do appear.[9]

7. Noble exploit (said ironically).   8. Serpent.   9. Anger based on misconception. *Passion:* violent feelings.   1. (1) Harder to bear; (2) more drowsy.   2. [Demetrius is saying that his sleepiness adds to the weariness caused by sorrow.]   3. That is, to a small extent I will be able to "pay back" and hence find some relief from sorrow, if I pause here a while (*make some stay*) while sleep "tenders" or offers itself by way of paying the debt owed to sorrow.   4. Mistake.   5. Faith.   6. That is, invalidating one oath with another.   7. Face. *Fancy-sick:* lovesick.   8. [An allusion to the physiological theory that each sigh costs the heart a drop of blood.]   9. In anticipation of her coming.

PUCK: I go, I go; look how I go,   100
   Swifter than arrow from the Tartar's bow.[1]   *[Exit.]*
OBERON: Flower of this purple dye,
     Hit with Cupid's archery.
     Sink in apple of his eye.   *[Applies love-juice to* DEMETRIUS's *eyes.]*
     When his love he doth espy,   105
     Let her shine as gloriously
     As the Venus of the sky.
     When thou wak'st, if she be by,
     Beg of her for remedy.

      [Enter PUCK.*]*

PUCK: Captain of our fairy band,   110
   Helena is here at hand,
   And the youth, mistook by me,
   Pleading for a lover's fee.[2]
   Shall we their fond pageant[3] see?
   Lord, what fools these mortals be!   115
OBERON: Stand aside. The noise they make
   Will cause Demetrius to awake.
PUCK: Then will two at once woo one;
   That must needs be sport alone[4];
   And those things do best please me   120
   That befall prepost'rously.[5]   *[They stand aside.]*

      [Enter LYSANDER *and* HELENA.*]*

LYSANDER: Why should you think that I should woo in scorn?
   Scorn and derision never come in tears.
   Look when[6] I vow, I weep; and vows so born,
   In their nativity all truth appears.[7]   125
   How can these things in me seem scorn to you,
   Bearing the badge[8] of faith, to prove them true?
HELENA: You do advance[9] your cunning more and more.
   When truth kills truth,[1] O devilish-holy fray!
   These vows are Hermia's. Will you give her o'er?
   Weigh oath with oath, and you will nothing weigh.   130
   Your vows to her and me, put in two scales,
   Will even weigh, and both as light as tales.[2]
LYSANDER: I had no judgment when to her I swore.
HELENA: Nor none, in my mind, now you give her o'er.   135

---

1. [Tartars were famed for their skill with the bow.]   2. Privilege, reward.   3. Foolish exhibition.
4. Unequaled.   5. Out of the natural order.   6. Whenever.   7. That is, vows made by one who is
weeping give evidence thereby of their sincerity.   8. Identifying device such as that worn on servants'
livery.   9. Carry forward, display.   1. That is, one of Lysander's vows must invalidate the other.
2. Lies.

LYSANDER: Demetrius loves her, and he loves not you.

DEMETRIUS: [*Awaking.*] O Helen, goddess, nymph, perfect, divine!
    To what, my love, shall I compare thine eyne?
    Crystal is muddy. O, how ripe in show[3]
140   Thy lips, those kissing cherries, tempting grow!
    That pure congealed white, high Taurus'[4] snow,
    Fann'd with the eastern wind, turns to a crow[5]
    When thou hold'st up thy hand. O, let me kiss
    This princess of pure white, this seal[6] of bliss!

145 HELENA: O spite! O hell! I see you all are bent
    To set against me for your merriment.
    If you were civil and knew courtesy,
    You would not do me thus much injury.
    Can you not hate me, as I know you do,
150   But you must join in souls to mock me too?
    If you were men, as men you are in show,
    You would not use a gentle lady so—
    To vow, and swear, and superpraise my parts,[7]
    When I am sure you hate me with your hearts.
155   You both are rivals, and love Hermia;
    And now both rivals, to mock Helena.
    A trim[8] exploit, a manly enterprise,
    To conjure tears up in a poor maid's eyes
    With your derision! None of noble sort
160   Would so offend a virgin and extort[9]
    A poor soul's patience, all to make you sport.

LYSANDER: You are unkind, Demetrius. Be not so;
    For you love Hermia; this you know I know.
    And here, with all good will, with all my heart,
165   In Hermia's love I yield you up my part;
    And yours of Helena to me bequeath,
    Whom I do love and will do till my death.

HELENA: Never did mockers waste more idle breath.

DEMETRIUS: Lysander, keep thy Hermia; I will none.[1]
170   If e'er I lov'd her, all that love is gone.
    My heart to her but as guest-wise sojourn'd,
    And now to Helen is it home return'd,
    There to remain.

LYSANDER: Helen, it is not so.

DEMETRIUS: Disparage not the faith thou dost not know,
175   Lest, to thy peril, thou aby[2] it dear.
    Look, where thy love comes; yonder is thy dear.

---

3. Appearance.   4. A lofty mountain range in Asia Minor.   5. That is, seems black by contrast.
6. Pledge.   7. Qualities. *Superpraise:* overpraise.   8. Pretty, fine (said ironically).   9. Twist, torture.
1. That is, wish none of her.   2. Pay for.

[*Enter* HERMIA.]

HERMIA: Dark night, that from the eye his[3] function takes,
   The ear more quick of apprehension makes;
   Wherein it doth impair the seeing sense,
   It pays the hearing double recompense.   180
   Thou art not by mine eye, Lysander, found;
   Mine ear, I thank it, brought me to thy sound.
   But why unkindly didst thou leave me so?
LYSANDER: Why should he stay, whom love doth press to go?
HERMIA: What love could press Lysander from my side?   185
LYSANDER: Lysander's love, that would not let him bide,
   Fair Helena, who more engilds the night
   Than all yon fiery oes[4] and eyes of light.
   Why seek'st thou me? Could not this make thee know,
   The hate I bear thee made me leave thee so?   190
HERMIA: You speak not as you think. It cannot be.
HELENA: Lo, she is one of this confederacy!
   Now I perceive they have conjoin'd all three
   To fashion this false sport, in spite of me.[5]
   Injurious Hermia, most ungrateful maid!   195
   Have you conspir'd, have you with these contriv'd[6]
   To bait[7] me with this foul derision?
   Is all the counsel[8] that we two have shar'd,
   The sisters' vows, the hours that we have spent,
   When we have chid the hasty-footed time   200
   For parting us—O, is all forgot?
   All school-days friendship, childhood innocence?
   We, Hermia, like two artificial[9] gods,
   Have with our needles created both one flower,
   Both on one sampler, sitting on one cushion,   205
   Both warbling of one song, both in one key,
   As if our hands, our sides, voices, and minds
   Had been incorporate. So we grew together,
   Like to a double cherry, seeming parted,
   But yet an union in partition;   210
   Two lovely[1] berries molded on one stem;
   So, with two seeming bodies, but one heart;
   Two of the first, like coats in heraldry,
   Due but to one and crowned with one crest.[2]
   And will you rent[3] our ancient love asunder,   215
   To join with men in scorning your poor friend?

3. Its.   4. That is, circles, orbs, stars.   5. To vex me.   6. Plotted.   7. Torment, as one sets on
dogs to bait a bear.   8. Confidential talk.   9. Skilled in art or creation.   1. Loving.   2. That is,
we have two separate bodies, just as a coat of arms in heraldry can be represented twice on a shield but
surmounted by a single crest.   3. Rend.

It is not friendly, 'tis not maidenly.
Our sex, as well as I, may chide you for it,
Though I alone do feel the injury.
220 HERMIA: I am amazed at your passionate words.
I scorn you not. It seems that you scorn me.
HELENA: Have you not set Lysander, as in scorn,
To follow me and praise my eyes and face?
And made your other love, Demetrius,
225 Who even but now did spurn me with his foot,
To call me goddess, nymph, divine and rare,
Precious, celestial? Wherefore speaks he this
To her he hates? And wherefore doth Lysander
Deny your love, so rich within his soul,
230 And tender[4] me, forsooth, affection,
But by your setting on, by your consent?
What though I be not so in grace[5] as you,
So hung upon with love, so fortunate,
But miserable most, to love unlov'd?
235 This you should pity rather than despise.
HERMIA: I understand not what you mean by this.
HELENA: Ay, do! Persever, counterfeit sad[6] looks,
Make mouths upon[7] me when I turn my back,
Wink each at other, hold the sweet jest up.
240 This sport, well carried,[8] shall be chronicled.
If you have any pity, grace, or manners,
You would not make me such an argument.[9]
But fare ye well. 'Tis partly my own fault,
Which death, or absence, soon shall remedy.
245 LYSANDER: Stay, gentle Helena; hear my excuse,
My love, my life, my soul, fair Helena!
HELENA: O excellent!
HERMIA: Sweet, do not scorn her so.
DEMETRIUS: If she cannot entreat,[1] I can compel.
LYSANDER: Thou canst compel no more than she entreat.
250 Thy threats have no more strength than her weak prayers.
Helen, I love thee, by my life, I do!
I swear by that which I will lose for thee,
To prove him false that says I love thee not.
DEMETRIUS: I say I love thee more than he can do.
255 LYSANDER: If thou say so, withdraw, and prove it too.
DEMETRIUS: Quick, come!
HERMIA: Lysander, whereto tends all this?

---

4. Offer.   5. Favor.   6. Grave, serious.   7. That is, makes mows, faces, grimaces at.   8. Managed.   9. Subject for a jest.   1. That is, succeed by entreaty.

LYSANDER: Away, you Ethiope![2]   [*He tries to break away from* HERMIA.]
DEMETRIUS: No, no; he'll
  Seem to break loose; take on as you would follow,
  But yet come not. You are a tame man, go!
LYSANDER: Hang off,[3] thou cat, thou burr! Vile thing, let loose,   260
  Or I will shake thee from me like a serpent!
HERMIA: Why are you grown so rude? What change is this,
  Sweet love?
LYSANDER: Thy love? Out, tawny Tartar, out!
  Out, loathed med'cine![4] O hated potion, hence!
HERMIA: Do you not jest?
HELENA: Yes, sooth,[5] and so do you.   265
LYSANDER: Demetrius, I will keep my word with thee.
DEMETRIUS: I would I had your bond, for I perceive
  A weak bond[6] holds you. I'll not trust your word.
LYSANDER: What, should I hurt her, strike her, kill her dead?
  Although I hate her, I'll not harm her so.   270
HERMIA: What, can you do me greater harm than hate?
  Hate me? Wherefore? O me, what news,[7] my love?
  Am not I Hermia? Are not you Lysander?
  I am as fair now as I was erewhile.[8]
  Since night you lov'd me; yet since night you left me.   275
  Why, then you left me—O, the gods forbid!—
  In earnest, shall I say?
LYSANDER: Ay, by my life!
  And never did desire to see thee more.
  Therefore be out of hope, of question, of doubt;
  Be certain, nothing truer. 'Tis no jest   280
  That I do hate thee and love Helena.
HERMIA: O me! You juggler! You cankerblossom![9]
  You thief of love! What, have you come by night
  And stol'n my love's heart from him?
HELENA: Fine, i' faith!
  Have you no modesty, no maiden shame,   285
  No touch of bashfulness? What, will you tear
  Impatient answers from my gentle tongue?
  Fie, fie! You counterfeit, you puppet,[1] you!
HERMIA: Puppet? Why so? Ay, that way goes the game.
  Now I perceive that she hath made compare   290
  Between our statures; she hath urg'd her height,
  And with her personage, her tall personage,

---

2. [Referring to Hermia's relatively dark hair and complexion; see also *tawny Tartar* six lines later.]
3. Let go.   4. That is, poison.   5. Truly.   6. That is, Hermia's arm (with a pun on *bond*, oath, in
the previous line).   7. What is the matter.   8. Just now.   9. Worm that destroys the flower bud (?).
1. (1) Counterfeit; (2) dwarfish woman (in reference to Hermia's smaller stature).

Her height, forsooth, she hath prevail'd with him.
And are you grown so high in his esteem,
295 Because I am so dwarfish and so low?
How low am I, thou painted maypole? Speak!
How low am I? I am not yet so low
But that my nails can reach unto thine eyes.

[*She flails at* HELENA, *but is restrained.*]

HELENA: I pray you, though you mock me, gentlemen,
300 Let her not hurt me. I was never curst;[2]
I have no gift at all in shrewishness;
I am a right[3] maid for my cowardice.
Let her not strike me. You perhaps may think,
Because she is something[4] lower than myself,
That I can match her.

305 HERMIA: Lower! Hark, again!

HELENA: Good Hermia, do not be so bitter with me.
I evermore did love you, Hermia,
Did ever keep your counsels, never wrong'd you;
Save that, in love unto Demetrius,
310 I told him of your stealth[5] unto this wood.
He followed you; for love I followed him.
But he hath chid me hence and threat'ned me
To strike me, spurn me, nay, to kill me too.
And now, so[6] you will let me quiet go,
315 To Athens will I bear my folly back
And follow you no further. Let me go.
You see how simple and how fond[7] I am.

HERMIA: Why, get you gone. Who is 't that hinders you?

HELENA: A foolish heart, that I leave here behind.

HERMIA: What, with Lysander?

320 HELENA: With Demetrius.

LYSANDER: Be not afraid; she shall not harm thee, Helena.

DEMETRIUS: No, sir, she shall not, though you take her part.

HELENA: O, when she is angry, she is keen and shrewd![8]
She was a vixen when she went to school;
325 And though she be but little, she is fierce.

HERMIA: "Little" again! Nothing but "low" and "little"!
Why will you suffer her to flout me thus?
Let me come to her.

LYSANDER: Get you gone, you dwarf!
You minimus, of hind'ring knot-grass[9] made!
You bead, you acorn!

2. Shrewish.   3. True.   4. Somewhat.   5. Stealing away.   6. If only.   7. Foolish.   8. Shrewish.
9. A weed, an infusion of which was thought to stunt the growth. *Minimus:* diminutive creature.

DEMETRIUS: You are too officious   330
  In her behalf that scorns your services.
  Let her alone. Speak not of Helena;
  Take not her part. For, if thou dost intend[1]
  Never so little show of love to her,
  Thou shalt aby[2] it.
LYSANDER: Now she holds me not;   335
  Now follow, if thou dar'st, to try whose right,
  Of thine or mine, is most in Helena.   *[Exit.]*
DEMETRIUS: Follow? Nay, I'll go with thee, cheek by jowl.[3]

                            [Exit, following LYSANDER.*]*

HERMIA: You, mistress, all this coil is 'long of[4] you.
  Nay, go not back.[5]
HELENA: I will not trust you, I,   340
  Nor longer stay in your curst company.
  Your hands than mine are quicker for a fray;
  My legs are longer, though, to run away.   *[Exit.]*
HERMIA: I am amaz'd, and know not what to say.   *[Exit.]*
OBERON: This is thy negligence. Still thou mistak'st,   345
  Or else committ'st thy knaveries willfully.
PUCK: Believe me, king of shadows, I mistook.
  Did not you tell me I should know the man
  By the Athenian garments he had on?
  And so far blameless proves my enterprise   350
  That I have 'nointed an Athenian's eyes;
  And so far am I glad it so did sort[6]
  As this their jangling I esteem a sport.
OBERON: Thou see'st these lovers seek a place to fight.
  Hie therefore, Robin, overcast the night;   355
  The starry welkin[7] cover thou anon
  With drooping fog as black as Acheron,[8]
  And lead these testy rivals so astray
  As[9] one come not within another's way.
  Like to Lysander sometime frame thy tongue,   360
  Then stir Demetrius up with bitter wrong;[1]
  And sometime rail thou like Demetrius.
  And from each other look thou lead them thus,
  Till o'er their brows death-counterfeiting sleep
  With leaden legs and batty[2] wings doth creep.   365
  Then crush this herb[3] into Lysander's eye,   *[Gives herb.]*
  Whose liquor hath this virtuous[4] property,

---

1. Give sign of.   2. Pay for.   3. That is, side by side.   4. On account of. *Coil:* turmoil, dissension.
5. That is, don't retreat (Hermia is again proposing a fight).   6. Turn out.   7. Sky.   8. River of
Hades (here representing Hades itself).   9. That.   1. Insults.   2. Batlike.   3. That is, the anti-
dote (mentioned in 2.1.184) to love-in-idleness.   4. Efficacious.

To take from thence all error with his[5] might
And make his eyeballs roll with wonted[6] sight.
370 When they next wake, all this derision[7]
Shall seem a dream and fruitless vision,
And back to Athens shall the lovers wend
With league whose date[8] till death shall never end.
Whiles I in this affair do thee employ,
375 I'll to my queen and beg her Indian boy;
And then I will her charmed eye release
From monster's view, and all things shall be peace.
PUCK: My fairy lord, this must be done with haste,
For night's swift dragons[9] cut the clouds full fast,
380 And yonder shines Aurora's harbinger,[1]
At whose approach, ghosts, wand'ring here and there,
Troop home to churchyards. Damned spirits all,
That in crossways and floods have burial,[2]
Already to their wormy beds are gone.
385 For fear lest day should look their shames upon,
They willfully themselves exile from light
And must for aye[3] consort with black-brow'd night.
OBERON: But we are spirits of another sort.
I with the Morning's love[4] have oft made sport,
390 And, like a forester,[5] the groves may tread
Even till the eastern gate, all fiery-red,
Opening on Neptune with fair blessed beams,
Turns into yellow gold his salt green streams.
But, notwithstanding, haste; make no delay.
395 We may effect this business yet ere day. [*Exit.*]
PUCK: Up and down, up and down,
I will lead them up and down.
I am fear'd in field and town.
Goblin, lead them up and down.
400 Here comes one.

[*Enter* LYSANDER.]

LYSANDER: Where art thou, proud Demetrius? Speak thou now.
PUCK: [*Mimicking* DEMETRIUS.] Here, villain, drawn[6] and ready. Where art thou?
LYSANDER: I will be with thee straight.[7]
PUCK: Follow me, then,

5. Its.   6. Accustomed.   7. Laughable business.   8. Term of existence.   9. [Supposed by Shakespeare to be yoked to the car of the goddess of night.]   1. The morning star, precursor of dawn.
2. [Those who had committed suicide were buried at crossways, with a stake driven through them; those drowned, that is, buried in floods or great waters, would be condemned to wander disconsolate for want of burial rites.]   3. Forever.   4. Cephalus, a beautiful youth beloved by Aurora; or perhaps the goddess of the dawn herself.   5. Keeper of a royal forest.   6. With drawn sword.   7. Immediately.

To plainer[8] ground.

[LYSANDER *wanders about,*[9] following the voice. *Enter* DEMETRIUS.]

DEMETRIUS: Lysander! Speak again!
 Thou runaway, thou coward, art thou fled?   405
 Speak! In some bush? Where dost thou hide thy head?
PUCK: [*Mimicking* LYSANDER.] Thou coward, art thou bragging to the stars,
 Telling the bushes that thou look'st for wars,
 And wilt not come? Come, recreant;[1] come, thou child,
 I'll whip thee with a rod. He is defil'd   410
 That draws a sword on thee.
DEMETRIUS: Yea, art thou there?
PUCK: Follow my voice. We'll try[2] no manhood here.   [*Exeunt.*]

[LYSANDER *returns.*]

LYSANDER: He goes before me and still dares me on.
 When I come where he calls, then he is gone.
 The villain is much lighter-heel'd than I.   415
 I followed fast, but faster he did fly,
 That fallen am I in dark uneven way,
 And here will rest me. [*Lies down.*] Come, thou gentle day!
 For if but once thou show me thy grey light,
 I'll find Demetrius and revenge this spite.   [*Sleeps.*] 420

[*Enter Robin* (PUCK) *and* DEMETRIUS.]

PUCK: Ho, ho, ho! Coward, why com'st thou not?
DEMETRIUS: Abide me, if thou dar'st; for well I wot[3]
 Thou runn'st before me, shifting every place,
 And dar'st not stand nor look me in the face.
 Where art thou now?
PUCK: Come hither. I am here.   425
DEMETRIUS: Nay, then, thou mock'st me. Thou shalt buy this dear,[4]
 If ever I thy face by daylight see.
 Now, go thy way. Faintness constraineth me
 To measure out my length on this cold bed.
 By day's approach look to be visited.   [*Lies down and sleeps.*] 430

[*Enter* HELENA.]

HELENA: O weary night, O long and tedious night,
 Abate[5] thy hours! Shine, comforts, from the east,
 That I may back to Athens by daylight,
 From these that my poor company detest;

---

8. Smoother. 9. [It is not clearly necessary that Lysander exit at this point; neither exit nor reentrance is indicated in the early texts.] 1. Cowardly wretch. 2. Test. 3. Know. 4. Pay dearly for this.
5. Lessen, shorten.

435   And sleep, that sometimes shuts up sorrow's eye,
       Steal me awhile from mine own company.   [*Lies down and sleeps.*]
PUCK: Yet but three? Come one more;
       Two of both kinds makes up four.
       Here she comes, curst and sad.
440   Cupid is a knavish lad,
       Thus to make poor females mad.

            [*Enter* HERMIA.]

HERMIA: Never so weary, never so in woe,
       Bedabbled with the dew and torn with briers,
       I can no further crawl, no further go;
445   My legs can keep no pace with my desires.
       Here will I rest me till the break of day.
       Heavens shield Lysander, if they mean a fray!   [*Lies down and sleeps.*]
PUCK: On the ground
       Sleep sound.
450   I'll apply
       To your eye,
       Gentle lover, remedy.   [*Squeezing the juice on* LYSANDER's *eyes.*]
       When thou wak'st,
       Thou tak'st
455   True delight
       In the sight
       Of thy former lady's eye;
       And the country proverb known,
       That every man should take his own,
460   In your waking shall be shown:
       Jack shall have Jill;
       Nought shall go ill;
       The man shall have his mare again, and all
          shall be well.   [*Exit. Manent the four lovers.*]

ACT IV

SCENE 1[6]

       Enter TITANIA, *Queen of Fairies, and* BOTTOM *the Clown, and* FAIRIES: *and* OBERON,
       the King, behind them.

TITANIA: Come, sit thee down upon this flow'ry bed,
       While I thy amiable cheeks do coy,[7]
       And stick musk-roses in thy sleek smooth head,
       And kiss thy fair large ears, my gentle joy.

---

6. Location: scene continues. The four lovers are still asleep on stage.   7. Caress. *Amiable:* lovely.

[*They recline.*]

BOTTOM: Where's Peaseblossom?   5

PEASEBLOSSOM: Ready.

BOTTOM: Scratch my head, Peaseblossom. Where's Mounsieur Cobweb?

COBWEB: Ready.

BOTTOM: Mounsieur Cobweb, good mounsieur, get you your weapons in your
    hand, and kill me a red-hipp'd humble-bee on the top of a thistle; and, good   10
    mounsieur, bring me the honey-bag. Do not fret yourself too much in the
    action, mounsieur; and, good mounsieur, have a care the honey-bag break
    not; I would be loath to have you overflown with a honey-bag, signior.
    Where's Mounsieur Mustardseed?   [*Exit* COBWEB.]

MUSTARDSEED: Ready.   15

BOTTOM: Give me your neaf,[8] Mounsieur Mustardseed. Pray you, leave your
    curtsy,[9] good mounsieur.

MUSTARDSEED: What's your will?

BOTTOM: Nothing, good mounsieur, but to help Cavalery Cobweb[1] to scratch. I
    must to the barber's, mounsieur; for methinks I am marvailes hairy about the   20
    face; and I am such a tender ass, if my hair do but tickle me, I must scratch.

TITANIA: What, wilt thou hear some music, my sweet love?

BOTTOM: I have a reasonable good ear in music. Let's have the tongs and the
    bones.[2]

      [*Music: tongs, rural music.*][3]

TITANIA: Or say, sweet love, what thou desirest to eat.   25

BOTTOM: Truly, a peck of provender. I could munch your good dry oats. Methinks
    I have a great desire to a bottle of hay. Good hay, sweet hay, hath no fellow.[4]

TITANIA: I have a venturous fairy that shall seek
    The squirrel's hoard, and fetch thee new nuts.

BOTTOM: I had rather have a handful or two of dried peas. But, I pray you, let none   30
    of your people stir me. I have an exposition[5] of sleep come upon me.

TITANIA: Sleep thou, and I will wind thee in my arms.
    Fairies, be gone, and be all ways[6] away.   [*Exeunt* FAIRIES.]
    So doth the woodbine the sweet honeysuckle
    Gently entwist; the female ivy so   35
    Enrings the barky fingers of the elm.
    Oh, how I love thee! How I dote on thee!   [*They sleep.*]

      [*Enter Robin Goodfellow* (PUCK).]

OBERON: [*Advancing.*] Welcome, good Robin. See'st thou this sweet sight?
    Her dotage now I do begin to pity.

---

8. Fist.   9. That is, put on your hat.   1. [Seemingly an error since Cobweb has been sent to bring
honey while Peaseblossom has been asked to scratch. *Cavalery:* form of address for a gentleman.]
2. Instruments for rustic music. (The tongs were played like a triangle, whereas the bones were held
between the fingers and used as clappers.)   3. [This stage direction is added from the Folio.]
4. Equal. *Bottle:* bundle.   5. [Bottom's word for *disposition.*]   6. In all directions.

40   For, meeting her of late behind the wood,
    Seeking sweet favors[7] for this hateful fool,
    I did upbraid her and fall out with her.
    For she his hairy temples then had rounded
    With coronet of fresh and fragrant flowers;
45   And that same dew, which sometime[8] on the buds
    Was wont to swell like round and orient pearls,[9]
    Stood now within the pretty flouriets'[1] eyes
    Like tears that did their own disgrace bewail.
    When I had at my pleasure taunted her,
50   And she in mild terms begg'd my patience,
    I then did ask of her her changeling child;
    Which straight she gave me, and her fairy sent
    To bear him to my bower in fairy land.
    And, now I have the boy, I will undo
55   This hateful imperfection of her eyes.
    And, gentle Puck, take this transformed scalp
    From off the head of this Athenian swain,
    That he, awaking when the other[2] do,
    May all to Athens back again repair,
60   And think no more of this night's accidents
    But as the fierce vexation of a dream.
    But first I will release the Fairy Queen.   [*Squeezes juice in her eyes.*]
        Be as thou wast wont to be;
        See as thou wast wont to see.
65   Dian's bud[3] o'er Cupid's flower
        Hath such force and blessed power.
    Now, my Titania, wake you, my sweet queen.
TITANIA: [*Waking.*] My Oberon! What visions have I seen!
    Methought I was enamor'd of an ass.
OBERON: There lies your love.
70 TITANIA: How came these things to pass?
    O, how mine eyes do loathe his visage now!
OBERON: Silence awhile. Robin, take off this head.
    Titania, music call, and strike more dead
    Than common sleep of all these five[4] the sense.
75 TITANIA: Music, ho! Music, such as charmeth sleep!

    [*Music.*]

PUCK: [*Removing the ass's head.*] Now, when thou wak'st, with thine own fool's
    eyes peep.

---

7. That is, gifts of flowers.   8. Formerly.   9. That is, the most beautiful of all pearls, those coming
from the Orient.   1. Flowerets'.   2. Others.   3. [Perhaps the flower of the *agnus castus,* or chaste-
tree, supposed to preserve chastity; or perhaps referring simply to Oberon's herb by which he can undo
the effects of "Cupid's flower," the love-in-idleness of 2.1.166 f.]   4. That is, the four lovers and Bottom.

OBERON: Sound, music! Come, my queen, take hands with me,
And rock the ground whereon these sleepers be.

[*Dance.*]
Now thou and I are new in amity, 80
And will tomorrow midnight solemnly[5]
Dance in Duke Theseus' house triumphantly
And bless it to all fair prosperity.
There shall the pairs of faithful lovers be
Wedded, with Theseus, all in jollity. 85
PUCK: Fairy King, attend, and mark:
I do hear the morning lark.
OBERON: Then, my queen, in silence sad,[6]
Trip we after night's shade.
We the globe can compass soon, 90
Swifter than the wand'ring moon.
TITANIA: Come, my lord, and in our flight
Tell me how it came this night
That I sleeping here was found
With these mortals on the ground. [*Exeunt.*] 95

[*Wind horn within. Enter* THESEUS *and all his train;* HIPPOLYTA, EGEUS.]

THESEUS: Go, one of you, find out the forester,
For now our observation[7] is perform'd;
And since we have the vaward[8] of the day,
My love shall hear the music of my hounds.
Uncouple in the western valley; let them go. 100
Dispatch, I say, and find the forester. [*Exit an Attendant.*]
We will, fair queen, up to the mountain's top
And mark the musical confusion
Of hounds and echo in conjunction.
HIPPOLYTA: I was with Hercules and Cadmus[9] once, 105
When in a wood of Crete they bay'd[1] the bear
With hounds of Sparta.[2] Never did I hear
Such gallant chiding; for, besides the groves,
The skies, the fountains, every region near
Seem'd all one mutual cry. I never heard 110
So musical a discord, such sweet thunder.
THESEUS: My hounds are bred out of the Spartan kind,
So flew'd, so sanded;[3] and their heads are hung
With ears that sweep away the morning dew;

---

5. Ceremoniously.   6. Sober.   7. That is, observance to a morn of May (1.1.167).   8. Vanguard,
that is, earliest part.   9. Mythical founder of Thebes. (This story about him is unknown.)   1. Brought
to bay.   2. [A breed famous in antiquity for its hunting skill.]   3. Of sandy color. *So flew'd:* similarly
having large hanging chaps or fleshy covering of the jaw.

115 Crook-knee'd, and dewlapp'd⁴ like Thessalian bulls;
 Slow in pursuit, but match'd in mouth like bells,
 Each under each. A cry more tuneable⁵
 Was never holla'd to, nor cheer'd with horn,
 In Crete, in Sparta, nor in Thessaly.
120 Judge when you hear. [*Sees the sleepers.*] But, soft! What nymphs are these?
 EGEUS: My lord, this' my daughter here asleep;
  And this, Lysander; this Demetrius is;
  This Helena, old Nedar's Helena.
  I wonder of their being here together.
125 THESEUS: No doubt they rose up early to observe
  The rite of May, and, hearing our intent,
  Came here in grace of our solemnity.⁶
  But speak, Egeus. Is not this the day
  That Hermia should give answer of her choice?
130 EGEUS: It is, my lord.
 THESEUS: Go, bid the huntsmen wake them with their horns.

             [*Exit an Attendant.*]

   [*Shout within. Wind horns. They all start up.*]

 Good morrow, friends. Saint Valentine⁷ is past.
 Begin these wood-birds but to couple now?
 LYSANDER: Pardon, my lord.   [*They kneel.*]
 THESEUS: I pray you all, stand up.
135 I know you two are rival enemies;
 How comes this gentle concord in the world,
 That hatred is so far from jealousy
 To sleep by hate and fear no enmity?
 LYSANDER: My lord, I shall reply amazedly,
140 Half sleep, half waking; but as yet, I swear,
 I cannot truly say how I came here.
 But, as I think—for truly would I speak,
 And now I do bethink me, so it is—
 I came with Hermia hither. Our intent
145 Was to be gone from Athens, where⁸ we might,
 Without⁹ the peril of the Athenian law—
 EGEUS: Enough, enough, my lord; you have enough.
 I beg the law, the law, upon his head.
 They would have stol'n away; they would, Demetrius,
150 Thereby to have defeated you and me,
 You of your wife and me of my consent,
 Of my consent that she should be your wife.

---

4. Having pendulous folds of skin under the neck. 5. Well tuned, melodious. *Match'd . . . each:* that is, harmoniously matched in their various cries like a set of bells, from treble down to bass. *Cry:* pack of hounds. 6. That is, observance of these same rites of May. 7. [Birds were supposed to choose their mates on St. Valentine's Day.] 8. Wherever, or to where. 9. Outside of, beyond.

DEMETRIUS: My lord, fair Helen told me of their stealth,
    Of this their purpose hither to this wood,
    And I in fury hither followed them,   155
    Fair Helena in fancy following me.
    But, my good lord, I wot not by what power—
    But by some power it is—my love to Hermia,
    Melted as the snow, seems to me now
    As the remembrance of an idle gaud[1]   160
    Which in my childhood I did dote upon;
    And all the faith, the virtue of my heart,
    The object and the pleasure of mine eye,
    Is only Helena. To her, my lord,
    Was I betroth'd ere I saw Hermia,   165
    But like a sickness did I loathe this food;
    But, as in health, come to my natural taste,
    Now I do wish it, love it, long for it,
    And will for evermore be true to it.
THESEUS: Fair lovers, you are fortunately met.   170
    Of this discourse we more will hear anon.
    Egeus, I will overbear your will;
    For in the temple, by and by, with us
    These couples shall eternally be knit.
    And, for the morning now is something[2] worn,   175
    Our purpos'd hunting shall be set aside.
    Away with us to Athens. Three and three,
    We'll hold a feast in great solemnity.
    Come, Hippolyta.   [*Exeunt* THESEUS, HIPPOLYTA, EGEUS, *and train.*]
DEMETRIUS: These things seem small and undistinguishable,   180
    Like far-off mountains turned into clouds.
HERMIA: Methinks I see these things with parted[3] eye,
    When every thing seems double.
HELENA: So methinks;
    And I have found Demetrius like a jewel,
    Mine own, and not mine own.[4]
DEMETRIUS: Are you sure   185
    That we are awake? It seems to me
    That yet we sleep, we dream. Do not you think
    The Duke was here, and bid us follow him?
HERMIA: Yea, and my father.
HELENA: And Hippolyta.
LYSANDER: And he did bid us follow to the temple.   190
DEMETRIUS: Why, then, we are awake. Let's follow him,
    And by the way let us recount our dreams.   [*Exeunt.*]
BOTTOM: [*Awaking.*] When my cue comes, call me, and I will answer. My next is,

---

1. Worthless trinket.   2. Somewhat. *For:* since.   3. Improperly focused.   4. That is, like a jewel
that one finds by chance and, therefore, possesses but cannot certainly consider one's own property.

"Most fair Pyramus." Heigh-ho! Peter Quince! Flute, the bellows-mender!
195 Snout, the tinker! Starveling! God's my life, stol'n hence, and left me asleep!
I have had a most rare vision. I have had a dream, past the wit of man to say
what dream it was. Man is but an ass, if he go about[5] to expound this dream.
Methought I was—there is no man can tell what. Methought I was—and
methought I had—but man is but a patch'd fool, if he will offer[6] to
200 say what methought I had. The eye of man hath not heard, the ear of man
hath not seen, man's hand is not able to taste, his tongue to conceive, nor
his heart to report, what my dream was. I will get Peter Quince to write a
ballad of this dream. It shall be called "Bottom's Dream," because it hath no
bottom; and I will sing it in the latter end of a play, before the Duke.
205 Peradventure, to make it the more gracious, I shall sing it at her[7] death.

[Exit.]

SCENE 2[8]

Enter QUINCE, FLUTE, SNOUT, *and* STARVELING.

QUINCE: Have you sent to Bottom's house? Is he come home yet?
STARVELING: He cannot be heard of. Out of doubt he is transported.[9]
FLUTE: If he come not, then the play is marr'd. It goes not forward, doth it?
QUINCE: It is not possible. You have not a man in all Athens able to discharge[1]
5 Pyramus but he.
FLUTE: No, he hath simply the best wit of any handicraft man in Athens.
QUINCE: Yea, and the best person too; and he is a very paramour for a sweet
voice.
FLUTE: You must say "paragon." A paramour is, God bless us, a thing of naught.

[*Enter* SNUG *the Joiner.*]

10 SNUG: Masters, the Duke is coming from the temple, and there is two or three
lords and ladies more married. If our sport had gone forward, we had all been
made men.
FLUTE: O sweet bully Bottom! Thus hath he lost sixpence a day[2] during his life; he
could not have scap'd sixpence a day. An the Duke had not given him
15 sixpence a day for playing Pyramus, I'll be hang'd. He would have deserv'd
it. Sixpence a day in Pyramus, or nothing.

[*Enter* BOTTOM.]

BOTTOM: Where are these lads? Where are these hearts?[3]
QUINCE: Bottom! O most courageous day! O most happy hour!
BOTTOM: Masters, I am to discourse wonders.[4] But ask me not what; for if I tell
20 you, I am no true Athenian. I will tell you everything, right as it fell out.

5. Attempt.   6. Venture. *Patch'd:* wearing motley, that is, a dress of various colors.   7. Thisby's (?).
8. Location: Athens. Quince's house (?).   9. Carried off by fairies or, possibly, transformed.   1. Perform.   2. That is, as a royal pension.   3. Good fellows.   4. Have wonders to relate.

QUINCE: Let us hear, sweet Bottom.

BOTTOM: Not a word of[5] me. All that I will tell you is, that the Duke hath din'd. Get your apparel together, good strings to your beards, new ribands[6] to your pumps; meet presently[7] at the palace; every man look o'er his part; for the short and the long is, our play is preferr'd.[8] In any case, let Thisby have clean   25
linen; and let not him that plays the lion pare his nails, for they shall hang out for the lion's claws. And, most dear actors, eat no onions nor garlic, for we are to utter sweet breath; and I do not doubt but to hear them say, it is a sweet comedy. No more words. Away! Go away!   [*Exeunt.*]

ACT V

SCENE 1[9]

Enter THESEUS, HIPPOLYTA, *and* PHILOSTRATE, *Lords, and Attendants.*

HIPPOLYTA: 'Tis strange, my Theseus, that[1] these lovers speak of.
THESEUS: More strange than true. I never may[2] believe
  These antic fables, nor these fairy toys.[3]
  Lovers and madmen have such seething brains,
  Such shaping fantasies,[4] that apprehend   5
  More than cool reason ever comprehends.
  The lunatic, the lover, and the poet
  Are of imagination all compact.[5]
  One sees more devils than vast hell can hold;
  That is the madman. The lover, all as frantic,   10
  Sees Helen's beauty in a brow of Egypt.[6]
  The poet's eye, in a fine frenzy rolling,
  Doth glance from heaven to earth, from earth to heaven;
  And as imagination bodies forth
  The forms of things unknown, the poet's pen   15
  Turns them to shapes and gives to airy nothing
  A local habitation and a name.
  Such tricks hath strong imagination
  That, if it would but apprehend some joy,
  It comprehends some bringer[7] of that joy;   20
  Or in the night, imagining some fear,[8]
  How easy is a bush suppos'd a bear!
HIPPOLYTA: But all the story of the night told over,
  And all their minds transfigur'd so together,

---

5. Out of.   6. Ribbons. *Strings:* that is, to attach the beards.   7. Immediately.   8. Selected for consideration.   9. Location: Athens. The palace of Theseus.   1. That which.   2. Can.   3. Trifling stories about fairies. *Antic:* strange, grotesque (with additional punning sense of *antique,* ancient). 4. Imaginations.   5. Formed, composed.   6. That is, face of a gypsy. *Helen's:* that is, of Helen of Troy, pattern of beauty.   7. That is, source.   8. Object of fear.

25   More witnesseth than fancy's images[9]
        And grows to something of great constancy;[1]
        But, howsoever, strange and admirable.[2]

        [*Enter lovers:* LYSANDER, DEMETRIUS, HERMIA, *and* HELENA.]

        THESEUS: Here come the lovers, full of joy and mirth.
        Joy, gentle friends! Joy and fresh days of love
        Accompany your hearts!
30   LYSANDER: More than to us
        Wait in your royal walks, your board, your bed!
        THESEUS: Come now, what masques, what dances shall we have,
        To wear away this long age of three hours
        Between our after-supper and bed-time?
35   Where is our usual manager of mirth?
        What revels are in hand? Is there no play,
        To ease the anguish of a torturing hour?
        Call Philostrate.
        PHILOSTRATE: Here, mighty Theseus.
        THESEUS: Say, what abridgement[3] have you for this evening?
40   What masque? What music? How shall we beguile
        The lazy time, if not with some delight?
        PHILOSTRATE: There is a brief[4] how many sports are ripe.
        Make choice of which your Highness will see first.   [*Giving a paper.*]
        THESEUS: [*Reads.*] "The battle with the Centaurs,[5] to be sung
45   By an Athenian eunuch to the harp."
        We'll none of that. That have I told my love,
        In glory of my kinsman[6] Hercules.
        [*Reads.*] "The riot of the tipsy Bacchanals,
        Tearing the Thracian singer in their rage."[7]
50   That is an old device; and it was play'd
        When I from Thebes came last a conqueror.
        [*Reads.*] "The thrice three Muses mourning for the death
        Of Learning, late deceas'd in beggary."[8]
        That is some satire, keen and critical,
55   Not sorting with[9] a nuptial ceremony.
        [*Reads.*] "A tedious brief scene of young Pyramus
        And his love Thisby; very tragical mirth."
        Merry and tragical? Tedious and brief?

9. Testifies to something more substantial than mere imaginings.   1. Certainty.   2. Source of wonder. *Howsoever:* in any case.   3. Pastime (to abridge or shorten the evening).   4. Short written statement, list.   5. [Probably refers to the battle of the Centaurs and the Lapithae, when the Centaurs
attempted to carry off Hippodamia, bride of Theseus's friend Pirothous.]   6. [Plutarch's *Life of Theseus*
states that Hercules and Theseus were near kinsmen. Theseus is referring to a version of the battle of the
Centaurs in which Hercules was said to be present.]   7. [This was the story of the death of Orpheus,
as told in *Metamorphoses* 11.]   8. [Possibly an allusion to Spenser's *Teares of the Muses* (1591), though
"satires" deploring the neglect of learning and the creative arts were commonplace.]   9. Befitting.

That is, hot ice and wondrous strange[1] snow.
How shall we find the concord of this discord? 60
PHILOSTRATE: A play there is, my lord, some ten words long,
Which is as brief as I have known a play;
But by ten words, my lord, it is too long,
Which makes it tedious. For in all the play
There is not one word apt, one player fitted. 65
And tragical, my noble lord, it is,
For Pyramus therein doth kill himself.
Which, when I saw rehears'd, I must confess,
Made mine eyes water; but more merry tears
The passion of loud laughter never shed. 70
THESEUS: What are they that do play it?
PHILOSTRATE: Hard-handed men that work in Athens here,
Which never labor'd in their minds till now,
And now have toil'd their unbreathed[2] memories
With this same play, against[3] your nuptial. 75
THESEUS: And we will hear it.
PHILOSTRATE: No, my noble lord,
It is not for you. I have heard it over,
And it is nothing, nothing in the world;
Unless you can find sport in their intents,
Extremely stretch'd and conn'd[4] with cruel pain, 80
To do you service.
THESEUS: I will hear that play;
For never anything can be amiss
When simpleness and duty tender it.
Go, bring them in; and take your places, ladies.

[PHILOSTRATE *goes to summon the players.*]

HIPPOLYTA: I love not to see wretchedness o'ercharg'd[5] 85
And duty in his service[6] perishing.
THESEUS: Why, gentle sweet, you shall see no such thing.
HIPPOLYTA: He says they can do nothing in this kind.[7]
THESEUS: The kinder we, to give them thanks for nothing.
Our sport shall be to take what they mistake; 90
And what poor duty cannot do, noble respect
Takes it in might, not merit.[8]
Where I have come, great clerks[9] have purposed
To greet me with premeditated welcomes;
Where I have seen them shiver and look pale, 95

---

1. [Seemingly an error for some adjective that would contrast with *snow,* just as *hot* contrasts with *ice.*]
2. Unexercised. *Toil'd:* taxed. 3. In preparation for. 4. Memorized. *Stretch'd:* strained. 5. Incompetence overburdened. 6. Its attempt to serve. 7. Kind of thing. 8. Values it for the effort made rather than for the excellence achieved. 9. Learned men.

Make periods in the midst of sentences,
Throttle their practic'd accent[1] in their fears,
And in conclusion dumbly have broke off,
Not paying me a welcome. Trust me, sweet,
100 Out of this silence yet I pick'd a welcome;
And in the modesty of fearful duty
I read as much as from the rattling tongue
Of saucy and audacious eloquence.
Love, therefore, and tongue-tied simplicity
105 In least speak most, to my capacity.[2]

[PHILOSTRATE *returns.*]

PHILOSTRATE: So please your Grace, the Prologue is address'd.[3]
THESEUS: Let him approach.

[*Flourish of trumpets. Enter the Prologue* (QUINCE).]

PROLOGUE: If we offend, it is with our good will.
That you should think, we come not to offend,
110 But with good will. To show our simple skill,
That is the true beginning of our end.
Consider, then, we come but in despite.
We do not come, as minding[4] to content you,
Our true intent is. All for your delight
115 We are not here. That you should here repent you,
The actors are at hand; and, by their show,
You shall know all that you are like to know.
THESEUS: This fellow doth not stand upon points.[5]
LYSANDER: He hath rid his prologue like a rough[6] colt; he knows not the stop.[7]
120 A good moral, my lord: it is not enough to speak, but to speak true.
HIPPOLYTA: Indeed he hath play'd on his prologue like a child on a recorder; a
sound, but not in government.[8]
THESEUS: His speech was like a tangled chain, nothing[9] impair'd, but all disorder'd.
Who is next?

[*Enter* PYRAMUS *and* THISBY, *and* WALL, *and* MOONSHINE, *and* LION.]

125 PROLOGUE: Gentles, perchance you wonder at this show;
But wonder on, till truth make all things plain.
This man is Pyramus, if you would know;
This beauteous lady Thisby is certain.
This man, with lime and rough-cast, doth present

---

1. That is, rehearsed speech, or usual way of speaking.   2. In my judgment and understanding. *Least:*
that is, saying least.   3. Ready. *Prologue:* speaker of the prologue.   4. Intending.   5. (1) Heed nice-
ties or small points; (2) pay attention to punctuation in his reading. (The humor of Quince's speech is
in the blunders of its punctuation.)   6. Unbroken.   7. (1) The stopping of a colt by reining it in; (2)
punctuation mark.   8. Control. *Recorder:* a wind instrument like a flute or flageolet.   9. Not at all.

Wall, that vile Wall which did these lovers sunder;   130
And through Wall's chink, poor souls, they are content
To whisper. At the which let no man wonder.
This man, with lantern, dog, and bush of thorn,
Presenteth Moonshine; for, if you will know,
By moonshine did these lovers think no scorn[1]   135
To meet at Ninus' tomb, there, there to woo.
This grisly beast, which Lion hight[2] by name,
The trusty Thisby, coming first by night,
Did scare away, or rather did affright;
And, as she fled, her mantle she did fall,[3]   140
Which Lion vile with bloody mouth did stain.
Anon comes Pyramus, sweet youth and tall,[4]
And finds his trusty Thisby's mantle slain;
Whereat, with blade, with bloody blameful blade,
He bravely broach'd[5] his boiling bloody breast.   145
And Thisby, tarrying in mulberry shade,
His dagger drew, and died. For all the rest,
Let Lion, Moonshine, Wall, and lovers twain
At large[6] discourse, while here they do remain.

                [*Exeunt* LION, THISBY, *and* MOONSHINE.]

THESEUS: I wonder if the lion be to speak.   150
DEMETRIUS: No wonder, my lord. One lion may, when many asses do.
WALL: In this same interlude it doth befall
  That I, one Snout by name, present a wall;
  And such a wall, as I would have you think,
  That had in it a crannied hole or chink,   155
  Through which the lovers, Pyramus and Thisby,
  Did whisper often very secretly.
  This loam, this rough-cast, and this stone doth show
  That I am that same wall; the truth is so.
  And this the cranny is, right and sinister,[7]   160
  Through which the fearful lovers are to whisper.
THESEUS: Would you desire lime and hair to speak better?
DEMETRIUS: It is the wittiest partition[8] that ever I heard discourse, my lord.

      [PYRAMUS *comes forward.*]

THESEUS: Pyramus draws near the wall. Silence!
PYRAMUS: O grim-look'd[9] night! O night with hue so black!   165
  O night, which ever art when day is not!
  O night, O night! Alack, alack, alack,

---

1. Think it no disgraceful matter.   2. Is called.   3. Let fall.   4. Courageous.   5. Stabbed.
6. In full, at length.   7. That is, the right side of it and the left; or running from right to left, horizontally.   8. (1) Wall; (2) section of a learned treatise or oration.   9. Grim-looking.

I fear my Thisby's promise is forgot.
And thou, O wall, O sweet, O lovely wall,
170 That stand'st between her father's ground and mine,
Thou wall, O wall, O sweet and lovely wall,
Show me thy chink, to blink through with mine eyne!

[WALL *holds up his fingers.*]

Thanks, courteous Wall. Jove shield thee well for this!
But what see I? No Thisby do I see.
175 O wicked wall, through whom I see no bliss!
Curs'd be thy stones for thus deceiving me!
THESEUS: The wall, methinks, being sensible,[1] should curse again.
PYRAMUS: No, in truth, sir, he should not. "Deceiving me" is Thisby's cue: she is
to enter now, and I am to spy her through the wall. You shall see, it will
180 fall pat as I told you. Yonder she comes.

[*Enter* THISBY.]

THISBY: O wall, full often hast thou heard my moans,
For parting my fair Pyramus and me.
My cherry lips have often kiss'd thy stones,
Thy stones with lime and hair knit up in thee.
185 PYRAMUS: I see a voice. Now will I to the chink,
To spy an[2] I can hear my Thisby's face.
Thisby!
THISBY: My love! Thou art my love, I think.
PYRAMUS: Think what thou wilt, I am thy lover's grace;[3]
190 And, like Limander, am I trusty still.
THISBY: And I like Helen,[4] till the Fates me kill.
PYRAMUS: Not Shafalus to Procrus[5] was so true.
THISBY: As Shafalus to Procrus, I to you.
PYRAMUS: O, kiss me through the hole of this vile wall!
195 THISBY: I kiss the wall's hole, not your lips at all.
PYRAMUS: Wilt thou at Ninny's tomb meet me straightway?
THISBY: 'Tide life, 'tide[6] death, I come without delay.

[*Exeunt* PYRAMUS *and* THISBY.]

WALL: Thus have I, Wall, my part discharged so;
And, being done, thus Wall away doth go.   [*Exit.*]
200 THESEUS: Now is the mural down between the two neighbors.
DEMETRIUS: No remedy, my lord, when walls are so willful to hear without
warning.[7]
HIPPOLYTA: This is the silliest stuff that ever I heard.

---

1. Capable of feeling.   2. If.   3. That is, gracious lover.   4. [Blunders for "Leander" (*Limander*) and
"Hero."]   5. [Blunders for "Cephalus" (*Shafalus*) and "Procris," also famous lovers.]   6. Betide, come.
7. That is, without warning the parents. *To hear:* as to hear.

THESEUS: The best in this kind are but shadows;[8] and the worst are no worse, if imagination amend them.   205

HIPPOLYTA: It must be your imagination then, and not theirs.

THESEUS: If we imagine no worse of them than they of themselves, they may pass for excellent men. Here come two noble beasts in, a man and a lion.

[*Enter* LION *and* MOONSHINE.]

LION: You, ladies, you, whose gentle hearts do fear
    The smallest monstrous mouse that creeps on floor,   210
    May now perchance both quake and tremble here,
    When lion rough in widest rage doth roar.
    Then know that I, as Snug the joiner, am
    A lion fell,[9] nor else no lion's dam;
    For, if I should as lion come in strife   215
    Into this place, 'twere pity on my life.

THESEUS: A very gentle beast, and of a good conscience.

DEMETRIUS: The very best at a beast, my lord, that e'er I saw.

LYSANDER: This lion is a very fox for his valor.[1]

THESEUS: True; and a goose for his discretion.[2]   220

DEMETRIUS: Not so, my lord; for his valor cannot carry his discretion; and the fox carries the goose.

THESEUS: His discretion, I am sure, cannot carry his valor; for the goose carries not the fox. It is well. Leave it to his discretion, and let us listen to the moon.

MOON: This lanthorn[3] doth the horned moon present—   225

DEMETRIUS: He should have worn the horns on his head.[4]

THESEUS: He is no crescent, and his horns are invisible within the circumference.

MOON: This lanthorn doth the horned moon present;
    Myself the man i' th' moon do seem to be.   230

THESEUS: This is the greatest error of all the rest. The man should be put into the lanthorn. How is it else the man i' th' moon?

DEMETRIUS: He dares not come there for the[5] candle; for, you see, it is already in snuff.[6]

HIPPOLYTA: I am aweary of this moon. Would he would change!   235

THESEUS: It appears, by his small light of discretion, that he is in the wane; but yet, in courtesy, in all reason, we must stay the time.

LYSANDER: Proceed, Moon.

MOON: All that I have to say is to tell you that the lanthorn is the moon, I, the man in the moon, this thorn-bush my thorn-bush, and this dog my dog.   240

---

8. Likenesses, representations. *In this kind:* of this sort.   9. Fierce lion (with a play on the idea of *lion skin*).   1. That is, his valor consists of craftiness and discretion.   2. That is, as discreet as a goose, meaning more foolish than discreet.   3. [This original spelling, *lanthorn,* may suggest a play on the *horn* of which lanterns were made, and also on a cuckold's horns; but the spelling *lanthorn* is not used consistently for comic effect in this play or elsewhere. At 5.1.133, for example, the word is *lantern* in the original.]   4. [As a sign of cuckoldry.]   5. Because of the.   6. (1) Offended; (2) in need of snuffing.

DEMETRIUS: Why, all these should be in the lanthorn; for all these are in the moon. But silence! Here comes Thisby.

[*Enter* THISBY.]

THISBY: This is old Ninny's tomb. Where is my love?
LION: [*Roaring.*] Oh— [THISBY *runs off, dropping her mantle.*]
245 DEMETRIUS: Well roar'd, Lion.
THESEUS: Well run, Thisby.
HIPPOLYTA: Well shone, Moon. Truly, the moon shines with a good grace.

[*The* LION *shakes* THISBY's *mantle, and exits.*]

THESEUS: Well mous'd,[7] Lion.
DEMETRIUS: And then came Pyramus.

[*Enter* PYRAMUS.]

250 LYSANDER: And so the lion vanish'd.
PYRAMUS: Sweet Moon, I thank thee for thy sunny beams;
I thank thee, Moon, for shining now so bright;
For, by thy gracious, golden, glittering gleams,
I trust to take of truest Thisby sight.

255   But stay, O spite!
      But mark, poor knight,
What dreadful dole[8] is here!
      Eyes, do you see?
      How can it be?
260   O dainty duck! O dear!
      Thy mantle good,
      What, stain'd with blood!
Approach, ye Furies fell![9]
      O Fates, come, come,
265   Cut thread and thrum;[1]
Quail, crush, conclude, and quell![2]

THESEUS: This passion, and the death of a dear friend, would go near to make a man look sad.[3]
HIPPOLYTA: Beshrew my heart, but I pity the man.
270 PYRAMUS: O wherefore, Nature, didst thou lions frame?
Since lion vile hath here deflow'r'd my dear,
Which is—no, no—which was the fairest dame
That liv'd, that lov'd, that lik'd, that look'd with cheer.[4]

274   Come, tears, confound,
275   Out, sword, and wound

---

7. Shaken.   8. Grievous event.   9. Fierce.   1. The warp in weaving and the loose end of the warp.
2. Kill, destroy. *Quail:* overpower.   3. That is, if one had other reason to grieve, one might be sad, but not from this absurd portrayal of passion.   4. Countenance.

The pap of Pyramus;
  Ay, that left pap,
  Where heart doth hop.   [*Stabs himself.*]
Thus die I, thus, thus, thus.
  Now am I dead,   280
  Now am I fled;
My soul is in the sky.
  Tongue, lose thy light;
  Moon, take thy flight.   [*Exit* MOONSHINE.]
Now die, die, die, die, die.   [*Dies.*]   285

DEMETRIUS: No die, but an ace,[5] for him; for he is but one.[6]
LYSANDER: Less than an ace, man; for he is dead, he is nothing.
THESEUS: With the help of a surgeon he might yet recover, and yet prove an ass.[7]
HIPPOLYTA: How chance Moonshine is gone before Thisby comes back and finds
  her lover?   290
THESEUS: She will find him by starlight. Here she comes; and her passion ends the
  play.

    [*Enter* THISBY.]

HIPPOLYTA: Methinks she should not use a long one for such a Pyramus. I hope
  she will be brief.
DEMETRIUS: A mote will turn the balance, which Pyramus, which[8] Thisby, is the   295
  better: he for a man, God warr'nt us; she for a woman, God bless us.
LYSANDER: She hath spied him already with those sweet eyes.
DEMETRIUS: And thus she means, videlicet:[9]
THISBY: Asleep, my love?
  What, dead, my dove?   300
O Pyramus, arise!
  Speak, speak. Quite dumb?
  Dead, dead? A tomb
Must cover thy sweet eyes.
  These lily lips,   305
  This cherry nose,
These yellow cowslip cheeks,
  Are gone, are gone!
  Lovers, make moan.
His eyes were green as leeks.   310
  O Sisters Three,[1]
  Come, come to me,
With hands as pale as milk;
  Lay them in gore,

---

5. The side of the die featuring the single pip, or spot. (The pun is on *die* as a singular of *dice;* Bottom's performance is not worth a whole *die* but rather one single face of it, one small portion.) 6. (1) An individual person; (2) unique. 7. [With a pun on *ace.*] 8. Whether . . . or. 9. To wit. *Means:* moans, laments. 1. The Fates.

315	Since you have shore[2]
	With shears his thread of silk.
	Tongue, not a word.
	Come, trusty sword,
	Come, blade, my breast imbrue![3] *[Stabs herself.]*
320	And farewell, friends.
	Thus Thisby ends.
	Adieu, adieu, adieu. *[Dies.]*

THESEUS: Moonshine and Lion are left to bury the dead.

DEMETRIUS: Ay, and Wall too.

325 BOTTOM: [*Starting up.*] No, I assure you; the wall is down that parted their fathers. Will it please you to see the epilogue, or to hear a Bergomask dance[4] between two of our company?

THESEUS: No epilogue, I pray you; for your play needs no excuse. Never excuse; for when the players are all dead, there need none to be blam'd. Marry, if he 330 that writ it had play'd Pyramus and hang'd himself in Thisby's garter, it would have been a fine tragedy; and so it is, truly, and very notably discharg'd. But, come, your Bergomask. Let your epilogue alone.   [*A dance.*]

The iron tongue of midnight hath told[5] twelve.
Lovers, to bed; 'tis almost fairy time.
335 I fear we shall outsleep the coming morn
As much as we this night have overwatch'd.[6]
This palpable-gross[7] play hath well beguil'd
The heavy[8] gait of night. Sweet friends, to bed.
A fortnight hold we this solemnity,
340 In nightly revels and new jollity.   [*Exeunt.*]

[*Enter* PUCK, *carrying a broom.*]

	PUCK: Now the hungry lion roars,
	And the wolf behowls the moon;
	Whilst the heavy ploughman snores,
	All with weary task fordone.[9]
345	Now the wasted brands[1] do glow,
	Whilst the screech-owl, screeching loud,
	Puts the wretch that lies in woe
	In remembrance of a shroud.
	Now it is the time of night
350	That the graves, all gaping wide,
	Every one lets forth his sprite,[2]
	In the churchway paths to glide.
	And we fairies, that do run

---

2. Shorn.   3. Stain with blood.   4. A rustic dance named from Bergamo, a province in the state of Venice.   5. Counted, struck ("tolled").   6. Stayed up too late.   7. Palpably gross, obviously crude.   8. Drowsy, dull.   9. Exhausted.   1. Burned-out logs.   2. Every grave lets forth its ghost.

By the triple Hecate's[3] team
From the presence of the sun,   355
   Following darkness like a dream,
Now are frolic.[4] Not a mouse
Shall disturb this hallowed house.
I am sent with broom before,
To sweep the dust behind[5] the door.   360

[*Enter* OBERON *and* TITANIA, *King and Queen of Fairies, with all their train.*]

OBERON: Through the house give glimmering light,
   By the dead and drowsy fire;
Every elf and fairy sprite
   Hop as light as bird from brier;
And this ditty, after me,   365
Sing, and dance it trippingly.
TITANIA: First, rehearse your song by rote,
To each word a warbling note.
Hand in hand, with fairy grace,
Will we sing, and bless this place.   370

[*Song and dance.*]

OBERON: Now, until the break of day,
Through this house each fairy stray.
To the best bride-bed will we,
Which by us shall blessed be;
And the issue there create[6]   375
Ever shall be fortunate.
So shall all the couples three
Ever true in loving be;
And the blots of Nature's hand
Shall not in their issue stand;   380
Never mole, hare lip, nor scar,
Nor mark prodigious,[7] such as are
Despised in nativity,
Shall upon their children be.
With this field-dew consecrate,[8]   385
Every fairy take his gait,[9]
And each several[1] chamber bless,
Through this palace, with sweet peace;
And the owner of it blest

3. [Hecate ruled in three capacities: as Luna or Cynthia in Heaven, as Diana on Earth, and as Proserpina in Hell.]   4. Merry.   5. From behind. (Robin Goodfellow was a household spirit who helped good housemaids and punished lazy ones.)   6. Created.   7. Monstrous, unnatural.   8. Consecrated. 9. Go his way.   1. Separate.

390   Ever shall in safety rest.
             Trip away; make no stay;
             Meet me all by break of day.   [*Exeunt* OBERON, TITANIA, *and train.*]
PUCK: If we shadows have offended,
             Think but this, and all is mended,
395   That you have but slumb'red here[2]
             While these visions did appear.
             And this weak and idle theme,
             No more yielding but[3] a dream,
             Gentles, do not reprehend.
400   If you pardon, we will mend.
             And, as I am an honest Puck,
             If we have unearned luck
             Now to scape the serpent's tongue,[4]
             We will make amends ere long;
405   Else the Puck a liar call.
             So, good night unto you all.
             Give me your hands,[5] if we be friends,
             And Robin shall restore amends.   [*Exit.*]

ca. 1594–1595

2. That is, that it is a "midsummer night's dream."   3. Yielding no more than.   4. That is, hissing.
5. Applaud.

Hamlet

CHARACTERS

CLAUDIUS, *King of Denmark*
HAMLET, *son of the former and*
    nephew to the present King
POLONIUS, *Lord Chamberlain*
HORATIO, *friend of Hamlet*
LAERTES, *son of Polonius*
VOLTEMAND
CORNELIUS
ROSENCRANTZ
GUILDENSTERN   } *courtiers*
OSRIC
A GENTLEMAN
A PRIEST

MARCELLUS }
BERNARDO   } *officers*
FRANCISCO, *a soldier*
REYNALDO, *servant to Polonius*
PLAYERS
TWO CLOWNS, *gravediggers*
FORTINBRAS, *Prince of Norway*
A NORWEGIAN CAPTAIN
ENGLISH AMBASSADORS
GERTRUDE, *Queen of Denmark, and*
    mother of Hamlet
OPHELIA, *daughter of Polonius*
GHOST OF HAMLET'S FATHER

LORDS, LADIES, OFFICERS, SOLDIERS, SAILORS, MESSENGERS, AND ATTENDANTS

SCENE: *The action takes place in or near the royal castle of Denmark at Elsinore.*

ACT I

SCENE 1

A guard station atop the castle. Enter BERNARDO *and* FRANCISCO, *two sentinels.*

BERNARDO: Who's there?

FRANCISCO: Nay, answer me. Stand and unfold yourself.

BERNARDO: Long live the king!

FRANCISCO: Bernardo?

BERNARDO: He.   5

FRANCISCO: You come most carefully upon your hour.

BERNARDO: 'Tis now struck twelve. Get thee to bed, Francisco.

FRANCISCO: For this relief much thanks. 'Tis bitter cold,
   And I am sick at heart.

BERNARDO: Have you had quiet guard?

FRANCISCO: Not a mouse stirring.   10

BERNARDO: Well, good night.
   If you do meet Horatio and Marcellus,
   The rivals[1] of my watch, bid them make haste.

       [*Enter* HORATIO *and* MARCELLUS.]

FRANCISCO: I think I hear them. Stand, ho! Who is there?

HORATIO: Friends to this ground.

MARCELLUS: And liegemen to the Dane.[2]   15

FRANCISCO: Give you good night.

MARCELLUS: O, farewell, honest soldier!
   Who hath relieved you?

FRANCISCO: Bernardo hath my place.
   Give you good night.   [*Exit* FRANCISCO.]

MARCELLUS: Holla, Bernardo!

BERNARDO: Say—
   What, is Horatio there?

HORATIO: A piece of him.

BERNARDO: Welcome, Horatio. Welcome, good Marcellus.   20

HORATIO: What, has this thing appeared again tonight?

BERNARDO: I have seen nothing.

MARCELLUS: Horatio says 'tis but our fantasy,
   And will not let belief take hold of him
   Touching this dreaded sight twice seen of us.   25
   Therefore I have entreated him along
   With us to watch the minutes of this night,

---

1. Companions.   2. The "Dane" is the king of Denmark, who is also called "Denmark," as in line 48 of this scene. In line 61 the same figure is used for the king of Norway.

That if again this apparition come,
He may approve[3] our eyes and speak to it.
HORATIO: Tush, tush, 'twill not appear.
30   BERNARDO: Sit down awhile,
And let us once again assail your ears,
That are so fortified against our story,
What we have two nights seen.
HORATIO: Well, sit we down.
And let us hear Bernardo speak of this.
35   BERNARDO: Last night of all,
When yond same star that's westward from the pole[4]
Had made his course t' illume that part of heaven
Where now it burns, Marcellus and myself,
The bell then beating one—

[*Enter* GHOST.]

40   MARCELLUS: Peace, break thee off. Look where it comes again.
BERNARDO: In the same figure like the king that's dead.
MARCELLUS: Thou art a scholar; speak to it, Horatio.
BERNARDO: Looks 'a[5] not like the king? Mark it, Horatio.
HORATIO: Most like. It harrows me with fear and wonder.
BERNARDO: It would be spoke to.
45   MARCELLUS: Speak to it, Horatio.
HORATIO: What art thou that usurp'st this time of night
Together with that fair and warlike form
In which the majesty of buried Denmark
Did sometimes march? By heaven I charge thee, speak.
MARCELLUS: It is offended.
50   BERNARDO: See, it stalks away.
HORATIO: Stay. Speak, speak. I charge thee, speak.   [*Exit* GHOST.]
MARCELLUS: 'Tis gone and will not answer.
BERNARDO: How now, Horatio! You tremble and look pale.
Is not this something more than fantasy?
55   What think you on't?
HORATIO: Before my God, I might not this believe
Without the sensible[6] and true avouch
Of mine own eyes.
MARCELLUS: Is it not like the king?
HORATIO: As thou art to thyself.
60   Such was the very armor he had on
When he the ambitious Norway combated.
So frowned he once when, in an angry parle,[7]
He smote the sledded Polacks on the ice.

---

3. Confirm the testimony of.   4. Polestar.   5. He.   6. Perceptible.   7. Parley.

'Tis strange.
MARCELLUS: Thus twice before, and jump[8] at this dead hour,
  With martial stalk hath he gone by our watch.   65
HORATIO: In what particular thought to work I know not,
  But in the gross and scope of mine opinion,
  This bodes some strange eruption to our state.
MARCELLUS: Good now, sit down, and tell me he that knows,
  Why this same strict and most observant watch   70
  So nightly toils the subject[9] of the land,
  And why such daily cast of brazen cannon
  And foreign mart for implements of war;
  Why such impress of shipwrights, whose sore task
  Does not divide the Sunday from the week.   75
  What might be toward that this sweaty haste
  Doth make the night joint-laborer with the day?
  Who is't that can inform me?
HORATIO: That can I.
  At last, the whisper goes so. Our last king,
  Whose image even but now appeared to us,   80
  Was as you know by Fortinbras of Norway,
  Thereto pricked on by a most emulate pride,
  Dared to the combat; in which our valiant Hamlet
  (For so this side of our known world esteemed him)
  Did slay this Fortinbras; who by a sealed compact   85
  Well ratified by law and heraldry,
  Did forfeit, with his life, all those his lands
  Which he stood seized of,[1] to the conqueror;
  Against the which a moiety competent[2]
  Was gagéd[3] by our king; which had returned   90
  To the inheritance of Fortinbras,
  Had he been vanquisher; as, by the same covenant
  And carriage of the article designed,
  His fell to Hamlet. Now, sir, young Fortinbras,
  Of unimprovéd mettle hot and full,   95
  Hath in the skirts of Norway here and there
  Sharked up a list of lawless resolutes
  For food and diet to some enterprise
  That hath a stomach in't; which is no other,
  As it doth well appear unto our state,   100
  But to recover of us by strong hand
  And terms compulsatory, those foresaid lands
  So by his father lost; and this, I take it,
  Is the main motive of our preparations,

---

8. Precisely.   9. People.   1. Possessed.   2. Portion of similar value.   3. Pledged.

105   The source of this our watch, and the chief head
        Of this post-haste and romage⁴ in the land.
    BERNARDO: I think it be no other but e'en so.
        Well may it sort⁵ that this portentous figure
        Comes arméd through our watch so like the king
110   That was and is the question of these wars.
    HORATIO: A mote⁶ it is to trouble the mind's eye.
        In the most high and palmy state of Rome,
        A little ere the mightiest Julius fell,
        The graves stood tenantless, and the sheeted dead
115   Did squeak and gibber in the Roman streets;
        As stars with trains of fire, and dews of blood,
        Disasters in the sun; and the moist star,
        Upon whose influence Neptune's empire stands,⁷
        Was sick almost to doomsday with eclipse.
120   And even the like precurse⁸ of feared events,
        As harbingers preceding still the fates
        And prologue to the omen coming on,
        Have heaven and earth together demonstrated
        Unto our climatures⁹ and countrymen.

          [Enter GHOST.]

125   But soft, behold, lo where it comes again!
        I'll cross it¹ though it blast me.—Stay, illusion.

          [It spreads (its) arms.]

        If thou hast any sound or use of voice,
        Speak to me.
        If there be any good thing to be done,
130   That may to thee do ease, and grace to me,
        Speak to me.
        If thou art privy to thy country's fate,
        Which happily foreknowing may avoid,
        O, speak!
135   Or if thou hast uphoarded in thy life
        Extorted treasure in the womb of earth,
        For which, they say, you spirits oft walk in death,

          [The cock crows.]

    Speak of it. Stay, and speak. Stop it, Marcellus.

---

4. Stir.   5. Chance.   6. Speck of dust.   7. Neptune was the Roman sea god; the "moist star" is the
moon.   8. Precursor.   9. Regions.   1. Horatio means either that he will move across the ghost's
path in order to stop him or that he will make the sign of the cross to gain power over him. The stage
direction that follows is somewhat ambiguous. "It" seems to refer to the ghost, but the movement would
be appropriate to Horatio.

MARCELLUS: Shall I strike at it with my partisan?[2]

HORATIO: Do, if it will not stand.

BERNARDO: 'Tis here.

HORATIO: 'Tis here.   140

MARCELLUS: 'Tis gone.   [*Exit* GHOST.]
   We do it wrong, being so majestical,
   To offer it the show of violence;
   For it is as the air, invulnerable,
   And our vain blows malicious mockery.   145

BERNARDO: It was about to speak when the cock crew.

HORATIO: And then it started like a guilty thing
   Upon a fearful summons. I have heard
   The cock, that is the trumpet to the morn,
   Doth with his lofty and shrill-sounding throat   150
   Awake the god of day, and at his warning,
   Whether in sea or fire, in earth or air,
   Th' extravagant and erring[3] spirit hies
   To his confine; and of the truth herein
   This present object made probation.[4]   155

MARCELLUS: It faded on the crowing of the cock.
   Some say that ever 'gainst that season comes
   Wherein our Savior's birth is celebrated,
   This bird of dawning singeth all night long,
   And then, they say, no spirit dare stir abroad,   160
   The nights are wholesome, then no planets strike,
   No fairy takes,[5] nor witch hath power to charm,
   So hallowed and so gracious is that time.

HORATIO: So have I heard and do in part believe it.
   But look, the morn in russet mantle clad   165
   Walks o'er the dew of yon high eastward hill.
   Break we our watch up, and by my advice
   Let us impart what we have seen tonight
   Unto young Hamlet, for upon my life
   This spirit, dumb to us, will speak to him.   170
   Do you consent we shall acquaint him with it,
   As needful in our loves, fitting our duty?

MARCELLUS: Let's do't, I pray, and I this morning know
   Where we shall find him most conveniently.   [*Exeunt.*]

SCENE 2

   A chamber of state. Enter KING CLAUDIUS, QUEEN GERTRUDE, HAMLET, POLONIUS, LAERTES, VOLTEMAND, CORNELIUS *and other members of the court.*

---

2. Halberd.   3. Wandering out of bounds.   4. Proof.   5. Enchants.

KING: Though yet of Hamlet our dear brother's death
    The memory be green, and that it us befitted
    To bear our hearts in grief, and our whole kingdom
    To be contracted in one brow of woe,
5   Yet so far hath discretion fought with nature
    That we with wisest sorrow think on him,
    Together with remembrance of ourselves.
    Therefore our sometime sister, now our queen,
    Th' imperial jointress[6] to this warlike state,
10   Have we, as 'twere with a defeated joy,
    With an auspicious and a dropping eye,
    With mirth in funeral, and with dirge in marriage,
    In equal scale weighing delight and dole,
    Taken to wife; nor have we herein barred
15   Your better wisdoms, which have freely gone
    With this affair along. For all, our thanks.
    Now follows that you know young Fortinbras,
    Holding a weak supposal of our worth,
    Or thinking by our late dear brother's death
20   Our state to be disjoint and out of frame,
    Colleaguéd with this dream of his advantage,
    He hath not failed to pester us with message
    Importing the surrender of those lands
    Lost by his father, with all bonds of law,
25   To our most valiant brother. So much for him.
    Now for ourself, and for this time of meeting,
    Thus much the business is: we have here writ
    To Norway, uncle of young Fortinbras—
    Who, impotent and bedrid, scarcely hears
30   Of this his nephew's purpose—to suppress
    His further gait[7] herein, in that the levies,
    The lists, and full proportions are all made
    Out of his subject; and we here dispatch
    You, good Cornelius, and you, Voltemand,
35   For bearers of this greeting to old Norway,
    Giving to you no further personal power
    To business with the king, more than the scope
    Of these dilated[8] articles allow.
    Farewell, and let your haste commend your duty.
CORNELIUS: ⎫
40 VOLTEMAND: ⎬ In that, and all things will we show our duty.
KING: We doubt it nothing, heartily farewell.

                        [*Exeunt* VOLTEMAND *and* CORNELIUS.]

---

6. A "jointress" is a widow who holds a *jointure* or life interest in the estate of her deceased husband.
7. Progress.   8. Fully expressed.

And now, Laertes, what's the news with you?
You told us of some suit. What is't, Laertes?
You cannot speak of reason to the Dane
And lose your voice. What wouldst thou beg, Laertes,   45
That shall not be my offer, not thy asking?
The head is not more native to the heart,
The hand more instrumental⁹ to the mouth,
Than is the throne of Denmark to thy father.
What wouldst thou have, Laertes?
LAERTES: My dread lord,   50
Your leave and favor to return to France,
From whence, though willingly, I came to Denmark
To show my duty in your coronation,
Yet now I must confess, that duty done,
My thoughts and wishes bend again toward France,   55
And bow them to your gracious leave and pardon.
KING: Have you your father's leave? What says Polonius?
POLONIUS: He hath, my lord, wrung from me my slow leave
By laborsome petition, and at last
Upon his will I sealed my hard consent.   60
I do beseech you give him leave to go.
KING: Take thy fair hour, Laertes. Time be thine,
And thy best graces spend it at thy will.
But now, my cousin¹ Hamlet, and my son—
HAMLET: [*Aside.*] A little more than kin, and less than kind.   65
KING: How is it that the clouds still hang on you?
HAMLET: Not so, my lord. I am too much in the sun.
QUEEN: Good Hamlet, cast thy nighted color off,
And let thine eye look like a friend on Denmark.
Do not for ever with thy vailéd lids²   70
Seek for thy noble father in the dust.
Thou know'st 'tis common—all that lives must die,
Passing through nature to eternity.
HAMLET: Ay, madam, it is common.
QUEEN: If it be,
Why seems it so particular with thee?   75
HAMLET: Seems, madam? Nay, it is. I know not "seems."
'Tis not alone my inky cloak, good mother,
Nor customary suits of solemn black,
Nor windy suspiration of forced breath,
No, nor the fruitful river in the eye,   80
Nor the dejected havior³ of the visage,
Together with all forms, moods, shapes of grief,

9. Serviceable.   1. "Cousin" is used here as a general term of kinship.   2. Lowered eyes.
3. Appearance.

That can denote me truly. These indeed seem,
For they are actions that a man might play,
85　　But I have that within which passes show—
These but the trappings and the suits of woe.
　　KING: 'Tis sweet and commendable in your nature, Hamlet,
To give these mourning duties to your father,
But you must know your father lost a father,
90　　That father lost, lost his, and the survivor bound
In filial obligation for some term
To do obsequious[4] sorrow. But to persever
In obstinate condolement is a course
Of impious stubbornness. 'Tis unmanly grief.
95　　It shows a will most incorrect to[5] heaven,
A heart unfortified, a mind impatient,
An understanding simple and unschooled.
For what we know must be, and is as common
As any the most vulgar thing to sense,
100　　Why should we in our peevish opposition
Take it to heart? Fie, 'tis a fault to heaven,
A fault against the dead, a fault to nature,
To reason most absurd, whose common theme
Is death of fathers, and who still hath cried,
105　　From the first corse[6] till he that died today,
"This must be so." We pray you throw to earth
This unprevailing woe, and think of us
As of a father, for let the world take note
You are the most immediate[7] to our throne,
110　　And with no less nobility of love
Than that which dearest father bears his son
Do I impart toward you. For your intent
In going back to school in Wittenberg,
It is most retrograde[8] to our desire,
115　　And we beseech you, bend you to remain
Here in the cheer and comfort of our eye,
Our chiefest courtier, cousin, and our son.
　　QUEEN: Let not thy mother lose her prayers, Hamlet.
I pray thee stay with us, go not to Wittenberg.
120　　HAMLET: I shall in all my best obey you, madam.
　　KING: Why, 'tis a loving and a fair reply.
Be as ourself in Denmark. Madam, come.
This gentle and unforced accord of Hamlet
Sits smiling to my heart, in grace whereof,
125　　No jocund health that Denmark drinks today

---

4. Suited for funeral obsequies.　　5. Uncorrected toward.　　6. Corpse.　　7. Next in line.　　8. Contrary.

But the great cannon to the clouds shall tell,
And the king's rouse the heaven shall bruit[9] again,
Respeaking earthly thunder. Come away.   [*Flourish. Exeunt all but* HAMLET.]
HAMLET: O, that this too too solid flesh would melt,
   Thaw, and resolve itself into a dew,   130
   Or that the Everlasting had not fixed
   His canon[1] 'gainst self-slaughter. O God, God,
   How weary, stale, flat, and unprofitable
   Seem to me all the uses of this world!
   Fie on't, ah, fie, 'tis an unweeded garden   135
   That grows to seed. Things rank and gross in nature
   Possess it merely.[2] That it should come to this,
   But two months dead, nay, not so much, not two.
   So excellent a king, that was to this
   Hyperion to a satyr,[3] so loving to my mother,   140
   That he might not beteem[4] the winds of heaven
   Visit her face too roughly. Heaven and earth,
   Must I remember? Why, she would hang on him
   As if increase of appetite had grown
   By what it fed on, and yet, within a month—   145
   Let me not think on't. Frailty, thy name is woman—
   A little month, or ere those shoes were old
   With which she followed my poor father's body
   Like Niobe,[5] all tears, why she, even she—
   O God, a beast that wants discourse of reason   150
   Would have mourned longer—married with my uncle,
   My father's brother, but no more like my father
   Than I to Hercules.[6] Within a month,
   Ere yet the salt of most unrighteous tears
   Had left the flushing in her gallèd eyes,   155
   She married. O, most wicked speed, to post
   With such dexterity to incestuous sheets!
   It is not, nor it cannot come to good.
   But break my heart, for I must hold my tongue.

     [*Enter* HORATIO, MARCELLUS, *and* BERNARDO.]

HORATIO: Hail to your lordship!
HAMLET: I am glad to see you well.   160
   Horatio—or I do forget myself.
HORATIO: The same, my lord, and your poor servant ever.

---

9. Echo. *Rouse:* carousal.   1. Law.   2. Entirely.   3. Hyperion, a Greek god, stands here for beauty
in contrast to the monstrous satyr, a lecherous creature, half man and half goat.   4. Permit.   5. In
Greek mythology, Niobe was turned to stone after a tremendous fit of weeping over the death of her
fourteen children, a misfortune brought about by her boasting over her fertility.   6. The demigod
Hercules was noted for his strength and the series of spectacular labors that it allowed him to accomplish.

HAMLET: Sir, my good friend, I'll change[7] that name with you.
    And what make you from Wittenberg, Horatio?
165   Marcellus?

MARCELLUS: My good lord!

HAMLET: I am very glad to see you. [*To* BERNARDO.] Good even, sir.—
    But what, in faith, make you from Wittenberg?

HORATIO: A truant disposition, good my lord.

170 HAMLET: I would not hear your enemy say so,
    Nor shall you do my ear that violence
    To make it truster of your own report
    Against yourself. I know you are no truant.
    But what is your affair in Elsinore?
175   We'll teach you to drink deep ere you depart.

HORATIO: My lord, I came to see your father's funeral.

HAMLET: I prithee do not mock me, fellow-student,
    I think it was to see my mother's wedding.

HORATIO: Indeed, my lord, it followed hard upon.

180 HAMLET: Thrift, thrift, Horatio. The funeral-baked meats
    Did coldly furnish forth the marriage tables.
    Would I had met my dearest[8] foe in heaven
    Or ever I had seen that day, Horatio!
    My father—methinks I see my father.

HORATIO: Where, my lord?

185 HAMLET: In my mind's eye, Horatio.

HORATIO: I saw him once, 'a was a goodly king.

HAMLET: 'A was a man, take him for all in all,
    I shall not look upon his like again.

HORATIO: My lord, I think I saw him yesternight.

190 HAMLET: Saw who?

HORATIO: My lord, the king your father.

HAMLET: The king my father?

HORATIO: Season your admiration[9] for a while
    With an attent ear till I may deliver[1]
    Upon the witness of these gentlemen
    This marvel to you.

195 HAMLET: For God's love, let me hear!

HORATIO: Two nights together had these gentlemen,
    Marcellus and Bernardo, on their watch
    In the dead waste and middle of the night
    Been thus encountered. A figure like your father,
200   Arméd at point exactly, cap-a-pe,[2]
    Appears before them, and with solemn march
    Goes slow and stately by them. Thrice he walked

---

7. Exchange.   8. Bitterest.   9. Moderate your wonder.   1. Relate. *Attent:* attentive.   2. From
head to toe. *Exactly:* completely.

By their oppressed and fear-surprisèd eyes
Within his truncheon's³ length, whilst they, distilled
Almost to jelly with the act of fear,   205
Stand dumb and speak not to him. This to me
In dreadful secrecy impart they did,
And I with them the third night kept the watch,
Where, as they had delivered, both in time,
Form of the thing, each word made true and good,   210
The apparition comes. I knew your father.
These hands are not more like.

HAMLET: But where was this?

MARCELLUS: My lord, upon the platform where we watch.

HAMLET: Did you not speak to it?

HORATIO: My lord, I did,
But answer made it none. Yet once methought   215
It lifted up it head and did address
Itself to motion, like as it would speak;
But even then the morning cock crew loud,
And at the sound it shrunk in haste away
And vanished from our sight.

HAMLET: 'Tis very strange.   220

HORATIO: As I do live, my honored lord, 'tis true,
And we did think it writ down in our duty
To let you know of it.

HAMLET: Indeed, sirs, but
This troubles me. Hold you the watch tonight?

ALL: We do, my lord.

HAMLET: Armed, say you?

ALL: Armed, my lord.   225

HAMLET: From top to toe?

ALL: My lord, from head to foot.

HAMLET: Then saw you not his face.

HORATIO: O yes, my lord, he wore his beaver⁴ up.

HAMLET: What, looked he frowningly?

HORATIO: A countenance more in sorrow than in anger.   230

HAMLET: Pale or red?

HORATIO: Nay, very pale.

HAMLET: And fixed his eyes upon you?

HORATIO: Most constantly.

HAMLET: I would I had been there.

HORATIO: It would have much amazed you.

HAMLET: Very like.
Stayed it long?   235

HORATIO: While one with moderate haste might tell a hundred.

___

3. Baton of office.   4. Movable face protector.

BOTH: Longer, longer.

HORATIO: Not when I saw't.

HAMLET: His beard was grizzled, no?

HORATIO: It was as I have seen it in his life,
   A sable silvered.

240 HAMLET: I will watch tonight.
   Perchance 'twill walk again.

HORATIO: I warr'nt it will.

HAMLET: If it assume my noble father's person,
   I'll speak to it though hell itself should gape[5]
   And bid me hold my peace. I pray you all,

245   If you have hitherto concealed this sight,
   Let it be tenable[6] in your silence still,
   And whatsomever else shall hap tonight,
   Give it an understanding but no tongue.
   I will requite your loves. So fare you well.

250   Upon the platform 'twixt eleven and twelve
   I'll visit you.

ALL: Our duty to your honor.

HAMLET: Your loves, as mine to you. Farewell.   [*Exeunt all but* HAMLET.]
   My father's spirit in arms? All is not well.
   I doubt[7] some foul play. Would the night were come!

255   Till then sit still, my soul. Foul deeds will rise,
   Though all the earth o'erwhelm them, to men's eyes.   [*Exit.*]

SCENE 3

The dwelling of POLONIUS. *Enter* LAERTES *and* OPHELIA.

LAERTES: My necessaries are embarked. Farewell.
   And, sister, as the winds give benefit
   And convoy is assistant,[8] do not sleep,
   But let me hear from you.

OPHELIA: Do you doubt that?

5 LAERTES: For Hamlet, and the trifling of his favor,
   Hold it a fashion and a toy in blood,
   A violet in the youth of primy[9] nature,
   Forward, not permanent, sweet, not lasting,
   The perfume and suppliance of a minute,
   No more.

OPHELIA: No more but so?

10 LAERTES: Think it no more.

---

5. Open (its mouth) wide.   6. Held.   7. Suspect.   8. Means of transport is available.   9. Of the spring.

For nature crescent[1] does not grow alone
In thews and bulk, but as this temple[2] waxes
The inward service of the mind and soul
Grows wide withal. Perhaps he loves you now,
And now no soil nor cautel[3] doth besmirch   15
The virtue of his will, but you must fear,
His greatness weighted,[4] his will is not his own,
For he himself is subject to his birth.
He may not, as unvalued persons do,
Carve for himself, for on his choice depends   20
The safety and health of this whole state,
And therefore must his choice be circumscribed
Unto the voice[5] and yielding of that body
Whereof he is the head. Then if he says he loves you,
It fits your wisdom so far to believe it   25
As he in his particular act and place
May give his saying deed, which is no further
Than the main voice of Denmark goes withal.
Then weigh what loss your honor may sustain
If with too credent ear you list[6] his songs,   30
Or lose your heart, or your chaste treasure open
To his unmastered importunity.
Fear it, Ophelia, fear it, my dear sister,
And keep you in the rear of your affection,
Out of the shot and danger of desire.   35
The chariest[7] maid is prodigal enough
If she unmask her beauty to the moon.
Virtue itself scapes not calumnious strokes.
The canker[8] galls the infants of the spring
Too oft before their buttons[9] be disclosed,   40
And in the morn and liquid dew of youth
Contagious blastments[1] are most imminent.
Be wary then; best safety lies in fear.
Youth to itself rebels, though none else near.
OPHELIA: I shall the effect of this good lesson keep   45
    As watchman to my heart. But, good my brother,
    Do not as some ungracious pastors do,
    Show me the steep and thorny way to heaven,
    Whiles like a puffed and reckless libertine
    Himself the primrose path of dalliance treads   50
    And recks not his own rede.[2]
LAERTES: O, fear me not.

---

1. Growing.   2. Body.   3. Deceit.   4. Rank considered.   5. Assent.   6. Too credulous an ear
you listen to.   7. Most circumspect.   8. Rose caterpillar.   9. Buds.   1. Blights.   2. Heedsnot
his own advice.

[*Enter* POLONIUS.]

I stay too long. But here my father comes.
A double blessing is a double grace;
Occasion smiles upon a second leave.

55 POLONIUS: Yet here, Laertes? Aboard, aboard, for shame!
The wind sits in the shoulder of your sail,
And you are stayed for. There—my blessing with thee,
And these few precepts in thy memory
Look thou character.³ Give thy thoughts no tongue,

60 Nor any unproportioned thought his act.
Be thou familiar, but by no means vulgar.
Those friends thou hast, and their adoption tried,
Grapple them unto thy soul with hoops of steel;
But do not dull⁴ thy palm with entertainment

65 Of each new-hatched, unfledged comrade. Beware
Of entrance to a quarrel, but being in,
Bear't that th' opposéd⁵ may beware of thee.
Give every man thy ear, but few thy voice;⁶
Take each man's censure, but reserve thy judgment.

70 Costly thy habit as thy purse can buy,
But not expressed in fancy; rich not gaudy,
For the apparel oft proclaims the man,
And they in France of the best rank and station
Are of a most select and generous chief⁷ in that.

75 Neither a borrower nor a lender be,
For loan oft loses both itself and friend,
And borrowing dulls th' edge of husbandry.
This above all, to thine own self be true,
And it must follow as the night the day

80 Thou canst not then be false to any man.
Farewell. My blessing season this in thee!
LAERTES: Most humbly do I take my leave, my lord.
POLONIUS: The time invests you. Go, your servants tend.⁸
LAERTES: Farewell, Ophelia, and remember well
What I have said to you.

85 OPHELIA: 'Tis in my memory locked,
And you yourself shall keep the key of it.
LAERTES: Farewell.   [*Exit.*]
POLONIUS: What is't, Ophelia, he hath said to you?
OPHELIA: So please you, something touching the Lord Hamlet.

90 POLONIUS: Marry, well bethought.
'Tis told me he hath very oft of late

3. Write.   4. Make callous.   5. Conduct it so that the opponent.   6. Approval.   7. Eminence.
8. Await.

Given private time to you, and you yourself
Have of your audience been most free and bounteous.
If it be so—as so 'tis put on me,
And that in way of caution—I must tell you,   95
You do not understand yourself so clearly
As it behooves my daughter and your honor.
What is between you? Give me up the truth.
OPHELIA: He hath, my lord, of late made many tenders
Of his affection to me.   100
POLONIUS: Affection? Pooh! You speak like a green girl,
Unsifted in such perilous circumstance.
Do you believe his tenders, as you call them?
OPHELIA: I do not know, my lord, what I should think.
POLONIUS: Marry, I will teach you. Think yourself a baby   105
That you have ta'en these tenders for true pay
Which are not sterling. Tender yourself more dearly,
Or (not to crack the wind of the poor phrase,
Running it thus) you'll tender me a fool.
OPHELIA: My lord, he hath importuned me with love   110
In honorable fashion.
POLONIUS: Ay, fashion you may call it. Go to, go to.
OPHELIA: And hath given countenance[9] to his speech, my lord,
With almost all the holy vows of heaven.
POLONIUS: Ay, springes[1] to catch woodcocks. I do know,   115
When the blood burns, how prodigal the soul
Lends the tongue vows. These blazes, daughter,
Giving more light than heat, extinct in both
Even in their promise, as it is a-making,
You must not take for fire. From this time   120
Be something scanter of your maiden presence.
Set your entreatments[2] at a higher rate
Than a command to parle. For Lord Hamlet,
Believe so much in him that he is young,
And with a larger tether may he walk   125
Than may be given you. In few, Ophelia,
Do not believe his vows, for they are brokers,[3]
Not of that dye which their investments[4] show,
But mere implorators[5] of unholy suits,
Breathing like sanctified and pious bawds,   130
The better to beguile. This is for all:
I would not, in plain terms, from this time forth
Have you so slander any moment leisure
As to give words or talk with the Lord Hamlet.

9. Confirmation.   1. Snares.   2. Negotiations before a surrender.   3. Panderers.   4. Garments.
5. Solicitors.

135   Look to't, I charge you. Come your ways.
   OPHELIA: I shall obey, my lord.   *[Exeunt.]*

SCENE 4

The guard station. Enter HAMLET, HORATIO *and* MARCELLUS.

HAMLET: The air bites shrewdly;[6] it is very cold.
HORATIO: It is a nipping and an eager[7] air.
HAMLET: What hour now?
HORATIO: I think it lacks of twelve.
MARCELLUS: No, it is struck.
HORATIO: Indeed? I heard it not.
5   It then draws near the season
   Wherein the spirit held his wont to walk.

      [A flourish of trumpets, and two pieces go off.]

   What does this mean, my lord?
HAMLET: The king doth wake tonight and takes his rouse,
   Keeps wassail, and the swagg'ring up-spring[8] reels,
10   And as he drains his draughts of Rhenish down,
   The kettledrum and trumpet thus bray out
   The triumph of his pledge.
HORATIO: Is it a custom?
HAMLET: Ay, marry, is't,
   But to my mind, though I am native here
15   And to the manner born, it is a custom
   More honored in the breach than the observance.
   This heavy-headed revel east and west
   Makes us traduced and taxed of other nations.
   They clepe[9] us drunkards, and with swinish phrase
20   Soil our addition,[1] and indeed it takes
   From our achievements, though performed at height,
   The pith and marrow of our attribute.[2]
   So oft it chances in particular men,
   That for some vicious mole of nature in them,
25   As in their birth, wherein they are not guilty
   (Since nature cannot choose his origin),
   By their o'ergrowth of some complexion,
   Oft breaking down the pales[3] and forts of reason,
   Or by some habit that too much o'er-leavens
30   The form of plausive[4] manners—that these men,

---

6. Sharply.   7. Keen.   8. A German dance.   9. Call.   1. Reputation.   2. Honor.   3. Barriers.   4. Pleasing.

Carrying, I say, the stamp of one defect,
Being nature's livery or fortune's star,
His virtues else, be they as pure as grace,
As infinite as man may undergo,
Shall in the general censure take corruption   35
From that particular fault. The dram of evil
Doth all the noble substance often doubt[5]
To his own scandal.

      [*Enter* GHOST.]

HORATIO: Look, my lord, it comes.
HAMLET: Angels and ministers of grace defend us!
  Be thou a spirit of health or goblin damned,   40
  Bring with thee airs from heaven or blasts from hell,
  Be thy intents wicked or charitable,
  Thou com'st in such a questionable[6] shape
  That I will speak to thee. I'll call thee Hamlet,
  King, father, royal Dane. O, answer me!   45
  Let me not burst in ignorance, but tell
  Why thy canonized[7] bones, hearséd in death,
  Have burst their cerements;[8] why the sepulchre
  Wherein we saw thee quietly inurned
  Hath oped his ponderous and marble jaws   50
  To cast thee up again. What may this mean
  That thou, dead corse, again in complete steel[9]
  Revisits thus the glimpses of the moon,
  Making night hideous, and we fools of nature
  So horridly to shake our disposition   55
  With thoughts beyond the reaches of our souls?
  Say, why is this? wherefore? What should we do?

      [GHOST *beckons*.]

HORATIO: It beckons you to go away with it,
  As if it some impartment[1] did desire
  To you alone.
MARCELLUS: Look with what courteous action   60
  It waves you to a more removéd[2] ground.
  But do not go with it.
HORATIO: No, by no means.
HAMLET: It will not speak; then I will follow it.
HORATIO: Do not, my lord.
HAMLET: Why, what should be the fear?

---

5. Put out.   6. Prompting question.   7. Buried in accordance with church canons.   8. Grave-
cloths.   9. Armor.   1. Communication.   2. Beckons you to a more distant.

65   I do not set my life at a pin's fee,[3]
    And for my soul, what can it do to that,
    Being a thing immortal as itself?
    It waves me forth again. I'll follow it
    HORATIO: What if it tempt you toward the flood, my lord,
70   Or to the dreadful summit of the cliff
    That beetles[4] o'er his base into the sea,
    And there assume some other horrible form,
    Which might deprive your sovereignty of reason[5]
    And draw you into madness? Think of it.
75   The very place puts toys of desperation,[6]
    Without more motive, into every brain
    That looks so many fathoms to the sea
    And hears it roar beneath.
    HAMLET: It wafts me still.
    Go on. I'll follow thee.
    MARCELLUS: You shall not go, my lord.
80   HAMLET: Hold off your hands.
    HORATIO: Be ruled. You shall not go.
    HAMLET: My fate cries out
    And makes each petty artere in this body
    As hardy as the Nemean lion's nerve.[7]
    Still am I called. Unhand me, gentlemen.
85   By heaven, I'll make a ghost of him that lets[8] me.
    I say, away! Go on. I'll follow thee.   [*Exeunt* GHOST *and* HAMLET.]
    HORATIO: He waxes desperate with imagination.
    MARCELLUS: Let's follow. 'Tis not fit thus to obey him.
    HORATIO: Have after. To what issue will this come?
90   MARCELLUS: Something is rotten in the state of Denmark.
    HORATIO: Heaven will direct it.
    MARCELLUS: Nay, let's follow him.   [*Exeunt.*]

SCENE 5

Near the guard station. Enter GHOST *and* HAMLET.

HAMLET: Whither wilt thou lead me? Speak. I'll go no further.
GHOST: Mark me.
HAMLET: I will.
GHOST: My hour is almost come,
    When I to sulph'rous and tormenting flames
    Must render up myself.

---

3. Price.   4. Juts out.   5. Rational power. *Deprive:* take away.   6. Desperate fancies.   7. The Nemean lion was a mythological monster slain by Hercules as one of his twelve labors.   8. Hinders.

HAMLET: Alas, poor ghost!
GHOST: Pity me not, but lend thy serious hearing   5
   To what I shall unfold.
HAMLET: Speak. I am bound to hear.
GHOST: So art thou to revenge, when thou shalt hear.
HAMLET: What?
GHOST: I am thy father's spirit,
   Doomed for a certain term to walk the night,   10
   And for the day confined to fast in fires,
   Till the foul crimes done in my days of nature[9]
   Are burnt and purged away. But that I am forbid
   To tell the secrets of my prison house,
   I could a tale unfold whose lightest word   15
   Would harrow up thy soul, freeze thy young blood,
   Make thy two eyes like stars start from their spheres,
   Thy knotted and combinéd[1] locks to part,
   And each particular hair to stand an end,
   Like quills upon the fretful porpentine.[2]   20
   But this eternal blazon[3] must not be
   To ears of flesh and blood. List, list, O, list!
   If thou didst every thy dear father love—
HAMLET: O God!
GHOST: Revenge his foul and most unnatural murder.   25
HAMLET: Murder!
GHOST: Murder most foul, as in the best it is,
   But this most foul, strange, and unnatural.
HAMLET: Haste me to know't, that I, with wings as swift
   As meditation or the thoughts of love,   30
   May sweep to my revenge.
GHOST: I find thee apt.
   And duller shouldst thou be than the fat weed
   That rots itself in ease on Lethe[4] wharf,—
   Wouldst thou not stir in this. Now, Hamlet, hear.
   'Tis given out that, sleeping in my orchard,   35
   A serpent stung me. So the whole ear of Denmark
   Is by a forgéd process[5] of my death
   Rankly abused. But know, thou noble youth,
   The serpent that did sting thy father's life
   Now wears his crown.
HAMLET: O my prophetic soul!   40
   My uncle!
GHOST: Ay, that incestuous, that adulterate beast,

---

9. That is, while I was alive.   1. Tangled.   2. Porcupine.   3. Description of eternity.   4. The waters of the Lethe, one of the rivers of the classical underworld, when drunk, induced forgetfulness. The "fat weed" is the asphodel that grew there; some texts have "roots" for "rots."   5. False report.

With witchcraft of his wits, with traitorous gifts—
O wicked wit and gifts that have the power
45   So to seduce!—won to his shameful lust
The will of my most seeming virtuous queen.
O Hamlet, what a falling off was there,
From me, whose love was of that dignity
That it went hand in hand even with the vow
50   I made to her in marriage, and to decline[6]
Upon a wretch whose natural gifts were poor
To those of mine!
But virtue, as it never will be moved,
Though lewdness court it in a shape of heaven,
55   So lust, though to a radiant angel linked,
Will sate itself in a celestial bed
And prey on garbage.
But soft, methinks I scent the morning air.
Brief let me be. Sleeping within my orchard,
60   My custom always of the afternoon,
Upon my secure hour thy uncle stole,
With juice of cursed hebona[7] in a vial,
And in the porches of my ears did pour
The leperous distilment, whose effect
65   Holds such an enmity with blood of man
That swift as quicksilver it courses through
The natural gates and alleys of the body,
And with a sudden vigor it doth posset[8]
And curd, like eager[9] droppings into milk,
70   The thin and wholesome blood. So did it mine,
And a most instant tetter barked about[1]
Most lazar-like[2] with vile and loathsome crust
All my smooth body.
Thus was I sleeping by a brother's hand
75   Of life, of crown, of queen at once dispatched,
Cut off even in the blossoms of my sin,
Unhouseled, disappointed, unaneled,[3]
No reck'ning made, but sent to my account
With all my imperfections on my head.
80   O, horrible! O, horrible! most horrible!
If thou hast nature in thee, bear it not.
Let not the royal bed of Denmark be
A couch of luxury[4] and damnéd incest.
But howsomever thou pursues this act,

---

6. Sink.   7. A poison.   8. Coagulate.   9. Acid. *Curd:* curdle.   1. Covered like bark. *Tetter:* a skin disease.   2. Leperlike.   3. The ghost means that he died without the customary rites of the church, that is, without receiving the Sacrament, without confession, and without Extreme Unction.   4. Lust.

Taint not thy mind, nor let thy soul contrive   85
Against thy mother aught. Leave her to heaven,
And to those thorns that in her bosom lodge
To prick and sting her. Fare thee well at once.
The glowworm shows the matin[5] to be near,
And gins to pale his uneffectual fire.   90
Adieu, adieu, adieu. Remember me.   [*Exit.*]
HAMLET: O all you host of heaven! O earth! What else?
  And shall I couple hell? O, fie! Hold, hold, my heart,
  And you, my sinews, grow not instant old,
  But bear me stiffly up. Remember thee?   95
  Ay, thou poor ghost, whiles memory holds a seat
  In this distracted globe.[6] Remember thee?
  Yea, from the table[7] of my memory
  I'll wipe away all trivial fond[8] records,
  All saws of books, all forms, all pressures past   100
  That youth and observation copied there,
  And thy commandment all alone shall live
  Within the book and volume of my brain,
  Unmixed with baser matter. Yes, by heaven!
  O most pernicious woman!   105
  O villain, villain, smiling, damnéd villain!
  My tables—meet it is I set it down
  That one may smile, and smile, and be a villain.
  At least I am sure it may be so in Denmark.
  So, uncle, there you are. Now to my word:[9]   110
  It is "Adieu, adieu. Remember me."
  I have sworn't.

        [*Enter* HORATIO *and* MARCELLUS.]

HORATIO: My lord, my lord!
MARCELLUS: Lord Hamlet!
HORATIO: Heavens secure him!
HAMLET: So be it!
MARCELLUS: Illo, ho, ho, my lord!   115
HAMLET: Hillo, ho, ho, boy![1] Come, bird, come.
MARCELLUS: How is't, my noble lord?
HORATIO: What news, my lord?
HAMLET: O, wonderful!
HORATIO: Good my lord, tell it.
HAMLET: No, you will reveal it.
HORATIO: Not I, my lord, by heaven.
MARCELLUS: Nor I, my lord.   120
HAMLET: How say you then, would heart of man once think it?

5. Morning.   6. Skull.   7. Writing tablet.   8. Foolish.   9. For my motto.   1. A falconer's cry.

But you'll be secret?

BOTH: Ay, by heaven, my lord.

HAMLET: There's never a villain dwelling in all Denmark
But he's an arrant knave.

125 HORATIO: There needs no ghost, my lord, come from the grave
To tell us this.

HAMLET: Why, right, you are in the right,
And so without more circumstance at all
I hold it fit that we shake hands and part,
You, as your business and desire shall point you,

130 For every man hath business and desire
Such as it is, and for my own poor part,
Look you, I'll go pray.

HORATIO: These are but wild and whirling words, my lord.

HAMLET: I am sorry they offend you, heartily;
Yes, faith, heartily.

135 HORATIO: There's no offence, my lord.

HAMLET: Yes, by Saint Patrick, but there is, Horatio,
And much offence too. Touching this vision here,
It is an honest ghost, that let me tell you.
For your desire to know what is between us,

140 O'ermaster't as you may. And now, good friends,
As you are friends, scholars, and soldiers,
Give me one poor request.

HORATIO: What is't, my lord? We will.

HAMLET: Never make known what you have seen tonight.

BOTH: My lord, we will not.

HAMLET: Nay, but swear't.

145 HORATIO: In faith,
My lord, not I.

MARCELLUS: Nor I, my lord, in faith.

HAMLET: Upon my sword.

MARCELLUS: We have sworn, my lord, already.

HAMLET: Indeed, upon my sword, indeed.

[GHOST *cries under the stage*.]

GHOST: Swear.

HAMLET: Ha, ha, boy, say'st thou so? Art thou there, truepenny?[2]

150 Come on. You hear this fellow in the cellarage.[3]
Consent to swear.

HORATIO: Propose the oath, my lord.

HAMLET: Never to speak of this that you have seen,
Swear by my sword.

GHOST: [*Beneath.*] Swear.

2. Old fellow.   3. Below.

HAMLET: Hic et ubique?⁴ Then we'll shift our ground.   155
  Come hither, gentlemen,
  And lay your hands again upon my sword.
  Swear by my sword
  Never to speak of this that you have heard.
GHOST: [*Beneath.*] Swear by his sword.   160
HAMLET: Well said, old mole! Canst work i' th' earth so fast?
  A worthy pioneer!⁵ Once more remove, good friends.
HORATIO: O day and night, but this is wondrous strange!
HAMLET: And therefore as a stranger give it welcome.
  There are more things in heaven and earth, Horatio,   165
  Than are dreamt of in your philosophy.
  But come.
  Here as before, never, so help you mercy,
  How strange or odd some'er I bear myself
  (As I perchance hereafter shall think meet   170
  To put an antic⁶ disposition on),
  That you, at such times, seeing me, never shall,
  With arms encumbered⁷ thus, or this head-shake,
  Or by pronouncing of some doubtful phrase,
  As "Well, we know," or "We could, and if we would"   175
  Or "If we list to speak," or "There be, and if they might"
  Or such ambiguous giving out, to note
  That you know aught of me—this do swear,
  So grace and mercy at your most need help you.
GHOST: [*Beneath.*] Swear.   [*They swear.*]   180
HAMLET: Rest, rest, perturbéd spirit! So, gentlemen,
  With all my love I do commend me to you,
  And what so poor a man as Hamlet is
  May do t'express his love and friending⁸ to you,
  God willing, shall not lack. Let us go in together,   185
  And still your fingers on your lips, I pray.
  The time is out of joint. O curséd spite
  That ever I was born to set it right!
  Nay, come, let's go together.   [*Exeunt.*]

ACT II

Scene 1

The dwelling of POLONIUS. *Enter* POLONIUS *and* REYNALDO.

POLONIUS: Give him this money and these notes, Reynaldo.
REYNALDO: I will, my lord.

---

4. Here and everywhere?   5. Soldier who digs trenches.   6. Mad.   7. Folded.   8. Friendship.

POLONIUS: You shall do marvellous wisely, good Reynaldo,
    Before you visit him, to make inquire[9]
    Of his behavior.
5 REYNALDO: My lord, I did intend it.
POLONIUS: Marry, well said, very well said. Look you, sir.
    Enquire me first what Danskers[1] are in Paris,
    And how, and who, what means, and where they keep,[2]
    What company, at what expense; and finding
10   By this encompassment[3] and drift of question
    That they do know my son, come you more nearer
    Than your particular demands[4] will touch it.
    Take you as 'twere some distant knowledge of him,
    As thus, "I know his father and his friends,
15   And in part him." Do you mark this, Reynaldo?
REYNALDO: Ay, very well, my lord.
POLONIUS: "And in part him, but," you may say, "not well,
    But if't be he I mean, he's very wild,
    Addicted so and so." And there put on him
20   What forgeries you please; marry, none so rank[5]
    As may dishonor him. Take heed of that.
    But, sir, such wanton, wild, and usual slips
    As are companions noted and most known
    To youth and liberty.
REYNALDO: As gaming, my lord.
25 POLONIUS: Ay, or drinking, fencing, swearing,
    Quarrelling, drabbing[6]—you may go so far.
REYNALDO: My lord, that would dishonor him.
POLONIUS: Faith, no, as you may season it in the charge.[7]
    You must not put another scandal on him,
30   That he is open to incontinency.[8]
    That's not my meaning. But breathe his faults so quaintly[9]
    That they may seem the taints of liberty,[1]
    The flash and outbreak of a fiery mind,
    A savageness in unreclaiméd[2] blood,
    Of general assault.[3]
35 REYNALDO: But, my good lord—
POLONIUS: Wherefore should you do this?
REYNALDO: Ay, my lord,
    I would know that.
POLONIUS: Marry, sir, here's my drift,
    And I believe it is a fetch of warrant.[4]
    You laying these slight sullies on my son,

9. Inquiry.   1. Danes.   2. Live.   3. Indirect means.   4. Direct questions.   5. Foul. *Forgeries:*
lies.   6. Whoring.   7. Soften the accusation.   8. Sexual excess.   9. With delicacy.   1. Faults
of freedom.   2. Untamed.   3. Touching everyone.   4. Permissible trick.

As 'twere a thing a little soiled wi' th' working,   40
Mark you,
Your party in converse,[5] him you would sound,
Having ever seen in the prenominate[6] crimes
The youth you breathe[7] of guilty, be assured
He closes with you in this consequence,   45
"Good sir," or so, or "friend," or "gentleman,"
According to the phrase or the addition
Of man and country.
REYNALDO: Very good, my lord.
POLONIUS: And then, sir, does 'a this—'a does—What was I about to say?
By the mass, I was about to say something.   50
Where did I leave?
REYNALDO: At "closes in the consequence."
POLONIUS: At "closes in the consequence"—ay, marry,
He closes thus: "I know the gentleman.
I saw him yesterday, or th' other day,   55
Or then, or then, with such, or such, and as you say,
There was 'a gaming, there o'ertook in's rouse,
There falling out at tennis," or perchance
"I saw him enter such a house of sale,"
Videlicet,[8] a brothel, or so forth.   60
See you, now—
Your bait of falsehood takes this carp of truth,
And thus do we of wisdom and of reach,[9]
With windlasses and with assays of bias,[1]
By indirections find directions out;   65
So by my former lecture and advice
Shall you my son. You have me, have you not?
REYNALDO: My lord, I have.
POLONIUS: God b'wi' ye; fare ye well.
REYNALDO: Good my lord.
POLONIUS: Observe his inclination in yourself.   70
REYNALDO: I shall, my lord.
POLONIUS: And let him ply[2] his music.
REYNALDO: Well, my lord.
POLONIUS: Farewell.   [*Exit* REYNALDO.]

    [*Enter* OPHELIA.]

         How now, Ophelia, what's the matter?
OPHELIA: O my lord, my lord, I have been so affrighted!
POLONIUS: With what, i' th' name of God?   75

5. Conversation.   6. Already named.   7. Speak.   8. Namely.   9. Ability.   1. Indirect tests.
2. Practice.

OPHELIA: My lord, as I was sewing in my closet,[3]
Lord Hamlet with his doublet all unbraced,[4]
No hat upon his head, his stockings fouled,
Ungartered and down-gyvéd[5] to his ankle,
80   Pale as his shirt, his knees knocking each other,
And with a look so piteous in purport
As if he had been looséd out of hell
To speak of horrors—he comes before me.
POLONIUS: Mad for thy love?
OPHELIA: My lord, I do not know,
But truly I do fear it.
85   POLONIUS: What said he?
OPHELIA: He took me by the wrist, and held me hard,
Then goes he to the length of all his arm,
And with his other hand thus o'er his brow,
He falls to such perusal of my face
90   As 'a would draw it. Long stayed he so.
At last, a little shaking of mine arm,
And thrice his head thus waving up and down,
He raised a sigh so piteous and profound
As it did seem to shatter all his bulk,[6]
95   And end his being. That done, he lets me go,
And with his head over his shoulder turned
He seemed to find his way without his eyes,
For out adoors he went without their helps,
And to the last bended[7] their light on me.
100   POLONIUS: Come, go with me. I will go seek the king.
This is the very ecstasy of love,
Whose violent property fordoes[8] itself,
And leads the will to desperate undertakings
As oft as any passion under heaven
105   That does afflict our natures. I am sorry.
What, have you given him any hard words of late?
OPHELIA: No, my good lord, but as you did command
I did repel[9] his letters, and denied
His access to me.
POLONIUS: That hath made him mad.
110   I am sorry that with better heed and judgment
I had not quoted[1] him. I feared he did but trifle,
And meant to wrack[2] thee; but beshrew my jealousy.
By heaven, it is as proper to our age
To cast beyond ourselves in our opinions
115   As it is common for the younger sort

---

3. Chamber.   4. Unlaced. *Doublet:* jacket.   5. Fallen down like fetters.   6. Body.   7. Directed.
8. Destroys. *Property:* character.   9. Refuse.   1. Observed.   2. Harm.

To lack discretion. Come, go we to the king.
This must be known, which being kept close, might move
More grief to hide than hate to utter love.
Come.   [*Exeunt.*]

SCENE 2

A public room. Enter KING, QUEEN, ROSENCRANTZ *and* GUILDENSTERN.

KING: Welcome, dear Rosencrantz and Guildenstern.
    Moreover that[3] we much did long to see you,
    The need we have to use you did provoke
    Our hasty sending. Something have you heard
    Of Hamlet's transformation—so call it,   5
    Sith[4] nor th' exterior nor the inward man
    Resembles that it was. What it should be,
    More than his father's death, that thus hath put him
    So much from th' understanding of himself,
    I cannot deem of. I entreat you both   10
    That, being of so young days[5] brought up with him,
    And sith so neighbored[6] to his youth and havior,
    That you vouchsafe your rest here in our court
    Some little time, so by your companies
    To draw him on to pleasures, and to gather   15
    So much as from occasion you may glean,
    Whether aught to us unknown afflicts him thus,
    That opened lies within our remedy.
QUEEN: Good gentlemen, he hath much talked of you,
    And sure I am two men there are not living   20
    To whom he more adheres. If it will please you
    To show us so much gentry[7] and good will
    As to expend your time with us awhile
    For the supply and profit of our hope,
    Your visitation shall receive such thanks   25
    As fits a king's remembrance.
ROSENCRANTZ: Both your majesties
    Might, by the sovereign power you have of us,
    Put your dread pleasures more into command
    Than to entreaty.
GUILDENSTERN: But we both obey,
    And here give up ourselves in the full bent[8]   30
    To lay our service freely at your feet,

3. In addition to the fact that.   4. Since.   5. From childhood.   6. Closely allied.   7. Courtesy.
8. Completely.

To be commanded.

KING: Thanks, Rosencrantz and gentle Guildenstern.

QUEEN: Thanks, Guildenstern and gentle Rosencrantz.

35   And I beseech you instantly to visit
      My too much changed son. Go, some of you,
      And bring these gentlemen where Hamlet is.

GUILDENSTERN: Heavens make our presence and our practices
      Pleasant and helpful to him!

QUEEN: Ay, amen!

        [*Exeunt* ROSENCRANTZ *and* GUILDENSTERN.]

      [*Enter* POLONIUS.]

40 POLONIUS: Th' ambassadors from Norway, my good lord,
      Are joyfully returned.

KING: Thou still⁹ hast been the father of good news.

POLONIUS: Have I, my lord? I assure you, my good liege,
      I hold my duty as I hold my soul,

45   Both to my God and to my gracious king;
      And I do think—or else this brain of mine
      Hunts not the trail of policy¹ so sure
      As it hath used to do—that I have found
      The very cause of Hamlet's lunacy.

50 KING: O, speak of that, that do I long to hear.

POLONIUS: Give first admittance to th' ambassadors.
      My news shall be the fruit² to that great feast.

KING: Thyself do grace to them, and bring them in.   [*Exit* POLONIUS.]
      He tells me, my dear Gertrude, he hath found

55   The head and source of all your son's distemper.

QUEEN: I doubt it is no other but the main,
      His father's death and our o'erhasty marriage.

KING: Well, we shall sift³ him.

        [*Enter Ambassadors* (VOLTEMAND *and* CORNELIUS) *with* POLONIUS.]

                        Welcome, my good friends,
      Say, Voltemand, what from our brother Norway?

60 VOLTEMAND: Most fair return of greetings and desires.
      Upon our first,⁴ he sent out to suppress
      His nephew's levies, which to him appeared
      To be a preparation 'gainst the Polack,
      But better looked into, he truly found

65   It was against your highness, whereat grieved,
      That so his sickness, age, and impotence
      Was falsely borne in hand, sends out arrests⁵

---

9. Ever.   1. Statecraft.   2. Dessert.   3. Examine.   4. That is, first appearance.   5. Orders to
stop. *Falsely borne in hand:* deceived.

On Fortinbras, which he in brief obeys,
Receives rebuke from Norway, and in fine,
Makes vow before his uncle never more   70
To give th' assay⁶ of arms against your majesty.
Whereon old Norway, overcome with joy,
Gives him three thousand crowns in annual fee,
And his commission to employ those soldiers,
So levied as before, against the Polack,   75
With an entreaty, herein further shown,   [*Gives* CLAUDIUS *a paper.*]
That it might please you to give quiet pass⁷
Through your dominions for this enterprise,
On such regards of safety and allowance
As therein are set down.
KING: It likes⁸ us well,   80
And at our more considered time⁹ we'll read,
Answer, and think upon this business.
Meantime we thank you for your well-took¹ labor.
Go to your rest; at night we'll feast together.
Most welcome home!   [*Exeunt* AMBASSADORS.]
POLONIUS: This business is well ended.   85
My liege and madam, to expostulate²
What majesty should be, what duty is,
Why day is day, night night, and time is time,
Were nothing but to waste night, day, and time.
Therefore, since brevity is the soul of wit,   90
And tediousness the limbs and outward flourishes,³
I will be brief. Your noble son is mad.
Mad call I it, for to define true madness,
What is't but to be nothing else but mad?
But let that go.
QUEEN: More matter with less art.   95
POLONIUS: Madam, I swear I use no art at all.
That he is mad, 'tis true: 'tis true 'tis pity,
And pity 'tis 'tis true. A foolish figure,
But farewell it, for I will use no art.
Mad let us grant him, then, and now remains   100
That we find out the cause of this effect,
Or rather say the cause of this defect,
For this effect defective comes by cause.
Thus it remains, and the remainder thus.
Perpend.⁴   105
I have a daughter—have while she is mine—
Who in her duty and obedience, mark,

6. Trial.   7. Safe conduct.   8. Pleases.   9. Time for more consideration.   1. Successful.   2. Discuss.   3. Adornments.   4. Consider.

Hath given me this. Now gather, and surmise.
   "To the celestial, and my soul's idol, the most beautified
110   Ophelia."—That's an ill phrase, a vile phrase, "beautified" is a
vile phrase. But you shall hear. Thus:
   "In her excellent white bosom, these, etc."
QUEEN: Came this from Hamlet to her?
POLONIUS: Good madam, stay awhile. I will be faithful.

115   "Doubt thou the stars are fire,
            Doubt that the sun doth move;
            Doubt truth to be a liar;
            But never doubt I love.

   O dear Ophelia, I am ill at these numbers.[5] I have not art to reck-
120   on my groans, but that I love thee best, O most best, believe it.
Adieu.
         Thine evermore, most dear lady, whilst this machine[6] is to him,
         Hamlet."
This in obedience hath my daughter shown me,
125   And more above, hath his solicitings,
As they fell out by time, by means, and place,
All given to mine ear.
KING: But how hath she
   Received his love?
POLONIUS: What do you think of me?
KING: As of a man faithful and honorable.
130 POLONIUS: I would fain prove so. But what might you think,
When I had seen this hot love on the wing.
(As I perceived it, I must tell you that,
Before my daughter told me), what might you,
Or my dear majesty your queen here, think,
135   If I had played the desk or table-book,
Or given my heart a winking, mute and dumb,
Or looked upon this love with idle sight,[7]
What might you think? No, I went round[8] to work,
And my young mistress thus I did bespeak:
140   "Lord Hamlet is a prince out of thy star.[9]
This must not be." And then I prescripts[1] gave her,
That she should lock herself from his resort,
Admit no messengers, receive no tokens.
Which done, she took[2] the fruits of my advice;
145   And he repelled, a short tale to make,

5. Verses.   6. Body.   7. Polonius means that he would have been at fault if, having seen Hamlet's
attention to Ophelia, he had winked at it or not paid attention, an "idle sight," and if he had remained
silent and kept the information to himself, as if it were written in a "desk" or "table-book."   8. Directly.
9. Beyond your sphere.   1. Orders.   2. Followed.

Fell into a sadness, then into a fast,
Thence to a watch, thence into a weakness,
Thence to a lightness, and by this declension,
Into the madness wherein now he raves,
And all we mourn for.
KING: Do you think 'tis this?   150
QUEEN: It may be, very like.
POLONIUS: Hath there been such a time—I would fain know that—
That I have positively said "Tis so,"
When it proved otherwise?
KING: Not that I know.
POLONIUS: [*Pointing to his head and shoulder.*] Take this from this, if this be
otherwise.   155
If circumstances lead me, I will find
Where truth is hid, though it were hid indeed
Within the centre.³
KING: How may we try it further?
POLONIUS: You know sometimes he walks four hours together
Here in the lobby.
QUEEN: So he does, indeed.   160
POLONIUS: At such a time I'll loose⁴ my daughter to him.
Be you and I behind an arras⁵ then.
Mark the encounter. If he love her not,
And be not from his reason fall'n thereon,
Let me be no assistant for a state,   165
But keep a farm and carters.
KING: We will try it.

[*Enter* HAMLET *reading a book.*]

QUEEN: But look where sadly the poor wretch comes reading.
POLONIUS: Away, I do beseech you both away,
I'll board⁶ him presently.   [*Exeunt* KING *and* QUEEN.]
O, give me leave.
How does my good Lord Hamlet?   170
HAMLET: Well, God-a-mercy.
POLONIUS: Do you know me, my lord?
HAMLET: Excellent well, you are a fishmonger.
POLONIUS: Not I, my lord.
HAMLET: Then I would you were so honest a man.   175
POLONIUS: Honest, my lord?
HAMLET: Ay, sir, to be honest as this world goes, is to be one man picked out of
ten thousand.
POLONIUS: That's very true, my lord.

3. Of the earth.   4. Let loose.   5. Tapestry.   6. Accost.

180   HAMLET: For if the sun breed maggots in a dead dog, being a god kissing carrion[7]—
          Have you a daughter?
      POLONIUS: I have, my lord.
      HAMLET: Let her not walk i' th' sun. Conception is a blessing, but as your daughter
          may conceive—friend, look to't.
185   POLONIUS: How say you by that? [*Aside.*] Still harping on my daughter. Yet he knew
          me not at first. 'A said I was a fishmonger. 'A is far gone. And truly in my
          youth I suffered much extremity for love. Very near this. I'll speak to him
          again.—What do you read, my lord?
      HAMLET: Words, words, words.
190   POLONIUS: What is the matter, my lord?
      HAMLET: Between who?
      POLONIUS: I mean the matter that you read, my lord.
      HAMLET: Slanders, sir; for the satirical rogue says here that old men have grey
          beards, that their faces are wrinkled, their eyes purging thick amber and
195   plum-tree gum, and that they have a plentiful lack of wit, together with most
          weak hams[8]—all which, sir, though I most powerfully and potently believe,
          yet I hold it not honesty to have it thus set down, for yourself, sir, shall grow
          old as I am, if like a crab you could go backward.
      POLONIUS: [*Aside.*] Though this be madness, yet there is method in't.—Will you
200   walk out of the air, my lord?
      HAMLET: Into my grave?
      POLONIUS: [*Aside.*] Indeed, that's out of the air. How pregnant sometime his replies
          are! a happiness that often madness hits on, which reason and sanity could
          not so prosperously be delivered of. I will leave him, and suddenly contrive
205   the means of meeting between him and my daughter.—My honorable lord.
          I will most humbly take my leave of you.
      HAMLET: You cannot take from me anything that I will more willingly part
          withal—except my life, except my life, except my life.

          [*Enter* GUILDENSTERN *and* ROSENCRANTZ.]

      POLONIUS: Fare you well, my lord.
210   HAMLET: These tedious old fools!
      POLONIUS: You go to seek the Lord Hamlet. There he is.
      ROSENCRANTZ: [*To* POLONIUS.] God save you, sir!   [*Exit* POLONIUS.]
      GUILDENSTERN: My honored lord!
      ROSENCRANTZ: My most dear lord!
215   HAMLET: My excellent good friends! How dost thou, Guildenstern?
          Ah, Rosencrantz! Good lads, how do you both?
      ROSENCRANTZ: As the indifferent[9] children of the earth.
      GUILDENSTERN: Happy in that we are not over-happy;
          On Fortune's cap we are not the very button.[1]
220   HAMLET: Nor the soles of her shoe?

---

7. A reference to the belief of the period that maggots were produced spontaneously by the action of sunshine on carrion.   8. Limbs.   9. Ordinary.   1. That is, on top.

ROSENCRANTZ: Neither, my lord.

HAMLET: Then you live about her waist, or in the middle of her favors?

GUILDENSTERN: Faith, her privates we.

HAMLET: In the secret parts of Fortune? O, most true, she is a strumpet.[2] What news?

ROSENCRANTZ: None, my lord, but that the world's grown honest.

HAMLET: Then is doomsday near. But your news is not true. Let me question more in particular. What have you, my good friends, deserved at the hands of Fortune, that she sends you to prison hither?

GUILDENSTERN: Prison, my lord?

HAMLET: Denmark's a prison.

ROSENCRANTZ: Then is the world one.

HAMLET: A goodly one, in which there are many confines, wards[3] and dungeons. Denmark being one o' th' worst.

ROSENCRANTZ: We think not so, my lord.

HAMLET: Why then 'tis none to you; for there is nothing either good or bad, but thinking makes it so. To me it is a prison.

ROSENCRANTZ: Why then your ambition makes it one. 'Tis too narrow for your mind.

HAMLET: O God, I could be bounded in a nutshell and count myself a king of infinite space, where it not that I have bad dreams.

GUILDENSTERN: Which dreams indeed are ambition; for the very substance of the ambitious is merely the shadow of a dream.

HAMLET: A dream itself is but a shadow.

ROSENCRANTZ: Truly, and I hold ambition of so airy and light a quality that it is but a shadow's shadow.

HAMLET: Then are our beggars bodies, and our monarchs and outstretched heroes the beggars' shadows. Shall we to th' court? for, by my fay,[4] I cannot reason.

BOTH: We'll wait upon you.

HAMLET: No such matter. I will not sort[5] you with the rest of my servants; for to speak to you like an honest man, I am most dreadfully attended. But in the beaten way of friendship, what make you at Elsinore?

ROSENCRANTZ: To visit you, my lord; no other occasion.

HAMLET: Beggar that I am, I am even poor in thanks, but I thank you; and sure, dear friends, my thanks are too dear a halfpenny.[6] Were you not sent for? Is it your own inclining? Is it a free visitation? Come, come, deal justly with me. Come, come, nay speak.

GUILDENSTERN: What should we say, my lord?

HAMLET: Anything but to th' purpose. You were sent for, and there is a kind of confession in your looks, which your modesties have not craft enough to color. I know the good king and queen have sent for you.

ROSENCRANTZ: To what end, my lord?

---

2. Prostitute. Hamlet is indulging in characteristic ribaldry. Guildenstern means that they are "privates" = ordinary citizens, but Hamlet takes him to mean "privates" = sexual organs and "middle of her favors" = waist = sexual organs. 3. Cells. 4. Faith. 5. Include. 6. Not worth a halfpenny.

HAMLET: That you must teach me. But let me conjure you by the rights of our
265   fellowship, by the consonancy of our youth, by the obligation of our ever-
preserved love, and by what more dear a better proposer can charge you
withal, be even and direct[7] with me whether you were sent for or no.

ROSENCRANTZ: [*Aside to* GUILDENSTERN.] What say you?

HAMLET: [*Aside.*] Nay, then, I have an eye of you.—If you love me, hold not off.

270 GUILDENSTERN: My lord, we were sent for.

HAMLET: I will tell you why; so shall my anticipation prevent your discovery,[8] and
your secrecy to the king and queen moult no feather. I have of late—but
wherefore I know not—lost all my mirth, forgone all custom of exercises;
and indeed it goes so heavily with my disposition, that this goodly frame the
275   earth seems to me a sterile promontory, this most excellent canopy the air,
look you, this brave o'er-hanging firmament, this majestical roof fretted[9] with
golden fire, why it appeareth nothing to me but a foul and pestilent congregation of vapors. What a piece of work is a man, how noble in reason, how
infinite in faculties, in form and moving, how express[1] and admirable in
280   action, how like an angel in apprehension, how like a god: the beauty of
the world, the paragon of animals. And yet to me, what is this quintessence
of dust? Man delights not me, nor woman neither, though by your smiling
you seem to say so.

ROSENCRANTZ: My lord, there was no such stuff in my thoughts.

285 HAMLET: Why did ye laugh, then, when I said "Man delights not me"?

ROSENCRANTZ: To think, my lord, if you delight not in man, what lenten entertainment the players shall receive from you. We coted[2] them on the way,
and hither are they coming to offer you service.

HAMLET: He that plays the king shall be welcome—his majesty shall have tribute
290   of me; the adventurous knight shall use his foil and target; the lover shall
not sigh gratis; the humorous[3] man shall end his part in peace; the clown
shall make those laugh whose lungs are tickle o' th' sere;[4] and the lady shall
say her mind freely, or the blank verse shall halt for't. What players are they?

ROSENCRANTZ: Even those you were wont to take such delight in, the tragedians
295   of the city.

HAMLET: How chances it they travel? Their residence, both in reputation and
profit, was better both ways.

ROSENCRANTZ: I think their inhibition comes by the means of the late innovation.

HAMLET: Do they hold the same estimation they did when I was in the city? Are
300   they so followed?

ROSENCRANTZ: No, indeed, are they not.

HAMLET: How comes it? Do they grow rusty?

ROSENCRANTZ: Nay, their endeavor keeps in the wonted pace; but there is, sir, an
eyrie of children, little eyases,[5] that cry out on the top of question,[6] and are
305   most tyrannically clapped for't. These are now the fashion, and so berattle

---

7. Straightforward.   8. Disclosure.   9. Ornamented with fretwork.   1. Well built.   2. Passed.
Lenten: scanty.   3. Eccentric. *Foil and target:* sword and shield.   4. Easily set off.   5. Little hawks.
6. With a loud, high delivery.

the common stages (so they call them) that many wearing rapiers are afraid of goose quills[7] and dare scarce come thither.[8]

HAMLET: What, are they children? Who maintains 'em? How are they escoted?[9] Will they pursue the quality no longer than they can sing? Will they not say afterwards, if they should grow themselves to common players (as it is most like, if their means are no better), their writers do them wrong to make them exclaim against their own succession?[1]   310

ROSENCRANTZ: Faith, there has been much todo on both sides; and the nation holds it no sin to tarre[2] them to controversy. There was for a while no money bid for argument,[3] unless the poet and the player went to cuffs[4] in the question.   315

HAMLET: Is't possible?

GUILDENSTERN: O, there has been much throwing about of brains.

HAMLET: Do the boys carry it away?

ROSENCRANTZ: Ay, that they do, my lord. Hercules and his load too.[5]   320

HAMLET: It is not very strange, for my uncle is King of Denmark, and those that would make mouths[6] at him while my father lived give twenty, forty, fifty, a hundred ducats apiece for his picture in little.[7] 'Sblood, there is something in this more than natural, if philosophy could find it out.

[A flourish.]

GUILDENSTERN: There are the players.   325

HAMLET: Gentlemen, you are welcome to Elsinore. Your hands. Come then, th' appurtenance of welcome is fashion and ceremony. Let me comply with you in this garb, lest my extent[8] to the players, which I tell you must show fairly outwards should more appear like entertainment[9] than yours. You are welcome. But my uncle-father and aunt-mother are deceived.   330

GUILDENSTERN: In what, my dear lord?

HAMLET: I am but mad north-north-west; when the wind is southerly I know a hawk from a handsaw.[1]

[Enter POLONIUS.]

POLONIUS: Well be with you, gentlemen.

HAMLET: Hark you, Guildenstern—and you too—at each ear a hearer.   335
That great baby you see there is not yet out of his swaddling clouts.[2]

ROSENCRANTZ: Happily he is the second time come to them, for they say an old man is twice a child.

---

7. Pens of satirical writers.   8. The passage refers to the emergence at the time of the play of theatrical companies made up of children from London choir schools. Their performances became fashionable and hurt the business of the established companies. Hamlet says that if they continue to act, "pursue the quality," when they are grown, they will find that they have been damaging their own future careers. 9. Supported.   1. Future careers.   2. Urge.   3. Paid for a play plot.   4. Blows.   5. During one of his labors Hercules assumed for a time the burden of the Titan Atlas, who supported the heavens on his shoulders. Also a reference to the effect on business at Shakespeare's theater, the Globe.   6. Sneer. 7. Miniature.   8. Fashion. Comply with: welcome.   9. Cordiality.   1. A "hawk" is a plasterer's tool; Hamlet may also be using "handsaw" = hernshaw = heron.   2. Wrappings for an infant.

HAMLET: I will prophesy he comes to tell me of the players. Mark it.
340   —You say right, sir, a Monday morning, 'twas then indeed.
POLONIUS: My lord, I have news to tell you.
HAMLET: My lord, I have news to tell you.
    When Roscius was an actor in Rome—[3]
POLONIUS: The actors are come hither, my lord.
345 HAMLET: Buzz, buzz.
POLONIUS: Upon my honor—
HAMLET: Then came each actor on his ass—
POLONIUS: The best actors in the world, either for tragedy, comedy, history, pasto-
    ral, pastoral-comical, historical-pastoral, tragical-historical, tragical-comical-
350   historical-pastoral, scene individable, or poem unlimited. Seneca cannot be
    too heavy nor Plautus too light. For the law of writ and the liberty, these are
    the only men.[4]
HAMLET: O Jephtha, judge of Israel, what a treasure hadst thou![5]
POLONIUS: What a treasure had he, my lord?
355 HAMLET: Why—

    "One fair daughter, and no more,
    The which he loved passing well."

POLONIUS: [*Aside.*] Still on my daughter.
HAMLET: Am I not i' th' right, old Jephtha?
360 POLONIUS: If you call me Jephtha, my lord, I have a daughter that I love passing
    well.
HAMLET: Nay, that follows not.
POLONIUS: What follows then, my lord?
HAMLET: Why—

365   "As by lot, God wot"

and then, you know,

    "It came to pass, as most like it was."

The first row of the pious chanson[6] will show you more, for look
where my abridgement[7] comes.

    [*Enter the* PLAYERS.]

370 You are welcome, masters; welcome, all.—I am glad to see thee well.—
    Welcome, good friends.—O, old friend! Why thy face is valanced[8] since I
    saw thee last. Com'st thou to beard me in Denmark?—What, my young lady

---

3. Roscius was the most famous actor of classical Rome.   4. Seneca and Plautus were Roman writers of
tragedy and comedy, respectively. The "law of writ" refers to plays written according to such rules as the
three unities; the "liberty" to those written otherwise.   5. To insure victory, Jephtha promised to sacrifice the first creature to meet him on his return. Unfortunately, his only daughter outstripped his dog
and was the victim of his vow. The biblical story is told in Judges 11.   6. Song. *Row:* stanza.   7. That
which cuts short by interrupting.   8. Fringed (with a beard).

and mistress? By'r lady, your ladyship is nearer to heaven than when I saw you last by the altitude of a chopine.[9] Pray God your voice, like a piece of uncurrent gold, be not cracked within the ring.—Masters, you are all wel- come. We'll e'en to't like French falconers, fly at anything we see. We'll have a speech straight. Come give us a taste of your quality,[1] come a passionate speech.

FIRST PLAYER: What speech, my good lord?

HAMLET: I heard thee speak me a speech once, but it was never acted, or if it was, not above once, for the play, I remember, pleased not the million; 'twas caviary to the general.[2] But it was—as I received it, and others whose judgments in such matters cried in the top of[3] mine—an excellent play, well digested[4] in the scenes, set down with as much modesty as cunning. I remember one said there were no sallets[5] in the lines to make the matter savory, nor no matter in the phrase that might indict the author of affectation, but called it an honest method, as wholesome as sweet, and by very much more handsome than fine. One speech in't I chiefly loved. 'Twas Æneas' tale to Dido, and thereabout of it especially where he speaks of Priam's slaughter.[6] If it live in your memory, begin at this line—let me see, let me see:

"The rugged Pyrrhus, like th' Hyrcanian beast"[7]—

'tis not so; it begins with Pyrrhus—

"The rugged Pyrrhus, he whose sable arms,
Black as his purpose, did the night resemble
When he lay couchéd in th' ominous horse,[8]
Hath now this dread and black complexion smeared
With heraldry more dismal; head to foot
Now is he total gules, horridly tricked[9]
With blood of fathers, mothers, daughters, sons,
Baked and impasted with the parching[1] streets,
That lend a tyrannous and a damnéd light
To their lord's murder. Roasted in wrath and fire,
And thus o'er-sizéd with coagulate[2] gore,
With eyes like carbuncles, the hellish Pyrrhus
Old grandsire Priam seeks."

So proceed you.

9. A reference to the contemporary theatrical practice of using boys to play women's parts. The company's "lady" has grown in height by the size of a woman's thick-soled shoe, "chopine," since Hamlet saw him last. The next sentence refers to the possibility, suggested by his growth, that the young actor's voice may soon begin to change. 1. Trade. 2. Masses. *Caviary*: caviar. 3. Were weightier than. 4. Arranged. 5. Spicy passages. 6. Aeneas, fleeing with his band from fallen Troy (Ilium), arrives in Carthage, where he tells Dido, the queen of Carthage, of the fall of Troy. Here he is describing the death of Priam, the aged king of Troy, at the hands of Pyrrhus, the son of the slain Achilles. 7. Tiger. 8. That is, the Trojan horse. 9. Adorned. *Total gules*: completely red. 1. Burning. *Impasted*: crusted. 2. Clotted. *O'er-sizéd*: glued over.

POLONIUS: Fore God, my lord, well spoken, with good accent and good discretion.

FIRST PLAYER: "Anon he finds him[3]
410   Striking too short at Greeks. His antique[4] sword,
           Rebellious[5] to his arm, lies where it falls,
           Repugnant to command. Unequal matched,
           Pyrrhus at Priam drives, in rage strikes wide.
           But with the whiff and wind of his fell sword
415   Th' unnervéd father falls. Then senseless[6] Ilium,
           Seeming to feel this blow, with flaming top
           Stoops[7] to his base, and with a hideous crash
           Takes prisoner Pyrrhus' ear. For, lo! his sword,
           Which was declining[8] on the milky head
420   Of reverend Priam, seemed i' th' air to stick.
           So as a painted tyrant Pyrrhus stood,
           And like a neutral to his will and matter,[9]
           Did nothing.
           But as we often see, against some storm,
425   A silence in the heavens, the rack[1] stand still,
           The bold winds speechless, and the orb below
           As hush as death, anon the dreadful thunder
           Doth rend the region; so, after Pyrrhus' pause,
           A rouséd vengeance sets him new awork,[2]
430   And never did the Cyclops' hammers fall
           On Mars's armor, forged for proof eterne,[3]
           With less remorse than Pyrrhus' bleeding sword
           Now falls on Priam.
           Out, out, thou strumpet, Fortune! All you gods,
435   In general synod take away her power,
           Break all the spokes and fellies[4] from her wheel,
           And bowl the round nave[5] down the hill of heaven
           As low as to the fiends."

POLONIUS: This is too long.
440   HAMLET: It shall to the barber's with your beard.—Prithee say on. He's for a jig,[6]
           or a tale of bawdry, or he sleeps. Say on; come to Hecuba.[7]

FIRST PLAYER: "But who, ah woe! had seen the mobléd[8] queen—"
HAMLET: "The mobléd queen"?
POLONIUS: That's good. "Mobléd queen" is good.
445   FIRST PLAYER: "Run barefoot up and down, threat'ning the flames

---

3. That is, Pyrrhus finds Priam.   4. Which he used when young.   5. Refractory.   6. Without feeling.   7. Falls.   8. About to fall.   9. Between his will and the fulfillment of it.   1. Clouds.
2. To work.   3. Mars, as befits a Roman war god, had armor made for him by the blacksmith god Vulcan
and his assistants, the Cyclopes. It was suitably impenetrable, of "proof eterne."   4. Parts of the rim.
5. Hub. *Bowl:* roll.   6. A comic act.   7. Hecuba was the wife of Priam and queen of Troy. Her "loins"
are described below as "o'erteemed" because of her unusual fertility. The number of her children varies
in different accounts, but twenty is a safe minimum.   8. Muffled (in a hood).

With bisson rheum, a clout[9] upon that head
Where late the diadem stood, and for a robe,
About her lank and all o'er-teeméd loins,
A blanket, in the alarm of fear caught up—
Who this had seen, with tongue in venom steeped, 450
'Gainst Fortune's state[1] would treason have pronounced.
But if the gods themselves did see her then,
When she saw Pyrrhus make malicious sport
In mincing[2] with his sword her husband's limbs,
The instant burst of clamor that she made, 455
Unless things mortal move them not at all,
Would have made milch[3] the burning eyes of heaven,
And passion in the gods."
POLONIUS: Look whe'r[4] he has not turned his color, and has tears in's eyes. Prithee
no more. 460
HAMLET: 'Tis well. I'll have thee speak out the rest of this soon.—Good my lord,
will you see the players well bestowed?[5] Do you hear, let them be well used,
for they are the abstract[6] and brief chronicles of the time; after your death
you were better have a bad epitaph than their ill report while you live.
POLONIUS: My lord, I will use them according to their desert. 465
HAMLET: God's bodkin, man, much better. Use every man after his desert, and who
shall 'scape whipping? Use them after your own honor and dignity. The less
they deserve, the more merit is in your bounty. Take them in.
POLONIUS: Come, sirs.
HAMLET: Follow him, friends. We'll hear a play tomorrow. [*Aside to* FIRST PLAYER.] 470
Dost thou hear me, old friend, can you play "The Murder of Gonzago"?
FIRST PLAYER: Ay, my lord.
HAMLET: We'll ha't tomorrow night. You could for a need study a speech of
some dozen or sixteen lines which I would set down and insert in't, could
you not? 475
FIRST PLAYER: Ay, my lord.
HAMLET: Very well. Follow that lord, and look you mock him not.
                                        [*Exeunt* POLONIUS *and* PLAYERS.]
My good friends, I'll leave you till night. You are welcome to Elsinore.
ROSENCRANTZ: Good my lord.
                                        [*Exeunt* ROSENCRANTZ *and* GUILDENSTERN.]
HAMLET: Ay, so God b'wi'ye. Now I am alone. 480
O, what a rogue and peasant slave am I!
Is it not monstrous that this player here,
But in a fiction, in a dream of passion,
Could force his soul so to his own conceit[7]
That from her working all his visage wanned;[8] 485

---

9. Cloth. *Bisson rheum:* blinding tears.   1. Government.   2. Cutting up.   3. Tearful (literally,
milk-giving).   4. Whether.   5. Provided for.   6. Summary.   7. Imagination.   8. Grew pale.

Tears in his eyes, distraction in his aspect[9]
A broken voice, and his whole function suiting
With forms to his conceit? And all for nothing,
For Hecuba!
490　What's Hecuba to him or he to Hecuba,
That he should weep for her? What would he do
Had he the motive and the cue for passion
That I have? He would drown the stage with tears,
And cleave the general ear with horrid speech,
495　Make mad the guilty, and appal the free,
Confound the ignorant, and amaze indeed
The very faculties of eyes and ears.
Yet I,
A dull and muddy-mettled rascal, peak[1]
500　Like John-a-dreams, unpregnant[2] of my cause,
And can say nothing; no, not for a king
Upon whose property and most dear life
A damned defeat was made. Am I a coward?
Who calls me villain, breaks my pate across,
505　Plucks off my beard and blows it in my face,
Tweaks me by the nose, gives me the lie i' th' throat
As deep as to the lungs? Who does me this?
Ha, 'swounds, I should take it; for it cannot be
But I am pigeon-livered and lack gall[3]
510　To make oppression bitter, or ere this
I should 'a fatted all the region kites[4]
With this slave's offal. Bloody, bawdy villain!
Remorseless, treacherous, lecherous, kindless[5] villain!
O, vengeance!
515　Why, what an ass am I! This is most brave,
That I, the son of a dear father murdered,
Prompted to my revenge by heaven and hell,
Must like a whore unpack[6] my heart with words,
And fall a-cursing like a very drab,
520　A scullion![7] Fie upon't! foh!
About, my brains. Hum—I have heard
That guilty creatures sitting at a play,
Have by the very cunning of the scene
Been struck so to the soul that presently
525　They have proclaimed[8] their malefactions;
For murder, though it have no tongue, will speak

---

9. Face.　1. Mope. *Muddy-mettled:* dull-spirited.　2. Not quickened by. *John-a-dreams:* a man dreaming.　3. Bitterness.　4. Birds of prey of the area.　5. Unnatural.　6. Relieve.　7. In some versions of the play, the word "stallion," a slang term for a prostitute, appears in place of "scullion."
8. Admitted.

With most miraculous organ. I'll have these players
Play something like the murder of my father
Before mine uncle. I'll observe his looks.
I'll tent him to the quick. If 'a do blench,⁹ 530
I know my course. The spirit that I have seen
May be a devil, and the devil hath power
T' assume a pleasing shape, yea, and perhaps
Out of my weakness and my melancholy,
As he is very potent with such spirits, 535
Abuses me to damn me. I'll have grounds
More relative¹ than this. The play's the thing
Wherein I'll catch the conscience of the king.   [*Exit.*]

ACT III

Scene 1

A room in the castle. Enter KING, QUEEN, POLONIUS, OPHELIA, ROSENCRANTZ *and*
GUILDENSTERN.

KING: And can you by no drift of conference²
  Get from him why he puts on this confusion,
  Grating so harshly all his days of quiet
  With turbulent³ and dangerous lunacy?
ROSENCRANTZ: He does confess he feels himself distracted, 5
  But from what cause 'a will by no means speak.
GUILDENSTERN: Nor do we find him forward to be sounded,⁴
  But with a crafty madness keeps aloof
  When we would bring him on to some confession
  Of his true state.
QUEEN: Did he receive you well? 10
ROSENCRANTZ: Most like a gentleman.
GUILDENSTERN: But with much forcing of his disposition.⁵
ROSENCRANTZ: Niggard of question, but of our demands⁶
  Most free in his reply.
QUEEN: Did you assay⁷ him
  To any pastime? 15
ROSENCRANTZ: Madam, it so fell out that certain players
  We o'er-raught⁸ on the way. Of these we told him,
  And there did seem in him a kind of joy
  To hear of it. They are here about the court,
  And as I think, they have already order 20
  This night to play before him.

---

9. Turn pale. *Tent:* try.   1. Conclusive.   2. Line of conversation.   3. Disturbing.   4. Questioned. *Forward:* eager.   5. Conversation.   6. To our questions.   7. Tempt.   8. Passed.

POLONIUS: 'Tis most true,
   And he beseeched me to entreat your majesties
   To hear and see the matter.⁹
KING: With all my heart, and it doth much content me
25   To hear him so inclined.
   Good gentlemen, give him a further edge,
   And drive his purpose¹ into these delights.
ROSENCRANTZ: We shall, my lord.   [*Exeunt* ROSENCRANTZ *and* GUILDENSTERN.]
KING: Sweet Gertrude, leave us too,
   For we have closely sent for Hamlet hither,
30   That he, as 'twere by accident, may here
   Affront² Ophelia.
   Her father and myself (lawful espials³)
   Will so bestow ourselves that, seeing unseen,
   We may of their encounter frankly judge,
35   And gather by him, as he is behaved,
   If't be th' affliction of his love or no
   That thus he suffers for.
QUEEN: I shall obey you.—
   And for your part, Ophelia, I do wish
   That your good beauties be the happy cause
40   Of Hamlet's wildness. So shall I hope your virtues
   Will bring him to his wonted⁴ way again,
   To both your honors.
OPHELIA: Madam, I wish it may.   [*Exit* QUEEN.]
POLONIUS: Ophelia, walk you here.—Gracious,⁵ so please you,
   We will bestow ourselves.—[*To* OPHELIA.] Read on this book,
45   That show of such an exercise may color⁶
   Your loneliness.—We are oft to blame in this,
   'Tis too much proved, that with devotion's visage
   And pious action we do sugar o'er
   The devil himself.
KING: [*Aside.*]   O, 'tis too true.
50   How smart a lash that speech doth give my conscience!
   The harlot's cheek, beautied with plast'ring⁷ art,
   Is not more ugly to the thing that helps it
   Than is my deed to my most painted word.
   O heavy burden!
55 POLONIUS: I hear him coming. Let's withdraw, my lord.
                                           [*Exeunt* KING *and* POLONIUS.]

      [*Enter* HAMLET.]

HAMLET: To be, or not to be, that is the question:
   Whether 'tis nobler in the mind to suffer

---

9. Performance.   1. Sharpen his intention.   2. Confront.   3. Justified spies.   4. Usual.   5. Majesty.   6. Explain. *Exercise:* act of devotion.   7. Thickly painted.

The slings and arrows of outrageous fortune,
Or to take arms against a sea of troubles,
And by opposing end them. To die, to sleep— 60
No more; and by a sleep to say we end
The heartache, and the thousand natural shocks
That flesh is heir to. 'Tis a consummation
Devoutly to be wished—to die, to sleep—
To sleep, perchance to dream, ay there's the rub; 65
For in that sleep of death what dreams may come
When we have shuffled off this mortal coil[8]
Must give us pause—there's the respect[9]
That makes calamity of so long life.
For who would bear the whips and scorns of time, 70
Th' oppressor's wrong, the proud man's contumely,[1]
The pangs of despised love, the law's delay,
The insolence of office, and the spurns[2]
That patient merit of th' unworthy takes,
When he himself might his quietus[3] make 75
With a bare bodkin? Who would fardels[4] bear,
To grunt and sweat under a weary life,
But that the dread of something after death,
The undiscovered country, from whose bourn[5]
No traveller returns, puzzles the will, 80
And makes us rather bear those ills we have
Than fly to others that we know not of?
Thus conscience does make cowards of us all;
And thus the native[6] hue of resolution
Is sicklied o'er with the pale cast of thought, 85
And enterprises of great pitch and moment[7]
With this regard their currents turn awry
And lose the name of action.—Soft you now,
The fair Ophelia.—Nymph, in thy orisons[8]
Be all my sins remembered.
OPHELIA: Good my lord, 90
   How does your honor for this many a day?
HAMLET: I humbly thank you, well, well, well.
OPHELIA: My lord, I have remembrances of yours
   That I have longéd long to re-deliver.
   I pray you now receive them.
HAMLET: No, not I, 95
   I never gave you aught.
OPHELIA: My honored lord, you know right well you did,
   And with them words of so sweet breath composed
   As made the things more rich. Their perfume lost,

8. Turmoil.   9. Consideration.   1. Insulting behavior.   2. Rejections.   3. Settlement.   4. Burdens. *Bodkin:* dagger.   5. Boundary.   6. Natural.   7. Importance. *Pitch:* height.   8. Prayers.

100   Take these again, for to the noble mind
        Rich gifts wax[9] poor when givers prove unkind.
        There, my lord.

HAMLET: Ha, ha! are you honest?[1]

OPHELIA: My lord?

105 HAMLET: Are you fair?

OPHELIA: What means your lordship?

HAMLET: That if you be honest and fair, your honesty should admit no discourse
    to your beauty.

OPHELIA: Could beauty, my lord, have better commerce[2] than with honesty?

110 HAMLET: Ay, truly, for the power of beauty will sooner transform honesty from
    what it is to a bawd than the force of honesty can translate beauty into his
    likeness. This was sometimes a paradox, but now the time gives it proof. I did
    love you once.

OPHELIA: Indeed, my lord, you made me believe so.

115 HAMLET: You should not have believed me, for virtue cannot so inoculate[3] our
    old stock but we shall relish of it. I loved you not.

OPHELIA: I was the more deceived.

HAMLET: Get thee to a nunnery.[4] Why wouldst thou be a breeder of sinners? I am
    myself indifferent[5] honest, but yet I could accuse me of such things that
120   it were better my mother had not borne me: I am very proud, revengeful,
    ambitious, with more offences at my beck[6] than I have thoughts to put them
    in, imagination to give them shape, or time to act them in. What should
    such fellows as I do crawling between earth and heaven? We are arrant[7]
    knaves all; believe none of us. Go thy ways to a nunnery. Where's your
125   father?

OPHELIA: At home, my lord.

HAMLET: Let the doors be shut upon him, that he may play the fool nowhere but
    in's own house. Farewell.

OPHELIA: O, help him, you sweet heavens!

130 HAMLET: If thou dost marry, I'll give thee this plague for thy dowry: be thou as
    chaste as ice, as pure as snow, thou shalt not escape calumny. Get thee to a
    nunnery, farewell. Or if thou wilt needs marry, marry a fool, for wise men
    know well enough what monsters[8] you make of them. To a nunnery, go, and
    quickly too. Farewell.

135 OPHELIA: Heavenly powers, restore him!

HAMLET: I have heard of your paintings, too, well enough. God hath given you
    one face, and you make yourselves another. You jig, you amble, and you lisp;
    [9] you nickname God's creatures, and make your wantonness your ignorance.[1]
    Go to, I'll no more on't, it hath made me mad. I say we will have no more
140   marriage. Those that are married already, all but one, shall live. The rest shall
    keep as they are. To a nunnery, go.   [Exit.]

---

9. Become.   1. Chaste.   2. Intercourse.   3. Change by grafting.   4. With typical ribaldry Hamlet uses "nunnery" in two senses, the second as a slang term for brothel.   5. Moderately.   6. Command.   7. Thorough.   8. Horned because cuckolded.   9. Walk and talk affectedly.   1. Hamlet
means that women call things by pet names and then blame the affectation on ignorance.

OPHELIA: O, what a noble mind is here o'erthrown!
  The courtier's, soldier's, scholar's, eye, tongue, sword,
  Th' expectancy and rose[2] of the fair state,
  The glass of fashion and the mould[3] of form,   145
  Th' observed of all observers, quite quite down!
  And I of ladies most deject and wretched,
  That sucked the honey of his music[4] vows,
  Now see that noble and most sovereign reason
  Like sweet bells jangled, out of time and harsh;   150
  That unmatched form and feature of blown[5] youth
  Blasted with ecstasy. O, woe is me
  T' have seen what I have seen, see what I see!

    [*Enter* KING *and* POLONIUS.]

KING: Love! His affections do not that way tend,
  Nor what he spake, though it lacked form a little,   155
  Was not like madness. There's something in his soul
  O'er which his melancholy sits on brood,[6]
  And I do doubt the hatch and the disclose[7]
  Will be some danger; which to prevent,
  I have in quick determination   160
  Thus set it down: he shall with speed to England
  For the demand of our neglected tribute.
  Haply the seas and countries different,
  With variable objects, shall expel
  This something-settled matter in his heart   165
  Whereon his brains still beating puts him thus
  From fashion of himself. What think you on't?
POLONIUS: It shall do well. But yet do I believe
  The origin and commencement of his grief
  Sprung from neglected love.—How now, Ophelia?   170
  You need not tell us what Lord Hamlet said,
  We heard it all.—My lord, do as you please,
  But if you hold it fit, after the play
  Let his queen-mother all alone entreat him
  To show his grief. Let her be round[8] with him,   175
  And I'll be placed, so please you, in the ear[9]
  Of all their conference. If she find him not,[1]
  To England send him; or confine him where
  Your wisdom best shall think.
KING: It shall be so.
  Madness in great ones must not unwatched go.   [*Exeunt.*] 180

---

2. Ornament. *Expectancy:* hope.   3. Model. *Glass:* mirror.   4. Musical.   5. Full-blown.   6. That
is, like a hen.   7. Result. *Doubt:* fear.   8. Direct.   9. Hearing.   1. Does not discover his problem.

Scene 2

A public room in the castle. Enter HAMLET *and three of the* PLAYERS.

HAMLET: Speak the speech, I pray you, as I pronounced it to you, trippingly on the tongue; but if you mouth it as many of our players do, I had as lief the town-crier spoke my lines. Nor do not saw the air too much with your hand thus, but use all gently, for in the very torrent, tempest, and as I may say,
5   whirlwind of your passion, you must acquire and beget a temperance that may give it smoothness. O, it offends me to the soul to hear a robustious periwig-pated² fellow tear a passion to tatters, to very rags, to split the ears of the groundlings, who for the most part are capable of³ nothing but inexplicable dumb shows and noise. I would have such a fellow whipped for
10   o'erdoing Termagant. It out-herods Herod.⁴ Pray you avoid it.

FIRST PLAYER: I warrant your honor.

HAMLET: Be not too tame neither, but let your own discretion be your tutor. Suit the action to the word, the word to the action, with this special observance, that you o'erstep not the modesty of nature; for anything so o'erdone is from⁵
15   the purpose of playing, whose end both at the first, and now, was and is, to hold as 'twere the mirror up to nature, to show virtue her own feature, scorn her own image, and the very age and body of the time his form and pressure.⁶ Now this overdone, or come tardy off, though it makes the unskilful⁷ laugh, cannot but make the judicious grieve, the censure⁸ of the which one must in
20   your allowance o'erweigh a whole theatre of others. O, there be players that I have seen play—and heard others praise, and that highly—not to speak it profanely, that neither having th' accent of Christians, nor the gait of Christian, pagan, nor man, have so strutted and bellowed that I have thought some of nature's journeymen⁹ had made men, and not made them well, they imi-
25   tated humanity so abominably.

FIRST PLAYER: I hope we have reformed that indifferently¹ with us, sir.

HAMLET: O, reform it altogether. And let those that play your clowns speak no more than is set down for them, for there be of them that will themselves laugh, to set on some quantity of barren² spectators to laugh too, though in
30   the meantime some necessary question of the play be then to be considered. That's villainous, and shows a most pitiful ambition in the fool that uses it. Go, make you ready.   [*Exeunt* PLAYERS.]

[*Enter* POLONIUS, GUILDENSTERN, *and* ROSENCRANTZ.]

How now, my lord? Will the king hear this piece of work?

POLONIUS: And the queen too, and that presently.

35   HAMLET: Bid the players make haste.   [*Exit* POLONIUS.]

Will you two help to hasten them?

---

2. Bewigged. *Robustious:* noisy.   3. That is, capable of understanding. *Groundlings:* the spectators who paid least.   4. Termagant, a "Saracen" deity, and the biblical Herod were stock characters in popular drama noted for the excesses of sound and fury used by their interpreters.   5. Contrary to.
6. Shape.   7. Ignorant.   8. Judgment.   9. Inferior   craftsmen.   1. Somewhat.   2. Dull-witted.

ROSENCRANTZ: Ay, my lord.   [*Exeunt they two.*]
HAMLET: What, ho, Horatio!

    [*Enter* HORATIO.]

HORATIO: Here, sweet lord, at your service.
HAMLET: Horatio, thou art e'en as just a man   40
  As e'er my conversation coped[3] withal.
HORATIO: O my dear lord!
HAMLET: Nay, do not think I flatter,
  For what advancement may I hope from thee,
  That no revenue hast but thy good spirits
  To feed and clothe thee? Why should the poor be flattered?   45
  No, let the candied tongue lick absurd pomp,
  And crook the pregnant[4] hinges of the knee
  Where thrift[5] may follow fawning. Dost thou hear?
  Since my dear soul was mistress of her choice
  And could of men distinguish her election,   50
  S'hath sealed thee for herself, for thou hast been
  As one in suff'ring all that suffers nothing,
  A man that Fortune's buffets and rewards
  Hast ta'en with equal thanks; and blest are those
  Whose blood and judgment are so well commingled   55
  That they are not a pipe[6] for Fortune's finger
  To sound what stop[7] she please. Give me that man
  That is not passion's slave, and I will wear him
  In my heart's core, ay, in my heart of heart,
  As I do thee. Something too much of this.   60
  There is a play tonight before the king.
  One scene of it comes near the circumstance
  Which I have told thee of my father's death.
  I prithee, when thou seest that act afoot,
  Even with the very comment[8] of thy soul   65
  Observe my uncle. If his occulted[9] guilt
  Do not itself unkennel[1] in one speech,
  It is a damnéd ghost that we have seen,
  And my imaginations are as foul
  As Vulcan's stithy. Give him heedful note,[2]   70
  For I mine eyes will rivet to his face,
  And after we will both our judgments join
  In censure of his seeming.[3]
HORATIO: Well, my lord.

---

3. Encountered.   4. Quick to bend.   5. Profit.   6. Musical instrument.   7. Note. *Sound:* play.
8. Keenest observation.   9. Hidden.   1. Break loose.   2. Careful attention. *Stithy:* smithy.
3. Manner.

If 'a steal aught the whilst this play in playing,
75   And 'scape detecting, I will pay[4] the theft.

[*Enter Trumpets and Kettledrums,* KING, QUEEN, POLONIUS, OPHELIA, ROSEN-
CRANTZ, GUILDENSTERN, *and other* LORDS *attendant.*]

HAMLET: They are coming to the play. I must be idle.
    Get you a place.
KING: How fares our cousin Hamlet?
HAMLET: Excellent, i' faith, of the chameleon's dish.[5] I eat the air, promise-
80   crammed. You cannot feed capons so.
KING: I have nothing with this answer, Hamlet. These words are not mine.
HAMLET: No, nor mine now. [*To* POLONIUS.] My lord, you played once i' th' uni-
    versity, you say?
POLONIUS: That did I, my lord, and was accounted a good actor.
85 HAMLET: What did you enact?
POLONIUS: I did enact Julius Cæsar. I was killed i' th' Capitol; Brutus killed
    me.[6]
HAMLET: It was a brute part of him to kill so capital a calf there. Be the players
    ready?
90 ROSENCRANTZ: Ay, my lord, they stay upon your patience.[7]
QUEEN: Come hither, my dear Hamlet, sit by me.
HAMLET: No, good mother, here's metal more attractive.
POLONIUS: [*To the* KING.] O, ho! do you mark that?
HAMLET: Lady, shall I lie in your lap?

[*Lying down at* OPHELIA's *feet.*]

95 OPHELIA: No, my lord.
HAMLET: I mean, my head upon your lap?
OPHELIA: Ay, my lord.
HAMLET: Do you think I meant country matters?[8]
OPHELIA: I think nothing, my lord.
100 HAMLET: That's a fair thought to lie between maids' legs.
OPHELIA: What is, my lord?
HAMLET: Nothing.
OPHELIA: You are merry, my lord.
HAMLET: Who, I?
105 OPHELIA: Ay, my lord.
HAMLET: O God, your only jig-maker![9] What should a man do but be merry?
    For look you how cheerfully my mother looks, and my father died within's
    two hours.

---

4. Repay.   5. A reference to a popular belief that the chameleon subsisted on a diet of air. Hamlet has
deliberately misunderstood the king's question.   6. The assassination of Julius Caesar by Brutus and
others is the subject of another play by Shakespeare.   7. Leisure. *Stay:* wait.   8. Presumably, rustic
misbehavior, but here and elsewhere in this exchange Hamlet treats Ophelia to some ribald double
meanings.   9. Writer of comic scenes.

OPHELIA: Nay, 'tis twice two months, my lord.

HAMLET: So long? Nay then, let the devil wear black, for I'll have a suit of sables. 110
O heavens! die two months ago, and not forgotten yet? Then there's hope a
great man's memory may outlive his life half a year, but by'r lady 'a must
build churches then, or else shall 'a suffer not thinking on, with the hobby-
horse, whose epitaph is "For O, for O, the hobby-horse is forgot!"[1]

> *The trumpets sound. Dumb Show follows. Enter a* KING *and a* QUEEN *very*
> *lovingly; the* QUEEN *embracing him and he her. She kneels, and makes show*
> *of protestation unto him. He takes her up, and declines[2] his head upon her*
> *neck. He lies him down upon a bank of flowers; she, seeing him asleep, leaves*
> *him. Anon come in another man, takes off his crown, kisses it, pours poison*
> *in the sleeper's ears, and leaves him. The* QUEEN *returns, finds the* KING *dead,*
> *makes passionate action. The* POISONER *with some three or four come in again,*
> *seem to condole with her. The dead body is carried away. The* POISONER *woos*
> *the* QUEEN *with gifts; she seems harsh awhile, but in the end accepts love.*
>
> *[Exeunt.]*

OPHELIA: What means this, my lord? 115

HAMLET: Marry, this is miching mallecho;[3] it means mischief.

OPHELIA: Belike this show imports the argument[4] of the play.

> *[Enter* PROLOGUE.*]*

HAMLET: We shall know by this fellow. The players cannot keep counsel; they'll
tell all.

OPHELIA: Will 'a tell us what this show meant? 120

HAMLET: Ay, or any show that you will show him. Be not you ashamed to show,
he'll not shame to tell you what it means.

OPHELIA: You are naught, you are naught. I'll mark[5] the play.

PROLOGUE: *For us, and for our tragedy,*
Here stooping to your clemency, 125
We beg your hearing patiently. *[Exit.]*

HAMLET: Is this a prologue, or the posy[6] of a ring?

OPHELIA: 'Tis brief, my lord.

HAMLET: As woman's love.

> *[Enter the* PLAYER KING *and* QUEEN.*]*

PLAYER KING: *Full thirty times hath Phœbus' cart gone round* 130
Neptune's salt wash and Tellus' orbéd ground,
And thirty dozen moons with borrowed sheen[7]
About the world have times twelve thirties been,

---

1. In traditional games and dances one of the characters was a man respresented as riding a horse. The
horse was made of something like cardboard and was worn about the "rider's" waist.   2. Lays.
3. Sneaking crime.   4. Plot. *Imports:* explains.   5. Attend to. *Naught:* obscene.   6. Motto engraved
inside.   7. Light.

Since love our hearts and Hymen did our hands
135   *Unite comutual in most sacred bands.*[8]
PLAYER QUEEN: *So many journeys may the sun and moon*
          Make us again count o'er ere love be done!
          But woe is me, you are so sick of late,
          So far from cheer and from your former state,
140   *That I distrust*[9] *you. Yet though I distrust,*
          Discomfort you, my lord, it nothing must.
          For women's fear and love hold quantity,[1]
          In neither aught, or in extremity.[2]
          Now what my love is proof hath made you know,
145   *And as my love is sized,*[3] *my fear is so.*
          Where love is great, the littlest doubts are fear;
          Where little fears grow great, great love grows there.
PLAYER KING: *Faith, I must leave thee, love, and shortly too;*
          My operant powers their functions leave[4] *to do.*
150   *And thou shalt live in this fair world behind,*
          Honored, beloved, and haply one as kind
          For husband shalt thou—
PLAYER QUEEN: *O, confound the rest!*
          Such love must needs be treason in my breast.
          In second husband let me be accurst!
155   *None wed the second but who killed the first.*[5]
HAMLET: That's wormwood.
PLAYER QUEEN: *The instances*[6] *that second marriage move*
          Are base respects[7] *of thrift, but none of love.*
          A second time I kill my husband dead,
160   *When second husband kisses me in bed.*
PLAYER KING: *I do believe you think what now you speak,*
          But what we do determine oft we break.
          Purpose is but the slave to memory,
          Of violent birth, but poor validity;
165   *Which now, like fruit unripe, sticks on the tree,*
          But fall unshaken when they mellow be.
          Most necessary 'tis that we forget
          To pay ourselves what to ourselves is debt.
          What to ourselves in passion we propose,
170   *The passion ending, doth the purpose lose.*
          The violence of either grief or joy

8. The speech contains several references to Greek mythology. Phoebus was the sun god, and his chariot
or "cart" is the sun. The "salt wash" of Neptune is the ocean; Tellus was an earth goddess, and her "orbed
ground" is the Earth, or globe. Hymen was the god of marriage. *Comutual:* mutually.   9. Fear for.
1. Agree in weight.   2. Without regard to too much or too little.   3. In size.   4. Cease. *Operant
powers:* active forces.   5. Though there is some ambiguity, she seems to mean that the only kind of
woman who would remarry is one who has killed or would kill her first husband.   6. Causes.
7. Concerns.

Their own enactures[8] with themselves destroy.
Where joy most revels, grief doth most lament;
Grief joys, joy grieves, on slender accident.
This world is not for aye,[9] nor 'tis not strange   175
That even our loves should with our fortunes change;
For 'tis a question left us yet to prove,
Whether love lead fortune, or else fortune love.
The great man down, you mark his favorite flies;
The poor advanced makes friends of enemies;   180
And hitherto doth love on fortune tend,
For who not needs shall never lack a friend,
And who in want a hollow[1] friend doth try,
Directly seasons him[2] his enemy.
But orderly to end where I begun,   185
Our wills and fates do so contrary run
That our devices[3] still are overthrown;
Our thoughts are ours, their ends none of our own.
So think thou wilt no second husband wed,
But die thy thoughts when thy first lord is dead.   190
PLAYER QUEEN: *Nor earth to me give food, nor heaven light,*
Sport and repose lock from me day and night,
To desperation turn my trust and hope,
An anchor's cheer[4] in prison be my scope,
Each opposite that blanks[5] the face of joy   195
Meet what I would have well, and it destroy,
Both here and hence[6] pursue me lasting strife,
If once a widow, ever I be wife!
HAMLET: If she should break it now!
PLAYER KING: *'Tis deeply sworn. Sweet, leave me here awhile.*   200
My spirits grow dull, and fain I would beguile
The tedious day with sleep.   [*Sleeps.*]
PLAYER QUEEN: *Sleep rock thy brain,*
And never come mischance between us twain!   [*Exit.*]
HAMLET: Madam, how like you this play?
QUEEN: The lady doth protest too much, methinks.   205
HAMLET: O, but she'll keep her word.
KING: Have you heard the argument? Is there no offence in't?
HAMLET: No, no, they do but jest, poison in jest; no offence i' th' world.
KING: What do you call the play?
HAMLET: "The Mouse-trap." Marry, how? Tropically.[7] This play is the image of a   210
murder done in Vienna. Gonzago is the duke's name; his wife, Baptista.
You shall see anon. 'Tis a knavish piece of work, but what of that? Your

---

8. Actions.   9. Eternal.   1. False.   2. Ripens him into.   3. Plans.   4. Anchorite's food.
5. Blanches.   6. In the next world.   7. Figuratively.

majesty, and we that have free souls, it touches us not. Let the galled jade wince, our withers are unwrung.[8]

[*Enter* LUCIANUS.]

215   This is one Lucianus, nephew to the king.

OPHELIA: You are as good as a chorus, my lord.

HAMLET: I could interpret between you and your love, if I could see the puppets dallying.

OPHELIA: You are keen, my lord, you are keen.

220   HAMLET: It would cost you a groaning to take off mine edge.

OPHELIA: Still better, and worse.

HAMLET: So you mistake your husbands.—Begin, murderer. Leave thy damnable faces and begin. Come, the croaking raven doth bellow for revenge.

LUCIANUS: *Thoughts black, hands apt, drugs fit, and time agreeing,*

225   *Confederate season,*[9] *else no creature seeing,*

Thou mixture rank, of midnight weeds collected,

With Hecate's ban thrice blasted, thrice infected,[1]

Thy natural magic[2] *and dire property*

On wholesome life usurp immediately.   [*Pours the poison in his ears.*]

230   HAMLET: 'A poisons him i' th' garden for his estate. His name's Gonzago. The story is extant, and written in very choice Italian. You shall see anon how the murderer gets the love of Gonzago's wife.

OPHELIA: The king rises.

HAMLET: What, frighted with false fire?

235   QUEEN: How fares my lord?

POLONIUS: Give o'er the play.

KING: Give me some light. Away!

POLONIUS: Lights, lights, lights!   [*Exeunt all but* HAMLET *and* HORATIO.]

HAMLET:

Why, let the strucken deer go weep,

240   The hart ungalléd[3] play.

For some must watch while some must sleep;

Thus runs the world away.

Would not this, sir, and a forest of feathers[4]—if the rest of my fortunes turn Turk with me—with two Provincial roses on my razed shoes, get me a fellow-

245   ship in a cry of players?[5]

HORATIO: Half a share.

HAMLET: A whole one, I.

8. A "galled jade" is a horse, particularly one of poor quality, with a sore back. The "withers" are the ridge between a horse's shoulders; "unwrung withers" are not chafed by the harness.   9. A helpful time for the crime.   1. Hecate was a classical goddess of witchcraft.   2. Native power.   3. Uninjured.   4. Plumes.   5. Hamlet asks Horatio if "this" recitation, accompanied with a player's costume, including plumes and rosettes on shoes that have been slashed for decorative effect, might not entitle him to become a shareholder in a theatrical company in the event that Fortune goes against him, "turn Turk." *Cry:* company.

> For thou dost know, O Damon dear,[6]
>   This realm dismantled was
> Of Jove himself, and now reigns here
>   A very, very—peacock.

HORATIO: You might have rhymed.

HAMLET: O good Horatio, I'll take the ghost's word for a thousand pound. Didst perceive?

HORATIO: Very well, my lord.

HAMLET: Upon the talk of the poisoning.

HORATIO: I did very well note[7] him.

HAMLET: Ah, ha! Come, some music. Come, the recorders.[8]

> For if the king like not the comedy.
> Why then, belike he likes it not, perdy.[9]

Come, some music.

    [*Enter* ROSENCRANTZ *and* GUILDENSTERN.]

GUILDENSTERN: Good my lord, vouchsafe me a word with you.

HAMLET: Sir, a whole history.

GUILDENSTERN: The king, sir—

HAMLET: Ay, sir, what of him?

GUILDENSTERN: Is in his retirement marvellous distempered.[1]

HAMLET: With drink, sir?

GUILDENSTERN: No, my lord, with choler.[2]

HAMLET: Your wisdom should show itself more richer to signify this to the doctor, for for me to put him to his purgation[3] would perhaps plunge him into more choler.

GUILDENSTERN: Good my lord, put your discourse into some frame,[4] and start not so wildly from my affair.

HAMLET: I am tame, sir. Pronounce.

GUILDENSTERN: The queen your mother, in most great affliction of spirit, hath sent me to you.

HAMLET: You are welcome.

GUILDENSTERN: Nay, good my lord, this courtesy is not of the right breed. If it shall please you to make me a wholesome[5] answer, I will do your mother's commandment. If not, your pardon and my return[6] shall be the end of my business.

HAMLET: Sir, I cannot.

ROSENCRANTZ: What, my lord?

HAMLET: Make you a wholesome answer; my wit's diseased. But, sir, such answer

---

6. Damon was a common name for a young man or a shepherd in lyric, especially pastoral poetry. Jove was the chief god of the Romans. Readers may supply for themselves the rhyme referred to by Horatio. 7. Observe.   8. Wooden, end-blown flutes.   9. *Par Dieu* (by God).   1. Vexed. *Retirement:* place to which he has retired.   2. Bile.   3. Treatment with a laxative.   4. Order. *Discourse:* speech. 5. Reasonable.   6. That is, to the queen.

285 as I can make, you shall command, or rather, as you say, my mother. Therefore no more, but to the matter. My mother, you say—

ROSENCRANTZ: Then thus she says: your behavior hath struck her into amazement and admiration.[7]

HAMLET: O wonderful son, that can so stonish a mother! But is there no sequel at
290 the heels of his mother's admiration? Impart.[8]

ROSENCRANTZ: She desires to speak with you in her closet[9] ere you go to bed.

HAMLET: We shall obey, were she ten times our mother. Have you any further trade[1] with us?

ROSENCRANTZ: My lord, you once did love me.

295 HAMLET: And do still, by these pickers and stealers.[2]

ROSENCRANTZ: Good my lord, what is your cause of distemper? You do surely bar the door upon your own liberty, if you deny your griefs to your friend.

HAMLET: Sir, I lack advancement.

ROSENCRANTZ: How can that be, when you have the voice of the king himself for
300 your succession in Denmark?

HAMLET: Ay, sir, but "while the grass grows"—the proverb[3] is something musty.

[Enter the PLAYERS with recorders.]

O, the recorders! Let me see one. To withdraw with you[4]—why do you go about to recover the wind of me, as if you would drive me into a toil?[5]

GUILDENSTERN: O my lord, if my duty be too bold, my love is too unmannerly.

305 HAMLET: I do not well understand that. Will you play upon this pipe?[6]

GUILDENSTERN: My lord, I cannot.

HAMLET: I pray you.

GUILDENSTERN: Believe me, I cannot.

HAMLET: I do beseech you.

310 GUILDENSTERN: I know no touch of it,[7] my lord.

HAMLET: It is as easy as lying. Govern these ventages[8] with your fingers and thumb, give it breath with your mouth, and it will discourse most eloquent music. Look you, these are the stops.[9]

GUILDENSTERN: But these cannot I command to any utt'rance of harmony. I have
315 not the skill.

HAMLET: Why, look you now, how unworthy a thing you make of me! You would play upon me, you would seem to know my stops, you would pluck out the heart of my mystery, you would sound[1] me from my lowest note to the top of my compass;[2] and there is much music, excellent voice, in this
320 little organ, yet cannot you make it speak. 'Sblood, do you think I am easier to be played on than a pipe? Call me what instrument you will, though you can fret[3] me, you cannot play upon me.

---

7. Wonder.   8. Tell me.   9. Bedroom.   1. Business.   2. Hands.   3. The proverb ends "the horse starves."   4. Let me step aside.   5. The figure is from hunting. Hamlet asks why Guildenstern is attempting to get windward of him, as if he would drive him into a net.   6. Recorder.   7. Have no ability.   8. Holes. *Govern:* cover and uncover.   9. Wind-holes.   1. Play.   2. Range. 3. "Fret" is used in a double sense, to annoy and to play a guitar or similar instrument using the "frets" or small bars on the neck.

[*Enter* POLONIUS.]

God bless you, sir!

POLONIUS: My lord, the queen would speak with you, and presently.[4]

HAMLET: Do you see yonder cloud that's almost in shape of a camel?   325

POLONIUS: By th' mass, and 'tis like a camel indeed.

HAMLET: Methinks it is like a weasel.

POLONIUS: It is backed like a weasel.

HAMLET: Or like a whale.

POLONIUS: Very like a whale.   330

HAMLET: Then I will come to my mother by and by. [*Aside.*] They fool me to the
    top of my bent.[5]—I will come by and by.

POLONIUS: I will say so.   [*Exit.*]

HAMLET: "By and by" is easily said. Leave me, friends.   [*Exeunt all but* HAMLET.]

    'Tis now the very witching time of night,   335

    When churchyards yawn, and hell itself breathes out

    Contagion to this world. Now could I drink hot blood,

    And do such bitter business as the day

    Would quake to look on. Soft, now to my mother.

    O heart, lose not thy nature; let not ever   340

    The soul of Nero[6] enter this firm bosom.

    Let me be cruel, not unnatural;

    I will speak daggers to her, but use none.

    My tongue and soul in this be hypocrites—

    How in my words somever she be shent,[7]   345

    To give them seals[8] never, my soul, consent!   [*Exit.*]

SCENE 3

A room in the castle. Enter KING, ROSENCRANTZ *and* GUILDENSTERN.

KING: I like him not,[9] nor stands it safe with us

    To let his madness range.[1] Therefore prepare you.

    I your commission will forthwith dispatch,

    And he to England shall along with you.

    The terms of our estate[2] may not endure   5

    Hazard so near's as doth hourly grow

    Out of his brows.

GUILDENSTERN: We will ourselves provide,[3]

    Most holy and religious fear it is

    To keep those many many bodies safe

    That live and feed upon your majesty.   10

---

4. At once.   5. Treat me as an utter fool.   6. The Roman emperor Nero, known for his excesses, was
believed to have been responsible for the death of his mother.   7. Shamed.   8. Fulfillment in action.
9. Distrust him.   1. Roam freely.   2. Condition of the state.   3. Equip (for the journey).

ROSENCRANTZ: The single and peculiar[4] life is bound
    With all the strength and armor of the mind
    To keep itself from noyance,[5] but much more
    That spirit upon whose weal[6] depends and rests
15   The lives of many. The cess[7] of majesty
    Dies not alone, but like a gulf[8] doth draw
    What's near it with it. It is a massy[9] wheel
    Fixed on the summit of the highest mount,
    To whose huge spokes ten thousand lesser things
20   Are mortised and adjoined,[1] which when it falls,
    Each small annexment, petty consequence,
    Attends[2] the boist'rous ruin. Never alone
    Did the king sigh, but with a general groan.
KING: Arm you, I pray you, to this speedy voyage,
25   For we will fetters put about this fear,
    Which now goes too free-footed.
ROSENCRANTZ: We will haste us.

                    [*Exeunt* ROSENCRANTZ *and* GUILDENSTERN.]

    [*Enter* POLONIUS.]

POLONIUS: My lord, he's going to his mother's closet.
    Behind the arras I'll convey[3] myself
    To hear the process. I'll warrant she'll tax him home,[4]
30   And as you said, and wisely was it said,
    'Tis meet that some more audience than a mother,
    Since nature makes them partial, should o'erhear
    The speech, of vantage.[5] Fare you well, my liege.
    I'll call upon you ere you go to bed,
    And tell you what I know.
35 KING: Thanks, dear my lord.   [*Exit* POLONIUS.]
    O, my offence is rank, it smells to heaven;
    It hath the primal eldest curse[6] upon't,
    A brother's murder. Pray can I not,
    Though inclination be as sharp as will.
40   My stronger guilt defeats my strong intent,
    And like a man to double business[7] bound,
    I stand in pause where I shall first begin,
    And both neglect. What if this cursèd hand
    Were thicker than itself with brother's blood,
45   Is there not rain enough in the sweet heavens
    To wash it white as snow? Whereto serves mercy
    But to confront the visage of offence?

---

4. Individual.   5. Harm.   6. Welfare.   7. Cessation.   8. Whirlpool.   9. Massive.   1. Attached.   2. Joins in.   3. Station.   4. Sharply. *Process:* proceedings.   5. From a position of vantage.   6. That is, of Cain.   7. Two mutually opposed interests.

And what's in prayer but this twofold force,
To be forestalléd[8] ere we come to fall,
Or pardoned being down?[9] Then I'll look up.   50
My fault is past, But, O, what form of prayer
Can serve my turn? "Forgive me my foul murder"?
That cannot be, since I am still possessed
Of those effects[1] for which I did the murder—
My crown, mine own ambition, and my queen.   55
May one be pardoned and retain th' offence?[2]
In the corrupted currents of this world
Offence's gilded[3] hand may shove by justice,
And oft 'tis seen the wicked prize itself
Buys out the law. But 'tis not so above.   60
There is no shuffling; there the action[4] lies
In his true nature, and we ourselves compelled,
Even to the teeth and forehead of[5] our faults,
To give in evidence. What then? What rests?[6]
Try what repentance can. What can it not?   65
Yet what can it when one cannot repent?
O wretched state! O bosom black as death!
O liméd[7] soul, that struggling to be free
Art more engaged! Help, angels! Make assay.
Bow, stubborn knees, and heart with strings of steel,   70
Be soft as sinews of the new-born babe.
All may be well.   [*He kneels.*]

    [*Enter* HAMLET.]

HAMLET: Now might I do it pat,[8] now 'a is a-praying,
    And now I'll do't—and so 'a goes to heaven,
    And so am I revenged. That would be scanned.[9]   75
    A villain kills my father, and for that,
    I, his sole son, do this same villain send
    To heaven.
    Why, this is hire and salary, not revenge.
    'A took my father grossly, full of bread,[1]   80
    With all his crimes broad blown, as flush[2] as May;
    And how his audit stands who knows save heaven?
    But in our circumstance and course of thought
    'Tis heavy with him; and am I then revenged
    To take him in the purging of his soul,   85
    When he is fit and seasoned[3] for his passage?

---

8. Prevented (from sin).   9. Having sinned.   1. Gains.   2. That is, benefits of the offense.
3. Bearing gold as a bribe.   4. Case at law.   5. Face-to-face with.   6. Remains   7. Caught as
with birdlime.   8. Easily.   9. Deserves consideration.   1. In a state of sin and without fasting.
2. Vigorous. *Broad blown:* full-blown.   3. Ready.

No.
Up, sword, and know thou a more horrid hent.⁴
When he is drunk, asleep, or in his rage,
90   Or in th' incestuous pleasure of his bed,
At game a-swearing, or about some act
That has no relish⁵ of salvation in't—
Then trip him, that his heels may kick at heaven,
And that his soul may be as damned and black
95   As hell, whereto it goes. My mother stays.
This physic⁶ but prolongs thy sickly days.   [*Exit.*]
KING: [*Rising.*] My words fly up, my thoughts remain below.
Words without thoughts never to heaven go.   [*Exit.*]

SCENE 4

The Queen's chamber. Enter QUEEN *and* POLONIUS.

POLONIUS: 'A will come straight. Look you lay home to⁷ him.
Tell him his pranks have been too broad⁸ to bear with,
And that your grace hath screen'd⁹ and stood between
Much heat and him. I'll silence me even here.
5   Pray you be round with him.
HAMLET: [*Within.*] Mother, mother, mother!
QUEEN: I'll warrant you. Fear¹ me not.
Withdraw, I hear him coming.

[POLONIUS *goes behind the arras. Enter* HAMLET.]

HAMLET: Now, mother, what's the matter?
10   QUEEN: Hamlet, thou hast thy father much offended.
HAMLET: Mother, you have my father much offended.
HAMLET: Come, come, you answer with an idle tongue.
HAMLET: Go, go, you question with a wicked tongue.
QUEEN: Why, how now, Hamlet?
HAMLET: What's the matter now?
QUEEN: Have you forgot me?
15   HAMLET: No, by the rood,² not so.
You are the queen, your husband's brother's wife,
And would it were not so, you are my mother.
QUEEN: Nay, then I'll set those to you that can speak.
HAMLET: Come, come, and sit you down. You shall not budge.
20   You go not till I set you up a glass³
Where you may see the inmost part of you.

___

4. Opportunity.   5. Flavor.   6. Medicine.   7. Be sharp with.   8. Outrageous.   9. Acted as a
fire screen.   1. Doubt.   2. Cross.   3. Mirror.

QUEEN: What wilt thou do? Thou wilt not murder me?
　Help, ho!
POLONIUS: [*Behind.*] What, ho! help!
HAMLET: [*Draws.*] How now, a rat?　　　　　　　　　　　　25
　Dead for a ducat, dead!

　　　　　[*Kills* POLONIUS *with a pass through the arras.*]

POLONIUS: [*Behind.*] O, I am slain!
QUEEN: O me, what hast thou done?
HAMLET:　　　　　　　　　　Nay, I know not.
　Is it the king?
QUEEN: O, what a rash and bloody deed is this!　　　　　30
HAMLET: A bloody deed!—almost as bad, good mother,
　As kill a king and marry with his brother.
QUEEN: As kill a king?
HAMLET:　　　　　Ay, lady, it was my word.　　　　[*Parting the arras.*]
　Thou wretched, rash, intruding fool, farewell!
　I took thee for thy better. Take thy fortune.　　　　35
　Thou find'st to be too busy[4] is some danger.—
　Leave wringing of your hands. Peace, sit you down
　And let me wring your heart, for so I shall
　If it be made of penetrable stuff,
　If damnéd custom have not brazed it[5] so　　　　　40
　That it be proof and bulwark against sense.[6]
QUEEN: What have I done that thou dar'st wag thy tongue
　In noise so rude against me?
HAMLET:　　　　　　　　Such an act
　That blurs the grace and blush of modesty,
　Calls virtue hypocrite, takes off the rose　　　　　45
　From the fair forehead of an innocent love.
　And sets a blister[7] there, makes marriage-vows
　As false as dicers' oaths. O, such a deed
　As from the body of contraction[8] plucks
　The very soul, and sweet religion makes　　　　　50
　A rhapsody of words. Heaven's face does glow
　O'er this solidity and compound mass[9]
　With heated visage, as against the doom[1]—
　Is thought-sick at the act.
QUEEN:　　　　　　Ay me, what act
　That roars so loud and thunders in the index?[2]　　　55
HAMLET: Look here upon this picture[3] and on this,
　The counterfeit presentment of two brothers.
　See what a grace was seated on this brow:

---

4. Officious.　　5. Plated it with brass.　　6. Feeling. *Proof:* armor.　　7. Brand.　　8. The marriage contract.　　9. Meaningless mass (Earth).　　1. Judgment Day.　　2. Table of contents.　　3. Portrait.

Hyperion's curls, the front[4] of Jove himself,
60   An eye like Mars, to threaten and command,
A station like the herald Mercury[5]
New lighted[6] on a heaven-kissing hill—
A combination and a form indeed
Where every god did seem to set his seal,[7]
65   To give the world assurance of a man.
This was your husband. Look you now what follows.
Here is your husband, like a mildewed ear
Blasting his wholesome brother. Have you eyes?
Could you on this fair mountain leave to feed,
70   And batten[8] on this moor? Ha! have you eyes?
You cannot call it love, for at your age
The heyday in the blood is tame, it's humble,
And waits upon the judgment, and what judgment
Would step from this to this? Sense sure you have
75   Else could you not have motion, but sure that sense
Is apoplexed[9] for madness would not err,
Nor sense to ecstasy was ne'er so thralled
But it reserved some quantity[1] of choice
To serve in such a difference. What devil was't
80   That thus hath cozened you at hoodman-blind?[2]
Eyes without feeling, feeling without sight,
Ears without hands or eyes, smelling sans[3] all,
Or but a sickly part of one true sense
Could not so mope.[4] O shame! where is thy blush?
85   Rebellious hell,
If thou canst mutine[5] in a matron's bones,
To flaming youth let virtue be as wax
And melt in her own fire. Proclaim no shame
When the compulsive ardor gives the charge,[6]
90   Since frost itself as actively doth burn,
And reason panders[7] will.
QUEEN: O Hamlet, speak no more!
Thou turn'st my eyes into my very soul;
And there I see such black and grainéd[8] spots
As will not leave their tint.[9]
HAMLET: Nay, but to live
95   In the rank sweat of an enseaméd[1] bed,
Stewed in curruption, honeying and making love
Over the nasty sty—

---

4. Forehead.   5. In Roman mythology, Mercury served as the messenger of the gods. *Station:* bearing.
6. Newly alighted.   7. Mark of approval.   8. Feed greedily.   9. Paralyzed.   1. Power.   2. Blind-
man's buff. *Cozened:* cheated.   3. Without.   4. Be stupid.   5. Commit mutiny.   6. Attacks.
7. Pimps for.   8. Ingrained.   9. Lose their color.   1. Greasy.

QUEEN: O, speak to me no more!
  These words like daggers enter in my ears;
  No more, sweet Hamlet.
HAMLET: A murderer and a villain,
  A slave that is not twentieth part the tithe[2]   100
  Of your precedent lord, a vice of kings,[3]
  A cutpurse[4] of the empire and the rule,
  That from a shelf the precious diadem stole
  And put it in his pocket—
QUEEN: No more.   105

    [*Enter* GHOST.]

HAMLET: A king of shreds and patches—
  Save me and hover o'er me with your wings,
  You heavenly guards! What would your gracious figure?
QUEEN: Alas, he's mad.
HAMLET: Do you not come your tardy[5] son to chide,   110
  That lapsed in time and passion lets go by
  Th' important acting of your dread command?
  O, say!
GHOST: Do not forget. This visitation
  Is but to whet thy almost blunted purpose.   115
  But look, amazement on thy mother sits.
  O, step between her and her fighting soul!
  Conceit[6] in weakest bodies strongest works.
  Speak to her, Hamlet.
HAMLET: How is it with you, lady?
QUEEN: Alas, how is't with you,   120
  That you do bend[7] your eye on vacancy,
  And with th' incorporal air do hold discourse?
  Forth at your eyes your spirits wildly peep,
  And as the sleeping soldiers in th' alarm,
  Your bedded hairs like life in excrements[8]   125
  Start up and stand an end. O gentle son,
  Upon the heat and flame of thy distemper
  Sprinkle cool patience. Whereon do you look?
HAMLET: On him, on him! Look you how pale he glares.
  His form and cause conjoined,[9] preaching to stones,   130
  Would make them capable.[1]—Do not look upon me,
  Lest with this piteous action you convert
  My stern effects.[2] Then what I have to do
  Will want true color—tears perchance for blood.

---

2. One-tenth.   3. The "Vice," a common figure in the popular drama, was a clown or buffoon. *Precedent lord:* first husband.   4. Pickpocket.   5. Slow to act.   6. Imagination.   7. Turn.   8. Nails and hair.   9. Working together.   1. Of responding.   2. Deeds.

135   QUEEN: To whom do you speak this?

    HAMLET: Do you see nothing there?

    QUEEN: Nothing at all, yet all that is I see.

    HAMLET: Nor did you nothing hear?

    QUEEN: No, nothing but ourselves.

140   HAMLET: Why, look you there. Look how it steals away.

       My father, in his habit[3] as he lived!

       Look where he goes even now out at the portal.   [*Exit* GHOST.]

    QUEEN: This is the very coinage[4] of your brain.

       Ths bodiless creation ecstasy[5]

       Is very cunning[6] in.

145   HAMLET: Ecstasy?

       My pulse as yours doth temperately keep time,

       And makes as healthful music. It is not madness

       That I have uttered. Bring me to the test,

       And I the matter will re-word, which madness

150   Would gambol[7] from. Mother, for love of grace,

       Lay not that flattering unction[8] to your soul,

       That not your trespass but my madness speaks.

       It will but skin and film the ulcerous place

       Whiles rank corruption, mining[9] all within,

155   Infects unseen. Confess yourself to heaven,

       Repent what's past, avoid what is to come.

       And do not spread the compost on the weeds,

       To make them ranker. Forgive me this my virtue,

       For in the fatness of these pursy[1] times

160   Virtue itself of vice must pardon beg,

       Yea, curb[2] and woo for leave to do him good.

    QUEEN: O Hamlet, thou hast cleft my heart in twain.

    HAMLET: O, throw away the worser part of it,

       And live the purer with the other half.

165   Good night—but go not to my uncle's bed.

       Assume a virtue, if you have it not.

       That monster custom[3] who all sense doth eat

       Of habits devil, is angel yet in this,

       That to the use of actions fair and good

170   He likewise gives a frock or livery

       That aptly[4] is put on. Refrain tonight,

       And that shall lend a kind of easiness

       To the next abstinence; the next more easy;

       For use almost can change the stamp of nature,

175   And either curb the devil, or throw him out

       With wondrous potency. Once more, good night,

---

3. Costume.   4. Invention.   5. Madness.   6. Skilled.   7. Shy away.   8. Ointment.   9. Undermining.   1. Bloated.   2. Bow.   3. Habit.   4. Easily.

And when you are desirous to be blest,
I'll blessing beg of you. For this same lord
I do repent; but heaven hath pleased it so,
To punish me with this, and this with me,   180
That I must be their scourge and minister.
I will bestow[5] him and will answer well
The death I gave him. So, again, good night.
I must be cruel only to be kind.
Thus bad begins and worse remains behind.   185
One word more, good lady.
QUEEN: What shall I do?
HAMLET: Not this, by no means, that I bid you do:
Let the bloat[6] king tempt you again to bed,
Pinch wanton[7] on your cheek, call you his mouse,
And let him, for a pair of reechy[8] kisses,   190
Or paddling in your neck with his damned fingers,
Make you to ravel[9] all this matter out,
That I essentially am not in madness,
But mad in craft. 'Twere good you let him know,
For who that's but a queen, fair, sober, wise,   195
Would from a paddock, from a bat, a gib,[1]
Such dear concernings hide? Who would so do?
No, in despite of sense and secrecy,
Unpeg the basket on the house's top,
Let the birds fly, and like the famous ape,   200
To try conclusions, in the basket creep
And break your own neck down.[2]
QUEEN: Be thou assured, if words be made of breath
And breath of life, I have no life to breathe
What thou hast said to me.   205
HAMLET: I must to England; you know that?
QUEEN: Alack,
I had forgot. 'Tis so concluded on.
HAMLET: There's letters sealed, and my two school-fellows,
Whom I will trust as I will adders fanged,
They bear the mandate; they must sweep[3] my way   210
And marshal me to knavery. Let it work,
For 'tis the sport to have the enginer
Hoist with his own petard; and't shall go hard
But I will delve[4] one yard below their mines
And blow them at the moon. O, 'tis most sweet   215

5. Dispose of.   6. Bloated.   7. Lewdly.   8. Foul.   9. Reveal.   1. Tomcat. *Paddock:* toad.
2. Apparently a reference to a now-lost fable in which an ape, finding a basket containing a cage of birds
on a housetop, opens the cage. The birds fly away. The ape, thinking that if he were in the basket he too
could fly, enters, jumps out, and breaks his neck.   3. Prepare. *Mandate:* command.   4. Dig.

When in one line two crafts directly meet.[5]
This man shall set me packing.
I'll lug the guts into the neighbor room.
Mother, good night. Indeed, this counsellor
220   Is now most still, most secret, and most grave,
Who was in life a foolish prating knave.
Come sir, to draw toward an end with you.
Good night, mother.   [*Exit the* QUEEN. *Then exit* HAMLET *tugging* POLONIUS.]

ACT IV

SCENE 1

A room in the castle. Enter KING, QUEEN, ROSENCRANTZ *and* GUILDENSTERN.

KING: There's matter in these sighs, these profound heaves,
You must translate;[6] 'tis fit we understand them.
Where is your son?
QUEEN: Bestow this place on us a little while.
                    [*Exeunt* ROSENCRANTZ *and* GUILDENSTERN.]
5   Ah, mine own lord, what have I seen tonight!
KING: What, Gertrude? How does Hamlet?
QUEEN: Mad as the sea and wind when both contend
Which is the mightier. In his lawless fit,
Behind the arras hearing something stir,
10   Whips out his rapier, cries "A rat, a rat!"
And in this brainish apprehension[7] kills
The unseen good old man.
KING: O heavy deed!
It had been so with us had we been there.
His liberty is full of threats to all—
15   To your yourself, to us, to every one.
Alas, how shall this bloody deed be answered?
It will be laid to us, whose providence[8]
Should have kept short, restrained, and out of haunt,[9]
This mad young man. But so much was our love,
20   We would not understand what was most fit;
But, like the owner of a foul disease,
To keep it from divulging, let it feed
Even on the pith of life. Where is he gone?
QUEEN: To draw apart the body he hath killed,

---

5. The "engineer," or engineer, is a military man who is here described as being blown up by a bomb of
his own construction, "hoist with his own petard." The military figure continues in the succeeding lines
where Hamlet describes himself as digging a countermine or tunnel beneath the one Claudius is digging
to defeat Hamlet. In line 214 the two tunnels unexpectedly meet.   6. Explain.   7. Insane notion.
8. Prudence.   9. Away from court.

O'er whom his very madness, like some ore   25
  Among a mineral of metals base,
  Shows itself pure: 'a weeps for what is done.
KING: O Gertrude, come away!
  The sun no sooner shall the mountains touch
  But we will ship him hence, and this vile deed   30
  We must with all our majesty and skill
  Both countenance and excuse. Ho, Guildenstern!

            [*Enter* ROSENCRANTZ *and* GUILDENSTERN.]

  Friends both, go join you with some further aid.
  Hamlet in madness hath Polonius slain,
  And from his mother's closet hath he dragged him.   35
  Go seek him out; speak fair, and bring the body
  Into the chapel. I pray you haste in this.
                              [*Exeunt* ROSENCRANTZ *and* GUILDENSTERN.]
  Come, Gertrude, we'll call up our wisest friends
  And let them know both what we mean to do
  And what's untimely done;   40
  Whose whisper o'er the world's diameter,
  As level as the cannon to his blank,[1]
  Transports his poisoned shot—may miss our name,
  And hit the woundless air. O, come away!
  My soul is full of discord and dismay.   [*Exeunt.*]   45

SCENE 2

    A passageway. Enter HAMLET.

HAMLET: Safely stowed.
ROSENCRANTZ *and* GUILDENSTERN: [*Within.*] Hamlet! Lord Hamlet!
HAMLET: But soft, what noise? Who calls on Hamlet?
  O, here they come.

            [*Enter* ROSENCRANTZ, GUILDENSTERN, *and* OTHERS.]

ROSENCRANTZ: What have you done, my lord, with the dead body?   5
HAMLET: Compounded it with dust, whereto 'tis kin.
ROSENCRANTZ: Tell us where 'tis, that we may take it thence
  And bear it to the chapel.
HAMLET: Do not believe it.
ROSENCRANTZ: Believe what?   10
HAMLET: That I can keep your counsel and not mine own. Besides, to be de-
  manded of a sponge—what replication[2] should be made by the son of a king?
ROSENCRANTZ: Take you me for a sponge, my lord?

---

1. Mark. *Level:* direct.   2. Answer. *Demanded of:* questioned by.

HAMLET: Ay, sir, that soaks up the king's countenance,[3] his rewards, his author-
15   ities. But such officers do the king best service in the end. He keeps them like
        an apple in the corner of his jaw, first mouthed to be last swallowed. When
        he needs what you have gleaned, it is but squeezing you and, sponge, you
        you shall be dry again.
ROSENCRANTZ: I understand you not, my lord.
20 HAMLET: I am glad of it. A knavish speech sleeps in a foolish ear.
ROSENCRANTZ: My lord, you must tell us where the body is, and go with us to the
        king.
HAMLET: The body is with the king, but the king is not with the body.
        The king is a thing—
25 GUILDENSTERN: A thing, my lord!
HAMLET: Of nothing. Bring me to him. Hide fox, and all after.[4]   [*Exeunt.*]

SCENE 3

A room in the castle. Enter KING.

KING: I have sent to seek him, and to find the body.
        How dangerous is it that this man goes loose!
        Yet must not we put the strong law on him.
        He's loved of the distracted[5] multitude,
5   Who like not in their judgment but their eyes,
        And where 'tis so, th' offender's scourge[6] is weighed,
        But never the offence. To bear all smooth and even,
        This sudden sending him away must seem
        Deliberate pause.[7] Diseases desperate grown
10   By desperate appliance are relieved,
        Or not at all.

        [*Enter* ROSENCRANTZ, GUILDENSTERN, *and all the rest.*]

                How now! what hath befall'n?
ROSENCRANTZ: Where the dead body is bestowed, my lord,
        We cannot get from him.
KING: But where is he?
ROSENCRANTZ: Without, my lord; guarded, to know[8] your pleasure.
KING: Bring him before us.
15 ROSENCRANTZ: Ho! bring in the lord.

        [*They enter with* HAMLET.]

KING: Now, Hamlet, where's Polonius?
HAMLET: At supper.

---

3. Favor.   4. Apparently a reference to a children's game like hide-and-seek.   5. Confused.
6. Punishment.   7. That is, not an impulse.   8. Await.

KING: At supper? Where?

HAMLET: Not where he eats, but where 'a is eaten. A certain convocation of politic[9]
worms are e'en at him. Your worm is your only emperor for diet. We fat all   20
creatures else to fat us, and we fat ourselves for maggots. Your fat king and
your lean beggar is but variable service—two dishes, but to one table. That's
the end.

KING: Alas, alas!

HAMLET: A man may fish with the worm that hath eat of a king, and eat of the   25
fish that hath fed of that worm.

KING: What dost thou mean by this?

HAMLET: Nothing but to show you how a king may go a progress through the guts
of a beggar.

KING: Where is Polonius?   30

HAMLET: In heaven. Send thither to see. If your messenger find him not there, seek
him i' th' other place yourself. But if, indeed, you find him not within this
month, you shall nose[1] him as you go up the stairs into the lobby.

KING: [To ATTENDANTS.] Go seek him there.

HAMLET: 'A will stay till you come.   [Exeunt ATTENDANTS.]   35

KING: Hamlet, this deed, for thine especial safety—
Which we do tender, as we dearly[2] grieve
For that which thou hast done—must send thee hence
With fiery quickness. Therefore prepare thyself.
The bark is ready, and the wind at help,   40
Th' associates tend, and everything is bent
For England.

HAMLET: For England?

KING: Ay, Hamlet.

HAMLET: Good.

KING: So it is, if thou knew'st our purposes.

HAMLET: I see a cherub that sees them. But come, for England!
Farewell, dear mother.   45

KING: Thy loving father, Hamlet.

HAMLET: My mother. Father and mother is man and wife, man and wife is one
flesh. So, my mother. Come, for England.   [Exit.]

KING: Follow him at foot;[3] tempt him with speed aboard.
Delay it not; I'll have him hence tonight.   50
Away! for everything is sealed and done
That else leans on th' affair. Pray you make haste.   [Exeunt all but the KING.]
And, England, if my love thou hold'st at aught—
As my great power thereof may give thee sense,[4]
Since yet thy cicatrice[5] looks raw and red   55
After the Danish sword, and thy free awe
Pays homage to us—thou mayst not coldly set[6]

---

9. Statesmanlike. *Convocation:* gathering.   1. Smell.   2. Deeply. *Tender:* consider.   3. Closely.
4. Of its value.   5. Wound scar.   6. Set aside.

Our sovereign process,[7] which imports at full
By letters congruing[8] to that effect
60   The present death of Hamlet. Do it, England,
For like the hectic[9] in my blood he rages,
And thou must cure me. Till I know 'tis done,
Howe'er my haps, my joys were ne'er begun.   [*Exit.*]

SCENE 4

Near Elsinore. Enter FORTINBRAS *with his army.*

FORTINBRAS: Go, captain, from me greet the Danish king.
Tell him that by his license Fortinbras
Craves the conveyance[1] of a promised march
Over his kingdom. You know the rendezvous.
5   If that his majesty would aught with us,
We shall express our duty in his eye,[2]
And let him know so.
CAPTAIN: I will do't, my lord.
FORTINBRAS: Go softly on.   [*Exeunt all but the* CAPTAIN.]

[*Enter* HAMLET, ROSENCRANTZ, GUILDENSTERN, *and* OTHERS.]

HAMLET: Good sir, whose powers are these?
10   CAPTAIN: They are of Norway, sir.
HAMLET: How purposed, sir, I pray you?
CAPTAIN: Against some part of Poland.
HAMLET: Who commands them, sir?
CAPTAIN: The nephew to old Norway, Fortinbras.
15   HAMLET: Goes it against the main[3] of Poland, sir,
Or for some frontier?
CAPTAIN: Truly to speak, and with no addition,[4]
We go to gain a little patch of ground
That hath in it no profit but the name.
20   To pay five ducats,[5] five, I would not farm it;
Nor will it yield to Norway or the Pole
A ranker rate should it be sold in fee.[6]
HAMLET: Why, then the Polack never will defend it.
CAPTAIN: Yes, it is already garrisoned.
25   HAMLET: Two thousand souls and twenty thousand ducats
Will not debate the question of this straw.
This is th' imposthume[7] of much wealth and peace,

---

7. Mandate.   8. Agreeing.   9. Chronic fever.   1. Escort.   2. Presence.   3. Central part.
4. Exaggeration.   5. That is, in rent.   6. Outright. *Ranker:* higher.   7. Abscess.

That inward breaks, and shows no cause without
Why the man dies. I humbly thank you, sir.
CAPTAIN: God b'wi'ye, sir.   [*Exit.*]
ROSENCRANTZ: Will't please you go, my lord?   30
HAMLET: I'll be with you straight. Go a little before.   [*Exeunt all but* HAMLET.]
    How all occasions do inform against me,
    And spur my dull revenge! What is a man,
    If his chief good and market[8] of his time
    Be but to sleep and feed? A beast, no more.   35
    Sure he that made us with such large discourse,[9]
    Looking before and after, gave us not
    That capability and godlike reason
    To fust[1] in us unused. Now, whether it be
    Bestial oblivion, or some craven scruple   40
    Of thinking too precisely on th' event[2]—
    A thought which, quartered, hath but one part wisdom
    And ever three parts coward—I do not know
    Why yet I live to say "This thing's to do,"
    Sith[3] I have cause, and will, and strength, and means,   45
    To do't. Examples gross as earth exhort me.
    Witness this army of such mass and charge,[4]
    Led by a delicate and tender prince,
    Whose spirit, with divine ambition puffed,
    Makes mouths at[5] the invisible event,   50
    Exposing what is mortal and unsure
    To all that fortune, death, and danger dare,
    Even for an eggshell. Rightly to be great
    Is not to stir without great argument,
    But greatly to find quarrel in a straw   55
    When honor's at the stake. How stand I then,
    That have a father killed, a mother stained,
    Excitements of my reason and my blood,
    And let all sleep, while to my shame I see
    The imminent death of twenty thousand men   60
    That for a fantasy and trick of fame
    Go to their graves like beds, fight for a plot
    Whereon the numbers cannot try the cause,
    Which is not tomb enough and continent
    To hide the slain?[6] O, from this time forth,   65
    My thoughts be bloody, or be nothing worth!   [*Exit.*]

---

8. Occupation.   9. Ample reasoning power.   1. Grow musty.   2. Outcome.   3. Since.   4. Expense.   5. Scorns.   6. The plot of ground involved is so small that it cannot contain the number of men involved in fighting or furnish burial space for the number of those who will die.

SCENE 5

A room in the castle. Enter QUEEN, HORATIO *and a* GENTLEMAN.

QUEEN: I will not speak with her.
GENTLEMAN: She is importunate, indeed distract.
  Her mood will needs to be pitied.
QUEEN: What would she have?
GENTLEMAN: She speaks much of her father, says she hears
5   There's tricks i' th' world, and hems, and beats her heart,
    Spurns enviously at straws,[7] speaks things in doubt
    That carry but half sense. Her speech is nothing,
    Yet the unshapéd use of it doth move
    The hearers to collection;[8] they yawn at it,
10   And botch the words up fit to their own thoughts,
    Which, as her winks and nods and gestures yield them,
    Indeed would make one think there might be thought,
    Though nothing sure, yet much unhappily.
HORATIO: 'Twere good she were spoken with, for she may strew
15 Dangerous conjectures in ill-breeding minds.
QUEEN: Let her come in.   [*Exit* GENTLEMAN.]
    [*Aside.*] To my sick soul, as sin's true nature is,
    Each toy seems prologue to some great amiss.[9]
    So full of artless jealousy is guilt,
20   It spills itself in fearing to be spilt.

            [*Enter* OPHELIA *distracted.*]

OPHELIA: Where is the beauteous majesty of Denmark?
QUEEN: How now, Ophelia!
OPHELIA:

        [*Sings.*]

    How should I your true love know
      From another one?
25   By his cockle hat and staff,[1]
      And his sandal shoon.[2]

QUEEN: Alas, sweet lady, what imports this song?
OPHELIA: Say you? Nay, pray you mark.

        [*Sings.*]

    He is dead and gone, lady,
30   He is dead and gone;

---

7. Takes offense at trifles.   8. An attempt to order.   9. Catastrophe. *Toy:* trifle.   1. A cockle hat, one decorated with a shell, indicated that the wearer had made a pilgrimage to the shrine of St. James at Compostela in Spain. The staff also marked the carrier as a pilgrim.   2. Shoes.

At his head a grass-green turf,
    At his heels a stone.

O, ho!
QUEEN: Nay, but Ophelia—
OPHELIA: Pray you mark.

    [*Sings.*]

White his shroud as the mountain snow—

    [*Enter* KING.]

QUEEN: Alas, look here, my lord.   35
OPHELIA:

    [*Sings.*]

    Larded all with sweet flowers;
    Which bewept to the grave did not go
        With true-love showers.

KING: How do you, pretty lady?
OPHELIA: Well, God dild³ you! They say the owl was a baker's daughter. Lord,   40
    we know what we are, but know not what we may be. God be at your table!
KING: Conceit⁴ upon her father.
OPHELIA: Pray let's have no words of this, but when they ask you what it means,
    say you this:

    [*Sings.*]

Tomorrow is Saint Valentine's day,   45
    All in the morning betime,
And I a maid at your window,
    To be your Valentine.

Then up he rose, and donn'd his clo'es,
    And dupped⁵ the chamber-door,   50
Let in the maid, that out a maid
    Never departed more.

KING: Pretty Ophelia!
OPHELIA: Indeed, without an oath, I'll make an end on't.

    [*Sings.*]

By Gis⁶ and by Saint Charity,   55
    Alack, and fie for shame!
Young men will do't, if they come to't;
    By Cock,⁷ they are to blame.

3. Yield.   4. Thought.   5. Opened.   6. Jesus.   7. God.

Quoth she "before you tumbled me,
60   You promised me to wed."

He answers:

"So would I'a done, by yonder sun,
An thou hadst not come to my bed."

KING: How long hath she been thus?
65   OPHELIA: I hope all will be well. We must be patient, but I cannot choose but weep
        to think they would lay him i' th' cold ground. My brother shall know of it,
        and so I thank you for your good counsel. Come, my coach! Good night,
        ladies, good night. Sweet ladies, good night, good night.   [Exit.]
KING: Follow her close; give her good watch, I pray you.

                                    [Exeunt HORATIO and GENTLEMAN.]

70   O, this is the poison of deep grief; it springs
        All from her father's death, and now behold!
        O Gertrude, Gertrude!
        When sorrows come, they come not single spies,
        But in battalions: first, her father slain;
75   Next, your son gone, and he most violent author
        Of his own just remove; the people muddied,[8]
        Thick and unwholesome in their thoughts and whispers
        For good Polonius' death; and we have done but greenly[9]
        In hugger-mugger[1] to inter him; poor Ophelia
80   Divided from herself and her fair judgment,
        Without the which we are pictures, or mere beasts;
        Last, and as much containing as all these,
        Her brother is in secret come from France,
        Feeds on his wonder, keeps himself in clouds,
85   And wants not buzzers to infect his ear
        With pestilent speeches of his father's death,
        Wherein necessity, of matter beggared,[2]
        Will nothing stick our person to arraign[3]
        In ear and ear.[4] O my dear Gertrude, this,
90   Like to a murd'ring piece,[5] in many places
        Gives me superfluous death.   [A noise within.]
QUEEN: Alack, what noise is this?
KING: Attend!
        Where are my Switzers?[6] Let them guard the door.
        What is the matter?
95   MESSENGER: Save yourself, my lord.
        The ocean, overpeering of his list,[7]
        Eats not the flats with more impiteous[8] haste

---

8. Disturbed.   9. Without judgment.   1. Haste.   2. Short on facts.   3. Accuse. *Stick:* hesitate.
4. From both sides.   5. A weapon designed to scatter its shot.   6. Swiss guards.   7. Towering
above its limits.   8. Pitiless.

Then young Laertes, in a riotous head,[9]
O'erbears your officers. The rabble call him lord,
And as the world were now but to begin,　　　　　　　　　　100
Antiquity forgot, custom not known,
The ratifiers and props of every word,
They cry "Choose we, Laertes shall be king."
Caps, hands, and tongues, applaud it to the clouds,
"Laertes shall be king, Laertes king."　　　　　　　　　　105
QUEEN: How cheerfully on the false trail they cry![1]

　　　　[*A noise within.*]

O, this is counter,[2] you false Danish dogs!
KING: The doors are broke.

　　　　[*Enter* LAERTES, *with* OTHERS.]

LAERTES: Where is this king?—Sirs, stand you all without.
ALL: No, let's come in.
LAERTES:　　　　　　　　I pray you give me leave.　　　　110
ALL: We will, we will.
LAERTES: I thank you. Keep[3] the door.　　　　　　[*Exeunt his followers.*]
　　　　　　　　　　　O thou vile king,
　　Give me my father!
QUEEN:　　　　　　　Calmly, good Laertes.
LAERTES: That drop of blood that's calm proclaims me bastard,
　　Cries cuckold to my father, brands the harlot　　　　　115
　　Even here between the chaste unsmirchéd brow
　　Of my true mother.
KING:　　　　　　　What is the cause, Laertes,
　　That thy rebellion looks so giant-like?
　　Let him go, Gertrude. Do not fear[4] our person.
　　There's such divinity doth hedge a king　　　　　　　120
　　That treason can but peep to[5] what it would,
　　Acts little of his will. Tell me, Laertes.
　　Why thou art thus incensed. Let him go, Gertrude.
　　Speak, man.
LAERTES:　　　Where is my father?
KING:　　　　　　　　　　Dead.
QUEEN: But not by him.
KING:　　　　　　　Let him demand[6] his fill.　　　　　125
LAERTES: How came he dead? I'll not be juggled with.
　　To hell allegiance, vows to the blackest devil,
　　Conscience and grace to the profoundest pit!
　　I dare damnation. To this point I stand,

---

9. With an armed band.　　1. As if following the scent.　　2. Backward.　　3. Guard.　　4. Fear for.
5. Look at over or through a barrier.　　6. Question.

130   That both the worlds I give to negligence,[7]
     Let come what comes, only I'll be revenged
     Most throughly for my father.
    KING: Who shall stay you?
    LAERTES: My will, not all the world's.
     And for my means, I'll husband[8] them so well
     They shall go far with little.
135   KING: Good Laertes,
     If you desire to know the certainty
     Of your dear father, is't writ in your revenge
     That, swoopstake,[9] you will draw both friend and foe,
     Winner and loser?
    LAERTES: None but his enemies.
140   KING: Will you know them, then?
    LAERTES: To his good friends thus wide I'll ope my arms,
     And like the kind life-rend'ring pelican,[1]
     Repast them with my blood.
    KING: Why, now you speak
     Like a good child and a true gentleman.
145   That I am guiltless of your father's death,
     And am most sensibly in grief for it,
     It shall as level[2] to your judgment 'pear
     As day does to your eye.

          [*A noise within:* "Let her come in."]

    LAERTES: How now? What noise is that?

          [*Enter* OPHELIA.]

150   O, heat dry up my brains! tears seven times salt
     Burn out the sense and virtue[3] of mine eye!
     By heaven, thy madness shall be paid with weight
     Till our scale turn the beam. O rose of May,
     Dear maid, kind sister, sweet Ophelia!
155   O heavens! is't possible a young maid's wits
     Should be as mortal as an old man's life?
     Nature is fine[4] in love, and where 'tis fine
     It sends some precious instances of itself
     After the thing it loves.[5]
    OPHELIA:

          [*Sings.*]

---

7. Disregard. *Both the worlds:* that is, this and the next.   8. Manage.   9. Sweeping the board.
1. The pelican was believed to feed her young with her own blood.   2. Plain.   3. Function. *Sense:*
feeling.   4. Refined.   5. Laertes means that Ophelia, because of her love for her father, gave up her
sanity as a token of grief at his death.

> They bore him barefac'd on the bier; 160
>> Hey non nonny, nonny, hey nonny;
> And in his grave rain'd many a tear—

Fare you well, my dove!

LAERTES: Hadst thou thy wits, and didst persuade revenge,
It could not move thus. 165

OPHELIA: You must sing "A-down, a-down, and you call him a-down-a." O,
how the wheel becomes it! It is the false steward, that stole his master's
daughter.[6]

LAERTES: This nothing's more than matter.

OPHELIA: There's a rosemary, that's for remembrance. Pray you, love, remember. 170
And there is pansies, that's for thoughts.

LAERTES: A document[7] in madness, thoughts and remembrance fitted.

OPHELIA: There's fennel for you, and columbines. There's rue for you, and here's
some for me. We may call it herb of grace a Sundays. O, you must wear your
rue with a difference. There's a daisy. I would give you some violets, but they 175
withered all when my father died. They say 'a made a good end.

> [*Sings.*]

> For bonny sweet Robin is all my joy.

LAERTES: Thought and affliction, passion, hell itself,
She turns to favor[8] and to prettiness.

OPHELIA:

> [*Sings.*]

> And will 'a not come again? 180
> And will 'a not come again?
>> No, no, he is dead,
>> Go to thy death-bed,
> He never will come again.

> His beard was as white as snow, 185
> All flaxen was his poll;[9]
>> He is gone, he is gone,
>> And we cast away moan:
> God-a-mercy on his soul!

And of all Christian souls, I pray God. God b'wi'you. [*Exit.*] 190

LAERTES: Do you see this, O God?

KING: Laertes, I must commune with your grief,
Or you deny me right. Go but apart,

---

6. The "wheel" refers to the "burden" or refrain of a song, in this case "A-down, a-down, and you call
him a-down-a." The ballad to which she refers was about a false steward. Others have suggested that the
"wheel" is the Wheel of Fortune, a spinning wheel to whose rhythm such a song might have been sung
or a kind of dance movement performed by Ophelia as she sings. 7. Lesson 8. Beauty. 9. Head.

Make choice of whom your wisest friends you will,
195   And they shall hear and judge 'twixt you and me.
        If by direct or by collateral[1] hand
        They find us touched,[2] we will our kingdom give,
        Our crown, our life, and all that we call ours,
        To you in satisfaction; but if not,
200   Be you content to lend your patience to us,
        And we shall jointly labor with your soul
        To give it due content.
LAERTES: Let this be so.
        His means of death, his obscure funeral—
        No trophy, sword, nor hatchment,[3] o'er his bones,
205   No noble rite nor formal ostentation[4]—
        Cry to be heard, as 'twere from heaven to earth,
        That I must call't in question.
KING: So you shall;
        And where th' offence is, let the great axe fall.
        I pray you go with me.   [*Exeunt.*]

SCENE 6

Another room in the castle. Enter HORATIO *and a* GENTLEMAN.

HORATIO: What are they that would speak with me?
GENTLEMAN: Sea-faring men, sir. They say they have letters for you.
HORATIO: Let them come in.   [*Exit* GENTLEMAN.]
        I do not know from what part of the world
5   I should be greeted, if not from Lord Hamlet.

        [*Enter* SAILORS.]

SAILOR: God bless you, sir.
HORATIO: Let him bless thee too.
SAILOR: 'A shall, sir, an't please him. There's a letter for you, sir—it came from th'
        ambassador that was bound for England—if your name be Horatio, as I am
10   let to know[5] it is.
HORATIO: [*Reads.*] "Horatio, when thou shalt have overlooked[6] this, give these
        fellows some means[7] to the king. They have letters for him. Ere we were two
        days old at sea, a pirate of very warlike appointment[8] gave us chase. Finding
        ourselves too slow of sail, we put on a compelled valor, and in the grapple I
15   boarded them. On the instant they got clear of our ship, so I alone became
        their prisoner. They have dealt with me like thieves of mercy, but they knew
        what they did; I am to do a good turn for them. Let the king have the letters

---

1. Indirect.   2. By guilt.   3. Coat of arms.   4. Pomp.   5. Informed.   6. Read through.
7. Access.   8. Equipment.

I have sent, and repair thou to me with as much speed as thou wouldest fly
death. I have words to speak in thine ear will make thee dumb; yet are they
much too light for the bore of the matter.[9] These good fellows will bring thee   20
where I am. Rosencrantz and Guildenstern hold their course for England. Of
them I have much to tell thee. Farewell.

He that thou knowest thine, Hamlet."

Come, I will give you way[1] for these your letters,
And do't the speedier that you may direct me   25
To him from whom you brought them.   [*Exeunt.*]

SCENE 7

Another room in the castle. Enter KING *and* LAERTES.

KING: Now must your conscience my acquittance seal,[2]
    And you must put me in your heart for friend,
    Sith you have heard, and with a knowing ear,
    That he which hath your noble father slain
    Pursued my life.
LAERTES: It well appears. But tell me   5
    Why you proceeded not against these feats,
    So criminal and so capital in nature,
    As by your safety, greatness, wisdom, all things else,
    You mainly were stirred up.
KING: O, for two special reasons,
    Which may to you, perhaps, seem much unsinewed,[3]   10
    But yet to me th' are strong. The queen his mother
    Lives almost by his looks, and for myself—
    My virtue or my plague, be it either which—
    She is so conjunctive[4] to my life and soul
    That, as the star moves not but in his sphere,[5]   15
    I could not but by her. The other motive,
    Why to a public count[6] I might not go,
    Is the great love the general gender[7] bear him,
    Who, dipping all his faults in their affection,
    Work like the spring that turneth wood to stone,[8]   20
    Convert his gyves[9] to graces; so that my arrows,
    Too slightly timbered[1] for so loud a wind,
    Would have reverted to my bow again,

9. A figure from gunnery, referring to shot that is too small for the size of the weapons to be fired.
1. Means of delivery.   2. Grant me innocent.   3. Weak.   4. Closely joined.   5. A reference to the
Ptolemaic cosmology, in which planets and stars were believed to revolve in crystalline spheres concen-
trically about the Earth.   6. Reckoning.   7. Common people.   8. Certain English springs contain so
much lime that a lime covering will be deposited on a log placed in one of them for a length of time.
9. Fetters.   1. Shafted.

But not where I had aimed them.

25   LAERTES: And so have I a noble father lost,
  A sister driven into desp'rate terms,
  Whose worth, if praises may go back again,
  Stood challenger on mount of all the age
  For her perfections. But my revenge will come.
30   KING: Break not your sleeps for that. You must not think
  That we are made of stuff so flat and dull
  That we can let our beard be shook with danger,
  And think it pastime. You shortly shall hear more.
  I loved you father, and we love our self,
35   And that, I hope, will teach you to imagine—

   [*Enter a* MESSENGER *with letters.*]

  How now? What news?
MESSENGER: Letters, my lord, from Hamlet.
  These to your majesty; this to the queen.
KING: From Hamlet! Who brought them?
MESSENGER: Sailors, my lord, they say. I saw them not.
40   They were given me by Claudio; he received them
  Of him that brought them.
KING: Laertes, you shall hear them.—
  Leave us.   [*Exit* MESSENGER.]
  [*Reads.*] "High and mighty, you shall know I am set naked on your king-
  dom. Tomorrow shall I beg leave to see your kingly eyes; when I shall, first
45   asking your pardon thereunto, recount the occasion of my sudden and more
  strange return.
     Hamlet."
  What should this mean? Are all the rest come back?
  Or is it some abuse,[2] and no such thing?
50   LAERTES: Know you the hand?
KING: 'Tis Hamlet's character.[3] "Naked"!
  And in a postscript here, he says "alone."
  Can you devise[4] me?
LAERTES: I am lost in it, my lord. But let him come.
55   It warms the very sickness in my heart
  That I shall live and tell him to his teeth
  "Thus didest thou."
KING: If it be so, Laertes—
  As how should it be so, how otherwise?—
  Will you be ruled by me?
LAERTES: Ay, my lord,
60   So you will not o'errule me to a peace.
KING: To thine own peace. If he be now returned,
  As checking at[5] his voyage, and that he means

2. Trick.   3. Handwriting.   4. Explain it to.   5. Turning aside from.

No more to undertake it, I will work him
To an exploit now ripe in my device,
Under the which he shall not choose but fall;   65
And for his death no wind of blame shall breathe
But even his mother shall uncharge[6] the practice
And call it accident.
LAERTES: My lord, I will be ruled;
    The rather if you could devise it so
    That I might be the organ.[7]
KING: It falls right.   70
    You have been talked of since your travel much,
    And that in Hamlet's hearing, for a quality
    Wherein they say you shine. Your sum of parts
    Did not together pluck such envy from him
    As did that one, and that, in my regard,   75
    Of the unworthiest siege.[8]
LAERTES: What part is that, my lord?
KING: A very riband in the cap of youth,
    Yet needful too, for youth no less becomes
    The light and careless livery that it wears
    Than settled age his sables and his weeds,[9]   80
    Importing health and graveness. Two months since
    Here was a gentleman of Normandy.
    I have seen myself, and served against, the French,
    And they can[1] well on horseback, but this gallant
    Had witchcraft in't. He grew unto his seat,   85
    And to such wondrous doing brought his horse,
    As had he been incorpsed and demi-natured
    With the brave beast. So far he topped my thought
    That I, in forgery[2] of shapes and tricks,
    Come short of what he did.[3]
LAERTES: A Norman was't?   90
KING: A Norman.
LAERTES: Upon my life, Lamord.
KING: The very same.
LAERTES: I know him well. He is the brooch indeed
    And gem of all the nation.
KING: He made confession[4] of you,   95
    And gave you such a masterly report
    For art and exercise in your defence,[5]
    And for your rapier most especial,

---

6. Not accuse.   7. Instrument.   8. Rank.   9. Dignified clothing.   1. Perform.   2. Imagination.
    3. The gentleman referred to was so skilled in horsemanship that he seemed to share one body with
the horse, "incorpsed." The king further extends the compliment by saying that he appeared like the
mythical centaur, a creature who was man from the waist up and horse from the waist down, therefore
"demi-natured."   4. Gave a report.   5. Skill in fencing.

That he cried out 'twould be a sight indeed
100   If one could match you. The scrimers[6] of their nation
He swore had neither motion, guard, nor eye,
If you opposed them. Sir, this report of his
Did Hamlet so envenom with his envy
That he could nothing do but wish and beg
105   Your sudden coming o'er, to play with you.
Now out of this—
LAERTES: What out of this, my lord?
KING: Laertes, was your father dear to you?
Or are you like the painting of a sorrow,
A face without a heart?
LAERTES: Why ask you this?
110   KING: Not that I think you did not love your father,
But that I know love is begun by time,
And that I see in passages of proof,[7]
Time qualifies the spark and fire of it.
There lives within the very flame of love
115   A kind of wick or snuff that will abate it,
And nothing is at a like goodness still,
For goodness, growing to a plurisy,[8]
Dies in his own too much.[9] That we would do,
We should do when we would; for this "would" changes,
120   And hath abatements and delays as many
As there are tongues, are hands, are accidents,
And then this "should" is like a spendthrift's sigh
That hurts by easing. But to the quick of th' ulcer—
Hamlet comes back; what would you undertake
125   To show yourself in deed your father's son
More than in words?
LAERTES: To cut his throat i' th' church.
KING: No place indeed should murder sanctuarize;[1]
Revenge should have no bounds. But, good Laertes,
Will you do this? Keep close within your chamber.
130   Hamlet returned shall know you are come home.
We'll put on those shall praise your excellence,
And set a double varnish[2] on the fame
The Frenchman gave you, bring you in fine[3] together,
And wager on your heads. He, being remiss,[4]
135   Most generous, and free from all contriving,
Will not peruse[5] the foils, so that with ease,
Or with a little shuffling, you may choose
A sword unbated,[6] and in a pass of practice

---

6. Fencers.   7. Tests of experience.   8. Fullness.   9. Excess.   1. Provide sanctuary for murder.
2. Gloss.   3. In short.   4. Careless.   5. Examine.   6. Not blunted.

Requite him for your father.

LAERTES: I will do't,
And for that purpose I'll anoint my sword.   140
I bought an unction of a mountebank
So mortal that but dip a knife in it,
Where it draws blood no cataplasm[7] so rare,
Collected from all simples[8] that have virtue
Under the moon, can save the thing from death   145
That is but scratched withal. I'll touch my point
With this contagion, that if I gall[9] him slightly,
It may be death.

KING: Let's further think of this,
Weigh what convenience both of time and means
May fit us to our shape. If this should fail,   150
And that our drift look[1] through our bad performance,
'Twere better not assayed. Therefore this project
Should have a back or second that might hold
If this did blast in proof.[2] Soft, let me see.
We'll make a solemn wager on your cunnings—   155
I ha't.
When in your motion you are hot and dry—
As make your bouts more violent to that end—
And that he calls for drink, I'll have prepared him
A chalice for the nonce, whereon but sipping,   160
If he by chance escape your venomed stuck,[3]
Our purpose may hold there.—But stay, what noise?

          [*Enter* QUEEN.]

QUEEN: One woe doth tread upon another's heel,
     So fast they follow. Your sister's drowned, Laertes.
LAERTES: Drowned? O, where?   165
QUEEN: There is a willow grows aslant the brook
     That shows his hoar leaves in the glassy stream.
     Therewith fantastic garlands did she make
     Of crowflowers, nettles, daisies, and long purples
     That liberal shepherds give a grosser[4] name,   170
     But our cold[5] maids do dead men's fingers call them.
     There on the pendent boughs her coronet weeds
     Clamb'ring to hang, an envious[6] sliver broke,
     When down her weedy trophies and herself
     Fell in the weeping brook. Her clothes spread wide,   175
     And mermaid-like awhile they bore her up,
     Which time she chanted snatches of old tunes,

---

7. Poultice.   8. Herbs.   9. Scratch.   1. Intent become obvious.   2. Fail when tried.   3. Thrust.
4. Coarser. *Liberal:* vulgar.   5. Chaste.   6. Malicious.

As one incapable[7] of her own distress,
Or like a creature native and indued[8]
180   Unto that element. But long it could not be
Till that her garments, heavy with their drink,
Pulled the poor wretch from her melodious lay
To muddy death.
LAERTES: Alas, then she is drowned?
QUEEN: Drowned, drowned.
185   LAERTES: Too much of water hast thou, poor Ophelia,
And therefore I forbid my tears; but yet
It is our trick; nature her custom holds,
Let shame say what it will. When these are gone,
The woman will be out. Adieu, my lord.
190   I have a speech o' fire that fain would blaze
But that this folly drowns it.   [Exit.]
KING: Let's follow, Gertrude.
How much I had to do to calm his rage!
Now fear I this will give it start again;
Therefore let's follow.   [Exeunt.]

ACT V

SCENE 1

A churchyard. Enter two CLOWNS.[9]

CLOWN: Is she to be buried in Christian burial when she wilfully seeks her own
        salvation?
OTHER: I tell thee she is. Therefore make her grave straight. The crowner hath sat
        on her,[1] and finds it Christian burial.
5   CLOWN: How can that be, unless she drowned herself in her own defence?
OTHER: Why, 'tis found so.
CLOWN: It must be "se offendendo";[2] it cannot be else. For here lies the point: if
        I drown myself wittingly, it argues an act, and an act hath three branches—
        it is to act, to do, to perform; argal,[3] she drowned herself wittingly.
10   OTHER: Nay, but hear you, Goodman Delver.
CLOWN: Give me leave. Here lies the water; good. Here stands the man; good. If
        the man go to this water and drown himself, it is, will he, nill he, he goes—
        mark you that. But if the water come to him and drown him, he drowns not
        himself. Argal, he that is not guilty of his own death shortens not his own
15   life.
OTHER: But is this law?
CLOWN: Ay, marry, is't; crowner's quest[4] law.

---

7. Unaware.   8. Habituated.   9. Rustics.   1. Held an inquest. *Crowner:* coroner.   2. An error for *se
defendendo,* in self-defense.   3. Therefore.   4. Inquest.

OTHER: Will you ha' the truth on't? If this had not been a gentlewoman, she should have been buried out o' Christian burial.

CLOWN: Why, there thou say'st. And the more pity that great folk should have count'nance[5] in this world to drown or hang themselves more than their even-Christen.[6] Come, my spade. There is no ancient gentlemen but gard'ners, ditchers, and grave-makers. They hold up Adam's profession.

OTHER: Was he a gentleman?

CLOWN: 'A was the first that ever bore arms.

OTHER: Why, he had none.

CLOWN: What, art a heathen? How dost thou understand the Scripture? The Scripture says Adam digged. Could he dig without arms? I'll put another question to thee. If thou answerest me not to the purpose, confess thyself—

OTHER: Go to.

CLOWN: What is he that builds stronger than either the mason, the shipwright, or the carpenter?

OTHER: The gallows-maker, for that frame outlives a thousand tenants.

CLOWN: I like thy wit well, in good faith. The gallows does well. But how does it well? It does well to those that do ill. Now thou dost ill to say the gallows is built stronger than the church. Argal, the gallows may do well to thee. To't again,[7] come.

OTHER: Who builds stronger than a mason, a shipwright, or a carpenter?

CLOWN: Ay tell me that, and unyoke.[8]

OTHER: Marry, now I can tell.

CLOWN: To't.

OTHER: Mass, I cannot tell.

CLOWN: Cudgel thy brains no more about it, for your dull ass will not mend his pace with beating. And when you are asked this question next, say "a grave maker." The houses he makes lasts till doomsday. Go, get thee in, and fetch me a stoup[9] of liquor. [*Exit* OTHER CLOWN.]

[*Enter* HAMLET *and* HORATIO *as* CLOWN *digs and sings.*]

In youth, when I did love, did love,
    Methought it was very sweet,
To contract the time for-a my behove,[1]
    O, methought there-a was nothing-a meet.[2]

HAMLET: Has this fellow no feeling of his business, that 'a sings in grave-making?

HORATIO: Custom hath made it in him a property of easiness.

HAMLET: 'Tis e'en so. The hand of little employment hath the daintier sense.

CLOWN:

[*Sings.*]

But age, with his stealing steps,
    Hath clawed me in his clutch,

---

5. Approval.   6. Fellow Christians.   7. Guess again.   8. Finish the matter.   9. Mug.   1. Advantage. *Contract:* shorten.   2. The gravedigger's song is a free version of "The aged lover renounceth love" by Thomas, Lord Vaux, published in *Tottel's Miscellany*, 1557.

And hath shipped me into the land,
As if I had never been such.

[*Throws up a skull.*]

HAMLET: That skull had a tongue in it, and could sing once. How the knave jowls³ it to the ground, as if 'twere Cain's jawbone, that did the first murder! This might be the pate of a politician, which this ass now o'erreaches;⁴ one that would circumvent God, might it not?

HORATIO: It might, my lord.

HAMLET: Or of a courtier, which could say, "Good morrow, sweet lord! How does thou, sweet lord?" This might be my Lord Such-a-one, that praised my Lord Such-a-one's horse, when 'a meant to beg it, might it not?

HORATIO: Ay, my lord.

HAMLET: Why, e'en so, and now my Lady Worm's, chapless,⁵ and knock'd about the mazzard⁶ with a sexton's spade. Here's fine revolution,⁷ an we had the trick to see't. Did these bones cost no more the breeding but to play at loggets with them?⁸ Mine ache to think on't.

CLOWN:

[*Sings.*]

A pick-axe and a spade, a spade,
For and a shrouding sheet:
O, a pit of clay for to be made
For such a guest is meet.

[*Throws up another skull.*]

HAMLET: There's another. Why may not that be the skull of a lawyer? Where be his quiddities now, his quillets, his cases, his tenures, and his tricks? Why does he suffer this mad knave now to knock him about the sconce⁹ with a dirty shovel, and will not tell him of his action of battery? Hum! This fellow might be in's time a great buyer of land, with his statutes, his recognizances, his fines, his double vouchers, his recoveries. Is this the fine¹ of his fines, and the recovery of his recoveries, to have his fine pate full of fine dirt? Will his vouchers vouch him no more of his purchases, and double ones too, than the length and breadth of a pair of indentures?² The very conveyances of his lands will scarcely lie in this box, and must th' inheritor himself have no more, ha?³

HORATIO: Not a jot more, my lord.

HAMLET: Is not parchment made of sheepskins?

HORATIO: Ay, my lord, and of calves' skins too.

HAMLET: They are sheep and calves which seek out assurance in that. I will speak to this fellow. Whose grave's this, sirrah?

CLOWN: Mine, sir.

---

3. Hurls.   4. Gets the better of.   5. Lacking a lower jaw.   6. Head.   7. Skill.   8. "Loggets" were small pieces of wood thrown as part of a game.   9. Head.   1. End.   2. Contracts.   3. In this speech Hamlet reels off a list of legal terms relating to property transactions.

[*Sings.*]

O, a pit of clay for to be made
For such a guest is meet.

HAMLET: I think it be thine indeed, for thou liest in't.

CLOWN: You lie out on't, sir, and therefore 'tis not yours. For my part, I do not lie 95
in't, yet it is mine.

HAMLET: Thou dost lie in't, to be in't and say it is thine. 'Tis for the dead, not for
the quick;[4] therefore thou liest.

CLOWN: 'Tis a quick lie, sir; 'twill away again from me to you.

HAMLET: What man dost thou dig it for? 100

CLOWN: For no man, sir.

HAMLET: What woman, then?

CLOWN: For none neither.

HAMLET: Who is to be buried in't?

CLOWN: One that was a woman, sir; but, rest her soul, she's dead. 105

HAMLET: How absolute the knave is! We must speak by the card,[5] or equivocation
will undo us. By the Lord, Horatio, this three years I have took note of it, the
age is grown so picked[6] that the toe of the peasant comes so near the heel of
the courtier, he galls his kibe.[7] How long hast thou been a grave-maker?

CLOWN: Of all the days i' th' year, I came to't that day that our last King Hamlet 110
overcame Fortinbras.

HAMLET: How long is that since?

CLOWN: Cannot you tell that? Every fool can tell that. It was that very day that
young Hamlet was born—he that is mad, and sent into England.

HAMLET: Ay, marry, why was he sent into England? 115

CLOWN: Why, because 'a was mad. 'A shall recover his wits there; or, if 'a do not,
'tis no great matter there.

HAMLET: Why?

CLOWN: 'Twill not be seen in him there. There the men are as mad as he.

HAMLET: How came he mad? 120

CLOWN: Very strangely, they say.

HAMLET: How strangely?

CLOWN: Faith, e'en with losing his wits.

HAMLET: Upon what ground?

CLOWN: Why, here in Denmark. I have been sexton here, man and boy, thirty 125
years.

HAMLET: How long will a man lie i' th' earth ere he rot?

CLOWN: Faith, if 'a be not rotten before 'a die—as we have many pocky[8] corses
now-a-days that will scarce hold the laying in—'a will last you some eight
year or nine year. A tanner will last you nine year. 130

HAMLET: Why he more than another?

CLOWN: Why, sir, his hide is so tanned with his trade that 'a will keep out water
a great while; and your water is a sore decayer of your whoreson dead body.

---

4. Living.   5. Exactly. *Absolute:* precise.   6. Refined.   7. Rubs a blister on his heel.   8. Corrupted by
syphilis.

Here's a skull now hath lien[9] you i' th' earth three and twenty years.

135 HAMLET: Whose was it?

CLOWN: A whoreson mad fellow's it was. Whose do you think it was?

HAMLET: Nay, I know not.

CLOWN: A pestilence on him for a mad rogue! 'A poured a flagon of Rhenish on
my head once. This same skull, sir, was, sir, Yorick's skull, the king's jester.

140 HAMLET: [*Takes the skull.*] This?

CLOWN: E'en that.

HAMLET: Alas, poor Yorick! I knew him, Horatio—a fellow of infinite jest, of most
excellent fancy. He hath bore me on his back a thousand times, and now
how abhorred in my imagination it is! My gorge[1] rises at it. Here hung those

145 lips that I have kissed I know not how oft. Where be your gibes now, your
gambols, your songs, your flashes of merriment that were wont to set the
table on a roar? Not one now to mock your own grinning? Quite chap-fall'n?[2]
Now get you to my lady's chamber, and tell her, let her paint an inch thick,
to this favor[3] she must come. Make her laugh at that. Prithee, Horatio, tell

150 me one thing.

HORATIO: What's that, my lord?

HAMLET: Dost thou think Alexander looked o' this fashion i' th' earth?

HORATIO: E'en so.

HAMLET: And smelt so? Pah!   [*Throws down the skull.*]

155 HORATIO: E'en so, my lord.

HAMLET: To what base uses we may return, Horatio! Why may not imagination
trace the noble dust of Alexander till 'a find it stopping a bung-hole?

HORATIO: 'Twere to consider too curiously[4] to consider so.

HAMLET: No, faith, not a jot, but to follow him thither with modesty[5] enough, and

160 likelihood to lead it. Alexander died, Alexander was buried, Alexander retur-
neth to dust; the dust is earth; of earth we make loam; and why of that loam
whereto he was converted might they not stop a beerbarrel?

Imperious Cæsar, dead and turned to clay,
Might stop a hole to keep the wind away.

165 O, that that earth which kept the world in awe
Should patch a wall t'expel the winter's flaw![6]

But soft, but soft awhile! Here comes the king,
The queen, the courtiers.

[*Enter* KING, QUEEN, LAERTES, *and the Corse with a* PRIEST *and* LORDS *attendant.*]

Who is this they follow?
And with such maiméd[7] rites? This doth betoken

170 The corse they follow did with desperate hand
Fordo its own life. 'Twas of some estate.[8]
Couch[9] we awhile and mark.   [*Retires with* HORATIO.]

---

9. Lain. *Whoreson:* bastard (not literally).   1. Throat.   2. Lacking a lower jaw.   3. Appearance.
4. Precisely.   5. Moderation.   6. Gusty wind.   7. Cut short.   8. Rank. *Fordo:* destroy.   9. Conceal
ourselves.

LAERTES: What ceremony else?[1]
HAMLET: That is Laertes, a very noble youth. Mark.
LAERTES: What ceremony else?   175
PRIEST: Here obsequies have been as far enlarged[2]
    As we have warranty. Her death was doubtful,
    And but that great command o'ersways the order,[3]
    She should in ground unsanctified been lodged
    Till the last trumpet. For charitable prayers,   180
    Shards, flints, and pebbles, should be thrown on her.
    Yet here she is allowed her virgin crants,[4]
    Her maiden strewments,[5] and the bringing home
    Of bell and burial.
LAERTES: Must there no more be done?
PRIEST: No more be done.   185
    We should profane the service of the dead
    To sing a requiem and such rest to her
    As to peace-parted souls.
LAERTES: Lay her i' th' earth,
    And from her fair and unpolluted flesh
    May violets spring! I tell thee, churlish priest,   190
    A minist'ring angel shall my sister be
    When thou liest howling.[6]
HAMLET: What, the fair Ophelia!
QUEEN: Sweets to the sweet. Farewell!   [Scatters flowers.]
    I hoped thou shouldst have been my Hamlet's wife.
    I thought thy bride-bed to have decked, sweet maid,   195
    And not t' have strewed thy grave.
LAERTES: O, treble woe
    Fall ten times treble on that cursèd head
    Whose wicked deed thy most ingenious sense[7]
    Deprived thee of! Hold off the earth awhile,
    Till I have caught her once more in mine arms.   [Leaps into the grave.]   200
    Now pile your dust upon the quick and dead,
    Till of this flat a mountain you have made
    T' o'er-top old Pelion or the skyish head
    Of blue Olympus.[8]
HAMLET: [Coming forward.] What is he whose grief   205
    Bears such an emphasis, whose phrase of sorrow
    Conjures[9] the wand'ring stars, and makes them stand
    Like wonder-wounded hearers? This is I,
    Hamlet the Dane.

---

1. More.   2. Extended.   3. Usual rules.   4. Wreaths.   5. Flowers strewn on the grave.   6. In Hell.
7. Lively mind.   8. The rivalry between Laertes and Hamlet in this scene extends even to their rhetoric.
Pelion and Olympus, mentioned here by Laertes, and Ossa, mentioned below by Hamlet, are Greek
mountains noted in mythology for their height. Olympus was the reputed home of the gods, and the
other two were piled one on top of the other by the Giants in an attempt to reach the top of Olympus
and overthrow the gods.   9. Casts a spell on.

[HAMLET *leaps into the grave and they grapple.*]

LAERTES: The devil take thy soul!

210   HAMLET: Thou pray'st not well.
       I prithee take thy fingers from my throat,
       For though I am not splenitive[1] and rash,
       Yet have I in me something dangerous,
       Which let thy wisdom fear. Hold off thy hand.

215   KING: Pluck them asunder.

       QUEEN: Hamlet! Hamlet!

       ALL: Gentlemen!

       HORATIO: Good my lord, be quiet.

[*The* ATTENDANTS *part them, and they come out of the grave.*]

       HAMLET: Why, I will fight with him upon this theme

220   Until my eyelids will no longer wag.[2]

       QUEEN: O my son, what theme?

       HAMLET: I loved Ophelia. Forty thousand brothers
           Could not with all their quantity of love
           Make up my sum. What wilt thou do for her?

225   KING: O, he is mad, Laertes.

       QUEEN: For love of God, forbear[3] him.

       HAMLET: 'Swounds, show me what th'owt do.
           Woo't[4] weep, woo't fight, woo't fast, woo't tear thyself,
           Woo't drink up eisel,[5] eat a crocodile?

230   I'll do't. Dost come here to whine?
           To outface[6] me with leaping in her grave?
           Be buried quick with her, and so will I.
           And if thou prate of mountains, let them throw
           Millions of acres on us, till our ground,

235   Singeing his pate against the burning zone,[7]
           Make Ossa like a wart! Nay, an thou'lt mouth,
           I'll rant as well as thou.

       QUEEN: This is mere madness;
           And thus awhile the fit will work on him.
           Anon, as patient as the female dove

240   When that her golden couplets[8] are disclosed,
           His silence will sit drooping.

       HAMLET: Hear you, sir.
           What is the reason that you use me thus?
           I loved you ever. But it is no matter.
           Let Hercules himself do what he may,

245   The cat will mew, and dog will have his day.   [*Exit.*]

       KING: I pray thee, good Horatio, wait upon[9] him.

---

1. Hot-tempered.   2. Move.   3. Bear with.   4. Will you.   5. Vinegar.   6. Get the best of.
7. Sky in the torrid zone.   8. Pair of eggs.   9. Attend.

[*Exit* HORATIO.]

[*To* LAERTES.] Strengthen your patience in our last night's speech.
We'll put the matter to the present push.¹—
Good Gertrude, set some watch over your son.—
This grave shall have a living monument.   250
An hour of quiet shortly shall we see;
Till then in patience our proceeding be.   [*Exeunt.*]

SCENE 2

A hall or public room. Enter HAMLET *and* HORATIO.

HAMLET: So much for this, sir; now shall you see the other.
    You do remember all the circumstance?
HORATIO: Remember it, my lord!
HAMLET: Sir, in my heart there was a kind of fighting
    That would not let me sleep. Methought I lay   5
    Worse than the mutines in the bilboes.² Rashly,
    And praised be rashness for it—let us know,
    Our indiscretion sometime serves us well,
    When our deep plots do pall; and that should learn³ us
    There's a divinity that shapes our ends,   10
    Rough-hew them how we will—
HORATIO: That is most certain.
HAMLET: Up from my cabin,
    My sea-gown scarfed⁴ about me, in the dark
    Groped I to find out them, had my desire,
    Fingered their packet, and in fine⁵ withdrew   15
    To mine own room again, making so bold,
    My fears forgetting manners, to unseal
    Their grand commission; where I found, Horatio—
    Ah, royal knavery!—an exact⁶ command,
    Larded⁷ with many several sorts of reasons,   20
    Importing Denmark's health, and England's too,
    With, ho! such bugs and goblins in my life,⁸
    That on the supervise,⁹ no leisure bated,
    No, not to stay the grinding of the axe,
    My head should be struck off.
HORATIO: Is't possible?   25
HAMLET: Here's the commission; read it at more leisure.
    But wilt thou hear now how I did proceed?
HORATIO: I beseech you.

---

1. Immediate trial.   2. Stocks. *Mutines:* mutineers.   3. Teach.   4. Wrapped.   5. Quickly. *Fingered:* stole.   6. Precisely stated.   7. Garnished.   8. Such dangers if I remained alive.   9. As soon as the commission was read.

HAMLET: Being thus benetted[1] round with villainies,
30   Ere I could make a prologue to my brains,
     They had begun the play. I sat me down,
     Devised a new commission, wrote it fair.[2]
     I once did hold it, as our statists[3] do,
     A baseness to write fair, and labored much
35   How to forget that learning; but sir, now
     It did me yeoman's service. Wilt thou know
     Th' effect[4] of what I wrote?
HORATIO: Ay, good my lord.
HAMLET: An earnest conjuration from the king,
     As England was his faithful tributary,[5]
40   As love between them like the palm might flourish,
     As peace should still her wheaten garland wear
     And stand a comma 'tween their amities[6]
     And many such like as's of great charge,[7]
     That on the view and knowing of these contents,
45   Without debatement[8] further more or less,
     He should those bearers put to sudden death,
     Not shriving-time allowed.[9]
HORATIO: How was this sealed?
HAMLET: Why, even in that was heaven ordinant,[1]
     I had my father's signet in my purse,
50   Which was the model of that Danish seal,
     Folded the writ up in the form of th' other,
     Subscribed it, gave't th' impression,[2] placed it safely,
     The changeling[3] never known. Now, the next day
     Was our sea-fight, and what to this was sequent[4]
55   Thou knowest already.
HORATIO: So Guildenstern and Rosencrantz go to't.
HAMLET: Why, man, they did make love to this employment.
     They are not near my conscience; their defeat[5]
     Does by their own insinuation grow.
60   'Tis dangerous when the baser nature comes
     Between the pass and fell[6] incensèd points
     Of mighty opposites.
HORATIO: Why, what a king is this!
HAMLET: Does it not, think thee, stand me now upon—
     He that hath killed my king and whored my mother,
65   Popped in between th' election and my hopes,
     Thrown out his angle[7] for my proper life,

1. Caught in a net.   2. Legibly. *Devised:* made.   3. Politicians.   4. Contents.   5. Vassal.   6. Link
friendships.   7. Import.   8. Consideration.   9. Without time for confession.   1. Operative.
2. Of the seal.   3. Alteration.   4. Followed.   5. Death. *Are not near:* do not touch.   6. Cruel.
Pass: thrust.   7. Fishhook.

And with such coz'nage[8]—is't not perfect conscience
To quit[9] him with this arm? And is't not to be damned
To let this canker of our nature come
   In further evil?   70
HORATIO: It must be shortly known to him from England
   What is the issue[1] of the business there.
HAMLET: It will be short;[2] the interim is mine.
   And a man's life's no more than to say "one."
   But I am very sorry, good Horatio,   75
   That to Laertes I forgot myself;
   For by the image of my cause I see
   The portraiture of his. I'll court his favors.
   But sure the bravery[3] of his grief did put me
   Into a tow'ring passion.
HORATIO: Peace; who comes here?   80

   [*Enter* OSRIC.]

OSRIC: Your lordship is right welcome back to Denmark.
HAMLET: I humbly thank you, sir. [*Aside to* HORATIO.] Dost know this water-fly?
HORATIO: [*Aside to* HAMLET.] No, my good lord.
HAMLET: [*Aside to* HORATIO.] Thy state is the more gracious, for 'tis a vice to
   know him. He hath much land, and fertile. Let a beast be lord of beasts, and   85
   his crib shall stand at the king's mess. 'Tis a chough,[4] but as I say, spacious
   in the possession of dirt.
OSRIC: Sweet lord, if your lordship were at leisure, I should impart a thing to you
   from his majesty.
HAMLET: I will receive it, sir, with all diligence of spirit. Put your bonnet to his   90
   right use. 'Tis for the head.
OSRIC: I thank your lordship, it is very hot.
HAMLET: No, believe me, 'tis very cold; the wind is northerly.
OSRIC: It is indifferent[5] cold, my lord, indeed.
HAMLET: But yet methinks it is very sultry and hot for my complexion.[6]   95
OSRIC: Exceedingly, my lord; it is very sultry, as 'twere—I cannot tell how. My
   lord, his majesty bade me signify to you that 'a has laid a great wager on your
   head. Sir, this is the matter—
HAMLET: I beseech you, remember.   [*Moves him to put on his hat.*]
OSRIC: Nay, good my lord; for my ease, in good faith. Sir, here is newly come to   100
   court Laertes; believe me, an absolute[7] gentleman, full of most excellent differences,[8] of very soft society and great showing.[9] Indeed, to speak feelingly
   of him, he is the card or calendar of gentry, for you shall find in him the
   continent[1] of what part a gentleman would see.

---

8. Trickery.   9. Repay.   1. Outcome.   2. Soon.   3. Exaggerated display.   4. Jackdaw.   5. Moderately.   6. Temperament.   7. Perfect.   8. Qualities.   9. Good manners.   1. Sum total. *Calendar:* measure.

105   HAMLET: Sir, his definement[2] suffers no perdition in you, though I know to divide
        him inventorially would dozy[3] th' arithmetic of memory, and yet but yaw[4]
        neither in respect of his quick sail. But in the verity of extolment, I take him
        to be a soul of great article,[5] and his infusion[6] of such dearth and rareness as,
        to make true diction of him, his semblage[7] is his mirror, and who else would
110   trace him, his umbrage,[8] nothing more.

      OSRIC: Your lordship speaks most infallibly of him.

      HAMLET: The concernancy,[9] sir? Why do we wrap the gentleman in our more rawer
        breath?[1]

      OSRIC: Sir?

115   HORATIO: Is't not possible to understand in another tongue? You will to't, sir,
        really.

      HAMLET: What imports the nomination[2] of this gentleman?

      OSRIC: Of Laertes?

      HORATIO: [*Aside.*] His purse is empty already. All's golden words are spent.

120   HAMLET: Of him, sir.

      OSRIC: I know you are not ignorant—

      HAMLET: I would you did, sir; yet, in faith, if you did, it would not much approve
        me. Well, sir.

      OSRIC: You are not ignorant of what excellence Laertes is—

125   HAMLET: I dare not confess that, lest I should compare[3] with him in excellence;
        but to know a man well were to know himself.

      OSRIC: I mean, sir, for his weapon; but in the imputation[4] laid on him by them,
        in his meed he's unfellowed.[5]

      HAMLET: What's his weapon?

130   OSRIC: Rapier and dagger.

      HAMLET: That's two of his weapons—but well.

      OSRIC: The king, sir, hath wagered with him six Barbary horses, against the which
        he has impawned,[6] as I take it, six French rapiers and poniards, with their
        assigns,[7] as girdle, hangers, and so. Three of the carriages, in faith, are very
135   dear to fancy,[8] very responsive to the hilts, most delicate carriages, and
        of very liberal conceit.[9]

      HAMLET: What call you the carriages?

      HORATIO: [*Aside to* HAMLET.] I knew you must be edified by the margent[1] ere you
        had done.

140   OSRIC: The carriages, sir, are the hangers.

      HAMLET: The phrase would be more germane to the matter if we could carry a
        cannon by our sides. I would it might be hangers till then. But on! Six Barbary
        horses against six French swords, their assigns, and three liberal conceited

---

2. Description.   3. Daze. *Divide him inventorially:* examine bit by bit.   4. Steer wildly.   5. Scope.
6. Nature.   7. Rival. *Diction:* telling.   8. Shadow. *Trace:* keep pace with.   9. Meaning.   1. Cruder
words.   2. Naming.   3. That is, compare myself.   4. Reputation.   5. Unequaled in his excellence.   6. Staked.   7. Appurtenances.   8. Finely designed.   9. Elegant design. *Delicate:* well
adjusted.   1. Marginal gloss.

carriages; that's the French bet against the Danish. Why is this all impawned, as you call it?   145

OSRIC: The king, sir, hath laid, sir, that in a dozen passes between yourself and him he shall not exceed you three hits; he hath laid on twelve for nine, and it would come to immediate trial if your lordship would vouchsafe the answer.

HAMLET: How if I answer no?

OSRIC: I mean, my lord, the opposition of your person in trial.   150

HAMLET: Sir, I will walk here in the hall. If it please his majesty, it is the breathing time[2] of day with me. Let the foils be brought, the gentleman willing, and the king hold his purpose; I will win for him an I can. If not, I will gain nothing but my shame and the odd hits.

OSRIC: Shall I deliver you so?   155

HAMLET: To this effect, sir, after what flourish your nature will.

OSRIC: I commend my duty to your lordship.

HAMLET: Yours, yours. [*Exit* OSRIC.] He does well to commend it himself; there are no tongues else for's turn.

HORATIO: This lapwing runs away with the shell on his head.[3]   160

HAMLET: 'A did comply, sir, with his dug[4] before 'a sucked it. Thus has he, and many more of the same bevy that I know the drossy age dotes on, only got the tune of the time; and out of an habit of encounter, a king of yesty[5] collection which carries them through and through the most fanned and winnowed opinions; and do but blow them to their trial, the bubbles are out.   165

[*Enter a* LORD.]

LORD: My lord, his majesty commended him to you by young Osric, who brings back to him that you attend[6] him in the hall. He sends to know if your pleasure hold to play with Laertes, or that you will take longer time.

HAMLET: I am constant to my purposes; they follow the king's pleasure. If his fitness speaks, mine is ready; now or whensoever, provided I be so able as   170 now.

LORD: The king and queen and all are coming down.

HAMLET: In happy time.

LORD: The queen desires you to use some gentle entertainment[7] to Laertes before you fall to play.   175

HAMLET: She well instructs me.   [*Exit* LORD.]

HORATIO: You will lose this wager, my lord.

HAMLET: I do not think so. Since he went into France I have been in continual practice. I shall win at the odds. But thou wouldst not think how ill[8] all's here about my heart. But it's no matter.   180

HORATIO: Nay, good my lord—

HAMLET: It is but foolery, but it is such a kind of gaingiving[9] as would perhaps trouble a woman.

---

2. Time for exercise.   3. The lapwing was thought to be so precocious that it could run immediately after being hatched, even, as here, with bits of the shell still on its head.   4. Mother's breast. *Comply:* deal formally.   5. Yeasty.   6. Await.   7. Cordiality.   8. Uneasy.   9. Misgiving.

HORATIO: If your mind dislike anything, obey it. I will forestall their repair[1]
hither, and say you are not fit.

HAMLET: Not a whit, we defy augury. There is special providence in the fall of a
sparrow. If it be now, 'tis not to come; if it be not to come, it will be now; if
it be not now, yet it will come. The readiness is all. Since no man of aught
he leaves knows, what is't to leave betimes? Let be.

[*A table prepared. Enter* TRUMPETS, DRUMS, *and* OFFICERS *with cushions;* KING,
QUEEN, OSRIC *and* ATTENDANTS *with foils, daggers, and* LAERTES.]

KING: Come, Hamlet, come and take this hand from me.

[*The* KING *puts* LAERTES' *hand into* HAMLET'S.]

HAMLET: Give me your pardon, sir. I have done you wrong,
But pardon 't as you are a gentleman.
This presence[2] knows, and you must needs have heard,
How I am punished with a sore distraction.
What I have done
That might your nature, honor, and exception,[3]
Roughly awake, I here proclaim was madness.
Was 't Hamlet wronged Laertes? Never Hamlet.
If Hamlet from himself be ta'en away,
And when he's not himself does wrong Laertes,
Then Hamlet does it not, Hamlet denies it.
Who does it then? His madness. If't be so,
Hamlet is of the faction that is wronged;
His madness is poor Hamlet's enemy.
Sir, in this audience,
Let my disclaiming from[4] a purposed evil
Free[5] me so far in your most generous thoughts
That I have shot my arrow o'er the house
And hurt my brother.

LAERTES: I am satisfied in nature,
Whose motive in this case should stir me most
To my revenge. But in my terms of honor
I stand aloof, and will no reconcilement
Till by some elder masters of known honor
I have a voice[6] and precedent of peace
To keep my name ungored.[7] But till that time
I do receive your offered love like love,
And will not wrong it.

HAMLET: I embrace it freely,
And will this brother's wager frankly[8] play.
Give us the foils. Come on.

1. Coming.   2. Company.   3. Resentment.   4. Denying of.   5. Absolve.   6. Authority.   7. Un-
shamed.   8. Without rancor.

LAERTES: Come, one for me.
HAMLET: I'll be your foil, Laertes. In mine ignorance   220
  Your skill shall, like a star i' th' darkest night,
  Stick fiery off[9] indeed.
LAERTES: You mock me, sir.
HAMLET: No, by this hand.
KING: Give them the foils, young Osric. Cousin Hamlet,
  You know the wager?
HAMLET: Very well, my lord;   225
  Your Grace has laid the odds o' th' weaker side.
KING: I do not fear it, I have seen you both;
  But since he is bettered[1] we have therefore odds.
LAERTES: This is too heavy; let me see another.
HAMLET: This likes me well. These foils have all a[2] length?   230

    [They prepare to play.]

OSRIC: Ay, my good lord.
KING: Set me the stoups of wine upon that table.
  If Hamlet give the first or second hit,
  Or quit in answer of[3] the third exchange,
  Let all the battlements their ordnance fire.   235
  The king shall drink to Hamlet's better breath,
  And in the cup an union[4] shall he throw,
  Richer than that which four successive kings
  In Denmark's crown have worn. Give me the cups,
  And let the kettle[5] to the trumpet speak,   240
  The trumpet to the cannoneer without,
  The cannons to the heavens, the heaven to earth,
  "Now the king drinks to Hamlet." Come, begin—

    [Trumpets the while.]

And you, the judges, bear a wary eye.
HAMLET: Come on, sir.
LAERTES: Come, my lord.

    [They play.]

HAMLET: One.
LAERTES: No.
HAMLET: Judgment?   245
OSRIC: A hit, a very palpable hit.

    [Drums, trumpets, and shot. Flourish; a piece goes off.]

LAERTES: Well, again.

9. Shine brightly.   1. Reported better.   2. The same. *Likes:* suits.   3. Repay.   4. Pearl.   5. Kettle-drum.

KING: Stay, give me drink. Hamlet, this pearl is thine.
    Here's to thy health. Give him the cup.
250 HAMLET: I'll play this bout first; set it by awhile.
    Come.

    [*They play.*]

    Another hit; what say you?
LAERTES: A touch, a touch, I do confess't.
KING: Our son shall win.
QUEEN: He's fat,[6] and scant of breath.
255   Here, Hamlet, take my napkin, rub thy brows.
    The queen carouses to thy fortune, Hamlet.
HAMLET: Good madam!
KING: Gertrude, do not drink.
QUEEN: I will, my lord; I pray you pardon me.
260 KING: [*Aside.*] It is the poisoned cup; it is too late.
HAMLET: I dare not drink yet, madam; by and by.
QUEEN: Come, let me wipe thy face.
LAERTES: My lord, I'll hit him now.
KING: I do not think't.
LAERTES: [*Aside.*] And yet it is almost against my conscience.
265 HAMLET: Come, for the third, Laertes. You do but dally.
    I pray you pass[7] with your best violence;
    I am afeard you make a wanton of me.[8]
LAERTES: Say you so? Come on.

    [*They play.*]

OSRIC: Nothing, neither way.
270 LAERTES: Have at you now!

    [LAERTES *wounds* HAMLET: *then, in scuffling, they change rapiers, and* HAMLET
    wounds LAERTES.]

KING: Part them. They are incensed.
HAMLET: Nay, come again.

    [*The* QUEEN *falls.*]

OSRIC: Look to the queen there, ho!
HORATIO: They bleed on both sides. How is it, my lord?
275 OSRIC: How is't, Laertes?
LAERTES: Why, as a woodcock to mine own springe,[9] Osric.
    I am justly killed with mine own treachery.
HAMLET: How does the queen?
KING: She swoons to see them bleed.
QUEEN: No, no, the drink, the drink! O my dear Hamlet!

6. Out of shape.   7. Attack.   8. Trifle with me.   9. Snare.

The drink, the drink! I am poisoned. *[Dies.]* 280
HAMLET: O, villainy! Ho! let the door be locked.
Treachery! seek it out.
LAERTES: It is here, Hamlet. Hamlet, thou art slain;
No med'cine in the world can do thee good.
In thee there is not half an hour's life. 285
The treacherous instrument is in thy hand,
Unbated[1] and envenomed. The foul practice
Hath turned itself on me. Lo, here I lie,
Never to rise again. Thy mother's poisoned.
I can no more. The king, the king's to blame. 290
HAMLET: The point envenomed too?
Then, venom, to thy work. *[Hurts the KING.]*
ALL: Treason! treason!
KING: O, yet defend me, friends. I am but hurt.[2]
HAMLET: Here, thou incestuous, murd'rous, damnéd Dane, 295
Drink off this potion. Is thy union here?
Follow my mother.

      [The KING dies.]

LAERTES: He is justly served.
It is a poison tempered[3] by himself.
Exchange forgiveness with me, noble Hamlet.
Mine and my father's death come not upon thee, 300
Nor thine on me! *[Dies.]*
HAMLET: Heaven make thee free of[4] it! I follow thee.
I am dead, Horatio. Wretched queen, adieu!
You that look pale and tremble at this chance,[5]
That are but mutes or audience to this act, 305
Had I but time, as this fell sergeant Death
Is strict in his arrest,[6] O, I could tell you—
But let it be. Horatio, I am dead:
Thou livest; report me and my cause aright
To the unsatisfied.[7]
HORATIO: Never believe it. 310
I am more an antique Roman than a Dane.
Here's yet some liquor left.
HAMLET: As th'art a man,
Give me the cup. Let go. By heaven, I'll ha't.
O God, Horatio, what a wounded name,
Things standing thus unknown, shall live behind me! 315
If thou didst ever hold me in thy heart,
Absent thee from felicity awhile,

1. Unblunted.   2. Wounded.   3. Mixed.   4. Forgive.   5. Circumstance.   6. Summons to court.
7. Uninformed.

And in this harsh world draw thy breath in pain,
To tell my story.

    [*A march afar off.*]

               What warlike noise is this?

320   OSRIC: Young Fortinbras, with conquest come from Poland,
        To th' ambassadors of England gives
        This warlike volley.[8]
    HAMLET: O, I die, Horatio!
        The potent poison quite o'er-crows[9] my spirit.
        I cannot live to hear the news from England,
325   But I do prophesy th' election lights
        On Fortinbras. He has my dying voice.[1]
        So tell him, with th' occurrents,[2] more and less,
        Which have solicited[3]—the rest is silence.   [*Dies.*]
    HORATIO: Now cracks a noble heart. Good night, sweet prince,
330   And flights of angels sing thee to thy rest!

    [*March within.*]

    Why does the drum come hither?

    [*Enter* FORTINBRAS, *with the* AMBASSADORS *and with drum, colors, and*
    ATTENDANTS.]

    FORTINBRAS: Where is this sight?
    HORATIO: What is it you would see?
        If aught of woe or wonder, cease your search.
    FORTINBRAS: This quarry cries on havoc.[4] O proud death,
335   What feast is toward[5] in thine eternal cell
        That thou so many princes at a shot
        So bloodily hast struck?
    AMBASSADORS: The sight is dismal;
        And our affairs from England come too late.
        The ears are senseless[6] that should give us hearing
340   To tell him his commandment is fulfilled,
        That Rosencrantz and Guildenstern are dead.
        Where should we have our thanks?
    HORATIO: Not from his mouth,
        Had it th' ability of life to thank you.
        He never gave commandment for their death.

---

8. The staging presents some difficulties here. Unless Osric is clairvoyant, he must have left the stage at some point and returned. One possibility is that he might have left to carry out Hamlet's order to lock the door (line 281) and returned when the sound of the distant march is heard.   9. Overcomes.
1. Support.   2. Circumstances.   3. Brought about this scene.   4. The game killed in the hunt proclaims a slaughter.   5. In preparation.   6. Without sense of hearing.

But since, so jump[7] upon this bloody question,   345
You from the Polack wars, and you from England,
Are here arrived, give orders that these bodies
High on a stage be placéd to the view,
And let me speak to th' yet unknowing world
How these things came about. So shall you hear   350
Of carnal, bloody, and unnatural acts;
Of accidental judgments, casual[8] slaughters;
Of deaths put on by cunning and forced cause;
And, in this upshot,[9] purposes mistook
Fall'n on th' inventors' heads. All this can I   355
Truly deliver.
FORTINBRAS: Let us haste to hear it,
And call the noblest to the audience.[1]
For me, with sorrow I embrace my fortune.
I have some rights of memory[2] in this kingdom,
Which now to claim my vantage[3] doth invite me.   360
HORATIO: Of that I shall have also cause to speak,
And from his mouth whose voice will draw on more.
But let this same be presently performed,
Even while men's minds are wild, lest more mischance
On plots and errors happen.
FORTINBRAS: Let four captains   365
Bear Hamlet like a soldier to the stage,
For he was likely, had he been put on,[4]
To have proved most royal; and for his passage
The soldier's music and the rite of war
Speak loudly for him.   370
Take up the bodies. Such a sight as this
Becomes the field, but here shows much amiss.
Go, bid the soldiers shoot.

                    [*Exeunt marching. A peal of ordnance shot off.*]

ca. 1600

---

7. Exactly.   8. Brought about by apparent accident.   9. Result.   1. Hearing.   2. Succession.
3. Position.   4. Elected king.

QUESTIONS

1. Carefully read over the first scene of *A Midsummer Night's Dream*, paying particular attention to Egeus's remarks about Hermia and Lysander and to the conversations between Hermia and Lysander and Hermia and Helena. How is love characterized in this scene? Why and how, for example, is love associated with dreams, with imagination? Why does Egeus object to his daughter's relationship with Lysander? What might his speeches and the scene as a whole suggest about the differences between the older and younger Athenians' views?

2. Look closely at the conversation between Theseus and Hippolyta that opens act 5, scene 1 of *A Midsummer Night's Dream*. What exactly is Theseus's argument here? What, for him, makes "[t]he lunatic, the lover, and the poet" alike (line 7)? What is his attitude toward all three? Given what has happened to the young Athenians in preceding acts, to what extent is Theseus's characterization of lovers accurate? inaccurate? In what way are Theseus's words and behavior in the rest of this scene, particularly his reactions to the mechanicals' play, consistent with this speech? How does Theseus's attitude toward plays compare to that of the mechanicals? For example, do the mechanicals seem to believe, as Theseus does, that the best plays "are but shadows" (5.1.204)?

3. Carefully read over *Hamlet's* first act and make a list of all the exposition given here— relationships between characters, events that have taken place before the play begins, conflicts of various kinds. What *else* happens in act 1? What emotions are aroused? What issues are raised? How exactly does the first scene prepare us for our introduction to Hamlet? What do we learn about Hamlet's character and concerns in the second scene— both before and after Horatio tells him about the ghost? How does your view of Hamlet develop over this act's subsequent scenes? What do these scenes suggest about what "is rotten in the state of Denmark" (1.4.90)? In these terms, what is the significance of the act's third scene (in which Hamlet never appears)?

4. How do the situations of Laertes, Fortinbras, and Ophelia resemble Hamlet's? How do their attitudes toward, and responses to, their situations compare to Hamlet's? Why might or might not they be good role models for Hamlet? Given the way Horatio talks and behaves throughout the play, how do you think he would act were he in Hamlet's shoes? Why might or might not he be a good role model for Hamlet?

5. In act 1, scene 3 of *Hamlet*, Laertes insists that a sovereign or a potential sovereign (like Hamlet) must be especially careful to make the right choices because "on his choice depends / The safety and health" of the "whole state" of which "he is the head" (20–24). How is this idea explored in both *A Midsummer Night's Dream* and *Hamlet*? In both plays, how do a sovereign's choices affect the safety and health of the state? What do the two plays suggest about how a sovereign should behave?

6. What similarities, if any, do you see in the way the mechanicals in *A Midsummer Night's Dream* and the clowns in *Hamlet* are characterized or represented? Why and how specifically are these socially humble characters important to the plays? What exactly do they contribute? How would the two plays be different were these characters not included?

WRITING SUGGESTIONS

1. List the references to eyes and to vision in *A Midsummer Night's Dream*. Write an essay in which you explore the significance of these references. What, through them, does the play suggest about both the power and the limitations of human vision?

2. Analyze the characterization of Ophelia and assess her function in *Hamlet*. If she were eliminated from the play, what specific things that seem crucial to the play's structure, effects, and theme would be missing?

3. In both *A Midsummer Night's Dream* and *Hamlet,* characters perform a play. Write an essay in which you explore the function and significance of these plays within plays. What are the functions and effects of this device? What issues does Shakespeare raise through it? What, for example, might the plays within plays suggest about the value of drama—or of plays like *A Midsummer Night's Dream* and *Hamlet?* What different attitudes toward drama are displayed by various characters in *A Midsummer Night's Dream* and *Hamlet?* What attitudes do the plays encourage us to adopt?

4. Death is obviously a major preoccupation of *Hamlet*: its first scene features the ghost of a dead man, its last portrays numerous deaths; in between, we get a great deal of talk about death, particularly from Hamlet. Though no deaths occur in *A Midsummer Night's Dream*, this play, too, opens and closes with references to death. Write an essay in which you explore why and how the specter of death looms so large in both plays. What do the plays suggest about why Shakespeare might want us to think about death (even as we watch a comedy)? What do the plays encourage us to think about it?

STUDENT WRITING

Rather than comparing *A Midsummer Night's Dream* and *Hamlet,* the following essay concentrates wholly on the latter, exploring how a single speech helps characterize the protagonist, foreshadow later events, and introduce key issues and themes.

The Play's the Thing: Deception in <u>Hamlet</u>

Jeanette Sperhac

Early in Act 1 we are introduced to the young Prince Hamlet, who, distraught over his father's death, is defending the utter sincerity of his grief. Alongside the wily banter of the court and the murky circumstances of his mother's marriage, Hamlet's distress is astonishingly genuine and true. But Hamlet's honesty does not appear to last; his hopelessness leads him to don an "antic disposition" and reciprocate the deceit of those around him. He is driven to feign madness, to toy with the sensibilities of courtiers, friends, and even his mother, and to plot the exposure of the king's monstrous crime; these acts seem to be breaches of his honesty, yet all actually uphold a higher end, avenging King Hamlet's murder. Hamlet's seeming descent from sincerity to deceit, and the nested plots and false appearances that ensnare him, can be traced to his first speech, that of an "honest" man.

Hamlet's opening speech resounds with his ideals. "I know not 'seems,' " he claims (1.2.76), seeking to dispel his mother's misgivings about his mourning. Not merely claiming sincerity, Hamlet is making a statement fundamental to his character; all that he knows, all that he recognizes, is <u>what</u> <u>is</u>. Appearances are transitory and fleeting; in his distracted state, Hamlet knows and acknowledges only that his father is dead, that his mother's remarriage is suspect, that his grief is <u>warranted</u>. When Hamlet learns later that his father's ghost desires revenge, that fact becomes Hamlet's warrant to do whatever he must to frame Claudius. Further insight into Hamlet's character can be ascertained from "I have that within which passes show" (1.2.85), which, on the surface, articulates the all-encompassing nature of his grief. Once again, there are strong undercurrents; Hamlet knows that he is able to project a false appearance, to act a part that still "passes show" and seems true. Hamlet's first speech makes evident two seemingly contradictory qualities, his conviction and honesty opposite his ability to lie and deceive.

It can hardly be surprising that Hamlet plunges into the rampant currents of deception, feigning madness and playing parts for those around him. The "actions that a man might play" to which Hamlet alluded in his opening speech (1.2.84) begin to unfold. Of Polonius he makes a "tedious old [fool]" (2.2.209) by bantering endlessly with the man until he is certain that the prince is mad with unrequited love; Hamlet is harsher with Polonius's daughter, berating Ophelia and mocking his own fond letters to her: "I did love you once [. . . but you] should not have believed me [. . .] I loved you not" (3.1.112–16). Hamlet is torn upon the subject of his mother; though he is tempted to reproach her, though she is playing along with Claudius, his father's ghost has warned him to leave her alone. With his mother, as throughout, Hamlet's justification for his actions and his play-acting lies in the genuine motive that lies paradoxically behind his antic disposition. The ghost of King Hamlet has given irrevocable orders; Hamlet, in his distress, is compelled to obey them, and is drawn deeper into his playing.

Most fundamental of all Hamlet's play-acting is that which involves Claudius, for revenge upon Claudius is Hamlet's true objective. Directly connected to the king is Hamlet's playing and counterplaying with Rosencrantz and Guildenstern, who, at Claudius's request, assume the guises of concerned friends. The perceptive prince cuts instantly through what "seems"; he knows that they are informers. His uncanny sense for what "is" identifies their true intent. In the course of their three-way playing, Hamlet taunts Rosencrantz and Guildenstern with his knowledge, continually mocks them, and even forces them to admit to their doings. "Though you can fret me, you cannot play upon me," Hamlet laughs (3.2.321–22); though Rosencrantz and Guildenstern are hired to spy on him, though it is purportedly their game, Hamlet is the one in control; it is he who plays upon them.

Of the final and most shattering instances of "playing," the framing of Claudius belongs completely to Hamlet; the exposure of the king's monstrous crime is Hamlet's great scheme. The prince's interest in the traveling players is misinterpreted by Claudius as a healthy diversion; the king never suspects that the crux of Hamlet's revenge lies in the players' art. Claudius's forced admission of the king's murder happens bizarrely, paradoxically, not acknowledged under confrontation, but whimpered in the dark in the response to posed figures on a stage. Hamlet has surpassed his own play-acting and the guile and tact of the court; he turns the false projection of an actor into a vehicle of justice. In his finest moment, Hamlet harnesses the actor's art to accuse Claudius; it is as if the prince has gone so far into playing that he must use puppets for his true intent.

The final scene could be viewed as Claudius's reply to the "Mousetrap." Challenged to an apparently harmless fencing match, Hamlet is doomed to lose his life, either to the tainted foil of Laertes, his "sporting" opponent, or to the poisoned goblet held by Claudius. The prince is hopelessly trapped; no guise can transport him now, no perception foresee the consequences of the scene. Deception heaped upon deception has caught up with Hamlet at last, and upstaged by Claudius's guile, the prince drags Denmark down with him.

Central to Hamlet are currents of deception: apparent truths, apparent sentiments, apparent relationships and the submerged realities which they misrepresent. Though the prince's opening speech shows a veneer of sincerity, it foreshadows the trickery that Hamlet is capable of, the playing and seeming that he will undertake to serve an ironically pure end. To obey his murdered father, a loyal son plays at deception, aiming to achieve justice; labyrinths of deceit produce a kind of final truth, once appearances are shed and the actual emerges. These entangled plots and jumbled motives within Hamlet are all evident from the prince's opening speech.

26

LITERARY CONTEXT: TRAGEDY AND COMEDY

Classifying literary texts serves a variety of purposes for historians and literary critics, who may need to "place" a literary work in history, suggest its relationship to other texts, or make a value judgment about its literary quality or cultural value. But classification is not just an activity for "professionals," and a knowledge of literary categories and definitions is useful not only for those who enjoy sorting and labeling. Classification can also be important to students and ordinary readers, for a knowledge of categories and what they stand for can aid in the enjoyment and interpretation of individual texts. Just as the generic divisions of poetry, fiction, and drama tell you something about what to expect when you pick up a text, so particular kinds of dramas—tragedies, for example, or comedies—provide certain expectations of what will go on and how. Knowing something about the nature of tragedy can make you a better, more attentive reader of *Oedipus the King,* and understanding the nature of literary categories can make your relationship with literary texts more generally satisfying.

Authors sometimes label their texts specifically to help readers know what to expect, thereby entering into a kind of contract of expectation with readers. When fiction writers call their books "romances," for example, they tell their readers to expect stories that are romantic, idealistic, improbable, full of fantasy, and characterized by love and emotional fulfillment. Playwrights too have historically labeled their texts to lure or warn readers. **Pastoral plays** promise to be about shepherds living in an idealized world reminiscent of the idealistic values of some primitive golden age. **Farces** promise broad humor and wild antics, perhaps slapstick or pratfalls or other physical humor or perhaps easy puns and verbal high jinks, but certainly something entertaining, not too taxing, and not too serious. **Satires** promise critical commentary on some person or situation or event, often political or involving some specific cultural or social situation of contemporary relevance. Not all pastoral plays, farces, and satires do exactly what they promise, but if they label themselves as such, they set up readers to expect a certain kind of text—a text that will treat predictable subject matter and behave in predictable fashion. Often these labels imply a certain kind of structure, a certain kind of language, and a value system. A title such as *The Tragedy of Hamlet, Prince of Denmark* gives us an idea, from the moment we read it, of what to expect—not just a plot, ending, and

1383

tone of a particular kind, but an imagined world that operates according to habits and laws.

Not all plays (or texts of any other kind) are given labels by their authors, but many unlabeled texts are nevertheless conceived along lines that have to do with previous practice and traditional classifications, and many texts are, therefore, classified by critics or by their earliest viewers and readers as belonging to traditional groups. We might, for example, describe a film as a whodunit or a spaghetti Western, or we might call a TV program a sitcom or a soap, and have a reasonable expectation that others would know, at least roughly speaking, what kind of thing we had been watching.

Tragedy and **comedy** are two of the oldest dramatic forms, and many contemporary playwrights and critics continue to apply these terms. Many people believe that tragedy and comedy still provide convenient ways to organize and present experience because they testify to, and reflect, basic ways of viewing human history. You can sometimes get into a pretty lively argument about whether a particular play should be called a tragedy; all kinds of critics, students, theatergoers, and readers once argued with Arthur Miller and with each other about whether *Death of a Salesman* was truly tragic, for example. But while individuals often disagree about the propriety of certain labels for particular texts, and often have somewhat different notions of everything that such labels imply, most people admit the necessity of labels and believe that some general agreement about definition is possible, despite quibbling over details.

> *Comedy aims at representing man as worse, Tragedy as better than in actual life.*
>
> —ARISTOTLE

The broad parameters of comedy and tragedy have been established since the time of Aristotle, who first tried to define tragedy by describing contemporary examples in the fourth century B.C. The most fundamental aspects of Aristotelian definition may be summarized as depending upon three categories of assumption—the order of values implicit in the play, the nature of character in the play, and the nature of the conclusion.

In a tragedy like *Oedipus the King,* values are universal and beyond the control of humankind. Right and wrong stem not from any agreement between individuals, but from the will of the gods or from some other preterhuman force. When the oracle tells Oedipus that he is fated to kill his father and marry his mother, Oedipus is revolted by the prospect. In human terms he must try to avoid such a fate—but in terms of the value system that rules the play, his attempt to circumvent the will of the gods must destroy him. In a comedy like *The Importance of Being Earnest,* on the other hand, values are social and determined by the general opinion of society. In moral terms Jack and Gwendolen, being healthy and single, might marry and begin the business of establishing a family. They face, however, a social problem, in that Gwendolen's children cannot achieve their "proper" place in society unless her husband is a suitable choice, a man of good family, some social position, and adequate means to provide an appropriate education for them. Implicit in this consideration is the fact that comedy tends to endorse the values of society, sometimes at the expense of individual needs or values. Lady Bracknell may be amusing, but she also understands how her society works, what is acceptable and what is not.

> *Tragic art, passionate art,*
> *. . . the confounder of*
> *understanding, moves us . . .*
> *almost to the intensity of*
> *trance. The persons upon the*
> *stage . . . greaten until they are*
> *humanity itself.*
>
> —W. B. YEATS

Tragedy and comedy also differ in their treatment of character. Tragedy, for example, tends to focus on a single individual, a person of high rank who confronts the universe and his or her fate as an individual, a hero. The tragic figure is ultimately doomed to defeat because, although good and noble, this person has a flaw of character or a limitation of knowledge—some mark of humanity—that offsets all his or her goodness. Oedipus wishes to know and to control his own destiny, but he learns too much and is destroyed. Had Oedipus been the son of a shepherd rather than of a king, perhaps the gods would not have taken such an unfortunate interest in his fate. By contrast, being concerned largely with society, comedies often define their characters in terms of social roles.

In *The Importance of Being Earnest* both Jack and Algernon are, for plot purposes, unmarried young men but not eminently eligible husbands-to-be, Jack because of his uncertain parentage and Algernon because of his lack of money. They have individual traits—Algernon eats too much and enjoys pretense, Jack is more straightforward or wishes to be—but what distinguishes them is not so important as what they have in common according to societal standards. Many comic characters go even further and become stereotypes. Lady Bracknell, for example, is a middle-aged, meddling matron, ideally placed by age and position to exert tremendous social influence. Other stereotypes in the same play include Miss Prism, the desperate spinster, and Dr. Chasuble, the slightly dim clergyman.

Finally, tragedy and comedy can be defined by their endings. In most tragedies, the hero is enlightened, coming to understand the meaning of his or her deeds and to accept an appropriate punishment. At the end of *Oedipus the King* the blind hero sees and understands. Accepting his ostracism, he leaves Thebes a chastened but wiser man. Many tragic heroes die, as Hamlet does, but understanding, not death itself, ends the tragedy. Hamlet understands what has happened and in his last moments tries to restore order to the kingdom, asking for himself only that people may know the truth about what he has done. In comedy, on the other hand, the resolution occurs when one or more characters take a proper social role. Most frequently, this means the marriage of an eligible young woman and an equally eligible young man. The society of *Earnest* believes that young men like Jack and Algernon and young women like Gwendolen and Cecily should marry and get about the business of having children and raising them to provide for the continuation of the society. Even the marriage of Miss Prism and Dr. Chasuble serves social purposes. The society of the play prefers married clergymen to celibates and has no really useful function for a middle-aged spinster.

The two plays that follow represent tragedy and comedy in something close to pure form, and each displays the assumptions and features of its genre. Many good plays provide less clear examples, and many other categories have been used over the centuries to describe the shape and conventions of groups of dramatic texts. In addition, many modern and postmodern plays consciously mix the genres. They tend to reflect and depict ordinary reality as their authors perceive it (that is, they aim to be *mimetic*) rather than following some predetermined shape or set of assumptions about some universal tone and standard kind of ending.

SOPHOCLES

Oedipus the King[1]

CHARACTERS

OEDIPUS, *King of Thebes*
JOCASTA, *His Wife*
CREON, *His Brother-in-Law*
TEIRESIAS, *an Old Blind Prophet*
A PRIEST

FIRST MESSENGER
SECOND MESSENGER
A HERDSMAN
A CHORUS *of Old Men of Thebes*

SCENE: *In front of the palace of* OEDIPUS *at Thebes. To the right of the stage near the altar stands the* PRIEST *with a crowd of children.* OEDIPUS *emerges from the central door.*

OEDIPUS: Children, young sons and daughters of old Cadmus,[2]
    why do you sit here with your suppliant crowns?
    The town is heavy with a mingled burden
    of sounds and smells, of groans and hymns and incense;
5   I did not think it fit that I should hear
    of this from messengers but came myself,—
    I Oedipus whom all men call the Great.

[*He turns to the* PRIEST.]

    You're old and they are young; come, speak for them.
    What do you fear or want, that you sit here
10   suppliant? Indeed I'm willing to give all
    that you may need; I would be very hard
    should I not pity suppliants like these.
PRIEST: O ruler of my country, Oedipus,
    you see our company around the altar;
15   you see our ages; some of us, like these,
    who cannot yet fly far, and some of us
    heavy with age; these children are the chosen
    among the young, and I the priest of Zeus.
    Within the market place sit others crowned
20   with suppliant garlands, at the double shrine
    of Pallas[3] and the temple where Ismenus
    gives oracles by fire. King, you yourself
    have seen our city reeling like a wreck
    already; it can scarcely lift its prow

---

1. Translated by David Grene.   2. The founder of Thebes.   3. Athena, the goddess of wisdom.

out of the depths, out of the bloody surf. 25
A blight is on the fruitful plants of the earth,
A blight is on the cattle in the fields,
a blight is on our women that no children
are born to them; a God that carries fire,
a deadly pestilence, is on our town, 30
strikes us and spares not, and the house of Cadmus
is emptied of its people while black Death
grows rich in groaning and in lamentation.
We have not come as suppliants to this altar
because we thought of you as of a God, 35
but rather judging you the first of men
in all the chances of this life and when
we mortals have to do with more than man.
You came and by your coming saved our city,
freed us from tribute which we paid of old 40
to the Sphinx, cruel singer. This you did
in virtue of no knowledge we could give you,
in virtue of no teaching; it was God
that aided you, men say, and you are held
with God's assistance to have saved our lives. 45
Now Oedipus, Greatest in all men's eyes,
here falling at your feet we all entreat you,
find us some strength for rescue.
Perhaps you'll hear a wise word from some God,
perhaps you will learn something from a man 50
(for I have seen that for the skilled of practice
the outcome of their counsels live the most).
Noblest of men, go, and raise up our city,
go,—and give heed. For now this land of ours
calls you its savior since you saved it once. 55
So, let us never speak about your reign
as of a time when first our feet were set
secure on high, but later fell to ruin.
Raise up our city, save it and raise it up.
Once you have brought us luck with happy omen; 60
be no less now in fortune.
If you will rule this land, as now you rule it,
better to rule it full of men than empty.
For neither tower nor ship is anything
when empty, and none live in it together. 65
OEDIPUS: I pity you, children. You have come full of longing,
but I have known the story before you told it
only too well. I know you are all sick,
yet there is not one of you, sick though you are,
that is as sick as I myself. 70

Your several sorrows each have single scope
and touch but one of you. My spirit groans
for city and myself and you at once.
You have not roused me like a man from sleep;
75 know that I have given many tears to this,
gone many ways wandering in thought,
but as I thought I found only one remedy
and that I took. I sent Menoeceus' son
Creon, Jocasta's brother, to Apollo,
80 to his Pythian temple,
that he might learn there by what act or word
I could save this city. As I count the days,
it vexes me what ails him; he is gone
far longer than he needed for the journey.
85 But when he comes, then, may I prove a villain,
if I shall not do all the God commands.
PRIEST: Thanks for your gracious words. Your servants here
signal that Creon is this moment coming.
OEDIPUS: His face is bright. O holy Lord Apollo,
90 grant that his news too may be bright for us
and bring us safety.
PRIEST: It is happy news,
I think, for else his head would not be crowned
with sprigs of fruitful laurel.
OEDIPUS: We will know soon,
95 he's within hail. Lord Creon, my good brother,
what is the word you bring us from the God?

[CREON *enters.*]

CREON: A good word,—for things hard to bear themselves
if in the final issue all is well
I count complete good fortune.
OEDIPUS: What do you mean?
100 What you have said so far
leaves me uncertain whether to trust or fear.
CREON: If you will hear my news before these others
I am ready to speak, or else to go within.
OEDIPUS: Speak it to all;
105 the grief I bear, I bear it more for these
than for my own heart.
CREON: I will tell you, then,
what I heard from the God.
King Phoebus[4] in plain words commanded us
to drive out a pollution from our land,

---

4. Apollo, the god of truth.

pollution grown ingrained within the land; 110
drive it out, said the God, not cherish it,
till it's past cure.
OEDIPUS: What is the rite
of purification? How shall it be done?
CREON: By banishing a man, or expiation
of blood by blood, since it is murder guilt 115
which holds our city in this destroying storm.
OEDIPUS: Who is this man whose fate the God pronounces?
CREON: My Lord, before you piloted the state
we had a king called Laius.
OEDIPUS: I know of him by hearsay. I have not seen him. 120
CREON: The God commanded clearly: let some one
punish with force this dead man's murderers.
OEDIPUS: Where are they in the world? Where would a trace
of this old crime be found? It would be hard
to guess where.
CREON: The clue is in this land; 125
that which is sought is found;
the unheeded thing escapes:
so said the God.
OEDIPUS: Was it at home,
or in the country that death came upon him,
or in another country travelling?
CREON: He went, he said himself, upon an embassy, 130
but never returned when he set out from home.
OEDIPUS: Was there no messenger, no fellow traveller
who knew what happened? Such a one might tell
something of use. 135
CREON: They were all killed save one. He fled in terror
and he could tell us nothing in clear terms
of what he knew, nothing, but one thing only.
OEDIPUS: What was it?
If we could even find a slim beginning 140
in which to hope, we might discover much.
CREON: This man said that the robbers they encountered
were many and the hands that did the murder
were many; it was no man's single power.
OEDIPUS: How could a robber dare a deed like this 145
were he not helped with money from the city,
money and treachery?
CREON: That indeed was thought.
But Laius was dead and in our trouble
there was none to help.
OEDIPUS: What trouble was so great to hinder you 150
inquiring out the murder of your king?

CREON: The riddling Sphinx induced us to neglect
    mysterious crimes and rather seek solution
    of troubles at our feet.
155 OEDIPUS: I will bring this to light again. King Phoebus
    fittingly took this care about the dead,
    and you too fittingly.
    And justly you will see in me an ally,
    a champion of my country and the God.
160   For when I drive pollution from the land
    I will not serve a distant friend's advantage,
    but act in my own interest. Whoever
    he was that killed the king may readily
    wish to dispatch me with his murderous hand;
165   so helping the dead king I help myself.

    Come, children, take your suppliant boughs and go;
    up from the altars now. Call the assembly
    and let it meet upon the understanding
    that I'll do everything. God will decide
170   whether we prosper or remain in sorrow.
  PRIEST: Rise, children—it was this we came to seek,
    which of himself the king now offers us.
    May Phoebus who gave us the oracle
    come to our rescue and stay the plague.

        [*Exeunt all but the* CHORUS.]

CHORUS: [*Strophe.*] What is the sweet spoken word of God from the shrine of
175   Pythorich in gold
    that has come to glorious Thebes?
    I am stretched on the rack of doubt, and terror and trembling hold
    my heart, O Delian Healer, and I worship full of fears
    for what doom you will bring to pass, new or renewed in the revolving years.
180   Speak to me, immortal voice,
    child of golden Hope.

        [*Antistrophe.*]

    First I call on you, Athene, deathless daughter of Zeus,
    and Artemis, Earth Upholder,
    who sits in the midst of the market place in the throne which men call Fame,
185   and Phoebus, the Far Shooter, three averters of Fate,
    come to us now, if ever before, when ruin rushed upon the state,
    you drove destruction's flame away
    out of our land.

        [*Strophe.*]

Our sorrows defy number;
all the ship's timbers are rotten;   190
taking of thought is no spear for the driving away of the plague.
There are no growing children in this famous land;
there are no women bearing the pangs of childbirth.
You may see them one with another, like birds swift on the wing,
quicker than fire unmastered,   195
speeding away to the coast of the Western God.

    [*Antistrophe.*]

In the unnumbered deaths
of its people the city dies;
those children that are born lie dead on the naked earth
unpitied, spreading contagion of death; and grey haired mothers and wives   200
everywhere stand at the altar's edge, suppliant, moaning;
the hymn to the healing God rings out but with it the wailing voices are
    blended.
From these our sufferings grant us, O golden Daughter of Zeus,
glad-faced deliverance.

    [*Strophe.*]

There is no clash of brazen shields but our fight is with the War God,   205
a War God ringed with the cries of men, a savage God who burns us;
grant that he turn in racing course backwards out of our country's bounds
to the great palace of Amphitrite[5] or where the waves of the Thracian sea
deny the stranger safe anchorage.
Whatsoever escapes the night   210
at last the light of day revisits;
so smite the War God, Father Zeus,
beneath your thunderbolt,
for you are the Lord of the lightning, the lightning that carries fire.

    [*Antistrophe.*]

And your unconquered arrow shafts, winged by the golden corded bow,   215
Lycean King, I beg to be at our side for help;
and the gleaming torches of Artemis with which she scours the Lycean hills,
and I call on the God with the turban of gold, who gave his name to this country
    of ours,
the Bacchic God with the wind flushed face,
Evian One, who travel   220
with the Maenad[6] company,
combat the God that burns us

5. The Atlantic Ocean.   6. Female worshipers of Bacchus.

with your torch of pine;
for the God that is our enemy is a God unhonoured among the Gods.

[OEDIPUS *returns*.]

225 OEDIPUS: For what you ask me—if you will hear my words,
and hearing welcome them and fight the plague,
you will find strength and lightening of your load
Hark to me; what I say to you, I say
as one that is a stranger to the story
230 as stranger to the deed. For I would not
be far upon the track if I alone
were tracing it without a clue. But now,
since after all was finished, I became
a citizen among you, citizens—
235 now I proclaim to all the men of Thebes:
who so among you knows the murderer
by whose hand Laius, son of Labdacus,
died—I command him to tell everything
to me,—yes, though he fears himself to take the blame
240 on his own head; for bitter punishment
he shall have none, but leave this land unharmed.
Or if he knows the murderer, another,
a foreigner, still let him speak the truth.
For I will pay him and be grateful, too.
245 But if you shall keep silence, if perhaps
some one of you, to shield a guilty friend,
or for his own sake shall reject my words—
hear what I shall do then:
I forbid that man, whoever he be, my land,
250 my land where I hold sovereignty and throne;
and I forbid any to welcome him
or cry him greeting or make him a sharer
in sacrifice or offering to the Gods,
or give him water for his hands to wash.
255 I command all to drive him from their homes,
since he is our pollution, as the oracle
of Pytho's God proclaimed him now to me.
So I stand forth a champion of the God
and of the man who died.
260 Upon the murderer I invoke this curse—
whether he is one man and all unknown,
or one of many—may he wear out his life
in misery to miserable doom!
If with my knowledge he lives at my hearth
265 I pray that I myself may feel my curse.
On you I lay my charge to fulfill all this

for me, for the God, and for this land of ours
destroyed and blighted, by the God forsaken.

Even were this no matter of God's ordinance
it would not fit you so to leave it lie,   270
unpurified, since a good man is dead
and one that was a king. Search it out.
Since I am now the holder of his office,
and have his bed and wife that once was his,
and had his line not been unfortunate   275
we would have common children—(fortune leaped
upon his head)—because of all these things,
I fight in his defence as for my father,
and I shall try all means to take the murderer
of Laius the son of Labdacus   280
the son of Polydorus and before him
of Cadmus and before him of Agenor.
Those who do not obey me, may the Gods
grant no crops springing from the ground they plough
nor children to their women! May a fate   285
like this, or one still worse than this consume them!
For you whom these words please, the other Thebans,
may Justice as your ally and all the Gods
live with you, blessing you now and for ever!
CHORUS: As you have held me to my oath, I speak: 290
  I neither killed the king nor can declare
  the killer; but since Phoebus set the quest
  it is his part to tell who the man is.
OEDIPUS: Right; but to put compulsion on the Gods
  against their will—no man can do that.   295
CHORUS: May I then say what I think second best?
OEDIPUS: If there's a third best, too, spare not to tell it.
CHORUS: I know that what the Lord Teiresias
  sees, is most often what the Lord Apollo
  sees. If you should inquire of this from him   300
  you might find out most clearly.
OEDIPUS: Even in this my actions have not been sluggard.
  On Creon's word I have sent two messengers
  and why the prophet is not here already
  I have been wondering.
CHORUS: His skill apart   305
  there is besides only an old faint story.
OEDIPUS: What is it?
  I look at every story.
CHORUS: It was said
  that he was killed by certain wayfarers.

310 OEDIPUS: I heard that, too, but no one saw the killer.
CHORUS: Yet if he has a share of fear at all,
his courage will not stand firm, hearing your curse.
OEDIPUS: The man who in the doing did not shrink
will fear no word.
CHORUS: Here comes his prosecutor:
315 led by your men the godly prophet comes
in whom alone of mankind truth is native.

[*Enter* TEIRESIAS, *led by a* LITTLE BOY.]

OEDIPUS: Teiresias, you are versed in everything,
things teachable and things not to be spoken,
things of the heaven and earth-creeping things.
320 You have no eyes but in your mind you know
with what a plague our city is afflicted.
My lord, in you alone we find a champion,
in you alone one that can rescue us.
Perhaps you have not heard the messengers,
325 but Phoebus sent in answer to our sending
an oracle declaring that our freedom
from this disease would only come when we
should learn the names of those who killed King Laius,
and kill them or expel from our country.
330 Do not begrudge us oracles from birds,
or any other way of prophecy
within your skill; save yourself and the city,
save me; redeem the debt of our pollution
that lies on us because of this dead man.
335 We are in your hands; pains are most nobly taken
to help another when you have means and power.
TEIRESIAS: Alas, how terrible is wisdom when
it brings no profit to the man that's wise!
This I knew well, but had forgotten it,
else I would not have come here.
340 OEDIPUS: What is this?
How sad you are now you have come!
TEIRESIAS: Let me
go home. It will be easiest for us both
to bear our several destinies to the end
if you will follow my advice.
OEDIPUS: You'd rob us
345 of this your gift of prophecy? You talk
as one who had no care for law nor love
for Thebes who reared you.
TEIRESIAS: Yes, but I see that even your own words
miss the mark; therefore I must fear for mine.

OEDIPUS: For God's sake if you know of anything,   350
    do not turn from us; all of us kneel to you,
    all of us here, your suppliants.
TEIRESIAS: All of you here know nothing. I will not
    bring to the light of day my troubles, mine—
    rather than call them yours.
OEDIPUS: What do you mean?   355
    You know of something but refuse to speak.
    Would you betray us and destroy the city?
TEIRESIAS: I will not bring this pain upon us both,
    neither on you nor on myself. Why is it
    you question me and waste your labour? I   360
    will tell you nothing.
OEDIPUS: You would provoke a stone! Tell us, you villain,
    tell us, and do not stand there quietly
    unmoved and balking at the issue.
TEIRESIAS: You blame my temper but you do not see   365
    your own that lives within you; it is me
    you chide.
OEDIPUS: Who would not feel his temper rise
    at words like these with which you shame our city?
TEIRESIAS: Of themselves things will come, although I hide them   370
    and breathe no word of them.
OEDIPUS: Since they will come
    tell them to me.
TEIRESIAS: I will say nothing further.
    Against this answer let your temper rage
    as wildly as you will.
OEDIPUS: Indeed I am
    so angry I shall not hold back a jot   375
    of what I think. For I would have you know
    I think you were complotter of the deed
    and doer of the deed save in so far
    as for the actual killing. Had you had eyes
    I would have said alone you murdered him.   380
TEIRESIAS: Yes? Then I warn you faithfully to keep
    the letter of your proclamation and
    from this day forth to speak no word of greeting
    to these nor me; you are the land's pollution.
OEDIPUS: How shamelessly you started up this taunt!   385
    How do you think you will escape?
TEIRESIAS: I have.
    I have escaped; the truth is what I cherish
    and that's my strength.
OEDIPUS: And who has taught you truth?
    Not your profession surely!

TEIRESIAS: You have taught me,
390   for you have made me speak against my will.
OEDIPUS: Speak what? Tell me again that I may learn it better.
TEIRESIAS: Did you not understand before or would you
        provoke me into speaking?
OEDIPUS: I did not grasp it,
        not so to call it known. Say it again.
395 TEIRESIAS: I say you are the murderer of the king
        whose murderer you seek.
OEDIPUS: Not twice you shall
        say calumnies like this and stay unpunished.
TEIRESIAS: Shall I say more to tempt your anger more?
OEDIPUS: As much as you desire; it will be said
        in vain.
400 TEIRESIAS: I say that with those you love best
        you live in foulest shame unconsciously
        and do not see where you are in calamity.
OEDIPUS: Do you imagine you can always talk
        like this, and live to laugh at it hereafter?
405 TEIRESIAS: Yes, if the truth has anything of strength.
OEDIPUS: It has, but not for you; it has no strength
        for you because you are blind in mind and ears
        as well as in your eyes.
TEIRESIAS: You are a poor wretch
        to taunt me with the very insults which
410   every one soon will heap upon yourself.
OEDIPUS: Your life is one long night so that you cannot
        hurt me or any other who sees the light.
TEIRESIAS: It is not fate that I should be your ruin,
        Apollo is enough; it is his care
        to work this out.
415 OEDIPUS: Was this your own design
        or Creon's?
TEIRESIAS: Creon is no hurt to you,
        but you are to yourself.
OEDIPUS: Wealth, sovereignty and skill outmatching skill
        for the contrivance of an envied life!
420   Great store of jealousy fill your treasury chests,
        if my friend Creon, friend from the first and loyal,
        thus secretly attacks me, secretly
        desires to drive me out and secretly
        suborns this juggling, trick devising quack,
425   this wily beggar who has only eyes
        for his own gains, but blindness in his skill.
        For, tell me, where have you seen clear, Teiresias,
        with your prophetic eyes? When the dark singer,

the sphinx, was in your country, did you speak
word of deliverance to its citizens?   430
And yet the riddle's answer was not the province
of a chance comer. It was a prophet's task
and plainly you had no such gift of prophecy
from birds nor otherwise from any God
to glean a word of knowledge. But I came,   435
Oedipus, who knew nothing, and I stopped her.
I solved the riddle by my wit alone.
Mine was no knowledge got from birds. And now
you would expel me,
because you think that you will find a place   440
by Creon's throne. I think you will be sorry,
both you and your accomplice, for your plot
to drive me out. And did I not regard you
as an old man, some suffering would have taught you
that what was in your heart was treason.   445
CHORUS: We look at this man's words and yours, my king,
and we find both have spoken them in anger.
We need no angry words but only thought
how we may best hit the God's meaning for us.
TEIRESIAS: If you are king, at least I have the right   450
no less to speak in my defence against you.
Of that much I am master. I am no slave
of yours, but Loxias', and so I shall not
enroll myself with Creon for my patron.
Since you have taunted me with being blind,   455
here is my word for you.
You have your eyes but see not where you are
in sin, nor where you live, nor whom you live with.
Do you know who your parents are? Unknowing
you are an enemy to kith and kin   460
in death, beneath the earth, and in this life.
A deadly footed, double striking curse,
from father and mother both, shall drive you forth
out of this land, with darkness on your eyes,
that now have such straight vision. Shall there be   465
a place will not be harbour to your cries,
a corner of Cithaeron[7] will not ring
in echo to your cries, soon, soon,—
when you shall learn the secret of your marriage,
which steered you to a haven in this house,—   470
haven no haven, after lucky voyage?
And of the multitude of other evils

7. The mountain where Oedipus was abandoned as a child.

establishing a grim equality
between you and your children, you know nothing.
475 So, muddy with contempt my words and Creon's!
Misery shall grind no man as it will you.

OEDIPUS: Is it endurable that I should hear
such words from him? Go and a curse go with you
Quick, home with you! Out of my house at once!

480 TEIRESIAS: I would not have come either had you not called me.

OEDIPUS: I did not know then you would talk like a fool—
or it would have been long before I called you.

TEIRESIAS: I am a fool then, as it seems to you—
but to the parents who have bred you, wise.

485 OEDIPUS: What parents? Stop! Who are they of all the world?

TEIRESIAS: This day will show your birth and will destroy you.

OEDIPUS: How needlessly your riddles darken everything.

TEIRESIAS: But it's in riddle answering you are strongest.

OEDIPUS: Yes. Taunt me where you will find me great.

490 TEIRESIAS: It is this very luck that has destroyed you.

OEDIPUS: I do not care, if it has saved this city.

TEIRESIAS: Well, I will go. Come, boy, lead me away.

OEDIPUS: Yes, lead him off. So long as you are here,
you'll be a stumbling block and a vexation;
once gone, you will not trouble me again.

495 TEIRESIAS: I have said
what I came here to say not fearing your
countenance: there is no way you can hurt me.
I tell you, king, this man, this murderer
(whom you have long declared you are in search of,
500 indicting him in threatening proclamation
as murderer of Laius)—he is here.
In name he is a stranger among citizens
but soon he will be shown to be a citizen
true native Theban, and he'll have no joy
505 of the discovery: blindness for sight
and beggary for riches his exchange,
he shall go journeying to a foreign country
tapping his way before him with a stick.
He shall be proved father and brother both
510 to his own children in his house; to her
that gave him birth, a son and husband both;
a fellow sower in his father's bed
with that same father that he murdered.
Go within, reckon that out, and if you find me
515 mistaken, say I have no skill in prophecy.

[*Exeunt separately* TEIRESIAS *and* OEDIPUS.]

CHORUS: [*Strophe.*] Who is the man proclaimed

by Delphi's prophetic rock
as the bloody handed murderer,
the doer of deeds that none dare name?
Now is the time for him to run   520
with a stronger foot
than Pegasus[8]
for the child of Zeus leaps in arms upon him
with fire and the lightning bolt,
and terribly close on his heels   525
are the Fates[9] that never miss.

    [*Antistrophe.*]

Lately from snowy Parnassus[1]
clearly the voice flashed forth,
bidding each Theban track him down,
the unknown murderer.   530
In the savage forests he lurks and in
the caverns like
the mountain bull.
He is sad and lonely, and lonely his feet
that carry him far from the navel of earth;   535
but its prophecies, ever living,
flutter around his head.

    [*Strophe.*]

The augur has spread confusion,
terrible confusion;
I do not approve what was said   540
nor can I deny it.
I do not know what to say;
I am in a flutter of foreboding;
I never heard in the present
nor past of a quarrel between   545
the sons of Labdacus and Polybus,[2]
that I might bring as proof
in attacking the popular fame
of Oedipus, seeking
to take vengeance for undiscovered   550
death in the line of Labdacus.

    [*Antistrophe.*]

Truly Zeus and Apollo are wise
and in human things all knowing;
but amongst men there is no

---

8. Winged horse.   9. Goddesses who decide the course of human life.   1. Mountain sacred to
Apollo.   2. King who adopted Oedipus.

555   distinct judgment, between the prophet
        and me—which of us is right.
        One man may pass another in wisdom
        but I would never agree
        with those that find fault with the king
560   till I should see the word
        proved right beyond doubt. For once
        in visible form the Sphinx
        came on him and all of us
        saw his wisdom and in that test
565   he saved the city. So he will not be condemned by my mind.

            [*Enter* CREON.]

        CREON: Citizens, I have come because I heard
        deadly words spread about me, that the king
        accuses me. I cannot take that from him.
        If he believes that in these present troubles
570   he has been wronged by me in word or deed
        I do not want to live on with the burden
        of such a scandal on me. The report
        injures me doubly and most vitally—
        for I'll be called a traitor to my city
575   and traitor also to my friends and you.
        CHORUS: Perhaps it was a sudden gust of anger
        that forced that insult from him, and no judgment.
        CREON: But did he say that it was in compliance
        with schemes of mine that the seer told him lies?
580   CHORUS: Yes, he said that, but why, I do not know.
        CREON: Were his eyes straight in his head? Was his mind right
        when he accused me in this fashion?
        CHORUS: I do not know; I have no eyes to see
        what princes do. Here comes the king himself.

            [*Enter* OEDIPUS.]

585   OEDIPUS: You, sir, how is it you come here? Have you so much
        brazen-faced daring that you venture in
        my house although you are proved manifestly
        the murderer of that man, and though you tried,
        openly, highway robbery of my crown?
590   For God's sake, tell me what you saw in me,
        what cowardice or what stupidity,
        that made you lay a plot like this against me?
        Did you imagine I should not observe
        the crafty scheme that stole upon me or
595   seeing it, take no means to counter it?
        Was it not stupid of you to make the attempt,

to try to hunt down royal power without
the people at your back or friends? For only
with the people at your back or money can
the hunt end in the capture of a crown.   600
CREON: Do you know what you're doing? Will you listen
   to words to answer yours, and then pass judgment?
OEDIPUS: You're quick to speak, but I am slow to grasp you,
   for I have found you dangerous,—and my foe.
CREON: First of all hear what I shall say to that.   605
OEDIPUS: At least don't tell me that you are not guilty.
CREON: If you think obstinacy without wisdom
   a valuable possession, you are wrong.
OEDIPUS: And you are wrong if you believe that one,
   a criminal, will not be punished only   610
   because he is my kinsman.
CREON: This is but just—
   but tell me, then, of what offense I'm guilty?
OEDIPUS: Did you or did you not urge me to send
   to this prophetic mumbler?
CREON: I did indeed,
   and I shall stand by what I told you.   615
OEDIPUS: How long ago is it since Laius . . .
CREON: What about Laius? I don't understand.
OEDIPUS: Vanished—died—was murdered?
CREON: It is long,
   a long, long time to reckon.
OEDIPUS: Was this prophet
   in the profession then?
CREON: He was, and honoured   620
   as highly as he is today.
OEDIPUS: At that time did he say a word about me?
CREON: Never, at least when I was near him.
OEDIPUS: You never made a search for the dead man?
CREON: We searched, indeed, but never learned of anything.   625
OEDIPUS: Why did our wise old friend not say this then?
CREON: I don't know; and when I know nothing, I
   usually hold my tongue.
OEDIPUS: You know this much,
   and can declare this much if you are loyal.
CREON: What is it? If I know, I'll not deny it.   630
OEDIPUS: That he would not have said that I killed Laius
   had he not met you first.
CREON: You know yourself
   whether he said this, but I demand that I
   should hear as much from you as you from me.
OEDIPUS: Then hear,—I'll not be proved a murderer.   635

CREON: Well, then. You're married to my sister.

OEDIPUS: Yes,
  that I am not disposed to deny.

CREON: You rule
  this country giving her an equal share
  in the government?

OEDIPUS: Yes, everything she wants
  she has from me.

640 CREON: And I, as thirdsman to you,
  am rated as the equal of you two?

OEDIPUS: Yes, and it's there you've proved yourself false friend.

CREON: Not if you will reflect on it as I do.
  Consider, first, if you think any one
645   would choose to rule and fear rather than rule
  and sleep untroubled by a fear if power
  were equal in both cases. I, at least,
  I was not born with such a frantic yearning
  to be a king—but to do what kings do.
650   And so it is with every one who has learned
  wisdom and self-control. As it stands now,
  the prizes are all mine—and without fear.
  But if I were the king myself, I must
  do much that went against the grain.
655   How should despotic rule seem sweeter to me
  than painless power and an assured authority?
  I am not so besotted yet that I
  want other honours than those that come with profit.
  Now every man's my pleasure; every man greets me;
660   now those who are your suitors fawn on me,—
  success for them depends upon my favour.
  Why should I let all this go to win that?
  My mind would not be traitor if it's wise;
  I am no treason lover, of my nature,
665   nor would I ever dare to join a plot.
  Prove what I say. Go to the oracle
  at Pytho and inquire about the answers,
  if they are as I told you. For the rest,
  if you discover I laid any plot
670   together with the seer, kill me, I say,
  not only by your vote but by my own.
  But do not charge me on obscure opinion
  without some proof to back it. It's not just
  lightly to count your knaves as honest men,
675   nor honest men as knaves. To throw away
  an honest friend is, as it were, to throw
  your life away, which a man loves the best.

In time you will know all with certainty;
time is the only test of honest men,
one day is space enough to know a rogue.   680
CHORUS: His words are wise, king, if one fears to fall.
Those who are quick of temper are not safe.
OEDIPUS: When he that plots against me secretly
moves quickly, I must quickly counterplot.
If I wait taking no decisive measure   685
his business will be done, and mine be spoiled.
CREON: What do you want to do then? Banish me?
OEDIPUS: No, certainly; kill you, not banish you.³
CREON: I do not think that you've your wits about you.
OEDIPUS: For my own interests, yes.
CREON: But for mine, too,   690
you should think equally.
OEDIPUS: You are a rogue.
CREON: Suppose you do not understand?
OEDIPUS: But yet
I must be ruler.
CREON: Not if you rule badly.
OEDIPUS: O, city, city!
CREON: I too have some share
in the city; it is not yours alone.   695
CHORUS: Stop, my lords! Here—and in the nick of time
I see Jocasta coming from the house;
with her help lay the quarrel that now stirs you.

[*Enter* JOCASTA.]

JOCASTA: For shame! Why have you raised this foolish squabbling
brawl? Are you not ashamed to air your private   700
griefs when the country's sick? Go in, you, Oedipus,
and you, too, Creon, into the house. Don't magnify
your nothing troubles.
CREON: Sister, Oedipus,
your husband, thinks he has the right to do
terrible wrongs—he has but to choose between   705
two terrors: banishing or killing me.
OEDIPUS: He's right, Jocasta; for I find him plotting
with knavish tricks against my person.
CREON: That God may never bless me! May I die
accursed, if I have been guilty of   710
one tittle of the charge you bring against me!

---

3. *Translator's note:* Two lines omitted here owing to the confusion in the dialogue consequent on the
loss of a third line. The lines as they stand in Jebb's edition (1902) are: OED.: That you may show what
manner of thing is envy. / CREON: You speak as one that will not yield or trust. / [OED. *lost line.*]

JOCASTA: I beg you, Oedipus, trust him in this,
    spare him for the sake of this his oath to God,
    for my sake, and the sake of those who stand here.
715 CHORUS: Be gracious, be merciful,
    we beg of you.
OEDIPUS: In what would you have me yield?
CHORUS: He has been no silly child in the past.
    He is strong in his oath now.
720   Spare him.
OEDIPUS: Do you know what you ask?
CHORUS: Yes.
OEDIPUS: Tell me then.
CHORUS: He has been your friend before all men's eyes; do not cast him
725   away dishonoured on an obscure conjecture.
OEDIPUS: I would have you know that this request of yours
    really requests my death or banishment.
CHORUS: May the Sun God, king of Gods, forbid! May I die without God's
    blessing, without friends' help, if I had any such thought. But my
730   spirit is broken by my unhappiness for my wasting country; and
    this would but add troubles amongst ourselves to the other troubles.
OEDIPUS: Well, let him go then—if I must die ten times for it,
    or be sent out dishonoured into exile.
    It is your lips that prayed for him I pitied,
735   not his; wherever he is, I shall hate him.
CREON: I see you sulk in yielding and you're dangerous
    when you are out of temper; natures like yours
    are justly heaviest for themselves to bear.
OEDIPUS: Leave me alone! Take yourself off, I tell you.
740 CREON: I'll go, you have not known me, but they have,
    and they have known my innocence.

        [Exit.]

CHORUS: Won't you take him inside, lady?
JOCASTA: Yes, when I've found out what was the matter.
CHORUS: There was some misconceived suspicion of a story, and on the other
745   side the sting of injustice.
JOCASTA: So, on both sides?
CHORUS: Yes.
JOCASTA: What was the story?
CHORUS: I think it best, in the interests of the country, to leave it where it ended.
750 OEDIPUS: You see where you have ended, straight of judgment
    although you are, by softening my anger.
CHORUS: Sir, I have said before and I say again—be sure that I would have been
    proved a madman, bankrupt in sane council, if I should put you away, you
    who steered the country I love safely when she was crazed with troubles. God
755   grant that now, too, you may prove a fortunate guide for us.

JOCASTA: Tell me, my lord, I beg of you, what was it
  that roused your anger so?
OEDIPUS: Yes, I will tell you.
  I honour you more than I honour them.
  It was Creon and the plots he laid against me.
JOCASTA: Tell me—if you can clearly tell the quarrel—
OEDIPUS: Creon says   760
  that I'm the murderer of Laius.
JOCASTA: Of his own knowledge or on information?
OEDIPUS: He sent this rascal prophet to me, since
  he keeps his own mouth clean of any guilt.
JOCASTA: Do not concern yourself about this matter;   765
  listen to me and learn that human beings
  have no part in the craft of prophecy.
  Of that I'll show you a short proof.
  There was an oracle once that came to Laius,—
  I will not say that it was Phoebus' own,   770
  but it was from his servants—and it told him
  that it was fate that he should die a victim
  at the hands of his own son, a son to be born
  of Laius and me. But, see now, he,
  the king, was killed by foreign highway robbers   775
  at a place where three roads meet—so goes the story;
  and for the son—before three days were out
  after his birth King Laius pierced his ankles
  and by the hands of others cast him forth
  upon a pathless hillside. So Apollo   780
  failed to fulfill his oracle to the son,
  that he should kill his father, and to Laius
  also proved false in that the thing he feared,
  death at his son's hands, never came to pass.
  So clear in this case were the oracles,   785
  so clear and false. Give them no heed, I say;
  what God discovers need of, easily
  he shows to us himself.
OEDIPUS: O dear Jocasta,
  as I hear this from you, there comes upon me
  a wandering of the soul—I could run mad.   790
JOCASTA: What trouble is it, that you turn again
  and speak like this?
OEDIPUS: I thought I heard you say
  that Laius was killed at a crossroads.
JOCASTA: Yes, that was how the story went and still
  that word goes round.
OEDIPUS: Where is this place, Jocasta,   795
  where he was murdered?

JOCASTA: Phocis is the country
     and the road splits there, one of two roads from Delphi,
     another comes from Daulia.

OEDIPUS: How long ago is this?

JOCASTA: The news came to the city just before
800   you became king and all men's eyes looked to you.
     What is it, Oedipus, that's in your mind?

OEDIPUS: What have you designed, O Zeus, to do with me?

JOCASTA: What is the thought that troubles your heart?

OEDIPUS: Don't ask me yet—tell me of Laius—
805   How did he look? How old or young was he?

JOCASTA: He was a tall man and his hair was grizzled
     already—nearly white—and in his form
     not unlike you.

OEDIPUS: O God, I think I have
     called curses on myself in ignorance.

810 JOCASTA: What do you mean? I am terrified
     when I look at you.

OEDIPUS: I have a deadly fear
     that the old seer had eyes. You'll show me more
     if you can tell me one more thing.

JOCASTA: I will.
     I'm frightened,—but if I can understand,
     I'll tell you all you ask.

815 OEDIPUS: How was his company?
     Had he few with him when he went this journey,
     or many servants, as would suit a prince?

JOCASTA: In all there were but five, and among them
     a herald; and one carriage for the king.

820 OEDIPUS: It's plain—it's plain—who was it told you this?

JOCASTA: The only servant that escaped safe home.

OEDIPUS: Is he at home now?

JOCASTA: No, when he came home again
     and saw you king and Laius was dead,
     he came to me and touched my hand and begged
825   that I should send him to the fields to be
     my shepherd and so he might see the city
     as far off as he might. So I
     sent him away. He was an honest man,
     as slaves go, and was worthy of far more
830   than what he asked of me.

OEDIPUS: O, how I wish that he could come back quickly!

JOCASTA: He can. Why is your heart so set on this?

OEDIPUS: O dear Jocasta, I am full of fears
     that I have spoken far too much; and therefore
     I wish to see this shepherd.

JOCASTA: He will come;   835
    but, Oedipus, I think I'm worthy too
    to know what it is that disquiets you.
OEDIPUS: It shall not be kept from you, since my mind
    has gone so far with its forebodings. Whom
    should I confide in rather than you, who is there   840
    of more importance to me who have passed
    through such a fortune?
    Polybus was my father, king of Corinth,
    and Merope, the Dorian, my mother.
    I was held greatest of the citizens   845
    in Corinth till a curious chance befell me
    as I shall tell you—curious, indeed,
    but hardly worth the store I set upon it.
    There was a dinner and at it a man,
    a drunken man, accused me in his drink   850
    of being bastard. I was furious
    but held my temper under for that day.
    Next day I went and taxed my parents with it;
    they took the insult very ill from him,
    the drunken fellow who had uttered it.   855
    So I was comforted for their part, but
    still this thing rankled always, for the story
    crept about widely. And I went at last
    to Pytho, though my parents did not know.
    But Phoebus sent me home again unhonoured   860
    in what I came to learn, but he foretold
    other and desperate horrors to befall me,
    that I was fated to lie with my mother,
    and show to daylight an accursed breed
    which men would not endure, and I was doomed   865
    to be murderer of the father that begot me.
    When I heard this I fled, and in the days
    that followed I would measure from the stars
    the whereabouts of Corinth—yes, I fled
    to somewhere where I should not see fulfilled   870
    the infamies told in that dreadful oracle.
    And as I journeyed I came to the place
    where, as you say, this king met with his death.
    Jocasta, I will tell you the whole truth.
    When I was near the branching of the crossroads,   875
    going on foot, I was encountered by
    a herald and a carriage with a man in it,
    just as you tell me. He that led the way
    and the old man himself wanted to thrust me
    out of the road by force. I became angry   880

and struck the coachman who was pushing me.
When the old man saw this he watched his moment,
and as I passed he struck me from his carriage,
full on the head with his two pointed goad.

885   But he was paid in full and presently
my stick had struck him backwards from the car
and he rolled out of it. And then I killed them
all. If it happened there was any tie
of kinship twixt this man and Laius,

890   who is then now more miserable than I,
what man on earth so hated by the Gods,
since neither citizen nor foreigner
may welcome me at home or even greet me,
but drive me out of doors? And it is I,

895   I and no other have so cursed myself.
And I pollute the bed of him I killed
by the hands that killed him. Was I not born evil?
Am I not utterly unclean? I had to fly
and in my banishment not even see

900   my kindred nor set foot in my own country,
or otherwise my fate was to be yoked
in marriage with my mother and kill my father,
Polybus who begot me and had reared me.
Would not one rightly judge and say that on me

905   these things were sent by some malignant God?
O no, no, no—O holy majesty
of God on high, may I not see that day!
May I be gone out of men's sight before
I see the deadly taint of this disaster

910   come upon me.

CHORUS: Sir, we too fear these things. But until you see this man face to face and
hear his story, hope.

OEDIPUS: Yes, I have just this much of hope—to wait until the herdsman comes.

JOCASTA: And when he comes, what do you want with him?

915   OEDIPUS: I'll tell you; if I find that his story is the same as yours, I at least will be
clear of this guilt.

JOCASTA: Why what so particularly did you learn from my story?

OEDIPUS: You said that he spoke of highway *robbers* who killed Laius. Now if he
uses the same number, it was not I who killed him. One man cannot be the

920   same as many. But if he speaks of a man travelling alone, then clearly the
burden of the guilt inclines towards me.

JOCASTA: Be sure, at least, that this was how he told the story. He cannot unsay it
now, for every one in the city heard it—not I alone. But, Oedipus, even if he
diverges from what he said then, he shall never prove that the murder of

925   Laius squares rightly with the prophecy—for Loxias declared that the king
should be killed by his own son. And that poor creature did not kill him

surely,—for he died himself first. So as far as prophecy goes, henceforward I
shall not look to the right hand or the left.

OEDIPUS: Right. But yet, send some one for the peasant to bring him here; do not
neglect it.   930

JOCASTA: I will send quickly. Now let me go indoors. I will do nothing except
what pleases you.

    [*Exeunt.*]

CHORUS: [*Strophe.*] May destiny ever find me
    pious in word and deed
    prescribed by the laws that live on high: 935
    laws begotten in the clear air of heaven,
    whose only father is Olympus;
    no mortal nature brought them to birth,
    no forgetfulness shall lull them to sleep;
    for God is great in them and grows not old.   940

    [*Antistrophe.*]

Insolence breeds the tyrant, insolence
    if it is glutted with a surfeit, unseasonable, unprofitable,
    climbs to the roof-top and plunges
    sheer down to the ruin that must be,
    and there its feet are no service.   945
But I pray that the God may never
    abolish the eager ambition that profits the state.
For I shall never cease to hold the God as our protector.

    [*Strophe.*]

If a man walks with haughtiness
    of hand or word and gives no heed   950
    to Justice and the shrines of Gods
    despises—may an evil doom
    smite him for his ill-starred pride of heart!—
    if he reaps gains without justice
    and will not hold from impiety   955
    and his fingers itch for untouchable things.
When such things are done, what man shall contrive
    to shield his soul from the shafts of the God?
When such deeds are held in honour,
    why should I honour the Gods in the dance?   960

    [*Antistrophe.*]

No longer to the holy place,
    to the navel of earth I'll go
    to worship, nor to Abae
    nor to Olympia,

965   unless the oracles are proved to fit,
    for all men's hands to point at.
    O Zeus, if you are rightly called
    the sovereign lord, all-mastering,
    let this not escape you nor your ever-living power!
970   The oracles concerning Laius
    are old and dim and men regard them not.
    Apollo is nowhere clear in honour; God's service perishes.

          [*Enter* JOCASTA, *carrying garlands.*]

JOCASTA: Princes of the land, I have had the thought to go
    to the Gods' temples, bringing in my hand
975   garlands and gifts of incense, as you see.
    For Oedipus excites himself too much
    at every sort of trouble, not conjecturing,
    like a man of sense, what will be from what was,
    but he is always at the speaker's mercy,
980   when he speaks terrors. I can do no good
    by my advice, and so I came as suppliant
    to you, Lycaean Apollo, who are nearest.
    These are the symbols of my prayer and this
    my prayer: grant us escape free of the curse.
985   Now when we look to him we are all afraid;
    he's pilot of our ship and he is frightened.

          [*Enter* MESSENGER.]

MESSENGER: Might I learn from you, sirs, where is the house of Oedipus? Or best of all, if you know, where is the king himself?

CHORUS: This is his house and he is within doors. This lady is his wife and mother
990   of his children.

MESSENGER: God bless you, lady, and God bless your household! God bless Oedipus' noble wife!

JOCASTA: God bless you, sir, for your kind greeting! What do you want of us that you have come here? What have you to tell us?

995 MESSENGER: Good news, lady. Good for your house and for your husband.

JOCASTA: What is your news? Who sent you to us?

MESSENGER: I come from Corinth and the news I bring will give you pleasure. Perhaps a little pain too.

JOCASTA: What is this news of double meaning?

1000 MESSENGER: The people of the Isthmus will choose Oedipus to be their king. That is the rumour there.

JOCASTA: But isn't their king still old Polybus?

MESSENGER: No. He is in his grave. Death has got him.

JOCASTA: Is that the truth? Is Oedipus' father dead?

1005 MESSENGER: May I die myself if it be otherwise!

JOCASTA: [*To a* SERVANT.] Be quick and run to the King with the news! O oracles of the Gods, where are you now? It was from this man Oedipus fled, lest he should be his murderer! And now he is dead, in the course of nature, and not killed by Oedipus.

[*Enter* OEDIPUS.]

OEDIPUS: Dearest Jocasta, why have you sent for me?   1010

JOCASTA: Listen to this man and when you hear reflect what is the outcome of the holy oracles of the Gods.

OEDIPUS: Who is he? What is his message for me?

JOCASTA: He is from Corinth and he tells us that your father Polybus is dead and gone.   1015

OEDIPUS: What's this you say, sir? Tell me yourself.

MESSENGER: Since this is the first matter you want clearly told: Polybus has gone down to death. You may be sure of it.

OEDIPUS: By treachery or sickness?

MESSENGER: A small thing will put old bodies asleep.   1020

OEDIPUS: So he died of sickness, it seems,—poor old man!

MESSENGER: Yes, and of age—the long years he had measured.

OEDIPUS: Ha! Ha! O dear Jocasta, why should one
    look to the Pythian hearth?[4] Why should one look
    to the birds screaming overhead? They prophesied   1025
    that I should kill my father! But he's dead,
    and hidden deep in earth, and I stand here
    who never laid a hand on spear against him,—
    unless perhaps he died of longing for me,
    and thus I am his murderer. But they,   1030
    the oracles, as they stand—he's taken them
    away with him, they're dead as he himself is,
    and worthless.

JOCASTA: That I told you before now.

OEDIPUS: You did, but I was misled by my fear.

JOCASTA: Then lay no more of them to heart, not one.   1035

OEDIPUS: But surely I must fear my mother's bed?

JOCASTA: Why should man fear since chance is all in all
    for him, and he can clearly foreknow nothing?
    Best to live lightly, as one can, unthinkingly.
    As to your mother's marriage bed,—don't fear it.   1040
    Before this, in dreams too, as well as oracles,
    many a man has lain with his own mother.
    But he to whom such things are nothing bears
    his life most easily.

OEDIPUS: All that you say would be said perfectly   1045
    if she were dead; but since she lives I must
    still fear, although you talk so well, Jocasta.

4. Delphi.

JOCASTA: Still in your father's death there's light of comfort?

OEDIPUS: Great light of comfort; but I fear the living.

1050 MESSENGER: Who is the woman that makes you afraid?

OEDIPUS: Merope, old man, Polybus' wife.

MESSENGER: What about her frightens the queen and you?

OEDIPUS: A terrible oracle, stranger, from the Gods.

MESSENGER: Can it be told? Or does the sacred law

1055 forbid another to have knowledge of it?

OEDIPUS: O no! Once on a time Loxias said

that I should lie with my own mother and

take on my hands the blood of my own father.

And so for these long years I've lived away

1060 from Corinth; it has been to my great happiness;

but yet it's sweet to see the face of parents.

MESSENGER: This was the fear which drove you out of Corinth?

OEDIPUS: Old man, I did not wish to kill my father.

MESSENGER: Why should I not free you from this fear, sir,

1065 since I have come to you in all goodwill?

OEDIPUS: You would not find me thankless if you did.

MESSENGER: Why, it was just for this I brought the news,—

to earn your thanks when you had come safe home.

OEDIPUS: No, I will never come near my parents.

MESSENGER: Son,

1070 it's very plain you don't know what you're doing.

OEDIPUS: What do you mean, old man? For God's sake, tell me.

MESSENGER: If your homecoming is checked by fears like these.

OEDIPUS: Yes, I'm afraid that Phoebus may prove right.

MESSENGER: The murder and the incest?

OEDIPUS: Yes, old man;

that is my constant terror.

1075 MESSENGER: Do you know

that all your fears are empty?

OEDIPUS: How is that,

if they are father and mother and I their son?

MESSENGER: Because Polybus was no kin to you in blood.

OEDIPUS: What, was not Polybus my father?

MESSENGER: No more than I but just so much.

1080 OEDIPUS: How can

my father be my father as much as one

that's nothing to me?

MESSENGER: Neither he nor I

begat you.

OEDIPUS: Why then did he call me son?

MESSENGER: A gift he took you from these hands of mine.

1085 OEDIPUS: Did he love so much what he took from another's hand?

MESSENGER: His childlessness before persuaded him.

OEDIPUS: Was I a child you bought or found when I
   was given to him?
MESSENGER: On Cithaeron's slopes
   in the twisting thickets you were found.
OEDIPUS: And why
   were you a traveller in those parts?
MESSENGER: I was   1090
   in charge of mountain flocks.
OEDIPUS: You were a shepherd?
   A hireling vagrant?
MESSENGER: Yes, but at least at that time
   the man that saved your life, son.
OEDIPUS: What ailed me when you took me in your arms?
MESSENGER: In that your ankles should be witnesses.   1095
OEDIPUS: Why do you speak of that old pain?
MESSENGER: I loosed you;
   the tendons of your feet were pierced and fettered,—
OEDIPUS: My swaddling clothes brought me a rare disgrace.
MESSENGER: So that from this you're called your present name.
OEDIPUS: Was this my father's doing or my mother's?   1100
   For God's sake, tell me.
MESSENGER: I don't know, but he
   who gave you to me has more knowledge than I.
OEDIPUS: You yourself did not find me then? You took me
   from someone else?
MESSENGER: Yes, from another shepherd.
OEDIPUS: Who was he? Do you know him well enough   1105
   to tell?
MESSENGER: He was called Laius' man.
OEDIPUS: You mean the king who reigned here in the old days?
MESSENGER: Yes, he was that man's shepherd.
OEDIPUS: Is he alive
   still, so that I could see him?
MESSENGER: You who live here
   would know that best.
OEDIPUS: Do any of you here   1110
   know of this shepherd whom he speaks about
   in town or in the fields? Tell me. It's time
   that this was found out once for all.
CHORUS: I think he is none other than the peasant
   whom you have sought to see already; but   1115
   Jocasta here can tell us best of that.
OEDIPUS: Jocasta, do you know about this man
   whom we have sent for? Is he the man he mentions?
JOCASTA: Why ask of whom he spoke? Don't give it heed;
   nor try to keep in mind what has been said.   1120

It will be wasted labour.

OEDIPUS: With such clues
I could not fail to bring my birth to light.

JOCASTA: I beg you—do not hunt this out—I beg you,
    if you have any care for your own life.
    What I am suffering is enough.

1125 OEDIPUS: Keep up
    your heart, Jocasta. Though I'm proved a slave,
    thrice slave, and though my mother is thrice slave,
    you'll not be shown to be of lowly lineage.

JOCASTA: O be persuaded by me, I entreat you;
1130   do not do this.

OEDIPUS: I will not be persuaded to let be
    the chance of finding out the whole thing clearly.

JOCASTA: It is because I wish you well that I
    give you this counsel—and it's the best counsel.

1135 OEDIPUS: Then the best counsel vexes me, and has
    for some while since.

JOCASTA: O Oedipus, God help you!
    God keep you from the knowledge of who you are!

OEDIPUS: Here, some one, go and fetch the shepherd for me;
    and let her find her joy in her rich family!

1140 JOCASTA: O Oedipus, unhappy Oedipus!
    that is all I can call you, and the last thing
    that I shall ever call you.

       [*Exit.*]

CHORUS: Why has the queen gone, Oedipus, in wild
    grief rushing from us? I am afraid that trouble
1145   will break out of this silence.

OEDIPUS: Break out what will! I at least shall be
    willing to see my ancestry, though humble.
    Perhaps she is ashamed of my low birth,
    for she has all a woman's high-flown pride.
1150   But I account myself a child of Fortune,
    beneficent Fortune, and I shall not be
    dishonoured. She's the mother from whom I spring;
    the months, my brothers, marked me, now as small,
    and now again as mighty. Such is my breeding,
1155   and I shall never prove so false to it,
    as not to find the secret of my birth.

CHORUS: [*Strophe.*] If I am a prophet and wise of heart
    you shall not fail, Cithaeron,
    by the limitless sky, you shall not!—
1160   to know at tomorrow's full moon
    that Oedipus honours you,

as native to him and mother and nurse at once;
and that you are honoured in dancing by us, as finding favour in sight of our
    king.
Apollo, to whom we cry, find these things pleasing!

    [*Antistrophe.*]

Who was it bore you, child? One of   1165
the long-lived nymphs who lay with Pan[5]—
the father who treads the hills?
Or was she a bride of Loxias, your mother? The grassy slopes
are all of them dear to him. Or perhaps Cyllene's[6] king
or the Bacchants' God[7] that lives on the tops   1170
of the hills received you a gift from some
one of the Helicon Nymphs,[8] with whom he mostly plays?

    [*Enter an* OLD MAN, *led by* OEDIPUS' *servants.*]

OEDIPUS: If some one like myself who never met him
    may make a guess,—I think this is the herdsman,
    whom we were seeking. His old age is consonant   1175
    with the other. And besides, the men who bring him
    I recognize as my own servants. You
    perhaps may better me in knowledge since
    you've seen the man before.
CHORUS: You can be sure
    I recognize him. For if Laius   1180
    had ever an honest shepherd, this was he.
OEDIPUS: You, sir, from Corinth, I must ask you first,
    is this the man you spoke of?
MESSENGER: This is he
    before your eyes.
OEDIPUS: Old man, look here at me
    and tell me what I ask you. Were you ever   1185
    a servant of King Laius?
HERDSMAN: I was,—
    no slave he bought but reared in his own house.
OEDIPUS: What did you do as work? How did you live?
HERDSMAN: Most of my life was spent among the flocks.
OEDIPUS: In what part of the country did you live?   1190
HERDSMAN: Cithaeron and the places near to it.
OEDIPUS: And somewhere there perhaps you knew this man?
HERDSMAN: What was his occupation? Who?
OEDIPUS: This man here

---

5. God of nature; half man, half goat.   6. Mountain reputed to be the birthplace of Hermes, the messenger of the gods.   7. Dionysus, the god of wine.   8. The Muses; nine sister goddesses who presided over poetry, music, and the arts.

have you had any dealings with him?

HERDSMAN: No—

1195   not such that I can quickly call to mind.

MESSENGER: That is no wonder, master. But I'll make him remember what he does not know. For I know, that he well knows the country of Cithaeron, how he with two flocks, I with one kept company for three years—each year half a year—from spring till autumn time and then when winter came I drove my

1200   flocks to our fold home again and he to Laius' steadings. Well—am I right or not in what I said we did?

HERDSMAN: You're right—although it's a long time ago.

MESSENGER: Do you remember giving me a child
  to bring up as my foster child?

HERDSMAN: What's this?
  Why do you ask this question?

1205 MESSENGER: Look old man,
  here he is—here's the man who was that child!

HERDSMAN: Death take you! Won't you hold your tongue?

OEDIPUS: No, no,
  do not find fault with him, old man. Your words
  are more at fault than his.

HERDSMAN: O best of masters,
  how do I give offense?

1210 OEDIPUS: When you refuse
  to speak about the child of whom he asks you.

HERDSMAN: He speaks out of his ignorance, without meaning.

OEDIPUS: If you'll not talk to gratify me, you
  will talk with pain to urge you.

HERDSMAN: O please, sir,
  don't hurt an old man, sir.

1215 OEDIPUS: [To the SERVANTS.]   Here, one of you,
  twist his hands behind him.

HERDSMAN: Why, God help me, why?
  What do you want to know?

OEDIPUS: You gave a child
  to him,—the child he asked you of?

HERDSMAN: I did.
  I wish I'd died the day I did.

OEDIPUS: You will
  unless you tell me truly.

1220 HERDSMAN: And I'll die
  far worse if I should tell you.

OEDIPUS: This fellow
  is bent on more delays, as it would seem.

HERDSMAN: O no, no! I have told you that I gave it.

OEDIPUS: Where did you get this child from? Was it your own or did you get it from another?

HERDSMAN: Not 1225
  my own at all; I had it from some one.
OEDIPUS: One of these citizens? or from what house?
HERDSMAN: O master, please—I beg you, master, please
  don't ask me more.
OEDIPUS: You're a dead man if I
  ask you again.
HERDSMAN: It was one of the children 1230
  of Laius.
OEDIPUS: A slave? Or born in wedlock?
HERDSMAN: O God, I am on the brink of frightful speech.
OEDIPUS: And I of frightful hearing. But I must hear.
HERDSMAN: The child was called his child; but she within,
  your wife would tell you best how all this was. 1235
OEDIPUS: *She* gave it to you?
HERDSMAN: Yes, she did, my lord.
OEDIPUS: To do what with it?
HERDSMAN: Make away with it.
OEDIPUS: She was so hard—its mother?
HERDSMAN: Aye, through fear
  of evil oracles.
OEDIPUS: Which?
HERDSMAN: They said that he
  should kill his parents.
OEDIPUS: How was it that you 1240
  gave it away to this old man?
HERDSMAN: O master,
  I pitied it, and thought that I could send it
  off to another country and this man
  was from another country. But he saved it
  for the most terrible troubles. If you are 1245
  the man he says you are, you're bred to misery.
OEDIPUS: O, O, O, they will all come,
  all come out clearly! Light of the sun, let me
  look upon you no more after today!
  I who first saw the light bred of a match 1250
  accursed, and accursed in my living
  with them I lived with, cursed in my killing.

  [*Exeunt all but the* CHORUS.]

CHORUS: [*Strophe.*] O generations of men, how I
  count you as equal with those who live
  not at all! 1255
  What man, what man on earth wins more
  of happiness than a seeming
  and after that turning away?

1260 Oedipus, you are my pattern of this,
Oedipus, you and your fate!
Luckless Oedipus, whom of all men
I envy not at all.

[*Antistrophe.*]

In as much as he shot his bolt
beyond the others and won the prize
1265 of happiness complete—
O Zeus—and killed and reduced to nought
the hooked taloned maid of the riddling speech,
standing a tower against death for my land:
hence he was called my king and hence
1270 was honoured the highest of all
honours; and hence he ruled
in the great city of Thebes.

[*Strophe.*]

But now whose tale is more miserable?
Who is there lives with a savager fate?
1275 Whose troubles so reverse his life as his?

O Oedipus, the famous prince
for whom a great haven
the same both as father and son
sufficed for generation,
1280 how, O how, have the furrows ploughed
by your father endured to bear you, poor wretch,
and hold their peace so long?

[*Antistrophe.*]

Time who sees all has found you out
against your will; judges your marriage accursed,
1285 begetter and begot at one in it.

O child of Laius,
would I had never seen you.
I weep for you and cry
a dirge of lamentation.

1290 To speak directly, I drew my breath
from you at the first and so now I lull
my mouth to sleep with your name.

[*Enter a* SECOND MESSENGER.]

SECOND MESSENGER: O Princes always honoured by our country,
what deeds you'll hear of and what horrors see,

what grief you'll feel, if you as true born Thebans 1295
care for the house of Labdacus's sons.
Phasis nor Ister cannot purge this house,
I think, with all their streams, such things
it hides, such evils shortly will bring forth
into the light, whether they will or not; 1300
and troubles hurt the most
when they prove self-inflicted.
CHORUS: What we had known before did not fall short
of bitter groaning's worth; what's more to tell?
SECOND MESSENGER: Shortest to hear and tell—our glorious queen 1305
Jocasta's dead.
CHORUS: Unhappy woman! How?
SECOND MESSENGER: By her own hand. The worst of what was done
you cannot know. You did not see the sight.
Yet in so far as I remember it
you'll hear the end of our unlucky queen. 1310
When she came raging into the house she went
straight to her marriage bed, tearing her hair
with both her hands, and crying upon Laius
long dead—Do you remember, Laius,
that night long past which bred a child for us 1315
to send you to your death and leave
a mother making children with her son?
And then she groaned and cursed the bed in which
she brought forth husband by her husband, children
by her own child, an infamous double bond. 1320
How after that she died I do not know,—
for Oedipus distracted us from seeing.
He burst upon us shouting and we looked
to him as he paced frantically around,
begging us always: Give me a sword, I say, 1325
to find this wife no wife, this mother's womb,
this field of double sowing whence I sprang
and where I sowed my children! As he raved
some god showed him the way—none of us there.
Bellowing terribly and led by some 1330
invisible guide he rushed on the two doors,—
wrenching the hollow bolts out of their sockets,
he charged inside. There, there, we saw his wife
hanging, the twisted rope around her neck.
When he saw her, he cried out fearfully 1335
and cut the dangling noose. Then, as she lay,
poor woman, on the ground, what happened after,
was terrible to see. He tore the brooches—
the gold chased brooches fastening her robe—

1340   away from her and lifting them up high
    dashed them on his own eyeballs, shrieking out
    such things as: they will never see the crime
    I have committed or had done upon me!
    Dark eyes, now in the days to come look on
1345   forbidden faces, do not recognize
    those whom you long for—with such imprecations
    he struck his eyes again and yet again
    with the brooches. And the bleeding eyeballs gushed
    and stained his beard—no sluggish oozing drops
1350   but a black rain and bloody hail poured down.

    So it has broken—and not on one head
    but troubles mixed for husband and for wife.
    The fortune of the days gone by was true
    good fortune—but today groans and destruction
1355   and death and shame—of all ills can be named
    not one is missing.
CHORUS: Is he now in any ease from pain?
SECOND MESSENGER: He shouts
    for some one to unbar the doors and show him
    to all the men of Thebes, his father's killer,
1360   his mother's—no I cannot say the word,
    it is unholy—for he'll cast himself,
    out of the land, he says, and not remain
    to bring a curse upon his house, the curse
    he called upon it in his proclamation. But
1365   he wants for strength, aye, and some one to guide him;
    his sickness is too great to bear. You, too,
    will be shown that. The bolts are opening.
    Soon you will see a sight to waken pity
    even in the horror of it.

         [*Enter the blinded* OEDIPUS.]

1370 CHORUS: This is a terrible sight for men to see!
    I never found a worse!
    Poor wretch, what madness came upon you!
    What evil spirit leaped upon your life
    to your ill-luck—a leap beyond man's strength!
1375   Indeed I pity you, but I cannot
    look at you, though there's much I want to ask
    and much to learn and much to see.
    I shudder at the sight of you.
OEDIPUS: O, O,
1380   where am I going? Where is my voice
    borne on the wind to and fro?

Spirit, how far have you sprung?
CHORUS: To a terrible place whereof men's ears
  may not hear, nor their eyes behold it.
OEDIPUS: Darkness!   1385
  Horror of darkness enfolding, resistless, unspeakable visitant sped by an ill
    wind in haste!
  madness and stabbing pain and memory
  of evil deeds I have done!
CHORUS: In such misfortunes it's no wonder
  if double weighs the burden of your grief.   1390
OEDIPUS: My friend,
  you are the only one steadfast, the only one that attends on me;
  you still stay nursing the blind man.
  Your care is not unnoticed. I can know
  your voice, although this darkness is my world.   1395
CHORUS: Doer of dreadful deeds, how did you dare
  so far to do despite to your own eyes?
  what spirit urged you to it?
OEDIPUS: It was Apollo, friends, Apollo,
  that brought this bitter bitterness, my sorrows to completion.   1400
  But the hand that struck me
  was none but my own.
  Why should I see
  whose vision showed me nothing sweet to see?
CHORUS: These things are as you say.   1405
OEDIPUS: What can I see to love?
  What greeting can touch my ears with joy?
  Take me away, and haste—to a place out of the way!
  Take me away, my friends, the greatly miserable,
  the most accursed, whom God too hates   1410
  above all men on earth!
CHORUS: Unhappy in your mind and your misfortune,
  would I had never known you!
OEDIPUS: Curse on the man who took
  the cruel bonds from off my legs, as I lay in the field.   1415
  He stole me from death and saved me,
  no kindly service.
  Had I died then
  I would not be so burdensome to friends.
CHORUS: I, too, could have wished it had been so.   1420
OEDIPUS: Then I would not have come
  to kill my father and marry my mother infamously.
  Now I am godless and child of impurity,
  begetter in the same seed that created my wretched self.
  If there is any ill worse than ill,   1425
  that is the lot of Oedipus.

CHORUS: I cannot say your remedy was good;
    you would be better dead than blind and living.
OEDIPUS: What I have done here was best done—don't tell me
1430   otherwise, do not give me further counsel.
    I do not know with what eyes I could look
    upon my father when I die and go
    under the earth, nor yet my wretched mother—
    those two to whom I have done things deserving
1435   worse punishment than hanging. Would the sight
    of children, bred as mine are, gladden me?
    No, not these eyes, never. And my city,
    its towers and sacred places of the Gods,
    of these I robbed my miserable self
1440   when I commanded all to drive *him* out,
    the criminal since proved by God impure
    and of the race of Laius.
    To this guilt I bore witness against myself—
    with what eyes shall I look upon my people?
1445   No. If there were a means to choke the fountain
    of hearing I would not have stayed my hand
    from locking up my miserable carcase,
    seeing and hearing nothing; it is sweet
    to keep our thoughts out of the range of hurt.

1450   Cithaeron, why did you receive me? why
    having received me did you not kill me straight?
    And so I had not shown to men my birth.

    O Polybus and Corinth and the house,
    the old house that I used to call my father's—
1455   what fairness you were nurse to, and what foulness
    festered beneath! Now I am found to be
    a sinner and a son of sinners. Crossroads,
    and hidden glade, oak and the narrow way
    at the crossroads, that drank my father's blood
1460   offered you by my hands, do you remember
    still what I did as you looked on, and what
    I did when I came here? O marriage, marriage!
    you bred me and again when you had bred
    bred children of your child and showed to men
1465   brides, wives and mothers and the foulest deeds
    that can be in this world of ours.

    Come—it's unfit to say what is unfit
    to do.—I beg of you in God's name hide me
    somewhere outside your country, yes, or kill me,
1470   or throw me into the sea, to be forever
    out of your sight. Approach and deign to touch me

for all my wretchedness, and do not fear.
No man but I can bear my evil doom.
CHORUS: Here Creon comes in fit time to perform
  or give advice in what you ask of us.   1475
  Creon is left sole ruler in your stead.
OEDIPUS: Creon! Creon! What shall I say to him?
  How can I justly hope that he will trust me?
  In what is past I have been proved towards him
  an utter liar.

       [*Enter* CREON.]

CREON: Oedipus, I've come   1480
  not so that I might laugh at you nor taunt you
  with evil of the past. But if you still
  are without shame before the face of men
  reverence at least the flame that gives all life,
  our Lord the Sun, and do not show unveiled   1485
  to him pollution such that neither land
  nor holy rain nor light of day can welcome.

       [*To a* SERVANT.]

Be quick and take him in. It is most decent
that only kin should see and hear the troubles
of kin.
OEDIPUS: I beg you, since you've torn me from   1490
  my dreadful expectations and have come
  in a most noble spirit to a man
  that has used you vilely—do a thing for me.
  I shall speak for your own good, not for my own.
CREON: What do you need that you would ask of me?   1495
OEDIPUS: Drive me from here with all the speed you can
  to where I may not hear a human voice.
CREON: Be sure, I would have done this had not I
  wished first of all to learn from the God the course
  of action I should follow.
OEDIPUS: But his word   1500
  has been quite clear to let the parricide,
  the sinner, die.
CREON: Yes, that indeed was said.
  But in the present need we had best discover
  what we should do.
OEDIPUS: And will you ask about
  a man so wretched?
CREON: Now even you will trust   1505
  the God.
OEDIPUS: So. I command you—and will beseech you—

to her that lies inside that house give burial
as you would have it; she is yours and rightly
you will perform the rites for her. For me—
1510   never let this my father's city have me
living a dweller in it. Leave me live
in the mountains where Cithaeron is, that's called
my mountain, which my mother and my father
while they were living would have made my tomb.
1515   So I may die by their decree who sought
indeed to kill me. Yet I know this much:
no sickness and no other thing will kill me.
I would not have been saved from death if not
for some strange evil fate. Well, let my fate
go where it will.
1520   Creon, you need not care
about my sons; they're men and so wherever
they are, they will not lack a livelihood.
But my two girls—so sad and pitiful—
whose table never stood apart from mine,
1525   and everything I touched they always shared—
O Creon, have a thought for them! And most
I wish that you might suffer me to touch them
and sorrow with them.

        [*Enter* ANTIGONE *and* ISMENE, OEDIPUS' *two daughters.*]

O my lord! O true noble Creon! Can I
1530   really be touching them, as when I saw?
What shall I say?
Yes, I can hear them sobbing—my two darlings!
and Creon has had pity and has sent me
what I loved most?
1535   Am I right?
CREON: You're right: it was I gave you this
because I knew from old days how you loved them
as I see now.
OEDIPUS: God bless you for it, Creon,
and may God guard you better on your road
than he did me!
1540   O children,
where are you? Come here, come to my hands,
a brother's hands which turned your father's eyes,
those bright eyes you knew once, to what you see,
a father seeing nothing, knowing nothing,
1545   begetting you from his own source of life.
I weep for you—I cannot see your faces—

I weep when I think of the bitterness
there will be in your lives, how you must live
before the world. At what assemblages
of citizens will you make one? to what   1550
gay company will you go and not come home
in tears instead of sharing in the holiday?
And when you're ripe for marriage, who will he be,
the man who'll risk to take such infamy
as shall cling to my children, to bring hurt   1555
on them and those that marry with them? What
curse is not there? "Your father killed his father
and sowed the seed where he had sprung himself
and begot you out of the womb that held him."
These insults you will hear. Then who will marry you?   1560
No one, my children; clearly you are doomed
to waste away in barrenness unmarried.
Son of Menoeceus, since you are all the father
left these two girls, and we, their parents, both
are dead to them—do not allow them wander   1565
like beggars, poor and husbandless.
They are of your own blood.
And do not make them equal with myself
in wretchedness; for you can see them now
so young, so utterly alone, save for you only.   1570
Touch my hand, noble Creon, and say yes.
If you were older, children, and were wiser,
there's much advice I'd give you. But as it is,
let this be what you pray: give me a life
wherever there is opportunity   1575
to live, and better life than was my father's.
CREON: Your tears have had enough of scope; now go within the house.
OEDIPUS: I must obey, though bitter of heart.
CREON: In season, all is good.
OEDIPUS: Do you know on what conditions I obey?
CREON: You tell me them,   1580
  and I shall know them when I hear.
OEDIPUS: That you shall send me out
  to live away from Thebes.
CREON: That gift you must ask of the God.
OEDIPUS: But I'm now hated by the Gods.
CREON: So quickly you'll obtain your prayer.
OEDIPUS: You consent then?
CREON: What I do not mean, I do not use to say.
OEDIPUS: Now lead me away from here.
CREON: Let go the children, then, and come.   1585
OEDIPUS: Do not take them from me.

CREON: Do not seek to be master in everything,
for the things you mastered did not follow you throughout your life.

[*As* CREON *and* OEDIPUS *go out.*]

CHORUS: You that live in my ancestral Thebes, behold this Oedipus,—
him who knew the famous riddles and was a man most masterful;
1590   not a citizen who did not look with envy on his lot—
see him now and see the breakers of misfortune swallow him!
Look upon that last day always. Count no mortal happy till
he has passed the final limit of his life secure from pain.

THE END

ca. 429 B.C.

QUESTIONS

1. Summarize the story before the play opens. What actually happens in the play itself? What period of time is covered? How important is setting to this play? In what specific ways?
2. How, exactly, does the chorus function in this play? What is the significance of the chorus being made up of Theban citizens? Which opinions of the chorus are most important to the effects of the play?
3. Characterize Teiresias. How much does the play itself actually tell us about Teiresias? What function does he perform in the plot? in the play's structure?
4. In what specific ways is the plot of *Oedipus the King* tragic?

WRITING SUGGESTIONS

1. In an essay of about three pages, compare Oedipus at the beginning of the play with Oedipus at the end. Explain the differences in terms of tragic form.
2. Try to recount the events of the play from the point of view of Jocasta. In what sense is the play a tragedy for her? Write a persuasive essay in which you argue that the play is Jocasta's story.
3. What are the more significant and distinctive elements in the character of Oedipus? In what sense is he responsible for his fate? In what sense is he a victim? How heroic is he? Write an essay appraising Oedipus's character and assessing his responsibility for the things that befall him.

OSCAR WILDE

The Importance of Being Earnest

CHARACTERS

ALGERNON MONCRIEFF	MISS PRISM
LANE	CECILY CARDEW
ERNEST WORTHING	CANON CHASUBLE
LADY AUGUSTA BRACKNELL	MERRIMAN
GWENDOLEN FAIRFAX	

ACT I

SCENE: *Morning room in* ALGERNON's *flat in Half-Moon Street.*[1]
The room is luxuriously and artistically furnished. The sound of a piano is heard in the adjoining room.

[LANE *is arranging afternoon tea on the table, and after the music has ceased,* ALGERNON *enters.*]

ALGERNON: Did you hear what I was playing, Lane?

LANE: I didn't think it polite to listen, sir.

ALGERNON: I'm sorry for that, for your sake. I don't play accurately—anyone can play accurately—but I play with wonderful expression. As far as the piano is concerned, sentiment is my forte. I keep science for Life.

LANE: Yes, sir.

ALGERNON: And, speaking of the science of Life, have you got the cucumber sandwiches cut for Lady Bracknell?

LANE: Yes, sir. [*Hands them on a salver.*]

ALGERNON: [*Inspects them, takes two, and sits down on the sofa.*] Oh! . . . by the way, Lane, I see from your book that on Thursday night, when Lord Shoreham and Mr. Worthing were dining with me, eight bottles of champagne are entered as having been consumed.

LANE: Yes, sir; eight bottles and a pint.

ALGERNON: Why is it that at a bachelor's establishment the servants invariably drink the champagne? I ask merely for information.

LANE: I attribute it to the superior quality of the wine, sir. I have often observed that in married households the champagne is rarely of a first-rate brand.

ALGERNON: Good heavens! Is marriage so demoralizing as that?

LANE: I believe it *is* a very pleasant state, sir. I have had very little experience of it myself up to the present. I have only been married once. That was in

---

1. Like many of the addresses in the play, Half-Moon Street is in Mayfair, a very fashionable section of London. It runs north from Piccadilly near Hyde Park.

consequence of a misunderstanding between myself and a young person.

ALGERNON: [*Languidly.*] I don't know that I am much interested in your family life, Lane.

LANE: No, sir; it is not a very interesting subject. I never think of it myself.

ALGERNON: Very natural, I am sure. That will do, Lane, thank you.

LANE: Thank you, sir. [LANE *goes out.*]

ALGERNON: Lane's views on marriage seem somewhat lax. Really, if the lower orders don't set us a good example, what on earth is the use of them? They seem, as a class, to have absolutely no sense of moral responsibility.

[*Enter* LANE.]

LANE: Mr. Ernest Worthing.

[*Enter* JACK. LANE *goes out.*]

ALGERNON: How are you, my dear Ernest? What brings you up to town?

JACK: Oh, pleasure, pleasure! What else should bring one anywhere? Eating as usual, I see, Algy!

ALGERNON: [*Stiffly.*] I believe it is customary in good society to take some slight refreshment at five o'clock. Where have you been since last Thursday?

JACK: [*Sitting down on the sofa.*] In the country.

ALGERNON: What on earth do you do there?

JACK: [*Pulling off his gloves.*] When one is in town one amuses oneself. When one is in the country one amuses other people. It is excessively boring.

ALGERNON: And who are the people you amuse?

JACK: [*Airily.*] Oh, neighbors, neighbors.

ALGERNON: Got nice neighbors in your part of Shropshire?

JACK: Perfectly horrid! Never speak to one of them.

ALGERNON: How immensely you must amuse them! [*Goes over and takes sandwich.*] By the way, Shropshire is your county, is it not?

JACK: Eh? Shropshire? Yes, of course.[2] Hallo! Why all these cups? Why cucumber sandwiches? Why such reckless extravagance in one so young? Who is coming to tea?

ALGERNON: Oh! merely Aunt Augusta and Gwendolen.

JACK: How perfectly delightful!

ALGERNON: Yes, that is all very well; but I am afraid Aunt Augusta won't quite approve of your being here.

JACK: May I ask why?

ALGERNON: My dear fellow, the way you flirt with Gwendolen is perfectly disgraceful. It is almost as bad as the way Gwendolen flirts with you.

JACK: I am in love with Gwendolen. I have come up to town expressly to propose to her.

ALGERNON: I thought you had come up for pleasure? . . . I call that business.

---

2. As we learn later, Jack's country place is in Hertfordshire, to the north of London. He is attempting to deceive Algernon by giving a false location to the west, on the Welsh border.

JACK: How utterly unromantic you are!

ALGERNON: I really don't see anything romantic in proposing. It is very romantic to be in love. But there is nothing romantic about a definite proposal. Why, one may be accepted. One usually is, I believe. Then the excitement is all over. The very essence of romance is uncertainty. If ever I get married, I'll certainly try to forget the fact.

JACK: I have no doubt about that, dear Algy. The divorce court was specially invented for people whose memories are so curiously constituted.

ALGERNON: Oh! there is no use speculating on that subject. Divorces are made in heaven— [JACK *puts out his hand to take a sandwich.* ALGERNON *at once interferes.*] Please don't touch the cucumber sandwiches. They are ordered specially for Aunt Augusta. [*Takes one and eats it.*]

JACK: Well, you have been eating them all the time.

ALGERNON: That is quite a different matter. She is my aunt. [*Takes plate from below.*] Have some bread and butter. The bread and butter is for Gwendolen. Gwendolen is devoted to bread and butter.

JACK: [*Advancing to table and helping himself.*] And very good bread and butter it is too.

ALGERNON: Well, my dear fellow, you need not eat as if you were going to eat it all. You behave as if you were married to her already. You are not married to her already, and I don't think you ever will be.

JACK: Why on earth do you say that?

ALGERNON: Well, in the first place, girls never marry the men they flirt with. Girls don't think it right.

JACK: Oh, that is nonsense!

ALGERNON: It isn't. It is a great truth. It accounts for the extraordinary number of bachelors that one sees all over the place. In the second place, I don't give my consent.

JACK: Your consent!

ALGERNON: My dear fellow, Gwendolen is my first cousin. And before I allow you to marry her, you will have to clear up the whole question of Cecily. [*Rings bell.*]

JACK: Cecily! What on earth do you mean? What do you mean, Algy, by Cecily? I don't know anyone of the name of Cecily.

[*Enter* LANE.]

ALGERNON: Bring me that cigarette case Mr. Worthing left in the smoking-room the last time he dined here.

LANE: Yes, sir. [LANE *goes out.*]

JACK: Do you mean to say you have had my cigarette case all this time? I wish to goodness you had let me know. I have been writing frantic letters to Scotland Yard about it. I was very nearly offering a large reward.

ALGERNON: Well, I wish you would offer one. I happen to be more than usually hard up.

JACK: There is no good offering a large reward now that the thing is found.

[*Enter* LANE *with the cigarette case on a salver.* ALGERNON *takes it at once.* LANE *goes out.*]

ALGERNON: I think that is rather mean of you, Ernest, I must say. [*Opens case and examines it.*] However, it makes no matter, for, now that I look at the inscription inside, I find that the thing isn't yours after all.

JACK: Of course it's mine. [*Moving to him.*] You have seen me with it a hundred times, and you have no right whatsoever to read what is written inside. It is a very ungentlemanly thing to read a private cigarette case.

ALGERNON: Oh! it is absurd to have a hard-and-fast rule about what one should read and what one shouldn't. More than half of modern culture depends on what one shouldn't read.

JACK: I am quite aware of the fact, and I don't propose to discuss modern culture. It isn't the sort of thing one should talk of in private. I simply want my cigarette case back.

ALGERNON: Yes; but this isn't your cigarette case. This cigarette case is a present from someone of the name of Cecily, and you said you didn't know anyone of that name.

JACK: Well, if you want to know, Cecily happens to be my aunt.

ALGERNON: Your aunt!

JACK: Yes. Charming old lady she is, too. Lives at Tunbridge Wells.[3] Just give it back to me, Algy.

ALGERNON: [*Retreating to back of sofa.*] But why does she call herself Cecily if she is your aunt and lives at Tunbridge Wells? [*Reading.*] "From little Cecily with her fondest love."

JACK: [*Moving to sofa and kneeling upon it.*] My dear fellow, what on earth is there in that? Some aunts are tall, some aunts are not tall. That is a matter that surely an aunt may be allowed to decide for herself. You seem to think that every aunt should be exactly like your aunt! That is absurd! For heaven's sake give me back my cigarette case. [*Follows* ALGY *round the room.*]

ALGERNON: Yes. But why does your aunt call you her uncle? "From little Cecily, with her fondest love to her dear Uncle Jack." There is no objection, I admit, to an aunt being a small aunt, but why an aunt, no matter what her size may be, should call her own nephew her uncle, I can't quite make out. Besides, your name isn't Jack at all; it is Ernest.

JACK: It isn't Ernest; it's Jack.

ALGERNON: You have always told me it was Ernest. I have introduced you to everyone as Ernest. You answer to the name of Ernest. You look as if your name was Ernest. You are the most earnest looking person I ever saw in my life. It is perfectly absurd your saying that your name isn't Ernest. It's on your cards. Here is one of them. [*Taking it from case.*] "Mr. Ernest Worthing, B. 4, The Albany."[4] I'll keep this as a proof that your name is Ernest if ever you attempt

---

3. A resort town in Kent, to the southeast of London.　　4. An apartment building for single gentlemen on Piccadilly, to the east of Algernon's flat.

to deny it to me, or to Gwendolen, or to anyone else. [*Puts the card in his pocket.*]

JACK: Well, my name is Ernest in town and Jack in the country, and the cigarette case was given to me in the country.

ALGERNON: Yes, but that does not account for the fact that your small Aunt Cecily, who lives at Tunbridge Wells, calls you her dear uncle. Come, old boy, you had much better have the thing out at once.

JACK: My dear Algy, you talk exactly as if you were a dentist. It is very vulgar to talk like a dentist when one isn't a dentist. It produces a false impression.

ALGERNON: Well, that is exactly what dentists always do. Now, go on! Tell me the whole thing. I may mention that I have always suspected you of being a confirmed and secret Bunburyist; and I am quite sure of it now.

JACK: Bunburyist? What on earth do you mean by a Bunburyist?

ALGERNON: I'll reveal to you the meaning of that incomparable expression as soon as you are kind enough to inform me why you are Ernest in town and Jack in the country.

JACK: Well, produce my cigarette case first.

ALGERNON: Here it is. [*Hands cigarette case.*] Now produce your explanation, and pray make it improbable. [*Sits on sofa.*]

JACK: My dear fellow, there is nothing improbable about my explanation at all. In fact it's perfectly ordinary. Old Mr. Thomas Cardew, who adopted me when I was a little boy, made me in his will guardian to his granddaughter, Miss Cecily Cardew. Cecily, who addresses me as her uncle from motives of respect that you could not possibly appreciate, lives at my place in the country under the charge of her admirable governess, Miss Prism.

ALGERNON: Where is that place in the country, by the way?

JACK: That is nothing to you, dear boy. You are not going to be invited. . . . I may tell you candidly that the place is not in Shropshire.

ALGERNON: I suspected that, my dear fellow! I have Bunburyed all over Shropshire on two separate occasions. Now, go on. Why are you Ernest in town and Jack in the country?

JACK: My dear Algy, I don't know whether you will be able to understand my real motives. You are hardly serious enough. When one is placed in the position of guardian, one has to adopt a very high moral tone on all subjects. It's one's duty to do so. And as a high moral tone can hardly be said to conduce very much to either one's health or one's happiness, in order to get up to town I have always pretended to have a younger brother of the name of Ernest, who lives in the Albany, and gets into the most dreadful scrapes. That, my dear Algy, is the whole truth pure and simple.

ALGERNON: The truth is rarely pure and never simple. Modern life would be very tedious if it were either, and modern literature a complete impossibility!

JACK: That wouldn't be at all a bad thing.

ALGERNON: Literary criticism is not your forte, my dear fellow. Don't try it. You should leave that to people who haven't been at a university. They do it so well in the daily papers. What you really are is a Bunburyist. I was quite right in saying you were a Bunburyist. You are one of the most advanced Bunburyists I know.

JACK: What on earth do you mean?

ALGERNON: You have invented a very useful young brother called Ernest, in order that you may be able to come up to town as often as you like. I have invented an invaluable permanent invalid called Bunbury, in order that I may be able to go down into the country whenever I choose. Bunbury is perfectly invaluable. If it wasn't for Bunbury's extraordinary bad health, for instance, I wouldn't be able to dine with you at Willis's[5] tonight, for I have been really engaged to Aunt Augusta for more than a week.

JACK: I haven't asked you to dine with me anywhere tonight.

ALGERNON: I know. You are absurdly careless about sending out invitations. It is very foolish of you. Nothing annoys people so much as not receiving invitations.

JACK: You had much better dine with your Aunt Augusta.

ALGERNON: I haven't the smallest intention of doing anything of the kind. To begin with, I dined there on Monday, and once a week is quite enough to dine with one's own relations. In the second place, whenever I do dine there I am always treated as a member of the family, and sent down with either no woman at all, or two. In the third place, I know perfectly well whom she will place me next to, tonight. She will place me next Mary Farquhar, who always flirts with her own husband across the dinner table. That is not very pleasant. Indeed, it is not even decent . . . and that sort of thing is enormously on the increase. The amount of women in London who flirt with their own husbands is perfectly scandalous. It looks so bad. It is simply washing one's clean linen in public. Besides, now that I know you to be a confirmed Bunburyist, I naturally want to talk to you about Bunburying. I want to tell you the rules.

JACK: I'm not a Bunburyist at all. If Gwendolen accepts me, I am going to kill my brother, indeed I think I'll kill him in any case. Cecily is a little too much interested in him. It is rather a bore. So I am going to get rid of Ernest. And I strongly advise you to do the same with Mr. . . . with your invalid friend who has the absurd name.

ALGERNON: Nothing will induce me to part with Bunbury, and if you ever get married, which seems to me extremely problematic, you will be very glad to know Bunbury. A man who marries without knowing Bunbury has a very tedious time of it.

JACK: That is nonsense. If I marry a charming girl like Gwendolen, and she is the only girl I ever saw in my life that I would marry, I certainly won't want to know Bunbury.

ALGERNON: Then your wife will. You don't seem to realize, that in married life three is company and two is none.

---

5. A well-known restaurant on King Street, off St. James's Street, near Piccadilly.

JACK: [*Sententiously.*] That, my dear young friend, is the theory that the corrupt French drama has been propounding for the last fifty years.[6]

ALGERNON: Yes; and that the happy English home has proved in half the time.

JACK: For heaven's sake, don't try to be cynical. It's perfectly easy to be cynical.

ALGERNON: My dear fellow, it isn't easy to be anything nowadays. There's such a lot of beastly competition about. [*The sound of an electric bell is heard.*] Ah! that must be Aunt Augusta. Only relatives, or creditors, ever ring in that Wagnerian manner.[7] Now, if I get her out of the way for ten minutes, so that you can have an opportunity for proposing to Gwendolen, may I dine with you tonight at Willis's?

JACK: I suppose so, if you want to.

ALGERNON: Yes, but you must be serious about it. I hate people who are not serious about meals. It is so shallow of them.

[*Enter* LANE.]

LANE: Lady Bracknell and Miss Fairfax.

[ALGERNON *goes forward to meet them. Enter* LADY BRACKNELL *and* GWENDOLEN.]

LADY BRACKNELL: Good afternoon, dear Algernon, I hope you are behaving very well.

ALGERNON: I'm feeling very well, Aunt Augusta.

LADY BRACKNELL: That's not quite the same thing. In fact the two things rarely go together. [*Sees* JACK *and bows to him with icy coldness.*]

ALGERNON: [*To* GWENDOLEN.] Dear me, you are smart!

GWENDOLEN: I am always smart! Aren't I, Mr. Worthing?

JACK: You're quite perfect, Miss Fairfax.

GWENDOLEN: Oh! I hope I am not that. It would leave no room for developments, and I intend to develop in many directions. [GWENDOLEN *and* JACK *sit down together in the corner.*]

LADY BRACKNELL: I'm sorry if we are a little late, Algernon, but I was obliged to call on dear Lady Harbury. I hadn't been there since her poor husband's death. I never saw a woman so altered; she looks quite twenty years younger. And now I'll have a cup of tea, and one of those nice cucumber sandwiches you promised me.

ALGERNON: Certainly, Aunt Augusta. [*Goes over to teatable.*]

LADY BRACKNELL: Won't you come and sit here, Gwendolen?

GWENDOLEN: Thanks, mamma, I'm quite comfortable where I am.

ALGERNON: [*Picking up empty plate in horror.*] Good heavens! Lane! Why are there no cucumber sandwiches? I ordered them specially.

---

6. Beginning in the middle of the nineteenth century, French drama produced plays dealing with subjects such as adultery, prostitution, and illegitimacy. The heavily censored English theater either avoided such subjects or dealt with them more circumspectly.   7. Many earlier listeners to the music of Richard Wagner found it extremely loud and, consequently, peremptory in demanding attention.

LANE: [*Gravely.*] There were no cucumbers in the market this morning, sir. I went down twice.

ALGERNON: No cucumbers!

LANE: No, sir. Not even for ready money.

ALGERNON: That will do, Lane, thank you.

LANE: Thank you, sir.

ALGERNON: I am greatly distressed, Aunt Augusta, about there being no cucumbers, not even for ready money.

LADY BRACKNELL: It really makes no matter, Algernon. I had some crumpets with Lady Harbury, who seems to me to be living entirely for pleasure now.

ALGERNON: I hear her hair has turned quite gold from grief.

LADY BRACKNELL: It certainly has changed its color. From what cause I, of course, cannot say. [ALGERNON *crosses and hands tea.*] Thank you. I've quite a treat for you tonight, Algernon. I am going to send you down with Mary Farquhar. She is such a nice woman, and so attentive to her husband. It's delightful to watch them.

ALGERNON: I am afraid, Aunt Augusta, I shall have to give up the pleasure of dining with you tonight after all.

LADY BRACKNELL: [*Frowning.*] I hope not, Algernon. It would put my table completely out. Your uncle would have to dine upstairs. Fortunately he is accustomed to that.

ALGERNON: It is a great bore, and, I need hardly say, a terrible disappointment to me, but the fact is I have just had a telegram to say that my poor friend Bunbury is very ill again. [*Exchanges glances with* JACK.] They seem to think I should be with him.

LADY BRACKNELL: It is very strange. This Mr. Bunbury seems to suffer from curiously bad health.

ALGERNON: Yes; poor Bunbury is a dreadful invalid.

LADY BRACKNELL: Well, I must say, Algernon, that I think it is high time that Mr. Bunbury made up his mind whether he was going to live or to die. This shilly-shallying with the question is absurd. Nor do I in any way approve of the modern sympathy with invalids. I consider it morbid. Illness of any kind is hardly a thing to be encouraged in others. Health is the primary duty of life. I am always telling that to your poor uncle, but he never seems to take much notice . . . as far as any improvement in his ailments goes. I should be obliged if you would ask Mr. Bunbury, from me, to be kind enough not to have a relapse on Saturday, for I rely on you to arrange my music for me. It is my last reception, and one wants something that will encourage conversation, particularly at the end of the season when everyone has practically said whatever they had to say, which, in most cases, was probably not much.

ALGERNON: I'll speak to Bunbury, Aunt Augusta, if he is still conscious, and I think I can promise you he'll be all right by Saturday. Of course the music is a great difficulty. You see, if one plays good music, people don't listen, and if one plays bad music, people don't talk. But I'll run over the program I've drawn out, if you will kindly come into the next room for a moment.

LADY BRACKNELL: Thank you, Algernon. It is very thoughtful of you. [*Rising, and following* ALGERNON.] I'm sure the program will be delightful, after a few expurgations. French songs I cannot possibly allow. People always seem to think that they are improper, and either look shocked, which is vulgar, or laugh, which is worse. But German sounds a thoroughly respectable language, and indeed, I believe is so. Gwendolen, you will accompany me.

GWENDOLEN: Certainly, mamma.

[LADY BRACKNELL *and* ALGERNON *go into the music room,* GWENDOLEN *remains behind.*]

JACK: Charming day it has been, Miss Fairfax.

GWENDOLEN: Pray don't talk to me about the weather, Mr. Worthing. Whenever people talk to me about the weather, I always feel quite certain that they mean something else. And that makes me so nervous.

JACK: I do mean something else.

GWENDOLWN: I thought so. In fact, I am never wrong.

JACK: And I would like to be allowed to take advantage of Lady Bracknell's temporary absence . . .

GWENDOLEN. I would certainly advise you to do so. Mamma has a way of coming back suddenly into a room that I have often had to speak to her about.

JACK: [*Nervously.*] Miss Fairfax, ever since I met you I have admired you more than any girl . . . I have ever met since . . . I met you.

GWENDOLEN: Yes, I am quite aware of the fact. And I often wish that in public, at any rate, you had been more demonstrative. For me you have always had an irresistible fascination. Even before I met you I was far from indifferent to you. [JACK *looks at her in amazement.*] We live, as I hope you know, Mr. Worthing, in an age of ideals. The fact is constantly mentioned in the more expensive monthly magazines, and has reached the provincial pulpits, I am told: and my ideal has always been to love someone of the name of Ernest. There is something in that name that inspires absolute confidence. The moment Algernon first mentioned to me that he had a friend called Ernest, I knew I was destined to love you.

JACK: You really love me, Gwendolen?

GWENDOLEN: Passionately!

JACK: Darling! You don't know how happy you've made me.

GWENDOLEN: My own Ernest!

JACK: But you don't really mean to say that you couldn't love me if my name wasn't Ernest?

GWENDOLEN: But your name is Ernest.

JACK: Yes, I know it is. But supposing it was something else? Do you mean to say you couldn't love me then?

GWENDOLEN: [*Glibly.*] Ah! that is clearly a metaphysical speculation, and like most metaphysical speculations has very little reference at all to the actual facts of real life, as we know them.

JACK: Personally, darling, to speak quite candidly, I don't much care about the name of Ernest . . . I don't think the name suits me at all.

GWENDOLEN: It suits you perfectly. It is a divine name. It has a music of its own. It produces vibrations.

JACK: Well, really, Gwendolen, I must say that I think there are lots of other much nicer names. I think Jack, for instance, a charming name.

GWENDOLEN: Jack? . . . No, there is very little music in the name Jack, if any at all, indeed. It does not thrill. It produces absolutely no vibrations. . . . I have known several Jacks, and they all, without exception, were more than usually plain. Besides, Jack is a notorious domesticity for John! And I pity any woman who is married to a man called John. She would probably never be allowed to know the entrancing pleasure of a single moment's solitude. The only really safe name is Ernest.

JACK: Gwendolen, I must get christened at once—I mean we must get married at once. There is no time to be lost.

GWENDOLEN: Married, Mr. Worthing?

JACK: [Astounded.] Well . . . surely. You know that I love you, and you led me to believe, Miss Fairfax, that you were not absolutely indifferent to me.

GWENDOLEN: I adore you. But you haven't proposed to me yet. Nothing has been said at all about marriage. The subject has not even been touched on.

JACK: Well . . . may I propose to you now?

GWENDOLEN: I think it would be an admirable opportunity. And to spare you any possible disappointment, Mr. Worthing, I think it only fair to tell you quite frankly beforehand that I am fully determined to accept you.

JACK: Gwendolen!

GWENDOLEN: Yes, Mr. Worthing, what have you got to say to me?

JACK: You know what I have got to say to you.

GWENDOLEN: Yes, but you don't say it.

JACK: Gwendolen, will you marry me? [Goes on his knees.]

GWENDOLEN: Of course I will, darling. How long you have been about it! I am afraid you have had very little experience in how to propose.

JACK: My own one, I have never loved anyone in the world but you.

GWENDOLEN: Yes, but men often propose for practice. I know my brother Gerald does. All my girlfriends tell me so. What wonderfully blue eyes you have, Ernest! They are quite, quite blue. I hope you will always look at me just like that, especially when there are other people present.

[Enter LADY BRACKNELL.]

LADY BRACKNELL: Mr. Worthing! Rise, sir, from this semi-recumbent posture. It is most indecorous.

GWENDOLEN: Mamma! [He tries to rise; she restrains him.] I must beg you to retire. This is no place for you. Besides, Mr. Worthing has not quite finished yet.

LADY BRACKNELL: Finished what, may I ask?

GWENDOLEN: I am engaged to Mr. Worthing, mamma.

[They rise together.]

LADY BRACKNELL: Pardon me, you are not engaged to anyone. When you do become engaged to someone, I, or you father, should his health permit him, will inform you of the fact. An engagement should come on a young girl as a surprise, pleasant or unpleasant, as the case may be. It is hardly a matter that she could be allowed to arrange for herself. . . . And now I have a few questions to put to you, Mr. Worthing. While I am making these inquiries, you, Gwendolen, will wait for me below in the carriage.

GWENDOLEN: [*Reproachfully.*] Mamma!

LADY BRACKNELL: In the carriage, Gwendolen! [GWENDOLEN *goes to the door. She and* JACK *blow kisses to each other behind* LADY BRACKNELL*'s back.* LADY BRACKNELL *looks vaguely about as if she could not understand what the noise was. Finally turns round.*] Gwendolen, the carriage!

GWENDOLEN: Yes, mamma. [*Goes out, looking back at* JACK.]

LADY BRACKNELL: [*Sitting down.*] You can take a seat, Mr. Worthing.

[*Looks in her pocket for notebook and pencil.*]

JACK: Thank you, Lady Bracknell, I prefer standing.

LADY BRACKNELL: [*Pencil and notebook in hand.*] I feel bound to tell you that you are not down on my list of eligible young men, although I have the same list as the dear Duchess of Bolton has. We work together, in fact. However, I am quite ready to enter your name, should your answers be what a really affectionate mother requires. Do you smoke?

JACK: Well, yes, I must admit I smoke.

LADY BRACKNELL: I am glad to hear it. A man should always have an occupation of some kind. There are far too many idle men in London as it is. How old are you?

JACK: Twenty-nine.

LADY BRACKNELL: A very good age to be married at. I have always been of opinion that a man who desires to get married should know either everything or nothing. Which do you know?

JACK: [*After some hesitation.*] I know nothing, Lady Bracknell.

LADY BRACKNELL: I am pleased to hear it. I do not approve of anything that tampers with natural ignorance. Ignorance is like a delicate exotic fruit; touch it and the bloom is gone. The whole theory of modern education is radically unsound. Fortunately in England, at any rate, education produces no effect whatsoever. If it did, it would prove a serious danger to the upper classes, and probably lead to acts of violence in Grosvenor Square.[8] What is your income?

JACK: Between seven and eight thousand a year.[9]

LADY BRACKNELL: [*Makes a note in her book.*] In land, or in investments?

JACK: In investments, chiefly.

LADY BRACKNELL: That is satisfactory. What between the duties expected of one during one's lifetime, and the duties exacted from one after one's death, land has ceased to be either a profit or a pleasure. It gives one position, and prevents one from keeping it up. That's all that can be said about land.

JACK: I have a country house with some land, of course, attached to it, about fifteen hundred acres, I believe; but I don't depend on that for my real income. In

---

8. A fashionable location in Mayfair.   9. A considerable income for the time.

fact, as far as I can make out, the poachers are the only people who make anything out of it.

LADY BRACKNELL: A country house! How many bedrooms? Well, that point can be cleared up afterwards. You have a town house, I hope? A girl with a simple, unspoiled nature, like Gwendolen, could hardly be expected to reside in the country.

JACK: Well, I own a house in Belgrave Square,[1] but it is let by the year to Lady Bloxham. Of course, I can get it back whenever I like, at six months' notice.

LADY BRACKNELL: Lady Bloxham? I don't know her.

JACK: Oh, she goes about very little. She is a lady considerably advanced in years.

LADY BRACKNELL: Ah, nowadays that is no guarantee of respectability of character. What number in Belgrave Square?

JACK: 149.

LADY BRACKNELL: [*Shaking her head.*] The unfashionable side. I thought there was something. However, that could easily be altered.

JACK: Do you mean the fashion, or the side?

LADY BRACKNELL: [*Sternly.*] Both, if necessary, I presume. What are your politics?

JACK: Well, I am afraid I really have none. I am a Liberal Unionist.

LADY BRACKNELL: Oh, they count as Tories.[2] They dine with us. Or come in the evening, at any rate. Now to minor matters. Are your parents living?

JACK: I have lost both my parents.

LADY BRACKNELL: Both? To lose one parent may be regarded as a misfortune—to lose *both* seems like carelessness. Who was your father? He was evidently a man of some wealth. Was he born in what the Radical papers call the purple of commerce, or did he rise from the ranks of aristocracy?

JACK: I am afraid I really don't know. The fact is, Lady Bracknell, I said I had lost my parents. It would be nearer the truth to say that my parents seem to have lost me. . . . I don't actually know who I am by birth. I was . . . well, I was found.

LADY BRACKNELL: Found!

JACK: The late Mr. Thomas Cardew, an old gentleman of a very charitable and kindly disposition, found me, and gave me the name of Worthing, because he happened to have a first-class ticket for Worthing in his pocket at the time. Worthing is a place in Sussex. It is a seaside resort.

LADY BRACKNELL: Where did the charitable gentleman who had a first-class ticket for this seaside resort find you?

JACK: [*Gravely.*] In a handbag.

LADY BRACKNELL: A handbag?

JACK: [*Very seriously.*] Yes, Lady Bracknell. I was in a handbag—a somewhat large, black leather handbag, with handles to it—an ordinary handbag, in fact.

LADY BRACKNELL: In what locality did this Mr. James, or Thomas, Cardew come across this ordinary handbag?

---

1. Near the southeast corner of Hyde Park in Belgravia, another fashionable section of London.
2. Members of the Conservative party. Opposed to home rule for Ireland, they joined forces with the Liberal Unionists, who had split from the Liberal party over the issue.

JACK: In the cloak room at Victoria Station.[3] It was given to him in mistake for his own.

LADY BRACKNELL: The cloak room at Victoria Station?

JACK: Yes. The Brighton line.

LADY BRACKNELL: The line is immaterial. Mr. Worthing, I confess I feel somewhat bewildered by what you have just told me. To be born, or at any rate, bred in a handbag, whether it had handles or not, seems to me to display a contempt for the ordinary decencies of family life that reminds one of the worst excesses of the French Revolution. And I presume you know what that unfortunate movement led to? As for the particular locality in which the handbag was found, a cloak room at a railway station might serve to conceal a social indiscretion—has probably, indeed, been used for that purpose before now—but it could hardly be regarded as an assured basis for a recognized position in good society.

JACK: May I ask you then what you would advise me to do? I need hardly say I would do anything in the world to ensure Gwendolen's happiness.

LADY BRACKNELL: I would strongly advise you, Mr. Worthing, to try and acquire some relations as soon as possible, and to make a definite effort to produce at any rate one parent, of either sex, before the season is quite over.

JACK: Well, I don't see how I could possibly manage to do that. I can produce the handbag at any moment, it is in my dressing room at home. I really think that should satisfy you, Lady Bracknell.

LADY BRACKNELL: Me, sir! What has it to do with me? You can hardly imagine that I and Lord Bracknell would dream of allowing our only daughter—a girl brought up with the utmost care—to marry into a cloak room, and form an alliance with a parcel? Good morning, Mr. Worthing!

[LADY BRACKNELL *sweeps out in majestic indignation.*]

JACK: Good morning! [ALGERNON, *from the other room, strikes up the Wedding March.* JACK *looks perfectly furious, and goes to the door.*] For goodness' sake don't play that ghastly tune, Algy! How idiotic you are!

[*The music stops, and* ALGERNON *enters cheerily.*]

ALGERNON: Didn't it go off all right, old boy? You don't mean to say Gwendolen refused you? I know it is a way she has. She is always refusing people. I think it is most ill-natured of her.

JACK: Oh, Gwendolen is as right as a trivet.[4] As far as she is concerned, we are engaged. Her mother is perfectly unbearable. Never met such a Gorgon[5] . . . I don't really know what a Gorgon is like, but I am quite sure that Lady Bracknell is one. In any case, she is a monster, without being a myth, which is rather unfair . . . I beg your pardon, Algy, I suppose I shouldn't talk about your own aunt in that way before you.

---

3. Major railroad terminus in London.   4. A proverbial expression, referring to the solidity of a tripod on its three legs.   5. A mythological creature of horrible aspect, the Gorgon had snakes in place of hair. According to myth, those who looked on a Gorgon were turned to stone by the experience.

ALGERNON: My dear boy, I love hearing my relations abused. It is the only thing that makes me put up with them at all. Relations are simply a tedious pack of people who haven't got the remotest knowledge of how to live, nor the smallest instinct about when to die.

JACK: Oh, that is nonsense!

ALGERNON: It isn't!

JACK: Well, I won't argue about the matter. You always want to argue about things.

ALGERNON: That is exactly what things were originally made for.

JACK: Upon my word, if I thought that, I'd shoot myself . . . [A pause.] You don't think there is any chance of Gwendolen becoming like her mother in about a hundred and fifty years, do you, Algy?

ALGERNON: All women become like their mothers. That is their tragedy. No man does. That's his.

JACK: Is that clever?

ALGERNON: It is perfectly phrased! and quite as true as any observation in civilized life should be.

JACK: I am sick to death of cleverness. Everybody is clever nowadays. You can't go anywhere without meeting clever people. The thing has become an absolute public nuisance. I wish to goodness we had a few fools left.

ALGERNON: We have.

JACK: I should extremely like to meet them. What do they talk about?

ALGERNON: The fools? Oh! about the clever people, of course.

JACK: What fools!

ALGERNON: By the way, did you tell Gwendolen the truth about your being Ernest in town, and Jack in the country?

JACK: [In a very patronizing manner.] My dear fellow, the truth isn't quite the sort of thing one tells to a nice sweet refined girl. What extraordinary ideas you have about the way to behave to a woman!

ALGERNON: The only way to behave to a woman is to make love to her, if she is pretty, and to someone else if she is plain.

JACK: Oh, that is nonsense.

ALGERNON: What about your brother? What about the profligate Ernest?

JACK: Oh, before the end of the week I shall have got rid of him. I'll say he died in Paris of apoplexy. Lots of people die of apoplexy, quite suddenly, don't they?

ALGERNON: Yes, but it's hereditary, my dear fellow. It's a sort of thing that runs in families. You had much better say a severe chill.

JACK: You are sure a severe chill isn't hereditary, or anything of that kind?

ALGERNON: Of course it isn't!

JACK: Very well, then. My poor brother Ernest is carried off suddenly in Paris, by a severe chill. That gets rid of him.

ALGERNON: But I thought you said that . . . Miss Cardew was a little too much interested in your poor brother Ernest? Won't she feel his loss a good deal?

JACK: Oh, that is all right. Cecily is not a silly romantic girl, I am glad to say. She has got a capital appetite, goes on long walks, and pays no attention at all to her lessons.

ALGERNON: I would rather like to see Cecily.

JACK: I will take very good care you never do. She is excessively pretty, and she is only just eighteen.

ALGERNON: Have you told Gwendolen yet that you have an excessively pretty ward who is only just eighteen?

JACK: Oh! one doesn't blurt these things out to people. Cecily and Gwendolen are perfectly certain to be extremely great friends. I'll bet you anything you like that half an hour after they have met, they will be calling each other sister.

ALGERNON: Women only do that when they have called each other a lot of other things first. Now, my dear boy, if we want to get a good table at Willis's, we really must go and dress. Do you know it is nearly seven?

JACK: [Irritably.] Oh! it always is nearly seven.

ALGERNON: Well, I'm hungry.

JACK: I never knew you when you weren't. . . .

ALGERNON: What shall we do after dinner? Go to the theater?

JACK: Oh no! I loathe listening.

ALGERNON: Well, let us go to the club?

JACK: Oh, no! I hate talking.

ALGERNON: Well, we might trot around to the Empire[6] at ten?

JACK: Oh no! I can't bear looking at things. It is so silly.

ALGERNON: Well, what shall we do?

JACK: Nothing!

ALGERNON: It is awfully hard work doing nothing. However, I don't mind hard work where there is no definite object of any kind.

[Enter LANE.]

LANE: Miss Fairfax.

[Enter GWENDOLEN. LANE goes out.]

ALGERNON: Gwendolen, upon my word!

GWENDOLEN: Algy, kindly turn your back. I have something very particular to say to Mr. Worthing.

ALGERNON: Really, Gwendolen, I don't think I can allow this at all.

GWENDOLEN: Algy, you always adopt a strictly immoral attitude towards life. You are not quite old enough to do that.

[ALGERNON retires to the fireplace.]

JACK: My own darling!

GWENDOLEN: Ernest, we may never be married. From the expression on mamma's face I fear we never shall. Few parents nowadays pay any regard to what their children say to them. The old-fashioned respect for the young is fast dying out. Whatever influence I ever had over mamma, I lost at the age of three. But although she may prevent us from becoming man and wife, and I may marry someone else, and marry often, nothing that she can possibly do can alter my eternal devotion to you.

JACK: Dear Gwendolen!

6. The Empire Theatre of Varieties, a music hall on Leicester Square.

GWENDOLEN: The story of your romantic origin, as related to me by mamma, with unpleasing comments, has naturally stirred the deeper fibers of my nature. Your Christian name has an irresistible fascination. The simplicity of your character makes you exquisitely incomprehensible to me. Your town address at the Albany I have. What is your address in the country?

JACK: The Manor House, Woolton, Hertfordshire.

[ALGERNON, *who has been carefully listening, smiles to himself, and writes the address on his shirt-cuff. Then picks up the Railway Guide.*]

GWENDOLEN: There is a good postal service, I suppose? It may be necessary to do something desperate. That of course will require serious consideration. I will communicate with you daily.

JACK: My own one!

GWENDOLEN: How long do you remain in town?

JACK: Till Monday.

GWENDOLEN: Good! Algy, you may turn round now.

ALGERNON: Thanks, I've turned round already.

GWENDOLEN: You may also ring the bell.

JACK: You will let me see you to your carriage, my own darling?

GWENDOLEN: Certainly.

JACK: [*To* LANE, *who now enters.*] I will see Miss Fairfax out.

LANE: Yes, sir.

[JACK *and* GWENDOLEN *go off.* LANE *presents several letters on a salver to* ALGERNON. *It is to be surmised that they are bills, as* ALGERNON, *after looking at the envelopes, tears them up.*]

ALGERNON: A glass of sherry, Lane.

LANE: Yes, sir.

ALGERNON: Tomorrow, Lane, I'm going Bunburying.

LANE: Yes, sir.

ALGERNON: I shall probably not be back till Monday. You can put up my dress clothes, my smoking jacket, and all the Bunbury suits . . .

LANE: Yes, sir. [*Handing sherry.*]

ALGERNON: I hope tomorrow will be a fine day, Lane.

LANE: It never is, sir.

ALGERNON: Lane, you're a perfect pessimist.

LANE: I do my best to give satisfaction, sir.

[*Enter* JACK. LANE *goes off.*]

JACK: There's a sensible, intellectual girl! the only girl I ever cared for in my life. [ALGERNON *is laughing immoderately.*] What on earth are you so amused at?

ALGERNON: Oh, I'm a little anxious about poor Bunbury, that is all.

JACK: If you don't take care, your friend Bunbury will get you into a serious scrape some day.

ALGERNON: I love scrapes. They are the only things that are never serious.

JACK: Oh, that's nonsense, Algy. You never talk anything but nonsense.

ALGERNON: Nobody ever does.

[JACK *looks indignantly at him, and leaves the room.* ALGERNON *lights a cigarette, reads his shirt-cuff, and smiles.*]

ACT-DROP

ACT II

SCENE: *Garden at the Manor House. A flight of gray stone steps leads up to the house. The garden, an old-fashioned one, full of roses. Time of year, July. Basket chairs, and a table covered with books, are set under a large yew tree.*

[MISS PRISM *discovered seated at the table.* CECILY *is at the back watering flowers.*]

MISS PRISM: [*Calling.*] Cecily, Cecily! Surely such a utilitarian occupation as the watering of flowers is rather Moulton's duty than yours? Especially at a moment when intellectual pleasures await you. Your German grammar is on the table. Pray open it at page fifteen. We will repeat yesterday's lesson.

CECILY: [*Coming over very slowly.*] But I don't like German. It isn't at all a becoming language. I know perfectly well that I look quite plain after my German lesson.

MISS PRISM: Child, you know how anxious your guardian is that you should improve yourself in every way. He laid particular stress on your German, as he was leaving for town yesterday. Indeed, he always lays stress on your German when he is leaving for town.

CECILY: Dear Uncle Jack is so very serious! Sometime he is so serious that I think he cannot be quite well.

MISS PRISM: [*Drawing herself up.*] Your guardian enjoys the best of health, and his gravity of demeanor is especially to be commended in one so comparatively young as he is. I know no one who has a higher sense of duty and responsibility.

CECILY: I suppose that is why he often looks a little bored when we three are together.

MISS PRISM: Cecily! I am surprised at you. Mr. Worthing has many troubles in his life. Idle merriment and triviality would be out of place in his conversation. You must remember his constant anxiety about that unfortunate young man his brother.

CECILY: I wish Uncle Jack would allow that unfortunate young man, his brother, to come down here sometimes. We might have a good influence over him, Miss Prism. I am sure you certainly would. You know German, and geology, and things of that kind influence a man very much. [CECILY *begins to write in her diary.*]

MISS PRISM: [*Shaking her head.*] I do not think that even I could produce any effect on a character that according to his own brother's admission is irretrievably weak and vacillating. Indeed I am not sure that I would desire to reclaim him. I am not in favor of this modern mania for turning bad people into good people at a moment's notice. As a man sows so let him reap. You must put away your diary, Cecily. I really don't see why you should keep a diary at all.

CECILY: I keep a diary in order to enter the wonderful secrets of my life. If I didn't write them down I should probably forget all about them.

MISS PRISM: Memory, my dear Cecily, is the diary that we all carry about with us.

CECILY: Yes, but it usually chronicles the things that have never happened, and couldn't possibly have happened. I believe that memory is responsible for nearly all the three-volume novels that Mudie sends us.[7]

MISS PRISM: Do not speak slightingly of the three-volume novel, Cecily. I wrote one myself in earlier days.

CECILY: Did you really, Miss Prism? How wonderfully clever you are! I hope it did not end happily? I don't like novels that end happily. They depress me so much.

MISS PRISM: The good ended happily, and the bad unhappily. That is what fiction means.

CECILY: I suppose so. But it seems very unfair. And was your novel ever published?

MISS PRISM: Alas! no. The manuscript unfortunately was abandoned. I use the word in the sense of lost or mislaid. To your work, child, these speculations are profitless.

CECILY: [Smiling.] But I see dear Dr. Chasuble coming up through the garden.

MISS PRISM: [Rising and advancing.] Dr. Chasuble! This is indeed a pleasure.

[Enter CANON CHASUBLE.]

CHASUBLE: And how are we this morning? Miss Prism, you are, I trust, well?

CECILY: Miss Prism has just been complaining of a slight headache. I think it would do her so much good to have a short stroll with you in the park, Dr. Chasuble.

MISS PRISM: Cecily, I have not mentioned anything about a headache.

CECILY: No, dear Miss Prism, I know that, but I felt instinctively that you had a headache. Indeed I was thinking about that, and not about my German lesson, when the Rector came in.

CHASUBLE: I hope, Cecily, you are not inattentive.

CECILY: Oh, I am afraid I am.

CHASUBLE: That is strange. Were I fortunate enough to be Miss Prism's pupil, I would hang upon her lips. [MISS PRISM glares.] I spoke metaphorically.—My metaphor was drawn from bees. Ahem! Mr. Worthing, I suppose, has not returned from town yet?

MISS PRISM: We do not expect him till Monday afternoon.

CHASUBLE: Ah yes, he usually likes to spend his Sunday in London. He is not one of those whose sole aim is enjoyment, as, by all accounts, that unfortunate young man his brother seems to be. But I must not disturb Egeria[8] and her pupil any longer.

MISS PRISM: Egeria? My name is Laetitia, Doctor.

---

7. From the 1840s to the 1890s most novels were published in three volumes. Because of the resultant price, most readers could not afford to buy copies and obtained them by subscription from lending libraries, of which Mudie's in London was by far the largest.   8. A nymph in classical mythology, famous as the wise counselor of Numa Pompilius, the second of the legendary kings of Rome.

CHASUBLE: [*Bowing.*] A classical allusion merely, drawn from the Pagan authors. I shall see you both no doubt at Evensong?[9]

MISS PRISM: I think, dear Doctor, I will have a stroll with you. I find I have a headache after all, and a walk might do it good.

CHASUBLE: With pleasure, Miss Prism, with pleasure. We might go as far as the schools and back.

MISS PRISM: That would be delightful. Cecily, you will read your Political Economy[1] in my absence. The chapter on the Fall of the Rupee you may omit. It is somewhat too sensational. Even these metallic problems have their melodramatic side. [*Goes down the garden with* CANON CHASUBLE.]

CECILY: [*Picks up books and throws them back on table.*] Horrid Political Economy! Horrid Geography! Horrid, horrid German!

[*Enter* MERRIMAN *with a card on a salver.*]

MERRIMAN: Mr. Ernest Worthing has just driven over from the station. He has brought his luggage with him.

CECILY: [*Takes the card and reads it.*] "Mr. Ernest Worthing, B. 4, The Albany, W." Uncle Jack's brother! Did you tell him Mr. Worthing was in town?

MERRIMAN: Yes, Miss. He seemed very much disappointed. I mentioned that you and Miss Prism were in the garden. He said he was anxious to speak to you privately for a moment.

CECILY. Ask Mr. Ernest Worthing to come here. I suppose you had better talk to the housekeeper about a room for him.

MERRIMAN: Yes, Miss. [MERRIMAN *goes off.*]

CECILY: I have never met any really wicked person before. I feel rather frightened. I am so afraid he will look just like everyone else. [*Enter* ALGERNON, *very gay and debonair.*] He does!

ALGERNON: [*Raising his hat.*] You are my little cousin Cecily, I'm sure.

CECILY: You are under some strange mistake. I am not little. In fact, I believe I am more than usually tall for my age. [ALGERNON *is rather taken aback.*] But I am your cousin Cecily. You, I see from your card, are Uncle Jack's brother, my cousin Ernest, my wicked cousin Ernest.

ALGERNON: Oh! I am not really wicked at all, cousin Cecily. You mustn't think that I am wicked.

CECILY: If you are not, then you have certainly been deceiving us all in a very inexcusable manner. I hope you have not been leading a double life, pretending to be wicked and being really good all the time. That would be hypocrisy.

ALGERNON: [*Looks at her in amazement.*] Oh! Of course I have been rather reckless.

CECILY: I am glad to hear it.

ALGERNON: In fact, now you mention the subject, I have been very bad in my own small way.

CECILY: I don't think you should be so proud of that, though I am sure it must have been very pleasant.

9. Evening church services.   1. That is, book about economics.

ALGERNON: It is much pleasanter being here with you.

CECILY: I can't understand how you are here at all. Uncle Jack won't be back till Monday afternoon.

ALGERNON: That is a great disappointment. I am obliged to go up by the first train on Monday morning. I have a business appointment that I am anxious . . . to miss.

CECILY: Couldn't you miss it anywhere but in London?

ALGERNON: No: the appointment is in London.

CECILY: Well, I know, of course, how important it is not to keep a business engagement, if one wants to retain any sense of the beauty of life, but still I think you had better wait till Uncle Jack arrives. I know he wants to speak to you about your emigrating.

ALGERNON: About my what?

CECILY: Your emigrating. He has gone up to buy your outfit.

ALGERNON: I certainly wouldn't let Jack buy my outfit. He has no taste in neckties at all.

CECILY: I don't think you will require neckties. Uncle Jack is sending you to Australia.

ALGERNON: Australia? I'd sooner die.

CECILY: Well, he said at dinner on Wednesday night, that you would have to choose between this world, the next world, and Australia.

ALGERNON: Oh, well! The accounts I have received of Australia and the next world are not particularly encouraging. This world is good enough for me, cousin Cecily.

CECILY: Yes, but are you good enough for it?

ALGERNON: I'm afraid I'm not that. That is why I want you to reform me. You might make that your mission, if you don't mind, cousin Cecily.

CECILY: I'm afraid I've no time, this afternoon.

ALGERNON: Well, would you mind my reforming myself this afternoon?

CECILY: It is rather Quixotic of you. But I think you should try.

ALGERNON: I will. I feel better already.

CECILY: You are looking a little worse.

ALGERNON: That is because I am hungry.

CECILY: How thoughtless of me. I should have remembered that when one is going to lead an entirely new life, one requires regular and wholesome meals. Won't you come in?

ALGERNON: Thank you. Might I have a buttonhole² first? I never have any appetite unless I have a buttonhole first.

CECILY: A Maréchal Niel? [*Picks up scissors.*]

ALGERNON: No, I'd sooner have a pink rose.

CECILY: Why? [*Cuts a flower.*]

ALGERNON: Because you are like a pink rose, cousin Cecily.

---

2. A flower to be worn on the lapel of a man's coat, in this case the Maréchal Niel, a popular yellow rose of the period.

CECILY: I don't think it can be right for you to talk to me like that. Miss Prism never says such things to me.

ALGERNON: Then Miss Prism is a shortsighted old lady. [CECILY *puts the rose in his buttonhole.*] You are the prettiest girl I ever saw.

CECILY: Miss Prism says that all good looks are a snare.

ALGERNON: They are a snare that every sensible man would like to be caught in.

CECILY: Oh! I don't think I would care to catch a sensible man. I shouldn't know what to talk to him about.

[*They pass into the house.* MISS PRISM *and* DR. CHASUBLE *return.*]

MISS PRISM: You are too much alone, dear Dr. Chasuble. You should get married. A misanthrope I can understand—a womanthrope, never!

CHASUBLE: [*With a scholar's shudder.*] Believe me, I do not deserve so neologistic a phrase. The precept as well as the practice of the Primitive Church was distinctly against matrimony.

MISS PRISM: [*Sententiously.*] That is obviously the reason why the Primitive Church has not lasted up to the present day. And you do not seem to realize, dear Doctor, that by persistently remaining single, a man converts himself into a permanent public temptation. Men should be more careful; this very celibacy leads weaker vessels astray.

CHASUBLE: But is a man not equally attractive when married?

MISS PRISM: No married man is ever attractive except to his wife.

CHASUBLE: And often, I've been told, not even to her.

MISS PRISM: That depends on the intellectual sympathies of the woman. Maturity can always be depended on. Ripeness can be trusted. Young women are green. [DR. CHASUBLE *starts.*] I spoke horticulturally. My metaphor was drawn from fruits. But where is Cecily?

CHASUBLE: Perhaps she followed us to the schools.

[*Enter* JACK *slowly from the back of the garden. He is dressed in the deepest mourning, with crape hat-band and black gloves.*]

MISS PRISM: Mr. Worthing!

CHASUBLE: Mr. Worthing?

MISS PRISM: This is indeed a surprise. We did not look for you till Monday afternoon.

JACK: [*Shakes* MISS PRISM'*s hand in a tragic manner.*] I have returned sooner than I expected. Dr. Chasuble, I hope you are well?

CHASUBLE: Dear Mr. Worthing, I trust this garb of woe does not betoken some terrible calamity?

JACK: My brother.

MISS PRISM: More shameful debts and extravagance?

CHASUBLE: Still leading his life of pleasure?

JACK: [*Shaking his head.*] Dead!

CHASUBLE: Your brother Ernest dead?

JACK: Quite dead.

MISS PRISM: What a lesson for him! I trust he will profit by it.

CHASUBLE: Mr. Worthing, I offer you my sincere condolence. You have at least the consolation of knowing that you were always the most generous and forgiving of brothers.

JACK: Poor Ernest! He had many faults, but it is a sad, sad blow.

CHASUBLE: Very sad indeed. Were you with him at the end?

JACK: No. He died abroad; in Paris, in fact. I had a telegram last night from the manager of the Grand Hotel.

CHASUBLE: Was the cause of death mentioned?

JACK: A severe chill, it seems.

MISS PRISM: As a man sows, so shall he reap.

CHASUBLE: [*Raising his hand.*] Charity, dear Miss Prism, charity! None of us are perfect. I myself am peculiarly susceptible to drafts. Will the interment take place here?

JACK: No. He seemed to have expressed a desire to be buried in Paris.

CHASUBLE: In Paris! [*Shakes his head.*] I fear that hardly points to any very serious state of mind at the last. You would no doubt wish me to make some slight allusion to this tragic domestic affliction next Sunday. [JACK *presses his hand convulsively.*] My sermon on the meaning of the manna in the wilderness can be adapted to almost any occasion, joyful, or, as in the present case, distressing. [*All sigh.*] I have preached it at harvest celebrations, christenings, confirmations, on days of humiliation and festal days. The last time I delivered it was in the Cathedral, as a charity sermon on behalf of the Society for the Prevention of Discontent among the Upper Orders. The Bishop, who was present, was much struck by some of the analogies I drew.

JACK: Ah! That reminds me, you mentioned christenings, I think, Dr. Chasuble? I suppose you know how to christen all right? [DR. CHASUBLE *looks astounded.*] I mean, of course, you are continually christening, aren't you?

MISS PRISM: It is, I regret to say, one of the Rector's most constant duties in this parish. I have often spoken to the poorer classes on the subject. But they don't seem to know what thrift is.

CHASUBLE: But is there any particular infant in whom you are interested, Mr. Worthing? Your brother was, I believe, unmarried, was he not?

JACK: Oh yes.

MISS PRISM: [*Bitterly.*] People who live entirely for pleasure usually are.

JACK: But it is not for any child, dear Doctor. I am very fond of children. No! the fact is, I would like to be christened myself, this afternoon, if you have nothing better to do.

CHASUBLE: But surely, Mr. Worthing, you have been christened already?

JACK: I don't remember anything about it.

CHASUBLE: But have you any grave doubts on the subject?

JACK: I certainly intend to have. Of course I don't know if the thing would bother you in any way, or if you think I am a little too old now.

CHASUBLE: Not at all. The sprinkling, and, indeed, the immersion of adults is a perfectly canonical practice.

JACK: Immersion!

CHASUBLE: You need have no apprehensions. Sprinkling is all that is necessary, or indeed I think advisable. Our weather is so changeable. At what hour would you wish the ceremony performed?

JACK: Oh, I might trot round about five if that would suit you.

CHASUBLE: Perfectly, perfectly! In fact I have two similar ceremonies to perform at that time. A case of twins that occurred recently in one of the outlying cottages on your own estate. Poor Jenkins the carter, a most hard-working man.

JACK: Oh! I don't see much fun in being christened along with other babies. It would be childish. Would half-past five do?

CHASUBLE: Admirably! Admirably! [*Takes out watch.*] And now, dear Mr. Worthing, I will not intrude any longer into a house of sorrow. I would merely beg you not to be too much bowed down by grief. What seem to us bitter trials are often blessings in disguise.

MISS PRISM: This seems to me a blessing of an extremely obvious kind.

[*Enter* CECILY *from the house.*]

CECILY: Uncle Jack! Oh, I am pleased to see you back. But what horrid clothes you have got on! Do go and change them.

MISS PRISM: Cecily!

CHASUBLE: My child! my child!

[CECILY *goes towards* JACK; *he kisses her brow in a melancholy manner.*]

CECILY: What is the matter, Uncle Jack? Do look happy! You look as if you had toothache, and I have got such a surprise for you. Who do you think is in the dining room? Your brother!

JACK: Who?

CECILY: Your brother Ernest. He arrived about half an hour ago.

JACK: What nonsense! I haven't got a brother!

CECILY: Oh, don't say that. However badly he may have behaved to you in the past he is still your brother. You couldn't be so heartless as to disown him. I'll tell him to come out. And you will shake hands with him, won't you, Uncle Jack? [*Runs back into the house.*]

CHASUBLE: These are very joyful tidings.

MISS PRISM: After we had all been resigned to his loss, his sudden return seems to me peculiarly distressing.

JACK: My brother is in the dining room? I don't know what it all means. I think it is perfectly absurd. [*Enter* ALGERNON *and* CECILY *hand in hand. They come slowly up to* JACK.] Good heavens! [*Motions* ALGERNON *away.*]

ALGERNON: Brother John, I have come down from town to tell you that I am very sorry for all the trouble I have given you, and that I intend to lead a better life in the future. [JACK *glares at him and does not take his hand.*]

CECILY: Uncle Jack, you are not going to refuse your own brother's hand?

JACK: Nothing will induce me to take his hand. I think his coming down here disgraceful. He knows perfectly well why.

CECILY: Uncle Jack, do be nice. There is some good in everyone. Ernest has just been telling me about his poor invalid friend Mr. Bunbury whom he goes to visit so often. And surely there must be much good in one who is kind to an invalid, and leaves the pleasures of London to sit by a bed of pain.

JACK: Oh! he has been talking about Bunbury, has he?

CECILY: Yes, he has told me all about poor Mr. Bunbury, and his terrible state of health.

JACK: Bunbury! Well, I won't have him talk to you about Bunbury or about anything else. It is enough to drive one perfectly frantic.

ALGERNON: Of course I admit that the faults were all on my side. But I must say that I think that Brother John's coldness to me is peculiarly painful. I expected a more enthusiastic welcome, especially considering it is the first time I have come here.

CECILY: Uncle Jack, if you don't shake hands with Ernest, I will never forgive you.

JACK: Never forgive me?

CECILY: Never, never, never!

JACK: Well, this is the last time I shall ever do it. [*Shakes hands with* ALGERNON *and glares.*]

CHASUBLE: It's pleasant, is it not, to see so perfect a reconciliation? I think we might leave the two brothers together.

MISS PRISM: Cecily, you will come with us.

CECILY: Certainly, Miss Prism. My little task of reconciliation is over.

CHASUBLE: You have done a beautiful action today, dear child.

MISS PRISM: We must not be premature in our judgments.

CECILY: I feel very happy.

[*They all go off.*]

JACK: You young scoundrel, Algy, you must get out of this place as soon as possible. I don't allow any Bunburying here.

[*Enter* MERRIMAN.]

MERRIMAN: I have put Mr. Ernest's things in the room next to yours, sir. I suppose that is all right?

JACK: What?

MERRIMAN: Mr. Ernest's luggage, sir. I have unpacked it and put it in the room next to your own.

JACK: His luggage?

MERRIMAN: Yes, sir. Three portmanteaus, a dressing case, two hat-boxes, and a large luncheon basket.

ALGERNON: I am afraid I can't stay more than a week this time.

JACK: Merriman, order the dogcart[3] at once. Mr. Ernest has been suddenly called back to town.

MERRIMAN: Yes, sir. [*Goes back into the house.*]

---

3. A light, two-wheeled carriage, usually drawn by one horse; it has two transverse seats positioned back to back.

ALGERNON: What a fearful liar you are, Jack. I have not been called back to town at all.

JACK: Yes, you have.

ALGERNON: I haven't heard anyone call me.

JACK: Your duty as a gentleman calls you back.

ALGERNON: My duty as a gentleman has never interfered with my pleasures in the smallest degree.

JACK: I can quite understand that.

ALGERNON: Well, Cecily is a darling.

JACK: You are not to talk of Miss Cardew like that. I don't like it.

ALGERNON: Well, I don't like your clothes. You look perfectly ridiculous in them. Why on earth don't you go up and change? It is perfectly childish to be in deep mourning for a man who is actually staying for a whole week with you in your house as a guest. I call it grotesque.

JACK: You are certainly not staying with me for a whole week as a guest or anything else. You have got to leave . . . by the four-five train.

ALGERNON: I certainly won't leave you so long as you are in mourning. It would be most unfriendly. If I were in mourning you would stay with me, I suppose. I should think it very unkind if you didn't.

JACK: Well, will you go if I change my clothes?

ALGERNON: Yes, if you are not too long. I never saw anybody take so long to dress, and with such little result.

JACK: Well, at any rate, that is better than being always overdressed as you are.

ALGERNON: If I am occasionally a little overdressed, I make up for it by being always immensely overeducated.

JACK: Your vanity is ridiculous, your conduct an outrage, and your presence in my garden utterly absurd. However, you have got to catch the four-five, and I hope you will have a pleasant journey back to town. This Bunbury-ing, as you call it, has not been a great success for you. [*Goes into the house.*]

ALGERNON: I think it has been a great success. I'm in love with Cecily, and that is everything. [*Enter* CECILY *at the back of the garden. She picks up the can and begins to water the flowers.*] But I must see her before I go, and make arrangements for another Bunbury. Ah, there she is.

CECILY: Oh, I merely came back to water the roses. I thought you were with Uncle Jack.

ALGERNON: He's gone to order the dogcart for me.

CECILY: Oh, is he going to take you for a nice drive?

ALGERNON: He's going to send me away.

CECILY: Then have we got to part?

ALGERNON: I am afraid so. It's very painful parting.

CECILY: It is always painful to part from people whom one has known for a very brief space of time. The absence of old friends one can endure with equanim-ity. But even a momentary separation from anyone to whom one has just been introduced is almost unbearable.

ALGERNON: Thank you.

[*Enter* MERRIMAN.]

MERRIMAN: The dogcart is at the door, sir. [ALGERNON *looks appealingly at* CECILY.]
CECILY: It can wait, Merriman . . . for . . . five minutes.
MERRIMAN: Yes, Miss. [*Exit* MERRIMAN.]
ALGERNON: I hope, Cecily, I shall not offend you if I state quite frankly and openly
    that you seem to me to be in every way the visible personification of absolute
    perfection.
CECILY: I think your frankness does you great credit, Ernest. If you will allow me
    I will copy your remarks into my diary. [*Goes over to table and begins writing
    in diary.*]
ALGERNON: Do you really keep a diary? I'd give anything to look at it. May I?
CECILY: Oh no. [*Puts her hand over it.*] You see, it is simply a very young girl's record
    of her own thoughts and impressions, and consequently meant for publica-
    tion. When it appears in volume form I hope you will order a copy. But pray,
    Ernest, don't stop. I delight in taking down from dictation. I have reached
    "absolute perfection." You can go on. I am quite ready for more.
ALGERNON: [*Somewhat taken aback.*] Ahem! Ahem!
CECILY: Oh, don't cough, Ernest. When one is dictating one should speak fluently
    and not cough. Besides, I don't know how to spell a cough. [*Writes as* ALGER-
    NON *speaks.*]
ALGERNON: [*Speaking very rapidly.*] Cecily, ever since I first looked upon your won-
    derful and incomparable beauty, I have dared to love you wildly, passion-
    ately, devotedly, hopelessly.
CECILY: I don't think that you should tell me that you love me wildly, passionately,
    devotedly, hopelessly. Hopelessly doesn't seem to make much sense, does it?
ALGERNON: Cecily!

[*Enter* MERRIMAN.]

MERRIMAN: The dogcart is waiting, sir.
ALGERNON: Tell it to come round next week, at the same hour.
MERRIMAN: [*Looks at* CECILY, *who makes no sign.*] Yes, sir. [MERRIMAN *retires.*]
CECILY: Uncle Jack would be very much annoyed if he knew you were staying on
    till next week, at the same hour.
ALGERNON: Oh, I don't care about Jack. I don't care for anybody in the whole world
    but you. I love you, Cecily. You will marry me, won't you?
CECILY: You silly boy! Of course. Why, we have been engaged for the last three
    months.
ALGERNON: For the last three months?
CECILY: Yes, it will be exactly three months on Thursday.
ALGERNON: But how did we become engaged?
CECILY: Well, ever since dear Uncle Jack first confessed to us that he had a younger
    brother who was very wicked and bad, you of course have formed the chief
    topic of conversation between myself and Miss Prism. And of course a man
    who is much talked about is always very attractive. One feels there must be

something in him after all. I daresay it was foolish of me, but I fell in love with you, Ernest.

ALGERNON: Darling! And when was the engagement actually settled?

CECILY: On the 14th of February last. Worn out by your entire ignorance of my existence, I determined to end the matter one way or the other, and after a long struggle with myself I accepted you under this dear old tree here. The next day I bought this little ring in your name, and this is the little bangle with the true lovers' knot I promised you always to wear.

ALGERNON: Did I give you this? It's very pretty, isn't it?

CECILY: Yes, you've wonderfully good taste, Ernest. It's the excuse I've always given for your leading such a bad life. And this is the box in which I keep all your dear letters. [*Kneels at table, opens box, and produces letters tied up with blue ribbon.*]

ALGERNON: My letters! But my own sweet Cecily, I have never written you any letters.

CECILY: You need hardly remind me of that, Ernest. I remember only too well that I was forced to write your letters for you. I always wrote three times a week, and sometimes oftener.

ALGERNON: Oh, do let me read them, Cecily?

CECILY: Oh, I couldn't possibly. They would make you far too conceited. [*Replaces box.*] The three you wrote me after I had broken off the engagement are so beautiful, and so badly spelled, that even now I can hardly read them without crying a little.

ALGERNON: But was our engagement ever broken off?

CECILY: Of course it was. On the 22nd of last March. You can see the entry if you like. [*Shows diary.*] "Today I broke off my engagement with Ernest. I feel it is better to do so. The weather still continues charming."

ALGERNON: But why on earth did you break it off? What had I done? I had done nothing at all. Cecily, I am very much hurt indeed to hear you broke it off. Particularly when the weather was so charming.

CECILY: It would hardly have been a really serious engagement if it hadn't been broken off at least once. But I forgave you before the week was out.

ALGERNON: [*Crossing to her, and kneeling.*] What a perfect angel you are, Cecily.

CECILY: You dear romantic boy. [*He kisses her, she puts her fingers through his hair.*] I hope your hair curls naturally, does it?

ALGERNON: Yes, darling, with a little help from others.

CECILY: I am so glad.

ALGERNON: You'll never break off our engagement again, Cecily?

CECILY: I don't think I could break it off now that I have actually met you. Besides, of course, there is the question of your name.

ALGERNON: Yes, of course. [*Nervously.*]

CECILY: You must not laugh at me, darling, but it had always been a girlish dream of mine to love someone whose name was Ernest. [ALGERNON *rises*, CECILY *also.*] There is something in that name that seems to inspire absolute confidence. I pity any poor married woman whose husband is not called Ernest.

ALGERNON: But, my dear child, do you mean to say you could not love me if I had some other name?

CECILY: But what name?

ALGERNON: Oh, any name you like—Algernon—for instance . . .

CECILY: But I don't like the name of Algernon.

ALGERNON: Well, my own dear, sweet, loving little darling, I really can't see why you should object to the name of Algernon. It is not at all a bad name. In fact, it is rather an aristocratic name. Half of the chaps who get into the Bankruptcy Court are called Algernon. But seriously, Cecily . . . [*Moving to her.*] . . . if my name was Algy, couldn't you love me?

CECILY: [*Rising.*] I might respect you, Ernest, I might admire your character, but I fear that I should not be able to give you my undivided attention.

ALGERNON: Ahem! Cecily! [*Picking up hat.*] Your Rector here is, I suppose, thoroughly experienced in the practice of all the rites and ceremonials of the Church?

CECILY: Oh, yes. Dr. Chasuble is a most learned man. He has never written a single book, so you can imagine how much he knows.

ALGERNON: I must see him at once on a most important christening—I mean on most important business.

CECILY: Oh!

ALGERNON: I shan't be away more than half an hour.

CECILY: Considering that we have been engaged since February the 14th, and that I only met you today for the first time, I think it is rather hard that you should leave me for so long a period as half an hour. Couldn't you make it twenty minutes?

ALGERNON: I'll be back in no time. [*Kisses her and rushes down the garden.*]

CECILY: What an impetuous boy he is! I like his hair so much. I must enter his proposal in my diary.

[*Enter* MERRIMAN.]

MERRIMAN: A Miss Fairfax has just called to see Mr. Worthing. On very important business, Miss Fairfax states.

CECILY: Isn't Mr. Worthing in his library?

MERRIMAN: Mr. Worthing went over in the direction of the rectory some time ago.

CECILY: Pray ask the lady to come out here; Mr. Worthing is sure to be back soon. And you can bring tea.

MERRIMAN: Yes, Miss. [*Goes out.*]

CECILY: Miss Fairfax! I suppose one of the many good elderly women who are associated with Uncle Jack in some of his philanthropic work in London. I don't quite like women who are interested in philanthropic work. I think it is so forward of them.

[*Enter* MERRIMAN.]

MERRIMAN: Miss Fairfax.

[*Enter* GWENDOLEN. *Exit* MERRIMAN.]

CECILY: [*Advancing to meet her.*] Pray let me introduce myself to you. My name is Cecily Cardew.

GWENDOLEN: Cecily Cardew? [*Moving to her and shaking hands.*] What a very sweet name! Something tells me that we are going to be great friends. I like you already more than I can say. My first impressions of people are never wrong.

CECILY: How nice of you to like me so much after we have known each other such a comparatively short time. Pray sit down.

GWENDOLEN: [*Still standing up.*] I may call you Cecily, may I not?

CECILY: With pleasure!

GWENDOLEN: And you will always call me Gwendolen, won't you?

CECILY: If you wish.

GWENDOLEN: Then that is all quite settled, is it not?

CECILY: I hope so. [*A pause. They both sit down together.*]

GWENDOLEN: Perhaps this might be a favorable opportunity for my mentioning who I am. My father is Lord Bracknell. You have never heard of papa, I suppose?

CECILY: I don't think so.

GWENDOLEN: Outside the family circle, papa, I am glad to say, is entirely unknown. I think that is quite as it should be. The home seems to me to be the proper sphere for the man. And certainly once a man begins to neglect his domestic duties he becomes painfully effeminate, does he not? And I don't like that. It makes men so very attractive. Cecily, mamma, whose views on education are remarkably strict, has brought me up to be extremely shortsighted; it is part of her system; so do you mind my looking at you through my glasses?

CECILY: Oh! not at all, Gwendolen. I am very fond of being looked at.

GWENDOLEN: [*After examining* CECILY *carefully through a lorgnette.*] You are here on a short visit, I suppose.

CECILY: Oh no! I live here.

GWENDOLEN: [*Severely.*] Really? Your mother, no doubt, or some female relative of advanced years, resides here also?

CECILY: Oh no! I have no mother, nor, in fact, any relations.

GWENDOLEN: Indeed?

CECILY: My dear guardian, with the assistance of Miss Prism, has the arduous task of looking after me.

GWENDOLEN: Your guardian?

CECILY: Yes, I am Mr. Worthing's ward.

GWENDOLEN: Oh! It is strange he never mentioned to me that he had a ward. How secretive of him! He grows more interesting hourly. I am not sure, however, that the news inspires me with feelings of unmixed delight. [*Rising and going to her.*] I am very fond of you, Cecily; I have liked you ever since I met you! But I am bound to state that now that I know that you are Mr. Worthing's ward, I cannot help expressing a wish you were—well just a little older than you seem to be—and not quite so very alluring in appearance. In fact, if I may speak candidly——

CECILY: Pray do! I think that whenever one has anything unpleasant to say, one should always be quite candid.

GWENDOLEN: Well, to speak with perfect candor, Cecily, I wish that you were fully forty-two, and more than usually plain for your age. Ernest has a strong upright nature. He is the very soul of truth and honor. Disloyalty would be as impossible to him as deception. But even men of the noblest possible moral character are extremely susceptible to the influence of the physical charms of others. Modern, no less than ancient history, supplies us with many most painful examples of what I refer to. If it were not so, indeed, history would be quite unreadable.

CECILY: I beg your pardon, Gwendolen, did you say Ernest?

GWENDOLEN: Yes.

CECILY: Oh, but it is not Mr. Ernest Worthing who is my guardian. It is his brother—his elder brother.

GWENDOLEN: [*Sitting down again.*] Ernest never mentioned to me that he had a brother.

CECILY: I am sorry to say they have not been on good terms for a long time.

GWENDOLEN: Ah! that accounts for it. And now that I think of it I have never heard any man mention his brother. The subject seems distasteful to most men. Cecily, you have lifted a load from my mind. I was growing almost anxious. It would have been terrible if any cloud had come across a friendship like ours, would it not? Of course you are quite, quite sure that it is not Mr. Ernest Worthing who is your guardian?

CECILY: Quite sure. [*A pause.*] In fact, I am going to be his.

GWENDOLEN: [*Inquiringly.*] I beg your pardon?

CECILY: [*Rather shy and confidingly.*] Dearest Gwendolen, there is no reason why I should make a secret of it to you. Our little county newspaper is sure to chronicle the fact next week. Mr. Ernest Worthing and I are engaged to be married.

GWENDOLEN: [*Quite politely, rising.*] My darling Cecily, I think there must be some slight error. Mr. Ernest Worthing is engaged to me. The announcement will appear in the *Morning Post* on Saturday at the latest.

CECILY: [*Very politely, rising.*] I am afraid you must be under some misconception. Ernest proposed to me exactly ten minutes ago. [*Shows diary.*]

GWENDOLEN: [*Examines diary through her lorgnette carefully.*] It is certainly very curious, for he asked me to be his wife yesterday afternoon at 5:30. If you would care to verify the incident, pray do so. [*Produces diary of her own.*] I never travel without my diary. One should always have something sensational to read in the train. I am so sorry, dear Cecily, if it is any disappointment to you, but I am afraid *I* have the prior claim.

CECILY: It would distress me more than I can tell you, dear Gwendolen, if it caused you any mental or physical anguish, but I feel bound to point out that since Ernest proposed to you he clearly has changed his mind.

GWENDOLEN: [*Meditatively.*] If the poor fellow has been entrapped into any foolish promise I shall consider it my duty to rescue him at once, and with a firm hand.

CECILY: [*Thoughtfully and sadly.*] Whatever unfortunate entanglement my dear boy may have got into, I will never reproach him with it after we are married.

GWENDOLEN: Do you allude to me, Miss Cardew, as an entanglement? You are presumptuous. On an occasion of this kind it becomes more than a moral duty to speak one's mind. It becomes a pleasure.

CECILY: Do you suggest, Miss Fairfax, that I entrapped Ernest into an engagement? How dare you? This is no time for wearing the shallow mask of manners. When I see a spade I call it a spade.

GWENDOLEN: [*Satirically.*] I am glad to say that I have never seen a spade. It is obvious that our social spheres have been widely different.

[*Enter* MERRIMAN, *followed by the footman. He carries a salver, tablecloth, and plate stand.* CECILY *is about to retort. The presence of the servants exercises a restraining influence, under which both girls chafe.*]

MERRIMAN: Shall I lay tea here as usual, Miss?

CECILY: [*Sternly, in a calm voice.*] Yes, as usual.

[MERRIMAN *begins to clear table and lay cloth. A long pause.* CECILY *and* GWENDOLEN *glare at each other.*]

GWENDOLEN: Are there many interesting walks in the vicinity, Miss Cardew?

CECILY: Oh! yes! a great many. From the top of one of the hills quite close one can see five counties.

GWENDOLEN: Five counties! I don't think I should like that. I hate crowds.

CECILY: [*Sweetly.*] I suppose that is why you live in town?

[GWENDOLEN *bites her lip, and beats her foot nervously with her parasol.*]

GWENDOLEN: [*Looking round.*] Quite a well-kept garden this is, Miss Cardew.

CECILY: So glad you like it, Miss Fairfax.

GWENDOLEN: I had no idea there were any flowers in the country.

CECILY: Oh, flowers are as common here, Miss Fairfax, as people are in London.

GWENDOLEN: Personally I cannot understand how anybody manages to exist in the country, if anybody who is anybody does. The country always bores me to death.

CECILY: Ah! This is what the newspapers call agricultural depression, is it not? I believe the aristocracy are suffering very much from it just at present. It is almost an epidemic amongst them, I have been told. May I offer you some tea, Miss Fairfax?

GWENDOLEN: [*With elaborate politeness.*] Thank you. [*Aside.*] Detestable girl! But I require tea!

CECILY: [*Sweetly.*] Sugar?

GWENDOLEN: [*Superciliously.*] No, thank you. Sugar is not fashionable any more.

[CECILY *looks angrily at her, takes up the tongs and puts four lumps of sugar into the cup.*]

CECILY: [*Severely.*] Cake or bread and butter?

GWENDOLEN: [*In a bored manner.*] Bread and butter, please. Cake is rarely seen at the best houses nowadays.

CECILY: [*Cuts a very large slice of cake, and puts it on the tray.*] Hand that to Miss Fairfax.

[MERRIMAN *does so, and goes out with footman.* GWENDOLEN *drinks the tea and makes a grimace. Puts down cup at once, reaches out her hand to the bread and butter, looks at it, and finds it is cake. Rises in indignation.*]

GWENDOLEN: You have filled my tea with lumps of sugar, and though I asked most distinctly for bread and butter, you have given me cake. I am known for the gentleness of my disposition, and the extraordinary sweetness of my nature, but I warn you, Miss Cardew, you may go too far.

CECILY: [*Rising.*] To save my poor, innocent, trusting boy from the machinations of any other girl there are no lengths to which I would not go.

GWENDOLEN: From the moment I saw you I distrusted you. I felt that you were false and deceitful. I am never deceived in such matters. My first impressions of people are invariably right.

CECILY: It seems to me, Miss Fairfax, that I am trespassing on your valuable time. No doubt you have many other calls of a similar character to make in the neighborhood.

[*Enter* JACK.]

GWENDOLEN: [*Catching sight of him.*] Ernest! My own Ernest!

JACK: Gwendolen! Darling! [*Offers to kiss her.*]

GWENDOLEN: [*Drawing back.*] A moment! May I ask if you are engaged to be married to this young lady? [*Points to* CECILY.]

JACK: [*Laughing.*] To dear little Cecily! Of course not! What could have put such an idea into your pretty little head?

GWENDOLEN: Thank you. You may! [*Offers her cheek.*]

CECILY: [*Very sweetly.*] I knew there must be some misunderstanding, Miss Fairfax. The gentleman whose arm is at present round your waist is my dear guardian, Mr. John Worthing.

GWENDOLEN: I beg your pardon?

CECILY: This is Uncle Jack.

GWENDOLEN: [*Receding.*] Jack! Oh!

[*Enter* ALGERNON.]

CECILY: Here is Ernest.

ALGERNON: [*Goes straight over to* CECILY *without noticing anyone else.*] My own love! [*Offers to kiss her.*]

CECILY: [*Drawing back.*] A moment, Ernest! May I ask you—are you engaged to be married to this young lady?

ALGERNON: [*Looking round.*] To what young lady? Good heavens! Gwendolen!

CECILY: Yes! to good heavens, Gwendolen, I mean to Gwendolen.

ALGERNON: [*Laughing.*] Of course not! What could have put such an idea into your pretty little head?

CECILY: Thank you. [*Presenting her cheek to be kissed.*] You may. [ALGERNON *kisses her.*]

GWENDOLEN: I felt there was some slight error, Miss Cardew. The gentleman who is now embracing you is my cousin, Mr. Algernon Moncrieff.

CECILY: [*Breaking away from* ALGERNON.] Algernon Moncrieff! Oh! [*The two girls move towards each other and put their arms round each other's waists as if for protection.*] Are you called Algernon?

ALGERNON: I cannot deny it.

CECILY: Oh!

GWENDOLEN: Is your name really John?

JACK: [*Standing rather proudly.*] I could deny it if I liked, I could deny anything if I liked. But my name certainly is John. It has been John for years.

CECILY: [*To* GWENDOLEN.] A gross deception has been practiced on both of us.

GWENDOLEN: My poor wounded Cecily!

CECILY: My sweet wronged Gwendolen!

GWENDOLEN: [*Slowly and seriously.*] You will call me sister, will you not?

[*They embrace.* JACK *and* ALGERNON *groan and walk up and down.*]

CECILY: [*Rather brightly.*] There is just one question I would like to be allowed to ask my guardian.

GWENDOLEN: An admirable idea! Mr. Worthing, there is just one question I would like to be permitted to put to you. Where is your brother Ernest? We are both engaged to be married to your brother Ernest, so it is a matter of some importance to us to know where your brother Ernest is at present.

JACK: [*Slowly and hesitatingly.*] Gwendolen—Cecily—it is very painful for me to be forced to speak the truth. It is the first time in my life that I have ever been reduced to such a painful position, and I am really quite inexperienced in doing anything of the kind. However I will tell you quite frankly that I have no brother Ernest. I have no brother at all. I never had a brother in my life, and certainly have not the smallest intention of ever having one in the future.

CECILY: [*Surprised.*] No brother at all?

JACK: [*Cheerily.*] None!

GWENDOLEN: [*Severely.*] Had you never a brother of any kind?

JACK: [*Pleasantly.*] Never. Not even of any kind.

GWENDOLEN: I am afraid it is quite clear, Cecily, that neither of us is engaged to be married to anyone.

CECILY: It is not a very pleasant position for a young girl suddenly to find herself in. Is it?

GWENDOLEN: Let us go into the house. They will hardly venture to come after us there.

CECILY: No, men are so cowardly, aren't they?

[*They retire into the house with scornful looks.*]

JACK: This ghastly state of things is what you call Bunburying, I suppose?

ALGERNON: Yes, and a perfectly wonderful Bunbury it is. The most wonderful Bunbury I have ever had in my life.

JACK: Well, you've no right whatsoever to Bunbury here.

ALGERNON: That is absurd. One has a right to Bunbury anywhere one chooses. Every serious Bunburyist knows that.

JACK: Serious Bunburyist! Good heavens!

ALGERNON: Well, one must be serious about something, if one wants to have any amusement in life. I happen to be serious about Bunburying. What on earth you are serious about I haven't got the remotest idea. About everything, I should fancy. You have such an absolutely trivial nature.

JACK: Well, the only small satisfaction I have in the whole of this wretched business is that your friend Bunbury is quite exploded. You won't be able to run down to the country quite so often as you used to do, dear Algy. And a very good thing too.

ALGERNON: Your brother is a little off-color, isn't he, dear Jack? You won't be able to disappear to London quite so frequently as your wicked custom was. And not a bad thing either.

JACK: As for your conduct towards Miss Cardew, I must say that your taking in a sweet, simple, innocent girl like that is quite inexcusable. To say nothing of the fact that she is my ward.

ALGERNON: I can see no possible defense at all for your deceiving a brilliant, clever, thoroughly experienced young lady like Miss Fairfax. To say nothing of the fact that she is my cousin.

JACK: I wanted to be engaged to Gwendolen, that is all. I love her.

ALGERNON: Well, I simply wanted to be engaged to Cecily. I adore her.

JACK: There is certainly no chance of your marrying Miss Cardew.

ALGERNON: I don't think there is much likelihood, Jack, of you and Miss Fairfax being united.

JACK: Well, that is no business of yours.

ALGERNON: If it was my business, I wouldn't talk about it. [*Begins to eat muffins.*] It is very vulgar to talk about one's business. Only people like stockbrokers do that, and then merely at dinner parties.

JACK: How can you sit there, calmly eating muffins when we are in this horrible trouble, I can't make out. You seem to me to be perfectly heartless.

ALGERNON: Well, I can't eat muffins in an agitated manner. The butter would probably get on my cuffs. One should always eat muffins quite calmly. It is the only way to eat them.

JACK: I say it's perfectly heartless your eating muffins at all, under the circumstances.

ALGERNON: When I am in trouble, eating is the only thing that consoles me. Indeed, when I am in really great trouble, as anyone who knows me intimately will tell you, I refuse everything except food and drink. At the present moment I am eating muffins because I am unhappy. Besides, I am particularly fond of muffins. [*Rising.*]

JACK: [*Rising.*] Well, that is no reason why you should eat them all in that greedy way. [*Takes muffins from* ALGERNON.]

ALGERNON: [*Offering tea cake.*] I wish you would have tea cake instead. I don't like tea cake.

JACK: Good heavens! I suppose a man may eat his own muffins in his own garden.

ALGERNON: But you have just said it was perfectly heartless to eat muffins.

JACK: I said it was perfectly heartless of you, under the circumstances. That is a very different thing.

ALGERNON: That may be. But the muffins are the same. [*He seizes the muffin dish from* JACK.]

JACK: Algy, I wish to goodness you would go.

ALGERNON: You can't possibly ask me to go without having some dinner. It's absurd. I never go without my dinner. No one ever does, except vegetarians and people like that. Besides I have just made arrangements with Dr. Chasuble to be christened at a quarter to six under the name of Ernest.

JACK: My dear fellow, the sooner you give up that nonsense the better. I made arrangements this morning with Dr. Chasuble to be christened myself at 5:30, and I naturally will take the name of Ernest. Gwendolen would wish it. We can't both be christened Ernest. It's absurd. Besides, I have a perfect right to be christened if I like. There is no evidence at all that I ever have been christened by anybody. I should think it extremely probable I never was, and so does Dr. Chasuble. It is entirely different in your case. You have been christened already.

ALGERNON: Yes, but I have not been christened for years.

JACK: Yes, but you have been christened. That is the important thing.

ALGERNON: Quite so. So I know my constitution can stand it. If you are not quite sure about your ever having been christened, I must say I think it rather dangerous your venturing on it now. It might make you very unwell. You can hardly have forgotten that someone very closely connected with you was very nearly carried off this week in Paris by a severe chill.

JACK: Yes, but you said yourself that a severe chill was not hereditary.

ALGERNON: It usen't to be, I know—but I daresay it is now. Science is always making wonderful improvements in things.

JACK: [*Picking up the muffin dish.*] Oh, that is nonsense; you are always talking nonsense.

ALGERNON: Jack, you are at the muffins again! I wish you wouldn't. There are only two left. [*Takes them.*] I told you I was particularly fond of muffins.

JACK: But I hate tea cake.

ALGERNON: Why on earth then do you allow tea cake to be served up for your guests? What ideas you have of hospitality!

JACK: Algernon! I have already told you to go. I don't want you here. Why don't you go!

ALGERNON: I haven't quite finished my tea yet! and there is still one muffin left.

[JACK *groans, and sinks into a chair.* ALGERNON *still continues eating.*]

ACT-DROP

ACT III

SCENE: *Morning room at the Manor House.*

[GWENDOLEN *and* CECILY *are at the window, looking out into the garden.*]

GWENDOLEN: The fact that they did not follow us at once into the house, as anyone else would have done, seems to me to show that they have some sense of shame left.
CECILY: They have been eating muffins. That looks like repentance.
GWENDOLEN: [*After a pause.*] They don't seem to notice us at all. Couldn't you cough?
CECILY: But I haven't got a cough.
GWENDOLEN: They're looking at us. What effrontery!
CECILY: They're approaching. That's very forward of them.
GWENDOLEN: Let us preserve a dignified silence.
CECILY: Certainly. It's the only thing to do now.

[*Enter* JACK *followed by* ALGERNON. *They whistle some dreadful popular air from a British Opera.*]

GWENDOLEN: This dignified silence seems to produce an unpleasant effect.
CECILY: A most distasteful one.
GWENDOLEN: But we will not be the first to speak.
CECILY: Certainly not.
GWENDOLEN: Mr. Worthing, I have something very particular to ask you. Much depends on your reply.
CECILY: Gwendolen, your common sense is invaluable. Mr. Moncrieff, kindly answer me the following question. Why did you pretend to be my guardian's brother?
ALGERNON: In order that I might have an opportunity of meeting you.
CECILY: [*To* GWENDOLEN.] That certainly seems a satisfactory explanation, does it not?
GWENDOLEN: Yes, dear, if you can believe him.
CECILY: I don't. But that does not affect the wonderful beauty of his answer.
GWENDOLEN: True. In matters of grave importance, style, not sincerity is the vital thing. Mr. Worthing, what explanation can you offer to me for pretending to have a brother? Was it in order that you might have an opportunity of coming up to town to see me as often as possible?
JACK: Can you doubt it, Miss Fairfax?
GWENDOLEN: I have the gravest doubts upon the subject. But I intend to crush

them. This is not the moment for German skepticism.[4] [*Moving to* CECILY.] Their explanations appear to be quite satisfactory, especially Mr. Worthing's. That seems to me to have the stamp of truth upon it.

CECILY: I am more than content with what Mr. Moncrieff said. His voice alone inspires one with absolute credulity.

GWENDOLEN: Then you think we should forgive them?

CECILY: Yes. I mean no.

GWENDOLEN: True! I had forgotten. There are principles at stake that one cannot surrender. Which of us should tell them? The task is not a pleasant one.

CECILY: Could we not both speak at the same time?

GWENDOLEN: An excellent idea! I nearly always speak at the same time as other people. Will you take the time from me?

CECILY: Certainly. [GWENDOLEN *beats time with uplifted finger.*]

GWENDOLEN AND CECILY: [*Speaking together.*] Your Christian names are still an insuperable barrier. That is all!

JACK AND ALGERNON: [*Speaking together.*] Our Christian names! Is that all? But we are going to be christened this afternoon.

GWENDOLEN: [*To* JACK.] For my sake you are prepared to do this terrible thing?

JACK: I am.

CECILY: [*To* ALGERNON.] To please me you are ready to face this fearful ordeal?

ALGERNON: I am!

GWENDOLEN: How absurd to talk of the equality of the sexes! Where questions of self-sacrifice are concerned, men are infinitely beyond us.

JACK: We are. [*Clasps hands with* ALGERNON.]

CECILY: They have moments of physical courage of which we women know absolutely nothing.

GWENDOLEN: [*To* JACK.] Darling!

ALGERNON: [*To* CECILY.] Darling. [*They fall into each other's arms.*]

[*Enter* MERRIMAN. *When he enters he coughs loudly, seeing the situation.*]

MERRIMAN: Ahem! Ahem! Lady Bracknell!

JACK: Good heavens!

[*Enter* LADY BRACKNELL. *The couples separate in alarm. Exit* MERRIMAN.]

LADY BRACKNELL: Gwendolen! What does this mean?

GWENDOLEN: Merely that I am engaged to be married to Mr. Worthing, mamma.

LADY BRACKNELL: Come here. Sit down. Sit down immediately. Hesitation of any kind is a sign of mental decay in the young, of physical weakness in the old. [*Turns to* JACK.] Apprised, sir, of my daughter's sudden flight by her trusty maid, whose confidence I purchased by means of a small coin, I followed her at once by a luggage train. Her unhappy father is, I am glad to say, under the

---

4. A reference to such philosophical movements as the Materialism of Ludwig Feuerbach (1804–1872) and such theological movements as the "Higher Criticism," which subjected the Bible to the same kind of study as that accorded other books.

impression that she is attending a more than usually lengthy lecture by the University Extension Scheme on the Influence of a permanent income on Thought. I do not propose to undeceive him. Indeed I have never undeceived him on any question. I would consider it wrong. But of course, you will clearly understand that all communication between yourself and my daughter must cease immediately from this moment. On this point, as indeed on all points, I am firm.

JACK: I am engaged to be married to Gwendolen, Lady Bracknell!

LADY BRACKNELL: You are nothing of the kind, sir. And now, as regards Algernon! . . . Algernon!

ALGERNON: Yes, Aunt Augusta.

LADY BRACKNELL: May I ask if it is in this house that your invalid friend Mr. Bunbury resides?

ALGERNON: [*Stammering.*] Oh! No! Bunbury doesn't live here. Bunbury is somewhere else at present. In fact, Bunbury is dead.

LADY BRACKNELL: Dead! When did Mr. Bunbury die? His death must have been extremely sudden.

ALGERNON: [*Airily.*] Oh! I killed Bunbury this afternoon. I mean poor Bunbury died this afternoon.

LADY BRACKNELL: What did he die of?

ALGERNON: Bunbury? Oh, he was quite exploded.

LADY BRACKNELL: Exploded! Was he the victim of a revolutionary outrage? I was not aware that Mr. Bunbury was interested in social legislation. If so, he is well punished for his morbidity.

ALGERNON: My dear Aunt Augusta, I mean he was found out! The doctors found out that Bunbury could not live, that is what I mean—so Bunbury died.

LADY BRACKNELL: He seems to have had great confidence in the opinion of his physicians. I am glad, however, that he made up his mind at the last to some definite course of action, and acted under proper medical advice. And now that we have finally got rid of this Mr. Bunbury, may I ask, Mr. Worthing, who is that young person whose hand my nephew Algernon is now holding in what seems to me a peculiarly unnecessary manner?

JACK: That lady is Miss Cecily Cardew, my ward.

[LADY BRACKNELL *bows coldly to* CECILY.]

ALGERNON: I am engaged to be married to Cecily, Aunt Augusta.

LADY BRACKNELL: I beg your pardon?

CECILY: Mr. Moncrieff and I are engaged to be married, Lady Bracknell.

LADY BRACKNELL: [*With a shiver, crossing to the sofa and sitting down.*] I do not know whether there is anything peculiarly exciting in the air of this particular part of Hertfordshire, but the number of engagements that go on seems to me considerably above the proper average that statistics have laid down for our guidance. I think some preliminary inquiry on my part would not be out of place. Mr. Worthing, is Miss Cardew at all connected with any of the larger railway stations in London? I merely desire information. Until yesterday I had no idea that there were any families or persons whose origin was a terminus.

[JACK *looks perfectly furious, but restrains himself.*]

JACK: [*In a clear, cold voice.*] Miss Cardew is the granddaughter of the late Mr. Thomas Cardew of 149, Belgrave Square, S.W.; Gervase Park, Dorking, Surrey; and the Sporran, Fifeshire, N.B.[5]

LADY BRACKNELL: That sounds not unsatisfactory. Three addresses always inspire confidence, even in tradesmen. But what proof have I of their authenticity?

JACK: I have carefully preserved the Court Guides of the period. They are open to your inspection, Lady Bracknell.

LADY BRACKNELL: [*Grimly.*] I have known strange errors in that publication.

JACK: Miss Cardew's family solicitors are Messrs. Markby, Markby, and Markby.

LADY BRACKNELL: Markby, Markby, and Markby? A firm of the very highest position in their profession. Indeed I am told that one of the Mr. Markbys is occasionally to be seen at dinner parties. So far I am satisfied.

JACK: [*Very irritably.*] How extremely kind of you, Lady Bracknell! I have also in my possession, you will be pleased to hear, certificates of Miss Cardew's birth, baptism, whooping cough, registration, vaccination, confirmation, and the measles; both the German and the English variety.

LADY BRACKNELL: Ah! A life crowded with incident, I see; though perhaps somewhat too exciting for a young girl. I am not myself in favor of premature experiences. [*Rises, looks at her watch.*] Gwendolen! the time approaches for our departure. We have not a moment to lose. As a matter of form, Mr. Worthing, I had better ask you if Miss Cardew has any little fortune?

JACK: Oh! about a hundred and thirty thousand pounds in the Funds.[6] That is all. Good-bye, Lady Bracknell. So pleased to have seen you.

LADY BRACKNELL: [*Sitting down again.*] A moment, Mr. Worthing. A hundred and thirty thousand pounds! And in the Funds! Miss Cardew seems to me a most attractive young lady, now that I look at her. Few girls of the present day have any really solid qualities, any of the qualities that last, and improve with time. We live, I regret to say, in an age of surfaces. [*To* CECILY.] Come over here, dear. [CECILY *goes across.*] Pretty child! your dress is sadly simple, and your hair seems almost as Nature might have left it. But we can soon alter all that. A thoroughly experienced French maid produces a really marvelous result in a very brief space of time. I remember recommending one to young Lady Lancing, and after three months her own husband did not know her.

JACK: [*Aside.*] And after six months nobody knew her.

LADY BRACKNELL: [*Glares at* JACK *for a few moments. Then bends, with a practiced smile, to* CECILY.] Kindly turn round, sweet child. [CECILY *turns completely round.*] No, the side view is what I want. [CECILY *presents her profile.*] Yes, quite as I

---

5. In addition to his London residence in Belgrave Square (already referred to in act 1), Mr. Cardew maintained establishments in the south of England (Dorking, Surrey) and in Scotland (Fifeshire; N.B.: North Britain).   6. Stock of the British National Debt.

expected. There are distinct social possibilities in your profile. The two weak points in our age are its want of principle and its want of profile. The chin a little higher, dear. Style largely depends on the way the chin is worn. They are worn very high, just at present. Algernon!

ALGERNON: Yes, Aunt Augusta!

LADY BRACKNELL: There are distinct social possibilities in Miss Cardew's profile.

ALGERNON: Cecily is the sweetest, dearest, prettiest girl in the whole world. And I don't care twopence about social possibilities.

LADY BRACKNELL: Never speak disrespectfully of Society, Algernon. Only people who can't get into it do that. [*To* CECILY.] Dear child, of course you know that Algernon has nothing but his debts to depend upon. But I do not approve of mercenary marriages. When I married Lord Bracknell I had no fortune of any kind. But I never dreamed for a moment of allowing that to stand in my way. Well, I suppose I must give my consent.

ALGERNON: Thank you, Aunt Augusta.

LADY BRACKNELL: Cecily, you may kiss me!

CECILY: [*Kisses her.*] Thank you, Lady Bracknell.

LADY BRACKNELL: You may also address me as Aunt Augusta for the future.

CECILY: Thank you, Aunt Augusta.

LADY BRACKNELL: The marriage, I think, had better take place quite soon.

ALGERNON: Thank you, Aunt Augusta.

CECILY: Thank you, Aunt Augusta.

LADY BRACKNELL: To speak frankly, I am not in favor of long engagements. They give people the opportunity of finding out each other's character before marriage, which I think is never advisable.

JACK: I beg your pardon for interrupting you, Lady Bracknell, but this engagement is quite out of the question. I am Miss Cardew's guardian, and she cannot marry without my consent until she comes of age. That consent I absolutely decline to give.

LADY BRACKNELL: Upon what grounds may I ask? Algernon is an extremely, I may almost say an ostentatiously, eligible young man. He has nothing, but he looks everything. What more can one desire?

JACK: It pains me very much to have to speak frankly to you, Lady Bracknell, about your nephew, but the fact is that I do not approve at all of his moral character. I suspect him of being untruthful.

[ALGERNON *and* CECILY *look at him in indignant amazement.*]

LADY BRACKNELL: Untruthful! My nephew Algernon? Impossible! He is an Oxonian.[7]

JACK: I fear there can be no possible doubt about the matter. This afternoon, during my temporary absence in London on an important question of romance, he obtained admission to my house by means of the false pretense of being my brother. Under an assumed name he drank, I've just been informed by the

7. A graduate of Oxford University.

butler, an entire pint bottle of my Perrier-Jouet, Brut, '89;[8] a wine I was specially reserving for myself. Continuing his disgraceful deception, he succeeded in the course of the afternoon in alienating the affections of my only ward. He subsequently stayed to tea, and devoured every single muffin. And what makes his conduct all the more heartless is, that he was perfectly well aware from the first that I have no brother, that I never had a brother, and that I don't intend to have a brother, not even of any kind. I distinctly told him so myself yesterday afternoon.

LADY BRACKNELL: Ahem! Mr. Worthing, after careful consideration I have decided entirely to overlook my nephew's conduct to you.

JACK: That is very generous of you, Lady Bracknell. My own decision, however, is unalterable. I decline to give my consent.

LADY BRACKNELL: [*To* CECILY.] Come here, sweet child. [CECILY *goes over*.] How old are you, dear?

CECILY: Well, I am really only eighteen, but I always admit to twenty when I go to evening parties.

LADY BRACKNELL: You are perfectly right in making some slight alteration. Indeed, no woman should ever be quite accurate about her age. It looks so calculating. . . . [*In a meditative manner*.] Eighteen, but admitting to twenty at evening parties. Well, it will not be very long before you are of age and free from the restraints of tutelage. So I don't think your guardian's consent is, after all, a matter of any importance.

JACK: Pray excuse me, Lady Bracknell, for interrupting you again, but it is only fair to tell you that according to the terms of her grandfather's will Miss Cardew does not come legally of age till she is thirty-five.

LADY BRACKNELL: That does not seem to me to be a grave objection. Thirty-five is a very attractive age. London society is full of women of the very highest birth who have, of their own free choice, remained thirty-five for years. Lady Dumbleton is an instance in point. To my own knowledge she has been thirty-five ever since she arrived at the age of forty, which was many years ago now. I see no reason why our dear Cecily should not be even still more attractive at the age you mention than she is at present. There will be a large accumulation of property.

CECILY: Algy, could you wait for me till I was thirty-five?

ALGERNON: Of course I could, Cecily. You know I could.

CECILY: Yes, I felt it instinctively, but I couldn't wait all that time. I hate waiting even five minutes for anybody. It always makes me rather cross. I am not punctual myself, I know, but I do like punctuality in others, and waiting, even to be married, is quite out of the question.

ALGERNON: Then what is to be done, Cecily?

CECILY: I don't know, Mr. Moncrieff.

LADY BRACKNELL: My dear Mr. Worthing, as Miss Cardew states positively that she cannot wait till she is thirty-five—a remark which I am bound to say seems

8. A very fine champagne.

to me to show a somewhat impatient nature—I would beg of you to reconsider your decision.

JACK: But my dear Lady Bracknell, the matter is entirely in your own hands. The moment you consent to my marriage with Gwendolen, I will most gladly allow your nephew to form an alliance with my ward.

LADY BRACKNELL: [*Rising and drawing herself up.*] You must be quite aware that what you propose is out of the question.

JACK: Then a passionate celibacy is all that any of us can look forward to.

LADY BRACKNELL: This is not the destiny I propose for Gwendolen. Algernon, of course, can choose for himself. [*Pulls out her watch.*] Come, dear; [GWENDOLEN *rises.*] we have already missed five, if not six, trains. To miss any more might expose us to comment on the platform.

[*Enter* CANON CHASUBLE.]

CHASUBLE: Everything is quite ready for the christenings.

LADY BRACKNELL: The christenings, sir! Is not that somewhat premature!

CHASUBLE: [*Looking rather puzzled, and pointing to* JACK *and* ALGERNON.] Both these gentlemen have expressed a desire for immediate baptism.

LADY BRACKNELL: At their age? The idea is grotesque and irreligious! Algernon, I forbid you to be baptized. I will not hear of such excesses. Lord Bracknell would be highly displeased if he learned that that was the way in which you wasted your time and money.

CHASUBLE: Am I to understand then that there are to be no christenings at all this afternoon?

JACK: I don't think that, as things are now, it would be of much practical value to either of us, Dr. Chasuble.

CHASUBLE: I am grieved to hear such sentiments from you, Mr. Worthing. They savor of the heretical views of the Anabaptists,[9] views that I have completely refuted in four of my unpublished sermons. However, as your present mood seems to be one peculiarly secular, I will return to the church at once. Indeed, I have just been informed by the pew-opener[1] that for the last hour and a half Miss Prism has been waiting for me in the vestry.

LADY BRACKNELL: [*Starting.*] Miss Prism! Did I hear you mention a Miss Prism?

CHASUBLE: Yes, Lady Bracknell. I am on my way to join her.

LADY BRACKNELL: Pray allow me to detain you for a moment. This matter may prove to be one of vital importance to Lord Bracknell and myself. Is this Miss Prism a female of repellent aspect, remotely connected with education?

CHASUBLE: [*Somewhat indignantly.*] She is the most cultivated of ladies, and the very picture of respectability.

---

9. A sixteenth-century religious group, most nearly like contemporary Mennonites. Dr. Chasuble, however, is probably using the term loosely to apply to a group more like contemporary Baptists.   1. An usher. Since most pews were completely enclosed, his duties would have included opening the gate that provided entrance for the worshipers. In addition, since most pews were rented for the use of specific persons, he would have been responsible for seeing that worshipers were seated in the correct pews.

LADY BRACKNELL: It is obviously the same person. May I ask what position she holds in your household?

CHASUBLE: [*Severely.*] I am a celibate, madam.

JACK: [*Interposing.*] Miss Prism, Lady Bracknell, has been for the last three years Miss Cardew's esteemed governess and valued companion.

LADY BRACKNELL: In spite of what I hear of her, I must see her at once. Let her be sent for.

CHASUBLE: [*Looking off.*] She approaches; she is nigh.

[*Enter* MISS PRISM *hurriedly.*]

MISS PRISM: I was told you expected me in the vestry, dear Canon. I have been waiting for you there for an hour and three quarters. [*Catches sight of* LADY BRACKNELL, *who has fixed her with a stony glare.* MISS PRISM *grows pale and quails. She looks anxiously round as if desirous to escape.*]

LADY BRACKNELL: [*In a severe, judicial voice.*] Prism! [MISS PRISM *bows her head in shame.*] Come here, Prism! [MISS PRISM *approaches in a humble manner.*] Prism! Where is that baby? [*General consternation.* THE CANON *starts back in horror.* ALGERNON *and* JACK *pretend to be anxious to shield* CECILY *and* GWENDOLEN *from hearing the details of a terrible public scandal.*] Twenty-eight years ago, Prism, you left Lord Bracknell's house, Number 104, Upper Grosvenor Street, in charge of a perambulator that contained a baby, of the male sex. You never returned. A few weeks later, through the elaborate investigations of the Metropolitan police, the perambulator was discovered at midnight, standing by itself in a remote corner of Bayswater.[2] It contained the manuscript of a three-volume novel of more than usually revolting sentimentality. [MISS PRISM *starts in involuntary indignation.*] But the baby was not there! [*Everyone looks at* MISS PRISM.] Prism! Where is that baby? [*A pause.*]

MISS PRISM: Lady Bracknell, I admit with shame that I do not know. I only wish I did. The plain facts of the case are these. On the morning of the day you mention, a day that is forever branded on my memory, I prepared as usual to take the baby out in its perambulator. I had also with me a somewhat old, but capacious handbag, in which I had intended to place the manuscript of a work of fiction that I had written during my few unoccupied hours. In a moment of mental abstraction, for which I never can forgive myself, I deposited the manuscript in the bassinette, and placed the baby in the handbag.

JACK: [*Who has been listening attentively.*] But where did you deposit the handbag?

MISS PRISM: Do not ask me, Mr. Worthing.

JACK: Miss Prism, this is a matter of no small importance to me. I insist on knowing where you deposited the handbag that contained that infant.

MISS PRISM: I left it in the cloak room of one of the larger railway stations in London.

JACK: What railway station?

MISS PRISM: [*Quite crushed.*] Victoria. The Brighton line. [*Sinks into a chair.*]

---

2. A fashionable residential section to the north of Hyde Park and Kensington Gardens.

JACK: I must retire to my room for a moment. Gwendolen, wait here for me.

GWENDOLEN: If you are not too long, I will wait here for you all my life.

[*Exit* JACK *in great excitement.*]

CHASUBLE: What do you think this means, Lady Bracknell?

LADY BRACKNELL: I dare not even suspect, Dr. Chasuble. I need hardly tell you that in families of high position strange coincidences are not supposed to occur. They are hardly considered the thing.

[*Noises heard overhead as if someone was throwing trunks about. Everyone looks up.*]

CECILY: Uncle Jack seems strangely agitated.

CHASUBLE: Your guardian has a very emotional nature.

LADY BRACKNELL: This noise is extremely unpleasant. It sounds as if he was having an argument. I dislike arguments of any kind. They are always vulgar, and often convincing.

CHASUBLE: [*Looking up.*] It has stopped now. [*The noise is redoubled.*]

LADY BRACKNELL: I wish he would arrive at some conclusion.

GWENDOLEN: This suspense is terrible. I hope it will last.

[*Enter* JACK *with a handbag of black leather in his hand.*]

JACK: [*Rushing over to* MISS PRISM.] Is this the handbag, Miss Prism? Examine it carefully before you speak. The happiness of more than one life depends on your answer.

MISS PRISM: [*Calmly.*] It seems to be mine. Yes, here is the injury it received through the upsetting of a Gower Street omnibus in younger and happier days. Here is the stain on the lining caused by the explosion of a temperance beverage, an incident that occurred at Leamington. And here, on the lock, are my initials. I had forgotten that in an extravagant mood I had had them placed there. The bag is undoubtedly mine. I am delighted to have it so unexpectedly restored to me. It has been a great inconvenience being without it all these years.

JACK: [*In a pathetic voice.*] Miss Prism, more is restored to you than this handbag. I was the baby you placed in it.

MISS PRISM: [*Amazed.*] You!

JACK: [*Embracing her.*] Yes . . . mother!

MISS PRISM: [*Recoiling in indignant astonishment.*] Mr. Worthing! I am unmarried!

JACK: Unmarried! I do not deny that is a serious blow. But after all, who has the right to cast a stone against one who has suffered? Cannot repentance wipe out an act of folly? Why should there be one law for men, and another for women? Mother, I forgive you. [*Tries to embrace her again.*]

MISS PRISM: [*Still more indignant.*] Mr. Worthing, there is some error. [*Pointing to* LADY BRACKNELL.] There is the lady who can tell you who you really are.

JACK: [*After a pause.*] Lady Bracknell, I hate to seem inquisitive, but would you kindly inform me who I am?

LADY BRACKNELL: I am afraid that the news I have to give you will not altogether please you. You are the son of my poor sister, Mrs. Moncrieff, and consequently Algernon's elder brother.

JACK: Algy's elder brother! Then I have a brother after all. I knew I had a brother! I always said I had a brother! Cecily—how could you have ever doubted that I had a brother? [*Seizes hold of* ALGERNON.] Dr. Chasuble, my unfortunate brother. Miss Prism, my unfortunate brother. Gwendolen, my unfortunate brother. Algy, you young scoundrel, you will have to treat me with more respect in the future. You have never behaved to me like a brother in all your life.

ALGERNON: Well, not till today, old boy, I admit. I did my best, however, though I was out of practice. [*Shakes hands.*]

GWENDOLEN: [*To* JACK.] My own! But what own are you? What is your Christian name, now that you have become someone else?

JACK: Good heavens! . . . I had quite forgotten that point. Your decision on the subject of my name is irrevocable, I suppose?

GWENDOLEN: I never change, except in my affections.

CECILY: What a noble nature you have, Gwendolen!

JACK: Then the question had better be cleared up at once. Aunt Augusta, a moment. At the time when Miss Prism left me in the handbag, had I been christened already?

LADY BRACKNELL: Every luxury that money could buy, including christening, had been lavished on you by your fond and doting parents.

JACK: Then I was christened! That is settled. Now, what name was I given? Let me know the worst.

LADY BRACKNELL: Being the eldest son you were naturally christened after your father.

JACK: [*Irritably*.] Yes, but what was my father's Christian name?

LADY BRACKNELL: [*Meditatively*.] I cannot at the present moment recall what the General's Christian name was. But I have no doubt he had one. He was eccentric, I admit. But only in later years. And that was the result of the Indian climate, and marriage, and indigestion, and other things of that kind.

JACK: Algy! Can't you recollect what our father's Christian name was?

ALGERNON: My dear boy, we were never even on speaking terms. He died before I was a year old.

JACK: His name would appear in the Army Lists of the period, I suppose, Aunt Augusta?

LADY BRACKNELL: The General was essentially a man of peace, except in his domestic life. But I have no doubt his name would appear in any military directory.

JACK: The Army Lists of the last forty years are here. These delightful records should have been my constant study. [*Rushes to bookcase and tears the books out.*] M. Generals . . . Mallam, Maxbohm, Magley, what ghastly names they have—Markby, Migsby, Mobbs, Moncrieff! Lieutenant 1840, Captain, Lieutenant Colonel, Colonel, General 1869, Christian names, Ernest John. [*Puts book very quietly down and speaks quite calmly.*] I always told you, Gwendolen, my name was Ernest, didn't I? Well it is Ernest after all. I mean it naturally is Ernest.

LADY BRACKNELL: Yes, I remember now that the General was called Ernest. I knew I had some particular reason for disliking the name.

GWENDOLEN: Ernest! My own Ernest! I felt from the first that you could have no other name!

JACK: Gwendolen, it is a terrible thing for a man to find out suddenly that all his life he has been speaking nothing but the truth. Can you forgive me?

GWENDOLEN: I can. For I feel that you are sure to change.

JACK: My own one!

CHASUBLE: [*To* MISS PRISM.] Laetitia! [*Embraces her.*]

MISS PRISM: [*Enthusiastically.*] Frederick! At last!

ALGERNON: Cecily! [*Embraces her.*] At last!

JACK: Gwendolen! [*Embraces her.*] At last!

LADY BRACKNELL: My nephew, you seem to be displaying signs of triviality.

JACK: On the contrary, Aunt Augusta, I've now realized for the first time in my life the vital Importance of Being Earnest.

CURTAIN

1899

QUESTIONS

1. What initial obstacles are there to a comic resolution of the romantic plot? How are they resolved? Trace the structure of the resolution, and show where the various structural parts of the play (exposition, rising action, climax, falling action, and conclusion) occur in the text.

2. Characterize Lady Bracknell. Trace the different ways that the character and her role are made clear. What is her structural role in the play?

3. What characters in the play seem simple stereotypes? Exactly how are attitudes toward these characters developed? Which characters rise "above" or go "beyond" stereotypes? What kinds of qualities separate the stereotypes from the more complex characters? Which names especially suggest their characters' natures? Which names are noncharacterizing or neutral?

4. Wilde is often praised for his wit and the skill with which he develops conversational repartee. Choose three speeches that seem especially witty, and explain in detail how they work, in what their wit consists. What patterns of verbal wit do you notice? How dependent is the tone on language? What human values does the play support? What has the preoccupation of the play with language to do with these values?

WRITING SUGGESTIONS

1. Recount in as few words as possible the plot of the play. Then retell the story structurally as a "typical" comic plot. On the basis of this retelling, write a two-page essay in which you show how Wilde structures his play along classical comic lines.

2. Choose one character in the play who seems not as fully developed as he or she might be. Construct a new scene for the play in which this character is allowed, through dialogue and action, to reveal him or herself more fully.

3. Defend the use of comic stereotypes in the play in an essay that suggests how the various stereotypical characters help create the basic comic plot.

27

CULTURE AS CONTEXT:
SOCIAL AND HISTORICAL SETTING

Time conditions all texts, but a sense of time is particularly important for readers of drama. Events in drama often seem more immediate than in poems or stories, and the demands of time seem more pressing. Immediacy is an important feature of drama, and not only in performance. Reading drama involves a strong sense of presentness as well, for all the action takes place in the present tense regardless of what time period is being represented. Nothing in drama is narrated or recounted: action is all in words and gestures happening right now. And all the action happens rather fast; novels often take many hours to read, but most plays can easily be read in the time it would take to perform them on stage—two or three hours—even when the action they represent covers several years.

But whatever the illusion of presentness, plays often deal with extensive and complicated dislocations in time, and readers of drama frequently must make sophisticated moves that involve an adjustment to more than the illusion of immediacy. Even though action seems to take place as we read, the plot may be set far in the past, and as readers we often must bring to bear specific historical information on the times being represented. Sensitive reading of a play may depend on making some fairly complicated distinctions between different time frames.

Three different levels of time operate in most plays. First, a play text represents some particular time—the temporal setting—in which the action takes place. We can call this **plot time.** Second, that text reflects the time when the author was writing, and the conditions and assumptions of that time find their way into the conception and style of the text. This feature of textual time we may call **authorial time.** Third, readers read in a particular time frame, when conditions and assumptions then may differ from those that obtain in either the text's present or the author's present. We may call this **reader time.**

These three levels of time often interact importantly in the way we interpret a text. When, for example, we read—as American readers in the 2000s—a play written by Shakespeare in the early seventeenth century about the Danish court of many centuries earlier, we have three time schemes operating at once. We read about a time (and place) very remote from us, and the text that represents these events also reflects values, writing conditions, habits of language, and dramatic conventions of a second time—centuries later than the action but still almost four centuries earlier than the time in which we read. Values in these three times will not be identical, and how we interpret the actions and thoughts of Hamlet in part depends not only on our own assumptions about what he ought to do or might do, but on what we know about the expectations of human events in two earlier ages. Suspending these three "settings" in our minds as we read—and consciously making comparisons when we perceive conflicts of values—is an important part of interpretation and response. We perceive at one and the same time three different Hamlets—ours (the reader's), Shakespeare's (the text's), and the "historical" Hamlet known to his contemporaries in medieval Denmark. In this particular case, the play does not ask us to know anything very specific about the historical Hamlet; we do not need to know, for example, the history of ancient Elsinore. All we really need to know is that the Danish monarchy passes within families but not necessarily to the eldest son.

Many plays explicitly invoke a particular era as the time of action, and often they specify (in stage directions or interjected comments) information about the era that is relevant to the interpretation of specific episodes. But sometimes we have to supply historical or cultural facts from outside the text, and often we have to adjust our expectations because the "world" of the play—its "present" time in some past age in some specific place—differs greatly from our own world. People may share some characteristics across ages and cultures, but behavior and motivation are often conditioned by present habits and situations, and often we have to think carefully about the particulars of a time and place very different from our own. Identifying the setting of a play—in both time and place—and considering carefully its historical situation can be crucial to understanding what happens and why.

Often, however, plays are aggressively contemporary—that is, they represent the times in which they are written—and thus they are not "historical" in the sense that they evoke earlier times that have to be consciously remembered or studied. When, for example, *A Raisin in the Sun* first appeared on Broadway in 1959, its audience watched scenes that might well have been occurring at virtually that same moment: Lorraine Hansberry wrote her play about current events and issues, and the temporal setting she represented on the stage was shortly before 1959 (she says explicitly that the action occurs "sometime between World War II and the present"). In such a play (and in plays, contemporary settings are very common, perhaps more so than in either stories or poems), almost no difference exists between plot time and authorial time. In fact the strategy of the play depends on the audience believing there is no distinction: playgoers (and readers) must accept that what they see (or read) is utterly contemporary, happening at the very moment of stage representation. Thus members of the audience feel as though they are confronting issues—and life itself—exactly as it is happening, that the play is dealing with the particular issues of that moment. And the choice of setting (the specific place where a play is set—in this case a South Side Chicago ghetto) usually involves a kind of representative setting—that is, a place broadly like other contemporary locations, though the specificity of setting is also important in itself.

Of course, a play such as *A Raisin in the Sun* remains "historical" in an important sense: the "history" that it represents is the moment of performance (or, technically, that moment of creation a few months or weeks just before the performances). In the case of *A Raisin in the Sun*, the historical time (both plot time and authorial time) represented is 1959, and for the first audiences and readers of the play 1959 was also reader time. Now, however, reading the play nearly forty years later, we will likely be quite conscious of it as "historical"—that is, it represents and preserves a particular moment in time when certain things happened that are now distanced from us and that we can now examine in a somewhat more detached way. But not totally. *A Raisin in the Sun* remains "relevant" for readers or viewers because issues of family, ambition, dignity, economic survival, American values, racial discrimination, and social attitudes continue to exist in very similar forms. A lot of what happens in *A Raisin in the Sun* could still happen in nearly the same way four generations later. But not everything.

Take, for example, the abortion that Ruth Younger contemplates near the end of act 1. In 1959, abortion was illegal in the United States; women who sought abortions had to either leave the country, usually traveling to Mexico or Puerto Rico, where abortion was more readily available, or resort to shady, back-alley practitioners like the one Ruth consults. Conditions in such operations were often unsanitary and unsavory, and medical expertise was sometimes poor; disease and mortality rates were high, and besides the social stigma of disobeying the law (which was very strong in middle-class, Christian, African American families), the fear of medical and physical consequences was powerful. However individuals might themselves feel about the ethics and emotional consequences of abortion, the law prohibited it, and public opinion—although beginning to be less rigid and censorious—weighed heavily against the practice. Some of the horror that the Younger family (and especially Mama) expresses here at the thought of abortion can be attributed to economic embarrassment and ideas of family unity and integrity, but to imagine how an audience responded to the idea in 1959 involves knowing about not only the legal situation but also social attitudes more generally, especially within a respectable, proud, and aspiring African American family like the Youngers.

Chicago, and especially the crowded African American neighborhoods on the South Side in the years after World War II, is an important part of the cultural context in the play, too. The migration of African Americans from the South to Chicago in early to mid century because of the availability of jobs there lies behind the conditions depicted in *A Raisin in the Sun,* as do the decreasing employment opportunities, worsening economic conditions, and urban crowding after World War II. If you know Richard Wright's novel *Native Son* or the film made from it, you will recognize the living conditions, racial segmentation, and rising social tensions expressed in *A Raisin in the Sun,* for Hansberry's play takes place in the very same Chicago neighborhood as Wright's novel. Just as any play depends on (or tries to create) some historical knowledge about plot time, the larger sense of culture in a particular time and place also can be crucial. Here a sense of culture and cultural context involves at least three distinct categories: America and American assumptions and values in the mid-twentieth century; the African American subculture in America, with all its social complexities and the brutal fruits of a long history of discrimination; and urban Chicago, with its specific versions of social, economic, and political values and problems. And each of these categories brings its own subcategories to think about. Consider, for example, the issues the play raises about matriarchal families and the "manhood" of characters like Walter.

Another aspect of cultural and historical context includes language. Language often involves subtle changes over time—changes that reflect broader social and cultural assumptions—and almost any gap between authorial time and reader time will turn up usages that have shifted. If you are an attentive student of American language, you may notice in the text a number of expressions that now require interpretation or at least an explanatory footnote. One example in *A Raisin in the Sun* involves the way the characters here refer to their racial identity, usually as "colored" Americans. You may not know quite how to take such a self-reference, but in 1959 it was the standard, approved, and respected self-designation. More complicated, of course, are the differentiations of attitude and language between generations in the play: the different languages of George Murchison and Joseph Asagai (or of Ruth and Beneatha) mirror different attitudes current in 1959 within the African American community and are reflected accurately here by the playwright. Readers conscious of how historical assumptions in a text may differ from assumptions within reader time still have to sort out carefully the way the text uses formal elements such as language to make class, generational, ethnic, and racial differentiations.

Negotiation of times in a play can often be complicated. Discovering the realities of an earlier time does not, however, exactly involve trying to project oneself into that earlier time; it would be as foolish as it is impossible to try to *be* an earlier reader or viewer. Understanding the difference—negotiating distances between what one knows or assumes now and what was known or assumed in an earlier historical moment—and taking that difference into account in interpretation is all a present reader can do.

Death of a Salesman was written ten years before *A Raisin in the Sun;* now half a century old, it seems contemporary in many ways because it draws on enduring assumptions within American culture about habits and values. Still, it is "dated": its specific notions about what salesmen want, how they talk, what they do remains rooted in the times just after World War II. As you read, you may want to pinpoint details that place the play firmly in the years around 1949, when it was first performed.

Like *A Raisin in the Sun, Death of a Salesman* pretty much collapses the difference between plot time and authorial time; both plays depict events that are virtually contemporary and that seem as if they could be taking place at the time of first performance. Both plays also draw heavily on the idea of the American Dream, a concept that is time- and culture-bound but not specifically tied to a particular year or decade and that could be represented as taking place in many different locations within U.S. culture. And like *A Raisin in the Sun, Death of a Salesman* both presents and questions the values involved in the Dream—wondering about the desire to be rich as well as the means commonly undertaken to achieve it. Both the plot and the characterization here are subservient to notions of Americanness and the pursuit of the Dream. In what ways does the play seem specifically characteristic of the mid twentieth century? How would a twenty-first-century character need to be represented differently (even if the American Dream was still his [or her] main preoccupation)? What particulars would need to be changed or updated? Would the sons need to be portrayed differently? Would the particulars of plot need to be varied? How, exactly? How would the character of Linda need to be changed? Willie? What details of the plot and action from 1949 do you have trouble understanding? What would you have to explain, in 1949 or now, to non-American readers?

> [Death of a Salesman] *is a tragedy modern and personal, not classic and heroic. Its central figure is a little man sentenced to discover his smallness rather than a big man undone by his greatness.*
>
> —JOHN MASON BROWN

All plays involve some historical adjustment and understanding on the parts of readers and viewers: time does not stand still, and with changes in habits come changes in values, behavior, and assumptions. All reading implicitly involves a kind of "double" response—the one readers feel from a present perspective and the one they may need to construct intellectually because of specific historical or cultural knowledge. One never bridges gaps of history completely, but conscious effort lessens the gap and makes it both understandable and negotiable in the reading process.

LORRAINE HANSBERRY

A Raisin in the Sun

What happens to a dream deferred?

Does it dry up
Like a raisin in the sun?
Or fester like a sore—
And then run?
Does it stink like rotten meat?
Or crust and sugar over—
Like a syrupy sweet?

Maybe it just sags
Like a heavy load.

Or does it explode?
—LANGSTON HUGHES[1]

CAST OF CHARACTERS

RUTH YOUNGER	JOSEPH ASAGAI
TRAVIS YOUNGER	GEORGE MURCHISON
WALTER LEE YOUNGER (BROTHER)	KARL LINDNER
BENEATHA YOUNGER	BOBO
LENA YOUNGER (MAMA)	MOVING MEN

The action of the play is set in Chicago's Southside, sometime between World War II and the present.

ACT I

SCENE ONE

The Younger living room would be a comfortable and well-ordered room if it were not for a number of indestructible contradictions to this state of being. Its furnishings are typical and undistinguished and their primary feature now is that they have clearly had to accommodate the living of too many people for too many years—and they are tired. Still, we can see that at some time, a time probably no longer remembered by the family (except perhaps for MAMA), the furnishings of this room were actually selected with care and love and even hope—and brought to this apartment and arranged with taste and pride.

That was a long time ago. Now the once loved pattern of the couch upholstery has to

---

1. Hughes's poem, published in 1951, is entitled "Harlem (A Dream Deferred)," and is about the classic New York ghetto.

fight to show itself from under acres of crocheted doilies and couch covers which have themselves finally come to be more important than the upholstery. And here a table or a chair has been moved to disguise the worn places in the carpet; but the carpet has fought back by showing its weariness, with depressing uniformity, elsewhere on its surface.

Weariness has, in fact, won in this room. Everything has been polished, washed, sat on, used, scrubbed too often. All pretenses but living itself have long since vanished from the very atmosphere of this room.

Moreover, a section of this room, for it is not really a room unto itself, though the landlord's lease would make it seem so, slopes backward to provide a small kitchen area, where the family prepares the meals that are eaten in the living room proper, which must also serve as dining room. The single window that has been provided for these "two" rooms is located in this kitchen area. The sole natural light the family may enjoy in the course of a day is only that which fights its way through this little window.

At left, a door leads to a bedroom which is shared by MAMA *and her daughter,* BENEA-THA. *At right, opposite, is a second room (which in the beginning of the life of this apartment was probably a breakfast room) which serves as a bedroom for* WALTER *and his wife,* RUTH.

Time: Sometime between World War II and the present.

Place: Chicago's Southside.

At Rise: It is morning dark in the living room. TRAVIS *is asleep on the make-down bed at center. An alarm clock sounds from within the bedroom at right, and presently* RUTH *enters from that room and closes the door behind her. She crosses sleepily toward the window. As she passes her sleeping son she reaches down and shakes him a little. At the window she raises the shade and a dusky Southside morning light comes in feebly. She fills a pot with water and puts it on to boil. She calls to the boy, between yawns, in a slightly muffled voice.*

RUTH *is about thirty. We can see that she was a pretty girl, even exceptionally so, but now it is apparent that life has been little that she expected, and disappointment has already begun to hang in her face. In a few years, before thirty-five even, she will be known among her people as a "settled woman."*

She crosses to her son and gives him a good, final, rousing shake.

RUTH: Come on now, boy, it's seven thirty! [*Her son sits up at last, in a stupor of sleepiness.*] I say hurry up, Travis! You ain't the only person in the world got to use a bathroom! [*The child, a sturdy, handsome little boy of ten or eleven, drags himself out of the bed and almost blindly takes his towels and "today's clothes" from drawers and a closet and goes out to the bathroom, which is in an outside hall and which is shared by another family or families on the same floor.* RUTH *crosses to the bedroom door at right and opens it and calls in to her husband.*] Walter Lee! . . . It's after seven thirty! Lemme see you do some waking up in there now! [*She waits.*] You better get up from there, man! It's after seven thirty I tell you. [*She waits again.*] All right, you just go ahead and lay there and next thing you know Travis be finished and Mr. Johnson'll be in there and you'll be fussing and cussing round here like a mad man! And be late too! [*She waits, at the end of patience.*] Walter Lee—it's time for you to get up!

[*She waits another second and then starts to go into the bedroom, but is apparently satisfied that her husband has begun to get up. She stops, pulls the door to, and returns to the kitchen area. She wipes her face with a moist cloth and runs her fingers through her sleep-disheveled hair in a vain effort and ties an apron around her housecoat. The bedroom door at right opens and her husband stands in the doorway in his pajamas, which are rumpled and mismated. He is a lean, intense young man in his middle thirties, inclined to quick nervous movements and erratic speech habits—and always in his voice there is a quality of indictment.*]

WALTER: Is he out yet?

RUTH: What you mean *out?* He ain't hardly got in there good yet.

WALTER: [*Wandering in, still more oriented to sleep than to a new day.*] Well, what was you doing all that yelling for if I can't even get in there yet? [*Stopping and thinking.*] Check coming today?

RUTH: They *said* Saturday and this is just Friday and I hopes to God you ain't going to get up here first thing this morning and start talking to me 'bout no money—'cause I 'bout don't want to hear it.

WALTER: Something the matter with you this morning?

RUTH: No—I'm just sleepy as the devil. What kind of eggs you want?

WALTER: Not scrambled. [RUTH *starts to scramble eggs.*] Paper come? [RUTH *points impatiently to the rolled up* Tribune *on the table, and he gets it and spreads it out and vaguely reads the front page.*] Set off another bomb yesterday.

RUTH: [*Maximum indifference.*] Did they?

WALTER: [*Looking up.*] What's the matter with you?

RUTH: Ain't nothing the matter with me. And don't keep asking me that this morning.

WALTER: Ain't nobody bothering you. [*Reading the news of the day absently again.*] Say Colonel McCormick[2] is sick.

RUTH: [*Affecting tea-party interest.*] Is he now? Poor thing.

WALTER: [*Sighing and looking at his watch.*] Oh, me. [*He waits.*] Now what is that boy doing in that bathroom all this time? He just going to have to start getting up earlier. I can't be late to work on account of him fooling around in there.

RUTH: [*Turning on him.*] Oh, no he ain't going to be getting up no earlier no such thing! It ain't his fault that he can't get to bed no earlier nights 'cause he got a bunch of crazy good-for-nothing clowns sitting up running their mouths in what is supposed to be his bedroom after ten o'clock at night . . .

WALTER: That's what you mad about, ain't it? The things I want to talk about with my friends just couldn't be important in your mind, could they?

[*He rises and finds a cigarette in her handbag on the table and crosses to the little window and looks out, smoking and deeply enjoying this first one.*]

RUTH: [*Almost matter of factly, a complaint too automatic to deserve emphasis.*] Why you always got to smoke before you eat in the morning?

---

2. Robert Rutherford McCormick (1880–1955), owner-publisher of the *Chicago Tribune*.

WALTER: [*At the window.*] Just look at 'em down there . . . Running and racing to work . . . [*He turns and faces his wife and watches her a moment at the stove, and then, suddenly.*] You look young this morning, baby.

RUTH: [*Indifferently.*] Yeah?

WALTER: Just for a second—stirring them eggs. It's gone now—just for a second it was—you looked real young again. [*Then, drily.*] It's gone now—you look like yourself again.

RUTH: Man, if you don't shut up and leave me alone.

WALTER: [*Looking out to the street again.*] First thing a man ought to learn in life is not to make love to no colored woman first thing in the morning. You all some evil people at eight o'clock in the morning.

[TRAVIS *appears in the hall doorway, almost fully dressed and quite wide awake now, his towels and pajamas across his shoulders. He opens the door and signals for his father to make the bathroom in a hurry.*]

TRAVIS: [*Watching the bathroom.*] Daddy, come on!

[WALTER *gets his bathroom utensils and flies out to the bathroom.*]

RUTH: Sit down and have your breakfast, Travis.

TRAVIS: Mama, this is Friday. [*Gleefully.*] Check coming tomorrow, huh?

RUTH: You get your mind off money and eat your breakfast.

TRAVIS: [*Eating.*] This is the morning we supposed to bring the fifty cents to school.

RUTH: Well, I ain't got no fifty cents this morning.

TRAVIS: Teacher say we have to.

RUTH: I don't care what teacher say. I ain't got it. Eat your breakfast, Travis.

TRAVIS: I *am* eating.

RUTH: Hush up now and just eat!

[*The boy gives her an exasperated look for her lack of understanding, and eats grudgingly.*]

TRAVIS: You think Grandmama would have it?

RUTH: No! And I want you to stop asking your grandmother for money, you hear me?

TRAVIS: [*Outraged.*] Gaaaleee! I don't ask her, she just gimme it sometimes!

RUTH: Travis Willard Younger—I got too much on me this morning to be—

TRAVIS: Maybe Daddy—

RUTH: *Travis!*

[*The boy hushes abruptly. They are both quiet and tense for several seconds.*]

TRAVIS: [*Presently.*] Could I maybe go carry some groceries in front of the supermarket for a little while after school then?

RUTH: Just hush, I said. [TRAVIS *jabs his spoon into his cereal bowl viciously, and rests his head in anger upon his fists.*] If you through eating, you can get over there and make up your bed.

[*The boy obeys stiffly and crosses the room, almost mechanically, to the bed and more or less carefully folds the covering. He carries the bedding into his mother's room and returns with his books and cap.*]

TRAVIS: [*Sulking and standing apart from her unnaturally.*] I'm gone.

RUTH: [*Looking up from the stove to inspect him automatically.*] Come here. [*He crosses to her and she studies his head.*] If you don't take this comb and fix this here head, you better! [TRAVIS *puts down his books with a great sigh of oppression, and crosses to the mirror. His mother mutters under her breath about his "slubborn-ness."*] 'Bout to march out of here with that head looking just like chickens slept in it! I just don't know where you get your slubborn ways . . . And get your jacket, too. Looks chilly out this morning.

TRAVIS: [*With conspicuously brushed hair and jacket.*] I'm gone.

RUTH: Get carfare and milk money—[*Waving one finger.*] —and not a single penny for no caps, you hear me?

TRAVIS: [*With sullen politeness.*] Yes'm.

[*He turns in outrage to leave. His mother watches after him as in his frustration he approaches the door almost comically. When she speaks to him, her voice has become a very gentle tease.*]

RUTH: [*Mocking; as she thinks he would say it.*] Oh, Mama makes me so mad some-times, I don't know what to do! [*She waits and continues to his back as he stands stock-still in front of the door.*] I wouldn't kiss that woman good-bye for nothing in this world this morning! [*The boy finally turns around and rolls his eyes at her, knowing the mood has changed and he is vindicated; he does not, however, move toward her yet.*] Not for nothing in this world! [*She finally laughs aloud at him and holds out her arms to him and we see that it is a way between them, very old and practiced. He crosses to her and allows her to embrace him warmly but keeps his face fixed with masculine rigidity. She holds him back from her presently and looks at him and runs her fingers over the features of his face. With utter gentleness—*] Now—whose little old angry man are you?

TRAVIS: [*The masculinity and gruffness start to fade at last.*] Aw gaalee—Mama . . .

RUTH: [*Mimicking.*] Aw—gaaaaalleeeee, Mama! [*She pushes him, with rough playful-ness and finality, toward the door.*] Get on out of here or you going to be late.

TRAVIS: [*In the face of love, new aggressiveness.*] Mama, could I *please* go carry groceries?

RUTH: Honey, it's starting to get so cold evenings.

WALTER: [*Coming in from the bathroom and drawing a make-believe gun from a make-believe holster and shooting at his son.*] What is it he wants to do?

RUTH: Go carry groceries after school at the supermarket.

WALTER: Well, let him go . . .

TRAVIS: [*Quickly, to the ally.*] I *have* to—she won't gimme the fifty cents . . .

WALTER: [*To his wife only.*] Why not?

RUTH: [*Simply, and with flavor.*] 'Cause we don't have it.

WALTER: [*To* RUTH *only.*] What you tell the boy things like that for? [*Reaching down into his pants with a rather important gesture.*] Here, son—

[*He hands the boy the coin, but his eyes are directed to his wife's.* TRAVIS *takes the money happily.*]

TRAVIS: Thanks, Daddy.

[*He starts out.* RUTH *watches both of them with murder in her eyes.* WALTER *stands and stares back at her with defiance, and suddenly reaches into his pocket again on an afterthought.*]

WALTER: [*Without even looking at his son, still staring hard at his wife.*] In fact, here's another fifty cents . . . Buy yourself some fruit today—or take a taxicab to school or something!

TRAVIS: Whoopee—

[*He leaps up and clasps his father around the middle with his legs, and they face each other in mutual appreciation; slowly* WALTER LEE *peeks around the boy to catch the violent rays from his wife's eyes and draws his head back as if shot.*]

WALTER: You better get down now—and get to school, man.
TRAVIS: [*At the door.*] O.K. Good-bye.

[*He exits.*]

WALTER: [*After him, pointing with pride.*] That's *my* boy. [*She looks at him in disgust and turns back to her work.*] You know what I was thinking 'bout in the bath-room this morning?
RUTH: No.
WALTER: How come you always try to be so pleasant!
RUTH: What is there to be pleasant 'bout!
WALTER: You want to know what I was thinking 'bout in the bathroom or not!
RUTH: I know what you thinking 'bout.
WALTER: [*Ignoring her.*] 'Bout what me and Willy Harris was talking about last night.
RUTH: [*Immediately—a refrain.*] Willy Harris is a good-for-nothing loud mouth.
WALTER: Anybody who talks to me has got to be a good-for-nothing loud mouth, ain't he? And what you know about who is just a good-for-nothing loud mouth? Charlie Atkins was just a "good-for-nothing loud mouth" too, wasn't he! When he wanted me to go in the dry-cleaning business with him. And now—he's grossing a hundred thousand a year. A hundred thousand dollars a year! You still call *him* a loud mouth!
RUTH: [*Bitterly.*] Oh, Walter Lee . . .

[*She folds her head on her arms over the table.*]

WALTER: [*Rising and coming to her and standing over her.*] You tired, ain't you? Tired of everything. Me, the boy, the way we live—this beat-up hole—everything. Ain't you? [*She doesn't look up, doesn't answer.*] So tired—moaning and groan-ing all the time, but you wouldn't do nothing to help, would you? You couldn't be on my side that long for nothing, could you?

RUTH: Walter, please leave me alone.

WALTER: A man needs for a woman to back him up . . .

RUTH: Walter—

WALTER: Mama would listen to you. You know she listen to you more than she do me and Bennie. She think more of you. All you have to do is just sit down with her when you drinking your coffee one morning and talking 'bout things like you do and— [*He sits down beside her and demonstrates graphically what he thinks her methods and tone should be.*] —you just sip your coffee, see, and say easy like that you been thinking 'bout that deal Walter Lee is so interested in, 'bout the store and all, and sip some more coffee, like what you saying ain't really that important to you—And the next thing you know, she be listening good and asking you questions and when I come home—I can tell her the details. This ain't no fly-by-night proposition, baby. I mean we figured it out, me and Willy and Bobo.

RUTH: [*With a frown.*] Bobo?

WALTER: Yeah. You see, this little liquor store we got in mind cost seventy-five thousand and we figured the initial investment on the place be 'bout thirty thousand, see. That be ten thousand each. Course, there's a couple of hundred you got to pay so's you don't spend your life just waiting for them clowns to let your license get approved—

RUTH: You mean graft?

WALTER: [*Frowning impatiently.*] Don't call it that. See there, that just goes to show you what women understand about the world. Baby, don't *nothing* happen for you in this world 'less you pay *somebody* off!

RUTH: Walter, leave me alone! [*She raises her head and stares at him vigorously—then says, more quietly.*] Eat your eggs, they gonna be cold.

WALTER: [*Straightening up from her and looking off.*] That's it. There you are. Man say to his woman: I got me a dream. His woman say: Eat your eggs. [*Sadly, but gaining in power.*] Man say: I got to take hold of this here world, baby! And a woman will say: Eat your eggs and go to work. [*Passionately now.*] Man say: I got to change my life, I'm choking to death, baby! And his woman say— [*In utter anguish as he brings his fists down on his thighs.*] —Your eggs is getting cold!

RUTH: [*Softly.*] Walter, that ain't none of our money.

WALTER: [*Not listening at all or even looking at her.*] This morning, I was lookin' in the mirror and thinking about it . . . I'm thirty-five years old; I been married eleven years and I got a boy who sleeps in the living room— [*Very, very quietly.*] —and all I got to give him is stories about how rich white people live . . .

RUTH: Eat your eggs, Walter.

WALTER: *Damn my eggs . . . damn all the eggs that ever was!*

RUTH: Then go to work.

WALTER: [*Looking up at her.*] See—I'm trying to talk to you 'bout myself— [*Shaking his head with the repetition.*] —and all you can say is eat them eggs and go to work.

RUTH: [*Wearily.*] Honey, you never say nothing new. I listen to you every day, every night and every morning, and you never say nothing new. [*Shrugging.*]

So you would rather *be* Mr. Arnold than be his chauffeur. So—I would *rather* be living in Buckingham Palace.[3]

WALTER: That is just what is wrong with the colored woman in this world . . . Don't understand about building their men up and making 'em feel like they somebody. Like they can do something.

RUTH: [*Drily, but to hurt.*] There *are* colored men who do things.

WALTER: No thanks to the colored woman.

RUTH: Well, being a colored woman, I guess I can't help myself none.

[*She rises and gets the ironing board and sets it up and attacks a huge pile of rough-dried clothes, sprinkling them in preparation for the ironing and then rolling them into tight fat balls.*]

WALTER: [*Mumbling.*] We one group of men tied to a race of women with small minds.

[*His sister* BENEATHA *enters. She is about twenty, as slim and intense as her brother. She is not as pretty as her sister-in-law, but her lean, almost intellectual face has a handsomeness of its own. She wears a bright-red flannel nightie, and her thick hair stands wildly about her head. Her speech is a mixture of many things; it is different from the rest of the family's insofar as education has permeated her sense of English—and perhaps the Midwest rather than the South has finally—at last—won out in her inflection; but not altogether, because over all of it is a soft slurring and transformed use of vowels which is the decided influence of the Southside. She passes through the room without looking at either* RUTH *or* WALTER *and goes to the outside door and looks, a little blindly, out to the bathroom. She sees that it has been lost to the Johnsons. She closes the door with a sleepy vengeance and crosses to the table and sits down a little defeated.*]

BENEATHA: I am going to start timing those people.

WALTER: You should get up earlier.

BENEATHA: [*Her face in her hands. She is still fighting the urge to go back to bed.*] Really— would you suggest dawn? Where's the paper?

WALTER: [*Pushing the paper across the table to her as he studies her almost clinically, as though he has never seen her before.*] You a horrible-looking chick at this hour.

BENEATHA: [*Drily.*] Good morning, everybody.

WALTER: [*Senselessly.*] How is school coming?

BENEATHA: [*In the same spirit.*] Lovely. Lovely. And you know, biology is the greatest. [*Looking up at him.*] I dissected something that looked just like you yesterday.

WALTER: I just wondered if you've made up your mind and everything.

BENEATHA: [*Gaining in sharpness and impatience.*] And what did I answer yesterday morning—and the day before that?

---

3. Where the queen of Great Britain resides.

RUTH: [*From the ironing board, like someone disinterested and old.*] Don't be so nasty, Bennie.

BENEATHA: [*Still to her brother.*] And the day before that and the day before that!

WALTER: [*Defensively.*] I'm interested in you. Something wrong with that? Ain't many girls who decide—

WALTER *and* BENEATHA: [*In unison.*] —"to be a doctor."

[*Silence.*]

WALTER: Have we figured out yet just exactly how much medical school is going to cost?

RUTH: Walter Lee, why don't you leave that girl alone and get out of here to work?

BENEATHA: [*Exits to the bathroom and bangs on the door.*] Come on out of there, please!

[*She comes back into the room.*]

WALTER: [*Looking at his sister intently.*] You know the check is coming tomorrow.

BENEATHA: [*Turning on him with a sharpness all her own.*] That money belongs to Mama, Walter, and it's for her to decide how she wants to use it. I don't care if she wants to buy a house or a rocket ship or just nail it up somewhere and look at it. It's hers. Not ours—*hers*.

WALTER: [*Bitterly.*] Now ain't that fine! You just got your mother's interest at heart, ain't you, girl? You such a nice girl—but if Mama got that money she can always take a few thousand and help you through school too—can't she?

BENEATHA: I have never asked anyone around here to do anything for me.

WALTER: No! And the line between asking and just accepting when the time comes is big and wide—ain't it!

BENEATHA: [*With fury.*] What do you want from me, Brother—that I quit school or just drop dead, which!

WALTER: I don't want nothing but for you to stop acting holy 'round here. Me and Ruth done made some sacrifices for you—why can't you do something for the family?

RUTH: Walter, don't be dragging me in it.

WALTER: You are in it—Don't you get up and go work in somebody's kitchen for the last three years to help put clothes on her back?

RUTH: Oh, Walter—that's not fair . . .

WALTER: It ain't that nobody expects you to get on your knees and say thank you, Brother; thank you, Ruth; thank you, Mama—and thank you, Travis, for wearing the same pair of shoes for two semesters—

BENEATHA: [*Dropping to her knees.*] Well—I *do*—all right?—thank everybody . . . and forgive me for ever wanting to be anything at all . . . forgive me, forgive me!

RUTH: Please stop it! Your mama'll hear you.

WALTER: Who the hell told you you had to be a doctor? If you so crazy 'bout messing 'round with sick people—then go be a nurse like other women—or just get married and be quiet . . .

BENEATHA: Well—you finally got it said . . . it took you three years but you finally got it said. Walter, give up; leave me alone—it's Mama's money.

WALTER: *He was my father, too!*

BENEATHA: So what? He was mine, too—and Travis' grandfather—but the insurance money belongs to Mama. Picking on me is not going to make her give it to you to invest in any liquor stores— [*Underbreath, dropping into a chair.*] — and I for one say, God bless Mama for that!

WALTER: [*To* RUTH.] See—did you hear? Did you hear!

RUTH: Honey, please go to work.

WALTER: Nobody in this house is ever going to understand me.

BENEATHA: Because you're a nut.

WALTER: Who's a nut?

BENEATHA: You—you are a nut. Thee is mad, boy.

WALTER: [*Looking at his wife and his sister from the door, very sadly.*] The world's most backward race of people, and that's a fact.

BENEATHA: [*Turning slowly in her chair.*] And then there are all those prophets who would lead us out of the wilderness— [WALTER *slams out of the house.*] —into the swamps!

RUTH: Bennie, why you always gotta be pickin' on your brother? Can't you be a little sweeter sometimes? [*Door opens.* WALTER *walks in.*]

WALTER: [*To* RUTH.] I need some money for carfare.

RUTH: [*Looks at him, then warms; teasing, but tenderly.*] Fifty cents? [*She goes to her bag and gets money.*] Here, take a taxi.

[WALTER *exits.* MAMA *enters. She is a woman in her early sixties, full-bodied and strong. She is one of those women of a certain grace and beauty who wear it so unobtrusively that it takes a while to notice. Her dark-brown face is surrounded by the total whiteness of her hair, and, being a woman who has adjusted to many things in life and overcome many more, her face is full of strength. She has, we can see, wit and faith of a kind that keep her eyes lit and full of interest and expectancy. She is, in a word, a beautiful woman. Her bearing is perhaps most like the noble bearing of the women of the Hereros of Southwest Africa—rather as if she imagines that as she walks she still bears a basket or a vessel upon her head. Her speech, on the other hand, is as careless as her carriage is precise—she is inclined to slur everything—but her voice is perhaps not so much quiet as simply soft.*]

MAMA: Who that 'round here slamming doors at this hour?

[*She crosses through the room, goes to the window, opens it, and brings in a feeble little plant growing doggedly in a small pot on the window sill. She feels the dirt and puts it back out.*]

RUTH: That was Walter Lee. He and Bennie was at it again.

MAMA: My children and they tempers. Lord, if this little old plant don't get more sun than it's been getting it ain't never going to see spring again. [*She turns from the window.*] What's the matter with you this morning, Ruth? You looks right peaked. You aiming to iron all them things? Leave some for me. I'll get to 'em this afternoon. Bennie honey, it's too drafty for you to be sitting 'round half dressed. Where's your robe?

BENEATHA: In the cleaners.

MAMA: Well, go get mine and put it on.

BENEATHA: I'm not cold, Mama, honest.

MAMA: I know—but you so thin . . .

BENEATHA: [Irritably.] Mama, I'm not cold.

MAMA: [Seeing the make-down bed as TRAVIS has left it.] Lord have mercy, look at that poor bed. Bless his heart—he tries, don't he?

[She moves to the bed TRAVIS has sloppily made up.]

RUTH: No—he don't half try at all 'cause he knows you going to come along behind him and fix everything. That's just how come he don't know how to do nothing right now—you done spoiled that boy so.

MAMA: Well—he's a little boy. Ain't supposed to know 'bout housekeeping. My baby, that's what he is. What you fix for his breakfast this morning?

RUTH: [Angrily.] I feed my son, Lena!

MAMA: I ain't meddling— [Underbreath; busy-bodyish.] I just noticed all last week he had cold cereal, and when it starts getting this chilly in the fall a child ought to have some hot grits or something when he goes out in the cold—

RUTH: [Furious.] I gave him hot oats—is that all right!

MAMA: I ain't meddling. [Pause.] Put a lot of nice butter on it? [RUTH shoots her an angry look and does not reply.] He likes lots of butter.

RUTH: [Exasperated.] Lena—

MAMA: [To BENEATHA. MAMA is inclined to wander conversationally sometimes.] What was you and your brother fussing 'bout this morning?

BENEATHA: It's not important, Mama.

[She gets up and goes to look out at the bathroom, which is apparently free, and she picks up her towels and rushes out.]

MAMA: What was they fighting about?

RUTH: Now you know as well as I do.

MAMA: [Shaking her head.] Brother still worrying hisself sick about that money?

RUTH: You know he is.

MAMA: You had breakfast?

RUTH: Some coffee.

MAMA: Girl, you better start eating and looking after yourself better. You almost thin as Travis.

RUTH: Lena—

MAMA: Un-hunh?

RUTH: What are you going to do with it?

MAMA: Now don't you start, child. It's too early in the morning to be talking about money. It ain't Christian.

RUTH: It's just that he got his heart set on that store—

MAMA: You mean that liquor store that Willy Harris want him to invest in?

RUTH: Yes—

MAMA: We ain't no business people, Ruth. We just plain working folks.

RUTH: Ain't nobody business people till they go into business. Walter Lee say colored people ain't never going to start getting ahead till they start gambling on some different kinds of things in the world—investments and things.

MAMA: What done got into you, girl? Walter Lee done finally sold you on investing.

RUTH: No. Mama, something is happening between Walter and me. I don't know what it is—but he needs something—something I can't give him any more. He needs this chance, Lena.

MAMA: [*Frowning deeply*.] But liquor, honey—

RUTH: Well—like Walter say—I spec people going to always be drinking themselves some liquor.

MAMA: Well—whether they drinks it or not ain't none of my business. But whether I go into business selling it to 'em *is*, and I don't want that on my ledger this late in life. [*Stopping suddenly and studying her daughter-in-law*.] Ruth Younger, what's the matter with you today? You look like you could fall over right there.

RUTH: I'm tired.

MAMA: Then you better stay home from work today.

RUTH: I can't stay home. She'd be calling up the agency and screaming at them, "My girl didn't come in today—send me somebody! My girl didn't come in!" Oh, she just have a fit . . .

MAMA: Well, let her have it. I'll just call her up and say you got the flu—

RUTH: [*Laughing*.] Why the flu?

MAMA: 'Cause it sounds respectable to 'em. Something white people get, too. They know 'bout the flu. Otherwise they think you been cut up or something when you tell 'em you sick.

RUTH: I got to go in. We need the money.

MAMA: Somebody would of thought my children done all but starved to death the way they talk about money here late. Child, we got a great big old check coming tomorrow.

RUTH: [*Sincerely, but also self-righteously*.] Now that's your money. It ain't got nothing to do with me. We all feel like that—Walter and Bennie and me—even Travis.

MAMA: [*Thoughtfully, and suddenly very far away*.] Ten thousand dollars—

RUTH: Sure is wonderful.

MAMA: Ten thousand dollars.

RUTH: You know what you should do, Miss Lena? You should take yourself a trip somewhere. To Europe or South America or someplace—

MAMA: [*Throwing up her hands at the thought*.] Oh, child!

RUTH: I'm serious. Just pack up and leave! Go on away and enjoy yourself some. Forget about the family and have yourself a ball for once in your life—

MAMA: [*Drily*.] You sound like I'm just about ready to die. Who'd go with me? What I look like wandering 'round Europe by myself?

RUTH: Shoot—these here rich white women do it all the time. They don't think nothing of packing up they suitcases and piling on one of them big steam-ships and—swoosh!—they gone, child.

MAMA: Something always told me I wasn't no rich white woman.

RUTH: Well—what are you going to do with it then?

MAMA: I ain't rightly decided. [*Thinking. She speaks now with emphasis.*] Some of it got to be put away for Beneatha and her schoolin'—and ain't nothing going to touch that part of it. Nothing. [*She waits several seconds, trying to make up her mind about something, and looks at* RUTH *a little tentatively before going on.*] Been thinking that we maybe could meet the notes on a little old two-story somewhere, with a yard where Travis could play in the summertime, if we use part of the insurance for a down payment and everybody kind of pitch in. I could maybe take on a little day work again, few days a week—

RUTH: [*Studying her mother-in-law furtively and concentrating on her ironing, anxious to encourage without seeming to.*] Well, Lord knows, we've put enough rent into this here rat trap to pay for four houses by now . . .

MAMA: [*Looking up at the words "rat trap" and then looking around and leaning back and sighing—in a suddenly reflective mood—*] "Rat trap"—yes, that's all it is. [*Smiling.*] I remember just as well the day me and Big Walter moved in here. Hadn't been married but two weeks and wasn't planning on living here no more than a year. [*She shakes her head at the dissolved dream.*] We was going to set away, little by little, don't you know, and buy a little place out in Morgan Park. We had even picked out the house. [*Chuckling a little.*] Looks right dumpy today. But Lord, child, you should know all the dreams I had 'bout buying that house and fixing it up and making me a little garden in the back— [*She waits and stops smiling.*] And didn't none of it happen.

[*Dropping her hands in a futile gesture.*]

RUTH: [*Keeps her head down, ironing.*] Yes, life can be a barrel of disappointments, sometimes.

MAMA: Honey, Big Walter would come in here some nights back then and slump down on that couch there and just look at the rug, and look at me and look at the rug and then back at me—and I'd know he was down then . . . really down. [*After a second very long and thoughtful pause; she is seeing back to times that only she can see.*] And then, Lord, when I lost that baby—little Claude—I almost thought I was going to lose Big Walter too. Oh, that man grieved hisself! He was one man to love his children.

RUTH: Ain't nothin' can tear at you like losin' your baby.

MAMA: I guess that's how come that man finally worked hisself to death like he done. Like he was fighting his own war with this here world that took his baby from him.

RUTH: He sure was a fine man, all right. I always liked Mr. Younger.

MAMA: Crazy 'bout his children! God knows there was plenty wrong with Walter Younger—hard-headed, mean, kind of wild with women—plenty wrong with him. But he sure loved his children. Always wanted them to have something—be something. That's where Brother gets all these notions, I reckon.

Big Walter used to say, he'd get right wet in the eyes sometimes, lean his head back with the water standing in his eyes and say, "Seem like God didn't see fit to give the black man nothing but dreams—but He did give us children to make them dreams seem worth while." [*She smiles.*] He could talk like that, don't you know.

RUTH: Yes, he sure could. He was a good man, Mr. Younger.

MAMA: Yes, a fine man—just couldn't never catch up with his dreams, that's all.

[BENEATHA *comes in, brushing her hair and looking up to the ceiling, where the sound of a vacuum cleaner has started up.*]

BENEATHA: What could be so dirty on that woman's rugs that she has to vacuum them every single day?

RUTH: I wish certain young women 'round here who I could name would take inspiration about certain rugs in a certain apartment I could also mention.

BENEATHA: [*Shrugging.*] How much cleaning can a house need, for Christ's sakes.

MAMA: [*Not liking the Lord's name used thus.*] Bennie!

RUTH: Just listen to her—just listen!

BENEATHA: Oh, God!

MAMA: If you use the Lord's name just one more time—

BENEATHA: [*A bit of a whine.*] Oh, Mama—

RUTH: Fresh—just fresh as salt, this girl!

BENEATHA: [*Drily.*] Well—if the salt loses its savor—[4]

MAMA: Now that will do. I just ain't going to have you 'round here reciting the scriptures in vain—you hear me?

BENEATHA: How did I manage to get on everybody's wrong side by just walking into a room?

RUTH: If you weren't so fresh—

BENEATHA: Ruth, I'm twenty years old.

MAMA: What time you be home from school today?

BENEATHA: Kind of late. [*With enthusiasm.*] Madeline is going to start my guitar lessons today.

[MAMA *and* RUTH *look up with the same expression.*]

MAMA: Your *what* kind of lessons?

BENEATHA: Guitar.

RUTH: Oh, Father!

MAMA: How come you done taken it in your mind to learn to play the guitar?

BENEATHA: I just want to, that's all.

MAMA: [*Smiling.*] Lord, child, don't you know what to do with yourself? How long it going to be before you get tired of this now—like you got tired of that little play-acting group you joined last year? [*Looking at* RUTH.] And what was it the year before that?

4. See Matthew 5.13 and Luke 14.34.

RUTH: The horseback-riding club for which she bought that fifty-five-dollar riding habit that's been hanging in the closet ever since!

MAMA: [*To* BENEATHA.] Why you got to flit so from one thing to another, baby?

BENEATHA: [*Sharply.*] I just want to learn to play the guitar. Is there anything wrong with that?

MAMA: Ain't nobody trying to stop you. I just wonders sometimes why you has to flit so from one thing to another all the time. You ain't never done nothing with all that camera equipment you brought home—

BENEATHA: I don't flit! I—I experiment with different forms of expression—

RUTH: Like riding a horse?

BENEATHA: —People have to express themselves one way or another.

MAMA: What is it you want to express?

BENEATHA: [*Angrily.*] Me! [MAMA *and* RUTH *look at each other and burst into raucous laughter.*] Don't worry—I don't expect you to understand.

MAMA: [*To change the subject.*] Who you going out with tomorrow night?

BENEATHA: [*With displeasure.*] George Murchison again.

MAMA: [*Pleased.*] Oh—you getting a little sweet on him?

RUTH: You ask me, this child ain't sweet on nobody but herself— [*Underbreath.*] Express herself!

[*They laugh.*]

BENEATHA: Oh—I like George all right, Mama. I mean I like him enough to go out with him and stuff, but—

RUTH: [*For devilment.*] What does *and stuff* mean?

BENEATHA: Mind your own business.

MAMA: Stop picking at her now, Ruth. [*A thoughtful pause, and then a suspicious sudden look at her daughter as she turns in her chair for emphasis.*] What *does* it mean?

BENEATHA: [*Wearily.*] Oh, I just mean I couldn't ever really be serious about George. He's—he's so shallow.

RUTH: Shallow—what do you mean he's shallow? He's *Rich!*

MAMA: Hush, Ruth.

BENEATHA: I know he's rich. He knows he's rich, too.

RUTH: Well—what other qualities a man got to have to satisfy you, little girl?

BENEATHA: You wouldn't even begin to understand. Anybody who married Walter could not possibly understand.

MAMA: [*Outraged.*] What kind of way is that to talk about your brother?

BENEATHA: Brother is a flip—let's face it.

MAMA: [*To* RUTH, *helplessly.*] What's a flip?

RUTH: [*Glad to add kindling.*] She's saying he's crazy.

BENEATHA: Not crazy. Brother isn't really crazy yet—he—he's an elaborate neurotic.

MAMA: Hush your mouth!

BENEATHA: As for George. Well. George looks good—he's got a beautiful car and he takes me to nice places and, as my sister-in-law says, he is probably the richest boy I will ever get to know and I even like him sometimes—but if the Youngers are sitting around waiting to see if their little Bennie is going to tie up the family with the Murchisons, they are wasting their time.

RUTH: You mean you wouldn't marry George Murchison if he asked you someday? That pretty, rich thing? Honey, I knew you was odd—

BENEATHA: No I would not marry him if all I felt for him was what I feel now. Besides, George's family wouldn't really like it.

MAMA: Why not?

BENEATHA: Oh, Mama—The Murchisons are honest-to-God-real-*live*-rich colored people, and the only people in the world who are more snobbish than rich white people are rich colored people. I thought everybody knew that. I've met Mrs. Murchison. She's a scene!

MAMA: You must not dislike people 'cause they well off, honey.

BENEATHA: Why not? It makes just as much sense as disliking people 'cause they are poor, and lots of people do that.

RUTH: [*A wisdom-of-the-ages manner. To* MAMA.] Well, she'll get over some of this—

BENEATHA: Get over it? What are you talking about, Ruth? Listen, I'm going to be a doctor. I'm not worried about who I'm going to marry yet—if I ever get married.

MAMA *and* RUTH: *If!*

MAMA: Now, Bennie—

BENEATHA: Oh, I probably will . . . but first I'm going to be a doctor, and George, for one, still thinks that's pretty funny. I couldn't be bothered with that. I am going to be a doctor and everybody around here better understand that!

MAMA: [*Kindly.*] 'Course you going to be a doctor, honey, God willing.

BENEATHA: [*Drily.*] God hasn't got a thing to do with it.

MAMA: Beneatha—that just wasn't necessary.

BENEATHA: Well—neither is God. I get sick of hearing about God.

MAMA: Beneatha!

BENEATHA: I mean it! I'm just tired of hearing about God all the time. What has He got to do with anything? Does He pay tuition?

MAMA: You 'bout to get your fresh little jaw slapped!

RUTH: That's just what she needs, all right!

BENEATHA: Why? Why can't I say what I want to around here, like everybody else?

MAMA: It don't sound nice for a young girl to say things like that—you wasn't brought up that way. Me and your father went to trouble to get you and Brother to church every Sunday.

BENEATHA: Mama, you don't understand. It's all a matter of ideas, and God is just one idea I don't accept. It's not important. I am not going out and be immoral or commit crimes because I don't believe in God. I don't even think about it. It's just that I get tired of Him getting credit for all the things the human race achieves through its own stubborn effort. There simply is no blasted God— there is only man and it is he who makes miracles!

[MAMA *absorbs this speech, studies her daughter and rises slowly and crosses to* BENEATHA *and slaps her powerfully across the face. After, there is only silence and the daughter drops her eyes from her mother's face, and* MAMA *is very tall before her.*]

MAMA: Now—you say after me, in my mother's house there is still God. [*There is a long pause and* BENEATHA *stares at the floor wordlessly.* MAMA *repeats the phrase with precision and cool emotion.*] In my mother's house there is still God.

BENEATHA: In my mother's house there is still God.

[*A long pause.*]

MAMA: [*Walking away from* BENEATHA, *too disturbed for triumphant posture. Stopping and turning back to her daughter.*] There are some ideas we ain't going to have in this house. Not long as I am at the head of this family.

BENEATHA: Yes, ma'am.

[MAMA *walks out of the room.*]

RUTH: [*Almost gently, with profound understanding.*] You think you a woman, Bennie—but you still a little girl. What you did was childish—so you got treated like a child.

BENEATHA: I see. [*Quietly.*] I also see that everybody thinks it's all right for Mama to be a tyrant. But all the tyranny in the world will never put a God in the heavens!

[*She picks up her books and goes out.*]

RUTH: [*Goes to* MAMA's *door.*] She said she was sorry.

MAMA: [*Coming out, going to her plant.*] They frightens me, Ruth. My children.

RUTH: You got good children, Lena. They just a little off sometimes—but they're good.

MAMA: No—there's something come down between me and them that don't let us understand each other and I don't know what it is. One done almost lost his mind thinking 'bout money all the time and the other done commence to talk about things I can't seem to understand in no form or fashion. What is it that's changing, Ruth?

RUTH: [*Soothingly, older than her years.*] Now . . . you taking it all too seriously. You just got strong-willed children and it takes a strong woman like you to keep 'em in hand.

MAMA: [*Looking at her plant and sprinkling a little water on it.*] They spirited all right, my children. Got to admit they got spirit—Bennie and Walter. Like this little old plant that ain't never had enough sunshine or nothing—and look at it . . .

[*She has her back to* RUTH, *who has had to stop ironing and lean against something and put the back of her hand to her forehead.*]

RUTH: [*Trying to keep* MAMA *from noticing.*] You . . . sure . . . loves that little old thing, don't you? . . .

MAMA: Well, I always wanted me a garden like I used to see sometimes at the back of the houses down home. This plant is close as I ever got to having one. [*She looks out of the window as she replaces the plant.*] Lord, ain't nothing as dreary as the view from this window on a dreary day, is there? Why ain't you singing this morning, Ruth? Sing that "No Ways Tired." That song always lifts me up so— [*She turns at last to see that* RUTH *has slipped quietly into a chair, in a state of semiconsciousness.*] Ruth! Ruth honey—what's the matter with you . . . Ruth!

[CURTAIN.]

SCENE TWO

It is the following morning; a Saturday morning, and house cleaning is in progress at the Youngers. Furniture has been shoved hither and yon and MAMA *is giving the kitchen-area walls a washing down.* BENEATHA, *in dungarees, with a handkerchief tied around her face, is spraying insecticide into the cracks in the walls. As they work, the radio is on and a Southside disk-jockey program is inappropriately filling the house with a rather exotic saxophone blues.* TRAVIS, *the sole idle one, is leaning on his arms, looking out of the window.*

TRAVIS: Grandmama, that stuff Bennie is using smells awful. Can I go downstairs, please?

MAMA: Did you get all them chores done already? I ain't seen you doing much.

TRAVIS: Yes'm—finished early. Where did Mama go this morning?

MAMA: [*Looking at* BENEATHA.] She had to go on a little errand.

TRAVIS: Where?

MAMA: To tend to her business.

TRAVIS: Can I go outside then?

MAMA: Oh, I guess so. You better stay right in front of the house, though . . . and keep a good lookout for the postman.

TRAVIS: Yes'm. [*He starts out and decides to give his aunt* BENEATHA *a good swat on the legs as he passes her.*] Leave them poor little old cockroaches alone, they ain't bothering you none.

[*He runs as she swings the spray gun at him both viciously and playfully.* WALTER *enters from the bedroom and goes to the phone.*]

MAMA: Look out there, girl, before you be spilling some of that stuff on that child!

TRAVIS: [*Teasing.*] That's right—look out now!

[*He exits.*]

BENEATHA: [*Drily.*] I can't imagine that it would hurt him—it has never hurt the roaches.

MAMA: Well, little boys' hides ain't as tough as Southside roaches.

WALTER: [*Into phone.*] Hello—Let me talk to Willy Harris.

MAMA: You better get over there behind the bureau. I seen one marching out of there like Napoleon yesterday.

WALTER: Hello, Willy? It ain't come yet. It'll be here in a few minutes. Did the lawyer give you the papers?

BENEATHA: There's really only one way to get rid of them, Mama—

MAMA: How?

BENEATHA: Set fire to this building.

WALTER: Good. Good. I'll be right over.

BENEATHA: Where did Ruth go, Walter?

WALTER: I don't know.

[*He exits abruptly.*]

BENEATHA: Mama, where did Ruth go?

MAMA: [*Looking at her with meaning.*] To the doctor, I think.

BENEATHA: The doctor? What's the matter? [*They exchange glances.*] You don't think—

MAMA: [*With her sense of drama.*] Now I ain't saying what I think. But I ain't never been wrong 'bout a woman neither.

[*The phone rings.*]

BENEATHA: [*At the phone.*] Hay-lo . . . [*Pause, and a moment of recognition.*] Well—when did you get back! . . . And how was it? . . . Of course I've missed you—in my way . . . This morning? No . . . house cleaning and all that and Mama hates it if I let people come over when the house is like this . . . You *have?* Well, that's different . . . What is it—Oh, what the hell, come on over . . . Right, see you then.

[*She hangs up.*]

MAMA: [*Who has listened vigorously, as is her habit.*] Who is that you inviting over here with this house looking like this? You ain't got the pride you was born with!

BENEATHA: Asagai doesn't care how houses look, Mama—he's an intellectual.

MAMA: *Who?*

BENEATHA: Asagai—Joseph Asagai. He's an African boy I met on campus. He's been studying in Canada all summer.

MAMA: What's his name?

BENEATHA: Asagai, Joseph. Ah-sah-guy . . . He's from Nigeria.

MAMA: Oh, that's the little country that was founded by slaves way back . . .

BENEATHA: No, Mama—that's Liberia.

MAMA: I don't think I never met no African before.

BENEATHA: Well, do me a favor and don't ask him a whole lot of ignorant questions about Africans. I mean, do they wear clothes and all that—

MAMA: Well, now, I guess if you think we so ignorant 'round here maybe you shouldn't bring your friends here—

BENEATHA: It's just that people ask such crazy things. All anyone seems to know about when it comes to Africa is Tarzan—

MAMA: [*Indignantly.*] Why should I know anything about Africa?

BENEATHA: Why do you give money at church for the missionary work?

MAMA: Well, that's to help save people.

BENEATHA: You mean save them from *heathenism*—

MAMA: [*Innocently.*] Yes.

BENEATHA: I'm afraid they need more salvation from the British and the French.

[RUTH *comes in forlornly and pulls off her coat with dejection. They both turn to look at her.*]

RUTH: [*Dispiritedly.*] Well, I guess from all the happy faces—everybody knows.

BENEATHA: You pregnant?

MAMA: Lord have mercy, I sure hope it's a little old girl. Travis ought to have a sister.

[BENEATHA *and* RUTH *give her a hopeless look for this grandmotherly enthusiasm.*]

BENEATHA: How far along are you?

RUTH: Two months.

BENEATHA: Did you mean to? I mean did you plan it or was it an accident?

MAMA: What do you know about planning or not planning?

BENEATHA: Oh, Mama.

RUTH: [*Wearily.*] She's twenty years old, Lena.

BENEATHA: Did you plan it, Ruth?

RUTH: Mind your own business.

BENEATHA: It is my business—where is he going to live, on the roof? [*There is silence following the remark as the three women react to the sense of it.*] Gee—I didn't mean that, Ruth, honest. Gee, I don't feel like that at all. I—I think it is wonderful.

RUTH: [*Dully.*] Wonderful.

BENEATHA: Yes—really.

MAMA: [*Looking at* RUTH, *worried.*] Doctor say everything going to be all right?

RUTH: [*Far away.*] Yes—she says everything is going to be fine . . .

MAMA: [*Immediately suspicious.*] "She"—What doctor you went to?

[RUTH *folds over, near hysteria.*]

MAMA: [*Worriedly hovering over* RUTH.] Ruth honey—what's the matter with you— you sick?

[RUTH *has her fists clenched on her thighs and is fighting hard to suppress a scream that seems to be rising in her.*]

BENEATHA: What's the matter with her, Mama?

MAMA: [*Working her fingers in* RUTH*'s shoulder to relax her.*] She be all right. Women gets right depressed sometimes when they get her way. [*Speaking softly, expertly, rapidly.*] Now you just relax. That's right . . . just lean back, don't think 'bout nothing at all . . . nothing at all—

RUTH: I'm all right . . .

[*The glassy-eyed look melts and then she collapses into a fit of heavy sobbing. The bell rings.*]

BENEATHA: Oh, my God—that must be Asagai.

MAMA: [*To* RUTH.] Come on now, honey. You need to lie down and rest awhile . . . then have some nice hot food.

[*They exit,* RUTH's *weight on her mother-in-law.* BENEATHA, *herself profoundly disturbed, opens the door to admit a rather dramatic-looking young man with a large package.*]

ASAGAI: Hello, Alaiyo—

BENEATHA: [*Holding the door open and regarding him with pleasure.*] Hello . . . [*Long pause.*] Well—come in. And please excuse everything. My mother was very upset about my letting anyone come here with the place like this.

ASAGAI: [*Coming into the room.*] You look disturbed too . . . Is something wrong?

BENEATHA: [*Still at the door, absently.*] Yes . . . we've all got acute ghettoitus. [*She smiles and comes toward him, finding a cigarette and sitting.*] So—sit down! How was Canada?

ASAGAI: [*A sophisticate.*] Canadian.

BENEATHA: [*Looking at him.*] I'm very glad you are back.

ASAGAI: [*Looking back at her in turn.*] Are you really?

BENEATHA: Yes—very.

ASAGAI: Why—you were quite glad when I went away. What happened?

BENEATHA: You went away.

ASAGAI: Ahhhhhhhh.

BENEATHA: Before—you wanted to be so serious before there was time.

ASAGAI: How much time must there be before one knows what one feels?

BENEATHA: [*Stalling this particular conversation. Her hands pressed together, in a deliberately childish gesture.*] What did you bring me?

ASAGAI: [*Handing her the package.*] Open it and see.

BENEATHA: [*Eagerly opening the package and drawing out some records and the colorful robes of a Nigerian woman.*] Oh, Asagai! . . . You got them for me! . . . How beautiful . . . and the records too! [*She lifts out the robes and runs to the mirror with them and holds the drapery up in front of herself.*]

ASAGAI: [*Coming to her at the mirror.*] I shall have to teach you how to drape it properly. [*He flings the material about her for the moment and stands back to look at her.*] Ah—Oh-pay-gay-day, oh-gbah-mu-shay. [*A Yoruba exclamation for admiration.*] You wear it well . . . very well . . . mutilated hair and all.

BENEATHA: [*Turning suddenly.*] My hair—what's wrong with my hair?

ASAGAI: [*Shrugging.*] Were you born with it like that?

BENEATHA: [*Reaching up to touch it.*] No . . . of course not.

[*She looks back to the mirror, disturbed.*]

ASAGAI: [*Smiling.*] How then?

BENEATHA: You know perfectly well how . . . as crinkly as yours . . . that's how.

ASAGAI: And it is ugly to you that way?

BENEATHA: [*Quickly.*] Oh, no—not ugly . . . [*More slowly, apologetically.*] But it's so hard to manage when it's, well—raw.

ASAGAI: And so to accommodate that—you mutilate it every week?

BENEATHA: It's not mutilation!

ASAGAI: [*Laughing aloud at her seriousness.*] Oh . . . please! I am only teasing you because you are so very serious about these things. [*He stands back from her and folds his arms across his chest as he watches her pulling at her hair and frowning in the mirror.*] Do you remember the first time you met me at school? . . . [*He laughs.*] You came up to me and you said—and I thought you were the most serious little thing I had ever seen—you said: [*He imitates her.*] "Mr. Asagai—I want very much to talk with you. About Africa. You see, Mr. Asagai, I am looking for my *identity!*"

[*He laughs.*]

BENEATHA: [*Turning to him, not laughing.*] Yes—

[*Her face is quizzical, profoundly disturbed.*]

ASAGAI: [*Still teasing and reaching out and taking her face in his hands and turning her profile to him.*] Well . . . it is true that this is not so much a profile of a Hollywood queen as perhaps a queen of the Nile— [*A mock dismissal of the importance of the question.*] But what does it matter? Assimilationism is so popular in your country.

BENEATHA: [*Wheeling, passionately, sharply.*] I am not an assimilationist!

ASAGAI: [*The protest hangs in the room for a moment and* ASAGAI *studies her, his laughter fading.*] Such a serious one. [*There is a pause.*] So—you like the robes? You must take excellent care of them—they are from my sister's personal wardrobe.

BENEATHA: [*With incredulity.*] You—you sent all the way home—for me?

ASAGAI: [*With charm.*] For you—I would do much more . . . Well, that is what I came for. I must go.

BENEATHA: Will you call me Monday?

ASAGAI: Yes . . . We have a great deal to talk about. I mean about identity and time and all that.

BENEATHA: Time?

ASAGAI: Yes. About how much time one needs to know what one feels.

BENEATHA: You never understood that there is more than one kind of feeling which can exist between a man and a woman—or, at least, there should be.

ASAGAI: [*Shaking his head negatively but gently.*] No. Between a man and a woman there need be only one kind of feeling. I have that for you . . . Now even . . . right this moment . . .

BENEATHA: I know—and by itself—it won't do. I can find that anywhere.

ASAGAI: For a woman it should be enough.

BENEATHA: I know—because that's what it says in all the novels that men write. But it isn't. Go ahead and laugh—but I'm not interested in being someone's little episode in America or— [*With feminine vengeance.*] —one of them! [ASA-GAI *has burst into laughter again.*] That's funny as hell, huh!

ASAGAI: It's just that every American girl I have known has said that to me. White— black—in this you are all the same. And the same speech, too!

BENEATHA: [*Angrily.*] Yuk, yuk, yuk!

ASAGAI: It's how you can be sure that the world's most liberated women are not liberated at all. You all talk about it too much!

> [MAMA *enters and is immediately all social charm because of the presence of a guest.*]

BENEATHA: Oh—Mama—this is Mr. Asagai.

MAMA: How do you do?

ASAGAI: [*Total politeness to an elder.*] How do you do, Mrs. Younger. Please forgive me for coming at such an outrageous hour on a Saturday.

MAMA: Well, you are quite welcome. I just hope you understand that our house don't always look like this. [*Chatterish.*] You must come again. I would love to hear all about— [*Not sure of the name.*] —your country. I think it's so sad the way our American Negroes don't know nothing about Africa 'cept Tarzan and all that. And all that money they pour into these churches when they ought to be helping you people over there drive out them French and En-glishmen done taken away your land.

> [*The mother flashes a slightly superior look at her daughter upon completion of the recitation.*]

ASAGAI: [*Taken aback by this sudden and acutely unrelated expression of sympathy.*] Yes . . . yes . . .

MAMA: [*Smiling at him suddenly and relaxing and looking him over.*] How many miles is it from here to where you come from?

ASAGAI: Many thousands.

MAMA: [*Looking at him as she would* WALTER.] I bet you don't half look after yourself, being away from your mama either. I spec you better come 'round here from time to time and get yourself some decent home-cooked meals . . .

ASAGAI: [*Moved.*] Thank you. Thank you very much. [*They are all quiet, then—*] Well . . . I must go. I will call you Monday, Alaiyo.

MAMA: What's that he call you?

ASAGAI: Oh—"Alaiyo." I hope you don't mind. It is what you would call a nick-name, I think. It is a Yoruba word. I am a Yoruba.

MAMA: [*Looking at* BENEATHA.] I—I thought he was from—

ASAGAI: [*Understanding.*] Nigeria is my country. Yoruba is my tribal origin—

BENEATHA: You didn't tell us what Alaiyo means . . . for all I know, you might be calling me Little Idiot or something . . .

ASAGAI: Well . . . let me see . . . I do not know how just to explain it . . . The sense of a thing can be so different when it changes languages.

BENEATHA: You're evading.

ASAGAI: No—really it is difficult . . . [*Thinking.*] It means . . . it means One for

Whom Bread—Food—Is Not Enough. [*He looks at her.*] Is that all right?

BENEATHA: [*Understanding, softly.*] Thank you.

MAMA: [*Looking from one to the other and not understanding any of it.*] Well . . . that's nice . . . You must come see us again—Mr.—

ASAGAI: Ah-sah-guy . . .

MAMA: Yes . . . Do come again.

ASAGAI: Good-bye.

[*He exits.*]

MAMA: [*After him.*] Lord, that's a pretty thing just went out here! [*Insinuatingly, to her daughter.*] Yes, I guess I see why we done commence to get so interested in Africa 'round here. Missionaries my aunt Jenny!

[*She exits.*]

BENEATHA: Oh, Mama! . . .

[*She picks up the Nigerian dress and holds it up to her in front of the mirror again. She sets the headdress on haphazardly and then notices her hair again and clutches at it and then replaces the headdress and frowns at herself. Then she starts to wriggle in front of the mirror as she thinks a Nigerian woman might. TRAVIS enters and regards her.*]

TRAVIS: You cracking up?

BENEATHA: Shut up.

[*She pulls the headdress off and looks at herself in the mirror and clutches at her hair again and squinches her eyes as if trying to imagine something. Then, suddenly, she gets her raincoat and kerchief and hurriedly prepares for going out.*]

MAMA: [*Coming back into the room.*] She's resting now. Travis, baby, run next door and ask Miss Johnson to please let me have a little kitchen cleanser. This here can is empty as Jacob's kettle.

TRAVIS: I just came in.

MAMA: Do as you told. [*He exits and she looks at her daughter.*] Where you going?

BENEATHA: [*Halting at the door.*] To become a queen of the Nile!

[*She exits in a breathless blaze of glory. RUTH appears in the bedroom doorway.*]

MAMA: Who told you to get up?

RUTH: Ain't nothing wrong with me to be lying in no bed for. Where did Bennie go?

MAMA: [*Drumming her fingers.*] Far as I could make out—to Egypt. [RUTH *just looks at her.*] What time is it getting to?

RUTH: Ten twenty. And the mailman going to ring that bell this morning just like he done every morning for the last umpteen years.

[TRAVIS *comes in with the cleanser can.*]

TRAVIS: She say to tell you that she don't have much.

MAMA: [*Angrily.*] Lord, some people I could name sure is tight-fisted! [*Directing her grandson.*] Mark two cans of cleanser down on the list there. If she that hard up for kitchen cleanser, I sure don't want to forget to get her none!

RUTH: Lena—maybe the woman is just short on cleanser—

MAMA: [*Not listening.*] —Much baking powder as she done borrowed from me all these years, she could of done gone into the baking business!

[*The bell sounds suddenly and sharply and all three are stunned—serious and silent—mid-speech. In spite of all the other conversations and distractions of the morning, this is what they have been waiting for, even* TRAVIS, *who looks helplessly from his mother to his grandmother.* RUTH *is the first to come to life again.*]

RUTH: [*To* TRAVIS.] *Get down them steps, boy!*

[TRAVIS *snaps to life and flies out to get the mail.*]

MAMA: [*Her eyes wide, her hand to her breast.*] You mean it done really come?

RUTH: [*Excited.*] Oh, Miss Lena!

MAMA: [*Collecting herself.*] Well . . . I don't know what we all so excited about 'round here for. We known it was coming for months.

RUTH: That's a whole lot different from having it come and being able to hold it in your hands . . . a piece of paper worth ten thousand dollars . . . [TRAVIS *bursts back into the room. He holds the envelope high above his head, like a little dancer, his face is radiant and he is breathless. He moves to his grandmother with sudden slow ceremony and puts the envelope into her hands. She accepts it, and then merely holds it and looks at it.*] Come on! Open it . . . Lord have mercy, I wish Walter Lee was here!

TRAVIS: Open it, Grandmama!

MAMA: [*Staring at it.*] Now you all be quiet. It's just a check.

RUTH: Open it . . .

MAMA: [*Still staring at it.*] Now don't act silly . . . We ain't never been no people to act silly 'bout no money—

RUTH: [*Swiftly.*] We ain't never had none before—*open it!*

[MAMA *finally makes a good strong tear and pulls out the thin blue slice of paper and inspects it closely. The boy and his mother study it raptly over* MAMA's *shoulders.*]

MAMA: *Travis!* [*She is counting off with doubt.*] Is that the right number of zeros.

TRAVIS: Yes'm . . . ten thousand dollars. Gaalee, Grandmama, you rich.

MAMA: [*She holds the check away from her, still looking at it. Slowly her face sobers into a mask of unhappiness.*] Ten thousand dollars. [*She hands it to* RUTH.] Put it away somewhere, Ruth. [*She does not look at* RUTH; *her eyes seem to be seeing something somewhere very far off.*] Ten thousand dollars they give you. Ten thousand dollars.

TRAVIS: [*To his mother, sincerely.*] What's the matter with Grandmama—don't she want to be rich?

RUTH: [*Distractedly.*] You go on out and play now, baby. [TRAVIS *exits.* MAMA *starts wiping dishes absently, humming intently to herself.* RUTH *turns to her, with kind exasperation.*] You've gone and got yourself upset.

MAMA: [*Not looking at her.*] I spec if it wasn't for you all . . . I would just put that money away or give it to the church or something.

RUTH: Now what kind of talk is that. Mr. Younger would just be plain mad if he could hear you talking foolish like that.

MAMA: [*Stopping and staring off.*] Yes . . . he sure would. [*Sighing.*] We got enough to do with that money, all right. [*She halts then, and turns and looks at her daughter-in-law hard;* RUTH *avoids her eyes and* MAMA *wipes her hands with finality and starts to speak firmly to* RUTH.] Where did you go today, girl?

RUTH: To the doctor.

MAMA: [*Impatiently.*] Now, Ruth . . . you know better than that. Old Doctor Jones is strange enough in his way but there ain't nothing 'bout him make somebody slip and call him "she"—like you done this morning.

RUTH: Well, that's what happened—my tongue slipped.

MAMA: You went to see that woman, didn't you?

RUTH: [*Defensively, giving herself away.*] What woman you talking about?

MAMA: [*Angrily.*] That woman who—

[WALTER *enters in great excitement.*]

WALTER: Did it come?

MAMA: [*Quietly.*] Can't you give people a Christian greeting before you start asking about money?

WALTER: [*To* RUTH.] Did it come? [RUTH *unfolds the check and lays it quietly before him, watching him intently with thoughts of her own.* WALTER *sits down and grasps it close and counts off the zeros.*] Ten thousand dollars— [*He turns suddenly, frantically to his mother and draws some papers out of his breast pocket.*] Mama— look. Old Willy Harris put everything on paper—

MAMA: Son—I think you ought to talk to your wife . . . I'll go on out and leave you alone if you want—

WALTER: I can talk to her later—Mama, look—

MAMA: Son—

WALTER: WILL SOMEBODY PLEASE LISTEN TO ME TODAY!

MAMA: [*Quietly.*] I don't 'low no yellin' in this house, Walter Lee, and you know it— [WALTER *stares at them in frustration and starts to speak several times.*] And there ain't going to be no investing in no liquor stores. I don't aim to have to speak on that again.

[*A long pause.*]

WALTER: Oh—so you don't aim to have to speak on that again? So you have decided . . . [*Crumpling his papers.*] Well, *you* tell that to my boy tonight when you put him to sleep on the living-room couch . . . [*Turning to* MAMA *and speaking directly to her.*] Yeah—and tell it to my wife, Mama, tomorrow when she has to go out of here to look after somebody else's kids. And tell it to *me*, Mama, every time we need a new pair of curtains and I have to watch *you* go out and work in somebody's kitchen. Yeah, you tell me then!

[WALTER *starts out.*]

RUTH: Where you going?

WALTER: I'm going out!

RUTH: Where?

WALTER: Just out of this house somewhere—

RUTH: [*Getting her coat.*] I'll come too.

WALTER: I don't want you to come!

RUTH: I got something to talk to you about, Walter.

WALTER: That's too bad.

MAMA: [*Still quietly.*] Walter Lee— [*She waits and he finally turns and looks at her.*] Sit down.

WALTER: I'm a grown man, Mama.

MAMA: Ain't nobody said you wasn't grown. But you still in my house and my presence. And as long as you are—you'll talk to your wife civil. Now sit down.

RUTH: [*Suddenly.*] Oh, let him go on out and drink himself to death! He makes me sick to my stomach! [*She flings her coat against him.*]

WALTER: [*Violently.*] And you turn mine too, baby! [RUTH *goes into their bedroom and slams the door behind her.*] That was my greatest mistake—

MAMA: [*Still quietly.*] Walter, what is the matter with you?

WALTER: Matter with me? Ain't nothing the matter with *me!*

MAMA: Yes there is. Something eating you up like a crazy man. Something more than me not giving you this money. The past few years I been watching it happen to you. You get all nervous acting and kind of wild in the eyes— [WALTER *jumps up impatiently at her words.*] I said sit there now, I'm talking to you!

WALTER: Mama—I don't need no nagging at me today.

MAMA: Seem like you getting to a place where you always tied up in some kind of knot about something. But if anybody ask you 'bout it you just yell at 'em and bust out the house and go out and drink somewheres. Walter Lee, people can't live with that. Ruth's a good, patient girl in her way—but you getting to be too much. Boy, don't make the mistake of driving that girl away from you.

WALTER: Why—what she do for me?

MAMA: She loves you.

WALTER: Mama—I'm going out. I want to go off somewhere and be by myself for a while.

MAMA: I'm sorry 'bout your liquor store, son. It just wasn't the thing for us to do. That's what I want to tell you about—

WALTER: I got to go out, Mama—

[*He rises.*]

MAMA: It's dangerous, son.

WALTER: What's dangerous?

MAMA: When a man goes outside his home to look for peace.

WALTER: [*Beseechingly.*] Then why can't there never be no peace in this house then?

MAMA: You done found it in some other house?

WALTER: No—there ain't no woman! Why do women always think there's a woman somewhere when a man gets restless. [*Coming to her.*] Mama— Mama—I want so many things . . .

MAMA: Yes, son—

WALTER: I want so many things that they are driving me kind of crazy . . . Mama— look at me.

MAMA: I'm looking at you. You a good-looking boy. You got a job, a nice wife, a fine boy and—

WALTER: A job. [*Looks at her.*] Mama, a job? I open and close car doors all day long. I drive a man around in his limousine and I say, "Yes, sir; no, sir; very good, sir; shall I take the Drive, sir?" Mama, that ain't no kind of job . . . that ain't nothing at all. [*Very quietly.*] Mama, I don't know if I can make you understand.

MAMA: Understand what, baby?

WALTER: [*Quietly.*] Sometimes it's like I can see the future stretched out in front of me—just plain as day. The future, Mama. Hanging over there at the edge of my days. Just waiting for me—a big, looming blank space—full of *nothing.* Just waiting for *me.* [*Pause.*] Mama—sometimes when I'm downtown and I pass them cool, quiet-looking restaurants where them white boys are sitting back and talking 'bout things . . . sitting there turning deals worth millions of dollars . . . sometimes I see guys don't look much older than me—

MAMA: Son—how come you talk so much 'bout money?

WALTER: [*With immense passion.*] Because it is life, Mama!

MAMA: [*Quietly.*] Oh— [*Very quietly.*] So now it's life. Money is life. Once upon a time freedom used to be life—now it's money. I guess the world really do change . . .

WALTER: No—it was always money, Mama. We just didn't know about it.

MAMA: No . . . something has changed. [*She looks at him.*] You something new, boy. In my time we was worried about not being lynched and getting to the North if we could and how to stay alive and still have a pinch of dignity too . . . Now here come you and Beneatha—talking 'bout things we ain't never even thought about hardly, me and your daddy. You ain't satisfied or proud of nothing we done. I mean that you had a home; that we kept you out of trouble till you was grown; that you don't have to ride to work on the back of nobody's streetcar—You my children—but how different we done become.

WALTER: You just don't understand, Mama, you just don't understand.

MAMA: Son—do you know your wife is expecting another baby? [WALTER *stands, stunned, and absorbs what his mother has said.*] That's what she wanted to talk to you about. [WALTER *sinks down into a chair.*] This ain't for me to be telling— but you ought to know. [*She waits.*] I think Ruth is thinking 'bout getting rid of that child.[5]

WALTER: [*Slowly understanding.*] No—no—Ruth wouldn't do that.

---

5. Abortions were illegal and dangerous in the United States at that time.

MAMA: When the world gets ugly enough—a woman will do anything for her family. *The part that's already living.*

WALTER: You don't know Ruth, Mama, if you think she would do that.

[RUTH *opens the bedroom door and stands there a little limp.*]

RUTH: [*Beaten.*] Yes I would too, Walter. [*Pause.*] I gave her a five-dollar down payment.

[*There is total silence as the man stares at his wife and the mother stares at her son.*]

MAMA: [*Presently.*] Well— [*Tightly.*] Well—son, I'm waiting to hear you say something . . . I'm waiting to hear how you be your father's son. Be the man he was . . . [*Pause.*] Your wife say she going to destroy your child. And I'm waiting to hear you talk like him and say we a people who give children life, not who destroys them— [*She rises.*] I'm waiting to see you stand up and look like your daddy and say we done give up one baby to poverty and that we ain't going to give up nary another one . . . I'm waiting.

WALTER: Ruth—

MAMA: If you a son of mine, tell her! [WALTER *turns, looks at her and can say nothing. She continues, bitterly.*] You . . . you are a disgrace to your father's memory. Somebody get me my hat.

[CURTAIN.]

ACT II

SCENE ONE

Time: Later the same day.

At rise: RUTH *is ironing again. She has the radio going. Presently* BENEATHA's *bedroom door opens and* RUTH's *mouth falls and she puts down the iron in fascination.*

RUTH: What have we got on tonight!

BENEATHA: [*Emerging grandly from the doorway so that we can see her thoroughly robed in the costume* ASAGAI *brought.*] You are looking at what a well-dressed Nigerian woman wears— [*She parades for* RUTH, *her hair completely hidden by the headdress; she is coquettishly fanning herself with an ornate oriental fan, mistakenly more like Butterfly[6] than any Nigerian that ever was.*] Isn't it beautiful? [*She promenades to the radio and, with an arrogant flourish, turns off the good loud blues that is playing.*] Enough of this assimilationist junk! [RUTH *follows her with her eyes as she goes to the phonograph and puts on a record and turns and waits ceremoniously for the music to come up. Then, with a shout—*] OCOMOGOSIAY!

---

6. Butterfly McQueen (1911–1995), African American actor who appeared in *Gone with the Wind.*

[RUTH *jumps. The music comes up, a lovely Nigerian melody.* BENEATHA *listens, enraptured, her eyes far away—"back to the past." She begins to dance.* RUTH *is dumbfounded.*]

RUTH: What kind of dance is that?

BENEATHA: A folk dance.

RUTH: [*Pearl Bailey.*][7] What kind of folks do that, honey?

BENEATHA: It's from Nigeria. It's a dance of welcome.

RUTH: Who you welcoming?

BENEATHA: The men back to the village.

RUTH: Where they been?

BENEATHA: How should I know—out hunting or something. Anyway, they are coming back now . . .

RUTH: Well, that's good.

BENEATHA: [*With the record.*]

> Alundi, alundi
> Alundi alunya
> Jop pu a jeepua
> Ang gu sooooooooooo
>
> Ai yai yae . . .
> Ayehaye—alundi . . .

[WALTER *comes in during this performance; he has obviously been drinking. He leans against the door heavily and watches his sister, at first with distaste. Then his eyes look off—"back to the past"—as he lifts both his fists to the roof, screaming.*]

WALTER: YEAH . . . AND ETHIOPIA STRETCH FORTH HER HANDS AGAIN! . . .

RUTH: [*Drily, looking at him.*] Yes—and Africa sure is claiming her own tonight. [*She gives them both up and starts ironing again.*]

WALTER: [*All in a drunken, dramatic shout.*] Shut up! . . . I'm digging them drums . . . them drums move me! . . . [*He makes his weaving way to his wife's face and leans in close to her.*] In my *heart of hearts*— [*He thumps his chest.*] —I am much warrior!

RUTH: [*Without even looking up.*] In your heart of hearts you are much drunkard.

WALTER: [*Coming away from her and starting to wander around the room, shouting.*] Me and Jomo . . . [*Intently, in his sister's face. She has stopped dancing to watch him in this unknown mood.*] That's my man, Kenyatta. [*Shouting and thumping his chest.*] FLAMING SPEAR! HOT DAMN! [*He is suddenly in possession of an imaginary spear and actively spearing enemies all over the room.*] OCOMOGOSIAY . . . THE LION IS WAKING . . . OWIMOWEH! [*He pulls his shirt open and leaps up on a table and gestures with his spear. The bell rings.* RUTH *goes to answer.*]

BENEATHA: [*To encourage* WALTER, *thoroughly caught up with this side of him.*] OCOMOGOSIAY, FLAMING SPEAR!

---

7. Popular African American singer and entertainer (1918–1990).

WALTER: [*On the table, very far gone, his eyes pure glass sheets. He sees what we cannot, that he is a leader of his people, a great chief, a descendant of Chaka, and that the hour to march has come.*] Listen, my black brothers—

BENEATHA: OCOMOGOSIAY!

WALTER: —Do you hear the waters rushing against the shores of the coastlands—

BENEATHA: OCOMOGOSIAY!

WALTER: —Do you hear the screeching of the cocks in yonder hills beyond where the chiefs meet in council for the coming of the mighty war—

BENEATHA: OCOMOGOSIAY!

WALTER: —Do you hear the beating of the wings of the birds flying low over the mountains and the low places of our land—

[RUTH *opens the door.* GEORGE MURCHISON *enters.*]

BENEATHA: OCOMOGOSIAY!

WALTER: —Do you hear the singing of the women, singing the war songs of our fathers to the babies in the great houses . . . singing the sweet war songs? OH, DO YOU HEAR, MY BLACK BROTHERS!

BENEATHA: [*Completely gone.*] We hear you, Flaming Spear—

WALTER: Telling us to prepare for the greatness of the time— [*To* GEORGE.] Black Brother!

[*He extends his hand for the fraternal clasp.*]

GEORGE: Black Brother, hell!

RUTH: [*Having had enough, and embarrassed for the family.*] Beneatha, you got company—what's the matter with you? Walter Lee Younger, get down off that table and stop acting like a fool . . .

[WALTER *comes down off the table suddenly and makes a quick exit to the bathroom.*]

RUTH: He's had a little to drink . . . I don't know what her excuse is.

GEORGE: [*To* BENEATHA.] Look honey, we're going *to* the theatre—we're not going to be *in* it . . . so go change, huh?

RUTH: You expect this boy to go out with you looking like that?

BENEATHA: [*Looking at* GEORGE.] That's up to George. If he's ashamed of his heritage—

GEORGE: Oh, don't be so proud of yourself, Bennie—just because you look eccentric.

BENEATHA: How can something that's natural be eccentric?

GEORGE: That's what being eccentric means—being natural. Get dressed.

BENEATHA: I don't like that, George.

RUTH: Why must you and your brother make an argument out of everything people say?

BENEATHA: Because I hate assimilationist Negroes!

RUTH: Will somebody please tell me what assimila-who-ever means!

GEORGE: Oh, it's just a college girl's way of calling people Uncle Toms—but that isn't what it means at all.

RUTH: Well, what does it mean?

BENEATHA: [*Cutting* GEORGE *off and staring at him as she replies to* RUTH.] It means someone who is willing to give up his own culture and submerge himself completely in the dominant, and in this case, *oppressive* culture!

GEORGE: Oh, dear, dear, dear! Here we go! A lecture on the African past! On our Great West African Heritage! In one second we will hear all about the great Ashanti empires; the great Songhay civilizations; and the great sculpture of Bénin—and then some poetry in the Bantu—and the whole monologue will end with the word *heritage!* [*Nastily.*] Let's face it, baby, your heritage is nothing but a bunch of raggedy-assed spirituals and some grass huts!

BENEATHA: *Grass huts!* [RUTH *crosses to her and forcibly pushes her toward the bedroom.*] See there . . . you are standing there in your splendid ignorance talking about people who were the first to smelt iron on the face of the earth! [RUTH *is pushing her through the door.*] The Ashanti were performing surgical operations when the English— [RUTH *pulls the door to, with* BENEATHA *on the other side, and smiles graciously at* GEORGE. BENEATHA *opens the door and shouts the end of the sentence defiantly at* GEORGE.] —were still tattooing themselves with blue dragons . . . [*She goes back inside.*]

RUTH: Have a seat, George. [*They both sit.* RUTH *folds her hands rather primly on her lap, determined to demonstrate the civilization of the family.*] Warm, ain't it? I mean for September. [*Pause.*] Just like they always say about Chicago weather: If it's too hot or cold for you, just wait a minute and it'll change. [*She smiles happily at this cliché of clichés.*] Everybody say it's got to do with them bombs and things they keep setting off.[8] [*Pause.*] Would you like a nice cold beer?

GEORGE: No, thank you. I don't care for beer. [*He looks at his watch.*] I hope she hurries up.

RUTH: What time is the show?

GEORGE: It's an eight-thirty curtain. That's just Chicago, though. In New York standard curtain time is eight forty.

[*He is rather proud of this knowledge.*]

RUTH: [*Properly appreciating it.*] You get to New York a lot?

GEORGE: [*Offhand.*] Few times a year.

RUTH: Oh—that's nice. I've never been to New York.

[WALTER *enters. We feel he has relieved himself, but the edge of unreality is still with him.*]

WALTER: New York ain't got nothing Chicago ain't. Just a bunch of hustling people all squeezed up together—being "Eastern."

[*He turns his face into a screw of displeasure.*]

GEORGE: Oh—you've been?

WALTER: *Plenty* of times.

8. In the 1950s, people commonly blamed weather fluctuations on atomic testing.

RUTH: [*Shocked at the lie.*] Walter Lee Younger!

WALTER: [*Staring her down.*] Plenty! [*Pause.*] What we got to drink in this house? Why don't you offer this man some refreshment. [*To* GEORGE.] They don't know how to entertain people in this house, man.

GEORGE: Thank you—I don't really care for anything.

WALTER: [*Feeling his head; sobriety coming.*] Where's Mama?

RUTH: She ain't come back yet.

WALTER: [*Looking* MURCHISON *over from head to toe, scrutinizing his carefully casual tweed sports jacket over cashmere V-neck sweater over soft eyelet shirt and tie, and soft slacks, finished off with white buckskin shoes.*] Why all you college boys wear them fairyish-looking white shoes?

RUTH: Walter Lee!

[GEORGE MURCHISON *ignores the remark.*]

WALTER: [*To* RUTH.] Well, they look crazy as hell—white shoes, cold as it is.

RUTH: [*Crushed.*] You have to excuse him—

WALTER: No he don't! Excuse me for what? What you always excusing me for! I'll excuse myself when I needs to be excused! [*A pause.*] They look as funny as them black knee socks Beneatha wears out of here all the time.

RUTH: It's the college *style*, Walter.

WALTER: Style, hell. She looks like she got burnt legs or something!

RUTH: Oh, Walter—

WALTER: [*An irritable mimic.*] Oh, Walter! Oh, Walter! [*To* MURCHISON.] How's your old man making out? I understand you all going to buy that big hotel on the Drive?[9] [*He finds a beer in the refrigerator, wanders over to* MURCHISON, *sipping and wiping his lips with the back of his hand, and straddling a chair backwards to talk to the other man.*] Shrewd move. Your old man is all right, man. [*Tapping his head and half winking for emphasis.*] I mean he knows how to operate. I mean he thinks *big*, you know what I mean, I mean for a *home*, you know? But I think he's kind of running out of ideas now. I'd like to talk to him. Listen, man, I got some plans that could turn this city upside down. I mean I think like he does. *Big*. Invest big, gamble big, hell, lose *big* if you have to, you know what I mean. It's hard to find a man on this whole Southside who understands my kind of thinking—you dig? [*He scrutinizes* MURCHISON *again, drinks his beer, squints his eyes and leans in close, confidential, man to man.*] Me and you ought to sit down and talk sometimes, man. Man, I got me some ideas . . .

GEORGE: [*With boredom.*] Yeah—sometimes we'll have to do that, Walter.

WALTER: [*Understanding the indifference, and offended.*] Yeah—well, when you get the time, man. I know you a busy little boy.

RUTH: Walter, please—

WALTER: [*Bitterly, hurt.*] I know ain't nothing in this world as busy as you colored college boys with your fraternity pins and white shoes . . .

RUTH: [*Covering her face with humiliation.*] Oh, Walter Lee—

WALTER: I see you all the time—with the books tucked under your arms—going

9. Lake Shore Drive, a scenic thoroughfare along Lake Michigan.

to your [*British A—a mimic.*] "clahsses." And for what! What the hell you learning over there? Filling up your heads— [*Counting off on his fingers.*] — with the sociology and the psychology—but they teaching you how to be a man? How to take over and run the world? They teaching you how to run a rubber plantation or a steel mill? Naw—just to talk proper and read books and wear white shoes . . .

GEORGE: [*Looking at him with distaste, a little above it all.*] You're all wacked up with bitterness, man.

WALTER: [*Intently, almost quietly, between the teeth, glaring at the boy.*] And you— ain't you bitter, man? Ain't you just about had it yet? Don't you see no stars gleaming that you can't reach out and grab? You happy?—You contented son-of-a-bitch—you happy? You got it made? Bitter? Man, I'm a volcano. Bitter? Here I am a giant—surrounded by ants! Ants who can't even understand what it is the giant is talking about.

RUTH: [*Passionately and suddenly.*] Oh, Walter—ain't you with nobody!

WALTER: [*Violently.*] No! 'Cause ain't nobody with me! Not even my own mother!

RUTH: Walter, that's a terrible thing to say!

[BENEATHA *enters, dressed for the evening in a cocktail dress and earrings.*]

GEORGE: Well—hey, you look great.

BENEATHA: Let's go, George. See you all later.

RUTH: Have a nice time.

GEORGE: Thanks. Good night. [*To* WALTER, *sarcastically.*] Good night, *Prometheus.*[1]

[BENEATHA *and* GEORGE *exit.*]

WALTER: [*To* RUTH.] Who is Prometheus?

RUTH: I don't know. Don't worry about it.

WALTER: [*In fury, pointing after* GEORGE.] See there—they get to a point where they can't insult you man to man—they got to go talk about something ain't nobody never heard of!

RUTH: How do you know it was an insult? [*To humor him.*] Maybe Prometheus is a nice fellow.

WALTER: Prometheus! I bet there ain't even no such thing! I bet that simple-minded clown—

RUTH: Walter—

[*She stops what she is doing and looks at him.*]

WALTER: [*Yelling.*] Don't start!

RUTH: Start what?

WALTER: Your nagging! Where was I? Who was I with? How much money did I spend?

RUTH: [*Plaintively.*] Walter Lee—why don't we just try to talk about it . . .

---

1. In Greek mythology, Prometheus represented the bold creative spirit; he stole fire from Olympus (the locale of the gods) and gave it to humankind.

WALTER: [*Not listening.*] I been out talking with people who understand me. People who care about the things I got on my mind.

RUTH: [*Wearily.*] I guess that means people like Willy Harris.

WALTER: Yes, people like Willy Harris.

RUTH: [*With a sudden flash of impatience.*] Why don't you all just hurry up and go into the banking business and stop talking about it!

WALTER: Why? You want to know why? 'Cause we all tied up in a race of people that don't know how to do nothing but moan, pray and have babies!

[*The line is too bitter even for him and he looks at her and sits down.*]

RUTH: Oh, Walter . . . [*Softly.*] Honey, why can't you stop fighting me?

WALTER: [*Without thinking.*] Who's fighting you? Who even cares about you?

[*This line begins the retardation of his mood.*]

RUTH: Well— [*She waits a long time, and then with resignation starts to put away her things.*] I guess I might as well go on to bed . . . [*More or less to herself.*] I don't know where we lost it . . . but we have . . . [*Then, to him.*] I—I'm sorry about this new baby, Walter. I guess maybe I better go on and do what I started . . . I guess I just didn't realize how bad things was with us . . . I guess I just didn't really realize— [*She starts out to the bedroom and stops.*] You want some hot milk?

WALTER: Hot milk?

RUTH: Yes—hot milk.

WALTER: Why hot milk?

RUTH: 'Cause after all that liquor you come home with you ought to have something hot in your stomach.

WALTER: I don't want no milk.

RUTH: You want some coffee then?

WALTER: No, I don't want no coffee. I don't want nothing hot to drink. [*Almost plaintively.*] Why you always trying to give me something to eat?

RUTH: [*Standing and looking at him helplessly.*] What else can I give you, Walter Lee Younger?

[*She stands and looks at him and presently turns to go out again. He lifts his head and watches her going away from him in a new mood which began to emerge when he asked her "Who cares about you?"*]

WALTER: It's been rough, ain't it, baby? [*She hears and stops but does not turn around and he continues to her back.*] I guess between two people there ain't never as much understood as folks generally thinks there is. I mean like between me and you— [*She turns to face him.*] How we gets to the place where we scared to talk softness to each other. [*He waits, thinking hard himself.*] Why you think it got to be like that? [*He is thoughtful, almost as a child would be.*] Ruth, what is it gets into people ought to be close?

RUTH: I don't know, honey. I think about it a lot.

WALTER: On account of you and me, you mean? The way things are with us. The way something done come down between us.

RUTH: There ain't so much between us, Walter . . . Not when you come to me and try to talk to me. Try to be with me . . . a little even.

WALTER: [*Total honesty.*] Sometimes . . . sometimes . . . I don't even know how to try.

RUTH: Walter—

WALTER: Yes?

RUTH: [*Coming to him, gently and with misgiving, but coming to him.*] Honey . . . life don't have to be like this. I mean sometimes people can do things so that things are better . . . You remember how we used to talk when Travis was born . . . about the way we were going to live . . . the kind of house . . . [*She is stroking his head.*] Well, it's all starting to slip away from us . . .

[MAMA *enters, and* WALTER *jumps up and shouts at her.*]

WALTER: Mama, where have you been?

MAMA: My—them steps is longer than they used to be. Whew! [*She sits down and ignores him.*] How you feeling this evening, Ruth?

[RUTH *shrugs, disturbed some at having been prematurely interrupted and watching her husband knowingly.*]

WALTER: Mama, where have you been all day?

MAMA: [*Still ignoring him and leaning on the table and changing to more comfortable shoes.*] Where's Travis?

RUTH: I let him go out earlier and he ain't come back yet. Boy, is he going to get it!

WALTER: Mama!

MAMA: [*As if she has heard him for the first time.*] Yes, son?

WALTER: Where did you go this afternoon?

MAMA: I went downtown to tend to some business that I had to tend to.

WALTER: What kind of business?

MAMA: You know better than to question me like a child, Brother.

WALTER: [*Rising and bending over the table.*] Where were you, Mama? [*Bringing his fists down and shouting.*] Mama, you didn't go do something with that insurance money, something crazy?

[*The front door opens slowly, interrupting him, and* TRAVIS *peeks his head in, less than hopefully.*]

TRAVIS: [*To his mother.*] Mama, I—

RUTH: "Mama I" nothing! You're going to get it, boy! Get on in that bedroom and get yourself ready!

TRAVIS: But I—

MAMA: Why don't you all never let the child explain hisself.

RUTH: Keep out of it now, Lena.

[MAMA *clamps her lips together, and* RUTH *advances toward her son menacingly.*]

RUTH: A thousand times I have told you not to go off like that—

MAMA: [*Holding out her arms to her grandson.*] Well—at least let me tell him something. I want him to be the first one to hear . . . Come here, Travis. [*The boy obeys, gladly.*] Travis— [*She takes him by the shoulder and looks into his face.*] — you know that money we got in the mail this morning?

TRAVIS: Yes'm—

MAMA: Well—what you think your grandmama gone and done with that money?

TRAVIS: I don't know, Grandmama.

MAMA: [*Putting her finger on his nose for emphasis.*] She went out and she bought you a house! [*The explosion comes from* WALTER *at the end of the revelation and he jumps up and turns away from all of them in a fury.* MAMA *continues, to* TRAVIS.] You glad about the house? It's going to be yours when you get to be a man.

TRAVIS: Yeah—I always wanted to live in a house.

MAMA: All right, gimme some sugar then— [TRAVIS *puts his arms around her neck as she watches her son over the boy's shoulder. Then, to* TRAVIS, *after the embrace.*] Now when you say your prayers tonight, you thank God and your grandfather—'cause it was him who give you the house—in his way.

RUTH: [*Taking the boy from* MAMA *and pushing him toward the bedroom.*] Now you get out of here and get ready for your beating.

TRAVIS: Aw, Mama—

RUTH: Get on in there— [*Closing the door behind him and turning radiantly to her mother-in-law.*] So you went and did it!

MAMA: [*Quietly, looking at her son with pain.*] Yes, I did.

RUTH: [*Raising both arms classically.*] Praise God! [*Looks at* WALTER *a moment, who says nothing. She crosses rapidly to her husband.*] Please, honey—let me be glad . . . you be glad too. [*She has laid her hands on his shoulders, but he shakes himself free of her roughly, without turning to face her.*] Oh, Walter . . . a home . . . *a home.* [*She comes back to* MAMA.] Well—where is it? How big is it? How much it going to cost?

MAMA: Well—

RUTH: When we moving?

MAMA: [*Smiling at her.*] First of the month.

RUTH: [*Throwing back her head with jubilance.*] Praise God!

MAMA: [*Tentatively, still looking at her son's back turned against her and* RUTH.] It's— it's a nice house too . . . [*She cannot help speaking directly to him. An imploring quality in her voice, her manner, makes her almost like a girl now.*] Three bedrooms—nice big one for you and Ruth . . . Me and Beneatha still have to share our room, but Travis have one of his own—and [*With difficulty.*] I figure if the—new baby—is a boy, we could get one of them double-decker outfits . . . And there's a yard with a little patch of dirt where I could maybe get to grow me a few flowers . . . And a nice big basement . . .

RUTH: Walter honey, be glad—

MAMA: [*Still to his back, fingering things on the table.*] 'Course I don't want to make it sound fancier than it is . . . It's just a plain little old house—but it's made good and solid—and it will be *ours.* Walter Lee—it makes a difference in a man when he can walk on floors that belong to *him* . . .

RUTH: Where is it?

MAMA: [*Frightened at this telling.*] Well—well—it's out there in Clybourne Park—[2]

[RUTH's *radiance fades abruptly, and* WALTER *finally turns slowly to face his mother with incredulity and hostility.*]

RUTH: Where?

MAMA: [*Matter-of-factly.*] Four o six Clybourne Street, Clybourne Park.

RUTH: Clybourne Park? Mama, there ain't no colored people living in Clybourne Park.

MAMA: [*Almost idiotically.*] Well, I guess there's going to be some now.

WALTER: [*Bitterly.*] So that's the peace and comfort you went out and bought for us today!

MAMA: [*Raising her eyes to meet his finally.*] Son—I just tried to find the nicest place for the least amount of money for my family.

RUTH: [*Trying to recover from the shock.*] Well—well—'course I ain't one never been 'fraid of no crackers[3] mind you—but—well, wasn't there no other houses nowhere?

MAMA: Them houses they put up for colored in them areas way out all seem to cost twice as much as other houses. I did the best I could.

RUTH: [*Struck senseless with the news, in its various degrees of goodness and trouble, she sits a moment, her fists propping her chin in thought, and then she starts to rise, bringing her fists down with vigor, the radiance spreading from cheek to cheek again.*] Well—well!—All I can say is—if this is my time in life—*my time*—to say good-bye— [*And she builds with momentum as she starts to circle the room with an exuberant, almost tearfully happy release.*] —to these Goddamned cracking walls!— [*She pounds the walls.*] —and these marching roaches!— [*She wipes at an imaginary army of marching roaches.*] —and this cramped little closet which ain't now or never was no kitchen! . . . then I say it loud and good, Hallelujah! and good-bye misery . . . I don't never want to see your ugly face again! [*She laughs joyously, having practically destroyed the apartment, and flings her arms up and lets them come down happily, slowly, reflectively, over her abdomen, aware for the first time perhaps that the life therein pulses with happiness and not despair.*] Lena?

MAMA: [*Moved, watching her happiness.*] Yes, honey?

RUTH: [*Looking off.*] Is there—is there a whole lot of sunlight?

MAMA: [*Understanding.*] Yes, child, there's a whole lot of sunlight.

[*Long pause.*]

RUTH: [*Collecting herself and going to the door of the room* TRAVIS *is in.*] Well—I guess I better see 'bout Travis. [*To* MAMA.] Lord, I sure don't feel like whipping nobody today!

[*She exits.*]

MAMA: [*The mother and son are left alone now and the mother waits a long time, considering deeply, before she speaks.*] Son—you—you understand what I done,

---

2. On Chicago's Near North Side.   3. Derogatory term for poor whites.

don't you? [WALTER *is silent and sullen.*] I—I just seen my family falling apart today . . . just falling to pieces in front of my eyes . . . We couldn't of gone on like we was today. We was going backwards 'stead of forwards—talking 'bout killing babies and wishing each other was dead . . . When it gets like that in life—you just got to do something different, push on out and do something bigger . . . [*She waits.*] I wish you say something, son . . . I wish you'd say how deep inside you you think I done the right thing—

WALTER: [*Crossing slowly to his bedroom door and finally turning there and speaking measuredly.*] What you need me to say you done right for? *You* the head of this family. You run our lives like you want to. It was your money and you did what you wanted with it. So what you need for me to say it was all right for? [*Bitterly, to hurt her as deeply as he knows is possible.*] So you butchered up a dream of mine—you—who always talking 'bout your children's dreams . . .

MAMA: Walter Lee—

[*He just closes the door behind him.* MAMA *sits alone, thinking heavily.*]

[CURTAIN.]

SCENE TWO

Time: Friday night. A few weeks later.

At rise: Packing crates mark the intention of the family to move. BENEATHA *and* GEORGE *come in, presumably from an evening out again.*

GEORGE: O.K. . . . O.K., whatever you say . . . [*They both sit on the couch. He tries to kiss her. She moves away.*] Look, we've had a nice evening; let's not spoil it, huh? . . .

[*He again turns her head and tries to nuzzle in and she turns away from him, not with distaste but with momentary lack of interest; in a mood to pursue what they were talking about.*]

BENEATHA: I'm *trying* to talk to you.

GEORGE: We always talk.

BENEATHA: Yes—and I love to talk.

GEORGE: [*Exasperated; rising.*] I know it and I don't mind it sometimes . . . I want you to cut it out, see—The moody stuff, I mean. I don't like it. You're a nice-looking girl . . . all over. That's all you need, honey, forget the atmosphere. Guys aren't going to go for the atmosphere—they're going to go for what they see. Be glad for that. Drop the Garbo[4] routine. It doesn't go with you. As for myself, I want a nice— [*Groping.*] —simple [*Thoughtfully.*] —sophisticated girl . . . not a poet—O.K.?

[*She rebuffs him again and he starts to leave.*]

---

4. Greta Garbo (1905–1990), Swedish-born American film star whose sultry, remote, and European femininity was widely imitated mid century.

BENEATHA: Why are you angry?

GEORGE: Because this is stupid! I don't go out with you to discuss the nature of "quiet desperation"[5] or to hear all about your thoughts—because the world will go on thinking what it thinks regardless—

BENEATHA: Then why read books? Why go to school?

GEORGE: [*With artificial patience, counting on his fingers.*] It's simple. You read books—to learn facts—to get grades—to pass the course—to get a degree. That's all—it has nothing to do with thoughts.

[*A long pause.*]

BENEATHA: I see. [*A longer pause as she looks at him.*] Good night, George.

[GEORGE *looks at her a little oddly, and starts to exit. He meets* MAMA *coming in.*]

GEORGE: Oh—hello, Mrs. Younger.

MAMA: Hello, George, how you feeling?

GEORGE: Fine—fine, how are you?

MAMA: Oh, a little tired. You know them steps can get you after a day's work. You all have a nice time tonight?

GEORGE: Yes—a fine time. Well, good night.

MAMA: Good night. [*He exits.* MAMA *closes the door behind her.*] Hello, honey. What you sitting like that for?

BENEATHA: I'm just sitting.

MAMA: Didn't you have a nice time?

BENEATHA: No.

MAMA: No? What's the matter?

BENEATHA: Mama, George is a fool—honest. [*She rises.*]

MAMA: [*Hustling around unloading the packages she has entered with. She stops.*] Is he, baby?

BENEATHA: Yes.

[BENEATHA *makes up* TRAVIS' *bed as she talks.*]

MAMA: You sure?

BENEATHA: Yes.

MAMA: Well—I guess you better not waste your time with no fools.

[BENEATHA *looks up at her mother, watching her put groceries in the refrigerator. Finally she gathers up her things and starts into the bedroom. At the door she stops and looks back at her mother.*]

BENEATHA: Mama—

MAMA: Yes, baby—

BENEATHA: Thank you.

MAMA: For what?

---

5. In *Walden* (1854), Henry Thoreau said that "the mass of men lead lives of quiet desperation."

BENEATHA: For understanding me this time.

[*She exits quickly and the mother stands, smiling a little, looking at the place where* BENEATHA *just stood.* RUTH *enters.*]

RUTH: Now don't you fool with any of this stuff, Lena—

MAMA: Oh, I just thought I'd sort a few things out.

[*The phone rings.* RUTH *answers.*]

RUTH: [*At the phone.*] Hello—Just a minute. [*Goes to door.*] Walter, it's Mrs. Arnold. [*Waits. Goes back to the phone. Tense.*] Hello. Yes, this is his wife speaking . . . He's lying down now. Yes . . . well, he'll be in tomorrow. He's been very sick. Yes—I know we should have called, but we were so sure he'd be able to come in today. Yes—yes, I'm very sorry. Yes . . . Thank you very much. [*She hangs up.* WALTER *is standing in the doorway of the bedroom behind her.*] That was Mrs. Arnold.

WALTER: [*Indifferently.*] Was it?

RUTH: She said if you don't come in tomorrow that they are getting a new man . . .

WALTER: Ain't that sad—ain't that crying sad.

RUTH: She said Mr. Arnold has had to take a cab for three days . . . Walter, you ain't been to work for three days! [*This is a revelation to her.*] Where you been, Walter Lee Younger? [WALTER *looks at her and starts to laugh.*] You're going to lose your job.

WALTER: That's right . . .

RUTH: Oh, Walter, and with your mother working like a dog every day—

WALTER: That's sad too—Everything is sad.

MAMA: What you been doing for these three days, son?

WALTER: Mama—you don't know all the things a man what got leisure can find to do in this city . . . What's this—Friday night? Well—Wednesday I borrowed Willy Harris' car and I went for a drive . . . just me and myself and I drove and drove . . . Way out . . . way past South Chicago, and I parked the car and I sat and looked at the steel mills all day long. I just sat in the car and looked at them big black chimneys for hours. Then I drove back and I went to the Green Hat. [*Pause.*] And Thursday—Thursday I borrowed the car again and I got in it and I pointed it the other way and I drove the other way—for hours—way, way up to Wisconsin, and I looked at the farms. I just drove and looked at the farms. Then I drove back and I went to the Green Hat. [*Pause.*] And today—today I didn't get the car. Today I just walked. All over the South-side. And I looked at the Negroes and they looked at me and finally I just sat down on the curb at Thirty-ninth and South Parkway and I just sat there and watched the Negroes go by. And then I went to the Green Hat. You all sad? You all depressed? And you know where I am going right now—

[RUTH *goes out quietly.*]

MAMA: Oh, Big Walter, is this the harvest of our days?

WALTER: You know what I like about the Green Hat? [*He turns the radio on and a steamy, deep blues pours into the room.*] I like this little cat they got there who blows a sax . . . He blows. He talks to me. He ain't but 'bout five feet tall and he's got a conked head[6] and his eyes is always closed and he's all music—

MAMA: [*Rising and getting some papers out of her handbag.*] Walter—

WALTER: And there's this other guy who plays the piano . . . and they got a sound. I mean they can work on some music . . . They got the best little combo in the world in the Green Hat . . . You can just sit there and drink and listen to them three men play and you realize that don't nothing matter worth a damn, but just being there—

MAMA: I've helped do it to you, haven't I, son? Walter, I been wrong.

WALTER: Naw—you ain't never been wrong about nothing, Mama.

MAMA: Listen to me, now. I say I been wrong, son. That I been doing to you what the rest of the world been doing to you. [*She stops and he looks up slowly at her and she meets his eyes pleadingly.*] Walter—what you ain't never understood is that I ain't got nothing, don't own nothing, ain't never really wanted nothing that wasn't for you. There ain't nothing as precious to me . . . There ain't nothing worth holding on to, money, dreams, nothing else—if it means—if it means it's going to destroy my boy. [*She puts her papers in front of him and he watches her without speaking or moving.*] I paid the man thirty-five hundred dollars down on the house. That leaves sixty-five hundred dollars. Monday morning I want you to take this money and take three thousand dollars and put it in a savings account for Beneatha's medical schooling. The rest you put in a checking account—with your name on it. And from now on any penny that come out of it or that go in it is for you to look after. For you to decide. [*She drops her hands a little helplessly.*] It ain't much, but it's all I got in the world and I'm putting it in your hands. I'm telling you to be the head of this family from now on like you supposed to be.

WALTER: [*Stares at the money.*] You trust me like that, Mama?

MAMA: I ain't never stop trusting you. Like I ain't never stop loving you.

[*She goes out, and* WALTER *sits looking at the money on the table as the music continues in its idiom, pulsing in the room. Finally, in a decisive gesture, he gets up, and, in mingled joy and desperation, picks up the money. At the same moment,* TRAVIS *enters for bed.*]

TRAVIS: What's the matter, Daddy? You drunk?

WALTER: [*Sweetly, more sweetly than we have ever known him.*] No, Daddy ain't drunk. Daddy ain't going to never be drunk again. . . .

TRAVIS: Well, good night, Daddy.

[*The father has come from behind the couch and leans over, embracing his son.*]

WALTER: Son, I feel like talking to you tonight.

TRAVIS: About what?

6. Straightened hair.

WALTER: Oh, about a lot of things. About you and what kind of man you going to be when you grow up . . . Son—son, what do you want to be when you grow up?

TRAVIS: A bus driver.

WALTER: [*Laughing a little.*] A what? Man, that ain't nothing to want to be!

TRAVIS: Why not?

WALTER: 'Cause, man—it ain't big enough—you know what I mean.

TRAVIS: I don't know then. I can't make up my mind. Sometimes Mama asks me that too. And sometimes when I tell you I just want to be like you—she says she don't want me to be like that and sometimes she says she does . . .

WALTER: [*Gathering him up in his arms.*] You know what, Travis? In seven years you going to be seventeen years old. And things is going to be very different with us in seven years, Travis . . . One day when you are seventeen I'll come home—home from my office downtown somewhere—

TRAVIS: You don't work in no office, Daddy.

WALTER: No—but after tonight. After what your daddy gonna do tonight, there's going to be offices—a whole lot of offices . . .

TRAVIS: What you gonna do tonight, Daddy?

WALTER: You wouldn't understand yet, son, but your daddy's gonna make a transaction . . . a business transaction that's going to change our lives . . . That's how come one day when you 'bout seventeen years old I'll come home and I'll be pretty tired, you know what I mean, after a day of conferences and secretaries getting things wrong the way they do . . . 'cause an executive's life is hell, man— [*The more he talks the farther away he gets.*] And I'll pull the car up on the driveway . . . just a plain black Chrysler, I think, with white walls— no—black tires. More elegant. Rich people don't have to be flashy . . . though I'll have to get something a little sportier for Ruth—maybe a Cadillac convertible to do her shopping in . . . And I'll come up the steps to the house and the gardener will be clipping away at the hedges and he'll say, "Good evening, Mr. Younger." And I'll say, "Hello, Jefferson, how are you this evening?" And I'll go inside and Ruth will come downstairs and meet me at the door and we'll kiss each other and she'll take my arm and we'll go up to your room to see you sitting on the floor with the catalogues of all the great schools in America around you . . . All the great schools in the world. And—and I'll say, all right son—it's your seventeenth birthday, what is it you've decided? . . . Just tell me where you want to go to school and you'll *go*. Just tell me, what it is you want to be—and you'll *be* it . . . Whatever you want to be— Yessir! [*He holds his arms open for* TRAVIS.] You just name it, son . . . [TRAVIS *leaps into them.*] and I hand you the world!

[WALTER's *voice has risen in pitch and hysterical promise and on the last line he lifts* TRAVIS *high.*]

[BLACKOUT.]

SCENE THREE

Time: Saturday, moving day, one week later.

Before the curtain rises, RUTH'*s voice, a strident, dramatic church alto, cuts through the silence.*

It is, in the darkness, a triumphant surge, a penetrating statement of expectation: "Oh, Lord, I don't feel no ways tired! Children, oh, glory hallelujah!"

As the curtain rises we see that RUTH *is alone in the living room, finishing up the family's packing. It is moving day. She is nailing crates and tying cartons.* BENEATHA *enters, carrying a guitar case, and watches her exuberant sister-in-law.*

RUTH: Hey!

BENEATHA: [*Putting away the case.*] Hi.

RUTH: [*Pointing at a package.*] Honey—look in that package there and see what I found on sale this morning at the South Center. [RUTH *gets up and moves to the package and draws out some curtains.*] Lookahere—hand-turned hems!

BENEATHA: How do you know the window size out there?

RUTH: [*Who hadn't thought of that.*] Oh—Well, they bound to fit something in the whole house. Anyhow, they was too good a bargain to pass up. [RUTH *slaps her head, suddenly remembering something.*] Oh, Bennie—I meant to put a special note on that carton over there. That's your mama's good china and she wants 'em to be very careful with it.

BENEATHA: I'll do it.

[BENEATHA *finds a piece of paper and starts to draw large letters on it.*]

RUTH: You know what I'm going to do soon as I get in that new house?

BENEATHA: What?

RUTH: Honey—I'm going to run me a tub of water up to here . . . [*With her fingers practically up to her nostrils.*] And I'm going to get in it—and I am going to sit . . . and sit . . . and sit in that hot water and the first person who knocks to tell *me* to hurry up and come out—

BENEATHA: Gets shot at sunrise.

RUTH: [*Laughing happily.*] You said it, sister! [*Noticing how large* BENEATHA *is absent-mindedly making the note.*] Honey, they ain't going to read that from no airplane.

BENEATHA: [*Laughing herself.*] I guess I always think things have more emphasis if they are big, somehow.

RUTH: [*Looking up at her and smiling.*] You and your brother seem to have that as a philosophy of life. Lord, that man—done changed so 'round here. You know—you know what we did last night? Me and Walter Lee?

BENEATHA: What?

RUTH: [*Smiling to herself.*] We went to the movies. [*Looking at* BENEATHA *to see if she understands.*] We went to the movies. You know the last time me and Walter went to the movies together?

BENEATHA: No.

RUTH: Me neither. That's how long it been. [*Smiling again.*] But we went last night.

The picture wasn't much good, but that didn't seem to matter. We went— and we held hands.

BENEATHA: Oh, Lord!

RUTH: We held hands—and you know what?

BENEATHA: What?

RUTH: When we come out of the show it was late and dark and all the stores and things was closed up . . . and it was kind of chilly and there wasn't many people on the streets . . . and we was still holding hands, me and Walter.

BENEATHA: You're killing me.

[WALTER *enters with a large package. His happiness is deep in him; he cannot keep still with his new-found exuberance. He is singing and wiggling and snapping his fingers. He puts his package in a corner and puts a phonograph record, which he has brought in with him, on the record player. As the music comes up he dances over to* RUTH *and tries to get her to dance with him. She gives in at last to his raunchiness and in a fit of giggling allows herself to be drawn into his mood and together they deliberately burlesque an old social dance of their youth.*]

BENEATHA: [*Regarding them a long time as they dance, then drawing in her breath for a deeply exaggerated comment which she does not particularly mean.*] Talk about— olddddddddddd-fashioneddddddd—Negroes!

WALTER: [*Stopping momentarily.*] What kind of Negroes?

[*He says this in fun. He is not angry with her today, nor with anyone. He starts to dance with his wife again.*]

BENEATHA: Old-fashioned.

WALTER: [*As he dances with* RUTH.] You know, when these *New Negroes* have their convention— [*Pointing at his sister.*] —that is going to be the chairman of the Committee on Unending Agitation. [*He goes on dancing, then stops.*] Race, race, race! . . . Girl, I do believe you are the first person in the history of the entire human race to successfully brainwash yourself. [BENEATHA *breaks up and he goes on dancing. He stops again, enjoying his tease.*] Damn, even the N double A C P takes a holiday sometimes! [BENEATHA *and* RUTH *laugh. He dances with* RUTH *some more and starts to laugh and stops and pantomimes someone over an operating table.*] I can just see that chick someday looking down at some poor cat on an operating table before she starts to slice him, saying . . . [*Pulling his sleeves back maliciously.*] "By the way, what are your views on civil rights down there? . . ."

[*He laughs at her again and starts to dance happily. The bell sounds.*]

BENEATHA: Sticks and stones may break my bones but . . . words will never hurt me!

[BENEATHA *goes to the door and opens it as* WALTER *and* RUTH *go on with the clowning.* BENEATHA *is somewhat surprised to see a quiet-looking middle-aged white man in a business suit holding his hat and a briefcase in his hand and consulting a small piece of paper.*]

MAN: Uh—how do you do, miss. I am looking for a Mrs.— [*He looks at the slip of paper.*] Mrs. Lena Younger?

BENEATHA: [*Smoothing her hair with slight embarrassment.*] Oh—yes, that's my mother. Excuse me [*She closes the door and turns to quiet the other two.*] Ruth! Brother! Somebody's here. [*Then she opens the door. The* MAN *casts a curious quick glance at all of them.*] Uh—come in please.

MAN: [*Coming in.*] Thank you.

BENEATHA: My mother isn't here just now. Is it business?

MAN: Yes . . . well, of a sort.

WALTER: [*Freely, the Man of the House.*] Have a seat. I'm Mrs. Younger's son. I look after most of her business matters.

[RUTH *and* BENEATHA *exchange amused glances.*]

MAN: [*Regarding* WALTER, *and sitting.*] Well—My name is Karl Lindner . . .

WALTER: [*Stretching out his hand.*] Walter Younger. This is my wife— [RUTH *nods politely.*[—and my sister.

LINDNER: How do you do.

WALTER: [*Amiably, as he sits himself easily on a chair, leaning with interest forward on his knees and looking expectantly into the newcomer's face.*] What can we do for you, Mr. Lindner!

LINDNER: [*Some minor shuffling of the hat and briefcase on his knees.*] Well—I am a representative of the Clybourne Park Improvement Association—

WALTER: [*Pointing.*] Why don't you sit your things on the floor?

LINDNER: Oh—yes. Thank you. [*He slides the briefcase and hat under the chair.*] And as I was saying—I am from the Clybourne Park Improvement Association and we have had it brought to our attention at the last meeting that you people— or at least your mother—has bought a piece of residential property at— [*He digs for the slip of paper again.*[—four o six Clybourne Street . . .

WALTER: That's right. Care for something to drink? Ruth, get Mr. Lindner a beer.

LINDNER: [*Upset for some reason.*] Oh—no, really. I mean thank you very much, but no thank you.

RUTH: [*Innocently.*] Some coffee?

LINDNER: Thank you, nothing at all.

[BENEATHA *is watching the man carefully.*]

LINDNER: Well, I don't know how much you folks know about our organization. [*He is a gentle man; thoughtful and somewhat labored in his manner.*] It is one of these community organizations set up to look after—oh, you know, things like block upkeep and special projects and we also have what we call our New Neighbors Orientation Committee . . .

BENEATHA: [*Drily.*] Yes—and what do they do?

LINDNER: [*Turning a little to her and then returning the main force to* WALTER.] Well— it's what you might call a sort of welcoming committee, I guess. I mean they, we, I'm the chairman of the committee—go around and see the new people who move into the neighborhood and sort of give them the lowdown on the way we do things out in Clybourne Park.

BENEATHA: [*With appreciation of the two meanings, which escape* RUTH *and* WALTER.] Un-huh.

LINDNER: And we also have the category of what the association calls— [*He looks elsewhere.*] —uh—special community problems . . .

BENEATHA: Yes—and what are some of those?

WALTER: Girl, let the man talk.

LINDNER: [*With understated relief.*] Thank you. I would sort of like to explain this thing in my own way. I mean I want to explain to you in a certain way.

WALTER: Go ahead.

LINDNER: Yes. Well. I'm going to try to get right to the point. I'm sure we'll all appreciate that in the long run.

BENEATHA: Yes.

WALTER: Be still now!

LINDNER: Well—

RUTH: [*Still innocently.*] Would you like another chair—you don't look comfortable.

LINDNER: [*More frustrated than annoyed.*] No, thank you very much. Please. Well—to get right to the point I— [*A great breath, and he is off at last.*] I am sure you people must be aware of some of the incidents which have happened in various parts of the city when colored people moved into certain areas— [BENEATHA *exhales heavily and starts tossing a piece of fruit up and down in the air.*] Well—because we have what I think is going to be a unique type of organization in American community life—not only do we deplore that kind of thing—but we are trying to do something about it. [BENEATHA *stops tossing and turns with a new and quizzical interest to the man.*] We feel— [*Gaining confidence in his mission because of the interest in the faces of the people he is talking to.*] —we feel that most of the trouble in this world, when you come right down to it— [*He hits his knee for emphasis.*] —most of the trouble exists because people just don't sit down and talk to each other.

RUTH: [*Nodding as she might in church, pleased with the remark.*] You can say that again, mister.

LINDNER: [*More encouraged by such affirmation.*] That we don't try hard enough in this world to understand the other fellow's problem. The other guy's point of view.

RUTH: Now that's right.

[BENEATHA *and* WALTER *merely watch and listen with genuine interest.*]

LINDNER: Yes—that's the way we feel out in Clybourne Park. And that's why I was elected to come here this afternoon and talk to you people. Friendly like, you know, the way people should talk to each other and see if we couldn't find some way to work this thing out. As I say, the whole business is a matter of *caring* about the other fellow. Anybody can see that you are a nice family of folks, hard working and honest I'm sure. [BENEATHA *frowns slightly, quizzically, her head tilted regarding him.*] Today everybody knows what it means to be on the outside of something. And of course, there is always somebody who is out to take the advantage of people who don't always understand.

WALTER: What do you mean?

LINDNER: Well—you see our community is made up of people who've worked hard as the dickens for years to build up that little community. They're not rich and fancy people; just hard-working, honest people who don't really have much but those little homes and a dream of the kind of community they want to raise their children in. Now, I don't say we are perfect and there is a lot wrong in some of the things they want. But you've got to admit that a man, right or wrong, has the right to want to have the neighborhood he lives in a certain kind of way. And at the moment the overwhelming majority of our people out there feel that people get along better, take more of a common interest in the life of the community, when they share a common background. I want you to believe me when I tell you that race prejudice simply doesn't enter into it. It is a matter of the people of Clybourne Park believing, rightly or wrongly, as I say, that for the happiness of all concerned that our Negro families are happier when they live in their *own* communities.

BENEATHA: [*With a grand and bitter gesture.*] This, friends, is the Welcoming Committee!

WALTER: [*Dumfounded, looking at* LINDNER.] Is this what you came marching all the way over here to tell us?

LINDNER: Well, now we've been having a fine conversation. I hope you'll hear me all the way through.

WALTER: [*Tightly.*] Go ahead, man.

LINDNER: You see—in the face of all things I have said, we are prepared to make your family a very generous offer . . .

BENEATHA: Thirty pieces and not a coin less![7]

WALTER: Yeah?

LINDNER: [*Putting on his glasses and drawing a form out of the briefcase.*] Our association is prepared, through the collective effort of our people, to buy the house from you at a financial gain to your family.

RUTH: Lord have mercy, ain't this the living gall!

WALTER: All right, you through?

LINDNER: Well, I want to give you the exact terms of the financial arrangement—

WALTER: We don't want to hear no exact terms of no arrangements. I want to know if you got any more to tell us 'bout getting together?

LINDNER: [*Taking off his glasses.*] Well—I don't suppose that you feel . . .

WALTER: Never mind how I feel—you got any more to say 'bout how people ought to sit down and talk to each other? . . . Get out of my house, man.

[*He turns his back and walks to the door.*]

LINDNER: [*Looking around at the hostile faces and reaching and assembling his hat and briefcase.*] Well—I don't understand why you people are reacting this way. What do you think you are going to gain by moving into a neighborhood

---

7. See Matthew 26.15.

where you just aren't wanted and where some elements—well—people can get awful worked up when they feel that their whole way of life and everything they've ever worked for is threatened.

WALTER: Get out.

LINDNER: [*At the door, holding a small card.*] Well—I'm sorry it went like this.

WALTER: Get out.

LINDNER: [*Almost sadly regarding* WALTER.] You just can't force people to change their hearts, son.

> [*He turns and put his card on a table and exits.* WALTER *pushes the door to with stinging hatred, and stands looking at it.* RUTH *just sits and* BENEATHA *just stands. They say nothing.* MAMA *and* TRAVIS *enter.*]

MAMA: Well—this all the packing got done since I left out of here this morning. I testify before God that my children got all the energy of the dead. What time the moving men due?

BENEATHA: Four o'clock. You had a caller, Mama.

> [*She is smiling, teasingly.*]

MAMA: Sure enough—who?

BENEATHA: [*Her arms folded saucily.*] The Welcoming Committee.

> [WALTER *and* RUTH *giggle.*]

MAMA: [*Innocently.*] Who?

BENEATHA: The Welcoming Committee. They said they're sure going to be glad to see you when you get there.

WALTER: [*Devilishly.*] Yeah, they said they can't hardly wait to see your face.

> [*Laughter.*]

MAMA: [*Sensing their facetiousness.*] What's the matter with you all?

WALTER: Ain't nothing the matter with us. We just telling you 'bout the gentleman who came to see you this afternoon. From the Clybourne Park Improvement Association.

MAMA: What he want?

RUTH: [*In the same mood as* BENEATHA *and* WALTER.] To welcome you, honey.

WALTER: He said they can't hardly wait. He said the one thing they don't have, that they just *dying* to have out there is a fine family of colored people! [*To* RUTH *and* BENEATHA.] Ain't that right!

RUTH *and* BENEATHA: [*Mockingly.*] Yeah! He left his card in case—

> [*They indicate the card, and* MAMA *picks it up and throws it on the floor—understanding and looking off as she draws her chair up to the table on which she has put her plant and some sticks and some cord.*]

MAMA: Father, give us strength. [*Knowingly—and without fun.*] Did he threaten us?

BENEATHA: Oh—Mama—they don't do it like that anymore. He talked Brotherhood. He said everybody ought to learn how to sit down and hate each other with good Christian fellowship.

[*She and* WALTER *shake hands to ridicule the remark.*]

MAMA: [*Sadly.*] Lord, protect us . . .

RUTH: You should hear the money those folks raised to buy the house from us. All we paid and then some.

BENEATHA: What they think we going to do—eat 'em?

RUTH: No, honey, marry 'em.

MAMA: [*Shaking her head.*] Lord, Lord, Lord . . .

RUTH: Well—that's the way the crackers crumble. Joke.

BENEATHA: [*Laughingly noticing what her mother is doing.*] Mama, what are you doing?

MAMA: Fixing my plant so it won't get hurt none on the way . . .

BENEATHA: Mama, you going to take *that* to the new house?

MAMA: Un-huh—

BENEATHA: That raggedy-looking old thing?

MAMA: [*Stopping and looking at her.*] It expresses *me.*

RUTH: [*With delight, to* BENEATHA.] So there, Miss Thing!

[WALTER *comes to* MAMA *suddenly and bends down behind her and squeezes her in his arms with all his strength. She is overwhelmed by the suddenness of it and, though delighted, her manner is like that of* RUTH *with* TRAVIS.]

MAMA: Look out now, boy! You make me mess up my thing here!

WALTER: [*His face lit, he slips down on his knees beside her, his arms still about her.*] Mama . . . you know what it means to climb up in the chariot?

MAMA: [*Gruffly, very happy.*] Get on away from me now . . .

RUTH: [*Near the gift-wrapped package, trying to catch* WALTER'S *eye.*] Psst—

WALTER: What the old song say, Mama . . .

RUTH: Walter—Now?

[*She is pointing at the package.*]

WALTER: [*Speaking the lines, sweetly, playfully, in his mother's face.*]

I got wings . . . you got wings . . .
All God's Children got wings[8] . . .

MAMA: Boy—get out of my face and do some work . . .

WALTER:

When I get to heaven gonna put on my wings,
Gonna fly all over God's heaven . . .

BENEATHA: [*Teasingly, from across the room.*] Everybody talking 'bout heaven ain't going there!

WALTER: [*To* RUTH, *who is carrying the box across to them.*] I don't know, you think we ought to give her that . . . Seems to me she ain't been very appreciative around here.

---

8. Lines from an African American spiritual. Walter's and Beneatha's next lines are also from the song.

MAMA: [*Eying the box, which is obviously a gift.*] What is that?

WALTER: [*Taking it from* RUTH *and putting it on the table in front of* MAMA.] Well— what you all think? Should we give it to her?

RUTH: Oh—she was pretty good today.

MAMA: I'll good you—

[*She turns her eyes to the box again.*]

BENEATHA: Open it, Mama.

[*She stands up, looks at it, turns and looks at all of them, and then presses her hands together and does not open the package.*]

WALTER: [*Sweetly.*] Open it, Mama. It's for you. [MAMA *looks in his eyes. It is the first present in her life without its being Christmas. Slowly she opens her package and lifts out, one by one, a brand-new sparkling set of gardening tools.* WALTER *continues, prodding.*] Ruth made up the note—read it . . .

MAMA: [*Picking up the card and adjusting her glasses.*] "To our own Mrs. Miniver[9]— Love from Brother, Ruth and Beneatha." Ain't that lovely . . .

TRAVIS: [*Tugging at his father's sleeve.*] Daddy, can I give her mine now?

WALTER: All right, son. [TRAVIS *flies to get his gift.*] Travis didn't want to go in with the rest of us, Mama. He got his own. [*Somewhat amused.*] We don't know what it is . . .

TRAVIS: [*Racing back in the room with a large hatbox and putting it in front of his grandmother.*] Here!

MAMA: Lord have mercy, baby. You done gone and bought your grandmother a hat?

TRAVIS: [*Very proud.*] Open it!

[*She does and lifts out an elaborate, but very elaborate, wide gardening hat, and all the adults break up at the sight of it.*]

RUTH: Travis, honey, what is that?

TRAVIS: [*Who thinks it is beautiful and appropriate.*] It's a gardening hat! Like the ladies always have on in the magazines when they work in their gardens.

BENEATHA: [*Giggling fiercely.*] Travis—we were trying to make Mama Mrs. Miniver— not Scarlett O'Hara![1]

MAMA: [*Indignantly.*] What's the matter with you all! This here is a beautiful hat! [*Absurdly.*] I always wanted me one just like it!

[*She pops it on her head to prove it to her grandson, and the hat is ludicrous and considerably oversized.*]

RUTH: Hot dog! Go, Mama!

WALTER: [*Doubled over with laughter.*] I'm sorry, Mama—but you look like you ready to go out and chop you some cotton sure enough!

---

9. The powerful and charismatic title character of a 1942 film starring Greer Garson.   1. The siren in *Gone with the Wind*.

[*They all laugh except* MAMA, *out of deference to* TRAVIS' *feelings.*]

MAMA: [*Gathering the boy up to her.*] Bless your heart—this is the prettiest hat I ever owned— [WALTER, RUTH and BENEATHA *chime in—noisily, festively and insincerely congratulating* TRAVIS *on his gift.*] What are we all standing around here for? We ain't finished packin' yet. Bennie, you ain't packed one book.

[*The bell rings.*]

BENEATHA: That couldn't be the movers . . . it's not hardly two good yet—

[BENEATHA *goes into her room.* MAMA *starts for door.*]

WALTER: [*Turning, stiffening.*] Wait—wait—I'll get it.

[*He stands and looks at the door.*]

MAMA: You expecting company, son?
WALTER: [*Just looking at the door.*] Yeah—yeah . . .

[MAMA *looks at* RUTH, *and they exchange innocent and unfrightened glances.*]

MAMA: [*Not understanding.*] Well, let them in, son.
BENEATHA: [*From her room.*] We need some more string.
MAMA: Travis—you run to the hardware and get me some string cord.

[MAMA *goes out and* WALTER *turns and looks at* RUTH. TRAVIS *goes to a dish for money.*]

RUTH: Why don't you answer the door, man?
WALTER: [*Suddenly bounding across the floor to her.*] 'Cause sometimes it hard to let the future begin! [*Stooping down in her face.*]

I got wings! You got wings!
All God's children got wings!

[*He crosses to the door and throws it open. Standing there is a very slight little man in a not too prosperous business suit and with haunted frightened eyes and a hat pulled down tightly, brim up, around his forehead.* TRAVIS *passes between the men and exits.* WALTER *leans deep in the man's face, still in his jubilance.*]

When I get to heaven gonna put on my wings,
Gonna fly all over God's heaven . . .

[*The little man just stares at him.*]

Heaven—

[*Suddenly he stops and looks past the little man into the empty hallway.*] Where's Willy, man?

BOBO: He ain't with me.
WALTER: [*Not disturbed.*] Oh—come on in. You know my wife.

BOBO: [*Dumbly, taking off his hat.*] Yes—h'you, Miss Ruth.

RUTH: [*Quietly, a mood apart from her husband already, seeing* BOBO.] Hello, Bobo.

WALTER: You right on time today . . . Right on time. That's the way! [*He slaps* BOBO *on his back.*] Sit down . . . lemme hear.

> [RUTH *stands stiffly and quietly in back of them, as though somehow she senses death, her eyes fixed on her husband.*]

BOBO: [*His frightened eyes on the floor, his hat in his hands.*] Could I please get a drink of water, before I tell you about it, Walter Lee?

> [WALTER *does not take his eyes off the man.* RUTH *goes blindly to the tap and gets a glass of water and brings it to* BOBO.]

WALTER: There ain't nothing wrong, is there?

BOBO: Lemme tell you—

WALTER: Man—didn't nothing go wrong?

BOBO: Lemme tell you—Walter Lee. [*Looking at* RUTH *and talking to her more than to* WALTER.] You know how it was. I got to tell you how it was. I mean first I got to tell you how it was all the way . . . I mean about the money I put in, Walter Lee . . .

WALTER: [*With taut agitation now.*] What about the money you put in?

BOBO: Well—it wasn't much as we told you—me and Willy— [*He stops.*] I'm sorry, Walter. I got a bad feeling about it. I got a real bad feeling about it . . .

WALTER: Man, what you telling me about all this for? . . . Tell me what happened in Springfield . . .

BOBO: Springfield.

RUTH: [*Like a dead woman.*] What was supposed to happen in Springfield?

BOBO: [*To her.*] This deal that me and Walter went into with Willy—Me and Willy was going to go down to Springfield and spread some money 'round so's we wouldn't have to wait so long for the liquor license . . . That's what we were going to do. Everybody said that was the way you had to do, you understand, Miss Ruth?

WALTER: Man—what happened down there?

BOBO: [*A pitiful man, near tears.*] I'm trying to tell you, Walter.

WALTER: [*Screaming at him suddenly.*] THEN TELL ME, GODDAMMIT . . . WHAT'S THE MATTER WITH YOU?

BOBO: Man . . . I didn't go to no Springfield, yesterday.

WALTER: [*Halted, life hanging in the moment.*] Why not?

BOBO: [*The long way, the hard way to tell.*] 'Cause I didn't have no reasons to . . .

WALTER: Man, what are you talking about!

BOBO: I'm talking about the fact that when I got to the train station yesterday morning—eight o'clock like we planned . . . Man—*Willy didn't never show up.*

WALTER: Why . . . where was he . . . where is he?

BOBO: That's what I'm trying to tell you . . . I don't know . . . I waited six hours . . . I called his house . . . and I waited . . . six hours . . . I waited in that train station six hours . . . [*Breaking into tears.*] That was all the extra money I had in the world . . . [*Looking up at* WALTER *with the tears running down his face.*] Man, *Willy is gone.*

WALTER: Gone, what you mean Willy is gone? Gone where? You mean he went by himself. You mean he went off to Springfield by himself—to take care of getting the license— [*Turns and looks anxiously at* RUTH.] You mean maybe he didn't want too many people in on the business down there? [*Looks to* RUTH *again, as before.*] You know Willy got his own ways. [*Looks back to* BOBO.] Maybe you was late yesterday and he just went on down there without you. Maybe—maybe—he's been callin' you at home tryin' to tell you what happened or something. Maybe—maybe—he just got sick. He's somewhere—he's got to be somewhere. We just got to find him—me and you got to find him. [*Grabs* BOBO *senselessly by the collar and starts to shake him.*] We got to!

BOBO: [*In sudden angry, frightened agony.*] What's the matter with you, Walter! *When a cat take off with your money he don't leave you no maps!*

WALTER: [*Turning madly, as though he is looking for* WILLY *in the very room.*] Willy! . . . Willy . . . don't do it . . . Please don't do it . . . Man, not with that money . . . Man, please, not with that money . . . Oh, God . . . Don't let it be true . . . [*He is wandering around, crying out for* WILLY *and looking for him or perhaps for help from God.*] Man . . . I trusted you . . . Man, I put my life in your hands . . . [*He starts to crumple down on the floor as* RUTH *just covers her face in horror.* MAMA *opens the door and comes into the room, with* BENEATHA *behind her.*] Man . . . [*He starts to pound the floor with his fists, sobbing wildly.*] That money is made out of my father's flesh . . .

BOBO: [*Standing over him helplessly.*] I'm sorry, Walter . . . [*Only* WALTER*'s sobs reply.* BOBO *puts on his hat.*] I had my life staked on this deal, too . . .

   [*He exits.*]

MAMA: [*To* WALTER.] Son— [*She goes to him, bends down to him, talks to his bent head.*] Son . . . Is it gone? Son, I gave you sixty-five hundred dollars. Is it gone? All of it? Beneatha's money too?

WALTER: [*Lifting his head slowly.*] Mama . . . I never . . . went to the bank at all . . .

MAMA: [*Not wanting to believe him.*] You mean . . . your sister's school money . . . you used that too . . . Walter? . . .

WALTER: Yessss! . . . All of it . . . It's all gone . . . [*There is total silence.* RUTH *stands with her face covered with her hands;* BENEATHA *leans forlornly against a wall, fingering a piece of red ribbon from the mother's gift.* MAMA *stops and looks at her son without recognition and then, quite without thinking about it, starts to beat him senselessly in the face.* BENEATHA *goes to them and stops it.*]

BENEATHA: Mama!

   [MAMA *stops and looks at both of her children and rises slowly and wanders vaguely, aimlessly away from them.*]

MAMA: I seen . . . him . . . night after night . . . come in . . . and look at that rug . . . and then look at me . . . the red showing in his eyes . . . the veins moving in his head . . . I seen him grow thin and old before he was

forty . . . working and working and working like somebody's old horse . . .
    killing himself . . . and you—you give it all away in a day . . .
BENEATHA: Mama—
MAMA: Oh, God . . . [*She looks up to Him.*] Look down here—and show me the
    strength.
BENEATHA: Mama—
MAMA: [*Folding over.*] Strength . . .
BENEATHA: [*Plaintively.*] Mama . . .
MAMA: Strength!

    [CURTAIN.]

ACT III

An hour later.
*At curtain, there is a sullen light of gloom in the living room, gray light not unlike
that which began the first scene of Act I. At left we can see* WALTER *within his room,
alone with himself. He is stretched out on the bed, his shirt out and open, his arms under
his head. He does not smoke, he does not cry out, he merely lies there, looking up at the
ceiling, much as if he were alone in the world.*
    In the living room BENEATHA *sits at the table, still surrounded by the now almost
ominous packing crates. She sits looking off. We feel that this is a mood struck perhaps
an hour before, and it lingers now, full of the empty sound of profound disappointment.
We see on a line from her brother's bedroom the sameness of their attitudes. Presently
the bell rings and* BENEATHA *rises without ambition or interest in answering. It is* ASAGAI,
*smiling broadly, striding into the room with energy and happy expectation and
conversation.*

ASAGAI: I came over . . . I had some free time. I thought I might help with the
    packing. Ah, I like the look of packing crates! A household in preparation for
    a journey! It depresses some people . . . but for me . . . it is another feeling.
    Something full of the flow of life, do you understand? Movement, progress
    . . . It makes me think of Africa.
BENEATHA: Africa!
ASAGAI: What kind of a mood is this? Have I told you how deeply you move me?
BENEATHA: He gave away the money, Asagai . . .
ASAGAI: Who gave away what money?
BENEATHA: The insurance money. My brother gave it away.
ASAGAI: Gave it away?
BENEATHA: He made an investment! With a man even Travis wouldn't have trusted.
ASAGAI: And it's gone?
BENEATHA: Gone!
ASAGAI: I'm very sorry . . . And you, now?
BENEATHA: Me? . . . Me? . . . Me, I'm nothing . . . Me. When I was very small . . .
    we used to take our sleds out in the wintertime and the only hills we had
    were the ice-covered stone steps of some houses down the street. And we

used to fill them in with snow and make them smooth and slide down them all day . . . and it was very dangerous you know . . . far too steep . . . and sure enough one day a kid named Rufus came down too fast and hit the sidewalk . . . and we saw his face just split open right there in front of us . . . And I remember standing there looking at his bloody open face thinking that was the end of Rufus. But the ambulance came and they took him to the hospital and they fixed the broken bones and they sewed it all up . . . and the next time I saw Rufus he just had a little line down the middle of his face . . . I never got over that . . .

[WALTER *sits up, listening on the bed. Throughout this scene it is important that we feel his reaction at all times, that he visibly respond to the words of his sister and* ASAGAI.]

ASAGAI: What?

BENEATHA: That that was what one person could do for another, fix him up—sew up the problem, make him all right again. That was the most marvelous thing in the world . . . I wanted to do that. I always thought it was the one concrete thing in the world that a human being could do. Fix up the sick, you know— and make them whole again. This was truly being God . . .

ASAGAI: You wanted to be God?

BENEATHA: No—I wanted to cure. It used to be so important to me. I wanted to cure. It used to matter. I used to care. I mean about people and how their bodies hurt . . .

ASAGAI: And you've stopped caring?

BENEATHA: Yes—I think so.

ASAGAI: Why?

[WALTER *rises, goes to the door of his room and is about to open it, then stops and stands listening, leaning on the door jamb.*]

BENEATHA: Because it doesn't seem deep enough, close enough to what ails man-kind—I mean this thing of sewing up bodies or administering drugs. Don't you understand? It was a child's reaction to the world. I thought that doctors had the secret to all the hurts . . . That's the way a child sees things—or an idealist.

ASAGAI: Children see things very well sometimes—and idealists even better.

BENEATHA: I know that's what you think. Because you are still where I left off— you still care. This is what you see for the world, for Africa. You with the dreams of the future will patch up all Africa—you are going to cure the Great Sore of colonialism with Independence——

ASAGAI: Yes!

BENEATHA: Yes—and you think that one word is the penicillin of the human spirit: "Independence!" But then what?

ASAGAI: That will be the problem for another time. First we must get there.

BENEATHA: And where does it end?

ASAGAI: End? Who even spoke of an end? To life? To living?

BENEATHA: An end to misery!

ASAGAI: [*Smiling.*] You sound like a French intellectual.

BENEATHA: No! I sound like a human being who just had her future taken right out of her hands! While I was sleeping in my bed in there, things were happening in this world that directly concerned me—and nobody asked me, consulted me—they just went out and did things—and changed my life. Don't you see there isn't any real progress, Asagai, there is only one large circle that we march in, around and around, each of us with our own little picture—in front of us—our own little mirage that we think is the future.

ASAGAI: That is the mistake.

BENEATHA: What?

ASAGAI: What you just said—about the circle. It isn't a circle—it is simply a long line—as in geometry, you know, one that reaches into infinity. And because we cannot see the end—we also cannot see how it changes. And it is very odd but those who see the changes are called "idealists"—and those who cannot, or refuse to think, they are the "realists." It is very strange, and amusing too, I think.

BENEATHA: You—you are almost religious.

ASAGAI: Yes . . . I think I have the religion of doing what is necessary in the world— and of worshipping man—because he is so marvelous, you see.

BENEATHA: Man is foul! And the human race deserves its misery!

ASAGAI: You see: *you* have become the religious one in the old sense. Already, and after such a small defeat, you are worshipping despair.

BENEATHA: From now on, I worship the truth—and the truth is that people are puny, small and selfish . . .

ASAGAI: Truth? Why is it that you despairing ones always think that only you have the truth? I never thought to see *you* like that. You! Your brother made a stupid, childish mistake—and you are grateful to him. So that now you can give up the ailing human race on account of it. You talk about what good is struggle; what good is anything? Where are we all going? And why are we bothering?

BENEATHA: *And you cannot answer it!* All your talk and dreams about Africa and Independence. Independence and then what? What about all the crooks and petty thieves and just plain idiots who will come into power to steal and plunder the same as before—only now they will be black and do it in the name of the new Independence—You cannot answer that.

ASAGAI: [*Shouting over her.*] *I live the answer!* [*Pause.*] In my village at home it is the exceptional man who can even read a newspaper . . . or who ever *sees* a book at all. I will go home and much of what I will have to say will seem strange to the people of my village . . . But I will teach and work and things will happen, slowly and swiftly. At times it will seem that nothing changes at all . . . and then again . . . the sudden dramatic events which make history leap into the future. And then quiet again. Retrogression even. Guns, murder, revolution. And I even will have moments when I wonder if the quiet was not better than all that death and hatred. But I will look about my village at the illiteracy and disease and ignorance and I will not wonder long. And perhaps . . . perhaps I will be a great man . . . I mean perhaps I will hold on

to the substance of truth and find my way always with the right course . . .
and perhaps for it I will be butchered in my bed some night by the servants
of empire . . .

BENEATHA: *The martyr!*

ASAGAI: . . . or perhaps I shall live to be a very old man, respected and esteemed
in my new nation . . . And perhaps I shall hold office and this is what I'm
trying to tell you, Alaiyo; perhaps the things I believe now for my country
will be wrong and outmoded, and I will not understand and do terrible things
to have things my way or merely to keep my power. Don't you see that there
will be young men and women, not British soldiers then, but my own black
countrymen . . . to step out of the shadows some evening and slit my then
useless throat? Don't you see they have always been there . . . that they always
will be. And that such a thing as my own death will be an advance? They
who might kill me even . . . actually replenish me!

BENEATHA: Oh, Asagai, I know all that.

ASAGAI: Good! Then stop moaning and groaning and tell me what you plan to do.

BENEATHA: Do?

ASAGAI: I have a bit of a suggestion.

BENEATHA: What?

ASAGAI: [*Rather quietly for him.*] That when it is all over—that you come home with
me—

BENEATHA: [*Slapping herself on the forehead with exasperation born of misunderstanding.*] Oh—Asagai—at this moment you decide to be romantic!

ASAGAI: [*Quickly understanding the misunderstanding.*] My dear, young creature of
the New World—I do not mean across the city—I mean across the ocean;
home—to Africa.

BENEATHA: [*Slowly understanding and turning to him with murmured amazement.*] To—
to Nigeria?

ASAGAI: Yes! . . . [*Smiling and lifting his arms playfully.*] Three hundred years later
the African Prince rose up out of the seas and swept the maiden back across
the middle passage over which her ancestors had come—

BENEATHA: [*Unable to play.*] Nigeria?

ASAGAI: Nigeria. Home. [*Coming to her with genuine romantic flippancy.*] I will show
you our mountains and our stars; and give you cool drinks from gourds and
teach you the old songs and the ways of our people—and, in time, we will
pretend that— [*Very softly.*] —you have only been away for a day—

[*She turns her back to him, thinking. He swings her around and takes her full
in his arms in a long embrace which proceeds to passion.*]

BENEATHA: [*Pulling away.*] You're getting me all mixed up—

ASAGAI: Why?

BENEATHA: Too many things—too many things have happened today. I must sit
down and think. I don't know what I feel about anything right this minute.

[*She promptly sits down and props her chin on her fist.*]

ASAGAI: [*Charmed.*] All right, I shall leave you. No—don't get up. [*Touching her,
gently, sweetly.*] Just sit awhile and think . . . Never be afraid to sit awhile and

think. [*He goes to door and looks at her.*] How often I have looked at you and said, "Ah—so this is what the New World hath finally wrought . . ."

[*He exits.* BENEATHA *sits on alone. Presently* WALTER *enters from his room and starts to rummage through things, feverishly looking for something. She looks up and turns in her seat.*]

BENEATHA: [*Hissingly.*] Yes—just look at what the New World hath wrought! . . . Just look! [*She gestures with bitter disgust.*] There he is! *Monsieur le petit bourgeois noir*—himself! There he is—Symbol of a Rising Class! Entrepreneur! Titan of the system! [WALTER *ignores her completely and continues frantically and destructively looking for something and hurling things to the floor and tearing things out of their place in his search.* BENEATHA *ignores the eccentricity of his actions and goes on with the monologue of insult.*] Did you dream of yachts on Lake Michigan, Brother? Did you see yourself on that Great Day sitting down at the Conference Table, surrounded by all the mighty bald-headed men in America? All halted, waiting, breathless, waiting for your pronouncements on industry? Waiting for you—Chairman of the Board? [WALTER *finds what he is looking for—a small piece of white paper—and pushes it in his pocket and puts on his coat and rushes out without ever having looked at her. She shouts after him.*] I look at you and I see the final triumph of stupidity in the world!

[*The door slams and she returns to just sitting again.* RUTH *comes quickly out of* MAMA'*s room.*]

RUTH: Who was that?
BENEATHA: Your husband.
RUTH: Where did he go?
BENEATHA: Who knows—maybe he has an appointment at U.S. Steel.
RUTH: [*Anxiously, with frightened eyes.*] You didn't say nothing bad to him, did you?
BENEATHA: Bad? Say anything bad to him? No—I told him he was a sweet boy and full of dreams and everything is strictly peachy keen, as the ofay[2] kids say!

[MAMA *enters from her bedroom. She is lost, vague, trying to catch hold, to make some sense of her former command of the world, but it still eludes her. A sense of waste overwhelms her gait; a measure of apology rides on her shoulders. She goes to her plant, which has remained on the table, looks at it, picks it up and takes it to the window sill and sits it outside, and she stands and looks at it a long moment. Then she closes the window, straightens her body with effort and turns around to her children.*]

MAMA: Well—ain't it a mess in here, though? [*A false cheerfulness, a beginning of something.*] I guess we all better stop moping around and get some work done. All this unpacking and everything we got to do. [RUTH *raises her head slowly in response to the sense of the line; and* BENEATHA *in similar manner turns very slowly to look at her mother.*] One of you all better call the moving people and tell 'em not to come.
RUTH: Tell 'em not to come?

2. White.

MAMA: Of course, baby. Ain't no need in 'em coming all the way here and having to go back. They charges for that too. [*She sits down, fingers to her brow, thinking.*] Lord, ever since I was a little girl, I always remembers people saying, "Lena—Lena Eggleston, you aims too high all the time. You needs to slow down and see life a little more like it is. Just slow down some." That's what they always used to say down home—"Lord, that Lena Eggleston is a high-minded thing. She'll get her due one day!"

RUTH: No, Lena . . .

MAMA: Me and Big Walter just didn't never learn right.

RUTH: Lena, no! We gotta go. Bennie—tell her . . . [*She rises and crosses to* BENEATHA *with her arms outstretched.* BENEATHA *doesn't respond.*] Tell her we can still move . . . the notes ain't but a hundred and twenty-five a month. We got four grown people in this house—we can work . . .

MAMA: [*To herself.*] Just aimed too high all the time—

RUTH: [*Turning and going to* MAMA *fast—the words pouring out with urgency and desperation.*] Lena—I'll work . . . I'll work twenty hours a day in all the kitchens in Chicago . . . I'll strap my baby on my back if I have to and scrub all the floors in America and wash all the sheets in America if I have to—but we got to move . . . We got to get out of here . . .

[MAMA *reaches out absently and pats* RUTH's *hand.*]

MAMA: No—I sees things differently now. Been thinking 'bout some of the things we could do to fix this place up some. I seen a second-hand bureau over on Maxwell Street[3] just the other day that could fit right there. [*She points to where the new furniture might go.* RUTH *wanders away from her.*] Would need some new handles on it and then a little varnish and then it look like something brand-new. And—we can put up them new curtains in the kitchen . . . Why this place be looking fine. Cheer us all up so that we forget trouble ever came . . . [*To* RUTH.] And you could get some nice screens to put up in your room round the baby's bassinet . . . [*She looks at both of them, pleadingly.*] Sometimes you just got to know when to give up some things . . . and hold on to what you got.

[WALTER *enters from the outside, looking spent and leaning against the door, his coat hanging from him.*]

MAMA: Where you been, son?

WALTER: [*Breathing hard.*] Made a call.

MAMA: To who, son?

WALTER: To The Man.

MAMA: What man, baby?

WALTER: The Man, Mama. Don't you know who The Man is?

RUTH: Walter Lee?

WALTER: *The Man.* Like the guys in the streets say—The Man. Captain Boss—Mistuh Charley . . . Old Captain Please Mr. Bossman . . .

3. A street market southwest of the Loop.

BENEATHA: [*Suddenly.*] Lindner!

WALTER: That's right! That's good. I told him to come right over.

BENEATHA: [*Fiercely, understanding.*] For what? What do you want to see him for!

WALTER: [*Looking at his sister.*] We going to do business with him.

MAMA: What you talking 'bout, son?

WALTER: Talking 'bout life, Mama. You all always telling me to see life like it is. Well—I laid in there on my back today . . . and I figured it out. Life just like it is. Who gets and who don't get. [*He sits down with his coat on and laughs.*] Mama, you know it's all divided up. Life is. Sure enough. Between the takers and the "tooken." [*He laughs.*] I've figured it out finally. [*He looks around at them.*] Yeah. Some of us always getting "tooken." [*He laughs.*] People like Willy Harris, they don't never get "tooken." And you know why the rest of us do? 'Cause we all mixed up. Mixed up bad. We get to looking 'round for the right and the wrong, and we worry about it and cry about it and stay up nights trying to figure out 'bout the wrong and the right of things all the time . . . And all the time, man, them takers is out there operating, just taking and taking. Willy Harris? Shoot—Willy Harris don't even count. He don't even count in the big scheme of things. But I'll say one thing for old Willy Harris . . . he's taught me something. He's taught me to keep my eye on what counts in this world. Yeah— [*Shouting out a little.*] Thanks, Willy!

RUTH: What did you call that man for, Walter Lee?

WALTER: Called him to tell him to come on over to the show. Gonna put on a show for the man. Just what he wants to see. You see, Mama, the man came here today and he told us that them people out there where you want us to move—well they so upset they willing to pay us not to move out there. [*He laughs again.*] And—and oh, Mama—you would of been proud of the way me and Ruth and Bennie acted. We told him to get out . . . Lord have mercy! We told the man to get out. Oh, we was some proud folks this afternoon, yeah. [*He lights a cigarette.*] We were still full of that old-time stuff . . .

RUTH: [*Coming toward him slowly.*] You talking 'bout taking them people's money to keep us from moving in that house?

WALTER: I ain't just talking 'bout it, baby—I'm telling you that's what's going to happen.

BENEATHA: Oh, God! Where is the bottom! Where is the real honest-to-God bottom so he can't go any farther!

WALTER: See—that's the old stuff. You and that boy that was here today. You all want everybody to carry a flag and a spear and sing some marching songs, huh? You wanna spend your life looking into things and trying to find the right and the wrong part, huh? Yeah. You know what's going to happen to that boy someday—he'll find himself sitting in a dungeon, locked in forever—and the takers will have the key! Forget it, baby! There ain't no causes—there ain't nothing but taking in this world, and he who takes most is smartest—and it don't make a damn bit of difference *how.*

MAMA: You making something inside me cry, son. Some awful pain inside me.

WALTER: Don't cry, Mama. Understand. That white man is going to walk in that door able to write checks for more money than we ever had. It's important to him and I'm going to help him . . . I'm going to put on the show, Mama.

MAMA: Son—I come from five generations of people who was slaves and share-croppers—but ain't nobody in my family never let nobody pay 'em no money that was a way of telling us we wasn't fit to walk the earth. We ain't never been that poor. [*Raising her eyes and looking at him.*] We ain't never been that dead inside.

BENEATHA: Well—we are dead now. All the talk about dreams and sunlight that goes on in this house. All dead.

WALTER: What's the matter with you all! I didn't make this world! It was give to me this way! Hell, yes, I want me some yachts someday! Yes, I want to hang some real pearls 'round my wife's neck. Ain't she supposed to wear no pearls? Somebody tell me—tell me, who decides which women is suppose to wear pearls in this world. I tell you I am a *man*—and I think my wife should wear some pearls in this world!

[*This last line hangs a good while and* WALTER *begins to move about the room. The word "Man" has penetrated his consciousness; he mumbles it to himself repeatedly between strange agitated pauses as he moves about.*]

MAMA: Baby, how you going to feel on the inside?

WALTER: Fine! . . . Going to feel fine . . . a man . . .

MAMA: You won't have nothing left then, Walter Lee.

WALTER: [*Coming to her.*] I'm going to feel fine, Mama. I'm going to look that son-of-a-bitch in the eyes and say— [*He falters.*] —and say, "All right, Mr. Lindner— [*He falters even more.*] —that's your neighborhood out there. You got the right to keep it like you want. You got the right to have it like you want. Just write the check and—the house is yours." And, and I am going to say— [*His voice almost breaks.*] And you—you people just put the money in my hand and you won't have to live next to this bunch of stinking niggers! . . . [*He straightens up and moves away from his mother, walking around the room.*] Maybe—maybe I'll just get down on my black knees . . . [*He does so;* RUTH *and* BENNIE *and* MAMA *watch him in frozen horror.*] Captain, Mistuh, Bossman. [*He starts crying.*] A-hee-hee-hee! [*Wringing his hands in profoundly anguished imitation.*] Yassss-suh! Great White Father, just gi' ussen de money, fo' God's sake, and we's ain't gwine come out deh and dirty up yo' white folks neighborhood . . .

[*He breaks down completely, then gets up and goes into the bedroom.*]

BENEATHA: That is not a man. That is nothing but a toothless rat.

MAMA: Yes—death done come in this here house. [*She is nodding, slowly, reflectively.*] Done come walking in my house. On the lips of my children. You what supposed to be my beginning again. You—what supposed to be my harvest. [*To* BENEATHA.] You—you mourning your brother?

BENEATHA: He's no brother of mine.

MAMA: What you say?

BENEATHA: I said that that individual in that room is no brother of mine.

MAMA: That's what I thought you said. You feeling like you better than he is today? [BENEATHA *does not answer.*] Yes? What you tell him a minute ago? That he wasn't a man? Yes? You give him up for me? You done wrote his epitaph too—like the rest of the world? Well, who give you the privilege?

BENEATHA: Be on my side for once! You saw what he just did, Mama! You saw him—down on his knees. Wasn't it you who taught me—to despise any man who would do that. Do what he's going to do.

MAMA: Yes—I taught you that. Me and your daddy. But I thought I taught you something else too . . . I thought I taught you to love him.

BENEATHA: Love him? There is nothing left to love.

MAMA: There is always something left to love. And if you ain't learned that, you ain't learned nothing. [*Looking at her.*] Have you cried for that boy today? I don't mean for yourself and for the family 'cause we lost the money. I mean for him; what he been through and what it done to him. Child, when do you think is the time to love somebody the most; when they done good and made things easy for everybody? Well then, you ain't through learning—because that ain't the time at all. It's when he's at his lowest and can't believe in hisself 'cause the world done whipped him so. When you starts measuring somebody, measure him right, child, measure him right. Make sure you done taken into account what hills and valleys he come through before he got to wherever he is.

[TRAVIS *bursts into the room at the end of the speech, leaving the door open.*]

TRAVIS: Grandmama—the moving men are downstairs! The truck just pulled up.

MAMA: [*Turning and looking at him.*] Are they, baby? They downstairs?

[*She sighs and sits.* LINDNER *appears in the doorway. He peers in and knocks lightly, to gain attention, and comes in. All turn to look at him.*]

LINDNER: [*Hat and briefcase in hand.*] Uh—hello . . . [RUTH *crosses mechanically to the bedroom door and opens it and lets it swing open freely and slowly as the lights come up on* WALTER *within, still in his coat, sitting at the far corner of the room. He looks up and out through the room to* LINDNER.]

RUTH: He's here.

[*A long minute passes and* WALTER *slowly gets up.*]

LINDNER: [*Coming to the table with efficiency, putting his briefcase on the table and starting to unfold papers and unscrew fountain pens.*] Well, I certainly was glad to hear from you people. [WALTER *has begun the trek out of the room, slowly and awkwardly, rather like a small boy, passing the back of his sleeve across his mouth from time to time.*] Life can really be so much simpler than people let it be most of the time. Well—with whom do I negotiate? You, Mrs. Younger, or your son here? [MAMA *sits with her hands folded on her lap and her eyes closed as* WALTER *advances.* TRAVIS *goes close to* LINDNER *and looks at the papers curiously.*] Just some official papers, sonny.

RUTH: Travis, you go downstairs.

MAMA: [*Opening her eyes and looking into* WALTER's.] No. Travis, you stay right here.

And you make him understand what you doing, Walter Lee. You teach him good. Like Willy Harris taught you. You show where our five generations done come to. Go ahead, son—

WALTER: [*Looks down into his boy's eyes.* TRAVIS *grins at him merrily and* WALTER *draws him beside him with his arm lightly around his shoulders.*] Well, Mr. Lindner. [BENEATHA *turns away.*] We called you— [*There is a profound, simple groping quality in his speech.*] —because, well, me and my family [*He looks around and shifts from one foot to the other.*] Well—we are very plain people . . .

LINDNER: Yes—

WALTER: I mean—I have worked as a chauffeur most of my life—and my wife here, she does domestic work in people's kitchens. So does my mother. I mean— we are plain people . . .

LINDNER: Yes, Mr. Younger—

WALTER: [*Really like a small boy, looking down at his shoes and then up at the man.*] And—uh—well, my father, well, he was a laborer most of his life.

LINDNER: [*Absolutely confused.*] Uh, yes—

WALTER: [*Looking down at his toes once again.*] My father almost beat a man to death once because this man called him a bad name or something, you know what I mean?

LINDNER: No, I'm afraid I don't.

WALTER: [*Finally straightening up.*] Well, what I mean is that we come from people who had a lot of pride. I mean—we are very proud people. And that's my sister over there and she's going to be a doctor—and we are very proud—

LINDNER: Well—I am sure that is very nice, but—

WALTER: [*Starting to cry and facing the man eye to eye.*] What I am telling you is that we called you over here to tell you that we are very proud and that this is— this is my son, who makes the sixth generation of our family in this country, and that we have all thought about your offer and we have decided to move into our house because my father—my father—he earned it. [MAMA *has her eyes closed and is rocking back and forth as though she were in church, with her head nodding the amen yes.*] We don't want to make no trouble for nobody or fight no causes—but we will try to be good neighbors. That's all we got to say. [*He looks the man absolutely in the eyes.*] We don't want your money.

[*He turns and walks away from the man.*]

LINDNER: [*Looking around at all of them.*] I take it then that you have decided to occupy.

BENEATHA: That's what the man said.

LINDNER: [*To* MAMA *in her reverie.*] Then I would like to appeal to you, Mrs. Younger. You are older and wiser and understand things better I am sure . . .

MAMA: [*Rising.*] I am afraid you don't understand. My son said we was going to move and there ain't nothing left for me to say. [*Shaking her head with double meaning.*] You know how these young folks is nowadays, mister. Can't do a thing with 'em. Good-bye.

LINDNER: [*Folding up his materials.*] Well—if you are that final about it . . . There is nothing left for me to say. [*He finishes. He is almost ignored by the family, who are concentrating on* WALTER LEE. *At the door* LINDNER *halts and looks around.*] I sure hope you people know what you're doing.

[*He shakes his head and exits.*]

RUTH: [*Looking around and coming to life.*] Well, for God's sake—if the moving men are here—LET'S GET THE HELL OUT OF HERE!

MAMA: [*Into action.*] Ain't it the truth! Look at all this here mess. Ruth, put Travis' good jacket on him . . . Walter Lee, fix your tie and tuck your shirt in, you look just like somebody's hoodlum. Lord have mercy, where is my plant? [*She flies to get it amid the general bustling of the family, who are deliberately trying to ignore the nobility of the past moment.*] You all start on down . . . Travis child, don't go empty-handed . . . Ruth, where did I put that box with my skillets in it? I want to be in charge of it myself . . . I'm going to make us the biggest dinner we ever ate tonight . . . Beneatha, what's the matter with them stockings? Pull them things up, girl . . .

[*The family starts to file out as two moving men appear and begin to carry out the heavier pieces of furniture, bumping into the family as they move about.*]

BENEATHA: Mama, Asagai—asked me to marry him today and go to Africa—

MAMA: [*In the middle of her getting-ready activity.*] He did? You ain't old enough to marry nobody— [*Seeing the moving men lifting one of her chairs precariously.*] Darling, that ain't no bale of cotton, please handle it so we can sit in it again. I had that chair twenty-five years . . .

[*The movers sigh with exasperation and go on with their work.*]

BENEATHA: [*Girlishly and unreasonably trying to pursue the conversation.*] To go to Africa, Mama—be a doctor in Africa . . .

MAMA: [*Distracted.*] Yes, baby—

WALTER: Africa! What he want you to go to Africa for?

BENEATHA: To practice there . . .

WALTER: Girl, if you don't get all them silly ideas out your head! You better marry yourself a man with some loot . . .

BENEATHA: [*Angrily, precisely as in the first scene of the play.*] What have you got to do with who I marry!

WALTER: Plenty. Now I think George Murchison—

[*He and* BENEATHA *go out yelling at each other vigorously;* BENEATHA *is heard saying that she would not marry* GEORGE MURCHISON *if he were Adam and she were Eve, etc. The anger is loud and real till their voices diminish.* RUTH *stands at the door and turns to* MAMA *and smiles knowingly.*]

MAMA: [*Fixing her hat at last.*] Yeah—they something all right, my children . . .

RUTH: Yeah—they're something. Let's go, Lena.

MAMA: [*Stalling, starting to look around at the house.*] Yes—I'm coming. Ruth—

RUTH: Yes?

MAMA: [*Quietly, woman to woman.*] He finally come into his manhood today, didn't he? Kind of like a rainbow after the rain . . .

RUTH: [*Biting her lip lest her own pride explode in front of* MAMA.] Yes, Lena.

[WALTER's *voice calls for them raucously.*]

MAMA: [*Waving* RUTH *out vaguely.*] All right, honey—go on down. I be down directly.

[RUTH *hesitates, then exits.* MAMA *stands, at last alone in the living room, her plant on the table before her as the lights start to come down. She looks around at all the walls and ceilings and suddenly, despite herself, while the children call below, a great heaving thing rises in her and she puts her fist to her mouth, takes a final desperate look, pulls her coat about her, pats her hat and goes out. The lights dim down. The door opens and she comes back in, grabs her plant, and goes out for the last time.*]

[CURTAIN.]

1959

QUESTIONS

1. Does the play ultimately answer Langston Hughes's question, "What happens to a dream deferred?" If so, how? Which of the different "dreams" in the play does the play as a whole endorse?
2. What role is played by the minor characters, especially George Murchison, Joseph Asagai, and Karl Lindner? What about Willy Harris, a character who never appears but who nonetheless becomes key to the plot?
3. What is the significance of the play's setting—"Chicago's Southside, sometime between World War II and the present" (i.e., 1959)—and of the action's all occurring within the Younger's apartment (which Hansberry describes in a very particular way in the play's initial stage directions)?
4. One of the few key props in the play is the flower that Lena keeps on the windowsill. Why is that prop important?
5. What is the significance of the play's various references to current events both in America and in Africa? What about the allusions to American popular culture and to classical myth? What kinds of references and allusions are most typical of particular characters, and what do they tell us about those characters?

WRITING SUGGESTIONS

1. Write an essay in which you explore the character of either Walter or Beneatha or Lena Younger, discussing the ways in which this character does or does not develop over the course of the play. If you see this character as developing, when and how does she or he do so? Which moments in the play seem especially revealing or significant from this point of view?
2. Explore the significance of the final scene, in which Walter and Beneatha's singing and dancing are interrupted by the arrival of George Murchison, or the final conversation between Beneatha and Joseph Asagai. What issues or questions are brought to the fore in this moment? How does this moment contribute—both structurally and thematically—to the play as a whole?

ARTHUR MILLER

Death of a Salesman

Certain Private Conversations in Two Acts and
a Requiem

CHARACTERS

WILLY LOMAN	UNCLE BEN
LINDA	HOWARD WAGNER
BIFF	JENNY
HAPPY	STANLEY
BERNARD	MISS FORSYTHE
THE WOMAN	LETTA
CHARLEY	

The action takes place in WILLY LOMAN's *house and yard and in various places he
visits in the New York and Boston of today.*

ACT I

*A melody is heard, playing upon a flute. It is small and fine, telling of grass and trees
and the horizon. The curtain rises.*

*Before us is the Salesman's house. We are aware of towering, angular shapes behind
it, surrounding it on all sides. Only the blue light of the sky falls upon the house and
forestage; the surrounding area shows an angry flow of orange. As more light appears,
we see a solid vault of apartment houses around the small, fragile-seeming home. An
air of the dream clings to the place, a dream rising out of reality. The kitchen at center
seems actual enough, for there is a kitchen table with three chairs, and a refrigerator.
But no other fixtures are seen. At the back of the kitchen there is a draped entrance,
which leads to the living-room. To the right of the kitchen, on a level raised two feet, is
a bedroom furnished only with a brass bedstead and a straight chair. On a shelf over
the bed a silver athletic trophy stands. A window opens onto the apartment house at the
side.*

*Behind the kitchen, on a level raised six and a half feet, is the boys' bedroom, at
present barely visible. Two beds are dimly seen, and at the back of the room a dormer
window. (This bedroom is above the unseen living-room.) At the left a stairway curves
up to it from the kitchen.*

*The entire setting is wholly or, in some places, partially transparent. The roof-line of
the house is one-dimensional; under and over it we see the apartment buildings. Before
the house lies an apron, curving beyond the forestage into the orchestra. This forward
area serves as the back yard as well as the locale of all* WILLY's *imaginings and of his
city scenes. Whenever the action is in the present the actors observe the imaginary wall-
lines, entering the house only through its door at the left. But in the scenes of the past*

*these boundaries are broken, and characters enter or leave a room by stepping "through"
a wall onto the forestage.*

From the right, WILLY LOMAN, *the Salesman, enters, carrying two large sample cases.
The flute plays on. He hears but is not aware of it. He is past sixty years of age, dressed
quietly. Even as he crosses the stage to the doorway of the house, his exhaustion is
apparent. He unlocks the door, comes into the kitchen, and thankfully lets his burden
down, feeling the soreness of his palms. A word-sigh escapes his lips—it might be "Oh,
boy, oh, boy." He closes the door, then carries his cases out into the living-room, through
the draped kitchen doorway.*

LINDA, *his wife, has stirred in her bed at the right. She gets out and puts on a robe,
listening. Most often jovial, she has developed an iron repression of her exceptions to*
WILLY's *behavior—she more than loves him, she admires him, as though his mercurial
nature, his temper, his massive dreams and little cruelties, served her only as sharp
reminders of the turbulent longings within him, longings which she shares but lacks the
temperament to utter and follow to their end.*

LINDA: [*Hearing* WILLY *outside the bedroom, calls with some trepidation.*] Willy!
WILLY: It's all right. I came back.
LINDA: Why? What happened? [*Slight pause.*] Did something happen, Willy?
WILLY: No, nothing happened.
LINDA: You didn't smash the car, did you?
WILLY: [*With casual irritation.*] I said nothing happened. Didn't you hear me?
LINDA: Don't you feel well?
WILLY: I'm tired to the death. [*The flute has faded away. He sits on the bed beside her,
  a little numb.*] I couldn't make it. I just couldn't make it, Linda.
LINDA: [*Very carefully, delicately.*] Where were you all day? You look terrible.
WILLY: I got as far as a little above Yonkers. I stopped for a cup of coffee. Maybe
  it was the coffee.
LINDA: What?
WILLY: [*After a pause.*] I suddenly couldn't drive any more. The car kept going off
  onto the shoulder, y'know?
LINDA: [*Helpfully.*] Oh. Maybe it was the steering again. I don't think Angelo knows
  the Studebaker.
WILLY: No, it's me, it's me. Suddenly I realize I'm goin' sixty miles an hour and I
  don't remember the last five minutes. I'm—I can't seem to—keep my mind
  to it.
LINDA: Maybe it's your glasses. You never went for your new glasses.
WILLY: No, I see everything. I came back ten miles an hour. It took me nearly four
  hours from Yonkers.
LINDA: [*Resigned.*] Well, you'll just have to take a rest, Willy, you can't continue
  this way.
WILLY: I just got back from Florida.
LINDA: But you didn't rest your mind. Your mind is overactive, and the mind is
  what counts, dear.
WILLY: I'll start out in the morning. Maybe I'll feel better in the morning. [*She is
  taking off his shoes.*] These goddam arch supports are killing me.

LINDA: Take an aspirin. Should I get you an aspirin? It'll soothe you.

WILLY: [*With wonder.*] I was driving along, you understand? And I was fine. I was even observing the scenery. You can imagine, me looking at scenery, on the road every week of my life. But it's so beautiful up there, Linda, the trees are so thick, and the sun is warm. I opened the windshield and just let the warm air bathe over me. And then all of a sudden I'm goin' off the road! I'm tellin' ya, I absolutely forgot I was driving. If I'd've gone the other way over the white line I might've killed somebody. So I went on again—and five minutes later I'm dreamin' again, and I nearly— [*He presses two fingers against his eyes.*] I have such thoughts, I have such strange thoughts.

LINDA: Willy, dear. Talk to them again. There's no reason why you can't work in New York.

WILLY: They don't need me in New York. I'm the New England man. I'm vital in New England.

LINDA: But you're sixty years old. They can't expect you to keep traveling every week.

WILLY: I'll have to send a wire to Portland. I'm supposed to see Brown and Morrison tomorrow morning at ten o'clock to show the line. Goddammit, I could sell them! [*He starts putting on his jacket.*]

LINDA: [*Taking the jacket from him.*] Why don't you go down to the place tomorrow and tell Howard you've simply got to work in New York? You're too accommodating, dear.

WILLY: If old man Wagner was alive I'da been in charge of New York now! That man was a prince, he was a masterful man. But that boy of his, that Howard, he don't appreciate. When I went north the first time, the Wagner Company didn't know where New England was!

LINDA: Why don't you tell those things to Howard, dear?

WILLY: [*Encouraged.*] I will, I definitely will. Is there any cheese?

LINDA: I'll make you a sandwich.

WILLY: No, go to sleep. I'll take some milk. I'll be up right away. The boys in?

LINDA: They're sleeping. Happy took Biff on a date tonight.

WILLY: [*Interested.*] That so?

LINDA: It was so nice to see them shaving together, one behind the other, in the bathroom. And going out together. You notice? The whole house smells of shaving lotion.

WILLY: Figure it out. Work a lifetime to pay off a house. You finally own it, and there's nobody to live in it.

LINDA: Well, dear, life is a casting off. It's always that way.

WILLY: No, no, some people—some people accomplish something. Did Biff say anything after I went this morning?

LINDA: You shouldn't have criticized him, Willy, especially after he just got off the train. You mustn't lose your temper with him.

WILLY: When the hell did I lose my temper? I simply asked him if he was making any money. Is that a criticism?

LINDA: But, dear, how could he make any money?

WILLY: [*Worried and angered.*] There's such an undercurrent in him. He became a moody man. Did he apologize when I left this morning?

LINDA: He was crestfallen, Willy. You know how he admires you. I think if he finds himself, then you'll both be happier and not fight any more.

WILLY: How can he find himself on a farm? Is that a life? A farmhand? In the beginning, when he was young, I thought, well, a young man, it's good for him to tramp around, take a lot of different jobs. But it's more than ten years now and he has yet to make thirty-five dollars a week!

LINDA: He's finding himself, Willy.

WILLY: Not finding yourself at the age of thirty-four is a disgrace!

LINDA: Shh!

WILLY: The trouble is he's lazy, goddammit!

LINDA: Willy, please!

WILLY: Biff is a lazy bum!

LINDA: They're sleeping. Get something to eat. Go on down.

WILLY: Why did he come home? I would like to know what brought him home.

LINDA: I don't know. I think he's still lost, Willy. I think he's very lost.

WILLY: Biff Loman is lost. In the greatest country in the world a young man with such—personal attractiveness, gets lost. And such a hard worker. There's one thing about Biff—he's not lazy.

LINDA: Never.

WILLY: [*With pity and resolve.*] I'll see him in the morning; I'll have a nice talk with him. I'll get him a job selling. He could be big in no time. My God! Remember how they used to follow him around in high school? When he smiled at one of them their faces lit up. When he walked down the street . . . [*He loses himself in reminiscences.*]

LINDA: [*Trying to bring him out of it.*] Willy, dear, I got a new kind of American-type cheese today. It's whipped.

WILLY: Why do you get American when I like Swiss?

LINDA: I just thought you'd like a change—

WILLY: I don't want a change! I want Swiss cheese. Why am I always being contradicted?

LINDA: [*With a covering laugh.*] I thought it would be a surprise.

WILLY: Why don't you open a window in here, for God's sake?

LINDA: [*With infinite patience.*] They're all open, dear.

WILLY: The way they boxed us in here. Bricks and windows, windows and bricks.

LINDA: We should've bought the land next door.

WILLY: The street is lined with cars. There's not a breath of fresh air in the neighborhood. The grass don't grow any more, you can't raise a carrot in the back yard. They should've had a law against apartment houses. Remember those two beautiful elm trees out there? When I and Biff hung the swing between them?

LINDA: Yeah, like being a million miles from the city.

WILLY: They should've arrested the builder for cutting those down. They massacred the neighborhood. [*Lost.*] More and more I think of those days, Linda. This time of year it was lilac and wisteria. And then the peonies would come out, and the daffodils. What fragrance in this room!

LINDA: Well, after all, people had to move somewhere.

WILLY: No, there's more people now.

LINDA: I don't think there's more people. I think—

WILLY: There's more people! That's what ruining this country! Population is getting out of control. The competition is maddening! Smell the stink from that apartment house! And another one on the other side . . . How can they whip cheese?

[*On* WILLY's *last line,* BIFF *and* HAPPY *raise themselves up in their beds, listening.*]

LINDA: Go down, try it. And be quiet.

WILLY: [*Turning to* LINDA, *guiltily.*] You're not worried about me, are you, sweetheart?

BIFF: What's the matter?

HAPPY: Listen!

LINDA: You've got too much on the ball to worry about.

WILLY: You're my foundation and my support, Linda.

LINDA: Just try to relax, dear. You make mountains out of mole-hills.

WILLY: I won't fight with him any more. If he wants to go back to Texas, let him go.

LINDA: He'll find his way.

WILLY: Sure. Certain men just don't get started till later in life. Like Thomas Edison, I think. Or B. F. Goodrich. One of them was deaf. [*He starts for the bedroom doorway.*] I'll put my money on Biff.

LINDA: And Willy—if it's warm Sunday we'll drive in the country. And we'll open the windshield, and take lunch.

WILLY: No, the windshields don't open on the new cars.

LINDA: But you opened it today.

WILLY: Me? I didn't. [*He stops.*] Now isn't that peculiar! Isn't that a remarkable— [*He breaks off in amazement and fright as the flute is heard distantly.*]

LINDA: What, darling?

WILLY: That is the most remarkable thing.

LINDA: What, dear?

WILLY: I was thinking of the Chevvy. [*Slight pause.*] Nineteen twenty-eight . . . when I had that red Chevvy— [*Breaks off.*] That funny? I coulda sworn I was driving that Chevvy today.

LINDA: Well, that's nothing. Something must've reminded you.

WILLY: Remarkable. *Ts.* Remember those days? The way Biff used to simonize that car? The dealer refused to believe there was eighty thousand miles on it. [*He shakes his head.*] Heh! [*To* LINDA.] Close your eyes, I'll be right up. [*He walks out of the bedroom.*]

HAPPY: [*To* BIFF.] Jesus, maybe he smashed up the car again!

LINDA: [*Calling after* WILLY.] Be careful on the stairs, dear! The cheese is on the middle shelf! [*She turns, goes over to the bed, takes his jacket, and goes out of the bedroom.*]

[*Light has risen on the boys' room. Unseen,* WILLY *is heard talking to himself, "Eighty thousand miles," and a little laugh.* BIFF *gets out of bed, comes downstage a bit, and stands attentively.* BIFF *is two years older than his brother* HAPPY, *well built, but in these days bears a worn air and seems less self-assured. He has succeeded less, and his dreams are stronger and less acceptable than* HAPPY's. HAPPY *is tall, powerfully made. Sexuality is like a visible color on him, or a scent that many women have discovered. He, like his brother, is lost, but in a different way, for he has never allowed himself to turn his face toward defeat and is thus more confused and hard-skinned, although seemingly more content.*]

HAPPY: [*Getting out of bed.*] He's going to get his license taken away if he keeps that up. I'm getting nervous about him, y'know, Biff?

BIFF: His eyes are going.

HAPPY: No, I've driven with him. He sees all right. He just doesn't keep his mind on it. I drove into the city with him last week. He stops at a green light and then it turns red and he goes. [*He laughs.*]

BIFF: Maybe he's color-blind.

HAPPY: Pop? Why he's got the finest eye for color in the business. You know that.

BIFF: [*Sitting down on his bed.*] I'm going to sleep.

HAPPY: You're not still sour on Dad, are you Biff?

BIFF: He's all right, I guess.

WILLY: [*Underneath them, in the living-room.*] Yes, sir, eighty thousand miles—eighty-two thousand!

BIFF: You smoking?

HAPPY: [*Holding out a pack of cigarettes.*] Want one?

BIFF: [*Taking a cigarette.*] I can never sleep when I smell it.

WILLY: What a simonizing job, heh!

HAPPY: [*With deep sentiment.*] Funny, Biff, y'know? Us sleeping in here again? The old beds. [*He pats his bed affectionately.*] All the talk that went across those two beds, huh? Our whole lives.

BIFF: Yeah. Lotta dreams and plans.

HAPPY: [*With a deep and masculine laugh.*] About five hundred women would like to know what was said in this room.

[*They share a soft laugh.*]

BIFF: Remember that big Betsy something—what the hell was her name—over on Bushwick Avenue?

HAPPY: [*Combing his hair.*] With the collie dog!

BIFF: That's the one. I got you in there, remember?

HAPPY: Yeah, that was my first time—I think. Boy, there was a pig! [*They laugh, almost crudely.*] You taught me everything I know about women. Don't forget that.

BIFF: I bet you forgot how bashful you used to be. Especially with girls.

HAPPY: Oh, I still am, Biff.

BIFF: Oh, go on.

HAPPY: I just control it, that's all. I think I got less bashful and you got more so. What happened, Biff? Where's the old humor, the old confidence? [*He shakes* BIFF'*s knee.* BIFF *gets up and moves restlessly about the room.*] What's the matter?

BIFF: Why does Dad mock me all the time?

HAPPY: He's not mocking you, he—

BIFF: Everything I say there's a twist of mockery on his face. I can't get near him.

HAPPY: He just wants you to make good, that's all. I wanted to talk to you about Dad for a long time, Biff. Something's—happening to him. He—talks to himself.

BIFF: I noticed that this morning. But he always mumbled.

HAPPY: But not so noticeable. It got so embarrassing I sent him to Florida. And you know something? Most of the time he's talking to you.

BIFF: What's he say about me?

HAPPY: I can't make it out.

BIFF: What's he say about me?

HAPPY: I think the fact that you're not settled, that you're still kind of up in the air . . .

BIFF: There's one or two things depressing him, Happy.

HAPPY: What do you mean?

BIFF: Never mind. Just don't lay it all to me.

HAPPY: But I think if you just got started—I mean—is there any future for you out there?

BIFF: I tell ya, Hap, I don't know what the future is. I don't know—what I'm supposed to want.

HAPPY: What do you mean?

BIFF: Well, I spent six or seven years after high school trying to work myself up. Shipping clerk, salesman, business of one kind or another. And it's a measly manner of existence. To get on that subway on the hot mornings in summer. To devote your whole life to keeping stock, or making phone calls, or selling or buying. To suffer fifty weeks of the year for the sake of a two-week vacation, when all you really desire is to be outdoors, with your shirt off. And always to have to get ahead of the next fella. And still—that's how you build a future.

HAPPY: Well, you really enjoy it on a farm? Are you content out there?

BIFF: [*With rising agitation.*] Hap, I've had twenty or thirty different kinds of jobs since I left home before the war, and it always turns out the same. I just realized it lately. In Nebraska when I herded cattle, and the Dakotas, and Arizona, and now in Texas. It's why I came home now, I guess, because I realized it. This farm I work on, it's spring there now, see? And they've got about fifteen new colts. There's nothing more inspiring or—beautiful than the sight of a mare and a new colt. And it's cool there now, see? Texas is cool now, and it's spring. And whenever spring comes to where I am, I suddenly get the feeling, my God, I'm not gettin' anywhere! What the hell am I doing, playing around with horses, twenty-eight dollars a week! I'm thirty-four years old. I oughta be makin' my future. That's when I come running home. And now, I get there, and I don't know what to do with myself. [*After a pause.*] I've always made a point of not wasting my life, and everytime I come back here I know that all I've done is to waste my life.

HAPPY: You're a poet, you know that, Biff? You're a—you're an idealist!

BIFF: No, I'm mixed up very bad. Maybe I oughta get married. Maybe I oughta get stuck into something. Maybe that's my trouble. I'm like a boy. I'm not married. I'm not in business, I just—I'm like a boy. Are you content, Hap? You're a success, aren't you? Are you content?

HAPPY: Hell, no!

BIFF: Why? You're making money, aren't you?

HAPPY: [*Moving about with energy, expressiveness.*] All I can do now is wait for the merchandise manager to die. And suppose I get to be merchandise manager? He's a good friend of mine, and he just built a terrific estate on Long Island. And he lived there about two months and sold it, and now he's building another one. He can't enjoy it once it's finished. And I know that's just what I would do. I don't know what the hell I'm workin' for. Sometimes I sit in my apartment—all alone. And I think of the rent I'm paying. And it's crazy. But then, it's what I always wanted. My own apartment, a car, and plenty of women. And still, goddammit, I'm lonely.

BIFF: [*With enthusiasm.*] Listen, why don't you come out West with me?

HAPPY: You and I, heh?

BIFF: Sure, maybe we could buy a ranch. Raise cattle, use our muscles. Men built like we are should be working out in the open.

HAPPY: [*Avidly.*] The Loman Brothers, heh?

BIFF: [*With vast affection.*] Sure, we'd be known all over the counties!

HAPPY: [*Enthralled.*] That's what I dream about, Biff. Sometimes I want to just rip my clothes off in the middle of the store and outbox that goddam merchandise manager. I mean I can outbox, outrun, and outlift anybody in that store, and I have to take orders from those common, petty sons-of-bitches till I can't stand it any more.

BIFF: I'm tellin' you, kid, if you were with me I'd be happy out there.

HAPPY: [*Enthused.*] See, Biff, everybody around me is so false that I'm constantly lowering my ideals . . .

BIFF: Baby, together we'd stand up for one another, we'd have someone to trust.

HAPPY: If I were around you—

BIFF: Hap, the trouble is we weren't brought up to grub for money. I don't know how to do it.

HAPPY: Neither can I!

BIFF: Then let's go!

HAPPY: The only thing is—what can you make out there?

BIFF: But look at your friend. Builds an estate and then hasn't the peace of mind to live in it.

HAPPY: Yeah, but when he walks into the store the waves part in front of him. That's fifty-two thousand dollars a year coming through the revolving door, and I got more in my pinky finger than he's got in his head.

BIFF: Yeah, but you just said—

HAPPY: I gotta show some of those pompous, self-important executives over there that Hap Loman can make the grade. I want to walk into the store the way he walks in. Then I'll go with you, Biff. We'll be together yet, I swear. But take those two we had tonight. Now weren't they gorgeous creatures?

BIFF: Yeah, yeah, most gorgeous I've had in years.

HAPPY: I get that any time I want, Biff. Whenever I feel disgusted. The only trouble is, it gets like bowling or something. I just keep knockin' them over and it doesn't mean anything. You still run around a lot?

BIFF: Naa. I'd like to find a girl—steady, somebody with substance.

HAPPY: That's what I long for.

BIFF: Go on! You'd never come home.

HAPPY: I would! Somebody with character, with resistance! Like Mom, y'know? You're gonna call me a bastard when I tell you this. That girl Charlotte I was with tonight is engaged to be married in five weeks. [*He tries on his new hat.*]

BIFF: No kiddin'!

HAPPY: Sure, the guy's in line for the vice-presidency of the store. I don't know what gets into me, maybe I just have an overdeveloped sense of competition or something, but I went and ruined her, and furthermore I can't get rid of her. And he's the third executive I've done that to. Isn't that a crummy characteristic? And to top it all, I go to their weddings! [*Indignantly, but laughing.*] Like I'm not supposed to take bribes. Manufacturers offer me a hundred-dollar bill now and then to throw an order their way. You know how honest I am, but it's like this girl, see. I hate myself for it. Because I don't want the girl, and, still, I take it and—I love it!

BIFF: Let's go to sleep.

HAPPY: I guess we didn't settle anything, heh?

BIFF: I just got one idea that I'm going to try.

HAPPY: What's that?

BIFF: Remember Bill Oliver?

HAPPY: Sure, Oliver is very big now. You want to work for him again?

BIFF: No, but when I quit he said something to me. He put his arm on my shoulder, and he said, "Biff, if you ever need anything, come to me."

HAPPY: I remember that. That sounds good.

BIFF: I think I'll go to see him. If I could get ten thousand or even seven or eight thousand dollars I could buy a beautiful ranch.

HAPPY: I bet he'd back you. 'Cause he thought highly of you, Biff. I mean, they all do. You're well liked, Biff. That's why I say to come back here, and we both have the apartment. And I'm tellin' you, Biff, any babe you want . . .

BIFF: No, with a ranch I could do the work I like and still be something. I just wonder though. I wonder if Oliver still thinks I stole that carton of basketballs.

HAPPY: Oh, he probably forgot that long ago. It's almost ten years. You're too sensitive. Anyway, he didn't really fire you.

BIFF: Well, I think he was going to. I think that's why I quit. I was never sure whether he knew or not. I know he thought the world of me, though. I was the only one he'd let lock up the place.

WILLY: [*Below.*] You gonna wash the engine, Biff?

HAPPY: Shh! [BIFF *looks at* HAPPY, *who is gazing down, listening.* WILLY *is mumbling in the parlor.*] You hear that?

[*They listen.* WILLY *laughs warmly.*]

BIFF: [*Growing angry.*] Doesn't he know Mom can hear that?

WILLY: Don't get your sweater dirty, Biff!

[*A look of pain crosses* BIFF'*s face.*]

HAPPY: Isn't that terrible? Don't leave again, will you? You'll find a job here. You gotta stick around. I don't know what to do about him, it's getting embarrassing.

WILLY: What a simonizing job!

BIFF: Mom's hearing that!

WILLY: No kiddin', Biff, you got a date? Wonderful!

HAPPY: Go on to sleep. But talk to him in the morning, will you?

BIFF: [*Reluctantly getting into bed.*] With her in the house. Brother!

HAPPY: [*Getting into bed.*] I wish you'd have a good talk with him.

[*The light on their room begins to fade.*]

BIFF: [*To himself in bed.*] That selfish, stupid . . .

HAPPY: Sh . . . Sleep, Biff.

[*Their light is out. Well before they have finished speaking,* WILLY'*s form is dimly seen below in the darkened kitchen. He opens the refrigerator, searches in there, and takes out a bottle of milk. The apartment houses are fading out, and the entire house and surroundings become covered with leaves. Music insinuates itself as the leaves appear.*]

WILLY: Just wanna be careful with those girls, Biff, that's all. Don't make any promises. No promises of any kind. Because a girl, y'know, they always believe what you tell 'em, and you're very young, Biff, you're too young to be talking seriously to girls. [*Light rises on the kitchen.* WILLY, *talking, shuts the refrigerator door and comes downstage to the kitchen table. He pours milk into a glass. He is totally immersed in himself, smiling faintly.*] Too young entirely, Biff. You want to watch your schooling first. Then when you're all set, there'll be plenty of girls for a boy like you. [*He smiles broadly at a kitchen chair.*] That so? The girls pay for you? [*He laughs.*] Boy, you must really be makin' a hit. [WILLY *is gradually addressing—physically—a point offstage, speaking through the wall of the kitchen, and his voice has been rising in volume to that of a normal conversation.*] I been wondering why you polish the car so careful. Ha! Don't leave the hubcaps, boys. Get the chamois to the hubcaps. Happy, use newspaper on the windows, it's the easiest thing. Show him how to do it, Biff! You see, Happy? Pad it up, use it like a pad. That's it, that's it, good work. You're doin' all right, Hap. [*He pauses, then nods in approbation for a few seconds, then looks upward.*] Biff, first thing we gotta do when we get time is clip that big branch over the house. Afraid it's gonna fall in a storm and hit the roof. Tell you what. We get a rope and sling her around, and then we climb up there with a couple of saws and take her down. Soon as you finish the car, boys, I wanna see ya. I got a surprise for you, boys.

BIFF: [*Offstage.*] Whatta ya got, Dad?

WILLY: No, you finish first. Never leave a job till you're finished—remember that. [*Looking toward the "big trees."*] Biff, up in Albany I saw a beautiful hammock. I think I'll buy it next trip, and we'll hang it right between those two elms. Wouldn't that be something? Just swingin' there under those branches. Boy, that would be . . .

[YOUNG BIFF *and* YOUNG HAPPY *appear from the direction* WILLY *was addressing.* HAPPY *carries rags and a pail of water.* BIFF, *wearing a sweater with a block "S," carries a football.*]

BIFF: [*Pointing in the direction of the car offstage.*] How's that, Pop, professional?

WILLY: Terrific. Terrific job, boys. Good work, Biff.

HAPPY: Where's the surprise, Pop?

WILLY: In the back seat of the car.

HAPPY: Boy! [*He runs off.*]

BIFF: What is it, Dad? Tell me, what'd you buy?

WILLY: [*Laughing, cuffs him.*] Never mind, something I want you to have.

BIFF: [*Turns and starts off.*] What is it, Hap?

HAPPY: [*Offstage.*] It's a punching bag!

BIFF: Oh, Pop!

WILLY: It's got Gene Tunney's[1] signature on it!

[HAPPY *runs onstage with a punching bag.*]

BIFF: Gee, how'd you know we wanted a punching bag?

WILLY: Well, it's the finest thing for the timing.

HAPPY: [*Lies down on his back and pedals with his feet.*] I'm losing weight, you notice, Pop?

WILLY: [*To* HAPPY.] Jumping rope is good too.

BIFF: Did you see the new football I got?

WILLY: [*Examining the ball.*] Where'd you get a new ball?

BIFF: The coach told me to practice my passing.

WILLY: That so? And he gave you the ball, heh?

BIFF: Well, I borrowed it from the locker room. [*He laughs confidentially.*]

WILLY: [*Laughing with him at the theft.*] I want you to return that.

HAPPY: I told you he wouldn't like it!

BIFF: [*Angrily.*] Well, I'm bringing it back!

WILLY: [*Stopping the incipient argument, to* HAPPY.] Sure, he's gotta practice with a

---

1. Tunney (1897–1978) was world heavyweight boxing champion from 1926 to 1928 and retired undefeated.

regulation ball, doesn't he? [*To* BIFF.] Coach'll probably congratulate you on your initiative!

BIFF: Oh, he keeps congratulating my initiative all the time, Pop.

WILLY: That's because he likes you. If somebody else took that ball there'd be an uproar. So what's the report, boys, what's the report?

BIFF: Where'd you go this time, Dad? Gee we were lonesome for you.

WILLY: [*Pleased, puts an arm around each boy and they come down to the apron.*] Lonesome, heh?

BIFF: Missed you every minute.

WILLY: Don't say? Tell you a secret, boys. Don't breathe it to a soul. Someday I'll have my own business, and I'll never have to leave home any more.

HAPPY: Like Uncle Charley, heh?

WILLY: Bigger than Uncle Charley! Because Charley is not—liked. He's liked, but he's not—well liked.

BIFF: Where'd you go this time, Dad?

WILLY: Well, I got on the road, and I went north to Providence. Met the Mayor.

BIFF: The Mayor of Providence!

WILLY: He was sitting in the hotel lobby.

BIFF: What'd he say?

WILLY: He said, "Morning!" And I said, "You got a fine city here, Mayor." And then he had coffee with me. And then I went to Waterbury. Waterbury is a fine city. Big clock city, the famous Waterbury clock. Sold a nice bill there. And then Boston—Boston is the cradle of the Revolution. A fine city. And a couple of other towns in Mass., and on to Portland and Bangor and straight home!

BIFF: Gee, I'd love to go with you sometime, Dad.

WILLY: Soon as summer comes.

HAPPY: Promise?

WILLY: You and Hap and I, and I'll show you all the towns. America is full of beautiful towns and fine, upstanding people. And they know me, boys, they know me up and down New England. The finest people. And when I bring you fellas up, there'll be open sesame for all of us, 'cause one thing, boys: I have friends. I can park my car in any street in New England, and the cops protect it like their own. This summer, heh?

BIFF and HAPPY: [*Together.*] Yeah! You bet!

WILLY: We'll take our bathing suits.

HAPPY: We'll carry your bags, Pop!

WILLY: Oh, won't that be something! Me comin' into the Boston stores with you boys carryin' my bags. What a sensation! [BIFF *is prancing around, practicing passing the ball.*] You nervous, Biff, about the game?

BIFF: Not if you're gonna be there.

WILLY: What do they say about you in school, now that they made you captain?

HAPPY: There's a crowd of girls behind him everytime the classes change.

BIFF: [*Taking* WILLY's *hand.*] This Saturday, Pop, this Saturday—just for you, I'm going to break through for a touchdown.

HAPPY: You're supposed to pass.

BIFF: I'm takin' one play for Pop. You watch me, Pop, and when I take off my helmet, that means I'm breakin' out. Then you watch me crash through that line!

WILLY: [*Kisses* BIFF.] Oh, wait'll I tell this in Boston!

[BERNARD *enters in knickers. He is younger than* BIFF, *earnest and loyal, a worried boy.*]

BERNARD: Biff, where are you? You're supposed to study with me today.

WILLY: Hey, looka Bernard. What're you lookin' so anemic about, Bernard?

BERNARD: He's gotta study, Uncle Willy. He's got Regents[2] next week.

HAPPY: [*Tauntingly, spinning* BERNARD *around.*] Let's box, Bernard!

BERNARD: Biff! [*He gets away from* HAPPY.] Listen, Biff, I heard Mr. Birnbaum say that if you don't start studyin' math he's gonna flunk you, and you won't graduate. I heard him!

WILLY: You better study with him, Biff. Go ahead now.

BERNARD: I heard him!

BIFF: Oh, Pop, you didn't see my sneakers! [*He holds up a foot for* WILLY *to look at.*]

WILLY: Hey, that's a beautiful job of printing!

BERNARD: [*Wiping his glasses.*] Just because he printed University of Virginia on his sneakers doesn't mean they've got to graduate him, Uncle Willy!

WILLY: [*Angrily.*] What're you talking about? With scholarships to three universities they're gonna flunk him?

BERNARD: But I heard Mr. Birnbaum say—

WILLY: Don't be a pest, Bernard! [*To his boys.*] What an anemic!

BERNARD: Okay, I'm waiting for you in my house, Biff.

[BERNARD *goes off. The* LOMANS *laugh.*]

WILLY: Bernard is not well liked, is he?

BIFF: He's liked, but he's not well liked.

HAPPY: That's right, Pop.

WILLY: That's just what I mean. Bernard can get the best marks in school, y'understand, but when he gets out in the business world, y'understand, you are going to be five times ahead of him. That's why I thank Almighty God you're both built like Adonises. Because the man who makes an appearance in the business world, the man who creates personal interest, is the man who gets ahead. Be liked and you will never want. You take me, for instance. I never have to wait in line to see a buyer. "Willy Loman is here!" That's all they have to know, and I go right through.

BIFF: Did you knock them dead, Pop?

WILLY: Knocked 'em cold in Providence, slaughtered 'em in Boston.

HAPPY: [*On his back, pedaling again.*] I'm losing weight, you notice, Pop?

[LINDA *enters, as of old, a ribbon in her hair, carrying a basket of washing.*]

LINDA: [*With youthful energy.*] Hello, dear!

---

2. An examination administered to New York State high-school students.

WILLY: Sweetheart!

LINDA: How'd the Chevvy run?

WILLY: Chevrolet, Linda, is the greatest car ever built. [*To the boys.*] Since when do you let your mother carry wash up the stairs?

BIFF: Grab hold there, boy!

HAPPY: Where to, Mom?

LINDA: Hang them up on the line. And you better go down to your friends, Biff. The cellar is full of boys. They don't know what to do with themselves.

BIFF: Ah, when Pop comes home they can wait!

WILLY: [*Laughs appreciatively.*] You better go down and tell them what to do, Biff.

BIFF: I think I'll have them sweep out the furnace room.

WILLY: Good work, Biff.

BIFF: [*Goes through wall-line of kitchen to doorway at back and calls down.*] Fellas! Everybody sweep out the furnace room! I'll be right down!

VOICES: All right! Okay, Biff.

BIFF: George and Sam and Frank, come out back! We're hangin' up the wash! Come on, Hap, on the double!

[*He and* HAPPY *carry out the basket.*]

LINDA: The way they obey him!

WILLY: Well, that training, the training. I'm tellin' you, I was sellin' thousands and thousands, but I had to come home.

LINDA: Oh, the whole block'll be at that game. Did you sell anything?

WILLY: I did five hundred gross in Providence and seven hundred gross in Boston.

LINDA: No! Wait a minute, I've got a pencil. [*She pulls pencil and paper out of her apron pocket.*] That makes your commission . . . Two hundred—my God! Two hundred and twelve dollars!

WILLY: Well, I didn't figure it yet, but . . .

LINDA: How much did you do?

WILLY: Well, I—I did—about a hundred and eighty gross in Providence. Well, no— it came to—roughly two hundred gross on the whole trip.

LINDA: [*Without hesitation.*] Two hundred gross. That's . . . [*She figures.*]

WILLY: The trouble was that three of the stores were half closed for inventory in Boston. Otherwise I woulda broke records.

LINDA: Well, it makes seventy dollars and some pennies. That's very good.

WILLY: What do we owe?

LINDA: Well, on the first there's sixteen dollars on the refrigerator—

WILLY: Why sixteen?

LINDA: Well, the fan belt broke, so it was a dollar eighty.

WILLY: But it's brand new.

LINDA: Well, the man said that's the way it is. Till they work themselves in, y'know.

[*They move through the wall-line into the kitchen.*]

WILLY: I hope we didn't get stuck on that machine.

LINDA: They got the biggest ads of any of them!

WILLY: I know, it's a fine machine. What else?

LINDA: Well, there's nine-sixty for the washing machine. And for the vacuum cleaner there's three and a half due on the fifteenth. Then the roof, you got twenty-one dollars remaining.

WILLY: It don't leak, does it?

LINDA: No, they did a wonderful job. Then you owe Frank for the carburetor.

WILLY: I'm not going to pay that man! That goddam Chevrolet, they ought to prohibit the manufacture of that car!

LINDA: Well, you owe him three and a half. And odds and ends, comes to around a hundred and twenty dollars by the fifteenth.

WILLY: A hundred and twenty dollars! My God, if business don't pick up I don't know what I'm gonna do!

LINDA: Well, next week you'll do better.

WILLY: Oh, I'll knock 'em dead next week. I'll go to Hartford. I'm very well liked in Hartford. You know, the trouble is, Linda, people don't seem to take to me.

[*They move onto the forestage.*]

LINDA: Oh, don't be foolish.

WILLY: I know it when I walk in. They seem to laugh at me.

LINDA: Why? Why would they laugh at you? Don't talk that way, Willy.

[WILLY *moves to the edge of the stage.* LINDA *goes into the kitchen and starts to darn stockings.*]

WILLY: I don't know the reason for it, but they just pass me by. I'm not noticed.

LINDA: But you're doing wonderful, dear. You're making seventy to a hundred dollars a week.

WILLY: But I gotta be at it ten, twelve hours a day. Other men—I don't know—they do it easier. I don't know why—I can't stop myself—I talk too much. A man oughta come in with a few words. One thing about Charley. He's a man of few words, and they respect him.

LINDA: You don't talk too much, you're just lively.

WILLY: [*Smiling.*] Well, I figure, what the hell, life is short, a couple of jokes. [*To himself.*] I joke too much! [*The smile goes.*]

LINDA: Why? You're—

WILLY: I'm fat. I'm very—foolish to look at, Linda. I didn't tell you, but Christmas time I happened to be calling on F. H. Stewarts, and a salesman I know, as I was going in to see the buyer I heard him say something about—walrus. And I—I cracked him right across the face. I won't take that. I simply will not take that. But they do laugh at me. I know that.

LINDA: Darling . . .

WILLY: I gotta overcome it. I know I gotta overcome it. I'm not dressing to advantage, maybe.

LINDA: Willy, darling, you're the handsomest man in the world—

WILLY: Oh, no, Linda.

LINDA: To me you are. [*Slight pause.*] The handsomest. [*From the darkness is heard the laughter of a woman.* WILLY *doesn't turn to it, but it continues through* LINDA's *lines.*] And the boys, Willy. Few men are idolized by their children the way you are.

[*Music is heard as behind a scrim, to the left of the house,* THE WOMAN, *dimly seen, is dressing.*]

WILLY: [*With great feeling.*] You're the best there is, Linda, you're a pal, you know that? On the road—on the road I want to grab you sometimes and just kiss the life outa you. [*The laughter is loud now, and he moves into a brightening area at the left, where* THE WOMAN *has come from behind the scrim and is standing, putting on her hat, looking into a "mirror" and laughing.*] 'Cause I get so lonely—especially when business is bad and there's nobody to talk to. I get the feeling that I'll never sell anything again, that I won't make a living for you, or a business, a business for the boys. [*He talks through* THE WOMAN's *subsiding laughter.* THE WOMAN *primps at the "mirror."*] There's so much I want to make for—

THE WOMAN: Me? You didn't make me, Willy. I picked you.

WILLY: [*Pleased.*] You picked me?

THE WOMAN: [*Who is quite proper-looking,* WILLY's *age.*] I did. I've been sitting at that desk watching all the salesmen go by, day in, day out. But you've got such a sense of humor, and we do have such a good time together, don't we?

WILLY: Sure, sure. [*He takes her in his arms.*] Why do you have to go now?

THE WOMAN: It's two o'clock . . .

WILLY: No, come on in! [*He pulls her.*]

THE WOMAN: . . . my sisters'll be scandalized. When'll you be back?

WILLY: Oh, two weeks about. Will you come up again?

THE WOMAN: Sure thing. You do make me laugh. It's good for me. [*She squeezes his arm, kisses him.*] And I think you're a wonderful man.

WILLY: You picked me, heh?

THE WOMAN: Sure. Because you're so sweet. And such a kidder.

WILLY: Well, I'll see you next time I'm in Boston.

THE WOMAN: I'll put you right through to the buyers.

WILLY: [*Slapping her bottom.*] Right. Well, bottoms up!

THE WOMAN: [*Slaps him gently and laughs.*] You just kill me, Willy. [*He suddenly grabs her and kisses her roughly.*] You kill me. And thanks for the stockings. I love a lot of stockings. Well, good night.

WILLY: Good night. And keep your pores open!

THE WOMAN: Oh, Willy!

[THE WOMAN *bursts out laughing, and* LINDA's *laughter blends in.* THE WOMAN *disappears into the dark. Now the area at the kitchen table brightens.* LINDA *is sitting where she was at the kitchen table, but now is mending a pair of her silk stockings.*]

LINDA: You are, Willy. The handsomest man. You've got no reason to feel that—

WILLY: [*Coming out of* THE WOMAN's *dimming area and going over to* LINDA.] I'll make it all up to you, Linda. I'll—

LINDA: There's nothing to make up, dear. You're doing fine, better than—

WILLY: [*Noticing her mending.*] What's that?

LINDA: Just mending my stockings. They're so expensive—

WILLY: [*Angrily, taking them from her.*] I won't have you mending stockings in this house! Now throw them out!

[LINDA *puts the stockings in her pocket.*]

BERNARD: [*Entering on the run.*] Where is he? If he doesn't study!

WILLY: [*Moving to the forestage, with great agitation.*] You'll give him the answers!

BERNARD: I do, but I can't on a Regents! That's a state exam! They're liable to arrest me!

WILLY: Where is he? I'll whip him, I'll whip him!

LINDA: And he'd better give back that football, Willy, it's not nice.

WILLY: Biff! Where is he? Why is he taking everything?

LINDA: He's too rough with the girls, Willy. All the mothers are afraid of him!

WILLY: I'll whip him!

BERNARD: He's driving the car without a license!

[THE WOMAN'*s laugh is heard.*]

WILLY: Shut up!

LINDA: All the mothers—

WILLY: Shut up!

BERNARD: [*Backing quietly away and out.*] Mr. Birnbaum says he's stuck up.

WILLY: Get outa here!

BERNARD: If he doesn't buckle down he'll flunk math! [*He goes off.*]

LINDA: He's right, Willy, you've gotta—

WILLY: [*Exploding at her.*] There's nothing the matter with him! You want him to be a worm like Bernard? He's got spirit, personality . . . [*As he speaks,* LINDA, *almost in tears, exits into the living room.* WILLY *is alone in the kitchen, wilting and staring. The leaves are gone. It is night again, and the apartment houses look down from behind.*] Loaded with it. Loaded! What is he stealing? He's giving it back, isn't he? Why is he stealing? What did I tell him? I never in my life told him anything but decent things.

[HAPPY *in pajamas has come down the stairs;* WILLY *suddenly becomes aware of* HAPPY'*s presence.*]

HAPPY: Let's go now, come on.

WILLY: [*Sitting down at the kitchen table.*] Huh! Why did she have to wax the floors herself? Everytime she waxes the floors she keels over. She knows that!

HAPPY: Shh! Take it easy. What brought you back tonight?

WILLY: I got an awful scare. Nearly hit a kid in Yonkers. God! Why didn't I go to Alaska with my brother Ben that time! Ben! That man was a genius, that man was success incarnate! What a mistake! He begged me to go.

HAPPY: Well, there's no use in—

WILLY: You guys! There was a man started with the clothes on his back and ended up with diamond mines!

HAPPY: Boy, someday I'd like to know how he did it.

WILLY: What's the mystery? The man knew what he wanted and went out and got it! Walked into a jungle, and comes out, the age of twenty-one, and he's rich! The world is an oyster, but you don't crack it open on a mattress!

HAPPY: Pop, I told you I'm gonna retire you for life.

WILLY: You'll retire me for life on seventy goddam dollars a week? And your women and your car and your apartment, and you'll retire me for life! Christ's sake, I couldn't get past Yonkers today! Where are you guys, where are you? The woods are burning! I can't drive a car!

[CHARLEY *has appeared in the doorway. He is a large man, slow of speech, laconic, immovable. In all he says, despite what he says, there is pity, and now, trepidation. He has a robe over pajamas, slippers on his feet. He enters the kitchen.*]

CHARLEY: Everything all right?

HAPPY: Yeah, Charley, everything's . . .

WILLY: What's the matter?

CHARLEY: I heard some noise. I thought something happened. Can't we do something about the walls? You sneeze in here, and in my house hats blow off.

HAPPY: Let's go to bed, Dad. Come on.

[CHARLEY *signals to* HAPPY *to go.*]

WILLY: You go ahead, I'm not tired at the moment.

HAPPY: [*To* WILLY.] Take it easy, huh? [*He exits.*]

WILLY: What're you doin' up?

CHARLEY: [*Sitting down at the kitchen table opposite* WILLY.] Couldn't sleep good. I had a heartburn.

WILLY: Well, you don't know how to eat.

CHARLEY: I eat with my mouth.

WILLY: No, you're ignorant. You gotta know about vitamins and things like that.

CHARLEY: Come on, let's shoot. Tire you out a little.

WILLY: [*Hesitantly.*] All right. You got cards?

CHARLEY: [*Taking a deck from his pocket.*] Yeah, I got them. Someplace. What is it with those vitamins?

WILLY: [*Dealing.*] They build up your bones. Chemistry.

CHARLEY: Yeah, but there's no bones in a heartburn.

WILLY: What are you talkin' about? Do you know the first thing about it?

CHARLEY: Don't get insulted.

WILLY: Don't talk about something you don't know anything about.

[*They are playing. Pause.*]

CHARLEY: What're you doin' home?

WILLY: A little trouble with the car.

CHARLEY: Oh. [*Pause.*] I'd like to take a trip to California.

WILLY: Don't say.

CHARLEY: You want a job?

WILLY: I got a job, I told you that. [*After a slight pause.*] What the hell are you offering me a job for?

CHARLEY: Don't get insulted.

WILLY: Don't insult me.

CHARLEY: I don't see no sense in it. You don't have to go on this way.

WILLY: I got a good job. [*Slight pause.*] What do you keep comin' in here for?

CHARLEY: You want me to go?

WILLY: [*After a pause, withering.*] I can't understand it. He's going back to Texas again. What the hell is that?

CHARLEY: Let him go.

WILLY: I got nothin' to give him, Charley, I'm clean, I'm clean.

CHARLEY: He won't starve. None a them starve. Forget about him.

WILLY: Then what have I got to remember?

CHARLEY: You take it too hard. To hell with it. When a deposit bottle is broken you don't get your nickel back.

WILLY: That's easy enough for you to say.

CHARLEY: That ain't easy for me to say.

WILLY: Did you see the ceiling I put up in the living-room?

CHARLEY: Yeah, that's a piece of work. To put up a ceiling is a mystery to me. How do you do it?

WILLY: What's the difference?

CHARLEY: Well, talk about it.

WILLY: You gonna put up a ceiling?

CHARLEY: How could I put up a ceiling?

WILLY: Then what the hell are you bothering me for?

CHARLEY: You're insulted again.

WILLY: A man who can't handle tools is not a man. You're disgusting.

CHARLEY: Don't call me disgusting, Willy.

> [UNCLE BEN, *carrying a valise and an umbrella, enters the forestage from around the right corner of the house. He is a stolid man, in his sixties, with a mustache and an authoritative air. He is utterly certain of his destiny, and there is an aura of far places about him. He enters exactly as* WILLY *speaks.*]

WILLY: I'm getting awfully tired, Ben.

> [BEN's *music is heard.* BEN *looks around at everything.*]

CHARLEY: Good, keep playing; you'll sleep better. Did you call me Ben?

> [BEN *looks at his watch.*]

WILLY: That's funny. For a second there you reminded me of my brother Ben.

BEN: I only have a few minutes. [*He strolls, inspecting the place.* WILLY *and* CHARLEY *continue playing.*]

CHARLEY: You never heard from him again, heh? Since that time?

WILLY: Didn't Linda tell you? Couple of weeks ago we got a letter from his wife in Africa. He died.

CHARLEY: That so.

BEN: [*Chuckling.*] So this is Brooklyn, eh?

CHARLEY: Maybe you're in for some of his money.

WILLY: Naa, he had seven sons. There's just one opportunity I had with that man . . .

BEN: I must make a train, William. There are several properties I'm looking at in Alaska.

WILLY: Sure, sure! If I'd gone with him to Alaska that time, everything would've been totally different.

CHARLEY: Go on, you'da froze to death up there.

WILLY: What're you talking about?

BEN: Opportunity is tremendous in Alaska, William. Surprised you're not up there.

WILLY: Sure, tremendous.

CHARLEY: Heh?

WILLY: There was the only man I ever met who knew the answers.

CHARLEY: Who?

BEN: How are you all?

WILLY: [*Taking a pot, smiling.*] Fine, fine.

CHARLEY: Pretty sharp tonight.

BEN: Is Mother living with you?

WILLY: No, she died a long time ago.

CHARLEY: Who?

BEN: That's too bad. Fine specimen of a lady, Mother.

WILLY: [*To* CHARLEY.] Heh?

BEN: I'd hoped to see the old girl.

CHARLEY: Who died?

BEN: Heard anything from Father, have you?

WILLY: [*Unnerved.*] What do you mean, who died?

CHARLEY: [*Taking a pot.*] What're you talkin' about?

BEN: [*Looking at his watch.*] William, it's half-past eight!

WILLY: [*As though to dispel his confusion he angrily stops* CHARLEY'*s hand.*] That's my build!

CHARLEY: I put the ace—

WILLY: If you don't know how to play the game I'm not gonna throw my money away on you!

CHARLEY: [*Rising.*] It was my ace, for God's sake!

WILLY: I'm through, I'm through!

BEN: When did Mother die?

WILLY: Long ago. Since the beginning you never knew how to play cards.

CHARLEY: [*Picks up the cards and goes to the door.*] All right! Next time I'll bring a deck with five aces.

WILLY: I don't play that kind of game!

CHARLEY: [*Turning to him.*] You ought to be ashamed of yourself!

WILLY: Yeah?

CHARLEY: Yeah! [*He goes out.*]

WILLY: [*Slamming the door after him.*] Ignoramus!

BEN: [As WILLY *comes toward him through the wall-line of the kitchen.*] So you're William.

WILLY: [*Shaking* BEN's *hand.*] Ben! I've been waiting for you so long! What's the answer? How did you do it?

BEN: Oh, there's a story in that.

> [LINDA *enters the forestage, as of old, carrying the wash basket.*]

LINDA: Is this Ben?

BEN: [*Gallantly.*] How do you do, my dear.

LINDA: Where've you been all these years? Willy's always wondered why you—

WILLY: [*Pulling* BEN *away from her impatiently.*] Where is Dad? Didn't you follow him? How did you get started?

BEN: Well, I don't know how much you remember.

WILLY: Well, I was just a baby, of course, only three or four years old—

BEN: Three years and eleven months.

WILLY: What a memory, Ben!

BEN: I have many enterprises, William, and I have never kept books.

WILLY: I remember I was sitting under the wagon in—was it Nebraska?

BEN: It was South Dakota, and I gave you a bunch of wild flowers.

WILLY: I remember you walking away down some open road.

BEN: [*Laughing.*] I was going to find Father in Alaska.

WILLY: Where is he?

BEN: At that age I had a very faulty view of geography, William. I discovered after a few days that I was heading due south, so instead of Alaska, I ended up in Africa.

LINDA: Africa!

WILLY: The Gold Coast!

BEN: Principally diamond mines.

LINDA: Diamond mines!

BEN: Yes, my dear. But I've only a few minutes—

WILLY: No! Boys! Boys! [*Young* BIFF *and* HAPPY *appear.*] Listen to this. This is your Uncle Ben, a great man! Tell my boys, Ben!

BEN: Why, boys, when I was seventeen I walked into the jungle, and when I was twenty-one I walked out. [*He laughs.*] And by God I was rich.

WILLY: [*To the boys.*] You see what I been talking about? The greatest things can happen!

BEN: [*Glancing at his watch.*] I have an appointment in Ketchikan Tuesday week.

WILLY: No, Ben! Please tell about Dad. I want my boys to hear. I want them to know the kind of stock they spring from. All I remember is a man with a big beard, and I was in Mamma's lap, sitting around a fire, and some kind of high music.

BEN: His flute. He played the flute.

WILLY: Sure, the flute, that's right!

> [*New music is heard, a high, rollicking tune.*]

BEN: Father was a very great and a very wild-hearted man. We would start in Boston, and he'd toss the whole family into the wagon, and then he'd drive the team right across the country; through Ohio, and Indiana, Michigan, Illinois, and all the Western states. And we'd stop in the towns and sell the flutes that he'd made on the way. Great inventor, Father. With one gadget he made more in a week than a man like you could make in a lifetime.

WILLY: That's just the way I'm bringing them up, Ben—rugged, well liked, all-around.

BEN: Yeah? [*To* BIFF.] Hit that, boy—hard as you can. [*He pounds his stomach.*]

BIFF: Oh, no, sir!

BEN: [*Taking boxing stance.*] Come on, get to me! [*He laughs.*]

WILLY: Go to it, Biff! Go ahead, show him!

BIFF: Okay! [*He cocks his fist and starts in.*]

LINDA: [*To* WILLY.] Why must he fight, dear?

BEN: [*Sparring with* BIFF.] Good boy! Good boy!

WILLY: How's that, Ben, heh?

HAPPY: Give him the left, Biff!

LINDA: Why are you fighting?

BEN: Good boy! [*Suddenly comes in, trips* BIFF, *and stands over him, the point of his umbrella poised over* BIFF's *eye.*]

LINDA: Look out, Biff!

BIFF: Gee!

BEN: [*Patting* BIFF's *knee.*] Never fight fair with a stranger, boy. You'll never get out of the jungle that way. [*Taking* LINDA's *hand and bowing.*] It was an honor and a pleasure to meet you, Linda.

LINDA: [*Withdrawing her hand coldly, frightened.*] Have a nice—trip.

BEN: [*To* WILLY.] And good luck with your—what do you do?

WILLY: Selling.

BEN: Yes. Well . . . [*He raises his hand in farewell to all.*]

WILLY: No, Ben, I don't want you to think . . . [*He takes* BEN's *arm to show him.*] It's Brooklyn, I know, but we hunt too.

BEN: Really, now.

WILLY: Oh, sure, there's snakes and rabbits and—that's why I moved out here. Why, Biff can fell any one of these trees in no time! Boys! Go right over to where they're building the apartment house and get some sand. We're gonna rebuild the entire front stoop right now! Watch this, Ben!

BIFF: Yes, sir! On the double, Hap!

HAPPY: [*As he and* BIFF *run off.*] I lost weight, Pop, you notice?

[CHARLEY *enters in knickers, even before the boys are gone.*]

CHARLEY: Listen, if they steal any more from that building the watchman'll put the cops on them!

LINDA: [*To* WILLY.] Don't let Biff . . .

[BEN *laughs lustily.*]

WILLY: You shoulda seen the lumber they brought home last week. At least a dozen six-by-tens worth all kinds a money.

CHARLEY: Listen, if that watchman—

WILLY: I gave them hell, understand. But I got a couple of fearless characters there.

CHARLEY: Willy, the jails are full of fearless characters.

BEN: [*Clapping* WILLY *on the back, with a laugh at* CHARLEY.] And the stock exchange, friend!

WILLY: [*Joining in* BEN'*s laughter.*] Where are the rest of your pants?

CHARLEY: My wife bought them.

WILLY: Now all you need is a golf club and you can go upstairs and go to sleep. [*To* BEN.] Great athlete! Between him and his son Bernard they can't hammer a nail!

BERNARD: [*Rushing in.*] The watchman's chasing Biff!

WILLY: [*Angrily.*] Shut up! He's not stealing anything!

LINDA: [*Alarmed, hurrying off left.*] Where is he? Biff, dear! [*She exits.*]

WILLY: [*Moving toward the left, away from* BEN.] There's nothing wrong. What's the matter with you?

BEN: Nervy boy. Good!

WILLY: [*Laughing.*] Oh, nerves of iron, that Biff!

CHARLEY: Don't know what it is. My New England man comes back and he's bleedin', they murdered him up there.

WILLY: It's contacts, Charley, I got important contacts!

CHARLEY: [*Sarcastically.*] Glad to hear it, Willy. Come in later, we'll shoot a little casino. I'll take some of your Portland money. [*He laughs at* WILLY *and exits.*]

WILLY: [*Turning to* BEN.] Business is bad, it's murderous. But not for me, of course.

BEN: I'll stop by on my way back to Africa.

WILLY: [*Longingly.*] Can't you stay a few days? You're just what I need, Ben, because I—I have a fine position here, but I—well, Dad left when I was such a baby and I never had a chance to talk to him and I still feel—kind of temporary about myself.

BEN: I'll be late for my train.

[*They are at opposite ends of the stage.*]

WILLY: Ben, my boys—can't we talk? They'd go into the jaws of hell for me, see, but I—

BEN: William, you're being first-rate with your boys. Outstanding, manly chaps!

WILLY: [*Hanging on to his words.*] Oh, Ben, that's good to hear! Because sometimes I'm afraid that I'm not teaching them the right kind of—Ben, how should I teach them?

BEN: [*Giving great weight to each word, and with a certain vicious audacity.*] William, when I walked into the jungle, I was seventeen. When I walked out I was twenty-one. And, by God, I was rich! [*He goes off into darkness around the right corner of the house.*]

WILLY: . . . was rich! That's just the spirit I want to imbue them with! To walk into a jungle! I was right! I was right! I was right!

[BEN *is gone, but* WILLY *is still speaking to him as* LINDA, *in nightgown and robe, enters the kitchen, glances around for* WILLY, *then goes to the door of the house, looks out and sees him. Comes down to his left. He looks at her.*]

LINDA: Willy, dear? Willy?

WILLY: I was right!

LINDA: Did you have some cheese? [*He can't answer.*] It's very late, darling. Come to bed, heh?

WILLY: [*Looking straight up.*] Gotta break your neck to see a star in this yard.

LINDA: You coming in?

WILLY: Whatever happened to that diamond watch fob? Remember? When Ben came from Africa that time? Didn't he give me a watch fob with a diamond in it?

LINDA: You pawned it, dear. Twelve, thirteen years ago. For Biff's radio correspondence course.

WILLY: Gee, that was a beautiful thing. I'll take a walk.

LINDA: But you're in your slippers.

WILLY: [*Starting to go around the house at the left.*] I was right! I was! [*Half to* LINDA, *as he goes, shaking his head.*] What a man! There was a man worth talking to. I was right!

LINDA: [*Calling after* WILLY.] But in your slippers, Willy!

[WILLY *is almost gone when* BIFF, *in his pajamas, comes down the stairs and enters the kitchen.*]

BIFF: What is he doing out there?

LINDA: Sh!

BIFF: God Almighty, Mom, how long has he been doing this?

LINDA: Don't, he'll hear you.

BIFF: What the hell is the matter with him?

LINDA: It'll pass by morning.

BIFF: Shouldn't we do anything?

LINDA: Oh, my dear, you should do a lot of things, but there's nothing to do, so go to sleep.

[HAPPY *comes down the stairs and sits on the steps.*]

HAPPY: I never heard him so loud, Mom.

LINDA: Well, come around more often; you'll hear him. [*She sits down at the table and mends the lining of* WILLY's *jacket.*]

BIFF: Why didn't you ever write me about this, Mom?

LINDA: How would I write to you? For over three months you had no address.

BIFF: I was on the move. But you know I thought of you all the time. You know that, don't you, pal?

LINDA: I know, dear, I know. But he likes to have a letter. Just to know that there's still a possibility for better things.

BIFF: He's not like this all the time, is he?

LINDA: It's when you come home he's always the worst.

BIFF: When I come home?

LINDA: When you write you're coming, he's all smiles, and talks about the future, and—he's just wonderful. And then the closer you seem to come, the more shaky he gets, and then, by the time you get here, he's arguing, and he seems angry at you. I think it's just that maybe he can't bring himself to—to open up to you. Why are you so hateful to each other? Why is that?

BIFF: [*Evasively.*] I'm not hateful, Mom.

LINDA: But you no sooner come in the door than you're fighting!

BIFF: I don't know why. I mean to change. I'm tryin', Mom, you understand?

LINDA: Are you home to stay now?

BIFF: I don't know. I want to look around, see what's doin'.

LINDA: Biff, you can't look around all your life, can you?

BIFF: I just can't take hold, Mom. I can't take hold of some kind of a life.

LINDA: Biff, a man is not a bird, to come and go with the springtime.

BIFF: Your hair . . . [*He touches her hair.*] Your hair got so gray.

LINDA: Oh, it's been gray since you were in high school. I just stopped dyeing it, that's all.

BIFF: Dye it again, will ya? I don't want my pal looking old. [*He smiles.*]

LINDA: You're such a boy! You think you can go away for a year and . . . You've got to get it into your head now that one day you'll knock on this door and there'll be strange people here—

BIFF: What are you talking about? You're not even sixty, Mom.

LINDA: But what about your father?

BIFF: [*Lamely.*] Well, I meant him too.

HAPPY: He admires Pop.

LINDA: Biff, dear, if you don't have any feeling for him, then you can't have any feeling for me.

BIFF: Sure I can, Mom.

LINDA: No. You can't just come to see me, because I love him. [*With a threat, but only a threat, of tears.*] He's the dearest man in the world to me, and I won't have anyone making him feel unwanted and low and blue. You've got to make up your mind now, darling, there's no leeway any more. Either he's your father and you pay him that respect, or else you're not to come here. I know he's not easy to get along with—nobody knows that better than me— but . . .

WILLY: [*From the left, with a laugh.*] Hey, hey, Biffo!

BIFF: [*Starting to go out after* WILLY.] What the hell is the matter with him? [HAPPY *stops him.*]

LINDA: Don't—don't go near him!

BIFF: Stop making excuses for him! He always, always wiped the floor with you. Never had an ounce of respect for you.

HAPPY: He's always had respect for—

BIFF: What the hell do you know about it?

HAPPY: [*Surlily.*] Just don't call him crazy!

BIFF: He's got no character—Charley wouldn't do this. Not in his own house— spewing out that vomit from his mind.

HAPPY: Charley never had to cope with what he's got to.

BIFF: People are worse off than Willy Loman. Believe me, I've seen them!

LINDA: Then make Charley your father, Biff. You can't do that, can you? I don't say he's a great man. Willy Loman never made a lot of money. His name was never in the paper. He's not the finest character that ever lived. But he's a human being, and a terrible thing is happening to him. So attention must be paid. He's not to be allowed to fall into his grave like an old dog. Attention, attention must be finally paid to such a person. You called him crazy—

BIFF: I didn't mean—

LINDA: No, a lot of people think he's lost his—balance. But you don't have to be very smart to know what his trouble is. The man is exhausted.

HAPPY: Sure!

LINDA: A small man can be just as exhausted as a great man. He works for a company thirty-six years this March, opens up unheard-of territories to their trademark, and now in his old age they take his salary away.

HAPPY: [Indignantly.] I didn't know that, Mom.

LINDA: You never asked, my dear! Now that you get your spending money someplace else you don't trouble your mind with him.

HAPPY: But I gave you money last—

LINDA: Christmas time, fifty dollars! To fix the hot water it cost ninety-seven fifty! For five weeks he's been on straight commission, like a beginner, an unknown!

BIFF: Those ungrateful bastards!

LINDA: Are they any worse than his sons? When he brought them business, when he was young, they were glad to see him. But now his old friends, the old buyers that loved him so and always found some order to hand him in a pinch—they're all dead, retired. He used to be able to make six, seven calls a day in Boston. Now he takes his valises out of the car and puts them back and takes them out again and he's exhausted. Instead of walking he talks now. He drives seven hundred miles, and when he gets there no one knows him any more, no one welcomes him. And what goes through a man's mind, driving seven hundred miles home without having earned a cent? Why shouldn't he talk to himself? Why? When he has to go to Charley and borrow fifty dollars a week and pretend to me that it's his pay? How long can that go on? How long? You see what I'm sitting here and waiting for? And you tell me he has no character? The man who never worked a day but for your benefit? When does he get the medal for that? Is this his reward—to turn around at the age of sixty-three and find his sons, who he loved better than his life, one a philandering bum—

HAPPY: Mom!

LINDA: That's all you are, my baby! [To BIFF.] And you! What happened to the love you had for him? You were such pals! How you used to talk to him on the phone every night! How lonely he was till he could come home to you!

BIFF: All right, Mom. I'll live here in my room, and I'll get a job. I'll keep away from him, that's all.

LINDA: No, Biff. You can't stay here and fight all the time.

BIFF: He threw me out of this house, remember that.

LINDA: Why did he do that? I never knew why.

BIFF: Because I know he's a fake and he doesn't like anybody around who knows!

LINDA: Why a fake? In what way? What do you mean?

BIFF: Just don't lay it all at my feet. It's between me and him—that's all I have to say. I'll chip in from now on. He'll settle for half my pay check. He'll be all right. I'm going to bed. [*He starts for the stairs.*]

LINDA: He won't be all right.

BIFF: [*Turning on the stairs, furiously.*] I hate this city and I'll stay here. Now what do you want?

LINDA: He's dying, Biff.

[HAPPY *turns quickly to her, shocked.*]

BIFF: [*After a pause.*] Why is he dying?

LINDA: He's been trying to kill himself.

BIFF: [*With great horror.*] How?

LINDA: I live from day to day.

BIFF: What're you talking about?

LINDA: Remember I wrote you that he smashed up the car again? In February?

BIFF: Well?

LINDA: The insurance inspector came. He said that they have evidence. That all these accidents in the last year—weren't—weren't—accidents.

HAPPY: How can they tell that? That's a lie.

LINDA: It seems there's a woman . . . [*She takes a breath as. . . .*]

⎰ BIFF: [*Sharply but contained.*] What woman?
⎱ LINDA: [*Simultaneously.*] . . . and this woman . . .

LINDA: What?

BIFF: Nothing. Go ahead.

LINDA: What did you say?

BIFF: Nothing. I just said what woman?

HAPPY: What about her?

LINDA: Well, it seems she was walking down the road and saw his car. She says that he wasn't driving fast at all, and that he didn't skid. She says he came to that little bridge, and then deliberately smashed into the railing, and it was only the shallowness of the water that saved him.

BIFF: Oh, no, he probably just fell asleep again.

LINDA: I don't think he fell asleep.

BIFF: Why not?

LINDA: Last month . . . [*With great difficulty.*] Oh, boys, it's so hard to say a thing like this! He's just a big stupid man to you, but I tell you there's more good in him than in many other people. [*She chokes, wipes her eyes.*] I was looking for a fuse. The lights blew out, and I went down the cellar. And behind the fuse box—it happened to fall out—was a length of rubber pipe—just short.

HAPPY: No kidding?

LINDA: There's a little attachment on the end of it. I knew right away. And sure enough, on the bottom of the water heater there's a new little nipple on the gas pipe.

HAPPY: [*Angrily.*] That—jerk.

BIFF: Did you have it taken off?

LINDA: I'm—I'm ashamed to. How can I mention it to him? Every day I go down and take away that little rubber pipe. But, when he comes home, I put it back where it was. How can I insult him that way? I don't know what to do. I live from day to day, boys. I tell you, I know every thought in his mind. It sounds so old-fashioned and silly, but I tell you he put his whole life into you and you've turned your backs on him. [*She is bent over in the chair, weeping, her face in her hands.*] Biff, I swear to God! Biff, his life is in your hands!

HAPPY: [*To* BIFF.] How do you like that damned fool!

BIFF: [*Kissing her.*] All right, pal, all right. It's all settled now. I've been remiss. I know that, Mom. But now I'll stay, and I swear to you, I'll apply myself. [*Kneeling in front of her, in a fever of self-reproach.*] It's just—you see, Mom, I don't fit in business. Not that I won't try. I'll try, and I'll make good.

HAPPY: Sure you will. The trouble with you in business was you never tried to please people.

BIFF: I know, I—

HAPPY: Like when you worked for Harrison's. Bob Harrison said you were tops, and then you go and do some damn fool thing like whistling whole songs in the elevator like a comedian.

BIFF: [*Against* HAPPY.] So what? I like to whistle sometimes.

HAPPY: You don't raise a guy to a responsible job who whistles in the elevator!

LINDA: Well, don't argue about it now.

HAPPY: Like when you'd go off and swim in the middle of the day instead of taking the line around.

BIFF: [*His resentment rising.*] Well, don't you run off? You take off sometimes, don't you? On a nice summer day?

HAPPY: Yeah, but I cover myself!

LINDA: Boys!

HAPPY: If I'm going to take a fade the boss can call any number where I'm supposed to be and they'll swear to him that I just left. I'll tell you something that I hate to say, Biff, but in the business world some of them think you're crazy.

BIFF: [*Angered.*] Screw the business world!

HAPPY: All right, screw it! Great, but cover yourself!

LINDA: Hap, Hap!

BIFF: I don't care what they think! They've laughed at Dad for years, and you know why? Because we don't belong in this nuthouse of a city! We should be mixing cement on some open plain, or—or carpenters. A carpenter is allowed to whistle!

[WILLY *walks in from the entrance of the house, at left.*]

WILLY: Even your grandfather was better than a carpenter. [*Pause. They watch him.*] You never grew up. Bernard does not whistle in the elevator, I assure you.

BIFF: [*As though to laugh* WILLY *out of it.*] Yeah, but you do, Pop.

WILLY: I never in my life whistled in an elevator! And who in the business world thinks I'm crazy?

BIFF: I didn't mean it like that, Pop. Now don't make a whole thing out of it, will ya?

WILLY: Go back to the West! Be a carpenter, a cowboy, enjoy yourself!

LINDA: Willy, he was just saying—

WILLY: I heard what he said!

HAPPY: [*Trying to quiet* WILLY.] Hey, Pop, come on now . . .

WILLY: [*Continuing over* HAPPY's *line*.] They laugh at me, heh? Go to Filene's, go to the Hub, go to Slattery's Boston. Call out the name Willy Loman and see what happens! Big shot!

BIFF: All right, Pop.

WILLY: Big!

BIFF: All right!

WILLY: Why do you always insult me?

BIFF: I didn't say a word. [*To* LINDA.] Did I say a word?

LINDA: He didn't say anything, Willy.

WILLY: [*Going to the doorway of the living-room*.] All right, good night, good night.

LINDA: Willy, dear, he just decided . . .

WILLY: [*To* BIFF.] If you get tired hanging around tomorrow, paint the ceiling I put up in the living-room.

BIFF: I'm leaving early tomorrow.

HAPPY: He's going to see Bill Oliver, Pop.

WILLY: [*Interestedly*.] Oliver? For what?

BIFF: [*With reserve, but trying, trying*.] He always said he'd stake me. I'd like to go into business, so maybe I can take him up on it.

LINDA: Isn't that wonderful?

WILLY: Don't interrupt. What's wonderful about it? There's fifty men in the City of New York who'd stake him. [*To* BIFF.] Sporting goods?

BIFF: I guess so. I know something about it and—

WILLY: He knows something about it! You know sporting goods better than Spalding, for God's sake! How much is he giving you?

BIFF: I don't know, I didn't even see him yet, but—

WILLY: Then what're you talkin' about?

BIFF: [*Getting angry*.] Well, all I said was I'm gonna see him, that's all!

WILLY: [*Turning away*.] Ah, you're counting your chickens again.

BIFF: [*Starting left for the stairs*.] Oh, Jesus, I'm going to sleep!

WILLY: [*Calling after him*.] Don't curse in this house!

BIFF: [*Turning*.] Since when did you get so clean?

HAPPY: [*Trying to stop them*.] Wait a . . .

WILLY: Don't use that language to me! I won't have it!

HAPPY: [*Grabbing* BIFF, *shouts*.] Wait a minute! I got an idea. I got a feasible idea. Come here, Biff, let's talk this over now, let's talk some sense here. When I was down in Florida last time, I thought of a great idea to sell sporting goods. It just came back to me. You and I, Biff—we have a line, the Loman Line. We train a couple of weeks, and put on a couple of exhibitions, see?

WILLY: That's an idea!

HAPPY: Wait! We form two basketball teams, see? Two water-polo teams. We play each other. It's a million dollars' worth of publicity. Two brothers, see? The

Loman Brothers. Displays in the Royal Palms—all the hotels. And banners over the ring and the basketball court: "Loman Brothers." Baby, we could sell sporting goods!

WILLY: That is a one-million-dollar idea!

LINDA: Marvelous!

BIFF: I'm in great shape as far as that's concerned.

HAPPY: And the beauty of it is, Biff, it wouldn't be like a business. We'd be out playin' ball again . . .

BIFF: [*Enthused.*] Yeah, that's . . .

WILLY: Million-dollar . . .

HAPPY: And you wouldn't get fed up with it, Biff. It'd be the family again. There'd be the old honor, and comradeship, and if you wanted to go off for a swim or somethin'—well, you'd do it! Without some smart cooky gettin' up ahead of you!

WILLY: Lick the world! You guys together could absolutely lick the civilized world.

BIFF: I'll see Oliver tomorrow. Hap, if we could work that out . . .

LINDA: Maybe things are beginning to—

WILLY: [*Wildly enthused, to* LINDA.] Stop interrupting! [*To* BIFF.] But don't wear sport jacket and slacks when you see Oliver.

BIFF: No, I'll—

WILLY: A business suit, and talk as little as possible, and don't crack any jokes.

BIFF: He did like me. Always liked me.

LINDA: He loved you!

WILLY: [*To* LINDA.] Will you stop! [*To* BIFF.] Walk in very serious. You are not applying for a boy's job. Money is to pass. Be quiet, fine, and serious. Everybody likes a kidder, but nobody lends him money.

HAPPY: I'll try to get some myself, Biff. I'm sure I can.

WILLY: I see great things for you kids, I think your troubles are over. But remember, start big and you'll end big. Ask for fifteen. How much you gonna ask for?

BIFF: Gee, I don't know—

WILLY: And don't say "Gee." "Gee" is a boy's word. A man walking in for fifteen thousand dollars does not say "Gee!"

BIFF: Ten, I think, would be top though.

WILLY: Don't be so modest. You always started too low. Walk in with a big laugh. Don't look worried. Start off with a couple of your good stories to lighten things up. It's not what you say, it's how you say it—because personality always wins the day.

LINDA: Oliver always thought the highest of him—

WILLY: Will you let me talk?

BIFF: Don't yell at her, Pop, will ya?

WILLY: [*Angrily.*] I was talking, wasn't I?

BIFF: I don't like you yelling at her all the time, and I'm tellin' you, that's all.

WILLY: What're you, takin' over this house?

LINDA: Willy—

WILLY: [*Turning on her.*] Don't take his side all the time, goddammit!

BIFF: [*Furiously.*] Stop yelling at her!

WILLY: [*Suddenly pulling on his cheek, beaten down, guilt ridden.*] Give my best to Bill Oliver—he may remember me. [*He exits through the living-room doorway.*]

LINDA: [*Her voice subdued.*] What'd you have to start that for? [BIFF *turns away.*] You see how sweet he was as soon as you talked hopefully? [*She goes over to* BIFF.] Come up and say good night to him. Don't let him go to bed that way.

HAPPY: Come on, Biff, let's buck him up.

LINDA: Please, dear. Just say good night. It takes so little to make him happy. Come. [*She goes through the living-room doorway, calling upstairs from within the living-room.*] Your pajamas are hanging in the bathroom, Willy!

HAPPY: [*Looking toward where* LINDA *went out.*] What a woman! They broke the mold when they made her. You know that, Biff?

BIFF: He's off salary. My God, working on commission!

HAPPY: Well, let's face it: he's no hot-shot selling man. Except that sometimes, you have to admit, he's a sweet personality.

BIFF: [*Deciding.*] Lend me ten bucks, will ya? I want to buy some new ties.

HAPPY: I'll take you to a place I know. Beautiful stuff. Wear one of my striped shirts tomorrow.

BIFF: She got gray. Mom got awful old. Gee, I'm gonna go in to Oliver tomorrow and knock him for a—

HAPPY: Come on up. Tell that to Dad. Let's give him a whirl. Come on.

BIFF: [*Steamed up.*] You know, with ten thousand bucks, boy!

HAPPY: [*As they go into the living-room.*] That's the talk, Biff, that's the first time I've heard the old confidence out of you! [*From within the living-room, fading off.*] You're gonna live with me, kid, and any babe you want just say the word . . .

[*The last lines are hardly heard. They are mounting the stairs to their parents' bedroom.*]

LINDA: [*Entering her bedroom and addressing* WILLY, *who is in the bathroom. She is straightening the bed for him.*] Can you do anything about the shower? It drips.

WILLY: [*From the bathroom.*] All of a sudden everything falls to pieces! Goddam plumbing, oughta be sued, those people. I hardly finished putting it in and the thing . . . [*His words rumble off.*]

LINDA: I'm just wondering if Oliver will remember him. You think he might?

WILLY: [*Coming out of the bathroom in his pajamas.*] Remember him? What's the matter with you, you crazy? If he'd've stayed with Oliver he'd be on top by now! Wait'll Oliver gets a look at him. You don't know the average caliber any more. The average young man today— [*He is getting into bed.*] —is got a caliber of zero. Greatest thing in the world for him was to bum around. [BIFF *and* HAPPY *enter the bedroom. Slight pause.* WILLY *stops short, looking at* BIFF.] Glad to hear it, boy.

HAPPY: He wanted to say good night to you, sport.

WILLY: [*To* BIFF.] Yeah. Knock him dead, boy. What'd you want to tell me?

BIFF: Just take it easy, Pop. Good night. [*He turns to go.*]

WILLY: [*Unable to resist.*] And if anything falls off the desk while you're talking to him—like a package or something—don't you pick it up. They have office boys for that.

LINDA: I'll make a big breakfast—

WILLY: Will you let me finish? [*To* BIFF.] Tell him you were in the business in the West. Not farm work.

BIFF: All right, Dad.

LINDA: I think everything—

WILLY: [*Going right through her speech.*] And don't undersell yourself. No less than fifteen thousand dollars.

BIFF: [*Unable to bear him.*] Okay. Good night, Mom. [*He starts moving.*]

WILLY: Because you got a greatness in you, Biff, remember that. You got all kinds of greatness . . . [*He lies back, exhausted.* BIFF *walks out.*]

LINDA: [*Calling after* BIFF.] Sleep well, darling!

HAPPY: I'm gonna get married, Mom. I wanted to tell you.

LINDA: Go to sleep, dear.

HAPPY: [*Going.*] I just wanted to tell you.

WILLY: Keep up the good work. [HAPPY *exits.*] God . . . remember that Ebbets Field[3] game? The championship of the city?

LINDA: Just rest. Should I sing to you?

WILLY: Yeah. Sing to me. [LINDA *hums a soft lullaby.*] When that team came out— he was the tallest, remember?

LINDA: Oh, yes. And in gold.

[BIFF *enters the darkened kitchen, takes a cigarette, and leaves the house. He comes downstage into a golden pool of light. He smokes, staring at the night.*]

WILLY: Like a young god. Hercules—something like that. And the sun, the sun all around him. Remember how he waved to me? Right up from the field, with the representatives of three colleges standing by? And the buyers I brought, and the cheers when he came out—Loman, Loman, Loman! God Almighty, he'll be great yet. A star like that, magnificent, can never really fade away!

[*The light on* WILLY *is fading. The gas heater begins to glow through the kitchen wall, near the stairs, a blue flame beneath red coils.*]

LINDA: [*Timidly.*] Willy dear, what has he got against you?

WILLY: I'm so tired. Don't talk any more.

[BIFF *slowly returns to the kitchen. He stops, stares toward the heater.*]

LINDA: Will you ask Howard to let you work in New York?

WILLY: First thing in the morning. Everything'll be all right.

[BIFF *reaches behind the heater and draws out a length of rubber tubing. He is horrified and turns his head toward* WILLY's *room, still dimly lit, from which the strains of* LINDA's *desperate but monotonous humming rise.*]

---

3. Stadium where the Dodgers, Brooklyn's major-league baseball team, played from 1913 to 1957.

WILLY: [*Staring through the window into the moonlight.*] Gee, look at the moon moving between the buildings!

[BIFF *wraps the tubing around his hand and quickly goes up the stairs.*]

CURTAIN

ACT II

Music is heard, gay and bright. The curtain rises as the music fades away. WILLY, *in shirt sleeves, is sitting at the kitchen table, sipping coffee, his hat in his lap.* LINDA *is filling his cup when she can.*

WILLY: Wonderful coffee. Meal in itself.

LINDA: Can I make you some eggs?

WILLY: No. Take a breath.

LINDA: You look so rested, dear.

WILLY: I slept like a dead one. First time in months. Imagine, sleeping till ten on a Tuesday morning. Boys left nice and early, heh?

LINDA: They were out of here by eight o'clock.

WILLY: Good work!

LINDA: It was so thrilling to see them leaving together. I can't get over the shaving lotion in this house!

WILLY: [*Smiling.*] Mmm—

LINDA: Biff was very changed this morning. His whole attitude seemed to be hopeful. He couldn't wait to get downtown to see Oliver.

WILLY: He's heading for a change. There's no question, there simply are certain men that take longer to get—solidified. How did he dress?

LINDA: His blue suit. He's so handsome in that suit. He could be a—anything in that suit!

[WILLY *gets up from the table.* LINDA *holds his jacket for him.*]

WILLY: There's no question, no question at all. Gee, on the way home tonight I'd like to buy some seeds.

LINDA: [*Laughing.*] That'd be wonderful. But not enough sun gets back there. Nothing'll grow any more.

WILLY: You wait, kid, before it's all over we're gonna get a little place out in the country, and I'll raise some vegetables, a couple of chickens . . .

LINDA: You'll do it yet, dear.

[WILLY *walks out of his jacket.* LINDA *follows him.*]

WILLY: And they'll get married, and come for a weekend. I'd build a little guest house. 'Cause I got so many fine tools, all I'd need would be a little lumber and some peace of mind.

LINDA: [*Joyfully.*] I sewed the lining . . .

WILLY: I could build two guest houses, so they'd both come. Did he decide how much he's going to ask Oliver for?

LINDA: [*Getting him into the jacket.*] He didn't mention it, but I imagine ten or fifteen thousand. You going to talk to Howard today?

WILLY: Yeah. I'll put it to him straight and simple. He'll just have to take me off the road.

LINDA: And Willy, don't forget to ask for a little advance, because we've got the insurance premium. It's the grace period now.

WILLY: That's a hundred . . . ?

LINDA: A hundred and eight, sixty-eight. Because we're a little short again.

WILLY: Why are we short?

LINDA: Well, you had the motor job on the car . . .

WILLY: That goddam Studebaker!

LINDA: And you got one more payment on the refrigerator . . .

WILLY: But it just broke again!

LINDA: Well, it's old, dear.

WILLY: I told you we should've bought a well-advertised machine. Charley bought a General Electric and it's twenty years old and it's still good, that son-of-a-bitch.

LINDA: But, Willy—

WILLY: Whoever heard of a Hastings refrigerator? Once in my life I would like to own something outright before it's broken! I'm always in a race with the junkyard! I just finished paying for the car and it's on its last legs. The refrigerator consumes belts like a goddam maniac. They time those things. They time them so when you finally paid for them, they're used up.

LINDA: [*Buttoning up his jacket as he unbuttons it.*] All told, about two hundred dollars would carry us, dear. But that includes the last payment on the mortgage. After this payment, Willy, the house belongs to us.

WILLY: It's twenty-five years!

LINDA: Biff was nine years old when we bought it.

WILLY: Well, that's a great thing. To weather a twenty-five year mortgage is—

LINDA: It's an accomplishment.

WILLY: All the cement, the lumber, the reconstruction I put in this house! There ain't a crack to be found in it any more.

LINDA: Well, it served its purpose.

WILLY: What purpose? Some stranger'll come along, move in, and that's that. If only Biff would take this house, and raise a family . . . [*He starts to go.*] Goodby, I'm late.

LINDA: [*Suddenly remembering.*] Oh, I forgot! You're supposed to meet them for dinner.

WILLY: Me?

LINDA: At Frank's Chop House on Forty-eighth near Sixth Avenue.

WILLY: Is that so! How about you?

LINDA: No, just the three of you. They're gonna blow you to a big meal!

WILLY: Don't say! Who thought of that?

LINDA: Biff came to me this morning, Willy, and he said, "Tell Dad, we want to blow him to a big meal." Be there six o'clock. You and your two boys are going to have dinner.

WILLY: Gee whiz! That's really somethin'. I'm gonna knock Howard for a loop, kid. I'll get an advance, and I'll come home with a New York job. Goddammit, now I'm gonna do it!

LINDA: Oh, that's the spirit, Willy!

WILLY: I will never get behind a wheel the rest of my life!

LINDA: It's changing, Willy, I can feel it changing!

WILLY: Beyond a question. G'by, I'm late. [*He starts to go again.*]

LINDA: [*Calling after him as she runs to the kitchen table for a handkerchief.*] You got your glasses?

WILLY: [*Feels for them, then comes back in.*] Yeah, yeah, got my glasses.

LINDA: [*Giving him the handkerchief.*] And a handkerchief.

WILLY: Yeah, handkerchief.

LINDA: And your saccharine?

WILLY: Yeah, my saccharine.

LINDA: Be careful on the subway stairs.

> [*She kisses him, and a silk stocking is seen hanging from her hand.* WILLY *notices it.*]

WILLY: Will you stop mending stockings? At least while I'm in the house. It gets me nervous. I can't tell you. Please.

> [LINDA *hides the stocking in her hand as she follows* WILLY *across the forestage in front of the house.*]

LINDA: Remember, Frank's Chop House.

WILLY: [*Passing the apron.*] Maybe beets would grow out there.

LINDA: [*Laughing.*] But you tried so many times.

WILLY: Yeah. Well, don't work hard today. [*He disappears around the right corner of the house.*]

LINDA: Be careful! [*As* WILLY *vanishes,* LINDA *waves to him. Suddenly the phone rings. She runs across the stage and into the kitchen and lifts it.*] Hello? Oh, Biff! I'm so glad you called, I just . . . Yes, sure, I just told him. Yes, he'll be there for dinner at six o'clock, I didn't forget. Listen, I was just dying to tell you. You know that little rubber pipe I told you about? That he connected to the gas heater? I finally decided to go down the cellar this morning and take it away and destroy it. But it's gone! Imagine? He took it away himself, it isn't there! [*She listens.*] When? Oh, then you took it. Oh—nothing, it's just that I'd hoped he'd taken it away himself. Oh, I'm not worried, darling, because this morning he left in such high spirits, it was like the old days! I'm not afraid any more. Did Mr. Oliver see you? . . . Well, you wait there then. And make a nice impression on him, darling. Just don't perspire too much before you see him. And have a nice time with Dad. He may have big news too! . . . That's right, a New York job. And be sweet to him tonight, dear. Be loving to him. Because he's only a little boat looking for a harbor. [*She is trembling with sorrow and joy.*] Oh, that's wonderful, Biff, you'll save his life. Thanks, darling.

Just put your arm around him when he comes into the restaurant. Give him a smile. That's the boy . . . Good-by, dear . . . You got your comb? . . . That's fine. Good-by, Biff dear.

[*In the middle of her speech,* HOWARD WAGNER, *thirty-six, wheels on a small typewriter table on which is a wire-recording machine and proceeds to plug it in. This is on the left forestage. Light slowly fades on* LINDA *as it rises on* HOWARD. HOWARD *is intent on threading the machine and only glances over his shoulder as* WILLY *appears.*]

WILLY: Pst! Pst!

HOWARD: Hello, Willy, come in.

WILLY: Like to have a little talk with you, Howard.

HOWARD: Sorry to keep you waiting. I'll be with you in a minute.

WILLY: What's that, Howard?

HOWARD: Didn't you ever see one of these? Wire recorder.

WILLY: Oh. Can we talk a minute?

HOWARD: Records things. Just got delivery yesterday. Been driving me crazy, the most terrific machine I ever saw in my life. I was up all night with it.

WILLY: What do you do with it?

HOWARD: I bought it for dictation, but you can do anything with it. Listen to this. I had it home last night. Listen to what I picked up. The first one is my daughter. Get this. [*He flicks the switch and "Roll out the Barrel" is heard being whistled.*] Listen to that kid whistle.

WILLY: That is lifelike, isn't it?

HOWARD: Seven years old. Get that tone.

WILLY: Ts, ts. Like to ask a little favor if you . . .

[*The whistling breaks off, and the voice of* HOWARD's *daughter is heard.*]

HIS DAUGHTER: "Now you, Daddy."

HOWARD: She's crazy for me! [*Again the same song is whistled.*] That's me! Ha! [*He winks.*]

WILLY: You're very good!

[*The whistling breaks off again. The machine runs silent for a moment.*]

HOWARD: Sh! Get this now, this is my son.

HIS SON: "The capital of Alabama is Montgomery; the capital of Arizona is Phoenix; the capital of Arkansas is Little Rock; the capital of California is Sacramento . . ." [*And on, and on.*]

HOWARD: [*Holding up five fingers.*] Five years old, Willy!

WILLY: He'll make an announcer some day!

HIS SON: [*Continuing.*] "The capital . . ."

HOWARD: Get that—alphabetical order! [*The machine breaks off suddenly.*] Wait a minute. The maid kicked the plug out.

WILLY: It certainly is a—

HOWARD: Sh, for God's sake!

HIS SON: "It's nine o'clock, Bulova watch time. So I have to go to sleep."

WILLY: That really is—

HOWARD: Wait a minute! The next is my wife.

[*They wait.*]

HOWARD'S VOICE: "Go on, say something." [*Pause.*] "Well, you gonna talk?"

HIS WIFE: "I can't think of anything."

HOWARD'S VOICE: "Well, talk—it's turning."

HIS WIFE: [*Shyly, beaten.*] "Hello." [*Silence.*] "Oh, Howard, I can't talk into this . . ."

HOWARD: [*Snapping the machine off.*] That was my wife.

WILLY: That is a wonderful machine. Can we—

HOWARD: I tell you, Willy, I'm gonna take my camera, and my bandsaw, and all my hobbies, and out they go. This is the most fascinating relaxation I ever found.

WILLY: I think I'll get one myself.

HOWARD: Sure, they're only a hundred and a half. You can't do without it. Supposing you wanna hear Jack Benny,[4] see? But you can't be at home at that hour. So you tell the maid to turn the radio on when Jack Benny comes on, and this automatically goes on with the radio . . .

WILLY: And when you come home you . . .

HOWARD: You can come home twelve o'clock, one o'clock, any time you like, and you get yourself a Coke and sit yourself down, throw the switch, and there's Jack Benny's program in the middle of the night!

WILLY: I'm definitely going to get one. Because lots of time I'm on the road, and I think to myself, what I must be missing on the radio!

HOWARD: Don't you have a radio in the car?

WILLY: Well, yeah, but who ever thinks of turning it on?

HOWARD: Say, aren't you supposed to be in Boston?

WILLY: That's what I want to talk to you about, Howard. You got a minute? [*He draws a chair in from the wing.*]

HOWARD: What happened? What're you doing here?

WILLY: Well . . .

HOWARD: You didn't crack up again, did you?

WILLY: Oh, no. No . . .

HOWARD: Geez, you had me worried there for a minute. What's the trouble?

WILLY: Well, tell you the truth, Howard. I've come to the decision that I'd rather not travel any more.

HOWARD: Not travel! Well, what'll you do?

WILLY: Remember, Christmas time, when you had the party here? You said you'd try to think of some spot for me here in town.

HOWARD: With us?

WILLY: Well, sure.

HOWARD: Oh, yeah, yeah. I remember. Well, I couldn't think of anything for you, Willy.

---

4. A vaudeville, radio, television, and motion picture star (1894–1974), who hosted America's most popular radio show from 1932 to 1955.

WILLY: I tell ya, Howard. The kids are all grown up, y'know. I don't need much any more. If I could take home—well, sixty-five dollars a week, I could swing it.

HOWARD: Yeah, but Willy, see I—

WILLY: I tell ya why, Howard. Speaking frankly and between the two of us, y'know—I'm just a little tired.

HOWARD: Oh, I could understand that, Willy. But you're a road man, Willy, and we do a road business. We've only got a half-dozen salesmen on the floor here.

WILLY: God knows, Howard, I never asked a favor of any man. But I was with the firm when your father used to carry you in here in his arms.

HOWARD: I know that, Willy, but—

WILLY: Your father came to me the day you were born and asked me what I thought of the name of Howard, may he rest in peace.

HOWARD: I appreciate that, Willy, but there just is no spot here for you. If I had a spot I'd slam you right in, but I just don't have a single solitary spot.

[*He looks for his lighter.* WILLY *has picked it up and gives it to him. Pause.*]

WILLY: [*With increasing anger.*] Howard, all I need to set my table is fifty dollars a week.

HOWARD: But where am I going to put you, kid?

WILLY: Look, it isn't a question of whether I can sell merchandise, is it?

HOWARD: No, but it's a business, kid, and everybody's gotta pull his own weight.

WILLY: [*Desperately.*] Just let me tell you a story, Howard—

HOWARD: 'Cause you gotta admit, business is business.

WILLY: [*Angrily.*] Business is definitely business, but just listen for a minute. You don't understand this. When I was a boy—eighteen, nineteen—I was already on the road. And there was a question in my mind as to whether selling had a future for me. Because in those days I had a yearning to go to Alaska. See, there were three gold strikes in one month in Alaska, and I felt like going out. Just for the ride, you might say.

HOWARD: [*Barely interested.*] Don't say.

WILLY: Oh, yeah, my father lived many years in Alaska. He was an adventurous man. We've got quite a little streak of self-reliance in our family. I thought I'd go out with my older brother and try to locate him, and maybe settle in the North with the old man. And I was almost decided to go, when I met a salesman in the Parker House. His name was Dave Singleman. And he was eighty-four years old, and he'd drummed merchandise in thirty-one states. And old Dave, he'd go up to his room, y'understand, put on his green velvet slippers—I'll never forget—and pick up his phone and call the buyers, and without ever leaving his room, at the age of eighty-four, he made a living. And when I saw that, I realized that selling was the greatest career a man could want. 'Cause what could be more satisfying than to be able to go, at the age of eighty-four, into twenty or thirty different cities, and pick up his phone and be remembered and loved and helped by so many different people? Do you know? when he died—and by the way he died the death of a salesman, in his green velvet slippers in the smoker of the New York, New Haven and Hartford, going into Boston—when he died, hundreds of salesmen and buyers were at his funeral. Things were sad on a lotta trains for months after that. [*He stands up.* HOWARD *has not looked at him.*] In those days there was personality in it, Howard. There was respect, and comradeship, and gratitude in it. Today, it's all cut and dried, and there's no chance for bringing friendship to bear—or personality. You see what I mean? They don't know me any more.

HOWARD: [*Moving away, toward the right.*] That's just the thing, Willy.

WILLY: If I had forty dollars a week—that's all I'd need. Forty dollars, Howard.

HOWARD: Kid, I can't take blood from a stone, I—

WILLY: [*Desperation is on him now.*] Howard, the year Al Smith[5] was nominated, your father came to me and—

HOWARD: [*Starting to go off.*] I've got to see some people, kid.

WILLY: [*Stopping him.*] I'm talking about your father! There were promises made across this desk! You mustn't tell me you've got people to see—I put thirty-four years into this firm, Howard, and now I can't pay my insurance! You can't eat the orange and throw the peel away—a man is not a piece of fruit! [*After a pause.*] Now pay attention. Your father—in 1928 I had a big year. I averaged a hundred and seventy dollars a week in commissions.

HOWARD: [*Impatiently.*] Now, Willy, you never averaged—

WILLY: [*Banging his hand on the desk.*] I averaged a hundred and seventy dollars a week in the year of 1928! And your father came to me—or rather, I was in the office here—it was right over this desk—and he put his hand on my shoulder—

HOWARD: [*Getting up.*] You'll have to excuse me, Willy, I gotta see some people. Pull yourself together. [*Going out.*] I'll be back in a little while.

[*On* HOWARD'*s exit, the light on his chair grows very bright and strange.*]

WILLY: Pull myself together! What the hell did I say to him? My God, I was yelling at him! How could I! [WILLY *breaks off, staring at the light, which occupies the chair, animating it. He approaches this chair, standing across the desk from it.*] Frank, Frank, don't you remember what you told me that time? How you put your hand on my shoulder, and Frank . . . [*He leans on the desk and as he speaks the dead man's name he accidentally switches on the recorder, and instantly.*]

HOWARD'S SON: ". . . of New York is Albany. The capital of Ohio is Cincinnati, the capital of Rhode Island is . . ." [*The recitation continues.*]

WILLY: [*Leaping away with fright, shouting.*] Ha! Howard! Howard! Howard!

HOWARD: [*Rushing in.*] What happened?

WILLY: [*Pointing at the machine, which continues nasally, childishly, with the capital cities.*] Shut it off! Shut it off!

HOWARD: [*Pulling the plug out.*] Look, Willy . . .

WILLY: [*Pressing his hands to his eyes.*] I gotta get myself some coffee. I'll get some coffee . . .

---

5. Alfred E. Smith (1873–1944), Democratic presidential nominee who lost to Herbert Hoover in 1928.

[WILLY *starts to walk out.* HOWARD *stops him.*]

HOWARD: [*Rolling up the cord.*] Willy, look . . .

WILLY: I'll go to Boston.

HOWARD: Willy, you can't go to Boston for us.

WILLY: Why can't I go?

HOWARD: I don't want you to represent us. I've been meaning to tell you for a long
    time now.

WILLY: Howard, are you firing me?

HOWARD: I think you need a good long rest, Willy.

WILLY: Howard—

HOWARD: And when you feel better, come back, and we'll see if we can work
    something out.

WILLY: But I gotta earn money, Howard. I'm in no position to—

HOWARD: Where are your sons? Why don't your sons give you a hand?

WILLY: They're working on a very big deal.

HOWARD: This is no time for false pride, Willy. You go to your sons and you tell
    them that you're tired. You've got two great boys, haven't you?

WILLY: Oh, no question, no question, but in the meantime . . .

HOWARD: Then that's that, heh?

WILLY: All right, I'll go to Boston tomorrow.

HOWARD: No, no.

WILLY: I can't throw myself on my sons. I'm not a cripple!

HOWARD: Look, kid, I'm busy, I'm busy this morning.

WILLY: [*Grasping* HOWARD's *arm.*] Howard, you've got to let me go to Boston!

HOWARD: [*Hard, keeping himself under control.*] I've got a line of people to see this
    morning. Sit down, take five minutes, and pull yourself together, and then
    go home, will ya? I need the office, Willy. [*He starts to go, turns, remembering
    the recorder, starts to push off the table holding the recorder.*] Oh, yeah. Whenever
    you can this week, stop by and drop off the samples. You'll feel better, Willy,
    and then come back and we'll talk. Pull yourself together, kid, there's people
    outside.

    [HOWARD *exits, pushing the table off left.* WILLY *stares into space, exhausted.
    Now the music is heard—*BEN's *music—first distantly, then closer, closer. As*
    WILLY *speaks,* BEN *enters from the right. He carries valise and umbrella.*]

WILLY: Oh, Ben, how did you do it? What is the answer? Did you wind up the
    Alaska deal already?

BEN: Doesn't take much time if you know what you're doing. Just a short business
    trip. Boarding ship in an hour. Wanted to say good-by.

WILLY: Ben, I've got to talk to you.

BEN: [*Glancing at his watch.*] Haven't the time, William.

WILLY: [*Crossing the apron to* BEN.] Ben, nothing's working out. I don't know what
    to do.

BEN: Now, look here, William. I've bought timberland in Alaska and I need a man
    to look after things for me.

WILLY: God, timberland! Me and my boys in those grand outdoors!

BEN: You've a new continent at your doorstep, William. Get out of these cities, they're full of talk and time payments and courts of law. Screw on your fists and you can fight for a fortune up there.

WILLY: Yes, yes! Linda, Linda!

[LINDA *enters as of old, with the wash.*]

LINDA: Oh, you're back?

BEN: I haven't much time.

WILLY: No, wait! Linda, he's got a proposition for me in Alaska.

LINDA: But you've got— [*To* BEN.] He's got a beautiful job here.

WILLY: But in Alaska, kid, I could—

LINDA: You're doing well enough, Willy!

BEN: [*To* LINDA.] Enough for what, my dear?

LINDA: [*Frightened of* BEN *and angry at him.*] Don't say those things to him! Enough to be happy right here, right now. [*To* WILLY, *while* BEN *laughs.*] Why must everybody conquer the world? You're well liked, and the boys love you, and someday— [*To* BEN.] —why, old man Wagner told him just the other day that if he keeps it up he'll be a member of the firm, didn't he, Willy?

WILLY: Sure, sure. I am building something with this firm, Ben, and if a man is building something he must be on the right track, mustn't he?

BEN: What are you building? Lay your hand on it. Where is it?

WILLY: [*Hesitantly.*] That's true, Linda, there's nothing.

LINDA: Why? [*To* BEN.] There's a man eighty-four years old—

WILLY: That's right, Ben, that's right. When I look at that man I say, what is there to worry about?

BEN: Bah!

WILLY: It's true, Ben. All he has to do is go into any city, pick up the phone, and he's making his living and you know why?

BEN: [*Picking up his valise.*] I've got to go.

WILLY: [*Holding* BEN *back.*] Look at this boy! [BIFF, *in his high school sweater, enters carrying suitcase.* HAPPY *carries* BIFF's *shoulder guards, gold helmet, and football pants.*] Without a penny to his name, three great universities are begging for him, and from there the sky's the limit, because it's not what you do, Ben. It's who you know and the smile on your face! It's contacts, Ben, contacts! The whole wealth of Alaska passes over the lunch table at the Commodore Hotel, and that's the wonder, the wonder of this country, that a man can end with diamonds here on the basis of being liked! [*He turns to* BIFF.] And that's why when you get out on that field today it's important. Because thousands of people will be rooting for you and loving you. [*To* BEN, *who has again begun to leave.*] And Ben! when he walks into a business office his name will sound out like a bell and all the doors will open to him! I've seen it, Ben, I've seen it a thousand times! You can't feel it with your hand like timber, but it's there!

BEN: Good-by, William.

WILLY: Ben, am I right? Don't you think I'm right? I value your advice.

BEN: There's a new continent at your doorstep, William. You could walk out rich. Rich! [*He is gone.*]

WILLY: We'll do it here, Ben! You hear me? We're gonna do it here!

[*Young* BERNARD *rushes in. The gay music of the Boys is heard.*]

BERNARD: Oh, gee, I was afraid you left already!

WILLY: Why? What time is it?

BERNARD: It's half-past one!

WILLY: Well, come on, everybody! Ebbets Field next stop! Where's the pennants?
[*He rushes through the wall-line of the kitchen and out into the living room.*]

LINDA: [*To* BIFF.] Did you pack fresh underwear?

BIFF: [*Who has been limbering up.*] I want to go!

BERNARD: Biff, I'm carrying your helmet, ain't I?

HAPPY: No, I'm carrying the helmet.

BERNARD: Oh, Biff, you promised me.

HAPPY: I'm carrying the helmet.

BERNARD: How am I going to get in the locker room?

LINDA: Let him carry the shoulder guards. [*She puts her coat and hat on in the kitchen.*]

BERNARD: Can I, Biff? 'Cause I told everybody I'm going to be in the locker room.

HAPPY: In Ebbets Field it's the clubhouse.

BERNARD: I meant the clubhouse, Biff!

HAPPY: Biff!

BIFF: [*Grandly, after a slight pause.*] Let him carry the shoulder guards.

HAPPY: [*As he gives* BERNARD *the shoulder guards.*] Stay close to us now.

[WILLY *rushes in with the pennants.*]

WILLY: [*Handing them out.*] Everybody wave when Biff comes out on the field.
[HAPPY *and* BERNARD *run off.*] You set now, boy?

[*The music has died away.*]

BIFF: Ready to go, Pop. Every muscle is ready.

WILLY: [*At the edge of the apron.*] You realize what this means?

BIFF: That's right, Pop.

WILLY: [*Feeling* BIFF's *muscles.*] You're comin' home this afternoon captain of the All-Scholastic Championship Team of the City of New York.

BIFF: I got it, Pop. And remember, pal, when I take off my helmet, that touchdown is for you.

WILLY: Let's go! [*He is starting out, with his arm around* BIFF, *when* CHARLEY *enters, as of old, in knickers.*] I got no room for you, Charley.

CHARLEY: Room? For what?

WILLY: In the car.

CHARLEY: You goin' for a ride? I wanted to shoot some casino.

WILLY: [*Furiously.*] Casino! [*Incredulously.*] Don't you realize what today is?

LINDA: Oh, he knows, Willy. He's just kidding you.

WILLY: That's nothing to kid about!

CHARLEY: No, Linda, what's goin' on?

LINDA: He's playing in Ebbets Field.

CHARLEY: Baseball in this weather?

WILLY: Don't talk to him. Come on, come on! [*He is pushing them out.*]

CHARLEY: Wait a minute, didn't you hear the news?

WILLY: What?

CHARLEY: Don't you listen to the radio? Ebbets Field just blew up.

WILLY: You go to hell! [CHARLEY *laughs. Pushing them out.*] Come on, come on! We're late.

CHARLEY: [*As they go.*] Knock a homer, Biff, knock a homer!

WILLY: [*The last to leave, turning to* CHARLEY.] I don't think that was funny, Charley. This is the greatest day of my life.

CHARLEY: Willy, when are you going to grow up?

WILLY: Yeah, heh? When this game is over, Charley, you'll be laughing out of the other side of your face. They'll be calling him another Red Grange.[6] Twenty-five thousand a year.

CHARLEY: [*Kidding.*] Is that so?

WILLY: Yeah, that's so.

CHARLEY: Well, then, I'm sorry, Willy. But tell me something.

WILLY: What?

CHARLEY: Who is Red Grange?

WILLY: Put up your hands. Goddam you, put up your hands! [CHARLEY, *chuckling, shakes his head and walks away, around the left corner of the stage.* WILLY *follows him. The music rises to a mocking frenzy.*] Who the hell do you think you are, better than everybody else? You don't know everything, you big, ignorant, stupid . . . Put up your hands!

> [*Light rises, on the right side of the forestage, on a small table in the reception room of* CHARLEY's *office. Traffic sounds are heard.* BERNARD, *now mature, sits whistling to himself. A pair of tennis rackets and an overnight bag are on the floor beside him.*]

WILLY: [*Offstage.*] What are you walking away for? Don't walk away! If you're going to say something say it to my face! I know you laugh at me behind my back. You'll laugh out of the other side of your goddam face after this game. Touchdown! Touchdown! Eighty thousand people! Touchdown! Right between the goal posts.

> [BERNARD *is a quiet, earnest, but self-assured young man.* WILLY's *voice is coming from right upstage now.* BERNARD *lowers his feet off the table and listens.* JENNY, *his father's secretary, enters.*]

JENNY: [*Distressed.*] Say, Bernard, will you go out in the hall?

BERNARD: What is that noise? Who is it?

JENNY: Mr. Loman. He just got off the elevator.

BERNARD: [*Getting up.*] Who's he arguing with?

---

6. Harold Edward Grange (1903–1991), All-American halfback at the University of Illinois from 1923 to 1925, who played professionally for the Chicago Bears.

JENNY: Nobody. There's nobody with him. I can't deal with him any more, and your father gets all upset everytime he comes. I've got a lot of typing to do, and your father's waiting to sign it. Will you see him?

WILLY: [*Entering.*] Touchdown! Touch— [*He sees* JENNY.] Jenny, Jenny, good to see you. How're ya? Workin'? Or still honest?

JENNY: Fine. How've you been feeling?

WILLY: Not much any more, Jenny. Ha, ha! [*He is surprised to see the rackets.*]

BERNARD: Hello, Uncle Willy.

WILLY: [*Almost shocked.*] Bernard! Well, look who's here! [*He comes quickly, guiltily to* BERNARD *and warmly shakes his hand.*]

BERNARD: How are you? Good to see you.

WILLY: What are you doing here?

BERNARD: Oh, just stopped by to see Pop. Get off my feet till my train leaves. I'm going to Washington in a few minutes.

WILLY: Is he in?

BERNARD: Yes, he's in his office with the accountant. Sit down.

WILLY: [*Sitting down.*] What're you going to do in Washington?

BERNARD: Oh, just a case I've got there, Willy.

WILLY: That so? [*Indicating the rackets.*] You going to play tennis there?

BERNARD: I'm staying with a friend who's got a court.

WILLY: Don't say. His own tennis court. Must be fine people, I bet.

BERNARD: They are, very nice. Dad tells me Biff's in town.

WILLY: [*With a big smile.*] Yeah, Biff's in. Working on a very big deal, Bernard.

BERNARD: What's Biff doing?

WILLY: Well, he's been doing very big things in the West. But he decided to establish himself here. Very big. We're having dinner. Did I hear your wife had a boy?

BERNARD: That's right. Our second.

WILLY: Two boys! What do you know!

BERNARD: What kind of a deal has Biff got?

WILLY: Well, Bill Oliver—very big sporting-goods man—he wants Biff very badly. Called him in from the West. Long distance, carte blanche, special deliveries. Your friends have their own private tennis court?

BERNARD: You still with the old firm, Willy?

WILLY: [*After a pause.*] I'm—I'm overjoyed to see how you made the grade, Bernard, overjoyed. It's an encouraging thing to see a young man really—really— Looks very good for Biff—very— [*He breaks off, then.*] Bernard— [*He is so full of emotion, he breaks off again.*]

BERNARD: What is it, Willy?

WILLY: [*Small and alone.*] What—what's the secret?

BERNARD: What secret?

WILLY: How—how did you? Why didn't he ever catch on?

BERNARD: I wouldn't know that, Willy.

WILLY: [*Confidentially, desperately.*] You were his friend, his boyhood friend. There's something I don't understand about it. His life ended after that Ebbets Field game. From the age of seventeen nothing good ever happened to him.

BERNARD: He never trained himself for anything.

WILLY: But he did, he did. After high school he took so many correspondence courses. Radio mechanics; television; God knows what, and never made the slightest mark.

BERNARD: [*Taking off his glasses.*] Willy, do you want to talk candidly?

WILLY: [*Rising, faces* BERNARD.] I regard you as a very brilliant man, Bernard. I value your advice.

BERNARD: Oh, the hell with the advice, Willy. I couldn't advise you. There's just one thing I've always wanted to ask you. When he was supposed to graduate, and the math teacher flunked him—

WILLY: Oh, that son-of-a-bitch ruined his life.

BERNARD: Yeah, but, Willy, all he had to do was go to summer school and make up that subject.

WILLY: That's right, that's right.

BERNARD: Did you tell him not to go to summer school?

WILLY: Me? I begged him to go. I ordered him to go!

BERNARD: Then why wouldn't he go?

WILLY: Why? Why! Bernard, that question has been trailing me like a ghost for the last fifteen years. He flunked the subject, and laid down and died like a hammer hit him!

BERNARD: Take it easy, kid.

WILLY: Let me talk to you—I got nobody to talk to. Bernard, Bernard, was it my fault? Y'see? It keeps going around in my mind, maybe I did something to him. I got nothing to give him.

BERNARD: Don't take it so hard.

WILLY: Why did he lay down? What is the story there? You were his friend!

BERNARD: Willy, I remember, it was June, and our grades came out. And he'd flunked math.

WILLY: That son-of-a-bitch!

BERNARD: No, it wasn't right then. Biff just got very angry, I remember, and he was ready to enroll in summer school.

WILLY: [*Surprised.*] He was?

BERNARD: He wasn't beaten by it at all. But then, Willy, he disappeared from the block for almost a month. And I got the idea that he'd gone up to New England to see you. Did he have a talk with you then? [WILLY *stares in silence.*] Willy?

WILLY: [*With a strong edge of resentment in his voice.*] Yeah, he came to Boston. What about it?

BERNARD: Well, just that when he came back—I'll never forget this, it always mystifies me. Because I'd thought so well of Biff, even though he'd always taken advantage of me. I loved him, Willy, y'know? And he came back after that month and took his sneakers—remember those sneakers with "University of Virginia" printed on them? He was so proud of those, wore them every day. And he took them down in the cellar, and burned them up in the furnace. We had a fist fight. It lasted at least half an hour. Just the two of us, punching each other down the cellar, and crying right through it. I've often thought of how strange it was that I knew he'd given up his life. What happened in Boston, Willy? [WILLY *looks at him as at an intruder.*] I just bring it up because you asked me.

WILLY: [*Angrily.*] Nothing. What do you mean, "What happened?" What's that got to do with anything?

BERNARD: Well, don't get sore.

WILLY: What are you trying to do, blame it on me? If a boy lays down is that my fault?

BERNARD: Now, Willy, don't get—

WILLY: Well, don't—don't talk to me that way! What does that mean, "What happened?"

[CHARLEY *enters. He is in his vest, and he carries a bottle of bourbon.*]

CHARLEY: Hey, you're going to miss that train. [*He waves the bottle.*]

BERNARD: Yeah, I'm going. [*He takes the bottle.*] Thanks, Pop. [*He picks up his rackets and bag.*] Good-by, Willy, and don't worry about it. You know, "If at first you don't succeed . . ."

WILLY: Yes, I believe in that.

BERNARD: But sometimes, Willy, it's better for a man just to walk away.

WILLY: Walk away?

BERNARD: That's right.

WILLY: But if you can't walk away?

BERNARD: [*After a slight pause.*] I guess that's when it's tough. [*Extending his hand.*] Good-by, Willy.

WILLY: [*Shaking* BERNARD's *hand.*] Good-by, boy.

CHARLEY: [*An arm on* BERNARD's *shoulder.*] How do you like this kid? Gonna argue a case in front of the Supreme Court.

BERNARD: [*Protesting.*] Pop!

WILLY: [*Genuinely shocked, pained, and happy.*] No! The Supreme Court!

BERNARD: I gotta run. 'By, Dad!

CHARLEY: Knock 'em dead, Bernard!

[BERNARD *goes off.*]

WILLY: [*As* CHARLEY *takes out his wallet.*] The Supreme Court! And he didn't even mention it!

CHARLEY: [*Counting out money on the desk.*] He don't have to—he's gonna do it.

WILLY: And you never told him what to do, did you? You never took any interest in him.

CHARLEY: My salvation is that I never took any interest in anything. There's some money—fifty dollars. I got an accountant inside.

WILLY: Charley, look . . . [*With difficulty.*] I got my insurance to pay. If you can manage it—I need a hundred and ten dollars. [CHARLEY *doesn't reply for a moment; merely stops moving.*] I'd draw it from my bank but Linda would know, and I . . .

CHARLEY: Sit down, Willy.

WILLY: [*Moving toward the chair.*] I'm keeping an account of everything, remember. I'll pay every penny back. [*He sits.*]

CHARLEY: Now listen to me, Willy.

WILLY: I want you to know I appreciate . . .

CHARLEY: [*Sitting down on the table.*] Willy, what're you doin'? What the hell is goin' on in your head?

WILLY: Why? I'm simply . . .

CHARLEY: I offered you a job. You can make fifty dollars a week. And I won't send you on the road.

WILLY: I've got a job.

CHARLEY: Without pay? What kind of job is a job without pay? [*He rises.*] Now, look kid, enough is enough. I'm no genius but I know when I'm being insulted.

WILLY: Insulted!

CHARLEY: Why don't you want to work for me?

WILLY: What's the matter with you? I've got a job.

CHARLEY: Then what're you walkin' in here every week for?

WILLY: [*Getting up.*] Well, if you don't want me to walk in here—

CHARLEY: I am offering you a job!

WILLY: I don't want your goddam job!

CHARLEY: When the hell are you going to grow up?

WILLY: [*Furiously.*] You big ignoramus, if you say that to me again I'll rap you one! I don't care how big you are! [*He's ready to fight. Pause.*]

CHARLEY: [*Kindly, going to him.*] How much do you need, Willy?

WILLY: Charley, I'm strapped, I'm strapped. I don't know what to do. I was just fired.

CHARLEY: Howard fired you?

WILLY: That snotnose. Imagine that? I named him. I named him Howard.

CHARLEY: Willy, when're you gonna realize that them things don't mean anything? You named him Howard, but you can't sell that. The only thing you got in this world is what you can sell. And the funny thing is that you're a salesman, and you don't know that.

WILLY: I've always tried to think otherwise, I guess. I always felt that if a man was impressive, and well liked, that nothing—

CHARLEY: Why must everybody like you? Who liked J. P. Morgan? Was he impressive? In a Turkish bath he'd look like a butcher. But with his pockets on he was very well liked. Now listen, Willy, I know you don't like me, and nobody can say I'm in love with you, but I'll give you a job because—just for the hell of it, put it that way. Now what do you say?

WILLY: I—I just can't work for you, Charley.

CHARLEY: What're you, jealous of me?

WILLY: I can't work for you, that's all, don't ask me why.

CHARLEY: [*Angered, takes out more bills.*] You been jealous of me all your life, you damned fool! Here, pay your insurance. [*He puts the money in* WILLY's *hand.*]

WILLY: I'm keeping strict accounts.

CHARLEY: I've got some work to do. Take care of yourself. And pay your insurance.

WILLY: [*Moving to the right.*] Funny, y'know? After all the highways and the trains, and the appointments, and the years, you end up worth more dead than alive.

CHARLEY: Willy, nobody's worth nothin' dead. [*After a slight pause.*] Did you hear what I said? [WILLY *stands still, dreaming.*] Willy!

WILLY: Apologize to Bernard for me when you see him. I didn't mean to argue with him. He's a fine boy. They're all fine boys, and they'll end up big—all of them. Someday they'll all play tennis together. Wish me luck, Charley. He saw Bill Oliver today.

CHARLEY: Good luck.

WILLY: [*On the verge of tears.*] Charley, you're the only friend I got. Isn't that a remarkable thing? [*He goes out.*]

CHARLEY: Jesus!

> [CHARLEY *stares after him a moment and follows. All light blacks out. Suddenly raucous music is heard, and a red glow rises behind the screen at right.* STANLEY, *a young waiter, appears, carrying a table, followed by* HAPPY, *who is carrying two chairs.*]

STANLEY: [*Putting the table down.*] That's all right, Mr. Loman, I can handle it myself. [*He turns and takes the chairs from* HAPPY *and places them at the table.*]

HAPPY: [*Glancing around.*] Oh, this is better.

STANLEY: Sure, in the front there you're in the middle of all kinds a noise. Whenever you got a party. Mr. Loman, you just tell me and I'll put you back here. Y'know, there's a lotta people they don't like it private, because when they go out they like to see a lotta action around them because they're sick and tired to stay in the house by theirself. But I know you, you ain't from Hackensack. You know what I mean?

HAPPY: [*Sitting down.*] So how's it coming, Stanley?

STANLEY: Ah, it's a dog life. I only wish during the war they'd a took me in the Army. I couda been dead by now.

HAPPY: My brother's back, Stanley.

STANLEY: Oh, he come back, heh? From the Far West.

HAPPY: Yeah, big cattle man, my brother, so treat him right. And my father's coming too.

STANLEY: Oh, your father too!

HAPPY: You got a couple of nice lobsters?

STANLEY: Hundred per cent, big.

HAPPY: I want them with the claws.

STANLEY: Don't worry, I don't give you no mice. [HAPPY *laughs.*] How about some wine? It'll put a head on the meal.

HAPPY: No. You remember, Stanley, that recipe I brought you from overseas? With the champagne in it?

STANLEY: Oh, yeah, sure. I still got it tacked up yet in the kitchen. But that'll have to cost a buck apiece anyways.

HAPPY: That's all right.

STANLEY: What'd you, hit a number or somethin'?

HAPPY: No, it's a little celebration. My brother is—I think he pulled off a big deal today. I think we're going into business together.

STANLEY: Great! That's the best for you. Because a family business, you know what I mean?—that's the best.

HAPPY: That's what I think.

STANLEY: 'Cause what's the difference? Somebody steals? It's in the family. Know what I mean? [*Sotto voce.*] Like this bartender here. The boss is goin' crazy what kinda leak he's got in the cash register. You put it in but it don't come out.

HAPPY: [*Raising his head.*] Sh!

STANLEY: What?

HAPPY: You notice I wasn't lookin' right or left, was I?

STANLEY: No.

HAPPY: And my eyes are closed.

STANLEY: So what's the—?

HAPPY: Strudel's comin'.

STANLEY: [*Catching on, looks around.*] Ah, no, there's no— [*He breaks off as a furred, lavishly dressed* GIRL *enters and sits at the next table. Both follow her with their eyes.*] Geez, how'd ya know?

HAPPY: I got radar or something. [*Staring directly at her profile.*] Oooooooo . . . Stanley.

STANLEY: I think, that's for you, Mr. Loman.

HAPPY: Look at that mouth. Oh, God. And the binoculars.

STANLEY: Geez, you got a life, Mr. Loman.

HAPPY: Wait on her.

STANLEY: [*Going to the* GIRL'*s table.*] Would you like a menu, ma'am?

GIRL: I'm expecting someone, but I'd like a—

HAPPY: Why don't you bring her—excuse me, miss, do you mind? I sell champagne, and I'd like you to try my brand. Bring her a champagne, Stanley.

GIRL: That's awfully nice of you.

HAPPY: Don't mention it. It's all company money. [*He laughs.*]

GIRL: That's a charming product to be selling, isn't it?

HAPPY: Oh, gets to be like everything else. Selling is selling, y'know.

GIRL: I suppose.

HAPPY: You don't happen to sell, do you?

GIRL: No, I don't sell.

HAPPY: Would you object to a compliment from a stranger? You ought to be on a magazine cover.

GIRL: [*Looking at him a little archly.*] I have been.

[STANLEY *comes in with a glass of champagne.*]

HAPPY: What'd I say before, Stanley? You see? She's a cover girl.

STANLEY: Oh, I could see, I could see.

HAPPY: [*To the* GIRL.] What magazine?

GIRL: Oh, a lot of them. [*She takes the drink.*] Thank you.

HAPPY: You know what they say in France, don't you? "Champagne is the drink of the complexion"—Hya, Biff!

[BIFF *has entered and sits with* HAPPY.]

BIFF: Hello, kid. Sorry I'm late.

HAPPY: I just got here. Uh, Miss—?

GIRL: Forsythe.

HAPPY: Miss Forsythe, this is my brother.

BIFF: Is Dad here?

HAPPY: His name is Biff. You might've heard of him. Great football player.

GIRL: Really? What team?

HAPPY: Are you familiar with football?

GIRL: No, I'm afraid I'm not.

HAPPY: Biff is quarterback with the New York Giants.

GIRL: Well, that's nice, isn't it? [*She drinks.*]

HAPPY: Good health.

GIRL: I'm happy to meet you.

HAPPY: That's my name, Hap. It's really Harold, but at West Point they called me Happy.

GIRL: [*Now really impressed.*] Oh, I see. How do you do? [*She turns her profile.*]

BIFF: Isn't Dad coming?

HAPPY: You want her?

BIFF: Oh, I could never make that.

HAPPY: I remember the time that idea would never come into your head. Where's the old confidence, Biff?

BIFF: I just saw Oliver—

HAPPY: Wait a minute. I've got to see that old confidence again. Do you want her? She's on call.

BIFF: Oh, no. [*He turns to look at the* GIRL.]

HAPPY: I'm telling you. Watch this. [*Turning to see the* GIRL.] Honey? [*She turns to him.*] Are you busy?

GIRL: Well, I am . . . but I could make a phone call.

HAPPY: Do that, will you, honey? And see if you can get a friend. We'll be here for a while. Biff is one of the greatest football players in the country.

GIRL: [*Standing up.*] Well, I'm certainly happy to meet you.

HAPPY: Come back soon.

GIRL: I'll try.

HAPPY: Don't try, honey, try hard. [*The* GIRL *exits.* STANLEY *follows, shaking his head in bewildered admiration.*] Isn't that a shame now? A beautiful girl like that? That's why I can't get married. There's not a good woman in a thousand. New York is loaded with them, kid!

BIFF: Hap, look—

HAPPY: I told you she was on call!

BIFF: [*Strangely unnerved.*] Cut it out, will ya? I want to say something to you.

HAPPY: Did you see Oliver?

BIFF: I saw him all right. Now look, I want to tell Dad a couple of things and I want you to help me.

HAPPY: What? Is he going to back you?

BIFF: Are you crazy? You're out of your goddam head, you know that?

HAPPY: Why? What happened?

BIFF: [*Breathlessly.*] I did a terrible thing today, Hap. It's been the strangest day I ever went through. I'm all numb, I swear.

HAPPY: You mean he wouldn't see you?

BIFF: Well, I waited six hours for him, see? All day. Kept sending my name in. Even tried to date his secretary so she'd get me to him, but no soap.

HAPPY: Because you're not showin' the old confidence, Biff. He remembered you, didn't he?

BIFF: [*Stopping* HAPPY *with a gesture.*] Finally, about five o'clock, he comes out. Didn't remember who I was or anything. I felt like such an idiot, Hap.

HAPPY: Did you tell him my Florida idea?

BIFF: He walked away. I saw him for one minute. I got so mad I could've torn the walls down! How the hell did I ever get the idea I was a salesman there? I even believed myself that I'd been a salesman for him! And then he gave me one look and—I realized what a ridiculous lie my whole life has been! We've been talking in a dream for fifteen years. I was a shipping clerk.

HAPPY: What'd you do?

BIFF: [*With great tension and wonder.*] Well, he left, see. And the secretary went out. I was all alone in the waiting-room. I don't know what came over me, Hap. The next thing I know I'm in his office—paneled walls, everything. I can't explain it. I—Hap, I took his fountain pen.

HAPPY: Geez, did he catch you?

BIFF: I ran out. I ran down all eleven flights. I ran and ran and ran.

HAPPY: That was an awful dumb—what'd you do that for?

BIFF: [*Agonized.*] I don't know, I just—wanted to take something, I don't know. You gotta help me, Hap, I'm gonna tell Pop.

HAPPY: You crazy? What for?

BIFF: Hap, he's got to understand that I'm not the man somebody lends that kind of money to. He thinks I've been spiting him all these years and it's eating him up.

HAPPY: That's just it. You tell him something nice.

BIFF: I can't.

HAPPY: Say you got a lunch date with Oliver tomorrow.

BIFF: So what do I do tomorrow?

HAPPY: You leave the house tomorrow and come back at night and say Oliver is thinking it over. And he thinks it over for a couple of weeks, and gradually it fades away and nobody's the worse.

BIFF: But it'll go on forever!

HAPPY: Dad is never so happy as when he's looking forward to something! [WILLY *enters.*] Hello, scout!

WILLY: Gee, I haven't been here in years!

[STANLEY *has followed* WILLY *in and sets a chair for him.* STANLEY *starts off but* HAPPY *stops him.*]

HAPPY: Stanley!

[STANLEY *stands by, waiting for an order.*]

BIFF: [*Going to* WILLY *with guilt, as to an invalid.*] Sit down, Pop. You want a drink?

WILLY: Sure, I don't mind.

BIFF: Let's get a load on.

WILLY: You look worried.

BIFF: N-no. [*To* STANLEY.] Scotch all around. Make it doubles.

STANLEY: Doubles, right. [*He goes.*]

WILLY: You had a couple already, didn't you?

BIFF: Just a couple, yeah.

WILLY: Well, what happened, boy? [*Nodding affirmatively, with a smile.*] Everything go all right?

BIFF: [*Takes a breath, then reaches out and grasps* WILLY'*s hand.*] Pal . . . [*He is smiling bravely, and* WILLY *is smiling too.*] I had an experience today.

HAPPY: Terrific, Pop.

WILLY: That so? What happened?

BIFF: [*High, slightly alcoholic, above the earth.*] I'm going to tell you everything from first to last. It's been a strange day. [*Silence. He looks around, composes himself as best he can, but his breath keeps breaking the rhythm of his voice.*] I had to wait quite a while for him, and—

WILLY: Oliver?

BIFF: Yeah, Oliver. All day, as a matter of cold fact. And a lot of—instances—facts, Pop, facts about my life came back to me. Who was it, Pop? Who ever said I was a salesman with Oliver?

WILLY: Well, you were.

BIFF: No, Dad, I was shipping clerk.

WILLY: But you were practically—

BIFF: [*With determination.*] Dad, I don't know who said it first, but I was never a salesman for Bill Oliver.

WILLY: What're you talking about?

BIFF: Let's hold on to the facts tonight, Pop. We're not going to get anywhere bullin' around. I was a shipping clerk.

WILLY: [*Angrily.*] All right, now listen to me—

BIFF: Why don't you let me finish?

WILLY: I'm not interested in stories about the past or any crap of that kind because the woods are burning, boys, you understand? There's a big blaze going on all around. I was fired today.

BIFF: [*Shocked.*] How could you be?

WILLY: I was fired, and I'm looking for a little good news to tell your mother, because the woman has waited and the woman has suffered. The gist of it is that I haven't got a story left in my head, Biff. So don't give me a lecture about facts and aspects. I am not interested. Now what've you got to say to me? [STANLEY *enters with three drinks. They wait until he leaves.*] Did you see Oliver?

BIFF: Jesus, Dad!

WILLY: You mean you didn't go up there?

HAPPY: Sure he went up there.

BIFF: I did. I—saw him. How could they fire you?

WILLY: [*On the edge of his chair.*] What kind of a welcome did he give you?

BIFF: He won't even let you work on commission?

WILLY: I'm out. [*Driving.*] So tell me, he gave you a warm welcome?

HAPPY: Sure, Pop, sure!

BIFF: [*Driven.*] Well, it was kind of—

WILLY: I was wondering if he'd remember you. [*To* HAPPY.] Imagine, man doesn't see him for ten, twelve years and gives him that kind of a welcome!

HAPPY: Damn right!

BIFF: [*Trying to return to the offensive.*] Pop, look—

WILLY: You know why he remembered you, don't you? Because you impressed him in those days.

BIFF: Let's talk quietly and get this down to the facts, huh?

WILLY: [*As though* BIFF *had been interrupting.*] Well, what happened? It's great news, Biff. Did he take you into his office or'd you talk in the waiting-room?

BIFF: Well, he came in, see and—

WILLY: [*With a big smile.*] What'd he say? Betcha he threw his arm around you.

BIFF: Well, he kinda—

WILLY: He's a fine man. [*To* HAPPY.] Very hard man to see, y'know.

HAPPY: [*Agreeing.*] Oh, I know.

WILLY: [*To* BIFF.] Is that where you had the drinks?

BIFF: Yeah, he gave me a couple of—no, no!

HAPPY: [*Cutting in.*] He told him my Florida idea.

WILLY: Don't interrupt. [*To* BIFF.] How'd he react to the Florida idea?

BIFF: Dad, will you give me a minute to explain?

WILLY: I've been waiting for you to explain since I sat down here! What happened? He took you into his office and what?

BIFF: Well—I talked. And—he listened, see.

WILLY: Famous for the way he listens, y'know. What was his answer?

BIFF: His answer was— [*He breaks off, suddenly angry.*] Dad, you're not letting me tell you what I want to tell you!

WILLY: [*Accusing, angered.*] You didn't see him, did you?

BIFF: I did see him!

WILLY: What'd you insult him or something? You insulted him, didn't you?

BIFF: Listen, will you let me out of it, will you just let me out of it!

HAPPY: What the hell!

WILLY: Tell me what happened!

BIFF: [*To* HAPPY.] I can't talk to him!

[*A single trumpet note jars the ear. The light of green leaves stains the house, which holds the air of night and a dream.* YOUNG BERNARD *enters and knocks on the door of the house.*]

YOUNG BERNARD: [*Frantically.*] Mrs. Loman, Mrs. Loman!
HAPPY: Tell him what happened!
BIFF: [*To* HAPPY.] Shut up and leave me alone!
WILLY: No, no. You had to go and flunk math!
BIFF: What math? What're you talking about?
YOUNG BERNARD: Mrs. Loman, Mrs. Loman!

[LINDA *appears in the house, as of old.*]

WILLY: [*Wildly.*] Math, math, math!
BIFF: Take it easy, Pop!
YOUNG BERNARD: Mrs. Loman!
WILLY: [*Furiously.*] If you hadn't flunked you'd've been set by now!
BIFF: Now, look, I'm gonna tell you what happened, and you're going to listen to me.
YOUNG BERNARD: Mrs. Loman!
BIFF: I waited six hours—
HAPPY: What the hell are you saying?
BIFF: I kept sending in my name but he wouldn't see me. So finally he . . . [*He continues unheard as light fades low on the restaurant.*]
YOUNG BERNARD: Biff flunked math!
LINDA: No!
YOUNG BERNARD: Birnbaum flunked him! They won't graduate him!
LINDA: But they have to. He's gotta go to the university. Where is he? Biff! Biff!
YOUNG BERNARD: No, he left. He went to Grand Central.
LINDA: Grand—You mean he went to Boston!
YOUNG BERNARD: Is Uncle Willy in Boston?
LINDA: Oh, maybe Willy can talk to the teacher. Oh, the poor, poor boy!

[*Light on house area snaps out.*]

BIFF: [*At the table, now audible, holding up a gold fountain pen.*] . . . so I'm washed up with Oliver, you understand? Are you listening to me?
WILLY: [*At a loss.*] Yeah, sure. If you hadn't flunked—
BIFF: Flunked what? What're you talking about?
WILLY: Don't blame everything on me! I didn't flunk math—you did! What pen?
HAPPY: That was awful dumb, Biff, a pen like that is worth—
WILLY: [*Seeing the pen for the first time.*] You took Oliver's pen?
BIFF: [*Weakening.*] Dad, I just explained it to you.
WILLY: You stole Bill Oliver's fountain pen!
BIFF: I didn't exactly steal it! That's just what I've been explaining to you!
HAPPY: He had it in his hand and just then Oliver walked in, so he got nervous and stuck it in his pocket!

WILLY: My God, Biff!

BIFF: I never intended to do it, Dad!

OPERATOR'S VOICE: Standish Arms, good evening!

WILLY: [*Shouting.*] I'm not in my room!

BIFF: [*Frightened.*] Dad, what's the matter? [*He and* HAPPY *stand up.*]

OPERATOR: Ringing Mr. Loman for you!

BIFF: [*Horrified, gets down on one knee before* WILLY.] Dad, I'll make good, I'll make good. [WILLY *tries to get to his feet.* BIFF *holds him down.*] Sit down now.

WILLY: No, you're no good, you're no good for anything.

BIFF: I am, Dad, I'll find something else, you understand? Now don't worry about anything. [*He holds up* WILLY's *face.*] Talk to me, Dad.

OPERATOR: Mr. Loman does not answer. Shall I page him?

WILLY: [*Attempting to stand, as though to rush and silence the* OPERATOR.] No, no, no!

HAPPY: He'll strike something, Pop.

WILLY: No, no . . .

BIFF: [*Desperately, standing over* WILLY.] Pop, listen! Listen to me! I'm telling you something good. Oliver talked to his partner about the Florida idea. You listening? He—he talked to his partner, and he came to me . . . I'm going to be all right, you hear? Dad, listen to me, he said it was just a question of the amount!

WILLY: Then you . . . got it?

HAPPY: He's gonna be terrific, Pop!

WILLY: [*Trying to stand.*] Then you got it, haven't you? You got it! You got it!

BIFF: [*Agonized, holds* WILLY *down.*] No, no. Look, Pop. I'm supposed to have lunch with them tomorrow. I'm just telling you this so you'll know that I can still make an impression, Pop. And I'll make good somewhere, but I can't go tomorrow, see?

WILLY: Why not? You simply—

BIFF: But the pen, Pop!

WILLY: You give it to him and tell him it was an oversight!

HAPPY: Sure, have lunch tomorrow!

BIFF: I can't say that—

WILLY: You were doing a crossword puzzle and accidentally used his pen!

BIFF: Listen, kid, I took those balls years ago, now I walk in with his fountain pen? That clinches it, don't you see? I can't face him like that! I'll try elsewhere.

PAGE'S VOICE: Paging Mr. Loman!

WILLY: Don't you want to be anything?

BIFF: Pop, how can I go back?

WILLY: You don't want to be anything, is that what's behind it?

BIFF: [*Now angry at* WILLY *for not crediting his sympathy.*] Don't take it that way! You think it was easy walking into that office after what I'd done to him? A team of horses couldn't have dragged me back to Bill Oliver!

WILLY: Then why'd you go?

BIFF: Why did I go? Why did I go! Look at you! Look at what's become of you!

[*Off left,* THE WOMAN *laughs.*]

WILLY: Biff, you're going to go to that lunch tomorrow, or—
BIFF: I can't go. I've got an appointment!
HAPPY: Biff, for . . . !
WILLY: Are you spiting me?
BIFF: Don't take it that way! Goddammit!
WILLY: [*Strikes* BIFF *and falters away from the table.*] You rotten little louse! Are you spiting me?
THE WOMAN: Someone's at the door, Willy!
BIFF: I'm no good, can't you see what I am?
HAPPY: [*Separating them.*] Hey, you're in a restaurant! Now cut it out, both of you! [*The* GIRLS *enter.*] Hello, girls, sit down.

[THE WOMAN *laughs, off left.*]

MISS FORSYTHE: I guess we might as well. This is Letta.
THE WOMAN: Willy, are you going to wake up?
BIFF: [*Ignoring* WILLY.] How're ya, miss, sit down. What do you drink?
MISS FORSYTHE: Letta might not be able to stay long.
LETTA: I gotta get up early tomorrow. I got jury duty. I'm so excited! Were you fellows ever on a jury?
BIFF: No, but I been in front of them! [*The* GIRLS *laugh.*] This is my father.
LETTA: Isn't he cute? Sit down with us, Pop.
HAPPY: Sit him down, Biff!
BIFF: [*Going to him.*] Come on, slugger, drink us under the table. To hell with it! Come on, sit down, pal.

[*On* BIFF'*s last insistence,* WILLY *is about to sit.*]

THE WOMAN: [*Now urgently.*] Willy, are you going to answer the door!

[THE WOMAN'*s call pulls* WILLY *back. He starts right, befuddled.*]

BIFF: Hey, where are you going?
WILLY: Open the door.
BIFF: The door?
WILLY: The washroom . . . the door . . . where's the door?
BIFF: [*Leading* WILLY *to the left.*] Just go straight down.

[WILLY *moves left.*]

THE WOMAN: Willy, Willy, are you going to get up, get up, get up, get up?

[WILLY *exits left.*]

LETTA: I think it's sweet you bring your daddy along.
MISS FORSYTHE: Oh, he isn't really your father!
BIFF: [*At left, turning to her resentfully.*] Miss Forsythe, you've just seen a prince walk by. A fine, troubled prince. A hardworking, unappreciated prince. A pal, you understand? A good companion. Always for his boys.

LETTA: That's so sweet.

HAPPY: Well, girls, what's the program? We're wasting time. Come on, Biff. Gather round. Where would you like to go?

BIFF: Why don't you do something for him?

HAPPY: Me!

BIFF: Don't you give a damn for him, Hap?

HAPPY: What're you talking about? I'm the one who—

BIFF: I sense it, you don't give a good goddam about him. [*He takes the rolled-up hose from his pocket and puts it on the table in front of* HAPPY.] Look what I found in the cellar, for Christ's sake. How can you bear to let it go on?

HAPPY: Me? Who goes away? Who runs off and—

BIFF: Yeah, but he doesn't mean anything to you. You could help him—I can't! Don't you understand what I'm talking about? He's going to kill himself, don't you know that?

HAPPY: Don't I know it! Me!

BIFF: Hap, help him! Jesus . . . help him . . . Help me, help me, I can't bear to look at his face! [*Ready to weep, he hurries out, up right.*]

HAPPY: [*Starting after him.*] Where are you going?

MISS FORSYTHE: What's he so mad about?

HAPPY: Come on, girls, we'll catch up with him.

MISS FORSYTHE: [*As* HAPPY *pushes her out.*] Say, I don't like that temper of his!

HAPPY: He's just a little overstrung, he'll be all right!

WILLY: [*Off left, as* THE WOMAN *laughs.*] Don't answer! Don't answer!

LETTA: Don't you want to tell your father—

HAPPY: No, that's not my father. He's just a guy. Come on, we'll catch Biff, and, honey, we're going to paint this town! Stanley, where's the check! Hey, Stanley!

[*They exit.* STANLEY *looks toward left.*]

STANLEY: [*Calling to* HAPPY *indignantly.*] Mr. Loman! Mr. Loman!

[STANLEY *picks up a chair and follows them off. Knocking is heard off left.* THE WOMAN *enters, laughing.* WILLY *follows her. She is in a black slip; he is buttoning his shirt. Raw, sensuous music accompanies their speech.*]

WILLY: Will you stop laughing? Will you stop?

THE WOMAN: Aren't you going to answer the door? He'll wake the whole hotel.

WILLY: I'm not expecting anybody.

THE WOMAN: Whyn't you have another drink, honey, and stop being so damn self-centered?

WILLY: I'm so lonely.

THE WOMAN: You know you ruined me, Willy? From now on, whenever you come to the office, I'll see that you go right through to the buyers. No waiting at my desk any more, Willy. You ruined me.

WILLY: That's nice of you to say that.

THE WOMAN: Gee, you are self-centered! Why so sad? You are the saddest, self-centeredest soul I ever did see-saw. [*She laughs. He kisses her.*] Come on inside, drummer boy. It's silly to be dressing in the middle of the night. [*As knocking is heard.*] Aren't you going to answer the door?

WILLY: They're knocking on the wrong door.

THE WOMAN: But I felt the knocking. And he heard us talking in here. Maybe the hotel's on fire!

WILLY: [*His terror rising.*] It's a mistake.

THE WOMAN: Then tell them to go away!

WILLY: There's nobody there.

THE WOMAN: It's getting on my nerves, Willy. There's somebody standing out there and it's getting on my nerves!

WILLY: [*Pushing her away from him.*] All right, stay in the bathroom here, and don't come out. I think there's a law in Massachusetts about it, so don't come out. It may be that new room clerk. He looked very mean. So don't come out. It's a mistake, there's no fire.

[*The knocking is heard again. He takes a few steps away from her, and she vanishes into the wing. The light follows him, and now he is facing* YOUNG BIFF, *who carries a suitcase.* BIFF *steps toward him. The music is gone.*]

BIFF: Why didn't you answer?

WILLY: Biff! What are you doing in Boston?

BIFF: Why didn't you answer? I've been knocking for five minutes, I called you on the phone—

WILLY: I just heard you. I was in the bathroom and had the door shut. Did anything happen home?

BIFF: Dad—I let you down.

WILLY: What do you mean?

BIFF: Dad . . .

WILLY: Biffo, what's this about? [*Putting his arm around* BIFF.] Come on, let's go downstairs and get you a malted.

BIFF: Dad, I flunked math.

WILLY: Not for the term?

BIFF: The term. I haven't got enough credits to graduate.

WILLY: You mean to say Bernard wouldn't give you the answers?

BIFF: He did, he tried, but I only got a sixty-one.

WILLY: And they wouldn't give you four points?

BIFF: Birnbaum refused absolutely. I begged him, Pop, but he won't give me those points. You gotta talk to him before they close the school. Because if he saw the kind of man you are, and you just talked to him in your way, I'm sure he'd come through for me. The class came right before practice, see, and I didn't go enough. Would you talk to him? He'd like you, Pop. You know the way you could talk.

WILLY: You're on. We'll drive right back.

BIFF: Oh, Dad, good work! I'm sure he'll change for you!

WILLY: Go downstairs and tell the clerk I'm checkin' out. Go right down.

BIFF: Yes, sir! See, the reason he hates me, Pop—one day he was late for class so I got up at the blackboard and imitated him. I crossed my eyes and talked with a lithp.

WILLY: [*Laughing.*] You did? The kids like it?

BIFF: They nearly died laughing!

WILLY: Yeah? What'd you do?

BIFF: The thquare root of thixthy twee is . . . [WILLY *bursts out laughing;* BIFF *joins him.*] And in the middle of it he walked in!

[WILLY *laughs and* THE WOMAN *joins in offstage.*]

WILLY: [*Without hesitation.*] Hurry downstairs and—

BIFF: Somebody in there?

WILLY: No, that was next door.

[THE WOMAN *laughs offstage.*]

BIFF: Somebody got in your bathroom!

WILLY: No, it's the next room, there's a party—

THE WOMAN: [*Enters laughing. She lisps this.*] Can I come in? There's something in the bathtub, Willy, and it's moving!

[WILLY *looks at* BIFF, *who is staring open-mouthed and horrified at* THE WOMAN.]

WILLY: Ah—you better go back to your room. They must be finished painting by now. They're painting her room so I let her take a shower here. Go back, go back . . . [*He pushes her.*]

THE WOMAN: [*Resisting.*] But I've got to get dressed, Willy, I can't—

WILLY: Get out of here! Go back, go back . . . [*Suddenly striving for the ordinary.*] This is Miss Francis, Biff, she's a buyer. They're painting her room. Go back, Miss Francis, go back . . .

THE WOMAN: But my clothes, I can't go out naked in the hall!

WILLY: [*Pushing her offstage.*] Get outa here! Go back, go back!

[BIFF *slowly sits down on his suitcase as the argument continues offstage.*]

THE WOMAN: Where's my stockings? You promised me stockings, Willy!

WILLY: I have no stockings here!

THE WOMAN: You had two boxes of size nine sheers for me, and I want them!

WILLY: Here, for God's sake, will you get outa here!

THE WOMAN: [*Enters holding a box of stockings.*] I just hope there's nobody in the hall. That's all I hope. [*To* BIFF.] Are you football or baseball?

BIFF: Football.

THE WOMAN: [*Angry, humiliated.*] That's me too. G'night. [*She snatches her clothes from* WILLY, *and walks out.*]

WILLY: [*After a pause.*] Well, better get going. I want to get to the school first thing in the morning. Get my suits out of the closet. I'll get my valise. [BIFF *doesn't move.*] What's the matter? [BIFF *remains motionless, tears falling.*] She's a buyer. Buys for J. H. Simmons. She lives down the hall—they're painting. You don't imagine— [*He breaks off. After a pause.*] Now listen, pal, she's just a buyer. She sees merchandise in her room and they have to keep it looking just so . . . [*Pause. Assuming command.*] All right, get my suits. [BIFF *doesn't move.*] Now stop crying and do as I say. I gave you an order. Biff, I gave you an order! Is that what you do when I give you an order? How dare you cry! [*Putting his arm around* BIFF.] Now look, Biff, when you grow up you'll understand about these things. You mustn't—you mustn't overemphasize a thing like this. I'll see Birnbaum first thing in the morning.

BIFF: Never mind.

WILLY: [*Getting down beside* BIFF.] Never mind! He's going to give you those points. I'll see to it.

BIFF: He wouldn't listen to you.

WILLY: He certainly will listen to me. You need those points for the U. of Virginia.

BIFF: I'm not going there.

WILLY: Heh? If I can't get him to change that mark you'll make it up in summer school. You've got all summer to—

BIFF: [*His weeping breaking from him.*] Dad . . .

WILLY: [*Infected by it.*] Oh, my boy . . .

BIFF: Dad . . .

WILLY: She's nothing to me, Biff. I was lonely, I was terribly lonely.

BIFF: You—you gave her Mama's stockings! [*His tears break through and he rises to go.*]

WILLY: [*Grabbing for* BIFF.] I gave you an order!

BIFF: Don't touch me, you—liar!

WILLY: Apologize for that!

BIFF: You fake! You phony little fake! You fake!

[*Overcome, he turns quickly and weeping fully goes out with his suitcase.* WILLY *is left on the floor on his knees.*]

WILLY: I gave you an order! Biff, come back here or I'll beat you! Come back here! I'll whip you! [STANLEY *comes quickly in from the right and stands in front of* WILLY. WILLY *shouts at* STANLEY.] I gave you an order . . .

STANLEY: Hey, let's pick it up, pick it up, Mr. Loman. [*He helps* WILLY *to his feet.*] Your boys left with the chippies. They said they'll see you home.

[*A* SECOND WAITER *watches some distance away.*]

WILLY: But we were supposed to have dinner together.

[*Music is heard,* WILLY's *theme.*]

STANLEY: Can you make it?

WILLY: I'll—sure, I can make it. [*Suddenly concerned about his clothes.*] Do I—I look all right?

STANLEY: Sure, you look all right. [*He flicks a speck off* WILLY's *lapel.*]

WILLY: Here—here's a dollar.

STANLEY: Oh, your son paid me. It's all right.

WILLY: [*Putting it in* STANLEY's *hand.*] No, take it. You're a good boy.

STANLEY: Oh, no, you don't have to . . .

WILLY: Here—here's some more, I don't need it any more. [*After a slight pause.*] Tell me—is there a seed store in the neighborhood?

STANLEY: Seeds? You mean like to plant?

[*As* WILLY *turns,* STANLEY *slips the money back into his jacket pocket.*]

WILLY: Yes. Carrots, peas . . .

STANLEY: Well, there's hardware stores on Sixth Avenue, but it may be too late now.

WILLY: [*Anxiously.*] Oh, I'd better hurry. I've got to get some seeds. [*He starts off to the right.*] I've got to get some seeds, right away. Nothing's planted. I don't have a thing in the ground.

[WILLY *hurries out as the light goes down.* STANLEY *moves over to the right after him, watches him off. The other* WAITER *has been staring at* WILLY.]

STANLEY: [*To the* WAITER.] Well, whatta you looking at?

[*The* WAITER *picks up the chairs and moves off right.* STANLEY *takes the table and follows him. The light fades on this area. There is a long pause, the sound of the flute coming over. The light gradually rises on the kitchen, which is empty.* HAPPY *appears at the door of the house, followed by* BIFF. HAPPY *is carrying a large bunch of long-stemmed roses. He enters the kitchen, looks around for* LINDA. *Not seeing her, he turns to* BIFF, *who is just outside the house door, and makes a gesture with his hands, indicating "Not here, I guess." He looks into the living-room and freezes. Inside,* LINDA, *unseen, is seated,* WILLY's *coat on her lap. She rises ominously and quietly and moves toward* HAPPY, *who backs up into the kitchen, afraid.*]

HAPPY: Hey, what're you doing up? [LINDA *says nothing but moves toward him implacably.*] Where's Pop? [*He keeps backing to the right, and now* LINDA *is in full view in the doorway to the living-room.*] Is he sleeping?

LINDA: Where were you?

HAPPY: [*Trying to laugh it off.*] We met two girls, Mom, very fine types. Here, we brought you some flowers. [*Offering them to her.*] Put them in your room, Ma. [*She knocks them to the floor at* BIFF's *feet. He has now come inside and closed the door behind him. She stares at* BIFF, *silent.*] Now what'd you do that for? Mom, I want you to have some flowers—

LINDA: [*Cutting* HAPPY *off, violently to* BIFF.] Don't you care whether he lives or dies?

HAPPY: [*Going to the stairs.*] Come upstairs, Biff.

BIFF: [*With a flare of disgust, to* HAPPY.] Go away from me! [*To* LINDA.] What do you mean, lives or dies? Nobody's dying around here, pal.

LINDA: Get out of my sight! Get out of here!

BIFF: I wanna see the boss.

LINDA: You're not going near him!

BIFF: Where is he? [*He moves into the living-room and* LINDA *follows.*]

LINDA: [*Shouting after* BIFF.] You invite him for dinner. He looks forward to it all

day— [BIFF *appears in his parents' bedroom, looks around and exits.*] —and then
  you desert him there. There's no stranger you'd do that to!
HAPPY: Why? He had a swell time with us. Listen, when I— [LINDA *comes back into
  the kitchen.*] —desert him I hope I don't outlive the day!
LINDA: Get out of here!
HAPPY: Now look, Mom . . .
LINDA: Did you have to go to women tonight? You and your lousy rotten whores!

> [BIFF *re-enters the kitchen.*]

HAPPY: Mom, all we did was follow Biff around trying to cheer him up! [*To* BIFF.]
  Boy, what a night you gave me!
LINDA: Get out of here, both of you, and don't come back! I don't want you tor-
  menting him any more. Go on now, get your things together! [*To* BIFF.] You
  can sleep in his apartment. [*She starts to pick up the flowers and stops herself.*]
  Pick up this stuff, I'm not your maid any more. Pick it up, you bum, you!
  [HAPPY *turns his back to her in refusal.* BIFF *slowly moves over and gets down on
  his knees, picking up the flowers.*] You're a pair of animals! Not one, not another
  living soul would have had the cruelty to walk out on that man in a
  restaurant!
BIFF: [*Not looking at her.*] Is that what he said?
LINDA: He didn't have to say anything. He was so humiliated he nearly limped
  when he came in.
HAPPY: But, Mom, he had a great time with us—
BIFF: [*Cutting him off violently.*] Shut up!

> [*Without another word,* HAPPY *goes upstairs.*]

LINDA: You! You didn't even go in to see if he was all right!
BIFF: [*Still on the floor in front of* LINDA, *the flowers in his hand; with self-loathing.*] No.
  Didn't. Didn't do a damned thing. How do you like that, heh? Left him bab-
  bling in a toilet.
LINDA: You louse. You . . .
BIFF: Now you hit it on the nose! [*He gets up, throws the flowers in the wastebasket.*]
  The scum of the earth, and you're looking at him!
LINDA: Get out of here!
BIFF: I gotta talk to the boss, Mom. Where is he?
LINDA: You're not going near him. Get out of this house!
BIFF: [*With absolute assurance, determination.*] No. We're gonna have an abrupt
  conversation, him and me.
LINDA: You're not talking to him! [*Hammering is heard from outside the house, off
  right.* BIFF *turns toward the noise. Suddenly pleading.*] Will you please leave him
  alone?
BIFF: What's he doing out there?
LINDA: He's planting the garden!
BIFF: [*Quietly.*] Now? Oh, my God!

> [BIFF *moves outside,* LINDA *following. The light dies down on them and comes
> up on the center of the apron as* WILLY *walks into it. He is carrying a flashlight,*

a hoe, and a handful of seed packets. He raps the top of the hoe sharply to fix it firmly, and then moves to the left, measuring off the distance with his foot. He holds the flashlight to look at the seed packets, reading off the instructions. He is in the blue of night.]

WILLY: Carrots . . . quarter-inch apart. Rows . . . one-foot rows. [*He measures it off.*] One foot. [*He puts down a package and measures off.*] Beets. [*He puts down another package and measures again.*] Lettuce. [*He reads the package, puts it down.*] One foot— [*He breaks off as* BEN *appears at the right and moves slowly down to him.*] What a proposition, ts, ts. Terrific, terrific. 'Cause she's suffered, Ben, the woman has suffered. You understand me? A man can't go out the way he came in, Ben, a man has got to add up to something. You can't, you can't— [BEN *moves toward him as though to interrupt.*] You gotta consider, now. Don't answer so quick. Remember, it's a guaranteed twenty-thousand-dollar proposition. Now look, Ben, I want you to go through the ins and outs of this thing with me. I've got nobody to talk to, Ben, and the woman has suffered, you hear me?

BEN: [*Standing still, considering.*] What's the proposition?

WILLY: It's twenty thousand dollars on the barrelhead. Guaranteed, gilt-edged, you understand?

BEN: You don't want to make a fool of yourself. They might not honor the policy.

WILLY: How can they dare refuse? Didn't I work like a coolie to meet every premium on the nose? And now they don't pay off! Impossible!

BEN: It's called a cowardly thing, William.

WILLY: Why? Does it take more guts to stand here the rest of my life ringing up a zero?

BEN: [*Yielding.*] That's a point, William. [*He moves, thinking, turns.*] And twenty thousand—that *is* something one can feel with the hand, it is there.

WILLY: [*Now assured, with rising power.*] Oh, Ben, that's the whole beauty of it! I see it like a diamond, shining in the dark, hard and rough, that I can pick up and touch in my hand. Not like—like an appointment! This would not be another damned-fool appointment, Ben, and it changes all the aspects. Because he thinks I'm nothing, see, and so he spites me. But the funeral— [*Straightening up.*] Ben, that funeral will be massive! They'll come from Maine, Massachusetts, Vermont, New Hampshire! All the old-timers with the strange license plates—that boy will be thunder-struck, Ben, because he never realized—I am known! Rhode Island, New York, New Jersey—I am known, Ben, and he'll see it with his eyes once and for all. He'll see what I am, Ben! He's in for a shock, that boy!

BEN: [*Coming down to the edge of the garden.*] He'll call you a coward.

WILLY: [*Suddenly fearful.*] No, that would be terrible.

BEN: Yes. And a damned fool.

WILLY: No, no, he mustn't, I won't have that! [*He is broken and desperate.*]

BEN: He'll hate you, William.

[*The gay music of the Boys is heard.*]

WILLY: Oh, Ben, how do we get back to all the great times? Used to be so full of light, and comradeship, the sleigh-riding in winter, and the ruddiness on his cheeks. And always some kind of good news coming up, always something nice coming up ahead. And never even let me carry the valises in the house, and simonizing, simonizing that little red car! Why, why can't I give him something and not have him hate me?

BEN: Let me think about it. [*He glances at his watch.*] I still have a little time. Remarkable proposition, but you've got to be sure you're not making a fool of yourself.

[BEN *drifts off upstage and goes out of sight.* BIFF *comes down from the left.*]

WILLY: [*Suddenly conscious of* BIFF, *turns and looks up at him, then begins picking up the packages of seeds in confusion.*] Where the hell is that seed? [*Indignantly.*] You can't see nothing out here! They boxed in the whole goddam neighborhood!

BIFF: There are people all around here. Don't you realize that?

WILLY: I'm busy. Don't bother me.

BIFF: [*Taking the hoe from* WILLY.] I'm saying good-by to you, Pop. [WILLY *looks at him, silent, unable to move.*] I'm not coming back any more.

WILLY: You're not going to see Oliver tomorrow?

BIFF: I've got no appointment, Dad.

WILLY: He put his arm around you, and you've got no appointment?

BIFF: Pop, get this now, will you? Everytime I've left it's been a fight that sent me out of here. Today I realized something about myself and I tried to explain it to you and I—I think I'm just not smart enough to make any sense out of it for you. To hell with whose fault it is or anything like that. [*He takes* WILLY'*s arm.*] Let's just wrap it up, heh? Come on in, we'll tell Mom. [*He gently tries to pull* WILLY *to left.*]

WILLY: [*Frozen, immobile, with guilt in his voice.*] No, I don't want to see her.

BIFF: Come on! [*He pulls again, and* WILLY *tries to pull away.*]

WILLY: [*Highly nervous.*] No, no, I don't want to see her.

BIFF: [*Tries to look into* WILLY'*s face, as if to find the answer there.*] Why don't you want to see her?

WILLY: [*More harshly now.*] Don't bother me, will you?

BIFF: What do you mean, you don't want to see her? You don't want them calling you yellow, do you? This isn't your fault; it's me, I'm a bum. Now come inside! [WILLY *strains to get away.*] Did you hear what I said to you?

[WILLY *pulls away and quickly goes by himself into the house.* BIFF *follows.*]

LINDA: [*To* WILLY.] Did you plant, dear?

BIFF: [*At the door, to* LINDA.] All right, we had it out. I'm going and I'm not writing any more.

LINDA: [*Going to* WILLY *in the kitchen.*] I think that's the best way, dear. 'Cause there's no use drawing it out, you'll just never get along.

[WILLY *doesn't respond.*]

BIFF: People ask where I am and what I'm doing, you don't know, and you don't care. That way it'll be off your mind and you can start brightening up again. All right? That clears it, doesn't it? [WILLY *is silent, and* BIFF *goes to him.*] You gonna wish me luck, scout? [*He extends his hand.*] What do you say?

LINDA: Shake his hand, Willy.

WILLY: [*Turning to her, seething with hurt.*] There's no necessity to mention the pen at all, y'know.

BIFF: [*Gently.*] I've got no appointment, Dad.

WILLY: [*Erupting fiercely.*] He put his arm around . . . ?

BIFF: Dad, you're never going to see what I am, so what's the use of arguing? If I strike oil I'll send you a check. Meantime forget I'm alive.

WILLY: [*To* LINDA.] Spite, see?

BIFF: Shake hands, Dad.

WILLY: Not my hand.

BIFF: I was hoping not to go this way.

WILLY: Well, this is the way you're going. Good-by. [BIFF *looks at him a moment, then turns sharply and goes to the stairs.* WILLY *stops him with.*] May you rot in hell if you leave this house!

BIFF: [*Turning.*] Exactly what is it that you want from me?

WILLY: I want you to know, on the train, in the mountains, in the valleys, wherever you go, that you cut down your life for spite!

BIFF: No, no.

WILLY: Spite, spite, is the word of your undoing! And when you're down and out, remember what did it. When you're rotting somewhere beside the railroad tracks, remember, and don't you dare blame it on me!

BIFF: I'm not blaming it on you!

WILLY: I won't take the rap for this, you hear?

[HAPPY *comes down the stairs and stands on the bottom step, watching.*]

BIFF: That's just what I'm telling you!

WILLY: [*Sinking into a chair at the table, with full accusation.*] You're trying to put a knife in me—don't think I don't know what you're doing!

BIFF: All right, phony! Then let's lay it on the line. [*He whips the rubber tube out of his pocket and puts it on the table.*]

HAPPY: You crazy—

LINDA: Biff!

[*She moves to grab the hose, but* BIFF *holds it down with his hand.*]

BIFF: Leave it there! Don't move it!

WILLY: [*Not looking at it.*] What is that?

BIFF: You know goddam well what that is.

WILLY: [*Caged, wanting to escape.*] I never saw that.

BIFF: You saw it. The mice didn't bring it into the cellar! What is this supposed to do, make a hero out of you? This supposed to make me sorry for you?

WILLY: Never heard of it.

BIFF: There'll be no pity for you, you hear it? No pity!

WILLY: [*To* LINDA.] You hear the spite!

BIFF: No, you're going to hear the truth—what you are and what I am!

LINDA: Stop it!

WILLY: Spite!

HAPPY: [*Coming down toward* BIFF.] You cut it now!

BIFF: [*To* HAPPY.] The man don't know who we are! The man is gonna know! [*To* WILLY.] We never told the truth for ten minutes in this house!

HAPPY: We always told the truth!

BIFF: [*Turning on him.*] You big blow, are you the assistant buyer? You're one of the two assistants to the assistant, aren't you?

HAPPY: Well, I'm practically—

BIFF: You're practically full of it! We all are! And I'm through with it. [*To* WILLY.] Now hear this, Willy, this is me.

WILLY: I know you!

BIFF: You know why I had no address for three months? I stole a suit in Kansas City and I was in jail. [*To* LINDA, *who is sobbing.*] Stop crying. I'm through with it.

[LINDA *turns away from them, her hands covering her face.*]

WILLY: I suppose that's my fault!

BIFF: I stole myself out of every good job since high school!

WILLY: And whose fault is that?

BIFF: And I never got anywhere because you blew me so full of hot air I could never stand taking orders from anybody! That's whose fault it is!

WILLY: I hear that!

LINDA: Don't, Biff!

BIFF: It's goddam time you heard that! I had to be boss big shot in two weeks, and I'm through with it!

WILLY: Then hang yourself! For spite, hang yourself!

BIFF: No! Nobody's hanging himself, Willy! I ran down eleven flights with a pen in my hand today. And suddenly I stopped, you hear me? And in the middle of that office building, do you hear this? I stopped in the middle of that building and I saw—the sky. I saw the things that I love in this world. The work and the food and time to sit and smoke. And I looked at the pen and said to myself, what the hell am I grabbing this for? Why am I trying to become what I don't want to be? What am I doing in an office, making a contemptuous, begging fool of myself, when all I want is out there, waiting for me the minute I say I know who I am! Why can't I say that, Willy? [*He tries to make* WILLY *face him, but* WILLY *pulls away and moves to the left.*]

WILLY: [*With hatred, threateningly.*] The door of your life is wide open!

BIFF: Pop! I'm a dime a dozen, and so are you!

WILLY: [*Turning on him now in an uncontrolled outburst.*] I am not a dime a dozen! I am Willy Loman, and you are Biff Loman!

[BIFF *starts for* WILLY, *but is blocked by* HAPPY. *In his fury,* BIFF *seems on the verge of attacking his father.*]

BIFF: I am not a leader of men, Willy, and neither are you. You were never anything but a hard-working drummer who landed in the ash can like all the rest of them! I'm one dollar an hour, Willy! I tried seven states and couldn't raise it. A buck an hour! Do you gather my meaning? I'm not bringing home any prizes any more, and you're going to stop waiting for me to bring them home!

WILLY: [*Directly to* BIFF.] You vengeful, spiteful mut!

[BIFF *breaks from* HAPPY. WILLY, *in fright, starts up the stairs.* BIFF *grabs him.*]

BIFF: [*At the peak of his fury.*] Pop, I'm nothing! I'm nothing, Pop. Can't you understand that? There's no spite in it any more. I'm just what I am, that's all.

[BIFF'*s fury has spent itself, and he breaks down, sobbing, holding on to* WILLY, *who dumbly fumbles for* BIFF'*s face.*]

WILLY: [*Astonished.*] What're you doing? What're you doing? [*To* LINDA.] Why is he crying?

BIFF: [*Crying, broken.*] Will you let me go, for Christ's sake? Will you take that phony dream and burn it before something happens? [*Struggling to contain himself, he pulls away and moves to the stairs.*] I'll go in the morning. Put him— put him to bed. [*Exhausted,* BIFF *moves up the stairs to his room.*]

WILLY: [*After a long pause, astonished, elevated.*] Isn't that—isn't that remarkable? Biff—he likes me!

LINDA: He loves you, Willy!

HAPPY: [*Deeply moved.*] Always did, Pop.

WILLY: Oh, Biff! [*Staring wildly.*] He cried! Cried to me. [*He is choking with his love, and now cries out his promise.*] That boy—that boy is going to be magnificent!

[BEN *appears in the light just outside the kitchen.*]

BEN: Yes, outstanding, with twenty thousand behind him.

LINDA: [*Sensing the racing of his mind, fearfully, carefully.*] Now come to bed, Willy. It's all settled now.

WILLY: [*Finding it difficult not to rush out of the house.*] Yes, we'll sleep. Come on. Go to sleep, Hap.

BEN: And it does take a great kind of man to crack the jungle.

[*In accents of dread,* BEN'*s idyllic music starts up.*]

HAPPY: [*His arm around* LINDA.] I'm getting married, Pop, don't forget it. I'm changing everything. I'm gonna run that department before the year is up. You'll see, Mom. [*He kisses her.*]

BEN: The jungle is dark but full of diamonds, Willy.

[WILLY *turns, moves, listening to* BEN.]

LINDA: Be good. You're both good boys, just act that way, that's all.

HAPPY: 'Night, Pop. [*He goes upstairs.*]

LINDA: [*To* WILLY.] Come, dear.

BEN: [*With greater force.*] One must go in to fetch a diamond out.

WILLY: [*To* LINDA, *as he moves slowly along the edge of the kitchen, toward the door.*] I just want to get settled down, Linda. Let me sit alone for a little.

LINDA: [*Almost uttering her fear.*] I want you upstairs.

WILLY: [*Taking her in his arms.*] In a few minutes, Linda. I couldn't sleep right now. Go on, you look awful tired. [*He kisses her.*]

BEN: Not like an appointment at all. A diamond is rough and hard to the touch.

WILLY: Go on now. I'll be right up.

LINDA: I think this is the only way, Willy.

WILLY: Sure, it's the best thing.

BEN: Best thing!

WILLY: The only way. Everything is gonna be—go on, kid, get to bed. You look so tired.

LINDA: Come right up.

WILLY: Two minutes. [LINDA *goes into the living-room, then reappears in her bedroom.* WILLY *moves just outside the kitchen door.*] Loves me. [*Wonderingly.*] Always loved me. Isn't that a remarkable thing? Ben, he'll worship me for it!

BEN: [*With promise.*] It's dark there, but full of diamonds.

WILLY: Can you imagine that magnificence with twenty thousand dollars in his pocket?

LINDA: [*Calling from her room.*] Willy! Come up!

WILLY: [*Calling into the kitchen.*] Yes! Yes. Coming! It's very smart, you realize that, don't you, sweetheart? Even Ben sees it. I gotta go, baby. 'By! 'By! [*Going over to* BEN, *almost dancing.*] Imagine? When the mail comes he'll be ahead of Bernard again!

BEN: A perfect proposition all around.

WILLY: Did you see how he cried to me? Oh, if I could kiss him, Ben!

BEN: Time, William, time!

WILLY: Oh, Ben, I always knew one way or another we were gonna make it, Biff and I!

BEN: [*Looking at his watch.*] The boat. We'll be late. [*He moves slowly off into the darkness.*]

WILLY: [*Elegiacally, turning to the house.*] Now when you kick off, boy, I want a seventy-yard boot, and get right down the field under the ball, and when you hit, hit low and hit hard, because it's important, boy. [*He swings around and faces the audience.*] There's all kinds of important people in the stands, and the first thing you know . . . [*Suddenly realizing he is alone.*] Ben! Ben, where do I . . . ? [*He makes a sudden movement of search.*] Ben, how do I . . . ?

LINDA: [*Calling.*] Willy, you coming up?

WILLY: [*Uttering a gasp of fear, whirling about as if to quiet her.*] Sh! [*He turns around as if to find his way; sounds, faces, voices, seem to be swarming in upon him and he flicks at them, crying.*] Sh! Sh! [*Suddenly music, faint and high, stops him. It rises in intensity, almost to an unbearable scream. He goes up and down on his toes, and rushes off around the house.*] Shhh!

LINDA: Willy? [*There is no answer.* LINDA *waits.* BIFF *gets up off his bed. He is still in his clothes.* HAPPY *sits up.* BIFF *stands listening.*] [*With real fear.*] Willy, answer me! Willy! [*There is the sound of a car starting and moving away at full speed.*] No!

BIFF: [*Rushing down the stairs.*] Pop!

[*As the car speeds off, the music crashes down in a frenzy of sound, which becomes the soft pulsation of a single cello string.* BIFF *slowly returns to his bedroom. He and* HAPPY *gravely don their jackets.* LINDA *slowly walks out of her room. The music has developed into a dead march. The leaves of day are appearing over everything.* CHARLEY *and* BERNARD, *somberly dressed, appear and knock on the kitchen door.* BIFF *and* HAPPY *slowly descend the stairs to the kitchen as* CHARLEY *and* BERNARD *enter. All stop a moment when* LINDA, *in clothes of mourning, bearing a little bunch of roses, comes through the draped doorway into the kitchen. She goes to* CHARLEY *and takes his arm. Now all move toward the audience, through the wall-line of the kitchen. At the limit of the apron,* LINDA *lays down the flowers, kneels, and sits back on her heels. All stare down at the grave.*]

REQUIEM

CHARLEY: It's getting dark, Linda.

[LINDA *doesn't react. She stares at the grave.*]

BIFF: How about it, Mom? Better get some rest, heh? They'll be closing the gate soon.

[LINDA *makes no move. Pause.*]

HAPPY: [*Deeply angered.*] He had no right to do that. There was no necessity for it. We would've helped him.

CHARLEY [*Grunting.*] Hmmm.

BIFF: Come along, Mom.

LINDA: Why didn't anybody come?

CHARLEY: It was a very nice funeral.

LINDA: But where are all the people he knew? Maybe they blame him.

CHARLEY: Naa. It's a rough world, Linda. They wouldn't blame him.

LINDA: I can't understand it. At this time especially. First time in thirty-five years we were just about free and clear. He only needed a little salary. He was even finished with the dentist.

CHARLEY: No man only needs a little salary.

LINDA: I can't understand it.

BIFF: There were a lot of nice days. When he'd come home from a trip; or on Sundays, making the stoop; finishing the cellar; putting on the new porch; when he built the extra bathroom; and put up the garage. You know something, Charley, there's more of him in that front stoop than in all the sales he ever made.

CHARLEY: Yeah. He was a happy man with a batch of cement.

LINDA: He was so wonderful with his hands.

BIFF: He had the wrong dreams. All, all, wrong.

HAPPY: [*Almost ready to fight* BIFF.] Don't say that!

BIFF: He never knew who he was.

CHARLEY: [*Stopping* HAPPY's *movement and reply. To* BIFF.] Nobody dast blame this man. You don't understand: Willy was a salesman. And for a salesman, there is no rock bottom to the life. He don't put a bolt to a nut, he don't tell you the law or give you medicine. He's a man way out there in the blue, riding on a smile and a shoeshine. And when they start not smiling back—that's an earthquake. And then you get yourself a couple of spots on your hat, and you're finished. Nobody dast blame this man. A salesman is got to dream, boy. It comes with the territory.

BIFF: Charley, the man didn't know who he was.

HAPPY: [*Infuriated.*] Don't say that!

BIFF: Why don't you come with me, Happy?

HAPPY: I'm not licked that easily. I'm staying right in this city, and I'm gonna beat this racket! [*He looks at* BIFF, *his chin set.*] The Loman Brothers!

BIFF: I know who I am, kid.

HAPPY: All right, boy. I'm gonna show you and everybody else that Willy Loman did not die in vain. He had a good dream. It's the only dream you can have— to come out number-one-man. He fought it out here, and this is where I'm gonna win it for him.

BIFF: [*With a hopeless glance at* HAPPY, *bends toward his mother.*] Let's go, Mom.

LINDA: I'll be with you in a minute. Go on, Charley. [*He hesitates.*] I want to, just for a minute. I never had a chance to say good-by. [CHARLEY *moves away, followed by* HAPPY. BIFF *remains a slight distance up and left of* LINDA. *She sits there, summoning herself. The flute begins, not far away, playing behind her speech.*] Forgive me, dear. I can't cry. I don't know what it is, but I can't cry. I don't understand it. Why did you ever do that? Help me, Willy, I can't cry. It seems to me that you're just on another trip. I keep expecting you. Willy, dear, I can't cry. Why did you do it? I search and search and I search, and I can't understand it, Willy. I made the last payment on the house today. Today, dear. And there'll be nobody home. [*A sob rises in her throat.*] We're free and clear. [*Sobbing more fully, released.*] We're free. [BIFF *comes slowly toward her.*] We're free . . . We're free . . .

[BIFF *lifts her to her feet and moves out up right with her in his arms.* LINDA *sobs quietly.* BERNARD *and* CHARLEY *come together and follow them, followed by* HAPPY. *Only the music of the flute is left on the darkening stage as over the house the hard towers of the apartment buildings rise into sharp focus.*]

CURTAIN

1949

QUESTIONS

1. How does Willy Loman understand the role of a salesman? What ideals does he hold? How fully does he live up to his ideals? In what ways does he noticeably fall short of them?

2. How do other characters in the play understand Willy's profession? In what ways are their interpretations different from Willy's? How do the other characters evaluate Willy? What seems to be their definition of success? What is Willy's definition?

3. What kind of dream does Willy have? How does it relate to the larger idea of an "American Dream"? In what ways does Willy's dream distort the values of the American Dream? In what ways is Willy's life a critique of the American Dream?

4. Describe Willy's character. What character "flaws" does he have? How much of his situation seems to be his own fault? How do you respond to Charley's words "Nobody dast blame this man"? Do you agree? Why should we (or should we not) agree with Charley? Does Arthur Miller seem to agree? Does the text of the play seem to give a definitive answer, or is the text indeterminate?

5. How consistent is Willy's thinking? What bothers you most about his inconsistencies? Do his inconsistencies make him more or less believable as a stage character? Why?

6. How fully is Willy differentiated from the other characters? What does Uncle Ben do for the play? How does Bernard clarify other characters and further the play's themes?

7. Describe the character of Biff. Of Happy. How do you keep them straight from each other? What devices differentiate them?

8. How "dated" does the play seem now? What particular episodes or references seem especially tied to the late 1940s? How would you define a "traveling salesman" in mid twentieth-century America? What social attitudes toward that kind of character seem built into the play? How fully do you understand the social and ethical status of Willy's profession?

9. What symbolic role does hosiery play on stage? If you were producing the play, how would you stage Linda's mending scenes?

WRITING SUGGESTIONS

1. In your college library, do some research on the idea of the "American Dream." What variations does it have in different eras and among different social or ethnic groups? Write a three- or four-page paper defining the American Dream as it manifested itself just after World War II, and describe how Willy's goals relate to the idea.

2. Consider carefully the character of Linda—how she is presented on stage, her relationship to Willy, the attitudes she displays toward the other characters. How important is her role in the play? Pretend you are Linda at the play's end: write a three- to four-hundred word "honest" summary of Willy's life and her own, a soliloquy she might speak only to the audience about her own ideals and dreams in relation to Willy's life and values.

3. At the beginning, *Death of a Salesman* states its setting as "today." In what ways has "today" changed since 1949? Write a three- or four-page paper in which you describe the most important changes since 1949 that affect your interpretation of the action and characters in the play. What habits have changed? What attitudes? What values?

STUDENT WRITING

In the following student paper, Sherry Schnake examines how characterization, sets and setting, and plot all contribute to a thematic analysis of the destructive clash between the American Dream and everyday reality.

Dream of a Salesman

Sherry Schnake

Success is an integral part of the American dream. However, as Arthur Miller points out in <u>Death of a Salesman</u>, when that dream is not based in reality it can lead to destruction. Miller demonstrates this through the character of Willy Loman, a salesman consumed by illusion. "He had all the wrong dreams," says his son Biff at Willy's funeral. Biff is right: Willy's dreams ruined his life and the lives of everyone he loved.

As the play opens, Willy is introduced as a tired man and gains sympathy from the reader. However, questions begin to arise about his integrity the first time he slips into the past. In this scene, when he learns his son Biff has stolen a football, Willy praises Biff for his initiative. He also tells his boys that as long as a person is well liked, it doesn't matter if he does poorly in school. As the play progresses, Willy reveals through his words and actions that being well liked is the center of his life's philosophy. Because Willy cannot fulfill this philosophy, he lives in an illusion. In this dream he is popular and successful, even though in reality he is a failure.

Although the action of the play occurs in a twenty-four hour period, much more of Willy's life is revealed through his memories of the past, which he continually relives. The staging of the play supports the theme and symbolizes Willy's life. The scenery is all transparent, just as Willy and his dreams are. In scenes of the past there are no boundaries, for during this time Willy knew no limits. The fact that Willy fluctuates so freely from the past to the present emphasizes his inability to distinguish illusion from reality. The flashbacks also allow the reader or viewer to see how Willy and his sons' lives were shaped by the past.

Near the beginning of the play, Willy suggests that Biff ask his former employer Bill Oliver for a loan to start a business. Willy assures Biff he will get it because Oliver always liked Biff. However, after being rejected by Oliver, Biff confronts Willy in the climax of the play. At this point Biff tries to make Willy see that the dream they had both been living by was phony. Biff knows now that being well liked is not the key to success and happiness. He tries to make his father realize that that outlook has gotten them nowhere by exclaiming, "I'm a dime a dozen and so are you!"

However, the dream is too deeply engraved in Willy's mind. It is ironic that Biff's attempt to make his father rid himself of his false dream only convinces Willy that his dream was right. When Biff cries to Willy in frustration, all Willy can see is that Biff likes him.

Biff's discontent with Willy began many years earlier. Through Willy's memories we learn that when Biff failed math he went to Boston to ask Willy to convince his teacher to pass him. There Biff found Willy with another woman. At that moment, Biff's image of his father was shattered. Because the false values Willy planted in his son were shattered also, Biff became a lost soul and didn't fully understand himself until his later confrontation with Willy.

Biff isn't the only one whose life is ruined by Willy's dream. Biff's brother, Happy, is usually ignored by Willy and overshadowed by Biff. Nonetheless, Happy enthusiastically embraces Willy's goals and will not

let go of them even when they have failed his father. In this sense, he
is less fortunate than Biff because he is destined to repeat his
father's life.

Willy's illusions also adversely affect his wife, Linda. She was
always supportive of him, yet he took out his frustrations on her in
the form of angry words and disrespect. His desire to be well liked led
him to betray her through an affair.

Willy's dreams are further challenged by his neighbor Charley and his
brother, Ben. Charley is the antithesis of Willy: he is unconcerned
with popularity, and yet is successful. Ben represents something Willy
could never attain: he grabbed success in an almost physical way and
never looked back.

Willy dies still clinging to his illusion. In fact, he kills himself
so that Biff can use his insurance money to succeed in life. His
painfully small funeral, which concludes the play, is a pathetic
reminder that his dreams, indeed, were wrong.

Thus, Willy's life and death were devoted to false goals. Because of
his inability to see reality, he left Linda alone, he left Biff
disillusioned, and, sadly, he left Happy to follow in his footsteps,
chasing the wrong dreams.

28

CRITICAL CONTEXTS: A DRAMA CASEBOOK

Even more than other forms of literature, drama has a relatively stable canon—that is, a select group of plays that the theater community thinks of as especially worthy of continued and frequent performance. New plays often join this canon, of course, but theater companies worldwide tend to perform the same plays over and over, especially plays by Shakespeare, Ibsen, and Sophocles. The reasons are many, involving the plays' themes and continued appeal across times and cultures as well as their formal literary and theatrical accomplishments. But their repeated performance means that a relatively small number of plays becomes a lot better known than all the others and that a tradition of "talk" about those plays becomes more intense, more concentrated, and more developed. A lot of this talk is informal and local, resulting from the fact that people see plays communally—that is, people are present together for a performance—and then often compare their responses afterward. But more permanent and more formal records of such responses also come to exist; critics almost always review individual productions of plays in newspapers and magazines, on radio and television, and on the Internet. Often this record of evaluation concentrates primarily on the details of a particular performance. But because every production of a play involves a particular interpretation of the text, cumulative accounts of performance add up to a body of interpretive criticism—that is, analytical commentary about many aspects of the play as text and as performance.

Any oral or written text can provoke a lot of disagreement, partly because of the slippery nature of both verbal and visual language and partly because different readers and listeners bring different interests, experiences, and perspectives to the text. Differences in response may result from different circumstances and cultural assumptions—all readers and viewers are to some extent influenced by the times and places in which they live—or by matters of individual temperament and preference. But plays in particular, because of their many productions in varied locations by many different acting companies and directors, carry with them an especially varied accumulation of critical responses. New productions of a play often draw consciously on previous productions, sometimes imitating particular features and sometimes reacting against particular well-known interpretations. The many famous productions of *Hamlet*, for example, consciously compare themselves to each other in their emphasis on political intrigue, mother/son and father/son relationships, the hesitations or "indecisiveness" of the hero, and so forth, as do interpretations of the main character in *A Doll House*. As a reader of plays in a textbook like this, you may or may not bring to your reading an awareness of what others have thought historically about a particular play, but that body of material is available to you if you choose to use it as a way of getting additional perspectives on the text.

Local critics may respond immediately to individual performances, but professional literary scholars, critics, and theorists think and write a lot about individual plays, too—again, perhaps, because such a relatively small number of plays are repeatedly in public view. Sophocles' *Antigone*, for instance, attracts attention from a wide variety of perspectives— from Greek scholars, who view it in relation to classical myth or the particulars of the ancient Greek language; from philosophers, who may see in it examinations of classic ideas and ethical problems; from theater historians, who may think about it in relation to traditions of staging and visualization or the particulars of gestures and stage business; or from historians of rhetoric, who may consider the interactions between the chorus and the players in their separate interpretations of the action.

A bust of Sophocles

Some of these examinations supply vast historical learning in the service of investigating particulars of the play; others depend more on working out a particular critical theory or simply a coherent interpretation. You don't necessarily have to read this accumulated criticism to understand what happens in a text, and sometimes you may feel that some of the intense and careful labor is over your head or at least irrelevant to you. But often, too, reading what others have said, from whatever point of view, about a text can help you—by offering historical information that you hadn't known about or hadn't considered relevant, by pointing to problems or possibilities of interpretation you had not yet thought of, or by supporting a reading you had already arrived at. In a sense, reading published criticism is a lot like talking with your fellow students or being involved in a formal class discussion. In general, you shouldn't read "the critics" until after

A play should give you
something to think about.
When I see a play and
understand it the first time,
then I know it can't be much
good.

—T. S. ELIOT

you have read the complete text of a play at least once, just as you should read the text in full before you discuss it with others. That way, your own reactions are fresh and straightforward; and if you don't understand some things, you can always manage to "footnote" them later through discussion or through reading criticism.

Reading critics can be especially helpful when you write a paper. Critics will often guide you to crucial points of debate or to a particular place in the text that is a kind of crux for deciding on a particular interpretation. You will likely get the most help if you read several critics with different perspectives and different conclusions—not because more is better, but because you will see their differences and, more important, the *grounds* for their differences in the kinds of evidence they use. Their disagreements will likely be most useful to you as a new interpreter; critics can be useful to you not as "authorities" (you should never regard a particular interpretation as true just because it is published or written by somebody famous), but as indicators of what the issues are.

Often, when you just begin to think about what kind of paper you want to write, turning to the critics can help you see some of the critical issues in the play. Critics frequently disagree on the interpretation of particular issues or passages or even on what the issues really are, but reading them can make your own thoughts concrete, especially when you have just started sorting things out and cannot yet articulate your own feelings. Reacting to someone else's view, especially one that it is strongly argued and opposes your own tentative feelings, can help you articulate and can suggest a line of interpretation and argument for your own writing.

Sorting out the important issues can be complicated, and issues do shift from era to era and culture to culture. But often the arguments posed in one era continue to interest subsequent critics in whatever age and from whatever perspective. *Antigone* has a performance history going back more than twenty-four centuries, and over that time readers and viewers have recorded many thousands of responses. Here we reprint only a small sample, and all of these come from the twentieth century. But earlier views are often referred to and sometimes still argued about vehemently. The famous comments of the German philosopher G. W. F. Hegel (1770–1831), for example, continue to set the agenda for an astonishing number of interpreters. Many answer him directly; others use him to sharpen, complicate, or detail their views or simply to position themselves in some larger debate about specific issues in the play or about literary criticism or philosophy more generally.

In the following selections you will find various views about how to interpret crucial scenes and issues in *Antigone*. Especially prominent are questions of how to read the opinions of the chorus, how to interpret the character of Antigone, and what the flaws of Creon consist of. As you read the critics, pay attention to the way they argue—the kinds of textual evidence they use to back up their points and the ways they structure their arguments—as well as the main interpretive points they make.

If you use published criticism in your papers (or to back up a point you make in class or in an argument with a fellow student), you will want to work the phrasing into your paper or your conversation the way you have learned to do with lines or phrases from the text. Sometimes a particular critic can be especially helpful in focusing your thoughts

A production of *Antigone* (New York Shakespeare Festival, 1982)

because you disagree so clearly or so violently with what she or he says. In that case, you may well get a good paper out of a rebuttal in which you answer or attack the argument there point by point. Pitting one critic against another—that is, sorting out the exact issues that different interpreters disagree on and showing exactly what their differences consist of—can also be a good way to focus on your own distinctive contribution. But the point in your reading the critics is to *use* them for your own interpretive purposes, to make your responses more sensitive and resonant, to make you a better reader of this play, and to make you a better reader in general.

SOPHOCLES

Antigone[1]

CHARACTERS

ANTIGONE	HAEMON
ISMENE	TEIRESIAS
CHORUS OF THEBAN ELDERS	A MESSENGER
CREON	EURYDICE
A SENTRY	SECOND MESSENGER

The two sisters ANTIGONE *and* ISMENE *meet in front of the palace gates in Thebes.*

ANTIGONE: Ismene, my dear sister,
    whose father was my father, can you think of any
    of all the evils that stem from Oedipus
    that Zeus does not bring to pass for us, while we yet live?
5   No pain, no ruin, no shame, and no dishonor
    but I have seen it in our mischiefs,
    yours and mine.
    And now what is the proclamation that they tell of
    made lately by the commander, publicly,
10   to all the people? Do you know it? Have you heard it?
    Don't you notice when the evils due to enemies
    are headed towards those we love?
ISMENE: Not a word, Antigone, of those we love,
    either sweet or bitter, has come to me since the moment
15   when we lost our two brothers,
    on one day, by their hands dealing mutual death.
    Since the Argive army fled in this past night,

1. Translated by David Grene.

I know of nothing further, nothing
of better fortune or of more destruction.
ANTIGONE: *I* knew it well; that is why I sent for you   20
    to come outside the palace gates
    to listen to me, privately.
ISMENE: What is it? Certainly your words
    come of dark thoughts.
ANTIGONE: Yes, indeed; for those two brothers of ours, in burial   25
    has not Creon honored the one, dishonored the other?
    Eteocles, they say he has used justly
    with lawful rites and hid him in the earth
    to have his honor among the dead men there.
    But the unhappy corpse of Polyneices   30
    he has proclaimed to all the citizens,
    they say, no man may hide
    in a grave nor mourn in funeral,
    but leave unwept, unburied, a dainty treasure
    for the birds that see him, for their feast's delight.   35
    That is what, they say, the worthy Creon
    has proclaimed for you and me—for me, I tell you—
    and he comes here to clarify to the unknowing
    his proclamation; he takes it seriously;
    for whoever breaks the edict death is prescribed,   40
    and death by stoning publicly.
    There you have it; soon you will show yourself
    as noble both in your nature and your birth,
    or yourself as base, although of noble parents.
ISMENE: If things are as you say, poor sister, how   45
    can I better them? how loose or tie the knot?
ANTIGONE: Decide if you will share the work, the deed.
ISMENE: What kind of danger is there? How far have your thoughts gone?
ANTIGONE: Here is this hand. Will you help it to lift the dead man?
ISMENE: Would you bury him, when it is forbidden the city?   50
ANTIGONE: At least he is my brother—and yours, too,
    though you deny him. *I* will not prove false to him.
ISMENE: You are so headstrong. Creon has forbidden it.
ANTIGONE: It is not for him to keep me from my own.
ISMENE: O God!   55
    Consider, sister, how our father died,
    hated and infamous; how he brought to light
    his own offenses; how he himself struck out
    the sight of his two eyes;
    his own hand was their executioner.   60
    Then, mother and wife, two names in one, did shame
    violently on her life, with twisted cords.
    Third, our two brothers, on a single day,

poor wretches, themselves worked out their mutual doom.
65 Each killed the other, hand against brother's hand.
    Now there are only the two of us, left behind,
    and see how miserable our end shall be
    if in the teeth of law we shall transgress
    against the sovereign's decree and power.
70 You ought to realize we are only women,
    not meant in nature to fight against men,
    and that we are ruled, by those who are stronger,
    to obedience in this and even more painful matters.
    I do indeed beg those beneath the earth
75 to give me their forgiveness,
    since force constrains me,
    that I shall yield in this to the authorities.
    Extravagant action is not sensible.
ANTIGONE: I would not urge you now; nor if you wanted
80 to act would I be glad to have you with me.
    Be as you choose to be; but for myself
    I myself will bury him. It will be good
    to die, so doing. I shall lie by his side,
    loving him as he loved me; I shall be
85 a criminal—but a religious one.
    The time in which I must please those that are dead
    is longer than I must please those of this world.
    For there I shall lie forever. You, if you like,
    can cast dishonor on what the gods have honored.
90 ISMENE: I will not put dishonor on them, but
    to act in defiance of the citizenry,
    my nature does not give me means for that.
ANTIGONE: Let that be your excuse. But I will go
    to heap the earth on the grave of my loved brother.
95 ISMENE: How I fear for you, my poor sister!
ANTIGONE: Do not fear for me. Make straight your own path to destiny.
ISMENE: At least do not speak of this act to anyone else;
    bury him in secret; I will be silent, too.
ANTIGONE: Oh, oh, no! shout it out. I will hate you still worse
100 for silence—should you not proclaim it,
    to everyone.
ISMENE: You have a warm heart for such chilly deeds.
ANTIGONE: I know I am pleasing those I should please most.
ISMENE: *If* you can do it. But you are in love
105 with the impossible.
ANTIGONE: No. When I can no more, then I will stop.
ISMENE: It is better not to hunt the impossible
    at all.
ANTIGONE: If you will talk like this I will loathe you,

and you will be adjudged an enemy—   110
justly—by the dead's decision. Let me alone
and my folly with me, to endure this terror.
No suffering of mine will be enough
to make me die ignobly.
ISMENE: Well, if you will, go on.   115
    Know this; that though you are wrong to go, your friends
    are right to love you.
CHORUS: Sun's beam, fairest of all
        that ever till now shone
        on seven-gated Thebes;   120
        O golden eye of day, you shone
        coming over Dirce's stream;[2]
        You drove in headlong rout
        the whiteshielded man from Argos,
        complete in arms;   125
        his bits rang sharper
        under your urging.

        Polyneices brought him here
        against our land, Polyneices,
        roused by contentious quarrel;   130
        like an eagle he flew into our country,
        with many men-at-arms,
        with many a helmet crowned with horsehair.

        He stood above the halls, gaping with murderous lances,
        encompassing the city's   135
        seven-gated mouth.
        But before his jaws would be sated
        with our blood, before the fire,
        pine fed, should capture our crown of towers,
        he went hence—   140
        such clamor of war stretched behind his back,
        from his dragon foe, a thing he could not overcome.

        For Zeus, who hates the most
        the boasts of a great tongue,
        saw them coming in a great tide,   145
        insolent in the clang of golden armor.
        The god struck him down with hurled fire,
        as he strove to raise the victory cry,
        now at the very winning post.

        The earth rose to strike him as he fell swinging.   150
        In his frantic onslaught, possessed, he breathed upon us

2. River near Thebes.

with blasting winds of hate.
Sometimes the great god of war was on one side,
and sometimes he struck a staggering blow on the other;
155   the god was a very wheel horse on the right trace.

At seven gates stood seven captains,
ranged equals against equals, and there left
their brazen suits of armor
to Zeus, the god of trophies.
160   Only those two wretches born of one father and mother
set their spears to win a victory on both sides;
they worked out their share in a common death.

Now Victory, whose name is great, has come
to Thebes of many chariots
165   with joy to answer her joy,
to bring forgetfulness of these wars;
let us go to all the shrines of the gods
and dance all night long.
Let Bacchus lead the dance,
170   shaking Thebes to trembling.

But here is the king of our land,
Creon, son of Menoeceus;
in our new contingencies with the gods,
he is our new ruler.
175   He comes to set in motion some design—
what design is it? Because he has proposed
the convocation of the elders.
He sent a public summons for our discussion.
CREON: Gentlemen: as for our city's fortune,
180   the gods have shaken her, when the great waves broke,
but the gods have brought her through again to safety.
For yourselves, I chose you out of all and summoned you
to come to me, partly because I knew you
as always loyal to the throne—at first,
185   when Laïus was king, and then again
when Oedipus saved our city and then again
when he died and you remained with steadfast truth
to their descendants,
until they met their double fate upon one day,
190   striking and stricken, defiled each by a brother's murder.
Now here I am, holding all authority
and the throne, in virtue of kinship with the dead.
It is impossible to know any man—

I mean his soul, intelligence, and judgment—
until he shows his skill in rule and law.   195
I think that a man supreme ruler of a whole city,
if he does not reach for the best counsel for her,
but through some fear, keeps his tongue under lock and key,
him I judge the worst of any;
I have always judged so; and anyone thinking   200
another man more a friend than his own country,
I rate him nowhere. For my part, God is my witness,
who sees all, always, I would not be silent
if I saw ruin, not safety, on the way
towards my fellow citizens. I would not count   205
any enemy of my country as a friend—
because of what I know, that she it is
which gives us our security. If she sails upright
and we sail on her, friends will be ours for the making.
In the light of rules like these, I will make her greater still.   210

In consonance with this, I here proclaim
to the citizens about Oedipus' sons.
For Eteocles, who died this city's champion,
showing his valor's supremacy everywhere,
he shall be buried in his grave with every rite   215
of sanctity given to heroes under earth.
However, his brother, Polyneices, a returned exile,
who sought to burn with fire from top to bottom
his native city, and the gods of his own people;
who sought to taste the blood he shared with us,   220
and lead the rest of us to slavery—
I here proclaim to the city that this man
shall no one honor with a grave and none shall mourn.
You shall leave him without burial; you shall watch him
chewed up by birds and dogs and violated.   225
Such is my mind in the matter; never by me
shall the wicked man have precedence in honor
over the just. But he that is loyal to the state
in death, in life alike, shall have my honor.
CHORUS: Son of Menoeceus, so it is your pleasure   230
to deal with foe and friend of this our city.
To use any legal means lies in your power,
both about the dead and those of us who live.
CREON: I understand, then, you will do my bidding.
CHORUS: Please lay this burden on some younger man.   235
CREON: Oh, watchers of the corpse I have already.
CHORUS: What else, then, do your commands entail?

CREON: That you should not side with those who disagree.

CHORUS: There is none so foolish as to love his own death.

240 CREON: Yes, indeed those are the wages, but often greed
has with its hopes brought men to ruin.

[*The* SENTRY *whose speeches follow represents a remarkable experiment in Greek tragedy in the direction of naturalism of speech. He speaks with marked clumsiness, partly because he is excited and talks almost colloquially. But also the royal presence makes him think apparently that he should be rather grand in his show of respect. He uses odd bits of archaism or somewhat stale poetical passages, particularly in catch phrases. He sounds something like lower-level Shakespearean characters, e.g. Constable Elbow, with his uncertainty about benefactor and malefactor.*]

SENTRY: My lord, I will never claim my shortness of breath
is due to hurrying, nor were there wings in my feet.
I stopped at many a lay-by in my thinking;
245 I circled myself till I met myself coming back.
My soul accosted me with different speeches.
"Poor fool, yourself, why are you going somewhere
when once you get there you will pay the piper?"
"Well, aren't you the daring fellow! stopping again?
250 and suppose Creon hears the news from someone else—
don't you realize that you will smart for that?"
I turned the whole matter over. I suppose I may say
"I made haste slowly" and the short road became long.
However, at last I came to a resolve:
255 I must go to you; even if what I say
is nothing, really, still I shall say it.
I come here, a man with a firm clutch on the hope
that nothing can betide him save what is fated.

CREON: What is it then that makes you so afraid?

260 SENTRY: No, I want first of all to tell you my side of it.
I didn't do the thing; I never saw who did it.
It would not be fair for me to get into trouble.

CREON: You hedge, and barricade the thing itself.
Clearly you have some ugly news for me.

265 SENTRY: Well, you know how disasters make a man
hesitate to be their messenger.

CREON: For God's sake, tell me and get out of here!

SENTRY: Yes, I *will* tell you. Someone just now
buried the corpse and vanished. He scattered on the skin
270 some thirsty dust; he did the ritual,
duly, to purge the body of desecration.

CREON: What! Now who on earth could have done that?

SENTRY: I do not know. For there was there no mark
of axe's stroke nor casting up of earth

of any mattock; the ground was hard and dry, 275
unbroken; there were no signs of wagon wheels.
The doer of the deed had left no trace.
But when the first sentry of the day pointed it out,
there was for all of us a disagreeable
wonder. For the body had disappeared; 280
not in a grave, of course; but there lay upon him
a little dust as of a hand avoiding
the curse of violating the dead body's sanctity.
There were no signs of any beast nor dog
that came there; he had clearly not been torn. 285
There was a tide of bad words at one another,
guard taunting guard, and it might well have ended
in blows, for there was no one there to stop it.
Each one of us was the criminal but no one
manifestly so; all denied knowledge of it. 290
We were ready to take hot bars in our hands
or walk through fire, and call on the gods with oaths
that we had neither done it nor were privy
to a plot with anyone, neither in planning
nor yet in execution. 295
At last when nothing came of all our searching,
there was one man who spoke, made every head
bow to the ground in fear. For we could not
either contradict him nor yet could we see how
if we did what he said we would come out all right. 300
His word was that we must lay information
about the matter to yourself; we could not cover it.
This view prevailed and the lot of the draw chose me,
unlucky me, to win that prize. So here
I am. I did not want to come, 305
and you don't want to have me. I know that.
For no one likes the messenger of bad news.
CHORUS: My lord: I wonder, could this be God's doing?
This is the thought that keeps on haunting me.
CREON: Stop, before your words fill even me with rage, 310
that you should be exposed as a fool, and you so old.
For what you say is surely insupportable
when you say the gods took forethought for this corpse.
Is it out of excess of honor for the man,
for the favors that he did them, they should cover him? 315
This man who came to burn their pillared temples,
their dedicated offerings—and this land
and laws he would have scattered to the winds?
Or do you see the gods as honoring
criminals? This is not so. But what I am doing 320

now, and other things before this, some men disliked,
within this very city, and muttered against me,
secretly shaking their heads; they would not bow
justly beneath the yoke to submit to me.
325 I am very sure that these men hired others
to do this thing. I tell you the worse currency
that ever grew among mankind is money. This
sacks cities, this drives people from their homes,
this teaches and corrupts the minds of the loyal
330 to acts of shame. This displays
all kinds of evil for the use of men,
instructs in the knowledge of every impious act.
Those that have done this deed have been paid to do it,
but in the end they will pay for what they have done.

335 It is as sure as I still reverence Zeus—
know this right well—and I speak under oath—
if you and your fellows do not find this man
who with his own hand did the burial
and bring him here before me face to face,
340 your death alone will not be enough for me.
You will hang alive till you open up this outrage.
That will teach you in the days to come from what
you may draw profit—safely—from your plundering.
It's not from anything and everything
345 you can grow rich. You will find out
that ill-gotten gains ruin more than they save.
SENTRY: Have I your leave to say something—or should I
    just turn and go?
CREON: Don't you know your talk is painful enough already?
350 SENTRY: Is the ache in your ears or in your mind?
CREON: Why do you dissect the whereabouts of my pain?
SENTRY: Because it is he who did the deed who hurts
    your mind. I only hurt your ears that listen.
CREON: I am sure you have been a chatterbox since you were born.
355 SENTRY: All the same, I did not do this thing.
CREON: You might have done this, too, if you sold your soul.
SENTRY: It's a bad thing if one judges and judges wrongly.
CREON: You may talk as wittily as you like of judgment.
    Only, if you don't bring to light those men
360 who have done this, you will yet come to say
    that your wretched gains have brought bad consequences.
SENTRY: [Aside.] It were best that he were found, but whether
    the criminal is taken or he isn't—
    for that chance will decide—one thing is certain,

you'll never see me coming here again.   365
I never hoped to escape, never thought I could.
But now I have come off safe, I thank God heartily.
CHORUS: Many are the wonders, none
         is more wonderful than what is man.
         This it is that crosses the sea   370
         with the south winds storming and the waves swelling,
         breaking around him in roaring surf.
         He it is again who wears away
         the Earth, oldest of gods, immortal, unwearied,
         as the ploughs wind across her from year to year   375
         when he works her with the breed that comes from horses.

         The tribe of the lighthearted birds he snares
         and takes prisoner the races of savage beasts
         and the brood of the fish of the sea,
         with the close-spun web of nets.   380
         A cunning fellow is man. His contrivances
         make him master of beasts of the field
         and those that move in the mountains.
         So he brings the horse with the shaggy neck
         to bend underneath the yoke;   385
         and also the untamed mountain bull;
         and speech and windswift thought
         and the tempers that go with city living
         he has taught himself, and how to avoid
         the sharp frost, when lodging is cold   390
         under the open sky
         and pelting strokes of the rain.
         He has a way against everything,
         and he faces nothing that is to come
         without contrivance.   395
         Only against death
         can he call on no means of escape;
         but escape from hopeless diseases
         he has found in the depths of his mind.
         With some sort of cunning, inventive   400
         beyond all expectation
         he reaches sometimes evil,
         and sometimes good.

         If he honors the laws of earth,
         and the justice of the gods he has confirmed by oath,   405
         high is his city; no city
         has he with whom dwells dishonor
         prompted by recklessness.

410　　　He who is so, may he never
　　　　share my hearth!
　　　　may he never think my thoughts!

　　　　Is this a portent sent by God?
　　　　I cannot tell.
　　　　I know her. How can I say
415　　　that this is not Antigone?
　　　　Unhappy girl, child of unhappy Oedipus,
　　　　what is this?
　　　　Surely it is not you they bring here
　　　　as disobedient to the royal edict,
420　　　surely not you, taken in such folly.

SENTRY: She is the one who did the deed;
　　　we took her burying him. But where is Creon?

CHORUS: He is just coming from the house, when you most need him.

CREON: What is this? What has happened that I come
425　　so opportunely?

SENTRY: My lord, there is nothing
　　　that a man should swear he would never do.
　　　Second thoughts make liars of the first resolution.
　　　I would have vowed it would be long enough
430　　before I came again, lashed hence by your threats.
　　　But since the joy that comes past hope, and against all hope,
　　　is like no other pleasure in extent,
　　　I have come here, though I break my oath in coming.
　　　I bring this girl here who has been captured
435　　giving the grace of burial to the dead man.
　　　This time no lot chose me; this was my jackpot,
　　　and no one else's. Now, my lord, take her
　　　and as you please judge her and test her; I
　　　am justly free and clear of all this trouble.

440　CREON: This girl—how did you take her and from where?

SENTRY: She was burying the man. Now you know all.

CREON: Do you know what you are saying? Do you mean it?

SENTRY: She is the one; I saw her burying
　　　the dead man you forbade the burial of.
445　　Now, do I speak plainly and clearly enough?

CREON: How was she seen? How was she caught in the act?

SENTRY: This is how it was. When we came there,
　　　with those dreadful threats of yours upon us,
　　　we brushed off all the dust that lay upon
450　　the dead man's body, heedfully
　　　leaving it moist and naked.
　　　We sat on the brow of the hill, to windward,
　　　that we might shun the smell of the corpse upon us.

Each of us wakefully urged his fellow
with torrents of abuse, not to be careless   455
in this work of ours. So it went on,
until in the midst of the sky the sun's bright circle
stood still; the heat was burning. Suddenly
a squall lifted out of the earth a storm of dust,
a trouble in the sky. It filled the plain,   460
ruining all the foliage of the wood
that was around it. The great empty air
was filled with it. We closed our eyes, enduring
this plague sent by the gods. When at long last
we were quit of it, why, then we saw the girl.   465

She was crying out with the shrill cry
of an embittered bird
that sees its nest robbed of its nestlings
and the bed empty. So, too, when she saw
the body stripped of its cover, she burst out in groans,   470
calling terrible curses on those that had done that deed;
and with her hands immediately
brought thirsty dust to the body; from a shapely brazen
urn, held high over it, poured a triple stream
of funeral offerings; and crowned the corpse.   475
When we saw that, we rushed upon her and
caught our quarry then and there, not a bit disturbed.
We charged her with what she had done, then and the first time.
She did not deny a word of it—to my joy,
but to my pain as well. It is most pleasant   480
to have escaped oneself out of such troubles
but painful to bring into it those whom we love.
However, it is but natural for me
to count all this less than my own escape.
CREON: You there, that turn your eyes upon the ground,   485
    do you confess or deny what you have done?
ANTIGONE: Yes, I confess; I will not deny my deed.
CREON: [*To the* SENTRY.] You take yourself off where you like.
    You are free of a heavy charge.
    Now, Antigone, tell me shortly and to the point,   490
    did you know the proclamation against your action?
ANTIGONE: I knew it; of course I did. For it was public.
CREON: And did you dare to disobey that law?
ANTIGONE: Yes, it was not Zeus that made the proclamation;
    nor did Justice, which lives with those below, enact   495
    such laws as that, for mankind. I did not believe
    your proclamation had such power to enable
    one who will someday die to override

God's ordinances, unwritten and secure.
500   *They* are not of today and yesterday;
       they live forever; none knows when first they were.
       These are the laws whose penalties I would not
       incur from the gods, through fear of any man's temper.

       I know that I will die—of course I do—
505   even if you had not doomed me by proclamation.
       If I shall die before my time, I count that
       a profit. How can such as I, that live
       among such troubles, not find a profit in death?
       So for such as me, to face such a fate as this
510   is pain that does not count. But if I dared to leave
       the dead man, my mother's son, dead and unburied,
       that would have been real pain. The other is not.
       Now, if you think me a fool to act like this,
       perhaps it is a fool that judges so.
515   CHORUS: The savage spirit of a savage father
       shows itself in this girl. She does not know
       how to yield to trouble.
       CREON: I would have you know the most fanatic spirits
       fall most of all. It is the toughest iron,
520   baked in the fire to hardness, you may see
       most shattered, twisted, shivered to fragments.
       I know hot horses are restrained
       by a small curb. For he that is his neighbor's slave cannot
       be high in spirit. This girl had learned her insolence
525   before this, when she broke the established laws.
       But here is still another insolence
       in that she boasts of it, laughs at what she did.
       I swear I am no man and she the man
       if she can win this and not pay for it.
530   No; though she were my sister's child or closer
       in blood than all that my hearth god acknowledges
       as mine, neither she nor her sister should escape
       the utmost sentence—death. For indeed I accuse her,
       the sister, equally of plotting the burial.
535   Summon her. I saw her inside, just now,
       crazy, distraught. When people plot
       mischief in the dark, it is the mind which first
       is convicted of deceit. But surely I hate indeed
       the one that is caught in evil and then makes
540   that evil look like good.
       ANTIGONE: Do you want anything
       beyond my taking and my execution?
       CREON: Oh, nothing! Once I have that I have everything.
       ANTIGONE: Why do you wait, then? Nothing that you say

pleases me; God forbid it ever should. 545
So my words, too, naturally offend you.
Yet how could I win a greater share of glory
than putting my own brother in his grave?
All that are here would surely say that's true,
if fear did not lock their tongues up. A prince's power 550
is blessed in many things, not least in this,
that he can say and do whatever he likes.

CREON: You are alone among the people of Thebes
to see things in that way.

ANTIGONE: No, these do, too, 555
but keep their mouths shut for the fear of you.

CREON: Are you not ashamed to think so differently
from them?

ANTIGONE: There is nothing shameful in honoring my brother.

CREON: Was not he that died on the other side your brother? 560

ANTIGONE: Yes, indeed, of my own blood from father and mother.

CREON: Why then do you show a grace that must be impious
in *his* sight?

ANTIGONE: *That* other dead man
would never bear you witness in what you say. 565

CREON: Yes he would, if you put him only on equality
with one that was a desecrator.

ANTIGONE: It was his brother, not his slave, that died.

CREON: He died destroying the country the other defended.

ANTIGONE: The god of death demands these rites for both. 570

CREON: But the good man does not seek an *equal* share only,
with the bad.

ANTIGONE: Who knows
if in that other world this is true piety?

CREON: My enemy is still my enemy, even in death.

ANTIGONE: My nature is to join in love, not hate. 575

CREON: Go then to the world below, yourself, if you
must love. Love *them*. When I am alive no woman shall rule.

CHORUS: Here before the gates comes Ismene
shedding tears for the love of a brother.
A cloud over her brow casts shame 580
on her flushed face, as the tears wet
her fair cheeks.

CREON: You there, who lurked in my house, viper-like—
secretly drawing its lifeblood; I never thought
that I was raising two sources of destruction, 585
two rebels against my throne. Come tell me now,
will you, too, say you bore a hand in the burial
or will you swear that you know nothing of it?

ISMENE: I did it, yes—if she will say I did it
I bear my share in it, bear the guilt, too. 590

ANTIGONE: Justice will not allow you what you refused
and I will have none of your partnership.
ISMENE: But in your troubles I am not ashamed
to sail with you the sea of suffering.
595 ANTIGONE: Where the act was death, the dead are witnesses.
I do not love a friend who loves in words.
ISMENE: Sister, do not dishonor me, denying me
a common death with you, a common honoring
of the dead man.
600 ANTIGONE: Don't die with me, nor make your own
what you have never touched. I that die am enough.
ISMENE: What life is there for me, once I have lost you?
ANTIGONE: Ask Creon; all your care was on his behalf.
ISMENE: Why do you hurt me, when you gain nothing by it?
605 ANTIGONE: I am hurt by my own mockery—if I mock you.
ISMENE: Even now—what can I do to help you still?
ANTIGONE: Save yourself; I do not grudge you your escape.
ISMENE: I cannot bear it! Not even to share your death!
ANTIGONE: Life was your choice, and death was mine.
610 ISMENE: You cannot say I accepted that choice in silence.
ANTIGONE: You were right in the eyes of one party, I in the other.
ISMENE: Well then, the fault is equally between us.
ANTIGONE: Take heart; you are alive, but my life died
long ago, to serve the dead.
615 CREON: Here are two girls; I think that one of them
has suddenly lost her wits—the other was always so.
ISMENE: Yes, for, my lord, the wits that they are born with
do not stay firm for the unfortunate.
They go astray.
CREON: Certainly yours do,
620 when you share troubles with the troublemaker.
ISMENE: What life can be mine alone without her?
CREON: Do not
speak of *her*. She isn't, anymore.
ISMENE: Will you kill your son's wife to be?
CREON: Yes, there are other fields for him to plough.
625 ISMENE: Not with the mutual love of him and her.
CREON: I hate a bad wife for a son of mine.
ANTIGONE: Dear Haemon, how your father dishonors you.
CREON: There is too much of you—and of your marriage!
CHORUS: Will you rob your son of this girl?
630 CREON: Death—it is death that will stop the marriage for me.
CHORUS: Your decision it seems is taken: she shall die.
CREON: Both you and I have decided it. No more delay.

[*He turns to the* SERVANTS.]

Bring her inside, you. From this time forth,
these must be women, and not free to roam.
For even the stout of heart shrink when they see 635
the approach of death close to their lives.

CHORUS: Lucky are those whose lives
　　　know no taste of sorrow.
　　　But for those whose house has been shaken by God
　　　there is never cessation of ruin; 640
　　　it steals on generation after generation
　　　within a breed. Even as the swell
　　　is driven over the dark deep
　　　by the fierce Thracian winds
　　　I see the ancient evils of Labdacus' house 645
　　　are heaped on the evils of the dead.
　　　No generation frees another, some god
　　　strikes them down; there is no deliverance.
　　　Here was the light of hope stretched
　　　over the last roots of Oedipus' house, 650
　　　and the bloody dust due to the gods below
　　　has mowed it down—that and the folly of speech
　　　and ruin's enchantment of the mind.

　　　Your power, O Zeus, what sin of man can limit?
　　　All-aging sleep does not overtake it, 655
　　　nor the unwearied months of the gods; and you,
　　　for whom time brings no age,
　　　you hold the glowing brightness of Olympus.

　　　For the future near and far,
　　　and the past, this law holds good: 660
　　　nothing very great
　　　comes to the life of mortal man
　　　without ruin to accompany it.
　　　For Hope, widely wandering, comes to many of mankind
　　　as a blessing, 665
　　　but to many as the deceiver,
　　　using light-minded lusts;
　　　she comes to him that knows nothing
　　　till he burns his foot in the glowing fire.
　　　With wisdom has someone declared 670
　　　a word of distinction:
　　　that evil seems good to one whose mind
　　　the god leads to ruin,
　　　and but for the briefest moment of time
　　　is his life outside of calamity. 675
　　　Here is Haemon, youngest of your sons.

Does he come grieving
for the fate of his bride to be,
in agony at being cheated of his marriage?

680 CREON: Soon we will know that better than the prophets.
My son, can it be that you have not heard
of my final decision on your betrothed?
Can you have come here in your fury against your father?
Or have I your love still, no matter what I do?

685 HAEMON: Father, I am yours; with your excellent judgment
you lay the right before me, and I shall follow it.
No marriage will ever be so valued by me
as to override the goodness of your leadership.

CREON: Yes, my son, this should always be
690 in your very heart, that everything else
shall be second to your father's decision.
It is for this that fathers pray to have
obedient sons begotten in their halls,
that they may requite with ill their father's enemy
695 and honor his friend no less than he would himself.
If a man have sons that are no use to him,
what can one say of him but that he has bred
so many sorrows to himself, laughter to his enemies?
Do not, my son, banish your good sense
700 through pleasure in a woman, since you know
that the embrace grows cold
when an evil woman shares your bed and home.
What greater wound can there be than a false friend?
No. Spit on her, throw her out like an enemy,
705 this girl, to marry someone in Death's house.
I caught her openly in disobedience
alone out of all this city and I shall not make
myself a liar in the city's sight. No, I will kill her.
So let her cry if she will on the Zeus of kinship;
710 for if I rear those of my race and breeding
to be rebels, surely I will do so with those outside it.
For he who is in his household a good man
will be found a just man, too, in the city.
But he that breaches the law or does it violence
715 or thinks to dictate to those who govern him
shall never have my good word.
The man the city sets up in authority
must be obeyed in small things and in just
but also in their opposites.
720 I am confident such a man of whom I speak
will be a good ruler, and willing to be well ruled.
He will stand on his country's side, faithful and just,

in the storm of battle. There is nothing worse
than disobedience to authority.
It destroys cities, it demolishes homes;   725
it breaks and routs one's allies. Of successful lives
the most of them are saved by discipline.
So we must stand on the side of what is orderly;
we cannot give victory to a woman.
If we must accept defeat, let it be from a man;   730
we must not let people say that a woman beat us.
CHORUS: We think, if we are not victims of Time the Thief,
that you speak intelligently of what you speak.
HAEMON: Father, the natural sense that the gods breed
in men is surely the best of their possessions.   735
I certainly could not declare you wrong—
may I never know how to do so!—Still there might
be something useful that some other than you might think.
It is natural for me to be watchful on your behalf
concerning what all men say or do or find to blame.   740
Your face is terrible to a simple citizen;
it frightens him from words you dislike to hear.
But what *I* can hear, in the dark, are things like these:
the city mourns for this girl; they think she is dying
most wrongly and most undeservedly   745
of all womenkind, for the most glorious acts.
Here is one who would not leave her brother unburied,
a brother who had fallen in bloody conflict,
to meet his end by greedy dogs or by
the bird that chanced that way. Surely what she merits   750
is golden honor, isn't it? That's the dark rumor
that spreads in secret. Nothing I own
I value more highly, father, than your success.
What greater distinction can a son have than the glory
of a successful father, and for a father   755
the distinction of successful children?
Do not bear this single habit of mind, to think
that what you say and nothing else is true
A man who thinks that he alone is right,
or what he says, or what he *is* himself,   760
unique, such men, when opened up, are seen
to be quite empty. For a man, though he be wise,
it is no shame to learn—learn many things,
and not maintain his views too rigidly.
You notice how by streams in wintertime   765
the trees that yield preserve their branches safely,
but those that fight the tempest perish utterly.
The man who keeps the sheet of his sail tight

and never slackens capsizes his boat
770   and makes the rest of his trip keel uppermost.
Yield something of your anger, give way a little.
If a much younger man, like me, may have
a judgment, I would say it were far better
to be one altogether wise by nature, but,
775   as things incline not to be so, then it is good
also to learn from those who advise well.
CHORUS: My lord, if he says anything to the point,
    you should learn from him, and you, too, Haemon,
    learn from your father. Both of you
780   have spoken well.
CREON: Should we that are my age learn wisdom
    from young men such as he is?
HAEMON: Not learn injustice, certainly. If I am young,
    do not look at my years but what I do.
CREON: Is what you do to have respect for rebels?
785   HAEMON: I
    would not urge you to be scrupulous
    towards the wicked.
CREON: Is *she* not tainted by the disease of wickedness?
HAEMON: The entire people of Thebes says no to that.
790   CREON: Should the city tell me how I am to rule them?
HAEMON: Do you see what a young man's words these are of yours?
CREON: Must I rule the land by someone else's judgment
    rather than my own?
HAEMON: There is no city
    possessed by one man only.
795   CREON: Is not the city thought to be the ruler's?
HAEMON: You would be a fine dictator of a desert.
CREON: It seems this boy is on the woman's side.
HAEMON: If you are a woman—my care is all for you.
CREON: You villain, to bandy words with your own father!
800   HAEMON: I see your acts as mistaken and unjust.
CREON: Am I mistaken, reverencing my own office?
HAEMON: There is no reverence in trampling on God's honor.
CREON: Your nature is vile, in yielding to a woman.
HAEMON: You will not find me yield to what is shameful.
805   CREON: At least, your argument is all for her.
HAEMON: Yes, and for you and me—and for the gods below.
CREON: You will never marry her while her life lasts.
HAEMON: Then she must die—and dying destroy another.
CREON: Has your daring gone so far, to threaten me?
810   HAEMON: What threat is it to speak against empty judgments?
CREON: Empty of sense yourself, you will regret
    your schooling of me in sense.

HAEMON: If you were not
    my father, I would say you are insane.
CREON: You woman's slave, do not try to wheedle me.
HAEMON: You want to talk but never to hear and listen.   815
CREON: Is that so? By the heavens above you will not—
    be sure of that—get off scot-free, insulting,
    abusing me.

          [*He speaks to the* SERVANTS.]

              You people bring out this creature,
    this hated creature, that she may die before
    his very eyes, right now, next her would-be husband.   820
HAEMON: Not at my side! Never think that! She will not
    die by my side. But you will never again
    set eyes upon my face. Go then and rage
    with such of your friends as are willing to endure it.
CHORUS: The man is gone, my lord, quick in his anger.   825
    A young man's mind is fierce when he is hurt.
CREON: Let him go, and do and think things superhuman.
    But these two girls he shall not save from death.
CHORUS: Both of them? Do you mean to kill them both?
CREON: No, not the one that didn't do anything.   830
    You are quite right there.
CHORUS: And by what form of death do you mean to kill her?
CREON: I will bring her where the path is loneliest,
    and hide her alive in a rocky cavern there.
    I'll give just enough of food as shall suffice   835
    for a bare expiation, that the city may avoid pollution.
    In that place she shall call on Hades, god of death,
    in her prayers. That god only she reveres.
    Perhaps she will win from him escape from death
    or at least in that last moment will recognize   840
    her honoring of the dead is labor lost.
CHORUS: Love undefeated in the fight,
      Love that makes havoc of possessions,
      Love who lives at night in a young girl's soft cheeks,
      Who travels over sea, or in huts in the countryside—   845
      there is no god able to escape you
      nor anyone of men, whose life is a day only,
      and whom you possess is mad.

      You wrench the minds of just men to injustice,
      to their disgrace; this conflict among kinsmen   850
      it is you who stirred to turmoil.
      The winner is desire. She gleaming kindles
      from the eyes of the girl good to bed.
      Love shares the throne with the great powers that rule.

855   For the golden Aphrodite[3] holds her play there
and then no one can overcome her.

Here I too am borne out of the course of lawfulness
when I see these things, and I cannot control
the springs of my tears
860   when I see Antigone making her way
to her bed—but the bed
that is rest for everyone.

ANTIGONE: You see me, you people of my country,
as I set out on my last road of all,
865   looking for the last time on this light of this sun—
never again. I am alive but Hades who gives sleep to everyone
is leading me to the shores of Acheron,[4]
though I have known nothing of marriage songs
nor the chant that brings the bride to bed.
870   My husband is to be the Lord of Death.

CHORUS: Yes, you go to the place where the dead are hidden,
but you go with distinction and praise.
You have not been stricken by wasting sickness;
you have not earned the wages of the sword;
875   it was your own choice and alone among mankind
you will descend, alive,
to that world of death.

ANTIGONE: But indeed I have heard of the saddest of deaths—
of the Phrygian stranger,[5] daughter of Tantalus,
880   whom the rocky growth subdued, like clinging ivy.
The rains never leave her, the snow never fails,
as she wastes away. That is how men tell the story.
From streaming eyes her tears wet the crags;
most like to her the god brings me to rest.

885 CHORUS: Yes, but she was a god, and god born,
and you are mortal and mortal born.
Surely it is great renown
for a woman that dies, that in life and death
her lot is a lot shared with demigods.

890 ANTIGONE: You mock me. In the name of our fathers' gods
why do you not wait till I am gone to insult me?
Must you do it face to face?
My city! Rich citizens of my city!
You springs of Dirce, you holy groves of Thebes,

---

3. Goddess of love and beauty.   4. River in Hades.   5. Niobe, whose children were slain because of her boastfulness and who was herself turned into a stone on Mount Siphylus. Her tears became the mountain's streams.

famed for its chariots! I would still have you as my witnesses,   895
  with what dry-eyed friends, under what laws
  I make my way to my prison sealed like a tomb.
  Pity me. Neither among the living nor the dead
  do I have a home in common—
  neither with the living nor the dead.   900
CHORUS: You went to the extreme of daring
  and against the high throne of Justice
  you fell, my daughter, grievously.
  But perhaps it was for some ordeal of your father
  that you are paying requital.   905
ANTIGONE: You have touched the most painful of my cares—
  the pity for my father, ever reawakened,
  and the fate of all of our race, the famous Labdacids;
  the doomed self-destruction of my mother's bed
  when she slept with her own son,   910
  my father.
  What parents I was born of, God help me!
  To them I am going to share their home,
  the curse on me, too, and unmarried.
  Brother, it was a luckless marriage you made,   915
  and dying killed my life.
CHORUS: There *is* a certain reverence for piety.
  But for him in authority,
  he cannot see that authority defied;
  it is your own self-willed temper   920
  that has destroyed you.
ANTIGONE: No tears for me, no friends, no marriage. Brokenhearted
  I am led along the road ready before me.
  I shall never again be suffered
  to look on the holy eye of the day.   925
  But my fate claims no tears—
  no friend cries for me.
CREON: [*To the* SERVANTS.] Don't you know that weeping and wailing before
     death
  would never stop if one is allowed to weep and wail?
  Lead her away at once. Enfold her   930
  in that rocky tomb of hers—as I told you to.
  There leave her alone, solitary,
  to die if she so wishes
  or live a buried life in such a home;
  we are guiltless in respect of her, this girl.   935
  But living above, among the rest of us, this life
  she shall certainly lose.
ANTIGONE: Tomb, bridal chamber, prison forever

dug in rock, it is to you I am going
940 to join my people, that great number that have died,
whom in their death Persephone[6] received.
I am the last of them and I go down
in the worst death of all—for I have not lived
the due term of my life. But when I come
945 to that other world my hope is strong
that my coming will be welcome to my father,
and dear to you, my mother, and dear to you,
my brother deeply loved. For when you died,
with my own hands I washed and dressed you all,
950 and poured the lustral offerings on your graves.
And now, Polyneices, it was for such care of your body
that I have earned these wages.
Yet those who think rightly will think I did right
in honoring you. Had I been a mother
955 of children, and my husband been dead and rotten,
I would not have taken this weary task upon me
against the will of the city. What law backs me
when I say this? I will tell you:
If my husband were dead, I might have had another,
960 and child from another man, if I lost the first.
But when father and mother both were hidden in death
no brother's life would bloom for me again.
That is the law under which I gave you precedence,
my dearest brother, and that is why Creon thinks me
965 wrong, even a criminal, and now takes me
by the hand and leads me away,
unbedded, without bridal, without share
in marriage and in nurturing of children;
as lonely as you see me; without friends;
970 with fate against me I go to the vault of death
while still alive. What law of God have I broken?
Why should I still look to the gods in my misery?
Whom should I summon as ally? For indeed
because of piety I was called impious.
975 If this proceeding is good in the gods' eyes
I shall know my sin, once I have suffered.
But if Creon and his people are the wrongdoers
let their suffering be no worse than the injustice
they are meting out to me.
980 CHORUS: It is the same blasts, the tempests of the soul,
possess her.
CREON: Then for this her guards,

6. Abducted by Pluto, god of the underworld.

who are so slow, will find themselves in trouble.

ANTIGONE: [*Cries out.*] Oh, that word has come
    very close to death.

CREON: I will not comfort you   985
    with hope that the sentence will not be accomplished.

ANTIGONE: O my father's city, in Theban land,
    O gods that sired my race,
    I am led away, I have no more stay.
    Look on me, princes of Thebes,   990
    the last remnant of the old royal line;
    see what I suffer and who makes me suffer
    because I gave reverence to what claims reverence.

CHORUS: Danae suffered, too, when, her beauty lost, she gave
        the light of heaven in exchange for brassbound walls,   995
        and in the tomb-like cell was she hidden and held;
        yet she was honored in her breeding, child,
        and she kept, as guardian, the seed of Zeus
        that came to her in a golden shower.[7]
    But there is some terrible power in destiny   1000
    and neither wealth nor war
    nor tower nor black ships, beaten by the sea,
    can give escape from it.

    The hot-tempered son of Dryas,[8] the Edonian king,
    in fury mocked Dionysus,   1005
    who then held him in restraint
    in a rocky dungeon.
    So the terrible force and flower of his madness
    drained away. He came to know the god
    whom in frenzy he had touched with his mocking tongue,   1010
    when he would have checked the inspired women
    and the fire of Dionysus,
    when he provoked the Muses[9] that love the lyre.
    By the black rocks, dividing the sea in two,
    are the shores of the Bosporus, Thracian Salmydessus.   1015
    There the god of war who lives near the city
    saw the terrible blinding wound
    dealt by his savage wife
    on Phineus' two sons.
    She blinded and tore with the points of her shuttle,   1020
    and her bloodied hands, those eyes
    that else would have looked on her vengefully.

---

7. Danae was locked away because it was prophesized that her son would kill her father. Zeus infiltrated her cell as a shower of gold, impregnated her, and thus fathered Perseus, the child who fulfilled the prophecy.   8. Stricken with madness by Dionysus.   9. Nine sister goddesses of poetry, music, and the arts.

As they wasted away, they lamented
their unhappy fate that they were doomed
1025 to be born of a mother cursed in her marriage.
She traced her descent from the seed
of the ancient Erechtheidae.
In far-distant caves she was raised
among her father's storms, that child of Boreas
1030 quick as a horse, over the steep hills,
a daughter of the gods.[1]
But, my child, the long-lived Fates[2]
bore hard upon her, too.

[*Enter* TEIRESIAS, *the blind prophet, led by a* BOY.]

TEIRESIAS: My lords of Thebes, we have come here together,
1035   one pair of eyes serving us both. For the blind
  such must be the way of going, by a guide's leading.
CREON: What is the news, my old Teiresias?
TEIRESIAS: I will tell you; and you, listen to the prophet.
CREON: Never in the past have I turned from your advice.
1040 TEIRESIAS: And so you have steered well the ship of state.
CREON: I have benefited and can testify to that.
TEIRESIAS: Then realize you are on the razor edge
  of danger.
CREON: What can that be? I shudder to hear those words.
1045 TEIRESIAS: When you learn the signs recognized by my art
  you will understand.
  I sat at my ancient place of divination
  for watching the birds, where every bird finds shelter;
  and I heard an unwonted voice among them;
1050   they were horribly distressed, and screamed unmeaningly.
  I knew they were tearing each other murderously;
  the beating of their wings was a clear sign.
  I was full of fear; at once on all the altars,
  as they were fully kindled, I tasted the offerings,
1055   but the god of fire refused to burn from the sacrifice,
  and from the thighbones a dark stream of moisture
  oozed from the embers, smoked and sputtered.
  The gall bladder burst and scattered to the air
  and the streaming thighbones lay exposed
1060   from the fat wrapped round them—
  so much I learned from this boy here,
  the fading prophecies of a rite that failed.

---

1. King Phineus's second wife blinded the children of his first wife, whom Phineus had imprisoned in a cave.   2. Supernatural forces, usually represented as three old women, who determine the quality and length of life.

This boy here is my guide, as I am others'.
This is the city's sickness—and your plans are the cause of it.   1065
For our altars and our sacrificial hearths
are filled with the carrion meat of birds and dogs,
torn from the flesh of Oedipus' poor son.
So the gods will not take our prayers or sacrifice
nor yet the flame from the thighbones, and no bird
cries shrill and clear, so glutted   1070
are they with fat of the blood of the killed man.
Reflect on these things, son. All men
can make mistakes; but, once mistaken,
a man is no longer stupid nor accursed
who, having fallen on ill, tries to cure that ill,   1075
not taking a fine undeviating stand.
It is obstinacy that convicts of folly.
Yield to the dead man; do not stab him—
now he is gone—what bravery is this,
to inflict another death upon the dead?   1080
I mean you well and speak well for your good.
It is never sweeter to learn from a good counselor
than when he counsels to your benefit.
CREON: Old man, you are all archers, and I am your mark.
I must be tried by your prophecies as well.   1085
By the breed of you I have been bought and sold
and made a merchandise, for ages now.
But I tell you: make your profit from silver-gold
from Sardis and the gold from India
if you will. But this dead man you shall not hide   1090
in a grave, not though the eagles of Zeus should bear
the carrion, snatching it to the throne of Zeus itself.
Even so, I shall not so tremble at the pollution
to let you bury him.
        No, I am certain
no human has the power to pollute the gods.   1095
They fall, you old Teiresias, those men,
—so very clever—in a bad fall whenever
they eloquently speak vile words for profit.
TEIRESIAS: I wonder if there's a man who dares consider—
CREON: What do you mean? What sort of generalization   1100
is this talk of yours?
TEIRESIAS: How much the best of possessions is the ability
to listen to wise advice?
CREON: As I should imagine that the worst
injury must be native stupidity.   1105
TEIRESIAS: Now that is exactly where your mind is sick.
CREON: I do not like to answer a seer with insults.

TEIRESIAS: But you do, when you say my prophecies are lies.

CREON: Well,
1110   the whole breed of prophets certainly loves money.

TEIRESIAS: And the breed that comes from princes loves to take
   advantage—base advantage.

CREON: Do you realize
   you are speaking in such terms of your own prince?

TEIRESIAS: I know. But it is through me you have saved the city.

1115 CREON: You are a wise prophet, but what you love is wrong.

TEIRESIAS: You will force me to declare what should be hidden
   in my own heart.

CREON: Out with it—
   but only if your words are not for gain.

TEIRESIAS: They won't be for *your* gain—that I am sure of.

1120 CREON: But realize you will not make a merchandise
   of my decisions.

TEIRESIAS: And you must realize
   that you will not outlive many cycles more
   of this swift sun before you give in exchange
   one of your own loins bred, a corpse for a corpse,
1125   for you have thrust one that belongs above
   below the earth, and bitterly dishonored
   a living soul by lodging her in the grave;
   while one that belonged indeed to the underworld
   gods you have kept on this earth without due share
1130   of rites of burial, of due funeral offerings,
   a corpse unhallowed. With all of this you, Creon,
   have nothing to do, nor have the gods above.
   These acts of yours are violence, on your part.
   And in requital the avenging Spirits
1135   of Death itself and the gods' Furies shall
   after *your* deeds, lie in ambush for you, and
   in their hands you shall be taken cruelly.
   Now, look at this and tell me I was bribed
   to say it! The delay will not be long
1140   before the cries of mourning in your house,
   of men and women. All the cities will stir in hatred
   against you, because their sons in mangled shreds
   received their burial rites from dogs, from wild beasts
   or when some bird of the air brought a vile stink
1145   to each city that contained the hearths of the dead.
   These are the arrows that archer-like I launched—
   you vexed me so to anger—at your heart.
   You shall not escape their sting. You, boy,
   lead me away to my house, so he may discharge
1150   his anger on younger men; so may he come to know

to bear a quieter tongue in his head and a better
mind than that now he carries in him.

CHORUS: That was a terrible prophecy, my lord.
The man has gone. Since these hairs of mine grew white
from the black they once were, he has never spoken   1155
a word of a lie to our city.

CREON: I know, I know.
My mind is all bewildered. To yield is terrible.
But by opposition to destroy my very being
with a self-destructive curse must also be reckoned   1160
in what is terrible.

CHORUS: You need good counsel, son of Menoeceus,
and need to take it.

CREON: What must I do, then? Tell me; I shall agree.

CHORUS: The girl—go now and bring her up from her cave,   1165
and for the exposed dead man, give him his burial.

CREON: That is really your advice? You would have me yield.

CHORUS: And quickly as you may, my lord. Swift harms
sent by the gods cut off the paths of the foolish.

CREON: Oh, it is hard; I must give up what my heart   1170
would have me do. But it is ill to fight
against what must be.

CHORUS: Go now, and do this;
do not give the task to others.

CREON: I will go,   1175
just as I am. Come, servants, all of you;
take axes in your hands; away with you
to the place you see, there.
For my part, since my intention is so changed,
as I bound her myself, myself will free her.   1180
I am afraid it may be best, in the end
of life, to have kept the old accepted laws.

CHORUS: You of many names,[3] glory of the Cadmeian
bride, breed of loud thundering Zeus;
you who watch over famous Italy;   1185
you who rule where all are welcome in Eleusis;
in the sheltered plains of Deo—
O Bacchus that dwells in Thebes,
the mother city of Bacchanals,
by the flowing stream of Ismenus,   1190
in the ground sown by the fierce dragon's teeth.

You are he on whom the murky gleam of torches glares,
above the twin peaks of the crag

3. Refers to Dionysus.

where come the Corycean nymphs
1195   to worship you, the Bacchanals;
and the stream of Castalia has seen you, too;
and you are he that the ivy-clad
slopes of Nisaean hills,
and the green shore ivy-clustered,
1200   sent to watch over the roads of Thebes,
where the immortal Evoe chant[4] rings out.

It is Thebes which you honor most of all cities,
you and your mother both,
she who died by the blast of Zeus' thunderbolt.
1205   And now when the city, with all its folk,
is gripped by a violent plague,
come with healing foot, over the slopes of Parnassus,
over the moaning strait.
You lead the dance of the fire-breathing stars,
1210   you are master of the voices of the night.
True-born child of Zeus, appear,
my lord, with your Thyiad attendants,
who in frenzy all night long
dance in your house, Iacchus,
1215   dispenser of gifts.
MESSENGER: You who live by the house of Cadmus and Amphion,[5]
hear me. There is no condition of man's life
that stands secure. As such I would not
praise it or blame. It is chance that sets upright;
1220   it is chance that brings down the lucky and the unlucky,
each in his turn. For men, that belong to death,
there is no prophet of established things.
Once Creon was a man worthy of envy—
of my envy, at least. For he saved this city
1225   of Thebes from her enemies, and attained
the throne of the land, with all a king's power.
He guided it right. His race bloomed
with good children. But when a man forfeits joy
I do not count his life as life, but only
1230   a life trapped in a corpse.
Be rich within your house, yes greatly rich,
if so you will, and live in a prince's style.
If the gladness of these things is gone, I would not
give the shadow of smoke for the rest,
1235   as against joy.

4. Come forth, come forth!   5. A name for Thebes.

CHORUS: What is the sorrow of our princes
    of which you are the messenger?
MESSENGER: Death; and the living are guilty of their deaths.
CHORUS: But who is the murderer? Who the murdered? Tell us.
MESSENGER: Haemon is dead; the hand that shed his blood   1240
    was his very own.
CHORUS: Truly his own hand? Or his father's?
MESSENGER: His own hand, in his anger
    against his father for a murder.
CHORUS: Prophet, how truly you have made good your word!   1245
MESSENGER: These things are so; you may debate the rest.
    Here I see Creon's wife Eurydice
    approaching. Unhappy woman!
    Does she come from the house as hearing about her son
    or has she come by chance?   1250
EURYDICE: I heard your words, all you men of Thebes, as I
    was going out to greet Pallas[6] with my prayers.
    I was just drawing back the bolts of the gate
    to open it when a cry struck through my ears
    telling of my household's ruin. I fell backward   1255
    in terror into the arms of my servants; I fainted.
    But tell me again, what is the story? I
    will hear it as one who is no stranger to sorrow.
MESSENGER: Dear mistress, I will tell you, for I was there,
    and I will leave out no word of the truth.   1260
    Why should I comfort you and then tomorrow
    be proved a liar? The truth is always best.
    I followed your husband, at his heels, to the end of the plain
    where Polyneices' body still lay unpitied,
    and torn by dogs. We prayed to Hecate, goddess   1265
    of the crossroads, and also to Pluto[7]
    that they might restrain their anger and turn kind.
    And him we washed with sacred lustral water
    and with fresh-cut boughs we burned what was left of him
    and raised a high mound of his native earth;   1270
    then we set out again for the hollowed rock,
    death's stone bridal chamber for the girl.
    Someone then heard a voice of bitter weeping
    while we were still far off, coming from that unblest room.
    The man came to tell our master Creon of it.   1275
    As the king drew nearer, there swarmed about him
    a cry of misery but no clear words.
    He groaned and in an anguished mourning voice
    cried "Oh, am I a true prophet? Is this the road

6. Athena, goddess of wisdom.   7. King of the underworld. *Hecate:* goddess of witchcraft.

1280　that I must travel, saddest of all my wayfaring?
　　It is my son's voice that haunts my ear. Servants,
　　get closer, quickly. Stand around the tomb
　　and look. There is a gap there where the stones
　　have been wrenched away; enter there, by the very mouth,
1285　and see whether I recognize the voice of Haemon
　　or if the gods deceive me." On the command
　　of our despairing master we went to look.
　　In the furthest part of the tomb we saw her, hanging
　　by her neck. She had tied a noose of muslin on it.
1290　Haemon's hands were about her waist embracing her,
　　while he cried for the loss of his bride gone to the dead,
　　and for all his father had done, and his own sad love.
　　When Creon saw him he gave a bitter cry,
　　went in and called to him with a groan: "Poor son!
1295　what have you done? What can you have meant?
　　What happened to destroy you? Come out, I pray you!"
　　The boy glared at him with savage eyes, and then
　　spat in his face, without a word of answer.
　　He drew his double-hilted sword. As his father
1300　ran to escape him, Haemon failed to strike him,
　　and the poor wretch in anger at himself
　　leaned on his sword and drove it halfway in,
　　into his ribs. Then he folded the girl to him,
　　in his arms, while he was conscious still,
1305　and gasping poured a sharp stream of bloody drops
　　on her white cheeks. There they lie,
　　the dead upon the dead. So he has won
　　the pitiful fulfillment of his marriage
　　within death's house. In this human world he has shown
1310　how the wrong choice in plans is for a man
　　his greatest evil.
　CHORUS: What do you make of this? My lady is gone,
　　without a word of good or bad.
　MESSENGER:　　　　　　　　　　　I, too,
　　am lost in wonder. I am inclined to hope
1315　that hearing of her son's death she could not
　　open her sorrow to the city, but chose rather
　　within her house to lay upon her maids
　　the mourning for the household grief. Her judgment
　　is good; she will not make any false step.
1320　CHORUS: I do not know. To me this over-heavy silence
　　seems just as dangerous as much empty wailing.
　MESSENGER: I will go in and learn if in her passionate
　　heart she keeps hidden some secret purpose.

You are right; there is sometimes danger in too much silence.

CHORUS: Here comes our king himself. He bears in his hands 1325
    a memorial all too clear;
    it is a ruin of none other's making,
    purely his own if one dare to say that.

CREON: The mistakes of a blinded man
    are themselves rigid and laden with death. 1330
    You look at us the killer and the killed
    of the one blood. Oh, the awful blindness
    of those plans of mine. My son, you were so young,
    so young to die. You were freed from the bonds of life
    through no folly of your own—only through mine. 1335

CHORUS: I think you have learned justice—but too late.

CREON: Yes, I have learned it to my bitterness. At this moment
    God has sprung on my head with a vast weight
    and struck me down. He shook me in my savage ways;
    he has overturned my joy, has trampled it, 1340
    underfoot. The pains men suffer
    are pains indeed.

SECOND MESSENGER: My lord, you have troubles and a store besides;
    some are there in your hands, but there are others
    you will surely see when you come to your house. 1345

CREON: What trouble can there be beside these troubles?

SECOND MESSENGER: The queen is dead. She was indeed true mother
    of the dead son. She died, poor lady,
    by recent violence upon herself.

CREON: Haven of death, you can never have enough. 1350
    Why, why do you destroy me?
    You messenger, who have brought me bitter news,
    what is this tale you tell?
    It is a dead man that you kill again—
    what new message of yours is this, boy? 1355
    Is this new slaughter of a woman
    a doom to lie on the pile of the dead?

CHORUS: You can see. It is no longer
    hidden in a corner.

       [*By some stage device, perhaps the so-called eccyclema, the inside of the palace
       is shown, with the body of the dead* QUEEN.]

CREON: Here is yet another horror 1360
    for my unhappy eyes to see.
    What doom still waits for me?
    I have but now taken in my arms my son,
    and again I look upon another dead face.
    Poor mother and poor son! 1365

SECOND MESSENGER: She stood at the altar, and with keen whetted knife
    she suffered her darkening eyes to close.
    First she cried in agony recalling the noble fate of Megareus,[8]
    who died before all this,
1370   and then for the fate of this son; and in the end
    she cursed you for the evil you had done
    in killing her sons.
CREON: I am distracted with fear. Why does not someone
    strike a two-edged sword right through me?
1375   I am dissolved in an agony of misery.
SECOND MESSENGER: You were indeed accused
    by her that is dead
    of Haemon's and of Megareus' death.
CREON: By what kind of violence did she find her end?
1380 SECOND MESSENGER: Her own hand struck her to the entrails
    when she heard of her son's lamentable death.
CREON: These acts can never be made to fit another
    to free me from the guilt. It was I that killed her.
    Poor wretch that I am, I say it is true!
1385   Servants, lead me away, quickly, quickly.
    I am no more a live man than one dead.
CHORUS: What you say is for the best—if there be a best
    in evil such as this. For the shortest way
    is best with troubles that lie at our feet.
1390 CREON: O, let it come, let it come,
    that best of fates that waits on my last day.
    Surely best fate of all. Let it come, let it come!
    That I may never see one more day's light!
CHORUS: These things are for the future. We must deal
1395   with what impends. What in the future is to care for
    rests with those whose duty it is
    to care for them.
CREON: At least, all that *I* want
    is in that prayer of mine.
1400 CHORUS: Pray for no more at all. For what is destined
    for us, men mortal, there is no escape.
CREON: Lead me away, a vain silly man
    who killed you, son, and you, too, lady.
    I did not mean to, but I did.
1405   I do not know where to turn my eyes
    to look to, for support.
    Everything in my hands is crossed. A most unwelcome fate
    has leaped upon me.

8. Another son of Creon.

CHORUS: Wisdom is far the chief element in happiness
   and, secondly, no irreverence towards the gods.   1410
   But great words of haughty men exact
   in retribution blows as great
   and in old age teach wisdom.

     THE END

                                      ca. 441 B.C.

RICHARD C. JEBB

From The *Antigone* of Sophocles*

The issue defined in the opening scene,—the conflict of divine with human law,—remains the central interest throughout. The action, so simple in plan, is varied by masterly character-drawing, both in the two principal figures, and in those lesser persons who contribute gradations of light and shade to the picture. There is no halting in the march of the drama; at each successive step we become more and more keenly interested to see how this great conflict is to end; and when the tragic climax is reached, it is worthy of such a progress.

    The simplicity of the plot is due to the clearness with which two principles are opposed to each other. *Creon represents the duty of obeying the State's laws; Antigone, the duty of listening to the private conscience.* The definiteness and the power with which the play puts the case on each side are conclusive proofs that the question had assumed a distinct shape before the poet's mind. It is the only instance in which a Greek play has for its central theme a practical problem of conduct, involving issues, moral and political, which might be discussed on similar grounds in any age and in any country of the world. Greek Tragedy, owing partly to the limitations which it placed on detail, was better suited than modern drama to raise such a question in a general form. The *Antigone,* indeed, raises the question in a form as nearly abstract as is compatible with the nature of drama. The case of Antigone is a thoroughly typical one for the private conscience, because the particular thing which she believes that she ought to do was, in itself, a thing which every Greek of that age recognised as a most sacred duty,—viz.,[1] to render burial rites to kinsfolk. This advantage was not devised by Sophocles; it came to him as part of the story which he was to dramatise; but it forms an additional reason for thinking that, when he dramatised that story in the precise manner which he has chosen, he had a consciously dialectical purpose. Such a purpose was wholly consistent, in this instance, with the artist's first aim,—to produce a

---

*From Sir Richard C. Jebb, ed., *The* Antigone *of Sophocles,* abr. by E. S. Shuckburgh (orig. ed., 1902; repr. Cambridge, Eng., and New York: Cambridge University Press, 1984), pp. xvii–xix.
1. Namely (abbreviation of the Latin *videlicet*) [Editor's note].

work of art. It is because Creon and Antigone are so human that the controversy which they represent becomes so vivid.

But how did Sophocles intend us to view the result? What is the drift of the words at the end, which say that "wisdom is the supreme part of happiness"? If this wisdom, or prudence, means, generally, the observance of due limit, may not the suggested moral be that both the parties to the conflict were censurable? As Creon overstepped the due limit when, by his edict, he infringed the divine law, so Antigone also overstepped it when she defied the edict. The drama would thus be a conflict between two persons, each of whom defends an intrinsically sound principle, but defends it in a mistaken way; and both persons are therefore punished. This view, of which Boeckh[2] is the chief representative, has found several supporters. Among them is Hegel:—"In the view of the Eternal Justice, both were wrong, because they were one-sided, but at the same time both were right."[3]

Or does the poet rather intend us to feel that Antigone is wholly in the right,— *i.e.,* that nothing of which the human lawgiver could complain in her was of a moment's account beside the supreme duty which she was fulfilling;—and that Creon was wholly in the wrong,—*i.e.,* that the intrinsically sound maxims of government on which he relies lose all validity when opposed to the higher law which he was breaking? If that was the poet's meaning, then the "wisdom" taught by the issue of the drama means the sense which duly subordinates human to divine law,—teaching that, if the two come into conflict, human law must yield.

A careful study of the play itself will suffice (I think) to show that the second of these two views is the true one. Sophocles has allowed Creon to put his case ably, and (in a measure from which an inferior artist might have shrunk) he has been content to make Antigone merely a nobly heroic woman, not a being exempt from human passion and human weakness; but none the less does he mean us to feel that, in this controversy, the right is wholly with her, and the wrong wholly with her judge.

MAURICE BOWRA

From Sophoclean Tragedy*

Modern critics who do not share Sophocles' conviction about the paramount duty of burying the dead and who attach more importance than he did to the claims of political authority have tended to underestimate the way in which he justifies Antigone against Creon. To their support they have called in the great name of Hegel, who was fascinated by the play and advanced remarkable views on it. His remarks have been taken out of their context, and he has been made responsible

2. August Boeckh (1785–1867), German classical scholar [Editor's note].   3. *Religionsphilosophie,* II. 114 [Jebb's note].
*From Sir Maurice Bowra, *Sophoclean Tragedy* (Oxford: Clarendon Press, 1944), pp. 65–67.

for the opinion that Sophocles dramatized a conflict not between right and wrong but between right and right, that Antigone and Creon are equally justified in their actions and that the tragedy arises out of this irreconcilable conflict. Hegel's own words lend some support to this view: "In the view of eternal justice both were wrong, because they were one-sided; but at the same time both were right." But if we look at Hegel's observations in their own place, we find that this summary hardly conveys his full meaning. He was thinking of something much vaster than the play, of the whole logic of history which is here symbolized in a concrete example. In this the conflict of opposites ends by producing a synthesis which is itself right. The conclusion is what matters, and that is different from saying that both sides in the conflict are themselves right. The tragic conclusion is, so to speak, a lesson of history, a fact which cannot be denied, real and therefore right, but the conflict which precedes it cannot be judged in isolation and neither side in it is right or wrong except in a relative sense. Hegel used the *Antigone* to illustrate his view of tragedy and his view of existence. He drew his own conclusions about the actions portrayed in it, as he was fully entitled to do. But his views are not those of Sophocles, and he should not be thought to maintain that Creon and Antigone were equally right in the eyes of their creator.

Sophocles leaves no doubt what conclusion should be drawn from the *Antigone*. He closes with a moral on the lips of the Chorus which tells the audience what to think:

> Wisdom has first place in happiness,
> And to fail not in reverence to the gods.
> The big words of the arrogant
> Lay big stripes on the boasters' backs.
> They pay the price
> And learn in old age to be wise.[1]

This can refer to no one but Creon, whose lack of wisdom has brought him to misery, who has shown irreverence to the gods in refusing burial to Polynices, been chastened for his proud words, and learned wisdom in his old age. To this lesson the preceding action in which Creon has lost son and wife and happiness has already made its effective contribution. We may be sure that the Chorus speak for the poet. It is as silent about Antigone as it is emphatic about Creon. There is no hint that she has in any way acted wrongly or that her death should be regarded as a righteous punishment. Of course the final words do not sum up everything important in the play, but we may reasonably assume that they pass judgement on its salient events as they appear in retrospect when the action is finished. There is no real problem about the ethical intention of the *Antigone*. It shows the fall of a proud man, and its lesson is that the gods punish pride and irreverence. But what matters much more than the actual conclusion is the means by which it is reached, the presentation of the different parties in the conflict, the view that we take of each, the feelings that are forced on us. The interest and power of the *Antigone* lie in the tangled issues which are unravelled in it.

1. Bowra's translation.

A conclusion so clear as this is only worth reaching if it has been preceded by a drama in which the issues are violent and complex. The rights and wrongs of the case must not throughout be so obvious as they are at the end; the audience must feel that the issue is difficult, that there is much to be said on both sides, that the ways of the gods are hard to discern. Without this the play will fail in dramatic and human interest. And Sophocles has taken great care to show the issues in their full difficulty before he provides a solution for them. He makes the two protagonists appear in such a light that at intervals we doubt if all the right is really with Antigone and all the wrong with Creon. To Creon, who defies the divine ordinance of burial, he gives arguments and sentiments which sound convincing enough when they are put forward, and many must feel that he has some good reason to act as he does. On the other hand Antigone, who fearlessly vindicates the laws of the gods, is by no means a gentle womanly creature who suffers martyrdom for the right. She may be right, but there are moments when we qualify our approval of her, when she seems proud and forbidding in her determination to do her duty and to do it alone. For these variations in our feelings Sophocles is responsible. He makes us find some right in Creon, some wrong in Antigone, even if we are misled about both. He built his play on a contrast not between obvious wrong and obvious right but between the real arrogance of Creon and the apparent arrogance of Antigone. The first deceives by its fine persuasive sentiments; the second works through Antigone's refusal to offer concessions or to consider any point of view but her own. This contrast runs through much of the play, accounts for misunderstandings of what takes place in it, provides false clues and suggests wrong conclusions, and adds greatly to the intensity of the drama. When a play is written round a moral issue, that issue must be a real problem about which more than one view is tenable until all the relevant facts are known. So the *Antigone* dramatizes a conflict which was familiar to the Periclean age, would excite divergent judgements and feelings, and make some support Antigone, some Creon, until the end makes all clear.

BERNARD KNOX

Introduction to Sophocles: The Three Theban Plays*

The opening scenes show us the conflicting claims and loyalties of the two adversaries, solidly based, in both cases, on opposed political and religious principles. This is of course the basic insight of Hegel's famous analysis of the play: he sees it as "a collision between the two highest moral powers." What is wrong with

---

*From Sophocles, *The Three Theban Plays: Antigone, Oedipus the King, Oedipus at Colonus*, trans. by Robert Fagles, intro. and notes by Bernard Knox (New York: Penguin, 1982), pp. 41–47, 53.

them, in his view, is that they are both "one-sided." But Hegel goes much further than that. He was writing in the first half of the nineteenth century, a period of fervent German nationalism in which the foundations of the unified German state were laid: his views on loyalty to the state were very much those of Creon. "Creon," he says, "is not a tyrant, he is really a moral power. He is not in the wrong."

However, as the action develops the favorable impression created by Creon's opening speech is quickly dissipated. His announcement of his decision to expose the corpse, the concluding section of his speech, is couched in violent, vindictive terms—"carrion for the birds and dogs to tear"[1]—which stand in shocking contrast to the ethical generalities that precede it. This hint of a cruel disposition underlying the statesmanlike façade is broadened by the threat of torture leveled at the sentry and the order to execute Antigone in the presence of Haemon, her betrothed. And as he meets resistance from a series of opponents—Antigone's contemptuous defiance, the rational, political advice of his son Haemon, the imperious summons to obedience of the gods' spokesman, Tiresias—he swiftly abandons the temperate rhetoric of his inaugural address for increasingly savage invective. Against the two sanctions invoked by Antigone, the demands of blood relationship, the rights and privileges of the gods below, he rages in terms ranging from near-blasphemous defiance to scornful mockery.

> Sister's child or closer in blood
> than all my family clustered at my altar
> worshiping Guardian Zeus—she'll never escape,
> . . . the most barbaric death.

He will live to regret this wholesale denial of the family bond, for it is precisely through that family clustered at his altar that his punishment will be administered, in the suicides of his son and his wife, both of whom die cursing him.

And for Antigone's appeals to Hades, the great god of the underworld to whom the dead belong, Creon has nothing but contempt; for him "Hades" is simply a word meaning "death," a sentence he is prepared to pass on anyone who stands in his way. He threatens the sentry with torture as a prelude: "simple death won't be enough for you." When asked if he really intends to deprive Haemon of his bride he answers sarcastically: "Death will do it for me." He expects to see Antigone and Ismene turn coward "once they see Death coming for their lives." With a derisive comment he tells his son to abandon Antigone: "Spit her out, / . . . Let her find a husband down among the dead [in Hades' house]." And he dismisses Antigone's reverence for Hades and the rights of the dead with mockery as he condemns her to be buried alive: "There let her pray to the one god she worships: / Death." But this Hades is not something to be so lightly referred to, used or mocked. In the great choral ode which celebrated Man's progress and powers this was the one insurmountable obstacle that confronted him:

---

1. Knox's references are to Robert Fagles's translation, printed in *The Three Theban Plays.*

> ready, resourceful man!
>   Never without resources
> never an impasse as he marches on the future—
> only Death, from Death alone he will find no rescue . . .

And Creon, in the end, looking at the corpse of his son and hearing the news of his wife's suicide, speaks of Hades for the first time with the fearful respect that is his due, not as an instrument of policy or a subject for sardonic word-play, but as a divine power, a dreadful presence: "harbor of Death, so choked, so hard to cleanse!— / why me? why are you killing me?"

Creon is forced at last to recognize the strength of those social and religious imperatives that Antigone obeys, but long before this happens he has abandoned the principles which he had proclaimed as authority for his own actions. His claim to be representative of the whole community is forgotten as he refuses to accept Haemon's report that the citizens, though they dare not speak out, disapprove of his action; he denies the relevance of such a report even if true—"And is Thebes about to tell me how to rule?"—and finally repudiates his principles in specific terms by an assertion that the city belongs to him—"The city *is* the king's—that's the law!" This autocratic phrase puts the finishing touch to the picture Sophocles is drawing for his audience: Creon has now displayed all the characteristics of the "tyrant," a despotic ruler who seizes power and retains it by intimidation and force. Athens had lived under the rule of a "tyrant" before the democracy was established in 508 B.C., and the name and institution were still regarded with abhorrence. Creon goes on to abandon the gods whose temples crown the city's high places, the gods he once claimed as his own, and his language is even more violent. The blind prophet Tiresias tells him that the birds and dogs are fouling the altars of the city's gods with the carrion flesh of Polynices; he must bury the corpse. His furious reply begins with a characteristic accusation that the prophet has been bribed (the sentry had this same accusation flung at him), but what follows is a hideously blasphemous defiance of those gods Creon once claimed to serve:

> You'll never bury that body in the grave,
> not even if Zeus's eagles rip the corpse
> and wing their rotten pickings off to the throne of god!

At this high point in his stubborn rage (he will break by the end of the scene and try, too late, to avoid the divine wrath), he is sustained by nothing except his tyrannical insistence on his own will, come what may, and his outraged refusal to be defeated by a woman. "No woman," he says, "is going to lord it over me." "I'm not the man, not now: she is the man / if this victory goes to her and she goes free."

Antigone, on her side, is just as indifferent to Creon's principles of action as he is to hers. She mentions the city only in her last agonized laments before she is led off to her living death:

> O my city, all your fine rich sons!
> . . . springs of the Dirce,
> holy grove of Thebes . . .

But here she is appealing for sympathy to the city over the heads of the chorus, the city's symbolic representative on stage. In all her arguments with Creon and Ismene she speaks as one wholly unconscious of the rights and duties membership in the city confers and imposes, as if no unit larger than the family existed. It is a position just as extreme as Creon's insistence that the demands of the city take precedence over all others, for the living and the dead alike.

Like Creon, she acts in the name of gods, but they are different gods. There is more than a little truth in Creon's mocking comment that Hades is "the one god she worships." She is from the beginning "much possessed by death"; together with Ismene she is the last survivor of a doomed family, burdened with such sorrow that she finds life hardly worth living. "Who on earth," she says to Creon, "alive in the midst of so much grief as I, / could fail to find his death a rich reward?" She has performed the funeral rites for mother, father and her brother Eteocles:

> I washed you with my hands,
> I dressed you all, I poured the cups
> across your tombs.

She now sacrifices her life to perform a symbolic burial, a handful of dust sprinkled on the corpse, for Polynices, the brother left to rot on the battlefield. She looks forward to her reunion with her beloved dead in that dark kingdom where Persephone, the bride of Hades, welcomes the ghosts. It is in the name of Hades, one of the three great gods who rule the universe, that she defends the right of Polynices and of all human beings to proper burial. "Death [Hades] longs for the same rites for all," she tells Creon—for patriot and traitor alike; she rejects Ismene's plea to be allowed to share her fate with an appeal to the same stern authority: "Who did the work? / Let the dead and the god of death bear witness!" In Creon's gods, the city's patrons and defenders, she shows no interest at all. Zeus she mentions twice: once as the source of all the calamities that have fallen and are still to fall on the house of Oedipus, and once again at the beginning of her famous speech about the unwritten laws. But the context here suggests strongly that she is thinking about Zeus in his special relationship to the underworld, Zeus *Chthonios* (Underworld Zeus). "It wasn't Zeus," she says,

> who made this proclamation. . . .
> Nor did that Justice, dwelling with the gods
> beneath the earth, ordain such laws for men.

From first to last her religious devotion and duty are to the divine powers of the world below, the masters of that world where lie her family dead, to which she herself, reluctant but fascinated, is irresistibly drawn.

But, like Creon, she ends by denying the great sanctions she invoked to justify her action. In his case the process was spread out over the course of several scenes, as he reacted to each fresh pressure that was brought to bear on him; Antigone turns her back on the claims of blood relationship and the nether gods in one sentence: three lines in Greek, no more. They are the emotional high point of the speech she makes just before she is led off to her death.

> Never, I tell you,
> if I had been the mother of children
> or if my husband died, exposed and rotting—
> I'd never have taken this ordeal upon myself,
> never defied our people's will.

These unexpected words are part of the long speech that concludes a scene of lyric lamentation and is in effect her farewell to the land of the living. They are certainly a total repudiation of her proud claim that she acted as the champion of the unwritten laws and the infernal gods, for, as she herself told Creon, those laws and those gods have no preferences, they long "for the same rites for all." And her assertion that she would not have done for her children what she has done for Polynices is a spectacular betrayal of that fanatical loyalty to blood relationship which she urged on Ismene and defended against Creon, for there is no closer relationship imaginable than that between the mother and the children of her own body. Creon turned his back on his guiding principles step by step, in reaction to opposition based on those principles; Antigone's rejection of her public values is just as complete, but it is the sudden product of a lonely, brooding introspection, a last-minute assessment of her motives, on which the imminence of death confers a merciless clarity. She did it because Polynices was her brother; she would not have done it for husband or child. She goes on to justify this disturbing statement by an argument which is more disturbing still: husband and children, she says, could be replaced by others but, since her parents are dead, she could never have another brother. It so happens that we can identify the source of this strange piece of reasoning; it is a story in the *Histories* of Sophocles' friend Herodotus (a work from which Sophocles borrowed material more than once). Darius the Great King had condemned to death for treason a Persian noble, Intaphrenes, and all the men of his family. The wife of Intaphrenes begged importunately for their lives; offered one, she chose her brother's. When Darius asked her why, she replied in words that are unmistakably the original of Antigone's lines. But what makes sense in the story makes less in the play. The wife of Intaphrenes saves her brother's life, but Polynices is already dead; Antigone's phrase "no brother could ever spring to light again" would be fully appropriate only if Antigone had managed to save Polynices' life rather than bury his corpse.

For this reason, and also because of some stylistic anomalies in this part of the speech, but most of all because they felt that the words are unworthy of the Antigone who spoke so nobly for the unwritten laws, many great scholars and also a great poet and dramatist, Goethe, have refused to believe that Sophocles wrote them. "I would give a great deal," Goethe told his friend Eckermann in

1827, "if some talented scholar could prove that these lines were interpolated, not genuine." Goethe did not know that the attempt had already been made, six years earlier; many others have tried since—Sir Richard Jebb, the greatest English editor of Sophocles, pronounced against them—and opinion today is still divided. Obviously a decision on this point is of vital significance for the interpretation of the play as a whole: with these lines removed, Antigone goes to her prison-tomb with no flicker of self-doubt, the flawless champion of the family bond and the unwritten laws, "whole as the marble, founded as the rock"—unlike Creon, she is not, in the end, reduced to recognizing that her motive is purely personal.

The gods do not praise Antigone, nor does anyone else in the play—except the young man who loves her so passionately that he cannot bear to live without her. Haemon tells his father what the Thebans are saying behind his back, the "murmurs in the dark": that Antigone deserves not death but "a glowing crown of gold!" Whether this is a true report (and the chorus does not praise Antigone even when they have been convinced that she was right) or just his own feelings attributed to others for the sake of his argument, it is a timely reminder of Antigone's heroic status. In the somber world of the play, against the background of so many sudden deaths and the dark mystery of the divine dispensation, her courage and steadfastness are a gleam of light; she is the embodiment of the only consolation tragedy can offer—that in certain heroic natures unmerited suffering and death can be met with a greatness of soul which, because it is purely human, brings honor to us all.

MARTHA C. NUSSBAUM

From The Fragility of Goodness: Luck and Ethics in Greek Tragedy and Philosophy*

[A]lmost all interpreters of [*Antigone*] have agreed that the play shows Creon to be morally defective, though they might not agree about the particular nature of his defect. The situation of Antigone is more controversial. Hegel assimilated her defect to Creon's; some more recent writers uncritically hold her up as a blameless heroine. Without entering into an exhaustive study of her role in the tragedy, I should like to claim (with the support of an increasing number of recent critics) that there is at least some justification for the Hegelian assimilation—though the criticism needs to be focused more clearly and specifically than it is in Hegel's brief remarks. I want to suggest that Antigone, like Creon, has engaged in a ruthless simplification of the world of value which effectively eliminates conflicting

*From Martha C. Nussbaum, *The Fragility of Goodness: Luck and Ethics in Greek Tragedy and Philosophy* (Cambridge, Eng., and New York: Cambridge University Press, 1986), pp. 63–67.

obligations. Like Creon, she can be blamed for refusal of vision. But there are important differences, as well, between her project and Creon's. When these are seen, it will also emerge that this criticism of Antigone is not incompatible with the judgment that she is morally superior to Creon.

> O kindred, own-sisterly head of Ismene, do you know that there is not one of the evils left by Oedipus that Zeus does not fulfill for us while we live? . . . Do you grasp anything? Have you heard anything? Or has it escaped your notice that the evils that belong to enemies are advancing against our friends?[1]

A person is addressed with a periphrasis that is both intimate and impersonal. In the most emphatic terms available, it characterizes her as a close relative of the speaker. And yet its attitude towards the addressee is strangely remote. Antigone sees Ismene simply as the form of a close family relation. As such, she presses on her, with anxious insistence, the knowledge of the family: that "loved ones" (*philoi*) are being penalized as if they were enemies (*echthroi*). Loving relatives must "see" the shame and dishonour of "the evils that are yours and mine."

There has been a war. On one side was an army led by Eteocles, brother of Antigone and Ismene. On the other side was an invading army, made up partly of foreigners, but led by a Theban brother, Polynices. This heterogeneity is denied, in different ways, by both Creon and Antigone. Creon's strategy is to draw, in thought, a line between the invading and defending forces. What falls to one side of this line is a foe, bad, unjust; what falls to the other (if loyal to the city's cause) becomes, indiscriminately, friend or loved one. Antigone, on the other hand, denies the relevance of this distinction entirely. She draws, in imagination, a small circle around the members of her family: what is inside (with further restrictions which we shall mention) is family, therefore loved one and friend; what is outside is non-family, therefore, in any conflict with the family, enemy. If one listened only to Antigone, one would not know that a war had taken place or that anything called "city" was ever in danger. To her it is a simple injustice that Polynices should not be treated like a friend.

"Friend" (*philos*) and "enemy," then, are functions solely of family relationship. When Antigone says, "It is my nature to join in loving, not to join in hating," she is expressing not a general attachment to love, but a devotion to the *philia* of the family. It is the nature of these *philia* bonds to make claims on one's commitments and actions regardless of one's occurrent desires. This sort of love is not something one decides about; the relationships involved may have little to do with liking or fondness. We might say (to use terminology borrowed from Kant[2]) that Antigone, in speaking of love, means "practical," not "pathological" love (a love that has its source in fondness or inclination). "He is my own brother," she says to Ismene in explanation of her defiance of the city's decree, "and yours too, even if you don't want it. I certainly will never be found a traitor to him." Relationship is itself a source of obligation, regardless of the feelings involved. When Antigone speaks of Polynices as "my dearest brother," even when she proclaims, "I shall lie with him as a loved one with a loved one," there is no

---

1. All translations are Nussbaum's, based on the Oxford Classical Text of A. C. Pearson.   2. Immanuel Kant (1724–1804), German philosopher, who uses these terms in his *Critique of Pure Reason*.

sense of closeness, no personal memory, no particularity animating her speech. Ismene, the one person who ought, historically, to be close to her, is treated from the beginning with remote coldness; she is even called enemy when she takes the wrong stand on matters of pious obligation. It is Ismene whom we see weeping "sister-loving tears," who acts out of commitment to a felt love. "What life is worth living for me, bereft of you?" she asks with an intensity of feeling that never animates her sister's piety. To Haemon, the man who passionately loves and desires her, Antigone never addresses a word throughout the entire play. It is Haemon, not Antigone, whom the Chorus views as inspired by *erōs*. Antigone is as far from *erōs* as Creon. For Antigone, the dead are "those whom it is most important to please." "You have a warm heart for the cold," observes her sister, failing to comprehend this impersonal and single-minded passion.

Duty to the family dead is the supreme law and the supreme passion. And Antigone structures her entire life and her vision of the world in accordance with this simple, self-contained system of duties. Even within this system, should a conflict ever arise, she is ready with a fixed priority ordering that will clearly dictate her choice. The strange speech in which she ranks duties to different family dead, placing duty to brother above duties to husband and children, is in this sense (if genuine) highly revealing: it makes us suspect that she is capable of a strangely ruthless simplification of duties, corresponding not so much to any known religious law as to the exigencies of her own practical imagination.

Other values fall into place, confirming these suspicions. Her single-minded identification with duties to the dead (and only some of these) effects a strange reorganization of piety, as well as of honor and justice. She is truly, in her own words, *hosia panourgēsasa*, one who will do anything for the sake of the pious; and her piety takes in only a part of conventional religion. She speaks of her allegiance to Zeus, but she refuses to recognize his role as guardian of the city and backer of Eteocles. The very expression of her devotion is suspect: "Zeus did not decree this, as far as I am concerned." She sets herself up as the arbiter of what Zeus can and cannot have decreed, just as Creon took it upon himself to say whom the gods could and could not have covered: no other character bears out her view of Zeus as single-mindedly backing the rights of the dead. She speaks, too, of the goddess *Dikē*, Justice; but *Dikē* for her is, simply, "the Justice who lives together with the gods below." The Chorus recognizes another *Dikē*. Later they will say to her, "Having advanced to the utmost limit of boldness, you struck hard against the altar of *Dikē* on high, o child." Justice is up here in the city, as well as below the earth. It is not as simple as she says it is. Antigone, accordingly, is seen by them not as a conventionally pious person, but as one who improvised her piety, making her own decisions about what to honor. She is a "maker of her own law"; her defiance is "self-invented passion." Finally they tell her unequivocally that her pious respect is incomplete: "[This] reverent action is a part of piety." Antigone's rigid adherence to a single narrow set of duties has caused her to misinterpret the nature of piety itself, a virtue within which a more comprehensive understanding would see the possibility of conflict.

Creon's strategy of simplification led him to regard others as material for his aggressive exploitation. Antigone's dutiful subservience to the dead leads to an equally strange, though different (and certainly less hideous) result. Her relation to others in the world above is characterized by an odd coldness. "You are alive," she tells her sister, "but my life is long since dead, to the end of serving the dead." The safely dutiful human life requires, or is, life's annihilation. Creon's attitude towards others is like necrophilia: he aspires to possess the inert and unresisting. Antigone's subservience to duty is, finally, the ambition to be a *nekros*, a corpse beloved of corpses. (Her apparent similarity to martyrs in our own tradition, who expect a fully active life after death, should not conceal from us the strangeness of this goal.) In the world below, there are no risks of failure or wrongdoing.

Neither Creon nor Antigone, then, is a loving or passionate being in anything like the usual sense. Not one of the gods, not one human being escapes the power of *erōs*, says the Chorus; but these two oddly inhuman beings do, it appears, escape. Creon sees loved persons as functions of the civic good, replaceable producers of citizens. For Antigone, they are either dead, fellow servants of the dead, or objects of complete indifference. No living being is loved for his or her personal qualities, loved with the sort of love that Haemon feels and Ismene praises. By altering their beliefs about the nature and value of persons, they have, it seems, altered or restructured the human passions themselves. They achieve harmony in this way; but at a cost. The Chorus speaks of *erōs* as a force as important and obligating as the ancient *thesmoi* or laws of right, a force against which it is both foolish and, apparently, blameworthy to rebel.

Antigone learns too—like Creon, by being forced to recognize a problem that lies at the heart of her single-minded concern. Creon saw that the city itself is pious and loving; that he could not be its champion without valuing what it values, in all its complexity. Antigone comes to see that the service of the dead requires the city, that her own religious aims cannot be fulfilled without civic institutions. By being her own law, she has not only ignored a part of piety, she has also jeopardized the fulfillment of the very pious duties to which she is so attached. Cut off from friends, from the possibility of having children, she cannot keep herself alive in order to do further service to the dead; nor can she guarantee the pious treatment of her own corpse. In her last speeches she laments not so much the fact of imminent death as, repeatedly, her isolation from the continuity of offspring, from friends and mourners. She emphasizes the fact that she will never marry; she will remain childless. Acheron will be her husband, the tomb her bridal chamber. Unless she can successfully appeal to the citizens whose needs as citizens she had refused to consider, she will die without anyone to mourn her death or to replace her as guardian of her family religion. She turns therefore increasingly, in this final scene, to the citizens and the gods of the city, until her last words closely echo an earlier speech made by Creon and blend his concerns with hers:

> O city of my fathers in this land of Thebes. O gods, progenitors of our race. I am led away, and wait no longer. Look, leaders of Thebes, the last of your royal line. Look what I suffer, at whose hands, for having respect for piety.

We have, then, two narrowly limited practical worlds, two strategies of avoidance and simplification. In one, a single human value has become *the* final end; in the other, a single set of duties has eclipsed all others. But we can now acknowledge that we admire Antigone, nonetheless, in a way that we do not admire Creon. It seems important to look for the basis of this difference.

First, in the world of the play, it seems clear that Antigone's actual choice is preferable to Creon's. The dishonour to civic values involved in giving pious burial to an enemy's corpse is far less radical than the violation of religion involved in Creon's act. Antigone shows a deeper understanding of the community and its values than Creon does when she argues that the obligation to bury the dead is an unwritten law, which cannot be set aside by the decree of a particular ruler. The belief that not all values are utility-relative, that there are certain claims whose neglect will prove deeply destructive of communal attunement and individual character, is a part of Antigone's position left untouched by the play's implicit criticism of her single-mindedness.

Furthermore, Antigone's pursuit of virtue is her own. It involves nobody else and commits her to abusing no other person. Rulership must be rulership *of* something; Antigone's pious actions are executed alone, out of a solitary commitment. She may be strangely remote from the world; but she does no violence to it.

Finally, and perhaps most important, Antigone remains ready to risk and to sacrifice her ends in a way that is not possible for Creon, given the singleness of his conception of value. There is a complexity in Antigone's virtue that permits genuine sacrifice *within* the defense of piety. She dies recanting nothing; but still she is torn by a conflict. Her virtue is, then, prepared to admit a contingent conflict, at least in the extreme case where its adequate exercise requires the cancellation of the conditions of its exercise. From within her single-minded devotion to the dead, she recognizes the power of these contingent circumstances and yields to them, comparing herself to Niobe wasted away by nature's snow and rain. (Earlier she had been compared, in her grief, to a mother bird crying out over an empty nest; so she is, while heroically acting, linked with the openness and vulnerability of the female.) The Chorus here briefly tries to console her with the suggestion that her bad luck does not really matter, in view of her future fame; she calls their rationalization a mockery of her loss. This vulnerability in virtue, this ability to acknowledge the world of nature by mourning the constraints that it imposes on virtue, surely contributes to making her the more humanly rational and the richer of the two protagonists: both active and receptive, neither exploiter nor simply victim.

REBECCA W. BUSHNELL

From Prophesying Tragedy: Sign and Voice in Sophocles' Theban Plays*

It is primarily through the power of speech, against silence, that Creon's suffering is distinguished from Antigone's, as Creon becomes "nothing" in his disaster,

*From Rebecca W. Bushnell, *Prophesying Tragedy: Sign and Voice in Sophocles' Theban Plays* (Ithaca and London: Cornell University Press, 1988), pp. 64–66. All notes are the editor's.

whereas Antigone leaves the stage as herself. She has clearly lost in her battle for any kind of political autonomy, in her effort to counteract Creon's *kērygma*[1] (the Chorus, not Antigone, makes him change his mind). Further, neither the other characters in the play nor the gods confer heroic status on her. While the "punishment" of Creon may be seen as her vindication, Creon never mentions her again, nor does Tiresias defend her directly in his prophecy. Yet she leaves the stage, neither abject nor resigned to oblivion, but proclaiming her importance as the last of the Cadmeans. While Creon speaks his "sentence" of death, Antigone responds by invoking the gods and the city of Thebes, calling upon the Chorus to look on her and acknowledge her right to have buried Polynices. Antigone's last act on stage is thus an act of apostrophe or invocation, meant to establish the presence and power of her own voice. For her, it matters little that neither god nor city responds; for one last time, Antigone relies on her voice to define herself, as she claims her link to her city, her lineage, and the gods of her race. Antigone is denied personal and political autonomy in the city of Thebes—what she cannot have as a woman; yet at the same time Antigone maintains her freedom of speech in public, which was the essence of freedom in Athens, where the worst punishment of exile was considered the loss of *parrēsia* or "free speech." Antigone speaks, too, as the bride of death, both in this world and beyond; like Hector, she has the authority that those on the brink of death possess over the living, and yet she already stands apart from the rest of the citizens, who must find a way to rule in the days to come.

Creon's loss of his power to invoke and command marks the loss of his role in the family and the city. Creon, too, laments his disaster, but his speech lacks the ceremony and self-reflection of Antigone's. Crying forth the ritual sound of wailing, *aiai*, he calls himself wretched (*deilaios*). Creon's penultimate gesture, matching Antigone's, is to utter a prayer for death. It may be addressed to the gods, but it is heard only by the Chorus, who refuse to answer the prayer: "That will come," they say, "but now we must do what is before us." When Creon protests that he prayed for what he desires most, the Chorus answers that he must not pray now. Creon thus ends in the world he created for himself, where "fate" is inflexible, yet there are no gods to hear his prayers. The gods will not help Creon, and he can no longer help himself. His words become meaningless when he himself becomes "nothing," having lost his family and his city. Earlier, Haemon compared Creon to writing tablets which, when unfolded, are blank. In the end, Creon fulfills that image, becoming someone who is nothing, a voice which is *asēmos*, "without significance."

In the *Iliad*, Hector's defiance of prophecy[2] plays out a conflict of discourse in the struggle between man and god for the right to declare *ananke*.[3] In *Antigone*, Sophocles dramatizes that conflict in the context of the city, where the king strives to emulate the gods in making the signs of "fate," and king, prophet, and citizen compete for the right to speak for the city's needs and future. Antigone loses this battle when Creon condemns her to death, just as Hector must die,

1. Proclamation. 2. Perhaps a reference to Book 22 of the *Iliad*, in which Hector mistakenly disbelieves Achilles' boast that Zeus will allow Achilles to kill Hector in battle. 3. Necessity, fate.

according to the sentence of "fate." But Creon is silenced by the gods—and by the playwright. Both Creon and Antigone threaten the order of the city and are destroyed, but Sophocles gives the victory to her, in the dramatic authority of her voice. Although the gods themselves never answer her pleas for recognition, her voice commands the audience's and Chorus' attention. Creon, however, trails off in inarticulate confusion, just as he has no recognizable "self" when stripped of his roles of *tyrannos*,[4] husband, and father. Antigone never loses her ability to speak for herself, and in this way, is given her freedom. Thus it is she, not Creon, who is Hector's heir, and she who most closely imitates his defiance of fatal authority. But Antigone is not only Hector's heir; she is also the forerunner[5] of her own father, Oedipus, who in *Oedipus the King* masters human speech in his pride and his shame.

MARY WHITLOCK BLUNDELL

From Helping Friends and Harming Enemies: A Study in Sophocles and Greek Ethics*

Creon and Antigone are alike in several ways, especially the inconsistency of their values and the way they are driven by passion below a surface of rational argument. Both are also one-sided in their commitments. The poet could have given the champion of the *polis*[1] a much stronger case. But he could also have let Antigone meet and conquer Creon on his own ground (for example by arguing that her two brothers were equally responsible for the war). The narrowness of both is revealed by their failure really to engage in argument. Creon's two main statements of principle actually occur in Antigone's absence. When they do confront each other, in the brief passage of stichomythia[2] with which we began, they argue at cross purposes, repeatedly missing each other's point.

This does not mean, however, that they are equally limited in the values to which they adhere. Antigone is sometimes accused of being as narrowly one-sided as Creon in her allegiance to the family and disregard for the interests and *nomoi*[3] of the *polis:* "If one listened only to Antigone, one would not know that a war had taken place or that anything called 'city' was ever in danger" (Nussbaum 63f.). Nor can it be denied that she ignores competing concepts of *nomos* and justice which have their claims, no matter how shoddily Creon may represent them. Creon's misapplication of his principles does not undermine their claim to consideration, and the rightness of Antigone's cause does not of itself justify the

4. Ruler.   5. In that the play *Antigone* was written and first performed more than ten years prior to *Oedipus the King*.
*From Mary Whitlock Blundell, *Helping Friends and Harming Enemies: A Study in Sophocles and Greek Ethics* (Cambridge, Eng., and New York: Cambridge University Press, 1989), pp. 145–48. All notes are the editor's.   1. City-state.   2. Dialogue delivered in alternating lines; often used to show vigorous dispute.
3. Laws, standards (singular, *nomos*) (Greek).

passionate narrowness with which she pursues it. But although she does not acknowledge the authority of the *polis*, she never explicitly rejects it, as Creon does the family. Moreover she acts ultimately to the city's advantage. As Creon himself so ironically puts it, "the man who is worthwhile in family matters will also turn out to be just in the *polis*." It is Creon's own scorn not just for the family but for public opinion which finally brings the *polis* "doom instead of *soteria*."[4] He who began by saving Thebes from its enemies ends by stirring up other cities with enmity. He tells Antigone she is alone in her views, but she retorts that, on the contrary, all those present (namely the chorus of the city's elders) are on her side. Moreover she foresees great glory from her deed, which the context suggests is to derive from none other than her fellow citizens. Creon can make no such claims for himself. Indeed Haemon will hint that his father's behaviour may be destroying a glorious reputation. With the loss of his son's loyalty, Creon also loses the last shreds of his claim to represent the *polis*. But Antigone's words are vindicated when Haemon reports the admiration of the ordinary citizens, echoing her own evaluation of her deed. Even the chorus, while withholding direct approval of Antigone's actions, promise her praise and glory for the manner of her death.

Antigone does once suggest that she is violating the will of the *polis* as represented by its citizens. But she does so only in the extremity of her isolation, lamenting that she is "friendless" and even questioning her divine support. She has cut herself off from her sister and quarrelled with the chorus, and has not, of course, heard Haemon's report of public sympathy for her fate. Under the circumstances it is not unreasonable that she should now believe she is defying the will of the citizens. But she claims that she would do so under the most extreme provocation, implying respect for the *polis* if not its present king. She restricts her defiance to the drastic circumstances of the present crisis, acknowledging the potential conflict between her own priorities and the demands of civic life.

As Antigone goes to her death, she emphatically calls the city itself, its gods and its most prominent citizens, the chorus, to bear witness to her fate. Does this tell us that she has learned the limitations of her own narrow principles? Or is it a reproach to the apathetic chorus? Surely the latter. She shows no sign of regret or new-found insight into the civic value of obedience. But she addresses the chorus in ways suggesting their special responsibility not just as citizens, but as Theban aristocrats who might be expected to play a role in public life. She calls them "citizens of the fatherland," "wealthy men of the *polis*," "leading men of Thebes." When she refers to herself as "the last remaining daughter of the royal house," she is reasserting her status as a member of the ruling family, to which the chorus are supposedly loyal, and to which Creon is tied only by marriage. This royal status is linked with her reverence for the gods, especially her ancestral gods. Her obligations to the *polis* and her dead family are not mutually exclusive. She has not failed the citizens, for the burial was both in their best interest and called for by their "established laws." But they, intimidated by Creon, have aban-

4. Salvation; the root, *soter*, means "savior."

doned her. She therefore accuses the chorus of mockery and *hubris*,[5] the same hostile laughter that she inflicted on her sister and (in his view) on Creon.

One-sided and "autonomous" though she may be, Antigone's obsession is less sterile and destructive than Creon's. He, as he so much likes to remind us, is the sole ruler of the *polis*. In order to achieve a just and stable social order, such a ruler must acknowledge and balance competing claims and values. If these are ultimately incommensurable, he must attempt a compromise, however uneasy. As Haemon eloquently insists, he must know how to bend with the storm. He must respect the ties of natural *philia*,[6] and at the same time promote political *philia* by adopting policies that meet the citizens' approval. Antigone abides heroically by the first variety of *philia* as she interprets it, and can make some claim to the second, but Creon is a failure at both.

5. A complex term in Greek ethical thought that implies an impious overreaching of human limits.
6. Love, affinity.

Evaluating Drama

How can you tell if a play is good? Why are some plays said to be "great"? On what grounds are plays like *Hamlet* or *Oedipus the King* judged so important that they are performed, season after season, in place after place, for hundreds or thousands of years? Why do actors try to build reputations on playing classic parts—Ophelia or Hamlet, Nora Helmer or Willy Loman—rather than staking their careers on new plays or less famous roles? Why do people continue to buy and read some plays over and over while other plays die on the shelf or never get printed at all? Is there a qualitative difference between "great" and "good" or between "good" and "satisfactory," or are such distinctions subjective or arbitrary? What criteria are useful in trying to assess the literary or dramatic quality of a play? What other kinds of values—political, cultural, social, moral, or ideological—are relevant in judging plays?

These questions are important ones, but the answers are not easy. No litmus test, unfortunately, turns a text blue if it is "great," red if it is "bad," or shades of purple if it is somewhere in between. Even intelligent, knowledgeable, and well-meaning people do not always agree about matters of pleasure, importance, or quality. Besides, judgments vary from age to age and culture to culture, and plays judged highly in one time and place do not necessarily hold their reputations later and elsewhere.

Still, quality matters, and if judgments are sometimes difficult and frustrating, they are also inevitable. We judge all the time, and the question is whether we judge by standards that we can communicate to others or whether we settle for gut feelings. Evaluating is not something that only critics or experts do. But how can we—students, teachers, editors—pretend to evaluate works that have been authoritatively established by the ages? One way, a way you probably already know, is to "fake it till you make it." You read a text that you don't like or don't understand, but, knowing that it is supposed to be "great" and that, therefore, you are supposed to admire it, you go through the motions. There may be a virtue in such pretense: humility. You temporarily suspend your opinion in the light of widespread, long-lasting judgment. Perhaps as you grow familiar with the text, you suddenly find yourself seeing things in it you did not see before, and you begin, in your fashion, to appreciate it. This chapter asks you to give established texts a chance and, without fakery, come to understand—whether or not you finally come to "like" them—why they have been popularly and critically "canonized." It also asks you to evaluate a successful, prizewinning play that is too recent to have become established.

The first play in this chapter, *A Streetcar Named Desire* by Tennessee Williams, is an American play written in the middle of the twentieth century. The second, *The Cherry Orchard* by Anton Chekhov, is a Russian play written at the beginning of the twentieth century. Most people consider these two plays classics. Though not everything that Williams or Chekhov wrote is as frequently performed or studied as *A Streetcar Named Desire* or *The Cherry Orchard*, an international consensus calls these two of the best plays—and playwrights—of the century. Both *A Streetcar Named Desire* and *The Cherry Orchard* are established in the literary canon, frequently performed and studied.

Pay attention to your own responses to these plays, listen to others' views, and try to arrive at interpretations and evaluations that you can support. The point is not to rank these plays in the "Top Hundred Plays of All Time" or to measure them against one another, though a fair assessment can benefit from comparisons among literary works. Evaluation is ultimately gut response. It is also *initially* gut response. But the initial and the ultimate response may not be—seldom are—the same. For feelings and impressions may be modified by clear thinking (aided by writing your thoughts down), by repeated readings, and by new information and perspectives gained by reading and speaking with others. Sorting out the reasons for a response is a useful part of learning to read effectively and resonantly. What this chapter suggests, then, is that after you read each play,

1. you should begin with an honest affective response: do you like it or not, how much or how little? If you don't like it, do you at least admire some things in it?
2. you should try to articulate that response in detail, preferably in writing;
3. you should listen to class discussion, and read what your classmates write and any critical commentary you are assigned or search out;
4. you should, when you have formulated your new, more informed judgment, write it down again;
5. you should then read the play again;
6. you should, finally (as medicine labels sometimes say), repeat as necessary.

Judgment does not wait for this process to run its course, however. Though we may "suspend our judgment" in the sense that we at first choose not to articulate what we think about a play, we begin judging, consciously or unconsciously, from the very beginning of our reading or viewing—and sometimes before. Even the title of *A Streetcar Named Desire* generates some kind of response. If we are coming to it for the first time, we can find it intriguing, and we may suspect that the strange notion of a streetcar having a name and that name being "Desire" will have something to do with the subject and theme of the play. If we see the title as carrying meaning but know that until 1948 New Orleans had a streetcar line named Desire, we may admire the playwright's ingenuity in blending the real and the "symbolic" (soon reinforced by the name Elysian Fields, which is also both real and symbolic). Or we might find the name a bit 1960s or "cutesy," or too obvious, like an allegory.

The Cherry Orchard similarly sets up expectations at the start, and some of your first responses may be misleading. Evidently we are in a country house, in Russia (May is still very cold, it is already light in the early hours of the morning), in an age of trains; but we know nothing about the disparate people moving about, or how they relate to each other or to the estate. Reading the play for the first time, you may find some of the lines stilted; remember that this is a translation. And what about all those confusing names? (According to Russian custom, each character has a first name [for example, Lyubov and Leonid, sister and brother heirs of the cherry orchard and estate]; a patronymic, or version of the father's name [Andreyevna and Andreyevich, literally daughter and son of Andrey]; and a public or family name, or surname [Ranevsky and Gaev].) Within a few scenes we learn who is who, but at first you may want to refer frequently to the list of "Characters in the Play." In actual performance it is easy enough to tell the characters apart.

Konstantin Stanislavsky, the founder of the Moscow Art Theatre who worked closely with Chekhov, warned against the first impression of a Chekhov play. Stanislavsky wrote in *My Life in Art* (1924),

The poetic power of Chekhov's plays does not manifest itself at the first reading. After having read them, you say to yourself: This is good, but . . . it's nothing special, nothing to stun you with admiration. . . . Familiar . . . truthful . . . nothing new. . . . The plot? The subject? You can explain them in a couple of words. Acting parts? Many are good, but none are striking enough to stimulate an ambitious actor.

Yet, as you recollect some phrases and scenes, you feel you want to think about them more, think about them longer. . . . You want to re-read it—and then you realize the depths hidden under the surface. . . . Chekhov is inexhaustible because, despite the everyday life which he appears to depict in his plays, he is really talking all the time not of the accidental and specific, but of the Human, with the capital "h."

In fact, Chekhov's plays are not particularly difficult to understand and to enjoy. Unlike such eminent playwrights of the past century as Bertolt Brecht and Samuel Beckett, but like a number of playwrights included in this anthology—Bernard Shaw, Henrik Ibsen, and Tennessee Williams among them—Chekhov depicts ordinary life and daily conversations; his characters are psychologically coherent, and the action is realistic and chronological. We might say that the poetry in *The Cherry Orchard* is less obvious than that in *A Streetcar Named Desire;* it is spoken in the tone of prose rather than of poetry, and we must put it together in our own minds rather than watch it acted out between characters.

In reading these plays, keep your first impressions flexible until you finish reading the whole and can think back on its parts—character, structure, setting, tone, theme— to see how they relate, to see the play as a whole. Discovering a play's wholeness—its fundamental direction and thrust—is not an easy matter. In fact, you cannot do it all at once. But you have been learning, in this course and in this book, how to think carefully about wholeness by looking systematically at parts. Ask yourself about the play's themes; the way it conceives character and presents changes within and interactions among characters; the kinds of conflicts it develops and resolves; the responses it calls for. Your considered evaluation involves first of all a close reading and a careful analysis of the relationship between parts and whole.

Of course, a literary work, being more than the sum of its parts, may trace more than one thematic pattern. As we read further in *A Streetcar Named Desire*, for example, we recognize that the opening motif of love/desire, with its elements of coarseness/aggressiveness and romance/sensuality, is reinforced with the arrival of Blanche, whose genteel finery can hardly find a place in these cramped two rooms in the squalid quarter of a steamy city. We observe the effects: Stanley's ominous line, "If I didn't know that you was my wife's sister I'd get ideas about you!"; the "dead boy's" love letters to her; her "unconsciously" standing half-undressed where she can be seen by the poker players. These effects are further complicated by the "courtship ritual"—her heart-to-heart conversation with Mitch about love—and the seemingly ordinary and sincere course of love between her and Mitch, destroyed by Stanley's exposure of her sad and ignoble life in Laurel and at the Flamingo Hotel, the sordid act that led to her being fired from her teaching job. Walking a thin line between a romantic ideal and sexual manipulation, Blanche provokes Stanley, who in his brutality also uses sex for power.

We can relate character, imagery, plot, setting (New Orleans, the Blue Piano sounds), and tone to the theme of desire; critical understanding usually requires that we relate elements and discrete details to a unifying theme. Most readers instinctively feel, however, that Tennessee Williams's play transcends simple thematic analysis of it. The love/desire reading, for example, leaves out the theme of class, of lost status, of a real or mythical Southern past—Belle Reve—that in some ways relates this play to Faulkner's "A Rose for Emily," O'Connor's "Everything That Rises Must Converge," and even *Gone with the Wind*; and it hardly explains why Williams once thought of calling the play *The Poker Night*. The theme of desire centers on Blanche (a role actresses covet), with reinforcement from Stella and Mitch. Why, then, was the sensation of the first performance, and of the 1951 film, Stanley Kowalski (other than the fact that he was played by the young Marlon Brando), and how does his centrality affect the complex of love and desire?

Even though evaluation may ultimately depend on subjective judgments and good readers may reasonably differ from each other, questions of evaluation, as we have seen, come close to analytical questions, and determining meaning and effect takes you quickly to questions of value. And vice versa. Often asking questions about how good a play is will get you closer to questions of what it is about and of what you value than you may at first be aware of. You must, then, in evaluating, in articulating your response— steps 1 and 2, above—"interpret"; that is, say what play, or what understanding of the play, you are responding to. As you may have noticed, the essays in "Critical Contexts" involve interpretation, singling out what the play says to the critic, often engaging with the readings of other critics—as in step 3, above. There will be no definitive interpretation; the reading in step 4 will be better and richer than that in step 1, but there will be no "perfect" reading. Even if you

> *For a writer who is not intentionally obscure, and never, in his opinion, obscure at all, I do get asked a hell of a lot of questions which I can't answer. I have never been able to say what was the theme of my play and I don't think I've ever been conscious of writing with a theme in mind. I am always surprised when, after a play has opened, I read in the papers what the play is about.*
>
> —TENNESSEE WILLIAMS

were to skip the third and fourth steps, when you read a play the second or third time your vision of it and your response to it will differ from those of your first reading.

Each critic is himself or herself part of a time, place, and culture, and that context also constrains the critical reading and evaluation. If theater reviewers from Moscow in 1904 or New York in 1947 were (through time travel) to attend an opening night in New York, 2002, they might feel almost as alienated and dumbfounded as if they had suddenly dropped into an ancient Athenian arena to watch a play by Sophocles. Though conflicts remain remarkably constant over thousands of years, social and dramatic conventions radically alter. You may find it easier to interpret and evaluate a recent play with a contemporary style and current themes. Or like many subscribers to repertory theaters, you may prefer classics of forty or a hundred years ago—or even four centuries ago, if it's Shakespeare you want. Or you may enjoy plays of many different contexts, reaching beyond your first reactions to engage with each work as much as possible on its own terms.

Samuel Johnson, the most respected arbiter of taste in England in the late eighteenth century, said that "nothing can please many and please long but just representations of general nature." Johnson was trying to explain why Shakespeare had continued to charm readers and playgoers for a century and a half, and his comments form both a commonsense argument about actual responses to texts (based on consensus and durability) and a proposition about the relation between literature and reality. Good literature, says Johnson, accurately reflects patterns that exist across culture and time; to last, literature must have something important ("just") to say about what does not change according to time or place ("general nature" or the Human with a capital "h").

Not everyone in Johnson's time agreed that such a universal standard could be found, and in the early twenty-first century's enlarged and varied world of cultural relativity, fewer still believe that universals exist. Yet his point interests even relativists. We still want to believe that literature has a vision of reality from which we can learn, even if we do not expect universal plots and characters that assure us that life and times are ever the same. We seek, to some degree, representations of the Human.

Anton Chekhov's last play, *The Cherry Orchard* has pleased many and pleased long—since its first production in 1904, weeks before the playwright's death from tuberculosis—and many admire its "just representations of general nature," in Samuel Johnson's terms. At the same time, it remains a distinctly Russian play, and its style and themes belong very much to modernist theater and to pre-Soviet, pre–World War I Europe. Celebrated from the 1880s as a short-story writer (see "The Lady with the Dog," in chapter 4), Chekhov had a reputation as a comic playwright when he began, after 1895, to produce the dramas for which he is known today: *The Seagull, Uncle Vanya, The Three Sisters,* and *The Cherry Orchard.* Each play had a precarious start, as regional and Moscow audiences had to grow accustomed to a new definition of drama and a new style of acting. Russians soon revered Chekhov as their quintessential national playwright, but then were puzzled at the enthusiasm of Parisian or London audiences in the mid twentieth century: how could the anguish and humor of the Russian spirit have international appeal? Chekhov's late plays have been steadily produced in regional theaters in the United States since World War II, yet as the critic Henry Popkin observes, Americans have a "caricature" of Chekhov, a "suspicion of total inaction, of a pervasive and peculiarly Russian gloom, or characters stumbling around ignoring each other, addressing their bitter complaints to convenient doors and windows, calling one another by indistinguishable three-barrelled Russian names." And badly performed, or carelessly read, Chekhov's plays may provoke impatience or unsolicited laughter.

Things for [Chekhov] were funny and sad at the same time, but you would not see their sadness if you did not see their fun, because both were linked up.

—VLADIMIR NABOKOV

Interpretation lies behind evaluation: our view of a work's meaning guides how we read or perform it and, hence, our response to its quality. A misguided interpretation can ruin even a well-made play for us. Some directors and actors, for example, deciding that Chekhov is a serious and mysterious playwright, present *The Cherry Orchard* as a tragedy and thus miss the point that it is chock-full of running jokes, such as the old butler's mumbling and deafness, Pishtchik's falling asleep midsentence or begging for money, Gaev's pretending to play billiards all the time, and Lyubov's constant squandering of cash. As he was writing the play, Chekhov asserted that it "will definitely be funny, very funny—at least in intention," but even without knowing this statement we can find within its words and action a delicate blend of the amusing with the wistful, foolish, cruel, hopeful, affectionate, sorrowful, deluded, generous, and selfish. We might think of the play as a small *Titanic* without special effects and with hints of a Marx Brothers farce. The members of this household, ordinary people, keep trying to deny that they have struck an iceberg, but sense that something infinitely precious is about to be wasted, that this is their last chance to say something that might be understood by a fellow being. Too often, the other person isn't listening. But we are.

Blanche DuBois, similarly, may be heard only by the audience. Like Arthur Miller's *Death of a Salesman,* which first appeared two years later, *A Streetcar Named Desire* depicts the destruction of an ordinary dreamer in a ruthless, competitive, modern world; both are often staged as tragedy. In their original Broadway productions, the sets of both *Streetcar* and *Salesman* showed the inside and outside of a cramped low-income home and conveyed the characters' confinement through invasive shadows or sounds. And with their intermixture of explicit psychological and sexual motivation, symbolic staging, poetic monologues or visions, and realistic, everyday action, Tennessee Williams and Arthur Miller together influenced postwar theater across the globe.

In the course of evaluating these plays, you can derive insights from further comparisons between them. Notice that they both focus on a similar problem, the loss of a family estate that represents an older, more hierarchical way of life, which depended on slavery (or serfdom) a couple of generations ago. In *The Cherry Orchard*, this problem drives the plot, rather than providing the background and a source of conflict as it does in *A Streetcar Named Desire*. Williams stages a violent confrontation between new and old social elements—a rape—whereas Chekhov postpones indefinitely the proposal of marriage between Lopahin and Varya. Sexuality drives Stanley and ruins Blanche in the 1947 play, whereas Chekhov's characters seem almost unaware of sex's appeal. Madame Ranevsky's lover appears only as a series of manipulative telegrams from Paris; the young couple, Anya and Trofimov, claim to be above love. On the other hand, Chekhov's characters seem aware of history, the social order, and coming political change in a way unimaginable in *Streetcar*. But in both plays, characters struggle to escape their narrow circumstances and their guilty or grieving memories.

Through a careful reading of details, connection of parts to the whole, interpretation of themes and the intended tone, whether tragic or comic, as well as comparison with other works, we approach a reasonably sound evaluation of a literary work. In the process, as in this chapter, we begin to place each work historically and to approach the spirit in which it was first created. If we ask a Disney cartoon to be a classical ballet, or imagine a Shakespeare play performed in the manner of *Star Trek*—or vice versa—the works lose their integrity, and we will be disappointed all around. Some sense of historical context is indispensable to an evaluation that goes beyond current fashions or personal likes and dislikes.

In addition to the other elements that *A Streetcar Named Desire* and *The Cherry Orchard* have in common, these works and their authors have a historical connection that accounts for some similarity of dramatic manner. Stanislavsky, the Russian actor and producer quoted above on Chekhov's art, wanted to cut through the prevailing style of acting around the turn of the twentieth century: the exaggerated, declamatory style of delivering lines, the conventionalized gestures and postures that seemed to remind no one of real people or emotions. He believed acting should physically express the emotional truth of a character; an actor should prepare by reconstructing a history for the character and, by drawing on his or her own memories of similar experiences, relive the feelings of that role. This technique, which became known as "method acting," focused on authentic inner motivation, from which convincing external behavior should intuitively follow. From the 1930s onward, particularly under the influence of Lee Strasberg's Actors' Studio in New York City, acting in the United States, whether in theater, film, or on television, has been based on the Stanislavskian method. Method acting was popularized, in fact, by Marlon Brando, who played Stanley in Elia Kazan's stage and movie versions of *Streetcar*. Try to see this 1951 film (available on video and DVD) to get an idea of the physicality and apparently natural, informal manners and speech that seemed new at the time—and which we have grown used to, whether from James Dean or from Robert De Niro. Then try to imagine Brando playing a part in *The Cherry Orchard*, perhaps the cocky servant Yasha, or the perpetual student Trofimov. For according to Stanislavsky's "Aphorisms for a New Theatre"—drawn up with Vladimir Nemiravich-Danchenko in 1897—anyone in an ensemble should be able to prepare any role:

1. There are no small parts, there are only small actors;
2. Today Hamlet, tomorrow an extra, but even as an extra the actor must be an artist;
3. The playwright, the actor, the scene-designer, the dresser and the stage-hand all serve one purpose, namely, to express the playwright's main idea in writing his play;
4. The theatre begins with the cloakroom;
5. Every violation of the creative life of the theatre is a crime;
6. Arriving late at the theatre, laziness, capriciousness, hysteria, ignorance of parts, the necessity of repeating the same thing twice, are all equally harmful and must be rooted out.

Since we have very few written records, and no film or video, of acting styles before the twentieth century, and since so many fine actors today are influenced by what we could call the Stanislavsky–Brando method, we must work to imagine what was startling about the new twentieth-century style in theater. Audiences at the premieres of Chekhov's plays had to learn to hear lines spoken in the manner of everyday conversation rather than of melodrama. At the same time, they had to recognize that the play was not just a slice of life, not just a reflection of social facts as in "naturalism"; they had to listen to the symbolic or universal implications of a Chekhov play. This new style helped prepare audiences for the plays of, for example, Tennessee Williams. But do we have to prefer this style? A great deal of important drama across the centuries and today has had nothing to do with realistic characterization. Actors in Britain and elsewhere enjoy excellent training without being taught to relive the fictitious emotional history of their parts. Introspection can be self-centered. It might strike audiences in a different century that the characters in a Chekhov or Williams play suffer isolation and anguish, or exert their brute force, because of a fatal egotism, perhaps the disease of modern individualism. Both plays extrapolate from individuals to the harm done by social systems: aristocratic impracticality (Mme. Ranevsky), peasant superstition (Firs), the extremes of femininity (Blanche) and masculinity (Stanley). An evaluation of both plays, together or separately, extends beyond the questions of whether they succeed on their own terms, to a historical perspective on the literary and theatrical conventions of their day as well as the ways of life and the values they portray.

Ultimately, evaluation is about what values we share and with whom. Sometimes, values shared throughout a whole culture or an entire age determine how a text will be received and evaluated; sometimes the sharing involves smaller, more local, or more select groups. Evaluations of some features of plays—of whether language is used precisely or effectively, for example, or whether characters are presented consistently and winningly—may sometimes seem almost value free. Can't we decide such issues without regard to our social, economic, religious, or political biases and presuppositions? The answer seems to be that what we bring to a text, and where we bring it from, will likely influence our judgment at every point. But the fact that our judgments are both highly subjective and influenced by the ideologies and cultural identities we participate in does not mean that evaluation is predetermined and beyond discussion or change. The better we can articulate our values and adduce evidence from the text, the more we will be able to learn, to grow, and to teach. Agreeing about the quality of a play is not ultimately the point. You may never convince someone else that a particular play is as good or bad as you think it is. And you may never be convinced by someone else's arguments. But having discussions about quality has virtues of its own. The grounds of judgment are ultimately more important than the judgment of any single play, and argument helps clarify the grounds of judgment. Knowing your own grounds of judgment may make a play more enjoyable and meaningful to you; certainly it will make you more aware of who you are as a reader and as a person.

Your challenge now is to read these three plays, imagining how you would see and hear them on a stage. Reading, you can pay extra attention to the words, which would fly by you in a theatrical performance. Pay attention as well to your changing responses and, as you respond, begin the open-ended process of evaluating.

TENNESSEE WILLIAMS

A Streetcar Named Desire

> And so it was I entered the broken world
> To trace the visionary company of love, its voice
> An instant in the wind (I know not whither hurled)
> But not for long to hold each desperate choice.
>
> —"The Broken Tower" by HART CRANE[1]

CHARACTERS

BLANCHE	PABLO
STELLA	A NEGRO WOMAN
STANLEY	A DOCTOR
MITCH	A NURSE (MATRON)
EUNICE	A YOUNG COLLECTOR
STEVE	A MEXICAN WOMAN

SCENE 1

The exterior of a two-story corner building on a street in New Orleans which is named Elysian Fields and runs between the L & N tracks and the river.[2] The section is poor but, unlike corresponding sections in other American cities, it has a raffish charm. The houses are mostly white frame, weathered grey, with rickety outside stairs and galleries and quaintly ornamented gables. This building contains two flats, upstairs and down. Faded white stairs ascend to the entrances of both.

It is first dark of an evening early in May. The sky that shows around the dim white building is a peculiarly tender blue, almost a turquoise, which invests the scene with a

---

1. American poet (1899–1932).   2. Elysian Fields is in fact a New Orleans street at the northern tip of the French Quarter, between the Louisville & Nashville railroad tracks and the Mississippi River. In Greek mythology, the Elysian Fields are the abode of the blessed in the afterlife; in Paris, the Champs-Élysées ("Elysian Fields") is a grand boulevard.

kind of lyricism and gracefully attenuates the atmosphere of decay. You can almost feel the warm breath of the brown river beyond the river warehouses with their faint redolences of bananas and coffee. A corresponding air is evoked by the music of Negro entertainers at a barroom around the corner. In this part of New Orleans you are practically always just around the corner, or a few doors down the street, from a tinny piano being played with the infatuated fluency of brown fingers. This "Blue Piano" expresses the spirit of the life which goes on here.

Two women, one white and one colored, are taking the air on the steps of the building. The white woman is EUNICE, *who occupies the upstairs flat; the* NEGRO WOMAN, *a neighbor, for New Orleans is a cosmopolitan city where there is a relatively warm and easy intermingling of races in the old part of town.*

Above the music of the "Blue Piano" the voices of people on the street can be heard overlapping.

> [*Two men come around the corner,* STANLEY KOWALSKI *and* MITCH. *They are about twenty-eight, or thirty years old, roughly dressed in blue denim work clothes.* STANLEY *carries his bowling jacket and a red-stained package from a butcher's. They stop at the foot of the steps.*]

STANLEY: [*Bellowing.*] Hey there! Stella, baby!

> [STELLA *comes out on the first floor landing, a gentle young woman, about twenty-five, and of a background obviously quite different from her husband's.*]

STELLA: [*Mildly.*] Don't holler at me like that. Hi, Mitch.
STANLEY: Catch!
STELLA: What?
STANLEY: Meat!

> [*He heaves the package at her. She cries out in protest but manages to catch it: then she laughs breathlessly. Her husband and his companion have already started back around the corner.*]

STELLA: [*Calling after him.*] Stanley! Where are you going?
STANLEY: Bowling!
STELLA: Can I come watch?
STANLEY: Come on. [*He goes out.*]
STELLA: Be over soon. [*To the* WHITE WOMAN.] Hello, Eunice. How are you?
EUNICE: I'm all right. Tell Steve to get him a poor boy's sandwich[3] 'cause nothing's left here.

> [*They all laugh; the* NEGRO WOMAN *does not stop.* STELLA *goes out.*]

NEGRO WOMAN: What was that package he th'ew at 'er? [*She rises from steps, laughing louder.*]
EUNICE: You hush, now!
NEGRO WOMAN: Catch *what!*

---

3. Usually called just "poor boy" or "po' boy." Similar to a hero or submarine sandwich.

[*She continues to laugh.* BLANCHE *comes around the corner, carrying a valise. She looks at a slip of paper, then at the building, then again at the slip and again at the building. Her expression is one of shocked disbelief. Her appearance is incongruous to this setting. She is daintily dressed in a white suit with a fluffy bodice, necklace and earrings of pearl, white gloves and hat, looking as if she were arriving at a summer tea or cocktail party in the garden district. She is about five years older than* STELLA. *Her delicate beauty must avoid a strong light. There is something about her uncertain manner, as well as her white clothes, that suggests a moth.*]

EUNICE: [*Finally.*] What's the matter, honey? Are you lost?

BLANCHE: [*With faintly hysterical humor.*] They told me to take a street-car named Desire, and then transfer to one called Cemeteries[4] and ride six blocks and get off at—Elysian Fields!

EUNICE: That's where you are now.

BLANCHE: At Elysian Fields?

EUNICE: This here is Elysian Fields.

BLANCHE: They mustn't have—understood—what number I wanted . . .

EUNICE: What number you lookin' for?

[BLANCHE *wearily refers to the slip of paper.*]

BLANCHE: Six thirty-two.

EUNICE: You don't have to look no further.

BLANCHE: [*Uncomprehendingly.*] I'm looking for my sister, Stella DuBois, I mean— Mrs. Stanley Kowalski.

EUNICE: That's the party.—You just did miss her, though.

BLANCHE: This—can this be—her home?

EUNICE: She's got the downstairs here and I got the up.

BLANCHE: Oh. She's—out?

EUNICE: You noticed that bowling alley around the corner?

BLANCHE: I'm—not sure I did.

EUNICE: Well, that's where she's at, watchin' her husband bowl. [*There is a pause.*] You want to leave your suitcase here an' go find her?

BLANCHE: No.

NEGRO WOMAN: I'll go tell her you come.

BLANCHE: Thanks.

NEGRO WOMAN: You welcome. [*She goes out.*]

EUNICE: She wasn't expecting you?

BLANCHE: No. No, not tonight.

EUNICE: Well, why don't you just go in and make yourself at home till they get back.

BLANCHE: How could I—do that?

EUNICE: We own this place so I can let you in.

[*She gets up and opens the downstairs door. A light goes on behind the blind,*

4. Desire is a street in New Orleans, Cemeteries the end of a streetcar line that stopped at a cemetery.

turning it light blue. BLANCHE *slowly follows her into the downstairs flat. The surrounding areas dim out as the interior is lighted. Two rooms can be seen, not too clearly defined. The one first entered is primarily a kitchen but contains a folding bed to be used by* BLANCHE. *The room beyond this is a bedroom. Off this room is a narrow door to a bathroom.*]

EUNICE: [*Defensively, noticing* BLANCHE's *look.*] It's sort of messed up right now but when it's clean it's real sweet.

BLANCHE: Is it?

EUNICE: Uh-huh, I think so. So you're Stella's sister?

BLANCHE: Yes. [*Wanting to get rid of her.*] Thanks for letting me in.

EUNICE: *Por nada,* as the Mexicans say, *por nada!*[5] Stella spoke of you.

BLANCHE: Yes?

EUNICE: I think she said you taught school.

BLANCHE: Yes.

EUNICE: And you're from Mississippi, huh?

BLANCHE: Yes.

EUNICE: She showed me a picture of your home-place, the plantation.

BLANCHE: Belle Reve?[6]

EUNICE: A great big place with white columns.

BLANCHE: Yes . . .

EUNICE: A place like that must be awful hard to keep up.

BLANCHE: If you will excuse me, I'm just about to drop.

EUNICE: Sure, honey. Why don't you set down?

BLANCHE: What I meant was I'd like to be left alone.

EUNICE: [*Offended.*] Aw. I'll make myself scarce, in that case.

BLANCHE: I didn't mean to be rude, but—

EUNICE: I'll drop by the bowling alley an' hustle her up. [*She goes out the door.*]

[BLANCHE *sits in a chair very stiffly with her shoulders slightly hunched and her legs pressed close together and her hands tightly clutching her purse as if she were quite cold. After a while the blind look goes out of her eyes and she begins to look slowly around. A cat screeches. She catches her breath with a startled gesture. Suddenly she notices something in a half opened closet. She springs up and crosses to it, and removes a whiskey bottle. She pours a half tumbler of whiskey and tosses it down. She carefully replaces the bottle and washes out the tumbler at the sink. Then she resumes her seat in front of the table.*]

BLANCHE: [*Faintly to herself.*] I've got to keep hold of myself!

[STELLA *comes quickly around the corner of the building and runs to the door of the downstairs flat.*]

STELLA: [*Calling out joyfully.*] Blanche!

---

5. It's nothing.   6. Beautiful Dream.

[*For a moment they stare at each other. Then* BLANCHE *springs up and runs to her with a wild cry.*]

BLANCHE: Stella, oh, Stella, Stella! Stella for Star! [*She begins to speak with feverish vivacity as if she feared for either of them to stop and think. They catch each other in a spasmodic embrace.*] Now, then, let me look at you. But don't you look at me, Stella, no, no, no, not till later, not till I've bathed and rested! And turn that over-light off! Turn that off! I won't be looked at in this merciless glare! [STELLA *laughs and complies.*] Come back here now! Oh, my baby! Stella! Stella for Star! [*She embraces her again.*] I thought you would never come back to this horrible place! What am I saying? I didn't mean to say that. I meant to be nice about it and say—Oh, what a convenient location and such— Ha-a-ha! Precious lamb! You haven't said a *word* to me.

STELLA: You haven't given me a chance to, honey! [*She laughs, but her glance at* BLANCHE *is a little anxious.*]

BLANCHE: Well, now you talk. Open your pretty mouth and talk while I look around for some liquor! I know you must have some liquor on the place! Where could it be, I wonder? Oh, I spy, I spy! [*She rushes to the closet and removes the bottle; she is shaking all over and panting for breath as she tries to laugh. The bottle nearly slips from her grasp.*]

STELLA: [*Noticing.*] Blanche, you sit down and let me pour the drinks. I don't know what we've got to mix with. Maybe a Coke in the icebox. Look'n see, honey, while I'm—

BLANCHE: No Coke, honey, not with my nerves tonight! Where—where—where is—?

STELLA: Stanley? Bowling! He loves it. They're having a—found some soda!— tournament . . .

BLANCHE: Just water, baby, to chase it! Now don't get worried, your sister hasn't turned into a drunkard, she's just all shaken up and hot and tired and dirty! You sit down, now, and explain this place to me! What are you doing in a place like this?

STELLA: Now, Blanche—

BLANCHE: Oh, I'm not going to be hypocritical, I'm going to be honestly critical about it! Never, never, never in my worst dreams could I picture—Only Poe! Only Mr. Edgar Allan Poe!—could do it justice! Out there I suppose is the ghoul-haunted woodland of Weir![7] [*She laughs.*]

STELLA: No, honey, those are the L & N tracks.

BLANCHE: No, now seriously, putting joking aside. Why didn't you tell me, why didn't you write me, honey, why didn't you let me know?

STELLA: [*Carefully, pouring herself a drink.*] Tell you what, Blanche?

BLANCHE: Why, that you had to live in these conditions!

STELLA: Aren't you being a little intense about it? It's not that bad at all! New Orleans isn't like other cities.

BLANCHE: This has got nothing to do with New Orleans. You might as well say—

---

7. From the refrain of Poe's gothic ballad *Ulalume* (1847).

forgive me, blessed baby! [*She suddenly stops short.*] The subject is closed!

STELLA: [*A little drily.*] Thanks.

[*During the pause,* BLANCHE *stares at her. She smiles at* BLANCHE.]

BLANCHE: [*Looking down at her glass, which shakes in her hand.*] You're all I've got in the world, and you're not glad to see me!

STELLA: [*Sincerely.*] Why, Blanche, you know that's not true.

BLANCHE: No?—I'd forgotten how quiet you were.

STELLA: You never did give me a chance to say much, Blanche. So I just got in the habit of being quiet around you.

BLANCHE: [*Vaguely.*] A good habit to get into . . . [*Then, abruptly.*] You haven't asked me how I happened to get away from the school before the spring term ended.

STELLA: Well, I thought you'd volunteer that information—if you wanted to tell me.

BLANCHE: You thought I'd been fired?

STELLA: No, I—thought you might have—resigned . . .

BLANCHE: I was so exhausted by all I'd been through my—nerves broke. [*Nervously tamping cigarette.*] I was on the verge of—lunacy, almost! So Mr. Graves—Mr. Graves is the high school superintendent—he suggested I take a leave of absence. I couldn't put all of those details into the wire . . . [*She drinks quickly.*] Oh, this buzzes right through me and feels so *good!*

STELLA: Won't you have another?

BLANCHE: No, one's my limit.

STELLA: Sure?

BLANCHE: You haven't said a word about my appearance.

STELLA: You look just fine.

BLANCHE: God love you for a liar! Daylight never exposed so total a ruin! But you— you've put on some weight, yes, you're just as plump as a little partridge! And it's so becoming to you!

STELLA: Now, Blanche—

BLANCHE: Yes, it is, it is or I wouldn't say it! You just have to watch around the hips a little. Stand up.

STELLA: Not now.

BLANCHE: You hear me? I said stand up! [STELLA *complies reluctantly.*] You messy child, you, you've spilt something on that pretty white lace collar! About your hair—you ought to have it cut in a feather bob with your dainty features. Stella, you have a maid, don't you?

STELLA: No. With only two rooms it's—

BLANCHE: What? *Two* rooms, did you say?

STELLA: This one and— [*She is embarrassed.*]

BLANCHE: The other one? [*She laughs sharply. There is an embarrassed silence.*] I am going to take just one little tiny nip more, sort of to put the stopper on, so to speak. . . . Then put the bottle away so I won't be tempted. [*She rises.*] I want you to look at *my* figure! [*She turns around.*] You know I haven't put on one ounce in ten years, Stella? I weigh what I weighed the summer you left

Belle Reve. The summer Dad died and you left us . . .

STELLA: [*A little wearily.*] It's just incredible, Blanche, how well you're looking.

BLANCHE: [*They both laugh uncomfortably.*] But, Stella, there's only two rooms, I don't see where you're going to put me!

STELLA: We're going to put you in here.

BLANCHE: What kind of bed's this—one of those collapsible things? [*She sits on it.*]

STELLA: Does it feel all right?

BLANCHE: [*Dubiously.*] Wonderful, honey. I don't like a bed that gives much. But there's no door between the two rooms, and Stanley—will it be decent?

STELLA: Stanley is Polish, you know.

BLANCHE: Oh, yes. They're something like Irish, aren't they?

STELLA: Well—

BLANCHE: Only not so—highbrow? [*They both laugh again in the same way.*] I brought some nice clothes to meet all your lovely friends in.

STELLA: I'm afraid you won't think they are lovely.

BLANCHE: What are they like?

STELLA: They're Stanley's friends.

BLANCHE: Polacks?

STELLA: They're a mixed lot, Blanche.

BLANCHE: Heterogeneous—types?

STELLA: Oh, yes. Yes, types is right!

BLANCHE: Well—anyhow—I brought nice clothes and I'll wear them. I guess you're hoping I'll say I'll put up at a hotel, but I'm not going to put up at a hotel. I want to be *near* you, got to be *with* somebody, I *can't* be *alone!* Because—as you must have noticed—I'm—*not* very well . . . [*Her voice drops and her look is frightened.*]

STELLA: You seem a little bit nervous or overwrought or something.

BLANCHE: Will Stanley like me, or will I be just a visiting in-law, Stella? I couldn't stand that.

STELLA: You'll get along fine together, if you'll just try not to—well—compare him with men that we went out with at home.

BLANCHE: Is he so—different?

STELLA: Yes. A different species.

BLANCHE: In what way; what's he like?

STELLA: Oh, you can't describe someone you're in love with! Here's a picture of him! [*She hands a photograph to* BLANCHE.]

BLANCHE: An officer?

STELLA: A Master Sergeant in the Engineers' Corps. Those are decorations!

BLANCHE: He had those on when you met him?

STELLA: I assure you I wasn't just blinded by all the brass.

BLANCHE: That's not what I—

STELLA: But of course there were things to adjust myself to later on.

BLANCHE: Such as his civilian background! [STELLA *laughs uncertainly.*] How did he take it when you said I was coming?

STELLA: Oh, Stanley doesn't know yet.

BLANCHE: [*Frightened.*] You—haven't told him?

STELLA: He's on the road a good deal.

BLANCHE: Oh. Travels?

STELLA: Yes.

BLANCHE: Good. I mean—isn't it?

STELLA: [*Half to herself.*] I can hardly stand it when he is away for a night . . .

BLANCHE: Why, Stella!

STELLA: When he's away for a week I nearly go wild!

BLANCHE: Gracious!

STELLA: And when he comes back I cry on his lap like a baby . . . [*She smiles to herself.*]

BLANCHE: I guess that is what is meant by being in love . . . [STELLA *looks up with a radiant smile.*] Stella—

STELLA: What?

BLANCHE: [*In an uneasy rush.*] I haven't asked you the things you probably thought I was going to ask. And so I'll expect you to be understanding about what *I* have to tell *you.*

STELLA: What, Blanche? [*Her face turns anxious.*]

BLANCHE: Well, Stella—you're going to reproach me, I know that you're bound to reproach me—but before you do—take into consideration—you left! I stayed and struggled! You came to New Orleans and looked out for yourself! *I* stayed at Belle Reve and tried to hold it together! I'm not meaning this in any reproachful way, but *all* the burden descended on *my* shoulders.

STELLA: The best I could do was make my own living, Blanche.

[BLANCHE *begins to shake again with intensity.*]

BLANCHE: I know, I know. But you are the one that abandoned Belle Reve, not I! I stayed and fought for it, bled for it, almost died for it!

STELLA: Stop this hysterical outburst and tell me what's happened? What do you mean fought and bled? What kind of—

BLANCHE: I knew you would, Stella. I knew you would take this attitude about it!

STELLA: About—what?—please!

BLANCHE: [*Slowly.*] The loss—the loss . . .

STELLA: Belle Reve? Lost, is it? No!

BLANCHE: Yes, Stella.

[*They stare at each other across the yellow-checked linoleum of the table.* BLANCHE *slowly nods her head and* STELLA *looks slowly down at her hands folded on the table. The music of the "Blue Piano" grows louder.* BLANCHE *touches her handkerchief to her forehead.*]

STELLA: But how did it go? What happened?

BLANCHE: [*Springing up.*] You're a fine one to ask me how it went!

STELLA: Blanche!

BLANCHE: You're a fine one to sit there *accusing me* of it!

STELLA: *Blanche!*

BLANCHE: I, I, *I* took the blows in my face and my body! All of those deaths! The long parade to the graveyard! Father, Mother! Margaret, that dreadful way!

So big with it, it couldn't be put in a coffin! But had to be burned like rubbish! You just came home in time for the funerals, Stella. And funerals are pretty compared to deaths. Funerals are quiet, but deaths—not always. Sometimes their breathing is hoarse, and sometimes it rattles, and sometimes they even cry out to you, "Don't let me go!" Even the old, sometimes, say, "Don't let me go." As if you were able to stop them! But funerals are quiet, with pretty flowers. And, oh, what gorgeous boxes they pack them away in! Unless you were there at the bed when they cried out, "Hold me!" you'd never suspect there was the struggle for breath and bleeding. You didn't dream, but I saw! *Saw! Saw!* And now you sit there telling me with your eyes that I let the place go! How in hell do you think all that sickness and dying was paid for? Death is expensive, Miss Stella! And old Cousin Jessie's right after Margaret's, hers! Why, the Grim Reaper had put up his tent on our doorstep! . . . Stella. Belle Reve was his headquarters! Honey—that's how it slipped through my fingers! Which of them left us a fortune? Which of them left a cent of insurance even? Only poor Jessie—one hundred to pay for her coffin. That was all, Stella! And I with my pitiful salary at the school. Yes, accuse me! Sit there and stare at me, thinking I let the place go! *I* let the place go? Where were *you!* In bed with your—Polack!

STELLA: [*Springing.*] Blanche! You be still! That's enough! [*She starts out.*]

BLANCHE: Where are you going?

STELLA: I'm going into the bathroom to wash my face.

BLANCHE: Oh, Stella, Stella, you're crying!

STELLA: Does that surprise you?

BLANCHE: Forgive me—I didn't mean to—

> [*The sound of men's voices is heard.* STELLA *goes into the bathroom, closing the door behind her. When the men appear, and* BLANCHE *realizes it must be* STAN- LEY *returning, she moves uncertainly from the bathroom door to the dressing table, looking apprehensively toward the front door.* STANLEY *enters, followed by* STEVE *and* MITCH. STANLEY *pauses near his door,* STEVE *by the foot of the spiral stair, and* MITCH *is slightly above and to the right of them, about to go out. As the men enter, we hear some of the following dialogue.*]

STANLEY: Is that how he got it?

STEVE: Sure that's how he got it. He hit the old weather-bird for 300 bucks on a six-number-ticket.

MITCH: Don't tell him those things; he'll believe it. [MITCH *starts out.*]

STANLEY: [*Restraining* MITCH.] Hey, Mitch—come back here.

> [BLANCHE, *at the sound of voices, retires in the bedroom. She picks up* STANLEY's *photo from dressing table, looks at it, puts it down. When* STANLEY *enters the apartment, she darts and hides behind the screen at the head of bed.*]

STEVE: [*To* STANLEY *and* MITCH.] Hey, are we playin' poker tomorrow?

STANLEY: Sure—at Mitch's.

MITCH: [*Hearing this, returns quickly to the stair rail.*] No—not at my place. My mother's still sick!

STANLEY: Okay, at my place . . . [MITCH *starts out again*.] But you bring the beer!

> [MITCH *pretends not to hear—calls out "Good night, all," and goes out, singing.*
> EUNICE'*s voice is heard, above*.]

EUNICE: Break it up down there! I made the spaghetti dish and ate it myself.

STEVE: [*Going upstairs*.] I told you and phoned you we was playing. [*To the men*.] Jax[8] beer!

EUNICE: You never phoned me once.

STEVE: I told you at breakfast—and phoned you at lunch . . .

EUNICE: Well, never mind about that. You just get yourself home here once in a while.

STEVE: You want it in the papers?

> [*More laughter and shouts of parting come from the men.* STANLEY *throws the screen door of the kitchen open and comes in. He is of medium height, about five feet eight or nine, and strongly, compactly built. Animal joy in his being is implicit in all his movements and attitudes. Since earliest manhood the center of his life has been pleasure with women, the giving and taking of it, not with weak indulgence, dependently, but with the power and pride of a richly feathered male bird among hens. Branching out from this complete and satisfying center are all the auxiliary channels of his life, such as his heartiness with men, his appreciation of rough humor, his love of good drink and food and games, his car, his radio, everything that is his, that bears his emblem of the gaudy seed-bearer. He sizes women up at a glance, with sexual classifications, crude images flashing into his mind and determining the way he smiles at them*.]

BLANCHE: [*Drawing involuntarily back from his stare*.] You must be Stanley. I'm Blanche.

STANLEY: Stella's sister?

BLANCHE: Yes.

STANLEY: H'lo. Where's the little woman?

BLANCHE: In the bathroom.

STANLEY: Oh. Didn't know you were coming in town.

BLANCHE: I—uh—

STANLEY: Where you from, Blanche?

BLANCHE: Why, I—live in Laurel.

> [*He has crossed to the closet and removed the whiskey bottle*.]

STANLEY: In Laurel, huh? Oh, yeah. Yeah, in Laurel, that's right. Not in my territory. Liquor goes fast in hot weather. [*He holds the bottle to the light to observe its depletion*.] Have a shot?

BLANCHE: No, I—rarely touch it.

STANLEY: Some people rarely touch it, but it touches them often.

BLANCHE: [*Faintly*.] Ha-ha.

---

8. A local brand.

STANLEY: My clothes're stickin' to me. Do you mind if I make myself comfortable? [*He starts to remove his shirt.*]

BLANCHE: Please, please do.

STANLEY: Be comfortable is my motto.

BLANCHE: It's mine, too. It's hard to stay looking fresh. I haven't washed or even powdered my face and—here you are!

STANLEY: You know you can catch cold sitting around in damp things, especially when you been exercising hard like bowling is. You're a teacher, aren't you?

BLANCHE: Yes.

STANLEY: What do you teach, Blanche?

BLANCHE: English.

STANLEY: I never was a very good English student. How long you here for, Blanche?

BLANCHE: I—don't know yet.

STANLEY: You going to shack up here?

BLANCHE: I thought I would if it's not inconvenient for you all.

STANLEY: Good.

BLANCHE: Traveling wears me out.

STANLEY: Well, take it easy.

[*A cat screeches near the window.* BLANCHE *springs up.*]

BLANCHE: What's that?

STANLEY: Cats . . . Hey, Stella!

STELLA: [*Faintly, from the bathroom.*] Yes, Stanley.

STANLEY: Haven't fallen in, have you? [*He grins at* BLANCHE. *She tries unsuccessfully to smile back. There is a silence.*] I'm afraid I'll strike you as being the unrefined type. Stella's spoke of you a good deal. You were married once, weren't you?

[*The music of the polka rises up, faint in the distance.*]

BLANCHE: Yes. When I was quite young.

STANLEY: What happened?

BLANCHE: The boy—the boy died. [*She sinks back down.*] I'm afraid I'm—going to be sick! [*Her head falls on her arms.*]

SCENE 2

It is six o'clock the following evening. BLANCHE is bathing. STELLA is completing her toilette. BLANCHE's dress, a flowered print, is laid out on STELLA's bed.

STANLEY enters the kitchen from outside, leaving the door open on the perpetual "Blue Piano" around the corner.

STANLEY: What's all this monkey doings?

STELLA: Oh, Stan! [*She jumps up and kisses him, which he accepts with lordly composure.*] I'm taking Blanche to Galatoire's[9] for supper and then to a show, because it's your poker night.

9. A famous old restaurant on Bourbon Street in the French Quarter.

STANLEY: How about my supper, huh? I'm not going to no Galatoire's for supper!

STELLA: I put you a cold plate on ice.

STANLEY: Well, isn't that just dandy!

STELLA: I'm going to try to keep Blanche out till the party breaks up because I don't know how she would take it. So we'll go to one of the little places in the Quarter afterward and you'd better give me some money.

STANLEY: Where is she?

STELLA: She's soaking in a hot tub to quiet her nerves. She's terribly upset.

STANLEY: Over what?

STELLA: She's been through such an ordeal.

STANLEY: Yeah?

STELLA: Stan, we've—lost Belle Reve!

STANLEY: The place in the country?

STELLA: Yes.

STANLEY: How?

STELLA: [*Vaguely.*] Oh, it had to be—sacrificed or something. [*There is a pause while* STANLEY *considers.* STELLA *is changing into her dress.*] When she comes in be sure to say something nice about her appearance. And, oh! Don't mention the baby. I haven't said anything yet, I'm waiting until she gets in a quieter condition.

STANLEY: [*Ominously.*] So?

STELLA: And try to understand her and be nice to her, Stan.

BLANCHE: [*Singing in the bathroom.*] "From the land of the sky blue water, They brought a captive maid!"

STELLA: She wasn't expecting to find us in such a small place. You see I'd tried to gloss things over a little in my letters.

STANLEY: So?

STELLA: And admire her dress and tell her she's looking wonderful. That's important with Blanche. Her little weakness!

STANLEY: Yeah. I get the idea. Now let's skip back a little to where you said the country place was disposed of.

STELLA: Oh!—yes . . .

STANLEY: How about that? Let's have a few more details on that subjeck.

STELLA: It's best not to talk much about it until she's calmed down.

STANLEY: So that's the deal, huh? Sister Blanche cannot be annoyed with business details right now!

STELLA: You saw how she was last night.

STANLEY: Uh-hum, I saw how she was. Now let's have a gander at the bill of sale.

STELLA: I haven't seen any.

STANLEY: She didn't show you no papers, no deed of sale or nothing like that, huh?

STELLA: It seems like it wasn't sold.

STANLEY: Well, what in hell was it then, give away? To charity?

STELLA: Shhh! She'll hear you.

STANLEY: I don't care if she hears me. Let's see the papers!

STELLA: There weren't any papers, she didn't show any papers, I don't care about papers.

STANLEY: Have you ever heard of the Napoleonic code?[1]

STELLA: No, Stanley, I haven't heard of the Napoleonic code and if I have, I don't see what it—

STANLEY: Let me enlighten you on a point or two, baby.

STELLA: Yes?

STANLEY: In the state of Louisiana we have the Napoleonic code according to which what belongs to the wife belongs to the husband and vice versa. For instance if I had a piece of property, or you had a piece of property—

STELLA: My head is swimming!

STANLEY: All right. I'll wait till she gets through soaking in a hot tub and then I'll inquire if *she* is acquainted with the Napoleonic code. It looks to me like you have been swindled, baby, and when you're swindled under the Napoleonic code I'm swindled *too.* And I don't like to be *swindled.*

STELLA: There's plenty of time to ask her questions later but if you do now she'll go to pieces again. I don't undertand what happened to Belle Reve but you don't know how ridiculous you are being when you suggest that my sister or I or anyone of our family could have perpetrated a swindle on anyone else.

STANLEY: Then where's the money if the place was sold?

STELLA: Not sold—*lost, lost!* [*He stalks into bedroom, and she follows him.*] Stanley!

[*He pulls open the wardrobe trunk standing in middle of room and jerks out an armful of dresses.*]

STANLEY: Open your eyes to this stuff! You think she got them out of a teacher's pay?

STELLA: Hush!

STANLEY: Look at these feathers and furs that she come here to preen herself in! What's this here? A solid-gold dress, I believe! And this one! What is these here? Fox-pieces! [*He blows on them.*] Genuine fox fur-pieces, a half a mile long! Where are your fox-pieces, Stella? Bushy snowwhite ones, no less! Where are your white fox-pieces?

STELLA: Those are inexpensive summer furs that Blanche has had a long time.

STANLEY: I got an acquaintance who deals in this sort of merchandise. I'll have him in here to appraise it. I'm willing to bet you there's thousands of dollars invested in this stuff here!

STELLA: Don't be such an idiot, Stanley!

[*He hurls the furs to the day bed. Then he jerks open small drawer in the trunk and pulls up a fistful of costume jewelry.*]

STANLEY: And what have we here? The treasure chest of a pirate!

STELLA: Oh, Stanley!

STANLEY: Pearls! Ropes of them! What is this sister of yours, a deep-sea diver? Bracelets of solid gold, too! Where are your pearls and gold bracelets?

STELLA: Shhh! Be still, Stanley!

---

1. This codification of French law (1802), made by Napoleon as emperor, is the basis for Louisiana's civil law.

STANLEY: And diamonds! A crown for an empress!

STELLA: A rhinestone tiara she wore to a costume ball.

STANLEY: What's rhinestone?

STELLA: Next door to glass.

STANLEY: Are you kidding? I have an acquaintance that works in a jewelry store. I'll have him in here to make an appraisal of this. Here's your plantation, or what was left of it, here!

STELLA: You have no idea how stupid and horrid you're being! Now close that trunk before she comes out of the bathroom!

[*He kicks the trunk partly closed and sits on the kitchen table.*]

STANLEY: The Kowalskis and the DuBoises have different notions.

STELLA: [*Angrily.*] Indeed they have, thank heavens!—*I'm* going outside. [*She snatches up her white hat and gloves and crosses to the outside door.*] You come out with me while Blanche is getting dressed.

STANLEY: Since when do you give me orders?

STELLA: Are you going to stay here and insult her?

STANLEY: You're damn tootin' I'm going to stay here.

[STELLA *goes out to the porch.* BLANCHE *comes out of the bathroom in a red satin robe.*]

BLANCHE: [*Airily.*] Hello, Stanley! Here I am, all freshly bathed and scented, and feeling like a brand new human being!

[*He lights a cigarette.*]

STANLEY: That's good.

BLANCHE: [*Drawing the curtains at the windows.*] Excuse me while I slip on my pretty new dress!

STANLEY: Go right ahead, Blanche.

[*She closes the drapes between the rooms.*]

BLANCHE: I understand there's to be a little card party to which we ladies are cordially *not* invited!

STANLEY: [*Ominously.*] Yeah?

[BLANCHE *throws off her robe and slips into a flowered print dress.*]

BLANCHE: Where's Stella?

STANLEY: Out on the porch.

BLANCHE: I'm going to ask a favor of you in a moment.

STANLEY: What could that be, I wonder?

BLANCHE: Some buttons in back! You may enter! [*He crosses through drapes with a smoldering look.*] How do I look?

STANLEY: You look all right.

BLANCHE: Many thanks! Now the buttons!

STANLEY: I can't do nothing with them.

BLANCHE: You men with your big clumsy fingers. May I have a drag on your cig?

STANLEY: Have one for yourself.

BLANCHE: Why, thanks! . . . It looks like my trunk has exploded.

STANLEY: Me an' Stella were helping you unpack.

BLANCHE: Well, you certainly did a fast and thorough job of it!

STANLEY: It looks like you raided some stylish shops in Paris.

BLANCHE: Ha-ha! Yes—clothes are my passion!

STANLEY: What does it cost for a string of fur-pieces like that?

BLANCHE: Why, those were a tribute from an admirer of mine!

STANLEY: He must have had a lot of—admiration!

BLANCHE: Oh, in my youth I excited some admiration. But look at me now! [*She smiles at him radiantly.*] Would you think it possible that I was once considered to be—attractive?

STANLEY: Your looks are okay.

BLANCHE: I was fishing for a compliment, Stanley.

STANLEY: I don't go in for that stuff.

BLANCHE: What—stuff?

STANLEY: Compliments to women about their looks. I never met a woman that didn't know if she was good-looking or not without being told, and some of them give themselves credit for more than they've got. I once went out with a doll who said to me, "I am the glamorous type, I am the glamorous type!" I said, "So what?"

BLANCHE: And what did she say then?

STANLEY: She didn't say nothing. That shut her up like a clam.

BLANCHE: Did it end the romance?

STANLEY: It ended the conversation—that was all. Some men are took in by this Hollywood glamor stuff and some men are not.

BLANCHE: I'm sure you belong in the second category.

STANLEY: That's right.

BLANCHE: I cannot imagine any witch of a woman casting a spell over you.

STANLEY: That's—right.

BLANCHE: You're simple, straightforward and honest, a little bit on the primitive side I should think. To interest you a woman would have to— [*She pauses with an indefinite gesture.*]

STANLEY: [*Slowly.*] Lay . . . her cards on the table.

BLANCHE: [*Smiling.*] Well, I never cared for wishy-washy people. That was why, when you walked in here last night, I said to myself—"My sister has married a man!"—Of course that was all that I could tell about you.

STANLEY: [*Booming.*] Now let's cut the re-bop![2]

BLANCHE: [*Pressing hands to her ears.*] Ouuuuu!

STELLA: [*Calling from the steps.*] Stanley! You come out here and let Blanche finish dressing!

BLANCHE: I'm through dressing, honey.

STELLA: Well, you come out, then.

STANLEY: Your sister and I are having a little talk.

2. Nonsense syllables (from "bop," a form of jazz).

BLANCHE: [*Lightly.*] Honey, do me a favor. Run to the drugstore and get me a lemon
Coke with plenty of chipped ice in it!—Will you do that for me, sweetie?

STELLA: [*Uncertainly.*] Yes. [*She goes around the corner of the building.*]

BLANCHE: The poor little thing was out there listening to us, and I have an idea
she doesn't understand you as well as I do. . . . All right; now, Mr. Kowalski,
let us proceed without any more double-talk. I'm ready to answer all questions. I've nothing to hide. What is it?

STANLEY: There is such a thing in this state of Louisiana as the Napoleonic code,
according to which whatever belongs to my wife is also mine—and vice versa.

BLANCHE: My, but you have an impressive judicial air!

> [*She sprays herself with her atomizer; then playfully sprays him with it. He
> seizes the atomizer and slams it down on the dresser. She throws back her head
> and laughs.*]

STANLEY: If I didn't know that you was my wife's sister I'd get ideas about you!

BLANCHE: Such as what!

STANLEY: Don't play so dumb. You know what!

BLANCHE: [*She puts the atomizer on the table.*] All right. Cards on the table. That
suits me. [*She turns to* STANLEY.] I know I fib a good deal. After all, a woman's
charm is fifty per cent illusion, but when a thing is important I tell the truth,
and this is the truth: I haven't cheated my sister or you or anyone else as long
as I have lived.

STANLEY: Where's the papers? In the trunk?

BLANCHE: Everything that I own is in that trunk. [STANLEY *crosses to the trunk, shoves
it roughly open and begins to open compartments*.] What in the name of heaven
are you thinking of! What's in the back of that little boy's mind of yours?
That I am absconding with something, attempting some kind of treachery
on my sister?—Let me do that! It will be faster and simpler . . . [*She crosses to
the trunk and takes out a box.*] I keep my papers mostly in this tin box. [*She
opens it.*]

STANLEY: What's them underneath? [*He indicates another sheaf of paper.*]

BLANCHE: These are love-letters, yellowing with antiquity, all from one boy. [*He
snatches them up. She speaks fiercely.*] Give those back to me!

STANLEY: I'll have a look at them first!

BLANCHE: The touch of your hands insults them!

STANLEY: Don't pull that stuff!

> [*He rips off the ribbon and starts to examine them.* BLANCHE *snatches them
> from him, and they cascade to the floor.*]

BLANCHE: Now that you've touched them I'll burn them!

STANLEY: [*Staring, baffled.*] What in hell are they?

BLANCHE: [*On the floor gathering them up.*] Poems a dead boy wrote. I hurt him the
way that you would like to hurt me, but you can't! I'm not young and vulnerable any more. But my young husband was and I—never mind about that!
Just give them back to me!

STANLEY: What do you mean by saying you'll have to burn them?

BLANCHE: I'm sorry, I must have lost my head for a moment. Everyone has something he won't let others touch because of their—intimate nature . . . [*She now seems faint with exhaustion and she sits down with the strong box and puts on a pair of glasses and goes methodically through a large stack of papers.*] Ambler & Ambler. Hmmmmm. . . . Crabtree. . . . More Ambler & Ambler.

STANLEY: What is Ambler & Ambler?

BLANCHE: A firm that made loans on the place.

STANLEY: Then it *was* lost on a mortgage?

BLANCHE: [*Touching her forehead.*] That must've been what happened.

STANLEY: I don't want no ifs, ands or buts! What's all the rest of them papers?

> [*She hands him the entire box. He carries it to the table and starts to examine the papers.*]

BLANCHE: [*Picking up a large envelope containing more papers.*] There are thousands of papers, stretching back over hundreds of years, affecting Belle Reve as, piece by piece, our improvident grandfathers and father and uncles and brothers exchanged the land for their epic fornications—to put it plainly! [*She removes her glasses with an exhausted laugh.*] The four-letter word deprived us of our plantation, till finally all that was left—and Stella can verify that!— was the house itself and about twenty acres of ground, including a graveyard, to which now all but Stella and I have retreated. [*She pours the contents of the envelope on the table.*] Here all of them are, all papers! I hereby endow you with them! Take them, peruse them—commit them to memory, even! I think it's wonderfully fitting that Belle Reve should finally be this bunch of old papers in your big, capable hands! . . . I wonder if Stella's come back with my lemon Coke . . . [*She leans back and closes her eyes.*]

STANLEY: I have a lawyer acquaintance who will study these out.

BLANCHE: Present them to him with a box of aspirin tablets.

STANLEY: [*Becoming somewhat sheepish.*] You see, under the Napoleonic code—a man has to take an interest in his wife's affairs—especially now that she's going to have a baby.

> [BLANCHE *opens her eyes. The "Blue Piano" sounds louder.*]

BLANCHE: Stella? Stella going to have a baby? [*Dreamily.*] I didn't know she was going to have a baby! [*She gets up and crosses to the outside door.* STELLA *appears around the corner with a carton from the drugstore.* STANLEY *goes into the bedroom with the envelope and the box. The inner rooms fade to darkness and the outside wall of the house is visible.* BLANCHE *meets* STELLA *at the foot of the steps to the sidewalk.*] Stella, Stella for star! How lovely to have a baby! It's all right. Everything's all right.

STELLA: I'm sorry he did that to you.

BLANCHE: Oh, I guess he's just not the type that goes for jasmine perfume, but maybe he's what we need to mix with our blood now that we've lost Belle Reve. We thrashed it out. I feel a bit shaky, but I think I handled it nicely, I laughed and treated it all as a joke. [STEVE *and* PABLO *appear, carrying a case of beer.*] I called him a little boy and laughed and flirted. Yes, I was flirting with your husband! [*As the men approach.*] The guests are gathering for the poker party. [*The two men pass between them, and enter the house.*] Which way do we go now, Stella—this way?

STELLA: No, this way. [*She leads* BLANCHE *away.*]

BLANCHE: [*Laughing.*] The blind are leading the blind!

[*A tamale* VENDOR *is heard calling.*]

VENDOR'S VOICE: Red-hot!

SCENE 3. THE POKER NIGHT

There is a picture of Van Gogh's of a billiard-parlor at night.[3] *The kitchen now suggests that sort of lurid nocturnal brilliance, the raw colors of childhood's spectrum. Over the yellow linoleum of the kitchen table hangs an electric bulb with a vivid green glass shade. The poker players—*STANLEY, STEVE, MITCH *and* PABLO—*wear colored shirts, solid blues, a purple, a red-and-white check, a light green, and they are men at the peak of their physical manhood, as coarse and direct and powerful as the primary colors. There are vivid slices of watermelon on the table, whiskey bottles and glasses. The bedroom is relatively dim with only the light that spills between the portieres and through the wide window on the street.*

For a moment, there is absorbed silence as a hand is dealt.

STEVE: Anything wild this deal?

PABLO: One-eyed jacks are wild.

STEVE: Give me two cards.

PABLO: You, Mitch?

MITCH: I'm out.

PABLO: One.

MITCH: Anyone want a shot?

STANLEY: Yeah. Me.

PABLO: Why don't somebody go to the Chinaman's and bring back a load of chop suey?

STANLEY: When I'm losing you want to eat! Ante up! Openers? Openers! Get y'r ass off the table, Mitch. Nothing belongs on a poker table but cards, chips and whiskey. [*He lurches up and tosses some watermelon rinds to the floor.*]

MITCH: Kind of on your high horse, ain't you?

STANLEY: How many?

STEVE: Give me three.

STANLEY: One.

MITCH: I'm out again. I oughta go home pretty soon.

STANLEY: Shut up.

MITCH: I gotta sick mother. She don't go to sleep until I come in at night.

---

3. *The Night Café,* by Vincent van Gogh (1853–1890), Dutch Postimpressionist painter. *The Poker Night* was Williams's first title for *A Streetcar Named Desire.*

STANLEY: Then why don't you stay home with her?

MITCH: She says to go out, so I go, but I don't enjoy it. All the while I keep wondering how she is.

STANLEY: Aw, for the sake of Jesus, go home, then!

PABLO: What've you got?

STEVE: Spade flush.

MITCH: You all are married. But I'll be alone when she goes.—I'm going to the bathroom.

STANLEY: Hurry back and we'll fix you a sugar-tit.

MITCH: Aw, go rut. [*He crosses through the bedroom into the bathroom.*]

STEVE: [*Dealing a hand.*] Seven card stud. [*Telling his joke as he deals.*] This ole farmer is out in back of his house sittin' down th'owing corn to the chickens when all at once he hears a loud cackle and this young hen comes lickety split around the side of the house with the rooster right behind her and gaining on her fast.

STANLEY: [*Impatient with the story.*] Deal!

STEVE: But when the rooster catches sight of the farmer th'owing the corn he puts on the brakes and lets the hen get away and starts pecking corn. And the old farmer says, "Lord God, I hopes I never gits *that* hongry!"

[STEVE *and* PABLO *laugh. The sisters appear around the corner of the building.*]

STELLA: The game is still going on.

BLANCHE: How do I look?

STELLA: Lovely, Blanche.

BLANCHE: I feel so hot and frazzled. Wait till I powder before you open the door. Do I look done in?

STELLA: Why no. You are as fresh as a daisy.

BLANCHE: One that's been picked a few days.

[STELLA *opens the door and they enter.*]

STELLA: Well, well, well. I see you boys are still at it?

STANLEY: Where you been?

STELLA: Blanche and I took in a show. Blanche, this is Mr. Gonzales and Mr. Hubbell.

BLANCHE: Please don't get up.

STANLEY: Nobody's going to get up, so don't be worried.

STELLA: How much longer is this game going to continue?

STANLEY: Till we get ready to quit.

BLANCHE: Poker is so fascinating. Could I kibitz?

STANLEY: You could not. Why don't you women go up and sit with Eunice?

STELLA: Because it is nearly two-thirty. [BLANCHE *crosses into the bedroom and partially closes the portieres.*] Couldn't you call it quits after one more hand?

[*A chair scrapes.* STANLEY *gives a loud whack of his hand on her thigh.*]

STELLA: [*Sharply.*] That's not fun, Stanley. [*The men laugh.* STELLA *goes into the bedroom.*] It makes me so mad when he does that in front of people.

BLANCHE: I think I will bathe.

STELLA: Again?

BLANCHE: My nerves are in knots. Is the bathroom occupied?

STELLA: I don't know.

[BLANCHE *knocks.* MITCH *opens the door and comes out, still wiping his hands on a towel.*]

BLANCHE: Oh!—good evening.

MITCH: Hello. [*He stares at her.*]

STELLA: Blanche, this is Harold Mitchell. My sister, Blanche DuBois.

MITCH: [*With awkward courtesy.*] How do you do, Miss DuBois.

STELLA: How is your mother now, Mitch?

MITCH: About the same, thanks. She appreciated your sending over that custard.— Excuse me, please.

[*He crosses slowly back into the kitchen, glancing back at* BLANCHE *and coughing a little shyly. He realizes he still has the towel in his hands and with an embarrassed laugh hands it to* STELLA. BLANCHE *looks after him with a certain interest.*]

BLANCHE: That one seems—superior to the others.

STELLA: Yes, he is.

BLANCHE: I thought he had a sort of sensitive look.

STELLA: His mother is sick.

BLANCHE: Is he married?

STELLA: No.

BLANCHE: Is he a wolf?

STELLA: Why, Blanche! [BLANCHE *laughs.*] I don't think he would be.

BLANCHE: What does—what does he do? [*She is unbuttoning her blouse.*]

STELLA: He's on the precision bench in the spare parts department. At the plant Stanley travels for.

BLANCHE: Is that something much?

STELLA: No. Stanley's the only one of his crowd that's likely to get anywhere.

BLANCHE: What makes you think Stanley will?

STELLA: Look at him.

BLANCHE: I've looked at him.

STELLA: Then you should know.

BLANCHE: I'm sorry, but I haven't noticed the stamp of genius even on Stanley's forehead.

[*She takes off the blouse and stands in her pink silk brassiere and white skirt in the light through the portieres. The game has continued in undertones.*]

STELLA: It isn't on his forehead and it isn't genius.

BLANCHE: Oh. Well, what is it, and where? I would like to know.

STELLA: It's a drive that he has. You're standing in the light, Blanche!

BLANCHE: Oh, am I!

[*She moves out of the yellow streak of light.* STELLA *has removed her dress and put on a light blue satin kimona.*]

STELLA: [*With girlish laughter.*] You ought to see their wives.

BLANCHE: [*Laughingly.*] I can imagine. Big, beefy things, I suppose.

STELLA: You know that one upstairs? [*More laughter.*] One time [*Laughing.*] the plaster— [*Laughing.*] cracked—

STANLEY: You hens cut out that conversation in there!

STELLA: You can't hear us.

STANLEY: Well, you can hear me and I said to hush up!

STELLA: This is my house and I'll talk as much as I want to!

BLANCHE: Stella, don't start a row.

STELLA: He's half drunk!—I'll be out in a minute.

[*She goes into the bathroom.* BLANCHE *rises and crosses leisurely to a small white radio and turns it on.*]

STANLEY: Awright, Mitch, you in?

MITCH: What? Oh!—No, I'm out!

[BLANCHE *moves back into the streak of light. She raises her arms and stretches, as she moves indolently back to the chair. Rhumba music comes over the radio.* MITCH *rises at the table.*]

STANLEY: Who turned that on in there?

BLANCHE: I did. Do you mind?

STANLEY: Turn it off!

STEVE: Aw, let the girls have their music.

PABLO: Sure, that's good, leave it on!

STEVE: Sounds like Xavier Cugat![4] [STANLEY *jumps up and, crossing to the radio, turns it off. He stops short at the sight of* BLANCHE *in the chair. She returns his look without flinching. Then he sits again at the poker table. Two of the men have started arguing hotly.*] I didn't hear you name it.

PABLO: Didn't I name it, Mitch?

MITCH: I wasn't listenin'.

PABLO: What were you doing, then?

STANLEY: He was looking through them drapes. [*He jumps up and jerks roughly at curtains to close them.*] Now deal the hand over again and let's play cards or quit. Some people get ants when they win.

[MITCH *rises as* STANLEY *returns to his seat.*]

STANLEY: [*Yelling.*] Sit down!

MITCH: I'm going to the "head." Deal me out.

PABLO: Sure he's got ants now. Seven five-dollar bills in his pants pocket folded up tight as spitballs.

4. Spanish-born Cuban bandleader (1900–1990), well known for composing and playing rhumbas.

STEVE: Tomorrow you'll see him at the cashier's window getting them changed into quarters.

STANLEY: And when he goes home he'll deposit them one by one in a piggy bank his mother give him for Christmas. [*Dealing.*] This game is Spit in the Ocean.

[MITCH *laughs uncomfortably and continues through the portieres. He stops just inside.*]

BLANCHE: [*Softly.*] Hello! The Little Boys' Room is busy right now.

MITCH: We've—been drinking beer.

BLANCHE: I hate beer.

MITCH: It's—a hot weather drink.

BLANCHE: Oh, I don't think so; it always makes me warmer. Have you got any cigs? [*She has slipped on the dark red satin wrapper.*]

MITCH: Sure.

BLANCHE: What kind are they?

MITCH: Luckies.

BLANCHE: Oh, good. What a pretty case. Silver?

MITCH: Yes. Yes; read the inscription.

BLANCHE: Oh, is there an inscription? I can't make it out. [*He strikes a match and moves closer.*] Oh! [*Reading with feigned difficulty.*] "And if God choose, / I shall but love thee better—after—death!" Why, that's from my favorite sonnet by Mrs. Browning![5]

MITCH: You know it?

BLANCHE: Certainly I do!

MITCH: There's a story connected with that inscription.

BLANCHE: It sounds like a romance.

MITCH: A pretty sad one.

BLANCHE: Oh?

MITCH: The girl's dead now.

BLANCHE: [*In a tone of deep sympathy.*] Oh!

MITCH: She knew she was dying when she give me this. A very strange girl, very sweet—very!

BLANCHE: She must have been fond of you. Sick people have such deep, sincere attachments.

MITCH: That's right, they certainly do.

BLANCHE: Sorrow makes for sincerity, I think.

MITCH: It sure brings it out in people.

BLANCHE: The little there is belongs to people who have experienced some sorrow.

MITCH: I believe you are right about that.

BLANCHE: I'm positive that I am. Show me a person who hasn't known any sorrow and I'll show you a shuperficial—Listen to me! My tongue is a little—thick! You boys are responsible for it. The show let out at eleven and we couldn't come home on account of the poker game so we had to go somewhere and

5. Elizabeth Barrett Browning (1806–1861), British poet, famous for her sequence of love poems, *Sonnets from the Portuguese.*

drink. I'm not accustomed to having more than one drink. Two is the limit—
and *three*! [*She laughs.*] Tonight I had three.

STANLEY: Mitch!

MITCH: Deal me out. I'm talking to Miss—

BLANCHE: DuBois.

MITCH: Miss DuBois?

BLANCHE: It's a French name. It means woods and Blanche means white, so the
two together mean white woods. Like an orchard in spring! You can remember it by that.

MITCH: You're French?

BLANCHE: We are French by extraction. Our first American ancestors were French
Huguenots.

MITCH: You are Stella's sister, are you not?

BLANCHE: Yes, Stella is my precious little sister. I call her little in spite of the fact
she's somewhat older than I. Just slightly. Less than a year. Will you do something for me?

MITCH: Sure. What?

BLANCHE: I bought this adorable little colored paper lantern at a Chinese shop on
Bourbon. Put it over the light bulb! Will you, please?

MITCH: Be glad to.

BLANCHE: I can't stand a naked light bulb, any more than I can a rude remark or
a vulgar action.

MITCH: [*Adjusting the lantern.*] I guess we strike you as being a pretty rough bunch.

BLANCHE: I'm very adaptable—to circumstances.

MITCH: Well, that's a good thing to be. You are visiting Stanley and Stella?

BLANCHE: Stella hasn't been so well lately, and I came down to help her for a while.
She's very run down.

MITCH: You're not—?

BLANCHE: Married? No, no. I'm an old maid schoolteacher!

MITCH: You may teach school but you're certainly not an old maid.

BLANCHE: Thank you, sir! I appreciate your gallantry!

MITCH: So you are in the teaching profession?

BLANCHE: Yes. Ah, yes . . .

MITCH: Grade school or high school or—

STANLEY: [*Bellowing.*] Mitch!

MITCH: Coming!

BLANCHE: Gracious, what lung-power! . . . I teach high school. In Laurel.

MITCH: What do you teach? What subject?

BLANCHE: Guess!

MITCH: I bet you teach art or music? [BLANCHE *laughs delicately.*] Of course I could
be wrong. You might teach arithmetic.

BLANCHE: Never arithmetic, sir; never arithmetic! [*With a laugh.*] I don't even know
my multiplication tables! No, I have the misfortune of being an English
instructor. I attempt to instill a bunch of bobby-soxers and drugstore Romeos
with reverence for Hawthorne and Whitman and Poe!

MITCH: I guess that some of them are more interested in other things.

BLANCHE: How very right you are! Their literary heritage is not what most of them treasure above all else! But they're sweet things! And in the spring, it's touching to notice them making their first discovery of love! As if nobody had ever known it before! [*The bathroom door opens and* STELLA *comes out.* BLANCHE *continues talking to* MITCH.] Oh! Have you finished? Wait—I'll turn on the radio.

[*She turns the knobs on the radio and it begins to play "Wien, Wien, nur du allein."*[6] BLANCHE *waltzes to the music with romantic gestures.* MITCH *is delighted and moves in awkward imitation like a dancing bear.* STANLEY *stalks fiercely through the portieres into the bedroom. He crosses to the small white radio and snatches it off the table. With a shouted oath, he tosses the instrument out the window.*]

STELLA: Drunk—drunk—animal thing, you! [*She rushes through to the poker table.*] All of you—please go home! If any of you have one spark of decency in you—
BLANCHE: [*Wildly.*] Stella, watch out, he's—

[STANLEY *charges after* STELLA.]

MEN: [*Feebly.*] Take it easy, Stanley. Easy, fellow.—Let's all—
STELLA: You lay your hands on me and I'll—

[*She backs out of sight. He advances and disappears. There is the sound of a blow,* STELLA *cries out.* BLANCHE *screams and runs into the kitchen. The men rush forward and there is grappling and cursing. Something is overturned with a crash.*]

BLANCHE: [*Shrilly.*] My sister is going to have a baby!
MITCH: This is terrible.
BLANCHE: Lunacy, absolute lunacy!
MITCH: Get him in here, men.

[STANLEY *is forced, pinioned by the two men, into the bedroom. He nearly throws them off. Then all at once he subsides and is limp in their grasp. They speak quietly and lovingly to him and he leans his face on one of their shoulders.*]

STELLA: [*In a high, unnatural voice, out of sight.*] I want to go away, I want to go away!
MITCH: Poker shouldn't be played in a house with women.

[BLANCHE *rushes into the bedroom.*]

BLANCHE: I want my sister's clothes! We'll go to that woman's upstairs!
MITCH: Where is the clothes?
BLANCHE: [*Opening the closet.*] I've got them! [*She rushes through to* STELLA.] Stella, Stella, precious! Dear, dear little sister, don't be afraid!

[*With her arm around* STELLA, BLANCHE *guides her to the outside door and upstairs.*]

6. "Vienna, Vienna, you are my only," a waltz from an operetta by Franz Lehár (1870–1948).

STANLEY: [*Dully.*] What's the matter; what's happened?

MITCH: You just blew your top, Stan.

PABLO: He's okay, now.

STEVE: Sure, my boy's okay!

MITCH: Put him on the bed and get a wet towel.

PABLO: I think coffee would do him a world of good, now.

STANLEY: [*Thickly.*] I want water.

MITCH: Put him under the shower!

> [*The men talk quietly as they lead him to the bathroom.*]

STANLEY: Let the rut go of me, you sons of bitches!

> [*Sounds of blows are heard. The water goes on full tilt.*]

STEVE: Let's get quick out of here!

> [*They rush to the poker table and sweep up their winnings on their way out.*]

MITCH: [*Sadly but firmly.*] Poker should not be played in a house with women.

> [*The door closes on them and the place is still. The Negro entertainers in the bar around the corner play "Paper Doll"⁷ slow and blue. After a moment STAN-LEY comes out of the bathroom dripping water and still in his clinging wet polka dot drawers.*]

STANLEY: Stella! [*There is a pause.*] My baby doll's left me! [*He breaks into sobs. Then he goes to the phone and dials, still shuddering with sobs.*] Eunice? I want my baby! [*He waits a moment; then he hangs up and dials again.*] Eunice! I'll keep on ringin' until I talk with my *baby!* [*An indistinguishable shrill voice is heard. He hurls phone to floor. Dissonant brass and piano sounds as the rooms dim out to darkness and the outer walls appear in the night light. The "Blue Piano" plays for a brief interval. Finally,* STANLEY *stumbles half-dressed out to the porch and down the wooden steps to the pavement before the building. There he throws back his head like a baying hound and bellows his wife's name:* "STELLA! STELLA, *sweetheart!* STELLA!"] Stell-*lahhhhh!*

EUNICE: [*Calling down from the door of her upper apartment.*] Quit that howling out there an' go back to bed!

STANLEY: I want my baby down here. Stella, Stella!

EUNICE: She ain't comin' down so you quit! Or you'll git th' law on you!

STANLEY: Stella!

EUNICE: You can't beat on a woman an' then call 'er back! She won't come! And her goin' t' have a baby! . . . You stinker! You whelp of a Polack, you! I hope they do haul you in and turn the fire hose on you, same as the last time!

STANLEY: [*Humbly.*] Eunice, I want my girl to come down with me!

EUNICE: Hah! [*She slams her door.*]

STANLEY: [*With heaven-splitting violence.*] STELL-LAHHHHH!

---

7. Popular song of the early 1940s.

[*The low-tone clarinet moans. The door upstairs opens again.* STELLA *slips down the rickety stairs in her robe. Her eyes are glistening with tears and her hair loose about her throat and shoulders. They stare at each other. Then they come together with low, animal moans. He falls to his knees on the steps and presses his face to her belly, curving a little with maternity. Her eyes go blind with tenderness as she catches his head and raises him level with her. He snatches the screen door open and lifts her off her feet and bears her into the dark flat.* BLANCHE *comes out the upper landing in her robe and slips fearfully down the steps.*]

BLANCHE: Where is my little sister? Stella? Stella?

[*She stops before the dark entrance of her sister's flat. Then catches her breath as if struck. She rushes down to the walk before the house. She looks right and left as if for a sanctuary. The music fades away.* MITCH *appears from around the corner.*]

MITCH: Miss DuBois?
BLANCHE: Oh!
MITCH: All quiet on the Potomac now?
BLANCHE: She ran downstairs and went back in there with him.
MITCH: Sure she did.
BLANCHE: I'm terrified!
MITCH: Ho-ho! There's nothing to be scared of. They're crazy about each other.
BLANCHE: I'm not used to such—
MITCH: Naw, it's a shame this had to happen when you just got here. But don't take it serious.
BLANCHE: Violence! Is so—
MITCH: Set down on the steps and have a cigarette with me.
BLANCHE: I'm not properly dressed.
MITCH: That don't make no difference in the Quarter.
BLANCHE: Such a pretty silver case.
MITCH: I showed you the inscription, didn't I?
BLANCHE: Yes. [*During the pause, she looks up at the sky.*] There's so much—so much confusion in the world . . . [*He coughs diffidently.*] Thank you for being so kind! I need kindness now.

SCENE 4

It is early the following morning. There is a confusion of street cries like a choral chant.

STELLA *is lying down in the bedroom. Her face is serene in the early morning sunlight. One hand rests on her belly, rounding slightly with new maternity. From the other dangles a book of colored comics. Her eyes and lips have that almost narcotized tranquility that is in the faces of Eastern idols.*

The table is sloppy with remains of breakfast and the debris of the preceding night, and STANLEY'*s gaudy pyjamas lie across the threshold of the bathroom. The outside door is slightly ajar on a sky of summer brilliance.*

BLANCHE *appears at this door. She has spent a sleepless night and her appearance entirely contrasts with* STELLA'*s. She presses her knuckles nervously to her lips as she looks through the door, before entering.*

BLANCHE: Stella?
STELLA: [*Stirring lazily.*] Hmmh?

> [BLANCHE *utters a moaning cry and runs into the bedroom, throwing herself down beside* STELLA *in a rush of hysterical tenderness.*]

BLANCHE: Baby, my baby sister!
STELLA: [*Drawing away from her.*] Blanche, what is the matter with you?

> [BLANCHE *straightens up slowly and stands beside the bed looking down at her sister with knuckles pressed to her lips.*]

BLANCHE: He's left?
STELLA: Stan? Yes.
BLANCHE: Will he be back?
STELLA: He's gone to get the car greased. Why?
BLANCHE: Why! I've been half crazy, Stella! When I found out you'd been insane enough to come back in here after what happened—I started to rush in after you!
STELLA: I'm glad you didn't.
BLANCHE: What were you thinking of? [STELLA *makes an indefinite gesture.*] Answer me! What? What?
STELLA: Please, Blanche! Sit down and stop yelling.
BLANCHE: All right, Stella. I will repeat the question quietly now. How could you come back in this place last night? Why, you must have slept with him!

> [STELLA *gets up in a calm and leisurely way.*]

STELLA: Blanche, I'd forgotten how excitable you are. You're making much too much fuss about this.
BLANCHE: Am I?
STELLA: Yes, you are, Blanche. I know how it must have seemed to you and I'm awful sorry it had to happen, but it wasn't anything as serious as you seem to take it. In the first place, when men are drinking and playing poker anything can happen. It's always a powder-keg. He didn't know what he was doing. . . . He was as good as a lamb when I came back and he's really very, very ashamed of himself.
BLANCHE: And that—that makes it all right?
STELLA: No, it isn't all right for anybody to make such a terrible row, but—people do sometimes. Stanley's always smashed things. Why, on our wedding night—soon as we came in here—he snatched off one of my slippers and rushed about the place smashing light bulbs with it.
BLANCHE: He did—*what?*

STELLA: He smashed all the lightbulbs with the heel of my slipper! [*She laughs.*]

BLANCHE: And you—you *let* him? Didn't *run*, didn't *scream?*

STELLA: I was—sort of—thrilled by it. [*She waits for a moment.*] Eunice and you had breakfast?

BLANCHE: Do you suppose I wanted any breakfast?

STELLA: There's some coffee left on the stove.

BLANCHE: You're so—matter-of-fact about it, Stella.

STELLA: What other can I be? He's taken the radio to get it fixed. It didn't land on the pavement so only one tube was smashed.

BLANCHE: And you are standing there smiling!

STELLA: What do you want me to do?

BLANCHE: Pull yourself together and face the facts.

STELLA: What are they, in your opinion?

BLANCHE: In my opinion? You're married to a madman!

STELLA: No!

BLANCHE: Yes, you are, your fix is worse than mine is! Only you're not being sensible about it. I'm going to *do* something. Get hold of myself and make myself a new life!

STELLA: Yes?

BLANCHE: But you've given in. And that isn't right, you're not old! You can get out.

STELLA: [*Slowly and emphatically.*] I'm not in anything I want to get out of.

BLANCHE: [*Incredulously.*] What—Stella?

STELLA: I said I am not in anything that I have a desire to get out of. Look at the mess in this room! And those empty bottles! They went through two cases last night! He promised this morning that he was going to quit having these poker parties, but you know how long such a promise is going to keep. Oh, well, it's his pleasure, like mine is movies and bridge. People have got to tolerate each other's habits, I guess.

BLANCHE: I don't understand you. [STELLA *turns toward her.*] I don't understand your indifference. Is this a Chinese philosophy you've—cultivated?

STELLA: Is what—what?

BLANCHE: This—shuffling about and mumbling—"One tube smashed—beer bottles—mess in the kitchen!"—as if nothing out of the ordinary has happened! [STELLA *laughs uncertainly and picking up the broom, twirls it in her hands.*] Are you deliberately shaking that thing in my face?

STELLA: No.

BLANCHE: Stop it. Let go of that broom. I won't have you cleaning up for him!

STELLA: Then who's going to do it? Are you?

BLANCHE: I? I!

STELLA: No, I didn't think so.

BLANCHE: Oh, let me think, if only my mind would function! We've got to get hold of some money, that's the way out!

STELLA: I guess that money is always nice to get hold of.

BLANCHE: Listen to me. I have an idea of some kind. [*Shakily she twists a cigarette into her holder.*] Do you remember Shep Huntleigh? [STELLA *shakes her head.*]

Of course you remember Shep Huntleigh. I went out with him at college and wore his pin for a while. Well—

STELLA: Well?

BLANCHE: I ran into him last winter. You know I went to Miami during the Christmas holidays?

STELLA: No.

BLANCHE: Well, I did. I took the trip as an investment, thinking I'd meet someone with a million dollars.

STELLA: Did you?

BLANCHE: Yes. I ran into Shep Huntleigh—I ran into him on Biscayne Boulevard, on Christmas Eve, about dusk . . . getting into his car—Cadillac convertible; must have been a block long!

STELLA: I should think it would have been—inconvenient in traffic!

BLANCHE: You've heard of oil wells?

STELLA: Yes—remotely.

BLANCHE: He has them, all over Texas. Texas is literally spouting gold in his pockets.

STELLA: My, my.

BLANCHE: Y'know how indifferent I am to money. I think of money in terms of what it does for you. But he could do it, he could certainly do it!

STELLA: Do what, Blanche?

BLANCHE: Why—set us up in a—shop!

STELLA: What kind of shop?

BLANCHE: Oh, a—shop of some kind! He could do it with half what his wife throws away at the races.

STELLA: He's married?

BLANCHE: Honey, would I be here if the man weren't married? [STELLA *laughs a little.* BLANCHE *suddenly springs up and crosses to phone. She speaks shrilly.*] How do I get Western Union?—Operator! Western Union!

STELLA: That's a dial phone, honey.

BLANCHE: I can't dial, I'm too—

STELLA: Just dial O.

BLANCHE: O?

STELLA: Yes, "O" for Operator!

[BLANCHE *considers a moment; then she puts the phone down.*]

BLANCHE: Give me a pencil. Where is a slip of paper? I've got to write it down first—the message, I mean . . . [*She goes to the dressing table, and grabs up a sheet of Kleenex and an eyebrow pencil for writing equipment.*] Let me see now . . . [*She bites the pencil.*] "Darling Shep. Sister and I in desperate situation."

STELLA: I beg your pardon!

BLANCHE: "Sister and I in desperate situation. Will explain details later. Would you be interested in—?" [*She bites the pencil again.*] "Would you be—interested—in . . ." [*She smashes the pencil on the table and springs up.*] You never get anywhere with direct appeals!

STELLA: [*With a laugh.*] Don't be so ridiculous, darling!

BLANCHE: But I'll think of something, I've *got* to think of—*some*thing! Don't laugh at me, Stella! Please, please don't—I—I want you to look at the contents of my purse! Here's what's in it! [*She snatches her purse open.*] Sixty-five measly cents in coin of the realm!

STELLA: [*Crossing to bureau.*] Stanley doesn't give me a regular allowance, he likes to pay bills himself, but—this morning he gave me ten dollars to smooth things over. You take five of it, Blanche, and I'll keep the rest.

BLANCHE: Oh, no. No, Stella.

STELLA: [*Insisting.*] I know how it helps your morale just having a little pocket-money on you.

BLANCHE: No, thank you—I'll take to the streets!

STELLA: Talk sense! How did you happen to get so low on funds?

BLANCHE: Money just goes—it goes places. [*She rubs her forehead.*] Sometime today I've got to get hold of a Bromo![8]

STELLA: I'll fix you one now.

BLANCHE: Not yet—I've got to keep thinking!

STELLA: I wish you'd just let things go, at least for a—while.

BLANCHE: Stella, I can't live with him! You can, he's your husband. But how could I stay here with him, after last night, with just those curtains between us?

STELLA: Blanche, you saw him at his worst last night.

BLANCHE: On the contrary, I saw him at his best! What such a man has to offer is animal force and he gave a wonderful exhibition of that! But the only way to live with such a man is to—go to bed with him! And that's your job—not mine!

STELLA: After you've rested a little, you'll see it's going to work out. You don't have to worry about anything while you're here. I mean—expenses . . .

BLANCHE: I have to plan for us both, to get us both—out!

STELLA: You take it for granted that I am in something that I want to get out of.

BLANCHE: I take it for granted that you still have sufficient memory of Belle Reve to find this place and these poker players impossible to live with.

STELLA: Well, you're taking entirely too much for granted.

BLANCHE: I can't believe you're in earnest.

STELLA: No?

BLANCHE: I understand how it happened—a little. You saw him in uniform, an officer, not here but—

STELLA: I'm not sure it would have made any difference where I saw him.

BLANCHE: Now don't say it was one of those mysterious electric things between people! If you do I'll laugh in your face.

STELLA: I am not going to say anything more at all about it!

BLANCHE: All right, then, don't!

STELLA: But there are things that happen between a man and a woman in the dark—that sort of make everything else seem—unimportant. [*Pause.*]

BLANCHE: What you are talking about is brutal desire—just—Desire!—the name of

8. Short for "Bromo Seltzer," a headache remedy.

that rattle-trap streetcar that bangs through the Quarter, up one old narrow street and down another . . .

STELLA: Haven't you ever ridden on that streetcar?

BLANCHE: It brought me here.—Where I'm not wanted and where I'm ashamed to be . . .

STELLA: Then don't you think your superior attitude is a bit out of place?

BLANCHE: I am not being or feeling at all superior, Stella. Believe me I'm not! It's just this. This is how I look at it. A man like that is someone to go out with— once—twice—three times when the devil is in you. But live with? Have a child by?

STELLA: I have told you I love him.

BLANCHE: Then I *tremble* for you! I just—*tremble* for you. . . .

STELLA: I can't help your trembling if you insist on trembling!

[*There is a pause.*]

BLANCHE: May I—speak—*plainly?*

STELLA: Yes, do. Go ahead. As plainly as you want to.

[*Outside, a train approaches. They are silent till the noise subsides. They are both in the bedroom. Under cover of the train's noise* STANLEY *enters from outside. He stands unseen by the women, holding some packages in his arms, and overhears their following conversation. He wears an undershirt and grease-stained seersucker pants.*]

BLANCHE: Well—if you'll forgive me—he's *common!*

STELLA: Why, yes, I suppose he is.

BLANCHE: Suppose! You can't have forgotten that much of our bringing up, Stella, that you just *suppose* that any part of a gentleman's in his nature! *Not one particle, no!* Oh, if he was just—*ordinary!* Just plain—but good and wholesome, but—*no.* There's something downright—*bestial*—about him! You're hating me saying this, aren't you?

STELLA: [*Coldly.*] Go on and say it all, Blanche.

BLANCHE: He acts like an animal, has an animal's habits! Eats like one, moves like one, talks like one! There's even something—sub-human—something not quite to the stage of humanity yet! Yes, something—ape-like about him, like one of those pictures I've seen in—anthropological studies! Thousands and thousands of years have passed him right by, and there he is—Stanley Kowalski—survivor of the Stone Age! Bearing the raw meat home from the kill in the jungle! And you—*you* here—*waiting* for him! Maybe he'll strike you or maybe grunt and kiss you! That is, if kisses have been discovered yet! Night falls and the other apes gather! There in the front of the cave, all grunting like him, and swilling and gnawing and hulking! His poker night! you call it—this party of apes! Somebody growls—some creature snatches at something—the fight is on! *God!* Maybe we are a long way from being made in God's image, but Stella—my sister—there has been *some* progress since then! Such things as art—as poetry and music—such kinds of new light have come into the world since then! In some kinds of people some tenderer feelings have had some little beginning! That we have got to make *grow!* And *cling* to, and hold as our flag! In this dark march toward whatever it is we're approaching. . . . *Don't—don't hang back with the brutes!*

[*Another train passes outside.* STANLEY *hesitates, licking his lips. Then suddenly he turns stealthily about and withdraws through front door. The women are still unaware of his presence. When the train has passed he calls through the closed front door.*]

STANLEY: Hey! Hey, Stella!
STELLA: [*Who has listened gravely to* BLANCHE.] Stanley!
BLANCHE: Stell, I—

[*But* STELLA *has gone to the front door.* STANLEY *enters casually with his packages.*]

STANLEY: Hiyuh, Stella. Blanche back?
STELLA: Yes, she's back.
STANLEY: Hiyuh, Blanche. [*He grins at her.*]
STELLA: You must've got under the car.
STANLEY: Them darn mechanics at Fritz's don't know their ass fr'm—*Hey!*

[STELLA *has embraced him with both arms, fiercely, and full in the view of* BLANCHE. *He laughs and clasps her head to him. Over her head he grins through the curtains at* BLANCHE. *As the lights fade away, with a lingering brightness on their embrace, the music of the "Blue Piano" and trumpet and drums is heard.*]

SCENE 5

BLANCHE *is seated in the bedroom fanning herself with a palm leaf as she reads over a just-completed letter. Suddenly she bursts into a peal of laughter.* STELLA *is dressing in the bedroom.*

STELLA: What are you laughing at, honey?
BLANCHE: Myself, myself, for being such a liar! I'm writing a letter to Shep. [*She picks up the letter.*] "Darling Shep. I am spending the summer on the wing, making flying visits here and there. And who knows, perhaps I shall take a sudden notion to *swoop* down on *Dallas!* How would you feel about that? Ha-ha! [*She laughs nervously and brightly, touching her throat as if actually talking to Shep.*] Forewarned is forearmed, as they say!"—How does that sound?
STELLA: Uh-huh . . .
BLANCHE: [*Going on nervously.*] "Most of my sister's friends go north in the summer but some have homes on the Gulf and there has been a continued round of entertainments, teas, cocktails, and luncheons—"

[*A disturbance is heard upstairs at the Hubbells' apartment.*]

STELLA: Eunice seems to be having some trouble with Steve. [EUNICE's *voice shouts in terrible wrath.*]

EUNICE: I heard about you and that blonde!

STEVE: That's a damn lie!

EUNICE: You ain't pulling the wool over my eyes! I wouldn't mind if you'd stay down at the Four Deuces, but you always going up.

STEVE: Who ever seen me up?

EUNICE: I seen you chasing her 'round the balcony—I'm gonna call the vice squad!

STEVE: Don't you throw that at me!

EUNICE: [*Shrieking.*] You hit me! I'm gonna call the police!

[*A clatter of aluminum striking a wall is heard, followed by a man's angry roar, shouts and overturned furniture. There is a crash; then a relative hush.*]

BLANCHE: [*Brightly.*] Did he *kill* her?

[EUNICE *appears on the steps in daemonic disorder.*]

STELLA: No! She's coming downstairs.

EUNICE: Call the police, I'm going to call the police! [*She rushes around the corner.*]

[*They laugh lightly.* STANLEY *comes around the corner in his green and scarlet silk bowling shirt. He trots up the steps and bangs into the kitchen.* BLANCHE *registers his entrance with nervous gestures.*]

STANLEY: What's a matter with Eun-uss?

STELLA: She and Steve had a row. Has she got the police?

STANLEY: Naw. She's gettin' a drink.

STELLA: That's much more practical!

[STEVE *comes down nursing a bruise on his forehead and looks in the door.*]

STEVE: She here?

STANLEY: Naw, naw. At the Four Deuces.

STEVE: That rutting hunk! [*He looks around the corner a bit timidly, then turns with affected boldness and runs after her.*]

BLANCHE: I must jot that down in my notebook. Ha-ha! I'm compiling a notebook of quaint little words and phrases I've picked up here.

STANLEY: You won't pick up nothing here you ain't heard before.

BLANCHE: Can I count on that?

STANLEY: You can count on it up to five hundred.

BLANCHE: That's a mighty high number. [*He jerks open the bureau drawer, slams it shut and throws shoes in a corner. At each noise* BLANCHE *winces slightly. Finally she speaks.*] What sign were you born under?

STANLEY: [*While he is dressing.*] Sign?

BLANCHE: Astrological sign. I bet you were born under Aries. Aries people are forceful and dynamic. They dote on noise! They love to bang things around! You must have had lots of banging around in the army and now that you're out, you make up for it by treating inanimate objects with such a fury!

[STELLA *has been going in and out of closet during this scene. Now she pops her head out of the closet.*]

STELLA: Stanley was born just five minutes after Christmas.

BLANCHE: Capricorn—the Goat!

STANLEY: What sign were *you* born under?

BLANCHE: Oh, my birthday's next month, the fifteenth of September; that's under Virgo.

STANLEY: What's Virgo?

BLANCHE: Virgo is the Virgin.

STANLEY: [*Contemptuously.*] Hah! [*He advances a little as he knots his tie.*] Say, do you happen to know somebody named Shaw?

[*Her face expresses a faint shock. She reaches for the cologne bottle and dampens her handkerchief as she answers carefully.*]

BLANCHE: Why, everybody knows somebody named Shaw!

STANLEY: Well, this somebody named Shaw is under the impression he met you in Laurel, but I figure he must have got you mixed up with some other party because this other party is someone he met at a hotel called the Flamingo.

[BLANCHE *laughs breathlessly as she touches the cologne-dampened handkerchief to her temples.*]

BLANCHE: I'm afraid he does have me mixed up with this "other party." The Hotel Flamingo is not the sort of establishment I would dare to be seen in!

STANLEY: You know of it?

BLANCHE: Yes, I've seen it and smelled it.

STANLEY: You must've got pretty close if you could smell it.

BLANCHE: The odor of cheap perfume is penetrating.

STANLEY: That stuff you use is expensive?

BLANCHE: Twenty-five dollars an ounce! I'm nearly out. That's just a hint if you want to remember my birthday! [*She speaks lightly but her voice has a note of fear.*]

STANLEY: Shaw must've got you mixed up. He goes in and out of Laurel all the time so he can check on it and clear up any mistake.

[*He turns away and crosses to the portieres.* BLANCHE *closes her eyes as if faint. Her hand trembles as she lifts the handkerchief again to her forehead.* STEVE *and* EUNICE *come around corner.* STEVE's *arm is around* EUNICE's *shoulder and she is sobbing luxuriously and he is cooing love-words. There is a murmur of thunder as they go slowly upstairs in a tight embrace.*]

STANLEY: [*To* STELLA.] I'll wait for you at the Four Deuces!

STELLA: Hey! Don't I rate one kiss?

STANLEY: Not in front of your sister.

[*He goes out.* BLANCHE *rises from her chair. She seems faint; looks about her with an expression of almost panic.*]

BLANCHE: Stella! What have you heard about me?

STELLA: Huh?

BLANCHE: What have people been telling you about me?

STELLA: Telling?

BLANCHE: You haven't heard any—unkind—gossip about me?

STELLA: Why, no, Blanche, of course not!

BLANCHE: Honey, there was—a good deal of talk in Laurel.

STELLA: About *you,* Blanche?

BLANCHE: I wasn't so good the last two years or so, after Belle Reve had started to slip through my fingers.

STELLA: All of us do things we—

BLANCHE: I never was hard or self-sufficient enough. When people are soft—soft people have got to shimmer and glow—they've got to put on soft colors, the colors of butterfly wings, and put a—paper lantern over the light. . . . It isn't enough to be soft *and attractive.* And I—I'm fading now! I don't know how much longer I can turn the trick. [*The afternoon has faded to dusk.* STELLA *goes into the bedroom and turns on the light under the paper lantern. She holds a bottled soft drink in her hand.*] Have you been listening to me?

STELLA: I don't listen to you when you are being morbid! [*She advances with the bottled Coke.*]

BLANCHE: [*With abrupt change to gaiety.*] Is that Coke for me?

STELLA: Not for anyone else!

BLANCHE: Why, you precious thing, you! Is it just Coke?

STELLA: [*Turning.*] You mean you want a shot in it!

BLANCHE: Well, honey, a shot never does a Coke any harm! Let me! You mustn't wait on me!

STELLA: I like to wait on you, Blanche. It makes it seem more like home. [*She goes into the kitchen, finds a glass and pours a shot of whiskey into it.*]

BLANCHE: I have to admit I love to be waited on . . . [*She rushes into the bedroom.* STELLA *goes to her with the glass.* BLANCHE *suddenly clutches* STELLA's *free hand with a moaning sound and presses the hand to her lips.* STELLA *is embarrassed by her show of emotion.* BLANCHE *speaks in a choked voice.*] You're—you're—so *good* to me! And I—

STELLA: Blanche.

BLANCHE: I know, I won't! You hate me to talk sentimental! But honey, *believe* I feel things more than I *tell* you! I *won't* stay long! I won't, I *promise* I—

STELLA: Blanche!

BLANCHE: [*Hysterically.*] I won't, I promise, *I'll* go! Go *soon!* I will *really!* I *won't* hang around until he—throws me out . . .

STELLA: Now will you stop talking foolish?

BLANCHE: Yes, honey. Watch how you pour—that fizzy stuff foams over!

[BLANCHE *laughs shrilly and grabs the glass, but her hand shakes so it almost slips from her grasp.* STELLA *pours the Coke into the glass. It foams over and spills.* BLANCHE *gives a piercing cry.*]

STELLA: [*Shocked by the cry.*] Heavens!

BLANCHE: Right on my pretty white skirt!

STELLA: Oh . . . Use my hanky. Blot gently.

BLANCHE: [*Slowly recovering.*] I know—gently—gently . . .

STELLA: Did it stain?

BLANCHE: Not a bit. Ha-ha! Isn't that lucky? [*She sits down shakily, taking a grateful drink. She holds the glass in both hands and continues to laugh a little.*]

STELLA: Why did you scream like that?

BLANCHE: I don't know why I screamed! [*Continuing nervously.*] Mitch—Mitch is coming at seven. I guess I am just feeling nervous about our relations. [*She begins to talk rapidly and breathlessly.*] He hasn't gotten a thing but a good-night kiss, that's all I have given him, Stella. I want his respect. And men don't want anything they get too easy. But on the other hand men lose interest quickly. Especially when the girl is over—thirty. They think a girl over thirty ought to—the vulgar term is—"put out." . . . And I—I'm not "putting out." Of course he—he doesn't know—I mean I haven't informed him—of my real age!

STELLA: Why are you sensitive about your age?

BLANCHE: Because of hard knocks my vanity's been given. What I mean is—he thinks I'm sort of—prim and proper, you know! [*She laughs out sharply.*] I want to *deceive* him enough to make him—want me . . .

STELLA: Blanche, do you want *him?*

BLANCHE: I want to *rest!* I want to breathe quietly again! Yes—I *want* Mitch . . . *very badly!* Just think! If it happens! I can leave here and not be anyone's problem . . .

[STANLEY *comes around the corner with a drink under his belt.*]

STANLEY: [*Bawling.*] Hey, Steve! Hey, Eunice! Hey, Stella!

[*There are joyous calls from above. Trumpet and drums are heard from around the corner.*]

STELLA: [*Kissing* BLANCHE *impulsively.*] It *will* happen!

BLANCHE: [*Doubtfully.*] It will?

STELLA: It *will!* [*She goes across into the kitchen, looking back at* BLANCHE.] It will, honey, *it will.* . . . But don't take another drink! [*Her voice catches as she goes out the door to meet her husband.*]

[BLANCHE *sinks faintly back in her chair with her drink.* EUNICE *shrieks with laughter and runs down the steps.* STEVE *bounds after her with goat-like screeches and chases her around corner.* STANLEY *and* STELLA *twine arms as they follow, laughing. Dusk settles deeper. The music from the Four Deuces is slow and blue.*]

BLANCHE: Ah, me, ah, me, ah, me . . . [*Her eyes fall shut and the palm leaf fan drops from her fingers. She slaps her hand on the chair arm a couple of times. There is a little glimmer of lightning about the building. A* YOUNG MAN *comes along the street and rings the bell.*] Come in. [*The* YOUNG MAN *appears through the portieres. She regards him with interest.*] Well, well! What can I do for *you?*

YOUNG MAN: I'm collecting for *The Evening Star.*

BLANCHE: I didn't know that stars took up collections.

YOUNG MAN: It's the paper.

BLANCHE: I know, I was joking—feebly! Will you—have a drink?

YOUNG MAN: No, ma'am. No, thank you. I can't drink on the job.

BLANCHE: Oh, well, now, let's see. . . . No, I don't have a dime! I'm not the lady of
the house. I'm her sister from Mississippi. I'm one of those poor relations
you've heard about.

YOUNG MAN: That's all right. I'll drop by later. [*He starts to go out. She approaches a
little.*]

BLANCHE: Hey! [*He turns back shyly. She puts a cigarette in a long holder.*] Could you
give me a light? [*She crosses toward him. They meet at the door between the two
rooms.*]

YOUNG MAN: Sure. [*He takes out a lighter.*] This doesn't always work.

BLANCHE: It's temperamental? [*It flares.*] Ah!—thank you. [*He starts away again.*]
Hey! [*He turns again, still more uncertainly. She goes close to him.*] Uh—what
time is it?

YOUNG MAN: Fifteen of seven, ma'am.

BLANCHE: So late? Don't you just love these long rainy afternoons in New Orleans
when an hour isn't just an hour—but a little piece of eternity dropped into
your hands—and who knows what to do with it? [*She touches his shoulders.*]
You—uh—didn't get wet in the rain?

YOUNG MAN: No, ma'am. I stepped inside.

BLANCHE: In a drugstore? And had a soda?

YOUNG MAN: Uh-huh.

BLANCHE: Chocolate?

YOUNG MAN: No, ma'am. Cherry.

BLANCHE: [*Laughing.*] Cherry!

YOUNG MAN: A cherry soda.

BLANCHE: You make my mouth water. [*She touches his cheek lightly, and smiles. Then
she goes to the trunk.*]

YOUNG MAN: Well, I'd better be going—

BLANCHE: [*Stopping him.*] Young man! [*He turns. She takes a large, gossamer scarf
from the trunk and drapes it about her shoulders. In the ensuing pause, the "Blue
Piano" is heard. It continues through the rest of this scene and the opening of
the next. The* YOUNG MAN *clears his throat and looks yearningly at the door.*]
Young man! Young, young, young man! Has anyone ever told you that
you look like a young Prince out of the Arabian Nights? [*The* YOUNG MAN
laughs uncomfortably and stands like a bashful kid. BLANCHE *speaks softly to
him.*] Well, you do, honey lamb! Come here. I want to kiss you, just once,
softly and sweetly on your mouth! [*Without waiting for him to accept, she
crosses quickly to him and presses her lips to his.*] Now run along, now, quickly!
It would be nice to keep you, but I've got to be good—and keep my hands
off children.

[*He stares at her a moment. She opens the door for him and blows a kiss at him as he goes down the steps with a dazed look. She stands there a little dreamily after he has disappeared. Then* MITCH *appears around the corner with a bunch of roses.*]

BLANCHE: [*Gaily.*] Look who's coming! My Rosenkavalier! Bow to me first . . . now present them! *Ahhhh—Merciiii!⁹* [*She looks at him over them, coquettishly pressing them to her lips. He beams at her self-consciously.*]

SCENE 6

It is about two A.M. *on the same evening. The outer wall of the building is visible.* BLANCHE *and* MITCH *come in. The utter exhaustion which only a neurasthenic personality can know is evident in* BLANCHE's *voice and manner.* MITCH *is stolid but depressed. They have probably been out to the amusement park on Lake Pontchartrain, for* MITCH *is bearing, upside down, a plaster statuette of Mae West, the sort of prize won at shooting galleries and carnival games of chance.*

BLANCHE: [*Stopping lifelessly at the steps.*] Well— [MITCH *laughs uneasily.*] Well . . .
MITCH: I guess it must be pretty late—and you're tired.
BLANCHE: Even the hot tamale man has deserted the street, and he hangs on till the end. [MITCH *laughs uneasily again.*] How will you get home?
MITCH: I'll walk over to Bourbon and catch an owl-car.
BLANCHE: [*Laughing grimly.*] Is that street-car named Desire still grinding along the tracks at this hour?
MITCH: [*Heavily.*] I'm afraid you haven't gotten much fun out of this evening, Blanche.
BLANCHE: I spoiled it for *you.*
MITCH: No, you didn't, but I felt all the time that I wasn't giving you much— entertainment.
BLANCHE: I simply couldn't rise to the occasion. That was all. I don't think I've ever tried so hard to be gay and made such a dismal mess of it. I get ten points for trying!—I *did* try.
MITCH: Why did you try if you didn't feel like it, Blanche?
BLANCHE: I was just obeying the law of nature.
MITCH: Which law is that?
BLANCHE: The one that says the lady must entertain the gentleman—or no dice! See if you can locate my door key in this purse. When I'm so tired my fingers are all thumbs!
MITCH: [*Rooting in her purse.*] This it?
BLANCHE: No, honey, that's the key to my trunk which I must soon be packing.
MITCH: You mean you are leaving here soon?
BLANCHE: I've outstayed my welcome.

---

9. *Merci:* thank you. *Rosenkavalier: Knight of the Rose,* title of a romantic opera (1911) by Richard Strauss (1864–1949).

MITCH: This it?

[*The music fades away.*]

BLANCHE: Eureka! Honey, you open the door while I take a last look at the sky. [*She leans on the porch rail. He opens the door and stands awkwardly behind her.*] I'm looking for the Pleiades,[1] the Seven Sisters, but these girls are not out tonight. Oh, yes they are, there they are! God bless them! All in a bunch going home from their little bridge party. . . . Y' get the door open? Good boy! I guess you—want to go now . . .

[*He shuffles and coughs a little.*]

MITCH: Can I—uh—kiss you—good night?
BLANCHE: Why do you always ask me if you may?
MITCH: I don't know whether you want me to or not.
BLANCHE: Why should you be so doubtful?
MITCH: That night when we parked by the lake and I kissed you, you—
BLANCHE: Honey, it wasn't the kiss I objected to. I liked the kiss very much. It was the other little—familiarity—that I—felt obliged to—discourage. . . . I didn't resent it! Not a bit in the world! In fact, I was somewhat flattered that you— desired me! But, honey, you know as well as I do that a single girl, a girl alone in the world, has got to keep a firm hold on her emotions or she'll be lost!
MITCH: [*Solemnly.*] Lost?
BLANCHE: I guess you are used to girls that like to be lost. The kind that get lost immediately, on the first date!
MITCH: I like you to be exactly the way that you are, because in all my—experi- ence—I have never known anyone like you. [BLANCHE *looks at him gravely; then she bursts into laughter and then claps a hand to her mouth.*] Are you laugh- ing at me?
BLANCHE: No, honey. The lord and lady of the house have not yet returned, so come in. We'll have a nightcap. Let's leave the lights off. Shall we?
MITCH: You just—do what you want to.

[BLANCHE *precedes him into the kitchen. The outer wall of the building disap- pears and the interiors of the two rooms can be dimly seen.*]

BLANCHE: [*Remaining in the first room.*] The other room's more comfortable—go on in. This crashing around in the dark is my search for some liquor.
MITCH: You want a drink?
BLANCHE: I want *you* to have a drink! You have been so anxious and solemn all evening, and so have I; we have both been anxious and solemn and now for these few last remaining moments of our lives together—I want to create— *joie de vivre!* I'm lighting a candle.
MITCH: That's good.
BLANCHE: We are going to be very Bohemian. We are going to pretend that we are sitting in a little artists' cafe on the Left Bank in Paris! [*She lights a candle stub*

1. The seven daughters of Atlas who were metamorphosed into stars.

and puts it in a bottle.] *Je suis la Dame aux Camellias! Vous êtes—Armand!*[2] Understand French?

MITCH: [*Heavily.*] Naw. Naw, I—

BLANCHE: *Voulez-vous couchez avec moi ce soir? Vous ne comprenez pas? Ah, quelle dommage!*[3]—I mean it's a damned good thing. . . . I've found some liquor! Just enough for two shots without any dividends, honey . . .

MITCH: [*Heavily.*] That's—good.

[*She enters the bedroom with the drinks and the candle.*]

BLANCHE: Sit down! Why don't you take off your coat and loosen your collar?

MITCH: I better leave it on.

BLANCHE: No. I want you to be comfortable.

MITCH: I am ashamed of the way I perspire. My shirt is sticking to me.

BLANCHE: Perspiration is healthy. If people didn't perspire they would die in five minutes. [*She takes his coat from him.*] This is a nice coat. What kind of material is it?

MITCH: They call that stuff alpaca.

BLANCHE: Oh. Alpaca.

MITCH: It's very light-weight alpaca.

BLANCHE: Oh. Light-weight alpaca.

MITCH: I don't like to wear a wash-coat even in summer because I sweat through it.

BLANCHE: Oh.

MITCH: And it don't look neat on me. A man with a heavy build has got to be careful of what he puts on him so he don't look too clumsy.

BLANCHE: You are not too heavy.

MITCH: You don't think I am?

BLANCHE: You are not the delicate type. You have a massive bone-structure and a very imposing physique.

MITCH: Thank you. Last Christmas I was given a membership to the New Orleans Athletic Club.

BLANCHE: Oh, good.

MITCH: It was the finest present I ever was given. I work out there with the weights and I swim and I keep myself fit. When I started there, I was getting soft in the belly but now my belly is hard. It is so hard now that a man can punch me in the belly and it don't hurt me. Punch me! Go on! See? [*She pokes lightly at him.*]

BLANCHE: Gracious. [*Her hand touches her chest.*]

MITCH: Guess how much I weigh, Blanche?

BLANCHE: Oh, I'd say in the vicinity of—one hundred and eighty?

MITCH: Guess again.

---

2. I am the Lady of the Camellias! You are—Armand! (Both are characters in the popular romantic play *La Dame aux Camélias* [1852] by the French author Alexandre Dumas [1824–1895]; she is a courtesan who gives up her true love, Armand.)   3. Would you like to sleep with me this evening? You don't understand? Ah, what a pity!

BLANCHE: Not that much?

MITCH: No. More.

BLANCHE: Well, you're a tall man and you can carry a good deal of weight without looking awkward.

MITCH: I weigh two hundred and seven pounds and I'm six feet one and one half inches tall in my bare feet—without shoes on. And that is what I weigh stripped.

BLANCHE: Oh, my goodness, me! It's awe-inspiring.

MITCH: [*Embarrassed.*] My weight is not a very interesting subject to talk about. [*He hesitates for a moment.*] What's yours?

BLANCHE: My weight?

MITCH: Yes.

BLANCHE: Guess!

MITCH: Let me lift you.

BLANCHE: Samson![4] Go on, lift me. [*He comes behind her and puts his hands on her waist and raises her lightly off the ground.*] Well?

MITCH: You are light as a feather.

BLANCHE: Ha-ha! [*He lowers her but keeps his hands on her waist.* BLANCHE *speaks with an affectation of demureness.*] You may release me now.

MITCH: Huh?

BLANCHE: [*Gaily.*] I said unhand me, sir. [*He fumblingly embraces her. Her voice sounds gently reproving.*] Now, Mitch. Just because Stanley and Stella aren't at home is no reason why you shouldn't behave like a gentleman.

MITCH: Just give me a slap whenever I step out of bounds.

BLANCHE: That won't be necessary. You're a natural gentleman, one of the very few that are left in the world. I don't want you to think that I am severe and old maid school-teacherish or anything like that. It's just—well—

MITCH: Huh?

BLANCHE: I guess it is just that I have—old-fashioned ideals! [*She rolls her eyes, knowing he cannot see her face.* MITCH *goes to the front door. There is a considerable silence between them.* BLANCHE *sighs and* MITCH *coughs self-consciously.*]

MITCH: [*Finally.*] Where's Stanley and Stella tonight?

BLANCHE: They have gone out. With Mr. and Mrs. Hubbell upstairs.

MITCH: Where did they go?

BLANCHE: I think they were planning to go to a midnight prevue at Loew's State.

MITCH: We should all go out together some night.

BLANCHE: No. That wouldn't be a good plan.

MITCH: Why not?

BLANCHE: You are an old friend of Stanley's?

MITCH: We was together in the Two-forty-first.[5]

BLANCHE: I guess he talks to you frankly?

MITCH: Sure.

BLANCHE: Has he talked to you about me?

MITCH: Oh—not very much.

4. Legendary strong man, in the Old Testament.   5. Battalion of engineers, in World War II.

BLANCHE: The way you say that, I suspect that he has.

MITCH: No, he hasn't said much.

BLANCHE: But what he *has* said. What would you say his attitude toward me was?

MITCH: Why do you want to ask that?

BLANCHE: Well—

MITCH: Don't you get along with him?

BLANCHE: What do you think?

MITCH: I don't think he understands you.

BLANCHE: That is putting it mildly. If it weren't for Stella about to have a baby, I wouldn't be able to endure things here.

MITCH: He isn't—nice to you?

BLANCHE: He is insufferably rude. Goes out of his way to offend me.

MITCH: In what way, Blanche?

BLANCHE: Why, in every conceivable way.

MITCH: I'm surprised to hear that.

BLANCHE: Are you?

MITCH: Well, I—don't see how anybody could be rude to you.

BLANCHE: It's really a pretty frightful situation. You see, there's no privacy here. There's just these portieres between the two rooms at night. He stalks through the rooms in his underwear at night. And I have to ask him to close the bathroom door. That sort of commonness isn't necessary. You probably wonder why I don't move out. Well, I'll tell you frankly. A teacher's salary is barely sufficient for her living expenses. I didn't save a penny last year and so I had to come here for the summer. That's why I have to put up with my sister's husband. And he has to put up with me, apparently so much against his wishes. . . . Surely he must have told you how much he hates he!

MITCH: I don't think he hates you.

BLANCHE: He hates me. Or why would he insult me? The first time I laid eyes on him I thought to myself, that man is my executioner! That man will destroy me, unless——

MITCH: Blanche—

BLANCHE: Yes, honey?

MITCH: Can I ask you a question?

BLANCHE: Yes. What?

MITCH: How old are you?

[*She makes a nervous gesture.*]

BLANCHE: Why do you want to know?

MITCH: I talked to my mother about you and she said, "How old is Blanche?" And I wasn't able to tell her. [*There is another pause.*]

BLANCHE: You talked to your mother about me?

MITCH: Yes.

BLANCHE: Why?

MITCH: I told my mother how nice you were, and I liked you.

BLANCHE: Were you sincere about that?

MITCH: You know I was.

BLANCHE: Why did your mother want to know my age?

MITCH: Mother is sick.

BLANCHE: I'm sorry to hear it. Badly?

MITCH: She won't live long. Maybe just a few months.

BLANCHE: Oh.

MITCH: She worries because I'm not settled.

BLANCHE: Oh.

MITCH: She wants me to be settled down before she— [*His voice is hoarse and he clears his throat twice, shuffling nervously around with his hands in and out of his pockets.*]

BLANCHE: You love her very much, don't you?

MITCH: Yes.

BLANCHE: I think you have a great capacity for devotion. You will be lonely when she passes on, won't you? [MITCH *clears his throat and nods.*] I understand what that is.

MITCH: To be lonely?

BLANCHE: I loved someone, too, and the person I loved I lost.

MITCH: Dead? [*She crosses to the window and sits on the sill, looking out. She pours herself another drink.*] A man?

BLANCHE: He was a boy, just a boy, when I was a very young girl. When I was sixteen, I made the discovery—love. All at once and much, much too completely. It was like you suddenly turned a blinding light on something that had always been half in shadow, that's how it struck the world for me. But I was unlucky. Deluded. There was something different about the boy, a nervousness, a softness and tenderness which wasn't like a man's, although he wasn't the least bit effeminate looking—still—that thing was there. . . . He came to me for help. I didn't know that. I didn't find out anything till after our marriage when we'd run away and come back and all I knew was I'd failed him in some mysterious way and wasn't able to give the help he needed but couldn't speak of! He was in the quicksands and clutching at me—but I wasn't holding him out, I was slipping in with him! I didn't know that. I didn't know anything except I loved him unendurably but without being able to help him or help myself. Then I found out. In the worst of all possible ways. By coming suddenly into a room that I thought was empty—which wasn't empty, but had two people in it . . . the boy I had married and an older man who had been his friend for years . . . [*A locomotive is heard approaching outside. She claps her hands to her ears and crouches over. The headlight of the locomotive glares into the room as it thunders past. As the noise recedes she straightens slowly and continues speaking.*] Afterward we pretended that nothing had been discovered. Yes, the three of us drove out to Moon Lake Casino, very drunk and laughing all the way. [*Polka music sounds, in a minor key faint with distance.*] We danced the "Varsouviana!"[6] Suddenly in the middle of the dance the boy I had married broke away from me and ran out of the casino. A few moments later—a shot! [*The polka stops abruptly.* BLANCHE

6. Fast Polish dance, similar to the polka.

rises stiffly. Then, the polka resumes in a major key.] I ran out—all did!—all ran and gathered about the terrible thing at the edge of the lake! I couldn't get near for the crowding. Then somebody caught my arm. "Don't go any closer! Come back! You don't want to see!" See? See what! Then I heard voices say— Allan! Allan! The Grey boy! He'd stuck the revolver into his mouth, and fired—so that the back of his head had been—blown away! [*She sways and covers her face.*] It was because—on the dance floor—unable to stop myself— I'd suddenly said—"I saw! I know! You disgust me . . ." And then the search-light which had been turned on the world was turned off again and never for one moment since has there been any light that's stronger than this— kitchen—candle . . .

[MITCH *gets up awkwardly and moves toward her a little. The polka music increases.* MITCH *stands beside her.*]

MITCH: [*Drawing her slowly into his arms.*] You need somebody. And I need some-body, too. Could it be—you and me, Blanche?

[*She stares at him vacantly for a moment. Then with a soft cry huddles in his embrace. She makes a sobbing effort to speak but the words won't come. He kisses her forehead and her eyes and finally her lips. The polka tune fades out. Her breath is drawn and released in long, grateful sobs.*]

BLANCHE: Sometimes—there's God—so quickly!

SCENE 7

It is late afternoon in mid-September.
The portieres are open and a table is set for a birthday supper, with cake and flowers.
STELLA *is completing the decorations as* STANLEY *comes in.*

STANLEY: What's all this stuff for?
STELLA: Honey, it's Blanche's birthday.
STANLEY: She here?
STELLA: In the bathroom.
STANLEY: [*Mimicking.*] "Washing out some things"?
STELLA: I reckon so.
STANLEY: How long she been in there?
STELLA: All afternoon.
STANLEY: [*Mimicking.*] "Soaking in a hot tub"?
STELLA: Yes.
STANLEY: Temperature 100 on the nose, and she soaks herself in a hot tub.
STELLA: She says it cools her off for the evening.
STANLEY: And you run out an' get her cokes, I suppose? And serve 'em to Her Majesty in the tub? [STELLA *shrugs.*] Set down here a minute.
STELLA: Stanley, I've got things to do.
STANLEY: Set down! I've got th' dope on your big sister, Stella.

STELLA: Stanley, stop picking on Blanche.

STANLEY: That girl calls *me* common!

STELLA: Lately you been doing all you can think of to rub her the wrong way, Stanley, and Blanche is sensitive and you've got to realize that Blanche and I grew up under very different circumstances than you did.

STANLEY: So I been told. And told and told and told! You know she's been feeding us a pack of lies here?

STELLA: No, I don't and—

STANLEY: Well, she has, however. But now the cat's out of the bag! I found out some things!

STELLA: What—things?

STANLEY: Things I already suspected. But now I got proof from the most reliable sources—which I have checked on!

> [BLANCHE *is singing in the bathroom a saccharine popular ballad which is used contrapuntally with* STANLEY'*s speech.*]

STELLA: [*To* STANLEY.] Lower your voice!

STANLEY: Some canary bird, huh!

STELLA: Now please tell me quietly what you think you've found out about my sister.

STANLEY: Lie Number One: All this squeamishness she puts on! You should just know the line she's been feeding to Mitch. He thought she had never been more than kissed by a fellow! But Sister Blanche is no lily! Ha-ha! Some lily she is!

STELLA: What have you heard and who from?

STANLEY: Our supply-man down at the plant has been going through Laurel for years and he knows all about her and everybody else in the town of Laurel knows all about her. She is as famous in Laurel as if she was the President of the United States, only she is not respected by any party! This supply-man stops at a hotel called the Flamingo.

BLANCHE: [*Singing blithely.*] "Say, it's only a paper moon, Sailing over a cardboard sea / —But it wouldn't be make-believe If you believed in me!"[7]

STELLA: What about the—Flamingo?

STANLEY: She stayed there, too.

STELLA: My sister lived at Belle Reve.

STANLEY: This is after the home-place had slipped through her lily-white fingers! She moved to the Flamingo! A second-class hotel which has the advantage of not interfering in the private social life of the personalities there! The Flamingo is used to all kinds of goings-on. But even the management of the Flamingo was impressed by Dame Blanche! In fact they was so impressed by Dame Blanche that they requested her to turn in her room key—for permanently! This happened a couple of weeks before she showed here.

BLANCHE: [*Singing.*] "It's a Barnum and Bailey world, Just as phony as it can be— / But it wouldn't be make-believe If you believed in me!"

---

7. From "It's Only a Paper Moon" (1933), a popular song by Harold Arlen.

STELLA: What—contemptible—lies!

STANLEY: Sure, I can see how you would be upset by this. She pulled the wool over your eyes as much as Mitch's!

STELLA: It's pure invention! There's not a word of truth in it and if I were a man and this creature had dared to invent such things in my presence—

BLANCHE: [*Singing.*] "Without your love, / it's a honky-tonk parade! / Without your love, / It's a melody played In a penny arcade . . ."

STANLEY: Honey, I told you I thoroughly checked on these stories! Now wait till I finish. The trouble with Dame Blanche was that she couldn't put on her act any more in Laurel! They got wised up after two or three dates with her and then they quit, and she goes on to another, the same old line, same old act, same old hooey! But the town was too small for this to go on forever! And as time went by she became a town character. Regarded as not just different but downright loco—nuts. [STELLA *draws back.*] And for the last year or two she has washed up like poison. That's why she's here this summer, visiting royalty, putting on all this act—because she's practically told by the mayor to get out of town! Yes, did you know there was an army camp near Laurel and your sister's was one of the places called "Out-of-Bounds"?

BLANCHE: "It's only a paper moon, Just as phony as it can be— / But it wouldn't be make-believe If you believed in me!"

STANLEY: Well, so much for her being such a refined and particular type of girl. Which brings us to Lie Number Two.

STELLA: I don't want to hear any more!

STANLEY: She's not going back to teach school! In fact I am willing to bet you that she never had no idea of returning to Laurel! She didn't resign temporarily from the high school because of her nerves! No, siree, Bob! She didn't. They kicked her out of that high school before the spring term ended—and I hate to tell you the reason that step was taken! A seventeen-year-old boy—she'd gotten mixed up with!

BLANCHE: "It's a Barnum and Bailey world, Just as phony as it can be—"

[*In the bathroom the water goes on loud; little breathless cries and peals of laughter are heard as if a child were frolicking in the tub.*]

STELLA: This is making me—sick!

STANLEY: The boy's dad learned about it and got in touch with the high school superintendent. Boy, oh, boy, I'd like to have been in that office when Dame Blanche was called on the carpet! I'd like to have seen her trying to squirm out of that one! But they had her on the hook good and proper that time and she knew that the jig was all up! They told her she better move on to some fresh territory. Yep, it was practickly a town ordinance passed against her!

[*The bathroom door is opened and* BLANCHE *thrusts her head out, holding a towel about her hair.*]

BLANCHE: Stella!

STELLA: [*Faintly.*] Yes, Blanche?

BLANCHE: Give me another bath-towel to dry my hair with. I've just washed it.

STELLA: Yes, Blanche. [*She crosses in a dazed way from the kitchen to the bathroom door with a towel.*]

BLANCHE: What's the matter, honey?

STELLA: Matter? Why?

BLANCHE: You have such a strange expression on your face!

STELLA: Oh— [*She tries to laugh.*] I guess I'm a little tired!

BLANCHE: Why don't you bathe, too, soon as I get out?

STANLEY: [*Calling from the kitchen.*] How soon is that going to be?

BLANCHE: Not so terribly long! Possess your soul in patience!

STANLEY: It's not my soul, it's my kidneys I'm worried about! [BLANCHE *slams the door.* STANLEY *laughs harshly.* STELLA *comes slowly back into the kitchen.*] Well, what do you think of it?

STELLA: I don't believe all of those stories and I think your supply-man was mean and rotten to tell them. It's possible that some of the things he said are partly true. There are things about my sister I don't approve of—things that caused sorrow at home. She was always—flighty!

STANLEY: Flighty!

STELLA: But when she was young, very young, she married a boy who wrote poetry. . . . He was extremely good-looking. I think Blanche didn't just love him but worshipped the ground he walked on! Adored him and thought him almost too fine to be human! But then she found out—

STANLEY: What?

STELLA: This beautiful and talented young man was a degenerate. Didn't your supply-man give you that information?

STANLEY: All we discussed was recent history. That must have been a pretty long time ago.

STELLA: Yes, it was—a pretty long time ago . . .

[STANLEY *comes up and takes her by the shoulders rather gently. She gently withdraws from him. Automatically she starts sticking little pink candles in the birthday cake.*]

STANLEY: How many candles you putting in that cake?

STELLA: I'll stop at twenty-five.

STANLEY: Is company expected?

STELLA: We asked Mitch to come over for cake and ice-cream.

[STANLEY *looks a little uncomfortable. He lights a cigarette from the one he has just finished.*]

STANLEY: I wouldn't be expecting Mitch over tonight.

[STELLA *pauses in her occupation with candles and looks slowly around at* STANLEY.]

STELLA: *Why?*

STANLEY: Mitch is a buddy of mine. We were in the same outfit together—Two-forty-first Engineers. We work in the same plant and now on the same bowling team. You think I could face him if—

STELLA: Stanley Kowalski, did you—did you repeat what that—?

STANLEY: You're goddam right I told him! I'd have that on my conscience the rest of my life if I knew all that stuff and let my best friend get caught!

STELLA: Is Mitch through with her?

STANLEY: Wouldn't you be if—?

STELLA: I said, *Is Mitch through with her?*

[BLANCHE's *voice is lifted again, serenely as a bell. She sings "But it wouldn't be make-believe If you believed in me."*]

STANLEY: No, I don't think he's necessarily through with her—just wised up!

STELLA: Stanley, she thought Mitch was—going to—going to marry her. I was hoping so, too.

STANLEY: Well, he's not going to marry her. Maybe he *was,* but he's not going to jump in a tank with a school of sharks—now! [*He rises.*] Blanche! Oh, Blanche! Can I please get in my bathroom? [*There is a pause.*]

BLANCHE: Yes, indeed, sir! Can you wait one second while I dry?

STANLEY: Having waited one hour I guess one second ought to pass in a hurry.

STELLA: And she hasn't got her job? Well, what will she do!

STANLEY: She's not stayin' here after Tuesday. You know that, don't you? Just to make sure I bought her ticket myself. A bus ticket.

STELLA: In the first place, Blanche wouldn't go on a bus.

STANLEY: She'll go on a bus and like it.

STELLA: No, she won't, no, she won't, Stanley!

STANLEY: *She'll go!* Period. P.S. She'll go *Tuesday!*

STELLA: [*Slowly.*] What'll—she—do? What on earth will she—*do!*

STANLEY: Her future is mapped out for her.

STELLA: What do you mean?

[BLANCHE *sings.*]

STANLEY: Hey, canary bird! Toots! Get *OUT* of the *BATHROOM!*

[*The bathroom door flies open and* BLANCHE *emerges with a gay peal of laughter, but as* STANLEY *crosses past her, a frightened look appears in her face, almost a look of panic. He doesn't look at her but slams the bathroom door shut as he goes in.*]

BLANCHE: [*Snatching up a hairbrush.*] Oh, I feel so good after my long, hot bath, I feel so good and cool and—rested!

STELLA: [*Sadly and doubtfully from the kitchen.*] Do you, Blanche?

BLANCHE: [*Snatching up a hairbrush.*] Yes, I do, so refreshed! [*She tinkles her highball glass.*] A hot bath and a long, cold drink always give me a brand new outlook on life! [*She looks through the portieres at* STELLA, *standing between them, and slowly stops brushing.*] Something has happened!—What is it?

STELLA: [*Turning away quickly.*] Why, nothing has happened, Blanche.

BLANCHE: You're lying! Something has! [*She stares fearfully at* STELLA, *who pretends to be busy at the table. The distant piano goes into a hectic breakdown.*]

SCENE 8

Three quarters of an hour later.

The view through the big windows is fading gradually into a still-golden dusk. A torch of sunlight blazes on the side of a big water-tank or oil-drum across the empty lot toward the business district which is now pierced by pinpoints of lighted windows or windows reflecting the sunset.

The three people are completing a dismal birthday supper. STANLEY *looks sullen.* STELLA *is embarrassed and sad.*

BLANCHE *has a tight, artificial smile on her drawn face. There is a fourth place at the table which is left vacant.*

BLANCHE: [*Suddenly.*] Stanley, tell us a joke, tell us a funny story to make us all laugh. I don't know what's the matter, we're all so solemn. Is it because I've been stood up by my beau? [STELLA *laughs feebly.*] It's the first time in my entire experience with men, and I've had a good deal of all sorts, that I've actually been stood up by anybody! Ha-ha! I don't know how to take it. . . . Tell us a funny little story, Stanley! Something to help us out.

STANLEY: I didn't think you liked my stories, Blanche.

BLANCHE: I like them when they're amusing but not indecent.

STANLEY: I don't know any refined enough for your taste.

BLANCHE: Then let me tell one.

STELLA: Yes, you tell one, Blanche. You used to know lots of good stories.

[*The music fades.*]

BLANCHE: Let me see, now. . . . I must run through my repertoire! Oh, yes—I love parrot stories! Do you all like parrot stories? Well, this one's about the old maid and the parrot. This old maid, she had a parrot that cursed a blue streak and knew more vulgar expressions than Mr. Kowalski!

STANLEY: Huh.

BLANCHE: And the only way to hush the parrot up was to put the cover back on its cage so it would think it was night and go back to sleep. Well, one morning the old maid had just uncovered the parrot for the day—when who should she see coming up the front walk but the preacher! Well, she rushed back to the parrot and slipped the cover back on the cage and then she let in the preacher. And the parrot was perfectly still, just as quiet as a mouse, but just as she was asking the preacher how much sugar he wanted in his coffee—the parrot broke the silence with a loud— [*She whistles.*] —and said—"God *damn*, but that was a short day!" [*She throws back her head and laughs.* STELLA *also makes an ineffectual effort to seem amused.* STANLEY *pays no attention to the story but reaches way over the table to spear his fork into the remaining chop which he eats with his fingers.*] Apparently Mr. Kowalski was not amused.

STELLA: Mr. Kowalski is too busy making a pig of himself to think of anything else!

STANLEY: That's right, baby.

STELLA: Your face and your fingers are disgustingly greasy. Go and wash up and then help me clear the table.

[*He hurls a plate to the floor.*]

STANLEY: That's how I'll clear the table! [*He seizes her arm.*] Don't ever talk that way to me! "Pig—Polack—disgusting—vulgar—greasy!"—them kind of words have been on your tongue and your sister's too much around here! What do you two think you are? A pair of queens? Remember what Huey Long[8] said—"Every Man is a King!" And I am the king around here, so don't forget it! [*He hurls a cup and saucer to the floor.*] My place is cleared! You want me to clear your places?

[STELLA *begins to cry weakly.* STANLEY *stalks out on the porch and lights a cigarette. The Negro entertainers around the corner are heard.*]

BLANCHE: What happened while I was bathing? What did he tell you, Stella?
STELLA: Nothing, nothing, nothing!
BLANCHE: I think he told you something about Mitch and me! You know why Mitch didn't come but you won't tell me! [STELLA *shakes her head helplessly.*] I'm going to call him!
STELLA: I wouldn't call him, Blanche.
BLANCHE: I am, I'm going to call him on the phone.
STELLA: [*Miserably.*] I wish you wouldn't.
BLANCHE: I intend to be given some explanation from someone!

[*She rushes to the phone in the bedroom.* STELLA *goes out on the porch and stares reproachfully at her husband. He grunts and turns away from her.*]

STELLA: I hope you're pleased with your doings. I never had so much trouble swallowing food in my life, looking at that girl's face and the empty chair! [*She cries quietly.*]
BLANCHE: [*At the phone.*] Hello. Mr. Mitchell, please. . . . Oh. . . . I would like to leave a number if I may. Magnolia 9047. And say it's important to call. . . . Yes, very important. . . . Thank you. [*She remains by the phone with a lost, frightened look.*]

[STANLEY *turns slowly back toward his wife and takes her clumsily in his arms.*]

STANLEY: Stell, it's gonna be all right after she goes and after you've had the baby. It's gonna be all right again between you and me the way that it was. You remember the way that it was? Them nights we had together? God, honey, it's gonna be sweet when we can make noise in the night the way that we used to and get the colored lights going with nobody's sister behind the curtains to hear us! [*Their upstairs neighbors are heard in bellowing laughter at something.* STANLEY *chuckles.*] Steve an' Eunice . . .
STELLA: Come on back in. [*She returns to the kitchen and starts lighting the candles on the white cake.*] Blanche?
BLANCHE: Yes. [*She returns from the bedroom to the table in the kitchen.*] Oh, those pretty, pretty little candles! Oh, don't burn them, Stella.

8. Demagogic Louisiana political leader, governor, and senator (1893–1935).

STELLA: I certainly will.

[STANLEY *comes back in.*]

BLANCHE: You ought to save them for baby's birthdays. Oh, I hope candles are going to glow in his life and I hope that his eyes are going to be like candles, like two blue candles lighted in a white cake!

STANLEY: [*Sitting down.*] What poetry!

BLANCHE: [*She pauses reflectively for a moment.*] I shouldn't have called him.

STELLA: There's lots of things could have happened.

BLANCHE: There's no excuse for it, Stella. I don't have to put up with insults. I won't be taken for granted.

STANLEY: Goddamn, it's hot in here with the steam from the bathroom.

BLANCHE: I've said I was sorry three times. [*The piano fades out.*] I take hot baths for my nerves. Hydrotherapy, they call it. You healthy Polack, without a nerve in your body, of course you don't know what anxiety feels like!

STANLEY: I am not a Polack. People from Poland are Poles, not Polacks. But what I am is a one-hundred-per-cent American, born and raised in the greatest country on earth and proud as hell of it, so don't ever call me a Polack.

[*The phone rings.* BLANCHE *rises expectantly.*]

BLANCHE: Oh, that's for me, I'm sure.

STANLEY: *I'm* not sure. Keep your seat. [*He crosses leisurely to phone.*] H'lo. Aw, yeh, hello, Mac.

[*He leans against wall, staring insultingly in at* BLANCHE. *She sinks back in her chair with a frightened look.* STELLA *leans over and touches her shoulder.*]

BLANCHE: Oh, keep your hands off me, Stella. What is the matter with you? Why do you look at me with that pitying look?

STANLEY: [*Bawling.*] QUIET IN THERE!—We've got a noisy woman on the place.— Go on, Mac. At Riley's? No, I don't wanta bowl at Riley's. I had a little trouble with Riley last week. I'm the team captain, ain't I? All right, then, we're not gonna bowl at Riley's, we're gonna bowl at the West Side or the Gala! All right, Mac. See you! [*He hangs up and returns to the table.* BLANCHE *fiercely controls herself, drinking quickly from her tumbler of water. He doesn't look at her but reaches in a pocket. Then he speaks slowly and with false amiability.*] Sister Blanche, I've got a little birthday remembrance for you.

BLANCHE: Oh, have you, Stanley? I wasn't expecting any, I—I don't know why Stella wants to observe my birthday! I'd much rather forget it—when you— reach twenty-seven! Well—age is a subject that you'd prefer to—ignore!

STANLEY: Twenty-seven?

BLANCHE: [*Quickly.*] What is it? Is it for *me?*

[*He is holding a little envelope toward her.*]

STANLEY: Yes, I hope you like it!

BLANCHE: Why, why—Why, it's a—

STANLEY: Ticket! Back to Laurel! On the Greyhound! Tuesday! [*The "Varsouviana" music steals in softly and continues playing.* STELLA *rises abruptly and turns her back.* BLANCHE *tries to smile. Then she tries to laugh. Then she gives both up and springs from the table and runs into the next room. She clutches her throat and then runs into the bathroom. Coughing, gagging sounds are heard.*] Well!

STELLA: You didn't need to do that.

STANLEY: Don't forget all that I took off her.

STELLA: You needn't have been so cruel to someone alone as she is.

STANLEY: Delicate piece she is.

STELLA: She is. She was. You didn't know Blanche as a girl. Nobody, nobody, was tender and trusting as she was. But people like you abused her, and forced her to change. [*He crosses into the bedroom, ripping off his shirt, and changes into a brilliant silk bowling shirt. She follows him.*] Do you think you're going bowling now?

STANLEY: Sure.

STELLA: You're not going bowling. [*She catches hold of his shirt.*] Why did you do this to her?

STANLEY: I done nothing to no one. Let go of my shirt. You've torn it.

STELLA: I want to know why. Tell me why.

STANLEY: When we first met, me and you, you thought I was common. How right you was, baby. I was common as dirt. You showed me the snapshot of the place with the columns. I pulled you down off them columns and how you loved it, having them colored lights going! And wasn't we happy together, wasn't it all okay till she showed here? [STELLA *makes a slight movement. Her look goes suddenly inward as if some interior voice had called her name. She begins a slow, shuffling progress from the bedroom to the kitchen, leaning and resting on the back of the chair and then on the edge of a table with a blind look and listening expression.* STANLEY, *finishing with his shirt, is unaware of her reaction.*] And wasn't we happy together? Wasn't it all okay? Till she showed here. Hoity-Toity, describing me as an ape. [*He suddenly notices the change in* STELLA.] Hey, what is it, Stell? [*He crosses to her.*]

STELLA: [*Quietly.*] Take me to the hospital.

[*He is with her now, supporting her with his arm, murmuring indistinguishably as they go outside.*]

SCENE 9

A while later that evening. BLANCHE *is seated in a tense hunched position in a bedroom chair that she has recovered with diagonal green and white stripes. She has on her scarlet satin robe. On the table beside chair is a bottle of liquor and a glass. The rapid, feverish polka tune, the "Varsouviana," is heard. The music is in her mind; she is drinking to escape it and the sense of disaster closing in on her, and she seems to whisper the words of the song. An electric fan is turning back and forth across her.*

MITCH *comes around the corner in work clothes: blue denim shirt and pants. He is unshaven. He climbs the steps to the door and rings.* BLANCHE *is startled.*

BLANCHE: Who is it, please?

MITCH: [*Hoarsely.*] Me. Mitch.

> [*The polka tune stops.*]

BLANCHE: Mitch!—Just a minute. [*She rushes about frantically, hiding the bottle in a closet, crouching at the mirror and dabbing her face with cologne and powder. She is so excited that her breath is audible as she dashes about. At last she rushes to the door in the kitchen and lets him in.*] Mitch!—Y'know, I really shouldn't let you in after the treatment I have received from you this evening! So utterly uncavalier! But hello, beautiful! [*She offers him her lips. He ignores it and pushes past her into the flat. She looks fearfully after him as he stalks into the bedroom.*] My, my, what a cold shoulder! And such uncouth apparel! Why, you haven't even shaved! The unforgivable insult to a lady! But I forgive you. I forgive you because it's such a relief to see you. You've stopped that polka tune that I had caught in my head. Have you ever had anything caught in your head? No, of course you haven't, you dumb angel-puss, you'd never get anything awful caught in your head!

> [*He stares at her while she follows him while she talks. It is obvious that he has had a few drinks on the way over.*]

MITCH: Do we have to have that fan on?

BLANCHE: No!

MITCH: I don't like fans.

BLANCHE: Then let's turn it off, honey. I'm not partial to them! [*She presses the switch and the fan nods slowly off. She clears her throat uneasily as* MITCH *plumps himself down on the bed in the bedroom and lights a cigarette.*] I don't know what there is to drink. I—haven't investigated.

MITCH: I don't want Stan's liquor.

BLANCHE: It isn't Stan's. Everything here isn't Stan's. Some things on the premises are actually mine! How is your mother? Isn't your mother well?

MITCH: Why?

BLANCHE: Something's the matter tonight, but never mind. I won't cross-examine the witness. I'll just— [*She touches her forehead vaguely. The polka tune starts up again.*] —pretend I don't notice anything different about you! That—music again . . .

MITCH: What music?

BLANCHE: The "Varsouviana"! The polka tune they were playing when Allan—Wait! [*A distant revolver shot is heard.* BLANCHE *seems relieved.*] There now, the shot! It always stops after that. [*The polka music dies out again.*] Yes, now it's stopped.

MITCH: Are you boxed out of your mind?

BLANCHE: I'll go and see what I can find in the way of— [*She crosses into the closet, pretending to search for the bottle.*] Oh, by the way, excuse me for not being dressed. But I'd practically given you up! Had you forgotten your invitation to supper?

MITCH: I wasn't going to see you any more.

BLANCHE: Wait a minute. I can't hear what you're saying and you talk so little that when you do say something, I don't want to miss a single syllable of it. . . . What am I looking around here for? Oh, yes—liquor! We've had so much excitement around here this evening that I *am* boxed out of my mind! [*She pretends suddenly to find the bottle. He draws his foot up on the bed and stares at her contemptuously.*] Here's something. Southern Comfort! What is that, I wonder?

MITCH: If you don't know, it must belong to Stan.

BLANCHE: Take your foot off the bed. It has a light cover on it. Of course you boys don't notice things like that. I've done so much with this place since I've been here.

MITCH: I bet you have.

BLANCHE: You saw it before I came. Well, look at it now! This room is almost— dainty! I want to keep it that way. I wonder if this stuff ought to be mixed with something? Ummm, it's sweet! It's terribly, terribly sweet! Why, it's a *liqueur*, I believe! Yes, that's what it *is*, a liqueur! [MITCH *grunts*.] I'm afraid you won't like it, but try it, and maybe you will.

MITCH: I told you already I don't want none of his liquor and I mean it. You ought to lay off his liquor. He says you been lapping it up all summer like a wild cat!

BLANCHE: What a fantastic statement! Fantastic of him to say it, fantastic of you to repeat it! I won't descend to the level of such cheap accusations to answer them, even!

MITCH: Huh.

BLANCHE: What's in your mind? I see something in your eyes!

MITCH: [*Getting up.*] It's dark in here.

BLANCHE: I like it dark. The dark is comforting to me.

MITCH: I don't think I ever seen you in the light. [BLANCHE *laughs breathlessly.*] That's a fact!

BLANCHE: Is it?

MITCH: I've never seen you in the afternoon.

BLANCHE: Whose fault is that?

MITCH: You never want to go out in the afternoon.

BLANCHE: Why, Mitch, you're at the plant in the afternoon!

MITCH: Not Sunday afternoon. I've asked you to go out with me sometimes on Sundays but you always make an excuse. You never want to go out till after six and then it's always some place that's not lighted much.

BLANCHE: There is some obscure meaning in this but I fail to catch it.

MITCH: What it means is I've never had a real good look at you, Blanche. Let's turn the light on here.

BLANCHE: [*Fearfully.*] Light? Which light? What for?

MITCH: This one with the paper thing on it.

[*He tears the paper lantern off the light bulb. She utters a frightened gasp.*]

BLANCHE: What did you do that for?

MITCH: So I can take a look at you good and plain!

BLANCHE: Of course you don't really mean to be insulting!

MITCH: No, just realistic.

BLANCHE: I don't want realism. I want magic! [MITCH *laughs.*] Yes, yes, magic! I try to give that to people. I misrepresent things to them. I don't tell truth, I tell what *ought* to be truth. And if that is sinful, then let me be damned for it!— Don't turn the light on!

[MITCH *crosses to the switch. He turns the light on and stares at her. She cries out and covers her face. He turns the lights off again.*]

MITCH: [*Slowly and bitterly.*] I don't mind you being older than what I thought. But all the rest of it—Christ! That pitch about your ideals being so old-fashioned and all the malarkey that you've dished out all summer. Oh, I knew you weren't sixteen any more. But I was a fool enough to believe you was straight.

BLANCHE: Who told you I wasn't—"straight"? My loving brother-in-law. And you believed him.

MITCH: I called him a liar at first. And then I checked on the story. First I asked our supply-man who travels through Laurel. And then I talked directly over long-distance to this merchant.

BLANCHE: Who is this merchant?

MITCH: Kiefaber.

BLANCHE: The merchant Kiefaber of Laurel! I know the man. He whistled at me. I put him in his place. So now for revenge he makes up stories about me.

MITCH: Three people, Kiefaber, Stanley and Shaw, swore to them!

BLANCHE: Rub-a-dub-dub, three men in a tub! And such a filthy tub!

MITCH: Didn't you stay at a hotel called The Flamingo?

BLANCHE: Flamingo? No! Tarantula was the name of it! I stayed at a hotel called The Tarantula Arms!

MITCH: [*Stupidly.*] Tarantula?

BLANCHE: Yes, a big spider! That's where I brought my victims. [*She pours herself another drink.*] Yes, I had many intimacies with strangers. After the death of Allan—intimacies with strangers was all I seemed able to fill my empty heart with. . . . I think it was panic, just panic, that drove me from one to another, hunting for some protection—here and there, in the most—unlikely places— even, at last, in a seventeen-year-old boy but—somebody wrote the super-intendent about it—"This woman is morally unfit for her position!" [*She throws back her head with convulsive, sobbing laughter. Then she repeats the statement, gasps, and drinks.*] True? Yes, I suppose—unfit somehow—anyway. . . . So I came here. There was nowhere else I could go. I was played out. You know what played out is? My youth was suddenly gone up the water-spout, and—I met you. You said you needed somebody. Well, I needed somebody, too. I thanked God for you, because you seemed to be gentle—a cleft in the rock of the world that I could hide in! But I guess I was asking, hoping—too much! Kiefaber, Stanley and Shaw have tied an old tin can to the tail of the kite.

[*There is a pause.* MITCH *stares at her dumbly.*]

MITCH: You lied to me, Blanche.

BLANCHE: Don't say I lied to you.

MITCH: Lies, lies, inside and out, all lies.

BLANCHE: Never inside, I didn't lie in my heart . . .

[*A vendor comes around the corner. She is a blind* MEXICAN WOMAN *in a dark shawl, carrying bunches of those gaudy tin flowers that lower-class Mexicans display at funerals and other festive occasions. She is calling barely audibly. Her figure is only faintly visible outside the building.*]

MEXICAN WOMAN: *Flores. Flores, Flores para los muertos.*[9] *Flores. Flores.*

BLANCHE: What? Oh! Somebody outside . . . [*She goes to the door, opens it and stares at the* MEXICAN WOMAN.]

MEXICAN WOMAN: [*She is at the door and offers* BLANCHE *some of her flowers.*] *Flores? Flores para los muertos?*

BLANCHE: [*Frightened.*] No, no! Not now! Not now! [*She darts back into the apartment, slamming the door.*]

MEXICAN WOMAN: [*She turns away and starts to move down the street.*] *Flores para los muertos.*

[*The polka tune fades in.*]

BLANCHE: [*As if to herself.*] Crumble and fade and—regrets—recriminations . . . "If you'd done this, it wouldn't've cost me that!"

MEXICAN WOMAN: *Corones*[1] *para los muertos. Corones* . . .

BLANCHE: Legacies! Huh. . . . And other things such as bloodstained pillow-slips—"Her linen needs changing"—"Yes, Mother. But couldn't we get a colored girl to do it?" No, we couldn't of course. Everything gone but the—

MEXICAN WOMAN: *Flores.*

BLANCHE: Death—I used to sit here and she used to sit over there and death was as close as you are. . . . We didn't dare even admit we had ever heard of it!

MEXICAN WOMAN: *Flores para los muertos, flores—flores* . . .

BLANCHE: The opposite is desire. So do you wonder? How could you possibly wonder! Not far from Belle Reve, before we had lost Belle Reve, was a camp where they trained young soldiers. On Sunday nights they would go in town to get drunk—

MEXICAN WOMAN: [*Softly.*] *Corones* . . .

BLANCHE: —and on the way back they would stagger onto my lawn and call—"Blanche! Blanche!"—the deaf old lady remaining suspected nothing. But sometimes I slipped outside to answer their calls. . . . Later the paddy-wagon would gather them up like daisies . . . the long way home . . . [*The* MEXICAN WOMAN *turns slowly and drifts back off with her soft mournful cries.* BLANCHE *goes to the dresser and leans forward on it. After a moment,* MITCH *rises and follows her*

9. Flowers for the dead.   1. Wreaths.

purposefully. The polka music fades away. He places his hands on her waist and tries to turn her about.] What do you want?

MITCH: [*Fumbling to embrace her.*] What I been missing all summer.

BLANCHE: Then marry me, Mitch!

MITCH: I don't think I want to marry you any more.

BLANCHE: No?

MITCH: [*Dropping his hands from her waist.*] You're not clean enough to bring in the house with my mother.

BLANCHE: Go away, then. [*He stares at her.*] Get out of here quick before I start screaming fire! [*Her throat is tightening with hysteria.*] Get out of here quick before I start screaming fire. [*He still remains staring. She suddenly rushes to the big window with its pale blue square of the soft summer light and cries wildly.*] Fire! Fire! Fire!

> [*With a startled gasp,* MITCH *turns and goes out the outer door, clatters awkwardly down the steps and around the corner of the building.* BLANCHE *staggers back from the window and falls to her knees. The distant piano is slow and blue.*]

SCENE 10

It is a few hours later that night.

BLANCHE *has been drinking fairly steadily since* MITCH *left. She has dragged her wardrobe trunk into the center of the bedroom. It hangs open with flowery dresses thrown across it. As the drinking and packing went on, a mood of hysterical exhilaration came into her and she has decked herself out in a somewhat soiled and crumpled white satin evening gown and a pair of scuffed silver slippers with brilliants set in their heels.*

Now she is placing the rhinestone tiara on her head before the mirror of the dressing-table and murmuring excitedly as if to a group of spectral admirers.

BLANCHE: How about taking a swim, a moonlight swim at the old rock-quarry? If anyone's sober enough to drive a car! Ha-ha! Best way in the world to stop your head buzzing! Only you've got to be careful to dive where the deep pool is—if you hit a rock you don't come up till tomorrow . . . [*Tremblingly she lifts the hand mirror for a closer inspection. She catches her breath and slams the mirror face down with such violence that the glass cracks. She moans a little and attempts to rise.* STANLEY *appears around the corner of the building. He still has on the vivid green silk bowling shirt. As he rounds the corner the honky-tonk music is heard. It continues softly throughout the scene. He enters the kitchen, slamming the door. As he peers in at* BLANCHE, *he gives a low whistle. He has had a few drinks on the way and has brought some quart beer bottles home with him.*] How is my sister?

STANLEY: She is doing okay.

BLANCHE: And how is the baby?

STANLEY: [*Grinning amiably.*] The baby won't come before morning so they told me to go home and get a little shut-eye.

BLANCHE: Does that mean we are to be alone in here?

STANLEY: Yep. Just me and you, Blanche. Unless you got somebody hid under the bed. What've you got on those fine feathers for?

BLANCHE: Oh, that's right. You left before my wire came.

STANLEY: You got a wire?

BLANCHE: I received a telegram from an old admirer of mine.

STANLEY: Anything good?

BLANCHE: I think so. An invitation.

STANLEY: What to? A fireman's ball?

BLANCHE: [Throwing back her head.] A cruise of the Caribbean on a yacht!

STANLEY: Well, well. What do you know?

BLANCHE: I have never been so surprised in my life.

STANLEY: I guess not.

BLANCHE: It came like a bolt from the blue!

STANLEY: Who did you say it was from?

BLANCHE: An old beau of mine.

STANLEY: The one that give you the white fox-pieces?

BLANCHE: Mr. Shep Huntleigh. I wore his ATO pin my last year at college. I hadn't seen him again until last Christmas. I ran in to him on Biscayne Boulevard. Then—just now—this wire—inviting me on a cruise of the Caribbean! The problem is clothes. I tore into my trunk to see what I have that's suitable for the tropics!

STANLEY: And come up with that—gorgeous—diamond—tiara?

BLANCHE: This old relic? Ha-ha! It's only rhinestones.

STANLEY: Gosh. I thought it was Tiffany diamonds. [He unbuttons his shirt.]

BLANCHE: Well, anyhow, I shall be entertained in style.

STANLEY: Uh-huh. It goes to show, you never know what is coming.

BLANCHE: Just when I thought my luck had begun to fail me—

STANLEY: Into the picture pops this Miami millionaire.

BLANCHE: This man is not from Miami. This man is from Dallas.

STANLEY: This man is from Dallas?

BLANCHE: Yes, this man is from Dallas where gold spouts out of the ground!

STANLEY: Well, just so he's from somewhere! [He starts removing his shirt.]

BLANCHE: Close the curtains before you undress any further.

STANLEY: [Amiably.] This is all I'm going to undress right now. [He rips the sack off a quart beer bottle.] Seen a bottle-opener? [She moves slowly toward the dresser, where she stands with her hands knotted together.] I used to have a cousin who could open a beer bottle with his teeth. [Pounding the bottle cap on the corner of table.] That was his only accomplishment, all he could do—he was just a human bottle-opener. And then one time, at a wedding party, he broke his front teeth off! After that he was so ashamed of himself he used t' sneak out of the house when company came . . . [The bottle cap pops off and a geyser of foam shoots up. STANLEY laughs happily, holding up the bottle over his head.] Ha-ha! Rain from heaven! [He extends the bottle toward her.] Shall we bury the hatchet and make it a loving-cup? Huh?

BLANCHE: No, thank you.

STANLEY: Well, it's a red-letter night for us both. You having an oil millionaire and me having a baby. [*He goes to the bureau in the bedroom and crouches to remove something from the bottom drawer.*]

BLANCHE: [*Drawing back.*] What are you doing in here?

STANLEY: Here's something I always break out on special occasions like this. The silk pyjamas I wore on my wedding night!

BLANCHE: Oh.

STANLEY: When the telephone rings and they say, "You've got a son!" I'll tear this off and wave it like a flag! [*He shakes out a brilliant pyjama coat.*] I guess we are both entitled to put on the dog. [*He goes back to the kitchen with the coat over his arm.*]

BLANCHE: When I think of how divine it is going to be to have such a thing as privacy once more—I could weep with joy!

STANLEY: This millionaire from Dallas is not going to interfere with your privacy any?

BLANCHE: It won't be the sort of thing you have in mind. This man is a gentleman and he respects me. [*Improvising feverishly.*] What he wants is my companionship. Having great wealth sometimes makes people lonely! A cultivated woman, a woman of intelligence and breeding, can enrich a man's life—immeasurably! I have those things to offer, and this doesn't take them away. Physical beauty is passing. A transitory possession. But beauty of the mind and richness of the spirit and tenderness of the heart—and I have all of those things—aren't taken away, but grow! Increase with the years! How strange that I should be called a destitute woman! When I have all of these treasures locked in my heart. [*A choked sob comes from her.*] I think of myself as a very, very rich woman! But I have been foolish—casting my pearls before swine!

STANLEY: Swine, huh?

BLANCHE: Yes, swine! Swine! And I'm thinking not only of you but of your friend, Mr. Mitchell. He came to see me tonight. He dared to come here in his work clothes! And to repeat slander to me, vicious stories that he had gotten from you! I gave him his walking papers . . .

STANLEY: You did, huh?

BLANCHE: But then he came back. He returned with a box of roses to beg my forgiveness! He implored my forgiveness. But some things are not forgivable. Deliberate cruelty is not forgivable. It is the one unforgivable thing in my opinion and it is the one thing of which I have never, ever been guilty. And so I told him, I said to him, "Thank you," but it was foolish of me to think that we could ever adapt ourselves to each other. Our ways of life are too different. Our attitudes and our backgrounds are incompatible. We have to be realistic about such things. So farewell, my friend! And let there be no hard feelings . . .

STANLEY: Was this before or after the telegram came from the Texas oil millionaire?

BLANCHE: What telegram? No! No, after! As a matter of fact, the wire came just as—

STANLEY: As a matter of fact there wasn't no wire at all!

BLANCHE: Oh, oh!

STANLEY: There isn't no millionaire! And Mitch didn't come back with roses 'cause I know where he is—

BLANCHE: Oh!

STANLEY: There isn't a goddam thing but imagination!

BLANCHE: Oh!

STANLEY: And lies and conceit and tricks!

BLANCHE: Oh!

STANLEY: And look at yourself! Take a look at yourself in that worn-out Mardi Gras outfit, rented for fifty cents from some ragpicker! And with the crazy crown on! What queen do you think you are?

BLANCHE: Oh—God . . .

STANLEY: I've been on to you from the start! Not once did you pull any wool over this boy's eyes! You come in here and sprinkle the place with powder and spray perfume and cover the light-bulb with a paper lantern, and lo and behold the place has turned into Egypt and you are the Queen of the Nile! Sitting on your throne and swilling down my liquor! I say—*Ha!—Ha!* Do you hear me? *Ha—ha—ha!* [*He walks into the bedroom.*]

BLANCHE: Don't come in here! [*Lurid reflections appear on the walls around* BLANCHE. *The shadows are of a grotesque and menacing form. She catches her breath, crosses to the phone and jiggles the hook.* STANLEY *goes into the bathroom and closes the door.*] Operator, operator! Give me long-distance, please. . . . I want to get in touch with Mr. Shep Huntleigh of Dallas. He's so well known he doesn't require any address. Just ask anybody who—Wait!!—No, I couldn't find it right now. . . . Please understand, I—No! No, wait! . . . One moment! Someone is—Nothing! Hold on, please! [*She sets the phone down and crosses warily into the kitchen. The night is filled with inhuman voices like cries in a jungle. The shadows and lurid reflections move sinuously as flames along the wall spaces. Through the back wall of the rooms, which have become transparent, can be seen the sidewalk. A prostitute has rolled a drunkard. He pursues her along the walk, overtakes her and there is a struggle. A policeman's whistle breaks it up. The figures disappear. Some moments later the* NEGRO WOMAN *appears around the corner with a sequined bag which the prostitute had dropped on the walk. She is rooting excitedly through it.* BLANCHE *presses her knuckles to her lips and returns slowly to the phone. She speaks in a hoarse whisper.*] Operator! Operator! Never mind long-distance. Get Western Union. There isn't time to be—Western—Western Union! [*She waits anxiously.*] Western Union? Yes! I—want to—Take down this message! "In desperate, desperate circumstances! Help me! Caught in a trap. Caught in—" Oh!

[*The bathroom door is thrown open and* STANLEY *comes out in the brilliant silk pyjamas. He grins at her as he knots the tassled sash about his waist. She gasps and backs away from the phone. He stares at her for a count of ten. Then a clicking becomes audible from the telephone, steady and rasping.*]

STANLEY: You left th' phone off th' hook.

[*He crosses to it deliberately and sets it back on the hook. After he has replaced it, he stares at her again, his mouth slowly curving into a grin, as he weaves* between BLANCHE *and the outer door. The barely audible "Blue Piano" begins to drum up louder. The sound of it turns into the roar of an approaching locomotive.* BLANCHE *crouches, pressing her fists to her ears until it has gone by.*]

BLANCHE: [*Finally straightening.*] Let me—let me get by you!
STANLEY: Get by me? Sure. Go ahead. [*He moves back a pace in the doorway.*]
BLANCHE: You—you stand over there! [*She indicates a further position.*]
STANLEY: You got plenty of room to walk by me now.
BLANCHE: Not with you there! But I've got to get out somehow!
STANLEY: You think I'll interfere with you? Ha-ha! [*The "Blue Piano" goes softy. She turns confusedly and makes a faint gesture. The inhuman jungle voices rise up. He takes a step toward her, biting his tongue, which protrudes between his lips. Softly.*] Come to think of it—maybe you wouldn't be bad to—interfere with . . .

[BLANCHE *moves backward through the door into the bedroom.*]

BLANCHE: Stay back! Don't you come toward me another step or I'll—
STANLEY: What?
BLANCHE: Some awful thing will happen! It will!
STANLEY: What are you putting on now?

[*They are now both inside the bedroom.*]

BLANCHE: I warn you, don't, I'm in danger!

[*He takes another step. She smashes a bottle on the table and faces him, clutching the broken top.*]

STANLEY: What did you do that for?
BLANCHE: So I could twist the broken end in your face!
STANLEY: I bet you would do that!
BLANCHE: I would! I will if you—
STANLEY: Oh! So you want some roughhouse! All right, let's have some roughhouse! [*He springs toward her, overturning the table. She cries out and strikes at him with the bottle top but he catches her wrist.*] Tiger—tiger! Drop the bottletop! Drop it! We've had this date with each other from the beginning!

[*She moans. The bottle-top falls. She sinks to her knees: He picks up her inert figure and carries her to the bed. The hot trumpet and drums from the Four Deuces sound loudly.*]

SCENE 11

It is some weeks later. STELLA *is packing* BLANCHE's *things. Sounds of water can be heard running in the bathroom.*

*The portieres are partly open on the poker players—*STANLEY, STEVE, MITCH *and* PABLO—*who sit around the table in the kitchen. The atmosphere of the kitchen is now the same raw, lurid one of the disastrous poker night.*

The building is framed by the sky of turquoise. STELLA *has been crying as she arranges the flowery dresses in the open trunk.*

EUNICE *comes down the steps from her flat above and enters the kitchen. There is an outburst from the poker table.*

STANLEY: Drew to an inside straight and made it, by God.

PABLO: *Maldita sea tu suerto!*

STANLEY: Put it in English, greaseball.

PABLO: I am cursing your rutting luck.

STANLEY: [*Prodigiously elated.*] You know what luck is? Luck is believing you're lucky. Take at Salerno.[2] I believed I was lucky. I figured that 4 out of 5 would not come through but I would . . . and I did. I put that down as a rule. To hold front position in this rat-race you've got to believe you are lucky.

MITCH: You . . . you . . . you . . . Brag . . . brag . . . bull . . . bull.

[STELLA *goes into the bedroom and starts folding a dress.*]

STANLEY: What's the matter with him?

EUNICE: [*Walking past the table.*] I always did say that men are callous things with no feelings but this does beat anything. Making pigs of yourselves. [*She comes through the portieres into the bedroom.*]

STANLEY: What's the matter with her?

STELLA: How is my baby?

EUNICE: Sleeping like a little angel. Brought you some grapes. [*She puts them on a stool and lowers her voice.*] Blanche?

STELLA: Bathing.

EUNICE: How is she?

STELLA: She wouldn't eat anything but asked for a drink.

EUNICE: What did you tell her?

STELLA: I—just told her that—we'd made arrangements for her to rest in the country. She's got it mixed in her mind with Shep Huntleigh.

[BLANCHE *opens the bathroom door slightly.*]

BLANCHE: Stella.

STELLA: Yes.

BLANCHE: That cool yellow silk—the bouclé. See if it's crushed. If it's not too crushed I'll wear it and on the lapel that silver and turquoise pin in the shape of a seahorse. You will find them in the heart-shaped box I keep my accessories in. And Stella . . . Try and locate a bunch of artificial violets in that box, too, to pin with the seahorse on the lapel of the jacket.

[*She closes the door.* STELLA *turns to* EUNICE.]

STELLA: I don't know if I did the right thing.

EUNICE: What else could you do?

STELLA: I couldn't believe her story and go on living with Stanley.

2. Important beachhead in the Allied invasion of Italy in World War II.

EUNICE: Don't ever believe it. Life has got to go on. No matter what happens, you've got to keep on going.

[*The bathroom door opens a little.*]

BLANCHE: [*Looking out.*] Is the coast clear?
STELLA: Yes, Blanche. [*To* EUNICE.] Tell her how well she's looking.
BLANCHE: Please close the curtains before I come out.
STELLA: They're closed.
STANLEY: —How many for you?
PABLO: Two.
STEVE: Three.

[BLANCHE *appears in the amber light of the door. She has a tragic radiance in her red satin robe following the sculptural lines of her body. The "Varsouviana" rises audibly as* BLANCHE *enters the bedroom.*]

BLANCHE: [*With faintly hysterical vivacity.*] I have just washed my hair.
STELLA: Did you?
BLANCHE: I'm not sure I got the soap out.
EUNICE: Such fine hair!
BLANCHE: [*Accepting the compliment.*] It's a problem. Didn't I get a call?
STELLA: Who from, Blanche?
BLANCHE: Shep Huntleigh . . .
STELLA: Why, not yet, honey!
BLANCHE: How strange! I—

[*At the sound of* BLANCHE'*s voice* MITCH'*s arm supporting his cards has sagged and his gaze is dissolved into space.* STANLEY *slaps him on the shoulder.*]

STANLEY: Hey, Mitch, come to!

[*The sound of this new voice shocks* BLANCHE. *She makes a shocked gesture, forming his name with her lips.* STELLA *nods and looks quickly away.* BLANCHE *stands quite still for some moments—the silver-backed mirror in her hand and a look of sorrowful perplexity as though all human experience shows on her face.* BLANCHE *finally speaks but with sudden hysteria.*]

BLANCHE: What's going on here? [*She turns from* STELLA *to* EUNICE *and back to* STELLA. *Her rising voice penetrates the concentration of the game.* MITCH *ducks his head lower but* STANLEY *shoves back his chair as if about to rise.* STEVE *places a restraining hand on his arm. Continuing.*] What's happened here? I want an explanation of what's happened here.
STELLA: [*Agonizingly.*] Hush! Hush!
EUNICE: Hush! Hush! Honey.
STELLA: Please, Blanche.
BLANCHE: Why are you looking at me like that? Is something wrong with me?
EUNICE: You look wonderful, Blanche. Don't she look wonderful?
STELLA: Yes.
EUNICE: I understand you are going on a trip.

STELLA: Yes, Blanche *is*. She's going on a vacation.

EUNICE: I'm green with envy.

BLANCHE: Help me, help me get dressed!

STELLA: [*Handing her dress.*] Is this what you—

BLANCHE: Yes, it will do! I'm anxious to get out of here—this place is a trap!

EUNICE: What a pretty blue jacket.

STELLA: It's lilac colored.

BLANCHE: You're both mistaken. It's Della Robbia blue.[3] The blue of the robe in the old Madonna pictures. Are these grapes washed? [*She fingers the bunch of grapes which* EUNICE *had brought in.*]

EUNICE: Huh?

BLANCHE: Washed, I said. Are they washed?

EUNICE: They're from the French Market.

BLANCHE: That doesn't mean they've been washed. [*The cathedral bells chime.*] Those cathedral bells—they're the only clean thing in the Quarter. Well, I'm going now. I'm ready to go.

EUNICE: [*Whispering.*] She's going to walk out before they get here.

STELLA: Wait, Blanche.

BLANCHE: I don't want to pass in front of those men.

EUNICE: Then wait'll the game breaks up.

STELLA: Sit down and . . .

[BLANCHE *turns weakly, hesitantly about. She lets them push her into a chair.*]

BLANCHE: I can smell the sea air. The rest of my time I'm going to spend on the sea. And when I die, I'm going to die on the sea. You know what I shall die of? [*She plucks a grape.*] I shall die of eating an unwashed grape one day out on the ocean. I will die—with my hand in the hand of some nice-looking ship's doctor, a very young one with a small blond mustache and a big silver watch. "Poor lady," they'll say, "the quinine did her no good. That unwashed grape has transported her soul to heaven." [*The cathedral chimes are heard.*] And I'll be buried at sea sewn up in a clean white sack and dropped overboard—at noon—in the blaze of summer—and into an ocean as blue as [*Chimes again.*] my first lover's eyes!

[*A* DOCTOR *and a* MATRON *have appeared around the corner of the building and climbed the steps to the porch. The gravity of their profession is exaggerated—the unmistakable aura of the state institution with its cynical detachment. The* DOCTOR *rings the doorbell. The murmur of the game is interrupted.*]

EUNICE: [*Whispering to* STELLA.] That must be them.

[STELLA *presses her fists to her lips.*]

BLANCHE: [*Rising slowly.*] What is it?

---

3. A shade of light blue seen in terra cottas made by the Della Robbia family during the Italian Renaissance.

EUNICE: [*Affectedly casual.*] Excuse me while I see who's at the door.
STELLA: Yes.

[EUNICE *goes into the kitchen.*]

BLANCHE: [*Tensely.*] I wonder if it's for me.

[*A whispered colloquy takes place at the door.*]

EUNICE: [*Returning, brightly.*] Someone is calling for Blanche.
BLANCHE: It *is* for me, then! [*She looks fearfully from one to the other and then to the portieres. The "Varsouviana" faintly plays.*] Is it the gentleman I was expecting from Dallas?
EUNICE: I think it is, Blanche.
BLANCHE: I'm not quite ready.
STELLA: Ask him to wait outside.
BLANCHE: I . . .

[EUNICE *goes back to the portieres. Drums sound very softly.*]

STELLA: Everything packed?
BLANCHE: My silver toilet articles are still out.
STELLA: Ah!
EUNICE: [*Returning.*] They're waiting in front of the house.
BLANCHE: They! Who's "they"?
EUNICE: There's a lady with him.
BLANCHE: I cannot imagine who this "lady" could be! How is she dressed?
EUNICE: Just—just a sort of a—plain-tailored outfit.
BLANCHE: Possibly she's— [*Her voice dies out nervously.*]
STELLA: Shall we go, Blanche?
BLANCHE: Must we go through that room?
STELLA: I will go with you.
BLANCHE: How do I look?
STELLA: Lovely.
EUNICE: [*Echoing.*] Lovely.

[BLANCHE *moves fearfully to the portieres.* EUNICE *draws them open for her.* BLANCHE *goes into the kitchen.*]

BLANCHE: [*To the men.*] Please don't get up. I'm only passing through.

[*She crosses quickly to outside door.* STELLA *and* EUNICE *follow. The poker players stand awkwardly at the table—all except* MITCH, *who remains seated, looking down at the table.* BLANCHE *steps out on a small porch at the side of the door. She stops short and catches her breath.*]

DOCTOR: How do you do?
BLANCHE: You are not the gentleman I was expecting. [*She suddenly gasps and starts back up the steps. She stops by* STELLA, *who stands just outside the door, and speaks in a frightening whisper.*] That man isn't Shep Huntleigh.

[*The "Varsouviana" is playing distantly.* STELLA *stares back at* BLANCHE. EUNICE *is holding* STELLA's *arm. There is a moment of silence—no sound but that of* STANLEY *steadily shuffling the cards.* BLANCHE *catches her breath again and slips back into the flat. She enters the flat with a peculiar smile, her eyes wide and brilliant. As soon as her sister goes past her,* STELLA *closes her eyes and clenches her hands.* EUNICE *throws her arms comfortingly about her. Then she starts up to her flat.* BLANCHE *stops just inside the door.* MITCH *keeps staring down at his hands on the table, but the other men look at her curiously. At last she starts around the table toward the bedroom. As she does,* STANLEY *suddenly pushes back his chair and rises as if to block her way. The* MATRON *follows her into the flat.*]

STANLEY: Did you forget something?
BLANCHE: [*Shrilly.*] Yes! Yes, I forgot something!

[*She rushes past him into the bedroom. Lurid reflections appear on the walls in odd, sinuous shapes. The "Varsouviana" is filtered into a weird distortion, accompanied by the cries and noises of the jungle.* BLANCHE *seizes the back of a chair as if to defend herself.*]

STANLEY: [*Sotto voce.*] Doc, you better go in.
DOCTOR: [*Sotto voce, motioning to the* MATRON.] Nurse, bring her out.

[*The* MATRON *advances on one side,* STANLEY *on the other. Divested of all the softer properties of womanhood, the* MATRON *is a peculiarly sinister figure in her severe dress. Her voice is bold and toneless as a firebell.*]

MATRON: Hello, Blanche.

[*The greeting is echoed and re-echoed by other mysterious voices behind the walls, as if reverberated through a canyon of rock.*]

STANLEY: She says that she forgot something.

[*The echo sounds in threatening whispers.*]

MATRON: That's all right.
STANLEY: What did you forget, Blanche?
BLANCHE: I—I—
MATRON: It don't matter. We can pick it up later.
STANLEY: Sure. We can send it along with the trunk.
BLANCHE: [*Retreating in panic.*] I don't know you—I don't know you. I want to be—left alone—please!
MATRON: Now, Blanche!
ECHOES: [*Rising and falling.*] Now, Blanche—now, Blanche—now, Blanche!
STANLEY: You left nothing here but spilt talcum and old empty perfume bottles—unless it's the paper lantern you want to take with you. You want the lantern?

[*He crosses to dressing table and seizes the paper lantern, tearing it off the light bulb, and extends it toward her. She cries out as if the lantern was herself. The*]

MATRON *steps boldly toward her. She screams and tries to break past the* MATRON. *All the men spring to their feet.* STELLA *runs out to the porch, with* EUNICE *following to comfort her, simultaneously with the confused voices of the men in the kitchen.* STELLA *rushes into* EUNICE'*s embrace on the porch.*]

STELLA: Oh, my God, Eunice help me! Don't let them do that to her, don't let them hurt her! Oh, God, oh, please God, don't hurt her! What are they doing to her? What are they doing? [*She tries to break from* EUNICE'*s arms.*]

EUNICE: No, honey, no, no, honey. Stay here. Don't go back in there. Stay with me and don't look.

STELLA: What have I done to my sister? Oh, God, what have I done to my sister?

EUNICE: You done the right thing, the only thing you could do. She couldn't stay here; there wasn't no other place for her to go.

[*While* STELLA *and* EUNICE *are speaking on the porch the voices of the men in the kitchen overlap them.* MITCH *has started toward the bedroom.* STANLEY *crosses to block him.* STANLEY *pushes him aside.* MITCH *lunges and strikes at* STANLEY. STANLEY *pushes* MITCH *back.* MITCH *collapses at the table, sobbing. During the preceding scenes, the* MATRON *catches hold of* BLANCHE'*s arm and prevents her flight.* BLANCHE *turns wildly and scratches at the* MATRON. *The heavy woman pinions her arms.* BLANCHE *cries out hoarsely and slips to her knees.*]

MATRON: These fingernails have to be trimmed. [*The* DOCTOR *comes into the room and she looks at him.*] Jacket, Doctor?

DOCTOR: Not unless necessary. [*He takes off his hat and now he becomes personalized. The unhuman quality goes. His voice is gentle and reassuring as he crosses to* BLANCHE *and crouches in front of her. As he speaks her name, her terror subsides a little. The lurid reflections fade from the walls, the inhuman cries and noises die out and her own hoarse crying is calmed.*] Miss DuBois. [*She turns her face to him and stares at him with desperate pleading. He smiles; then he speaks to the* MATRON.] It won't be necessary.

BLANCHE: [*Faintly.*] Ask her to let go of me.

DOCTOR: [*To the* MATRON.] Let go.

[*The* MATRON *releases her.* BLANCHE *extends her hands toward the* DOCTOR. *He draws her up gently and supports her with his arm and leads her through the portieres.*]

BLANCHE: [*Holding tight to his arm.*] Whoever you are—I have always depended on the kindness of strangers.

[*The poker players stand back as* BLANCHE *and the* DOCTOR *cross the kitchen to the front door. She allows him to lead her as if she were blind. As they go out on the porch,* STELLA *cries out her sister's name from where she is crouched a few steps up on the stairs.*]

STELLA: Blanche! Blanche, Blanche!

[BLANCHE *walks on without turning, followed by the* DOCTOR *and the* MATRON. *They go around the corner of the building.* EUNICE *descends to* STELLA *and places the child in her arms. It is wrapped in a pale blue blanket.* STELLA *accepts the child, sobbingly.* EUNICE *continues downstairs and enters the kitchen where the men, except for* STANLEY, *are returning silently to their places about the table.* STANLEY *has gone out on the porch and stands at the foot of the steps looking at* STELLA.]

STANLEY: [*A bit uncertainly.*] Stella? [*She sobs with inhuman abandon. There is something luxurious in her complete surrender to crying now that her sister is gone. Voluptuously, soothingly.*] Now, honey. Now, love. Now, now, love. [*He kneels beside her and his fingers find the opening of her blouse.*] Now, now, love. Now, love. . . .

[*The luxurious sobbing, the sensual murmur fade away under the swelling music of the "Blue Piano" and the muted trumpet.*]

STEVE: This game is seven-card stud.

CURTAIN

1947

ANTON CHEKHOV

The Cherry Orchard[1]

CHARACTERS IN THE PLAY

MADAME RANEVSKY (LYUBOV ANDREYEVNA), *the owner of the Cherry Orchard*
ANYA, *her daughter, aged 17*
VARYA, *her adopted daughter, aged 24*
SEMYONOV-PISHTCHIK, *a landowner*
CHARLOTTA IVANOVNA, *a governess*
EPIHODOV (SEMYON PANTALEYEVITCH), *a clerk*
DUNYASHA, *a maid*
FIRS, *an old valet, aged 87*

GAEV (LEONID ANDREYEVITCH), *brother of Madame Ranevsky*
LOPAHIN (YERMOLAY ALEXEYEVITCH), *a merchant*
TROFIMOV (PYOTR SERGEYEVITCH), *a student*
YASHA, *a young valet*
A WAYFARER
THE STATION MASTER
A POST-OFFICE CLERK
VISITORS, SERVANTS

The action takes place on the estate of MADAME RANEVSKY.

ACT I

A room, which has always been called the nursery. One of the doors leads into ANYA's *room. Dawn, sun rises during the scene. May, the cherry trees in flower, but it is cold in the garden with the frost of early morning. Windows closed.*
    Enter DUNYASHA *with a candle and* LOPAHIN *with a book in his hand.*

LOPAHIN: The train's in, thank God. What time is it?
DUNYASHA: Nearly two o'clock. [*Puts out the candle.*] It's daylight already.
LOPAHIN: The train's late! Two hours, at least. [*Yawns and stretches.*] I'm a pretty one; what a fool I've been. Came here on purpose to meet them at the station and dropped asleep. . . . Dozed off as I sat in the chair. It's annoying. . . . You might have waked me.
DUNYASHA: I thought you had gone. [*Listens.*] There, I do believe they're coming!
LOPAHIN: [*Listens.*] No, what with the luggage and one thing and another. [*A pause.*] Lyubov Andreyevna has been abroad five years; I don't know what she is like now. . . . She's a splendid woman. A good-natured, kind-hearted woman. I remember when I was a lad of fifteen, my poor father—he used to keep a little shop here in the village in those days—gave me a punch in the face with his fist and made my nose bleed. We were in the yard here, I forget what we'd come about—he had had a drop. Lyubov Andreyevna—I can see her now—she was a slim young girl then—took me to wash my face, and

1. Translated by Constance Garnett.

then brought me into this very room, into the nursery. "Don't cry, little peasant," says she, "it will be well in time for your wedding day." . . . [A pause.] Little peasant. . . . My father was a peasant, it's true, but here am I in a white waistcoat and brown shoes, like a pig in a bun shop. Yes, I'm a rich man, but for all my money, come to think, a peasant I was, and a peasant I am. [Turns over the pages of the book.] I've been reading this book and I can't make head or tail of it. I fell asleep over it. [A pause.]

DUNYASHA: The dogs have been awake all night, they feel that the mistress is coming.

LOPAHIN: Why, what's the matter with you, Dunyasha?

DUNYASHA: My hands are all of a tremble. I feel as though I should faint.

LOPAHIN: You're a spoilt soft creature, Dunyasha. And dressed like a lady too, and your hair done up. That's not the thing. One must know one's place.

[Enter EPIHODOV with a nosegay; he wears a pea-jacket and highly polished creaking topboots; he drops the nosegay as he comes in.]

EPIHODOV: [Picking up the nosegay.] Here! the gardener's sent this, says you're to put it in the dining-room. [Gives DUNYASHA the nosegay.]

LOPAHIN: And bring me some kvass.

DUNYASHA: I will. [Goes out.]

EPIHODOV: It's chilly this morning, three degrees of frost, though the cherries are all in flower. I can't say much for our climate. [Sighs.] I can't. Our climate is not often propitious to the occasion. Yermolay Alexeyevitch, permit me to call your attention to the fact that I purchased myself a pair of boots the day before yesterday, and they creak, I venture to assure you, so that there's no tolerating them. What ought I to grease them with?

LOPAHIN: Oh, shut up! Don't bother me.

EPIHODOV: Every day some misfortune befalls me. I don't complain, I'm used to it, and I wear a smiling face.

[DUNYASHA comes in, hands LOPAHIN the kvass.]

EPIHODOV: I am going. [Stumbles against a chair, which falls over.] There! [As though triumphant.] There you see now, excuse the expression, an accident like that among others. . . . It's positively remarkable. [Goes out.]

DUNYASHA: Do you know, Yermolay Alexeyevitch, I must confess, Epihodov has made me a proposal.

LOPAHIN: Ah!

DUNYASHA: I'm sure I don't know. . . . He's a harmless fellow, but sometimes when he begins talking, there's no making anything of it. It's all very fine and expressive, only there's no understanding it. I've a sort of liking for him too. He loves me to distraction. He's an unfortunate man; every day there's something. They tease him about it—two and twenty misfortunes they call him.

LOPAHIN: [Listening.] There! I do believe they're coming.

DUNYASHA: They are coming! What's the matter with me? . . . I'm cold all over.

LOPAHIN: They really are coming. Let's go and meet them. Will she know me? It's five years since I saw her.

DUNYASHA: [*In a flutter.*] I shall drop this very minute. . . . Ah, I shall drop.

> [*There is a sound of two carriages driving up to the house.* LOPAHIN *and* DUN-
> YASHA *go out quickly. The stage is left empty. A noise is heard in the adjoining
> rooms.* FIRS, *who has driven to meet* MADAME RANEVSKY, *crosses the stage hur-
> riedly leaning on a stick. He is wearing old-fashioned livery and a high hat. He
> says something to himself, but not a word can be distinguished. The noise
> behind the scenes goes on increasing. A voice: "Come, let's go in here." Enter*
> LYUBOV ANDREYEVNA, ANYA, *and* CHARLOTTA IVANOVNA *with a pet dog on a
> chain, all in traveling dresses.* VARYA *in an out-door coat with a kerchief over
> her head,* GAEV, SEMYONOV-PISHTCHIK, LOPAHIN, DUNYASHA *with bag and par-
> asol, servants with other articles. All walk across the room.*]

ANYA: Let's come in here. Do you remember what room this is, mamma?

LYUBOV: [*Joyfully, through her tears.*] The nursery!

VARYA: How cold it is, my hands are numb. [*To* LYUBOV ANDREYEVNA.] Your rooms,
the white room and the lavender one, are just the same as ever, mamma.

LYUBOV: My nursery, dear delightful room. . . . I used to sleep here when I was
little. . . . [*Cries.*] And here I am, like a little child. . . . [*Kisses her brother and*
VARYA, *and then her brother again.*] Varya's just the same as ever, like a nun.
And I knew Dunyasha. [*Kisses* DUNYASHA.]

GAEV: The train was two hours late. What do you think of that? Is that the way
to do things?

CHARLOTTA: [*To* PISHTCHIK.] My dog eats nuts, too.

PISHTCHIK: [*Wonderingly.*] Fancy that!

> [*They all go out except* ANYA *and* DUNYASHA.]

DUNYASHA: We've been expecting you so long. [*Takes* ANYA's *hat and coat.*]

ANYA: I haven't slept for four nights on the journey. I feel dreadfully cold.

DUNYASHA: You set out in Lent, there was snow and frost, and now? My darling!
[*Laughs and kisses her.*] I *have* missed you, my precious, my joy. I must tell
you . . . I can't put it off a minute. . . .

ANYA: [*Wearily.*] What now?

DUNYASHA: Epihodov, the clerk, made me a proposal just after Easter.

ANYA: It's always the same thing with you. . . . [*Straightening her hair.*] I've lost all
my hairpins. . . . [*She is staggering from exhaustion.*]

DUNYASHA: I don't know what to think, really. He does love me, he does love me
so!

ANYA: [*Looking towards her door, tenderly.*] My own room, my windows just as
though I had never gone away. I'm home! To-morrow morning I shall get up
and run into the garden. . . . Oh, if I could get to sleep! I haven't slept all the
journey, I was so anxious and worried.

DUNYASHA: Pyotr Sergeyevitch came the day before yesterday.

ANYA: [*Joyfully.*] Petya!

DUNYASHA: He's asleep in the bath house, he has settled in there. I'm afraid of
being in their way, says he. [*Glancing at her watch.*] I was to have waked him,
but Varvara Mihalovna told me not to. Don't you wake him, says she.

[*Enter* VARYA *with a bunch of keys at her waist.*]

VARYA: Dunyasha, coffee and make haste. . . . Mamma's asking for coffee.

DUNYASHA: This very minute. [*Goes out.*]

VARYA: Well, thank God, you've come. You're home again. [*Petting her.*] My little darling has come back! My precious beauty has come back again!

ANYA: I have had a time of it!

VARYA: I can fancy.

ANYA: We set off in Holy Week—it was so cold then, and all the way Charlotta would talk and show off her tricks. What did you want to burden me with Charlotta for?

VARYA: You couldn't have traveled all alone, darling. At seventeen!

ANYA: We got to Paris at last, it was cold there—snow. I speak French shockingly. Mamma lives on the fifth floor, I went up to her and there were a lot of French people, ladies, an old priest with a book. The place smelt of tobacco and so comfortless. I felt sorry, oh! so sorry for mamma all at once, I put my arms round her neck, and hugged her and wouldn't let her go. Mamma was as kind as she could be, and she cried. . . .

VARYA: [*Through her tears.*] Don't speak of it, don't speak of it!

ANYA: She had sold her villa at Mentone, she had nothing left, nothing. I hadn't a farthing left either, we only just had enough to get here. And mamma doesn't understand! When we had dinner at the stations, she always ordered the most expensive things and gave the waiters a whole rouble. Charlotta's just the same. Yasha too must have the same as we do; it's simply awful. You know Yasha is mamma's valet now, we brought him here with us.

VARYA: Yes, I've seen the young rascal.

ANYA: Well, tell me—have you paid the arrears on the mortgage?

VARYA: How could we get the money?

ANYA: Oh, dear! Oh, dear!

VARYA: In August the place will be sold.

ANYA: My goodness!

LOPAHIN: [*Peeps in at the door and moos like a cow.*] Moo! [*Disappears.*]

VARYA: [*Weeping.*] There, that's what I could do to him. [*Shakes her fist.*]

ANYA: [*Embracing* VARYA, *softly.*] Varya, has he made you an offer? [VARYA *shakes her head.*] Why, but he loves you. Why is it you don't come to an understanding? What are you waiting for?

VARYA: I believe that there never will be anything between us. He has a lot to do, he has no time for me . . . and takes no notice of me. Bless the man, it makes me miserable to see him. . . . Everyone's talking of our being married, everyone's congratulating me, and all the while there's really nothing in it; it's all like a dream. [*In another tone.*] You have a new brooch like a bee.

ANYA: [*Mournfully.*] Mamma bought it. [*Goes into her own room and in a lighthearted childish tone.*] And you know, in Paris I went up in a balloon!

VARYA: My darling's home again! My pretty is home again!

[DUNYASHA *returns with the coffee-pot and is making the coffee.*]

VARYA: [*Standing at the door.*] All day long, darling, as I go about looking after the house, I keep dreaming all the time. If only we could marry you to a rich man, then I should feel more at rest. Then I would go off by myself on a pilgrimage to Kiev, to Moscow . . . and so I would spend my life going from one holy place to another. . . . I would go on and on. . . . What bliss!

ANYA: The birds are singing in the garden. What time is it?

VARYA: It must be nearly three. It's time you were asleep, darling. [*Going into* ANYA's *room.*] What bliss!

[YASHA *enters with a rug and a traveling bag.*]

YASHA: [*Crosses the stage, mincingly.*] May one come in here, pray?

DUNYASHA: I shouldn't have known you, Yasha. How you have changed abroad.

YASHA: H'm! . . . And who are you?

DUNYASHA: When you went away, I was that high. [*Shows distance from floor.*] Dunyasha, Fyodor's daughter. . . . You don't remember me!

YASHA: H'm! . . . You're a peach! [*Looks round and embraces her: she shrieks and drops a saucer.* YASHA *goes out hastily.*]

VARYA: [*In the doorway, in a tone of vexation.*] What now?

DUNYASHA: [*Through her tears.*] I have broken a saucer.

VARYA: Well, that brings good luck.

ANYA: [*Coming out of her room.*] We ought to prepare mamma: Petya is here.

VARYA: I told them not to wake him.

ANYA: [*Dreamily.*] It's six years since father died. Then only a month later little brother Grisha was drowned in the river, such a pretty boy he was, only seven. It was more than mamma could bear, so she went away, went away without looking back. [*Shuddering.*] . . . How well I understand her, if only she knew! [*A pause.*] And Petya Trofimov was Grisha's tutor, he may remind her.

[*Enter* FIRS: *he is wearing a pea-jacket and a white waistcoat.*]

FIRS: [*Goes up to the coffee-pot, anxiously.*] The mistress will be served here. [*Puts on white gloves.*] Is the coffee ready? [*Sternly to* DUNYASHA.] Girl! Where's the cream?

DUNYASHA: Ah, mercy on us! [*Goes out quickly.*]

FIRS: [*Fussing round the coffee-pot.*] Ech! you good-for-nothing! [*Muttering to himself.*] Come back from Paris. And the old master used to go to Paris too . . . horses all the way. [*Laughs.*]

VARYA: What is it, Firs?

FIRS: What is your pleasure? [*Gleefully.*] My lady has come home! I have lived to see her again! Now I can die. [*Weeps with joy.*]

[*Enter* LYUBOV ANDREYEVNA, GAEV *and* SEMYONOV-PISHTCHIK; *the latter is in a short-waisted full coat of fine cloth, and full trousers.* GAEV, *as he comes in, makes a gesture with his arms and his whole body, as though he were playing billiards.*]

LYUBOV: How does it go? Let me remember. Cannon off the red!

GAEV: That's it—in off the white! Why, once, sister, we used to sleep together in this very room, and now I'm fifty-one, strange as it seems.

LOPAHIN: Yes, time flies.

GAEV: What do you say?

LOPAHIN: Time, I say, flies.

GAEV: What a smell of patchouli!

ANYA: I'm going to bed. Good-night, mamma. [*Kisses her mother.*]

LYUBOV: My precious darling. [*Kisses her hands.*] Are you glad to be home? I can't believe it.

ANYA: Good-night, uncle.

GAEV: [*Kissing her face and hands.*] God bless you! How like you are to your mother! [*To his sister.*] At her age you were just the same, Lyuba.

> [ANYA *shakes hands with* LOPAHIN *and* PISHTCHIK, *then goes out, shutting the door after her.*]

LYUBOV: She's quite worn out.

PISHTCHIK: Aye, it's a long journey, to be sure.

VARYA: [*To* LOPAHIN *and* PISHTCHIK.] Well, gentlemen? It's three o'clock and time to say good-bye.

LYUBOV: [*Laughs.*] You're just the same as ever, Varya. [*Draws her to her and kisses her.*] I'll just drink my coffee and then we will all go and rest. [FIRS *puts a cushion under her feet.*] Thanks, friend. I am so fond of coffee, I drink it day and night. Thanks, dear old man. [*Kisses* FIRS.]

VARYA: I'll just see whether all the things have been brought in. [*Goes out.*]

LYUBOV: Can it really be me sitting here? [*Laughs.*] I want to dance about and clap my hands. [*Covers her face with her hands.*] And I could drop asleep in a moment! God knows I love my country, I love it tenderly; I couldn't look out of the window in the train, I kept crying so. [*Through her tears.*] But I must drink my coffee, though. Thank you, Firs, thanks, dear old man. I'm so glad to find you still alive.

FIRS: The day before yesterday.

GAEV: He's rather deaf.

LOPAHIN: I have to set off for Harkov directly, at five o'clock. . . . It is annoying! I wanted to have a look at you, and a little talk. . . . You are just as splendid as ever.

PISHTCHIK: [*Breathing heavily.*] Handsomer, indeed. . . . Dressed in Parisian style . . . completely bowled me over.

LOPAHIN: Your brother, Leonid Andreyevitch here, is always saying that I'm a low-born knave, that I'm a money-grubber, but I don't care one straw for that. Let him talk. Only I do want you to believe in me as you used to. I do want your wonderful tender eyes to look at me as they used to in the old days. Merciful God! My father was a serf of your father and of your grandfather, but you—you—did so much for me once, that I've forgotten all that; I love you as though you were my kin . . . more than my kin.

LYUBOV: I can't sit still, I simply can't. . . . [*Jumps up and walks about in violent agitation.*] This happiness is too much for me. . . . You may laugh at me,

I know I'm silly. . . . My own bookcase. [*Kisses the bookcase.*] My little table.

GAEV: Nurse died while you were away.

LYUBOV: [*Sits down and drinks coffee.*] Yes, the Kingdom of Heaven be hers! You wrote me of her death.

GAEV: And Anastasy is dead. Squinting Petruchka has left me and is in service now with the police captain in the town. [*Takes a box of caramels out of his pocket and sucks one.*]

PISHTCHIK: My daughter, Dashenka, wishes to be remembered to you.

LOPAHIN: I want to tell you something very pleasant and cheering. [*Glancing at his watch.*] I'm going directly . . . there's no time to say much . . . well, I can say it in a couple of words. I needn't tell you your cherry orchard is to be sold to pay your debts; the 22nd of August is the date fixed for the sale; but don't you worry, dearest lady, you may sleep in peace, there is a way of saving it. . . . This is what I propose. I beg your attention! Your estate is not twenty miles from the town, the railway runs close by it, and if the cherry orchard and the land along the river bank were cut up into building plots and then let on lease for summer villas, you would make an income of at least 25,000 roubles a year out of it.

GAEV: That's all rot, if you'll excuse me.

LYUBOV: I don't quite understand you, Yermolay Alexeyevitch.

LOPAHIN: You will get a rent of at least 25 roubles a year for a three-acre plot from summer visitors, and if you say the word now, I'll bet you what you like there won't be one square foot of ground vacant by the autumn, all the plots will be taken up. I congratulate you; in fact, you are saved. It's a perfect situation with that deep river. Only, of course, it must be cleared—all the old buildings, for example, must be removed, this house too, which is really good for nothing and the old cherry orchard must be cut down.

LYUBOV: Cut down? My dear fellow, forgive me, but you don't know what you are talking about. If there is one thing interesting—remarkable indeed—in the whole province, it's just our cherry orchard.

LOPAHIN: The only thing remarkable about the orchard is that it's a very large one. There's a crop of cherries every alternate year, and then there's nothing to be done with them, no one buys them.

GAEV: This orchard is mentioned in the *Encyclopædia*.

LOPAHIN: [*Glancing at his watch.*] If we don't decide on something and don't take some steps, on the 22nd of August the cherry orchard and the whole estate too will be sold by auction. Make up your minds! There is no other way of saving it, I'll take my oath on that. No, no!

FIRS: In old days, forty or fifty years ago, they used to dry the cherries, soak them, pickle them, make jam too, and they used——

GAEV: Be quiet, Firs.

FIRS: And they used to send the preserved cherries to Moscow and to Harkov by the wagon-load. That brought the money in! And the preserved cherries in those days were soft and juicy, sweet and fragrant. . . . They knew the way to do them then. . . .

LYUBOV: And where is the recipe now?

FIRS: It's forgotten. Nobody remembers it.

PISHTCHIK: [*To* LYUBOV ANDREYEVNA.] What's it like in Paris? Did you eat frogs there?

LYUBOV: Oh, I ate crocodiles.

PISHTCHIK: Fancy that now!

LOPAHIN: There used to be only the gentlefolks and the peasants in the country, but now there are these summer visitors. All the towns, even the small ones, are surrounded nowadays by these summer villas. And one may say for sure, that in another twenty years there'll be many more of these people and that they'll be everywhere. At present the summer visitor only drinks tea in his verandah, but maybe he'll take to working his bit of land too, and then your cherry orchard would become happy, rich and prosperous. . . .

GAEV: [*Indignant.*] What rot!

[*Enter* VARYA *and* YASHA.]

VARYA: There are two telegrams for you, mamma. [*Takes out keys and opens an old-fashioned bookcase with a loud crack.*] Here they are.

LYUBOV: From Paris. [*Tears the telegrams, without reading them.*] I have done with Paris.

GAEV: Do you know, Lyuba, how old that bookcase is? Last week I pulled out the bottom drawer and there I found the date branded on it. The bookcase was made just a hundred years ago. What do you say to that? We might have celebrated its jubilee. Though it's an inanimate object, still it is a *book* case.

PISHTCHIK: [*Amazed.*] A hundred years! Fancy that now.

GAEV: Yes. . . . It is a thing. . . . [*Feeling the bookcase.*] Dear, honored, bookcase! Hail to thee who for more than a hundred years hast served the pure ideals of good and justice; thy silent call to fruitful labor has never flagged in those hundred years, maintaining [*In tears.*] in the generations of man, courage and faith in a brighter future and fostering in us ideals of good and social consciousness. [*A pause.*]

LOPAHIN: Yes. . . .

LYUBOV: You are just the same as ever, Leonid.

GAEV: [*A little embarrassed.*] Cannon off the right into the pocket!

LOPAHIN: [*Looking at his watch.*] Well, it's time I was off.

YASHA: [*Handing* LYUBOV ANDREYEVNA *medicine.*] Perhaps you will take your pills now.

PISHTCHIK: You shouldn't take medicines, my dear madam . . . they do no harm and no good. Give them here . . . honored lady. [*Takes the pill-box, pours the pills into the hollow of his hand, blows on them, puts them in his mouth and drinks off some kvass.*] There!

LYUBOV: [*In alarm.*] Why, you must be out of your mind!

PISHTCHIK: I have taken all the pills.

LOPAHIN: What a glutton! [*All laugh.*]

FIRS: His honor stayed with us in Easter week, ate a gallon and a half of cucumbers. . . . [*Mutters.*]

LYUBOV: What is he saying?

VARYA: He has taken to muttering like that for the last three years. We are used to it.

YASHA: His declining years!

[CHARLOTTA IVANOVNA, *a very thin, lanky figure in a white dress with a lorgnette in her belt, walks across the stage.*]

LOPAHIN: I beg your pardon, Charlotta Ivanovna, I have not had time to greet you. [*Tries to kiss her hand.*]

CHARLOTTA: [*Pulling away her hand.*] If I let you kiss my hand, you'll be wanting to kiss my elbow, and then my shoulder.

LOPAHIN: I've no luck to-day! [*All laugh.*] Charlotta Ivanovna, show us some tricks!

LYUBOV: Charlotta, do show us some tricks!

CHARLOTTA: I don't want to. I'm sleepy. [*Goes out.*]

LOPAHIN: In three weeks' time we shall meet again. [*Kisses* LYUBOV ANDREYEVNA's *hand.*] Good-bye till then—I must go. [*To* GAEV.] Good-bye. [*Kisses* PISHTCHIK.] Good-bye. [*Gives his hand to* VARYA, *then to* FIRS *and* YASHA.] I don't want to go. [*To* LYUBOV ANDREYEVNA.] If you think over my plan for the villas and make up your mind, then let me know; I will lend you 50,000 roubles. Think of it seriously.

VARYA: [*Angrily.*] Well, do go, for goodness sake.

LOPAHIN: I'm going, I'm going. [*Goes out.*]

GAEV: Low-born knave! I beg pardon, though . . . Varya is going to marry him, he's Varya's fiancé.

VARYA: Don't talk nonsense, uncle.

LYUBOV: Well, Varya, I shall be delighted. He's a good man.

PISHTCHIK: He is, one must acknowledge, a most worthy man. And my Dashenka . . . says too that . . . she says . . . various things. [*Snores, but at once wakes up.*] But all the same, honored lady, could you oblige me . . . with a loan of 240 roubles . . . to pay the interest on my mortgage to-morrow?

VARYA: [*Dismayed.*] No, no.

LYUBOV: I really haven't any money.

PISHTCHIK: It will turn up. [*Laughs.*] I never lose hope. I thought everything was over, I was a ruined man, and lo and behold—the railway passed through my land and . . . they paid me for it. And something else will turn up again, if not to-day, then to-morrow . . . Dashenka'll win two hundred thousand . . . she's got a lottery ticket.

LYUBOV: Well, we've finished our coffee, we can go to bed.

FIRS: [*Brushes* GAEV, *reprovingly.*] You have got on the wrong trousers again! What am I to do with you?

VARYA: [*Softly.*] Anya's asleep. [*Softly opens the window.*] Now the sun's risen, it's not a bit cold. Look, mamma, what exquisite trees! My goodness! And the air! The starlings are singing!

GAEV: [*Opens another window.*] The orchard is all white. You've not forgotten it, Lyuba? That long avenue that runs straight, straight as an arrow, how it shines on a moonlight night. You remember? You've not forgotten?

LYUBOV: [*Looking out of the window into the garden.*] Oh, my childhood, my innocence! It was in this nursery I used to sleep, from here I looked out into the orchard, happiness waked with me every morning and in those days the orchard was just the same, nothing has changed. [*Laughs with delight.*] All, all white! Oh, my orchard! After the dark gloomy autumn, and the cold winter; you are young again, and full of happiness, the heavenly angels have never left you. . . . If I could cast off the burden that weighs on my heart, if I could forget the past!

GAEV: H'm! and the orchard will be sold to pay our debts; it seems strange. . . .

LYUBOV: See, our mother walking . . . all in white, down the avenue! [*Laughs with delight.*] It is she!

GAEV: Where?

VARYA: Oh, don't, mamma!

LYUBOV: There is no one. It was my fancy. On the right there, by the path to the arbor, there is a white tree bending like a woman. . . .

[*Enter* TROFIMOV *wearing a shabby student's uniform and spectacles.*]

LYUBOV: What a ravishing orchard! White masses of blossom, blue sky. . . .

TROFIMOV: Lyubov Andreyevna! [*She looks round at him.*] I will just pay my respects to you and then leave you at once. [*Kisses her hand warmly.*] I was told to wait until morning, but I hadn't the patience to wait any longer. . . .

[LYUBOV ANDREYEVNA *looks at him in perplexity.*]

VARYA: [*Through her tears.*] This is Petya Trofimov.

TROFIMOV: Petya Trofimov, who was your Grisha's tutor. . . . Can I have changed so much?

[LYUBOV ANDREYEVNA *embraces him and weeps quietly.*]

GAEV: [*In confusion.*] There, there, Lyuba.

VARYA: [*Crying.*] I told you, Petya, to wait till to-morrow.

LYUBOV: My Grisha . . . my boy . . . Grisha . . . my son!

VARYA: We can't help it, mamma, it is God's will.

TROFIMOV: [*Softly through his tears.*] There . . . there.

LYUBOV: [*Weeping quietly.*] My boy was lost . . . drowned. Why? Oh, why, dear Petya? [*More quietly.*] Anya is asleep in there, and I'm talking loudly . . . making this noise. . . . But, Petya? Why have you grown so ugly? Why do you look so old?

TROFIMOV: A peasant-woman in the train called me a mangy-looking gentleman.

LYUBOV: You were quite a boy then, a pretty little student, and now your hair's thin—and spectacles. Are you really a student still? [*Goes towards the door.*]

TROFIMOV: I seem likely to be a perpetual student.

LYUBOV: [*Kisses her brother, then* VARYA.] Well, go to bed. . . . You are older too, Leonid.

PISHTCHIK: [*Follows her.*] I suppose it's time we were asleep. . . . Ugh! my gout. I'm staying the night! Lyubov Andreyevna, my dear soul, if you could . . . to-morrow morning . . . 240 roubles.

GAEV: That's always his story.

PISHTCHIK: 240 roubles . . . to pay the interest on my mortgage.

LYUBOV: My dear man, I have no money.

PISHTCHIK: I'll pay it back, my dear . . . a trifling sum.

LYUBOV: Oh, well, Leonid will give it you. . . . You give him the money, Leonid.

GAEV: Me give it him! Let him wait till he gets it!

LYUBOV: It can't be helped, give it him. He needs it. He'll pay it back.

[LYUBOV ANDREYEVNA, TROFIMOV, PISHTCHIK *and* FIRS *go out.* GAEV, VARYA *and* YASHA *remain.*]

GAEV: Sister hasn't got out of the habit of flinging away her money. [*To* YASHA.] Get away, my good fellow, you smell of the hen-house.

YASHA: [*With a grin.*] And you, Leonid Andreyevitch, are just the same as ever.

GAEV: What's that? [*To* VARYA.] What did he say?

VARYA: [*To* YASHA.] Your mother has come from the village; she has been sitting in the servants' room since yesterday, waiting to see you.

YASHA: Oh, bother her!

VARYA: For shame!

YASHA: What's the hurry? She might just as well have come to-morrow. [*Goes out.*]

VARYA: Mamma's just the same as ever, she hasn't changed a bit. If she had her own way, she'd give away everything.

GAEV: Yes. [*A pause.*] If a great many remedies are suggested for some disease, it means that the disease is incurable. I keep thinking and racking my brains; I have many schemes, a great many, and that really means none. If we could only come in for a legacy from somebody, or marry our Anya to a very rich man, or we might go to Yaroslavl and try our luck with our old aunt, the Countess. She's very, very rich, you know.

VARYA: [*Weeps.*] If God would help us.

GAEV: Don't blubber. Aunt's very rich, but she doesn't like us. First, sister married a lawyer instead of a nobleman. . . .

[ANYA *appears in the doorway.*]

GAEV: And then her conduct, one can't call it virtuous. She is good, and kind, and nice, and I love her, but, however one allows for extenuating circumstances, there's no denying that she's an immoral woman. One feels it in her slightest gesture.

VARYA: [*In a whisper.*] Anya's in the doorway.

GAEV: What do you say? [*A pause.*] It's queer, there seems to be something wrong with my right eye. I don't see as well as I did. And on Thursday when I was in the district Court . . .

[*Enter* ANYA.]

VARYA: Why aren't you asleep, Anya?

ANYA: I can't get to sleep.

GAEV: My pet. [*Kisses* ANYA's *face and hands.*] My child. [*Weeps.*] You are not my niece, you are my angel, you are everything to me. Believe me, believe. . . .

ANYA: I believe you, uncle. Everyone loves you and respects you . . . but, uncle dear, you must be silent . . . simply be silent. What were you saying just now about my mother, about your own sister? What made you say that?

GAEV: Yes, yes. . . . [*Puts his hand over his face.*] Really, that was awful! My God, save me! And to-day I made a speech to the bookcase . . . so stupid! And only when I had finished, I saw how stupid it was.

VARYA: It's true, uncle, you ought to keep quiet. Don't talk, that's all.

ANYA: If you could keep from talking, it would make things easier for you, too.

GAEV: I won't speak. [*Kisses* ANYA's *and* VARYA's *hands.*] I'll be silent. Only this is about business. On Thursday I was in the district Court; well, there was a large party of us there and we began talking of one thing and another, and this and that, and do you know, I believe that it will be possible to raise a loan on an I.O.U. to pay the arrears on the mortgage.

VARYA: If the Lord would help us!

GAEV: I'm going on Tuesday; I'll talk of it again. [*To* VARYA.] Don't blubber. [*To* ANYA.] Your mamma will talk to Lopahin; of course, he won't refuse her. And as soon as you're rested you shall go to Yaroslavl to the Countess, your great-aunt. So we shall all set to work in three directions at once, and the business is done. We shall pay off arrears, I'm convinced of it. [*Puts a caramel in his mouth.*] I swear on my honor, I swear by anything you like, the estate shan't be sold. [*Excitedly.*] By my own happiness, I swear it! Here's my hand on it, call me the basest, vilest of men, if I let it come to an auction! Upon my soul I swear it!

ANYA: [*Her equanimity has returned, she is quite happy.*] How good you are, uncle, and how clever! [*Embraces her uncle.*] I'm at peace now! Quite at peace! I'm happy!

[*Enter* FIRS.]

FIRS: [*Reproachfully.*] Leonid Andreyevitch, have you no fear of God? When are you going to bed?

GAEV: Directly, directly. You can go, Firs. I'll . . . yes, I will undress myself. Come, children, bye-bye. We'll go into details to-morrow, but now go to bed. [*Kisses* ANYA *and* VARYA.] I'm a man of the eighties. They run down that period, but still I can say I have had to suffer not a little for my convictions in my life, it's not for nothing that the peasant loves me. One must know the peasant! One must know how. . . .

ANYA: At it again, uncle!

VARYA: Uncle dear, you'd better be quiet!

FIRS: [*Angrily.*] Leonid Andreyevitch!

GAEV: I'm coming. I'm coming. Go to bed. Potted the shot—there's a shot for you! A beauty! [*Goes out,* FIRS *hobbling after him.*]

ANYA: My mind's at rest now. I don't want to go to Yaroslavl, I don't like my great-aunt, but still my mind's at rest. Thanks to uncle. [*Sits down.*]

VARYA: We must go to bed. I'm going. Something unpleasant happened while you were away. In the old servants' quarters there are only the old servants, as you know—Efimyushka, Polya and Yevstigney—and Karp too. They began letting stray people in to spend the night—I said nothing. But all at once I heard they had been spreading a report that I gave them nothing but pease pudding to eat. Out of stinginess, you know. . . . And it was all Yevstigney's doing. . . . Very well, I said to myself. . . . If that's how it is, I thought, wait a bit. I sent for Yevstigney. . . . [*Yawns.*] He comes. . . . "How's this, Yevstigney," I said, "you could be such a fool as to? . . ." [*Looking at* ANYA.] Anitchka! [*A pause.*] She's asleep. [*Puts her arm around* ANYA.] Come to bed . . . come along! [*Leads her.*] My darling has fallen asleep! Come. . . . [*They go.*]

> [*Far away beyond the orchard a shepherd plays on a pipe.* TROFIMOV *crosses the stage and, seeing* VARYA *and* ANYA, *stands still.*]

VARYA: 'Sh! asleep, asleep. Come, my own.

ANYA: [*Softly, half asleep.*] I'm so tired. Still those bells. Uncle . . . dear . . . mamma and uncle. . . .

VARYA: Come, my own, come along.

> [*They go into* ANYA's *room.*]

TROFIMOV: [*Tenderly.*] My sunshine! My spring.

CURTAIN

ACT II

The open country. An old shrine, long abandoned and fallen out of the perpendicular; near it a well, large stones that have apparently once been tombstones, and an old garden seat. The road to GAEV's *house is seen. On one side rise dark poplars; and there the cherry orchard begins. In the distance a row of telegraph poles and far, far away on the horizon there is faintly outlined a great town, only visible in very fine clear weather. It is near sunset.* CHARLOTTA, YASHA *and* DUNYASHA *are sitting on the seat.* EPIHODOV *is standing near, playing something mournful on a guitar. All sit plunged in thought.* CHARLOTTA *wears an old forage cap; she has taken a gun from her shoulder and is tightening the buckle on the strap.*

CHARLOTTA: [*Musingly.*] I haven't a real passport of my own, and I don't know how old I am, and I always feel that I'm a young thing. When I was a little girl, my father and mother used to travel about to fairs and give performances— very good ones. And I used to dance *salto-mortale*[2] and all sorts of things. And when papa and mamma died, a German lady took me and had me educated. And so I grew up and become a governess. But where I came from, and who I am, I don't know. . . . Who my parents were, very likely they weren't married. . . . I don't know. [*Takes a cucumber out of her pocket and eats.*] I know nothing at all. [*A pause.*] One wants to talk and has no one to talk to. . . . I have nobody.

---

2. *Salto mortal*, literally "deadly leap," is Spanish for "somersault."

EPIHODOV: [*Plays on the guitar and sings.*] "What care I for the noisy world! What care I for friends or foes!" How agreeable it is to play on the mandoline!

DUNYASHA: That's a guitar, not a mandoline. [*Looks in a hand-mirror and powders herself.*]

EPIHODOV: To a man mad with love, it's a mandoline. [*Sings.*] "Were her heart but aglow with love's mutual flame." [YASHA *joins in.*]

CHARLOTTA: How shockingly these people sing! Foo! Like jackals!

DUNYASHA: [*To* YASHA.] What happiness, though, to visit foreign lands.

YASHA: Ah, yes! I rather agree with you there. [*Yawns, then lights a cigar.*]

EPIHODOV: That's comprehensible. In foreign lands everything has long since reached full complexion.

YASHA: That's so, of course.

EPIHODOV: I'm a cultivated man, I read remarkable books of all sorts, but I can never make out the tendency I am myself precisely inclined for, whether to live or to shoot myself, speaking precisely, but nevertheless I always carry a revolver. Here it is. . . . [*Shows revolver.*]

CHARLOTTA: I've had enough, and now I'm going. [*Puts on the gun.*] Epihodov, you're a very clever fellow, and a very terrible one too, all the women must be wild about you. Br-r-r! [*Goes.*] These clever fellows are all so stupid; there's not a creature for me to speak to. . . . Always alone, alone, nobody belonging to me . . . and who I am, and why I'm on earth, I don't know. [*Walks away slowly.*]

EPIHODOV: Speaking precisely, not touching upon other subjects, I'm bound to admit about myself, that destiny behaves mercilessly to me, as a storm to a little boat. If, let us suppose, I am mistaken, then why did I wake up this morning, to quote an example, and look round, and there on my chest was a spider of fearful magnitude . . . like this. [*Shows with both hands.*] And then I take up a jug of kvass, to quench my thirst, and in it there is something in the highest degree unseemly of the nature of a cockroach. [*A pause.*] Have you read Buckle?[3] [*A pause.*] I am desirous of troubling you, Dunyasha, with a couple of words.

DUNYASHA: Well, speak.

EPIHODOV: I should be desirous to speak with you alone. [*Sighs.*]

DUNYASHA: [*Embarrassed.*] Well—only bring me my mantle first. It's by the cupboard. It's rather damp here.

EPIHODOV: Certainly. I will fetch it. Now I know what I must do with my revolver. [*Takes guitar and goes off playing on it.*]

YASHA: Two and twenty misfortunes! Between ourselves, he's a fool. [*Yawns.*]

DUNYASHA: God grant he doesn't shoot himself! [*A pause.*] I am so nervous, I'm always in a flutter. I was a little girl when I was taken into our lady's house, and now I have quite grown out of peasant ways, and my hands are white, as white as a lady's. I'm such a delicate, sensitive creature, I'm afraid of every-

---

3. Henry Thomas Buckle, a learned but eccentric historian, whose *History of Civilization in England* (1857) was the talk of Moscow a generation earlier. His work, highly respected initially for its empirical methods, quickly fell into disrepute in sophisticated intellectual circles.

thing. I'm so frightened. And if you deceive me, Yasha, I don't know what will become of my nerves.

YASHA: [*Kisses her.*] You're a peach! Of course a girl must never forget herself; what I dislike more than anything is a girl being flighty in her behavior.

DUNYASHA: I'm passionately in love with you, Yasha; you are a man of culture— you can give your opinion about anything. [*A pause.*]

YASHA: [*Yawns.*] Yes, that's so. My opinion is this: if a girl loves anyone, that means that she has no principles. [*A pause.*] It's pleasant smoking a cigar in the open air. [*Listens.*] Someone's coming this way . . . it's the gentlefolk. [DUNYASHA *embraces him impulsively.*] Go home, as though you had been to the river to bathe; go by that path, or else they'll meet you and suppose I have made an appointment with you here. That I can't endure.

DUNYASHA: [*Coughing softly.*] The cigar has made my head ache. . . . [*Goes off.*]

[YASHA *remains sitting near the shrine. Enter* LYUBOV ANDREYEVNA, GAEV *and* LOPAHIN.]

LOPAHIN: You must make up your mind once for all—there's no time to lose. It's quite a simple question, you know. Will you consent to letting the land for building or not? One word in answer: Yes or no? Only one word!

LYUBOV: Who is smoking such horrible cigars here? [*Sits down.*]

GAEV: Now the railway line has been brought near, it's made things very convenient. [*Sits down.*] Here we have been over and lunched in town. Cannon off the white! I should like to go home and have a game.

LYUBOV: You have plenty of time.

LOPAHIN: Only one word! [*Beseechingly.*] Give me an answer!

GAEV: [*Yawning.*] What do you say?

LYUBOV: [*Looks in her purse.*] I had quite a lot of money here yesterday, and there's scarcely any left to-day. My poor Varya feeds us all on milk soup for the sake of economy; the old folks in the kitchen get nothing but pease pudding, while I waste my money in a senseless way. [*Drops purse, scattering gold pieces.*] There, they have all fallen out! [*Annoyed.*]

YASHA: Allow me, I'll soon pick them up. [*Collects the coins.*]

LYUBOV: Pray do, Yasha. And what did I go off to the town to lunch for? Your restaurant's a wretched place with its music and the tablecloth smelling of soap. . . . Why drink so much, Leonid? And eat so much? And talk so much? To-day you talked a great deal again in the restaurant, and all so inappropriately. About the era of the seventies, about the decadents. And to whom? Talking to waiters about decadents!

LOPAHIN: Yes.

GAEV: [*Waving his hand.*] I'm incorrigible; that's evident. [*Irritably to* YASHA.] Why is it you keep fidgeting about in front of us!

YASHA: [*Laughs.*] I can't help laughing when I hear your voice.

GAEV: [*To his sister.*] Either I or he. . . .

LYUBOV: Get along! Go away, Yasha.

YASHA: [*Gives* LYUBOV ANDREYEVNA *her purse.*] Directly. [*Hardly able to suppress his laughter.*] This minute. . . . [*Goes off.*]

LOPAHIN: Deriganov, the millionaire, means to buy your estate. They say he is coming to the sale himself.

LYUBOV: Where did you hear that?

LOPAHIN: That's what they say in town.

GAEV: Our aunt in Yaroslavl has promised to send help; but when, and how much she will send, we don't know.

LOPAHIN: How much will she send? A hundred thousand? Two hundred?

LYUBOV: Oh, well! . . . Ten or fifteen thousand, and we must be thankful to get that.

LOPAHIN: Forgive me, but such reckless people as you are—such queer, unbusiness-like people—I never met in my life. One tells you in plain Russian your estate is going to be sold, and you seem not to understand it.

LYUBOV: What are we to do? Tell us what to do.

LOPAHIN: I do tell you every day. Every day I say the same thing. You absolutely must let the cherry orchard and the land on building leases; and do it at once, as quick as may be—the auction's close upon us! Do understand! Once make up your mind to build villas, and you can raise as much money as you like, and then you are saved.

LYUBOV: Villas and summer visitors—forgive me saying so—it's so vulgar.

GAEV: There I perfectly agree with you.

LOPAHIN: I shall sob, or scream, or fall into a fit. I can't stand it! You drive me mad! [To GAEV.] You're an old woman!

GAEV: What do you say?

LOPAHIN: An old woman! [Gets up to go.]

LYUBOV: [In dismay.] No, don't go! Do stay, my dear friend! Perhaps we shall think of something.

LOPAHIN: What is there to think of?

LYUBOV: Don't go, I entreat you! With you here it's more cheerful, anyway. [A pause.] I keep expecting something, as though the house were going to fall about our ears.

GAEV: [In profound dejection.] Potted the white! It fails—a kiss.

LYUBOV: We have been great sinners. . . .

LOPAHIN: You have no sins to repent of.

GAEV: [Puts a caramel in his mouth.] They say I've eaten up my property in caramels. [Laughs.]

LYUBOV: Oh, my sins! I've always thrown my money away recklessly like a lunatic. I married a man who made nothing but debts. My husband died of champagne—he drank dreadfully. To my misery I loved another man, and immediately—it was my first punishment—the blow fell upon me, here, in the river . . . my boy was drowned and I went abroad—went away for ever, never to return, not to see that river again . . . I shut my eyes, and fled, distracted, and he after me . . . pitilessly, brutally. I bought a villa at Mentone, for he fell ill there, and for three years I had no rest day or night. His illness wore me out, my soul was dried up. And last year, when my villa was sold to pay my debts, I went to Paris and there he robbed me of everything and abandoned me for another woman; and I tried to poison myself. . . . So stupid, so shameful! . . . And suddenly I felt a yearning for Russia, for my country, for my little girl. . . . [*Dries her tears.*] Lord, Lord, be merciful! Forgive my sins! Do not chastise me more! [*Takes a telegram out of her pocket.*] I got this to-day from Paris. He implores forgiveness, entreats me to return. [*Tears up the telegram.*] I fancy there is music somewhere. [*Listens.*]

GAEV: That's our famous Jewish orchestra. You remember, four violins, a flute and a double bass.

LYUBOV: That still in existence? We ought to send for them one evening, and give a dance.

LOPAHIN: [*Listens.*] I can't hear. . . . [*Hums softly.*] "For money the Germans will turn a Russian into a Frenchman." [*Laughs.*] I did see such a piece at the theater yesterday! It was funny!

LYUBOV: And most likely there was nothing funny in it. You shouldn't look at plays, you should look at yourselves a little oftener. How gray your lives are! How much nonsense you talk.

LOPAHIN: That's true. One may say honestly, we live a fool's life. [*Pause.*] My father was a peasant, an idiot; he knew nothing and taught me nothing, only beat me when he was drunk, and always with his stick. In reality I am just such another blockhead and idiot. I've learnt nothing properly. I write a wretched hand. I write so that I feel ashamed before folks, like a pig.

LYUBOV: You ought to get married, my dear fellow.

LOPAHIN: Yes . . . that's true.

LYUBOV: You should marry our Varya, she's a good girl.

LOPAHIN: Yes.

LYUBOV: She's a good-natured girl, she's busy all day long, and what's more, she loves you. And you have liked her for ever so long.

LOPAHIN: Well? I'm not against it. . . . She's a good girl. [*Pause.*]

GAEV: I've been offered a place in the bank: 6,000 roubles a year. Did you know?

LYUBOV: You would never do for that! You must stay as you are.

[*Enter* FIRS *with overcoat.*]

FIRS: Put it on, sir, it's damp.

GAEV: [*Putting it on.*] You bother me, old fellow.

FIRS: You can't go on like this. You went away in the morning without leaving word. [*Looks him over.*]

LYUBOV: You look older, Firs!

FIRS: What is your pleasure?

LOPAHIN: You look older, she said.

FIRS: I've had a long life. They were arranging my wedding before your papa was born. . . . [*Laughs.*] I was the head footman before the emancipation came. I wouldn't consent to be set free then; I stayed on with the old master. . . . [*A pause.*] I remember what rejoicings they made and didn't know themselves what they were rejoicing over.

LOPAHIN: Those were fine old times. There was flogging anyway.

FIRS: [*Not hearing.*] To be sure! The peasants knew their place, and the masters knew theirs; but now they're all at sixes and sevens, there's no making it out.

GAEV: Hold your tongue, Firs. I must go to town to-morrow. I have been promised
an introduction to a general, who might let us have a loan.

LOPAHIN: You won't bring that off. And you won't pay your arrears, you may rest
assured of that.

LYUBOV: That's all his nonsense. There is no such general.

[*Enter* TROFIMOV, ANYA *and* VARYA.]

GAEV: Here come our girls.

ANYA: There's mamma on the seat.

LYUBOV: [*Tenderly.*] Come here, come along. My darlings! [*Embraces* ANYA *and*
VARYA.] If you only knew how I love you both. Sit beside me, there, like that.
[*All sit down.*]

LOPAHIN: Our perpetual student is always with the young ladies.

TROFIMOV: That's not your business.

LOPAHIN: He'll soon be fifty, and he's still a student.

TROFIMOV: Drop your idiotic jokes.

LOPAHIN: Why are you so cross, you queer fish?

TROFIMOV: Oh, don't persist!

LOPAHIN: [*Laughs.*] Allow me to ask you what's your idea of me?

TROFIMOV: I'll tell you my idea of you, Yermolay Alexeyevitch: you are a rich man,
you'll soon be a millionaire. Well, just as in the economy of nature a wild
beast is of use, who devours everything that comes in his way, so you too
have your use.

[*All laugh.*]

VARYA: Better tell us something about the planets, Petya.

LYUBOV: No, let us go on with the conversation we had yesterday.

TROFIMOV: What was it about?

GAEV: About pride.

TROFIMOV: We had a long conversation yesterday, but we came to no conclusion.
In pride, in your sense of it, there is something mystical. Perhaps you are
right from your point of view; but if one looks at it simply, without subtlety,
what sort of pride can there be, what sense is there in it, if man in his physiological formation is very imperfect, if in the immense majority of cases he
is coarse, dull-witted, profoundly unhappy? One must give up glorification
of self. One should work, and nothing else.

GAEV: One must die in any case.

TROFIMOV: Who knows? And what does it mean—dying? Perhaps man has a hundred senses, and only the five we know are lost at death, while the other
ninety-five remain alive.

LYUBOV: How clever you are, Petya!

LOPAHIN: [*Ironically.*] Fearfully clever!

TROFIMOV: Humanity progresses, perfecting its powers. Everything that is beyond
its ken now will one day become familiar and comprehensible; only we must
work, we must with all our powers aid the seeker after truth. Here among us
in Russia the workers are few in number as yet. The vast majority of the

intellectual people I know, seek nothing, do nothing, are not fit as yet for work of any kind. They call themselves intellectual, but they treat their servants as inferiors, behave to the peasants as though they were animals, learn little, read nothing seriously, do practically nothing, only talk about science and know very little about art. They are all serious people, they all have severe faces, they all talk of weighty matters and air their theories, and yet the vast majority of us—ninety-nine per cent—live like savages, at the least thing fly to blows and abuse, eat piggishly, sleep in filth and stuffiness, bugs everywhere, stench and damp and moral impurity. And it's clear all our fine talk is only to divert our attention and other people's. Show me where to find the *crèches* there's so much talk about, and the reading-rooms?[4] They only exist in novels: in real life there are none of them. There is nothing but filth and vulgarity and Asiatic apathy. I fear and dislike very serious faces. I'm afraid of serious conversations. We should do better to be silent.

LOPAHIN: You know, I get up at five o'clock in the morning, and I work from morning to night; and I've money, my own and other people's, always passing through my hands, and I see what people are made of all round me. One has only to begin to do anything to see how few honest, decent people there are. Sometimes when I lie awake at night, I think: "Oh! Lord, thou hast given us immense forests, boundless plains, the widest horizons, and living here we ourselves ought really to be giants."

LYUBOV: You ask for giants! They are no good except in story-books; in real life they frighten us.

[EPIHODOV *advances in the background, playing on the guitar.*]

LYUBOV: [*Dreamily.*] There goes Epihodov.
ANYA: [*Dreamily.*] There goes Epihodov.
GAEV: The sun has set, my friends.
TROFIMOV: Yes.
GAEV: [*Not loudly, but, as it were, declaiming.*] O nature, divine nature, thou art bright with eternal luster, beautiful and indifferent! Thou, whom we call mother, thou dost unite within thee life and death! Thou dost give life and dost destroy!
VARYA: [*In a tone of supplication.*] Uncle!
ANYA: Uncle, you are at it again!
TROFIMOV: You'd much better be cannoning off the red!
GAEV: I'll hold my tongue, I will.

[*All sit plunged in thought. Perfect stillness. The only thing audible is the muttering of* FIRS. *Suddenly there is a sound in the distance, as it were from the sky—the sound of a breaking harp-string, mournfully dying away.*]

LYUBOV: What is that?

4. Nursery schools and centers offering free reading material, that is, the social services and civilizing influences that have been imagined but never created.

LOPAHIN: I don't know. Somewhere far away a bucket fallen and broken in the pits. But somewhere very far away.

GAEV: It might be a bird of some sort—such as a heron.

TROFIMOV: Or an owl.

LYUBOV: [Shudders.] I don't know why, but it's horrid. [A pause.]

FIRS: It was the same before the calamity—the owl hooted and the samovar hissed all the time.

GAEV: Before what calamity?

FIRS: Before the emancipation. [A pause.]

LYUBOV: Come, my friends, let us be going; evening is falling. [To ANYA.] There are tears in your eyes. What is it, darling? [Embraces her.]

ANYA: Nothing, mamma; it's nothing.

TROFIMOV: There is somebody coming.

> [The WAYFARER appears in a shabby white forage cap and an overcoat; he is slightly drunk.]

WAYFARER: Allow me to inquire, can I get to the station this way?

GAEV: Yes. Go along that road.

WAYFARER: I thank you most feelingly. [Coughing.] The weather is superb. [Declaims.] My brother, my suffering brother! . . . Come out to the Volga! Whose groan do you hear? . . . [To VARYA.] Mademoiselle, vouchsafe a hungry Russian thirty kopecks.

> [VARYA utters a shriek of alarm.]

LOPAHIN: [Angrily.] There's a right and a wrong way of doing everything!

LYUBOV: [Hurriedly.] Here, take this. [Looks in her purse.] I've no silver. No matter—here's gold for you.

WAYFARER: I thank you most feelingly! [Goes off.]

> [Laughter.]

VARYA: [Frightened.] I'm going home—I'm going. . . . Oh, mamma, the servants have nothing to eat, and you gave him gold!

LYUBOV: There's no doing anything with me. I'm so silly! When we get home, I'll give you all I possess. Yermolay Alexeyevitch, you will lend me some more! . . .

LOPAHIN: I will.

LYUBOV: Come, friends, it's time to be going. And Varya, we have made a match of it for you. I congratulate you.

VARYA: [Through her tears.] Mamma, that's not a joking matter.

LOPAHIN: "Ophelia, get thee to a nunnery!"[5]

GAEV: My hands are trembling; it's a long while since I had a game of billiards.

LOPAHIN: "Ophelia! Nymph, in thy orisons be all my sins remember'd."

LYUBOV: Come, it will soon be supper-time.

VARYA: How he frightened me! My heart's simply throbbing.

---

5. For this quotation and the one below, see *Hamlet* 3.1.

LOPAHIN: Let me remind you, ladies and gentlemen: on the 22nd of August the cherry orchard will be sold. Think about that! Think about it!

[*All go off, except* TROFIMOV *and* ANYA.]

ANYA: [*Laughing.*] I'm grateful to the wayfarer! He frightened Varya and we are left alone.

TROFIMOV: Varya's afraid we shall fall in love with each other, and for days together she won't leave us. With her narrow brain she can't grasp that we are above love. To eliminate the petty and transitory which hinder us from being free and happy—that is the aim and meaning of our life. Forward! We go forward irresistibly towards the bright star that shines yonder in the distance. Forward! Do not lag behind, friends.

ANYA: [*Claps her hands.*] How well you speak! [*A pause.*] It is divine here today.

TROFIMOV: Yes, it's glorious weather.

ANYA: Somehow, Petya, you've made me so that I don't love the cherry orchard as I used to. I used to love it so dearly. I used to think that there was no spot on earth like our garden.

TROFIMOV: All Russia is our garden. The earth is great and beautiful—there are many beautiful places in it. [*A pause.*] Think only, Anya, your grandfather, and great-grandfather, and all your ancestors were slave-owners—the owners of living souls—and from every cherry in the orchard, from every leaf, from every trunk there are human creatures looking at you. Cannot you hear their voices? Oh, it is awful! Your orchard is a fearful thing, and when in the evening or at night one walks about the orchard, the old bark on the trees glimmers dimly in the dusk, and the old cherry trees seem to be dreaming of centuries gone by and tortured by fearful visions. Yes! We are at least two hundred years behind, we have really gained nothing yet, we have no definite attitude to the past, we do nothing but theorize or complain of depression or drink vodka. It is clear that to begin to live in the present we must first expiate our past, we must break with it; and we can expiate it only by suffering, by extraordinary unceasing labor. Understand that, Anya.

ANYA: The house we live in has long ceased to be our own, and I shall leave it, I give you my word.

TROFIMOV: If you have the house keys, fling them into the well and go away. Be free as the wind.

ANYA: [*In ecstasy.*] How beautifully you said that!

TROFIMOV: Believe me, Anya, believe me! I am not thirty yet, I am young, I am still a student, but I have gone through so much already! As soon as winter comes I am hungry, sick, careworn, poor as a beggar, and what ups and downs of fortune have I not known! And my soul was always, every minute, day and night, full of inexplicable forebodings. I have a foreboding of happiness, Anya. I see glimpses of it already.

ANYA: [*Pensively.*] The moon is rising.

[EPIHODOV *is heard playing still the same mournful song on the guitar. The moon rises. Somewhere near the poplars* VARYA *is looking for* ANYA *and calling* "Anya! where are you?"]

TROFIMOV: Yes, the moon is rising. [*A pause.*] Here is happiness—here it comes! It is coming nearer and nearer; already I can hear its footsteps. And if we never see it—if we may never know it—what does it matter? Others will see it after us.

VARYA'S VOICE: Anya! Where are you?

TROFIMOV: That Varya again! [*Angrily.*] It's revolting!

ANYA: Well, let's go down to the river. It's lovely there.

TROFIMOV: Yes, let's go. [*They go.*]

VARYA'S VOICE: Anya! Anya!

CURTAIN

ACT III

A drawing-room divided by an arch from a larger drawing-room. A chandelier burning. The Jewish orchestra, the same that was mentioned in Act II, is heard playing in the ante-room. It is evening. In the larger drawing-room they are dancing the grand chain. The voice of SEMYONOV-PISHTCHIK: "Promenade à une paire!"[6] *Then enter the drawing-room in couples first* PISHTCHIK *and* CHARLOTTA IVANOVA, *then* TROFIMOV *and* LYUBOV ANDREYEVNA, *thirdly* ANYA *with the* POST-OFFICE CLERK, *fourthly* VARYA *with the* STATION MASTER, *and other guests.* VARYA *is quietly weeping and wiping away her tears as she dances. In the last couple is* DUNYASHA. *They move across the drawing-room.* PISHTCHIK *shouts:* "Grand rond, balancez!" *and* "Les Cavaliers à genou et remerciez vos dames."

FIRS *in a swallow-tail coat brings in seltzer water on a tray.* PISHTCHIK *and* TROFIMOV *enter the drawing-room.*

PISHTCHIK: I am a full-blooded man; I have already had two strokes. Dancing's hard work for me, but as they say, if you're in the pack, you must bark with the rest. I'm as strong, I may say, as a horse. My parent, who would have his joke—may the Kingdom of Heaven be his!—used to say about our origin that the ancient stock of the Semyonov-Pishtchiks was derived from the very horse that Caligula made a member of the senate.[7] [*Sits down.*] But I've no money, that's where the mischief is. A hungry dog believes in nothing but meat. [*Snores, but at once wakes up.*] That's like me . . . I can think of nothing but money.

TROFIMOV: There really is something horsy about your appearance.

PISHTCHIK: Well . . . a horse is a fine beast . . . a horse can be sold.

[*There is the sound of billiards being played in an adjoining room.* VARYA *appears in the arch leading to the larger drawing-room.*]

6. In this French phrase and those quoted below, Semyonov-Pishtchik is calling out the moves in the "grand chain" dance: promenade (walk) to a couple; grand circle, step to the side (that is, *balancez* as in ballet); and gentlemen (knights), kneel and thank your ladies. 7. Caligula (A.D. 12–41), Roman emperor known for tyrannical cruelty, is said to have gone insane and to have appointed his horse as a consul.

TROFIMOV: [*Teasing.*] Madame Lopahin! Madame Lopahin!

VARYA: [*Angrily.*] Mangy-looking gentleman!

TROFIMOV: Yes, I am a mangy-looking gentleman, and I'm proud of it!

VARYA: [*Pondering bitterly.*] Here we have hired musicians and nothing to pay them! [*Goes out.*]

TROFIMOV: [*To* PISHTCHIK.] If the energy you have wasted during your lifetime in trying to find the money to pay your interest had gone to something else, you might in the end have turned the world upside down.

PISHTCHIK: Nietzsche, the philosopher, a very great and celebrated man . . . of enormous intellect . . . says in his works, that one can make forged bank-notes.

TROFIMOV: Why, have you read Nietzsche?

PISHTCHIK: What next . . . Dashenka told me. . . . And now I am in such a position, I might just as well forge banknotes. The day after to-morrow I must pay 310 roubles—130 I have procured. [*Feels in his pockets, in alarm.*] The money's gone! I have lost my money! [*Through his tears.*] Where's the money? [*Glee-fully.*] Why, here it is behind the lining. . . . It has made me hot all over.

[*Enter* LYUBOV ANDREYEVNA *and* CHARLOTTA IVANOVNA.]

LYUBOV: [*Hums the Lezginka.*] Why is Leonid so long? What can he be doing in town? [*To* DUNYASHA.] Offer the musicians some tea.

TROFIMOV: The sale hasn't taken place, most likely.

LYUBOV: It's the wrong time to have the orchestra, and the wrong time to give a dance. Well, never mind. [*Sits down and hums softly.*]

CHARLOTTA: [*Gives* PISHTCHIK *a pack of cards.*] Here's a pack of cards. Think of any card you like.

PISHTCHIK: I've thought of one.

CHARLOTTA: Shuffle the pack now. That's right. Give it here, my dear Mr. Pishtchik. *Ein, zwei, drei*—now look, it's in your breast pocket.

PISHTCHIK: [*Taking a card out of his breast pocket.*] The eight of spades! Perfectly right! [*Wonderingly.*] Fancy that now!

CHARLOTTA: [*Holding pack of cards in her hands, to* TROFIMOV.] Tell me quickly which is the top card.

TROFIMOV: Well, the queen of spades.

CHARLOTTA: It is! [*To* PISHTCHIK.] Well, which card is uppermost?

PISHTCHIK: The ace of hearts.

CHARLOTTA: It is! [*Claps her hands, pack of cards disappears.*] Ah! what lovely weather it is to-day!

[*A mysterious feminine voice which seems coming out of the floor answers her.* "Oh, yes, it's magnificent weather, madam."]

CHARLOTTA: You are my perfect ideal.

VOICE: And I greatly admire you too, madam.

STATION MASTER: [*Applauding.*] The lady ventriloquist—bravo!

PISHTCHIK: [*Wonderingly.*] Fancy that now! Most enchanting Charlotta Ivanovna. I'm simply in love with you.

CHARLOTTA: In love? [*Shrugging shoulders.*] What do you know of love, *guter Mensch, aber schlechter Musikant.*[8]

TROFIMOV: [*Pats* PISHTCHIK *on the shoulder.*] You dear old horse. . . .

CHARLOTTA: Attention, please! Another trick! [*Takes a traveling rug from a chair.*] Here's a very good rug; I want to sell it. [*Shaking it out.*] Doesn't anyone want to buy it?

PISHTCHIK: [*Wonderingly.*] Fancy that!

CHARLOTTA: *Ein, zwei, drei!* [*Quickly picks up rug she has dropped; behind the rug stands* ANYA; *she makes a curtsey, runs to her mother, embraces her and runs back into the larger drawing-room amidst general enthusiasm.*]

LYUBOV: [*Applauds.*] Bravo! Bravo!

CHARLOTTA: Now again! *Ein, zwei, drei!* [*Lifts up the rug; behind the rug stands* VARYA, *bowing.*]

PISHTCHIK: [*Wonderingly.*] Fancy that now!

CHARLOTTA: That's the end. [*Throws the rug at* PISHTCHIK, *makes a curtsey, runs into the larger drawing-room.*]

PISHTCHIK: [*Hurries after her.*] Mischievous creature! Fancy! [*Goes out.*]

LYUBOV: And still Leonid doesn't come. I can't understand what he's doing in the town so long! Why, everything must be over by now. The estate is sold, or the sale has not taken place. Why keep us so long in suspense?

VARYA: [*Trying to console her.*] Uncle's bought it. I feel sure of that.

TROFIMOV: [*Ironically.*] Oh, yes!

VARYA: Great-aunt sent him an authorization to buy it in her name, and transfer the debt. She's doing it for Anya's sake, and I'm sure God will be merciful. Uncle will buy it.

LYUBOV: My aunt in Yaroslavl sent fifteen thousand to buy the estate in her name, she doesn't trust us—but that's not enough even to pay the arrears. [*Hides her face in her hands.*] My fate is being sealed to-day, my fate. . . .

TROFIMOV: [*Teasing* VARYA.] Madame Lopahin.

VARYA: [*Angrily.*] Perpetual student! Twice already you've been sent down from the University.

LYUBOV: Why are you angry, Varya? He's teasing you about Lopahin. Well, what of that? Marry Lopahin if you like, he's a good man, and interesting; if you don't want to, don't! Nobody compels you, darling.

VARYA: I must tell you plainly, mamma, I look at the matter seriously; he's a good man, I like him.

LYUBOV: Well, marry him. I can't see what you're waiting for.

VARYA: Mamma. I can't make him an offer myself. For the last two years, every-one's been talking to me about him. Everyone talks; but he says nothing or else makes a joke. I see what it means. He's growing rich, he's absorbed in business, he has no thoughts for me. If I had money, were it ever so little, if

8. A good man, but a poor musician (performer, player). As when she counts to three in German above and below, Charlotta speaks the language she associates with her childhood of performing at carnivals.

I had only a hundred roubles, I'd throw everything up and go far away. I would go into a nunnery.

TROFIMOV: What bliss!

VARYA: [*To* TROFIMOV.] A student ought to have sense! [*In a soft tone with tears.*] How ugly you've grown, Petya! How old you look! [*To* LYUBOV ANDREYEVNA, *no longer crying.*] But I can't do without work, mamma; I must have something to do every minute.

[*Enter* YASHA.]

YASHA: [*Hardly restraining his laughter.*] Epihodov has broken a billiard cue! [*Goes out.*]

VARYA: What is Epihodov doing here? Who gave him leave to play billiards? I can't make these people out. [*Goes out.*]

LYUBOV: Don't tease her, Petya. You see she has grief enough without that.

TROFIMOV: She is so very officious, meddling in what's not her business. All the summer she's given Anya and me no peace. She's afraid of a love affair between us. What's it to do with her? Besides, I have given no grounds for it. Such triviality is not in my line. We are above love!

LYUBOV: And I suppose I am beneath love. [*Very uneasily.*] Why is it Leonid's not here? If only I could know whether the estate is sold or not! It seems such an incredible calamity that I really don't know what to think. I am distracted . . . I shall scream in a minute . . . I shall do something stupid. Save me, Petya, tell me something, talk to me!

TROFIMOV: What does it matter whether the estate is sold to-day or not? That's all done with long ago. There's no turning back, the path is overgrown. Don't worry yourself, dear Lyubov Andreyevna. You mustn't deceive yourself; for once in your life you must face the truth!

LYUBOV: What truth? You see where the truth lies, but I seem to have lost my sight, I see nothing. You settle every great problem so boldly, but tell me, my dear boy, isn't it because you're young—because you haven't yet understood one of your problems through suffering? You look forward boldly, and isn't it that you don't see and don't expect anything dreadful because life is still hidden from your young eyes? You're bolder, more honest, deeper than we are, but think, be just a little magnanimous, have pity on me. I was born here, you know, my father and mother lived here, my grandfather lived here, I love this house. I can't conceive of life without the cherry orchard, and if it really must be sold, then sell me with the orchard. [*Embraces* TROFIMOV, *kisses him on the forehead.*] My boy was drowned here. [*Weeps.*] Pity me, my dear kind fellow.

TROFIMOV: You know I feel for you with all my heart.

LYUBOV: But that should have been said differently, so differently. [*Takes out her handkerchief, telegram falls on the floor.*] My heart is so heavy to-day. It's so noisy here, my soul is quivering at every sound, I'm shuddering all over, but I can't go away; I'm afraid to be quiet and alone. Don't be hard on me, Petya . . . I love you as though you were one of ourselves. I would gladly let you marry Anya—I swear I would—only, my dear boy, you must take your degree, you do nothing—you're simply tossed by fate from place to place. That's so strange. It is, isn't it? And you must do something with your beard to make it grow somehow. [*Laughs.*] You look so funny!

TROFIMOV: [*Picks up the telegram.*] I've no wish to be a beauty.

LYUBOV: That's a telegram from Paris. I get one every day. One yesterday and one to-day. That savage creature is ill again, he's in trouble again. He begs forgiveness, beseeches me to go, and really I ought to go to Paris to see him. You look shocked, Petya. What am I to do, my dear boy, what am I to do? He is ill, he is alone and unhappy, and who'll look after him, who'll keep him from doing the wrong thing, who'll give him his medicine at the right time? And why hide it or be silent? I love him, that's clear. I love him! I love him! He's a millstone about my neck, I'm going to the bottom with him, but I love that stone and can't live without it. [*Presses* TROFIMOV's *hand.*] Don't think ill of me, Petya, don't tell me anything, don't tell me. . . .

TROFIMOV: [*Through his tears*] For God's sake forgive my frankness: why, he robbed you!

LYUBOV: No! No! No! You mustn't speak like that. [*Covers her ears.*]

TROFIMOV: He is a wretch! You're the only person that doesn't know it! He's a worthless creature! A despicable wretch!

LYUBOV: [*Getting angry, but speaking with restraint.*] You're twenty-six or twenty-seven years old, but you're still a schoolboy.

TROFIMOV: Possibly.

LYUBOV: You should be a man at your age! You should understand what love means! And you ought to be in love yourself. You ought to fall in love! [*Angrily.*] Yes, yes, and it's not purity in you, you're simply a prude, a comic fool, a freak.

TROFIMOV: [*In horror.*] The things she's saying!

LYUBOV: I am above love! You're not above love, but simply as our Firs here says, "You are a good-for-nothing." At your age not to have a mistress!

TROFIMOV: [*In horror.*] This is awful! The things she is saying! [*Goes rapidly into the larger drawing-room clutching his head.*] This is awful! I can't stand it! I'm going. [*Goes off, but at once returns.*] All is over between us! [*Goes off into the ante-room.*]

LYUBOV: [*Shouts after him.*] Petya! Wait a minute! You funny creature! I was joking! Petya! [*There is a sound of somebody running quickly downstairs and suddenly falling with a crash.* ANYA *and* VARYA *scream, but there is a sound of laughter at once.*]

LYUBOV: What has happened?

[ANYA *runs in.*]

ANYA: [*Laughing.*] Petya's fallen downstairs! [*Runs out.*]

LYUBOV: What a queer fellow that Petya is!

[*The* STATION MASTER *stands in the middle of the larger room and reads* The Magdalene, *by Alexey Tolstoy. They listen to him, but before he has recited many lines strains of a waltz are heard from the ante-room and the reading is broken off. All dance.* TROFIMOV, ANYA, VARYA *and* LYUBOV ANDREYEVNA *come in from the ante-room.*]

LYUBOV: Come, Petya—come, pure heart! I beg your pardon. Let's have a dance! [*Dances with* PETYA.]

[ANYA *and* VARYA *dance.* FIRS *comes in, puts his stick down near the side door.* YASHA *also comes into the drawing-room and looks on at the dancing.*]

YASHA: What is it, old man?

FIRS: I don't feel well. In old days we used to have generals, barons and admirals dancing at our balls, and now we send for the post-office clerk and the station master and even they're not overanxious to come. I am getting feeble. The old master, the grandfather, used to give sealing-wax for all complaints. I have been taking sealing-wax for twenty years or more. Perhaps that's what's kept me alive.

YASHA: You bore me, old man! [*Yawns.*] It's time you were done with.

FIRS: *Ach,* you're a good-for-nothing! [*Mutters.*]

[TROFIMOV *and* LYUBOV ANDREYEVNA *dance in larger room and then on to the stage.*]

LYUBOV: *Merci.* I'll sit down a little. [*Sits down.*] I'm tired.

[*Enter* ANYA.]

ANYA: [*Excitedly.*] There's a man in the kitchen has been saying that the cherry orchard's been sold to-day.

LYUBOV: Sold to whom?

ANYA: He didn't say to whom. He's gone away.

[*She dances with* TROFIMOV, *and they go off into the larger room.*]

YASHA: There was an old man gossiping there, a stranger.

FIRS: Leonid Andreyevitch isn't here yet, he hasn't come back. He has his light overcoat on, *demi-saison,* he'll catch cold for sure. *Ach!* Foolish young things!

LYUBOV: I feel as though I should die. Go, Yasha, find out to whom it has been sold.

YASHA: But he went away long ago, the old chap. [*Laughs.*]

LYUBOV: [*With slight vexation.*] What are you laughing at? What are you pleased at?

YASHA: Epihodov is so funny. He's a silly fellow, two and twenty misfortunes.

LYUBOV: Firs, if the estate is sold, where will you go?

FIRS: Where you bid me, there I'll go.

LYUBOV: Why do you look like that? Are you ill? You ought to be in bed.

FIRS: Yes. [*Ironically.*] Me go to bed and who's to wait here? Who's to see to things without me? I'm the only one in all the house.

YASHA: [*To* LYUBOV ANDREYEVNA.] Lyubov Andreyevna, permit me to make a request of you; if you go back to Paris again, be so kind as to take me with you. It's positively impossible for me to stay here. [*Looking about him; in an undertone.*] There's no need to say it, you see for yourself—an uncivilized country, the people have no morals, and then the dullness! The food in the kitchen's abominable, and then Firs runs after one muttering all sorts of unsuitable words. Take me with you, please do!

[*Enter* PISHTCHIK.]

PISHTCHIK: Allow me to ask you for a waltz, my dear lady. [LYUBOV ANDREYEVNA *goes with him.*] Enchanting lady, I really must borrow of you just 180 roubles, [*Dances.*] only 180 roubles. [*They pass into the larger room.*]

[*In the larger drawing-room, a figure in a gray top hat and in check trousers is gesticulating and jumping about. Shouts of "Bravo, Charlotta Ivanovna."*]

DUNYASHA: [*She has stopped to powder herself.*] My young lady tells me to dance. There are plenty of gentlemen, and too few ladies, but dancing makes me giddy and makes my heart beat. Firs, the post-office clerk said something to me just now that quite took my breath away.

[*Music becomes more subdued.*]

FIRS: What did he say to you?

DUNYASHA: He said I was like a flower.

YASHA: [*Yawns.*] What ignorance! [*Goes out.*]

DUNYASHA: Like a flower. I am a girl of such delicate feelings, I am awfully fond of soft speeches.

FIRS: Your head's being turned.

[*Enter* EPIHODOV.]

EPIHODOV: You have no desire to see me, Dunyasha. I might be an insect. [*Sighs.*] Ah! life!

DUNYASHA: What is it you want?

EPIHODOV: Undoubtedly you may be right. [*Sighs.*] But, of course, if one looks at it from that point of view, if I may so express myself, you have, excuse my plain speaking, reduced me to a complete state of mind. I know my destiny. Every day some misfortune befalls me and I have long ago grown accustomed to it, so that I look upon my fate with a smile. You gave me your word, and though I——

DUNYASHA: Let us have a talk later, I entreat you, but now leave me in peace, for I am lost in reverie. [*Plays with her fan.*]

EPIHODOV: I have a misfortune every day, and if I may venture to express myself, I merely smile at it, I even laugh.

[VARYA *enters from the larger drawing-room.*]

VARYA: You still have not gone, Epihodov. What a disrespectful creature you are, really! [*To* DUNYASHA.] Go along, Dunyasha! [*To* EPIHODOV.] First you play billiards and break the cue, then you go wandering about the drawing-room like a visitor!

EPIHODOV: You really cannot, if I may so express myself, call me to account like this.

VARYA: I'm not calling you to account, I'm speaking to you. You do nothing but wander from place to place and don't do your work. We keep you as a counting-house clerk, but what use you are I can't say.

EPIHODOV: [*Offended.*] Whether I work or whether I walk, whether I eat or whether I play billiards, is a matter to be judged by persons of understanding and my elders.

VARYA: You dare to tell me that! [*Firing up.*] You dare! You mean to say I've no understanding. Begone from here! This minute!

EPIHODOV: [*Intimidated.*] I beg you to express yourself with delicacy.

VARYA: [*Beside herself with anger.*] This moment! get out! away! [*He goes towards the door, she following him.*] Two and twenty misfortunes! Take yourself off! Don't let me set eyes on you! [EPIHODOV *has gone out, behind the door his voice,* "I shall lodge a complaint against you."] What! You're coming back? [*Snatches up the stick* FIRS *has put down near the door.*] Come! Come! Come! I'll show you! What! you're coming? Then take that! [*She swings the stick, at the very moment that* LOPAHIN *comes in.*]

LOPAHIN: Very much obliged to you!

VARYA: [*Angrily and ironically.*] I beg your pardon!

LOPAHIN: Not at all! I humbly thank you for your kind reception!

VARYA: No need of thanks for it. [*Moves away, then looks round and asks softly.*] I haven't hurt you?

LOPAHIN: Oh, no! Not at all! There's an immense bump coming up, though!

VOICES FROM LARGER ROOM: Lopahin has come! Yermolay Alexeyevitch!

PISHTCHIK: What do I see and hear? [*Kisses* LOPAHIN.] There's a whiff of cognac about you, my dear soul, and we're making merry here too!

[*Enter* LYUBOV ANDREYEVNA.]

LYUBOV: Is it you, Yermolay Alexeyevitch? Why have you been so long? Where's Leonid?

LOPAHIN: Leonid Andreyevitch arrived with me. He is coming.

LYUBOV: [*In agitation.*] Well! Well! Was there a sale? Speak!

LOPAHIN: [*Embarrassed, afraid of betraying his joy.*] The sale was over at four o'clock. We missed our train—had to wait till half-past nine. [*Sighing heavily.*] Ugh! I feel a little giddy.

[*Enter* GAEV. *In his right hand he has purchases, with his left hand he is wiping away his tears.*]

LYUBOV: Well, Leonid? What news? [*Impatiently, with tears.*] Make haste, for God's sake!

GAEV: [*Makes her no answer, simply waves his hand. To* FIRS, *weeping.*] Here, take them; there's anchovies, Kertch herrings. I have eaten nothing all day. What

I have been through! [*Door into the billiard room is open. There is heard a knocking of balls and the voice of* YASHA *saying* "Eighty-seven." GAEV's *expression changes, he leaves off weeping.*] I am fearfully tired. Firs, come and help me change my things. [*Goes to his own room across the larger drawing-room.*]

PISHTCHIK: How about the sale? Tell us, do!

LYUBOV: Is the cherry orchard sold?

LOPAHIN: It is sold.

LYUBOV: Who has bought it?

LOPAHIN: I have bought it. [*A pause.* LYUBOV *is crushed; she would fall down if she were not standing near a chair and table.*]

> [VARYA *takes keys from her waistband, flings them on the floor in middle of drawing-room and goes out.*]

LOPAHIN: I have bought it! Wait a bit, ladies and gentlemen, pray. My head's a bit muddled, I can't speak. [*Laughs.*] We came to the auction. Deriganov was there already. Leonid Andreyevitch only had 15,000 and Deriganov bid 30,000, besides the arrears, straight off. I saw how the land lay. I bid against him. I bid 40,000, he bid 45,000, I said 55, and so he went on, adding 5 thousands and I adding 10. Well . . . So it ended. I bid 90, and it was knocked down to me. Now the cherry orchard's mine! Mine! [*Chuckles.*] My God, the cherry orchard's mine! Tell me that I'm drunk, that I'm out of my mind, that it's all a dream. [*Stamps with his feet.*] Don't laugh at me! If my father and my grandfather could rise from their graves and see all that has happened! How their Yermolay, ignorant, beaten Yermolay, who used to run about barefoot in winter, how that very Yermolay has bought the finest estate in the world! I have bought the estate where my father and grandfather were slaves, where they weren't even admitted into the kitchen. I am asleep, I am dreaming! It is all fancy, it is the work of your imagination plunged in the darkness of ignorance. [*Picks up keys, smiling fondly.*] She threw away the keys; she means to show she's not the housewife now. [*Jingles the keys.*] Well, no matter. [*The orchestra is heard tuning up.*] Hey, musicians! Play! I want to hear you. Come, all of you, and look how Yermolay Lopahin will take the ax to the cherry orchard, how the trees will fall to the ground! We will build houses on it and our grandsons and great-grandsons will see a new life springing up there. Music! Play up!

> [*Music begins to play.* LYUBOV ANDREYEVNA *has sunk into a chair and is weeping bitterly.*]

LOPAHIN: [*Reproachfully.*] Why, why didn't you listen to me? My poor friend! Dear lady, there's no turning back now. [*With tears.*] Oh, if all this could be over, oh, if our miserable disjointed life could somehow soon be changed!

PISHTCHIK: [*Takes him by the arm, in an undertone.*] She's weeping, let us go and leave her alone. Come. [*Takes him by the arm and leads him into the larger drawing-room.*]

LOPAHIN: What's that? Musicians, play up! All must be as I wish it. [*With irony.*] Here comes the new master, the owner of the cherry orchard! [*Accidentally tips over a little table, almost upsetting the candelabra.*] I can pay for everything! [*Goes out with* PISHTCHIK. *No one remains on the stage or in the larger drawing-room except* LYUBOV, *who sits huddled up, weeping bitterly. The music plays softly.* ANYA *and* TROFIMOV *come in quickly.* ANYA *goes up to her mother and falls on her knees before her.* TROFIMOV *stands at the entrance to the larger drawing-room.*]

ANYA: Mamma! Mamma, you're crying, dear, kind, good mamma! My precious! I love you! I bless you! The cherry orchard is sold, it is gone, that's true, that's true! But don't weep, mamma! Life is still before you, you have still your good, pure heart! Let us go, let us go, darling, away from here! We will make a new garden, more splendid than this one; you will see it, you will understand. And joy, quiet, deep joy, will sink into your soul like the sun at evening! And you will smile, mamma! Come, darling, let us go!

    CURTAIN

ACT IV

    SCENE: *Same as in First Act. There are neither curtains on the windows nor pictures on the walls: only a little furniture remains piled up in a corner as if for sale. There is a sense of desolation; near the outer door and in the background of the scene are packed trunks, traveling bags, etc. On the left the door is open, and from here the voices of* VARYA *and* ANYA *are audible.* LOPAHIN *is standing waiting.* YASHA *is holding a tray with glasses full of champagne. In front of the stage* EPIHODOV *is tying up a box. In the background behind the scene a hum of talk from the peasants who have come to say good-bye. The voice of* GAEV: "Thanks, brothers, thanks!"*

YASHA: The peasants have come to say good-bye. In my opinion, Yermolay Alexeyevitch, the peasants are good-natured, but they don't know much about things.

    [*The hum of talk dies away. Enter across front of stage* LYUBOV ANDREYEVNA *and* GAEV. *She is not weeping, but is pale; her face is quivering—she cannot speak.*]

GAEV: You gave them your purse, Lyuba. That won't do—that won't do!
LYUBOV: I couldn't help it! I couldn't help it!

    [*Both go out.*]

LOPAHIN: [*In the doorway, calls after them.*] You will take a glass at parting? Please do. I didn't think to bring any from the town, and at the station I could only get one bottle. Please take a glass. [*A pause.*] What? You don't care for any? [*Comes away from the door.*] If I'd known, I wouldn't have bought it. Well, and I'm not going to drink it. [YASHA *carefully sets the tray down on a chair.*] You have a glass, Yasha, anyway.
YASHA: Good luck to the travelers, and luck to those that stay behind! [*Drinks.*] This champagne isn't the real thing, I can assure you.
LOPAHIN: It cost eight roubles the bottle. [*A pause.*] It's devilish cold here.

YASHA: They haven't heated the stove today—it's all the same since we're going. [*Laughs.*]

LOPAHIN: What are you laughing for?

YASHA: For pleasure.

LOPAHIN: Though it's October, it's as still and sunny as though it were summer. It's just right for building! [*Looks at his watch; says in doorway.*] Take note, ladies and gentlemen, the train goes in forty-seven minutes; so you ought to start for the station in twenty minutes. You must hurry up!

[TROFIMOV *comes in from out of doors wearing a great-coat.*]

TROFIMOV: I think it must be time to start, the horses are ready. The devil only knows what's become of my goloshes; they're lost. [*In the doorway.*] Anya! My goloshes aren't here. I can't find them.

LOPAHIN: And I'm getting off to Harkov. I am going in the same train with you. I'm spending all the winter at Harkov. I've been wasting all my time gossiping with you and fretting with no work to do. I can't get on without work. I don't know what to do with my hands, they flap about so queerly, as if they didn't belong to me.

TROFIMOV: Well, we're just going away, and you will take up your profitable labors again.

LOPAHIN: Do take a glass.

TROFIMOV: No, thanks.

LOPAHIN: Then you're going to Moscow now?

TROFIMOV: Yes. I shall see them as far as the town, and to-morrow I shall go on to Moscow.

LOPAHIN: Yes, I daresay, the professors aren't giving any lectures, they're waiting for your arrival.

TROFIMOV: That's not your business.

LOPAHIN: How many years have you been at the University?

TROFIMOV: Do think of something newer than that—that's stale and flat. [*Hunts for goloshes.*] You know we shall most likely never see each other again, so let me give you one piece of advice at parting: don't wave your arms about—get out of the habit. And another thing, building villas, reckoning up that the summer visitors will in time become independent farmers—reckoning like that, that's not the thing to do either. After all, I am fond of you: you have fine delicate fingers like an artist, you've a fine delicate soul.

LOPAHIN: [*Embraces him.*] Good-bye, my dear fellow. Thanks for everything. Let me give you money for the journey, if you need it.

TROFIMOV: What for? I don't need it.

LOPAHIN: Why, you haven't got a half-penny.

TROFIMOV: Yes, I have, thank you. I got some money for a translation. Here it is in my pocket, [*Anxiously.*] but where can my goloshes be!

VARYA: [*From the next room.*] Take the nasty things! [*Flings a pair of goloshes on to the stage.*]

TROFIMOV: Why are you so cross, Varya? h'm! . . . but those aren't my goloshes.

LOPAHIN: I sowed three thousand acres with poppies in the spring, and now I have cleared forty thousand profit. And when my poppies were in flower, wasn't it a picture! So here, as a I say, I made forty thousand, and I'm offering you a loan because I can afford to. Why turn up your nose? I am a peasant—I speak bluntly.

TROFIMOV: Your father was a peasant, mine was a chemist—and that proves absolutely nothing whatever. [LOPAHIN *takes out his pocket-book.*] Stop that—stop that. If you were to offer me two hundred thousand I wouldn't take it. I am an independent man, and everything that all of you, rich and poor alike, prize so highly and hold so dear, hasn't the slightest power over me—it's like so much fluff fluttering in the air. I can get on without you. I can pass by you. I am strong and proud. Humanity is advancing towards the highest truth, the highest happiness, which is possible on earth, and I am in the front ranks.

LOPAHIN: Will you get there?

TROFIMOV: I shall get there. [*A pause.*] I shall get there, or I shall show others the way to get there.

[*In the distance is heard the stroke of an ax on a tree.*]

LOPAHIN: Good-bye, my dear fellow; it's time to be off. We turn up our noses at one another, but life is passing all the while. When I am working hard without resting, then my mind is more at ease, and it seems to me as though I too know what I exist for; but how many people there are in Russia, my dear boy, who exist, one doesn't know what for. Well, it doesn't matter. That's not what keeps things spinning. They tell me Leonid Andreyevitch has taken a situation. He is going to be a clerk at the bank—6,000 roubles a year. Only, of course, he won't stick to it—he's too lazy.

ANYA: [*In the doorway.*] Mamma begs you not to let them chop down the orchard until she's gone.

TROFIMOV: Yes, really, you might have the tact. [*Walks out across the front of the stage.*]

LOPAHIN: I'll see to it! I'll see to it! Stupid fellows! [*Goes out after him.*]

ANYA: Has Firs been taken to the hospital?

YASHA: I told them this morning. No doubt they have taken him.

ANYA: [*To* EPIHODOV, *who passes across the drawing-room.*] Semyon Pantaleyevitch, inquire, please, if Firs has been taken to the hospital.

YASHA: [*In a tone of offence.*] I told Yegor this morning—why ask a dozen times?

EPIHODOV: Firs is advanced in years. It's my conclusive opinion no treatment would do him good; it's time he was gathered to his fathers. And I can only envy him. [*Puts a trunk down on a cardboard hat-box and crushes it.*] There, now, of course—I knew it would be so.

YASHA: [*Jeeringly.*] Two and twenty misfortunes!

VARYA: [*Through the door.*] Has Firs been taken to the hospital?

ANYA: Yes.

VARYA: Why wasn't the note for the doctor taken too?

ANYA: Oh, then, we must send it after them. [*Goes out.*]

VARYA: [*From the adjoining room.*] Where's Yasha? Tell him his mother's come to say good-bye to him.

YASHA: [*Waves his hand.*] They put me out of all patience! [DUNYASHA *has all this time been busy about the luggage. Now, when* YASHA *is left alone, she goes up to him.*]

DUNYASHA: You might just give me one look, Yasha. You're going away. You're leaving me. [*Weeps and throws herself on his neck.*]

YASHA: What are you crying for? [*Drinks the champagne.*] In six days I shall be in Paris again. To-morrow we shall get into the express train and roll away in a flash. I can scarcely believe it! *Vive la France!* It doesn't suit me here—it's not the life for me; there's no doing anything. I have seen enough of the ignorance here. I have had enough of it. [*Drinks champagne.*] What are you crying for? Behave yourself properly, and then you won't cry.

DUNYASHA: [*Powders her face, looking in a pocket-mirror.*] Do send me a letter from Paris. You know how I loved you, Yasha—how I loved you! I am a tender creature, Yasha.

YASHA: Here they are coming!

[*Busies himself about the trunks, humming softly. Enter* LYUBOV ANDREYEVNA, GAEV, ANYA *and* CHARLOTTA IVANOVNA.]

GAEV: We ought to be off. There's not much time now. [*Looking at* YASHA.] What a smell of herrings!

LYUBOV: In ten minutes we must get into the carriage. [*Casts a look about the room.*] Farewell, dear house, dear old home of our fathers! Winter will pass and spring will come, and then you will be no more; they will tear you down! How much those walls have seen! [*Kisses her daughter passionately.*] My treasure, how bright you look! Your eyes are sparkling like diamonds! Are you glad? Very glad?

ANYA: Very glad! A new life is beginning, mamma.

GAEV: Yes, really, everything is all right now. Before the cherry orchard was sold, we were all worried and wretched, but afterwards, when once the question was settled conclusively, irrevocably, we all felt calm and even cheerful. I am a bank clerk now—I am a financier—cannon off the red. And you, Lyuba, after all, you are looking better; there's no question of that.

LYUBOV: Yes. My nerves are better, that's true. [*Her hat and coat are handed to her.*] I'm sleeping well. Carry out my things, Yasha. It's time. [*To* ANYA.] My darling, we shall soon see each other again. I am going to Paris. I can live there on the money your Yaroslavl auntie sent us to buy the estate with—hurrah for auntie—but that money won't last long.

ANYA: You'll come back soon, mamma, won't you? I'll be working up for my examination in the high school, and when I have passed that, I shall set to work and be a help to you. We will read all sorts of things together, mamma, won't we? [*Kisses her mother's hands.*] We will read in the autumn evenings. We'll read lots of books, and a new wonderful world will open out before us. [*Dreamily.*] Mamma, come soon.

LYUBOV: I shall come, my precious treasure. [*Embraces her.*]

[*Enter* LOPAHIN. CHARLOTTA *softly hums a song.*]

GAEV: Charlotta's happy; she's singing!

CHARLOTTA: [*Picks up a bundle like a swaddled baby.*] Bye, bye, my baby. [*A baby is heard crying: "Ooah! ooah!"*] Hush, hush, my pretty boy! [*Ooah! ooah!*] Poor little thing! [*Throws the bundle back.*] You must please find me a situation. I can't go on like this.

LOPAHIN: We'll find you one, Charlotta Ivanovna. Don't you worry yourself.

GAEV: Everyone's leaving us. Varya's going away. We have become of no use all at once.

CHARLOTTA: There's nowhere for me to be in the town. I must go away. [*Hums.*] What care I . . .

[*Enter* PISHTCHIK.]

LOPAHIN: The freak of nature!

PISHTCHIK: [*Gasping.*] Oh! . . . let me get my breath. . . . I'm worn out . . . my most honored . . . Give me some water.

GAEV: Want some money, I suppose? Your humble servant! I'll go out of the way of temptation. [*Goes out.*]

PISHTCHIK: It's a long while since I have been to see you . . . dearest lady. [*To* LOPAHIN.] You are here . . . glad to see you . . . a man of immense intellect . . . take . . . here. [*Gives* LOPAHIN.] 400 roubles. That leaves me owing 840.

LOPAHIN: [*Shrugging his shoulders in amazement.*] It's like a dream. Where did you get it?

PISHTCHIK: Wait a bit . . . I'm hot . . . a most extraordinary occurrence! Some Englishmen came along and found in my land some sort of white clay. [*To* LYUBOV ANDREYEVNA.] And 400 for you . . . most lovely . . . wonderful. [*Gives money.*] The rest later. [*Sips water.*] A young man in the train was telling me just now that a great philosopher advises jumping off a house-top. "Jump!" says he; "the whole gist of the problem lies in that." [*Wonderingly.*] Fancy that, now! Water, please!

LOPAHIN: What Englishmen?

PISHTCHIK: I have made over to them the rights to dig the clay for twenty-four years . . . and now, excuse me . . . I can't stay . . . I must be trotting on. I'm going to Znoikovo . . . to Kardamanovo. . . . I'm in debt all round. [*Sips.*] . . . To your very good health! . . . I'll come in on Thursday.

LYUBOV: We are just off to the town, and to-morrow I start for abroad.

PISHTCHIK: What! [*In agitation.*] Why to the town? Oh, I see the furniture . . . the boxes. No matter . . . [*Through his tears.*] . . . no matter . . . men of enormous intellect . . . these Englishmen. . . . Never mind . . . be happy. God will succor you . . . no matter . . . everything in this world must have an end. [*Kisses* LYUBOV ANDREYEVNA's *hand.*] If the rumor reaches you that my end has come, think of this . . . old horse, and say: "There once was such a man in the world . . . Semyonov-Pishtchik . . . the Kingdom of Heaven be his!" . . . most extraordinary weather . . . yes. [*Goes out in violent agitation, but at once returns and says in the doorway.*] Dashenka wishes to be remembered to you. [*Goes out.*]

LYUBOV: Now we can start. I leave with two cares in my heart. The first is leaving Firs ill. [*Looking at her watch.*] We have still five minutes.

ANYA: Mamma, Firs has been taken to the hospital. Yasha sent him off this morning.

LYUBOV: My other anxiety is Varya. She is used to getting up early and working; and now, without work, she's like a fish out of water. She is thin and pale, and she's crying, poor dear! [*A pause.*] You are well aware, Yermolay Alexey-evitch, I dreamed of marrying her to you, and everything seemed to show that you would get married. [*Whispers to* ANYA *and motions to* CHARLOTTA *and both go out.*] She loves you—she suits you. And I don't know—I don't know why it is you seem, as it were, to avoid each other. I can't understand it!

LOPAHIN: I don't understand it myself, I confess. It's queer somehow, altogether. If there's still time, I'm ready now at once. Let's settle it straight off, and go ahead; but without you, I feel I shan't make her an offer.

LYUBOV: That's excellent. Why, a single moment's all that's necessary. I'll call her at once.

LOPAHIN: And there's champagne all ready too. [*Looking into the glasses.*] Empty! Someone's emptied them already. [YASHA *coughs.*] I call that greedy.

LYUBOV: [*Eagerly.*] Capital! We will go out. Yasha, *allez!*[9] I'll call her in. [*At the door.*] Varya, leave all that; come here. Come along! [*Goes out with* YASHA.]

LOPAHIN: [*Looking at his watch.*] Yes.

[*A pause. Behind the door, smothered laughter and whispering, and, at last, enter* VARYA.]

VARYA: [*Looking a long while over the things.*] It is strange, I can't find it anywhere.

LOPAHIN: What are you looking for?

VARYA: I packed it myself, and I can't remember. [*A pause.*]

LOPAHIN: Where are you going now, Varvara Mihailova?

VARYA: I? To the Ragulins. I have arranged to go to them to look after the house—as a housekeeper.

LOPAHIN: That's in Yashnovo? It'll be seventy miles away. [*A pause.*] So this is the end of life in this house!

VARYA: [*Looking among the things.*] Where is it? Perhaps I put it in the trunk. Yes, life in this house is over—there will be no more of it.

LOPAHIN: And I'm just off to Harkov—by this next train. I've a lot of business there. I'm leaving Epihodov here, and I've taken him on.

VARYA: Really!

LOPAHIN: This time last year we had snow already, if you remember; but now it's so fine and sunny. Though it's cold, to be sure—three degrees of frost.

VARYA: I haven't looked. [*A pause.*] And besides, our thermometer's broken. [*A pause.*]

[*Voice at the door from the yard:* "Yermolay Alexeyevitch!"]

9. Go! (French, the language of the upper classes in pre-Soviet Russia).

LOPAHIN: [*As though he had long been expecting this summons.*] This minute!

> [LOPAHIN *goes out quickly.* VARYA *sitting on the floor and laying her head on a bag full of clothes, sobs quietly. The door opens.* LYUBOV ANDREYEVNA *comes in cautiously.*]

LYUBOV: Well? [*A pause.*] We must be going.

VARYA: [*Has wiped her eyes and is no longer crying.*] Yes, mamma, it's time to start. I shall have time to get to the Ragulins to-day, if only you're not late for the train.

LYUBOV: [*In the doorway.*] Anya, put your things on.

> [*Enter* ANYA, *then* GAEV *and* CHARLOTTA IVANOVNA. GAEV *has on a warm coat with a hood. Servants and cabmen come in.* EPIHODOV *bustles about the luggage.*]

LYUBOV: Now we can start on our travels.

ANYA: [*Joyfully.*] On our travels!

GAEV: My friends—my dear, my precious friends! Leaving this house for ever, can I be silent? Can I refrain from giving utterance at leave-taking to those emotions which now flood all my being?

ANYA: [*Supplicatingly.*] Uncle!

VARYA: Uncle, you mustn't!

GAEV: [*Dejectedly.*] Cannon and into the pocket . . . I'll be quiet. . . .

> [*Enter* TROFIMOV *and afterwards* LOPAHIN.]

TROFIMOV: Well, ladies and gentlemen, we must start.

LOPAHIN: Epihodov, my coat!

LYUBOV: I'll stay just one minute. It seems as though I have never seen before what the walls, what the ceilings in this house were like, and now I look at them with greediness, with such tender love.

GAEV: I remember when I was six years old sitting in that window on Trinity Day watching my father going to church.

LYUBOV: Have all the things been taken?

LOPAHIN: I think all. [*Putting on overcoat, to* EPIHODOV.] You, Epihodov, mind you see everything is right.

EPIHODOV: [*In a husky voice.*] Don't you trouble, Yermolay Alexeyevitch.

LOPAHIN: Why, what's wrong with your voice?

EPIHODOV: I've just had a drink of water, and I choked over something.

YASHA: [*Contemptuously.*] The ignorance!

LYUBOV: We are going—and not a soul will be left here.

LOPAHIN: Not till the spring.

VARYA: [*Pulls a parasol out of a bundle, as though about to hit someone with it.* LOPAHIN *makes a gesture as though alarmed.*] What is it? I didn't mean anything.

TROFIMOV: Ladies and gentlemen, let us get into the carriage. It's time. The train will be in directly.

VARYA: Petya, here they are, your goloshes, by that box. [*With tears.*] And what dirty old things they are!

TROFIMOV: [*Putting on his goloshes.*] Let us go, friends!

GAEV: [*Greatly agitated, afraid of weeping.*] The train—the station! Double baulk, ah!

LYUBOV: Let us go!

LOPAHIN: Are we all here? [*Locks the side-door on left.*] The things are all here. We must lock up. Let us go!

ANYA: Good-bye, home! Good-bye to the old life!

TROFIMOV: Welcome to the new life!

[TROFIMOV *goes out with* ANYA. VARYA *looks round the room and goes out slowly.* YASHA *and* CHARLOTTA IVANOVNA, *with her dog, go out.*]

LOPAHIN: Till the spring, then! Come, friends, till we meet! [*Goes out.*]

[LYUBOV ANDREYEVNA *and* GAEV *remain alone. As though they had been waiting for this, they throw themselves on each other's necks, and break into subdued smothered sobbing, afraid of being overheard.*]

GAEV: [*In despair.*] Sister, my sister!

LYUBOV: Oh, my orchard!—my sweet, beautiful orchard! My life, my youth, my happiness, good-bye! good-bye!

VOICE OF ANYA: [*Calling gaily.*] Mamma!

VOICE OF TROFIMOV: [*Gaily, excitedly.*] Aa—oo!

LYUBOV: One last look at the walls, at the windows. My dear mother loved to walk about this room.

GAEV: Sister, sister!

VOICE OF ANYA: Mamma!

VOICE OF TROFIMOV: Aa—oo!

LYUBOV: We are coming. [*They go out.*]

[*The stage is empty. There is the sound of the doors being locked up, then of the carriages driving away. There is silence. In the stillness there is the dull stroke of an ax in a tree, clanging with a mournful lonely sound. Footsteps are heard.* FIRS *appears in the doorway on the right. He is dressed as always—in a pea-jacket and white waistcoat, with slippers on his feet. He is ill.*]

FIRS: [*Goes up to the doors, and tries the handles.*] Locked! They have gone . . . [*Sits down on sofa.*] They have forgotten me. . . . Never mind . . . I'll sit here a bit. . . . I'll be bound Leonid Andreyevitch hasn't put his fur coat on and has gone off in his thin overcoat. [*Sighs anxiously.*] I didn't see after him. . . . These young people . . . [*Mutters something that can't be distinguished.*] Life has slipped by as though I hadn't lived. [*Lies down.*] I'll lie down a bit. . . . There's no strength in you, nothing left you—all gone! Ech! I'm good for nothing. [*Lies motionless.*]

[*A sound is heard that seems to come from the sky, like a breaking harp-string, dying away mournfully. All is still again, and there is heard nothing but the strokes of the ax far away in the orchard.*]

CURTAIN

1903–04

Appendices

Appendices

Writing about Literature

Writing about literature ought to be easier than writing about anything else. When you write about painting, for example, you have to translate shapes and colors and textures into words. When you write about music, you have to translate various aspects and combinations of sounds into words. When you write about that complex, mysterious, fleeting thing called "reality" or "life," you have an even more difficult task. Worst of all, perhaps, is trying to put into words all that is going on at any given moment inside your particular and unique self. So you ought to be relieved to know that you are going to write about literature—that is, use words to write about words.

But writing about literature will not be easy if you haven't learned to *read* literature, for in order to write about anything you have to know that something rather well. Helping you learn to read literature is what the earlier chapters of this book are about; this chapter is about the writing. (But, as you will see, you cannot fully separate the writing from the reading.)

Another thing keeps writing about literature from being easy: writing itself is not easy. Writing well requires a variety of language skills—a good working vocabulary, for example—and a sense of how to order your ideas, of how to link one idea or statement to another, of what to put in and what to leave out. Worse, writing is not a finite or definite skill or art; you never really "know how to write," you just learn how to write a little better about a little more. The very words you are reading have been written and revised several times, even though the authors have had many years of practice.

Writing about
Literature

REPRESENTING THE LITERARY TEXT

COPYING

If writing about literature is using words about words, what words should you use? Since most writers work very hard to get each word exactly right and in exactly the right order, there are no better words to use in discussing what the literature is about than those of the literary work itself. Faced with writing about a story, then, you could just write the story over again, word for word:

> Once upon a time there was a Siamese cat who pretended to be a lion and spoke inappropriate Zebraic . . .

and so on until the end. Copying texts was useful in medieval monasteries, but in our electronic age, with all the technology available to us, it doesn't seem very useful. Besides, if you try to copy a text, you will probably find that spelling or punctuation errors, reversed word order, and missing or added or just different words seem mysteriously to appear. Still, it's a good exercise for teaching yourself accuracy and attention to detail, and you will probably discover things about the text you are copying that you would likely miss otherwise. Early in a literature course, particularly, copying can be a useful step in learning how to read and write about fiction, poetry, or drama; later, being able to copy a passage accurately will help when you want to quote a passage to illustrate or prove a point you are making. But copying is not, in itself, writing *about* literature.

Reading aloud, a variation of copying, may be a more original and interpretive exercise than copying itself, since by tone, emphasis, and pace you can clarify the text or indicate the way you understand it. But this, too, is not *writing* about literature, and you will not long be satisfied with merely repeating someone else's words. You will want to express your perceptions, responses, and ideas about what you are reading. And having something to say and wanting to say or write it is the first and most significant step in learning to write about literature.

PARAPHRASE

If you look away from the text for a while and then write the same material but in your own words, you are writing a paraphrase.

For example, let's paraphrase the first sentence of Jane Austen's *Pride and Prejudice:* "It is a truth universally acknowledged that a single man in possession of a good fortune, must be in want of a wife." We can start by making "It is a truth" a little less formal: *It's true that,* perhaps. Now "universally acknowledged": *everybody acknowledges* or, a little more loosely, *everybody agrees.* Now we may drop the whole first clause and begin, *Everybody agrees that* "a single man"—*a bachelor*—"in possession of a good fortune"—*rich*—"must be in want of a wife"—*wants a wife.* Or is it *needs a wife?* Okay, *Everybody agrees that a rich bachelor needs* (or *wants*) *a wife.* The process of paraphrase resembles that of translation, and we are translating Austen's nineteenth-century formal English prose into twentieth-century informal American prose.

But what good is that? First of all, it enables us to test whether we really understand what we are reading. Second, certain elements of the text become clearer: we may see now that Austen means her sentence to be ironic or humorous, and we now understand the two possible meanings of "in want of." Third, we can check our paraphrase against those of others—classmates' versions, for example—to compare our understanding of the passage with theirs. Finally, we have learned how much literature depends on words. A paraphrase, no matter how precise, can render only an approximate equivalent of a text's meaning—how *good* Austen's sentence is, how *flat* our paraphrase.

Paraphrasing, like copying, is not in itself an entirely satisfactory way of writing about literature, but, like copying, it can be a useful tool. To explain or clarify a literary text for someone, to illustrate a point about that text, or to remind your readers of or acquaint them with a text or passage, you will at times want to paraphrase. Unlike an exact copy, a paraphrase, being in your own words, adds something of yours to the text or passage—your emphasis, your perspective, your understanding.

SUMMARY

Paraphrase follows faithfully the outlines of the text. But if you stand back far enough from the text so as not to see its specific words or smaller details and put down briefly in your own words what you believe the work is about, you will have a summary. How briefly? You could, for example, summarize the 108 lines of Poe's "The Raven" in about 180 words or so:

> The speaker of Poe's "The Raven" is sitting in his room late at night reading in order to forget the death of his beloved Lenore. There's a tap at the door; after some hesitation he opens it and calls Lenore's name, but there is only an echo. When he goes back into his room he hears the rapping again, this time at his window, and when he opens it a raven enters. He asks the raven its name, and it answers very clearly, "Nevermore." When the speaker says that the bird, like his friends, will leave, the raven again says, "Nevermore." As the speaker's thoughts run back to Lenore, he realizes the aptness of the raven's word: she shall sit there nevermore. But, he says, sooner or later he will forget her and the grief will lessen. "Nevermore," the raven says again, too aptly. Now the speaker wants the bird to leave, but "Nevermore," the raven says once again. At the end, the speaker knows he'll never escape the raven or its dark message.

Or you could summarize the story of *Hamlet* in a single sentence: "A young man, seeking to avenge the murder of his father by his uncle, kills his uncle, but he himself and others die in the process." Has *too* much been left out? What do you feel it essential to add? Let's try again: "In Denmark, many centuries ago, a young prince avenged the murder of his father, the king, by his uncle, who had usurped the throne, but the prince himself was killed as were others, and a well-led foreign army had no trouble successfully invading the decayed and troubled state." A classmate may have written this summary: "From the ghost of his murdered father a young prince learns that his uncle, who has married the prince's mother, much to the young man's shame and disgust, is the father's murderer, and the prince plots revenge, feigning madness, acting erratically— even insulting the woman he loves—and, though gaining his revenge, causes the suicide of his beloved and the deaths of others and, finally, of himself."

The last two, though accurate enough, sound like two different plays, don't they? To summarize means to select and emphasize and so to interpret: that is, not to replicate the text in miniature, as a reduced photograph might replicate the original, but while reducing it to change the angle of vision and even the filter, to represent the essentials as the reader or summarizer sees them. When you write a summary, you should try to be as objective as possible; nevertheless, your summary will reflect not only the literary text but also your own understanding and attitudes. There's nothing wrong with your fingerprints or "mindprints" appearing on the summary, so long as you recognize that in summarizing you are doing more than copying, paraphrasing, or merely reflecting the literary text. You might learn something about both literature and yourself by comparing your summaries of, say, three or four short poems, a couple of short stories, or a play with summaries of the same works by several of your classmates. As you read their summaries, try to understand how each viewed the text differently from you. You might then write a composite summary that would include all that any one reader felt important. You might try the same exercise again on different texts. Has the practice made you more careful? More inclusive? Is there a greater degree of uniformity or inclusiveness in your summaries?

A good summary can be a form of literary criticism. Though you will seldom be called upon merely to summarize a work, a good deal of writing about literature requires that at some point or other you do summarize—a whole work, a particular incident or aspect, a stanza, chapter, or scene. But beware: a mere summary, no matter how accurate, will seldom fulfill an assignment for a critical essay.

REPLYING TO THE TEXT

IMITATION AND PARODY

While paraphrase is something like translation—a faithful following of the original text but in different words—and summary is the faithful, but inevitably interpretive, reduction of the text, another kind of writing about literature faithfully follows the manner or matter or both of a literary text, but it does so for different ends. It's called imitation.

For many generations, students were taught to write by "writing from models"—imitating good writing. Many serious works are, in one way or another, imitations: the *Aeneid*, for example, may be seen as an imitation of the *Odyssey*, and, in a very different way, so might James Joyce's *Ulysses*. You, too, may be able to learn a good deal about writing—and reading—by trying your hand at an imitation.

To write an imitation, first analyze the original—that is, break it down into its characteristics or qualities—and decide just what you want to preserve in your version. Sometimes you can poke fun at a work by imitating it but at the same time exaggerating its style or prominent characteristics, or placing it in an inappropriate context; that kind of imitation, a kind that is still popular, is called a parody. The list of qualities and the model might be much the same for a serious imitation and for a parody, only in a parody you can exaggerate a little—or a lot.

To parody Poe's "The Raven," we might stick closely to its rhythms, its use of repetitive mood words or of several words that mean almost the same thing, and its frequent use of alliteration (words that begin with the same sound). We might exaggerate the characteristic stylistic devices, as C. L. Edson does in his parody:

> Once upon a midnight dreary, eerie, scary,
> I was wary, I was weary, full of worry, thinking of my lost Lenore,
> Of my cheery, airy, faerie, fierie Dearie—(Nothing more).

We might choose another kind of parody, keeping the form as close as possible to the original but applying it to a ludicrously unsuitable subject, as Pope does in his mock epic "The Rape of the Lock," where he uses pretentious epic machinery in a poem about cutting off a lock of a woman's hair. In writing such a parody of "The Raven," we will keep the rhythm closer to Poe's and the subject matter less close. How about this?

> Once upon a midday murky, crunching on a Christmas turkey,
> And guzzling giant Jereboams of gin . . .

And maybe we could use the "Nevermore" refrain as if this were an antacid commercial.

To write a good imitation or parody, you must read and reread the original very carefully, examine it, and identify just those elements and qualities that make it a unique and recognizable text. Since you admire works you wish to imitate, such close study should be a pleasure. You may or may not admire a work you wish to parody, but parody itself is fun to do and fun to read. In either case, you should have fun while gaining a deeper, more intimate knowledge of the nature and details of a work of literature. Moreover, such close attention to how a professional piece of writing is put together and how its parts function together along with your effort to reproduce the effects in your own imitation or parody are sure to help you understand the process of writing and so help you improve your own ability to write about literature knowledgeably.

RE-CREATION AND REPLY

Sometimes a story, poem, or play will seem so partial, biased, or unrealistic that it will stimulate a response that is neither an imitation nor a parody, but a retort. While Christopher Marlowe's "shepherd" in "The Passionate Shepherd to His Love" paints an idyllic scene of love in the country for his beloved and pleads, "Come live with me and be my love," Sir Walter Ralegh apparently feels obliged to reply in the name of the beloved "nymph": it won't always be spring, she says in "The Nymph's Reply to the Shepherd"; we won't always be young, and, besides, I can scarcely trust myself to someone who offers me such a phony view of reality.

Ralegh's nymph confronts the invitation and the words of Marlowe's shepherd directly and almost detail for detail. In fiction the reply probably won't be so direct and verbal a retort and will likely involve a shift in perspective. It may tell the same story as the original but from a different angle, not only giving a different view of the same events and people, but also adding details that the original focus ignored or could not perceive. In *Jane Eyre* (1847), for example, Bertha Mason Rochester is the hero's bestial, mad wife, whom he has locked away upstairs and whose existence, when it comes to light, prevents for a time our heroine, our Jane, from marrying her heart's desire; Bertha is, in effect, the villainess. In *Wide Sargasso Sea* (1966), Jean Rhys not only gives Bertha's side of Charlotte Brontë's story, but tells us more details about Bertha's earlier life: poor Bertha was more sinned against than sinning, it turns out.

We may respond to a work whose view seems partial or distorted by shifting the perspective in time as well as in space. At the end of John Cheever's "The Country Husband," are Francis Weed's marital and other problems solved by his recognition that life in the suburbs can be, in its own way, as adventurous as more romantic kinds of existence? What will happen to him next spring? On his fortieth birthday? As he lies dying? What will the speaker of Theodore Roethke's "My Papa's Waltz" be thinking about as he plays or dances with *his* daughter?

You may have noticed that while retorts can often be witty, they are also serious. Usually they say not merely, "That's not how the story went," but "That's not what life is really like." Try to read literature initially with the aim of understanding it and taking it at its highest value (rather than reducing it and quibbling). Try to "hear" what it is saying; avoid imposing your own notions of reality prematurely upon a work. Open your mind to learning from the work, and let it broaden your views. Finally, read it critically as well, asking, "Is this the way things *really* are?" or, more generously, "If I were standing over there, where the story (author, character) is, would things really look that way?"

Perhaps the most familiar kind of literary re-creation or reply is the adaptation, especially that of fiction into film. (Among the stories in this anthology that have been made into feature-length films are Richard Connell's "The Most Dangerous Game," Ambrose Bierce's "An Occurrence at Owl Creek Bridge," and Anton's Chekhov's "The Lady with the Dog.") In adaptation, the contradictory demands of faithfulness to the original and appropriateness to the new medium can teach us a great deal about both the content and the medium of the original. Although in this course you most likely won't have the opportunity to make a film based on a story, you can still try your hand at adapting a work or piece of a work to a new medium. You might want to turn Poe's "The Cask of Amontillado" into verse (probably as a dramatic monologue) or write a short story called *Hamlet* or a one-act play called "Young Goodman Brown." You very likely will learn not only about the nature of the original work, but also about the nature of the medium in which you are working.

EXPLAINING THE TEXT

DESCRIPTION

To give an account of the form of a work or passage rather than merely a brief version of its content or plot (and a plot summary, even of a poem, is usually what we mean by "summary") you may wish to write a description. We have given a summary of Poe's "The Raven" earlier, concentrating there, as summaries tend to do, on subject and plot. A description, on the other hand, may concentrate on the form of the stanzas, the lines, the rhyme scheme, perhaps like this:

> Poe's "The Raven" is a poem of 108 lines divided into eighteen six-line stanzas. If in describing the rhyme scheme you were to look just at the ends of the lines, you would notice only one or two unusual features: not only is there only one rhyme sound per stanza—lines 2, 4, 5, and 6 rhyming—but one rhyme sound is the same in all eighteen stanzas, so that seventy-two lines end with the sound "ore"; in addition, the fourth and fifth lines of each stanza end with the identical word, and in six of the stanzas that word is "door" and in four others "Lenore." There is even more repetition: the last line of six of the first seven stanzas ends with the words "nothing more," and the last eleven stanzas end with the word "Nevermore." The rhyming lines—other than the last, which is very short—in each stanza are fifteen syllables long, the unrhymed lines sixteen. The longer lines give the effect of shorter ones, however, and add still further to the frequency of repeated sounds, for the first half of each opening line rhymes with the second half of the line, and so do the halves of line 3. There is still more: the first half of line 4 rhymes with the halves of line 3 (in the first stanza the rhymes are "dreary" / "weary" and "napping" / "tapping" / "rapping"). So at least nine words in each eight-line stanza are involved in the regular rhyme scheme, and many stanzas have added instances of rhyme or repetition. As if this were not enough, all the half-line rhymes are rich feminine rhymes, where both the accented and the following unaccented syllables rhyme—"drēārў" / "wēārў."

This is a detailed and complicated description of a complex and unusual pattern of rhymes. Though we could describe many other elements of the poem—images and symbols, for example—the unusual and dominant element is clearly the intricate and insistent pattern of rhyme and repetition. Moreover, this paragraph shows how you can describe at length, in depth, and with considerable complexity certain aspects of a work without mentioning the content at all. You can describe a play in comparable terms— acts, scenes, settings, time lapses perhaps—and you might describe a novel in terms of chapters, books, summary narration, dramatized scenes. In addition to describing the narrative structure or focus and voice of a short story, you might also describe the diction (word choice), the sentence structure, the amount of description of the characters or landscape, and so on.

ANALYSIS

Like copying, paraphrase, and summary, a description of a work or passage rarely stands alone as a piece of writing about literature. It is, instead, a tool, a means of supporting a point or opinion. Even the description we have given above borders on analysis. To analyze is to break something down into its parts to discover what they are and, usually, how they function in and relate to the whole. The description of the rhyme scheme of "The Raven" tells you what that scheme or pattern is but says nothing about how it functions in the poem. If you were to add such an account to the description, then, you would have analyzed one aspect of the poem. In order to do so, however, you would first have to decide what, in general, the poem is about: what its *theme* is. If you defined the theme of "The Raven" as "inconsolable grief," you could then write an analytical paper suggesting how the rhyme scheme reinforces that theme. You might begin like this:

Obsessive Rhyme in "The Raven"

We all know that gloomy poem with that gloomy bird, Edgar Allan Poe's "The Raven." The time is midnight, the room is dark, the bird is black, and the poem is full of words like "dreary," "sad," "mystery," and "ghastly." We all know, too, it has a rather singsong rhythm and repeated rhymes, but we do not often stop to think how the rhymes contribute to the mood or meaning. Before we do so here, perhaps it would be a good idea to describe in detail just what that rhyme scheme is.

Then follow with the description of the rhyme scheme, and go on like this:

Of course, the most obvious way in which the rhyme scheme reinforces the theme of inconsolable loss is through the emphatic repetition of "Nevermore." Since this refrain comes at the very end of each of the last stanzas it is even more powerful in its effect.

What is not so obvious as the effect of repeating "Nevermore" is the purpose of the overall abundance and richness of rhyme. Some might say it is not abundant and rich, but excessive and cloying. These harsh critics cynically add that in a way the rhymes and repetitions are appropriate because the whole poem is excessive and cloying: grief over loss, even intense grief, does pass away. This criticism is just, however, only if we have accurately defined the theme of the poem as "inconsolable sorrow." The very insistence of the rhyme and repetition, however, suggests that we may need to adjust slightly our definition of that theme. Perhaps the poem is not about "inconsolable sorrow" in so neutral a way but rather about obsessive grief. Then the insistent, pounding rhyme and repetition make sense (just as the closed-in dark chamber does). Obsessive repetition of words and sounds thus helps to create the meaning of the poem almost as much as the words themselves do.

INTERPRETATION

PRINCIPLES AND PROCEDURES

If you have been reading carefully, you may have noticed what looks like a catch: to turn description into analysis, you must relate what you are describing to the theme, overall effect, and meaning of the text. But how do you know what the theme is? If analysis relates the part to the whole, how can you know the "whole" before you have analyzed each part? And how can you analyze each part and relate it to the whole if you don't know what that whole is?

Interpretation, or the expression of your understanding of a literary work and its meaning, involves an initial general impression that is then supported and often modified by analysis of the particulars. It involves looking at the whole, the part, the whole, the part, the whole, the part in a series of approximations and adjustments. (Note, in particular, the need to keep your mind open for modifications or changes, rather than forcing your analysis to confirm your first impressions.)

This procedure should, in turn, suggest something of the nature and even the form of the critical essay, or essay of interpretation. The essay should present the overall theme and support that generalization with close analyses of the major elements of the text (or, in some essays, an analysis of one significant element)—showing how one or more such elements as rhyme or speaker, plot or setting reinforce, define, or modify the theme of the story. Often the conclusion of such an essay will be a fuller, more refined statement of the theme.

Both the definition of and the procedures for interpreting a work suggest that a literary text is unified, probably around a theme, a meaning, and an effect. In interpreting, you therefore ask of each element or detail, "How does it fit? How does it contribute to *the* theme or whole?" In most instances, especially when you write on shorter works, if you dig hard and deep enough you will find a satisfactory interpretation or central theme. Even after you have done your best, however, you must hold your "reading" or interpretation as a hypothesis rather than a final truth. Your experience of reading criticism has probably already shown you that more than one reading of a literary work is possible and that no reading exhausts the meaning and totality of a work. Nonetheless, you will want to begin reading a literary text as if it were going to make a central statement and create a single effect, no matter how complex. Try as conscientiously as you can to make sense of the work, to analyze it, to show how its elements work together. In analyzing elements, you kept your initial sense of the whole as hypothesis and did not try to force evidence to fit your first impression. Here, too, you will want to hold your interpretation as a hypothesis even in its final stages, even at the end. It is, you must be sure, the fullest and best "reading" of the text you are capable of at this time, with the evidence and knowledge you have at this moment—but only that. In other words, an interpretation is "only an opinion." But just as your political and other opinions are not lightly held but are what you really feel and believe based on all you know and have experienced and all you have thought and felt, so your opinion or interpretation of a literary work should be as responsible as you can make it. Your opinions are a measure of your knowledge, intelligence, and sensibility. They should not be lightly changed, but neither should they be obstinately and inflexibly held.

READING AND THEME MAKING

Because you need a sense of the whole text before you can analyze it, analysis and interpretation would seem to be possible only after repeated readings. Though obvious, logical, and partially true, this may not be *entirely* true. In reading, we actually anticipate theme or meaning much as we anticipate what will happen next. Often this anticipation or expectation of theme or effect begins with our first opening a book—or even before, in reading the title. If you were to read *Hamlet* in an edition that gives its full title, *The Tragedy of Hamlet, Prince of Denmark*—even if you had never heard of the play or its author before—you would have some idea or hypothesis about who the protagonist is, where the action will more than likely be set, how the play will end, and even some of the feelings it will arouse.

Such anticipation of theme and effect, projecting and modifying understanding and response, continues as you read. When you see the first four words of "The Zebra Storyteller"—"Once upon a time"—the strange title is to some extent explained and the kind of story you are about to read and its relation to everyday reality have been established. The title and the first short section of "The Most Dangerous Game" arouse expectations of the supernatural, the frightening, the adventurous, and thus create suspense: "What will happen next?" we ask as we read the first few paragraphs. The brief conversation about hunting, toward the end of that section, not only educates our expectations but also generates a moral and thematic question: "If there really are two animal classes, the hunters and the hunted, does one's luck in being among the hunters justify insensitivity toward the feelings of the hunted?" While the question may recede from the foreground of our attention for a while, it has nonetheless been raised. It is, in addition, reinforced by the break on the page, which forces us to pause and, even if momentarily, reflect. It comes forward again when General Zaroff introduces the subject of hunting. At these two points, at least, a thematic hypothesis based on hunters and hunted begins forming, however faintly, in our minds. That is enough to give us grounds—even as we read the story for the first time—for an analysis of elements and their relationship to our tentatively formulated theme, and perhaps for beginning to modify or modulate our articulation of that theme. Many details in the story indicate a political coloring to the theme: Zaroff is a Cossack—his people were noted for fierceness—and is, or was, a czarist general; he keeps a giant Cossack servant who was an official flogger under the czar; he refers to the Russian Revolution of 1917 as a "debacle"; he is clearly a racist. We may want to alter "hunter" and "hunted" in our first version of the anticipated theme to something broader—"strong" and "weak," perhaps, or "privileged" and "underprivileged"—or we may need fuller definitions of the terms "hunter" and "hunted."

Just as we have more than one expectation of what may happen next as we read a story, poem, or play, so we may have more than one expectation of what it is going to be "about" in the more general sense: as we read along we have expectations or hypotheses of meaning, and so we consciously or unconsciously try to fit together the pieces or elements of what we are reading into a pattern of significance. By the end of our first reading we should have a fairly well-defined sense of what the work is "about," what it means, even how some of the elements have worked together to produce that meaning and effect. Indeed, isn't this the way we read when we are not reading for a class or performance? Don't most people read most stories, poems, plays only once? And don't we usually think we have understood what we have read? Shouldn't we be able to read a very short story in class just once and immediately write an interpretive paper based on that first reading?

This is not to say that we cannot understand more about a work by repeated readings or that some virtue or purity of response in the naïve first reading will be lost in closer study. Our first "reading"—"reading" in the sense of both "casting our eye over" and "interpretation"—will almost certainly be modified or refined by rereading: if nothing else, we know from the beginning what will happen next—what the most dangerous game is, for example. The theme or meaning will likely be modulated by later readings, the way the elements function in defining or embodying meaning will likely be clearer; the effect of the second reading will certainly differ from that of the first. It may be instructive to reread several times the short work we interpreted in class after a single reading, then write a new interpretive essay and see how our understanding has been changed and enriched by subsequent readings.

OPINIONS, RIGHT AND WRONG

Just as each of our separate readings differs, so naturally one reader's fullest and "final" reading, interpretation, or opinion will differ somewhat from another's. Seldom will readers agree entirely with any full statement of a literary text's theme. Nor is one of these interpretations entirely "right" and all the others necessarily "wrong." For no thematic summary, no analysis or interpretation, no matter how full, can exhaust the affective or intellectual significance of a major literary text. Every major work will support various approximate readings of diverse degrees of acceptability, various competent or "good" readings, not just one single "right" reading.

Anyone who has heard two accomplished musicians faithfully perform the same work, playing all the same notes, or anyone who has seen two performances of *Hamlet* will recognize how "interpretations" can be both correct and different. You might try to get hold of several (audio or video) recordings of one or more of Hamlet's soliloquies— by John Barrymore, Sir John Gielgud, Richard Burton, Sir Laurence Olivier, Mel Gibson, Kenneth Branagh, or Ethan Hawke, for example—and notice how each of these actors lends to identical passages his own emphasis, pacing, tone, color, effect, and so, ultimately, his own meaning. These actors reading the identical words are, in effect, "copying." They are not paraphrasing or putting Shakespeare's Elizabethan poetry into modern American prose, not "interpreting" as we have defined it, or putting his play into their own words. If merely performing or reading the words aloud generates significant differences in interpretation, it is no wonder that when you write an interpretive essay about literature, when you give your conception of the meaning and effect of the literary text in your own words, your interpretation will differ from other interpretations, even when each of the different interpretations is competent and "correct."

Any communication, even a work of literature, is refracted—that is, interpreted and modified—by the recipient. In one sense, it is not complete until it is received, just as, in a sense, a musical score is not "music" until it is played. The novelist Philip Roth once reported how perturbed he was at first by what the critics and other readers said of his first novel, *Goodbye, Columbus*—they had missed what he intended, what the novel really was. But then he realized that once he had had his say in the novel, it was "out there," and each reader had to understand it within the limits and range of his or her own perspectives and literary and life experiences. His novel, once in print, was no longer merely "his," and rightly so.

That different interpretations may be "correct" is not to say, with Alice's (or is that Lewis Carroll's?) Humpty-Dumpty, that a word or a work "means just what I choose it to mean." Though no single "right" reading may exist, some readings are more appropriate and convincing than others and some readings are demonstrably wrong.

What would you say about this reading of *Hamlet*?

The play is about the hero's sexual love for his mother. He sees his father's "ghost" because he feels guilty, somehow responsible for his father's death, more than likely because he had often wished his father dead. To free himself from this feeling of guilt, he imagines that he sees his father's ghost and that the ghost tells him that his uncle murdered his father. He focuses upon his uncle because he is fiercely jealous that it is his uncle, not himself, who has replaced his father in his mother's bed. He so resents his mother's choice of so unworthy a mate, he attributes it not to love but to mere lust, clearly a projection of his own lust for his mother, which he calls love. His mother's lust so disgusts him that he hates all women now, even Ophelia. When his father was alive he could be fond of Ophelia, for his sexual feeling for his mother was deflected by his father-the-king's powerful presence. Now, however, he must alienate Ophelia not only because of his new hatred of women but because he has a chance of winning his mother, especially if he can get rid of Claudius, his uncle.

Such a reading explains more or less convincingly certain details in the play, but it wrenches some out of context and leaves a good deal out and a good deal unexplained: why, for example, do others see the ghost of Hamlet's father if it is just a figment of his imagination? What are Horatio and Fortinbras and the political elements doing in the play? *If* you accept certain Freudian premises about human psychology and see life in Freudian terms (see "Freudian Criticism," p. A21), *if* you see literary texts as the *author's* psychic fantasy stimulating your own psychic fantasies and believe that interpretation of *Hamlet* is not merely a reading of the play itself but an analysis of Shakespeare's psyche, you may find this reading somewhat convincing. You will perhaps explain away some of the details of the play that do not seem to fit your Freudian reading as a cover-up, an attempt by Shakespeare to disguise the true but hidden meaning of his dramatic fantasy from others—and from himself. Such a reading is probably neither right nor wrong but only a way of interpreting *Hamlet* based on certain assumptions about psychology and about the way literature *means,* and so it could seem "right" or acceptable to those who share those assumptions.

Suppose one of your ingenious classmates were to argue that the real subject of *Hamlet* is that the hero has tuberculosis. This would explain, your classmate would say, the hero's moodiness, his pretended madness that sometimes seems real, his rejection of Ophelia (he wouldn't want their children to suffer from the disease), his father's ghost (he, too, died of consumption), his anger at his uncle (who carries the disease, of course) for marrying Hamlet's mother, and so on. Your classmate might even argue that the text of the play is flawed, that it was just copied down during a performance by someone in the audience or was printed from an actor's imperfect copy. Therefore, "O that this too too *solid flesh"* should read *"sullied flesh,"* as many scholars have argued (and might not "sullied flesh" suggest tuberculosis?). And, therefore, isn't it quite possible that the most famous soliloquy in the play really began or was meant to begin, "TB or not TB"? "No way!" we'd say. We would be reasonably sure that this is not just "not proved" but just plain *wrong*. It might be interesting and illuminating to rebut that reading in a paper of your own and to notice what kinds of evidence you bring to bear on an interpretive argument.

READER AND TEXT

If we find it difficult to say exactly what a particular piece of literature *says,* it is usually not because that work is vague or meaning*less* but because it is too specific and meaning*ful* to paraphrase satisfactorily in any language other than its own. Since no two human beings are identical and no two people can inhabit the same space at the same time, no two people can see exactly the same reality from the same angle and vantage point. Most of us get around this awkward truth by saying that we see what we are "supposed" to see, a generalized, commonsense approximation of reality. We are all, in effect, like Polonius in the third act of *Hamlet,* who sees in a cloud, a camel, a weasel, a whale—whatever Hamlet tells him he sees.

Some individuals struggle to see things as fully and clearly as possible from their unique vantage points and to communicate to others their particular—even peculiar—visions. But here, too, we are individuated, for though we speak of our "common language," we each speak a unique language, made up of "dialects" that are not only regional and ethnic but also conditioned by our age group, our profession, our education, travel, reading—all our experiences. Yet if we want to express our unique vision to others who have different visions and different "languages," we have to find some medium that is both true to ourselves and understandable to others.

For these individuals—these writers of literature—a constant tug-of-war exists between the uniqueness of their individual visions and the generalizing nature of language. The battle does not always result in sheer loss, however. Often, in the very struggle to get their own perceptions into language, writers sharpen those perceptions or discover what they themselves did not know when they began to write. You have probably made similar discoveries in the process of writing a letter or an assigned paper. But writers also find that what they have written does not perfectly embody what they meant it to, just as you perhaps have found that your finished papers have been not quite as brilliant as your original idea.

"Understanding" is not a passive reception of a text, but an active reaching out from our own experiences toward the text. At least at first we need to do so by meeting the author on the ground of a common or general language and set of conventions—things that everybody "knows." The first task of the reader, therefore, is to get not to the author's intention, but to the general statement that the work itself makes—that is, its theme or thesis. After a few readings we can usually make a stab at articulating the theme of a text. What a work says in the way of a general theme, however, is not necessarily its full or ultimate meaning; otherwise we would read theme summaries and not stories. The theme is the meaning accessible to all through close reading of the text and common to all, but a literary text is not all statement. Often we find cloudy areas in the text where we cannot be sure what is implication, the suggestion of the text, and what is our inference or interpretation. Why does Doris Lessing's Judith prefer having a tomcat put to death to having him neutered, but does not suggest that the female kitten who has been ruined for procreation be put to death? Does this suggest that males, including human males, exist only to fertilize eggs, but that females have other functions as well? Or, at least, that this is what Judith believes? Does this give us more insight into Judith's life, her singleness, her refusal to marry the Greek professor, her ultimate flight from Luigi? The story does not *say* this, but many readers will find this inference convincing. If accepted, this changes the meaning of the story to some degree. Still, it need not be accepted; the story does not, will never, say. The meaning of the story for the reader who is convinced will differ from the meaning for the reader who is not convinced.

The full meaning of a work for you is not only in its stated theme, one that everyone can agree on, but in the meaning you derive by bringing together that generalized theme, the precise language of the text, and your own response and experiences—including reading experience—and imagination. That "meaning" is not the total meaning of the work, not what the author originally perceived and "meant to say"; it is the vision of the author as embodied in the work *and re-viewed from your own angle of vision.*

Your role in producing a meaning from the text does not free you from paying very close attention to the precise language of the text, the words and their meanings, their order, the syntax of the sentences, and even such mundane details as punctuation. You cannot impose a meaning on the text, no matter how sincerely and intensely you feel it, in defiance of the rules of grammar and the nature of the language.

Still, the reader has to be an artist too, trying to experience the reality of the work as the author experienced reality, and with the same reverence and sense of responsibility for the original. To write about literature you need to embody your reading experience— or interpretation—of the work in language. Alas, writing about literature, using words about words, is not as easy as it sounds at first. But it is more exciting, giving you a chance to see with another's eyes, to explore another's perceptions or experiences, and to explore and more fully understand your own in the process, thus expanding the horizon of your experience, perception, consciousness.

When some rich works of literature, like *Hamlet,* seem to have more than one meaning or no entirely satisfactory meaning or universally agreed-on single theme, they are saying something, something very specific, but what they are saying is too specific and complex and profound (and true, perhaps) to be generalized or paraphrased in a few dozen words. The literary work is meaning*ful*—that is, full of meaning or meanings; but the reader must produce each particular meaning from the work, using the work itself, the language of the community and of the work, and his or her own language, experience, and imagination.

As a reader trying to understand the unique perception and language of the author, you should try to translate the text as best you can into terms you can understand. Do your best to approach the text with an open, receptive mind.

An interpretation, then, is not a clarification of what the writer "was trying to say"; it is a process that itself says, in effect, "The way I am trying to understand this work is. . . ."

CRITICAL APPROACHES

The way you read and talk about a literary text depends on your assumptions, usually unconscious or unarticulated, about what a work of literature is, what it is supposed to do, and what makes it good. Literary critics, however, often define their assumptions about literature and the proper way to go about reading it and writing about it. The results are critical theories or critical approaches. Looking at a few of these, you may recognize some of your own assumptions, see new and exciting ways of looking at literature, or, at the very least, become aware of your own critical premises and prejudices.

OBJECTIVISM

We might begin by asking just what, literally, a work of literature is. Some critics think of it as a fixed and freestanding object made up of words on a page. It is "freestanding" in that it has no connection, on the one hand, with the author or his or her intention or life or, on the other hand, with the historical or cultural context of the author or the reader. These we might call objectivist critics; they believe that a text is an independent object, free from the subjectivity of author and reader.

FORMALISM

Among the objectivist critics are the formalists. One common formalist conception is that a work is *autotelic,* that is, complete in itself, written for its own sake, and unified by its form—that which makes it a work of art. Content is less important than form. Literature involves a special kind of language that sets it apart from merely utilitarian writing; the formal strategies that organize and animate that language elevate literature and give it a special, almost religious character.

NEW CRITICISM One group of formalists, the New Critics, dominated literary criticism in the middle of the twentieth century, and New Criticism remains an important influence today. Their critical practice is to demonstrate formal unity by showing how every part of a work—every word, every image, every element—contributes to a central unifying theme. Because the details of the work relate to a theme or idea, they are generally treated as *symbolic,* as figurative or allegorical, representations of that central, unifying idea. The kind of unity thus demonstrated, in which every part is related to the whole and the whole is reflected in each part, is called organic unity. The New Critics differentiate organic unity from (and much prefer it to) mechanical unity, the external, preconceived structure or rules that arise not from the individuality of the work, but from the type or genre. New Critical analysis, or explication of the text, is especially effective in the critical reading of lyric poetry. It has become so universally accepted as *at least the first step* in the understanding of literature that it is almost everywhere the critical approach taught in introductory literature courses, even in those that do not share its fundamental autotelic assumption. It is, indeed, the basic approach of the "Understanding the Text" sections in *The Norton Introduction to Literature.*

The New Critics' focus on theme or meaning as well as form signifies that for them literature is referential: it points to something outside itself, things in the real, external world or in human experience—a tree, a sound wave, love. The New Critics, in general, do not question the reality of the phenomenal world or the ability of language to represent it.

STRUCTURALISM

For many formalists, however, literature is not referential. The words in a story, poem, or play no longer point outward to the things, people, or world they are supposed to denote, as they might do in ordinary, "nonliterary" discourse, but point inward to each other and to the formal system they create. The critic still focuses on interrelatedness, but is less concerned with "meaning"; words are treated not as referential symbols, but as natural numbers; poetry is likened to mathematics or music.

Structuralism focuses on the text as an independent aesthetic object and also tends to detach literature from history and social and political implications, but (much more than New Criticism) structuralism emphasizes systematic analysis, aspiring to make literary criticism a branch of scientific inquiry. It sees every literary work as a separate "system" and seeks to discover the principles or general laws that govern the interaction of parts within the system. Structuralism has its roots in modern linguistic theory; it looks especially to the work of Ferdinand de Saussure (1857–1913), who founded structural linguistics early in the twentieth century. Structuralism in criticism did not, however, flourish internationally until the early 1960s, when a combination of space-age preoccupation with science and cold-war fear of implication led to a view of literature as intellectually challenging yet socially and politically noncontroversial.

Although based on linguistic theory, structuralism tries to extend newly discovered principles about language to other aspects of literature. Drawing on the semiotic principle that a vast and intricate system of signs enables human beings to communicate through language, structuralism asks readers to consider the way that other kinds of sign systems within a work—structures all—combine to produce meaning. Language and its characteristic habits are important to structuralists, but it is not enough to consider any single part of a work or any single kind of sign—linguistic or otherwise—within it. Structuralism aspires to elucidate the meaning of a work of literature by seeing the way all of its parts work together toward some wholeness of structure and meaning. Like formalism, it shows little interest in the creative process as such and has virtually no interest in authors, their intentions, or the circumstances or contexts of creation. It takes texts to represent interactions of words and ideas apart from individual human identities or sociopolitical commitments, and concentrates its analytical attention on what can be said about how different elements or processes in a text operate in relation to one another. Structuralists are less likely than formalists to concentrate their attention on some single all-explaining characteristic of literature (such as Cleanth Brooks's "tension" or William Empson's "ambiguity"), and its practitioners are less likely to privilege a particular text for its revelation or authority. Structuralism may be seen as a sort of secular equivalent of formalism; it is less mysterious and authoritarian, and it has both the advantage and the disadvantage of seeming to be less arbitrary and more "objectively" reliable. But in some ways it seems to promise too much for method and "objectivity," and by the 1970s its insights into the ways of language were already being used against it to attack the certitudes it appeared to promise and to emphasize instead the uncertainties and indeterminateness of texts.

POSTSTRUCTURALISM

Poststructuralism is the broad term used to designate the several directions of literary criticism that, while depending crucially on the insights of science-based theory, attack the very idea that any kind of certitude can exist about the meaning, understandability, or shareability of texts. Poststructuralists, disturbed at the optimism of positivist philosophy in suggesting that the world is knowable and explainable, ultimately doubt the possibility of certainties of any kind, and they see language as especially elusive and unfaithful. Much of poststructuralism involves undoing; the best-known variety of poststructuralism, deconstruction, suggests as much in its very name.

DECONSTRUCTION Deconstruction takes the observations of structuralism to their logical conclusion, arguing that the elaborate web of semiotic differentiations created by the principle of difference in language means that no text can ultimately have any stable, definite, or discoverable meaning.

For the deconstructionist, language consists just in black marks on a page that repeat or differ from each other and the reader is the only author, one who can find whatever can be found in, or be made to appear in, those detached, isolated marks. The deconstructionist conception of literature is thus very broad—almost any writing will do. While this may seem "subjective" in that the critical reader has great freedom, it is the object—the black marks on the blank page—that is the sole subject/object of intention/attention.

As practiced by its most famous proponent, the French philosopher Jacques Derrida (1930–), deconstruction endeavors to trace the way texts challenge or cancel their explicit meanings and wrestle themselves into stasis or neutrality. Many deconstructionists have strong radical political commitments (it is possible to argue that the radical counterculture of the 1960s and especially the political events in Paris of 1968 are the crucial context for understanding the origins of deconstructionism), but the retreat from meaning and denial of clear signification that characterize deconstruction also have affinities with formalism and structuralism, particularly as deconstruction is practiced by American critics. Rather than emphasizing form over content, however, deconstruction tries to deny the possibility of content and places value instead on verbal play as a characteristic outlet of a fertile, adroit, and supple human mind. Like structuralism, it lives almost completely in a self-referential verbal world rather than a world in which texts represent some larger or other reality, but unlike structuralism it denies that the verbal world adds up to anything coherent, consistent, or meaningful in itself. Deconstruction also influences other varieties of poststructuralism with different kinds of interests in history and ideology. Michel Foucault (1926–1984), Julia Kristeva (1941–), and Jacques Lacan (1901–1981), though their disciplinary interests are in social history, feminist philosophy, and psychoanalysis, respectively, all come out of deconstructionist assumptions and carry the indeterminacies of poststructuralism (and of postmodernism more generally) into kinds of literary criticism with interests fundamentally different from those of structuralism.

SUBJECTIVISM

Opposed to objectivism is what might be called subjectivism. This loose term can be used to embrace many forms of psychological and self-, subject-, or reader-centered criticism.

PSYCHOLOGICAL CRITICISM

The assumption is that literature is the expression of the author's psyche, often his or her unconscious, and, like dreams, needs to be interpreted.

FREUDIAN CRITICISM The dominant school is the Freudian, based on the work of Sigmund Freud (1856–1939). Many of its practitioners assert that the meaning of a literary work exists not on its surface but in the psyche (some would even claim, in the neuroses) of the author. The value of the work, then, lies in how powerfully and convincingly it expresses the author's unconscious and how universal its psychological elements are. A well-known Freudian reading of *Hamlet,* for example, insists that Hamlet is troubled because he is jealous of his uncle, for Hamlet, *like all male children,* unconsciously wants to sleep with his mother. The ghost may then be a manifestation of Hamlet's unconscious desire; his madness is not just acting, but is the result of this frustrated desire; his cruelly gross mistreatment of Ophelia is a deflection of his disgust at his mother's being "lecherous," "unfaithful" in her love for him. A Freudian critic may assume then that Hamlet suffers from an Oedipus complex, a Freudian term for the desire of the son for his mother, its name derived from the Greek myth that is the basis of Sophocles' play *Oedipus the King.*

Some Freudian critics stress the author's psyche and find *Hamlet* the expression of Shakespeare's own Oedipus complex. Others stress the effect on the reader, the work having a purgative or cleansing effect by expressing in socially and morally acceptable ways unconscious desires that would be unacceptable if expressed directly.

LACANIAN CRITICISM As it absorbs the indeterminacies of poststructuralism under the influence of thinkers such as Jacques Lacan, psychological criticism has become increasingly complex. Accepting the Oedipal paradigm and the unconscious as the realm of repressed desire, Lacanian psychology (and the critical theory that comes from that psychology) conflates these concepts with the deconstructionist emphasis on language as expressing absence—you use a word to represent an absent object but you cannot make it present. The word, then, like the unconscious desire, is something that cannot be fulfilled. Language, reaching out with one word after the other, striving for but never reaching its object, is the arena of desire.

JUNGIAN CRITICISM Just as a Freudian assumes that human psyches have similar histories and structures, the Jungian critic assumes that we all share a universal or collective unconscious (as well as having a racial and individual unconscious). According to Carl Gustav Jung (1875–1961) and his followers, in the collective unconscious and in our individual unconsciouses are universal images, patterns, and forms of human experiences, or archetypes. We can never know these archetypes directly, but they surface in art in an imperfect, shadowy way, taking the form of archetypal images—the snake with its tail in its mouth, rebirth, mother, the double, the descent into Hell. To get a sense of the archetype beneath the archetypal images or shadows in the characters, plot, language, and images of a work, to bring these together in an archetypal interpretation, is the function of the Jungian critic. Just as, for the Freudian literary critic, the "family romance"—out of which the Oedipus story comes—is central, so the Jungian assumes that a monomyth underlies the archetypal images. In that all-encompassing myth, called the quest, the hero struggles to free himself (the gender of the pronoun is specific and significant) from the Great Mother, to become a separate, self-sufficient being, who is then rewarded by union with his ideal other, the feminine anima.

PHENOMENOLOGICAL CRITICISM

Another kind of subjectivist criticism is phenomenology, especially as it is practiced by critics of consciousness. They consider all the writings of an author—shopping lists and letters as well as lyrics—the expression of his or her mind-set or way of looking at reality. Such critics look for repeated or obsessive use of certain key words, incidents, patterns, and angles of vision, and use these to map out the inner world of the writer.

READER-RESPONSE CRITICISM

The formalists focus on the text. Though the psychological critics focus most frequently on the author, their assumptions about the similarity or universality of the human mind make them consider as well the role of the reader. Another approach, while not psychological in the usual sense of the word, also focuses on the reception of the text, on reader response. The conventional notion of reading is that a writer or speaker has an "idea," encodes it—that is, turns it into words—and the reader or listener decodes it, deriving, when successful, the writer or speaker's "idea." The reader-response critic assumes, however, that such equivalency between sender and receiver is impossible. The literary work, therefore, does *not* exist on the page; that is only the text. The text becomes a work only when it is read, just as a score becomes music only when it is played. And just as every musical performance, even of exactly the same notes, is somewhat different, a different "interpretation," so no two readers read or perform exactly the same work from identical texts. Individual readers differ, of course, and gaps in a text itself provide space for different readings or interpretations. Some of these lacunae are temporary—such as the withholding of the murderer's name until the end—and are closed by the text sooner or later, though each reader will in the meantime fill them differently. But others are permanent and can never be filled with certainty; they result in a degree of uncertainty or indeterminacy in the text.

The reader-response critic's focus on the reading process is especially useful in the study of long works such as novels. The critic follows the text sequentially, observing the expectations being aroused, how they are satisfied or modified, how the reader recapitulates "evidence" from the text to project forward a configuration, a tentative assumption of what the work as a whole will be and mean once it is done. The expectations come partly from the text and partly from the reader's repertoire—that is, the reader's reading experience plus his or her social and cultural knowledge.

HISTORICAL CRITICISM

DIALOGISM

Largely identified with the work of Mikhail Bakhtin (1895–1975), this critical approach also gives a significant role to the reader and is particularly useful for long fiction. Dialogic critics base the study of language and literature on the individual utterance, taking into account the specific time, the place, the speaker, and the listener or reader. Such critics thus see language as a continuous dialogue, each utterance being a reply to what has gone before. Thought, which they define as inner speech, is a dialogue between utterances that you have taken in. Even your own language is dialogic, for it is made up of the dialogue in which you engage; that which you have heard from parents and peers, teachers and television; all kinds of social and professional discourse and reading. Indeed, you speak many "languages"—those of your ethnic, social, economic, national, professional, gender, and other identities. Your individual language consists in the combination of those languages. The literary form in which the dialogic is most interesting, complex, and significant is the novel, for it includes the languages not only of the characters (as in drama), but also of a mediator or narrator and passages of description or analysis or information that seem to come from other voices—newspapers, whaling manuals, legal cases, what have you. Because the world is growing ever more interrelated, with multiple voices rather than one dominant voice or language, the novel has become the most appropriate form for the representation of the world.

The dialogic sees utterances, including literary utterances or works, as specific to a time and place, so one of its dimensions (unlike formalist, structuralist, or psychological criticism) is *historical.* Nineteenth-century historical criticism took the obvious fact that a work is created in a specific historical and cultural context and that the author is a part of that context as reason to treat literature as a product of the culture. Formalists and others emphasizing the aesthetic value of literature saw this as reducing the literary work to the status of a mere historical document and the abandonment of literary study to history. The dialogic critic sees the work in relation to its host context, a part of the culture's dialogue. The work in turn helps create the context for other utterances, literary and otherwise. Some consider dialogic criticism a form of sociological criticism.

SOCIOLOGICAL CRITICISM

More recently, as scientists from psychology to physics recognized the role of the perceiver in perception, historians realized that they were not only discovering and looking at facts, but were finding what they were looking for, selecting facts to fit preconceived views or interpretations. Literary historians or historical critics began to see literature not as a mere passive product of "history," but as a contributor to and even creator of history. An early form of this kind of historicism was sociological criticism, which sees literature as one aspect of the larger processes of history, especially those processes involving people in social groups or as members of social institutions or movements. Much sociological criticism uses literary texts to illustrate social attitudes and tendencies—and, therefore, has been strongly resisted by formalists, structuralists, and other "objectivist" critics as not being properly literary—but sociological criticism also attempts to relate what happens in texts to social events and patterns, and is as concerned about the effects of texts on human events as about the effects of historical events on texts. Sociological criticism assumes that the most significant aspects of human beings are social and that the most important functions of literature thus involve the way that literature both portrays and influences human interactions. Much sociological criticism centers its attention on contemporary life and texts, seeking to affect both societal directions and literary ones in the present, but some sociological criticism is historical, concerned with differences in different times and places, and anxious to interpret directions of literature in terms of historical emphases and patterns.

MARXIST CRITICISM

The most insistent and vigorous historicism through most of the twentieth century has been Marxism, based on the work of Karl Marx (1818–1883). Marxist criticism, like other historical critical methods in the nineteenth century, treated literature as a passive product of the culture, specifically of the economic aspect, and, therefore, of class warfare. Economics, the underlying cause of history, was thus the *base,* and culture, including literature and the other arts, the *superstructure.* Viewed from the Marxist perspective, the literary works of a period would, then, reveal the state of the struggle between classes in the historical place and moment.

Marxist critics, however, early on recognized the role of perception. They insisted that all use of language, including literary and critical language, is ideological—that is, that it derives from and expresses preconceived ideas, particularly economic or class values. Criticism is thus not just the product of the culture but also part of the discourse or "conversation" that we call history. Formalism and even the extreme apolitical position of aestheticism, "art for art's sake," by placing art in a realm above the grubbiness of everyday life—above such mundane things as politics and money—removes art from having any importance in that life. According to Marxists, this "bourgeois mystification of art" tends to support the class in power. Marxism has traditionally been sensitive to and articulate about power politics in both life and literature, and both its social and literary analyses have often been based on an explicit or implicit political agenda, though many Marxist critics are motivated more by theoretical than practical aims. In recent years, especially in the wake of poststructuralism and the psychoanalytical criticism of the 1970s and '80s, Marxist criticism has become increasingly theoretical and less doctrinaire politically. Critics such as Raymond Williams, Fredric Jameson, Terry Eagleton, Pierre Macherey, Walter Benjamin, and Louis Althusser have gained wide audiences among readers with a variety of political and literary commitments. Over the course of the century, Marxism has most often and most consistently raised referential and historical issues about literature, and readers interested in the interactive relationship between literature and life have most often turned for their guidance on such issues to Marxist analysts, whether or not they share their philosophical or political assumptions. In the past decades, however, two other critical schools with strong commitments to historical and cultural issues have become very powerful intellectually and have attracted many practitioners and adherents. These two, feminism and new historicism, have (along with Marxism and, in its way, dialogism) turned critical attention powerfully toward historical and representational issues, and since the mid 1980s they have set the dominant directions in literary criticism.

FEMINIST CRITICISM

Like Marxist criticism, feminist criticism derives from firm political and ideological commitments and insists that literature both reflects and influences human behavior in the larger world. Feminist criticism often, too, has practical and political aims. Strongly conscious that most of recorded history has given grossly disproportionate attention to the interests, thoughts, and actions of men, feminist thought endeavors both to extend contemporary attention to distinctively female concerns, ideas, and accomplishments and to recover the largely unrecorded and unknown history of women in earlier times. Not all directions of feminist criticism are historical; feminism has, in fact, taken many different directions and forms in recent years, and it has many different concerns. French feminist criticism, for example, has been deeply influenced by psychoanalysis, especially Lacanian psychoanalysis, and by French poststructuralist emphasis on language. Beyond their common aim of explicating and furthering specifically female interests, feminist critics may differ substantially in their assumptions and emphases. Like Marxism, feminism draws creatively on various other approaches and theories for its several methodologies. The most common historical directions of American feminism in particular involve the recovery of neglected or forgotten texts written by women in earlier times, the redrawing of literary values to include forms of writing (letters and autobiography, for example) that women were able to create when more public and accepted forms were denied to them, the discovery of the roles (positive and negative) that reading played in the lives and consciousnesses of women when they were unable to pursue more "active" and "public" courses, and the sorting out of cultural values implicit in the way women are represented in the texts of particular times and places.

NEW HISTORICISM

New historicism has less obvious ideological commitments than Marxism or feminism, but it shares their interest in the investigation of how power is distributed and used in different cultures. Drawing on the insights of modern anthropology (and especially on the work of Clifford Geertz), new historicism wishes to isolate the fundamental values in texts and cultures, and it regards texts both as evidence of basic cultural patterns and as forces in cultural and social change. Many of the most influential practitioners of the new historicism come out of the ranks of Marxism and feminism, and new historicists are usually knowledgeable about most varieties of literary theory. Like Marxists and feminists, they wish to uncover the ideological commitments in texts, and they care deeply about historical and cultural difference and the way texts represent it. But their personal commitments and specific political agendas usually are less important—at least explicitly—to their work, and one of the main disagreements between feminists and new historicists, or between Marxists and new historicists, involves the role that one's own politics should play in the practice of criticism. Many observers regard new historicism as politically to the left in its analysis of traditional cultural values; but critics on the left are suspicious of new historicism, especially of its reluctance to state its premises openly, and they generally regard its assumptions as conservative. Whatever its fundamental political commitments, however (or whether its commitments can be fairly described as having a consistent and specifiable bias), new historicism is far more interested than any other literary approach in social groups generally ignored by literary historians, and it refuses to privilege "literature" over other printed, oral, or material texts. "Popular literature" often gets major attention in the work of new historicists, who see all texts in a culture as somehow expressing its values and directions, and thus as equally useful in determining the larger intellectual, epistemological, and ethical system of which any text is a part. New historicists thus see texts as less specifically individual and distinctive than do most objectivist critics; and although they sometimes consider the psychology of authors or readers, they mainly examine the prevailing tendencies shared across a culture and thus shared across all kinds of texts, whatever their class status, literary value, or political aim.

PLURALISM

Since these classifications are not pigeonholes, critics' approaches often overlap: many feminists, especially French feminists, are Lacanian or poststructuralist as well, while many British feminists lean toward sociological, especially Marxist, criticism; dialogic critics accept many of the starting points and methods of reader-response and sociological critics; and so on. These crossovers or combinations, generally enriching, cause problems only when critics seem to operate out of contradictory assumptions.

Critics and theorists disagree about whether readers should bring together the insights and methods of different schools or whether they should commit themselves whole-heartedly to a single system. Pluralists, as the mixers of methods usually are called, contend that they make use of promising insights or methods wherever they find them and argue that putting together the values of different approaches leads to a fairer and more balanced view of texts and their uses. Opponents—those who insist on a consistency of ideological commitment—argue that pluralists are simply unwilling to state or admit their real commitments, and that any mixing of methods leads to confusion, uncertainty, and inconsistency rather than fairness. Readers, conscious or not of their assumptions and their methods, make this basic choice—to follow one lead or many—and the kind of reading they do and the conclusions they come to depend not only on this basic choice, but on many others suggested by the dominant strands of recent criticism that have been described here. Not all critics are aware of their assumptions, methodologies, or values, and some would even deny that they begin with any particular assumptions or biases. But readers newly learning to practice literary criticism often find it useful to sort out their own beliefs carefully and see exactly what kind of difference it makes in the way they read literature and ask questions of it.

FURTHER READING ON CRITICAL APPROACHES

For good introductions to the issues discussed here, see the following books, from which we have drawn in our discussion and definitions:

Alter, Robert. *The Pleasure of Reading in an Ideological Age.* New York: Norton, 1996. Rpt. of *The Pleasures of Reading: Thinking about Literature in an Ideological Age.* 1989.

Culler, Jonathan. *On Deconstruction: Theory and Criticism after Structuralism.* Ithaca, NY: Cornell UP, 1982.

---. *The Pursuit of Signs: Semiotics, Literature, Deconstruction.* Ithaca, NY: Cornell UP, 1981.

Davis, Robert Con, and Ronald Schleifer, *Contemporary Literary Criticism: Literary and Cultural Studies.* 4th ed. New York: Addison-Wesley, 1999.

Eagleton, Mary, ed. *Feminist Literary Theory: A Reader.* 2nd ed. Malden, MA: Blackwell, 1996.

Eagleton, Terry. *Literary Theory: An Introduction.* 2nd rev. ed. Minneapolis: U of Minnesota P, 1996.

Groden, Michael, and Martin Kreiswirth. *The Johns Hopkins Guide to Literary Theory and Criticism.* Baltimore: Johns Hopkins UP, 1994.

Keohane, Nannerl, Michelle Z. Rosaldo, and Barbara C. Gelpi, eds. *Feminist Theory: A Critique of Ideology.* Chicago: U of Chicago P, 1982.

LaCapra, Dominick. *History and Criticism.* Ithaca, NY: Cornell UP, 1987.

Leitch, Vincent B. *American Literary Criticism from the Thirties to the Eighties.* New York: Columbia UP, 1989.

Lentricchia, Frank. *After the New Criticism.* Chicago UP, 1981.

Lentricchia, Frank, and Thomas McLaughlin, eds. 2nd ed. *Critical Terms for Literary Study.* Chicago: U of Chicago P, 1995.

Macksey, Richard, and Eugenio Donato, eds. *The Structuralist Controversy: The Languages of Criticism and the Sciences of Man.* 1972. Ann Arbor: Books on Demand, n.d.

Moi, Toril. *Sexual-Textual Politics.* New York: Routledge, 1985.

Piaget, Jean. *Structuralism.* Trans. and ed. Chaninah Maschler. New York: Basic, 1970.

Selden, Raman, and Peter Widdowson. *A Reader's Guide to Contemporary Literary Theory.* 3rd ed. Lexington: UP of Kentucky, 1993.

Todorov, Tzvetan. *Mikhail Bakhtin: The Dialogic Principle.* Trans. Wlad Godzich. Minneapolis: U of Minnesota P, 1984.

Veeser, Harold, ed. *The New Historicism.* New York: Routledge, 1989.

---. *The New Historicism Reader.* New York: Routledge, 1994.

WRITING ABOUT FICTION, POETRY, DRAMA

So far we have been discussing writing about literature in general, rather than writing about a story, a poem, or a play in particular, though we have used specific works as examples. Some topics may be equally applicable to all three genres: you could study the imagery, symbols, or themes, for example, in a story, a poem, or a play. For that matter, you could study imagery, symbols, or themes in a story, a poem, *and* a play—comparing the water imagery in Baldwin's story "Sonny's Blues," say, with the air or wind imagery in Shelley's poem "Ode to the West Wind" and with the fire or burning imagery in Sophocles' play *Antigone*. Since fiction and drama also have action and character in common, you have the option not only of writing about a story or a play in isolation, but of comparing aspects—writing about the plot of a story and that of a play, analyzing a character or characterization from each, and so on.

NARRATIVE

A story not only has elements common to all three genres, such as plot and character; it also has something special: a narrator, someone who tells the story. Everything in fiction—action, character, theme, structure, even the language—is mediated: everything comes to us through an intervening mind or voice; we often see the story from a particular vantage point or several vantage points *(focus)* and always are told the story by someone, whether that someone is identified or is merely a disembodied *voice*. We must be aware of the narration, the means by which the story comes to us. We must be aware that someone exists between us and the story, and that this mediation contributes greatly to the meaning, structure, and effect of the story. Who tells us the story of "The Lame Shall Enter First"? What is the physical and emotional relationship of that story's narrator to its characters? How can we describe the language or voice of the narration? In answering these essential questions, you could write a paper called "The Narrator in 'The Lame Shall Enter First' " (or, to be more dramatic, "The Ghostly Reporter of 'The Lame Shall Enter First' "). Since a story is told *to* someone as well as *by* someone, you might ask yourself about the relationship between us—the audience—and the narrator. To what kind of audience is the narrator of Lessing's "Our Friend Judith" telling her story? How do we, as readers, differ from that audience? What impression of the narrator do we form that she does not intend? Such questions might lead to an analysis of that story's tone—and a paper sardonically titled "With Friends Like Judith's. . . ." These kinds of questions follow from the simple but central fact that stories do not come to us directly but are narrated; they are the kinds of questions writing about fiction frequently centers on.

Even the conventional past tense, which we often take for granted, often implies a narrator. Since the story is not happening "now," in the present, is not being enacted before us but is over with, having already happened in the past, someone must be recalling it, someone who knows what happened and how it all came out. That someone, the narrator, has been able to select and shape all the events and details. For that reason everything in a well-constructed story proves relevant and significant.

Even narrative time is purposefully structured. Stories, unlike actual time as we know it, have beginnings and endings, but they do not have to begin at the beginning and proceed in a uniform direction at a uniform pace toward the end. They can be told from end to beginning, or even from middle to beginning to end, as in Baldwin's "Sonny's Blues." An hour, a day, or a decade can be skipped or condensed into a narrative moment (a phrase or a sentence), or a moment can be expanded to fill pages. Since this manipulation of time affects the meaning and effect of the story, we must pay close attention to it and question its significance. For example, the beginning of the third section of Bierce's "An Occurrence at Owl Creek Bridge" follows immediately from the end of the first section, so what purpose does the second section serve? Why does the first section cover only a few minutes of action but the third, only a little longer, cover what seems to be a whole day? Can you explain why—in terms of meaning and effect—Chekhov's "Lady with the Dog" dwells on each of its long scenes? why it briefly summarizes or skips other, longer periods? Why do some stories cover only a very short period of time, while others cover years and years? Why are some stories presented largely through dialogue, while others are "told" rather than presented, with few dramatized scenes and little dialogue?

DRAMATIZATION

Scenes presented more or less immediately (that is, without mediation) through dialogue and action, taking place over a short period of time, are said to be *dramatized*. Though gaps of time may exist *between* the *scenes* or *acts* of a play, once the action begins it takes exactly as much time on the stage as it would in actuality: the actors speak and move in "real" time. Though a playwright, of course, knew how it would all come out and has shaped the play accordingly, the language of the play comes to us in the present tense; the dialogue and action happen right before our eyes. And though the playwright has written all the lines, we do not hear his or her voice directly: only the characters speak. Neither the playwright nor a surrogate in the form of a narrator tells us who are the good guys and who the bad, what each character is like or whether what is being said is true, distorted, false. Only very rarely—as in the Shakespearean soliloquy or aside—do we know what a character is thinking. Plays such as *Oedipus the King* and even *Hamlet* provide only very brief indications of setting, costume, movement of characters, tone of voice, if they are present at all. Such stage directions—which may be as elaborate as the detailed description of setting and costumes and the instructions for action and tone in *A Doll House*—are not, in a sense, purely dramatic. Watching a play being performed on a stage, we do not see or hear these words at all. On the page, they are usually distinguished from the text of the play by italics, brackets, or some other typographical device, so as we read we register—or should register—them as separate from "the play itself." They seem to belong to some other dimension and clearly belong to a voice other than that of any character.

When we read a play, we tend to imagine it—in the literal sense of putting it into images—in our minds as if it were being performed on a stage. We act, as it were, as our own directors; if we were to put into words all that would be necessary to stage the play as we see it in our minds, we would be writing the stage directions, or narrative, of the play. The relative absence of such narrative in drama makes our part in the imaging or staging of a play as we read more crucial than it is in reading fiction. How you would stage a play or a scene to bring out its full meaning and effect as you imagined it can serve as a significant topic for writing about drama. You might ask yourself such questions as, What scene or passage would I use as the best example of how the play should be read? How would I costume Oedipus in the first and last scenes to bring out the main movement and theme of the play? How can I, in the early scenes, subtly reveal that Oedipus has an injured ankle without detracting from the power and majesty of his presence at that time? In *The Cherry Orchard*'s final stage direction, Chekhov calls for "a sound . . . that seems to come from the sky, like a breaking harp-string, dying away mournfully." How, exactly, would you create this sound? How do you interpret its significance, and how would you convey that significance to the audience? *Would* you attempt to convey it?

Though you may wish to write on the theme, characters, action, imagery, or language of a play from time to time, one central element you will certainly want to write about sooner or later is the staging, or dramatization—the set, costumes, acting, moving of characters about on the stage, even lighting—and how this can enhance the effect and meaning of the play on the page.

WORDS

Some plays, like *Hamlet,* are written partly or entirely in verse. Though we may be able to make a distinction between poetry and verse, we might also say that as the term is generally used, poetry is not so much a literary genre as it is a medium. Thus we might more logically break literature down into "prose" and "poetry" rather than into "fiction," "drama," and "poetry." For besides poetic dramas like *Hamlet,* there are dramatic poems, such as Browning's "My Last Duchess" and Donne's "The Flea," poems in which a distinguishable character speaks in a definable, almost "stageable" situation. There are also narrative poems, those that tell a story through a narrator, such as "Sir Patrick Spens" or Milton's *Paradise Lost.* What these and other poems—lyrics, for example—have in common is rhythmic language (and, some people would add, highly figurative language).

All writing is embodied in words, of course, but poetry uses words most intensely, most fully. It uses not only the statements words make, what they signify or *denote,* using them with great precision; not only what words suggest or *connote,* usually with wide-ranging sensitivity and inclusiveness; but the very sounds of the words themselves. Not all poems have highly patterned or very regular meter, but almost all poetry is more highly patterned than almost any prose. Not all poems rhyme, but all extensively rhymed works are poems. So much writing about poetry concentrates on the words themselves:

some papers treat the patterns of sounds, the rhythms or rhymes; some, the precision or suggestiveness of the language; and some, the relation of sounds to shades of meaning. This is not to say that you can't write excellent papers on the themes, characters, settings of poems, or that you can't compare aspects of poems with aspects of stories or plays: the theme of Arnold's "Dover Beach" with the theme of Chekhov's "Lady with the Dog," for example, or the theme of Hughes's "Harlem (A Dream Deferred)" with that of Hansberry's *A Raisin in the Sun*. But in writing about poetry, even when discussing theme or other elements, at some point we usually concentrate on the medium itself, the sound, precision, suggestiveness of the language (see, for example, the student paper on Sharon Olds's "The Victims," in chapter 17).

SAMPLE TOPICS AND TITLES

We have been stressing, on the one hand, writing about the most characteristic elements of stories, plays, and poems—narration, dramatization, and words—and, on the other hand, writing about the elements common to all three genres, such as theme or symbol. For further hints about likely topics, you might look at the chapter headings in this book's table of contents and read the introductory material to the chapter or chapters that look most interesting or most promising for your immediate purpose. You might look, too, at the "Writing Suggestions" at the end of each chapter, the sample student papers, and the list of sample topics that follows, not so much for the topic that you will actually come to write on, but as a trigger for your own imagination and ideas.

FICTION

1. A Plotless Story about Plot: Paley's "A Conversation with My Father"
2. The Selection and Ordering of the Scenes in Cheever's "The Country Husband"
3. Voice in Erdrich's "Love Medicine"
4. Who Am I?: The Nature of the Narrator in Lessing's "Our Friend Judith"
5. The Self-Characterization of Montresor in Poe's "The Cask of Amontillado"
6. Sonny's Brother's Character in Baldwin's "Sonny's Blues"
7. Another Ending to Atwood's "Happy Endings"
8. The Image and Import of the Sea in Chekhov's "The Lady with the Dog"
9. "Only a Girl": The Theme of Munro's "Boys and Girls"

POETRY

1. Attitudes toward Authority in "Sir Patrick Spens"
2. Scene, Sequence, and Time in "Sir Patrick Spens"
3. Sir Patrick Spens as a Tragic Hero
4. Why "Facts" Are Missing in "Western Wind"
5. Birth and Death Imagery in Jarrell's "The Death of the Ball Turret Gunner"
6. Varieties of Violence in Frost's "Range-Finding"
7. The Idea of Flight in Keats's "Ode to a Nightingale"
8. Attitudes toward the Past in Robinson's "Mr. Flood's Party" and Wyatt's "They Flee from Me"
9. Satire of Distinctive American Traits in Nemerov's "Boom!," Fearing's "Dirge," and Van Duyn's "What the Motorcycle Said"

DRAMA

1. The Effect of Offstage Action in Sophocles' *Oedipus the King*
2. Rosencrantz and Guildenstern as Half-Men in Shakespeare's *Hamlet*
3. The Past Recaptured: What We Know (or Can Infer) about Blanche's Life in Williams's *A Streetcar Named Desire*
4. Varieties of Verbal Wit as a Device of Characterization in Wilde's *The Importance of Being Earnest*
5. Realistic Drama versus Comedy: Love and Marriage in Ibsen's *A Doll House* and Wilde's *The Importance of Being Earnest*
6. Staging Polonius: Language and Cliché as Guides to Gestures, Facial Expression, and Character in Shakespeare's *Hamlet*

INTERGENERIC TOPICS

1. Motivation in Lessing's "Our Friend Judith" and Rich's "Aunt Jennifer's Tigers"
2. The Power of Music in Michael Harper's "Dear John, Dear Coltrane" and August Wilson's *The Piano Lesson*
3. Francis Weed and Willy Loman: A Comparison
4. The Murderer Confesses: Browning's Duke of Ferrara and Poe's Montresor

CREATIVE TOPICS

1. The speaker in Browning's "My Last Duchess" has been charged with the murder of his last duchess. On the basis of his words in the poem, prepare a case for the prosecution.
2. Write a "reply" to the speaker of Marvell's "To His Coy Mistress," declining his invitation and picking out the flaws in his argument.
3. Write a soliloquy for Gertrude *(Hamlet)* in which she defends herself against the most serious charges made against her motives and conduct.
4. Reconstruct the events and sentiments in Arnold's "Dover Beach" as a short mood play by writing dialogue and stage directions for a scene between the speaker and the woman.
5. Retell (in poetry or prose) the story in Dickey's "Cherrylog Road" from the woman's perspective as she looks back on the experience twenty years later.
6. What would happen in your neighborhood (town, city) if one morning a very old man with enormous wings appeared?
7. Select three scenes for a one-act play called "Dressing Down."
8. Choose a story from *Reading More Fiction* that you have not read before, read to a crucial point or a pause marked by the author, and describe your expectations of how the story will develop and conclude.

DECIDING WHAT TO WRITE ABOUT

HAVING SOMETHING TO SAY

Deciding what to write about—what approach to use, which questions to ask—seems like the first step in the process of writing a paper about a work of literature. It isn't. Before that, you have to feel confident that you have something to say. If you are a beginner at this kind of writing, you will likely have deep doubts about that. Developing confidence is not, at first, easy. You may feel as if you can *never* begin and want to put off the paper forever, or you may want to plunge in fast and get it over with. Either of these approaches, though common and tempting, is a mistake. Instead, you should begin preparing for the paper as soon as possible—the moment you know you have one to write—but not hurry into the writing itself.

First, get close enough to the work to feel comfortable with it. Before you can tell anyone else about what you have read—and writing about literature is just another form of talking about literature, although a more formal and organized one—you need to "know" the work, to have a sure sense of what the work itself is like, how its parts function, what ideas it expresses, how it creates particular effects, and what your responses are. And the only way you will get to know the work is to spend time with it, reading it carefully and thoughtfully and turning it over in your mind. There is no substitute for reading, several times and with care, the work you will write about *before* you pick up a pen or sit at the keyboard. And read the *work itself,* not something *about* that work; later, your instructor may steer you to background materials or to critical readings about the work, but at first you should encounter the work alone and become aware of your own responses to it.

Begin, then, by reading, several times, the work you will write about. The first time, read it straight through at one sitting: read slowly, pausing at its natural divisions—between paragraphs or stanzas, or at the ends of scenes—to consider how you respond to the work. Later, when your knowledge of the work is more nearly complete and when you have the "feel" of the whole, you can compare your early responses with your more considered thoughts, in effect "correcting" your first impressions in whatever way seems necessary on the basis of new and better knowledge. But if you are noncommittal at first, refusing to notice what you think and feel, you will have nothing to correct, and you may cut yourself off from the most direct routes of response. Feelings are not always reliable—about literature or anything else—but they are always the first point of contact with a literary work: you feel before you think. Start with your mind open, as if it were a blank sheet of paper ready to receive an impression from what you read.

When you have finished that first reading, think about your first impressions. Think about how the work began, how it gained your interest, how it generated expectations, how its conflicts and issues were resolved, how it ended, how it made you feel from beginning to end. Write down any phrases or events that you remember especially vividly, anything you might forget. Look back at any parts that puzzled you at first. Write down in one sentence what you think the work is about. Then read it again, this time much more slowly, making notes as you go on any passages that seem especially significant and pausing over any features or passages that puzzle you. Then write a longer statement—three or four sentences—summarizing the work and suggesting more fully what it seems to be about. Try to write the kind of summary described above on pages A5–A6. If you get stuck, try brainstorming all of your ideas about the work for fifteen minutes, and then write the summary.

Stop. Do something else for a while, something as different as possible—see a movie, work on math problems, ride a bicycle, listen to music, eat a meal, take a nap. Do *not* catch up on other reading. When you return to the work and finish reading it for the third time—rapidly and straight through—write down in a sentence the most important thing you would want to tell someone else who was about to read it for the first time: not just whether you liked it or not, but what exactly you liked, how the whole thing seems to have worked.

Now you are ready to choose a topic.

CHOOSING A TOPIC

Once you are ready to choose a topic, you may already—quietly and unconsciously—have chosen one. The clue is in the last statement you wrote, for the desire to tell someone about a work of literature is a wonderful place to begin. Good papers almost always grow out of a desire to communicate. Desire is not enough—the substance (and most of the work, sentence by sentence) remains ahead of you; but desire will get you started. What you wrote down—the one thing you most wanted to say—is the issue you will write about, or is very close to it. Your statement will become, perhaps, in somewhat revised form, your thesis.

Next, you need to convert your personal feelings and desire to communicate into a sentence or two that states your purpose—into an "objective" statement about the work, a statement that will mean something to someone else. This will be your thesis. Again, you may already be further along than you realize. Look at the "summary" you wrote after your second reading. The summary will probably sound factual, objective, and general about the work; the personal statement you wrote after the third reading will be more emotional, subjective, and particular about some aspect of the work. Combining the two successfully is the key to a good paper: you need to write a persuasive elaboration and explanation of the last statement so that your reader comes to share the "objective" view of the whole work that your summary expresses. The summary you have written will, in short, be implicit in the whole essay; your total essay will suggest to your reader the wholeness of the work you are writing about, but it will do so by focusing its attention on some particular aspect of the work—on a part that leads to, or suggests, or represents the whole. You want to build the essay on the basis of your first statement, taking a firm hold on the handle you have found. The summary is your limit and guide: it reminds you of where you will come out. Any good topic ultimately leads back to the crucial perceptions involved in a summary. Ultimately, any good writing about literature leads to a full and resonant sense of the central thrust of the work, but you will find that center most effectively by discovering a pathway that particularly interests you. The best writing about literature presents a clear, well-argued thesis about a work or works and does so from the perspective of individual perception. But the thesis should clarify the central thrust of the work, helping readers to open it up more completely and more satisfyingly.

Topics often suggest themselves after a second or third reading simply because one feature or problem stands out so prominently that it almost demands to be talked about. What is real in James's "The Real Thing"? Will the love between Gurov and the lady with the dog last? Sometimes you may be lucky: your instructor may *assign* a topic instead of asking you to choose your own. At first glance, that may not seem like a good break; it often feels confining to follow specific directions or to operate within limits and rules prescribed by someone else. It may, however, save a lot of time and prevent floundering around. If your instructor assigns a topic, it almost certainly will work, will have a payoff if you approach it creatively and without resentment at being directed so closely and precisely. It is time-consuming to think through the implications of a topic and be sure it works; and an instructor's directions, especially if they are detailed and call attention to particular questions or passages, may help you focus on important issues or lead you to crucial evidence.

If your instructor does *not* give you a topic and if no topic suggests itself to you after you have read a particular work three or four times, you may sometimes have to settle for the kind of topic that will—more or less—be safe for any literary work. Some topics are almost all-purpose. You can always analyze devices of characterization in a story, showing how descriptive detail, dialogue, and the reactions of other people combine to present a particular character and evoke the reader's response to him or her; you can almost always analyze rhythm, verse form, imagery, or the connotations of key words in a poem. Such "fall-back" topics are, however, best used only as last resorts, when your instincts have failed you in a particular instance. When you have free choice you will much more likely build a lively and committed paper from a particular insight or question, something that grabs you and makes you want to say something, or solve a problem, or formulate a thesis. The best papers are usually very personal in origin; even when a topic is set by the assignment, the best papers come from a sense of having personally found an answer to a significant question. To turn a promising idea into a good paper, however, personal responses usually need to be supported by a considerable mass of evidence; the process often resembles the testing of "evidence" in a laboratory or the formulation of hypotheses and arguments in a law case. You may need to narrow your topic so that your thesis is focused and can be supported by examples from through-out the text. If your topic is too broad, your paper will likely become long, unwieldy, and overly general.

CONSIDERING YOUR AUDIENCE

Thinking of your paper as an argument or an explanation will also help with one of the most sensitive issues in writing about literature. The issue: for whom are you writing? Who is your audience? The obvious answer is your instructor, but in an important sense, that is the wrong answer. It is wrong because, although your instructor could literally be the only other person who will ever read your paper, you write about literature to learn how to write for an audience of peers, people a lot like yourself who are sensible, are educated, and appreciate having something (in this case a literary work) explained so that they will understand it more fully. Picture your ideal reader as someone about your own age and with about the same educational background. Assume the person is intelligent and has some idea of what literature is like and how it works, but that he or she has just read this particular literary work for the first time and has not yet had a chance to think about it carefully. Don't be insulting and explain the obvious, but don't assume either that your reader has noticed and considered every detail. The object is to inform and convince your reader, not to impress.

Should you, then, altogether ignore the obvious fact that an instructor—probably one with a master's degree or Ph.D. in literature—is your actual reader? Not altogether: you don't want to get so carried away with speaking to people of your own age and interests that you slip into slang, or feel the need to explain what a stanza is, or leave an allusion to a rock star unexplained, and you do want to learn from the kind of advice your instructor has given in class, or from comments he or she may have made on other papers you have written. But don't become preoccupied with the idea that you are writing for someone in "authority" or someone you need to please. Most of all, don't think of yourself as writing for a captive audience, for a reader who *has* to read what you write. It is not always easy to know exactly who your audience is or how interested your readers may be, so you have to make the most of every single word. You must get the reader's attention, and you will have to do it subtly, making conscious assumptions about what your reader already knows and what he or she can readily understand. The tone of your paper should be serious and straightforward and its attitude respectful toward the reader as well as toward the literary work. But its approach and vocabulary, while formal enough for academic writing, should be readily understandable by some-one with your own background and reading experience. And it should be lively enough to interest someone like you. Try to imagine, as your ideal reader, the person in your class whom you most respect. Write to grab, and hold, that person's serious attention. Try to communicate, to teach.

FROM TOPIC TO ROUGH DRAFT

Writing about literature is very much like talking about literature, with one important difference. When we talk, we organize as we go—trying to get a handle, experimenting, working toward an understanding. And the early stages of preparing a paper—the note-taking, the outlining, the rough drafts—can be much like that. A "finished" paper, however, has the uncertainties and tentativeness worked out and presents an argument that moves carefully and compellingly toward a conclusion. How do you move from here to there?

Once you have decided on a topic, the process of planning is fairly straightforward, but it can be time-consuming and (often) frustrating. First you gather the evidence, then you sort it into order, and finally you develop it into a convincing argument. The easiest way is to take these steps one by one.

GATHERING EVIDENCE

The first step involves accumulating evidence that supports the statement you have decided to make about your topic (that is, your thesis) and that takes you back to the text. But before you read the text again, look over the notes you have already made in the margins of that text or on separate pieces of paper. Which of them have something to do with the topic you have now defined? Which of them say something about your main point? Which ones can you now set aside as irrelevant to your topic?

Reading over the notes you have already made is a good preparation for rereading the work again, for this time as you read you will look at it in a new and specific way, searching for all the things in it that relate to your topic. This time you will, in effect, flag everything—words, phrases, structural devices, changes of tone, and so forth—that bears on your topic. As you read—very slowly and single-mindedly, with your topic always in mind—keep your pen constantly poised to mark useful points. Be ready to say something about the points as you come upon them; write down immediately any sentences that occur to you as you read. Some of these sentences will be useful when you write your paper. Some will appear in your paper, but some will not: a lot of your notes, like a lot of the footage shot in making a film, will end up on the cutting-room floor.

No one can tell you exactly how to take notes, especially because the notes you need and how you take them will depend on the particular paper you want to write. But here are five general hints toward successful notetaking:

1. Keep your topic and your thesis about your topic constantly in mind as you reread and take notes. Mark all passages in the text that bear on your topic, and for each one write on a note card a single sentence that describes how the passage relates to your topic and thesis. Add a "key" word that identifies the note at the top of the card to help you organize the cards into clusters later in the process. Then indicate, for each passage, the specific location in the text—by page or paragraph number if you are working on a story; by line number if you are writing about a poem; by act, scene, and line number (if any) if you are writing about a play. If you are working on a computer, put page breaks between each note, so that you can print one note per page.

2. Keep rereading and taking notes until one of five things happens:
   a. You get too tired and lose your concentration. (If that happens, stop and then start again later, preferably the next day.)
   b. You stop finding relevant passages or perceive a noticeable drying up of your ideas. (Again, time to pause; give the work at least one more reading later when your mind is fresh and see whether the juices start anew. If they don't, you may be ready to outline and write.)
   c. You find yourself annotating every sentence or line, and the evidence all runs together into a single blob. (If this happens, your thesis is probably too broad. Simplify and narrow it so that you don't try to include everything. Then go back to your notetaking and discriminate more carefully between what actually is important to your thesis and what only relates at some distance.)
   d. You become impatient with your notetaking and can't wait to get started writing. (Start writing. Be prepared to go back to systematic notetaking if your ideas stop coming or your energy fades. The prose passages you write this way may find a place in your paper, but they may not belong exactly where you think they do when you first write them down.)
   e. You find that the evidence is insufficient for your thesis, that it points in another direction, or that it contradicts your thesis. (Revise your topic to reflect the evidence, and begin rereading once more.)

3. When you think you have finished your notetaking, read all your note cards over slowly, one by one, and jot down any further ideas as they occur to you, each one on a separate note card. Computer users can either read the file on screen and add notes as they wish or print out all the notes and read through them on paper. (Sometimes note cards seem to beget note cards. Don't worry if you have too many notes and too much material, because too much is better than too little at the notetaking stage: you can always discard them before the final draft. But later, when you boil down to essentials, you will have to be ruthless and omit some of your favorite ideas.)

4. Transfer all of your notes to pieces of paper—or note cards—that are all the same size, one note on each. You will find it easier to sort them this way when you get ready to organize and outline. If you like to write notes in the margin of your text (or on the backs of envelopes, or on dinner napkins, or on shirtsleeves), systematically transfer every note to uniform sheets of paper or cards before you outline. Having everything easily recorded on sortable cards that you can move from one pile to another will make organizing easier later, especially when you change your mind (as you will) and decide to move a point from one part of your paper to another. Index cards—either 3" × 5", if you write small and make economical notes, or 4" × 6", if you need more space—are ideal for notetaking and sorting.

5. When you think you have finished taking notes (because you are out of ideas, or out of time, or getting beyond a manageable number of pieces of evidence), read through the whole pile one more time, again letting any new ideas—or ideas that take on a fresh look because you combine them in a new way—spawn new sentences.

How many times should you read a story, poem, or play before you stop taking notes? There is no right answer. If you have read the work three times before settling on a topic, two more readings may do. But it could take several more. Common sense, endurance, and deadlines will all have an effect on how many rereadings you do. Let your conscience, your judgment, and your clock be your guides.

ORGANIZING YOUR NOTES

The notes you have taken will become almost the whole content of your paper. In the next few hours (or days), you have to give that content the form and shape that will make it appealing and persuasive, but this is not an easy task: the best content in the world isn't worth much if it isn't effectively presented. The key is getting all your ideas into the right order—that is, into a sequence that allows them to argue your thesis most persuasively.

To put your notes into a proper order, you will need (ironically) to get a little distance from them. (Good planning and writing—like so many other pursuits—involves knowing when to back away and get some perspective.) Set your notes aside, but not too far away. On a fresh sheet of paper or in a separate document on your computer, write all the major points you want to make. Write them randomly, as they occur to you. Now read quickly through your pack of notes and add to your list any important points you have left out. Then decide which ideas should go first, which should go second, and so on.

Putting your points in order is something of a guess at this point. You may want to reorder them before you begin to write—or later, when you write a first (or second or third) draft. But make your best guess. Try out an order by taking your random list and putting a "1" in front of the point you will probably begin with, a "2" before the probable second point, and so on. Then copy the list, in numerical order, revising (if you need to) as you go; do not be surprised if later you have to revise your list further. Next, match up your notes (and the examples they contain) with the points on your outline. If you've added "key" words to the top of each card or file, you can make a "rough cut" according to these words.

Putting things in a particular order is a spatial problem, and by having your notes on cards or pieces of paper of a uniform size you can do much of your organizing physically. Work on a large table, or sit in the middle of the floor. Prepare a title card for each point in your outline, writing on it the point and its probable place in your paper, then line them up on the table or floor in order before you begin writing. If you're working on a computer, you can use the search function to find each instance of a key word, phrase, or name, and arrange your electronic "cards" under the headings on your list by blocking and moving your "cards" to new parts of the document.

Two-thirds of this exercise is quite easy: most examples and ideas you have written down will match quite easily with a particular point. Some cards will resist classification, however. Some cards will belong in two or more places; others will not belong at all. If a card belongs to more than one point, put it in the pile with the lowest number (but write on it the number or numbers of other possible locations). If, for example, a card might belong in point 2 but could also belong in point 6 or 9, put it in the pile of 2s and add the phrase "maybe 6 or 9" to the card; if you don't use it in writing about point 2, move it to pile 6; if you don't use it in 6, move it to 9. You will work your way through the piles in numerical order, so you have a safety system for notes that don't belong where you first thought but that still belong somewhere in your paper. Move them to a possible later point, or put them in a special file (marked "?" or "use in revised draft") and, once you have completed a first draft of your paper, go through this file, carefully looking for places in your paper where these ideas may belong. Almost never will everything fit neatly into your first draft. If everything seems to fit exactly as you had originally planned, you have either done an incredible job of planning and guessing about the organization of your paper, or you are forcing things into inappropriate places.

Don't be surprised if you have a large number of leftover notes—that is, ideas you haven't yet used—after you have written your first draft. You will probably find places for many of these ideas later, but some just won't fit and won't be needed for the paper you ultimately write, no matter how good the ideas are. No paper will do everything it could do. Writing a paper is a *human* project; it has limits.

Before you actually start writing, you may want to develop a more elaborate outline, incorporating your examples and including topic sentences for each paragraph, or you may wish to work from your sketchy outline and the accompanying packs of cards. Do the more detailed outline if it seems right to you, but don't delay the writing too long. You are probably ready right now, and any exercises you invent to delay writing are probably just excuses.

DEVELOPING AN ARGUMENT

Once you have decided on your major points and assembled your evidence, you have to decide how you want to present your argument and how you want to present *yourself*. What you say is, of course, more important than how you say it, but your manner of presentation can make a world of difference. Putting your evidence together effectively—in a coherent and logical order so that you satisfy your readers' curiosity and answer their questions systematically and fully—is half the task in developing a persuasive argument. The other half involves choosing a voice and tone that will make readers want to read on—and make them favorably disposed toward what you say.

The tone of your paper is the basis of your relationship with your readers. "I will be just *me*," you may say, "and write naturally." But writing is not a "natural" act, any more than swinging a tennis racket, carrying a football, or executing a pirouette is. The "me" you choose to present will be only one of several possible me's; you will project a certain mood, a certain attitude toward your subject, a certain confidence. How do you want your readers to feel about you and your argument? Being too positive can make your audience feel stupid and inadequate and can turn them into defensive, resistant readers who will rebel at your every point. Friendship with your readers is better than an adversarial relationship. Sounding like a nice person who is talking reasonably and sensibly will not be enough if you don't make sense or have nothing to say, but the right tone should make readers receptive to your content, not hostile. The rest of the job depends on the argument itself.

It has been said that all good papers should be organized in the same way:

1. Tell 'em what you're going to tell 'em.
2. Tell 'em.
3. Tell 'em what you told 'em.

That description fits—in pretty general terms—the most common kind of organization, which includes an introduction, a body of argument, and a conclusion, but if you follow it too simplistically your paper may seem simple-minded. Your beginning does need to introduce the subject, sort out the essential issues, and suggest what your perspective will be, and the conclusion does need to sum up what you have said in the main part of your paper, but the first paragraph shouldn't give *everything* away, nor should the final one simply repeat the points you've made. Lead into your subject clearly but with a little subtlety; arrange your main points in the most effective manner you can think of, building a logical argument and supporting your general points with clear textual evidence, concisely phrased and presented; and at the end *show how* your argument has added up—don't just *say* that it did.

You can organize in other ways, of course, but this basic Tell-3 method will allow you to exercise practically unlimited imagination and originality.

WRITING THE FIRST DRAFT

When you set pen to paper or fingers to keyboard, the main thing is to get started right, with a clear first sentence that expresses your sense of direction and arrests the attention of your readers. (If you can't think of a good first sentence, don't pause over it too long. Write down a paraphrase of what you want it to say—something like the statement you wrote down after your third reading—and then start writing about your main points. Your "first" sentence may sometimes be the last one you will write.) And then inch along, word by word and sentence by sentence, as you follow your outline from one paragraph to another. Keep at it. Struggle. Stare into space. Bite your pen when you feel like it. Get up and stride about the room. Scratch your head. Sharpen a pencil. Run your fingers through your hair. Groan. Snap your fingers. But keep writing.

You may feel frustrated as you search for the right word or struggle to decide how the next sentence begins, but you will feel equally satisfied when you get it right. If you become stuck, try working out your ideas on a separate piece of paper or freewriting for a while. Sometimes, working out an idea, away from your draft, can be helpful. Stay with your draft until you're reasonably satisfied with it. Breathe a sigh of relief, then put it away until tomorrow.

FROM ROUGH DRAFT TO COMPLETED PAPER

REVISING

This final stage of the process, the most important of all, is the easiest one to misman-age. A world of difference exists between a bunch of ideas that present a decent inter-pretation of a literary work and a cogent, coherent essay that stirs readers to a nod of agreement and shared pleasure in a moment of insight. If you haven't done solid literary analysis and sorted out your insights earlier, nothing you do at this stage will help much; but if you have done a satisfactory job so far, this stage can turn your paper into some-thing special.

Don't allow yourself to be too easily satisfied. If you have struggled with earlier stages, you may want to think you are finished when you have put a period to the last sentence in your first draft. Often you will feel done: drained, tired of the subject, anxious to move on to other things, such as sleep or food or friends or another project. And you should take a break once you've finished a draft; let your work settle for a few hours, preferably overnight. (The Roman poet and critic Horace suggested putting a draft aside for nine years, but most instructors won't wait that long.) Rereading it "cold" may be discouraging, though: all those sentences that felt so good when you wrote them often seem flat and stale, or even worthless, when a little time has elapsed. Your biggest struggle in moving from a first draft to a second one will be to keep from throwing what you have written into a wastebasket. You've spent a lot of time on this already, and with some more work you'll have a paper you can be proud of.

You may need *several* more drafts to produce your best work. Often you will want to cut corners—to smooth out a troublesome paragraph by obscuring the issue or by omitting the difficult point altogether instead of confronting it, or to ask a roommate or friend for help in figuring out what is wrong with a particular passage. But you will learn more in the long run—and probably do better in the short run as well—if you make yourself struggle a bit. When a particular word or phrase you have used turns out to be imprecise or misleading or ambiguous, search until you find the *right* word or phrase. (At the least put a big X in the margin so that you will come back and fix it later.) If a paragraph is incomplete or poorly organized, fill it in or reorganize it. If a transition from one point to another does not work, look again at your outline and see if another way of ordering your points would help. *Never* decide that you can best solve the problem by hoping your readers will not notice. The satisfaction of finally solving the problem will build your confidence and sooner or later make your writing easier and better.

REVIEWING YOUR WORK AND REVISING AGAIN

Precisely how you move from one draft to another is up to you and will depend on the ways you work best. However you do it, find all the things that bother you (and that *should* bother you) and then gradually correct them, moving toward a better paper with each succeeding draft. Here are some things to watch for:

Thesis and central thrust: Is your main point clear? Do you state it effectively and early? Do you make clear what the work is about? Are you fair to the spirit and emphasis of the work? Do you make clear the relationship between your thesis and the central thrust of the work? Do you explain *how* the work creates its effect rather than just asserting that it does?

Organization: Does your paper move logically from beginning to end? Does your first paragraph set up the main issue you are going to discuss and suggest the direction of your discussion? Do your paragraphs follow each other in a coherent and logical order? Does the first sentence of each paragraph accurately suggest what that paragraph will contain? Does your final paragraph draw a conclusion that follows from the body of your paper? Do you resolve the issues you say you resolve?

Use of evidence: Do you use enough examples? Too many? Does each example prove what you say it does? Do you explain each example fully enough? Are the examples sufficiently varied? Are any of them labored, or overexplained, or made to bear more weight than they can stand? Have you left out any examples useful to your thesis? Do you include any gratuitous ones just because you like them? Have you achieved a good balance between examples and generalizations?

Tone: How does your voice sound in the paper? Confident? Does it show off too much? Is it too timid or self-effacing? Do you ever sound smug? Too tentative? Too dogmatic? Would a neutral reader be put off by any of your assertions? By your way of arguing? By your choice of examples? By the language you use?

Sentences: Does each sentence read clearly and crisply? Have you rethought and rewritten any sentences you can't explain? Is the first sentence of your paper a strong, clear one likely to interest a neutral reader? Is the first sentence of each paragraph an especially vigorous one? Are your sentences varied enough? Do you avoid the passive voice and "there is/there are" sentences?

Word choice: Have you used any words whose meaning you are not sure of? In any cases in which you were not sure of what word to use, did you stay with the problem until you found the exact word? Do your metaphors and figures of speech make literal sense? Are all the idioms used correctly? Is your terminology correct? Do your key words always mean *exactly* the same things? Have you avoided repetition by varying your sentences rather than using several different terms to mean precisely the same thing?

Conciseness: Have you eliminated all the padding you put in when you didn't think your paper would be long enough? Have you gone through your paper, sentence by sentence, to eliminate all the unnecessary words and phrases? Have you looked for sentences (or even paragraphs) that essentially repeat what you have already said, then eliminated all repetition? Have you checked for multiple examples and pared down to the best and most vivid ones? Have you gotten rid of all inflated phrasing calculated to impress readers? Have you eliminated all roundabout phrases and rewritten long, complicated, or confusing sentences into shorter, clearer ones? Are *you* convinced that you have trimmed every possible bit of excess and that you cannot say what you have to say any more economically?

Punctuation and mechanics: Have you checked the syntax in each *separate* sentence? Have you checked the spelling of any words you are not sure of or that look funny? Have you confirmed the punctuation of each sentence? Have you read every quotation word by word against the original? Have you given proper credit for all material—written or oral—that you have borrowed from others? Have you followed the directions your instructor gave you for citations, notes, and form?

As you begin to revise, look first at the larger issues (your thesis, organization, and supporting evidence) to make sure you find and solve any major problems early on. Then you will be in a better position to work on your tone, sentences, choice of words, and punctuation and mechanics. In the final stages, reread through your paper looking for one problem at a time—that is, go through it once looking at paragraphing, another time looking at individual sentences, still another for word choice or problems of grammar. You cannot really check too many things too often—although you can get so absorbed with little things that you overlook larger matters. With practice, you will learn to watch carefully for the kinds of mistakes you are most prone to; everyone has individual weaknesses and flaws. Here are some of the most common stumbling blocks for beginning writers:

1. Haste. (Don't start too late, or finish too soon after you begin.)
2. Pretentiousness. (Don't use words you don't understand, tackle problems that are too big for you, or write sentences you can't explain. Aim to make sense, not a big, empty impression.)
3. Boredom. (The quickest way to bore others is to be bored yourself. If you think your paper will be a drag, you are probably right. Rather than faking interest in something you can't get excited about, keep at it until you find a spark.)
4. Randomness. (Don't string together half a dozen unrelated ideas or insights and con yourself into thinking that you have written a paper.)
5. Imprecision. (Don't settle for approximation, either in words or ideas. Being 50 percent right means being 50 percent wrong.)
6. Universalism. (Don't try to be a philosopher and make grand statements about life. Stick to what is in the work you are writing about.)
7. Vagueness. (Don't settle for a general "sense" of the work you are talking about. Get it detailed, get it right.)
8. Wandering. (Don't lose track of your subject or the work you are talking about.)
9. Sloppiness. (Don't sabotage all your hard work on analysis and writing by failing to notice misspelled words, grammatical mistakes, misquotations, incorrect citations or references, or typographical errors. Little oversights make readers suspicious.)
10. Impatience. (Don't be too anxious to get done. Enjoy the experience; savor the process. Have fun watching yourself learn.)

Being flexible—being willing to rethink your ideas and reorder your argument as you go—is crucial to success in writing, especially in writing about literature. You will find different (and better) ways to express your ideas and feelings as you struggle with revisions, and you will also find that—in the course of analyzing the work, preparing to write, writing, and rewriting—your response to the work itself will grow and shift somewhat. For one thing, you will have become more knowledgeable as a result of the time and effort you have spent, and you will have a more subtle understanding of the work. For another, the work itself will have changed. Just as a work is a little different for every reader, it is also a little different with every successive reading by the *same* reader; and you will be capturing in your words some of the work's subtlety, its capacity to produce effects that are alive and that are, therefore, always changing just slightly. Thus you need not—indeed, cannot—say the final word about the work you are writing about, though you must make your case in the best possible way.

You can turn all this into a full-time job, of course, but you needn't. It is hard work, and at first the learning seems slow and the payoff questionable. A golf novice watching the magic of Tiger Woods may find it hard to see the point of practicing putts, but even creative geniuses go through the basic steps. Those awful moments of sitting down and putting pen to paper (and then crossing out and rewriting again and again) are how you learn to make it seem easy. Art is mostly craft, and craft means methodical work.

It *will* come more easily with practice. But you needn't aspire to professional writing to take pleasure in what you accomplish. Learning to write well about literature will help you with all sorts of tasks, some of them having little to do with writing. Writing trains the mind, creates habits, teaches you procedures that will have all kinds of long-range effects that you may not immediately recognize or be able to predict. And ultimately it is very satisfying, even if it is not easy, to stand back and say, "That is mine. Those are my words. I know what I'm talking about. I understand, and I can make someone else understand."

One final bit of advice: do not follow, too rigidly or too closely, anyone's advice, including ours. We have suggested some general strategies and listed some common pitfalls. But writing is a very personal experience, and your talents (and faults) are a little different from anyone else's. Learn to play to your own strengths and avoid the weaknesses you are especially prone to. Pay attention to your instructor's comments; learn from your own mistakes.

SECONDARY SOURCES

Always form your own opinion about a story, poem, or play before consulting the opinions of others. Sometimes, however, you will want or need to read and then quote from commentary written by professional critics. These critiques and scholarly studies, called *secondary sources,* may enlarge and complement your sense and appreciation of a work, and they can provide you with valuable evidence that confirms or modifies your thesis.

You probably shouldn't consult secondary sources until you've completed the first stage of your writing (see "Stage One," page A51). Once you've written the one-paragraph "promise" of what your paper will argue and you've taken notes from the text in support of that argument, then you are prepared to read the critical materials selectively, analytically, and intelligently.

The steps involved in writing a literary research paper are nearly identical to those involved in writing a paper based on your personal response to a work, for writing a research paper involves the same careful and deliberate process of reading and reread-ing, taking notes, ordering your thoughts, writing an outline, drafting, revising, and proofreading that is involved in writing a personal response. But because a research paper uses other materials in addition to the primary text (that is, the story, poem, or play), you need to be even more precise and diligent in your notetaking, and you must take on the additional responsibility of fairly and accurately citing your sources.

FINDING SOURCES

Before you can begin reading secondary sources, you must find them. The best place to find them is, of course, the library. But where do you begin? Two types of resources in particular are especially useful: the library catalog and scholarly bibliographies.

ONLINE AND CARD CATALOGS The library catalog will guide you to books about the author and the work, but very often the titles of potentially useful books will be too general for you to determine whether or not the book covers the topic you're writing about. If your library's catalog is online, use "keyword searches" to limit the number and range of books that the computer finds. For example, if you're writing about William Faulkner's "A Rose for Emily," first limit your search to items that include "Faulkner" AND "A Rose for Emily." If you find no matches or too few, broaden your search to include all books about William Faulkner.

Most likely, the books you find through a catalog search will lead you to a section of the library where other books on the subject are filed. Even if you locate the books you were looking for right away, take a moment to browse the shelves nearby. The books on either side of your source probably cover the same topic, and they may prove even more useful than the ones you sought out.

BIBLIOGRAPHIES Scholarly bibliographies, most of which appear annually, provide comprehensive lists of scholarly books and articles published during the preceding year. In most libraries, these guides are kept in the reference area (that is, they're not available for checkout), but often they are also online. Two bibliographies in particular—*The MLA International Bibliography* and the *Readers' Guide to Periodical Literature*—are especially useful to students of literature and the humanities. When you consult bibliographies, start with the most recent year and work backward. You will find references not only to relevant books, but also to articles published in scholarly journals. Most journal articles have very specific titles, so you'll be able to see quickly which articles are most useful to you. Give yourself enough time in the library to consult journal articles; unlike books, periodicals may not be checked out on most campuses. If you don't have enough time to read these in the library, photocopy them. As you read the books and articles, check the footnotes for sources that your author, title, and word searches did not find.

USING THE INTERNET With its innumerable links and pathways, the Internet seems at first to be the perfect resource for research work. And in fact, some very good resources are available for students of literature. One in particular, called "The Voice of the Shuttle" (*http://vos.ucsb.edu/*), is a great starting point for students and scholars alike. "Voice of the Shuttle" provides links to thousands of other sites that offer valuable and interesting information on authors, genres, specific works, cultural and historical contexts, literary periods, and critical approaches. If you don't find an appropriate link at "Voice of the Shuttle," you will probably want to conduct a search using one of the commonly available "search engines"—such as Yahoo (*www.yahoo.com/*) or AltaVista (*www.altavista.com/*). Using keywords such as "Faulkner" or "poetry" in your Internet searches will lead you to hundreds of possible matches, however, so you should limit your search by creating search strings longer than one word. As you do so, read the on-screen directions carefully to make sure that your search engine treats the search string as a unit and doesn't find every mention of each individual word.

Despite the obvious benefits of the Internet, you should be cautious in your use of online sources for research for two reasons. First, although many sites provide solid information, many more provide misinformation or unsubstantiated opinion. Unlike journal articles and books, which are systematically reviewed and critiqued by scholars and other experts before being published, many Internet sources are posted without any sort of review process. (Though you can usually rely on refereed journals for information, remember that not everything in print is "true." Cross-checking and confirming sources, as good newspaper reporters do, is always a good idea.) Second, because the Internet allows you to jump from one site to another by clicking a button and to copy whole pages of text merely by "cutting and pasting," you may lose your place and be unable to provide your readers with a precise citation of your source. Make sure, therefore, to carefully note the specific address of each site you quote; and if the text you use has been taken from a printed source such as a book or magazine, note all of the particulars about that original source as well. In other words, ensure that readers can retrace your steps and check your sources. The brief guide to MLA citation formats that follows (page A48) includes examples of citations from electronic sources. If you need further information, ask your instructor about an appropriate style guide to follow.

TAKING NOTES FROM SOURCES

Taking notes from secondary sources begins with creating a "Works Cited" entry for each source you consult, either in a computer file (one page per citation) or on an index card. Here is a citation for one of the scholarly sources Willow Crystal quoted in her research paper on Faulkner's "A Rose for Emily" (chapter 11):

Sample citation note

Fetterley, Judith. "A Rose for 'A Rose for Emily.'" *The Resisting Reader: A Feminist Approach to American Fiction.* Bloomington: Indiana UP, 1978. 34–45.

You'll find guidelines for citing just about any research source in *The MLA Handbook for Writers of Research Papers,* but starting on page A49, we provide examples of some of the most common sources.

Read an article all the way through before taking notes from it. During this reading, evaluate the article's relevance to your topic. If an article doesn't apply directly to your topic but nonetheless interests you, create a brief citation of the publication information and write a one-sentence summary of the article's main argument. You will find the citation useful if you later alter your topic to include some of what's covered in this source.

Once you have read your potential sources and made a short list of those you'll use in your paper, you can begin the serious work of taking notes. Taking notes from sources involves three tasks:

1. Noting publication information for your "Works Cited" page (see above);
2. Creating a summary or outline (sometimes called a précis) of the critic's argument;
3. Directly quoting or summarizing a passage in your source.

Creating a summary of the author's argument ensures that you've understood your source and can accurately convey its sense to your reader. Once you're confident of that, you can use quotations either to support your argument or to take issue with the author's interpretation if it challenges your own.

If you're using a computer to take notes, you will be able to mingle your summary of the author's argument with direct quotations. This works especially well if you've formatted your summary in outline form: simply type the quotation along with its page reference under the appropriate heading within the outline. If you're taking notes on cards, you'll want to keep your outline separate from your quotations, and you should use only one card for each quotation. This gives you the freedom to arrange and re-arrange the quotations as necessary. Make sure, however, to bind quotations from the same source together with a paper clip or rubber band and to note the author's last name somewhere on each quotation card.

USING SOURCES IN YOUR PAPER

You use sources in your paper to provide evidence that supports your thesis or to exemplify an interpretation with which you don't completely agree. Either way, bear in mind that the sources shouldn't dominate your paper; they should flesh out and verify your thesis, as a supplement to, not a replacement for, your own interpretation. Evidence without interpretation, just as in a court of law, is not convincing in itself. Unlike the practice in law, however, merely citing "authorities" or precedents is also not sufficient.

CITING SOURCES

As you use secondary sources, through either direct quotation or summary of a critic's argument, you must signal to your reader the specific source in each case. Your instructor may have guidelines for citing sources within the body of your paper, but if not, you should follow the guidelines found in the *The MLA Handbook for Writers of Research Papers.* Here is a brief summary of the MLA's guidelines:

IN-TEXT CITATION
- If you use the author's name to introduce the material, give only the page number in parentheses.

  Example:

  As Judith Fetterley notes, "Emily, like Georgiana, is a man-made object" (35).

- If you don't use the author's name to introduce the source, put the name and page number(s) in parentheses.

  Example:

  One critic points out that "Emily, like Georgiana, is a man-made object" (Fetterley 35).

- If you cite another work by the same author elsewhere in the paper, use a title word before the page number(s).

Example:

As Judith Fetterley notes, "Emily, like Georgiana, is a man-made object" ("A Rose" 35).

- If you don't use the author's name to introduce your source and you cite another work by the same author, use both name and title with the page number(s).

Example:

One critic points out that "Emily, like Georgiana, is a man-made object" (Fetterley, "A Rose" 35).

THE "WORKS CITED" PAGE In addition, every literary research paper must include a "Works Cited" page that lists, alphabetically by author's last name, all secondary sources used in the paper. See Willow Crystal's paper on Faulkner (at the end of chapter 11) for a properly formatted "Works Cited" page. Here is a brief guide to the proper format for some of the most common sources:

A book by one author or editor:

Morgan, Kathryn A. Myth and Philosophy from the Presocratics to Plato. New York: Cambridge UP, 2000.

A book by two or three authors or editors:

Wellek, René, and Austin Warren. Theory of Literature. 3rd ed. Orlando: Harcourt, 1956.

A book by more than three authors or editors:

Greenblatt, Stephen, et al., eds. The Norton Shakespeare. New York: Norton, 1997.

or

Greenblatt, Stephen, Walter Cohen, Jean E. Howard, and Katharine Eisaman Maus. The Norton Shakespeare. New York: Norton, 1997

Editor's introduction to a book:

O'Prey, Paul. Introduction. Heart of Darkness. By Joseph Conrad. New York: Viking, 1983. 7-24.

A translated book:

Boccaccio, Giovanni. The Decameron. Trans. G. H. McWilliam. London: Penguin, 1972.

Essay or any other short work in a book:

Wihl, Gary. "Marxist Theory and Criticism." The Johns Hopkins Guide to

Literary Theory and Criticism. Ed. Michael Groden and Martin
   Kreiswirth. Baltimore: Johns Hopkins UP, 1994.

Article in a reference book:

"Gnostic." Merriam-Webster's Collegiate Dictionary. 10th ed. 1994.

Article in a newspaper:

McNulty, Charles. "All the World's a Stage Door." Village Voice 13 Feb.
   2001:69.

Article in a magazine:

Fenton, James. "Becoming Marianne Moore." New York Review of Books 24 Apr.
   1997: 40–45.

Article in a scholarly journal with continuous pagination:

(Each *volume* of a journal includes a full year of *issues.* The page numbers of some
journals begin with "1" in the first issue and run continuously through subsequent
issues—that is, issue 1 runs from page 1 to page 323, issue 2 runs from 324 to
656, and so forth.)

Dickey, Stephen. "Shakespeare's Mastiff Comedy." Shakespeare Quarterly
   42 (1991): 255–75.

Article in a scholarly journal with separate pagination for each issue:

Sosnoski, James. "The Theory Junkyard." Minnesota Review 96.41 (1996): 80–
   94.

INTERNET SOURCES Here is the general format for citing online sources:

1. Author of Web site should come first, if the name is available.
2. Title of Web site. (If author's name is not available, begin with title of site.)
3. Date site was last revised or, if that is unavailable, original publication date.

- If site is an online version of a published journal, give original publication date first
  and online publication date second.
- If no date is available, indicate with *n.d.*

4. Date site was accessed.
5. Web site address (URL).

Web site:

Padgett, John B. "William Faulkner." The Mississippi Writers Page.29 Mar.
   1999. 8 Feb. 2001 <http://www.olemiss.edu/depts/english/ms-
   writers/dir/faulkner_william/>.

A SUMMARY OF THE PROCESS

Here is a step-by-step summary of the stages we have suggested you move through in preparing a paper about literature:

Stage One: Deciding what to write about

- Read the work straight through, thoughtfully. Make notes at the end on any points that caught your attention.
- Read the work again more slowly, pausing to think through all the parts you don't understand. When you finish, write a three- or four-sentence summary.
- Read the work again, carefully but quickly. Decide what you feel most strongly about in the work. Write down the one thing you would most want to explain to a friend about how the story, poem, or play works, or (if the work still puzzles you) the one question you would most like to answer.
- Decide how the statement you made at the end of your third reading relates to the summary you wrote after the second reading.
- Write a one-paragraph "promise" of what your paper will argue.

Stage Two: Planning and drafting your paper

- Read the work at least twice more. Take notes on anything that relates to your thesis.
- Read through all your notes so far. For each, write a sentence articulating how it relates to your thesis.
- Transfer all your notes to cards of uniform size.
- Read through all your notes again. Record any new observations or ideas on additional note cards.
- Set aside your note cards for the moment. Make a brief outline of the major points you intend to make.
- Sort the note cards into piles corresponding to the major points in your outline. Sort the cards in each pile into the most likely order of their use in the paper.
- Make a more detailed outline (including the most significant examples) from your pile of note cards on each point.

- Reconsider your order of presentation; make any necessary adjustments.
- Write a first draft.

Stage Three: Rewriting

- Go over your writing, word by word, sentence by sentence, and paragraph by paragraph, in draft after draft until your paper expresses your ideas clearly and concisely.

Stage Four: Final preparation

- If you have not been working on a computer, type or word-process your paper.
- Proofread carefully for errors of all kinds—spelling, typing, and so forth.
- Proofread again. Find your mistakes before someone else does.
- Congratulate yourself on a job well done.

Glossary

Words set **boldface** within definitions are themselves defined in the glossary.

acting: the last of the four steps in **characterization** in a performed play.

action: an imagined event or series of events; an event may be verbal as well as physical, so that saying something or telling a story within the story may be an event.

allegory: as in **metaphor,** one thing (usually nonrational, abstract, religious) is implicitly spoken of in terms of something concrete, usually sensuous, but in an allegory the comparison is extended to include an entire work or large portion of a work.

alliteration: the repetition of initial consonant sounds through a sequence of words— for example, "While I nodded, nearly napping" in Edgar Allan Poe's "The Raven."

allusion: a reference—whether explicit or implicit, to history, the Bible, myth, literature, painting, music, and so on—that suggests the meaning or generalized implication of details in the story, poem, or play.

ambiguity: the use of a word or expression to mean more than one thing.

amphitheater: the design of classical Greek theaters, consisting of a stage area surrounded by a semicircle of tiered seats.

analogy: a comparison based on certain resemblances between things that are otherwise unlike.

anapestic: a metrical form in which each foot consists of two unstressed syllables followed by a stressed one.

antagonist: a neutral term for a **character** who opposes the leading male or female character. *See* **hero/heroine** and **protagonist.**

antihero: a leading **character** who is not, like a **hero,** perfect or even outstanding, but is rather ordinary and representative of the more or less average person.

archetype: a **plot** or **character** element that recurs in cultural or cross-cultural **myths** such as "the quest" or "descent into the underworld" or "scapegoat."

arena stage: a stage design in which the audience is seated all the way around the acting area; actors make their entrances and exits through the auditorium.

assonance: the repetition of vowel sounds in a sequence of words with different endings—for example, "The death of the poet was kept from his poems" in W. H. Auden's "In Memory of W. B. Yeats."

aubade: a morning song in which the coming of dawn is either celebrated or denounced as a nuisance.

auditor: someone other than the reader—a **character** within the fiction—to whom the story or "speech" is addressed.

authorial time: distinct from **plot time** and **reader time,** authorial time denotes the influence that the time in which the author was writing had upon the **conception** and **style** of the text.

ballad: a narrative poem that is, or originally was, meant to be sung. Characterized by repetition and often by a repeated refrain (recurrent phrase or series of phrases), ballads were originally a folk creation, transmitted orally from person to person and age to age.

ballad stanza: a common **stanza** form, consisting of a quatrain that alternates four-beat and three-beat lines; lines 1 and 3 are unrhymed iambic tetrameter (four beats), and lines 2 and 4 are rhymed iambic trimeter (three beats).

blank verse: the verse form most like everyday human speech, blank verse consists of unrhymed lines in iambic pentameter. Many of Shakespeare's plays are in blank verse.

canon: when applied to an individual author, *canon* (like **oeuvre**) means the sum total of works verifiably written by that author. When used generally, it means the range of works that a consensus of scholars, teachers, and readers of a particular time and culture consider "great" or "major." This second sense of the word is a matter of much debate since the literary canon in Europe and America has long been dominated by the works of white men. During the last thirty years, the canon in the United States has expanded considerably to include more women and writers from various ethnic and racial backgrounds.

casting: the third step in the creation of a **character** on the stage; deciding which actors are to play which parts.

centered (central) consciousness: a limited third-person **point of view,** one tied to a single **character** throughout the story, often revealing his or her inner thoughts but unable to read the thoughts of others.

character: (1) a fictional personage who acts, appears, or is referred to in a work; (2) a combination of a person's qualities, especially moral qualities, so that such terms as "good" and "bad," "strong" and "weak," often apply. *See* **nature** and **personality.**

characterization: the fictional or artistic presentation of a fictional personage. A term like "a good character" can, then, be ambiguous—it may mean that the personage is virtuous or that he or she is well presented regardless of his or her characteristics or moral qualities.

chorus: in classical Greek plays, a group of actors who commented on and described the **action** of a play. Members of the chorus were often masked and relied alternatively on song, dance, and recitation to make their commentary.

classical unities: as derived from Aristotle's *Poetics,* the principles of structure that require a play to have one action that occurs in one place and within one day.

climax: also called the **turning point,** the third part of **plot structure,** the point at which the **action** stops rising and begins falling or reversing.

colloquial diction: a level of language in a work that approximates the speech of ordinary people. The language used by characters in Toni Cade Bambara's "Gorilla, My Love" is a good example.

comedy: a broad category of dramatic works that are intended primarily to entertain and amuse an audience. Comedies take many different forms, but they all share three basic characteristics: (1) the values that are expressed and that typically present the conflict within the play are social and determined by the general opinion of society (as opposed to universal and beyond the control of humankind, as in **tragedy**); (2) **characters** in comedies are often defined primarily in terms of their society and their role within it; (3) comedies often end with a restoration of social order in which one or more characters take a proper social role.

conception: the first step in the creation of any work of art, but especially used to indicate the first step in the creation of a dramatic **character,** whether for written text or performed play; the original idea, when the playwright first begins to construct (or even dream about) a **plot,** the **characters,** the **structure,** or a **theme.**

conclusion: the fifth part of **plot structure,** the point at which the situation that was destabilized at the beginning of the story becomes stable once more.

concrete poetry: poetry shaped to look like an object. George Herbert's "Easter Wings," for example, is arranged to look like a pair of wings. Also called **shaped verse.**

confessional poem: a relatively recent (or recently defined) **kind** in which the speaker describes a state of mind, which becomes a **metaphor** for the larger world.

conflict: a struggle between opposing forces, such as between two people, between a person and something in nature or society, or even between two drives, impulses, or parts of the self.

connotation: what is suggested by a word, apart from what it explicitly describes. *See* **denotation.**

controlling metaphors: metaphors that dominate or organize an entire poem. In Linda Pastan's "Marks," for example, the controlling metaphor is of marks (grades) as a way of talking about the speaker's performance of roles within her family.

conventions: standard or traditional ways of saying things in literary works, employed to achieve certain expected effects.

cosmic irony: implies that a god or fate controls and toys with human actions, feelings, lives, outcomes.

criticism: the evaluative or interpretive work written by professional interpreters of texts. It is "criticism" not because it is negative or corrective, but rather because those who write criticism ask hard, analytical, crucial, or "critical" questions about the works they read.

culture: a broad and relatively indistinct term that implies a commonality of history and some cohesiveness of purpose within a group. One can speak of southern culture, for example, or urban culture, or American culture, or rock culture; at any one time, each of us belongs to a number of these cultures.

curiosity: the desire to know what is happening or has happened.

dactylic: the metrical pattern in which each foot consists of a stressed syllable followed by two unstressed ones.

denotation: a direct and specific meaning. *See* **connotation.**

descriptive structure: a textual organization determined by the requirements of describing someone or something.

diction: an author's choice of words.

discriminated occasion: the first specific event in a story, usually in the form of a specific scene.

discursive structure: a textual organization based on the form of a treatise, argument, or essay.

dramatic irony: a **plot** device in which a **character** holds a position or has an expectation that is reversed or fulfilled in a way that the character did not expect but that we, as readers or as audience members, have anticipated because our knowledge of events or individuals is more complete than the character's.

dramatic monologue: a monologue set in a specific situation and spoken to an imaginary audience.

dramatic structure: a textual organization based on a series of scenes, each of which is presented vividly and in detail.

dramatis personae: the list of **characters** that appears either in the play's program or at the top of the first page of the written play.

echo: a verbal reference that recalls a word, phrase, or sound in another text.

elegy: in classical times, any poem on any subject written in "elegiac" **meter;** since the Renaissance, usually a formal lament on the death of a particular person.

English sonnet: also called a **Shakespearean sonnet;** a **sonnet** form that divides the poem into three units of four lines each and a final unit of two lines (4+4+4+2 structure). Its classic rhyme scheme is *abab cdcd efef gg,* but variations exist.

epic: a poem that celebrates, in a continuous narrative, the achievements of mighty **heroes** and **heroines,** usually in founding a nation or developing a **culture,** and uses elevated language and a grand, high style.

epigram: originally any poem carved in stone (on tombstones, buildings, gates, and so forth), but in modern usage a very short, usually witty verse with a quick turn at the end.

existential character: a person, real or fictional, who, whatever his or her past or conditioning, can change by an act of will.

expectation: the anticipation of what is to happen next (*see* **curiosity** and **suspense**), what a **character** is like or how he or she will develop, what the **theme** or meaning of the story will prove to be, and so on.

exposition: that part of the **structure** that sets the scene, introduces and identifies **characters,** and establishes the situation at the beginning of a story or play. Additional exposition is often scattered throughout the work.

extended metaphor: a detailed and complex **metaphor** that stretches through a long section of a work.

falling action: the fourth part of **plot structure,** in which the complications of the **rising action** are untangled.

farce: a play characterized by broad humor, wild antics, and often slapstick, pratfalls, or other physical humor.

figurative: usually applied to language that uses **figures of speech.** Figurative language heightens meaning by implicitly or explicitly representing something in terms of some other thing, the assumption being that the "other thing" will be more familiar to the reader.

figures of speech: comparisons in which something is pictured or figured in other, more familiar terms.

first-person narrator: a **character,** "I," who tells the story and necessarily has a **limited point of view;** may also be an **unreliable narrator.**

flashback: a **plot-structuring** device whereby a scene from the fictional past is inserted into the fictional present or dramatized out of order.

flat character: a fictional **character,** often but not always a minor character, who is relatively simple; who is presented as having few, though sometimes dominant, traits; and who thus does not change much in the course of a story. See **round character.**

focus: the point from which people, events, and other details in a story are viewed. *See* **point of view.**

foil: one **character** that serves as a contrast to another.

formal diction: language that is lofty, dignified, and impersonal. *See* **colloquial diction** and **informal diction.**

free verse: poetry characterized by varying line lengths, lack of traditional **meter,** and nonrhyming lines.

genre: the largest category for classifying literature—fiction, poetry, drama. *See* **kind** and **subgenre.**

haiku: an unrhymed poetic form, Japanese in origin, that contains seventeen syllables arranged in three lines of five, seven, and five syllables, respectively.

hero/heroine: the leading male/female **character,** usually larger than life, sometimes almost godlike. *See* **antihero, protagonist,** and **villain.**

heroic couplet: rhymed pairs of lines in iambic pentameter.

high (verbal) comedy: humor that employs subtlety, wit, or the representation of refined life. *See* **low (physical) comedy.**

history: the imaginary people, places, chronologically arranged events that we assume exist in the world of the author's imagination, a world from which he or she chooses and arranges or rearranges the story elements.

hyperbole: overstatement characterized by exaggerated language.

iambic: a metrical form in which each foot consists of an unstressed syllable followed by a stressed one.

imagery: broadly defined, any sensory detail or evocation in a work; more narrowly, the use of **figurative** language to evoke a feeling, to call to mind an idea, or to describe an object.

imitative structure: a textual organization that mirrors as exactly as possible the structure of something that already exists as an object and can be seen.

informal diction: language that is not as lofty or impersonal as **formal diction;** similar to everyday speech. *See* **colloquial diction,** which is one variety of informal diction.

initiation story: a kind of short story in which a **character**—often but not always a child or young person—first learns a significant, usually life-changing truth about the universe, society, people, himself or herself.

in medias res: "in the midst of things"; refers to opening a story in the middle of the **action,** necessitating filling in past details by **exposition** or **flashback.**

irony: a situation or statement characterized by a significant difference between what is expected or understood and what actually happens or is meant. *See* **cosmic irony** and **dramatic irony.**

Italian sonnet: a **sonnet** form that divides the poem into one section of eight lines and a second section of six lines, usually following the *abbaabba cdecde* rhyme scheme.

kind: a species or subcategory within a **subgenre; initiation story** is a subcategory of the subgenre *short story.*

limerick: a light or humorous verse form of mainly **anapestic** verses of which the first, second, and fifth lines are of three feet; the third and fourth lines are of two feet; and the rhyme scheme is *aabba.*

limited point of view or **limited focus:** a perspective pinned to a single **character,** whether a first-person- or a third-person-centered consciousness, so that we cannot know for sure what is going on in the minds of other characters; thus, when the focal character leaves the room in a story we must go, too, and cannot know what is going on while our "eyes" or "camera" is gone. A variation on this, which generally has no name and is often lumped with the **omniscient point of view,** is the **point of view** that can wander like a camera from one character to another and close in or move back but cannot (or at least does not) get inside anyone's head, does not present from the inside any character's thoughts.

literary critics: professional "interpreters" (and often implicitly or explicitly evaluators) of literary texts.

litotes: a figure of speech that emphasizes its subject by conscious **understatement.** An example from common speech is to say "Not bad" as a form of high praise.

low (physical) comedy: humor that employs burlesque, horseplay, or the representation of unrefined life. *See* **high (verbal) comedy.**

lyric: originally, poems meant to be sung to the accompaniment of a lyre; now, any short poem in which the **speaker** expresses intense personal emotion rather than describing a narrative or dramatic situation.

major (main) characters: those **characters** whom we see and learn about the most.

meditation: a contemplation of some physical object as a way of reflecting upon some larger truth, often (but not necessarily) a spiritual one.

memory devices: also called **mnemonic devices;** these devices—including rhyme, repetitive phrasing, and **meter**—when part of the structure of a longer work, make that work easier to memorize.

message: a misleading term for **theme,** the central idea or statement of a story or area of inquiry or explanation, misleading because it suggests a simple, packaged statement that preexists and that explains the story.

metaphor: (1) one thing pictured as if it were something else, suggesting a likeness or **analogy** between them; (2) an implicit comparison or identification of one thing with another unlike itself without the use of a verbal signal. Sometimes used as a general term for **figure of speech.**

meter: the more or less regular pattern of stressed and unstressed syllables in a line of poetry. This is determined by the kind of "foot" (**iambic** and **dactylic,** for example) and by the number of feet per line (five feet=pentameter, six feet=hexameter, for example).

minor characters: those figures who fill out the story but who do not figure prominently in it.

mode: style, manner, way of proceeding, as in "tragic mode"; often used synonymously with **genre, kind,** and **subgenre.**

motif: a recurrent device, formula, or situation that deliberately connects a poem with common patterns of existing thought.

myth: like **allegory,** myth usually is symbolic and extensive, including an entire work or story. Though it no longer is necessarily specific to or pervasive in a single **culture**—individual authors may now be said to create myths—myth still seems communal or cultural, while the symbolic can often involve private or personal myths. Thus stories more or less universally shared within a culture to explain its history and traditions are frequently called myths.

narrative structure: a textual organization based on sequences of connected events usually presented in a straightforward chronological framework.

narrator: the **character** who "tells" the story.

nature: as it refers to a person—"it is his (or her) nature"—a rather old term suggesting something inborn, inherent, fixed, and thus predictable. *See* **character, personality.**

occasional poem: a poem written about or for a specific occasion, public or private.

oeuvre: the sum total of works verifiably written by an author. See **canon.**

omniscient point of view: also called **unlimited focus;** a perspective that can be seen from one **character**'s view, then another's, then another's, or can be moved in or out of any character's mind at any time. Organization in which the reader has access to the perceptions and thoughts of all the characters in the story.

onomatopoeia: a word capturing or approximating the sound of what it describes; *buzz* is a good example.

orchestra: in classical Greek theater, a semicircular area used mostly for dancing by the **chorus.**

overplot: a main **plot** in fiction or drama.

overstatement: exaggerated language; also called **hyperbole.**

oxymoron: a **figure of speech** that combines two apparently contradictory elements, as in *wise fool (sophomore)*.

parable: a short fiction that illustrates an explicit moral lesson.

paradox: a statement that seems contradictory but may actually be true, such as "That I may rise and stand, o'erthrow me" in Donne's "Batter My Heart, Three-personed God."

parody: a work that imitates another work for comic effect by exaggerating the style and changing the content of the original.

pastoral: a poem (also called an eclogue, a bucolic, or an idyll) that describes the simple life of country folk, usually shepherds who live a timeless, painless (and sheepless) life in a world full of beauty, music, and love.

pastoral play: a play that features the sort of idyllic world described in the definition for **pastoral.**

persona: the voice or figure of the author who tells and structures the story and who may or may not share the values of the actual author.

personality: that which distinguishes or individualizes a person; its qualities are judged not so much in terms of their moral value, as in **character,** but as to whether they are "pleasing" or "unpleasing."

personification (or *prosopopeia*): treating an abstraction as if it were a person by endowing it with humanlike qualities.

Petrarchan sonnet: also called **Italian sonnet;** a **sonnet** form that divides the poem into one section of eight lines and a second section of six lines, usually following the *abbaabba cdecde* rhyme scheme or, more loosely, an *abbacddc* pattern.

plot/plot structure: the arrangement of the **action.**

plot summary: a description of the arrangement of the **action** in the order in which it actually appears in a story. The term is popularly used to mean the description of the history, or chronological order, of the action as it would have appeared in reality. It is important to indicate exactly in which sense you are using the term.

plot time: the temporal setting in which the **action** takes place in a story or play.

point of view: also called **focus;** the point from which people, events, and other details in a story are viewed. This term is sometimes used to include both focus and **voice.**

precision: exactness, accuracy of language or description.

presentation: the second step in the creation of a **character** for the written text and the performed play; the representation of the character by the playwright in the words and actions specified in the text.

props: articles and objects used on the stage.

proscenium arch: an arch over the front of a stage; the proscenium serves as a "frame" for the **action** on stage.

protagonist: the main **character** in a work, who may be male or female, heroic or not heroic. *See* **antagonist, antihero,** and **hero/heroine.** *Protagonist* is the most neutral term.

protest poem: a poetic attack, usually quite direct, on allegedly unjust institutions or social injustices.

psychological realism: a modification of the concept of **realism,** or telling it like it is, which recognizes that what is real to the individual is that which he or she perceives. It is the ground for the use of the **centered consciousness,** or the first-person narrator, since both of these present reality only as something perceived by the focal **character.**

reader time: the actual time it takes a reader to read a work.

realism: the practice in literature of attempting to describe nature and life without idealization and with attention to detail.

red herring: a false lead, something that misdirects expectations.

referential: when used to describe a poem, play, or story, *referential* means making textual use of a specific historical moment or event or, more broadly, making use of external, "natural," or "actual" detail.

reflective (meditative) structure: a textual organization based on the pondering of a **subject, theme,** or event, and letting the mind play with it, skipping from one sound to another, or to related thoughts or objects as the mind receives them.

represent: to verbally depict an image so that readers can "see" it.

rhetorical trope: traditional **figure of speech,** used for specific persuasive effects.

rhythm: the modulation of weak and strong (or stressed and unstressed) elements in the flow of speech. In most poetry written before the twentieth century, rhythm was often expressed in regular, metrical forms; in prose and in **free verse,** rhythm is present but in a much less predictable and regular manner.

rising action: the second of the five parts of **plot structure,** in which events complicate the situation that existed at the beginning of a work, intensifying the **conflict** or introducing new conflict.

rite of passage: a ritual or ceremony marking an individual's passing from one stage or state to a more advanced one, or an event in one's life that seems to have such significance; a formal initiation. Rites of passage are common in **initiation stories.**

round characters: complex **characters,** often **major characters,** who can grow and change and "surprise convincingly"—that is, act in a way that you did not expect from what had gone before but now accept as possible, even probable, and "realistic."

sarcasm: a form of **verbal irony** in which apparent praise is actually harshly or bitterly critical.

satire: a literary work that holds up human failings to ridicule and censure.

scanning/scansion: *Scansion* is the process of *scanning* a poem, analyzing the verse to show its **meter,** line by line.

second-person narrator: a **character,** "you," who tells the story and necessarily has a **limited point of view;** may be seen as an extension of the reader, an external figure acting out a story, or an **auditor;** may also be an **unreliable narrator.**

selection: the process by which authors leave out some aspects of the **history** of the story or play for dramatic or thematic effect.

sestina: an elaborate verse **structure** written in **blank verse** that consists of six **stanzas** of six lines each followed by a three-line stanza. The final words of each line in the first stanza appear in variable order in the next five stanzas, and are repeated in the middle and at the end of the three lines in the final stanza, as in Elizabeth Bishop's "Sestina."

set: the design, decoration, and scenery of the stage during a play.

setting: the time and place of the **action** in a story, poem, or play.

Shakespearean sonnet: also called an **English sonnet;** a **sonnet** form that divides the poem into three units of four lines each and a final unit of two lines (4+4+4+2 structure). Its classic rhyme scheme is *abab cdcd efef gg,* but there are variations.

shaped verse: another name for **concrete poetry;** poetry that is shaped to look like an object.

simile: a direct, explicit comparison of one thing to another, usually using the words *like* or *as* to draw the connection. *See* **metaphor.**

situation: the context of the literary work's **action,** what is happening when the story, poem, or play begins.

skene: a low building in the back of the stage area in classical Greek theaters. It represented the palace or temple in front of which the **action** took place.

soliloquy: a monologue in which the **character** in a play is alone and speaking only to him- or herself.

sonnet: a fixed verse form consisting of fourteen lines usually in iambic pentameter. *See* **Italian sonnet** and **Shakespearean sonnet.**

spatial setting: the place of a poem, story, or play.

speaker: the person, not necessarily the author, who is the voice of a poem.

Spenserian stanza: a **stanza** that consists of eight lines of iambic pentameter (five feet) followed by a ninth line of iambic hexameter (six feet). The rhyme scheme is *ababbcbcc.*

stanza: a section of a poem demarcated by extra line spacing. Some distinguish between a stanza, a division markedby a single pattern of **meter** or rhyme, and a verse paragraph, a division governed by thought rather than sound pattern.

stereotype: a **characterization** based on conscious or unconscious assumptions that some one aspect—such as gender, age, ethnic or national identity, religion, occupation, marital status, and so on—is predictably accompanied by certain **character** traits, actions, even values.

stock character: a **character** that appears in a number of stories or plays, such as the cruel stepmother, the braggart, and so forth.

structure: the organization or arrangement of the various elements in a work.

style: a distinctive manner of expression; each author's style is expressed through his/ her **diction, rhythm, imagery,** and so on.

subgenre: division within the category of a **genre;** *novel, novella,* and *short story* are subgenres of the genre *fiction.*

subject: (1) the concrete and literal description of what a story is about; (2) the general or specific area of concern of a poem—also called **topic;** (3) also used in fiction commentary to denote a **character** whose inner thoughts and feelings are recounted.

subplot: another name for an **underplot;** a subordinate **plot** in fiction or drama.

suspense: the expectation of and doubt about what is going to happen next.

syllabic verse: a form in which the poet establishes a precise number of syllables to a line and repeats it in subsequent **stanzas.**

symbol: a person, place, thing, event, or pattern in a literary work that designates itself and at the same time figuratively represents or "stands for" something else. Often the thing or idea represented is more abstract, general, non- or superrational; the symbol, more concrete and particular.

symbolic poem: a poem in which the use of **symbols** is so pervasive and internally consistent that the larger referential world is distanced, if not forgotten.

syntax: the way words are put together to form phrases, clauses, and sentences.

technopaegnia: the art of "shaped" poems in which the visual force is supposed to work spiritually or magically.

temporal setting: the time of a story, poem, or play.

terza rima: a verse form consisting of three-line **stanzas** in which the second line of each stanza rhymes with the first and third of the next.

tetrameter couplet: rhymed pairs of lines that contain (in classical **iambic, trochaic,** and **anapestic** verse) four measures of two feet or (in modern English verse) four metrical feet.

theme: (1) a generalized, abstract paraphrase of the inferred central or dominant idea or concern of a work; (2) the statement a poem makes about its subject.

third-person narrator: a **character,** "he" or "she," who "tells" the story; may have either a **limited point of view** or an **omniscient point of view;** may also be an **unreliable narrator.**

thrust stage: a stage design that allows the audience to sit around three sides of the major acting area.

tone: the attitude a literary work takes toward its **subject** and **theme.**

topic: (1) the concrete and literal description of what a story is about; (2) a poem's general or specific area of concern. Also called **subject.**

tradition: an inherited, established, or customary practice.

traditional symbols: symbols that, through years of usage, have acquired an agreed-upon significance, an accepted meaning. *See* **archetype.**

tragedy: a drama in which a **character** (usually a good and noble person of high rank) is brought to a disastrous end in his or her confrontation with a superior force (fortune, the gods, social forces, universal values), but also comes to understand the meaning of his or her deeds and to accept an appropriate punishment. Often the **protagonist's** downfall is a direct result of a fatal flaw in his or her character.

trochaic: a metrical form in which each foot consists of a stressed syllable followed by an unstressed one.

turning point: the third part of **plot structure,** the point at which the **action** stops rising and begins falling or reversing. Also called **climax.**

underplot: a subordinate **plot** in fiction or drama. Also called a **subplot.**

understatement: language that avoids obvious emphasis or embellishment; **litotes** is one form of it.

unity of time: one of the three unities of drama as described by Aristotle in his *Poetics.* Unity of time refers to the limitation of a play's action to a short period—usually the time it takes to present the play or, at any rate, no longer than a day. *See* **classical unities.**

unlimited focus: also called **omniscient point of view;** a perspective that can be seen from one **character's** view, then another's, then another's, or can be moved in or out of any character's mind at any time. Organization in which the reader has access to the perceptions and thoughts of all the characters in the story.

unreliable narrator: a **speaker** or **voice** whose vision or version of the details of a story are consciously or unconsciously deceiving; such a **narrator's** version is usually subtly undermined by details in the story or the reader's general knowledge of facts outside the story. If, for example, the narrator were to tell you that Columbus was Spanish and that he discovered America in the fourteenth century when his ship the *Golden Hind* landed on the coast of Florida near present-day Gainesville, you might not trust other things he tells you.

verbal irony: a statement in which the literal meaning differs from the implicit meaning. *See* **dramatic irony.**

verse paragraph: *see* **stanza.**

villain: the one who opposes the hero and heroine—that is, the "bad guy." *See* **antagonist** and **hero/heroine.**

villanelle: a verse form consisting of nineteen lines divided into six **stanzas**—five tercets (three-line stanzas) and one quatrain (four-line stanza). The first and third lines of the first tercet rhyme, and this rhyme is repeated through each of the next four tercets and in the last two lines of the concluding quatrain. The villanelle is also known for its repetition of select lines. A good example of a twentieth-century villanelle is Dylan Thomas's "Do Not Go Gentle into That Good Night."

voice: the acknowledged or unacknowledged source of a story's words; the **speaker;** the "person" telling the story.

word order: the positioning of words in relation to one another.

Biographical Sketches

Sketches are included for all fiction writers and playwrights and for poets represented by two or more poems.

Margaret Atwood (1939–)

Margaret Atwood spent her first eleven years in sparsely populated areas of northern Ontario and Quebec, where her father worked as an entomologist. After her education at the University of Toronto and Harvard, she held various jobs in Canada, the United States, England, and Italy. Atwood published her first poem at nineteen, and she has won numerous prizes for her poetry as well as for her fiction—including the Booker Prize for her multilayered novel *The Blind Assassin* (2000). Her novels, which have become increasingly political over the years, include *The Edible Woman* (1969), *Surfacing* (1972), *Lady Oracle* (1976), *Life before Man* (1979), *Bodily Harm* (1982), *The Handmaid's Tale* (1985), *Cat's Eye* (1988), *The Robber Bride* (1993), and *Alias Grace* (1996). Many of her stories have been collected in *Dancing Girls and Other Stories* (1978), *Murder in the Dark* (1983), *Bluebeard's Egg* (1983), and *Wilderness Tips* (1991).

W. H. Auden (1907–1973)

Wystan Hugh Auden was born in York, England, to a medical officer and a nurse. Auden studied at Oxford; traveled during the 1930s in Germany, Iceland, Spain, and China; and taught at various universities in the United States, where he became a naturalized citizen in 1946. A prolific writer of poems, plays, essays, and criticism, he won the Pulitzer Prize in 1948 for his collection of poems *Age of Anxiety*. He is regarded as a masterly poet of political and intellectual conscience.

Nicholson Baker (1957–)

A bassoonist, Nicholson Baker studied at the Eastman School of Music, Haverford College, before becoming a writer. Thanks to his literary fascination with time and the minutiae of daily existence, he has been hailed as "a subatomic physicist of fiction, a quantum suburban Proust." His publications include *The Mezzanine* (1988), *Room Temperature* (1990), *U & I* (1991), *Vox* (1992), *The Fermata* (1994), *The Size of Thoughts* (1996), *The Everlasting Story of Nory* (1997), and *Double Fold: Libraries and the Assault on Paper* (2001).

James Baldwin (1924–1987)

James Baldwin was for some time a leading literary spokesman for black Americans. Born in New York City but long a resident of France, he first attracted critical attention with two extraordinary novels, *Go Tell It on the Mountain* (1953) and *Giovanni's Room* (1956), which dealt, somewhat autobiographically, with religious awakening (Baldwin was a minister at fourteen but later left his church) and the anguish of being black and homosexual in a white and heterosexual society. Baldwin was also a dramatist and an outstanding essayist, his best-known nonfiction prose being *Notes of a Native Son* (1955), *Nobody Knows My Name* (1961), and *The Fire Next Time* (1963), aimed at unraveling the repressive myths of white society and at healing the disastrous estrangement he found in the lives of black people in America. His stories are collected in *Going to Meet the Man* (1965).

Toni Cade Bambara (1939–1995)

Born in New York City, Toni Cade Bambara grew up in Harlem and Bedford-Stuyvesant, two of its poorest neighborhoods, and began writing as a child. After graduating from Queens College, she worked at various jobs while studying for her M.A. at the City College of New York, writing fiction all the while in "the predawn in-betweens." Bambara began to publish her stories in 1962. She had also been a dancer, a teacher, an editor, and a critic, and had worked in psychiatric and drug therapy, youth organizing, and settlement houses. Her work includes two anthologies, *The Black Woman* (1970) and *Stories for Black Folks* (1971), and two collections of stories, *Gorilla, My Love* (1972) and *The Sea Birds Are Still Alive* (1977). She also wrote two novels, *The Salt Eaters* (1980) and *If Blessing Comes* (1987).

Bashō (1644–1694)

Born Matsuo Munefusa, the second son of a low-ranking provincial samurai, the haiku poet who came to be known as Bashō at first put aside his literary interests and entered into service with the local ruling military house. In 1666, following the feudal lord's death, Bashō left for Edo (now Tokyo), the military capital of the shogun's new government, to pursue a career as a professional poet. He supported himself as a teacher and corrector of other people's poetry but ultimately earned a following and a sizable group of students. A seasoned traveler, Bashō maintained an austere existence on the road as well as at home, casting himself in travel narratives such as *Oku no hosomichi* (*The Narrow Road to the Interior*, 1694) as a pilgrim devoted to nature and Zen.

Ann Beattie (1947–)

Ann Beattie grew up in the Washington suburb of Chevy Chase, Maryland. She received a B.A. from American University and went on to graduate study in English at the University of Connecticut. After publishing "A Rose for Judy Garland" in 1972, she began placing stories in such magazines as *The New Yorker,* in the process becoming a kind of spokesperson for the generation that came of age in the 1960s. Many of her stories have been collected in *Distortions* (1976), *Secrets and Surprises* (1979), *Jacklighting* (1981), *The Burning House* (1982), *Where You'll Find Me* (1986), *What Was Mine: Stories* (1990), and *Park City: New and Selected Stories* (1999). Her novels are *Chilly Scenes of Winter* (1976), *Falling in Place* (1980), *Love Always* (1985), *Picturing Will* (1990), *Another You* (1995), and *My Life, Starring Dara Falcon* (1997).

Ambrose Bierce (1842–1914?)

The tenth child of a poor Ohio family, Ambrose Bierce served in the Union Army during the Civil War, rising to the rank of major. He stayed in the army for a time after the war, then was a journalist in California and London, where his boisterous western mannerisms and savage wit made him a celebrity and earned him the name "Bitter Bierce." He published two volumes of stories: *Tales of Soldiers and Civilians* (1891; later called *In the Midst of Life*) and *Can Such Things Be?* (1893). The deaths of his two sons in 1889 and 1901, along with his divorce in 1891, might well have led him to Mexico, where he reportedly rode with Pancho Villa's revolutionaries. He disappeared and is presumed to have died there. Bierce is well known as the author of *The Cynic's Wordbook* (1906; later called *The Devil's Dictionary*), but his short stories are considered his finest achievement.

Elizabeth Bishop (1911–1979)

Born in Worcester, Massachusetts, Elizabeth Bishop endured the death of her father before she was a year old and the institutionalization of her mother when she was five. Bishop was raised by her maternal grandmother in Nova Scotia, then by her paternal grandparents back in Worcester. At Vassar College she met the poet Marianne Moore, who encouraged her to give up plans for medical school and pursue the life of a poet. Bishop traveled through Canada, Europe, and South America, finally settling in Rio de Janeiro, where she lived for nearly twenty years. Her four volumes of poetry are *North and South* (1946); *A Cold Spring* (1955), which won the Pulitzer Prize; *Questions of Travel* (1965); and *Geography III* (1976), which won the National Book Critics' Circle Award. *Complete Poems 1929–1979* and *Collected Prose* gather most of her published work.

William Blake (1757–1828)

The son of a London haberdasher and his wife, William Blake studied drawing at ten and at fourteen was apprenticed to an engraver for seven years. After a first book of poems, *Poetical Sketches* (1783), he began experimenting with what he called "illuminated printing"—the words and pictures of each page were engraved in relief on copper and the printed sheets partly colored by hand—a laborious and time-consuming process that resulted in books of singular beauty, no two of which were exactly alike. His great *Songs of Innocence* (1789) and *Songs of Experience* (1794) were printed in this manner, as were his increasingly mythic and prophetic books, which include *The Marriage of Heaven and Hell* (1793), *The Four Zoas* (1803), *Milton* (1804), and *Jerusalem* (1809). Blake devoted his later life to pictorial art, illustrating *The Canterbury Tales,* the Book of Job, and *The Divine Comedy,* on which he was hard at work when he died.

Jorge Luis Borges (1899–1986)

Often considered Latin America's foremost author, Jorge Luis Borges was born and raised in Argentina, where he spoke English and Spanish. Traveling in Europe, his family was trapped in Geneva at the outbreak of World War I, and Borges attended the Collège de Genève, where he learned French, German, and Latin. Before returning to Argentina in 1921, he spent two years in Spain, where he wrote his first poems under the influence of the Ultraists, a group of young writers rebelling against the decadence of the previous generation. Credited with establishing the Ultraist movement in South America, Borges also advocated "art for art's sake," an apolitical attitude at odds with his persistent and outspoken opposition to the military dictatorship of Juan Perón. A prolific writer as well as the director of the national library of Argentina, Borges published such works as *Fervor de Buenos Aires: Poemas* (1923), *Evaristo Carriego* (1930), *Ficciones, 1935–1944* (1944), *El Aleph* (1949), *Otras Inquisiciones, 1937–1952*

(1952), *El Hacedor* (1960), *El Libro de los Seres Imaginarios* (1967), *El Informe de Brodie* (1970) and *El Libro de Arena* (1955). English-translation collections include *Labyrinths: Selected Stories and Other Writings* (1988), *Ficciones* (1989), *Collected Fictions* (1999), *Selected Non-Fictions* (1999), and *Selected Poems* (2000).

Roo Borson (1952–)

Though considered a Canadian poet, Ruth Elizabeth Borson was born in Berkeley, California. She attended the University of California at Santa Barbara and earned her B.A. from Gordon College. In 1977, she published her first book, *Landfall*, in addition to receiving her M.F.A. from the University of British Columbia, where she was awarded the Macmillan Prize for Poetry. Her work suggests what she calls the "intricacy of the physical world," and it recognizes the powers of sensuality and memory. Collections include *The Whole Night Coming Home* (1984), *Intent, or the Weight of the World* (1989), and *Water Memory* (1996).

Gwendolyn Brooks (1917–2000)

Gwendolyn Brooks was born in Topeka, Kansas, and raised in Chicago, where she began writing poetry at the age of seven, and where she graduated from Wilson Junior College in 1936. Shortly after beginning her formal study of modern poetry at Chicago's Southside Community Art Center, Brooks produced her first book of poems, *A Street in Bronzeville* (1945). With her second book, *Annie Allen* (1949), she became the first African American to win the Pulitzer Prize. Though her early work focused on what Langston Hughes called the "ordinary aspects of black life," during the mid 1960s she devoted her poetry to raising African American consciousness and to social activism. In 1968, she was named the poet laureate of Illinois; from 1985 to 1986, she served as poetry consultant to the Library of Congress. Her publications include *The Bean Eaters* (1960), *In the Mecca* (1968), *The Tiger Who Wore White Gloves; Or, What You Are You Are* (1974), and *Selected Poems* (1999).

Elizabeth Barrett Browning (1806–1861)

Elizabeth Barrett was born into a wealthy family in Durham, England, and raised in Herefordshire. She received no formal schooling, but was very well educated at home and published her first volume of poetry at the age of thirteen. Despite her status as a prominent woman of letters, deteriorating health forced Barrett to live in semiseclusion. Her collection *Poems* (1844) inspired the poet Robert Browning to write to her in May 1845, and thus began a courtship that resulted in their elopement to Italy in 1846. Following the publication of *Sonnets from the Portuguese* (1850), Barrett Browning received serious consideration to succeed Wordsworth as poet laureate (although the laureateship went to Tennyson). Her most admired work is *Aurora Leigh* (1857), a nine-book verse novel.

Robert Browning (1812–1889)

Born in London, Robert Browning attended London University but was largely self-educated. He was an aspiring but unknown poet and playwright when he began courting the already famous poet Elizabeth Barrett. After their elopement to Italy in 1846, the Brownings separately wrote most of their great poems. Robert returned to England with their son in 1861, following Elizabeth's death, and for the rest of his life enjoyed great literary and social success. His major collections are *Men and Women* (1855) and *Dramatis Personae* (1864), which contains some of his finest dramatic monologues.

Buson (1716–1784)

Born into a wealthy family in Kemu, Settsu province, Japan, Taniguchi Buson renounced a life of privilege to pursue a career in the arts. In 1751, after several years of traveling and studying under masters of haiku in northeastern Japan, he settled in Kyoto and established himself as a professional painter. Known in later life as Yosa Buson, or simply Buson, he was responsible for a revival of the work of his prominent predecessor, Bashō. In his own work, Buson was particularly attentive to visual detail and pioneered an experimental form of verse based on and incorporating Chinese poetry.

Angela Carter (1940–1992)

Born in Eastbourne, Sussex, England, Angela Carter chose to work in journalism rather than attend Oxford University, though she later studied medieval literature at the University of Bristol. Her novels include *The Magic Toyshop* (1967), *Several Perceptions* (1968), *The Infernal Desire Machines of Dr. Hoffman* (1972), *The Passion of New Eve* (1977), *Love* (1988), and *Wise Children* (1991). Her stories are collected in *Burning Your Boats* (1997). Carter's writing gained widespread popularity after the release of the film *The Company of Wolves* (1984), which was based on a story from *The Bloody Chamber* (1979), a collection of macabre and erotic retellings of fairy tales. Her chief nonfiction work is *The Sadeian Woman: An Exercise in Cultural History* (1979).

Raymond Carver (1938–1988)

Born in the logging town of Clatskanie, Oregon, to a family of the working poor, Raymond Carver married at nineteen and had two children by the time he was twenty-one. Despite these early responsibilities and a (lifelong) struggle with alcoholism, Carver published his first story in 1961 and graduated from Humboldt State College in 1963. He published his first book, a collection of poetry entitled *Near Klamath,* in 1968, and thereafter supported himself with visiting lectureships at the University of California at Berkeley and the Iowa Writer's Workshop, among other institutions. His short-story collections include *What We Talk About When We Talk About Love* (1981), *Will You Please Be Quiet, Please?* (1976), *Cathedral* (1983), *My Father's Life* (1986), and *Where I'm Calling From* (1989). His poetry is collected in *All of Us* (2000).

Helen Chasin (ca. 1940–)

Helen Chasin was born in New York and attended Radcliffe College. Her first book of poems, *Coming Close* (1968), was chosen for the Yale Series of Younger Poets. In this collection and her next, *Casting Stones* (1975), Chasin employed a compressed voice dense with meaning: many of her poems are a mere ten or fifteen lines long, yet every colloquial word and one-syllable line resonates. A student of Robert Lowell's, she has taught poetry at the University of Iowa. Most recently, Chasin served as editor for *Likeness and Unlikeness: Selected Paintings* (1997), a volume of visual art by the modern Chinese painter and poet Qi Baishi.

John Cheever (1912–1982)

John Cheever was born in Quincy, Massachusetts. His formal education ended when he was expelled from Thayer Academy at seventeen; thereafter he devoted himself to fiction writing, except for brief interludes of teaching at Barnard College and the University of Iowa and of writing scripts for television. Cheever published his first story when he was sixteen, and until his first novel, *The Wapshot Chronicle*, won the National Book Award in 1958, he was known primarily as a prolific writer of superb short stories. Built around a strong moral core and tinged with melancholy nostalgia for the past, his stories form a running commentary on the tensions, manners, and crippled aspirations of urban and suburban life. Collections include *The Way Some People Live* (1943), *The Enormous Radio* (1953), and *The Stories of John Cheever* (1978), which won the Pulitzer Prize.

Anton Chekhov (1860–1904)

The son of a grocer and the grandson of an emancipated serf, Anton Chekhov was born in the Russian town of Taganrog. In 1875, his father, facing bankruptcy and imprisonment, fled to Moscow; shortly after, the rest of the family lost their house to a former friend and lodger from the bureaucratic class, a situation that Chekhov would revisit in his play *The Cherry Orchard*. In 1884, Chekhov received his M.D. from the University of Moscow; in the early 1890s, he purchased an estate near Moscow and became both an industrious landowner and doctor to the local peasants. After contributing stories to magazines and journals throughout the 1880s, he began writing for the stage in 1887. His plays were generally ill-received in his lifetime: *The Wood Demon* (later rewritten as *Uncle Vanya*) was performed only a few times in 1889 before closing, while the 1896 premiere of *The Seagull* turned into a riot when an audience expecting comedy was confronted with an experimental tragedy. Konstantin Stanislavsky, director at the Moscow Art Theater, helped restore Chekhov's reputation with successful productions of *The Seagull* and *Uncle Vanya* in 1899 and *The Cherry Orchard* in 1904.

Kate Chopin (1850–1904)

Katherine O'Flaherty was born in St. Louis, Missouri, to a family that enjoyed a high place in society. Her father died when she was four, and Kate was raised by her mother, grandmother, and great-grandmother. Very well read at a young age, she received her formal education at the St. Louis Academy of the Sacred Heart. In 1870, she married Oscar Chopin and moved with him to Louisiana. Following her husband's sudden death, in 1884, she returned to St. Louis, where she raised her six children and began her literary career. In slightly more than a decade she produced a substantial body of work, including the story collections *Bayou Folk* (1894) and *A Night in Acadie* (1897) and the classic novel *The Awakening* (1899).

Samuel Taylor Coleridge (1772–1834)

Born in the small town of Ottery St. Mary in rural Devonshire, England, Samuel Taylor Coleridge was one of the greatest and most original of the nineteenth-century Romantic poets. He wrote three of the most haunting poems in the English tradition—*The Rime of the Ancient Mariner* (1798), *Christabel* (1816), and *Kubla Khan* (1816)—as well as immensely influential literary criticism and a revolutionary treatise on biology, *Hints towards the Formation of a More Comprehensive Theory of Life*. In 1795, in the midst of a failed experiment to establish a "Pantisocracy" (his form of ideal community), he met William Wordsworth, and in 1798 they published together their *Lyrical Ballads*, which influenced the course of English Romanticism for decades. Coleridge's physical ailments, addiction to opium, and profound sense of despair have to this day shaped our sense of the poet suffering for the sake of art.

Richard Connell (1893–1949)

A native of Poughkeepsie, New York, Richard Connell began his writing career as a journalist. At sixteen, he was city editor of the *Poughkeepsie News-Press;* later, he was editor of both the *Crimson* and the *Lampoon* at Harvard, from which he graduated in 1915. After leaving his New York job as an advertising editor to become a freelance writer, Connell traveled to Paris and London and finally settled in Beverly Hills, California. His works include the short-story collections *Apes and Angels* (1924), *The Sin of Monsieur Pettipon* (1925), *Variety* (1925), and *Ironies* (1930) and the novels *Mad Lover* (1927), *Murder at Sea* (1929), *Playboy* (1936), and *What Ho!* (1937).

Joseph Conrad (1857–1924)

Jozeph Teodor Konrad Nalecz Korzeniowski was born in Berdyczew, Polish Ukraine. At five, he accompanied his parents into exile in northern Russia and later near Kiev; he was left an orphan at eleven. Before he was seventeen, he was off to Marseilles, making several trips to the West Indies as an apprentice seaman. After some troubles in France involving gambling debts and an apparent suicide attempt, he sailed on a British ship, landed in England in 1878, and spent the next sixteen years in the British merchant service, rising to master in 1886, the year he became a British subject. In 1890, he worked on a boat that sailed up the Congo, a trip that inspired his novel *Heart of Darkness* (1899). Although he began writing in 1889, he did not publish his first novel, *Almayer's Folly,* until 1896, and was not truly popular or financially independent until the publication of *Chance* in 1912–13. Among his major novels are *The Nigger of the "Narcissus"* (1897), *Lord Jim* (1900), *Nostromo* (1904), *Under Western Eyes* (1910), and *Victory* (1915). His short-story collections include *Tales of Unrest* (1898), *Typhoon* (1903), *'Twixt Land and Sea* (1912), and *Within the Tides: Tales* (1915).

Stephen Crane (1871–1900)

Stephen Crane was one of fourteen children, and his family moved frequently before settling, after his father's death in 1880, in Asbury Park, New Jersey. Crane sporadically attended different preparatory schools and colleges, without excelling in much besides baseball. During his teenage years he became interested in journalism, and he left school for the last time in 1891 and began contributing pieces to New York newspapers. His city experiences led him to write *Maggie: A Girl of the Streets,* a realist social-reform novel published in 1893 at his own expense. His most famous novel, *The Red Badge of Courage* (1895), presented a stark picture of the Civil War. Crane later reported on the Cuban insurrection, the Greco-Turkish War, and the Spanish-American War. Suffering from tuberculosis, he eventually settled in England. Many of his stories were published in the collections *The Open Boat and Other Tales of Adventure* (1898) and *The Monster and Other Stories* (1899).

E. E. Cummings (1894–1962)

Born in Cambridge, Massachusetts, the son of a Congregationalist minister, Edward Estlin Cummings attended Harvard University, where he wrote poetry in the Pre-Raphaelite and Metaphysical traditions. He joined the ambulance corps in France the day after the United States entered World War I and was imprisoned by his own side for his outspoken letters and disdain for bureaucracy; he transmuted the experience into his first literary success, the novel *The Enormous Room* (1922). After the war, Cummings established himself as a poet and artist in Greenwich Village, made frequent trips to France and New Hampshire, and showed little interest in wealth or his growing celebrity. His variety of modernism was distinguished by its playfulness, its formal experimentation, its lyrical directness, and above all its celebration of the individual against mass society. His poetry is collected in *Complete Poems 1904–62* (1991).

James Dickey (1923–1997)

James Dickey did not become seriously interested in poetry until he joined the Air Force in 1942. When he returned from World War II, he earned a B.A. and an M.A. at Vanderbilt University, publishing his first poem in *Sewanee Review* in his senior year. Following the publication of his first book of poems, *Into the Stone* (1960), Dickey, while primarily a poet, engaged in diverse careers ranging from advertising writer and novelist to poetry teacher at various universities. His 1965 collection, *Buckdancer's Choice*, received the National Book Award, and from 1967 to 1969 Dickey was consultant in poetry to the Library of Congress. He is more popularly known for his best-selling novel, *Deliverance* (1970), which he later adapted for Hollywood. Other publications include *The Whole Motion: Collected Poems 1949–1992* (1992) and a novel, *To the White Sea* (1993).

Emily Dickinson (1830–1886)

From childhood on, Emily Dickinson's life was sequestered and obscure. Yet her verse had a power and influence that has traveled far beyond the cultured yet relatively circumscribed environment in which she lived: her room, her father's house, her family, a few close friends, and the small town of Amherst, Massachusetts. Indeed, along with Walt Whitman, her far more public contemporary, she all but invented American poetry. Born in Amherst, the daughter of a respected lawyer and revered father ("His heart was pure and terrible," she once wrote), Dickinson studied for less than a year at the Mount Holyoke Female Seminary, returning permanently to Amherst. In later life she became more and more of a recluse, dressing in white, seeing no visitors, yet working without stint at her poems—nearly eighteen hundred in all, only a few of which were published during her lifetime.

John Donne (1572–1631)

The first and greatest of what came to be known as the Metaphysical poets, John Donne wrote in a revolutionary style that combined highly intellectual conceits with complex, compressed phrasing. Born into an old Roman Catholic family at a time when Catholics were subject to constant harassment, Donne quietly abandoned his religion and had a brilliant early career until a politically disastrous marriage ruined his worldly hopes and forced him to struggle for years to support a large and growing family; impoverished and despairing, he even wrote a treatise (*Biathanatos*) on the lawfulness of suicide. King James (who had ambitions for him as a preacher) eventually forced Donne to take Anglican orders in 1615, and indeed he became one of the great sermonizers of his day, rising to dean of St. Paul's Cathedral in 1621. Donne's private devotions were published in 1624, and he continued to write sacred poetry until a few years before his death.

Rita Dove (1952–)

A native of Akron, Ohio, Rita Dove attended Miami University in Ohio, studied for a year in West Germany as a Fulbright scholar, and received an M.F.A. in creative writing from the University of Iowa. She taught creative writing at Arizona State University and is now a professor of English at the University of Virginia as well as associate editor of *Callaloo,* a journal of African American arts and letters. In 1987, Dove became the second African American poet (after Gwendolyn Brooks, in 1950) to win the Pulitzer Prize (for *Thomas and Beulah*). In 1993, she was appointed poet laureate of the United States. Her books include *The Yellow House on the Corner* (1980), *Museum* (1983), *Grace Notes* (1989), *Mother Love* (1995), and *On the Bus with Rosa Parks* (1999). She is the editor of *The Best American Poetry 2000.*

Paul Laurence Dunbar (1872–1906)

Paul Laurence Dunbar was born the son of former slaves in Dayton, Ohio. He attended a white high school, where he showed an early talent for writing and was elected class president, but was employed as an elevator operator after being unable to fund further education. Writing poems and newspaper articles when he could find the time, Dunbar took out a loan to subsidize the printing of his first book, *Oak and Ivy* (1893). With the publication of *Majors and Minors* (1895) and *Lyrics of Lowly Life* (1896), his reputation as a poet grew, and he was able to support himself by writing and lecturing in the United States and England. Acclaimed during his lifetime for his lyrical use of black dialect and his tributes to the experiences of rural blacks in volumes such as *Candle-Lightin' Time* (1902) and *Lyrics of Sunshine and Shadow* (1905), Dunbar was later criticized for adopting white literary conventions and frequently pandering to racist images of slaves and ex-slaves. The author of four novels and four books of short stories in addition to collections of poetry, he wrote frankly about racial injustice in works such as *The Sport of the Gods* (1903) and *The Fourth of July and Race Outrages* (1903).

James A. Emanuel (1921–)

Raised in Nebraska, James A. Emanuel spent the 1950s and early 1960s solidifying an academic career: he earned a B.A. from Howard University, an M.A. from Northwestern, and a Ph.D. from Columbia, then became an assistant professor of English at the City College of New York. As the 1960s passed, Emanuel became increasingly committed to reading and writing practices grounded in consciousness of his own racial identity, and he began to write poetry as well as literary criticism. His collections include *The Treehouse and Other Poems* (1968), *Panther Man* (1970), *Black Man Abroad: The Toulouse Poems* (1978), *A Chisel in the Dark: Poems Selected and New* (1980), *The Broken Bowl: New and Uncollected Poems* (1983), *Deadly James and Other Poems* (1987), *Whole Grain: Collected Poems 1958–1989* (1991), and *Jazz: From the Haiku King* (1999). For many years, he has lived in Paris.

Louise Erdrich (1954–)

Born in Minnesota of German-American and French-Chippewa descent, Louise Erdrich grew up in Wahpeton, North Dakota, as a member of the Turtle Mountain Band of Chippewa. She attended Dartmouth College and received an M.F.A. in creative writing from Johns Hopkins University. Her first novel, *Love Medicine* (1984), a collection of linked stories, won the National Book Critics Circle Award. Her subsequent publications, including *The Beet Queen* (1986), *Tracks* (1988), *The Bingo Palace* (1993), and *Tales of Burning Love* (1996), continued to tell stories from the lives of Native American characters in contemporary North Dakota. In 1991, she jointly authored the best-selling novel *The Crown of Columbus* with her husband, Michael Dorris; that year, their eldest child was killed in a car accident. Erdrich and Dorris separated in 1995, Dorris committed suicide two years later, and Erdrich's novel *The Antelope Wife* (1998) is dedicated to him. Her most recent novel is *The Last Report on the Miracles at Little No Horse* (2001).

William Faulkner (1897–1962)

William Faulkner spent most of his life in his native state of Mississippi, though he spent time in Hollywood (writing a screenplay for *The Big Sleep*, among other films) and lived his last years in Charlottesville, Virginia. He left high school without graduating, joined the Royal Canadian Air Force in 1918, and in the mid-1920s lived briefly in New Orleans, where he was encouraged as a writer by Sherwood Anderson. He then spent a few miserable months as a clerk in a New York bookstore; published a collection of poems, *The Marble Faun*, in 1924; and took a long walking tour of Europe in 1925. With the publication of *Sartoris* in 1929, Faulkner began a cycle of works interrelated by his fictional Yoknapatawpha County and the reappearance of characters or families from work to work. These include *The Sound and the Fury* (1929), *As I Lay Dying* (1930), *Light in August* (1932), *Absalom, Absalom!* (1936), *The Hamlet* (1940), and *Go Down, Moses* (1942). His short fiction can be found in *The Collected Stories of William Faulkner* (1950). He received the Nobel Prize for Literature in 1950.

David Ferry (1924–)

Born in Orange, New Jersey, David Ferry received a B.A. from Amherst College and both an M.A. and a Ph.D. from Harvard. A professor of English at Wellesley College, he has published acclaimed translations: *Gilgamesh* (1992), *The Odes of Horace* (1997), *The Eclogues of Virgil* (1999), and *The Epistles of Horace* (2001). His own poetry, informed by his multilingual scholarship, has been published in such collections as *On the Way to the Island* (1960), *A Letter and Some Photographs: A Group of Poems* (1981), *Strangers: A Book of Poems* (1983), *Dwelling Places: Poems and Translations* (1993), and *Of No Country I Know: New and Selected Poems and Translations* (1999), which won the 2000 Lenore Marshall Prize.

Timothy Findley (1930–)

A Toronto native, Timothy Findley was a student of dance and drama and a successful Shakespearean actor before the publication of his first short story convinced him to concentrate on writing fiction. Although his first two novels, *The Last of the Crazy People* (1967) and *The Butterfly Plague* (1969) were rejected by Canadian publishers and eventually published in Britain, Findley's third work, *The Wars* (1977), received critical acclaim and established his reputation in Canada. In addition to novels such as *Famous Last Words* (1981), *Not Wanted on the Voyage* (1985), *The Telling of Lies: A Mystery* (1987), *Headhunter* (1993), and *The Piano Man's Daughter* (1995), Findley has published *You Went Away* (1996), a novella; two volumes of personal and literary memoirs; several collections of short fiction; and numerous scripts, screenplays, and plays. His most recent novel is *Pilgrim* (1999).

Robert Frost (1874–1963)

Though his poetry forever identifies Frost with rural New England, he was born and lived to the age of eleven in San Francisco. Coming to New England after his father's death, Frost studied classics in high school, entered and dropped out of both Dartmouth and Harvard, and spent difficult years as an unrecognized poet before his first book, *A Boy's Will* (1913), was accepted and published in England. Frost's character was full of contradiction—he held "that we get forward as much by hating as by loving"—yet by the end of his long life he was one of the most honored poets of his time. In 1961, two years before his death, he was invited to read a poem at John F. Kennedy's presidential inauguration ceremony. His poems are collected in *The Poetry of Robert Frost* (1969).

Gabriel García Márquez (1928–)

Born in Aracataca, a remote town in Magdalena province near the Caribbean coast of Colombia, Gabriel García Márquez studied law at the University of Bogotá and then worked as a journalist in Latin America, Europe, and the United States. In 1967, he took up permanent residence in Barcelona, Spain. His first published book, *Leaf Storm* (1955, translated 1972), is set in the fictional small town of Macondo and is based on the myths and legends of his childhood home. His most famous novel, *One Hundred Years of Solitude* (1967, translated 1970), presents six generations of one family in Macondo, fusing magic, reality, fable, and fantasy in a way that also allows the town to serve as a microcosm of many of the social, political, and economic problems of Latin America. Among his works are *The Autumn of the Patriarch* (1975, translated 1976), *Innocent Eréndira and Other Stories* (1972, translated 1978), *Chronicle of a Death Foretold* (1981, translated 1982), *Love in the Time of Cholera* (1987, translated 1988), and *Of Love and Other Demons* (1994, translated 1995). He won the Nobel Prize for Literature in 1982.

Charlotte Perkins Gilman (1860–1935)

Charlotte Anna Perkins was born in Hartford, Connecticut. After a painful, lonely childhood and several years of supporting herself as a governess, art teacher, and designer of greeting cards, Perkins married the artist Charles Stetson. Following several extended periods of depression, she was put by her husband into the hands of Dr. S. Weir Mitchell, who "sent me home with the solemn advice to 'live as domestic a life as . . . possible,' to 'have but two hours' intellectual life a day,' and 'never to touch pen, brush, or pencil again' as long as I lived." Three months of this, ending "near the borderline of utter mortal ruin," became the inspiration for "The Yellow Wallpaper." In 1900, she married George Houghton Gilman, having divorced Stetson in 1892. Her nonfiction works, which placed her at the center of the early women's movement, include *Women and Economics* (1898) and *Man-Made World* (1911). She also wrote several utopian novels, including *Moving the Mountain* (1911) and *Herland* (1915).

Allen Ginsberg (1926–1997)

After a childhood in Paterson, New Jersey, overshadowed by his mother's severe mental illness, Allen Ginsberg enrolled at Columbia University, intent upon following his father's advice and becoming a labor lawyer. He soon befriended fellow students Lucien Carr and Jack Kerouac, as well as locals William S. Burroughs and Neal Cassady, and with them he developed an alternative lifestyle and literary vision. After graduating from Columbia in 1948, Ginsberg joined a burgeoning poetry movement in San Francisco. In 1956, he published *Howl and Other Poems,* with an introduction by his mentor William Carlos Williams. The title poem, which condemned bourgeois culture and celebrated the emerging counterculture, became a manifesto for the Beat movement and catapulted Ginsberg to fame. Deeply involved in radical politics and Eastern spiritualism, Ginsberg wrote such prose works as *Declaration of Independence for Dr.*

Timothy Leary (1971) in addition to numerous volumes of poetry, including *Kaddish and Other Poems* (1961), *Reality Sandwiches* (1963), *Planet News, 1961–1967* (1968), *The Fall of America, Poems of These States, 1965–1971* (1973), and *White Shroud: Poems, 1980–1985* (1986). His *Collected Poems, 1947–1980* appeared in 1984; *Selected Poems 1947–1995*, in 1996.

Susan Glaspell (1876–1948)

Born and raised in Davenport, Iowa, Susan Glaspell graduated from Drake University and worked on the staff of the *Des Moines Daily News* until her stories began appearing in magazines such as *Harper's* and the *Ladies' Home Journal*. In 1911, Glaspell moved to New York City, where, two years later, she married the theater director George Cram Cook. In 1915, they founded the Provincetown Playhouse on Cape Cod, an extraordinary gathering of actors, directors, and playwrights, including Eugene O'Neill, Edna St. Vincent Millay, and John Reed. Glaspell spent the last part of her life in Provincetown, devoting herself to writing fiction; among her books are *Visioning* (1911), *Lifted Masks: Stories* (1912), *Fidelity* (1915), and *The Morning Is Near Us* (1940). Her plays include *The Verge* (1921), *Bernice* (1924), and *Alison's House* (1930).

Thom Gunn (1929–)

With the irony that characterizes much of his poetry, Thom Gunn once claimed, "I am a completely anonymous person—my life contains no events, and I lack any visible personality." Nevertheless, Gunn has impressed himself on American poetry, having produced more than thirty volumes and having won the Lenore Marshall Prize for *The Man with Night Sweats* (1992). He has lived and worked in California for many years, although he was born and educated in England, earning by 1958 both a B.A. and an M.A. from Trinity College, Cambridge. His work combines a refined appreciation for formal tradition with frank treatments of such subjects as homosexuality and hallucinogens. Many of his best pieces can be found in selective editions, which include *Selected Poems 1950–1975* (1979) and *Collected Poems* (1994). His latest collection is *Boss Cupid* (2000).

Lorraine Hansberry (1930–1965)

The first African American woman to have a play produced on Broadway, Lorraine Hansberry was born in Chicago to a prominent family and showed an interest in writing from a young age. She attended the University of Wisconsin, the Art Institute of Chicago, and Roosevelt University, then moved to New York City, where she continued to concentrate on her writing. After extensive fund-raising, Hansberry's play *A Raisin in the Sun* (loosely based on events involving her own family) opened in 1959 at the Ethel Barrymore Theatre on Broadway, received critical acclaim, and won the New York Drama Critics' Circle Award for Best Play of the Year. Hansberry's second production, *The Sign in Sidney Brustein's Window*, had a short run on Broadway in 1964. Shortly after, Hansberry lost her battle with cancer. *To Be Young, Gifted, and Black*, adapted from her writing, was produced Off Broadway in 1969 and published the next year, when her drama *Les Blancs* was also produced.

Thomas Hardy (1840–1928)

In a preface dated 1901, Thomas Hardy called his poems "unadjusted impressions," which nevertheless might, by "humbly recording diverse readings of phenomena as they are forced upon us by chance and change," lead to a philosophy. Indeed, though he was essentially retrospective in his outlook, Hardy anticipated the concerns of modern poetry by treating the craft as an awkward, often skeptical means of penetrating the facade of language. Born at Upper Bockhampton in Dorset, England, the son of a master mason and his wife, Hardy began to write while in the midst of an architectural career. After a long and successful career as a novelist, he turned exclusively to poetry; he died while preparing his last book, *Winter Words* (1929), for publication. His major novels include *Far from the Madding Crowd* (1887) and *Tess of the D'Urbervilles* (1891); his poems have been selected and collected in various editions.

Nathaniel Hawthorne (1804–1864)

Nathaniel Hawthorne was born in Salem, Massachusetts, a descendant of Puritan immigrants; one ancestor had been a judge in the Salem witchcraft trials. Educated at Bowdoin College, he was agonizingly slow in winning acclaim for his work, and supported himself from time to time in government service—working in the customhouses of Boston and Salem and serving as the United States consul in Liverpool. His early collections of stories, *Twice-Told Tales* (1837) and *Mosses from an Old Manse* (1846), did not sell well, and it was not until the publication of his most famous novel, *The Scarlet Letter* (1850), that his fame spread beyond a discerning few. His other novels include *The House of the Seven Gables* (1851) and *The Blithedale Romance* (1852).

Robert Hayden (1913–1980)

Robert Hayden was born Asa Bundy Sheffey, in Detroit, Michigan, and raised by foster parents in a Detroit ghetto. He studied at Detroit City College (later Wayne State University), but left in 1936 to work for the Federal Writers' Project, where he researched black history and folk culture. He received an M.A. from the University of Michigan, taught at Fisk University from 1949 until 1969, and then taught at Michigan until his retirement. Although he published ten volumes of poetry, he did not receive acclaim until late in life. His collections include *Heart-Shape in the Dust* (1940), *The Lion and the Archer, Figures of Time* (1955), *A Ballad of Remembrance* (1962), *Selected Poems* (1966), *Words in the Mourning Time* (1970), *Night-Blooming Cereus* (1972), *Angle of Ascent* (1975), *American Journal* (1978 and 1982), and *Collected Poems* (1985).

Lillian Hellman (1905–1984)

Born into a Jewish family in New Orleans, Lillian Hellman was raised in New York and Louisiana. She attended New York and Columbia universities and briefly worked in publishing before writing short stories and reviewing books; in the early 1930s she read scripts for MGM in Hollywood. As a playwright she first gained success with *The Children's Hour* (1934), which ran on Broadway for nearly seven hundred performances, though its follow-up, *Days to Come* (1936), failed; her best-known work is *The Little Foxes* (1939). In 1952, called to appear before the House of Representatives Committee on Un-American Activities, Hellman refused to inform on other writers, and as a result she was blacklisted until the 1960s. During this time she taught writing at New York University, Yale, Harvard, and the Massachusetts Institute of Technology. After the death of her longtime companion, writer Dashiell Hammett, Hellman began work on her memoirs, which were published in three volumes: *An Unfinished Woman* (1969), *Pentimento* (1973), and *Scoundrel Time* (1976).

Ernest Hemingway (1899–1961)

Born in Oak Park, Illinois, Ernest Hemingway became a reporter after graduating from high school. During World War I, he served as an ambulance-service volunteer in France and an infantryman in Italy, where he was wounded and decorated for valor. After the war, he lived for a time in Paris, working as a journalist, polishing his writing, and socializing with American expatriates such as Gertrude Stein and F. Scott Fitzgerald. Two volumes of stories, *In Our Time* (1925) and *Death in the Afternoon* (1932), and two major novels, *The Sun Also Rises* (1926) and *A Farewell to Arms* (1929), established his international reputation. Hemingway later helped the Loyalists in the Spanish Civil War—the subject of *For Whom the Bell Tolls* (1940)—served as a war correspondent during World War II, and from 1950 until his death lived in Cuba. His novel *The Old Man and the Sea* (1952) won a Pulitzer Prize, and Hemingway was awarded the Nobel Prize for Literature in 1954. He committed suicide.

George Herbert (1593–1633)

After the early death of his Welsh father, George Herbert was raised by his mother, a literary patron of John Donne. Herbert graduated with honors from Cambridge and was subsequently elected public orator at the university. He twice served as a member of Parliament in the 1620s, but his political career never flourished. Instead, he began to work for the church in 1626, married, and took holy orders in 1630. While living in Bemerton, he became known as "Holy Mr. Herbert" for his diligent care of the members of his ministry. He died of consumption, and his most famous poetry collection, *The Temple* (1633), was published posthumously by a friend.

Robert Herrick (1591–1674)

The son of a London goldsmith and his wife, Robert Herrick would have liked nothing better than to live a life of leisured study, discussing literature and drinking sack with his hero, Ben Jonson. For a number of reasons, though, he took religious orders and moved to a parish in Devonshire. Herrick eventually made himself at home there, inventing dozens of imaginary mistresses with exotic names and practicing, half-seriously, his own peculiar form of paganism. When the Puritans came to power, Herrick was driven from his post to London, where in 1648 he published a volume of over fourteen hundred poems with two titles, *Hesperides* for the secular poems and *Noble Numbers* for those with sacred subjects. Though they did not survive the harsh atmosphere of Puritanism and were virtually forgotten until the nineteenth century, Herrick was eventually restored to his post in Devonshire, where he lived out his last years quietly.

Spencer Holst (1926–)

A legendary New York storyteller, well known in the literary underground, Spencer Holst has published his short stories and poetry in numerous periodicals. He has translated the work of German poet Vera Lachmann, and his own books include *The Language of Cats and Other Stories* (1971); *Spencer Holst Stories* (1976), a collection of humorous fables that play with reality and fantasy; *The Zebra Storyteller: Collected Stories* (1997); and *Brilliant Silence* (2000).

Gerard Manley Hopkins (1844–1889)

Born the eldest of eight children of a marine-insurance adjuster and his wife, Gerard Manley Hopkins attended Oxford, where his ambition was to become a painter—until he was converted to Catholicism. He taught for a time, decided to become a Jesuit, burnt all his early poetry as too worldly, and was ordained in 1877. Near the end of his life, Hopkins was appointed professor of Greek at University College, Dublin. Out of place and miserable, he died there of typhoid. His verse, in all its superbly controlled tension, strong rhythm, and sheer exuberance, has been championed by a number of modern poets—yet he made few attempts to publish what many of his contemporaries found nearly incomprehensible, and he was all but unknown until long after his death.

Langston Hughes (1902–1967)

Born in Joplin, Missouri, Langston Hughes was raised mainly by his maternal grandmother, though he lived intermittently with each of his parents. He studied at Columbia University, but left to travel and work at various jobs. Having already published poems in periodicals, anthologies, and his own first collection, *The Weary Blues* (1926), he graduated from Lincoln University; published a successful novel, *Not without Laughter* (1930); and became a public figure—a major writer in the intellectual and literary movement called the Harlem Renaissance. During the 1930s, he became absorbed in radical politics and traveled the world as a correspondent and columnist; but during the 1950s, the FBI classified him as a security risk and limited his ability to travel. In addition to poems and novels, he wrote essays, plays, screenplays, and an autobiography; he also edited anthologies of literature and folklore. His *Collected Poems* appeared in 1994.

Henrik Ibsen (1828–1906)

Born in Skien, Norway, Henrik Ibsen was apprenticed to an apothecary until 1850, when he left for Oslo and published his first play, *Catilina,* under a pseudonym. Two of his early works, written in Rome, were in verse—*Brand* (1866) and *Peer Gynt* (1867). During the course of his career, he turned to more realistic plays—including *Ghosts* (1881) and *An Enemy of the People* (1882)—that explored contemporary social problems; they won him a reputation throughout Europe as a controversial and outspoken advocate of moral and social reform. Near the end of his life, Ibsen explored the human condition in the symbolic terms of *The Master Builder* (1892) and *When We Dead Awaken* (1899), plays that anticipated many of the concerns of twentieth-century drama.

David Ives (1950–)

A native of Chicago, David Ives worked as the assistant editor of *Foreign Affairs* before graduating from the Yale School of Drama. While plays such as *Don Juan in Chicago* (1995) and *Ancient History* (1995) have established his place among contemporary dramatists, Ives is also an accomplished journalist and the author of fiction, screenplays, and opera. In 1993, his series of one-act plays, *All in the Timing*, received the Outer Critics Circle Award for playwriting, and it became the most performed play nationally after Shakespeare productions during the 1995–96 season. A Guggenheim fellow in playwriting, Ives adapted magician David Copperfield's *Dreams and Nightmares* (1996) for the stage.

Henry James (1843–1916)

Son of a writer and religious philosopher and his wife, brother of the philosopher William James, Henry James was born in New York and entered Harvard Law School in 1862, after private study, art school, and study and residence abroad. Thereafter his American home was in Cambridge, Massachusetts, but he lived in England from 1876 until his death forty years later, having become a British subject in 1915. James's fiction often centers on the confrontation of Americans with Europe or Europeans; he treats the two as moral or value systems as much as geographical entities. His practice and theory of fiction, set forth mainly in the prefaces to his novels, dominated fiction criticism for generations. Among his works are *The American* (1877), *Daisy Miller* (1879), *Portrait of a Lady* (1881), *The Turn of the Screw* (1898), *The Wings of the Dove* (1902), *The Ambassadors* (1903), and *The Golden Bowl* (1904).

Ben Jonson (1572?–1637)

Poet, playwright, actor, scholar, critic, translator, and leader, for the first time in English, of a literary "school" (the "Cavalier" poets), Ben Jonson was born the posthumous son of a clergyman; his mother's second marriage was to a master bricklayer of Westminster. Jonson had an eventful early career, going to war against the Spanish, working as an actor, killing an associate in a duel, and converting to Catholicism (which made him an object of deep suspicion after Guy Fawkes's Gunpowder Plot, in 1605). Jonson wrote a number of plays in the midst of all this, including *Every Man in His Humour* (in which Shakespeare acted a leading role; 1598), *Volpone* (1606), and *The Alchemist* (1610). He spent the latter part of his life at the center of a vast literary circle. When he published *The Works of Benjamin Jonson*, it was the first time an English author had been so presumptuous as to consider writing a profession.

James Joyce (1882–1941)

In 1902, after graduating from University College, Dublin, James Joyce left his native city for Paris, only to return in April 1903 to teach school. In October 1904, he eloped with Nora Barnacle and left Ireland again, this time for Trieste, where he taught English for the Berlitz school. Though he lived abroad the rest of his life, that first abortive trip proved symbolic: in his fiction the expatriate could never leave Dublin. Joyce had more than his share of difficulties with publication and censorship. His volume of short stories, *Dubliners*, completed in 1905, was not published until 1914. His novel *Portrait of the Artist as a Young Man*, dated "Dublin 1904, Trieste 1914," appeared first in America, in 1916. His great novel, *Ulysses* (1921), was banned for a dozen years in the United States and as long or longer elsewhere. In addition, Joyce published a play, *Exiles*, (1918); two collections of poetry, *Chamber Music* (1907) and *Pomes Penyeach* (1927); and the monumental, experimental, and puzzling novel *Finnegans Wake* (1939).

Franz Kafka (1883–1924)

Born in Prague into a middle-class Jewish family, Franz Kafka earned a doctorate in law from the German University in that city and held an inconspicuous position in the civil service for many years. Emotionally and physically ill for the last seven or eight years of his short life, he died of tuberculosis in Vienna, never having married (though he was twice engaged to the same woman and lived with an actress in Berlin for some time before he died) and not having published his three major novels, *The*

Trial (1925), *The Castle* (1926), and *Amerika* (1927). Indeed, he ordered his friend Max Brod to destroy them and other works he had left in manuscript. Fortunately, Brod did not; and not long after Kafka's death, his work was world-famous and widely influential. His stories in English translation are collected in *The Great Wall of China* (1933), *The Penal Colony* (1948), and *The Complete Stories* (1976).

Yasunari Kawabata (1899–1972)

Born in Osaka, Japan, to a prosperous family, Yasunari Kawabata graduated from Tokyo Imperial University in 1924 and had his first literary success with the semiautobiographical novella *The Izu Dancer* (1926). He cofounded the journal *Contemporary Literature* in support of the Neosensualist movement, which had much in common with the European literary movements of Dadaism, Expressionism, and Cubism. His best-known works include *The Snow Country* (1948), *Thousand Cranes* (1952), *The Sound of the Mountain* (1954), and the collection *Palm-of-the-Hand Stories* (translated in 1988). Kawabata was awarded the Nobel Prize for Literature in 1968. After long suffering from poor health, he committed suicide.

John Keats (1795–1821)

John Keats was born in London, the son of a livery stable owner and his wife; reviewers would later disparage his working-class background by calling him a "Cockney poet." At fifteen he was apprenticed to a surgeon, and at twenty-one he became a licensed druggist—in the same year that his first two published poems, including the sonnet "On First Looking into Chapman's Homer," appeared in *The Examiner,* a journal edited by the critic and poet Leigh Hunt. Hunt introduced Keats to such literary figures as the poet Percy Bysshe Shelley and helped him publish his *Poems by John Keats* (1817). When his second book, the long poem *Endymion* (1818), was fiercely attacked by critics, Keats, suffering from a steadily worsening case of tuberculosis, felt that he would not live to realize his poetic promise. In July 1820, he published *Lamia, Isabella, The Eve of St. Agnes, and Other Poems,* which contained the poignant lyric "To Autumn" and three grand odes: "Ode on a Grecian Urn," "Ode on Melancholy," and "Ode to a Nightingale"; a few months later, he died in Rome. In the years after his death, his letters became almost as famous as his poetry.

Jamaica Kincaid (1949–)

Born in St. John's, Antigua, Elaine Potter Richardson left her native island and her family at seventeen. Changing her name to Jamaica Kincaid, she worked in New York City as an au pair and a receptionist before studying photography at the New School for Social Research, then briefly studying at Franconia College. After returning to New York, she became a regular contributor to *The New Yorker,* for which she wrote from 1976 until 1995. Her publications include a collection of short stories, *At the Bottom of the River* (1983); a book-length essay about Antigua, *A Small Place* (1988); a book for children, *Annie, Gwen, Lilly, Pam, and Tulip* (1986); the novels *Annie John* (1985), *Lucy* (1990), and *The Autobiography of My Mother* (1996); the memoir *My Brother* (1997); and a collection of her *New Yorker* pieces, *Talk Stories* (2001).

Galway Kinnell (1927–)

Born in Providence, Rhode Island, Galway Kinnell earned a B.A. from Princeton and an M.A. from the University of Rochester. He served in the navy and has been a journalist, a civil-rights field-worker, and a teacher at numerous colleges and universities. His early poetry, collected in *What a Kingdom It Was* (1960) and *First Poems 1946–1954* (1970), is highly formal; his subsequent work employs a more colloquial style. He received both a Pulitzer Prize and the American Book Award for *Selected Poems* (1982), and in 2000 he culled *A New Selected Poems* from eight collections spanning twenty-four years. He lives in New York and Vermont.

Etheridge Knight (1931–1991)

A native of Corinth, Mississippi, Etheridge Knight spent much of his adolescence carousing in pool halls, bars, and juke joints, developing a skillful oratorical style in an environment that prized verbal agility. During this time he also became addicted to narcotics. He served in the U.S. Army from 1947 to 1951, but in 1960 he was sentenced to eight years in prison for robbery. At the Indiana State Prison in Michigan City he began to write poetry, and by 1968, thanks to acclaim and support from such established African American artists as Dudley Randall and Gwendolyn Brooks, his first collection, *Poems from Prison,* was published. After his release, Knight joined the Black Arts movement and taught at several universities, all the while championing the role of oral artistry in maintaining the functional and communal aspects of poetry. His works include *Black Voices from Prison* (1970, originally published in Italian as *Voce negre dal carcere* two years earlier), *Belly Song and Other Poems* (1973), and *Born of a Woman* (1980).

Jhumpa Lahiri (1967–)

Born in London and raised in Rhode Island, Jhumpa Lahiri is the daughter of Bengali parents; much of her fiction addresses the difficulty of reconciling an Indian heritage with life in the United States. Lahiri earned a B.A. from Barnard College and several degrees from Boston University: an M.A. in English, an M.F.A. in creative writing, an M.A. in comparative studies in literature and the arts, and a Ph.D. in renaissance studies. She has published many stories in well-known periodicals such as *The New Yorker* and won the 2000 Pulitzer Prize for her first collection, *Interpreter of Maladies* (1999). She currently lives in New York City and is working on a novel.

D. H. Lawrence (1885–1930)

Son of a coal miner and a middle-class schoolteacher, David Herbert Lawrence won a scholarship to Nottingham High School at thirteen but had to leave a few years later when his elder brother died. He worked for a surgical-appliance manufacturer, attended Nottingham University College, and taught school in Croydon, near London. After publishing his first novel, *The White Peacock* (1911), he devoted his time to writing, and *Sons and Lovers* (1913) established him as a major literary figure. In 1912, he eloped to the Continent with Frieda von Richthofen, and in 1914, after her divorce, they were married. During World War I, both his novels and his wife's being German gave him trouble: *The Rainbow* was published in September 1915 and suppressed in November. In November 1919, the Lawrences left England and began years of wandering: first Italy, then Ceylon and Australia, Mexico and New Mexico, then back to England and Italy. Lawrence published *Women in Love* in New York in 1920 and *Lady Chatterley's Lover,* his most sexually explicit and controversial novel, eight years later. Through it all he suffered from tuberculosis, the disease from which he finally died, in France. Lawrence's stories are collected in a three-volume edition, first published in 1961.

Ursula K. Le Guin (1929–)

Born in Berkeley, California, to a writer/folklorist mother and an anthropologist father, Ursula Kroeber earned a B.A. from Radcliffe College and an M.A. from Columbia University. In 1952, she married the historian Charles Le Guin. Although she began publishing fiction in the early 1960s, Le Guin established her literary reputation with the philosophical fantasy *A Wizard of Earthsea* (1968), which formed a trilogy with *The Tombs of Atuan* (1971) and *The Farthest Shore* (1972). Read by both adolescents and adults, her work often depicts complex fictional societies with folkloric or anthropological attention. Her publications include *The Left Hand of Darkness* (1969), *The Dispossessed* (1974), *Malafrena* (1979), *The Compass Rose* (1982), and *The Telling* (2000). In addition, she has written essays, children's books, and poetry; collaborated on multimedia work; and edited collections of science fiction.

Doris Lessing (1919–)

Born in Persia (now Iran), to English parents, Doris Tayler lived for twenty-five years in Southern Rhodesia (now Zimbabwe), where she left school at fourteen to work as a nursemaid and secretary. After marriages to Frank Wisdom and Gottfried Lessing, she moved to England and soon thereafter published her first novel, *The Grass Is Singing* (1950). Some of her work is set in Africa, much of it is political (she was briefly a Communist), and much of it examines the inner lives of women in modern society. Her major works of fiction include the five Martha Quest novels, *Children of Violence* (1952–69); *The Golden Notebook* (1962); a five-volume science-fiction collection, *Canopus in Argos: Archives* (1979–83); *The Good Terrorist* (1985); and *The Fifth Child* (1988). She has also published collections of short fiction, plays, teleplays, poetry, memoirs, essays, and two volumes of an autobiography. Her most recent novel is *Ben, in the World: The Sequel to* The Fifth Child (2000).

Andrew Marvell (1621–1678)

The son of a clergyman and his wife, Andrew Marvell was born in Yorkshire, England, and educated at Trinity College, Cambridge. There is no evidence that he fought in the English Civil War, which broke out in 1642, but his poem "An Horatian Ode upon Cromwell's Return from Ireland" appeared in 1650, shortly after the beheading of King Charles I in 1649, and may represent straightforward praise of England's new Puritan leader. Some regard it as strong satire, however, and Marvell was known in his day for such satires in prose and verse. Today he is better known for lyric poems, such as the carpe diem manifesto "To His Coy Mistress," that he wrote probably while serving as tutor to a Yorkshire noble's daughter. In 1657, upon the recommendation of John Milton, Marvell accepted a position in Cromwell's government, which he held for two years until his election to Parliament in 1659. After helping restore the monarchy in 1660, he continued to write and to serve as a member of Parliament until the end of his life.

Guy de Maupassant (1850–1893)

Born Henri René Albert in Normandy, France, Maupassant was expelled at sixteen from a Rouen seminary and finished his education at a public high school. After serving in the Franco-Prussian War, he was a government clerk in Paris for ten years. A protégé of Flaubert, he published during the 1880s some three hundred stories, half a dozen novels, and plays. The short stories, which appeared regularly in popular periodicals, sampled military and peasant life, the decadent world of politics and journalism, prostitution, the supernatural, and the hypocrisies of solid citizens; with Chekhov, he may be said to have created the modern short story. His life ended somewhat like one of his own stories: he died of syphilis in an asylum. His novels include *Une Vie* (*A Life,* 1883), *Bel Ami* (*Handsome Friend,* 1885), and *Pierre et Jean* (1888). His stories are available in various collections.

Herman Melville (1819–1891)

When his father died in debt, twelve-year-old Herman Melville moved from a life of privilege to one of struggle. At eighteen, Melville left his native New York to teach in a backwoods Massachusetts school, then trained as a surveyor; finding no work, he became a sailor in 1839. After voyaging through the South Seas for five years, he wrote *Typee* (1846), a sensationalized account of his travels. Both this work and the similar *Omoo* (1847) were hungrily read and loudly praised, but they proved the pinnacle of Melville's career in his lifetime. His books became either too abstruse for his audience, as in *Mardi* (1849), or too listless, as in the recycled travel narratives of *Redburn* (1849) and *White-Jacket* (1850). Melville's magnum opus, *Moby-Dick* (1851), was alternately shunned and condemned. Other novels—*Pierre* (1852), *Israel Potter* (1853), and *The Confidence-Man* (1856)—met similar fates; his poetry collection *Battle-Pieces* (1866) was hardly read. Melville fared better writing magazine stories such as "Bartleby, the Scrivener," collecting some into *The Piazza Tales* in 1856. Growing increasingly morose and erratic, he spent the Civil War years in New York with his wife and children, who suspected that he was insane. In later years, several legacies improved his finances; and the novel *Billy Budd, Sailor* (1924), nearly finished at his death, was judged one of his finest works.

Edna St. Vincent Millay (1892–1950)

Born in Rockland, Maine, Edna St. Vincent Millay published her first poem at twenty, her first poetry collection at twenty-five. After graduating from Vassar College, she moved to New York City's Greenwich Village, where she extended her reputation as a poet, became notorious for her bohemian life, and associated with many prominent artists, writers, and radicals. In 1923, she won the Pulitzer Prize for her collection *The Ballad of the Harp-Weaver;* in 1925, she and her husband moved to Austerlitz, New York, where she lived for the rest of her life. Her poetry has been collected and selected in various editions.

Arthur Miller (1915–)

Born and raised in New York City, Arthur Miller studied history, economics, and journalism at the University of Michigan, began writing plays, and went to work—in the middle of the Depression—with the Federal Theater Project, a fertile proving ground for some of the best playwrights of the period. He had his first Broadway success, *All My Sons,* in 1947, followed only two years later by his masterpiece, *Death of a Salesman.* With Senator Joseph McCarthy's Communist "witch-hunts" of the early 1950s as his inspiration, Miller fashioned another modern parable, basing his Tony Award–winning *The Crucible* (1953) on the seventeenth-century Salem witch trials. His major works since then have included *After the Fall* (1964) and *The Ride Down Mt. Morgan* (1991). In 1984, Miller was given the John F. Kennedy Award for Lifetime Achievement; in 1987, he published his autobiography, *Timebends: A Life.*

John Milton (1608–1674)

Born in London, the elder son of a self-made businessman and his wife, John Milton exhibited unusual literary and scholarly gifts at an early age; before entering Cambridge University, he was already adept at Latin and Greek and was well on his way to mastering Hebrew and most of the European languages. After graduation, he spent six more years reading, day and night, just about everything of importance written in English, Italian, Latin, and Greek—after which his father sent him abroad for another year of travel and study. Returning to England, Milton immediately embroiled himself in political controversy, writing pamphlets defending everything from free speech to the execution of Charles I by Cromwell and his followers. In the midst of this feverish activity, the monarchy was restored, Milton was imprisoned, and his property was confiscated—worst of all, he lost his sight. Blind, impoverished, and isolated, he set about writing the great works of his later years: *Paradise Lost* (1667), *Paradise Regained* (1671), and *Samson Agonistes* (1671).

Lorrie Moore (1957–)

Born in Glens Falls, New York, Marie Lorena Moore was nicknamed "Lorrie" by her parents. At nineteen, while attending St. Lawrence University, she published her first story, in *Seventeen* magazine. After graduating, she worked as a paralegal in New York City before earning her M.F.A. in creative writing from Cornell. She followed her first book, *Self-Help* (1985), a collection of short stories satirizing the stern and generic imperatives aimed at modern women, with the novels *Anagrams* (1986) and *Who Will Run the Frog Hospital?* (1994) and the short-story collections *Like Life* (1990) and *Birds of America* (1998). Since 1984, she has been a professor of English at the University of Wisconsin at Madison.

Marianne Moore (1887–1972)

Born in Kirkwood, Missouri, Marianne Moore was raised in Carlisle, Pennsylvania. After receiving a degree in biology from Bryn Mawr College, she studied business at Carlisle Commercial College; taught stenography at the U.S. Industrial Indian School in Carlisle; and traveled to Europe. She and her mother moved to New Jersey and New York's Greenwich Village before settling, in 1918, in Brooklyn, New York. From 1921 to 1925, Moore was a librarian at the New York Public Library. She had written and published poetry while still in college, but did not publish her first collection until 1921. A prolific critic, she also edited the influential modernist magazine *Dial* from 1926 to 1929. Her *Collected Poems* (1951) won the Bollingen Prize, the Pulitzer Prize, and a National Book Award and made her a public figure. Her *Complete Poems* appeared in 1967.

Pat Mora (1942–)

Born to Mexican American parents in El Paso, Texas, Pat Mora earned both her B.A. and her M.A. from the University of Texas at El Paso. She has been a consultant on U.S.–Mexico youth exchanges; a museum director and administrator at her alma mater; and a teacher of English at all levels. Her poetry—collected in *Chants* (1985), *Borders* (1986), *Communion* (1991), *Agua Santa* (1995), and *Aunt Carmen's Book of Practical Saints* (1997)—reflects and addresses her Chicana and southwestern background. Mora's other publications include many works for children; *Nepantla: Essays from the*

Land in the Middle (1993); and a family memoir, *House of Houses* (1997). She divides her time between the Southwest and the Cincinnati area.

Bharati Mukherjee (1940–)

Born to wealthy parents in Calcutta, India, Bharati Mukherjee attended private schools in India, London, and Switzerland before studying English at the University of Iowa. There, she met and married Canadian novelist Clark Blaise, with whom she has lived in Canada and the United States, and with whom she wrote *Days and Nights in Calcutta* (1977), an acclaimed account of their visit to her native country in 1972. In addition to her novels *The Tiger's Daughter* (1971), *Wife* (1975), *Jasmine* (1989), *The Holder of the World* (1993), and *Leave It to Me* (1997), Mukherjee has published the short-story collections *Darkness* (1985) and *The Middleman* (1988). She teaches at the University of California at Berkeley.

Alice Munro (1931–)

Alice Laidlaw was born in Wingham, Ontario, Canada, on a farm near Lake Huron. While attending the University of Western Ontario, she began publishing stories. When her two-year scholarship ran out, she left the university, married James Munro, and moved to Vancouver. During the 1950s, her stories appeared sporadically, and she did not publish her first collection, the Governor General's Award–winning *Dance of the Happy Shades,* until 1968. Divorced, remarried, returned to Ontario, and widely considered Canada's best writer of short stories, she went on to publish the novel *Lives of Girls and Women* (1971) and the collections *Something I've Been Meaning to Tell You* (1974), *Who Do You Think You Are?* (1978, published in the United States as *The Beggar Maid* in 1979), *The Moons of Jupiter* (1983), *The Progress of Love* (1986), *Friend of My Youth* (1990), *Open Secrets* (1994), *Selected Stories* (1996), and *The Love of a Good Woman* (1998).

Howard Nemerov (1920–1991)

Born and raised in New York City, Howard Nemerov graduated from Harvard University, served in the air force during World War II, and returned to New York to complete his first book, *The Image and the Law* (1948). He taught at a number of colleges and universities and published books of poetry, plays, short stories, novels, and essays. His *Collected Poems* won the Pulitzer Prize and the National Book Award in 1978. Consultant in poetry to the Library of Congress from 1963 to 1964, he served as poet laureate of the United States from 1988 to 1990. *Trying Conclusions: New and Selected Poems 1961–1991* was published in 1991.

Flannery O'Connor (1925–1964)

Mary Flannery O'Connor was born in Savannah, Georgia, studied at the Georgia State College for Women, and won a fellowship to the Writer's Workshop of the University of Iowa, from which she received her M.F.A. Her first novel, *Wise Blood,* was published in 1952, and her first collection of stories, *A Good Man Is Hard to Find,* in 1955. She was able to complete only one more novel, *The Violent Bear It Away* (1960), and a second collection of stories, *Everything That Rises Must Converge* (1965), before dying of lupus, in Milledgeville, Georgia. Her reputation has grown steadily since her untimely death. A collection of letters, edited by Sally Fitzgerald under the title *The Habit of Being,* appeared in 1979.

Sharon Olds (1942–)

Born in San Francisco, Sharon Olds earned a B.A. from Stanford University and a Ph.D. from Columbia University. A founding chair of the Writing Program at Goldwater Hospital (a public facility for the severely physically disabled), she currently chairs New York University's Creative Writing Program. She has received a National Endowment for the Arts Grant and a Guggenheim Fellowship and was named New York State Poet in 1998. Her books include *Satan Says* (1980), the National Book Critics Circle Award–winning *The Dead and the Living* (1983), *The Gold Cell* (1987), *The Father* (1992), *The Wellspring* (1997), and *Blood, Tin, Straw* (1999).

Grace Paley (1922–)

Born to Russian immigrants in the Bronx, New York, Grace Paley studied at Hunter College and New York University but never finished college because she was too busy reading and writing. Her short stories, first published in *The Little Disturbances of Man: Stories of Men and Women at Love* (1959), *Enormous Changes at the Last Minute* (1974), and *Later the Same Day* (1985), are assembled in *The Collected Stories* (1994); her poetry, in *Begin Again: Collected Poems* (2000); and her essays, reviews, and lectures, in *Just as I Thought* (1998). Designated the first official New York State Author (in 1988), Paley has been conferred an honorary doctorate and has taught at various colleges and universities.

Dorothy Parker (1893–1967)

Born in West End, New Jersey, Dorothy Rothschild worked briefly on the editorial staff of *Vogue* and slightly longer as a drama critic for *Vanity Fair* before becoming a freelance writer. In 1917, she married Edwin Pond Parker II, whom she divorced in 1928. Her first book of verse, *Enough Rope* (1926), was a best-seller and was followed by *Sunset Gun* (1928), *Death and Taxes* (1931), and *Collected Poems: Not So Deep as a Well* (1936). In 1927, Parker became a book reviewer for *The New Yorker,* to which she contributed for most of her career. At the "Algonquin Round Table" at the Algonquin Hotel in Manhattan, she associated with other prominent writers and humorists of the day; a number of her brief, witty aphorisms from the period remain in circulation. In 1933, Parker and her second husband, Alan Campbell, moved to Hollywood and collaborated as film writers. In addition, Parker wrote news reports from the Spanish Civil War, criticism, two plays, and short stories. In 1963, following her husband's death, she returned to New York.

Linda Pastan (1932–)

Linda Pastan was born in New York City and raised in nearby Westchester County. After graduating from Radcliffe College, she received an M.A. in literature from Brandeis University. Although her first published poems appeared in *Mademoiselle* in 1955, Pastan spent years concentrating on her husband and children—indeed, much of her poetry deals with her own family life. Her many collections include *A Perfect Circle of Sun* (1971), *The Five Stages of Grief* (1978), *PM/AM: New and Selected Poems* (1982; nominated for the American Book Award), *A Fraction of Darkness* (1985), *The Imperfect Paradise* (1988), *An Early Afterlife* (1995), and *Carnival Evening: New and Selected Poems 1968–1998* (1998). She lives in Potomac, Maryland, and was chosen as the poet laureate of Maryland in 1991.

Marge Piercy (1936–)

Born and raised in Detroit, Marge Piercy received her B.A. from the University of Michigan and her M.A. from Northwestern University. She taught for some time before the success of her novels allowed her to live a semirural life on Cape Cod. While her early poetry forcefully juxtaposed the personal and the political, her later work expresses also the interconnection of all living things. Her many books include the poetry collections *Living in the Open* (1976), *The Moon Is Always Female* (1980), *Stone, Paper, Knife* (1983), *Available Light* (1988), *Mars and Her Children* (1992), *What Are Big Girls Made Of?* (1997), and *The Art of Blessing the Day: Poems with a Jewish Theme* (2000); a collection of essays on poetry, *Parti-Colored Blocks for a Quilt* (1982); and her most recent novel, *Three Women* (1999). She lives in Wellfleet, Massachusetts.

Sylvia Plath (1932–1963)

Sylvia Plath was born in Boston, Massachusetts; her father, a Polish immigrant, died when she was eight. After graduating from Smith College, Plath attended Cambridge University on a Fulbright scholarship, and there she met and married the poet Ted Hughes, with whom she had two children. As she documented in her novel *The Bell Jar* (1963), in 1953—between her junior and senior years of college—Plath went through a serious depression, a suicide attempt, and a period of hospitalization. In 1963, following the break-up of her marriage, Plath suffered a similar episode, which ended with her suicide. She has attained the status of a cult figure as much for the beautiful agony of her poems as for her "martyrdom" to art and life. In addition to her first collection of poetry, *The Colossus* (1960), Plath's works include *Ariel* (1966), *Crossing the Water* (1971), and *Winter Trees* (1972). Her selected letters were published in 1975; her expurgated journals, in 1983; and her unabridged journals, in 2000.

Edgar Allan Poe (1809–1849)

Edgar Poe's father, an actor, deserted his wife and son when Edgar was less than a year old, and Poe's mother died before he was three. He and his younger sister were separated and taken into different families; and in 1815, the Allans (who gave Poe his middle name) moved to England, where Edgar had his early schooling. He also studied briefly at the University of Virginia. In 1827, he paid to have a volume of poems published in Boston (his birthplace); a second volume appeared in 1829 in Baltimore (where he was to die twenty years later). Having served for two years in the army, he was appointed to West Point in 1830 but was expelled within the year for cutting classes. Living in Baltimore with his grandmother, aunt, and cousin Virginia (whom he married in 1835, when she was thirteen), Poe attracted critical attention but made very little money. For the twelve years before his wife died, he wrote, worked as journalist and editor, and drank. He died suddenly, during a period of apparent sobriety. His poems and stories have been selected and collected in many editions.

Katherine Anne Porter (1890–1980)

Born in Indian Creek, Texas, Katherine Anne Porter supported herself with hackwork in Denver, Chicago, and elsewhere before establishing her literary reputation. She published her first story in 1922; her first collection *Flowering Judas* (1930), helped make her a leading American writer. A writer-in-residence at a succession of universities and colleges, Porter won several awards for her work, including both a Pulitzer Prize and a

National Book Award for her *Collected Short Stories* (1965) and a Gold Medal from the National Institute of Arts and Letters. Among her works are *Pale Horse, Pale Rider* (1939), *The Leaning Tower* (1944), and *The Never-Ending Wrong* (1977), dealing with the controversial murder trial of Sacco and Vanzetti. Her only full-length novel, *Ship of Fools* (1962), was met with both popular and critical acclaim.

Ezra Pound (1885–1972)

Born in Hailey, Idaho, Ezra Loomis Pound studied at the University of Pennsylvania and Hamilton College before traveling to Europe in 1908. He remained there, living in Ireland, England, France, and Italy, for much of his life. Pound's tremendous ambition—to succeed in his own work and to influence the development of poetry and Western culture in general—led him to found the Imagist school of poetry, to advise and assist a galaxy of great writers (Eliot, Joyce, Williams, Frost, and Hemingway, to name a few), and to write a number of highly influential critical works. It also led to a charge of treason (he served as a propagandist for Mussolini during World War II), a diagnosis of insanity, and twelve years at St. Elizabeth's, an institution for the criminally insane. His verse is collected in *Personae: The Collected Poems* (1949) and *The Cantos* (1976).

Jarold Ramsey (b. 1937)

Jarold Ramsey grew up on a ranch in central Oregon, and his work is deeply influenced by the mythology and culture of Northwest Indians. He is currently a professor of English at the University of Rochester. His books include *Reading the Fire: Essays in the Traditional Indian Literatures of the Far West* (1983) and *Hand-Shadows* (1989).

Adrienne Rich (1929–)

Adrienne Rich was born in Baltimore. Since the selection of her first volume by W. H. Auden for the Yale Series of Younger Poets (1951), her work has continually broken new ground, moving from closed forms to a poetics of change rooted in a radical imagination and politics. Her books of poetry include *Collected Early Poems 1950–1970* (1993), *The Dream of a Common Language* (1978), *Your Native Land, Your Life* (1986), *Time's Power* (1988), *An Atlas of the Difficult World* (1991), *Dark Fields of the Republic* (1995), *Midnight Salvage* (1999), and *Fox* (2001). Her prose works include *Of Woman Born: Motherhood as Experience and Institution* (1976), *On Lies, Secrets and Silence* (1979), and *Blood, Bread, and Poetry* (1986), all influential feminist texts; *What Is Found There: Notebooks on Poetry and Politics* (1993); and *Arts of the Possible: Essays and Conversations* (2001). Her work as a writer has received numerous recognitions including the Los Angeles Times Book Award, the Lambda Literary Award, the Lenore Marshall/NATION Award, a MacArthur Fellowship, the Dorothea Tanning Prize, and a Lanning Foundation Lifetime Achievement Award. Since 1984, she has lived in California.

William Shakespeare (1564–1616)

Considering the great and deserved fame of his work, surprisingly little is known of William Shakespeare's life. Between 1585 and 1592, he left his birthplace of Stratford for London to begin a career as playwright and actor. No dates of his professional career are recorded, however, nor is the order in which he composed his plays and poetry certain. By 1594, he had established himself as a poet with two long works—*Venus and Adonis* and *The Rape of Lucrece*—but he made his strongest reputation in the theater.

Shakespeare produced perhaps thirty-five plays in twenty-five years, proving himself a master of many genres in works such as *Macbeth, King Lear, Othello,* and *Antony and Cleopatra* (tragedy); *Richard III* and *Henry IV* (historical drama); *Twelfth Night* and *As You Like It* (comedy); and *The Tempest* (romance). His more than 150 sonnets are supreme expressions of the form.

Carol Shields (1935–2003)

Born in Oak Park, Illinois, Carol Shields received her B.A. from Hanover College and her M.A. from the University of Ottawa. She taught at several Canadian universities; in 1996, she became the chancellor of the University of Winnipeg. Her writing was slow to earn critical appreciation, although novels such as *Small Ceremonies* (1976), *The Box Garden* (1977), *Happenstance* (1980), and *A Fairly Conventional Woman* (1982) were popular with Canadian readers. With her first story collection, *Various Miracles* (1985), Shields began to experiment with multiple narrators. She refined this technique in the triumphantly successful novel *The Stone Diaries* (1993), a fictional biography that won the Pulitzer Prize and was short-listed for the Booker Prize. In addition to such plays as *Thirteen Hands* (1993), she wrote another innovative biographical novel, *Larry's Party* (1997); a collection of stories, *Dressing Up for the Carnival* (2000); and the short biography *Jane Austen* (2001).

Sophocles (496?–406? B.C.)

Sophocles lived at a time when Athens and Greek civilization had reached the peak of their power and influence. He not only served as a general under Pericles and played a prominent role in the city's affairs, but was also arguably the greatest of the Greek tragic playwrights, an innovator who fundamentally changed the form of dramatic performance. He was also the model Aristotle turned to when he discussed the nature of tragedy in his *Poetics*. Today only seven of Sophocles' tragedies survive—the Oedipus trilogy (*Oedipus the King, Oedipus at Colonus,* and *Antigone*), *Philoctetes, Ajax, Trachiniae,* and *Electra*—though he may have written over 120 plays.

Wallace Stevens (1879–1955)

Born and raised in Reading, Pennsylvania, Wallace Stevens attended Harvard University and New York Law School. In New York City, he worked for a number of law firms; published poems in magazines; and befriended such literary figures as William Carlos Williams and Marianne Moore. In 1916, Stevens moved to Connecticut and began working for the Hartford Accident and Indemnity Company, where he became a vice-president in 1934 and where he remained for the rest of his life, writing poetry at night and during vacations. He published his first collection, *Harmonium,* in 1923, and followed it with a series of volumes from 1935 until 1950, in the process becoming one of the century's most important poets. His lectures were collected in *The Necessary Angel: Essays on Reality and Imagination* (1951); his *Collected Poems* appeared in 1954.

Elizabeth Tallent (1954–)

Born in Washington, D.C., and raised in the Midwest, Elizabeth Tallent earned a B.A. in anthropology from Illinois State University. Abandoning plans to do graduate work in anthropology, she devoted herself to writing; in 1980, she published her first story in *The New Yorker*. Tallent has taught creative writing at the University of Nevada at Reno, the University of Iowa, and the University of California at Davis; she currently teaches at Stanford University. Her first book, *Married Men and Magic Tricks,* was a collection of essays on the novelist John Updike; a year later, she published a collection of her own stories, *In Constant Flight* (1983). In addition to the novel *Museum Pieces* (1985), she has published two more story collections: *Time with Children* (1987) and *Honey* (1994).

Amy Tan (1952–)

Amy Tan was born in Oakland, California, just two and a half years after her parents immigrated there from China. She received her M.A. in linguistics from San Jose State University and has worked as a consultant to programs for disabled children and as a freelance writer. In 1987, she visited China for the first time—"As soon as my feet touched China, I became Chinese"—and returned to write her first book, *The Joy Luck Club* (1989). Tan has since published three more novels—*The Kitchen God's Wife* (1991), *The Hundred Secret Senses* (1995), and *The Bonesetter's Daughter* (2000)—and coauthored two children's books.

Alfred, Lord Tennyson (1809–1892)

Perhaps the most important and certainly the most popular of the Victorian poets, Alfred, Lord Tennyson demonstrated his talents at an early age; he published his first volume in 1827. Encouraged to devote his life to poetry by a group of undergraduates at Cambridge University known as the "Apostles," Tennyson was particularly close to Arthur Hallam, whose sudden death in 1833 inspired the long elegy *In Memoriam* (1850). With that poem he achieved lasting fame and recognition; he was appointed poet laureate the year of its publication. Whatever the popularity of his "journalistic" poetry—"The Charge of the Light Brigade" (1854) is perhaps his best known—Tennyson's great theme was always the past, both personal (*In the Valley of Cauteretz*, 1864) and national (*Idylls of the King*, 1869).

Dylan Thomas (1914–1953)

Born in Swansea, Wales, into what he called "the smug darkness of a provincial town," Dylan Thomas published his first book at twenty, in the same year that he moved to London. Thereafter he had a successful, though turbulent, career publishing poetry, short stories, and plays, including the highly successful *Under Milk Wood* (1954). In his last years he supported himself with lecture tours and poetry readings in the United States, but his extravagant drinking caught up with him and he died in New York City of chronic alcoholism. His work has been selected and collected in various editions.

Derek Walcott (1930–)

Born of mixed heritage on the West Indian island of St. Lucia, Derek Walcott grew up speaking French and patois but was educated in English and studied classical languages. In 1953, he earned his B.A. in English, French, and Latin from the University College of the West Indies in Jamaica. In 1950, with his twin brother, Roderick, he founded the St. Lucia Arts Guild, a dramatic society; nine years later, he founded the Little Carib Theatre Workshop in Trinidad, which he ran until 1976, writing many plays for production there. He also continued to write poetry, which he had been publishing since the age of eighteen; and in collections including *In a Green Night* (1962), *The Castaway* (1965), *Another Life* (1973), *Sea Grapes* (1976), *The Fortunate Traveller* (1981), *Omeros* (1990), *The Bounty* (1997), and *Tiepolo's Hound* (2000), Walcott draws on diverse influences from West Indian folk tales to Homer to Yeats. The first

Caribbean poet to have won the Nobel Prize (in 1992), Walcott now lives in the United States and lectures at various universities, including Yale and Rutgers.

Eudora Welty (1909–2001)

Eudora Welty was born and raised in Jackson, Mississippi, attended Mississippi State College for Women, and earned a B.A. from the University of Wisconsin. Among the countless awards she received were two Guggenheim Fellowships, three O. Henry Awards, a Pulitzer Prize, the National Medal for Literature, and the Presidential Medal of Freedom. Although she wrote five novels, including *The Robber Bridegroom* (1942), *Ponder Heart* (1954), and *The Optimist's Daughter* (1972), she is best known for her short stories, many of which have been published in *The Collected Stories of Eudora Welty* (1980). Among her nonfiction works are *One Writer's Beginnings* (1984) and *A Writer's Eye: Collected Book Reviews* (1994).

Walt Whitman (1819–1892)

Walt Whitman was born on a farm in West Hills, Long Island, to a British father and a Dutch mother. After working as a journalist throughout New York for many years, he taught for a while; founded his own newspaper, *The Long Islander*, in 1838; then left journalism to work on *Leaves of Grass*, which he originally intended as a poetic treatise on American democratic idealism. Published privately in multiple editions from 1855 to 1874, the book originally failed to reach a mass audience. In 1881, Boston's Osgood and Company published another edition of *Leaves of Grass*, which sold well until the district attorney called it "obscene literature" and stipulated that Whitman remove certain poems and phrases. He refused, and many years later his works were published, this time in Philadelphia. His poetry creates tension between the self-conscious and the political, the romantic and the realistic, the mundane and the mystical, the collective and the individual.

Richard Wilbur (1921–)

Born in New York City and raised in New Jersey, Richard Wilbur received his B.A. from Amherst College and his M.A. from Harvard. He started to write while serving as an army cryptographer during World War II, and his collections *The Beautiful Changes* (1947) and *Ceremony* (1950) established his reputation as a significant new poet. In addition to subsequent volumes such as the Pulitzer Prize–winning *Things of This World* (1956), *Walking to Sleep* (1969), *The Mind Reader* (1976), the Pulitzer Prize–winning *New and Collected Poems* (1988), and *Mayflies: New Poems and Translations* (2000), he has published children's books, critical essays, and numerous translations of classic French works by Racine and Molière. He has taught at various colleges and universities, including Harvard, Wellesley, Wesleyan, and Smith. In 1987, he was chosen as poet laureate of the United States.

Oscar Wilde (1854–1900)

Born and raised in Dublin, Oscar Wilde majored in classical studies at Trinity College and took his degree from Oxford in 1878. While at Oxford, he was influenced by the "aesthetic movement" as theorized by John Ruskin and Walter Pater. Upon graduation, he moved to London to write and became a major proponent of the "art for art's sake" school. In addition to drama, Wilde wrote criticism, poetry, and fiction, most notably *The Picture of Dorian Gray* (1891). However, he is most remembered for his comic dramas, especially *The Importance of Being Earnest*, which was performed in 1895. That same year, Wilde was accused of homosexuality, and while he sued for libel, he lost the case and was imprisoned. Public sentiment in England and America was unsupportive, and during his two years in jail, Wilde's writing became more serious. Upon his release, he emigrated to France under an assumed name. He is buried in Paris.

Tennessee Williams (1911–1983)

Born in Columbus, Mississippi, Thomas Lanier Williams moved to St. Louis with his family at the age of seven. Williams's father was a violent drinker, his mother was ill, and his sister, Rose, suffered from a variety of mental illnesses. Each of them became a model for the domineering men and genteel women of his plays. He attended the University of Missouri and Washington University in St. Louis, but earned his B.A. from the University of Iowa. While there, Williams won prizes for his fiction and began writing plays. His extensive body of work confronts issues usually marginalized by society: adultery, homosexuality, incest, and mental illness. In 1944, his drama *The Glass Menagerie* won the New York Drama Critics' Circle Award. In 1948, he earned his first Pulitzer Prize with *A Streetcar Named Desire*; in 1955, he won a second Pulitzer Prize, for *Cat on a Hot Tin Roof*. His other dramas include *Camino Real* (1953), *Suddenly Last Summer* (1958), *The Night of the Iguana* (1961), *The Two-Character Play* (1969; later revised as *Out Cry*), and *Clothes for a Summer Hotel* (1980).

William Carlos Williams (1883–1963)

Born in Rutherford, New Jersey, William Carlos Williams attended school in Switzerland and New York and studied medicine at the University of Pennsylvania, where he met Hilda Doolittle (H.D.) and Ezra Pound. Thereafter, he spent most of his life in Rutherford, practicing medicine and crafting a poetry of palpable immediacy, written in vital, local language, that influenced a generation of American poets. His long poem, *Paterson* (completed in 1963), vividly expresses what lies at the heart of his work: "No ideas but in things." His poems, stories, plays, and so on, have been selected and collected in various editions.

August Wilson (1945–)

Frederick August Kittel was born in a lower-class black neighborhood of Pittsburgh, Pennsylvania. Rejecting his white father, he adopted his black mother's surname. At fifteen, he left school permanently after a racist incident involving a teacher. A black nationalist and participant in the black arts movement during the 1960s, Wilson cofounded in 1968 the Black Horizons Theater Company, in St. Paul, Minnesota; he later founded the Playwrights Center, in Minneapolis. The 1984 Broadway production of *Ma Rainey's Black Bottom* established his theatrical reputation, and since then he has been writing a series of ten full-length plays dealing with the black experience in America, each one set during a different decade of the twentieth century. Among his plays are *Jitney* (1982); *Fences* (1983); *Joe Turner's Come and Gone* (1986); *The Piano Lesson* (1987), which won a Tony Award, the Drama Critics Circle Award, the American Theater Critics Outstanding Play Award, and the Pulitzer Prize; *Two Trains Running* (1992); *Seven Guitars* (1995); and *King Hedley II* (2001).

William Wordsworth (1770–1850)

Born in Cockermouth in the sparsely populated English Lake District (which Coleridge and he would immortalize), William Wordsworth spent his early years taking in a rural environment that would provide material for much of his later poetry. After studying at Cambridge University, he spent a year in France, hoping to witness firsthand the French Revolution's "glorious renovation." Remarkably, he was able to establish "a saving intercourse with my true self"—and to write some of his finest poetry—after a love affair with a French woman whose sympathies were Royalist, his own disillusionment at the Revolution, a forced return to England, and near emotional collapse. Perhaps because he was, above all, a poet of remembrance (of "emotion recollected in tranquility"), and his own early experience was not an inexhaustible resource, Wordsworth had written most of his great work—including his masterpiece, *The Prelude*—by the time he was forty.

William Butler Yeats (1865–1939)

William Butler Yeats was born in Dublin, but spent much of his life away from Ireland. He attended art school for a time, but left to devote himself to poetry (at the start of his career, a self-consciously romantic poetry, dreamy and ethereal). His reading of Nietzsche, his involvement with the Nationalist cause, and his desperate love for the actress (and Nationalist) Maud Gonne led to a tighter, more actively passionate verse and a number of innovative dramatic works. Bitter and disillusioned at the results of revolution and the rise of the Irish middle class, Yeats later withdrew from contemporary events to "Thoor Ballylee," his Norman Tower in the country, there to construct an elaborate mythology and to write poetry, at once realist, symbolist, and metaphysical, which explored what were, for Yeats, fundamental questions of history and identity. His works, in many genres, have been selected and collected in various editions.

Permissions Acknowledgments

POETRY

BASHŌ: "This road" and "A village without bells" from *The Essential Haiku*, edited and with verse translations by Robert Hass. Copyright © 1994 by Robert Hass.

CHARLES BERNSTEIN: "Of Time and the Line" from *Rough Trade* by Charles Bernstein. Reprinted by permission of the author.

JOHN BETJEMAN: "In Westminster Abbey" from *Collected Poems* by John Betjeman. Reprinted by permission of John Murray (Publishers) Ltd.

EARLE BIRNEY: "Anglosaxon Street" from *Selected Poems* by Earle Birney. Used by permission of McClelland & Stewart, Inc., Toronto, The Canadian Publishers.

ELIZABETH BISHOP: "Casabianca," "Exchanging Hats," and "Sestina" from *The Collected Poems 1927–1979* by Elizabeth Bishop. Copyright © 1979, 1980 by Alice Helen Methfessel. Reprinted by permission of Farrar, Straus & Giroux, Inc.

EAVAN BOLAND: "The Necessity for Irony" from *The Lost Land* by Eavan Boland. Copyright © 1998 by Eavan Boland. Used by permission of W. W. Norton & Company, Inc.

ROO BORSON: "After a Death" and "Save Us From" from *Night Walk: Selected Poems* by Roo Borson, Oxford University Press, Toronto, 1994. Used by permission of the author.

MARY LYNN BROE: excerpt from *Protean Poetic: The Poetry of Sylvia Plath* by Mary Lynn Broe. Copyright © 1980 by the Curators of the University of Missouri Press. Reprinted by permission of the publisher.

GWENDOLYN BROOKS: "First Fight, Then Fiddle" and "We Real Cool" from *Blacks* by Gwendolyn Brooks. "To the Diaspora" from *Children Coming Home* by Gwendolyn Brooks. Copyright © 1991 by Gwendolyn Brooks. Reprinted by permission of The Estate of Gwendolyn Brooks.

LEE ANN BROWN: "Foolproof Loofah" from *Polyverse*, published by Sun & Moon Press.

BUSON: "Coolness" and "Listening to the Moon" from *The Essential Haiku*, edited and with verse translations by Robert Hass. Copyright © 1994 by Robert Hass. Reprinted by permission of the Ecco Press.

HELEN CHASIN: "Joy Sonnet in a Random Universe" and "The Word *Plum*" from *Coming Close and Other Poems* by Helen Chasin. Copyright © 1968 by Helen Chasin. Reprinted by permission of Yale University Press.

KELLY CHERRY: "Alzheimer's" from *Death and Transfiguration*. Copyright © 1997. Reprinted by permission of Louisiana State University Press.

MARILYN CHIN: "Summer Love" from *The Phoenix Gone, The Terrace Empty* by Marilyn Chin (Milkweed Editions, 1994). Copyright © 1994 by Marilyn Chin. Reprinted by permission of Milkweed Editions.

CHIYOJO: "Whether astringent I do not know" from *One Hundred Famous Haiku*, selected and translated by Daniel Buchanan. Reprinted by permission of Japan Publications, Inc.

MARTHA COLLINS: "Lies" from *Some Things Words Can Do*. Copyright © 1998 by Martha Collins. Reprinted by permission of the author.

WENDY COPE: "Emily Dickinson" from *Making Cocoa for Kingsley Amis* by Wendy Cope. Reprinted by permission of Faber & Faber Ltd.

COUNTEE CULLEN: "Yet Do I Marvel" from *Color* by Countee Cullen. Copyright © 1925 by Harper & Brothers, copyright renewed 1953 by Ida M. Cullen. Reprinted by permission of GRM Associates, agents for the Estate of Ida M. Cullen.

E. E. CUMMINGS: "l(a," and "(ponder, darling, these busted statues" from *Complete Poems: 1904–1962* by E. E. Cummings, edited by George J. Firmage. "l(a," copyright © 1958, 1986, 1991 by the Trustees for the E. E. Cummings Trust. "(ponder, darling, these busted statues," copyright © 1926, 1954, 1991 by the Trustees for the E. E. Cummings Trust. Copyright © 1985 by George James Firmage. "Buffalo Bill's" and "in Just-" from *Complete Poems: 1904–1962* by E. E. Cummings, edited by George J. Firmage. Copyright © 1923, 1951, 1991 by the Trustees for the E. E. Cummings Trust. Copyright © 1976 by George James Firmage. Reprinted by permission of Liveright Publishing Corporation.

WALTER DE LA MARE: "Slim Cunning Hands" from *The Complete Poems of Walter de la Mare*. Reprinted by permission of the Literary Trustees of Walter de la Mare and the Society of Authors as their representative.

BABETTE DEUTSCH: "The Falling Flower . . ." from *Poetry Handbook: A Dictionary of Terms* by Babette

ETHERIDGE KNIGHT: "Eastern guard tower" from *The Essential Etheridge Knight* by Etheridge Knight, copyright © 1986. Reprinted by permission of the University of Pittsburgh Press. "Hard Rock Returns to Prison from the Hospital for the Criminal Insane" from *Poems from Prison* by Etheridge Knight. Permission to reprint granted by Broadside Press.

KENNETH KOCH: "Variations on a Theme by William Carlos Williams" from *Thank You and Other Poems* by Kenneth Koch. Copyright © 1962 and 1994 by Kenneth Koch. Reprinted by permission of the author.

JUDITH KROLL: "Rituals of Exorcism: 'Daddy' " from *Chapters in a Mythology: The Poetry of Sylvia Plath* by Judith Kroll (HarperCollins, 1976). Copyright © 1997 by Judith Kroll.

MAXINE KUMIN: "Woodchucks" from *Selected Poems 1960–1990* by Maxine Kumin. Copyright © 1972 by Maxine Kumin. Reprinted by permission of W. W. Norton & Company, Inc.

PHILIP LARKIN: "Church Going" from *The Less Deceived* by Philip Larkin. Reprinted by permission of The Marvell Press, England and Australia.

D. H. LAWRENCE: "I Am Like a Rose" from *The Complete Poems of D. H. Lawrence.* Copyright © 1964, 1971 by the Estate of D. H. Lawrence, renewed by the Executors of the Estate of Frieda Lawrence Ravagli. Used by permission of Laurence Pollinger Limited and the Estate of Frieda Lawrence Ravagli.

IRVING LAYTON: "From Colony to Nation" from *Collected Poems of Irving Layton* by Irving Layton. Used by permission of McClelland & Stewart, Inc., The Canadian Publishers.

LI-YOUNG LEE: "Persimmons" from *Rose* by Li-Young Lee. Copyright © 1986 by Li-Young Lee. Reprinted by permission of BOA Editions, Ltd.

DENISE LEVERTOV: "Wedding Ring" from *Life in the Forest* by Denise Levertov. Copyright © 1978 by Denise Levertov. Reprinted by permission of New Directions Publishing Corp.

AUDRE LORDE: "Hanging Fire" from *The Black Unicorn* by Audre Lorde. Copyright © 1978 by Audre Lorde. Reprinted by permission of W. W. Norton & Company, Inc.

ROBERT LOWELL: "Skunk Hour" from *Life Studies* by Robert Lowell. Copyright © 1956, 1959 by Robert Lowell. Copyright renewed © 1987 by Harriet Lowell, Sheridan Lowell, and Caroline Lowell. Reprinted by permission of Farrar, Straus & Giroux, Inc.

CLAUDE MCKAY: "The White House." Used by permission of The Archives of Claude McKay, Carl Cowl, Administrator.

ARCHIBALD MACLEISH: "Ars Poetica" from *Collected Poems 1917–1982* by Archibald MacLeish. Copyright © 1985 by the Estate of Archibald MacLeish. Reprinted by permission of Houghton Mifflin Company. All rights reserved.

GAIL MAZUR: "Bluebonnets" from *The Common.* Reprinted by permission of the author.

JAMES MERRILL: "Watching the Dance" from *Nights and Days* by James Merrill. Copyright © 1966, 1992 by James Merrill. *Selected Poems 1946–1985* by James Merrill, published by Alfred A. Knopf in 1992. Reprinted with permission of Alfred A. Knopf, Inc.

EDNA ST. VINCENT MILLAY: "I, being born a woman and distressed" and "What lips my lips have kissed" by Edna St. Vincent Millay. From *Collected Poems,* HarperCollins. Copyright © 1923, 1951, 1954, 1982 by Edna St. Vincent Millay and Norma Millay Ellis. "Sonnet XXVI [Women have loved before as I love now]" from *Fatal Interview* by Edna St. Vincent Millay. From *Collected Poems,* HarperCollins. Copyright © 1922, 1931, 1950, 1958 by Edna St. Vincent Millay and Norma Millay Ellis. All rights reserved. Reprinted by permission of Elizabeth Barnett, literary executor.

EARL MINER: "The still old pond" from *Japanese Linked Poetry* by Earl Miner. Copyright © 1979 by Earl Miner. Reprinted by permission of the author.

MARIANNE MOORE: "Love in America?" from *The Complete Poems of Marianne Moore* by Marianne Moore. Copyright © 1981 by Clive E. Driver, Literary Executor of the Estate of Marianne Moore. Used by permission of Viking Penguin, a division of Penguin Books USA, Inc. "Poetry" from *The Complete Poems of Marianne Moore.* Copyright © 1935 by Marianne Moore; copyright renewed © 1963 by Marianne Moore and T. S. Eliot. Reprinted with the permission of Simon & Schuster.

PAT MORA: "Gentle Communion" from *Communion* (Houston: Arte Publico Press–University of Houston, 1991) by Pat Mora. "Sonrisas" from *Borders* by Pat Mora (Houston: Arte Publico Press–University of Houston, 1986). Reprinted with permission from the publisher.

EDWIN MORGAN: "Opening the Cage" from *Collected Poems* by Edwin Morgan. Reprinted by permission of Carcanet Press Limited.

SUSAN MUSGRAVE: "You Didn't Fit" from *Embalmer's Art* by Susan Musgrave. Copyright © 1991 and 1985 by Susan Musgrave. Reprinted by permission of the author.

MARILYN NELSON: "How I Discovered Poetry" from *The Yellow Shoe Poets.* Copyright © 1999. Reprinted by permission of Louisiana State University Press.

HOWARD NEMEROV: "Boom!," "The Goose Fish," "The Town Dump," "The Vacuum," and "A Way of Life" from *The Collected Poems of Howard Nemerov.* Copyright © 1977 by Howard Nemerov. Reprinted by permission of Margaret Nemerov.

SHARON OLDS: "The Lifting" from *The Father* by Sharon Olds. Copyright © 1992 by Sharon Olds. "I Go Back to May 1937" from *The Gold Cell* by Sharon Olds. Copyright © 1987 by Sharon Olds. "Sex Without Love" and "The Victims" from *The Dead and the Living* by Sharon Olds. Copyright © 1983 by Sharon Olds. Reprinted by permission of Alfred A. Knopf, Inc. "Leningrad Cemetery, Winter of 1941" from *The New Yorker,* December 31, 1979. Copyright © 1979 by The New Yorker Magazine, Inc. Reprinted by permission of the publisher.

MARY OLIVER: "Singapore" from *House of Light* by Mary Oliver. Copyright © 1990 by Mary Oliver. Reprinted by permission of Beacon Press, Boston.

MICHAEL ONDAATJE: "King Kong Meets Wallace Stevens" from *The Cinammon Peeler* by Michael Ondaatje. Copyright © 1979 by Michael Ondaatje. Reprinted by permission of Michael Ondaatje.

DOROTHY PARKER: "A Certain Lady" and "One Perfect Rose" copyright © 1926, renewed 1954 by Dorothy Parker from *The Portable Dorothy Parker* by Dorothy Parker. Copyright © 1928, renewed 1956 by Dorothy Parker. Used by permission of Viking Penguin, a division of Penguin Putnam, Inc.

LINDA PASTAN: "love poem" and "To a Daughter Leaving Home" from *The Imperfect Paradise* by Linda Pastan. Copyright © 1988 by Linda Pastan. "Marks" from *PM/AM: New and Selected Poems* by Linda Pastan. Copyright © 1978 by Linda Pastan. Reprinted by permission of W. W. Norton & Company, Inc.

WILLIE PERDOMO: "123rd Street Rap" from *Where a Nickel Costs a Dime* by Willie Perdomo. Copyright © 1996 by Willie Perdomo. Used by permission of W. W. Norton & Company, Inc.

MARGE PIERCY: "Barbie Doll" and "What's That Smell in the Kitchen?" from *Circles on the Water* by Marge Piercy. Copyright © 1982 by Marge Piercy. Reprinted by permission of Alfred A. Knopf, Inc.

SYLVIA PLATH: "Point Shirley" from *The Colossus and Other Poems* by Sylvia Plath. Copyright © 1959 by Sylvia Plath. Reprinted by permission of Alfred A. Knopf, Inc. "Black Rook in Rainy Weather" (all lines) from *Crossing the Water* by Sylvia Plath. Copyright © 1960 by Ted Hughes. "Morning Song" (all lines) copyright © 1961 by Ted Hughes, copyright renewed; "Daddy" (all lines) copyright © 1963 by Ted Hughes; from *Ariel* by Sylvia Plath. Copyright © 1963 by Ted Hughes, copyright renewed. "Barren Women" from *The Collected Poems of Sylvia Plath* edited by Ted Hughes. Copyright © 1960, 1965, 1971, 1981 by the Estate of Sylvia Plath. Editorial material copyright © 1981 by Ted Hughes. Reprinted by permission of HarperCollins Publishers, Inc., and Faber & Faber Ltd.

EZRA POUND: "In a Station of the Metro," "The River-Merchant's Wife: A Letter," and "A Virginal" from *Personae* by Ezra Pound. Copyright © 1926 by Ezra Pound. Reprinted by permission of New Directions Publishing Corp.

JAROLD RAMSEY: "The Tally Stick." Reprinted by permission of the author.

DUDLEY RANDALL: "Ballad of Birmingham" from *Poem Counter Poem* by Dudley Randall (Michigan: Broadside Press, 1969). Reprinted by permission of the publisher.

JOHN CROWE RANSOM: "Bells for John Whiteside's Daughter" from *Selected Poems* by John Crowe Ransom. Copyright © 1924 by Alfred A. Knopf, Inc., and renewed 1952 by John Crowe Ransom. Reprinted by permission of the publisher.

ADRIENNE RICH: "At a Bach Concert," "Aunt Jennifer's Tigers," "Diving into the Wreck," "For the Record," "Planetarium," "Snapshots of a Daughter-in-Law," "Storm Warnings," and "Two Songs" from *The Fact of a Doorframe, Poems Selected and New 1950–1984* by Adrienne Rich. Copyright © 1984 by Adrienne Rich. Copyright © 1975, 1978 by W. W. Norton & Company, Inc.

DRAMA

ART ACKNOWLEDGMENTS

Tom Keats. Sketch by Joseph Severn. Reprinted with the kind permission of the Keats–Shelley Memorial House, Rome.

John Hamilton Reynolds. Miniature by Joseph Severn. Reprinted by permission of the Corporation of London from the Collections at Keats House, Hampstead.

Adrienne Rich, circa 1970. Photograph by Sissy Krook. Reprinted by permission of the photographer.

Adrienne Rich in the classroom, circa 1978. Photograph by Linda Koolish, Ph.D. Reprinted by permission of the photographer.

Adrienne Rich today. Copyright © by Jason Langer, photographer. Reprinted by permission.

Sylvia Plath. Courtesy of the Sylvia Plath Collection, Mortimer Rare Book Room, Smith College.

Sylvia Plath's father, Otto Plath. Courtesy of the Sylvia Plath Collection, Mortimer Rare Book Room, Smith College.

DRAMA

Sophocles. Greek playwright of the fifth century B.C., head-and-shoulders sculpture. Reprinted by permission of Corbis-Bettmann.

Production of *Antigone* (The New York Shakespeare Festival, 1982). Photo by Martha Swope. Reprinted by the courtesy of Time, Inc.

Shakespeare's Birthplace. Copyright © Michael Maslan Historic Photographs/CORBIS. Courtesy of Corbis.

Laurence Olivier in *Hamlet.* Copyright © Bettman/CORBIS. Courtesy of Corbis.

William Shakespeare. Droeshout engraving. Copyright © Chris Hellier/CORBIS. Courtesy of Corbis.

Bottom from *Midsummer Night's Dream.* Nineteenth-century print. Copyright © CORBIS. Courtesy of Corbis.

The Globe Theatre. Copyright © Bettman/CORBIS. Courtesy of Corbis.

Index of Authors

Index of Titles and First Lines